PSYCHOLOGY

SIXTH EDITION

Douglas A. Bernstein
University of South Florida
University of Surrey

Louis A. Penner
University of South Florida

Alison Clarke-Stewart
University of California, Irvine

Edward J. Roy
University of Illinois at Urbana-Champaign

Houghton Mifflin Company   Boston   New York

To the researchers, past and present, whose work embodies psychology today, and to the students who will follow in their footsteps to shape the psychology of tomorrow.

Senior Sponsoring Editor: Kerry T. Baruth
Development Editors: Marianne Stepanian/Rita Lombard
Editorial Assistant: Nirmal Trivedi
Senior Project Editor: Aileen Mason
Editorial Assistant: Lindsay Frost
Senior Production/Design Coordinator: Sarah Ambrose
Senior Manufacturing Coordinator: Marie Barnes
Senior Marketing Manager: Katherine Greig
Text Designer: Henry Rachlin
Cover Design Coordinator: Diana Coe

Anatomical illustrations by Pat Rossi

CREDITS
Credits begin after the References, on page C-1.

Copyright © 2003 by Houghton Mifflin Company.

All rights reserved. No part of this work may be reproduced or transmitted in any form or by any means, electronic or mechanical, including photocopying and recording, or by any information storage or retrieval system without the prior written permission of Houghton Mifflin Company unless such copying is expressly permitted by federal copyright law. Address inquiries to College Permissions, Houghton Mifflin Company, 222 Berkeley Street, Boston, MA 02116-3764.

Printed in the U.S.A.

Library of Congress Control Number: 2001133226

ISBN (Student Edition): 0-618-21374-0

ISBN (Instructor's Annotated Edition): 0-618-21990-0

4 5 6 7 8 9-QWV-06 05 04

BRIEF CONTENTS

Preface xv

Chapter 1 Introducing Psychology 1

Chapter 2 Research in Psychology 25

Chapter 3 Biological Aspects of Psychology 54

Chapter 4 Sensation 99

Chapter 5 Perception 143

Chapter 6 Learning 184

Chapter 7 Memory 224

Chapter 8 Cognition and Language 264

Chapter 9 Consciousness 308

Chapter 10 Cognitive Abilities 344

Chapter 11 Motivation and Emotion 380

Chapter 12 Human Development 431

Chapter 13 Health, Stress, and Coping 485

Chapter 14 Personality 517

Chapter 15 Psychological Disorders 552

Chapter 16 Treatment of Psychological Disorders 603

Chapter 17 Social Cognition 646

Chapter 18 Social Influence 679

Appendix: Behavioral Genetics A-1

Appendix: Statistics in Psychological Research A-10

References R-1

Credits C-1

Name Index NI-1

Subject Index/Glossary SIG-1

CONTENTS

Preface xv

1 Introducing Psychology 1

The World of Psychology: An Overview 2
  Subfields of Psychology 3
  Linkages Within Psychology and Beyond 7
  Research: The Foundation of Psychology 9
  A Brief History of Psychology 11

Unity and Diversity in Psychology 15
  Approaches to Psychology 16
  Human Diversity and Psychology 21
  SUMMARY 24

2 Research in Psychology 25

Thinking Critically About Psychology (or Anything Else) 26
  Critical Thinking and Scientific Research 29
  The Role of Theories 30

Research Methods in Psychology 31
  Selecting Human Participants for Research 32
  Naturalistic Observation: Watching Behavior 33
  Case Studies: Taking a Closer Look 34
  Surveys: Looking at the Big Picture 35
  Experiments: Exploring Cause and Effect 36

Statistical Analysis of Research Results 42
  Descriptive Statistics 42
  Inferential Statistics 46
  Statistics and Research Methods as Tools in Critical Thinking 47

Ethical Guidelines for Psychologists 48

■ **LINKAGES: Psychological Research and Behavioral Genetics** 49
  LINKAGES 52
  SUMMARY 53

3 Biological Aspects of Psychology 54

The Nervous System 56
  Cells of the Nervous System 57
  Action Potentials 58
  Synapses and Communication Between Neurons 60
  Organization and Functions of the Nervous System 62

The Peripheral Nervous System: Keeping in Touch with the World 64
  The Somatic Nervous System 64
  The Autonomic Nervous System 65

The Central Nervous System: Making Sense of the World 66
  The Spinal Cord 67
  The Brain 68

■ **FOCUS ON RESEARCH METHODS: Manipulating Genes in Animal Models of Human Disease** 73
  The Cerebral Cortex 75
  The Divided Brain in a Unified Self 79
  Plasticity: Repairing Damage in the Central Nervous System 82

■ **LINKAGES: Human Development and the Changing Brain** 84

The Chemistry of Psychology 86
    Three Classes of Neurotransmitters 87
- **THINKING CRITICALLY: Are There Drugs That Can Make You Smarter?** 90

The Endocrine System: Coordinating the Internal World 92

The Immune System: Defending the Body 95
    LINKAGES 96
    SUMMARY 97

4 Sensation 99

Sensory Systems 101

The Problem of Coding 102
- **LINKAGES: Sensation and Biological Aspects of Psychology** 103

Hearing 104
    Sound 104
    The Ear 106
    Coding Intensity and Frequency 108
    Auditory Pathways and Representations 109

Vision 111
    Light 111
    Focusing Light 112
    Converting Light into Images 113
    Visual Pathways 116 
    Visual Representations 117
    Seeing Color 120
    The Interaction of Vision and Hearing: Synesthesia 125

The Chemical Senses: Smell and Taste 126
    Olfaction 126
    Gustation 128
    Smell, Taste, and Flavor 129

Somatic Senses and the Vestibular System 130
    Touch and Temperature 131
    Pain 132
- **THINKING CRITICALLY: Does Acupuncture Relieve Pain?** 135
    Proprioception 137
    Vestibular Sense 137
- **FOCUS ON RESEARCH METHODS: The Case of the Disembodied Woman** 138
    LINKAGES 140
    SUMMARY 140

5 Perception 143

The Perception Paradox 144

Three Approaches to Perception 145

Psychophysics 146
    Absolute Thresholds: Is Something Out There? 147
- **THINKING CRITICALLY: Can Subliminal Stimuli Influence Your Behavior?** 147
    Signal-Detection Theory 149
    Judging Differences: Has Anything Changed? 152
    Magnitude Estimation: How Intense Is That? 153

Organizing the Perceptual World 154
    Basic Processes in Perceptual Organization 155
    Perception of Location and Distance 157
    Perception of Motion 161
    Perceptual Constancy 162
    Culture, Experience, and Perception 165

Recognizing the Perceptual World 165
    Bottom-Up Processing 166
    Top-Down Processing 168
    Network Processing 170
- **LINKAGES: Perception and Human Development** 171

Attention 173
- **FOCUS ON RESEARCH METHODS: An Experiment in "Mind Reading"** 174
  - Directing Attention 175
  - Ignoring Information 176
  - Divided Attention 177
  - Attention and Automatic Processing 177
  - Attention and the Brain 178

Applications of Research on Perception 178
- Aviation Psychology 179
- Human-Computer Interaction 180
- Traffic Safety 180
- LINKAGES 181
- SUMMARY 181

6 Learning 184

Learning About Stimuli 186

Classical Conditioning: Learning Signals and Associations 187
- Pavlov's Discovery 187
- Conditioned Responses over Time: Extinction and Spontaneous Recovery 189
- Stimulus Generalization and Discrimination 190
- The Signaling of Significant Events 190
- Some Applications of Classical Conditioning 193

Instrumental and Operant Conditioning: Learning the Consequences of Behavior 195
- From the Puzzle Box to the Skinner Box 195
- Basic Components of Operant Conditioning 197
- Forming and Strengthening Operant Behavior 200
- Why Reinforcers Work 204
- Punishment 205
- Some Applications of Operant Conditioning 207

Cognitive Processes in Learning 208
- Learned Helplessness 209
- **FOCUS ON RESEARCH METHODS: A Two-Factor Experiment on Human Helplessness** 209
  - Latent Learning and Cognitive Maps 211
  - Insight and Learning 212
  - Observational Learning: Learning by Imitation 213
- **THINKING CRITICALLY: Does Watching Violence on Television Make People More Violent?** 215
- **LINKAGES: Neural Networks and Learning** 217

Using Research on Learning to Help People Learn 218
- Classrooms Across Cultures 218
- Active Learning 219
- Skill Learning 220
- LINKAGES 221
- SUMMARY 222

7 Memory 224

The Nature of Memory 225
- Basic Memory Processes 225
- Types of Memory 226
- Explicit and Implicit Memory 227
- **FOCUS ON RESEARCH METHODS: Measuring Explicit Versus Implicit Memory** 228
  - Models of Memory 229

Storing New Memories 232
- Sensory Memory 232
- Short-Term Memory and Working Memory 233
- Long-Term Memory 236
- Distinguishing Between Short-Term and Long-Term Memory 238

Retrieving Memories 239
- Retrieval Cues and Encoding Specificity 239
- Context and State Dependence 239

Contents

Retrieval from Semantic Memory 240
Constructing Memories 243
■ LINKAGES: **Memory, Perception, and Eyewitness Testimony** 245

Forgetting 247
How Do We Forget? 247
Why Do We Forget? The Roles of Decay and Interference 248
■ THINKING CRITICALLY: **Can Traumatic Memories Be Repressed, Then Recovered?** 250

Biological Bases of Memory 253
The Biochemistry of Memory 254
Brain Structures and Memory 255

Applications of Memory Research 258
Improving Your Memory 258
Design for Memory 260
LINKAGES 261
SUMMARY 261

8 Cognition and Language 264

Basic Functions of Thought 266
The Circle of Thought 266
Measuring Information Processing 267

Mental Representations: The Ingredients of Thought 270
Concepts 270
Propositions 271
Schemas, Scripts, and Mental Models 271
Images and Cognitive Maps 273

Thinking Strategies 274
Formal Reasoning 274
Informal Reasoning 276

Problem Solving 279
Strategies for Problem Solving 279
■ FOCUS ON RESEARCH METHODS: **Locating Analogical Thinking** 280
Obstacles to Problem Solving 282
Building Problem-Solving Skills 285
Problem Solving by Computer 286

Decision Making 288
Evaluating Options 288
Biases and Flaws in Decision Making 289

Naturalistic Decision Making 291
■ LINKAGES: **Group Processes in Problem Solving and Decision Making** 291

Language 292
The Elements of Language 293
Understanding Speech 294
The Development of Language 296
How Is Language Acquired? 299
■ THINKING CRITICALLY: **Can Nonhumans Use Language?** 301
Culture, Language, and Thought 303
LINKAGES 305
SUMMARY 305

9 Consciousness 308

Analyzing Consciousness 309
Some Functions of Consciousness 310
Levels of Consciousness 311
Mental Processing Without Awareness 312
■ FOCUS ON RESEARCH METHODS: **Subliminal Messages in Rock Music** 314
The Neuropsychology of Consciousness 315
States of Consciousness 317

Sleeping and Dreaming 318
Stages of Sleep 318
Sleep Disorders 320

Why Do People Sleep? 322
Dreams and Dreaming 325

Hypnosis 327
Experiencing Hypnosis 327
Explaining Hypnosis 327
Applications of Hypnosis 329

■ **Linkages: Meditation, Health, and Stress** 329

Psychoactive Drugs 330
Psychopharmacology 330
The Varying Effects of Drugs 331
Depressants 333
Stimulants 335
Opiates 337
Hallucinogens 337

■ **Thinking Critically: Is Marijuana Dangerous?** 339
LINKAGES 342
SUMMARY 342

10 Cognitive Abilities 344

Testing for Intelligence 346
A Brief History of Intelligence Tests 346
Intelligence Tests Today 348
Aptitude and Achievement Tests 350

Measuring the Quality of Tests 350
Reliability 351
Validity 351

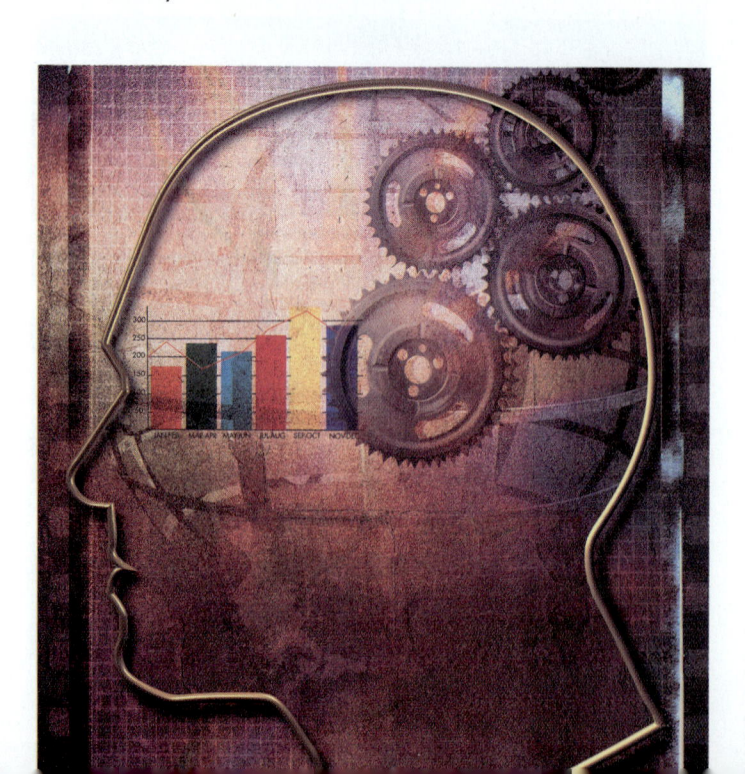

Evaluating IQ Tests 352
The Reliability and Validity of IQ Tests 352

■ **Thinking Critically: Are IQ Tests Unfairly Biased Against Certain Groups?** 354
IQ Scores as a Measure of Innate Ability 356
Group Differences in IQ Scores 358
Conditions That Can Raise IQ Scores 361
IQ Scores in the Classroom 362

■ **Linkages: Emotionality and the Measurement of Cognitive Abilities** 364

Understanding Intelligence 365
The Psychometric Approach 365
The Information-Processing Approach 366
The Triarchic Theory of Intelligence 366
Multiple Intelligences 369

■ **Focus on Research Methods: Tracking Cognitive Abilities over the Life Span** 370

Diversity in Cognitive Abilities 373
Creativity 373
Unusual Cognitive Ability 374
LINKAGES 377
SUMMARY 378

11 Motivation and Emotion 380

Concepts and Theories of Motivation 381
Sources of Motivation 382
Instinct Theory and Its Descendants 383
Drive Reduction Theory 385
Arousal Theory 386
Incentive Theory 387

Hunger and Eating 388
Biological Signals for Hunger and Satiety 388
Hunger and the Brain 390
Flavor, Cultural Learning, and Food Selection 391
Eating Disorders 392

Sexual Behavior 395

■ **Focus on Research Methods: A Survey of Human Sexual Behavior** 396
The Biology of Sex 398
Social and Cultural Factors in Sexuality 399
Sexual Orientation 400

■ **Thinking Critically: Does Biology Determine Sexual Orientation?** 400
Sexual Dysfunctions 403

Achievement Motivation 404
    Need for Achievement 404
    Goal Setting and Achievement Motivation 406
    Achievement and Success in the Workplace 407
    Achievement and Subjective Well-Being 408

Relations and Conflicts Among Motives 409
■ LINKAGES: **Conflicting Motives and Stress** 410
    Opponent Processes, Motivation, and Emotion 411

The Nature of Emotion 412
    Defining Characteristics 412
    The Biology of Emotion 413

Theories of Emotion 417
    James's Peripheral Theory 417
    Cannon's Central Theory 421
    Cognitive Theories 422

Communicating Emotion 424
    Innate Expressions of Emotion 425
    Social and Cultural Influences on Emotional Expression 426
    LINKAGES 428
    SUMMARY 428

12 Human Development 431

Exploring Human Development 432

Beginnings 435
    Prenatal Development 435
    The Newborn 436

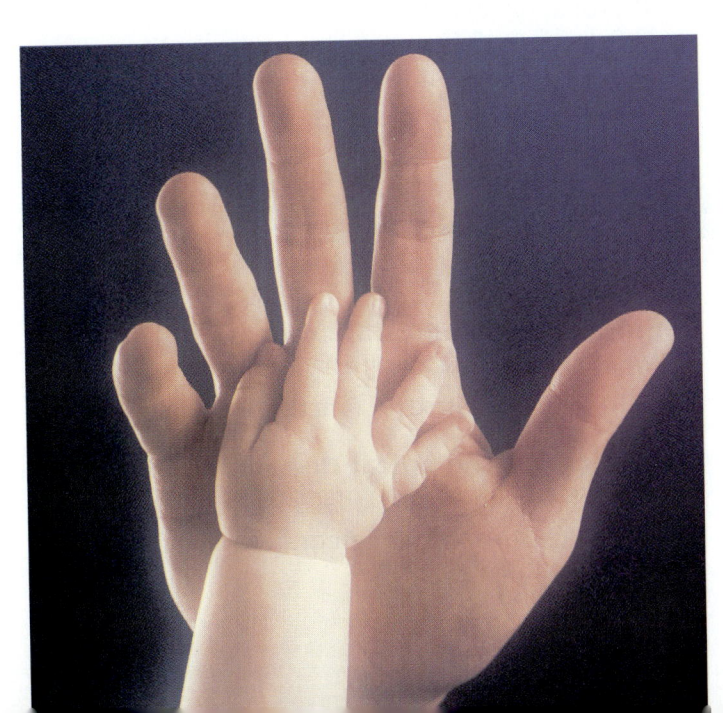

Infancy and Childhood: Cognitive Development 439
    Changes in the Brain 439
    The Development of Knowledge: Piaget's Theory 439
■ FOCUS ON RESEARCH METHODS: **Experiments on Developing Minds** 443
    Modifying Piaget's Theory 446
    Information Processing During Childhood 447
■ LINKAGES: **Development and Memory** 449
    Culture and Cognitive Development 450
    Variations in Cognitive Development 451

Infancy and Childhood: Social and Emotional Development 453
    Individual Temperament 454
    The Infant Grows Attached 455
■ THINKING CRITICALLY: **Does Day Care Harm the Emotional Development of Infants?** 457
    Relationships with Parents and Peers 459
    Social Skills 463
    Gender Roles 464
    Risk and Resilience 466

Adolescence 467
    The Challenges of Change 467
    Identity and Development of the Self 469
    Abstract Thought and Moral Reasoning 471

Adulthood 474
    Physical Changes 474
    Cognitive Changes 474
    Social Changes 477
    Death and Dying 481
    Longevity 481
    LINKAGES 482
    SUMMARY 482

13 Health, Stress, and Coping 485

Health Psychology 486

Stress and Stressors 487
    Psychological Stressors 488
    Measuring Stressors 489

Stress Responses 490
    Physical Responses 491
    Psychological Responses 493

■ **LINKAGES: Stress and Psychological Disorders** 495

Stress Mediators: Interactions Between People and Stressors 496
- How Stressors Are Appraised 496
- Predictability and Control 497
- Coping Resources and Coping Methods 498
- Social Support 499
- Stress, Personality, and Gender 501

■ **FOCUS ON RESEARCH METHODS: Personality and Health** 501

The Physiology and Psychology of Health and Illness 504
- Stress, Illness, and the Immune System 504
- Stress, Illness, and the Cardiovascular System 506

■ **THINKING CRITICALLY: Does Hostility Increase the Risk of Heart Disease?** 506
- Risking Your Life: Health-Endangering Behaviors 508

Promoting Healthy Behavior 509
- Health Beliefs and Health Behaviors 510
- Changing Health Behaviors: Stages of Readiness 511
- Programs for Coping with Stress and Promoting Health 512
- LINKAGES 515
- SUMMARY 515

14 Personality 517

The Psychodynamic Approach 519
- The Structure and Development of Personality 519
- Variations on Freud's Personality Theory 522
- Contemporary Psychodynamic Theories 523
- Evaluation of the Psychodynamic Approach 523

The Trait Approach 525
- Allport's Trait Theory 526
- The Big-Five Model of Personality 526
- Biological Trait Theories 528

■ **THINKING CRITICALLY: Are Personality Traits Inherited?** 530
- Evaluation of the Trait Approach 532

The Social-Cognitive Approach 533
- Roots of the Social-Cognitive Approach 533
- Prominent Social-Cognitive Theories 534
- Evaluation of the Social-Cognitive Approach 536

The Humanistic Approach 537
- Prominent Humanistic Theories 538
- Evaluation of the Humanistic Approach 540

■ **LINKAGES: Personality, Culture, and Human Development** 541

■ **FOCUS ON RESEARCH METHODS: Longitudinal Studies of Temperament and Personality** 543

Assessing Personality 545
- Objective Personality Tests 545
- Projective Personality Tests 548
- Personality Tests and Employee Selection 549
- LINKAGES 550
- SUMMARY 550

15 Psychological Disorders 552

Defining Psychological Disorders 554
- What Is Abnormal? 554
- Behavior in Context: A Practical Approach 555

Explaining Psychological Disorders 556
- The Biopsychosocial Model 556
- Diathesis-Stress as an Integrative Explanation 559

Classifying Psychological Disorders 560
A Classification System: *DSM-IV* 561
Purposes and Problems of Diagnosis 561
■ **THINKING CRITICALLY: Is Psychological Diagnosis Biased?** 563

Anxiety Disorders 565
Types of Anxiety Disorders 566
Causes of Anxiety Disorders 569
■ **LINKAGES: Anxiety Disorders and Learning** 570

Somatoform Disorders 572

Dissociative Disorders 573

Mood Disorders 576
Depressive Disorders 576
Bipolar Disorders 578
Causes of Mood Disorders 579

Schizophrenia 582
Symptoms of Schizophrenia 583
Categorizing Schizophrenia 584
Causes of Schizophrenia 586

Personality Disorders 589
■ **FOCUS ON RESEARCH METHODS: Exploring Links Between Childhood Abuse and Antisocial Personality Disorder** 591

A Sampling of Other Psychological Disorders 593
Psychological Disorders of Childhood 593
Substance-Related Disorders 595

Mental Illness and the Law 598
LINKAGES 600
SUMMARY 601

16 Treatment of Psychological Disorders 603

Basic Features of Treatment 604

Psychodynamic Psychotherapy 606
Classical Psychoanalysis 606
Contemporary Variations on Psychoanalysis 607

Humanistic Psychotherapy 610
Client-Centered Therapy 610
Gestalt Therapy 612

Behavior Therapy 613
Techniques for Modifying Behavior 614
Cognitive-Behavior Therapy 618

Group, Family, and Couples Therapy 620
Group Therapy 620
Family and Couples Therapy 621

Evaluating Psychotherapy 623
■ **THINKING CRITICALLY: Are All Forms of Therapy Equally Effective?** 624
■ **FOCUS ON RESEARCH METHODS: Which Therapies Work Best for Which Problems?** 626
Addressing the "Ultimate Question" 628
Cultural Factors in Psychotherapy 629
Rules and Rights in the Therapeutic Relationship 631

Biological Treatments 632
Electroconvulsive Therapy 633
Psychosurgery 634
Psychoactive Drugs 634
Evaluating Psychoactive Drug Treatments 639
Drugs and Psychotherapy 640
■ **LINKAGES: Biological Aspects of Psychology and the Treatment of Psychological Disorders** 641

Community Psychology: From Treatment to Prevention 642
LINKAGES 643
SUMMARY 644

17 Social Cognition 646

Social Influences on the Self 647
- Social Comparison 647
- ■ FOCUS ON RESEARCH METHODS: Self-Esteem and the Ultimate Terror 649
- Social Identity Theory 650
- Self-Schemas 651

Social Perception 652
- The Role of Schemas 652
- First Impressions 653
- Explaining Behavior: Attribution 655
- Biases in Attribution 657
- The Self-Protective Functions of Social Cognition 659

Attitudes 660
- The Structure of Attitudes 660
- Forming Attitudes 661
- Changing Attitudes 662

■ LINKAGES: Biological and Social Psychology 665

Prejudice and Stereotypes 666
- Theories of Prejudice and Stereotyping 666
- Reducing Prejudice 668

■ THINKING CRITICALLY: Is Ethnic Prejudice Too Ingrained Ever to Be Eliminated? 669

Interpersonal Attraction 671
- Keys to Attraction 672
- Intimate Relationships and Love 673

LINKAGES 677
SUMMARY 677

18 Social Influence 679

Social Influence 680
■ LINKAGES: Motivation and the Presence of Others 682

Conformity and Compliance 684
- The Role of Norms 685
- Why Do People Conform? 685
- When Do People Conform? 686
- Inducing Compliance 687

Obedience 689
- Factors Affecting Obedience 690
- Evaluating Milgram's Studies 692

Aggression 694
- Why Are People Aggressive? 695
- When Are People Aggressive? 697

■ THINKING CRITICALLY: Does Pornography Cause Aggression? 699

Altruism and Helping Behavior 702
- Why Do People Help? 703

■ FOCUS ON RESEARCH METHODS: Does Family Matter? 707

Cooperation, Competition, and Conflict 710
- Social Dilemmas 710
- Fostering Cooperation 712
- Interpersonal Conflict 712

Group Processes 714
- Group Leadership 714
- Groupthink 715

LINKAGES 716
SUMMARY 716

Appendix: Behavioral Genetics A-1

Appendix: Statistics in Psychological Research A-10

References R-1

Credits C-1

Name Index NI-1

Subject Index/Glossary SIG-1

FEATURES

LINKAGES

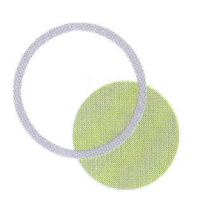

Psychological Research and Behavioral Genetics 49
Human Development and the Changing Brain 84
Sensation and Biological Aspects of Psychology 103
Perception and Human Development 171
Neural Networks and Learning 217
Memory, Perception, and Eyewitness Testimony 245
Group Processes in Problem Solving and Decision Making 291
Meditation, Health, and Stress 329
Emotionality and the Measurement of Cognitive Abilities 364
Conflicting Motives and Stress 410
Development and Memory 449
Stress and Psychological Disorders 495
Personality, Culture, and Human Development 541
Anxiety Disorders and Learning 570
Biological Aspects of Psychology and the Treatment of Psychological Disorders 641
Biological and Social Psychology 665
Motivation and the Presence of Others 682

FOCUS ON RESEARCH METHODS

Manipulating Genes in Animal Models of Human Disease 73
The Case of the Disembodied Woman 138
An Experiment in "Mind Reading" 174
A Two-Factor Experiment on Human Helplessness 209
Measuring Explicit Versus Implicit Memory 228
Locating Analogical Thinking 280
Subliminal Messages in Rock Music 314
Tracking Cognitive Abilities over the Life Span 370
A Survey of Human Sexual Behavior 396
Experiments on Developing Minds 443
Personality and Health 501
Longitudinal Studies of Temperament and Personality 543
Exploring Links Between Child Abuse and Antisocial Personality Disorder 591
Which Therapies Work Best for Which Problems? 626
Self-Esteem and the Ultimate Terror 649
Does Family Matter? 707

THINKING CRITICALLY

Are There Drugs That Can Make You Smarter? 90
Does Acupuncture Relieve Pain? 135
Can Subliminal Stimuli Influence Your Behavior? 147
Does Watching Violence on Television Make People More Violent? 215
Can Traumatic Memories Be Repressed, Then Recovered? 250
Can Nonhumans Use Language? 301
Is Marijuana Dangerous? 339
Are IQ Tests Unfairly Biased Against Certain Groups? 354
Does Biology Determine Sexual Orientation? 400
Does Day Care Harm the Emotional Development of Infants? 457
Does Hostility Increase the Risk of Heart Disease? 506
Are Personality Traits Inherited? 530
Is Psychological Diagnosis Biased? 563
Are All Forms of Therapy Equally Effective? 624
Is Ethnic Prejudice Too Ingrained Ever to Be Eliminated? 669
Does Pornography Cause Aggression? 699

PREFACE

In revising *Psychology* we have rededicated ourselves to the goals we pursued in the first five editions:

- To explore the full range of psychology, from cell to society, in an eclectic manner as free as possible of theoretical bias.
- To balance our need to explain the content of psychology with an emphasis on the doing of psychology, through a blend of conceptual discussion and description of research studies.
- To foster scientific attitudes and to help students learn to think critically by examining the ways that psychologists have solved, or failed to solve, fascinating puzzles of behavior and mental processes.
- To produce a text that, without oversimplifying psychology, is clear, accessible, and enjoyable to read.
- To demonstrate that, in spite of its breadth and diversity, psychology is an integrated discipline in which each subfield is linked to other subfields by common interests and overarching research questions. The productive cross-fertilization among social, clinical, and biological psychologists in researching health and illness is just one example of how different types of psychologists benefit from and build on one another's work.

Preparing the Sixth Edition provided us with new ways to do justice to our goals. We sought to respond to the needs of instructors who wanted us to reduce or expand coverage of various topics. For example, many instructors asked us to increase the amount of material on applied psychology without losing the book's emphasis on basic research in psychology. As a result, we have added material relating to applied areas such as industrial/organizational and forensic psychology throughout the book, wherever appropriate.

As always, we sought to strike an ideal balance between classic and current research. The important historic findings of psychological research are here, but so is coverage of much recent work. Approximately one third of the research citations are new to the Sixth Edition, and we have added the latest information on such topics as

- Methods for evaluating claims for the effectiveness of eye movement desensitization ("Research in Psychology")
- Techniques for studying the brain ("Biological Aspects of Psychology")
- The interaction of senses in synesthesia ("Sensation")
- Perceptual grouping principles such as synchrony and connectedness ("Perception")
- Applying learning principles to help diagnose Alzheimer's disease ("Learning")
- Biological bases of memory ("Memory")
- Locating brain areas involved in analogical thinking ("Cognition and Language")
- The controversy over using marijuana for medical purposes ("Consciousness")
- How anxiety over ethnic stereotypes can affect cognitive test performance ("Cognitive Abilities")
- Achievement and happiness ("Motivation and Emotion")
- The challenges facing adults in twenty-first-century families ("Human Development")
- Psychological reactions to stress ("Health, Stress, and Coping")
- Gray's Approach-Inhibition Theory ("Personality")
- The biopsychosocial model of psychological disorder ("Psychological Disorders")
- Empirically validated psychotherapies ("Treatment of Psychological Disorders")
- Terror management theory and social cognitive neuroscience ("Social Cognition")
- Obedience and social power ("Social Influence")

The Sixth Edition also contains substantial material on culture and human diversity. Throughout the text students will encounter recent research on multicultural phenomena occurring in North America and around the world. We introduce this multicultural emphasis in the chapter on introducing psychology, and we follow up on it in other chapters through such topics as

- Selecting human participants for research ("Research in Psychology")
- Culture, experience, and perception ("Perception")
- Classrooms across cultures ("Learning")
- Culture, language, and thought ("Cognition and Language")
- Ethnic differences in IQ ("Cognitive Abilities")
- Flavor, cultural learning, and food selection ("Motivation and Emotion")
- Social and cultural factors in sexuality ("Motivation and Emotion")
- Cultural and gender differences in achievement motivation ("Motivation and Emotion")
- Cultural aspects of emotional expression ("Motivation and Emotion")
- Culture and cognitive development ("Human Development")

- Sociocultural factors in adult development ("Human Development")
- Cultural background and heart disease ("Health, Stress, and Coping")
- Personality, culture, and human development ("Personality")
- Ethnic bias in psychodiagnosis ("Psychological Disorders")
- Sociocultural factors in psychological disorders ("Psychological Disorders")
- Gender and cultural differences in depression and suicide ("Psychological Disorders")
- Cultural factors in psychotherapy ("Treatment of Psychological Disorders")
- Ethnic differences in responses to drug treatment ("Treatment of Psychological Disorders")
- Cultural differences in attribution ("Social Cognition")
- The roots of ethnic stereotyping and prejudice ("Social Cognition")
- Cultural factors and love ("Social Cognition")
- Cultural factors in social norms ("Social Influence")
- Culture and conformity ("Social Influence")
- Culture and social loafing ("Social Influence")
- Cultural factors in aggression ("Social Influence")

We also have updated our coverage of behavioral genetics and evolutionary psychology beginning in the chapters on introducing psychology and research in psychology and in a revised behavioral genetics appendix. They are also explored wherever appropriate—for example, when we discuss

- Gene manipulation research on the causes of Alzheimer's disease ("Biological Aspects of Psychology")
- Biopreparedness for learning ("Learning")
- Genetic components of intelligence ("Cognitive Abilities")
- Genetic components of sexual orientation ("Motivation and Emotion")
- Evolutionary explanations of mate selection ("Motivation and Emotion")
- Innate expressions of emotion ("Motivation and Emotion")
- The genetics of prenatal development ("Human Development")
- The heritability of personality ("Personality")
- Genetic factors in psychological disorders ("Psychological Disorders")
- Evolutionary/genetic explanations for aggression, helping, and altruism ("Social Influence")

Chapter Organization

As always, we have refrained from grouping the book's eighteen chapters into more general sections. We designed each chapter to be a freestanding unit so that you may assign chapters in any order you wish. For example, many instructors prefer to teach the material on human development relatively late in the course, which is why it appears as Chapter 12 in the Sixth Edition. But that chapter can be comfortably assigned earlier in the course as well.

Special Features

Psychology contains a number of special features designed to promote efficient learning and students' mastery of the material. Most of the features from previous editions have been revised and enhanced in the Sixth; two features are entirely new to the Sixth Edition.

Linkages

In our experience, most students enter the introductory course thinking that psychology concerns itself mainly with personality, psychological testing, mental disorders, psychotherapy, and other aspects of clinical psychology. They have little or no idea of how broad and multifaceted psychology is. Many students are surprised, therefore, when we ask them to read about neuroanatomy, neural communication, the endocrine system, sensory and perceptual processes and principles, prenatal risk factors, and many other topics that they tend to associate with disciplines other than psychology.

We have found that students are better able to appreciate the scope of psychology when they see it not as a laundry list of separate topics but as an interrelated set of subfields, each of which contributes to and benefits from the work going on in all of the others. To help students see these relationships, we have built into the book an integrating tool called "Linkages." There are four elements in the Linkages program:

1. Beginning with the chapter on research in psychology, a Linkages diagram presents a set of questions that illustrate three of the ways in which material in the chapter is related to other chapters in the book. For example, the Linkages diagram in the chapter on biological aspects of psychology contains questions that show how biological psychology is related to human development ("How do our brains change over a lifetime?"), consciousness ("Does the brain shut down when we sleep?"), and treatment of psychological disorders ("How do drugs help people who suffer from schizophrenia?").

2. The Linkages diagrams are placed at the end of each chapter so that students will be more familiar with the material to which each linkage refers when they encounter this feature. To help students notice the Linkages diagrams and appreciate their purpose, we provide an explanatory caption with each.

3. The page numbers following each question in the Linkages diagram direct the student to pages that carry further discussion of that question. The relevant material is marked by a Linkages logo in the margin next to the discussion.

4. One of the questions in each chapter's Linkages diagram is treated more fully in a special section in the chapter titled, appropriately enough, Linkages.

The Linkages elements combine with the text narrative to highlight the network of relationships among psychology's subfields. This Linkages program is designed to help students see the "big picture" that is psychology—no matter how many chapters their instructor assigns or in what sequence.

Thinking Critically

We try throughout the book to describe research on psychological phenomena in a way that reveals the logic of the scientific enterprise, that identifies possible flaws in design or interpretation, and that leaves room for more questions and further research. In other words, we try to display critical thinking processes. The Thinking Critically sections in each chapter are designed to make these processes more explicit and accessible by providing a framework for analyzing evidence before drawing conclusions. The framework is built around five questions that the reader should find useful in analyzing not only studies in psychology but other forms of communication as well. These questions, first introduced when we discuss the importance of critical thinking in the chapter on research in psychology, are

1. What am I being asked to believe or accept?
2. What evidence is available to support the assertion?
3. Are there alternative ways of interpreting the evidence?
4. What additional evidence would help to evaluate the alternatives?
5. What conclusions are most reasonable?

All the Thinking Critically sections retained from the Fifth Edition have been extensively revised and updated.

Focus on Research Methods

This feature, appearing in the chapter on biological aspects of psychology through the chapter on social influence, examines the ways in which the research methods described in the chapter on research in psychology have been applied to help advance our understanding of some aspect of behavior and mental processes. To make this feature more accessible, it is organized around the following questions:

1. What was the researcher's question?
2. How did the researcher answer the question?
3. What did the researcher find?
4. What do the results mean?
5. What do we still need to know?

Examples of these Focus on Research Methods sections include the use of neuroimaging technology to locate areas of the brain involved in analogical thinking ("Cognition and Language"), the use of experiments to study attention ("Perception"), learned helplessness ("Learning"), the development of physical knowledge ("Human Development"), and self-esteem ("Social Cognition"). Other sections illustrate the use of quasi-experimental, survey, longitudinal, and laboratory analogue designs. All the Focus on Research Methods sections retained from the Fifth Edition were revised and updated and some new ones were added. A full list of topics appears on p. xiii.

An Emphasis on Active Learning

To help students become active learners, not just passive readers of the material in the Sixth Edition, we have added two features to each chapter that encourage students to become more deeply involved with that material. These "Try This" features include

- Dozens of new figure and photo captions that help students understand and remember a psychological principle or phenomenon by suggesting ways in which they can demonstrate it for themselves. In the chapter on memory, for example, a photo caption suggests that students show the photo to a friend and then ask the friend questions about it to illustrate the operation of constructive memory. These captions are all identified with a "Try This" symbol.

- Placement of "Try This" symbols in page margins at the many places throughout the book where active learning opportunities are encouraged in the narrative. At these points, we ask students to stop reading and try doing something to illustrate or highlight the psychological principle or phenomenon under discussion. For example, in the chapter on perception, we ask the student to focus attention on various targets as a way of appreciating the difference between overt and covert shifts in attention.

Behavioral Genetics Appendix

This feature is designed to amplify the coverage of behavioral genetics methodology that is introduced in the chapter on research in psychology. The revised appendix includes a discussion of the impact of the Human Genome Project. It also includes a section on the basic principles of genetics and heredity, a brief history of genetic research in psychology, a discussion of what it means to say that genes influence behavior, and an analysis of what behavioral genetics research can—and cannot—tell us about the origins of such human attributes as intelligence, personality, and mental disorders.

In Review Charts

In Review charts summarize information in a convenient tabular format. We have placed two or three In Review charts strategically in each chapter to help students synthesize and assimilate large chunks of information—for example, on drug effects, key elements of personality theories, and stress responses and mediators.

Key Terms

New to the Sixth Edition is the listing of key terms and their definitions in the margin where the terms are first used. As always, key terms and their definitions also appear in the glossary at the end of the book.

Teaching and Learning Support Package

Many useful materials have been developed to support *Psychology*. Designed to enhance the teaching and learning experience, they are well integrated with the text and include some of the latest technologies. Several components are new to this edition.

Instructor's Annotated Edition

To help instructors coordinate the many print, software, and video supplements available with the text, an Instructor's Annotated Edition shows which materials correlate to and support the content on every page of the student text. These materials include learning objectives, test questions, discussion and lecture ideas, handouts, active learning and critical thinking activities from the *Study Guide*, videodisc segments and stills, lecture starter videos, overhead transparencies and PowerPoint images, as well as three psychology readers.

Print Ancillaries

Accompanying this book are, among other ancillaries, a *Test Bank*, an *Instructor's Resource Manual*, and a *Study Guide*. Because the lead author and a number of colleagues who have worked with him over the years at the University of Illinois psychology department prepared these items, you will find an especially high level of coordination between the textbook and these supplements. All three are unified by a shared set of learning objectives, and all three have been revised and enhanced for the Sixth Edition.

Test Bank The *Test Bank*, by Ted Powers, David Spurlock, and Douglas A. Bernstein, contains more than 3,000 multiple-choice items plus three essay questions for each chapter of the text. Half the multiple-choice questions are new; in all others, the response alternatives have been scrambled. All multiple-choice items are keyed to pages in the textbook and to the learning objectives listed in the *Instructor's Resource Manual* and *Study Guide*. In addition, questions that ask students to apply their knowledge of the concepts are distinguished from those that require factual recall. More than 2,100 questions have already been class-tested with between 500 and 2,500 students and are accompanied by data indicating the question's discriminative power and level of difficulty, the percentage of students who chose each response, and the relationship between students' performance on a given item and their overall performance on the test in which the item appeared.

Instructor's Resource Manual The *Instructor's Resource Manual*, by Amanda Allman, Sandra Goss Lucas, and Douglas A. Bernstein, contains for each chapter a complete set of learning objectives, detailed chapter outlines, suggested readings, and numerous specific teaching aids—many of them new to the Sixth Edition—including ideas for discussion, class activities, focus on research sections, and the accompanying handouts. It also contains sections on pedagogical strategies such as how to implement active learning and critical thinking techniques and how to make full use of the Linkages and Focus on Research supplements. In addition, it contains material geared toward teachers of large introductory courses, including a section on classroom management and another on the administration of multisection courses.

Study Guide The *Study Guide*, by Kelly Bouas Henry, Linda Lebie, and Douglas A. Bernstein, employs numerous techniques that help students to learn. Each chapter contains a detailed outline, a key terms section that presents fresh examples and aids to remembering, plus a fill-in-the-blank test, learning objectives, a concepts and exercises section that shows students how to apply their knowledge of psychology to everyday issues and concerns, a critical thinking exercise, and personal learning activities. In addition, each chapter concludes with a two-part self-quiz consisting of forty multiple-choice questions. An answer key tells the student not only which response is correct but also why each of the other choices is wrong, and quiz analysis tables enable students to track patterns to their wrong answers, either by topic or by type of question—definition, comprehension, or application.

Succeed in College! *Succeed in College!* is a skills-building booklet containing selected chapters from Walter Pauk's best-selling study skills text *How to Study in College*. This booklet, which offers time-tested advice on notetaking,

Preface

test-taking, and other topics, as well as a section on careers in psychology by John P. Fiore, can be shrink-wrapped free of charge with new copies of the student text.

Introductory Psychology Readers *Psychology in Context: Voices and Perspectives*, Second Edition, by David N. Sattler and Virginia Shabatay, contains engaging first-person narratives and essays keyed to major psychological concepts. Coursewise Publishing offers two readers by Laura Freberg. *Perspectives: Introductory Psychology* comprises articles relating to key topics in introductory psychology courses, and *Stand! Introductory Psychology* contains articles that explore contending ideas and opinions relating to fundamental issues in introductory psychology courses.

Electronic and Video Ancillaries

In keeping with the technological needs of today's campus, we provide the following electronic and video supplements to *Psychology*:

For the Student

PsychStart CD-ROM This brand-new CD-ROM, which comes packaged with the textbook, contains study guide content to help students study for exams. This consists of The Big Picture (chapter summary), Chapter Walkthough (students answer different types of questions to build their own detailed chapter summary), What's That? (labeling exercises), Critical Thinking Questions, Practice Tests, and a glossary with pronunciation guide. The CD is intended especially for students whose reading skills and study habits are poor. It should also help ESL students, not only because of the pronunciation guide with the glossary but also because of the different activities that help students rehearse the content.

Student Web Site The student web site contains additional study aids, such as self-tests and flashcards, as well as activities that ask the student to evaluate materials that they find on the web. Additionally, multimedia tutorials are included on topics instructors have identified as the most difficult to teach and the most appropriate for multimedia treatment. These help students learn difficult concepts by experiencing activities in different media and by being asked to respond interactively. All web resources are keyed to the textbook and can be found at **psychology.college.hmco.com/students**.

For the Instructor

Online Quizzes Powered by eduSpace Instructors can assign these quizzes, with multiple-choice, true/false, and fill-in questions, and track student's results in the gradebook.

HMClassPrep CD-ROM with Computerized Test Bank This instructor CD-ROM collects in one place materials that instructors might want to have available electronically. It contains PowerPoint lecture outlines and art from the textbook, as well as electronic versions of much of the IRM and SG materials to make it easy to incorporate into a web site or lecture/activity. It also makes the Test Bank questions available in the HMTesting 6.0 package, a new version of our testing software that offers complete delivery over the Internet; a new, easy-to-use interface; complete cross-platform flexibility; and well as other new features to make the product flexible and easy to use.

Instructor's Web Site Much of the material from the HMClassPrep CD-ROM is also available on the web at **psychology.college.hmco.com/instructors**, as well as information on how to integrate the students' technology package into the course.

Course Cartridges for WebCT and Blackboard Ask your Houghton Mifflin representative for details about these course management cartridges. You can utilize many of the instructor resources available with this edition including chapter outlines, PowerPoint slides, and handouts. Additionally, you can access a wealth of testing material specifically developed for this edition including multiple-choice quizzes, NetLabs, Critical Thinking exercises, and Evaluating Research web exercises.

Lecture Starter Video and Guide The Lecture Starter Video contains a series of high-interest, concise segments that instructors can use to begin a class meeting or change to a new topic. The accompanying guide briefly describes each segment, indicates concepts that can be addressed using each segment, and offers suggestions on how to use each segment.

Lecture Starter CD-ROM An additional set of video clips is available on CD-ROM.

The Psychology Show Houghton Mifflin's video supplement for introductory psychology is available in both videodisc and videotape formats to qualified adopters. Containing nineteen motion segments plus nearly 100 still images, The Psychology Show is designed to expand on text coverage and to stimulate class discussion through the length of the course. An accompanying instructor's guide offers information on each motion segment and still image and provides bar codes for videodisc use.

Transparencies The accompanying transparency set contains more than 150 full-color images from both the text and sources outside the text.

Online Teaching Tools Useful and practical information on online teaching tools can be found on the Bernstein 6/e web site, including a link to *Research Online: A Practical*

Guide. Houghton Mifflin also offers a useful print resource *Teaching Online: A Practical Guide* (0-618-00042-9).

Other Multimedia Offerings A range of videos, CD-ROMs, and other multimedia materials relevant to psychology are available free to qualified adopters. Houghton Mifflin sales representatives have further details.

Acknowledgments

Many people provided us with the help, criticism, and encouragement we needed to create the Sixth Edition.

Once again we must thank Katie Steele, who got the project off the ground in 1983 by encouraging us to stop talking about this book and start writing it.

We are indebted to a number of our colleagues for their expert help and advice on the revisions of a number of chapters for the Sixth Edition. These colleagues include, for Chapter 5, Melody Carswell, University of Kentucky; for Chapter 6, J. Bruce Overmier, University of Minnesota; for Chapter 7, Kathleen McDermott, Washington University; for Chapter 8, Paul Whitney, Washington State University; for Chapter 10, Deborah Beidel, University of Maryland; for Chapter 11, Steve Brown, Rockhurst University; for Chapter 13, Catherine Stoney, The Ohio State University; for Chapter 15, Ronald Kleinknecht, Western Washington University; for Chapter 16, Robert DeRubeis, University of Pennsylvania; and for the behavioral genetics appendix, Robert Plomin, University of London.

We also owe an enormous debt to the colleagues who provided prerevision evaluations of, or reviewed the manuscript for, the Sixth Edition as it was being developed: David R. Barkmeier, Northeastern University; Mitchell Berman, University of Southern Mississippi; Evelyn W. Chisholm, Spelman College; Douglas L. Chute, Drexel University; Lawrence D. Cohn, University of Texas at El Paso; Teresa K. Elliott, American University; Keegan D. Greenier, Mercer University; Barry Haimson, University of Massachusetts, Dartmouth; Rona McCall, Regis University; Ann Merriwether, University of Michigan; Michelle Merwin, University of Tennessee at Martin; and Kathleen A. Flannery, Saint Anselm College. Their advice and suggestions for improvement were responsible for many of the good qualities you will find in the book. If you have any criticisms, they probably involve areas these people warned us about. We especially want to thank these friends and colleagues for their help: Sandra Goss Lucas, University of Illinois at Urbana-Champaign; Elizabeth Loftus, University of Washington, and Scott Tindale, Loyola University, Chicago.

The process of creating the Sixth Edition was greatly facilitated by the work of many dedicated people in the College Division at Houghton Mifflin Company. From the sales representatives and sales managers who told us of faculty members' suggestions for improvement, to the marketing staff who developed innovative ways of telling our colleagues about the changes we have made, it seems that everyone in the division had a hand in shaping and improving the Sixth Edition. Several people deserve special thanks, however. Former senior associate editor Jane Knetzger, senior sponsoring editor Kerry Baruth, and former editor-in-chief Kathi Prancan gave us invaluable advice about structural, pedagogical, and content changes for the new edition. Jennifer Wall, our developmental editor, applied her editorial expertise and disciplined approach to helping us create this manuscript. Aileen Mason, senior project editor, contributed her considerable organizational skills and a dedication to excellence that was matched by a wonderfully helpful and cooperative demeanor. We also wish to thank Jessyca Broekman for her stellar work in the creation and updating of the art program for the Sixth Edition, and Naomi Kornhauser for her creativity in developing new photo ideas and for her diligence in selecting and locating them. A big thank-you goes to Mary Berry for her outstanding job of copyediting the manuscript. Thanks also to Debbie Prato, who checked page proof to ensure its typographical accuracy. Without these people, and those who worked with them, this revision simply could not have happened. Finally, we want to express our deepest appreciation to our families and friends. Once again, their love saw us through an exhilarating but demanding period of our lives. They endured our hours at the computer, missed meals, postponed vacations, and occasional irritability during the creation of the First Edition of this book, and they had to suffer all over again during the lengthy process of revising it once more. Their faith in us is more important than they realize, and we will cherish it forever.

D.A.B.

L.A.P.

A.C.-S.

E.J.R.

The authors of this comprehensive, research-oriented text have rededicated themselves to exploring "the full range of psychology from cell to society, as free as possible from theoretical bias." The Sixth Edition emphasizes updates and improvements in applied psychology—such as new findings in organizational and forensic psychology; culture and human diversity; and behavioral genetics and evolutionary psychology.

Written in a lively, contemporary style, *Psychology* offers a skillful balance of classic and contemporary topics. The extensive supplement package has been improved, to provide complete learning and teaching solutions for instructors, students, and teaching assistants.

▶ **New!** An improved technology package includes a student CD free with all new books; psychology quizzes powered by eduSpace; all-new, extensive PowerPoint slides available on an instructor CD or on the web; plus more depth and variety of student and instructor materials on the web site.

▶ **New!** The art program has undergone a thorough revision, making illustrations clearer, more effective teaching tools and creating a contemporary, stimulating learning environment.

▶ **New!** *Try This* icons appear in the margin to encourage active learning in the following ways: figure and photo captions which enable students to demonstrate psychological principles for themselves, and marginal symbols alert students to stop reading and engage in an activity that illustrates the principle or phenomenon under discussion.

▶ **New!** A Margin Glossary defines key terms in the margin of the page to reinforce key concepts without interrupting the flow of reading or the text.

▶ **New!** The subject index and glossary have been combined to make information easier to locate.

> "Bernstein et al. is a comprehensive overview of the field of psychology. The research discussed is current, and the text is far more accurate than many other books on the market. A strong emphasis on the critical evaluation of research is a central theme, and is presented so the subtleties of psychological research are accessible to the average student."
> —Mitchell Berman, University of Southern Mississippi

Thinking Critically

Do your students understand the need for and process of critical thinking?

These dedicated sections in every chapter model the critical-thinking process and encourage students to analyze research studies before drawing conclusions.

The same five questions are repeated in every feature, reinforcing the process:

1. What am I being asked to believe or accept?
2. Is there evidence available to support the claim?
3. Can that evidence be interpreted another way?
4. What evidence would help to evaluate the alternatives?
5. What conclusions are most reasonable?

---

figure 7.17
Retrieval Failures and Forgetting
In Tulving and Psotka's experiment, people's ability to recall a list of items was strongly affected by the number of other lists they learned before being tested on the first one. When item-category (retrieval) cues were provided on a second test, however, retroactive interference from the intervening lists almost disappeared.

Source: Tulving & Psotka (1971).

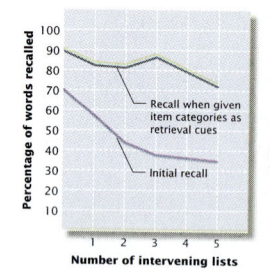

was due to a failure in retrieval. So putting more and more information in long-term memory may be like putting more and more CDs into a storage case. None of the CDs disappears, but it becomes increasingly difficult to find the specific one you are looking for.

Some theorists have concluded that all forgetting from long-term memory is due to some form of retrieval failure (Ratcliff & McKoon, 1989). Does this mean that everything in long-term memory remains there until death, even if you cannot always, or ever, recall it? No one knows for sure, but as described in the next section, this question lies at the heart of some highly controversial court cases.

LINKAGES (a link to Consciousness)

THINKING CRITICALLY

Can Traumatic Memories Be Repressed, Then Recovered?

In 1989, Eileen Franklin-Lipsker told police in California that when she looked into her young daughter's eyes one day, she suddenly remembered seeing her father kill her childhood friend more than twenty years earlier. Her father, George Franklin, Sr., was sent to prison for murder on the basis of her testimony about that memory (Loftus & Ketcham, 1994). This case sparked a debate that has continued to grow in intensity and involves not only psychologists but the North American legal system as well. The controversy concerns the validity of claims of recovered memory. Some psychologists accept the idea that it is possible for people to *repress*, or push into unconsciousness, memories of traumatic incidents and then recover these memories many years later. Other psychologists are skeptical about recovered memory claims.

What am I being asked to believe or accept?

The prosecution in the Franklin case successfully argued that Eileen had repressed, and then recovered, her memory of a murder. Similar arguments in a number of other cases tried in the early 1990s resulted in the imprisonment of other parents whose now-adult children claimed to have recovered childhood memories of being physically or sexually abused by them. The juries in these trials accepted the assertion that all memory of shocking events can be repressed, or pushed into an inaccessible corner of the mind where for decades, subconscious processes keep it out of awareness, yet potentially subject to accurate recollection (Hyman, 2000). Jurors are not the only believers in this phenomenon. A few years ago a large American news organization reported that the United States had illegally used nerve gas during the war in Vietnam. The story was based, in part, on a Vietnam

---

"I enjoyed these features very much and feel that students who read them will gain an excellent perspective on critically evaluating research. Ultimately, the experience that students gain from these segments may make them better consumers of scientific information in general."

—Dr. Barry Hamison, University of Massachusetts–Dartmouth

Focus on Research Methods

How can you help students analyze evidence before drawing conclusions?

In these sections, focused attention on a particular study helps students understand the value of empirical research, the creativity with which it is conducted, and how it furthers understanding of behavior and mental processes.

Five focus questions consistently ask students to make connections between research questions and results:

1. What was the researcher's question?
2. How did the researcher answer the question?
3. What did the researcher find?
4. What do the results mean?
5. What do we still need to know?

---

in review: Body Senses

Sense	Energy	Conversion of Physical Energy to Nerve Activity	Pathways and Characteristics
Touch	Mechanical deformation of skin	Skin receptors (may be stimulated by hair on the skin)	Nerve endings respond to changes in weight (intensity) and location of touch.
Temperature	Heat	Sensory neurons in the skin	Changes in temperature are detected by warm-sensing and cool-sensing fibers. Temperature interacts with touch.
Pain	Increases with intensity of touch or temperature	Free nerve endings in or near the skin surface	Changes in intensity cause the release of chemicals detected by receptors in pain neurons. Some fibers convey sharp pain; others convey dull aches and burning sensations.
Kinesthesia	Mechanical energy of joint and muscle movement	Receptors in muscle fibers	Information from muscle fibers is sent to the spinal cord, thalamus, cerebellum, and cortex.

changes, receptors in the joints transduce this mechanical energy into neural activity, providing information about both the rate of change and the angle of the bones. This coded information goes to the spinal cord and is sent from there to the thalamus, along with sensory information from the skin. Eventually the information goes to the cerebellum and to the somatosensory cortex (see Figures 3.13 and 3.16), both of which are involved in the smooth coordination of movements

Proprioception is a critical sense for success in physical therapy and rehabilitative medicine, especially for people who have to relearn how to move their muscles after strokes or other problems. Research in a branch of physics called *nonlinear dynamics* has been applied to problems in proprioception. Utilizing the discovery that the right amount of random, background noise can actually improve the detection of signals, rehabilitation neurologists have found that adding a small amount of vibration (or "noise") to muscle and joint sensations dramatically increases patients' ability to detect joint movements and position (Glanz, 1997). (See "In Review: Body Senses" for a summary of our discussion of touch, temperature, pain, and kinesthesia.)

FOCUS ON RESEARCH METHODS

The Case of the Disembodied Woman

Early in this chapter we discussed the problem of coding sensation—of translating the physical properties of some stimulus into neural signals that make sense to the brain. In later sections we described how this problem is "solved" for the different senses. But what happens when the brain does not receive the sensory information it needs? The most common examples of this situation are deafness and blindness, but in the case study described next, a person suffered the loss of a proprioceptive sense.

● **What was the researcher's question?**

Oliver Sacks, a well-known clinical neurologist, has spent years treating people with "neurological deficits"—that is, impairments or incapacities of neurological functions. One of his most memorable cases was that of "Christina," who had apparently lost the sense of kinesthesia and, thus, was unable to feel the position of her own body.

In 1977, Christina was a healthy young woman who entered a hospital in preparation for some minor surgery. The night before her operation, she dreamt that she was unsteady on her feet, "could hardly feel anything in her hands . . . and kept dropping whatever she picked up" (Sacks, 1985, p. 43). Her dream soon became a horrible reality. The next day, Christina tried to get out of bed but flopped onto the floor like a rag doll. She was unable to hold onto objects and had trouble moving. She felt "weird—disembodied." A psychiatrist diagnosed Christina's problem as *conversion disorder*, a psychological condition described in the chapter on psychological disorders as involving apparent, but not actual, damage to sensory or motor systems. Sacks, however, wondered if there might be another reason for Christina's strange symptoms.

● **How did the researcher answer the question?**

Sacks tested Christina's nerve and muscle functions, performed a spinal tap to examine the fibers that carry sensory information to the brain, and studied the portion of her brain that receives proprioceptive information. His approach exemplifies the *case study* method of research. As noted in the chapter on research in psychology, case studies focus intensively on a particular individual, group, or situation. Sometimes they lead to important insights about clinical problems or other phenomena that occur so rarely that they cannot be studied through surveys or controlled experiments.

● **What did the researcher find?**

Sacks's examination of Christina ruled out a psychological disorder. His tests of her nerves and muscles disclosed that the signals they normally sent to tell her brain about the location of her body parts were simply not being transmitted. The spinal tap revealed why: The sensory neurons that carry proprioceptive information had, for unknown reasons, degenerated. As a result, Christina seemed to have become disconnected from her body. On one occasion, for example, she became annoyed at a visitor who she thought was tapping her fingers on a table top. But it was Christina, not the visitor, who was doing it. Her hands were acting on their own; her body was doing things she did not know about.

● **What do the results mean?**

In his analysis of this case, Sacks noted that the sense we have of our bodies is provided partly through our experience of seeing it, but also partly through proprioception. Christina put it this way: "Proprioception is like the eyes of the body, the way the body sees itself. And if it goes, it's like the body's blind." With great effort and determination, Christina was ultimately able to regain some of her ability to move about. If she looked intently at her arms and legs, she could coordinate their movement to some degree. Eventually, she left the hospital and resumed many of her normal activities. But Christina never recovered her sense of self. She still feels like a stranger in her own body.

● **What do we still need to know?**

The story of Christina and the other fascinating case studies in Sacks's popular

---

"The fact that Psychology is well organized with key points clearly identified seems to help students grasp the relevant conceptual framework, and also feel more relaxed and ready to explore more challenging concepts. Within this framework, interesting examples and research points are well paced to keep the student engaged and thinking creatively."

—Teresa K. Elliott, American University

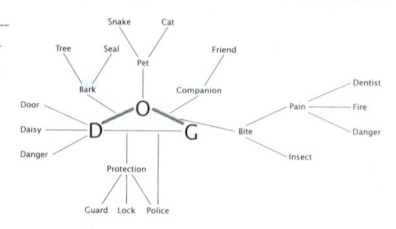

Linkages

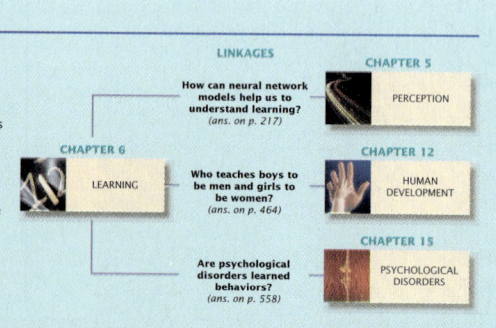

How well do your students grasp the scope of psychology and the network of relationships among the subfields?

▶ Linkages features help students understand psychology as a whole, linking the content in each chapter and showing how the subfields contribute to and benefit from one another.

▶ Wherever a linkage is discussed in the text, a marginal callout directs students to further discussion.

▶ Every chapter explores one linkage in depth.

▶ Within the active review, a diagram plots out the relationship among the linkages in that chapter.

"These linkages increase and reinforce the content presented in a different format. [Because] we emphasize interdisciplinarity and attempt to illustrate the interconnectedness of psychology, these sections provide me an opportunity to have students look beyond the topics immediately being considered."

—Evelyn W. Chisolm, Spelman College

Introducing Psychology

1

The World of Psychology: An Overview
Subfields of Psychology
Linkages Within Psychology and Beyond
Research: The Foundation of Psychology
A Brief History of Psychology
Unity and Diversity in Psychology
Approaches to Psychology
Human Diversity and Psychology
Summary

See if you can figure out what the following people have in common:

- Kristen Beyer works for the Federal Bureau of Investigation, where she develops questionnaires and conducts interviews aimed at identifying common features in the backgrounds of serial killers.
- David Buss, a professor at the University of Texas, conducts research and teaches courses on how evolution influences aggression, the choice of sexual partners, and other aspects of people's social behavior.
- Anne Marie Apanovitch is employed by a major drug company to study which of the company's marketing strategies are most effective in promoting sales.
- Michael Moon's job at a software company is to find new ways to make Internet web sites more informative and easier for consumers to use.
- Marissa Reddy, co-director of the U.S. Secret Service's Safe Schools initiative, tries to prevent school shootings by identifying risk factors for violent behavior in high school students.
- Sharon Lundgren, founder of Lundgren Trial Consulting, Inc., helps prepare witnesses to testify in court, conducts mock trials in which attorneys rehearse their questioning strategies, and teaches attorneys how to present themselves and their evidence in the most convincing way.
- Evan Byrne works at the National Transportation Safety Board, where he investigates the role of memory lapses, disorientation, errors in using equipment, and other human factors in causing airplane crashes.
- Karen Orts, a captain in the U.S. Air Force, is chief of mental health services at an air base, where among other things, she provides psychotherapy to military personnel suffering combat-related stress disorders and teaches leadership courses to commissioned and noncommissioned officers.

Because Captain Orts offers psychotherapy, you probably guessed that she is a psychologist, but the fact is that *all* these people are psychologists! They may not all fit your image of what psychologists do, but as you will see in this chapter, and throughout this book, psychology is much broader and more diverse than you might have expected.

There are many different kinds of psychologists, doing all sorts of interesting work in one or more of psychology's many *subfields*. Most of these people took their first psychology course without realizing how many of these subfields there are or how many different kinds of jobs are open to psychologists. But like the people we described here, they found something in psychology—perhaps something unexpected—that captured their interest, and they were hooked. And who knows? By the time you have finished this book and this course, you may have found some aspect of psychology so fascinating that you will want to make it your life's work, too. Or not. At the very least, we hope you enjoy learning about psychology, about the work of psychologists, and about how that work benefits people everywhere.

In this chapter, we offer an overview of psychology and its subfields, and how these subfields are linked to one another and to other disciplines. We then tell the story of how psychology came to be and the various ways in which psychologists approach their work.

The World of Psychology: An Overview

Psychology is the science that seeks to understand behavior and mental processes, and to apply that understanding in the service of human welfare. It is a science that covers a lot of territory, as illustrated by the vastly different jobs that occupy the

TRY THIS

eight psychologists we described. They are all psychologists, because they are all involved in studying, predicting, improving, or explaining some aspect of behavior and mental processes (Conner, 2001a).

To begin to appreciate all that can fall within the realm of *behavior and mental processes*, take a moment to jot down an answer to this question: Who are you?

Now review your answer. Perhaps you described your personality or your 20/20 vision, your interests or your aspirations, your skills or your accomplishments, your IQ or your cultural background. You could have listed these and dozens of other things about yourself, and every one of them would reflect some aspect of what psychologists mean by behavior and mental processes. It is no wonder, then, that this book's table of contents includes so many different topics, including some—such as vision and hearing—that you might not have expected to see in a book about psychology. The topics have to be diverse in order to capture the full range of behaviors and mental processes that make you who you are and that come together in other ways in people of every culture around the world.

Subfields of Psychology

Let's see what psychologists working in different subfields would emphasize about you.

Biological Psychology

From a biological point of view, you are a collection of cells that form your bones and muscles, your skin and hair, your liver and brain. Your heart beats and your lungs breathe because of activity in these cells, and because the cells are able to communicate with one another. **Biological psychologists,** also called *physiological psychologists,* use high-tech scanning devices and other methods to study how biological processes in the brain and other organs affect, and are affected by, behavior and mental processes (see Figure 1.1). Biological psychologists have found, for example, that when mental patients "hear voices" or "see things" that are not really there, activity appears in regions of the brain that help process information about real sounds and sights (Silbersweig et al., 1995). In the chapter on biological aspects of psychology, you can read more about biological psychologists' research on the processes that allow you to maintain blood pressure, move, speak, cope with stress, fight disease, and perform many other vital functions.

figure 1.1

Visualizing Brain Activity

Magnetic resonance imaging (MRI) techniques allow biological psychologists to study the brain activity accompanying various mental processes. This study found that males (left) and females (right) show different patterns of brain activity (indicated by the brightly colored areas) while reading (Shaywitz et al., 1995).

psychology The science of behavior and mental processes.

biological psychologists Psychologists who analyze the biological factors influencing behavior and mental processes.

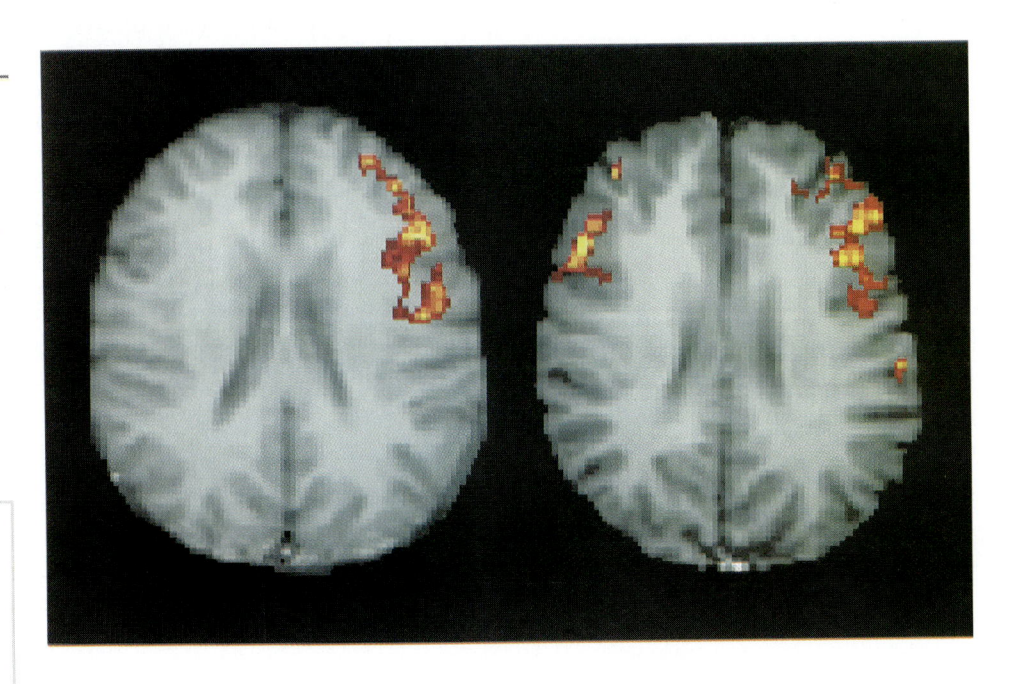

figure 1.2
Where Would You Put a Third Eye?
In a study of how thinking processes develop, children were asked to show where they would place a third eye, if they could have one. Nine-year-old children, who were still in an early stage of mental development, drew the extra eye between their existing eyes, "as a spare." Having developed more advanced thinking abilities, eleven-year-olds drew the third eye in more creative places, such as the palm of their hand "so I can see around corners" (Shaffer, 1973).

Source: Shaffer (1973). Box 4-2.

Drawing by a nine-year-old   Drawing by an eleven-year-old

---

developmental psychologists Psychologists who seek to understand, describe, and explore how behavior and mental processes change over the course of a lifetime.

cognitive psychologists Psychologists who study the mental processes underlying judgment, decision making, problem solving, imagining, and other aspects of human thought or cognition.

engineering psychology A field in which psychologists study human factors in the use of equipment and help designers create better versions of that equipment.

personality psychologists Psychologists who study the characteristics that make individuals similar to, or different from, one another.

clinical and counseling psychologists Psychologists who seek to assess, understand, and change abnormal behavior.

community psychologists Psychologists who work to obtain psychological services for people in need of help and to prevent psychological disorders by changing in social systems.

Developmental Psychology
Your cells' ability to divide and take on specific functions allowed you to blossom from the single fertilized cell you once were into the complex human being you are now. **Developmental psychologists** describe these changes, from birth through old age, and try to understand their causes and effects (see Figure 1.2). Their research on the development of memory and other mental abilities, for example, is used by judges and attorneys in deciding how old a child has to be in order to serve as a reliable witness in court, or to responsibly choose which divorcing parent to live with. The chapter on human development describes more research by developmental psychologists and how it is applied in areas such as parenting, evaluating day care, and preserving mental capacity in elderly people.

Cognitive Psychology
Stop reading for a moment, and look left and right. Your ability to follow this suggestion, to recognize whatever you saw, and to understand the words you are reading right now are the result of mental, or *cognitive,* abilities that allow you to receive information from the outside world, understand it, and act on it. **Cognitive psychologists** (some of whom prefer to be called **experimental psychologists**) focus on these and other mental abilities, including sensation and perception, learning and memory, thinking, consciousness, intelligence, and creativity. Cognitive psychologists have found, for example, that we don't just passively receive incoming information—we mentally manipulate it. Thus, although the drawing in Figure 1.3 does not physically change, two different versions emerge, depending on which of its features *you* emphasize.

Applications of cognitive psychologists' research are all around you. For instance, research by those whose special interest is **engineering psychology**—also known as *human factors*—has helped designers create computer keyboards, Internet web sites, aircraft instrument panels, nuclear power plant controls, and even on-screen VCR programming systems that are logical, easy to use, and less likely to cause errors (Mumford, 2000; Segal & Suri, 1999). The need for human factors consultants on the design of medical equipment was underscored in September 1999, in the neonatal intensive care unit of a hospital in Bournemouth, England. A nurse intended to shut off the alarm on a pump delivering a painkiller to a three-day-old baby, but accidentally pressed a nearby button that increased the drug flow. The infant died twelve hours later (Rayner, 2000). Many chapters of this book deal with human factors and many other interesting aspects of cognitive psychology.

Personality Psychology

Although you may be like other people in some ways, you are in other ways different from everyone else on earth. **Personality psychologists** study these similarities and differences, often using tests and interviews to create profiles that describe how one individual compares with others in terms of characteristics such as openness to experience, emotionality, reliability, agreeableness, and sociability. Some personality psychologists apply their research by examining these profiles for what they might teach us about identifying people who are most likely to develop mental or physical health problems in the face of stress, or who are at greatest risk for becoming violent or abusing drugs. Others use personality assessment tools to better understand the characteristics of people who are prejudiced against others, who tend to be pessimistic or depressed, or even who claim to have been abducted by space aliens. And as part of a recent focus on *positive psychology* (Seligman & Csikszentmihalyi, 2000), personality psychologists have also become involved in identifying the characteristics of people who maintain optimism, even in the face of stress or tragedy, and have achieved happiness in life (Lykken, 1999). You can read more about personality psychology and its applications in the chapter on personality.

Clinical, Counseling, Community, and Health Psychology

Part of your uniqueness as an individual includes the stresses you face and the problems that you might have, whether they be insomnia, academic difficulties, trouble with overeating or smoking, a lack of confidence, or maybe a tendency toward depression or anxiety. **Clinical psychologists** and **counseling psychologists** conduct research on the causes of various kinds of behavior disorders and offer services to help troubled people overcome those disorders. They have found, for example, that many irrational fears, called *phobias*, are learned through the bad experiences people have with dogs, public speaking, or whatever, and that fearful people can literally be taught to overcome their fears (Robbins, 2000). Other clinicians have worked at summarizing research on treatment methods to help therapists choose those methods that have been shown most effective with particular kinds of disorders (DeRubeis & Crits-Christoph, 1998).

Community psychologists work to ensure that psychological services reach the homeless and others who need help but tend not to seek it. They also try to *prevent* psychological disorders by working for changes in schools and other social systems

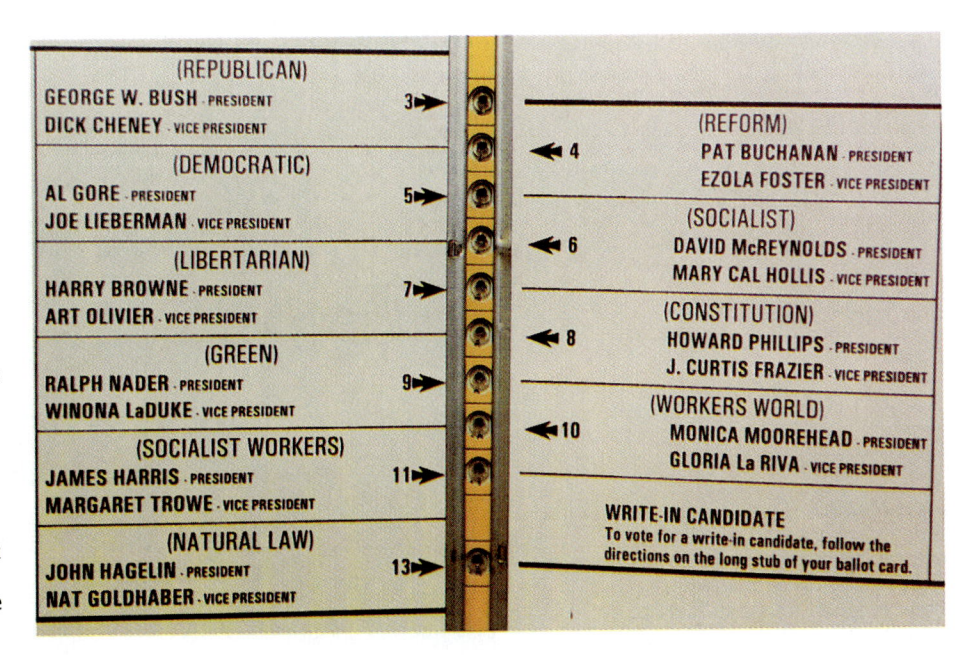

figure 1.3

Husband and Father-in-Law
TRY THIS — This figure is labeled "husband and father-in-law" (Botwinick, 1961) because you can see an old man or a young man, depending upon how you mentally organize its features. The elderly father-in-law faces to your right, and he is turned slightly toward you. He has a large nose, and the dark areas represent his coat pulled up to his protruding chin. However, the tip of his nose can also be seen as the tip of a younger man's chin; the younger man is in profile, also looking to your right, but away from you. The old man's mouth is the young man's neck band. Both men are wearing a broad-brimmed hat.

A Bad Design Consultation by human factors psychologists would probably have resulted in changes in the design of the "butterfly" ballot used in Palm Beach County, Florida, and elsewhere, during the U.S. presidential election in November 2000. The candidates' names appeared in two columns to allow for a more readable type size, but many voters said this layout was so confusing that they may have accidentally voted for the wrong candidate (Baron, Roediger, & Anderson, 2000).

in hopes of reducing the poverty and other stresses of life that so often lead to disorders. **Health psychologists** study the effects of behavior on health, as well as the effects that illness has on people's behavior and emotions. Their research is applied, for example, in programs that help people reduce the risk of heart disease and stroke by giving up smoking, eating a low-fat diet, and exercising more. You can read more about the work of clinical, counseling, community, and health psychologists in the chapters on health, stress, and coping; psychological disorders; and treatment of psychological disorders.

Social Psychology

Although you are an individual, you live in a social world. **Social psychologists** study several aspects of this world, focusing especially on how we think about, relate to, influence, and are influenced by other people. They have found, for example, that though we may pride ourselves on not being prejudiced, we may actually hold unconscious beliefs about certain ethnic groups that negatively affect the way we relate to people from those groups (Abreu, 1999; Chen & Bargh, 1997). Social psychologists also study persuasion; their research has been applied by advertisers, not only to make television commercials more effective (Kardes, 1999) but also to increase the impact of campaigns to keep young people away from smoking, drugs, and unsafe sex. The chapters on social cognition and social influence describe these and many other examples of research in social psychology.

Other Subfields

Psychologists in still other subfields might think of you in the many social roles you play—perhaps as an employee, a student, an athlete, the occupant of a residence hall or apartment building, or even as a defendant in a lawsuit. In the workplace, for example, **industrial/organizational psychologists** blend research on cooperation, competition, and other aspects of social psychology with studies of motivation, job stress, leadership, and other topics of interest to employers and employees. They explore the ways in which businesses and industrial organizations work—or fail to work—and they make recommendations for improving the efficiency, productivity, and satisfaction of workers, teams, and the organizations that employ them (Krumm, 2001). If you have ever taken a test of skill in order to get a new job, it may have been because an industrial/organizational psychologist recommended it to the company as a way of choosing employees who are most likely to succeed at that job.

In school systems, **educational psychologists** conduct research and develop theories about teaching and learning. The results of their work are applied to improving

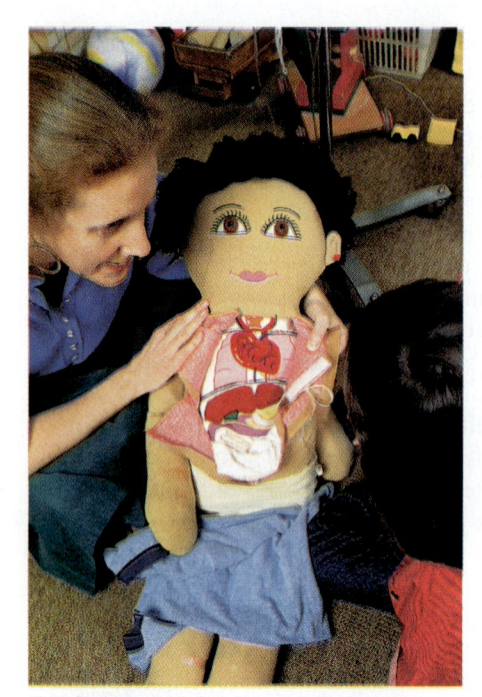

Getting Ready for Surgery Health psychologists have learned that when patients are mentally prepared for a surgical procedure, they are less stressed by it and recover more rapidly. Their research is now routinely applied in hospitals through programs in which children and adults are given more information about what to expect before, during, and after their operations.

Essay Q 1.1

Got a Match? Some commercial dating services apply social psychologists' research on interpersonal attraction in an effort to pair up people whose characteristics are most likely to be compatible.

Working Underground Before putting its new data-processing center in the basement of a new office building, one large corporation asked an environmental psychologist how employees' performance and morale would be affected by working in a windowless space like this. The psychologist described the possible negative effects and, to combat those effects, recommended the creation of shafts that let in natural light, as well as the installation of plants and artwork depicting nature's beauty (Sommer, 1999).

health psychologists Psychologists who study the effects of behavior and mental processes on health and illness, and vice versa.

social psychologists Psychologists who study how people influence one another's behavior and attitudes, individually and in groups.

industrial/organizational psychologists Psychologists who study ways to improve efficiency, productivity, and satisfaction among workers and the organizations that employ them.

educational psychologists Psychologists who study methods by which instructors teach and students learn, and who apply their results to improving such methods.

school psychologists Psychologists who test IQs, diagnose students' academic problems, and set up programs to improve students' achievement.

sport psychologists Psychologists who explore the relationships between athletic performance and such psychological variables as motivation and emotion.

forensic psychologists Psychologists who create criminal profiles, assist in jury selection, evaluate defendants' mental competence to stand trial, and deal with other issues involving psychology and the law.

environmental psychologists Psychologists who study the effects of the physical environment on behavior and mental processes.

teacher training and to helping students learn more efficiently (Hoy, 1999). For example, they have supported the use of the "jigsaw" technique, a type of classroom activity in which children from various ethnic groups must work cooperatively to complete a task or solve a problem. Research indicates that these cooperative experiences not only promote learning but also generate mutual respect and minimize prejudicial attitudes (Aronson, Wilson, & Akert, 2002). **School psychologists** traditionally specialized in IQ testing, diagnosing learning disabilities and other academic problems, and setting up programs to improve students' achievement and satisfaction in school. Today, however, they are also involved in early detection of students' mental health problems, in crisis intervention following school violence, and the like (DeAngelis, 2000).

In the competitive arena, **sport psychologists** use visualization and relaxation training programs, for example, to help athletes reduce excessive anxiety, focus attention, and make other changes that let them perform at their best (Roberts & Treasure, 1999). In the legal system, **forensic psychologists** create criminal profiles, assist in jury selection, evaluate defendants' mental competence to stand trial, and deal with other issues involving psychology and the law (Otto & Heilbrun, 2002). Finally, **environmental psychologists** study the effects of environmental characteristics on people's behavior and mental processes. The results of their research help architects and interior designers plan or remodel residence halls, shopping malls, auditoriums, hospitals, prisons, offices, and other spaces to make them more comfortable and functional for the people who will occupy them (Sommer, 1999). Our list of psychology's subfields is long, but it is not complete. You can read about more of them in books such as *Psychology: Fields of Application* (Stec & Bernstein, 1999).

Where do the psychologists in all these subfields work? Table 1.1 contains the latest figures on where the approximately 160,000 psychologists in the United States find employment, as well as the kinds of things they typically do in each setting.

Linkages Within Psychology and Beyond

We have listed psychology's subfields as though they were separate, but they often overlap, as do the activities of the psychologists working in them. When developmental psychologists study the growth of children's thinking skills or friendships,

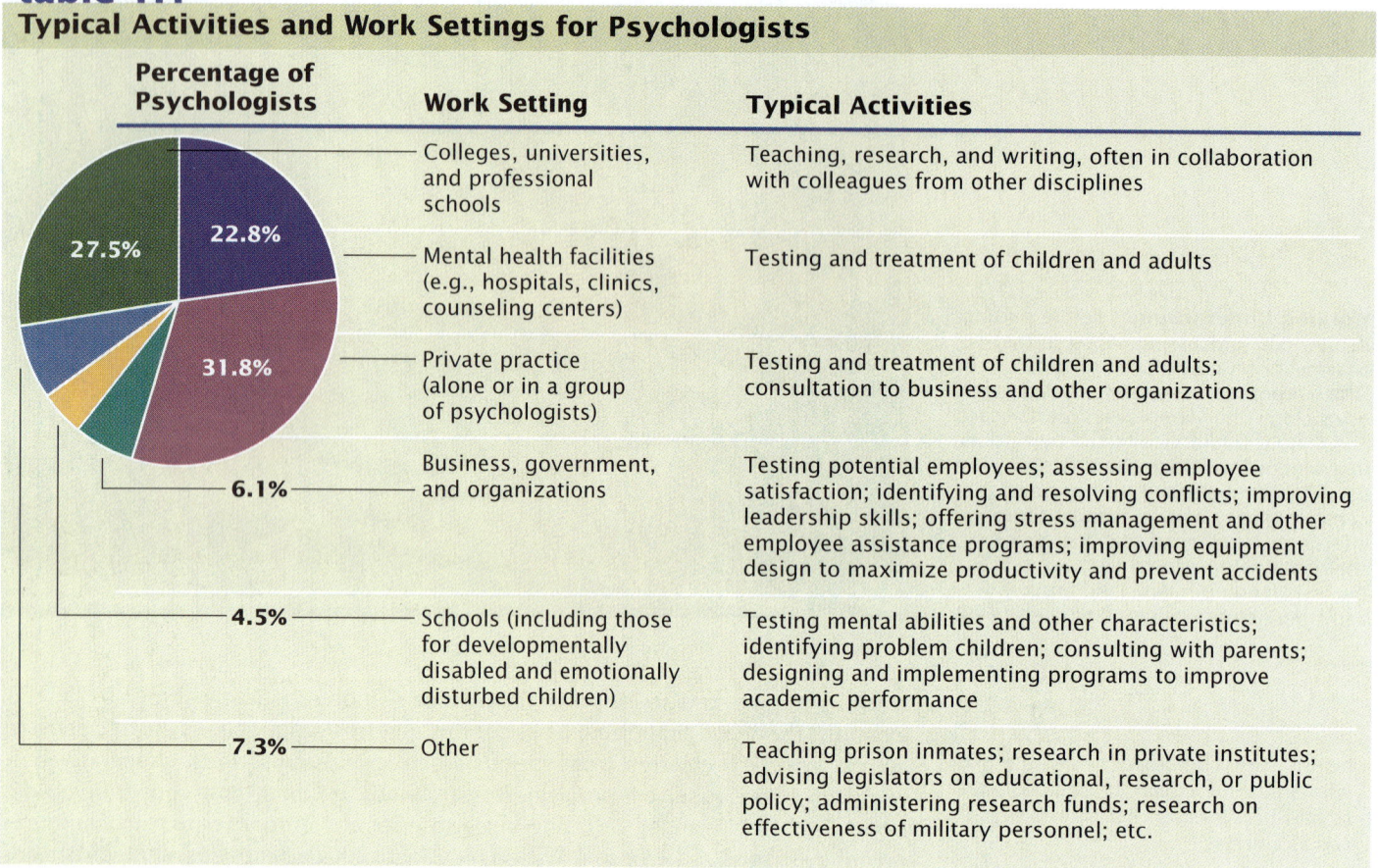

table 1.1
Typical Activities and Work Settings for Psychologists

Percentage of Psychologists	Work Setting	Typical Activities
22.8%	Colleges, universities, and professional schools	Teaching, research, and writing, often in collaboration with colleagues from other disciplines
27.5%	Mental health facilities (e.g., hospitals, clinics, counseling centers)	Testing and treatment of children and adults
31.8%	Private practice (alone or in a group of psychologists)	Testing and treatment of children and adults; consultation to business and other organizations
6.1%	Business, government, and organizations	Testing potential employees; assessing employee satisfaction; identifying and resolving conflicts; improving leadership skills; offering stress management and other employee assistance programs; improving equipment design to maximize productivity and prevent accidents
4.5%	Schools (including those for developmentally disabled and emotionally disturbed children)	Testing mental abilities and other characteristics; identifying problem children; consulting with parents; designing and implementing programs to improve academic performance
7.3%	Other	Teaching prison inmates; research in private institutes; advising legislators on educational, research, or public policy; administering research funds; research on effectiveness of military personnel; etc.

The fact that psychologists can work in such a wide variety of settings and do so many interesting—and often well-paying—jobs helps account for the popularity of psychology as an undergraduate major (APA, 2000; National Center for Education Statistics, 1998; Williams, 2000). Psychology courses also provide excellent background for students planning to enter medicine, law, business, and many other fields (Kohout, 2000).

Source: Data from 1999 APA Directory Survey.

for example, their research is linked to that of cognitive or social psychologists. Similarly, biological psychologists are working partly in clinical psychology when they look to problems in brain chemistry as a cause of mental disorder. And when social psychologists apply research on persuasion or cooperation to improve antismoking campaigns or group activities in the classroom, they are linking up with health psychology or educational psychology.

Even when psychologists do not themselves conduct research that crosses subfields, they often draw on, and contribute to, the knowledge developed in other subfields (Conner, 2001b). Recognizing the linkages among subfields is an important part of understanding psychology as a whole. We illustrate three of these linkages at the end of each chapter in a diagram similar to the one shown here. Each question in these Linkages diagrams illustrates a way in which the topics of two chapters are connected to each other; the number in parentheses tells you the page on which you can find a discussion of each question (look for the linked rings in the margin of that page). One linkage is given special attention in the Linkages section of each chapter. By examining the Linkages diagram in each chapter, you can more easily see how the topic of that chapter is related to other subfields of psychology. We hope that the diagrams will lead you to look for still other linkages that we did not mention. This kind of detective work can be enjoyable, and you may find it easier to remember material in one chapter by relating it to linked material in other chapters.

Much as psychology's subfields are linked to one another, psychology is linked to many other academic disciplines. Sometimes these linkages occur because psychologists and researchers from other disciplines have common interests. For example, *neuroscience* is a multidisciplinary research enterprise that examines

LINKAGES

By staying alert to the many linkages among psychology's subfields as you read this book, you will come away with not only threads of knowledge about each subfield but also an appreciation of the fabric of psychology as a whole. We discuss one linkage in detail in each chapter in a special Linkages section.

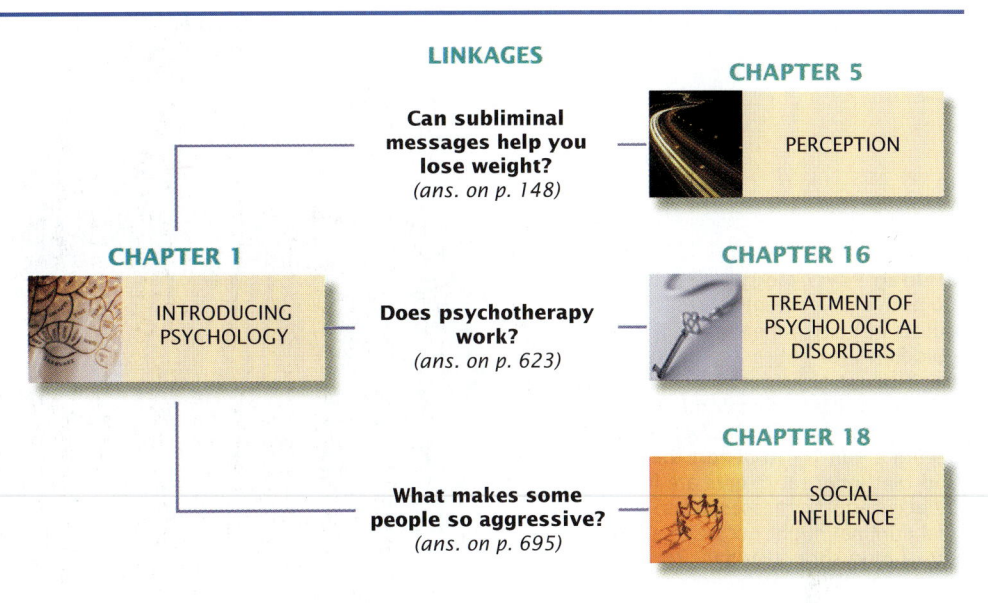

LINKAGES

CHAPTER 1 — INTRODUCING PSYCHOLOGY

- Can subliminal messages help you lose weight? (ans. on p. 148) → **CHAPTER 5** PERCEPTION
- Does psychotherapy work? (ans. on p. 623) → **CHAPTER 16** TREATMENT OF PSYCHOLOGICAL DISORDERS
- What makes some people so aggressive? (ans. on p. 695) → **CHAPTER 18** SOCIAL INFLUENCE

the structure and function of the nervous system in animals and humans, at levels ranging from the individual cell to overt behavior. This integrated field includes biological psychologists as well as specialists in neuroanatomy, neurophysiology, neurochemistry, genetics, and computer science. Someday, biological psychologists, like the colleagues with whom they work, may be known simply as "neuroscientists."

Psychology is also linked to other disciplines because research and theory from one discipline are applicable to another. For example, psychologists have applied chaos theory—which was developed in physics and mathematics to understand natural systems such as weather—to detect underlying order in apparently random patterns of brain activity, violence, drug abuse, depression, or family conflict (e.g., Dafilis, Liley, & Cadusch, 2001). Economists and political scientists apply social psychologists' research on cooperation, conflict, and negotiation to help them understand economic trends and explain international tensions. And genetic counselors use psychological knowledge about decision making and stress management to help clients decide whether, given a risky gene profile, they should have children.

This book is filled with examples of other ways in which psychological theories and research have been applied to fields as diverse as medicine, dentistry, law, business, engineering, architecture, aviation, public health, and sports. Cognitive psychologists' research on memory has influenced how lineups are displayed to eyewitnesses attempting to identify criminals, how attorneys question eyewitnesses in court, and how judges instruct juries (e.g., Casell & Bernstein, 2001; Kassin, 1997). Developmental psychologists' work on understanding the social and emotional aspects of aging is reshaping nursing-home policies on sexual behavior, and research by industrial/organizational psychologists is helping Web-based companies and other businesses adjust and survive in an economy under the threat of terrorism in the new millennium.

Research: The Foundation of Psychology

To help face the challenge of dealing with so many aspects of behavior and mental processes, most psychologists rely on a philosophical view known as *empiricism*. Empiricists see knowledge as coming through experience and observation, not through speculation. Accordingly, psychologists use the methods of science to conduct *empirical research*, meaning that they perform experiments and other scientific procedures to systematically gather and analyze information about psychological phenomena.

Linking Psychology and Law
Cognitive psychologists' research on the quirks of human memory has led to new guidelines for police and prosecutors (U.S. Department of Justice, 1999). The guidelines note that asking crime witnesses leading questions (e.g., "Do you remember seeing a gun?") can distort their memory, and that innocent people are less likely to be accused if witnesses are told that the real criminal might not be in a lineup or a set of mug shots (Foxhall, 2000).

For example, Michael Morris and Kaiping Peng (1994) were interested in learning more about how people explain other people's actions. Previous research in North America and other Western cultures had shown that people in those cultures tend to see other people's behavior as caused mainly by their personality traits and other individual characteristics. Morris and Peng wondered if this tendency occurred in all cultures. They had reason to believe it did not. North American cultures tend to place great emphasis on self-esteem, personal achievement, and other individual traits and goals. In other cultures, such as those in China and Japan, individuals tend to be seen as less important than the groups to which they belong. These cultural differences affect the way people think about what is important in life, but could they also affect the way people explain other people's behavior? Morris and Peng predicted that whereas North Americans would tend to see behavior as caused by *personal* characteristics such as laziness or bravery, people from China would tend to see behavior as caused by social pressure, lack of money, or other *situational* factors.

To test this idea, Morris and Peng gave North American students and Chinese students (who were studying in the United States) newspaper stories about two real murders. In one, the murderer was Chinese; in the other, he was North American. After reading the articles, both groups of students were asked to rate the extent to which each murder was due to the personal attributes of the murderer (e.g., personality problems) and the extent to which it was due to the situation in which the murderer found himself (e.g., being provoked by the victim).

The results of this study are presented in Figure 1.4. As Morris and Peng had predicted, North American students were more inclined to attribute the murders to the murderer's personality than to the situation he was in. In contrast, the Chinese students gave more weight to the situation as the cause of the murderer's actions. This study, along with many others described in later chapters, provides part of the empirical basis for psychologists' assertion that cultural factors can have a strong influence on people's thoughts, feelings, and actions.

In other words, psychologists do more than speculate about behavior and mental processes; they also use scientific methods to test the validity of their theories and to reach informed conclusions. Even psychologists who do not personally engage in research are constantly applying the results of their colleagues' studies to enhance the quality, currency, and effectiveness of their own teaching, writing, or service to clients and organizations.

The rules and methods of science that guide psychologists in their research are summarized in the chapter on research in psychology. We have placed our discussion of research methods early in the book to underscore the fact that without scientific methods and the foundation of empirical data they provide, psychologists' statements and recommendations would be no more credible than those of astrologers, tabloid newspapers, or talk-show guests who offer empirically unsupported opinions. Indeed, throughout this book, the results of scientific research in psychology shape our presentation of what psychologists have discovered so far about behavior and mental processes, as well as our evaluation of their efforts to apply that knowledge to improve the quality of human life.

A Brief History of Psychology

Psychologists have been studying behavior and mental processes for almost 125 years. The birth date of modern psychology is usually given as 1879, the year that Wilhelm Wundt (pronounced "voont") established the first formal psychology research laboratory at the University of Leipzig, Germany (Benjamin, 2000). However, the roots of psychology can be traced back through centuries of history in philosophy and science. Since at least the time of Socrates, Plato, and Aristotle, there has been debate about such topics as the source of human knowledge, the nature of mind and soul, the relationship of mind to body, and the possibility of scientifically studying these matters (Wertheimer, 1987).

The philosophy of empiricism was particularly important to the development of scientific psychology. Beginning in the seventeenth century, proponents of empiricism—especially the British philosophers John Locke, George Berkeley, and David Hume—challenged the view, held by philosophers from Plato to Descartes, that some knowledge is innate. As mentioned earlier, empiricists see everything we know as coming through the experience of our senses. At birth, they said, our minds are like a blank slate (*tabula rasa,* in Latin) upon which experience writes a lifelong story.

Wundt and the Structuralism of Titchener
By the nineteenth century, a number of German physiologists, including Hermann von Helmholtz and Gustav Fechner (pronounced "FECK-ner"), were conducting scientific studies of the structure and function of vision, hearing, and the other sensory systems and perceptual processes that empiricism identified as the basis of human knowledge. Fechner's work was especially valuable because he realized that one could study these mental processes by observing people's reactions to changes in sensory stimuli. By exploring, for example, how much brighter a light must become before we see it as twice as bright, Fechner discovered complex, but predictable, relationships between changes in the *physical* characteristics of stimuli and changes in our *psychological experience* of them. Fechner's approach, which he called *psychophysics,* paved the way for much of the research described in the chapter on perception.

As a physiologist, Wundt, too, analyzed sensory-perceptual systems using the methods of laboratory science, but his goal was to study *consciousness,* the immediate experience arising from these systems. Wundt wanted to describe the basic elements of consciousness, how they are organized, and how they relate to one another (Schultz & Schultz, 2000). He developed ingenious laboratory methods to study these elements, including the speed at which decisions and other mental events take place. In an attempt to observe conscious experience, Wundt used the technique of *introspection,* which means "inward looking." He trained research participants in this method, then repeatedly exposed them to a light or sound and asked them to describe the sensations and feelings the stimuli created. Wundt concluded that "quality" (e.g., cold or blue) and "intensity" (e.g., brightness or loudness) are the two essential elements of any sensation and that feelings can be described in terms of pleasure-displeasure, tension-relaxation, and excitement-depression (Schultz &

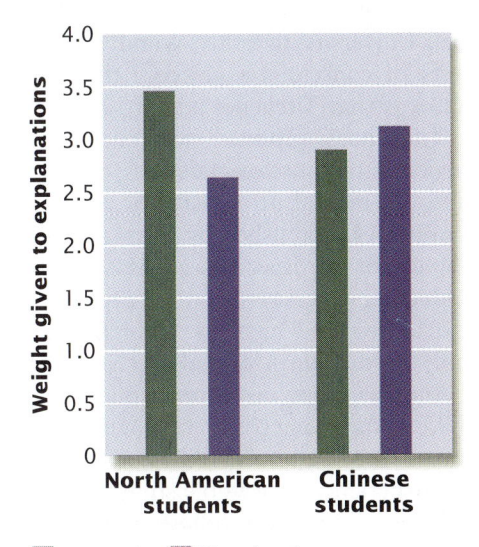

figure 1.4

North American and Chinese Students' Explanations of a Murder

When North American students were asked to explain why someone committed a murder, they tended to attribute the act to the murderer's personal characteristics. Chinese students tended to attribute it to the circumstances in which the murderer found himself. The experiment illustrates how psychologists can design empirical research to objectively study virtually any kind of behavior or mental process. It also illustrates how cultural background can affect people's mental processes.

Source: Morris & Peng (1994); adapted from Figure 8.

Wilhelm Wundt (1832–1920) In a classic experiment on the speed of mental processes, Wundt (third from left) first measured how quickly people could respond to a light by releasing a button they had been holding down. He then measured how much longer the response took when they held down one button with each hand and had to decide—based on the color of the light—which one to release. Wundt reasoned that the additional time taken reflected how long it took to perceive the color and decide which hand to move. As noted in the chapter on cognition and language, the logic behind this experiment remains a part of research on cognitive processes today.

Source: Psychology Archives—The University of Akron

Schultz, 2000). In short, with Wundt's work, psychology had evolved from the *philosophy* of mental processes to the *science* of mental processes.

Edward Titchener, an Englishman who had been a student of Wundt's, used introspection in his own laboratory at Cornell University to study Wundt's basic elements, as well as images and other aspects of conscious experience that are harder to quantify (see Figure 1.5). One result was that Titchener added "clarity" as an element of sensation (Watson, 1963). Titchener's approach was known as *structuralism* because he tried to define the structure of consciousness.

Wundt was not alone in the scientific study of mental processes, nor was his work universally accepted. In psychology laboratories established by German contemporaries such as Hermann Ebbinghaus, the use of introspection to dissect consciousness was seen as less important than conducting experiments on the capacities and limitations of mental processes such as learning and memory. Ebbinghaus's experiments—in which he himself was the only participant—formed the basis for some of what we know about memory today. Another group of German colleagues, including Max Wertheimer, Kurt Koffka, and Wolfgang Köhler, criticized Wundt on the grounds that introspection can be misleading. Pointing to visual illusions of the type shown in Figure 1.3, they argued that our experience of a whole stimulus pattern is not the same as the sum of its parts. These Gestalt psychologists (*Gestalt* means, roughly, "unified whole" in German) claimed that consciousness can be best understood by observing it as a total experience, not by breaking it down into its component elements. Take movies, for example. Imagine how boring it would be to browse slowly through the thousands of still images that are printed on a reel of film. Yet when those same images are projected onto a screen at just the right speed, they combine to create a rich, emotional experience.

Freud and Psychoanalysis

While Wundt and his colleagues in Leipzig were conducting scientific research on consciousness, Sigmund Freud (1856–1939) was in Vienna, beginning to explore the unconscious. As a physician, Freud had presumed that all behavior and mental processes have *physical* causes somewhere in the nervous system. He began to question that assumption in the late 1800s, however, after encountering a series of patients who displayed a variety of physical ailments that had no apparent physical cause. Using hypnosis and other methods, Freud found evidence that convinced him that the roots of these people's "neuroses" lay in shocking experiences from the distant past that the patients had pushed out of

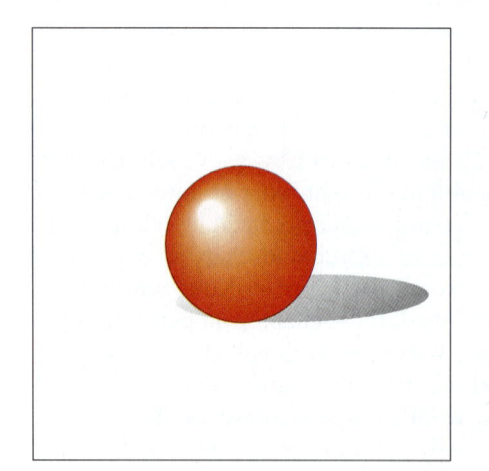

figure 1.5

A Stimulus for Introspection

TRY THIS Look at this object, and try to describe not what it is but only the intensity and clarity of the sensations and images (such as redness, brightness, and roundness) that you experience. If you can do this, you would have been an excellent research participant in Titchener's laboratory.

consciousness (Breuer & Freud, 1896). He eventually came to believe that all behavior—from everyday slips of the tongue to severe forms of mental disorder—is motivated by *psychological* processes, especially conflicts within ourselves that occur without our awareness, at an unconscious level. For the next forty years, Freud developed his ideas into a body of work known as *psychoanalysis*, which included a theory of personality and mental disorder, as well as a set of treatment methods. Freud's ideas were (and still are) controversial, but they have had an undeniable influence on the thinking of many psychologists around the world.

James and Functionalism

It was also during the late 1800s that scientific research in psychology took root outside Europe, especially in the United States and Canada. The first U.S. psychology laboratory was founded by William James at Harvard University, at around the same time Wundt established his laboratory in Leipzig. Most historians believe that James used his laboratory mainly for conducting demonstrations for his students; it was not until 1883 that G. Stanley Hall, at Johns Hopkins University, established the first psychology research laboratory in the United States. Six years later, in 1889, the first Canadian laboratory was established at the University of Toronto by James Mark Baldwin, Canada's first modern psychologist and a pioneer in research on child development.

Like the Gestalt psychologists, William James rejected both Wundt's approach and Titchener's structuralism. Influenced by Charles Darwin's theory of evolution, James was more interested in understanding how consciousness *functions* to help people adapt to their environments (James, 1890, 1892). This idea came to be called *functionalism*, and it focused on the ongoing "stream" of consciousness—the ever-changing pattern of images, sensations, memories, and other mental events. James wanted to know how the whole process works for the individual. Why, for example, do we usually remember recent events better than things that happened in the remote past?

James's focus on the *functions* of mental processes encouraged North American psychologists to look not only at how those processes work to our advantage but also at how they vary from person to person. Accordingly, some psychologists began to measure individual differences in learning, memory, and other mental processes associated with intelligence, made recommendations for improving educational practices in the schools, and even worked with teachers on programs tailored to children in need of special help (Nietzel et al., 2003).

William James's Lab William James (1842–1910) established this psychology demonstration laboratory at Harvard University in the late 1870s. Like the Gestalt psychologists, James saw the approach used by Wundt and Titchener as a scientific dead end; he noted that trying to understand consciousness by studying its components is like trying to understand a house by looking at individual bricks (James, 1884). He preferred to study instead the functions served by consciousness.

Watson and Behaviorism
Besides fueling James's functionalism, Darwin's theory of evolution led psychologists—especially those in North America after 1900—to study animals as well as humans. If all species evolved in similar ways, perhaps their behavior and mental processes followed similar laws. If so, we could learn something about people by studying animals. Psychologists could not expect cats or rats or chickens to introspect, so they observed animal behavior in mazes and other experimental situations. From these observations, they made *inferences* about conscious experience and about what they hoped would become general laws of learning, memory, and other mental processes.

John B. Watson, a psychology professor at Johns Hopkins University, agreed that overt behavior in animals and humans was the most important source of scientific information for psychology. However, Watson believed it was utterly unscientific to use behavior as the basis for making inferences about consciousness, as structuralists and functionalists did—let alone about the unconscious, as Freudians did. In 1913, Watson published an article called "Psychology As the Behaviorist Views It." In it, he argued that psychologists should ignore mental events and base psychology only on what they can actually observe about overt behavior and its response to various stimuli (Watson, 1913, 1919). Watson's *behaviorism* recognized the existence of consciousness but considered it useless as a target of research, because it would always be private and unobservable by scientific methods. Preoccupation with consciousness, said Watson, would prevent psychology from ever being a true science. Influenced by Ivan Pavlov's research on classical conditioning in dogs (described in the chapter on learning), Watson believed that *learning* is the most important determinant of behavior, and that it is through learning that organisms are able to adapt to their environments. He was famous for claiming that with enough control over the environment, he could create learning experiences that would turn any infant into a doctor, a lawyer, or even a criminal.

American psychologist B. F. Skinner was another early champion of behaviorism. From the 1930s until his death in 1990, Skinner worked on mapping out the details of how rewards and punishments shape, maintain, and change behavior through what he termed "operant conditioning." His *functional analysis of behavior* helped explain, for example, how children's tantrums are sometimes inadvertently encouraged by the attention they attract from parents and teachers, and how a virtual addiction to gambling can result from the occasional and unpredictable rewards it brings.

Many psychologists were drawn to Watson's and Skinner's vision of psychology as the learning-based science of observable behavior. Behaviorism dominated psychological research from the 1920s through the 1960s, whereas the study of consciousness received less attention, especially in the United States. ("In Review: The Development of Psychology" summarizes behaviorism and the other schools of thought that have influenced psychologists in the last century.)

Psychology Today
Psychologists continue to study all kinds of overt behavior in humans and in animals. By the 1960s, however, many had become dissatisfied with the limitations imposed by behaviorism (some, especially in Europe, had never accepted it in the first place). They grew uncomfortable ignoring mental processes that might be important in more fully understanding behavior (e.g., Ericsson & Simon, 1994). With the dawn of the computer age, these psychologists began to think about mental activity in a new way—as information processing. Computers also enabled psychologists to measure mental activity far more accurately than ever before. At the same time, progress in computer-supported biotechnology began to offer psychologists exciting new ways to study the biological bases of mental processes—to literally see what is going on in the brain when, for example, a person thinks or makes decisions (see Figure 1.1).

Armed with ever more sophisticated research tools, psychologists today are striving to do what Watson thought was impossible: to study mental processes with

in review	The Development of Psychology		
School of Thought	**Founders**	**Goals**	**Methods**
Structuralism	Edward Titchener, trained by Wilhelm Wundt	To study conscious experience and its structure	Experiments; introspection
Gestalt psychology	Max Wertheimer	To describe organization of mental processes: "The whole is greater than the sum of its parts."	Observation of sensory/perceptual phenomena
Psychoanalysis	Sigmund Freud	To explain personality and behavior; to develop techniques for treating mental illness	Study of individual cases
Functionalism	William James	To study how the mind works in allowing an organism to adapt to the environment	Naturalistic observation of animal and human behavior
Behaviorism	John B. Watson, B. F. Skinner	To study only observable behavior and explain behavior via learning principles	Observation of the relationship between environmental stimuli and behavioral responses

precision and scientific objectivity. In fact, there are probably as many contemporary psychologists studying cognitive and biological processes as there are those studying observable behaviors. So mainstream psychology has come full circle, once again accepting consciousness—in the form of cognitive processes—as a legitimate topic for scientific research and justifying the definition of psychology as the science of behavior and mental processes (Kimble, 2000; Robins, Gosling, & Craik, 1999).

Unity and Diversity in Psychology

Psychologists today are unified by their commitment to empiricism and scientific research, by their linked interests in behavior and mental processes, and by the debt they owe to predecessors whose work has shaped psychology over its 125-year history (Kimble, 1999). In other ways, however, psychologists are an amazingly diverse group. This diversity is reflected not only in the many subfields they choose but also in who they are and how they approach their work.

Our photographs of psychology's founders might suggest that all psychologists are Caucasian men, but this is certainly not the case. White males did dominate in psychology—much as they did in other academic disciplines—through the early part of the twentieth century. However, almost from the beginning, women and people of color made important contributions to psychology (Schultz & Schultz, 2000). Throughout this book you will find the work of their modern counterparts. Psychology research, service, and teaching by women and members of ethnic minority groups have all increased in tandem with their growing representation in the field.

In the United States, women now constitute about 46.1 percent of all psychologists holding doctoral degrees (National Science Foundation, 2001), and they are earning 66 percent of the new psychology doctorates awarded each year (National Science Foundation, 2000). Moreover, 16 percent of new doctoral degrees in psychology are being earned by members of ethnic minority groups (National Science Foundation, 2000). These numbers reflect continuing efforts by psychological organizations and governmental bodies, especially in the United States and Canada, to promote the recruitment, graduation, and employment of women and ethnic minorities in psychology (O'Conner, 2001; Rabasca, 2000).

Mary Whiton Calkins (1863–1930)
Mary Whiton Calkins studied psychology at Harvard University, where William James described her as "brilliant." Because she was a woman, though, Harvard refused to grant her a doctoral degree. They offered her the degree through Radcliffe, an affiliated school, but she refused it and went on to do research on memory. In 1905, she became the first woman president of the American Psychological Association (APA). Margaret Washburn (1871–1939) encountered similar sex discrimination at Columbia University, so she transferred to Cornell University, became the first woman to earn a doctorate in psychology, and in 1921 became the second woman president of the APA.

Approaches to Psychology

Diversity among psychologists can also be seen in the different ways in which they think about, study, and try to change behavior and mental processes. Suppose, for example, that you are a psychologist, and you want to know why some people stop to help a sick or injured stranger and others just keep walking. Where would you start? You could look for answers in people's brain cells and hormones, in their genetic background, in their personality traits, and in what they have learned from family, friends, and cultural traditions, to name just a few possibilities. With so many research directions available, you'd have to decide which sources of information were most likely to explain helping behavior.

Psychologists have to make the same kinds of decisions, not only about where to focus their research but also about what kind of treatment methods to use, or what other services to provide to schools, businesses, government agencies, or other clients. Their decisions are guided mainly by their overall *approach* to psychology—that is, by the assumptions, questions, and methods they believe will be most helpful in their work. The approaches we described earlier as structuralism and functionalism are gone now, but the psychodynamic and behavioral approaches remain, along with others known as biological, evolutionary, cognitive, and humanistic approaches. Some psychologists adopt just one of these approaches, but most psychologists are *eclectic*. This means that they blend assumptions and methods from two or more approaches in an effort to more fully understand behavior and mental processes (e.g., Cacioppo et al., 2000). Some approaches to psychology are more influential than others these days, but we should review the main features of all of them so you understand the differences among them, and how they have affected psychologists' work over the years.

The Biological Approach

As its name implies, the **biological approach** to psychology assumes that behavior and mental processes are largely shaped by biological processes. Psychologists who take this approach study the psychological effects of hormones, genes, and the activity of the nervous system, especially the brain. So if they are studying memory, they might try to identify the changes taking

The Biology of Emotion Robert Levenson, a biological psychologist at the University of California at Berkeley, measures heart rate, muscle tension, and other physical reactions in couples as they discuss problems in their relationships.

Gilbert Haven Jones (1883–1966)
When Gilbert Haven Jones graduated from the University of Jena in Germany in 1909, he became one of the first African Americans to earn a doctorate in psychology. Many others were to follow, including J. Henry Alston, who was the first African American to publish research in a major U.S. psychology journal (Alston, 1920).

place in the brain as information is stored there (Figure 7.18, in the chapter on memory, shows an example of these changes). Or if they are studying thinking, they might look for patterns of brain activity associated with, say, making quick decisions or reading a foreign language.

Research discussed in nearly every chapter of this book reflects the enormous influence of the biological approach on psychology today. To help you better understand the terms and concepts used in that research, we have included an appendix on the principles of genetics and a chapter on biological aspects of psychology.

The Evolutionary Approach

Biological processes also figure prominently in the **evolutionary approach** to psychology. The foundation for this approach was Charles Darwin's book *The Origin of Species*. Darwin argued that the forms of life we see today are the result of *evolution*—of changes in life forms that occur over many generations—and more specifically, that evolution occurs through *natural selection*. Darwin believed that natural selection operates at the level of individuals, but most evolutionists now see it operating at the level of genes. At either level, the process is the same. Genes that result in characteristics and behaviors that are adaptive and useful in a certain environment will enable the creatures that inherited them to survive and reproduce, thereby passing those genes on to subsequent generations. Genes that result in characteristics that are not adaptive in that environment are not passed on to subsequent generations, because the creatures possessing them don't survive to reproduce. Thus, evolutionary theory says that many (but not all) of the genes we possess today are the result of natural selection.

In psychology, the evolutionary approach assumes that the *behavior* of animals and humans today is also the result of evolution through natural selection. Psychologists who take this approach see aggression, for example, as a form of territory protection, and gender differences in mate-selection preferences as reflecting different ways of helping one's genes to survive in future generations. The evolutionary approach has generated a growing body of research (Buss, 1999; Kurzban & Leary, 2001). You will encounter it again in later chapters in relation to topics such as helping and altruism, mental disorders, temperament, and interpersonal attraction.

A Father's Love Mothers are solely responsible for the care and protection of their offspring in 95 percent of mammalian species. If all these species survive without male involvement in parenting, why are some human fathers so active in child rearing? Do evolutionary forces make fathering more adaptive for humans? Is it a matter of learning to care? Is it a combination of both? Psychologists who take an evolutionary approach study these questions and others relating to the origins of human social behavior (Buss, 1999; Geary, 2000).

biological approach An approach to psychology in which behavior and behavior disorders are seen as the result of physical processes, especially those relating to the brain and to hormones and other chemicals.

evolutionary approach An approach to psychology that emphasizes the inherited, adaptive aspects of behavior and mental processes.

figure 1.6

What Do You See?

TRY THIS Take a moment to jot down what you see in these clouds. According to the psychodynamic approach to psychology, what we see in cloud formations and other vague patterns reflects wishes, impulses, and other mental processes of which we may be unaware. The chapter on personality discusses the value of personality tests based on this assumption.

psychodynamic approach A view developed by Freud that emphasizes the interplay of unconscious mental processes in determining human thought, feelings, and behavior.

behavioral approach An approach to psychology emphasizing that human behavior is determined mainly by what a person has learned, especially from rewards and punishments.

cognitive approach A way of looking at human behavior that emphasizes research on how the brain takes in information, creates perceptions, forms and retrieves memories, processes information, and generates integrated patterns of action.

The Psychodynamic Approach

The **psychodynamic approach** to psychology offers a different slant on the role of inherited instincts and other biological forces in human behavior. Rooted in Freud's psychoanalysis, this approach asserts that all behavior and mental processes reflect constant, and mostly unconscious, psychological struggles raging within each person (see Figure 1.6). Usually, these struggles involve conflict between the impulse to satisfy instincts (such as for food, sex, or aggression) and the need to abide by the restrictions imposed by society. Psychologists taking the psychodynamic approach would see aggression, for example, as a case of primitive urges overcoming a person's defenses against expressing those urges. They would see anxiety, depression, or other disorders as overt signs of inner turmoil.

Freud's original theories are not as influential today as they once were (Robins, Gosling, & Craik, 1999), but as you will see in later chapters, modern versions of the psychodynamic approach still appear in various theories of personality, psychological disorders, and psychotherapy.

The Behavioral Approach

The assumptions of the **behavioral approach** to psychology contrast sharply with those of the psychodynamic, biological, and evolutionary approaches. As founded by John Watson, behaviorism characterizes behavior as primarily the result of *learning*. From a strict behaviorist point of view, biological, genetic, and evolutionary factors simply provide "raw material," which is then shaped by learning experiences into what we see in each individual's actions. So behaviorists would seek to understand all behavior—whether it is aggression or drug abuse, shyness or sociability, confidence or anxiety—by looking at the individual's learning history, especially the patterns of reward and punishment the person has experienced. They also believe that people can change problematic behaviors, from overeating to criminality, by unlearning old habits and developing new ones.

Many of today's behaviorists have broadened their approach to include thoughts, or cognitions, as well as overt behavior. Those who take this *cognitive-behavioral*, or *social-cognitive*, approach explore how learning affects the development of thoughts and beliefs and, in turn, how these learned cognitive patterns affect overt behavior.

The Cognitive Approach

The growth of the cognitive-behavioral perspective reflects the influence of a broader **cognitive approach** to psychology. The

Why Is He So Aggressive?
Psychologists taking the cognitive-behavioral approach suggest that children *learn* to be aggressive. They say it happens partly through seeing family and friends acting aggressively, but also through hearing people talking about others as being threatening and about aggression as the only way to deal with disagreements (Shahinfar, Kupersmidt, & Matza, 2001).

cognitive approach focuses on how people take in, mentally represent, and store information; how they perceive and process that information; and how cognitive processes are related to the behavior we see. In other words, the cognitive approach leads psychologists to study the rapid series of mental events—including those taking place outside of awareness—that accompany overt behavior. Here is how a psychologist would use the cognitive approach to describe the information processing that occurs during an aggressive incident outside a movie theater: The aggressor (1) *perceives* that someone has cut into the theater line, (2) uses information stored in memory to *decide* that this act is inappropriate, (3) *attributes* the act to the culprit's obnoxious personality, (4) *considers* possible responses and their likely consequences, (5) *decides* that shoving the person is the best response, and (6) *executes* that response.

Psychologists who adopt the cognitive approach explore how people process information in domains ranging from decision making and interpersonal attraction to intelligence testing and group problem solving, to name but a few. Some of them work with researchers from computer science, the biological sciences, engineering, linguistics, philosophy, and other disciplines in a multidisciplinary field called *cognitive science*. Cognitive scientists attempt to discover the building blocks of cognition and to determine how these components produce complex behaviors such as remembering a fact, naming an object, or writing a word (Reisberg, 1997).

The Humanistic Approach
Mental events play a different role in the **humanistic approach** to psychology (also known as the *phenomenological approach*). Psychologists who favor the humanistic perspective see behavior as determined primarily by each person's capacity to choose how to think and act. They see these choices as dictated not by instincts, biological processes, or rewards and punishments, but by each individual's unique perceptions of the world. So if, to you, the world is a friendly place, you are likely to be optimistic and secure. If you perceive it as full of hostile people, you will probably be defensive and anxious.

Like their cognitively oriented colleagues, psychologists who choose the humanistic approach would see aggression in a theater line as stemming from a perception that aggression is justified. But where those favoring the cognitive approach search for general laws governing *all* people's thoughts and actions, humanistic psychologists try to understand how each individual's immediate and unique experiences guide *that* person's thoughts and actions. In fact, many proponents of the humanistic approach say that behavior and mental processes can be fully understood *only*

humanistic approach An approach to psychology that views behavior as controlled by the decisions that people make about their lives based on their perceptions of the world.

Cognitive Science at Work
Psychologists and other cognitive scientists are working on a "computational theory of the mind," in which they create computer programs that simulate how humans process information. In the chapter on cognition and language, we discuss their progress in creating artificial intelligence in computers that can help make medical diagnoses and perform other complex cognitive tasks.

by appreciating the perceptions and feelings experienced by each individual. Humanistic psychologists also believe that people are essentially good, that they are in control of themselves, and that their main innate tendency is to grow toward their highest potential.

The humanistic approach began to attract attention in North America in the 1940s through the writings of Carl Rogers (1902–1987), a psychologist who had been trained in, but later rejected, the psychodynamic approach. We describe his views on personality and his psychotherapy methods in the chapters on personality and the treatment of psychological disorders. The humanistic approach also shaped the famous hierarchy-of-needs theory of motivation proposed by Abraham Maslow (1908–1970) and discussed in the chapters on motivation and emotion and

in review: Approaches to Psychology

Approach	Characteristics
Biological	Emphasizes activity of the nervous system, especially of the brain; the action of hormones and other chemicals; and genetics.
Evolutionary	Emphasizes the ways in which behavior and mental processes are adaptive for survival.
Psychodynamic	Emphasizes internal conflicts, mostly unconscious, which usually pit sexual or aggressive instincts against environmental obstacles to their expression.
Behavioral	Emphasizes learning, especially each person's experience with rewards and punishments.
Cognitive	Emphasizes mechanisms through which people receive, store, retrieve, and otherwise process information.
Humanistic	Emphasizes individual potential for growth and the role of unique perceptions in guiding behavior and mental processes.

personality. Today, however, the impact of the humanistic approach to psychology is limited, mainly because many psychologists find humanistic concepts and predictions too vague to be expressed and tested scientifically. (For a summary of the approaches we have discussed, see "In Review: Approaches to Psychology.")

Human Diversity and Psychology

A final aspect of the diversity in psychology can be seen in the range of people whom psychologists study and serve. This was not always the case. Many psychologists once presumed that all people are essentially the same, and that whatever principles emerged from research with local volunteer research participants would apply to everyone, everywhere. Since about 90 percent of researchers in psychology work at universities in North America and Europe, they tended to study local college students, mostly white and middle-class, and more often men than women (Graham, 1992). Most of the psychologists, too, tended to be white, middle-class, and male (Walker, 1991).

From one perspective, studying a narrow sample of people need not limit the usefulness of psychological research, because in many ways, people *are* very much alike. They tend to live in groups; have religious beliefs; and create social rules, music, dances, and games. And reactions to heat or a sour taste are the same in men and women the world over, as is their recognition of a smile.

But are people's moral values, motivation to achieve, or patterns of interpersonal communication universal as well? Do the principles derived from research on European American males living in the midwestern United States apply to African American women or to people in Greece, Korea, Argentina, or Egypt? Not always. What people experience and what they learn from that experience are shaped by *sociocultural factors*, including differences in gender, ethnicity, social class, and culture. As in the study about how people from different countries explained a murderer's actions, these variables create many significant differences in behavior and mental processes, especially from one culture to another (Cross & Markus, 1999; Sue et al., 1999).

Culture has been defined as the accumulation of values, rules of behavior, forms of expression, religious beliefs, occupational choices, and the like for a group of people who share a common language and environment (Fiske et al., 1998). Culture is an organizing and stabilizing influence. It encourages or discourages particular behaviors and mental processes; it also allows people to understand and anticipate the behavior of others in that culture. It is a kind of group adaptation, passed along by tradition and example rather than by genes from one generation to the next. Culture determines, for example, whether children's education will focus on skill at hunting or reading, how close people stand when they converse, and whether or not they form lines in public places (Munroe & Munroe, 1994).

Psychologists and anthropologists have isolated many respects in which cultures differ (Triandis, 1998). Table 1.2 outlines one way of analyzing these differences; it shows that many cultures can be described as either individualist or collectivist. Many people in *individualist* cultures, such as those typical of North America and Western Europe, tend to value personal rather than group goals and achievement. Competitiveness to distinguish oneself from others is common in these cultures, as is a sense of isolation. By contrast, many people in *collectivist* cultures, such as Japan, tend to think of themselves mainly as part of family or work groups. Cooperative effort aimed at advancing the welfare of such groups is highly valued, and whereas loneliness is seldom a problem, fear of rejection by the group is common. Many aspects of U.S. culture—from self-reliant cowboy heroes and bonuses for "top" employees to the invitation to "help yourself" at a buffet table—reflect its tendency toward an individualist orientation (see Table 1.3).

Culture is often associated with a particular country, but in fact most countries are *multicultural;* in other words, they host many *subcultures* within their borders.

---

culture The accumulation of values, rules of behavior, forms of expression, religious beliefs, occupational choices, and the like for a group of people who share a common language and environment.

The Impact of Culture Culture helps shape virtually every aspect of our behavior and mental processes, from how we dress to how we think to what we think is important. Because we grow up immersed in our culture, we may be unaware of its influence on our own thoughts and actions until—like these participants at a United Nations World Conference on Women—we encounter people whose culture has shaped them in different ways.

Often, these subcultures are formed by people of various ethnic origins. The population of the United States, for instance, encompasses African Americans, Hispanic Americans, Asian Americans, and American Indians, as well as European Americans whose families came from Italy, Germany, Britain, Poland, Ireland, and many other places (see Figure 1.7). In each of these groups, the individuals who identify with their cultural heritage tend to share behaviors, values, and beliefs based on their culture of origin and, thus, form a subculture (Phinney, 1996).

Like fish unaware of the water in which they are immersed, people often fail to notice how their culture or subculture has shaped their patterns of thinking and behavior until they come in contact with people whose culture or subculture has shaped different patterns. For example, an American teaching in Korea discovered

Cultures don't make everyone in them exactly the same, but they do create certain tendencies in behavior and mental processes (Fiske et al., 1998; Oyserman, Coon, & Kemmelmeier, 2002). For example, individualist cultures support the idea of placing one's personal goals before the goals of the extended family or work group, whereas collectivist cultures tend to encourage putting the goals of those groups ahead of personal goals (Smith & Bond, 1999). Cultures also vary in the degree to which they impose tight or loose rules for social behavior, value achievement or self-awareness, seek dominance over nature or integration with it, and emphasize the importance of time (Abi-Hashem, 2000; Triandis, 1996).

table 1.2
Some Characteristics of Behavior and Mental Processes Typical of Individualist Versus Collectivist Cultures

Variable	Individualist	Collectivist
Personal identity	Separate from others	Connected to others
Major goals	Self-defined; be unique; realize your personal potential; compete with others	Defined by others; belong; occupy your proper place; meet your obligations to others; be like others
Criteria for self-esteem	Ability to express unique aspects of the self; ability to be self-assured	Ability to restrain the self and be part of a social unit; ability to be self-effacing
Sources of success and failure	Success comes from personal effort; failure, from external factors	Success is due to help from others; failure is due to personal faults
Major frame of reference	Personal attitudes, traits, and goals	Family, work group

TRY THIS — The statements listed here appeared in advertisements in Korea and the United States. Those from Korea reflect collectivist values, whereas those from the United States emphasize a more individualist orientation (Han & Shavitt, 1994). See if you can tell which are which; then check the bottom of the next page for the answers. You can follow up on this exercise by identifying cultural values in ads you see in newspapers and magazines, as well as on billboards and television. By surfing the Web or scanning international newspapers, you can compare the values conveyed by ads in your culture with those in ads from other cultures.

table 1.3
Cultural Values in Advertising

1. "She's got a style all her own."
2. "You, only better."
3. "A more exhilarating way to provide for your family."
4. "We have a way of bringing people closer together."
5. "Celebrating a half-century of partnership."
6. "How to protect the most personal part of the environment: Your skin."
7. "Our family agrees with this selection of home furnishings."
8. "A leader among leaders."
9. "Make your way through the crowd."
10. "Your business success: Harmonizing with (company name)."

Source: Brehm, Kassin, & Fein (2002).

that some people there believe it is in poor taste to write a student's name in red ink (Stevens, 1999). He was told that doing so conveys a prediction or wish that the person will die, because red ink was traditionally used to record new names in official death registers. Even some of the misunderstandings that occur between men and women in the same culture are traceable to subtle, culturally influenced differences in their communication patterns (Tannen, 1994). In the United States, for example, women's efforts to connect with others by talking may be perceived by many men as "pointless" unless the discussion is aimed at solving a specific problem; thus women often feel frustrated and misunderstood by men, who tend to offer, instead of conversation, well-intentioned but unwanted advice.

For decades, psychologists interested in cross-cultural research have studied cultural differences (Triandis, 1964), but now the influence of sociocultural variables is of growing interest to psychologists in general (Miller, 1999; Sampson, 2000). As psychology strives to be the science of *all* behavior and mental processes, researchers are increasingly taking into account gender, nationality, and other sociocultural variables (Miller, 1999). You will see this trend in much of the research described in the chapters to come.

figure 1.7
Cultural Diversity in the United States

The people of the United States represent a wide array of cultural backgrounds. Notice that these figures total more than 100 percent because many people see themselves belonging to two or more groups.

Source: U.S. Bureau of the Census (2001).

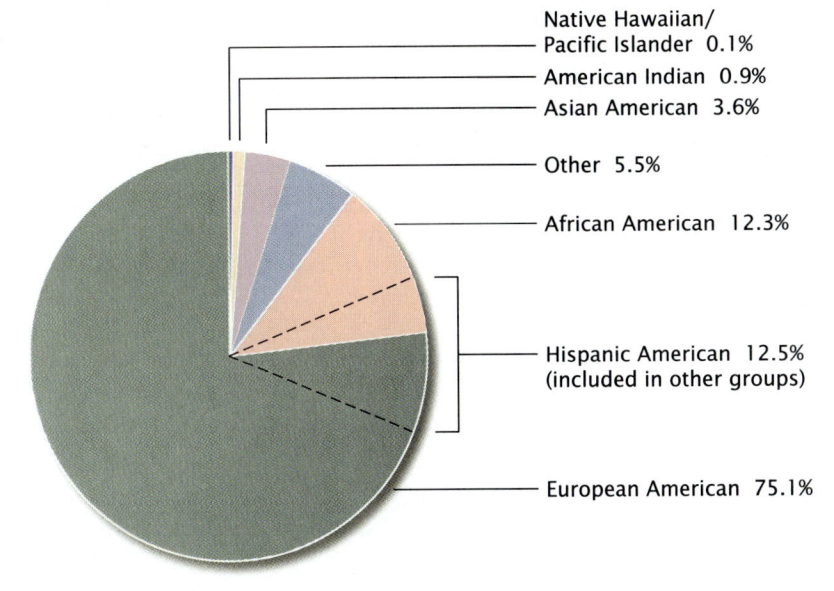

- Native Hawaiian/Pacific Islander 0.1%
- American Indian 0.9%
- Asian American 3.6%
- Other 5.5%
- African American 12.3%
- Hispanic American 12.5% (included in other groups)
- European American 75.1%

SUMMARY

Psychology is the science that seeks to understand behavior and mental processes, and to apply that understanding in the service of human welfare.

The World of Psychology: An Overview

The concept of "behavior and mental processes" is a broad one, encompassing virtually all aspects of what it means to be a human being.

Subfields of Psychology

Because the subject matter of psychology is so diverse, most psychologists work in particular subfields within the discipline. For example, *biological psychologists,* also called *physiological psychologists,* study topics such as the role played by the brain in regulating normal and disordered behavior. *Developmental psychologists* specialize in trying to understand the development of behavior and mental processes over a lifetime. *Cognitive psychologists,* some of whom prefer to be called *experimental psychologists,* focus on basic psychological processes such as learning, memory, and perception; they also study judgment, decision making, and problem solving. *Engineering psychology,* the study of human factors in the use of equipment, helps designers create better versions of that equipment. *Personality psychologists* focus on characteristics that set people apart from one another. *Clinical psychologists* and *counseling psychologists* provide direct service to troubled people and conduct research on abnormal behavior. *Community psychologists* work to prevent mental disorders and to extend mental health services to those who need them. *Health psychologists* study the relationship between behavior and health and help promote healthy lifestyles. *Social psychologists* examine questions regarding how people influence one another. *Industrial/organizational psychologists* study ways to increase efficiency and productivity in the workplace. *Educational psychologists* conduct and apply research on teaching and learning, whereas *school psychologists* specialize in assessing and alleviating children's academic problems. *Sport psychologists, forensic psychologists,* and *environmental psychologists* exemplify some of psychology's many other subfields.

Linkages Within Psychology and Beyond

Psychologists often work in more than one subfield and usually share knowledge with colleagues in many subfields. Psychologists also draw on, and contribute to, knowledge in other disciplines, such as physics, economics, and political science.

Research: The Foundation of Psychology

Psychologists use the methods of science to conduct empirical research. This means that they perform experiments and use other scientific procedures to systematically gather and analyze information about psychological phenomena.

A Brief History of Psychology

The founding of modern psychology is usually marked as 1879, when Wilhelm Wundt established the first psychology research laboratory. Wundt used laboratory methods to study consciousness in a manner that, as expanded by Edward Titchener, became known as *structuralism.* It was in the late 1800s, too, that Freud, in Vienna, began his study of the unconscious, while in the United States, William James's perspective, known as functionalism, suggested that psychologists should study how consciousness functions to help us adapt to our environments. In 1913, John B. Watson founded behaviorism, arguing that to be scientific, psychologists should study only the behavior they can see, not private mental events. Behaviorism dominated psychology for decades, but psychologists are once again studying consciousness in the form of cognitive processes.

Unity and Diversity in Psychology

Psychologists are unified by their commitment to empirical research and scientific methods, by their linked interests, and by the legacy of psychology's founders, but they are diverse in their backgrounds, in their activities, and in the approaches they take to their work. Most of the prominent figures in psychology's early history were white males, but women and members of minority groups made important contributions from the start, and continue to do so.

Approaches to Psychology

Psychologists differ in their approaches to psychology—that is, in the assumptions, questions, and methods they believe will be most helpful in their work. Some adopt one particular approach; many combine features of two or more approaches. Those adopting a *biological approach* focus on how physiological processes shape behavior and mental processes. Psychologists who prefer the *evolutionary approach* emphasize the inherited, adaptive aspects of behavior and mental processes. In the *psychodynamic approach,* behavior and mental processes are seen as reflecting struggles to resolve conflicts between impulses and the demands made by society to control those impulses. Psychologists who take the *behavioral approach* view behavior as determined primarily by learning based on experiences with rewards and punishments. The *cognitive approach* assumes that behavior can be understood through analysis of the basic mental processes that underlie it. To those adopting the *humanistic approach,* behavior is controlled by the decisions that people make about their lives based on their perceptions of the world.

Human Diversity and Psychology

Psychologists are increasingly taking into account the influence of culture and other sociocultural variables such as gender and ethnicity in shaping human behavior and mental processes.

Answer key for Table 1.3: U.S. ads are numbers 1, 2, 6, 8, and 9.

Research in Psychology

Thinking Critically About Psychology (or Anything Else)
Critical Thinking and Scientific Research
The Role of Theories

Research Methods in Psychology
Selecting Human Participants for Research
Naturalistic Observation: Watching Behavior
Case Studies: Taking a Closer Look
Surveys: Looking at the Big Picture
Experiments: Exploring Cause and Effect

Statistical Analysis of Research Results
Descriptive Statistics
Inferential Statistics
Statistics and Research Methods as Tools in Critical Thinking

Ethical Guidelines for Psychologists

LINKAGES: **Psychological Research and Behavioral Genetics**

Linkages

Summary

Francine Shapiro, a clinical psychologist in northern California, had an odd experience one day in 1987 while taking a walk. She had been thinking about some distressing events when she noticed that her emotional reaction to them was fading away (Shapiro, 1989a). In trying to figure out why this should be, she realized that she had been moving her eyes from side to side. Could these eye movements have caused the change in her emotions? To test this possibility, she made more deliberate eye movements and found that the emotion-reducing effect was even stronger. Was this a fluke, or would the same thing happen to others? Curious, she first tested the effects of side-to-side eye movements with friends and colleagues, and then with clients who had suffered traumatic experiences such as sexual abuse, military combat, or rape. She asked these people to think about unpleasant experiences in their lives while keeping their eyes on her finger as she moved it rapidly back and forth in front of them. Like her, they found that during and after these eye movement sessions, their reactions to unpleasant thoughts faded away. Most notably, her clients reported that their emotional flashbacks, nightmares, fears, and other trauma-related problems had decreased dramatically (Shapiro, 1989a).

Based on the success of these cases, Shapiro developed a treatment method she calls *eye movement desensitization and reprocessing*, or *EMDR* (Shapiro, 1991). Since 1990, she and her associates at EMDR Institute, Inc., have trained more than 30,000 therapists in 52 countries to use EMDR in the treatment of adults and children with problems ranging from simple phobias to severe emotional disorders (EMDR Institute, 2001; Greenwald, 1999; Smith & Yule, 1999).

Suppose you had an anxiety-related problem. Would the growth of EMDR be enough to convince you to spend your own money on it? If not, what would you want to know about EMDR before deciding? As a cautious person, you would probably ask some of the same questions that have occurred to many scientists in psychology: Are the effects of EMDR caused by the treatment itself, or by the faith that clients might have in *any* new and impressive treatment? And are EMDR's effects faster, stronger, and longer lasting than those of other treatments?

Asking questions about cause and effect, quality, and value are part of a *critical thinking* process that can help us make informed decisions, not only about psychotherapy options but also about all sorts of other things—such as which pain reliever or Internet service to choose, which college to attend, what apartment to rent, which candidate to vote for, and whether we believe that cell phones can cause cancer or that shark cartilage can cure it. Finding answers to these kinds of questions requires us to translate critical thinking into research. For most people, this means reading *Consumer Reports,* surfing the Web, listening to speeches, or tapping other sources for information about the products, services, institutions, people, and issues we are considering. For psychologists, research means using scientific methods to gather information about behavior and mental processes.

In the pages that follow, we summarize some basic questions that emerge from thinking critically about psychology, describe the scientific research methods psychologists use, and show how some of those methods have been applied in evaluating EMDR. We end the chapter by considering the importance of research ethics in psychology.

Thinking Critically About Psychology (or Anything Else)

Ask several friends and relatives if humans and animals are more aggressive during the full moon, if psychics help the police solve crimes, and if people sometimes suddenly burst into flames for no reason. Most people you ask will probably agree with at least one of these statements, even though not one of them is true (see Table 2.1). Perhaps you already knew that, but don't feel too smug. At one time or another, we all accept something we are told simply because the information seems to come

table 2.1
Some Popular Myths

Myth	Fact
Many children are injured each year in the United States when razor blades, needles, or poison is put in Halloween candy.	Reported cases are rare, most turn out to be hoaxes, and in the only documented case of a child dying from poisoned candy, the culprit was the child's own parent (Brunvald, 1989).
If your roommate commits suicide during the school term, you automatically get A's in all your classes for that term.	No college or university anywhere has ever had such a rule.
People have been known to burst into flames and die from fire erupting within their own bodies.	In rare cases, humans have been consumed by fires that caused little or no damage to the surrounding area. However, this phenomenon has been duplicated in a laboratory, and each alleged case of "spontaneous human combustion" has been traced to an external source of ignition (Benecke, 1999; Nienhuys, 2001).
Most big-city police departments rely on the advice of psychics to help them solve murders, kidnappings, and missing persons cases.	Only about 35% of urban police departments ever seek psychics' advice, and that advice is virtually never more helpful than other means of investigation (Nickell, 1997; Wiseman, West, & Stemman, 1996).
Murders, suicides, animal bites, and episodes of mental disorder are more likely to occur when the moon is full.	Records of crimes, dog bites, and mental hospital admissions do not support this common belief (Bickis, Kelly, & Byrnes, 1995; Chapman & Morrell, 2000; Rotton & Kelly, 1985).
You can't fool a lie detector.	Lie detectors can be helpful in solving crimes, but they are not perfect; their results can free a guilty person or send an innocent person to jail (see the chapter on motivation and emotion).
Viewers never see David Letterman walking to his desk after the opening monologue because his contract prohibits him from showing his backside on TV.	When questioned about this story on the air, Letterman denied it and, to prove his point, lifted his jacket and turned a full circle in front of the cameras and studio audience (Brunvald, 1989).
Psychics have special abilities to see into the future.	Even the most famous psychics are almost always wrong, as in these predictions for the year 2000: "Prince Charles will fly in the space shuttle," "An earthquake will destroy Los Angeles and San Francisco," and "O. J. Simpson will admit his guilt." None predicted the September 11, 2001, terrorist attacks on New York and Washington. The few correct predictions are usually vague ("Dolly Parton *may* write a book") or obvious ("Brad Pitt and Jennifer Aniston will marry") (Emery, 2001).

Many people believe in the statements listed here, but critical thinkers who take the time to investigate them will discover that they are not true.

from a reliable source or because "everyone knows" it is true. If this were not the case, advertisers, politicians, salespeople, social activists, and others who seek our money, our votes, or our loyalty would not be as successful as they are. These people want you to believe their promises or claims without careful thought; they don't want you to think critically.

Often, they get their wish. Millions of people waste billions of dollars every year on worthless predictions by telephone "psychics"; on bogus cures for cancer, heart

Uncritically accepting claims for the value of "psychic" readings, "get-rich-quick" schemes, new therapies, or proposed government policies can be embarrassing, expensive, and dangerous. Critical thinkers carefully evaluate evidence for *and* against such claims before reaching a conclusion about them.

Doonesbury © 1993 G. B. Trudeau. Reprinted with permission of Universal Press Syndicate. All rights reserved.

disease, and arthritis; on phony degrees offered by nonexistent Internet "universities"; and on "miracle" defrosting trays, eat-all-you-want weight-loss programs, "effortless" exercise gadgets, and other consumer products that simply don't work—not to mention the millions more lost in investment scams and fraudulent charity appeals (Cassel & Bernstein, 2001).

Critical thinking is the process of assessing claims and making judgments on the basis of well-supported evidence (Wade, 1988). We can apply critical thinking to EMDR—or to any other topic—by asking the following five questions:

1. *What am I being asked to believe or accept?* In this case, the assertion to be examined is that EMDR causes the reduction or elimination of anxiety-related problems.

2. *What evidence is available to support the assertion?* Shapiro experienced a reduction in her own emotional distress following certain kinds of eye movements. Later, she found the same effect in others.

3. *Are there alternative ways of interpreting the evidence?* The dramatic effects experienced by Shapiro and others might be due not to EMDR itself but instead to the motivation of these individuals to change or their desire to prove her right. And who knows? They might have eventually improved on their own, without any treatment. Even the most remarkable evidence cannot be accepted as confirming an assertion until equally plausible alternative assertions like these have been ruled out. Doing that leads to the next step in critical thinking: conducting scientific research.

4. *What additional evidence would help to evaluate the alternatives?* The ideal method for collecting further evidence about the value of EMDR would be to identify three groups of emotionally troubled people who were alike in every way except for the anxiety treatment they received. Now suppose the people in the EMDR group improved much more than those getting an equally motivating, but useless, treatment or no treatment at all. Such results would make it less likely that the improvements seen following EMDR can be explained by client motivation or the mere passage of time.

5. *What conclusions are most reasonable?* So far, additional research evidence has not ruled out alternative explanations for the effects of EMDR. People's belief in EMDR, rather than the treatment itself, may be largely responsible for its positive effects. So the only reasonable conclusions to be drawn at this point are that (a) EMDR seems to have a positive impact on some clients and (b) further research is needed in order to understand the nature and origins of those effects (Herbert et al., 2000).

Does that sound wishy-washy? Critical thinking sometimes does seem indecisive, because even though scientists would prefer to find quick, clear, and final answers, their conclusions must be tempered by the evidence available. In the long run, though, critical thinking opens the way to understanding. To help you hone your

critical thinking The process of assessing claims and making judgments on the basis of well-supported evidence.

Taking Your Life in Your Hands?
Does exposure to microwave radiation from cell phone antennas cause brain tumors (Carlo & Schram, 2001)? And what about the possible dangers and benefits of herbal remedies, dietary supplements, and other controversial treatments for cancer, AIDS, and depression? These questions have generated intense speculation, strong opinions, and a lot of wishful thinking, but the best answers will depend on scientific research based on critical thinking. For example, although there is no evidence that cell phones cause tumors, scientists continue to study the effects of long-term or heavy exposure (e.g., Carlo & Thibodeau, 2001; Inskip et al., 2001).

own critical thinking skills, we include in each subsequent chapter of this book a section called "Thinking Critically," in which we examine an issue by asking the same five questions we raised here about EMDR.

Critical Thinking and Scientific Research

Scientific research often begins with curious questions, such as "Can eye movements reduce anxiety?" Like many seemingly simple questions, however, this one is actually rather complex. Are we talking about horizontal, vertical, or diagonal eye movements? How long do they continue in each session, and how many sessions should there be? What kind of anxiety will we address, and how will we measure improvement? In other words, a scientist must ask *specific* questions in order to get meaningful answers.

Psychologists and other scientists clarify their questions about behavior and mental processes by phrasing them in terms of a **hypothesis**—a specific, testable proposition about something they want to study. Researchers state hypotheses in order to establish in clear, precise terms what they think may be true, and how they will know if it is not. In the case of EMDR, the hypothesis might be as follows: *EMDR treatment causes significant reduction in anxiety*. To make it easier to understand and objectively evaluate hypotheses, scientists employ **operational definitions**, which are statements describing the exact operations or methods they will use in their research. In the hypothesis just presented, "EMDR treatment" might be operationally defined as inducing a certain number of back-and-forth eye movements per second for a particular period of time, whereas "significant reduction in anxiety" might be operationally defined as a decline of ten points or more on a scale that measures clients' self-reported anxiety. The kind of treatment a client is given (say, EMDR versus no treatment) and the results of that treatment (how much anxiety

hypothesis In scientific research, a prediction stated as a specific, testable proposition about a phenomenon.

operational definitions Statements that define the exact operations or methods used in research.

reduction occurred) are examples of research **variables**, the specific factors or characteristics that are manipulated and measured in research.

To evaluate whether the results of a study support a hypothesis, the researcher usually looks at objective, quantifiable evidence—numbers or scores that represent the variables of interest and provide the basis for conclusions. This kind of evidence is usually called **data** (which is the plural of *datum*), or a *data set*. Even though data themselves are objective, it is all too easy for scientists to look only for those numbers or scores that confirm a hypothesis, especially if they expect the hypothesis to be true or hope that it is. This common human failing, called *confirmation bias*, is described in the chapter on cognition and language. Scientists have a special responsibility to combat confirmation bias by looking for evidence that contradicts their hypotheses, not just evidence that supports those hypotheses.

Scientists must also assess the *quality* of the evidence they collect. Usually, the quality of evidence is evaluated in terms of two characteristics: reliability and validity. *Reliability* is the degree to which the data are stable and consistent; the *validity* of data is the degree to which they accurately represent the topic being studied. For example, the initial claims for EMDR stemmed from Shapiro's use of this treatment with colleagues and clients. If she had not been able to repeat, or *replicate*, the initial effects—if clients sometimes showed improvement and sometimes did not—she would have had to question the reliability of her data. Alternatively, if the clients' reports of improvement were not supported by, say, the reports of their close relatives, she would have had to doubt the validity of her data.

The Role of Theories

After examining the evidence from research on particular phenomena, scientists often begin to favor certain explanations. Sometimes, they organize these explanations into a **theory**, which is a set of statements designed to account for, predict, and even suggest ways of controlling certain phenomena. For example, Shapiro's theory about the effects of EMDR suggests that eye movements activate parts of the brain

I Love It! When we want something—or someone—to be perfect, we may ignore all evidence to the contrary. This is one reason why people end up in faulty used cars—or in bad relationships. Psychologists and other scientists must be especially careful to keep this confirmation bias from distorting the conclusions they draw from their research.

---

variables Factors or characteristics that are manipulated or measured in research.
data Numbers that represent research findings and provide the basis for research conclusions.
theory An integrated set of propositions that can be used to account for, predict, and even control certain phenomena.

Where Does Prejudice Come From? In September 2001, local Protestants shouted insults, threw rocks, and even exploded a bomb as terrified Catholic children were escorted by their parents to classes at Holy Cross Primary school in Belfast, Northern Ireland. Researchers have proposed several theories about the causes of such prejudice—and how to prevent it (see the chapter on social cognition). The testing of these theories by other researchers is an example of how theory and research go hand in hand. Without research results, there would be nothing to explain; without explanatory theories, the results might never be organized in a useful way. The knowledge generated by psychologists over the past 125 years has been based on this constant interaction of theory and research.

where information about trauma or other unpleasant experiences has been stored but never fully processed. EMDR, she says, promotes the "accelerated information processing" required for the resolution of emotional and behavioral problems (Shapiro, 1995, 1999). In the chapter on introducing psychology, we reviewed broader and more famous examples of explanatory theories, including Charles Darwin's theory of evolution and Sigmund Freud's theory of psychoanalysis.

Theories are tentative explanations that must be subjected to scientific evaluation based on critical thinking. For example, Shapiro's theory about EMDR has been criticized as being vague; lacking empirical support; and being less plausible than other, simpler explanations (e.g., Herbert et al., 2000; Keane, 1998). In other words, theories are based on research results, but they also generate hypotheses for further research. The predictions of one psychologist's theory will be tested by many other psychologists. If research does not support a theory, the theory will be revised or abandoned.

The constant formulation, evaluation, reformulation, and abandonment of psychological theories have resulted in several competing explanations for color vision, memory, sleep, aggression, and many other behaviors and mental processes. A sometimes frustrating consequence of this continuing search for answers in psychology is that we cannot offer as many definite conclusions as you might want. The conclusions we *do* draw about many of the phenomena described in this book are always based on what is known so far, and we always cite the need for additional research. This is because research often raises at least as many questions as it answers. The results of one study might not apply in every situation, or to all people. For example, herbal remedies containing St.-John's-Wort appear to reduce mild depression but have little or no impact on severe depression (Shelton et al., 2001). Keep this point in mind the next time you hear a talk-show guest confidently offering simple solutions to complex problems such as depression or anxiety, or presenting easy formulas for a happy marriage and perfect children. These self-proclaimed experts—called "pop" (for *popular*) psychologists by the scientific community—tend to oversimplify issues, cite evidence for their views without concern for its reliability or validity, and ignore good evidence that contradicts the pet theories that they live on.

Psychological scientists must be far more cautious. It is often necessary that they suspend final judgments about complex aspects of behavior and mental processes until they have enough high-quality data to make responsible statements and recommendations. Still, psychological research has led to an enormous body of knowledge that is being put to good use in many ways. And psychologists in all subfields are using today's knowledge as the foundation for the research that will increase tomorrow's understanding of behavior and mental processes. In the rest of this chapter, we describe their research methods and some of the pitfalls that lie in the path of progress toward their goals.

Research Methods in Psychology

Like other scientists, psychologists strive to achieve four main goals in their research: to *describe* a phenomenon, to make *predictions* about it, and to introduce enough *control* over the variables in their research to allow them to *explain* the phenomenon with some degree of confidence. Certain methods are especially useful for gathering the evidence needed to attain each of these goals. Specifically, psychologists tend to use *naturalistic observation, case studies,* and *surveys* to describe and predict behavior and mental processes. They use *experiments* to control variables and thus establish *cause-effect relationships,* in which one variable can be shown to have actually caused a change in another. Thus, Shapiro initially *described* the effects of EMDR on the basis of observations of her own reactions; then she tested her *prediction* that similar results might occur in other people. Later we discuss an experiment designed to introduce enough *control* over the variables of interest to begin evaluating alternative explanations for EMDR effects, and thus to explore whether the treatment is actually the cause of clients' improvement. Let's look at how these goals and methods are blended in psychologists' work, beginning with how researchers select the participants in their studies.

Selecting Human Participants for Research

Just as visitors from another galaxy would be wildly mistaken if they tried to describe the typical earthling after meeting only Jackie Chan, Michael Jackson, Madonna, and Sparky the Wonder Dog, psychologists can go astray in their research if the participants they choose to study are not typical of the larger population of people or animals about which they want to draw conclusions.

The process of selecting participants for research is called **sampling.** Sampling is an extremely important component of the research enterprise because it can affect not only what results a psychologist gets but also what those results mean. If all the participants in a study come from a particular subgroup (say, male Asian American musicians), the research results might apply, or *generalize,* only to people like them. This outcome would be especially likely if the researcher is studying a behavior or mental process that is affected by age, gender, ethnicity, cultural background, socioeconomic status, sexual orientation, disability, or other characteristics specific to the participants. When, as is often the case, these variables are likely to have an impact on research results, the sample of participants studied must be representative of people in general if the researcher wants results that are applicable to people in general.

If every member of a population to be studied has the same chance of being chosen as a research participant, the individuals selected constitute a **random sample.** If not everyone has a chance of participating, those selected constitute a **biased sample.** Because it is so difficult and expensive to select a truly random sample from, say, "all college students," "all Canadians," or any other large group, most researchers draw their participants, as randomly as possible, from the population available to them. Depending on their research budget, this population might include, for example, all college students on a local campus or on several campuses around the country, all citizens in the Toronto phone book, or the like. Participants chosen in this way provide a *representative sample* of the population from which they were selected. These samples might represent an even larger population as well, but researchers cannot merely assume that. Before drawing broad conclusions from their research, they must conduct additional studies to show that those conclusions apply to people who differ on sociocultural characteristics such as age, gender, and ethnicity (APA Office of Ethnic Minority Affairs, 2000; Case & Smith, 2000; Gray-Little & Hafdahl, 2000).

Sometimes, however, representative samples of the general population are not necessary, or even desirable. If you are studying unusual mental abilities, it might be more valuable to focus on those rare individuals who can do complex math problems in their heads than to test a representative sample of adults. Further, if you *want* to learn about male Asian American musicians, or pregnant teenagers, or Hispanic American women executives, all your participants should be randomly selected from those groups, not from among people in general.

No matter how they select their samples, psychologists must guard against allowing their preconceptions about people to influence the questions they ask; the research designs they create; and the way they analyze, interpret, and report their data (Denmark et al., 1988; Hall, 1997). When designing a study on gender and job commitment, for example, the researcher must be sure to sample men and women in jobs of equal status. Comparing male executives with female secretaries might create a false impression of greater male commitment, because people in lower-status positions tend to change jobs more often, regardless of gender. Similarly, researchers who use an all-male sample should give this fact the same prominence

sampling The process of selecting participants who are members of the population that the researcher wishes to study.

random sample A group of research participants selected from a population, each of whose members had an equal chance of being chosen.

biased sample A group of research participants selected from a population each of whose members did not have an equal chance of being chosen.

Selecting Research Participants Imagine that as a social psychologist, you want to study people's willingness to help each other. You have developed a method for testing helpfulness, but now you want a random sample of people to test. Take a minute to think about the steps necessary to select a truly random sample; then ask yourself how you might obtain a representative sample, instead.

in their research report as is customarily the case when only females are studied (Ader & Johnson, 1994). To do otherwise would imply that males provide a standard against which females' behavior and mental processes are to be compared. Finally, researchers must report whatever results appear. After all, it is just as valuable to know that men and women, or African Americans and European Americans, did *not* differ on a test of leadership ability as to know that they did. Stephanie Riger (1992) suggests that one of psychologists' greatest challenges is to "disengage themselves sufficiently from commonly shared beliefs so that those beliefs do not predetermine research findings" (p. 732).

Let's now consider some specific research methods that psychologists use to describe, predict, control, and explain the behavior and mental processes of the participants they select for study.

Naturalistic Observation: Watching Behavior

Sometimes, the best way to describe behavior is through **naturalistic observation**, the process of watching without interfering as behavior occurs in the natural environment. This method is especially valuable in cases where other methods are likely to be disruptive or misleading. For example, if you studied animals only by observing them in the laboratory, you might conclude that learning determines most of what they do. If you saw them in the wild, however, you might realize that they also display unlearned actions that are automatically triggered by signals in their natural habitat.

Naturalistic observation of people can be just as important. For example, much of what we know about gender differences in how children play and communicate has come from psychologists' observations in classrooms and playgrounds. Observations of adults have helped psychologists see that the gender differences evident in childhood might underlie some of the conflict and miscommunication that occurs later in intimate relationships (Bradbury, Campbell, & Fincham, 1995). And understanding gender differences that first came to light through observational research helps therapists who work with couples in conflict.

naturalistic observation The process of watching without interfering as a phenomenon occurs in the natural environment.

Although naturalistic observation can provide large amounts of information, it is not problem-free (Nietzel et al., 2003). For one thing, when people know they are being observed (and ethics usually requires that they do know), they tend to act differently than they otherwise would. Researchers typically combat this problem by observing long enough for participants to get used to the situation and begin behaving more naturally. Observational data can also be distorted if observers *expect* to see certain behaviors. If, in a study of EMDR's effects on anxiety, observers know which participants received EMDR and which did not, they might tend to rate the treated participants as less anxious, no matter how they actually behave. To get the most out of naturalistic observation, psychologists must counteract problems such as these. In the treatment study just mentioned, for example, the researchers might ask observers to rate participants' anxiety as seen in videotaped interviews, and without telling them which participants had been given treatment.

Case Studies: Taking a Closer Look

Observations are often an important part of a **case study**, which is an intensive examination of behavior or mental processes in a particular individual, group, or situation. Case study examinations may also include tests; interviews; and analysis of letters, school transcripts, or other written records. Case studies are especially useful when studying something that is new, complex, or relatively rare. Shapiro's EMDR treatment, for example, first attracted psychologists' attention through case studies of its remarkable effects on her clients (Shapiro, 1989a).

Case studies have a long tradition in clinical work. Freud's theory of psychoanalysis, for example, was largely developed from case studies of people whose paralysis or other physical symptoms disappeared when they were hypnotized or asleep. Case studies have also played a special role in *neuropsychology*, the study of the relationships among brain activity, thinking, and behavior. Consider the case of Dr. P., a patient described by Oliver Sacks (1985). A distinguished musician with superior intelligence, Dr. P. began to display odd symptoms, such as the inability to recognize familiar people or to distinguish between people and objects. During a visit to a neurologist, Dr. P. mistook his foot for his shoe. When he rose to leave, he tried to lift off his wife's head—like a hat—and put it on his own. He could not

An Ethologist at Work Konrad Lorenz helped to found *ethology*, the scientific study of animal behavior in the natural environment. Using naturalistic observation, Lorenz described many examples of inborn, but environmentally triggered, behaviors. For example, baby geese follow their mother because her movement and honking provide signals that are naturally attractive. After Lorenz squatted and made mother-goose noises in front of orphaned newborn geese, the goslings began following him wherever he went.

TRY THIS **Naturalistic Observation** Observing people in natural settings can provide important clues to understanding social interaction, but it is not easy. Imagine you are studying these children at play. Make a list of the *exact* behaviors you would count as "aggressive," "cooperative," and "competitive."

Learning from Rare Cases Dustin Hoffman's character in *Rain Man* was based on the case of "Joseph," an autistic man who can, for example, mentally multiply or divide six-digit numbers. Other case studies have described *autistic savants* who can correctly identify the day of the week for any date in the past or the future, or tell at a glance that, say, exactly 125 paper clips are scattered on the floor. By carefully studying such rare cases, cognitive psychologists are learning more about human mental capacities and how they might be maximized in everyone (L. K. Miller, 1999; Snyder & Mitchell, 1999).

name common objects when he looked at them, although he could describe them. When handed a glove, for example, he said, "A continuous surface, infolded on itself. It appears to have . . . five outpouchings, if this is the word. . . . A container of some sort." Only later, when he put it on his hand, did he exclaim, "My God, it's a glove!" (Sacks, 1985, p. 13).

Using case studies like this one, pioneers in neuropsychology noted the difficulties suffered by people with particular kinds of brain damage or disease (Banich, 2003). Eventually, neuropsychologists were able to tie specific disorders to certain types of injuries, tumors, poisons, and other causes. (Dr. P.'s symptoms may have been caused by a large brain tumor.) Case studies do have their limitations, however. They may contain only the evidence that a particular researcher considered important, and of course, they are unlikely to be representative of people in general. Nonetheless, case studies can provide valuable raw material for further research. They can also be vital sources of information about particular people, and they serve as the testing ground for new treatments, training programs, and other applications of research.

Surveys: Looking at the Big Picture

Whereas case studies provide close-up views of individuals, surveys provide wide-angle portraits of large groups. In a **survey**, researchers use interviews or questionnaires to ask people about their behavior, attitudes, beliefs, opinions, or intentions. Just as politicians and advertisers rely on opinion polls to gauge the popularity of policies or products, psychologists use surveys to gather descriptive data on just about anything related to behavior and mental processes, from parenting practices to sexual behavior. However, the validity of survey data depends partly on how questions are worded (Schwarz, 1999). This point was illustrated in the results of a 1998 Gallup poll conducted just after then-president Bill Clinton admitted to an adulterous affair with White House intern Monica Lewinsky. This survey suggested that only 40 percent of a national sample had a favorable opinion of Clinton—a 20-point drop from previous polls assessing his popularity. However, the wording of the question differed from the previous surveys. The 1998 poll asked, "Thinking

case study A research method involving the intensive examination of some phenomenon in a particular individual, group, or situation.

survey A research method that involves giving people questionnaires or special interviews designed to obtain descriptions of their attitudes, beliefs, opinions, and intentions.

of Bill Clinton *as a person,* do you have a favorable or unfavorable opinion of him?" The earlier polls had presented respondents with the names of several well-known people, including Clinton. As each name was read, respondents were asked, "Do you have a favorable or unfavorable opinion *of this person*?" When this original wording was used again in a survey conducted one day later, 55 percent of respondents said they had a favorable opinion of Clinton. This figure represented a drop of only 5 percentage points from earlier polls (New York Times, August 20, 1998).

A survey's validity also depends on the sample of people surveyed. As mentioned earlier in relation to all research methods, if you want to draw conclusions about a large population, the sample of people surveyed must be representative of that population. If only people who had voted for Bill Clinton had been sampled in the post-Lewinsky survey, his favorability rating would probably have been even higher than it was. But that result would have reflected the views of Clinton supporters, not U.S. citizens in general.

Other limitations of the survey method are more difficult to avoid. For example, the American Society for Microbiology found that 95 percent of the 1,021 U.S. adults it surveyed said that they wash their hands after using toilet facilities. However, naturalistic observations of 7,836 people in public restrooms across the United States revealed that the figure is closer to 67 percent (ASM, 2000). In short, people may be reluctant to admit undesirable or embarrassing things about themselves, or they may say what they believe they *should* say about an issue. And sometimes, those who respond to a survey hold views that differ from those who do not respond (Rogelberg & Luong, 1998). Survey results—and the conclusions drawn from them—will be distorted to the extent that such tendencies distort people's responses and researchers' access to responses (Turner, Miller, & Rogers, 1998). Still, surveys provide an efficient way to gather large amounts of data about people's attitudes, beliefs, or other characteristics.

Experiments: Exploring Cause and Effect

Naturalistic observation, case studies, and surveys provide valuable descriptions of behavior and mental processes. The relationships revealed by these research methods help psychologists to evaluate existing explanations—and to form new

TRY THIS — **Designing Survey Research** How do people feel about gay men and lesbians serving openly in the U.S. military? To appreciate the difficulties of survey research, try writing a question about this issue that you think is clear enough and neutral enough to generate valid data. Then ask some friends whether or not they agree it would be a good survey question, and why.

Research Methods in Psychology

hypotheses—about why people think and act as they do. For example, observations that children who watch a lot of violence on television tend to be more aggressive than other children led to the hypothesis that exposure to media violence can cause aggressiveness (see the chapter on learning.). Surveys showing that sex criminals consume more pornography than other men do suggested that exposure to pornography might cause rape and other sex-related crimes (see the chapter on social influence). And observations that children in day care for more than thirty hours a week are more aggressive than those who stay home with their mothers raised concerns that day care can cause behavior problems (see the chapter on human development).

Establishing Cause and Effect

Do violent television, pornography, and day care actually *cause* the problems with which they are associated? They might, but the most obvious explanations of what is causing what in observational, case study, and survey results may not always be the correct ones (see Figure 2.1). Accordingly, psychologists must consider and test a number of hypotheses to determine which one best explains their research results. Perhaps children who are most aggressive in the first place are the ones who watch the most violent television; maybe sex criminals exaggerate the impact of pornography in hope of escaping punishment; and the aggressiveness seen in day care might have something to do with certain children's pre-existing characteristics, not just their separation from a parent.

One way to evaluate possibilities like these is to analyze observations, case studies, and surveys for trends that support or conflict with certain hypotheses. One trend in the day-care study, for example, was for the most aggressive preschoolers to be the ones who spent the most time in day care each week. This trend supports the hypothesis that separation from the mother can cause aggressiveness. However, it was also the case that 83 percent of the children in day care did *not* show any behavior problems. This second trend suggests that whatever effect separation has, it may be different for different children. It would have been ideal if the children in day care and those at home had been the same in every way except for where they spent their time, but this was not the case. It was the parents, not the researchers, who decided whether to place a particular child in day care, and for how long. The researchers could only describe the results of these decisions and then try to figure out the most reasonable explanation for those results.

The Experimental Method

A better way to evaluate explanatory hypotheses and establish cause-effect relationships is to exert some *control* over research variables ahead of time, not just describe them after the fact. This kind of research usually takes the form of an experiment. **Experiments** are situations in which the researcher manipulates one variable and then observes the effect of that manipulation on another variable, while holding all other variables constant. The variable controlled by the experimenter is called the **independent variable**. The variable to be observed is called the **dependent variable** because it is affected by, or depends on, the independent variable.

Consider the experiment Shapiro conducted in an attempt to better understand the effects of EMDR. As illustrated in Figure 2.2, she first identified twenty-two people suffering the ill effects of traumas such as rape or military combat. These were her research participants. She assigned the participants to two groups. The first group received a single fifty-minute session of EMDR treatment; the second group focused on their unpleasant memories for eight minutes, but without moving their eyes back and forth (Shapiro, 1989b). The experimenter controlled whether EMDR treatment was administered to each participant, so the presence or absence of treatment was the independent variable. The participants' anxiety level while thinking about their traumatic memories was the dependent variable.

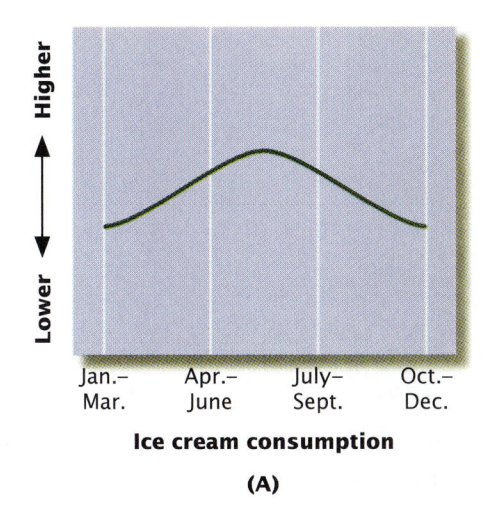

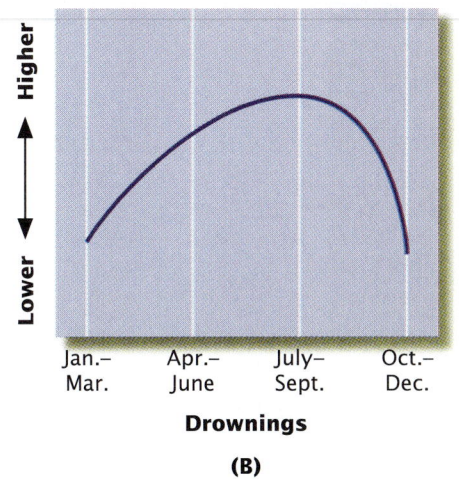

figure 2.1

What Is Causing What?

As these graphs show, ice cream consumption and drownings in the United States tend to rise and fall together. Does this mean that eating ice cream *causes* drowning? No. The relationship between them probably reflects a third variable—time of year—that affects both ice cream sales and the likelihood of swimming and boating (Brenner et al., 2001).

---

experiments Situations in which the researcher manipulates one variable and then observes the effect of that manipulation on another variable, while holding all other variables constant.

independent variable The variable manipulated by the researcher in an experiment.

dependent variable In an experiment, the factor affected by the independent variable.

Unthinkable Experiments It would be much easier to draw cause-effect conclusions about the impact of day care if researchers assigned similar children to either day care or home care. And keeping one group of pregnant women drug-free while giving others varying amounts of alcohol would allow firmer conclusions about the amount of alcohol it takes to cause birth defects. But these controlled experiments would be utterly unethical, which is why psychologists explore some important research questions only by comparing the outcomes of people's differing decisions about day care, drug use, dropping out of school, and the like.

---

experimental group In an experiment, the group that receives the experimental treatment.

control group In an experiment, the group that receives no treatment or provides some other baseline against which to compare the performance or response of the experimental group.

confounding variable In an experiment, any factor that affects the dependent variable, along with or instead of the independent variable

random variables In an experiment, confounding variables in which uncontrolled or uncontrollable factors affect the dependent variable, along with or instead of the independent variable.

random assignment The procedure by which random variables are evenly distributed in an experiment by putting participants into various groups through random process.

placebo A physical or psychological treatment that contains no active ingredient but produces an effect because the person receiving it believes it will.

The group that receives the experimental treatment is called, naturally enough, the **experimental group.** The group that receives no treatment or some other treatment is called the **control group.** Control groups provide baselines against which to compare the performance of other groups. In Shapiro's experiment, having a control group allowed her to measure how much change in anxiety could be expected from exposure to bad memories without EMDR treatment. If everything about the two groups was exactly the same *before* the experiment, then any difference in anxiety between the groups *afterward* should have been due to the treatment given. At the same time, hypotheses about alternative causes of improvement, such as the mere passage of time, became less plausible.

The results of the Shapiro (1989b) experiment showed that participants who received EMDR treatment experienced a complete and nearly immediate reduction in anxiety related to their traumatic memories, whereas those in the control group showed no change. This difference suggests that EMDR caused the improvement. But look again at the structure, or design, of the experiment. The EMDR group's session lasted about fifty minutes, but the control group focused on their memories for only eight minutes. Would the people in the control group have improved, too, if they had spent fifty minutes focusing on their memories? We don't know, because the experiment did not compare methods of equal duration.

Anyone who conducts or relies on research must be on guard for such flaws in experimental design and control. Before drawing any conclusions from research, experimenters must consider other factors—especially variables that could confound, or confuse, interpretation of the results. Any factor that might have affected the dependent variable, along with or instead of the independent variable, may be such a **confounding variable.** When confounding variables are present, the experimenter cannot know whether the independent variable or the confounding variable produced the results. Let's examine three sources of confounding: random variables, participants' expectations, and experimenter bias.

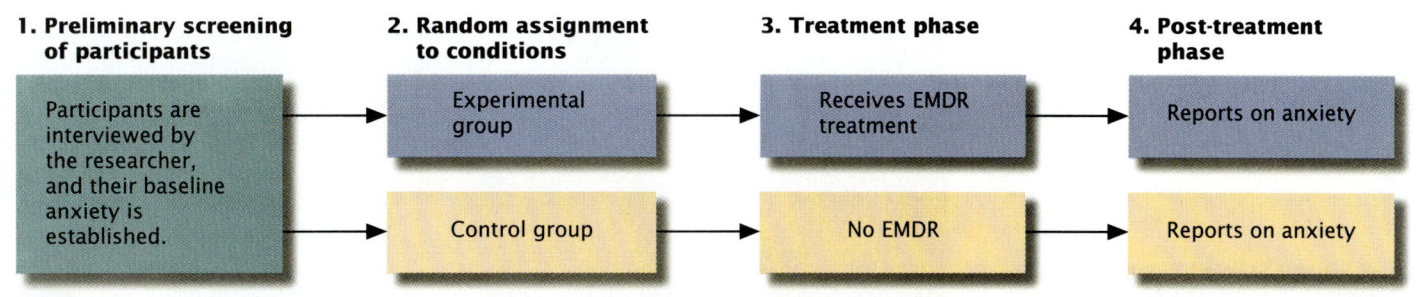

figure 2.2
A Simple Two-Group Experiment

1. Preliminary screening of participants: Participants are interviewed by the researcher, and their baseline anxiety is established.

2. Random assignment to conditions: Experimental group / Control group

3. Treatment phase: Receives EMDR treatment / No EMDR

4. Post-treatment phase: Reports on anxiety / Reports on anxiety

Ideally, the only difference between the experimental and control groups in experiments like this one is whether the participants receive the treatment the experimenter wishes to evaluate. Under such ideal circumstances, any difference in the two groups' reported levels of anxiety (the dependent variable) at the end of the experiment would be due only to whether or not they received treatment (the independent variable).

Random Variables In an ideal research world, everything about the experimental and control groups would be identical except for their exposure to the independent variable (such as whether or not they received treatment). In reality, however, there are always other differences, especially those introduced by **random variables**. Random variables are uncontrolled, sometimes uncontrollable, factors such as differences among the participants—in terms of their backgrounds, personalities, physical health, or vulnerability to stress, for example—as well as differences in research conditions such as the time of day, temperature, or noise level.

Differences among participants can be so numerous that no experimenter can create groups that are equivalent on all of them. A common solution to this problem is to flip a coin or use some other random process to assign each research participant to experimental or control groups. Such procedures—called **random assignment**—are intended to distribute the impact of these uncontrolled variables randomly (and probably about equally) across groups, thus minimizing the chance that they will distort the results of the experiment (Shadish, Cook, & Campbell, 2002).

Notice that although the names are similar, *random assignment* is not the same as *random sampling*. As mentioned earlier, random sampling is used in many kinds of research to ensure that the people studied are representative of some larger group, whereas random assignment is used in experiments to create equivalence among various groups.

They Are All the Same Scientists in Hawaii succeeded in cloning dozens of mice and then creating a second generation of clones from the original group. Having lots of genetically identical animals is important because they can be assigned to various experimental and control groups without having to worry about the effects of individual differences on the dependent variable. Ethical concerns rule out creating a pool of cloned people, so random assignment will remain a vital component of psychological research with human beings.

Participants' Expectations After eight minutes of focusing on unpleasant memories, participants in the control group in Shapiro's (1989b) experiment were asked to begin moving their eyes. At that point they, too, started to experience a reduction in anxiety. Was this improvement caused by the eye movements themselves, or could it be that the instructions made the participants feel more confident that they were now getting "real" treatment? This question illustrates a second source of confounding: differences in what people *think* about the experimental situation. If participants who receive an impressive treatment expect that it will help them, they may try harder to improve than those in a control group who receive no treatment or a less impressive one. Improvement created by a participant's knowledge and expectations is called the *placebo effect*. A **placebo** (pronounced "pla-SEE-boe") is a treatment that contains nothing known to be helpful, but that nevertheless produces benefits because a person believes it will be beneficial.

How can researchers determine the extent to which a result is caused by the independent variable or by a placebo effect? Usually, they include a special control group that receives *only* a placebo treatment. Then they compare results for the experimental group, the placebo group, and those receiving no treatment. In one smoking-cessation study, for example, participants in a placebo group took sugar

Ever Since I Started Wearing These Magnets... Placebo-controlled experiments are vital for establishing cause-effect relationships between treatment and outcome with human participants. For example, many people swear that magnets held against their joints relieve the pain of sports injuries and even arthritis. But experiments show that magnets are no more effective than placebo treatment with an identical, but nonmagnetic, metal object (e.g., Carter et al., 2002; Collacott et al., 2000). Something other than magnets—wishful thinking, perhaps—appears to be causing the reported benefits.

pills described by the experimenter as "fast-acting tranquilizers" that would help them learn to endure the stress of giving up cigarettes (Bernstein, 1970). These people did far better at quitting than did those in a no-treatment group; in fact, they did as well as participants in the experimental group, who received extensive treatment. This result suggested that the success of the experimental group may have been due largely to the participants' expectations, not to the treatment methods. Placebo effects may not be as strong as experimenters once assumed (Hrobjartsson & Gotzsche, 2001), but some people do improve after receiving medical or psychological treatment, not because of the treatment itself but because they believe that it will help them.

Research on EMDR treatment suggests that the eye movements themselves may not be responsible for improvement, inasmuch as staring, finger tapping, or listening to rapid clicks or tones while focusing on traumatic memories has also produced benefits (e.g., Carrigan & Levis, 1999; Cusack & Spates, 1999; Rosen, 1999). In fact, although EMDR appears to have some positive effects on some clients (e.g., Feske & Goldstein, 1997), its failure to outperform impressive placebo treatments (or other established methods for helping clients deal with unpleasant images) has led many researchers to conclude that EMDR should not be a first-choice treatment for anxiety-related disorders (Davison & Parker, 2001; Goldstein et al., 2000; Herbert et al., 2000). Accordingly, mental health professionals volunteering to work with traumatized people in the days following the September 11, 2001, terrorist attack on the World Trade Center were asked by New York authorities not to use EMDR (P. Fraenkel, personal communication, October 28, 2001).

Experimenter Bias

Another potential confounding variable comes from **experimenter bias**, the unintentional effect that experimenters may exert on their results. Robert Rosenthal (1966) was one of the first to demonstrate the power of one kind of experimenter bias: *experimenter expectancies*. His research participants were laboratory assistants whose job was to place rats in a maze. Rosenthal told some of the assistants that their rats had been bred to be particularly "maze-bright"; he told the others that their rats were "maze-dull." In fact, both groups of rats were randomly drawn from the same population and had equal maze-learning capabilities. But the "maze-bright" animals learned the maze significantly faster than the "maze-dull" rats. Why? Rosenthal concluded that the result had nothing to do with

experimenter bias A confounding variable that occurs when an experimenter unintentionally encourages participants to respond in a way that supports the hypothesis.

double-blind design A research design in which neither the experimenter nor the participants know who is in the experimental group and who is in the control group.

Try This — Keeping Experimenters "Blind" Suppose you are a sport psychologist conducting an experiment in which the independent variable is coaching style (standard methods versus a new relaxation-based technique) for reducing athletic performance anxiety (the dependent variable). How would you create a double-blind design to prevent experimenter bias? Would it be possible to keep coaches in the dark about which method is expected to produce the best results?

the rats and everything to do with the experimenters. He suggested that the assistants' expectations about their rats' supposedly superior (or inferior) capabilities caused them to slightly alter their training and handling techniques, which in turn speeded (or slowed) the animals' learning. Similarly, when administering different kinds of anxiety treatments to different groups, experimenters who believe one treatment will be the best may do a slightly better job with that treatment and thus unintentionally improve its effects.

To prevent experimenter bias from confounding results, experimenters often use a **double-blind design.** In this arrangement, both the research participants and those giving the treatments are unaware of, or "blind" to, who is receiving a placebo, and they do not know what results are expected from various treatments. Only the director of the study—a person who makes no direct contact with participants—has this information, and he or she does not reveal it until the experiment is over. The fact that double-blind studies of EMDR have not yet been conducted is another reason for caution in drawing conclusions about this treatment.

In short, experiments are vital tools for examining cause-effect relationships between variables, but like the other methods we have described (see "In Review: Methods of Psychological Research"), they are vulnerable to error. To maximize the value of their experiments, psychologists try to eliminate as many confounding variables as possible, replicate their work to ensure consistent results, and then temper their interpretation of the results to take into account the limitations or problems that remain.

To best control for participant expectancies and experimenter bias, neither experimenters nor participants should know who is getting the experimental treatment and who is getting placebo treatment.

By permission of Johnny Hart and Creators Syndicate, Inc.

THE WIZARD OF ID — Brant parker and Johnny hart

in review | Methods of Psychological Research

Method	Features	Strengths	Pitfalls
Naturalistic observation	Observation of human or animal behavior in the environment where it typically occurs	Provides descriptive data about behavior presumably uncontaminated by outside influences	Observer bias and participant self-consciousness can distort results
Case studies	Intensive examination of the behavior and mental processes associated with a specific person or situation	Provide detailed descriptive analyses of new, complex, or rare phenomena	May not provide representative picture of phenomena
Surveys	Standard sets of questions asked of a large number of participants	Gather large amounts of descriptive data relatively quickly and inexpensively	Sampling errors, poorly phrased questions, and response biases can distort results
Experiments	Manipulation of an independent variable and measurement of its effects on a dependent variable	Can establish a cause-effect relationship between independent and dependent variables	Confounding variables may prevent valid conclusions

Statistical Analysis of Research Results

Naturalistic observations, case studies, surveys, and experiments generate a large amount of information, or data. *Statistical analyses* are the methods most often used to summarize and analyze those data. These methods include **descriptive statistics**, which are the numbers that psychologists use to describe and present their data, and **inferential statistics**, which are mathematical procedures used to draw conclusions from data and to make inferences about what they mean. Here, we describe a few statistical terms that you will encounter in later chapters; you can find more information about these terms in the statistics appendix.

Descriptive Statistics

The three most important *descriptive statistics* are *measures of central tendency*, which describe the typical score (or value) in a set of data; *measures of variability*, which describe the spread, or dispersion, among the scores in a set of data; and *correlation coefficients*, which describe relationships between variables.

Measures of Central Tendency

Suppose you wanted to test the effects of EMDR treatment on fear of the dark. Looking for participants, you collect the eleven self-ratings of anxiety listed on the left side of Table 2.2. What is the typical score, the central tendency, that best represents the anxiety level of this group of people? There are three measures designed to capture this typical score: the mode, the median, and the mean.

The **mode** is the value or score that occurs most frequently in a data set. You can find it by arranging the scores from lowest to highest. On the left side of Table 2.2, the mode is 50, because the score of 50 occurs more often than any other. Notice, however, that in this data set the mode is actually an extreme score. Sometimes, the mode acts like a microphone for a small but vocal minority that, though it speaks most frequently, does not represent the views of the majority.

Unlike the mode, the median takes all of the scores into account. The **median** is the halfway point in a set of data: Half the scores fall above the median, and half

---

descriptive statistics Numbers that summarize a set of research data.

inferential statistics A set of procedures that provides a measure of how likely it is that research results came about by chance.

mode A measure of central tendency that is the value or score that occurs most frequently in a data set.

median A measure of central tendency that is the halfway point in a set of data: Half the scores fall above the median, and half fall below it.

mean A measure of central tendency that is the arithmetic average of the scores in a set of data.

Here are scores representing people's self-ratings, on a 1–100 scale, of their fear of the dark.

table 2.2
A Set of Pretreatment Anxiety Ratings

Data from 11 Participants		Data from 12 Participants	
Participant Number	Anxiety Rating	Participant Number	Anxiety Rating
1	20	1	20
2	22	2	22
3	28	3	28
4	35	4	35
5	40	5	40
6	45 (Median)	6	45
7	47	7	47 (Median = 46*)
8	49	8	49
9	50	9	50
10	50	10	50
11	50	11	50
		12	100

Measures of central tendency
Mode = 50
Median = 45
Mean = 436/11 = 39.6

Measures of variability
Range = 30
Standard deviation = 11.064

Measures of central tendency
Mode = 50
Median = 46
Mean = 536/12 = 44.7

Measures of variability
Range = 80
Standard deviation = 19.763

*When there is an even number of scores, the exact middle of the list lies between two numbers. The median is the value halfway between those numbers.

fall below it. For the scores on the left side of Table 2.2, the halfway point—the median—is 45.

The third measure of central tendency is the **mean**, which is the *arithmetic average* of a set of scores. When people talk about the "average" in everyday conversation, they are usually referring to the mean. To find the mean, add the scores and divide by the number of scores. For the data on the left side of Table 2.2, the mean is 436/11 = 39.6.

Like the median (and unlike the mode), the mean reflects all the data to some degree, not just the most frequent data. Notice, however, that the mean reflects the actual values of all the scores, whereas the median gives each score equal weight, whatever its value. This distinction can have a big effect on how well the mean and median represent the scores in a particular set of data. Suppose, for example, that

Descriptive statistics are valuable for summarizing research results, but we must evaluate them carefully before drawing conclusions about what they mean. Given this executive's reputation for uncritical thinking, you can bet that Dogbert's impressive-sounding restatement of the definition of *median* will win him an extension of his pricey consulting contract.

DILBERT reprinted by permission of United Feature Syndicate, Inc.

you add to your sample a twelfth participant, whose anxiety rating is 100. When you re-analyze the anxiety data (see the right side of Table 2.2), the median hardly changes, because the new participant counts as just one more score. However, when you compute the new mean, the actual *amount* of the new participant's rating is added to everyone else's ratings; as a result, the mean jumps five points. Sometimes, as in this example, the median is a better measure of central tendency than the mean because the median is less sensitive to extreme scores. But because the mean is more representative of the values of all the data, it is often the preferred measure of central tendency.

Measures of Variability

The variability (also known as *spread* or *dispersion*) in a set of data is described by statistics known as the *range* and the *standard deviation*. The **range** is simply the difference between the highest and the lowest scores in a data set (it would be 30 for the data on the left side of Table 2.2 and 80 for the data on the right side). In contrast, the **standard deviation**, or **SD**, measures the average difference between each score and the mean of the data set. It provides information on the extent to which scores in a data set vary, or differ, from one another. The more variable the data are, the higher the standard deviation will be. For example, the SD for the eleven participants on the left side of Table 2.2 is 11.064, but it rises to 19.763 once the very divergent twelfth score is added on the right side. In the statistics appendix, we show how to calculate the standard deviation.

Correlation and Correlation Coefficients

Does the number of fears people have tend to decrease with age? In general, yes (Kleinknecht, 1991);

TRY THIS **The Impact of Variability** Suppose that on your first day as a substitute teacher at a new school, you are offered either of two classes. The mean IQ score in both classes is 100, but the standard deviation (SD) of scores is 16 in one class and 32 in the other. Before you read the next sentence, ask yourself which class you would choose if you wanted an easy day's work, or a tough challenge. (Higher standard deviation means more variability, so students in the class with the SD of 32 will vary more in ability, thus creating a greater challenge.)

range A measure of variability that is the difference between the highest and the lowest values in a data set.

standard deviation (SD) A measure of variability that is the average difference between each score and the mean of the data set.

correlation In research, the degree to which one variable is related to another.

correlation coefficient A statistic, *r*, that summarizes the strength and direction of a relationship between two variables.

but to test hypotheses about questions such as this, psychologists must have a way to measure how, and to what extent, variables such as age and fearfulness are correlated.

Correlation means just what it says: "co-relation." In statistics, correlation refers both to how strongly one variable is related to another and to the direction of the relationship. A *positive correlation* means that two variables increase together or decrease together. A *negative correlation* means that the variables move in opposite directions: When one increases, the other decreases. For example, James Schaefer observed 4,500 customers in 65 bars and found that the tempo of jukebox music was negatively correlated with the rate at which the customers drank alcohol; the slower the tempo, the faster the drinking (Schaefer et al., 1988).

Does this mean Schaefer could wear a blindfold and predict exactly how fast people are drinking by timing the music? Or could he plug his ears and determine the musical tempo by watching how fast people drink? No and no, because the accuracy of predictions about one variable from knowledge of another depends on the strength of the correlation. Only a perfect correlation between two variables would allow you to predict the exact value of one from a knowledge of the other. The weaker the correlation, the less one variable can tell you about the other.

To describe the strength of a correlation, psychologists use a statistic called the **correlation coefficient** (the statistics appendix shows how to calculate it). The correlation coefficient is given the symbol r, and it can vary from $+1.00$ to -1.00. Thus, the coefficient includes (1) an absolute value, such as .20 or .50, and (2) either a plus sign or a minus sign.

The actual value of r indicates the strength of the relationship. An r of $+.01$ between people's shoe size and the age of their cars, for example, indicates that there is virtually no relationship between the variables, whereas an r of $+1.00$ indicates a perfectly predictable relationship between two variables (see Figure 2.3).

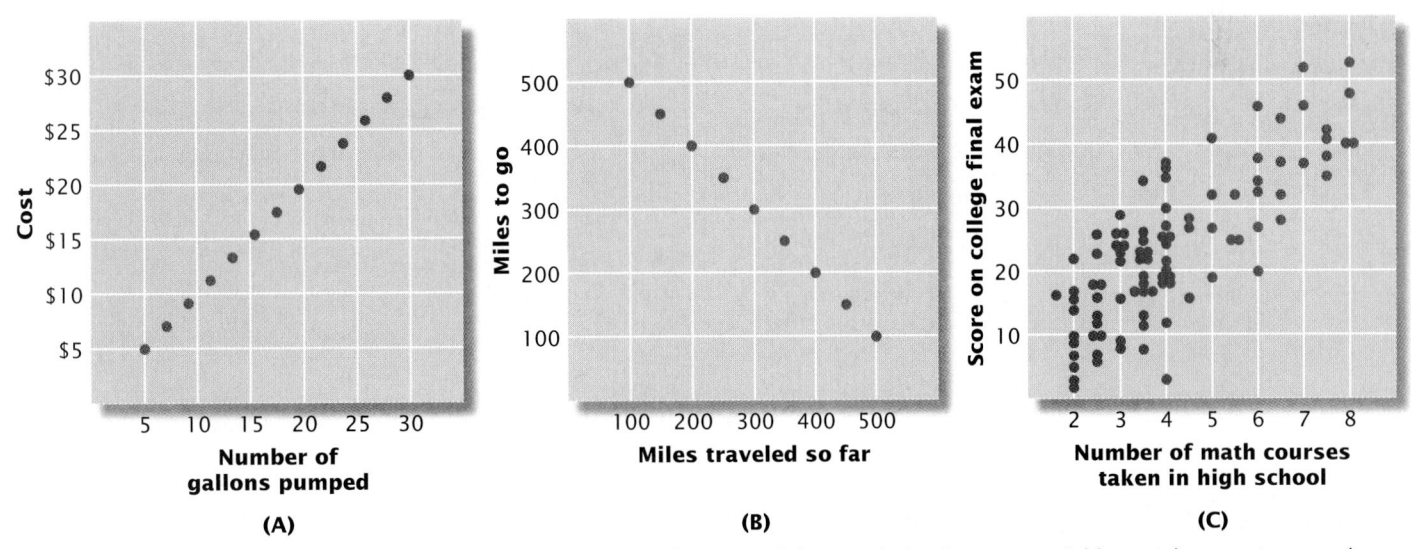

figure 2.3

Three Correlations

The strength and direction of the correlation between variables can be seen in a graph called a *scatterplot*. Here are three examples. In Part A, we have plotted the cost of a gasoline purchase against the number of gallons pumped. The number of gallons is *positively* and perfectly correlated with their cost, so the scatterplot appears as a straight line, and you can predict the value of either variable from a knowledge of the other. Part B shows a perfect *negative* correlation between the number of miles you have traveled toward a destination and the distance remaining. Again, one variable can be exactly predicted from the other. Part C illustrates a correlation of $+.81$ between the number of math courses students had in high school and their scores on a college math exam; each dot represents one student (Hays, 1981). As correlations decrease, they are represented by ever-greater dispersion in the pattern of dots. A correlation of 0.00 would appear as a shapeless cloud.

Unfortunately, the variables of interest in psychology are seldom perfectly correlated. Throughout this book, you will find many correlation coefficients whose absolute values range from .20 to .90, reflecting relationships of intermediate strength in which knowing about one variable tells us something, but not everything, about the other.

The *sign* of a correlation coefficient indicates its direction. A plus sign signifies a *positive* correlation between variables; a minus sign indicates a *negative* correlation.

Psychologists use correlation coefficients to help them describe the results of their research, to evaluate existing hypotheses, and often, to generate new hypotheses. As mentioned earlier, however, they must be very careful when drawing conclusions about what correlations mean. Think back to that positive correlation between watching violent television programs and behaving violently. Does seeing violence on TV cause viewers to be violent, or does being violent to begin with cause a preference for violent shows? Perhaps neither causes the other; violent behavior and TV choices could both be due to some third factor, such as examples set by friends. Finding that two variables are *correlated* doesn't guarantee that one is *causing* an effect on the other. And even if one *does* affect the other, a correlation coefficient can't tell us which variable is influencing which. In short, correlations can reveal and describe relationships, but correlations alone cannot explain them.

Inferential Statistics

The task of understanding the meaning of research results summarized in correlations or other descriptive statistics is not an easy one. For example, how did researchers conclude that compared with other anxiety treatments or a placebo, the benefits of EMDR were not great enough to justify recommending it as a treatment of choice (Goldstein et al., 2000)? Such conclusions are based largely on the results of analyses that use *inferential statistics*.

in review: Descriptive and Inferential Statistics

Statistic	Characteristics	Information Provided
Mode	Describes the central tendencies of a set of scores	The score that occurs most frequently in a data set
Median	Describes the central tendencies of a set of scores	The halfway point in a data set; half the scores fall above this score, half below
Mean	Describes the central tendencies of a set of scores	The arithmetic average of the scores in a data set
Range	Describes the variability of a set of scores	The difference between the highest and lowest scores in a data set
Standard deviation	Describes the variability of a set of scores	The average difference between each score and the mean of a data set
Correlation coefficient	Describes the relationship between two variables	How strongly the two variables are related and whether the relationship is positive (variables move in same direction) or negative (variables move in opposite directions)
Tests of significance	Help make inferences about the relationships between descriptive statistics	How likely it is that the difference between measures of central tendencies or the size of a correlation coefficient is due to chance alone

Inferential statistics employ certain rules to evaluate the possibility that a correlation or a difference between groups represents a real and reliable phenomenon rather than the operation of chance factors of some kind. Suppose, for example, that participants who received EMDR showed a mean decrease of 10 points on an anxiety test, whereas the scores of a no-treatment control group decreased by a mean of 7 points. Does this difference reflect the greater impact of EMDR or some random fluctuation in people's scores that made EMDR appear more powerful than it actually is? Traditionally, psychologists have answered questions like this by using tests of statistical significance to estimate how likely it is that an observed difference was due to chance alone (Krueger, 2001). When such tests show that a correlation coefficient or the difference between two means is larger than would be expected by chance alone, that correlation or difference is said to be **statistically significant.** In the statistics appendix we describe some of these tests and discuss the factors that affect their results.

Keep in mind, however, that statistical significance tests alone do not necessarily constitute proof that a particular treatment is effective or ineffective. In fact, some psychologists have begun to suggest that other methods of analysis be used in addition to, or instead of, such tests to evaluate research findings (e.g., Cohen, 1994; Hunter, 1997; Krueger, 2001; Loftus, 1996). But whatever quantitative methods are used, psychological scientists are more confident in, and pay the most attention to, correlations or other research findings that statistical analyses suggest are robust and not flukes. (For a review of the statistical measures discussed in this section, see "In Review: Descriptive and Inferential Statistics.")

Statistics and Research Methods as Tools in Critical Thinking

As you think critically about evidence for or against any hypothesis, remember that part of the process is to ask whether a researcher's results have withstood careful statistical analysis—and whether they can be replicated. Using your critical thinking skills to evaluate the statistical and methodological aspects of research becomes especially important when you encounter results that are dramatic or unexpected. This point was well illustrated when Douglas Biklen (1990) began promoting a procedure called "facilitated communication (FC)" to help people with severe autistic disorder use language for the first time (autistic disorder is described in the chapter on psychological disorders). Biklen claimed that these people have language skills and coherent thoughts, but no way to express them. He reported case studies in which autistic people were apparently able to answer questions and speak intelligently using a special keyboard, but only when assisted by a "facilitator" who physically supported their unsteady hands. Controlled experiments showed this claim to be groundless, however (Jacobson, Mulick, & Schwartz, 1995). The alleged communication abilities of these autistic people disappeared under conditions in which the facilitator (1) did not know the question being asked of the participant or (2) could not see the keyboard (Delmolino & Romanczyk, 1995). The discovery that facilitators were—perhaps inadvertently (Spitz, 1997)—guiding participants' hand movements has allowed those who work with autistic people to see FC in a different light.

The role of experiments and other scientific research methods in understanding behavior and mental processes is so important that in each chapter to come, we include a special feature called "Focus on Research Methods." These features describe in detail the specific procedures employed in a particularly interesting research project. Our hope is that by reading these sections, you will see how the research methods discussed in this chapter are applied in every subfield of psychology.

---

statistically significant A term used to describe the results of an experiment when the outcome of a statistical test indicates that the probability of those results occurring by chance is small.

The Social Impact of Research The impact of research in psychology depends partly on the quality of the results and partly on how people feel about those results. Despite negative results of controlled experiments on facilitated communication, the Facilitated Communication Institute's web site continues to announce training for the many professionals and relatives of autistic people who still believe in its value (Gorman, 1999). The fact that some people ignore, or even attack, research results that challenge cherished beliefs reminds us that scientific research has always affected, and been affected by, the social and political values of the society in which it takes place (Bjork, 2000; Hagen, 2001; Hunt, 1999; Oellerich, 2000; Tavris, 1998).

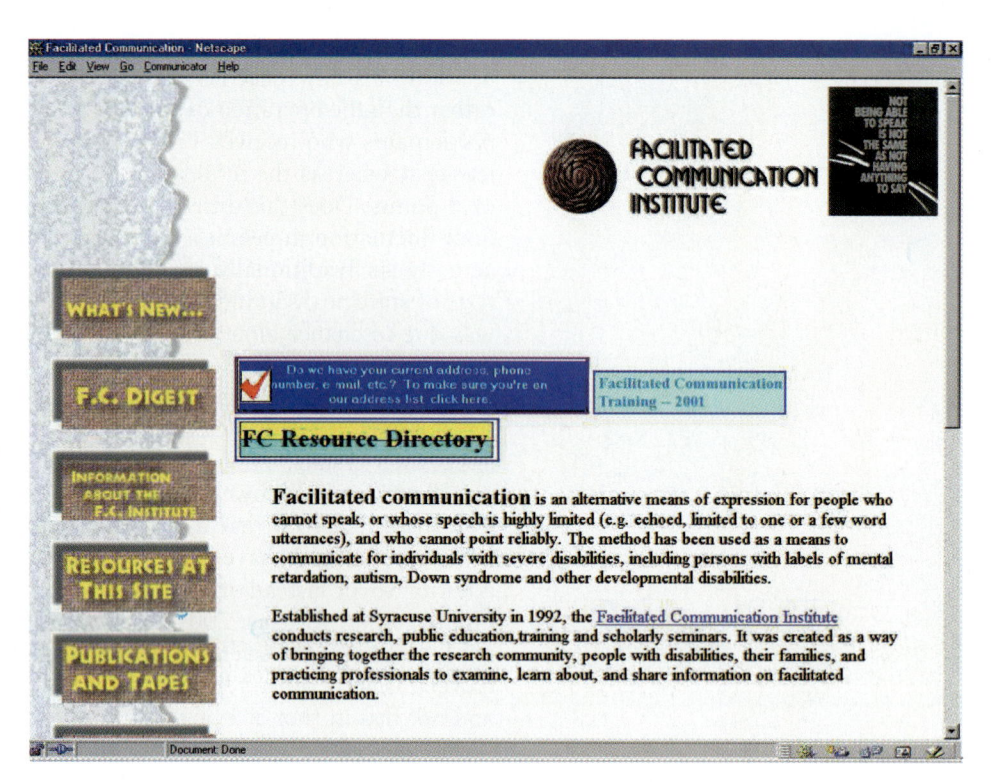

Ethical Guidelines for Psychologists

The obligation to analyze and report research fairly and accurately is one of the many ethical requirements that guide psychologists in their work. Preserving the welfare and dignity of research participants, both animal and human, is another. So although researchers *could* measure severe anxiety by putting a loaded gun to people's heads, or study marital conflicts by telling one partner that the other has been unfaithful, such methods are potentially harmful and therefore unethical. Whatever their research topic, psychologists' first priority is to investigate it in accordance with the highest ethical standards. They must find ways to protect their participants from harm while still gathering data that will have potential benefits for everyone. To measure anxiety, for example, a researcher might ask people to enter a situation that is anxiety provoking, but not traumatic (e.g., approaching a feared animal, riding in an elevator, or sitting in a dark room). And research on marital conflict usually involves observing couples as they discuss controversial issues in their relationship.

Psychologists take very seriously their obligation to minimize any discomfort or risk involved in their research projects, as well as the need to protect participants from long-term negative consequences. Accordingly, they take care to inform potential participants about every aspect of the study that might influence their decision to participate and ensure that each person's involvement is voluntary. But what if the purpose of the study is to, say, measure emotional reactions to being insulted? Participants might not react as they otherwise would if they know ahead of time that an "insult" will be part of the experiment. When some deception is necessary to create certain experimental conditions, ethical standards require the researcher to "debrief" participants as soon as the study is over by revealing all relevant information about the research and correcting any misconceptions it created.

Local review committees—and standards issued by organizations such as the Association for the Accreditation of Human Research Protection Programs—help psychologists think through these and other ethical implications of any research that might have the slightest risk of harm to human participants. Their review

Caring for Animals in Research Psychologists are careful to protect the welfare of animal participants in research. They do not wish to see animals suffer, and besides, undue stress on animals can create reactions that can act as confounding variables. For example, in a study of how learning is affected by food rewards, the researcher could starve animals to make them hungry enough to want the rewards. But this would introduce discomfort that would make it impossible to separate the effects of the reward from the effects of starvation.

determines whether the planned project's potential benefits, in terms of new knowledge and human welfare, outweigh any potential harm.

The obligation to protect participants' welfare also extends to animals, which are used in a small percentage of psychological research studies (Plous, 1996). Psychologists study animals partly because their behavior is interesting in and of itself and partly because research with animals can yield information that would be impossible or unethical to collect from humans (Mason, 1997). For example, researchers can randomly assign animals to live alone or with others, and then look at how these conditions affect later social interactions. The same thing could not ethically be done with people, but studies like this can provide clues about how social isolation might affect humans (see the chapter on motivation and emotion).

Contrary to the claims of some animal-rights activists, animals used in psychological research are not routinely subjected to extreme pain, starvation, or other inhumane conditions (Novak, 1991). Even in the small proportion of studies that require the use of electric shock, the discomfort created is mild, brief, and not harmful. The *Animal Welfare Act*, the National Institutes of Health's *Guide for the Care and Use of Laboratory Animals*, the American Psychological Association's *Principles on Animal Use*, and other laws and regulations set high standards for the care and treatment of animal participants. In those relatively rare studies that require animals to undergo short-lived pain or other forms of moderate stress, legal and ethical standards require that funding agencies—as well as local committees charged with monitoring animal research—first determine that the discomfort is justified by the expected benefits to human welfare.

The responsibility for conducting research in the most humane fashion is just one aspect of the *Ethical Principles of Psychologists and Code of Conduct* developed by the American Psychological Association (1992b). This document not only emphasizes the importance of ethical behavior but also describes specific ways in which psychologists can protect and promote the welfare of society and the particular people with whom they work in any capacity. Here are some examples: As teachers, psychologists should give students complete, accurate, and up-to-date coverage of each topic rather than a narrow, biased point of view. Psychologists should perform only those services and use only those techniques for which they are adequately trained; a psychologist untrained in clinical methods, for example, should not try to offer psychotherapy. Except in the most unusual circumstances (discussed in the chapter on treatment of psychological disorders), psychologists should not reveal information obtained from clients or students, and they should avoid situations in which a conflict of interest might impair their judgment or harm someone else. They should not, for example, have sexual relations with their clients, their students, or their employees.

Despite these guidelines, doubt and controversy arise in some cases about whether a proposed experiment or a particular practice, such as deceiving participants, is ethical (e.g., D. N. Bersoff, 1999). The American Psychological Association has published a casebook to help psychologists resolve such issues (Nagy, 1999). The ethical principles themselves must continually be updated to deal with complex new questions—such as how to protect the confidentiality of e-mail communications—that psychologists face in their ever-expanding range of work (Jones, 2001).

LINKAGES

LINKAGES (a link to Biological Aspects of Psychology)

Psychological Research and Behavioral Genetics

One of the most fascinating and difficult challenges in psychology is to find research methods that can help us understand the ways in which people's genetic inheritance (their biological *nature*) intertwines with environmental events and conditions before and after birth (often called *nurture*) to shape their behavior and mental processes. In the chapters to come, you will encounter questions about nature and nurture in relation to perception, personality, mental ability, mental disorder, and many other topics. Psychologists' efforts to explore the influences of nature and nurture in relation to these phenomena have taken them into the field of **behavioral genetics**, the study of how genes and heredity affect behavior. In this section, we describe the logic—and some results—of research methods in behavioral genetics. The basic principles of genetics and heredity that underlie these methods are described as part of a more detailed discussion in the behavioral genetics appendix.

Researchers in behavioral genetics realize that most behavioral tendencies can be influenced by many different genes, but also by the environment. Accordingly, research in behavioral genetics is designed to explore the relative roles of genetic and environmental factors in creating differences in behavioral tendencies and, most recently, to identify specific genes that contribute to hereditary influences.

Early research in behavioral genetics relied on the selective breeding of animals. For example, Robert Tryon (1940) mated rats who were fast maze learners with other fast learners and mated slower learners with other slow learners. After repeating this procedure for several generations, he found that the offspring of the fast learners were significantly better at maze learning than those of the slow learners.

Selective-breeding studies must be interpreted with caution, however, because it is not specific behaviors that are inherited but rather differing sets of physical structures, capacities, and the like, which in turn make certain behaviors more or less likely. These behavioral tendencies are often narrow, and they can be altered by the environment (Gottlieb, 2000). For example, "maze-dull" rats performed just as well as "maze-bright" rats on many tasks other than maze learning (Searle, 1949). And when raised in an environment containing tunnels and other stimulating features, "dull" animals did as well at maze learning as "bright" ones; both groups did equally poorly in the maze after being raised in an environment that lacked stimulating features (Cooper & Zubek, 1958).

Research on behavioral genetics in humans must be interpreted with even more caution, because environmental influences have an enormous impact on human behavior and because legal, moral, and ethical considerations prohibit manipulations such as selective breeding. Instead, research in human behavioral genetics depends on studies where control is imperfect. Some of the most important designs in behavioral genetics research are family studies, twin studies, and adoption studies (Plomin et al., 2001; Rutter et al., 2001).

In *family studies*, researchers examine whether similarities in behavior and mental processes are greater among people who are closely related than among more distant relatives or unrelated individuals. If increasing similarity is associated with closer family ties, the similarities might be inherited. For example, data from family studies suggest a genetic basis for schizophrenia because this severe mental disorder appears much more often in the closest relatives of schizophrenics than in other people (see Figure 2.4). But family studies alone cannot establish the role of genetic factors in mental disorders or other characteristics, because close relatives tend to share environments, as well as genes. So similarities among close relatives might stem from environmental factors instead of, or in addition to, genetic ones.

Twin studies explore the heredity-environment mix by comparing the similarities seen in identical twins with those of nonidentical pairs. Twins usually share the same environment and may also be treated very much the same by parents and others. Therefore, if identical twins (whose genes are exactly the same) are more alike on some characteristic than nonidentical twins (whose genes are no more similar than those of other siblings), that characteristic may have a significant genetic component. As we will see in later chapters, this pattern of results holds for a number of characteristics, including some measures of intelligence and some mental disorders. For example, Figure 2.4 shows that if one member of an identical twin pair is schizophrenic, the chances are about 45 percent that the other

behavioral genetics The study of the effect of genes on behavior.

figure 2.4

Family and Twin Studies of Schizophrenia

The risk of developing schizophrenia, a severe mental disorder described in the chapter on psychological disorders, is highest for the siblings and children of schizophrenics and lowest for those genetically unrelated to a schizophrenic. Does this mean that schizophrenia is inherited? These results are consistent with that interpretation, but the question cannot be answered through family studies alone. Environmental factors, such as stressors that close relatives share, could also play an important role. Studies comparing identical and nonidentical twins also suggest a genetic influence on schizophrenia, but even twin studies do not eliminate the role of environmental influences.

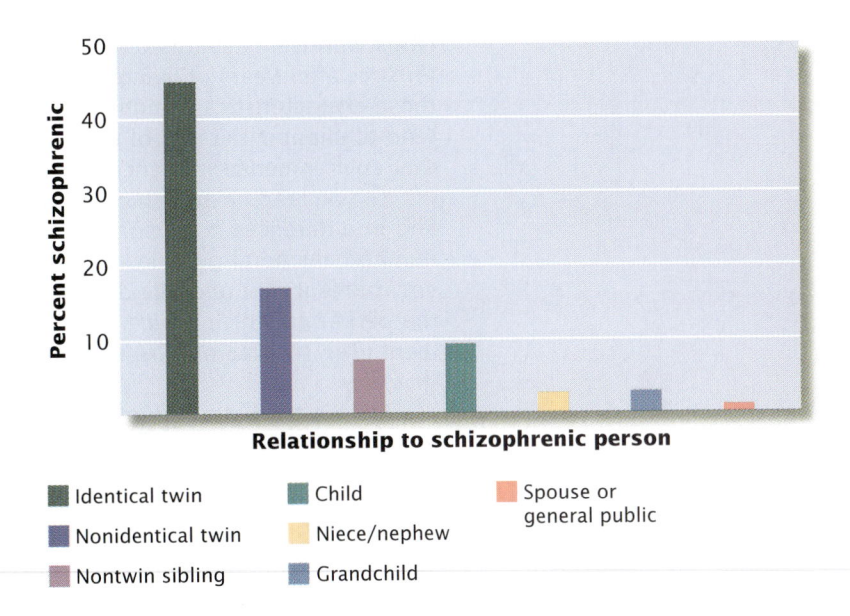

- Identical twin
- Nonidentical twin
- Nontwin sibling
- Child
- Niece/nephew
- Grandchild
- Spouse or general public

twin will be schizophrenic, too. Those chances drop to about 17 percent if the twins are nonidentical.

Adoption studies take scientific advantage of cases in which babies are adopted very early in life. The logic underlying these studies is that if adopted children's characteristics are more like those of their biological parents than those of their adoptive parents, genetically inherited ingredients in the nature-nurture mix play a clear role in those characteristics. For example, as described in the chapter on personality, the personalities of young adults who were adopted at birth tend to be more like those of their biological parents than those of their adoptive parents. Adoption studies can be especially valuable when they focus on identical

Research in Behavioral Genetics Like other identical twins, each member of this pair has identical genes. Twin studies and adoption studies help to reveal the interaction of genetic and environmental influences on human behavior and mental processes. Cases in which identical twins who had been separated at birth are found to have similar interests, personality traits, and mental abilities suggest that these characteristics have a significant genetic component.

twins who were separated at or near birth. If identical twins show similar characteristics after years of living in very different environments, the role of heredity in those characteristics is highlighted. Adoption studies of intelligence, for example, tend to support the role of genetics in variations in mental ability, but they show that environmental influences are important as well.

As you read in later chapters about the role of genetics in human development and in differences in personality and mental abilities, remember that research on human behavioral genetics can help illuminate the relative roles of heredity and environment that underlie differences *among* individuals, but it cannot determine the degree to which a *particular* person's behavior is due to heredity or environment. The two factors are too closely entwined in an individual to be separated that way.

Family, twin, and adoption studies will continue to be an important part of behavioral genetics research, but the future of behavioral genetics will also be shaped by the results of the Human Genome Project, which has now deciphered the genetic code contained in the DNA that makes each human being unique (International Human Genome Sequencing Consortium, 2001; Venter et al., 2001; see the behavioral genetics appendix). This achievement has allowed behavioral geneticists and other scientists to begin pinpointing some of the many genes that contribute to individual differences in disorders such as autism, learning disabilities, hyperactivity, and Alzheimer's disease, as well as to the normal variations in personality and mental abilities that we see all around us. Finding the DNA differences responsible for the role of heredity in psychology will eventually make it possible to understand exactly how heredity interacts with the environment as development unfolds. Analysis of DNA—collected by rubbing a cotton swab inside an individual's cheek—may someday be used not only in behavioral genetics research but also in clinics where it will help psychologists more precisely diagnose clients' problems and choose the most appropriate treatments (Plomin & Crabbe, 2000).

LINKAGES

As noted in the chapter on introducing psychology, all of psychology's subfields are related to one another. Our discussion of behavioral genetics illustrates just one way in which the topic of this chapter, research in psychology, is linked to the subfield of biological psychology (see the chapter on biological aspects of psychology). The Linkages diagram shows ties to two other subfields as well, and there are many more ties throughout the book. Looking for linkages among subfields will help you see how they all fit together and help you better appreciate the big picture that is psychology.

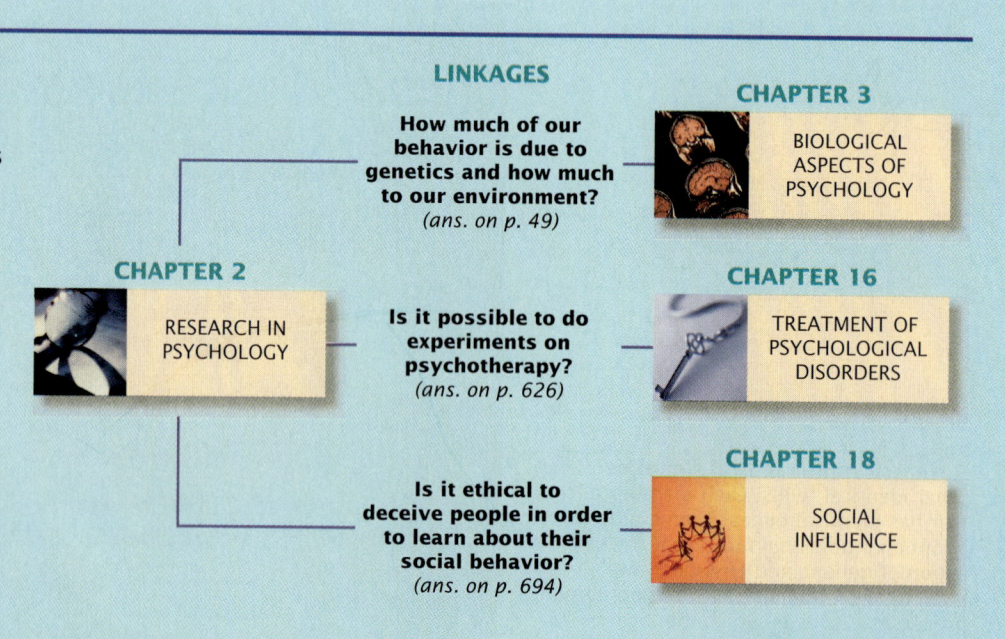

LINKAGES

CHAPTER 2
RESEARCH IN PSYCHOLOGY

- How much of our behavior is due to genetics and how much to our environment? *(ans. on p. 49)* → **CHAPTER 3** BIOLOGICAL ASPECTS OF PSYCHOLOGY
- Is it possible to do experiments on psychotherapy? *(ans. on p. 626)* → **CHAPTER 16** TREATMENT OF PSYCHOLOGICAL DISORDERS
- Is it ethical to deceive people in order to learn about their social behavior? *(ans. on p. 694)* → **CHAPTER 18** SOCIAL INFLUENCE

SUMMARY

Thinking Critically About Psychology (or Anything Else)

Critical thinking is the process of assessing claims and making judgments on the basis of well-supported evidence.

Critical Thinking and Scientific Research

Often, questions about behavior and mental processes are phrased in terms of *hypotheses* about *variables* that have been specified by *operational definitions*. Tests of hypotheses are based on objective, quantifiable evidence, or *data*, representing the variables of interest. If data are to be useful, they must be evaluated for reliability and validity.

The Role of Theories

Explanations of phenomena often take the form of a *theory*, which is a set of statements that can be used to account for, predict, and even suggest ways of controlling certain phenomena. Theories must be subjected to rigorous evaluation.

Research Methods in Psychology

Research in psychology, as in other sciences, focuses on four main goals: description, prediction, control, and explanation.

Selecting Human Participants for Research

Psychologists' research can be limited if their *sampling* procedures do not give them a fair cross-section of the population they want to study and about which they want to draw conclusions. Anything other than a *random sample* is said to be a *biased sample* of participants. In most cases, samples consist of people who are representative of specified target populations rather than of the general population.

Naturalistic Observation: Watching Behavior

Naturalistic observation entails watching without interfering as behavior occurs in the natural environment. This method can be revealing, but care must be taken to ensure that observers are unbiased and do not alter the behavior being observed.

Case Studies: Taking a Closer Look

Case studies are intensive examinations of a particular individual, group, or situation. They are useful for studying new or rare phenomena and for evaluating new treatments or training programs.

Surveys: Looking at the Big Picture

Surveys ask questions, through interviews or questionnaires, about behavior, attitudes, beliefs, opinions, and intentions. They provide an efficient way to gather large amounts of data from many people at a relatively low cost, but their results can be distorted if questions are poorly phrased, if answers are not given honestly, or if respondents do not constitute a representative sample.

Experiments: Exploring Cause and Effect

In *experiments*, researchers manipulate an *independent variable* and observe the effect of that manipulation on a *dependent variable*. Participants receiving experimental treatment are called the *experimental group*; those in comparison conditions are called *control groups*. Experiments can reveal cause-effect relationships between variables, but only if researchers use *random assignment*, *placebo* conditions, *double-blind designs*, and other strategies to avoid being misled by *random variables*, participants' expectations, *experimenter bias*, and other *confounding variables*.

Statistical Analysis of Research Results

Psychologists use *descriptive statistics* and *inferential statistics* to summarize and analyze data.

Descriptive Statistics

Descriptive statistics include measures of central tendency (such as the *mode*, *median*, and *mean*), measures of variability (such as the *range* and *standard deviation*, or *SD*), and *correlation coefficients*. Although valuable for describing relationships, *correlations* alone cannot establish that two variables are causally related, nor can they determine which variable might affect which, or why.

Inferential Statistics

Psychologists employ inferential statistics to guide conclusions about data and, especially, to determine if correlations or differences between means are *statistically significant*—that is, larger than would be expected by chance alone.

Statistics and Research Methods as Tools in Critical Thinking

Scientific evaluation of research requires the use of critical thinking to carefully assess the statistical and methodological aspects of even the most dramatic or desirable results.

Ethical Guidelines for Psychologists

Ethical guidelines promote the protection of humans and animals in psychological research. They also set the highest standards for behavior in all other aspects of psychologists' scientific and professional lives.

Biological Aspects of Psychology

3

The Nervous System
Cells of the Nervous System
Action Potentials
Synapses and Communication Between Neurons
Organization and Functions of the Nervous System

The Peripheral Nervous System: Keeping in Touch with the World
The Somatic Nervous System
The Autonomic Nervous System

The Central Nervous System: Making Sense of the World
The Spinal Cord
The Brain

FOCUS ON RESEARCH METHODS: Manipulating Genes in Animal Models of Human Disease
The Cerebral Cortex
The Divided Brain in a Unified Self
Plasticity: Repairing Damage in the Central Nervous System

LINKAGES: Human Development and the Changing Brain

The Chemistry of Psychology
Three Classes of Neurotransmitters

THINKING CRITICALLY: Are There Drugs That Can Make You Smarter?

The Endocrine System: Coordinating the Internal World

The Immune System: Defending the Body

Linkages

Summary

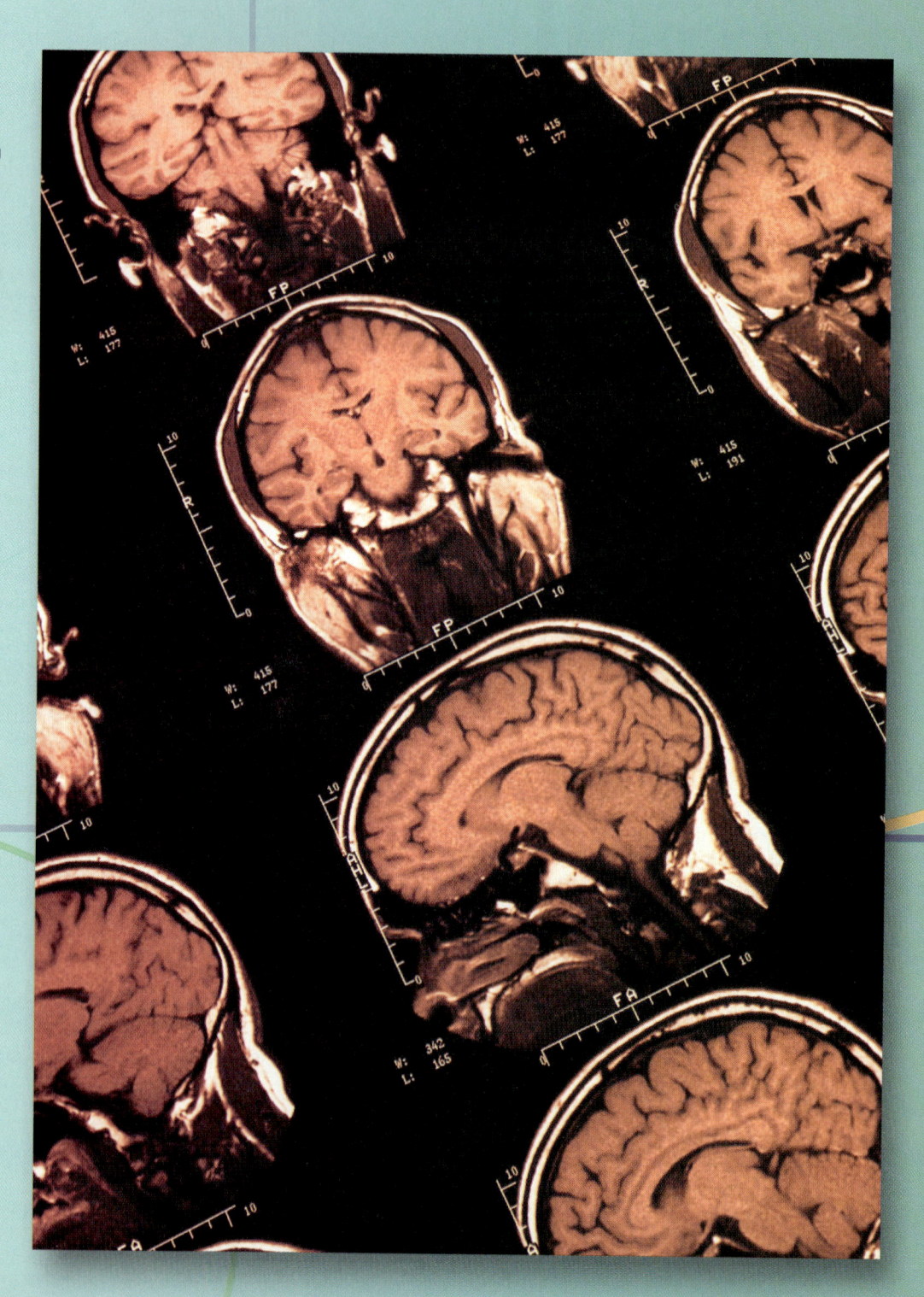

Do you drink coffee? Do you like beer or wine? Are you still unable to quit smoking? If so, you know that caffeine, alcohol, and nicotine can change the way you feel. The effects of these substances are based largely on their ability to change the chemistry of your brain. There are many other examples of how our mental experiences, and our identity as individuals, are rooted in biological processes. Each year, millions of people who suffer anxiety, depression, and other psychological disorders take prescription drugs that alter brain chemistry in ways that relieve their distress. And severe brain disorders such as Alzheimer's disease cause their victims to "lose themselves" as they become progressively less able to think clearly, to express themselves, to remember events, or even to recognize members of their families.

These examples of biological influences on behavior and mental processes reflect the biological approach to psychology discussed in the chapter on introducing psychology. The popularity and impact of that approach stems from the fact that brain cells, hormones, genes, and other biological factors are intimately related to everything you think and feel and do, from the fleeting memory you had a minute ago, to the anxiety or excitement or fatigue you felt last night, to the movements of your eyes as you read right now. In this chapter, we describe these biological factors in more detail. Reading it will take you into the realm of **biological psychology**, which is the study of the cells and organs of the body and the physical and chemical changes involved in behavior and mental processes. It is here that we begin to consider the relationship between your body and your mind, your brain and your behavior.

It is a complex relationship. Scientific psychologists are no doubt correct when they say that every thought, every feeling, and every action are represented somehow in the nervous system and that none of these events could occur without it. However, we must be careful not to oversimplify or overemphasize biological explanations in psychology. Many people assume, for example, that if a behavior or mental process has a strong biological *basis*, it is beyond our control—that "biology is destiny." Accordingly, many smokers do not even try to quit, simply because they assume that their biological addiction to nicotine will doom them to failure. This is not necessarily true, as millions of ex-smokers can attest. The fact that all behavior and mental processes are *based* on biological processes does not mean that they can be fully understood through the study of biological processes alone.

Reducing all of psychology to the analysis of brain chemicals would vastly underestimate the complexity of the interactions between our biological selves and our psychological experiences, between our genes and our environments. Just as all behaviors and mental processes are influenced by biology, all biological processes are influenced by the environment. We will see later, for example, that the experiences we have in the environment can change our brain chemistry and even our brain anatomy. Similarly, your height is a biological characteristic, but how tall you actually become depends heavily on nutrition and other environmental factors (Tanner, 1992). As described in the chapter on research in psychology and the behavioral genetics appendix, hereditary and environmental influences also combine to determine intelligence, personality, mental disorders, and all our other characteristics.

In short, understanding behavior and mental processes requires that we combine information mined at many levels of analysis, ranging from the activity of cells and organ systems to the activity of individuals and groups in social contexts. This chapter focuses on the biological level, not because it reveals the whole story of psychology but because it tells an important part of that story.

We begin by considering your **nervous system**, a complex combination of cells that tells you what is going on inside and outside your body and allows you to make appropriate responses. For example, if you are jabbed with a pin, your nervous system gets the message and immediately causes you to flinch. But your nervous system can do far more than detect information and execute responses. When information

---

biological psychology The psychological specialty that researches the physical and chemical changes that cause, and occur in response to, behavior and mental processes.

nervous system A complex combination of cells whose primary function is to allow an organism to gain information about what is going on inside and outside the body and to respond appropriately.

figure 3.1

Three Functions of the Nervous System

The nervous system's three main functions are to receive information (input), integrate that information with past experiences (processing), and guide actions (output). When the alarm clock goes off, this person's nervous system, like yours, gets the message, recognizes what it means, decides what to do, and then takes action, by getting out of bed or perhaps hitting the snooze button.

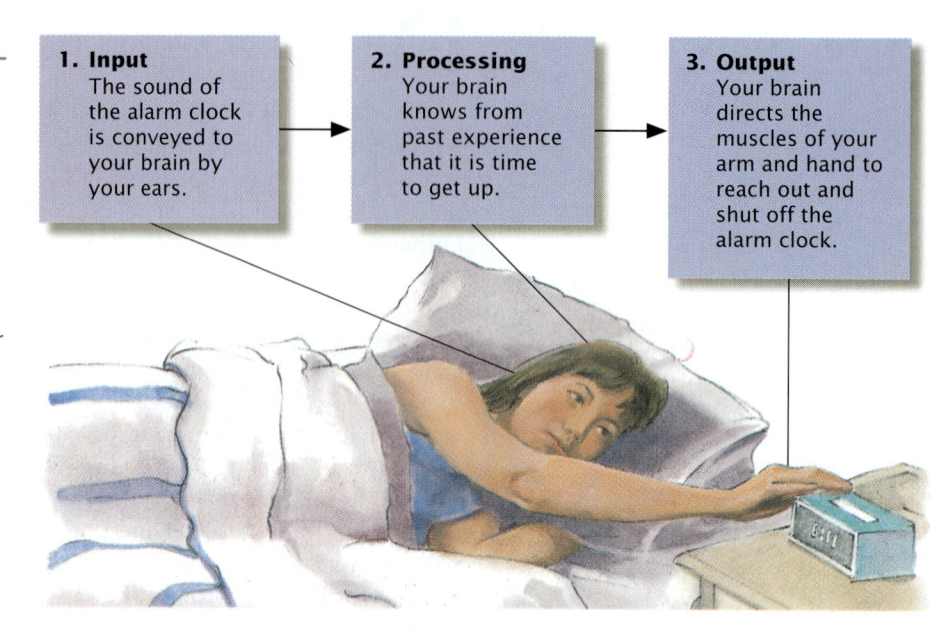

1. Input The sound of the alarm clock is conveyed to your brain by your ears.

2. Processing Your brain knows from past experience that it is time to get up.

3. Output Your brain directs the muscles of your arm and hand to reach out and shut off the alarm clock.

about the world reaches the brain, that information is *processed*—meaning that it is combined with information about past experiences and current wants and needs to make a decision about how to respond. The chosen action is then taken (see Figure 3.1). In other words, your nervous system displays the characteristics of an information-processing system: it has input, processing, and output capabilities.

The processing capabilities of this system are especially important, not only because the brain interprets information, makes decisions, and guides action but also because the brain can actually adjust the impact of incoming information. This phenomenon helps explain why you can't tickle yourself. In one study, simply telling ticklish people that they were about to be touched on the bottom of their feet caused marked activation in the brain region that receives sensory input from the foot (Carlsson et al., 2000). The *anticipation* of being touched made these people all the more sensitive to that touch. However, when they were asked to touch the bottom of their *own* feet, there was far less advance activation of this brain region, and they did not overreact to their touch. Why? The explanation is that when the brain plans a movement, it also predicts which of its own touch-detecting regions will be affected by that movement. So predictable, self-controlled touches, even in a normally "ticklish" spot, reduce activation of the sensory regions associated with that spot (Blakemore et al., 2000).

The nervous system is able to do what it does partly because it is made up of cells that *communicate with each other*. Like all cells in the body—indeed, like all living cells—those in the nervous system can respond to outside influences. Many of the signals that cells respond to come in the form of *chemicals* released by other cells. So even as various cells specialize during prenatal development to become skin, bone, hair, and other tissues, they still "stay in touch" through chemical signals. Bone cells, for example, add or drop calcium in response to hormones secreted in another part of the body. Cells in the bloodstream respond to viruses and other invaders by destroying them. We focus first on the cells of the nervous system, because their ability to communicate is the most efficient and complex.

The Nervous System

Scientists have studied many aspects of the nervous system, from the workings of molecules and cells to the wonders of how vast networks of brain cells accomplish such tasks as recognizing visual patterns and learning a language. We begin our exploration of the nervous system at the "bottom," with a description of the individual cells and molecules that compose it. Then we consider how these cells are organized to form the structures of the human nervous system.

Cells of the Nervous System

One of the most striking findings of research on the cells of the nervous system is how similar they are to other cells in the body, and how similar all cells are in all living organisms, from bacteria to plants to humans. For example, bacteria, plant cells, and brain cells all synthesize similar proteins when they are subjected to reduced oxygen or elevated temperatures. Because of this similarity, we can learn much about humans by studying animals, and much about brain cells by studying cells in simple organisms. For example, recent studies of cells in simple worms have provided clues to the causes of Alzheimer's disease (Okochi et al., 2000).

Figure 3.2 illustrates three of the characteristics that cells of the nervous system share with every other kind of cell in the body. First, they have an *outer membrane* that, like a fine screen, lets some substances pass in and out while blocking others. Second, nervous system cells have a *cell body*, which contains a *nucleus*. The nucleus carries the genetic information that determines how a cell will function. Third, nervous system cells contain *mitochondria*, which are structures that turn oxygen and glucose into energy. This process is especially vital to brain cells. Although the brain accounts for only 2 percent of the body's weight, it consumes more than 20 percent of the body's oxygen (Sokoloff, 1981). All of this energy is required because brain cells transmit signals among themselves to an even greater extent than do cells in the rest of the body.

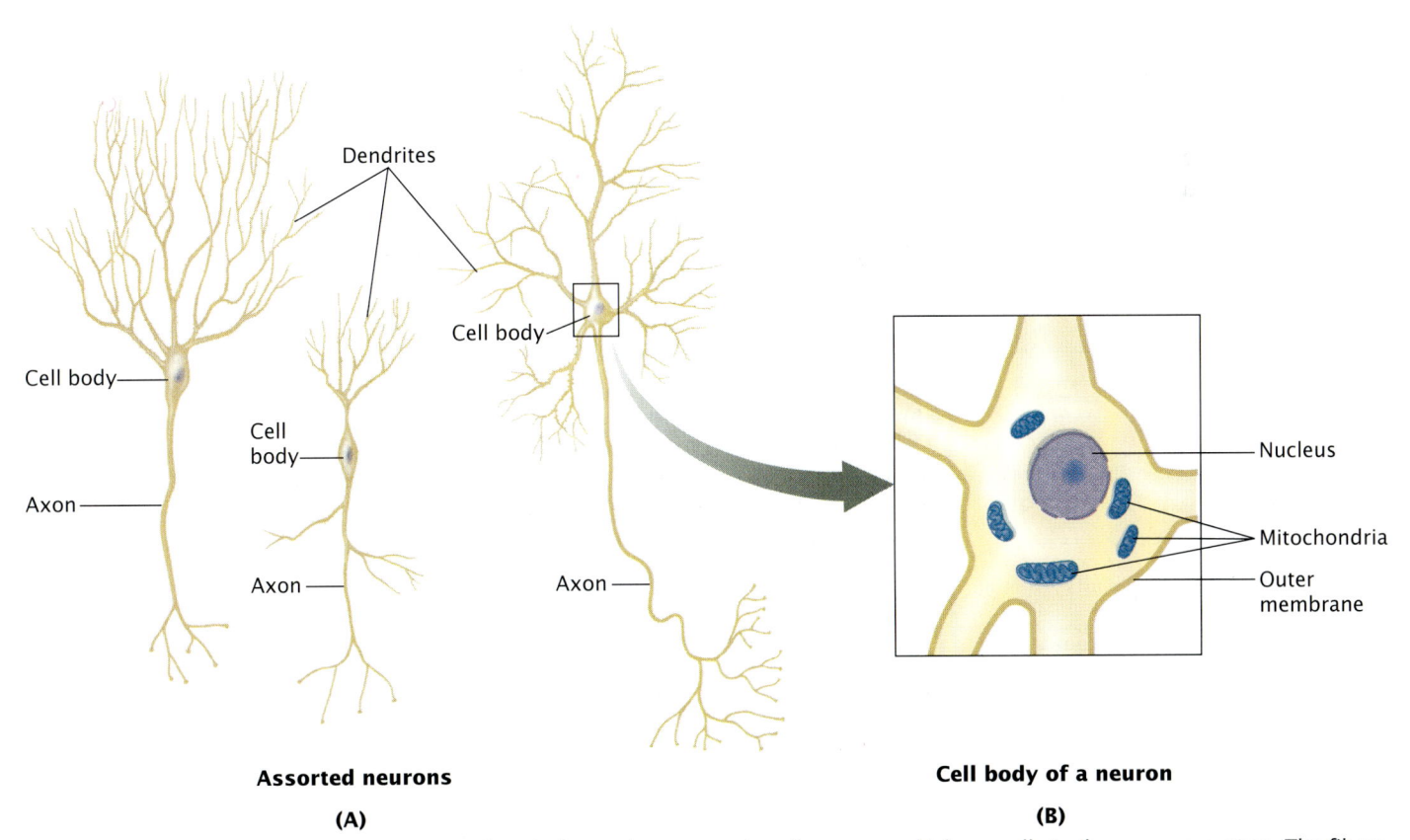

Assorted neurons
(A)

Cell body of a neuron
(B)

figure 3.2
The Neuron

Part A shows three examples of neurons, which are cells in the nervous system. The fibers extending outward from the cell body—the axons and dendrites—are among the features that make neurons unique. Part B is an enlarged drawing of the cell body of a neuron. The cell body of every neuron has typical cell elements, including an outer membrane, a nucleus, and mitochondria.

Two major types of cells—neurons and glial cells—allow the nervous system to carry out its complex signaling tasks so efficiently. **Neurons** are cells that are specialized to rapidly respond to signals and quickly send signals of their own. Most of our discussion of brain cells will be about neurons, but glial cells are important as well. *Glial* means "glue," and scientists had long believed that glial cells did no more than hold neurons together. Recent research shows, however, that **glial cells** also help neurons communicate by directing their growth, keeping their chemical environment stable, providing energy, secreting chemicals to help restore damage, and even responding to signals from neurons (Laming et al., 2000; Smit et al., 2001). Without glial cells, neurons could not function.

Neurons have three special features that enable them to communicate signals efficiently. The first is their structure. Although neurons come in many shapes and sizes, they all have long, thin fibers that extend outward from the cell body (see Figure 3.2). When these fibers get close to other neurons, communication between the cells can occur. The intertwining of all these fibers with fibers from other neurons allows each neuron to be in close proximity to thousands or even hundreds of thousands of other neurons.

The fibers extending from a neuron's cell body are called axons and dendrites. **Axons** are the fibers that carry signals away from the cell body, out to where communication occurs with other neurons. Each neuron generally has only one axon leaving the cell body, but that one axon may have many branches. Axons can be very short or several feet long, like the axon that sends signals from your spinal cord all the way down to your big toe. **Dendrites** are the fibers that receive signals from the axons of other neurons and carry those signals to the cell body. A neuron can have many dendrites. Dendrites, too, usually have many branches. Remember that *a*xons carry signals *a*way from the cell body, whereas *d*endrites *d*etect signals from other cells.

The neuron's ability to communicate efficiently also depends on two other features: the "excitable" surface membrane of some of its fibers and the tiny gap between neurons, called a **synapse**. In the following sections we examine how these features allow a signal to be sent rapidly from one end of a neuron to the other and from one neuron to another.

Action Potentials

To understand how signals are sent in the nervous system, you first need to know something about nerve cell membranes and the chemicals within and outside these cells. As we mentioned earlier, the cell membrane lets some chemical molecules pass through, but excludes others. Many of these molecules carry a positive or negative electrical charge. Normally, the cell pumps positively charged molecules out through its membrane, making the inside of the cell slightly more negative than the outside. When this happens, the cell membrane is said to be *polarized*. Molecules with a positive charge are attracted to those with a negative charge, creating a force called an *electrochemical potential,* which drives positively charged molecules toward the inside of the cell.

Many of these positively charged molecules are kept out by the cell membrane, but some enter by passing through special openings, or *channels,* in the membrane. These channels are distributed along the axon and dendrites and act as gates that can be opened or closed. Normally the channels along the axon are closed, but changes in the environment around the cell can *depolarize* part of its membrane, causing the gates in that area to swing open and allowing positively charged molecules to rush in (see Figure 3.3). When this happens, the next area of the axon becomes depolarized, causing the neighboring gate to open. This sequence continues, creating a wave of changes in electrochemical potential that spreads rapidly all the way down the axon.

neurons Fundamental units of the nervous system; nerve cells.

glial cells Cells in the nervous system that hold neurons together and help them communicate with one another.

axons Fibers that carry signals from the body of a neuron out to where communication occurs with other neurons.

dendrites Neuron fibers that receive signals from the axons of other neurons and carry those signals to the cell body.

synapse The tiny gap between neurons across which they communicate.

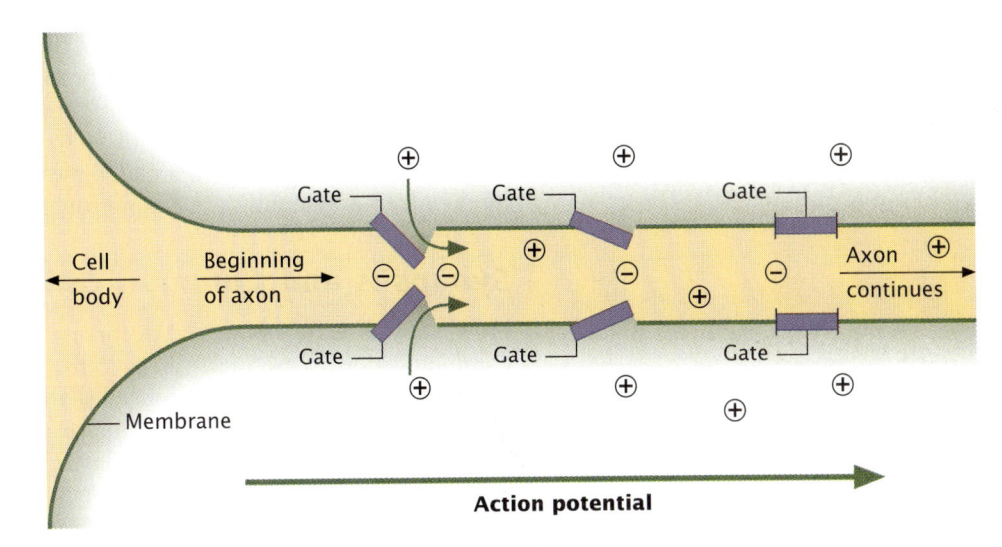

figure 3.3
The Beginning of an Action Potential

This highly simplified view of a polarized nerve cell shows the normally closed gates in the cell membrane. The electrochemical potential across the membrane is generated by an uneven distribution of positively and negatively charged molecules. For example, there are more positively charged molecules on the outside than on the inside. There are also more negatively charged molecules on the inside than on the outside. If stimulation causes depolarization near a particular gate, that gate may swing open, allowing positively charged molecules to rush through the membrane; this, in turn, depolarizes the neighboring region of the membrane and stimulates the next gate to open, and so on down the axon. This wave of depolarization is called an *action potential*. Membrane gates allow action potentials to spread along dendrites in a similar fashion.

This abrupt wave of electrochemical changes in the axon is called an **action potential**. When an action potential shoots down an axon, the neuron is said to have "fired." This term is appropriate because action potentials in axons are like gunshots: the cell either fires at full strength or it does not fire at all. For many years, scientists believed that only axons were capable of generating action potentials. However, more recent research has revealed that action potentials also occur in dendrites (Magee & Johnston, 1997). In many neurons, action potentials beginning in the axon go in both directions—down the axon and also "backward" through the cell body and into the dendrites. Action potentials that spread into the dendrites from the cell body appear to reach some dendritic branches and not others, leading scientists to conclude that these messages may be important in strengthening particular connections between neurons that are important to learning and memory (Stuart & Hausser, 2001).

The speed of the action potential as it moves down an axon is constant for a particular cell, but in different cells the speed ranges from 0.2 meters per second to 120 meters per second (about 260 miles per hour). The speed depends on the diameter of the axon—larger ones are faster—and on whether myelin is present. **Myelin** (pronounced "MY-a-lin") is a fatty substance that wraps around some axons and speeds action potentials. Larger, myelinated cells are usually found in parts of the nervous system that carry the most urgently needed information. For example, the sensory neurons that receive information from the environment about oncoming cars, hot irons, and other dangers are fast-acting, myelinated cells. Multiple sclerosis (MS), a severe brain disorder that destroys myelin, probably occurs because some viruses are very similar to components of myelin (Martin et al., 2001). When the MS victim's immune system attacks such viruses, it attacks and destroys vital myelin as well, resulting in disruption of vision, speech, balance, and other important functions.

Although each neuron fires or does not fire in an "all-or-none" fashion, its *rate* of firing can vary. It can fire over and over, because the membrane gates open only

action potential An abrupt wave of electrochemical changes traveling down an axon when a neuron becomes depolarized.

myelin A fatty substance that wraps around some axons and increases the speed of action potentials.

briefly and then close. Between firings there is a very short rest, called a **refractory period,** during which the membrane becomes repolarized. At that point the neuron can fire again. Because the refractory period is so short, a neuron can send action potentials down its axon at rates of up to 1,000 per second. The *pattern* of repeated action potentials amounts to a coded message. We describe some of the codes used by the nervous system in the chapter on sensation

Synapses and Communication Between Neurons

How does an action potential occurring in one neuron affect other neurons? For communication to occur *between* cells, a signal must be transmitted across the synapse, or gap, between neurons. Usually, the axon of one cell delivers its signals across a synapse to the dendrites of a second cell; those dendrites, in turn, transmit the signal to their cell body, which may relay the signal down its axon to a third cell, and so on. But other communication patterns also occur. Axons can signal to other axons or even directly to the cell body of another neuron; dendrites of one cell can send signals to the dendrites of other cells (Didier et al., 2001). These varied communication patterns allow the brain to conduct extremely complex information-processing tasks.

Neurotransmitters
Communication between neurons across the synapse relies first on chemical messengers called **neurotransmitters.** These chemicals are stored in numerous little "bags," called *vesicles*, at the tips of axons (see Figure 3.4). When an action potential reaches the end of an axon, a neurotransmitter is released into the synapse, where it spreads to reach the next, or *postsynaptic*, cell (see Figure 3.5).

When they reach the membrane of the postsynaptic cell, neurotransmitters attach to proteins called **receptors.** Like a puzzle piece fitting into its proper place, a neurotransmitter snugly fits, or "binds" to, its own receptors but not to receptors for other neurotransmitters (see Figure 3.6). Although each receptor "recognizes" only one type of neurotransmitter, each neurotransmitter type can bind to several different receptor types. As a result, the same neurotransmitter can have different effects depending on the type of receptor to which it binds.

When a neurotransmitter binds to a receptor, it stimulates channels in the membrane of the postsynaptic cell to open, allowing charged molecules to flow in or out. The flow of these charged molecules into and out of the postsynaptic cell produces a change in its membrane potential; thus, the *chemical* signal that crosses the synapse creates an *electrochemical* signal in the postsynaptic cell.

figure 3.4

A Synapse
This photograph taken through an electron microscope shows part of a neural synapse magnified 50,000 times. The mitochondria show up as green ovals, and the neurotransmitter-containing vesicles near the ending of the presynaptic cell's axon appear as small red dots. The synapse itself is the narrow gap between the greenish axon of the presynaptic cell and the bluish dendrite of the postsynaptic cell.

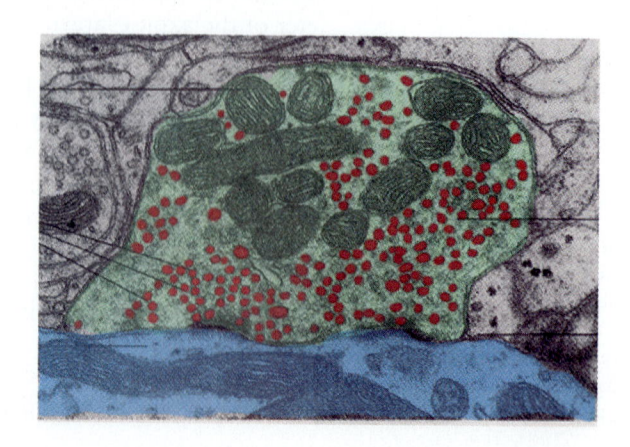

figure 3.5

Communication Between Neurons

When a neuron fires, an action potential shoots to the end of its axon, triggering the release of a neurotransmitter into the synapse. This process stimulates neighboring neurons and may cause them to fire their own action potentials.

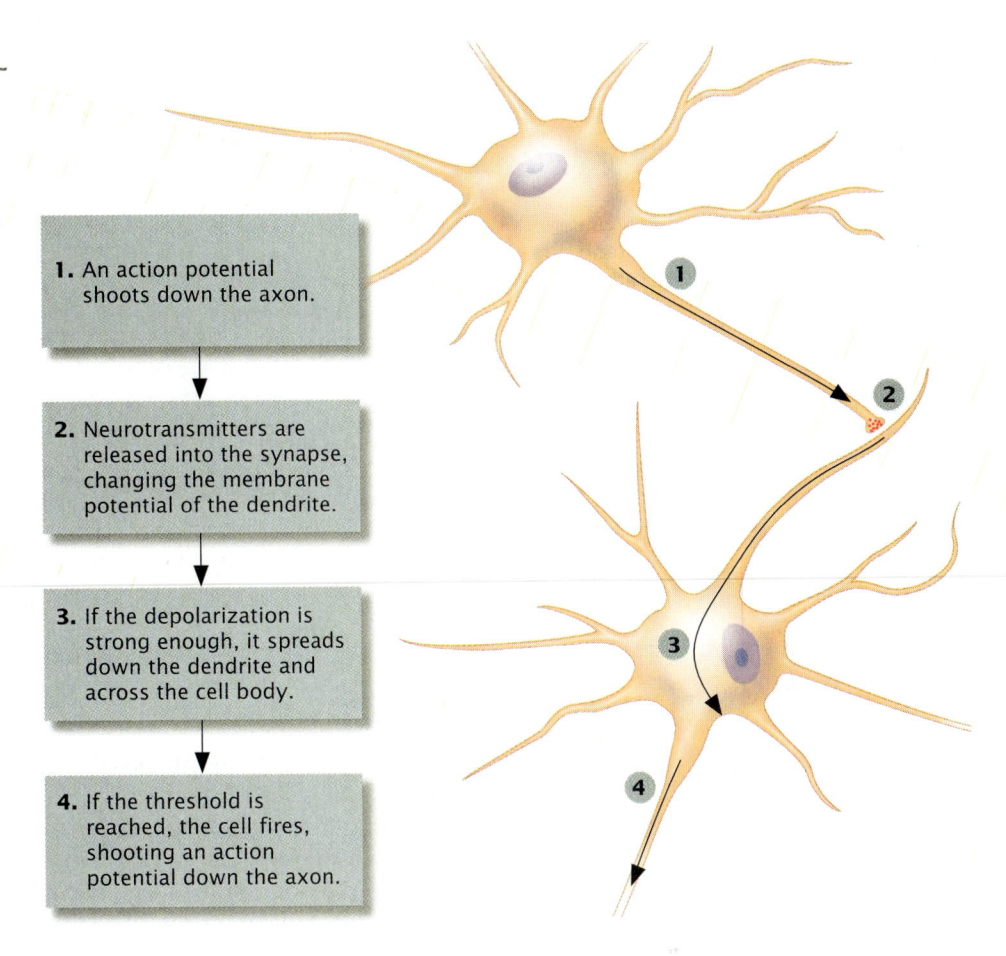

1. An action potential shoots down the axon.

2. Neurotransmitters are released into the synapse, changing the membrane potential of the dendrite.

3. If the depolarization is strong enough, it spreads down the dendrite and across the cell body.

4. If the threshold is reached, the cell fires, shooting an action potential down the axon.

refractory period A short rest period between action potentials.

neurotransmitters Chemicals that assist in the transfer of signals from one neuron to another.

receptors Sites on the surface of cells that allow only one type of neurotransmitter to fit into them, triggering a chemical response that may lead to an action potential.

postsynaptic potential The change in the membrane potential of a neuron that has received stimulation from another neuron.

excitatory postsynaptic potential A postsynaptic potential that depolarizes the neuronal membrane, bringing the cell closer to the threshold for firing an action potential.

inhibitory postsynaptic potential A postsynaptic potential that hyperpolarizes the neuronal membrane, making a cell less likely to fire an action potential.

Excitatory and Inhibitory Signals

The change taking place in the membrane potential of the dendrite or cell body of the postsynaptic cell is called the **postsynaptic potential**. The change can make the cell either more likely or less likely to fire. For example, if positively charged molecules of chemicals such as sodium or calcium flow *into* the neuron, it becomes slightly *less* polarized. Because this *depolarization* of the membrane can lead the neuron to fire an action potential, a depolarizing postsynaptic potential is called an **excitatory postsynaptic potential**, or **EPSP**. However, if positively charged molecules (such as potassium) flow *out* of the neuron, or if negatively charged molecules flow in, the neuron becomes slightly *more* polarized. This *hyperpolarization* makes it less likely that the neuron will fire an action potential. For this reason, a hyperpolarizing postsynaptic potential is called an **inhibitory postsynaptic potential**, or **IPSP**.

The postsynaptic potential spreads along the membrane of the postsynaptic cell. But unlike the action potential in an axon, which remains at a constant strength, the postsynaptic potential fades as it goes along. Usually, it is not strong enough to pass all the way along the dendrite and through the cell body to the axon, so a single EPSP will not cause a neuron to fire. However, each neuron is constantly receiving EPSPs and IPSPs. The combined effect of rapidly repeated potentials or potentials from many locations can create a signal strong enough to reach the junction of the axon and cell body, a specialized region where new action potentials are generated.

Whether or not the postsynaptic cell fires and how rapidly it fires depend on whether, at a given moment, there are more excitatory ("fire") or more inhibitory ("don't fire") signals from other neurons at this junction (see Figure 3.7). So as neurotransmitters transfer information across many neurons, each neuron constantly integrates or processes this information.

figure 3.6

The Relationship Between Neurotransmitters and Receptors

Neurotransmitters influence postsynaptic cells by stimulating special receptors on the surface of those cells' membranes. Each type of receptor receives only one type of neurotransmitter; the two fit together like puzzle pieces or like a lock and its key. Stimulation of a cell's receptors by their neurotransmitter causes them to either help or hinder the generation of a wave of depolarization in that cell's dendrites.

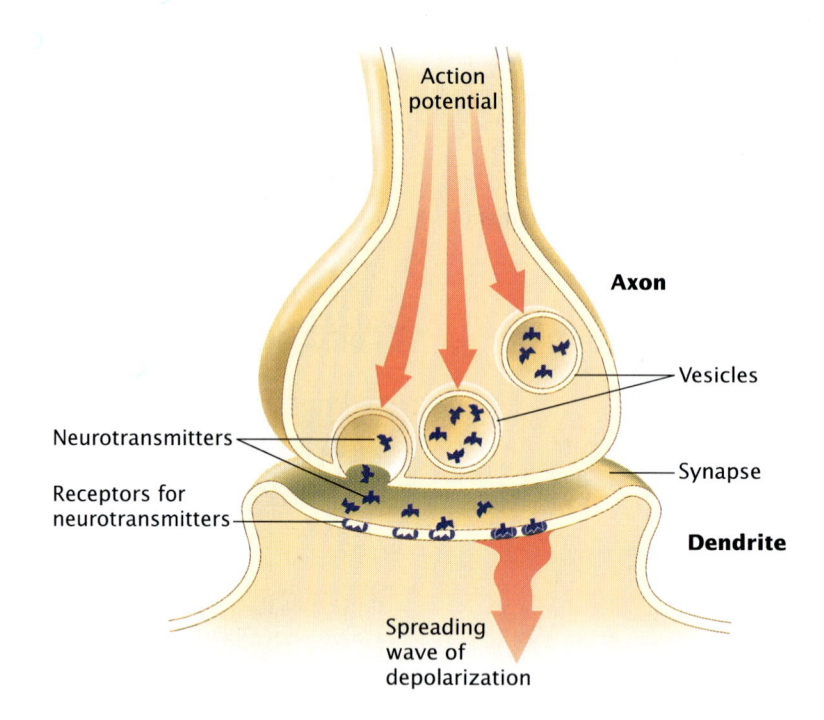

Neurotransmitters are involved in every aspect of behavior and mental processes, as you will see later in this chapter and in other chapters, too. In the chapter on sensation, for example, we describe some of the neurotransmitters used in pathways that convey pain messages throughout the brain and spinal cord. In the chapter on psychological disorders, we discuss the role that neurotransmitters play in schizophrenia and depression. And in the chapter on the treatment of psychological disorders, we consider how prescription drugs act on neurotransmitters and the cells they affect.

Organization and Functions of the Nervous System

Impressive as individual neurons are (see "In Review: Neurons, Neurotransmitters, and Receptors"), we can best understand their functions by looking at how they operate in groups. In the brain and spinal cord, neurons are organized into groups called **neural networks.** Many neurons in a network are closely connected, sending axons to the dendrites of many other neurons in the network. Signals from one network also go to other networks, and small networks are organized into bigger

figure 3.7

Integration of Neural Signals

Most of the signals that a neuron receives arrive at its dendrites or at its cell body. These signals, which typically come from many neighboring cells, can contain conflicting messages. Some are excitatory, telling the cell to fire; others are inhibitory, telling the cell not to fire. Whether or not the cell actually fires at any given moment depends on whether excitatory or inhibitory messages predominate at the junction of the cell body and the axon.

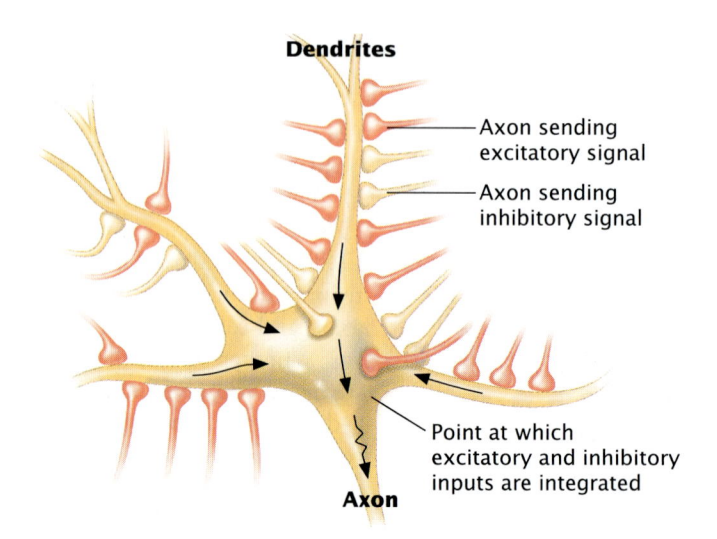

in review: Neurons, Neurotransmitters, and Receptors

Part	Function	Type of Signal Carried
Axon	Carries signals away from the cell body	The action potential, an all-or-nothing electrochemical signal that shoots down the axon to vesicles at the tip of the axon, releasing neurotransmitters
Dendrite	Detects and carries signals to the cell body	The postsynaptic potential, an electrochemical signal moving toward the cell body
Synapse	Provides an area for the transfer of signals between neurons, usually between axon and dendrite	Chemicals that cross the synapse and reach receptors on another cell
Neurotransmitter	A chemical released by one cell that binds to the receptors on another cell	A chemical message telling the next cell to fire or not to fire its own action potential
Receptor	Protein on the cell membrane that receives chemical signals	Recognizes certain neurotransmitters, thus allowing it to begin a postsynaptic potential in the dendrite

collections. By studying these networks, neuroscientists have begun to see that the nervous system conveys information not so much by the activity of single neurons sending single messages with a particular meaning, but by the activity of *groups* of neurons firing together in varying combinations. So the same neurons may be involved in producing different patterns of behavior, depending on which combinations of them are active.

The groups of neurons in the nervous system that provide input about the environment are known as the senses, or **sensory systems**. These systems—including hearing, vision, taste, smell, and touch—are described in the chapter on sensation. Integration and processing of information occur mainly in the brain. Output flows through **motor systems**, which are the parts of the nervous system that influence muscles and other organs to respond to the environment.

Still a Super Man If axons, dendrites, or other components of the nervous system are damaged or disordered, serious problems can result. For example, the spinal cord injury that actor Christopher Reeve suffered in a riding accident cut the neural communication lines that had allowed him to feel most of his body and to move most of his muscles.

---

neural networks Neurons that operate together to perform complex functions.
sensory systems The parts of the nervous system that provide information about the environment.
motor systems The parts of the nervous system that influence muscles and other organs to respond to the environment in some way.

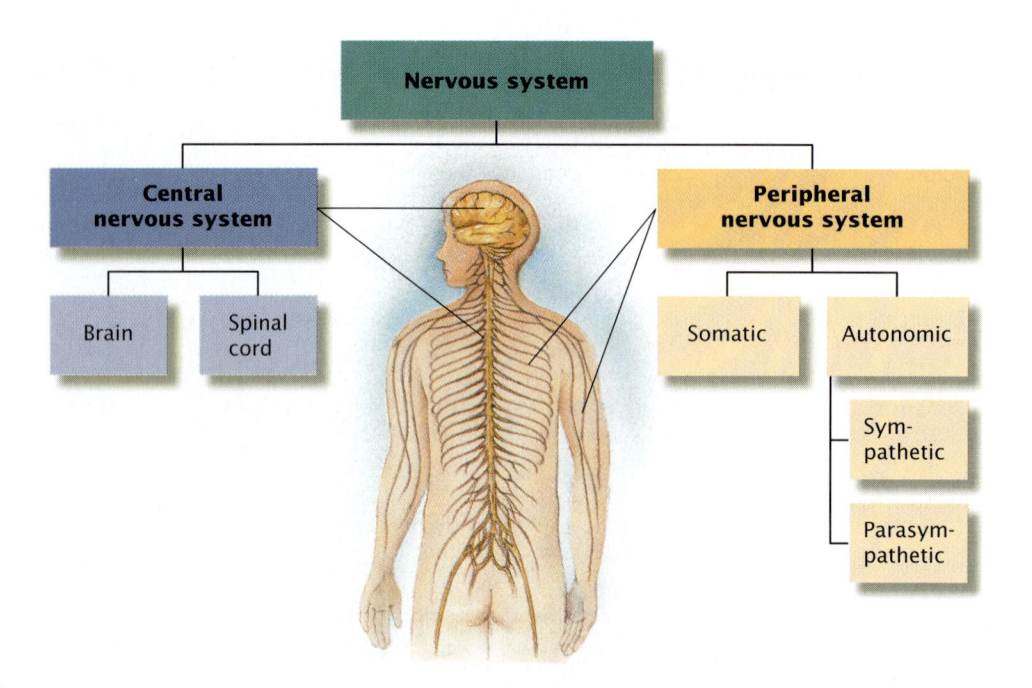

figure 3.8
Organization of the Nervous System

The brain and spinal cord make up the bone-encased central nervous system (CNS), the body's central information processor, decision maker, and director of actions. The peripheral nervous system, which is not housed in bone, functions mainly to carry messages. The somatic subsystem of the peripheral nervous system transmits information to the CNS from the outside world and conveys instructions from the CNS to the muscles. The autonomic subsystem conveys messages from the CNS that alter the activity of organs and glands, and it sends information about that activity back to the brain.

The nervous system has two major divisions, which work together: the peripheral nervous system and the central nervous system (see Figure 3.8). The **peripheral nervous system** (**PNS**), which includes all of the nervous system that is not housed in bone, carries out sensory and motor functions. The **central nervous system** (**CNS**) is the part encased in bone. It includes the brain, which is inside the skull, and the spinal cord, which is inside the spinal column (backbone). The CNS is often called the "central executive" of the body because information is usually sent to the CNS to be processed and acted on. Let's take a closer look at these divisions of the nervous system.

The Peripheral Nervous System: Keeping in Touch with the World

As shown in Figure 3.8, the peripheral nervous system has two components, each of which performs both sensory and motor functions.

The Somatic Nervous System

The first of these components is the **somatic nervous system**; it transmits information from the senses to the CNS and carries signals from the CNS to the muscles that move the skeleton. For example, when you lie in the sun at the beach, the somatic nervous system sends signals from the skin to the brain that become sensations of warmth. The somatic nervous system is also involved in every move you make. Neurons extend from the spinal cord to the muscles, where the release of a neurotransmitter onto them causes the muscles to contract. In fact, much of what we

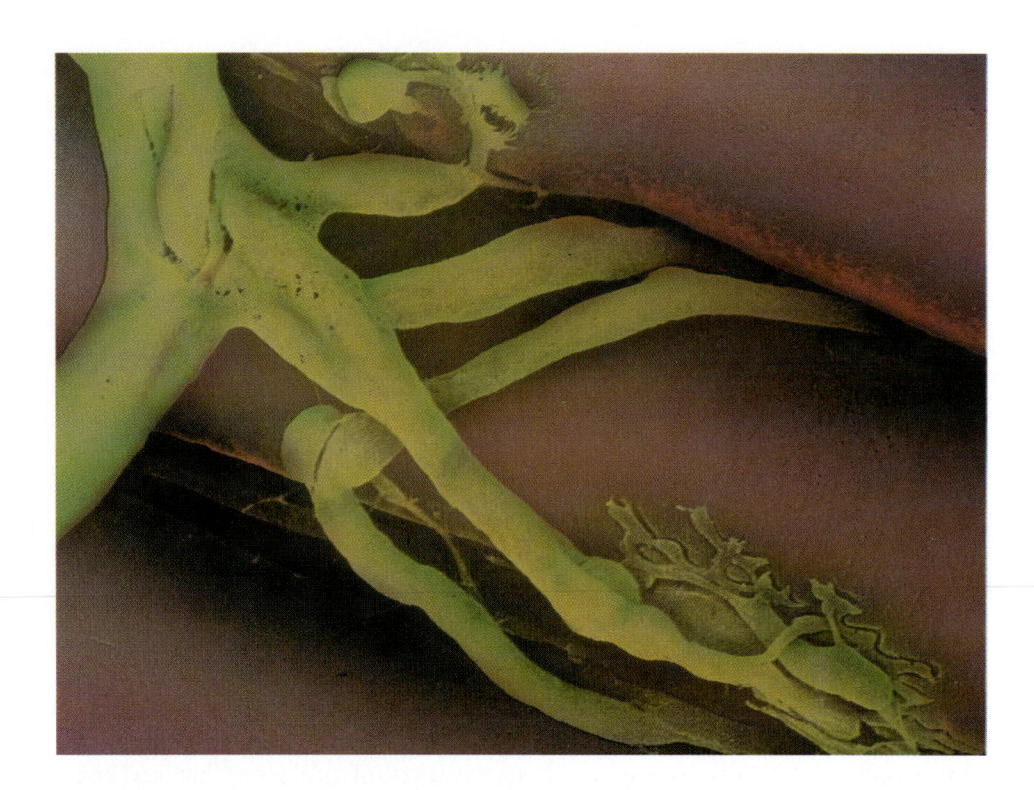

The Neuromuscular Junction When nerve cells (shown here as green fibers) release neurotransmitters onto muscle tissue, the muscle contracts.

know about neurotransmitters was discovered in laboratory studies of this "neuromuscular junction," especially in the frog's hind leg. At the neuromuscular junction, the action of a neurotransmitter allows a quick response that can mean the difference between life and death, for a frog or any other animal, including humans.

The Autonomic Nervous System

The second component of the peripheral nervous system, the **autonomic nervous system**, carries messages back and forth between the CNS and the heart, lungs, and other organs and glands (Berthoud & Neuhuber, 2000). These messages increase or decrease the activity of the organs and glands to meet varying demands placed on the body. As you lie on the beach, it is your autonomic nervous system that makes your heart beat a little faster when an attractive person walks by and smiles.

The name *autonomic* means "autonomous" and suggests independent operation. This term is appropriate because, although the autonomic nervous system is influenced by the brain, it controls activities that are normally outside of conscious control, such as digestion and perspiration (sweating). The autonomic nervous system exercises this control through its two divisions: the sympathetic and parasympathetic branches. Generally, the *sympathetic system* mobilizes the body for action in the face of stress; the responses that result are sometimes collectively referred to as the *fight-or-flight response*. The *parasympathetic system* regulates the body's functions to conserve energy. These two branches often create opposite effects. For example, the sympathetic nervous system can make your heart beat faster, whereas the parasympathetic nervous system can slow it down.

The functions of the autonomic nervous system may not get star billing, but you would miss them if they were gone. Just as a race-car driver is nothing without a good pit crew, the somatic nervous system depends on the autonomic nervous system to get its job done. For example, when you want to move your muscles, you create a demand for energy; the autonomic nervous system fills the bill by increasing sugar fuels in the bloodstream. If you decide to stand up, you need increased blood pressure so that your blood does not flow out of your brain and settle in your legs. Again, the autonomic nervous system makes the adjustment. Disorders of the

---

peripheral nervous system The parts of the nervous system not housed in bone.

central nervous system The parts of the nervous system encased in bone, including the brain and the spinal cord.

somatic nervous system The subsystem of the peripheral nervous system that transmits information from the senses to the central nervous system and carries signals from the central nervous system to the muscles.

autonomic nervous system A subsystem of the peripheral nervous system that carries messages between the central nervous system and the heart, lungs, and other organs and glands.

autonomic nervous system can make people sweat uncontrollably or faint whenever they stand up; they can also lead to other problems, such as an inability to have sex. We examine the autonomic nervous system in more detail in the chapter on motivation and emotion.

The Central Nervous System: Making Sense of the World

The amazing speed and efficiency of the neural networks that make up the central nervous system—the brain and spinal cord—have prompted many people to compare it to the central processor in a computer. In fact, to better understand how human and other brains work and how they relate to sensory and motor systems, *computational neuroscientists* have created neural network models on computers (Koch & Davis, 1994). Figure 3.9 shows an example of how the three components of the nervous system (input, processing, and output) might be represented in a neural network model. Notice that input simultaneously activates several paths in the network, so information is processed in various places at the same time. Accordingly, the activity of these models is described as *parallel distributed processing*. In the chapters on sensation, perception, learning, and memory, we describe how parallel distributed processing often characterizes the activity of the brain.

Although neural network models were initially intended to help scientists better understand the nervous system, the principles of neural networks have been applied to a variety of problems that are not directly related to neurons or the brain. Specifically, neural network models can be programmed into computers, allowing them to perform functions that previously only humans could do. For example, computers using neural networks are able to determine the quality of pork from scans of pig carcasses (Berg, Engel, & Forrest, 1998) and to predict which cancer patients will relapse after chemotherapy (Burke et al., 1998).

Neural network models are neatly laid out like computer circuits or the carefully planned streets of a new suburb, but the flesh-and-blood central nervous system is more difficult to follow. In fact, the CNS looks more like Boston or Paris, with distinct neighborhoods, winding back streets, and multilaned expressways. Its "neighborhoods" are collections of neuronal cell bodies called **nuclei**. The "highways" of the central nervous system are made up of axons that travel together in bundles called **fiber tracts** or **pathways**. Like a freeway ramp, the axon from a given cell may merge with and leave fiber tracts, and it may send branches into other tracts. The pathways travel from one nucleus to other nuclei, and scientists have learned much about how the brain works by tracing the connections among nuclei. To begin our description of some of these nuclei and anatomical connections, let's consider a practical example of nervous system functioning.

At 6 A.M., your alarm goes off. The day begins innocently enough with what appears to be a simple case of information processing. Input in the form of sound

figure 3.9

A Neural Network Model

This simple computer-based neural network model includes three basic components: an input layer, a processing layer, and an output layer. Notice that each element in each layer is connected to every other element in each of the other layers. As in the brain itself, these connections can be either excitatory or inhibitory, and the strength of the connections between elements can be modified depending on the results of the output; in other words, a computerized neural network model has the capacity to learn.

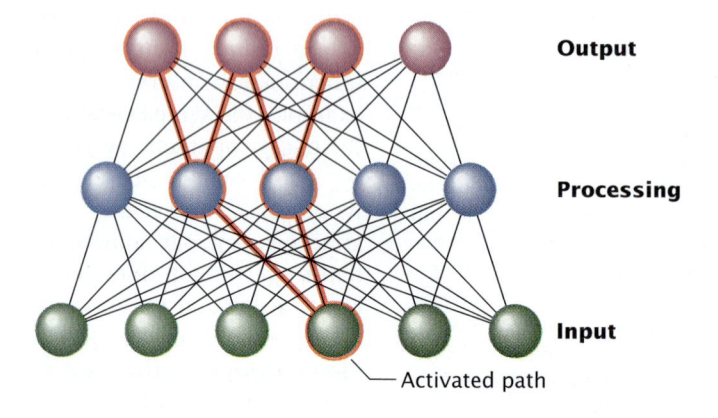

figure 3.10

A Reflex Pathway

TRY THIS Sit on a chair, cross one leg over the other, and then use the handle of a butter knife or some other solid object to gently tap your top knee, just below the joint, until you get a "knee jerk" reaction. Tapping your knee at just the right spot sets off an almost instantaneous sequence of events that begins with stimulation of sensory neurons that respond to stretch. When those neurons fire, their axons, which end within the spinal cord, cause spinal neurons to fire. This, in turn, stimulates the firing of motor neurons with axons ending in your thigh muscles. The result is a contraction of those muscles and a kicking of the lower leg and foot. Information about the knee tap and about what the leg has done also goes to your cerebral cortex, but the reflex is completed without waiting for guidance from the brain.

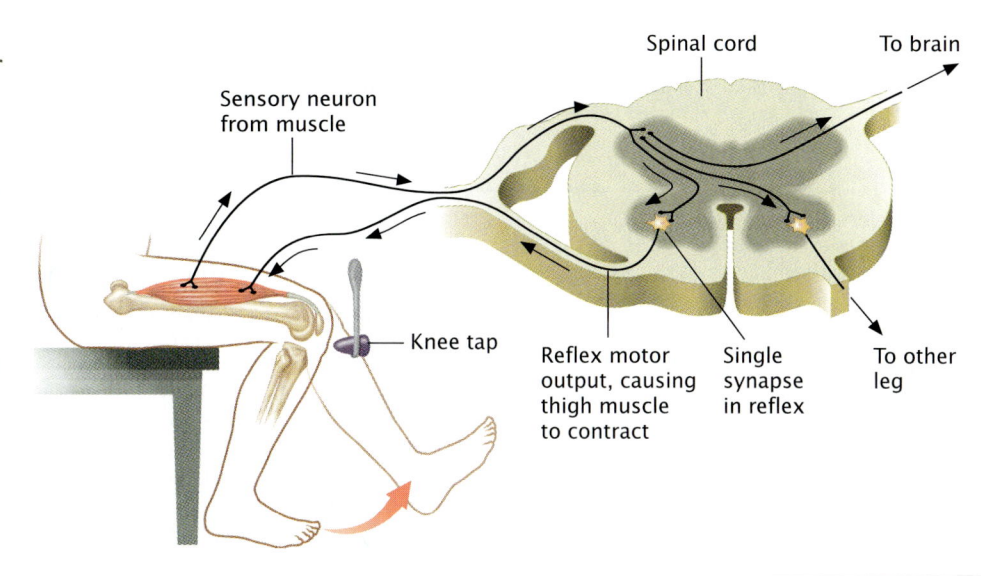

nuclei Collections of nerve cell bodies in the central nervous system.

fiber tracts Axons in the central nervous system that travel together in bundles.

spinal cord The part of the central nervous system within the spinal column that relays signals from peripheral senses to the brain and conveys messages from the brain to the rest of the body.

reflexes Involuntary, unlearned reactions in the form of swift, automatic, and finely coordinated movements in response to external stimuli.

from the alarm clock is received by your ears, which convert the sound into neural signals that reach your brain. Your brain compares these signals with previous experiences stored in memory and correctly associates the sound with "alarm clock." However, your output is somewhat impaired because your brain's activity has not yet reached the waking state. It directs your muscles poorly: You get out of bed and shuffle into the kitchen, where, in your drowsy condition, you touch a hot burner as you reach for the coffeepot. Now things get more lively. Heat energy activates sensory neurons in your fingers, and action potentials flash along fiber tracts going into the spinal cord.

The Spinal Cord

The **spinal cord** receives signals from peripheral senses, including pain and touch from the fingertips, and relays those signals to the brain through fibers within the cord. Neurons in the spinal cord also carry signals downward, from the brain to the muscles. In addition, cells of the spinal cord can direct some simple behaviors without instructions from the brain. These behaviors are called **reflexes** because the response to an incoming signal is directly "reflected" back out (see Figure 3.10).

For example, when you touched that hot burner, impulses from sensory neurons in your fingers reflexively activated motor neurons, which caused muscles in your arm to contract and quickly withdraw your hand. Because spinal reflexes like this one include few time-consuming synaptic links, they are very fast. And because spinal reflexes occur without instructions from the brain, they are considered involuntary; but they also send action potentials along fiber tracts going to the brain. Thus, you officially "know" you have been burned a fraction of a second after your reflex got you out of further trouble.

The story does not end there, however. When a simple reflex set off by touching something hot causes one set of arm muscles to contract, an opposing set of muscles relaxes. If this did not happen, the arm would go rigid. Furthermore, muscles have receptors that send impulses to the spinal cord to let it know how extended they are, so that a reflex pathway can adjust the muscle contraction to allow smooth movement. This is an example of a *feedback system*, a series of processes in which information about the consequences of an action goes back to the source of the action so that adjustments can be made.

In the spinal cord, sensory neurons are often called *afferent* neurons and motor neurons are termed *efferent* neurons, because *afferent* means "coming toward" and *efferent* means "going away." To remember these terms, notice that *afferent* and *approach* both begin with *a*; *efferent* and *exit* both begin with *e*.

table 3.1
Techniques for Studying Human Brain Function and Structure

Technique	What It Shows	Advantages (+) and Disadvantages (−)
EEG (electroencephalography) Multiple electrodes are pasted to the outside of the head	Lines that chart the summated electrical fields resulting from the activity of billions of neurons	+ Detects very rapid changes in electrical activity, allowing analysis of stages of cognitive processing − Provides poor spatial resolution of the source of electrical activity
PET (positron emission tomography) and SPECT (single photon emission computed tomography): Positrons and photons are emissions from radioactive substances	An image of the amount and localization of any molecule that can be injected in radioactive form, such as neurotransmitters, drugs, or tracers for blood flow or glucose use (which indicates specific changes in neuronal activity)	+ Allows functional and biochemical studies + Provides visual image corresponding to anatomy − Requires exposure to low levels of radioactivity − Provides spatial resolution better than that of EEG but poorer than that of MRI − Cannot follow rapid changes (faster than 30 seconds)
MRI (magnetic resonance imaging): Exposes the brain to a magnetic field and measures radiofrequency waves	The traditional MRI provides a high-resolution image of brain anatomy, and the newer functional MRI (fMRI) provides images of changes in blood flow (which indicate specific changes in neuronal activity)	+ Requires no exposure to radioactivity + Provides high spatial resolution of anatomical details (<1 mm) + Provides high temporal resolution ($<\frac{1}{10}$ second)
MEG (magnetoencephalography)	Detects the magnetic fields produced by electrical currents in neurons; detects and localizes brain activity, usually combined with a structural image from MRI	+ Like EEG, detects very rapid changes in electrical activity, allowing analysis of cognitive processing + Allows millimeter resolution of source of electrical activity for surface sources such as cerebral cortex − Has poor spatial resolution of brain activity in structures below the cortex − Requires very expensive equipment

The Brain

The brain has three major subdivisions: the hindbrain, the midbrain, and the forebrain. Table 3.1 and Figures 3.11 and 3.12 describe and illustrate some of the techniques scientists use to learn about these structures and how they function.

The Hindbrain

Incoming signals first reach the **hindbrain**, which is actually a continuation of the spinal cord. As you can see in Figure 3.13, the hindbrain lies just inside the skull. Blood pressure, heart rate, breathing, and many other vital autonomic functions are controlled by nuclei in the hindbrain, particularly in an area called the **medulla**. Threading throughout the hindbrain and into the midbrain

---

hindbrain An extension of the spinal cord contained inside the skull where nuclei control blood pressure, heart rate, breathing, and other vital functions.

medulla An area in the hindbrain that controls blood pressure, heart rate, breathing, and other vital functions.

figure 3.11

Combining a PET Scan and an MRI
Researchers have superimposed images from PET scans and MRI to construct a three-dimensional view of the living brain. Here you can see the brain of a young epileptic girl. The picture of the outer surface of the brain is from the MRI; the pink area is from the PET scan and shows the source of epileptic activity. The images at the right are the MRI and PET images at one plane, or "slice," through the brain (indicated by the line on the brain at the left).

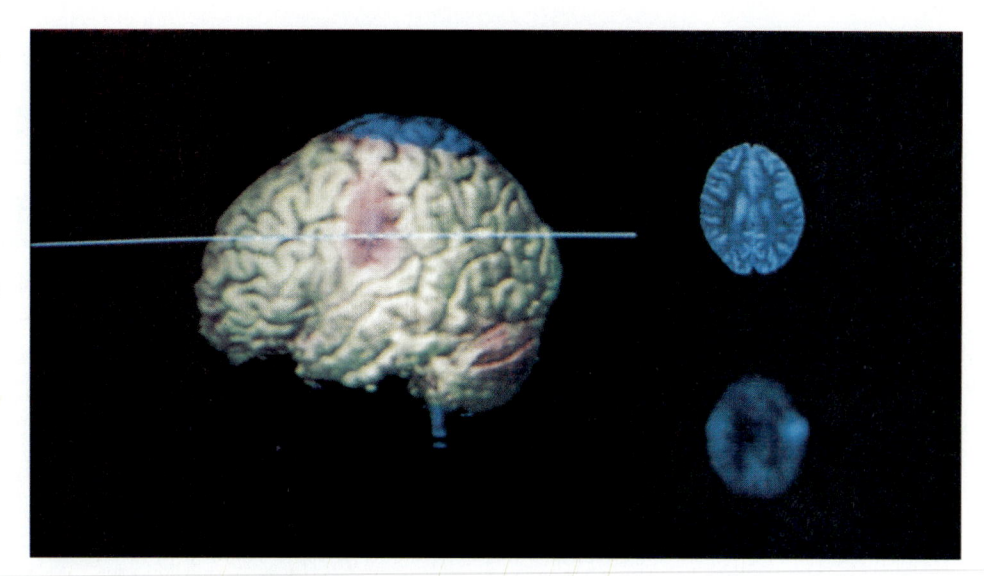

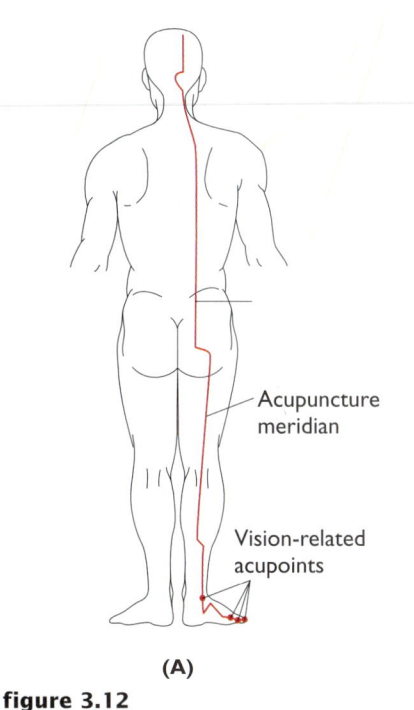

figure 3.12

Linking Eastern Medicine and Western Neuroscience Through Functional MRI

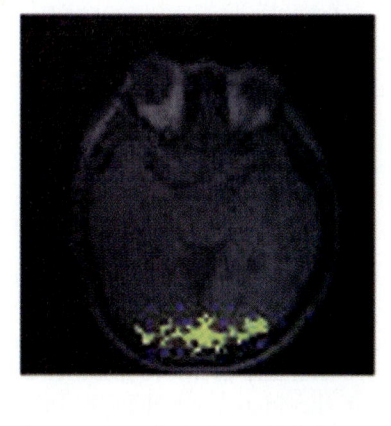

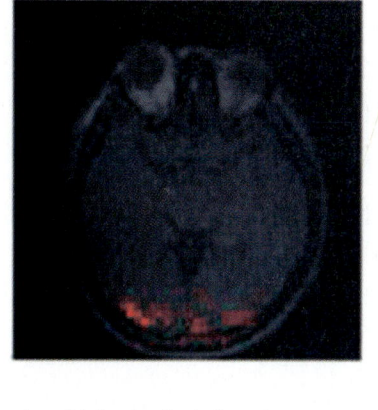

Acupuncture is an ancient Asian medical practice in which physical disorders are treated by stimulating specific locations in the skin with needles. Most acupuncture points are distant from the organ being treated. For example, vision and hearing problems are treated by inserting needles at different "acupoints" in the foot (Part A). Scientists have begun to investigate the role of the brain in the effects of acupuncture (Cho et al., 1998). In Part B, similar areas of the brain are activated by direct sensory stimulation and stimulation of the related acupoints on the foot. The MRI images on the left are produced by visual stimuli. On the right is the MRI image showing activation of the same brain areas in response to acupuncture at a vision-related spot in the foot. These acupoints are located near nerves, but the pathways to the specific parts of the brain have not been charted.

reticular formation A network of cells and fibers threaded throughout the hindbrain and midbrain that alters the activity of the rest of the brain.

locus coeruleus A small nucleus in the reticular formation that contains about half of the cell bodies of neurons in the brain that use norepinephrine.

is a collection of cells that are not arranged in any well-defined nucleus. Because the collection resembles a net, it is called the **reticular formation** (*reticular* means "net-like"). This network is very important in altering the activity of the rest of the brain. It is involved, for example, in arousal and attention; if the fibers from the reticular system are disconnected from the rest of the brain, a permanent coma results. Some of the fibers carrying pain signals from the spinal cord make connections in the reticular formation, which immediately arouses the rest of the brain from sleep. Within seconds, the hindbrain causes your heart rate and blood pressure to increase.

Activity of the reticular formation also leads to activity in a small nucleus within it called the **locus coeruleus** (pronounced "LO-kus seh-ROO-lee-us"), which means

figure 3.13

Major Structures of the Brain (with Hindbrain Highlighted)

This side view of a section cut down the middle of the human brain reveals the forebrain, midbrain, hindbrain, and spinal cord. Many of these subdivisions do not have clear-cut borders, because they are all interconnected by fiber tracts. The anatomy of the mammalian brain reflects its evolution over millions of years. Newer structures (such as the cerebral cortex, which is the outer surface of the forebrain) that handle higher mental functions were built on older ones (such as the medulla) that coordinate heart rate, breathing, and other more basic functions.

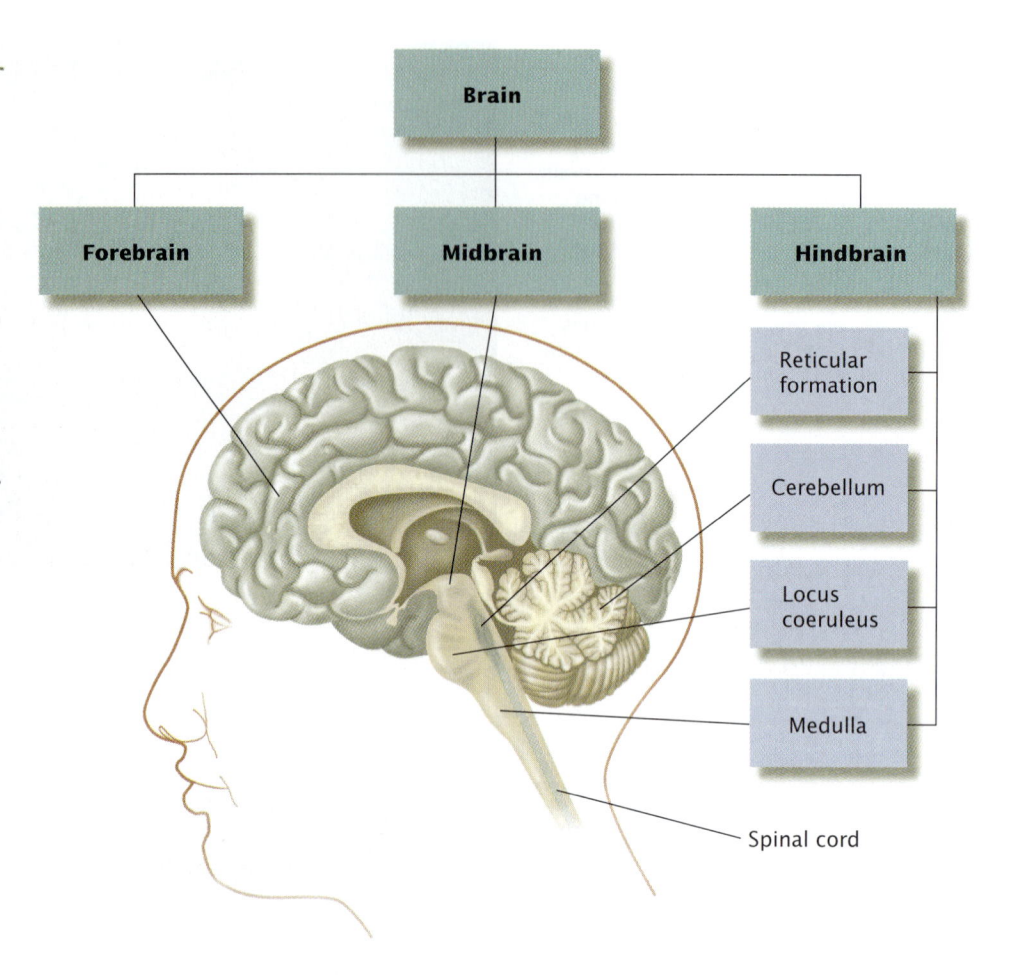

cerebellum The part of the hindbrain whose function is to control finely coordinated movements and to store learned associations that involve movement.

"blue spot" (see Figure 3.13). There are relatively few cells in the locus coeruleus—only about 30,000 of the 100 billion or so in the human brain (Foote, Bloom, & Aston-Jones, 1983)—but each sends out an axon that branches extensively, making contact with as many as 100,000 other cells. Studies of rats, monkeys, and humans suggest that the locus coeruleus is involved in directing attention (Aston-Jones, Chiang, & Alexinsky, 1991; Smythies, 1997). In humans, abnormalities in the locus coeruleus have been linked to depression (Leonard, 1997).

The **cerebellum** is also part of the hindbrain. It allows the eyes to track a moving target accurately (Krauzlis & Lisberger, 1991), and it may be the storehouse for well-rehearsed movements, such as those associated with ballet, piano playing, and athletics (McCormick & Thompson, 1984). For a long time its primary function was thought to be control of finely coordinated movements, such as threading a needle. But compared with other species, the human cerebellum has grown more in size than any other brain structure, so researchers have begun to rethink and reinvestigate the cerebellum's role in more uniquely human tasks such as language and symbolic thought.

Recent work on the function of the cerebellum highlights the fact that there are different ways to think about what various parts of the brain do. For instance, you can think of coordinated movements simply as "motor functioning" or as an example of the more general activity of "sequencing and timing" (Gibbon et al., 1997). The importance of sequencing has become increasingly apparent in the study of nonmovement activities, particularly language. To speak fluently, you must put together a sequence of words rapidly and in the correct order and temporal rhythm. It appears that the cerebellum plays a vital role in normal speech by integrating moment-to-moment feedback about vocal sounds with a sequence of precise movements of the lips and tongue (Leiner, Leiner, & Dow, 1993). When this process of

A Field Sobriety Test The cerebellum is involved in the balance and coordination required for walking. When the cerebellum's activity is impaired by alcohol, these skills are disrupted, which is why the police ask people suspected of driving under the influence of alcohol to walk a straight line.

integration and sequencing is disrupted, stuttering can result. Even nonstutterers who hear their own speech with a slight delay begin to stutter. (This is why radio talk-show hosts ask callers to turn off their radios. A momentary gap occurs before the shows are actually broadcast, and listening to the delayed sound of their own voice on the radio can cause callers to stutter.) Recent magnetic resonance imaging (MRI) studies indicate that the cerebellum is one of a number of brain regions that are concurrently involved in stuttering (Fox et al., 2000).

Reflexes and feedback systems are important to the functioning of the hindbrain, just as they are in the spinal cord. For example, if blood pressure drops, heart action increases reflexively to compensate for that drop. If you stand up very quickly, your blood pressure can drop so suddenly that it produces lightheadedness until the hindbrain reflex "catches up." If the hindbrain does not activate autonomic nervous system mechanisms to increase blood pressure, you will faint.

The Midbrain

Above the hindbrain is the **midbrain.** In humans it is a small structure, but it serves some very important functions. Certain types of automatic behaviors that integrate simple movements with sensory input are controlled there. For example, when you move your head, midbrain circuits allow you to move your eyes smoothly in the opposite direction, so that you can keep your eyes focused on an object despite the movement of your head. And when a loud noise causes you to turn your head reflexively and look in the direction of the sound, your midbrain circuits are at work.

One vital nucleus in the midbrain is the **substantia nigra,** meaning "black substance." This small area and its connections to the **striatum** (named for its "striped" appearance) in the forebrain are necessary in order to smoothly begin movements. Without them, you would find it difficult, if not impossible, to get up out of a chair, lift your hand to swat a fly, move your mouth to form words, or reach for that coffeepot at 6:00 A.M.

The Forebrain

Like the cerebellum, the human **forebrain** is another region that has grown out of proportion to the rest of the brain, so much so that it folds back over and completely covers the other parts. It is responsible for the most complex aspects of behavior and mental life. As Figure 3.14 shows, the forebrain includes a variety of structures.

midbrain A small structure, between the hindbrain and forebrain, that relays information from the eyes, ears, and skin and that controls certain types of automatic behaviors.

substantia nigra An area of the midbrain involved in the smooth initiation of movement.

striatum A structure within the forebrain that is involved in the smooth initiation of movement.

forebrain The most highly developed part of the brain; it is responsible for the most complex aspects of behavior and mental life.

figure 3.14

Major Structures of the Forebrain

The structures of the forebrain are covered by an outer "bark" known as the *cerebral cortex*. This diagram shows some of the structures that lie within the forebrain. The amygdala, the hippocampus, the septum, and portions of the cerebral cortex are part of the limbic system.

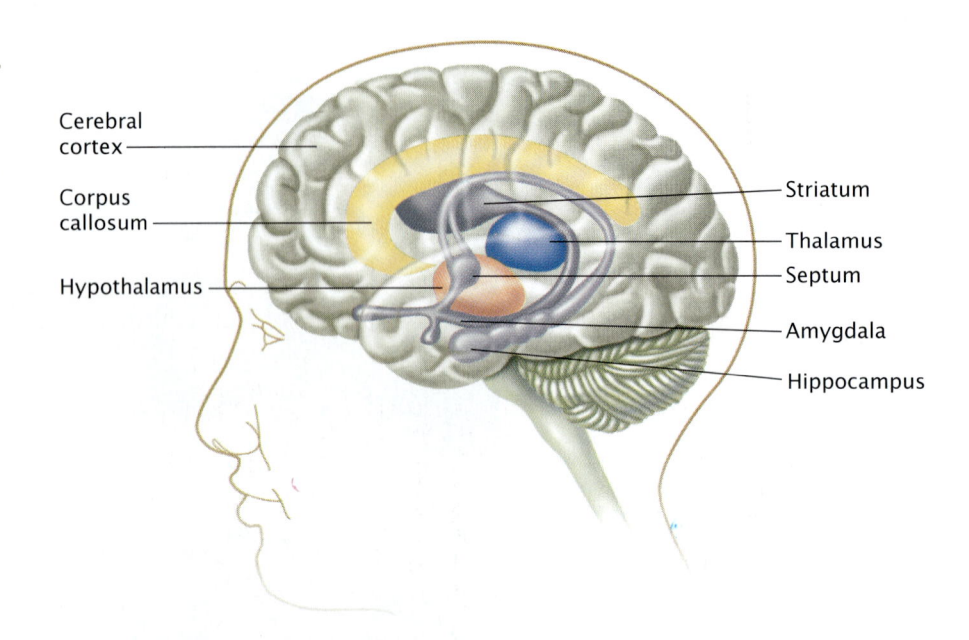

Labels: Cerebral cortex, Corpus callosum, Hypothalamus, Striatum, Thalamus, Septum, Amygdala, Hippocampus

thalamus A forebrain structure that relays signals from most sense organs to higher levels in the brain and plays an important role in processing and making sense out of this information.

hypothalamus A structure in the forebrain that regulates hunger, thirst, and sex drives.

suprachiasmatic nuclei Nuclei in the hypothalamus that generate biological rhythms.

amygdala A structure in the forebrain that, among other things, associates features of stimuli from two sensory modalities.

hippocampus A structure in the forebrain associated with the formation of new memories.

limbic system A set of brain structures that play important roles in regulating emotion and memory.

Two of these structures lie deep within the brain. The first is the **thalamus,** which relays pain signals from the spinal cord, as well as signals from the eyes and most other sense organs, to upper levels in the brain. It also plays an important role in processing and making sense out of this information. The other is the **hypothalamus,** which lies under the thalamus (*hypo* means "under") and is involved in regulating hunger, thirst, and sex drives. It has many connections to and from the autonomic nervous system, as well as to other parts of the brain. Destruction of one section of the hypothalamus results in an overwhelming urge to eat (see the chapter on motivation and emotion). Damage to another area of a male's hypothalamus causes his sex organs to degenerate and his sex drive to decrease drastically. There is also a fascinating part of the hypothalamus that contains the brain's own timepiece: the **suprachiasmatic nuclei.** The suprachiasmatic (pronounced "soo-pra-kye-as-MAT-ik") nuclei keep an approximately twenty-four-hour clock that determines your biological rhythms. We discuss these rhythms in the chapter on consciousness

Two other forebrain structures, the **amygdala** (pronounced "ah-MIG-duh-luh") and the **hippocampus,** are important in memory and emotion. For example, the amygdala associates features of stimuli from two different senses, as when we link the shape and feel of objects in memory (Murray & Mishkin, 1985). It is also involved in fear and other emotions (LeDoux, 1995; Whalen, 1998); its activity has been found to be altered in people suffering from posttraumatic stress disorder (Shin et al., 1997; see the chapter on health, stress, and coping). Damage to the hippocampus results in an inability to form new memories of events. In one case, a patient known as R.B. suffered a stroke (an interruption of blood flow in the brain) that damaged only his hippocampus. Although tests indicated that his intelligence was above average and he could recall old memories, he was almost totally unable to build new memories (Squire, 1986). Research using MRI scans and tests of the decline of memory function in normal elderly people suggests that memory ability is correlated with the size of the hippocampus (Golomb et al., 1994); a small hippocampus predicts severe memory problems even before they are evident (Kaye et al., 1997). Animal studies have also shown that damage to the hippocampus within a day of a mildly painful experience erases memories of the experience, but that removal of the hippocampus several days after the experience has no effect on the memory. So memories are not permanently stored in the hippocampus but are transferred elsewhere. As described in the chapter on memory, your storehouse of memories depends on the activities of many parts of the brain.

figure 3.15

Alzheimer's Disease and Brain Atrophy

These human brains, photographed after death, show that compared with a normal brain (bottom), the brain of a person with Alzheimer's disease (top) shows considerable degeneration, especially in limbic regions and the cerebral cortex (Callan et al., 2001). For example, the hippocampus of a person with Alzheimer's disease is about 40 percent smaller than normal. In fact, a smaller-than-average hippocampus in the elderly predicts the onset of the disease (Jack et al., 1999).

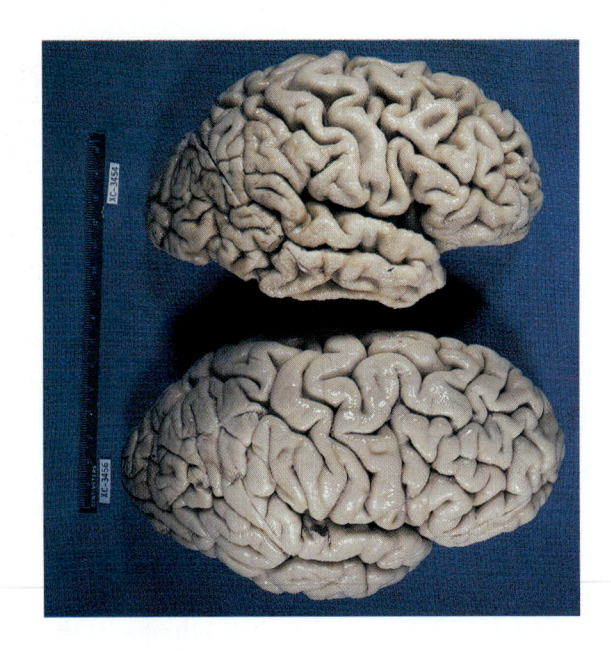

The hippocampus and amygdala, and other interconnected structures such as the hypothalamus and the septum, are part of the **limbic system**. The limbic system plays an important role in regulating emotion and memory. Studies of the brains of people who died from Alzheimer's disease have found severe degeneration of neurons in the hippocampus and other limbic structures (see Figure 3.15). This may explain why Alzheimer's disease is a major cause of *dementia*, the deterioration of cognitive capabilities often associated with aging. About 10 percent of people over the age of sixty-five, and more than 47 percent of people over eighty-five, suffer from this disorder (Small et al., 1997; U.S. Surgeon General, 1999). The financial cost of Alzheimer's disease in the United States alone is more than $100 billion a year (Small et al., 1997); the cost in human suffering is incalculable. It is no wonder, then, that the search for its causes and cures has a high priority among researchers who study the brain.

FOCUS ON RESEARCH METHODS

Manipulating Genes in Animal Models of Human Disease

Alzheimer's disease is named for Alois Alzheimer, a German neurologist. Almost a century ago, Alzheimer examined the brain of a woman who had died after years of progressive mental deterioration and dementia. He was looking for the cause of her disorder, and he found that cells in her cerebral cortex were bunched up like a rope tied in knots and that cellular debris had collected around the affected nerves. These features came to be known as tangles and plaques. *Tangles* are twisted fibers within neurons; their main protein component is called *tau*. *Plaques* are deposits of protein and parts of dead cells found between neurons. The major component of plaques was found to be a small protein called *beta-amyloid*, which is produced from a larger protein called *beta-amyloid precursor protein*. Ever since Alzheimer described plaques and tangles, researchers have been trying to learn about the role they play in Alzheimer's disease.

● **What was the researchers' question?**

One specific question that researchers have addressed is whether the biochemicals found in plaques and tangles actually *cause* Alzheimer's disease.

As noted in the chapter on research in psychology, a causal relationship cannot be inferred from a correlation. Therefore, to discover if beta-amyloid and tau might cause the death of neurons seen in Alzheimer's disease, researchers needed to conduct controlled experiments, which means manipulating an independent variable and measuring its effect on a dependent variable. In this case, the experiment would involve creating plaques and tangles (the independent variable) and looking for their effects on memory (the dependent variable). Because such experiments cannot ethically be conducted on humans, scientists began looking for Alzheimer's-like conditions in some other species of animal. Progress in finding the causes of Alzheimer's disease depended on their finding an "animal model" of the disease.

● How did the researchers answer the question?

Previous studies of the genes of people with Alzheimer's disease had revealed that a mutation in the beta-amyloid precursor protein was associated with the disease. However, many Alzheimer's patients exhibited mutations not in this protein but in another one, which researchers called *presenilin* because it was associated with senility. (It turns out that presenilin is related to Alzheimer's disease because it affects the way in which beta-amyloid precursor protein is modified.) At this point, the researchers hoped to determine whether these mutated proteins actually cause the brain damage and memory impairment associated with Alzheimer's disease. Armed with new genetic engineering tools, they began to create, literally, an animal model of Alzheimer's disease with mutated human genes.

The first attempts to create this animal model involved the insertion of a mutant form of beta-amyloid precursor protein into the cells of mice. If Alzheimer's disease is caused by faulty beta-amyloid precursor protein, so the logic went, inserting the gene for this faulty protein into mouse cells should cause deposits of beta-amyloid and the loss of neurons in the same parts of the brain as those seen in human Alzheimer's victims. No such changes should be observed in a control group of untreated animals.

● What did the researchers find?

Of course, finding this result just once is not enough; an experiment's results must be replicable in order to be reliable. This principle was reinforced in 1992, when a group of scientists reported success in creating a model of Alzheimer's disease in mice, only to retract their statements when they could not repeat their results. Three years later, researchers at a biotechnology company encountered a different problem. Although they succeeded in implanting the faulty protein into mice and found damage characteristic of Alzheimer's disease (Games et al, 1995), they did not observe any memory impairment in the mice.

Since then, however, other scientists have found that a variety of different mutations of beta-amyloid precursor protein inserted into mice produce both brain damage and memory impairment (Hsiao et al., 1996; Nalbantoglu et al., 1997). One group subsequently claimed that the best animal model of Alzheimer's disease appears to involve mice with mutations in both beta-amyloid precursor protein and presenilin. These mice exhibit both severe brain pathology and memory impairment at a younger age than that seen in other experiments (Arendash et al., 2001; Holcomb et al., 1998). Another group has claimed that its model better mimics the tau-containing tangles of Alzheimer's disease in humans (Sturchler-Pierrat et al., 1997).

Unfortunately, none of these "transgenic" mouse models yet fully reproduces the brain pathology seen in Alzheimer's disease (Chapman et al., 2001). Nevertheless, these mice have paved the way for an exciting new possibility for the treatment for Alzheimer's disease: a vaccine against beta-amyloid. Transgenic mice given this vaccine have shown not only improvements in memory but also a reversal of beta-amyloid deposits in their brains (Morgan et al., 2000; Younkin 2001). Researchers have begun clinical trials of beta-amyloid vaccines in humans, but it is too soon to tell how beneficial they might be. At first they appeared safe (Ingram, 2001), but serious side effects have halted some trials.

Gene Manipulation in Mice In one study, the gene for a particular type of neurotransmitter receptor was "knocked out" in these black mice. As shown here, these animals were much more aggressive than a control group of brown mice (Nelson et al., 1995).

• What do the results mean?

Regardless of whether this particular vaccine works, scientists will continue to use transgenic mice to evaluate the roles of mutations in beta-amyloid precursor protein, presenilin, *tau*, and other proteins in causing Alzheimer's disease. This research is important not only because it might eventually solve the mystery of this terrible disorder but also because it illustrates the power of experimental modification of animal genes for testing all kinds of hypotheses about biological factors influencing behavior. Besides inserting new or modified genes into brain cells, scientists also can manipulate an independent variable by "knocking out" specific genes, then looking at the effect on dependent variables. One research team has shown, for example, that knocking out a gene for a particular type of neurotransmitter receptor causes mice to become obese and to overeat even when given appetite-suppressant drugs (Tecott et al., 1995). And genetic elimination of proteins that modify neurotransmitter activity in mice canceled out the stimulating effects of cocaine (Sora et al., 2001).

Of course, researchers must be careful not to inadvertently affect other genes while modifying the particular gene they are interested in. And they must be sure that the modified gene has not influenced the mice's behavior in unexpected and important ways. For example, if the gene significantly affects sensory or motor functions, a behavioral change could mistakenly be attributed to a change in brain function. (After all, a mouse with defective legs cannot run through a memory-testing maze.) Careful behavioral analyses of the mouse model of Alzheimer's disease will also be needed to determine what components of memory processes are impaired.

• What do we still need to know?

The scarcity of animal models of obesity, drug addiction, and other problems has impeded progress in finding biological treatments for them. As animal models for these conditions become more available through gene modification techniques, they will pave the way for new types of animal studies that are directly relevant to human problems. The next challenge will be to use these animal models to develop and test treatments that might effectively be applied to humans.

The Cerebral Cortex

So far, we have described some key structures *within* the forebrain; now we turn to a discussion of other structures on its surface. The outermost part of the brain appears rather round and has right and left halves that are similar in appearance. These halves are called the **cerebral hemispheres.** The outer part of the cerebral hemispheres, the **cerebral cortex,** has a surface area of one to two square feet—an area that is larger than it looks because of the folds that allow the cortex to fit compactly inside the skull. The cerebral cortex is much larger in humans than in most other animals (dolphins are an exception). It is associated with the analysis of information from all the senses, control of voluntary movements, higher-order thought, and other complex aspects of human behavior and mental processes.

The left side of Figure 3.16 shows the *anatomical* or physical features of the cerebral cortex. The folds of the cortex give the surface of the human brain its wrinkled appearance—its ridges and valleys. The ridges are called *gyri* (pronounced "ji-rye"), and the valleys are called *sulci* (pronounced "sulk-eye") or *fissures*. As you can see in the figure, several deep sulci divide the cortex into four areas: the *frontal, parietal, occipital,* and *temporal* lobes. Thus, the gyri and sulci provide landmarks for describing the appearance of the cortex. The right side of Figure 3.16 depicts the areas of the cerebral cortex in which various *functions* or activities occur. The functional areas do not exactly match the anatomical areas, inasmuch as some functions

---

cerebral hemispheres The left and right halves of the rounded, outermost part of the brain.

cerebral cortex The outer surface of the brain.

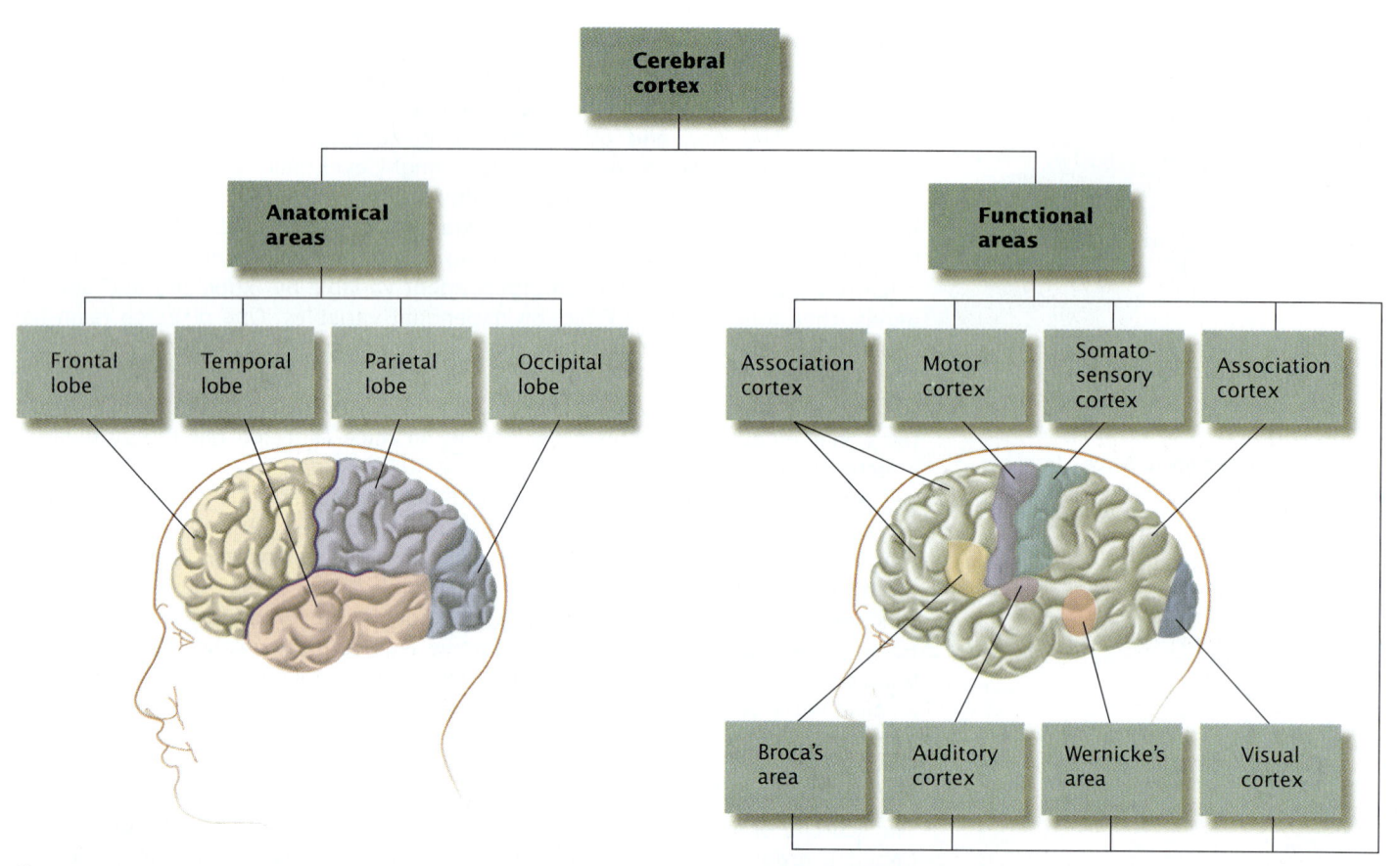

figure 3.16

The Cerebral Cortex (Viewed from the Left Side)

The brain's ridges (gyri) and valleys (sulci) are landmarks that divide the cortex into four lobes: the frontal, parietal, occipital, and temporal. These terms describe where the regions are (the lobes are named for the skull bones that cover them), but the cortex is also divided in terms of function. These functional areas are the motor cortex (which controls movement), sensory cortex (including somatosensory, auditory, and visual areas that receive information from the senses), and association cortex (which integrates information). Also labeled are Wernicke's area and Broca's area, two regions that are found only on the left side of the cortex and that are vital to the interpretation and production of speech.

occur in more than one area. Three of these functional areas—the sensory cortex, the motor cortex, and the association cortex—are discussed below, along with related areas.

Sensory Cortex The **sensory cortex** lies in the parietal, occipital, and temporal lobes and is the part of the cerebral cortex that receives information from our senses. Different regions of the sensory cortex receive information from different senses. Visual information is received by the *visual cortex*, made up of cells in the occipital lobe; auditory information is received by the *auditory cortex*, made up of cells in the temporal lobe; and information from the skin about touch, pain, and temperature is received in the *somatosensory cortex*, made up of cells in the parietal lobe.

Information about skin sensations from neighboring parts of the body comes to neighboring parts of the somatosensory cortex, as Figure 3.17 illustrates. It is as if the outline of a tiny person, dangling upside down, determined the location of the information. This pattern is called the *homunculus*, which is Latin for "little man." The organization of the homunculus has long been assumed to be unchanging, but recent work has shown that the amount of sensory cortex that responds to particular sensory inputs can be modified by experience. The experience may be as traumatic as the loss of a limb (whereby sensory areas of the brain formerly stimulated

---

sensory cortex The parts of the cerebral cortex that receive stimulus information from the senses.

motor cortex The part of the cerebral cortex whose neurons control voluntary movements in specific parts of the body.

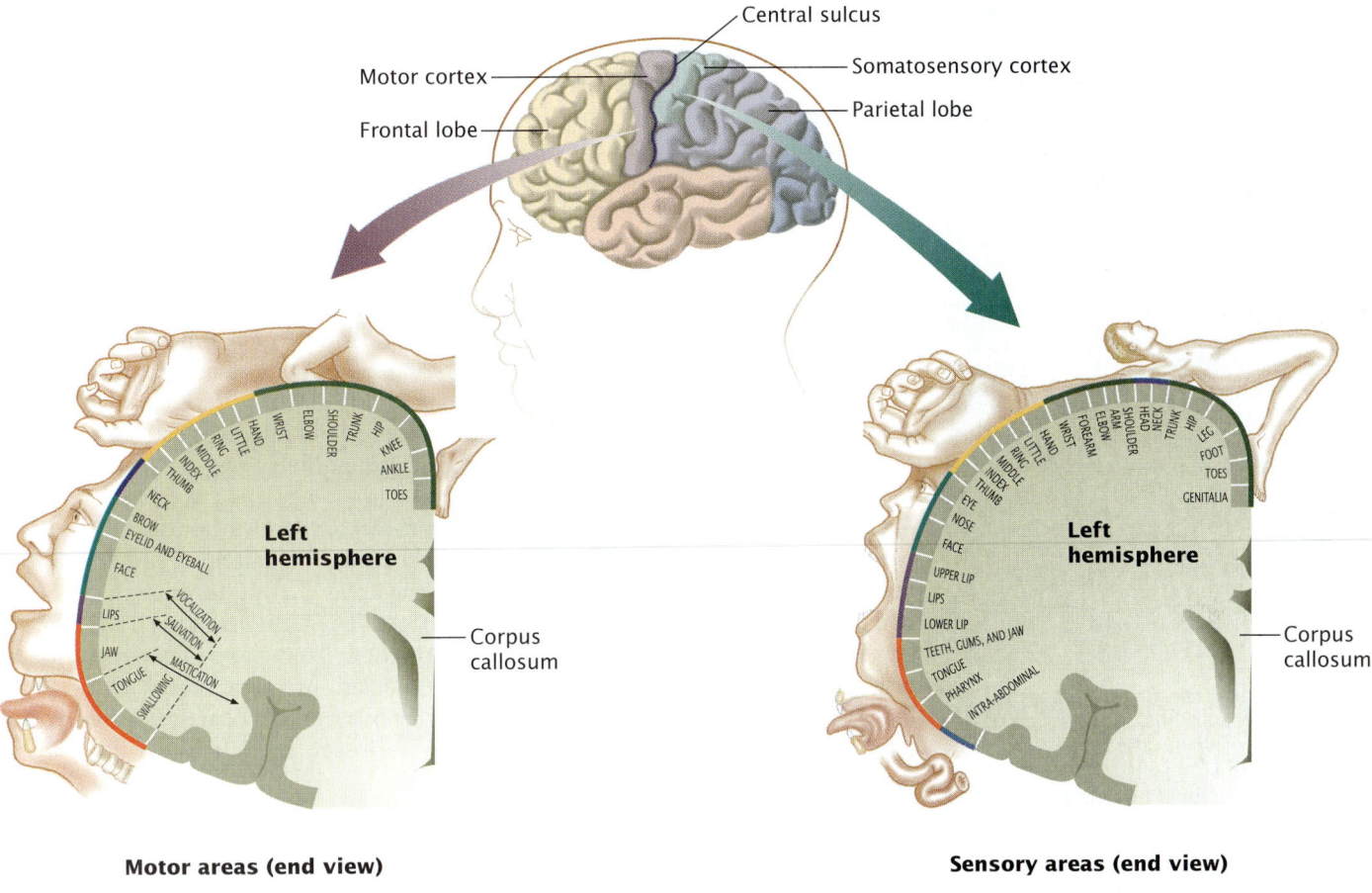

The Central Nervous System: Making Sense of the World

figure 3.17

Motor and Somatosensory Cortex

The areas of cortex that move parts of the body (motor cortex) and receive sensory input from body parts (somatosensory cortex) appear in both hemispheres of the brain. Here we show cross-sections of only those on the left side, looking from the back of the brain toward the front. Areas controlling movement of neighboring parts of the body, such as the foot and leg, occupy neighboring parts of the motor cortex. Areas receiving input from neighboring body parts, such as the lips and tongue, are near one another in the somatosensory cortex. Notice that the size of these areas is uneven; the larger the area devoted to each body part, the larger that body part appears on the "homunculus."

Note: Did you notice the error in this class drawing? (The figure shows the right side of the body, but the left hand and left side of the face.)

Source: Penfield & Rasmussen (1968).

THE FAR SIDE By GARY LARSON

"Whoa! *That* was a good one! Try it, Hobbs — just poke his brain right where my finger is."

The Far Side® by Gary Larson © 1986 FarWorks, Inc. All rights reserved. Used with permission.

by that limb are now stimulated by other regions of skin) or something as mundane as practicing the violin (which can increase the number of neurons responding to touch). These changes appear to be coordinated partly by brain areas outside the cerebral cortex, which reassign more neurons to process particular sensory inputs. For example, activity in the basal nucleus of the forebrain can generate a massive reorganization of the sensory cortex involved in sound processing (Kilgard & Merzenich, 1998).

Motor Cortex Neurons in specific areas of the **motor cortex**, which is in the frontal lobe, create voluntary movements in specific parts of the body. Some control movement of the hand; others stimulate movement of the foot, the knee, the head, and so on. The specific muscles activated by these regions are linked not to specific neurons but, as mentioned earlier, to the patterned activity of many neurons. For example, some of the same neurons are active in moving more than one finger. In other words, different parts of the motor cortex homunculus overlap somewhat

(Indovina & Sanes, 2001). As you can see in Figure 3.17, the motor homunculus mirrors the somatosensory homunculus; the parts of the motor cortex that control the hands, for instance, are near parts of the somatosensory cortex that receive sensory information from the hands.

Controlling the movement of the body may seem simple: You have a map of body parts in the motor cortex, and you activate cells in the hand region if you want to move your hand. But the actual process is much more complex. Recall again your sleepy reach for the coffeepot. The motor cortex must first translate the coffeepot's location in space into a location relative to your body; for example, your hand might have to be moved forward and a certain number of degrees to the right or to the left of your body. Next, the motor cortex must determine which muscles must be contracted to produce those movements. Populations of neurons work together to produce just the right combinations of direction and force in the particular muscle groups necessary to create the desired effects. Many interconnected areas of the motor cortex are involved in making these determinations.

Association Cortex The parts of the cerebral cortex not directly involved with either receiving specific sensory information or initiating movement are referred to as **association cortex**. These are the areas that perform complex cognitive tasks, such as associating words with images. The term *association* is appropriate because these areas either receive information from more than one sense or combine sensory and motor information. Association cortex occurs in all of the lobes and forms a large part of the cerebral cortex in human beings. For this reason, damage to association areas can create severe losses, or deficits, in all kinds of mental abilities.

One of the most devastating deficits, called *aphasia*, creates difficulty in understanding or producing speech and can involve all the functions of the cerebral cortex. Language information comes from the auditory cortex (for spoken language) or from the visual cortex (for written language); areas of the motor cortex produce speech (Geschwind, 1979). But the complex function known as language also involves activity in association cortex.

In the 1800s, two areas of association cortex involved in different aspects of language were delineated. Paul Broca described the difficulties that result from damage to the association cortex in the frontal lobe near motor areas that control facial muscles, an area now called *Broca's area* (see Figure 3.16). When Broca's area is damaged, the mental organization of speech suffers. Victims have great difficulty speaking, and what they say is often grammatically incorrect. Each word comes slowly. Other language problems result from damage to a portion of the association cortex first described by Carl Wernicke (pronounced "VER-nick-ee") and thus called *Wernicke's area*. As Figure 3.16 shows, it is located in the temporal lobe, near an area of the cortex that receives information from the ears and eyes. Wernicke's area is involved in the interpretation of both speech and written words. Damage to this area can leave a person able to speak, but it disrupts the ability to understand the meaning of words or to speak comprehensibly.

One study illustrates the different effects of damage to each area (Lapointe, 1990). In response to the request "Tell me what you do with a cigarette," a person with chronic Broca's aphasia replied, "Uh . . . uh . . . cigarette (pause) smoke it." Though halting and ungrammatical, this speech was meaningful. In response to the same request, a person with chronic Wernicke's aphasia replied, "This is a segment of a pegment. Soap a cigarette." This speech, by contrast, was fluent but without meaning. A fascinating aspect of Broca's aphasia is that when a person with the disorder sings, the words come fluently and correctly. Presumably, words set to music are handled by a different part of the brain than spoken words (Besson et al., 1998). Capitalizing on this observation, "melodic intonation" therapy helps Broca's aphasia patients gain fluency in speaking by teaching them to speak in a "singsong" manner (Lapointe, 1990).

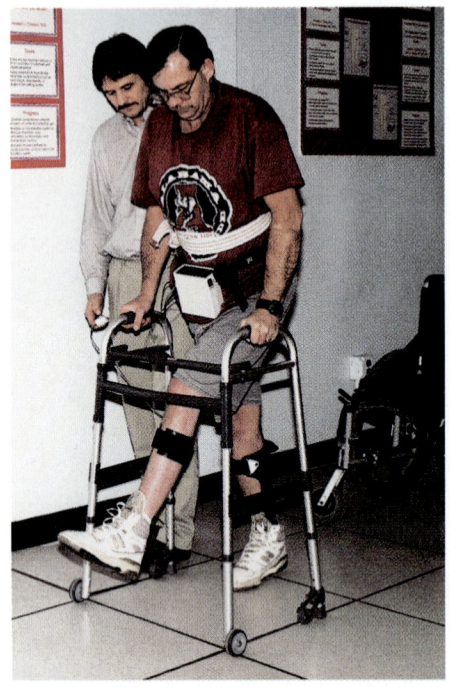

Movement and the Brain Smooth movements require the coordination of neural activity in both the brain and the spinal cord. This presents a challenge to researchers developing devices to restore movement in paralyzed individuals. Delivering computer-controlled electrical stimulation to the leg muscles allows walking movements to occur, but they are jerkier than movements that the brain normally produces.

LINKAGES (a link to Cognition and Language)

association cortex Those parts of the cerebral cortex that receive information from more than one sense or that combine sensory and motor information to perform complex cognitive tasks.

corpus callosum A massive bundle of fibers that connects the right and left cerebral hemispheres and allows them to communicate with each other.

It appears that differing areas of association cortex are activated, depending on whether language is spoken or written and whether particular grammatical and conceptual categories are involved. For example, consider the cases of two women who had strokes that damaged different language-related parts of their association cortex (Caramazza & Hillis, 1991). Neither woman had difficulty speaking or writing nouns, but both had difficulty with verbs. One woman could write verbs but could not speak them: She had difficulty pronouncing *watch* when it was used as a verb in the sentence "I watch TV," but she spoke the same word easily when it appeared as a noun in "My watch is slow." The other woman could speak verbs but had difficulty writing them. Another odd language abnormality following brain damage, known as "foreign accent syndrome," was illustrated by a thirty-two-year-old stroke victim whose native language was English. His speech was slurred immediately after the stroke, but as it improved, he began to speak with a Scandinavian accent, adding syllables to some words ("How are you today-ah?") and pronouncing *hill* as "heel." His normal accent did not fully return for four months (Takayama et al., 1993). Case studies of "foreign accent syndrome" suggest that specific regions of the brain are involved in the sound of language, whereas others are involved in various aspects of its meaning.

Regions of association cortex long assumed to be involved mainly with spoken or written language also appear to be involved in processing the "language" of music. For example, recent studies using magnetoencephalography have found that Broca's area is activated when people hear a chord in a progression that disobeys musical "rules of grammar" (Maess et al., 2001).

The Divided Brain in a Unified Self

A striking idea emerged from observations of people with damage to the language areas of the brain. Researchers noticed that damage to limited areas of the *left hemisphere* impaired the ability to use or comprehend language, whereas damage to corresponding parts of the *right hemisphere* usually did not. Perhaps, they reasoned, the right and left halves of the brain serve different functions.

This concept was not entirely new. It had long been understood, for example, that most sensory and motor pathways cross over as they enter or leave the brain. As a result, the *left hemisphere* receives information from, and controls movements of, the *right* side of the body, whereas the *right hemisphere* receives input from and controls the *left* side of the body. However, both sides of the brain perform these functions. In contrast, the fact that language centers, such as Broca's area and Wernicke's area, are almost exclusively on the left side of the brain suggested that each hemisphere might be specialized to perform some functions almost independently of the other hemisphere.

Split-Brain Studies

As far back as the late 1800s, scientists had wanted to test the hypothesis that the cerebral hemispheres might be specialized, but they had no techniques for doing so. Then, during the 1960s, Roger Sperry, Michael Gazzaniga, and their colleagues began to study *split-brain* patients—people who had undergone a surgical procedure in an attempt to control severe epilepsy. Before the surgery, their seizures began in one hemisphere and then spread to engulf the whole brain. As a last resort, surgeons isolated the two hemispheres from each other by severing the **corpus callosum**, a massive bundle of more than a million fibers that connects the two hemispheres (see Figure 3.18).

After the surgery, researchers used a special apparatus to present visual images to only one side of these patients' split brains (see Figure 3.19). They found that severing the tie between the hemispheres had dramatically affected the way these people thought about and dealt with the world. For example, when the image of a spoon was presented to the left, language-oriented side of one patient's split brain, she could say what the spoon was; but when the spoon was presented to the right

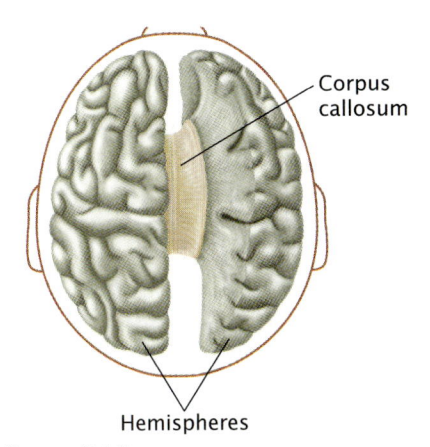

figure 3.18

The Brain's Left and Right Hemispheres

The brain's two hemispheres are joined by a core bundle of nerve fibers known as the *corpus callosum*; in this figure the corpus callosum has been cut, and the hemispheres are separated. The two cerebral hemispheres look nearly the same but perform somewhat different tasks. For one thing, the left hemisphere receives sensory input from, and controls movement on, the right side of the body. The right hemisphere senses and controls the left side of the body.

figure 3.19

Apparatus for Studying Split-Brain Patients

When the person stares at the dot on the screen, images briefly presented on one side of the dot go to only one side of the brain. For example, a picture of a spoon presented on the left side of the screen goes to the right side of the brain. The right side of the brain can find the spoon and direct the left hand to touch it; but because the language areas on the left side of the brain did not see it, the person is not able to say what it is.

side of her brain, she could not describe the spoon in words. She still knew what the object was, however. Using her left hand (controlled by the right hemisphere), she could pick out the spoon from a group of other objects by its shape. But when asked what she had just grasped, she replied, "A pencil." The right hemisphere recognized the object, but the patient could not describe it because the left (language) half of her brain did not see or feel it (Sperry, 1968).

Although the right hemisphere has no control over spoken language in split-brain patients, it does have important capabilities, including some related to nonspoken language. For example, a split-brain patient's right hemisphere can guide the left hand in spelling out words with Scrabble tiles (Gazzaniga & LeDoux, 1978). Thanks to this ability, researchers discovered that the right hemisphere of split-brain patients has self-awareness and normal learning abilities. In addition, it is superior to the left hemisphere on tasks dealing with spatial relations (especially drawing three-dimensional shapes) and at recognizing human faces.

Lateralization of Normal Brains Sperry (1974) concluded from his studies that each hemisphere in the split-brain patient has its own "private sensations, perceptions, thoughts, and ideas all of which are cut off from the corresponding experiences in the opposite hemisphere. . . . In many respects each disconnected hemisphere appears to have a separate mind of its own." But when the hemispheres are connected normally, are certain functions, such as mathematical reasoning or language skills, lateralized? A **lateralized** task is one that is performed more efficiently by one hemisphere than by the other.

To find out, researchers presented images to just one hemisphere of people with normal brains and then measured how fast they could analyze information. If information is presented to one side of the brain and that side is specialized to analyze that type of information, a person's responses will be faster than if the information must first be transferred to the other hemisphere for analysis. These studies have confirmed that the left hemisphere has better logical and language abilities than the right, whereas the right hemisphere has better spatial, artistic, and musical abilities (Springer & Deutsch, 1989). Positron emission tomography (PET) scans of normal people receiving varying kinds of auditory stimulation also demonstrate these asymmetries of function (see Figure 3.20). We know that the language abilities of the left

lateralized Referring to the tendency for one cerebral hemisphere to excel at a particular function or skill compared with the other hemisphere.

figure 3.20

Lateralization of the Cerebral Hemispheres: Evidence from PET Scans

These PET scans show overhead views of a section of a person's brain that was receiving different kinds of stimulation. At the upper left, the person was resting, with eyes open and ears plugged. Note that the greatest brain activity (as indicated by the red color) was in the visual cortex, which was receiving input from the eyes. As shown at the lower left, when the person listened to spoken language, the auditory cortex in the left temporal lobe became more active, but the right temporal lobe did not. When the person listened to music (lower right), there was intense activity in the right temporal lobe but little in the left. When the person heard both words and music, the temporal cortex on both sides of the brain became activated. Here is visual evidence of the involvement of each side of the brain in processing different kinds of information (Phelps & Mazziotta, 1985).

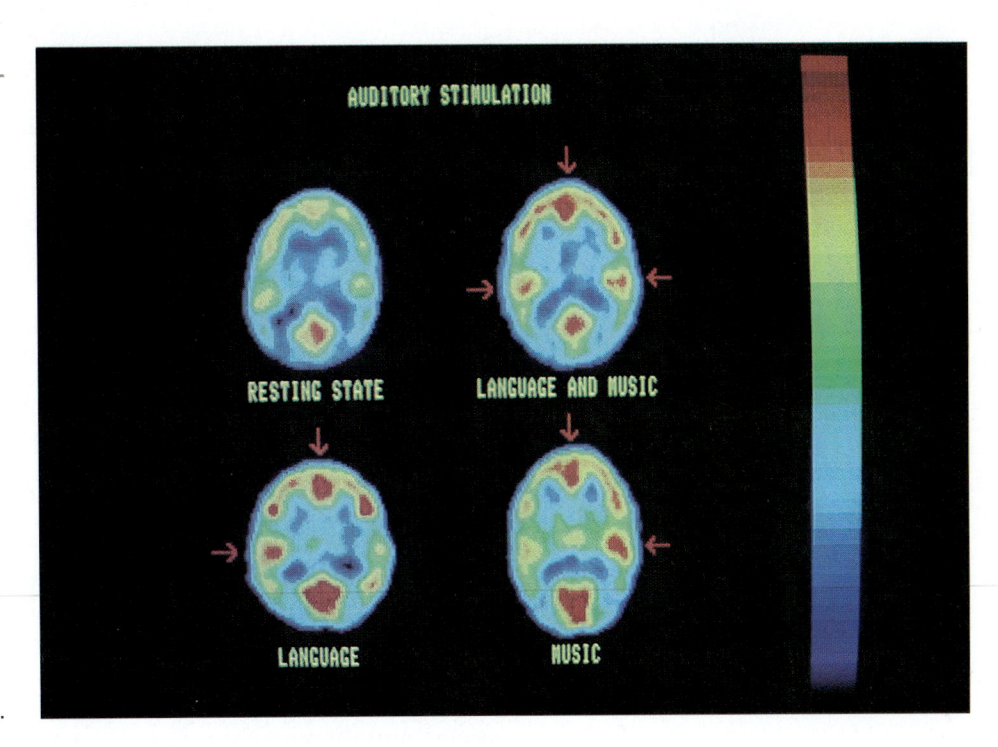

hemisphere are not specifically related to auditory information, though, because people who are deaf also use the left hemisphere more than the right for sign language (Hickok, Bellugi, & Klima, 1996).

The precise nature and degree of lateralization vary quite a bit among individuals. For example, in about a third of left-handed people, either the right hemisphere or both hemispheres control language functions (Springer & Deutsch, 1989). In contrast, only about 5 percent of right-handed people have language controlled by the right hemisphere. Evidence about sex differences in brain laterality comes from studies on the cognitive abilities of normal men and women, the effects of brain damage on cognitive function, and anatomical differences between the sexes. Among normal individuals there are sex differences in the ability to perform tasks that are known to be lateralized in the brain. For example, women tend to do better than men at perceptual fluency tasks, such as rapidly identifying matching items, and at arithmetic calculations. Men tend to be better at imagining the rotation of an object in space and tasks involving target-directed motor skills, such as guiding projectiles or intercepting them, in real or virtual-reality situations (Halperin, 1992; Waller, 2000).

Damage to just one side of the brain is more debilitating to men than to women. In particular, men show larger deficits in language ability than women when the left side is damaged (McGlone, 1980). This difference may reflect a wider distribution of language abilities in the brains of women compared with those of men. When participants in one study performed language tasks, such as thinking about whether particular words rhyme, MRI scans showed increased activity on the left side of the brain for men but on both sides for women (Shaywitz et al., 1995; see also Figure 1.1 in the chapter on introducing psychology). Women appear to have proportionately more of their association cortex devoted to language tasks (Harasty et al., 1997). Note, however, that although humans and animals show definite sex differences in brain anatomy and metabolism (Allen et al., 1989; Gur et al., 1995), no particular anatomical feature has been identified as underlying sex differences in lateralization. One highly publicized report claimed that the corpus callosum is larger in women than men (de Lacoste-Utamsing & Holloway, 1982), but numerous subsequent investigations have all failed to replicate this finding (Olivares et al., 2000). (The original report of a sex difference in the corpus callosum continues to be cited, however, despite overwhelming evidence against it, suggesting that scientists are sometimes not entirely unbiased.)

Having two somewhat specialized hemispheres allows the brain to more efficiently perform some tasks, particularly difficult ones (Hoptman & Davidson, 1994), but the differences between the hemispheres should not be exaggerated. The corpus callosum usually integrates the functions of the "two brains"; this role is particularly important in tasks that require sustained attention (Rueckert et al., 1999). As a result, the hemispheres work so closely together, and each makes up so well for whatever lack of ability the other may have, that people are normally unaware that their brains are made up of two partially independent, somewhat specialized halves (Banich & Heller, 1998; Staudt et al., 2001).

Plasticity: Repairing Damage in the Central Nervous System

The central nervous system has a remarkable property called **synaptic plasticity**, which is the ability to strengthen neural connections at synapses, as well as to establish new synapses. This ability, which depends partly on neurons and partly on glial cells (Ullian et al., 2001), provides the basis for the learning and memory processes described in other chapters. Plasticity occurs continuously throughout the nervous system; even the simplest reflex in the spinal cord can be modified by experience (Feng-Chen & Wolpaw, 1996).

Unfortunately, plasticity is limited when it comes to repairing damage to the brain and spinal cord. Although there are cases of heroic recovery from brain damage following a stroke, for example, most victims are permanently disabled in some way. In fact, until recently, scientists had good reason to be skeptical that a damaged central nervous system could ever heal its own wounds. For one thing, available evidence suggested that neurons divide and multiply during prenatal development, but that they virtually stop dividing by adulthood. They can still grow new axons, but except in the case of canaries and certain other songbirds (Nottebohm, 1985; Scharff et al., 2000), adult neurons appeared incapable of dividing into new ones, even in response to injury (Eriksson et al., 1998). Second, even if adults *could* generate new neurons, their axons and dendrites would have to reestablish all their former communication links. In the peripheral nervous system, glial cells form "tunnels" that guide the regrowth of axons. But in the central nervous system, reestablishing communication links is almost impossible, because glial cells actively suppress new connections (Olson, 1997).

Still, the brain does try to heal itself. Healthy neurons attempt to take over for damaged ones, partly by changing their own function and partly by sprouting axons whose connections help neighboring regions take on new functions (Cao et al., 1994). Although these changes rarely result in total restoration of lost functions, recent research is creating hope for better outcomes and optimism about finding ways to help the process along.

For example, special mental and physical exercise programs appear helpful in "re-wiring" the brains of stroke victims so as to reverse some forms of paralysis and improve some cognitive abilities (Blakeslee, 2001; Liepert et al., 2000; Robertson & Murre, 1999). Scientists have also discovered a protein called Nogo that prevents newly sprouted axons from making connections with other neurons in the central nervous system. Blocking the action of Nogo in rats allowed surviving neurons to make new axonal connections and actually repair spinal cord damage (Chen et al., 2000). The regeneration process can be greatly accelerated by inserting genes for growth proteins into adult neurons (Bomze et al., 2001; Condic, 2001). And in a preliminary study from the newly developing field *of tissue engineering,* immature cells from an adult rat's spinal cord were stimulated to grow and then implanted into the gap in other rats' severed spinal cords. Within a few months, some of these

---

synaptic plasticity The ability to create new synapses and to change the strength of synapses.

A Patient with Parkinson's Disease
Cells from a person's own adrenal gland have been used as an alternative to brain tissue in a transplant treatment for Parkinson's disease. Adrenal gland cells act like neurons when placed in the brain, and the benefits appear to be enhanced when the adrenal tissue is mixed with peripheral nerve tissue (Watts et al., 1997). Considered radical just ten years ago, the treatment is now well established, but only partly effective (Lopez-Lozano, Mata, & Bravo, 2000). Scientists hope that stem cells will work even better (Sawamoto et al., 2001).

previously paralyzed rats were able to stand and walk (Noble, 2000). Much more research is needed on methods such as these, of course, but if they are successful and found to apply to the human central nervous system, they might someday help people like Christopher Reeve to walk again (Schwab, 2002).

Another approach to repairing brain damage involves replacing lost tissue with tissue from another brain. Scientists have transplanted, or grafted, tissue from a still-developing fetal brain into the brain of an adult animal of the same species. If the receiving animal does not reject it, the graft sends axons out into the brain and makes some functional connections. This treatment has reversed animals' learning difficulties, movement disorders, and other results of brain damage. The technique has also been used to treat a small number of people with *Parkinson's disease*—a disorder characterized by tremors, rigidity of the arms and legs, difficulty in initiating movements, and poor balance (Lindvall & Hagell, 2001). The initial results were encouraging, but improvement faded after a year, and some patients suffered side effects involving uncontrollable movements (Freed et al., 2001).

Exciting new work with animals has shown that the effectiveness of brain-tissue grafts can be greatly enhanced by adding naturally occurring proteins called *growth factors*, or *neurotrophic factors*, which promote the survival of neurons (Hoglinger et al., 2001). One of the most effective of these proteins is glial cell line-derived neurotrophic factor, or GDNF, which actually causes neurons to produce the neurotransmitter needed to reverse the effects of Parkinson's disease (Kordower et al., 2000; Theofilopoulos et al., 2001).

The brain-tissue transplant procedure is promising, but because its use with humans requires tissue from aborted fetuses, it has generated considerable controversy. Two newer transplant treatments are designed to get around this problem. In one, Russian physicians transplanted neural tissue from fruit flies into the brains of Parkinson's patients, with therapeutic benefits and no reported side effects (Saveliev et al., 1997). In the other, U.S. researchers found that immune-resistant cells taken from testes have growth-promoting effects on some neurotransmitters, and that cells from the testes transplanted into the brains of rats with Parkinson's disease reduced their symptoms (Willing et al., 1999).

In yet another approach to treating brain diseases and damage, researchers have "engineered" cells from rats to produce *nerve growth factor*, a substance that helps stimulate and guide the growth of newly sprouted axons in the central nervous system. When the engineered cells were implanted into the brains of rats with brain damage or disease, the cells secreted nerve growth factor. In many cases, brain damage was reversed, with surviving neurons sprouting axons that grew toward the graft (Rosenberg et al., 1988). Based on these animal studies, nerve growth factor has been infused directly into the brain of a person with Alzheimer's disease (Seiger et al., 1993). The results were encouraging, and trials with other patients are in progress.

Most promising of all is recent research showing that new neurons can appear not only in adult songbirds but also in the brains of adult mammals, including mice, rabbits, primates, and humans (Blakeslee, 2000; Eriksson et al., 1998; Gould et al., 1999). These new cells have been found in areas such as the hippocampus, which is critical to the formation of new memories and is vulnerable to degeneration through Alzheimer's disease. The rate at which new neurons form in these areas appears to be affected by chemicals naturally secreted during stress, and possibly by those contained in certain drugs (Gould et al., 2000). For example, running in an activity wheel caused new neurons to form in mice, and these additional neurons apparently improved the animals' ability to learn (van Praag et al., 1999). Drugs normally prescribed to fight depression have also been shown to increase the formation of new hippocampal neurons (Malberg et al., 2000).

New neurons in mammals' central nervous system arise from a special type of glial cell called a *neural stem cell* (Alvarez-Buylla et al., 2001), which many scientists now believe may hold the key to reversing the consequences of brain damage and neurodegenerative diseases. They hope that someday, patients suffering from Parkinson's disease and Alzheimer's disease might be cured by treatments that replace damaged or dying neurons with new ones grown from stem cells (Kondo & Raff, 2000; Lennard & Jackson, 2000; Phillips et al., 2000; Sanchez-Ramos et al., 2000; Woodbury et al., 2000).

LINKAGES

LINKAGES (a link to Human Development)

Human Development and the Changing Brain

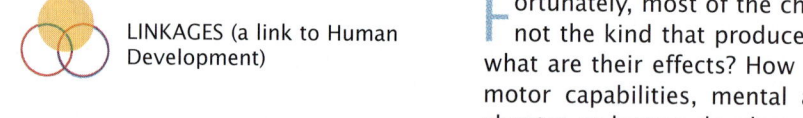

Fortunately, most of the changes that take place in the brain throughout life are not the kind that produce degenerative diseases. What are these changes, and what are their effects? How are they related to the developments in sensory and motor capabilities, mental abilities, and other characteristics described in the chapter on human development?

Classical anatomical studies—and more recently, PET scans and functional MRI scans—are beginning to answer these questions. They have uncovered some interesting correlations between changes in neural activity and the behavior of human newborns and young infants. Among newborns, activity is relatively high in the thalamus but low in the striatum. This pattern may be related to the way newborns move: They make nonpurposeful, sweeping movements of the arms and legs, much like adults who have a hyperactive thalamus and a degenerated striatum (Chugani & Phelps, 1986). During the second and third months after birth, activity increases in many regions of the cortex, a change that is correlated with the loss of subcortically controlled reflexes such as the grasping reflex. When infants are around eight or nine months old, activity in the frontal cortex increases, a development that correlates well with the apparent beginnings of cognitive activity in infants (Chugani & Phelps, 1986). The brain continues to mature even through adolescence, showing evidence of ever more efficient neural communication in its major fiber tracts (Paus et al., 1999; Thompson et al., 2000).

These changes mainly reflect brain plasticity, not the appearance of new cells. After birth, the number of dendrites and synapses increases. In one area of the cortex, the number of synapses increases tenfold from birth to twelve months of age

figure 3.21

Changes in Neurons of the Cerebral Cortex During Development

During childhood, the brain overproduces neural connections, establishes the usefulness of certain connections, and then "prunes" the extra connections. Overproduction of synapses, especially in the frontal cortex, may be essential for infants to develop certain intellectual abilities. Some scientists believe that connections that are used survive, whereas others die.

Source: Reprinted by permission of the publisher from *The Postnatal Development of the Human Cerebral Cortex,* Vol. I–VIII by Jesse LeRoy Conel, Cambridge, Mass.: Harvard University Press, Copyright © 1939–1975 by the President and Fellows of Harvard College.

At birth
(A)

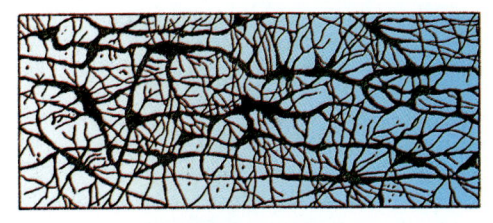

Six years old
(B)

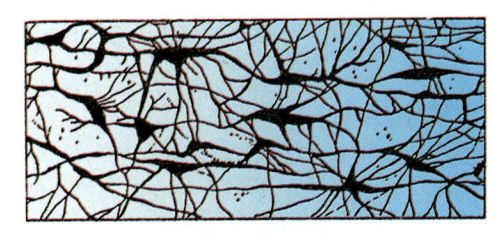

Fourteen years old
(C)

(Huttenlocher, 1990). By the time children are six or seven years old, their brains have more dendrites and use twice as much metabolic fuel as those of adults (Chugani & Phelps, 1986). Then, in early adolescence, the number of dendrites and neural connections begins to drop, so that the adult level is reached by about the age of fourteen (see Figure 3.21). MRI scans show an actual loss of gray-matter volume in the cortex throughout the adolescent years as adult cognitive abilities develop (Sowell et al., 2001). In other words, as we reach adulthood, we develop more brainpower with less brain.

Even as dendrites are reduced, the brain retains its plasticity and "rewires" itself to form new connections throughout life. Our genes apparently determine the basic pattern of growth and the major lines of connections—the "highways" of the brain and its general architecture. (For a summary of this architecture, see "In Review: Organization of the Brain.") But the details of the connections depend on experience, including such factors as how complex and interesting the environment is. For example, researchers have compared the brains of rats raised alone with only a boring view of the side of their cages to the brains of rats raised with interesting toys and stimulating playmates. The cerebral cortex of those from the enriched environment had more and longer dendrites, as well as more synapses and neurotrophic factors, than the cortex of animals from barren, individual housing (Klintsova & Greenough, 1999; Torasdotter et al., 1998). Furthermore, the number of cortical synapses increased when isolated animals were moved to an enriched environment. To the extent that these ideas and research findings apply

in review: Organization of the Brain

Major Division	Some Important Structures	Some Major Functions
Hindbrain	Medulla	Regulation of breathing, heart rate, and blood pressure
	Reticular formation (also extends into midbrain)	Regulation of arousal and attention
	Cerebellum	Control of finely coordinated movements and sequences
Midbrain	Various nuclei	Relay of sensory signals to forebrain; creation of automatic responses to certain stimuli
	Substantia nigra	Smooth initiation of movement
Forebrain	Hypothalamus	Regulation of hunger, thirst, and sex drives
	Thalamus	Interpretation and relaying of sensory information
	Hippocampus	Formation of new memories
	Amygdala	Connection of sensations and emotions
	Cerebral cortex	Analysis of sensory information; control over voluntary movements, abstract thinking, and other complex cognitive activity
	Corpus callosum	Transfer of information between the two cerebral hemispheres

to humans, they hold obvious implications for how people raise children and treat the elderly.

In any event, this line of research highlights the interaction of environmental and genetic factors. Some overproduced synapses may reflect genetically directed preparation for certain types of experiences. Generation of these synapses is an "experience-expectant" process, and it accounts for sensitive periods during development when certain things can be most easily learned. But overproduction of synapses also occurs in response to totally new experiences; this process is "experience dependent" (Greenough, Black, & Wallace, 1987). Within constraints set by genetics, interactions with the world mold the brain itself.

The Chemistry of Psychology

So far, we have described how the cells of the nervous system communicate by releasing neurotransmitters at their synapses, and we have outlined some of the basic structures of the nervous system and their functions. Let's now pull these topics together by considering two questions about neurotransmitters and the nervous system. First, which neurotransmitters occur in which structures? As noted earlier, different sets of neurons use different neurotransmitters; a group of neurons that communicates using the same neurotransmitter is called a **neurotransmitter system**. Second, how do neurotransmitter systems affect behavior? It appears that certain

The Chemistry of Psychology

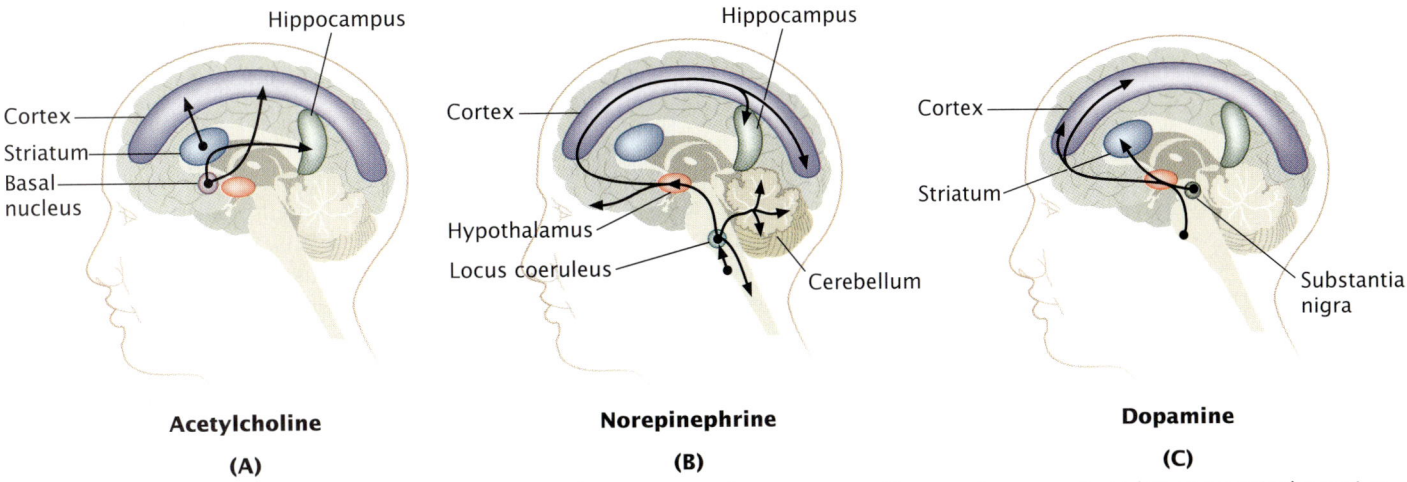

figure 3.22

Examples of Neurotransmitter Pathways

[Acetylcholine (A): Cortex, Striatum, Basal nucleus, Hippocampus]
[Norepinephrine (B): Cortex, Hippocampus, Hypothalamus, Locus coeruleus, Cerebellum]
[Dopamine (C): Cortex, Striatum, Substantia nigra]

Neurons that use a certain neurotransmitter may be concentrated in one particular region (indicated by dots) and send fibers into other regions with which they communicate (see arrows). Here are examples for three major neurotransmitters.

neurotransmitter systems play a dominant role in particular functions, such as emotion or memory, and in particular problems, such as Alzheimer's disease. Our discussion will also reveal that certain drugs affect behavior and mental processes by altering these systems. Details about how these *psychoactive drugs* work are presented in other chapters, where we discuss drugs of abuse—such as cocaine and heroin (see the chapter on consciousness)—and drugs used in treating mental disorders (see the chapter on the treatment of psychological disorders).

Chemical neurotransmission was first demonstrated, in frogs, by Otto Loewi in 1921. Since then, more than a hundred different neurotransmitters have been identified. Some of the chemicals that act on receptors at synapses have been called *neuromodulators*, because they act slowly and often modify or "modulate" a cell's response to other neurotransmitters. The distinction between neurotransmitter and neuromodulator is not always clear, however. Depending on the type of receptor it acts on at a given synapse, the same substance can function as either a neuromodulator or a neurotransmitter.

Three Classes of Neurotransmitters

The neurotransmitters used in the nervous system fall into three main categories, based on their chemical structure: *small molecules*, *peptides*, and *gases*. In the following sections we discuss some examples found in each category.

Small Molecules

The *small-molecule* neurotransmitters were discovered first, partly because they occur in both the central nervous system and the peripheral nervous system. For example, **acetylcholine** (pronounced "a-see-tull- KO-leen") is used by neurons of the parasympathetic nervous system to slow the heartbeat and activate the gastrointestinal system, and by neurons that make muscles contract. In the brain, neurons that use acetylcholine (called *cholinergic* neurons) are especially plentiful in the midbrain and striatum, where they occur in circuits that are important for movement (see Figure 3.22). Axons of cholinergic neurons also make up major pathways in the limbic system, including the hippocampus, and in other areas of the forebrain that are involved in memory. Drugs that interfere with acetylcholine prevent the formation of new memories. In Alzheimer's disease, there is a nearly complete loss of cholinergic neurons in a nucleus in the forebrain that sends fibers to the cerebral cortex and hippocampus—a nucleus that normally enhances plasticity in these regions (Kilgard & Merzenich, 1998).

---

neurotransmitter system A group of neurons that communicates by using the same neurotransmitter.

acetylcholine A neurotransmitter used by neurons in the peripheral and central nervous systems in the control of functions ranging from muscle contraction and heart rate to digestion and memory.

Three other small-molecule neurotransmitters are known as *catecholamines* (pronounced "cat-ah-KO-lah-meens"). They include *norepinephrine, serotonin,* and *dopamine.* **Norepinephrine** (pronounced "nor-eppa-NEF-rin"), also called *noradrenaline,* occurs in both the central and peripheral nervous systems; in both places, it contributes to arousal. Norepinephrine (and its close relative, epinephrine, or adrenaline) are the neurotransmitters used by the sympathetic nervous system to activate you and prepare you for action. Approximately half of the norepinephrine in the entire brain is contained in cells of the locus coeruleus, which is near the reticular formation in the hindbrain (see Figure 3.22). Because norepinephrine systems cover a lot of territory, it is logical that norepinephrine would affect several broad categories of behavior. Indeed, norepinephrine is involved in the appearance of wakefulness and sleep, in learning, and in the regulation of mood.

Serotonin is similar to norepinephrine in several ways. First, most of the cells that use it as a neurotransmitter occur in an area along the midline of the hindbrain. Second, axons from neurons that use serotonin send branches throughout the forebrain, including the hypothalamus, the hippocampus, and the cerebral cortex. Third, serotonin affects sleep and mood. Serotonin differs from norepinephrine, however, in that the brain can get one of the substances from which it is made, *tryptophan,* directly from food. As a result, what you eat can affect the amount of serotonin in your brain. Carbohydrates increase the amount of tryptophan getting into the brain and therefore affect how much serotonin is made; so a meal high in carbohydrates produces increased levels of serotonin. Serotonin, in turn, normally causes a reduction in the desire for carbohydrates. Some researchers suspect that malfunctions in the serotonin feedback system are responsible for the disturbances of mood and appetite seen in certain types of obesity, premenstrual tension, and depression (Wurtman & Wurtman, 1995). Serotonin has also been implicated in aggression and impulse control. One of the most consistently observed relationships between a particular neurotransmitter system and a particular behavior is the low level of serotonin metabolites in the brains of suicide victims, who tend to show a combination of depressed mood, self-directed aggression, and impulsivity (Oquendo & Mann, 2000).

Dopamine is the neurotransmitter used in the substantia nigra and striatum, which are important for movement. Malfunctioning of the dopamine-using (or *dopaminergic*) system in these regions contributes to movement disorders, including Parkinson's disease. As dopamine cells in the substantia nigra degenerate, Parkinson's disease victims experience severe shakiness and difficulty in beginning movements. Parkinson's disease is most common in elderly people, and it may result in part from sensitivity to environmental toxins. These toxins have not yet been identified, but there is evidence from animal studies that chemicals in some common garden pesticides damage dopaminergic neurons (Jenner 2001). Parkinson's disease has been treated, with partial success, using drugs that enable neurons to make more dopamine (Chase, 1998). Malfunctioning of dopaminergic neurons whose axons go to the cerebral cortex may be partly responsible for schizophrenia, a severe disorder in which perception, emotional expression, and thought are severely distorted (Marenco & Weinberger, 2000).

Other dopaminergic systems that send axons from the midbrain to the forebrain are important in the experience of reward or pleasure (Wise & Rompre, 1989). Animals will work intensively to receive a direct infusion of dopamine into the forebrain. These dopamine systems play a role in the rewarding properties of many drugs, including cocaine.

Two other small-molecule neurotransmitters—*GABA* and *glutamate*—are amino acids. Neurons in widespread regions of the brain use **GABA**, or gamma-amino butyric acid. GABA reduces the likelihood that postsynaptic neurons will fire an action potential; in fact, it is the major inhibitory neurotransmitter in the central nervous system. When you fall asleep, neurons that use GABA deserve part of the credit.

norepinephrine A neurotransmitter involved in arousal, as well as in learning and mood regulation.

serotonin A neurotransmitter used by cells in parts of the brain involved in the regulation of sleep, mood, and eating.

dopamine A neurotransmitter used in the parts of the brain involved in regulating movement and experiencing pleasure.

GABA A neurotransmitter that inhibits the firing of neurons.

Malfunctioning of GABA systems has been implicated in a variety of disorders, including severe anxiety and *Huntington's disease*, an inherited and incurable disorder in which the victim is plagued by uncontrollable jerky movement of the arms and legs, along with dementia. Huntington's disease results in the loss of many GABA-containing neurons in the striatum. Normally these GABA systems inhibit dopamine systems; so when they are lost through Huntington's disease, the dopamine systems may run wild, impairing many motor and cognitive functions. Because drugs that block GABA receptors produce intense repetitive electrical discharges, known as *seizures*, researchers suspect that malfunctioning GABA systems probably contribute to *epilepsy*, a brain disorder associated with seizures and convulsive movements. Repeated or sustained seizures can result in permanent brain damage; drug treatments can reduce their frequency and severity, but completely effective drugs are not yet available.

Glutamate is the major excitatory neurotransmitter in the central nervous system. Glutamate is used by more neurons than any other neurotransmitter; its synapses are especially plentiful in the cerebral cortex and the hippocampus. Glutamate is particularly important because it plays a major role in the ability of the brain to "strengthen" its synaptic connections—that is, to allow messages to cross the synapse more efficiently. This process is necessary for normal development and may be at the root of learning and memory (Pennartz et al., 2000). At the same time, overactivity of glutamate synapses can cause neurons to die. In fact, this overactivity is the main cause of the brain damage that occurs when oxygen is cut off from neurons during a stroke. Glutamate can "excite neurons to death," so blocking glutamate receptors immediately after a brain trauma can prevent permanent brain damage (Dawson et al., 2001). Glutamate may also contribute to the loss of cells from the hippocampus that occurs in Alzheimer's disease (Cha et al., 2001).

Peptides

Hundreds of chemicals called *peptides* have been found to act as neurotransmitters. The first of these were discovered in the 1970s, when scientists were investigating *opiates*, which are substances derived from poppy flowers. Opiates such as morphine and heroin can relieve pain, produce euphoria, and in high doses, bring on sleep. After marking morphine with a radioactive substance, researchers traced where it became concentrated in the brain. They found that opiates bind to receptors that were not associated with any known neurotransmitter. Because it was unlikely that the brain had developed opiate receptors just in case a person might want to use morphine or heroin, researchers reasoned that the body must contain a substance similar to opiates. This hypothesis led to the search for a naturally occurring, or endogenous, morphine, which was called *endorphin* (short for endogenous morphine). As it turned out, there are many natural opiate-like compounds. So the term **endorphin** refers to any neurotransmitter that can bind to the same receptors stimulated by opiates. Neurons in several parts of the brain use endorphin, including neuronal pathways that modify pain signals to the brain.

Gases

The concept of what neurotransmitters can be was radically altered following the recent discovery that *nitric oxide* and *carbon monoxide*—two toxic gases that contribute to air pollution—can act as neurotransmitters (Baranano et al., 2001). When nitric oxide or carbon monoxide is released by a neuron, it spreads to nearby neurons, sending a signal that affects chemical reactions inside those neurons rather than binding to receptors on their surface. Nitric oxide is not stored in vesicles, as most other neurotransmitters are; it can be released from any part of the neuron. Nitric oxide appears to be one of the neurotransmitters responsible for such diverse functions as penile erection and the formation of memories—not at the same site, obviously. (For a summary of the main neurotransmitters and the consequences of malfunctioning neurotransmitter systems, see "In Review: Classes of Neurotransmitters.")

---

glutamate An excitatory neurotransmitter that helps strengthen synaptic connections between neurons.

endorphin One of a class of neurotransmitters that bind to opiate receptors and moderate pain.

in review	Classes of Neurotransmitters	
Neurotransmitter Class	**Normal Function**	**Disorder Associated with Malfunction**
Small Molecules		
Acetylcholine	Memory, movement	Alzheimer's disease
Norepinephrine	Mood, sleep, learning	Depression
Serotonin	Mood, appetite, impulsivity	Depression
Dopamine	Movement, reward	Parkinson's disease, schizophrenia
GABA	Sleep, movement	Anxiety, Huntington's disease, epilepsy
Glutamate	Memory	Damage after stroke
Peptides		
Endorphins	Pain control	No established disorder
Gases		
Nitric oxide	Memory	No established disorder

THINKING CRITICALLY

Are There Drugs That Can Make You Smarter?

Neurotransmitter systems provide humans with all sorts of remarkable capabilities. It is hard not to be impressed by how effectively and efficiently these systems work to affect behavior and mental processes. And it is hard not to be concerned by the severe disorders that occur when major neurotransmitter systems malfunction, as is the case with Alzheimer's disease. Some people believe that drugs designed to correct these malfunctions might also improve the functioning of neurotransmitters in normal individuals. Advertisements and articles in many health magazines and on tens of thousands of web sites describe an incredible array of "smart drugs" and dietary supplements. (The drugs are called *nootropics*—from *noos*, which is Greek for "mind.") It is claimed that these substances will improve mental sharpness and reduce or slow the effects of degenerative brain diseases. Belief in the value of nootropics is not confined to health-food fanatics, however; many respected scientists agree with some of the less extreme claims about some of these substances. The use of "smart drugs" is increasing in the United States, and in some other countries (India, for example), it is even more common (Geary, 1997). Are "smart drugs" really effective, or are they modern-day snake oil, giving no more than the illusion of a sharpened mind?

- **What am I being asked to believe or accept?**

Proponents of "smart drugs" and dietary supplements claim that these substances can enhance memory and reverse the effects of degenerative brain diseases. This notion was popularized in the 1990s by two books by John Morgenthaler and Ward Dean. In an interview, Morgenthaler said he had been taking "smart drugs" for ten years, about eight pills twice a day. He explained, "It's not a scientific study; I may have gotten smarter just from growing up, educating myself and stimulating my brain. But I do stop taking the drugs every now and then, and I know that I have better concentration, attention and memory when I'm on them" (Greenwald, 1991).

- **What evidence is available to support the assertion?**

There is certainly an element of truth to the idea that some of these drugs can improve cognitive performance under some circumstances. Animals given the drugs under controlled conditions show statistically significant improvements in performance on tasks requiring attention and memory. The chemicals used in these drugs include *piracetam,* extracts from the herb *Ginkgo biloba,* and *vasopressin.* The drugs not only affect behavior but also have measurable biochemical effects on the brain. Some have general effects on brain metabolism and also increase blood sugar levels; others affect specific neurotransmitters such as acetylcholine, glutamate, serotonin, and dopamine (Dormehl et al., 1999; Pepeu, 1994).

Do "smart drugs" work with humans? One review of the scientific literature on the effects of nootropics in elderly people describes improvement in cognitive functioning associated with forty-five different medications (van Reekum et al., 1997). One study of elderly people with general brain impairment found improvement after twelve weeks of treatment with "smart drugs." Other studies have shown memory improvement in elderly people whose problems were due to poor blood circulation to the brain (Balestreri, Fontana, & Astengo, 1987). Positive effects have also been reported in younger people. In one study, college students did better on tests of memory after taking some of these drugs (File, Fluck, & Fernandes, 1999). In other words, you can probably find a study supporting the effectiveness of virtually any nootropic drug.

● Are there alternative ways of interpreting the evidence?

One alternative explanation of the data on nootropics is that they represent *placebo effects.* As noted in the chapter on research in psychology, placebo effects occur when a person's *beliefs* about a drug, not the drug itself, are responsible for any changes that occur. In their first book on "smart drugs," Morgenthaler and Dean (1990) acknowledge the possibility that placebo effects may be responsible for many of the glowing testimonials about these drugs; but then they themselves present such testimonials to help readers decide which substances to take, and they encourage readers to send in their own accounts of the benefits they have derived from a particular food or dietary supplement. This is hardly the kind of objective, empirical evidence that psychologists seek when evaluating theories and treatments.

Steven Rose (1993) suggests other serious flaws in many of the experiments that apparently show the benefits of nootropic drugs. Specifically, some researchers used only small numbers of participants in their studies, and others failed to test whether positive findings could be reproduced in their own or other researchers' laboratories. Studies that have examined whether the effects of "smart drugs" can be reproduced have yielded mixed results. For example, some experimenters have reported positive effects of *Ginkgo biloba,* while others—using exactly the same dosages and memory tasks—have not (Warot et al., 1991).

One's view of the effects of "smart drugs" must also be tempered by the fact that these effects are not very substantial. For example, the first drug (*tacrine*) approved by the U.S. Food and Drug Administration for the treatment of Alzheimer-related memory problems has repeatedly been shown to "significantly" improve memory, but the actual improvement is always minor. Other nootropic drugs that have positive effects on memory or other cognitive abilities primarily affect attentiveness; they are no more effective than coffee, or even lemonade (Metzger, 2000; Service, 1994). Overall, the evidence from properly designed studies shows nootropic drugs to be a major disappointment (Lobaugh et al., 2001; Riedel & Jolles, 1996).

Finally, the effects of "smart drugs" must be interpreted in light of their possible side effects. For example, tacrine carries the risk of potentially fatal liver damage. Aricept, a similar drug, does not damage the liver, but does cause nausea and diarrhea (Dunn et al., 2000). Even "natural" remedies that people assume are safe can have unwanted effects. For example, ephedrine, a common ingredient in herbal remedies, is a potent stimulant that has lead to cardiac arrest and death in some cases. Ephedrine, *Ginkgo biloba,* and several other herbal substances can also interfere with the action of prescription drugs and raise the risk of bleeding during surgical procedures (Ang-Lee, Moss, & Yuan, 2001).

- **What additional evidence would help to evaluate the alternatives?**

Researchers are evaluating several promising new categories of nootropic drugs in animals (Qizilbash & Emre, 2001). However, it will take years of study to determine which drugs are truly effective for memory enhancement, and under what circumstances. It will also take time to learn whether the results with animals are applicable to humans. Research with humans will require carefully controlled double-blind studies that eliminate the effects of participants' and investigators' expectancies so that the direct effects of the drugs or other treatments can be separated from placebo effects. One critical question to be addressed in such research is whether drugs that can reduce the memory loss associated with Alzheimer's disease will also improve the memories of normal, healthy people and vice versa. And of course, we still need to determine how these drugs work, what their potential side effects are, and whether they affect memory alone or also related processes such as motivation or attention.

- **What conclusions are most reasonable?**

The scientific community is somewhat divided regarding the present benefits and the long-term potential of nootropic drugs. It is much too soon to hail them as the long-sought cure for all sorts of problems in cognitive functioning, but also too soon to write them off as a pseudoscientific fad. Moreover, although the drugs currently available for improving memory are limited in effectiveness, proponents argue that even if such drugs only delay the institutionalization of Alzheimer's patients for several months, the savings to society are substantial. Accordingly, researchers continue to investigate new nootropic drugs, while the scientific jury continues to deliberate about the value of existing ones.

The same wait-and-see attitude is not justified by evidence about the herbs, potions, and drinks that are supposed to make normal people smarter. You can buy them in health-food stores and "smart bars," but their effect on mental powers is minimal. In fact, the strategies described in the chapter on memory are likely to be far more effective in helping you remember information and do well in school. There is also evidence that "exercising your brain" has long-term benefits on memory and brain function. For example, educational achievement and a life of working at a job that engages the mind have been associated with a lowered risk for Alzheimer's disease (Evans et al., 1997), perhaps because education and other factors that increase cerebral blood flow reduce the risk of this disorder (Crawford, 1998).

The Endocrine System: Coordinating the Internal World

As noted earlier, neurons are not the only cells that can use chemicals to communicate with one another in ways that affect behavior and mental processes. Another class of cells with this ability resides in the **endocrine system** (pronounced "EN-doh-krinn"), which regulates functions ranging from stress responses to physical growth. The cells of endocrine organs, or **glands**, communicate by secreting chemicals, much as neurons do. In the case of endocrine organs, the chemicals are called **hormones**. Figure 3.23 shows the location and functions of some of the major endocrine glands.

Hormones secreted from the endocrine organs are similar to neurotransmitters. In fact, many of these chemicals, including norepinephrine and the endorphins, act both as hormones and as neurotransmitters. However, whereas neurons release neurotransmitters into synapses, endocrine organs put their chemicals into the bloodstream, which carries them throughout the body. In this way, endocrine glands can stimulate cells with which they have no direct connection. But not all cells receive the hormonal message. Hormones, like neurotransmitters, can influence only those cells with receptors capable of receiving them (McEwen, 1994). Organs whose cells have receptors for a hormone are called *target organs*.

---

endocrine system Cells that form organs called glands and that communicate with one another by secreting chemicals called hormones.

glands Organs that secrete hormones into the bloodstream.

hormones Chemicals secreted by a gland into the bloodstream, which carries them throughout the body.

figure 3.23

Some Major Glands of the Endocrine System

Each of the glands shown releases its hormones into the bloodstream. Even the hypothalamus, a part of the brain, regulates the nearby pituitary gland by secreting hormones.

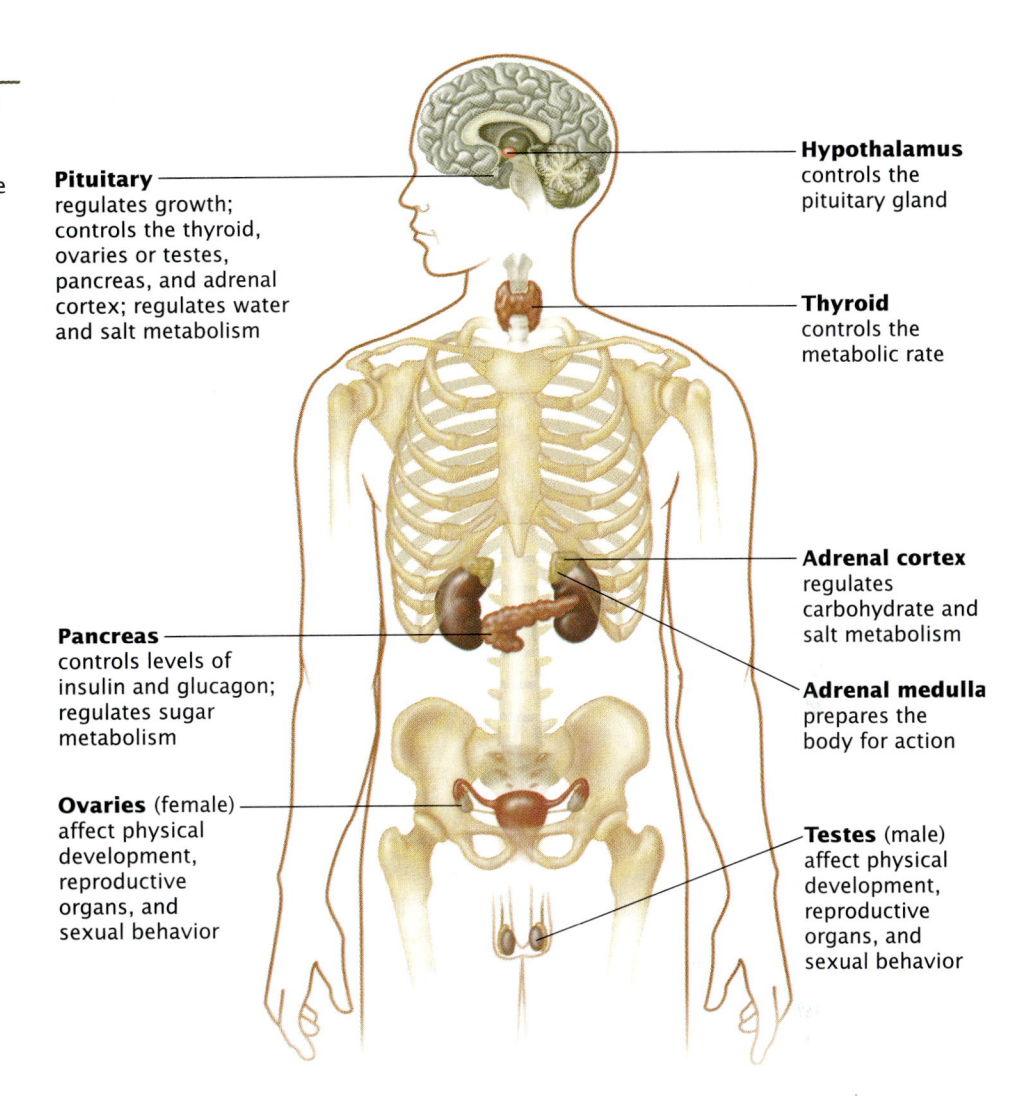

Pituitary regulates growth; controls the thyroid, ovaries or testes, pancreas, and adrenal cortex; regulates water and salt metabolism

Hypothalamus controls the pituitary gland

Thyroid controls the metabolic rate

Adrenal cortex regulates carbohydrate and salt metabolism

Pancreas controls levels of insulin and glucagon; regulates sugar metabolism

Adrenal medulla prepares the body for action

Ovaries (female) affect physical development, reproductive organs, and sexual behavior

Testes (male) affect physical development, reproductive organs, and sexual behavior

Each hormone acts on many target organs, producing coordinated effects throughout the body. For example, when the sex hormone *estrogen* is secreted by a woman's ovaries, it activates her reproductive system. It causes the uterus to grow in preparation for nurturing an embryo; it enlarges the breasts to prepare them for nursing; it stimulates the brain to enhance interest in sexual activity; and it stimulates the pituitary gland to release another hormone that causes a mature egg to be released by the ovary for fertilization. Pituitary hormones cause the male sex organs to secrete *androgens* (which are sex hormones such as testosterone), stimulate the maturation of sperm, increase a male's motivation for sexual activity, and increase his aggressiveness (Rubinow & Schmidt, 1996).

Can differences between hormones in men and women account for some of the differences between the sexes? During development and in adulthood, sex differences in hormones are relative rather than absolute: Both men and women have androgens and estrogens, but men have relatively higher concentrations of androgens, whereas women have relatively higher concentrations of estrogens. There is plenty of evidence from animal studies that the presence of higher concentrations of androgens in males during development creates both structural sex differences in the brain and sex differences in adult behaviors. Humans, too, may be similarly affected by hormones early in development. For example, studies of girls who were exposed to high levels of androgens before birth found that they were later more aggressive than their sisters who had not had such exposure (Berenbaum & Resnick, 1997). And as shown in Figure 1.1, MRI studies have revealed specific brain regions that function differently in men and women. However, such sex differences may not be simple, inevitable, or due to the actions of hormones alone. For example, just the act of practicing finger tapping for ten minutes a day over several weeks can create alterations in the activity of the motor cortex that are detectable with functional MRI (Karni et al., 1998). Most likely, the sex differences we see in behavior depend not only on hormones but also on complex interactions of biological and social forces, as described in the chapter on motivation and emotion.

The brain has ultimate control over the secretion of hormones. Through the hypothalamus, it controls the pituitary gland, which in turn controls endocrine organs in the body. The brain is also one of the target organs for most endocrine secretions. In fact, the brain creates some of the same hormones that are secreted in the endocrine system, and uses them for neural communication (Compagnone & Mellon, 2000). In summary, the endocrine system typically involves four elements: the brain, the pituitary gland, an endocrine organ, and the target organs, which include the brain. Each element in the system uses hormones to signal to the next element, and the secretion of each hormone is stimulated or suppressed by other hormones.

For example, in stress-hormone systems, the brain controls the pituitary gland by signaling the hypothalamus to release hormones that stimulate receptors of the pituitary gland, which secretes another hormone, which stimulates another endocrine gland to secrete its hormones. Specifically, when the brain interprets a situation as threatening, the pituitary releases *adrenocorticotropic hormone (ACTH)*, which causes the adrenal glands to release the hormone *cortisol* into the bloodstream. These hormones, in turn, act on cells throughout the body, including the brain. One effect of cortisol, for example, is to activate the emotion-related limbic system, making it more likely that you will remember stressful or traumatic events (Cahill & McGaugh, 1998). The combined effects of the adrenal hormones and the activation of the sympathetic system result in a set of responses called the **fight-or-flight syndrome**, which, as mentioned earlier, prepares the animal or person for action in response to danger or other stress. The heart beats faster, the liver releases glucose into the bloodstream, fuels are mobilized from fat stores, and the organism usually enters a state of high arousal.

The hormones provide feedback to the brain, as well as to the pituitary gland. Just as a thermostat and furnace regulate heat, this feedback system regulates hor-

Hormones at Work The appearance of a threat activates a pattern of hormonal secretions and other physiological responses that prepare animals and humans to confront, or flee, the danger. This pattern is known as the *fight-or-flight syndrome*.

fight-or-flight syndrome Physical reactions initiated by the sympathetic nervous system that prepare the body to fight or to run from a threatening situation.

mone secretion so as to keep it within a certain range. If a hormone rises above a certain level, feedback about this situation signals the brain and pituitary to stop stimulating that hormone's secretion. So after the immediate threat is over, feedback about cortisol's action in the brain and in the pituitary terminates the secretion of ACTH and, in turn, cortisol. Because the feedback suppresses further action, this arrangement is called a *negative feedback system*.

The Immune System: Defending the Body

Like the nervous system and endocrine system, the **immune system** serves as both a sensory system and a security system. It monitors the internal state of the body and detects unwanted cells and toxic substances that may have invaded. It recognizes and remembers foreign substances, and it engulfs and destroys foreign cells as well as cancer cells. Individuals whose immune system is impaired—AIDS patients, for example—face death from invading bacteria or malignant tumors. However, if the system becomes overactive, the results can be just as devastating: Many diseases, including arthritis, diabetes, and multiple sclerosis, are now recognized as **autoimmune disorders**, in which cells of the immune system attack normal cells of the body, including brain cells (Marrack, Kappler, & Kotzin, 2001).

The immune system is as complex as the nervous system, and it contains as many cells as the brain. Some of these cells are in organs such as the thymus and

figure 3.24

Relations Among the Nervous System, Endocrine System, and Immune System

All three systems interact and influence one another. The nervous system affects the endocrine system by controlling the secretion of hormones via the pituitary gland. It also affects the immune system through the autonomic nervous system's action on the thymus gland. The thymus, spleen, and bone marrow are sites of generation and development of immune cells. Hormones of the pituitary gland and adrenal gland modulate immune cells. Immune cells secrete cytokines and antibodies to fight foreign invaders; cytokines are blood-borne messengers that regulate the development of immune cells and also influence the central nervous system.

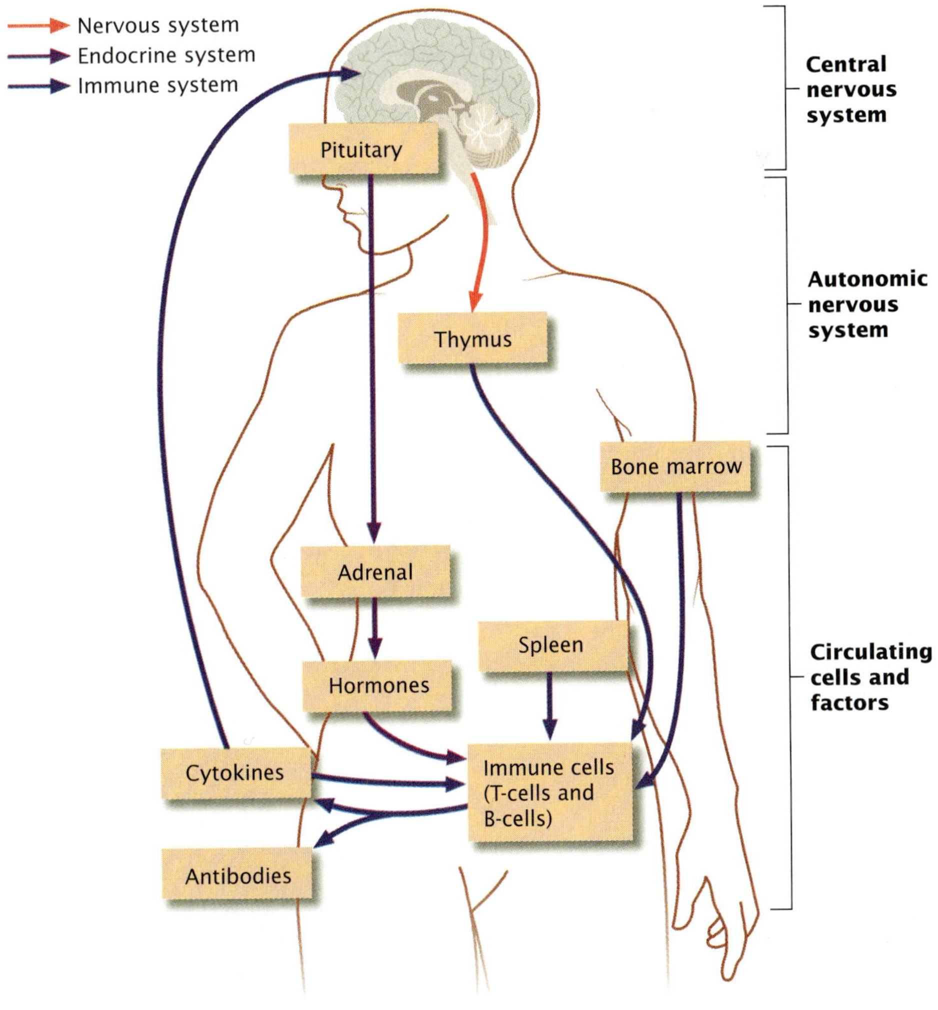

immune system The body's system of defense against invading substances and microorganisms.

autoimmune disorders Physical problems caused when cells of the body's immune system attack normal body cells as if they were foreign invaders.

spleen, whereas others circulate in the bloodstream and enter tissues throughout the body (see Figure 3.24). In the chapter on health, stress, and coping, we describe a few of the immune system's many cell types and how they work.

The nervous system and the immune system were once thought of as completely separate (Ader, Felten, & Cohen, 1990). However, five lines of evidence suggest important interactions between the two. First, stress can alter the outcome of disease in animals, and as discussed in the chapter on health, stress, and coping, there is growing evidence that psychological stressors also affect disease processes in humans (Sternberg, 2001). Second, immune responses can be "taught" using some of the principles outlined in the chapter on learning. In one study with humans, for example, exposure to the taste of sherbet was repeatedly associated with an injection of epinephrine, which increases immune system activity. Later, an increase in immune system activity could be prompted by the taste of sherbet alone (Exton et al., 2000). Third, animal studies have shown that stimulating or damaging specific parts of the hypothalamus, the cortex, or the brainstem that control the autonomic nervous system can enhance or impair immune functions (Felten et al., 1998). Fourth, activation of the immune system can produce changes in the electrical activity of the brain, in neurotransmitter activity, in hormonal secretion, and in behavior—including symptoms of sickness (Kronfol & Remick, 2000). Finally, some of the same chemical messengers are found in both the brain and the immune system (Maier & Watkins, 1998).

These converging lines of evidence point to important relationships that illustrate the intertwining of biological and psychological functions, the interaction of body and mind. They highlight the ways in which the immune system, nervous system, and endocrine system—all systems of communication between and among cells—are integrated to form the biological basis for a smoothly functioning self that is filled with interacting thoughts, emotions, and memories and is capable of responding to life's challenges and opportunities with purposeful and adaptive behavior.

The Common Cold The interaction of the immune system and the nervous system can be seen in some of the symptoms associated with routine "sickness." Sleepiness, nausea, and fever are actually a result of chemicals released by immune cells, collectively called *cytokines,* which act directly on the brain through specific receptors (Pousset, 1994).

LINKAGES

As noted in the chapter on introducing psychology, all of psychology's subfields are related to one another. Our discussion of developmental changes in the brain illustrates just one way in which the topic of this chapter, biological aspects of psychology, is linked to the subfield of developmental psychology, which is described in the chapter on human development. The Linkages diagram shows ties to two other subfields as well, and there are many more ties throughout the book. Looking for linkages among subfields will help you see how they all fit together and help you better appreciate the big picture that is psychology.

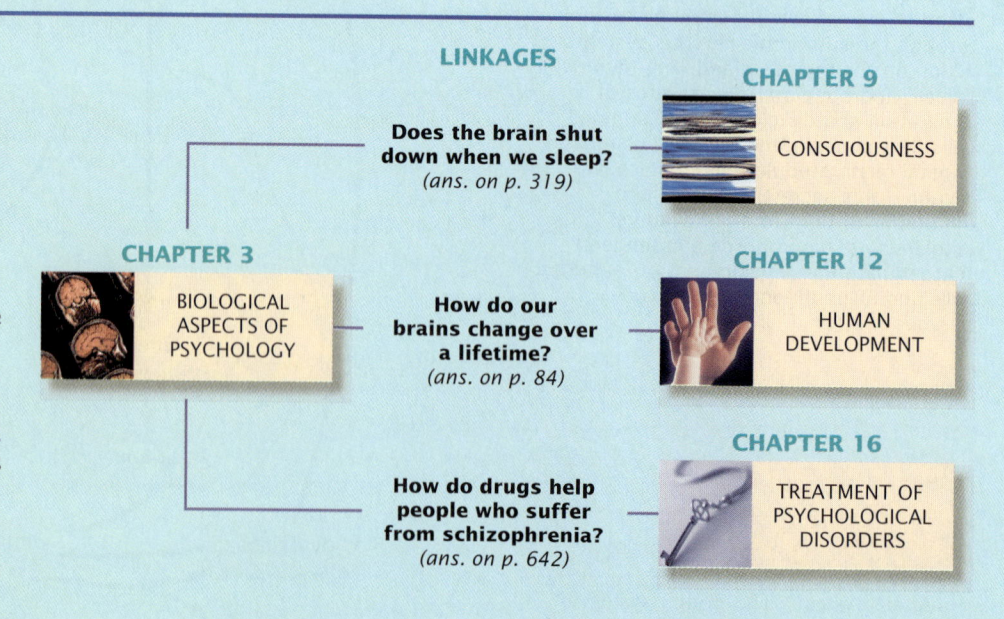

LINKAGES

CHAPTER 3 — BIOLOGICAL ASPECTS OF PSYCHOLOGY

- Does the brain shut down when we sleep? (ans. on p. 319) — **CHAPTER 9** CONSCIOUSNESS
- How do our brains change over a lifetime? (ans. on p. 84) — **CHAPTER 12** HUMAN DEVELOPMENT
- How do drugs help people who suffer from schizophrenia? (ans. on p. 642) — **CHAPTER 16** TREATMENT OF PSYCHOLOGICAL DISORDERS

SUMMARY

Biological psychology focuses on the biological aspects of our being, including the nervous system, which provide the physical basis for behavior and mental processes. The *nervous system* is a system of cells that allows an organism to gain information about what is going on inside and outside the body and to respond appropriately.

The Nervous System

Much of our understanding of the biological aspects of psychology has stemmed from research on animal and human nervous systems at levels ranging from single cells to complex organizations of cells.

Cells of the Nervous System

The main units of the nervous system are cells called *neurons* and *glial cells*. Neurons are especially good at receiving signals from, and transmitting signals to, other neurons. Neurons have cell bodies and two types of fibers, called *axons* and *dendrites*. Axons usually carry signals away from the cell body, whereas dendrites usually carry signals to the cell body. Neurons can transmit signals because of the structure of these fibers, the excitable surface of some of the fibers, and the *synapses*, or gaps, between cells.

Action Potentials

The membranes of neurons normally keep the distribution of electrically charged molecules uneven between the inside of cells and the outside, creating an electrochemical force, or potential. The membrane surface of the axon can transmit a disturbance in this potential, called an *action potential*, from one end of the axon to the other. The speed of the action potential is fastest in neurons sheathed in *myelin*. Between firings there is a very brief rest, called a *refractory period*.

Synapses and Communication Between Neurons

When an action potential reaches the end of an axon, the axon releases a chemical called a *neurotransmitter*. This chemical crosses the synapse and interacts with the postsynaptic cell at special sites called *receptors*. This interaction creates *a postsynaptic potential*—either an *excitatory postsynaptic potential (EPSP)* or an *inhibitory postsynaptic potential (IPSP)*—that makes the postsynaptic cell more likely or less likely to fire an action potential. So whereas communication within a neuron is electrochemical, communication between neurons is chemical. Because the fibers of neurons have many branches, each neuron can interact with thousands of other neurons. Each neuron constantly integrates signals received at its many synapses; the result of this integration determines how often the neuron fires an action potential.

Organization and Functions of the Nervous System

Neurons are organized in *neural networks* of closely connected cells. *Sensory systems* receive information from the environment, and *motor systems* influence the actions of muscles and other organs. The two major divisions of the nervous system are the *peripheral nervous system (PNS)* and the *central nervous system (CNS)*, which includes the brain and spinal cord.

The Peripheral Nervous System: Keeping in Touch with the World

The peripheral nervous system has two components.

The Somatic Nervous System

The first component of the peripheral nervous system is the *somatic nervous system*, which transmits information from the senses to the CNS and carries signals from the CNS to the muscles that move the skeleton.

The Autonomic Nervous System

The second component of the peripheral nervous system is the *autonomic nervous system*; it carries messages back and forth between the CNS and the heart, lungs, and other organs and glands.

The Central Nervous System: Making Sense of the World

The CNS is laid out in interconnected groups of neuronal cell bodies, called *nuclei*, whose collections of axons travel together in *fiber tracts*, or *pathways*.

The Spinal Cord

The *spinal cord* receives information from the peripheral senses and sends it to the brain; it also relays messages from the brain to the periphery. In addition, cells of the spinal cord can direct simple behaviors, called *reflexes*, without instructions from the brain.

The Brain

The brain's major subdivisions are the *hindbrain*, *midbrain*, and *forebrain*. The hindbrain includes the *medulla*, the *cerebellum*, and the *locus coeruleus*. The midbrain includes the *substantia nigra*. The *reticular formation* is found in both the hindbrain and the midbrain. The forebrain is the largest and most highly developed part of the brain; it includes many structures, including the *hypothalamus* and *thalamus*. A part of the hypothalamus called the *suprachiasmatic nuclei* maintains a clock that determines biological rhythms. Other forebrain structures include the *striatum*, *hippocampus*, and *amygdala*. Several of these structures form the *limbic system*, which plays an important role in regulating emotion and memory.

The Cerebral Cortex

The outer surface of the *cerebral hemispheres* is called the *cerebral cortex*; it is responsible for many of the higher functions of the brain, including speech and reasoning. The functional areas of the cortex include the *sensory cortex*, *motor cortex*, and *association cortex*.

The Divided Brain in a Unified Self

The right and left hemispheres of the cerebral cortex are specialized to some degree in their functions. In most people, the left hemisphere is more active in language and logical tasks and the right hemisphere, in spatial, musical, and artistic tasks. A task that is performed more efficiently by one hemisphere than the other is said to be *lateralized*. The hemispheres are connected through the *corpus callosum*, allowing them to operate in a coordinated fashion.

Plasticity: Repairing Damage in the Central Nervous System

The brain's *synaptic plasticity*, the ability to strengthen neural connections at its synapses as well as to establish new synapses, forms the basis for learning and memory. Scientists are studying ways to increase plasticity following brain damage.

The Chemistry of Psychology

Neurons that use the same neurotransmitter form a *neurotransmitter system*.

Three Classes of Neurotransmitters

There are three classes of neurotransmitters: small-molecules, peptides, and gases. *Acetylcholine* systems in the brain influence memory processes and movement. *Norepinephrine* is released by neurons whose axons spread widely throughout the brain; it is involved in arousal, mood, and learning. *Serotonin*, another pervasive neurotransmitter, is active in systems regulating mood and appetite. *Dopamine* systems are involved in movement and higher cognitive activities; both Parkinson's disease and schizophrenia involve a disturbance of dopamine systems.

GABA is an inhibitory neurotransmitter involved in anxiety and epilepsy. *Glutamate* is the most common excitatory neurotransmitter; it is involved in learning and memory and, in excess, may cause neuronal death. *Endorphins* are peptide neurotransmitters that affect pain pathways. Nitric oxide and carbon monoxide are gases that function as neurotransmitters.

The Endocrine System: Coordinating the Internal World

Like nervous system cells, those of the *endocrine system* communicate by releasing a chemical that signals to other cells. However, the chemicals released by endocrine organs, or *glands*, are called *hormones* and are carried by the bloodstream to remote target organs. The target organs often produce a coordinated response to hormonal stimulation. One of these responses is the *fight-or-flight syndrome*, which is set off by adrenal hormones that prepare for action in times of stress. Hormones also modulate the development of the brain, contributing to sex differences in the brain and behavior. Negative feedback systems are involved in the control of most endocrine functions. The brain is the main controller: Through the hypothalamus, it controls the pituitary gland, which in turn controls endocrine organs in the body. The brain is also a target organ for most endocrine secretions.

The Immune System: Defending the Body

The *immune system* serves both as a sensory system that monitors the internal state of the body and as a protective system for detecting, and then destroying, unwanted cells and toxic substances that may invade the body. *Autoimmune disorders* result when cells of the immune system attack normal cells of the body. There are important reciprocal relationships among the immune system, nervous system, and endocrine system.

Sensation

4

Sensory Systems
The Problem of Coding
LINKAGES: **Sensation and Biological Aspects of Psychology**

Hearing
Sound
The Ear
Coding Intensity and Frequency
Auditory Pathways and Representations

Vision
Light
Focusing Light
Converting Light into Images
Visual Pathways
Visual Representations
Seeing Color
The Interaction of Vision and Hearing: Synesthesia

The Chemical Senses: Smell and Taste
Olfaction
Gustation
Smell, Taste, and Flavor

Somatic Senses and the Vestibular System
Touch and Temperature
Pain
THINKING CRITICALLY: **Does Acupuncture Relieve Pain?**
Proprioception
Vestibular Sense
FOCUS ON RESEARCH METHODS: **The Case of the Disembodied Woman**

Linkages

Summary

Years ago, Fred Aryee lost his right arm below the elbow in a boating accident, yet he still "feels" his missing arm and hand (Shreeve, 1993). Like Aryee, many people who have lost an arm or a leg continue to experience itching and other sensations from a "phantom limb." When asked to "move" it, they can feel it move, and some people feel intense pain when their missing hand spontaneously tightens into a fist, digging nonexistent fingernails into a phantom palm. Worse, they may be unable to "open" their hand to relieve the pain. In an effort to help these people, scientists have seated them at a table in front of a mirror, then angled the mirror to create the illusion that their amputated arm and hand have been restored. When these patients moved their real hand while looking in the mirror, they not only "felt" movement occurring in their phantom hand but could now "unclench" their phantom fist and stop their excruciating pain (Ramachandran & Rogers-Ramachandran, 2000). This clever strategy arose from research on how vision interacts with the sense of touch. To experience this interaction yourself, sit across a table from someone, and ask that person to stroke the tabletop while stroking your knee under the table in exactly the same way, in exactly the same direction. If you watch the person's hand stroking the table, you will soon experience the touch sensations coming from the table, not your knee! If the person's two hands do not move in synch, however, the illusion will not occur.

This illusion illustrates several points about our senses. It shows, first, that the streams of information coming from different senses can interact. Second, it reveals that experience can change the sensations we receive. Third, and most important, the illusion suggests that "reality" differs from person to person. This last point sounds silly if you assume that there is an "objective reality" that is the same for everyone. After all, the seat you sit on and the book you are reading are solid objects. You can see and feel them with your senses, so they must look and feel the same to you as they would to anyone else. But sensory psychologists tell us that reality is not that simple—that the senses do not reflect an objective reality. Just as people can feel a hand that is not objectively "there," the senses of each individual actively shape information about the outside world to create a *personal reality*. The sensory experiences of different species—and individual humans—vary. You do not see the same world a fly sees, people from California may not hear music quite the same way as do people from Singapore, and different people experience color differently.

In order to understand how sensory systems create reality, consider some basic information about the senses. A **sense** is a system that translates information from outside the nervous system into neural activity. For example, vision is the system through which the eyes convert light into neural activity. This neural activity tells the brain something about the source of the light (e.g., that it is bright) or about objects from which the light is reflected (e.g., that there is a round, red object out there). These messages from the senses are called **sensations**. Because they provide the link between the self and the world outside the brain, sensations help shape many of the behaviors and mental processes studied by psychologists.

Traditionally, psychologists have distinguished between *sensation*—the initial message from the senses—and *perception*, the process through which messages from the senses are given meaning. They point out, for example, that you do not actually sense a cat lying on the sofa; you sense shapes and colors—visual sensations. You use your knowledge of the world to interpret, or perceive, these sensations as a cat. However, it is impossible to draw a clear line between sensation and perception. This is partly because the process of interpreting sensations begins in the sense organs themselves. For example, a frog's eye immediately interprets any small black object as "fly!"—thus enabling the frog to attack the fly with its tongue without waiting for its brain to process the sensory information (Lettvin et al., 1959).

This chapter covers the first steps of the sensation-perception process; the chapter on perception deals with the later phases. Together, these chapters illustrate how we human beings, with our sense organs and brains, create our own realities. In

---

sense A system that translates information from outside the nervous system into neural activity.

sensations Messages from the senses that make up the raw information that affects many kinds of behavior and mental processes.

accessory structures Structures, such as the lens of the eye, that modify a stimulus.

transduction The process of converting incoming energy into neural activity through receptors.

sensory receptors Specialized cells that detect certain forms of energy.

adaptation The process through which responsiveness to an unchanging stimulus decreases over time.

this chapter we explore how sensations are produced, received, and acted upon. First, we consider what sensations are and how they inform us about the world. Then we examine the physical and psychological mechanisms involved in the auditory, visual, and chemical senses. And finally, we turn to a discussion of the somatic senses, which enable us to feel things, to experience temperature and pain, and to know where our body parts are in relation to one another. Together, these senses play a critical role in our ability as humans to adapt to and survive in our environment.

Sensory Systems

The senses gather information about the world by detecting various forms of energy, such as sound, light, heat, and physical pressure. Specifically, the eyes detect light energy, the ears detect the energy of sound, and the skin detects the energy of heat and pressure. Humans depend primarily on vision, hearing, and the skin senses to gain information about the world; they depend less than other animals on smell and taste. To your brain, "the world" also includes the rest of your body, and there are sensory systems that provide information about the location and position of your body parts.

All of these senses must detect stimuli, encode them into neural activity, and transfer this coded information to the brain. Figure 4.1 illustrates these basic steps in sensation. At each step, sensory information is "processed" in some way: The information that arrives at one point in the system is not the same as the information that goes to the next step.

In some sensory systems, the first step in sensation involves **accessory structures**, which modify the energy created by something in the environment—such as a person talking or a flashing sign (Step 1 in Figure 4.1). The outer part of the ear is an accessory structure that collects sound; the lens of the eye is an accessory structure that changes incoming light by focusing it.

The second step in sensation is **transduction,** which is the process of converting incoming energy into neural activity (Step 2 in Figure 4.1). Just as a radio receives energy and transduces it into sounds, the ears receive sound energy and transduce it into neural activity that people recognize as voices, music, and other auditory experiences. Transduction takes place at structures called **sensory receptors,** specialized cells that detect certain forms of energy. Sensory receptors are somewhat like the neurons that we describe in the chapter on biological aspects of psychology; they respond to incoming energy by firing an action potential and releasing neurotransmitters that send a signal to neighboring cells. (However, some sensory receptors do not have axons and dendrites, as neurons do.) Sensory receptors respond best to changes in energy. A constant level of stimulation usually produces **adaptation,** a process through which responsiveness to an unchanging stimulus decreases over time. This is why the touch sensations you get from items such as glasses or a wristwatch disappear shortly after you have put them on.

Energy contains information about the world.

↓

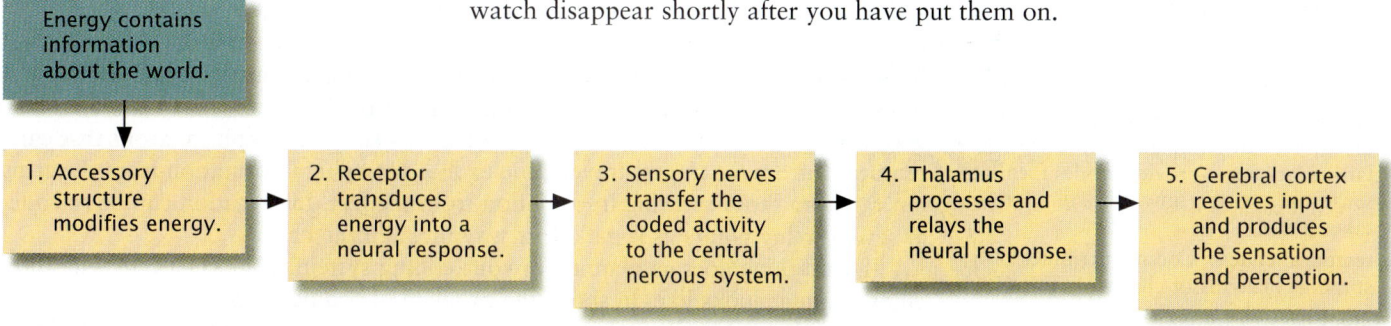

1. Accessory structure modifies energy. → 2. Receptor transduces energy into a neural response. → 3. Sensory nerves transfer the coded activity to the central nervous system. → 4. Thalamus processes and relays the neural response. → 5. Cerebral cortex receives input and produces the sensation and perception.

figure 4.1

Elements of a Sensory System

Objects in the world generate energy that is focused by accessory structures and detected by sensory receptors, which convert the energy into neural signals. The signals are then relayed through parts of the brain, which process them into perceptual experiences.

Next, sensory nerves carry the output from receptors to the central nervous system, including the brain (Step 3 in Figure 4.1). For all the senses except smell, the information is taken first to the thalamus (Step 4), which relays it to the sensory portion of the cerebral cortex (Step 5). It is in the sensory cortex that the most complex processing occurs.

The Problem of Coding

When receptors transduce energy, they must somehow code the physical properties of the stimulus into patterns of neural activity that, when analyzed by the brain, allow you to make sense of the stimulus—to determine, for example, whether you are looking at a cat, a dog, or a person. For each psychological dimension of a sensation, such as the brightness or color of light, there must be a corresponding physical dimension coded by sensory receptors.

As a way of thinking about the problem of coding, imagine that for your birthday you receive a Pet Brain. You are told that your Pet Brain is alive, but it does not respond when you open the box and talk to it. You remove it from the box and show it a hot-fudge sundae; no response. You show it pictures of other attractive brains; still no response. You are about to deposit your Pet Brain in the trash when you suddenly realize that the two of you are probably not talking the same language. As described in the chapter on biological aspects of psychology, the brain usually receives information from sensory neurons and responds via motor neurons. So if you want to communicate with your Pet Brain, you will have to stimulate its sensory nerves (so that you can send it messages) and record signals from its motor nerves (so that you can read its responses).

After having this brilliant insight and setting up an electric stimulator and recorder, you are faced with an awesome problem. How do you describe a hot-fudge sundae to sensory nerves so that they will pass on the correct information to the brain? This is the problem of coding. **Coding** is the translation of the physical properties of a stimulus into a pattern of neural activity that specifically identifies those physical properties.

If you want the brain to visualize the sundae, you should stimulate the optic nerve (the nerve from the eye to the brain) rather than the auditory nerve (the nerve from the ear to the brain). This idea is based on the **doctrine of specific nerve energies**: Stimulation of a particular sensory nerve provides codes for that one sense, no matter how the stimulation takes place. For example, if you apply gentle pressure to your eyeball, you will produce activity in the optic nerve and sense little spots of light.

Having chosen the optic nerve to convey visual information, you must next develop a code for the specific attributes of the sundae: the soft white curves of the vanilla ice cream, the dark richness of the chocolate, the bright red roundness of the cherry on top. These dimensions must be coded in the language of neural activity—that is, in the firing of action potentials.

Some attributes of a stimulus are coded relatively simply. For example, a bright light will cause some neurons in the visual system to fire faster than will a dim light. This is a **temporal code**, because it involves changes in the *timing* of firing. Temporal codes can be more complex as well; for example, a burst of firing followed by a slower firing rate means something different than a steady rate. The other basic type of code is a **spatial code**, in which the *location* of firing neurons relative to their neighbors provides information about the stimulus. For example, neurons that carry sensations from the fingers travel close to those carrying information from the arms, but far from those carrying information from the feet. Information can be re-coded at several relay points as it makes its way through the brain.

If everything goes as planned in your coding system, your Pet Brain will know what a sundae looks like. In short, the problem of coding is solved by means of sensory systems, which allow the brain to receive detailed, accurate, and useful information about stimuli in its environment. Later, we discuss how this remarkable feat is accomplished.

---

coding Translating the physical properties of a stimulus into a pattern of neural activity that specifically identifies those properties.

doctrine of specific nerve energies The discovery that stimulation of a particular sensory nerve provides codes for that sense, no matter how the stimulation takes place.

temporal codes Coding attributes of a stimulus in terms of changes in the timing of neural firing.

spatial codes Coding attributes of a stimulus in terms of the location of firing neurons relative to their neighbors.

What Is It? In the split second before you recognized this stimulus as a hot-fudge sundae, sensory neurons in your visual system detected the light reflected off this page and transduced it into a neural code that your brain could interpret. This amazing process of coding occurs so quickly and efficiently in all our senses that we are seldom aware of it.

LINKAGES (a link to Biological Aspects of Psychology)

Sensation and Biological Aspects of Psychology

As sensory systems transfer information to the brain, they also organize that information. This organized information is called a *representation.* If you have read the chapter on biological aspects of psychology, you are already familiar with some characteristics of sensory representations. In humans, representations of vision, hearing, and the skin senses in the cerebral cortex share the following features:

1. The information from each of these senses reaches the cortex via the thalamus. (Figure 3.14 shows where these areas of the brain are.)

2. The representation of the sensory world in the cortex is *contralateral,* or opposite, to the part of the world being sensed. For example, the left side of the visual cortex "sees" the right side of the world, whereas the right side of that cortex "sees" the left side of the world. This happens because nerve fibers from each side of the body cross on their way to the thalamus. Why they cross is still a mystery.

3. The cortex contains maps, or *topographical representations,* of each sense. Accordingly, features that are next to each other in the world stimulate neurons that are next to each other in the brain. For example, two notes that are similar in pitch activate neighboring neurons in the auditory cortex, and the neurons that respond to sensations in the elbow and in the forearm are relatively close to one another in the somatosensory cortex. There are multiple maps representing each sense, but the area that receives input directly from the thalamus is called the *primary cortex* for that sense.

4. The density of nerve fibers in any part of a sense organ determines its representation in the cortex. For example, the skin on a fingertip, which has a higher density of receptors for touch than the skin on the back, has a larger area of cortex representing it than does the back.

5. Each region of primary sensory cortex is divided into columns of cells that have similar properties. For example, some columns of cells in the visual cortex respond most to diagonal lines.

6. For each of the senses, regions of cortex other than the primary areas do additional processing of sensory information. As described in the chapter on biological aspects of psychology, these areas of *association cortex* may contain representations of more than one sense, thus setting the stage for the interaction of sensory information described at the beginning of this chapter.

In summary, sensory systems convert some form of energy into neural activity, as described in Figure 4.1. Often the energy is first modified by accessory structures; then a sensory receptor converts the energy to neural activity. The pattern of neural activity encodes physical properties of the energy. The codes are modified as the information is transferred to the brain and processed further. In the remainder of this chapter we describe these processes in specific sensory systems.

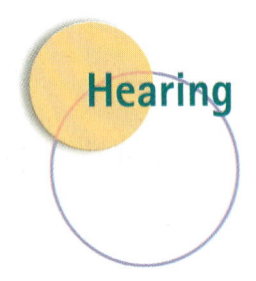

Hearing

In 1969, when Neil Armstrong became the first human to step onto the moon, millions of people back on earth heard his radio transmission: "That's one small step for a man, one giant leap for mankind." But if Armstrong had taken off his space helmet and shouted, "Whoo-ee! I can moonwalk!" another astronaut, a foot away, would not have heard him. Why? Because Armstrong would have been speaking into airless, empty space. **Sound** is a repetitive fluctuation in the pressure of a medium, such as air. In a place like the moon, which has almost no atmospheric medium, sound cannot exist.

Sound

Vibrations of an object produce the fluctuations in pressure that constitute sound. Each time the object moves outward, it increases the pressure in the medium around it. As the object moves back, the pressure drops. In speech, for example, the vibrating object is the vocal cord, and the medium is air. When you speak, your vocal cords vibrate, producing fluctuations in air pressure that spread as waves. A *wave* is a repetitive variation in pressure that spreads out in three dimensions. The wave can move great distances, but the air itself barely moves. Imagine a jam-packed line of people waiting to get into a rock concert. If someone at the rear of the line shoves the next person, a wave of people jostling against people may spread all the way to the front of the line, but the person who shoved first is still no closer to getting into the theater.

Physical Characteristics of Sound

Sound is represented graphically by waveforms like those in Figure 4.2. A *waveform* represents a wave in two-dimensions, but remember that waves actually move through the air in all directions.

Three characteristics of the waveform are important in understanding sounds. First, the difference in air pressure from the baseline to the peak of the wave is the **amplitude** of the sound, or its intensity. Second, the distance from one peak to the next is called the **wavelength**. Third, a sound's **frequency** is the number of complete waveforms, or cycles, that pass by a given point in space every second. Frequency is described in a unit called *hertz*, abbreviated *Hz* (for Heinrich Hertz, a nineteenth-century physicist). One cycle per second is 1 hertz. Because the speed of sound is constant in a given medium, wavelength and frequency are related: The longer the wavelength, the lower the frequency; the shorter the wavelength, the higher the frequency. Most sounds are mixtures of many different frequencies and amplitudes. In contrast, a pure tone is made up of only one frequency and can be represented, by what is known as a *sine wave* (Figure 4.2 shows such sine waves).

sound A repetitive fluctuation in the pressure of a medium like air.
amplitude The difference between the peak and the baseline of a waveform.
wavelength The distance from one peak to the next in a waveform.
frequency The number of complete waveforms, or cycles, that pass by a given point in space every second.
loudness A psychological dimension of sound determined by the amplitude of a sound wave.
pitch How high or low a tone sounds.
timbre The mixture of frequencies and amplitudes that make up the quality of sound.

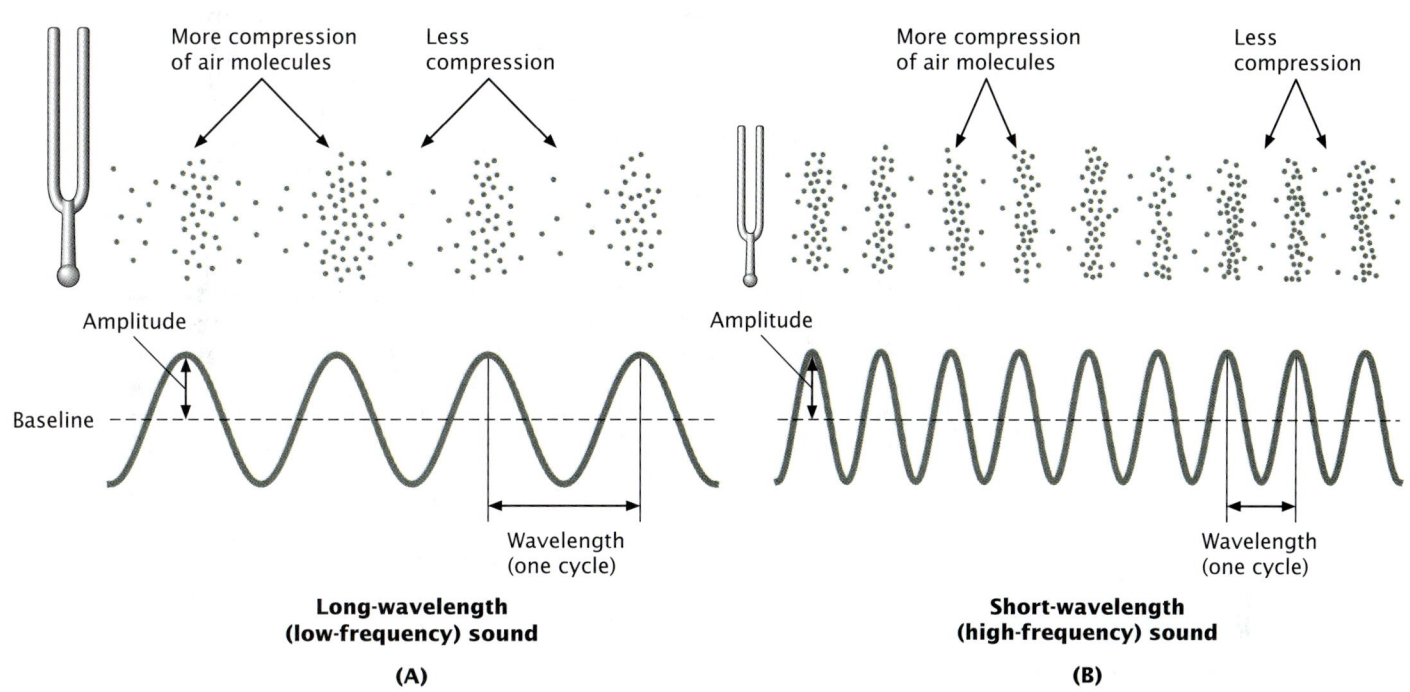

figure 4.2
Sound Waves and Waveforms

Sound is created when objects, such as a tuning fork, vibrate. These vibrating objects create alternating regions of greater and lesser compression of air molecules, which can be represented as a waveform. The point of greatest compression is the peak of the graph. The lowest point, or trough, is where compression is least.

Noise Eliminators Complex sound, including noise, can be analyzed into its component, simple sine waves by means of a mathematical process called *Fourier analysis*. This technique can be used to eliminate engine and wind noise in airplanes, trains, and other moving vehicles. After the waveforms are analyzed, a sound synthesizer produces the opposite waveforms. The opposing waves cancel each other out, and the amazing result is silence. Several versions of these noise eliminators are now sold to the public, and related devices are being developed to treat chronic tinnitus, or "ringing in the ear."

Psychological Dimensions of Sound
The amplitude and frequency of sound waves determine the sounds that you hear. These physical characteristics of the waves produce the psychological dimensions of sound known as *loudness*, *pitch*, and *timbre*.

Loudness is determined by the amplitude of the sound wave; waves with greater amplitude produce sensations of louder sounds. Loudness is described in units called *decibels*, abbreviated *dB*. By definition, 0 decibels is the minimal detectable sound for normal hearing. Table 4.1 gives examples of the loudness of some common sounds.

Pitch, or how high or low a tone sounds, depends on the frequency of sound waves. High-frequency waves are sensed as sounds of high pitch. The highest note on a piano has a frequency of about 4,000 hertz; the lowest note has a frequency of about 50 hertz. Humans can hear sounds ranging from about 20 hertz to about 20,000 hertz. Almost everyone experiences pitch as a relative dimension; that is, they can tell whether one note is higher than, lower than, or equal to another note. However, some people have *perfect pitch*, which means they can identify specific frequencies and the notes they represent. They can say, for example, that a 262-hertz tone is middle C. It was once thought that perfect pitch occurs only in gifted people; but we now know that children who are taught before the age of six can learn that specific frequencies are particular notes (Takeuchi & Hulse, 1993).

Timbre (pronounced "tam-ber") is the quality of sound; it is determined by complex wave patterns that are added onto the lowest, or *fundamental*, frequency of a sound. The extra waves allow you to tell, for example, the difference between a note played on a flute and the same note played on a clarinet.

Sound intensity varies across an extremely wide range. A barely audible sound is, by definition, 0 decibels. Every increase of 20 decibels reflects a tenfold increase in the amplitude of sound waves. So the 40-decibel sounds of an office are actually 10 times as intense as a 20-decibel whisper, and traffic noise of 100 decibels is 10,000 times as intense as that whisper.

table 4.1
Intensity of Sound Sources

Source	Sound Level (dB)
Spacecraft launch (from 45 m)	180
Loudest rock band on record	160
Pain threshold (approximate)	140
Large jet motor (at 22 m)	120
Loudest human shout on record	111
Heavy auto traffic	100
Conversation (at about 1 m)	60
Quiet office	40
Soft whisper	20
Threshold of hearing	0

An Accessory Structure Some animals, like Annie here, have a large pinna that can be rotated to help localize the source of a sound.

tympanic membrane A membrane in the middle ear that generates vibrations that match the sound waves striking it.

cochlea A fluid-filled spiral structure in the ear in which auditory transduction occurs.

basilar membrane The floor of the fluid-filled duct that runs through the cochlea.

auditory nerve The bundle of axons that carries stimuli from the hair cells of the cochlea to the brain.

The Ear

The human ear converts sound energy into neural activity through a series of accessory structures and transduction mechanisms.

Auditory Accessory Structures Sound waves are collected in the outer ear, beginning with the *pinna*, the crumpled part of the ear visible on the side of the head. The pinna funnels sound down through the ear canal (see Figure 4.3). At the end of the ear canal, the sound waves reach the middle ear, where they strike a tightly stretched membrane known as the *eardrum*, or **tympanic membrane**. The sound waves set up matching vibrations in the tympanic membrane.

Next, the vibrations of the tympanic membrane are passed on by a chain of three tiny bones: the *malleus*, or *hammer*; the *incus*, or *anvil*; and the *stapes* (pronounced "STAY-peez"), or *stirrup* (see Figure 4.3). These bones amplify the changes in pressure produced by the original sound waves, by focusing the vibrations of the tympanic membrane onto a smaller membrane, the *oval window*.

Auditory Transduction When sound vibrations pass through the oval window, they enter the inner ear, reaching the **cochlea** (pronounced "COCK-lee-ah"), the structure in which transduction occurs. The cochlea is wrapped into a coiled spiral. (*Cochlea* is derived from the Greek word for "snail.") If you unwrapped the spiral, you would see that a fluid-filled tube runs down its length. The **basilar membrane** forms the floor of this long tube (see Figure 4.4). Whenever a sound wave passes through the fluid in the tube, it moves the basilar membrane, and this movement deforms *hair cells* of the *organ of Corti*, a group of cells that rests on the membrane. These hair cells connect with fibers from the **auditory nerve**, a bundle of axons that goes into the brain. Mechanical deformation of the hair cells stimulates the auditory nerve, changing the electrical activity of some of its neurons and thus sending a coded signal to the brain about the amplitude and frequency of sound waves, which you sense as loudness and pitch.

Deafness Problems with the three tiny bones of the middle ear are one cause of deafness. Sometimes the bones fuse together, preventing accurate reproduction of vibrations. This condition is called *conduction deafness*. It may be treated by breaking the bones apart or by replacing the natural bones with plastic ones; a hearing aid that amplifies the input can also be helpful.

If the auditory nerve or, more commonly, the hair cells are damaged, *nerve deafness* results. Hair cell damage occurs gradually with age, but it can also be

figure 4.3

Structures of the Ear

The outer ear (pinna and ear canal) channels sounds into the middle ear, where the vibrations of the tympanic membrane are amplified by the delicate bones that stimulate the cochlea. In the cochlea in the inner ear, the vibrations are transduced into changes in neural activity, which are sent along the auditory nerve to the brain.

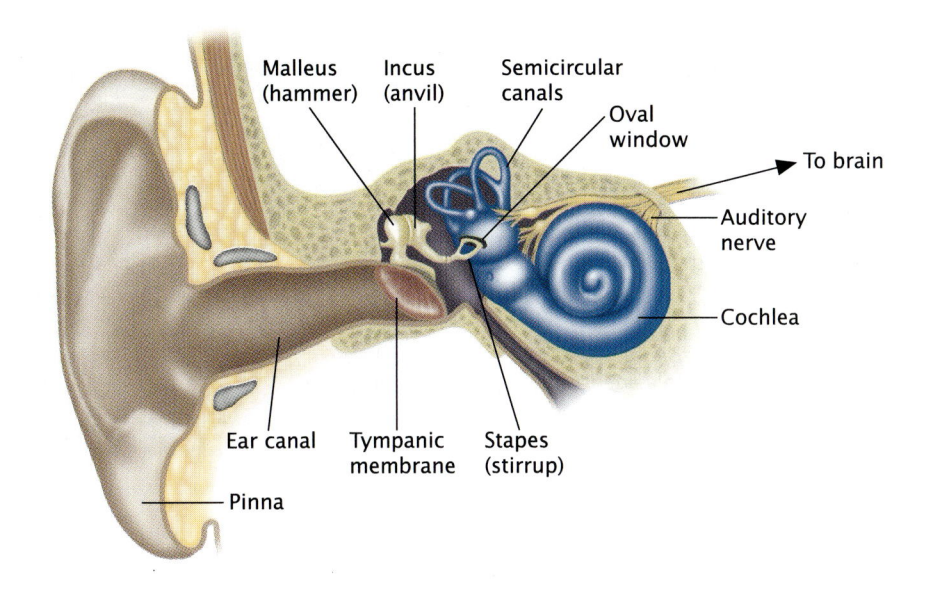

caused by loud noise, such as that created by jet engines, noisy equipment, and intense rock music (Goldstein, 1999; see Figure 4.5). For example, some rock musicians from the 1970s, including Stephen Stills and Pete Townshend, have become partially deaf as a result of their many years of performing extremely loud music (Ackerman, 1995). In the United States and other industrialized countries, people born after World War II are experiencing hearing loss at a younger age than did their forebears, possibly because noise pollution has increased during the past fifty years (Levine, 1999).

Although hair cells can regenerate in chickens (who seldom listen to rock music), such regeneration was long believed to be impossible in mammals (Salvi et al., 1998). However, recent evidence that mammals can regenerate a related kind of inner-ear hair cell has fueled optimism about finding a way to stimulate regeneration of human auditory hair cells (Malgrange et al., 1999). The feat might be accomplished by treating damaged areas with growth factors similar to those used to repair damaged brain cells (see the chapter on biological aspects of psychology). Hair cell regeneration could revolutionize the treatment of nerve deafness, because this form of deafness cannot be overcome by conventional hearing aids. Meanwhile, scientists have developed an artificial cochlea for use as *cochlear implants* that can stimulate the auditory nerve in cases involving congenital nerve deafness (Lee et al., 2001). However, implanting these devices in deaf children is controversial. Some members of the deaf community argue that cochlear implants prevent children from fully entering the deaf culture while at the same time failing to adequately repair the children's hearing deficit (Clay, 1997).

figure 4.4

The Cochlea

This drawing shows how vibrations of the stapes, or stirrup, set up vibrations in the fluid inside the cochlea. The coils of the cochlea are unfolded in this illustration to show the path of the fluid waves along the basilar membrane. Movements of the basilar membrane stimulate the hair cells of the organ of Corti, which transduce the vibrations into changes in neural firing patterns.

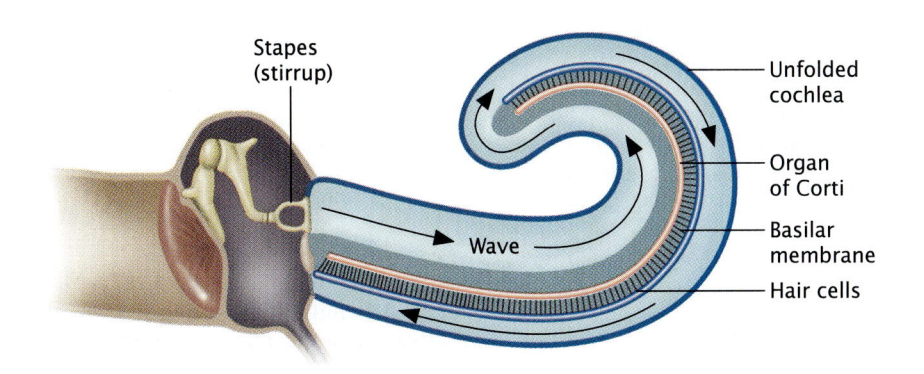

figure 4.5
Effects of Loud Sounds
High-intensity sounds can actually destroy the hair cells of the inner ear. Part A shows the organ of Corti of a normal guinea pig. Part B shows the damage caused by exposure to 24 hours of 2,000-hertz sound at 120 decibels. Generally, any sound loud enough to produce tinnitus (ringing in the ears) causes some damage. In humans, small amounts of damage can accumulate over time to produce a significant hearing loss by middle age—as many middle-aged rock musicians can attest.

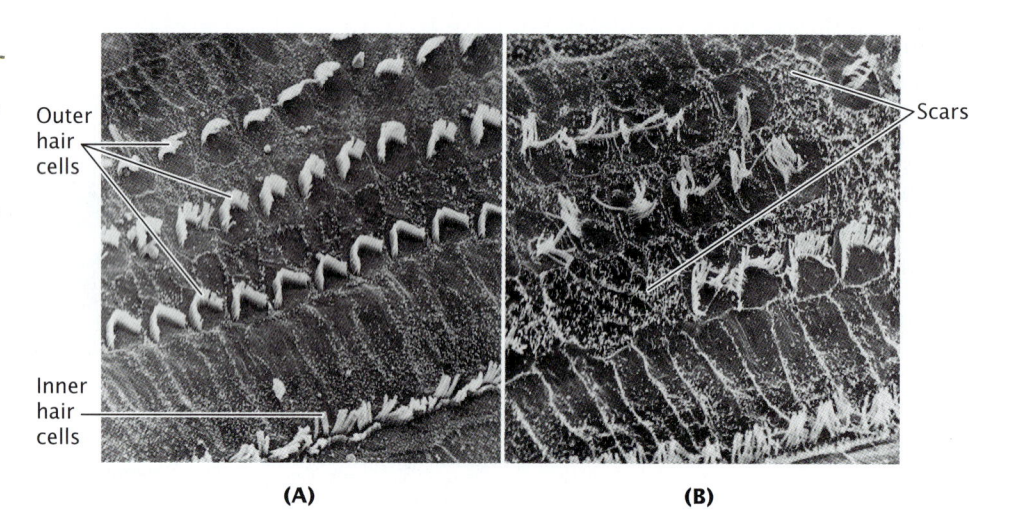

Coding Intensity and Frequency

People can hear an incredibly wide range of sound intensities. The faintest sound that can be heard moves the hair cells less than the diameter of a single hydrogen atom (Hudspeth, 1997). Sounds more than a trillion times more intense can also be heard. Between these extremes, the auditory system codes intensity in a straightforward way: The more intense the sound, the more rapid the firing of a given neuron.

Recall that the pitch of a sound depends on its frequency. How do people tell the differences among frequencies? Differences in frequency appear to be coded in two ways, which are described by place theory and frequency-matching theory.

Place Theory
Georg von Bekesy performed some pioneering experiments in the 1930s and 1940s to figure out how frequency is coded (von Bekesy, 1960). Studying human cadavers, he made a hole in the cochlear wall and observed the basilar membrane. He then presented sounds of different frequencies by vibrating a rubber membrane that was installed in place of the oval window. With sensitive optical instruments, von Bekesy observed ripples of waves moving down the basilar membrane. He noticed that the outline of the waves, called the *envelope*, grows and reaches a peak; then it quickly tapers off to smaller and smaller fluctuations, much like an ocean wave that crests and then dissolves.

As shown in Figure 4.6, the critical feature of this wave is that the place on the basilar membrane where the envelope peaks depends on the frequency of the sound. High-frequency sounds produce a wave that peaks soon after it starts down the basilar membrane. Lower-frequency sounds produce a wave that peaks farther along the basilar membrane, farther from the oval window.

How does the location of the peak affect the coding of frequency? According to **place theory**, also called *traveling wave theory*, the greatest response by hair cells occurs at the peak of the wave. Because the location of the peak varies with the frequency of the sound, it follows that hair cells at a particular place on the basilar membrane respond most to a particular frequency of sound, called a *characteristic frequency*. In other words, place theory describes a *spatial*, or place-related, code for frequency. One important result of this arrangement is that if extended exposure to a very loud sound of a particular frequency destroys hair cells at one spot on the basilar membrane, the ability to hear sounds of that frequency is lost as well.

Frequency-Matching Theory
Although place theory accounts for a great deal of data on hearing, it cannot explain the coding of very low frequencies, such as that of a deep bass note, because there are no auditory nerve fibers that have very low characteristic frequencies. Because humans can hear frequencies as low as

---

place theory A theory that hair cells at a particular place on the basilar membrane respond most to a particular frequency of sound.

frequency-matching theory The view that some sounds are coded in terms of the frequency of neural firing.

primary auditory cortex The area in the brain's temporal lobe that is first to receive information about sounds from the thalamus.

figure 4.6

Movements of the Basilar Membrane
As vibrations of the cochlear fluid spread along the basilar membrane, the membrane is bent and then recovers. As shown in these three examples, the point at which the bending of the basilar membrane reaches a maximum is different for each sound frequency. According to place theory, these are the locations at which the hair cells receive the greatest stimulation.

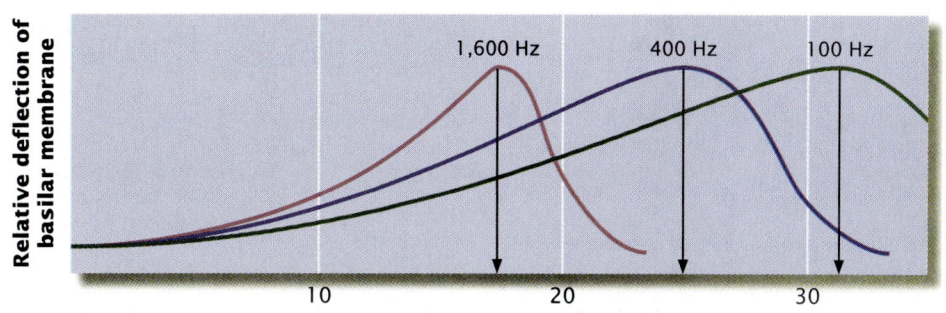

20 hertz, however, the frequencies must be coded somehow. The answer is provided by **frequency-matching theory,** which is based on the fact that the firing rate of a neuron in the auditory nerve matches the frequency of a sound wave. Frequency matching provides a *temporal,* or timing-related, code for frequency. For example, one neuron might fire at every peak of a wave. So a sound of 20 hertz could be coded by a neuron that fires 20 times per second.

Frequency matching by individual neurons would apply only up to about 1,000 hertz, however, because no neuron can fire faster than 1,000 times per second. However, frequency matching can code frequencies somewhat above 1,000 hertz because these moderately higher frequencies are matched not by the firing of a single neuron but by the summed activity of a group of neurons. Some neurons in the group might fire, for example, at every other wave peak, others at every fifth peak, and so on, producing a *volley* of firing at a combined frequency higher than any could manage alone. Accordingly, frequency-matching theory is sometimes called the *volley theory* of frequency coding.

In summary, the nervous system uses more than one way to code the range of audible frequencies. The lowest sound frequencies are coded by frequency matching, whereby the frequency is matched by the firing rate of auditory nerve fibers. Low to moderate frequencies are coded by both frequency matching and the place on the basilar membrane where the wave peaks. High frequencies are coded exclusively by the place where the wave peaks.

Auditory Pathways and Representations

Before sounds can be heard, the information coded in the activity of auditory nerve fibers must be conveyed to the brain and processed further. (For a review of how changes in air pressure become signals in the brain that are perceived as sounds, see "In Review: Hearing.") The auditory nerve, the bundle of axons that conveys this information, crosses the brain's midline and reaches the thalamus. From the thalamus, the information is relayed to the **primary auditory cortex.** As discussed in the chapter on biological aspects of psychology, this is an area located in the temporal lobe of the cerebral cortex, close to areas of the brain involved in language perception and production (see Figure 3.16).

Various aspects of sound are processed separately as the auditory nerve stimulates the auditory cortex. For example, information about the source of a sound and information about the sound's frequency components are processed in different regions of the cortex (Rauschecker, 1997). Neighboring cells in the cortex have similar preferred frequencies and are arranged so that they create at least three separate maps of sound frequencies (Kaas & Hackett, 2000). In the auditory nerve, too, each neuron has a characteristic frequency to which it best responds, though each also responds to some extent to a range of frequencies. The auditory cortex must examine the pattern of activity of a number of neurons in order to determine the

in review	Hearing	
Aspect of Sensory System	**Elements**	**Key Characteristics**
Energy	Sound—pressure fluctuations of air produced by vibrations	The amplitude, frequency, and complexity of sound waves determine the loudness, pitch, and timbre of sounds.
Accessory structures	Ear—pinna, tympanic membrane, malleus, incus, stapes, oval window, basilar membrane	Changes in pressure produced by the original wave are amplified.
Transduction mechanism	Hair cells of the organ of Corti	Frequencies are coded by the location of the hair cells receiving the greatest stimulation (place theory) and by the firing rate of neurons (frequency-matching theory).
Pathways and representations	Auditory nerve to thalamus to primary auditory cortex	Neighboring cells in the auditory cortex have similar preferred frequencies, thus providing a map of sound frequencies

Shaping the Brain The primary auditory cortex is larger in trained musicians than in people whose jobs are less focused on fine gradations of sound. How much larger this area becomes is correlated with how long the musicians have studied their art. This finding reminds us that, as described in the chapter on biological aspects of psychology, the brain can literally be shaped by experience and other environmental factors (Pantev et al., 1998).

frequency of a sound. Certain parts of the auditory cortex process certain types of sounds. One part, for example, specializes in responding to information coming from human voices (Belin et al., 2000).

Sensing the pitch of sound is not always as simple as you might expect, because most sounds are mixtures of frequencies. The mixtures that make up musical chords and voices, for example, can produce sounds of ambiguous pitch. As a result, different individuals may perceive the "same" sound as different pitches (Patel & Balaban, 2001). In fact, a given sequence of chords can sound like an ascending scale to one person and a descending scale to another. Pitch-recognition abilities are influenced by genetics (Drayna et al., 2001), but cultural factors are partly responsible for the way in which pitch is sensed. For instance, people in the United States tend to hear *ambiguous scales* as progressing in directions that are opposite to the way they are heard by people from Canada and England (Dawe, Platt, & Welsh, 1998). This cross-cultural difference appears to be a reliable one, though researchers do not yet know exactly why it occurs.

Analysis of the location of sound sources is based partly on the very slight difference in when a sound arrives at each of your two ears (it reaches the closer ear slightly earlier) and on the difference in its intensity at each ear (sounds that are closer to one ear are slightly louder in that ear). As a result, you can determine where a voice or other sound is coming from even when you can't see its source. The brain determines the location of the sound source by analyzing the activities of groups of neurons that, individually, signal only a rough approximation of the location (Fitzpatrick, Olsen, & Suga, 1998). The combined firing frequencies of these many neurons in the auditory cortex thus create a *temporal* "Morse code" that describes where a sound is coming from (Middlebrooks et al., 1994; Wright & Fitzgerald, 2001).

Hearing and Language Language is the auditory stimulation that humans depend upon most, and scientists are learning how the cortex processes

Processing Language As this student and teacher communicate using American Sign Language, the visual information they receive from each other's hand movements is processed by the same areas of their brains that allow hearing people to understand spoken language. Studies show that the primary auditory cortex is also activated when you watch someone speak (but not when the person makes other facial movements). This is the biological basis for the lip reading that helps you to hear what people say (Calvert et al., 1997).

sound signals that we recognize as words. We already know, for example, that temporal processing is particularly important in distinguishing some consonants; in fact, research suggests that children with language learning problems often have deficits in the temporal processing of sounds in general (Merzenich et al., 1996). Fortunately, these children can be trained to more efficiently process the temporal aspects of sounds. Such training dramatically improves their language acquisition (Tallal et al., 1996). It is interesting to note that the brain regions involved in processing language are the same whether the language comes to hearing individuals in the form of sounds or to deaf individuals in the form of sign language (Neville et al., 1998).

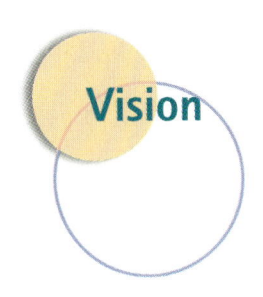

Vision

Soaring eagles have the incredible ability to see a mouse move in the grass from a mile away. Cats have special "reflectors" at the back of their eyes that help them to see even in very dim light. Through natural selection, over eons of time, each species has developed a visual system uniquely adapted to its way of life. The human visual system is also adapted to do many things well: It combines great sensitivity and great sharpness, enabling people to see objects near and far, during the day and at night. Our night vision is not as acute as that of some animals, but our color vision is excellent. This is not a bad tradeoff; being able to appreciate a sunset's splendor seems worth an occasional stumble in the dark. In this section, we consider the human visual sense and how it responds to light.

Light

Light is a form of energy known as *electromagnetic radiation*. Most electromagnetic radiation—including x-rays, radio waves, television signals, and radar—passes through space undetected by the human eye. **Visible light** is electromagnetic radiation that has a wavelength from just under 400 nanometers to about 750 nanometers (a *nanometer* is one-billionth of a meter; see Figure 4.7). Unlike sound, light does not need a medium to pass through. So, even on the airless moon, astronauts can see one another, even if they can't hear one another without radios. Light waves

visible light Electromagnetic radiation that has a wavelength of about 400 nanometers to about 750 nanometers.

figure 4.7

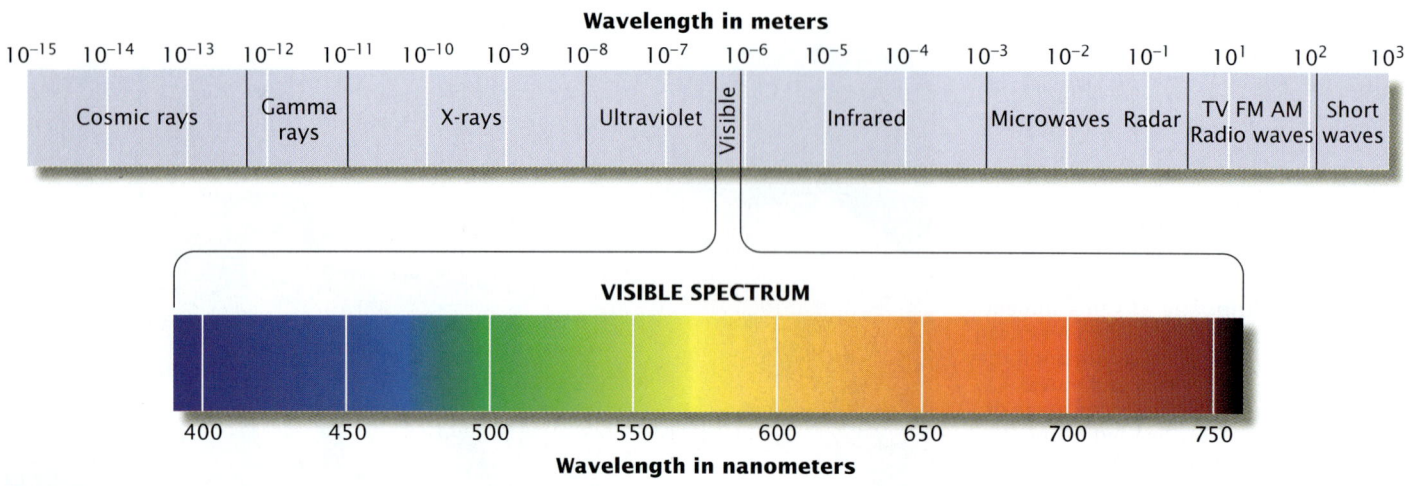

The Spectrum of Electromagnetic Energy

The range of wavelengths that the human eye can see as visible light is very limited—encompassing a band of only about 370 nanometers within the overall spectrum of electromagnetic energy. To detect energy outside this range, people rely on electronic instruments such as radios, TV sets, radar, and infrared night-vision scopes that can "see" this energy, just as the eye sees visible light.

are like particles that pass through space, but they vibrate with a certain wavelength. Thus, light has some properties of waves and some properties of particles, and it is correct to refer to light as either *light waves* or *light rays*.

Sensations of light depend on two physical dimensions of light waves: intensity and wavelength. **Light intensity** refers to how much energy the light contains; it determines the brightness of light, much as the amplitude of sound waves determines the loudness of sound. What color you sense depends mainly on **light wavelength.** At a given intensity, different wavelengths produce sensations of different colors, much as different sound frequencies produce sensations of different pitch. For instance, 440-nanometer light appears violet blue, and 700-nanometer light appears orangish red.

Focusing Light

Just as sound energy is converted to neural activity in the ear, light energy is transduced into neural activity in the eye. First, the accessory structures of the human eye focus light rays into a sharp image. The light rays enter the eye by passing through the curved, transparent, protective layer called the **cornea** (see Figure 4.8). Then the light passes through the **pupil,** the opening just behind the cornea. The **iris,** which gives the eye its color, adjusts the amount of light allowed into the eye by constricting to reduce the size of the pupil or relaxing to enlarge it. Directly behind the pupil is the **lens.** The cornea and the lens of the human eye are both curved so that, like the lens of a camera, they bend light rays. The light rays are focused into an image on the surface at the back of the eye; this surface is called the **retina.**

The lens of the human eye bends light rays from a point source so that they meet at a point on the retina (see Figure 4.9). If the rays meet either in front of the retina or behind it, the image will be out of focus. The muscles that hold the lens adjust its shape so that either near or far objects can be focused on the retina. If you peer at something very close, for example, your muscles must tighten the lens, making it more curved, to obtain a focused image. This ability to change the shape of the lens to bend light rays is called **accommodation.** Over time, the lens loses some of its flexibility, and accommodation becomes more difficult. This is why most older people become "farsighted," seeing distant objects clearly but needing glasses for

light intensity A physical dimension of light waves that refers to how much energy the light contains; it determines the brightness of light.

light wavelength The distance between peaks in light waves.

cornea The curved, transparent, protective layer through which light rays enter the eye.

pupil An opening in the eye, just behind the cornea, through which light passes.

iris The colorful part of the eye, which constricts or relaxes to adjust the amount of light entering the eye.

lens The part of the eye behind the pupil that bends light rays, focusing them on the retina.

retina The surface at the back of the eye onto which the lens focuses light rays.

accommodation The ability of the lens to change its shape and bend light rays so that objects are in focus.

photoreceptors Nerve cells in the retina that code light energy into neural activity.

photopigments Chemicals in photoreceptors that respond to light and assist in converting light into neural activity.

dark adaptation The increasing ability to see in the dark as time in the dark increases.

figure 4.8

Major Structures of the Eye

As shown in this top view of the eye, light rays bent by the combined actions of the cornea and the lens are focused on the retina, where the light energy is transduced into neural activity. Nerve fibers known collectively as the *optic nerve* pass out the back of the eye and continue to the brain.

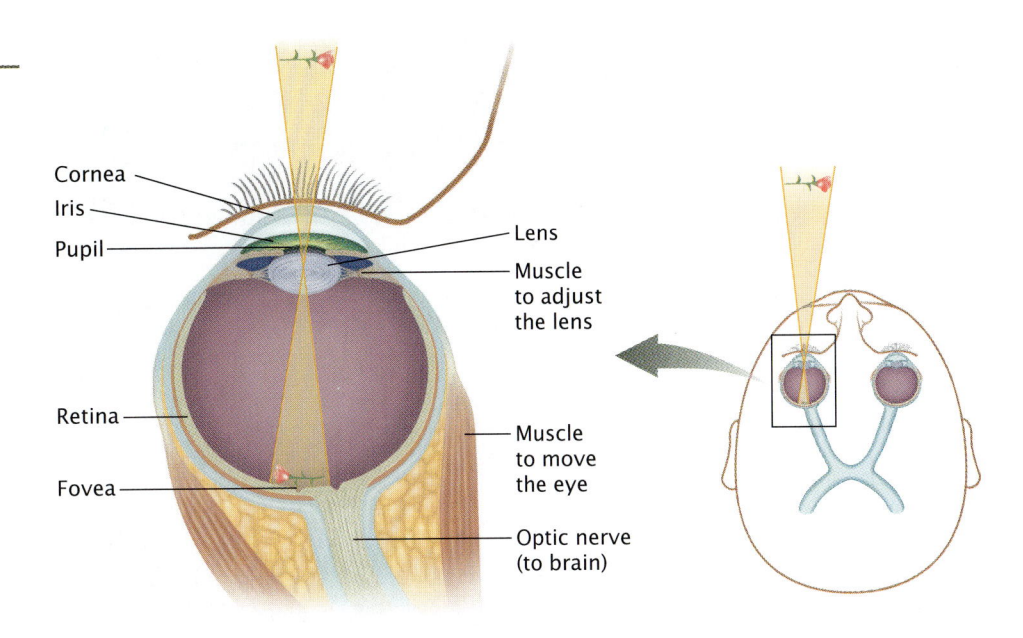

reading or close work. A more common problem in younger people is nearsightedness, in which close objects are in focus but distant ones are blurry. This condition has a genetic component, but it may be influenced by the environment, too (Quinn et al., 1999; Zadnik, 2001).

Converting Light into Images

Visual transduction, the conversion of light energy into neural activity, takes place in the retina. The word *retina* is Latin for "net"; the retina is an intricate network of cells. Before transduction can occur, light rays must actually pass through several layers in this network to reach photoreceptor cells.

Photoreceptors

Photoreceptors are specialized cells in the retina that convert light energy into neural activity. They contain **photopigments**, chemicals that respond to light. When light strikes a photopigment, the photopigment breaks apart, changing the membrane potential of the photoreceptor cell. This change in membrane potential provides a signal that can be transferred to the brain.

After a photopigment has broken down in response to light, new photopigment molecules are put together. This takes a little time, however. So when you first come from bright sunshine into, say, a dark theater, you cannot see because your photoreceptors do not yet have enough photopigment. In the dark, your photoreceptors synthesize more photopigments, and your ability to see gradually increases. This increasing ability to see in the dark as time passes is called **dark adaptation**. Overall,

figure 4.9

The Lens and the Retinal Image

Light rays from the top of an object are focused at the bottom of the image on the retinal surface, whereas rays from the right side of the object end up on the left side of the retinal image. The brain rearranges this upside-down and reversed image so that people see the object as it really is.

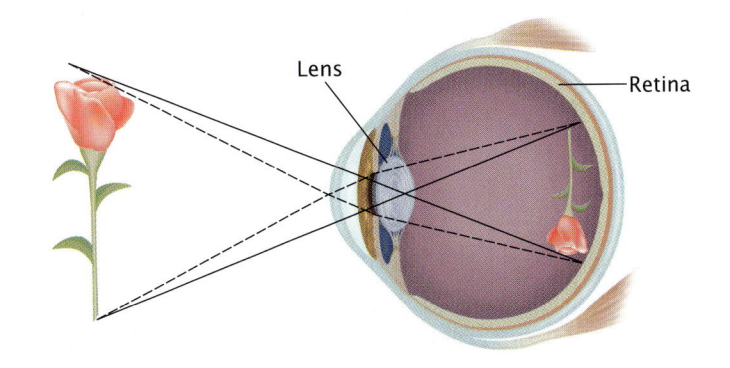

Reading and Nearsightedness Visual experience can modify the eye. When chicks are raised with goggles that allow only diffused, unpatterned light through, their eyeballs become elongated and they become nearsighted (Wallman et al., 1987). Humans may be vulnerable to the same elongation because reading presents areas around the fovea with a constant, relatively unpatterned image.

your sensitivity to light increases about 10,000-fold after about half an hour in a darkened room.

The retina has two basic types of photoreceptors: **rods** and **cones**. As their names imply, these cells differ in shape. They also differ in composition and response to light. The photopigment in rods includes a substance called *rhodopsin* (pronounced "row-DOP-sin"), whereas the photopigment in cones includes one of three varieties of *iodopsin*. The multiple forms of iodopsin provide the basis for color vision, which we explain later. Because rods have only one pigment, they are unable to discriminate colors. However, the rods are more sensitive to light than cones. So rods allow you to see even when there is very little light, as on a moonlit night. In dim light, you are seeing with your rods, which cannot discriminate colors; at higher light intensities, the cones, with their ability to detect colors, become most active. As a result, you may put on what you thought was a matched pair of socks in a darkened bedroom, only to go outside and discover that one is dark blue and the other is dark green.

Rods and cones also differ in their distribution in the eye. Cones are concentrated in the center of the retina, a region called the **fovea**, where the eye focuses the light coming from objects you look at. This concentration makes the ability to see details, or **acuity**, greatest in the fovea. Variations in the density of cones in the fovea probably account for individual differences in visual acuity (Curcio et al., 1987). There are no rods in the human fovea. With increasing distance from the fovea, though, the number of cones gradually decreases, and the proportion of rods gradually increases. So, if you are trying to detect a small amount of light, like that from a faint star, it is better to look slightly away from where you expect to see it. This focuses the weak light on the rods outside the fovea, which are very sensitive to light. Because cones do not work well in low light, looking directly at the star will make it seem to disappear.

Interactions in the Retina

If the eye simply transferred to the brain the stimuli that are focused on the retina, the resulting images would resemble a somewhat blurred TV picture. Instead, the eye actually sharpens visual images. How? The key lies in the interactions among the cells of the retina, which are illustrated in Figure 4.10. The most direct connections from the photoreceptor cells to the brain go first to *bipolar cells* and then to *ganglion cells*; the axons of the ganglion cells form the optic nerve, which extends out of the eye and into the brain. However, this direct path to the brain is modified by interactions with other cells.

rods Highly light-sensitive, but color-insensitive, photoreceptors in the retina that allow vision even in dim light.

cones Photoreceptors in the retina whose color-sensitive photopigment helps us to distinguish colors.

fovea A region in the center of the retina where cones are highly concentrated.

acuity Visual clarity, which is greatest in the fovea because of its large concentration of cones.

lateral inhibition A process in which lateral connections allow one photoreceptor to inhibit the responsiveness of its neighbor, thus enhancing the sensation of visual contrast.

Rods and Cones This electron microscope view of rods (blue) and cones (aqua) shows what your light receptors look like. Rods are more light sensitive, but they do not detect color. Cones can detect color, but they require more light in order to be activated. To experience the difference in how these cells work, look at an unfamiliar color photograph in a room where there is barely enough light to see. Even this dim light will activate your rods and allow you to make out images in the picture. But because there is not enough light to activate your cones, you will not be able to see colors in the photo.

These interactions change the information reaching the brain, enhancing the sensation of contrast, for example. How? Most of the time, the amount of light reaching any two photoreceptors will differ slightly. When this happens, the photoreceptor receiving more light inhibits the output to the brain from the photoreceptor receiving less light, making it seem as if there is less light at that cell than there really is. This process, called **lateral inhibition**, is aided by *interneurons*, which are cells that make sideways, or lateral, connections between photoreceptors (see Figure 4.10). In other words, the brain actually receives a *comparison* of the light hitting two neighboring points, and whatever difference that exists between the light

figure 4.10

Cells in the Retina

Light rays actually pass through several layers of cells before striking photoreceptors, the rods and cones. Signals generated by the rods and cones then go back toward the surface of the retina, passing through bipolar cells and ganglion cells, and on to the brain. Interconnections among interneurons, bipolar cells, and ganglion cells allow the eye to begin analyzing visual information even before that information leaves the retina.

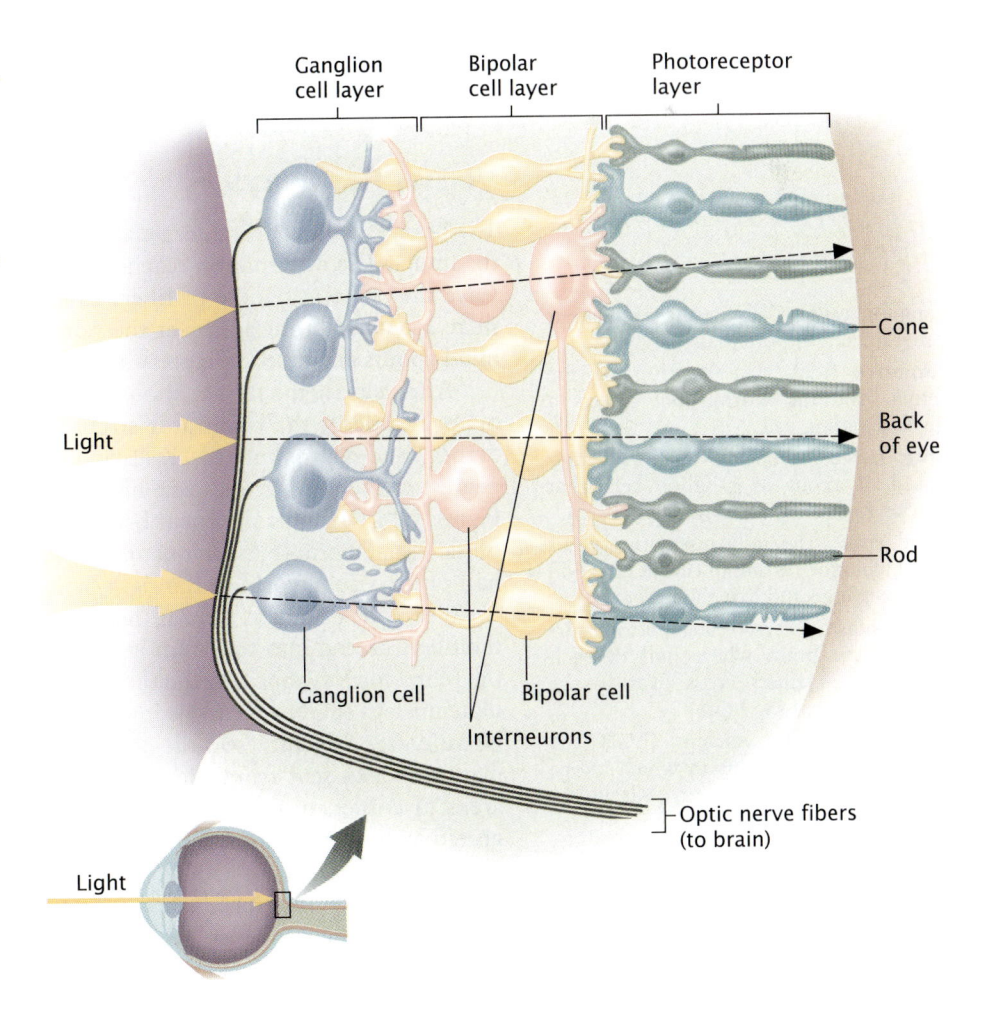

reaching the two photoreceptors is exaggerated. This exaggeration is important, because specific features of objects can create differences in amounts of incoming light. For example, the visual image of the edge of a table contains a transition from a lighter region to a darker region. Lateral inhibition in the retina amplifies this difference, creating contrast that sharpens the edge and makes it more noticeable.

Ganglion Cells and Their Receptive Fields

Photoreceptors and bipolar cells communicate by releasing neurotransmitters. But as discussed in the chapter on biological aspects of psychology, neurotransmitters cause only small, graded changes in the membrane potential of the next cell, which cannot travel the distance from eye to brain. The cells in the retina that generate action potentials capable of traveling that distance are the **ganglion cells,** whose axons extend out of the retina to the brain.

What message do ganglion cells send to the brain? The answer depends on each cell's **receptive field,** which is the part of the retina and the corresponding part of the visual world to which a cell responds (Sekuler & Blake, 1994). Most ganglion cells have *center-surround receptive fields.* That is, most ganglion cells compare the amount of light stimulating the photoreceptors in the center of their receptive fields with the amount of light stimulating the photoreceptors in the area surrounding the center. This comparison results from the interactions in the retina that enhance contrast. Some center-surround ganglion cells *(center-on cells)* are activated by light in the center of their receptive field; light in the regions surrounding the center inhibits their activity (see Figure 4.11). Other center-surround ganglion cells *(center-off cells)* work in just the opposite way. They are inhibited by light in the center and activated by light in the surrounding area.

The center-surround receptive fields of ganglion cells make it easier for you to see edges and, as illustrated in Figure 4.12, also create a sharper contrast between darker and lighter areas than actually exists. By enhancing the sensation of important features, the retina gives your brain an "improved" version of the visual world.

Visual Pathways

The brain performs even more elaborate processing of visual information than does the retina. The information reaches the brain via the axons of ganglion cells, which leave the eye as a bundle of fibers called the **optic nerve** (see Figure 4.8). Because there are no photoreceptors at the point where the optic nerve exits the eyeball, a **blind spot** is created, as Figure 4.13 shows.

After leaving the retina, about half the fibers of the optic nerve cross over to the opposite side of the brain at a structure called the **optic chiasm.** (*Chiasm* means "cross" and is pronounced "KYE-az-um.") Fibers from the inside half of each eye, nearest to the nose, cross over; fibers from the outside half of each eye do not (see Figure 4.14). This arrangement brings all the visual information about the right half of the visual world to the left hemisphere of the brain and information about the left half of the visual world to the right hemisphere of the brain.

The optic chiasm is part of the bottom surface of the brain; beyond the chiasm, the fibers ascend into the brain itself. The axons from most of the ganglion cells in the retina form synapses in the thalamus, in a specific region called the **lateral geniculate nucleus (LGN).** Neurons in the LGN then send the visual input to the **primary visual cortex,** which lies in the occipital lobe at the back of the brain. Visual information is also sent from the primary visual cortex for processing in many other areas of cortex. In studies of monkeys, thirty-two separate visual areas interconnected by more than three hundred pathways have been identified so far (Van Essen, Anderson, & Felleman, 1992).

The retina is organized to create a topographical map of the visual world, such that neighboring points on the retina receive information from neighboring points

---

ganglion cells Cells in the retina that generate action potentials.

receptive field The portion of the retina, and the world, that affects a given ganglion cell.

optic nerve A bundle of fibers composed of axons of ganglion cells that carries visual information to the brain.

blind spot The light-insensitive point at which axons from all of the ganglion cells converge and exit the eyeball.

optic chiasm Part of the bottom surface of the brain where half of each optic nerve's fibers cross over to the opposite side of the brain.

lateral geniculate nucleus (LGN) A region of the thalamus in which axons from most of the ganglion cells in the retina end and form synapses.

primary visual cortex An area at the back of the brain, to which neurons in the lateral geniculate nucleus relay visual input.

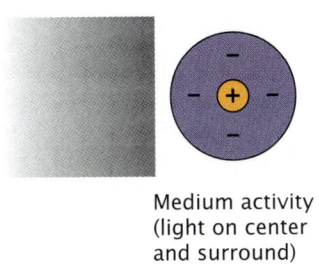

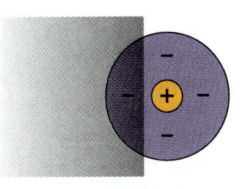

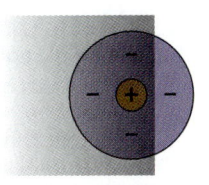

Medium activity (light on center and surround)   Higher activity (light on center; dark on surround)   Low activity (dark on both center and surround)

figure 4.11

Center-Surround Receptive Fields of Ganglion Cells

Center-surround receptive fields allow ganglion cells to act as edge detectors. An edge is a region of light next to a region of relative darkness. If, as shown at the left, an edge is outside the receptive field of a center-on ganglion cell, there will be a uniform amount of light on both the excitatory center and the inhibitory surround, thus creating a moderate amount of activity. If, as shown in the middle drawing, the dark side of an edge covers a large portion of the inhibitory surround but leaves light on the excitatory center, the output of the cell will be high, signaling an edge in its receptive field. When, as shown at right, the dark area covers both the center and the surround of the ganglion cell, its activity will be lower, because neither segment of the cell's receptive field is receiving much stimulation.

in the visual world. This topographical map is also maintained in the brain, in the primary visual cortex, and in each of the many other visual areas of the cortex. So neighboring points in the retina are represented in neighboring cells in the brain. (This is a spatial coding system.) The map is a distorted one, however. A larger area of cortex is devoted to the areas of the retina that have many photoreceptors. For example, the fovea, which is densely packed with photoreceptors, is represented in an especially large segment of cortex.

Visual Representations

So the apparently effortless experience of sight is due to a very complex system, in which visual sensations are transmitted from the retina through various cortical regions. We can appreciate some of these complexities by considering the receptive fields of neurons at each point along the way. Two of the processes that characterize these receptive fields are *parallel processing of visual properties* and *hierarchical processing of visual information.*

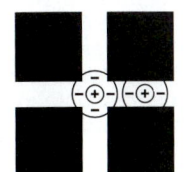

figure 4.12

The Hermann Grid

There seem to be dark spots at the intersections of the *Hermann grid,* until you look directly at them. To understand why, look at the black boxes in the smaller grid at right. The circles superimposed on this smaller grid represent the receptive fields of two center-on ganglion cells. At the intersections, a center-on ganglion cell has more whiteness shining on its inhibitory surround. Because its output is reduced compared with that of the cell on the right, the spot on the left appears darker. The spot disappears when you look directly at the intersection because ganglion cells in the fovea have smaller receptive fields than do ganglion cells elsewhere in the retina, so more excitatory centers are being stimulated, creating a greater sensation of whiteness.

figure 4.13

Find Your Blind Spot

TRY THIS There is a blind spot where axons from the ganglion cells leave the eye and become the optic nerve. To "see" your blind spot, cover your left eye, and stare at the cross inside the circle. Move the page closer and then farther away, and at some point the dot to the right should disappear. However, the vertical lines around the dot will probably look continuous, because the brain tends to fill in visual information at the blind spot. We are normally unaware of this "hole" in our vision because the blind spot of one eye is in the visual field of the other eye.

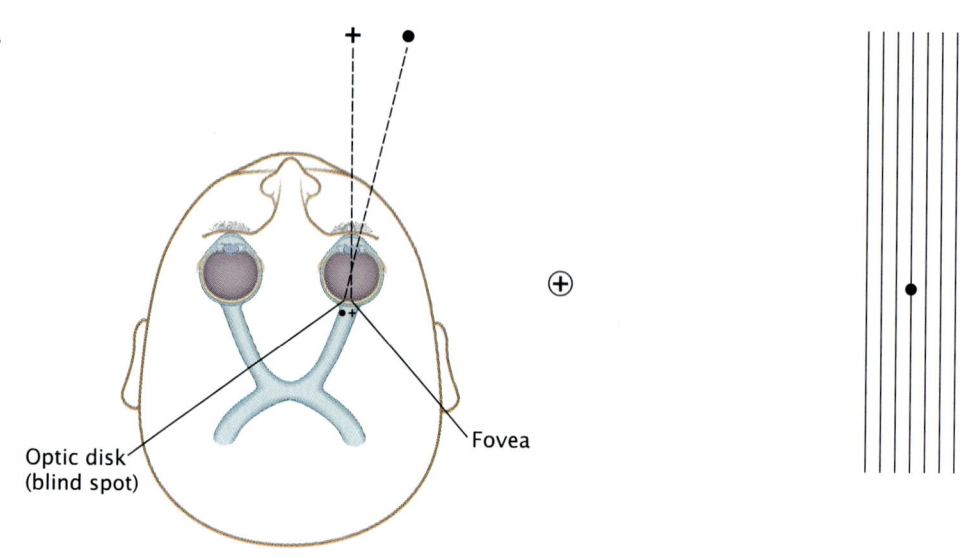

Parallel Processing of Visual Properties

Like ganglion cells, neurons of the LGN in the thalamus have center-surround receptive fields. However, the LGN is organized in multiple layers of neurons, and each layer contains a complete map of the retina. Neurons in different layers respond to particular aspects of visual stimuli. In fact, four separate aspects of a visual scene are simultaneously handled by *parallel processing systems* (Livingstone & Hubel, 1987). The *form* of objects and their *color* are handled by one system (the "what" system), whereas their *movement* and *cues to distance* are handled by another (the "where" system).

These sensations are then sent to the cortex, but the question of where in the cortex they are finally assembled into a unified conscious experience is still being debated. Some researchers argue that there is no one region where all the separate streams of processing converge (Engel et al., 1992). Instead, they say, connections among the regions of cortex that process separate aspects of visual sensation appear to integrate their activity, making possible a distributed, but unified, experience (Gilbert, 1992).

figure 4.14

Pathways from the Ganglion Cells into the Brain

Light rays from the right side of the visual field (the right side of what you are looking at) end up on the left half of each retina (shown in red). Light rays from the left visual field end up on the right half of each retina (shown in blue). From the right eye, axons from the nasal side of the retina (the side nearer the nose, which receives information from the right visual field) cross over the midline and travel to the left side of the brain with those fibers from the left eye that also receive input from the right side of the visual world. A similar arrangement unites left visual-field information from both eyes in the right side of the brain.

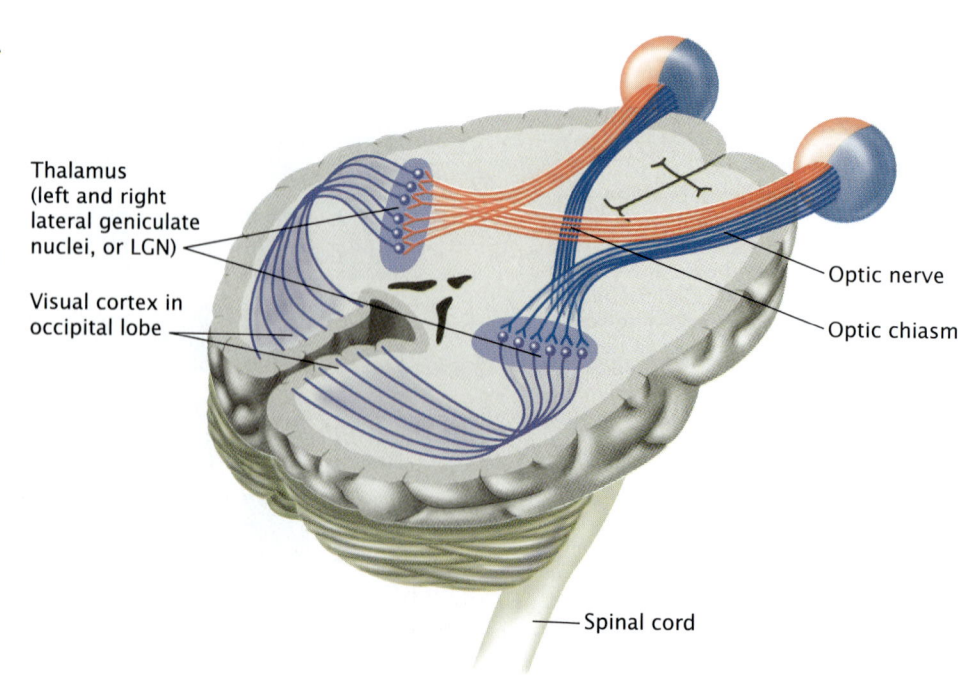

figure 4.15

Construction of a Feature Detector

The output from several center-on ganglion cells goes to cells in the lateral geniculate nucleus (LGN) and is then fed into one cell in the cortex. This "wiring" makes the cortical cell respond best when all of its LGN cells are excited, and they are most excited when light falls on the center of the receptive fields of their ganglion cells. Because those receptive fields lie in an angled row, it takes a bar-shaped light at that angle to stimulate all their centers. In short, this cortical cell responds best when it detects a bar-shaped feature at a particular angle. Rotating the bar to a different orientation would no longer stimulate this particular cortical cell.

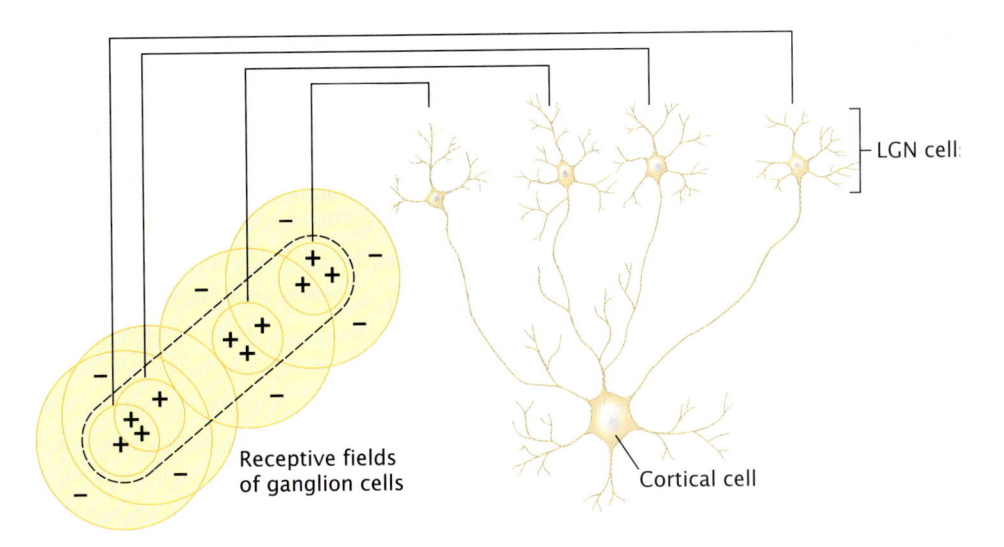

Positron emission tomography (PET) scans, too, have provided evidence of separate processing channels in humans. One area of visual cortex is activated when a person views a colorful painting; a different area is activated by viewing black-and-white moving images (Zeki, 1992). Brain damage may also reveal these separate channels. Damage in one area can leave a person unable to see colors or even remember them, but still able to see and recognize objects. Damage in another area can leave a person able to see only stationary objects; as soon as the object moves, it disappears. People with brain damage in still other regions can see only moving objects, not stationary ones (Zeki, 1992). Even in visual imagination, the same separate processing channels apparently operate. So some patients with brain damage can recall parts of a visual image, but not their correct spatial relationship. For example, they may be able to "see" a mental image of a bull's horns and ears but be unable to assemble them mentally to form a bull's head (Kosslyn, 1988).

Hierarchical Processing of Visual Information

Multiple inputs from the LGN converge on single cells of the cortex, as Figure 4.15 illustrates. Cells of the cortex that receive input from the LGN in the thalamus have more complex receptive fields than the center-surround fields of LGN cells. For example, a specific cell in the cortex might respond only to vertical edges, but it responds to vertical edges anywhere in its receptive field. Another class of cells responds only to moving objects; a third class responds only to objects with corners. Because cortical cells respond to specific characteristics of objects in the visual field, they have been described as **feature detectors** (Hubel & Wiesel, 1979).

Feature detectors illustrate how cortical processing is partly *hierarchical*, or stepwise, in nature. Complex feature detectors may be built up out of more and more complex connections among simpler feature detectors (Hubel & Wiesel, 1979). For example, several center-surround cells might feed into one cortical cell to make a line detector, and several line detectors might feed into another cortical cell to make a cell that responds to a particular spatial orientation, such as vertical. With further connections, a more complex detector, such as a "box detector," might be built from simpler line and corner detectors.

Cells with similar receptive-field properties are organized into columns in the cortex. The columns are arranged at right angles to the surface of the cortex. For example, if you locate a cell that responds to diagonal lines in a particular spot in the visual field, most of the cells in a column above and below that cell will also respond to diagonal lines. Other properties, too, are represented by whole columns of cells; for example, there are columns in which all of the cells are most sensitive

---

feature detectors Cells in the cortex that respond to a specific feature of an object.

in review: Seeing

Aspect of Sensory System	Elements	Key Characteristics
Energy	Light—electromagnetic radiation from about 400 nm to about 750 nm	The intensity and wavelength of light waves determine the brightness and color of visual sensations.
Accessory structures	Eye—cornea, pupil, iris, lens	Light rays are bent to focus on the retina.
Transduction mechanism	Photoreceptors (rods and cones) in the retina	Rods are more sensitive to light than cones, but cones discriminate among colors. Sensations of color depend first on the cones, which respond differently to different light wavelengths. Interactions among cells of the retina exaggerate differences in the light stimuli reaching the photoreceptors, enhancing the sensation of contrast.
Pathways and representations	Optic nerve to optic chiasm to LGN of thalamus to primary visual cortex	Neighboring points in the visual world are represented at neighboring points in the LGN and primary visual cortex. Neurons there respond to particular aspects of the visual stimulus—such as color, movement, distance, or form.

to a particular color. Research has also revealed that individual neurons in the cortex perform several different tasks, allowing complex visual processing (Schiller, 1996). ("In Review: Seeing" summarizes how the nervous system gathers the information that allows people to see.)

Seeing Color

Like beauty, color is in the eye of the beholder. Many animals see only shades of gray, even when they look at a rainbow, but for humans color is a prominent feature of vision. A marketer might tell you about the impact of color on buying preferences, a poet might tell you about the emotional power of color, but we will tell you about how you see colors—a process that is itself a thing of beauty and elegance.

Wavelengths and Color Sensations

We noted earlier that at a given intensity, each wavelength of light is sensed as a certain color (look again at Figure 4.7). However, the eye is seldom, if ever, presented with pure light of a single wavelength. Sunlight, for example, is a mixture of all wavelengths of light. When sunlight passes through a droplet of water, the different wavelengths of light are bent to different degrees, separating into a colorful rainbow. The spectrum of color found in the rainbow illustrates an important concept: The sensation produced by a mixture of different wavelengths of light is not the same as the sensations produced by separate wavelengths. So just as most sounds are a mixture of sound waves of different frequencies, most colors are a mixture of light of different wavelengths.

Characteristics of the mixture of wavelengths striking the eyes determine the color sensation. There are three separate aspects of this sensation: hue, saturation, and brightness. These are *psychological* dimensions that correspond roughly to the

hue The essential "color," determined by the dominant wavelength of light.
saturation The purity of a color.
brightness The overall intensity of all of the wavelengths that make up light.

physical properties of light. **Hue** is the essential "color," determined by the dominant wavelength in the mixture of the light. For example, the wavelength of yellow is about 570 nanometers, and that of red is about 700 nanometers. Black, white, and gray are not considered hues, because no wavelength predominates in them. **Saturation** is related to the purity of a color. A color is more saturated and more pure if just one wavelength is relatively more intense—contains more energy—than other wavelengths. If many wavelengths are added to a pure hue, the color is said to be *desaturated*. For example, pastels are colors that have been desaturated by the addition of whiteness. **Brightness** refers to the overall intensity of all of the wavelengths making up light.

The color circle shown in Figure 4.16 arranges hues according to their perceived similarities. If lights of two different wavelengths but equal intensity are mixed, the color you sense is at the midpoint of a line drawn between the two original colors on the color circle. This process is known as *additive color mixing*, because the effects of the wavelengths from each light are added together. If you keep adding different colored lights, you eventually get white (the combination of all wavelengths). You are probably more familiar with a different form of color mixing, called *subtractive color mixing*, which occurs when paints are combined. Like other physical objects, paints reflect certain wavelengths and absorb all others. For example, grass is green because it absorbs all wavelengths except wavelengths that are sensed as green. White objects are white because they reflect all wavelengths. Light reflected from paints or other colored objects is seldom a pure wavelength, so predicting the color resulting from mixing paint is not as straightforward as combining pure wavelengths of light. But if you keep combining different colored paints, all of the wavelengths will eventually be subtracted, resulting in black. (The discussion that follows refers to *additive color mixing*, the mixing of light.)

By mixing lights of just a few wavelengths, we can produce different color sensations. How many wavelengths are needed to create any possible color? Figure 4.17 illustrates an experiment that addresses this question, using a piece of white paper, which reflects all wavelengths and therefore appears to be the color of the light shined upon it. The answer to the question of how many lights are needed to create all colors helped lead scientists to an important theory of how people sense color.

figure 4.16

The Color Circle

Ordering colors according to their psychological similarities creates a color circle that predicts the result of additive mixing of two colored lights. The resulting color will be on a line between the two starting colors, the exact location on the line depending on the relative proportions of the two colors. For example, mixing equal amounts of pure green and pure red light will produce yellow, the color that lies at the midpoint of the line connecting red and green. (*Nm* stands for *nanometers,* the unit in which wavelengths are measured.)

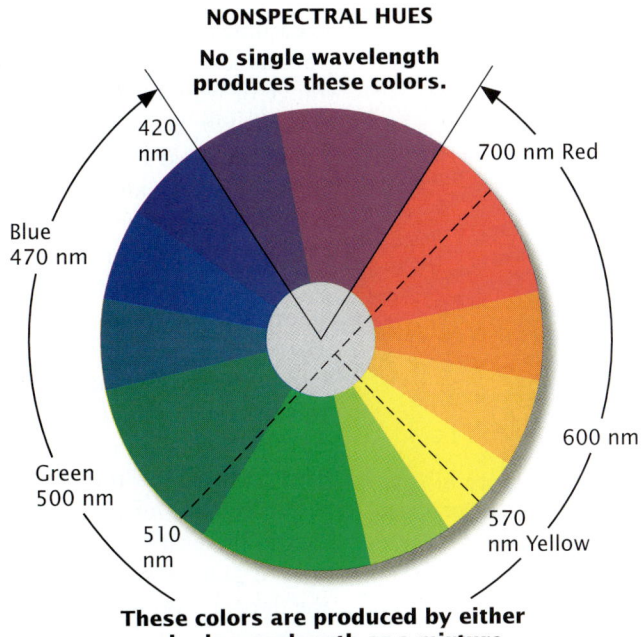

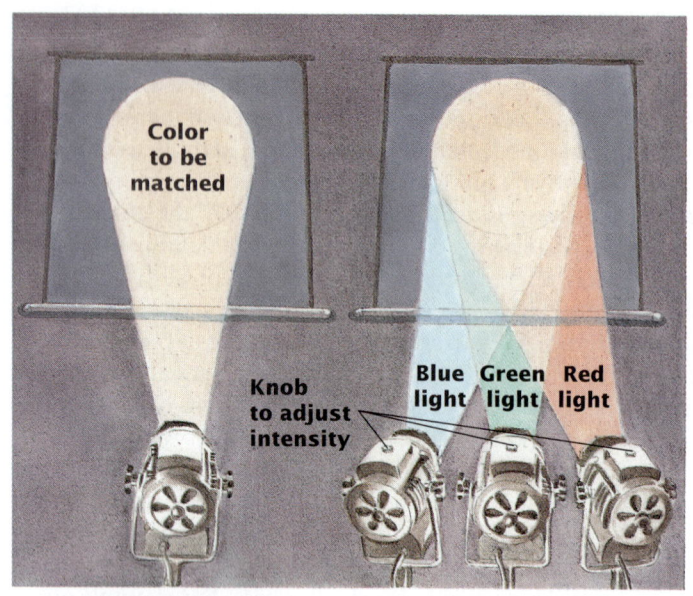

figure 4.17

Matching a Color by Mixing Lights of Pure Wavelengths

A target color is presented on the left side of this display; the participant's task is to adjust the intensity of different pure-wavelength lights until the resulting mixture looks exactly like the target. A large number of colors can be matched with just two mixing lights, but *any* color can be matched by mixing three pure-wavelength lights. Experiments like this generated the information that led to the trichromatic theory of color vision.

trichromatic theory A theory of color vision identifying three types of visual elements, each of which is most sensitive to different wavelengths of light.

opponent-process theory A theory of color vision stating that color-sensitive visual elements are grouped into red-green, blue-yellow, and black-white elements.

The Trichromatic Theory of Color Vision

Early in the nineteenth century, Thomas Young and, later, Hermann von Helmholtz established that they could match any color by mixing pure lights of only three wavelengths. For example, by mixing blue light (about 440 nanometers), green light (about 510 nanometers), and red light (about 700 nanometers) in different ratios, they could produce *any* other color. Young and Helmholtz interpreted this evidence to mean that there must be three types of visual elements, each of which is most sensitive to different wavelengths, and that information from these three elements combines to produce the sensation of color. This theory of color vision is called the *Young-Helmholtz theory*, or the **trichromatic theory**.

Support for the trichromatic theory has come from recordings of the responses of individual photoreceptors to particular wavelengths of light and from electrical recordings from human cones (Schnapf, Kraft, & Baylor, 1987). This research reveals that there are three types of cones. Although each type responds to a broad range of wavelengths, each type is most sensitive to particular wavelengths. *Short-wavelength* cones respond most to light in the blue range. *Medium-wavelength* cones are most sensitive to light in the green range. Finally, *long-wavelength* cones respond best to light in the reddish yellow range (although these have traditionally been called "red cones").

Note that no single cone, by itself, can signal the color of a light. It is the *ratio* of the activities of the three types of cones that indicates what color will be sensed. In other words, color vision is coded by the *pattern of activity* of the different cones. For example, a light is sensed as yellow if it has a pure wavelength of about 570 nanometers; this light stimulates both medium- and long-wavelength cones, as illustrated by arrow A in Figure 4.18. But yellow is also sensed whenever any mixture of other lights stimulates the same pattern of activity in these two types of cones. The trichromatic theory was applied in the creation of color television screens, which contain microscopic elements of red, green, and blue. A television broadcast excites these elements to varying degrees, mixing their colors to produce many other colors. You see color mixtures—not patterns of red, green, and blue dots—because the dots are too small and close together to be seen individually.

The Opponent-Process Theory of Color Vision

Brilliant as it is, the trichromatic theory in its simplest form cannot explain some aspects of color

figure 4.18

Relative Responses of Three Cone Types to Different Wavelengths of Light

Each type of cone responds to a range of wavelengths but responds more to some wavelengths than to others. This makes it possible to generate the same pattern of output—and hence the same sensation of color—by more than one combination of wavelengths. For example, a pure light of 570 nanometers (A in the figure) stimulates long-wavelength cones at 1.0 relative units and medium-wavelength cones at about 0.7 relative units. This ratio of cone activity (1/0.7 = 1.4) yields the sensation of yellow. Any combination of wavelengths at the proper intensity that generates the same ratio of activity in these cone types will produce the sensation of yellow.

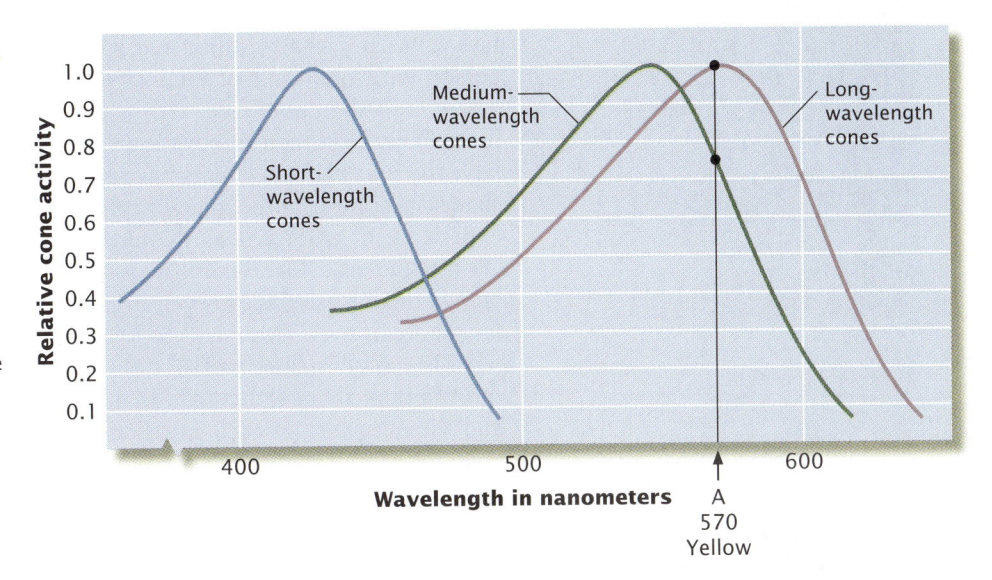

vision. For example, it cannot account for the fact that if you stare at the flag in Figure 4.19 for thirty seconds and then look at the blank white space below it, you will see a color afterimage. What was yellow in the original image will be blue in the afterimage, what was green before will appear red, and what was black will now appear white.

This type of phenomenon led Ewald Hering to offer an alternative to the trichromatic theory of color vision, called the **opponent-process theory**. It holds that the visual elements sensitive to color are grouped into three pairs and that the members of each pair oppose, or inhibit, each other. The three pairs are a *red-green element*, a *blue-yellow element*, and a *black-white element*. Each element signals one color or the other—red or green, for example—but never both. This theory explains color afterimages. When one part of an opponent pair is no longer stimulated, the other is activated. So, as in Figure 4.19, if the original image you look at is green, the afterimage will be red.

The opponent-process theory also explains the phenomenon of complementary colors. Two colors are *complementary* if gray results when lights of the two colors are mixed together. Actually, the neutral color of gray can appear as anything from white to gray to black, depending on the intensity of the light. On the color circle shown in Figure 4.16, complementary colors are roughly opposite each other. Red and green lights are complementary, as are yellow and blue. Notice that complementary colors are *opponent* colors in Hering's theory. According to opponent-process theory, complementary colors stimulate the same visual element (e.g., red-green) in opposite directions, canceling each other out. This theory helps explain why mixing lights of complementary colors produces gray.

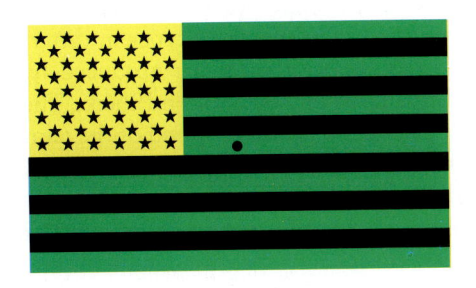

A Synthesis and an Update

The trichromatic and opponent-process theories seem quite different, but both are correct to some extent, and together they can explain most of what is known about color vision. Electrical recordings made from different types of cells in the retina paved the way for a synthesis of the two theories.

At the level of the photoreceptors, a slightly revised version of the trichromatic theory is correct. As a general rule, there *are* three types of cones that have three different photopigments. However, molecular biologists who isolated the genes for cone pigments have found variations in the genes for the cones sensitive to middle-wavelength and long-wavelength light. These variants have slightly different sensitivities to different wavelengths of light. So a person can have two, three, or even four genes for long-wavelength pigments (Neitz & Neitz, 1995). Individual differences in people's long-wavelength pigments become apparent in color-matching

figure 4.19

Afterimages Produced by the Opponent-Process Nature of Color Vision

TRY THIS Stare at the dot in the center of the flag for at least thirty seconds; then fixate on the dot in the white space below it.

tasks. When asked to mix a red light and a green light to match a yellow light, a person with one kind of long-wavelength pigment will choose a different red-to-green ratio than someone with a different long-wavelength pigment. Women are more likely than men to have four distinct photopigments, and the women who do have the four photopigments have a richer experience of color. They can detect more shades of color than people with the more common three photopigments, but their experience of color pales in comparison to that of certain shrimp. These tropical shrimp live on colorful coral reefs and have twelve different photopigments, which allows them to see colors even in the ultraviolet range, which no human—male or female—can sense (Marshall & Oberwinkler, 1999).

But color vision works a little differently at the level of ganglion cells. Information about light from many photoreceptors feeds into each ganglion cell, and the output from each ganglion cell goes to the brain. Recall that the receptive fields of most ganglion cells are arranged in center-surround patterns. The center and the surround are color coded, as illustrated in Figure 4.20. The center responds best to one color, and the surround responds best to a different color. This color coding arises because varying proportions of the three cone types feed into the center and the surround of the ganglion cell.

When either the center or the surround of a ganglion cell is stimulated, the other area is inhibited. In other words, the colors to which the center and the surround of a given ganglion cell are most responsive are opponent colors. Recordings from many ganglion cells show that three very common pairs of opponent colors are those predicted by Hering's opponent-process theory: red-green, blue-yellow, and black-white. Stimulating both the center and the surround cancels the effects of either light, producing gray. Black-white cells receive input from all types of cones, so it does not matter what color stimulates them. Cells in specific regions of the visual cortex, too, respond in opponent pairs sensitive to the red-green and blue-yellow input coming from ganglion cells in the retina (Engel, Zhang, & Wandell, 1997).

In summary, color vision is possible because the three types of cones have different sensitivities to different wavelengths, as the trichromatic theory suggests. The sensation of different colors results from stimulating the three cone types in different ratios. Because there are three types of cones, any color can be produced by mixing three different wavelengths of light. But the story does not end there. The output from cones is fed into ganglion cells, and the center and surround of the ganglion cells respond to different colors and inhibit each other. This activity provides the basis for afterimages. Therefore, the trichromatic theory describes the properties of the photoreceptors, whereas the opponent-process theory describes the properties of the ganglion cells. Both theories are needed to account for the complexity of visual sensations of color.

figure 4.20

Color Coding and the Ganglion Cells

The center-surround receptive fields of ganglion cells form the anatomical basis for opponent colors. Some ganglion cells, like G_2, have a center whose photoreceptors respond best to red wavelengths and a surround whose photoreceptors respond best to green wavelengths. Other ganglion cells pair blue and yellow, whereas still others receive input from all types of photoreceptors.

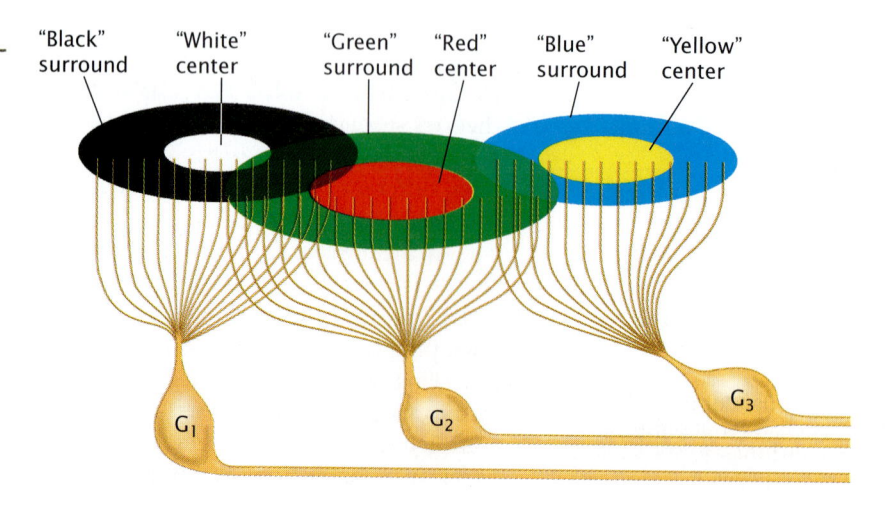

figure 4.21

Are You Colorblind?

TRY THIS At the upper left is a photo as it appears to people who have all three cone photopigments. The other photos simulate how colors appear to people who are missing photopigments for short wavelengths (lower left), long wavelengths (upper right), or medium wavelengths (lower right). If any of these photos look to you just like the one at the upper left, you may have a form of colorblindness.

Colorblindness People who have cones containing only two of the three possible color-sensitive pigments are described as *colorblind* (see Figure 4.21). They are not actually blind to all color; they simply discriminate fewer colors than other people. Two centuries ago, a colorblind chemist named John Dalton carefully described the colors he sensed—to him, a red ribbon appeared the same color as mud—and hypothesized that the fluid in his eyeball must be tinted blue. He instructed his doctor to examine the fluid after he died, but it turned out to be clear. His preserved retinas were examined recently by molecular biologists. The scientists were not surprised to find that just as most colorblind people today lack the genes that code one or more of the pigments, Dalton had no gene for medium-wavelength pigments (Hunt et al., 1995).

The Interaction of Vision and Hearing: Synesthesia

At the beginning of this chapter, we gave examples of the interaction of two senses, namely, vision and touch. Vision also interacts with hearing. For example, hearing a brief sound just as lights are flashed can make it appear that there are more lights than there actually are (Shams, Kamitani, & Shimojo, 2000). And hearing a sound as objects collide can affect your perception of their motion (Watanabe & Shimojo, 2001). Sound can also improve your ability to see an object at the sound's source, which could be a vital aid in avoiding or responding to danger (McDonald, Teder-Salejarvi, & Hillyard, 2000). These interactions occur in everyone, but some people also report **synesthesia** (pronounced "sin-ess-THEE-zhah"), a more unusual mixing of sensory modalities or dimensions within modalities. These people may say that they "feel" colors or sounds as touches, or that they "taste" shapes; others claim that they sense certain colors, such as red, when they hear certain sounds, such as a trumpet. Some report experiencing certain tastes, numbers, or letters as vivid patterns or particular colors.

Once dismissed as poetic delusions, some of these claims have recently received scientific support from experiments such as the one illustrated in Figure 4.22 (Mattingly et al., 2001; Ramachandran & Hubbard, 2001). Researchers speculate that synesthesia occurs partly because brain areas that process colors are near areas that process letters and numbers, and partly because the connections between these neighboring areas may be more extensive in people who experience synesthesia.

synesthesia A blending of sensory experience that causes some people to "see" sounds or "taste" colors, for example.

figure 4.22

Synesthesia

In this experiment on synesthesia, a triangular pattern of H's was embedded in a background of other letters, as shown at left. Most people find it difficult to detect the triangle, but "J.C.," a person with synesthesia, easily picked it out because, as depicted at right, he saw the H's as green, the F's as yellow, and the P's as red (Ramachandran & Hubbard, 2001).

Source: Figure 3 from Ramachandran & Hubbard (2001).

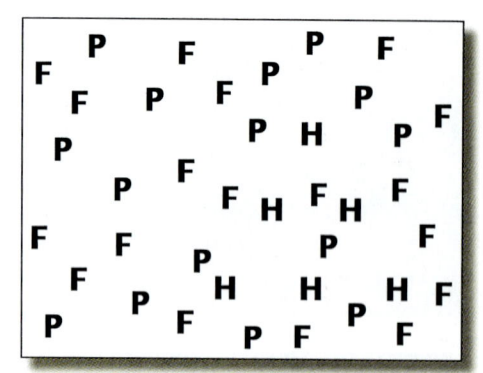

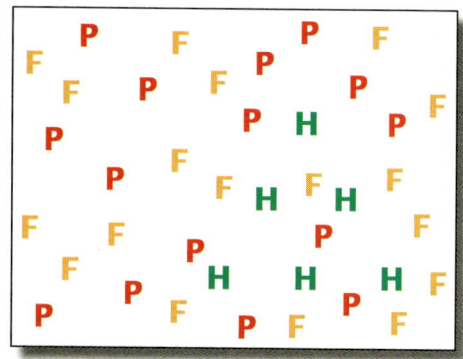

They suggest that similar, but less extensive, connections may underlie widely used metaphors, such as saying that a shirt is "loud," that a cheese is "sharp," or as one wine expert put it, that the taste of a particular wine had "a light straw color with greenish hues" (Martino & Marks, 2001).

The Chemical Senses: Smell and Taste

There are animals without vision, and there are animals without hearing, but there are no animals without some form of chemical sense—some sense that arises from the interaction of chemicals and receptors. **Olfaction** (our sense of smell) detects chemicals that are airborne, or volatile. **Gustation** (our sense of taste) detects chemicals in solution that come into contact with receptors inside the mouth.

Olfaction

People sense odors in the upper part of the nose (see Figure 4.23). Odor molecules can reach olfactory receptors there either by passing directly through the nostrils or by rising through an opening in the palate at the back of the mouth, allowing us to sample odors from food as we eat it. The olfactory receptors themselves are located on the dendrites of specialized neurons that extend into the moist lining of the nose. Odor molecules bind to these receptors, causing depolarization of the dendrites' membrane, which in turn leads to changes in the firing rates of the neurons. A single molecule of an odorous substance can cause a change in the membrane potential of an olfactory neuron, but detection of the odor by a human normally requires about fifty such molecules (Menini, Picco, & Firestein, 1995); the average hot pizza generates lots more than that.

Olfactory neurons are continuously replaced with new ones, as each lives only about two months. Scientists are very interested in this process because, as noted in the chapter on biological aspects of psychology, most neurons cannot divide to create new ones. An understanding of how new olfactory neurons are generated—and how they make appropriate connections in the brain—may someday be helpful in treating brain damage.

Substances that have similar chemical structures tend to have similar odors. The precise means by which olfactory receptors in the nose discriminate various smells and send coded messages about them to the brain has only recently been determined (Buck, 1996). In contrast to vision, which makes use of only four basic receptor types (rods and three kinds of cones), the olfactory system employs about a thousand different types of receptors. The genes for these olfactory receptors make up about 1 to 2 percent of the human genome. A given odor stimulates these receptors to varying degrees, and the combination of receptors stimulated creates codes for a particular odor (Kajiya et al., 2001). The many combinations possible allow humans to discriminate tens of thousands of different odors.

olfaction The sense of smell.
gustation The sense of taste.
olfactory bulb A brain structure that receives messages regarding olfaction.
pheromones Chemicals released by one animal and detected by another that shape the second animal's behavior or physiology.
vomeronasal organ A portion of the mammalian olfactory system that is sensitive to pheromones.

The Chemical Senses: Smell and Taste

figure 4.23

The Olfactory System: The Nose and the Rose
Airborne chemicals from the rose reach the olfactory area through the nostrils and through the back of the mouth. Fibers pass directly from the olfactory area to the olfactory bulb in the brain, and from there signals pass to areas such as the hypothalamus and amygdala, which are involved in emotion.

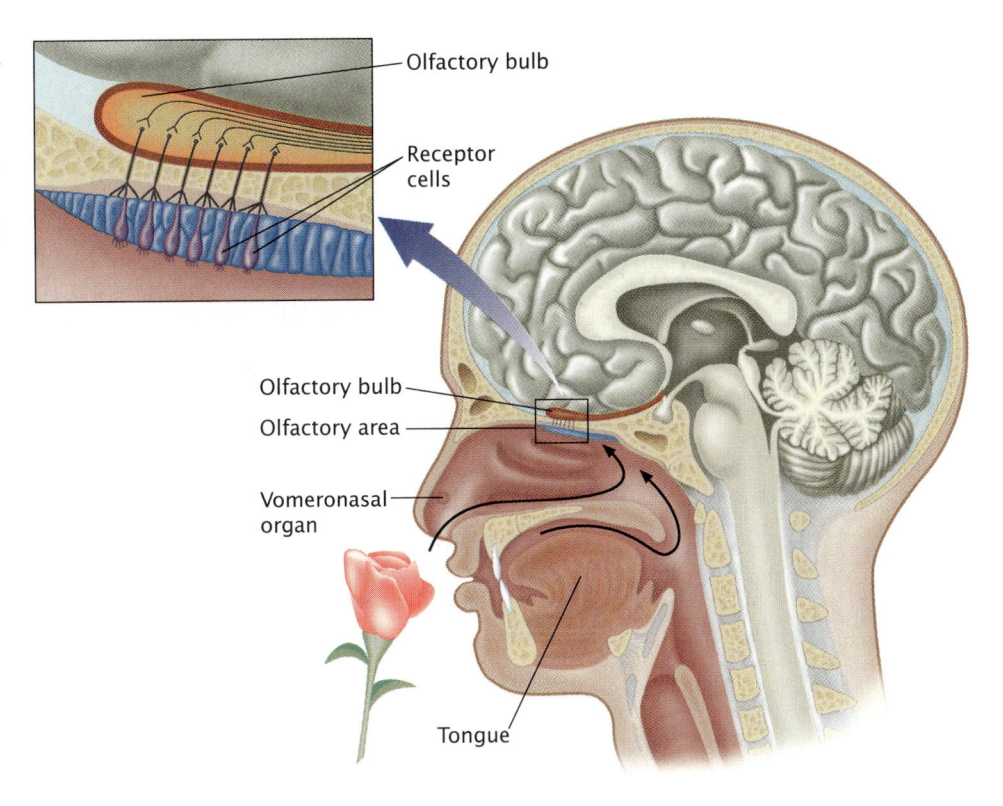

A "Mating Ball" Among snakes there is intense competition for females. Dozens of males will wrap themselves around a single female in a "mating ball." Snakes' forked tongues allow them to sample airborne chemicals at two different points and, hence, to follow an olfactory trail (Schwenk, 1994). Males with the best olfactory tracking abilities are the ones most likely to reach a female first, enabling them to pass on their genes to the next generation.

Olfaction is the only sense that does not send its messages through the thalamus. Instead, axons from neurons in the nose extend through a bony plate and directly into the brain, where they have a synapse in a structure called the **olfactory bulb.** Connections from the olfactory bulb spread diffusely through the brain's olfactory cortex (Zou et al., 2001), and connections are especially plentiful in the amygdala, a part of the brain involved in emotional experience.

These features of the olfactory system may account for the strong relationship between olfaction and emotional memory. For example, associations between a certain experience and a particular odor are not weakened much by time or subsequent experiences (Lawless & Engen, 1977). So catching a whiff of the scent once worn by a lost loved one can reactivate intense feelings of love or sadness associated with that person. Odors can also bring back accurate memories of significant experiences linked with them (Engen, Gilmore, & Mair, 1991).

The mechanisms of olfaction are remarkably similar in species ranging from humans to worms. Different species vary considerably, however, in their sensitivity to smell, and in the degree to which they depend on it for survival. For example, humans have about 9 million olfactory neurons, whereas there are about 225 million such neurons in dogs, which are far more dependent on smell to identify food, territory, and receptive mates. In addition, dogs and many other species have an accessory olfactory system that is able to detect pheromones. **Pheromones** (pronounced "FAIR-o-mones") are chemicals that are released by one animal and, when detected by another, can shape the second animal's behavior or physiology. For example, when male snakes detect a chemical exuded on the skin of female snakes, they are stimulated to "court" the female.

In mammals, pheromones can be nonvolatile chemicals that animals lick and pass into a portion of the olfactory system called the **vomeronasal organ.** In female mice, for example, the vomeronasal organ detects chemicals in the male's urine; by this means a male can cause a female to ovulate and become sexually receptive, and an unfamiliar male can cause a pregnant female to abort her pregnancy (Bruce, 1969).

The role of pheromones in humans is much more controversial. Some perfume companies want potential customers to believe that they have created sexual attractants that act as pheromones to subconsciously influence the behavior of desirable partners. At the other extreme are those who argue that in humans, the vomeronasal organ is an utterly nonfunctional vestige, like the appendix. The best current scientific evidence suggests that the human vomeronasal organ is capable of responding to certain hormonal substances and can influence certain hormonal secretions (Berliner et al., 1996). Further, odorants that cannot be consciously detected have been shown to influence mood, suggesting a pheromone-like action (Jacob & McClintock, 2000), and a possible gene for pheromone receptors has been found in humans (Rodriguez et al., 2000). Pheromones themselves are definitely capable of producing physiological changes in humans that are related to reproduction. For example, pheromonal signals secreted in the perspiration of a woman can shorten or prolong the menstrual cycle of other women nearby (Stern & McClintock, 1998). In such cases, pheromones are responsible for *menstrual synchrony*, the tendency of women living together to menstruate at the same time. However, despite some suggestive findings (e.g., Cutler, Friedmann, & McCoy, 1998), there is still no solid evidence for a sexual attractant pheromone in humans, or even in nonhuman primates.

Nevertheless, learned associations between certain odors and emotional experiences may enhance a person's readiness for sex. People also use olfactory information in other social situations. For example, after just a few hours of contact, mothers can usually identify their newborn babies by the infants' smell (Porter, Cernich, & McLaughlin, 1983). And if infants are breastfed, they can discriminate their own mothers' odor from that of other breastfeeding women, and appear to be comforted by it (Porter, 1991). In fact, individual mammals, including humans, have a distinct "odortype," which is determined by their immune cells and other inherited physiological factors (Beauchamp et al., 1995). During pregnancy, a woman's own odortype combines with the odortype of her fetus to form a third odortype. Each of these three odors is distinguishable, suggesting that recognition of odortypes may help establish the mother-infant bonds discussed in the chapter on human development.

Gustation

The chemical sense system in the mouth is gustation, or taste. The receptors for taste are in the taste buds, which are grouped together in structures called **papillae** (pronounced "pa-PILL-ee"). Normally, there are about 10,000 taste buds in a person's mouth, mostly on the tongue but also on the roof of the mouth and on the back of the throat.

In contrast to the olfactory system, which can discriminate thousands of different odors, the human taste system detects only a few elementary sensations. The most familiar of these are sweet, sour, bitter, and salty. Each taste bud responds best to one or two of these categories, but it also responds weakly to others. The sensation of a particular substance appears to result from the responses of taste buds that are relatively sensitive to a specific category. Behavioral studies and electrical recordings from taste neurons have also established two additional taste sensations (Rolls, 1997). One, called *umami*, enhances other tastes and is produced by certain proteins, as well as by monosodium glutamate (MSG). The other, called *astringent*, is the taste produced by tannins, which are found in teas, for example.

Different tastes are transduced into neural activity by quite different types of taste receptors, and in different ways (Stewart, DeSimone, & Hill, 1997). For example, sweet and bitter are signaled when chemicals fit into specific receptor sites (Montmayeur et al., 2001), whereas sour and salty act through more direct effects on the ion channels in membranes of taste cells. Knowledge of the chemistry of sweetness is allowing scientists to design new chemicals that fit into sweetness receptors and taste thousands of times sweeter than sugar. Many of these substances are

---

papillae Structures on the tongue containing groups of taste receptors, or taste buds.

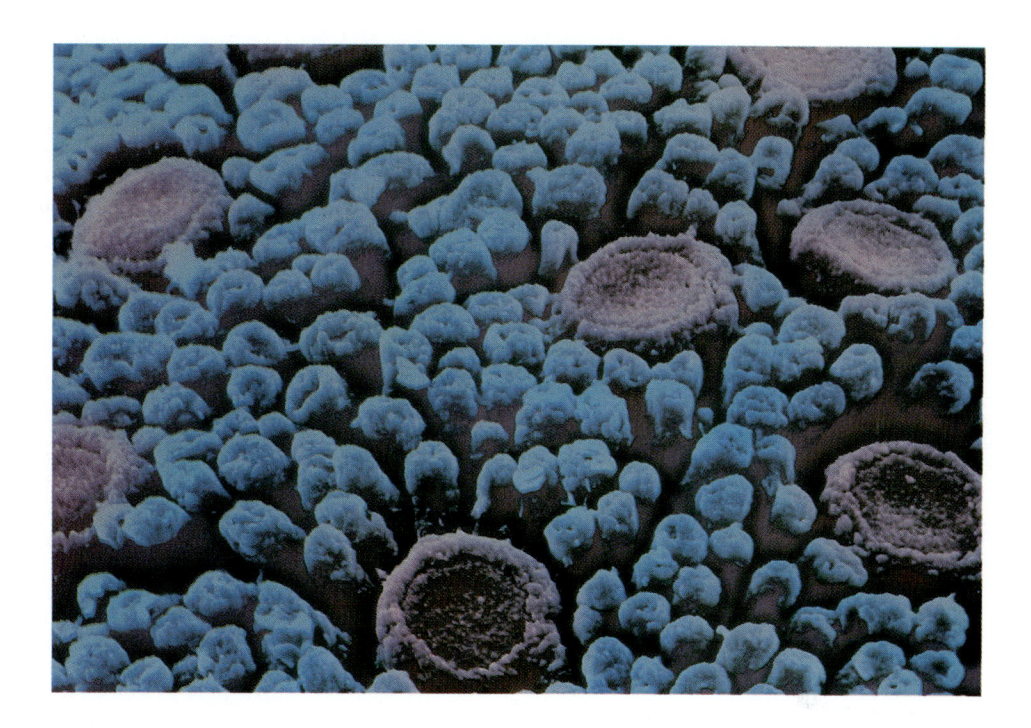

Taste Receptors Taste buds are grouped into structures called *papillae*. Two kinds of papillae are visible in this greatly enlarged photo of the surface of the human tongue.

figure 4.24

Are You a Supertaster?

TRY THIS This photo shows the large number of papillae on the tongue of a "supertaster." If you don't mind a temporary stain on your mouth and teeth, you can look at your own papillae by painting the front of your tongue with a cotton swab soaked in blue food coloring. Distribute the dye by moving your tongue around and swallowing; then look into a magnifying mirror as you shine a flashlight on your tongue. The pink circles you see against the blue background are papillae, each of which has about six taste buds buried in its surface. Get several friends to do this test, and you will see that genes create wide individual differences in taste bud density.

now being tested for safety and may soon allow people to enjoy low-calorie hot-fudge sundaes.

A taste component in its own right, saltiness also enhances the taste of food by suppressing bitterness (Breslin & Beauchamp, 1997). In animals, taste responses to salt are determined during early development, before and after birth. Research with animals has shown that if mothers are put on a low-salt diet, their offspring are less likely to prefer salt (Hill & Przekop, 1988). In humans, experiences with salty foods over the first four years of life may alter the sensory systems that detect salt and contribute to enduring preferences for salty foods (Hill & Mistretta, 1990).

There may be genetically determined differences in the ability to taste things. About 25 percent of the population are "supertasters"—individuals who have an especially large number of papillae on their tongues (Bartoshuk, 2000). Supertasters have thousands of taste buds, whereas "nontasters" have only hundreds of buds (see Figure 4.24). Most people fall between these extremes. Supertasters are more sensitive than other people to bitterness, as revealed in their reaction to foods such as broccoli, soy products, and grapefruit. Having different numbers of taste buds may help account for differences in people's food intake, as well as weight problems. For example, Linda Bartoshuk has found that compared with overweight people, thin people have many more taste buds (Duffy et al., 1999). Perhaps they do not have to eat as much to experience the good tastes of food.

Smell, Taste, and Flavor

If you have a stuffy nose, everything tastes like cardboard. Why? Because smell and taste act as two components of a single system, known as *flavor* (Rozin, 1982). Most of the properties that make food taste good are actually odors detected by the olfactory system, not activities of the taste system. The olfactory and gustatory pathways converge in the *orbitofrontal cortex* (Rolls, 1997), where neurons also respond to the sight and texture of food. The responses of neurons in this "flavor cortex" are also influenced by conditions of hunger and satiety ("fullness").

Both tastes and odors prompt strong emotional responses. For tastes, the reaction to bitter flavors is inborn, but the associations of emotions with odors are all learned (Bartoshuk, 1991). Many animals easily learn taste aversions to particular

in review	Smell and Taste	
Aspect of Sensory System	**Elements**	**Key Characteristics**
Energy	Smell: volatile chemicals Taste: chemicals in solution	The amount, intensity, and location of the chemicals determine taste and smell sensations.
Structures of taste and smell	Smell: chemical receptors in the mucous membrane of the nose Taste: taste buds grouped in papillae in the mouth	Odor and taste molecules stimulate chemical receptors.
Pathways to the brain	Olfactory bulb and taste buds	Axons from the nose bypass the thalamus and extend directly to the olfactory bulb.

foods when the taste is associated with nausea, but humans learn aversions to odors more readily than to tastes (Bartoshuk & Wolfe, 1990).

Variations in one's nutritional state affect taste and flavor, as well as the motivation to consume particular foods. For example, food deprivation or salt deficiency makes sweet or salty things taste better. Intake of protein and fat are influenced more indirectly. Molecules of protein and fat have no inherent taste or smell; the tastes and smells of foods that contain these nutrients actually come from small amounts of other volatile substances. So adjustments in the intake of these nutrients are based on associations between olfactory cues from the volatile substances and the nutritional consequences of eating the foods (Bartoshuk, 1991). These findings have implications for dieting, which is discussed in the chapter on motivation and emotion.

Flavor includes other characteristics of food as well: its tactile properties (how it feels in your mouth) and, especially, its temperature. Temperature does not alter saltiness, but warm foods are experienced as sweeter; in fact, simply warming a person's taste receptors creates a sensation of sweetness (Cruz & Green, 2000). Aromas released from warm food rise from the mouth into the nose and create more flavor sensations. This is why some people find hot pizza delicious and cold pizza disgusting. Spicy "hot" foods actually stimulate pain fibers in the mouth because they contain a substance called *capsaicin* (pronounced "kap-SAY-uh-sin"), which opens specific ion channels in pain neurons that are also opened by heat. As a result, these foods are experienced as physiologically "hot" (Caterina et al., 1997). Why do people eat spicy foods even though they stimulate pain? The practice may have originated because many "hot" spices have antibacterial properties. In fact, researchers have found a strong correlation between frequent use of antibacterial spices and living in climates that promote bacterial contamination (Billing & Sherman, 1998). ("In Review: Smell and Taste" summarizes our discussion of these senses.)

Somatic Senses and the Vestibular System

Some senses are not located in a specific organ, such as the eye or the ear. These are the **somatic senses**, also called *somatosensory systems*, which are spread throughout the body. The somatic senses include the skin senses of touch, temperature, and pain, as well as kinesthesia, the sense that tells the brain where the parts of the body are. Closely related to kinesthesia is the vestibular system, which tells the brain about the position and movements of the head. Although not strictly a somatosensory system, the vestibular system will also be considered in this section.

Touch and Temperature

Touch is crucial. People can function and prosper without vision, hearing, or smell, but a person without touch would have difficulty surviving. Without a sense of touch, you could not even swallow food, because you could not tell where it was in your mouth and throat.

Stimulus and Receptors for Touch

The energy detected by the sense of touch is the mechanical deformation of tissue, usually of the skin. The skin covers nearly two square yards of surface and weighs more than twenty pounds. The hairs distributed virtually everywhere on the skin do not sense anything directly, but when bent, they deform the skin beneath them. The receptors that transduce this deformation into neural activity are in, or just below, the skin.

Many nerve endings in the skin are candidates for the role of touch receptor. Some neurons come from the spinal cord, enter the skin, and simply end; these are called *free nerve endings*. Many other neurons end in a variety of elaborate, specialized structures. However, there is generally little relationship between the type of nerve ending and the type of sensory information carried by the neuron. Many types of nerve endings respond to mechanical stimuli, but the exact process through which they transduce mechanical energy is still unknown. These somatosensory neurons are unusual in that they have no dendrites. Their cell bodies are outside the spinal cord, and their axon splits and extends both to the skin and to the spinal cord. Action potentials travel from the nerve endings in the skin to the spinal cord, where they communicate across a synapse to dendrites of other neurons.

We do more than just passively respond to whatever happens to come in contact with our bodies. For humans, touch is also an active sense that is used to get specific information. In much the same way as you can look as well as just see, you can also touch as well as feel. When people are involved in active sensing, they usually use the part of the sensory apparatus that has the greatest sensitivity. For vision, this is the fovea; for touch, the fingertips. (The area of primary somatosensory cortex devoted to the fingertips is correspondingly large.) Fingertip touch is the principal way people explore the textures of surfaces. It can be extremely sensitive, as evidenced by blind people who can read Braille as rapidly as 200 words per minute (Foulke, 1991).

Adaptation of Touch Receptors

Constant input from all your touch neurons would provide an abundance of unnecessary information. Once you get dressed, for example, you do not need to be constantly reminded that you are wearing clothes. Thanks in part to the process of adaptation mentioned earlier, you do not continue to feel your clothes against your skin.

Changes in touch (as when a shoelace breaks, making your shoe feel loose) constitute the most important sensory information. The touch sense emphasizes these changes and filters out the excess information. How? Typically, a touch neuron responds with a burst of firing when a stimulus is applied, then quickly returns to baseline firing rates, even though the stimulus may still be in contact with the skin. If the touch pressure increases, the neuron again responds with an increase in firing rate, but then it again slows down. A few neurons adapt more slowly, continuing to fire at an elevated rate as long as pressure is applied to the skin. By attending to this input, you can sense a constant stimulus (try doing this by focusing on sensations from your glasses or shoes).

---

somatic senses Senses of touch, temperature, pain, and kinesthesia.

Coding and Representation of Touch Information The sense of touch codes information about two aspects of an object in contact with the skin: its weight and its location. The *intensity* of the stimulus—how heavy it is—is coded by both the firing rate of individual neurons and the number of neurons stimulated. A heavy object produces a higher rate of firing and stimulates more neurons than a light object. The *location* of touch is coded much as it is for vision: by the spatial organization of the information.

Touch information is organized such that signals from neighboring points on the skin stay next to one another other, even as they ascend from the skin through the spinal cord to the thalamus and on to the somatosensory cortex. So just as there is a topographical map of the visual field in the brain, the area of cortex that receives touch information resembles a map of the surface of the body (see Figure 3.17). As with the other senses, these representations are contralateral; that is, input from the left side of the body goes to the right side of the brain, and vice versa. In nonhuman primates, however, touch information from each hand is sent to both sides of the brain. This arrangement appears to amplify information from manual exploration of objects and to improve feedback from hand movements (Iwamura, Iriki, & Tanaka, 1994).

Temperature

When you dig your toes into a sandy summer beach, the pleasant experience you get comes partly from the sensation of warmth. Touch and temperature seem to be separate senses, and to some extent they are; but the difference between the two senses is not always clear.

Some of the skin's sensory neurons respond to a change in temperature, but not to simple contact. There are "warm fibers," which are nerve fibers that increase their firing rates when the temperature changes in the range of about 95 to 115°F (35 to 47°C). Temperatures above this range are painful and stimulate different fibers. Other nerve fibers are "cold fibers"; they respond to a broad range of cool temperatures. However, many of the fibers that respond to temperature also respond to touch, so sensations of touch and temperature sometimes interact. For example, warm and cold objects can feel up to 250 percent heavier than body-temperature objects (Stevens & Hooper, 1982). Also, if you touch an object made up of alternating warm and cool bars, you will have the sensation of intense heat (Thunberg, 1896, cited in Craig & Bushnell, 1994).

Stimulation of the touch sense can have some interesting psychological and physiological effects. For example, premature infants gain weight 47 percent faster when they are given massages; they do not eat more but, rather, process the food more efficiently. In children with asthma, massage therapy increases air flow (Field et al., 1998); in children with arthritis, it reduces pain and lowers stress hormone levels (Field et al., 1997). In adults, massage can reduce anxiety, increase brainwave (EEG) patterns associated with alertness, and improve performance on math tests (Field et al., 1996).

Pain

The skin senses can convey a great deal of pleasure, but a change in the intensity of the same kind of stimulation can create a distinctly different sensation: pain. Pain provides you with information about the impact of the world on your body; it can tell you, "A hammer just crushed your left thumb." Pain also has a distinctly negative emotional component. Researchers have focused on the information-carrying aspects of pain, its emotional components, and the various ways that the brain can adjust the amount of pain that reaches consciousness.

Pain as an Information Sense The information-carrying aspect of pain is very similar to that of touch and temperature. The receptors for pain are free nerve endings. As mentioned earlier, for example, capsaicin, the active ingredient in

The Complex Nature of Pain If pain were based only on the nature of incoming stimuli, this participant in a purification ceremony in Singapore would be hurting. However, as described in the chapter on consciousness, the experience of pain is a complex phenomenon affected by psychological and biological variables that can make it more, or as in this case less, intense.

Somatic Senses and the Vestibular System

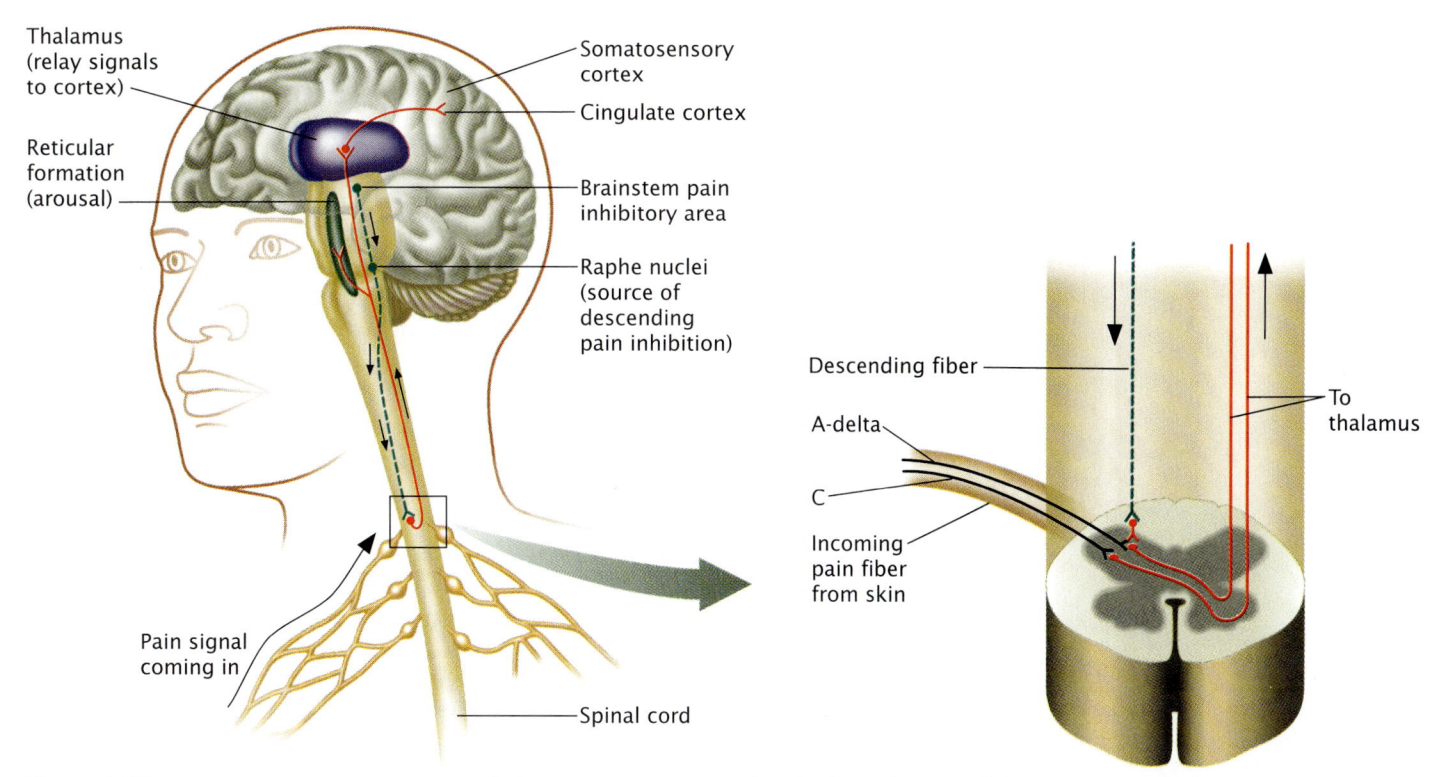

figure 4.25
Pain Pathways

Pain messages are carried to the brain by way of the spinal cord. Myelinated *A-delta fibers* carry information about sharp pain. Unmyelinated *C fibers* carry several types of pain, including chronic, dull aches. Pain fibers make synapses in the reticular formation, causing arousal. They also project to the thalamus and from there to the cortex.

chili peppers, creates pain in the mouth by specifically stimulating these pain nerve endings. Painful stimuli cause the release of chemicals that fit into specialized receptors in pain neurons, causing them to fire. The axons of pain-sensing neurons release neurotransmitters not only near the spinal cord, sending information to the brain, but also near the skin, causing local inflammation.

Two types of nerve fibers carry pain signals from the skin to the spinal cord. *A-delta fibers* carry sharp, pricking pain sensations; they are myelinated to carry the sharp pain message quickly. *C fibers* carry chronic, dull aches and burning sensations. Some of these same C fibers also respond to nonpainful touch, but with a different pattern of firing.

Both A-delta and C fibers carry pain impulses into the spinal cord, where they form synapses with neurons that carry the pain signals to the thalamus and other parts of the brain (see Figure 4.25). Different pain neurons are activated by different degrees of painful stimulation. Numerous types of neurotransmitters are used by different pain neurons, a phenomenon that has allowed the development of a variety of new drugs for pain management.

The role of the cerebral cortex in experiencing pain is still being explored. Earlier studies of humans undergoing brain surgery for epilepsy concluded that pain has little, if any, cortical representation (Penfield & Rasmussen, 1968). More recently, functional magnetic resonance imaging (MRI) studies of healthy volunteers have compared cortical activity during a pain experience with cortical activity during an attention-demanding task (Davis et al., 1997). The scans showed activation of the somatosensory cortex under both conditions, and additional activity during pain in the *anterior cingulate cortex,* an evolutionarily primitive region thought to be important in emotions. When hypnosis has been used to manipulate the unpleasantness of pain, there are corresponding changes in cingulate cortex activity but not in somatosensory cortex activity. This is yet another finding consistent with the hypothesized role of this brain region in pain perception (Rainville et al., 1997).

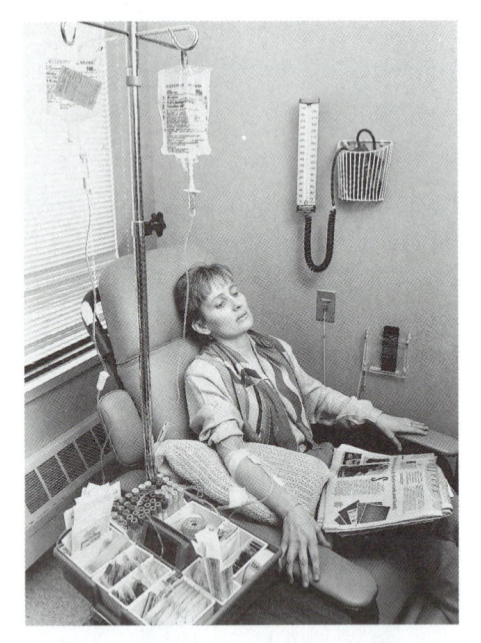

Easing Pain Candy containing capsaicin is sometimes given for the treatment of painful mouth sores associated with cancer chemotherapy (Berger et al., 1995). Capsaicin is what makes chili peppers "hot," but eating enough of it results in desensitization and a corresponding reduction in pain sensations (Bevan & Geppetti, 1994).

Natural Analgesia The stress of athletic exertion causes the release of endorphins, natural painkillers that have been associated with pleasant feelings nicknamed "runner's high."

Research also suggests that pain can be experienced without any external stimulation of pain receptors. In such cases, the pain appears to originate in the thalamus and in cortical regions of the brain (Canavero & Bonicalzi, 1998; Gawande, 1998).

Emotional Aspects of Pain

All senses can have emotional components, most of which are learned responses. For example, the smell of baking cookies can make you feel good if it has been associated with happy childhood times. The emotional response to pain is more direct. Specific pathways carry an emotional component of the painful stimulus to areas of the hindbrain and reticular formation (see Figure 4.25), as well as to the cingulate cortex via the thalamus (Craig et al., 1994; Johansen, Fields, & Manning, 2001).

Nevertheless, the overall emotional response to pain depends greatly on cognitive factors (Keefe & France, 1999; Pincus & Morley, 2001). For example, experimenters compared responses to a painful stimulus in people who were informed about the nature of the stimulus, and when to expect it, with responses in people who were not similarly informed. Knowing about pain seemed to make it less objectionable, even though the sensation was reported to be just as noticeable (Mayer & Price, 1982). Another factor affecting emotional responses to pain sensations is the use of pain-reducing strategies, such as focusing on distracting thoughts (Young et al., 1995).

Modulation of Pain: The Gate Control Theory

Pain is extremely useful, because in the long run it protects you from harm. However, there are times when enough is enough. Fortunately, the nervous system has several mechanisms for controlling the experience of pain.

One explanation of how the nervous system controls the amount of pain that reaches the brain is the **gate control theory** (Melzack & Wall, 1965). It holds that there is a "gate" in the spinal cord that either lets pain impulses travel upward to the brain or blocks their progress. The details of the original formulation of this theory turned out to be incorrect, but later work supports the idea that natural mechanisms can block pain sensations (Stanton-Hicks & Salamon, 1997). For example, input from other skin senses can come into the spinal cord at the same time the pain gets there and "take over" the pathways that the pain impulses would have used. This appears to be why rubbing the skin around a wound temporarily reduces the pain that is felt, and why electrical stimulation of the skin around a painful spot relieves the pain. Gate control theory may also partially explain why scratching relieves itching, because itch sensations involve activity in fibers located close to pain fibers (Andrew & Craig, 2001).

The brain can also close the gate to pain impulses by sending signals down the spinal cord. The control of sensation by messages descending from the brain is a common aspect of sensory systems (Willis, 1988). In the case of pain, these messages from the brain block incoming pain signals at spinal cord synapses. The result is **analgesia**, the absence of the sensation of pain in the presence of a normally painful stimulus. For example, if part of a rat's hindbrain is electrically stimulated, pain signals generated in the skin never reach the brain (Reynolds, 1969). Permanently implanting stimulating electrodes in the same region of the human brain has reduced severe pain in some patients, but unfortunately it also produces a profound sense of impending doom (Hoffert, 1992).

Natural Analgesics

At least two substances play a role in the brain's ability to block pain signals: (1) the neurotransmitter *serotonin*, which is released by neurons descending from the brain, and (2) natural opiates called *endorphins*. As described in the chapter on biological aspects of psychology, endorphins are natural painkillers that act as neurotransmitters at many levels of the pain pathway, including the spinal cord, where they block the synapses of the fibers that carry pain signals. Endorphins may also relieve pain when the adrenal and pituitary glands secrete them into the bloodstream as hormones. The more endorphin receptors a person has inherited, the more pain tolerance that person has (Benjamin, Wilson, & Mogil, 1999; Uhl, Sora, & Wang, 1999).

Several conditions are known to cause the body to ease its own pain. For example, endorphins are released by immune cells that arrive at sites of inflammation (Cabot, 2001). And during the late stages of pregnancy, an endorphin system is activated that will reduce the mother's labor pains (Dawson-Basoa & Gintzler, 1997). An endorphin system is also activated when people believe they are receiving a painkiller even when they are not (Benedetti & Amanzio, 1997); this may be one reason for the placebo effect, discussed in the chapter on research in psychology. Remarkably, the resulting pain inhibition is experienced in the part of the body where it was expected to occur, but not elsewhere (Benedetti, Arduino, & Amanzio, 1999). Physical or psychological stress, too, can activate natural analgesic systems. Stress-induced release of endorphins may account for cases in which injured soldiers and athletes continue to perform in the heat of battle or competition with no apparent pain.

There are also mechanisms for reactivating pain sensitivity once a crisis is past. Studies with animals show that they can learn that certain situations signal "safety," and that these safety signals prompt the release of a neurotransmitter that counteracts endorphins' analgesic effects (Wiertelak, Maier, & Watkins, 1992). Blocking these "safety signals" increases the painkilling effects brought on by a placebo (Benedetti & Amanzio, 1997).

THINKING CRITICALLY

Does Acupuncture Relieve Pain?

Acupuncture is an ancient and widely used treatment in Asian medicine that is alleged to relieve pain. The method is based on the idea that body energy flows along lines called *channels* (Vincent & Richardson, 1986). There are fourteen main channels, and a person's health supposedly depends on the balance of energy flowing in them. Stimulating the channels by inserting very thin needles into the skin and twirling them is said to restore a balanced flow of energy. The needles produce an aching and tingling sensation called *Teh-ch'i* at the site of stimulation, but they relieve pain at distant, seemingly unrelated parts of the body.

- **What am I being asked to believe or accept?**

Acupuncturists assert that twirling a needle in the skin can relieve pain caused by everything from tooth extraction to cancer.

- **What evidence is available to support the assertion?**

There is no scientific evidence for the existence of energy channels as described in the theory underlying acupuncture. However, as described in the chapter on biological aspects of psychology, some of the sites for stimulation are very near peripheral nerves, and there is evidence from MRI scans that stimulating these sites changes activity in brain regions related to the targets of treatment (Cho et al., 1998).

What about the more specific assertions that acupuncture relieves pain and that it does so through direct physical mechanisms? Numerous studies show positive results in 50 to 80 percent of patients treated by acupuncture for various kinds of pain (Richardson & Vincent, 1986). In one controlled study of headache pain, for example, 33 percent of the patients in a placebo group improved following mock electrical nerve stimulation (which is about the usual proportion of people responding to a placebo), but 53 percent reported reduced pain following real acupuncture (Dowson, Lewith, & Machin, 1985). Another headache study found both acupuncture and drugs to be superior to a placebo. Each reduced the frequency of headaches, but the drugs were more effective than acupuncture at

gate control theory A theory suggesting that a functional "gate" in the spinal cord can either let pain impulses travel upward to the brain or block their progress.

analgesia The absence of pain sensations in the presence of a normally painful stimulus.

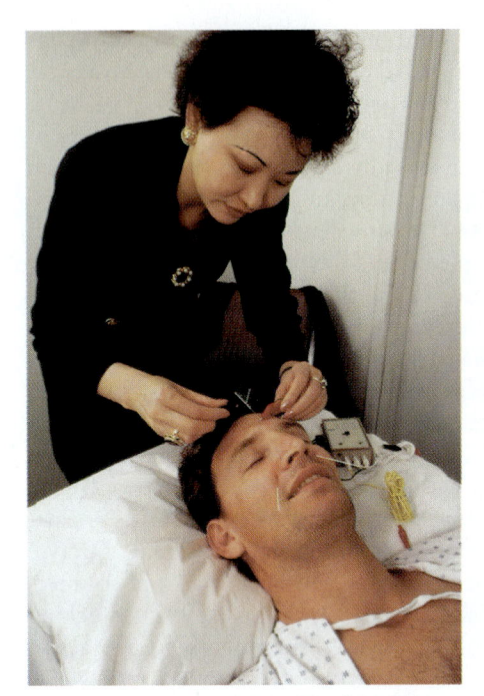

How Does Acupuncture Work? This acupuncturist is inserting fine needles in her patient's face in hopes of treating poor blood circulation in his hands and feet. Acupuncture treatments appear to alleviate a wide range of problems, including many kinds of pain, but the mechanisms through which it works are not yet determined.

reducing the severity of headache pain (Hesse, Mogelvang, & Simonsen, 1994). Such well-controlled studies are rare, however, and their results are often contradictory (Ter Riet, Kleijnen, & Knipschild, 1990). Recent studies of patients with back or neck pain, for example, found acupuncture to be no better than a placebo or massage therapy (Cherkin et al., 2001; Irnich et al., 2001).

There is evidence that acupuncture activates the endorphin system. It is associated with the release of endorphins in the brain, and drugs that slow the breakdown of opiates also prolong the analgesia produced by acupuncture (He, 1987). Furthermore, the pain-reducing effects of acupuncture during electrical stimulation of a tooth can be reversed by *naloxone,* a substance that blocks the painkilling effects of endorphins (and other opiate drugs). This finding suggests that acupuncture somehow activates the body's natural painkilling system. In cases where acupuncture activates endorphins, is this activation brought about only through the placebo effect? Probably not entirely, because acupuncture produces naloxone-reversible analgesia in monkeys and rats, who could not have developed positive expectancies by reading about acupuncture (Ha et al., 1981; Kishioka et al., 1994).

• Are there alternative ways of interpreting the evidence?

Yes. Evidence about acupuncture might be interpreted as simply confirming that the body's painkilling system can be stimulated by external means. Acupuncture may merely provide one activating method; there may be other, even more efficient methods for doing so. We already know, for example, that successful placebo treatments for human pain appear to operate by activating the endorphin system.

• What additional evidence would help to evaluate the alternatives?

More placebo-controlled studies of acupuncture are needed, but it is difficult to control for the placebo effect in acupuncture treatment, especially in double-blind fashion (e.g., Kaptchuk, 2001). (How could a therapist not know whether the treatment being given was acupuncture or not? And from the patient's perspective, what placebo treatment could look and feel like having a needle inserted and twirled in the skin?) Nevertheless, researchers have tried to separate the psychological and physical effects of acupuncture—for example, by using sham needles; mock electrical nerve stimulation, in which electrodes are attached to the skin but no electrical stimulation is given; or stimulation at other sites on the skin (Park, White, & Ernst, 2001).

Researchers also need to go beyond focusing on the effects of acupuncture to consider the general relationship between internal painkilling systems and external methods for stimulating them. Regarding acupuncture itself, scientists do not yet know what factors govern whether it will activate the endorphin system. Other important unknowns include the types of pain for which acupuncture is most effective, the types of patients who respond best, and the precise procedures that are most effective.

• What conclusions are most reasonable?

There seems little doubt that in some circumstances, acupuncture relieves pain. It is not a panacea, however. For example, committees convened in the United States and the United Kingdom have concluded that acupuncture can be effective for the treatment of pain and nausea (British Medical Association, 2000; National Institutes of Health, 1998), but more than $2 million in research has failed to show that acupuncture is better than the best antinausea drugs or conventional painkilling procedures (Taub, 1998). While critics argue that further expenditures for acupuncture research are not warranted, proponents point out that acupuncture's effects can go beyond pain reduction. One study, for example, found that preoperative acupuncture reduced postoperative pain and nausea, decreased the need for pain-relieving drugs, and reduced patients' stress responses (Kotani et al., 2001). Further studies are likely to continue; the quality of their methodology and the nature of their results will determine whether acupuncture finds a prominent place in Western medicine.

Balancing Act The smooth coordination of all physical movement, from scratching your nose to complex feats of balance, depends on kinesthesia, the sense that provides information about where each part of the body is in relation to all the others.

proprioceptive senses The sensory systems that allow us to know about where we are and what each part of our body is doing.

vestibular sense The proprioceptive sense that provides information about the position of the head (and hence the body) in space and about its movements.

vestibular sacs Organs in the inner ear that connect the semicircular canals and the cochlea, and contribute to the body's sense of balance.

otoliths Small crystals in the fluid-filled vestibular sacs of the inner ear that, when shifted by gravity, stimulate nerve cells that inform the brain of the position of the head.

semicircular canals Tubes in the inner ear whose fluid, when shifted by head movements, stimulates nerve cells that tell the brain about those movements.

kinesthesia The sense that tells you where the parts of your body are with respect to one another.

Proprioception

Most sensory systems receive information from the external world, such as the light reflected from a flower or the feeling of cool water. But as far as the brain is concerned, the rest of the body is "out there," too. You know about the position of your body and what each of its parts is doing only because sensory systems provide this information to the brain. These sensory systems are called **proprioceptive senses** (*proprioceptive* means "received from one's own").

Vestibular Sense

The **vestibular sense** tells the brain about the position of the head (and hence the body) in space and about its general movements. It is often thought of as the *sense of balance*. People usually become aware of the vestibular sense only when they overstimulate it and become dizzy.

The organs for the vestibular sense are two vestibular sacs and three semicircular canals that are part of the inner ear. (You can see the semicircular canals in Figure 4.3; the vestibular sacs connect these canals and the cochlea.) The **vestibular sacs** are filled with fluid and contain small crystals called **otoliths** ("ear stones") that rest on hair endings. The **semicircular canals** are fluid-filled, arc-shaped tubes; tiny hairs extend into the fluid in the canals. When your head moves, the otoliths shift in the vestibular sacs and the fluid moves in the semicircular canals, stimulating hair endings. This process activates neurons that travel with the auditory nerve, signaling to the brain the amount and direction of head movement.

The vestibular system has neural connections to the cerebellum, to the part of the autonomic nervous system (ANS) that affects the digestive system, and to the muscles of the eyes. The connections to the cerebellum help coordinate bodily movements. The connections to the ANS are partly responsible for the nausea that sometimes follows overstimulation of the vestibular system—on amusement park rides, for example. Finally, the connections to the eye muscles create *vestibular-ocular reflexes*. For instance, when your head moves in one direction, your eyes reflexively move in the opposite direction. This reflex allows your eyes to fixate on a point in space even when your head is moving, so you can track a ball in flight as you are running to catch it. You can experience this reflex by having a friend spin you around on a stool for a while; when you stop, try to fix your gaze on one point in the room. You will be temporarily unable to do so, because the excitation of the vestibular system will cause your eyes to move repeatedly in the direction opposite to that in which you were spinning. Because vestibular reflexes adapt to the lack of gravity in outer space, astronauts returning to earth have postural and movement difficulties until their vestibular systems readjust to the effects of gravity (Paloski, 1998).

Kinesthesia

The sense that tells you where the parts of your body are with respect to one another is **kinesthesia** (pronounced "kin-es-THEE-zha"). You probably do not think much about kinesthetic information, but you definitely use it, and you can demonstrate it for yourself. Close your eyes, hold your arms out in front of you, and try to touch your two index fingertips together. You probably did this well because your kinesthetic sense told you where each finger was with respect to your body. You also depend on kinesthetic information to guide all your movements. Otherwise, it would be impossible to develop or improve any motor skill, from basic walking to complex athletic movements. These movement patterns become simple and fluid because with practice, the brain uses kinesthetic information automatically.

Normally, kinesthetic information comes primarily from the joints but it also comes from muscles. Receptors in muscle fibers send information to the brain about the stretching of muscles (McCloskey, 1978). When the position of the bones

in review: Body Senses

Sense	Energy	Conversion of Physical Energy to Nerve Activity	Pathways and Characteristics
Touch	Mechanical deformation of skin	Skin receptors (may be stimulated by hair on the skin)	Nerve endings respond to changes in weight (intensity) and location of touch.
Temperature	Heat	Sensory neurons in the skin	Changes in temperature are detected by warm-sensing and cool-sensing fibers. Temperature interacts with touch.
Pain	Increases with intensity of touch or temperature	Free nerve endings in or near the skin surface	Changes in intensity cause the release of chemicals detected by receptors in pain neurons. Some fibers convey sharp pain; others convey dull aches and burning sensations.
Kinesthesia	Mechanical energy of joint and muscle movement	Receptors in muscle fibers	Information from muscle fibers is sent to the spinal cord, thalamus, cerebellum, and cortex.

changes, receptors in the joints transduce this mechanical energy into neural activity, providing information about both the rate of change and the angle of the bones. This coded information goes to the spinal cord and is sent from there to the thalamus, along with sensory information from the skin. Eventually the information goes to the cerebellum and to the somatosensory cortex (see Figures 3.13 and 3.16), both of which are involved in the smooth coordination of movements

Proprioception is a critical sense for success in physical therapy and rehabilitative medicine, especially for people who have to relearn how to move their muscles after strokes or other problems. Research in a branch of physics called *nonlinear dynamics* has been applied to problems in proprioception. Utilizing the discovery that the right amount of random, background noise can actually improve the detection of signals, rehabilitation neurologists have found that adding a small amount of vibration (or "noise") to muscle and joint sensations dramatically increases patients' ability to detect joint movements and position (Glanz, 1997). (See "In Review: Body Senses" for a summary of our discussion of touch, temperature, pain, and kinesthesia.)

FOCUS ON RESEARCH METHODS

The Case of the Disembodied Woman

Early in this chapter we discussed the problem of coding sensation—of translating the physical properties of some stimulus into neural signals that make sense to the brain. In later sections we described how this problem is "solved" for the different senses. But what happens when the brain does not receive the sensory information it needs? The most common examples of this situation are deafness and blindness, but in the case study described next, a person suffered the loss of a proprioceptive sense.

Summary

Sound

The *frequency* (which is related to *wavelength*) and *amplitude* of sound waves approximately correspond to the psychological dimensions of *pitch* and *loudness*, respectively. *Timbre*, the quality of sound, depends on complex wave patterns added to the lowest frequency of the sound.

The Ear

The energy from sound waves is collected and transmitted to the *cochlea* through a series of accessory structures, including the *tympanic membrane*. Transduction occurs when sound energy stimulates hair cells of the organ of Corti on the *basilar membrane* of the cochlea, which in turn stimulate the *auditory nerve*.

Coding Intensity and Frequency

The intensity of a sound stimulus is coded by the firing rate of auditory neurons. *Place theory* describes the coding of higher frequencies: They are coded by the place on the basilar membrane where the wave envelope peaks. Each neuron in the auditory nerve is most sensitive to a specific frequency (its characteristic frequency). Very low frequencies are coded by frequency matching, which refers to the fact that the firing rate of a neuron matches the frequency of a sound wave; according to *frequency-matching theory*, or volley theory, some frequencies may be matched by the firing rate of a group of neurons. Low to moderate frequencies are coded through a combination of these methods.

Auditory Pathways and Representations

Auditory information is relayed through the thalamus to the *primary auditory cortex* and to other areas of auditory cortex. Sounds of similar frequency activate neighboring cells in the cortex, but loudness is coded temporally.

Vision

Light

Visible light is electromagnetic radiation with a wavelength of about 400 nanometers to about 750 nanometers. *Light intensity*, or the amount of energy in light, determines its brightness. Differing *light wavelengths* are sensed as different colors.

Focusing Light

Accessory structures of the eye include the *cornea, pupil, iris,* and *lens*. Through *accommodation* and other means, these structures focus light rays on the *retina*, the netlike structure of cells at the back of the eye.

Converting Light into Images

Photoreceptors in the retina—*rods* and *cones*—have *photopigments* and can transduce light into neural activity. Rods and cones differ in their shape, their sensitivity to light, their ability to discriminate colors, and their distribution across the retina. The *fovea*, the area of highest *acuity*, has only cones, which are color sensitive. Rods are more sensitive to light but do not discriminate colors; they are distributed in areas around the fovea. Both types of photoreceptors contribute to *dark adaptation*. From the photoreceptors, energy transduced from light is transferred to bipolar cells and then to *ganglion cells*, aided by lateral connections between photoreceptors, bipolar cells, and ganglion cells. Through *lateral inhibition*, the retina enhances the contrast between dark and light areas. Most ganglion cells, in effect, compare the amount of light falling on the center of their *receptive fields* with that falling on the surrounding area.

Visual Pathways

The ganglion cells send action potentials out of the eye, at a point where a *blind spot* is created. Axons of ganglion cells leave the eye as a bundle of fibers called the *optic nerve*; half of these fibers cross over at the *optic chiasm* and terminate in the *lateral geniculate nucleus (LGN)* of the thalamus. Neurons in the LGN send visual information on to the *primary visual cortex*.

Visual Representations

Visual form, color, movement, and distance are processed by parallel systems. Complex *feature detectors* in the visual cortex are hierarchically built out of simpler units that detect and respond to features such as lines, edges, and orientations.

Seeing Color

The color of an object depends on which of the wavelengths striking it are absorbed and which are reflected. The sensation of color has three psychological dimensions: *hue, saturation*, and *brightness*. According to the *trichromatic* (or Young-Helmholtz) *theory*, color vision results from the fact that the eye includes three types of cones, each of which is most sensitive to short, medium, or long wavelengths; information from the three types combines to produce the sensation of color. Individuals may have variations in the number and sensitivity of their cone pigments. According to the *opponent-process* (or Hering) *theory*, there are red-green, blue-yellow, and black-white visual elements; the members of each pair inhibit each other so that only one member of a pair may produce a signal at a time. This theory explains color afterimages, as well as the fact that lights of complementary colors cancel each other out and produce gray when mixed together.

The Interaction of Vision and Hearing: Synesthesia

Various dimensions of vision interact, and vision can also interact with hearing and other senses in a process known as *synesthesia*. For example, some people experience certain colors when stimulated by certain letters, numbers, or sounds.

The Chemical Senses: Smell and Taste

The chemical senses include olfaction (smell) and gustation (taste).

Olfaction

Olfaction detects volatile chemicals that come into contact with olfactory receptors in the nose. Olfactory signals are sent to the *olfactory bulb* in the brain without passing through the thalamus. *Pheromones* are odors from one animal that change the physiology or behavior of another animal; in mammals, pheromones act through the *vomeronasal organ*.

Gustation

Gustation detects chemicals that come into contact with taste receptors in *papillae* on the tongue. Elementary taste sensations are limited to sweet, sour, bitter, salty, umami, and astringent. The combined responses of many taste buds determine a taste sensation.

Smell, Taste, and Flavor

The senses of smell and taste interact to produce flavor.

Somatic Senses and the Vestibular System

The *somatic senses,* or somatosensory systems, include skin senses and proprioceptive senses. The skin senses include touch, temperature, and pain.

Touch and Temperature

Nerve endings in the skin generate touch sensations when they are mechanically stimulated. Some nerve endings are sensitive to temperature, and some respond to both temperature and touch. Signals from neighboring points on the skin stay next to one another all the way to the cortex.

Pain

Pain provides information about damaging stimuli. Sharp pain and dull, chronic pain are carried by different fibers—A-delta and C fibers, respectively. The emotional response to pain depends on how the painful stimulus is interpreted. According to the *gate control theory*, incoming pain signals can be blocked by a "gate" in the spinal cord; messages sent from the brain down the spinal cord also can block pain signals, producing *analgesia*. Endorphins act at several levels of the pain systems to reduce sensations of pain.

Proprioception

Proprioceptive senses provide information about the body. The *vestibular sense* provides information about the position of the head in space through the *otoliths* in *vestibular sacs* and the *semicircular canals,* and *kinesthesia* provides information about the positions of body parts with respect to one another.

Perception

5

The Perception Paradox

Three Approaches to Perception

Psychophysics
Absolute Thresholds: Is Something Out There?
THINKING CRITICALLY: Can Subliminal Stimuli Influence Your Behavior?
Signal-Detection Theory
Judging Differences: Has Anything Changed?
Magnitude Estimation: How Intense Is That?

Organizing the Perceptual World
Basic Processes in Perceptual Organization
Perception of Location and Distance
Perception of Motion
Perceptual Constancy
Culture, Experience, and Perception

Recognizing the Perceptual World
Bottom-Up Processing
Top-Down Processing
Network Processing

LINKAGES: Perception and Human Development

Attention
FOCUS ON RESEARCH METHODS: An Experiment in "Mind Reading"
Directing Attention
Ignoring Information
Divided Attention
Attention and Automatic Processing
Attention and the Brain

Applications of Research on Perception
Aviation Psychology
Human-Computer Interaction
Traffic Safety

Linkages

Summary

At a traffic circle in Scotland, fourteen fatal accidents occurred in a single year, partly because drivers failed to slow down as they approached the circle. When warning signs failed to solve the problem, Gordon Denton, a British psychologist, proposed an ingenious solution. White lines were painted across the road leading to the circle, in a pattern that looked something like this:

/   /   /   /   /   / / /

Drivers crossing these progressively more closely spaced lines at a constant speed got the impression that they were speeding up, and their automatic response was to slow down (Denton, 1980). During the fourteen months after Denton's idea was implemented, there were only two fatalities at the traffic circle. The same striping is now being used to slow drivers on roads approaching small towns in the United States (Associated Press, 1999). Denton's solution to this problem relied heavily on his knowledge of the principles of human perception.

Perception is the process through which sensations are interpreted, using knowledge and understanding of the world, so that they become meaningful experiences. Perception is not a passive process of simply absorbing and decoding incoming sensations. If it were, our experience of the environment would be a constantly changing, utterly confusing mosaic of light and color. Instead, our brains take sensations and create a coherent world, often by filling in missing information and using past experience to give meaning to what we see, hear, or touch. For example, the raw sensations coming from the stimuli in Figure 5.1 convey only the information that there is a series of intersecting lines. But your perceptual system automatically interprets this image as a rectangle (or window frame) on its side.

We begin this chapter by considering these perceptual processes and the various approaches that psychologists have taken in trying to understand them. Then we explore how people detect incoming sensory stimuli, organize these sensations into distinct and stable patterns, and recognize those patterns. We also examine the role of attention in guiding the perceptual system to analyze some parts of the world more closely than others. Finally, we provide some examples of how research on perception has been applied to some practical problems.

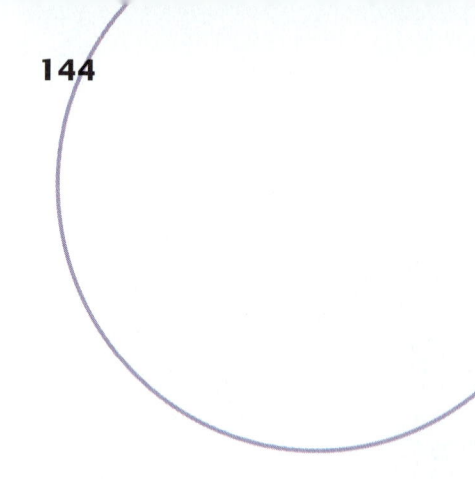

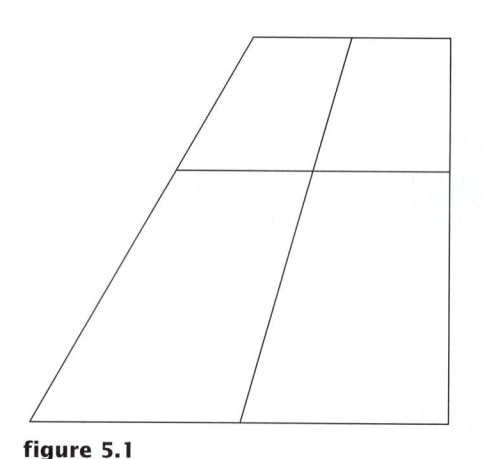

figure 5.1

What Do You See?

The Perception Paradox

As discovered by drivers who find themselves slowing because of lines painted on pavement, a lot of our perceptual work is done automatically, without conscious awareness. This quick, often effortless aspect of perceptual processing suggests that perception is a rather simple affair, but it contains a basic contradiction, or paradox: What is so easy for the perceiver to do is not easy for psychologists to understand and explain. The difficulty lies in the fact that to function so effectively and efficiently, our perceptual systems must be exceedingly complex.

To illustrate the workings of these complex systems, psychologists draw attention to *perceptual failures*, cases in which our perceptual experience differs from the actual characteristics of some stimulus. Figure 5.2 provides a good example. Perceptual errors provide clues to the problems that perception must solve, such as estimating length, and to the solutions that it achieves. Ask yourself, for example, why you saw the two lines in Figure 5.2 as differing in length even though they are the same. Part of the answer is that your visual system tries to interpret all stimuli as three-dimensional, even when they are not. A three-dimensional interpretation of this drawing would lead you to see the two lines as defining the edges of two parallel paths, one of which ends closer to you than the other. Because your eyes tell you that the two paths originate from about the same point (the castle entrance), you solve the perceptual problem by assuming that the closer line must be the longer of the two.

perception The process through which people take raw sensations from the environment and interpret them, using knowledge, experience, and understanding of the world, so that the sensations become meaningful experiences.

figure 5.2
Misperceiving Reality

TRY THIS Which line is longer—line A-C or line A-B? They are exactly the same length, but you probably perceived A-C as longer. Understanding why our perceptual systems make this kind of error has helped psychologists understand the basic principles of perception.

Three Approaches to Perception

Psychologists have taken three main approaches in their efforts to understand human perception. Those who take the **computational approach** try to determine the *computations* that a machine would have to perform to solve perceptual problems. Understanding these computations in machines, they believe, will help explain how complex computations within the nervous systems of humans and animals might turn raw sensory stimulation into a representation of the world (Green, 1991). The computational approach owes much to two earlier, but still influential, views of perception: the constructivist approach and the ecological approach.

Psychologists who take the **constructivist approach** argue that our perceptual systems construct a representation of reality from fragments of sensory information.

Is Anything Missing? Because you know what animals look like, you perceive a whole cat in this picture even though its midsection is hidden from view. The constructivist approach to perception emphasizes our ability to use knowledge and expectations to fill in the gaps in incomplete objects and to perceive them as unified wholes, not disjointed parts.

computational approach An approach to perception that focuses on how computations by the nervous system translate raw sensory stimulation into an experience of reality.

constructivist approach A view of perception taken by those who argue that the perceptual system uses fragments of sensory information to construct an image of reality.

They are particularly interested in situations in which the same stimulus creates different perceptions in different people. Stimuli such as those in Figure 5.2, for example, create optical illusions in some cultures but may not do so in those where people have not had experience with the objects or perspectives shown (Leibowitz et al., 1969). Constructivists emphasize that perception is strongly influenced by past experiences and prior knowledge, and by the expectations and inferences that arise from them (Rock, 1983). So if a desk prevents you from seeing the lower half of a person seated behind it, you still "see" the person as a complete human being. Experience tells you to expect that people remain intact even when parts of them are obscured.

Researchers influenced by the **ecological approach** to perception claim that rather than depending on interpretations, inferences, and expectations, most of our perceptual experience is due directly to the wealth of information contained in the stimuli presented by the environment. For example, J. J. Gibson (1979), founder of the ecological approach, argues that the primary goal of perception is to *support actions,* such as walking, grasping, or driving, by "tuning in" to the part of the environmental stimulus array that is most important for performing those actions. These researchers would be less interested in our *inferences* about the person behind the desk than in how we would *use* visual information from that person, from the desk, and from other objects in the room to guide us as we walk toward a chair and sit down (Nakayama, 1994).

In summary: To explain perception, the computational approach focuses on the nervous system's manipulations of incoming signals, the constructivist approach emphasizes the inferences that people make about the environment, and the ecological approach emphasizes the information provided by the environment. Later, we discuss evidence in support of each of these approaches.

Psychophysics

How can psychologists measure people's perceptions when there is no way to get inside people's heads to experience what they are experiencing? One solution to this problem is to present people with lights, sounds, and other stimuli and ask them to report their perception of the stimuli, using special scales of measurement. This

ecological approach An approach to perception maintaining that humans and other species are so well adapted to their natural environment that many aspects of the world are perceived without requiring higher-level analysis and inferences.

psychophysics An area of research focusing on the relationship between the physical characteristics of environmental stimuli and the psychological experiences those stimuli produce.

subliminal stimuli Stimuli that are too weak or brief to be perceived.

supraliminal stimuli Stimuli that fall above the absolute threshold and thus are consistently perceived.

absolute threshold The minimum amount of stimulus energy that can be detected 50 percent of the time.

table 5.1
Some Absolute Thresholds

Human Sense	Absolute Threshold Is Equivalent to:
Vision	A candle flame seen at 30 miles on a clear night
Hearing	The tick of a watch under quiet conditions at 20 feet
Taste	1 teaspoon of sugar in 2 gallons of water
Smell	1 drop of perfume diffused into the entire volume of air in a 6-room apartment
Touch	The wing of a fly falling on your cheek from a distance of 1 centimeter

TRY THIS Absolute thresholds can be amazingly low. Here are examples of stimulus equivalents at the absolute threshold for the five primary senses in humans. Set up the conditions for testing the absolute threshold for sound, and see if you can detect this minimal amount of auditory stimulation. If you can't hear it, the signal-detection theory we discuss later in this chapter may help explain why.

Source: Galanter (1962).

figure 5.3

The Absolute Threshold

The curve shows the relationship between the physical intensity of a signal and the likelihood that it will be detected. If the absolute threshold were truly absolute, all signals at or above a particular intensity would always be detected, and no signal below that intensity would ever be detected (see green line). But this response pattern almost never occurs, so the "absolute" threshold is defined as the intensity at which the signal is detected with 50 percent accuracy.

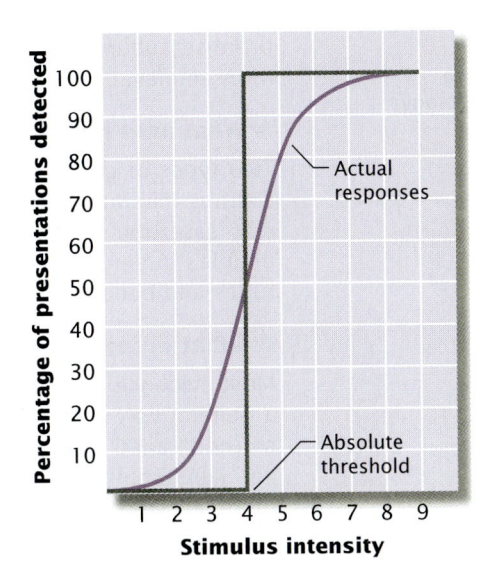

method of studying perception, called **psychophysics,** describes the relationship between *physical energy* in the environment and our *psychological experience* of that energy.

Absolute Thresholds: Is Something Out There?

How much stimulus energy is needed to trigger a conscious perceptual experience? The minimum amount of light, sound, pressure, or other physical energy we can detect is called the *absolute threshold* (see Table 5.1). Stimuli below this threshold—stimuli that are too weak or too brief for us to notice—are traditionally referred to as **subliminal stimuli.** Stimuli that fall above the absolute threshold—stimuli that are consistently perceived—are referred to as **supraliminal stimuli.**

If you were participating in a typical experiment to measure the absolute threshold for vision, you would sit in a darkened laboratory. After your eyes adapted to the darkness, you would be presented with many brief flashes of light that varied in brightness. After each one, you would be asked if you saw the stimulus. If your absolute threshold were truly "absolute," your detection accuracy should jump from 0 to 100 percent at the exact level of brightness where your threshold is; this is illustrated by the point at which the green line in Figure 5.3 suddenly rises. But research shows that the average of your responses over many trials would actually form a curve much like the purple line in that figure. In other words, the "absolute" threshold is not really an all-or-nothing phenomenon. Notice in Figure 5.3 that a flash whose brightness (intensity) is 3 is detected 20 percent of the time and missed 80 percent of the time. Is that stimulus *subliminal* or *supraliminal*? Psychologists have dealt with questions of this sort by redefining the **absolute threshold** as the minimum amount of stimulus energy that can be detected 50 percent of the time.

THINKING CRITICALLY

Can Subliminal Stimuli Influence Your Behavior?

In 1957, an adman named James Vicary claimed that a New Jersey theater flashed messages such as "buy popcorn" and "drink Coke" on a movie screen, too briefly to be noticed, while customers watched the movie *Picnic*. He said that these subliminal messages caused a 15 percent rise in sales of Coca-Cola and a 58 percent increase in popcorn sales. Can such "mind control" really work? Many people seem to think so: They spend millions of dollars each year on audiotapes and videos that

LINKAGES (a link to Introducing Psychology)

promise subliminal help to lose weight, raise self-esteem, quit smoking, make more money, or achieve other goals.

● What am I being asked to believe or accept?

Two types of claims have been made about subliminal stimuli. The more general claim is that subliminal stimuli can influence our behavior. The second, more specific assertion is that subliminal stimuli provide an effective means of changing people's buying habits, political opinions, self-confidence, and other complex attitudes and behaviors, with or without their awareness or consent.

● What evidence is available to support the assertion?

Most evidence for the first claim—that subliminal stimuli can influence behavior in a general way—comes from research on visual perception. For example, using a method called *subliminal priming*, participants are shown clearly visible (supraliminal) stimuli, such as pictures of people, and then asked to make some sort of judgment about them. Unbeknownst to the participants, however, each of the visible pictures is preceded by other pictures or words flashed so briefly that the participants are unaware of them. The critical question is whether the information in the subliminal stimuli influences—or, more specifically, has a "priming effect" on—participants' responses to the supraliminal stimuli that follow them.

In one subliminal priming study, supraliminal pictures of individuals were preceded by subliminal pictures that were either "positive" (e.g., happy children) or "negative" (e.g., a monster). The participants in this study judged the people in the visible pictures as more likable, polite, friendly, successful, and reputable when their pictures had been preceded by a subliminal picture that was positive rather than negative (Krosnick et al., 1992). Another study found that people with eating disorders ate more crackers after being exposed to a subliminal presentation of the phrase "Mama is leaving me" than after either a supraliminal presentation of that phrase or a subliminal presentation of the neutral phrase "Mama is loaning it" (Masling, 1992). More recently, researchers have found that subliminally presented words can influence decisions about the meaning of words. For example, after being exposed to subliminal presentations of a man's name (e.g., "*Tom*"), participants were able to decide more rapidly whether a supraliminal stimulus (e.g., "*John*") was a man's or woman's name. However, the impact of the subliminally presented name lasted for only about one-tenth of a second (Greenwald, Draine, & Abrams, 1996).

Other research shows that subliminal stimuli can lead to a change in people's physiological responses. In one study, participants were shown words at subliminal speed while researchers recorded their *galvanic skin resistance (GSR)*, a measure of physiological arousal. Although the words were flashed too quickly to be perceived consciously, participants had higher GSR measurements following words such as "No one loves me" than after nonemotional messages such as "No one lifts it" (Masling & Bornstein, 1991). In another study, participants were exposed to subliminal photos of snakes, spiders, flowers, and mushrooms. Even though the photos were impossible to perceive at a conscious level, participants who were afraid of snakes or spiders showed increased GSR measurements (and reported fear) in response to snake and spider photos (Öhman & Soares, 1994).

The results of studies like these support the claim that subliminal information can have at least a temporary impact on judgment and emotion, but they say little or nothing about the effects of subliminal advertising or the value of subliminal self-help tapes. We have only the claims of people who believe in subliminal selling and the reports of satisfied customers (e.g., Key, 1973; McGarvey, 1989).

● Are there alternative ways of interpreting the evidence?

Many claims for subliminal advertising—including those reported in the New Jersey theater case we mentioned—have turned out to be publicity stunts using fabricated data (Haberstroh, 1995; Pratkanis, 1992). And testimonials from people who have purchased subliminal tapes may be biased by what these people *want* to believe about the product they bought. This interpretation is supported by experiments that manipulate the beliefs of participants regarding the messages on subliminal tapes. In one study, half the participants were told that they would be hearing tapes whose subliminal messages would improve their memory; the other half were told that the subliminal messages would improve their self-esteem. However, half the participants expecting self-esteem tapes actually received memory-improvement tapes, and half the participants expecting memory-improvement tapes actually received self-esteem tapes. Regardless of which tapes they actually heard, participants who *thought* they had heard memory-enhancement messages reported improved memory; those who *thought* they had heard self-esteem messages said that their self-esteem had improved (Pratkanis, Eskenazi, & Greenwald, 1994). In other words, the effects of the tapes were determined by the listeners' expectations—not by the tapes' subliminal content.

- **What additional evidence would help to evaluate the alternatives?**

To fully evaluate the effectiveness of subliminal products such as self-help tapes, researchers must conduct further experiments—like the one just mentioned—that carefully control for expectations. For example, in a *double-blind, placebo-controlled experiment,* some participants would hear a tape whose subliminal content was consistent with the stated purpose of the tapes (e.g., weight control). Others would hear a tape whose subliminal content was irrelevant to the tapes' stated purpose (e.g., French grammar), or that contained no subliminal messages. Further, neither the participants nor the researchers would know who listened to which tape until after all the results were in. Ultimately, the effects of the three types of tapes would be compared with one another and with the effects of tapes containing supraliminal (audible) self-help messages.

- **What conclusions are most reasonable?**

Available scientific evidence suggests that subliminal perception does occur, but that it has no potential for "mind control" (Greenwald, Klinger, & Schuh, 1995). Subliminal effects are usually small and short-lived, and they mainly affect simple judgments and general measures of overall arousal. Most researchers agree that subliminal messages have no special power to induce major changes in people's needs, goals, skills, or actions (Pratkanis, 1992). In fact, advertisements, political speeches, and other messages that people *can* perceive consciously have far stronger persuasive effects.

Signal-Detection Theory

Look again at Figure 5.3. It shows that stimuli just above and just below the absolute threshold are sometimes detected and sometimes missed. For example, a stimulus at intensity level 3 appears to be subliminal, even though you will perceive it 20 percent of the time; a stimulus at level 5 is above threshold, but it will be missed 20 percent of the time. Why should the "absolute" threshold vary this way? The two most important reasons have to do with sensitivity and our response criterion.

Sensitivity refers to our ability to pick out a particular stimulus, or *signal*. Sensitivity is influenced by the *intensity of the signal* (stronger ones are easier to detect), the *capacity of sensory systems* (good vision or hearing makes us more sensitive), and the *amount of background stimulation*, or *noise*, arriving at the same time. Some noise comes from outside the person, as when electrical equipment hums or overhead lights flicker. There is also noise coming from the spontaneous, random firing of cells of our own nervous system. Varying amounts of this *internal noise* is always occurring, whether or not we are stimulated by physical energy. You might think of it as a little like "snow" on a television screen or static between radio stations.

---

sensitivity The ability to detect a stimulus.

Detecting Vital Signals According to signal-detection theory, the likelihood that security personnel will detect the outline of a bomb or other weapon in x-ray images of a passenger's luggage depends partly on the sensitivity of their visual systems and partly on their response criterion. That criterion is affected by their expectations that weapons might appear, as well as by how motivated they are to look carefully for them. To help keep inspectors' response criteria sufficiently low, airport security officials occasionally attempt to smuggle a simulated weapon through a checkpoint. This procedure both evaluates the inspectors and helps keep them focused on their vital task.

The second source of variation in absolute threshold comes from the **response criterion**, which reflects our willingness to respond to a stimulus. Motivation—wants and needs—as well as expectancies affect the response criterion. For example, if you would be punished for reporting that a faint light appeared when it did not, then you might be motivated to raise your response criterion. That is, you would report the light only when you were sure you saw it. Similarly, expecting a faint stimulus to occur lowers the response criterion. Suppose, for example, that you worked at an airport security checkpoint, where you spent hours looking at x-ray images of people's handbags, briefcases, and luggage. The signal to be detected in this situation is a weapon, whereas the "noise" consists of harmless objects in a person's luggage, vague or distorted images on the viewing screen, and anything else that is not a weapon. If there has been a recent terrorist attack, or if the threat of one has just been issued, your airport will be on special alert. Accordingly, your response criterion for saying that some questionable object on the x-ray image might be a weapon will be much lower than if terrorism were not so likely. In other words, expecting a stimulus makes it more likely that you will detect it than if it is unexpected.

When researchers realized that detecting a signal depends on a combination of each person's sensitivity *and* response criterion, they concluded that the measurement of absolute thresholds could never be more precise than the 50 percent rule mentioned earlier. As a result, they abandoned the notion of absolute thresholds and focused instead on **signal-detection theory,** a mathematical model of how our personal sensitivity and response criterion combine to determine decisions about whether or not a near-threshold stimulus has occurred (Green & Swets, 1966).

Once again, imagine that you are participating in a threshold experiment. When presented with faint signals, you may find it impossible to distinguish accurately between trials involving noise alone and those involving a signal plus noise. Sometimes, external or internal noise levels may be so high that you think something must surely be "out there," in which case you report that the stimulus is present when, in fact, it is not. This type of error is called a *false alarm*. At other times, the signal is so faint that it does not produce enough stimulation for you to detect it—causing an error known as a *miss*. But a person with a more sensitive sensory system might correctly detect the stimulus—a situation called a *hit*.

Because it allows precise measurement of people's sensitivity to stimuli of any kind, signal-detection theory provides a way to understand and predict responses in

response criterion The internal rule a person uses to decide whether or not to report a stimulus.

signal-detection theory A mathematical model of what determines a person's report that a near-threshold stimulus has or has not occurred.

Psychophysics

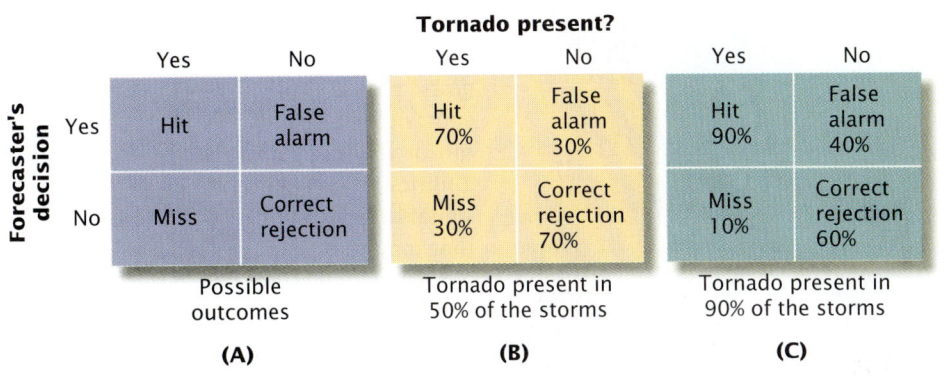

	Tornado present?					
Forecaster's decision	Yes	No	Yes	No	Yes	No
Yes	Hit	False alarm	Hit 70%	False alarm 30%	Hit 90%	False alarm 40%
No	Miss	Correct rejection	Miss 30%	Correct rejection 70%	Miss 10%	Correct rejection 60%
	Possible outcomes		Tornado present in 50% of the storms		Tornado present in 90% of the storms	
	(A)		(B)		(C)	

figure 5.4

Signal Detection

Part A shows the possible outcomes of examining a radar display for signs of a tornado: a *hit* (correctly detecting the tornado), a *miss* (failing to detect the tornado), a *correct rejection* (seeing no tornado when there is none), or a *false alarm* (reporting a tornado when none exists). The rest of the figure illustrates the impact of two different response criteria: Part B represents outcomes of a high response criterion, which is set under conditions where tornadoes are seen only 50 percent of the time; Part C represents outcomes of a low response criterion, which operates under conditions where tornadoes are seen 90 percent of the time.

a wide range of situations (Swets, 1992). Consider weather forecasting. Signal-detection theory can be valuable in understanding why weather forecasters, using the latest radar systems, sometimes fail to warn of a tornado that local residents can see with the naked eye (Stevens, 1995). The forecaster's task is not easy, because the high-tech systems they use may respond not only to dangerous shifts in wind direction (wind shear) and a tornado's spinning funnel, but also to such trivial stimuli as swirling dust and swarming insects. So the telltale radar "signature" of a tornado appears against a potentially confusing background of visual "noise." Whether or not that signature will be picked out and reported depends both on the forecaster's sensitivity to the signal and on the response criterion being used. In establishing the criterion for making a report, the forecaster must consider certain consequences. Setting the criterion too high might cause a tornado to go unnoticed. Such a miss could cost many lives if it left a populated area with no warning of danger. If the response criterion were set too low, however, the forecaster might deliver a false alarm that would unnecessarily disrupt people's lives, activate costly emergency plans, and reduce the credibility of future tornado warnings (see Figure 5.4A). In short, there is a tradeoff. To minimize false alarms, the forecaster could set a very high response criterion, but doing so would also make misses more likely.

Let's examine how various kinds of expectations or assumptions can change the response criterion and how those changes might affect the accuracy of a forecaster's decisions. If a forecaster knows it's a time of year when tornadoes exist in only about 50 percent of the storm systems seen on radar, a rather high response criterion is likely to be used; it will take relatively strong evidence to trigger a tornado warning. The hypothetical data in Figure 5.4(B) show that under these conditions, the forecaster correctly detected 70 percent of actual tornadoes but missed 30 percent of them; also, 30 percent of the tornado reports were false alarms. Now suppose the forecaster learns that a different kind of storm system is on the way, and that about 90 percent of such systems spawn tornadoes. This information is likely to increase the forecaster's expectancy for seeing a tornado signature, thus lowering the response criterion. The forecaster will now require less visual evidence of a tornado before reporting one. Under these conditions, the hit rate might rise from 70 percent to, say, 90 percent, but the false-alarm rate might also increase from 30 percent to 40 percent (see Figure 5.4C).

Sensitivity to tornado signals will also affect a forecaster's hit rate and false-alarm rate. Forecasters with greater sensitivity to these signals will have high hit

Perfect! This chef's ability to taste the difference in his culinary creation before and after he has adjusted the spices depends on psychophysical laws that also apply to judging differences in visual, auditory, and other sensory stimuli.

table 5.2
Weber's Fraction (K) for Different Stimuli

Stimulus	K
Pitch	.003
Brightness	.017
Weight	.02
Odor	.05
Loudness	.10
Pressure on skin	.14
Saltiness of taste	.20

The value of Weber's fraction, K, differs from one sense to another. Differences in K demonstrate the adaptive nature of perception. Humans, who depend more heavily on vision than on taste for survival, are more sensitive to vision than to taste.

rates and low false-alarm rates. Forecasters with less sensitivity are still likely to have high hit rates, but their false-alarm rates will also be higher. As Figure 5.4 suggests, people do sometimes make mistakes at signal detection, whether it involves spotting tornadoes, inspecting luggage, diagnosing medical conditions, searching for oil, or looking for clues at a crime scene. Research on these and other perceptual abilities has led psychologists to suggest ways of improving people's performance on signal-detection tasks (Wickens, 1992a). For example, psychologists recommend that manufacturers occasionally place flawed items among a batch of objects to be inspected. This strategy increases inspectors' expectations of seeing flaws, thus lowering the response criterion and raising the hit rate.

Judging Differences: Has Anything Changed?

Sometimes our perceptual task is not to detect a faint stimulus but rather to notice small differences as a stimulus changes, or to judge whether there are differences between two stimuli. For example, when tuning up, musicians are concerned about whether the notes played by two instruments are the same or different. When repainting part of a wall, you must judge whether the new color matches the old. And you have to decide if your soup tastes any spicier after you have added some pepper.

The smallest difference between stimuli that we can detect is called the **difference threshold** or **just-noticeable difference** (JND). How small is that difference? The size of a JND is determined by two factors. The first is how much of a stimulus there was to begin with. The weaker the stimuli are, the easier it is to detect small differences between them. For example, if you are comparing the weight of two envelopes, you will be able to detect a difference of as little as a fraction of an ounce. But if you are comparing two boxes weighing around fifty pounds, you may not notice a difference unless it is a pound or more. The second factor affecting people's ability to detect differences is which sense is being stimulated.

The relationship between these two factors is described by one of the oldest laws in psychology. Named after the nineteenth-century German physiologist Ernst Weber (pronounced "VAY-ber"), **Weber's law** states that the smallest detectable difference in stimulus energy is a constant fraction of the intensity of the stimulus. This fraction, often called *Weber's constant* or *Weber's fraction*, is given the symbol K. As shown in Table 5.2, K is different for each of the senses. The smaller K is, the more sensitive a sense is to stimulus differences.

Specifically, Weber's law says that $JND = KI$, where K is the Weber's constant for a particular sense, and I is the amount, or intensity, of the stimulus. To compute the JND for a particular stimulus, we must know its intensity and what sense it is stimulating. For example, as shown in Table 5.2, the value of K for weight is .02. If an object weighs 25 pounds *(I)*, the JND is only half a pound (.02 × 25 pounds). So while carrying a 25-pound bag of groceries, you would have to add or remove a half a pound before you would be able to detect a change in heaviness. But candy snatchers beware: It takes a change of only two-thirds of an ounce to determine that someone has been into a 2-pound box of chocolates!

Weber's constants vary somewhat among individuals, and as we get older we tend to become less sensitive to stimulus differences. There are exceptions to this rule, however. If you like candy, you will be happy to know that Weber's fraction for sweetness stays fairly constant throughout life (Gilmore & Murphy, 1989). Weber's law does not hold when stimuli are very intense or very weak, but it does apply to complex, as well as simple, stimuli. We all tend to have our own personal Weber's fractions that describe how much prices can increase before we notice or worry about the change. For example, if your Weber's fraction for cost is .10, then you would surely notice, and perhaps protest, a fifty-cent increase in a one-dollar bus fare. But the same fifty-cent increase in monthly rent would be less than a JND and thus unlikely to cause notice, let alone concern.

figure 5.5
Length Illusions
People can usually estimate line lengths very accurately, but this ability can be impaired under certain conditions. The pairs of lines marked A and B are the same length in each drawing, but most people report that line A appears longer than line B. These optical illusions, like the one in Figure 5.2, occur partly because of our tendency to see two-dimensional figures as three-dimensional. With the exception of the "top hat," all or part of line A in each drawing can easily be interpreted as being farther away than line B. When two equal-sized objects appear to be at different distances, the visual system tends to infer that the more distant object must be larger.

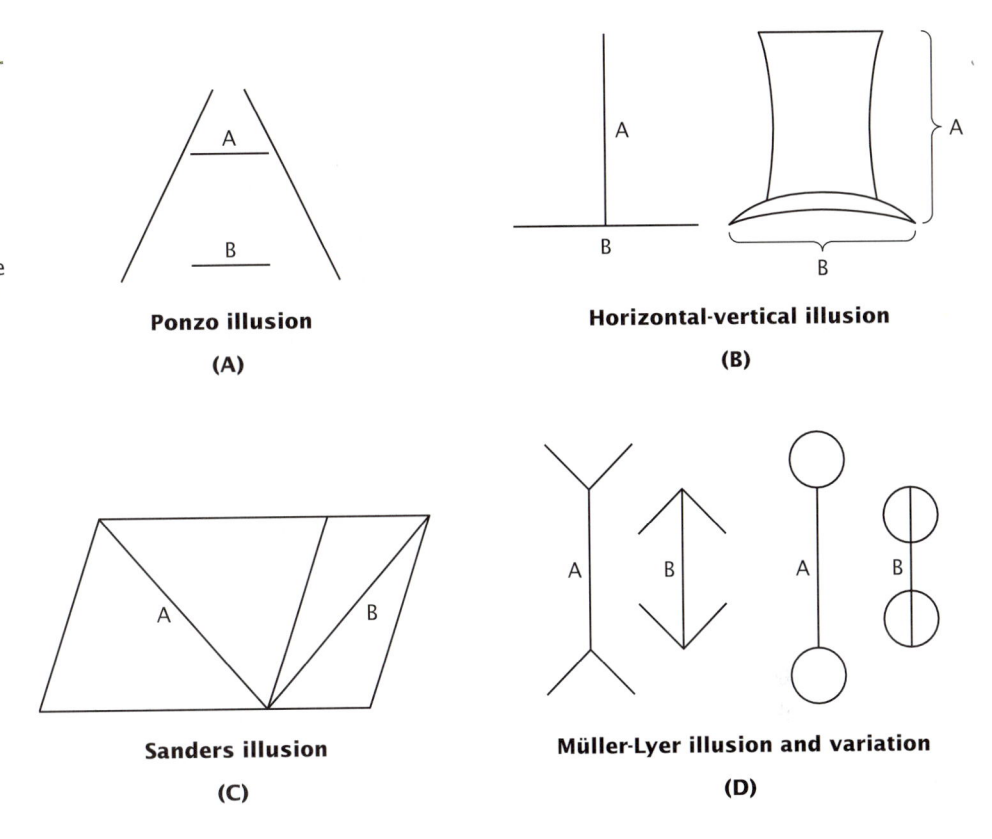

Ponzo illusion
(A)

Horizontal-vertical illusion
(B)

Sanders illusion
(C)

Müller-Lyer illusion and variation
(D)

Magnitude Estimation: How Intense Is That?

How much would you have to increase the volume on your stereo to make it sound twice as loud as your neighbor's? How much would you have to turn it down to make it sound only half as loud as it was before your neighbor complained? These are questions about *magnitude estimation*—about how our perception of stimulus intensity is related to actual stimulus strength. In 1860, Gustav Fechner (pronounced "FECK-ner") used Weber's law to study the relationship between the *physical* magnitude of a stimulus and its *perceived* magnitude. He reasoned that if just-noticeable differences get progressively larger as stimulus magnitude increases, then so, too, must the amount of change in the stimulus required to double or triple the perceived intensity of the stimulus. He was right. For example, it takes only a small increase in volume to make a soft sound seem twice as loud, but imagine how much additional volume it would take to make a rock band seem twice as loud. To put it another way, constant increases in physical energy will produce progressively smaller increases in perceived magnitude. This observation, when expressed as a mathematical equation relating actual stimulus intensity to perceived intensity, became known as *Fechner's law*.

Fechner's law applies to most, but not all, stimuli. Whereas it takes larger and larger increases in light or sound to create the same amount of change in perceived magnitude, the reverse is true for the perceived intensity of electric shock. It takes a relatively large increase in shock intensity to make a weak shock seem twice as intense, but if the shock is already painful, it takes only a small increase in intensity before you would perceive it was twice as strong. S. S. Stevens offered another formula (known as *Stevens's power law*) for magnitude estimation that works for a wider array of stimuli, including electric shock, temperature, and sound and light intensity. Stevens's law is still used today by psychologists who want to determine how much larger, louder, longer, or more intense a stimulus must be for people to perceive a specific difference or amount of change.

---

just-noticeable difference (JND) The smallest detectable difference in stimulus energy.

Weber's law A law stating that the smallest detectable difference in stimulus energy is a constant fraction of the intensity of the stimulus.

Overall, people do well at estimating differences between stimuli. For example, we are very good at estimating how much longer one line is than another. Yet as shown in Figure 5.2, this perceptual comparison process can be disrupted when the lines are embedded in more complex figures. (See Figure 5.5 for some additional examples of lines that appear to be different lengths but are not.) The perceptual laws that we have discussed, as well as the exceptions to these laws, emphasize a central principle in perception—that perception is not absolute, but relative. Our experience of one stimulus depends on its relationship to others. The way in which the human perceptual system relates one stimulus to another is the focus of research on our next topic, perceptual organization.

Organizing the Perceptual World

Suppose you are driving on a busy road while searching for Barney's Diner, an unfamiliar restaurant where you are to meet a friend. The roadside is crammed with signs of all shapes and colors, some flashing and some rotating. If you are ever to recognize the sign that says "Barney's Diner," you must impose some sort of organization on this overwhelming array of visual information.

Perceptual organization is the task performed by the perceptual system to determine what edges and other stimuli go together to form an object. In this case, the object would be the sign for Barney's Diner. It is perceptual organization, too, that makes it possible for you to separate the sign from its background of lights, colors, letters, and other competing stimuli. Figure 5.6 shows some of the ways in which your perceptual system can organize stimuli. For example, the figure appears as a hollow cube, but notice that you can see it from two angles: either looking down at the top of the cube or looking up toward the bottom of the cube. And notice that the "cube" is not really a cube at all but rather a series of unconnected arrows and Ys. Your perceptual system organized these elements into a cube by creating imaginary connecting lines called *subjective contours*. That system can also change the apparent location of the cube. You probably saw it first as "floating" in front of a background of large black dots, but those dots can also be "holes" through which you see the cube against a solid black background "behind" the page. It may take a little time to see this second perceptual organization, but when you do, notice that the subjective contours you saw earlier are gone. They disappear because your perceptual system adjusts for the fact that when an object is partially obscured, we should not be able to see all of it.

figure 5.6

Organize This!

Psychologists have employed the principles of figure-ground organization and grouping to help explain how your visual system allows you to perceive these disconnected lines as a cube, as well as to see this cube from above or below, and as being in front of the page or behind it.

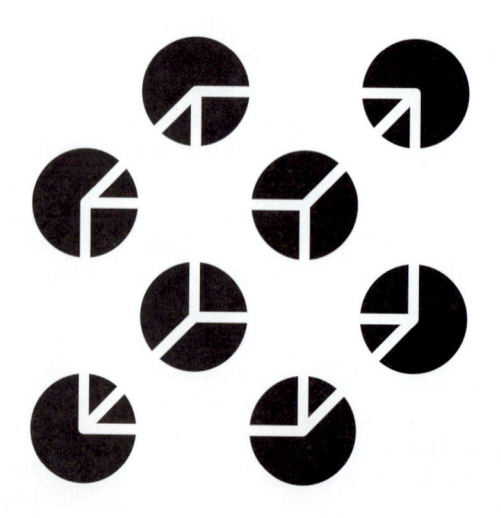

Organizing the Perceptual World

Basic Processes in Perceptual Organization

To explain phenomena like these and to understand the way our perceptual systems organize more naturalistic scenes, psychologists have focused on two basic processes: *figure-ground organization* and *grouping*.

Figure-Ground Organization When you look at a complex scene or listen to a noisy environment, your perceptual apparatus automatically picks out certain features, objects, or sounds to be emphasized and relegates others to be *ground*—the less relevant background. For example, as you drive toward an intersection, a stop sign becomes a figure, standing out clearly against the background of trees, houses, and cars. A *figure* is the part of the visual field that has meaning, stands in front of the rest, and always seems to include the contours or edges that separate it from the less relevant background (Rubin, 1915). As described in the chapter on sensation, edges are one of the most basic features detected by our visual system; they combine to form figures.

To fully appreciate the process of figure-ground organization, look at the drawings in Figure 5.7. These drawings are called *reversible figures*, because you can repeatedly reverse your perceptual organization of what is figure and what is ground. Your ability to do this shows that perception is not only an active process but a categorical one as well. People usually organize sensory stimulation into one perceptual category or another, but rarely into both or into something in between. In Figure 5.7, for instance, you cannot easily see both faces *and* a vase, or the words *figure* and *ground*, at the same time.

Grouping To distinguish figure from ground, our perceptual system must first identify stimulus elements in the environment, such as the edges of a stop sign or billboard, that belong together as figures. We tend to group certain elements together more or less automatically; in the early 1900s, several German psychologists began to study how this happens. They argued first of all that people perceive sights and sounds as organized wholes. These wholes, they said, are different from, and more than, just the sum of the individual sensations, much as water is something more than just an assortment of hydrogen and oxygen atoms. Because the German word meaning (roughly) "whole figure" is *Gestalt* (pronounced "ge-SHTALT"), these researchers became known as *Gestalt psychologists*. They proposed a number of principles, or "Gestalt laws," that describe how perceptual systems group stimuli into a world of shapes and objects. Some of the most enduring of these principles are the following:

1. *Proximity.* The closer objects or events are to one another, the more likely they are to be perceived as belonging together, as Figure 5.8(A) illustrates.

2. *Similarity.* Similar elements are perceived to be part of a group, as in Figure 5.8(B).

3. *Continuity.* Sensations that appear to create a continuous form are perceived as belonging together, as in Figure 5.8(C).

4. *Closure.* We tend to fill in missing contours to form a complete object, as in Figure 5.8(D). The gaps are easy to see, but as illustrated in Figure 5.6, the tendency to fill in missing contours can be so strong that you may see faint connections that are not really there.

5. *Common fate.* Sets of objects that are moving in the same direction at the same speed are perceived together. Choreographers and marching-band directors often use the principle of common fate, arranging for groups of dancers or musicians to move identically, creating the illusion of waves of motion or of large moving objects.

figure 5.7

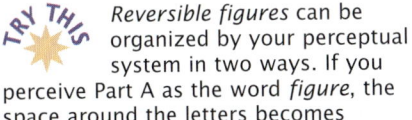

Reversible Figures

TRY THIS *Reversible figures* can be organized by your perceptual system in two ways. If you perceive Part A as the word *figure*, the space around the letters becomes meaningless background. Now emphasize the word *ground*, and what had stood out a moment ago now becomes background. In Part B, when you emphasize the white vase, the two black profiles become background; if you organize the faces as the figure, what had been a vase now becomes background.

perceptual organization The task of determining what edges and other stimuli go together to form an object.

figure 5.8

Gestalt Principles of Perceptual Grouping

We tend to perceive Part A as two groups of two circles plus two single circles, rather than as, say, six single circles. In Part B, we see two columns of Xs and two columns of Os, not four rows of XOXO. We see the X in Part C as being made out of two continuous lines, not a combination of the odd forms shown. We perceive the disconnected segments in Part D as a triangle and a circle. In Part E, we tend to pair up dots in the same oval, even though they are far apart. Part F shows that connected objects are grouped together.

Proximity (A)

Similarity (B)

Continuity (C)

Closure (D)

Common Region (E)

Connectedness (F)

THE FAR SIDE By GARY LARSON

"Wait! Wait! . . . Cancel that, I guess it says 'help.'"

The principle of closure allows us to fill in the blanks in what we see and hear. Without it, the world would appear as fragmented images and sounds that would confuse everyone, including would-be rescuers.

The Far Side® by Gary Larson © 1982 FarWorks, Inc. All rights reserved. Used with permission.

---

auditory scene analysis The perceptual process through which sounds are mentally represented and interpreted.

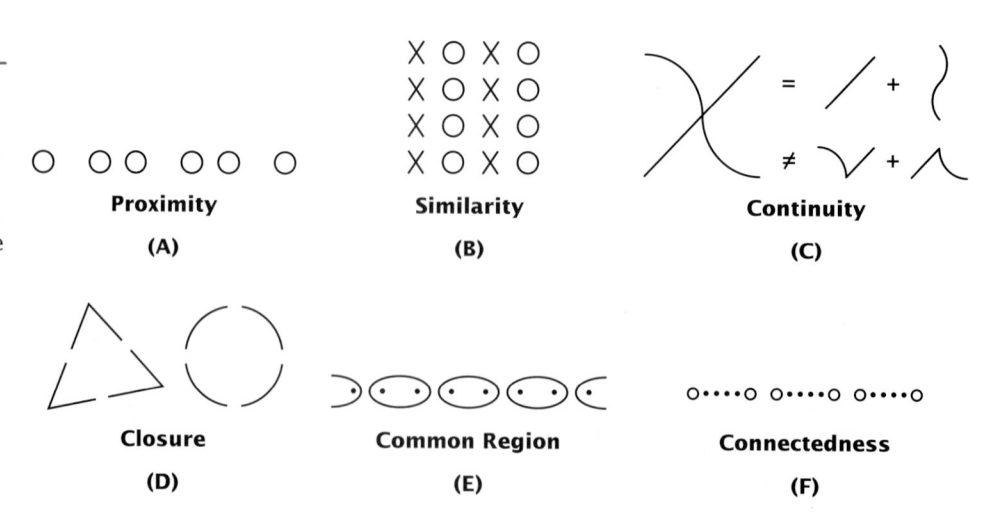

Stephen Palmer (1999) has introduced the following three additional grouping principles, which may be more important than many of the traditional laws:

1. *Synchrony.* Stimuli that occur at the same time are likely to be perceived as belonging together. For example, if you see a car ahead stop violently at the same instant you hear a crash, you will probably perceive these visual and auditory stimuli as part of the same event.

2. *Common region.* Elements located within some boundary tend to be grouped together. The boundary can be created by an enclosing perimeter, as in Figure 5.8(E); a region of color; or other factors.

3. *Connectedness.* Elements that are connected by other elements tend to be grouped together. Figure 5.8(F) demonstrates how important this law is. The circles connected by dotted lines seem to go together even though they are farther apart than some pairs of unconnected circles. In this situation, the principle of connectedness appears more important than the principle of proximity.

Why do these grouping principles guide human perceptual organization? One answer is that they reflect the way stimuli are likely to be organized in the natural world. Two nearby elements are, in fact, more likely to be part of an object than are widely separated elements. Likewise, stimulus elements moving in the same direction at the same rate are likely to be part of the same object. Your initial impression of the cube in Figure 5.6 reflects this *likelihood principle* in action. At first glance, you probably saw the cube as being below you rather than above you. This tendency makes adaptive sense, because cubes (such as boxes) are more likely to be on the ground than hanging in midair. The likelihood principle is consistent with both the ecological and constructivist approaches to perception. From the ecological perspective, the likelihood principle evolved because it worked, giving our ancestors reliable information about how the world is most likely to be organized, and thus increasing their chances of survival. Constructivists point out, however, that our personal experiences in the world also help determine the likelihood of interpreting a stimulus array in one way over another. The likelihood principle operates automatically and accurately most of the time. As shown in Figure 5.9, however, when we try using it to organize very *unlikely* stimuli, it can lead to frustrating misperceptions.

Complementing the likelihood principle is the *simplicity principle,* which says that we organize stimulus elements in a way that gives us the simplest possible perception (Pomerantz & Kubovy, 1986). Your visual system, for example, will group stimulus elements so as to reduce the amount of information that you must process.

Organizing the Perceptual World

You can see the simplicity principle in action in Figure 5.6; it was simpler to see a single cube than an assortment of separate, unrelated arrows and Ys.

Auditory Scene Analysis
Grouping principles such as similarity, proximity, closure, and continuity apply to what we hear as well as to what we see (Bartlett, 1993). For example, sounds that are similar in pitch tend to be grouped together, much like sounds that come close together in time. Through closure, we hear a tone as continuous even if it is repeatedly interrupted by bursts of static. **Auditory scene analysis** (Bregman, 1990) is the perceptual process of mentally representing and interpreting sounds. First, the flow of sound energy is organized into a series of segments based on characteristics such as frequency, intensity, location, and the like. Sounds with similar characteristics are then grouped into separate *auditory streams,* which are sounds perceived as coming from the same source. It is through auditory scene analysis that the potentially overwhelming world of sound is organized into separate, coherent patterns of speech, music, or even noise.

Perception of Location and Distance

One of the most important perceptual tasks we face is to determine where objects and sound sources are located. This task involves knowing both their two-dimensional position (left or right, up or down) and their distance from us.

Two-Dimensional Location
Visually determining whether an object is to your right or your left appears to be simple. All the perceptual system has to do, it seems, is determine where the object's image falls on the retina. For example, if the image falls on the center of the retina, then the object must be straight ahead. But when an object is, say, far to your right, and you focus its image on the center of your retina by turning your head and eyes toward it, you do not assume it is straight ahead. A computational approach to this location problem suggests that your brain estimates the object's true location relative to your body using an equation that takes information about where an image strikes the retina and adjusts it based on information about the movement of your eyes and head.

As mentioned in the chapter on sensation, localization of sounds depends on cues about differences in the information received by your two ears. If a sound is

Common Fate When numerous objects, such as a large flock of birds, move together, we see them as a group or even as a single large object in the sky. Marching-band directors put this perceptual grouping process to good use. By arranging for musicians to move together, they make it appear as though huge letters and other large "objects" are in motion on the field during half-time shows at football games.

figure 5.9

Impossible Objects

These objects can exist as two-dimensional drawings, but not as the three-dimensional objects that experience tells us to expect them to be. When we try to use the likelihood principle to organize them in three-dimensional space, we eventually discover that they are "impossible."

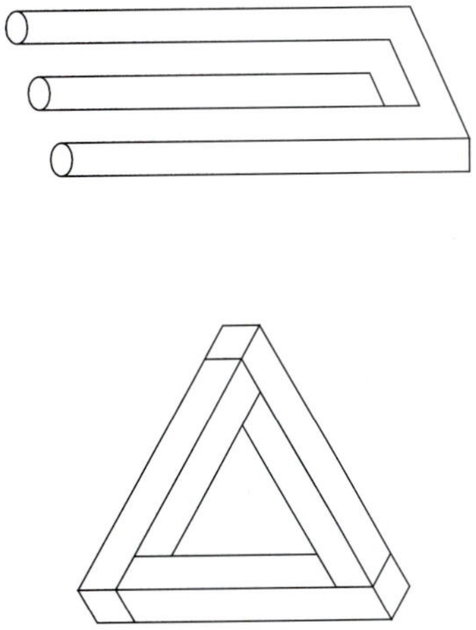

LINKAGES (a link to Sensation)

TRY THIS

continuous, sound waves coming toward the right side of your head will reach the right ear before reaching the left ear. Similarly, a sound coming toward the right side of your head will seem a little bit louder to the right ear than to the left ear, because the head blocks some of the sound to the latter. The brain uses these slight differences in the timing and the intensity of a sound as cues to locate its source. Visual cues are often integrated with auditory cues to determine the exact identity and location of the sound source. Most often, information from the eyes and the ears converges on the same likely sound source. However, there are times when the two senses produce conflicting impressions; in such cases, we tend to believe our eyes rather than our ears. This bias toward using visual information is known as *visual dominance*. The phenomenon is illustrated by our impression that the sound of a television program is coming from the screen rather than the speaker. Next time you are watching someone talking on TV, close your eyes. If your television has a single speaker below or to the side of the screen, you will notice that the sound no longer seems to be coming from the screen but instead seems to be coming from the speaker itself. As soon as you open your eyes, however, the false impression resumes; words once again seem to come from the obvious visual source of the sound—the person on the screen.

Depth Perception One of the oldest puzzles in psychology relates to **depth perception,** our ability to perceive distance. How are we able to experience the world in three-dimensional depth even though the visual information we receive from it is projected onto two-dimensional retinas? The answer lies in the many

figure 5.10

Stimulus Cues for Depth Perception

TRY THIS See if you can identify the cues of relative size, interposition, linear perspective, height in the visual field, textural gradient, and shadows that combine to create a sense of three-dimensional depth in this drawing.

depth perception Perception of distance, one of the most important factors underlying size and shape constancy.

interposition A depth cue whereby closer objects block one's view of things farther away.

relative size A depth cue whereby larger objects are perceived as closer than smaller ones.

Organizing the Perceptual World

depth cues provided by the environment and by some special properties of the visual system.

To some extent, people perceive depth through the same cues that artists use to create the impression of depth and distance on a two-dimensional canvas. These cues are actually characteristics of visual stimuli and therefore illustrate the ecological approach to perception. Figure 5.10 demonstrates several of these cues:

- One of the most important depth cues is **interposition,** or *occlusion:* Closer objects block the view of things farther away. This cue is illustrated in Figure 5.10 by the person walking nearest the car; because his body blocks out part of the car, we perceive him as being closer than the car.

- The two people at the far left side of Figure 5.10 illustrate the cue of **relative size:** When two objects are assumed to be about equal in size, the one that casts the larger image on the retina is perceived to be closer.

- Another cue comes from **height in the visual field:** On the ground, more distant objects are usually higher in the visual field than those nearby. Because the buildings in Figure 5.10 are higher than the people in the foreground, the buildings appear to be farther away.

- A cue known as **texture gradient** involves a graduated change in the "grain" of the visual field. Texture appears less detailed as distance increases, so as the texture of a surface changes across the retinal image, people perceive a change in distance. In Figure 5.10, you can see a texture gradient as the grass, the sidewalk, and the street become less distinct toward the "back" of the drawing.

- The small figure crossing the center line in Figure 5.10 is seen as very far away, partly because she is near the horizon line, which we know is quite distant. She appears far away also because she is near a point where the road's edges, like all parallel lines that recede into the distance, appear to converge toward a single point. This apparent convergence provides a cue called **linear perspective.** Objects that are nearer the point of convergence are seen as farther away.

Still other depth cues depend on *clarity, color,* and *shadows.* Distant objects often appear hazier and tend to take on a bluish tone. (Art students are taught to

A Case of Depth Misperception The runner in this photo is actually farther away than the man on the pitcher's mound. But because he is lower, not higher, in the visual field—and because his leg can be seen as being in front of, not behind, the pitcher's leg—the runner appears smaller than normal rather than farther away.

Texture Gradient The details of a scene fade gradually as distance increases. This texture gradient helps us to perceive the less detailed birds in this photo as farther away.

height in the visual field A depth cue whereby objects higher in the visual field are perceived as more distant.

texture gradient A graduated change in the texture, or grain, of the visual field, whereby objects with finer, less detailed textures are perceived as more distant.

linear perspective A depth cue whereby objects closer to the point where two lines appear to converge are perceived as being at a greater distance.

figure 5.11

Light, Shadow, and Depth Perception

TRY THIS The shadows cast by these protruding rivets and deep dents make it easy to see them in three dimensions. But if you turn the book upside down, the rivets now look like dents, and the dents look like bumps. This reversal in depth perception occurs partly because people normally assume that illumination comes from above and interpret the pattern of light and shadow accordingly. With the picture upside down, light coming from the top would produce the observed pattern of shadows only if the circles were dents, not rivets.

add a little blue when mixing paint for distant background features.) Light and shadow also contribute to the perception of depth (Ramachandran, 1988). The buildings in the background of Figure 5.10 are seen as three-dimensional, not flat, because of the shadows on their right faces. Figure 5.11 offers a more dramatic example of shadows' effect on depth perception.

An important visual depth cue that cannot be demonstrated in Figure 5.10, or in any other still picture, comes from looking at moving objects. You may have noticed, for example, that when you look out the window of a moving car, objects nearer to you seem to speed across your visual field, whereas objects in the distance seem to move slowly, if at all. This difference in the apparent rate of movement is called **motion parallax,** and it provides cues to differences in the distance of various objects.

Several additional depth cues result from the way human eyes are built and positioned. One of these cues is related to facts discussed in the chapter on sensation. To bring an image into focus on the retina, the lens of the eye changes shape, or *accommodates,* so as to bend light rays. To accomplish this feat, muscles surrounding the lens either tighten, to make the lens more curved for focusing on close objects, or relax, to flatten the lens for focusing on more distant objects. Information about that muscle activity is relayed to the brain, and this **accommodation** cue helps create the perception of distance.

The relative location of our two eyes produces two other depth cues. One is **convergence:** Because each eye is located at a slightly different place on the skull, the eyes must converge, or rotate inward, to project an image on each retina. The brain receives and processes information from the eye muscles about this activity. The closer the object, the more the eyes must converge, which sends more intense stimulation to the brain.

Second, because of their differing locations, each eye receives a slightly different view of the world. The difference between the two retinal images of an object is called **binocular disparity.** For any particular object, this difference gets smaller as distance increases. The brain combines the two images, processes information about the amount of disparity, and generates the impression of a single object having depth as well as height and width. View-Master slide viewers and 3-D movies create the appearance of depth by displaying to each eye a separate photograph of a scene, each taken from a slightly different angle.

motion parallax A depth cue whereby a difference in the apparent rate of movement of different objects provides information on the relative distance of those objects.

accommodation The ability of the lens of the eye to change its shape and bend light rays so that objects are in focus.

convergence A depth cue involving the rotation of the eyes to project the image of an object on each retina.

binocular disparity A depth cue based on the difference between two retinal images of the world.

The wealth of depth cues available to us is consistent with the ecological approach to perception. However, researchers taking the constructivist and computational approaches argue that even when temporarily deprived of these depth cues, we can still move about and locate objects in an environment. In one study, for example, participants viewed an object from a particular vantage point. Then, with their eyes closed, they were guided to a point well to the side of the object and asked to walk toward it from this new position. The participants were amazingly accurate at this task, leading the researchers to suggest that seeing an object at some point in space creates a spatial model in our minds—a model that remains intact even when immediate depth cues are removed.

Perception of Motion

Sometimes an object's most important property is not its size or shape or distance but its motion—how fast it is going and where it is heading. For example, a car in front of you may change speed or direction, requiring that you change your own speed or direction, often in a split second.

How are you able to perceive such changes in motion? As with the detection of location and depth, the answer seems to be that you can efficiently "tune in" to a host of useful cues. Many of these cues make use of *optical flow*, or the changes in retinal images across the entire visual field. One particularly meaningful pattern of optical flow is known as **looming**, the rapid expansion in the size of an image so that it fills the retina. When an image looms, you tend to interpret it as an approaching stimulus. Your perceptual system quickly assesses whether the expansion on the retina is about equal in all directions or greater to one side than to the other. If it is greater to the right, for example, the approaching stimulus will miss you and pass to your right. However, if the retinal expansion is approximately equal in all directions, then duck!

Two questions, in particular, have interested psychologists who study motion perception. First, how do we know whether the flow of images across the retina is due to the movement of objects in the environment or to our own movements? If changes in retinal images were the only factor contributing to motion perception, then moving your eyes would create the perception that everything in the visual field was moving. This is not the case, though, because as noted earlier, the brain also receives and processes information about the motion of the eyes and head. If you look around the room right now, tables, chairs, and other stationary objects will not appear to move, because your brain determines that all the movement of images on your retinas is due to your eye and head movements. But now close one eye, and wiggle your open eyeball by gently pushing your lower eyelid. Because your brain receives no signals that your eye is being moved by its own muscles, everything in the room will appear to move.

A second question about motion perception involves the time lag of about one-twentieth of a second between the moment when an image is registered on the retina and the moment when messages about that image reach the brain. In theory, each momentary perception of, say, a dog running toward you is actually a perception of where the dog was approximately one-twentieth of a second earlier. How does the perceptual system deal with this time lag so as to accurately interpret information about both motion and location? Psychologists have found that when a stimulus is moving along a relatively constant path, the brain corrects for the image delay by predicting where the stimulus should be one-twentieth of a second in the future (Nijhawan, 1997).

Motion perception is of great interest to sport psychologists. They try to understand, for example, why some individuals are so proficient at perceiving motion. One team of British psychologists discovered a number of cues and computations apparently used by "expert catchers." In catching a ball, these individuals seem to be especially sensitive to the angle between their "straight ahead" gaze (i.e., a

TRY THIS **Binocular Disparity** The difference between each eye's view of an object is smaller for distant objects and greater for closer ones. These binocular disparity cues help to create our perception of distance. To see how distance affects binocular disparity, hold a pencil vertically about six inches in front of your nose; then close one eye and notice where the pencil is in relation to the background. Now open that eye, close the other one, and notice how much the pencil "shifts." These are the two different views your eyes have of the pencil. Repeat the procedure while holding the pencil at arm's length. There is now less disparity, or "shift," because there is less difference in the angles from which your two eyes see the pencil.

looming A motion cue involving a rapid expansion in the size of an image so that it fills the available space on the retina.

Stroboscopic Motion If this series of still photographs of an athlete's handspring were presented to you, one at a time, in quick succession, an illusion called *stroboscopic motion* would cause you to perceive him to be moving.

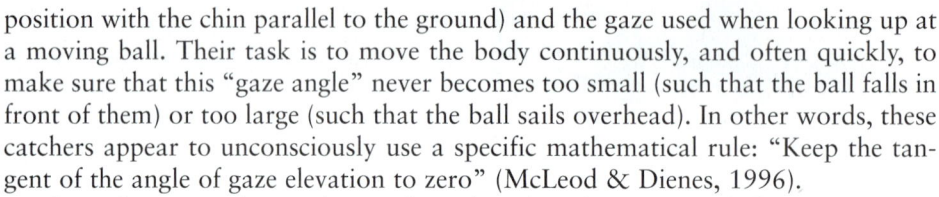

LINKAGES (a link to Sensation)

stroboscopic motion An illusion in which lights or images flashed in rapid succession are perceived as moving.

perceptual constancy The perception of objects as constant in size, shape, color, and other properties despite changes in their retinal image.

position with the chin parallel to the ground) and the gaze used when looking up at a moving ball. Their task is to move the body continuously, and often quickly, to make sure that this "gaze angle" never becomes too small (such that the ball falls in front of them) or too large (such that the ball sails overhead). In other words, these catchers appear to unconsciously use a specific mathematical rule: "Keep the tangent of the angle of gaze elevation to zero" (McLeod & Dienes, 1996).

Sometimes, people perceive motion when there is none. Psychologists are interested in these motion illusions because they can tell us something about how the brain processes various kinds of movement-related information. When you accelerate in a car, for example, the experience of motion does not come only from the flow of visual information across your retinas; it also comes from touch information as you are pressed against the seat and vestibular information as your head tilts backward. If a visual flow suggests that you are moving, but you don't receive appropriate sensations from other parts of your body, particularly the vestibular senses, you may experience a nauseating movement illusion. This form of motion sickness often occurs when people watch some 3-D movies; operate motion simulators; or play certain video games, especially those with virtual reality technology.

Other illusions of motion are much less unpleasant. The most important of these, called **stroboscopic motion,** occurs because of our tendency to interpret as continuous motion a series of still images flashed in rapid succession. Stroboscopic motion is the basis for our ability to see movement in the still images on films and videos. Films consist of sequences of snapshots presented at a rate of twenty-four per second. Each snapshot is slightly different from the preceding one, and each is separated by a brief blank-out produced by the shutter of the film projector. Videotapes show thirty snapshots per second. As we watch, the "memory" of each image lasts long enough in the brain to bridge the gap until the next image appears. Thus, we are usually unaware that we are seeing a series of still pictures and that, about half the time, there is actually no image on the screen!

Perceptual Constancy

Suppose that one sunny day you are watching someone walking toward you along a tree-lined sidewalk. The visual sensations produced by this person are actually rather bizarre, if you think about them. For one thing, the size of the image on your retinas keeps getting larger as the person gets closer. To see this for yourself, hold out a hand at arm's length and look at someone far away. The retinal image of that person will be so small that you can cover it with your hand. If you do the same

figure 5.12
A Size Illusion
The monster that is higher in the drawing probably appears larger than the other one, but they are actually the same size. Why does this illusion occur? The converging lines of the tunnel provide strong depth cues telling us that the higher monster is farther away, but because that monster casts an image on our retinas that is just as big as the "nearer" one, we assume that the more distant monster must be bigger. (Look again at Figure 5.5 for other examples of this illusion.)

TRY THIS **Shape Constancy** Trace the outline of this floating object onto a piece of paper. The tracing will be oval shaped, but shape constancy leads you to perceive it as the circular life ring that it actually is. Sometimes, constancy mechanisms are so good at creating perceptions of a stable world that they can keep us from seeing changes. In one study, for example, participants looking at a computer display of a person's head failed to notice that as the head turned, it morphed gradually into the head of a different person (Wallis & Bülthoff, 2001).

when the person is three feet away, the retinal image will be much larger than your hand, but you will perceive the person as being closer now, not bigger. Similarly, if you watch people pass from bright sunshine through the shadows of trees, your retinas receive images that are darker, then lighter, then darker again. Still, you perceive individuals whose coloring remains the same.

These examples illustrate **perceptual constancy,** the perception of objects as constant in size, shape, color, and other properties despite changes in their retinal image. Without perceptual constancy, the world would be an Alice-in-Wonderland kind of place in which objects continuously changed their properties.

Size Constancy
Why does the perceived size of objects remain more or less constant, no matter what changes occur in the size of their retinal image? One explanation emphasizes the computational aspects of perception. It suggests that as objects move closer or farther away, the brain perceives the change in distance and automatically adjusts the perception. More specifically, the *perceived size* of an object is equal to the size of the retinal image multiplied by the perceived distance (Holway & Boring, 1941). As an object moves closer, its retinal image increases, but the perceived distance decreases at the same rate, so the perceived size remains constant. If, instead, a balloon is inflated in front of your eyes, perceived distance remains constant, and the perceived size (correctly) increases as the retinal image size increases.

The computational perspective is reasonably good at explaining most aspects of size constancy, but it cannot fully account for the fact that people are better at judging the true size (and distance) of familiar rather than unfamiliar objects. This phenomenon suggests that there is an additional mechanism for size constancy—one that is consistent with the constructivists' emphasis on the knowledge-based aspects of perception: Your knowledge and experience tell you that most objects (aside from balloons) do not suddenly change size.

The perceptual system usually produces size constancy correctly and automatically, but it can sometimes fail, resulting in size illusions such as the one illustrated in Figure 5.12. Because this figure contains strong linear perspective cues (lines converging in the "distance"), and because objects nearer the point of convergence are interpreted as farther away, we perceive the monster near the top of the figure as the bigger of the two, even though it is exactly the same size as the other one. The consequences of such illusions can be far more serious when the objects involved are, say, moving automobiles. If there are few other depth cues available, we may perceive objects with smaller retinal images to be farther away than those with larger images. This error may explain why in countries where cars vary greatly in size, small cars have higher accident rates than large ones (Eberts & MacMillan, 1985). A small car produces a smaller retinal image than a large one at the same distance, easily causing the driver of a following vehicle to overestimate the distance to the small car (especially in dim light) and therefore fail to brake in time to avoid a collision. Such misjudgments illustrate the *inferential* nature of perception emphasized by constructivists: People make logical inferences or hypotheses about the world based on the available cues. Unfortunately, if the cues are misleading or the inferences are wrong, perceptual errors may occur.

Shape Constancy
The principles behind shape constancy are closely related to those of size constancy. To see shape constancy at work, remember what page you are on, close this book, and tilt it toward and away from you several times. The book will continue to look rectangular, even though the shape of its retinal image changes dramatically as you move it. The brain automatically integrates information about retinal images and distance as movement occurs. In this case, the distance information involves the difference in distance between the near and far edges of the book.

figure 5.13

Brightness Contrast

TRY THIS At first glance, the inner rectangle on the left probably looks lighter than the inner rectangle on the right. But carefully examine the inner rectangles alone (covering their surroundings), and you will see that both are of equal intensity. The brighter surround in the right-hand figure leads you to perceive its inner rectangle as relatively darker.

As with size constancy, much of the ability to judge shape constancy depends on automatic computational mechanisms in the nervous system, but expectations about the shape of objects also play a role. For example, in Western cultures, most corners are at right angles. Knowledge of this fact helps make "rectangle" the most likely interpretation of the retinal image shown in Figure 5.1.

Brightness Constancy Even with dramatic changes in the amount of light striking an object, the object's perceived brightness remains relatively constant (MacEvoy & Paradiso, 2001). Place a piece of charcoal in sunlight and a piece of white paper in nearby shade. The charcoal will look very dark and the paper very bright, even though a light meter would reveal much more light energy reflected from the sun-bathed coal than from the shaded paper. One reason the charcoal continues to look dark, no matter what the illumination, is that you *know* that charcoal is nearly black, illustrating once again the knowledge-based nature of perception. Another reason is that the charcoal is still the darkest object relative to

in review: Principles of Perceptual Organization and Constancy

Principle	Description	Example
Figure-ground processing	Certain objects or sounds are automatically identified as figures, whereas others become meaningless background.	You see a person standing against a building, not a building with a person-shaped hole in it.
Grouping (Gestalt laws)	Properties of stimuli lead us to automatically group them together. These include proximity, similarity, continuity, closure, common fate, synchrony, common region, and connectedness.	People who are sitting together, or who are dressed similarly, are perceived as a group.
Perception of location and depth	Knowing an object's two-dimensional position position (left and right, up and down) and distance enables us to locate it. The image on the retina and the orientation of the head position provide information about the two-dimensional position of visual stimuli; auditory localization relies on differences in the information received by the ears. Depth or distance perception uses stimulus cues such as interposition, relative size, height in the visual field, texture gradients, linear perspective, clarity, color, and shadow.	Large, clear objects appear closer than small, hazy objects.
Perceptual constancy	Objects are perceived as constant in size, shape, brightness, color, and other properties, despite changes in their retinal images.	A train coming toward you is perceived as getting closer, not larger; a restaurant sign is perceived as rotating, not changing shape.

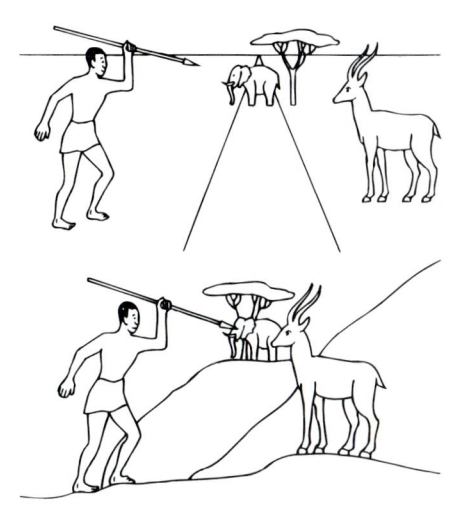

figure 5.14

Culture and Depth Cues

Participants in research on the influence of experience on perception were shown drawings like these and asked to judge which animal is closer to the hunter. People in cultures where pictured depth cues are familiar choose the antelope, which is at the same distance from the viewer as the hunter. People in cultures less familiar with such cues might choose the elephant, which though closer to the hunter on the page, is more distant when depth cues are considered (Hudson, 1960).

Source: Hudson (1960).

its background in the sunlight, and the paper is the brightest object relative to its background in the shade. As shown in Figure 5.13, the brightness of an object is perceived in relation to its background.

For a summary of this discussion, see "In Review: Principles of Perceptual Organization and Constancy."

Culture, Experience, and Perception

So far, we have talked as if all aspects of perception work or fail in the same way for everyone. Differing experiences, however, do affect people's perceptions. To the extent that people in different cultures are exposed to substantially different visual environments, some of their perceptual experiences may be different as well. For example, researchers have compared responses to depth cues by people from cultures that do and do not use pictures and paintings to represent reality (Derogowski, 1989). This research suggests that people in cultures that provide minimal experience with pictorial representations, such as the Me'n or the Nuba in Africa, have a more difficult time judging distances shown in pictures (see Figure 5.14). These individuals also tend to have a harder time sorting pictures of three-dimensional objects into categories, even though they can easily sort the objects themselves (Derogowski, 1989).

Other research shows that the perception of optical illusions varies from culture to culture and is related to cultural differences in perceptual experiences. In one study, researchers enhanced the Ponzo illusion, shown in Figure 5.5(A), by superimposing its horizontal lines on a picture of railroad tracks. This familiar image added depth cues for participants in the United States, but not for people in Guam, which had no railroad tracks at the time of the research (Leibowitz et al., 1969). In short, although the structure and principles of human perceptual systems tend to create generally similar views of the world for all of us, our perception of reality is also shaped by experience, including the experience of living in a particular culture. Unfortunately, as more and more cultures are "westernized," the visual stimulation they present to their children will become less distinctive; eventually, research on the impact of differential experience on perception may become impossible.

Recognizing the Perceptual World

In discussing how people organize the perceptual world, we have set the stage for addressing one of the most vital questions that perception researchers must answer: How do people recognize what objects are? If you are driving in search of Barney's Diner, exactly what happens when your eyes finally locate the pattern of light that spells out its name?

To know that you have finally found what you have been looking for, your brain must analyze incoming patterns of information and compare them with information stored in memory. If your brain finds a match, recognition takes place, and the stimulus is classified into a *perceptual category*. Once recognition occurs, your perception of a stimulus may never be the same again. Look at Figure 5.15. Do you see anything familiar? If not, turn to Figure 5.20, later in the chapter; then look at Figure 5.15 again. You should now see it in an entirely new light. The difference between your "before" and "after" experiences of Figure 5.15 is the difference between the sensory world before and after a perceptual match occurs and recognition takes place.

Exactly how does such matching occur? Some aspects of recognition are guided by knowledge, expectations, and other psychological factors. This phenomenon is called **top-down processing,** because it involves higher-level, knowledge-based information. Other aspects of recognition rely on specific, detailed information elements

top-down processing Aspects of recognition that are guided by higher-level cognitive processes and psychological factors such as expectations.

figure 5.15

Categorizing Perceptions

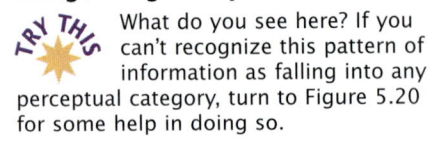

TRY THIS What do you see here? If you can't recognize this pattern of information as falling into any perceptual category, turn to Figure 5.20 for some help in doing so.

from the sensory receptors that are integrated and assembled into a whole. This latter phenomenon is called **bottom-up processing,** because it begins with basic information units that serve as a foundation for recognition. Let's consider the contributions of bottom-up and top-down processing to recognition, as well as the use of neural network models to understand both.

Bottom-Up Processing

Research on the visual system is providing a detailed picture of how bottom-up processing works. As described in the chapter on sensation, all along the path from the eye to the brain, certain cells respond to selected features of a stimulus so that the stimulus is actually analyzed into basic features before these features are recombined to create the perceptual experience.

What features undergo separate analysis? As also noted in the chapter on sensation, certain cells specialize in responding to stimuli having specific orientations in space (Hubel & Wiesel, 1979). For example, one cell in the cerebral cortex might

figure 5.16

Feature Analysis

Feature detectors operating at lower levels of the visual system detect such features of incoming stimuli as the corners and angles shown in the center of this figure. Later in the perceptual sequence, bottom-up processing might recombine these features to aid in pattern recognition, as in the examples on the right.

Presented stimulus → Features detected → Features combined → Patterns recognized

bottom-up processing Aspects of recognition that depend first on the information about the stimulus that comes up to the brain from the sensory receptors.

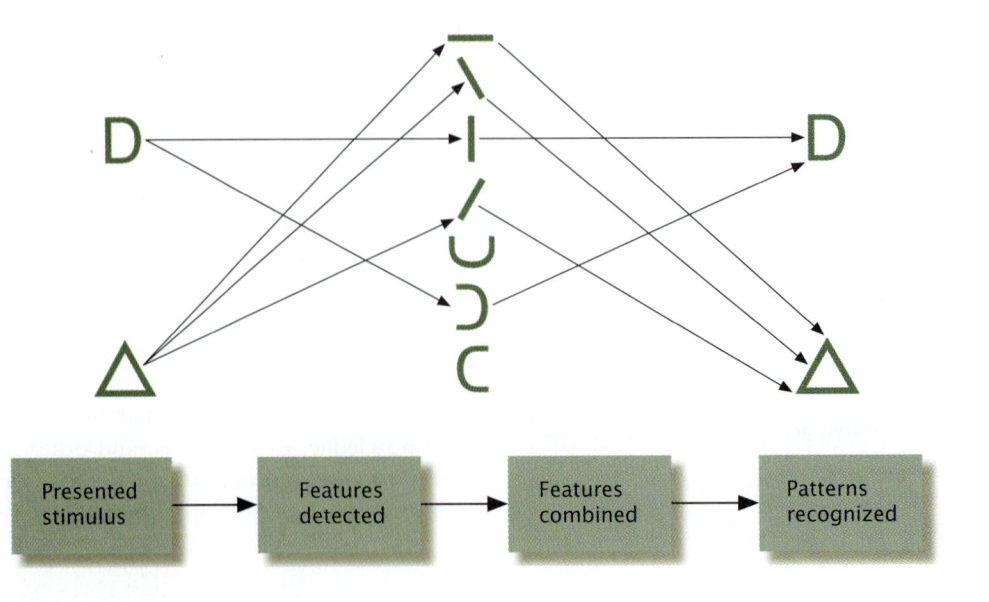

figure 5.17
The Face Looks Familiar
Who are these people? Most people first see Vice President Dick Cheney and President George W. Bush, but look more closely. The image on the left is actually a composite, combining the head shape and glasses of Cheney with the facial features of Bush. The tendency to identify this composite as Cheney suggests that large-scale features, such as overall shape, may be more important than eyes or other small-scale features in the initial recognition of people.

fire only in response to a diagonal line, so it acts as a *feature detector* for diagonal lines. Figure 5.16 illustrates how the analysis by such feature detectors, early in the information-processing sequence, may contribute to recognition of letters or judgments of shape. Color, motion, and even corners are other sensory features that appear to be analyzed separately in different parts of the brain prior to full perceptual recognition (Beatty, 1995; Cowey, 1994).

Features such as color, motion, overall shape, and fine details can all contribute to our ability to recognize objects, but some carry more weight than others in various situations. In the case of face recognition, for example, not all features are equally weighted when we decide who it is that we are seeing (Sinha & Poggio, 1996). Take just a quick look at Figure 5.17, and see if you recognize the person on the *left*. If you are like most people, it will take a second look to realize that your first glance led you to an erroneous conclusion. Such recognition errors are evidence that at least initially, we tend to rely on large-scale features, such as hair and head shape, to recognize people.

How do psychologists know that feature analysis is actually involved in pattern recognition? Recordings of brain activity indicate that the sensory features we have listed here cause particular sets of neurons to fire. In fact, scientists have recently shown that it is possible to determine what category of object a person is looking at (e.g., a face vs. a house) based on the pattern of activity occurring in visual processing areas of the person's brain (Haxby et al., 2001). Further, as described in the chapter on sensation, people with certain kinds of brain damage show selective impairment in the ability to perceive certain sets of sensory features, such as an object's color or movement (Banks & Krajicek, 1991). Irving Biederman (1987) has

figure 5.18
Recognizing Objects from Geons

TRY THIS   Research suggests that we use geons—the forms in the top row—to recognize complex objects. Some examples of objects that can be recognized based on the layout and combination of only two or three geons are shown in the bottom row. The cup, for example, is made up of geons 2 and 4. Other combinations, such as an elongated cylinder (geon 2) on top of a cone (geon 3), might produce a broom. Can you make a kettle out of these geons? The solution is on page 168.

Source: Taken from Belderman, I., Matching Image Edges to Object Memory, from the Proceedings of the IEEE First International Conference on Computer Vision, pp. 364–382, 1987, IEEE © 1997 IEEE.

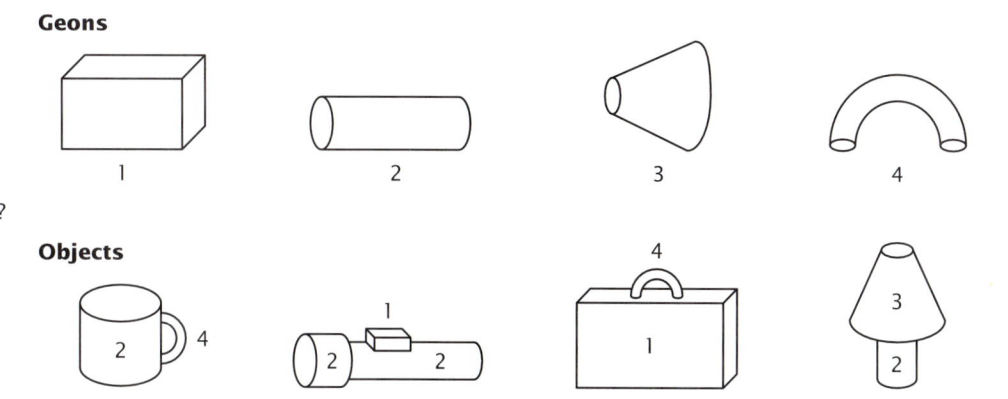

figure 5.19

Recognition of Objects With and Without Their Geons Destroyed

The drawings in columns 2 and 3 have had the same amount of ink removed, but in column 3 the deletions have destroyed many of the geons used in object recognition. The drawings in column 2 are far easier to recognize, because their geons are intact.

proposed that people recognize three-dimensional objects by detecting and then combining simple forms, which he calls *geons*; Figure 5.18 shows some of these geons and how they can be combined to form a variety of recognizable objects. Evidence for Biederman's theory comes from experiments in which people must identify drawings when some of the details have been eliminated. Recognition becomes particularly difficult when the geons are no longer intact, as Figure 5.19 demonstrates.

Top-Down Processing

Bottom-up feature analysis can explain why you recognize the letters in a sign for Barney's Diner. But why is it that you will recognize the sign more easily if it appears where you were told to expect it rather than a block earlier? And why can you recognize it even if a few letters are missing from the sign? Top-down processing seems

figure 5.20

Another Version of Figure 5.15

Now that you can identify a dog in this figure, it should be much easier to recognize when you look back at the original version.

In figure 5.18 you can create a kettle by adding a cone (geon 3) to a combination of geons 2 and 4 (the cup).

Recognizing the Perceptual World

figure 5.21

What Does It Look Like to You?

TRY THIS Many people have reported seeing a demonic face in the smoke pouring from New York's World Trade Center after terrorists attacked it on September 11, 2001. This perceptual categorization results from a combination of bottom-up and top-down recognition processes. Feature detectors automatically register the edges and colors of images, whereas knowledge, beliefs, and expectancies give meaning to these features. A person who does not expect to see a face in the smoke—or whose cultural background does not include the concept of "the devil"—might not see one until that interpretation is suggested. To assess that possibility, show this photo to people from various religious and cultural backgrounds who have not seen it before (don't tell them what to look for) and make a note of which individuals require prompting in order to identify a demonic face.

© 2001 stellarimages.com/Mark D. Phillips. All rights reserved.

schemas Mental representations of what we know and have come to expect about the world.

to be at work in these cases. Fo- ex-mp-e, y-u c-n r-ad -hi- se-te-ce -it- ev-ry -hi-d l-tt-r m-ss-ng. In top-down processing, people use their knowledge in making inferences or "educated guesses" to recognize objects, words, or melodies, especially when sensory information is vague or ambiguous (DeWitt & Samuel, 1990; Rock, 1983). Once you knew that there was a dog in Figure 5.15, it became much easier for you to perceive it in Figure 5.20. Similarly, police officers find it easy to recognize familiar people on blurry security camera videos, but it is much more difficult for them to recognize strangers (Burton et al., 1999).

Many aspects of perception can best be explained by higher-level cognitive influences, especially by expectancy and context. Consider again the two faces in Figure 5.17. Do you think that you'd have been as likely to mistakenly identify the man on the left as Dick Cheney if the person on the right had been, say, British prime minister Tony Blair or John Travolta? Probably not. Through bottom-up processing you correctly identified the combination of features on the right as President Bush; and given your knowledge of him, you reasonably expected to see certain individuals at his side, such as Cheney. In other words, your perceptual system made a quick "educated guess" that turned out to be wrong.

Top-down processing is also involved in sightings of unusual images or "visions." For example, look at Figure 5.21, which shows the World Trade Center under attack. Some people see an image of the devil in the smoke. This interpretation requires some knowledge of paintings and other representations of the devil. Expectancy plays a role, too. Many people who have not heard about the image through the news media do not see a demonic face in this photo.

These examples illustrate that top-down processing can have a strong influence on pattern recognition. Our experiences create **schemas**, which are mental representations of what we know and have come to expect about the world. Schemas can bias our perception toward one recognition or another by creating a *perceptual set*, a readiness or predisposition to perceive a stimulus in a certain way. This predisposition can also be shaped by the immediate context in which a stimulus occurs. In one case we know of, a woman saw a masked man in the darkened hallway of a house she was visiting. Her first perception was that the man who lived there was playing a joke; in fact, she had confronted a burglar. Context has biasing effects for sounds as well as sights. Gunfire heard in public places is often perceived as firecrackers or a car backfiring; at a rifle range, it would immediately be interpreted as shots. In short, top-down processing saves time. It allows us to identify objects even before examination of features is complete, or even when features are missing, distorted, or ambiguous; but as in Figure 5.17, it can sometimes lead us to jump to false conclusions.

The Eye of the Beholder Top-down processing can affect our perception of people, as well as objects. As noted in the chapter on social cognition, for example, if you expect everyone in a certain ethnic or social group to behave in a certain way, you may perceive a particular group member's behavior in line with this prejudice. In contrast, have you ever come to perceive someone as physically more attractive or less attractive as you got to know the person better? This change in perception occurs largely because new information alters, in top-down fashion, your interpretation of the raw sensations you get from the person.

Motivation is another aspect of top-down processing that can affect perception. A hungry person might misperceive a sign for "Burger's Body Shop" as indicating a place to eat. Similarly, if you have ever watched an athletic contest, you probably remember a time when an obviously demented referee incorrectly called a foul on your favorite team. You knew the call was wrong because you clearly saw the other team's player at fault. But suppose you had been cheering for that other team. The chances are good that you would have seen the referee's call as the right one.

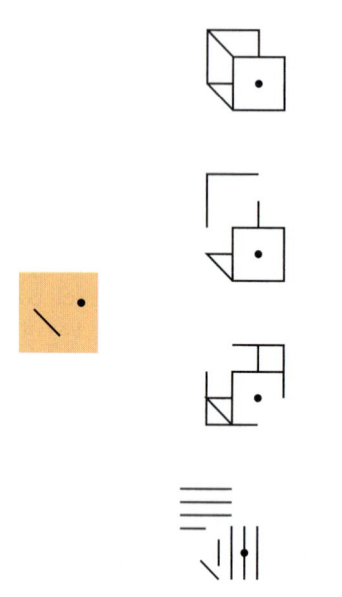

Network Processing

Researchers taking a computational approach to perception have attempted to explain various aspects of object recognition in terms of both top-down *and* bottom-up processing. In one study, participants were asked to say whether a particular feature, like the dot and angle at the left side of Figure 5.22, appeared within a pattern that was briefly flashed on a computer screen. The participants detected this feature faster when it was embedded in a pattern resembling a three-dimensional object than when it appeared within a random pattern of lines (Purcell & Stewart, 1991). This result is called the *object superiority effect*. There is also a *word superiority effect*: When strings of letters are briefly flashed on a screen, people's ability to detect target letters is better if the string forms a word than if it is a nonword (Prinzmetal, 1992).

Neural network models have been used to explain findings such as these. As described in the chapter on biological aspects of psychology, each element in these networks is connected to every other element, and each connection has a specific strength. Applying network processing models to pattern recognition involves focusing on the interactions among the various feature analyzers we have discussed (Rumelhart & Todd, 1992). More specifically, some researchers explain recognition using **parallel distributed processing (PDP) models** (Rumelhart & McClelland, 1986). According to PDP models, the units in a network operate in parallel—simultaneously. Connections between units either excite or inhibit other units. If the connection is excitatory, activating one unit spreads the activation to connected units. Using a connection may strengthen it.

How does this process apply to recognition? According to PDP models, recognition occurs as a result of the simultaneous operation of connected units. Units are

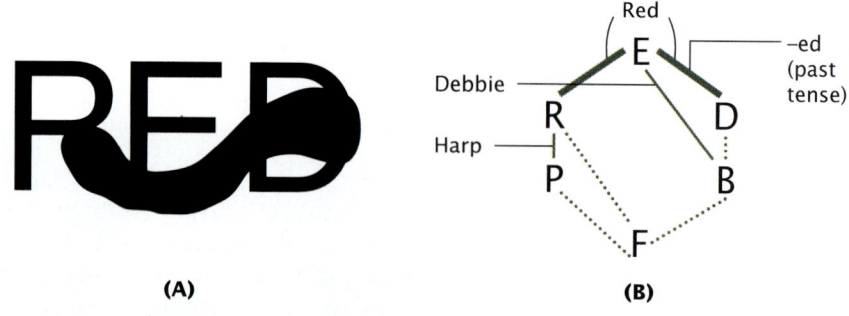

figure 5.22
The Object Superiority Effect

When people are asked to say whether the feature at the left appears in patterns briefly flashed on a computer screen, the feature is more likely to be detected when it appears in patterns like those at the top right, which most resemble three-dimensional objects. This object superiority effect supports the importance of network processing in perception.

Source: Reprinted with permission from figures by Weisstein & Harris, *Science*, 1974, 186, 752–755. Copyright © 1974 by American Association of the Advancement of Science.

figure 5.23
Recognizing a Word

You probably recognized the pattern shown in Part A as the word *RED*, even though the first letter of the word shown could be *R* or *P*; the second, *E* or *F*; and the third, *D* or *B*. According to PDP models, your recognition occurred because, together, the letters excite each other's correct interpretation. This mutual excitation process is illustrated in Part B by a set of letter "nodes" (corresponding to activity sites in the brain) and some of the words they might activate. These nodes will be activated if the feature they detect appears in the stimulus array. They will also be activated if nodes to which they are linked become active. All six letter nodes shown in Part B will initially be excited when the stimulus in Part A is presented, but mutual excitement along the strongest links will guarantee that the word *RED* is perceived (Rumelhart & McClelland, 1985).

Source: Rumelhart & McClelland (1986).

in review: Mechanisms of Pattern Recognition

Mechanism	Description	Example
Bottom-up processing	Raw sensations from the eye or the ear are analyzed into basic features, such as form, color, or movement; these features are then recombined at higher brain centers, where they are compared with stored information about objects or sounds.	You recognize a dog as a dog because its features—four legs, barking, panting—match your perceptual category for "dog."
Top-down processing	Knowledge of the world and experience in perceiving allow people to make inferences about the identity of stimuli, even when the quality of raw sensory information is low.	On a dark night, what you see as a small, vague blob pulling on the end of a leash is recognized as a dog because the stimulus occurs at a location where you would expect a dog to be.
Network, or PDP, processing	Recognition depends on communication among feature-analysis systems operating simultaneously and enlightened by past experience.	A dog standing behind a picket fence will be recognized as a dog even though each disjointed "slice" of the stimulus may not look like a dog.

activated when matched by features in a stimulus. To the extent that features, such as the letters in a word or the angles in a box, have occurred together in the past, their connective links will be stronger, and detection of any of them will be made more likely by the presence of all the others. This appears to be what happens in the word and object superiority effects, and the same phenomenon is illustrated in Figure 5.23. PDP models, sometimes called *connectionist models*, clearly represent the computational approach to perception. Researchers have achieved many advances in theories of pattern recognition by programming computers to carry out the kinds of complex computations that neural networks are assumed to perform in the human perceptual system (Grossberg, 1988). These computers have "learned" to read and recognize speech, and even faces, in a manner that is strikingly similar to the way humans learn and perform the same perceptual tasks (see "In Review: Mechanisms of Pattern Recognition").

LINKAGES (a link to Human Development)

Perception and Human Development

We have seen the important role that knowledge and experience play in recognition, but are they also required for more basic aspects of perception? Which perceptual abilities are babies born with, and which do they acquire by seeing, hearing, smelling, touching, and tasting things? How do their perceptions compare with those of adults? To learn about infants' perception, psychologists have studied two inborn patterns, *habituation* and *dishabituation*. For example, infants stop looking when they repeatedly see stimuli that are perceived to be the same. This is habituation. If a stimulus appears that is perceived to be different, infants resume looking. This is dishabituation. Researchers have used the habituation and dishabituation phenomena, along with measurements of electrical responses in the brain, to study color perception in infants. It seems that newborns can perceive differences among stimuli showing different amounts of black-and-white contrast, but they are unable to distinguish among particular hues (Burr, Morrone, & Fiorentini, 1996). Other researchers have used similar methods to show that newborns can perceive differences in the angles of lines (Slater et al., 1991). These

parallel distributed processing (PDP) models An approach to understanding object recognition in which various elements of the object are thought to be simultaneously analyzed by a number of widely distributed, but connected, neural units in the brain.

figure 5.24

Infants' Perceptions of Human Faces

Newborns show significantly greater interest in the face-like pattern at the far left than in any of the other patterns. Evidently, some aspects of face perception are innate.

Source: Johnson et al. (1991).

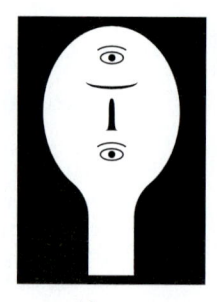

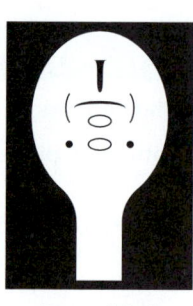

Face   Configuration   Linear   Scrambled

studies and others suggest that we are born with some, but not all, of the basic components of feature detection.

Do we also have an innate ability to combine features into perceptions of whole objects? This question generates lively debate among specialists in infant perception. Some research indicates that at one month of age, infants concentrate their gaze on one part of an object, such as the corner of a triangle (Goldstein, 1999). By two months, though, the eyes systematically scan all the edges of the object, suggesting that only then has the infant begun to perceive the pattern of the object, or its shape, rather than just its component features. However, other researchers have found that once newborns have become habituated to specific combinations of features, they show dishabituation (i.e., they pay attention) when those features are combined in a novel way. The implication is that even newborns notice, and keep track of, the way some features are put together (Slater et al., 1991).

There is evidence that infants may be innately tuned to perceive at least one important complex pattern—the human face. In one study of newborns, some less than an hour old, patterns like those in Figure 5.24 were moved slowly past the infants' faces (Johnson et al., 1991). The infants moved their heads and eyes to follow these patterns, but they tracked the face-like pattern shown on the left side of Figure 5.24 significantly farther than any of the nonfaces. The difference in tracking indicates that the infants could discriminate between faces and nonfaces and were more interested in the faces. Why should this be? The investigators suggest that interest in human faces is adaptive, in evolutionary terms, because it helps newborns focus on their only source of food and care.

Other research on perceptual development suggests that our ability to use certain distance cues develops more slowly than our recognition of object shapes (see Figure 5.25). For example, infants' ability to use binocular disparity and relative

figure 5.25

The Visual Cliff

The *visual cliff* is a glass-topped table that creates the impression of a sudden drop-off. A ten-month-old placed at what looks like the edge will calmly crawl across the shallow side to reach a parent but will hesitate and cry rather than crawl over the "cliff" (Gibson & Walk, 1960). Changes in heart rate show that infants too young to crawl also perceive the depth but are not frightened by it. Here again, nature and nurture interact adaptively: Depth perception appears shortly after birth, but fear and avoidance of dangerous depths do not develop until an infant is old enough to crawl into trouble.

motion cues to judge depth appears to develop some time after about three months of age (Yonas, Arterberry, & Granrud, 1987). Infants do not use texture gradients and linear perspective as cues about depth until they are five to seven months old (Arterberry, Yonas, & Bensen, 1989).

In summary, there is little doubt that many of the basic building blocks of perception are present within the first few days after birth. The basics include organ-based cues to depth, such as accommodation and convergence. Maturation of the visual system adds to these basics as time goes by. For example, over the first few months after birth, the eye's fovea gradually develops the number of cone cells necessary for high visual acuity and perception of small differences in hue (Goldstein, 1999). However, visual experience may also be necessary if the infant is to recognize some unified patterns and objects in frequently encountered stimuli, to interpret depth and distance cues, and to use them in moving safely through the world. In other words, like so many aspects of human psychology, perception is the result of a blending of heredity and environment. From infancy onward, the perceptual system creates a personal reality based in part on the experience that shapes each individual's feature-analysis networks and knowledge-based expectancies.

Attention

Believe it or not, you still haven't found Barney's Diner! By now, you understand *how* you will recognize the right sign when you perceive it, but how can you be sure you *will* perceive it? As you drive, the diner's sign will appear as but one piece in a sensory puzzle that also includes road signs, traffic lights, sirens, talk radio, and dozens of other stimuli. You can't perceive all of them at once, so to find Barney's you are going to have to be sure that the information you select for perceptual processing includes the stimuli that will help you reach your goal. In short, you are going to have to pay attention.

Attention is the process of directing and focusing certain psychological resources to enhance perception, performance, and mental experience. We use attention to *direct* our sensory and perceptual systems toward certain stimuli, to *select* specific information for further processing, to *ignore* or screen out unwanted stimuli, to *allocate* the mental energy required to process selected stimuli, and to *regulate* the flow of resources necessary for performing a task or coordinating several tasks at once (Wickens & Carswell, 1997).

Psychologists have discovered three important characteristics of attention. First, it *improves mental processing*; you often need to concentrate attention on a task to do your best at it. If your attentional system temporarily malfunctions, you might drive right past Barney's Diner. Second, attention takes *effort*. Prolonged concentration of attention can be draining (McNay, McCarty, & Gold, 2001), and when you are tired, focusing attention on anything becomes more difficult. Third, attentional resources are *limited*. When your attention is focused on reading this book, for example, you have less attention left over to listen to a conversation in the next room.

TRY THIS To experience attention as a process, try "moving it around" a bit. When you finish reading this sentence, look at something behind you, then face forward and notice the next sound you hear, then visualize your best friend, and then focus on how your tongue feels. You just used attention to direct your perceptual systems toward different aspects of your external and internal environments. Sometimes, as when you looked behind you, shifting attention involves *overt orienting*—pointing sensory systems at a particular stimulus. But you were able to shift attention to an image of your friend's face without having to move a muscle; this is called *covert orienting*. There is a rumor that students sometimes use covert orienting to shift their attention from their lecturer to thoughts that have nothing to do with the lecture.

attention The process of directing and focusing certain psychological resources to enhance perception, performance, and mental experience.

FOCUS ON RESEARCH METHODS

An Experiment in "Mind Reading"

Everyone knows what it is like to covertly shift attention, but how can we tell when someone else is doing it? The study of covert attention requires the sort of "mind reading" that has been made possible by innovative experimental research methods. These techniques are helping psychologists to measure where a person's attention is focused.

• What was the researchers' question?

Michael Posner and his colleagues were interested in finding out what changes in perceptual processing occur when people covertly shift their attention to a specific location in space (Posner, Nissen, & Ogden, 1978). Specifically, the researchers addressed the question of whether these attentional shifts lead to more sensitive processing of stimuli in the location attended to.

• How did the researchers answer the question?

Posner and his colleagues took advantage of an important property of mental events: Even though such events do not produce movements that can be observed and recorded, they do take time. Moreover, the time taken by mental events can vary considerably, thus providing important clues about internal processes such as covert attention.

The researchers designed a study in which participants were asked to focus their eyes on a fixation point that appeared at the center of a computer screen. One second later, a tiny square appeared at either the right or left edge of the screen. The participants were then asked to indicate, by pressing a key as quickly as possible, when they detected the square. However, because their vision was focused on the fixation point, they could detect the square only out of the "corners" of their eyes.

On any given trial, a participant could never be sure where the square would be located. However, the researchers provided "hints" on some of the trials. At the start of some trials, participants were given a cue at the fixation point. Sometimes, the cue was an arrow pointing to the right edge of the screen (→). This cue was correct 80 percent of the time. On other trials, participants were presented with an arrow pointing to the left edge of the screen (←); this cue was also correct 80 percent of the time. On still other trials, participants saw a plus sign (+), which indicated that the square was equally likely to appear on the left or the right.

The researchers reasoned that when the plus sign appeared, the best strategy for quickly detecting the square would be to maintain visual attention on the center of the screen and to shift it only after the square appeared. However, when one of the arrow cues was presented, the best strategy would involve covertly shifting attention in the direction indicated by the arrow before the square appeared. If the participants were actually using covert attention shifts, they should have been able to detect the square fastest when the cue provided accurate information about the location of the target square, even though they were not actually moving their eyes.

The dependent variable in this study was the speed of target detection, measured in milliseconds. The independent variable was the type of cue given: valid, invalid, or neutral. Valid cues were arrows that correctly predicted the target location; invalid ones were arrows that pointed the wrong way. Neutral cues gave no guidance.

• What did the researchers find?

As shown in Figure 5.26, the square stimulus was detected significantly faster when the cue gave valid information about where the square would appear. Invalid

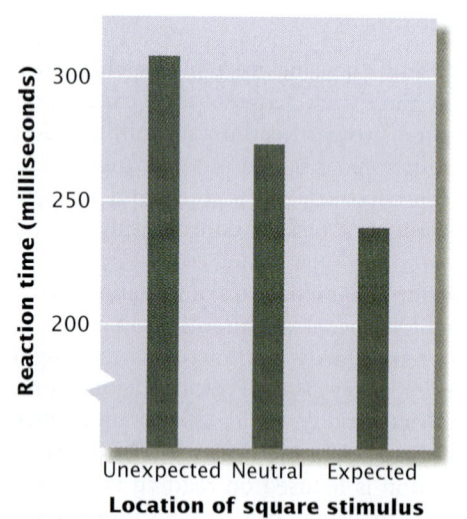

figure 5.26

Measuring Covert Shifts in Attention

It took people less time (measured in thousandths of a second) to detect a square appearing at an expected location than at an unexpected location on a computer screen. This result suggests that even though their eyes did not move, they covertly shifted attention to the expected location before the stimulus was presented.

cues, however, resulted in a distinct cost to performance: When participants were led to shift their attention in the wrong direction, they were much slower in detecting the square.

● **What do the results mean?**

The data provide evidence that the participants used cues to shift their attention to the expected location, thus readying their perceptual systems to detect information there. When a cue led them to shift their attention to the wrong location, they were less ready to detect information at the correct location, and their detection was slowed. In short, attention can enhance the processing of information at one retinal location, but it does so at the expense of processing information elsewhere.

● **What do we still need to know?**

More recent research on the costs and benefits associated with perceptual expectancies has been generally consistent with the findings of Posner's pioneering team (e.g., Ball & Sekuler, 1992; Carrasco & McElree, 2001). However, there are still many unanswered questions about how covert attention actually operates. How quickly can we shift attention from one location to another? And how quickly can we shift attention between sensory modalities, say, from watching to listening? These questions are methodologically difficult to address, but they are fundamental to understanding our ability to deal with the potentially overwhelming load of stimuli that reaches our sensory receptors. Experiments designed to answer such questions not only expand our understanding of attention but also illustrate the possibility of measuring hidden mental events through observation of overt behavior (Wolfe, Alvarez, & Horowitz, 2000).

Directing Attention

As shown in Posner's experiment on "mind reading," attending to some stimuli makes us less able to attend to others. In other words, attention is *selective*; it is like a spotlight that can illuminate only a part of the external or internal environment at any particular moment. How do you control, or allocate, your attention?

Control over attention can be voluntary or involuntary (Yantis, 1993). *Voluntary*, or goal-directed, attention control occurs when you purposely focus your attention in order to perform a task, such as reading a book in a noisy room or watching for a friend in a crowd. Voluntary control reflects top-down processing, because attention is guided by knowledge-based factors such as intentions, beliefs, expectations, and motivation. As people learn certain skills, they voluntarily direct their attention to information they once ignored. For example, when rounding a bend, a newly licensed driver will attend to the outside of the curve; the experienced driver will attend to the inside of the curve, which actually conveys more information about where to steer. If you are watching a sports event, learning where to allocate your attention is important if you are to understand what is going on. And if you are a competitor, the proper allocation of attention is absolutely essential for success on the playing field (Moran, 1996).

When, in spite of these top-down factors, some aspect of the environment—such as a loud noise—diverts your attention, attentional control is said to be *involuntary*. In this case, it is a bottom-up, or stimulus-driven, process. Stimulus characteristics that tend to capture attention include abrupt changes in lighting or color (such as flashing signs), movement, and the appearance of unusual shapes (Folk, Remington, & Wright, 1994). Some psychologists use the results of attention research to help design advertisements, logos, and product packaging that "grab" potential customers' attention.

Ignoring Information

When the spotlight of your attention is voluntarily or involuntarily focused on one part of the environment, you may ignore stimuli occurring in other parts. This ability, called *inattentional blindness* (Mack & Rock, 1998), can be helpful when it allows us to ignore construction noise while we are taking an exam, but it can also endanger us if we ignore information—such as a stop sign—that we should be attending to. Inattentional blindness can result in our missing some rather dramatic changes in our environment (Most et al., 2001). In one study, a researcher asked college students for directions to a campus building (Simons & Levin, 1997). During each conversation, two other researchers dressed as workmen passed between the first researcher and the student, carrying a large door. As the door hid the researcher from the student's view, one of the "workmen" took his place. This new person then resumed the conversation with the student as though nothing had happened.

figure 5.27

Change Blindness

TRY THIS These two photos are almost, but not exactly, alike. If you can't see the difference, or if it took you a while, you may have been focusing your attention on the similarity of main features, resulting in blindness to one small, but obvious, change. (See page 179 for the answer.)

Amazing as it seems, only half of the students noticed that they were suddenly talking to a new person! The rest had apparently been paying so much attention to the researcher's question or to the map he was showing that they did not notice his appearance. And half the participants in another study were so focused on their assigned task of counting the passes made during a videotaped basketball game that they did not notice a woman in a gorilla suit who walked in front of the camera, beat her chest, and walked away (Simons & Chabris, 1999). Magicians take advantage of this phenomenon whenever they direct our attention elsewhere while making switches that we would otherwise clearly see. To experience a type of inattentional blindness known as "change blindness," take a look at the photographs in Figure 5.27.

Divided Attention

In many situations, people can divide their attention efficiently enough to allow them to perform more than one activity at a time (Damos, 1992). In fact, as Figure 5.28 illustrates, it is sometimes difficult to keep our attention focused rather than divided. We can walk while talking or drive while listening to music, but we find it virtually impossible to read and talk at the same time. Why is it sometimes so easy and at other times so difficult to do two things at once?

When one task is so *automatic* that it requires little or no attention, it is usually easy to do something else at the same time, even if the other task takes some attention (Schneider, 1985). When two tasks both require attention, it may still be possible to perform them simultaneously, as long as each taps into different kinds of attentional resources (Wickens, 1992a). For example, some attentional resources are devoted to perceiving incoming stimuli, whereas others handle making responses. This specialization of attention allows a skilled pianist to read musical notes and press keys simultaneously, even the first time through a piece. Apparently, the human brain has more than one type of attentional resource and more than one spotlight of attention (Wickens, 1989). This notion of different types of attention also helps explain why a driver can listen to the radio while steering safely and why voice control can be an effective way of performing a second task in an aircraft while the pilot's hands are busy manipulating the controls (Wickens, 1992a). If two tasks require the same kind of attention, however, performance on both tasks will suffer (Just et al., 2001)

Attention and Automatic Processing

Your search for Barney's Diner will be aided by your ability to voluntarily allocate attention to a certain part of the environment, but it would be even easier if you knew that Barney's had the only bright red sign on that stretch of road (see "In Review: Attention"). Your search would not take much effort in this case because you could simply "set" your attention to filter out all signs except red ones. The process of actively ignoring certain information will help you find Barney's, but it will also continue to affect your perceptions for some time afterward. Suppose, for example, that while you are ignoring blue signs, you pass one showing a giant blue palm tree. Researchers have found that your efforts to ignore certain stimuli may create *negative priming* (Rock & Gutman, 1981), making you slightly less able than before to identify palm trees of any color for several minutes, hours, or days (Deschepper & Treisman, 1996).

Psychologists describe the ability to search for targets rapidly and automatically as *parallel processing*; it is as if you can examine all nearby locations at once (in parallel) and rapidly detect the target no matter where it appears. So if the sign you are looking for is bright red and twice as large as any other one on the road, you could conduct a parallel search, and it would quickly "pop out." The automatic, parallel processing that allows detection of color or size suggests that these features are

BLUE   **GREEN**
GREEN **ORANGE**
PURPLE **ORANGE**
GREEN **BLUE**
RED   **RED**
GRAY   **GRAY**
RED   **BLUE**
BLUE   **PURPLE**

figure 5.28

The Stroop Task

TRY THIS Look at these words, and as rapidly as possible, call out the *color of the ink* in which each word is printed. This Stroop task (Stroop, 1935) is not easy, because your brain automatically processes the *meaning* of each word, which then competes for attention with the response you are supposed to give. To do well, you must focus on the ink color and not allow your attention to be divided between color and meaning. Children just learning to read have less trouble with this task, because they do not yet process word meanings as automatically as experienced readers do.

in review: Attention

Characteristics	Functions	Mechanisms
Improves mental functioning	Directs sensory and perceptual systems toward stimuli	Overt orienting (e.g., cupping your ear to hear a whisper)
Requires effort	Selects specific information for further processing	Covert orienting (e.g., thinking about spring break while looking at the notes in front of you)
Has limits	Allows us to ignore some information	Voluntary control (e.g., purposefully looking for cars before crossing a street)
	Allocates mental energy to process information	Involuntary control (e.g., losing your train of thought when you're interrupted by a thunderclap)
	Regulates the flow of resources necessary for performing a task or coordinating multiple tasks	Automatic processing (e.g., no longer thinking about grammar rules as you become fluent in a foreign language)
		Divided attention (e.g., looking for an open teammate while you dribble a soccer ball down the field)

analyzed before the point at which attention is required. However, if the target you seek shares many features with others nearby, you must conduct a slower, serial search, examining each one in turn (Treisman, 1988).

Attention and the Brain

If directing attention to a task causes extra mental work to be done, there should be evidence of that work in brain activity. Such evidence has been provided by positron emission tomography (PET) and magnetic resonance imaging (MRI) scans, which reveal increased blood flow and greater neural activity in regions of the brain associated with the mental processing necessary for the task. In one study, for example, people were asked either to focus attention on reporting only the color of a stimulus or to divide attention in order to report its color, speed of motion, and shape (Corbetta et al., 1991). When attention was focused on color alone, increased blood flow appeared only in the part of the brain where that stimulus feature was analyzed; when attention was divided, the added supply of blood was shared between two locations. Similarly, increased neural activity occurs in two different areas of the brain when participants perform two different tasks, such as deciding whether sentences are true while also deciding whether two three-dimensional objects are the same or different (Just et al., 2001).

Because attention appears to be a linked set of resources that improve information processing at several levels and locations in the brain, it is not surprising that no single brain region has been identified as an "attention center" (Posner & Peterson, 1990; Sasaki et al., 2001). However, scientists have found regions in the base of the brain and in the parietal lobe of the cerebral cortex that are involved in the *switching* of visual attention from one stimulus element or location to another (Posner & Raichle, 1994).

Applications of Research on Perception

Throughout this chapter we have mentioned ways in which perceptual systems shape people's ability to handle a variety of tasks, from recognizing restaurant signs to detecting tornadoes. We have also seen how research on perception explains the

Avoiding Perceptual Overload The pilot of a modern commercial jetliner is faced with a potentially overwhelming array of visual and auditory signals that must be correctly perceived and interpreted to ensure a safe flight. Engineering psychologists are helping to design instrument displays, warning systems, and communication links that make this task easier and make errors less likely.

principles behind movies and videos and affects the design of advertisements. In this section we examine three other areas in which perception research has been applied: aviation, human-computer interaction, and traffic safety.

Aviation Psychology

Much of the research on perception in aviation has stemmed from efforts to understand accidents that were caused in part by failures of perception (O'Hare & Roscoe, 1991; Wiener & Nagel, 1988). To land an aircraft safely, for example, pilots must make accurate judgments of how far they are from the ground, as well as how fast and from what angle they are approaching the runway. The ecological approach to perception emphasizes that the perceptual cues providing this information are rich and redundant. Normally, this is the case, and pilots' perceptions are correct (Gibson, 1979). Consistent with the constructivist view, pilots can also use their experience-based expectations about the approaching ground surface, thus adding top-down processing to produce an accurate perception of reality.

But suppose there are few depth cues because the landing occurs at night, and suppose the lay of the land differs from what the pilot normally experiences. With both bottom-up and top-down processing impaired, the pilot's interpretation of reality may be disastrously incorrect. If, for example, the runway is much smaller than a pilot expects, it might be perceived as farther away than it actually is—especially at night—and thus may be approached too fast (O'Hare & Roscoe, 1991). (This illusion is similar to the one mentioned earlier in which drivers overestimate their distance from small cars.) Or if a pilot expects the runway to be perfectly flat but it actually slopes upward, the pilot might falsely perceive that the aircraft is too high. Misguided attempts to "correct" a plane's altitude under these circumstances have caused pilots to fly in too low, resulting in a series of major nighttime crashes in the 1960s (Kraft, 1978). Psychologists have helped to prevent similar tragedies by recommending that airline training programs remind pilots about the dangers of visual illusions and the importance of relying on their flight instruments during landings, especially at night.

Unfortunately, the instruments in a traditional aircraft cockpit present information that bears little resemblance to the perceptual world. A pilot depending on these instruments must do a lot of time-consuming and effortful serial processing to perceive and piece together the information necessary to understand the aircraft's position and movement. To address this problem, engineering psychologists have helped to develop displays that present a realistic three-dimensional image of the flight environment—similar in some ways to a video-game display. This image more accurately captures the many cues for depth perception that the pilot needs (Haskell & Wickens, 1993; Lintern, 1991; Theunisson, 1994).

Research on auditory perception has also contributed to aviation safety, both in the creation of warning signals that are most likely to catch the pilot's attention and in efforts to minimize errors in cockpit communications. Air-traffic control communications use a special vocabulary and standardized phrases to avoid misunderstandings. But as a result, these communications are usually short, with little of the built-in redundancy that in normal conversation allows people to understand a sentence even if some words are missing. For example, if a pilot eager to depart on time perceives an expected message as "clear for takeoff" when the actual message is "hold for takeoff," the results can be catastrophic. Problems like these are being addressed "bottom up," through "noise-canceling" microphones and visual message displays (Kerns, 1991), as well as through the use of slightly longer messages that aid top-down processing by providing more contextual cues.

The difference between the photos in Figure 5.27 is that in the top photo, there is a clump of trees just to the left of the sphinx.

Human-Computer Interaction

The principles of perception are also being applied by engineering psychologists who serve as key members of design teams at various computer manufacturers and software companies. For example, in line with the ecological approach to perception, they are trying to duplicate in the world of computer displays many of the depth cues that help people navigate in the physical world (Preece et al., 1994). The next time you use a word-processing or spreadsheet program, notice how shading cues make the "buttons" on the application toolbar at the top or bottom of the screen seem to protrude from their background, as real buttons would. Similarly, when you open several documents or spreadsheets, notice that interposition cues make them appear to be lying on top of one another.

The results of research on attention have even been applied to your cursor. It blinks to attract your attention, making it possible to do a quick parallel search rather than a slow serial search when you are looking for it amid all the other stimuli on the screen (Schneiderman, 1992). Perceptual principles have also guided creation of the pictorial images, or icons, that are used to represent objects, processes, and commands in your computer programs (Preece et al., 1994). These icons speed your use of the computer if their features are easy to detect, recognize, and interpret (McDougall, de Bruijn, & Curry, 2000; Niemela & Saarinen, 2000). This is why a little trash-can icon is used in some software programs to show you where to click when you want to delete a file; a tiny eraser or paper shredder would also work, but its features might be harder to recognize, making the program confusing. In short, psychologists are applying research on perception to make computers easier to use.

Traffic Safety

Research on perception is being applied in many ways to enhance traffic safety. For example, psychologists are involved in the design of automotive night vision displays that make it easier for drivers to see low-visibility targets, such as pedestrians dressed in dark clothing, or animals (Essock, et al., 1999). Further, research on divided attention is informing the debate over the use of cell phones while driving. The demands of traffic safety groups and the example set by countries such as Britain and Japan have led the state of New York to outlaw drivers' use of cell phones; thirty-four other U.S. states are considering such bans (Clines, 2001). Cell phone manufacturers agree that phone use while driving can be dangerous, but only

Driven to Distraction? About 85 percent of the more than 110 million cell phone owners in the United States use their phones while driving (Clines, 2001). Some cell phone manufacturers claim that hands-free models can eliminate any dangers associated with using a phone while driving, but perception research indicates that using any kind of phone can create distractions that impair driving performance and may contribute to accidents.

because looking at the handset, pushing its buttons, and holding it in place during the call can distract the driver from steering and watching the road. They claim that hands-free phones that feature headsets and voice-controlled dialing eliminate any dangers associated with cell phone use. That argument is contradicted by recent research showing that driving performance is impaired while talking on *any* cell phone, even if it is a hands-free model (Strayer & Johnston, 2001). The research also suggests that the dangers of driving while using a phone do not stem simply from listening to someone speak, or even from talking. The driving performance of research participants was not impaired by listening to books on tape or by repeating words that they heard. Performance *did* decline, though, when participants were asked to do more elaborate processing of auditory information, such as rephrasing what they heard. (You may have experienced similar effects if you have ever missed a turn or had a near-accident while deeply engaged in conversation with a passenger.) These results suggest that using a cell phone while driving is dangerous not only because it can take your eyes off the road and a hand off the wheel but also because the phone conversation competes for the cognitive/attentional resources you need to drive safely. Perception researchers suggest that this competition and the dangers associated with it are unlikely to be reduced by hands-free car phones (Just et al., 2001).

LINKAGES

As noted in the chapter on introducing psychology, all of psychology's subfields are related to one another. Our discussion of how perceptual processes develop in infants illustrates just one way in which the topic of this chapter, perception, is linked to the subfield of developmental psychology (which is the topic of the chapter on human development). The Linkages diagram shows ties to two other subfields as well, and there are many more ties throughout the book. Looking for linkages among subfields will help you see how they all fit together and help you better appreciate the big picture that is psychology.

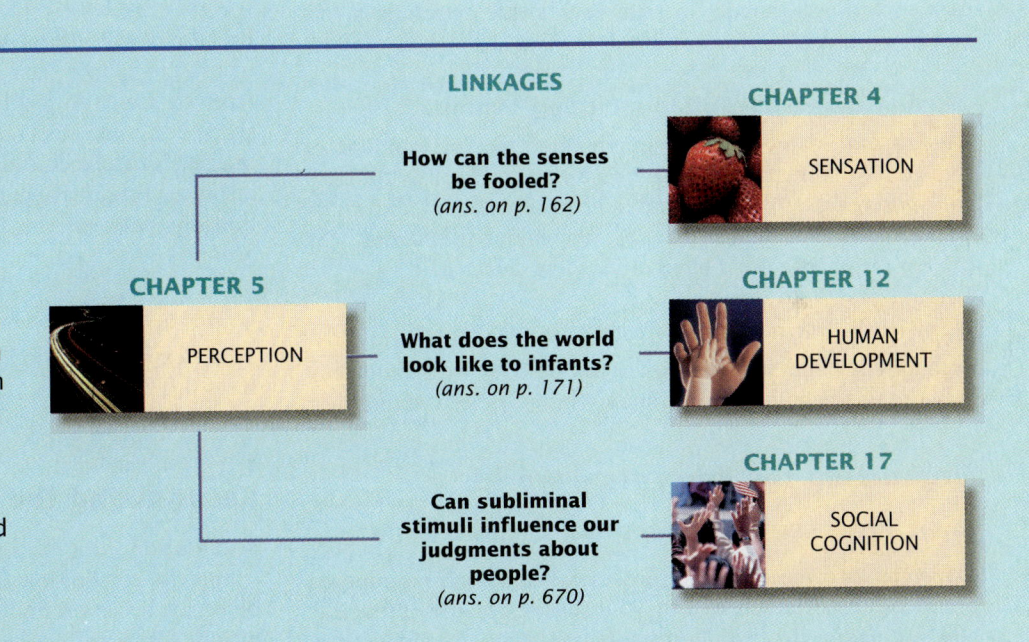

LINKAGES

CHAPTER 5 — PERCEPTION

- How can the senses be fooled? (ans. on p. 162) — **CHAPTER 4** SENSATION
- What does the world look like to infants? (ans. on p. 171) — **CHAPTER 12** HUMAN DEVELOPMENT
- Can subliminal stimuli influence our judgments about people? (ans. on p. 670) — **CHAPTER 17** SOCIAL COGNITION

SUMMARY

Perception is the process through which people actively use knowledge and understanding of the world to interpret sensations as meaningful experiences.

The Perception Paradox

Because perception often seems so rapid and effortless, it appears to be a rather simple operation; however, this is not the case. An enormous amount of processing is required to transform energy received by receptors into perceptual experience. The complexity of perception is revealed by various perceptual errors (e.g., illusions).

Three Approaches to Perception

The *computational approach* to perception emphasizes the computations performed by the nervous system. The *constructivist approach* suggests that the perceptual system constructs the experience of reality, making inferences and applying knowledge in order to interpret sensations. The *ecological approach* holds that the environment itself provides the cues that people use to form perceptions.

Psychophysics

Psychophysics is the study of the relationship between stimulus energy and the psychological experience of that energy.

Absolute Thresholds: Is Something Out There?

Psychophysics has traditionally been concerned with matters such as determining absolute thresholds for the detection of stimuli. Research shows that this threshold is not, in fact, absolute. Thus, the *absolute threshold* has been redefined as the minimum amount of stimulus energy that can be detected 50 percent of the time. *Supraliminal stimuli* fall above this threshold; *subliminal stimuli* fall below it.

Signal-Detection Theory

Signal-detection theory describes how people respond to faint or ambiguous stimuli. Detection of a signal is affected by external and internal noise, *sensitivity*, and the *response criterion*. Signal-detection theory has been applied to understanding decision making and performance in areas such as the detection of tornadoes on radar.

Judging Differences: Has Anything Changed?

Weber's law states that the minimum detectable amount of change in a stimulus—the *difference threshold*, or *just-noticeable difference (JND)*—increases in proportion to the initial amount of the stimulus. The less the initial stimulation, the smaller the change must be in order to be detected.

Magnitude Estimation: How Intense Is That?

Fechner's law and Stevens's power law describe the relationship between the magnitude of a stimulus and its perceived intensity.

Organizing the Perceptual World

Basic Processes in Perceptual Organization

Perceptual organization is the process whereby order is imposed on the information received by your senses. The perceptual system automatically distinguishes figure from ground, and it groups stimuli into patterns. Gestalt psychologists and others identified laws or principles that guide such grouping: proximity, similarity, continuity, closure, common fate, synchrony, common region, and connectedness. These laws appear to ensure that perceptual organization creates interpretations of incoming information that are simple and most likely to be correct. The process of mentally representing and interpreting sounds is called *auditory scene analysis*.

Perception of Location and Distance

Visual localization requires information about the position of the body and eyes, as well as information about where a stimulus falls on the retinas. Auditory localization depends on detecting differences in the information that reaches the two ears, including differences in timing and intensity. Perception of distance, or *depth perception*, depends partly on stimulus cues and partly on the physical structure of the visual system. Some of the stimulus cues for depth perception are *interposition*, *relative size*, *height in the visual field*, *texture gradient*, *linear perspective*, and *motion parallax*. Cues based on the structure of the visual system include *accommodation* (the change in the shape of the lenses as objects are brought into focus), *convergence* (the fact that the eyes must move to focus on the same object), and *binocular disparity* (the fact that the eyes are set slightly apart).

Perception of Motion

The perception of motion results, in part, from the movement of stimuli across the retina. Expanding or *looming* stimulation is perceived as an approaching object. Movement of the retinal image is interpreted along with information about movement of the head, eyes, and other parts of the body so that one's own movement can be discriminated from the movement of external objects. *Stroboscopic motion* is an illusion that accounts for our ability to see smooth motion in films and videos.

Perceptual Constancy

Because of *perceptual constancy*, the brightness, size, and shape of objects can be seen as constant even though the sensations received from those objects may change. Size constancy and shape constancy depend on the relationship between the retinal image of an object and the knowledge-based perception of its distance. Brightness constancy depends on the perceived relationship between the brightness of an object and its background.

Culture, Experience, and Perception

To the extent that visual environments of people in different cultures differ, their perceptual experiences—as evidenced by their responses to perceptual illusions—may differ as well.

Recognizing the Perceptual World

Both *bottom-up processing* and *top-down processing* may contribute to recognition of the world. The ability to recognize objects is based on finding a match between the pattern of sensations organized by the perceptual system and a pattern that is stored in memory.

Bottom-Up Processing

Bottom-up processing seems to be accomplished by the analysis of stimulus features or combinations of features, such as form, color, and motion.

Top-Down Processing

Top-down processing is influenced by expectancy and motivation. *Schemas* based on past experience can create a perceptual set, the readiness or predisposition to perceive stimuli in certain ways. Expectancies can also be created by the context in which a stimulus appears.

Network Processing

Research on pattern recognition has focused attention on network models, or *parallel distributed processing (PDP) models*, of perception. These emphasize the simultaneous activation and interaction of feature-analysis systems and the role of experience.

Attention

Attention is the process of focusing psychological resources to enhance perception, performance, and mental experience. We can shift attention overtly—by moving the eyes, for example—or covertly, without any movement of sensory systems.

Directing Attention

Attention is selective; it is like a spotlight that illuminates different parts of the external environment or various mental processes. Control over attention can be voluntary and knowledge based or involuntary and driven by environmental stimuli.

Ignoring Information

Sometimes attention can be so focused that it results in inattentional blindness, a failure to detect or identify normally noticeable stimuli.

Divided Attention

Although there are limits to how well people can divide attention, they can sometimes attend to two tasks at once. For example, tasks that have become automatic can often be performed along with more demanding tasks, and tasks that require very different types of processing, such as gardening and talking, can be performed together because each task depends on a different supply of mental resources.

Attention and Automatic Processing

Some information can be processed automatically, in parallel, whereas other situations demand focused attention and a serial search.

Attention and the Brain

Although the brain plays a critical role in attention, no single brain region has been identified as the main attention center.

Applications of Research on Perception

Research on human perception has numerous practical applications.

Aviation Psychology

Accurate size and distance judgments, top-down processing, and attention are all important to safety in aviation.

Human-Computer Interaction

Perceptual principles relating to recognition, depth cues, and attention are being applied by psychologists who work with designers of computers and computer programs.

Traffic Safety

Research on divided attention is being applied to help understand the potential dangers of driving while using various kinds of cell phones.

6 Learning

Learning About Stimuli
Classical Conditioning: Learning Signals and Associations
Pavlov's Discovery
Conditioned Responses Over Time: Extinction and Spontaneous Recovery
Stimulus Generalization and Discrimination
The Signaling of Significant Events
Some Applications of Classical Conditioning

Instrumental and Operant Conditioning: Learning the Consequences of Behavior
From the Puzzle Box to the Skinner Box
Basic Components of Operant Conditioning
Forming and Strengthening Operant Behavior
Why Reinforcers Work
Punishment
Some Applications of Operant Conditioning

Cognitive Processes in Learning
Learned Helplessness
Focus on Research Methods: A Two-Factor Experiment on Human Helplessness
Latent Learning and Cognitive Maps
Insight and Learning
Observational Learning: Learning by Imitation
Thinking Critically: Does Watching Violence on Television Make People More Violent?
Linkages: Neural Networks and Learning

Using Research on Learning to Help People Learn
Classrooms Across Cultures
Active Learning
Skill Learning

Linkages
Summary

Can you recall how you felt on your first day of kindergarten? Like many young children, you may have been bewildered, even frightened, as the comforting familiarity of home or day care was suddenly replaced by an environment filled with new names and faces, rules and events. But like most youngsters, you probably adjusted to this new environment within a few days, much as you did again when you started middle school, high school, and college.

Your adjustment, or *adaptation,* to these new environments occurred in many ways. Ringing bells, lunch lines, midterm grades, and other once-strange new school events not only became part of your expectations about the world but also began to serve as signals. You soon realized that if a note was delivered to your teacher during class, someone would be called to the main office. If a substitute teacher appeared, it meant an easy lesson, or a chance to act up. And if your teacher arrived with a box of papers, you'd know the tests had been graded. Adapting to school also meant developing new knowledge about what behaviors were appropriate and inappropriate in the new situations you encountered. Although your parents might have encouraged you to talk whenever you wanted to at home, perhaps you found that at school, you had to raise your hand first. And the messy finger painting that got you in trouble at home might have earned you praise in art class. You found, too, that there were things you could do—such as paying attention in class and getting to school on time—to reap rewards and avoid punishment. Finally, of course, you adapted to school by absorbing facts about the world and developing skills ranging from kickball and reading to writing and debating.

The entire process of development, from birth to death, involves adapting to increasingly complex, ever-changing environments, using continuously updated knowledge gained through experience. Although perhaps most highly developed in humans, the ability to adapt to changing environments appears to varying degrees in members of all species. According to the evolutionary approach to psychology, it is individual variability in the capacity to adapt that shapes the evolution of appearance and behavior in animals and humans. As Charles Darwin noted, individuals who don't adapt may not survive to reproduce.

Many forms of animal and human adaptation follow the principles of learning. **Learning** is the process through which experience modifies pre-existing behavior and understanding. The pre-existing behavior and understanding may have been present at birth, acquired through maturation, or learned earlier. Learning plays a central role in the development of most aspects of human behavior, from the motor skills we need to walk or tie a shoe to the language skills we use to communicate to the object categories—such as "food," "vehicle," or "animal"—that help us organize our perceptions and think logically about the world. Sayings such as "Once burned, twice shy" and "Fool me once, shame on you; fool me twice, shame on me" reflect this vital learning process. If you want to know who you are and how you became the person you are today, examining what and how you have learned is a good place to start.

People learn primarily by experiencing events, observing relationships between those events, and noting the regularity in the world around them. When two events repeatedly take place together, people can predict the occurrence of one from knowledge of the other. They learn that a clear blue sky means dry weather, that too little sleep makes them irritable, that they can reach someone via e-mail by typing a certain address, and that screaming orders motivates some people and angers others. Some learning takes place consciously, as when we study for an exam, but as mentioned later, we can also learn things without being aware we are doing so (Watanabe, Náñez, & Sasaki, 2001).

Psychological research on learning has been guided by three main questions: (1) Which events and relationships do people learn about? (2) What circumstances determine whether and how people learn? and (3) Is learning a slow process requiring lots of practice, or does it involve sudden flashes of insight? In this chapter we provide some of the answers to these questions.

learning The modification through experience of pre-existing behavior and understanding.

We first consider the simplest forms of learning—learning about sights, sounds, and other individual stimuli. Then we examine the two major kinds of learning that involve *associations* between events—classical conditioning and operant conditioning. Next we consider some higher forms of learning and cognition, and we conclude by discussing how research on learning might help people learn better. As you read, notice that learning principles operate in education, the workplace, medical treatment, psychotherapy, and many other aspects of people's lives.

Learning About Stimuli

In a changing world, people are constantly bombarded by stimuli. If we tried to pay attention to every sight and sound, our information-processing systems would be overloaded, and we would be unable to concentrate on anything. People appear to be genetically tuned to attend to certain kinds of events, such as loud sounds, special tastes, or pain. *Novel* stimuli—stimuli we have not experienced before—also tend to attract our attention. By contrast, our response to *unchanging* stimuli decreases over time. This aspect of adaptation is a simple form of learning called **habituation**, which can occur in relation to sights, sounds, smells, tastes, or touches, including ones that originally caused excitement, fear, or even a startle reaction. Through habituation, you eventually fail to notice that you are wearing glasses or a watch. And after having been in a room for a while, you no longer smell that musty or flowery odor or hear that loudly ticking clock. In fact, you may become aware of the clock again only when it stops, because now, something in your environment has changed. Habituation occurs in all animals, from simple sea snails to humans (Pinel, 1993).

Habituation provides organisms with a useful way to adapt to their environments, but notice that this kind of learning results from the impact of one particular stimulus, not because a person or animal learned to associate one stimulus with another (Barker, 1997). For this reason, habituation is an example of *nonassociative learning*. In another form of nonassociative learning called *sensitization*, people and animals show exaggerated responses to unexpected, potentially threatening sights or sounds, especially if they are emotionally aroused at the time. So while breathlessly exploring a dark, spooky house, you might scream, run, or violently throw something in response to the unexpected creaking of a door.

According to Richard Solomon's *opponent-process theory*, habituation may help explain some of the dangers associated with certain drugs. Consider, for example, what happens as someone continues to use a drug such as heroin. The pleasurable reaction (the high) obtained from a particular dose of the drug begins to decrease with repeated doses. This habituation occurs, Solomon says, because the initial, pleasurable reaction to the drug is eventually followed by an unpleasant, opposing reaction that counteracts the drug's primary effects. The opposing reaction becomes quicker and stronger the longer the drug is taken. As drug users become habituated, they must take progressively larger doses to get the same high. According to Solomon, these opponent processes form the basis of drug tolerance and addiction.

Solomon's analysis may also explain some accidental drug overdoses. Suppose the unpleasant reaction that counteracts a drug's initial effects becomes associated with a particular room, person, or other stimulus that is always present when the drug is taken. This stimulus may eventually come to trigger the counteracting process, allowing tolerance of larger doses. Now suppose that a person takes this larger drug dose in an environment where this stimulus is not present. The strength of the drug's primary effect will remain the same, but without the familiar environmental stimulus, the counteracting process may be weaker. The net result may be a stronger-than-usual drug reaction, possibly leading to an overdose (Siegel et al., 1982; Turkkan, 1989).

Learning to Live with It People who move to a big city may be distracted at first by the din of traffic, low-flying aircraft, and other urban sounds, but after a while the process of habituation makes all this noise far less noticeable.

Sensitization The documentary film makers portrayed in *The Blair Witch Project* demonstrated the nonassociative learning process called *sensitization* as their behavioral reactions to sudden stimuli became more and more extreme.

Notice that this explanation of drug overdoses is based not just on simple habituation and sensitization but also on a *learned association* between certain environmental stimuli and certain responses. Indeed, the nonassociative processes of habituation and sensitization cannot, by themselves, explain many of the behaviors and mental processes that are the focus of psychology. To better understand how learning affects our thoughts and behaviors, we need to consider forms of learning that involve the building of associations between various stimuli, as well as between stimuli and responses. One major type of associative learning is called *classical conditioning*.

Classical Conditioning: Learning Signals and Associations

At the opening bars of the national anthem, a young ballplayer's heart may start pounding; those sounds signal that the game is about to begin. A flashing light on a control panel may make an airplane pilot's adrenaline flow, because it means that something may be wrong. People are not born with these reactions; they learn them by observing relationships or *associations* between events in the world. The experimental study of this kind of learning was begun, almost by accident, by Ivan Petrovich Pavlov.

Pavlov's Discovery

Pavlov is one of the best-known figures in psychology, but he was not a psychologist. A Russian physiologist, Pavlov won a Nobel Prize in 1904 for his research on the digestive processes of dogs. In the course of this work, Pavlov noticed a strange phenomenon: The first stage of the digestive process—salivation—sometimes occurred when no food was present. His dogs salivated, for example, when they saw the assistant who normally brought their food, even if the assistant was empty-handed.

Pavlov devised a simple experiment to determine why salivation occurred in the absence of an obvious physical cause. First he performed a simple operation to

habituation The process of adapting to stimuli that do not change.

figure 6.1

Apparatus for Measuring Conditioned Responses

In this more elaborate version of Pavlov's original apparatus, the amount of saliva flowing from a dog's cheek is measured and then recorded on a slowly revolving drum of paper.

---

divert a dog's saliva into a container so that the amount of salivation could be measured precisely. He then placed the dog in an apparatus similar to the one shown in Figure 6.1. The experiment had three phases.

In the first phase of the experiment, Pavlov and his associates (Anrep, 1920) confirmed that when meat powder was placed on the dog's tongue, the dog salivated, but that it did not salivate in response to a neutral stimulus—a musical tone, for example. Thus, the researchers established the existence of the two basic components for Pavlov's experiment: a natural reflex (the dog's salivation when meat powder was placed on its tongue) and a neutral stimulus (the sound of the tone). A *reflex* is the swift, automatic response to a stimulus, such as shivering in the cold or jumping when you are jabbed with a needle. A *neutral stimulus* is a stimulus that initially does not trigger the reflex being studied, although it may cause other responses. For example, when the tone is first sounded, the dog will prick up its ears, turn toward the sound, and sniff around, but it will not salivate.

It was the second and third phases of the experiment that showed how one type of associative learning can occur. In the second phase, the tone sounded, and then a few seconds later meat powder was placed in the dog's mouth. The dog salivated. This *pairing*—the tone followed immediately by meat powder—was repeated several times. The tone predicted that the meat powder was coming, but the question remained: Would the animal learn this relationship and associate the tone with the meat powder? Yes. In the third phase of the experiment, the tone was sounded, and even though no meat powder was presented, the dog again salivated. In other words, the tone by itself now elicited salivation.

Pavlov's experiment was the first laboratory demonstration of a basic form of associative learning. Today, it is called **classical conditioning**—a procedure in which a neutral stimulus is repeatedly paired with a stimulus that already triggers a reflexive response until the neutral stimulus alone comes to evoke a similar response. Figure 6.2 shows the basic elements of classical conditioning. The stimulus that elicits a response without conditioning, like the meat powder in Pavlov's experiment, is called the **unconditioned stimulus** (UCS). The automatic, unlearned reaction to this stimulus is called the **unconditioned response** (UCR). The new stimulus being paired with the unconditioned stimulus is called the **conditioned stimulus** (CS), and the response it comes to elicit is the **conditioned response** (CR).

---

classical conditioning A procedure in which a neutral stimulus is paired with a stimulus that elicits a reflex or other response until the neutral stimulus alone comes to elicit a similar response.

unconditioned stimulus (UCS) A stimulus that elicits a response without conditioning.

unconditioned response (UCR) The automatic or unlearned reaction to a stimulus.

conditioned stimulus (CS) The originally neutral stimulus that, through pairing with the unconditioned stimulus, comes to elicit a conditioned response.

conditioned response (CR) The response that the conditioned stimulus elicits.

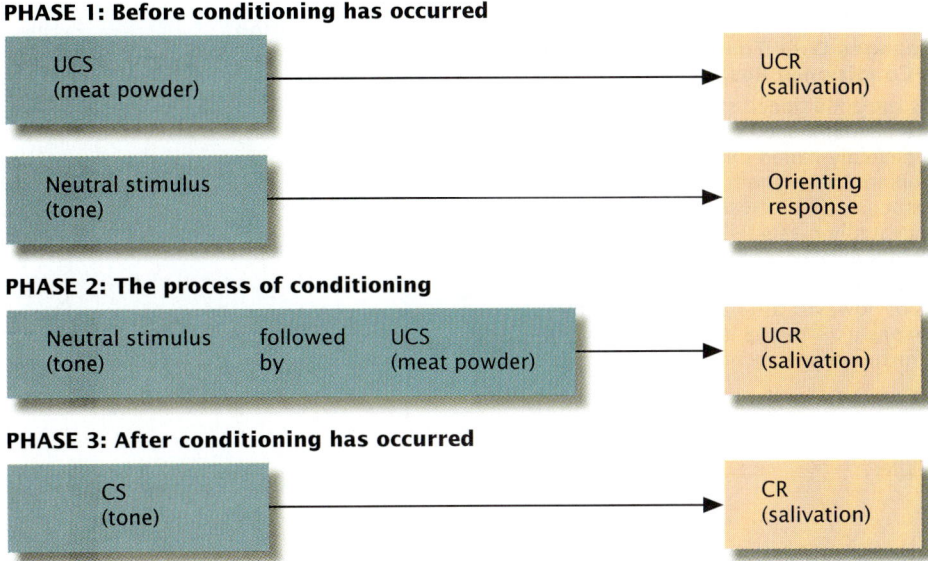

Classical Conditioning: Learning Signals and Associations

PHASE 1: Before conditioning has occurred

UCS (meat powder) → UCR (salivation)

Neutral stimulus (tone) → Orienting response

PHASE 2: The process of conditioning

Neutral stimulus (tone) followed by UCS (meat powder) → UCR (salivation)

PHASE 3: After conditioning has occurred

CS (tone) → CR (salivation)

figure 6.2
Classical Conditioning

Before classical conditioning has occurred, meat powder on a dog's tongue produces salivation, but the sound of a tone—a neutral stimulus—does not. During the process of conditioning, the tone is repeatedly paired with the meat powder. After classical conditioning has taken place, the sound of the tone alone acts as a conditioned stimulus, producing salivation.

Conditioned Responses over Time: Extinction and Spontaneous Recovery

Continued pairings of a conditioned stimulus with an unconditioned stimulus strengthen conditioned responses. The curve on the left side of Figure 6.3 shows an example: Repeated associations of a tone (CS) with meat powder (UCS) caused Pavlov's dogs to increase their salivation (CR) to the tone alone.

What if the meat powder is no longer given? In general, unless the unconditioned stimulus continues to be paired at least occasionally with the conditioned stimulus, the conditioned response will gradually disappear through a process known as **extinction** (see the center section of Figure 6.3). If the conditioned stimulus and the unconditioned stimulus are again paired after the conditioned response has been extinguished, the conditioned response returns to its original strength very quickly, often after only one or two trials. This quick relearning of a conditioned response after extinction is called **reconditioning**. Because reconditioning takes much less time than the original conditioning, extinction must not have completely erased the learned association.

Additional evidence for this conclusion is illustrated on the right side of Figure 6.3: An extinguished conditioned response will temporarily reappear if, after some time delay, the conditioned stimulus is presented again—even without the unconditioned stimulus. This reappearance of the conditioned response after extinction (and without further CS-UCS pairings) is called **spontaneous recovery**. In general, the longer the time between extinction and the re-presentation of the conditioned stimulus, the stronger the recovered conditioned response. (However, unless the UCS is again paired with the CS, extinction rapidly occurs again.) Spontaneous recovery is at work when a person hears a song or smells a scent associated with a long-lost lover and experiences a ripple of emotion—a conditioned response. Through its association with that person, the song or fragrance, which originally had no particular significance, became a conditioned stimulus that—even years later—can provoke conditioned emotional reactions.

extinction The gradual disappearance of a conditioned response due to elimination of the association between conditioned and unconditioned stimuli.

reconditioning The quick relearning of a conditioned response following extinction.

spontaneous recovery The reappearance of the conditioned response after extinction and without further pairings of the conditioned and unconditioned stimuli.

figure 6.3
Changes Over Time in the Strength of a Conditioned Response (CR)

As the conditioned stimulus (CS) and the unconditioned stimulus (UCS) are repeatedly paired during initial conditioning, the strength of the conditioned response (CR) increases. If the CS is repeatedly presented without the UCS, the CR weakens—and eventually disappears—through a process called *extinction*. However, after a brief period the CR reappears if the CS is again presented, which is called *spontaneous recovery*.

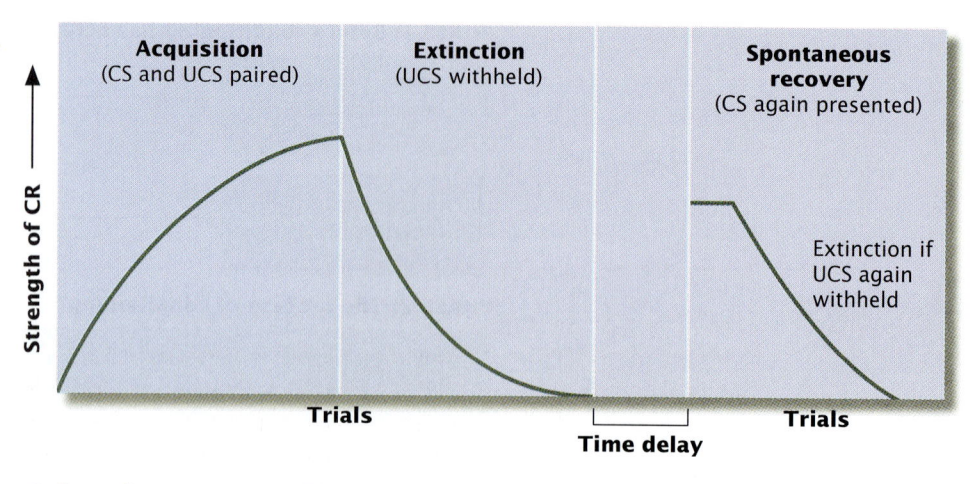

Stimulus Generalization and Discrimination

After a conditioned response is learned, stimuli that are similar but not identical to the conditioned stimulus also elicit the response—but to a lesser degree. This phenomenon is called **stimulus generalization**. Usually the greater the similarity between a new stimulus and the conditioned stimulus, the stronger the conditioned response will be. Figure 6.4 shows an example.

Stimulus generalization has obvious adaptive advantages. For example, it is important for survival that a person who becomes sick after drinking sour-smelling milk later avoids dairy products that give off an odor resembling the smell associated with the illness. Generalization, however, would be a problem if it had no limits. Like most people, you would probably be frightened if you found a lion in your home, but imagine the disruption if your fear response generalized so widely that you were panicked by a picture of a lion, or even by reading the word *lion*.

Stimulus generalization does not run wild because it is balanced by a complementary process called **stimulus discrimination**. Through stimulus discrimination, people and animals learn to differentiate among similar stimuli. Many parents find that the sound of their own baby whimpering may become a conditioned stimulus that triggers a conditioned response that wakes them up. That conditioned response might not occur if a visiting friend's baby whimpers.

The Signaling of Significant Events

Is classical conditioning entirely automatic? Pavlov's research suggested that it is—that classical conditioning allows the substitution of one stimulus (the CS) for another (the UCS) in producing an automatic, reflexive response. This kind of learning helps animals and people prepare for events involving food, pain, or other unconditioned stimuli. For years the study of classical conditioning focused mainly on its role in the control of such automatic, involuntary behavior. However, psychologists now recognize the wider implications of classical conditioning (Hollis, 1997). Some argue that organisms acquire conditioned responses when one event reliably predicts, or *signals*, the appearance of another. These psychologists believe that instead of giving rise to simple robot-like reflexes, classical conditioning leads to responses based on the information provided by conditioned stimuli. As a result, animals and people develop *mental representations* of the relationships between important events in their environment and expectancies about when such events will occur (Rescorla, 1988). These representations and expectancies aid adaptation and survival (Williams, Butler, & Overmier, 1990).

What determines whether and how a conditioned response is learned? Important factors include the timing, predictability, and strength of signals; the amount of attention they receive; and how easily the signals can be associated with other stimuli.

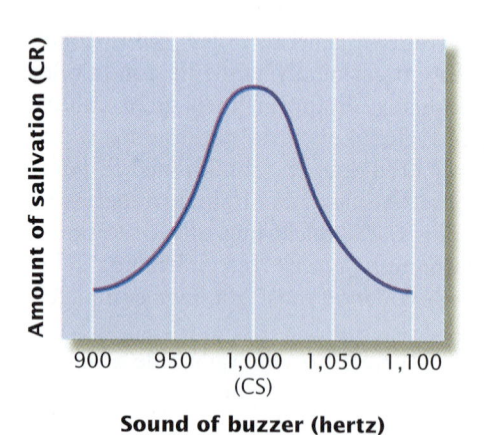

figure 6.4
Stimulus Generalization

The strength of a conditioned response (CR) is greatest when the original conditioned stimulus (CS) occurs, but the CR also appears following stimuli that closely resemble the CS. Here, the CS is the sound of a buzzer at 1,000 hertz, and the CR is salivation. Notice that the CR generalizes well to stimuli at 990 or 1,010 hertz, but it gets weaker and weaker following stimuli that are less and less similar to the CS.

Timing
If your instructor always dismisses class at 9:59 and a bell rings at 10:00, the bell cannot act as a signal to prepare you for the dismissal. For the same reason, classical conditioning works best when the conditioned stimulus precedes the unconditioned stimulus. In this arrangement, known as *forward conditioning*, the conditioned stimulus signals that the unconditioned stimulus is coming.

There is also an arrangement, called *backward conditioning*, in which the conditioned stimulus *follows* the unconditioned stimulus. When this happens, however, a conditioned response develops very slowly, if at all. (Part of the explanation is that the CS in backward conditioning comes too late to signal the approach of the UCS. In fact, the CS signals the *absence* of the UCS and eventually triggers a response that is opposite to the conditioned response, thus inhibiting its development.)

When the conditioned stimulus and unconditioned stimulus occur at the same time (an arrangement known as *simultaneous conditioning*), conditioning is much less likely to take place than it is in either forward or backward conditioning, and special techniques are required to detect its occurrence.

Research shows that forward conditioning usually works best when there is an interval between the conditioned stimulus and the unconditioned stimulus. This interval can range from a fraction of a second to a few seconds to more than a minute, depending on the particular CS, UCS, and UCR involved (Longo, Klempay, & Bitterman, 1964; Ross & Ross, 1971). Classical conditioning will always be weaker if the interval between the CS and the UCS is longer than what is ideal for the stimuli and responses in a given situation. This makes adaptive sense. Normally, the appearance of food, predators, or other significant events is most reliably predicted by smells, growls, or other stimuli that occur at varying intervals before those events (Einhorn & Hogarth, 1982). So it is logical that organisms are "wired" to form associations most easily between things that occur in a relatively tight time sequence.

Predictability
Is it enough that the conditioned stimulus precedes the unconditioned stimulus—that the two events are close together in time—in order for classical conditioning to occur? Think about it. Suppose two dogs, Moxie and Fang, have very different personalities. When Moxie growls, she sometimes bites, but sometimes she doesn't. Other times, she bites without growling first. Fang, however, growls *only* before biting. Your conditioned fear response to Moxie's growl will probably occur slowly, if at all, because her growl is a stimulus that does not reliably signal the danger of a bite. But you are likely to quickly develop a classically conditioned fear response to Fang's growl, because classical conditioning proceeds most rapidly when the conditioned stimulus *always* signals the unconditioned stimulus, and *only* the unconditioned stimulus. So even if both dogs provide the same number of pairings of the conditioned stimulus (growl) and the unconditioned stimulus (bite), it is only in Fang's case that the conditioned stimulus *reliably* predicts the unconditioned stimulus (Rescorla, 1968).

Signal Strength
A conditioned response will be greater if the unconditioned stimulus is strong than if it is weak. So a predictive signal associated with a strong UCS, such as an intense shock, will come to evoke more fear than one associated with a weak shock. As with timing and predictability, the effect of signal strength on classical conditioning makes adaptive sense: It is more important to be prepared for major events than for events that have little impact.

How quickly a conditioned response is learned also depends on the strength of the conditioned stimulus. As described in the chapter on perception, louder tones, brighter lights, or other, more intense stimuli events tend to get attention, so they are most rapidly associated with an unconditioned stimulus—as long as they remain reliable predictive signals.

Attention
In the laboratory, a single neutral stimulus is presented, followed shortly by an unconditioned stimulus. In the natural environment, however, several

---

stimulus generalization A phenomenon in which a conditioned response is elicited by stimuli that are similar but not identical to the conditioned stimulus.

stimulus discrimination A process through which individuals learn to differentiate among similar stimuli and respond appropriately to each one.

stimuli might be present just before an unconditioned stimulus occurs. Suppose you are at the beach, sipping lemonade, reading a magazine, listening to a Sting CD, and inhaling the scent of sunscreen, when you are suddenly bitten by a wasp. Where your attention was focused at that moment can influence which potential conditioned stimulus—lemonade, magazine, Sting, or sunscreen—becomes associated with that painful unconditioned stimulus. The stimulus you were attending to most closely—and thus most fully perceiving—is the one likely to be more strongly associated with pain than any of the others (Hall, 1991).

Second-Order Conditioning

When a child suffers the pain of an injection (an unconditioned stimulus) at a doctor's office, noticeable stimuli—such as the doctor's white coat—that precede and predict the unconditioned stimulus can become conditioned stimuli for fear. Once the white coat can trigger a conditioned fear response, it may take on some properties of an unconditioned stimulus. So at future visits, the once-neutral sight of the doctor's waiting room can become a conditioned stimulus for fear because it signals the appearance of the doctor's white coat, which in turn signals pain. When a conditioned stimulus acts like an unconditioned stimulus, creating conditioned stimuli out of events associated with it, the phenomenon is called **second-order conditioning**.

Conditioned fear, along with the second-order conditioning that can be based on it, illustrates one of the most important adaptive characteristics of classical conditioning: the ability to prepare a person or an animal for threatening events—unconditioned stimuli—that are reliably signaled by a conditioned stimulus. Unfortunately, second-order conditioning can also cause problems. For example, medical patients known as *white coat hypertensives* (Myers et al., 1996) appear to have high blood pressure because the presence of a doctor or nurse has become a conditioned stimulus for fear. This conditioned fear response includes a temporary rise in blood pressure.

Biopreparedness

After Pavlov's initial demonstration of classical conditioning, many psychologists believed that associations formed through classical conditioning were like Velcro. Just as Velcro pieces of any size or shape can be attached

The Power of Second-Order Conditioning Cancer patients may feel queasy when they enter a chemotherapy room because they have associated the room with nausea-producing treatment. Through second-order conditioning, almost anything associated with that *room* can also become a conditioned stimulus for nausea. One cancer patient, flying out of town on a business trip, became nauseated just by seeing her hospital from the air.

© Herb Lingl/aerialarchives.com

Taste Aversions Humans can develop classically conditioned taste aversions, even to preferred foods. Ilene Bernstein (1978) gave one group of cancer patients Mapletoff ice cream an hour before they received nausea-provoking chemotherapy. A second group ate the same kind of ice cream on a day they did not receive chemotherapy. A third group got no ice cream. Five months later, the patients were asked to taste several ice cream flavors. Those who had never tasted Mapletoff and those who had not eaten it in association with chemotherapy chose it as their favorite. Those who had eaten Mapletoff before receiving chemotherapy found it very distasteful.

with equal ease, it was believed that any conditioned stimulus—such as the taste of food, the pain of an insect bite, or the sight of a dog—has an equal potential for becoming associated with any unconditioned stimulus, as long as the two stimuli occur in the right time sequence. This view, called *equipotentiality*, was later challenged by experiments showing that certain signals or events are especially suited to form associations with other events (Logue, 1985). This apparent natural tendency for certain events to become linked suggests that humans and animals are "biologically prepared" or "genetically tuned" to develop certain conditioned associations.

The most dramatic example of this *biopreparedness* is seen in conditioned taste aversion. Consider the results of a study in which rats were either shocked or made nauseous in the combined presence of a bright light, a loud buzzer, and saccharin-flavored water. Only certain conditioned associations were formed. Specifically, the animals that had been shocked developed a conditioned fear response to the light and the buzzer, but not to the flavored water. Those animals that had been made nauseous developed a conditioned aversion to the flavored water but showed no particular response to the light or buzzer (Garcia & Koelling, 1966). Notice that these associations are useful and adaptive: Nausea is more likely to be produced by something that is eaten or drunk than by a noise or some other external stimulus. Accordingly, nausea is more likely to become a conditioned response to an internal stimulus, such as a saccharine flavor, than to an external stimulus, such as a light or buzzer. In contrast, sudden pain is more likely to have been caused by an external stimulus, so it makes evolutionary sense that organisms should be "tuned" to associate pain with external stimuli like sights or sounds.

Notice, too, that strong conditioned taste aversion can develop despite the fact that poisons or other nausea-producing substances do not usually produce their effects until minutes or hours after being ingested. These intervals are far longer than what is optimal for producing conditioning in most other situations, but people who experience food poisoning may never again eat the type of food that made them ill. This makes sense in evolutionary terms, because organisms that are biologically prepared to link taste signals with illness, even if it occurs after a considerable delay, are more likely to survive than organisms not so prepared.

Evidence from several sources suggests other ways in which animals and people are innately prepared to learn associations between certain stimuli and certain responses. For example, people are much more likely to develop a conditioned fear of harmless dogs, snakes, and rats than of equally harmless doorknobs or stereos (Kleinknecht, 1991). And experiments with animals suggest that they are prone to learn the type of associations that are most common in, or most relevant to, their environments (Staddon & Ettinger, 1989). For example, birds of prey, so strongly dependent upon their vision in searching for food, may develop taste aversions on the basis of visual stimuli. Coyotes and rats, more dependent on their sense of smell, tend to develop aversions related to odor.

Some Applications of Classical Conditioning

"In Review: Basic Phenomena in Classical Conditioning" summarizes the principles of classical conditioning. These principles have proven useful in overcoming fears, controlling predators, and diagnosing Alzheimer's disease, to name just a few examples.

Phobias
Classical conditioning can play a role in the development not only of mild fears (such as a child's fear of doctors in white coats) but also of phobias (Bouton, Mineka, & Barlow, 2001). *Phobias* are extreme fears of objects or situations that either are not objectively dangerous—public speaking, for example—or are less dangerous than the phobic person's reaction suggests. In some instances, phobias can seriously disrupt a person's life. A child who is frightened by a large dog may learn a dog phobia that is so intense and generalized that it creates avoidance

second-order conditioning A phenomenon in which a conditioned stimulus acts like an unconditioned stimulus, creating conditioned stimuli out of events associated with it.

in review: Basic Phenomena in Classical Conditioning

Process	Description	Example
Acquisition	A neutral stimulus and an unconditioned stimulus (UCS) are paired. The neutral stimulus becomes a conditioned stimulus (CS), eliciting a conditioned response (CR).	A child learns to fear (conditioned response) the doctor's office (conditioned stimulus) by associating it with the reflexive emotional reaction (unconditioned response) to a painful injection (unconditioned stimulus).
Stimulus generalization	A conditioned response is elicited not only by the conditioned stimulus but also by stimuli similar to the conditioned stimulus.	A child fears most doctors' offices and places that smell like them.
Stimulus discrimination	Generalization is limited so that some stimuli similar to the conditioned stimulus do not elicit the conditioned response.	A child learns that his mother's doctor's office is not associated with the unconditioned stimulus.
Extinction	The conditioned stimulus is presented alone, without the unconditioned stimulus. Eventually the conditioned stimulus no longer elicits the conditioned response.	A child visits the doctor's office several times for a checkup but does not receive an injection. Fear may eventually cease.

of all dogs. Dangerous situations, too, can produce classical conditioning of very long lasting fears. Decades after their war experiences, some military veterans still respond to simulated battle sounds with large changes in heart rate, blood pressure, and other signs of emotional arousal (Edwards & Acker, 1972). These symptoms, combined with others such as distressing dreams about the troubling events, characterize posttraumatic stress disorder (PTSD, described in the chapter on health, stress, and coping).

LINKAGES (a link to Treatment of Psychological Disorders)

Classical conditioning procedures can be employed to treat phobias, and even PTSD. Joseph Wolpe (1958; Wolpe & Plaud, 1997) pioneered the development of this methodology. Using techniques first developed with laboratory animals, Wolpe showed that irrational fears could be relieved through *systematic desensitization,* which involves two conditioning components: (1) extinction of classically conditioned fear responses through harmless exposure to the feared stimulus and (2) classical conditioning of a new response, such as relaxation, to the feared stimulus. Desensitization is discussed in more detail in the chapter on the treatment of psychological disorders.

Predator Control The power of classically conditioned taste aversion has been put to work to help ranchers who are plagued by wolves and coyotes that kill and eat their sheep. To alleviate this problem without killing the predators, some ranchers have set out lithium-laced mutton for marauding wolves and coyotes to eat. The dizziness and nausea caused by the lithium becomes associated with the smell and taste of mutton, thus making sheep an undesirable meal for these predators and protecting the ranchers' livelihood (Garcia, Rusiniak, & Brett, 1977; Gustavson et al., 1974).

Diagnosis of Alzheimer's Disease A puff of air directed at your eye is an unconditioned stimulus that causes the reflexive unconditioned response we call an *eye blink* (Hilgard & Marquis, 1936). If each air puff is preceded by a flash of light, the light will become a conditioned stimulus that can then cause an eye blink on its own. Recent research with animals has demonstrated that the hippocampus, a brain structure that is damaged in the early stages of Alzheimer's disease, is involved in the development of this type of conditioned response (Green &

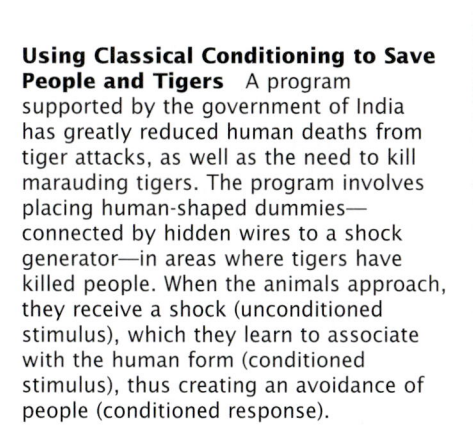

Using Classical Conditioning to Save People and Tigers A program supported by the government of India has greatly reduced human deaths from tiger attacks, as well as the need to kill marauding tigers. The program involves placing human-shaped dummies—connected by hidden wires to a shock generator—in areas where tigers have killed people. When the animals approach, they receive a shock (unconditioned stimulus), which they learn to associate with the human form (conditioned stimulus), thus creating an avoidance of people (conditioned response).

Woodruff-Pak, 2000). That research is now being applied in the identification of people who are at high risk for this devastating brain disorder. One study found that elderly people whose eye blink conditioning was impaired were the ones most likely to develop Alzheimer's disease in the next two or three years (Downey-Lamb & Woodruff-Pak, 1999). Knowing who is at risk for Alzheimer's disease is important because it allows doctors to offer these people medication that can delay the emergence of the disease.

Instrumental and Operant Conditioning: Learning the Consequences of Behavior

Much of what people learn cannot be described in terms of classical conditioning. In classical conditioning, neutral and unconditioned stimuli are predictably paired, and the result is an association between the two. The association is shown by the conditioned response that occurs when the conditioned stimulus appears. Notice that both stimuli occur *before* or *along with* the conditioned response. But people also learn associations between specific actions or responses and the stimuli that *follow* them—in other words, between behavior and its consequences (Colwill, 1994). A child learns to say "Please" to get a piece of candy; a headache sufferer learns to take a pill to escape pain; a dog learns to "shake hands" to get a treat. This form of learning is called *operant conditioning*, and it constitutes the second major type of associative learning.

From the Puzzle Box to the Skinner Box

Much of the groundwork for research on the consequences of behavior was done by Edward L. Thorndike, an American psychologist. While Pavlov was exploring classical conditioning in animals, Thorndike was studying animals' intelligence and ability to solve problems. He would place an animal, usually a hungry cat, in a *puzzle box*, where it had to learn some response—say, stepping on a pedal—in order to unlock the door and get to some food (see Figure 6.5). The animal would solve the

figure 6.5

Thorndike's Puzzle Box

This drawing illustrates the kind of puzzle box used in Thorndike's research. His cats learned to open the door and reach food by stepping on the pedal, but the learning occurred gradually. Some cats actually took longer to get out of the box on one trial than on a previous trial.

puzzle, but very slowly. It did not appear to understand, or suddenly gain *insight* into, the problem (Thorndike, 1898).

So what were Thorndike's cats learning? Thorndike argued that any response (such as pressing the pedal) that produces a satisfying effect (such as access to food) gradually becomes stronger, whereas any response (such as pacing or meowing) that does not produce a satisfying effect gradually becomes weaker. The cats' learning, said Thorndike, is governed by the **law of effect.** According to this law, if a response made in the presence of a particular stimulus is followed by satisfaction (such as a reward), that response is more likely to be made the next time the stimulus is encountered. Conversely, responses that produce discomfort are less likely to be performed again. Thorndike described this kind of learning as **instrumental conditioning,** because responses are strengthened when they are instrumental in producing rewards (Thorndike, 1905).

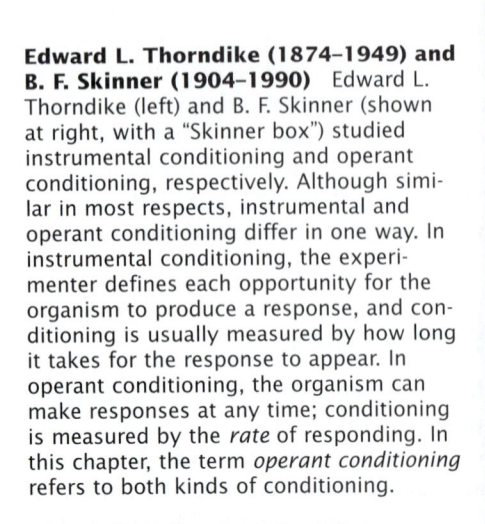

Edward L. Thorndike (1874–1949) and B. F. Skinner (1904–1990) Edward L. Thorndike (left) and B. F. Skinner (shown at right, with a "Skinner box") studied instrumental conditioning and operant conditioning, respectively. Although similar in most respects, instrumental and operant conditioning differ in one way. In instrumental conditioning, the experimenter defines each opportunity for the organism to produce a response, and conditioning is usually measured by how long it takes for the response to appear. In operant conditioning, the organism can make responses at any time; conditioning is measured by the *rate* of responding. In this chapter, the term *operant conditioning* refers to both kinds of conditioning.

Edward Thorndike photo: Psychology Archives—The University of Akron

About forty years after Thorndike published his work, B. F. Skinner extended and formalized many of Thorndike's ideas. Skinner (1938) emphasized that during instrumental conditioning, an organism learns a response by *operating on* the environment, so he called the process of learning these responses **operant conditioning**. His primary aim was to analyze *how* behavior is changed by its consequences. To study operant conditioning, Skinner devised a chamber that became known as the *Skinner box*. The Skinner box differed from Thorndike's puzzle box in one way: The puzzle box measured learning in terms of whether an animal successfully completed a trial (i.e., got out of the box), and how long it took. The Skinner box measures learning in terms of how often an animal responds during a specified period of time (Barker, 1997).

Basic Components of Operant Conditioning

The tools Skinner devised allowed him and other researchers to precisely arrange relationships between a response and its consequences and then to analyze how those consequences affected behavior over time. They found that the basic phenomena seen in classical conditioning—such as stimulus generalization, stimulus discrimination, extinction, and spontaneous recovery—also occur in operant conditioning. However, operant conditioning involves additional concepts and processes as well. Let's consider these now.

Operants and Reinforcers

Skinner introduced the term *operant* or *operant response* to distinguish the responses in operant conditioning from those in classical conditioning. Recall that in classical conditioning, the conditioned response does not affect whether or when the stimulus occurs. Dogs salivated when a buzzer sounded, but the salivation had no effect on the buzzer or on whether food was presented. In contrast, an **operant** is a response that has some effect on the world; it is a response that *operates on* the environment. For example, when a child says, "Momma, I'm hungry," and is then fed, the child has made an operant response that influences when food will appear.

A **reinforcer** increases the probability that an operant behavior will occur again. There are two main types of reinforcers: positive and negative. **Positive reinforcers** strengthen a response if they are experienced after that response occurs. They are roughly equivalent to rewards. The food given to a hungry pigeon after it pecks at a switch is a positive reinforcer; its presentation increases the pigeon's switch pecking. For people, positive reinforcers can include food, smiles, money, and other desirable outcomes. Presentation of a positive reinforcer after a response is called *positive reinforcement*. **Negative reinforcers** are the *removal* of unpleasant stimuli such as pain, noise, threats, or a disapproving frown. Like positive reinforcers, negative reinforcers also strengthen responses. For example, if taking aspirin removes your headache pain, you are more likely to take aspirin the next time you have a headache. When a response is strengthened by the *removal* of an unpleasant stimulus, the process is called *negative reinforcement*. So whether reinforcement takes the form of presenting something pleasant or removing something unpleasant, it always *increases* the strength of the behavior that precedes it (see Figure 6.6).

Escape and Avoidance Conditioning

The effects of negative reinforcement can be seen in escape conditioning and avoidance conditioning. **Escape conditioning** occurs as a person or animal learns to make a response in order to stop an aversive stimulus. As shown in Figure 6.7, dogs will learn to jump over the barrier in a shuttle box to escape shock. And parents may learn to give in to a child's demands because doing so stops the child's whining. Now let's consider avoidance conditioning. Look again at Figure 6.7, and imagine that a buzzer sounds a few seconds before one side of the shuttle box is electrified. The animal will soon learn to jump over the barrier when the buzzer sounds, thus avoiding the shock. (In a

---

law of effect A law stating that if a response made in the presence of a particular stimulus is followed by a reward, that response is more likely the next time the stimulus is encountered.

instrumental conditioning A process through which responses are learned that produce some rewarding effect.

operant conditioning A process through which an organism learns to respond to the environment in a way that produces positive consequences.

operant A response that has some effect on the world.

reinforcer A stimulus event that increases the probability that the response that immediately preceded it will occur again.

positive reinforcers Stimuli that strengthen a response if they follow that response.

negative reinforcers The removal of unpleasant stimuli, such as pain.

escape conditioning A type of learning in which an organism learns to make a particular response in order to terminate an aversive stimulus.

figure 6.6

Positive and Negative Reinforcement

TRY THIS Behavior is strengthened through *positive reinforcement* when something pleasant or desirable follows the behavior. Behavior is strengthened through *negative reinforcement* when the behavior results in the removal of something unpleasant. To see how these operant learning principles apply in your own life, list two situations in which your behavior was affected by positive reinforcement and two in which it was affected by negative reinforcement.

POSITIVE REINFORCEMENT

Behavior You put coins into a vending machine. → **Presentation of a pleasant or positive stimulus** You receive a cold can of soda. → **Frequency of behavior increases** You put coins in vending machines in the future.

NEGATIVE REINFORCEMENT

Behavior In the middle of a boring date, you say you have a headache. → **Removal of an unpleasant stimulus** The date ends early. → **Frequency of behavior increases** You use the same tactic on future boring dates.

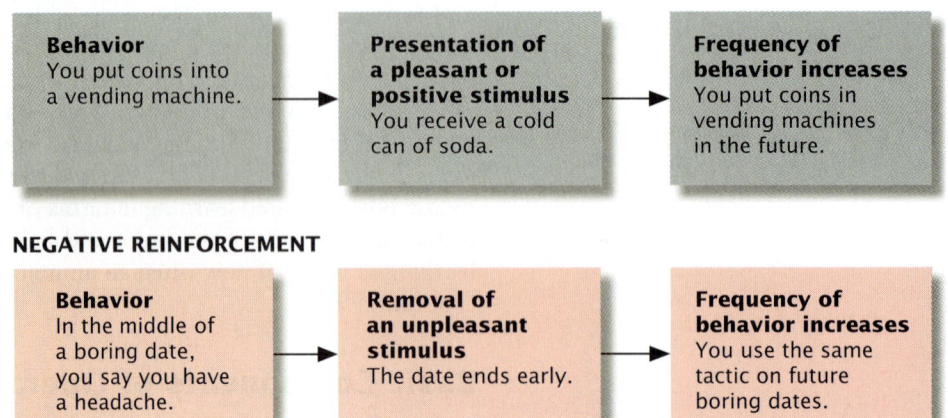

similar way, some children learn that they can avoid getting in trouble for misbehavior by apologizing as soon as they see their parent's frown.) When an animal or person responds to a signal in a way that avoids an impending aversive stimulus, **avoidance conditioning** has occurred. Remember that in escape conditioning the learned response *stops* an aversive stimulus, whereas in avoidance conditioning the learned response *prevents* the aversive stimulus from occurring in the first place.

Notice that avoidance conditioning involves both classical and operant conditioning. In the shuttle box, for example, the buzzer signals the onset of an *unconditioned stimulus* (shock). Through classical conditioning, this signal becomes a *conditioned stimulus* that triggers fear, a *conditioned response*. Like the shock itself, fear is unpleasant. Once the animal learns to jump over the barrier to avoid shock, this operant response is reinforced by its consequences—the reduction of fear. In short, avoidance conditioning takes place in two steps. The first step involves classical conditioning (a signal is repeatedly paired with shock); the second step involves operant conditioning (learning to make a response that reduces fear).

Along with positive reinforcement, avoidance conditioning is one of the most important influences on everyday behavior. Most people go to work even when they would rather stay in bed, and they stop at red lights even when they are in a hurry. Each of these behaviors reflects avoidance conditioning, because each behavior allows people to avoid a negative consequence, such as lost pay or a traffic ticket.

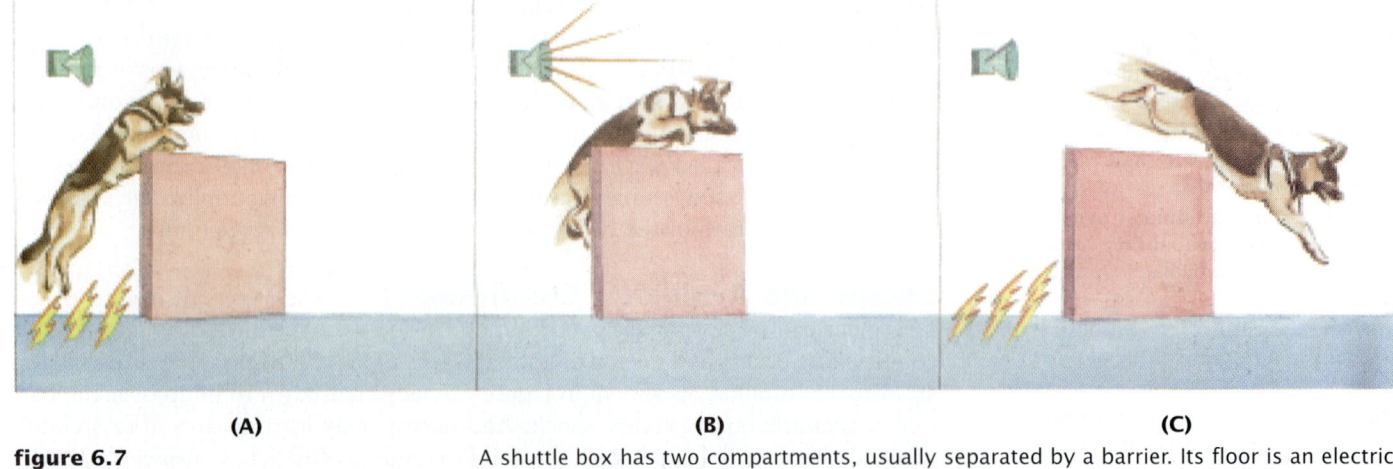

(A) (B) (C)

figure 6.7

A Shuttle Box

A shuttle box has two compartments, usually separated by a barrier. Its floor is an electric grid, so that shock can be delivered to either compartment. In escape conditioning (A), the animal feels a shock but can get away from it by jumping over the barrier when the shock occurs. In avoidance conditioning (B), a buzzer signals that the shock is coming, and the animal can avoid the shock if it jumps as soon as the buzzer sounds (C).

Avoidance is a difficult habit to break, partly because avoidance responses continue to be reinforced by fear reduction even if the aversive stimulus never appears (Solomon, Kamin, & Wynne, 1953). In fact, avoidance responses prevent the opportunity to learn that avoidance is no longer necessary. If you fear escalators and therefore avoid them, you will never discover that they hold no real danger. Avoidance conditioning can also prevent people from learning new, more desirable behaviors. For example, fear of doing something embarrassing may cause people with limited social skills to shy away from social situations, thus depriving themselves of the chance to become more skilled in those situations.

Discriminative Stimuli and Stimulus Control

One of the most important benefits of operant conditioning is that it enables organisms to adapt quickly to changes in their environment—an ability that has survival value in the real world. For example, even pigeons easily learn when they should respond and when they should not. If they are reinforced with food for pecking at a switch when a red light is on but are not reinforced for pecking when a green light is on, they will eventually peck only when they see a red light. Their behavior demonstrates the effect of **discriminative stimuli,** which are stimuli that signal whether reinforcement is available if a certain response is made. When an organism learns to make a particular response in the presence of one stimulus but not another, *stimulus discrimination* has occurred (see Figure 6.8). Another way to say this is that the response is now under *stimulus control*. In general, stimulus discrimination allows people or animals to learn what is appropriate (reinforced) and inappropriate (not reinforced) in particular situations. For both animals and humans, discrimination develops fastest when the discriminative stimulus signals that a behavior is appropriate, and it develops slowest when the stimulus signals that a behavior is inappropriate (Newman, Wolff, & Hearst, 1980).

Stimulus generalization also occurs in operant conditioning; that is, an animal or a person often performs a response in the presence of a stimulus that is similar, but not identical, to the one that previously signaled the availability of reinforcement. As in classical conditioning, the more similar the new stimulus is to the old, the more likely it is that the response will be performed. Suppose you ate a wonderful meal at a restaurant built to look like a big boat. In the future, you might be attracted to another restaurant that looks something like the one where you had that great meal.

figure 6.8

Stimulus Discrimination

In this experiment the rat could jump from a stand through any of three doors, but it was reinforced only if it jumped through the door that differed from the other two. The rat learned to do this quite well: On this trial, it discriminated vertical from horizontal stripes.

avoidance conditioning A type of learning in which an organism responds to a signal in a way that avoids exposure to an aversive stimulus.

discriminative stimuli Stimuli that signal whether reinforcement is available if a certain response is made.

Although the artist may not have intended it, this cartoon nicely illustrates one way in which discriminative stimuli can affect behavior.

"Oh, not bad. The light comes on, I press the bar, they write me a check. How about you?"

©The New Yorker Collection 1993 Tom Cheney from cartoonbank.com. All Rights Reserved.

As in classical conditioning, stimulus discrimination and stimulus generalization often complement each other in operant conditioning. In one study, for example, pigeons received food for pecking at a switch, but only when they saw certain works of art. When other paintings were shown, pecking was not reinforced (Watanabe, Sakamoto, & Wakita, 1995). As a result, these birds learned to *discriminate* the works of the impressionist painter Claude Monet from those of the cubist painter Pablo Picasso. Later, when the birds were shown new paintings by other impressionist and cubist artists, they were able to *generalize* from the original artists to other artists who painted in the same style. In other words, they had learned what paintings fall into the "impressionist" and "cubist" categories. Humans learn to place people and things into even more finely detailed categories, such as "honest," "dangerous," or "tax deductible." We discriminate one stimulus from another and then, through generalization, respond similarly to all stimuli we perceive to be in a particular category. This ability to respond in a similar way to all members of a category can save us considerable time and effort, but it can also lead to the development of unwarranted prejudice against certain groups of people (see the chapter on social cognition).

Forming and Strengthening Operant Behavior

Daily life is full of examples of operant conditioning. People go to movies, parties, classes, and jobs primarily because doing so brings reinforcement. What is the effect of the type or timing of the reinforcers? How can new responses be established through operant conditioning?

Shaping

Imagine that you want to train your dog, Henry, to sit and to "shake hands." The basic method using positive reinforcement is obvious: Every time Henry sits and shakes hands, you give him a treat. But the problem is also obvious: Smart as Henry is, he may never spontaneously make the desired response, so you will never be able to give the reinforcer. Instead of your teaching and Henry's learning, the two of you will just stare at each other (and he'll probably wag his tail).

shaping The process of reinforcing responses that come successively closer to the desired response.
primary reinforcers Reinforcers that meet an organism's basic needs, such as food and water.
secondary reinforcer A reward that people or animals learn to like.

Getting the Hang of It Learning to eat with a spoon is, as you can see, a hit-or-miss process at first. However, this child will learn to hit the target more and more often as the food reward gradually shapes a more efficient, and far less messy, pattern of behavior.

The way around this problem is to *shape* Henry's behavior. **Shaping** is accomplished by reinforcing *successive approximations*—that is, responses that come successively closer to the desired response. For example, you might first give Henry a treat whenever he sits down. Then you might reinforce him only when he sits and partially lifts a paw. Next, you might reinforce more complete paw lifting. Eventually, you would require that Henry perform the entire sit-lift-shake sequence before giving the treat. Shaping is an extremely powerful, widely used tool. Animal trainers have used it to teach chimpanzees to roller-skate, dolphins to jump through hoops, and pigeons to play Ping-Pong (Coren, 1999).

Secondary Reinforcement

Often, operant conditioning begins with the use of **primary reinforcers,** events or stimuli—such as food or water—that are inherently rewarding. But Henry's training will be slowed if he must stop and eat every time he makes a correct response. Furthermore, once he is full, food will no longer act as an effective reinforcer. To avoid these problems, animal trainers and others in the teaching business rely on the principle of secondary reinforcement.

A **secondary reinforcer** is a previously neutral stimulus that, if paired with a stimulus that is already reinforcing, will itself take on reinforcing properties. In other words, secondary reinforcers are rewards that people or animals learn to like. For example, if you say, "Good boy!" a moment before you give Henry each food reward, these words will become associated with the food and can then be used alone to reinforce Henry's behavior (as long as the words are again paired with food now and then). Does this remind you of classical conditioning? It should, because the primary reinforcer (food) is an unconditioned stimulus; if the sound of "Good boy!" predictably precedes, and thus signals, food, it becomes a conditioned stimulus. For this reason, secondary reinforcers are sometimes called *conditioned reinforcers*.

Secondary reinforcement greatly expands the power of operant conditioning (Schwartz & Reisberg, 1991). Money is the most obvious secondary reinforcer; some people will do anything for it (even though it tastes terrible!). Its reinforcing power lies in its association with the many rewards it can buy. Smiles and other forms of social approval (like the words "Good job!") are also important secondary reinforcers for human beings. However, what becomes a secondary reinforcer can vary a great deal from person to person and culture to culture. For example, tickets to a rock concert are an effective secondary reinforcer for some people, but not everyone. A ceremony honoring outstanding job performance might be highly reinforcing to most employees in individualist cultures, but it might be embarrassing for some employees from cultures in which group cooperation is valued more than personal distinction (Fiske et al., 1998). Still, when chosen carefully, secondary reinforcers can build or maintain behavior even when primary reinforcement is absent for long periods.

Secondary Reinforcers A touch or a smile, words of praise or thanks, and a loving or approving look are just a few of the social stimuli that can serve as secondary reinforcers for humans. Parents have used these reinforcers for generations to shape the behavior of children in accordance with their cultural values.

Delay and Size of Reinforcement

Much of human behavior is learned and maintained because it is regularly reinforced. But many people overeat, smoke, drink too much, or procrastinate, even though they know these behaviors are bad for them and even though they want to eliminate them. They just cannot seem to change; they seem to lack "self-control." If behavior is controlled by its consequences, why do people perform acts that are ultimately self-defeating?

Part of the answer lies in the *timing* of reinforcers. In general, the effect of a reinforcer is stronger when it comes soon after a response occurs (Kalish, 1981). The good feelings (positive reinforcers) that follow, say, drinking too much are immediate; hangovers and other negative consequences are usually delayed, which weakens their impact. Under some conditions, delaying a positive reinforcer for even a few seconds can decrease the effectiveness of positive reinforcement. (An advantage of praise or other secondary reinforcers is that they can easily be delivered immediately after a desired response occurs.)

The *size* of a reinforcer is also important. In general, operant conditioning generates more vigorous behavior when the reinforcer is large than when it is small. For example, a strong electrical shock will elicit a faster avoidance or escape response than a weak one.

Schedules of Reinforcement

We flip a light switch, and the light comes on. We put money in a vending machine, and we receive the item we want. When a reinforcer is delivered every time a particular response occurs, the arrangement is called a **continuous reinforcement schedule**. Quite often, however, reinforcement is administered only some of the time; the result is a **partial reinforcement schedule**, or *intermittent reinforcement schedule*.

Most partial reinforcement schedules can be classified according to (1) whether the delivery of reinforcers depends on the number of responses made or on the time that has elapsed since the last reinforcer and (2) whether the number of responses or the time lapse required for delivery of reinforcers is fixed or variable. Accordingly, there are four basic types of intermittent reinforcement schedules:

1. *Fixed-ratio (FR) schedules* provide a reinforcer following a fixed number of responses. So rats might receive food after every tenth time they press the lever in a Skinner box (FR 10) or after every twentieth time (FR 20); factory workers might be paid for every five computers they assemble (FR 5) or for every fiftieth (FR 50).

2. *Variable-ratio (VR) schedules* also provide a reinforcer after a given number of responses, but that number can vary. So on a VR 30 schedule, a rat might sometimes be reinforced after ten lever presses, sometimes after fifty, and sometimes after five, but the *average* number of responses required to get a reinforcer would be thirty. Gambling offers a variable-ratio schedule. A slot machine, for example, pays off only after a frustratingly unpredictable number of lever pulls, averaging perhaps one in twenty.

3. *Fixed-interval (FI) schedules* provide a reinforcer for the first response that occurs after some fixed time has passed since the last reward, regardless of how many responses have been made during that interval. For example, on an FI 60 schedule, the first response after sixty seconds have passed will be rewarded. Some radio stations use fixed-interval schedules to discourage "professional contestants" by stating that listeners cannot win a prize more than once every thirty days.

4. *Variable-interval (VI) schedules* reinforce the first response after some period of time, but the amount of time varies. On a VI 60 schedule, for example, the first response to occur after an *average* of 60 seconds is reinforced, but the actual time between reinforcements might vary from, say, 1 second to 120 seconds. Teachers use VI schedules when they give "points"—at unpredictably varying intervals—to children who are in their seats. A VI schedule has also been successfully used to encourage seat belt use: During a 10-week test in Illinois, police stopped drivers at random times and awarded prizes to those who were buckled up (Mortimer et al., 1988).

Different schedules of reinforcement produce different patterns of responding, as Figure 6.9 shows (Skinner, 1961a). The figure illustrates two important points. First, both fixed-ratio and variable-ratio schedules produce high rates of behavior, because in both cases the frequency of the reward depends directly on the rate of responding. Industrial/organizational psychologists have applied this principle to help companies increase worker productivity and lower absenteeism. Workers who are paid on the basis of the number of items they produce or the number of days they show up for work usually produce more items and miss fewer workdays (Muchinsky, 1993; Yukl, Latham, & Purcell, 1976). Similarly, gamblers reinforced

TRY THIS — **Reinforcement Schedules on the Job** Make a list of all the jobs you have ever held, along with the reinforcement schedule on which you received your pay for each. Now consider which of the four types of schedules (FR, FI, VR, or VI) was most common, and which was most satisfying to you.

figure 6.9
Schedules of Reinforcement

These curves illustrate the patterns of behavior typically seen under different reinforcement schedules. The steeper the curve, the faster the response rate; the thin diagonal lines crossing the curves show when reinforcement was given. In general, the rate of responding is higher under ratio schedules than under interval schedules.

Source: Adapted from Skinner (1961).

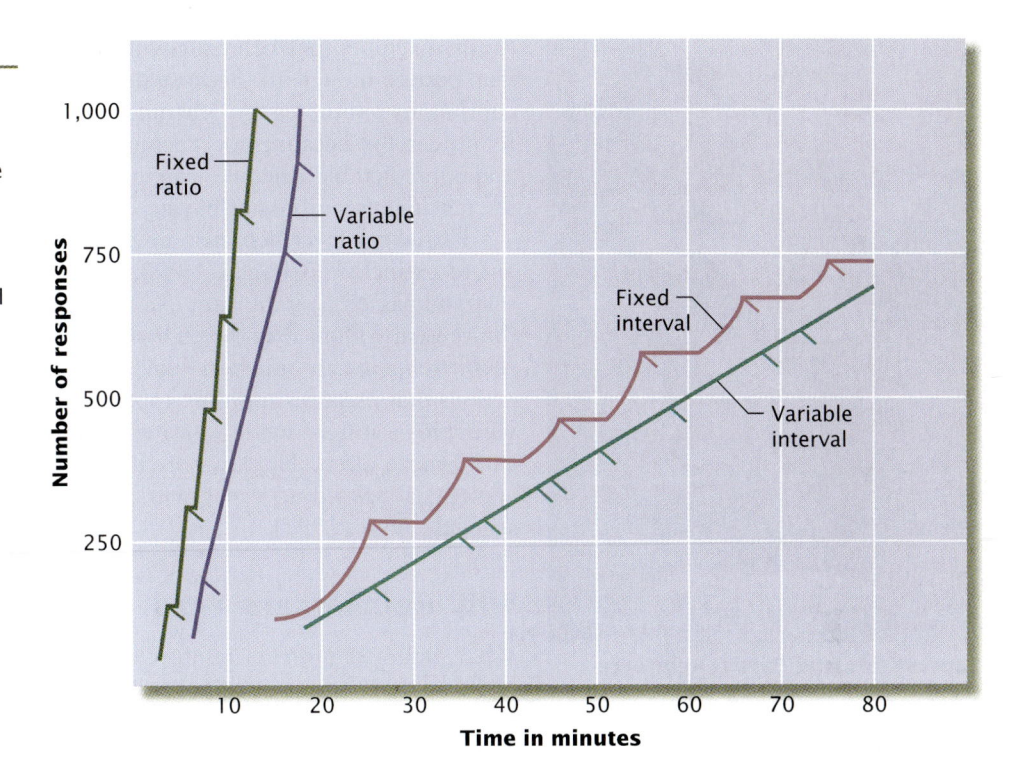

on a variable-ratio schedule for pulling a slot machine handle, rolling dice, or playing other games of chance tend to maintain a high rate of responding—some so-called gambling addicts appear unable to stop.

The second important aspect of Figure 6.9 relates to the "scallops" shown in the fixed-interval schedule. Under this schedule, it does not matter how many responses are made during the time between rewards. As a result, the rate of responding typically drops dramatically immediately after a reinforcer occurs and then increases as the time for another reward approaches. When teachers schedule all their quizzes in advance, for example, some students study just before each quiz and then virtually stop studying in that course until just before the next quiz. Behavior rewarded on variable-interval schedules looks quite different. The unpredictable timing of rewards typically generates slow, steady responding. So if you know that your teacher might give a pop quiz at any class session, you might be more inclined to study more steadily from day to day (Ruscio, 2001).

Schedules and Extinction

Just as breaking the predictive link between a conditioned and an unconditioned stimulus weakens a classically conditioned response, ending the relationship between an operant response and its reinforcers weakens that response. In other words, failure to reinforce a response *extinguishes* that response; the response occurs less often and eventually may disappear. If lever pressing no longer brings food, a rat stops pressing; if repeated e-mail messages to a friend are not answered, you eventually stop sending them. As in classical conditioning, **extinction** in operant conditioning does not totally erase learned relationships. If a signaling stimulus reappears at some time after an operant response has been extinguished, that response may recur (spontaneously recover), and if it is again reinforced, it will be quickly relearned.

In general, behaviors learned under a partial reinforcement schedule are far more difficult to extinguish than those learned on a continuous reinforcement schedule. This phenomenon—called the **partial reinforcement extinction effect**—is easy to understand if you imagine yourself in a gambling casino, standing near a broken slot machine and a broken candy machine. If you deposit money in the

---

continuous reinforcement schedule A pattern in which a reinforcer is delivered every time a particular response occurs.

partial reinforcement schedule A pattern in which a reinforcer is administered only some of the time after a particular response occurs.

fixed-ratio (FR) schedule A partial reinforcement schedule that provides reinforcement following a fixed number of responses.

variable-ratio (VR) schedule A partial reinforcement schedule that provides reinforcement after a varying number of responses.

fixed-interval (FI) schedule A partial reinforcement schedule that provides reinforcement for the first response that occurs after some fixed time has passed since the last reward.

variable-interval (VI) schedule A partial reinforcement schedule that provides reinforcement for the first response after some varying period of time.

extinction The gradual disappearance of operant behavior due to elimination of rewards for that behavior.

partial reinforcement extinction effect A phenomenon in which behaviors learned under a partial reinforcement schedule are more difficult to extinguish than behaviors learned on a continuous reinforcement schedule.

candy machine, that behavior will probably be extinguished quickly (i.e., you will stop putting money in). Because the machine is supposed to deliver its goodies on a continuous reinforcement schedule, it is easy to tell that it is not going to provide a reinforcer. But because slot machines are known to offer rewards on an intermittent and unpredictable schedule, you might put in coin after coin, on the assumption that the machine is simply not paying off at the moment.

Partial reinforcement also helps explain why superstitious behavior is so resistant to extinction (Chance, 1988). Suppose you take a shower just before hearing that you passed an important exam. The shower did nothing to cause this outcome; the reward followed it through sheer luck. Still, for some people, this *accidental reinforcement* can function like a partial reinforcement schedule, strengthening actions that precede, and thus appear to cause, reward (Chance, 1988). So someone who wins a lottery while wearing a particular shirt may begin wearing the "lucky shirt" more often. The laws of chance dictate that if you wear a lucky shirt often enough, a rewarding event will follow now and then, on a very sparse partial schedule (Vyse, 1997).

Why Reinforcers Work

What makes reinforcers reinforcing? For primary reinforcers, at least, the reason could be that they satisfy hunger, thirst, and other physiological needs basic to survival. This explanation is incomplete, however, because substances like saccharin, which have no nutritional value, can have as much reinforcing power as sugar, which is nutritious. Further, addictive drugs are powerful reinforcers even though they pose a long-term threat to the health of people who use them. So psychologists have sought other explanations for the mechanisms of reinforcement.

Some psychologists have argued that reinforcement is based not on a stimulus itself but on the opportunity to engage in an activity that involves the stimulus. According to David Premack (1965), for example, at any moment each person maintains a list of behavioral preferences, ranked from most desirable to least desirable, like a kind of psychological "Top Ten." The higher on the list an activity is, the greater is its power as a reinforcer. This means that a preferred activity can serve as a reinforcer for any other activity that is less preferred at the moment. For example, when parents allow their teenage daughter to use the car in return for mowing the lawn, they are using something high on her preference list (driving) to reinforce an activity that is lower on the list (lawn mowing). This idea is known as the *Premack principle*.

Taking the Premack principle a step further, some psychologists have suggested that virtually any activity can become a reinforcer if a person or animal has not been allowed to perform that activity for a while (Timberlake, 1980; Timberlake & Farmer-Dougan, 1991). To understand how this *disequilibrium hypothesis* works, suppose that you would rather study than work out at the gym. Now suppose that the gym has been closed for several weeks, and you have been unable to have a workout. According to the disequilibrium hypothesis, because your opportunity to exercise has been held below its normal level, its value as a reinforcer has been raised. In fact, it might have become so preferred that it could be used to reinforce studying! In short, under certain circumstances, even activities that are normally not strongly preferred can become reinforcers for normally more preferred activities. The disequilibrium hypothesis helps explain why money is such a powerful secondary reinforcer: It can be exchanged for whatever a person finds reinforcing at the moment. In fact, some researchers believe that the disequilibrium hypothesis may provide a better overall explanation of why reinforcers work than the Premack principle does (Hergenhahn & Olson, 1997).

Psychologists taking a biological approach suggest that the stimuli and activities we know as reinforcers may work by exerting particular effects within the brain. This possibility was suggested when James Olds and Peter Milner (1954) discovered

Superstition and Partial Reinforcement Partial reinforcement often creates superstitious athletic rituals—such as a fixed sequence of actions prior to hitting a golf ball or shooting a free throw in basketball. If the ritual has preceded success often enough, failure to execute the action may upset the player and disrupt performance. One professional baseball player, Wade Boggs, ate chicken before every game and warmed up by catching exactly one hundred ground balls; pitcher Mike Hamilton, shown here, always sits in a certain spot on the dugout steps between innings.

figure 6.10

Two Kinds of Punishment

In one form of punishment, a behavior is followed by an aversive or unpleasant stimulus. In a second form of punishment, sometimes called *penalty*, a pleasant stimulus is removed following a behavior. In either case, punishment decreases the chances that the behavior will occur in the future. When a toddler reaches toward an electric outlet and her father says "NO!" and gently taps her hand, is that punishment or negative reinforcement? (If you said *punishment*, you are right, because it will *reduce* the likelihood of touching outlets in the future.)

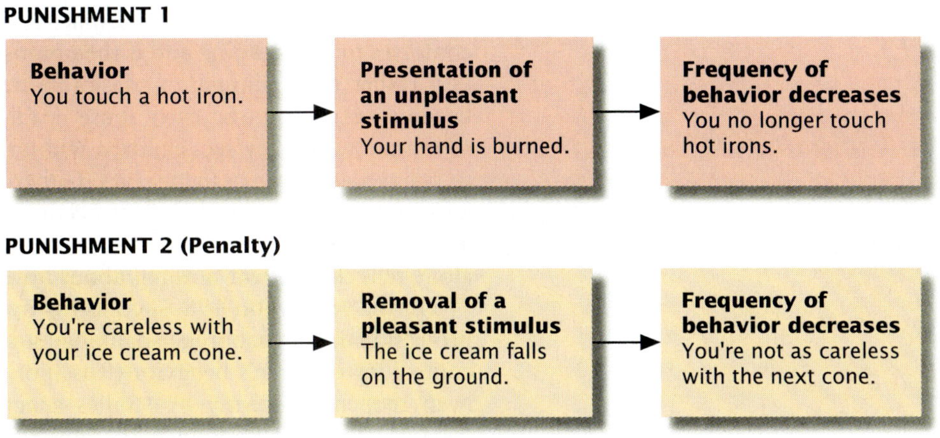

PUNISHMENT 1

| Behavior: You touch a hot iron. | → | Presentation of an unpleasant stimulus: Your hand is burned. | → | Frequency of behavior decreases: You no longer touch hot irons. |

PUNISHMENT 2 (Penalty)

| Behavior: You're careless with your ice cream cone. | → | Removal of a pleasant stimulus: The ice cream falls on the ground. | → | Frequency of behavior decreases: You're not as careless with the next cone. |

that mild electrical stimulation of certain areas of the hypothalamus can be such a powerful reinforcer that a hungry rat will ignore food in a Skinner box, preferring to spend hours pressing a lever that stimulates these "pleasure centers" in its brain (Olds, 1973). It is not yet clear whether physiological mechanisms underlie the power of all reinforcers, but evidence available so far suggests that these mechanisms are important components of the process (Waelti, Dickinson, & Schultz, 2001). For example, as mentioned in the chapter on biological aspects of psychology, the activation of dopamine systems is associated with the pleasure of many stimuli, including food; music; sex; the uncertainty involved in gambling; and some addictive drugs, such as cocaine (Berns et al., 2001; Blood & Zatorre, 2001; Breiter et al., 2001; Cardinal et al., 2001; Ciccocioppo, Sanna, & Weiss, 2001).

Punishment

So far, we have discussed positive and negative reinforcement, both of which *increase* the frequency of a response, either by presenting something pleasurable or by removing something unpleasant. In contrast, **punishment** *reduces* the frequency of an operant behavior by presenting an unpleasant stimulus or removing a pleasant one. Shouting "No!" and swatting your dog when he begins chewing on the rug illustrates punishment that presents an unpleasant stimulus following a response. Taking away a child's TV privileges because of rude behavior is a kind of punishment—sometimes called *penalty*—that removes a positive stimulus (see Figure 6.10).

Punishment is often confused with negative reinforcement, but they are actually quite different. Reinforcement of any sort always *strengthens* behavior; punishment *weakens* it. If shock is *turned off* when a rat presses a lever, that is negative reinforcement; it increases the probability that the rat will press the lever when shock occurs again. But if shock is *turned on* when the rat presses the lever, that is punishment; the rat will be less likely to press the lever again.

Although punishment can change behavior, it has several potential drawbacks. First, it does not "erase" an undesirable habit; it merely suppresses it. This suppression usually occurs in response to stimuli (such as a parent or teacher) that were present at the time of punishment, so people may repeat previously punished acts when they think they can avoid detection. This problem is summed up in the adage "When the cat's away, the mice will play." Second, punishment sometimes produces unwanted side effects. For example, if you punish a child for swearing, the child may associate the punisher with the punishment and end up being afraid of you. Third, punishment is often ineffective, especially with animals or young children, unless it is given immediately after the response and each time the response is made. If a child gets into a cookie jar and enjoys a few cookies before being discovered and

punishment Presentation of an aversive stimulus or the removal of a pleasant stimulus.

punished, the effect of the punishment will be greatly reduced. Similarly, if a child confesses to wrongdoing and is then punished, the punishment may discourage honesty rather than eliminate undesirable behavior. Fourth, physical punishment can become aggression and even abuse if administered in anger. Because children tend to imitate what they see, children who are frequently punished may be more likely to behave aggressively themselves (Gilbert, 1997). Finally, although punishment signals that inappropriate behavior occurred, it does not specify what should be done instead. An F on a term paper says the assignment was poorly done, but the grade alone tells the student nothing about how to improve.

In the 1970s and 1980s, concerns over these drawbacks led many parents and professionals to discourage spanking and other forms of punishment as a means of controlling children's behavior (Rosellini, 1998). The debate about punishment has been reopened recently by studies suggesting that spanking can be an effective behavior control technique with children three to thirteen years of age. These studies found that occasional spanking is not detrimental to children's development, if used in combination with other disciplinary practices such as requiring that the children pay some penalty for their misdeeds, having them provide some sort of restitution to the victims of their actions, and making them aware of what they did wrong (Gunnoe & Mariner, 1997; Larzelere, 1996).

When used *properly*, then, punishment can work, and in some instances it may be the only alternative. For example, some children suffer developmental disabilities in which they strike or mutilate themselves or display other potentially life threatening behaviors. As shown in Figure 6.11, punishing these behaviors has sometimes proven to be the only effective treatment (e.g., Flavell et al., 1982). Whatever the case, punishment is most effective when it is administered in accordance with several guidelines. First, the person giving punishment should specify *why* it is being given and that its purpose is to change the person's behavior, not to harm or demean the person. This step helps prevent a general fear of the punisher. Second, without being abusive, punishment should be immediate and noticeable enough to eliminate the undesirable behavior. A halfhearted "Quit it" may actually reinforce a child's misbehavior, because almost any attention is reinforcing to some children. Moreover, if children become habituated to very mild punishment, the parent may end up using substantially more severe punishment to stop inappropriate behavior than would have been necessary if a stern, but moderate, punishment had been used in the first place. (You may have witnessed this *escalation effect* in grocery stores or restaurants, where parents are often not initially firm enough in dealing with their children's misbehavior.) Finally, the use of punishment alone is usually not enough

figure 6.11

Life-Saving Punishment

This child suffered from chronic ruminative disorder, a condition in which he vomited everything he ate. At left, the boy was approximately one year old and had been vomiting for four months. At right is the same child thirteen days after punishment with electric shock had eliminated the vomiting behavior; his weight had increased 26 percent. He was physically and psychologically healthy when tested six months, one year, and two years later (Lang & Melamed, 1969).

Source: Lang & Melamed (1969).

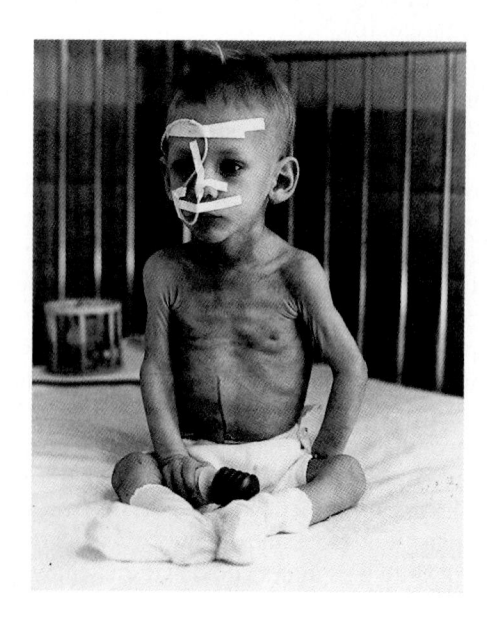

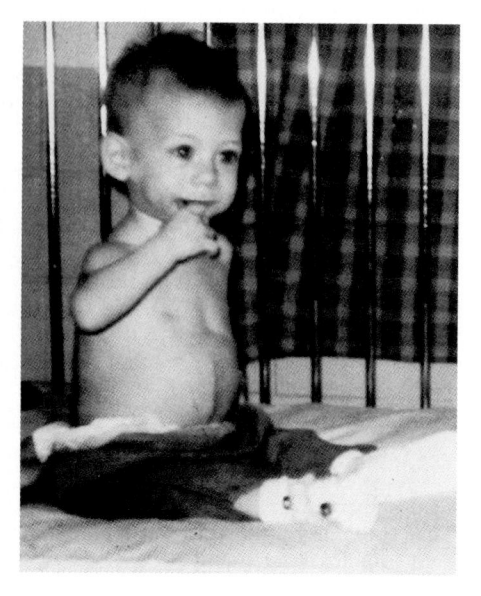

to change behavior in the long run. It is important also to identify what the person should do instead of the punished act, and then reinforce the appropriate behavior when it occurs. As the frequency of appropriate behavior increases through reinforcement, the frequency of undesirable responses (and the need for further punishment) should decline.

When these guidelines are not followed, the potentially beneficial effects of punishment may disappear or be only temporary (Hyman, 1995). As illustrated in many countries' justice systems, punishment for criminal acts is typically administered long after the acts have occurred, and initial punishments are often relatively mild—as when offenders are repeatedly given probation. Even being sent to jail or prison rarely leads to rehabilitation, because this punishment is usually not supplemented by efforts to teach and reinforce noncriminal lifestyles (Brennan & Mednick, 1994; Cassel & Bernstein, 2001). It is no wonder, then, that of the more than 2 million criminals in prison in the United States alone, about two-thirds are likely to be rearrested for serious crimes within three years of completing their sentences, and about 40 percent of them will return to prison (Cassel & Bernstein, 2001; U.S. Department of Justice, 1997).

Some Applications of Operant Conditioning

The principles of operant conditioning were originally developed with animals in the laboratory, but they are valuable for understanding human behavior in an endless variety of everyday situations. ("In Review: Reinforcement and Punishment" summarizes some key principles of operant conditioning.) The unscientific but effective use of rewards and punishments by parents, teachers, and peers is vital to helping children learn what is and is not appropriate behavior at the dinner table, in the classroom, or at a birthday party. People learn how to be "civilized" in their own culture partly through positive ("Good!") and negative ("Stop that!") responses from others. As described in the chapter on human development, differing patterns

in review: Reinforcement and Punishment

Concept	Description	Example or Comment
Positive reinforcement	Increasing the frequency of a behavior by following it with the presentation of a positive reinforcer—a pleasant, positive stimulus or experience	You say "Good job!" after someone works hard to perform a task.
Negative reinforcement	Increasing the frequency of a behavior by following it with the removal of an unpleasant stimulus or experience	You learn to use the "mute" button on the TV remote control to remove the sound of an obnoxious commercial.
Escape conditioning	Learning to make a response that removes an unpleasant stimulus	A little boy learns that crying will cut short the time that he must stay in his room.
Avoidance conditioning	Learning to make a response that avoids an unpleasant stimulus	You slow your car to the speed limit when you spot a police car, thus avoiding being stopped and reducing the fear of a fine; very resistant to extinction.
Punishment	Decreasing the frequency of a behavior by either presenting an unpleasant stimulus (punishment 1) or removing a pleasant one (punishment 2, or penalty)	You swat the dog after it steals food from the table, or you take a favorite toy away from a child who misbehaves. A number of cautions should be kept in mind before using punishment.

Learning Cultural Values As described in the chapter on social influence, the prevalence of aggressive behavior varies considerably from culture to culture, in part because some cultures reward it more than others do. In some Inuit cultures, for example, aggressive behavior is actively discouraged and extremely rare (Banta, 1997). In many other cultures, it is all too common.

of rewards and punishments for boys and girls also underlie the development of behaviors that fit culturally approved *gender roles*.

The scientific study of operant conditioning has led to numerous treatment programs for altering problematic behavior. Behavioral programs that combine the use of rewards for appropriate actions and extinction, or carefully administered punishment, for inappropriate behaviors have helped countless mental patients, mentally retarded individuals, autistic children, and hard-to-manage youngsters to develop the behavior patterns they need to live happier and more productive lives (Ayllon, 1999; Morisse et al., 1996). These same methods have been used successfully to help keep former drug addicts drug-free and to help patients with alcohol-related memory problems to recognize and remember new faces and names—including those of their own grandchildren (Hochhalter et al., 2001; Silverman et al., 2001). Many self-help books also incorporate principles of positive reinforcement, recommending self-reward following each small victory in efforts to lose weight, stop smoking, avoid procrastination, or reach other goals (e.g., Rachlin, 2000).

When people cannot do anything about the consequences of a behavior, discriminative stimuli may hold the key to changing the behavior. For example, people trying to quit smoking often find it easier to avoid smoking if they stay away from bars and other places that contain discriminative stimuli for smoking. Stimulus control can also help alleviate insomnia. Insomniacs are much more likely than other people to use their beds for nonsleeping activities, such as watching television, writing letters, reading magazines, worrying, and so on. Soon the bedroom becomes a discriminative stimulus for so many activities that relaxation and sleep become less and less likely. But if insomniacs begin to use their beds only for sleeping, there is a good chance that they will sleep better (Jacobs, 1999; Lichstein & Morin, 2000).

Cognitive Processes in Learning

During the first half of the twentieth century, psychologists in North America tended to look at classical and operant conditioning through the lens of behaviorism, the theoretical approach that was dominant in psychology at the time. As described in the chapter on introducing psychology, behaviorism stresses the importance of empirical observation of lawful relationships in animal and human behavior. Behaviorists tried to identify the stimuli, responses, and consequences that build and alter overt behavior. In other words, they saw learning as resulting from the automatic, unthinking formation or modification of associations between observable events. Behaviorists paid almost no attention to the role of conscious mental activity that might accompany the learning process.

This strictly behavioral view of classical and operant conditioning is challenged by the cognitive approach, which has become increasingly influential in recent decades. Cognitive psychologists see a common thread in these apparently different forms of learning. Both classical and operant conditioning, they argue, help animals and people to detect causality—to understand what causes what (Schwartz & Robbins, 1995). By extension, both types of conditioning may result not only from automatic associations but also from more complex mental processes that organisms use to understand their environments and to interact with them adaptively (Dickinson, 2001).

Certainly there is evidence that cognitive processes—how people represent, store, and use information—play an important role in learning. This evidence includes research on learned helplessness, latent learning, cognitive maps, insight, and observational learning.

Learned Helplessness

Babies learn that crying brings parental attention, children learn which button turns on the TV, and adults learn what behaviors bring success in the workplace. On the basis of this learning, people come to expect that certain actions on their part cause certain consequences. If this learning is disrupted, problems may result. One such problem is **learned helplessness,** a tendency to give up any effort to control the environment (Seligman, 1975).

Learned helplessness was first demonstrated in animals. As described earlier, dogs placed in a shuttle box (see Figure 6.7) will normally learn to jump over a partition to escape a shock. However, if the dogs are first placed in a restraining harness and receive shocks that they cannot escape, they later do not even try to escape when a shock is turned on in the shuttle box (Overmier & Seligman, 1967). It is as if the animals had learned that "shock happens, and there is nothing I can do to control it."

FOCUS ON RESEARCH METHODS

A Two-Factor Experiment on Human Helplessness

The results of animal studies on learned helplessness led psychologists to wonder whether learned helplessness might play a role in human psychological problems, but they had to deal with more basic questions first. One of the most important of these questions is whether lack of control over the environment can lead to helplessness in humans.

- **What was the researcher's question?**

Donald Hiroto (1974) conducted an experiment to test the hypothesis that people would develop learned helplessness after either experiencing lack of control or simply being told that their control was limited.

- **How did the researcher answer the question?**

The first independent variable Hiroto manipulated in his experiment was whether or not volunteer participants could control a series of thirty randomly timed bursts of loud, obnoxious noise. Like dogs receiving inescapable shock, one group of participants had no way to stop the noise. A second group did have control; they could press a button to turn off the noise. A third group heard no noise at all.

learned helplessness A failure to try to exert control over the environment when an organism has, or believes that it has, no such control.

After this preliminary phase, all participants were exposed to eighteen more bursts of obnoxious noise, each preceded by a red warning light. During this second phase, *all* participants could stop the noise by moving a lever to the left or right, and if they acted quickly enough, they could even prevent it from starting. However, the participants did not know which lever direction would be correct on any given trial.

Before these new trials began, the experimenter manipulated a second independent variable: the participants' *expectation* about control. Half the participants were told that avoiding or escaping the noise depended on their *skill* at moving the lever. The other participants were told that no matter how hard they tried, success at avoiding or escaping noise would be a matter of *chance*. This was a *two-factor experiment,* because the dependent variable—the participants' efforts to control noise—could be affected by either or both of two independent variables: prior experience with noise (control, lack of control, or no noise) and expectation (skill or chance) about the ability to influence the noise.

● What did the researcher find?

On the average, participants who had previously experienced lack of control now failed to control noise on almost four times as many trials (50 percent versus 13 percent) as did participants who had earlier been in control. Further, regardless of whether participants had experienced control before, those who expected control to depend on their skill exerted control on significantly more trials than did those who expected chance to govern the outcome.

● What do the results mean?

These results supported Hiroto's hypothesis that people, like animals, tend to make less effort to control their environment when prior experience leads them to expect their efforts to be in vain. Unlike animals, however, people can develop expectations of helplessness either through personally experiencing lack of control or through being *told* that they are powerless. Hiroto's (1974) results appear to reflect a general phenomenon: When people's prior experience leads them to *believe* that nothing they do can change their lives or control their destiny, they generally stop trying to improve their lot (Dweck, Chiu, & Hong, 1995; Peterson, Maier, & Seligman, 1993). Instead, they tend to passively endure aversive situations and, at the cognitive level, to attribute negative events to their own permanent and general shortcomings rather than to changeable external circumstances (Abramson, Metalsky, & Alloy, 1989; Seligman, Klein, & Miller, 1976).

● What do we still need to know?

Although it seems clear that helplessness can be learned, not all of its consequences are known or understood. For example, Martin Seligman (1975) originally proposed that learned helplessness was a major cause of depression and other mental disorders in humans, but subsequent research (Abramson, Metalsky, & Alloy, 1989; Metalsky et al., 1993) indicates that the causal picture is more complicated. One study suggests that learned-helplessness experiences give rise to a more general *pessimistic explanatory style* that can produce depression and other mental disorders (Peterson & Seligman, 1984). People with this style tend to see the good things that happen to them as temporary and due to external factors such as luck, and the bad things as permanent and due to internal factors such as lack of ability. A pessimistic explanatory style, in fact, has been associated with negative outcomes, such as poor grades, poor sales performance, and health problems (Peterson & Barrett, 1987; Seligman & Schulman, 1986; Taylor, 1998). However, the mechanism responsible for this connection remains unknown (Wiebe & Smith, 1997); understanding how pessimistic (or optimistic) explanatory styles can lead to negative (or positive) consequences remains an important focus of research (Salovey, Rothman, & Rodin, 1998).

figure 6.12

Latent Learning

Notice that when the rats in Group C did not receive food reinforcement, they continued to make many errors in locating the goal box of a maze. The day after first finding food there, however, they took almost no wrong turns! The reinforcement, argued Tolman, affected only the rats' *performance*; they must have learned the maze earlier, without reinforcement.

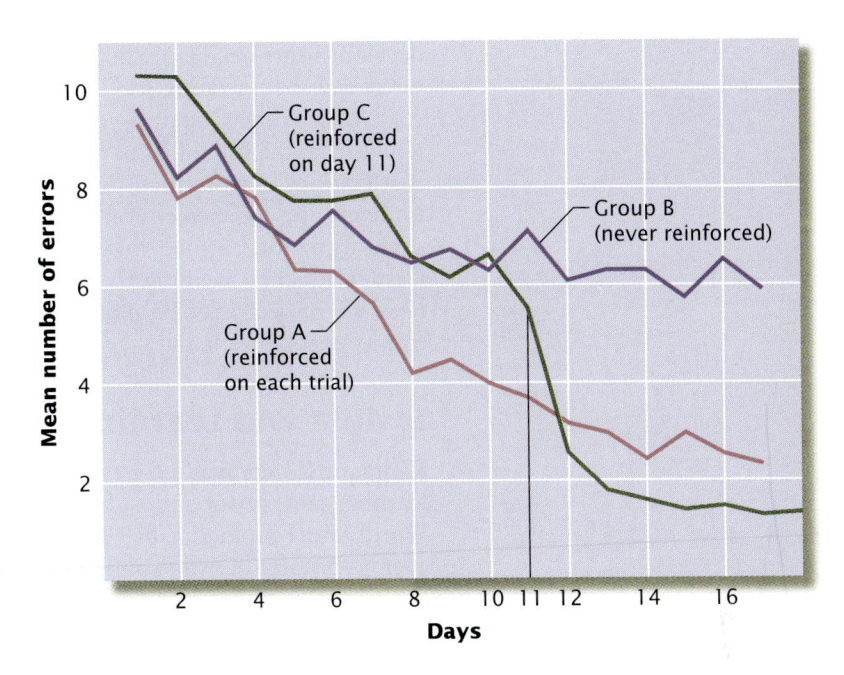

Latent Learning and Cognitive Maps

The study of cognitive processes in learning goes back at least to the 1920s and Edward Tolman's research on maze learning in rats. The rats' task was to find the goal box of the maze, where food awaited them. The rats typically took many wrong turns, but over the course of many trials they made fewer and fewer mistakes. The behavioral interpretation was that the rats learned a long chain of turning responses that were ultimately reinforced by the food. Tolman disagreed and offered evidence for a cognitive interpretation.

In one of Tolman's studies, three groups of rats were placed in the same maze once a day for several consecutive days (Tolman & Honzik, 1930). For Group A, food was placed in the goal box on each trial. As shown in Figure 6.12, these rats gradually improved their performance so that by the end of the experiment, they made only one or two mistakes as they ran through the maze. Group B also ran the maze once a day, but there was never any food in their goal box. These animals continued to make many errors throughout the experiment. Neither of these results is surprising, and each is consistent with a behavioral view of learning.

The third group of rats, Group C, was the critical one. For the first ten days, they received no reinforcement for running the maze and continued to make many mistakes. But on the eleventh day, food was placed in their goal box for the first time. Then a very surprising thing happened: On the day after receiving reinforcement, these rats made almost no mistakes. In fact, their performance was as good as that of the rats who had been reinforced every day. In other words, for Group C the single reinforcement trial on day 11 produced a dramatic change in performance the next day.

Tolman argued that these results supported two conclusions. First, the reinforcement on day 11 could not have significantly affected the rats' *learning* of the maze itself; it simply changed their subsequent *performance*. They must have learned the maze earlier. Therefore, the rats demonstrated **latent learning**—learning that is not evident when it first occurs. Second, because the rats' performance changed immediately after the first reinforcement trial, the results obtained could occur only if the rats had earlier developed a **cognitive map**—that is, a mental representation of how the maze was arranged.

Tolman concluded that cognitive maps develop naturally through experience with the world, even if there is no overt response or reinforcement. Research on learning in the natural environment has supported these views. For example, we

latent learning Learning that is not demonstrated at the time it occurs.

cognitive map A mental representation, or picture, of the environment.

develop mental maps of shopping malls and city streets, even when we receive no direct reward for doing so (Tversky & Kahneman, 1991).

Much as the Gestalt psychologists argued that the whole of a perception is different from the sum of its parts (see the chapter on perception), cognitive views hold that learning is more than just the effects of associations, reinforcements, and punishments. Just as perception may depend on the meaning attached to sensations, some forms of learning involve higher mental processes and depend on how the learner attaches meaning to events. To take just one example, being praised by a boss we respect may be more reinforcing than getting the same good evaluation from someone we hate.

Insight and Learning

Wolfgang Köhler was a Gestalt psychologist whose work on the cognitive aspects of learning came about almost by accident. He was visiting the island of Tenerife when World War I broke out in 1914. As a German in an area controlled by Germany's enemy, Britain, he was confined to the island for the duration of the war, and he devoted his time to studying problem solving by chimpanzees housed there (Köhler, 1924).

For example, Köhler would put a chimpanzee in a cage and place a piece of fruit so that it was visible, but out of the animal's reach. He sometimes hung the fruit from a string too high to reach or laid it on the ground too far outside the cage to be retrieved. Many of the chimps overcame these obstacles easily. If the fruit was out of reach on the ground outside the cage, some chimps looked around the cage and,

figure 6.13
Insight

Here are three impressive examples of problem solving by chimpanzees. At left, the animal fixed a fifteen-foot pole in the ground, climbed to the top, and dropped down after grabbing fruit that had previously been out of its reach. In the center photo, the chimp stacked two boxes from different areas of the compound, climbed to the top, and used a pole to knock down the fruit. The chimp at right stacked three boxes and climbed them to reach the fruit.

Source: Köhler (1976).

Cognitive Processes in Learning

finding a long stick, used it to rake in the fruit. Surprised that the chimpanzees could solve these problems, Köhler tried more difficult tasks. Again, the chimps proved very adept, as Figure 6.13 illustrates.

In contrast to Thorndike, who thought that animals learn gradually through the consequences of their actions, Köhler argued that animals' problem solving does not have to depend on automatic associations developing slowly through trial and error. He supported his claim with three observations. First, once a chimpanzee solved a particular problem, it would immediately do the same thing in a similar situation. In other words, it acted as if it understood the problem. Second, Köhler's chimpanzees rarely tried a solution that did not work. Third, they often reached a solution suddenly. When confronted with a piece of fruit hanging from a string, for example, a chimp might jump for it several times. Then it would stop jumping, look up, and pace back and forth. Finally it would run over to a wooden crate, place it directly under the fruit, and climb on top of it to reach the fruit. Once, when there were no other objects available, a chimp went over to Köhler, dragged him by the arm until he stood beneath the fruit, and then started climbing up his back!

Köhler believed that the only explanation for these results was that the chimpanzees had sudden **insight**, an understanding of the problem as a whole, not just growing associations among its specific elements. However, demonstrating that a particular performance is the product of sudden insight requires experiments more sophisticated than those conducted by Köhler. Some cases of "insight" might actually be the result of a process known as *learning to learn*, in which previous experiences in problem solving are applied to new ones in a way that makes their solution seem to be instantaneous (Harlow, 1949). In other cases, according to some cognitive psychologists, insight may actually result from a "mental trial-and-error" process in which people (and some animals) envision a course of action, mentally simulate its results, compare it with the imagined outcome of other alternatives, and settle on the course of action most likely to aid complex problem solving and decision making (Klein, 1993).

Observational Learning: Learning by Imitation

Research on the role of cognitive processes in learning has been further stimulated by the finding that learning can occur not only by doing but also by observing what others do. Learning by watching others—called **observational learning**, or *social*

TRY THIS — **Learning by Imitation** Much of our behavior is learned by imitating others, especially those who serve as role models. To appreciate the impact of social learning in your life, list five examples of how your own actions, speech, mannerisms, or appearance have come to match those of a parent, a sibling, a friend, a teacher, or even a celebrity.

insight A sudden understanding about what is required to solve a problem.

observational learning Learning how to perform new behaviors by watching others.

IN THE BLEACHERS By Steve Moore

In spite of the power of observational learning, some people just have to learn things the hard way.

IN THE BLEACHERS © 1999 Moore. Reprinted with permission of UNIVERSAL PRESS SYNDICATE. All rights reserved.

learning—is efficient and adaptive. It occurs in both animals and humans. For example, young chimpanzees learn how to use a stone to crack open nuts by watching their mothers perform this action (Inoue-Nakamura & Matsuzawa, 1997). And we don't have to find out for ourselves that a door is locked or an iron is hot if we have just seen someone else try the door or suffer a burn.

Children are particularly influenced by the adults and peers who act as models for appropriate behavior in various situations. In one classic experiment, Albert Bandura showed nursery school children a film featuring an adult and a large, inflatable, bottom-heavy "Bobo" doll (Bandura, 1965). The adult in the film punched the Bobo doll in the nose, kicked it, threw objects at it, and hit its head with a hammer while saying things like "Sockeroo!" There were different endings to the film. Some children saw an ending in which the aggressive adult was called a "champion" by a second adult and rewarded with candy and soft drinks. Some saw the aggressor scolded and called a "bad person." Some saw a neutral ending in which there was neither reward nor punishment. After the film, each child was allowed to play alone with a Bobo doll. How the children played in this and similar studies led to some important conclusions about learning and about the role of cognitive factors in it.

Bandura found that children who saw the adult rewarded for aggression showed the most aggressive acts in play; they had received **vicarious conditioning,** a kind of observational learning in which one is influenced by seeing or hearing about the consequences of others' behavior. Those who had seen the adult punished for aggressive acts initially showed less aggression, but they still learned something. When later offered rewards for all the aggressive acts they could perform, these children displayed just as many as the children who had watched the rewarded adult. Observational learning can occur even when there are no vicarious consequences; many children in the neutral condition also imitated the model's aggression (see Figure 6.14).

figure 6.14

Observational Learning

Albert Bandura found that after observing an aggressive model, many children imitate the model's acts precisely, especially if the model's aggression was rewarded.

Source: Bandura, Ross, & Ross (1963).

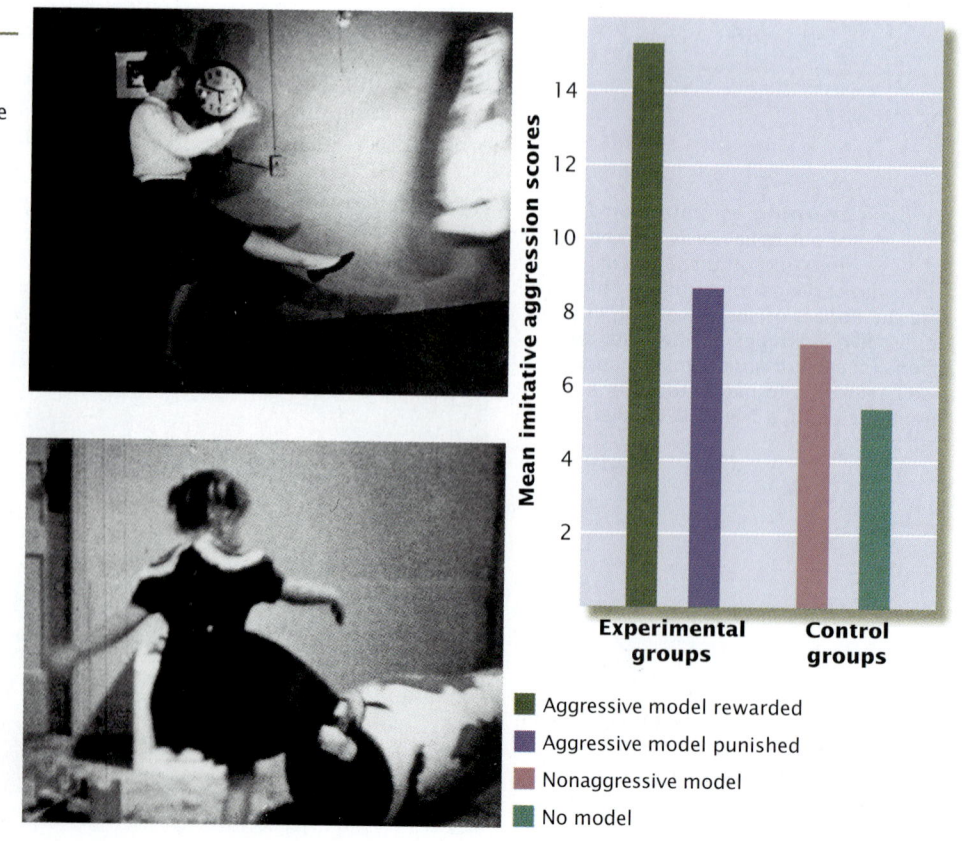

- Aggressive model rewarded
- Aggressive model punished
- Nonaggressive model
- No model

vicarious conditioning Learning conditioned responses by watching what happens to others.

Observational learning seems to be a powerful source of the *socialization* process through which children learn about which behaviors are—and are not—appropriate in their culture (Bandura, 1999). Experiments show, for example, that children are more willing to help and share after seeing a demonstration of helping by a friendly, powerful model—even after some months have elapsed (Schroeder et al., 1995). Still other studies suggest that anxiety disorders such as phobias may be learned through observation of fearful models (Cook & Mineka, 1987; Kleinknecht, 1991).

THINKING CRITICALLY

Does Watching Violence on Television Make People More Violent?

If observational learning is important, then surely television—and televised violence—must teach children a great deal. For one thing, it is estimated that the average child in the United States spends more time watching television than attending school (Hepburn, 1995; Nielsen Media, 1990). Much of what children see is violent; prime-time programs in the United States present an average of 5 violent acts per hour; some Saturday morning cartoons include 20 to 25 per hour (American Psychological Association, 1993; Seppa, 1997). As a result, the average child will have witnessed at least 8,000 murders and more than 100,000 other acts of televised violence *before graduating from elementary school,* and twice that many by age 18 (Feshbach et al., 1993; Kunkel et al., 1996).

Psychologists have speculated that watching so much violence might be emotionally arousing, making viewers more likely to react violently to frustration (Huston & Wright, 1989). In fact, there is evidence that exposure to media violence can trigger or amplify viewers' aggressive thoughts and feelings, thus increasing the likelihood that they will act aggressively (Anderson & Dill, 2000; Bushman, 1998). Televised violence might also provide models that viewers imitate, particularly if the violence is carried out by attractive, powerful models—the "good guys," for example (Bandura, 1983). Finally, prolonged viewing of violent TV programs might "desensitize" viewers, making them less distressed when they see others suffer and less disturbed about inflicting pain on others (Aronson, 1999; Donnerstein et al., 1995). Concern over the influence of violence on television has recently led to the development of a violence-blocking V-Chip for new television sets in the United States.

• **What am I being asked to believe or accept?**

Many have argued that through one or more of the mechanisms just listed, watching violence on television causes violent behavior in viewers (Eron et al., 1996; Huesmann, 1998). A 1993 report by the National Academy of Science concluded that "overall, the vast majority of studies, whatever their methodology, showed that exposure to television violence resulted in increased aggressive behavior, both contemporaneously and over time" (Reiss & Roth, 1993, p. 371). An American Psychological Association Commission on Violence and Youth reached the same conclusion (American Psychological Association, 1993).

• **What evidence is available to support the assertion?**

Three types of evidence support the claim that watching violent television programs increases violent behavior. Some evidence comes from anecdotes and case studies. Children have poked one another in the eye after watching the Three Stooges appear to do so on television, and adults have claimed that watching TV shows prompted them to commit murders or other violent acts matching those seen on the shows.

Second, many longitudinal studies have found a correlation between watching violent television programs and later acts of aggression and violence. One such study tracked people from the time they were six or seven (in 1977) until they reached their early twenties (in 1992). Those who watched more violent television as children were significantly more aggressive as adults (Huesmann et al., 1997) and more likely to engage in criminal activity (Huesmann, 1995). They were also more likely to use physical punishment on their own children, who themselves tended to be much more aggressive than average. These latter results have been found not only in the United States, but in Israel, Australia, Poland, the Netherlands, and even Finland, where the number of violent TV shows is very small (Centerwall, 1990; Huesmann & Eron, 1986).

Finally, the results of numerous laboratory experiments also support the view that TV violence increases aggression among viewers (American Psychological Association, 1993; Paik & Comstock, 1994; Reiss & Roth, 1993). In one study, groups of boys watched violent or nonviolent programs in a controlled setting and then played floor hockey (Josephson, 1987). Boys who had watched the violent shows were more likely than those who had watched nonviolent programs to behave aggressively on the hockey floor. This effect was greatest for those boys who had the most aggressive tendencies to begin with. More extensive experiments in which children are exposed for long periods to carefully controlled types of television programs also suggest that exposure to large amounts of violent activity on television results in aggressive behavior (Eron et al., 1996).

- **Are there alternative ways of interpreting the evidence?**

Anecdotal reports and case studies are certainly open to different interpretations. When people face imprisonment or execution for their violent acts, how much credibility can we give to their claims that their actions were triggered by television programs? And how many other people might say that the same programs made them *less* likely to be violent? Anecdotes alone do not provide a good basis for drawing solid scientific conclusions.

What about the correlational evidence from longitudinal studies? As discussed in the chapter on research in psychology, a *correlation* between two variables does not necessarily mean that one is *causing* an effect on the other; both might be affected by a third factor. Why, for example, are certain people watching so much television violence in the first place? This question suggests a possible third factor that might account for the observed relationship between watching TV violence and acting aggressively: People who tend to be aggressive may prefer to watch more violent TV programs *and* behave aggressively toward others. In other words, personality may account for the observed correlations (e.g., Aluja-Fabregat & Torrubia-Beltri, 1998).

The results of controlled experiments on the effects of televised violence have been criticized as well (Geen, 1998). The major objection is that both the independent and dependent variables in these experiments are artificial, so they may not apply beyond the laboratory (Anderson, Lindsay, & Bushman, 1999). For example, the kinds of violent shows viewed by the participants during some of these experiments, as well as the ways in which their aggression has been measured, may not reflect what goes on in the real-world situations we most want to know about.

- **What additional evidence would help to evaluate the alternatives?**

Given the difficulty of interpreting correlational evidence, it would be useful to have evidence from controlled experiments in which equivalent groups of people were exposed for years to differing "doses" of the violence actually portrayed on TV, and the effects on their subsequent behavior were observed in real-world situations. Such experiments could also explore the circumstances under which different people (e.g., children versus adults) were affected by various forms of violence. However, studies like these create an ethical dilemma. If watching violent television programs *does* cause violent behavior, are psychologists justified in creating conditions that might lead some people to be more violent? If such violence occurred, would the researchers be partly responsible to the victims and to society? Difficulty in answering questions like these is one reason why there are so many short-term experiments and correlational studies in this area and why there is still some uncertainty about the effects of television violence.

- **What conclusions are most reasonable?**

The preponderance of evidence collected so far, including statistical analyses of correlational findings (e.g., Huesmann et al., 1997), makes it reasonable to conclude that watching TV violence may be one cause of violent behavior (Bushman & Anderson, 2001; Robinson et al., 2001; Smith & Donnerstein, 1998). Playing violent video games may be another (Anderson & Bushman, 2001). However, a causal relationship between watching TV violence and acting violently is not inevitable, and there are many circumstances in which the effect does not occur (Charleton, Gunter, & Coles, 1998; Freedman, 1992). Parents, peers, and other environmental influences, along with personality factors, may dampen or amplify the effect of watching televised violence. The viewers most likely to be affected by TV violence may be those who are most aggressive or violence-prone in the first place, a trait that could well have been acquired by observing the behavior of parents or peers (Huesmann et al., 1997). Still, the fact that violence on television *can* have a causal impact on violent behavior is reason for serious concern and continues to influence public debate about what should and should not be aired on television (Glod, 1998).

LINKAGES (a link to Perception)

Neural Networks and Learning

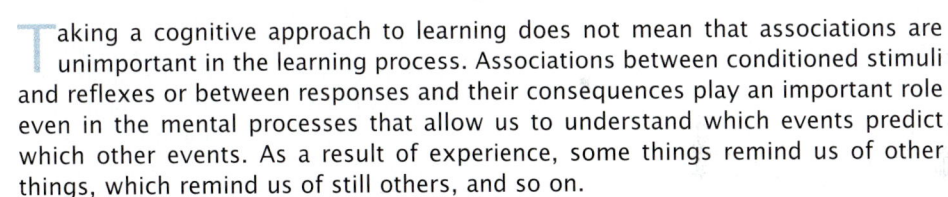

Taking a cognitive approach to learning does not mean that associations are unimportant in the learning process. Associations between conditioned stimuli and reflexes or between responses and their consequences play an important role even in the mental processes that allow us to understand which events predict which other events. As a result of experience, some things remind us of other things, which remind us of still others, and so on.

How are associations actually stored in the brain? No one yet knows for sure, but the neural network models discussed in the chapter on perception provide a good way of thinking about this process. Networks of neural connections are believed to play a critical role not only in the rapid and accurate recognition of objects (Hintzman, 1991), but also in the learning process itself (Hergenhahn & Olson, 1997). These associative networks can be very complex. Consider the word *dog*. As shown in Figure 6.15, each person's experience builds many associations to this word, and the strength of each association will reflect the frequency with

figure 6.15

An Associative Network

Here is an example of a network of associations to the word *dog*. Network theorists suggest that the connections shown here represent patterns of neural connections in the brain.

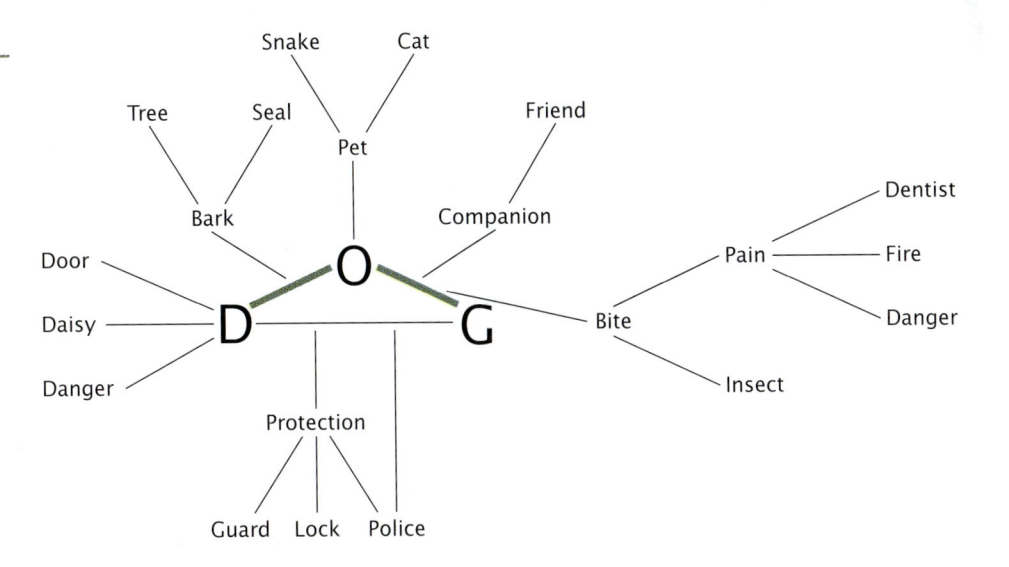

which *dog* has been mentally linked to the other objects, events, and ideas in that person's life.

Using what they know about the laws of learning and about the way neurons communicate and alter their synaptic connections, psychologists have been trying to develop models of how these associations are established (Messinger et al., 2001). We discuss some of these efforts in the chapter on perception in terms of *neural networks* and *parallel distributed processing* models of perception. A crucial aspect of such models is the idea of *distributed memory* or *distributed knowledge*. These models suggest, for example, that the knowledge of "dog" does not lie in a single location, or node, within your brain. Instead, knowledge is distributed throughout the network of associations that connect the letters *D, O,* and *G,* along with other "dog-like" experiences. In addition, as shown in Figure 6.15, each of the interconnected nodes that make up your knowledge of "dog" is connected to many other nodes as well. So the letter *D* will be connected to "Daisy," "Danger," and a host of other concepts. Networks of connections also appear to be the key to explaining how people come to understand the words and sentences they read (Wolman, van den Broek, & Lorch, 1997).

Neural network models of learning focus on how these connections are developed through experience (Hanson & Burr, 1990). For example, suppose you are learning a new word in a foreign language. Each time you read the word and associate it with its English equivalent, you strengthen the neural connections between the sight of the letters forming that word and all of the nodes activated when its English equivalent is brought to mind. Neural network, or *connectionist,* models of learning predict how much the strength of each linkage grows (in terms of the likelihood of neural communication between the two connected nodes) each time the two words are experienced together.

The details of various theories about how these connections grow are very complex (see Hanson & Burr, 1990; Schwartz & Reisberg, 1991), but a theme common to many is that the weaker the connection between two items, the greater the increase in connection strength when they are experienced together. So in a simple classical conditioning experiment, the connections between the nodes characterizing the conditioned stimulus and those characterizing the unconditioned stimulus will show the greatest increase in strength during the first few learning trials. Notice that this prediction nicely matches the typical learning curve shown in Figure 6.3 (Rescorla & Wagner, 1972).

Neural network models have yet to fully explain the learning of complex tasks, nor can they easily account for how people adapt when the "rules of the game" are suddenly changed and old habits must be unlearned and replaced (Hintzman, 1991). Nevertheless, a better understanding of what we mean by *associations* may very well lie in future research on neural network models (Anthony & Bartlett, 1999; Goldblum, 2001).

Using Research on Learning to Help People Learn

Teaching and training—explicit efforts to assist learners in mastering a specific skill or body of material—are major aspects of socialization in virtually every culture. So the study of how people learn has important implications for improved teaching in our schools (Lambert, 1999; Woolfolk-Hoy, 1999) and for helping people develop skills ranging from typing to tennis.

Classrooms Across Cultures

Many people are concerned that schools in the United States are not doing a very good job (Associated Press, 1997; Carnegie Task Force, 1996; Penner et al., 1994).

Reciprocal Teaching Ann Brown and her colleagues (1992) demonstrated the success of reciprocal teaching, in which children take turns teaching one another. This technique is similar to the cooperative arrangements seen in Japanese education.

The average performance of U.S. students on tests of reading, math, and other basic academic skills has tended to fall short of that of youngsters in other countries, especially some Asian countries (International Association for the Evaluation of Education Achievement, 1999; National Center for Education Statistics, 2000). In one comparison study, Harold Stevenson (1992) followed a sample of pupils in Taiwan, Japan, and the United States from first grade, in 1980, to eleventh grade, in 1991. In first grade, the Asian students scored no higher than their U.S. peers on tests of mathematical aptitude and skills, nor did they enjoy math more. However, by fifth grade the U.S. students had fallen far behind. Corresponding differences were seen in reading skills.

Some possible causes of these differences were found in the classroom itself. In a typical U.S. classroom session, teachers talked to students as a group; then students worked at their desks independently. Reinforcement or other feedback about performance on their work was usually delayed until the next day or, often, not provided at all. In contrast, the typical Japanese classroom placed greater emphasis on cooperative work among students (Kristof, 1997). Teachers provided more immediate feedback on a one-to-one basis. And there was an emphasis on creating teams of students with varying abilities, an arrangement in which faster learners help teach slower ones. However, before concluding that the differences in performance are the result of social factors alone, we must consider another important distinction: The Japanese children practiced more. They spent more days in school during the year and on average spent more hours doing homework. It is interesting to note that they were also given longer recesses than U.S. students and had more opportunities to get away from the classroom during a typical school day.

Although the significance of these cultural differences in learning and teaching is not yet clear, the educational community in the United States is paying attention to them. Psychologists and educators are also considering how other principles of learning can be applied to improve education (Bransford, Brown, & Cocking, 1999; Woolfolk-Hoy, 1999). Anecdotal and experimental evidence suggests that some of the most successful educational techniques are those that apply basic principles of operant conditioning, offering frequent testing, positive reinforcement for correct performance, and immediate corrective feedback following mistakes (Kass, 1999; Oppel, 2000; Walberg, 1987). Research in cognitive psychology (e.g., Bjork, 1979, 1999) also suggests that students are more likely to retain what they learn if they engage in numerous study sessions rather than in a single "cramming" session on the night before a quiz or exam. To encourage this more beneficial "distributed practice" pattern, researchers say, teachers should give enough exams and quizzes (some unannounced, perhaps) that students will be reading and studying more or less continuously. And because learning is aided by repeated opportunities to use new information, these exams and quizzes should cover material from throughout the term, not just from recent classes. Such recommendations are not necessarily popular with students, but there is good evidence that they promote long-term retention of course material (e.g., Bjork, 1999).

Active Learning

The importance of cognitive processes in learning is apparent in instructional methods that emphasize *active learning* (Bonwell & Eison, 1991). These methods take many forms, such as small-group problem-solving tasks, discussion of "one-minute essays" written in class, use of "thumbs up" or "thumbs down" to indicate agreement or disagreement with the instructor's lecture, and multiple-choice questions that give students feedback about their understanding of the previous fifteen minutes of lecture (Heward, 1997). There is little doubt that for many students, the inclusion of active learning experiences makes classes more interesting and enjoyable (Moran, 2000; Murray, 2000). Active learning methods also provide

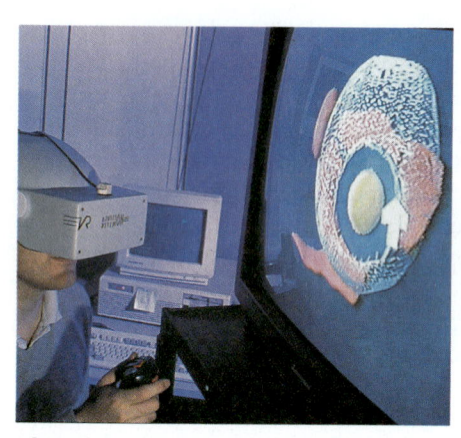

Virtual Surgery Using a virtual reality system called "Surgery in 3-D," this medical student can actively learn and practice eye surgery skills before working with real patients.

immediate reinforcement and help students to go beyond memorizing isolated facts by encouraging them to think more deeply about new information, consider how it relates to what they already know, and apply it in new situations.

The elaborate mental processing associated with active learning makes new information not only more personally meaningful but also easier to remember. Active learning strategies have been found to be superior to passive teaching methods in a number of experiments with children and adults (Meyers & Jones, 1993). In one study, a fifth-grade science teacher spent some class periods calling on only those students whose hands were raised; the rest listened passively. On other days, all students were required to answer every question by holding up a card on which they had written their response. Scores on next-day quizzes and biweekly tests showed that students remembered more of the material covered on the active learning days than on the "passive" days (Gardner, Heward, & Grossi, 1994). Studies with students in high school, as well as with community college and university students, have found that active learning approaches result in better test performance and greater class participation compared with standard instructional techniques (e.g., Kellum, Carr, & Dozier, 2001). For example, students who passively listened to a physics lecture received significantly lower scores on a test of lecture content than did those who participated in a virtual reality lab that allowed them to "interact" actively with the physical forces covered in the lecture (Brelsford, 1993). Results like these have fueled the development of other science education programs that place students in virtual laboratory environments where they can actively manipulate materials and test hypotheses (e.g., Horwitz & Christie, 2000). Despite the enthusiasm generated by active learning methods, rigorous experimental research is still needed to compare their short- and long-term effects with those of more traditional methods in teaching various kinds of course content.

Skill Learning

The complex action sequences, or *skills*, that people learn to perform in everyday life—tying a shoe, opening a door, operating a computer, shooting a basketball, driving a car—develop through direct and vicarious learning processes involving imitation, instructions, reinforcement, and of course, lots of practice. Some skills, like those of a basketball player or violinist, demand exceptional perceptual-motor coordination. Others, like those involved in scientific thinking, have a large cogni-

Active Learning Field trips provide students with first-hand opportunities to see and interact with the things they study in the classroom. Such experiences are just one example of the active learning exercises that can help students become more deeply involved in the learning process.

tive component, requiring rapid understanding. In either case, the learning of skills usually involves practice and feedback.

Practice—the repeated performance of a skill—is the most critical component of skill learning (Howe, Davidson, & Sloboda, 1998). For perceptual-motor skills, both physical and mental practice are beneficial (Druckman & Bjork, 1994). To be most effective, practice should continue past the point of correct performance until the skill can be performed automatically, with little or no need for attention. As mentioned earlier, in learning many cognitive skills, what counts most seems to be practice in retrieving relevant information from memory. Trying to recall and write down facts that you have read, for example, is a more effective learning tool than simply reading the facts a second time.

Feedback about the correctness of responses is also necessary. As with any learning process, the feedback should come soon enough to be effective, but not so quickly that it interferes with the learner's efforts to learn independently. Large amounts of guidance may produce very good performance during practice, but too much guidance may impair later performance (Wickens, 1992). Coaching students about correct responses in math, for example, may impair their ability later to retrieve the correct response from memory on their own. And in coaching athletes, if feedback is given too soon after an action occurs or while it is still taking place, it may divert the learner's attention from understanding how that action was achieved and what it felt like to perform it (Schmidt & Bjork, 1992). Independent practice at retrieving previously learned responses or information requires more effort, but it is critical for skill development (Ericsson & Charness, 1994). There is little or no evidence to support "sleep learning" or other schemes designed to make learning effortless (Druckman & Bjork, 1994; Phelps & Exum, 1992). In short, "no pain, no gain."

Try It This Way Good coaches provide enough guidance and performance feedback to help budding athletes develop their skills to the fullest, but not so much that the guidance interferes with the learning process. Striking this delicate balance is one of the greatest challenges faced by coaches, and by teachers in general.

LINKAGES

As noted in the chapter on introducing psychology, all of psychology's many subfields are related to one another. Our discussion of neural networks as possible models of learning illustrates just one way in which the topic of this chapter, learning, is linked to the subfield of perception, which is covered in the chapter on that topic. The Linkages diagram shows ties to two other subfields as well, and there are many more ties throughout the book. Looking for linkages among subfields will help you see how they all fit together and better appreciate the big picture that is psychology.

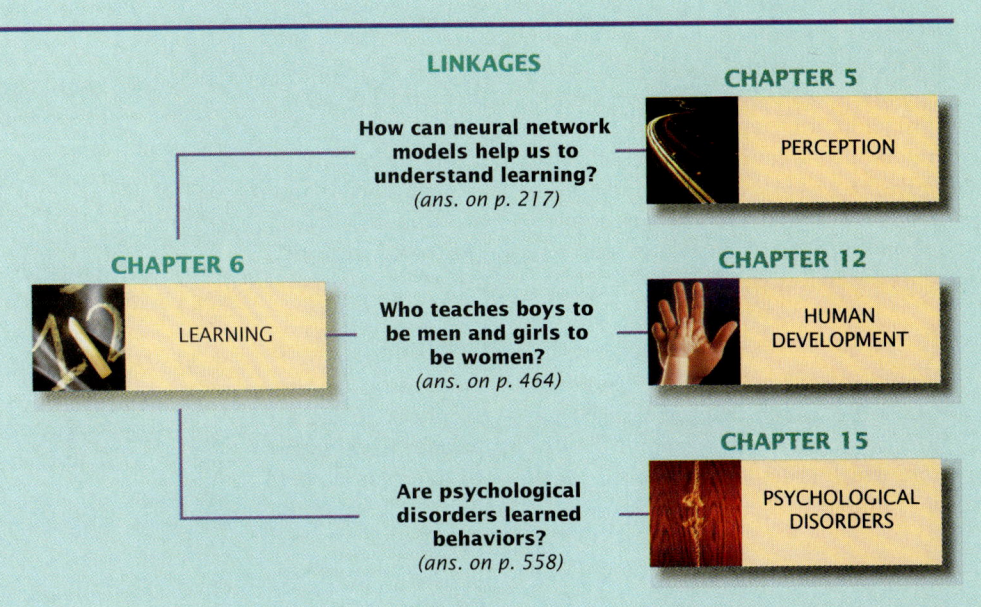

LINKAGES

CHAPTER 6
LEARNING

How can neural network models help us to understand learning?
(ans. on p. 217)
→ CHAPTER 5
PERCEPTION

Who teaches boys to be men and girls to be women?
(ans. on p. 464)
→ CHAPTER 12
HUMAN DEVELOPMENT

Are psychological disorders learned behaviors?
(ans. on p. 558)
→ CHAPTER 15
PSYCHOLOGICAL DISORDERS

SUMMARY

Individuals adapt to changes in the environment through the process of *learning,* which is the modification through experience of pre-existing behavior and understanding.

Learning About Stimuli

One kind of learning is *habituation,* which is reduced responsiveness to a repeated stimulus. According to Richard Solomon's opponent-process theory, habituation results as two processes balance each other. The first process is a relatively automatic response to some stimulus. The second, or opponent, process follows and counteracts the first. This theory may help explain drug tolerance and some overdose cases.

Classical Conditioning: Learning Signals and Associations

Pavlov's Discovery

One form of associative learning is *classical conditioning.* It occurs when a *conditioned stimulus,* or *CS* (such as a tone), is repeatedly paired with an *unconditioned stimulus,* or *UCS* (such as meat powder on a dog's tongue), which naturally brings about an *unconditioned response,* or *UCR* (such as salivation). Eventually the conditioned stimulus will elicit a response, known as the *conditioned response,* or *CR,* even when the unconditioned stimulus is not presented.

Conditioned Responses Over Time: Extinction and Spontaneous Recovery

In general, the strength of a conditioned response grows as CS-UCS pairings continue. If the unconditioned stimulus is no longer paired with the conditioned stimulus, the conditioned response eventually disappears; this is *extinction.* Following extinction, the conditioned response often reappears if the conditioned stimulus is presented after some time; this is *spontaneous recovery.* In addition, if the conditioned and unconditioned stimuli are paired once or twice after extinction, *reconditioning* occurs; that is, the conditioned response reverts to its original strength.

Stimulus Generalization and Discrimination

Because of *stimulus generalization,* conditioned responses are elicited by stimuli that are similar, but not identical, to conditioned stimuli. Generalization is limited by *stimulus discrimination,* which prompts conditioned responses to some stimuli but not to others.

The Signaling of Significant Events

Classical conditioning involves learning that the conditioned stimulus is an event that predicts the occurrence of another event, the unconditioned stimulus. The conditioned response is not just an automatic reflex but also a means through which animals and people develop mental models of the relationships between events. Classical conditioning works best when the conditioned stimulus precedes the unconditioned stimulus, an arrangement known as forward conditioning. Conditioned responses develop best when the conditioned stimulus precedes the unconditioned stimulus by intervals ranging from less than a second to a minute or more, depending on the stimuli involved. Conditioning is also more likely when the conditioned stimulus reliably signals the unconditioned stimulus. In general, the strength of a conditioned response and the speed of conditioning increase as the intensity of the unconditioned stimulus increases. Stronger conditioned stimuli also speed conditioning. The particular conditioned stimulus likely to be linked to a subsequent unconditioned stimulus depends in part on which stimulus was being attended to when the unconditioned stimulus occurred. *Second-order conditioning* occurs when a conditioned stimulus becomes powerful enough to make conditioned stimuli out of stimuli associated with it. Some stimuli are easier to associate than others; organisms seem to be biologically prepared to learn certain associations, as exemplified by taste aversions.

Some Applications of Classical Conditioning

Classical conditioning plays a role in the development and treatment of phobias, in the humane control of predators in the wild, and in procedures for identifying people at risk for Alzheimer's disease.

Instrumental and Operant Conditioning: Learning the Consequences of Behavior

Learning occurs not only through associating stimuli but also through associating behavior with its consequences.

From the Puzzle Box to the Skinner Box

Edward L. Thorndike's *law of effect* holds that any response that produces satisfaction becomes more likely to occur again when the same stimulus is encountered, and any response that produces discomfort becomes less likely to occur again. Thorndike called this type of learning *instrumental conditioning.* B. F. Skinner called the same basic process *operant conditioning.* In operant conditioning the organism is free to respond at any time, and conditioning is measured by the rate of responding.

Basic Components of Operant Conditioning

An *operant* is a response that has some effect on the world. A *reinforcer* increases the probability that the operant preceding it will occur again; in other words, reinforcers strengthen behavior. There are two types of reinforcers: *positive reinforcers,* which strengthen a response if they are presented after that response occurs, and *negative reinforcers,* which are the removal of an unpleasant stimulus following some response. Both kinds of reinforcers strengthen the behaviors that precede them. *Escape conditioning* results when behavior terminates an aversive event. *Avoidance conditioning* results when behavior prevents or avoids an aversive stimulus; it reflects both classical and operant conditioning. Behaviors learned through avoidance conditioning are highly resistant to extinction. *Discriminative*

Summary

stimuli indicate whether reinforcement is available for a particular behavior.

Forming and Strengthening Operant Behavior

Complex responses can be learned through *shaping*, which involves reinforcing successive approximations of the desired response. *Primary reinforcers* are inherently rewarding; *secondary reinforcers* are rewards that people or animals learn to like because of their association with primary reinforcers. In general, operant conditioning proceeds more quickly when the delay in receiving reinforcement is short rather than long, and when the reinforcer is large rather than small. Reinforcement may be delivered on a *continuous reinforcement schedule* or on one of four basic types of *partial reinforcement schedules* (also called intermittent reinforcement schedules): *fixed-ratio (FR) schedules*, *variable-ratio (VR) schedules*, *fixed-interval (FI) schedules*, and *variable-interval (VI) schedules*. Ratio schedules lead to a rapid rate of responding. Behavior learned through partial reinforcement, particularly through variable schedules, is very resistant to extinction; this phenomenon is called the *partial reinforcement extinction effect*. Partial reinforcement is involved in superstitious behavior, which results when a response is coincidentally followed by a reinforcer.

Why Reinforcers Work

Research suggests that reinforcers are rewarding because they provide an organism with the opportunity to engage in desirable activities, which may change from one situation to the next. Another possibility is that activity in the brain's pleasure centers plays a role in reinforcement.

Punishment

Punishment decreases the frequency of a behavior by following it with either an unpleasant stimulus or the removal of a pleasant stimulus. Punishment modifies behavior but has several drawbacks. It only suppresses behavior; fear of punishment may generalize to the person doing the punishing; it is ineffective when delayed; it can be physically harmful and may teach aggressiveness; and it teaches only what not to do, not what should be done to obtain reinforcement.

Some Applications of Operant Conditioning

The principles of operant conditioning have been used in many spheres of life, including the teaching of everyday social skills, the treatment of sleep disorders, the development of self-control, and the improvement of classroom education.

Cognitive Processes in Learning

Cognitive processes—how people represent, store, and use information—play an important role in learning.

Learned Helplessness

Learned helplessness appears to result when people believe that their behavior has no effect on the world.

Latent Learning and Cognitive Maps

Both animals and humans display *latent learning*, learning that is not obvious at the time it occurs. They also form *cognitive maps* of their environments, even in the absence of any reinforcement for doing so.

Insight and Learning

Experiments on *insight* also support the idea that cognitive processes and learned strategies play an important role in learning, perhaps even by animals.

Observational Learning: Learning by Imitation

The process of learning by watching others is called *observational learning*, or social learning. Some observational learning occurs through *vicarious conditioning*, in which an individual is influenced by seeing or hearing about the consequences of others' behavior. Observational learning is more likely to occur when the person observed is rewarded for the observed behavior. Observational learning is a powerful source of socialization.

Using Research on Learning to Help People Learn

Research on how people learn has implications for improved teaching and for the development of a wide range of skills.

Classrooms Across Cultures

The degree to which immediate reinforcement and extended practice are used in teaching varies considerably from culture to culture, but research suggests that the application of these and other basic learning principles is important to promoting effective teaching and learning.

Active Learning

The importance of cognitive processes in learning is seen in active learning methods designed to encourage people to think deeply about and apply new information instead of just memorizing isolated facts.

Skill Learning

Observational learning, practice, and corrective feedback play important roles in the learning of skills.

7 Memory

The Nature of Memory
Basic Memory Processes
Types of Memory
Explicit and Implicit Memory
FOCUS ON RESEARCH METHODS: Measuring Explicit Versus Implicit Memory
Models of Memory

Storing New Memories
Sensory Memory
Short-Term Memory and Working Memory
Long-Term Memory
Distinguishing Between Short-Term and Long-Term Memory

Retrieving Memories
Retrieval Cues and Encoding Specificity
Context and State Dependence
Retrieval from Semantic Memory
Constructing Memories
LINKAGES: Memory, Perception, and Eyewitness Testimony

Forgetting
How Do We Forget?
Why Do We Forget? The Roles of Decay and Interference
THINKING CRITICALLY: Can Traumatic Memories Be Repressed, Then Recovered?

Biological Bases of Memory
The Biochemistry of Memory
Brain Structures and Memory

Applications of Memory Research
Improving Your Memory
Design for Memory

Linkages

Summary

Several years ago an air-traffic controller at Los Angeles International Airport cleared a US Airways flight to land on runway 24L. A couple of minutes later, the US Airways pilot radioed the control tower that he was on approach for runway 24L, but the controller did not reply because she was preoccupied by a confusing exchange with another pilot. After finishing that conversation, the controller told a Sky West commuter pilot to taxi onto runway 24L for takeoff, completely forgetting about the US Airways plane that was about to land on the same runway. The US Airways jet hit the commuter plane, killing thirty-four people. The controller's forgetting was so complete that she assumed the fireball from the crash was an exploding bomb. How could her memory have failed her at such a crucial time?

Memory is full of paradoxes. It is common, for example, for people to remember the name of their first-grade teacher but not the name of someone they met just a minute before. Like perception, memory is selective. So although we retain a great deal of information, we also lose a great deal (Bjork & Vanhuele, 1992). Consider Rajan Mahadevan, who once set a world's record by reciting from memory the first 31,811 places of pi (the ratio of the circumference of a circle to its diameter). On repeated visits to the psychology building at the University of Minnesota, Mahadevan had trouble recalling the location of the nearest restroom (Biederman et al., 1992)! Similarly, Tatiana Cooley, the U.S. National Memory Champion for three years in a row, says that she is so absent-minded that she relies on Post-it Notes to remember everyday errands (Schacter, 2001). Cases like these show that memory is made up of many component abilities, some of which may operate much more effectively, or less efficiently, than others.

Memory plays a critical role in your life. Without memory, you would not know how to shut off your alarm clock, take a shower, get dressed, or recognize objects. You would be unable to communicate with other people, because you would not remember what words mean, or even what you had just said. You would be unaware of your own likes and dislikes, and you would have no idea of who you are (Craik et al., 1999). In this chapter we describe what is known about both memory and forgetting. First, we discuss what memory is—the different kinds of memory and the different ways we remember things. Then we examine how new memories are acquired and later recalled, and why they are sometimes forgotten. We continue with a discussion of the biological bases of memory, and we conclude with some practical advice for improving memory and studying skills.

The Nature of Memory

Mathematician John Griffith estimated that in an average lifetime, each of us will have stored roughly five hundred times as much information as can be found in all the volumes of the *Encyclopaedia Britannica* (Hunt, 1982). The impressive capacity of human memory depends on the operation of a complex mental system (Schacter, 1999).

Basic Memory Processes

We know a psychologist who sometimes drives to work and sometimes walks. On one occasion, he drove, forgot that he had driven, and walked home. When his car was not in the driveway the next morning, he reported the car stolen. The police soon called to say that "some college kids" had probably stolen the car, because it was found on campus (next to the psychology building!). What went wrong? There are several possibilities, because memory depends on three basic processes: encoding, storage, and retrieval (see Figure 7.1).

First, information must be put into memory, a step that requires **encoding**. Just as incoming sensory information must be coded so that it can be communicated to the brain, information to be remembered must be put in a form that the memory

encoding The process of putting information into a form that the memory system can accept and use.

figure 7.1

Basic Memory Processes
Remembering something requires, first, that the item be encoded—put in a form that can be placed in memory. It then must be stored and, finally, retrieved, or recovered. If any of these processes fails, forgetting will occur.

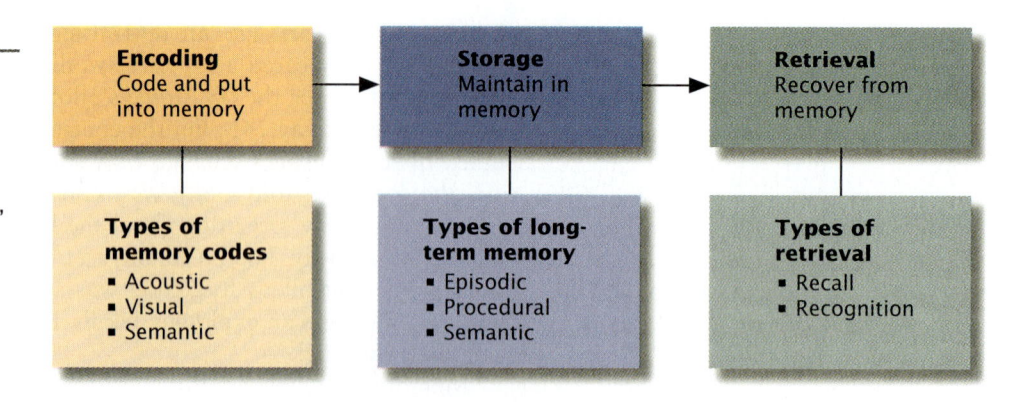

Encoding — Code and put into memory → **Storage** — Maintain in memory → **Retrieval** — Recover from memory

- **Types of memory codes**
  - Acoustic
  - Visual
  - Semantic
- **Types of long-term memory**
  - Episodic
  - Procedural
  - Semantic
- **Types of retrieval**
  - Recall
  - Recognition

---

system can accept and use. Sensory information is put into various *memory codes*, which are mental representations of physical stimuli. Suppose you see a billboard that reads "Huey's Going-Out-of-Business Sale," and you want to remember it so you can take advantage of the sale later. If you encode the sound of the words as if they had been spoken, you are using **acoustic encoding**, and the information is represented in your memory as a sequence of sounds. If you encode the image of the letters as they were arranged on the sign, you are using **visual encoding**, and the information is represented in your memory as a picture. Finally, if you encode the fact that you saw an ad for Huey's, you are using **semantic encoding**, and the information is represented in your memory by its general meaning. The type of encoding used can influence what is remembered. For example, semantic encoding might allow you to remember that a car was parked in your neighbors' driveway just before their house was robbed. If there was little or no other encoding, however, you might not be able to remember the make, model, or color of the car.

The second basic memory process is **storage**, which refers to the maintenance of information in memory over time—often over a very long time. When you find you can still use a pogo stick you haven't seen since you were a child or recall a vacation from many years ago, you are depending on the storage capacity of your memory.

The third process, **retrieval**, occurs when you locate information stored in memory and bring it into consciousness. Retrieving stored information such as your address or telephone number is usually so fast and effortless that it seems automatic. Only when you try to retrieve other kinds of information—such as the answer to a quiz question that you know but cannot quite recall—do you become aware of the searching process. Retrieval processes include both recall and recognition. To *recall* information, you have to retrieve it from memory without much help; this is what is required when you answer an essay test question or play *Jeopardy!* In *recognition*, retrieval is aided by clues, such as the response alternatives given on multiple-choice tests and the questions on *Who Wants to Be a Millionaire*. Accordingly, recognition tends to be easier than recall.

Types of Memory

When was the last time you charged something on your credit card? What part of speech is used to modify a noun? How do you keep your balance when you are skiing? To answer these questions, you must use your memory. However, each answer may require a different type of memory (Baddeley, 1998). To answer the first question, you must remember a particular event in your life; to answer the second one, you must recall a piece of general knowledge that is unlikely to be tied to a specific event. And the answer to the final question is difficult to put into words but appears in the form of remembered actions when you get up on skis. How many types of memory are there? No one is sure, but most research suggests that there are at least three basic types. Each type is named for the kind of information it handles: episodic, semantic, and procedural (Best, 1999).

---

acoustic encoding The mental representation of information as a sequence of sounds.
visual encoding The mental representation of information as images.
semantic encoding The mental representation of an experience by its general meaning.
storage The process of maintaining information in memory over time.
retrieval The process of recalling information stored in memory.
episodic memory Memory of an event that happened while one was present.
semantic memory A type of memory containing generalized knowledge of the world.
procedural memory A type of memory containing information about how to do things.
explicit memory The process in which people intentionally try to remember something.
implicit memory The unintentional influence of prior experiences.

Memory of a specific event that happened while you were present—that is, during an "episode" in your life—is called **episodic memory** (Tulving, 1983, in press). Remembering what you had for dinner yesterday, what you did last summer, or where you were last Friday night all require episodic memory. Generalized knowledge of the world that does not involve memory of a specific event is called **semantic memory.** For instance, you can answer a question like "Are wrenches pets or tools?" without remembering any specific event in which you learned that wrenches are tools. As a general rule, people convey episodic memories by saying, "I remember when . . . ," whereas they convey semantic memories by saying, "I know that . . ." (Tulving, 1995). Finally, memory of how to do things, such as riding a bike or tying a shoelace, is called **procedural memory.** Often, procedural memory consists of a complicated sequence of movements that cannot be described adequately in words. For example, a gymnast might find it impossible to describe the exact motions in a particular routine.

Many activities require all three types of memory. Consider the game of tennis. Knowing the official rules or how many sets are needed to win a match involves semantic memory. Remembering which side served last requires episodic memory. Knowing how to lob or volley involves procedural memory.

How Does She Do That? As she practices, this young violinist is developing procedural memories of how to play her instrument that will be difficult to put into words. To appreciate the special nature of procedural memory, try writing a step-by-step description of *exactly* how you tie a shoe.

Explicit and Implicit Memory

Memory can also be categorized in terms of its effects on thoughts and behaviors. For example, you make use of **explicit memory** when you intentionally try to remember something and are consciously aware of doing so (Masson & MacLeod, 1992). Suppose someone asks you about your last vacation. As you think about where you went, you are using explicit memory to recall this episode from your past. Similarly, when responding to an exam question, you use explicit memory to retrieve the information needed to give a correct answer. In contrast, **implicit memory** is the unintentional influence of prior experiences (McDermott, 2000; Nelson, 1999; Schacter, Chiu, & Ochsner, 1993). For example, if you were to read this chapter a second time, implicit memories of its content would help you to read it more quickly than you did the first time. For the same reason, you can solve a puzzle faster if you have solved it in the past. This facilitation of performance (often

Making Implicit Memories By the time they reach adulthood, these boys may have no explicit memories of the interactions they had in early childhood with friends from differing ethnic groups, but research suggests that their implicit memories of such experiences could have an unconscious effect on their attitudes toward, and judgments about, members of those groups.

called *priming*) is automatic, and it occurs without conscious effort. Perhaps you've found yourself disliking someone you just met, but you didn't know why. One explanation is that implicit memory may have been at work. Specifically, you may have reacted in this way because the person bore a resemblance to someone from your past who treated you badly. In such instances, people are usually unable to recall the person from the past and are unaware of any connection between the two individuals (Lewicki, 1985). Episodic, semantic, and procedural memories can be explicit or implicit, but procedural memory usually operates implicitly. This is why, for example, you can skillfully ride a bike even though you cannot explicitly remember all the procedures necessary to do so.

It is not surprising that experience affects how people behave. What is surprising is that they are often unaware that their actions have been influenced by previous events. Because some influential events cannot be recalled even when people try to do so, implicit memory has been said to involve "retention without remembering" (Roediger, 1990).

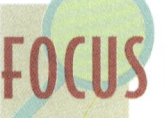

FOCUS ON RESEARCH METHODS

Measuring Explicit Versus Implicit Memory

In Canada, Endel Tulving and his colleagues undertook a series of experiments to map the differences between explicit and implicit memory (Tulving, Schacter, & Stark, 1982).

● What was the researcher's question?

Tulving knew he could measure explicit memory by giving a recognition test in which participants simply said which words on a list they remembered seeing on a previous list. The question was, How would it be possible to measure implicit memory?

● How did the researcher answer the question?

First, Tulving asked the participants in his experiment to study a long list of words—the "study list." An hour later, they took a recognition test involving explicit memory—saying which words on a new list had been on the original study list. Then, to test their implicit memory, Tulving asked them to perform a "fragment completion" task (Warrington & Weiskrantz, 1970). In this task, participants were shown a "test list" of word fragments, such as *d_li__u_*, and asked to complete the word (in this case, *delirium*). On the basis of priming studies such as those described in the chapter on consciousness, Tulving assumed that memory from a previous exposure to the correct word would improve the participants' ability to complete the fragment, even if they were unable to consciously recall having seen the word before. A week later, all participants took a second test of their explicit memory (recognition) and implicit memory (fragment completion) of the study list. Some of the words on this second test list had been on the original study list, but none had been used in the first set of memory tests. The independent variable in this experiment, then, was the amount of time that had elapsed since the participants read the study list (one hour versus one week), and the dependent variable was performance on each of the two types of memory tests, explicit and implicit.

● What did the researcher find?

As shown in Figure 7.2, explicit memory for the study list decreased dramatically over time, but implicit memory (or priming) was virtually unchanged. Results from several other experiments also show that the passage of time affects explicit memory more than implicit memory (Komatsu & Naito, 1992; Mitchell, 1991). For example, it appears that the aging process has fewer negative effects on implicit memory than on explicit memory (Light, 1991).

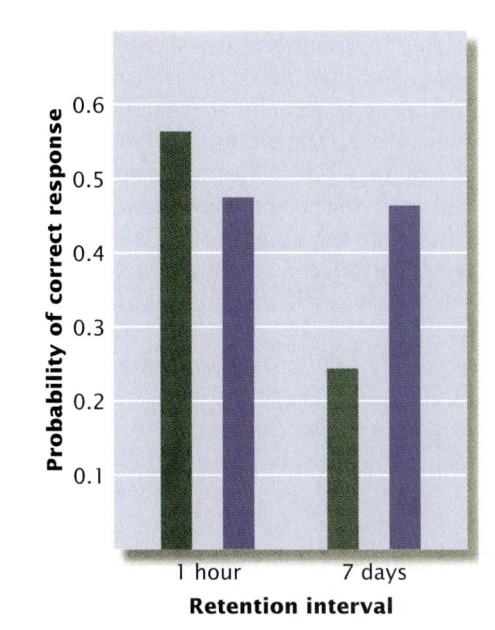

figure 7.2

Measures of Explicit and Implicit Memory

This experiment showed that the passage of time greatly affected people's recognition (explicit memory) of a word list but left fragment completion (implicit memory) essentially intact. Results such as these suggest that explicit and implicit memory may be different memory systems.

Source: Tulving, Schacter, & Stark (1982).

- **What do the results mean?**

The work of Tulving and others supports the idea of a dissociation, or independence, between explicit and implicit memory, suggesting that the two may operate on different principles (Gabrieli et al., 1995). In fact, some researchers believe that explicit and implicit memory may involve the activity of distinct neural systems in the brain (Squire, 1987; Tulving & Schacter, 1990). Others argue that the two types of memory are best described as requiring different cognitive processes (Nelson, McKinney, & Bennett, 1999; Roediger, Guynn, & Jones, 1995; Roediger & McDermott, 1995).

- **What do we still need to know?**

Psychologists are studying the role of implicit memory (and dissociations between explicit and implicit memory) in such important psychological phenomena as amnesia (Schacter, Church, & Treadwell, 1994; Tulving, 1993), depression (Elliott & Greene, 1992), problem solving (Jacoby, Marriott, & Collins, 1990), prejudice and stereotyping (Fiske, 1998), the development of self-concept in childhood (Nelson, 1993), and even the power of ads to associate brand names with good feelings (Duke & Carlson, 1994). The results of these studies should shed new light on implicit memory and how it operates in the real world.

For example, some social psychologists are trying to determine whether consciously held attitudes are independent of *implicit social cognitions*—past experiences that unconsciously influence a person's judgments about a group of people (Greenwald & Banaji, 1995). A case in point would be a person whose explicit thoughts about members of some ethnic group are positive but whose implicit thoughts are negative. Early work on implicit memory for stereotypes seemed to indicate that explicit and implicit stereotypes are independent (Devine, 1989), but more recent research suggests that they are related to some extent (Lepore & Brown, 1997). Further research is needed to determine what mechanisms are responsible for implicit versus explicit memory and how these two kinds of memory are related to one another (Lustig & Hasher, 2001; Nelson et al., 1998). That research will be facilitated by functional neuroimaging techniques. As described later, these techniques allow scientists to "watch" the brain's activity during various memory tasks, and to determine which areas are associated with the explicit and implicit cognitive processes involved in these tasks (Roediger, Buckner, & McDermott, 1999).

Models of Memory

We remember some information far better than other information. For example, suppose your friends throw a surprise party for you. When you enter the room, you might barely notice, and later fail to recall, the flash from a camera. And you might forget in a few seconds the name of a person you met at the party. But if you live to be a hundred, you will never forget where the party took place or how surprised and pleased you were. Why do some stimuli leave no more than a fleeting impression and others remain in memory forever? Each of four models of memory provides a somewhat different explanation. Let's see how the levels-of-processing, transfer-appropriate processing, parallel distributed processing, and information-processing models look at memory.

Levels of Processing

The **levels-of-processing model** suggests that the most important determinant of memory is how extensively information is encoded or processed when it is first received (Craik & Lockhart, 1972; Craik & Tulving, 1975). Consider situations in which people try to memorize something by mentally rehearsing it. There appear to be two basic types of mental rehearsal: maintenance and elaborative. **Maintenance rehearsal** involves simply repeating an item over and

levels-of-processing model A view stating that how well something is remembered depends on the degree to which incoming information is mentally processed.

maintenance rehearsal Repeating information over and over to keep it active in short-term memory.

over. This method can be effective for remembering information for a short time. If you look up a phone number, pick up the phone, and then make the call, maintenance rehearsal works just fine. But what if you need to remember something for hours or months or years? In these cases, you are better off using **elaborative rehearsal**, which involves thinking about how new material relates to information already stored in memory. For example, instead of trying to remember a new person's name by simply repeating it to yourself, try thinking about how the name is related to something you already know. If you are introduced to a man named Jim Crews, for example, you might think, "He is as tall as my Uncle Jim, who always wears a crew cut."

Study after study has shown that memory is enhanced when people use elaborative rather than maintenance rehearsal (Jahnke & Nowaczyk, 1998). According to the levels-of-processing model, this enhancement occurs because of the degree or "depth" to which incoming information is mentally processed during elaborative rehearsal (Lockhart & Craik, 1990). The more you think about new information, organize it, and relate it to existing knowledge, the "deeper" the processing, and the better your memory of it becomes. Teachers use this idea when they ask their students not only to define a new word but also to use it in a sentence. Figuring out how to use the new word takes deeper processing than merely defining it. (The next time you come across an unfamiliar word in this book, don't just read its definition. Try to use the word in a sentence by coming up with an example of the concept that relates to your knowledge and experience.)

Transfer-Appropriate Processing The level of processing is not the only factor affecting what we remember (Baddeley, 1992). Another critical factor, suggested by the **transfer-appropriate processing model**, is how well the processes involved during retrieval match the way in which the information was initially encoded. Consider an experiment in which people were shown sentences with a word missing and were then asked one of two types of questions about the missing word (Morris, Bransford, & Franks, 1977). Some questions were designed so that participants would encode the target word using its meaning (semantic encoding). For example, one sentence read, "A _____ is a building," and participants were asked whether the target word *house* should go in the blank space. Other questions were designed to create a rhyming code. For example, participants were shown the sentence "_____ rhymes with legal" and asked whether the target word *eagle* rhymed with *legal*.

Later, the participants were given two kinds of memory tasks. On one task, they were asked to select from a list the target words they had been shown earlier. As Figure 7.3 shows, the participants did much better at recognizing the words for which they had used a semantic code rather than a rhyming code. On the other task, they were asked to pick out words that *rhymed* with the ones they had seen (e.g., *grouse*, which rhymes with *house*). Here, they did much better at identifying words that *rhymed* with those for which they had used a rhyming code rather than a semantic code. Results like these illustrate the concept of *transfer-appropriate processing*, which suggests that memory is better when the processes people use during retrieval match the processes they used during encoding

Parallel Distributed Processing A third approach to memory is based on **parallel distributed processing (PDP) models** of memory (Rumelhart & McClelland, 1986). These models suggest that new experiences don't just provide new facts that are later retrieved individually; those facts are also integrated with existing knowledge or memories, changing our overall knowledge base and altering in a more general way our understanding of the world and how it operates. For example, when you first arrived at college, you learned specific facts, such as where classes are held, what time the library closes, and where to get the best pizza. Over

---

elaborative rehearsal A memorization method that involves thinking about how new information relates to information already stored in long-term memory.

transfer-appropriate processing model A model of memory that suggests that a critical determinant of memory is how well the retrieval process matches the original encoding process.

parallel distributed processing (PDP) models Memory models in which new experiences change one's overall knowledge base.

information-processing model A model of memory in which information is seen as passing through sensory memory, short-term memory, and long-term memory.

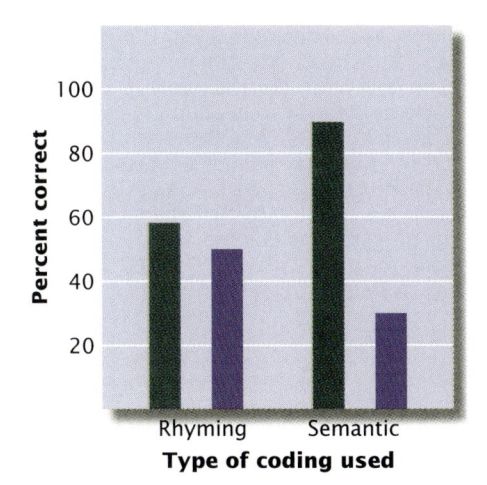

figure 7.3
The Match Between Encoding and Retrieval

People who were asked to recognize words seen earlier did better if they had encoded the words on the basis of their meaning (semantic coding) rather than on the basis of what they rhymed with. But if asked to identify words that *rhymed* with those seen before, they did better on those that had been encoded using a rhyming code. These results support the transfer-appropriate processing model of memory.

time, these and many other facts of college life form a network of information that creates a more general understanding of how the whole college system works. Developing this network makes you more knowledgeable, but also more sophisticated. It allows you to, say, allocate your study time so as to do well in your most important courses, and to plan a schedule that avoids conflicts between classes, work, and recreational activities. In other words, your knowledge of college life changes day by day in a way that is much more general than any single new fact you learned.

PDP models of memory reflect this notion of knowledge networks. PDP memory theorists begin by considering how *neural networks*—described in the chapters on perception and learning—might provide a functional memory system (Anderson, 1990b). They suggest that each unit of knowledge is ultimately connected to every other unit, and that the connections between units become stronger as they are experienced together more frequently. From this perspective, then, "knowledge" is distributed across a dense network of associations. When this network is activated, *parallel processing* occurs; that is, different portions of the network operate simultaneously, allowing people to quickly and efficiently draw inferences and make generalizations. Just seeing the word *sofa*, for example, allows us immediately to gain access to knowledge about what a sofa looks like, what it is used for, where it tends to be located, who might buy one, and the like. PDP models of memory explain this process very effectively.

Information Processing Historically, the most influential and comprehensive theories of memory have been based on a general **information-processing model** (Roediger, 1990). The information-processing model originally suggested that in order for information to become firmly embedded in memory, it must pass through three stages of mental processing: sensory memory, short-term memory, and long-term memory (Atkinson & Shiffrin, 1968; see Figure 7.4).

In *sensory memory*, information from the senses—sights or sounds, for example—is held in sensory registers for a very brief period of time, often for less than one second. Information in the sensory registers may be attended to, analyzed, and encoded as a meaningful pattern; this is the process of perception, as discussed in the chapter on that topic. If the information in sensory memory is perceived, it can enter *short-term memory*. If nothing further is done, the information will disappear in less than twenty seconds. But if the information in short-term memory is further processed, it may be encoded into *long-term memory*, where it may remain indefinitely.

Contemporary versions of the information-processing model emphasize the constant interactions among sensory, short-term, and long-term memory (Massaro & Cowan, 1993; Wagner, 1999). For example, sensory memory can be thought of as that part of your knowledge base (or long-term memory) that is momentarily activated by information sent to the brain via the sensory nerves. And short-term memory can be thought of as that part of your knowledge base that is the focus of attention at any given moment. Like perception, memory is an active process, and what is already in long-term memory influences how new information is encoded (Cowan, 1988). To understand this interaction better, try the exercise in Figure 7.5.

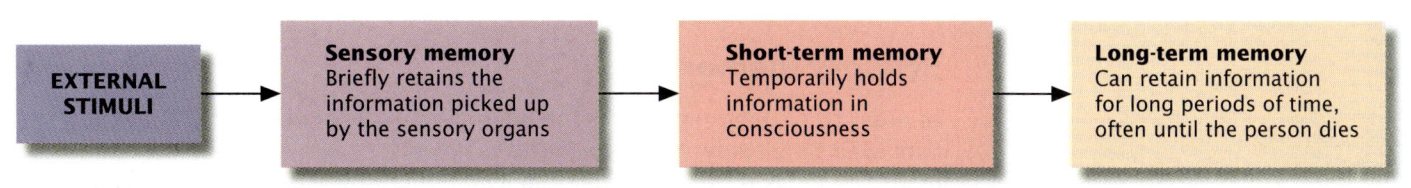

figure 7.4
The Three Stages of Memory

This traditional information-processing model describes three stages in the memory system.

EXTERNAL STIMULI → **Sensory memory** Briefly retains the information picked up by the sensory organs → **Short-term memory** Temporarily holds information in consciousness → **Long-term memory** Can retain information for long periods of time, often until the person dies

figure 7.5
The Role of Memory in Comprehension

TRY THIS Read the passage shown here; then turn away and try to recall as much of it as possible. Then read the footnote on page 234, and reread the passage. The second reading probably made a lot more sense and was much easier to remember, because knowing the title of the passage allowed you to retrieve from long-term memory your knowledge about the topic.

Source: Bransford & Johnson (1972).

> The procedure is actually quite simple. First, you arrange items into different groups. Of course, one pile may be sufficient, depending on how much there is to do. If you have to go somewhere else due to lack of facilities that is the next step; otherwise, you are pretty well set. It is important not to overdo things. That is, it is better to do too few things at once than too many. In the short run, this may not seem important, but complications can easily arise. A mistake can be expensive as well. At first, the whole procedure will seem complicated. Soon, however, it will become just another facet of life. It is difficult to foresee any end to the necessity for this task in the immediate future, but then, one never can tell. After the procedure is completed, one arranges the materials into different groups again. Then they can be put into their appropriate places. Eventually they will be used once more, and the whole cycle will then have to be repeated. However, that is part of life.

in review Models of Memory

Model	Assumptions
Levels of processing	The more deeply material is provessed, the better the memory of it.
Transfer-appropriate processing	Retrieval is improved when we try to recall material in a way that matches how the material was encoded.
Parallel distributed processing (PDP)	New experiences add to and alter our overall knowledge base; they are not separate, unconnected facts. PDP networks allow us to draw inferences and make generalizations about the world.
Information processing	Information is processed in three stages: sensory, short-term, and long-term memory.

For a summary of the four models we have discussed, see "In Review: Models of Memory." Each of these models provides an explanation of why we remember some things and forget others, but which one offers the best explanation? The answer is that more than one model may be required to understand memory. Just as it is helpful for physicists to characterize light in terms of both waves and particles, psychologists find it useful to think of memory as both a serial or sequential process, as suggested by the information-processing model, and as a parallel process, as suggested by parallel distributed processing models.

Storing New Memories

The information-processing model suggests that sensory, short-term, and long-term memory each provide a different type of storage system.

Sensory Memory

In order to recognize incoming stimuli, the brain must analyze and compare them with what is already stored in long-term memory. Although this process is very quick, it still takes time. The major function of **sensory memory** is to hold information long enough for it to be processed further. This maintenance is the job of the **sensory registers**, whose storage capability retains an almost complete representation of a sensory stimulus (Best, 1999). There is a separate register for each of the

Sensory Memory at Work In a darkened room, ask a friend to hold a small flashlight, and move it very slowly in a circle. You will see a moving point of light. If it appears to have a "tail," like a comet, that is your sensory memory of the light before the memory fades. Now ask your friend to speed up the movement. You should now see a complete circle of light, because as the light moves, its impression on your sensory memory does not have time to fade before the circle is completed. A similar process allows us to see "sparkler circles" and still images that "move" when we watch a film or video (see our discussion of stroboscopic motion in the chapter on sensation).

sensory memory A type of memory that holds large amounts of incoming information very briefly, but long enough to connect one impression to the next.

sensory registers Memory systems that hold incoming information long enough for it to be processed further.

selective attention The focusing of mental resources on only part of the stimulus field.

short-term memory (STM) The maintenance component of working memory, which holds unrehearsed information for a limited time.

working memory The part of the memory system that allows us to mentally work with, or manipulate, information being held in short-term memory.

five senses, and every register is capable of storing a relatively large amount of stimulus information.

Memories held in the sensory registers are fleeting, but they last long enough for stimulus identification to begin (Eysenck & Keane, 1995). As you read a sentence, for example, you identify and interpret the first few words. At the same time, subsequent words are being scanned, and these are maintained in your visual sensory register until you can process them as well.

Sensory memory helps bring coherence and continuity to your world. To appreciate this fact, turn your head slowly from left to right. Your eyes may seem to be moving smoothly, like a movie camera scanning a scene, but this is not what is happening. Your eyes fixate at one point for about one-fourth of a second and then rapidly jump to a new position. The sensation of smoothness occurs because the scene is held in the visual sensory register until your eyes fixate again. Similarly, when you listen to someone speak, the auditory sensory register allows you to experience a smooth flow of information. Information persists for varying amounts of time in the five sensory registers. For example, information in the auditory sensory register lasts longer than information in the visual sensory register.

The fact that sensory memories quickly fade if they are not processed further is an adaptive characteristic of the memory system (Martindale, 1991). One simply cannot deal with all of the sights, sounds, odors, tastes, and tactile sensations that impinge on the sense organs at any given moment. As mentioned in the chapter on perception, **selective attention** focuses mental resources on only part of the stimulus field, thus controlling what information is processed further. It is through the process of perception that the elusive impressions of sensory memory are captured and transferred to short-term memory.

Short-Term Memory and Working Memory

The sensory registers allow your memory system to develop a representation of a stimulus, but they do not allow the more thorough representation and analysis needed if the information is going to be used in some way. These functions are accomplished by short-term memory and working memory.

Short-term memory (STM) is the part of our memory system that stores limited amounts of information for a limited amount of time. When you check *TV Guide* for the channel number of a show and then switch to that channel, you are using short-term memory. **Working memory** is the part of the memory system that allows us to mentally work with, or manipulate, the information being held in short-term memory. So short-term memory is actually a component of working memory. Together, they enable us to do many kinds of mental work (Baddeley, 1992; Engle & Oransky, 1999). Suppose you are buying something for 83 cents, and you go through your change and pick out two quarters, two dimes, two nickels, and three pennies. To do this, you use both short-term and working memory to remember the price, retrieve the rules of addition from long-term memory, *and* keep a running count of how much change you have so far. Now try to recall how many windows there are on the front of the house or apartment where you grew up. In attempting to answer this question, you probably formed a mental image of the building, which required one kind of working-memory process, and then, while maintaining that image in short-term memory, you "worked" on it by counting the windows. In short, working memory has at least two components: *maintenance* (holding information in short-term memory) and *manipulation* (working on that information).

Encoding in Short-Term Memory
The encoding of information in short-term memory is much more elaborative and varied than that in the sensory registers (Brandimonte, Hitch, & Bishop, 1992). *Acoustic encoding* (by sound) seems to dominate. Evidence in support of this assertion comes from analyzing the mistakes people make when encoding information in short-term memory. These

figure 7.6

Capacity of Short-Term Memory

TRY THIS Here is a test of your immediate memory span. Ask someone to read to you the numbers in the top row at the rate of about one per second; then try to repeat them back in the same order. Then try the next row, and the one after that, until you make a mistake. Your immediate memory span is the maximum number of items you can repeat back perfectly. Similar tests can be performed using the rows of letters and words.

```
9 2 5                    G M N
8 6 4 2                  S L R R
3 7 6 5 4                V O E P G
6 2 7 4 1 8              X W D X Q O
0 4 0 1 4 7 3            E P H H J A E
1 9 2 2 3 5 3 0          Z D O F W D S V
4 8 6 8 5 4 3 3 2        D T Y N R H E H Q
2 5 3 1 9 7 1 7 6 8      K H W D A G R O F Z
8 5 1 2 9 6 1 9 4 5 0    U D F F W H D Q D G E
9 1 8 5 4 6 9 4 2 9 3 7  Q M R H X Z D P R R E H
```

CAT BOAT RUG
RUN BEACH PLANT LIGHT
SUIT WATCH CUT STAIRS CAR
JUNK LONE GAME CALL WOOD HEART
FRAME PATCH CROSS DRUG DESK HORSE LAW
CLOTHES CHOOSE GIFT DRIVE BOOK TREE HAIR THIS
DRESS CLERK FILM BASE SPEND SERVE BOOK LOW TIME
STONE ALL NAIL DOOR HOPE EARL FEEL BUY COPE GRAPE
AGE SOFT FALL STORE PUT TRUE SMALL FREE CHECK MAIL LEAF
LOG DAY TIME CHESS LAKE CUT BIRD SHEET YOUR SEE STREET WHEEL

mistakes tend to be acoustically related, which means that they involve the substitution of similar sounds. For example, Robert Conrad (1964) showed people strings of letters and asked them to repeat the letters immediately. Their mistakes tended to involve replacing the correct letter (say, C) with another that *sounded* like it (such as D, P, or T). These mistakes occurred even though the letters were presented visually, without any sound.

Evidence for acoustic coding in short-term memory also comes from studies showing that items are more difficult to remember if their spoken sounds are similar. For example, native English speakers do less well when asked to remember a string of letters like *ECVTGB* (which all have similar sounds) than when asked to remember one like *KRLDQS* (which have distinct sounds). Encoding in short-term memory is not *always* acoustic, however. Visual codes are also used (Zhang & Simon, 1985), but information coded visually tends to fade much more quickly from short-term memory than information that is encoded acoustically (Cornoldi, DeBeni, & Baldi, 1989). There is also evidence for kinesthetic encoding, which involves physical movements (Best, 1999). In one study, deaf people were shown a list of words and then asked to immediately write them down from memory (Shand, 1982). When these people made errors, they wrote words that are expressed through similar *hand movements* in American Sign Language, rather than words that *sounded* similar to the correct words. Apparently, these individuals had encoded the words on the basis of the movements they would use when signing them.

Storage Capacity of Short-Term Memory

You can easily determine the capacity of short-term memory by conducting the simple experiment shown in Figure 7.6 (Howard, 1983). Your **immediate memory span** is the maximum number of items you are able to recall perfectly after one presentation. If your memory span is like most people's, you can repeat about six or seven items from the test in this figure. The interesting thing is that you should come up with about

---

immediate memory span The maximum number of items a person can recall perfectly after one presentation of the items.

chunks Stimuli that are perceived as one unit or as a meaningful grouping of information.

The title of the passage in Figure 7.5 is "Washing Clothes."

the same number whether you estimate your immediate memory span with digits, letters, words, or virtually any type of unit (Pollack, 1953). George Miller (1956) noticed that studies of a wide variety of tasks showed the same limit on the ability to process information. This "magic number," which is seven plus or minus two, appears to be the capacity of short-term memory. In addition, the "magic number" refers not only to discrete elements, such as words or digits, but also to meaningful *groupings* of information, called **chunks.**

TRY THIS — To appreciate the difference between discrete elements and chunks, read the following letters to a friend, pausing at each dash: *FB-IAO-LM-TVI-BMB-MW.* The chances are very good that your friend will not be able to repeat this string of letters perfectly. Why? There are fifteen letters, which exceeds most people's immediate memory span. Now, give your friend the test again, but group the letters like this: *FBI-AOL-MTV-IBM-BMW.* Your friend will probably repeat that string easily because, even though the same fifteen letters are involved, they will be processed as only five meaningful chunks of information (Bower, 1975).

The Power of Chunking

Chunks of information can become very complex. If someone read to you, "The boy in the red shirt kicked his mother in the shin," you could probably repeat the sentence very easily. Yet it contains twelve words and forty-three letters. How can you repeat the sentence so effortlessly? The answer is that people can build bigger and bigger chunks of information (Ericsson & Staszewski, 1989). In this case, you might represent "the boy in the red shirt" as one chunk of information rather than as six words or nineteen letters. Similarly, "kicked his mother" and "in the shin" represent separate chunks of information.

Learning to use bigger and bigger chunks of information can enhance short-term memory. Children's memories improve in part because they gradually become able to hold as many as seven chunks in memory, but also because they become better able to group information into chunks (Servan-Schreiber & Anderson, 1990). Adults, too, can greatly increase the capacity of their short-term memory by more appropriate chunking (Waldrop, 1987); one college student increased his immediate memory span from seven digits to eighty digits (Neisser, 2000). In short, although the capacity of short-term memory is more or less constant—five to nine chunks of meaningful information—the size of those chunks can vary tremendously.

Chunking in Action People who provide instantaneous translation of speeches—such as this one by Kofi Annan, the Nobel Prize–winning secretary general of the United Nations—must store long, often complicated segments of speech in short-term memory while searching long-term memory for the equivalent second-language expressions. The task is made easier by chunking the speaker's words into phrases and sentences.

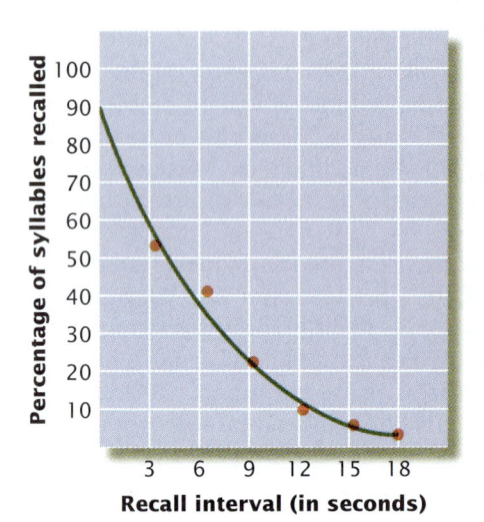

figure 7.7

Forgetting in Short-Term Memory
This graph shows the percentage of nonsense syllables recalled after various intervals during which rehearsal was prevented. Notice that virtually complete forgetting occurred after a delay of eighteen seconds.

Source: Data from Peterson & Peterson (1959).

Brown-Peterson procedure A method for determining how long unrehearsed information remains in short-term memory.

long-term memory (LTM) A relatively long-lasting stage of memory whose capacity to store new information is believed to be unlimited.

Duration of Short-Term Memory

Imagine how hard it would be to, say, mentally calculate the tip you should leave in a restaurant if your short-term memory was cluttered with every other bill you had ever paid, every phone number you had ever called, and every conversation you had ever heard. This problem doesn't come up because—unless you continue repeating information to yourself (maintenance rehearsal) or use elaborative rehearsal to transfer it to long-term memory—information in short-term memory is usually forgotten quickly. You may have experienced this adaptive, though sometimes inconvenient, phenomenon if you have ever been interrupted while repeating to yourself a new phone number you were about to call, and then couldn't remember the number.

How long does unrehearsed information remain in short-term memory? To answer this question, John Brown (1958) and Lloyd and Margaret Peterson (1959) devised the **Brown-Peterson procedure**, which is a method for preventing rehearsal. A person is presented with a group of three letters, such as *GRB*, and then counts backward by threes from some number until a signal is given. Counting prevents the person from rehearsing the letters. At the signal, the person stops counting and tries to recall the letters. By varying the number of seconds that the person counts backward, the experimenter can determine how much forgetting takes place over a certain amount of time. As you can see in Figure 7.7, information in short-term memory is forgotten gradually but rapidly: After eighteen seconds, participants can remember almost nothing. Evidence from these and other experiments suggests that unrehearsed information can be maintained in short-term memory for no more than about eighteen seconds. However, if the information is rehearsed or processed further, it may be encoded into long-term memory.

Long-Term Memory

When people talk about memory, they are in fact usually talking about **long-term memory (LTM)**, which is the part of the memory system whose encoding and storage capabilities can produce memories that last a lifetime.

Encoding in Long-Term Memory

Some information is encoded into long-term memory without any conscious attempt to memorize it (Ellis, 1991). However, putting information into long-term memory is often the result of a relatively deep level of conscious processing, which usually involves some degree of *semantic encoding*. In other words, encoding in long-term memory often ignores details and instead encodes the general, underlying meaning of the information.

Jacqueline Sachs (1967) demonstrated the dominance of semantic encoding in long-term memory in a classic study. She first asked people to listen to tape-recorded passages. She then showed them sentences and asked them to say which contained the exact wording heard in the taped passage. People did very well when they were tested *immediately* (using mainly short-term memory). However, after only twenty-seven seconds, at which point the information had to be retrieved from long-term memory, they could not determine which of two sentences they had heard if both sentences expressed the same meaning. For example, they could not determine whether they had heard "He sent a letter about it to Galileo, the great Italian scientist" or "A letter about it was sent to Galileo, the great Italian scientist." In short, they remembered the general meaning of what they had heard, but not the exact wording.

Perhaps you are thinking, "So what?" After all, the two sentences mean the same thing. However, psychologists have found that when people encode the general meaning of information, they may make mistakes about the specifics of what they have heard. For example, after hearing "The karate champion hit the cinderblock," people often remember having heard "The karate champion broke the cinderblock" (Brewer, 1977). When recalling exact words is important—such as in the courtroom, during business negotiations, and in discussions between parents

figure 7.8

Encoding into Long-Term Memory

TRY THIS Which is the correct image of a U.S. penny? (See page 238 for the answer.) Although most people often cannot explicitly remember the specific details of information stored in long-term memory, priming studies suggest that they do retain some implicit memory of them (e.g., Srinivas, 1993).

Source: Nickerson & Adams (1979).

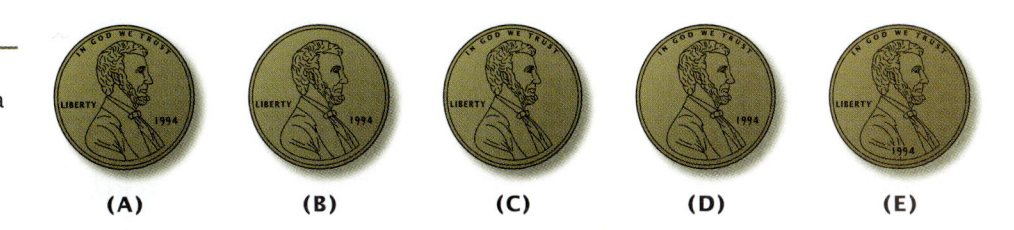

and children about previous agreements—people are often wrong about what someone actually said. As discussed later in this chapter, these errors occur partly because people encode into long-term memory not only the general meaning of information but also what they think and assume about that information (Hannigan & Reinitz, 2001). Those expectations and assumptions—that karate champions always break what they hit, for example—may color what is recalled.

Counterfeiters depend on the fact that people encode only the general meaning of visual, as well as auditory, stimuli. For example, look at Figure 7.8, and find the correct drawing of the U.S. penny (Nickerson & Adams, 1979). Most people from the United States are unsuccessful at this task, just as people from Great Britain do poorly at recognizing their country's coins (Jones, 1990). Research showing that people fail to remember specific details about visual information has prompted the U.S. Treasury to begin using more distinctive drawings on the paper currencies it distributes.

Although long-term memory normally involves semantic encoding, people can also use visual encoding to process images into long-term memory. In one study, people viewed 2,500 pictures. It took 16 hours just to present the stimuli, but the participants later correctly recognized more than 90 percent of the pictures tested (Standing, Conezio, & Haber, 1970). *Dual coding theory* suggests that the reason pictures tend to be remembered better than words is that pictures are represented in two codes—visual and semantic—rather than in only one (Paivio, 1986). This assertion is supported by neuroimaging studies showing that when people are asked to memorize pictures, they tend to create a semantic label for the picture (e.g., *frog*), as well as look at the drawing's visual features (Kelley et al., 1998).

Storage Capacity of Long-Term Memory

Whereas the capacity of short-term memory is limited, the capacity of long-term memory is extremely large; in fact, most theorists believe it to be unlimited (Matlin, 1998). The unlimited capacity of long-term memory is impossible to prove, but there are no cases of people being unable to learn something new because they had too much information stored in long-term memory. We do know for sure that people store vast quantities of information in long-term memory, and that they often remember it remarkably well for long periods of time. For example, people are amazingly accurate at recognizing the faces of their high school classmates after not having seen them for over twenty-five years (Bruck, Cavanagh, & Ceci, 1991), and they do surprisingly well on tests of a foreign language or high school algebra fifty years after having formally studied these subjects (Bahrick & Hall, 1991; Bahrick et al., 1994).

However, long-term memories are also subject to distortion. In one study, college students were asked to recall their high school grades. Even though the students were motivated to be accurate, they correctly remembered 89 percent of their A grades but only 29 percent of their D grades. And perhaps it should not be surprising that when they made errors, these usually involved recalling grades as being higher than they actually were (Bahrick, Hall, & Berger, 1996). In another study, students were asked to describe where they were and what they were doing at the moment they heard about the verdict in the O. J. Simpson murder trial (Schmolck, Buffalo, & Squire, 2000). The students reported their recollections three times, first just three days after the verdict, and then again after

A Photographic Memory Franco Magnani had been away from his hometown in Italy for more than thirty years, but he could still paint it from memory (see comparison photo; Sacks, 1992). People like Magnani display *eidetic imagery*, commonly called *photographic memory*; they have automatic, detailed, and vivid images of virtually everything they have ever seen. About 5 percent of all school-age children have eidetic imagery, but almost no adults have it (Haber, 1979).

fifteen and thirty-two months. At the final reporting, almost all the students claimed they could still remember accurately where they were and what they were doing, but more than 70 percent of their memories were distorted, inaccurate, or both. For example, three days after the verdict, one student said he heard about it while in a campus lounge with many other students around him. Thirty-two months later, the same student recalled hearing the news in the living room of his home with his father and sister. Most of the students whose memories had been substantially distorted over time were unaware that this distortion had occurred; they were very confident that their reports were accurate. Later, we will see that such overconfidence can also appear in courtroom testimony by eyewitnesses to crime.

Distinguishing Between Short-Term and Long-Term Memory

Some psychologists claim that there is no need to distinguish between short-term and long-term memory: What people call short-term (and working) memory is simply that part of memory that they happen to be thinking about at any particular time, whereas long-term memory is the part of memory that they are not thinking about at any given moment. ("In Review: Storing New Memories" summarizes the characteristics of these systems.) However, other psychologists argue that short-term and long-term memory are qualitatively different—that they obey different laws (Cowan, 1988). Evidence that information is transferred from short-term memory to a distinct storage system comes from experiments on recall.

Experiments on Recall
To conduct your own recall experiment, look at the following list of words for thirty seconds, then look away and write down as many of the words as you can, in any order: desk, chalk, pencil, chair, paperclip, book, eraser, folder, briefcase, essays. Which words you remember depends in part on their *serial position*—that is, where the words are in the list, as Figure 7.9 shows. This figure is a *serial-position curve*, which shows the chances of recalling words appearing in each position in a list. For the first two or three words in a list, recall tends to be very good—a characteristic that is called the **primacy effect**. The

figure 7.9
A Serial-Position Curve
The probability of recalling an item is plotted here as a function of its serial position in a list of items. Generally, the first several items and the last several items are the most likely to be recalled.

Drawing (A) shows the correct penny image in Figure 7.8.

in review	Storing New Memories			
Storage System	**Function**	**Capacity**	**Duration**	
Sensory memory	Briefly holds representations of stimuli from each sense for further processing	Large: absorbs all sensory input from a particular stimulus	Less than 1 second	
Short-term and working memory	Holds information in awareness and manipulates it to accomplish mental work	Five to nine distinct items or chunks of information	About 18 seconds	
Long-term memory	Stores new information indefinitely	Unlimited	Unlimited	

probability of recall decreases for words in the middle of the list and then rises dramatically for the last few words. The ease of recalling words near the end of a list is called the **recency effect**. It has been suggested that the primacy effect reflects rehearsal that puts early words into *long-term memory*, and that the recency effect occurs because the last few words are still in *short-term memory* when we try to recall the list (Glanzer & Cunitz, 1966; Koppenaal & Glanzer, 1990).

Retrieving Memories

Have you ever been unable to recall the name of an old television show or movie star, only to think of it the next day? Remembering something requires not only that it be appropriately encoded and stored but also that you have the ability to bring it into consciousness—in other words, to *retrieve* it.

Retrieval Cues and Encoding Specificity

Stimuli that help people retrieve information from long-term memory are called **retrieval cues.** They allow people to recall things that were once forgotten and help them to recognize information stored in memory. In general, recognition tasks are easier than recall tasks, because they contain more retrieval cues. As noted earlier, it is usually easier to recognize the correct alternative on a multiple-choice exam than to recall material for an essay test.

The effectiveness of cues in aiding retrieval depends on the degree to which they tap into information that was encoded at the time of learning (Tulving, 1983). This rule, known as the **encoding specificity principle**, is consistent with the transfer-appropriate processing model of memory. Because long-term memories are often encoded semantically, cues related to the *meaning* of the stored information tend to work best. For example, imagine you have learned a long list of sentences, one of which is either (1) "The man lifted the piano" or (2) "The man tuned the piano." Having the cue "something heavy" during a recall test would probably help you remember the first sentence, because you probably encoded something about the weight of a piano, but "something heavy" would probably not help you recall the second sentence. Similarly, the cue "makes nice sounds" would be likely to help you recall the second sentence, but not the first (Barclay et al., 1974).

Context and State Dependence

Have you ever taken a test in a classroom other than the one in which you learned the material for that test? If so, your performance may have been affected (Smith,

primacy effect A characteristic of memory in which recall of the first two or three items in a list is particularly good.

recency effect A characteristic of memory in which recall is particularly good for the last few items in a list.

retrieval cues Stimuli that allow people to recall or recognize information stored in memory.

encoding specificity principle A principle stating that the ability of a cue to aid retrieval depends on the degree to which it taps into information that was encoded at the time of the original learning.

Glenberg, & Bjork, 1978). In general, people remember more when their efforts at recall take place in the same environment in which they learned, because they tend to encode features of the environment where the learning occurred (Richardson-Klavehn & Bjork, 1988). These features may later act as retrieval cues. In one experiment, people studied a series of photos while in the presence of a particular odor. Later, they reviewed a larger set of photos and tried to identify the ones they had seen earlier. Half of these people were tested in the presence of the original odor and half in the presence of a different odor. Those who smelled the same odor during learning and testing did significantly better on the recognition task than those who were tested in the presence of a different odor. The matching odor served as a powerful retrieval cue (Cann & Ross, 1989).

When memory can be helped or hindered by similarities in environmental context, it is called **context-dependent memory**. This context-dependency effect is not always strong (Saufley, Otaka, & Bavaresco, 1985; Smith, Vela, & Williamson, 1988), but some students do find it helpful to study for a test in the classroom where the test will be given.

Like the external environment, the internal psychological environment can be encoded when people learn, and thus it can act as a retrieval cue When a person's internal state can aid or impede retrieval, the person has what is called **state-dependent memory**. For example, if people learn new material while under the influence of marijuana, they tend to recall it better if they are also tested under the influence of marijuana (Eich et al., 1975). Similar effects have been found with alcohol (Overton, 1984) and other drugs (Eich, 1989), although memory is best overall when people are not under the influence of any drug! Mood states, too, can affect memory (Eich & Macaulay, 2000). People tend to remember more positive incidents from their past when they are in a positive mood at the time of recall and more negative events when they are in a negative mood (Ehrlichman & Halpern, 1988; Lewinsohn & Rosenbaum, 1987). These *mood congruency effects* are strongest when people try to recall personally meaningful episodes, because such events were most likely to be colored by their mood (Eich & Metcalfe, 1989).

Retrieval from Semantic Memory

All of the retrieval situations we have discussed so far are relevant to episodic memory. ("In Review: Factors Affecting Retrieval from Long-Term Memory" summarizes this material.) But how do we retrieve information from semantic memory, where our general knowledge about the world is stored? Researchers studying this process typically ask participants general-knowledge questions, such as (1) Are fish

Context-Dependent Memories Some parents find that being in their child's schoolroom for a teacher conference provides context cues that bring back memories of their own grade school days.

context-dependent memory Memory that can be helped or hindered by similarities or differences between the context in which it is learned and the context in which it is recalled.

state-dependent memory Memory that is aided or impeded by a person's internal state.

spreading activation A principle that explains how information is retrieved in semantic network theories of memory.

in review: Factors Affecting Retrieval from Long-Term Memory

Process	Effect on Memory
Encoding specificity	Retrieval cues are effective only to the extent that they tap into information that was originally encoded.
Context dependence	Retrieval is most successful when it occurs in the same environment in which the information was originally learned.
State dependence	Retrieval is most successful when people are in the same psychological state as when they originally learned the information.

minerals? (2) Is a beagle a dog? (3) Do birds fly? and (4) Does a car have legs? As you might imagine, most people almost always respond correctly to such questions. By measuring the amount of time people take to answer the questions, however, psychologists gain important clues about how semantic memory is organized and how we retrieve information from it.

Semantic Networks   One of the most influential theories of semantic memory suggests that concepts are represented in a dense network of associations (Collins & Loftus, 1975). Figure 7.10 presents a fragment of what a *semantic memory network* might look like. In general, semantic network theories suggest that information is retrieved from memory through **spreading activation** (Medin, Ross, & Markman, 2001). So whenever you think about some concept, that concept becomes activated in the network, and this activation—in the form of neural energy—begins to spread along all the paths related to it. For example, if a person is asked to say whether "A robin is a bird" is true or false, the concepts of both "robin" and "bird" will become activated, and the spreading activation from each will intersect in the middle of the path between them.

Some associations within the network are stronger than others. Differing strengths are depicted by the varying thicknesses of the lines in Figure 7.10; spreading activation travels faster along thick paths than along thin ones. For example, most people probably have a stronger association between "bat" and "can fly" or "has wings" than between "bat" and "is a mammal." Accordingly, most people respond more quickly to "Can a bat fly?" than to "Is a bat a mammal?"

Because of the tight organization of semantic networks and the speed at which activation spreads through them, we can gain access to an enormous body of knowledge about the world quickly and effortlessly. We can retrieve not only the facts we have learned directly but also the knowledge that allows us to infer or compute other facts about the world (Matlin, 1998). For example, imagine answering the following two questions: (1) Is a robin a bird? and (2) Is a robin a living thing? You can probably answer the first question "directly," because you probably learned this

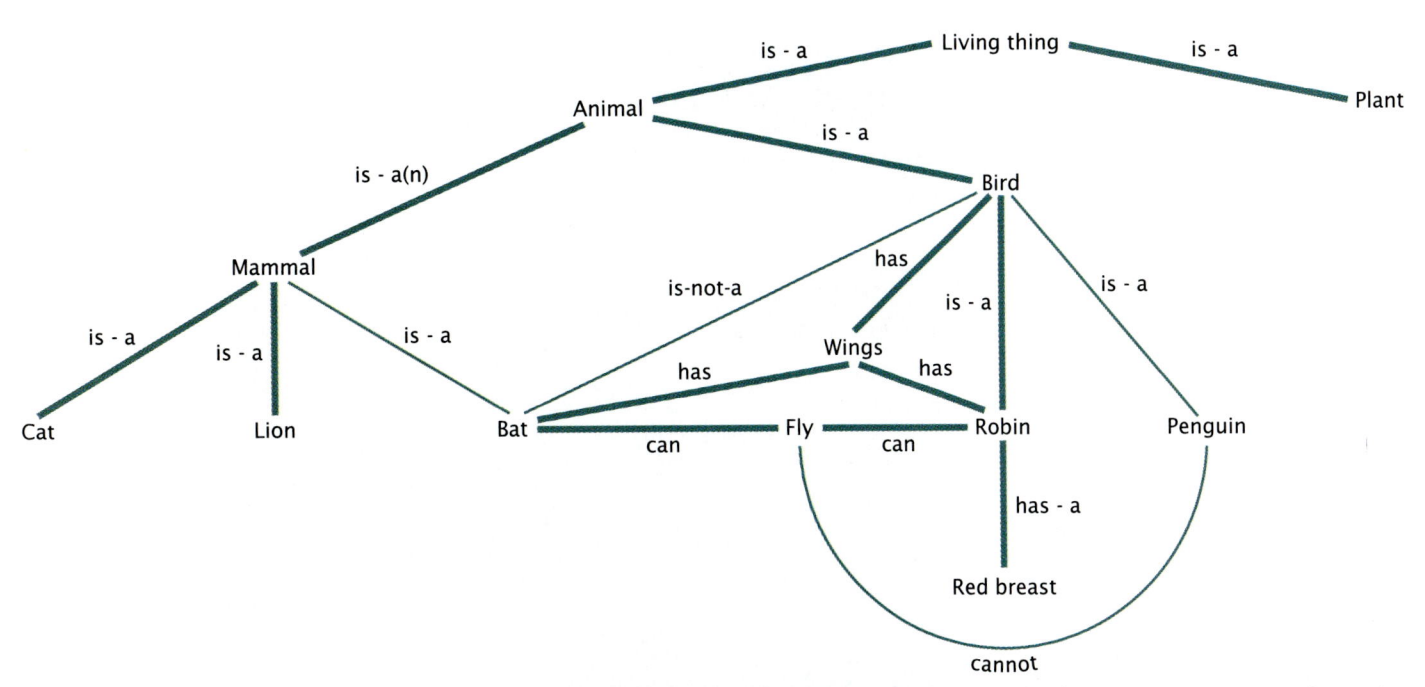

figure 7.10

Semantic Networks

This drawing represents just a small part of a network of semantic associations. Semantic network theories of memory suggest that networks like these allow us to retrieve specific pieces of previously learned information and to make new inferences about concepts.

fact at some point in your life. However, you may never have consciously thought about the second question, so answering it requires you to make an inference. Figure 7.10 illustrates the path to that inference. Because you know that a robin is a bird, a bird is an animal, and animals are living things, you can infer that a robin must be a living thing. As you might expect, however, it takes slightly longer to answer the second question than the first.

Retrieving Incomplete Knowledge

Figure 7.10 also shows that concepts—such as "bird"—are represented in semantic memory as collections of features or attributes. When you can retrieve some features of a concept from your semantic network, but not enough of them to identify what the concept is, you are said to have retrieved *incomplete knowledge*. For example, you might know that there is an animal that has wings, can fly, but is not a bird, and yet be unable to retrieve its name (Connor, Balota, & Neely, 1992).

You have probably experienced a particular example of incomplete knowledge called the *tip-of-the-tongue phenomenon*. In a typical experiment on this phenomenon, people listen to dictionary definitions of words and are then asked to name each defined word (Brown & McNeill, 1966). If they cannot recall a particular word, they are asked whether they can recall any feature of it, such as its first letter or how many syllables it has. People are surprisingly good at this task, indicating that they are able to retrieve at least some knowledge of the word (Brennen et al., 1990). Most people experience the tip-of-the-tongue phenomenon about once a week (Brown, 1991).

Another example of retrieving incomplete knowledge is the *feeling-of-knowing experience,* which is often studied by asking people trivia questions (Reder & Ritter, 1992). When they cannot answer a question, they are asked to estimate the probability that they could recognize the correct answer if they were given several options. Again, people are remarkably good at this task; even though they cannot recall the answer, they can retrieve enough knowledge to determine whether the answer is actually stored in their memory (Costermans, Lories, & Ansay, 1992).

TRY THIS **Constructive Memory** Ask a friend to examine this photo for a minute or so (cover the caption). Then take the book away and ask whether each of the following items appeared in the photo: chair, wastebasket, bottle, typewriter, coffeepot, and book. If your friend reports having seen a wastebasket or book, you will have demonstrated constructive memory.

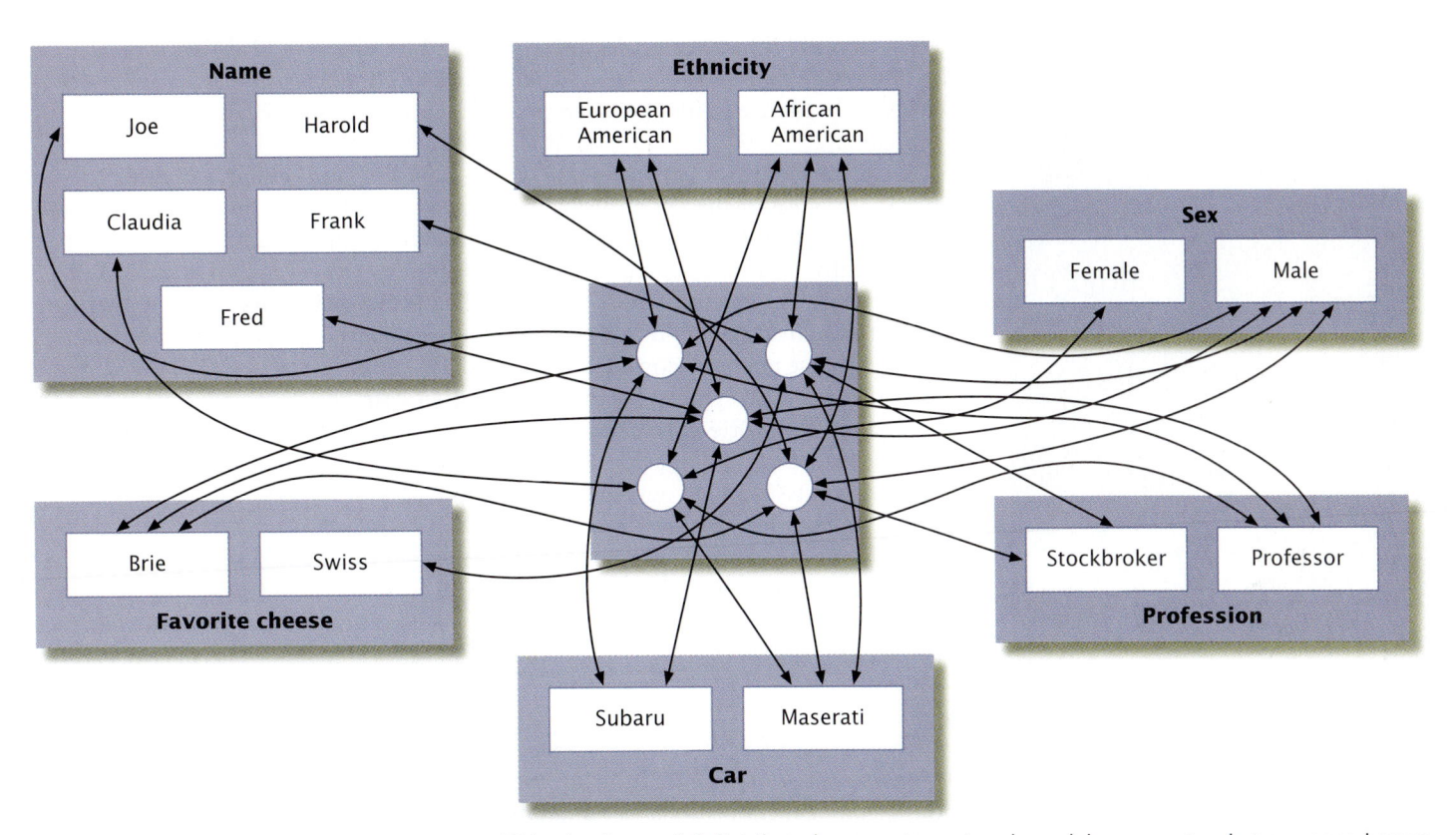

figure 7.11

A PDP Network Model

This simple parallel distributed processing network model represents what someone knows about the characteristics of five people and how these characteristics are related to one another. Note that each arrow between a rectangle and a circle connects a characteristic with a person. More complex versions of such networks are capable of accounting not only for what people know but also for the inferences and generalizations they tend to make.

Source: From *Cognitive Psychology,* 1st Edition, by C. Martindale, © 1991. Reprinted with permission of Wadsworth Publishing, a division of International Thomson Publishing. Fax 800-730-2215.

Constructing Memories

The generalized knowledge about the world that each person has stored constantly affects memory (Schacter, Norman, & Koutstaal, 1998). We use our existing knowledge to organize new information as we receive it and to fill in gaps in the information we encode and retrieve (Sherman & Bessennoff, 1999). In this way, memories are constructed.

To study this process, which is sometimes called *constructive memory,* William Brewer and James Treyens (1981) asked undergraduates to wait for several minutes in the office of a graduate student. When later asked to recall everything that was in the office, most of the students mistakenly "remembered" that books were present, even though there were none. Apparently, the general knowledge that graduate students read many books influenced the participants' memory of what was in the room.

Relating Semantic and Episodic Memory: PDP Models
Parallel distributed processing models offer one way of explaining how semantic and episodic information become integrated in constructive memories. As mentioned earlier, PDP models suggest that newly learned facts alter our general knowledge of what the world is like. Figure 7.11 shows a simple PDP network model of just a tiny part of someone's knowledge of the world (Martindale, 1991). At its center lie the intersections of several learned associations between specific facts about five people, each of whom is represented by a circle. This network "knows" that Joe is a

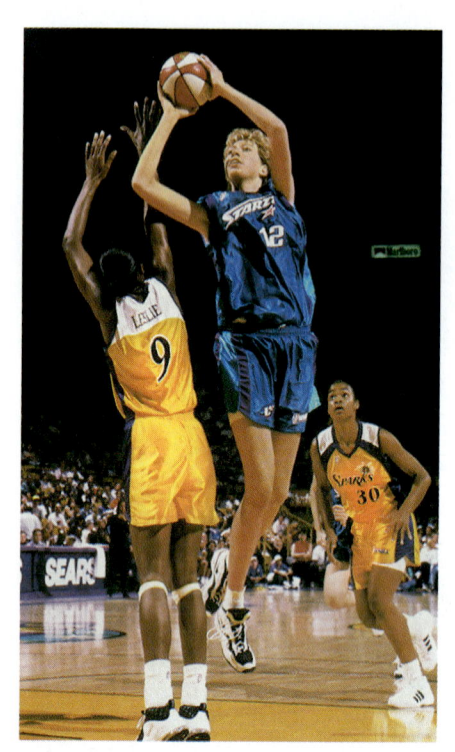

PDP Models and Constructive Memory If you were to hear that "our basketball team won last night," your schema about basketball might prompt you to encode, and later retrieve, the fact that the players were men. Such spontaneous, though often incorrect, generalizations associated with PDP models of memory help account for constructive memory.

male European American professor who likes Brie cheese and drives a Subaru. It also "knows" that Claudia is a female African American professor who drives a Maserati. Notice that the network has never learned what type of cheese she prefers.

Suppose Figure 7.11 represents your memory, and you now think about Claudia. Because of the connections in the network, the facts that she is a female African American professor and drives a Maserati would be activated; you would automatically remember these facts about Claudia. However, "likes Brie cheese" would also be activated, because it is linked to other professors in the network. If the level of activation for Brie cheese were low, then the proposition that Claudia likes Brie cheese might be considered a hypothesis or an educated guess. But suppose every other professor you know likes Brie. In that case, the connection between professors and "likes Brie cheese" would be strong, and the conclusion that Claudia likes Brie cheese would be held so confidently that it would take overwhelming evidence for you to change your mind (Rumelhart & McClelland, 1986).

PDP networks also produce spontaneous generalizations. If a friend told you she just bought a new car, you would know without asking that—like all other cars you have seen—it has four wheels. However, spontaneous generalizations can create significant errors if the network is based on limited or biased experience with a class of objects. For example, if the network in Figure 7.11 were asked what European American males are like, it would think that all of them drive Japanese cars.

This aspect of PDP networks—generalizing from scanty information—is actually an accurate reflection of human thought and memory. Virtually everyone makes spontaneous generalizations about males, females, European Americans, African Americans, and many other categories (Martindale, 1991).

Schemas Parallel distributed processing models also help us understand constructive memory by explaining the operation of the schemas that guide it. **Schemas** are mental representations of categories of objects, events, and people. For example, for people who have a schema for *baseball game*, simply hearing these words is likely to activate whole clusters of information in long-term memory, including the rules of the game, images of players, bats, balls, a green field, summer days, and perhaps hot dogs and stadiums. The generalized knowledge contained in schemas

figure 7.12

The Effect of Schemas on Recall

	Group 1		Group 2	
Figure shown to participants	Label given	Figure drawn by participants	Label given	Figure drawn by participants
⊙—⊙	Eyeglasses	⊙⊙	Dumbbell	⊙—⊙
⋈	Hourglass	⋈	Table	⋈
7	Seven	7	Four	4
⊥	Gun	⌐──	Broom	⊥

In one early experiment, participants were shown figures like these, along with labels designed to activate certain schemas (Carmichael, Hogan, & Walter, 1932). For example, when showing the top figure, the experimenter said either "This resembles eyeglasses" or "This resembles a dumbbell." When the participants were asked to reproduce the figures from memory, their drawings tended to resemble the items mentioned by the experimenter. In other words, their memory had been altered by the labels.

schemas Mental representations of categories of objects, events, and people.

provides a basis for making inferences about incoming information during the encoding stage. So if you hear that a baseball player was injured, your schema about baseball might prompt you to encode the incident as game related, even though the cause was not mentioned. As a result, you are likely to recall the injury as having occurred during a game (see Figure 7.12 for another example).

LINKAGES

Memory, Perception, and Eyewitness Testimony

There are few situations in which accurate retrieval of memories is more important—and constructive memory is more dangerous—than when an eyewitness testifies in court about a crime. Eyewitnesses provide the most compelling evidence in many trials, but they can sometimes be mistaken (Kassin et al., 2001; Loftus & Ketcham, 1991). In 1984, for example, a North Carolina college student, Jennifer Thompson, confidently identified Ronald Cotton as the man who had raped her at knifepoint. Mainly on the basis of Thompson's testimony, Cotton was convicted of rape and sentenced to life in prison. He was released eleven years later, when DNA evidence revealed that he was innocent (and it identified another man as the rapist). The eyewitness-victim's certainty had convinced a jury, but her memory had been faulty (O'Neill, 2000). Let's consider the accuracy of eyewitness memory and how it can be distorted (Loftus, 1993).

Like the rest of us, eyewitnesses can remember only what they perceive, and they can perceive only what they attend to (Backman & Nilsson, 1991). As described in the perception chapter, perception is influenced by a combination of the stimulus features we find "out there" in the world and what we already know, expect, or want—that is, by both bottom-up and top-down processing.

LINKAGES (a link to Perception)

Witnesses are asked to report exactly what they saw or heard; but no matter how hard they try to be accurate, there are limits to how faithful their reports can be (Kassin, Rigby, & Castillo, 1991). As mentioned earlier, semantic encoding into long-term memory may result in the loss of certain details. Further, new information, including questions posed by police or lawyers, can alter a witness's memory (Loftus, 1979). For example, when witnesses were asked, "How fast was the blue car going when it *smashed into* the truck?" they were likely to recall a higher speed than when they were asked, "How fast was the blue car going when it *hit* the truck?" (Loftus & Palmer, 1974; see Figure 7.13). There is also evidence that an object mentioned after the fact is often mistakenly remembered as having been

figure 7.13

The Impact of Leading Questions on Eyewitness Memory

After seeing a filmed traffic accident, people were asked, "About how fast were the cars going when they (smashed, hit, or contacted) each other?" As shown here, the witnesses' responses were influenced by the verb used in the question; *smashed* was associated with the highest average speed estimates. A week later, people who heard the question that used *smashed* remembered the accident as being more violent than did people in the other two groups (Loftus & Palmer, 1974).

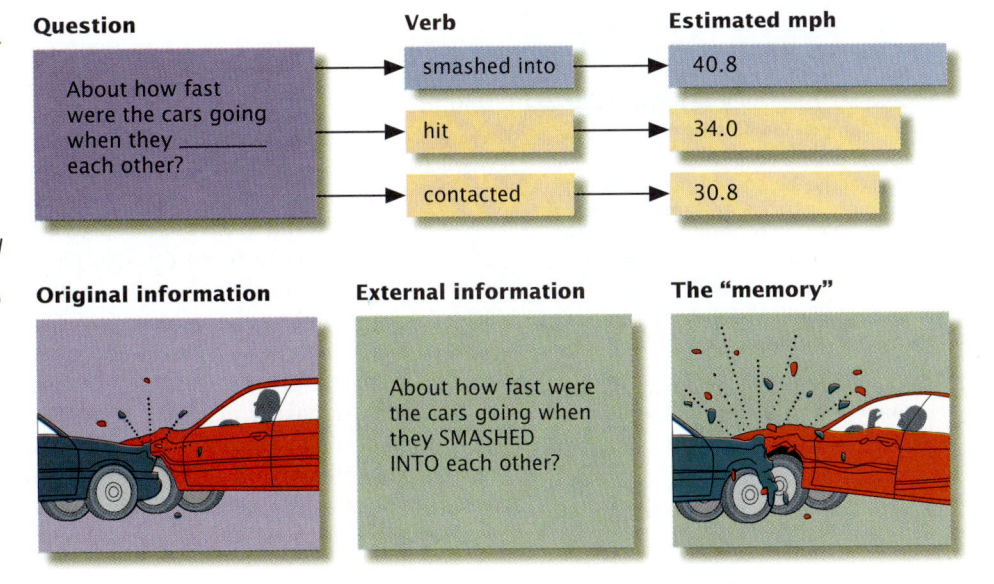

Question	Verb	Estimated mph
About how fast were the cars going when they _____ each other?	smashed into	40.8
	hit	34.0
	contacted	30.8

Original information | External information: About how fast were the cars going when they SMASHED INTO each other? | The "memory" there in the first place (Dodson & Reisberg, 1991). So if a lawyer says that a screwdriver was lying on the ground (when it was not), witnesses often recall with great certainty having seen it (Ryan & Geiselman, 1991). Some theorists have speculated that mentioning a new object makes the original memory more difficult to retrieve (Tversky & Tuchin, 1989). However, there is now considerable evidence that when new objects are mentioned, they are integrated into the old memory representation and subsequently are not distinguished from what was originally seen (Loftus, 1992).

For jurors, the believability of a witness often depends as much (or even more) on *how* the witness presents evidence as on the content or relevance of that evidence (Leippe, Manion, & Romanczyk, 1992). Many jurors are impressed, for example, by witnesses who give lots of details about what they saw or heard. Extremely detailed testimony from prosecution witnesses is especially likely to lead to guilty verdicts, even when the details reported are irrelevant (Bell & Loftus, 1989). When a witness gives very detailed testimony, such as the exact time of the crime or the color of the criminal's shoes, jurors apparently infer that the witness paid especially close attention or has a particularly accurate memory. At first glance, these inferences might seem reasonable. However, as discussed in the chapter on perception, the ability to divide attention is limited. As a result, witnesses might focus attention on the crime and the criminal, or on the surrounding details, but probably not on both—particularly if they were emotionally aroused and the crime happened quickly. So witnesses who accurately remember unimportant details of a crime scene may not accurately recall the criminal's facial features or other identifying characteristics (Backman & Nilsson, 1991).

Juries also tend to believe witnesses who are confident (Leippe, Manion, & Romanczyk, 1992), but witnesses' confidence about their testimony is frequently much higher than its accuracy (Shaw, 1996). Repeated exposure to misinformation and the repeated recall of misinformation can increase a witness's confidence in objectively incorrect testimony (Lamb, 1998; Mitchell & Zaragoza, 1996; Roediger, Jacoby, & McDermott, 1996). In other words, as in the Jennifer Thompson case, even witnesses who are confident about their testimony are not always correct.

The weaknesses inherent in eyewitness memory can be amplified by the use of police lineups and certain other criminal identification procedures. In one study, for example, participants watched a videotaped crime and then tried to identify the criminal from a set of photographs (Wells & Bradfield, 1999). None of the photos showed the person who had committed the crime, but some participants nevertheless identified one of them as the criminal they saw on tape. When these mistaken participants were led to believe that they had correctly identified the criminal, they became even more confident in the accuracy of their false identification. These incorrect, but confident, witnesses became more likely than other participants to claim that it had been easy for them to identify the criminal from the photos because they had had a good view of him and had paid careful attention to him.

As of 2000, at least 96 people, including Ronald Cotton, have been released from U.S. prisons after DNA tests or other evidence revealed that they had been falsely convicted—mostly on the basis of faulty eyewitness testimony (Death Penalty Information Center, 2001; Scheck, Neufeld, & Dwyer, 2000; Wells et al., 2000). DNA evidence freed Charles Fain, who had been convicted of murder and spent almost eighteen years on death row in Idaho (Bonner, 2001). Frank Lee Smith, too, would have been set free after the sole eyewitness at his murder trial retracted her testimony, but he had already died of cancer while awaiting execution in a Florida prison. Research on memory and perception helps explain how these miscarriages of justice can occur, and it is also guiding efforts to prevent such errors in the future. The U.S. Department of Justice has recently acknowledged the potential for errors in eyewitness evidence, as well as the dangers of asking witnesses to identify suspects from lineups and photo arrays. The result is *Eyewitness Evidence: A Guide for Law Enforcement* (U.S. Department of Justice,

HERMAN

"Can you identify the man who punched you in the knee?"

This is exactly the sort of biased lineup that the new Justice Department *Guide for Law Enforcement* (1999) is designed to avoid. Based on research on memory and perception, this guide recommends that no suspect should stand out from all the others in a lineup, that witnesses should not assume the real criminal is in the lineup, and that they should not be encouraged to base identification on their "best guess."

HERMAN® is reprinted with permission from LaughingStock Licensing Inc., Ottawa, Canada. All rights reserved.

Forgetting

1999), the first-ever guide for police and prosecutors involved in obtaining eyewitness evidence. The guide warns these officials that asking leading questions about what witnesses saw can distort their memory, that witnesses should examine mug shots of possible suspects one at a time, and that false identifications are less likely if witnesses viewing suspects in a lineup are told that the real perpetrator might not be included (Foxhall, 2000; Wells et al., 2000).

The frustrations of forgetting—where you left your keys, the answer to a test question, an anniversary—are apparent to most people nearly every day (Neisser, 2000). In this section we look more closely at the nature of forgetting and at some of the mechanisms that are responsible for it.

How Do We Forget?

In the late 1800s, Hermann Ebbinghaus, a German psychologist, began the systematic study of memory and forgetting, using only himself as the subject of his research. His aim was to study memory in its "pure" form, uncontaminated by emotional reactions and other pre-existing associations between new material and what was already in memory. To eliminate such associations, Ebbinghaus created the *nonsense syllable*, a meaningless set of two consonants and a vowel, such as *POF, XEM,* and *QAL*. He read a list of nonsense syllables aloud at a constant rate and then tried to recall the syllables.

To measure forgetting, Ebbinghaus devised the **method of savings**, which involves computing the difference between the number of repetitions needed to learn a list of items and the number of repetitions needed to relearn it after some time has elapsed. This difference is called the *savings*. If it took Ebbinghaus ten trials to learn a list and ten more trials to relearn it, there would be no savings, and forgetting would have been complete. If it took him ten trials to learn the list and only five trials to relearn it, there would be a savings of 50 percent.

As you can see in Figure 7.14, Ebbinghaus found a decline in savings (and an increase in forgetting) as time passes. However, the most dramatic drop in what people retain in long-term memory occurs during the first nine hours, especially in the first hour. After this initial decline, the rate of forgetting slows down considerably. In Ebbinghaus's study, some savings existed even thirty-one days after the original learning.

Ebbinghaus's research had some important limitations, but it produced two lasting discoveries. One is the shape of the forgetting curve, depicted in Figure 7.14. Psychologists have subsequently substituted words, sentences, and even stories for nonsense syllables. In virtually all cases the forgetting curve shows the same strong initial drop in memory, followed by a much more moderate decrease over time (Slamecka & McElree, 1983). Of course, people remember sensible stories better than nonsense syllables, but the *shape* of the curve is the same no matter what type of material is involved (Davis & Moore, 1935). Even the forgetting of events from daily life tends to follow Ebbinghaus's forgetting curve (Thomson, 1982).

The second of Ebbinghaus's important discoveries is just how long-lasting savings in long-term memory can be. Psychologists now know from the method of savings that information about everything from algebra to bike riding is often retained for decades (Matlin, 1998). You may forget something you have learned if you do not use the information, but it is easy to relearn the material if the need arises, indicating that the forgetting was not complete (Hall & Bahrick, 1998).

Durable Memories This man probably had not used a pogo stick since he was ten. His memory of how to do it is not entirely gone, however, so he showed some "savings": It took him less time to relearn the skill now than it took to learn it initially.

method of savings Measuring forgetting by computing the difference between the number of repetitions needed to learn and, after a delay, relearn the same material.

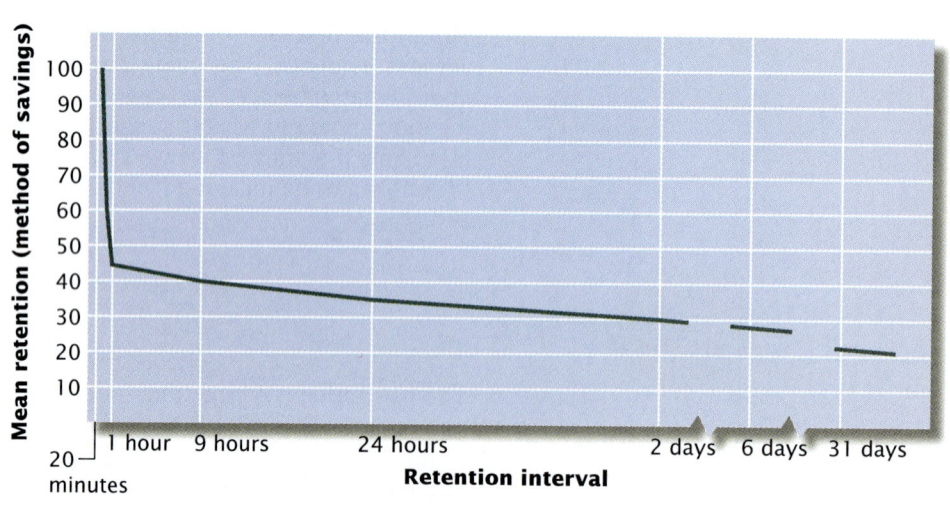

figure 7.14
Ebbinghaus's Curve of Forgetting

TRY THIS Select thirty words at random from a dictionary, and spend a few minutes memorizing them. After an hour has passed, write down as many words as you can remember, but don't look at the original list again. Do the same self-test eight hours later, a day later, and two days later. Now look at the original list, and see how well you did on each recall test. Ebbinghaus found that most forgetting occurs during the first nine hours after learning, and especially during the first hour. If this was not the case for you, why do you think your results were different?

Why Do We Forget? The Roles of Decay and Interference

Nothing we have said so far explains *why* forgetting occurs. In principle, either of two processes can be responsible (Best, 1999). One process is **decay**, the gradual disappearance of the mental representation of a stimulus. Decay occurs in memory much as the inscription engraved on a ring or bracelet wears away and becomes less distinct over time. Forgetting might also occur because of **interference**, a process through which either the storage or retrieval of information is impaired by the presence of other information. Interference might occur either because one piece of information actually *displaces* other information, pushing it out of memory, or because one piece of information makes storing or recalling other information more difficult.

In the case of short-term memory, we noted that if an item is not rehearsed or elaborated, memory of it decreases consistently over the course of about eighteen seconds. So decay appears to play a prominent role in forgetting information in short-term memory. But interference through displacement also produces forgetting from short-term memory. Like a desktop, short-term memory can hold only so much. When additional items are added, the old ones tend to "fall off" and are no longer available (Haberlandt, 1999). Displacement is one reason why the phone number you just looked up is likely to drop out of short-term memory if you read another number before making your call. Rehearsal prevents displacement by continually re-entering the same information into short-term memory.

The causes of forgetting from long-term memory are more complicated. In long-term memory there can be **retroactive interference**, in which learning of new information interferes with recall of older information, or **proactive interference**, in which old information interferes with learning or remembering new information. For example, retroactive interference would help explain why studying French vocabulary this term might make it more difficult to remember the Spanish words you learned last term. And because of proactive interference, the French words you are learning now might make it harder to learn German next term. Figure 7.15 outlines the types of experiments used to study the influence of each form of interference in long-term memory.

decay The gradual disappearance of the mental representation of a stimulus.
interference The process through which either the storage or the retrieval of information is impaired by the presence of other information.
retroactive interference A cause of forgetting in which new information placed in memory interferes with the ability to recall information already in memory.
proactive interference A cause of forgetting in which information already in long-term memory interferes with the ability to remember new information.

PROACTIVE INTERFERENCE

Group	Time 1	Time 2	Time 3	Result
Experimental	Learn list A	Learn list B	Recall list B	The experimental group will suffer from proactive interference, and the control group will be able to recall more material from list B.
Control		Learn list B	Recall list B	

RETROACTIVE INTERFERENCE

Group	Time 1	Time 2	Time 3	Result
Experimental	Learn list A	Learn list B	Recall list A	The experimental group will suffer from retroactive interference, and the control group will be able to recall more material from list A.
Control	Learn list A		Recall list A	

figure 7.15

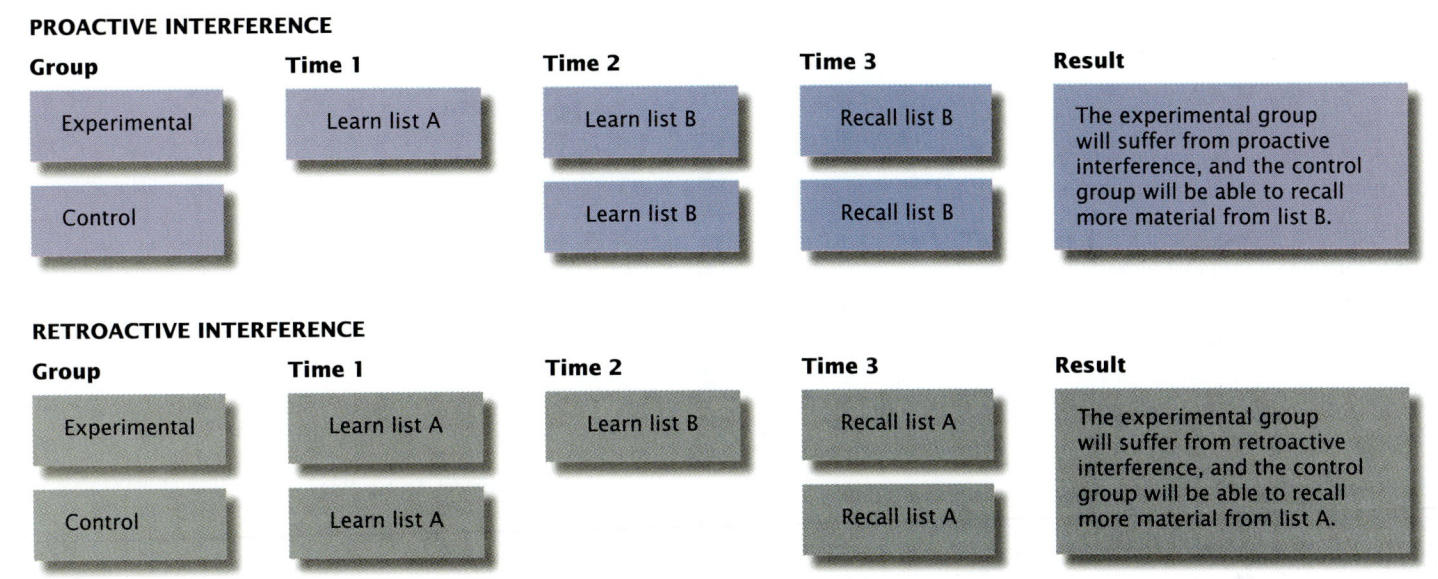

Procedures for Studying Interference

To recall the two types of interference, remember that the prefixes—*pro* and *retro*—indicate directions in time. In *pro*active interference, previously learned material interferes with *future* learning; *retro*active interference occurs when new information interferes with the recall of *past* learning.

Suppose a person learns something and then, when tested on it after various intervals, remembers less and less as the delay becomes longer. Is this forgetting due to decay or to interference? It is not easy to tell, because longer delays produce both more decay and more retroactive interference as the person is exposed to further information while waiting. To separate the effects of decay from those of interference, Karl Dallenbach sought to create situations in which time passed but there was no accompanying interference. Evidence of forgetting in such a situation would suggest that decay, not interference, was operating.

In one of Dallenbach's studies, college students learned a list of nonsense syllables and then either continued with their waking routine or were sheltered from interference by going to sleep (Jenkins & Dallenbach, 1924). Although the delay (and thus the potential for decay) was held constant for both groups, the greater interference associated with being awake produced much more forgetting (see Figure 7.16).

Results like these suggest that although decay sometimes occurs, interference is the major cause of forgetting from long-term memory. But does interference actually push the forgotten information out of memory, or does it just impair the retrieval process? To find out, Endel Tulving and Joseph Psotka (1971) presented people with different numbers of word lists. Each list contained words from one of six categories, such as types of buildings *(hut, cottage, tent, hotel)* or earth formations *(cliff, river, hill, volcano)*. Some people learned a list and then recalled as many of the words as possible. Other groups learned the first list and then learned different numbers of other lists before trying to recall the first one.

The results were dramatic. As the number of intervening lists increased, the number of words that people could recall from the original list declined. This finding reflected strong retroactive interference. Then the researchers gave a second test, in which they provided people with a *retrieval cue* by telling them the category of the words (such as types of buildings) to be recalled. Now the number of intervening lists had almost no effect on the number of words recalled from the original list, as Figure 7.17 shows. These results indicate that the words were still in long-term memory; they had not been pushed out, but the participants had been unable to recall them without appropriate retrieval cues. In other words, the original forgetting

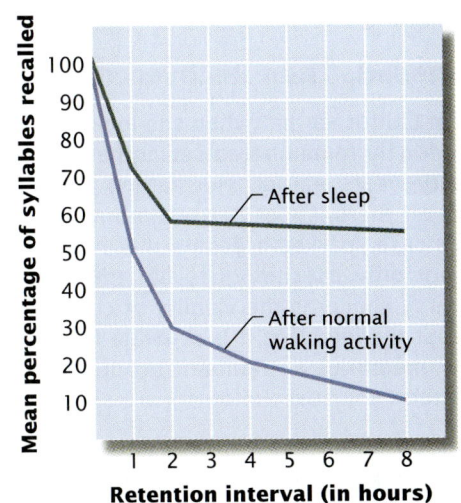

figure 7.16

Interference and Forgetting

In this study, college students' forgetting was more rapid if they engaged in normal activity after learning than if they spent the time asleep. These results suggest that interference is more important than decay in forgetting information in long-term memory.

Source: Minimi & Dallenbach (1946).

figure 7.17

Retrieval Failures and Forgetting

In Tulving and Psotka's experiment, people's ability to recall a list of items was strongly affected by the number of other lists they learned before being tested on the first one. When item-category (retrieval) cues were provided on a second test, however, retroactive interference from the intervening lists almost disappeared.

Source: Tulving & Psotka (1971).

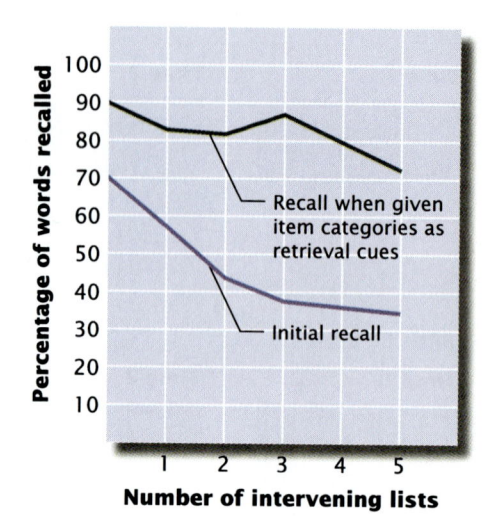

was due to a failure in retrieval. So putting more and more information in long-term memory may be like putting more and more CDs into a storage case. None of the CDs disappears, but it becomes increasingly difficult to find the specific one you are looking for.

Some theorists have concluded that all forgetting from long-term memory is due to some form of retrieval failure (Ratcliff & McKoon, 1989). Does this mean that everything in long-term memory remains there until death, even if you cannot always, or ever, recall it? No one knows for sure, but as described in the next section, this question lies at the heart of some highly controversial court cases.

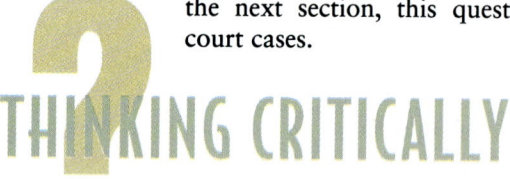

THINKING CRITICALLY

LINKAGES (a link to Consciousness)

Can Traumatic Memories Be Repressed, Then Recovered?

In 1989, Eileen Franklin-Lipsker told police in California that when she looked into her young daughter's eyes one day, she suddenly remembered seeing her father kill her childhood friend more than twenty years earlier. Her father, George Franklin, Sr., was sent to prison for murder on the basis of her testimony about that memory (Loftus & Ketcham, 1994). This case sparked a debate that has continued to grow in intensity and involves not only psychologists but the North American legal system as well. The controversy concerns the validity of claims of recovered memory. Some psychologists accept the idea that it is possible for people to *repress*, or push into unconsciousness, memories of traumatic incidents and then recover these memories many years later. Other psychologists are skeptical about recovered memory claims.

• **What am I being asked to believe or accept?**

The prosecution in the Franklin case successfully argued that Eileen had repressed, and then recovered, her memory of a murder. Similar arguments in a number of other cases tried in the early 1990s resulted in the imprisonment of other parents whose now-adult children claimed to have recovered childhood memories of being physically or sexually abused by them. The juries in these trials accepted the assertion that all memory of shocking events can be repressed, or pushed into an inaccessible corner of the mind where for decades, subconscious processes keep it out of awareness, yet potentially subject to accurate recollection (Hyman, 2000). Jurors are not the only believers in this phenomenon. A few years ago a large American news organization reported that the United States had illegally used nerve gas during the war in Vietnam. The story was based, in part, on a Vietnam veteran's account of recovered memories of having been subjected to a nerve gas attack.

- **What evidence is available to support the assertion?**

Proponents of the recovered memory argument point to several lines of evidence to support their claims. First, there is evidence that a substantial amount of mental activity occurs outside conscious awareness (Kihlstrom, 1999; see the chapter on consciousness). Second, research on implicit memory shows that information of which we are unaware can influence our behavior (Schacter, Chiu, & Ochsner, 1993). Third, research on *motivated forgetting* suggests that people are able to willfully suppress information so that it is no longer accessible on a later memory test (Anderson & Green, 2001). Even suppressing one's emotional reactions to events can interfere with memories of those events (Richards & Gross, 2000). And people appear more likely to forget unpleasant rather than pleasant events (Erdelyi, 1985). In one study, a psychologist kept a detailed record of his daily life over a six-year period. When he later tried to recall those experiences, he remembered more than half of the positive ones, but only one-third of the negative ones. In another study, 38 percent of women who, as children, had been brought to a hospital because of sexual abuse did not report the incident as adults (Williams, 1994). Fourth, retrieval cues can help people recall memories that had previously been inaccessible to conscious awareness (Andrews et al., 2000; Landsdale & Laming, 1995). For example, these cues have helped soldiers remember for the first time the circumstances under which they had been wounded many years before (Karon & Widener, 1997). Finally, there is the confidence with which people report recovered memories; they say they are just too vivid to be anything but real.

- **Are there alternative ways of interpreting the evidence?**

Those who are skeptical about recovered memories do not deny the operation of subconscious memory and retrieval processes (Kihlstrom, 1999). They also recognize that unfortunately, child abuse and other traumas are all too common. But to these psychologists, the available evidence is not strong enough to support the conclusion that traumatic memories can be repressed and then accurately recalled (Pope, 1998; Pope & Hudson, 1995). Any given "recovered" memory, they say, might actually be a distorted, or constructed, memory (Clancy et al., 2000; Hyman, 2000; Loftus, 1998). As already mentioned, our recall of past events is affected by what happened at the time, what we knew beforehand, and everything we have experienced since. The people described earlier who "remembered" nonexistent books in a graduate student's office constructed that memory based on what prior knowledge led them to *assume* was there. Similarly, the "recovered memory" of the Vietnam veteran mentioned earlier appears to have no basis in fact; the news story about the alleged nerve gas attack was later retracted.

Research shows that *false memories*—distortions of actual events and the recall of events that didn't actually happen—can be at least as vivid as accurate ones, and people can be just as confident in them (Brainerd & Reyna, 1998; Brainerd, Reyna, & Brandse, 1995; Roediger & McDermott, 1995, 2000). Most of us have experienced everyday versions of false memories; it is common for people to "remember" turning off the coffeepot or mailing the rent check, only to discover later that they did not. Researchers have demonstrated that false memories can occur in relation to more emotional events, too. In one case study, a teenager named Chris was given descriptions of four incidents from his childhood and asked to write about each of them every day for five days (Loftus, 1997a). One of those incidents—being lost in a shopping mall at age five—never really happened. Yet Chris not only eventually "remembered" this event but added many details about the mall and the stranger whose hand he was supposedly found holding. He also rated this (false) memory as being more vivid than two of the other three (real) incidents. Similar results occurred in about half of seventy-seven child participants in a more recent set of case studies (Porter, Yuille, & Lehman, 1999). The same pattern of results has appeared in formal experiments on the planting of emotion-laden false memories (Hyman & Pentland, 1996). Researchers have been able to

Exploring Memory Processes
Research by Elizabeth Loftus (shown here with a student) and other cognitive psychologists has demonstrated mechanisms through which false memories can be created. The researchers have shown, for example, that false memories appear even in research participants who are told about them and asked to avoid them (McDermott & Roediger, 1998). Their work has helped to focus scientific scrutiny on reports of recovered memories, especially those arising from contact with therapists who assume that most people have repressed memories of abuse.

create vivid and striking, but *completely false*, memories of events that people thought they experienced when they were one day old (DuBreuil, Garry, & Loftus, 1998). In other experiments, children who were repeatedly asked about a nonexistent trauma (getting a hand caught in a mousetrap) eventually developed a vivid and unshakable false memory of experiencing it (Ceci et al., 1994).

In other words, people sometimes have a difficult time distinguishing between what has happened to them and what they have only imagined, or have come to believe, has happened (Garry & Polaschek, 2000; Johnson & Raye, 1998; Zaragosa et al., 2001). Some studies indicate that people who score high on tests of introversion, fantasy-proneness, and dissociation—the latter of which includes a tendency toward lapses of memory and attention—are more likely than others to develop false memories and may also be more likely to report the recovery of repressed memories (McNally et al., 2000b; Porter et al., 2000). Also, two studies have found that women who have suffered physical or sexual abuse are more likely to falsely remember words on a laboratory recall test (Bremner, Shobe, & Kihlstrom, 2000; Zoellner et al., 2000). This tendency appears strongest among abused women who show signs of posttraumatic stress disorder (Bremner, Shobe, & Kihlstrom, 2000). Another study found that susceptibility to false memory in a word recall task was greater in women who reported recovered memories of sexual abuse than in nonabused women or in those who had always remembered the abuse they suffered (Clancy et al., 2000).

Why would anyone "remember" a traumatic event that did not actually occur? Elizabeth Loftus (1997b) suggests that for one thing, popular books such as *The Courage to Heal* (Bass & Davis, 1994) and *Secret Survivors* (Blume, 1998) may lead people to believe that anyone who experiences guilt, depression, low self-esteem, overemotionality, or any of a long list of other problems is harboring repressed memories of abuse. This message, says Loftus, tends to be reinforced and extended by therapists who specialize in using guided imagination, hypnosis, and other methods to "help" clients recover repressed memories (Polusny & Follette, 1996; Poole et al., 1995). These therapists may influence people to construct false memories by encouraging them to imagine experiencing events that might never have actually occurred, or that occurred only in a dream (Mazzoni & Loftus, 1996; Olio, 1994). As one client described her therapy, "I was rapidly losing the ability to differentiate between my imagination and my real memory" (Loftus & Ketcham, 1994, p. 25). To such therapists, a client's failure to recover memories of abuse, or refusal to accept their existence, is evidence of "denial" of the truth (Loftus, 1997a).

The possibility that recovered memories might actually be false memories has led to dismissed charges or not-guilty verdicts for defendants in some repressed memory cases. In others, previously convicted defendants have been set free. (George Franklin's conviction was overturned, but only after he served five years in prison.) Concern over the potential damage resulting from false memories led to the establishment of the False Memory Syndrome Foundation, a support group for families affected by abuse accusations stemming from allegedly repressed memories. More than a hundred of these families (including Franklin's family) have filed lawsuits against hospitals and therapists (False Memory Syndrome Foundation, 1997). In 1994, California winery executive Gary Ramona received $500,000 in damages from two therapists who had "helped" his daughter recall alleged sexual abuse at his hands. More recent suits led to a $2 million judgment against a Minnesota therapist whose client realized that her "recovered" memories of childhood abuse were false; a similar case in Wisconsin brought a $5 million judgment against two therapists. And an Illinois case resulted in a $10.6 million settlement and the suspension of the license of the psychiatrist who had "found" his patient's "lost" memories (Loftus, 1998).

● **What additional evidence would help to evaluate the alternatives?**

Evaluating reports of recovered memories would be aided by more information about whether it is possible for people to repress traumatic events. If it is possible, we also need to know how common it is and how accurate recovered memories might be. So far, we know that some people apparently do forget intense emotional experiences, but that most people's memories of them are vivid and long lasting (Pope et al., 1998; Strongman & Kemp, 1991). Some are called *flashbulb memories* because they preserve particular experiences in great detail (Brown & Kulik, 1977). In fact, many people who live through trauma are *unable* to forget it. In the sexual abuse study mentioned earlier, for example (Williams, 1994a), 62 percent of the abuse victims did recall their trauma (some of the others may have recalled it, but chose not to report it). More studies like that one—studies that track the fate of memories in known abuse cases—not only would help estimate the prevalence of this kind of forgetting but also might offer clues as to the kinds of people and events most likely to be associated with it.

It would also be valuable to know more about the processes through which repression might occur and how they are related to empirically established theories and models of human memory. Is there a mechanism that specifically pushes traumatic memories out of awareness, then keeps them at a subconscious level for long periods and allows them to be accurately recalled? So far, cognitive psychologists have not found evidence for such a mechanism (Loftus, 1997a; McNally, Clancy, & Schacter, 2001; McNally et al., 2000a; Pope et al., 1998).

- **What conclusions are most reasonable?**

An objective reading of the available research evidence supports the view that recovery of memories of trauma is at least possible, but that the implantation of false memories is also possible—and has been demonstrated experimentally. Accordingly, it may be difficult to decide whether any particular case is an instance of recovered memory or false memory, especially in the absence of objective corroborating evidence.

The intense conflict between the False Memory Syndrome Foundation and those psychologists who accept as genuine most of the memories recovered in therapy reflects a fundamental disagreement about recovered memories: Client reports constitute "proof" for therapists who deal daily with victims of sexual abuse and other traumas, and who rely more on personal experiences than on scientific research findings. Those reports are viewed with far more skepticism by psychologists who engage in, or rely on, empirical research on the processes of memory and forgetting (Pope, 1998).

So whether or not one believes a claim of recovered memory may be determined by the relative weight one assigns to personal experiences and intuition versus empirical evidence. Still, the apparent ease with which false memories can be created should lead judges, juries, and the general public to exercise great caution before accepting as valid unverified memories of traumatic events. At the same time, we should not automatically and uncritically reject the claims of people who appear to have recovered memories. Perhaps the wisest course is to use all the scientific and circumstantial evidence available to carefully and critically examine such claims, while keeping in mind that constructive memory processes *might* have influenced them. This careful, scientific approach is vital if we are to protect the rights and welfare of those who report recovered memories, as well as of those who face accusations arising from them.

Biological Bases of Memory

Many psychologists study memory by exploring the physical, electrical, and chemical changes that take place in the brain when people encode, store, and retrieve information (Cabeza & Nyberg, 2000; Smith, 2000). The story of the scientific search for the biological bases of memory begins with the work of Karl Lashley and Donald Hebb, who spent many years studying how memory is related to brain structures and processes. Lashley (1950) taught rats new behaviors and then observed how damage to various parts of the rats' brains changed their ability to perform the tasks they had learned. Lashley hoped that his work would identify the brain area that contained the "engram"—the physical manifestation of memory in the brain. However, after many experiments, he concluded that memories are not localized in one specific region, but instead are distributed throughout large areas of brain tissue (Lashley, 1950).

Hebb, who was a student of Lashley's, proposed another biological theory of memory. Hebb believed that a given memory is represented by a group of interconnected neurons in the brain. This set of neurons, which he called a *cell assembly*, form a network in the cortex. The connections among these neurons were strengthened, he said, when the neurons were simultaneously stimulated through sensory experiences (Hebb, 1949). Though not correct in all its details, Hebb's theory stimulated research and contributed to an understanding of the physical basis of memory. His theory is also consistent, in many respects, with contemporary parallel distributed processing models of memory (Hergenhahn & Olson, 1997).

Let's consider more recent research on the biochemical mechanisms and brain structures that are most directly involved in memory processes.

The Biochemistry of Memory

As described in the chapter on biological aspects of psychology, communication among brain cells takes place at the synapses between axons and dendrites, and it depends on chemicals, called *neurotransmitters*, released at the synapses. The formation and storage of new memories are associated with at least two kinds of changes in synapses.

The first kind of change occurs when stimulation from the environment promotes the formation of *new* synapses, thus increasing the complexity of the communication networks through which neurons receive information (Black & Greenough, 1991; Rosenzweig & Bennett, 1996). Scientists have now actually seen this process occur. As shown in Figure 7.18, repeatedly sending signals across a particular synapse increases the number of special little branches, called *spines*, that appear on the receiving cell's dendrites (Toni et al., 1999).

The second kind of change occurs as new experiences alter the functioning of *existing* synapses. Researchers have discovered that when two neurons fire at the same time and together stimulate a third neuron, that third neuron will later be more responsive than before to stimulation by either neuron alone (Sejnowski, Chattarji, & Stanton, 1990). This process of "sensitizing" synapses is called *long-term potentiation* (Rioult-Pedotti, Friedman, & Donoghue, 2000). Changing patterns of electrical stimulation can also weaken synaptic connections (Malenka,

figure 7.18

Building Memories

These models of synapses are based on electron microscope images of neurons in the brain. Notice that before the synapse has been "sensitized," just one spine (shown in white) appears on this part of the dendrite. Afterward, there are two spines. The creation and changing of many individual synapses in the brain appear to underlie the formation and storage of new memories.

Source: Toni et al. (1999).

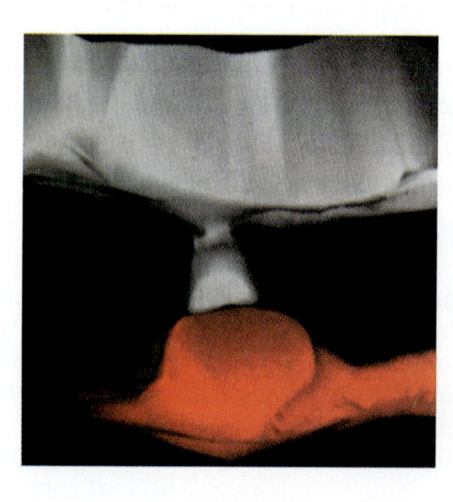

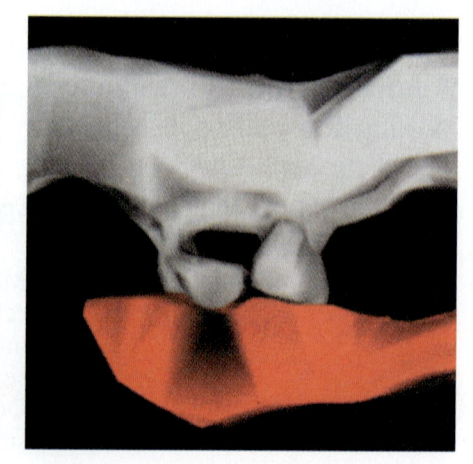

figure 7.19
Some Brain Structures Involved in Memory
Combined neural activity in many parts of the brain allows us to encode, store, and retrieve memories. The complexity of the biological bases of these processes is underscored by research showing that different aspects of a memory—such as the sights and sounds associated with some event—are stored in different parts of the cerebral cortex (Gallagher & Chiba, 1996).

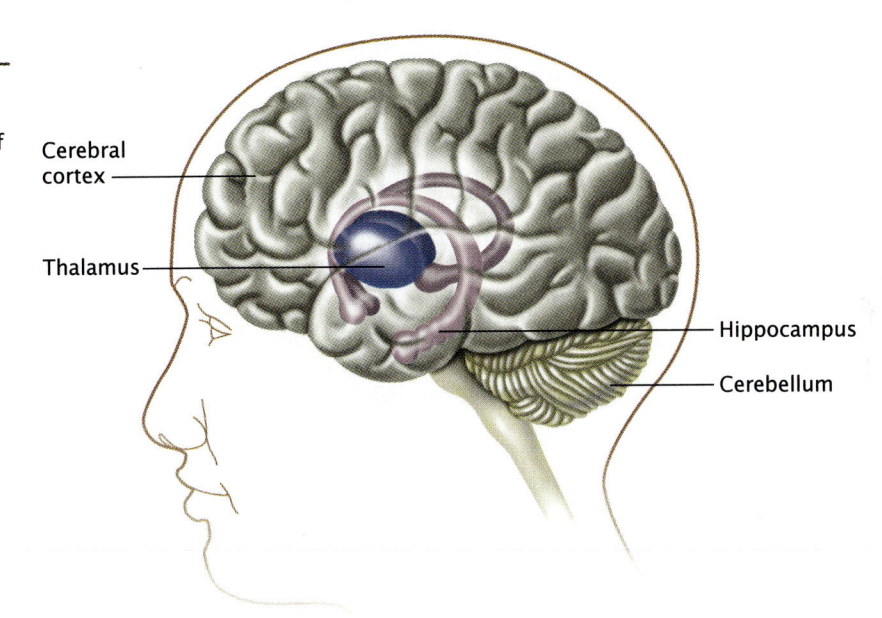

LINKAGES (a link to Biological Aspects of Psychology)

1995). Such changes in sensitivity could account for the development of conditioned responses and other types of learning.

In the hippocampus (see Figure 7.19), these changes appear to occur at synapses that use the neurotransmitter glutamate (Malenka & Nicoll, 1999). Other neurotransmitters, such as acetylcholine, also play important roles in memory formation (e.g., Furey, Pietrini, & Haxby, 2000). The memory problems seen in people with Alzheimer's disease are related to a deficiency in neurons that use acetylcholine and send fibers to the hippocampus and the cortex (Muir, 1997). Drugs that interfere with the action of acetylcholine impair memory, and drugs that increase the amount of acetylcholine in synapses improve memory in aging animals and humans (Pettit, Shao, & Yakel, 2001; Sirvio, 1999).

In short, research has shown that the formation of memories is associated with changes in many individual synapses that, together, strengthen and improve the communication in networks of neurons (Malleret et al., 2001; Rosenzweig & Bennett, 1996). These findings provide some support for the ideas formulated by Hebb many years ago.

Brain Structures and Memory

Are the biochemical processes involved in memory concentrated in certain regions, or are they distributed throughout the brain? The latest research suggests that memory involves both specialized regions for various types of memory formation and widespread areas for storage. Several of the brain regions shown in Figure 7.19, including the hippocampus and nearby parts of the cortex and the thalamus, are vital to the formation of new memories (Brewer et al., 1998; Squire & Zola, 1996; Wagner et al., 1998). Evidence for the memory-related functions of these regions comes from two main sources. First, there are case studies of patients with brain injuries that allow neuropsychologists to determine how damage to specific brain areas is related to specific kinds of memory problems. Second, studies using PET scans, functional MRI, and other neuroimaging methods (described in the chapter on biological aspects of psychology) have allowed neuroscientists to observe where brain activity is concentrated as normal people perform various memory tasks.

The Impact of Brain Damage
Both kinds of research have confirmed that the hippocampus, which is part of the limbic system, is among the brain regions involved in the formation of new memories. Damage to the hippocampus often

results in **anterograde amnesia**, a loss of memory for any event occurring *after* the injury. The case of H.M. provides a striking example of anterograde amnesia (Milner, 1966). When H.M. was twenty-seven years old, part of his hippocampus was removed to end his severe epileptic seizures. Afterward, both his long-term and short-term memory appeared normal, but he had a severe problem. Two years after the operation, he still believed that he was twenty-seven. When his family moved into a new house, H.M. could not remember the new address or even how to get there. When told that his uncle had died, he grieved in a normal way. But soon afterward, he began to ask why his uncle had not visited him. He had to be repeatedly reminded of the death, and each time, he became just as upset as when he was first told. The surgery had apparently destroyed the mechanism that transfers information from short-term to long-term memory.

Although such patients cannot form episodic memories following hippocampal damage, they may still be able to form implicit memories. For example, H.M. was presented with a complicated puzzle on which mistakes are common and performance gradually improves with practice. Over several days his performance steadily improved, just as it does with normal people, and eventually it became virtually perfect. But each time he tried the puzzle, he insisted that he had never seen it before (Cohen & Corkin, 1981; see Figure 9.4). A musician with a similar kind of brain damage was able to use his implicit memory to continue leading choral groups (Vattano, 2000). Other researchers, too, have found intact implicit memory in patients who have anterograde amnesia for new episodic material (Squire & McKee, 1992; Tulving, Hayman, & Macdonald, 1991). These patients are also able to keep information temporarily in working memory, which depends on the activity of dopamine neurons in the prefrontal cortex (Williams & Goldman-Rakic, 1995). So the hippocampus is crucial in the formation of new episodic memories, but implicit memory, procedural memory, and working memory appear to be governed by other regions of the brain (Squire, 1992).

Retrograde amnesia, which involves a loss of memory for events *prior* to a brain injury, is also consistent with the idea that memory processes are widely distributed. Often, a person with this condition is unable to remember anything that took place in the months, or even years, before the injury (Kapur, 1999). In 1994, head injuries from a car crash left thirty-six-year-old Perlene Griffith-Barwell with retrograde amnesia so severe that she forgot virtually everything she had learned about everything and everybody over the previous twenty years. She thought she was still sixteen and did not recognize her husband, Malcolm, or her four children. She said, "The children were sweet, but they didn't seem like mine," and she "didn't feel anything" for Malcolm. Her memories of the last twenty years have never fully returned. She is divorced, but she still lives with her children and holds a job in a bank (Weinstein, 1999). Unlike Perlene, most victims of retrograde amnesia gradually recover their memories. The most distant events are recalled first, and the person gradually regains memory for events leading up to the injury. Recovery is seldom complete, however, and the person may never remember the last few seconds before the injury. One man received a severe blow to the head after being thrown from his motorcycle. After regaining consciousness, he claimed that he was eleven years old. Over the next three months, he gradually recovered his memory right up until the time he was riding his motorcycle the day of the accident. But he was never able to remember what happened just before the accident (Baddeley, 1982). Those final events must have been encoded into short-term memory, but apparently they were never transferred into long-term memory.

An additional clue to the role of specific brain areas in memory comes from research on people with *Korsakoff's syndrome,* a disorder that usually occurs in chronic alcoholics. These people's brains become unable to use glucose as fuel, resulting in severe and widespread brain damage. Damage to the mediodorsal nucleus of the thalamus is particularly implicated in the memory problems typical

---

anterograde amnesia A loss of memory for any event that occurs after a brain injury.

retrograde amnesia A loss of memory for events prior to a brain injury.

A Case of Retrograde Amnesia Trevor Rees-Jones, a bodyguard for Diana, Princess of Wales, is the sole survivor of the 1997 car crash that killed Diana, her companion Dodi al-Fayed, and her driver. Investigators had hoped that Rees-Jones could shed light on what caused the accident, but the head injury he received left him with retrograde amnesia. It was months before he could begin to recall anything about the events leading up to the accident, and he still cannot remember the accident itself. This type of amnesia is relatively common following concussions, so if you ride a motorcycle, wear that helmet!

of these patients, which can include both anterograde and retrograde amnesia (Squire, Amara, & Press, 1992). Moreover, like patients with hippocampal damage, Korsakoff's patients show impairments in the ability to form new episodic memories but retain some implicit memory abilities. Research has demonstrated that damage to the prefrontal cortex (also common in Korsakoff's patients) is related to disruptions in remembering the order in which events occur (Squire, 1992). Other studies have found that regions within the prefrontal cortex are involved in working memory in both animals and humans (D'Esposito et al., 1995; Goldman-Rakic, 1994, 1995; Smith, 2000).

Multiple Storage Areas It seems clear that neither the hippocampus nor the thalamus provides permanent long-term memory storage (Rosenbaum et al., 2000). However, both structures send nerve fibers to the cerebral cortex, suggesting that memory is impaired following hippocampal and thalamic damage at least in part because injury to these areas disrupts pathways leading to the cortex. Memories are probably stored in and around the cortex—but not all in one place (Gabrieli, 1998; Miceli et al., 2001).

As described in the chapters on biological aspects of psychology and on sensation, messages from different senses are represented in different regions of the cortex, so information about specific aspects of an experience is probably stored in or near these regions. This arrangement would explain why damage to the auditory cortex disrupts memory for sounds (Colombo et al., 1990). A memory, however, involves more than one sensory system. Even in the simple case of a rat remembering a maze, the experience of the maze includes vision, smell, movement, and emotions, each of which may be stored in different regions of the brain (Gallagher & Chiba, 1996). So memories are both localized and distributed; certain brain areas store specific aspects of each remembered event, but many brain regions are involved in experiencing a whole event (Brewer et al., 1998). The cerebellum, for instance (see Figure 7.19), is involved in the storage of procedural memories, such as dance steps and other movements.

The memory deficits observed in cases of damage to various brain areas are consistent with the view that short-term and long-term memory are distinct systems, and that the deficits themselves result from an inability to transfer information from one system to the other. However, the precise physiological processes involved in this transfer are not yet clear. According to one line of thought, a physiological trace that codes the experience must be gradually transformed and stabilized, or consolidated, if the memory is to endure (Shimizu, Tang, & Tsien, 2000; Verfaellie & Cermak, 1991). Recent research with animals also suggests that when emotional (fear-related) memories are recalled, they are subject to a biological re-storage process during which they are open to alteration (Nader, Schafe, & Le Doux, 2000). Future research on this phenomenon may eventually shed additional light on the processes of constructive memory and the bases for false memories.

It seems likely that memory consolidation depends primarily on the movement of electrochemical impulses within clusters of neurons in the brain (Berman, 1991; Taubenfeld et al., 2001). Events that suppress neural activity in the brain (e.g., physical blows to the head, anesthetics, and carbon monoxide and other types of poisoning) can disrupt the transfer of information from short-term to long-term memory—as can strong but random sets of electrical impulses, such as those that occur in the electroshock treatments sometimes used to treat psychological disorders. The information being transferred from short-term to long-term memory seems to be particularly vulnerable to destruction during the first minute or so (Donegan & Thompson, 1991).

What happens in the brain as we retrieve memories? Functional neuroimaging studies consistently show that the hippocampus, as well as regions of the parietal cortex and prefrontal cortex, are active during memory retrieval (Buckner &

Wheeler, 2001; Cabeza & Nyberg, 2000; Cabeza et al., 2001; Eldridge et al., 2000; McDermott & Buckner, in press; Rugg & Wilding, 2000). There is also evidence to suggest that retrieving memories of certain experiences, such as a conversation or a tennis game, reactivates the sensory and motor regions of the brain that had been involved during the event itself (Nyberg et al., 2001). Cognitive neuroscientists are currently trying to learn more about the retrieval process, including whether different patterns of brain activity are associated with the retrieval of accurate versus inaccurate memories (Gonsalves & Paller, 2000). This research will have obvious applications in areas such as lie detection and the evaluation of recovered memory claims.

Applications of Memory Research

Even though some questions about what memory is and how it works resist final answers, the results of memory research offer many valuable guidelines to help people improve their memories and function more effectively (Neisser, 2000).

Improving Your Memory

The most valuable memory enhancement strategies are based on the elaboration of incoming information, and especially on linking new information to what you already know.

Mnemonics
Psychologists have found that people with normal memory skills, and even those with brain damage, can improve their memory through the use of *mnemonics* (pronounced "nee-MON-ix"). Named for Mnemosyne, the Greek goddess of memory, **mnemonics** are strategies for placing information into an organized context in order to remember it. For example, to remember the names of the Great Lakes, you might use the acronym HOMES (for Huron, Ontario, Michigan, Erie, and Superior). Verbal organization is the basis for many mnemonics. You can link items by weaving them into a story, a sentence, or a rhyme. To help customers remember where they have parked their cars, some large garages have replaced section designations such as "A1" or "G8" with labels that use colors, animal names, or months. Customers can then tie the location of their cars to information already in long-term memory—for example, "I parked in the month of my mother's birthday."

One simple but powerful mnemonic is called the *method of loci* (pronounced "LOW-sigh"), or the method of places. To use this method, first think about a set of familiar locations—in your home, for example. You might imagine walking through the front door, around all four corners of the living room, and through each of the other rooms. Next, imagine that each item to be remembered is in one of these locations. Whenever you want to remember a list, use the same locations, in the same order. Creating vivid, unusual images of how these items appear in each location seems to be particularly effective (Kline & Groninger, 1991). For example, tomatoes smashed against the front door or bananas hanging from the bedroom ceiling might be helpful in recalling these items on a grocery list.

Guidelines for More Effective Studying
The success of mnemonic strategies demonstrates again the importance of relating new information to knowledge already stored in memory. All mnemonic systems require that you have a well-learned body of knowledge (such as locations) that can be used to provide a context for organizing incoming information (Hilton, 1986). When you want to remember more complex material, such as a textbook chapter, the same principles apply (Palmisano & Herrmann, 1991). You can improve your memory for text material by

mnemonics Strategies for placing information in an organized context in order to remember it.

first creating an outline or some other overall context for learning, rather than by just reading and rereading (Glover et al., 1990). Repetition may *seem* effective, because it keeps material in short-term memory; but for retaining information over long periods, repetition alone tends to be ineffective, no matter how much time you spend on it (Bjork, 1999; Bjorklund & Green, 1992). In short, "work smarter, not harder."

In addition, spend your time wisely. *Distributed practice* is much more effective than *massed practice* for learning new information. If you are going to spend ten hours studying for a test, you will be much better off studying for ten one-hour blocks (separated by periods of sleep and other activity) than "cramming" for one ten-hour block. By scheduling more study sessions, you will stay fresh and tend to think about the material from a new perspective at each session. This method will help you elaborate on the material (elaborative rehearsal) and remember it.

Reading a Textbook

More specific advice for remembering textbook material comes from a study that examined how successful and unsuccessful college students approach their reading (Whimbey, 1976). Unsuccessful students tend to read the material straight through; they do not slow down when they reach a difficult section; and they keep going even when they do not understand what they are reading. In contrast, successful college students monitor their understanding, reread difficult sections, and periodically stop to review what they have learned. In other words, effective learners engage in a deep level of processing. They are active learners, thinking of each new fact in relation to other material, and they develop a context in which many new facts can be organized effectively.

Research on memory suggests two specific guidelines for reading a textbook. First, make sure that you understand what you are reading before moving on (Herrmann & Searleman, 1992). Second, use the *PQ4R method* (Thomas & Robinson, 1972), which is one of the most successful strategies for remembering textbook material (Anderson, 1990b; Chastain & Thurber, 1989). *PQ4R* stands for six activities to engage in when you read a chapter: *preview, question, read, reflect, recite,* and *review*. These activities are designed to increase the depth to which you process the information you read and should be done as follows:

1. *Preview.* First, take a few minutes to skim the chapter. Look at the section headings and any boldfaced or italicized terms. Get a general idea of what material will be discussed, the way it is organized, and how its topics relate to one another and to what you already know. Some students find it useful to survey the entire chapter once and then survey each major section in a little more detail before reading it.

2. *Question.* Before reading each section, ask yourself what content will be covered and what information you should be getting from it.

3. *Read.* Now read the text, but *think about* the material as you read. Are you understanding the material? Are the questions you raised earlier being answered?

4. *Reflect.* As you read, think of your own examples—and create visual images—of the concepts and phenomena you encounter. Ask yourself what the material means, and consider how each section relates to other sections in the chapter and to other chapters in the book (this book's Linkages features are designed to promote this kind of reflection).

5. *Recite.* At the end of each section, recite the major points. Resist the temptation to be passive and say, "Oh, I'll remember that." Be active. Put the ideas into your own words by reciting them aloud.

6. *Review.* Finally, at the end of the chapter, review all the material. You should see connections not only within each section but also among sections. The

Understand and Remember Research on memory suggests that students who simply read their textbooks will not remember as much as those who, like this woman, read for understanding using the PQ4R method. Further, memory for the material is likely to be better if you read and study it over a number of weeks rather than in one marathon session on the night before a test.

objective is to see how the material is organized. Once you grasp the organization, the individual facts will be far easier to remember.

By following these procedures you will learn and remember the material better, and you will also save yourself considerable time.

Lecture Notes   Effective note-taking during lectures is vital, but it is an acquired skill. Research on memory suggests some simple strategies for taking and using notes effectively.

Realize first that in note-taking, more is not necessarily better. Taking detailed notes of everything you hear requires that you pay close attention to unimportant, as well as important, content, leaving little time for thinking about the material. Note-takers who concentrate on expressing the major ideas in relatively few words remember more than those who try to catch every detail (Pauk & Fiore, 2000). The best way to take notes is to think about what is being said, draw connections with other material in the lecture, and then summarize the major points clearly and concisely (Kiewra, 1989).

Once you have a set of lecture notes, review them as soon as possible after the lecture so that you can fill in missing details. (Remember that most forgetting from long-term memory occurs within the first few hours after learning.) When the time comes for serious study, use your notes as if they were a chapter in a textbook. Write a detailed outline. Think about how various points are related. Once you have organized the material, the details will make more sense and will be much easier to remember. ("In Review: Improving Your Memory" summarizes tips for studying.)

Design for Memory

The scientific study of memory has influenced the design of the electronic and mechanical devices that play an increasingly important role in our lives. Those who design computers, VCRs, DVD players, digital cameras, and even stoves are faced with a choice: Either place the operating instructions on the devices themselves, or assume that users will remember how to operate them. Understanding the limits of both working memory and long-term memory has helped designers distinguish between information that is likely to be stored in (and easily retrieved from) the user's memory, and information that should be presented in the form of labels,

in review   Improving Your Memory

Goal	Helpful Techniques
Remembering lists of items	Use mnemonics. Look for meaningful acronyms. Try the method of loci.
Remembering textbook material	Follow the PQ4R system. Allocate your time to allow for distributed practice. Read actively, not passively.
Taking lecture notes	Take notes, but record only the main points. Think about the overall organization of the material. Review your notes as soon after the lecture as possible in order to fill in missing points.
Studying for exams	Write a detailed outline of your lecture notes rather than passively reading them.

instructions, or other cues that reduce memory demands (Norman, 1988). Placing unfamiliar or hard-to-recall information in plain view makes it easier to use the device as intended, and with less chance of errors (Segal & Suri, 1999).

Psychologists have influenced advertisers and designers to create many other "user-friendly" systems (Wickens, Gordon, & Liu, 1998). As a result, toll-free numbers are designed to take advantage of chunking, which, as mentioned earlier, provides an efficient way to maintain information in working memory. Which do you think would be easier to remember: 1-800-438-4357 or 1-800-GET-HELP? Obviously, the more meaningful "get help" number is more memorable (there are web sites that can help you translate any phone number into words or a phrase). In the automotive arena, designers ensure that turn signals emit an audible cue when activated, a feature that reduces your memory load while driving and leaves you with enough working memory capacity to keep in mind that there is a car in your "blind spot."

As ever more complex devices appear in the marketplace, it will be increasingly important that instructions about how to operate them are presented clearly and memorably. With guidance from research on memory it should be possible for almost anyone to operate these devices efficiently. Yes, even the programming of a VCR will no longer be a mystery!

LINKAGES

As noted in the chapter on introducing psychology, all of psychology's subfields are related to one another. Our discussion of the accuracy of eyewitnesses' memories illustrates just one way in which the topic of this chapter, memory, is linked to the subfield of perception (see the chapter on perception). The Linkages diagram shows ties to two other subfields as well, and there are many more ties throughout the book. Looking for linkages among subfields will help you see how they all fit together and help you better appreciate the big picture that is psychology.

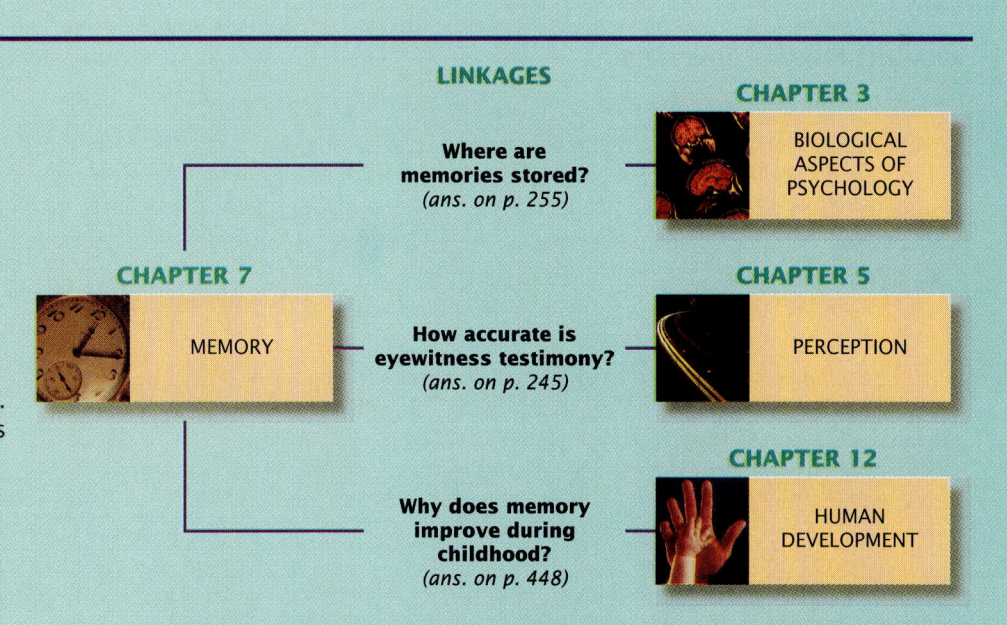

LINKAGES

CHAPTER 7 — MEMORY

- Where are memories stored? (ans. on p. 255) → **CHAPTER 3** BIOLOGICAL ASPECTS OF PSYCHOLOGY
- How accurate is eyewitness testimony? (ans. on p. 245) → **CHAPTER 5** PERCEPTION
- Why does memory improve during childhood? (ans. on p. 448) → **CHAPTER 12** HUMAN DEVELOPMENT

SUMMARY

The Nature of Memory

Human memory depends on a complex mental system.

Basic Memory Processes

There are three basic memory processes. *Encoding* transforms information into some type of mental representation. Encoding can be *acoustic* (by sound), *visual* (by appearance), or *semantic* (by meaning). *Storage* maintains information in the memory system over time. *Retrieval* is the process of gaining access to previously stored information.

Types of Memory

Most psychologists agree that there are at least three types of memory. *Episodic memory* contains information about specific events in a person's life. *Semantic memory* contains generalized knowledge about the world. *Procedural memory* contains information about how to do various things.

Explicit and Implicit Memory

Some research on memory concerns *explicit memory*, the processes through which people intentionally try to remember something. Psychologists also examine *implicit memory*, which refers to the unintentional influence of prior experiences.

Models of Memory

Four theoretical models of memory have guided most research. According to the *levels-of-processing model*, the most important determinant of memory is how extensively information is encoded or processed when it is first received. In general, *elaborative rehearsal* is more effective than *maintenance rehearsal* in learning new information, because it represents a deeper level of processing. According to the *transfer-appropriate processing model*, the critical determinant of memory is not how deeply information is encoded but whether processes used during retrieval match those used during encoding. *Parallel distributed processing (PDP) models* of memory suggest that new experiences not only provide specific information but also become part of, and alter, a whole network of associations. And the *information-processing model* suggests that in order for information to become firmly embedded in memory, it must pass through three stages of processing: sensory memory, short-term memory, and long-term memory.

Storing New Memories

Sensory Memory

Sensory memory maintains incoming information in the *sensory registers* for a very brief time. *Selective attention*, which focuses mental resources on only part of the stimulus field, controls what information in the sensory registers is actually perceived and transferred to short-term and working memory.

Short-Term Memory and Working Memory

Working memory is a system that allows us to store, organize, and manipulate information in order to think, solve problems, and make decisions. The storage, or maintenance, component of working memory is referred to as *short-term memory*. Remembering a phone number long enough to call it involves simple maintenance of the information in short-term memory.

Various memory codes can be used in short-term memory, but acoustic codes seem to dominate in most verbal tasks. Studies of the *immediate memory span* indicate that the storage capacity of short-term memory is approximately seven *chunks*, or meaningful groupings of information. Studies using the *Brown-Peterson procedure* show that information in short-term memory is usually forgotten within about eighteen seconds if it is not rehearsed.

Long-Term Memory

Long-term memory normally involves semantic encoding, which means that people tend to encode the general meaning of information, not specific details, in long-term memory. The capacity of long-term memory to store new information is extremely large, and perhaps even unlimited.

Distinguishing Between Short-Term and Long-Term Memory

According to some psychologists, there is no need to distinguish between short-term and long-term memory. Still, some evidence suggests that these systems are distinct. For example, the *primacy* and *recency effects* that occur when people try to recall a list of words may indicate the presence of two different systems.

Retrieving Memories

Retrieval Cues and Encoding Specificity

Retrieval cues help people remember things that they would otherwise not be able to recall. The effectiveness of retrieval cues follows the *encoding specificity principle:* Cues help retrieval only if they match some feature of the information that was originally encoded.

Context and State Dependence

All else being equal, memory may be better when one attempts to retrieve information in the same environment in which it was learned; this is called *context-dependent memory*. When a person's internal state can aid or impede retrieval, the person is said to have *state-dependent memory*.

Retrieval from Semantic Memory

Researchers usually study retrieval from semantic memory by examining how long it takes people to answer world knowledge questions. It appears that ideas are represented as associations in a dense semantic memory network, and that the retrieval of information occurs by a process of *spreading activation*. Each concept in the network is represented as a collection of features or attributes. The tip-of-the-tongue phenomenon and the feeling-of-knowing experience represent the retrieval of incomplete knowledge.

Constructing Memories

In the process of constructive memory, people use their existing knowledge to fill in gaps in the information they encode and retrieve. Parallel distributed processing models provide one explanation of how people make spontaneous generalizations about the world. They also explain the *schemas* that shape the memories people construct.

Forgetting

How Do We Forget?

In his research on long-term memory and forgetting, Hermann Ebbinghaus introduced the *method of savings*. He found that most forgetting from long-term memory occurs during the first several hours after learning and that savings can be extremely long lasting.

Why Do We Forget?: The Roles of Decay and Interference

Decay and *interference* are two mechanisms of forgetting. Although there is evidence of both decay and interference in short-term memory, it appears that most forgetting from long-term memory is due to either *retroactive interference* or *proactive interference*.

Biological Bases of Memory

The Biochemistry of Memory

Research has shown that memory can result as new synapses are formed in the brain and as communication at existing synapses is improved. Several neurotransmitters appear to be involved in the strengthening that occurs at synapses.

Brain Structures and Memory

Neuroimaging studies of normal people, as well as research with patients whose brain damage has resulted in *anterograde amnesia*, *retrograde amnesia*, Korsakoff's syndrome, and other memory problems, provide valuable information about the brain structures involved in memory. The hippocampus and thalamus are known to play a role in the formation of memories. These structures send nerve fibers to the cerebral cortex, which is where memories are probably stored and which is activated during memory retrieval. Memories appear to be both localized and distributed throughout the brain.

Applications of Memory Research

Improving Your Memory

Among the many applications of memory research are *mnemonics*, devices that are used to remember things better. One of the simplest but most powerful mnemonics is the method of loci. It is useful because it provides a context for organizing material more effectively. Guidelines for effective studying have also been derived from memory research. For example, the key to remembering textbook material is to read actively rather than passively. One of the most effective ways to do this is to follow the PQ4R method: preview, question, read, reflect, recite, and review. To take good lecture notes and to study them effectively, organize the points into a meaningful framework, and think about how each main point relates to the others.

Design for Memory

Research on the limits of memory has helped product designers to create electronic and mechanical systems and devices that are "user-friendly."

8

Cognition and Language

Basic Functions of Thought
The Circle of Thought
Measuring Information Processing

Mental Representations: The Ingredients of Thought
Concepts
Propositions
Schemas, Scripts, and Mental Models
Images and Cognitive Maps

Thinking Strategies
Formal Reasoning
Informal Reasoning

Problem Solving
Strategies for Problem Solving
FOCUS ON RESEARCH METHODS: Locating Analogical Thinking
Obstacles to Problem Solving
Building Problem-Solving Skills
Problem Solving by Computer

Decision Making
Evaluating Options
Biases and Flaws in Decision Making
Naturalistic Decision Making

LINKAGES: **Group Processes in Problem Solving and Decision Making**

Language
The Elements of Language
Understanding Speech
The Development of Language
How Is Language Acquired?

THINKING CRITICALLY: **Can Nonhumans Use Language?**
Culture, Language, and Thought

Linkages

Summary

Dr. Joyce Wallace, a New York City internist, was trying to figure out what was the matter with a forty-three-year-old patient, "Laura McBride." Laura reported pains in her stomach and abdomen, aching muscles, irritability, dizzy spells, and fatigue (Rouéché, 1986). The doctor's first hypothesis was that the patient had iron-deficiency anemia, a condition in which there is too little oxygen-carrying hemoglobin in the blood. There was some evidence to support that hypothesis. Laura's spleen was somewhat enlarged, and blood tests showed low hemoglobin and high production of red blood cells, suggesting that Laura's body was attempting to compensate for the loss of hemoglobin. However, other tests revealed normal iron levels. Perhaps she was losing blood through internal bleeding, but an additional test ruled that out. Had Laura been vomiting blood? She said no. Blood in the urine? No. Abnormally heavy menstrual flow? No. During the next week, as Dr. Wallace puzzled over the problem, Laura reported more intense pain, cramps, shortness of breath, and severe loss of energy. Her blood was becoming less and less capable of sustaining her, but if it was not being lost, what was happening to it? When the doctor looked at a smear of Laura's blood under the microscope, she saw that some kind of poison was destroying the red blood cells. What could it be? Laura spent most of her time at home, but her teenage daughters, who lived with her, were healthy. Dr. Wallace asked herself, "What does Laura do that the girls don't?" She repairs and restores paintings. Paint. Lead! She might be suffering from lead poisoning! When a blood test showed a lead level seven times higher than normal, Dr. Wallace knew she had solved this medical mystery at last.

To do so, Dr. Wallace relied on her ability to think, solve problems, and make judgments and decisions. She used these higher mental processes to weigh the pros and cons of various hypotheses and to reach decisions about what tests to order and how to interpret them. She also consulted with the patient and other physicians, using that remarkable human ability known as *language*.

As described in the chapter on biological aspects of psychology, these vital skills depend on the proper functioning of the brain; anything that disrupts that functioning can drastically impair cognitive abilities. For example, "Elliot," an intelligent and successful young businessman, had a cancerous tumor removed from the frontal area of his brain. After the surgery, neurologist Antonio Damasio found that Elliot's language, memory, and perceptual processes remained intact, but his ability to make complex business decisions and rational plans was virtually gone. In fact, a series of reckless, impulsive business schemes had already forced him into bankruptcy (Damasio, 1994).

These cases highlight the fact that our success as individuals depends largely on our cognitive and language skills. When those skills are impaired, by biological or other factors, we become vulnerable to all sorts of failures and errors. What pitfalls threaten the effectiveness of human cognition? What factors influence our success? How are our thoughts transformed into language? Many of the answers to these questions come from **cognitive psychology**, the study of the mental processes by which the information humans receive from their environment is modified, made meaningful, stored, retrieved, used, and communicated to others (Neisser, 1967).

In this chapter we examine two major aspects of human cognition: thought and language. First we consider what thought is and what functions it serves. Then we examine the basic ingredients of thought and the cognitive processes people use as they interact with their environment. These cognitive processes include reasoning, problem solving, and decision making. Next, we discuss language and how it is acquired and used. We discuss thought and language in the same chapter because thinking and communicating often involve the same cognitive processes. Learning about thought helps us to better understand language, and learning about language helps us to better understand thought.

---

cognitive psychology The study of the mental processes by which information from the environment is modified, made meaningful, stored, retrieved, used, and communicated to others.

Basic Functions of Thought

Let's begin our exploration of human cognition by considering the five core functions of thought, which are to *describe, elaborate, decide, plan,* and *guide action.* These functions can be seen as forming a *circle of thought* (see Figure 8.1).

The Circle of Thought

Consider how the circle of thought operated in Dr. Wallace. It began when she received the information about Laura's symptoms that allowed her to *describe* the problem. Next, she *elaborated* on this information by using her knowledge and experience to consider what disorders might cause such symptoms. Then she made a *decision* to investigate a possible cause, such as anemia. To implement this decision, she made a *plan*—to order a blood test—and then *acted* on that plan. But the circle of thought did not stop there. Information from the blood test provided new descriptive information, which Dr. Wallace *elaborated* further to reach another decision, create a new plan, and guide her next action.

Because the circle of thought spins constantly and rapidly and cannot be observed directly, it is difficult to study scientifically. One way to do so is to approach mental processes as a kind of information-processing system. An **information-processing system** receives information, represents the information with symbols, and then manipulates those representations. According to this information-processing model, then, **thinking** is defined as the manipulation of mental representations. Figure 8.2 shows how an information-processing model might view the sequence of events that form each cycle in the circle of thought. Notice that according to this model, information from the world is transformed somewhat as it passes through each stage of processing (Wickens, Gordon, & Liu, 1998).

figure 8.1
The Circle of Thought

The circle of thought begins as our sensory systems take in information from the world. Our perceptual system describes and elaborates this information, which is represented in the brain in ways that allow us to make decisions, formulate plans, and guide our actions. As those actions change our world, we receive new information—and the circle of thought begins again.

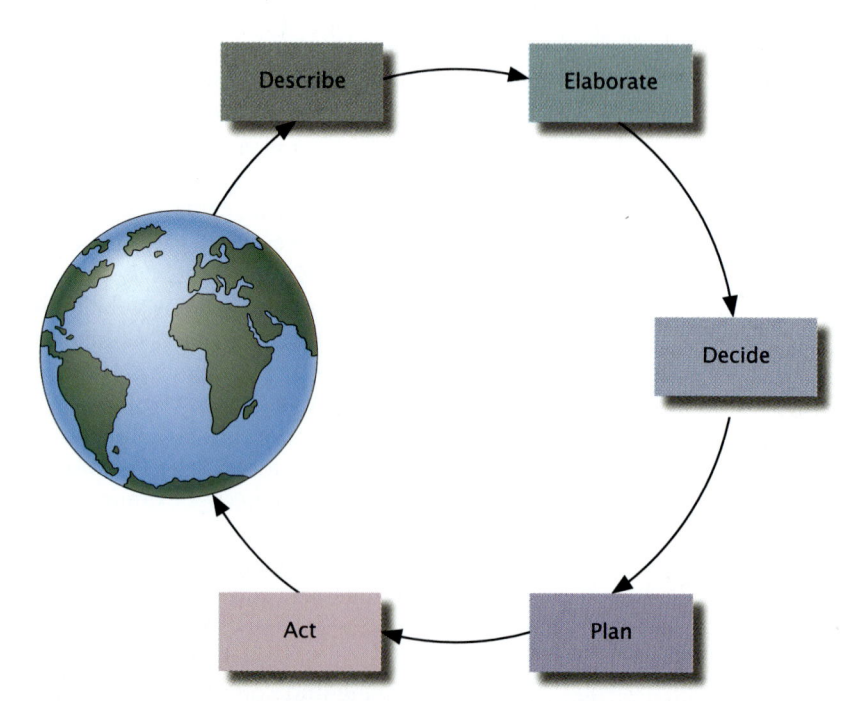

information-processing system Mechanisms for receiving information, representing it with symbols, and manipulating it.

thinking The manipulation of mental representations.

reaction time The time between the presentation of a stimulus and an overt response to it.

In the first stage, information about the world reaches the brain by way of the sensory receptors described in the chapter on sensation. This stage does not require attention. In the second stage, the information must be perceived and recognized, using the attentional and perceptual processes described in the chapter on perception. It is also during this stage that the information is consciously elaborated, using short-term and working memory processes that allow us to think about it in relation to knowledge stored in long-term memory. Once the information has been elaborated in this way, we must decide what to do with it. This third stage—decision making—also demands attention. The decision may be simply to store the information in memory. If, however, a decision is made to take some action, a response must be planned in the third stage and then carried out through a coordinated pattern of responses—the action itself—in the fourth and fifth stages. As suggested in Figure 8.1, this action usually affects the environment, providing new information that, in turn, is "fed back" to the system for processing in the ongoing circle of thought.

Measuring Information Processing

The brain damage suffered by Dr. Damasio's patient Elliot appeared to have mainly affected the decision-making and response selection stages of information processing. Analyzing the effects of brain damage is just one of several methods that scientists use to study the details of how the entire information-processing sequence normally works and what can interfere with it.

Mental Chronometry

Drivers and video-game players know that there is always a slight delay between seeing a red light or a space alien and hitting the brakes or firing the laser gun. The delay occurs because each of the processes described in Figure 8.2 takes some time. Psychologists began the laboratory investigation of thinking by exploring *mental chronometry,* the timing of mental events (Posner, 1978). Specifically, they examined **reaction time,** the time elapsing between the presentation of a stimulus and the appearance of an overt response to it. Reaction time, they reasoned, would give us an idea of how long it takes for all the processes shown in Figure 8.2 to occur. In a typical reaction-time experiment, a person is asked to say a word or to push a button as rapidly as possible after a stimulus appears. Even in such simple situations, several factors influence reaction times (Wickens, Gordon, & Liu, 1998).

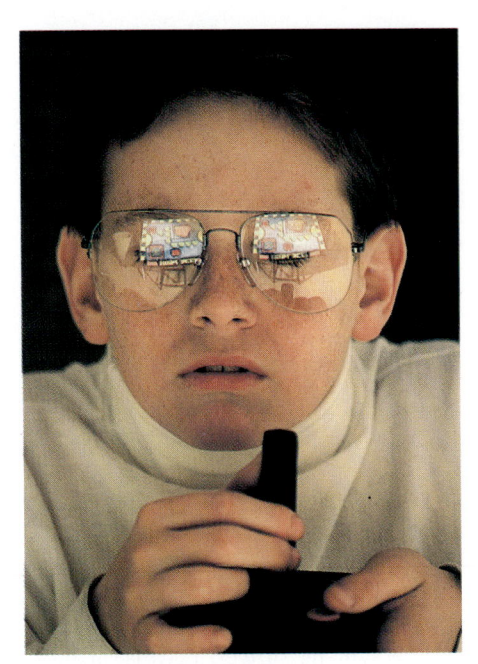

"Automatic" Thinking The sensory, perceptual, decision-making, and response-planning components that make up the circle of thought often occur so rapidly that we may be unaware of anything other than incoming information and our quick response to it. This is especially likely in skilled computer-game players, because as described in the chapter on perception, well-practiced tasks can be performed automatically.

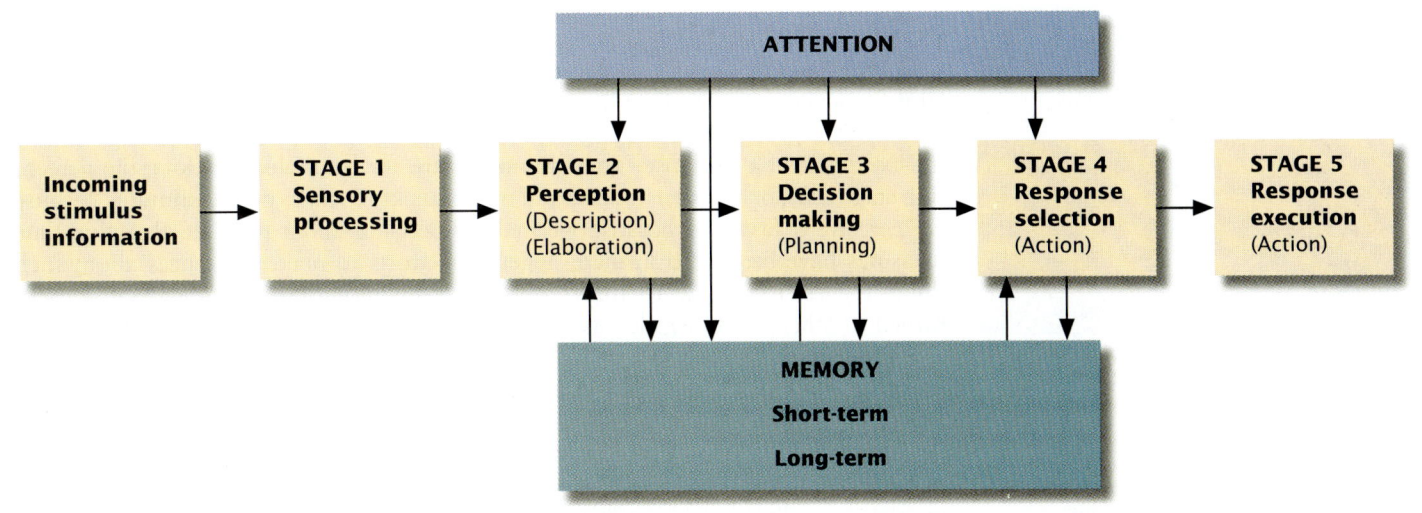

figure 8.2

An Information-Processing Model

According to the information-processing model, each stage in the circle of thought takes a certain amount of time. Some stages depend heavily on both short-term and long-term memory and require some attention—that limited supply of mental energy required for information processing to be carried out efficiently.

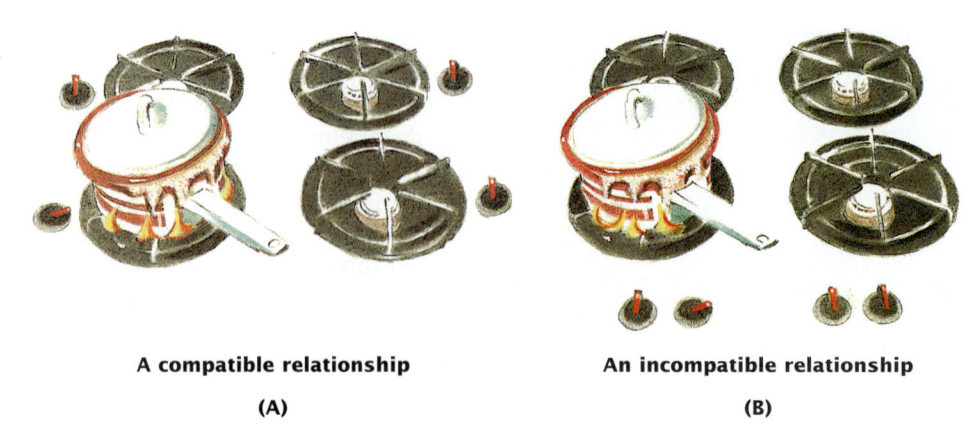

figure 8.3

Stimulus-Response Compatibility
Imagine standing in front of an unfamiliar stove when a pot starts to boil over. Your reaction time in turning down the heat will depend in part on the stove's design. The response you make will be quicker on the stove in Part A, because each knob is next to the burner it controls; there is compatibility between the source of the stimulus and the location of the response. The stove in Part B shows less compatibility; here, which knob you should turn is not as obvious, so your reaction time will be slower.

A compatible relationship
(A)

An incompatible relationship
(B)

One important factor in reaction time is the *complexity* of the decision. The larger the number of possible actions that might be carried out in response to a set of stimuli, the longer the reaction time. The tennis player who knows that her opponent usually serves to a particular spot on the court will have a simple decision to make when the serve is completed and will react rapidly. But if she faces an opponent whose serve is less predictable, her reaction will be slower, because a more complex decision about which way to move is now required.

Reaction time is also influenced by *stimulus-response compatibility*. If the relationship between a set of stimuli and possible responses is a natural or compatible one, reaction time will be fast. If not, reaction time will be slower. Figure 8.3 illustrates compatible and incompatible relationships. Incompatible stimulus-response relationships are major culprits in causing errors in the use of all kinds of equipment (Proctor & Van Zandt, 1994; Segal & Suri, 1999).

Expectancy, too, affects reaction time. People respond faster to stimuli that they expect to occur and more slowly to stimuli that surprise them. So your reaction time will be shorter when braking for a traffic light that you knew might turn red than when dodging a ball thrown at you unexpectedly.

Finally, in any reaction-time task there is a *speed-accuracy tradeoff*. If you try to respond quickly, errors increase; if you try for an error-free performance, reaction time increases (Wickens & Carswell, 1997). Sprinters who try too hard to anticipate the starting gun may have especially quick starts but may also have especially frequent false starts that disqualify them.

On Your Mark . . . The runner who reacts quickest when the starting gun is fired will have an advantage over other competitors, but too much eagerness can cause an athlete to literally jump the gun and lose the race before it starts. At the same time, too much concern over avoiding a false start can slow reaction time and cost precious time in getting off the mark. This is the speed-accuracy tradeoff in action.

Evoked Brain Potentials Research on reaction time has helped establish the time required for information processing to occur; it has also revealed how the entire sequence can be made faster or slower. But reaction times alone cannot provide a detailed picture of what goes on between the presentation of a stimulus and the execution of a response. They do not tell us, for example, how long the perception stage lasts, or whether we respond more quickly to an expected stimulus because we perceive it faster or because we make a decision about it faster. Reaction-time measures have been used in many ingenious efforts to make inferences about such things (Coles, 1989); but to analyze mental events more directly, psychologists have turned to other methods, such as the analysis of evoked brain potentials.

The **evoked brain potential** is a small, temporary change in voltage on an *electroencephalogram (EEG)* that occurs in response to specific events (Rugg & Coles, 1995). Figure 8.4 shows an example. Each peak reflects the firing of large groups of neurons, within different regions of the brain, at different times during the information-processing sequence. The pattern of the peaks provides information that is more precise than overall reaction time. For example, a large positive peak, called the P300, occurs 300 to 500 milliseconds after a stimulus is presented. The exact timing of the P300 depends in part on factors that affect the speed of perceptual processes, such as the difficulty of detecting a stimulus. But the timing of the P300 is not affected by factors—such as changes in stimulus-response compatibility—that merely alter the speed with which a response is selected and executed (Rugg & Coles, 1995; Siddle et al., 1991). Thus, the length of time before a P300 occurs may reflect the duration of the first two stages of information processing shown in Figure 8.2.

Neuroimaging Using positron emission tomography (PET), functional magnetic resonance imaging (fMRI), and other neuroimaging techniques described in the chapter on biological aspects of psychology, cognitive psychologists and other cognitive neuroscientists are finding ways to watch what happens in the brain during information processing (e.g., Miller & Cohen, 2001; Posner & DiGirolamo, 2001). In one study, for example, participants performed a task that required complex problem-solving skills. As shown by the red-shaded areas in Figure 8.5, the frontal lobe of the brain was especially active when this task was still relatively new and difficult. As the participants learned the skills, however, this frontal lobe involvement decreased. When the task was well learned, the hippocampus became especially active (see the green-shaded areas in the bottom panel of Figure 8.5). Activation in the hippocampus suggests that the participants were no longer struggling with a problem-solving task but instead were performing it from memory.

A number of other studies of brain activity during the performance of cognitive tasks have also found that the frontal lobes are especially important for problem solving and other cognitive tasks that place heavy demands on attention and working memory (Duncan & Owen, 2000; Wallis, Anderson, & Miller, 2001; this chapter's Focus on Research Methods shows another example). It is no wonder, then, that the damage Elliot suffered in the frontal area of his brain disrupted his decision-making abilities.

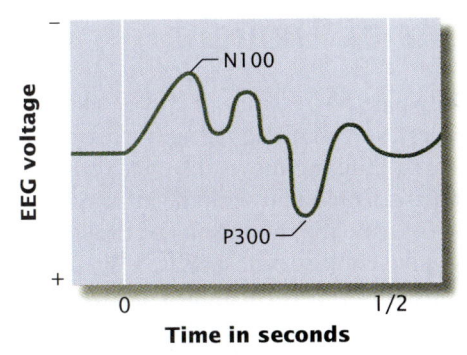

figure 8.4

Evoked Potentials

Here is the average EEG, or brain wave tracing, produced from several trials on which a participant's name was presented. Evoked potentials are averaged in this way so as to eliminate random variations in the tracings. The result is the appearance of a *negative* peak (N100) followed by a large *positive* peak (P300). Traditionally, positive peaks are shown as decreases on such tracings, whereas negative ones are shown as increases.

figure 8.5

Watching People Think

Cognitive psychologists can now actually watch information processing as it takes place in the brain. These fMRI pictures show activity in two "slices" of the brain of a research participant who was practicing a complex problem-solving task. The areas shown in red were activated early in the learning process; as skill developed, the areas shown in green became activated.

Source: Anderson (2000).

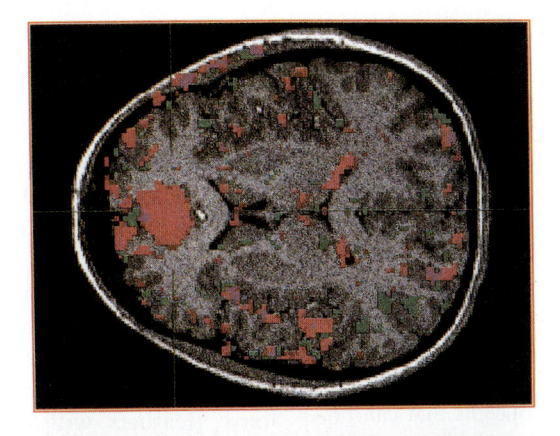

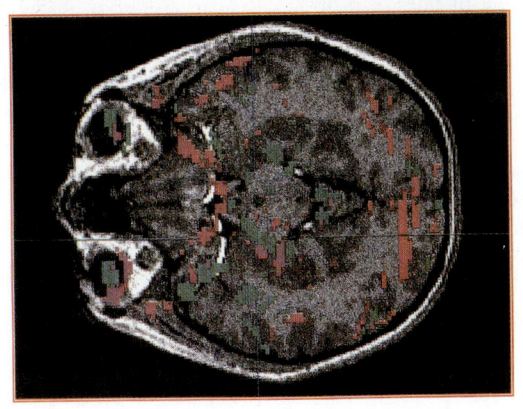

evoked brain potential A small, temporary change in EEG voltage that is evoked by some stimulus.

Mental Representations: The Ingredients of Thought

Just as measuring, stirring, and baking are only part of the story of cookie making, so timing, describing, and visualizing the processes of thinking tell only part of the story behind the circle of thought. To understand thinking more fully, we also need to know what it is that these processes manipulate. Consistent with the information-processing model, most psychologists usually describe the ingredients of thought as *information*. But this is like saying that you make cookies with "stuff." What specific forms does information take in our minds? In other words, how do we mentally represent information? Researchers in cognitive psychology have found that information can be mentally represented in many ways, including as *concepts, propositions, schemas, scripts, mental models, images,* and *cognitive maps.* Let's consider each of these ingredients of thought and how people manipulate them as they think.

Concepts

The most fundamental building blocks of thought are **concepts**, which are categories of objects, events, or ideas with common properties (Jahnke & Nowaczyk, 1998; Katz & Fodor, 1963). To "have a concept" is to recognize the properties, or *features,* that tend to be shared by the members of the category. For example, the concept "bird" includes such properties as having feathers, laying eggs, and being able to fly. The concept "scissors" includes such properties as having two blades, a connecting hinge, and a pair of hand holes. Concepts allow you to relate each object, event, or idea you encounter to a category you already know. Concepts also make it possible to think logically. If you have the concepts "whale" and "bird," you can decide whether a whale is bigger than a bird without having either creature in the room with you.

Some concepts—called **formal concepts**—can be clearly defined by a set of rules or properties such that each member of the concept has all of the defining properties, and no nonmember does. For example, the concept "square" can be defined as "a shape with four equal sides and four right-angle corners." Any object that does not have all of these features simply is not a square, and any object with all these features is a square. To study concept learning in the laboratory, psychologists often use formal concepts, because the members of the concept can be neatly defined (Trabasso & Bower, 1968).

TRY THIS — In contrast, try to define the concept "home" or "game." These are examples of **natural concepts**, concepts that have no fixed set of defining features but instead share a set of typical, or characteristic, features. Members of a natural concept need not have all of these characteristic features. One characteristic feature of the natural concept "bird," for example, is the ability to fly; but an ostrich is a bird even though it cannot fly, because it possesses enough other characteristic features of "bird" (feathers, wings, and the like). Having just one bird property is not enough; a snake lays eggs and a bat flies, but neither is a bird. It is usually a combination of properties that defines a concept. Outside the laboratory, most of the concepts people use in thinking are natural rather than formal concepts. Natural concepts include relatively concrete object categories, such as "bird" or "house"; abstract idea categories, such as "honesty" or "justice"; and temporary goal-related categories that help people make plans, such as "things I need to pack in my suitcase" (Barsalou, 1991, 1993).

The boundaries of a natural concept are fuzzy, and some members of it are better examples of the concept than others because they share more of its characteristic features (Rosch, 1975). A robin, a chicken, an ostrich, and a penguin are all birds. But a robin is a better example than the other three, because a robin can fly and is closer to the size and proportion of what most people, through experience,

concepts Categories of objects, events, or ideas that have common properties.
formal concepts Concepts that can be clearly defined by a set of rules or properties.
natural concepts Concepts that have no fixed set of defining features but instead share a set of characteristic features.
prototype A member of a natural concept that possesses all or most of its characteristic features.
propositions Mental representations of the relationship between concepts.
schemas Generalizations about categories of objects, places, events, and people.

A Natural Concept A space shuttle and a hot-air balloon are two examples of the natural concept "aircraft," but most people think of the space shuttle, with its wings, as the better example. A prototype of the concept is probably an airplane.

think of as a typical bird. A member of a natural concept that possesses all or most of its characteristic features is called a **prototype,** or is said to be *prototypical* (Smith, 1998). A robin, then, is a prototypical bird. The more prototypical a member of a concept is, the more quickly people can decide if it is an example of the concept. Thus, it takes less time to answer the question "Is a robin a bird?" than "Is a penguin is a bird?"

Propositions

We often combine concepts in units known as **propositions.** A proposition is a mental representation that expresses a relationship between concepts. Propositions can be true or false. Suppose you hear someone say that your friend Heather broke up with her boyfriend, Jason. Your mental representation of this event will include a proposition that links your concepts of "Heather" and "Jason" in a particular way. This proposition could be diagrammed (using unscientific terms) as follows: Heather—dumped→Jason.

The diagram looks like a sentence, but it is not. Propositions can be expressed as sentences, but they are actually general ideas that can be conveyed in any number of specific ways. In this case, "Jason was dumped by Heather" and "Heather is not dating Jason anymore" would all express the same proposition. If you later discover that it was Jason who caused the breakup, your proposition about the event would become the following: Heather←dumped—Jason. Propositions are part of the network of associations that many psychologists see as the basis for our knowledge of the world (see Figures 7.10 and 7.11 in the chapter on memory). So hearing the name Heather, for example, will activate lots of associated information about her, including the proposition about her relationship to Jason.

Schemas, Scripts, and Mental Models

Sets of propositions are often so closely associated that they form more complex mental representations called **schemas.** As described in the chapters on perception, memory, and human development, schemas are generalizations that we develop about categories of objects, places, events, and people. Our schemas help us to understand the world. If you borrow a friend's car, your "car" schema will give you

You Can't Judge a Book by Its Cover
Does this person look like a millionaire to you? Our schemas tell us what to expect about objects, events, and people, but those expectations can sometimes be wrong. This fact was dramatically illustrated in October 1999 when Gordon Elwood died. The Medford, Oregon, man, who dressed in rags and collected cans, left over $9 million to charity (McMahon, 2000).

a good idea of where to put the ignition key, where the accelerator and brake are, and how to raise and lower the windows. Schemas also generate expectations about objects, places, events, and people—telling us that stereo systems have speakers, that picnics occur in the summer, that rock concerts are loud, and so on.

Scripts Schemas about familiar activities, such as going to a restaurant, are known as **scripts** (Anderson, 2000). Your "restaurant" script represents the sequence of events you can expect when you go out to eat (see Figure 8.6). That script tells you what to do when you are in a restaurant and helps you to understand stories involving restaurants (Whitney, 2001). Scripts also shape your interpretation of events. For example, on your first day of college, you no doubt assumed that the person standing at the front of the class was a teacher, not a mugger.

If our scripts are violated, however, it is easy to misinterpret events. In 1993, a heart attack victim in London lay for nine hours in the hallway of an apartment building after an ambulance crew smelled alcohol on his breath and assumed he was "sleeping it off." The crew's script for what happens in the poorer sections of big cities told them that someone slumped in a hallway is drunk, not sick. Because script-violating events are unexpected, our reactions to them tend to be slower and less effective than are our reactions to expected events. Your "grocery shopping" script, for example, probably includes pushing a cart, putting items in it, going to the checkout stand, and paying for your purchases. But suppose you are at the back of the store when a robber near the entrance fires a gun and shouts at the manager to open the safe. People sometimes ignore these script-violating events, interpreting gunshots as a car backfiring and shouted orders as "someone fooling around." Others simply "freeze," unsure of what to do.

scripts Mental representations of familiar sequences of activity.
mental model A cluster of propositions representing our understanding of objects and processes that guides our interaction with those things.
images Mental representations of visual information.
cognitive map A mental representation of familiar parts of the environment.

Mental Models Sets of propositions can be organized not only as schemas and scripts but also as **mental models** (Johnson-Laird, 1983). For example, suppose someone tells you, "My living room has blue walls, a white ceiling, and an oval window across from the door." You will mentally represent this information as propositions about how the concepts "wall," "blue," "ceiling," "white," "door," "oval," and "window" are related. However, you will also combine these propositions to create in your mind a three-dimensional model of the room. As more infor-

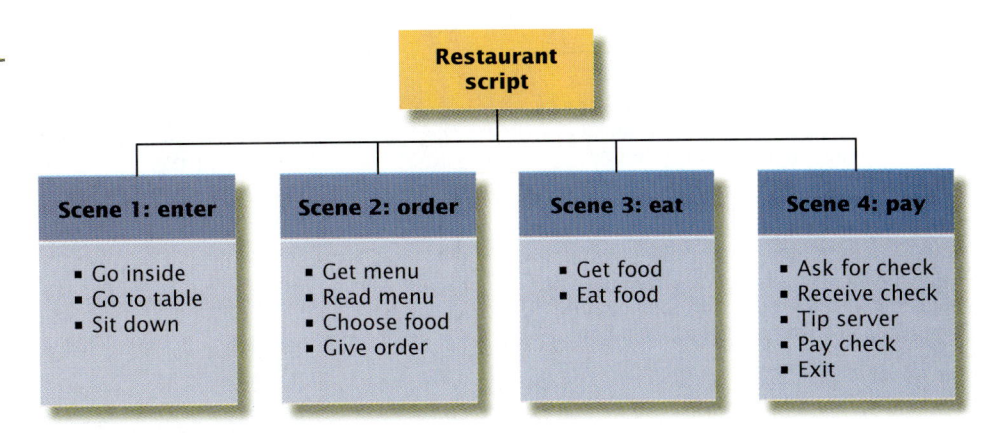

figure 8.6
Eating at a Restaurant

Schemas about what happens in restaurants and how to behave in them take the form of a *script*, represented here in four "scenes." Scripts guide our actions in all sorts of familiar situations and also help us to understand descriptions of events occurring in those situations (e.g., "Our service was really slow").

Source: Whitney (2001).

Restaurant script

Scene 1: enter
- Go inside
- Go to table
- Sit down

Scene 2: order
- Get menu
- Read menu
- Choose food
- Give order

Scene 3: eat
- Get food
- Eat food

Scene 4: pay
- Ask for check
- Receive check
- Tip server
- Pay check
- Exit

mation about the world becomes available, either from existing memories or from new information we receive, our mental models become more complete.

Accurate mental models are excellent guides for thinking about, and interacting with, many of the things we encounter (Galotti, 1999). If a mental model is incorrect, however, we are likely to make mistakes (see Figure 8.7). For example, people who hold an incorrect mental model of how physical illness is cured might stop taking an antibiotic when their symptoms begin to disappear, well before the bacteria causing those symptoms have been eliminated (Medin, Ross, & Markman, 2001). Others overdose on medication because according to their faulty mental model, "if taking three pills a day is good, taking six would be even better."

Images and Cognitive Maps

Think about how your best friend would look in a clown suit. The "mental picture" you just got illustrates that often, thinking involves the manipulation of **images**—which are mental representations of visual information. Cognitive psychologists refer to mental images as *analogical representations,* because we manipulate these images in a way that is similar, or *analogous* to, manipulating the objects themselves (Reed, 2000). This similarity was demonstrated in a classic study by Roger Shepard and Jacqueline Metzler (1971). They measured how long it took people to decide whether pairs of objects like those in Figure 8.8 were the same or different. They found that decision time depended on how far one object had to be "mentally rotated" to compare it with the other. The more rotation required, the longer the decision took. In other words, rotating the mental image of an object was like rotating the real object. More recent studies using neuroimaging have confirmed that manipulating mental images activates some of the same visual and spatial areas of the brain that are active during comparable tasks with real objects (Farah, 2000).

Our ability to think using images extends beyond the manipulation of stimuli like those in Figure 8.8. We also create mental images from written or spoken descriptions, as you probably did a minute ago when you read about that blue-walled room. The same thing happens when someone gives you directions to that new pizza place in town. In this case, you scan your **cognitive map**—a mental representation of familiar parts of your world—to find the location. In doing so, you use a mental process similar to the visual process of scanning a paper map (Anderson, 2000; Taylor & Tversky, 1992). Manipulating images on another cognitive map would help you if a power failure left your home pitch dark. Even though you couldn't see a thing, you could still find a flashlight or candle, because your cognitive map would show the floor plan, furniture placement, door locations, and other physical features of your home. You would not have this mental map in an unfamiliar house; there, you would have to walk slowly, arms outstretched, to avoid wrong turns and painful collisions. In the chapter on learning we describe how experience shapes cognitive maps that help animals navigate mazes and people navigate shopping malls.

figure 8.7
Applying a Mental Model

TRY THIS Try to imagine the path that the marble will follow when it leaves the curved tube. In one study, most people drew the incorrect (curved) path indicated by the dotted line rather than the correct (straight) path indicated by the dashed line (McClosky, 1983). Their error was based on a faulty mental model of the behavior of physical objects.

figure 8.8

Manipulating Images

TRY THIS Are these pairs of objects the same or different? To decide, you will have to rotate one member of each pair. Because manipulating mental images, like manipulating actual objects, takes some time, the speed of your decision will depend on how far you have to mentally rotate one object to line it up with the other for comparison. (The top pair matches; the bottom pair does not.)

Source: Shepard & Metzler (1971).

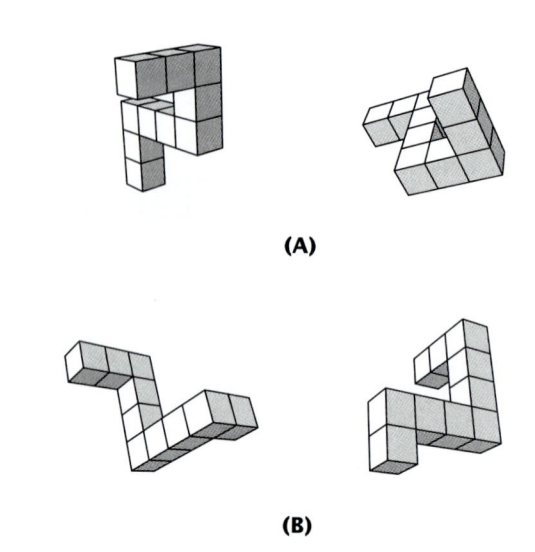

(A)

(B)

Thinking Strategies

We have seen that our thinking capacity is based largely on our ability to manipulate mental representations—the ingredients of thought—much as a baker manipulates the ingredients of cookies (see "In Review: Ingredients of Thought" for a summary of these representations). But whereas the baker's food-processing system combines and transforms flour, sugar, milk, eggs, and chocolate into a delicious treat, our information-processing system combines, transforms, and elaborates mental representations in ways that allow us to engage in reasoning, problem solving, and decision making. Let's begin our discussion of these thinking strategies by considering **reasoning,** the process through which we generate and evaluate arguments, as well as reach conclusions about them.

Formal Reasoning

Astronomers tell us that the temperature at the core of the sun is about 27 million degrees Fahrenheit. They can't put a temperature probe inside the sun, so how can they be so confident about this assertion? Their estimate is based on *inferences* from other things that they know about the sun and about physical objects in general. Telescopic observations of the sun's volume and mass allowed astronomers to calculate its density, using the formula Density = Mass ÷ Volume. These observations also enabled them to measure the energy coming from one small region of the sun and—using what geometry told them about the surface area of spheres—to estimate the energy output from the sun as a whole. Further calculations told them how hot a body would have to be to generate that much energy.

In short, the astronomers' highly educated guess about the sun's core temperature was based on **formal reasoning** (also called *logical reasoning*), the process of following a set of rigorous procedures to reach valid, or correct, conclusions. Some of these procedures included the application of specific mathematical formulas to existing data in order to generate new data. Such formulas are examples of **algorithms,** systematic methods that always produce a correct solution to a problem, if a solution exists (Jahnke & Nowaczyk, 1998). The astronomers also followed the **rules of logic,** sets of statements that provide a formula for drawing valid conclusions about the world. For example, each step in the astronomers' thinking took the form of "if-then" statements: If we know how much energy comes from one part of the sun's surface, and if we know how big the whole surface is, then we can calculate the total energy output. You use the same formal reasoning processes when you conclude, for example, that if your friend José is two years older than you are, then

---

reasoning The process by which people generate and evaluate arguments and reach conclusions about them.

formal reasoning The process of following a set of rigorous procedures for reaching valid conclusions.

algorithms Systematic procedures that cannot fail to produce a correct solution to a problem, if a solution exists.

rules of logic Sets of statements that provide a formula for drawing valid conclusions.

in review: Ingredients of Thought

Ingredient	Description	Examples
Concepts	Categories of objects, events, or ideas, with common properties; basic building blocks of thought	"Square" (a formal concept); "game" (a natural concept).
Propositions	Mental representations that express relationships between concepts; can be true or false	Assertions such as "The cow jumped over the the moon."
Schemas	Sets of propositions that create generalizations and expectations about categories of objects, places, events, and people	A schema might suggest that all grandmothers are elderly, gray haired, and bake a lot of cookies.
Scripts	Schemas about familiar activities and situations; guide behavior in those situations	You pay before eating in fast-food restaurants and after eating in fancier restaurants.
Mental models	Sets of propositions about how things relate to each other in the real world; can be correct or incorrect	Assuming that airflow around an open car will send thrown objects upward, a driver tosses a lighted cigarette butt overhead, causing it to land in the back seat.
Images	Mental representations of visual information	Hearing a description of your blind date creates a mental picture of him or her.
Cognitive maps	Mental representations of familiar parts of the world	You can get to class by an alternate route even if your usual route is blocked by construction.

his twin brother, Juan, will be two years older, too. This kind of reasoning is called *deductive* because it takes a general rule (e.g., twins are the same age) and applies it to deduce conclusions about specific cases (e.g., José and Juan).

The rules of logic, which are traceable to the Greek philosopher Aristotle, have evolved into a system for drawing correct conclusions from a set of statements known as *premises*. Consider, for example, what conclusion can be drawn from the following premises:

Premise 1: People who study hard do well in this course.

Premise 2: You have studied hard.

According to the rules of logic, it would be valid to conclude that you will do well in this course. Logical arguments containing two or more premises and a conclusion are known as **syllogisms** (pronounced "SILL-o-jisms"). Notice that the conclusion in a syllogism goes beyond what the premises actually say. The conclusion is an inference based on the premises and on the rules of logic. In this case, the logical rule was that if something is true of all members of a category, and A is in that category, then that something will also be true of A.

Most of us try to use formal reasoning to reach valid conclusions and avoid false ones (Rips, 1994), but we have to watch out for two pitfalls: incorrect premises and violations of the rules of logic. Consider this example:

Premise 1: All psychologists are brilliant.

Premise 2: The authors of this book are psychologists.

Conclusion: The authors of this book are brilliant.

syllogisms Arguments made up of two or more propositions, called *premises*, and a conclusion based on those premises.

Do you agree? The conclusion follows logically from the premises, but because the first premise is false, we cannot determine whether or not the conclusion is true. Now consider this syllogism:

Premise 1: All gun owners are people.

Premise 2: All criminals are people.

Conclusion: All gun owners are criminals.

Here, the premises are correct, but the logic is faulty. If *all As are B* and *all Cs are B*, it does not follow that *all As are C*. In other words, even conclusions based on correct premises can be false if they do not follow the rules of logic.

Psychologists have discovered that both kinds of pitfalls lead people to make errors in formal reasoning, which is one reason why misleading advertisements or speeches can still attract sales and votes (Cialdini, 2001). At least two related factors can also promote errors in logical reasoning (Ashcraft, 2002):

1. *Bias about conclusions.* Consider this syllogism: *The United States is a free country. In a free country all people have equal opportunity. Therefore, in the United States all people have equal opportunity.* People who agree with this conclusion often do so not because they have carefully considered the premises but because they hold a prior belief about it. This example illustrates **confirmation bias,** the tendency to seek evidence and reach conclusions that confirm existing beliefs. Confirmation bias can affect thinking in many situations. When people first fall in love, they often focus only on their loved one's best qualities and ignore evidence of less desirable ones. In the courtroom, jurors may pay little attention to evidence of a defendant's guilt if that defendant is, say, a beloved celebrity or a harmless-looking senior citizen. In such cases, prosecutors' logical arguments based on true premises may not lead to conviction, because the logical conclusion ("guilty") does not match jurors' beliefs about celebrities, the elderly, or some other favored group. Similarly, if jurors believe the defendant represents a category of people who tend to commit crimes, they may not be swayed much by evidence suggesting innocence. In other words, the conclusions that people reach are often based on both logical and wishful thinking (Evans et al., 1999).

2. *Limits on working memory. Some As are B. All Bs are C. Therefore, some As are C.* Do you agree? This syllogism is correct, but evaluating it requires you to hold a lot of material in short-term memory while mentally manipulating it. This task is particularly difficult if elements in a syllogism involve negatives, as in *No dogs are nonanimals.* If the amount of material to be mentally manipulated exceeds the capacity of short-term memory (see the chapter on memory), logical errors can easily result.

Informal Reasoning

The use of algorithms and logic to discover new facts and draw inferences is only one kind of reasoning. A second kind, **informal reasoning,** comes into play in situations where we are trying to assess the *believability* of a conclusion based on the evidence available to support it. Informal reasoning is also known as *inductive reasoning,* because its goal is to induce a general conclusion to appear on the basis of specific facts or examples. Psychologists use this kind of reasoning when they design experiments and other research methods whose results will provide evidence for (or against) a theory; jurors use informal reasoning when weighing evidence for the guilt or innocence of a defendant.

Formal reasoning is guided by algorithms and the rules of logic, but there are no foolproof methods for informal reasoning. Consider, for example, how many white swans you would have to see before concluding that all swans were white.

---

confirmation bias The tendency to pay more attention to evidence in support of one's beliefs than to evidence that refutes them.

informal reasoning The process of evaluating a conclusion, theory, or course of action on the basis of the believability of evidence.

heuristics Time-saving mental shortcuts used in reasoning.

anchoring heuristic A mental shortcut that involves basing judgments on existing information.

Pitfalls in Logical Reasoning *Elderly people cannot be astronauts. This is an elderly man. Therefore, he cannot be an astronaut.* The logic of this syllogism is correct, but because the first premise is wrong, so is the conclusion. John Glenn, the astronaut who in 1962 became the first American to orbit the earth, returned to space in 1998 at the age of seventy-seven as a full-fledged member of the crew of the space shuttle *Discovery*.

Fifty? A hundred? A million? A strictly formal, algorithmic approach would require that you observe every swan in existence to be sure they are all white, but such a task would be impossible. A more practical approach is to base your conclusion on the number of observations that you *believe* is "enough." In other words, you would take a mental "shortcut" to reach a conclusion that is probably, but not necessarily, correct (there are, in fact, black swans). Such mental shortcuts are called **heuristics** (pronounced "hyoor-IST-ix").

Suppose you are about to leave home but cannot find your watch. Applying an algorithm would mean searching in every possible location, room by room, until you find the watch. But you can reach the same outcome more quickly by using a heuristic—that is, by searching only where your experience suggests you might have left the watch. In short, heuristics are often valuable in guiding judgments about which events are probable or which hypotheses are likely to be true. They are easy to use and frequently work well (Gigerenzer et al., 2000).

However, heuristics can also bias cognitive processes and result in errors. For example, if a heuristic leads you to vote for all the candidates in a particular political party instead of researching the views of each candidate, you might help elect someone with whom you strongly disagree on some issues. The degree to which heuristics are responsible for important errors in judgment and decision making is a matter of continuing research and debate by cognitive psychologists (Medin & Bazerman, 1999; Mellers, Schwartz, & Cooke, 1998). Amos Tversky and Daniel Kahneman (1974, 1993) have described three potentially problematic heuristics that people seem to use intuitively in making judgments. We discuss these heuristics in the following sections.

The Anchoring Heuristic

People use the **anchoring heuristic** when they estimate the probability of an event not by starting from scratch but by adjusting an earlier estimate (Rottenstreich & Tversky, 1997). This strategy sounds reasonable,

Formal reasoning follows the rules of logic, but there are no foolproof rules for informal reasoning, as this fool demonstrates.

DILBERT reprinted by permission of United Feature Syndicates, Inc.

but the starting value biases the final estimate. Once people have fixed a starting point, their adjustments of the initial judgment tend to be too small. It is as if they drop a "mental anchor" at one hypothesis or estimate and then are reluctant to move very far from that original judgment. For example, if you thought that the probability of being mugged in Los Angeles is 90 percent and then heard evidence that the figure was closer to 1 percent, you might reduce your estimate, but only to 80 percent, so your judgment would still be way off. The anchoring heuristic presents a challenge for defense attorneys in U.S. courtrooms because once jurors have been affected by the prosecution's evidence (which is presented first), it may be difficult to alter their belief in a defendant's guilt or in the amount of money the defendant should have to pay (Greene & Loftus, 1998; Hogarth & Einhorn, 1992). Similarly, our first impressions of people are not easily shifted by later evidence.

The Representativeness Heuristic Using the **representativeness heuristic**, people decide whether an example belongs in a certain class on the basis of how similar it is to other items in that class. For example, suppose you encounter a man who is tidy, small in stature, wears glasses, speaks quietly, and is somewhat shy. If asked whether this person is more likely to be a librarian or a farmer, what would you say? Tversky and Kahneman (1974) found that most of their research participants chose *librarian*. The chances are that this answer would be wrong, though. Why? Because of differences in the *base rates,* or commonness, of the two occupations. True, the description is more similar to the prototypical librarian than to the prototypical farmer, but because there are many more farmers in the world than librarians, there are probably more farmers than librarians who match this description. Therefore, a man matching this description is more likely to be a farmer than a librarian. In fact, almost any set of physical features is more likely to belong to a farmer than to a librarian.

Another study found that jurors' decisions to convict or acquit a defendant may depend partly on the degree to which the defendant's actions were representative of a crime category. For example, someone who abducts a child and asks for ransom (actions that clearly fit the crime category of "kidnapping") is more likely to be convicted than someone who abducts an adult and demands no ransom—even though both crimes constitute kidnapping, and the evidence is equally strong in each case (Smith, 1991).

The Availability Heuristic Even when people use probability information to help them judge group membership or to assess a hypothesis, a third heuristic can bias their thinking. The **availability heuristic** involves judging the probability that an event may occur or that a hypothesis may be true by how easily the hypothesis or examples of the event can be brought to mind (Reed, 2000). People tend to choose the hypothesis or alternative that is most mentally "available" to them, much as you might choose which T-shirt to wear on the basis of which one is on top in the drawer.

Like other heuristics, this shortcut tends to work well. After all, what people remember most easily are frequent events or likely hypotheses. However, the availability heuristic can lead to biased judgments, especially when mental availability does not reflect actual frequency. For example, television news reports showing the grisly aftermath of urban shootings and train wrecks may make these relatively rare events so memorable that some people avoid certain cities or avoid train travel because they overestimate the frequency of crime or the probability of a crash (Carmody, 1998; Slovic, 1984).

The heuristics we have discussed represent only three of the many mental shortcuts that people use, and they describe only some of the biases and limitations that affect human reasoning (Hogarth & Einhorn, 1992). Some other biases and limitations are described in the following sections as we consider two important goals of thinking: problem solving and decision making.

---

representativeness heuristic A mental shortcut that involves judging whether something belongs in a given class on the basis of its similarity to other members of that class.

availability heuristic A mental shortcut through which judgments are based on information that is most easily brought to mind.

Problem Solving

If where you are is not where you want to be, and when the path to getting there is not obvious, you have a *problem*. As suggested by the circle of thought, the most efficient approach to problem solving would be first to diagnose the problem in the elaboration stage, then to formulate a plan for solving it, then to execute the plan, and finally to evaluate the results to determine whether the problem remains (Bransford & Stein, 1993). But people's problem-solving efforts are not always so systematic, which is one reason why medical tests are sometimes given unnecessarily, diseases are sometimes misdiagnosed, and auto parts are sometimes replaced when there is nothing wrong with them.

Strategies for Problem Solving

When you are trying to get from a starting point to some goal, the best path may not necessarily be a straight line. In fact, obstacles may dictate going in the opposite direction. So it is with problem solving. Sometimes, the best strategy is not to take mental steps aimed straight at your goal. For example, when a problem is especially difficult, it can sometimes be helpful to allow it to "incubate" by setting it aside for a while. A solution that once seemed out of reach may suddenly appear after you think about other things for a time. The benefits of incubation probably arise from forgetting incorrect ideas that may have been blocking the path to a correct solution (Anderson, 2000). Psychologists have identified several other useful problem-solving strategies.

Means-End Analysis

One of the most generally applicable of these strategies is called *means-end analysis*. It involves continuously asking where you are in relation to your final goal, and then deciding on the means by which you can get one step closer to the end that you desire (Newell & Simon, 1972). In other words, rather than trying to solve the problem all at once, you identify a subgoal that will take you toward a solution (this process is also referred to as *decomposition*). After reaching that subgoal, you identify another one that will get you even closer to the solution, and you continue this step-by-step process until the problem is solved. Some students apply this approach to the problem of writing a major term paper. The task might seem overwhelming at first, but their first subgoal is simply to write an outline of what they think the paper should cover. When the outline is complete, they decide whether a paper based on it will satisfy the assignment. If so, the next subgoal might be to search the library and the Internet for information about each section. If they decide that this information is adequate, the next subgoal would be to write a rough draft of the introduction, and so on.

Working Backward

A second problem-solving strategy is to *work backward*. Many problems are like a tree. The trunk is the information you are given;

Simply knowing about problem-solving strategies, such as means-end analysis, is not enough. As described in the chapter on motivation and emotion, people must perceive the effort involved to be worth the rewards it is likely to bring.

CALVIN AND HOBBES © 1993 Watterson. Reprinted by permission of UNIVERSAL PRESS SYNDICATE. All rights reserved.

Working Backward to Forge Ahead
Whether you are organizing a family vacation or, as Ellen MacArthur did recently, sailing alone in an around-the-world race, working backward from the final goal through all the steps necessary to reach that goal is a helpful approach to solving complex problems.

the solution is a twig on one of the limbs. If you work forward by taking the "givens" of the problem and trying to find the solution, it will be easy to branch off in the wrong direction. A more efficient approach may be to start at the twig end and work backward toward your goal (Galotti, 1999). Consider, for example, the problem of planning a climb to the summit of Mount Everest. The best strategy is to figure out, first, what equipment and supplies are needed at the highest camp on the night before the summit attempt, then how many people are needed to stock that camp the day before, then how many people are needed to supply those who must stock the camp, and so on until a plan for the entire expedition is established. It is easy to overlook the working-backward strategy, however, because it runs counter to the way we have learned to think. It is hard to imagine that the first step in solving a problem could be to assume that you have already solved it. Unfortunately, six climbers died on Mount Everest in 1996 in part because of failure to apply this strategy (Krakauer, 1997).

Using Analogies   A third problem-solving strategy is trying to find *analogies*, or similarities between today's problem and others you have encountered before. A supervisor may find, for example, that a seemingly hopeless problem between co-workers may be resolved by the same compromise that worked during a recent family squabble. To take advantage of analogies, we must first recognize the similarities between current and previous problems and then recall the solution that worked before. Although it may be surprising, most people are not very good at drawing analogies from one problem to another (Anderson, 2000). They tend to concentrate on the surface features that make problems appear different.

FOCUS ON RESEARCH METHODS

Locating Analogical Thinking

The value of using analogies in problem solving was beautifully illustrated after the Hubble Space Telescope was placed in orbit around the Earth in 1990. It was designed to take detailed photographs of distant galaxies, but because its main mirror was not focusing light properly, the pictures were blurry. Then NASA engineer James Crocker happened to notice the way a hotel room showerhead pivoted, and it gave him the idea for a system of movable mirrors to correct for the

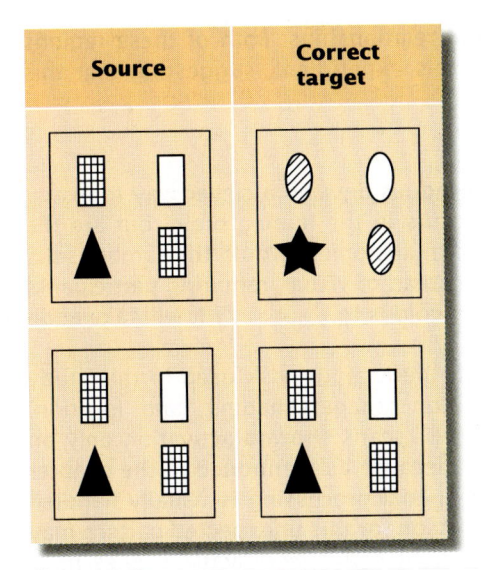

figure 8.9

Comparing Stimulus Patterns

The top row shows examples of the stimulus patterns that were compared in an analogy task. Participants had to say whether the pattern on the right is similar, or *analogous*, to the one on the left. (In this case it is, because even though the specific shapes used in one pattern differ from those in the other pattern, their shading and physical arrangement are similar.) The bottom row shows examples of the patterns that were compared in a "same-different" task. Here, participants were asked only to decide whether the two patterns are exactly the same (Wharton et al., 2000).

flaw in the Hubble's mirror. When shuttle astronauts installed these mirrors in 1993, the problem was solved (Stein, 1993).

- **What was the researchers' question?**

Charles Wharton and his colleagues wanted to know what goes on in the brain when people do this kind of *analogical mapping*—recognizing similarities between things that appear to be different and even unrelated (Wharton et al., 2000).

- **How did the researchers answer the question?**

The researchers knew that PET scan technology could show brain activity while participants performed an analogy task, but how could the researchers separate the activity associated with analogical mapping from everything else going on in the brain at the same time? Their answer was to use a *subtraction technique*. They asked people to perform two tasks—one after the other—that involved making comparisons between patterns of rectangles, ovals, triangles, and other shapes. Both tasks placed similar demands on the brain, but only one of them required the participants to *make analogies* between the patterns (see Figure 8.9). The researchers then compared the resulting PET scans, looking for areas of the brain that were active in the analogy task but not in the other one. What their computers did, in essence, was to take all brain activity that occurred during the analogy task and "subtract" from it all the activity that occurred during the other task. The activity remaining was presumed to reflect analogical mapping.

- **What did the researchers find?**

As you can see in Figure 8.10, the brain areas uniquely activated during the analogy task were in the left hemisphere, particularly in the frontal and parietal areas. Other neuroimaging studies have shown activation of similar areas during abstract problem solving and reasoning (e.g., Osherson et al., 1998).

- **What do the results mean?**

These results show that it is possible to locate specific brain activities associated with a specific kind of cognitive activity. They also fit well into what we already know about where certain brain functions are localized. As mentioned earlier, the frontal areas of the brain are involved in complex processing tasks, including those requiring coordination of information in working memory with information coming from the senses. There is also evidence that parietal areas are involved in our

figure 8.10

Brain Activity During Analogical Mapping

Comparing PET scans of brain activity during an analogy task and a task not requiring analogical thinking revealed that making analogies appears to involve areas of the left frontal and parietal lobes, as seen here from below and highlighted in red.

Source: Wharton et al. (2000).

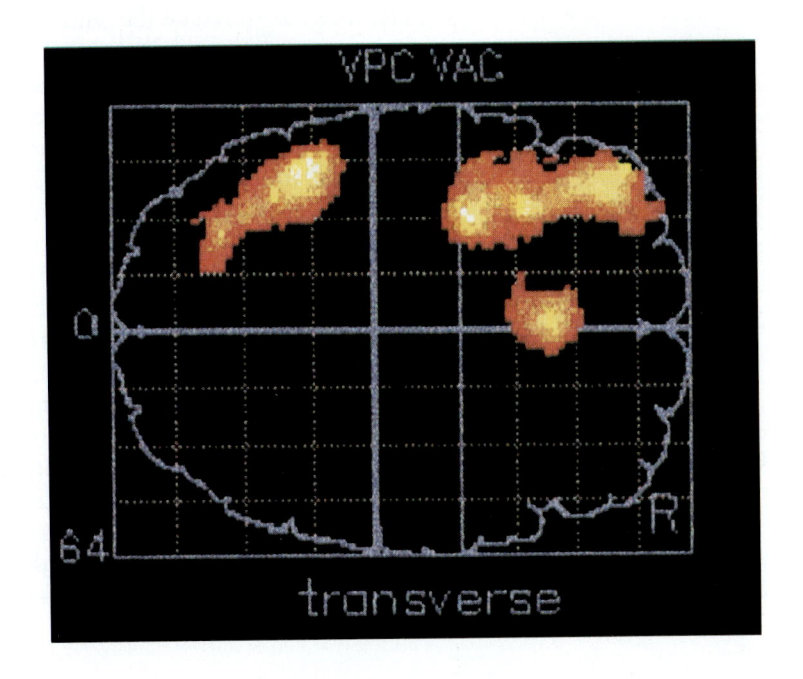

ability to perceive spatial arrangements and relationships. Both of these regions were activated during the analogy task in this experiment, suggesting that this task required both kinds of abilities.

● **What do we still need to know?**

There is no doubt that Wharton and his colleagues devised a clever way to examine the analogical mapping process as it occurs in the human brain, but are the brain areas identified the only ones involved in analogies? Would the same results appear if the analogy task had been verbal instead of visual, requiring participants to make analogies such as "Dark is to light as cold is to _____"? It will take additional research to answer this question.

Consider also the fact that even though the analogy task used in this study involved processing visual-spatial information (shape, shading, and location) rather than verbal information (words), the PET scans showed activation only on the left side of the brain. This is surprising, because as mentioned in the chapter on biological aspects of psychology, visual-spatial processing is usually handled mainly in the brain's right hemisphere. One reason for this unexpected pattern may be that, as noted in that same chapter, the right hemisphere actually does have some verbal processing abilities. However, the results also warn us to be careful about misinterpreting PET scan activity. Increased activity in a particular brain region doesn't always mean that the region is performing the processing we are trying to locate. The activity observed might also result if the area were being suppressed so as not to interfere with processing going on elsewhere. The study of brain activity during higher-level thinking is still quite new, so it will take some time, and a lot more research, to learn how to correctly interpret the data coming from neuroimaging techniques.

Obstacles to Problem Solving

Failing to use analogies is just one example of the obstacles that face problem solvers every day. Difficulties frequently occur at the start, during the diagnosis stage, when a person forms and then tests hypotheses about a problem.

As a case in point, consider this true story: In September 1998, John Gatiss was in the kitchen of his rented house in Cheltenham, England, when he heard a faint meowing sound. He could not find the source of the sound, but he assumed that a kitten had become trapped in the walls or under the flooring, so he called for the fire brigade to rescue the animal. The sound seemed to be coming from the electric oven, so the rescuers dismantled it, disconnecting the power cord in the process. The sound stopped, but everyone assumed that wherever the kitten was, it had become too frightened to meow. The search was reluctantly abandoned, and the oven was reconnected. Four days later, though, the meowing began anew. This time, Gatiss and his landlord called the Royal Society for the Prevention of Cruelty to Animals (RSPCA), whose inspectors heard the kitten in distress and asked the fire brigade to return. They spent the next three days searching for the cat. First, they dismantled parts of the kitchen walls and ripped up the floorboards. Next, they called in plumbing and drainage specialists, who used cables tipped with fiber-optic cameras to search remote cavities where a kitten might hide. Rescuers then brought in a disaster search team, which tried to find the kitten using acoustic and ultrasonic equipment designed to locate victims trapped in the debris of earthquakes and explosions. Not a sound could be heard. Increasingly concerned about how much longer the kitten could survive, the fire brigade tried to coax it from hiding with the finest-quality fish, but to no avail. Suddenly, there was a burst of "purring," which to everyone's surprise (and the landlord's dismay), the ultrasonic equipment traced to the clock in the electric oven! Later, the landlord commented that everyone had assumed that Gatiss's hypothesis was correct—that the meowing sound came from a cat trapped

figure 8.11

The Luchins Jar Problem

TRY THIS The problem is to obtain the quantities of liquid shown in the first column by using jars with the capacities shown in the next three columns. Each line represents a different problem. See if you can solve the first six problems without looking at the answer in the text; then try the last one. In dealing with such problems, people often fall prey to mental sets that prevent them from using the most efficient solution.

Quantity	Jar A	Jar B	Jar C
1. 21 quarts	8	35	3
2. 10 quarts	6	18	1
3. 19 quarts	5	32	4
4. 21 quarts	20	57	8
5. 18 quarts	8	40	7
6. 6 quarts	7	17	2
7. 15 quarts	12	33	3

Problem: Measure out the quantities listed in the first column using jars with the stated capacities (in quarts).

somewhere in the kitchen. "I just let them carry on. If there is an animal in there, you have to do what it takes. The funniest thing was that it seemed to reply when we called out to it" (*London Daily Telegraph,* September 19, 1998).

How could fifteen fire-rescue workers, three RSPCA inspectors, four drainage workers, and two acoustics experts waste eight days and cause nearly $2,000 in damage to a house in pursuit of a nonexistent kitten? The answer lies in the fact that they, like the rest of us, are prone to four main obstacles to efficient problem solving, described in the following sections.

Multiple Hypotheses Often, people begin to solve a problem with only a vague notion of which hypotheses to test. Suppose you heard a strange sound in your kitchen. It could be caused by several things, but which hypotheses should you test, and in what order?

People have a difficult time considering more than two or three hypotheses at a time (Mehle, 1982). The limited capacity of short-term memory may be part of the reason. As discussed in the chapter on memory, we can hold only about seven chunks of information in short-term memory; because a single hypothesis, let alone two or three, might include many more than seven chunks, it might be difficult or impossible to keep them all in mind at once. As a result, the correct hypothesis is often neglected. Which hypothesis a person considers may depend on the availability heuristic. In other words, the particular hypothesis considered may be the one that most easily comes to mind, not the one most likely to be correct (Tversky & Kahneman, 1974). Thus, Gatiss diagnosed the sound he heard as a kitten, not a clock, because such sounds usually come from kittens, not clocks.

Mental Sets Sometimes people are so blinded by one hypothesis or strategy that they continue to apply it even when better alternatives should be obvious (a clear case of the anchoring heuristic at work). Once Gatiss reported hearing a "trapped kitten," his description created an assumption that everyone else accepted and no one challenged.

A laboratory example of this phenomenon devised by Abraham Luchins (1942) is shown in Figure 8.11. The object of each problem in the figure is to use three jars with specified capacities to obtain a certain amount of liquid. For example, in the first problem you are to obtain 21 quarts by using 3 jars that have capacities of 8, 35, and 3 quarts, respectively. The solution is to fill Jar B to its capacity, 35 quarts, and then use its contents to fill Jar A to its capacity of 8 quarts, leaving 27 quarts in Jar B. Then pour liquid from Jar B to fill Jar C to its capacity twice, leaving

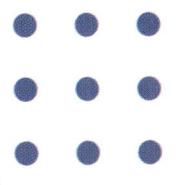

figure 8.12

The Nine-Dot Problem

TRY THIS The problem is to draw no more than four straight lines that run through all nine dots on the page without lifting your pencil from the paper. Figure 8.14 shows two ways of going beyond mental constraints to solve this problem.

TRY THIS

21 quarts in Jar B [27 − (2 × 3) = 21]. In other words, the general solution is B − A − 2C. Now solve the remaining problems before reading further.

If you solved all the problems in Figure 8.11, you found that a similar solution worked each time. By the time you reached Problem 7, you had probably developed a **mental set,** a tendency for old patterns of problem solving to persist (Sweller & Gee, 1978). That mental set may have caused you to use the same solution formula (B − A − 2C) for Problem 7 even though a simpler one (A + C) would have worked just as well. Figures 8.12 and 8.14 show that a mental set can also restrict your perception of the problem itself.

Another restriction on problem solving may come from experience with objects. Once people are accustomed to using an object for one purpose, they may be blinded to its other possible functions. Long experience may produce **functional fixedness,** a tendency to use familiar objects in familiar rather than creative ways. Figure 8.13 illustrates an example. An incubation strategy often helps to break mental sets.

Confirmation Bias

Anyone who has had a series of medical tests knows that diagnosis is not a one-shot decision. Instead, physicians choose their first hypothesis on the basis of observed symptoms and then order tests or evaluate additional symptoms to confirm or refute that hypothesis (Trillin, 2001). This process can be distorted by the *confirmation bias* mentioned earlier: Humans have a strong bias to confirm rather than to refute the hypothesis they have chosen, even in the face of strong evidence against it (Aronson, Wilson, & Akert, 1999; Groopman, 2000). Confirmation bias can be seen as a form of the anchoring heuristic, in that it involves "anchoring" to an initial hypothesis and being unwilling to abandon it. The would-be rescuers of the "trapped kitten" were so intent on their efforts to pinpoint its location that they never stopped to question its existence.

Ignoring Negative Evidence

On September 26, 1983, Soviet Lt. Col. Stanislav Petrov was in command of a facility that analyzed information from his country's early-warning satellites. Suddenly, alarms went off as computers detected evidence of five U.S. missiles being launched toward the Soviet Union. There was great tension between the two countries at the time, so based on the availability heuristic, Petrov hypothesized that a nuclear attack was under way. He was about

figure 8. 13

An Example of Functional Fixedness

TRY THIS Before reading further, consider how you would fasten together two strings that are hanging from the ceiling but are out of reach of each other. Several tools are available, yet most people do not think of attaching, say, the pliers to one string and swinging it like a pendulum until it can be reached while holding the other string. This solution is not obvious because we tend to fixate on the function of pliers as a tool rather than as a weight. People are more likely to solve this problem if the tools are scattered around the room. When the pliers are in a toolbox, their function as a tool is emphasized, and functional fixedness becomes nearly impossible to break.

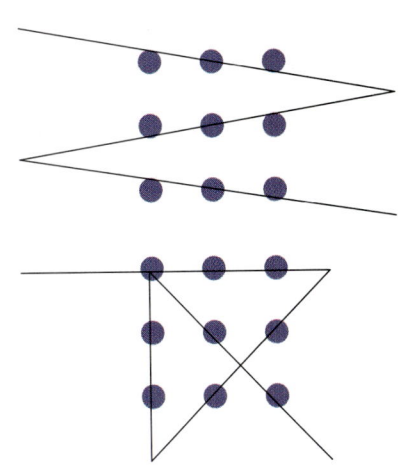

figure 8.14

Two Creative Solutions to the Nine-Dot Problem

Many people find puzzles like this difficult because their mental sets create artificial constraints on the range of solutions. In this case, the mental sets involve the tendency to draw within the frame of the dots and the tendency to draw through the middle of each dot. As shown here, however, there are other possibilities.

mental set The tendency for old patterns of problem solving to persist, even when they might not always be the most efficient alternative.

functional fixedness A tendency to think about familiar objects in familiar ways that may prevent using them in other ways.

to alert his superiors to launch a counterattack on the United States when it occurred to him that if this were a real nuclear attack, there should be evidence of many more than five missiles. Fortunately for everyone, he realized that the "attack" was a false alarm (Hoffman, 1999). As this near-disaster shows, the absence of symptoms or events can sometimes provide important evidence for or against a hypothesis. Compared with evidence that is present, however, symptoms or events that do not occur are less likely to be noticed (Hunt & Rouse, 1981).

People have a difficult time using the absence of evidence to help eliminate hypotheses from consideration (Ashcraft, 1989). In the "trapped kitten" case, when the "meowing" stopped for several days after the stove was reconnected, rescuers assumed that the animal was frightened into silence. They ignored the possibility that their hypothesis was incorrect in the first place.

Building Problem-Solving Skills

Some psychologists suggest that it should be possible to train people to avoid the biases that impair problem solving, and their efforts to do so have produced some modest benefits. In one study, cautioning people against their tendency to anchor on a hypothesis reduced the magnitude of confirmation bias and increased participants' openness to alternative evidence (Lopes, 1982).

How do experts avoid obstacles to problem solving? What do they bring to a situation that a beginner does not? Knowledge based on experience is particularly important (Mayer, 1992). Experts frequently proceed by looking for analogies between current and past problems. Compared with beginners, they are better able to relate new information and new experiences to past experiences and existing knowledge (Anderson, 1995b; Bedard & Chi, 1992). Accordingly, experts can use existing knowledge to organize new information into chunks, a process described in the chapter on memory. By chunking many elements of a problem into a smaller number of units, experts apparently can visualize problems more clearly and efficiently than beginners (Reingold et al., 2001).

Experts can use their experience as a guide because they tend to perceive the similarity between new and old problems more deeply than beginners (Hardimann, Dufresne, & Mestre, 1989). Specifically, experts see the similarity of underlying principles, whereas beginners perceive similarity only in surface features. As a result, experts can more quickly and easily apply these principles to solve the new problem. In one study, expert physicists and beginning physics students sorted physics problems into groups (Chi, Feltovitch, & Glaser, 1981). The beginners grouped together problems that looked similar (such as those involving blocks lying on an inclined plane), whereas the experts grouped together problems that could be solved by the same principle (such as Newton's second law of motion).

Experience also gives experts a broader perspective on the problem domain, allowing them to perceive the whole problem "tree" so that they can work forward without error, thus avoiding the slower "working backward" strategy more suited to the beginner. Finally, successful problem solvers can explain each step in the solution, and they can remain aware of precisely what is and is not understood along the way (Medin, Ross, & Markman, 2001).

Although experts are often better problem solvers than beginners, expertise also carries a danger: Using past experience can lead to the traps of functional fixedness and mental sets. Top-down, knowledge-driven processes can bias you toward seeing what you expect or want to see and prevent you from seeing a problem in new ways. As in the case of the "trapped kitten," confirmation bias sometimes prevents experts from appreciating that a proposed solution is incorrect (Fischoff & Slovic, 1980). Several studies have shown that although experts may be more confident in their solutions (Payne, Bettman, & Johnson, 1992), they are not always more accurate than others in such areas as medical diagnosis, accounting, and pilot judgment (Wickens et al., 1992).

Experts typically have a large store of knowledge about their area of expertise, but even confidently stated opinions based on this knowledge can turn out to be wrong. In 1768, one expert critic called William Shakespeare's now-revered play *Hamlet* "the work of a drunken savage" (Henderson & Bernard, 1998). Here are some equally incorrect expert pronouncements from *The Experts Speak* (Cerf & Navasky, 1998).

table 8.1
Some Expert Opinions

On the possibility of painless surgery through anesthesia:
"'Knife' and 'pain' are two words in surgery that must forever be associated.... To this compulsory combination we shall have to adjust ourselves." (Dr. Alfred Velpeau, professor of surgery, Paris Faculty of Medicine, 1839)

On the hazards of cigarette smoking:
"If excessive smoking actually plays a role in the production of lung cancer, it seems to be a minor one." (Dr. W. C. Heuper, National Cancer Institute, 1954)

On the stock market (one week before the disastrous 1929 crash that wiped out over $50 billion in investments):
"Stocks have reached what looks like a permanently high plateau." (Irving Fisher, professor of economics, Yale University, 1929)

On the prospects of war with Japan (three years before the December 1941 Japanese attack on Pearl Harbor):
"A Japanese attack on Pearl Harbor is a strategic impossibility." (Maj. George F. Eliot, military science writer, 1938)

On the value of personal computers:
"There is no reason for any individual to have a computer in their home." (Ken Olson, president, Digital Equipment Corporation, 1977)

On the concept of the airplane:
"Heavier-than-air flying machines are impossible." (Lord Kelvin, mathematician, physicist, and president of the British Royal Society, 1895)

In short, there is a fine line between using past experience and being trapped by it. Experience alone does not ensure excellence at problem solving, and practice may not make perfect (see Table 8.1). (For a summary of our discussion of human problem solving, see "In Review: Solving Problems.")

Problem Solving by Computer

Medical and scientific researchers have created artificial limbs, retinas, cochleae, and even hearts to help disabled people move, see, hear, and live more normally. They are developing artificial brains, too, in the form of computer systems that not only see, hear, and manipulate objects but also reason and solve problems. These systems are the product of research in **artificial intelligence** (**AI**), a field that seeks to develop computers that imitate the processes of human perception and thought. For problems such as those involved in making certain kinds of medical diagnoses, locating minerals, forecasting solar flares, or evaluating loan applications, computerized *expert systems* can already perform just as well as humans, and sometimes better (e.g., Gawande, 1998a; Khan et al., 2001).

Symbolic Reasoning and Computer Logic
Early efforts at developing artificial intelligence focused on computers' enormous capabilities for formal reasoning and symbol manipulation and on their abilities to follow general problem-solving strategies, such as working backward (Newell & Simon, 1972). Valuable as it is, this logic-based approach to AI has important limitations. For one thing, expert systems are successful only in narrowly defined fields, and even within a specific domain, computers show limited ability. There are no ways of putting into computer code all aspects of the reasoning of human experts. Sometimes, the experts can only say, "I know it when I see it, but I can't put it into words." Second, the vital ability to draw analogies and make other connections among remote knowledge

artificial intelligence (AI) The field that studies how to program computers to imitate the products of human perception, understanding, and thought.

in review: Solving Problems

Steps	Pitfalls	Remedies
Define the problem	Inexperience: the tendency to see each problem as unique.	Gain experience and practice in seeing the similarity between present problems and previous problems.
Form hypotheses about solutions	Availability heuristic: the tendency to recall the hypothesis or solution that is most available to memory.	Force yourself to entertain different hypotheses.
	Anchoring heuristic or mental set: the tendency to anchor on the first solution or hypothesis and not adjust your beliefs in light of new evidence or failures of the current approach.	Break the mental set, stop, and try a fresh approach.
Test hypotheses	The tendency to ignore negative evidence.	In evaluating a hypothesis, consider the things you should be seeing (but are not) if the hypothesis is true.
	Confirmation bias: the tendency to seek only evidence that confirms your hypothesis.	Look for disconfirming evidence that, if found, would show your hypothesis to be false.

domains is still beyond the grasp of current expert systems, partly because the builders of the systems seldom know ahead of time which other areas of knowledge might lead to insight. They can't always tell computers where to look for new ideas or how to use them. Finally, logic-based AI systems depend on "if-then" rules, and it is often difficult to tell a computer how to recognize the "if" condition in the real world (Dreyfus & Dreyfus, 1988). Consider just one example: *If it's a clock, then set it.* Humans can recognize all kinds of clocks because they have the natural concept of "clock," but computers perform this task very poorly. As discussed earlier, forming natural concepts requires putting into the same category many examples that may have very different physical features—from a bedside digital alarm clock to Big Ben.

Neural Network Models

Recognizing the problems posed by the need to teach computers to form natural concepts, many researchers in AI have shifted to the *connectionist,* or *neural network,* approach discussed in earlier chapters

Artificial Intelligence Chess master Garry Kasparov had his hands full when he was challenged by "Deep Blue," a chess-playing computer that was programmed so well that it has won games against the world's best competitors, including Kasparov. Still, even the most sophisticated computers cannot perceive and think about the world in general anywhere near as well as humans can. Some observers believe that this situation will eventually change as progress in computer technology—and a deepening understanding of human cognitive processes—leads to dramatic breakthroughs in artificial intelligence.

(Anderson, 1995b). This approach—which simulates the information processing taking place at many different, but interconnected, locations in the brain—is very effective for modeling many aspects of perceptual recognition. It has contributed to the development of computers that are able to recognize voices, understand speech, read print, guide missiles, and perform many other complex tasks. One program, called PAPNET, actually outperforms human technicians at detecting abnormal cells in smears collected during cervical examinations (Kok & Boon, 1996).

The capacities of current computer models of neural networks still fall well short of those of the human perceptual system, however. For example, computers are slow to learn how to classify visual patterns, and they do not show sudden insight when a key common feature is identified. Even though neural networks are far from perfect "thinking machines," however, they are sure to play an important role in psychologists' efforts to build ever more intelligent systems and to better understand the principles of human problem solving.

Computer-Assisted Problem Solving One approach to minimizing the limitations of both computers and humans is to have them work together in ways that create a better outcome than either could achieve alone. In medical diagnosis, for example, the human's role is to establish the presence and nature of a patient's symptoms. The computer then combines this information in a completely unbiased way to identify the most likely diagnosis (Swets, Dawes, & Monahan, 2000). Similarly, laboratory technologists who examine blood samples for the causes of disease are assisted by computer programs that serve to reduce errors and memory lapses by (1) keeping track of the findings from previous tests, (2) listing possible tests that remain to be tried, and (3) indicating either that certain tests have been left undone or that a new sequence of tests should be done (Guerlain, 1993, 1995). This kind of teamwork can also help in the assessment of psychological problems (Nietzel et al., 2003).

Decision Making

Dr. Wallace's patient, Laura McBride, faced a simple decision: risk death by doing nothing or protect herself from lead poisoning. Most decisions are not so easy. Patients must decide whether to undergo a dangerous operation; a college graduate must choose a career; a corporate executive must decide whether to shut down a factory. Unlike the high-speed decisions discussed earlier, these decisions require considerable time, planning, and mental effort.

Even carefully considered decisions sometimes lead to undesirable outcomes, however, because the world is uncertain. Decisions made when the outcome is uncertain are called *risky decisions* or *decisions under uncertainty*. Psychologists have discovered many reasons why human decisions may lead to unsatisfactory outcomes, and we describe some of them here.

Evaluating Options

Suppose that you must choose between (1) a fascinating academic major that is unlikely to lead to a good job and (2) a boring major that virtually guarantees a high-paying job. The fact that each option has positive and negative features, or *attributes,* greatly complicates decision making. Deciding which car to buy, which college to attend, or even how to spend the evening are all examples of *multi-attribute decision making* (Edwards, 1987). Often these decisions are further complicated by difficulties in comparing the attributes and in estimating the probabilities of various outcomes.

Comparing Attributes Multi-attribute decisions can be difficult in part because the limited storage capacity of short-term memory does not permit us to keep in mind all of the attributes of all of our options long enough to compare them (Bettman, Johnson, & Payne, 1990). Instead, people tend to focus on the one attribute that is most important to them (Kardes, 1999; Tversky, 1972). If, for instance, finishing a degree quickly is most important to you, then you might choose courses based mainly on graduation requirements, without giving much consideration to professors' reputations. (Listing the pros and cons of each option offers a helpful way of keeping them all in mind as you think about decisions.)

Furthermore, the attributes of the options involved in most important decisions cannot be measured in dollars or other objective terms. We are often forced to compare "apples and oranges." Psychologists use the term **utility** to describe the subjective value that each attribute holds for each of us. In deciding on a major, for example, you have to think about the positive and negative utilities of each attribute—such as the job prospects and interest level—of each major. Then you must somehow weigh and combine these utilities. Will the positive utility of enjoying your courses be higher than the negative utility of risking unemployment?

Estimating Probabilities Uncertainty adds other difficulties to the decision-making process: To make a good decision, you should take into account not only the attributes of each option but also the probabilities and risks of their possible outcomes. For example, the economy could change by the time you graduate, closing many of today's job opportunities in one of the majors you are considering and perhaps opening opportunities in another.

In studying risky decision making, psychologists begin by assuming that the best decision is the one that maximizes **expected value,** or the total amount of benefit you could expect if the decision were repeated on several occasions. Suppose someone asks you to buy a charity raffle ticket. You know that it costs $2 to enter and that the probability of winning the $100 prize is one in ten (.10). Assuming you are more interested in the prize money than in donating to the charity, should you enter the contest? The expected value of entering is determined by multiplying the probability of gain (.10) by the size of the gain ($100); this is the average benefit you would receive if you entered the raffle many times. Next, from this product you subtract the probability of loss, which is 1.0 (the entry fee is a certain loss), multiplied by the amount of the loss ($2). That is, $(.10 \times \$100) - (1.0 \times \$2) = \$8$. Because this $8 expected value is greater than the expected value of not entering (which is zero), you should enter. However, if the odds of winning the raffle were one in a hundred (.01), then the expected value of entering would be $(.01 \times \$100) - (1.0 \times \$2) = -\$1$. In this case, the expected value is negative, so you should not enter the raffle.

Biases and Flaws in Decision Making

Most people think of themselves as logical and rational, but in making decisions about everything from giving up smoking to investing in the stock market, they do not always act in ways that maximize expected value (Arkes & Ayton, 1999; Gilovich, 1997; Shiller, 2001). Why not?

Gains, Losses, and Probabilities For one thing, positive utilities are not mirror images of negative utilities. People usually feel worse about losing a certain amount than they feel good about gaining the same amount, a phenomenon known as *loss aversion* (Dawes, 1998; Mellers, Schwartz, & Cooke, 1998; Tversky & Kahneman, 1991). They may be willing to exert more effort to try collecting a $100 debt, for example, than to try winning a $100 prize.

It also appears that the utility of a specific gain depends not on how large the gain actually is but on what the starting point was. Suppose you can do something

---

utility A subjective measure of value.
expected value The total benefit to be expected if a decision were to be repeated several times.

to receive a coupon for a free dinner worth $10. Does this gain have the same utility as having an extra $10 added to your paycheck? The amount of gain is the same, but people tend to behave as if the difference in utility between $0 and $10 is much greater than the difference between, say, $300 and $310. So the person who refuses to do an after-work errand across town for an extra $10 on payday might gladly make the same trip to pick up a $10 coupon. This tendency conforms to Weber's law of psychophysics, discussed in the chapter on perception. The subjective value of a gain depends on how much you already have (Dawes, 1998); the more you have, the less it means.

Biases in our perception of probabilities are also a source of less-than-optimal decisions. One of these biases comes into play when decisions involve extremely likely or extremely unlikely events. In making such decisions, we tend to overestimate the probability of very unlikely events and to underestimate the probability of very likely ones (Kahneman & Tversky, 1984). This bias helps explain why people gamble and enter lotteries, even though the odds are against them and the decision to do so has a negative expected value. According to the formula for expected value, buying a $1 lottery ticket when the probability of winning $4 million is 1 in 10 million yields an expected value of −60 cents. But because people overestimate the probability of winning, they believe there is a positive expected value. The tendency to overestimate the likelihood of unlikely events is amplified by the availability heuristic: Vivid memories of rare gambling successes and the publicity given to lottery winners help people recall gains rather than losses when deciding about future gambles (Wagenaar, 1989).

Another bias relating to probability is called the *gambler's fallacy:* People believe that events in a random process will correct themselves. This belief is false. If you flip a coin and it comes up heads ten times in a row, the chance that it will come up heads on the eleventh try is still 50 percent. Some gamblers, however, will continue feeding a slot machine that hasn't paid off much for hours, assuming it is "due." This assumption may be partly responsible for the resistance to extinction of intermittently reinforced behaviors, as described in the chapter on learning.

Yet another factor underlying flaws in human decision making is the tendency for people to be unrealistically confident in the accuracy of their predictions. Baruch Fischoff and Donald MacGregor (1982) used an ingenious approach to study this bias. They asked people whether they believed that a certain event would occur—for example, that a certain sports team would win—and how confident they were about this prediction. After the events took place, the accuracy of the forecasts was compared with the confidence these people had had in those forecasts. Sure enough, people's confidence in their predictions was consistently greater than their accuracy.

This kind of overconfidence appears in many cultures, but it is more common in some than others. For example, Chinese students are more likely to show this bias than students in North America (Wright & Phillips, 1980; Yates et al., 1989). One possible explanation is that students in China are discouraged from challenging what they are told by teachers, so they may be less likely than North Americans to question what they tell themselves and thus more likely to be overconfident (Yates, Lee, & Shinotsuka, 1992).

The moral of the story is to be wary when people in any culture express confidence that a forecast or decision is correct. They will be wrong more often than they think.

A Highly Unlikely Outcome By focusing public attention on the very few people who win big prizes, lottery agencies take advantage of the human tendency to overestimate the probability of rare events. Lottery ads never show the millions of people whose tickets turn out to be worthless.

How Biased Are We?

Almost everyone makes decisions they later regret, but psychologists are divided on the extent to which cognitive biases are to blame (Cohen, 1993; Payne, Bettman, & Johnson, 1992). Some decisions are not intended to maximize expected value but rather to satisfy other criteria, such as minimizing expected loss, producing a quick and easy resolution, or preserving a moral principle (Arkes & Ayton, 1999; Zsambok & Klein, 1997). For example, decisions may depend not just on how likely we are to gain or lose a certain amount of something but also on what that something is. So a decision that could cost or save a human life might be made differently than one that could cost or gain a few dollars, even though the probabilities of each outcome were exactly the same in both cases.

Even the "goodness" or "badness" of decisions can be difficult to measure. Many of them depend on personal values (utilities), which can vary from person to person and from culture to culture. People in individualist cultures, for example, may tend to assign high utilities to attributes that promote personal goals, whereas people in collectivist cultures might place greater value on attributes that bring group harmony and the approval of family and friends (Markus, Kitayama, & Heiman, 1996).

Naturalistic Decision Making

Circumstances in the real world often make it difficult or impossible to go through all the steps needed to complete a successful multi-attribute decision process (Zsambok & Klein, 1997). An alternative approach, called *naturalistic decision making*, is used when experts—working in organizational teams and facing limitations on time and resources—must find solutions to complex problems (Klein, 1997).

Naturalistic decision making involves the use of prior experiences to develop mental representations of how organizational systems really work. Suppose that a production team needs some computer graphics to complete a brochure for a sales meeting to be held in three days. The company's stated policy is that all computer graphics work will be completed in two days, but company veterans know that it always takes at least a week to get the work done. On the basis of prior organizational experience, the production team will probably decide to use an outside service to do the graphics task.

Although naturalistic decision making models vary somewhat, most of them predict that experts make decisions based on mental representations that they have developed as a consequence of prior experiences with similar problems. Based on the perceived parallels between current and past experiences, these experts develop what is known as *situation awareness*—the ability to appreciate all elements of a problem, as well as all elements of the environment within which it appears, and to make decisions that take them all into account. Situation awareness is vital to effective decision making and problem solving in the real world.

LINKAGES

LINKAGES (a link to Social Influence)

Group Processes in Problem Solving and Decision Making

As with the production team we just described, problem solving and decision making are often done in groups. The processes that influence an individual's problem solving and decision making continue to operate when the individual is in a group, but group interactions also shape the outcome.

When groups are trying to choose from among several options, for example, the discussions typically follow a consistent pattern (Hastie, Penrod, & Pennington, 1983). First, various options are proposed and debated until the group sees that no one has strong objections to one option. That option becomes the *minimally acceptable solution*. From then on, the group criticizes any other proposal and argues more and more strongly for the minimally acceptable solution, which is likely to become the group's decision. This sequence is an example of the anchoring heuristic operating in a group, and it suggests that the order in which options are considered can determine decisions (Wittenbaum & Stasser, 1996).

Groups Working at a Distance
Research on group problem solving and decision making is beginning to focus on "electronic groups," whose members use e-mail and teleconferencing to work together from a distance. Some evidence suggests that compared with meeting in person, communication via e-mail tends to be slower, more explicit, and blunt (sometimes qualifying as "flaming"), and it may result in especially extreme decisions (Kiesler & Sproull, 1992).

Group discussions often result in decisions that are more extreme than the group members would make individually. This tendency toward extreme decisions by groups is called *group polarization* (Kaplan, 1987). Two mechanisms appear to underlie group polarization. First, most arguments presented during the discussion favor the majority view, most criticisms are directed at the minority view, and (influenced by confirmation bias) group members tend to seek additional information that supports the majority position (Schulz-Hardt et al., 2000). So it seems rational to those favoring the majority view to adopt an even stronger version of it (Stasser, 1991). Second, once some group members begin to agree that a particular decision is desirable, other members may try to associate themselves with that decision, perhaps by advocating an even more extreme version (Kaplan & Miller, 1987).

Are people better at problem solving and decision making when they work in groups than when on their own? This is one of the questions about human thought studied by social psychologists. In a typical experiment, a group of people is asked to solve a problem like the one in Figure 8.12 or to make a decision about the guilt or innocence of a fictional defendant. Each person is asked to reach an individual answer and then to join with the others in the group to try to reach a consensus. These studies have found that when problems have solutions that can be demonstrated easily to all members, groups will usually outperform individuals at solving them (Laughlin, 1999). When problems have less obvious solutions, though, groups may be somewhat better at solving them than their average member, but usually no better than their most talented member (Hackman, 1998). And because of a phenomenon called *social loafing* (discussed in the chapter on social influence), people working in a group are often less productive than people working alone (Williams & Sommer, 1997).

Other research (e.g., Stasser, Stewart, & Wittenbaum, 1995) suggests that a critical element in successful group problem solving is the sharing of individual members' unique information and expertise. For example, when asked to diagnose an illness, groups of physicians were much more accurate when they pooled the information possessed by each doctor (Larson et al., 1998). However, *brainstorming,* a popular strategy that supposedly encourages group members to generate innovative solutions to a problem, may actually produce fewer ideas than are generated by individuals working alone (Levine & Moreland, 1998)—possibly because the comments of other group members interfere with the creative process in individuals. Group members who are confident or have high status are most likely to influence a group's deliberations (Levine & Moreland, 1998), but whether these people will help or hurt the group's output depends on whether they have good ideas (Hinsz, 1990). Unfortunately, there is little evidence that members with the best ideas or greatest competence (as opposed to the highest status) always contribute more to group deliberations (Littlepage et al., 1995).

As they work to solve a problem, the members of a group manipulate their own concepts, propositions, images, and other mental representations. How does each member share these private events so as to help the group perform its task? The answer lies in the use of language.

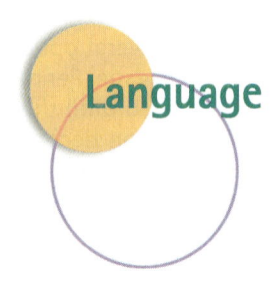

Language

LSV: Language

Language is the primary means through which we communicate our thoughts to others. We use language not only to share the thoughts we have at the moment but also to pass on cultural information and traditions from one generation to the next. In this section, we describe the elements that make up a language, the ways that people use language to communicate, the means by which language is learned, and how language influences our thinking.

The Elements of Language

A **language** has two basic elements: (1) symbols, such as words, and (2) a set of rules, called **grammar,** for combining those symbols. These two components allow human language to be at once rule bound and creative. With their knowledge of approximately 50,000 to 100,000 words (Miller, 1991), humans can create and understand an infinite number of sentences. All of the sentences ever spoken are created from just a few dozen categories of sounds. The power of language comes from the way these rather unimpressive raw materials are organized according to rules. This organization occurs at several levels.

From Sounds to Sentences

Organization occurs first at the level of sounds. A **phoneme** is the smallest unit of sound that affects the meaning of speech. Changing a phoneme changes the meaning of a spoken word, much as changing a letter in a printed word changes its meaning. *Tea* has a meaning different from *sea*, and *sight* is different from *sigh*.

The number of phonemes in the world's languages varies from a low of thirteen (Hawaiian) to a high of over sixty (Hindi). Most languages have between thirty and fifty phonemes; English uses about forty. With forty basic sounds and an alphabet of only twenty-six letters, you can see that the same letters must sometimes signal different sounds. For example, the letter *a* stands for different phonemes in the words *cat* and *cake*.

Although changing a phoneme affects the meaning of speech, phonemes themselves are not meaningful. We combine them to form a higher level of organization: morphemes. A **morpheme** is the smallest unit of language that has meaning. For example, because they have meaning, *dog* and *run* are morphemes; but so are prefixes like *un-* and suffixes like *-ed*, because they, too, have meaning, even though they cannot stand alone.

Words are made up of one or more morphemes. Words, in turn, are combined to form phrases and sentences according to a set of grammatical rules called **syntax** (Fromkin & Rodman, 1992). According to English syntax, a subject and a verb must be combined in a sentence, adjectives typically appear before the nouns that they modify, and so on. Compare the following sentences:

Fatal accidents deter careful drivers.

Snows sudden floods melting cause.

The first sentence makes sense, but the second sentence violates English syntax. If the words were reordered, however, they would produce the perfectly acceptable sentence "Melting snows cause sudden floods."

Even if you use English phonemes combined in proper ways to form morphemes strung together according to the laws of English syntax, you may not end up with an acceptable English sentence. Consider the sentence "Rapid bouquets deter sudden neighbors." It somehow sounds right, but it is nonsense. Why? It has syntax, but it ignores the set of rules, called **semantics,** that govern the meaning of words and sentences. For example, because of its meaning, the noun *bouquets* cannot be modified by the word *rapid*.

Surface Structure and Deep Structure

So far, we have discussed elements of language that are apparent in the sentences people produce. These elements were the focus of study by linguists for many decades. Then, in 1965, Noam Chomsky started a revolution in the study of language. He argued that if linguists studied only the language that people produce, they would never uncover the principles that account for all aspects of language. They could not explain, for example, how the sentence "This is my old friend" has more than one meaning. Nor could they account for the close relationship between the meanings of such sentences as "Don't give up just because things look bad" and "It ain't over 'til it's over."

---

language Symbols and a set of rules for combining them that provide a vehicle for communication.

grammar A set of rules for combining the words used in a given language.

phoneme The smallest unit of sound that affects the meaning of speech.

morpheme The smallest unit of language that has meaning.

words Units of language composed of one or more morphemes.

syntax The set of rules that govern the formation of phrases and sentences in a language.

semantics Rules governing the meaning of words and sentences.

figure 8.15

Surface Structure and Deep Structure
The listener on the right has interpreted the speaker's message in a way that differs from the speaker's intended deep structure. Obviously, identical surface structures can correspond to quite different deep structures.

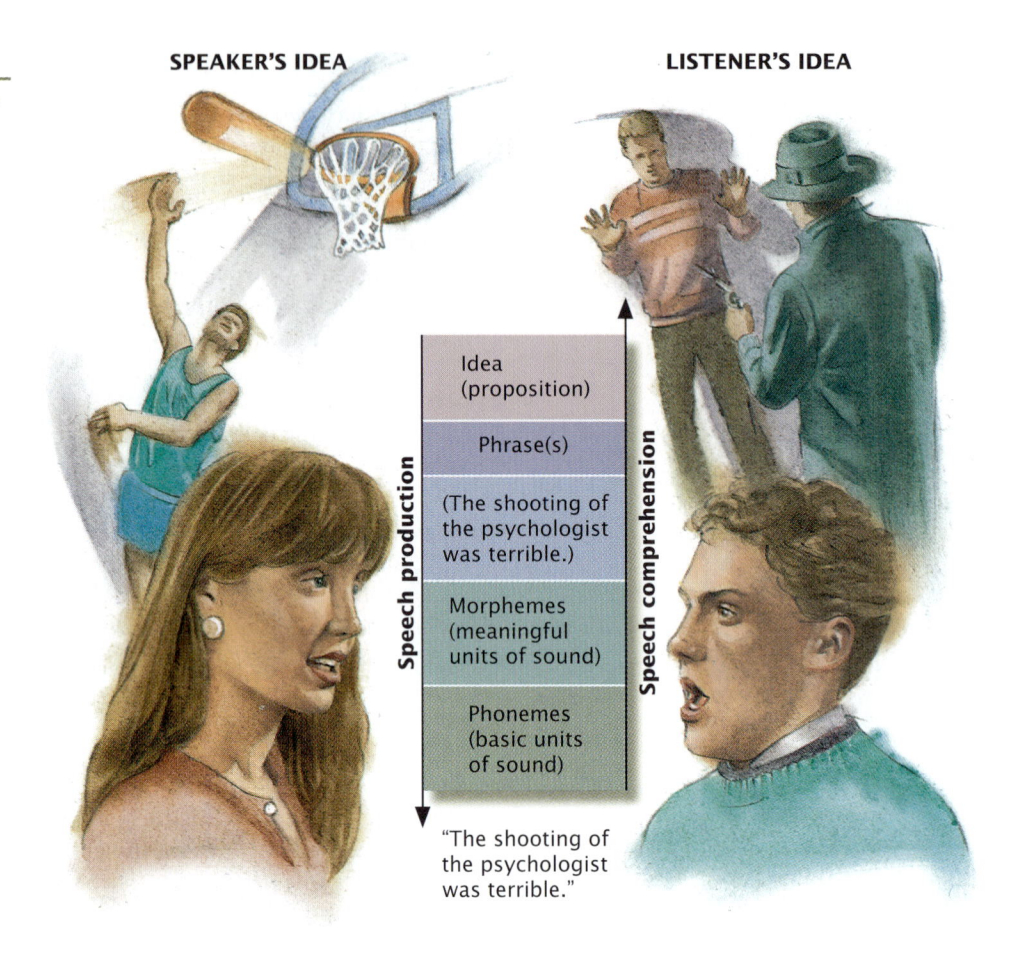

SPEAKER'S IDEA — LISTENER'S IDEA

Speech production →
- Idea (proposition)
- Phrase(s) (The shooting of the psychologist was terrible.)
- Morphemes (meaningful units of sound)
- Phonemes (basic units of sound)

← Speech comprehension

"The shooting of the psychologist was terrible."

To take these aspects of language into account, Chomsky proposed a more abstract level of analysis. Behind the word strings that people produce, called **surface structures,** there is, he said, a **deep structure,** an abstract representation of the relationships expressed in a sentence. For example, as Figure 8.15 illustrates, the surface structure "The shooting of the psychologist was terrible" can represent either of two deep structures: (1) that the psychologist had terrible aim or (2) that it was terrible that someone shot the psychologist. Chomsky's original analysis of deep and surface structures was important because it encouraged psychologists to analyze not just verbal behavior and grammatical rules but also mental representations.

Understanding Speech

When someone speaks to you in your own language, your sensory, perceptual, and other cognitive systems reconstruct the sounds of speech in a way that allows you to detect, recognize, and understand what the person is saying. The process may seem effortless, but it involves amazingly complex feats of information processing. Scientists trying to develop speech-recognition software systems have discovered just how complex the process is. After decades of effort, the accuracy and efficiency of these systems are still not much better than those of the average five-year-old child. What makes understanding speech so complicated?

One factor is that the physical features of a particular speech sound are not always the same. This phenomenon is illustrated in Figure 8.16, which shows how the sounds of particular letters differ depending on the sounds that follow them. A second factor complicating our understanding of speech is that each of us creates

---

surface structures The order in which words are arranged in sentences.

deep structure An abstract representation of the underlying meanings of a given sentence.

Making sure that the surface structures we create accurately convey the deep structures we intend is one of the greatest challenges people face when communicating through language.

© The New Yorker Collection 1989 Danny Shanahan from cartoonbank.com. All Rights Reserved.

slightly different speech sounds, even when saying the same words. Third, as people speak, their words are not usually separated by silence. So if the speech spectrograms in Figure 8.16 showed whole sentences, you would not be able to tell where one word ended and the next began.

Perceiving Words and Sentences   Despite these challenges, humans can instantly recognize and understand the words and sentences produced by almost anyone speaking a familiar language. In contrast, even the best voice-recognition software must learn to recognize words spoken by a new voice, and even then may make many mistakes. (A man we know recently requested the toll-free number for the Maglite Corporation, and the voice-recognition software in a directory assistance computer gave him the number for Metlife insurance.)

Scientists have yet to discover all the details about how people overcome the challenges of understanding speech, but some general answers are emerging. Just as we recognize objects by analyzing their visual features (see the chapter on perception), it appears that humans identify and recognize the specific—and changing—features of the sounds created when someone speaks. And as in visual perception, this *bottom-up processing* of stimulus features combines with *top-down processing* guided by knowledge-based factors, such as context and expectation, to aid understanding (Samuel, 2001). For example, knowing the general topic of conversation helps you to recognize individual words that might otherwise be hard to understand (Cole & Jakimik, 1978).

Finally, we are often guided to an understanding of speech by nonverbal cues. The frown, the enthusiastic nod, or the bored yawn that accompanies speech each carries information that helps you understand what the person is saying. So if someone says "Wow, are you smart!" but really means "I think you're a jerk," you will detect the true meaning based on the context, facial expression, and tone of voice. No wonder it is usually easier to understand someone in a face-to-face conversation than on the telephone or via e-mail (Massaro & Stork, 1998).

figure 8.16
Speech Spectrograms

These speech spectrograms show what the sound frequencies of speech look like as people say various words. Notice how the shape of the whole speech signal differs from one word to another, even when the initial consonant (*b* or *d*) is the same.

Source: Jusczyk et al. (1981).

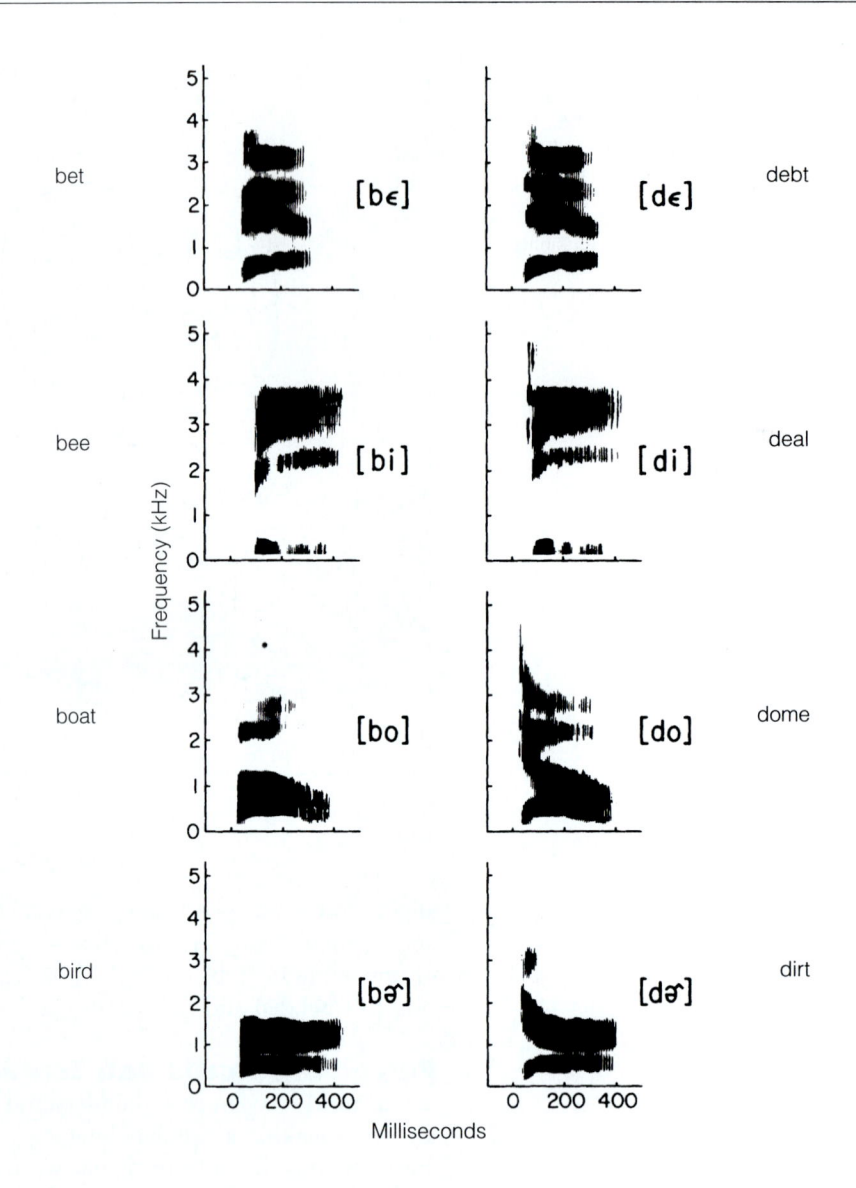

The Development of Language

Children the world over develop language with impressive speed; the average six-year-old already has a vocabulary of about 13,000 words (Pinker, 1994). But acquiring a language involves more than just learning vocabulary. We also have to learn how words are combined and how to produce and understand sentences. Psychologists who study the development of language have found that the process begins in the earliest days of a child's life and follows some predictable steps (Saffran, Senghas, & Trueswell, 2001).

The First Year Within the first few months of life, babies can tell the difference between the sounds of their native language and those of other languages (Gerken, 1994), and by ten months of age they pay closer attention to speech in

LINKAGES (a link to Human Development)

babblings The first sounds infants make that resemble speech.

Understanding Spoken Language
Top-down perceptual processes, described in the chapter on perception, help explain why speech in a language you do not understand sounds like a continuous stream being spoken faster than speech in your own language. You do not know where each unfamiliar word starts and stops, so without perceived gaps, the speech sounds run together at what seems to be a faster-than-normal rate. To people unfamiliar with your language, your speech, too, sounds extremely fast!

their native language (Werker et al., 1996). In the first year, then, infants become more and more attuned to the sounds that will be important in acquiring their native language.

The first year is also the time when babies begin to produce **babblings,** which are patterns of meaningless sounds that first resemble speech. Infants of all nationalities begin with the same set of babbling sounds. At about nine months, however, babies who hear only English start to lose their German gutturals and French nasals. At this time, babbling becomes more complex and begins to sound like "sentences" in the babies' native language. Starting around this time, too, babies who hear English begin to shorten some of their vocalizations to "da," "duh," and "ma." These sounds seem very much like language, and babies use them in specific contexts and with obvious purpose (Blake & de Boysson-Bardies, 1992). Accompanied by appropriate gestures, they may be used to express joy ("oohwow") or anger ("uh-uh-uh"), to get something that is out of reach ("engh-engh"), or to point out something interesting ("dah!").

By ten to twelve months of age, babies can understand several words—certainly more words than they can say (Fenson et al., 1994). Proper names and object labels

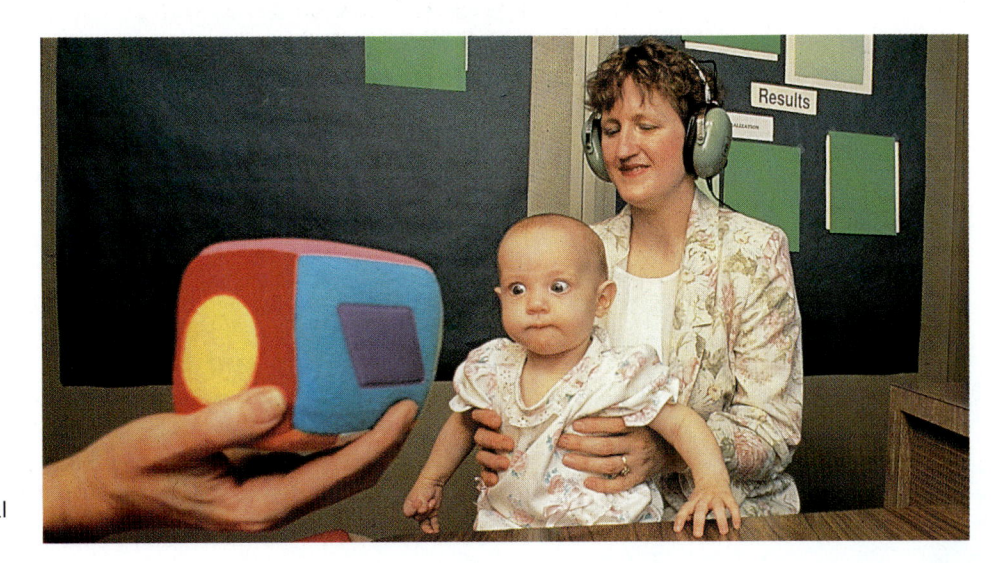

Getting Ready to Talk Long before they utter their first words, babies are getting ready to talk. Experiments in Patricia Kuhl's laboratory show that even six-month-olds tend to look longer at faces whose lip movements match the sounds of spoken words. This tendency reflects babies' abilities to focus on, recognize, and discriminate among the sounds of speech, especially in their native language. These abilities are crucial to the development of language.

are among the earliest words they understand. Often the first word they understand is a pet's name.

Proper names and object words—such as *mama, daddy, cookie, doggy,* and *car*—are also among the first words children are likely to say when, at around twelve months of age, they begin to talk (some do this a little earlier and some a little later). Nouns for simple object categories *(dog, flower)* are acquired before more general nouns *(animal, plant)* or more specific names *(collie, rose)* (Rosch et al., 1976).

Of course, these early words do not sound exactly like adult language. English-speaking babies usually reduce them to a shorter, easier form, like "duh" for *duck* or "mih" for *milk*. Children make themselves understood, however, by using gestures, intonations, facial expressions, and endless repetitions. If they have a word for an object, they may "overextend" it to cover more ground. So they might use *dog* for cats, bears, and horses; they might use *fly* for all insects and perhaps for other small things like raisins and M&Ms (Clark, 1983, 1993). Children make these "errors" because their vocabularies are limited, not because they fail to notice the difference between dogs and cats or because they want to eat a fly (Fremgen & Fay, 1980; Rescorla, 1981).

Until they can say the conventional words for objects, children overextend the words they have, use all-purpose sounds (like "dat" or "dis"), and coin new words (like *pepping* for "shaking the pepper shaker") (Becker, 1994). Being around people who don't understand these overextensions encourages children to learn and use more precise words (Markman, 1994). During this period, children build up their vocabularies one word at a time. They also use their limited vocabulary one word at a time; they cannot yet put words together into sentences.

The Second Year

The **one-word stage** of speech lasts for about six months. Then, sometime around eighteen months of age, children's vocabularies expand dramatically (Gleitman & Landau, 1994). They may learn several new words each day, and by the age of two, most youngsters can use fifty to well over one hundred words. They also start using two-word combinations to form efficient little sentences. These two-word sentences are called *telegraphic* because they are brief and to the point, leaving out anything that is not absolutely essential. So if she wants her mother to give her a book, a twenty-month-old might first say, "Give book," then "Mommy give," and if that does not work, "Mommy book." The child also uses rising tones to indicate a question ("Go out?") and puts stress on certain words to indicate location ("Play *park*") or new information ("*Big* car").

Three-word sentences come next in the development of language. They are still telegraphic, but more nearly complete: "Mommy give book." The child can now speak in sentences that have the usual subject-verb-object form of adult sentences. Other words and word endings begin appearing, too, such as the suffix *-ing,* the prepositions *in* and *on,* the plural *-s,* and irregular past tenses ("It broke," "I ate") (Brown, 1973; Dale, 1976). Children learn to use the suffix *-ed* for the past tense ("I walked"), but then they often overapply this rule to irregular verbs that they previously used correctly, saying, for example, "It breaked," "It broked," or "I eated" (Marcus, 1996).

Children also expand their sentences with adjectives, although at first they make some mistakes. For example, they are likely to use both *less* and *more* to mean "more" or both *tall* and *short* to mean "tall" (Smith & Sera, 1992).

The Third Year and Beyond

By age three or so, children begin to use auxiliary verbs ("Adam is going") and to ask questions using *wh-* words, such as *what, where, who,* and *why.* They begin to put together clauses to form complex sentences ("Here's the ball I was looking for"). By age five, children have acquired most of the grammatical rules of their native language.

---

one-word stage A stage of language development during which children tend to use one word at a time.

How Is Language Acquired?

Despite all that has been discovered about the steps children follow in acquiring language, mystery and debate still surround the question of just how they do it. Obviously, children pick up the specific content of language from the speech they hear around them; English children learn English, and French children learn French. As parents and children share meals, playtime, and conversations, children learn that words refer to objects and actions and what the labels for them are. But how do children learn syntax, the rules of grammar?

Conditioning, Imitation, and Rules

Our discussion of conditioning in the chapter on learning would suggest that children learn syntax because their parents reinforce them for using it. This sounds reasonable, but observational studies show that positive reinforcement does not tell the whole story. Parents are usually more concerned about what is said than about its grammatical form (Hirsch-Pasek, Treiman, & Schneiderman, 1984). So when the little boy with chocolate crumbs on his face says, "I not eat cookie," his mother is more likely to say, "Yes, you did" than to ask the child to say, "I did not eat the cookie" and then reinforce him for grammatical correctness.

Learning through modeling, or imitation, appears to be more influential. Children learn grammar most rapidly when adults demonstrate the correct syntax in the course of a conversation, as in the following example:

CHILD: Mommy fix.

MOTHER: Okay, Mommy will fix the truck.

CHILD: It breaked.

MOTHER: Yes, it broke.

CHILD: Truck broke.

MOTHER: Let's see if we can fix it.

But if children learn syntax by imitation, why would they overgeneralize rules, such as the rule for making the past tense? Why, for example, do children who at one time said "I went" later say "I goed"? Adults never use this form of speech. Its sudden appearance indicates that the child either has mastered the rule of adding *-ed* or has generalized from similar-sounding words (such as *mowed* or *rowed*). In short, neither conditioning nor imitation seems entirely adequate to explain how children learn language. Children must still analyze for themselves the underlying patterns in the language examples they hear around them (Bloom, 1995).

Innate Sources of Language Acquisition

The ease with which children everywhere discover these underlying patterns and learn language has led some to argue that language acquisition is at least partly innate. For example, Chomsky believes that we have a built-in *universal grammar*, a mechanism that allows us to identify the basic dimensions of language (Baker, 2002; Chomsky, 1986; Nowak, Komarova, & Niyogi, 2001). One of these dimensions is how important word order is in the syntax of a particular language. For example, in English, word order tells us who is doing what to whom (the sentences "Heather dumped Jason" and "Jason dumped Heather" contain the same words, but they have different meanings). In languages such as Russian, however, word order is less important than modifiers attached to the word, also called *inflections*. According to Chomsky, a child's universal grammar might initially be "set" to assume that word order is important to syntax, but it would change if the child hears language in which word order is not crucial. In Chomsky's system, then, we don't entirely learn language—we develop it as genetic predispositions interact with experience (Senghas & Coppola, 2001).

Other theorists disagree with Chomsky, arguing that the development of language reflects the development of more general cognitive skills rather than innate, language-specific mechanisms (e.g., Bates, 1993). Still, there is other evidence to support the existence of biological factors in language acquisition. For example, the unique speech-generating properties of the human mouth and throat, the language-related brain regions such as Broca's area and Wernicke's area (see Figure 3.16), and recent genetic research all suggest that humans are innately "prewired," or biologically programmed, for language (Buxhoeveden et al., 2001; Lai et al., 2001). In addition, there appears to be a *critical period* in childhood during which we can learn language more easily than at any other time (Ridley, 2000). The existence of this critical period is supported by the difficulties adults have in learning a second language (e.g., Lenneberg, 1967), and also by cases in which unfortunate children spent their early years in isolation from human contact and the sound of adult language. Even after years of therapy and language training, these individuals are not able to combine ideas into sentences (Rymer, 1993b). These cases suggest that in order to acquire the complex features of our language, we must be exposed to speech before a certain age.

Bilingualism   Does trying to learn two languages at once, even before the critical period is over, impair the learning of either? Research suggests just the opposite. Although their early language utterances may be confused or delayed, children who are raised in a bilingual environment before the end of the critical period seem to show enhanced performance in each language (deHouwer, 1995). There is also some evidence that *balanced bilinguals*—people who developed roughly equal mastery of two languages as children—are superior to others in cognitive flexibility, concept formation, and creativity. It is as if each language offers a slightly different perspective on thinking, and this dual perspective makes the brain more flexible (Hong et al., 2000).

The apparent benefits of bilingualism have important implications for U.S. school systems, where children from non-English-speaking homes often receive instruction in their native language while taking classes in English. Although lack of control over school environments makes it difficult to perform true experiments on the effects of this practice, available evidence suggests that these bilingual programs

Learning a Second Language The notion of a critical period for language acquisition is supported by the fact that after the age of thirteen or fourteen, people learn a second language more slowly (Johnson & Newport, 1989) and virtually never learn to speak it without an accent (Lenneberg, 1967).

facilitate educational achievement (Cavaliere, 1996). The evidence also suggests that rapid immersion in an English-only program may do considerable educational harm to children who enter school with no English-language background (Crawford, 1989).

THINKING CRITICALLY

Can Nonhumans Use Language?

Some psychologists say that it is the ability of humans to acquire and use language that sets them apart from all other creatures. Yet those creatures, too, use symbols to communicate. Bees perform a dance that tells other bees where they found sources of nectar; the grunts and gestures of chimpanzees signify varying desires and emotions. These forms of communication do not necessarily have the grammatical characteristics of language, however (Rendall, Cheney, & Seyfarth, 2000). Are any animals other than humans capable of learning language?

- **What am I being asked to believe or accept?**

Over the last forty years, several researchers have asserted that nonhumans can master language. Chimpanzees and gorillas have been the most popular targets of study, because at maturity they are estimated to have the intelligence of two- or three-year-old children, who are usually well on their way to learning language. Dolphins, too, have been studied because they have a complex communication system and exceptionally large brains relative to their body size (Janik, 2000; Reiss & Marino, 2001). It would seem that if these animals were unable to learn language, their general intelligence could not be blamed. Instead, failure would be attributed to the absence of a genetic makeup that permits language learning.

- **What evidence is available to support the assertion?**

The question of whether nonhuman mammals can learn to use language is not a simple one, for at least two reasons. First, language is more than just communication, but defining just when animals are exhibiting that "something more" is a source of debate. What seems to set human language apart from the gestures, grunts, chirps, whistles, or cries of other animals is grammar—a formal set of rules for combining words. Also, because of their anatomical structures, nonhuman mammals will never be able to "speak" in the same way that humans do (Lieberman, 1991). To test these animals' ability to learn language, investigators therefore must devise novel ways for them to communicate.

David and Ann Premack taught their chimp, Sarah, to communicate by placing differently shaped chips, each symbolizing a word, on a magnetic board (Premack, 1971). Lana, a chimpanzee studied by Duane Rumbaugh (1977), learned to communicate by pressing keys on a specially designed computer. American Sign Language (ASL), the hand-gesture language used by people who are deaf, has been used by Beatrice and Allen Gardner with the chimp Washoe, and by Herbert Terrace with Nim Chimsky, a chimp named after Noam Chomsky. And Kanzi, a bonobo (commonly known as a pygmy chimpanzee) studied by Sue Savage-Rumbaugh (1990; Savage-Rumbaugh et al., 1993), learned to recognize spoken words and to communicate by both gesturing and pressing word-symbol keys on a computer that would "speak" them. Kanzi was a special case: He learned to communicate by listening and watching as his mother, Matata, was being taught and then used what he had learned to interact with her trainers.

Studies of these animals suggested that they could spontaneously use combinations of words to refer to things that were not present. Washoe, Lana, Sarah, Nim, and Kanzi all mastered between 130 and 500 words. Their vocabulary included names for concrete objects, such as *apple* or *me*; verbs, such as *tickle* and *eat*; adjectives, such as *happy* and *big*; and adverbs, such as *again*. The animals combined the words in sentences, expressing wishes such as "You tickle me" or "If

Sarah good, then apple." Sometimes the sentences referred to things in the past. When an investigator called attention to a wound that Kanzi had received, the animal produced the sentence "Matata hurt," referring to a disciplinary bite his mother had recently given him (Savage-Rumbaugh, 1990). Finally, all these animals seemed to enjoy their communication tools and used them spontaneously to interact with their caretakers and with other animals.

Most of the investigators mentioned here have argued that their animals mastered a crude grammar (Premack & Premack, 1983; Savage-Rumbaugh, Shankar, & Taylor, 1999). For example, if Washoe wanted to be tickled, she would gesture, "You tickle Washoe." But if she wanted to do the tickling, she would gesture, "Washoe tickle you." The correct placement of object and subject in these sentences suggested that Washoe was following a set of rules for word combination—in other words, a grammar (Gardner & Gardner, 1978). Louis Herman and his colleagues documented similar grammatical sensitivity in dolphins, who rarely confused subject-verb order in following instructions given by human hand signals (Herman, Richards, & Wolz, 1984). Furthermore, Savage-Rumbaugh observed several hundred instances in which Kanzi understood sentences he had never heard before. Once, for example, while his back was turned to the speaker, Kanzi heard the sentence "Jeanie hid the pine needles in her shirt." He turned around, approached Jeanie, and searched her shirt to find the pine needles. His actions would seem to indicate that he understood this new sentence the first time he heard it.

- **Are there alternative ways of interpreting the evidence?**

Many of the early conclusions about primate language learning were challenged by Herbert Terrace and his colleagues in their investigation of Nim (Terrace et al., 1979). Terrace noticed many subtle characteristics of Nim's communications that seemed quite different from a child's use of language, and he argued that animals in other studies demonstrated these same characteristics.

First, he said, their sentences were always very short. Nim could combine two or three gestures but never used strings that conveyed more sophisticated messages. The ape was never able to say anything equivalent to a three-year-old child's "I want to go to Wendy's for a hamburger, OK?" Second, Terrace questioned whether the animals' use of language demonstrated the spontaneity, creativity, and expanding complexity characteristic of children's language. Many of the animals' sentences were requests for food, tickling, baths, pets, and other pleasurable objects and experiences. Is such behavior different from the kind of behavior shown by the family dog who learns to sit up and beg for table scraps? Other researchers also pointed out that chimps are not naturally predisposed to associate seen objects with heard words, as human infants are (Savage-Rumbaugh et al., 1983). Finally, Terrace questioned whether experimenter bias influenced the reports of the chimps' communications. Consciously or not, experimenters who want to conclude that chimps learn language might tend to ignore strings that violate grammatical order or to reinterpret ambiguous strings so that they make grammatical sense. If Nim sees someone holding a banana and signs, "Nim banana," the experimenter might assume the word order is correct and means "Nim wants the banana" rather than, for example, "That banana belongs to Nim," in which case the word order would be wrong.

- **What additional evidence would help to evaluate the alternatives?**

Studies of animals' ability to learn language are expensive and take many years. Accordingly, the amount of evidence in the area is small—just a handful of studies, each based on a few animals. Obviously, more data are needed from more studies that use a common methodology.

It is important, as well, to study the extent to which limits on the length of primates' spontaneous sentences result from limits on short-term and working memory (Savage-Rumbaugh & Brakke, 1996). If memory is in fact the main limiting factor, then the failure to produce progressively longer sentences does not necessarily reflect an inability to master language.

Animal Language? Here, a gorilla named Koko makes the American Sign Language (ASL) sign for "smoke" as her trainer, Penny Patterson, holds a cat named Smoky. Koko recently responded to questions sent to her on the Internet. Because Koko can't read or type, her trainer relayed the questions in ASL and typed the gorilla's signed responses. This procedure left some questioners wondering whether they were talking to Koko or her trainer.

Research on how primates might spontaneously acquire language by listening and imitating, as Kanzi did, as well as naturalistic observations of communications among primates in their natural habitat, would also help scientists better understand primates' capacity to communicate (Savage-Rumbaugh, Shankar, & Taylor, 1999; Sevcik & Savage-Rumbaugh, 1994).

● **What conclusions are most reasonable?**

Psychologists are still not in full agreement about whether our sophisticated mammalian cousins can learn language. Two things are clear, however. First, whatever the chimp, gorilla, and dolphin have learned is a much more primitive and limited form of communication than that learned by children. Second, their level of communication does not do justice to their overall intelligence; these animals are smarter than their "language" production suggests. In short, the evidence to date favors the view that humans have language abilities that are unique (Buxhoeveden et al., 2001), but that under the right circumstances, and with the right tools, other animals can master many language-like skills.

Culture, Language, and Thought

When ideas from one language are translated into another, the intended meaning can easily be distorted, as shown in Table 8.2. But differences in language and culture may have more serious and important implications as well. The language that people speak forms part of their knowledge of the world, and that knowledge, as noted in the chapter on perception, guides perceptions. This relationship raises the question of whether differences among languages create differences in the ways that people perceive and think about the world.

Benjamin Whorf (1956) claimed that language actually determines how we can think, a process he called *linguistic determinism*. He noted, for example, that Inuit Eskimos have several different words for "snow" and proposed that this feature of their language should lead to a greater perceptual ability to discriminate among varieties of snow. When these discrimination abilities of Inuits and other people are

Sometimes a lack of familiarity with the formal and informal aspects of other languages get American advertisers in trouble. Here are three examples.

table 8.2
Lost in Translation

When the Clairol Company introduced its "Mist Stick" curling iron in Germany, it was unaware that *mist* is a German slang word meaning "manure." Not many people wanted to buy a manure stick.

In Chinese, the Kentucky Fried Chicken slogan "Finger lickin' good" came out as "Eat your fingers off."

In Chinese, the slogan for Pepsi, "Come alive with the Pepsi Generation," became "Pepsi brings your ancestors back from the grave."

---

compared, there are indeed significant differences. But are these differences in perception the *result* of differences in language?

One of the most interesting tests of Whorf's ideas was conducted by Eleanor Rosch (1975). She compared the perception of colors by North Americans with that by members of the Dani tribe of New Guinea. In the language of the Dani, there are only two color names—one for dark, "cold" colors and one for lighter, "warm" ones. In contrast, English speakers have names for a vast number of different hues. Of these, it is possible to identify eleven focal colors; these are prototypes, the particular wavelengths of light that are the best examples of the eleven major categories (red, yellow, green, blue, black, gray, white, purple, orange, pink, and brown). Fire-engine red is the focal color for red. Rosch reasoned that if Whorf's views were correct, then English speakers, who have verbal labels for focal colors, should recognize them better than nonfocal colors, but that for the Dani, the focal-nonfocal distinction should make no difference. In fact, however, Rosch found that both the Dani and the English-speaking North Americans perceived focal colors more efficiently than nonfocal ones (Heider, 1972).

Although our language may not determine what we think about, it does appear to influence how we think. For example, Alfred Bloom (1981) reported that Chinese-speaking residents of Hong Kong had a hard time thinking about questions such as "How would you react if the government were to pass a law requiring people to make weekly reports of their activities?" Responding to such questions requires dealing with *counterfactual arguments*—which are propositions that could be true but are not. The problem, he said, is that the Chinese language does not have an easy way to express such arguments. Bloom's results do not mean that the Chinese are incapable of counterfactual thinking (Au, 1992; Chan, 2000; Liu, 1985); rather, they remind us that thinking habits are shaped by our culture, including the language in which we do our thinking (Nisbett et al., 2002).

Another example of the influence of language on thinking comes from a study showing that compared with children who speak Japanese or Korean, English- and French-speaking children have more trouble understanding the mathematical concept of "place value"—such as that the number *eleven* means "one 10 and one 1" (Miura et al., 1993). As described in the chapter on human development, one important reason for this difference is that some languages make place values more obvious than others. The Korean word for *eleven*, which is *shib-il*, means "ten-one." English speakers have to remember what *eleven* refers to every time they hear it.

TRY THIS — Even within a culture, language can affect reasoning, problem solving, and decision making. For example, consider whether you would choose A or B in each of the following situations:

> *The government is preparing for the outbreak of an unusual disease, which you know will kill 600 people if nothing is done. Two programs are proposed. If program A is adopted, 200 people will be saved. If program B is adopted, there is a one-third chance that all 600 people will be saved and a two-thirds chance that no people will be saved.*

A ship hits a mine in the middle of the ocean, and 600 passengers on board will die if action is not taken immediately. There are two options. If option A is adopted, 400 passengers will die. If option B is adopted, there is a one-third chance that no passengers will die and a two-thirds chance that no passengers will be saved.

The logic of each situation is the same (program A and option A will both save 200 lives), so people who choose program A in one case should choose option A in the other. But this is not what happens. In one study, 72 percent of participants chose program A in the disease situation, but 78 percent chose option B in the shipwreck situation (Kahneman & Tversky, 1984). Their choices were not logically consistent, because people's thinking tends to be influenced by the words used to describe situations. Here, program A was framed in terms of lives saved; option B was framed in terms of lives lost. Advertisers are well aware of how this *framing effect* alters decisions; as a result, your grocer stocks ground beef labeled as "75 percent lean," not "25 percent fat."

LINKAGES

As noted in the chapter on introducing psychology, all of psychology's subfields are related to one another. Our discussion of group processes in problem solving illustrates just one way in which the topic of this chapter, cognition and language, is linked to the subfield of social psychology (especially to the chapter on social influence). The Linkages diagram shows ties to two other subfields as well, and there are many more ties throughout the book. Looking for linkages among subfields will help you see how they all fit together and help you better appreciate the big picture that is psychology.

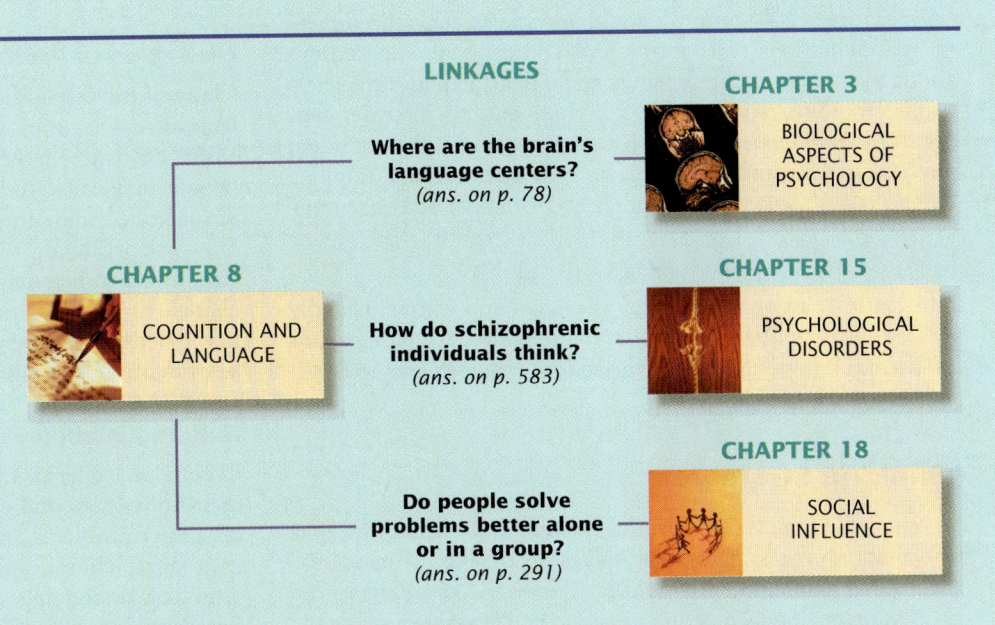

LINKAGES

CHAPTER 8 — COGNITION AND LANGUAGE

- Where are the brain's language centers? (ans. on p. 78) → **CHAPTER 3** BIOLOGICAL ASPECTS OF PSYCHOLOGY
- How do schizophrenic individuals think? (ans. on p. 583) → **CHAPTER 15** PSYCHOLOGICAL DISORDERS
- Do people solve problems better alone or in a group? (ans. on p. 291) → **CHAPTER 18** SOCIAL INFLUENCE

SUMMARY

Cognitive psychology is the study of the mental processes by which the information humans receive from their environment is modified, made meaningful, stored, retrieved, used, and communicated to others.

Basic Functions of Thought

The five core functions of thought are to describe, elaborate, decide, plan, and guide action.

The Circle of Thought

Many psychologists think of the components of the circle of thought as constituting an *information-processing system* that receives, represents, transforms, and acts on incoming stimuli. *Thinking*, then, is defined as the manipulation of mental representations by this system.

Measuring Information Processing

The time elapsing between the presentation of a stimulus and an overt response to it is the *reaction time*. Among the factors affecting reaction times are the complexity of the choice of a response, stimulus-response compatibility, expectancy, and the tradeoff between speed and accuracy. Using methods such as the EEG and neuroimaging techniques, psychologists can also measure mental events as reflected in *evoked brain potentials* and other brain activity.

Mental Representations: The Ingredients of Thought

Mental representations take the form of concepts, propositions, schemas, scripts, mental models, images, and cognitive maps.

Concepts

Concepts are categories of objects, events, or ideas with common properties. They may be formal or natural. *Formal concepts* are precisely defined by the presence or absence of certain features. *Natural concepts* are fuzzy; no fixed set of defining properties determines membership in a natural concept. A member of a natural concept that displays all or most of its characteristic features is called a *prototype*.

Propositions

Propositions are assertions that state how concepts are related. Propositions can be true or false.

Schemas, Scripts, and Mental Models

Schemas are sets of propositions that serve as generalized mental representations of concepts and also generate expectations about them. *Scripts* are schemas of familiar activities that help people to think about those activities and to interpret new events. *Mental models* are clusters of propositions that represent physical objects and processes, as well as guide our thinking about those things; mental models may or may not be accurate.

Images and Cognitive Maps

Information can be represented as *images* and can be mentally rotated, inspected, and otherwise manipulated. *Cognitive maps* are mental representations of the spatial arrangements in familiar parts of the world.

Thinking Strategies

By combining and transforming mental representations, our information-processing system makes it possible for us to reason, solve problems, and make decisions. *Reasoning* is the process through which people generate and evaluate arguments, as well as reach conclusions about them.

Formal Reasoning

Formal reasoning seeks valid conclusions through the application of rigorous procedures. These procedures include formulas, or *algorithms*, which are guaranteed to produce correct solutions if they exist, and the *rules of logic*, which are useful in evaluating sets of premises and conclusions called *syllogisms*. To reach a sound conclusion, we must consider both the truth or falsity of the premises and the logic of the argument itself. People are prone to logical errors; their belief in a conclusion is often affected by the extent to which the conclusion is consistent with their attitudes, as well as by other factors, including *confirmation bias* and limits on working memory.

Informal Reasoning

People use *informal reasoning* to assess the believability of a conclusion based on the evidence for it. Errors in informal reasoning often stem from the misuse of *heuristics,* or mental shortcuts. Three important heuristics are the *anchoring heuristic* (estimating the probability of an event by adjusting a starting value), the *representativeness heuristic* (categorizing an event by how representative it is of a category of events), and the *availability heuristic* (estimating probability by how available an event is in memory).

Problem Solving

Steps in problem solving include diagnosing the problem and then planning, executing, and evaluating a solution.

Strategies for Problem Solving

Especially when solutions are not obvious, problem solving can be aided by the use of strategies such as incubation, means-end analysis, working backward, and using analogies.

Obstacles to Problem Solving

Many of the difficulties that people experience in solving problems arise when they are dealing with hypotheses. People do not easily entertain multiple hypotheses. Because of *mental sets,* people may stick to a particular hypothesis even when it is unsuccessful and, through *functional fixedness,* may tend to miss opportunities to use familiar objects in unusual ways. Confirmation bias may lead people to be reluctant to revise or change hypotheses, especially cherished ones, on the basis of new evidence, and they may fail to use the absence of symptoms as evidence in solving problems.

Building Problem-Solving Skills

Experts are superior to beginners in problem solving because of their knowledge and experience. They can draw on knowledge of similar problems, visualize related components of a problem as a single chunk, and perceive relations among problems in terms of underlying principles rather than surface features. Extensive knowledge is the main component of expertise, yet expertise itself can prevent the expert from seeing problems in new ways.

Problem Solving by Computer

Some specific problems can be solved by computer programs known as expert systems. These systems are one application of *artificial intelligence (AI).* One approach to AI focuses on programming computers to imitate the logical manipulation of symbols that occurs in human thought; another approach (involving connectionist, or neural network, models) attempts to imitate the connections among neurons in the human brain. Current problem-solving computer systems deal most successfully with specific domains. Often, the best outcomes occur when humans and computers work together.

Decision Making

Evaluating Options

Decisions are sometimes difficult because there are too many alternatives and too many attributes of each alternative to consider at one time. Furthermore, decisions often involve comparisons of *utility*, not objective value. Decision making is also complicated by the fact that the world is unpredictable, which makes decisions risky. In risky decision making, the best decision is one that maximizes *expected value*.

Biases and Flaws in Decision Making

People often fail to maximize expected value in their decisions for two reasons: First, losses are perceived differently from gains of equal size; second, people tend to overestimate the probability of unlikely events, underestimate the probability of likely events, and feel overconfident in the accuracy of their forecasts. The gambler's fallacy leads people to believe that outcomes in a random process are affected by previous outcomes. People sometimes make decisions aimed at goals other than maximizing expected value; these goals may be determined by personal and cultural factors.

Naturalistic Decision Making

Many real-world circumstances require naturalistic decision making, in which prior experiences are used to develop mental representations of how organizational systems really work.

Language

The Elements of Language

Language consists of symbols such as words and rules for their combination—a *grammar*. Spoken *words* are made up of *phonemes*, which are combined to make *morphemes*. Combinations of words must have both *syntax* (grammar) and *semantics* (meaning). Behind the word strings, or *surface structures*, is an underlying representation, or *deep structure*, that expresses the relationship among the ideas in a sentence. Ambiguous sentences occur when one surface structure reflects two or more deep structures.

Understanding Speech

When people listen to speech, their perceptual system allows them to perceive gaps between words, even when those gaps are not physically present. To understand language generally, and conversations in particular, people use their knowledge of the context and of the world. In addition, understanding is guided by nonverbal cues.

The Development of Language

Children develop grammar according to an orderly pattern. *Babblings* and the *one-word stage* of speech come first, then telegraphic two-word sentences. Next come three-word sentences and certain grammatical forms that appear in a somewhat predictable order. Once children learn certain regular verb forms and plural endings, they may overgeneralize rules. Children acquire most of the syntax of their native language by the time they are five years old.

How Is Language Acquired?

Conditioning and imitation both play a role in a child's acquisition of language, but neither can provide a complete explanation of how children acquire syntax. Humans may be biologically programmed to learn language. In any event, it appears that language must be learned during a certain critical period if normal language is to occur. The critical-period notion is supported by research on second-language acquisition.

Culture, Language, and Thought

Research across cultures, and within North American culture, suggests that although language does not determine what we can think, it does influence how we think, solve problems, and make decisions.

9 Consciousness

Analyzing Consciousness
Some Functions of Consciousness
Levels of Consciousness
Mental Processing Without Awareness
FOCUS ON RESEARCH METHODS: Subliminal Messages in Rock Music
The Neuropsychology of Consciousness
States of Consciousness

Sleeping and Dreaming
Stages of Sleep
Sleep Disorders
Why Do People Sleep?
Dreams and Dreaming

Hypnosis
Experiencing Hypnosis
Explaining Hypnosis
Applications of Hypnosis

LINKAGES: Meditation, Health, and Stress

Psychoactive Drugs
Psychopharmacology
The Varying Effects of Drugs
Depressants
Stimulants
Opiates
Hallucinogens
THINKING CRITICALLY: Is Marijuana Dangerous?

Linkages

Summary

There is an old *Sesame Street* episode in which Ernie is trying to find out whether Bert is asleep or awake. In other words, Ernie is trying to determine Bert's state of consciousness. Ernie observes that Bert's eyes are closed, and he comments that Bert usually closes his eyes when he is asleep. Ernie also notes that when Bert is asleep, he does not respond to pokes, so naturally, he delivers a few pokes. At first, Bert does not respond; but after being poked a few times, he awakes, very annoyed, and yells at Ernie for waking him. Ernie then informs Bert that he just wanted to let him know it was time for his nap.

In a way, doctors face a similar situation in dealing with the more than 30 million people each year who receive general anesthesia during surgery. These patients certainly appear to go to sleep, but it may surprise you to learn that there is no reliable way of knowing whether they are actually unconscious. It turns out that about 1 percent of them retain some degree of consciousness during the surgical procedure (Ranta, Jussila, & Hynynen, 1990; Sandin et al., 2000). In rare cases, patients have conscious awareness of surgical pain and remember the trauma. Although their surgical incisions heal, these people may be psychologically scarred by the experience and may even show symptoms of posttraumatic stress disorder (Schwender et al., 1995).

The fact that people can be conscious while "asleep" under the influence of powerful anesthetic drugs obviously makes defining consciousness quite difficult. After decades of discussion and research by philosophers, psychologists, and even physicists, some believe that consciousness is still not yet understood well enough to be precisely defined (Crick & Koch, 1998; King & Pribram, 1995). Given the ethical and legal concerns raised by the need to ensure that patients are not subjected to pain during surgery, doctors tend to define *consciousness* as awareness that is demonstrated by either explicit or implicit recall (Schwender et al., 1995). In psychology, the definition is somewhat broader: **Consciousness** is generally defined as your awareness of the outside world and of your thoughts, feelings, perceptions, and other mental processes (Metzinger, 2000). This definition suggests that consciousness is a property of many mental processes rather than a unique mental process unto itself. For example, memories can be conscious, but consciousness is not just memory. Perceptions can be conscious, but consciousness is not just perception. This definition also allows for the possibility that humans are not the only creatures that experience consciousness. It would appear that some animals whose brains are similar to our own have self-awareness, even though they do not have the language abilities to tell us about it. One way to assess this awareness is to determine if a creature recognizes itself in a mirror. Children can do so at about two years of age. Monkeys never display this ability, but chimpanzees do, and it has recently been discovered that dolphins do, too (Reiss & Marino, 2001). Although consciousness may not be a uniquely human capacity, it is central to our experience of life.

In this chapter we begin by analyzing the nature of consciousness and the ways in which it affects mental activity and behavior. Then we examine what happens when consciousness is altered by sleep, hypnosis, and meditation. Finally, we explore the changes in consciousness that occur when people use certain drugs.

A "Self-aware" Dolphin? Scientists have provided evidence that animals other than humans have aspects of self-awareness such as mirror-recognition. For example, this dolphin is said to recognize itself because it showed self-directed behaviors at a mirror and used the mirror to view specific parts of its body that had been marked (Reiss & Marino, 2001).

Analyzing Consciousness

Psychologists have been fascinated by the study of consciousness for more than a century, but only in the last thirty years or so has consciousness emerged as an active and vital research area in psychology. This is because, as described in the chapter on introducing psychology, behaviorism dominated psychological research in the United States from the 1920s through the 1960s. Accordingly, little research was conducted on mental processes, including the structure and functions of consciousness. But since the late 1960s, as CT scans, PET scans, MRI, and other new techniques described in the biological psychology chapter allowed ever more precise

consciousness Awareness of external stimuli and one's own mental activity.

analysis of brain activity, the study of consciousness has returned to the mainstream of research in psychology. Scientists who study consciousness sometimes describe their work as *cognitive science* or *cognitive neuroscience,* because their research is so closely tied to the subfields of biological psychology, sensation, perception, memory, and human cognition. In fact, many cognitive psychologists can be said to study consciousness through their work on memory, reasoning, problem solving, and decision making.

Other psychologists study consciousness more directly by addressing three central questions about it. First, like the philosophers who preceded them, psychologists have grappled with the *mind-body problem:* What is the relationship between the conscious mind and the physical brain? One approach, known as *dualism,* sees the mind and brain as different entities. This idea was championed in the seventeenth century by French philosopher René Descartes. Descartes claimed that a person's soul, or consciousness, is separate from the brain but can "view" and interact with brain events through the pineal gland, a brain structure about the size of a grape. Once a popular point of view, dualism has virtually disappeared from psychology.

Another perspective, known as *materialism,* suggests that mind is brain. Materialists argue that complex interactions among the brain's nerve cells create consciousness, much as hardware and software interact to create the image that appears on a computer screen. A good deal of support for the materialist view comes from case studies in which disruptions of consciousness occur following brain damage.

A second question focuses on whether or not consciousness is a unitary entity: Does consciousness occur as a single "point" in mental processing or as several parallel mental operations that occur independently? According to the *"theater"* view, consciousness is a single phenomenon, a kind of "stage" on which all the different events of awareness converge to "play" before the "audience" of your mind. Those adopting this view say it is supported by the fact that the subjective intensities of lights, sounds, weights, and other stimuli follow similar psychophysical laws (described in the chapter on perception), as if each sensory system passes its inputs to a single "monitor" that coordinates the experience of magnitude (Teghtsoonian, 1992).

In contrast, the *parallel distributed processing (PDP) models* described in the perception chapter describe the mind as processing many parallel streams of information, which interact somehow to create the unitary experience we know as consciousness (Devinsky, 1997). PDP models became influential when research on sensation, perception, memory, cognition, and language suggested that components of these processes are analyzed in separate brain regions. For example, perception of a visual scene involves activity in a number of separate brain regions that analyze "what" each object is, "where" it is, and whether the object is actually there or merely imagined (Ishai et al., 2000). Scientists still do not know whether these parallel streams of information ever unite in a common brain region.

A third question about consciousness addresses the relationship between nonconscious mental activities and conscious awareness. More than a century ago, Sigmund Freud theorized that some mental processes occur without our awareness and that these processes can affect us in many ways. Most aspects of Freud's theory are not supported by modern laboratory research, but studies have shown that many important mental activities do occur outside of awareness. Let's examine some of these activities and consider the functions they serve.

Some Functions of Consciousness

Francis Crick and Christof Koch have suggested that one function of consciousness is to produce the best current interpretation of sensory information in light of past experience, and to make this interpretation available to those parts of the brain that

---

conscious level The level at which mental activities that people are normally aware of occur.

nonconscious level A level of mental activity that is inaccessible to conscious awareness.

preconscious level A level of mental activity that is not currently conscious, but of which we can easily become conscious.

can act on it (Crick & Koch, 1998). Having a *single* conscious representation, rather than multiple ones, allows us to be less hesitant and more decisive in taking action. The conscious brain, then, experiences a representation of the sensory world that is the result of many complex computations; it has access to the *results* of these computational processes but not to the processes themselves. The conscious representation experienced is not necessarily the quickest processing available, however. For example, tennis players may respond to a hard serve before they consciously "see" the ball. However, for complex problems, consciousness allows the most adaptive and efficient interactions among sensory input, motor responses, and a range of knowledge resources in the brain (Baars, 1998).

As described in the chapter on memory, the contents of consciousness at any given moment are limited by the capacity of short-term memory, but the overall process of consciousness allows access to a vast store of memories and other information. In one study, for example, participants paid brief conscious attention to ten thousand different pictures over several days. A week later they were able to recognize more than 90 percent of the photographs. Evidently, mere consciousness of an event helps to store a recognizable memory that can later be brought into consciousness (Kosslyn, 1994).

Almost a hundred years ago William James compared consciousness to a stream, describing it as ever changing, multilayered, and varying in both quantity and quality. Variations in quantity—in the degree to which one is aware of mental events—result in different *levels of consciousness*. Variations in quality—in the nature of the mental processing available to awareness—lead to different *states of consciousness*. Appreciating the difference between levels of consciousness and states of consciousness takes a little thought. When you are alert and aware of your mental activity and of incoming sensations, you are fully conscious, and experiencing yourself as "I." At the same time, however, other mental activity is taking place within your brain at varying "distances" from your conscious awareness. These activities are occurring at differing *levels* of consciousness. It is when your experience of yourself as "I" varies in focus and clarity—as when you sleep or are under the influence of a mind-altering drug—that there are variations in your *state* of consciousness. Let's first consider various levels of consciousness.

Levels of Consciousness

At any moment, the mental events that you are aware of are said to exist at the **conscious level**. For example, look at the Necker cube in Figure 9.1. If you are like most people, you can hold the cube in one configuration for only a few seconds before the other configuration "pops out" at you. The configuration that you experience at any moment is at your conscious level of awareness for that moment.

Some mental events, however, cannot be experienced consciously. For example, you are not directly aware of the fact that your brain constantly regulates your blood pressure. Such mental processing occurs at the **nonconscious level**, totally removed from conscious awareness. Other mental events are not conscious, but they can either become conscious or influence conscious experience; these mental events make up the *cognitive unconscious* (Reber, 1992), which is further divided into preconscious and unconscious (or subconscious) levels. Mental events at the **preconscious level** are outside of awareness but can easily be brought into awareness. For example, stop reading for a moment, and think about last night's dinner. As you do so, you become aware of what and where you ate, and with whom. But moments ago, you were probably not thinking about that information; it was preconscious, ready to be brought to the conscious level. Varying amounts of effort may be required to bring preconscious information into consciousness. In a trivia game you may draw on your large storehouse of preconscious memories to come up with obscure facts, sometimes easily and sometimes only with difficulty.

figure 9.1

The Necker Cube

TRY THIS   Each of the two squares in the Necker cube can be perceived as either the front or rear surface of the cube. Try to make the cube switch back and forth between these two configurations. Now try to hold only one configuration. You probably cannot maintain the whole cube in consciousness for longer than about three seconds before it "flips" from one configuration to the other.

Evidence for the operation of subconscious mental processing includes research showing that surgery patients may be able to hear and later comply with instructions or suggestions given while they are under anesthesia and of which they have no memory (Bennett, Giannini, & Davis, 1985). In another study, people showed physiological arousal to emotionally charged words even when they were not paying attention to them (Von Wright, Anderson, & Stenman, 1975).

Reprinted by permission of International Creative Management, Inc. Copyright © 2002 Berke Breathed.

LINKAGES (a link to Sensation)

There are still other mental activities that can alter thoughts, feelings, and actions but are more difficult to bring into awareness (Ratner, 1994). As described in the chapter on personality, Freud suggested that mental events at the **unconscious level**—especially those involving unacceptable sexual and aggressive urges—are actively kept out of consciousness. Many psychologists do not accept this view but still use the term *unconscious* (or *subconscious*) to describe the level of mental activity that influences consciousness but is not conscious.

Mental Processing Without Awareness

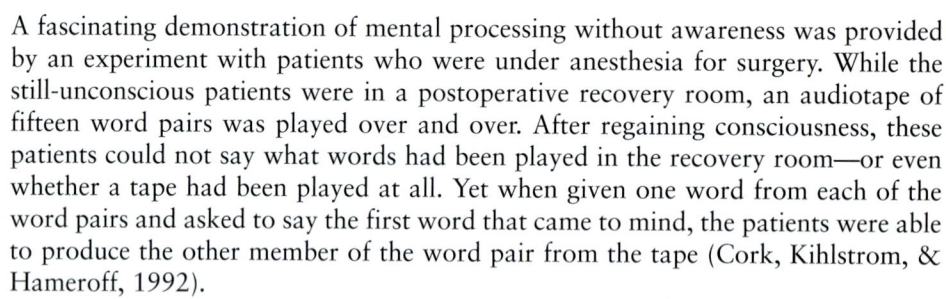

A fascinating demonstration of mental processing without awareness was provided by an experiment with patients who were under anesthesia for surgery. While the still-unconscious patients were in a postoperative recovery room, an audiotape of fifteen word pairs was played over and over. After regaining consciousness, these patients could not say what words had been played in the recovery room—or even whether a tape had been played at all. Yet when given one word from each of the word pairs and asked to say the first word that came to mind, the patients were able to produce the other member of the word pair from the tape (Cork, Kihlstrom, & Hameroff, 1992).

Even when people are conscious and alert, information can sometimes be processed and used without their awareness (Ward, 1997). In one study of this phenomenon, participants watched a computer screen as an X flashed in one of four locations. The participants' task was to indicate where the X appeared by rapidly pushing one of four buttons. The X's location seemed to vary randomly, but the placement sequence actually followed a set of complex rules, such as "If the X moves horizontally twice in a row, then it will move vertically next." The participants' responses became progressively faster and more accurate, but their performance instantly deteriorated when the rules were dropped and the Xs began appearing in truly random locations. Without being aware of doing so, these participants had apparently learned a complex rule-bound strategy to improve their performance. However, even when offered $100 to state the rules that had guided the location sequence, they could not do so, nor were they sure that any such rules existed (Lewicki, 1992).

Visual processing without awareness may also occur in cases of blindness caused by damage that is limited to the primary visual cortex. In such cases, fibers from the eyes are still connected to other brain areas that process visual information. Some of these surviving pathways may permit visual processing, but without visual awareness—a condition known as *blindsight* (Gazzaniga, Fendrich, & Wessinger, 1994). Even though such patients say they see nothing, if forced to guess, they can still locate visual targets, identify the direction and orientation of moving images, reach for objects, name the color of lights, and even discriminate happy from fearful faces that they cannot consciously see (Morris et al., 2001).

unconscious level A level of mental activity that influences consciousness, but is not conscious.

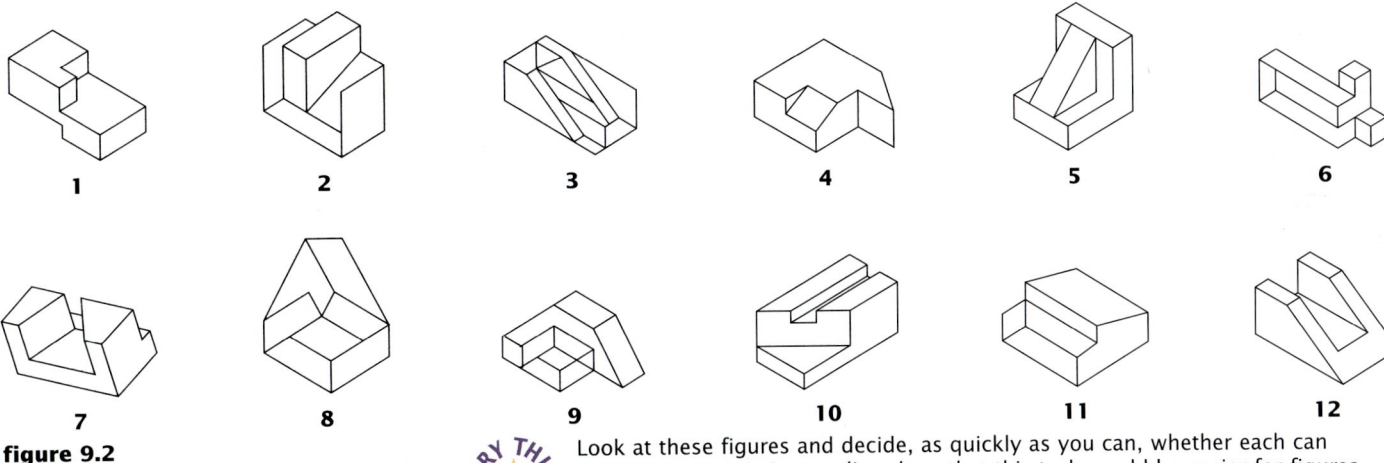

figure 9.2
Possible or Impossible?

Look at these figures and decide, as quickly as you can, whether each can actually exist. Priming studies show that this task would be easier for figures you have seen in the past, even if you don't recall seeing them. How did you do? (The correct answers appear on page 314.)

Source: Schacter et al. (1991).

Research on *priming* also demonstrates mental processing without awareness. In a typical priming study, people tend to respond faster or more accurately to previously seen stimuli, even when they cannot consciously recall having seen those stimuli (Abrams & Greenwald, 2000; Arndt et al., 1997; Bar & Biederman, 1998; Schacter & Cooper, 1993). In one study, people were asked to look at a set of drawings like those in Figure 9.2 and decide which of the objects depicted could actually exist in three-dimensional space and which could not. The participants were better at classifying pictures that they had seen before, even when they could not remember having seen them (Cooper et al., 1992b; Schacter et al., 1991).

Other studies show how priming can alter certain behaviors even when participants are not consciously aware of being influenced. In one such study, for example (Bargh, Chen, & Burrows, 1996), participants were asked to unscramble sentences in which the words were out of order (e.g., "He it finds instantly."). In one condition of the experiment, the scrambled sentences contained words associated with the attribute of rudeness (e.g., *rude, bother,* and *annoying*); in a second condition, the scrambled words were associated with politeness (e.g., *respect, honor,* and *polite*); and in a third condition, the words were neutral (e.g., *normally, sends,* and *rapidly*). After completing the unscrambling task, the participants were asked to go to another room to get further instructions from the experimenter. But by design, the experimenter was always found talking to a research assistant. The dependent variable in this experiment was whether participants in the three conditions would interrupt the experimenter. As shown in Figure 9.3, the participants in the "rude priming" condition were most likely to interrupt, whereas those in the "polite priming" condition were least likely to do so. Those in the "neutral" condition fell in between the other two groups.

The results of priming studies challenge some of the traditional Freudian views about the unconscious. According to Freud, unconscious processes function mainly to protect us from painful or frightening thoughts, feelings, and memories by keeping them out of consciousness (Pervin, 1996). However, many psychologists studying unconscious processes now believe that, in fact, one of the primary functions of these processes is to help us more effectively carry out mundane, day-to-day mental activities.

Numerous questions about the relationship between conscious and unconscious processes remain to be answered. One of the most significant of these questions is whether conscious and unconscious thoughts occur independently of each other.

figure 9.3
Priming Behavior Without Awareness

Participants in this study were primed with rude, polite, or neutral words before being confronted with the problem of interrupting an ongoing conversation. Although they were not consciously aware of the priming process, participants previously exposed to rude words were most likely to interrupt, whereas those previously exposed to polite words were least likely to do so.

Source: Bargh, Chen, & Burrows (1996, Figure 1).

Priming studies seem to suggest that they are independent, but other research suggests that they may not be. For example, one study found a correlation between unconscious indicators of age prejudice—as seen in implicit memory for negative stereotypes about the elderly—and consciously held attitudes toward the elderly (Hense, Penner, & Nelson, 1995). Another study (Lepore & Brown, 1997) also found similarity between unconscious and conscious forms of ethnic prejudice. Overall, however, if there is a relationship between explicit and implicit cognitions, it appears to be weak and not yet clearly understood (Dovidio, Kawakami, & Beach, 2001). We consider this issue further in the chapter on social cognition.

FOCUS ON RESEARCH METHODS

Subliminal Messages in Rock Music

Numerous Internet web sites present claims that Satanic or drug-related messages have been embedded in the recorded music of rock bands such as Marilyn Manson, Nine Inch Nails, Judas Priest, Led Zeppelin, and the Rolling Stones. The story goes that because these alleged messages were recorded backward, they are *subliminal* (not consciously perceived), but they have supposedly influenced listeners to commit suicide or murder. For this assertion to be true, however, the content of the subliminal backward message would have to be perceived at some level of consciousness.

- **What was the researchers' question?**

There is no compelling evidence that backward messages are actually present in most of the music cited. However, John R. Vokey and J. Don Read (1985) asked whether any backward messages that might exist could be perceived and understood when the music is playing forward. They also asked whether such messages have any effect on behavior.

- **How did the researchers answer the question?**

Vokey and Read conducted a series of multiple case studies of the impact of backward-recorded messages. They first recorded readings of portions of the Twenty-third Psalm and Lewis Carroll's poem "The Jabberwocky." This poem includes many nonsense words, but it follows grammar rules (e.g., "'Twas brillig and the slithy toves . . ."). These recordings were then played backward to groups of college students. The students were asked to judge whether what they heard would have been nonsensical or meaningful if played forward.

- **What did the researchers find?**

When the students heard the material played backward, they could not discriminate sense from nonsense. They could not tell the difference between declarative sentences and questions. They could not even identify the original material on which the recordings were based. In short, the participants could not make sense of the backward messages at a conscious level. Could they do so subconsciously? To find out, the researchers asked the participants to sort the backward statements they heard into one of five categories: nursery rhymes, Christian, Satanic, pornographic, or advertising. They reasoned that if some sort of meaning could be subconsciously understood, the participants would be able to sort the statements nonrandomly. As it turned out, however, the accuracy of the participants' category judgments was no better than chance.

Can even *unperceived* backward messages unconsciously shape behavior? To answer this question, Vokey and Read presented a backward version of a message whose sentences contained homophones (words that sound alike but have two spellings and two different meanings, such as *feat* and *feet*). When heard in the

---

Answer key for Figure 9.2: Figures 1, 4, 5, 7, 10, and 12 can exist in three-dimensional space.

Subliminal Messages in Rock Music? Picketers in Florida hold up a large cross as they protest outside a Marilyn Manson concert. Some believe that Manson's music, as well as that of rock stars ranging from Michael Jackson to Madonna, contains subliminal messages advocating drug use, violence, and Satanism.

normal forward direction, such messages affect people's spelling of ambiguous words that are read aloud to them at a later time. (For example, people tend to spell out *f-e-a-t* rather than *f-e-e-t* if they previously heard the sentence "It was a great feat of strength.") This example of priming occurs even if people do not recall having heard the message. After hearing a backward version of the message, however, the participants in this study did not produce the expected spelling bias.

- **What do the results mean?**

Obviously, it wasn't possible for the participants to subconsciously understand meaning in the backward messages. Backward messages are evidently not consciously or unconsciously understood, nor do they influence behavior.

- **What do we still need to know?**

Researchers would like to understand why the incorrect idea persists that backward messages can influence behavior. Beliefs and suspicions do not simply disappear in the face of contrary scientific evidence (Vyse, 1997). Perhaps such evidence needs to be publicized more widely in order to lay the misconceptions to rest, but it seems likely that some people so deeply want to believe in the existence and power of backward messages in rock music that such beliefs will forever hold the status of folk myths in Western culture.

The Neuropsychology of Consciousness

The nature of various levels of consciousness and the role of the brain regions that support them have been illuminated by studies of the results of brain damage. Consider the case of Karen Ann Quinlan. After drug-induced heart failure starved her brain of oxygen, Quinlan entered a coma; she was unconscious, unresponsive, and—in medical terms—brain-dead. Amid worldwide controversy, her parents obtained a court order that allowed them to shut off their daughter's life-support machines; but to everyone's surprise, she continued to live in a vegetative state for ten more years. A detailed study of her autopsied brain revealed that it had sustained damage mainly in the thalamus, an area described in the chapter on biological psychology as a "relay station" for most sensory signals entering the brain (Kinney et al., 1994). Some researchers have used this finding to argue that the thalamus may be critical for the experience of consciousness (e.g., Bogen, 1995). Given the discovery of reciprocal feedback between the thalamus and the cortex, there is reason to believe that the thalamus does, in fact, play a role in directing the spotlight of conscious attention to information in particular parts of the cortex "where the action is" (Baars, 1998).

A condition known as *prosopagnosia* provides an example of how brain damage can also cause more limited impairments in consciousness. People with prosopagnosia cannot consciously recognize faces—including their own face in the mirror—yet they can still see and recognize many other objects and can still recognize people by their voices (Young & De Haan, 1992). This deficit may reflect a more general inability to recognize curved objects (Laeng & Caviness, 2001), but in practice the problem is relatively specific for faces. One individual with prosopagnosia who became a farmer could recognize and name his sheep, but he never was able to recognize humans (McNeil & Warrington, 1993). Still, when such people see a familiar—but not consciously recognized—face, they show eye movement patterns, changes in brain activity, and autonomic nervous system responses that do not occur when viewing an unfamiliar face (Bruyer, 1991). So some vestige of face

figure 9.4

Memory Formation in Anterograde Amnesia

"H.M.," a patient with anterograde amnesia, was asked to trace the outline of an object while using only a mirror (which reverses left and right) to guide him. His performance on this difficult task improved daily, indicating that he learned and remembered how to do the task. Yet he had no conscious memory of the practice sessions that allowed his skill to develop (Milner, 1965).

Source: Data from Milner (1965).

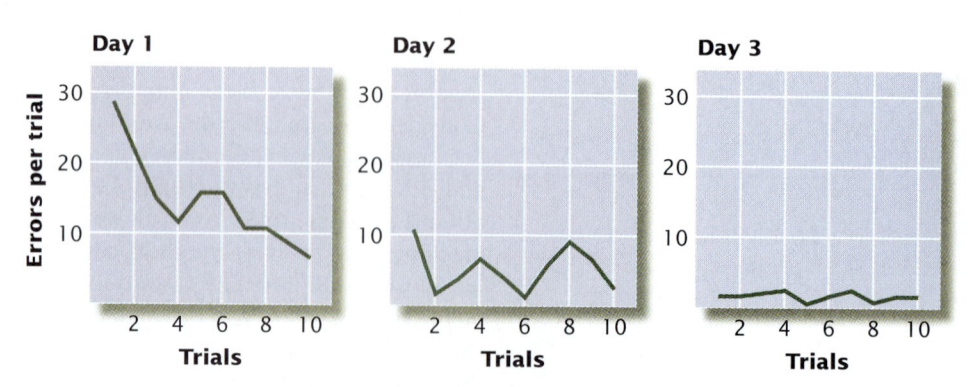

recognition is preserved in prosopagnosia, but it remains unavailable to conscious experience.

Brain damage can also impair conscious access to other mental abilities. Consider *anterograde amnesia*, the inability to form new memories, which often accompanies damage to the hippocampus (Eichenbaum, Otto, & Cohen, 1994). Anterograde amnesics seem unable to remember any new information, even about the passage of time. One man who developed this condition in 1957 still needed to be reminded more than thirty years later that it was no longer 1957 (Smith, 1988). Yet as Figure 9.4 shows, anterograde amnesics can learn new skills, even though they cannot consciously recall the practice sessions (Milner, 1965). Their brain activity, too, shows different reactions to words they have recently studied than to other words, even though they have no memory of studying them (Düzel et al., 2001).

States of Consciousness

Mental activity is always changing. The features of consciousness at any instant—what reaches your awareness, the decisions you are making, and so on—make up your **state of consciousness** at that moment. States of consciousness can range from deep sleep to alert wakefulness; they can also be affected by drugs and other influences. Consider, for example, the varying states of consciousness that might occur aboard an airplane en route from New York to Los Angeles. In the cockpit, the pilot calmly scans instrument displays while talking to an air-traffic controller. In seat 9B, a lawyer has just finished her second cocktail while planning a courtroom strategy. Nearby, a young father gazes out a window, daydreaming, while his small daughter sleeps in his lap, dreaming dreams of her own.

All these people are experiencing different states of consciousness. Some states are active and some are passive (Hilgard, 1980). The daydreaming father is letting his mind wander, passively noting images, memories, and other mental events that come unbidden to mind. The lawyer is actively directing her mental activity, evaluating various options and considering their likely outcomes.

Most people spend most of their time in a *waking* state of consciousness. Mental processing in this state varies with changes in attention or arousal. While reading, for example, you may temporarily ignore sounds around you. Similarly, if you are upset, or bored, or talking on a cell phone, you may miss important environmental cues, making it dangerous to drive a car.

When changes in mental processes are great enough for you or others to notice significant differences in how you function, you have entered an **altered state of consciousness**. In an altered state, mental processing shows distinct changes unique to that state. Cognitive processes or perceptions of yourself or the world may change, and normal inhibitions or self-control may weaken (Martindale, 1981).

The phrase *altered states of consciousness* recognizes waking consciousness as the most common state, a baseline against which "altered" states are compared. However, this is not to say that waking consciousness is universally considered more normal, proper, or valued than other states. In fact, value judgments about different states of consciousness vary considerably across cultures (Ward, 1994).

Consider, for instance, *hallucinations*, which are perceptual experiences—such as hearing voices—that occur in the absence of sensory stimuli. In the United States, hallucinations are viewed as undesirable. Mental patients who hallucinate often feel stress and self-blame; many may choose not to report their hallucinations. Those who do so tend to be considered more disturbed and may receive more drastic treatments than patients who do not report hallucinations (Wilson et al., 1996). Among the Moche of Peru, however, hallucinations have a culturally approved place. When someone is beset by illness or misfortune, a healer conducts an elaborate ritual to find causes and treatments. During the ceremony, the healer ingests mescaline, a drug that causes hallucinations. These hallucinations are thought to give the healer

state of consciousness The characteristics of consciousness at any particular moment.

altered state of consciousness A condition in which changes in mental processes are extensive enough that a person or others notice significant differences in psychological and behavioral functioning.

Altered States and Cultural Values
Cultures define which altered states of consciousness are approved. Here we see members of a Brazilian spirit possession cult in various stages of trance, and in Peru, a Moche *curandero* (curer) attempting to heal a patient by using fumes from a potion—and a drug derived from the San Pedro cactus—to put himself in an altered state of consciousness.

spiritual insight into the patient's problems (de Rios, 1992). In the context of many other tribal cultures, too, purposeful hallucinations are revered, not demeaned (Grob & Dobkin-de-Rios, 1992).

In other words, states of consciousness differ not only in their basic characteristics but also in their value to members of particular cultures. In the sections to follow, we describe some of the most interesting altered states of consciousness, beginning with the most common one, sleep.

Sleeping and Dreaming

According to ancient myths, sleepers lose control of their minds, flirting with death as their souls wander freely. Early researchers thought sleep was a time of mental inactivity. In fact, however, sleep is an active, complex state.

Stages of Sleep

Sleep researchers use an *electroencephalograph*, or *EEG*, to record the brain's electrical activity during sleep. EEG recordings, often called *brain waves*, vary in height (amplitude) and speed (frequency) as behavior or mental processes change. The brain waves of an awake, alert person have high frequency and low amplitude. They appear as small, closely spaced, irregular EEG spikes. A relaxed person with closed eyes shows *alpha waves*, which are more rhythmic brain waves occurring at speeds of eight to twelve cycles per second. During a normal night's sleep, brain waves show distinctive and systematic changes in amplitude and frequency as you pass through various stages of sleep (Guevara et al., 1995).

Slow-Wave Sleep

Imagine that you are participating in a sleep study. You are hooked up to an EEG and various monitors, and filmed as you sleep through the night. If you were to watch that film, here's what you'd see: At first, you are relaxed, with eyes closed, but awake. At this point, your muscle tone and eye movements are normal, and your EEG shows the slow brain waves associated with relaxation. You then drift into what is called **slow-wave sleep,** which is named for the fact that your EEG shows even slower brain waves. Your breathing deepens,

slow-wave sleep Sleep stages 1 through 4, which are accompanied by slow, deep breathing; a calm, regular heartbeat; and reduced blood pressure.

rapid eye movement (REM) sleep A stage of sleep in which brain activity and other functions resemble the waking state, but that is accompanied by rapid eye movements and virtual muscle paralysis.

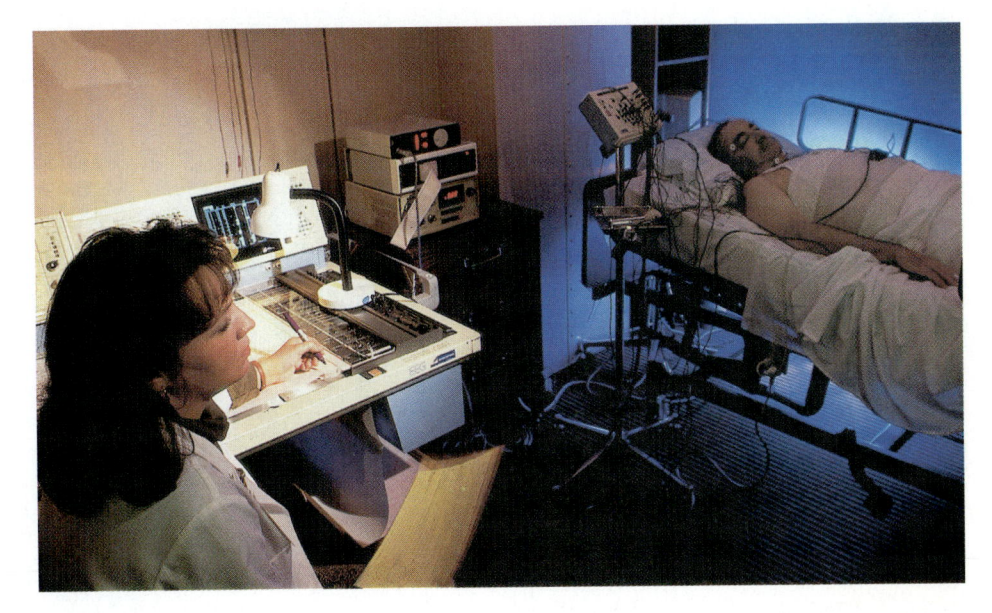

A Sleep Lab The electroencephalograph (EEG) allows scientists to record brain activity through electrodes attached to the skull. The advent of this technology opened the door to the scientific study of sleep.

LINKAGES (a link to Biological Aspects of Psychology)

your heartbeat slows, and your blood pressure drops. Over the next half hour, you descend ever deeper into stages of sleep that are characterized by even slower brain waves with even higher amplitude (see Figure 9.5). When you reach stage 4, the deepest stage of slow-wave sleep, it is quite difficult to be awakened. If you were roused from this stage of deep sleep, you would be groggy and confused.

REM Sleep

After thirty to forty-five minutes in stage 4, you quickly return to stage 2 and then enter a special stage in which your eyes move rapidly under your closed eyelids. This is called **rapid eye movement (REM) sleep,** or *paradoxical sleep*.

figure 9.5

EEG Recordings Typical of Various Sleep Stages

EEG recordings of brain wave activity disclose four relatively distinct stages of slow-wave sleep. Notice the regular patterns of alpha waves that occur just before a person goes to sleep, followed by the slowing of brain waves as sleep becomes deeper (stages 1 through 4). In rapid eye movement (REM) sleep, the frequency of brain waves increases dramatically and in some ways resembles patterns seen in people who are awake.

Source: Horne (1988).

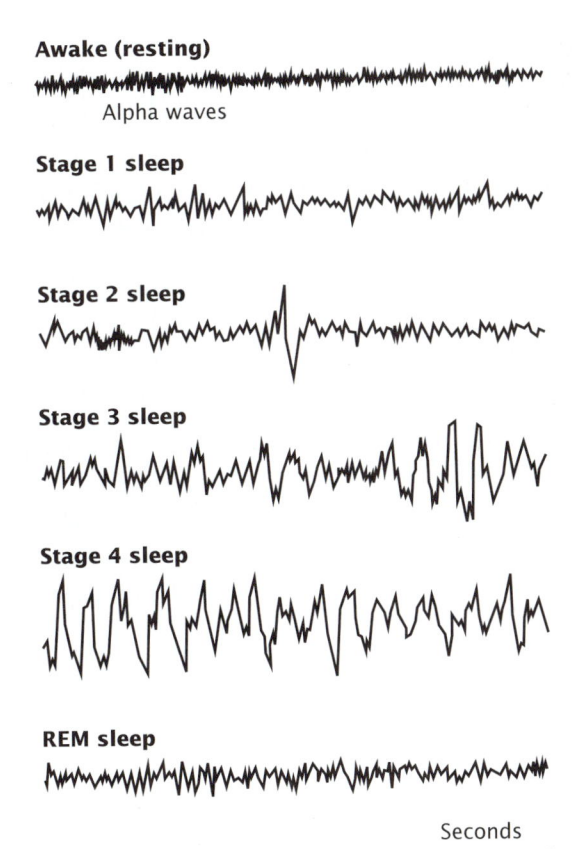

figure 9.6

A Night's Sleep

During a typical night a sleeper goes through this sequence of EEG stages. Notice that sleep is deepest during the first part of the night and more shallow later on, when REM sleep becomes more prominent.

Source: Cartwright (1978).

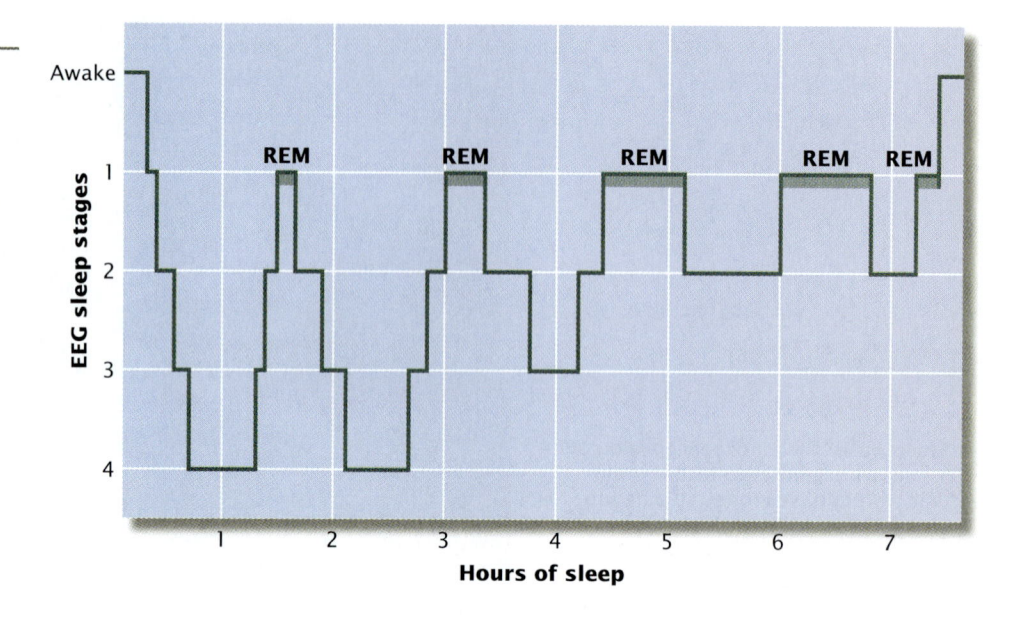

It is called *paradoxical* because its characteristics pose a paradox, or contradiction. In REM sleep, your EEG resembles that of an awake, alert person, and your physiological arousal—heart rate, breathing, and blood pressure—is also similar to when you are awake. However, your muscles are nearly paralyzed. Sudden, twitchy spasms appear, especially in your face and hands, but your brain actively suppresses other movements (Blumberg & Lucas, 1994).

In other words, there are two different types of sleep, REM sleep and slow-wave sleep (which is sometimes called *non-REM,* or *NREM,* sleep).

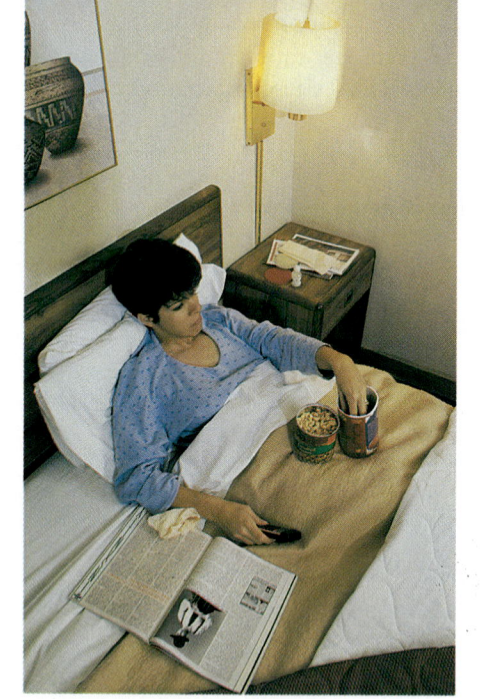

A Night's Sleep

Most people pass through the cycle of sleep stages four to six times each night. Each cycle lasts about ninety minutes, but with a somewhat changing pattern of stages and stage duration. Early in the night, most of the time is spent in the deeper stages of slow-wave sleep, with only a few minutes in REM sleep (see Figure 9.6). As sleep continues, though, it is dominated by stage 2 and REM sleep, from which sleepers finally awaken.

Sleep patterns change with age. The average infant sleeps about sixteen hours a day, and the average seventy-year-old sleeps only about six hours (Roffwarg, Muzio, & Dement, 1966). The composition of sleep changes, too (see Figure 9.7). REM sleep accounts for half of total sleep at birth but less than 25 percent in young adults. People may vary widely from these averages, however; some people feel well rested after four hours of sleep, whereas others of similar age require ten hours to feel satisfied (Clausen, Sersen, & Lidsky, 1974). There are also wide variations among cultural and socioeconomic groups in the tendency to take daytime naps. Contrary to the stereotype about the popularity of siestas in Latin and South American countries, urban Mexican college students actually nap less than many other college populations (Valencia-Flores et al., 1998).

Sleep Disorders

Most people experience sleep-related problems at some point in their lives. These problems range from occasional nights of tossing and turning to more serious and long-term *sleep disorders*. The most common sleeping problem is **insomnia,** in which one feels daytime fatigue due to trouble falling asleep or staying asleep. If you have difficulty getting to sleep or staying asleep that persists for longer than one month at a time, you may be suffering from insomnia. Besides being tiring, insomnia is tied to mental distress and impaired functioning. Insomnia is especially associated with depressive and anxiety disorders (U.S. Surgeon General, 1999);

Stimulus Control Therapy Insomnia can often be reduced through a combination of relaxation techniques and *stimulus control therapy,* in which the person goes to bed only when sleepy and gets out of bed if sleep does not come within fifteen to twenty minutes. The goal is for one's bed to become a stimulus associated with sleeping, and perhaps sex, but not with reading, eating, watching television, worrying, or anything else that is incompatible with sleep (Edinger et al., 2001).

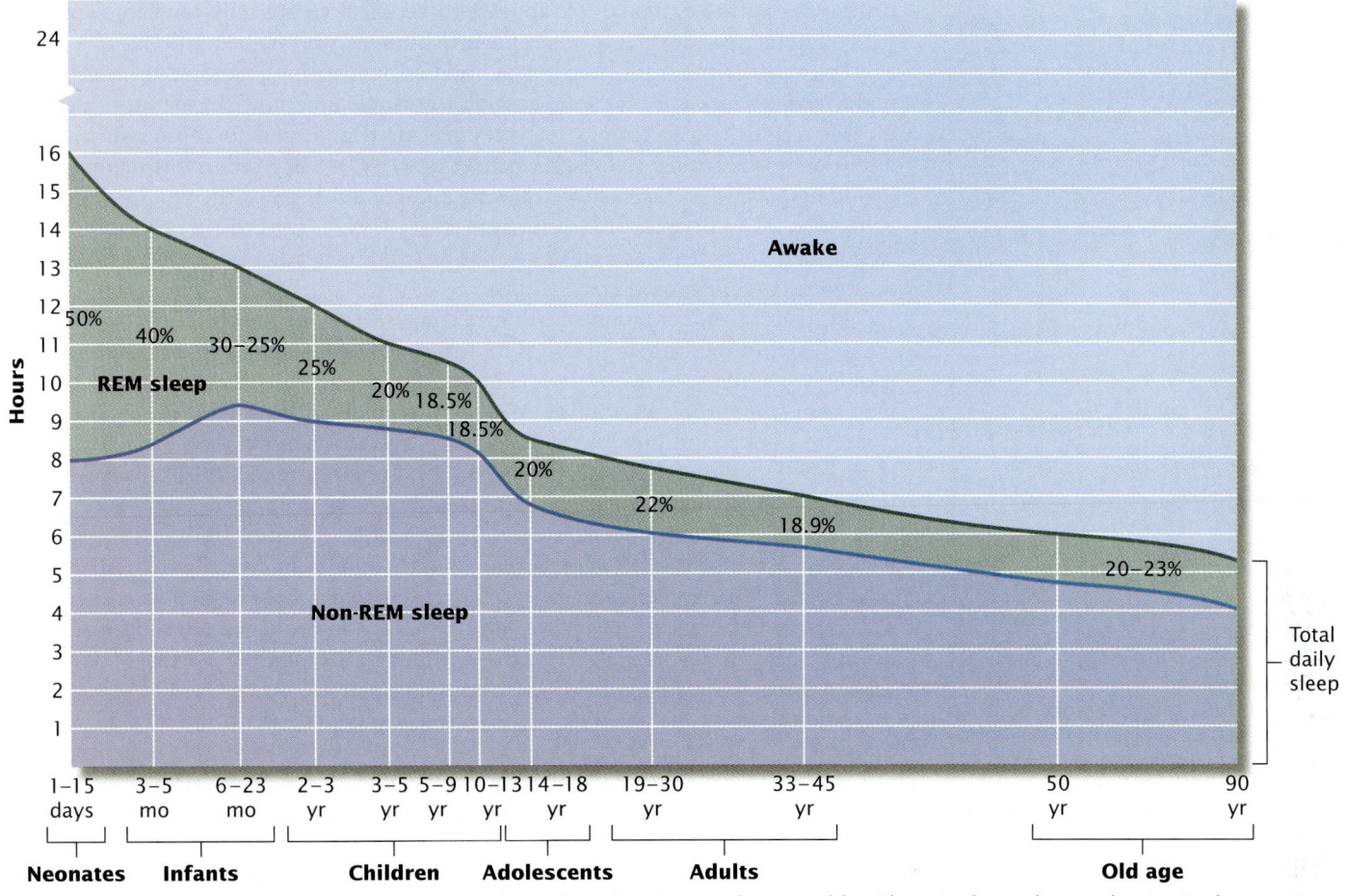

figure 9.7

Sleep and Dreaming over the Life Span

People tend to sleep less as they get older. There is also a sharp reduction in the percentage of REM sleep, from about eight hours per day in infancy to about an hour per day by age seventy. Non-REM sleep time also decreases but, compared with the drop in REM, remains relatively stable. After age twenty, however, non-REM sleep contains less and less of the deepest, or stage 4, sleep.

Note: Percentages indicate portion of total sleep time in REM sleep.

Source: Roffwarg, Muzio, & Dement (1966/1969).

overall, insomniacs are three times as likely to show a mental disorder as those with no sleep complaints. It is unclear from such correlations, however, whether insomnia causes mental disorders, mental disorders cause insomnia, or some other factor causes both.

Sleeping pills can relieve insomnia, but they are dangerous when a person also drinks alcohol and may eventually lead to *increased* sleeplessness (Ashton, 1995). In the long run, methods based on learning principles may be more helpful (Stepanski & Perlis, 2000). For example, stress management techniques such as relaxation training have been shown to help insomniacs reduce unusually strong physiological reactions to stress, thus allowing sleep (Bernstein, Borkovec, & Hazlette-Stevens, 2000).

Narcolepsy is a disturbing daytime sleep disorder that usually begins when a person is between fifteen and twenty-five years old (Choo & Guilleminault, 1998). Its victims abruptly switch from active, often emotional waking states into a few minutes of REM sleep. Because of the loss of muscle tone in REM, the narcoleptic collapses and remains briefly immobile even after awakening. The cause of narcolepsy may involve genetic factors and lack of a neurotransmitter called *hypocretin* (Krahn et al., 2001). Planned napping can be a helpful treatment, as can stimulant

insomnia A sleep disorder in which a person feels tired during the day because of trouble falling asleep or staying asleep at night.

narcolepsy A daytime sleep disorder in which a person switches abruptly from an active, often emotional waking state into several minutes of REM sleep.

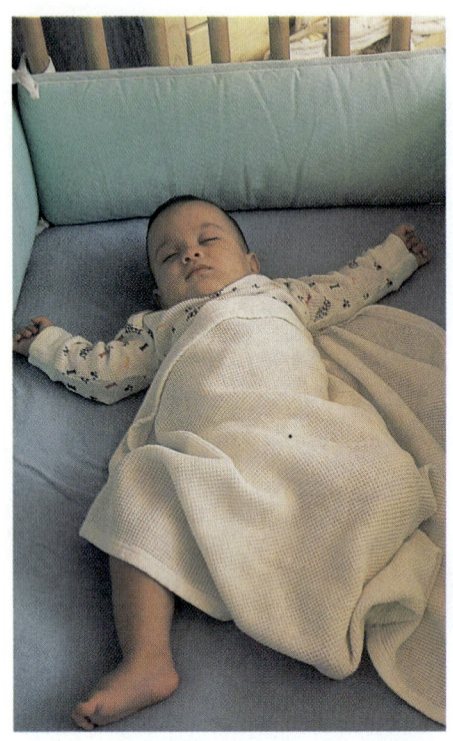

Sudden Infant Death Syndrome (SIDS) In SIDS cases, seemingly healthy infants stop breathing while asleep in their cribs. All the causes of SIDS are not known, but the "Back to Sleep" program promoted by health authorities suggests that infants should sleep on their backs, as this baby demonstrates.

drugs. One of these, modafinil, appears to be effective not only for narcolepsy but for counteracting the effects of sleep deprivation as well (Silber, 2001).

People suffering from **sleep apnea** briefly stop breathing hundreds of times every night, waking up each time long enough to resume breathing. In the morning, they do not recall the awakenings, yet they feel tired and tend to show reductions in attention and learning ability (Naëgelé et al., 1995). Sleep apnea has many causes, including genetic predisposition, obesity, and compression of the windpipe (Dixon, Schachter, & O'Brien, 2001; Kadotani et al., 2001). Effective treatments include weight loss and use of a nasal mask that provides a steady stream of air (Davies & Stradling, 2000; Peppard et al., 2000).

In cases of **sudden infant death syndrome (SIDS),** sleeping infants stop breathing and die. In the United States, SIDS strikes about two of every thousand infants, usually when they are two to four months old (Hirschfeld, 1995). Some SIDS cases may stem from problems with brain systems regulating breathing, from exposure to cigarette smoke, and possibly from genetic causes (Ackerman et al., 2001; Harper et al., 1988; Klonoff-Cohen & Edelstein, 1995; Narita et al., 2001). Because SIDS is less common in cultures where infants and parents sleep in the same bed, it may also be that sleeping position is involved in sudden infant death (Gessner, Ives, & Perham-Hester, 2001). It has been estimated that about half of apparent SIDS cases might actually be accidental suffocations caused when infants sleep facedown on a soft surface (Guntheroth & Spiers, 1992). Since doctors began advising parents to be sure their babies sleep faceup, the number of infants dying from SIDS in the United States has dropped by 40 percent (Gibson et al., 2000).

Nightmares are frightening REM sleep dreams that occur in 4 to 8 percent of the general population, but in a much higher percentage of people suffering posttraumatic stress disorder following military combat or rape (Kryger et al., 2000). Imagery therapy, in which people repeatedly imagine new and less frightening outcomes to their nightmares, has been effective in reducing their frequency (Forbes et al., 2001; Krakow et al., 2001). Whereas nightmares occur during REM sleep, **night terrors** are horrific dream images that occur during stage 3 or 4 sleep. Sleepers often awake from a night terror with a bloodcurdling scream and remain intensely frightened for up to thirty minutes, yet they may not recall the episode in the morning. Night terrors are especially common in boys, but adults can suffer milder versions. The condition is sometimes treatable with drugs (Lillywhite, Wilson, & Nutt, 1994).

Like night terrors, **sleepwalking** occurs during non-REM sleep, usually in childhood (Masand, Popli, & Welburg, 1995). By morning, most sleepwalkers have forgotten their travels. Despite myths to the contrary, waking a sleepwalker is not harmful. One adult sleepwalker was cured when his wife blew a whistle whenever he began a nocturnal stroll (Meyer, 1975). Drugs help reduce sleepwalking, but most children simply outgrow the problem.

In **REM behavior disorder,** the near paralysis that normally accompanies REM sleep is absent, so sleepers move as if acting out their dreams (Watanabe & Sugita, 1998). The disorder can be dangerous to the dreamer or those nearby. In January 2001, a nine-year-old boy in New York City was seriously injured when he jumped from a third floor window while dreaming that his parents were being murdered. In another case, a man grabbed his wife's throat during the night because, he claimed, he was dreaming about breaking a deer's neck. The disorder sometimes occurs along with daytime narcolepsy (Schenck & Mahowald, 1992). Fortunately, drug treatments are usually effective.

Why Do People Sleep?

In trying to understand sleep, psychologists have studied both the functions that sleep serves and the ways in which brain mechanisms shape its characteristics.

---

sleep apnea A sleep disorder in which people briefly, but repeatedly, stop breathing during the night.

sudden infant death syndrome (SIDS) A disorder in which a sleeping baby stops breathing and suffocates.

nightmares Frightening dreams that take place during REM sleep.

night terrors Horrific dreams that cause rapid awakening from stage 3 or 4 sleep and intense fear for up to thirty minutes.

sleepwalking A phenomenon occurring in non-REM sleep in which people walk while asleep.

REM behavior disorder A sleep disorder in which there is no loss of muscle tone during REM sleep, allowing the person to act out dreams.

figure 9.8

Westward/Eastward Travel and Jet Lag

Changing time zones causes more intense symptoms of jet lag after eastward travel (when time is lost) than after westward travel (when time is gained). These data show how long it took people flying between London and Detroit (a five-hour time change) to fall asleep once in bed, both on the night before the trip (B1) and on the five nights afterward. Those who flew eastward, from Detroit to London, needed more time to fall asleep than those who flew westward, from London to Detroit (Nicholson et al., 1986).

Source: Data from Nicholson et al. (1986).

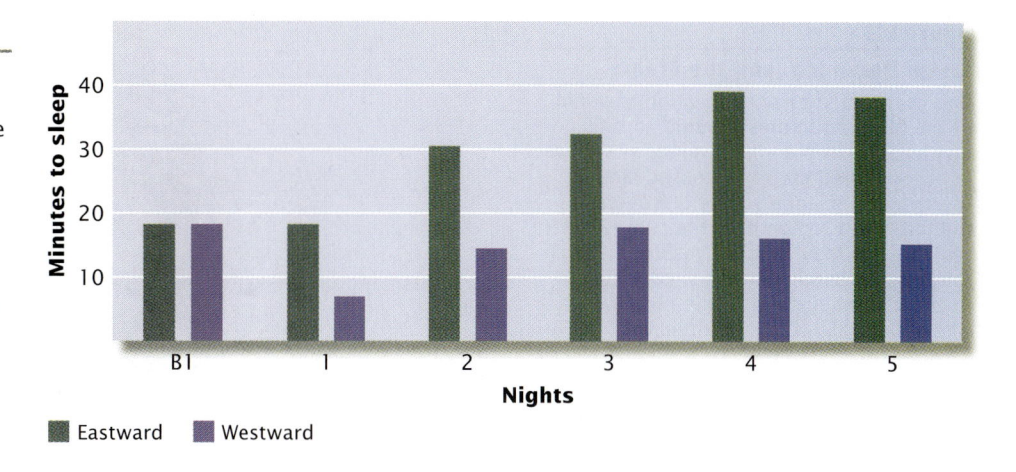

circadian rhythm A cycle, such as waking and sleeping, that repeats about once a day.

jet lag A syndrome of fatigue, irritability, inattention, and sleeping problems caused by air travel across several time zones.

Sleep as a Circadian Rhythm

The sleep-wake cycle is one example of the rhythmic nature of life. Almost all animals (including humans) display cycles of behavior and physiology that repeat about every twenty-four hours in a pattern called a **circadian rhythm** (from the Latin *circa dies*, meaning "about a day"). Longer and shorter rhythms also occur, but they are less common. Circadian (pronounced "sir-KAY-dee-en") rhythms are linked, or *entrained*, to signals such as the light and dark of day and night, but most of them continue even without such time cues. Volunteers living for months without external cues maintain daily rhythms in sleeping and waking, hormone release, eating, urination, and other physiological functions. Under such conditions, these cycles repeat about every twenty-four hours (Czeisler et al., 1999).

Disrupting the sleep-wake cycle can create problems. For example, air travel across several time zones often causes **jet lag**, a pattern of fatigue, irritability, inattention, and sleeping problems that can last several days. The traveler's body feels ready to sleep at the wrong time for the new locale. Similar problems affect workers changing between day and night shifts. Because it tends to be easier to stay awake longer than usual than to go to sleep earlier than usual, sleep-wake rhythms readjust to altered light-dark cycles more easily when sleep is shifted to a later, rather than an earlier, time (see Figure 9.8).

Because circadian-like rhythms continue without external cues, an internal "biological clock" in the brain must keep track of time. This clock is in the *suprachiasmatic nuclei (SCN)* of the hypothalamus (see Figure 9.9). Signals from the SCN reach areas in the hindbrain that initiate sleep or wakefulness (Moore, 1997). SCN neurons show a firing rhythm of twenty-four to twenty-five hours, even when removed from the brain and put in a laboratory dish (Gillette, 1986). And when animals with SCN damage receive transplanted SCN cells, the restored circadian rhythms are similar to those of the donor animal (Menaker & Vogelbaum, 1993). SCN neurons also regulate the release of the hormone *melatonin* from the pineal gland, via an autonomic pathway. Melatonin, in turn, appears to be important in maintaining circadian rhythms; timely injections of melatonin may reduce fatigue and disorientation stemming from jet lag or other sleep-wake cycle changes by acting on melatonin receptors in the SCN (Liu et al., 1997; Sack et al., 1997). The length of circadian rhythms can vary from person to person such that some have a natural tendency to stay up later at night ("owls") or to wake up earlier in the morning ("larks"). Scientists have recently discovered that extreme variations in these rhythms are associated with mutations in the genes that code for biological clock proteins, and that certain variations can help in distinguishing Alzheimer's disease from other brain disorders (Harper et al., 2001; Toh et al., 2001).

figure 9.9

Sleep, Dreaming, and the Brain
This diagram shows the location of some of the brain structures thought to be involved in sleep and dreaming, as well as in other altered states discussed later in the chapter. Scientists have discovered that cells in a region near the suprachiasmatic nuclei may act as a "master switch" for sleep by sending signals that shut down arousal systems in the hindbrain (Gallopin et al., 2000; Sherin et al., 1996).

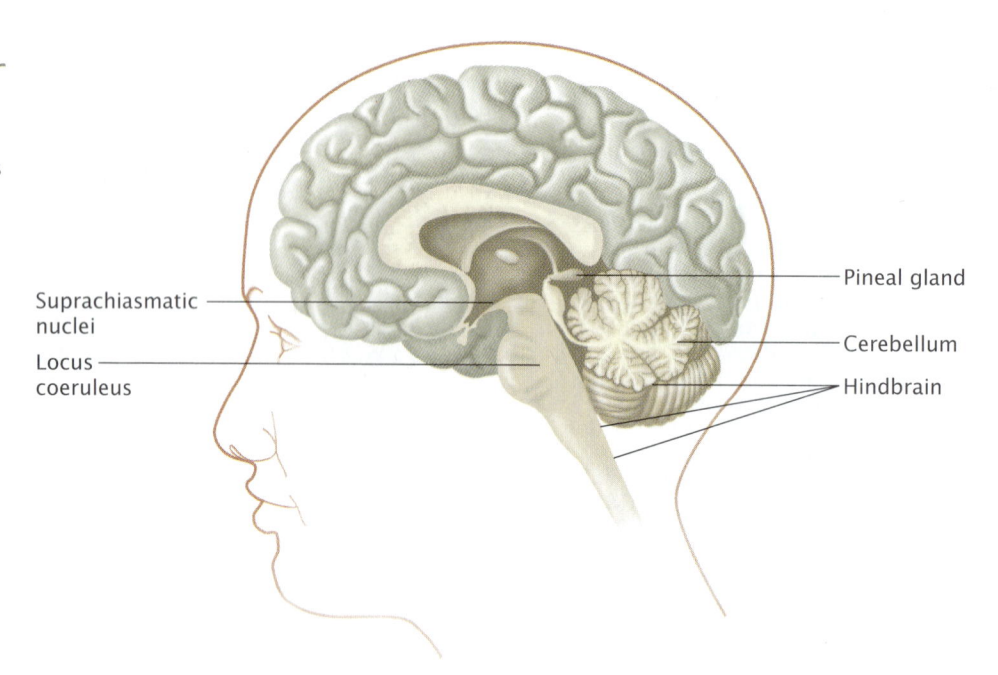

- Suprachiasmatic nuclei
- Locus coeruleus
- Pineal gland
- Cerebellum
- Hindbrain

The Functions of Sleep Examining the effects of sleep deprivation may help explain why people sleep at all. People who go without sleep for as long as a week usually do not suffer serious long-term effects, but sleeplessness does lead to fatigue, irritability, and inattention (Drummond et al., 2000; Smith & Maben, 1993). The effects of short-term sleep deprivation—which is a common condition among busy adolescents and adults—can also take their toll (Stapleton, 2001). For example, most fatal auto accidents in the United States occur during the "fatigue hazard" hours of midnight to 6 A.M. (Coleman, 1992), leading some researchers to consider "sleepy driving" to be as dangerous as drunk driving. Fatigue has been implicated as the primary cause of up to 25 percent of all auto accidents (Philip et al., 2001; Summala & Mikkola, 1994) and of many injuries suffered by sleepy young children at play or in day care (Valent, Brusaferro, & Barbone, 2001). Learning, too, is more difficult after sleep deprivation, but certain parts of the

The Effects of Sleep Deprivation
Here, scientists at Loughborough University, England, test the effects of sleep deprivation on motor coordination. Driving while sleep deprived can be dangerous, but some other functions may not suffer as much. One man reportedly stayed awake for 231 hours and was still lucid and capable of serious intellectual work, including the creation of a lovely poem on his tenth day without sleep (Katz & Landis, 1935).

cerebral cortex actually increase their activity when a sleep-deprived person faces a learning task, so the person is able to compensate for a while (Drummond et al., 2000).

Some researchers believe that sleep, especially non-REM sleep, helps restore the body and the brain for future activity (Porkka-Heiskanen et al., 1997). The waking brain uses more metabolic fuel than the sleeping brain, and during wakefulness, the byproducts of metabolism accumulate. The accumulation of one such byproduct, *adenosine*, inhibits cholinergic systems in the forebrain and hindbrain, inducing sleepiness (Porkka-Heiskanen et al., 1997). During sleep, adenosine levels gradually decline.

Sleep-deprived people do not make up lost sleep hour for hour. Instead, they sleep about 50 percent more than usual, then awake feeling rested. But if people are deprived only of REM sleep, they later compensate more directly. In a classic study, participants were awakened whenever their EEG tracings showed REM sleep. When allowed to sleep uninterrupted the next night, the participants "rebounded," nearly doubling the percentage of time spent in REM sleep (Dement, 1960). Even after *total* sleep deprivation, the next night of uninterrupted sleep includes an unusually high percentage of REM sleep (Feinberg & Campbell, 1993). This apparent need for REM sleep suggests that it has special functions.

What these special functions might be is still unclear, but there are several possibilities. First, REM sleep may improve the functioning of neurons that use norepinephrine (Siegel & Rogawski, 1988). Norepinephrine is a neurotransmitter released by cells in the *locus coeruleus* (see Figure 9.9); during waking hours, it affects alertness and mood. But the brain's neurons lose sensitivity to norepinephrine if it is released continuously for too long. Because the locus coeruleus is almost completely inactive during REM sleep, researchers suggest that REM helps restore sensitivity to norepinephrine and thus its ability to keep us alert (Steriade & McCarley, 1990). Animals deprived of REM sleep show unusually high norepinephrine levels and decreased daytime alertness (Brock et al., 1994).

REM sleep may also be a time for developing, checking, and expanding the brain's nerve connections (Roffwarg, Muzio, & Dement, 1966). If so, it would explain why children and infants, whose brains are still developing, spend so much time in REM sleep (see Figure 9.7). Evidence favoring this possibility comes from recent research showing that REM sleep enhances the creation of neural connections (synaptic plasticity) in response to altered visual experience during the development of the visual cortex (Frank et al., 2001). REM sleep may also help solidify and assimilate the day's experiences in adults. In one study, people who were REM deprived showed poorer retention of a skill learned the day before than people who were either deprived of non-REM sleep or allowed to sleep normally (Karni et al., 1994). In another study, establishing memories of emotional information was particularly dependent on REM sleep (Wagner et al., 2001). Certain types of skill learning, too, may improve overnight, but only if both REM and slow-wave sleep occur (Sejnowski & Destexhe, 2000; Stickgold et al., 2000).

Dreams and Dreaming

We have seen that the brain is active in all sleep stages, but **dreams** differ from other mental activity in sleep because they are usually story-like, lasting from seconds to minutes. Dreams may be organized or chaotic, realistic or fantastic, tranquil or exciting (Hobson & Stickgold, 1994). Sometimes, dreams lead to creative insights about waking problems. For example, after trying for days to write a story about good and evil in the same person, author Robert Louis Stevenson dreamed about a man who drank a potion that turned him into a monster (Hill, 1968). This dream inspired *The Strange Case of Dr. Jekyll and Mr. Hyde*. On the whole, however, there are no scientific data indicating that dreams lead to more creative insights than do waking thoughts.

dreams Story-like sequences of images, sensations, and perception that occur mainly during REM sleep.

Some dreaming occurs during non-REM sleep, but most dreams—and the most bizarre and vivid dreams—occur during REM sleep (Casagrande et al., 1996; Dement & Kleitman, 1957; Stickgold, Rittenhouse, & Hobson, 1994). Even when they seem to make no sense, dreams may contain a certain amount of logic. In one study, for example, when segments from dream reports were randomly reordered, readers could correctly say which had been rearranged and which were intact (Stickgold, Rittenhouse, & Hobson, 1994). And although dreams often involve one person becoming another person or one object turning into another object, it is rare that objects become people or vice versa (Stickgold, Rittenhouse, & Hobson, 1994).

Daytime activities may influence the content of dreams, though their impact is probably minor (Foulkes, 1985). In one study, when people wore red-tinted goggles for a few minutes before going to sleep, they reported more red images in their dreams than people who had not worn the goggles (Roffwarg, Hermann, & Bowe-Anders, 1978). It is also sometimes possible to intentionally direct dream content, especially during **lucid dreaming,** in which the sleeper is aware of dreaming while a dream is happening (Stickgold et al., 2000).

Research leaves little doubt that everyone dreams during the course of every normal night's sleep. Even blind people dream, although their perceptual experiences are usually not visual. Whether you remember a dream depends on how you sleep and wake up. Recall is better if you awaken abruptly and lie quietly while writing or tape-recording your recollections.

Why do we dream? Theories abound. Some see dreaming as a fundamental process by which all mammals analyze and consolidate information that has personal significance or survival value (Porte & Hobson, 1996). This view is supported by the fact that dreaming appears to occur in most mammals, as indicated by the appearance of REM sleep. For example, after researchers disabled the neurons that cause REM sleep paralysis, sleeping cats ran around and attacked, or seemed alarmed by, unseen objects, presumably the images from dreams (Winson, 1990).

According to Freud (1900), dreams are a disguised form of *wish fulfillment*, a way to satisfy unconscious urges or resolve unconscious conflicts that are too upsetting to deal with consciously. Seeing patients' dreams as a "royal road to a knowledge of the unconscious," Freud interpreted their meaning as part of his psychoanalytic therapy (see the chapter on treatment of psychological disorders).

In contrast, the *activation-synthesis theory* sees dreams as the meaningless, random byproducts of REM sleep (Hobson, 1997). According to this theory, hindbrain arousal during REM sleep creates random messages that *activate* the brain, especially the cerebral cortex. Dreams result as the cortex *synthesizes* these random messages as best it can, using stored memories and current feelings to impose a coherent perceptual organization on confusingly random inputs. From this perspective, dreams represent the brain's attempt to make sense of meaningless stimulation during sleep, much as it does when a person, while awake, tries to find meaningful shapes in cloud formations (Bernstein & Roberts, 1995).

Even if dreams arise from random physiological activity, their content can still have psychological significance. Some psychologists believe that dreams give people a chance to review and address some of the problems they face during waking hours (Cartwright, 1993). This view is supported by evidence that people's current concerns can affect both the content of their dreams and the ways in which dreams are organized and recalled (Domhoff, 1996; Stevens, 1996). However, research using brain imaging techniques shows that while we are asleep, brain areas involved in emotion tend to be overactivated, whereas areas controlling logical thought tend to be suppressed (Braun, Balkin, & Wesensten, 1998; Hobson et al., 1998). In fact, as we reach deeper sleep stages, and then enter REM sleep, thinking subsides and hallucinations increase (Fosse, Stickgold, & Hobson, 2001). This is probably why dreams rarely provide realistic, logical solutions to our problems (Blagrove, 1996).

lucid dreaming Awareness that a dream is a dream while it is happening.

hypnosis A phenomenon brought on by special induction techniques and characterized by varying degrees of responsiveness to suggestions for changes in experience and behavior.

Hypnosis

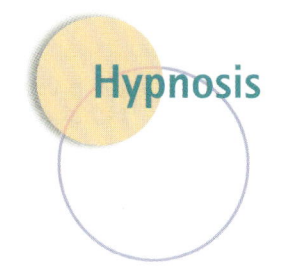

The word *hypnosis* comes from the Greek word *hypnos*, meaning "sleep," but hypnotized people are not sleeping. People who have been hypnotized say that their bodies felt "asleep," but their minds were active and alert. **Hypnosis** has traditionally been defined as an altered state of consciousness brought on by special techniques and producing responsiveness to suggestions for changes in experience and behavior (Kirsch, 1994b). Most hypnotized people do not feel forced to follow the hypnotist's instructions; they simply see no reason to refuse (Hilgard, 1965).

Experiencing Hypnosis

Usually, hypnosis begins with suggestions that the participant feels relaxed and sleepy. The hypnotist then gradually focuses the participant's attention on a restricted, often monotonous set of stimuli while suggesting that the participant should ignore everything else and imagine certain feelings.

Not everyone can be hypnotized. Special tests measure *hypnotic susceptibility,* the degree to which people respond to hypnotic suggestions (Gfeller, 1994). Such tests categorize about 10 percent of adults as difficult or impossible to hypnotize (Hilgard, 1982). Hypnotically susceptible people, in contrast, typically differ from others in several ways. They have a better ability to focus attention and ignore distraction (Crawford, Brown, & Moon, 1993), a more active imagination (Spanos, Burnley, & Cross, 1993), a tendency to fantasize (Lynn & Rhue, 1986), a capacity for processing information quickly and easily (Dixon, Brunet, & Lawrence, 1990), a tendency to be suggestible (Kirsch & Braffman, 2001), and more positive attitudes toward hypnosis (Gfeller, 1994; Spanos, Burnley, & Cross, 1993). Their *willingness* to be hypnotized is the most important factor of all; contrary to myth, people cannot be hypnotized against their will.

The results of hypnosis can be fascinating. People told that their eyes cannot open may struggle fruitlessly to open them. They may appear deaf or blind or insensitive to pain. They may forget their own names. Some appear to remember forgotten things. Others show *age regression,* apparently recalling or reenacting their childhood. Hypnotic effects can last for hours or days through *posthypnotic suggestions*—instructions about behavior that is to take place after hypnosis has ended (such as smiling whenever someone says "England"). Some participants show *posthypnotic amnesia,* an inability to recall what happened while they were hypnotized, even after being told what happened.

Ernest Hilgard (1965, 1992) described the main changes that people display during hypnosis. First, hypnotized people show *reduced planfulness*. They tend not to begin actions on their own, waiting instead for the hypnotist's instructions. One participant said, "I was trying to decide if my legs were crossed, but I couldn't tell, and didn't quite have the initiative to move to find out" (Hilgard, 1965, p. 6). Second, they tend to ignore all but the hypnotist's voice and whatever it points out; their *attention is redistributed*. Third, hypnosis enhances the *ability to fantasize,* so participants more vividly imagine a scene or relive a memory. Fourth, hypnotized people display *increased role taking;* they more easily act like a person of a different age or a member of the opposite sex, for example. Fifth, hypnotic participants show *reduced reality testing,* tending not to question if statements are true and more willingly accepting apparent distortions of reality. A hypnotized person might shiver in a warm room if a hypnotist says it is snowing.

Explaining Hypnosis

Hypnotized people look and act differently from nonhypnotized people (Hilgard, 1965). Do these differences actually indicate an altered state of consciousness?

Inducing Hypnosis In the late 1700s, an Austrian physician named Franz Anton Mesmer became famous for his treatment of physical disorders using *mesmerism,* a forerunner of hypnosis. His patients touched their afflicted body parts to magnetized metal rods extending from a tub of water and then, when touched by Mesmer, fell into a curative "crisis" or trance, sometimes accompanied by convulsions. We now know that hypnosis can be induced more easily, often simply by asking a person to stare at an object.

figure 9.10
Can Hypnosis Produce Blindness?

E H M T W X Z M I 2 D T H 6 9 N 6 X M D W

F H N V   X T M I 2   D N 6 N C L V D A

The top row looks like gibberish, but you could read it as the numbers and letters in the lower row if you closed one eye and viewed it through special glasses. Yet when hypnotized subjects who had been given suggestions for blindness in one eye wore the glasses, they were unable to read the display (as they should have been able to do if one eye were blind), indicating that both eyes were in fact working normally (Pattie, 1935).

Source: Pattie (1935).

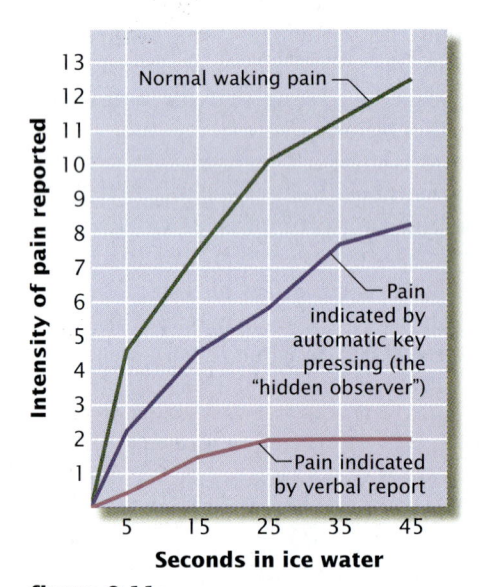

figure 9.11
Reports of Pain in Hypnosis

This graph shows average reports of pain when people's hands were immersed in painfully cold water under three different conditions. The green line represents the oral reports by nonhypnotized participants. The pink line represents the reports by hypnotized participants who were told they would feel no pain. The purple line represents the responses by hypnotized participants who were told they would feel no pain but were asked to press a key if "any part of them" felt pain. The key pressing by this "hidden observer" suggests that under hypnosis, the experience of pain was dissociated from conscious awareness (Hilgard, 1977).

---

state theory A theory that hypnosis is an altered state of consciousness.

role theory A theory that hypnotized people act in accordance with a social role that provides a reason to follow the hypnotist's suggestions.

dissociation theory A theory defining hypnosis as a socially agreed upon opportunity to display one's ability to let mental functions become dissociated.

Advocates of the **state theory** of hypnosis say that they do. They point to the dramatic effects that hypnosis can produce, including insensitivity to pain and the disappearance of warts (Noll, 1994). They also note that there are subtle differences in the way hypnotized and nonhypnotized people carry out suggestions. In one study, hypnotized people and those who had been asked to simulate hypnosis were told to run their hands through their hair whenever they heard the word *experiment* (Orne, Sheehan, & Evans, 1968). Simulators did so only when the hypnotist said the cue word. Hypnotized participants complied no matter who said it. Another study found that hypnotized people complied more often than simulators with a posthypnotic suggestion to mail postcards to the experimenter (Barnier & McConkey, 1998).

Proponents of the **role theory** of hypnosis argue that hypnosis is *not* a special state of consciousness, and that hypnotized people are merely complying with social demands and acting in accordance with a special social role (Kirsch, 1994a). In other words, they say, hypnosis provides a socially acceptable reason to follow someone's suggestions, much as a doctor's white coat provides a good reason for patients to remove clothing on command.

Support for role theory comes from several sources. For example, laboratory experiments show that motivated, but nonhypnotized, volunteers can duplicate many, if not all, aspects of hypnotic behavior, from arm rigidity to age regression (Dasgupta et al., 1995; Orne & Evans, 1965). Other studies using special tests have found that people rendered blind or deaf by hypnosis can still see or hear, even though their actions and beliefs suggest that they cannot (Bryant & McConkey, 1989; Pattie, 1935; see Figure 9.10).

Hilgard (1992) proposed a **dissociation theory** of hypnosis to blend role and state theories. He suggested that hypnosis is not one specific state but a general condition in which our normally centralized control of thoughts and actions is temporarily reorganized, or broken up, through a process called *dissociation*, meaning a split in consciousness (Hilgard, 1979). As a result, body movements normally under voluntary control can occur on their own, and normally involuntary processes (such as overt reactions to pain) can be controlled voluntarily. Hilgard argued that this relaxation of central control occurs as part of a *social agreement* to share control with the hypnotist. In other words, people usually decide for themselves how to act or what to attend to, perceive, or remember, but during hypnosis, the hypnotist is "allowed" to control some of these experiences and actions. So Hilgard saw hypnosis as a socially agreed upon display of dissociated mental functions. Compliance with a social role may account for part of the story, he said, but hypnosis also leads to significant changes in mental processes.

Evidence for dissociation theory comes from a study in which hypnotized participants immersed one hand in ice water after being told that they would feel no pain (Hilgard, Morgan, & MacDonald, 1975). With the other hand, participants were to press a key to indicate if "any part of them" felt pain. Participants' oral reports indicated almost no pain, but their key pressing told a different story (see Figure 9.11). Hilgard concluded that a "hidden observer" was reporting on pain that was reaching the person but had been separated, or dissociated, from conscious awareness (Hilgard, 1977). Contemporary research continues to test the validity of various explanatory theories of hypnosis, but traditional distinctions between state and role theories have become less relevant as researchers focus on larger questions, such as the impact of social and cognitive factors in hypnotic phenomena, the nature of the hypnotic experience, and the psychological and physiological basis for hypnotic susceptibility (Kirsch & Lynn, 1995).

Applications of Hypnosis

Whatever hypnosis is, it has proven useful, especially in relation to pain. Hypnosis seems to be the only anesthetic some people need to block the pain of dental work, childbirth, burns, and abdominal surgery (Van Sickel, 1992). For others, hypnosis relieves chronic pain from arthritis, nerve damage, migraine headaches, and cancer (Nolan et al., 1995). MRI studies of hypnotized pain patients show altered activity in the anterior cingulate cortex, a brain region mentioned in the chapter on sensation as being associated with the emotional component of pain (Faymonville et al., 2000). Hypnotic suggestions can also reduce nausea and vomiting due to chemotherapy (Redd, 1984) and can help reduce surgical bleeding (Gerschman, Reade, & Burrows, 1980).

Other applications of hypnosis are more controversial, especially the use of hypnosis to aid memory. For example, hypnotic age regression is sometimes attempted in an effort to help people recover lost memories. In actuality, however, the memories of past events reported by age-regressed individuals are less accurate than those of nonhypnotized individuals (Lynn, Myers, & Malinoski, 1997). Similarly, it is doubtful that hypnosis can improve the ability of witnesses to recall details of a crime (Lynn, Myers, & Malinoski, 1997). Instead, their expectations about, and confidence in, hypnosis may cause them to unintentionally distort information or reconstruct memories for the events in question (Garry & Loftus, 1994; Weekes et al., 1992). These distortions can be especially problematic because although hypnosis may not enhance people's memory for information, it may make them more confident about their reports, even if they are inaccurate.

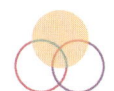

Surgery Under Hypnosis Bernadine Coady, of Wimblington, England, has a condition that makes it dangerous for her to have general anesthesia. So in April 1999, when a hypnotherapist failed to show up to help her through a foot operation, she used self-hypnosis as her only anesthetic. The surgery would have been extremely painful without anesthesia, but she said that she imagined the pain as "waves lashing against a sea wall . . . [and] going away, like the tide." Coady's report that the operation was painless is believable because in December 2000 she underwent the same operation on her other foot, again using only self-hypnosis for pain control (Morris, 2000).

LINKAGES (a link to Health, Stress, and Coping)

Meditation, Health, and Stress

Meditation provides a set of techniques intended to create an altered state of consciousness characterized by inner peace and tranquility (Shapiro & Walsh, 1984). Some claim that meditation increases awareness and understanding of themselves and their environment, reduces anxiety, improves health, and aids performance in everything from work to tennis (Bodian, 1999; Mahesh Yogi, 1994).

The techniques used to achieve a meditative state differ, depending on belief and philosophy (for example, Eastern meditation, Sufism, yoga, or prayer). However, in the most common meditation methods, attention is focused on just one thing—a word, sound, or object—until the meditator stops thinking about anything and experiences nothing but "pure awareness" (Benson, 1975). In this way, the individual becomes more fully aware of the present moment rather than being caught up in the past or the future.

What a meditator focuses on is far less important than doing so with a passive attitude. To organize attention, meditators might inwardly name every sound or

"Are you not thinking what I'm not thinking?"

thought that reaches consciousness, focus on the sound of their own breathing, or slowly repeat a *mantra,* which is a soothing word or phrase. During a typical meditation session, breathing, heart rate, muscle tension, blood pressure, and oxygen consumption decrease (Wallace & Benson, 1972). Most forms of meditation induce alpha-wave EEG activity, the brain wave pattern commonly found in a relaxed, eyes-closed, waking state (see Figure 9.5).

Meditators often report significant reductions in stress-related problems such as general anxiety, high blood pressure, and insomnia (Beauchamp-Turner & Levinson, 1992). More generally, meditators' scores on personality tests indicate increases in general mental health, self-esteem, and social openness (Janowiak & Hackman, 1994; Sakairi, 1992). Exactly how meditation produces its effects is unclear. Many of its effects can also be achieved by biofeedback, hypnosis, and just relaxing (Beyerstein, 1999; Holmes, 1984).

Psychoactive Drugs

Every day, most people in the world use drugs that alter brain activity and consciousness (Levinthal, 1996). For example, 80 to 90 percent of people in North America use caffeine, the stimulant found in coffee (Gilbert, 1984). A drug is a chemical not usually needed for physiological activity and that can affect the body upon entering it. (Some people use the word *drug* to mean therapeutic medicines but refer to nonmedicinal drugs as *substances,* as in *substance abuse*). Drugs that affect the brain, changing consciousness and other psychological processes, are called **psychoactive drugs.** The study of psychoactive drugs is called **psychopharmacology.**

Psychopharmacology

Most psychoactive drugs affect the brain by altering the interactions between neurotransmitters and receptors, as described in the chapter on biological aspects of

psychoactive drugs Substances that act on the brain to create some psychological effect.

psychopharmacology The study of psychoactive drugs and their effects.

Psychoactive Drugs

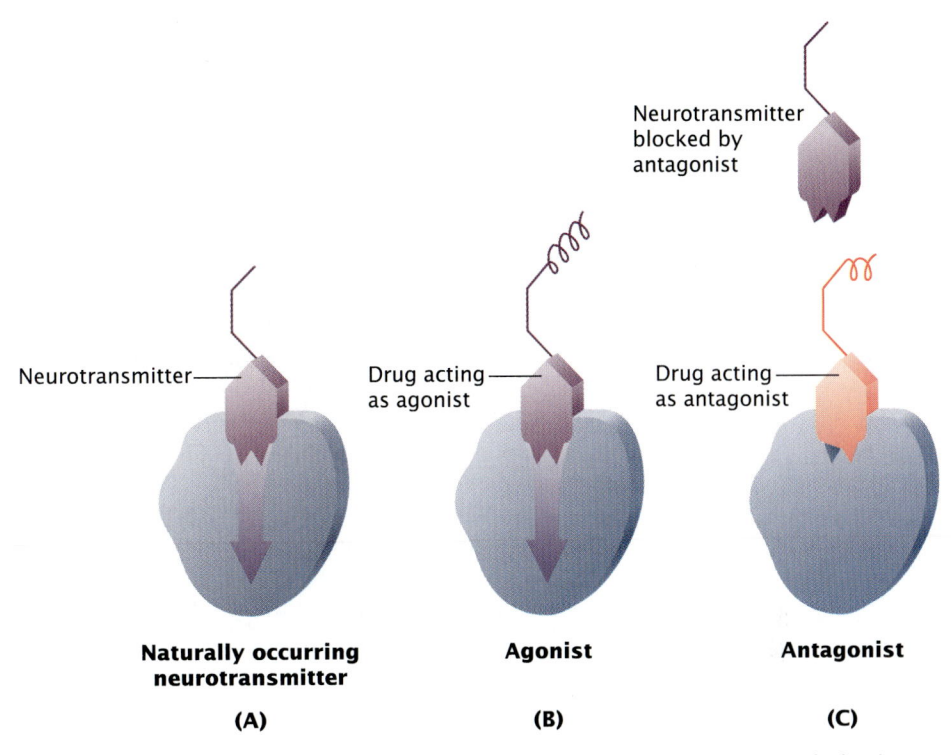

figure 9.12
Agonists and Antagonists

In Part A, a molecule of neurotransmitter interacts with a receptor on a neuron's dendrites by fitting into and stimulating it. Part B shows a drug molecule acting as an *agonist*, affecting the receptor in the same way a neurotransmitter would. Part C depicts an *antagonist* drug molecule blocking a natural neurotransmitter from reaching and acting upon the receptor.

psychology. To create their effects, these drugs must cross the **blood-brain barrier**, a feature of blood vessels in the brain that prevents some substances from entering brain tissue. Once past this barrier, a psychoactive drug's effects depend on several factors: With which neurotransmitter systems does the drug interact? How does the drug affect these neurotransmitters or their receptors? What psychological functions are performed by the brain systems that use these neurotransmitters?

Drugs can affect neurotransmitters or their receptors through several mechanisms. As Figure 9.12 shows, neurotransmitters fit into their own receptors; however, some drugs are similar enough to a particular neurotransmitter to fool its receptors. These drugs, called **agonists**, bind to the receptor and mimic the effects of the normal neurotransmitter. Other drugs are similar enough to a neurotransmitter to occupy its receptors but cannot mimic its effects; they bind to a receptor and prevent the normal neurotransmitter from binding. These drugs are called **antagonists**. Still other drugs work by increasing or decreasing the release of a specific neurotransmitter. Finally, some drugs work by speeding or slowing the *removal* of a neurotransmitter from synapses.

Predicting a drug's behavioral effects is complicated by the fact that some drugs interact with many neurotransmitter systems. Also, the nervous system may compensate for a disturbance. For example, repeated exposure to a drug that blocks receptors for a certain neurotransmitter often leads to a compensatory increase in the number of receptors available to accept the neurotransmitter.

The Varying Effects of Drugs

Drugs affect biological systems in accordance with their chemical properties. Unfortunately, their medically desirable *main effects*, such as pain relief, are often accompanied by undesirable *side effects*, which may include the potential for abuse.

blood-brain barrier A feature of blood vessels in the brain that allows only certain substances to leave the blood and interact with brain tissue.

agonists Drugs that mimic the effects of the neurotransmitter that normally binds to a neural receptor.

antagonists Drugs that bind to a receptor and prevent the normal neurotransmitter from binding to it.

Substance abuse is a pattern of use that causes serious social, legal, or interpersonal problems for the user (American Psychiatric Association, 1994).

Substance abuse may lead to psychological or physical dependence. **Psychological dependence** is a condition in which a person continues drug use despite adverse effects, needs the drug for a sense of well-being, and becomes preoccupied with obtaining the drug. However, the person can still function without the drug. Psychological dependence can occur with or without **physical dependence,** or **addiction,** which is a physiological state in which drug use is needed to prevent a **withdrawal syndrome.** Withdrawal symptoms vary across drugs but often include an intense craving for the drug and effects generally opposite to those of the drug itself. Eventually, *drug tolerance* may appear. **Tolerance** is a condition in which increasingly larger drug doses are needed to produce the same effect. With the development of tolerance, many addicts need the drug just to prevent the negative effects of not taking it. However, most researchers believe that a craving for the positive effects of drugs is what keeps addicts coming back to drug use (Weiss et al., 2001). MRI studies of addicts imagining cocaine or alcohol use reveal that craving activates regions of the brain related to the rewards, positive emotions, and other pleasures they have learned to associate with using the drug (George et al., 2001; Kilts et al., 2001). Stimulating these regions in the brains of rats that had once been physically dependent on cocaine causes them to again seek out the drug (Vorel et al., 2001).

It is tempting to think of "addicts" as being unlike ourselves, but we should never underestimate the potential for "normal" people to develop drug dependence. Physical dependence can develop gradually, without a person's awareness. In fact, scientists now believe that the changes in the brain that underlie addiction may be similar to those that occur during learning (Overton et al., 1999). All addictive drugs stimulate the brain's "pleasure centers," regions that are sensitive to the neurotransmitter dopamine. Neuronal activity in these areas produces intensely pleasurable feelings; it also helps generate the pleasant feelings of a good meal, a "runner's high," or sex (Grunberg, 1994; Harris & Aston-Jones, 1995). Neuroscientists long believed that these feelings stem directly from the action of dopamine itself, but activity in dopamine systems may actually be more involved in responding to the novelty associated with pleasurable events than in actually creating the experience of pleasure (Bevins, 2001; Garris et al., 1999). In any case, by affecting dopamine regulation and related biochemical processes in "pleasure centers," addictive drugs have the capacity to create tremendously rewarding effects in most people.

Expectations and Drug Effects

Drug effects are determined by more than biochemistry. *Learned expectations* also play a role (Cumsille, Sayer, & Graham, 2000; Goldman, Del Boca, & Darkes, 1999; Stein, Goldman, & Del Boca, 2000). In one experiment, for example, college students reported being drunk after consuming drinks that tasted and smelled like alcohol—even though the drinks contained no alcohol (Darkes & Goldman, 1993). Other studies have demonstrated that people's expectancies about the effects of alcohol had a greater influence on their aggressive behavior than did alcohol itself (e.g., Lang et al., 1975). Expectations about drug effects develop, in part, as people watch other people react to drugs. Because what they see can be different from one individual and culture to the next, drug effects vary considerably throughout the world (MacAndrew & Edgerton, 1969). For example, the loss of inhibition and the violence commonly associated with alcohol use in the United States is partly attributable to custom, inasmuch as these effects are not universal. Consider the contrasting example of Bolivia's Camba culture, in which people drink, in extended bouts, a brew that is 89 percent alcohol. These people repeatedly pass out, wake up, and start drinking again—all the while maintaining tranquil social relations. Other studies have shown that learned expectancies also contribute to the effects of heroin, cocaine, and marijuana (Robbins & Everitt, 1999; Schafer & Brown, 1991; Smith et al., 1992).

---

substance abuse The self-administration of psychoactive drugs in ways that deviate from a culture's social norms.

psychological dependence A condition in which a person uses a drug despite adverse effects, needs the drug for a sense of well-being, and becomes preoccupied with obtaining it.

physical dependence Development of a physical need for a psychoactive drug.

withdrawal syndrome Symptoms associated with discontinuing the use of a drug.

tolerance A condition in which increasingly larger drug doses are needed to produce a given effect.

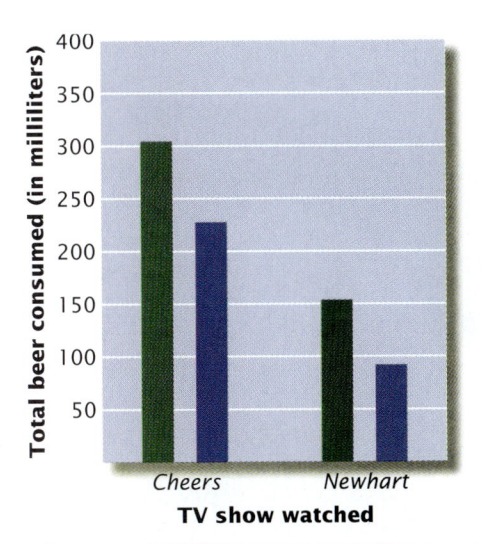

The learned nature of responses to alcohol is also demonstrated by cases in which people are exposed to new ideas about what those responses can be. For example, when Europeans brought alcohol to Tahiti in the 1700s, the Tahitians' initial response to drinking it was to become relaxed and befuddled, much as when consuming *kava*, their traditional nonalcoholic tranquilizing drink. But after years of watching European sailors' drunken violence, Tahitian alcohol drinkers became violent themselves. Fortunately, subsequent learning experiences once again made their response to alcohol more peaceful (MacAndrew & Edgerton, 1969).

Expectations about a drug's effects can also influence how much of it people will consume (Goldman, Darkes, & Del Boca, 1999). In one study, for example, participants thought they were taking part in a memory experiment, but in fact, their expectations about the positive effects of alcohol were being primed, without their awareness, in one or both of two ways (Roehrich & Goldman, 1995): (1) Participants viewed an episode of a television show *(Cheers)* that portrayed alcohol consumption in a positive light, and/or (2) they were subtly exposed to positive adjectives associated with alcohol consumption (e.g., *funny, happy,* and *talkative*). Later, the participants were given an opportunity to drink what they thought was alcohol (but was actually nonalcoholic beer) as part of a separate "taste-rating study." Figure 9.13 shows the results of this experiment. Although the participants saw no connection between the priming stages of the study and the subsequent taste test, those who had watched *Cheers* drank more than those who had watched a TV show not related to alcohol. Those who were exposed to the positive alcohol-consumption adjectives drank more than those who were exposed to neutral adjectives.

These examples and experiments show that the effects of psychoactive drugs are complex and variable. In the chapter on treatment of psychological disorders, we discuss some of the psychoactive drugs being used to help people who display psychopathology. Here, we consider several major categories of psychoactive drugs that are used primarily for the alterations they produce in consciousness, including depressants, stimulants, opiates, and hallucinogens.

figure 9.13

Expectancies and Alcohol Consumption

People may drink more when their expectancies about the positive effects of alcohol have been primed. In this study, participants who (1) watched a TV show in which the characters enjoyed themselves while drinking alcohol and (2) were exposed to adjectives associated with positive expectancies about alcohol subsequently drank more (nonalcoholic) beer than participants who watched a show not related to alcohol and who were not exposed to the adjectives.

Source: Roehrich & Goldman (1995, Figure 1).

Depressants

Depressants are drugs that reduce activity of the central nervous system. Examples are alcohol and barbiturates, both of which increase the activity of GABA, a neurotransmitter described in the chapter on biological aspects of psychology. Because GABA reduces, or inhibits, neuron activity, enhancing GABA function reduces the excitability of many neural circuits. Because of the impact of depressants on GABA, using them creates feelings of relaxation, drowsiness, and sometimes depression (Hanson & Venturelli, 1995).

Alcohol In the United States, over 100 million people drink *alcohol;* it is equally popular worldwide (Alvarez, Delrio, & Prada, 1995). Alcohol affects several neurotransmitters, including dopamine, endorphins, glutamate, serotonin, and most notably, GABA (Koob et al., 1998). For this reason, drugs that interact with GABA receptors can block some of alcohol's effects, as shown in Figure 9.14 (Suzdak et al., 1986). Alcohol also enhances the effect of endorphins (the body's natural painkillers, described in the chapter on sensation). This action may underlie the "high" that people feel when drinking alcohol and may explain why *naltrexone* and *naloxone,* which are endorphin antagonists, are better than placebos at reducing alcohol craving and relapse rates in recovering alcoholics (Salloum et al., 1998). Alcohol also interacts with dopamine systems, a component of the brain's reward mechanisms (Thanos et al., 2001). Prolonged alcohol use can have lasting effects on the brain's ability to regulate dopamine levels (Tiihonen et al., 1995), and dopamine agonists reduce alcohol craving and withdrawal effects (Lawford et al., 1995).

depressants Psychoactive drugs that inhibit the functioning of the central nervous system.

figure 9.14

GABA Receptors and Alcohol

Both of these rats received the same amount of alcohol, enough to incapacitate them with drunkenness. However, the rat on the right then received a drug that reverses alcohol's intoxicating effects by blocking the ability of alcohol to stimulate GABA receptors. Within two minutes, the rat was completely sober. Researchers found a serious problem with the drug, however: It did not reverse the effects of alcohol on the brain's breathing centers. So if people were drinking to get intoxicated, the drug would frustrate their efforts, and they might consume a lethal overdose of alcohol. Accordingly, the drug's manufacturer has discontinued its development.

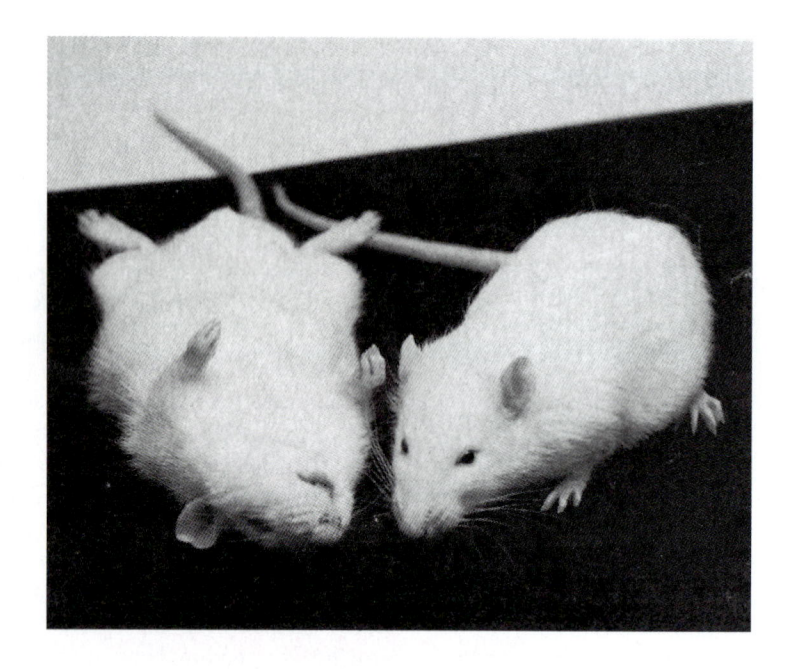

Alcohol affects specific brain regions. For example, it depresses activity in the locus coeruleus, an area that helps activate the cerebral cortex (Koob & Bloom, 1988). Reduced cortical activity tends to cause cognitive changes and a release of inhibitions. Some drinkers begin talking loudly, acting silly, or telling others what they think of them. Emotional reactions range from euphoria to despair. Normally shy people may become impulsive or violent. Alcohol's impairment of the hippocampus causes memory problems, making it more difficult to form memories for new information (Givens, 1995). And its suppression of the cerebellum causes poor motor coordination (Rogers et al., 1986). Alcohol's ability to depress hindbrain mechanisms that control breathing and heartbeat can make overdoses fatal.

As mentioned earlier, some effects of alcohol—such as anger and aggressiveness—depend on both biochemical factors and learned expectations (Goldman, Darkes, & Del Boca, 1999; Kushner et al., 2000). But other effects—especially disruptions in motor coordination, speech, and thought—result from biochemical factors alone. These biological effects depend on the amount of alcohol the blood carries to the brain. It takes the liver about an hour to break down one ounce of alcohol (the amount in one average drink), so alcohol has milder effects if consumed slowly. Effects increase with faster drinking, or if you drink on an empty stomach, thereby speeding absorption into the blood. Even after allowing for differences in average male and female body weight, researchers have found metabolic differences that allow male bodies to tolerate somewhat higher amounts of alcohol. As a result, equal doses of alcohol may create greater effects in women compared with men (York & Welte, 1994).

Genetics also seems to play a role in determining the biochemical effects of alcohol. Some people appear to have a genetic predisposition toward alcohol dependence (Agarwal, 1997), although the specific genes involved have not yet been identified. Others, such as the Japanese, may have inherited metabolic characteristics that increase the adverse effects of alcohol, thus possibly inhibiting the development of alcohol abuse (Iwahashi et al., 1995).

Barbiturates Sometimes called "downers" or "sleeping pills," *barbiturates* are extremely addictive. Small doses cause relaxation, mild euphoria, loss of muscle coordination, and lowered attention. Higher doses cause deep sleep, but continued use actually distorts sleep patterns (Kales & Kales, 1973). Obviously, then, long-

Drinking and Driving Don't Mix
Although practice makes it seem easy, driving a car is a complex information-processing task. As described in the chapter on cognition and language, such tasks require constant vigilance, quick decisions, and skillful execution of responses. Alcohol can impair all these processes, as well as the ability to judge the degree of impairment—thus making drinking and driving a deadly combination that kills tens of thousands of people each year in the United States alone.

term use of barbiturates as sleeping pills is unwise. Overdoses can be fatal. Withdrawal symptoms are among the most severe for any drug and can include intense agitation, violent outbursts, convulsions, hallucinations, and even sudden death.

Stimulants

Amphetamines, cocaine, caffeine, and nicotine are all examples of **stimulants,** drugs that increase behavioral and mental activity.

Amphetamines
Also called "uppers" or "speed," *amphetamines* (Benzedrine, for example) increase the release and decrease the removal of norepinephrine and dopamine at synapses, causing increased activity at these neurotransmitters' receptors. These drugs' rewarding properties are probably due in part to their activation of dopamine systems, because taking dopamine antagonists reduces amphetamine use (Holman, 1994).

Amphetamines stimulate both the brain and the sympathetic branch of the autonomic nervous system, raising heart rate and blood pressure, constricting blood vessels, shrinking mucous membranes (thus relieving stuffy noses), and reducing appetite. Amphetamines also increase alertness and response speed, especially in tasks requiring prolonged attention (Koelega, 1993), and they may improve memory for verbal material (Soetens et al., 1995).

Amphetamine abuse usually begins as an effort to lose weight, stay awake, or experience a "high." Continued use leads to anxiety, insomnia, heart problems, brain damage, movement disorders, confusion, paranoia, nonstop talking, and psychological and physical dependence (Volkow et al., 2001). In some cases, the symptoms of amphetamine abuse are virtually identical to those of paranoid schizophrenia, a serious mental disorder associated with malfunctioning dopamine systems.

Cocaine
Like amphetamines, *cocaine* increases norepinephrine and dopamine activity, and thus it produces many amphetamine-like effects. Cocaine's particularly powerful effect on dopamine activity and its rapid onset may underlie its remarkably addictive nature (Holman, 1994; Ungless et al., 2001). Drugs with rapid onset

stimulants Psychoactive drugs that have the ability to increase behavioral and mental activity.

Deadly Drug Use In his short career as a comedian, Chris Farley starred on *Saturday Night Live* and in several movies. At the age of thirty-three, he died from an overdose of cocaine and opium.

and short duration are generally more addictive than others (Kato, Wakasa, & Yamagita, 1987), which may explain why *crack*—a purified, fast-acting, highly potent, smokable form of cocaine—is especially addictive.

Cocaine stimulates self-confidence, a sense of well-being, and optimism. But continued use brings nausea, overactivity, insomnia, paranoia, a sudden depressive "crash," hallucinations, sexual dysfunction, and seizures (Lacayo, 1995). Overdoses, especially of crack, can be deadly, and even small doses can cause a fatal heart attack or stroke (Marzuk et al., 1995). There is now little doubt that a pregnant woman who uses cocaine harms her fetus (Hurt et al., 1995; Konkol et al., 1994; Snodgrass, 1994). However, many of the severe, long-term behavioral problems seen in "cocaine babies" may have at least as much to do with poverty and neglect after birth as with the mother's cocaine use beforehand. Early intervention can reduce the effects of both cocaine and the hostile environment that confronts most cocaine babies (Wren, 1998).

Ending a cocaine addiction is difficult. One possible treatment involves *buprenorphine*, an opiate antagonist that suppresses cocaine self-administration in addicted monkeys (Mello et al., 1989). Other drugs that affect selective types of dopamine receptors have been found effective in preventing relapse when mice previously addicted to cocaine were exposed to drug-related cues, but these drugs have not yet been tested in humans (Beardsley et al., 2001). The results of other methods have been mixed; fewer than 25 percent of human cocaine addicts who have undergone even long-term pharmacological and psychological treatments are drug-free five years later (*Harvard Mental Health Letter*, 2001).

Caffeine *Caffeine* may be the world's most popular drug. It is found in coffee, tea, chocolate, and many soft drinks. Caffeine reduces drowsiness by inhibiting receptors for the neuromodulator adenosine, which we discussed earlier in relation to sleep (Nehlig, Daval, & Debry, 1992). It improves problem solving, increases the capacity for physical work, and raises urine production (Warburton, 1995). At high doses it induces anxiety and tremors. Caffeine use can result in tolerance, as well as physical dependence (Strain et al., 1994). Withdrawal symptoms—including headaches, fatigue, anxiety, shakiness, and craving—appear on the first day of abstinence and last about a week (Silverman et al., 1992). Caffeine may make it harder for women to become pregnant and may increase the risk of miscarriage (Alderete, Eskenazi, & Sholtz, 1995; Cnattingius et al., 2000), but overall, moderate daily caffeine use appears to have few, if any, negative effects (Kleemola et al., 2000; Thompson, 1995).

Nicotine A powerful stimulant of the autonomic nervous system, *nicotine* is the psychoactive ingredient in tobacco. Nicotine is an acetylcholine agonist, but it also increases neuronal release of glutamate, the brain's primary excitatory neurotransmitter (McGehee et al., 1995). Nicotine has many psychoactive effects, including elevated mood and improved memory and attention (Ernst et al., 2001; Pomerleau & Pomerleau, 1992). Its ability to create dependence is now well established (White, 1998). This claim is supported by evidence of a nicotine withdrawal syndrome, which includes craving, anxiety, irritability, lowered heart rate, and weight gain (Hughes, Higgins, & Bickel, 1994). Although nicotine does not create the "rush" characteristic of many drugs of abuse, withdrawal from it reduces activity in the brain's reward pathways (Epping-Jordan et al., 1998). Other research suggests that nicotine creates more psychological than physical dependence (Robinson & Pritchard, 1995), but whatever blend of physical and psychological dependence may be involved, there is no doubt that smoking is a difficult habit for most smokers to break (Shiffman et al., 1997). As discussed in the chapter on health, stress, and coping, it is also clearly recognized as a major risk factor for cancer, heart disease, and respiratory disorders (U.S. Department of Health and Human Services, 2001b).

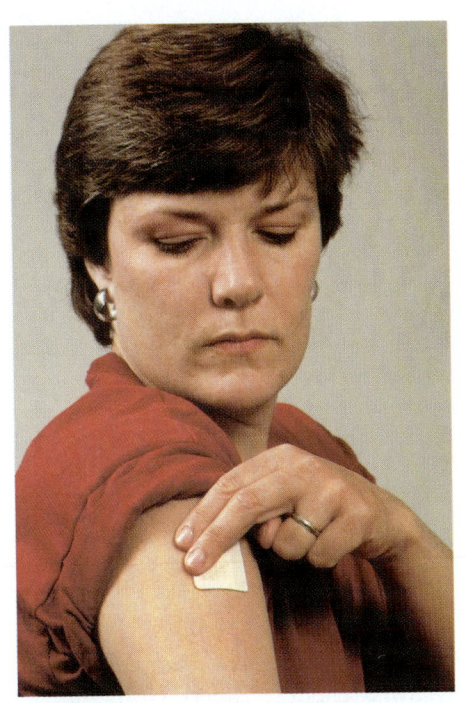

Giving Up Smoking The chemical effects of nicotine, combined with strong learned associations between smoking and relaxation, stimulation, mealtimes, alcohol, and a wide variety of pleasant social interactions, make it extremely difficult for most smokers to give up their unhealthy habit. One of the more promising treatment programs available today combines nicotine administration (through a patch like the one this woman is wearing) with antidepressant medication and behavioral training in how to cope with smoking-related situations—and with the stress of quitting.

opiates Psychoactive drugs, such as opium, morphine, or heroin, that produce both sleep-inducing and pain-relieving effects.

hallucinogens Psychoactive drugs that alter consciousness by producing a temporary loss of contact with reality and changes in emotion, perception, and thought.

MDMA

"Ecstasy," or *MDMA* (short for 3,4-methylenedioxymethamphetamine), causes visual hallucinations, a feeling of greater closeness to others, dry mouth, hyperactivity, and jaw muscle spasms resulting in "lockjaw." Because MDMA increases the activity of dopamine-releasing neurons, it leads to some of the same effects as those produced by cocaine and amphetamines (Steele, McCann, & Ricaurte, 1994). At serotonin synapses, MDMA is a receptor agonist and also causes neurotransmitter release, thus possibly accounting for the drug's hallucinatory effects (Green, Cross, & Goodwin, 1995). On the day after using MDMA—also known as "XTC," "clarity," "essence," "E," and "Adam"—people often experience muscle aches, fatigue, depression, and poor concentration (Peroutka, Newman, & Harris, 1988). With continued use, MDMA's positive effects decrease, but its negative effects persist.

Although it does not appear to be physically addictive, MDMA is a dangerous, potentially deadly drug (National Institute on Drug Abuse, 2000b). For one thing, it permanently damages the brain, killing neurons that use serotonin (Green, Cross, & Goodwin, 1995); the damage increases with higher doses and continued use (Battaglia, Yeh, & De Souza, 1988). MDMA impairs memory, even after its use is discontinued (Reneman et al., 2001; Rodgers, 2000; Zakzanis & Young, 2001), and users may develop *panic disorder,* a problem whose symptoms include intense anxiety and a sense of impending death (see the chapter on psychological disorders).

Opiates

The **opiates** (opium, morphine, heroin, and codeine) are unique in their capacity for inducing sleep and relieving pain (Julien, 2001). *Opium,* derived from the poppy plant, relieves pain and causes feelings of well-being and dreamy relaxation. One of its most active ingredients, *morphine,* was first isolated in the early 1800s and is used worldwide for pain relief. Percodan and Demerol are two common morphine-like drugs. *Heroin* is derived from morphine but is three times more powerful, causing intensely pleasurable reactions when first taken.

Opiates have complex effects on consciousness. Drowsy, cloudy feelings occur because opiates depress activity in areas of the cerebral cortex. But they also create excitation in other parts, causing some users to experience euphoria (Bozarth & Wise, 1984). Opiates exert many of their effects through their role as agonists for endorphins. When opiates activate endorphin receptors, they are "tricking" the brain into an exaggerated activation of its painkilling and mood-altering systems (Julien, 2001).

Opiates are highly addictive, perhaps because they stimulate a particular type of glutamate receptor in the brain that can bring physical changes in a neuron's structure. It may be, then, that opiates alter neurons so that they come to require the drug to function properly. Supporting this idea are data showing that glutamate antagonists appear to prevent morphine dependence yet leave the drug's painkilling effects intact (Trujillo & Akil, 1991). Beyond the hazards of addiction itself, heroin addicts risk death through overdoses, contaminated drugs, or AIDS contracted by sharing drug-injection needles (Hser et al., 2001).

Hallucinogens

Hallucinogens, also called *psychedelics*, create a loss of contact with reality and alter other aspects of emotion, perception, and thought. They can cause distortions in body image (the user may feel gigantic or tiny), loss of identity (confusion about who one actually is), dream-like fantasies, and hallucinations. Because these effects resemble many severe forms of mental disorder, hallucinogens are also called *psychotomimetics* (mimicking psychosis).

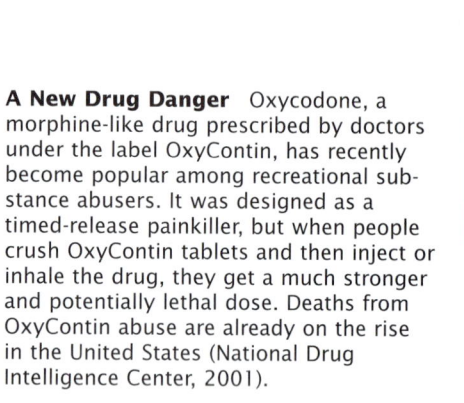

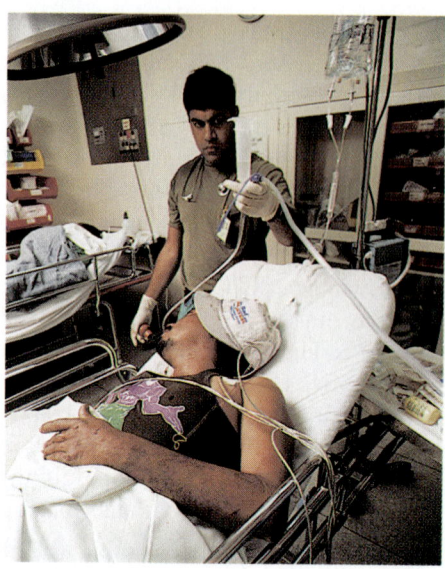

A New Drug Danger Oxycodone, a morphine-like drug prescribed by doctors under the label OxyContin, has recently become popular among recreational substance abusers. It was designed as a timed-release painkiller, but when people crush OxyContin tablets and then inject or inhale the drug, they get a much stronger and potentially lethal dose. Deaths from OxyContin abuse are already on the rise in the United States (National Drug Intelligence Center, 2001).

LSD One of the most powerful psychedelics is *lysergic acid diethylamide*, or *LSD*, first synthesized from a rye fungus by Swiss chemist Albert Hofmann. In 1938, after Hofmann accidentally ingested a minuscule amount of the substance, he discovered the drug's strange effects in the world's first LSD "trip" (Julien, 1995). LSD's hallucinations can be quite bizarre. Time may seem distorted, sounds may cause visual sensations, and users may feel as if they have left their bodies.

LSD's hallucinatory effects are probably due to its ability to stimulate a specific type of receptor in the forebrain, called 5-HT_{2a} receptors, that normally respond to serotonin (Carlson, 1998; Leonard, 1992). Supporting this assertion is evidence that serotonin antagonists greatly reduce LSD's hallucinatory effects (Leonard, 1992).

The precise effects of LSD on a particular individual are unpredictable. Unpleasant hallucinations and delusions can occur during a person's first—or two hundredth—LSD experience. Although LSD is not addictive, tolerance to its effects does develop. Some users suffer lasting adverse effects, including severe short-term memory loss, paranoia, violent outbursts, nightmares, and panic attacks (Gold, 1994). Distortions in visual sensations can remain years after the end of heavy use (Abraham & Wolf, 1988). Sometimes flashbacks occur, in which a person suddenly returns to an LSD-like state of consciousness weeks or even years after using the drug.

Ketamine *Ketamine* is an anesthetic widely used by veterinarians to ease pain in their animal patients, but because it also has hallucinogenic effects, it is being stolen and sold as a recreational drug known as "Special K." Its effects include dissociative feelings that create what some users describe as an "out-of-body" or "near death" experience. Unfortunately, ketamine also causes enduring memory impairment (Curran & Monaghan, 2001), which may result from damage to memory-related brain structures such as the hippocampus (Jevtovic-Todorovic et al., 2001).

Marijuana A mixture of the crushed leaves, flowers, and stems from the hemp plant *(Cannabis sativa)* makes up *marijuana*. The active ingredient is *tetrahydrocannabinol*, or *THC*. When inhaled, THC is absorbed in minutes by many organs, including the brain, and it continues to affect consciousness for a few hours. THC tends to collect in fatty deposits of the brain and reproductive organs, where it can be detected for weeks. The specific receptors for THC include those sensitive to *anandamide* (from a Sanskrit word meaning "bliss"), a naturally occurring brain substance that research suggests may be a neurotransmitter (Fride & Mechoulam,

in review: Major Classes of Psychoactive Drugs

Drug	Trade/Street Name	Main Effects	Potential for Physical/Psychological Dependence
Depressants			
Alcohol	"booze"	Relaxation, anxiety reduction, sleep	High/high
Barbiturates	Seconal, Tuinal, Nembutal ("downers")		High/high
Stimulants			
Amphetamines	Benzedrine, Dexedrine, Methadrine ("speed," "uppers," "ice")	Alertness, euphoria	Moderate/high
Cocaine	"coke," "crack"		Moderate to high/high
Caffeine		Alertness	Moderate/moderate
Nicotine	"smokes," "coffin nails"	Alertness	High (?)/high
MDMA	ecstasy, clarity	Hallucinations	Low/(?)
Opiates			
Opium		Euphoria	High/high
Morphine	Percodan, Demerol	Euphoria, pain control	High/high
Heroin	"junk," "smack"	Euphoria, pain control	High/high
Hallucinogens			
LSD/Ketamine	"acid"/"Special K"	Altered perceptions, hallucinations	Low/low
Marijuana (cannabis)	"pot," "dope," "reefer"	Euphoria, relaxation	Low/moderate

1993). Another substance in the brain that binds to THC receptors is called *2-AG*, which may affect the neural basis of memory in the hippocampus (Stella, Schweitzer, & Piomelli, 1997).

Low doses of marijuana may initially create restlessness and hilarity, followed by a dreamy, carefree relaxation, an expanded sense of space and time, more vivid sensations, food cravings, and subtle changes in thinking (Kelly et al., 1990). For a summary of the effects of marijuana and other psychoactive drugs, see "In Review: Major Classes of Psychoactive Drugs."

THINKING CRITICALLY

Is Marijuana Dangerous?

A large-scale study of U.S. teenagers indicated a dramatic rise in their use of marijuana from 1991 to 1996. Usage almost tripled among eighth-graders (from 4 to 11 percent) and more than doubled among tenth-graders (from 9 to 20 percent). During this same period, the number of students who believed that there is a "great risk" associated with using marijuana declined in about the same proportions (Hall, 1997). Marijuana use has continued to increase in recent years (National Institute on Drug Abuse, 2000a), and in response to these trends, U.S. government officials have condemned marijuana use as "dangerous, illegal, and wrong." Concern about the drug has also been voiced in many other countries.

At the same time, the medical community has been engaged in serious discussion about whether marijuana should be used for medicinal purposes, and in the United States and around the world many individuals and organizations continue to argue for the decriminalization of marijuana use (Hall, 1997; Iversen & Snyder, 2000; Strang, Witten, & Hall, 2000).

Those who support legalization of marijuana cite its medical benefits; some doctors claim to have successfully used marijuana in the treatment of asthma,

The Cannabis Controversy Marijuana is illegal in North America and in many other places, too, but the question of whether it should remain so is a matter of hot debate between those who see the drug as a dangerous gateway to more addictive substances and those who view it as a benign source of pleasure that may also have important medical benefits.

glaucoma, epilepsy, chronic pain, and nausea from cancer chemotherapy (Tramer et al., 2001; Voelker, 1997). But critics insist that medical legalization of marijuana is premature, because its medicinal value has not been clearly established (Bennet, 1994) and because—even though patients may prefer marijuana-based drugs—other medications may be equally effective and less dangerous (e.g., Campbell et al., 2001).

- **What am I being asked to believe or accept?**

Those who see marijuana as dangerous usually assert four beliefs: (1) that marijuana is addictive; (2) that it leads to the use of "hard drugs," such as heroin; (3) that marijuana intoxication endangers the user and other individuals; and (4) that long-term marijuana use leads to undesirable behavioral changes, disruption of brain functions, and other adverse effects on health.

- **What evidence is available to support the assertion?**

Without a doubt, some people do use marijuana to such an extent that it disrupts their lives. According to the criteria normally used to define alcohol abuse, these people are dependent on marijuana—at least psychologically (Stephens, Roffman, & Simpson, 1994). The question of physical dependence (addiction) is less clear, inasmuch as withdrawal from chronic marijuana use has long been thought not to produce any severe physical symptoms. However, some evidence of a mild withdrawal syndrome has been reported in rats, and in humans, withdrawal from marijuana may be accompanied by increases in anxiety, depression, and aggressiveness (Budney et al., 2001; Haney et al., 1999; Kouri, Pope, & Lukas, 1999; Rodriguez de Fonseca et al., 1997). Other research (e.g., Tanda, Pontieri, & Di Chiara, 1997) has found that marijuana interacts with the same dopamine and opiate receptors as does heroin, implying that marijuana could be a "gateway drug" to the use of more addictive drugs.

Regardless of whether marijuana is addicting or leads to "harder drugs," it can create a number of problems. It disrupts memory formation, making it difficult to carry out complex tasks (Lichtman, Dimen, & Martin, 1995; Pope et al., 2001). And because marijuana affects muscle coordination, driving while under its influence is quite hazardous. Compounding the danger is the fact that motor impairment continues long after the obvious effects of the drug have worn off. In one study, for example, pilots had difficulty landing a simulated aircraft even a full day after smoking one marijuana cigarette (Yesavage et al., 1985). As for marijuana's effects on intellectual and cognitive performance, long-term use can lead to lasting impairments in reasoning and memory (Solowij et al., 2002). One study found that adults who frequently used marijuana scored lower on a twelfth-grade academic achievement test than did nonusers with the same IQs (Block & Ghoneim, 1993).

● Are there alternative ways of interpreting the evidence?

Those who see marijuana as a benign or even beneficial substance criticize studies like those just mentioned as providing an inaccurate or incomplete picture of marijuana's effects (Grinspoon, 1999). They argue, for example, that the same dopamine receptors activated by marijuana and heroin are also activated by sex and chocolate—and that few people would call for the criminalization of those pleasures (Grinspoon et al., 1997). Moreover, the correlation between early marijuana use and later use of hard drugs could be due more to the people with whom users become involved than to any property of the drug per se (Fergusson & Horwood, 1997).

The question of marijuana's long-term effects on memory and reasoning is also difficult to resolve, partly because studies of academic achievement scores and marijuana use tend to be correlational in nature. As noted in the chapter on research in psychology, cause and effect cannot easily be determined in such studies. Does marijuana use lead to poor academic performance, or does poor academic performance lead to increased marijuana use? Both possibilities are credible.

● What additional evidence would help to evaluate the alternatives?

More definitive evidence on marijuana's short- and long-term effects is obviously needed, but evaluating the meaning of that evidence will be difficult. The issues involved in the marijuana debate involve questions of degree and relative risk. For example, is the risk of marijuana dependence greater than that of alcohol dependence? There are clearly differences among people in the extent to which marijuana use poses a risk for them. So far, however, we have not determined what personal characteristics account for such differences. Nor do we know why some people use marijuana only occasionally, whereas others use it so often and in such quantities that it seriously disrupts their ability to function in a normal and adaptive manner. The physical and psychological factors underlying these differences have yet to be identified.

● What conclusions are most reasonable?

Those who would decriminalize the use of marijuana argue that when marijuana was declared illegal in the United States in the 1930s, there was no evidence that it was any more harmful than alcohol or tobacco. Scientific evidence supports that claim, but more by illuminating the dangers of alcohol and tobacco than by exonerating marijuana. Although marijuana is less dangerous than, say, cocaine or heroin, it is by no means totally benign. Marijuana easily reaches a developing fetus and should not be used by pregnant women (Fried, Watkinson, & Gray, 1992); it suppresses some immune functions in humans (Cabral & Dove Pettit, 1998); and marijuana smoke is as irritating to lungs as tobacco smoke (Roth et al., 1998). Further, because possession of marijuana is still a crime almost everywhere in the United States, as well as in many other countries throughout the world, it would be foolish to flaunt existing laws without regard for the legal consequences of such actions.

However, in Canada, it is legal to grow and use marijuana for medicinal purposes, and despite federal laws to the contrary, the same is true in eight U.S. states. Although the American Medical Association has recently rejected the idea of medical uses for marijuana, scientists are intent on objectively studying its potential value in the treatment of certain diseases, as well as its dangers (or lack thereof). Their work is being encouraged by bodies such as the National Institute of Medicine (Joy, Watson, & Benson, 1999), and a British company is working on new cannabis-based medicines (Altman, 2000). The United Nations, too, has recommended that governments worldwide sponsor additional work on the medical uses of marijuana (Wren, 1999). Ultimately, the most reasonable conclusions about marijuana use must await the outcome of this research (Joy, Watson, & Benson, 1999).

LINKAGES

As noted in the chapter on introducing psychology, all of psychology's subfields are related to one another. Our discussion of meditation, health, and stress illustrates just one way in which the topic of this chapter, consciousness, is linked to the subfield of health psychology (which is a focus of the chapter on health, stress, and coping). The Linkages diagram shows ties to two other subfields as well, and there are many more ties throughout the book. Looking for linkages among subfields will help you see how they all fit together and help you better appreciate the big picture that is psychology.

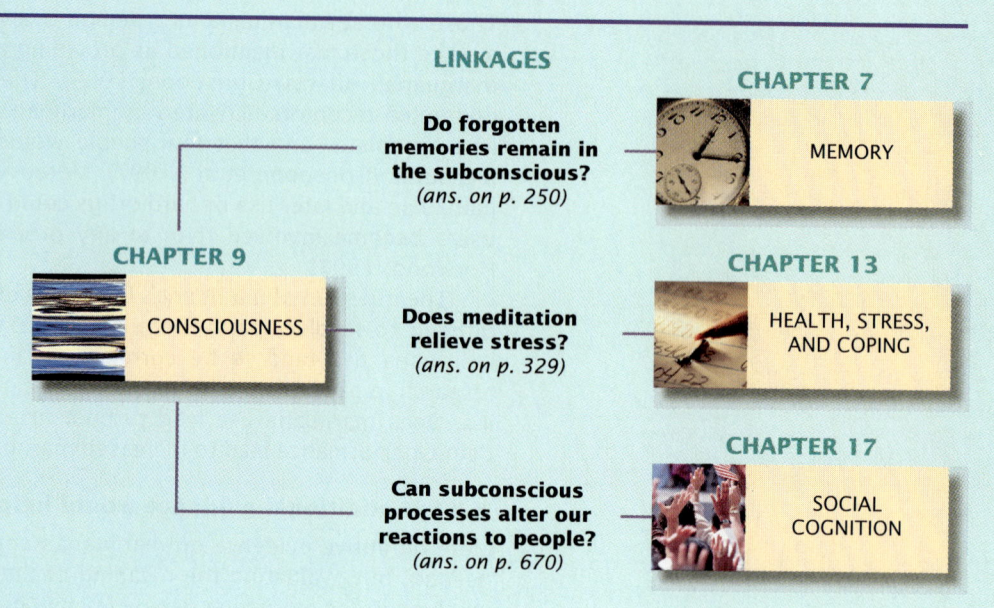

LINKAGES

CHAPTER 9 — CONSCIOUSNESS

Do forgotten memories remain in the subconscious? (ans. on p. 250) — **CHAPTER 7** MEMORY

Does meditation relieve stress? (ans. on p. 329) — **CHAPTER 13** HEALTH, STRESS, AND COPING

Can subconscious processes alter our reactions to people? (ans. on p. 670) — **CHAPTER 17** SOCIAL COGNITION

SUMMARY

Consciousness can be defined as awareness of the outside world and of one's own thoughts, feelings, perceptions, and other mental processes.

Analyzing Consciousness

Current research on consciousness focuses on three main questions. First, what is the relationship between the mind and the brain? Second, does consciousness occur as a single "point" in mental processing or as several parallel mental operations that operate independently? Third, what mental processes are outside awareness, and how do they affect conscious processes?

Some Functions of Consciousness

Consciousness produces the best current interpretation of sensory information in light of past experience and makes this interpretation available to the parts of the brain that plan voluntary actions and speech.

Levels of Consciousness

Variations in how much awareness you have for a mental function are described by different levels of consciousness. The *preconscious level* includes mental activities that are outside of awareness but can easily be brought to the *conscious level*. The *unconscious level* involves thoughts, memories, and processes that are more difficult to bring to awareness. Mental processes that cannot be brought into awareness occur at the *nonconscious level*.

Mental Processing Without Awareness

Awareness is not always required for mental operations. Priming studies show that people's responses to some stimuli can be sped up, improved, or modified, even when the people are not consciously aware of the priming stimuli.

The Neuropsychology of Consciousness

Brain injuries often reveal ways in which mental processing can occur without conscious awareness. For instance, patients with anterograde amnesia continue to acquire new skills without later awareness of learning them.

States of Consciousness

A person's *state of consciousness* is constantly changing. When the changes are particularly noticeable, they are called *altered states of consciousness*. Examples include sleep, hypnosis, meditation, and some drug-induced states. Different cultures vary considerably in the value placed on different states of consciousness.

Sleeping and Dreaming

Sleep is an active and complex state.

Stages of Sleep

Different stages of sleep are defined on the basis of changes in brain activity (as recorded by an electroencephalograph, or EEG) and physiological arousal. Sleep normally begins with stage 1 sleep and progresses gradually to stage 4 sleep. Sleep stages 1 through 4 constitute *slow-wave sleep*, or non-REM sleep. Most dreaming occurs when people enter *rapid eye movement (REM) sleep*. The sleeping person cycles through these stages several times each night, gradually spending more time in stage 2 and REM sleep later in the night.

Summary

Sleep Disorders

Sleep disorders can disrupt the natural rhythm of sleep. Among the most common is *insomnia*, in which one feels tired because of trouble falling asleep or staying asleep. *Narcolepsy* produces sudden daytime sleeping episodes. In *sleep apnea*, people briefly, but repeatedly, stop breathing during sleep. *Sudden infant death syndrome (SIDS)* may be due to brain abnormalities or accidental suffocation. *Nightmares* and *night terrors* are different kinds of frightening dreams. *Sleepwalking* occurs most frequently during childhood. *REM behavior disorder* is potentially dangerous because it allows people to act out REM dreams.

Why Do People Sleep?

The cycle of waking and sleeping is a natural *circadian rhythm*, controlled by the suprachiasmatic nuclei in the brain. *Jet lag* can be one result of disrupting the normal sleep-wake cycle. The purpose of sleep is much debated. Non-REM sleep may aid bodily rest and repair. REM sleep may help maintain activity in brain areas that provide daytime alertness, or it may allow the brain to "check circuits" and solidify learning from the previous day.

Dreams and Dreaming

Dreams are story-like sequences of images, sensations, and perceptions that occur during sleep. Evidence from research on *lucid dreaming* suggests that people may sometimes be able to control their own dream content. Some claim that dreams are the meaningless byproducts of brain activity, but dreams may still have psychological significance.

Hypnosis

Hypnosis is a well-known but still poorly understood phenomenon.

Experiencing Hypnosis

Tests of hypnotic susceptibility suggest that some people cannot be hypnotized. Hypnotized people tend to focus attention on the hypnotist and passively follow instructions. They become very good at fantasizing and role taking. They may exhibit apparent age regression, experience posthypnotic amnesia, and obey posthypnotic suggestions.

Explaining Hypnosis

State theory sees hypnosis as a special state of consciousness. *Role theory* suggests that hypnosis creates a special social role that gives people permission to act in unusual ways. *Dissociation theory* combines aspects of role and state theories, suggesting that hypnotic participants enter into a social contract with the hypnotist to allow normally integrated mental processes to become dissociated and to share control over these processes.

Applications of Hypnosis

Hypnosis is useful in the control of pain and the reduction of nausea associated with cancer chemotherapy. Its use as a memory aid is open to serious question.

Psychoactive Drugs

Psychoactive drugs affect the brain, changing consciousness and other psychological processes. *Psychopharmacology* is the field that studies drug effects and their mechanisms.

Psychopharmacology

Psychoactive drugs exert their effects primarily by influencing specific neurotransmitter systems and, hence, certain brain activities. To reach brain tissue, drugs must cross the *blood-brain barrier*. Drugs that mimic the receptor effects of a neurotransmitter are called *agonists*, and drugs that block the receptor effects of a neurotransmitter are called *antagonists*. Some drugs alter the release or removal of specific neurotransmitters, thus affecting the amount of neurotransmitter available for receptor effects.

The Varying Effects of Drugs

Adverse effects such as *substance abuse* often accompany the use of psychoactive drugs. *Psychological dependence, physical dependence (addiction), tolerance,* and a *withdrawal syndrome* may result. Drugs that produce dependence share the property of directly stimulating certain areas of the brain known as pleasure centers. The consequences of using a psychoactive drug depend both on how the drug affects neurotransmitters and on the user's expectations.

Depressants

Alcohol and barbiturates are examples of *depressants*. They reduce activity in the central nervous system, often by enhancing the action of inhibitory neurotransmitters. They have considerable potential for producing both psychological and physical dependence.

Stimulants

Stimulants such as amphetamines and cocaine increase behavioral and mental activity mainly by increasing the action of dopamine and norepinephrine. These drugs can produce both psychological and physical dependence. Caffeine, one of the world's most popular stimulants, may also create dependency. Nicotine is a potent stimulant. MDMA is one of several psychoactive drugs that can permanently damage brain tissue.

Opiates

Opiates such as opium, morphine, and heroin are highly addictive drugs that induce sleep and relieve pain.

Hallucinogens

LSD, ketamine, and marijuana are examples of *hallucinogens*, or psychedelics. Hallucinogens alter consciousness by producing a temporary loss of contact with reality and changes in emotion, perception, and thought.

10 Cognitive Abilities

Testing for Intelligence
A Brief History of Intelligence Tests
Intelligence Tests Today
Aptitude and Achievement Tests

Measuring the Quality of Tests
Reliability
Validity

Evaluating IQ Tests
The Reliability and Validity of IQ Tests
THINKING CRITICALLY: Are IQ Tests Unfairly Biased Against Certain Groups?
IQ Scores as a Measure of Innate Ability
Group Differences in IQ Scores
Conditions That Can Raise IQ Scores
IQ Scores in the Classroom
LINKAGES: Emotionality and the Measurement of Cognitive Abilities

Understanding Intelligence
The Psychometric Approach
The Information-Processing Approach
The Triarchic Theory of Intelligence
Multiple Intelligences
FOCUS ON RESEARCH METHODS: Tracking Cognitive Abilities over the Life Span

Diversity in Cognitive Abilities
Creativity
Unusual Cognitive Ability

Linkages

Summary

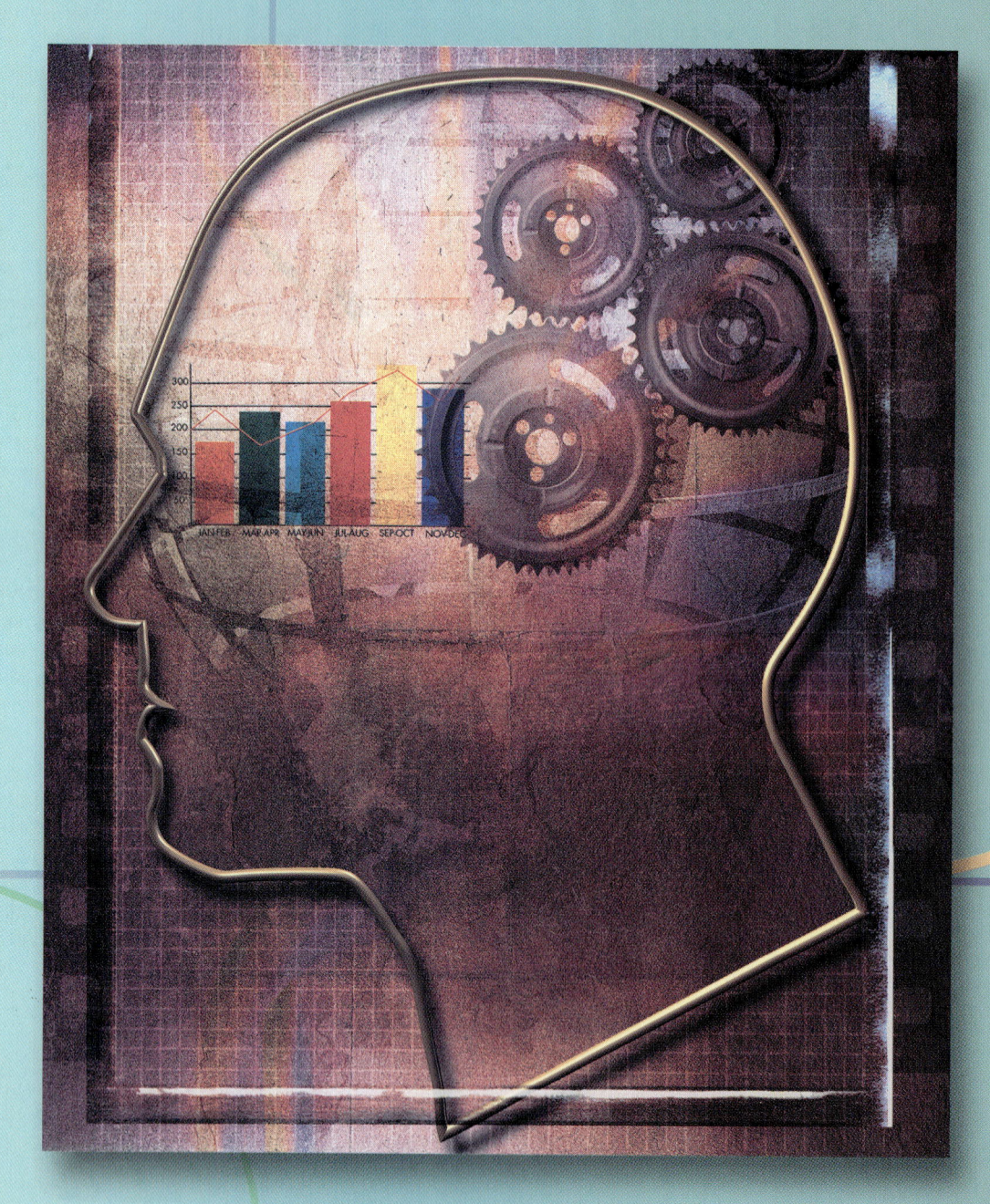

Consider the following sketches of four college seniors and their varying abilities and interests. Do any of these descriptions remind you of anyone you know? Do any of them sound like you?

Jack's big-city "street smarts" were not reflected in his high school grades. After testing revealed a learning disability, Jack worked to compensate for it, graduating with a grade-point average (GPA) of 3.78; but when he took the Scholastic Aptitude Test (SAT), his score was only 860 out of a possible 1600. He attended a local college, where he was given extra time to complete exams because of his learning disability. He held a half-time job throughout all four years, and his GPA was 2.95. When he completes his undergraduate degree, Jack will apply to master's degree programs in special education.

Deneace earned straight As in public grade school. She attended a private high school, where she placed in the top fifth of her class and played the violin. Her SAT score was 1340, but because her school did not give letter grades, she had no grade-point average to include in college applications. Instead, she submitted teachers' evaluations and a portfolio containing papers and class projects. Deneace was accepted at several prestigious small colleges, but not at major research universities. She is enrolled in a pre-med program, and with a GPA of 3.60, Deneace is hoping to be accepted by a medical school.

Ruthie has a wide range of interests and many friends, loves physical activities, and can talk to anybody about almost anything. Her high school grades, however, were only fair, averaging 2.60; but she played four sports, was captain of the state champion volleyball team, and was vice president of her senior class. She scored rather poorly on the SAT but received an athletic scholarship at a large university. She majored in sociology and minored in sport psychology. Focusing on just one sport helped her achieve a 3.25 GPA. She has applied to graduate schools but has also looked into a job as a city recreation director.

George showed an early interest in computers. In high school, he earned straight As in math, art, and shop, but his overall GPA was only 2.55, and he didn't get along with other students. Everyone was surprised when he scored 1320 on the SAT and went on to major in math and computer science at a large public university. His grades suffered initially as he began to spend time with people who shared his interests, but his GPA is now 3.33. He writes computer animation software and has applied to graduate programs in fields relating to artificial intelligence and human factors engineering.

TRY THIS — Before reading further, rank these four people on **cognitive ability**—the capacity to reason, remember, understand, solve problems, and make decisions. Who came out on top? Now ask a friend to do the same, and see if your rankings match. They may not, because each of the four students excels in different ways.

Deneace might score highest on general intelligence tests, which emphasize remembering, reasoning, and verbal and mathematical abilities. But would these tests measure Ruthie's social skills, Jack's street smarts, or George's artistic ability? If you were hiring an employee or evaluating a student, what characteristics would you want a test to measure? Can test scores be compared without consideration of social and academic background? The answers to these questions are important. Research on cognitive abilities helps us to understand human cognition and which factors help or hinder people's ability to learn from and adapt to their environment; and as our examples illustrate, measures of cognitive abilities often determine the educational and employment opportunities people have or don't have.

cognitive ability The capacity to reason, remember, understand, solve problems, and make decisions.

As you can see from its definition, *cognitive ability* is a very broad term. In this chapter, we will focus mainly on one aspect of it, known as *intelligence*. Like many other concepts in psychology, intelligence cannot be directly observed. Therefore, we must draw inferences about it from what can be observed and measured—namely, from scores on tests designed to assess intelligence.

Testing for Intelligence

There is no universally agreed upon definition of *intelligence*, but Robert Sternberg (1985) has offered one that is accepted by many psychologists. Sternberg says that **intelligence** includes three main characteristics: having knowledge, efficiently using that knowledge to reason about the world, and using that reasoning adaptively in different environments. Standard tests of intelligence measure some of these characteristics, but they don't address all of them. Accordingly, some psychologists argue that these tools are not able to capture all that should be tested if we want to get a complete picture of someone's intelligence in its broadest sense. To better understand the controversy, let's take a look at how standard intelligence tests were created, what they are designed to measure, and how well they do their job.

A Brief History of Intelligence Tests

The story of modern intelligence tests begins in France in 1904, when the French government appointed psychologist Alfred Binet to a commission charged with identifying, studying, and providing special educational programs for children who were not doing well in school. As part of his work, Binet developed a set of test items that provided the model for today's intelligence tests. Binet assumed that intelligence is involved in many reasoning, thinking, and problem-solving activities. Therefore, he looked for tasks that would highlight differences in children's ability to reason, judge, and solve problems (Binet & Simon, 1905). His test included tasks such as unwrapping a piece of candy, repeating numbers or sentences from memory, and identifying familiar objects (Rogers, 1995). Binet also assumed that children's abilities increase with age. He tested the items on children of various ages and then categorized items according to the age at which the typical child could respond correctly. For example, a "six-year-old item" was one that a substantial majority of six-year-olds could answer. Binet's test was thus a set of age-graded items. It measured a child's "mental level"—now called *mental age*—by determining the age level of the most advanced items a child could consistently answer correctly. Children whose mental age equaled their actual age, or *chronological age*, were considered to be of "regular" intelligence (Schultz & Schultz, 2000).

About a decade after Binet published his test, Lewis Terman at Stanford University developed an English version known as the **Stanford-Binet** (Terman, 1916). Table 10.1 gives examples of the kinds of items included on this test. Terman added items to measure the intelligence of adults and revised the scoring procedure. Mental age was divided by chronological age, and the result, multiplied by 100, was called the *intelligence quotient*, or *IQ*. So a child whose mental age and chronological age were equal would have an IQ of 100, which is considered "average" intelligence. A ten-year-old who scored at the mental age of twelve would have an IQ of $12/10 \times 100 = 120$. From this method of scoring came the term **IQ test**, a name that is widely used for any test designed to measure intelligence on an objective, standardized scale.

This scoring method allowed testers to rank people on IQ, which was seen as an important advantage by Terman and others who promoted the test in the United States. Unlike Binet—who believed that intelligence improved with practice—they saw intelligence as a fixed and inherited entity, and they believed that IQ tests could pinpoint who did and who did not have a suitable amount of intelligence. These

---

intelligence Those attributes that center around reasoning skills, knowledge of one's culture, and the ability to arrive at innovative solutions to problems.

Stanford-Binet A test for determining a person's intelligence quotient, or IQ.

IQ test A test designed to measure intelligence on an objective, standardized scale.

Here are samples of the types of items included on Lewis Terman's original Stanford-Binet test. As in Alfred Binet's test, an age level was assigned to each item.

table 10.1
The Stanford-Binet

Age	Task
2	Place geometric shapes into corresponding openings; identify body parts; stack blocks; identify common objects.
4	Name objects from memory; complete analogies (e.g., fire is hot; ice is _____); identify objects of similar shape; answer simple questions (e.g., "Why do we have schools?").
6	Define simple words; explain differences (e.g., between a fish and a horse); identify missing parts of a picture; count out objects.
8	Answer questions about a simple story; identify absurdities (e.g., in statements like "John had to walk on crutches because he hurt his arm"); explain similarities and differences among objects; tell how to handle certain situations (e.g., finding a stray puppy).
10	Define more difficult words; give explanations (e.g., about why people should be quiet in a library); list as many words as possible; repeat 6-digit numbers.
12	Identify more difficult verbal and pictured absurdities; repeat 5-digit numbers in reverse order; define abstract words (e.g., *sorrow*); fill in a missing word in a sentence.
14	Solve reasoning problems; identify relationships among points of the compass; find similarities in apparently opposite concepts (e.g., "high" and "low"); predict the number of holes that will appear when folded paper is cut and then opened.
Adult	Supply several missing words for incomplete sentences; repeat 6-digit numbers in reverse order; create a sentence, using several unrelated words (e.g., *forest, business-like,* and *dismayed*); describe similarities between concepts (e.g., "teaching" and "business").

Source: Nietzel & Bernstein (1987).

beliefs were controversial because in some instances, they led to prejudicial attitudes and acts of discrimination as enthusiasm for testing outpaced understanding of what was being tested.

Actually, controversy over intelligence testing arose even before the Stanford-Binet was published. In 1910, the U.S. government asked Henry Goddard to help identify immigrants who might be mentally defective. Goddard (1917) created an English translation of Binet's test and then administered it to immigrants by orally translating each item into their native languages. Scores resulting from this error-prone procedure led to the conclusion that 83 percent of Jews, 80 percent of Hungarians, 87 percent of Russians, and 79 percent of Italians immigrating to America were "feeble-minded"! The fact that this was not a fair test is painfully obvious today; even Goddard came to doubt the accuracy of his conclusions and eventually retracted them (Schultz & Schultz, 2000). Some of the same testing problems remained when the United States entered World War I, in 1918. To assess the cognitive abilities of military recruits, the government asked a team of psychologists to develop the first group-administered intelligence tests. The Army Alpha test assessed abilities such as arithmetic, analogies, and general knowledge among recruits who could read English. The Army Beta test was for recruits who could not read or did not speak English; it measured ability using nonverbal tasks, such as

Coming to America Early in the twentieth century, immigrants to the United States, including these new arrivals at Ellis Island in New York Harbor, were tested for both physical and mental frailties. Especially for those who could not read, speak, or understand English, the intelligence tests they took tended to greatly underestimate their intellectual capacity.

visualizing three-dimensional objects and solving mazes. Unfortunately, the verbal tests contained items that were unfamiliar to many recruits. Further, both versions were given in crowded rooms, where instructions were not always audible or, for non-English speakers, understandable. When 47 percent of the recruits scored at a mental age of thirteen years or lower (Yerkes, 1921), C. C. Brigham (1923) arrived at the incorrect conclusion that (1) from 1890 to 1915 the mental age of immigrants to America had declined and (2) the main source of this decline was the increase in immigration from southern and eastern Europe. Like Goddard, however, Brigham (1930) later retracted his statements (Gould, 1983).

In the late 1930s, David Wechsler (1939, 1949) developed new tests designed to improve on the earlier ones in three key ways. First, both verbal and nonverbal subtests were completed by all test takers. Second, knowing correct answers depended less on familiarity with a particular culture. Third, each subtest was scored separately, producing a profile that described an individual's performance in terms of several cognitive abilities.

Intelligence Tests Today

Today's editions of the Wechsler tests and the Stanford-Binet are the most widely used individually administered intelligence tests. The Wechsler Adult Intelligence Scale–Third Edition (WAIS-III) includes fourteen subtests. Seven of them measure verbal skills such as remembering a series of digits, solving arithmetic problems, defining vocabulary words, and understanding and answering general-information questions (e.g., What did Shakespeare do?). The other seven subtests have little or no verbal content; they are designed to measure performance skills such as manipulating materials and understanding the relationships between objects. These nonverbal subtests include tasks such as assembling blocks, solving mazes, arranging pictures to form a story, and completing unfinished pictures (Figure 10.1 shows examples of such performance items from a Wechsler test designed for children). Using the WAIS-III, the tester can calculate a verbal IQ, performance IQ, and a full-

intelligence quotient An index of intelligence that reflects the degree to which a person's score on an intelligence test deviates from the average score of others in the same age group.

figure 10.1

Performance Items Similar to Those on the Wechsler Intelligence Scale for Children (WISC-III-R)

Items like these are designed to measure aspects of intelligence that involve little or no verbal ability. The WISC-III-R contains six verbal subtests and seven performance tests.

Source: Simulated items similar to those in the Wechsler Intelligence Scales for Adults and Children. Copyright © 1949, 1955, 1974, 1981, 1991 by the Psychological Corporation. Reproduced by permission. All rights reserved.

PICTURE COMPLETION
What part is missing from this picture?

PICTURE ARRANGEMENT
These pictures tell a story, but they are in the wrong order. Put them in the right order so that they tell a story.

BLOCK DESIGN

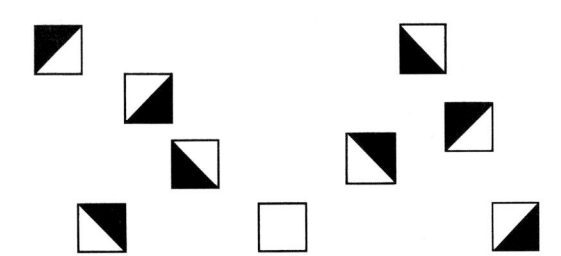

Put the blocks together to make this picture.

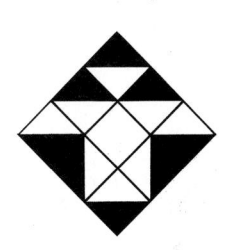

scale IQ, as well as factor scores that reflect a person's *cognitive processing speed, working memory, perceptual organization,* and *verbal comprehension.*

Like the Wechsler scales, the latest edition of the Stanford-Binet also uses subtests. It provides scores on *verbal reasoning* (e.g., What is similar about an orange, an apple, and a grape?), *quantitative reasoning* (e.g., math problems), *abstract/visual reasoning* (e.g., explaining why you should wear a coat in winter), and *working memory* (e.g., repeating a string of numbers in reverse order), along with an overall IQ score (Thorndike, Hagan, & Sattler, 2001).

If you take an IQ test today, your score will not be calculated by dividing your mental age by your chronological age and multiplying by 100. Instead, the points you earn for each correct answer are summed. Then the summed score is compared with the scores earned by other people. The average score obtained by people at each age level is *assigned* the IQ value of 100. Other scores are assigned IQ values that reflect how far each score deviates from that average. If you do better on the test than the average person in your age group, you will receive an IQ score above 100; how far above depends on how much better than average you do. Similarly, a person scoring below the age-group average will have an IQ below 100. This procedure may sound arbitrary, but it is based on a well-documented assumption about many characteristics: Most people's scores fall in the middle of the range of possible scores, creating a bell-shaped curve known as the *normal distribution,* shown in Figure 10.2. (The statistics appendix provides a fuller explanation of the normal distribution and how IQ tests are scored.) As a result of this scoring method, your **intelligence quotient,** or **IQ score,** reflects your *relative* standing within a population of your age.

figure 10.2

The Normal Distribution of IQ Scores in a Population

When the IQ scores in the overall population are plotted on a graph, a bell-shaped curve appears. The average IQ score of any given age group is 100. Half of the scores are higher than 100, and half are lower than 100. Approximately two-thirds of the IQ scores of any age group fall between 84 and 116; about one-sixth fall below 84, and one-sixth fall above 116.

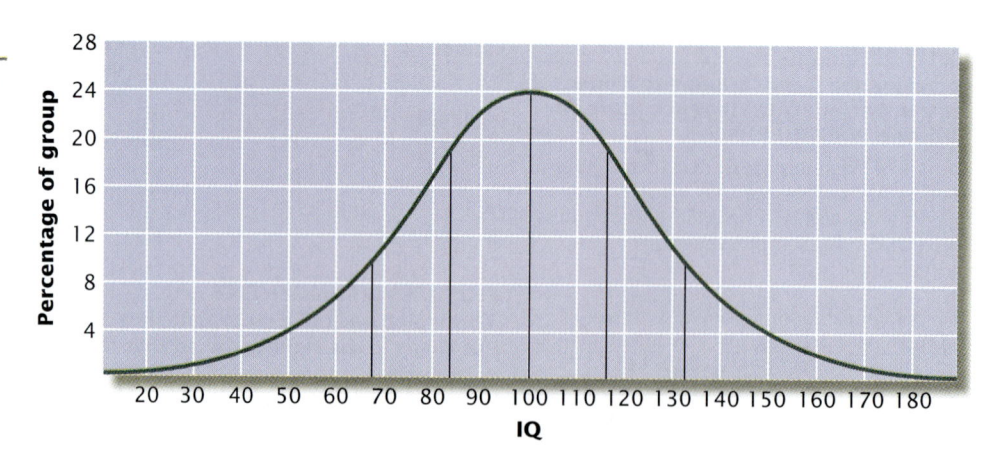

Aptitude and Achievement Tests

Closely related to intelligence tests are aptitude and achievement tests. **Aptitude tests** are designed to measure a person's capability to learn certain things or perform certain tasks. Although such tests may contain questions about what you already know, their ultimate goal is to assess your *potential* to learn (Aiken, 1994). The *SAT* (originally called the *Scholastic Aptitude Test*), the *American College Testing Assessment (ACT)*, and the verbal, quantitative, and analytic components of the *Graduate Records Examination (GRE)* are the aptitude tests most commonly used by colleges and universities in the United States to help guide decisions about which applicants to admit (e.g., Kuncel, Hezlett, & Ones, 2001). Corporations also use aptitude tests as part of the process of selecting new employees. These tests usually involve brief assessments of cognitive abilities; examples include the Otis-Lennon Mental Abilities Test and the Wonderlic Personnel Test (Aiken, 1994). Corporations may also use the General Aptitude Test Battery (GATB) to assess both general and specific skills ranging from learning ability and verbal aptitude to motor coordination and finger dexterity at computer or clerical tasks.

Schools and employers also commonly administer **achievement tests,** which measure what a person has accomplished or learned in a particular area. For example, schoolchildren are tested on what they have learned about language, mathematics, and reading (Rogers, 1995). Their performance on these tests is then compared with that of other students in the same grade to evaluate their educational progress. Similarly, college students' scores on the Graduate Record Examination's Subject Tests assess how much they have learned about the field in which they wish to pursue graduate work.

Measuring the Quality of Tests

A **test** is a systematic procedure for observing behavior in a standard situation and describing it with the help of a numerical scale or a system of categories (Cronbach, 1990). Any test, including an IQ test, should fairly and accurately measure a person's performance. Accordingly, schools and employers in the United States are required by law to use fair and accurate tests for placing students in particular classes and for choosing new employees.

Tests have two major advantages over interviews and other means of evaluating people. First, they are *standardized;* that is, conditions surrounding a test are as similar as possible for everyone who takes it. Standardization helps ensure, for example, that test results will not be significantly affected by who gives and scores the test. Incidental factors, such as variations in how a question is phrased, are also less likely to affect the results of standardized tests. Because the biases of those giving or scoring the test do not influence the results, a standardized test is said to be *objective*. Second, tests summarize the test taker's performance with a specific number, known as a *score*. Scores, in turn, allow the calculation of **norms**, which describe the frequency of particular scores. Norms tell us, for example, what percentage of high school students obtained each possible score on a college entrance exam and whether a particular person's score is above or below the average.

The two most important things to know about when determining the value of a test are its reliability and validity.

Reliability

If you stepped on a scale, checked your weight, stepped off, stepped back on, and found that your weight had increased by twenty pounds, you would know it was time to buy a new scale. A good scale, like a good test, must have **reliability**; in other words, the results must be repeatable or stable. A test must measure the same thing in the same way every time. If you received a very high score on a reasoning test the first time you took it but a very low score when the test was repeated the next day, the test is probably unreliable. The higher the reliability of a test, the less likely it is that its scores will be affected by temperature, hunger, or other irrelevant changes in the environment or the test taker.

To estimate the reliability of a test, researchers usually get two sets of scores on the same test from the same people and then compute a *correlation coefficient* between the two (see the chapter on research in psychology and the statistics appendix). If the correlation is high and positive (usually above +.80 or so), the test is considered reliable. The two sets of scores can be obtained in several ways. In the *test-retest* method, a group of people take the same test twice. Using this method assumes, of course, that whatever is being measured will not change much between the two testings. If you practiced on your keyboard before taking a second test of typing skill, your second score would be higher than the first, but not because the test was unreliable. Using an *alternate form* of the test at the second testing can reduce this practice effect, but great care must be taken to ensure that the second test is truly equivalent to the first. Perhaps the most common approach is the *split-half* method, in which a correlation coefficient is calculated between each person's scores on two comparable halves of the test (Thorndike & Dinnel, 2001). Some researchers employ more than one of these methods to check the reliability of their tests.

Validity

Imagine that your scale is reliable, giving you the same reading every time you step on it, but that it says you weigh thirty pounds. Unless you are a small child, this scale would provide a reliable but incorrect, or *invalid*, measure of your weight. Tests, like scales, can be reliable without being valid. In simplest terms, the **validity** of a test is reflected in the degree to which it measures what it is supposed to measure and leads to correct inferences about people (American Educational Research Association, American Psychological Association, and National Council on Measurement in Education, 1999; Anastasi, 1997). Assessing validity is not easy, partly because tests do not have "high" or "low" validity built into them. *The validity of a test depends on how it is used.* Suppose, for example, that you test people's intelligence by seeing how long they can hold their hands in ice water. This test's validity *as an intelligence test* would be low, because it does not measure what most of us think of as intelligence; it would not allow us to make accurate inferences about the cognitive abilities of the people tested. However, this same test might be a valid test of *pain tolerance*, because its results allow us to make accurate statements about people's sensitivity to discomfort. In other words, a test can be valid for one purpose but invalid for another.

aptitude tests Tests designed to measure a person's capacity to learn certain things or perform certain tasks.

achievement tests Measures of what a person has accomplished or learned in a particular area.

test A systematic procedure for observing behavior in a standard situation and describing it with the help of a numerical scale or a category system.

norms Descriptions of the frequency at which particular scores occur, allowing scores to be compared statistically.

reliability The degree to which a test can be repeated with the same results.

validity The degree to which a test measures what it is supposed to measure and leads to correct inferences about people.

A test's validity can be measured in several ways. For example, we can look at *content validity,* the degree to which the test's content is related to what the test is supposed to measure. If an instructor spends only five minutes out of forty lectures discussing the mating behavior of the tree frog and then devotes half of the final exam to this topic, that exam would be low on content validity. It would not allow us to make accurate inferences about students' learning in the course as a whole. Similarly, a test that measures only math skills would not have acceptable content validity as an intelligence test. A content-valid test includes items relating to the entire area of interest, not just a narrow slice (Lanyon & Goodstein, 1997).

Another way to evaluate a test's validity is to determine how well it correlates with an independent measure of whatever the test is supposed to assess. This independent measure is called a *criterion.* For example, a test of eye-hand coordination would have high *criterion validity* for hiring diamond cutters if scores on the test were highly correlated with a hands-on test of actual skill at diamond cutting. Why give a test if there is an independent criterion we can measure? The reasons often relate to convenience and cost. It would be silly to hire all job applicants and then fire those who are unskilled, if a ten-minute test could identify the best candidates. Criterion validity is called *predictive validity* when test scores are correlated with a criterion that cannot be measured until some time in the future—such as success in a pilot training program or grade-point average at graduation.

Evaluating IQ Tests

Criteria for assessing the reliability and validity of tests have been incorporated into the testing standards established by the American Psychological Association and other organizations (American Educational Research Association, American Psychological Association, and National Council on Measurement in Education, 1999). These standards are designed to maintain quality in educational and psychological testing by providing guidelines for the administration, interpretation, and application of tests in such areas as therapy, education, employment, certification or licensure, and program evaluation (Turner et al., 2001). Despite the best efforts of testers and test developers, however, scores on IQ tests must still be interpreted with caution, mainly because no one test can accurately measure all aspects of what various people think of as intelligence. So what does an IQ score say about you? Can it predict your performance in school or on the job? Is it a fair summary of your cognitive abilities? To scientifically answer questions like these, we must take into account not only the reliability and validity of the tests from which IQ scores come but also a number of sociocultural factors that might influence those scores.

The Reliability and Validity of IQ Tests

The reliability and validity of IQ tests are generally evaluated on the basis of the stability, or consistency, of IQ scores (reliability) and the accuracy of these scores in measuring cognitive abilities associated with intelligence (validity).

How Reliable Are IQ Tests?
IQ scores obtained before the age of seven typically do not correlate very well with scores on IQ tests given later, for two key reasons: (1) Test items used with very young children are different from those used with older children, and (2) cognitive abilities change rapidly in the early years (see the chapter on human development). During the school years, however, IQ scores tend to remain stable (Mayer & Sutton, 1996). For teenagers and adults, the reliability of IQ tests is high, generally above +.90.

Of course, a person's score may vary from one time to another if testing conditions, degree of motivation or anxiety, physical status, or other factors change. For

If only measuring intelligence were this easy!

this reason, testers today do not make decisions about a person's abilities on the basis of a single score. Overall, though, modern IQ tests usually provide exceptionally consistent results—especially compared with most other kinds of mental tests.

How Valid Are IQ Tests?

If everyone agreed on exactly what intelligence is (having a good memory, for example), we could evaluate the validity of IQ tests simply by correlating people's IQ scores with their performance on particular tasks (in this case, memory tasks). IQ tests whose scores correlated most highly with scores on memory tests would be the most valid measures of intelligence. But because psychologists do not fully agree on a single definition of intelligence, they don't have a single standard against which to compare IQ tests. Therefore, they cannot say whether IQ tests are valid measures of intelligence. They can only assess the validity of IQ tests for *specific purposes*.

IQ tests appear to be most valid for assessing aspects of intelligence that are related to schoolwork, such as abstract reasoning and verbal comprehension. Their validity—as measured by correlating IQ scores with high school grades—is reasonably good, about +.50 (Brody & Ehrlichman, 1998).

In addition, there is evidence that employees who score high on tests of verbal and mathematical reasoning tend to perform better on the job (and are paid more) than those who earned lower scores (Borman, Hanson, & Hedge, 1997; Johnson & Neal, 1998). Later, we describe a study that kept track of people for sixty years and found that children with high IQ scores tended to be well above average in terms of academic and financial success in adulthood (Oden, 1968; Terman & Oden, 1947). IQ scores also appear to be highly correlated with performance on "real-life" tasks such as reading medicine labels and using the telephone book (Gottfredson, 1997).

So, by the standard measures for judging psychological tests, IQ tests have good reliability and reasonably good validity for predicting certain abilities, such as success in school. As noted earlier, however, an IQ score is not an infallible measure of how "smart" a person is. Because IQ tests do not measure the full array of cognitive abilities, a particular test score tells only part of the story, and even that part may be distorted. Many factors other than cognitive ability—including response to the tester—can influence test performance. Children might not do as well if they

IQ and Job Performance IQ scores are reasonably good at predicting the ability to learn job-relevant information and to deal with unpredictable, changing aspects of the work environment (Hunter, 1986)—characteristics that are needed for success in complex jobs such as the ones these Navy navigator trainees will undertake.

are suspicious of strangers, for example (Jones & Appelbaum, 1989). Test scores can also be affected by anxiety, motor disabilities, and language differences and other cultural barriers (Fagan, 2000; Steele, 1997). For example, older adults who worry about making mistakes in unfamiliar situations may fail to even try to answer some questions, thus artificially lowering their IQ scores (Zelinski, Schaie, & Gribben, 1977).

How Fair Are IQ Tests? Our review of the history of intelligence testing in the United States suggests that early IQ tests were biased against people who were unfamiliar with English or with the vocabulary and experiences associated mainly with middle-class culture at the time. For example, consider the question "Which is most similar to a xylophone? (violin, tuba, drum, marimba, piano)." No matter how intelligent children are, if they have never had a chance to see an orchestra or to learn about these instruments, they may miss the question. Test designers today try to avoid obviously biased questions (American Educational Research Association, American Psychological Association, and National Council on Measurement in Education, 1999; Serpell, 2000). Furthermore, because IQ tests now include more than one scale, areas that are most influenced by culture, such as vocabulary, can be assessed separately from areas that are less vulnerable to cultural bias.

The solutions to many of the technical problems in IQ tests, however, have not resolved the controversy over the fairness of intelligence *testing*. The debate continues partly because results of IQ tests can have important consequences (Messick, 1982, 1989). Recall that intelligence tests were initially developed to identify and assist children with special educational needs. Yet today, such children may find themselves in special classes that not only isolate them from other students but also carry negative social labels. Obviously, the social consequences of testing can be evaluated separately from the quality of the tests themselves (Maguire, Hattie, & Haig, 1994); but those consequences cannot be ignored, especially if they tend to affect some groups more than others.

THINKING CRITICALLY

Are IQ Tests Unfairly Biased Against Certain Groups?

Despite attempts to eliminate cultural bias from IQ tests, there are differences in the average scores of various ethnic and cultural groups in the United States (e.g., Fagan, 2000; Herrnstein & Murray, 1994; Lynn, 1996; Taylor & Richards, 1991). Asian Americans typically score highest, followed, in order, by European Americans, Hispanic Americans, and African Americans. Similar patterns appear on a number of other tests of cognitive ability (e.g., Bobko, Roth, & Potosky, 1999; Sackett et al., 2001).

● **What am I being asked to believe or accept?**

Some critics of IQ tests argue that a disproportionately large number of people in some ethnic minority groups score low on IQ tests for reasons that are unrelated to cognitive ability, job potential, or other criteria that the tests are supposed to predict (Helms, 1992; Kwate, 2001; Neisser et al., 1996). They say that using IQ tests—and related cognitive aptitude tests—to make decisions about people may unfairly deprive members of some ethnic minority groups of equal employment or educational opportunities.

● **What evidence is available to support the assertion?**

Research reveals several possible sources of bias in tests of cognitive abilities. First, as noted earlier, noncognitive factors such as motivation, trust, and anxiety influence performance on IQ tests and may put certain groups at a disadvantage. Children from some minority groups may be less motivated to perform well on standardized tests and less likely to trust the adult tester (Bradley-Johnson, Graham, & Johnson, 1986; Jones & Appelbaum, 1989; Steele, 1997). Consequently, differences in test scores may reflect motivational differences among various groups.

Second, many test items are still drawn from the vocabulary and experiences of the dominant middle-class culture in the United States. As a result, these tests often measure *achievement* in acquiring knowledge valued by that culture. Not all cultures value the same things, however (Serpell, 1994). A study of Cree Indians in northern Canada revealed that words and phrases associated with *competence* included *good sense of direction;* at the incompetent end of the scale was the phrase *lives like a white person* (Berry & Bennett, 1992). A European American might not perform well on a Cree intelligence test based on these criteria. In fact, as illustrated in Table 10.2, poor performance on a culture-specific test is probably due more to unfamiliarity with culture-based concepts than to lack of cognitive ability. "Culture-fair" tests—such as the Universal Nonverbal Intelligence Test—that reduce, if not eliminate, dependence on language skills and other knowledge of a specific culture do indeed produce smaller differences between majority and minority groups than more traditional measures (Bracken & McCallum, 1998).

Third, some tests may reward those who interpret questions as expected by the test designer. Conventional IQ tests have clearly defined "right" and "wrong" answers. Yet a person may interpret test questions in a manner that is "intelligent" or "correct," but that produces a "wrong" answer. For example, when one child was asked, "In what way are an apple and a banana alike?" he replied, "Both give me diarrhea." The fact that you don't give the answer that the test designer was looking for does not mean that you *can't*. When rice farmers from Liberia were asked to sort objects, they tended to put a knife in the same group as vegetables. This was the clever way to do it, they said, because the knife is used to cut vegetables. When asked to sort the objects as a "stupid" person would, they grouped the cutting tools together, the vegetables together, and so on, much as most North Americans would (Segall et al., 1990).

- **Are there alternative ways of interpreting the evidence?**

The evidence might be interpreted as showing that although IQ tests do not provide an unbiased measure of cognitive abilities in general, they do provide a fair test of whether a person is likely to succeed in school or in certain jobs. In short, they may be biased—but not in a way that discriminates *unfairly* among groups. Perhaps familiarity with the culture reflected in IQ tests is just as important for success at school or work in that culture as it is for success on the tests themselves. After all, the ranking among groups on measures of academic achievement is similar to the ranking for average IQ scores (Sue & Okazaki, 1990). According to this view, it doesn't matter very much if tests that are supposed to measure intellectual aptitude actually measure culture-related achievement, as long as they are useful

TRY THIS How did you do on this "intelligence test"? If, like most people, you are unfamiliar with the material being tested by these rather obscure questions, your score was probably low. Would it be fair to say, then, that you are not very intelligent?

table 10.2
An Intelligence Test?

Take a minute to answer each of these questions, and check your answers against the key below.

1. What fictional detective was created by Leslie Charteris?
2. What planet travels around the sun every 248 years?
3. What vegetable yields the most pounds of produce per acre?
4. What was the infamous pseudonym of broadcaster Iva Toguri d'Aquino?
5. What kind of animal is Dr. Dolittle's pushmi-pullyu?

Answers: (1) Simon Templar (2) Pluto (3) Cabbage (4) Tokyo Rose (5) A two-headed llama.

in predicting whatever criterion is of interest. In fact, "culture-fair" tests do not predict academic achievement as well as conventional IQ tests do (Aiken, 1994; Humphreys, 1988).

- **What additional evidence would help to evaluate the alternatives?**

Evaluation of whether tests fairly or unfairly differentiate among people depends on whether the sources of test-score differences are relevant to predicting performance in the environment for which the test is intended. To take an extreme example, perhaps average differences in IQ scores between ethnic groups result entirely from certain test items that have nothing to do with how well the test as a whole predicts academic success. It is important to conduct research on this possibility.

Alternative tests must also be explored, particularly those that include assessment of problem-solving skills and other abilities not measured by most IQ tests (e.g., Sternberg & Kaufman, 1998). If new tests prove to be less biased than traditional tests but have equal or better predictive validity, many of the issues discussed in this section will have been resolved.

- **What conclusions are most reasonable?**

The effort to reduce unfair cultural biases in tests is well founded, but "culture-fair" tests will be of little benefit if they fail to predict success as well as conventional tests do. Whether one considers this circumstance good or bad, fair or unfair, it is important for people to have information and skills that are valued by the culture in which they live and work. As long as this is the case, tests designed to predict success in such areas are reasonable insofar as they measure a person's skills and access to the information valued by that culture.

Stopping at that conclusion, however, would mean freezing the status quo, whereby members of certain groups are denied many educational and economic benefits. As discussed later, if more attention were focused on combating poverty, poor schools, inadequate nutrition, lack of health care, and other conditions that result in lower average IQ scores and reduced economic opportunities for certain groups of people, many of the reasons for concern about test bias might be eliminated. In the meantime, researchers are working to develop ways to reduce unnecessary culture-specific content on IQ and other cognitive ability tests, to motivate test takers to do their best on these tests, and to base ability-related decisions on a combination of cognitive ability tests and other relevant measures. The goal of this work is to maximize the predictive validity of the testing process while also maximizing the ethnic diversity of the people selected through that process for important educational and occupational opportunities (Sackett et al., 2001).

IQ Scores as a Measure of Innate Ability

Years of research have led psychologists to conclude that both hereditary and environmental factors interact to influence cognitive abilities. For example, by asking many questions, bright children help generate an enriching environment for themselves; thus, innate abilities allow people to take better advantage of their environment (Scarr & Carter-Saltzman, 1982). In addition, if their own biologically influenced intelligence allows bright parents to give their children an environment that helps the development of intelligence, their children are favored by both heredity and environment.

Psychologists have explored the influence of genetics on individual differences in IQ by comparing the correlation between the IQ scores of people who have differing degrees of similarity in their genetic makeup and environment. For example, they have examined the IQ scores of identical twins—pairs with exactly the same genetic makeup—who were separated when very young and reared in different environments. They have also examined the scores of identical twins raised together.

(You may want to review the Linkages section of the chapter on research in psychology, as well as the behavioral genetics appendix, for more on the research designs typically used to analyze hereditary and environmental influences.)

These studies find, first, that hereditary factors are strongly related to IQ scores. When identical twins who were separated at birth and adopted by different families are tested many years later, the correlation between their scores is usually high and positive, at least +.60 (Bouchard et al., 1990; McGue et al., 1993; Pederson et al., 1992). If one twin receives a high IQ score, the other probably will, too; if one is low, the other is likely to be low as well. However, studies of IQ correlations also highlight the importance of the environment (Scarr, 1998). Consider any two people—twins, siblings, or unrelated children—brought together in a foster home. No matter what the degree of genetic similarity in these pairs, the correlation between their IQ scores is higher if they share the same home than if they are raised in different environments, as Figure 10.3 shows (Scarr & Carter-Saltzman, 1982).

The role of environmental influences is also seen in the results of studies that compare children's IQ scores before and after environmental changes such as adoption. Generally, when children from relatively impoverished backgrounds were adopted into homes offering a more enriching intellectual environment—including interesting materials and experiences, as well as a supportive, responsive adult—they showed modest increases in IQ scores (Weinberg, Scarr, & Waldman, 1992).

A study of French children who were adopted soon after birth demonstrates the importance of both genetic and environmental influences. These children were tested after years of living in their adopted homes. Children whose biological parents were from upper socioeconomic groups (where higher IQ scores are more common) had higher IQ scores than children whose biological parents came from lower socioeconomic groups, regardless of the socioeconomic status of the adoptive homes (Capron & Duyme, 1989). These findings were supported by data from the Colorado Adoption Project (Cardon & Fulker, 1993; Cardon et al., 1992), and they suggest that a genetic component of children's cognitive abilities continues to exert an influence even in their adoptive environment. At the same time, when children from low socioeconomic backgrounds were adopted by parents who provided academically enriched environments, their IQ scores rose by twelve to fifteen points (Capron & Duyme, 1989). Other studies have also found that the IQ scores of adopted children were an average of fourteen points higher than those of siblings who remained with their biological parents in poorer, less enriching environments (Schiff et al., 1978).

figure 10.3

Correlations of IQ Scores

The correlation in IQ scores between pairs increases with increasing similarity in heredity or environment.

Source: Reprinted with permission from "Familial Studies of Intelligence: A Review," T. Bouchard et al., *Science,* Vol. 212, #4498, pp. 1055–9, 29 May 1981. Copyright © 1981 American Association for the Advancement of Science.

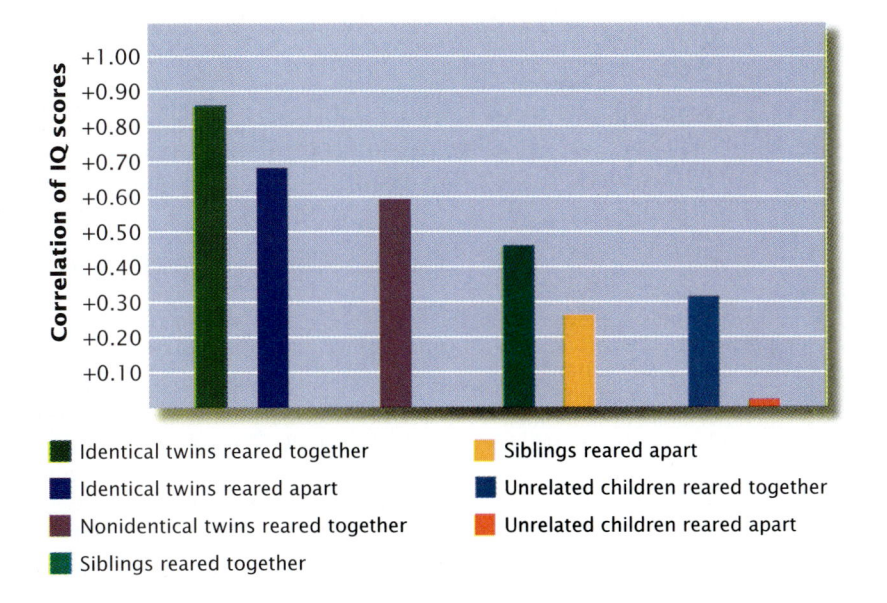

- Identical twins reared together
- Identical twins reared apart
- Nonidentical twins reared together
- Siblings reared together
- Siblings reared apart
- Unrelated children reared together
- Unrelated children reared apart

figure 10.4

IQ Test Scores, Then and Now

Comparisons of performance on the Stanford-Binet IQ test reveal that today's children are answering more questions correctly than did children in the 1930s. In fact, the average child today would receive an IQ score of 120 on the 1932 test, a very high score! No one is sure why this increase in performance has occurred, but some psychologists suspect that better nutrition and improvements in education programs are partly responsible.

Source: Neisser (1998).

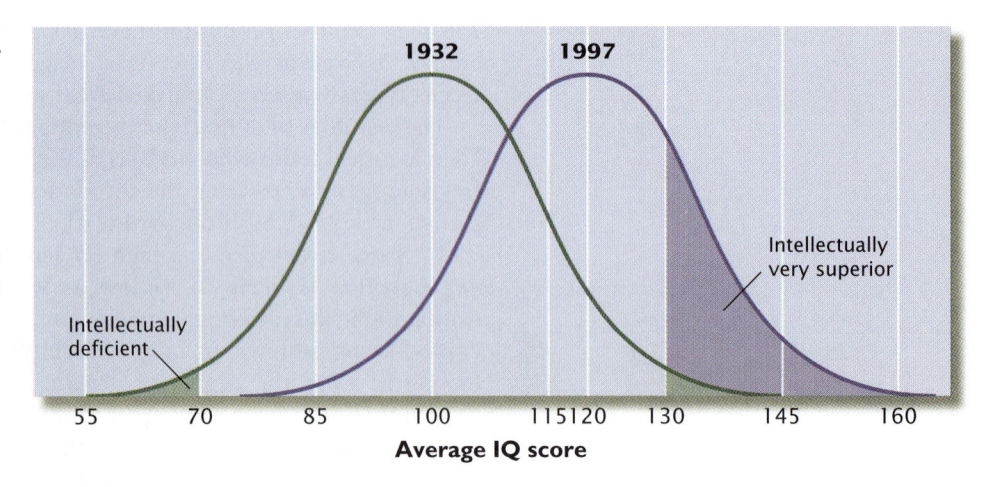

Research on genetic and environmental influences can help us understand the differences we see *among* people in terms of cognitive abilities and other characteristics, but it cannot tell us how strong each influence is in any *particular* person.

© 2002 Leo Cullum from cartoonbank.com. All Rights Reserved.

Other factors that may have negative effects on cognitive abilities include poor nutrition, exposure to lead or alcohol, low birth weight, and complications during birth (Matte et al., 2001; Strathearn et al., 2001). In contrast, exposure to early interventions that improve school readiness and academic ability tend to improve children's scores on tests of intelligence (Neisser et al., 1996; Ripple et al., 1999). These intervention programs, some of which are described later, may be responsible for the steady increase in average IQ scores throughout the world over the past six decades (Flynn, 1999; Neisser, 1998). Note that this increase cannot be due to the influence of new and "better" genes, because genetic changes or mutations do not occur this rapidly in humans (see Figure 10.4).

Some researchers have concluded that the influence of heredity and environment on differences in cognitive abilities appears to be about equal; others see a somewhat larger role for heredity (Herrnstein & Murray, 1994; Loehlin, 1989; Petrill et al., 1998; Plomin, 1994b). One research team has even suggested that specific genes are associated with extremely high IQs (Chorney et al., 1998). Still, it must be emphasized that such estimates of the relative contributions of heredity and environment apply only to groups, not to individuals. It would be inaccurate to say that 50 percent of *your* IQ score is inherited and 50 percent learned. It is far more accurate to say that about half of the *variability* in the IQ scores of a group of people can be attributed to hereditary influences, and about half can be attributed to environmental influences.

Intelligence provides yet another example of nature and nurture working together to shape behavior and mental processes. It also illustrates how the relative contributions of genetic and environmental influences can change over time. Environmental influences, for example, seem to be greater at younger ages (Plomin, 1994b) and tend to diminish over the years. So IQ differences in a group of children will probably be affected more by parental help with preschool reading than by, say, the courses they take in junior high school ten years later.

Group Differences in IQ Scores

Much of the controversy over the roles played by genes and the environment in intelligence has been sparked by efforts to explain differences in the average IQ scores earned by particular groups of people. As noted earlier, for example, the average scores of Asian Americans are typically the highest among various ethnic groups in the U.S. (e.g., Taylor & Richards, 1991). Further, the average IQ scores of people from high-income areas in the United States and elsewhere are consistently higher than those of people from low-income communities with the same ethnic makeup (Fergusson, Lloyd, & Horwood, 1991; Jordan, Huttenlocher, & Levine, 1992; McLoyd, 1998; Murthy & Panda, 1987; Rowe, Jacobson, & Van den Oord, 1999).

To correctly interpret these differences and analyze their sources, we must remember two things. First, group scores are just that; they do not describe individuals. Although the mean IQ score of Asian Americans is higher than the mean score of European Americans, there will still be large numbers of European Americans who score well above the Asian American mean and large numbers of Asian Americans who score below the European American mean (see Figure 10.5).

Second, increases in IQ scores over the past sixty years (Flynn, 1999; Neisser, 1998) and other similar findings suggest that inherited characteristics are not necessarily fixed. A favorable environment may improve a child's performance somewhat, even if the inherited influences on that child's IQ are negative (Humphreys, 1984).

Socioeconomic Differences

Why should there be a relationship between IQ scores and socioeconomic status? Four factors seem to be involved. First, parents' jobs and status depend on characteristics related to their own intelligence, and this intelligence is partly determined by a genetic component that, in turn, contributes to their children's IQ scores. Second, parents' income affects their children's environment in ways that can increase or decrease IQ scores (Bacharach & Baumeister, 1998; MacKenzie, 1984; Suzuki & Valencia, 1997). Third, motivational differences may play a role. Parents in upper- and middle-income families tend to provide more financial and psychological support for their children's motivation to succeed and excel in academic endeavors (Atkinson & Raynor, 1974; Nelson-LeGall & Resnick, 1998). As a result, children from middle- and upper-class families may exert more effort in testing situations and therefore obtain higher scores (Bradley-Johnson, Graham, & Johnson, 1986; Zigler & Seitz, 1982). Some suggest that this effect is strongest in smaller families, where each individual child, or an only child, can receive more parental support for academic achievement (Downey, 2001), while others see siblings themselves as a potential source of additional motivation (Zajonc, 2001a). Fourth, because colleges, universities, and businesses usually select people who score high on various cognitive ability tests, those with higher IQs—who tend to do better on such tests—may have greater opportunities to earn more money (Sackett et al., 2001).

Ethnic Differences

Some have argued that the average differences in IQ scores among various ethnic groups in the United States are due mostly to heredity. Note, however, that the existence of hereditary differences *within* groups does not indicate whether differences *among* groups result from similar genetic causes (Lewontin, 1976). As shown in Figure 10.5, variation within ethnic groups is much greater than variation among the mean scores of those groups (Zuckerman, 1990).

figure 10.5

A Representation of Ethnic Group Differences in IQ Scores

The average IQ score of Asian Americans is about four to six points higher than the average score of European Americans, who average twelve to fifteen points higher than African Americans and Hispanic Americans. Notice, however, that the variation *within* these groups is much greater than the differences among their average scores.

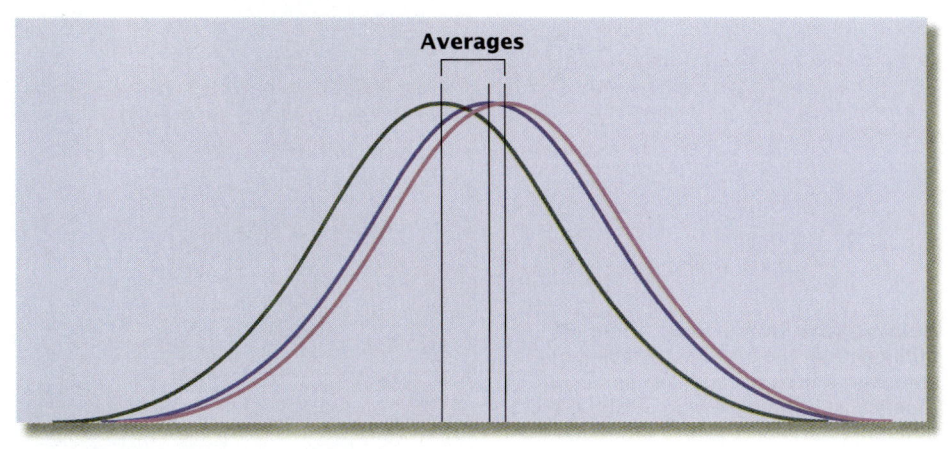

— African Americans and Hispanic Americans
— European Americans
— Asian Americans

We must also take into account the significantly different environments in which the average child in various ethnic groups grows up. To take only the most blatant evidence, the latest U.S. Census Bureau figures show 22.1 percent of African American families and 21.2 percent of Hispanic American families living below the poverty level, compared with 9.4 percent of European American families (U.S. Census Bureau, 2001). Among children under age sixteen, the figures show about 15 percent of European Americans, 36 percent of African Americans, and about 36 percent of Hispanic Americans living below the poverty line. Compared with European Americans, African Americans are more likely to have parents with poor educational backgrounds, as well as inferior nutrition, health care, and schools (Wilson, 1997). All of these conditions are likely to pull down scores on IQ tests (Brooks-Gunn, Klebanov, & Duncan, 1996).

Evidence for the influence of environmental factors on the average black-white difference in IQ scores is supported by data from adoption studies. One such study involved African American children from disadvantaged homes who were adopted by middle- to upper-class European American families in the first years of their lives (Scarr & Weinberg, 1976). When measured a few years later, the mean IQ score of these children was 110. A comparison of this mean score with that of nonadopted children from similar backgrounds suggests that the new environment raised the children's IQ scores at least ten points. A ten-year follow-up study of these youngsters showed that their average IQ scores were still higher than the average scores of African American children raised in disadvantaged homes (Weinberg, Scarr, & Waldman, 1992).

As discussed in the chapter on human development, cultural factors may also contribute to differences among the mean scores of various ethnic groups. For example, those means may partly reflect differences in motivation based on how much value is placed on academic achievement. In one study of 15,000 African American, Asian American, Hispanic American, and European American high school students, parental and peer influences related to achievement tended to vary by ethnic group (Steinberg, Dornbusch, & Brown, 1992). The Asian American students received strong support for academic pursuits from both their parents and

Helping with Homework There are differences in the average IQ scores of European Americans and African Americans, but people who attribute these differences primarily to hereditary factors are ignoring a number of environmental, social, and other nongenetic factors that are important in creating, and that are now narrowing, this IQ gap.

their peers. European American students whose parents expected high academic achievement tended to associate with peers who also encouraged achievement, and they tended to do better academically than African American and Hispanic American students. The parents of the African American students in the study supported academic achievement, but because these students' peers did not, the students may have been less motivated, and their performance may have suffered. The performance of the Hispanic American students may have suffered because, in this study at least, they were more likely than the others to have authoritarian parents, whose emphasis on obedience (see the chapter on human development) may have created conflicts with the schools' emphasis on independent learning.

In short, it appears that some important nongenetic factors decrease the mean scores of African American and Hispanic American children. The currently narrowing gap between African American and European American children on tests of intelligence and mathematical aptitude may be related to changing environmental conditions for many African American children (College Board, 1994; Vincent, 1991). Whatever heredity might contribute to children's performance, it may be possible for them to improve greatly, given the right conditions.

Conditions That Can Raise IQ Scores

A number of environmental conditions can help or deter cognitive development (see the chapter on human development). For example, lack of caring attention or of normal intellectual stimulation can inhibit a child's mental growth. Low test scores have been linked with poverty, chaos, and noise in the home; poor schools; and inadequate nutrition and health care (Alaimo, Olson, & Frongillo, 2001; Kwate, 2001; Serpell, 2000; Weinberg, 1989). Can the effects of bad environments be reversed? Not always, but efforts to intervene in the lives of children and enrich their environments have had some success. Conditions for improving children's performance include rewards for progress, encouragement of effort, and creation of expectations for success.

In the United States, the best-known attempt to enrich children's environments is Project Head Start, a set of programs established by the federal government in the 1960s to help preschoolers from lower-income backgrounds. In some of these programs, teachers visit the home and work with the child and parents on cognitive skills. In others, the children attend classes in nursery schools. Some programs emphasize health and nutrition and, in recent years, family mental health and social skills as well (Murray, 1995). Head Start has brought measurable benefits to children's health, as well as improvements in their academic and intellectual skills (Barnett, 1998; Lee, Brooks-Gunn, & Schnur, 1988; Ramey, 1999). Closely related to Project Head Start are intervention programs for infants at risk because of low birth weight, low socioeconomic status, or low parental IQ scores. Such programs appear to enhance IQ scores by as much as nine points by the age of three; the effects appear especially strong for the infants of mothers with a high school education or less (Brooks-Gunn et al., 1992; Ramey et al., 2000; Wasik et al., 1990).

Do the gains achieved by preschool enrichment programs last? Although program developers sometimes claim long-term benefits (Schweinhart & Weikart, 1991), such claims are disputed (Spitz, 1991). Various findings from more than a thousand such programs are often contradictory, but the effect on IQ scores typically diminishes after a year or two (Woodhead, 1988). A study evaluating two of the better preschool programs concluded that their effects are at best only temporary (Locurto, 1991a). The fading of effects is probably due to reduced motivation, not loss of cognitive ability (Zigler & Seitz, 1982). Children may lose motivation when they leave a special preschool program and enter the substandard schools that often serve poor children.

Fading effects were also seen in programs such as the Abecedarian Project (Ramey, 1992). Children at risk for mental retardation were identified while they

Project Head Start This teacher is working in Project Head Start, a U.S. government program designed to enrich the academic environments of preschoolers from lower-income backgrounds and improve their chances of succeeding in grade school.

were still in the womb. They then received five years of intense interventions to improve their chances of success once they entered school. When they started school, children in this enrichment program had IQ scores that were seven points higher than the scores of at-risk children who were not in the program. At age twelve, they still scored higher on IQ tests, but the size of the difference at that time was just five points. This difference was still evident nearly a decade later, when the participants were assessed recently at the age of twenty-one (Campbell et al., 2001).

Martin Woodhead (1988) concluded that the primary benefits of early-enrichment programs probably lie in their effect on children's attitudes toward school. One consistent, though very small, effect is that children who have taken part in enrichment programs are less likely to be held back in school or to need special-education programs (Locurto, 1991b; Palmer & Anderson, 1979). Especially in borderline cases, favorable attitudes toward school may help reduce the chances that children will be held back a grade or placed in special-education classes. Children who avoid these experiences may retain positive attitudes about school and enter a cycle in which gains due to early enrichment are maintained and amplified on a long-term basis (Myerson et al., 1998; Zigler & Styfco, 1994).

IQ Scores in the Classroom

IQ scores do not act as a crystal ball that can infallibly predict a person's destiny, nor are they a measure of some fixed quantity of cognitive ability. However, they can subtly affect how people are treated and how they behave. Decades ago, Robert Rosenthal and Lenore Jacobson (1968) argued that labels placed on students create teacher *expectancies* that can become self-fulfilling prophecies. This assertion was based on what happened after they gave grade school teachers the names of students who were about to enter a "blooming" period of rapid academic growth. These students had supposedly scored high on a special test, but the researchers had actually selected the "bloomers" at random. During the next year, however, the IQ scores of two-thirds of the bloomers dramatically increased, whereas only one-quarter of the other children showed the same increase. Apparently, the teachers' expectancies about certain children influenced those children in ways that showed up on IQ tests.

Some attempts to replicate Rosenthal and Jacobson's findings have failed (Elashoff, 1979); others have found that the effect of teacher expectancies, though statistically significant, is relatively small (Jussim, 1989; Snow, 1995). Still, there is little doubt that IQ-based teacher expectancies can have an effect on students (Rosenthal, 1994b). To find out how, Alan Chaiken and his colleagues (1974) videotaped teacher-child interactions in a classroom in which teachers had been informed (falsely) that certain pupils were particularly bright. They found that the teachers tended to favor the supposedly brighter students—smiling at them more often than at other students, making more eye contact, and reacting more positively to their comments. Children receiving extra social reinforcement not only get more intense teaching but are also more likely to enjoy school, to have their mistakes corrected, and to continue trying to improve. Later research found that teachers provide a wider range of classroom activities for students for whom they have higher expectations, suggesting another way in which expectancies might influence IQ scores (Blatchford et al., 1989).

These results suggest that the "rich get richer": Those perceived to be blessed with better cognitive abilities are given better opportunities to improve those abilities. There may also be a "poor get poorer" effect. Some studies have found that teachers tend to be less patient, less encouraging, and less likely to try teaching as much material to students whom they do not consider bright (Cooper, 1979; Trujillo, 1986). Further, differential expectations among teachers—and even parents—about the academic potential of boys and girls may contribute to gender differences in performance in certain areas, such as science (e.g., Crowley et al., 2001).

IQ tests have been criticized for being biased and for labeling people on the basis of scores or profiles. ("In Review: Influences on IQ Scores" lists the factors that can shape IQ scores.) "Summarizing" a person through an IQ score does indeed run the risk of oversimplifying reality and making errors, but intelligence tests can also *prevent* errors by reducing the number of important educational and employment decisions that are made on the basis of inaccurate stereotypes, false preconceptions, and faulty generalizations. For example, boredom or lack of motivation at school might make a child appear mentally slow, or even retarded. But a test of cognitive abilities conducted under the right conditions is likely to reveal the child's potential. The test can prevent the mistake of moving a child of average intelligence to a class for the mentally handicapped. And as Alfred Binet had hoped, intelligence tests have been enormously helpful in identifying children who need special educational attention. So despite their limitations and potential for bias, IQ tests can minimize the likelihood of assigning children to remedial work they do not need or to advanced work they cannot yet handle.

in review: Influences on IQ Scores

Source of Effect	Description	Examples of Evidence for Effect
Genetics	Genes appear to play a significant role in differences among people on IQ test performance.	The IQ scores of siblings who share no common environment are positively correlated. There is a greater correlation between scores of identical twins than between those of nonidentical twins.
Environment	Environmental conditions interact with genetic inheritance. Nutrition, medical care, sensory and intellectual stimulation, interpersonal relations, and influences on motivation are all significant features of the environment.	IQ scores have risen among children who are adopted into homes that offer a stimulating, enriching environment. Correlations between IQs of identical twins reared together are higher than for those reared apart.

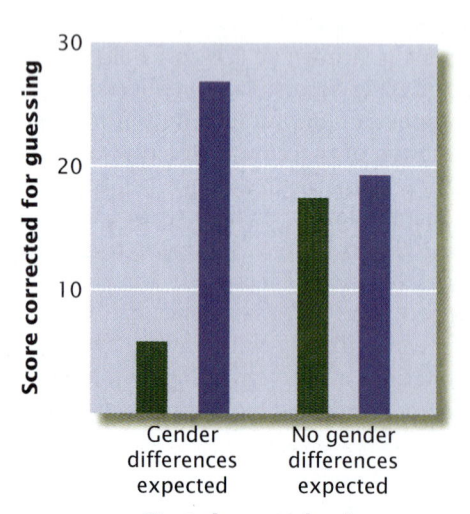

LINKAGES

LINKAGES (a link to Motivation and Emotion)

Emotionality and the Measurement of Cognitive Abilities

As mentioned earlier, factors other than cognitive ability can potentially influence scores on cognitive ability tests. One of the most important of these factors is emotional arousal. In the chapter on motivation and emotion, we note that people tend to perform best when their arousal level is moderate, whereas too much arousal, or even too little, tends to result in decreased performance. People whose overarousal impairs their ability to do well in testing situations are said to suffer from *test anxiety*.

These people fear that they will do poorly on the test and that others will think they are "stupid." In a testing situation, they may experience physical symptoms such as heart palpitations and sweating, as well as negative thoughts such as "I am going to blow this exam" or "They are going to think I am a real idiot." In the most severe cases of test anxiety, individuals may be so distressed that they are unable to successfully complete the test.

Test anxiety may affect up to 40 percent of elementary school students and about the same percentage of college students. It afflicts boys and girls equally (Turner et al., 1993). High test anxiety is correlated with lower IQ scores, and even among people with high IQ scores, those who experience severe test anxiety do poorly on achievement tests such as the SAT. Test-anxious grade school students are likely to receive low grades and to perform poorly on evaluated tasks and on those that require new learning (Campbell, 1986). Some children with test anxiety refuse to attend school or they "play sick" on test days, thus becoming caught up in a vicious circle that further harms their performance on standardized achievement tests.

Anxiety, frustration, and other emotions may also be at work in a testing phenomenon identified by Claude Steele and his colleagues. In one study, when test instructions were written in such a way as to cause bright African American students to become more sensitive to negative stereotypes about the intelligence of their ethnic group, these students performed less well on a standardized test than equally bright African American students whose sensitivity to the stereotypes had not been increased (Steele & Aronson, 1995). In another study, math-proficient women were randomly divided into two groups. The first group was given information that elicited concern over the stereotype that women are less good at math than men; specifically, they were told that men usually do better on the difficult math test they were about to take. The second group was not given such information. As shown in Figure 10.6, the women in the second group performed much better on the test than did those in the first. In fact, their performance was equal to that of men who took the same test (Spencer, Steele, & Quinn, 1997). Steele refers to this phenomenon as *stereotype threat* (Steele & Aronson, 2000): Concern over negative stereotypes about the cognitive abilities of the group to which they belong can impair the performance of some women—and some members of ethnic minorities—such that the test scores they earn underestimate their cognitive abilities (Blascovich et al., 2001; Inzlicht & Ben-Zeev, 2000).

The good news for people who suffer from test anxiety is that the counseling centers at most colleges and universities have effective programs for dealing with it. Test anxiety can be remedied through some of the same procedures used to treat other anxiety disorders (see the chapter on treatment of psychological disorders). There is also reason to be cautiously optimistic about reducing the impact of the stereotype threat phenomenon on the academic performance of African Americans and other minority groups. A program at the University of Michigan that directly addresses this phenomenon has produced substantial improvements in the grades of first-year minority students (Steele, 1997).

figure 10.6

The Stereotype Threat Effect

In this experiment, male and female college students took a difficult math test. Beforehand, some of the students were told that men usually outscore women on such tests. Women who heard this gender-stereotype information scored lower than women who did not hear it; they also scored lower than the men, even though their mathematical ability was equal to that of the men. Men's scores were not significantly affected by gender-stereotype information.

These and other research findings indicate that the relationship between anxiety and test performance is a complex one, but one generalization seems to hold true: People who are severely test anxious do not perform to the best of their ability on IQ tests.

Understanding Intelligence

We have said that standard IQ tests such as the Stanford-Binet and the Wechsler do not measure all aspects of intelligence. This is true because psychologists have taken several approaches to studying intelligence, some of which include a wider array of cognitive abilities than those focused on by Binet, Terman, and Wechsler. Let's consider these approaches and a few of the nontraditional intelligence tests that have emerged from some of them.

The Psychometric Approach

Standard IQ tests are associated with the **psychometric approach,** which is a way of studying intelligence that emphasizes the *products* of intelligence, including IQ scores. Researchers taking this approach ask whether intelligence is one general trait or a bundle of more specific abilities. The answer matters, because if intelligence is a single "thing," an employer might assume that someone with a low IQ could not do any tasks well. But if intelligence is composed of many independent abilities, a poor showing in one area—say, spatial abilities—would not rule out good performance in others, such as understanding information or solving word problems.

Early in the twentieth century, statistician Charles Spearman made a suggestion that began the modern debate about the nature of intelligence. Spearman noticed that scores on almost all tests of cognitive abilities were positively correlated (Spearman, 1904, 1927). That is, people who did well on one test also tended to do well on all of the others. Spearman concluded that these correlations were created by general cognitive ability, which he called **g,** for *general intelligence,* and a group of special intelligences, which he collectively referred to as *s.* The *s*-factors, he said, are the specific information and skills needed for particular tasks.

Spearman argued that people's scores on a particular test depend on both *g* and *s.* Further examination of test scores, however, revealed correlations that could not be explained by either *g* or *s* and were called *group factors.* Although Spearman modified his theory to accommodate these factors, he continued to assert that *g* represented a measure of mental force, or intellectual power.

In 1938, L. L. Thurstone published a paper criticizing Spearman's mathematical methods. Using the statistical technique of factor analysis, he analyzed the correlations among IQ tests to identify the underlying factors, or abilities, being measured by those tests. Thurstone's analyses did not reveal a single, dominating *g*-factor; instead, he found seven relatively independent *primary mental abilities*: numerical ability, reasoning, verbal fluency, spatial visualization, perceptual ability, memory, and verbal comprehension. Thurstone did not deny that *g* exists, but he argued that it was not as important as primary mental abilities in describing a particular person. Similarly, Spearman did not deny the existence of special abilities, but he maintained that *g* tells us most of what we need to know about a person's cognitive ability.

Raymond B. Cattell (1963) agreed with Spearman, but his own factor analyses suggested that there are two kinds of *g*, which he labeled *fluid* and *crystallized.* **Fluid intelligence,** he said, is the basic power of reasoning and problem solving. **Crystallized intelligence,** in contrast, involves specific knowledge gained as a result of applying fluid intelligence. It produces, for example, a good vocabulary and familiarity with the multiplication tables.

psychometric approach A way of studying intelligence that emphasizes analysis of the products of intelligence, especially scores on intelligence tests.

g A general intelligence factor that Charles Spearman postulated as accounting for positive correlations between people's scores on all sorts of mental ability tests.

s A group of special abilities that Charles Spearman saw as accompanying general intelligence (*g*).

fluid intelligence The basic power of reasoning and problem solving.

crystallized intelligence The specific knowledge gained as a result of applying fluid intelligence.

Who is right? After decades of research and debate, most psychologists today agree that there is a positive correlation among various tests of cognitive ability, a correlation that is due to a factor known as *g*. However, the brain probably does not contain some unified "thing" corresponding to what people call intelligence. Instead, it is suggested, cognitive abilities may be organized in "layers," beginning with skills that are narrow and specific and progressing through those that are broader and more general; *g* is the most general of all (Carroll, 1993).

The Information-Processing Approach

The **information-processing approach** analyzes the *processes* involved in intelligent behavior, rather than test scores and other *products* of intelligence (Das, 2002; Hunt, 1983; Naglieri et al., 1991; Vernon, 1987). Researchers taking this approach ask, What mental operations are necessary to perform intellectual tasks? What aspects depend on past learning, and what aspects depend on attention, working memory, and processing speed? In other words, the information-processing approach relates the basic mental processes discussed in the chapters on perception, learning, memory, and cognition to the concept of intelligence. Are there individual differences in these processes that correlate with measures of intelligence? More specifically, are measures of intelligence related to differences in the attention available for basic mental processes or in the speed of these processes?

The notion that intelligence may be related to attention builds on the results of research by Earl Hunt and others (Ackerman, 1994; Eysenck, 1987; Hunt, 1980). As discussed in the chapter on perception, attention represents a pool of resources or mental energy. When people perform difficult tasks or perform more than one task at a time, they must call on greater amounts of these resources. Does intelligent behavior depend on the amount of attention that can be mobilized? Early research by Hunt (1980) suggests that it does—that people with greater intellectual ability have more attentional resources available. There is also evidence of a positive correlation between IQ scores and performance on tasks requiring attention, such as mentally tallying the frequency of words in the "animal" category while reading a list of varied terms aloud (Stankov, 1989).

Another possible link between differences in information processing and differences in intelligence relates to processing speed. Perhaps intelligent people have "faster brains" than other people—perhaps they carry out basic mental processes more quickly. When a task is complex, having a "fast brain" might decrease the chance that information will disappear from memory before it can be used (Jensen, 1993; Larson & Saccuzzo, 1989). A fast brain might also allow people to do a better job of mastering material in everyday life and therefore to build up a good knowledge base (Miller & Vernon, 1992). Hans Eysenck (1986) even proposed that intelligence can be defined as the error-free transmission of information through the brain. Following his lead, some researchers have attempted to measure various aspects of intelligence by looking at electrical activity in particular parts of the brain (Deary & Caryl, 1993; Eysenck, 1994).

These hypotheses sound reasonable, but research suggests that only about 25 percent of the variation seen in people's performance on general cognitive abilities tests can be accounted for by differences in speed of access to long-term memory, the capacity of short-term and working memory, or other information-processing abilities (Baker, Vernon, & Ho, 1991; Miller & Vernon, 1992).

The Triarchic Theory of Intelligence

According to Robert Sternberg (1988b, 1999), a complete theory of intelligence must deal with three different types of intelligence: analytic, creative, and practical intelligence. *Analytic intelligence,* the kind that is measured by traditional IQ tests, would help you solve a physics problem; *creative intelligence* is what you would use

---

information-processing approach An approach to the study of intelligence that focuses on mental operations, such as attention and memory, that underlie intelligent behavior.

Brainpower and Intelligence The information-processing approach to intelligence suggests that people with the most rapid information processors (the "fastest brains") should do best on cognitive ability tests, including IQ tests and college entrance exams. Research suggests, however, that there is more to intelligent behavior than sheer processing speed.

to compose music; and you would draw on *practical intelligence* to figure out what to do if you were stranded on a lonely road during a blizzard. Sternberg's **triarchic theory of intelligence** deals with all three types of intelligence.

Sternberg acknowledges the importance of analytic intelligence for success at school and in other areas, but he argues that universities and employers should not select people solely on the basis of tests of this kind of intelligence (Sternberg, 1996; Sternberg & Williams, 1997). Why? Because the tasks posed by tests of analytic intelligence are often of little interest to the people taking them and typically have little relationship to their daily experience; each task is usually clearly defined and comes with all the information needed to find the one right answer (Neisser, 1996). In contrast, the practical problems people face every day are generally of personal interest and are related to their actual experiences; they are ill-defined and do not contain all the information necessary to solve them; they typically have more than one correct solution; and there may be several methods by which one can arrive at a solution (Sternberg et al., 1995).

It is no wonder, then, that children who do poorly in school can nevertheless show high degrees of practical intelligence. Some Brazilian street children, for example, are capable of doing the math required for their street business, despite having failed mathematics in school (Carraher, Carraher, & Schliemann, 1985). And a study of avid race-track bettors revealed that even bettors whose IQ scores were as low as 82 were highly accurate at predicting race odds at post time by combining many different kinds of complex information about horses, jockeys, and track conditions (Ceci & Liker, 1986). In other words, their practical intelligence was unrelated to measures of their IQ.

Sternberg's theory is important because it extends the concept of intelligence into areas that most psychologists traditionally did not examine and emphasizes what intelligence means in everyday life. The theory is so broad, however, that many parts of it are difficult to test. Determining exactly how to measure practical "street smarts," for example, is a challenge that is now being addressed (Sternberg et al., 1995, 2001). Sternberg and his colleagues have developed new intelligence tests designed to assess analytic, practical, and creative intelligence, and there is some evidence that scores on these tests can predict success at some jobs at least as well as standard IQ tests (Leonhardt, 2000; Sternberg & Kaufman, 1998; Sternberg et al., 1995). Figure 10.7 provides examples of several items from Sternberg's test that are designed to measure practical and creative aspects of intelligence.

triarchic theory of intelligence Robert Sternberg's theory that describes intelligence as having analytic, creative, and practical dimensions.

figure 10.7

Testing for Practical and Creative Intelligence

TRY THIS Robert Sternberg argues that traditional IQ tests measure mainly analytic intelligence. Here are sample items from tests he developed that test practical and creative intelligence as well. The answers are given at the bottom of the figure. How did you do?

Source: Sternberg (1996).

PRACTICAL

1. Think of a problem that you are currently experiencing in real life. Briefly describe the problem, including how long it has been present and who else is involved (if anyone). Then describe three different practical things you could do to try to solve the problem. *(Students are given up to 15 minutes and up to 2 pages.)*

2. Choose the answer that provides the **best** solution, given the specific situation and desired outcome.

    John's family moved to Iowa from Arizona during his junior year in high school. He enrolled as a new student in the local high school two months ago but still has not made friends and feels bored and lonely. One of his favorite activities is writing stories. What is likely to be the most effective solution to this problem?

    A. Volunteer to work on the school newspaper staff.
    B. Spend more time at home writing columns for the school newsletter.
    C. Try to convince his parents to move back to Arizona.
    D. Invite a friend from Arizona to visit during Christmas break.

3. Each question asks you to use information about everyday things. Read each question carefully and choose the best answer.

    Mike wants to buy two seats together and is told there are pairs of seats available only in Rows 8, 12, 49, and 95–100. Which of the following is not one of his choices for the total price of the two tickets?

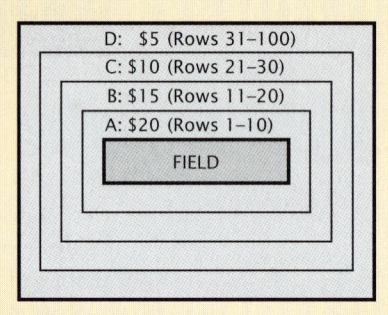

    ```
    D: $5 (Rows 31–100)
    C: $10 (Rows 21–30)
    B: $15 (Rows 11–20)
    A: $20 (Rows 1–10)
        FIELD
    ```

    A. $10. **B.** $20. **C.** $30. **D.** $40.

CREATIVE

1. Suppose you are the student representative to a committee that has the power and the money to reform your school system. Describe your ideal school system, including buildings, teachers, curriculum, and any other aspects you feel are important. *(Students are given up to 15 minutes and up to 2 pages.)*

2. Each question has a "Pretend" statement. You must suppose that this statement is true. Decide which word goes with the third underlined word in the same way that the first two underlined words go together.

    Colors are audible.
    <u>flavor</u> is to <u>tongue</u> as <u>shade</u> is to

    A. ear. **B.** light. **C.** sound. **D.** hue.

3. First, read how the operation is defined. Then, decide what is the correct answer to the question.

    There is a new mathematical operation called **flix**.
    It is defined as follows:
    A flix $B = A + B$, if $A > B$
    but A flix $B = A \times B$, if $A < B$
    and A flix $B = A / B$, if $A = B$
    How much is 4 flix 7?

    A. 28. **B.** 11. **C.** 3. **D.** −11.

ANSWERS: Practical: (2) A, (3) B. Creative: (2) A, (3) A.

---

multiple intelligences Eight semi-independent kinds of intelligence postulated by Howard Gardner.

Multiple Intelligences

Some people whose IQ scores are only average, or even below-average, may have exceptional ability in specific areas (Miller, 1999). One child whose IQ score was 50 could correctly state the day of the week for any date between 1880 and 1950 (Scheerer, Rothmann, & Goldstein, 1945). He could also play melodies on the piano by ear and sing Italian operatic pieces he had heard. In addition, he could spell—forward or backward—any word spoken to him and could memorize long speeches, although he had no understanding of what he was doing.

Cases of remarkable ability in specific areas constitute part of the evidence cited by Howard Gardner in support of his theory of **multiple intelligences** (Gardner, 1993). To study intelligence, Gardner focused on how people learn and use symbol systems such as language, mathematics, and music. He asked, Do these systems all require the same abilities and processes, the same "intelligence"? According to Gardner, the answer is no. All people, he says, possess a number of intellectual potentials, or intelligences, each of which involves a somewhat different set of skills. Biology provides raw capacities; cultures provide symbolic systems—such as language—to mobilize those raw capacities. Although the intelligences normally interact, they can function with some independence, and individuals may develop certain intelligences further than others. ("In Review: Analyzing Cognitive Abilities" summarizes Gardner's theory, along with the other views of intelligence we have discussed.)

The specific intelligences that Gardner (1998) proposes are (1) *linguistic* intelligence (reflected in good vocabulary and reading comprehension), (2) *logical-mathematical* intelligence (as indicated by skill at arithmetic and certain kinds of reasoning), (3) *spatial* intelligence (seen in understanding relationships between objects), (4) *musical* intelligence (as in abilities involving rhythm, tempo, and sound identification), (5) *body-kinesthetic* intelligence (reflected in skill at dancing,

A Musical Prodigy? According to Gardner's theory of multiple intelligences, skilled artists, athletes, and musicians—such as the young pianist shown here—display forms of intelligence not assessed by standard intelligence tests.

in review: Analyzing Cognitive Abilities

Approach	Method	Key Findings or Propositions
Psychometric	Define the structure of intelligence by examining factor analyses of the correlations between scores on tests of mental abilities.	Performance on many tests of mental abilities is highly correlated, but this correlation, represented by g, reflects a bundle of abilities, not just one trait.
Information processing	Understand intelligence by examining the mental operations involved in intelligent behavior.	The speed of basic processes and the amount of attentional resources available make significant contributions to performance on IQ tests.
Sternberg's triarchic theory	Understand intelligence by examining the information processing involved in thinking, changes with experience, and effects in different environments.	There are three distinct kinds of intelligence: analytic, creative, and practical. IQ tests measure only analytic intelligence, but creative intelligence (which involves dealing with new problems) and practical intelligence (which involves adapting to one's environment) may also be important to success in school and at work.
Gardner's theory of multiple intelligences	Understand intelligence by examining test scores, information processing, biological and developmental research, the skills valued by different cultures, and exceptional people.	Biology provides the capacity for eight distinct "intelligences": linguistic, logical-mathematical, spatial, musical, body-kinesthetic, intrapersonal, interpersonal, and naturalistic.

athletics, and eye-hand coordination), (6) *intrapersonal* intelligence (displayed by self-understanding), (7) *interpersonal intelligence* (seen in the ability to understand and interact with others), and (8) *naturalistic* intelligence (the ability to see patterns in nature). Other researchers have suggested that people also possess *emotional* intelligence, which involves the capacity to perceive emotions and to link them to one's thinking (Meyer & Salovey, 1997). Gardner says that traditional IQ tests sample only the first three of these intelligences, mainly because these are the forms of intelligence most valued in school. To measure intelligences not tapped by standard IQ tests, Gardner suggests collecting samples of children's writing, assessing their ability to appreciate or produce music, and obtaining teacher reports of their strengths and weaknesses in athletic and social skills.

Gardner's view of intelligence is appealing, partly because it allows virtually everyone to be highly intelligent in at least one way. However, critics argue that including athletic or musical skill dilutes the validity and usefulness of the intelligence concept, especially as it is applied in school and in many kinds of jobs. Nevertheless, Gardner and his colleagues are working on new ways to assess potentially important multiple intelligences that are ignored by traditional IQ tests (Kornhaber, Krechevsky, & Gardner, 1990). The value of these methods will be decided by further research.

FOCUS ON RESEARCH METHODS

Tracking Cognitive Abilities over the Life Span

As described in the chapter on human development, significant changes in cognitive abilities occur from infancy through adolescence, but development does not stop there. One major study has focused specifically on the changes in cognitive abilities that occur during adulthood.

• **What was the researchers' question?**

The researchers began by asking what appears to be a relatively simple question: How do adults' cognitive abilities change over time?

• **How did the researchers answer the question?**

LINKAGES (a link to Research in Psychology)

Answering this question is extremely difficult because findings about age-related changes in cognitive abilities depend to some extent on the methods that are used to observe those changes. None of the methods includes true experiments, because psychologists cannot randomly assign people to be a certain age and then give them mental tests. So changes in cognitive abilities must be explored through a number of other research designs.

One of these, the *cross-sectional study,* compares data collected simultaneously from people of different ages. However, cross-sectional studies contain a major confounding variable: Because people are born at different times, they may have had very different educational, cultural, nutritional, and medical experiences. This confounding variable is referred to as a *cohort effect.* Suppose two cohorts, or age groups, are given a test of their ability to imagine the rotation of an object in space. The cohort born around 1940 might not do as well as the one born around 1980, but the difference may not be due so much to declining spatial ability in the older people as to the younger group's greater experience with video games and other spatial tasks. In short, it may be differences in experience, and not just age, that account for differences in ability among older and younger people in a cross-sectional study.

Changes associated with age can also be examined through *longitudinal studies,* in which a group of people are repeatedly tested as they grow older. But longitudinal designs have their own inherent problems. For one thing, fewer and fewer members of an age cohort can be tested over time as death, physical disability, relocation, and lack of interest reduce the sample size. Researchers call this problem the *mortality effect*. Further, the remaining members are likely to be the healthiest in the group and may also have retained better mental powers than the dropouts (Botwinick, 1977). As a result, longitudinal studies may underestimate the degree to which abilities decline with age. Another confounding factor can come from the *history effect*. Here, some event—such as a reduction in health care benefits for senior citizens—might have an effect on cognitive ability scores that is mistakenly attributed to age. Finally, longitudinal studies may be confounded by *testing effects*, meaning that participants may improve over time because of what they learn during repeated testing procedures. People who become "test wise" in this way might even remember answers from one testing session to the next.

As part of the Seattle Longitudinal Study of cognitive aging, K. Warner Schaie (1993) developed a design that measures the impact of the confounding variables we have discussed and thus allows corrections to be made for them. In 1956, Schaie identified a random sample of five thousand members of a health maintenance organization and invited some of them to volunteer for his study. These volunteers, who ranged in age from twenty to eighty, were given a battery of intelligence tests designed to measure Thurstone's primary mental abilities (PMA). The cross-sectional comparisons allowed by this first step were, of course, confounded by cohort effects. To control for those effects, the researchers retested the same participants seven years later, in 1963. Thus, the study combined cross-sectional with longitudinal methods in what is called a *cross-sequential with resampling design*. This design allowed the researchers to compare the size of the *difference* in PMA scores between, say, the twenty-year-olds and twenty-seven-year-olds tested in 1956 with the size of the *change* in PMA scores for these same people as they aged from twenty to twenty-seven and from twenty-seven to thirty-four. Schaie reasoned that if the size of the longitudinal change was about the same as the size of the cross-sectional difference, the cross-sectional difference could probably be attributed to aging, not to the era in which the participants were born.

What about the effect of confounding variables on the longitudinal changes themselves? To measure the impact of testing effects, the researchers randomly drew a new set of participants from their original pool of five thousand. These people were of the same age range as the first sample, but they had not yet been tested. If people from the first sample did better on their second PMA testing than the people of the same age who now took the PMA for the first time, a testing effect would be suggested. (In this case, the size of the difference would indicate the size of the testing effect.) To control for history effects, the researchers examined the scores of people who were the same age in different years. For example, they compared people who were thirty in 1956 with those who were thirty in 1963, people who were forty in 1956 with those who were forty in 1963, and so on. If PMA scores were the same for people of the same age no matter what year they were tested, it is unlikely that events that happened in any particular year would have influenced test results. The researchers tested participants six times between 1956 and 1991; on each occasion they retested some previous participants and tested others for the first time.

● **What did the researchers find?**

The results of the Seattle Longitudinal Study and other, more limited longitudinal studies suggest a reasonably consistent conclusion: Unless people are impaired by Alzheimer's disease or other brain disorders, their cognitive abilities usually remain about the same from early adulthood until about sixty to seventy years of age. Some components of intelligence, but not others, then begin to fail.

Crystallized intelligence, which depends on retrieving information and facts about the world from long-term memory, may continue to grow well into old age. *Fluid intelligence,* which involves rapid and flexible manipulations of ideas and

The Voice of Experience Even in old age, most people's crystallized intelligence remains intact. Their extensive storehouse of knowledge, experience, and wisdom makes older people a valuable resource for the young.

symbols, remains stable during adulthood and then declines in later life (Horn, 1982; Schaie, 1996). Among people over sixty-five or seventy, problems in several areas of information processing may impair problem-solving ability (Sullivan & Stankov, 1990). This decline shows up in the following areas:

1. ***Working memory.*** The ability to hold and organize material in working memory declines beyond age fifty or sixty, particularly when attention must be redirected (Parkin & Walter, 1991).

2. ***Processing speed.*** There is a general slowing of all mental processes (Salthouse, 1996, 2000). Research has not yet isolated whether this slowing is due to reduced storage capacity, impaired processing efficiency, problems in coordinating simultaneous activities, or some combination of these factors (Babcock & Salthouse, 1990; Salthouse, 1990). For many tasks, this slowing does not create obstacles. But if a problem requires manipulating material in working memory, quick processing of information is critical (Rabbitt, 1977). To multiply two 2-digit numbers mentally, for example, you must combine the subsums before you forget them.

3. ***Organization.*** Older people seem to be less likely to solve problems by adopting specific strategies, or mental shortcuts (Charness, 1987; Young, 1971). For example, to locate a wiring problem, you might perform a test that narrows down the regions where the problem might be. The tests carried out by older people tend to be more random and haphazard (Young, 1971). This result may occur partly because many older people are out of practice at solving such problems.

4. ***Flexibility.*** Older people tend to be less flexible in problem solving than their younger counterparts. They are less likely to consider alternative solutions (Salthouse & Prill, 1987), and they require more information before making a tentative decision (Rabbitt, 1977). Laboratory studies suggest that older people are also more likely than younger ones to choose conservative, risk-free options (Botwinick, 1966).

5. ***Control of attention.*** The ability to direct or control attention declines with age (Kramer et al., 1999). When required to switch their attention from one task to another, older participants typically perform less well than younger ones.

● **What do the results mean?**

This study indicates that different kinds of cognitive abilities change in different ways throughout our lifetime. In general, there is a gradual, continual accumulation of knowledge about the world, some systematic changes in the limits of cognitive processes, and qualitative changes in the way those processes are carried out. This finding suggests that a general decline in cognitive abilities during adulthood is neither inevitable nor universal.

● **What do we still need to know?**

An important question that the Schaie (1993) study leaves unanswered is why age-related changes in cognitive abilities occur. Some researchers suggest that these changes are largely due to a decline in the speed with which older people process information (Salthouse, 2000). If this interpretation is correct, it would explain why some older people are less successful than younger ones at tasks that require rapidly integrating several pieces of information in working memory prior to making a choice or a decision. Finally, it is vital that we learn why some people do *not* show declines in cognitive abilities—even when they reach their eighties. By understanding the biological and psychological factors responsible for these exceptions to the general rule, we might be able to reverse or delay some of the intellectual consequences of growing old.

Diversity in Cognitive Abilities

Although psychologists still don't agree on the details of what intelligence is, the study of IQ tests and intelligent behavior has yielded many insights into human cognitive abilities. It also has highlighted the diversity of those abilities. In this section we briefly examine some of that diversity.

Creativity

If you watch *The Simpsons* on television, you have probably noticed that Bart writes a different "punishment" sentence on the blackboard at the beginning of every episode. To maintain this tradition, the show's writers have had to create a unique—and funny—gag sentence for each of the more than two hundred shows that have aired since 1989. In every area of human endeavor, there are people who demonstrate **creativity**, the ability to produce new, high-quality ideas or products (Simonton, 1999; Sternberg, 2001). Whether a corporate executive or a homemaker, a scientist or an artist, everyone is more or less creative (Klahr & Simon, 1999). Yet like *intelligence, creativity* is difficult to define (Amabile, Goldfarb, & Brackfield, 1990). Does creativity include innovation based on previous ideas, or must it be utterly new? And must it be new to the world, as in Pablo Picasso's paintings, or only new to the creator, as when a child "makes up" the word *waterbird* without having heard it before? As with intelligence, psychologists have defined *creativity* not as a "thing" that people have or don't have but rather as a process or cognitive activity that can be inferred from performance on creativity tests, as well as from the books and artwork and other products resulting from the creative process (Sternberg & Dess, 2001)

To measure creativity, some psychologists have generated tests of **divergent thinking**, the ability to think along many paths to generate many solutions to a problem (Guilford & Hoepfner, 1971). The Consequences Test is an example. It contains items such as "Imagine all of the things that might possibly happen if all national and local laws were suddenly abolished" (Guilford, 1959). Divergent-thinking tests are scored by counting the number of reasonable responses that a person can list for each item, and how many of those responses differ from other people's responses.

Of course, the ability to come up with different answers or different ways of looking at a situation does not guarantee that anything creative will be produced. Creative behavior requires divergent thinking that is *appropriate* for a given situation or problem. To be productive rather than just weird, a creative person must be firmly anchored to reality, understand society's needs, and learn from the experience and knowledge of others (Sternberg & Lubert, 1992). Teresa Amabile has identified three kinds of cognitive and personality characteristics necessary for creativity (Amabile, 1996; Amabile, Hennessey, & Grossman, 1986):

1. *Expertise* in the field of endeavor, which is directly tied to what a person has learned. For example, a painter or composer must know the paints, techniques, or instruments available.

2. A set of *creative skills,* including willingness to work hard, persistence at problem solving, capacity for divergent thinking, ability to break out of old problem-solving habits, and willingness to take risks. Amabile believes that training can influence many of these skills (some of which are closely linked to the strategies for problem solving discussed in the chapter on cognition and language).

3. The *motivation* to pursue creative production for internal reasons, such as satisfaction, rather than for external reasons, such as prize money. In fact,

---

creativity The capacity to produce new, high-quality ideas or products.

divergent thinking The ability to think along many alternative paths to generate many different solutions to a problem.

Amabile and her colleagues found that external rewards can deter creativity (e.g., Amabile, Hennessey, & Grossman, 1986). In one study, they asked groups of children or adults to create artistic products such as collages or stories. Some were simply asked to work on the project. Others were told that their project would be judged for its creativity and excellence and that rewards would be given or winners announced. Experts, who had no idea which products were created by which group, judged those from the "reward" group to be significantly less creative. Similar effects have been found in many other studies (Deci, Koestner, & Ryan, 1999, 2001).

Is creativity inherited? To some extent, perhaps it is; but there is evidence that a person's environment—including the social, economic, and political forces in it—can influence creative behavior at least as much as it influences intelligence (Amabile, 2001; Nakamura & Csikszentmihalyi, 2001). For example, the correlation between the creativity scores of identical twins reared apart is lower than that between their IQ scores (Nichols, 1978). Do you have to be smart to be creative? Creativity does appear to require a certain degree of intelligence (Simonton, 1984; Sternberg, 2001), but it may not necessarily appear as an extremely high IQ score (Simonton, 1984). Correlations between scores on IQ tests and on tests of creativity are only modest, between +.10 and +.30 (Barron & Harrington, 1981; Rushton, 1990; Simonton, 1999). This result is not surprising, because creativity as psychologists measure it requires broad, divergent thinking, whereas traditional IQ tests assess **convergent thinking**—the ability to apply logic and knowledge in order to *narrow down* the number of possible solutions to a problem. The pace of research on creativity, and its relationship to intelligence, has picked up lately (Sternberg & Dess, 2001). One result of that research has been to define the combination of intelligence and creativity in the same person as *wisdom* (Sternberg, 2001; Sternberg & O'Hara, 1999).

Unusual Cognitive Ability

Our understanding of cognitive abilities has been advanced by research on people whose cognitive abilities are unusual—people who are gifted, mentally retarded, or have learning disabilities (Robinson, Zigler, & Gallagher, 2000).

Giftedness

People with especially high IQ scores are often referred to as *gifted*, but this does not mean that they share exactly the same pattern of exceptional cognitive abilities. In one study, Robert Sternberg (2000) found that gifted people can display at least seven different combinations of the analytic, creative, and practical skills measured by his Triarchic Abilities Test.

Do all people with unusually high IQs become famous and successful in their chosen fields? One of the best-known studies of the intellectually gifted was conducted by Louis Terman and his colleagues (Oden, 1968; Sears, 1977; Terman & Oden, 1947, 1959). This study began in 1921 with the identification of more than 1,500 children whose IQ scores were very high—most higher than 135 by age 10. Periodic interviews and tests over the next 60 years revealed that few, if any, became truly creative geniuses—such as world-famous inventors, authors, artists, or composers—but only 11 failed to graduate from high school, and more than two-thirds graduated from college. Ninety-seven earned Ph.D.s; 92, law degrees; and 57, medical degrees. In 1955 their median family income was well above the national average (Terman & Oden, 1959). In general, they were physically and mentally healthier than the nongifted people and appear to have led happier, or at least more fortunate, lives (see the Focus on Research Methods section of the chapter on health, stress, and coping).

In short, although high IQ scores tend to predict longer, more successful lives (Whalley & Deary, 2001), an extremely high IQ does not guarantee special

---

convergent thinking The ability to apply logic and knowledge to narrow down the number of possible solutions to a problem or perform some other complex cognitive task.

distinction. Some research suggests that gifted children are not fundamentally different from other children; they just have "more" of the same basic cognitive abilities seen in all children (Dark & Benbow, 1993). Other work suggests that there may be other differences as well, such as an unusually intense motivation to master certain tasks or areas of intellectual endeavor (Lubinski et al., 2001; Winner, 2000).

Mental Retardation People whose score on an IQ test is less than about 70 *and* who fail to display the skill at daily living, communication, and other tasks expected of those their age have traditionally been described as *mentally retarded* (American Psychiatric Association, 1994). They now are often referred to as *developmentally disabled* or *mentally challenged*. People within this very broad category differ greatly in their cognitive abilities, as well as in their ability to function independently in daily life. Table 10.3 shows a classification that divides the range of low IQ scores into categories that reflect these differences.

Some cases of mental retardation have a clearly identifiable origin. The best-known example is *Down syndrome*, which occurs when an abnormality during conception results in an extra twenty-first chromosome (Hattori et al., 2000). Children with Down syndrome typically have IQ scores in the range of 40 to 55, though some may score higher than that. There are also several inherited causes of mental retardation. The most common of these is *Fragile X* syndrome, caused by a defect on chromosome 23 (known as the *X chromosome*). More rarely, retardation is caused by inheriting *Williams syndrome* (a defect on chromosome 7) or by inheriting a gene for *phenylketonuria*, or *PKU* (which causes the body to create toxins out of milk and other foods). Retardation can also result from environmental causes, such as exposure to German measles (rubella) or alcohol or other toxins before birth; oxygen deprivation during birth; and head injuries, brain tumors, and infectious diseases (such as meningitis or encephalitis) in childhood (U.S. Surgeon General, 1999).

These categories are approximate. Especially at the upper end of the scale, many retarded persons can be taught to handle tasks well beyond what their IQ scores might suggest. Furthermore, IQ is not the only diagnostic criterion for retardation. Many people with IQs lower than 70 can function adequately in their communities and so would not be classified as mentally retarded.

table 10.3
Categories of Mental Retardation

Level of Retardation	IQ Scores	Characteristics
Mild	50–70	A majority of all the mentally retarded. Usually show no physical symptoms of abnormality. Individuals with higher IQs can marry, maintain a family, and work in unskilled jobs. Abstract reasoning is difficult for those with the lower IQs of this category. Capable of some academic learning to a sixth-grade level.
Moderate	35–49	Often lack physical coordination. Can be trained to take care of themselves and to acquire some reading and writing skills. Abilities of a 4- to 7-year-old. Capable of living outside an institution with their families.
Severe	20–34	Only a few can benefit from any schooling. Can communicate vocally after extensive training. Most require constant supervision.
Profound	Below 20	Mental age less than 3. Very limited communication. Require constant supervision. Can learn to walk, utter a few simple phrases, and feed themselves.

The Eagle Has Landed In February 2000, Richard Keebler, twenty-seven, became an Eagle Scout, the highest rank in the Boy Scouts of America. His achievement is notable not only because only 4 percent of all Scouts reach this pinnacle but also because Keebler has Down syndrome. As we come to better understand the potential, and not just the limitations, of mentally retarded people, their opportunities and their role in society will continue to expand.

LINKAGES (a link to Memory)

metacognition The knowledge of what strategies to apply, when to apply them, and how to deploy them in new situations.

Familial retardation refers to the 30 to 40 percent of (usually mild) cases in which there is no obvious genetic or environmental cause (American Psychiatric Association, 1994). In these cases, retardation appears to result from a complex, and as yet unknown, interaction between heredity and environment that researchers are continuing to explore (Croen, Grether, & Selvin, 2001).

In what ways are the cognitive skills of mentally retarded people deficient? Actually, they are just as good as others at recognizing simple stimuli, and their rate of forgetting information from short-term memory is no more rapid (Belmont & Butterfield, 1971). But mildly retarded people do differ from other people in three important ways (Campione, Brown, & Ferrara, 1982):

1. They perform certain mental operations more slowly, such as retrieving information from long-term memory. When asked to repeat something they have learned, they are not as quick as a person of normal intelligence.

2. They simply know fewer facts about the world. It is likely that this deficiency is a consequence of the third problem.

3. They are not very good at using particular mental strategies that may be important in learning and problem solving. For example, they do not spontaneously rehearse material that must be held in short-term memory.

What are the reasons for these deficiencies? In some ways, the differences between normal and retarded children resemble the differences between older and younger children discussed in the chapter on human development. Both younger children and retarded children show deficiencies in *metamemory*—the knowledge of how their memory works. More generally, retarded children are deficient in **metacognition:** the knowledge of what strategies to apply, when to apply them, and how to deploy them in new situations so that new specific knowledge can be gained and different problems mastered (Ferretti & Butterfield, 1989).

It is their deficiencies in metacognition that most limit the intellectual performance of mildly retarded people. For example, if retarded children are simply taught a strategy, they are not likely to use it again on their own or to transfer the strategy to a different task. It is important, therefore, to teach retarded children to evaluate the appropriateness of strategies (Wong, 1986) and to monitor the success of their strategies. Finally, like other children, retarded children must be shown that effort, combined with effective strategies, pays off (Borkowski, Weyhing, & Turner, 1986).

Despite such difficulties, the intellectual abilities of mentally retarded people can be improved to some extent. One program emphasizing positive parent-child communications began when the children were as young as thirty months old. It ultimately helped children with Down syndrome to master reading skills at a second-grade level, providing the foundation for further achievement (Rynders & Horrobin, 1980; Turkington, 1987). However, designing effective programs for retarded children is complicated because the way people learn depends not just on cognitive skills but also on social and emotional factors, including *where* they learn. Currently, there is debate about *mainstreaming,* the policy of teaching children with disabilities, including those who are retarded, in regular classrooms with children who do not have disabilities. Is mainstreaming good for retarded children? A number of studies of the cognitive and social skills of students who have been mainstreamed and those who were separated show few significant differences overall, although it appears that students at higher ability levels may gain more from being mainstreamed than their less mentally able peers (Cole et al., 1991).

Learning Disabilities People who show a significant discrepancy between their measured intelligence and their academic performance may have a *learning disability* (National Information Center for Children and Youth with Disabilities, 2000). Learning disabilities are often seen in people with average or

Summary

An Inventive Genius When, as in the case of inventor Thomas Edison, students' academic performance falls short of what intelligence tests say they are capable of, a learning disability may be present. However, poor study skills, lack of motivation, and even the need for eyeglasses are among the many factors other than learning disabilities that can create a discrepancy between IQ scores and academic achievement. Accordingly, accurately diagnosing learning disabilities is not an easy task.

above-average IQs. For example, the problems with reading, writing, and math that Leonardo da Vinci and Thomas Edison had as children may have been due to such a disability; the problems certainly did not reflect a lack of cognitive ability!

There are several kinds of learning disabilities (Myers & Hammill, 1990; Wadsworth et al., 2000). People with *dyslexia* find it difficult to understand the meaning of what they read; they may also have difficulty in sounding out and identifying written words. *Dysphasia* is difficulty with understanding spoken words or with recalling the words one needs for effective speech. *Dysgraphia*—problems with writing—appears as an inability to form letters or as the omission or reordering of words and parts of words in one's writing. The least common learning disability, *dyscalculia*, is a difficulty with arithmetic that reflects not poor mathematical ability but rather an impairment in the understanding of quantity and/or in the comprehension of basic arithmetic principles and operations, such as addition and subtraction.

The National Joint Committee on Learning Disabilities (1994) suggests that these disorders are caused by dysfunctions in the brain; however, although brain imaging studies are helping to locate areas of dysfunction (e.g., Pugh et al., 2000; Richards et al., 2000), specific neurological causes have not yet been found. Accordingly, most researchers describe learning disabilities in terms of dysfunctional information processing (Kujala et al., 2001; Shaw et al., 1995). Diagnosis of a learning disability includes several steps. First, it is important to look for significant weaknesses in a person's listening, speaking, reading, writing, reasoning, or arithmetic skills (Brinckerhoff, Shaw, & McGuire, 1993). The person's actual ability is compared with that predicted by the person's IQ score. Tests for brain damage are also given. To help rule out alternative explanations of poor academic performance, the person's hearing, vision, and other sensory systems are tested, and factors such as poverty, family conflicts, and inadequate instruction are reviewed. Finally, alternative diagnoses such as attention deficit disorder (see the chapter on psychological disorders) must be eliminated.

LINKAGES

As noted in the chapter that introduced psychology, all of psychology's subfields are related to one another. Our discussion of test anxiety illustrates just one way in which the topic of this chapter, cognitive abilities, is linked to the subfield of motivation and emotion (which is the focus of the chapter by that name). The Linkages diagram shows ties to two other subfields as well, and there are many more ties throughout the book. Looking for linkages among subfields will help you see how they all fit together and help you better appreciate the big picture that is psychology.

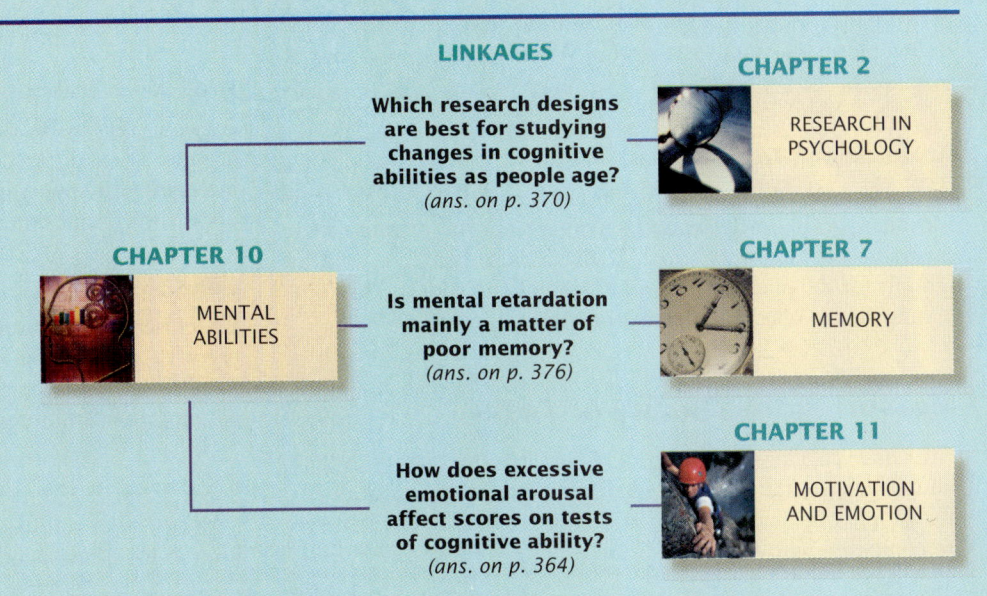

LINKAGES

CHAPTER 10 — MENTAL ABILITIES

- Which research designs are best for studying changes in cognitive abilities as people age? (ans. on p. 370) — **CHAPTER 2** RESEARCH IN PSYCHOLOGY
- Is mental retardation mainly a matter of poor memory? (ans. on p. 376) — **CHAPTER 7** MEMORY
- How does excessive emotional arousal affect scores on tests of cognitive ability? (ans. on p. 364) — **CHAPTER 11** MOTIVATION AND EMOTION

SUMMARY

Cognitive ability refers to the capacity to perform the higher mental processes of reasoning, remembering, understanding, problem solving, and decision making.

Testing for Intelligence

Psychologists have not reached a consensus on how best to define *intelligence*. A working definition describes intelligence in terms of reasoning, problem solving, and dealing with the environment.

A Brief History of Intelligence Tests

Alfred Binet's pioneering test of intelligence included questions that required reasoning and problem solving of varying levels of difficulty, graded by age. Lewis Terman developed a revision of Binet's test that became known as the *Stanford-Binet*; it included items designed to assess the intelligence of adults as well as children and became the model for *IQ tests*. Early IQ tests in the United States required not just cognitive ability but also knowledge of U.S. culture. David Wechsler's tests remedied some of the deficiencies of the earlier IQ tests. Made up of subtests, some of which have little verbal content, these tests allowed testers to generate scores for different aspects of cognitive ability.

Intelligence Tests Today

The Stanford-Binet and Wechsler tests are the most popular individually administered intelligence tests. Both include subtests and provide scores for parts of the test as well as an overall score. For example, the Wechsler tests yield verbal, performance, and full-scale IQ as well as scores reflecting cognitive processing speed, working memory, perceptual organization, and verbal comprehension. Currently, a person's *intelligence quotient*, or *IQ score*, reflects how far that person's performance on the test deviates from the average performance by people in the same age group. An average performance is assigned an IQ score of 100.

Aptitude and Achievement Tests

Aptitude tests are intended to measure a person's potential to learn new skills; *achievement tests* are intended to measure what a person has already learned. Both kinds of tests are used by schools for the placement or admission of students and by companies for the selection of new employees.

Measuring the Quality of Tests

Tests have two key advantages over other techniques of evaluation. They are standardized, so that the performances of different people can be compared, and they produce scores that can be compared with *norms*.

Reliability

A good test must be *reliable*, which means that the results for each person are consistent, or stable. Reliability can be measured by the test-retest, alternate-form, and split-half methods.

Validity

A test is said to be *valid* if it measures what it is supposed to measure and leads to correct inferences about people. A test's *validity* for a particular purpose can be evaluated in several ways, including the measurement of content validity or criterion validity; the latter entails measuring the correlation between the test score and some criterion. If the criterion is not measured until after the test is given, criterion validity is considered to be predictive validity.

Evaluating IQ Tests

The Reliability and Validity of IQ Tests

IQ tests are reasonably reliable, and they do a good job of predicting academic success. However, IQ tests assess only some of the abilities that might be considered aspects of intelligence, and they may favor people most familiar with middle-class culture. Nonetheless, this familiarity is important for academic and occupational success.

IQ Scores as a Measure of Innate Ability

Both heredity and the environment influence IQ scores, and their effects interact. The influence of heredity is shown by the high correlation between IQ scores of identical twins raised in separate households and by the similarity in the IQ scores of children adopted at birth and their biological parents. The influence of the environment is revealed by the higher correlation of IQ scores among siblings who share the same environment than among siblings who do not, as well as by the effects of environmental changes such as adoption.

Group Differences in IQ Scores

Average IQ scores differ across socioeconomic and ethnic groups. These differences appear to be due to numerous factors, including differences in motivation, family support, educational opportunity, and other environmental conditions.

Conditions That Can Raise IQ Scores

An enriched environment sometimes raises IQ scores. Initial gains in cognitive performance that result from interventions like Project Head Start may decline over time, but the programs may improve children's attitudes toward school.

IQ Scores in the Classroom

Like any label, an IQ score can generate expectations that affect both how other people respond to a person and how that

Summary

person behaves. Children labeled with low IQ scores may be offered fewer or lower-quality educational opportunities. However, IQ scores help educators to identify a student's strengths and weaknesses and to offer the curriculum that will best serve that student.

Understanding Intelligence

The Psychometric Approach

The *psychometric approach* attempts to analyze the structure of intelligence by examining correlations between tests of cognitive ability. Because scores on almost all tests of cognitive ability are positively correlated, Charles Spearman concluded that such tests measure a general factor of mental ability, called *g*, as well as more specific factors, called *s*. As a result of factor analysis, other researchers have concluded that intelligence is not a single general ability but a collection of abilities and subskills needed to succeed on any test of intelligence. Raymond B. Cattell distinguished between *fluid intelligence*, the basic power of reasoning and problem solving, and *crystallized intelligence*, the specific knowledge gained as a result of applying fluid intelligence.

The Information-Processing Approach

The *information-processing approach* to intelligence focuses on the process of intelligent behavior. Varying degrees of correlation have been found between IQ scores and measures of the flexibility and capacity of attention, and between IQ scores and measures of the speed of information processing.

The Triarchic Theory of Intelligence

According to Robert Sternberg's *triarchic theory of intelligence*, there are three different types of intelligence: analytic, creative, and practical. IQ tests typically focus on analytic intelligence, but recent research has suggested ways to assess practical and creative intelligence.

Multiple Intelligences

Howard Gardner's approach to intelligence suggests that biology equips us with the capacities for *multiple intelligences* that can function with some independence—specifically, linguistic, logical-mathematical, spatial, musical, body-kinesthetic, intrapersonal, interpersonal, and naturalistic intelligences.

Diversity in Cognitive Abilities

Creativity

Tests of *divergent thinking* are used to measure differences in *creativity*. In contrast, IQ tests typically require *convergent thinking*. Although creativity and IQ scores are not highly correlated, creative behavior requires a certain amount of intelligence, along with expertise in a creative field, skills at problem solving and divergent thinking, and motivation to pursue a creative endeavor for its own sake.

Unusual Cognitive Ability

Knowledge about cognitive abilities has been expanded by research on giftedness, mental retardation, and learning disabilities. People with very high IQ scores tend to be successful in life, but they are not necessarily geniuses. People are considered mentally retarded if their IQ score is below about 70 and if their communication and daily living skills are less than expected of people their age. Some cases of retardation have a known cause; in familial retardation the mix of genetic and environmental causes is unknown. Compared with people of normal intelligence, retarded people process information more slowly, know fewer facts, and are deficient at *metacognition*—that is, at knowing and using mental strategies. Mentally retarded people can be taught strategies, but they must also be taught how and when to use those strategies. People who show a significant discrepancy between their measured intelligence and their academic performance may have a learning disability. Learning disabilities can take several forms and must be carefully diagnosed.

11 Motivation and Emotion

Concepts and Theories of Motivation
Sources of Motivation
Instinct Theory and Its
 Descendants
Drive Reduction Theory
Arousal Theory
Incentive Theory

Hunger and Eating
Biological Signals for Hunger
 and Satiety
Hunger and the Brain
Flavor, Cultural Learning, and
 Food Selection
Eating Disorders

Sexual Behavior

FOCUS ON RESEARCH METHODS:
 A Survey of Human
 Sexual Behavior
The Biology of Sex
Social and Cultural Factors in
 Sexuality
Sexual Orientation

THINKING CRITICALLY: Does
 Biology Determine Sexual
 Orientation?
Sexual Dysfunctions

Achievement Motivation
Need for Achievement
Goal Setting and
 Achievement Motivation
Achievement and Success in
 the Workplace
Achievement and Subjective
 Well-Being

**Relations and Conflicts
 Among Motives**

LINKAGES: Conflicting
 Motives and Stress
Opponent Processes,
 Motivation, and Emotion

The Nature of Emotion
Defining Characteristics
The Biology of Emotion

Theories of Emotion
James's Peripheral Theory
Cannon's Central Theory
Cognitive Theories

Communicating Emotion
Innate Expressions of
 Emotion

Social and Cultural Influences
 on Emotional Expression
Linkages
Summary

In January 1994, despite temperatures reaching 30 degrees below zero, Brian Carr caught 155 fish, beating out 36 competitors to win the annual ice-fishing contest at upstate New York's Lake Como Fish and Game Club. He also netted the grand prize of $8 (Shepherd, 1994). Why would these people endure such harsh conditions in pursuit of such a paltry reward? Why, for that matter, do any of us do what we do? Why do we help others or ignore them, overeat or diet, haunt art museums or sleazy bars, attend college or drop out of high school?

These are questions about **motivation,** the factors that influence the initiation, direction, intensity, and persistence of behavior (Reeve, 1996). Psychologists who study motivation ask questions such as these: What prompts a person to start looking for food, to register for dance lessons, or to act in any other particular way? What determines whether a person chooses to go mountain climbing or to stay home and read? What makes some people go all out to reach a goal while others exert only halfhearted efforts and quit at the first obstacle?

Part of the motivation for behavior is to feel certain emotions, such as the joy of scaling a lofty peak or of becoming a parent. Motivation also affects emotion, as when hunger makes you more likely to become angry if people annoy you. In short, motivation and emotion are closely intertwined.

The first part of this chapter concerns motivation. We begin with some general theories of motivation and then discuss three specific motives—hunger, sexual desire, and the need for achievement. Next, we examine the nature of human emotion, as well as some major theories of how and why certain emotions are experienced. The chapter concludes with a discussion of how humans communicate their emotions to one another.

Concepts and Theories of Motivation

The concept of motivation helps psychologists accomplish what Albert Einstein once called the whole purpose of science: to discover unity in diversity. Suppose that a man works two jobs, refuses party invitations, wears old clothes, drives a beat-up car, eats food others leave behind at lunch, never gives to charity, and keeps his furnace set at sixty degrees all winter. In trying to explain why he does what he does, you could propose a separate reason for each behavior: Perhaps he likes to work hard, hates parties, despises shopping for clothes and cars, enjoys other people's leftovers, has no concern for the poor, and loves cold air. Or you could suggest a **motive,** a reason or purpose that provides a single explanation for this man's diverse and apparently unrelated behaviors. That unifying motive might be the man's desire to save as much money as possible.

This example illustrates the fact that motivation cannot be observed directly; its presence is inferred from what we *can* observe. Psychologists think of motivation, whether it be hunger or thirst or love or greed, as an *intervening variable*—something that is used to explain the relationships between environmental stimuli and behavioral responses. The three different responses shown in Figure 11.1, for example, can be understood as guided by a single unifying motive: thirst. In order for an intervening variable to be considered a motive, it must be able to change behavior in some way. For example, suppose we arrange for some party guests to eat only salted peanuts and other guests to eat only unsalted peanuts. We will probably find that the people who ate salted peanuts drink more liquids, and perhaps take longer sips, than do those who ate the unsalted nuts. We can then explain differences in the initiation and intensity of drinking behavior in terms of differences in thirst.

Figure 11.1 shows that motivation can help explain why different stimuli can lead to the same response, and why the same stimulus can evoke different responses. Motivation also helps explain why behavior varies over time. For example, many people cannot bring themselves to lose weight, quit smoking, or exercise until they

---

motivation The influences that account for the initiation, direction, intensity, and persistence of behavior.

motive A reason or purpose for behavior.

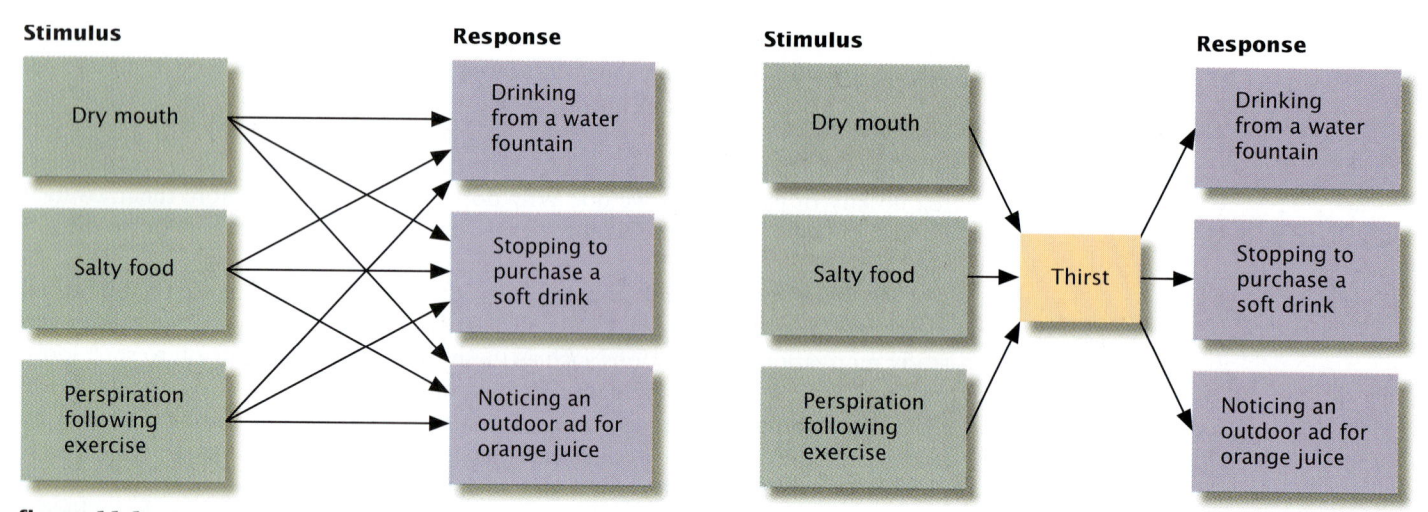

figure 11.1

Motives as Intervening Variables

Motives can act as explanatory links between apparently unrelated stimuli and responses. In this example, seeing thirst as the common motive provides an explanation for why each stimulus triggers the responses shown.

experience a heart attack or symptoms of other serious health problems. At that point, these people may suddenly start eating a low-fat diet, give up tobacco, and exercise regularly. In other words, because of changes in motivation, particular stimuli—such as ice cream, cigarettes, and health clubs—elicit different responses at different times.

Sources of Motivation

The number of possible motives for human behavior seems endless. People are motivated to satisfy their needs for food and water, of course, but they have many other needs as well. Some people seek the pleasures of creativity, whereas many others are motivated by money or praise or power. And as social creatures, people are also influenced by motives to form emotional attachments to others, to become parents, and to join groups.

These and many other sources of human motivation fall into four general, somewhat overlapping categories. First, human behavior is motivated by basic *biological factors*, particularly the need for food, water, sex, and temperature regulation (Tinbergen, 1989). *Emotional factors* are a second source of motivation (Izard, 1993). Panic, fear, anger, love, and hatred can influence behavior ranging from selfless giving to brutal murder. Third, *cognitive factors* can motivate human behavior (Weiner, 1993). People behave in certain ways—becoming arrogant or timid, for example—partly because of these cognitive factors, which include their perceptions of the world, their beliefs about what they can or cannot do, and their expectations about how others will respond to them. Fourth, motivation may stem from *social factors*, that is, from reactions to parents, teachers, siblings, friends, television, and other sociocultural forces. The combined influence of these social factors in motivation has a profound effect on almost all human behavior (Baumeister & Leary, 1995). For example, have you ever bought a jacket or tried a particular hairstyle not because you liked it but because it was in fashion?

Psychologists have used various combinations of these factors to develop four prominent theories of human motivation. None of these theories can completely explain all aspects of how and why we behave as we do, but each of them—instinct theory, drive reduction theory, arousal theory, and incentive theory—helps tell part of the story.

Motivation and Emotion The link between motivation and emotion is obvious in many everyday situations. For example, her motivation to win the U.S. National Spelling Bee creates strong emotions in this contestant as she struggles with a tough word. And emotions can create motivation, as when anger leads a parent to become aggressive toward a child or when love leads that parent to provide for the child.

Fixed Action Patterns The male three-spined stickleback fish attacks aggressively when it sees the red underbelly of another male. This automatic response is called a *fixed action pattern,* because it can be triggered by almost any red stimulus. These fish have been known to fly into an aggressive frenzy in response to a wooden fish model sporting a red spot, or even in response to a red truck driving past a window near their tank!

Instinct Theory and Its Descendants

Early in the twentieth century, many psychologists favored **instinct theory** as an explanation for the motivation of humans and animals alike. **Instincts** are automatic, involuntary behavior patterns consistently triggered, or "released," by particular stimuli (Tinbergen, 1989). Such behaviors are often called *fixed-action patterns* because they are unlearned, genetically coded responses to specific "releaser" stimuli. For example, these stimuli cause birds to build nests or engage in complex mating dances, and the birds do so perfectly the first time they try.

In 1908, William McDougall listed eighteen human instincts, including self-assertion, reproduction, pugnacity, and gregariousness. Within a few years, McDougall and others had named more than ten thousand more, prompting one critic to suggest that his colleagues had "an instinct to produce instincts" (Bernard, 1924). The problem was that instincts had become labels that simply describe what people do. Saying that someone gambles because of a gambling instinct, golfs because of a golfing instinct, and works because of a work instinct explains nothing about why these behaviors do or do not occur, how they developed, or the like.

Despite the shortcomings of early instinct theories, psychologists have continued to explore the possibility that at least some aspects of human motivation are innate. Their interest has been stimulated partly by research showing that a number of human behaviors are present at birth. Among these are sucking and other reflexes, as well as certain facial expressions, such as smiling. There is also the fact that people do not have to learn to be hungry or thirsty or to want to stay warm, and—as discussed in the chapters on learning and psychological disorders—that they appear to be biologically prepared to fear snakes and other potentially dangerous stimuli. Psychologists who take the evolutionary approach suggest that all such behaviors have evolved because they were adaptive for promoting individual survival; the individuals who possessed these behavioral predispositions were more likely than others to father or give birth to offspring. We are the descendants of these ancestral human survivors, so to the extent that our ancestors' behavioral predispositions were transmitted genetically, we should show similar predispositions. Even many aspects of human social behavior, such as helping and aggression, are seen by evolutionary psychologists as motivated by inborn factors—especially by the desire to maximize our genetic contribution to the next generation (Buss, 1999). We may not be aware of this specific desire, they say, but we nevertheless behave in ways that promote it (Geary, 2000). So you are more likely to hear someone say "I can't wait to have children" than to say "I want to contribute genes to the next generation."

The evolutionary approach suggests, for example, that the choice of a marriage partner has a biological basis; heterosexual love and marriage are seen as the result of inborn desires to create and nurture offspring so that parents' genes will survive in their children. According to this view, the mating strategies of males and females

instinct theory A view that explains human behavior as motivated by automatic, involuntary, and unlearned responses.

instincts Innate, automatic dispositions toward responding in a particular way when confronted with a specific stimulus.

differ in ways that reflect traditional differences in how much males and females invest in their offspring (Bjorklund & Shackelford, 1999; Trivers, 1972). Because women can produce relatively few children in their lifetime, they are more psychologically invested than men are in the survival and development of those children (Townsend, Kline, & Wasserman, 1995). This greater investment motivates women to choose mates more cautiously, seeking males who are not only genetically fit but also able to provide the protection and resources necessary to ensure children's survival. The search for genetic fitness, say evolutionary psychologists, helps account for the fact that women tend to prefer men who display athleticism and facial symmetry (Barber, 1995; Gangestad & Thornhill, 1997). But good looks and well-built bodies may not be enough; women are also drawn to men who have demonstrated an ability to acquire resources, as signified by maturity, ambition, and earning power. It takes some time to assess these resource-related characteristics (He drives a nice car, but can he afford it?), which is why, according to the evolutionary view, women are more likely than men to prefer a period of courtship prior to mating. Men tend to want to begin a sexual relationship sooner than women (Buss & Schmitt, 1993) because, compared with their female partners, they have little to lose from doing so. On the contrary, their eagerness to engage in sex early in a relationship is seen as reflecting their evolutionary ancestors' tendency toward casual sex as a means of maximizing their genetic contribution to the next generation. In fact, evolutionary psychologists see the desire to produce as many children as possible as motivating males' preference to mate with women whose reproductive capacity and genetic fitness are signified by youth, attractiveness, and good health (Symons, 1995).

These controversial speculations have received some support. For instance, according to a survey of more than ten thousand men and women in thirty-three countries on six continents and five isolated islands, males generally preferred youth and good health in prospective female mates, and females generally preferred males who were mature and wealthy (Kenrick, 1994). One example of this sex difference is illustrated in Figure 11.2, which shows the age preferences of men and women who advertised for dates in the personal sections of newspapers in the United States. In general, men were interested in women younger than themselves, but women were interested in older men (Kenrick et al., 1995).

Critics argue that such preferences could stem from cultural traditions, not genetic programming. Among the Zulu of South Africa, where women are expected to build houses, carry water, and perform other physically demanding tasks, men tend to value maturity and ambition in a mate more than women do (Buss, 1989).

figure 11.2

Age Preferences Reflected in Personal Advertisements

An analysis of 486 personal section ads placed in newspapers around the United States showed a sex difference in age preferences. As men got older, their preferences for younger women increased, whereas women, regardless of age, preferred men who were about their own age or older.

Source: Kenrick et al. (1995, Figure 1).

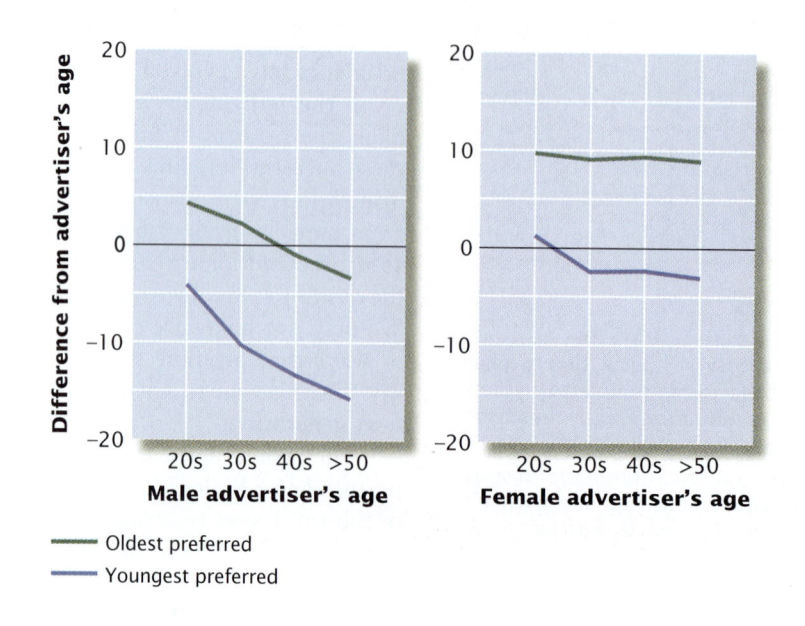

Evolution at Work? Film stars Michael Douglas and Catherine Zeta-Jones married when he was 57 and she was 32, exemplifying the worldwide tendency for older men to prefer younger women, and vice versa. This tendency has been interpreted as evidence supporting an evolutionary explanation of mate selection, but skeptics see social and economic forces at work in establishing these preference patterns.

The fact that women have been systematically denied economic and political power in many cultures may also account for their tendency to rely on the security and economic power provided by men (Silverstein, 1996).

Drive Reduction Theory

Like instinct theory, drive reduction theory emphasizes biological factors, but it is based on the concept of homeostasis. **Homeostasis** is the tendency for organisms to keep physiological systems at a steady level, or *equilibrium*, by constantly making adjustments in response to change. We describe a version of this concept in the chapter on biological aspects of psychology, in relation to feedback loops that keep hormones at desirable levels.

According to **drive reduction theory,** an imbalance in homeostasis creates a **need**—a biological requirement for well-being. The brain responds to such needs, in the service of homeostasis, by creating a psychological state called a **drive**—a feeling of arousal that prompts an organism to take action, restore the balance, and as a result, reduce the drive (Hull, 1943). For example, if you have had no water for some time, the chemical balance of your body fluids is disturbed, creating a biological need for water. One consequence of this need is a drive—thirst—that motivates you to find and drink water. After you drink, the need for water is met, so the drive to drink is reduced. In other words, drives push people to satisfy needs, thus reducing the drives as well as the arousal they create (see Figure 11.3).

Drive reduction theory recognizes the influence of learning on motivation by distinguishing between primary and secondary drives. **Primary drives** stem from biological needs, such as the need for food or water. (In the chapter on learning, we note that food, water, and other things that satisfy primary drives are called *primary reinforcers.*) People do not have to learn either these basic biological needs or the primary drives to satisfy them (Hull, 1951). However, we do learn other drives, called *secondary drives*. Once acquired, **secondary drives** motivate us to act *as if* we have an unmet basic need. For example, as people learn to associate money with the satisfaction of primary drives for food, shelter, and so on, having money may become a secondary drive. Having too little money then motivates many behaviors—from hard work to thievery—to obtain more funds.

---

homeostasis The tendency for organisms to keep their physiological systems at a stable, steady level by constantly adjusting themselves in response to change.

drive reduction theory A theory of motivation stating that much motivation arises from constant imbalances in homeostasis.

need A biological requirement for well-being that is created by an imbalance in homeostasis.

drive A psychological state of arousal created by an imbalance in homeostasis that prompts an organism to take action to restore the balance and reduce the drive.

primary drives Drives that arise from basic biological needs.

secondary drives Stimuli that acquire the motivational properties of primary drives through classical conditioning or other learning mechanisms.

figure 11.3

Drive Reduction Theory and Homeostasis

Homeostatic mechanisms, such as the regulation of body temperature or food and water intake, are often compared to thermostats. If the temperature in a house drops below the thermostat setting, the furnace comes on and brings the temperature up to that preset level, achieving homeostasis. When the temperature reaches the preset point, the furnace shuts off.

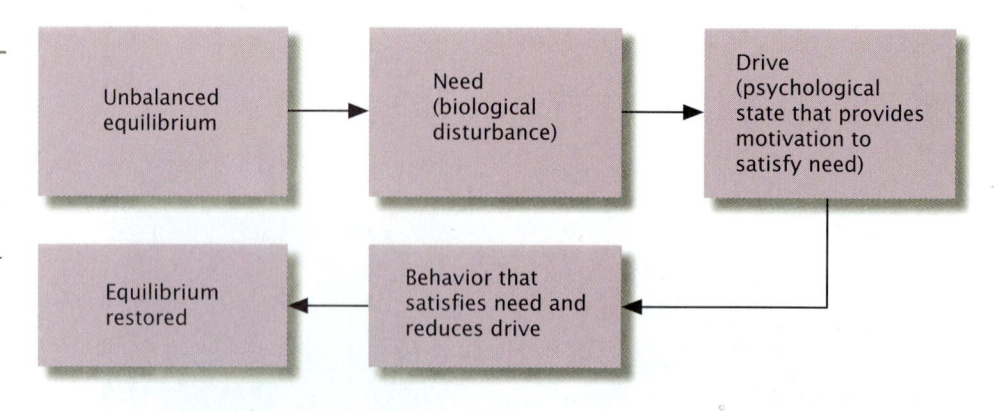

Unbalanced equilibrium → Need (biological disturbance) → Drive (psychological state that provides motivation to satisfy need) → Behavior that satisfies need and reduces drive → Equilibrium restored

By recognizing secondary as well as primary drives, drive reduction theory can account for a wider range of behaviors than instinct theory. But humans and animals often go to great lengths to do things that do not appear to reduce any drive. Consider curiosity. Animals explore and manipulate their surroundings, even though such activities do not lead to drive reduction. They will also exert considerable effort simply to enter a new environment, especially if it is complex and full of novel objects (Bolles, 1975; Loewenstein, 1994). People are no less curious. Most of us cannot resist checking out anything new or unusual. We go to the new mall, read the newspaper, surf the Web, and travel the world just to see what there is to see.

Arousal Theory

People also go out of their way to ride roller coasters, skydive, drive racecars, and do countless other things that, like curiosity-motivated behaviors, do not reduce any known drive (Zuckerman, 1996). In fact, these behaviors *increase* people's levels of activation, or arousal. The realization that people sometimes try to decrease arousal and sometimes try to increase it has led theorists to argue that motivation is tied to the regulation of arousal.

Most of these theorists think of **arousal** as a general level of activation reflected in the state of several physiological systems (Plutchik & Conte, 1997). Your level of arousal can be measured by your brain's electrical activity, by heart action, or by muscle tension (Deschaumes et al., 1991). Normally, arousal is lowest during deep sleep and highest during panic or great excitement. Many factors increase arousal, including hunger, thirst, intense stimuli, unexpected events, and stimulants (such as amphetamines). It is interesting to note that people who tend to actively seek novelty in life also tend to be at increased risk for abusing stimulants. This phenomenon may be related to individual differences in the brain's dopamine system, which is activated by novelty and by most drugs of abuse (Bardo, Donohew, & Harrington, 1996; Berns et al., 2001). Through especially creative applications of brain imaging techniques, researchers have found that the dopamine system is activated even when a person gambles or plays a video game (Breiter et al., 2001; Koepp et al., 1998).

People perform best, and may feel best, when arousal is moderate (Teigen, 1994). Figure 11.4 illustrates the general relationship between arousal and performance. Overarousal can be harmful to performance; it can also disrupt activities ranging from intellectual tasks to athletic competition (Penner & Craiger, 1992; Smith et al., 2000; Wright et al., 1995).

Arousal theories of motivation suggest that people are motivated to behave in ways that keep them at their own *optimal* level of arousal (Hebb, 1955). This optimal level is higher for some people than for others (Zuckerman, 1984). Generally, however, people try to increase arousal when it is too low and decrease it when it is

Optimal Arousal and Personality
People whose optimal arousal is high are likely to smoke, drink alcohol, engage in frequent sexual activity, listen to loud music, eat spicy foods, and do things that are novel and risky (Farley, 1986; Zuckerman, 1979). Those with lower optimal arousal tend to behave in ways that bring less intense stimulation and to take fewer risks. Most of the differences in optimal arousal have a strong biological basis and, as discussed in the chapter on personality, may help shape broader differences, such as introversion-extraversion.

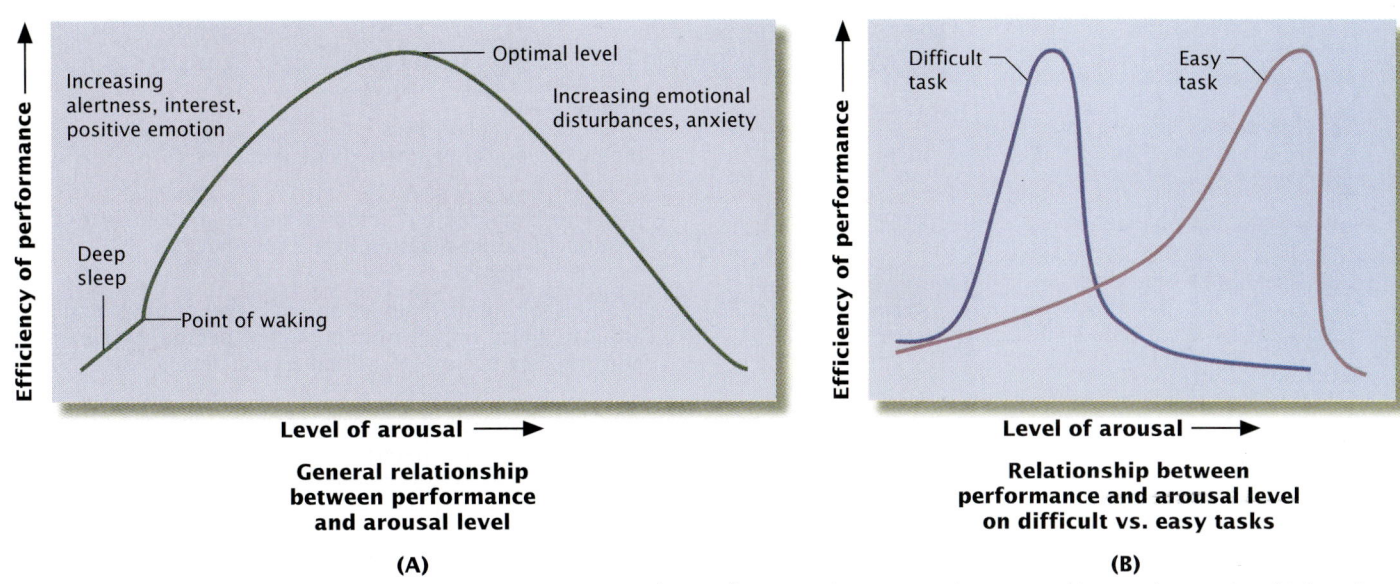

figure 11.4
The Arousal-Performance Relationship

(A) General relationship between performance and arousal level

(B) Relationship between performance and arousal level on difficult vs. easy tasks

Notice in Part A that performance is poorest when arousal is very low or very high and best when arousal is at some intermediate level. When you are either nearly asleep or overly excited, for example, it may be difficult to think clearly or to be physically coordinated. In general, optimal performance comes at a lower level of arousal on difficult or complex tasks and at a higher level of arousal on easy tasks, as shown in Part B. So even a relatively small amount of overarousal can cause students to perform far below their potential on difficult tests (Sarason, 1984). Because animal research early in this century by Robert Yerkes and his colleagues provided supportive evidence, this arousal-performance relationship is sometimes referred to as the *Yerkes-Dodson law,* even though Yerkes never actually discussed performance as a function of arousal (Teigen, 1994).

too high. They seek excitement when bored and relaxation when overaroused. After classes and studying, for example, you may want to see an exciting movie. But if your day was spent playing baseball, fiercely debating a political issue, and helping a friend move, an evening of quiet relaxation may seem ideal.

Incentive Theory

Instinct, drive reduction, and arousal theories of motivation all focus on internal processes that prompt people to behave in certain ways. By contrast, **incentive theory** emphasizes the role of environmental stimuli that can motivate behavior by pulling us toward them or pushing us away from them. According to this view, people act to obtain positive incentives and avoid negative incentives. Differences in behavior from one person to another, or in the same person from one situation to another, can be traced to the incentives available and the value a person places on them at the time. So if you expect a behavior (such as buying a lottery ticket) to lead to a valued outcome (winning money), you will want to engage in that behavior. The value of an incentive is influenced by biological as well as cognitive factors. For example, food is a more motivating incentive when you are hungry than when you are full (Balleine & Dickinson, 1994).

Today, incentive theorists distinguish between two incentive-related systems: wanting and liking. *Wanting* is the process of being attracted to stimuli, whereas *liking* is the immediate evaluation of how pleasurable a stimulus is (Berridge, 1999). Studies with animals have shown that these two systems involve separate parts of the brain, that the wanting system guides behavior to a greater extent than does the liking system, and that the operation of the wanting system varies according to whether an individual has been deprived or not (Nader, Bechara, & Van der Kooy,

arousal A general level of activation that is reflected in several physiological systems.

arousal theories Theories of motivation stating that people are motivated to behave in ways that maintain what is, for them, an optimal level of arousal.

incentive theory A theory of motivation stating that behavior is directed toward attaining desirable stimuli and avoiding unwanted stimuli.

in review: Theories of Motivation

Theory	Main Points
Instinct	Innate biological instincts guide behavior.
Drive reduction	Behavior is guided by biological needs and learned ways of reducing drives arising from those needs.
Arousal	People seek to maintain an optimal level of physiological arousal, which differs from person to person. Maximum performance occurs at optimal arousal levels.
Incentive	Behavior is guided by the lure of positive incentives and the avoidance of negative incentives. Cognitive factors influence expectations of the value of various rewards and the likelihood of attaining them.

1997). For example, different brain regions would affect the motivation to consume a piece of apple pie, depending on whether it is served as an appetizer or as a dessert.

The theoretical approaches we have outlined (see "In Review: Theories of Motivation") complement one another. Each emphasizes different sources of motivation, and each has helped to guide research into motivated behaviors such as eating, sex, and achievement-related activities, which we consider in the sections that follow.

Hunger and Eating

Hunger is deceptively simple; you get hungry when you do not eat. Much as a car needs gas, you need fuel from food. Is there a bodily mechanism that, like a car's gas gauge, signals the need for fuel? What causes hunger? What determines which foods you eat, and how do you know when to stop? The answers to these questions involve not only interactions between the brain and the rest of the body but also learning, social, and environmental factors (Hill & Peters, 1998).

Biological Signals for Hunger and Satiety

A variety of mechanisms underlie **hunger,** the general state of wanting to eat, and **satiety** (pronounced "se-TY-a-tee"), the general state of no longer wanting to eat. In order to maintain body weight, we must have ways to regulate food intake over the short term (a question of how often we eat and when we stop eating a given meal) and to regulate the body's stored energy reserves (fat) over the long term.

Signals from the Stomach
The stomach would seem to be a logical source of signals for hunger and satiety. After all, people say they feel "hunger pangs" from an "empty" stomach, and they complain of a "full stomach" after overeating. True, the stomach does contract during hunger pangs, and increased pressure within the stomach can reduce appetite (Cannon & Washburn, 1912; Houpt, 1994). But people who have lost their stomachs due to illness still get hungry when they do not eat and still eat normal amounts of food (Janowitz, 1967). So stomach cues can affect eating, but they do not play a major role in the normal control of eating. These cues appear to operate mainly when you are very hungry or very full.

hunger The general state of wanting to eat.

satiety The condition of no longer wanting to eat.

LINKAGES (a link to Biological Aspects of Psychology)

Signals from the Blood   The most important signals about the body's fuel level and nutrient needs are sent to the brain from the blood. The brain's ability to "read" blood-borne signals about the body's nutritional needs was shown years ago when researchers deprived rats of food for a long period and then injected them with blood from rats that had just eaten. When offered food, the injected rats ate little or nothing (Davis et al., 1969); something in the injected blood of the well-fed animals apparently signaled the hungry rats' brains that there was no need to eat. What sent that satiety signal? Subsequent research has shown that the brain constantly monitors both the level of food *nutrients* absorbed into the bloodstream from the stomach and the level of *hormones* released into the blood in response to those nutrients and from stored fat.

Some blood-borne signals affect short-term intake—telling us when to start and stop eating a meal—whereas others reflect and regulate the body's long-term supply of fat. The short-term signals are called *satiety factors*. One such signal comes from *cholecystokinin (CCK)* (pronounced "cole-ee-sis-toe-KY-nin"), which regulates meal size (Woods et al., 1998). During a meal, cholecystokinin is released as a hormone in the gut and as a neurotransmitter in the brain (Crawley & Corwin, 1994). The activation of CCK in the brain causes animals to stop eating (Parrott, 1994), and even a well-fed animal will start to eat if receptors in the brain for CCK are blocked (Brenner & Ritter, 1995). Moderate doses of CCK given to humans cause them to eat less of a given meal, whereas high doses can cause nausea—thus possibly explaining why people sometimes feel sick after overeating. However, research with animals suggests that simply increasing production of CCK would probably not result in weight loss, because the animals made up for smaller meals by eating more often. This phenomenon reflects the fact that the brain monitors the long-term storage of fat, as well as the short-term status of nutrients.

The nutrients that the brain monitors include *glucose*, the main form of sugar used by body cells. Decades ago, researchers noted that when the level of blood glucose drops, eating increases sharply (e.g., Mogenson, 1976). More recent work has shown that glucose acts indirectly by affecting certain chemical messengers. For example, when glucose levels rise, the pancreas releases *insulin*, a hormone that most body cells need in order to use the glucose they receive. Insulin may enhance the brain's satiety response to CCK. In one study, animals receiving CCK preceded by insulin infusions into the brain ate less food and gained less weight than animals getting either CCK or insulin alone (Riedy et al., 1995). Insulin itself may also provide a satiety signal by acting directly on brain cells (Brüning et al., 2000; Schwartz et al., 2000).

The long-term regulation of fat stores involves a hormone called *leptin* (from the Greek word *leptos*, meaning "thin"). The process works like this: Cells that store fat have genes that produce leptin in response to increases in fat supplies. The leptin is released into the bloodstream, and when it reaches special receptors for it in the hypothalamus, it provides information to the brain about the increasing fat supplies (Farooqi et al., 2001; Huang & Li, 2000; Tartaglia et al., 1996). When leptin levels are high, hunger decreases, helping to reduce food intake. When leptin levels are low, hunger increases, as illustrated in animals that are obese because of defects in leptin-producing genes (Zhang et al., 1994). Researchers have found that injections of leptin cause these animals to lose weight and body fat rapidly, with no effect on muscle or other body tissue (Forbes et al., 2001). Leptin injections can produce the same effects in normal animals, too (e.g., Campfield et al., 1995; Fox & Olster, 2000). At first, these results raised hope that leptin might be a "magic bullet" for treating obesity, or severe overweight, in humans, but this is not the case. It can help those rare individuals who are obese because their cells make no leptin (Farooqi et al., 1999), but leptin injections are far less effective for people whose obesity results from a high-fat diet (Gura, 1999; Heymsfield et al., 1999). In these far more common cases of obesity, the brain appears to become less sensitive to leptin's signals (Ahima & Flier, 2000; Lin et al., 2000).

Hunger and the Brain

Many parts of the brain contribute to the control of hunger and eating, but research has focused on several regions of the hypothalamus that may play primary roles in detecting and reacting to the blood's signals about the need to eat (see Figure 11.5). Some regions of the hypothalamus detect leptin and insulin; these regions generate signals that either increase hunger and reduce energy expenditure, or else reduce hunger and increase energy expenditure. At least twenty neurotransmitters and *neuromodulators*—substances that modify the action of neurotransmitters—convey these signals to networks in other parts of the hypothalamus and in the rest of the brain (Woods et al., 1998, 2000).

Activity in a part of the network that passes through the *ventromedial nucleus* of the hypothalamus tells an animal that there is no need to eat. So if a rat's ventromedial nucleus is electrically or chemically stimulated, the animal will stop eating (Kent et al., 1994). However, if the ventromedial nucleus is destroyed, the animal will eat continuously, increasing its weight up to threefold.

In contrast, the *lateral hypothalamus* contains networks that stimulate eating. When the lateral hypothalamus is electrically or chemically stimulated, rats eat huge quantities, even if they have just had a large meal (Stanley et al., 1993). When the lateral hypothalamus is destroyed, however, rats stop eating almost entirely.

One theory suggests that, much as a thermostat maintains a constant temperature in a house, these two hypothalamic regions interact to create a *set point* based on food intake or related metabolic signals that keeps body weight within a narrow range (Cabanac & Morrissette, 1992). According to this *range theory*, normal animals (and people) eat until their set point is reached, then stop eating until desirable intake falls below the set point. Destroying or stimulating the lateral or ventromedial hypothalamus may alter the set point.

However, research on other regions of the hypothalamus suggests that the brain's control of eating involves more than just the interaction of "stop-eating" and

figure 11.5

The Hypothalamus and Hunger

Regions of the hypothalamus generate signals that either increase hunger and reduce energy expenditure, called *anabolic effects,* or reduce hunger and increase energy expenditure, called *catabolic effects.*

Source: Adapted from Schwartz et al. (2000).

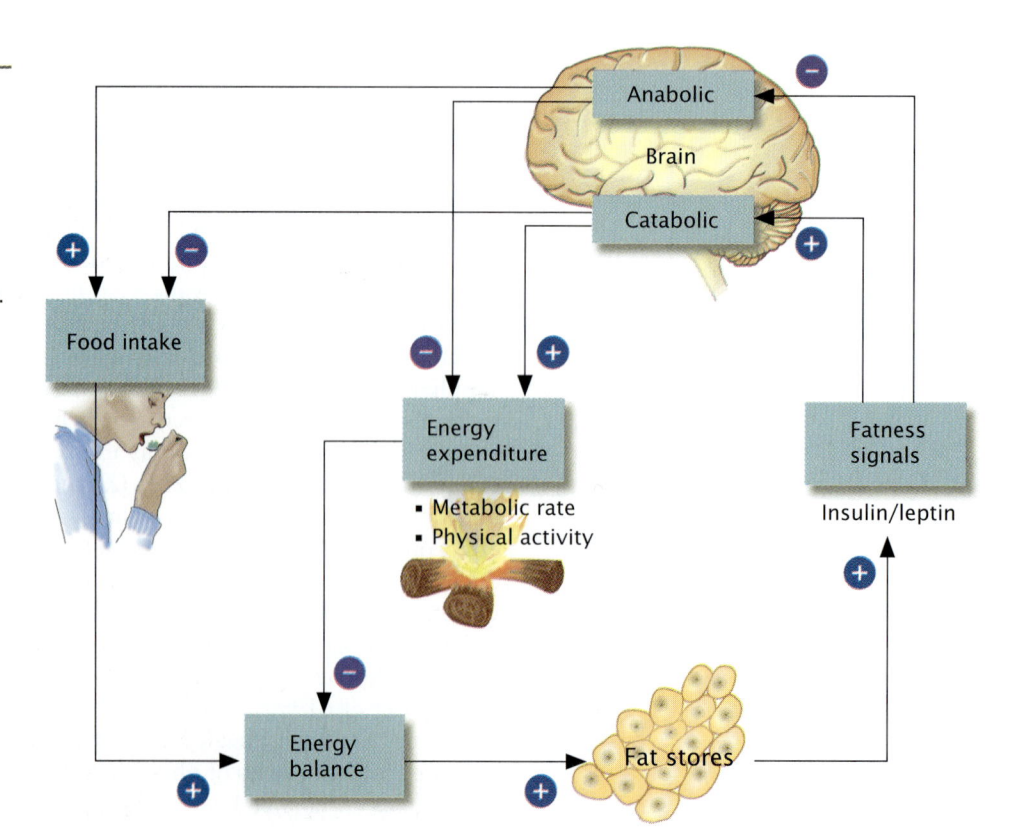

One Fat Mouse After surgical destruction of its ventromedial nucleus, this mouse ate enough to triple its body weight. Such animals become picky eaters, choosing only foods that taste good and ignoring all others.

"start-eating" areas (Winn, 1995). For example, hunger—and hunger for particular types of food—is also related to the effects of certain neurotransmitters on certain neurons (Lee, Schiffman, & Pappas, 1994; Woods et al., 1998). One of these neurotransmitters, called *neuropeptide Y*, stimulates carbohydrate eating (Jhanwar et al., 1993), whereas another, *serotonin*, suppresses it (Blundell & Halford, 1998). Similarly, *galanin* motivates the eating of high-fat food (Krykouli et al., 1990), and *enterostatin* reduces it (Lin et al., 1998). *Endocannabinoids* stimulate eating in general. They affect the same hypothalamic receptors as does the active ingredient in marijuana, which may account for "the munchies," a sudden hunger that marijuana often creates (Di Marzo et al., 2001).

In short, several brain regions and many brain chemicals help to regulate hunger and eating. And although eating is controlled by processes that suggest the existence of a set point, that set point appears variable enough to be overridden by other factors.

Flavor, Cultural Learning, and Food Selection

One factor that can override a set point is the *flavor* of food. In one experiment, some animals were offered just a single type of food while others were offered foods of several different flavors. The group getting the varied menu ate nearly four times more than the one-food group. As each new food appeared, the animals began to eat voraciously, regardless of how much they had already eaten (Peck, 1978). Humans behave similarly. All things being equal, people eat more food during a multicourse meal than when only one food is served (Raynor & Epstein, 2001). Apparently, the flavor of any particular food becomes less enjoyable as more of it is eaten (Swithers & Hall, 1994). In one study, for example, people rated how much they liked four kinds of food; then they ate one of the foods and rated all four again. The food they had just eaten now got a lower rating, whereas liking increased for all the rest (Johnson & Vickers, 1993).

Another factor that can override blood-borne signals about satiety is *appetite*, the motivation to seek food's pleasures. For example, the appearance and aroma of certain foods come to elicit conditioned physiological responses—such as secretion of saliva, gastric juices, and insulin—in anticipation of eating those foods. (The process is based on the principles of classical conditioning described in the chapter on learning.) These responses then increase appetite. So merely seeing a pizza on television may prompt you to order one—even if you hadn't been feeling hungry—and if you see a delicious-looking cookie, you do not have to be hungry to start eating it. In fact, brain-damaged patients who cannot remember anything for more than a minute will eat a full meal ten to thirty minutes after finishing one just like it, and may even start a third meal ten to thirty minutes later, simply because the food looks good (Rozin et al., 1998). In other words, people eat not only to satisfy nutritional needs but also to experience enjoyment.

A different mechanism appears to be responsible for *specific hungers*, or desires for particular foods at particular times. These hungers appear to reflect the biological need for the nutrients contained in certain foods. In one study, rats were allowed to eat from a bowl of carbohydrate-rich but protein-free food and also from a bowl of protein-rich but carbohydrate-free food. These animals learned to eat from both bowls in amounts that gave them a proper balance of carbohydrates and protein (Miller & Teates, 1985). In another study, rats were given three bowls of tasty, protein-free food and one bowl of food that tasted bad but was rich in protein. Again, the rats learned to eat enough of the bad-tasting food to get a proper supply of dietary protein (Galef & Wright, 1995).

These results are remarkable in part because food nutrients such as carbohydrates, fats, and proteins have no taste or odor. How, then, can they guide food choices that maintain nutritional balance? As with appetite, learning principles are probably involved. It may be that *volatile odorants* (odor molecules) in foods come to be associated with the nutritional value of their fat and protein content. Evidence for this kind of learning comes from experiments in which rats received infusions of liquid directly into their stomachs. Some of these infusions consisted of plain water; others included nutritious cornstarch. Each kind of infusion was paired with a different taste—either sour or bitter—in the animals' normal supply of drinking water. After all the infusions were completed, both sour water and bitter water were made available. When the animals became hungry, they showed a strong preference for the water whose taste had been associated with the cornstarch infusions (Drucker, Ackroff, & Sclafani, 1994). Related research shows that children come to prefer flavors that have been associated with high-fat ingredients (Johnson, McPhee, & Birch, 1991).

The role of learning in food selection is also seen in the social rules and cultural traditions that influence eating. Munching popcorn at movies and hot dogs at baseball games are common examples from North American culture of how certain social situations can stimulate appetite for particular food items. Similarly, how much you eat may depend on what others do. Courtesy or custom might prompt you to select foods you might otherwise have avoided. Generally, the mere presence of others, even strangers, tends to increase consumption: Most people consume 60 to 75 percent more food when they are with others than when eating alone (Clendenen, Herman, & Polivy, 1995; Redd & de Castro, 1992).

Eating and food selection are central to the way people function within their cultures. Celebrations, holidays, vacations, and even daily family interactions often revolve around food and what some call a *food culture* (Rozin, 1996). As any world traveler knows, there are wide cultural and subcultural variations in food selection. For example, chewing coca leaves is popular in the Bolivian highlands but illegal in the United States (Burchard, 1992). In China, people in urban areas eat a high-cholesterol diet rich in animal meat, whereas those in rural areas eat so little meat as to be cholesterol deficient (Tian et al., 1995). And the insects known as *palm weevils*, a popular food for people in Papua New Guinea (Paoletti, 1995), are regarded by many Westerners as disgusting (Springer & Belk, 1994). Even within the same general culture, different groups may have sharply contrasting food traditions. Squirrel brains won't be found on most dinner tables in the United States, but some people in the rural South consider them to be a tasty treat. In short, eating serves functions beyond nutrition—functions that help to remind us of who we are and with whom we identify.

Eating Disorders

Problems in the processes regulating hunger and eating may cause an *eating disorder*. The most common and dangerous examples are obesity, anorexia nervosa, and bulimia nervosa.

Obesity

The World Health Organization defines **obesity** as a condition in which a person's body-mass index, or BMI, is greater than 30. People whose BMI is 25 to 29.9 are considered to be overweight. (BMI is determined by dividing a person's weight in kilograms by the square of the person's height in meters. So someone who is 5 feet 2 inches tall and weighs 164 pounds would be classified as obese, as would someone 5 feet 10 inches tall who weighs 207 pounds. BMI calculators appear on web sites such as www.consumer.gov/weightloss/bmi.htm.) Using these BMI criteria, 36 percent of adults in the United States are overweight, and another 27 percent are obese (USDHHS, 2000a). Worse yet, obesity appears to be on the rise, not only in the United States but also in regions as diverse as Europe, Asia, South America, and Africa (Kopelman, 2000; Lewis et al., 2000; Mokdad et al., 2000, 2001; Rudolph et al., 2001; Taubes, 1998). It is associated with health problems such as diabetes, high blood pressure, pancreatic cancer, and increased risk of

TRY THIS **Bon Appétit!** The definition of *delicacy* differs from culture to culture. At this elegant restaurant in Mexico, diners pay to feast on baby alligators, insects, and other dishes that some people from other cultures would not eat even if the restaurant paid *them*. To appreciate your own food culture, make a list of foods that are traditionally valued by your family or cultural group but that people from other groups do not, or might even be unwilling, to eat.

obesity A condition in which a person is severely overweight, as measured by a body-mass index greater than 30.

heart attack (Field et al., 2001; Michaud et al., 2001; Sturm & Wells, 2001). With nearly 300,000 deaths in the United States alone attributed to obesity each year, it has been described as at least as dangerous as smoking and alcohol abuse (Allison et al., 1999; Sturm & Wells, 2001).

The precise reasons for this obesity epidemic are unknown (Hill & Peters, 1998), but possible causes include increased portion sizes at fast-food outlets, greater prevalence of high-fat foods, and decreases in physical activity associated with both work and recreation. These are important factors, because the body maintains a given weight through a combination of food intake and energy output (Keesey & Powley, 1986). Obese people get more energy from food than their body *metabolizes*, or "burns up"; the excess energy, measured in *calories*, is stored as fat. Metabolism declines during sleep and rises with physical activity. Because women tend to have a lower metabolic rate than men, even when equally active, they tend to gain weight more easily than do men with similar diets (Ferraro et al., 1992). Most obese people have normal resting metabolic rates, but they tend to eat above-average amounts of high-calorie, tasty foods and below-average amounts of less tasty foods (Kauffman, Herman, & Polivy, 1995; Peck, 1978). Further, some obese people are less active than lean people, a pattern that often begins in childhood (Strauss & Pollack, 2001). Spending long hours watching television or playing computer games is a major cause of the inactivity seen in overweight children (USDHHS, 1996; Vioque, Torres, & Quiles, 2000). In short, inadequate physical activity, combined with overeating—especially of the high-fat foods so prevalent in most Western cultures—has a lot to do with obesity.

But not everyone who is inactive and eats a high-fat diet becomes obese, and some obese people are as active as lean people, so other factors must also be involved (Blundell & Cooling, 2000). Some people probably have a genetic predisposition toward obesity (Arner, 2000; Rosmond, Bouchard, & Björntorp, 2001). For example, although most obese people have the genes to make leptin, they may not be sensitive to its weight-suppressing effects—perhaps because of a genetic defect in leptin receptors in the hypothalamus. Recent brain-imaging studies also suggest that obese people's brains may be slower to "read" satiety signals coming from their blood, thus causing them to continue eating when leaner people would have stopped (Liu et al., 2000). These factors, along with the presence of one or more recently discovered viruses in the body (Dhurandhar et al., 2000), may help explain obese people's tendency to eat more, to accumulate fat, and to feel more hunger than lean people.

Psychological explanations for obesity focus on factors such as learning from examples set by parents who overeat (Hood et al., 2000) and maladaptive reactions to stress. Many people do tend to eat more when under stress, a reaction that may be especially extreme among those who become obese (Friedman & Brownell, 1995). However, obese people are no more likely than other people to display mental disorders (Stunkard & Wadden, 1992).

Losing weight, and keeping it off for at least five years, is extremely difficult for many people, especially those who are obese (Lewis et al., 2000; McGuire et al., 1999). Part of the problem may be due to metabolic changes that accompany weight loss. When food intake is reduced, the process of homeostasis leads to a drop in metabolic rate, thus saving energy and curbing weight loss (Leibel, Rosenbaum, & Hirsch, 1995). This response makes evolutionary sense; conservation of energy during famine, for example, is adaptive for survival. But when obese people try to lose weight, their metabolic rate drops below normal. As a result, they can gain weight even while eating amounts that would maintain constant weight in other people.

These facts suggest that attempts to lose a great deal of weight quickly will be met with compensatory changes in one's set point (Brownell & Rodin, 1994). Animal studies show that losing and then regaining large amounts of weight, a process called *cycling*, actually leads to a gradual rise in average weight

Thin Is In In Western cultures today, thinness is a much-sought-after ideal, especially among young women who are dissatisfied with their appearance. That ideal is seen in fashion models, as well as in Miss America pageant winners, whose body-mass index has decreased from the "normal" range of 20 to 25 in the 1920s to an "undernourished" 18.5 in recent years (Rubinstein & Caballero, 2000). In the United States, 35 percent of normal-weight girls—and 12 percent of underweight girls!—begin dieting when they are as young as nine or ten. Many of these children try to lose weight in response to criticism by their mothers (Schreiber et al., 1996); for some, the result is anorexia.

anorexia nervosa An eating disorder characterized by self-starvation and dramatic weight loss.

bulimia nervosa An eating disorder that involves eating massive amounts of food and then eliminating the food by self-induced vomiting or the use of strong laxatives.

(Archambault et al., 1989). Moreover, people whose body weight "cycles" tend to experience more depression and stress-related symptoms than do people whose weight does not fluctuate (Foreyt et al., 1995).

Several anti-obesity drugs have been developed recently, including one that prevents fat in foods from being digested (e.g., Finer et al., 2000; Hauptman et al., 2000). Another drug has been found to interfere with an enzyme that forms fat. This "fatty acid synthase inhibitor" not only caused rapid weight loss in mice but also reduced their hunger (Loftus et al., 2000). The drug has not yet been tested for safety and effectiveness in humans, but researchers hope that it may someday be possible to give obese people medications that alter brain mechanisms involved in overeating and fat storage (Abu-Elheiga et al., 2001; Arterburn & Noël, 2001; Halford & Blundell, 2000).

Even the best drug treatments are unlikely to solve the problem of obesity on their own, however. To achieve the kind of gradual weight loss that is most likely to last, obese people are advised to increase exercise, because it burns calories without slowing metabolism (Tremblay & Bueman, 1995). In fact, a regular regimen of aerobic exercise and weight training *raises* the metabolic rate (Binzen, Swan, & Manore, 2001; McCarty, 1995). The most effective weight-loss programs include components designed to reduce food intake, change eating habits and attitudes toward food, and increase energy expenditure through exercise (Bray & Tartaglia, 2000; National Task Force on the Prevention and Treatment of Obesity, 2000; Wadden et al., 2001).

Anorexia Nervosa

At the opposite extreme from obesity is **anorexia nervosa**, an eating disorder characterized by some combination of self-starvation, self-induced vomiting, and laxative use that results in weight loss to below 85 percent of normal (Kaye et al., 2000; U.S. Surgeon General, 1999). About 95 percent of people who suffer from anorexia are young females. Anorexic individuals often feel hungry, and many are obsessed with food and its preparation, yet they refuse to eat. Anorexic self-starvation causes serious, often irreversible physical damage, including reduction in bone density that enhances the risk of fractures (Grinspoon et al., 2000). Between 4 and 30 percent of anorexics die of starvation, biochemical imbalances, or suicide; their risk of death is twelve times higher than that of other young women (Herzog et al., 2000; Sullivan, 1995). Anorexia tends to appear in adolescence, when concern over appearance becomes intense. The incidence of anorexia appears to be on the increase; it now affects about 1 percent of young women in the United States and is a growing problem in many other industrialized nations as well (Feingold & Mazzella, 1998; Thompson, 1996a).

The causes of anorexia are not yet clear. Anorexic individuals do have abnormally low levels of certain neurotransmitters; but because these levels return to normal when weight is restored, the deficit may be a response to starvation, not its cause (Kaye et al., 1988). Genetic factors may be involved in anorexia, but their strength is not yet determined (Bulik et al., 2000; Vink et al., 2001). Psychological factors that may contribute to the problem include a self-punishing, perfectionistic personality and a culturally reinforced obsession with thinness and attractiveness (Thompson & Stice, 2001; Tiller et al., 1995). People with anorexia appear to develop a fear of being fat, which they take to dangerous extremes (de Castro & Goldstein, 1995). Many anorexics continue to view themselves as fat or misshapen even as they are wasting away.

Drugs, hospitalization, and psychotherapy are all used to treat anorexia. In most cases, some combination of treatment and the passage of time brings recovery and maintenance of normal weight (Herzog et al., 1999).

Bulimia Nervosa

Like anorexia, bulimia nervosa involves intense fear of being fat, but the person may be thin, normal in weight, or even overweight (U.S. Surgeon General, 1999). **Bulimia nervosa** involves eating huge amounts of food

in review: Major Factors Controlling Hunger and Eating

	Stimulate Eating	Inhibit Eating
Biological factors	Levels of glucose and insulin in the blood provide signals that stimulate eating; neurotransmitters that affect neurons in different regions of the hypothalamus also stimulate food intake and influence hungers for specific kinds of foods, such as fats and carbohydrates. Stomach contractions are associated with subjective feelings of hunger, but they do not play a substantial role in the stimulation of eating.	Hormones released into the bloodstream produce signals that inhibit eating; hormones such as leptin, CCK, and insulin act as neurotransmitters or neuromodulators and affect neurons in the hypothalamus and inhibit eating. The ventromedial nucleus of the hypothalamus may be a "satiety center" that monitors these hormones.
Nonbiological factors	Sights and smells of particular foods elicit eating because of prior associations; family customs and social occasions often include norms for eating in particular ways; stress is often associated with eating more.	Values in contemporary U.S. society encourage thinness, and thus can inhibit eating.

(say, several boxes of cookies, a half-gallon of ice cream, and a bucket of fried chicken) and then getting rid of the food through self-induced vomiting or strong laxatives. These "binge-purge" episodes may occur as often as twice a day (Weltzin et al., 1995).

Like people with anorexia, bulimic individuals are usually female, and like anorexia, bulimia usually begins with a desire to be slender. However, bulimia and anorexia are separate disorders (Pryor, 1995). For one thing, most bulimics see their eating habits as problematic, whereas most anorexics do not. In addition, bulimia nervosa is usually not life threatening (Thompson, 1996b). There are consequences, however, including dehydration, nutritional problems, and intestinal damage. Many bulimics develop dental problems from the acids associated with vomiting. Frequent vomiting and the insertion of objects to trigger it can also cause damage to the throat. More generally, a preoccupation with eating and avoiding weight gain prevents many bulimics from working productively (Herzog, 1982).

Estimates of the frequency of bulimia range from 1 to 3 percent of adolescent and college-age women (Thompson, 1996a; U.S. Surgeon General, 1999). It appears to be caused by a combination of factors, including perfectionism, low self-esteem, stress, culturally encouraged preoccupation with being thin, depression and other emotional problems, and as-yet-undetermined biological problems that might include defective satiety mechanisms (Crowther et al., 2001; Steiger et al., 2001; Stice, 2001; Wade, Martin, & Tiggemann, 1998). Treatment for bulimia typically includes individual or group therapy and, sometimes, antidepressant drugs; these treatments help the vast majority of bulimic people to eat more normally (Herzog et al., 1999; Wilson et al., 1999).

(For a summary of the processes involved in hunger and eating, see "In Review: Major Factors Controlling Hunger and Eating.")

Sexual Behavior

Unlike food, sex is not necessary for individual survival. A strong desire for reproduction does help ensure the survival of a species, however (Keeling & Roger, 1995). The various factors shaping sexual motivation and behavior differ in strength across species, but they often include a combination of the individual's physiology, learned behavior, and physical and social environment. For example, one species of desert bird requires adequate sex hormones, a suitable mate, and a particular environment before it begins sexual behavior. As long as the dry season lasts, it shows no interest in sex, but within ten minutes of the first rainfall the birds vigorously copulate.

Rainfall is obviously much less influential as a sexual trigger for humans. People show a staggering diversity of *sexual scripts,* or patterns of behavior that lead to sex. One survey of college-age men and women identified 122 specific acts and 34 different tactics used for promoting sexual encounters (Greer & Buss, 1994). What happens next? The matter is exceedingly difficult to address scientifically, because most people are reluctant to respond to specific questions about their sexual practices, let alone to allow researchers to observe their sexual behavior (Bancroft, 1997). Yet having valid information about the nature of human sexual behavior is a vital first step for psychologists and other scientists who study such topics as individual differences in sexuality, sources of sexual orientation, types of sexual dysfunctions, and the pathways through which AIDS and other sexually transmitted diseases (STDs) reach new victims. This information also has important implications for helping people understand themselves, alleviating sexual problems, and curbing the spread of STDs.

FOCUS ON RESEARCH METHODS

A Survey of Human Sexual Behavior

The first extensive studies of sexual behavior in the United States were done by Alfred Kinsey during the late 1940s and early 1950s (Kinsey, Pomeroy, & Martin, 1948; Kinsey et al., 1953), followed in the 1960s by the work of William Masters and Virginia Johnson. The Kinsey studies surveyed people about their sex lives; Masters and Johnson actually measured sexual arousal and behavior in volunteers who received natural or artificial stimulation in a laboratory. These studies broke new ground in the exploration of human sexuality, but the people who volunteered for them probably did not constitute a representative sample of humankind. Accordingly, the results—and any conclusions drawn from them—may

Do They Look Ready? Research on sexual behavior provides psychologists, public health officials, and others who are concerned about poverty and child abuse with important information that helps them to more precisely tailor advertising campaigns and other efforts to prevent these problems.

not apply to people in general. The results of more recent surveys, such as reader polls in *Cosmopolitan* and other magazines, are also flawed by the use of unrepresentative samples (Davis & Smith, 1990).

● What was the researchers' question?

Is there a way to gather data on sexual behavior that is more representative and thus more revealing about people in general? A team of researchers at the University of Chicago believe there is, so they undertook the National Health and Social Life Survey, the first extensive survey of sexual behavior in the United States since the Kinsey studies (Laumann et al., 1994).

● How did the researchers answer the question?

This survey included important design features that had been neglected in most other surveys of sexual behavior. First, the study did not depend on self-selected volunteers. The researchers sought out a particular sample of 3,432 people, ranging in age from eighteen to fifty-nine. Second, careful construction of the sample made it reflective of the sociocultural diversity of the U.S. population in terms of gender, ethnicity, socioeconomic status, geographical location, and the like. Third, unlike previous mail-in surveys, the Chicago study was based on face-to-face interviews. This approach made it easier to ensure that the participants understood each question and could explain their responses. To encourage honesty, the researchers allowed participants to answer some questions anonymously, by placing written responses in a sealed envelope.

● What did the researchers find?

For one thing, the researchers found that people in the United States have sex less often and with fewer people than many had assumed. For most, sex occurs about once a week, and only with a partner with whom they share a stable relationship. About a third of the participants reported having sex only a few times, or not at all, in the past year. And in contrast to certain celebrities' splashy tales of dozens, even hundreds, of sexual partners per year, the average male survey participant had only six sexual partners in his entire life. The average female respondent reported a lifetime total of two. Further, the survey data suggested that people in committed, one-partner relationships had the most frequent and the most satisfying sex. And although a wide variety of specific sexual practices were reported, the overwhelming majority of heterosexual couples said they tend to engage mainly in penis-vagina intercourse.

● What do the results mean?

The Chicago survey challenges some of the cultural and media images of sexuality in the United States. In particular, it suggests that people in the United States may be more sexually conservative than one might think on the basis of magazine reader polls and the testimony of guests on daytime talk shows.

● What do we still need to know?

Many questions remain. The Chicago survey did not ask about some of the more controversial aspects of human sexuality, such as the effects of pornography, the nature and incidence of pedophilia (sexual attraction to children), and the role in sexual activity of sexual fetishes such as shoes or other clothing. Had the researchers asked about such topics, their results might have painted a less conservative picture. Further, because the Chicago survey focused on people in the United States, it told us little or nothing about the sexual practices, traditions, and values of people in the rest of the world.

The Chicago team has continued to conduct interviews, and the results are beginning to fill in the picture about sexual behavior in the United States and around the world. They have found, for example, that nearly one quarter of U.S. women prefer to achieve sexual satisfaction without partners of either sex. And although people in the United States tend to engage in a wider variety of sexual behaviors than those in Britain, there is less tolerance in the United States of disapproved sexual practices (Laumann & Michael, 2000; Michael et al., 1998).

Even the best survey methods—like the best of all other research methods—usually yield results that raise as many questions as they answer. When do people become interested in sex, and why? How do they choose to express these desires, and why? What determines their sexual likes and dislikes? How do learning and sociocultural factors modify the biological forces that seem to provide the raw material of human sexual motivation? These are some of the questions about human sexual behavior that a survey cannot easily or accurately explore.

The Biology of Sex

Some aspects of the sexual behavior observed by Masters and Johnson in their laboratory may not have reflected exactly what goes on when people have sex in more familiar surroundings. Still, those observations led to important findings about the **sexual response cycle**, the pattern of physiological arousal during and after sexual activity (see Figure 11.6).

People's motivation to engage in sexual activity has biological roots in **sex hormones**. The female sex hormones are **estrogens** and **progestins**; the main ones are *estradiol* and *progesterone*. The male hormones are **androgens**; the principal example is *testosterone*. Each sex hormone flows in the blood of both sexes, but males have relatively more androgens, and women have relatively more estrogens and progestins. Sex hormones have both organizational and activational effects. The *organizational* effects are permanent changes in the brain that alter the way a person thereafter responds to hormones. The *activational* effects are temporary behavioral changes that last only during the time a hormone level remains elevated, such as during puberty or in the ovulation phase of the monthly menstrual cycle.

The organizational effects of hormones occur around the time of birth, when certain brain areas are sculpted into a "male-like" or "female-like" pattern. These areas are thus described as *sexually dimorphic*. In rodents, for example, a sexually dimorphic area of the hypothalamus appears to underlie specific sexual behaviors. When these areas are destroyed in male gerbils, the animals can no longer copulate; yet damage to other nearby brain regions does not affect sexual behavior (Yahr & Jacobsen, 1994). Sexually dimorphic areas also exist in the human hypothalamus and elsewhere in the brain (Breedlove, 1994; Kimura, 1999). For example, a hypothalamic area called *BSTc* is generally smaller in women than in men. Its possible role in some aspects of human sexuality was suggested by a study of transsexual men—genetic males who feel like women and who may request sex-change surgery in order to "be" female. The BSTc in these men was smaller than in other men; in fact, it was about the size usually seen in women (Zhou et al., 1995).

Rising levels of sex hormones during puberty have activational effects, resulting in increased sexual desire and interest in sexual behavior. Generally, estrogens and androgens stimulate females' sexual interest (Burleson, Gregory, & Trevarthen, 1995; Sherwin & Gelfand, 1987). Androgens raise males' sexual interest (Davidson, Camargo, & Smith, 1979). The activational effects of hormones are also seen in reduced sexual motivation and behavior among people whose hormone-secreting ovaries or testes have been removed for medical reasons. Injections of hormones help restore these people's sexual interest and activity.

Generally, hormones affect sexual *desire*, not the physical *ability* to have sex (Wallen & Lovejoy, 1993). This fact may explain why castration does not prevent sex crimes in male offenders. Men with low testosterone levels due to medical problems or castration show less sexual desire, but they still experience physiological responses to erotic stimuli (Kwan et al., 1983). So a sex offender treated with androgen antagonists or castration would be less likely to seek out sex, but he would still respond as before to his favorite sexual stimuli (Wallen & Lovejoy, 1993).

sexual response cycle The pattern of physiological arousal during and after sexual activity.

sex hormones Chemicals in the blood of males and females that have both organizational and activational effects on sexual behavior.

estrogens Feminine hormones that circulate in the bloodstream of both men and women; relatively more estrogens circulate in women.

progestins Feminine hormones that circulate in the bloodstream of both men and women; relatively more progestins circulate in women.

androgens Masculine hormones that circulate in the bloodstream and regulate sexual motivation in both sexes; relatively more androgens circulate in men than in women.

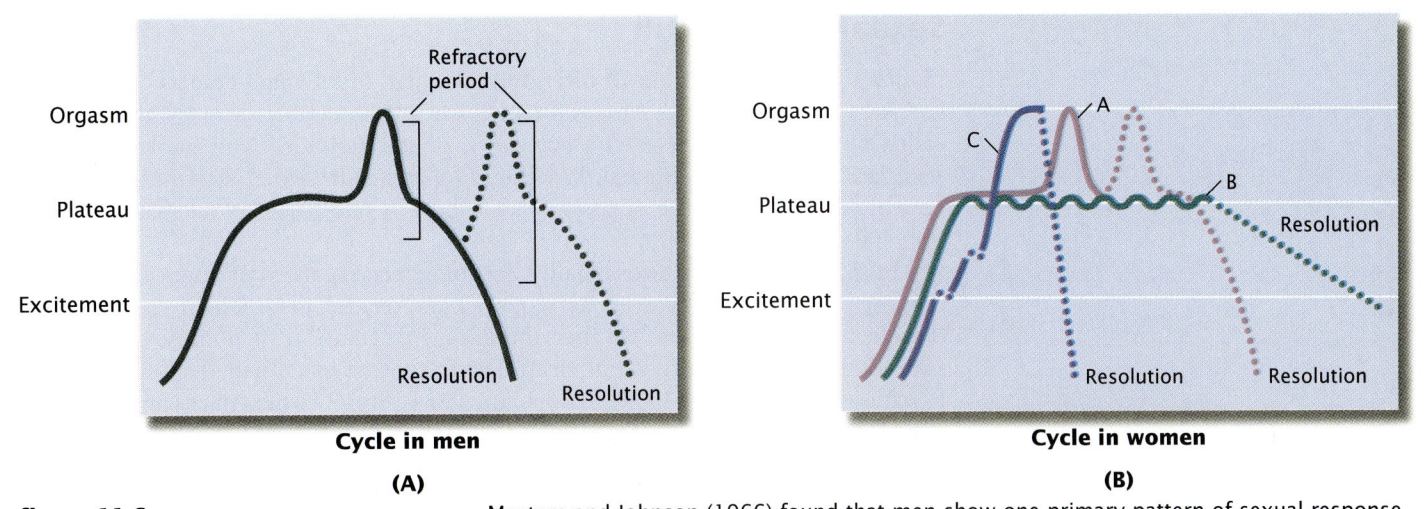

figure 11.6
The Sexual Response Cycle

Cycle in men (A) / **Cycle in women (B)**

Masters and Johnson (1966) found that men show one primary pattern of sexual response, depicted in Part A, and that women display at least three different patterns from time to time—labeled A, B, and C in Part B. For both men and women, the *excitement* phase begins with sexual stimulation from the environment or one's own thoughts. Continued stimulation leads to intensified excitement in the *plateau* phase and, if stimulation continues, to the intensely pleasurable release of tension in the *orgasmic* phase. During the *resolution* phase, both men and women experience a state of relaxation. Following resolution, men enter a *refractory* phase, during which they are unresponsive to sexual stimulation; women are capable of immediately repeating the cycle.

Source: Adapted from Masters & Johnson (1966).

Social and Cultural Factors in Sexuality

In humans, sexuality is profoundly shaped by a lifetime of learning and thinking that modifies the biological "raw materials" provided by hormones. For example, children learn some of their sexual attitudes and behaviors as part of the development of *gender roles,* which we discuss in the chapter on human development. The specific attitudes and behaviors learned depend partly on the nature of gender roles in their culture (Baumeister, 2000; Hyde & Durik, 2000). One survey of the sexual experiences of more than 1,500 college students in the United States, Japan, and Russia found numerous cross-cultural differences in the ways that men and women behave in sexual situations (Sprecher et al., 1994). For example, the results indicated that more women than men in the United States had consented to sex when they did not really want it; in both Russia and Japan, men and women were about equally likely to have had this experience.

Sexual behavior is also shaped by a variety of other sociocultural forces. In the United States, for example, concern over transmission of the AIDS virus during sex has prompted mass-media campaigns and school-based educational programs to encourage sexual abstinence prior to marriage or "safe sex" using condoms (e.g., Smith & DiClemente, 2000; some examples of such programs are described in the chapter on health, stress, and coping). These efforts seem to be shaping young people's sexual attitudes and practices. At the beginning of one sex education program, only 36 percent of 1,800 students in grades 7 through 10 thought premarital sex was a bad idea, and only 35 percent saw many benefits in premarital abstinence from sex. By the end of the semester-long program, these figures had risen to 66 percent and 58 percent, respectively (Eisenman, 1994). Another survey of 1,100 adolescents and young adults in the United States found that prior to 1985, first-time intercourse seldom included use of a condom. With growing AIDS awareness since 1985, however, condom use has become far more common in first-time intercourse and in later sexual activity (Everett et al., 2000; Leigh, Schafer, & Temple, 1995).

Sexual Orientation

Human sexual activity is most often **heterosexual,** involving members of the opposite sex. When sexual behavior is directed toward a member of one's own sex, it is called **homosexual.** People who engage in sexual activities with partners of both sexes are described as **bisexual.** Whether you engage in sexual activities with members of your own sex, the opposite sex, or both is one part of your *sexual orientation* (Ellis & Mitchell, 2000).

In many cultures, heterosexuality has long been regarded as a moral norm, and homosexuality has been seen as a disease, a mental disorder, or even a crime (Hooker, 1993). Attempts to alter the sexual orientation of homosexuals—using psychotherapy, brain surgery, or electric shock—were usually ineffective (American Psychiatric Association, 1999; Haldeman, 1994). In 1973 the American Psychiatric Association dropped homosexuality from the *Diagnostic and Statistical Manual of Mental Disorders,* thus ending its official status as a form of psychopathology. The same change was made by the World Health Organization in its *International Classification of Diseases* in 1993, by Japan's psychiatric organization in 1995, and by the Chinese Psychiatric Association in 2001.

Nevertheless, some people still disapprove of homosexuality. Because homosexuals and bisexuals are often the victims of discrimination and even hate crimes, many are reluctant to let their sexual orientation be known (Bernat et al., 2001). It is difficult, therefore, to obtain an accurate picture of the mix of heterosexual, homosexual, and bisexual orientations in a population. In the Chicago sex survey mentioned earlier, 1.4 percent of women and 2.8 percent of men identified themselves as exclusively homosexual (Laumann et al., 1994), figures much lower than the 10 percent found in Kinsey's studies. However, that survey did not allow respondents to give anonymous answers to questions about sexual orientation. It has been suggested that if anonymous responses to those questions had been permitted, the prevalence figures for homosexual and bisexual orientations would have been higher (Bullough, 1995). In fact, studies that have allowed anonymous responding estimate the percentage of homosexual people in the United States, Canada, and Western Europe at between 5 and 15 percent (Bagley & Tremblay, 1998; Diamond, 1993; Rogers & Turner, 1991; Sell, Wells, & Wypij, 1995).

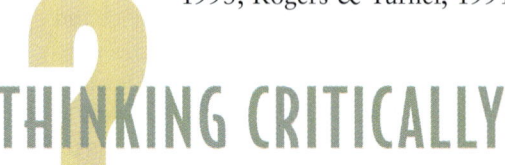

THINKING CRITICALLY

Does Biology Determine Sexual Orientation?

The question of where sexual orientation comes from is a topic of intense debate in scientific circles, on talk shows, in everyday conversations, and even in the halls of the U.S. Congress.

- **What am I being asked to believe or accept?**

One point of view suggests that genes dictate sexual orientation. According to this view, we do not learn a sexual orientation but rather are born with it.

- **What evidence is available to support the assertion?**

In 1995, a report by a respected research group suggested that one kind of sexual orientation—namely, homosexuality in males—was associated with a particular gene on the X chromosome (Hu et al., 1995). This finding was not supported by later studies (Rice et al., 1999), but a growing body of evidence from research in behavioral genetics (see the chapter on research in psychology) suggests that genes might influence sexual orientation (Kendler et al., 2000; Pillard & Bailey, 1998). One study examined pairs of monozygotic male twins (whose genes are

---

heterosexual A description of sexual motivation that is focused on members of the opposite sex.

homosexual A description of sexual motivation that is focused on members of one's own sex.

bisexual A description of people who engage in sexual activities with partners of both sexes.

identical), nonidentical twin pairs (whose genes are no more alike than those of any brothers), and pairs of adopted brothers (who are genetically unrelated). To participate in this study, at least one brother in each pair had to be homosexual. As it turned out, the other brother was also homosexual or bisexual in 52 percent of the identical-twin pairs, but in only 22 percent of the nonidentical twin pairs and in just 11 percent of the pairs of adopted brothers (Bailey & Pillard, 1991). Similar findings have been reported for male identical twins raised apart; in such cases, a shared sexual orientation cannot be attributed to the effects of a shared environment (Whitam, Diamond, & Martin, 1993). The few available studies of female sexual orientation have yielded similar results (Bailey & Benishay, 1993; Bailey, Dunne, & Martin, 2000).

Evidence for the role of other biological factors in sexual orientation comes from research on the impact of sex hormones. In adults, differences in the level of these hormones are not generally associated with differences in sexual orientation. However, hormonal differences during prenatal development might be involved in the shaping of sexual orientation (Williams et al., 2000). Support for this view is provided by research on a congenital disorder that causes the adrenal glands to secrete extremely high levels of androgens prior to birth (Carlson, 1998). Women who suffered from this disorder, and who thus had been exposed to high levels of androgens during their fetal development, were much more likely to become lesbians than their sisters who had not been exposed (Meyer et al., 1995). In animals, such hormonal influences alter the structure of the hypothalamus, a brain region known to underlie some aspects of sexual functioning (Swaab & Hofman, 1995). In humans, hormones may likewise be responsible for anatomical differences in the hypothalamus that are seen not only in males versus females but in homosexual versus heterosexual men as well (LeVay, 1991; Swaab & Hofman, 1990). The anterior commissure, an area near the hypothalamus, also appears to differ in people with differing sexual orientations (Allen & Gorski, 1992; Gladue, 1994).

Further support for the influence of hormones on sexual orientation comes from a study of *otoacoustic emissions,* which are faint sounds that come from the human ear (McFadden & Pasanen, 1998). These sounds, known to be affected by hormones during prenatal development, are louder in heterosexual women than in men. In lesbians, however, the sounds are more similar to men's than to heterosexual women's, suggesting a biological process of sexual differentiation. This study did *not* find a difference between homosexual and heterosexual men, which is contrary to what would be expected if sexual orientation were invariably associated with otoacoustic emissions.

Finally, a biological basis for sexual orientation is suggested by the fact that environmental factors have a relatively weak impact on it. For example, several studies have shown that the sexual orientation of children's caregivers has little or no effect on those children's own sexual orientation.

● Are there alternative ways of interpreting the evidence?

Correlations between genetics and sexual orientation, like all correlational data, are open to alternative interpretations. As discussed in the chapter on research in psychology, a correlation describes the strength and direction of a relationship between variables, but it does not guarantee that one variable is actually influencing the other. Consider again the data showing that brothers who shared the most genes were also most likely to share a homosexual orientation. It is possible that what the brothers shared was not a gene for homosexuality but rather a set of genes that influenced their activity level, emotionality, aggressiveness, or the like. One example is "gender nonconformity" in childhood, the tendency for some boys to display "feminine" behaviors and for some girls to behave in "masculine" ways (Bailey, Dunne, & Martin, 2000). It could be such general aspects of temperament or personality—and other people's reactions to them—that influence the likelihood of a particular sexual orientation (Bem, 1996). In other words, sexual orientation could arise as a reaction to the way people respond to a genetically

A Committed Relationship Heterosexual and homosexual relationships can be brief and stormy, or stable and long lasting. These gay men are committed to each other for the long haul, as evidenced by their decision to adopt two children together. The strong role of biological factors in sexual orientation is seen in research showing that these children's orientation will not be influenced much, if at all, by that of their adopted parents (e.g., Bailey et al., 1995; Stacey & Biblarz, 2001; Tasker & Golombok, 1995).

determined, but nonsexual, aspect of personality. Prenatal hormone levels, too, could influence sexual orientation by shaping aggressiveness or other nonsexual aspects of behavior.

It is also important to look at behavioral genetics evidence for what it can tell us about the role of *environmental factors* in sexual orientation. When we read that both members of identical twin pairs have a homosexual or bisexual orientation 52 percent of the time, it is easy to ignore the fact that the orientation of the twin pair members was *different* in nearly half the cases. Viewed in this way, the results suggest that genes do not tell the entire story of sexual orientation.

So even if sexual orientation has a biological base, it is probably not determined by genetic and hormonal forces alone. As described in the chapter on biological aspects of psychology, the bodies we inherit are quite responsive to environmental input; the behaviors we engage in and the environmental experiences we have often result in physical changes in the brain and elsewhere (Wang et al., 1995). For example, changes occur in the brain's synapses as we form new memories. So differences in the brains of people with differing sexual orientations could be the effect, not the cause, of their behavior or experiences.

● **What additional evidence would help to evaluate the alternatives?**

Much more evidence is needed regarding the extent to which genetic characteristics directly determine sexual orientation, as well as the extent to which genes and hormones shape physical and psychological characteristics that lead to the social construction of various sexual orientations. For example, the few available reports of sexual dimorphism in human brains have yet to be replicated. In studying this issue, researchers need to learn more not only about the genetic characteristics of people with different sexual orientations but also about their mental and behavioral styles. Are there personality characteristics associated with different sexual orientations? If so, do those characteristics have a strong genetic component? To what extent are heterosexuals, bisexuals, and homosexuals similar—and to what extent are they different—in terms of cognitive styles, biases, coping skills, developmental histories, and the like? And are there any differences in how sexual orientation is shaped in males versus females (Bailey, Dunne, & Martin, 2000)?

The more we learn about sexual orientation generally, the easier it will be to interpret data relating to its origins; but even defining sexual orientation is not simple. Alfred Kinsey and his colleagues (1948) viewed sexual orientation as occurring along a continuum rather than falling into a few discrete categories. Should a man who identifies himself as gay be considered bisexual because he occasionally has heterosexual daydreams? What sexual orientation label would be appropriate for a forty-year-old woman who experienced a few lesbian encounters in her teens but has engaged in exclusively heterosexual sex since then? Progress in understanding the origins of sexual orientation would be enhanced by a generally accepted system for describing and defining what is meant by *sexual orientation* (Stein, 1999).

- **What conclusions are most reasonable?**

Given the antagonism and physical danger often faced by people with nonheterosexual orientations (Cramer, 1999), it seems unlikely that a homosexual or bisexual identity is entirely a matter of choice. On the contrary, much of the evidence reviewed suggests that our sexual orientation chooses us, rather than the other way around. In light of this evidence, a reasonable hypothesis is that genetic factors, probably operating through prenatal hormones, create differences in the brains of people with different sexual orientations. Even if this hypothesis is correct, however, the manner in which a person expresses a genetically influenced sexual orientation will be profoundly shaped by what that person learns through social and cultural experiences (Bancroft, 1994). In short, sexual orientation most likely results from the complex interplay of both genetic and nongenetic mechanisms—both nature and nurture. Those who characterize sexual orientation as being either all "in the genes" or entirely a matter of choice are probably wrong.

Sexual Dysfunctions

The same biological, social, and psychological factors that shape human sexual behavior can also result in **sexual dysfunctions**, problems in a person's desire for or ability to have satisfying sexual activity. Fortunately, most of these problems—which affect 30 to 40 percent of U.S. adults (Laumann, Paik, & Rosen, 1999)—respond to psychotherapy, drugs, or both (de Silva, 1994). For men, a common problem is *erectile disorder* (once called *impotence*), a persistent inability to have or maintain an erection adequate for sex. Physical causes—such as fatigue, diabetes, hypertension, aging, and alcohol or other drugs—account for some cases, but psychological causes such as anxiety are also common (Everaerd & Laan, 1994). Viagra, a drug that increases blood flow in the penis, is effectively treating many cases of erectile disorder (Lue, 2000), and other drugs are in development. *Premature ejaculation,* another common dysfunction, involves a recurring tendency to ejaculate during sex sooner than the man or his partner desires. Most men experience episodes of at least one of these problems at some point in their lives, but such episodes are considered dysfunctions only if they become a distressing obstacle to sexual functioning (American Psychiatric Association, 1994).

For women, the most common sexual dysfunction is *arousal disorder* (once called *frigidity*), which is characterized by a recurring inability to become physiologically aroused during sexual activity (Phillips, 2000; Wilson et al., 1996). Arousal disorder can stem from inadequate genital stimulation, insufficient vaginal lubrication, or inadequate blood flow to the clitoris (Mansfield, Voda, & Koch, 1995; Wilson et al., 1996). However, it is also often tied to psychological factors such as guilt or self-consciousness, which can affect men as well as women (Davidson & Moore, 1994; Laan et al., 1993).

---

sexual dysfunctions Problems with sex that involve sexual motivation, arousal, or orgasmic response.

Achievement Motivation

This sentence was written at 6 A.M. on a beautiful Sunday in June. Why would someone get up that early to work on a weekend? Why do people take their work seriously and try to do the best that they can? People work hard partly due to *extrinsic motivation*, a desire for external rewards such as money. But work and other human behaviors also reflect *intrinsic motivation*, a desire to attain internal satisfaction.

The next time you visit someone's home or office, look at the mementos displayed there. You may see framed diplomas and awards, trophies and ribbons, pictures of memorable personal events, and photos of children and grandchildren. These badges of achievement affirm that a person has accomplished tasks that merit approval or establish worth. Much of our behavior is motivated by a desire for approval, admiration, and achievement—in short, for *esteem*—from others and from ourselves. In this section, we examine two of the most common avenues to esteem: achievement in general and a job in particular.

Need for Achievement

Many athletes who already hold world records still train intensely; many people who have built multimillion-dollar businesses still work fourteen-hour days. What motivates these people?

One possible answer is a motive called **need achievement** (Murray, 1938). People with a high need for achievement seek to master tasks—be they sports, business ventures, intellectual puzzles, or artistic creations—and feel intense satisfaction from doing so. They exert strenuous efforts in striving for excellence, enjoy themselves in the process, and take great pride in achieving at a high level (McClelland, 1985).

Individual Differences

How do people with strong achievement motivation differ from others? To find out, researchers gave children a test to measure their need for achievement (Figure 11.7 shows a test for adults) and then asked them to play a ring-toss game. Children scoring low on the need-achievement test usually stood so close to, or so far away from, the ring-toss target that they either could not fail or could not succeed. In contrast, children scoring high on the need-achievement test stood at a moderate distance from the target, making the game challenging but not impossible (McClelland, 1958). These and other experiments suggest that people with high achievement needs tend to set challenging—but realistic—goals. They actively seek success, take risks when necessary, and are intensely satisfied with success. But if they feel they have tried their best, people with high achievement motivation are not too upset by failure. Those with low achievement motivation also like to succeed, but instead of joy, success tends to bring them relief at having avoided failure (Winter, 1996).

Differences in achievement motivation also appear in people's goals in achievement-related situations (Molden & Dweck, 2000). Some people tend to adopt *learning goals*. When they play golf, take piano lessons, work at puzzles and problems, go to school, and get involved in other achievement-oriented activities, they do so mainly to develop competence in those activities. Realizing that they may not yet possess the skills necessary to achieve at a high level, they tend to learn by watching others and to struggle with problems on their own rather than asking for help (Mayer & Sutton, 1996). When they do seek help, people with learning goals are likely to ask for explanations, hints, and other forms of task-related information, not for quick, easy answers that remove the challenge from the situation. In contrast, people who adopt *performance goals* are usually more concerned with demonstrating the competence they believe they already possess. They tend to seek information about how well they have performed compared with others rather than

figure 11.7
Assessment of Need Achievement
This picture is from the Thematic Apperception Test, or TAT (Morgan & Murray, 1935). The strength of people's achievement motivation is inferred from the stories they tell about TAT pictures. A response such as "The young woman is hoping that she will be able to make her grandmother proud of her" would be seen as reflecting high achievement motivation.

Source: Murray (1971).

Helping Them Do Their Best
Learning-oriented goals are especially appropriate in classrooms, where students typically have little knowledge of the subject matter. This is why most teachers tolerate errors and reward gradual improvement. They do not usually encourage performance goals, which emphasize doing better than others and demonstrating immediate competence (Reeve, 1996). Still, to help students do their best in the long run, teachers sometimes promote performance goals, too. The proper combination of both kinds of goals may be more motivating than either kind alone (Barron & Harackiewicz, 2001).

about how to improve their performance (Butler, 1999). When they seek help, it is usually to ask for "the right answer" rather than for tips on how to find the answer themselves. Because their primary goal is to demonstrate their competence, people with performance goals tend to avoid new challenges if they are not confident that they will be successful, and they tend to quit in response to failure (Weiner, 1980).

Development of Achievement Motivation

Achievement motivation tends to be learned in early childhood, especially from parents. For example, in one study young boys were given a very hard task at which they were sure to fail. Fathers whose sons scored low on achievement motivation tests often became annoyed as they watched their boys, discouraged them from continuing, and interfered or even completed the task themselves (Rosen & D'Andrade, 1959). A different pattern of behavior emerged among parents of children who scored high on tests of achievement motivation. Those parents tended to (1) encourage the child to try difficult tasks, especially new ones; (2) give praise and other rewards for success; (3) encourage the child to find ways to succeed rather than merely complaining about failure; and (4) prompt the child to go on to the next, more difficult challenge (McClelland, 1985).

More general cultural influences also affect the development of achievement motivation. For example, subtle messages about a culture's view of how achievement occurs often appear in the books children read and the stories they hear. Does the story's main character work hard and overcome obstacles (creating expectations of a payoff for persistence) or loaf and then win the lottery (suggesting that rewards come randomly, regardless of effort)? If the main character succeeds, is this outcome the result of personal initiative (typical of an individualist culture) or of ties to a cooperative and supportive group (typical of a collectivist culture)? These themes appear to act as blueprints for reaching culturally approved goals. It should not be surprising, then, that ideas about how people achieve differ from culture to culture. In one study, for example, individuals from Saudi Arabia and from the United States were asked to comment on short stories describing people succeeding at various tasks. Saudis tended to see the people in the stories as having succeeded because of the help they got from others, whereas Americans tended to attribute success to the internal characteristics of each story's main character (Zahrani & Kaplowitz, 1993). Achievement motivation is also influenced by how much a particular culture *values*

need achievement A motive influenced by the degree to which a person establishes specific goals, cares about meeting those goals, and experiences feelings of satisfaction by doing so.

achievement. For example, in cultures where demanding standards lead students to fear rejection for failure to attain high grades, the motivation to excel is likely to be especially strong (Eaton & Dembo, 1997; Hess, Chih-Mei, & McDevitt, 1987).

It is possible to increase achievement motivation among people whose cultural training did not foster it in childhood (Mayer & Sutton, 1996). In one study, high school and college students with low achievement motivation were helped to develop fantasies about their own success. They imagined setting goals that were difficult, but not impossible. Then they imagined themselves concentrating on breaking a complex problem into small, manageable steps. They fantasized about working hard, failing but not being discouraged, continuing to work, and finally feeling elated at success. Afterward, the students' grades and academic success improved, suggesting an increase in their achievement motivation (McClelland, 1985). In short, achievement motivation is strongly influenced by social and cultural learning experiences, as well as by the beliefs about oneself that these experiences help to create. People who come to believe in their ability to achieve are more likely to do so than those who expect to fail (Butler, 1998; Dweck, 1998; Wigfield & Eccles, 2000).

Goal Setting and Achievement Motivation

Why are you reading this chapter instead of watching television or hanging out with your friends? Your motivation to study is probably based on your goal of doing well in a psychology course, which relates to broader goals, such as attaining a degree, having a career, and the like. Psychologists have found that we set goals when we recognize a discrepancy between our current situation and how we want that situation to be (Oettingen, Pak, & Schnetter, 2001). Establishing a goal motivates us to engage in behaviors designed to reduce the discrepancy we have identified. The kinds of goals we set can influence the amount of effort, persistence, attention, and planning we devote to a task.

In general, the more difficult a goal, the harder people will try to reach it. This rule assumes, of course, that the goal is seen as attainable. Goals that are impossibly difficult may not motivate maximum effort. It also assumes that the person accepts the goal. If a difficult goal is set by someone else—as when a parent assigns a teenager to keep a large lawn and garden trimmed and weeded—people may not accept it as their own and may not work very hard to attain it. Setting goals that are

Children raised in environments that support the development of strong achievement motivation tend not to give up on difficult tasks—even if all the king's horses and all the king's men do!

"Maybe they didn't try hard enough."

Motivated by a Goal People are more motivated to persist in efforts to improve their appearance and avoid health risks when they are pursuing a clear, specific goal such as "lose twenty pounds," "do aerobics three times a week," or "quit smoking" rather than pursuing a vague goal such as "get in shape."

clear and specific tends to increase people's motivation to persist at a task. For example, you are more likely to keep reading this chapter if your goal is to "read the motivation and emotion chapter today" than if it is to "do some studying." Clarifying your goal makes it easier to know when you have reached it, and when it is time to stop. Without clear goals, a person can be more easily distracted by fatigue, boredom, or frustration and more likely to give up before completing a task. Goals, especially clear goals, also tend to focus people's attention on creating plans for pursuing them, on the activities they believe will lead to goal attainment, and on evaluating their progress. In short, the process of goal setting is more than just wishful thinking. It is an important first step in motivating all kinds of behavior.

Achievement and Success in the Workplace

In the workplace, there is usually less concern with employees' general level of achievement motivation than with their motivation to work hard during business hours. In fact, employers tend to set up jobs in accordance with their ideas about how intrinsic and extrinsic motivation combine to shape their employees' performance (Riggio, 1989). Employers who see workers as lazy, untrustworthy creatures with no ambition tend to offer highly structured, heavily supervised jobs that give employees little say in deciding what to do or how to do it. These employers assume that workers are motivated mainly by extrinsic rewards—money, in particular. So they tend to be surprised when, in spite of good pay and benefits, employees sometimes express dissatisfaction with their jobs and show little motivation to work hard (Amabile et al., 1994; Igalens & Roussel, 2000).

If good pay and benefits alone do not bring job satisfaction and the desire to excel on the job, what does? Research suggests that low worker motivation in Western cultures comes largely from the feeling of having little or no control over the work environment (Rosen, 1991). Compared with those in rigidly structured jobs, workers tend to be more satisfied and productive if they are (1) encouraged to participate in decisions about how work should be done; (2) given problems to solve, without being told how to solve them; (3) taught more than one skill; (4) given individual responsibility; and (5) given public recognition, not just money, for good performance.

Allowing people to set and achieve clear goals is one way to increase both job performance and job satisfaction (Abramis, 1994). As suggested by our earlier discussion, some goals are especially effective at maintaining work motivation (Katzell

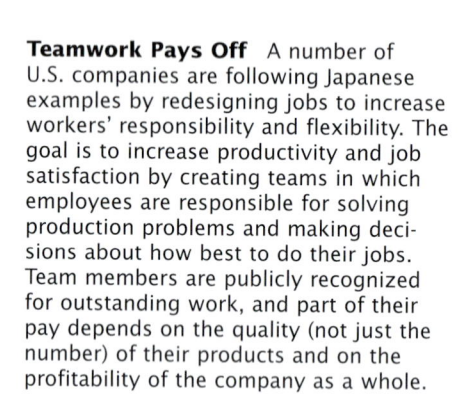

Teamwork Pays Off A number of U.S. companies are following Japanese examples by redesigning jobs to increase workers' responsibility and flexibility. The goal is to increase productivity and job satisfaction by creating teams in which employees are responsible for solving production problems and making decisions about how best to do their jobs. Team members are publicly recognized for outstanding work, and part of their pay depends on the quality (not just the number) of their products and on the profitability of the company as a whole.

& Thompson, 1990). First, they are personally meaningful. When a memo from a remote administrator decrees that employees should increase production, they tend to feel put upon and not particularly motivated to meet the goal. Before assigning difficult goals, good managers try to ensure that employees accept those goals (Klein et al., 1999). They include employees in the goal-setting process, make sure that the employees have the skills and resources to reach the goal, and emphasize the benefits to be gained from success—perhaps including financial incentives (Jenkins et al., 1998; Locke & Latham, 1990). Second, effective goals are specific and concrete. The goal of "doing better" is usually not a strong motivator, because it provides no direction about how to proceed and also fails to specify when the goal has been met. A specific target, such as increasing sales by 10 percent, is a far more motivating goal; it can be measured objectively, allowing feedback on progress, and it tells workers whether the goal has been reached. Finally, goals are most effective if management supports the workers' own goal setting, offers special rewards for reaching goals, and gives encouragement for renewed efforts after failure (Kluger & DeNisi, 1998).

In summary, motivating jobs offer personal challenges, independence, and both intrinsic and extrinsic rewards. They provide enough satisfaction for people to feel excitement and pleasure in working hard. For employers, meanwhile, the rewards are more productivity, less absenteeism, and lower turnover (Ilgen & Pulakos, 1999).

Achievement and Subjective Well-Being

Some people believe that the more they achieve at work and elsewhere, and the more money and other material goods they acquire as a result, the happier they will be. Will they? As part of a recent focus on *positive psychology* (Seligman & Csikszentmihalyi, 2000; Sheldon & King, 2001), researchers have become increasingly interested in studying what it actually takes to achieve happiness, or more formally, subjective well-being. **Subjective well-being** is a combination of a cognitive judgment of satisfaction with life, the frequent experiencing of positive moods and emotions, and the relatively infrequent experiencing of unpleasant moods and emotions (Diener, 2000).

Research on subjective well-being indicates that, as you might expect, people living in extreme poverty or in war-torn or politically chaotic countries are less

subjective well-being A combination of a cognitive judgment of satisfaction with life, the frequent experiencing of positive moods and emotions, and the relatively infrequent experiencing of unpleasant moods and emotions.

happy than people in better circumstances. And people everywhere react to good or bad events with corresponding changes in mood. As described in the chapter on health, stress, and coping, for example, severe or long-lasting stressors—such as the death of a loved one—can lead to psychological and physical problems. But although events do have an impact, the saddening or elevating effects of major changes, such as being promoted or fired, or even being imprisoned or seriously injured, tend not to last as long as we might think they would. In other words, how happy you are may have less to do with what happens to you than you might expect (Gilbert & Wilson, 1998).

Most event-related changes in mood subside within days or weeks, and most people then return to their previous level of happiness (Suh, Diener, & Fujita, 1996). Even when events create permanent changes in circumstances, most people adapt by changing their expectancies and goals, not by radically and permanently changing their baseline level of happiness. For example, people may be thrilled after getting a big salary increase, but as they get used to having it, the thrill fades, and they may eventually feel just as underpaid as before. In fact, people's level of subjective well-being tends to be remarkably stable throughout their lives. This stable baseline may be related to temperament, or personality, and it has been likened to a set point for body weight (Lykken, 1999). Like many other aspects of temperament, our baseline level of happiness may be influenced by genetics. Twin studies have shown, for example, that individual differences in happiness are more strongly associated with inherited personality characteristics than with environmental factors such as money, popularity, or physical attractiveness (Lykken, 1999; Tellegen et al., 1988).

Beyond inherited tendencies, the things that appear to matter most in generating happiness are close social ties (especially a satisfying marriage or partnership and good friends), religious faith, and having the resources necessary to allow progress toward one's goals (Diener, 2000; Myers, 2000b). So you don't have to be a rich, physically attractive high achiever to be happy, and it turns out that most people in Western cultures are relatively happy (Diener & Diener, 1995).

These results are consistent with the views expressed over many centuries by philosophers, psychologists, and wise people in all cultures. For example, decades ago, Abraham Maslow (1970) noted that when people in Western cultures experience unhappiness and psychological problems, those problems can often be traced to a *deficiency orientation*. That is, these people tend to seek happiness by trying to acquire the goods and reach the status they *don't* have—but think they need—rather than by appreciating life itself and the value of the material and nonmaterial riches they *already* have. Others have amplified this point, suggesting that efforts to get more of the things we think will bring happiness may actually contribute to unhappiness if what we get is never "enough" (Csikszentmihalyi, 1999; Myers, 2000a; Srivastava, Locke, & Bartol, 2001).

Relations and Conflicts Among Motives

Maslow's views about deficiency motivation stemmed from his more general model, in which human behavior is seen as based on a hierarchy of needs, or motives (see Figure 11.8). Needs at the lowest level of the hierarchy, he said, must be at least partially satisfied before people can be motivated by higher-level goals. From the bottom to the top of Maslow's hierarchy, these five motives are as follows:

1. *Biological,* such as the need for food, water, oxygen, activity, and sleep.

2. *Safety,* such as the need to be cared for as a child and have a secure income as an adult.

3. *Belongingness and love,* such as the need to be part of social groups and to participate in affectionate sexual and nonsexual relationships.

figure 11.8

Maslow's Hierarchy of Motives

Abraham Maslow (1970) saw human motives as organized in a hierarchy in which motives at lower levels take precedence over those at higher levels. According to this view, self-actualization is the essence of mental health; but Maslow recognized that only rare individuals, such as Mother Teresa or Dr. Martin Luther King, Jr., approach full self-actualization.

Source: Adapted from Maslow (1943).

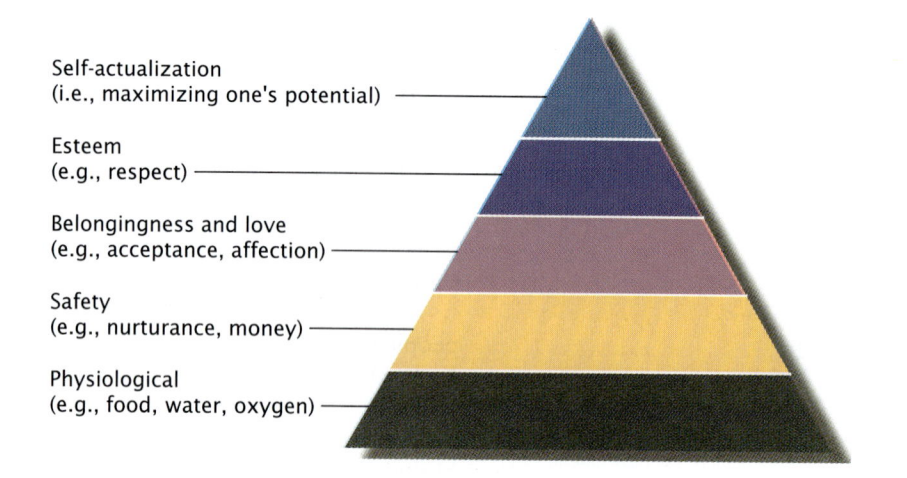

Self-actualization (i.e., maximizing one's potential)
Esteem (e.g., respect)
Belongingness and love (e.g., acceptance, affection)
Safety (e.g., nurturance, money)
Physiological (e.g., food, water, oxygen)

4. *Esteem,* such as the need to be respected as a useful, honorable individual.

5. *Self-actualization,* which means reaching one's fullest potential. People motivated by this need explore and enhance relationships with others; follow interests for intrinsic pleasure rather than for money, status, or esteem; and are concerned with issues affecting all people, not just themselves.

Maslow's theoretical hierarchy has been very influential over the years, but critics see it as far too simplistic (Hall, Lindsay, & Campbell, 1998; Neher, 1991). It does not predict or explain, for example, the motivation of people who starve themselves to death to draw attention to political or moral causes. Further, people may not have to satisfy one kind of need before addressing others; we can seek several needs at once. And though the needs associated with basic survival and security do generally take precedence over those related to self-enhancement or personal growth (Baumeister & Leary, 1995; Oishi et al., 1999), the needs that are most important to people's satisfaction with life do not always correspond to Maslow's hierarchy. One set of studies with college students found that the needs for autonomy (independence), relatedness to others, competence, and self-esteem were more important than the need for luxury *or* self-actualization (Sheldon et al., 2001). Further, the ordering of needs within the survival/security and enhancement/growth categories differs from culture to culture, suggesting that there may not be a single, universal hierarchy of needs.

LINKAGES (a link to Health, Stress, and Coping)

Conflicting Motives and Stress

As in the case of hunger strikes, human motives can sometimes conflict. The usual result is some degree of discomfort. For example, imagine that you are alone and bored on a Saturday night, and you think about going to the store to buy some snacks. What are your motives? Hunger might prompt you to go out, as might the prospect of increased arousal that a change of scene will provide. Even sexual motivation might be involved, as you fantasize about meeting someone exciting in the snack-food aisle. But safety-related motives may also kick in—what if you get mugged? Even an esteem motive might come into play, making you hesitate to be seen alone on a weekend night.

These are just a few motives that may shape a trivial decision. When the decision is more important, the number and strength of motivational pushes and pulls are often greater, creating far more internal conflict. Four basic types of motivational conflict have been identified (Miller, 1959):

1. **Approach-approach conflicts.** When a person must choose only one of two desirable activities—say, going to a movie or going to a play—an *approach-approach conflict* exists. As the importance of the choice increases, so does the difficulty of making it.

2. **Avoidance-avoidance conflicts.** An *avoidance-avoidance conflict* arises when a person must select one of two undesirable alternatives. Someone forced either to sell the family farm or to declare bankruptcy faces an avoidance-avoidance conflict. Such conflicts are very difficult to resolve and often create intense emotions.

3. **Approach-avoidance conflicts.** If someone you couldn't stand had tickets to your favorite group's sold-out concert and invited you to come along, what would you do? When a single event or activity has both attractive and unattractive features, an *approach-avoidance conflict* is created. Conflicts of this type are also difficult to resolve and often result in long periods of indecision.

4. **Multiple approach-avoidance conflicts.** Suppose you must choose between two jobs. One offers a high salary with a well-known company, but it requires long hours and relocation to a miserable climate. The other boasts advancement opportunities, fringe benefits, and a better climate, but it offers lower pay and an unpredictable work schedule. This is an example of a *multiple approach-avoidance conflict,* in which two or more alternatives each have both positive and negative features. Such conflicts are difficult to resolve partly because the attributes of each option are often difficult to compare. For example, how many dollars a year does it take to compensate you for living in a bad climate?

Each of these conflicts can create a significant amount of stress, a topic described at length in the chapter on health, stress, and coping. Most people in the midst of motivational conflicts are tense, irritable, and more vulnerable than usual to physical and psychological problems. These reactions are especially likely when there is no obviously "right" choice, when conflicting motives have approximately equal strength, and when the choice can have serious consequences (as in decisions to marry, to divorce, or to approve disconnection of a relative's life-support system). People may take a long time to resolve these conflicts, or they may act impulsively and thoughtlessly, if only to end the discomfort of uncertainty. And even after a conflict is resolved, stress responses may continue in the form of anxiety about the wisdom of the decision or self-blame over bad choices. These and other consequences of conflicting motives can even lead to depression or other serious disorders.

Opponent Processes, Motivation, and Emotion

Resolving approach-avoidance conflicts is often complicated by the fact that some behaviors have more than one emotional effect, and those effects may be opposite to one another. People who ride roller coasters or skydive, for example, often say that the experience is scary, but also thrilling. How do they decide whether or not to repeat these behaviors? One answer lies in the changing value of incentives and the regulation of arousal described in Richard Solomon's *opponent-process theory,* which is discussed in the chapter on learning (Solomon & Corbit, 1974). Opponent-process theory is based on two assumptions. The first is that any reaction to a stimulus is followed by an opposite reaction, called the *opponent process.* For example, being startled by a sudden sound is typically followed by relaxation and relief. Second, after repeated exposure to the same stimulus, the initial reaction weakens, and the opponent process becomes quicker and stronger.

Research on opponent-process theory has revealed a predictable pattern of emotional changes that helps explain some people's motivation to repeatedly engage in arousing but fearsome activities, such as skydiving. Prior to the first several episodes, people usually experience stark terror, followed by intense relief when they reach the ground. With more experience, however, the terror becomes mild anxiety, and what had been relief grows to a euphoria that can appear *during* the activity (Solomon, 1980). As a result, says Solomon, some people's motivation to pursue such activities can become a virtual addiction.

The emotions associated with motivational conflicts and with the operation of opponent processes provide just two examples of the intimate links between motivation and emotion. Motivation can intensify emotion, as when a normally timid person's hunger results in an angry phone call about a late pizza delivery. But emotions can also create motivation. Happiness, for example, is an emotion that people want to feel, so they engage in whatever behaviors—studying, creating art, investing, beachcombing—they think will achieve it. Similarly, as an emotion that most people want to avoid, anxiety prompts many behaviors, from leaving the scene of an accident to avoiding poisonous snakes. In the next section of this chapter, we take a closer look at emotions.

The Nature of Emotion

Everyone seems to agree that joy, sorrow, anger, fear, love, and hate are emotions, but it is hard to identify exactly what it is that makes these experiences emotions rather than, say, thoughts or impulses. In fact, some cultures see emotion and thought as the same thing. The Chewong of Malaysia, for example, consider the liver the seat of both what we call thoughts and feelings (Russell, 1991).

Defining Characteristics

Most psychologists in Western cultures tend to see emotions as organized psychological and physiological reactions to changes in our relationship to the world. These reactions are partly inner, or *subjective,* experiences and partly objectively measurable patterns of behavior and physiological arousal. The subjective experience of emotion has several characteristics:

Winners and Losers Emotional experiences depend in part on our interpretation of situations and how those situations relate to our goals. A single stimulus—the announcement of the results of a cheerleading contest—triggered drastically different emotional reactions in these women, depending on whether they perceived it as making them winners or losers.

The Nature of Emotion

1. Emotion is usually *temporary;* it tends to have a relatively clear beginning and end, as well as a relatively short duration. Moods, by contrast, tend to last longer.

2. Emotional experience is either *positive* or *negative,* that is, pleasant or unpleasant.

3. Emotional experience is elicited partly by a *cognitive appraisal* of how a situation relates to your goals. The same event can bring about different emotions depending on your interpretation of what the event means. An exam score of 75 percent could excite you if your previous score had been 50 percent, but it might upset you if you had never before scored below 90 percent and you saw the result as a disaster.

4. Emotional experience *alters thought processes,* often by directing attention toward some things and away from others. The anguish of parents whose child is killed by a drunken driver, for example, might change their perception of the importance of drunk-driving laws.

5. Emotional experience triggers an *action tendency,* the motivation to behave in certain ways. The grieving parents' anger, for example, might motivate them to harm the driver or to work for stronger penalties for drunk driving.

6. Emotional experiences are *passions* that happen to you, usually whether you want them to or not. You can exert at least some control over emotions in the sense that they depend partly on how you interpret situations (Gross, 2001). For example, your emotional reaction might be less extreme after a house fire if you remind yourself that no one was hurt and you are insured. Still, such control is limited. You cannot *decide* to experience joy or sorrow; instead, you "fall in love" or are "overcome by grief." Emotional experiences, much like personality traits, have a different relation to the self than do conscious thoughts.

In other words, the subjective aspects of emotions are both *triggered* by the thinking self and felt as *happening* to the self. They reveal each individual as both agent and object, both I and me, both the controller of thoughts and the recipient of passions. The extent to which we are "victims" of our passions versus rational designers of our emotions is a central dilemma of human existence, as much a subject of literature as of psychology.

The *objective* aspects of emotion include learned and innate *expressive displays* and *physiological responses.* Expressive displays—a smile, a frown—communicate feelings to others. Physiological responses—changes in heart rate, for example—are the biological adjustments needed to perform the action tendencies generated by emotional experience. If you throw a temper tantrum or jump for joy, your heart must deliver additional oxygen and fuel to your muscles.

In summary, an **emotion** is a temporary experience with either positive or negative qualities. It is felt with some intensity as happening to the self, generated in part by a cognitive appraisal of situations, and accompanied by both learned and innate physical responses. Through emotion, people communicate their internal states and intentions to others, but emotion also functions to direct and energize a person's own thoughts and actions. Emotion often disrupts thought and behavior, but it also triggers and guides cognitions and organizes, motivates, and sustains behavior and social relations.

emotion A transitory positive or negative experience that is felt as happening to the self, is generated in part by cognitive appraisal of a situation, and is accompanied by both learned and reflexive physical responses.

The Biology of Emotion

The role of biology in emotion is seen in mechanisms of the central nervous system and the autonomic nervous system. In the *central nervous system,* specific brain areas are involved in the generation of emotions as well as in our experience of those

figure 11.9

Brain Regions Involved in Emotion

Incoming sensory information alerts the brain to an emotion-evoking situation. Most of the information goes through the thalamus; the cingulate cortex and hippocampus are involved in the interpretation of this sensory input. Output from these areas goes to the amygdala and hypothalamus, which control the autonomic nervous system via hindbrain connections. There are also connections from the thalamus directly to the amygdala. The locus coeruleus is an area of the hindbrain that causes both widespread arousal of cortical areas and changes in autonomic activity.

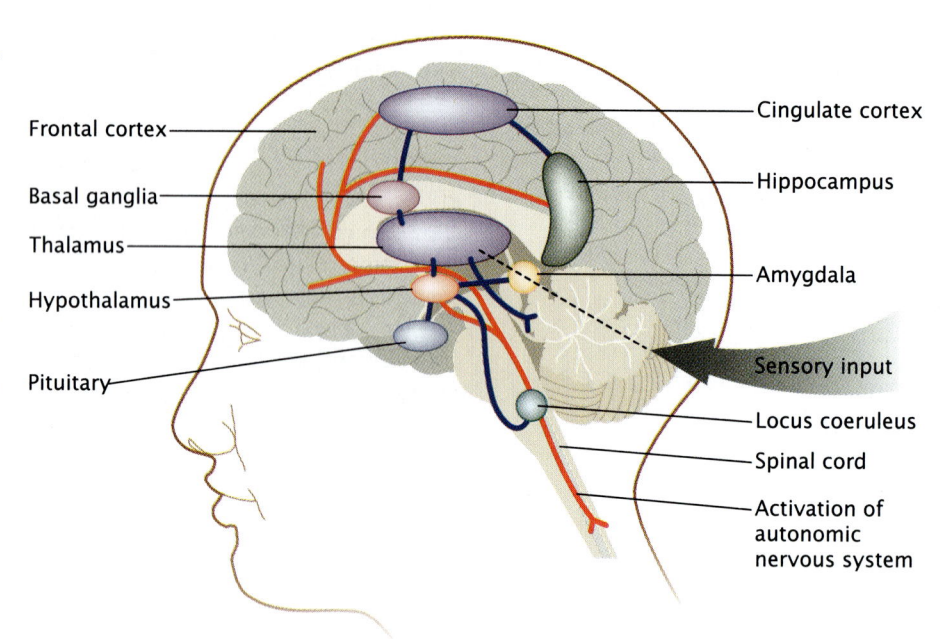

emotions. The *autonomic nervous system (ANS)* gives rise to many of the physiological changes associated with emotional arousal.

Brain Mechanisms

Although many questions remain, researchers have described three basic features of the brain's control of emotion. First, it appears that activity in the *limbic system,* especially in the *amygdala,* is central to various aspects of emotion (LeDoux, 1996; see Figure 11.9). Disruption of the amygdala's functioning prevents animals from being able to associate fear with a negative stimulus (Davis et al., 1993). In humans, too, the amygdala plays a critical role in the ability to learn emotional associations, recognize emotional expressions, and perceive emotionally charged words (e.g., Anderson & Phelps, 2001). In one functional magnetic resonance imaging study, when researchers paired an aversively loud noise with pictures of faces, the participants' brains revealed activation of the amygdala while the noise-picture association was being learned (LaBar et al., 1998). In another study, victims of a disease that destroys only the amygdala were found to be unable to judge other people's emotional states by looking at their faces (Adolphs et al., 1994). Faces that normal people rated as expressing strong negative emotions were rated by the amygdala-damaged individuals as approachable and trustworthy (Adolphs, Tranel, & Damasio, 1998).

TRY THIS — A second aspect of the brain's involvement in emotion is seen in its control over emotional and nonemotional facial expressions (Rinn, 1984). Take a moment to look in a mirror and put on your best fake smile. The voluntary facial movements you just made, like all voluntary movements, are controlled by the *pyramidal motor system,* a brain system that includes the motor cortex (see Figure 3.17). However, a smile that expresses genuine happiness is involuntary. That kind of smile, like the other facial movements associated with emotions, is governed by the *extrapyramidal motor system,* which depends on areas beneath the cortex. Brain damage can disrupt either system (see Figure 11.10). People with pyramidal motor system damage show normal facial expressions during genuine emotion, but they cannot fake a smile. In contrast, people with damage to the extrapyramidal system can pose facial expressions at will, but they remain straight-faced even when feeling genuine joy or profound sadness (Hopf, Muller, & Hopf, 1992).

A third aspect of the brain's role in emotion is revealed by research on the cerebral cortex and the differing contributions of its two cerebral hemispheres to the perception, experience, and expression of emotion (Davidson, 2000). For example, after suffering damage to the right, but not the left, hemisphere, people no longer

figure 11.10

Control of Voluntary and Emotional Facial Movements

This man has a tumor in his motor cortex that prevents him from voluntarily moving the muscles on the left side of his face. In the photograph at the left he is trying to smile in response to instructions from the examiner. He cannot smile on command, but he can smile with happiness, as the photograph at the right shows, because the movements associated with genuine emotion are controlled by the extrapyramidal motor system.

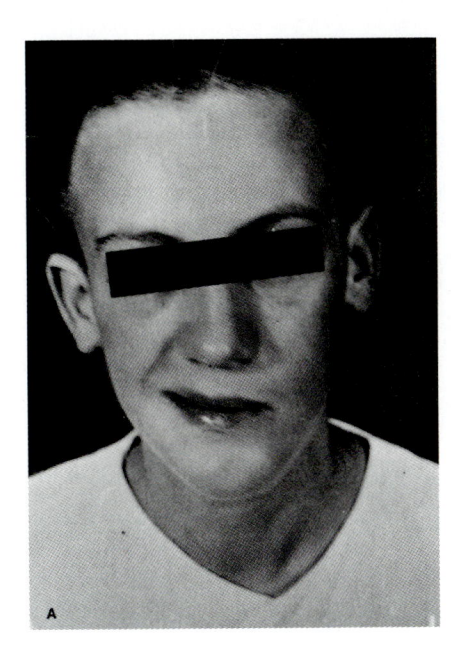

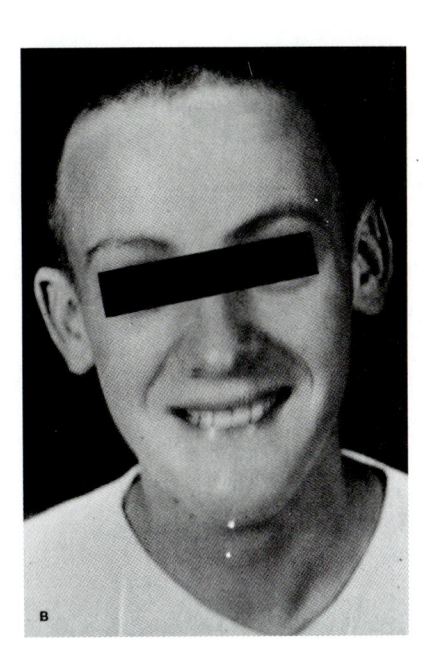

laugh at jokes—even though they can still understand the jokes' words, the logic (or illogic) underlying them, and the punch lines (Critchley, 1991). Further, when people are asked to name the emotions shown in slides of facial expressions, blood flow increases in the right hemisphere more than in the left hemisphere (Gur, Skolnic, & Gur, 1994). People are also faster and more accurate at this emotion-naming task when the facial expressions are presented to the brain's right hemisphere than when they are presented to the left (Hahdahl, Iversen, & Jonsen, 1993). Finally, compared with normal people, depressed people display greater electrical activity in the right frontal cortex (Schaffer, Davidson, & Saron, 1983) and perform more poorly on tasks that depend especially on the right hemisphere (Banich et al., 1992; Heller, Etienne, & Miller, 1995).

There is some debate about how hemispheric differences relate to emotion. Research has demonstrated that the right hemisphere is activated during many displays of emotion (Heller, 1993), including negative emotion. But some investigators argue that the experiencing of positive emotion depends on the left frontal cortex. For example, EEG recordings show that smiling during an experience of genuine positive emotion correlates with greater left frontal activity (Davidson et al., 1990). And consider the findings from a case study of a sixteen-year-old girl. When an area of her left frontal cortex was given mild electrical stimulation, she began to smile, and stimulation at a higher intensity elicited robust laughter (Fried et al., 1998). She attributed her laughing to whatever external stimulus was present ("You guys are just so funny . . . standing around"). Generally, however, most other aspects of emotion—the experiencing of negative emotion, the perception of any emotion exhibited in faces or other stimuli, and the facial expression of any emotion—depend on the right hemisphere more than on the left (Heller, Nitschke, & Miller, 1998; Kawasaki et al., 2001).

If the right hemisphere is relatively dominant in emotion, which side of the face would you expect to be somewhat more involved in expressing emotion? If you said the left side, you are correct, because movements of each side of the body are controlled by the opposite side of the brain (see the chapter on biological aspects of psychology).

Mechanisms of the Autonomic Nervous System

The autonomic nervous system is involved in many of the physiological changes that accompany emotions (Vernet, Robin, & Dittmar, 1995). If your hands get cold and clammy when you are nervous, it is because the ANS has increased perspiration and decreased the blood flow in your hands.

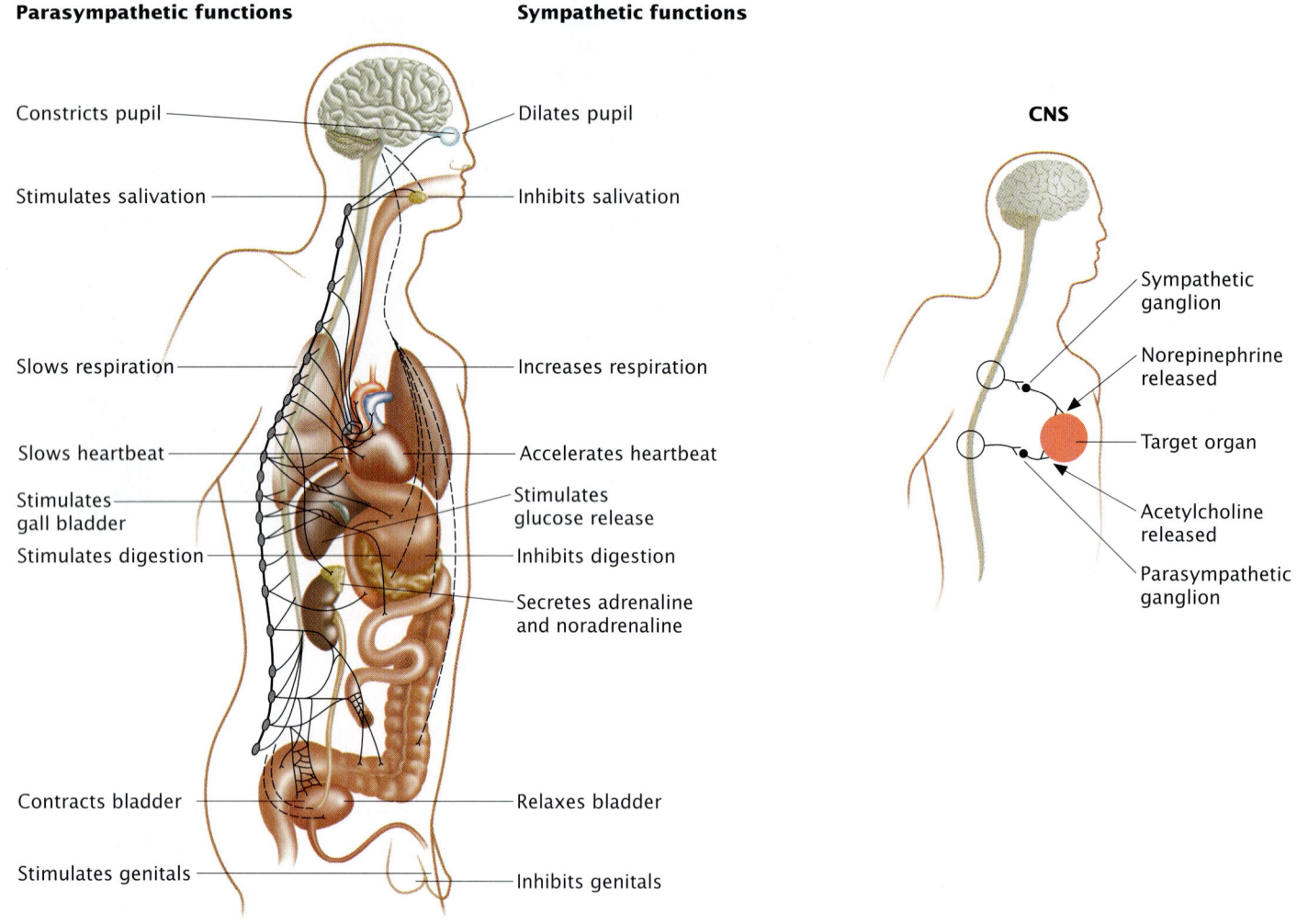

figure 11.11
The Autonomic Nervous System

Emotional responses involve activation of the autonomic nervous system, which includes sympathetic and parasympathetic subsystems. Which of the bodily responses depicted here do you associate with emotional experiences?

Parasympathetic functions: Constricts pupil; Stimulates salivation; Slows respiration; Slows heartbeat; Stimulates gall bladder; Stimulates digestion; Contracts bladder; Stimulates genitals.

Sympathetic functions: Dilates pupil; Inhibits salivation; Increases respiration; Accelerates heartbeat; Stimulates glucose release; Inhibits digestion; Secretes adrenaline and noradrenaline; Relaxes bladder; Inhibits genitals.

CNS; Sympathetic ganglion; Norepinephrine released; Target organ; Acetylcholine released; Parasympathetic ganglion.

As described in the chapter on biological aspects of psychology, the ANS carries information between the brain and most organs of the body—the heart and blood vessels, the digestive system, and so on. Each of these organs has its own ongoing activity, but ANS input affects this activity, increasing or decreasing it. By doing so, the ANS coordinates the functioning of these organs to meet the body's general needs and to prepare it for change (Porges, Doussard, & Maita, 1995). If you are aroused to take action—to run to catch a bus, say—you need more glucose to fuel your muscles. The ANS frees needed energy by stimulating secretion of glucose-generating hormones and promoting blood flow to the muscles.

Figure 11.11 shows that the autonomic nervous system is organized into two divisions: the sympathetic nervous system and the parasympathetic nervous system. Emotions can activate either of these divisions, both of which send axon fibers to each organ in the body. Generally, the sympathetic and parasympathetic fibers have opposite effects on these so-called *target organs*. Axons from the **parasympathetic system** release *acetylcholine* onto target organs, leading to activity related to the protection, nourishment, and growth of the body. For example, parasympathetic activity increases digestion by stimulating movement of the intestinal system so that more nutrients are taken from food. Axons from the **sympathetic system** release a different neurotransmitter, *norepinephrine*, onto target organs, helping to prepare

parasympathetic system The subsystem of the autonomic nervous system that typically influences activity related to the protection, nourishment, and growth of the body.

sympathetic system The subsystem of the autonomic nervous system that usually prepares the organism for vigorous activity.

the body for vigorous activity. When one part of the sympathetic system is stimulated, other parts are activated "in sympathy" with it (Gellhorn & Loofbourrow, 1963). For example, input from sympathetic neurons to the adrenal medulla causes that gland to dump norepinephrine and epinephrine into the bloodstream, thereby activating all sympathetic target organs (see Figure 13.3). The result is the **fight-or-flight syndrome,** a pattern of increased heart rate and blood pressure, rapid or irregular breathing, dilated pupils, perspiration, dry mouth, increased blood sugar, piloerection ("goose bumps"), and other changes that help prepare the body to combat or run from a threat.

The ANS is not directly connected to brain areas involved in consciousness, so sensations about organ activity reach the brain at a nonconscious level. You may hear your stomach grumble, but you can't actually feel it secrete acids. Similarly, you can't consciously experience the brain mechanisms that alter the activity of your autonomic nervous system. This is why most people cannot exert direct, conscious control over blood pressure or other aspects of ANS activity. However, there are things you can do that have indirect effects on the ANS. For example, to arouse autonomic innervation of your sex organs, you might imagine an erotic situation. And to raise your blood pressure, you might hold your breath or strain your muscles.

Theories of Emotion

How does all this activity in the brain and the autonomic nervous system relate to the emotions we actually experience? Are autonomic responses to events enough to *create* the experience of emotion, or are those responses the *result* of emotional experiences that begin in the brain? And how does our cognitive interpretation of events affect our emotional reactions to them? Psychologists have worked on the answers to these questions for over a century; in the process, they have developed a number of theories that explain emotion mainly in terms of biological or cognitive factors. The main biological theories are those of William James and Walter Cannon. The most prominent cognitive theories are those of Stanley Schachter and Richard Lazarus. In this section we review these theories, along with some research designed to evaluate them.

James's Peripheral Theory

Suppose you are camping in the woods when a huge bear approaches your tent. Scared to death, you run for dear life. Do you run because you are afraid, or are you afraid because you run? The example and the question come from William James, who offered one of the first formal accounts of how physiological responses relate to emotional experience. James argued that you are afraid *because* you run. Your running and other physiological responses, he said, follow directly from your perception of the bear. Without some form of these responses, you would feel no fear, because, said James, recognition of physiological responses *is* fear. Because James saw activity in the peripheral nervous system, not the central nervous system, as the cause of emotional experience, his theory is known as a *peripheral theory* of emotion.

On the surface, James's theory might seem preposterous. It defies common sense, which says that it would be silly to run from something unless you already fear it. James concluded otherwise after examining his own mental processes. He decided that once you strip away all physiological responses, nothing remains of the experience of an emotion (James, 1890). Emotion, he reasoned, must therefore be the result of experiencing a particular set of physiological responses. A similar argument was offered by Carle Lange, a Danish physician, so James's view is sometimes called the *James-Lange theory* of emotion.

fight-or-flight syndrome The physical reactions initiated by the sympathetic nervous system that prepare the body to fight or to run from a threatening situation.

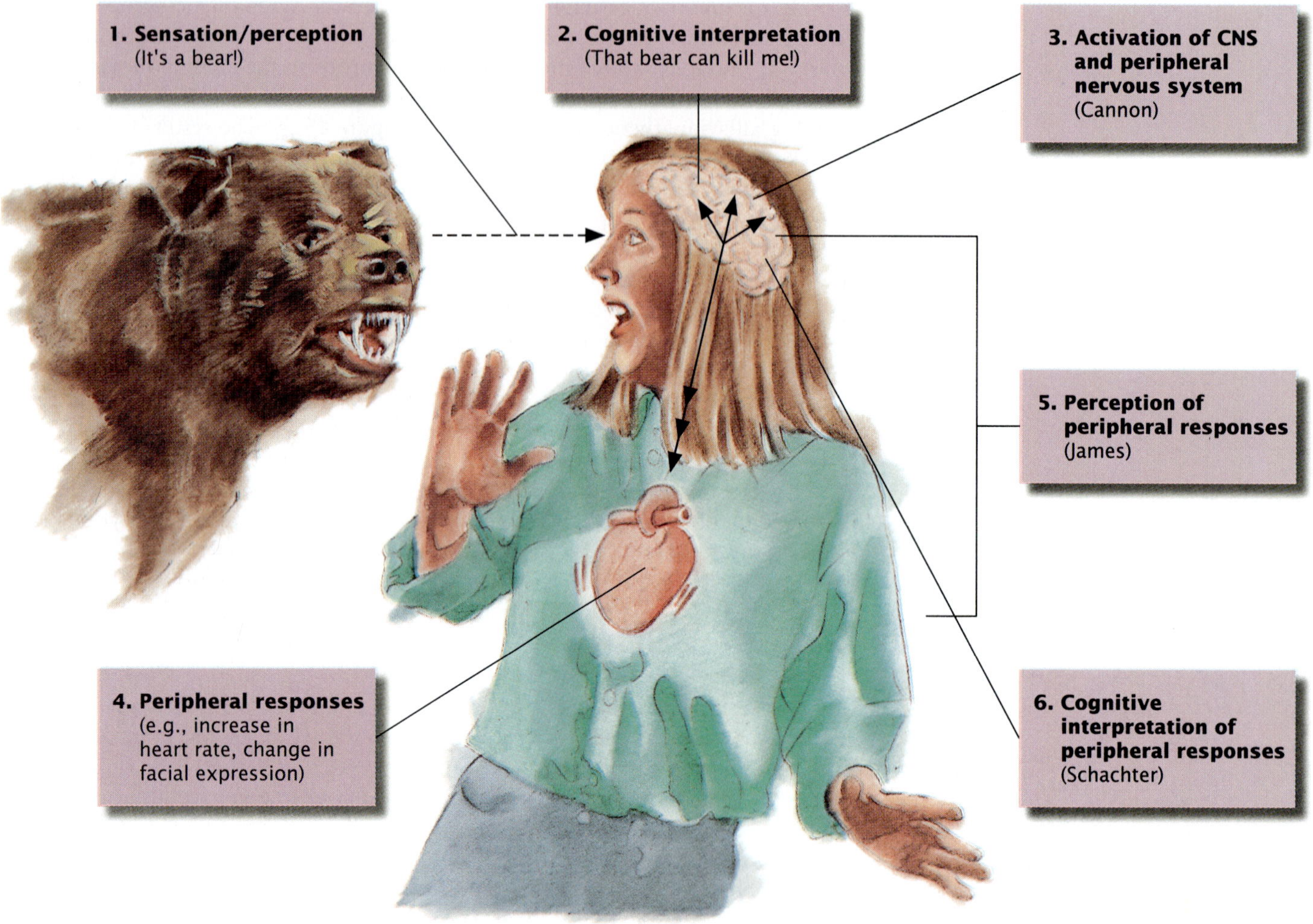

1. Sensation/perception
(It's a bear!)

2. Cognitive interpretation
(That bear can kill me!)

3. Activation of CNS and peripheral nervous system
(Cannon)

5. Perception of peripheral responses
(James)

4. Peripheral responses
(e.g., increase in heart rate, change in facial expression)

6. Cognitive interpretation of peripheral responses
(Schachter)

figure 11.12
Components of Emotion

Emotion is associated with activity in the central nervous system (the brain and spinal cord), with responses elsewhere in the body (called *peripheral* responses), and with cognitive interpretations of events. Different theories of emotion place differing emphasis on each of these components. William James emphasized the perception of peripheral responses, such as changes in heart rate. Walter Cannon asserted that emotion could occur entirely within the brain. Stanley Schachter emphasized cognitive factors, including how we interpret events and how we label our peripheral responses to them.

Observing Peripheral Responses Figure 11.12 outlines the components of emotional experience, including those emphasized by James. First, a perception affects the cerebral cortex, said James; "then quick as a flash, reflex currents pass down through their pre-ordained channels, alter the condition of muscle, skin, and viscus; and these alterations, perceived, like the original object, in as many portions of the cortex, combine with it in consciousness and transform it from an object-simply-apprehended into an object-emotionally-felt" (James, 1890, p. 759). In other words, the brain interprets a situation and automatically directs a particular set of peripheral physiological changes—a palpitating heart, sinking stomach, facial grimace, perspiration, and certain patterns of blood flow. We are not conscious of the process, said James, until we become aware of these bodily changes; at that point, we experience an emotion. In other words, James's theory holds that reflexive peripheral responses precede the subjective experience of emotion, and that each particular emotion is created by a particular pattern of physiological responses. For example, fear would follow from one pattern of bodily responses, and anger would follow from a different pattern.

Notice that according to James's view, there is no emotional experience generated by activity in the brain alone—no special "emotion center" in the brain where the firing of neurons creates a direct experience of emotion. If this theory is accurate, it might account for the difficulty we sometimes have in knowing our true feelings: We must figure out what emotions we feel by perceiving subtle differences in specific physiological response patterns.

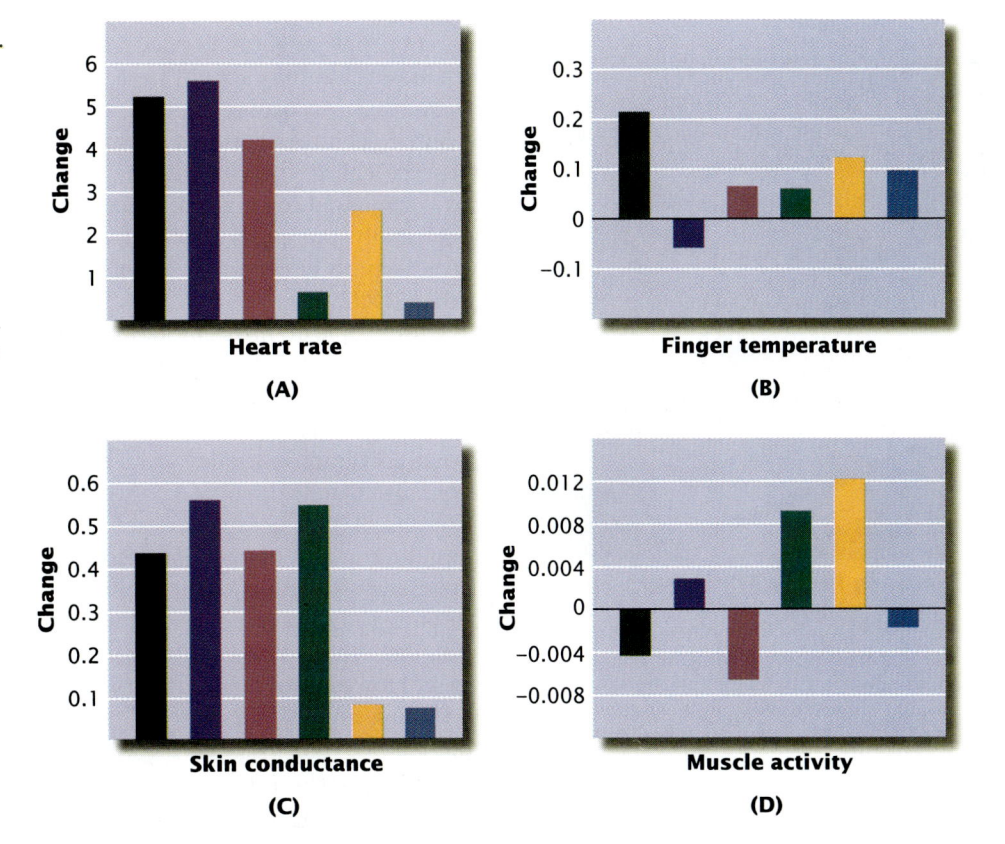

Evaluating James's Theory

There are more than five hundred labels for emotions in the English language (Averill, 1980). Does a distinctly different pattern of physiological activity precede each of these emotions? Research shows that certain emotional states are indeed associated with different patterns of autonomic changes (Damasio et al., 2000; Kelter & Buswell, 1996; Sinha & Parsons, 1996). For example, blood flow to the hands and feet increases in association with anger and declines in association with fear (Levenson, Ekman, & Friesen, 1990). So fear involves "cold feet"; anger does not. A pattern of activity associated with disgust includes increased muscle activity, but no change in heart rate. Even when people mentally re-live different kinds of emotional experiences, they show different patterns of autonomic activity (Ekman, Levenson, & Friesen, 1983). Such emotion-specific patterns of physiological activity have been found in widely different cultures (Levenson et al., 1992).

Furthermore, different patterns of autonomic activity are closely tied to specific emotional facial expressions, and vice versa (Ekman, 1993). In one study, when participants were told to make certain facial movements, autonomic changes occurred that resembled those normally accompanying emotion (Ekman, Levenson, & Friesen, 1983; see Figure 11.13). Almost all these participants also reported *feeling the emotion*—such as fear, anger, disgust, sadness, or happiness—associated with the expression they had created, even though they could not see their own expressions and did not realize that they had portrayed a specific emotion. Other studies, too, have shown that people feel emotions such as anger or sadness, for example, when simply making an "angry" or "sad" face. They can also ease these feelings just by relaxing their faces (Duclos & Laird, 2001). The emotional effects of this "face making" appear strongest in people who are the most sensitive to internal bodily cues. The emotions created by posed facial expressions can be significant enough to affect social judgments. Research participants who were asked to smile, for example, tended to form more positive impressions of other people than did those who received no special instructions (Ohira & Kurono, 1993).

figure 11.13

Patterns of Physiological Change Associated with Different Emotions

In this experiment, facial movements characteristic of different emotions produced different patterns of change in (A) heart rate; (B) peripheral blood flow, as measured by finger temperature; (C) skin conductance; and (D) muscle activity (Levenson, Ekman, & Friesen, 1990). For example, making an angry face caused heart rate and finger temperature to rise, whereas making a fearful face raised heart rate but lowered finger temperature.

Source: Levenson, Ekman, & Friesen (1990).

■ Anger   ■ Sadness   ■ Happiness
■ Fear   ■ Disgust   ■ Surprise

James's theory implies that the experience of emotion would be blocked if a person were unable to detect physiological changes occurring in the body's periphery. For example, spinal cord injuries that reduce feedback from peripheral responses should reduce the intensity of emotional experiences. This was the result reported in a study performed during the 1960s (Hohmann, 1966). More recently, however, studies have shown that when people with spinal injuries actively pursue their life goals, they experience a full range of emotions, including as much happiness as noninjured people (Bermond et al., 1991; Chwalisz, Diener, & Gallagher, 1988). These people report that their emotional experiences are just as intense as before their injuries, even though they notice less intense physiological changes associated with their emotions.

Such reports seem to contradict James's theory. But spinal cord injuries do not usually affect facial expressions, which James included among the bodily responses that are experienced as emotions. Some researchers have proposed a variant of James's theory, the *facial feedback hypothesis,* which maintains that involuntary facial movements provide enough peripheral information to create emotional experience (Ekman & Davidson, 1993). This hypothesis helps to explain why posed facial expressions generate the emotions normally associated with them. (The next time you want to cheer yourself up, it might help to smile—even though you don't feel like it.)

Lie Detection James's view that different patterns of physiological activity are associated with different emotions forms the basis for the lie detection industry. If people experience anxiety or guilt when they lie, specific patterns of physiological activity accompanying these emotions should be detectable on instruments, called *polygraphs,* that record heart rate, breathing, skin conductance (which is affected by slight changes in perspiration), and other autonomic responses.

To identify the perpetrator of a crime using the *control question test,* a polygraph operator may ask questions specific to the crime, such as "Did you stab anyone on July 3, 2002?" Responses to such *relevant questions* are then compared with responses to *control questions,* such as "Have you ever tried to hurt someone?" Innocent people might have tried to hurt someone at some time and might feel guilty when asked, but they should have no reason to feel guilty about what they did on July 3, 2002. Accordingly, an innocent person should have a stronger emotional response to control questions than to relevant questions (Rosenfeld, 1995). Another approach, called the *directed lie test,* compares a person's physiological reactions when asked to lie about something and when telling what is known to be the truth. Finally, the *guilty knowledge test* seeks to determine if a person reacts in a notable way to information about a crime that only the perpetrator would know (Lykken, 1992).

Most people do have emotional responses when they lie, but statistics about the accuracy of polygraphs are difficult to obtain. Estimates vary widely, from those suggesting that polygraphs detect 90 percent of guilty, lying individuals (Honts & Quick, 1995; Kircher, Horowitz, & Raskin, 1988; Raskin, 1986) to those suggesting that polygraphs mislabel as many as 40 percent of truthful, innocent persons as guilty liars (Ben-Shakhar & Furedy, 1990; Saxe & Ben-Shakhar, 1999). Obviously, the results of a polygraph test are not determined entirely by whether a person is telling the truth. What people think about the act of lying, and about the value of the test, can also influence the accuracy of its results. For example, people who consider lying to be acceptable—and who do not believe in the power of polygraphs—are unlikely to display emotion-related physiological responses while lying during the test. However, an innocent person who believes in such tests and who thinks that "everything always goes wrong" might show a large fear response when asked about a crime, thus wrongly suggesting guilt.

Polygraphs can catch some liars, but most researchers agree that a guilty person can "fool" a polygraph lie detector, and that some innocent people can be misla-

Searching for the Truth Polygraph tests are not foolproof, though they may intimidate people who believe that they are. In a small town where the police could not afford a polygraph, one guilty suspect confessed his crime when a "lie detector" consisting of a kitchen colander was placed on his head and attached by wires to a copy machine (Shepherd, Kohut, & Sweet, 1989).

beled as guilty (Lykken, 1998). Accordingly, a large majority of psychologists in the United States have expressed serious reservations about the use of polygraph tests to detect deception (Abeles, 1985; Iacono & Lykken, 1997) and do not support their use as evidence in court.

Cannon's Central Theory

For James, the experience of emotion depends on feedback from physiological responses occurring outside the brain, but Walter Cannon disagreed (Cannon, 1927/1987). According to Cannon, you feel fear at the sight of a wild bear even before you start to run because emotional experience starts in the central nervous system—specifically, in the thalamus, the brain structure that relays information from most sense organs to the cortex.

According to Cannon's *central theory* (also known as the *Cannon-Bard theory*, in recognition of Philip Bard's contribution), when the thalamus receives sensory information about emotional events and situations, it sends signals *simultaneously* to the autonomic nervous system and to the cerebral cortex, where the emotion becomes conscious. So when you see a bear, the brain receives sensory information about it, perceives it as a bear, and *directly* creates the experience of fear while at the same time sending messages to the heart, lungs, and muscles to do what it takes to run away. In other words, Cannon said that the experience of emotion appears directly in the brain, with or without feedback from peripheral responses (see Figure 11.12).

Updating Cannon's Theory

Research conducted since Cannon proposed his theory indicates that the thalamus is actually not the "seat" of emotion, but through its connections to the amygdala (see Figure 11.9), the thalamus does participate in some aspects of emotional processing (Lang, 1995). For example, studies in animals and humans show that the emotion of fear is generated by connections from the thalamus to the amygdala (Anderson & Phelps, 2000; LeDoux, 1995). The implication is that strong emotions can sometimes bypass the cortex without requiring conscious thought to activate them. One study showed, for example, that people presented with stimuli such as angry faces display physiological signs of arousal even if they are not conscious of seeing those stimuli (Morris et al., 1998). The same processes might explain why people find it so difficult to overcome an intense fear, or phobia, even though they may consciously know the fear is irrational.

An updated version of Cannon's theory suggests that specific brain areas produce the feelings of pleasure or pain associated with emotion. This idea arose from studies mentioned in the chapter on learning, showing that electrical stimulation of certain brain areas is rewarding. Researchers found that rats kept returning to the place in their cage where they received this kind of stimulation. When the animals were allowed to control delivery of the stimulation by pressing a bar, they pressed it until they were physically exhausted, ignoring even food and water (Olds & Milner, 1954). Stimulation of other brain regions is so unpleasant that animals work hard to avoid it. The areas of the brain in which stimulation is experienced as especially pleasurable include the dopamine systems, which are activated by drugs such as cocaine (Bardo, 1998). When animals are given drugs that block the action of dopamine, this kind of brain stimulation is no longer experienced as pleasurable (Wise & Rompre, 1989).

Presumably, part of the direct central experience of emotions involves areas of the brain whose activity is experienced as either pleasurable or aversive. The areas of the brain activated by the kind of events that elicit emotion in humans have widespread connections throughout the brain. Therefore, the central nervous system's experience of emotion is probably widely distributed, not narrowly localized in any one "emotion center" (Derryberry & Tucker, 1992). Still, there is evidence to support the main thrust of Cannon's theory: that emotion occurs through the activation of specific parts of the central nervous system. What Cannon did not foresee is that different parts of the central nervous system may be activated for different emotions and for different aspects of the total emotional experience.

Cognitive Theories

Suppose you are about to be interviewed for your first job, or go out on a blind date, or fly in a hot-air balloon for the first time. In such situations, it is not always easy to be sure of what you are feeling. Is it fear, excitement, anticipation, worry, happiness, dread, or what? Stanley Schachter suggested that the emotions we experience every day are shaped partly by how we interpret the arousal we feel. His cognitive theory of emotion, known as the *Schachter-Singer theory* in recognition of the contributions of Jerome Singer, took shape in the early 1960s, when many psychologists were raising questions about the validity of James's theory of emotion. Schachter argued that the theory was essentially correct—but required a few modifications (Cornelius, 1996). In Schachter's view, feedback about physiological changes may not vary enough to create the many subtle shades of emotion that people can experience. He argued instead that all these emotions emerge from a combination of feedback from peripheral responses and the *cognitive interpretation* of those responses, and of what caused them (Schachter & Singer, 1962). Cognitive interpretation first comes into play, said Schachter, when you perceive the stimulus that leads to bodily responses ("It's a bear!") and again when you identify feedback from those responses as a particular emotion (see Figure 11.12). The same physiological responses might be given many different labels, depending on how you interpret those responses. So, according to Schachter, the emotion you experience when that bear approaches your campsite might be fear, excitement, astonishment, or surprise, depending on how you label your bodily reactions to seeing it.

The labeling of arousal depends, in turn, on **attribution,** the process of identifying the cause of an event. People may attribute their physiological arousal to different emotions based on the information available about the situation. If you are watching the final seconds of a close ball game, you might attribute your racing heart, rapid breathing, and perspiration to excitement; but you might attribute the same physiological reactions to anxiety if you are waiting for a big exam to begin. Schachter predicted that our emotional experiences will be less intense if we attribute arousal to a nonemotional cause. So if you notice your heart pounding before an exam but say to yourself, "Sure my heart's pounding—I just drank five cups of coffee!" then you should feel "wired" from caffeine rather than afraid or worried. This prediction has received some support (Mezzacappa, Katkin, & Palmer, 1999; Sinclair et al., 1994), but other aspects of Schachter's theory have not.

Few researchers today fully accept the Schachter-Singer theory, but it did stimulate an enormous amount of valuable research, including studies of **transferred excitation,** a phenomenon in which physiological arousal from one experience carries over to affect emotion in an independent situation (Reisenzein, 1983; Zillman, 1984). For example, people who have been aroused by physical exercise become more angry when provoked, or experience more intense sexual feelings when in the company of an attractive person, than do people who have been less physically active (Allen et al., 1989). This transfer is most likely to occur when the overt signs of physiological arousal have subsided but the sympathetic nervous system is still active. In one study, people were emotionally "primed" by reading words that were cheerful, neutral, or depressing. Next, they either engaged in physical exercise or sat quietly and then rated their mood, either immediately or after a short delay. Those who had not exercised, as well as those who rated themselves immediately after exercise, reported being in no particular mood. However, the mood of those whose reports came several minutes after exercising tended to be positive, neutral, or negative, depending on which priming words they had read earlier. Apparently, the

attribution The process of explaining the causes of an event.

transferred excitation The process of carrying over arousal from one experience to an independent situation.

people in this latter group were still somewhat aroused; but because the delay had been long enough to keep them from attributing their lingering arousal to exercise, they instead used the emotional tone of the word list as a guide to labeling their mood (Sinclair et al., 1994).

Schachter's theory also led to the development of theories emphasizing the role of other cognitive processes in emotion (Cornelius, 1996). Schachter focused on the cognitive interpretation of our *bodily responses* to events, but other theorists have argued that it is our cognitive interpretation of *events themselves* that are most important in shaping emotional experiences. For example, as we mentioned earlier, a person's emotional reaction to receiving exam results can depend partly whether the score is seen as a sign of improvement or a grade worthy of shame. According to Richard Lazarus's (1966, 1991) *cognitive appraisal* theory of emotion, these differing reactions can be best explained by how we think exam scores, job interviews, blind dates, bear sightings, and other events will affect our personal well-being. According to Lazarus, the process of cognitive appraisal, or evaluation, begins when we decide whether or not an event is relevant to our well-being; that is, do we even care about it? If we don't, as might be the case if an exam doesn't count toward our grade, we are unlikely to have an emotional experience when we get the results. If the event *is* relevant to our well-being, we will experience an emotional reaction to it. That reaction will be positive or negative, said Lazarus, depending on whether we appraise the event as advancing our personal goals or obstructing them. The *specific* emotion we experience depends on our individual goals, needs, standards, expectations, and past experiences. As a result, a particular exam score can create contentment in one person, elation in another, mild disappointment in someone else, and despair in yet another. Individual differences in goals and standards are at work, too, when a second-place finisher in a marathon race experiences bitter disappointment at having "lost," while someone at the back of the pack may be thrilled just to have completed the race alive.

"In Review: Theories of Emotion" summarizes key elements of the theories we have discussed. It appears that both peripheral autonomic responses (including facial responses) and the cognitive interpretation of those responses add to emotional experience. So does cognitive appraisal of events themselves. In addition, the brain can apparently generate emotional experience on its own, independent of

in review: Theories of Emotion

Theory	Source of Emotions	Example
James-Lange	Emotions are created by awareness of specific patterns of peripheral (autonomic) responses.	Anger is associated with increased blood flow in the hands and feet; fear is associated with decreased blood flow in these areas.
Cannon-Bard	The brain generates direct experiences of emotion.	Stimulation of certain brain areas can create pleasant or unpleasant emotions.
Cognitive (Schachter-Singer and Lazarus)	Cognitive interpretation of events, and of physiological reactions to them, shapes emotional experiences.	Autonomic arousal can be experienced as anxiety or excitement, depending on how it is labeled. A single event can lead to different emotions, depending on whether it is perceived as threatening or challenging.

physiological arousal. In short, emotion is probably both in the heart and in the head (including the face). The most basic emotions probably occur directly within the brain, whereas the many shades of discernible emotions probably arise from attributions and other cognitive interpretations of physiological responses and environmental events. No theory has completely resolved the issue of which, if any, component of emotion is primary. However, the theories we have discussed have helped psychologists better understand how these components interact to produce emotional experience. Cognitive appraisal theories, in particular, have been especially useful in studying and treating stress-related emotional problems (see the chapters on health, stress, and coping; psychological disorders; and treatment of psychological disorders).

Communicating Emotion

Imagine a woman watching television. You can see her face, but not what she sees on the screen. She might be engaged in complex thought, perhaps comparing her investments with those of the experts on *Wall Street Week*. Or she might be thinking of nothing at all as she loses herself in a rerun of *The Drew Carey Show*. In other words, your observation is not likely to tell you much about what the woman is thinking. If the television program creates an emotional experience, however, you will be able to make a reasonably accurate guess about which emotion she feels just by looking at the expression on her face. So far, we have described emotion from the inside, as people experience their own emotions. In this section, we examine the social organization of emotion—how people communicate emotions to one another.

Humans communicate emotions partly through tone of voice and body posture or movement, but mainly through facial movements and expressions. The human face can create thousands of different expressions (Zajonc, 1998), and people are good at detecting them. Observers can notice even tiny facial movements—a twitch of the mouth or eyebrow can carry a lot of information. Females consistently

TRY THIS What Are They Feeling? People's emotions are usually "written on their faces." Jot down the emotions you think these people are feeling, and then look at the footnote on page 426 to see how well you "read" their emotions.

outperform males in identifying and interpreting the nonverbal emotion cues conveyed by facial expressions (Hall, 1984). This gender difference also appears in adolescents, children, and even infants (McClure, 2000), suggesting that it may be rooted in biology as well as in gender-specific socialization. Are emotional facial expressions innate as well, or are they learned? And how are they used in communicating emotion?

Innate Expressions of Emotion

Charles Darwin observed that some facial expressions seem to be universal (Darwin, 1872/1965). He proposed that these expressions are genetically determined, passed on biologically from one generation to the next. The facial expressions seen today, said Darwin, are those that have been most effective at telling others something about how a person is feeling. If someone is scowling with teeth clenched, for example, you will probably assume that he or she is angry, and you will be unlikely to choose that particular moment to ask for a loan.

Infants provide one source of evidence that some facial expressions are innate. Newborns do not need to be taught to grimace in pain or to smile in pleasure or to blink when startled (Balaban, 1995). Even blind infants, who cannot imitate adults' expressions, show the same emotional expressions as do sighted infants (Goodenough, 1932).

A second line of evidence for innate facial expressions comes from studies showing that for the most basic emotions, people in all cultures show similar facial responses to similar emotional stimuli (Hejmadi, Davidson, & Rozin, 2000; Zajonc, 1998). Participants in these studies look at photographs of people's faces and then try to name the emotion each person is feeling. The pattern of facial movements we call a smile, for example, is universally related to positive emotions. Sadness is almost always accompanied by slackened muscle tone and a "long" face. Likewise, in almost all cultures, people contort their faces in a similar way when shown something they find disgusting. And a furrowed brow is frequently associated with frustration (Ekman, 1994).

Anger is also linked with a facial expression recognized by almost all cultures. One study examined artwork—including ceremonial masks—of various Western and non-Western cultures (Aronoff, Barclay, & Stevenson, 1988). The angry, threatening masks of all eighteen cultures contained similar elements, such as triangular eyes and diagonal lines on the cheeks. In particular, angular and diagonal elements carry the impression of threat (see Figure 11.14). One study with high school students found that threat is conveyed most strongly by the eyebrows, followed by the mouth and eyes (Lundqvist, Esteves, & Öhman, 1999).

The Universal Smile The idea that some emotional expressions are innate is supported by the fact that the facial movement pattern we call a smile is related to happiness, pleasure, and other positive emotions in human cultures throughout the world.

Social and Cultural Influences on Emotional Expression

Whereas some basic emotional expressions are innate, many others are neither innate nor universal (Ekman, 1993). Even innate expressions are flexible and modifiable, changing as necessary in the social contexts within which they occur (Fernández-Dols & Ruiz-Belda, 1995). For example, facial expressions become more intense and change more frequently while people are imagining social scenes as opposed to solitary scenes (Fridlund et al., 1990). Similarly, facial expressions in response to odors tend to be more intense when others are watching than when people are alone (Jancke & Kaufmann, 1994).

Further, although a core of emotional responses is recognized by all cultures (Hejmadi, Davidson, & Rozin, 2000), there is a certain degree of cultural variation in recognizing some emotions (Russell, 1995). In one study, for example, Japanese and North American people agreed about which facial expressions signaled happiness, surprise, and sadness, but they frequently disagreed about which faces showed anger, disgust, and fear (Matsumoto & Ekman, 1989). Members of preliterate cultures, such as the Fore of New Guinea, agree even less with people in Western cultures on the labeling of facial expressions (Russell, 1994). In addition, there are variations in how people in different cultures interpret emotions expressed by tone of voice (Mesquita & Frijda, 1992). For instance, Taiwanese participants were best at recognizing a sad tone of voice, whereas Dutch participants were best at recognizing happy tones (Van Bezooijen, Otto, & Heenan, 1983).

People learn how to express certain emotions in particular ways, as specified by cultural rules. Suppose you say, "I just bought a new car," and all your friends stick their tongues out at you. In North America, this would mean that they are envious or resentful. But in some regions of China, such a display expresses surprise.

Even smiles can vary as people learn to use them to communicate certain feelings. Paul Ekman and his colleagues categorized seventeen types of smiles, including "false smiles," which fake enjoyment, and "masking smiles," which hide unhappiness. They called the smile that occurs with real happiness the *Duchenne* (pronounced "do-SHEN") *smile,* after the French researcher who first noticed a difference between spontaneous, happy smiles and posed smiles. A genuine, Duchenne smile includes contractions of the muscles around the eyes (creating a distinctive wrinkling of the skin in these areas), as well as of the muscles that raise the lips and cheeks. Few people can successfully contract the muscles around the eyes during a posed smile, so this feature can be used to distinguish "lying smiles" from genuine ones (Frank, Ekman, & Friesen, 1993). In one study, the Duchenne smile was highly correlated with reports of positive emotions experienced while people watched a movie, as well as with a pattern of brain waves known to be associated with positive emotions. These relationships did not appear for other types of smiles (Ekman, Davidson, & Friesen, 1990).

Learning About Emotions The effects of learning are seen in a child's growing range of emotional expressions. Although infants begin with an innate set of emotional responses, they soon learn to imitate facial expressions and use them for more and more emotions. In time, these expressions become more precise and personalized, so that a particular expression conveys a clear emotional message to anyone who knows that person well.

If facial expressions become *too* personalized, however, no one will know what the expressions mean. Operant shaping (described in the chapter on learning)

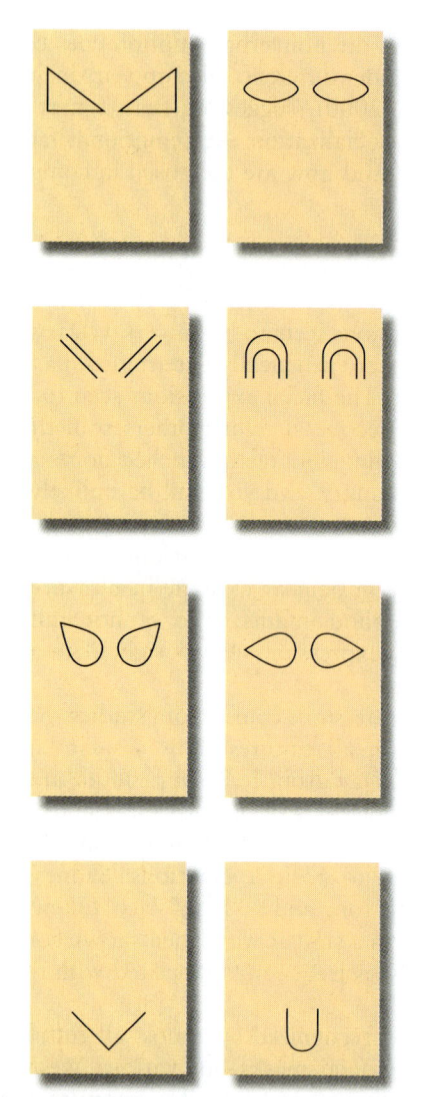

figure 11.14

Elements of Ceremonial Facial Masks That Convey Threat

Certain geometric patterns are common to threatening masks in many cultures. When people in various cultures were asked which member of each of these pairs was more threatening, they consistently chose those, shown here on the left, containing triangular and diagonal elements. "Scary" Halloween pumpkins tend to have such elements as well.

The people pictured on page 424 were waiting to hear whether Chile's former dictator Augusto Pinochet would be brought to trial in Britain for torturing their relatives in Chilean prisons. Their emotions probably included anxiety, worry, dread, uncertainty, excitement, hope, and perhaps anger. Pinochet was allowed to return to Chile, where he was found mentally unfit to stand trial.

probably helps keep emotional expressions within certain limits. If you could not see other people's facial expressions or observe their responses to yours, you might show fewer, or less intense, facial signs of emotion. Indeed, as congenitally blind people grow older, their facial expressions tend to become less animated (Izard, 1977).

As children grow, they learn an *emotion culture*—rules that govern what emotions are appropriate in what circumstances and what emotional expressions are allowed. These rules can vary from culture to culture. For example, TV news cameras showed that men in the U.S. military leaving for duty in Kosovo in 1999 tended to keep their emotions in check as they said goodbye to wives, girlfriends, and parents. However, in Italy—where mother-son ties are particularly strong—many male soldiers wailed with dismay and wept openly as they left. In a laboratory study, when viewing a distressing movie with a group of peers, Japanese students exhibited much more control over their facial expressions than did North American students. When they watched the film while alone, however, the Japanese students' faces showed the same emotional expressions as those of the North American students (Ekman, Friesen, & Ellsworth, 1972).

Emotion cultures shape how people describe and categorize feelings, resulting in both similarities and differences across cultures (Russell, 1991). At least five of the seven basic emotions listed in an ancient Chinese book called the *Li Chi*—joy, anger, sadness, fear, love, disliking, and liking—are considered primary emotions by most Western theorists. Yet while English has over five hundred emotion-related words, some emotion words in other languages have no English equivalent. The Czech word *litost* apparently has no English word equivalent: "It designates a feeling as infinite as an open accordion, a feeling that is the synthesis of many others: grief, sympathy, remorse, and an indefinable longing" (quoted in Russell, 1991). The Japanese word *ijirashii* also has no English equivalent; it describes the feeling of seeing a praiseworthy person overcoming an obstacle (Russell, 1991).

Similarly, other cultures have no equivalent for some English emotion words. Many cultures do not see anger and sadness as different, for example. The Ilongot, a Philippine head-hunting group, have only one word, *liget,* for both anger and grief (Russell, 1991). Tahitians have words for forty-six different types of anger, but no word for sadness and, apparently, no concept of it. One Westerner described a Tahitian man as sad over separation from his wife and child, but the man himself felt *pe'a pe'a*—a generic word for feeling ill, troubled, or fatigued—and did not attribute it to the separation.

Social Referencing

Facial expressions, tone of voice, body postures, and gestures not only communicate information about the emotion someone is experiencing; they can also influence others' behavior, especially the behavior of people who are not sure what to do. An inexperienced chess player, for instance, might reach out to move the queen, catch sight of a spectator's grimace, and infer that another move would be better. The process of letting another person's emotional state guide our own behavior is called **social referencing** (Campos, 1980).

The visual-cliff studies described in the chapter on perception have been used to create an uncertain situation for infants. To reach its mother, an infant in these experiments must cross the visual cliff (see Figure 5.25). If the apparent drop-off is very small or very large, there is no question about what to do; a one-year-old knows to crawl across in the first case and to stay put in the second case. However, if the apparent drop-off is shallow enough (say, two feet) to create uncertainty, the infant relies on its mother's facial expression to decide what to do. In one study, mothers were asked to make either a fearful or a happy face. When the mothers made a fearful face, no infant crossed the glass floor. But when they posed a happy face, most infants crossed (Sorce et al., 1981). Here is yet another example of the adaptive value of sending, and receiving, emotional communications.

social referencing A phenomenon in which other people's facial expressions, tone of voice, and bodily gestures serve as guidelines for how to proceed in uncertain situations.

LINKAGES

As noted in the chapter on introducing psychology, all of psychology's subfields are related to one another. Our discussion of conflicting motives and stress illustrates just one way in which the topic of this chapter, motivation and emotion, is linked to the subfield of health psychology (which is discussed in the chapter on health, stress, and coping). The Linkages diagram shows ties to two other subfields as well, and there are many more ties throughout the book. Looking for linkages among sub-fields will help you see how they fit together and help you better appreciate the big picture that is psychology.

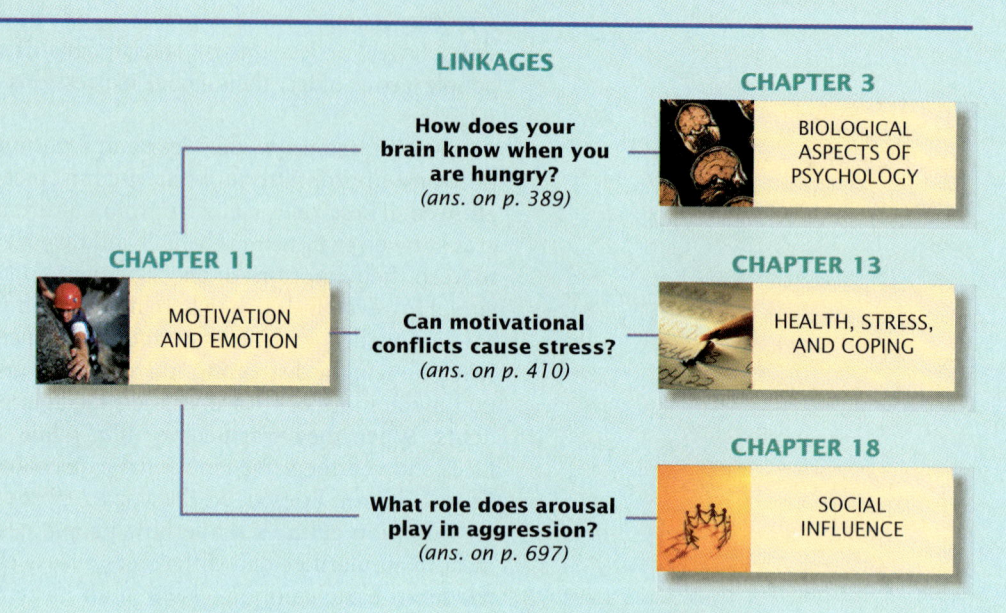

LINKAGES

CHAPTER 11 — MOTIVATION AND EMOTION

- How does your brain know when you are hungry? (ans. on p. 389) → **CHAPTER 3** BIOLOGICAL ASPECTS OF PSYCHOLOGY
- Can motivational conflicts cause stress? (ans. on p. 410) → **CHAPTER 13** HEALTH, STRESS, AND COPING
- What role does arousal play in aggression? (ans. on p. 697) → **CHAPTER 18** SOCIAL INFLUENCE

SUMMARY

Motivation refers to factors that influence the initiation, direction, intensity, and persistence of behavior. Emotion and motivation are often linked: Motivation can influence emotion, and people are often motivated to seek certain emotions.

Concepts and Theories of Motivation

Focusing on a *motive* often reveals a single theme within apparently diverse behaviors. Motivation is said to be an intervening variable, a way of linking various stimuli to the behaviors that follow them.

Sources of Motivation

The many sources of motivation fall into four categories: biological factors, emotional factors, cognitive factors, and social factors.

Instinct Theory and Its Descendants

An early argument held that motivation follows from *instincts*, which are automatic, involuntary, and unlearned behavior patterns consistently "released" by particular stimuli. Modern versions of *instinct theory* are seen in evolutionary accounts of helping, aggression, mate selection, and other aspects of social behavior.

Drive Reduction Theory

Drive reduction theory is based on *homeostasis*, a tendency to maintain equilibrium in a physical or behavioral process. When disruption of equilibrium creates a *need* of some kind, people are motivated to reduce the resulting *drive* by behaving in some way that satisfies the need and restores balance. *Primary drives* are unlearned; *secondary drives* are learned.

Arousal Theory

According to *arousal theories* of motivation, people are motivated to behave in ways that maintain a level of *arousal* that is optimal for their functioning.

Incentive Theory

Incentive theory highlights behaviors that are motivated by attaining desired stimuli (positive incentives) and avoiding undesirable ones (negative incentives).

Hunger and Eating

Hunger and eating are controlled by a complex mix of learning, culture, and biology.

Biological Signals for Hunger and Satiety

The desire to eat *(hunger)* or to stop eating *(satiety)* depends primarily on signals from blood-borne substances such as cholecystokinin (CCK), glucose, insulin, and leptin.

Hunger and the Brain

Activity in the ventromedial nucleus of the hypothalamus results in satiety, whereas activity in the lateral hypothalamus results in hunger. These brain regions might be acting together to maintain a set point of body weight, but control of eating is more complex than that. For example, a variety of neurotransmitters act in various regions of the hypothalamus to create hunger for specific types of foods.

Flavor, Cultural Learning, and Food Selection

Eating may also be influenced by the flavor of food and by appetite for the pleasure of food. Food selection is influenced by biological needs (specific hungers) for certain nutrients, as well as by food cravings, social contexts, and cultural traditions.

Eating Disorders

Obesity has been linked to overconsumption of certain kinds of foods, to low energy metabolism, and to genetic factors. People suffering from *anorexia nervosa* starve themselves to avoid becoming fat. Those who suffer from *bulimia nervosa* engage in binge eating, followed by purging through self-induced vomiting or laxatives.

Sexual Behavior

Sexual motivation and behavior result from a rich interplay of biology and culture.

The Biology of Sex

Sexual stimulation generally produces a stereotyped *sexual response cycle*, a pattern of physiological arousal during and after sexual activity. *Sex hormones*, which include male hormones *(androgens)* and female hormones *(estrogens* and *progestins)*, occur in different relative amounts in both sexes. They can have organizational effects, such as physical differences in the brain, and activational effects, such as increased desire for sex.

Social and Cultural Factors in Sexuality

Gender-role learning and educational experiences are examples of cultural factors that can bring about variations in sexual attitudes and behaviors.

Sexual Orientation

Sexual orientation—*heterosexual, homosexual,* or *bisexual*—is increasingly viewed as a sociocultural variable that affects many other aspects of behavior and mental processes. Though undoubtedly shaped by a lifetime of learning, sexual orientation appears to have strong biological roots.

Sexual Dysfunctions

Common male *sexual dysfunctions* include erectile disorder and premature ejaculation. Females may experience such problems as arousal disorder.

Achievement Motivation

People gain esteem from achievement in many areas, including the workplace.

Need for Achievement

The motive to succeed is called *need achievement*. Individuals with high achievement motivation strive for excellence, persist despite failures, and set challenging but realistic goals.

Goal Setting and Achievement Motivation

Goals influence motivation, especially the amount of effort, persistence, attention, and planning we devote to a task.

Achievement and Success in the Workplace

Workers are most satisfied when they are working toward their own goals and are getting concrete feedback. Jobs that offer clear and specific goals, a variety of tasks, individual responsibility, and other intrinsic rewards are the most motivating.

Achievement and Subjective Well-Being

People tend to have a characteristic level of happiness, or *subjective well-being*, which is not necessarily related to the attainment of money, status, or other material goals.

Relations and Conflicts Among Motives

Human behavior reflects many motives, some of which may be in conflict. Abraham Maslow proposed a hierarchy of five classes of human motives, from meeting basic biological needs to attaining a state of self-actualization. Motives at the lowest levels, according to Maslow, must be at least partially satisfied before people can be motivated by higher-level goals.

Opponent Processes, Motivation, and Emotion

Motivated behavior sometimes gives rise to opponent emotional processes, such as the fear and excitement associated with a roller coaster ride. Opponent-process theory illustrates the close link between motivation and emotion.

The Nature of Emotion

Defining Characteristics

An *emotion* is a temporary experience with positive or negative qualities that is felt with some intensity as happening to the self, is generated in part by a cognitive appraisal of a situation, and is accompanied by both learned and reflexive physical responses.

The Biology of Emotion

Several brain mechanisms are involved in emotion. The amygdala, in the limbic system, is deeply involved in various aspects of emotion. The expression of emotion through involuntary facial movement is controlled by the extrapyramidal motor system. Voluntary facial movements are controlled by the pyramidal motor system. The brain's right and left hemispheres play somewhat different roles in emotional expression. In addition to specific brain mechanisms, both branches of the autonomic nervous system, the *sympathetic system* and the *parasympathetic system*, are involved in physiological changes that accompany emotional activation. The *fight-or-flight syndrome*, for example, follows from activation of the sympathetic system.

Theories of Emotion

James's Peripheral Theory
William James's theory of emotion holds that peripheral physiological responses are the primary source of emotion and that self-observation of these responses constitutes emotional experience. James's theory is supported by evidence that, at least for several basic emotions, physiological responses are distinguishable enough for emotions to be generated in this way. Distinct facial expressions are linked to particular patterns of physiological change.

Cannon's Central Theory
Walter Cannon's theory of emotion proposes that emotional experience occurs independent of peripheral physiological responses and that there is a direct experience of emotion based on activity of the central nervous system. Updated versions of this theory suggest that various parts of the central nervous system may be involved in different emotions and different aspects of emotional experience. Some pathways in the brain, such as that from the thalamus to the amygdala, allow strong emotions to occur before conscious thought can take place. And specific parts of the brain appear to be responsible for the feelings of pleasure or pain in emotion.

Cognitive Theories
Stanley Schachter's modification of James's theory proposes that physiological responses are primary sources of emotion but that the cognitive labeling of those responses—a process that depends partly on *attribution*—strongly influences the emotions we experience. Schachter's theory stimulated research on *transferred excitation*. Other cognitive theories, such as that of Richard Lazarus, emphasize that emotional experience depends heavily on how we think about the situations and events we encounter.

Communicating Emotion

Humans communicate emotions mainly through facial movement and expressions, but also through voice tones and bodily movements.

Innate Expressions of Emotion
Charles Darwin suggested that certain facial expressions of emotion are innate and universal and that these expressions evolved because they effectively communicate one creature's emotional condition to other creatures. Some facial expressions of basic emotions do appear to be innate. Even blind infants smile when happy and frown when experiencing discomfort. And certain facial movements are universally associated with certain emotions.

Social and Cultural Influences on Emotional Expression
Many emotional expressions are learned, and even innate expressions are modified by learning and social contexts. As children grow, they learn an emotion culture, the rules of emotional expression appropriate to their culture. Accordingly, the same emotion may be communicated by different facial expressions in different cultures. Especially in ambiguous situations, other people's emotional expressions may serve as a guide about what to do or what not to do, a phenomenon called *social referencing*.

Human Development

12

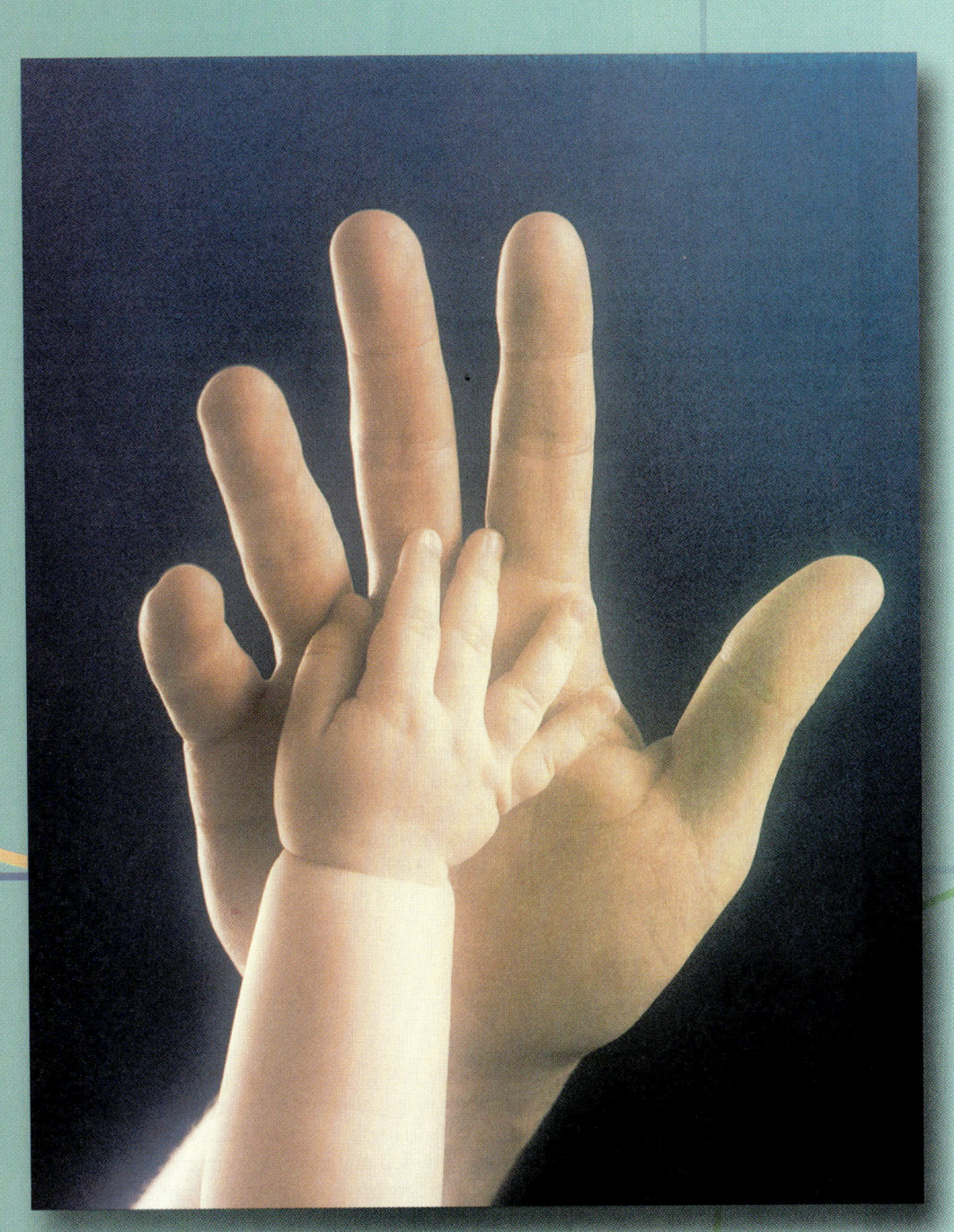

Exploring Human Development

Beginnings
Prenatal Development
The Newborn

Infancy and Childhood: Cognitive Development
Changes in the Brain
The Development of Knowledge: Piaget's Theory

Focus on Research Methods: Experiments on Developing Minds
Modifying Piaget's Theory
Information Processing During Childhood

Linkages: Development and Memory
Culture and Cognitive Development
Variations in Cognitive Development

Infancy and Childhood: Social and Emotional Development
Individual Temperament
The Infant Grows Attached

Thinking Critically: Does Day Care Harm the Emotional Development of Infants?
Relationships with Parents and Peers
Social Skills
Gender Roles
Risk and Resilience

Adolescence
The Challenges of Change
Identity and Development of the Self
Abstract Thought and Moral Reasoning

Adulthood
Physical Changes
Cognitive Changes
Social Changes
Death and Dying
Longevity

Linkages

Summary

Santee, California; Littleton, Colorado; Springfield, Oregon; Jonesboro, Arkansas; West Paducah, Kentucky; Edinboro, Pennsylvania; Bethel, Alaska; Pearl, Mississippi; and Taber, Alberta. These towns have shared a common tragedy—the shooting deaths of students and teachers at local schools. Overall, the number of school homicides has been dropping, but that statistic is of little solace to the friends and families of the fifty-one people who were killed and the sixty-eight others who were injured in these school shooting sprees. With each new tragedy the cry became louder: *Why do these things happen?* All the killers were boys, ranging in age from eleven to eighteen. Had they watched too many violent movies and television programs? Were their actions the fault of a "gun culture" that allows children access to firearms? Had they been victims of abuse and neglect? Were their parents too strict—or not strict enough? Did they come from "broken homes," or had they witnessed violence within their own families? Did they behave violently because they were going through a difficult "stage," because they had not been taught right from wrong, because they wanted to impress their peers, because males are more aggressive in general, or because their brains were "defective"? Were they just "bad kids"?

These are the kinds of questions developmental psychologists try to answer. They investigate when certain behaviors first appear and how they change with age. They explore how development in one area, such as moral reasoning, relates to development in other areas, such as aggressive behavior. They attempt to discover whether most people develop at the same rate and, if not, whether slow starters ever catch up to early bloomers. They ask why some children become well-adjusted, socially competent, nurturant, and empathic individuals, whereas others become murderers, and why some adolescents go on to win honors in college, whereas others drop out of high school. They seek to explain how development throughout the life span is affected by both genetics and the environment, analyzing the extent to which development is a product of what we arrive with at birth (our inherited, biological *nature*) and the extent to which it is a product of what the world provides (the *nurture* of the environment). And they pursue development into adulthood, examining the changes that occur over the years and determining how these changes are related to earlier abilities and later events. In short, **developmental psychology** is concerned with the course and causes of developmental changes over a person's lifetime.

In this chapter we examine many such changes. We begin by describing the physical and biological changes that occur from the moment of conception to the time a child is born. Then we discuss cognitive, social, and emotional development during infancy and childhood. Next, we examine the changes and challenges that confront humans during their adolescence. And we conclude by considering the significant physical, intellectual, and social changes that occur as people move through early, middle, and late adulthood.

Exploring Human Development

The question of whether development is the result of nature or nurture was the subject of philosophical debate centuries before psychologists began studying it scientifically. In essays published in the 1690s, British philosopher John Locke argued for nurture. He believed that experiences provided by the environment during childhood have a profound and permanent effect. As mentioned in the chapter that introduced psychology, Locke thought of the newborn as a blank slate, or *tabula rasa*. Adults write on that slate, he said, as they teach children about the world and how to behave in it. Some seventy years later, French philosopher Jean-Jacques Rousseau made the opposite argument. He claimed that children are capable of discovering how the world operates and how they should behave without instruction from adults, and he advocated letting children grow as their natures dictate, with little guidance or pressure from parents.

developmental psychology The psychological specialty that documents the course of social, emotional, moral, and intellectual development over the life span.

maturation Natural growth or change that unfolds in a fixed sequence relatively independent of the environment.

figure 12.1

Motor Development

When did you start walking? The left end of each bar indicates the age at which 25 percent of the infants tested were able to perform the behavior; 50 percent of the babies were performing the behavior at the age indicated by the vertical line in the bars; the right end indicates the age at which 90 percent could do so (Frankenberg & Dodds, 1967). Although different infants, especially in different cultures, achieve milestones of motor development at slightly different ages, all infants—regardless of their ethnicity, social class, or temperament—achieve them in the same order.

A Deadly Child Andrew Golden was barely out of diapers when he was given camouflage clothing and taught to fire a hunting rifle. In March 1998, at the age of eleven, he and his thirteen-year-old friend Mitchell Johnson used their shooting skills to kill four classmates and a teacher at their elementary school in Jonesboro, Arkansas. Many youngsters learn to hunt; what led these two to commit murder? Researchers in developmental psychology are studying the genetic and environmental factors that underlie the emergence of violent aggression and many other patterns of behavior and mental processes.

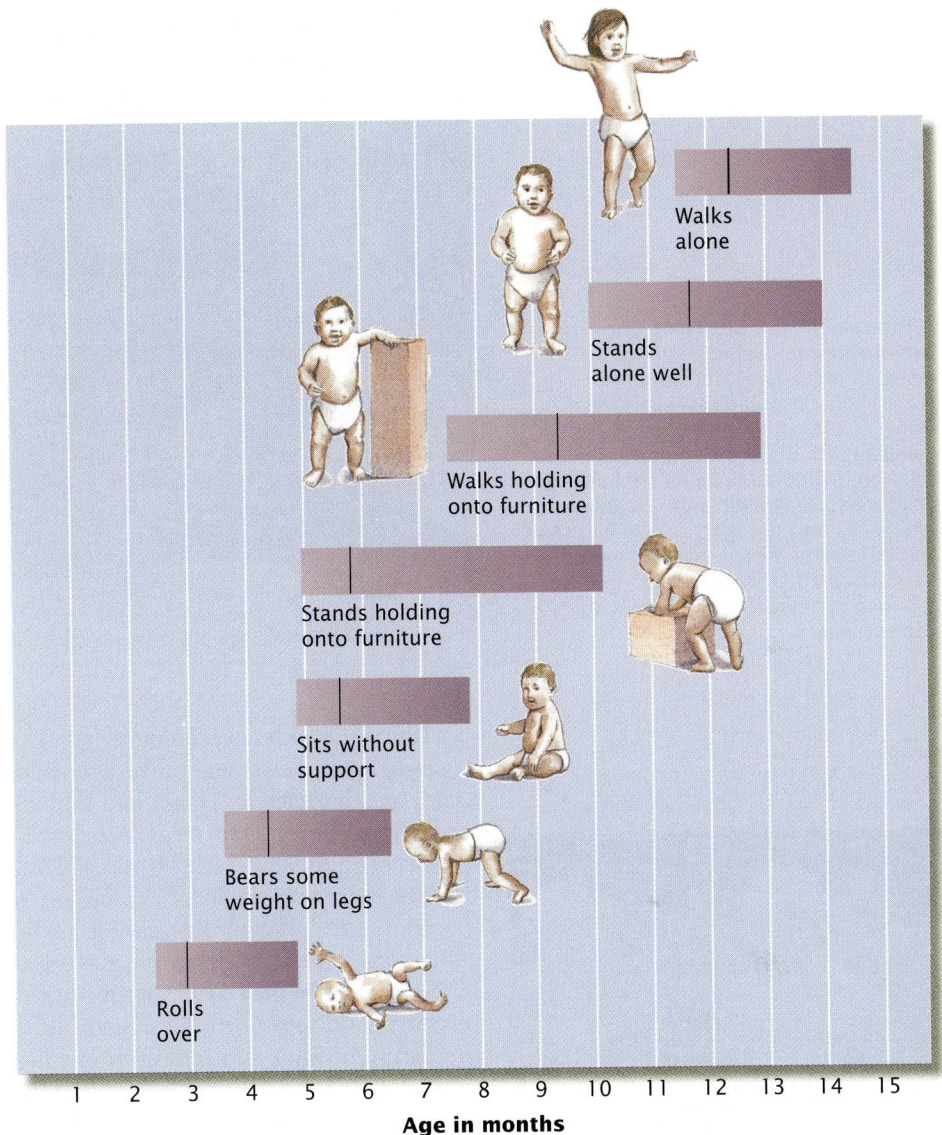

The first psychologist to systematically investigate the role of nature in behavior was Arnold Gesell. In the early 1900s, Gesell (pronounced "geh-ZELL") observed many children of all ages. He found that their motor skills, such as standing and walking, picking up a cube, and throwing a ball, developed in a fixed sequence of stages, as Figure 12.1 illustrates. The order of the stages and the age at which they develop, he suggested, are determined by nature and relatively unaffected by nurture. Only under extreme conditions, such as famine, war, or poverty, he claimed, are children thrown off their biologically programmed timetable. Gesell referred to this type of natural growth or change, which unfolds in a fixed sequence relatively independent of the environment, as **maturation**. The broader term *development* encompasses not only maturation but also the behavioral and mental processes that are due to learning.

John B. Watson, founder of the behaviorist approach to psychology, disagreed with Gesell. He claimed that the environment, not nature, molds and shapes development. Early in the twentieth century Watson began conducting experiments with children. From these experiments he inferred that children learn everything, from skills to fears.

A Pioneer in the Study of Cognitive Development Using a variety of research procedures, including his remarkable observational skills, Jean Piaget (1896–1980) investigated the development of cognitive processes in children, including his own son and daughters. He wove his observations and inferences into the most comprehensive and influential theory that had yet been formulated about how thought and knowledge develop from infancy to adolescence.

A Tiger in Training Human behavior develops as a function of both heredity and environment—of both nature and nurture. The joint and inseparable influence of these two factors in development is nicely illustrated in the case of professional golfer Tiger Woods, shown here as a youngster with his father, who not only provided some of Tiger's genes but also served as his golf teacher.

It was the Swiss psychologist Jean Piaget (pronounced "p-ah-ZHAY") who first suggested that nature and nurture work together, and that their influences are inseparable and interactive. Piaget had a lifelong interest in human intellectual and cognitive development. His ideas, presented in numerous books and articles published from the 1920s until his death in 1980, influenced the field of developmental psychology more than those of any other person before or since (Flavell, 1996).

Most developmental psychologists now accept the idea that nature and nurture contribute jointly to development—in two ways. First, they operate together to make all people alike as human beings. For example, we all achieve milestones of physical development in the same order and at roughly the same rate as a result of the nature of biological maturation supported by the nurture of basic care, nutrition, and exercise. Second, nature and nurture also both operate to make each person unique. The nature of inherited genes and the nurture of widely different family and cultural environments produce differences among individuals in such dimensions as athletic abilities, intelligence, and personality (Cross & Markus, 1999; Plomin & Caspi, 1999). Heredity creates *predispositions* that interact with environmental influences, including family and teachers, friends and random events, books and computers. It is this interaction that produces the developmental outcomes we see in individuals. So Michael Jordan, Eminem, and Prince William are different from one another and from other men because of both their genes and their experiences.

Just how much nature and nurture contribute varies from one characteristic to another. Nature shapes some characteristics, such as physical size and appearance, so strongly that only extreme environmental conditions can affect them. Variation in height, for example, has been estimated to be 80 to 95 percent genetic. This means that 80 to 95 percent of the differences in height that we see among people are due to their genes. Less than 20 percent of the differences are due to prenatal or postnatal diet, or to early illness or other growth-stunting environmental factors. Nature's influence on other characteristics, such as intelligence or personality, is not as strong. Complex traits like these are influenced by genes, but by many environmental factors as well (Plomin et al., 2000).

It is impossible for researchers to identify the separate influences that nature and nurture exert on such complex traits, partly because heredity and environment are *correlated*. For instance, highly intelligent biological parents give their children genes for intelligence and typically also provide a stimulating environment. Heredity and environment also influence each other. Just as the environment promotes or hampers an individual's abilities, those inherited abilities to some extent determine the individual's environment. For example, a stimulating environment full of toys, books, and lessons encourages children's mental development and increases the chances that their full inherited intelligence will emerge. At the same time, more intelligent children seek out environments that are more stimulating, ask more questions, draw more attention from adults, and ultimately, learn more from these experiences.

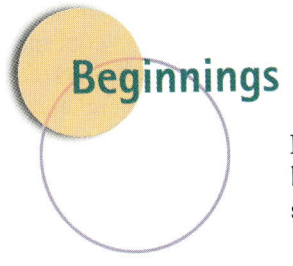

Beginnings

Let's now consider how nature and nurture interact to affect human development, before and after birth. Nowhere is this interaction clearer than in the womb, as a single fertilized egg becomes a functioning infant.

Prenatal Development

The process of development begins when a sperm from the father-to-be penetrates, or fertilizes, the ovum of the mother-to-be, and a brand-new cell, called a **zygote**, is formed. This new cell carries a genetic heritage from both mother and father (see the behavioral genetics appendix).

Stages of Development

In the first stage of prenatal development, called the *germinal stage,* the zygote divides into many more cells, which by the end of the second week have formed an **embryo** (pronounced "EM-bree-oh"). What follows is the *embryonic stage* of development, during which the embryo quickly develops a heart, nervous system, stomach, esophagus, and ovaries or testes. By two months after conception, when the embryonic stage ends, the inch-long embryo has developed eyes, ears, a nose, a jaw, a mouth, and lips. The tiny arms have elbows, hands, and stubby fingers; the legs have knees, ankles, and toes.

During the remaining seven-month period until birth, called the *fetal stage* of prenatal development, the organs grow and start to function. By the end of the third month, the **fetus** can kick, make a fist, turn its head, open its mouth, swallow, and frown. In the sixth month, the eyelids, which have been sealed, open. The fetus now has taste buds and a well-developed grasp and, if born prematurely, can breathe regularly for as long as twenty-four hours at a time. By the end of the seventh month, the organ systems, though immature, are all functional. In the eighth and ninth months, fetuses respond to light and touch, and they can hear what is going on outside. They can also learn. For example, they will ignore a stimulus, such as a vibration or sound, after it has been repeated a number of times. In such cases, they have *habituated* to the stimulus.

Habituation, described in the chapter on learning, predicts cognitive abilities after birth; babies who habituate faster display higher mental abilities later on.

Nature determines the timing and stages of prenatal development, but that development is also affected by the nurture provided by the environment of the womb.

Prenatal Risks

During prenatal development, a spongy organ called the *placenta,* formed from the outside layer of the zygote, sends nutrients from the mother to the fetus and carries away wastes. It also screens out many potentially harmful substances, including most bacteria. This screening is imperfect, however: Gases and viruses, as well as nicotine, alcohol, and other drugs, can pass through.

---

zygote A new cell, formed from a father's sperm and a mother's ovum.

embryo The developing individual from the fourteenth day after fertilization until the end of the second month after conception.

fetus The developing individual from the third month after conception until birth.

A Fetus at Twelve Weeks At this point in prenatal development, the fetus can kick its legs, curl its toes, make a fist, turn its head, squint, open its mouth, swallow, and take a few "breaths" of amniotic fluid.

Severe damage can occur if the baby's mother takes certain drugs, is exposed to toxic substances, or has certain illnesses while organs are forming in the embryonic stage.

Harmful external substances that invade the womb and result in birth defects are called **teratogens** (pronounced "ta-RAT-a-jens"). Teratogens are especially damaging during the embryonic stage, because it is a **critical period** in prenatal development, a time when certain kinds of growth must occur if the infant's development is to proceed normally. If the heart, eyes, ears, hands, and feet do not appear during this period, they cannot form later on; and if they form incorrectly, the defects are permanent. So even before a mother knows she is pregnant, she may accidentally damage her infant by exposing it to teratogens. A baby whose mother has rubella (German measles) during the third or fourth week after conception, for example, has a 50 percent chance of being blind, deaf, or mentally retarded, or of having a malformed heart. If the mother has rubella later in the pregnancy, after the infant's eyes, ears, brain, and heart have formed, the likelihood that the baby will have one of these defects drops substantially. Later, during the fetal stage, teratogens affect the baby's size, behavior, intelligence, and health, rather than the formation of organs and limbs.

Of special concern today are the effects of drugs on infants' development. Pregnant women who use substances such as cocaine create a substantial risk for their fetuses, which do not yet have the enzymes necessary to break down the drugs. "Cocaine babies" or "crack babies" may be born premature, underweight, tense, and fussy (Inciardi, Surratt, & Saum, 1997); they may also suffer delayed physical growth and motor development (Tarr & Pyfer, 1996). Current research suggests, however, that although cocaine babies are more likely to have behavioral and learning problems (Singer et al., 2001), their mental abilities are not substantially different from those of any baby born into an impoverished environment (Frank et al., 2001). How well they ultimately do in school depends on how supportive that environment turns out to be (Begley, 1997).

Alcohol is another dangerous teratogen. Pregnant women who drink as little as a glass or two of wine a day can harm their infants' intellectual functioning (Streissguth et al., 1999). Almost half the children born to expectant mothers who abuse alcohol will develop **fetal alcohol syndrome,** a pattern of defects that includes mental retardation and malformations of the face, such as a flattened nose and an underdeveloped upper lip (Jenkins & Culbertson, 1996). Smoking, too, can affect the developing fetus. Smokers' babies are usually born underweight and often suffer from respiratory problems (Gilliland, Li, & Peters, 2001). They may also be irritable and display problems with attention later on (Milberger et al., 1997).

Defects due to teratogens are most likely to appear when the negative effects of nature and nurture combine—when a genetically susceptible infant receives a strong dose of a damaging substance during a critical period of prenatal development. Fortunately, mental or physical problems resulting from all harmful prenatal factors affect fewer than 10 percent of the babies born in Western nations. Mechanisms built into the human organism maintain normal development under all but the most adverse conditions. The vast majority of fetuses arrive at the end of their nine-month gestation averaging a healthy seven pounds and ready to continue a normal course of development in the world.

The Newborn

Determining what newborns are able to see, hear, and do is one of the most fascinating—and frustrating—research challenges in developmental psychology. Young infants are very difficult to study. About 70 percent of the time, they are asleep; and when they are not sleeping, they may be drowsy, crying, or restlessly moving about. It is only when they are in a state of quiet alertness, which occurs infrequently and only for a few minutes at a time, that researchers can assess infants' abilities.

teratogens Harmful substances that can cause birth defects.

critical period An interval during which certain kinds of growth must occur if development is to proceed normally.

fetal alcohol syndrome A pattern of physical and mental defects found in babies born to women who abused alcohol during pregnancy.

A Baby's-Eye View of the World The photograph on the left simulates what the mother on the right looks like to her newborn infant. Although their vision is blurry, infants particularly seem to enjoy looking at faces. As mentioned in the chapter on perception, their eyes will follow a moving face-like drawing (Johnson et al., 1991a, 1991b), and they will stare at a human face longer than at other figures (Valenza et al., 1996).

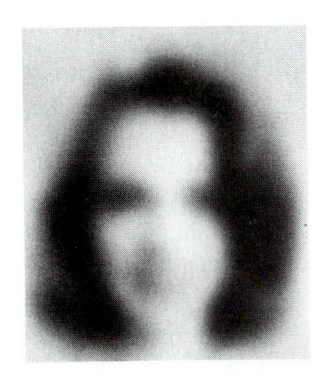

During these brief periods, psychologists show infants objects or pictures, or present sounds to them, and watch where they look and for how long. They film the infants' eye movements and record changes in their heart rates, sucking rates, brain waves, body movements, and skin conductance (a measure of perspiration associated with emotion) to learn what infants can see and hear (Aslin, Jusczyk, & Pisoni, 1998; Kellman & Banks, 1998).

Vision and Other Senses

Infants can see at birth, but their vision is blurry. Researchers estimate that newborns have 20/300 eyesight; that is, an object 20 feet away looks as clear as it would if viewed from 300 feet by an adult with normal vision. The reason infants' vision is so limited is that their eyes and brains still need time to grow and develop. Newborns' eyes are smaller than those of adults, and the cells in their foveas—the area of each retina on which images are focused—are fewer and far less sensitive. Their eye movements are slow and jerky. And pathways connecting the eyes to the brain are still inefficient, as is the processing of visual information within the brain.

Although infants cannot see small objects on the other side of the room, they are able to see large objects close up. They stare longest at objects that have large visible elements, movement, clear contours, and a lot of contrast—all qualities that exist in the human face. In fact, from the time they are born, infants will redirect their eyes to follow a moving drawing of a face, and they stare at a human face longer than at other figures (Johnson et al., 1991a, 1991b; Valenza et al., 1996). They also exhibit a degree of *size constancy*—the ability to perceive the correct physical size of an object despite changes in the size of its image on the retina (see the chapter on perception). So a baby perceives Mother's face as remaining about the same size, whether she is looking over the edge of the crib or close enough to kiss the baby's cheek. Newborns do not experience *depth perception* until some time later, however; it takes about seven months before they develop the ability to use the pictorial cues to depth described in the chapter on perception.

The course of development for hearing is similar to that of vision. Infants at birth are not deaf, but they hear poorly. At two or three days of age, they can hear soft voices and notice the difference between tones about one note apart on the musical scale; they also turn their heads toward sounds (Clifton, 1992). But their hearing is not as sharp as that of adults until well into childhood. Infants' hearing is particularly attuned to the sounds of speech. When they hear voices, babies open their eyes wider and look for the speaker. By four months of age, they can discriminate differences among almost all of the more than fifty phonetic contrasts in adult languages. Infants also prefer certain kinds of speech. They like rising tones spoken by women or children, and they like speech that is high pitched, exaggerated, and expressive. In other words, they like to hear the "baby talk" used by most adults when they talk to babies.

Newborns' sense of smell is similar to that of adults, but again, less acute. Certain smells and tastes appeal to them more than others. For instance, they like the smell of flowers and the taste of sweet drinks (Ganchrow, Steiner, & Daher,

1983). Contrary to popular myth, however, they dislike the smell of ammonia (in wet diapers). Research indicates that within a few days after birth, breastfed babies prefer the odor of their own mother to that of another mother (Porter et al., 1992). They also develop preferences for the food flavors consumed by their mothers (Mennella & Beauchamp, 1996).

Although limited, these inborn sensory abilities—smell, taste, hearing, and vision—are important for survival and development because they focus the infant's attention on the caregiver. For example, the attraction of newborns to the sweet smell and taste of mother's milk helps them locate appropriate food and identify their caregiver. Their sensitivity to speech allows them to focus on language and encourages the caregiver to talk to them. And because their vision is limited to the distance at which most interaction with a caregiver takes place and is tuned to the special qualities of faces, the caregiver's face is especially noticeable to them. Accordingly, infants are exposed to emotional expressions and come to recognize the caregiver by sight, further encouraging the caregiver to interact. As infants physically mature and learn from their environment, their sensory capacities become more complex and adult-like.

Reflexes and Motor Skills In the first few weeks and months after birth, babies demonstrate involuntary, unlearned motor behaviors called *reflexes*. These are swift, automatic movements that occur in response to external stimuli. Figure 12.2 illustrates the *grasping reflex;* more than twenty other reflexes have been observed in newborn infants. For example, the *rooting reflex* causes the infant to turn its mouth toward a nipple (or anything else) that touches its cheek, and the *sucking reflex* causes the newborn to suck on anything that touches its lips. Many of these reflexes evolved because, like seeing and hearing, they were important for infants' survival. But infants' behavior does not remain under the control of these reflexes for long. Most reflexes disappear after the first three or four months, when infants' brain development allows them to control their muscles voluntarily. At that point, infants can develop motor skills, so they are soon able to roll over, sit up, crawl, stand, and by the end of the year, walk (see Figure 12.1).

Until a few years ago, most developmental psychologists accepted Gesell's view that barring extreme environmental conditions, these motor abilities occur spontaneously as the central nervous system and muscles mature. Recent research demonstrates, however, that maturation does not tell the whole story. Consider the fact that many babies today aren't learning to crawl on time—or at all. Why? A decade ago, in an effort to prevent sudden infant death syndrome, described in the chapter on consciousness, public health officials launched the "Back to Sleep" campaign, which urged parents to put babies to sleep on their backs rather than facedown. The campaign was successful, but researchers have discovered that many babies who were never placed on their tummies went directly from sitting to toddling, skipping the crawling stage but reaching all other motor milestones on schedule (Kolata & Markel, 2001). Observation of infants who do learn to crawl has shown that it does not happen suddenly. It takes the development of enough muscle strength to support the abdomen—and some active experimentation—to get the job done (Thelen, 1995). Six infants in one study tried various crawling techniques—moving backward, moving one limb at a time, using the arms only, and so on (Freedland & Bertenthal, 1994). It was only after a week or two of trial and error that all six arrived at the same method: moving diagonal limbs (right arm and left leg, left arm and right leg) together. This pattern turned out to be the most efficient way of getting around quickly without tipping over. Such observations suggest that as maturation increases infants' strength, they try out motor patterns and select the ones that work best (Nelson, 1999).

In short, motor development results from a combination of maturation and experience. It is not the result of an entirely automatic sequence genetically etched in the brain. Yet again, we see that nature and nurture influence each other.

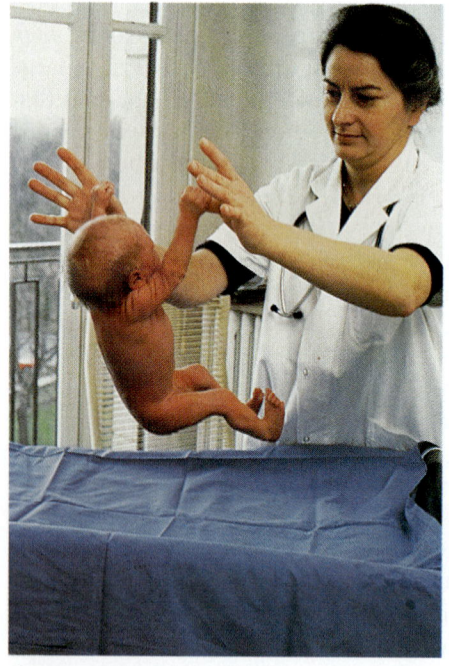

figure 12.2

Reflexes in the Newborn

When a finger is pressed into a newborn's palm, the *grasping reflex* causes the infant to hold on tightly enough to suspend its entire weight. And when a newborn is held upright over a flat surface, the *stepping reflex* leads to walking movements.

Infancy and Childhood: Cognitive Development

Over the first ten years of life, the tiny infant becomes a competent child who can read a book, write a poem, and argue for access to the family's new computer. Several changes lead to the dramatic shifts in thinking, knowing, and remembering that occur between early infancy and later childhood.

Changes in the Brain

One factor that underlies the cognitive leaps of infancy and childhood is continued growth and development of the brain. When infants are born, they already have a full quota of brain cells, but the neural networks connecting the cells are immature. With time, the connections grow increasingly complex and then, with pruning, more efficient. Studies reveal how, as different regions of the brain develop more complex and efficient neural networks, new cognitive abilities appear (Nelson, 1997).

In the first few months of infancy, the area of the brain that is most mature is the cerebellum. Its early maturation allows infants to display simple associative abilities such as sucking more when they see their mother's face or hear her voice. Between six and twelve months of age, neurological development in the medial temporal lobe of the cortex makes it possible for infants to remember and imitate an action they have seen earlier, or to recognize a picture of an object they have never seen before but have held in their hands. And neurological development in the frontal cortex, which occurs later in childhood, allows the individual to develop higher cognitive functions such as reasoning. Brain structures thus provide the "hardware" for children's *cognitive development*. How does the "software" of thinking develop, and how does it modify the "wiring" of the brain's "hardware"? These questions have been pursued by many developmental psychologists, beginning with Piaget.

The Development of Knowledge: Piaget's Theory

Piaget dedicated his life to a search for the origins of intelligence in infancy and the factors that lead to changes in knowledge over the life span. He was the first to chart the fascinating journey from the simple reflexes of the newborn to the complex understandings of the adolescent. Piaget's theory was not correct in every respect—later we discuss some of its weaknesses—but the fact remains that his ideas about cognitive development still guide much research in the field (Fischer & Hencke, 1996).

Piaget proposed that cognitive development proceeds through a series of distinct *periods* or *stages* (outlined in Table 12.1). He believed that all children's thinking goes through the same stages, in the same order, without skipping—building on previous stages, then moving progressively to higher ones. According to Piaget, the thinking of infants is different from the thinking of children, and the thinking of children is different from that of adolescents. He concluded that children are not just miniature adults, and they are not dumber than adults; they just think in different ways. Entering each stage involves a *qualitative* change from the previous stage, much as a caterpillar is transformed into a butterfly. What drives children to higher stages is their constant struggle to make sense of their experiences. They are active thinkers who are always trying to construct more advanced understandings of the world.

Building Blocks of Development

To explain how infants and children move to ever-higher stages of understanding and knowledge, Piaget used the concept of **schemas**. As noted in the chapters on perception, memory, and cognition, schemas are the generalizations that form as people experience the world; they organize past experiences and provide a framework for understanding future experiences. Piaget

schemas Generalizations based on experience that form the basic units of knowledge.

According to Piaget, a predictable set of features characterizes each period of children's cognitive development. The ages associated with the stages are approximate; Piaget realized that some children move through the stages slightly faster or slower than others.

table 12.1
Piaget's Periods of Cognitive Development

Period	Activities and Achievements
Sensorimotor Birth–2 years	Infants discover aspects of the world through their sensory impressions, motor activities, and coordination of the two.
	They learn to differentiate themselves from the external world. They learn that objects exist even when they are not visible and that objects are independent of the infant's own actions. They gain some appreciation of cause and effect.
Preoperational 2–4 years 4–7 years	Children cannot yet manipulate and transform information in logical ways, but they now can think in images and symbols.
	They become able to represent something with something else, acquire language, and play games that involve pretending. Intelligence at this stage is said to be intuitive, because children cannot make general, logical statements.
Concrete operational 7–11 years	Children can understand logical principles that apply to concrete external objects.
	They can appreciate that certain properties of an object remain the same despite changes in appearance, and they can sort objects into categories. They can appreciate the perspective of another viewer. They can think about two concepts, such as longer and wider, at the same time.
Formal operational Over 11 years	Only adolescents and adults can think logically about abstractions, can speculate, and can consider what might or what ought to be.
	They can work in probabilities and possibilities. They can imagine other worlds, especially ideal ones. They can reason about purely verbal or logical statements. They can relate any element or statement to any other, manipulate variables in a scientific experiment, and deal with proportions and analogies. They reflect on their own activity of thinking.

saw schemas as organized patterns of action or thought that children construct as they adapt to the environment; they are the basic units of knowledge, the building blocks of intellectual development. Schemas, he said, can involve behaviors (e.g., tying a shoelace or sucking), mental symbols (e.g., words or images), or mental activities (e.g., doing arithmetic "in our head" or imagining actions).

At first, infants form simple schemas. For example, a sucking schema consolidates their experiences of sucking into images of what objects can be sucked on (bottles, fingers, pacifiers) and what kinds of sucking can be done (soft and slow, speedy and vigorous). Later, children form more complex schemas, such as a schema for tying a knot or making a bed. Still later, adolescents form schemas about what it is to be in love.

Two complementary processes guide the development of schemas: assimilation and accommodation. In the process of **assimilation,** infants and children take in information about new objects by using existing schemas that will fit the new objects. An infant is given a new toy. He sucks on it, assimilating it into the sucking schema he has developed with his bottle and pacifier. A toddler sees a butterfly for

assimilation The process of trying out existing schemas on objects that fit those schemas.

figure 12.3

Accommodation

Because the bars of the playpen are in the way, this child discovers that her schema for grasping and pulling objects toward her will not work. She then adjusts, or accommodates, her schema to achieve her goal.

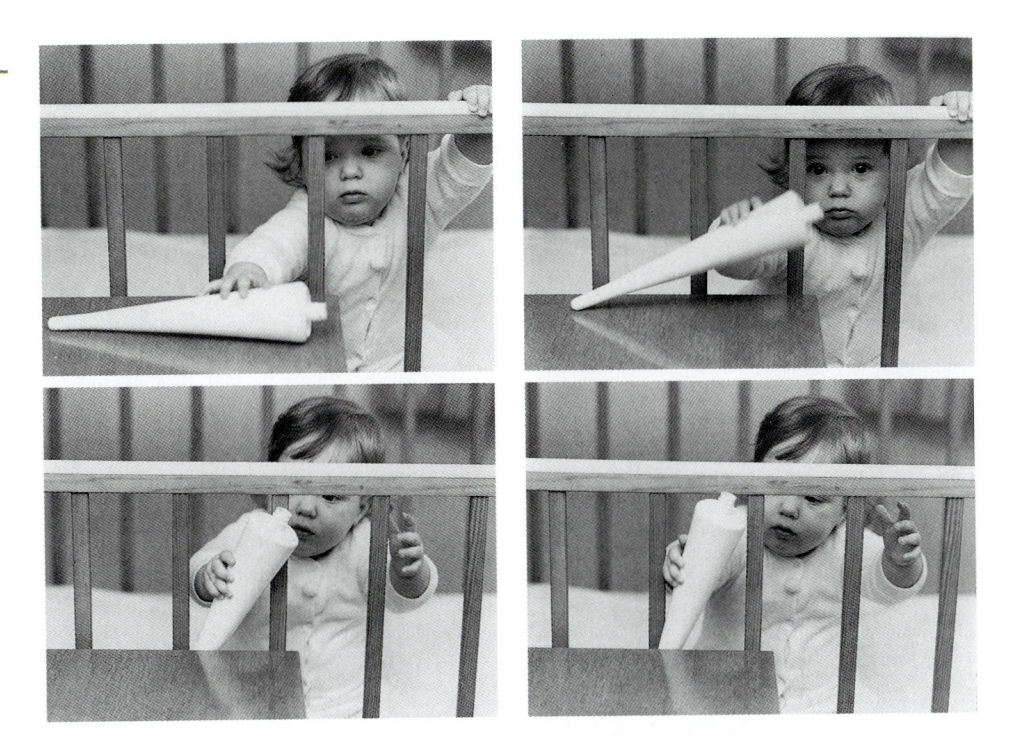

the first time. It's colorful and flies, like a bird, so she assimilates it into her "birdie" schema. An older child encounters a large dog. How she assimilates this new creature depends on her existing schema of dogs. If she has had positive experiences with a family pet, she will expect the dog to behave like her pet, and she will greet it enthusiastically. If she has been frightened by dogs in the past, she may have a negative schema and react with fear to the dog she has just met.

Sometimes, like Cinderella's sisters squeezing their oversized feet into the glass slipper, people distort information about a new object to make it fit their existing schema. When squeezing won't work, though, they are forced to change, or accommodate, their schema to the new object. In **accommodation,** a person finds that a familiar schema cannot be made to fit a new object, and changes it (see Figure 12.3). So when the infant discovers that another new toy—a squeaker—is more fun when it makes a noise, he accommodates his sucking schema and starts munching on the squeaker instead. When the toddler realizes that butterflies are not birds because they don't have beaks and feathers, she accommodates her "birdie" schema to include two kinds of "flying animals"—birds and butterflies. And if the child with the positive "doggie" schema meets a snarling stray, she discovers that her original schema does not extend to all dogs, and she refines it to distinguish between friendly dogs and those that are aggressive. Through assimilation and accommodation, said Piaget, we build our knowledge of the world, block by block.

Sensorimotor Development

Piaget (1952) called the first stage of cognitive development the **sensorimotor period** because, he claimed, the infant's mental activity and schemas are confined to sensory functions, like seeing and hearing, and motor skills, like grasping and sucking. According to Piaget, during this stage, infants can form schemas only of objects and actions that are present—things they can see or hear or touch. They cannot think about absent objects because they cannot act on them; thinking, for infants, is doing. They do not lie in the crib thinking about their mother or their teddy bear, because they are not yet able to form schemas that are *mental representations* of objects and actions.

The sensorimotor period ends when infants can form mental representations and thus can think about objects and actions even while the objects are not visible or the actions are not occurring. This is a remarkable milestone, according to Piaget;

accommodation The process of modifying schemas when familiar schemas do not work.

sensorimotor period The first of Piaget's stages of cognitive development, when the infant's mental activity is confined to sensory perception and motor skills.

it frees the child from the here-and-now of the sensory environment and allows for the development of thought. One sign that children have reached this milestone is their ability to find a hidden object. This behavior was of particular interest to Piaget because, for him, it reflected infants' knowledge that they do not have to look at, touch, or suck an object to know that it exists; it exists even when out of sight. Piaget called this knowledge **object permanence.**

Before they acquire a knowledge of object permanence, infants do not search for objects that are placed out of their sight. They act as if out of sight is literally out of mind. The first evidence of developing object permanence appears when infants are four to eight months old. At this age, for the first time, they recognize a familiar object even if part of it is hidden. They know it's their bottle even if they can see only the nipple peeking out from under the blanket. In Piaget's view, infants now have some primitive mental representation of objects. If an object is completely hidden, however, they will not search for it.

Several months later, infants will search briefly for a hidden object, but their search is random and ineffective. Not until they are eighteen to twenty-four months old, said Piaget, do infants appear able to picture and follow events in their minds. They look for the object in places other than where they saw it last, sometimes in completely new places. According to Piaget, their concept of the object as permanent is now fully developed; they have a mental representation of the object that is completely separate from their immediate perception of it.

New Views of Infants

In the years since Piaget's death, psychologists have found new ways to measure what is going on in infants' minds—infrared photography to record infants' eye movements, time-lapse photography to detect subtle hand movements, special equipment to measure infants' sucking rates, and computer technology to track and analyze it all. Their research shows that infants know a lot more, and know it sooner, than Piaget ever thought they did.

Infants are not just sensing and moving in the sensorimotor period; they are already thinking as well. For example, they are able to integrate sights with sounds. In one study, infants were shown two different videotapes at the same time, while the soundtrack for one of them was played through a speaker placed between the two video screens. The infants tended to look at the video that went with the soundtrack—at a toy bouncing in time with a tapping sound or at a pair of cymbals accompanied by clanging (Walker-Andrews et al., 1991). Infants can remember, too. As young as two to three months of age, they can recall a particular mobile that was hung over their crib a few days before (Rovee-Collier, 1999; see Figure 12.4).

Young babies also seem to have a sense of object permanence. Piaget had required infants to demonstrate object permanence through rather grand movements, such as removing a cover that had been placed over a hidden object. However, when experimenters simply turn off the lights, infants as young as five months of age have been shown to reach for now-unseen objects in the dark (Clifton et al., 1991). Researchers now recognize that finding a hidden object under a cover requires several abilities: mentally representing the hidden object, figuring out where it might be, and pulling off the cover. Piaget's tests did not allow for the possibility that infants know a hidden object still exists but do not have adequate strategies for finding it or memory skills for remembering it while they search. In research situations where infants merely have to stare to indicate that they know where an object is hidden, they demonstrate this cognitive ability even before the age of one (Ahmed & Ruffman, 1998; Hespos & Baillargeon, 2001).

In short, developmental psychologists now generally agree that infants develop some mental representations earlier than Piaget had suggested. They disagree, however, about whether this knowledge is "programmed" in infants (Spelke et al., 1992), quickly develops through interactions with the outside world (Baillargeon, 1995), or is constructed through the recombination of old schemas into new ones (Fischer & Bidell, 1991).

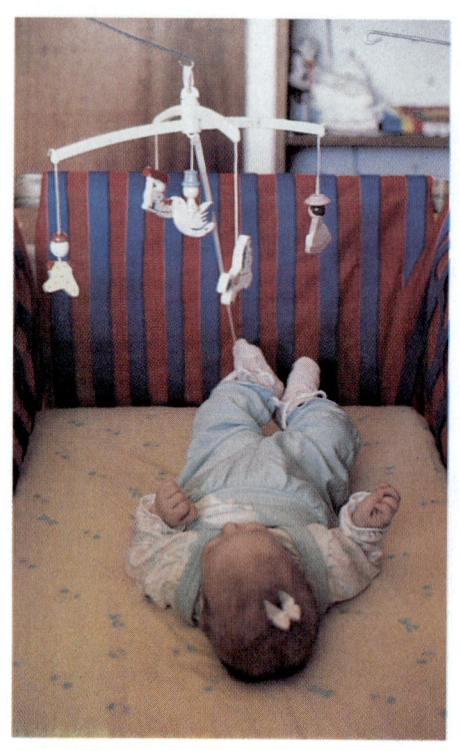

figure 12.4

Infant Memory

This three-month-old infant learned to move a mobile by kicking her left foot, which is tied to the mobile with a ribbon. Even a month later, the baby will show recognition of this particular mobile by kicking more vigorously when she sees it than when she sees another one.

object permanence The knowledge that objects exist even when they are not in view.

FOCUS ON RESEARCH METHODS

Experiments on Developing Minds

To explore how infants develop mental representations, Renee Baillargeon (pronounced "by-ar-ZHAN") investigated infants' early understanding of the principles of physics. Whether you realize it or not, you know a lot about physics. You know about gravity and balance, for example. But when did you first understand that "what goes up must come down" and that an unbalanced tray will tip over? Are these things you have always known, or did you figure them out through trial and error?

● What was the researcher's question?

Baillargeon wanted to know when and how babies first develop knowledge about balance and gravity—specifically, about the tendency of unsupported objects to fall.

● How did the researcher answer the question?

Baillargeon (1994a, 1994b) devised a creative experimental method to probe infants' knowledge. She showed infants pairs of events, one of which was physically possible and the other, physically impossible. She then determined the infants' interest in each kind of event by measuring the amount of time they spent looking at it. Their tendency to look longer at unexpected events provided an indication of which events violated what the babies knew about the world. Using this method, Baillargeon studied infants' knowledge of balance and gravity.

The independent variable in her studies was the amount of physical support applied to objects; the dependent variable was the length of time the infants looked at the objects. Specifically, the infants viewed a bright-red gloved hand pushing a box from left to right along the top of a platform. On some trials, they saw physically possible events. For example, the hand pushed the box until its edge reached the end of the platform (see event A in Figure 12.5). On other trials, they saw impossible events, as when the hand pushed the box until only the end of its bottom surface rested on the platform or the box was beyond the platform altogether (see events B and C in the figure). On still other trials, the gloved hand held onto the box while pushing it beyond the edge of the platform (as shown in event D). Trials continued until the infants had seen at least four pairs of possible and impossible events in alternating order.

● What did the researcher find?

Baillargeon found that three-month-old infants looked longest at impossible event C, in which the box was entirely off the platform, whereas they were not particularly interested in either event D (box held by the gloved hand) or event A (box still on the platform). At six and a half months, infants stared intently at both event C (box off the platform) and event B (in which only the end of the box was resting on the platform).

● What do the results mean?

According to Baillargeon (1998), these results suggest that three-month-old babies know something about physical support: They expect the box to fall if it is entirely off the platform and act surprised when it does not. But they do not yet know that a box should fall if its center of gravity is unsupported, as in event B. By the time they are six and a half months old, however, infants apparently know about centers of gravity—that most of the box must be on the platform or it will fall.

Other researchers have questioned whether infants' tendency to stare longer at a particular display necessarily indicates "surprise" (Bogartz, Shinskey, & Speaker, 1997). Perhaps they simply recognize that the image is different from what they remember it to be or find the impossible image more noticeable.

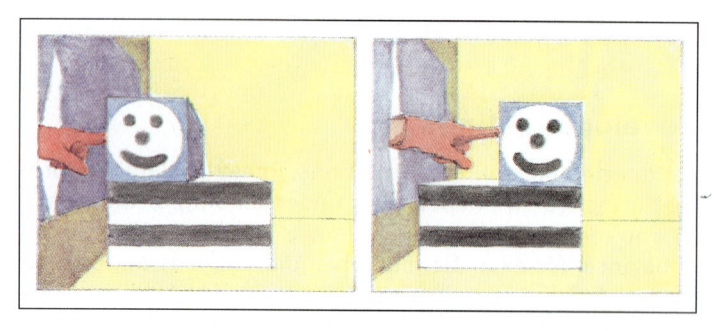

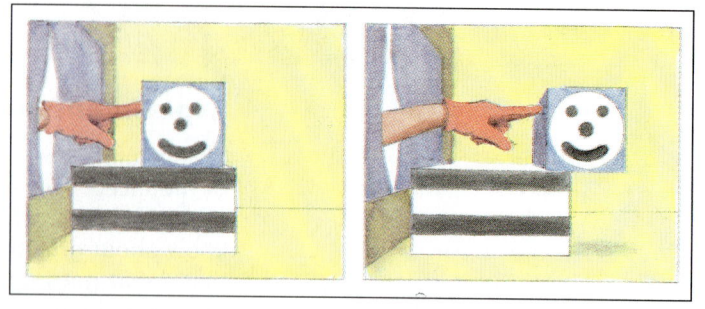

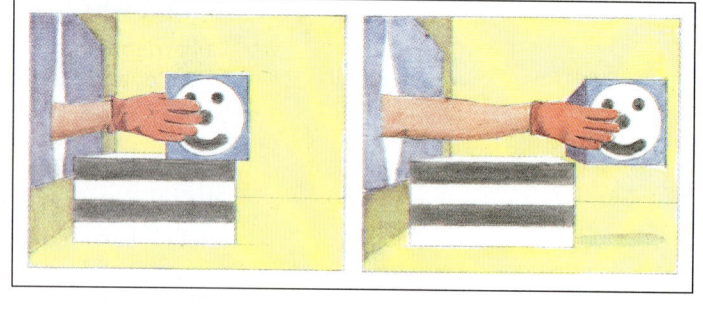

figure 12.5

Events Demonstrating Infants' Knowledge of Physics

Infants look longer at things that interest them—that is, at new things rather than things they have seen before and find boring. In her research on the development of knowledge, Renee Baillargeon (1995) has found that physically impossible events B and C—made possible by an experimenter reaching through a hidden door to support a moving box—attract the most attention from infants. These results suggest that humans understand some basic laws of physics quite early in life.

Source: Baillargeon (1992).

• What do we still need to know?

The question remains as to which of these interpretations is correct. Do infants possess fundamental knowledge about the world that implies an understanding of complex physical principles, or are they just staring at something because it is novel or vivid? The answer to this question will require further research using varied visual stimuli that allows researchers to determine whether infants stare longer at physically possible events that are just as novel and vivid as physically impossible events.

Whether or not such research confirms Baillargeon's view, psychologists are still faced with the task of discovering *how* babies know about physics (Wynn & Chiang, 1998). Does their increasing understanding of physical principles result from their experience with objects, or is the knowledge innate?

In an attempt to answer this question, Baillargeon conducted another experiment in which she manipulated object-experience. She randomly assigned infants, ranging in age from three months to six and a half months, to receive either normal or extra experience with objects (the independent variable) and observed the effect on the infants' understanding of gravity (the dependent variable). After only a few demonstrations in which unsupported objects fell off platforms, infants in the extra object-experience group stared longer at a display of an unsupported object that did not fall. Other studies found similar results (Needham & Baillargeon, 1999).

It is still too early to say for sure whether Baillargeon's hypothesis about the importance of experience in developing knowledge is correct, but her results seem to support it.

Preoperational Development

According to Piaget, the sensorimotor stage of development is followed by the **preoperational period**. During the first half of this period, children begin to understand, create, and use *symbols* (words, images, and objects) to represent things that are not present. As described in the chapter on cognition and language, they begin to use words to stand for objects: *Mommy, cup, me*. They also begin to play "pretend." They make their fingers "walk" or "shoot" and use a spoon to make a bridge. By the age of three or four, children can symbolize roles and play "house" or "doctor." They also can use drawing symbolically: Pointing to their scribble, they might say, "This is Mommy and Daddy and me going for a walk." The ability to use and understand symbols opens up vast domains for two- to four-year-olds.

During the second half of the preoperational stage, according to Piaget, four- to seven-year-olds begin to make intuitive guesses about the world as they try to figure out how things work. They claim that dreams are real: "Last night there was a circus in my room." And they believe that inanimate objects are alive and have intentions, feelings, and consciousness, a belief called *animism*: "Clouds go slowly because they have no legs" and "Empty cars feel lonely." In short, said Piaget, preoperational children cannot distinguish between the seen and the unseen, between the physical and the mental world. They are also highly *egocentric*, meaning that they appear to believe that the way things look to them is also how they look to everyone else. (This helps to explain why they may stand so as to block your view when both of you are trying to watch TV or ask "What's this?" as they look at a picture book in the back seat of the car while you're driving.)

Children's thinking is so dominated by what they can see and touch for themselves, Piaget said, that they do not realize that something is the same if its appearance changes. In one study, for example, preoperational children thought that a cat wearing a dog mask was actually a dog—because that's what it looked like (DeVries, 1969). These children do not yet have what Piaget called **conservation**, the ability to recognize that important properties of a substance or object—including its volume, weight, and species—remain constant despite changes in its shape.

In a test of conservation, Piaget first showed children equal amounts of water in two identical containers. He then poured one of them into a tall, thin glass and the other into a short, wide glass and asked whether one glass contained more water

During the second half of the preoperational period, according to Piaget, children believe that inanimate objects are alive and have feelings, intentions, and consciousness.

"I think the moon likes us. It keeps on followin' us."

preoperational period According to Piaget, the second stage of cognitive development, during which children begin to use symbols to represent things that are not present.

conservation The ability to recognize that the important properties of a substance remain constant despite changes in shape, length, or position.

Testing for Conservation If you know a child who is between the ages of four and seven, get permission to test the child for what Piaget called *conservation.* Show the child two identical lumps of clay, and ask which lump is bigger. The child will probably say they are the same. Now roll one lump into a long "rope," and again ask which lump is bigger. If the child says that they are still the same, this is evidence of conservation. If the longer one is seen as bigger, conservation has not yet developed—at least not for this task. The older the child, the more likely it is that conservation will appear, but some children display conservation much earlier than Piaget thought was possible.

than the other. Children at the preoperational stage of development said that one glass (usually the taller one) contained more. They were dominated by the evidence of their eyes. If the glass looked bigger, they thought it contained more. In other words, they did not understand the logical concepts of *reversibility* (you just poured the water from one container to another, so you can pour it back, and it will still be the same amount) or *complementarity* (one glass is taller but also narrower; the other is shorter but also wider). Piaget named this stage "*pre*operational" because children at this stage do not yet understand logical mental operations such as these.

Concrete Operational Thought

Sometime around the age of six or seven, Piaget observed, children do develop the ability to conserve number and amount. When they do so, they enter what Piaget called the stage of **concrete operations.** Now, he said, they can count, measure, add, and subtract; their thinking is no longer dominated by the appearance of things. They can use simple logic and perform simple mental manipulations and mental operations on things. They can also sort objects into classes (such as tools, fruit, and vehicles) or series (such as largest to smallest).

Still, concrete operational children can perform their logical operations only on real, concrete objects—sticks and glasses, tools and fruit—not on abstract concepts like justice and freedom. They can reason about what is, but not yet about what is possible. The ability to think logically about abstract ideas comes in the next stage of cognitive development, the *formal operational period,* which we discuss later in relation to adolescence.

Modifying Piaget's Theory

Piaget was right in pointing out that there are significant shifts with age in children's thinking, and that thinking becomes more systematic, consistent, and integrated as children get older. His idea that children are active explorers and constructors of knowledge has been absorbed into contemporary ways of thinking about childhood. And he inspired many other psychologists to test his findings and theory with experiments of their own. The results of these experiments have suggested that Piaget's theory needs some modification.

concrete operations According to Piaget, the third stage of cognitive development, during which children's thinking is no longer dominated by visual appearances.

What needs to be modified most is Piaget's notion of developmental stages. Researchers have shown that changes from one stage to the next are less consistent and global than Piaget thought. For example, three-year-olds can sometimes make the distinction between physical and mental phenomena; they know the characteristics of real dogs versus pretend dogs (Woolley, 1997). Moreover, they are not invariably egocentric; as one study demonstrated, children of this age knew that a white card, which looked pink to them because they were wearing rose-colored glasses, still looked white to someone who was not wearing the glasses (Liben, 1978). Preoperational children can even do conservation tasks if they are allowed to count the number of objects or have been trained to focus on relevant dimensions such as number, height, and width (Gelman & Baillargeon, 1983).

Taken together, these studies suggest that children's knowledge and mental strategies develop at different ages in different areas, and in "pockets" rather than at global levels of understanding (Sternberg, 1989). Knowledge in particular areas is demonstrated sooner in children who are given specific experience in those areas or who are presented with very simple questions and tasks. Children's reasoning depends not only on their general level of development but also on (1) how easy the task is, (2) how familiar they are with the objects involved, (3) how well they understand the language being used, and (4) what experiences they have had in similar situations (Siegal, 1997). Research has also shown that the level of a child's thinking varies from day to day and may even shift when the child solves the same problem twice in the same day (Siegler, 1994).

In summary, psychologists today tend to think of cognitive development in terms of rising and falling "waves," not fixed stages—in terms of changing frequencies in children's use of different ways of thinking, not sudden, permanent shifts from one way of thinking to another (Siegler, 1995). Psychologists now suggest that children systematically try out many different solutions to problems and gradually come to select the best of them.

Information Processing During Childhood

An alternative to Piaget's theory of cognitive development is based on the *information-processing approach* discussed in the chapters on memory and on cognition and language. This approach describes cognitive activities in terms of how people take in information, use it, and remember it. Developmental psychologists taking this approach focus on gradual increases in children's mental capacities, rather than on dramatic changes in their stages of development. Their research demonstrates that as children get older, their information-processing skills gradually get better, and they can perform more complex tasks faster and easier.

First, older children have longer attention spans and are better at filtering out irrelevant information. These skills help them overcome distractions and concentrate intently on a variety of tasks, from hobbies to homework. Second, older children take in information more rapidly and can shift their attention from one task to another more quickly. (This is how they manage to do their homework while watching TV.) Third, older children can process the information they take in more rapidly and efficiently (Halford et al., 1994; Miller & Vernon, 1997). Compared with younger children, they code information into fewer dimensions and divide tasks into steps that can be processed one after another. This helps them to organize and complete their homework assignments.

Children's memory also markedly improves with age (Schneider & Bjorklund, 1998). Whereas preschoolers can keep only two or three pieces of information in their short-term memory at the same time, older children can hold four or five pieces of information. Older children can also put more information into their long-term memory storage, so they remember things longer than younger children. After about age seven, children can remember information that is more complex and abstract, such as the gist of what several people have said during a conversation. Their

in review: Milestones of Cognitive Development in Infancy and Childhood

Age*	Achievement	Description
3–4 months	Maturation of senses	Immaturities that limit the newborn's vision and hearing are overcome.
	Voluntary movement	Reflexes disappear, and infants begin to gain voluntary control over their movements.
12–18 months	Mental representation	Infants can form images of objects and actions in their minds.
	Object permanence	Infants understand that objects exist even when out of sight.
18–24 months	Symbolic thought	Young children use symbols to represent things that are not present in their pretend play, drawing, and talk.
4 years	Intuitive thought	Children reason about events, real and imagined, by guessing rather than by engaging in logical analysis.
6–7 years	Concrete operations / Conservation	Children can apply simple logical operations to real objects. For example, they recognize that important properties of a substance, such as number or amount, remain constant despite changes in shape or position.
7–8 years	Information processing	Children can remember more information; they begin to learn strategies for memorization.

*These ages are approximate; they indicate the order in which children first reach these milestones of cognitive development rather than the exact ages.

memories are more accurate, extensive, and well organized. And because they have accumulated more knowledge during their years of learning about the world, older children can integrate new information into a more complete network of facts. This makes it easier for them to understand and remember new information. (See "In Review: Milestones of Cognitive Development in Infancy and Childhood.")

LINKAGES (a link to Memory)

What accounts for these increases in children's attention, information processing, and memory capacities? It should not be surprising that it's nature plus nurture. As mentioned earlier, maturation of the brain contributes to better and faster information processing as children grow older. Experience also contributes. The importance of experience has been demonstrated by researchers who have tested children's cognitive abilities using familiar versus unfamiliar materials. In one study, for example, Mayan children in Mexico lagged behind their age-mates in the United States on standard memory tests for pictures and nouns that the Mexican children had not seen before. But the children did much better when researchers gave them a more familiar task, such as recalling the objects they saw in a model of a Mayan village (Rogoff & Waddell, 1982). The children's memory for these familiar objects was better, presumably because they could process information about them more easily and quickly.

Knowing how to memorize things also improves children's memories. To a great extent, children acquire memorization strategies in school. They learn to repeat information over and over to help fix it in memory, to place information into categories, and to use memory aids like "*i* before *e* except after *c*" to help them remember. They also learn what situations call for deliberate memorization and what factors, such as the length of a list, affect memory.

LINKAGES

Development and Memory

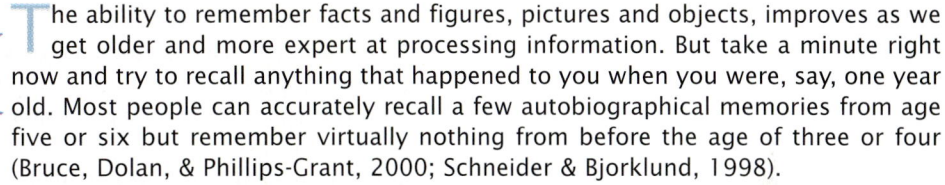

The ability to remember facts and figures, pictures and objects, improves as we get older and more expert at processing information. But take a minute right now and try to recall anything that happened to you when you were, say, one year old. Most people can accurately recall a few autobiographical memories from age five or six but remember virtually nothing from before the age of three or four (Bruce, Dolan, & Phillips-Grant, 2000; Schneider & Bjorklund, 1998).

Psychologists have not yet found a fully satisfactory explanation for this "infantile amnesia." Some have suggested that young children lack the memory encoding and storage processes described in the chapter on memory. Yet children two or three years old can clearly recall experiences that happened weeks or even months earlier (Bauer, 1996). Others suggest that infantile amnesia occurs because very young children lack a sense of self. They don't recognize themselves in a mirror, so they may not have a framework for organizing memories about what happens to them (Howe, 1995). However, this explanation cannot apply to the entire period up to three years of age, because children do recognize themselves in the mirror by the time they are two. In fact, research suggests that infants even younger than two can recognize their own faces, as well as their voices on tape (Legerstee, Anderson, & Schaffer, 1998).

Another possibility is that early memories, though "present," are implicit rather than explicit. As described in the chapter on memory, *implicit memories* form automatically and can affect our emotions and behavior even when we do not consciously recall them. Toddlers' implicit memories were demonstrated in a study in which two-and-a-half-year-olds apparently remembered a strange, pitch-dark room where they had participated in an experiment two years earlier (Perris, Myers, & Clifton, 1990). Unlike children who had never been in the room, these children were unafraid and reached for noisy objects in the dark, just as they had learned to do at the previous session. However, children's implicit memories of their early years, like their explicit memories, are quite limited. In one study, researchers showed photographs of young children to a group of ten-year-olds (Newcombe & Fox, 1994). Some of the photos were of preschool classmates whom the children had not seen since they were five years old. They explicitly recalled 21 percent of their former classmates, and their skin conductance (an index of emotion) indicated that they had implicit memories of an additional 5 percent. Yet these children had *no* memory of 74 percent of their preschool pals, as compared with adults in another study who correctly identified 90 percent of the photographs of high school classmates they had not seen in thirty years (Bahrick, Bahrick, & Wittlinger, 1975).

Other psychologists have proposed that our early memories are lost because in those years we did not yet have the language skills to talk about, and thus solidify, our memories. Nor could we be reminded of past events when others talked about them (Fivush, Haden, & Adam, 1995; Hudson & Sheffield, 1998). Still others say that early memories were stored, but because the schemas we used in early childhood to mentally represent them changed in later years, we no longer possess the retrieval cues necessary to recall them. Another possibility is that early experiences tend to be fused into *generalized event representations,* such as "going to Grandma's" or "playing at the beach," so it becomes difficult to remember any specific event. Research on hypotheses such as these may someday unravel the mystery of infantile amnesia (Eacott, 1999; Newcombe et al., 2000; Rovee-Collier, 1999).

Culture and Cognitive Development

Whereas Piaget focused on the physical world of objects in explaining development, the Russian psychologist Lev Vygotsky (pronounced "vah-GOT-ski") focused on the social world of people. He viewed cognitive abilities as the product of cultural history. The child's mind, said Vygotsky, grows through interaction with other minds. Dramatic support for this idea comes from cases such as the "Wild Boy of Aveyron," a French child who, in the late 1700s, was apparently lost or abandoned by his parents at an early age and had grown up with animals. At about eleven years of age, he was captured by hunters and sent to Paris, where scientists observed him. What the scientists saw was a dirty, frightened creature who trotted like a wild animal and spent most of his time silently rocking. Although the scientists worked with the boy for more than ten years, he was never able to live unguarded among other people, and he never learned to speak.

Consistent with Vygotsky's ideas, this tragic case suggests that without society, children's minds would not develop much beyond those of animals—that children acquire their ideas through interaction with parents, teachers, and other representatives of their culture. Vygotsky's followers have studied the effects of the social world on children's cognitive development—how participation in social routines affects children's developing knowledge of the world (Gauvain, 2001). In Western societies, such routines include shopping, eating at McDonald's, going to birthday parties, and attending religious services. In other cultures they might include helping to make pottery, going hunting, and weaving baskets (Larson & Verma, 1999). Quite early, children develop mental representations, called *scripts,* for these activities (see the chapter on cognition and language). By the time they are three, children can accurately describe the scripts for their routine activities (Nelson, 1986). Scripts, in turn, affect children's knowledge and understanding of cognitive tasks. So suburban children can understand conservation problems earlier than inner-city children if the problems are presented, as Piaget's were, like miniature science experiments; but the performance of inner-city children is improved when the task is presented via a script that is more familiar to them, such as one involving what a "slick trickster" would do to fool someone (White & Glick, 1978).

From a remarkably young age, children's cognitive abilities are influenced by the language of their culture. Consider, for instance, the way people think about relations between objects in space. Children who learn a language that has no words for spatial concepts—such as *in, on, in front of, behind, to the left,* and *to the right*—will acquire cognitive categories that are different from those of people in North America. Research indicates that such individuals do, in fact, have difficulty distinguishing between the left and right sides of objects, and they tend not to invoke the symbolic associations with left and right hands that North Americans do (Bowerman, 1996; Levinson, 1996).

As a cultural tool, language can also affect academic achievement. For example, Korean and Chinese children show exceptional ability at adding and subtracting large numbers (Fuson & Kwon, 1992; Miller et al., 1995). As third-graders, they can do in their heads three-digit problems (such as 702 minus 125) that would stump most North American children. The difference seems traceable in part to the clear and explicit way that Asian languages label numbers from eleven to nineteen. In English, the meaning of the words *eleven* and *twelve,* for instance, is not as clear

Encouraging Academic Achievement
Asian American children tend to do better in school than European American children partly because Asian American children's families tend to provide especially strong support for academic achievement.

as the Asian *ten-one* and *ten-two*. A related cultural difference supports this mathematical expertise: Asians use the metric system of measurement and a manual computing device called the *abacus*, both of which are structured around the number ten. Korean math textbooks emphasize this tens structure by presenting the ones digits in red, the tens in blue, and the hundreds in green. Above all, in Asian cultures, educational achievement, especially in mathematics, is encouraged at home and strongly encouraged in school (Crystal et al., 1994; Naito & Miura, 2001).

In short, children's cognitive development is affected in ways large and small by the culture in which they live (Tomasello, 2000).

Variations in Cognitive Development

Even within a single culture, some children are mentally advanced, whereas others lag behind their peers. Why? As already suggested, heredity is an important factor, but experience also plays a role. To explore the significance of that role, psychologists have studied the cognitive development of children who are exposed to differing environments.

Cognitive development is profoundly delayed if children are raised in environments that deprive them of the everyday sights, sounds, and feelings provided by conversation and loving interaction with family members, by pictures and books, even by toys and television. Children subjected to this kind of severe deprivation show marked impairment in intellectual development by the time they are two or three years old, and they may never fully recover even if they are given special attention later on. These effects were seen in the "Wild Boy," and also in more recent cases of youngsters whose abusive parents deliberately isolated them from contact with the world (Rymer, 1993a, 1993b), or who grew up in the understaffed and understimulating orphanages of Russia and Romania (O'Conner et al., 2000). Cognitive development is also impaired by less extreme conditions of deprivation, including the neglect, malnourishment, noise, and chaos that occur in many poor households. One study found that children raised in poverty scored nine points lower on IQ tests by the time they were five years old than did children in families

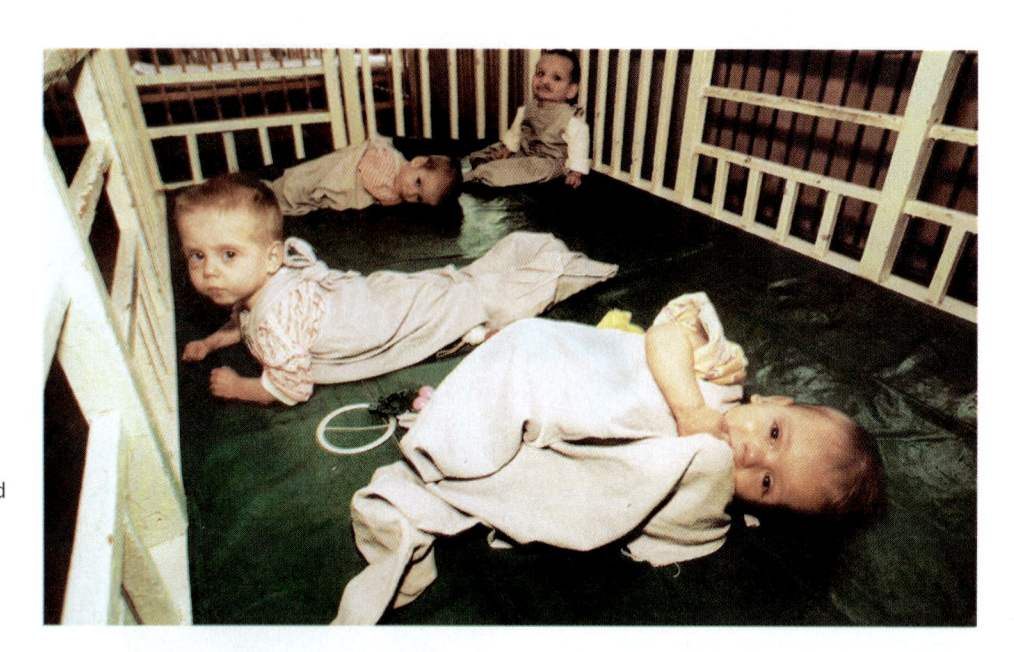

Babies at Risk The cognitive development of infants raised in this understaffed Russian orphanage will be permanently impaired if they are not given far more stimulation in the orphanage or, better yet, adopted into a loving family at a young age.

whose incomes were twice the poverty level (Duncan, Brooks-Gunn, & Klebanov, 1994). These differences continue as poor children enter school (Stipek & Ryan, 1997). Children who remain in poverty have lower IQs and poorer school achievement, the result of a buildup of problems that often begins with prenatal complications and continues through childhood with exposure to lead, lack of cognitive stimulation, and harsh and inconsistent parenting (McLoyd, 1998).

In families above the poverty line, too, children's cognitive development is related to their surroundings, their experiences, and most notably, their parents' behavior. One longitudinal study, for instance, revealed that the parents of gifted children started stimulating their children's cognitive activity very early on (Gottfried, 1997). When they were infants, the parents read to them. When they were toddlers, the parents provided them with reference books, computerized teaching aids, and trips to museums. And when they were preschoolers and older, the parents drew out their children's natural curiosity about the world and encouraged their tendency to seek out new learning opportunities themselves. In another study, researchers examined how interactions between parents and children are related to IQ scores (Fagot & Gauvain, 1997). When the children were eighteen to thirty months old, they were asked to solve a problem—specifically, to use a hook to remove a stuffed animal from a box. The researchers recorded how the mothers interacted with their children during this task. Later, at the age of five, the children were given IQ tests. It turned out that the mothers of children with the highest IQ scores had been the ones who provided cognitive guidance by offering numerous hints and suggestions. In contrast, the mothers of children with the lowest IQ scores had forcefully told them what they needed to do to complete the task.

To improve the cognitive skills of children who do not get the optimum stimulation and guidance at home, developmental psychologists have provided extra lessons, materials, and educational contact with sensitive adults. In a variety of such programs, ranging from weekly home visits to daily preschools, children's cognitive abilities have been enhanced (Ramey & Ramey, 1998), and some effects can last into adulthood (Campbell et al., 2001). Music lessons have also been shown to promote children's cognitive development (Rauscher et al., 1997). Even electronic games, though no substitute for adult attention, can provide opportunities for school-age children to hone spatial skills that help improve their performance in math and science (Subrahmanyam & Greenfield, 1994). It appears that the earlier the stimulation begins, the better; and for some cognitive abilities, stimulation affects both the brain and behavior throughout much of the life span (Greenough, 1997).

Infancy and Childhood: Social and Emotional Development

Life for the child is more than learning about objects, doing math problems, and getting good grades. It is also about social relationships and emotional reactions. From the first months onward, infants are both attracted by and attractive to other people.

During the first hour or so after birth, mothers gaze into their infants' eyes and give them gentle touches (Klaus & Kennell, 1976). This is the first opportunity for the mother to display her *bond* to her infant—an emotional tie that begins even before the baby is born. Psychologists once believed that this immediate postbirth contact was critical—that the mother-infant bond would never be strong if the opportunity for early interaction was missed. Research has revealed, however, that such interaction in the first few hours is not a requirement for a close relationship (Myers, 1987). With or without early contact, mothers (and nowadays many fathers as well), whether biological or adoptive, gradually form close attachments to their infants by interacting with them day after day.

As the mother gazes at her baby, the baby is gazing back (Klaus & Kennell, 1976). By the time infants are two days old, they recognize—and like—their mother's face; they will suck more vigorously to see a videotaped image of her face than to see that of a stranger (Walton, Bower, & Bower, 1992). Soon, they begin to respond to the mother's facial expressions as well. By the time they are a year old, children use their mothers' emotional expressions to guide their own behavior in ambiguous situations (Saarni, Mummer, & Campos, 1998; Thompson, 1998). If the mother looks frightened when a stranger approaches, for example, the child is more likely to avoid the stranger. As mentioned in the chapter on motivation and emotion, this phenomenon is called *social referencing*.

Infants also communicate their feelings to their parents. They do so by crying and screaming, but also by more subtle behavior. When they want to interact, they look and smile; when they do **not** want to interact, they turn away and suck their thumbs (Tronick, 1989).

Forming a Bond Mutual eye contact, exaggerated facial expressions, and shared "baby talk" are an important part of the early social interactions that promote an enduring bond of attachment between parent and child.

Individual Temperament

From the moment infants are born, they differ from one another in the emotions they express most often. Some infants are happy, active, and vigorous; they splash, thrash, and wriggle. Others are usually quiet. Some infants approach new objects with enthusiasm; others turn away or fuss. Some infants whimper; others kick, scream, and wail. Characteristics like these make up the infant's disposition or **temperament**—the individual style of expressing needs and emotions. Temperament has long been known to reflect heredity's influence on the beginning of an individual's personality. But temperament may itself be affected by the prenatal environment—for example, by the mother's level of stress; her intrauterine hormones; and her health habits, such as smoking.

Early research on infant temperament indicated that most babies fall into one of three general temperament patterns (Thomas & Chess, 1977). *Easy babies* are the most common kind. They get hungry and sleepy at predictable times, react to new situations cheerfully, and seldom fuss. In contrast, *difficult babies* are irregular and irritable. And *slow-to-warm-up babies* react warily to new situations but eventually come to enjoy them.

Traces of these early temperament patterns weave their way throughout childhood (Rothbart, Ahadi, & Evans, 2000): Easy infants usually stay easy; difficult infants often remain difficult, sometimes developing attention and aggression problems in childhood (Guerin, Gottfried, & Thomas, 1997); timid, or slow-to-warm-up, toddlers tend to become shy preschoolers, restrained and inhibited eight-year-olds, and somewhat anxious teenagers (Schwartz, Kagan, & Snidman, 1995). However, these tendencies are not set in stone. In temperament, as in cognitive development, nature interacts with nurture. Many events take place between infancy and adulthood that can shift an individual's development in one direction or another. For instance, if parents are patient enough to allow their difficult baby to respond to changes in daily routines at a more relaxed pace, the child may become less difficult over time.

If the characteristics of parent and infant are in synch, chances increase that temperamental qualities will be stable. Consider, for example, the temperament patterns of Chinese American and European American children. At birth, Chinese American infants are calmer, less changeable, less perturbable, and more easily consoled when upset than is typical of European American infants. This pattern suggests that there may be an inherited predisposition toward self-control among the Chinese (Kagan et al., 1994). This tendency is then powerfully reinforced by the Chinese culture. Compared with European American parents, Chinese parents are less likely to reward and stimulate babbling and smiling, and more likely to maintain close control of their young children. The children, in turn, are more dependent on their mothers and less likely to play by themselves; by and large, they are less vocal, noisy, and active than European American children (Smith & Freedman, 1983).

These temperamental differences between children in different ethnic groups illustrate the combined contributions of nature and nurture. There are many other illustrations as well. Mayan infants, for example, are relatively inactive from birth. The Zinacantecos, a Mayan group in southern Mexico, reinforce this innate predisposition toward restrained motor activity by swaddling their infants and by nursing at the slightest sign of movement (Greenfield & Childs, 1991). This combination of genetic predisposition and cultural reinforcement is culturally adaptive: Quiet Mayan infants do not kick off their covers at night, which is important in the cold highlands where they live; inactive infants are able to spend long periods on their mother's back as she works at the loom; infants who do not begin to walk until they can understand some language do not wander into the open fire at the center of the house. This adaptive interplay of innate and cultural factors in the development of temperament operates in all cultures.

---

temperament An individual's basic disposition, which is evident from infancy.

attachment A deep and enduring relationship with the person with whom a baby has shared many experiences.

The Infant Grows Attached

During the first year of life, as infants and caregivers watch and respond to one another, the infant begins to form an **attachment**—a deep, affectionate, close, and enduring relationship—to these important figures. John Bowlby, a British psychoanalyst, drew attention to the importance of attachment after he observed children who had been orphaned in World War II. These children's depression and other emotional scars led Bowlby to develop a theory about the importance of developing a strong attachment to one's primary caregivers, a tie that normally keeps infants close to their caregivers and, therefore, safe (Bowlby, 1973). Soon after Bowlby first described his theory, researchers began to investigate how such attachments are formed and what happens when they are not formed, or when they are broken by loss or separation. Some of the most dramatic of these studies were conducted by Harry Harlow.

Motherless Monkeys—and Children

Harlow (1959) explored two hypotheses about what leads infants to develop attachments to their mothers. The first hypothesis was that attachment occurs because mothers feed their babies; food, along with the experience of being fed, creates an emotional bond to the mother. Harlow's second hypothesis was that attachment is based on the warm, comforting contact the baby gets from the mother. To evaluate these hypotheses, Harlow separated newborn monkeys from their mothers and raised them in cages containing two artificial mothers. One "mother" was made of wire, but it featured a rubber nipple from which the infant could get milk (see Figure 12.6); it provided food but no physical comfort. The other artificial mother had no nipple but was made of soft, comfortable terrycloth. Harlow found that the infants preferred the terrycloth mother; they spent most of their time with it, especially when frightened. The terrycloth mother provided feelings of softness and cuddling, which were things the infants needed when they sensed danger.

Harlow also investigated what happens when attachments do not form. He isolated some newborn monkeys from all social contact. After a year of this isolation,

figure 12.6
Wire and Terrycloth "Mothers"

Here are the two types of artificial mothers used in Harlow's research. Although baby monkeys received milk from the wire mother, they spent most of their time with the terrycloth version, and they clung to it when frightened.

the monkeys showed dramatic disturbances. When visited by normally active, playful monkeys, they withdrew to a corner, huddling or rocking for hours. As adults, they were unable to have normal sexual relations; but when some of the females did have babies (through artificial insemination), they tended to ignore them. When their infants became distressed, the mothers physically abused and sometimes even killed them.

Humans who spend their first few years without a consistent caregiver react in a tragically similar manner. At the Romanian and Russian orphanages mentioned earlier, where many children were neglected by institutional caregivers, visitors have discovered that the children, like Harlow's deprived monkeys, were withdrawn and engaged in constant rocking (Holden, 1996). These effects continued even after the children were adopted. In one study, researchers observed the behaviors of four-year-old children who had been in a Romanian orphanage for at least eight months before being adopted and compared them with the behaviors of children in two other groups matched for age and gender: those who had been adopted before the age of four months, and those who had remained with their biological parents (Chisholm, 1997). The late-adopted children were found to have many more serious problems. Depressed or withdrawn, they stared blankly, demanded attention, and could not control their tempers (Holden, 1996). They also interacted poorly with their adopted mothers but were indiscriminately friendly with strangers, trying to cuddle and kiss them. Neurologists suggest that the dramatic problems observed in isolated monkeys and humans are the result of developmental brain dysfunction and damage brought on by a lack of touch and body movement in infancy (Prescott, 1996).

Forming an Attachment

Fortunately, most infants do have a consistent caregiver, usually the mother, to whom they can form an attachment. By the age of six or seven months, infants show signs of preferring their mother to anyone else—watching her closely, crawling after her, clambering up into her lap, protesting when she leaves, and brightening when she returns (Ainsworth, 1973). After an attachment has been formed, separation from the mother for even thirty minutes can be a stressful experience (Larson, Gunnar, & Hertsgaard, 1991).

Later on, infants develop attachments to their fathers as well (Lamb, 1997). However, interaction with fathers is typically less frequent, and of a somewhat different nature, than with mothers (Parke, 2002). Mothers tend to feed, bathe, dress, cuddle, and talk to their infants, whereas fathers are more likely to play, jiggle, and toss them, especially sons.

Variations in Attachment

The amount of closeness and contact infants seek with either their mother or father depends to some extent on the infant. Those who are ill, tired, or slow to warm up may require more closeness. Closeness also depends to some extent on the parent. An infant whose parent has been absent, aloof, or unresponsive is likely to need more closeness than one whose parent is accessible and responsive.

Researchers have studied the differences in infants' attachments in a special situation that simulates the natural comings and goings of parents—the so-called *Strange Situation Test* (Ainsworth et al., 1978). Mother and infant come to an unfamiliar room where they can be videotaped through a one-way window. Here the infant interacts with the mother and an unfamiliar woman in brief episodes: The infant plays with the mother and the stranger, the mother leaves the baby with the stranger for a few minutes, the mother and the stranger leave the baby alone in the room briefly, and the mother returns to the room.

Researchers have found that most infants display a *secure attachment* to the mother in the Strange Situation Test (Thompson, 1998). In the unfamiliar room, they use the mother as a home base, leaving her side to explore and play but returning to her periodically for comfort or contact. And when the mother returns after

Infancy and Childhood: Social and Emotional Development

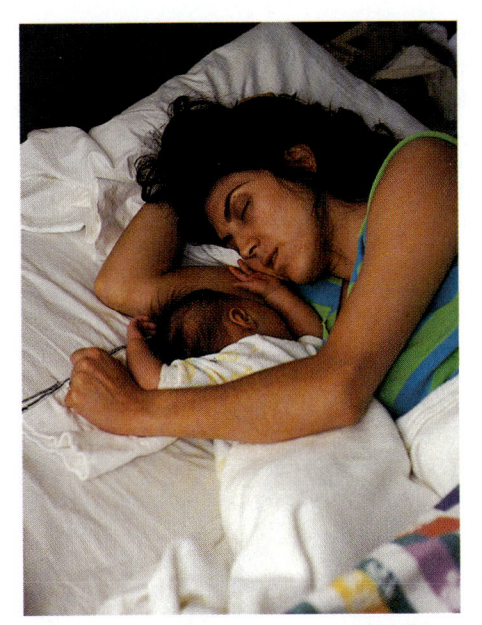

Cultural Differences in Parent-Child Relations Variations in the intimacy of family interactions, including whether infants sleep in their parents' bed, may contribute to cross-cultural differences in attachment patterns.

the brief separation, these infants are invariably happy to see her and receptive when she initiates contact. These mother-child pairs also tend to have harmonious interactions at home. The mothers themselves are generally sensitive and responsive to their babies' needs and signals (DeWolff & van IJzendoorn, 1997).

Some infants, however, display an *insecure attachment*. Their relationship with their mother may be (1) *avoidant*—they avoid or ignore their mother when she approaches or when she returns after the brief separation; (2) *ambivalent*—they are upset when their mother leaves, but when she returns they act angry and reject her efforts at contact, and when picked up they squirm to get down; or (3) *disorganized*—their behavior is inconsistent, disturbed, and disturbing; they may begin to cry again after their mother has returned and comforted them, or they may reach out for their mother while looking away from her.

The nature of a child's attachment to parents can have long-term and far-reaching effects. For example, unless disrupted by the loss of a parent, abuse by a family member, chronic depression in the mother, or some other severe negative event (Weinfield, Sroufe, & Egeland, 2000), an infant's secure attachment continues into young adulthood—and probably throughout life (Hamilton, 2000; Waters et al., 2000). A secure attachment to the mother is also reflected in relationships with other people. Children who are securely attached receive more positive reactions from other children when they are toddlers (Fagot, 1997) and have better relations with peers in middle childhood and adolescence (Schneider, Atkinson, & Tardif, 2001). Attachment to the mother also affects the way children process emotional information. Securely attached children tend to remember positive events more accurately than negative events, whereas insecurely attached children tend to do the opposite (Belsky, Spritz, & Crnic, 1996).

Patterns of attachment vary widely in different parts of the world and are related to how parents treat their children. In northern Germany, for example, where parents promote children's independence with strict discipline, the proportion of infants who display avoidant attachments is quite high (Spangler et al., 1996). Kibbutz babies in Israel, who sleep in infant houses away from their parents, are likely to show insecure attachment, as well as other attachment difficulties, later in life (Aviezer et al., 1999). And in Japan, where mothers are completely devoted to their young children and are seldom apart from them, including at night, children develop an attachment relationship that emphasizes harmony and union (Rothbaum et al., 2000). These attachment patterns differ from the secure one that is most common in the United States: with their parents' encouragement, U.S. children balance closeness and proximity with exploration and autonomy.

THINKING CRITICALLY

Does Day Care Harm the Emotional Development of Infants?

With about 60 percent of mothers now working outside the home, concern has been expressed about how daily separations from their mothers might affect children, especially infants. Some have argued that leaving infants with a baby sitter or putting them in a day-care center damages the quality of the mother-infant relationship and increases the babies' risk for psychological problems later on (Gallagher, 1998).

- **What am I being asked to believe or accept?**

The claim to be evaluated is that daily separations brought about by the need for day care undermine the infant's ability to form a secure attachment, as well as inflict emotional harm.

- **What evidence is available to support the assertion?**

There is clear evidence that separation from the mother is painful for young children. Furthermore, if separation lasts a week or more, young children may become apathetic and mournful and eventually lose interest in the missing mother (Robertson & Robertson, 1971). But day care does not involve such lasting separations, and research has shown that infants in day care do form attachments to their mothers. In fact, they prefer their mothers to their daytime caregivers (Clarke-Stewart & Fein, 1983).

But are their attachments as secure as the attachments formed by infants whose mothers do not work outside the home? Researchers first examined this question by comparing infants' behavior in the Strange Situation Test. A review of the data disclosed that, on average, infants in full-time day care were somewhat more likely to be classified as insecurely attached. Specifically, 36 percent of the infants in full-time care received this classification, compared with 29 percent of the infants not in full-time day care (Clarke-Stewart, 1989). These results appear to support the suggestion that day care hinders the development of infants' attachments to their mothers.

- **Are there alternative ways of interpreting the evidence?**

Perhaps factors other than day care could explain this difference between infants in day care and those at home with their mothers. One such factor could be the method used to assess attachment—the Strange Situation Test. Infants in these studies were judged insecure if they did not run to their mothers after a brief separation. But maybe infants who experience daily separations from their mothers are less disturbed by the separations in the Strange Situation Test and therefore seek out less closeness with their mothers. A second factor could be differences between the infants' mothers: Working mothers may value independence in themselves and their children, whereas mothers who value closeness may choose to stay home.

- **What additional evidence would help to evaluate the alternatives?**

Finding a heightened rate of insecure attachment among the infants of working mothers does not, by itself, prove that day care is harmful. To judge the effects of day care, we must use other measures of emotional adjustment. If infants in day care show consistent signs of impaired emotional relations in other situations (at home, say) and with other caregivers (such as the father), this evidence would support the argument that day care harms children's emotional development. Another

The Effects of Day Care Parents are understandably concerned that leaving their infants in a day-care center all day long might interfere with the mother-infant attachment or with other aspects of the children's development. Research shows that most infants in day care do form healthy bonds with their parents, but that if children spend many hours in day care between infancy and kindergarten, they are more likely to have behavior problems in school, such as talking back to the teacher or getting into fights with other children (NICHD Early Child Care Research Network, 2001).

useful method would be to statistically control for differences in the attitudes and behaviors of parents who do and do not use day care and then examine the differences in their children.

In fact, this research design has already been employed. In 1990 the U.S. government funded a study of infant day care in ten sites around the country. The psychological and physical development of more than 1,300 randomly selected infants was tracked from birth through age three. The results showed that when factors such as parents' education, income, and attitudes were statistically controlled for, infants in day care were no more likely to have emotional problems or to be insecurely attached to their mothers than infants not in day care. However, in cases where infants were placed in poor-quality day care, where the caregivers were insensitive and unresponsive, and where mothers were insensitive to their babies' needs at home, the infants were less likely to develop a secure attachment to their mothers (NICHD Early Child Care Research Network, 1997, 1998, 1999).

- **What conclusions are most reasonable?**

Based on available evidence, the most reasonable conclusion appears to be that day care by itself does not lead to insecure attachment or cause emotional harm to infants. But if the care is of poor quality, it can worsen a risky situation at home and increase the likelihood that infants will have problems forming a secure attachment to their mothers. The U.S. government study is still under way, and the children's progress is being followed into elementary school. Time will tell if other problems develop in the future.

Relationships with Parents and Peers

Erik Erikson (1968) saw the first year of life as the time when infants develop a feeling of basic trust (or mistrust) about the world. According to his theory, an infant's first year represents the first of eight stages of lifelong psychosocial development (see Table 12.2). Each stage focuses on an issue or crisis that is especially important at that time of life. Erikson believed that the ways in which people resolve these issues shape their personalities and social relationships. Positive resolution of an issue provides the foundation for characteristics such as trust, autonomy, initiative, and industry. But if the crisis is not resolved positively, according to Erikson, the person will be psychologically troubled and cope less effectively with later crises. In Erikson's theory, then, forming basic feelings of trust during infancy is the bedrock for all future emotional development.

After children have formed strong emotional attachments to their parents, their next psychological task is to begin to develop a more independent, or autonomous, relationship with them. This task is part of Erikson's second stage, when children begin to exercise their wills, develop some independence from their parents, and initiate activities on their own. According to Erikson, children who are not allowed to exercise their wills or initiate their own activities will feel uncertain about doing things for themselves and guilty about seeking independence. The extent to which parents allow or encourage their children's autonomy depends largely on their parenting style.

Parenting Styles
Parents try to channel children's impulses into socially accepted outlets and teach them the skills and rules needed to function in their society. This process, called *socialization,* is shaped by cultural values. Parents in Hispanic cultures of Mexico, Puerto Rico, and Central America, for example, tend to be influenced by the collectivist tradition, in which family and community interests are emphasized over individual goals. Children in these cultures are expected to respect and obey their elders and to do less of the questioning, negotiating, and arguing that is encouraged—or at least allowed—in many middle-class European and European American families (Greenfield, 1995). When parents from Hispanic

In each of Erikson's stages of development, a different psychological issue presents a new crisis for the person to resolve. The person focuses attention on that issue and, by the end of the period, has worked through the crisis and resolved it either positively, in the direction of healthy development, or negatively, hindering further psychological development.

table 12.2
Erikson's Stages of Psychosocial Development

Age	Central Psychological Issue or Crisis
First year	**Trust versus mistrust** Infants learn to trust that their needs will be met by the world, especially by the mother—or they learn to mistrust the world.
Second year	**Autonomy versus shame and doubt** Children learn to exercise will, to make choices, and to control themselves—or they become uncertain and doubt that they can do things by themselves.
Third to fifth year	**Initiative versus guilt** Children learn to initiate activities and enjoy their accomplishments, acquiring direction and purpose. Or, if they are not allowed initiative, they feel guilty for their attempts at independence.
Sixth year through puberty	**Industry versus inferiority** Children develop a sense of industry and curiosity and are eager to learn—or they feel inferior and lose interest in the tasks before them.
Adolescence	**Identity versus role confusion** Adolescents come to see themselves as unique and integrated persons with an ideology—or they become confused about what they want out of life.
Early adulthood	**Intimacy versus isolation** Young people become able to commit themselves to another person—or they develop a sense of isolation and feel they have no one in the world but themselves.
Middle age	**Generativity versus stagnation** Adults are willing to have and care for children and to devote themselves to their work and the common good—or they become self-centered and inactive.
Old age	**Integrity versus despair** Older people enter a period of reflection, becoming assured that their lives have been meaningful and ready to face death with acceptance and dignity. Or they are in despair for their unaccomplished goals, failures, and ill-spent lives.

cultures immigrate to the United States, they may find that some of their values conflict with those of their children's European American teachers (Raeff, Greenfield, & Quiroz, 1995), and their own parenting efforts may become inconsistent (Harwood, Schulze, & Wilson, 1995).

European and European American parents tend to employ one of three distinct parenting styles, as described by Diana Baumrind (1971). **Authoritarian parents** are relatively strict, punitive, and unsympathetic. They value obedience and try to shape their children's behavior to meet a set standard and to curb the children's wills. They do not encourage independence. They are detached and seldom praise their youngsters. In contrast, **permissive parents** give their children lax discipline and a great deal of freedom. **Authoritative parents** fall between these two extremes. They reason with their children, encouraging give and take. They allow the children increasing responsibility as they get older and better at making decisions. They are firm but

authoritarian parents Firm, punitive, and unsympathetic parents who value obedience from their child and authority for themselves.

permissive parents Parents who give their child great freedom and lax discipline.

authoritative parents Parents who reason with their child, encourage give and take, and are firm but understanding.

understanding. They set limits but also encourage independence. Their demands are reasonable, rational, and consistent.

In her research with middle-class parents, Baumrind found that these three parenting styles were related to young children's social and emotional development. The children of authoritarian parents tended to be unfriendly, distrustful, and withdrawn. Children of permissive parents tended to be immature, dependent, and unhappy; they were likely to have tantrums or to ask for help when they encountered even slight difficulties. Children raised by authoritative parents tended to be friendly, cooperative, self-reliant, and socially responsible (Baumrind, 1986).

Other researchers have found authoritative parenting styles to be associated with additional positive outcomes, including better school achievement (Steinberg et al., 1994), higher sociometric status (Hinshaw et al., 1997), and better psychological adjustment to parental divorce (Hetherington & Clingempeel, 1992). In contrast, children of authoritarian parents are more likely to cheat and to be aggressive, and less likely to be empathic or to experience guilt or accept blame after doing something wrong (Eisenberg & Fabes, 1998).

The results of these studies of parenting styles are interesting, but they have some limitations. First, they involve *correlations*, which, as discussed in the chapter on research in psychology, do not prove causation. Finding consistent correlations between parenting styles and children's behavior does not establish that the parents' behavior is causing the differences seen in their children. In fact, parents' behavior is, itself, often shaped by their children to some extent. For example, parents may react differently to children of different ages. Children's temperament, size, and appearance may also influence the way parents treat them (Bugental & Goodnow, 1998). Second, some psychologists have suggested that it is not the parents' behavior itself that influences children but rather how the children perceive the discipline they receive—as stricter or more lenient than what an older sibling received, for example (Reiss et al., 2000).

A third limitation of these studies is that the correlations between parenting styles and children's behavior, though statistically significant, are usually not terribly strong. Expected relationships between parenting styles and children's behavior do not always appear. For example, Baumrind (1971) found a small group of "harmonious" families in which she never observed the parents disciplining the children, yet the children were thriving.

In all likelihood, it is the "fit" between parenting style and children's characteristics that affects children the most. There is no universally "best" style of parenting (Parke & Buriel, 1998, 2002). For example, authoritative parenting, so consistently linked with positive outcomes in European American families, is not related to better school performance in African American or Asian American youngsters (Steinberg, Dornbusch, & Brown, 1992; Wang & Phinney, 1998). One possible explanation is that different disciplinary styles have different meanings in different cultures. Chinese American parents use authoritarian discipline more than European American parents, but their goal is usually to "train" *(chiao shun)* and "govern" *(guan)* children so that they will know what is expected of them (Chao, 1994). By contrast, European American parents who use authoritarian discipline are more likely to do so to "break the child's will." In other words, each parenting style must be evaluated in its cultural context.

There are no hard and fast rules about how to discipline children, even when it comes to things like spanking. In her longitudinal study of children from preschool through adolescence, Baumrind found that although severe punishment was linked with negative outcomes, there were no detrimental effects of occasional mild to moderate spanking. Accordingly, Baumrind (2001) argues that parents should be free to raise their children in accordance with their own values and traditions.

Some people have suggested that parenting styles are a less significant influence on children's social development than are the influences the children encounter outside the home—especially by interacting with peers (Harris, 1995, 1998). Research

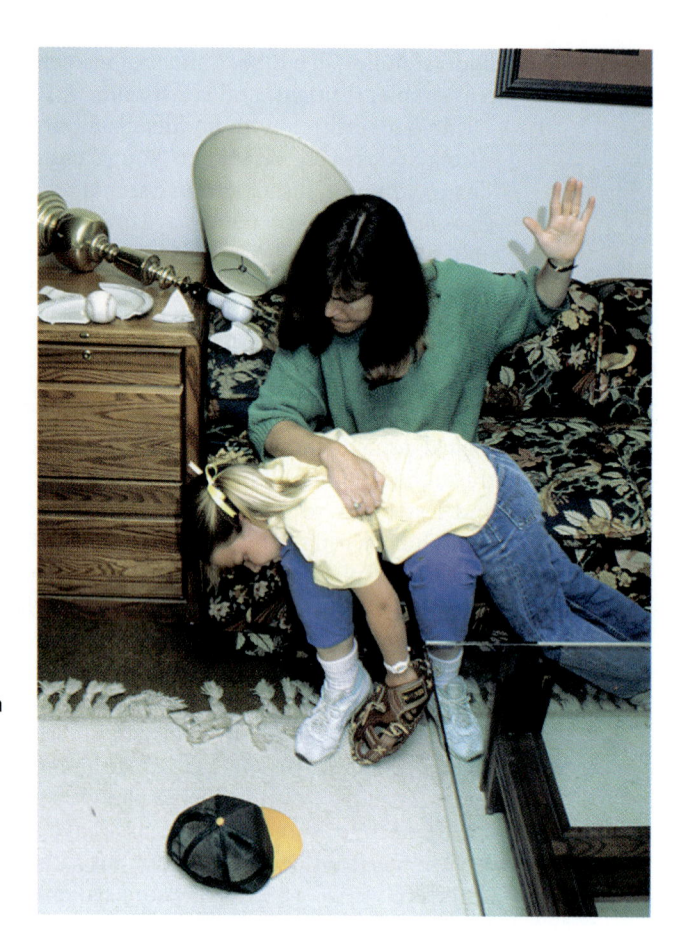

Parent-Training Programs Research in developmental psychology on the relationship between parents' socialization styles and children's behavior has helped shape parent-training programs based on both the social-cognitive and the humanistic approaches described in the chapter on personality. These programs are designed to teach parents authoritative methods that can avoid scenes like this.

evidence does not justify dismissing the impact of parenting styles, but there is no denying the impact of peer influences, either (Collins et al., 2000; Leventhal & Brooks-Gunn, 2000).

Relationships with Peers Social development over the years of childhood occurs in a social world that broadens to include brothers, sisters, playmates, and classmates. Relationships with other children start very early (Rubin, Bukowski, & Parker, 1998). By two months of age, infants engage in mutual gazing. By six months, they vocalize and smile at each other. By eight months, they prefer to look at another child rather than at an adult (Bigelow et al., 1990). So people are interested in one another, even as infants, but it's a long journey from interest to intimacy.

Observations of two-year-olds show that the most they can do with their peers is to look at them, imitate them, and exchange—or grab—toys. By age four, they begin to play "pretend" together, agreeing about roles and themes. This "sociodramatic" play is important because it provides a context for communicating meaning and offers an opportunity to form first "friendships" (Dunn & Hughes, 2001; Rubin, Bukowski, & Parker, 1998).

In the school years, peer interaction becomes more frequent, complex, and structured. Children play games with rules, join teams, tutor each other, and cooperate—or compete—in achieving goals. Friends become more important and friendships longer lasting as school-age children find that friends are a source of companionship, stimulation, support, and affection (Hartup & Stevens, 1997). In fact, companionship and fun are the most important aspects of friendship for children at this age; psychological intimacy does not enter the picture until adolescence (Parker et al., 2001).

Children's Friendships Although relationships with peers may not always be this cordial, they are often among the closest and most positive in a child's life. Friends are more interactive than nonfriends. They smile and laugh together more; pay closer attention to equality in their conversation; and talk about mutual, rather than just personal, goals. Having at least one close friend in childhood predicts good psychological functioning later on.

LINKAGES (a link to Social Cognition)

Friends also help children to establish their sense of self-worth. For example, through friendships children can compare their own strengths and weaknesses with those of others in a supportive and accepting atmosphere. Unfortunately, about 10 percent of schoolchildren do not have friends. These children report extremely high levels of loneliness and rejection (Asher & Hopmeyer, 2001). They do poorly in school and usually experience psychological and behavior problems in later life (Asher & Hopmeyer, 2001; Bagwell, Newcomb, & Bukowski, 1998). It appears that having just one close, stable friend can protect schoolchildren from loneliness and other problems (Parker et al., 2001); having more than one friend does not seem to provide further benefits.

Social Skills

The changes in peer interactions and the formation of friendships over the years of childhood can be traced in part to children's increasing social competencies and skills. *Social skills,* like cognitive skills, must be learned (Rubin, Bukowski, & Parker, 1998).

One social skill is the ability to engage in sustained, responsive interactions with peers. Such interactions require cooperation, sharing, and taking turns—behaviors that first appear in the preschool years. Parents can aid their children's development of these skills by initiating lots of "pretend" play and other prosocial activities (Ladd & LeSieur, 1995; Parke & O'Neil, 2000) and by helping the children express their emotions constructively (Eisenberg, 1998). Older siblings, too, can help by acting out social roles during play and by talking about their feelings (Ruffman et al., 1998). Children who have been abused by their parents tend to lack these important interactional skills and are thus more likely to be victimized by their peers (Bolger & Patterson, 2001; Crick, 1997).

A second social skill learned by children is the ability to detect and interpret other people's emotional signals. In fact, effective performance in social situations depends on this ability to process information about other people (Slomkowski & Dunn, 1996). Research indicates that girls are able to read emotional signals at younger ages than boys (Dunn et al., 1991). Children who understand another person's perspective, who appreciate how that person might be feeling, and who behave accordingly tend to be the most popular members of a peer group (Izard et al., 2001; Rubin, Bukowski, & Parker, 1998). Children who do not have these skills are rejected or neglected; they may become bullies or the victims of bullies.

A related social skill is the ability to feel what another person is feeling, or something close to it, and to respond with comfort or help if the person is in distress. This skill allows children to develop both *empathy* and *sympathy*. Affectionate mothers who discuss emotions openly, and who provide clear messages about the consequences of their child's hurtful behavior, effectively encourage the child to be empathic and sympathetic (Eisenberg, 1997).

Yet another social skill that develops in childhood is the ability to control one's emotions and behavior—an ability known as **self-regulation** (Rothbart & Bates, 1998). In the first few years of life, children learn to calm or console themselves by sucking their thumbs or cuddling their favorite blanket. Later, they learn more sophisticated strategies of self-regulation, such as planning ahead to avoid a problem (e.g., getting on the first bus if the school bully usually takes the second one) and recruiting social support (e.g., casually joining a group of big kids to walk past the bully on the playground). Children who cannot regulate their emotions tend to experience anxiety and distress and have trouble recovering from stressful events. They become emotionally overaroused when they see someone in distress and are often unsympathetic and unhelpful (Eisenberg & Fabes, 1998). Further, boys who are easily aroused and have difficulty regulating this arousal become less and less popular with their peers as the months go by (Fabes et al., 1997).

Self-regulation is most effectively learned by children who experience harmonious interactions at home under the guidance of supportive and competent parents (Saarni, Mummer, & Campos, 1998). One study revealed that children skilled at regulating their emotions had parents who had soothed them in infancy by holding them, talking to them, and providing distractions. As the children grew older, the parents gradually began to introduce them to new and potentially uncomfortable events (such as their first haircut), all the while remaining close by as a safe base (Fox, 1997). Another study, specifically involving North American children, found that self-regulation and empathy are fostered by parents who talk about their own feelings and encourage their children to express emotions (Eisenberg, 1997). This phenomenon is not universal, however. For example, Japanese children are usually better emotion regulators than North American children, even though Japanese parents tend not to encourage the expression of strong emotion. (Zahn-Waxler et al., 1996).

In recent years, psychologists in the United States have been encouraging schools to teach children the social skills of self-regulation, as well as understanding, empathy, and cooperation (Goleman, 1995; Salovey & Sluyter, 1997). It is their hope that this "emotional literacy" will reduce the prevalence of childhood depression and aggression.

Gender Roles

LINKAGES (a link to Learning)

An important aspect of understanding other people and being socially skilled is knowing about social roles, including **gender roles**—the general patterns of work, appearance, and behavior associated with being a man or a woman. One survey of gender roles in twenty-five countries found that children learn these roles earliest in Muslim countries (where gender roles are perhaps most extreme), but children in all twenty-five countries eventually develop them (Williams & Best, 1990).

Gender roles persist because they are deeply rooted in both nature and nurture. Small physical and behavioral differences between the sexes are evident early on and tend to increase over the years (Eagly, 1996). For example, girls tend to speak and write earlier and to be better at grammar and spelling (Halpern, 1997), whereas boys tend to be more skilled than girls at manipulating objects, constructing three-dimensional forms, and mentally manipulating complex figures and pictures. Girls are likely to be more kind, considerate, and empathic. Their play tends to be more orderly. Boys are more physically active and aggressive; they play in larger groups and spaces, enjoying noisier, more strenuous physical games (Eisenberg & Fabes, 1998).

self-regulation The ability to control one's emotions and behavior.

gender roles Patterns of work, appearance, and behavior that a society associates with being male or female.

Learning Gender Roles Socialization by parents and others typically encourages interests and activities traditionally associated with a child's own gender.

The presence of a biological contribution to these male-female differences is supported by studies of differences in anatomy, hormones, and brain organization and functioning (Geary, 1999; Ruble & Martin, 1998), as well as by cross-cultural research that finds consistent gender patterns even in the face of differing socialization practices (Simpson & Kenrick, 1997). Consider the phenomenon of violence. In one survey, there was not a single culture in which the number of women who killed women was even one-tenth as great as the number of men who killed men; on average, men's homicides outnumbered women's by more than thirty to one (Cassel & Bernstein, 2001; Daly & Wilson, 1988).

At the same time, there is strong evidence that socialization influences gender roles. From the moment they are born, boys and girls are treated differently. Adults usually play more gently and talk more to infants they believe to be girls than to infants they believe to be boys. They often shower their daughters with dolls and doll clothes, their sons with trucks and tools. They tend to encourage boys to achieve, compete, explore, control their feelings, act independent, and assume personal responsibility. They more often encourage girls to be reflective, dependent, domestic, obedient, and unselfish (Ruble & Martin, 1998). They talk more, and use more supportive speech, with daughters than with sons (Leaper, Anderson, & Sanders, 1998). In these and many other ways, parents, teachers, and television role models consciously or inadvertently pass on their ideas about "appropriate" behaviors for boys and girls (Witt, 1997).

Children also pick up notions of what is gender-appropriate behavior from their peers (Martin & Fabes, 2001). Peer pressure exaggerates whatever differences may already exist. For example, boys tend to be better than girls at computer and video games (Greenfield, 1994), but this difference stems in part from the fact that boys encourage and reward each other for skilled performance at these games more than girls do (Law, Pellegrino, & Hunt, 1993). Children are also more likely to play with other children of the same sex, and to act in gender-typical ways, when they are on the playground than when they are at home or in the classroom (Luria, 1992). On the playground, boys are the overtly aggressive ones; they push and they punch (Hyde, 1986). Among girls, the aggression is less obvious and more "relational." Although unlikely to hit other children, girls hurt with nasty words and threats to withdraw friendship (Crick, Casas, & Mosher, 1997; Crick et al., 1999; Zuger, 1998).

Children are also influenced by **gender schemas,** the generalizations they develop about what toys and activities are "appropriate" for boys versus girls and what jobs are "meant" for men versus women (Fagot, 1995). For example, by the time they are three years old, children tend to believe that dolls are for girls and trucks are for boys. Once they have developed these gender schemas and know that they themselves are male or female, children tend to choose activities, toys, and behaviors that are "appropriate" for their own gender (Ruble & Martin, 1998). They become "sexist self-socializers" as they work at developing the masculine or feminine attributes they view as consistent with their self-image as a male or a female. By the age of eight or nine, they may have become more flexible about what's okay for members of each sex to do—but most still say they wouldn't be friends with a boy who wore lipstick or a girl who played football (Levy et al., 1995).

In short, social training by both adults and peers, along with the child's own cognitions about the world, tends to bolster and amplify any biological predispositions that distinguish boys and girls. This process, in turn, creates gender roles that are the joint—and inextricably linked—products of nature and nurture. This and other elements of early development are summarized in "In Review: Social and Emotional Development During Infancy and Childhood."

The efforts of some parents to de-emphasize gender roles in their children's upbringing may be helping to reduce the magnitude of gender differences in areas such as verbal and quantitative skills (Hyde, 1994). However, some observers believe that other gender differences—such as males' greater ability to visualize the

gender schemas The generalizations children develop about what toys, activities, and occupations are "appropriate" for males versus females.

in review: Social and Emotional Development During Infancy and Childhood

Age	Relationships with Parents	Relationships with Other Children	Social Understanding
Birth–2 years	Infants form an attachment to the primary caregiver.	Play focuses on toys, not on other children.	Infants respond to emotional expressions of others.
2–4 years	Children become more autonomous and no longer need their parents' constant attention.	Toys are a way of eliciting responses from other children.	Young children can recognize emotions of others.
4–10 years	Parents actively socialize their children.	Children begin to cooperate, compete, play games, and form friendships with peers.	Children learn social rules, like politeness, and roles, like being a male or female; they learn to control their emotions.

rotation of objects in space and females' greater ability to read facial expressions—are unlikely to change much. Evolutionary psychologists see these differences as deeply rooted in our evolutionary past, when males' major activity was hunting and females' was child rearing (Buss, 1999). Other psychologists have suggested that prenatal exposure to male or female hormones influences the organization of male and female brains in ways that make boys more receptive to spatial activities and girls more susceptible to social exchanges (Halpern, 1997).

Risk and Resilience

Family instability, child abuse, homelessness, poverty, substance abuse, and domestic violence put many children at risk for various problems in social and emotional development. When parents divorce, for example, their children often develop serious interpersonal problems. By two or three years after the divorce, the intense psychological stress is over, and most children are functioning competently (Hetherington & Kelly, 2002), but there can be long-lasting effects. Adults whose parents had divorced when they were children may not live as long as those from intact families (Friedman et al., 1995b), and a high proportion of people who were young adolescents when their parents divorced are unable to form committed relationships even years later (Wallerstein, Lewis, & Blakeslee, 2000). Children are also at risk if their parents have violent fights. Nearly half the children exposed to marital violence exhibit various forms of psychological disorder—a rate six times higher than that in the general population (Garber, 1992).

How well children ultimately adjust to their parents' fighting or divorce, as well as whether they lead happy and successful lives, is influenced by numerous factors, including the intensity and duration of the parents' marital conflict and how well divorcing parents work out a harmonious arrangement that allows both to have regular contact with their children (Hetherington & Kelley, 2002). Even when the odds are against them, though, some children are left virtually unscathed by even the most dangerous risk factors. These children are said to be *resilient*. **Resilience** is a characteristic that permits successful development in the face of significant challenge (Luthar, Cicchetti, & Becker, 2000). It has been studied in a wide variety of adverse situations throughout the world, including war, natural disaster, family violence, and poverty. This research has consistently identified certain qualities in children and their environments that are associated with resilience. Specifically, resilient children tend to be intelligent and to have easy dispositions, high self-esteem, talent, and faith (Masten & Coatsworth, 1998). They are cheerful,

resilience A quality allowing children to develop normally in spite of severe environmental risk factors.

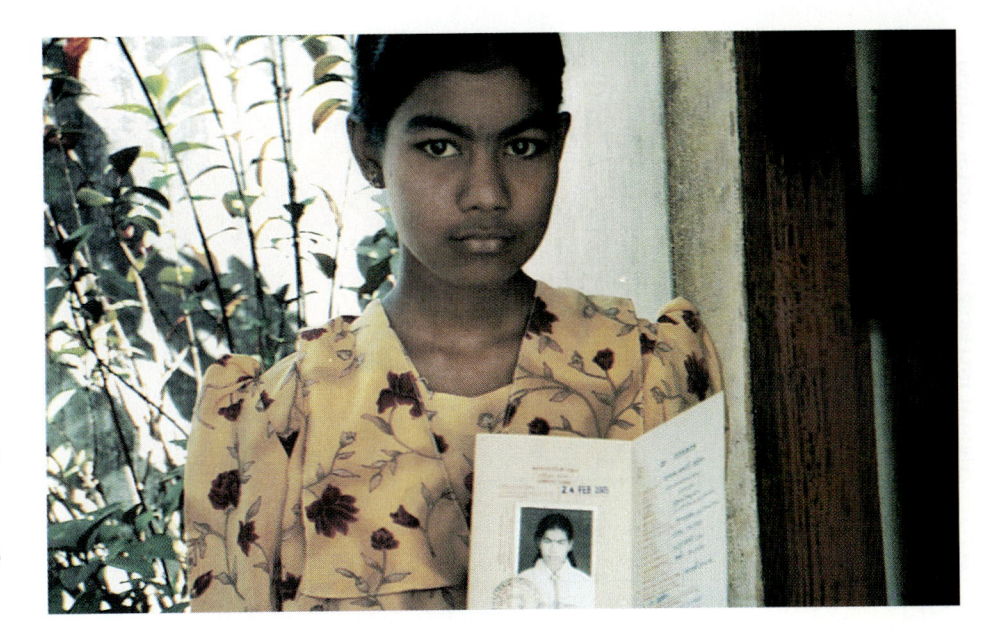

Beating the Odds Some children are able to overcome the difficulties and risks associated with poverty, war, family violence, homelessness, and other circumstances to make a success of their lives. These children are said to be *resilient*. This 15-year-old girl grew up in a war zone, but retains her dream of becoming a doctor.

focused, and persistent in completing a task (Wills et al., 2001). They also typically have significant relationships with a warm and authoritative parent; with someone in their extended family; or with other caring adults outside the family, at school or in clubs or religious organizations.

Adolescence

The years of middle childhood usually pass smoothly, but adolescence changes things drastically. All adolescents undergo significant changes in size, shape, and physical capacities. Many also experience substantial changes in their social life, reasoning abilities, and views of themselves.

The Challenges of Change

A sudden spurt in physical growth is the most visible sign that adolescence has begun. This growth spurt peaks at about age twelve for girls and age fourteen for boys (Tanner, 1978; see Figure 12.7). Suddenly, adolescents find themselves in new bodies. At the end of the growth spurt, females begin to menstruate, and males produce live sperm. This state of being able for the first time to reproduce is called **puberty**.

In Western cultures, *early adolescence*, the period from ages eleven to fourteen or so, is filled with challenges. Sexual interest stirs, and there are opportunities to smoke, drink alcohol, and take other drugs. All of this can be disorienting. Adolescents may experience bouts of depression and other psychological problems. Early-maturing girls are the most likely to be depressed (Ge, Conger, & Elder, 2001). This is also the time when eating disorders are likely to first appear (Wilson et al., 1996) and when the incidence of attempted and completed suicides rises (Centers for Disease Control and Prevention, 1999a). Between 15 and 30 percent of adolescents drop out of school; their arrest rate is the highest of any age group (Zigler & Stevenson, 1993). About 30 percent of twelfth graders report having had at least five drinks in a row in the previous two weeks, and about 25 percent report having used drugs in the previous month (Federal Interagency Forum on Children and Family Statistics, 2001). For some children, then, early adolescence marks the beginning of a downward spiral that ends up in academic failure, dropping out of school, delinquency, and substance abuse.

puberty The condition of being able, for the first time, to reproduce.

figure 12.7

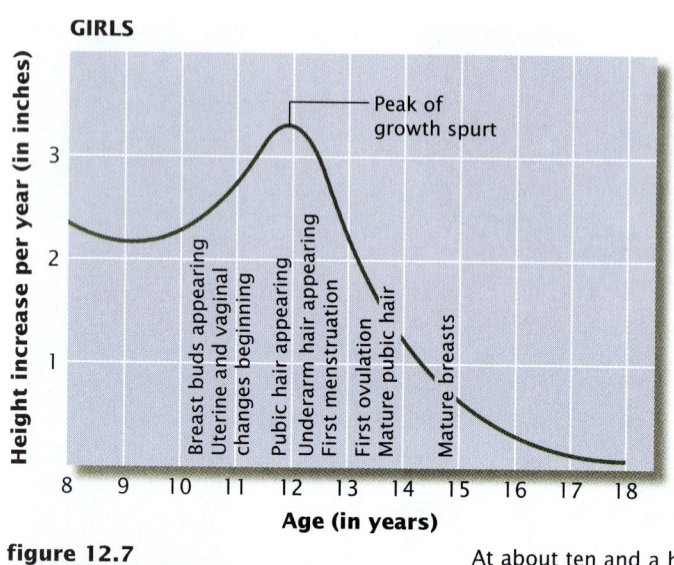

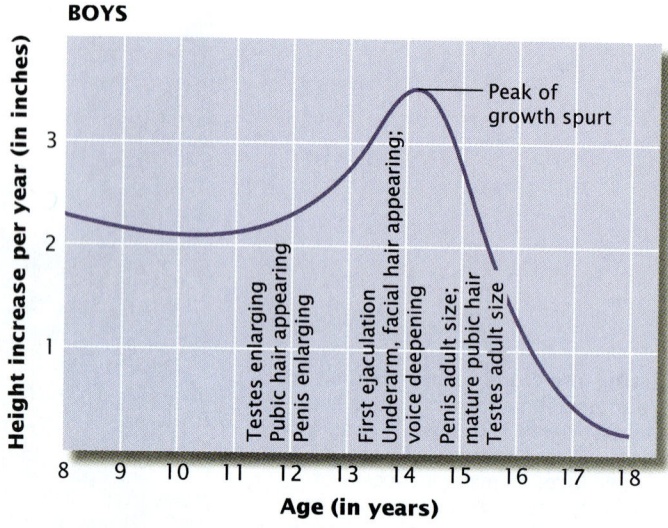

Physical Changes in Adolescence

At about ten and a half years of age, girls begin their growth spurt, and by age twelve, they are taller than their male peers. When boys, at about twelve and a half years of age, begin their growth spurt, they usually grow faster and for a longer period of time than girls. Adolescents may grow as much as five inches a year. The development of sexual characteristics accompanies these changes in height. The ages at which these changes occur vary considerably across individuals, but their sequence is the same.

Many of the problems of adolescence are associated with challenges to young people's *self-esteem*, their sense of being worthy, capable, and deserving of respect (Harter, 1998). Adolescents are especially vulnerable if many stressors occur at the same time (DuBois et al., 1992; Kling et al., 1999). The switch from elementary school to middle school is particularly challenging. Grades tend to drop, especially for students who were already having trouble in school or who don't have confidence in their own abilities (Rudolph et al., 2001). But grades do not affect self-esteem in all teens. Some base their self-esteem on athletic success and on their peers' opinions of them rather than on their academic achievement (Osborne, 1997). In fact, adolescents' academic performance is strongly affected by the peers with whom they spend their time. For example, adolescents whose grades and motivation decline from the end of elementary school to the end of their first year in middle school tend to be those who affiliated themselves with other academic underachievers (Ryan, 2001).

The transition from elementary school to junior high or middle school can be a rude awakening for an eleven- or twelve-year-old (Eccles, Lord, & Buchanan, 1996). At the new school, teachers may be less friendly and less likely to have time for nurturing relationships with students. They may also exert more control, impose higher standards, and set up more public evaluation of students' work. In addition, junior high school teachers may not be aware of their students' anxieties or insecurities, and they may assume that students are adjusting well as long as they are doing well academically (Eccles, Lord, & Roeser, 1996).

The changes and pressures of adolescence are often played out at home, as adolescents try to have a greater say in a parent-child relationship once ruled mainly by their parents. National surveys of more than 90,000 adolescents from 80 high schools and middle schools in the United States found that teens who do not feel close to their parents are more likely to engage in risky behaviors such as smoking, taking drugs, attempting suicide, and having sex (Blum, Beuhring, & Rinehart, 2000; Resnick, 1997). Fortunately, such closeness is not uncommon; there are also programs that can teach parents what is "normal" behavior for adolescents and how to respond to it. In one study, for example, low-income parents of young adolescents participated in a parenting program in which they learned how to listen and communicate; to invite their children to participate in family decision making; and to reduce nonsupportive behaviors such as scolding, criticizing, and interrogating. The children of these parents adjusted well to the transition to middle school and showed more positive functioning than children in a control group. In addition, their grades remained stable (whereas the control kids' grades declined), and they exhibited fewer problem behaviors (Bronstein et al., 1998).

When troubles arise, they often involve sex. Surveys suggest that about 50 percent of teens in the United States have had sexual intercourse by age sixteen (National Center for Health Statistics, 1997). Teens who have sex differ from those who do not in a number of ways. They hold less conventional attitudes and values, and they are more likely to smoke, drink alcohol, and use other drugs. Their parents tend to be less educated, to have less control over them, and to not talk openly with them. Sexual activity in adolescence is also related to ethnicity. For instance, teens from Asian American families are less likely to be sexually active than those from European American families (McLaughlin et al., 1997).

All too often, sexual activity leads to declining school achievement and interest, sexually transmitted diseases, and unplanned and unwanted pregnancies. Teenagers have the highest rates of gonorrhea, chlamydia, pelvic inflammatory disease, and other sexually transmitted diseases than any other age group (Grady, 1998). One-fifth of all AIDS cases start in adolescence (Brody, 1998). And although teenage pregnancy rates have been declining lately, nearly 10 percent of all teenage girls in the United States become pregnant before the age of nineteen (National Center for Health Statistics, 2000). More than half of them decide to keep their babies and become single mothers.

A teenage pregnancy can create problems for the mother, the baby, and others in the family. Teenage parents tend to be less positive and stimulating with their children, and more likely to abuse them, than older parents (Brooks-Gunn & Chase-Lansdale, 2002). The children of teenage parents, in turn, are more likely to develop behavior problems and to do poorly in school than those whose parents are older (Furstenberg, Brooks-Gunn, & Chase-Lansdale, 1989). They do better if they have strong attachments to their fathers and if their mothers are prepared for their new responsibilities and know about children and parenting even before the baby is born (Miller et al., 1996; Whitman et al., 2001). The younger sisters of teenage mothers are also affected by the birth. Often, they must take time away from schoolwork to help care for the child, and they are at increased risk for drug and alcohol use and for becoming pregnant themselves (East & Jacobson, 2001).

Fortunately, despite all the dangers and problems of adolescence, most teens in Western cultures do not experience major personal turmoil or family conflicts (Peterson, 1987; Steinberg, 1990). In fact, research suggests that in Western cultures, more than half of today's teens find early adolescence relatively trouble-free (Arnett, 1999). Only about 15 percent of the adolescents studied experience serious turmoil (Steinberg, 1990). The vast majority of adolescents cope well with the changes puberty brings and soon find themselves in the midst of perhaps the biggest challenge of their young lives—preparing themselves for the transition to young adulthood.

Identity and Development of the Self

In many less developed countries today, as in the United States a century ago, the end of early adolescence, around the age of fifteen, marks the beginning of adulthood: of work, parenting, and grown-up responsibilities. In modern North America, though, the transition from childhood to adulthood often lasts well into the twenties. This lengthened adolescence has created special problems—among them, the matter of finding or forming an identity.

Forming a Personal and Ethnic Identity

Most adolescents have not previously thought deeply about who they are. When preschool children are asked to describe themselves, they often mention a favorite or habitual activity: "I watch TV" or "I do the dishes" (Keller, Ford, & Meacham, 1978). At age eight or nine, children identify themselves by giving facts such as their sex, age, name, physical appearance, likes, and dislikes. They may still describe themselves in terms of what they do, but they now include how well they do it compared with other children (Secord & Peevers, 1974). Then, at about age eleven, children begin to describe themselves in terms of social relationships, personality traits, and other general, stable psychological characteristics (Damon & Hart, 1982). By the end of early adolescence, they are ready to develop a personal identity as a unique individual.

Their personal identity may be affected by their **ethnic identity**—the part of a person's identity that reflects the racial, religious, or cultural group to which he or she belongs. In melting-pot nations such as the United States, some members of ethnic minorities may identify with their ethnic group—Chinese, Mexican, or Italian, for example—even more than with their national citizenship. Children are aware of ethnic cues such as skin color before they reach the age of three and prefer to play with children from their own group. Minority-group children reach this awareness earlier than other children (Milner, 1983). In high school, most students hang out with members of their own ethnic group. They tend not to know classmates in other ethnic groups well, seeing them more as members of those groups than as individuals (Steinberg, Dornbusch, & Brown, 1992). A positive ethnic identity contributes to self-esteem; seeing their own group as superior makes people feel good about themselves (Fiske, 1998). However, as described in the chapter on social cognition, the same processes that foster ethnic identity can also sow the seeds of ethnic prejudice. Adolescents who have more extensive contact with members of other ethnic groups in school tend to develop more mature ethnic identities and more favorable attitudes toward people of other ethnicities (Phinney, Ferguson, & Tate, 1997).

Facing the Identity Crisis

According to Erikson (1968), identity formation is the central task of adolescence. Events of late adolescence, such as graduating from high school, going to college, and forging new relationships, challenge the adolescent's self-concept and precipitate an **identity crisis** (see Table 12.2). In this crisis, the adolescent must develop an integrated self-image as a unique person by pulling together self-knowledge acquired during childhood. If infancy and childhood

Ethnic Identity Ethnic identity is that part of our personal identity that reflects the racial, religious, or cultural group to which we belong. Ethnic identity often leads people to interact mainly with others who share that same identity.

brought trust, autonomy, and initiative, according to Erikson, the adolescent will resolve the identity crisis positively, feeling self-confident and competent. If infancy and childhood resulted in feelings of mistrust, shame, guilt, and inferiority, the adolescent will be confused about his or her identity and goals.

In Western cultures there is some limited empirical support for Erikson's ideas about the identity crisis. In late adolescence, young people do consider alternative identities (Waterman, 1982). They "try out" being rebellious, studious, or detached as they attempt to resolve questions about sexuality, self-worth, industriousness, and independence. Adolescents who explore matters of identity more extensively tend to have had opportunities to express and develop their own points of view in a supportive environment at home, at school, and in the community (Grotevant, 1998). By the time they are twenty-one, about half of the adolescents studied resolve the identity crisis in a way that is consistent with their self-image and the historical era in which they are living. They are ready to enter adulthood with self-confidence. Basically the same people who entered adolescence, they now have more mature attitudes and behavior, more consistent goals and values, and a clearer idea of who they are (Savin-Williams & Demo, 1984). For those who fail to resolve identity issues—either because they avoided an identity crisis by accepting whatever identity their parents set for them or because they postponed dealing with the crisis and remain uncommitted and lacking in direction—there are often problems ahead (Hart & Yates, 1997).

Abstract Thought and Moral Reasoning

One reason that adolescents can develop a conscious identity is that they are able to think and reason about abstract concepts. In terms of Piaget's theory, they have reached the **formal operational period.** This stage is marked by the ability to engage in hypothetical thinking, including the imagining of logical consequences. For example, adolescents who have reached this level can consider various strategies for finding a part-time job and recognize that some methods are more likely to succeed than others. They can form general concepts and understand the impact of the past on the present and the present on the future. They can question social institutions; think about the world as it might be and ought to be; and consider the consequences and complexities of love, work, politics, and religion. They can think logically and systematically about symbols and propositions.

Piaget explored adolescents' formal operational abilities by asking them to perform science experiments that involved formulating and systematically investigating hypotheses. Research indicates that only about half the people in Western cultures ever reach the formal operational level necessary to succeed in Piaget's experiments; people who have not studied high school level science and math are less likely to do well in those experiments (Keating, 1990). In other cultures, too, people who have not gone to school are less likely to exhibit formal operations. Consider the following exchange, in which a researcher explores the formal operations of an illiterate Kpelle farmer in a Liberian village by giving him a test of logic (Scribner, 1977):

RESEARCHER: All Kpelle men are rice farmers. Mr. Smith is not a rice farmer. Is he a Kpelle man?

KPELLE FARMER: I don't know the man. I have not laid eyes on the man myself.

Kpelle villagers who had completed some formal schooling answered the question logically by saying, "No, Mr. Smith is not a Kpelle man."

Even people who have been to school do not use a single mode of thinking in all situations. In adulthood, people are more likely to use formal operations for problems based on their own occupations; this is one reason why people whose logic is impeccable at work may still become victims of a home-repair or investment scam (Cialdini, 2001).

ethnic identity The part of a person's identity associated with the racial, religious, or cultural group to which the person belongs.

identity crisis A phase during which an adolescent attempts to develop an integrated self-image.

formal operational period According to Piaget, the fourth stage in cognitive development, usually beginning around age eleven, when abstract thinking first appears.

Kohlberg's Stages of Moral Reasoning

Adolescents are capable of applying their advanced cognitive skills not only to science and logic but also to questions of morality. To examine how people think about morality, psychologists have asked them how they would resolve various moral dilemmas. Perhaps the most famous of these is the "Heinz dilemma." It requires people to decide whether a man named Heinz should steal a rare and unaffordable drug in order to save his wife from cancer. Using moral dilemmas like this one, Lawrence Kohlberg found that the reasons people give for their moral choices change systematically and consistently with age (Kohlberg & Gilligan, 1971). Kohlberg proposed that moral reasoning develops in six stages, which are summarized in Table 12.3. These stages, he said, are not tightly linked to a person's age; there is a range of ages for reaching each stage, and not everyone reaches the highest level.

Stage 1 and Stage 2 moral judgments, which are most typical of children under the age of nine, tend to be selfish. Kohlberg called this level **preconventional moral reasoning** because reasoning at this level is not yet based on the conventions or rules that guide social interactions in society. People at this level of moral development are concerned with avoiding punishment or following rules when it is to their own advantage. At the **conventional moral reasoning** level, Stages 3 and 4, people are concerned about other people; they think that morality consists of following rules and conventions such as duty to the family, to marriage vows, and to the country. A conventional thinker would never think it was proper to burn the flag in protest, for example. The moral reasoning of children and adolescents from ages nine to

Kohlberg's stages of moral reasoning describe differences in how people think about moral issues. Here are some examples of answers that people at different stages of development might give to the "Heinz dilemma" described in the text. This dilemma is more realistic than you might think. In 1994, a man was arrested for robbing a bank after being turned down for a loan to pay for his wife's cancer treatments.

table 12.3
Kohlberg's Stages of Moral Development

Stage	What Is Right?	Should Heinz Steal the Drug?
Preconventional		
1	Obeying, and avoiding punishment from, a superior authority	Heinz should not steal the drug because he will be jailed.
2	Making a fair exchange, a good deal	Heinz should steal the drug because his wife will repay him later.
Conventional		
3	Pleasing others and getting their approval	Heinz should steal the drug because he loves his wife and because she and the rest of the family will approve.
4	Doing your duty, following rules and social order	Heinz should steal the drug for his wife because he has a duty to care for her, or he should not steal the drug because stealing is illegal.
Postconventional		
5	Respecting rules and laws, but recognizing that they may have limits	Heinz should steal the drug because life is more important than property.
6	Following universal ethical principles, such as justice, reciprocity, equality, and respect for human life and rights	Heinz should steal the drug because of the principle of preserving and respecting life.

nineteen is most often at this level. Stages 5 and 6 represent the highest level of moral reasoning, which Kohlberg called **postconventional moral reasoning** because it occurs after conventional reasoning. Moral judgments at this level are based on personal standards or universal principles of justice, equality, and respect for human life rather than on the dictates of authority figures or society. People who have reached this level view rules and laws as arbitrary but respect them because they protect human welfare. They believe that individual rights can sometimes supersede these laws if the laws become destructive. People do not usually reach this level until sometime in young adulthood—if at all. Stage 6 is seen only rarely in extraordinary individuals. Studies of Kohlberg's stages generally support the sequence he proposed (Colby et al., 1983; Walker, 1989).

Limitations of Kohlberg's Stages

Kohlberg's first four stages appear to be universal; evidence of them has been found in twenty-seven cultures from Alaska to Zambia. Stages 5 and 6, however, do not always appear (Snarey, 1987). Further, some people in collectivist cultures—Papua New Guinea, Taiwan, and Israeli kibbutzim, for example—explained their answers to moral dilemmas by pointing to the importance of the community rather than to personal standards. People in India included in their moral reasoning the importance of acting in accordance with one's gender and caste and with maintaining personal purity (Shweder et al., 1994). As in other areas of cognitive development, culture plays a significant role in shaping moral judgments.

Gender may also play a role. Carol Gilligan (1982, 1993) has suggested that for females, the moral ideal is not the abstract, impersonal concept of justice that Kohlberg documented in males but, rather, the need to protect enduring relationships and fulfill human needs. Gilligan questioned Kohlberg's assumption that the highest level of morality is based on justice. When she asked her research participants about moral conflicts, the majority of men focused on justice, but only half of the women did. The other half focused on caring. Although this difference between men and women has not been found in many studies (Jaffe & Hyde, 2000), there does seem to be an overall tendency for females to focus on caring more than males and for males to focus on justice more than females when they are resolving hypothetical moral dilemmas (Turiel, 1998). When resolving real-life moral issues, both men and women focus more on caring than on justice (Walker, 1995).

Taken together, the results of research in many countries and with both genders suggest that moral ideals are not absolute and universal. Moral development is apparently an adaptation to the moral world in which one lives, a world that differs from place to place (D. M. Bersoff, 1999). Formal operational reasoning may be necessary for people to reach the highest level of moral reasoning, but formal operational reasoning alone is not sufficient. To some extent, at the highest levels, moral reasoning is a product of culture and history.

Moral Reasoning and Moral Action

There is some evidence that moral reasoning is related to moral behavior. In one study, adolescents who committed crimes ranging from burglary to murder tended to see obedience to laws mainly as a way of avoiding jail—a Stage 1 belief—whereas their nondelinquent peers, who showed Stage 4 reasoning, believed that one should obey laws because they prevent chaos in society (Gregg, Gibbs, & Basinger, 1994). But having high moral reasoning ability is no guarantee that a person will always act morally; other factors, such as the likelihood of being caught, also affect behavior (Krebs, 1967).

Children and adolescents can be encouraged to move to higher levels of moral reasoning through exposure to arguments at a higher stage, perhaps as they argue about issues with one another. Hearing about moral reasoning that is one stage higher than their own or encountering a situation that requires more advanced reasoning seems to push people into moral reasoning at a higher level (Enright, Lapsley, & Levy, 1983). The development of moral behavior takes more than abstract

---

preconventional moral reasoning Reasoning that is not yet based on the conventions or rules that guide social interactions in society.

conventional moral reasoning Reasoning that reflects the belief that morality consists of following rules and conventions.

postconventional moral reasoning Reasoning that reflects moral judgments based on personal standards or universal principles of justice, equality, and respect for human life.

knowledge, however. Consider a study of inner-city adolescents who were required to take a high school class that involved community service—working at a soup kitchen for the needy (Youniss & Yates, 1997). As part of the course they also had to write essays on their experience. Over time, the students' essays became more sophisticated, going beyond discussion of, say, homelessness to observations about the distribution of wealth in society and other ideological matters. By the end of the course, the behavior of the students had also changed; they were going to the soup kitchen more often than the course required.

For children and adolescents, learning to behave in moral ways requires (1) consistent modeling of moral reasoning and behavior by parents and peers, (2) parents and teachers who promote moral behavior, (3) real-life experience with moral issues, and (4) situational factors that support moral actions. Moral reasoning and moral behavior both tend to be lower when situational factors—such as excessive use of alcohol—do not support them (Denton & Krebs, 1990). Not only do we sometimes fail to act at the highest level of which we are capable; we sometimes fail even to reason at this level (Batson & Thompson, 2001).

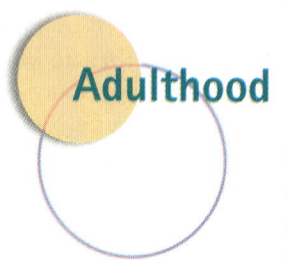

Adulthood

Development does not end with adolescence. Adults, too, go through transitions and experience physical, cognitive, and social changes. It has been suggested that adulthood emerges as early as eighteen (Arnett, 2000), but for our purposes, adulthood can be divided into three periods: early adulthood (ages twenty to thirty-nine), middle adulthood (ages forty to sixty-five), and late adulthood (older than age sixty-five).

Physical Changes

In *early adulthood,* physical growth continues. Shoulder width, height, and chest size increase. People continue to develop their athletic abilities. For most people, the years of early adulthood are the prime of life.

In *middle adulthood,* one of the most common physical changes is the loss of sensory acuity (Fozard et al., 1977). By this time, nearly everyone shows some hearing impairment. People in their early forties become less sensitive to light, and their vision deteriorates somewhat. Increased farsightedness is an inevitable change that usually results in a need for reading glasses. Inside the body, bone mass is dwindling, the risk of heart disease is increasing, and fertility declines. In their late forties or early fifties, women generally experience the shutdown of reproductive capability, a process known as **menopause.** Estrogen and progesterone levels drop, and the menstrual cycle eventually ceases.

In *late adulthood,* men shrink about an inch, and women about two inches, as their posture changes and cartilage disks between the spinal vertebrae become thinner. Hardening of the arteries and a buildup of fat deposits on the artery walls may lead to heart disease. The digestive system slows down and becomes less efficient. In addition, the brain shrinks and the flow of blood to the brain slows. The few reflexes that remained after infancy (such as the knee-jerk reflex) weaken or disappear. But as in earlier years, many of these changes can be delayed or diminished by a healthy diet and exercise.

Cognitive Changes

Despite the aging of the brain, cognitive abilities do not normally decline until late adulthood. In fact, except in cases where limitations are imposed by brain disorders such as Alzheimer's disease, the adult nervous system appears considerably more open to positive change throughout the life span than was previously thought

---

menopause The process whereby a woman's reproductive capacity ceases.

(Nelson & Bloom, 1997). Alert older people can think just as quickly as alert younger people. In fact, older adults may function as well as, or better than, younger adults in situations that tap their long-term memories and well-learned skills. The experienced teacher may deal with an unruly child more skillfully than the novice, and the senior lawyer may understand the implications of a new law more quickly than the recent graduate. Their years of accumulating and organizing information can make older adults practiced, skillful, and wise.

Early and Middle Adulthood

In early and middle adulthood, until age sixty at least, important cognitive abilities improve. During this period, adults do better on tests of vocabulary, comprehension, and general knowledge, especially if they use these abilities in their daily lives (Eichorn et al., 1981; Park, 2001). Young and middle-aged adults learn new information and new skills; they remember old information and hone old skills. It is in their forties through their early sixties that people tend to put in the best performance of their lives on complex mental tasks such as reasoning, verbal memory, and vocabulary (Willis & Schaie, 1999).

The nature of thought may also change during adulthood. Adult thought is often more complex and adaptive than adolescent thought (Labouvie-Vief, 1992). Adults can understand, as adolescents cannot, the contradictions inherent in thinking. They see both the possibilities and the problems in every course of action (Riegel, 1975)—in deciding whether to start a new business or to move to a new house, for example. Middle-aged adults are more adept than adolescents or young adults at making rational decisions and at relating logic and abstractions to actions, emotions, social issues, and personal relationships (Tversky & Kahneman, 1981). As they appreciate these relationships, their thought becomes more global, more concerned with broad moral and practical concerns (Labouvie-Vief, 1982). It has been suggested that the achievement of these new kinds of thinking reflects a stage of cognitive development that goes beyond Piaget's formal operational period (Lutz & Sternberg, 1999). In this stage, people's thinking becomes *dialectical,* which means they understand that knowledge is relative, not absolute—such that what is seen as wise today may have been thought foolish in times past. They see life's contradictions as an inevitable part of reality, and they tend to weigh various solutions to problems rather than just accepting the first one that springs to mind.

Late Adulthood

It is not until late adulthood—after sixty-five or so—that some intellectual abilities decline in some people. Generally, these are abilities that require rapid and flexible manipulation of ideas and symbols, active thinking and reasoning, and sheer mental effort (Baltes, 1993, 1994; see Figure 12.8). Older adults do just as well as younger ones at tasks they know well, like naming familiar objects (Radvansky, 1999). It is when they are asked to perform an unfamiliar task or to solve a complex problem they have not seen before that older adults are generally slower and less effective than younger ones (Craik & Rabinowitz, 1984). When facing complex problems, older people apparently suffer from having too much information to sift through. They have trouble considering, choosing, and executing solutions (Arenberg, 1982). As people age, they grow less efficient at organizing the elements of a problem and at holding and manipulating more than one idea at a time. They have difficulty doing tasks that require them to divide their attention between two activities (Smith et al., 2001) and are slower at shifting their attention back and forth between two activities (Korteling, 1991). If older adults have enough time, though, and can separate the two activities, they can perform just as well as younger adults (Hawkins, Kramer, & Capaldi, 1993).

Older people also have the ability to think deeply and wisely about life. Psychologists define *wisdom* as expert knowledge in the fundamental, practical aspects of life, permitting exceptional insight and judgment involving complex and uncertain matters of the human condition (Smith & Baltes, 1990). Old age does not in itself guarantee wisdom, but if it is combined with experiences conducive to the

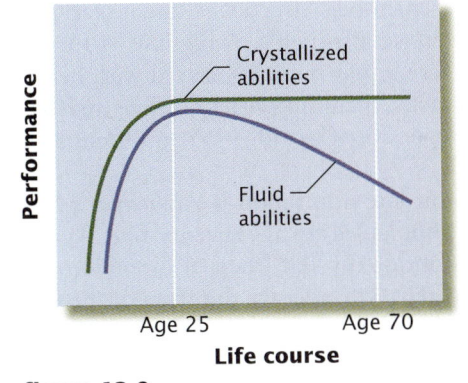

figure 12.8

Mental Abilities over the Life Span

Mental abilities collectively known as "fluid" intelligence—speed and accuracy of information processing, for example—begin to decline quite early in adult life. Changes in these biologically based aspects of thinking are usually not marked until late adulthood, however. "Crystallized" abilities learned over a lifetime—such as reading, writing, comprehension of language, and professional skills—do not diminish even in old age (see the chapter on cognitive abilities).

Source: Adapted from Baltes (1994).

accumulation and refinement of wisdom-related knowledge, growing old can be associated with high levels of wisdom (Baltes et al., 1995). Researchers have found that one component of wisdom—the ability to infer what other people are thinking—remains intact and sometimes even improves over the later adult years. For example, when asked to explain why a burglary suspect in a story surrendered to the police, seventy-year-olds gave better answers than younger adults. Their answers included inferences about the suspect's motives, such as "the burglar surrendered because he thought the policeman knew he had robbed the shop" (Happe, Winner, & Brownell, 1998).

Usually the loss of intellectual abilities in older adults is slow and need not cause severe problems (Bashore & Ridderinkhoff, 2002). A study of Swedish adults (Nilsson, 1996) found that memory problems among older adults are largely confined to *episodic memory* (e.g., what they ate for lunch yesterday, or what was on a list of words they read half an hour ago) rather than to *semantic memory* (general knowledge, such as the name of the capital of France). In short, everyday competencies that involve verbal processes are likely to remain intact into advanced old age (Freedman, Aykan, & Martin, 2001; Willis & Schaie, 1999). Unfortunately, however, there is one way in which older adults' declining memories can have negative effects: They may be more likely than younger adults to recall false information as being true (Park, 2001), making some of them especially prone to victimization by scam artists. For example, the more warnings they hear about a false medical claim—such as a claim that shark cartilage cures arthritis—the more likely they are to believe that the claim is true. Because the often-repeated false claim seems familiar, it eventually comes to seem true. As described in the chapter on memory, younger people are also vulnerable to memory distortions, but they are more likely to remember that false information is false, even when it is familiar.

People who are healthy and psychologically flexible; who have a high level of education, income, and occupation; and who live in an intellectually stimulating environment with mentally able spouses or companions have a significantly lower risk of cognitive decline (Albert et al., 1995; Shimamura et al., 1995). Continued mental exercise—such as doing puzzles, painting, and talking to intelligent friends—can help older adults think and remember effectively and creatively (Wilson et al., 2002). Continued physical exercise also helps. A lifetime of fitness through dancing or other forms of aerobic exercise has been associated with better maintenance of skills on a variety of mental tasks, including reaction time, reasoning, and divided attention (Hawkins, Kramer, & Capaldi, 1993; Offenbach, Chodzko-Zajko, & Ringel, 1990).

The greatest threat to cognitive abilities in late adulthood is *Alzheimer's disease*, which strikes 3 percent of the world's population by age seventy-five. As the disease runs its course, its victims become emotionally flat, then disoriented, and then mentally vacant; they finally die prematurely. The average duration of the disease, from onset to death, is seven years. But the rate of deterioration depends on a number of factors, such as gender (Molsa, Marttila, & Rinne, 1995), education (Stern et al., 1995), and age of onset (Jagger, Clarke, & Stone, 1995). Women, well-educated people, and those who develop Alzheimer's at an older age deteriorate more slowly.

One ongoing study of the risk factors for Alzheimer's disease is focused on a group of nuns from the School Sisters of Notre Dame. When they took their vows, at ages ranging from eighteen to thirty-two, they had written autobiographies. Years later, when the women were seventy-five to ninety-five years old, they were given cognitive tests, and they gave permission for their brains to be examined after death. The Nun Study has found that the women whose autobiographies indicated more limited linguistic abilities—as seen in vague, repetitious, and less complex writing—

Staying Alert, Staying Active, Staying Alive Sisters Alcantara, 91, Claverine, 87, and Nicolette, 94, of the School Sisters of Notre Dame convent, stay alert by reading, solving puzzles, playing cards, and participating in vocabulary quizzes. Along with the other nuns at this convent, these women are participating in a study of aging and the brain.

did less well on the cognitive tests, were more likely to develop Alzheimer's, and died at younger ages than those with richer linguistic abilities (Kemper et al., 2001). Similar findings appeared in a Scottish study of childhood mental ability and dementia in late adulthood (Whalley et al., 2000). These results suggest that the seeds of Alzheimer's disease may be planted early in life, even though it may not appear for many decades.

Social Changes

In adulthood, people develop new relationships, assume new positions, and take on new roles. These changes do not come in neat, predictable stages but instead follow various paths, depending on each individual's experiences (Lieberman, 1996). Transitions—such as initiating a divorce, getting fired from a job, going back to school, remarrying, losing a spouse to death, being hospitalized, getting arrested, or retiring—are turning points that can redirect a person's life path and lead to changes in personality (Caspi, 1998). Sometimes these events create radical turnarounds. More often, they involve gradual and incremental change.

Early Adulthood
Men and women in Western cultures typically enter the adult world in their twenties. They decide on an occupation, or at least take a job,

and often become preoccupied with their careers. They also become more concerned with matters of love (Whitbourne et al., 1992). They reach the sixth of Erikson's stages of psychosocial development noted in Table 12.2: intimacy versus isolation. This intimacy may include sexual intimacy, friendship, or mutual intellectual stimulation. It may lead to marriage or some other form of committed relationship. Today, intimacy occurs at earlier ages than it did when Erikson formulated his theory three decades ago. Specifically, intimate and sexual peer relationships now become important in late adolescence, as well as in early adulthood. Adolescents whose parents are accepting and supportive of their children's growing independence tend to develop more mature and comfortable relationships (Dresner & Grolnick, 1996).

Intimate commitments are also related to the young adult's earlier attachment relationships. Although the kind of attachment infants form may not necessarily color all their subsequent intimate relationships, researchers have discovered that young adults' views of intimate relationships parallel the patterns of infant attachment that we described earlier (Horowitz, Rosenberg, & Bartholomew, 1993). If their view reflects a secure attachment, they tend to feel valued and worthy of support and affection; develop closeness easily; and have relationships characterized by joy, trust, and commitment. If their view reflects an insecure attachment, however, they tend to be preoccupied with relationships and may feel misunderstood, underappreciated, and worried about being abandoned; their relationships are often negative, obsessive, and jealous. In one study, individuals whose attachment was avoidant were found to engage in more "one-night stands" and less cuddling than did those whose attachment was secure (Tidwell, Reis, & Shaver, 1996).

For many young adults, the experience of becoming parents represents entry into a major new developmental phase that is accompanied by personal, social, and occupational changes. Often, marital satisfaction declines after a baby is born (Belsky & Kelly, 1994). Young mothers may experience particular dissatisfaction, especially if they resent the constraints an infant brings, if they see their career as important, if the infant is temperamentally difficult, if the partnership is not strong, and if the partner is not supportive (Shapiro, Gottman, & Carrere, 2000). Researchers have found that when the father does not do his share of caring for the baby, both mothers and fathers are dissatisfied (Levy-Shiff, 1994). The ability of young parents to provide adequate care for their babies is related to their own attachment histories. New mothers whose attachment to their own mother was secure are more responsive to their infants, and the infants, in turn, are more likely to develop secure attachments to them (van IJzendoorn, 1995).

The challenges of young adulthood are complicated by the nature of family life in the twenty-first century. Forty years ago, about half of North American households consisted of married couples in their twenties and thirties—a breadwinner husband and a homemaker wife—raising at least two children together. This picture now describes only about 10 percent of households (Demo, Allen, & Fine, 2000; Hernandez, 1997). Today, parents are older because young adults are delaying marriage longer and waiting longer to have children. And many are having children without marrying. About 75 percent of African American women become single mothers, and 11 percent of European American college-educated women in their thirties are also choosing single-motherhood, a dramatic increase over past decades (Weinraub, Horuath, & Gringlas, 2002). Most of these women become pregnant "the old-fashioned way," but some are taking advantage of technological advances that allow them to conceive through *in vitro fertilization* (Hahn & DiPietro, 2001). Many gay men and lesbians are becoming parents, too. Current estimates suggest that at least four million families in the United States are headed by openly gay or lesbian adults who became parents by retaining custody of children born in a previous heterosexual marriage, adopting a child, or having a child through artificial

midlife transition A point at around age forty when adults take stock of their lives.

generativity Adult concerns about producing or generating something.

insemination or surrogacy (Patterson, 2002). Young adult homosexuals face special challenges in making the transition to parenthood. For example, they often confront antigay prejudice in health care organizations and employer policies that do not recognize their parental role. They may also experience pervasive hostility, even from members of their own extended families.

Whether they are homosexual or heterosexual, the 60 percent of mothers who hold full-time jobs outside the home often find that the demands of children and career pull them in opposite directions. Devotion to their jobs leaves many of these mothers feeling guilty about spending too little time with their children (Booth et al., 2002), but placing too much emphasis on home life may impair their productivity at work and threaten their advancement. This stressful balancing act can lead to anxiety, frustration, and conflicts at home and on the job. It affects fathers, too. The husbands of employed women are more involved in child care (Booth et al., 2002), and their contributions to housework have doubled since 1970 (Coltrane, 2001). They can be effective caregivers (Parke, 2002), but mothers still do most of the child care and housework. Research indicates that gay and lesbian parents share duties more equally—and are more satisfied with the division of labor—than is typically the case in heterosexual families (Patterson, 2002).

Nearly half of all marriages in the United States end in divorce (National Center for Health Statistics, 2001), creating yet another set of challenges for adults. Although freeing people from bad relationships, divorce can leave them feeling anxious, guilty, incompetent, depressed, and lonely (Hetherington & Stanley-Hagan, 2002). Divorce is also correlated with health problems and, ultimately, with earlier mortality (Friedman et al., 1995b). Often, divorce creates new stressors, including money problems, changes in living circumstances and working hours, and for custodial parents, a dramatic increase in housework and child-care tasks. One study found that two years after divorcing, most women were happier than during the final year of their marriage, but more distressed than mothers in two-parent families (Hetherington & Stanley-Hagan, 2002). How effectively divorced people deal with these stressors depends on many factors, such as social support, their general psychological stability and coping skills, their ability to form new relationships, and whether or not they continue to have conflicts with their ex-spouse.

In short, the changes seen in families and family life over the past several decades have made it more challenging than ever to successfully navigate the years of early adulthood.

Middle Adulthood

At around age forty, women as well as men go through a **midlife transition**, during which they may reappraise and modify their lives and relationships. Many feel invigorated and liberated; some may feel upset and have a "midlife crisis" (Beck, 1992; Levinson et al., 1978). The contrast between youth and middle age may be especially upsetting for men who matured early in adolescence and were sociable and athletic rather than intellectual (Block, 1971). Women who chose a career over a family now hear the biological clock ticking out their last childbearing years. Women who have had children, however, become more independent and confident, and more oriented toward achievement and events outside the family (Helson & Moane, 1987). For both men and women, the emerging sexuality of their teenage children, the emptiness of the nest as children leave home, or the declining health of a parent may precipitate a crisis. Results from a study of over seven thousand adults suggest that the degree of happiness and healthiness people experience during middle adulthood depends on how much control they feel they have over their work, finances, marriage, children, and sex life, as well as how many years of education they completed and what kind of job they have (Azar, 1996a).

Following the midlife transition, the middle years of adulthood are often a time of satisfaction and happiness (MacArthur Foundation, 1999). Many people become concerned with producing something that will outlast them—usually through parenthood or job achievements. Erikson called this concern the crisis of **generativity**,

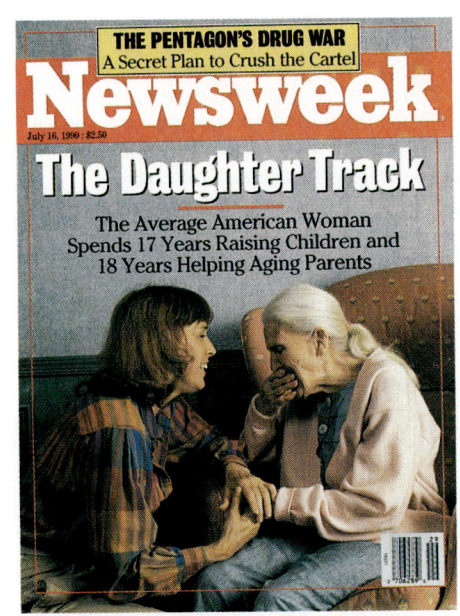

The "Sandwich" Generation People in the midlife transition may feel caught between the generations, pressured by the expenses of college on one side and the needs of their aging parents on the other.

because people begin to focus on producing or generating something. If they do not resolve this crisis, he suggested, people stagnate. A recent study found that after the age of forty, people are indeed more likely than before to say they are striving for generativity goals (Sheldon & Kasser, 2001). These included writing a book, helping those in need, developing closer relationships with children and being a good role model for them, and trying to make a lasting contribution to society.

In their fifties, most people become grandparents (Smith & Drew, 2002). This new status often amazes them. One study of male and female professionals in their fifties found that they could not quite believe they were no longer young (Karp, 1991). Most described themselves as healthy but acknowledged that their bodies were slowing down.

Late Adulthood Even when they are sixty-five to seventy-five, most people think of themselves as middle-aged, not old (Neugarten, 1977). They are active and influential politically and socially; they often are physically vigorous. Ratings of life satisfaction, well-being, and self-esteem are, on average, as high in old age as during any other period of adulthood (Mroczek & Kolarz, 1998; Sheldon & Kasser, 2001; Volz, 2000). This is the time when men and women usually retire from their jobs, but research shows that many people underestimate older people's ability and willingness to work (Clay, 1996b). This misperception was once codified in laws that forced workers to retire at sixty-five regardless of their abilities. Thanks to changes in those laws, most people can now continue working as long as they wish. Being forced to retire can result in psychological and physical problems. In one study of cardiovascular disease, men who retired involuntarily were found to be more depressed, more unhealthy, and more poorly adjusted than those who retired voluntarily (Swan, 1996). Such problems may also occur when husbands retire before their wives (Rubin, 1998). Men tend to view retirement as a time to wind down,

in review: Milestones of Adolescence and Adulthood

Age	Physical Changes	Cognitive Changes	Social Events and Psychological Changes
Early adolescence (11–15 years)	Puberty brings reproductive capacity and marked bodily changes.	Formal operations and principled moral reasoning become possible for the first time. (This occurs only for some people.)	Social and emotional changes result from growing sexual awareness; adolescents experience mood swings, physical changes, and conflicts with parents.
Late adolescence (16–19 years)	Physical growth continues.	Formal operations and principled moral reasoning become more likely.	An identity crisis accompanies graduation from high school.
Early adulthood (20–39 years)	Physical growth continues.	Increases continue in knowledge, problem-solving ability, and moral reasoning.	People choose a job and often a mate; they may become parents.
Middle adulthood (40–65 years)	Size and muscle mass decrease; fat increases; eyesight declines; reproductive capacity in women ends.	Thought becomes more complex, adaptive, and global.	Midlife transition may lead to change; for most, the middle years are satisfying.
Late adulthood (over 65 years)	Size decreases; organs become less efficient.	Reasoning, mathematical ability, comprehension, novel problem solving, and memory may decline.	Retirement requires adjustments; people look inward; awareness of death precipitates life review.

Gray Power Actor Paul Newman, seventy-six, is a famous example of the thousands of people whose late adulthood is healthy and vigorous. In January 2000, Newman received bruised ribs in a minor accident while preparing to drive his racecar in the 24 Hours of Daytona. He was racing again the following month.

whereas women see it as a time to try new things, to reinvent themselves (Helgesen, 1998). In a longitudinal study that followed people from childhood through adulthood, researchers found that when previously employed women reached their seventies, they were more active and more concerned about maintaining their independence and continuing their achievements than women who had been homemakers. They were also happier, as well as less depressed and anxious (Holahan, 1994). In general, it seems, retirees are more likely to be satisfied with their lives than people who continue to work through their sixties and seventies (Moen et al., 2000).

More people than ever are reaching old age. In fact, people over 75 make up the fastest-growing segment of the population. This group is 25 times larger today than it was a hundred years ago. Today, 77,000 people in the United States are older than 100, and the Census Bureau predicts that number will rise to 834,000 by 2050 (Volz, 2000). Old age is not necessarily a time of loneliness and desolation, but it is a time when people generally become more inward looking, cautious, and conforming (Reedy, 1983). It is a time when people develop coping strategies that increasingly take into account the limits of their control—accepting chronic health problems and other things they cannot change (Brandtstadter & Renner, 1990).

In old age, people interact with others less frequently, but they enjoy their interactions more (Carstensen, 1997). They find relationships more satisfying, supportive, and fulfilling than they did earlier in life. As they sense that time is running out, they value positive interactions and become selective about their social partners. During the last twenty years of their lives, people gradually restrict their social network to loved ones. As long as there are at least three close friends or relatives in their network, they tend to be content.

The many changes associated with adolescence and adulthood are summarized in "In Review: Milestones of Adolescence and Adulthood."

Death and Dying

With the onset of old age, people become aware that death is approaching. They watch as their friends disappear. They feel their health deteriorating, their strength waning, and their intellectual capabilities declining. A few years or a few months before death, people may experience a sharp decline in mental functioning known as **terminal drop** (Small & Bäckman, 1999).

The awareness of impending death brings about the last psychological crisis, according to Erikson's theory, in which people evaluate their lives and accomplishments and affirm them as meaningful (leading to a feeling of integrity) or meaningless (leading to a feeling of despair). People at this stage tend to become more philosophical and reflective. They attempt to put their lives into perspective. They reminisce, resolve past conflicts, and integrate past events. They may also become more interested in the religious and spiritual side of life. This "life review" may trigger anxiety, regret, guilt, and despair, or it may allow people to face their own death and the deaths of friends and relatives with a feeling of peace and acceptance (Lieberman & Tobin, 1983).

Even the actual confrontation with death does not have to bring despair and depression. People generally want to be told if they are dying (Hinton, 1967). When death finally is imminent, old people strive for a death with dignity, love, affection, physical contact, and no pain (Schulz, 1978). As they think about death, they are comforted by their religious faith, their achievements, and the love of their friends and family (Kastenbaum, Kastenbaum, & Morris, 1989).

Longevity

Facing death with dignity and openness helps people complete the life cycle with a sense of life's meaningfulness and unity, but most of us want to live as long as possible. How can we do so? Researchers studying the factors associated with longer

terminal drop A sharp decline in mental functioning that tends to occur in late adulthood, a few years or months before death.

life have discovered that longevity is greater in women, in people without histories of heavy drinking or heart problems, and in those who live independently. Longevity is also related to personality characteristics such as conscientiousness as a child (Friedman et al., 1995a) and curiosity as an adult. One study of more than two thousand adults revealed that those who, at age seventy, expressed more curiosity were more likely to still be alive five years later (Swan & Carmelli, 1996). However, the secret of extreme longevity—one hundred years or more—may lie in a group of genes on chromosome 4 that appears to somehow slow the aging process (Puca et al., 2001).

Older adults can be helped to feel better physically and psychologically if they continue to be socially active and useful. For example, old people who are given parties, plants, or pets are happier and more alert than those who receive less attention, and they do not die as soon (Clark et al., 2001). People who restrict their caloric intake, engage in regular physical and mental exercise, and have a sense of control over important aspects of their lives are also likely to live longer (Krause & Shaw, 2000; Yaffe et al., 2001).

So eat your veggies, stay physically fit, and continue to think actively—not just to live longer later, but to live better now.

LINKAGES

As noted in the chapter on introducing psychology, all of psychology's subfields are related to one another. Our discussion of infantile amnesia illustrates just one way in which the topic of this chapter, human development, is linked to the subfield of memory (which is the focus of the memory chapter). The Linkages diagram shows ties to two other subfields as well, and there are many more ties throughout the book. Looking for linkages among subfields will help you see how they all fit together and help you better appreciate the big picture that is psychology.

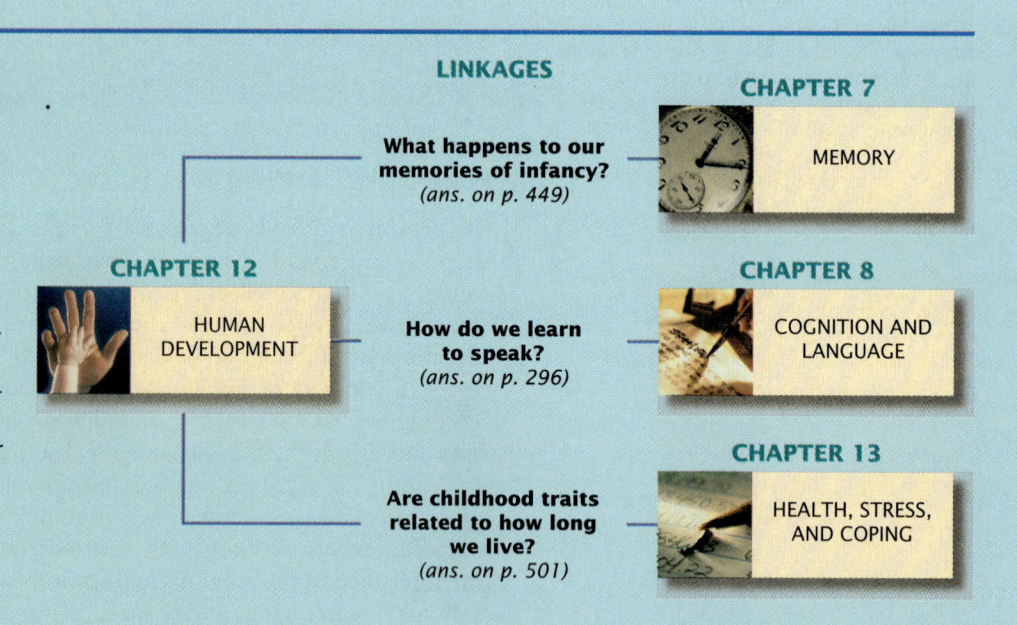

LINKAGES

CHAPTER 12 — HUMAN DEVELOPMENT

What happens to our memories of infancy? (ans. on p. 449) — CHAPTER 7 MEMORY

How do we learn to speak? (ans. on p. 296) — CHAPTER 8 COGNITION AND LANGUAGE

Are childhood traits related to how long we live? (ans. on p. 501) — CHAPTER 13 HEALTH, STRESS, AND COPING

SUMMARY

Developmental psychology is the study of the course and causes of age-related changes in mental abilities, social relationships, emotions, and moral understanding over the life span.

Exploring Human Development

A central question in developmental psychology concerns the relative influences of nature and nurture, a theme that has its origins in the philosophies of John Locke and Jean-Jacques Rousseau. In the twentieth century, Arnold Gesell stressed nature in his theory of development, proposing that development is *maturation*—the natural unfolding of abilities with age. John B. Watson took the opposite view, claiming that development is learning—shaped by the external environment. In his theory of cognitive development, Jean Piaget described how nature and nurture work together. Today we accept the notion that both nature and nurture affect development and ask how and to what extent each contributes.

Beginnings

Prenatal Development

Development begins with the union of an ovum and a sperm to form a *zygote,* which develops into an *embryo.* The embryonic stage is a *critical period* for development, a time when certain organs must develop properly, or they never will. Development of organs at this stage is irrevocably affected by harmful *teratogens,* such as drugs and alcohol. After the embryo develops into a *fetus,* adverse conditions during the fetal stage may harm the infant's size, behavior, intelligence, or health. Babies born to women who drink heavily have a strong chance of suffering from *fetal alcohol syndrome.*

The Newborn

Newborns have limited but effective senses of vision, hearing, taste, and smell. They exhibit many reflexes, or swift, automatic responses to external stimuli. Motor development proceeds as the nervous system matures, muscles grow, and the infant experiments with and selects the most efficient movement patterns.

Infancy and Childhood: Cognitive Development

Cognitive development includes the development of thinking, knowing, and remembering.

Changes in the Brain

The development of increasingly complex and efficient neural networks in various regions of the brain provides the "hardware" for the increasingly complex cognitive abilities that arise during infancy and childhood.

The Development of Knowledge: Piaget's Theory

According to Piaget, cognitive development occurs in a fixed sequence of stages, as *schemas* are modified through the complementary processes of *assimilation* (fitting new objects or events into existing schemas) and *accommodation* (changing schemas when new objects will not fit existing ones). During the *sensorimotor period,* infants progress from using only simple senses and reflexes to forming mental representations of objects and actions. Thus, the child becomes capable of thinking about objects that are not immediately present. The ability to recognize that objects continue to exist even when they are hidden from view is what Piaget called *object permanence.* During the *preoperational period,* children can use symbols, but they do not have the ability to think logically and rationally. Their understanding of the world is intuitive and egocentric. They do not understand the logical operations of reversibility or complementarity. When children develop the ability to think logically about concrete objects, they enter the period of *concrete operations.* At this time they can solve simple problems. They also have an understanding of *conservation,* recognizing that, for example, the amount of a substance is not altered even when its shape changes.

Modifying Piaget's Theory

Recent research reveals that Piaget underestimated infants' mental abilities. Developmental psychologists now also believe that new levels of cognition are reached not in sharply marked stages of global understanding but more gradually, and in specific areas. Children's reasoning is affected by factors such as task difficulty and degree of familiarity with the objects and language involved.

Information Processing During Childhood

Psychologists who explain cognitive development in terms of information processing have documented age-related improvements in children's attention, their abilities to explore and focus on features of the environment, and their memories.

Culture and Cognitive Development

The specific content of cognitive development, including the development of scripts, depends on the cultural context in which children live.

Variations in Cognitive Development

How fast children develop cognitive abilities depends to a certain extent on how stimulating and supportive their environments are. Children growing up in poverty are likely to have delayed or impaired cognitive abilities.

Infancy and Childhood: Social and Emotional Development

Infants and their caregivers, from the early months, respond to each other's emotional expressions. When an infant's behavior in an ambiguous situation is affected by the caregiver's emotional expression, social referencing is said to have occurred.

Individual Temperament

Most infants can be classified as having easy, difficult, or slow-to-warm-up *temperaments.* Whether they retain these temperamental styles depends to some extent on their parents' expectations and demands.

The Infant Grows Attached

Over the first year of life, infants form a deep and abiding emotional *attachment* to their mother or other primary caregiver. This attachment may be secure or insecure.

Relationships with Parents and Peers

Parents teach their children the skills and rules needed in their culture using various parenting styles; they can be described as *authoritarian, permissive,* or *authoritative parents.* Among European and European American parents, those with an authoritative style tend to have more competent and cooperative children. Parenting styles depend upon the culture and conditions in which parents find themselves. Over the childhood years, interactions with peers evolve into cooperative and competitive encounters, and friendships become more important.

Social Skills

Children become increasingly able to interpret and understand social situations and emotional signals. They begin to express empathy and sympathy, and to engage in the *self-regulation* of their emotions and behavior. They also learn social rules and roles.

Gender Roles

Children develop *gender roles* that are based both on biological differences between the sexes and on implicit and explicit socialization by parents, teachers, and peers. Children are also influenced by *gender schemas*, which affect their choices of activities and toys.

Risk and Resilience

Children who lead successful lives despite such adversities as family instability, child abuse, homelessness, poverty, or war are described as having *resilience*. Factors associated with this characteristic include good intellectual functioning and strong relationships with caring adults.

Adolescence

Adolescents undergo significant changes not only in size, shape, and physical capacity but also, typically, in their social lives, reasoning abilities, and views of themselves.

The Challenges of Change

Puberty brings about physical changes that lead to psychological changes. Early adolescence is a period of shaky self-esteem. It is also a time when conflict with parents, as well as closeness and conformity to friends, is likely to rise. A particularly difficult challenge for adolescents is the transition from elementary school to junior high or middle school.

Identity and Development of the Self

Late adolescence focuses on finding an answer to the question, Who am I? Events such as graduating from high school and going to college challenge the adolescent's self-concept, precipitating an *identity crisis*. To resolve this crisis the adolescent must develop an integrated self-image as a unique person, an image that often includes *ethnic identity*.

Abstract Thought and Moral Reasoning

For many people, adolescence begins a stage of cognitive development that Piaget called the *formal operational period*. Formal abstract reasoning now becomes more sophisticated, and moral reasoning may begin its progress through *preconventional, conventional,* and *postconventional moral reasoning* stages. Principled moral judgment—shaped by gender and culture—becomes possible for the first time in adolescence. Such advanced understanding may be reflected in moral action.

Adulthood

Physical, cognitive, and social changes occur throughout adulthood.

Physical Changes

Middle adulthood sees changes that include decreased acuity of the senses, increased risk of heart disease, and the end of fertility *(menopause)*. Nevertheless, major health problems may not appear until late adulthood.

Cognitive Changes

The cognitive changes that occur in early and middle adulthood are generally positive, including improvements in reasoning and problem-solving ability. In late adulthood, some intellectual abilities decline—especially those involved in tasks that are unfamiliar, complex, or difficult. Other abilities, such as recalling facts or making wise decisions, tend not to decline. Individuals with Alzheimer's disease become disoriented and mentally vacant, and they die prematurely.

Social Changes

In their twenties, young adults make occupational choices and form intimate commitments. In middle adulthood they become concerned with *generativity*—with producing something that will outlast them. Sometime around age forty, adults experience a *midlife transition,* which may or may not be a crisis. The forties and fifties are often a time of satisfaction. In their sixties, people contend with retirement. They generally become more inward looking, cautious, and conforming. Adults' progress through these ages is influenced by the unique personal events that befall them.

Death and Dying

In their seventies and eighties, people confront their own mortality. They may become more philosophical and reflective as they review their lives. A few years or months before death, individuals may experience a sharp decline in mental functioning known as *terminal drop*. They strive for a death with dignity, love, and no pain.

Longevity

Death is inevitable, but certain factors—including healthy diets, exercise, personality qualities such as conscientiousness and curiosity, a sense of control over one's life, and genetics—are associated with living longer and happier lives. Older adults feel better and live longer if they receive attention from other people, maintain an open attitude toward new experiences, and keep their minds active.

Health, Stress, and Coping

13

Health Psychology
Stress and Stressors
Psychological Stressors
Measuring Stressors
Stress Responses
Physical Responses
Psychological Responses
LINKAGES: **Stress and Psychological Disorders**
Stress Mediators: Interactions Between People and Stressors
How Stressors Are Appraised
Predictability and Control
Coping Resources and Coping Methods
Social Support
Stress, Personality, and Gender
FOCUS ON RESEARCH METHODS: **Personality and Health**
The Physiology and Psychology of Health and Illness
Stress, Illness, and the Immune System
Stress, Illness, and the Cardiovascular System
THINKING CRITICALLY: **Does Hostility Increase the Risk of Heart Disease?**
Risking Your Life: Health-Endangering Behaviors
Promoting Healthy Behavior
Health Beliefs and Health Behaviors
Changing Health Behaviors: Stages of Readiness
Programs for Coping with Stress and Promoting Health
Linkages
Summary

Two decades ago, acquired immune deficiency syndrome (AIDS) was a rare and puzzling medical condition. Today, it threatens everyone and is one of the major causes of death in the United States. In some African countries, the infection rate among adults from the human immunodeficiency virus (HIV), which causes AIDS, is as high as 20 percent (Centers for Disease Control and Prevention, 2001a). As medical researchers race against time to find a cure for AIDS and a vaccine against HIV, others work to find ways to prolong the lives of people infected with HIV or suffering with AIDS.

One important factor that may affect how long AIDS patients live is their expectations about survival. Geoffrey Reed and his associates asked seventy-four male AIDS patients about the extent to which they had accepted their situation and prepared themselves for the worst (Reed et al., 1994). Acknowledging the reality of a terminal illness has been considered by some to be a psychologically healthy adaptation (e.g., Kübler-Ross, 1975); however, Reed and his associates found that the men who had accepted their situation and prepared themselves for death died an average of nine months earlier than those who had neither accepted nor resigned themselves to their situation. This statistically significant difference is all the more impressive because it cannot be accounted for by differences in the patients' general health status, immune system functioning, psychological distress, or other factors that might have affected the time of death. Here is evidence that compared with those who are "fighters," terminally ill patients who resign themselves to decline and death might actually hasten both.

Research like this has made psychologists and the medical community more aware than ever of psychological factors that can affect health and illness. It also reflects the growth of **health psychology,** "a field within psychology devoted to understanding psychological influences on how people stay healthy, why they become ill, and how they respond when they do get ill" (Taylor, 1998, p. 4). Health psychologists use knowledge from many subfields of psychology to enhance understanding of the psychological and behavioral processes associated with health and illness. In this chapter we describe some of the ways in which health is related to psychological, social, and behavioral factors, as well as what health psychologists are doing to understand these relationships and to apply their research to prevent illness and promote better health. We begin by examining the nature of stressors and people's physical, psychological, and behavioral responses to stress. Then we consider factors that might alter the impact of stressful life events on a person. Next, we examine the psychological factors responsible for specific physical disorders and some behaviors that endanger people's health. We conclude by discussing health psychologists' recommendations for coping with stress and promoting health, and some of their programs for doing so.

Health Psychology

Although the field of health psychology is relatively new, its underlying themes are ancient. For thousands of years, in many cultures around the world, people have believed that their mental state, their behavior, and their health are linked. Today, there is scientific evidence to support this belief (Taylor, 1999). We know, for example, that through their impact on psychological and physical processes, the stresses of life can influence physical health. Researchers have also associated anger, hostility, pessimism, depression, and hopelessness with the appearance of physical illnesses, and traits such as optimism with good health. Similarly, poor health has been linked to lack of exercise, inadequate diet, smoking, alcohol and drug abuse, and other behavioral factors, whereas good health has been associated with behaviors such as physical activity and following medical advice.

Health psychology has become increasingly prominent in North America, in part because of changing patterns of illness. Until the middle of the twentieth

health psychology A field in which psychologists conduct and apply research aimed at promoting human health and preventing illness.

This table shows five of the leading causes of death in the United States today, along with behavioral factors that contribute to their development.

table 13.1
Lifestyle Behaviors That Affect the Leading Causes of Death in the United States

Cause of Death	Contributing Behavioral Factor				
	Alcohol	Smoking	Diet	Exercise	Stress
Heart disease	x	x	x	x	x
Cancer	x	x	x		?
Stroke	x	x	x	?	?
Lung disease		x			
Accidents and Injury	x	x			x

Source: Data from USDHHS (1990); Centers for Disease Control and Prevention (1999a).

Running for Your Life Health psychologists have developed programs to help people increase exercise, stop smoking, eat healthier diets, and make other lifestyle changes that lower their risk of illness and death. They have even helped to insure community blood supplies by finding ways to make blood donation less stressful (Bonk, France, & Taylor, 2001).

century, the major causes of illness and death in the United States and Canada were acute infectious diseases, such as influenza, tuberculosis, and pneumonia. With these afflictions now less threatening, chronic illnesses—such as coronary heart disease, cancer, and diabetes—have joined accidents and injuries as the leading causes of disability and death (Guyer et al., 2000). Further, psychological, lifestyle, and environmental factors play substantial roles in determining whether a person will fall victim to these modern-day killers (Taylor, 1999). For example, lifestyle choices, such as whether a person smokes, affect the risk for the five leading causes of death for men and women in the United States (D'Agostino et al., 2001; Lichtenstein et al., 2000; see Table 13.1). Further, the psychological and behavioral factors that contribute to these illnesses can be altered by psychological interventions, including programs that promote nonsmoking and low-fat diets. As many as half of all deaths in the United States are due to potentially preventable lifestyle behaviors (National Cancer Institute, 1994).

Health psychologists have been active in helping people understand the role they can play in controlling their own health and life expectancy (Baum, Revenson, & Singer, 2001). For example, they have promoted early detection of disease by educating people about the warning signs of cancer, heart disease, and other serious illnesses and encouraging them to seek medical attention while lifesaving treatment is still possible. Health psychologists also study, and help people to understand, the role played by stress in physical health and illness.

Stress and Stressors

You have probably heard that death and taxes are the only two things you can be sure of in life. If there is a third, it must surely be stress. Stress is basic to life—no matter how wealthy, powerful, attractive, or happy you might be. It comes in many forms—a difficult exam, an automobile accident, waiting in a long line, a day on which everything goes wrong. Mild stress can be stimulating, motivating, and sometimes desirable. But as it becomes more severe, stress can bring on physical, psychological, and behavioral problems.

Stress is the negative emotional and physiological process that occurs as individuals try to adjust to or deal with **stressors**, which are environmental circumstances that disrupt, or threaten to disrupt, individuals' daily functioning and cause

stress The process of adjusting to circumstances that disrupt, or threaten to disrupt, a person's equilibrium.

stressors Events or situations to which people must adjust.

figure 13.1
The Process of Stress

Stressful events, people's reactions to those events, and interactions between people and the situations they face are all important components of stress. Notice the two-way relationships in the stress process. For example, if a person has effective coping skills, stress responses will be less severe. Having milder stress responses will act as a "reward" that will strengthen those skills. Further, as coping skills (such as refusing unreasonable demands) improve, certain stressors (such as a boss's unreasonable demands) may become less frequent.

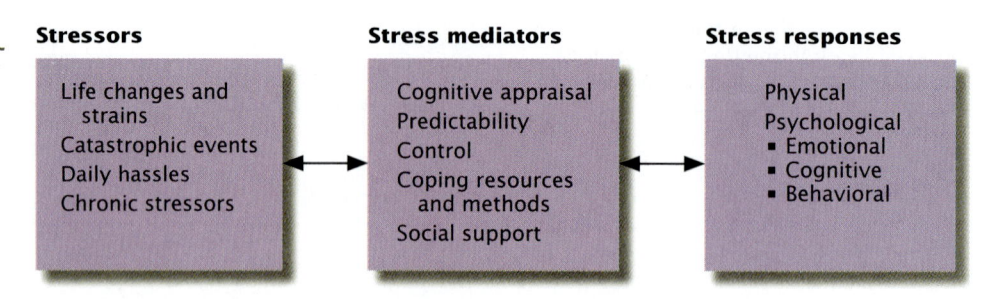

Stressors
- Life changes and strains
- Catastrophic events
- Daily hassles
- Chronic stressors

↔

Stress mediators
- Cognitive appraisal
- Predictability
- Control
- Coping resources and methods
- Social support

↔

Stress responses
- Physical
- Psychological
  - Emotional
  - Cognitive
  - Behavioral

people to make adjustments (Taylor, 1999). In other words, stress involves a *transaction* between people and their environment. Figure 13.1 lists the main types of stressors and illustrates that when confronted by stressors, people respond physically (e.g., with nervousness, nausea, and fatigue), as well as psychologically.

As also shown in Figure 13.1, the transaction between people and their environment can be influenced by *stress mediators,* which include such variables as the extent to which people can predict and control their stressors, how they interpret the threat involved, the social support they get, and their stress-coping skills. (We discuss these mediators in greater detail later.) So stress is not a specific event but a *process* in which the nature and intensity of stress responses depend to a large degree on factors such as the way people think about stressors and the skills and resources they have to cope with them.

For humans, most stressors have both physical and psychological components. Students, for example, are challenged by psychological demands to do well in their courses, as well as by the physical fatigue that can result from a heavy load of classes, combined perhaps with a job and family responsibilities. Similarly, for victims of arthritis, AIDS, and other chronic illnesses, physical pain is accompanied by worry and other forms of psychological distress (Melzack, 1973; Salovey et al., 1992). Here, we focus on psychological stressors, which can stimulate some of the same physiological responses as physical stressors (Cacioppo et al., 1995).

Psychological Stressors

Any event that forces people to accommodate or change can be a psychological stressor. Accordingly, even pleasant events can be stressful (Brown & McGill, 1989). For example, the increased salary and status associated with a promotion may be desirable, but the upgrade usually brings new pressures as well (Schaubroeck, Jones, & Xie, 2001). Similarly, people often feel exhausted after a vacation. Still, it is typically negative events that have the most adverse psychological and physical effects (Kessler, 1997). These circumstances include catastrophic events, life changes and strains, chronic stressors, and daily hassles (Baum, Gatchel, & Krantz, 1997).

Catastrophic events are sudden, unexpected, potentially life-threatening experiences or traumas, such as physical or sexual assault, military combat, natural disasters, terrorist attacks, and accidents. *Life changes* and *strains* include divorce, illness in the family, difficulties at work, moving to a new place, and other circumstances that create demands to which people must adjust (Price, 1992; see Table 13.2). *Chronic stressors*—those that continue over a long period of time—include circumstances such as living near a noisy airport, having a serious illness, being unable to earn a decent living, residing in a high-crime neighborhood, being the victim of discrimination, and even enduring years of academic pressure (Evans, Hygge, & Bullinger, 1995; Levenstein, Smith, & Kaplan, 2001). *Daily hassles* include irritations, pressures, and annoyances that might not be significant stressors by themselves but whose cumulative effects can be significant (Evans & Johnson, 2000).

Here are some items from the Undergraduate Stress Questionnaire, which asks students to indicate whether various stressors have occurred during the previous week (Crandall, Preisler, & Aussprung, 1992).

table 13.2
The Undergraduate Stress Questionnaire

Has this stressful event happened to you at any time during the last week? If it has, please check the space next to it. If it has not, please leave it blank.

____ 1. Assignments in all classes due the same day
____ 2. Having roommate conflicts
____ 3. Lack of money
____ 4. Trying to decide on a major
____ 5. Can't understand your professor
____ 6. Stayed up late writing a paper
____ 7. Sat through a boring class
____ 8. Went into a test unprepared
____ 9. Parents getting divorced
____ 10. Incompetence at the registrar's office

Measuring Stressors

Which stressors are most harmful? To study stress more precisely, psychologists have tried to measure the impact of particular stressors. In 1967, Thomas Holmes and Richard Rahe (pronounced "ray") made a pioneering effort to find a standard way of measuring the stress in a person's life. Working on the assumption that all change, positive or negative, is stressful, they asked a large number of people to rate—in terms of *life change events,* or *LCUs*—the amount of change and demand for adjustment represented by events such as divorcing, being fired, retiring, losing a loved one, or becoming pregnant. (Getting married, the event against which raters were told to compare all other stressors, came in as slightly more stressful than losing one's job.) On the basis of these ratings, Holmes and Rahe created the *Social Readjustment Rating Scale,* or *SRRS*. People taking the SRRS receive a stress score equal to the sum of the LCUs for the events they have recently experienced.

Another Catastrophe Catastrophic events such as explosions, hurricanes, plane crashes, school shootings, and other traumas are stressors that can be psychologically devastating for victims, their families, and rescue workers. As was the case in the wake of the September 11, 2001, terrorist attacks on the World Trade Center and the Pentagon, health psychologists and other professionals provide on-the-spot counseling and follow-up sessions to help people deal with the consequences of trauma.

Numerous studies show that people scoring high on the SRRS and other life-change scales are more likely to suffer physical or mental disorders than those with lower scores (e.g., Monroe, Thase, & Simons, 1992). However, other researchers questioned whether life changes alone tell the whole story about the effects of stress. Accordingly, investigators developed scales such as the *Life Experiences Survey,* or *LES* (Sarason, Johnson, & Siegel, 1978), that go beyond the SRRS to measure not just what life events have occurred but also people's perceptions, or cognitive appraisal, of how positive or negative the events were, and how well they were able to cope with the events. This is particularly important for understanding the impact of life experiences that may have very different meanings to different individuals. For example, a woman eager to have a baby is likely to see pregnancy as a positive event; for someone who does not wish to become pregnant, a positive pregnancy test can be an intensely negative event. Still other researchers have measured stressors and their impact via face-to-face interviews (e.g., Dohrenwend et al., 1993). Different measures yield somewhat differing results (McQuaid et al., 2000), but as you might expect, they generally show that events appraised as negative have a stronger negative impact on health than do those appraised as positive (De Benedittis, Lornenzetti, & Pieri, 1990).

The LES also gives respondents the opportunity to write in and rate any stressors they have experienced that are not on the printed list. This personalized approach is particularly valuable for capturing the differing impact and meaning that experiences may have for men compared with women and for individuals from various cultural or subcultural groups. Divorce, for example, may have very different meanings to people of different religious or cultural backgrounds. Similarly, members of certain ethnic groups are likely to experience stressors—such as prejudice and discrimination—that are not felt by other groups (Contrada et al., 2000).

Stress Responses

Physical and psychological responses to stress often occur together, especially as stressors become more intense. Furthermore, one type of stress response can set off a stress response in another dimension. For example, a physical stress response—such as mild chest pain—may lead to the psychological stress response of worrying

A Daily Hassle Relatively minor daily hassles can accumulate to create significant physical and psychological stress responses. The frustrations of daily commuting in heavy traffic, for example, can become so intense for some drivers that they may display a pattern of anger and aggression called "road rage" (Levy et al., 1997). Between 1990 and 1996, more than 10,000 road rage incidents in the United States alone resulted in 218 deaths and 12,610 injuries (Rathbone & Huckabee, 1999).

figure 13.2

The General Adaptation Syndrome
Hans Selye found that physical reactions to stressors include an initial alarm reaction, followed by resistance and then exhaustion. During the alarm reaction, the body's resistance to stress temporarily drops below normal as the body absorbs a stressor's initial impact. Resistance increases and then levels off in the resistance stage, but it ultimately declines if the exhaustion stage is reached.

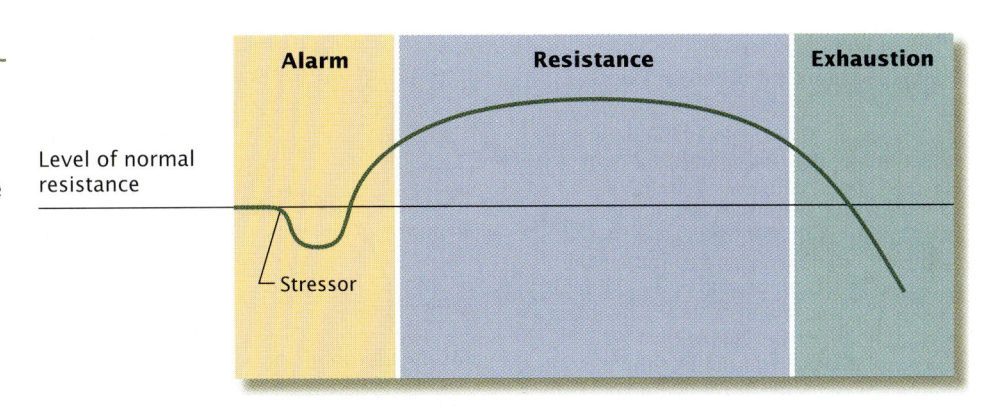

about having a heart attack. Still, it is useful to analyze separately each category of stress responses.

Physical Responses

Anyone who has experienced a near accident or some other sudden, frightening event knows that the physical responses to stressors include rapid breathing, increased heartbeat, sweating, and a little later, shakiness. These reactions are part of a general pattern known as the *fight-or-flight syndrome*. As described in the chapters on biological aspects of psychology and on motivation and emotion, this syndrome prepares the body to face or to flee an immediate threat. When the danger has passed, fight-or-flight responses subside. However, when stressors are long lasting, these responses are only the beginning of a sequence of reactions.

The General Adaptation Syndrome

Careful observation of animals and humans led Hans Selye (pronounced "SELL-yay") to suggest that the sequence of physical responses to stress occurs in a consistent pattern and is triggered by the effort to adapt to any stressor. Selye called this sequence the **general adaptation syndrome,** or **GAS** (Selye, 1956, 1976). The GAS has three stages, as shown in Figure 13.2.

The first stage is the *alarm reaction*, which involves some version of the fight-or-flight syndrome. In the face of a mild stressor such as a hot room, the reaction may simply involve changes in heart rate, respiration, and perspiration that help the body regulate its temperature. More severe stressors prompt more dramatic alarm reactions, rapidly mobilizing the body's adaptive energy, much as a burglar alarm alerts the police to take action (Kiecolt-Glaser et al., 1998).

Alarm reactions are controlled by the sympathetic branch of the autonomic nervous system (ANS) through organs and glands that make up the *sympatho-adreno-medullary (SAM) system*. As shown on the right side of Figure 13.3, environmental demands (stressors) trigger a process in the brain in which the hypothalamus activates the sympathetic branch of the ANS, which stimulates the medulla (inner part) of the adrenal gland. The adrenal gland, in turn, secretes *catecholamines*—especially adrenaline and noradrenaline—which circulate in the bloodstream, activating various organs, including the liver, kidneys, heart, and lungs. The results are increased blood pressure, enhanced muscle tension, increased blood sugar, and other physical changes needed to cope with stressors. Even brief exposure to a mild stressor can produce major changes in these coordinated regulatory physiological mechanisms (Cacioppo et al., 1995).

As shown on the left side of Figure 13.3, stressors also activate the *hypothalamic-pituitary-adrenocortical (HPA) system*, in which the hypothalamus stimulates the pituitary gland in the brain. The pituitary, in turn, secretes hormones such as adrenocorticotropic hormone (ACTH). Among other things, ACTH stimulates the

general adaptation syndrome (GAS) A three-stage pattern of responses triggered by the effort to adapt to any stressor.

figure 13.3

Organ Systems Involved in the GAS

Stressors produce a variety of physiological responses that begin in the brain and spread to organs throughout the body. Through the hypothalamic-pituitary-adrenocortical system (HPA; purple arrows), for example, the hypothalamus causes the pituitary gland to trigger the release of endorphins, the body's natural painkillers. The HPA also stimulates the release of corticosteroids, which help resist stress but also tend to suppress the immune system. In the sympatho-adreno-medullary system (SAM; blue arrows), the hypothalamus stimulates the release of catecholamines, which mobilize the body for action.

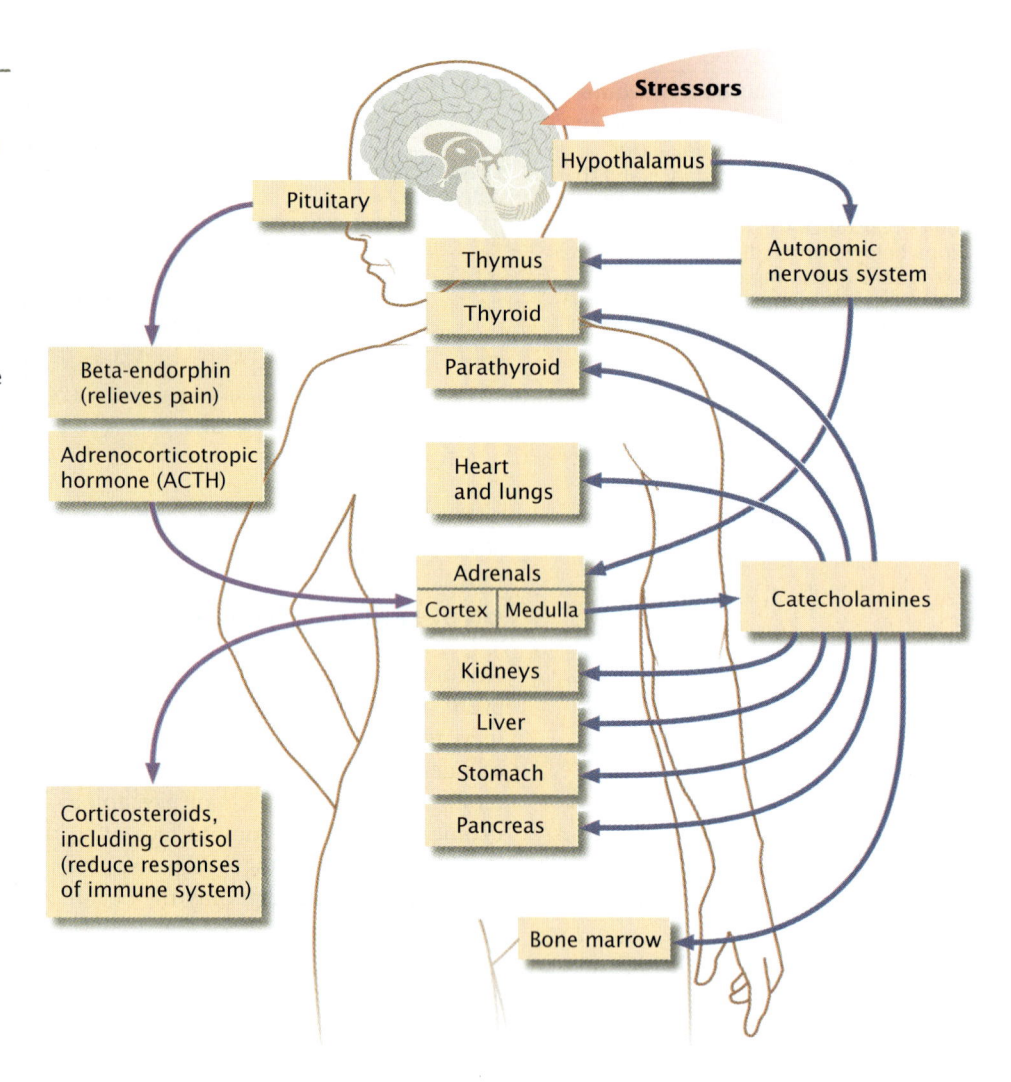

cortex (outer surface) of the adrenal glands to secrete *corticosteroids;* these hormones release the body's energy supplies and fight inflammation. The pituitary gland also triggers the release of endorphins, the body's natural painkillers.

The overall effect of these stress systems is to generate emergency energy. The more stressors there are and the longer they last, the more resources the body must expend in response.

If stressors persist, the *resistance stage* of the GAS begins. Here, obvious signs of the initial alarm reaction diminish as the body settles in to resist the stressor on a long-term basis. The drain on adaptive energy is slower during the resistance stage than it was during the alarm reaction, but the body is still working hard, physiologically.

This continued campaign of biochemical resistance is costly. It slowly but surely uses up the body's reserves of adaptive energy. The body then enters the third GAS stage, known as *exhaustion.* In extreme cases, such as prolonged exposure to freezing temperatures, the result is death. More commonly, the exhaustion stage brings signs of physical wear and tear, especially in organ systems that were weak in the first place or heavily involved in the resistance process. For example, if adrenaline and cortisol, which help fight stressors during the resistance stage, remain at high levels for an extended time, they can damage the heart and blood vessels; suppress the functioning of the body's disease-fighting immune system; and promote illnesses ranging from heart disease, high blood pressure, and arthritis to colds and flu (Carney et al., 1998; Light et al., 1999; McEwen, 1998). Selye referred to illnesses that are caused or worsened by stressors as **diseases of adaptation.**

diseases of adaptation Illnesses that are caused or worsened by stressors.

Psychological Responses

Selye's model has been very influential, but it has also been criticized for underestimating the role of psychological factors in stress, such as a person's emotional state or the way a person thinks about stressors. These criticisms led to the development of *psychobiological models,* which emphasize the importance of psychological as well as biological variables in regulating and producing stress responses (Lazarus & Folkman, 1984). Psychological responses to stress can appear as changes in emotions, thoughts (cognition), and behaviors.

Emotional Responses

The physical stress responses we have described are usually accompanied by emotional stress responses. If someone shows a gun and demands your money, you will no doubt experience the GAS alarm reaction, but you will also feel some strong emotion, probably fear and maybe anger. In fact, when people describe stress, they are more likely to say, "I was angry and frustrated!" than "My heart rate increased and my blood pressure went up." In other words, they are likely to mention changes in the emotions they are experiencing.

In most cases, emotional stress responses subside soon after the stressors are gone. However, if stressors continue for a long time or occur in a tight sequence, emotional stress reactions may persist. When people do not have a chance to recover their emotional equilibrium, they commonly report feeling tense, irritable, short-tempered, or anxious more and more of the time.

Cognitive Responses

In 1995, in the busy, noisy intensive care unit of a London hospital, a doctor misplaced a decimal point while calculating the amount of morphine a one-day-old premature baby should receive. The child died of a massive overdose (Davies, 1999). Reductions in the ability to concentrate, to think clearly, or to remember accurately are typical cognitive stress responses. Sometimes, these problems appear because of *ruminative thinking,* the recurring intrusion of thoughts about stressful events (Lyubomirsky & Nolen-Hoeksma, 1995). Ruminative thoughts about problems in a romantic relationship, for example, can seriously interfere with studying for a test. A related phenomenon is *catastrophizing,* which means dwelling on and overemphasizing the potential consequences of negative events (Sarason et al., 1986). During examinations, test-anxious college students are likely to say to themselves, "I'm falling behind" or "Everyone else is

Yet Another Funeral Even severe emotional stress responses usually ease eventually, but people plagued by numerous stressful events in quick succession—such as people living in strife-torn areas of the Middle East, where violent death is all too frequent—may experience increasingly intense feelings of fear, sadness, and helplessness. These reactions can become severe enough to be diagnosed as generalized anxiety disorder, major depressive disorder, or other stress-related mental disorders described in the chapter on psychological disorders.

Reprinted by permission of International Creative Management, Inc. Copyright © 2002 Berke Breathed.

BLOOM COUNTY by Berke Breathed

doing better than I am." As catastrophizing or ruminative thinking impairs cognitive functioning, a person may experience anxiety and other emotional arousal that adds to the total stress response and further hampers performance (Dougell, Craig, & Baum, 1999).

Overarousal created by stressors also tends to narrow the scope of attention, making it harder to scan the full range of possible solutions to complex problems (Keinan, Friedland, & Ben-Porath, 1987). In addition, stress-narrowed attention may increase the problem-solving errors described in the chapter on cognition and language. People under stress are more likely to cling to *mental sets*, which are well learned, but not always efficient, approaches to problems. Stress can also intensify *functional fixedness*, the tendency to use objects for only one purpose. Victims of hotel fires, for example, sometimes die trapped in their rooms because, in the stress of the moment, it did not occur to them to use the telephone or a piece of furniture to break a window.

Stressors may also impair decision making. People who normally consider all aspects of a situation before making a decision may, under stress, act impulsively and sometimes foolishly. High-pressure salespeople try to take advantage of this phenomenon by creating artificially time-limited offers or by telling customers that others are waiting to buy the item they are considering (Cialdini, 1995).

Behavioral Responses

Clues about people's physical and emotional stress responses come from changes in how they look, act, or talk. Strained facial

Stress for $500, Alex The effects of stress on memory, clear thinking, decision making, and other cognitive functions are often displayed by players on *Jeopardy!* and other TV game shows. Under the intense pressure of time, competition, and the scrutiny of millions of viewers, contestants may miss questions that seem ridiculously easy to those calmly recalling the correct answers at home. The hosts of some shows, such as *Weakest Link*, add to this pressure for the sake of entertainment.

expressions, a shaky voice, tremors or spasms, and jumpiness are common behavioral stress responses. Posture can also convey information about stress, a fact well known to skilled interviewers.

Even more obvious behavioral stress responses appear as people attempt to escape or avoid stressors. Some quit their jobs, drop out of school, turn to alcohol, or even attempt suicide. Unfortunately, as discussed in the chapter on learning, escape and avoidance tactics deprive people of the opportunity to learn more adaptive ways of coping with stressful environments, including college (Cooper et al., 1992). Aggression is another common behavioral response to stressors. All too often, this response is directed at members of one's own family (Polusny & Follette, 1995). In the months after Hurricane Andrew hit south Florida in 1992, for example, the rate of domestic-violence reports in the devastated area doubled (Rotton, 1990).

LINKAGES (a link to Psychological Disorders)

Stress and Psychological Disorders

Physical, psychological, and behavioral stress responses sometimes appear together in patterns known as *burnout* and *posttraumatic stress disorder.* **Burnout** is an increasingly intense pattern of physical and psychological dysfunction in response to a continuous flow of stressors or to chronic stress (Maslach & Goldberg, 1998). As burnout approaches, previously reliable workers or once-attentive spouses may become indifferent, disengaged, impulsive, or accident-prone. They may miss work frequently; oversleep; perform their jobs poorly; abuse alcohol or other drugs; and become irritable, suspicious, withdrawn, depressed, and unwilling to talk about stress or anything else (Taylor, 1999). Burnout is particularly common among individuals who do "people work," such as teachers and nurses (Schultz & Schultz, 1998). Each year, it accounts for a significant percentage of occupational disease claims by U.S. workers (Sauter et al., 1999).

A different pattern of severe stress reactions is illustrated by the case of "Mary," a thirty-three-year-old nurse who was raped at knifepoint by an intruder in her apartment (Spitzer et al., 1983). In the weeks following the attack, she became afraid of being alone and was preoccupied with the attack and with the fear that it might happen again. She had additional locks installed on her doors and windows but experienced difficulty concentrating and could not immediately return to work. She was repelled by the thought of sex.

Mary suffered from **posttraumatic stress disorder (PTSD),** a pattern of adverse reactions following a traumatic and threatening event. Among the characteristic reactions are anxiety, depression, irritability, jumpiness, inability to concentrate or work productively, sexual dysfunction, and difficulty in getting along with others (e.g., Goenjian et al., 2001). People suffering from posttraumatic stress disorder may also experience sleep disturbances and intense startle responses to noise or other sudden stimuli, and long-term suppression of their immune system (Kawamura, Kim, & Asukai, 2001; Shalev et al., 2000). The most common feature of posttraumatic stress disorder is re-experiencing the trauma through nightmares or vivid memories. In rare cases, *flashbacks* occur in which the person behaves for minutes, hours, or days as if the trauma were occurring again. Posttraumatic stress disorder is most commonly associated with events such as war, terrorism, assault, or rape (Schnurr et al., 2000), but researchers now believe that some PTSD symptoms can be triggered by any major stressor, from car accidents to being stalked (Ironson et al., 1997; Kamphuis & Emmelkamp, 2001).

Posttraumatic stress disorder may appear immediately following a trauma, or it may not occur until weeks, months, or—rarely—even years later (Gilboa-Schechtman & Foa, 2001; Heim et al., 2000; Port, Engdahl, & Frazier, 2001). The majority of people affected require professional help, although some seem

---

burnout A gradually intensifying pattern of physical, psychological, and behavioral dysfunction in response to a continuous flow of stressors.

posttraumatic stress disorder (PTSD) A pattern of adverse and disruptive reactions following a traumatic event.

Life Hanging in the Balance Symptoms of burnout and posttraumatic stress disorder often plague firefighters, police officers, emergency medical personnel, and others who are repeatedly exposed to time pressure, trauma, danger, and other stressors (DeAngelis, 1995a).

to recover without it. For most, improvement takes time; for nearly all, the support of family and friends is vital to recovery (Foa et al., 1999; Shalev, Bonne, & Eth, 1996).

Stress has also been implicated in the development of a number of other psychological disorders, including depression and schizophrenia (see the chapter on psychological disorders). The *diathesis-stress model* suggests that certain people are predisposed to these disorders, but that whether or not individuals actually display them depends on the frequency, nature, and intensity of the stressors they encounter.

Stress Mediators: Interactions Between People and Stressors

The interaction of particular people with particular stressors can be important in many ways. For example, in Afghanistan in 2001, three U.S. special forces soldiers and several anti-Taliban fighters were killed when an error in communicating target coordinates caused a U.S. B-52 to drop a bomb on their position. The stress of combat is partly responsible for similarly tragic "friendly fire" errors in almost every military operation (Adler, 1993). But why does stress disrupt the performance of some individuals and not others? And why does one individual survive, and even thrive, under the same circumstances that lead another to break down, give up, and burn out? A number of the mediating factors listed in Figure 13.1 help determine how much impact a given stressor will have (McEwen & Seeman, 1999).

How Stressors Are Appraised

As discussed in the chapter on perception, our view of the world depends on which stimuli we attend to and how we interpret, or appraise, them. Any potential stressor, whether it is a hot elevator or a deskful of work, usually has more negative impact on those who perceive it as a threat than on those who see it as a challenge (Goode et al., 1998; Lazarus, 1999).

figure 13.4

Cognitive Influences on Stress Responses

Richard Lazarus and his colleagues found that students' physiological stress reactions to a film showing bloody industrial accidents were affected by the way they thought about the film. Those who had been instructed to remain detached from the film (the "intellectualizers") or to think of it as unreal (the "denial" group) were less upset—as measured by sweat-gland activity—than those in an "unprepared" group. These results were among the first to show that people's cognitive appraisal of stressors can affect their responses to those stressors.

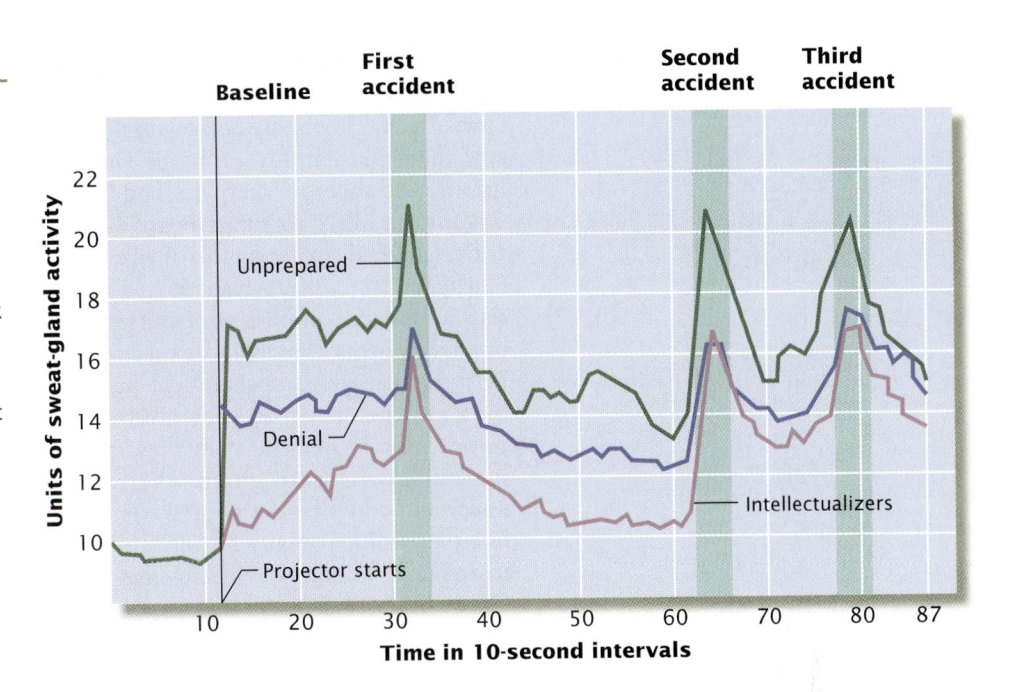

Evidence for the effects of cognitive factors on stress responses comes from both laboratory experiments and surveys. Figure 13.4 shows the results of a classic experiment that demonstrated these effects. In this case, the intensity of physiological arousal during a film depended on how the viewers were instructed to think about the film (Lazarus et al., 1965). Similarly, physical and psychological symptoms associated with the stress of airport noise, of learning about toxins in local soil, or of bioterrorism threats are more common in people who engage in more catastrophic thinking about these problems (Kjellberg et al., 1996; Matthies, Hoeger, & Guski, 2000).

The influence of cognitive factors weakens somewhat as stressors become more extreme. For example, if chronic-pain patients feel a sense of control over their pain, they tend to show higher levels of physical activity; but this effect does not hold for patients whose pain is severe (Jensen & Karoly, 1991). Still, even the impact of natural disasters or major stressors such as divorce may be less severe for those who think of them as challenges to be overcome. In short, many stressful events are not inherently stressful; their impact depends partly on how people perceive them (Wiedenfeld et al., 1990). An important aspect of this appraisal is the degree to which the stressors are perceived to be predictable or controllable.

Predictability and Control

Knowing that a particular stressor *might* occur but being uncertain whether it will tends to increase the stressor's impact (Boss, 1999; Sorrentino & Roney, 2000). In other words, predictable stressors tend to have less impact than those that are unpredictable (Lazarus & Folkman, 1984; Lejuez et al., 2000), especially when the stressors are intense and occur for relatively brief periods (Abbott, Schoen, & Badia, 1984). Rats given a reliable warning signal every time they are to receive a shock show less severe physiological responses than animals given no warnings (Weinberg & Levine, 1980). Among humans, men and women whose spouses died suddenly tend to display more immediate disbelief, anxiety, and depression than those who had weeks or months to prepare for the loss (Parkes & Weiss, 1983; Schulz et al., 2001). This is not to say that predictability provides total protection against stressors. Laboratory research with animals has shown that predictable stressors, even if relatively mild, can be more damaging than unpredictable ones if they occur over long periods of time (Abbott, Schoen, & Badia, 1984).

The *perception of control* can also mediate the effects of stressors. If people can exert some control over them, stressors usually have less impact on health (e.g., Christensen, Stephens, & Townsend, 1998; Krause & Shaw, 2000). Studies of several thousand employees in the United States, Sweden, and the United Kingdom have found that workers who had little or no control over their work environment were more likely to suffer heart disease and other health problems than workers with a high degree of control over their work environment (Bosma et al., 1997; Cheng et al., 2000; Hancock, 1996). In another study, researchers randomly selected a group of patients awaiting surgery and gave them a full explanation of the procedures that they could expect to undergo, along with information that would help them manage postsurgical pain (Egbert et al., 1964). After the surgery was over, patients who had been given this information and who felt they had at least some control over the pain they experienced were not only better adjusted than patients in a control group who received no special preparation, but also healed faster and could be discharged from the hospital sooner. So impressive are findings like these that, at many hospitals, it is now standard practice to teach patients how to manage or control the adverse effects of surgery (Chamberlin, 2000; Kiecolt-Glaser et al., 1998).

Simply believing that a stressor is controllable, even if it isn't, can also reduce its impact (Thompson et al., 1993). In one study of the cause of panic disorder (discussed in the chapter on psychological disorders), clients inhaled a mixture of carbon dioxide and oxygen that typically causes such clients to experience intense fear and other symptoms of a panic attack (Sanderson, Rapee, & Barlow, 1989). Half the clients were led to believe (falsely) that they could control the concentration of the mixture. Compared with those who believed they had no control, significantly fewer of the "in control" clients experienced full-blown panic attacks during the session, and their panic symptoms were fewer and less severe.

People who feel they have no control over negative events appear especially prone to physical and psychological problems. They often experience feelings of helplessness and hopelessness that, in turn, may promote depression or other mental disorders (Taylor & Aspinwall, 1996).

Coping Resources and Coping Methods

People usually suffer fewer ill effects from a stressor if they have adequate coping resources and effective coping methods. *Coping resources* include, for example, the money and time to deal with stressful events. Your physical and psychological responses to your car breaking down are likely to be more negative if you are low on cash and pressed for time than if you have money for repairs and the freedom to take a day off from work.

The impact of stressors can also be reduced by the use of effective *coping methods* (Benight et al., 1999). Most of these methods can be categorized as either *problem focused*, involving efforts to alter or eliminate a source of stress, or *emotion focused*, involving attempts to regulate the negative emotional consequences of the stressor (Folkman et al., 1986b). These two forms of coping sometimes work together. For example, you might deal with the problem of noise from a nearby airport by forming a community action group to push for tougher noise regulations and, at the same time, calm your anger when noise occurs by mentally focusing on the group's efforts to improve the situation (Folkman & Moskowitz, 2000). Susan Folkman and Richard Lazarus (1988) have devised a widely used questionnaire to assess the specific ways in which people cope with stressors; Table 13.3 shows some examples of responses to their questionnaire.

Particularly when a stressor is difficult to control, it is sometimes helpful to express fully, and think about, the emotions you are experiencing in relation to the stressful event (Pennebaker, 1993). For example, although people may not be able to do very much about stressors such as the death of a family member, attempting

TRY THIS *Coping* is defined as the cognitive and behavioral efforts to manage specific demands that people perceive as taxing their resources (Folkman et al., 1986b). This table illustrates two major approaches to coping measured by the Ways of Coping questionnaire: problem-focused and emotion-focused coping. To get an idea of your own coping style, rank-order the skills under each major approach in terms of how often you tend to use each skill. Do you rely on just one or two, or do you adjust your coping strategies to fit different kinds of stressors?

table 13.3
Ways of Coping

Coping Skills	Example
Problem-focused coping	
Confronting	"I stood my ground and fought for what I wanted."
Seeking social support	"I talked to someone to find out more about the situation."
Planful problem solving	"I made a plan of action, and I followed it."
Emotion-focused coping	
Self-controlling	"I tried to keep my feelings to myself."
Distancing	"I didn't let it get to me; I tried not to think about it too much."
Positive reappraisal	"I changed my mind about myself."
Accepting responsibility	"I realized I brought the problem on myself."
Escape/avoidance (wishful thinking)	"I wished that the situation would go away or somehow be over with."

Source: Adapted from Folkman et al. (1986a); S. E. Taylor (1995).

to see the meaning of the death in relation to their own lives may help them cope more successfully (Bower et al., 1999). The benefits of this cognitive strategy have been observed among many individuals whose religious beliefs allow them to bring meaning to events that might otherwise be deemed senseless tragedies (Seybold & Hill, 2001; Smith et al., 2000). Humor may also play a role. Some individuals who use humor to help them cope show better adjustment and lower physiological reactivity to stressful events (Lefcourt et al., 1997; Martin, 2001).

Social Support

If you have ever benefited from the comforting presence of a good friend during troubled times, you know about another factor that mediates the impact of stressful events—*social support*. Social support consists of resources provided by other people; the friends and social contacts on whom you can depend for support constitute your **social support network** (Burleson, Albrecht, & Sarason, 1994). The support may take many forms, from eliminating the stressor (as when a friend helps you fix your car) to easing its impact with companionship, ideas for coping, or reassurance that you are cared about and valued and that everything will be all right (Sarason, Sarason, & Gurung, 1997).

The stress-reducing effects of social support have been documented for a wide range of stressors, including cancer, military combat, loss of loved ones, natural disasters, arthritis, AIDS, and even ethnic discrimination (e.g., Foster, 2000; Holahan et al., 1997; Penner, Dovidio, & Albrecht, 2001; Savelkoul et al., 2000). Students clearly benefit from social support. Compared with those who are part of a supportive network, students with the least adequate social support suffer more emotional distress and are more vulnerable to upper respiratory infections during times of high academic stress (Lepore, 1995b). Some researchers have concluded that having inadequate social support can be as dangerous as smoking, obesity, or lack of exercise in that it nearly doubles a person's risk of dying from disease, suicide, or other causes (House, Landis, & Umberson, 1988; Kiecolt-Glaser & Newton, 2001).

Having strong social support can reduce the likelihood of illness, improve recovery from existing illness, promote healthier behaviors (Grassi et al., 2000;

social support network The friends and social contacts on whom one can depend for help and support.

You've Got a Friend Even when social support cannot eliminate stressors, it can help people, such as these breast cancer survivors, to feel less anxious, more optimistic, more capable of control, and more willing to try new ways of dealing with stressors.

Uchino, Uno, & Holt-Lunstad, 1999), and even reduce the intensity of stress responses. In laboratory studies, for example, participants tended to show smaller heart rate changes in response to a stressor if a friend was present than if they experienced the stressor alone (Gerin et al., 1995; Kamarck, Annunziato, & Amateau, 1995).

However, the relationship between social support and the impact of stressors is more complex than it might appear. First, just as the quality of social support may influence people's ability to cope with stress, the reverse may also be true: People's ability to cope may determine the quality of social support they receive (McLeod, Kessler, & Landis, 1992). For example, people who complain endlessly about stressors but never try to do anything about them may discourage social support, whereas those with an optimistic, action-oriented approach may attract support.

Second, *social support* refers not only to relationships with others but also to the recognition that others care and will help (Pierce, Sarason, & Sarason, 1991). Some relationships in a social support network may be stormy and fragile, resulting in interpersonal conflicts that can have an adverse effect on health (Malarkey et al., 1994).

Finally, having too much support or the wrong kind of support can be as bad as not having enough. For example, people whose friends and family are overprotective may actually put less energy into coping efforts. And in one study of people with physical disabilities, nearly 40 percent of them were found to have experienced emotional distress in response to the well-intentioned help they received from their spouses. This distress, in turn, was a predictor of depression nearly a year later (Newsome & Schulz, 1998). Similarly, people living in crowded conditions might initially perceive the situation as providing lots of social support, but these conditions may eventually become an added source of stress (Lepore, Evans, & Schneider, 1991). Further, the value of social support may depend on the kind of stressor being encountered. So although having a friend present might reduce the impact of some stressors, it might amplify the impact of others. In one study, for example, participants faced with speaking in public experienced it as more threatening—and showed stronger physical and psychological stress responses—when a friend was watching than when they were alone (Stoney & Finney, 2000). In short, the efforts or presence of members of a social support network can sometimes become annoying, disruptive, or interfering, thereby increasing stress and intensifying psychological problems (Newsome, 1999; Newsome & Schulz, 1998).

Stress, Personality, and Gender

The impact of stress on health appears to depend not only on how people think about particular stressors but, to some extent, on how they think about and react to the world in general (Prior, 1999). For instance, stress-related health problems are more common among people who tend to be angry, anxious, or depressed; who persist at mentally evading perceived stressors; who perceive stressors as long-term, catastrophic threats that they brought on themselves; and who are pessimistic about their ability to overcome negative situations (e.g., Penninx et al., 2001; Peterson et al., 1998; Segerstrom et al., 1998; Suinn, 2001).

Other cognitive styles, such as those characteristic of "disease-resistant" personalities, help insulate people from the ill effects of stress. These people tend to think of stressors as temporary challenges to be overcome, not catastrophic threats, and they do not constantly blame themselves for bringing them about. One particularly important component of the disease-resistant personality seems to be *dispositional optimism,* the belief or expectation that things will work out positively (Folkman & Moskowitz, 2000; Taylor et al., 2000a). Optimistic students, for example, experience fewer physical symptoms at the end of the academic term (Aspinwall & Taylor, 1992). Optimistic coronary bypass surgery patients have been shown to heal faster than pessimists (Scheier et al., 1989) and to experience a higher quality of life following coronary surgery than those with less optimistic outlooks (Fitzgerald et al., 1993). And among HIV-positive men, dispositional optimism has been associated with less psychological distress, fewer worries, and lower perceived risk of acquiring full-blown AIDS (Taylor et al., 1992). These effects appear to be due in part to optimists' tendency to use challenge-oriented, problem-focused coping strategies that attack stressors directly, in contrast to pessimists' tendency to use emotion-focused coping, such as denial and avoidance (Taylor, 1999).

Recent research suggests that gender may also play a role in responses to stress. In a review of two hundred studies of stress responses and coping methods, Shelley Taylor and her colleagues found that males under stress tended to get angry, avoid stressors, or both, whereas females were more likely to help others and to make use of their social support network (Taylor et al., 2000b). This was not true in every case, of course, but why should a significant difference show up at all? The gender-role learning discussed in the chapter on human development surely plays a part (Eagly & Wood, 1999). But Taylor also proposes that women's "tend and befriend" style differs from the "fight-or-flight" pattern so often seen in men because of gender differences in how hormones combine under stress. For example, oxytocin (pronounced "ok-see-TOE-sin"), a hormone released in both sexes as part of the general adaptation syndrome, interacts differently with male and female sex hormones—amplifying men's physical stress responses and reducing women's. This difference could lead to the more intense emotional and behavioral stress responses typical of men, and it might be partly responsible for their greater vulnerability to heart disease and other stress-related illnesses. If that is the case, gender differences in stress responses may help to explain why women in North America live an average of 7.5 years longer than men.

FOCUS ON RESEARCH METHODS

LINKAGES (a link to Human Development)

Personality and Health

The way people think and act in the face of stressors, the ease with which they attract social support, and their tendency to be optimists or pessimists are but a few aspects of *personality.*

- **What was the researchers' question?**

Are there other personality characteristics that protect or threaten people's health?

This was the research question asked by Howard Friedman and his associates (1995a, 1995b). In particular, they attempted to identify aspects of personality that increase the likelihood that people will develop heart disease or hypertension and die prematurely from these disorders.

● **How did the researchers answer the question?**

Friedman suspected that an answer might lie in earlier research—specifically, in the Terman Life Cycle Study of Intelligence, named after Louis Terman, author of the Stanford-Binet intelligence test. As described in the chapter on cognitive abilities, the study was originally designed to document the long-term development of 1,528 gifted California children (856 boys and 672 girls)—nicknamed the "Termites" (Terman & Oden, 1947). Friedman and his colleagues found ways of using data from this study to explore the relationship between personality and health.

Starting in 1921, and every five to ten years thereafter, Terman's research team had gathered information about the Termites' personality traits, social relationships, stressors, health habits, and many other variables. The data were collected through questionnaires and interviews with the Termites themselves, as well as with their teachers, parents, and other family members. When, by the early 1990s, about half of the Termites had died, Friedman realized that the Terman Life Cycle Study was really a longitudinal study in health psychology. As in most such studies, the independent variable (in this case, personality characteristics) was not actually manipulated (the Termites had obviously not been randomly assigned different personalities by the researchers), but the various personality traits identified in these people could still be related to a dependent variable (namely, how long they lived). So Friedman and his colleagues gathered the death certificates of the Termites, noted the dates and causes of death, and then looked for associations between personality and longevity.

● **What did the researchers find?**

One of the most important predictors of long life turned out to be where people fell on a personality dimension known as *conscientiousness,* or social dependability (see the chapter on personality). Termites who, in childhood, had been seen as truthful, prudent, reliable, hard-working, and free from vanity tended to live longer than those whose parents and teachers had identified them as impulsive and lacking in self-control.

Friedman and his colleagues also used the Terman Life Cycle Study to investigate the relationship between social support and health. They compared the life spans of Termites whose parents had divorced or who had been in unstable marriages themselves with those who grew up in stable homes and who had stable marriages. The researchers found that people who had experienced parental divorce during childhood or who themselves had unstable marriages died an average of four years earlier than those whose close social relationships had been less stressful.

● **What do the results mean?**

The research of Friedman and his co-workers was based mainly on correlational analyses, so it is difficult to draw conclusions about whether differences in personality traits and social support actually caused the observed differences in life span. Nevertheless, Friedman and his colleagues searched the Terman data for clues to mechanisms through which personality and other factors might have exerted a causal influence on longevity (Peterson et al., 1998). For example, they evaluated the hypothesis that conscientious, dependable Termites who lived socially stable lives might have followed healthier lifestyles than their impulsive and socially stressed age-mates. People in the latter group did indeed tend to eat less healthy diets and were more likely to smoke, drink to excess, or use drugs; but these behaviors alone did not fully account for their shorter average life spans. Another possible explanation is that conscientiousness and stability in social relationships create a general attitude of caution that goes beyond eating right and avoiding substance abuse. The researchers found some support for this idea in the Terman data. Termites who were impulsive or low on conscientiousness were somewhat more likely to die from accidents or violence than those who were less impulsive. (A similar finding is reported in the Focus on Research Methods section of the chapter on personality.)

● **What do we still need to know?**

Although the Terman Life Cycle Study cannot provide definite answers about the relationship between personality and health, it has generated some important clues and a number of intriguing hypotheses to be evaluated in future research with more representative samples of people. Further, Friedman's decision to reanalyze a set of data on psychosocial development as a way of exploring issues in health psychology stands as a fine example of how a creative researcher can pursue answers to complex questions that are difficult or impossible to study via controlled experiments.

Our review of personality and other factors that can alter the impact of stressors should make it obvious that what is stressful for a particular individual is not determined simply by predispositions, coping styles, or situations. (See "In Review: Stress Responses and Stress Mediators.") Even more important are interactions

in review: Stress Responses and Stress Mediators

Category	Examples
Responses	
Physical	Fight-or-flight syndrome (increased heart rate, respiration, and muscle tension; sweating; pupillary dilation); SAM and HPA activation (involving release of catecholamines and corticosteroids); eventual breakdown of organ systems involved in prolonged resistance to stressors.
Psychological	*Emotional:* anger, anxiety, depression, and other emotional states. *Cognitive:* inability to concentrate or think logically, ruminative thinking, catastrophizing. *Behavioral:* aggression and escape/avoidance tactics (including suicide attempts).
Mediators	
Appraisal	Thinking of a difficult new job as a challenge will create less discomfort than focusing on the threat of failure.
Predictability	A tornado that strikes without warning may have a more devastating emotional impact than a long-predicted hurricane.
Control	Repairing a disabled spacecraft may be less stressful for the astronauts doing the work than for their loved ones on Earth, who can do nothing to help.
Coping resources and methods	Having no effective way to relax after a hard day may prolong tension and other stress responses.
Social support	Having no one to talk to about a rape or other trauma may amplify the negative impact of the experience.

between the person and the situation, the mixture of each individual's coping resources and the specific characteristics of the situations encountered (Smith, 1993).

The Physiology and Psychology of Health and Illness

Several studies mentioned so far have suggested that stress shapes the development of physical illness by affecting cognitive, physiological, and behavioral processes. Those studies are part of a much larger body of research in health psychology that sheds light on the relationship between stress and illness. In the following sections we focus on some of the ways in which stress can, directly or indirectly, lead to physical illnesses by affecting the *immune system* and the *cardiovascular system*.

Stress, Illness, and the Immune System

LINKAGES (a link to Biological Aspects of Psychology)

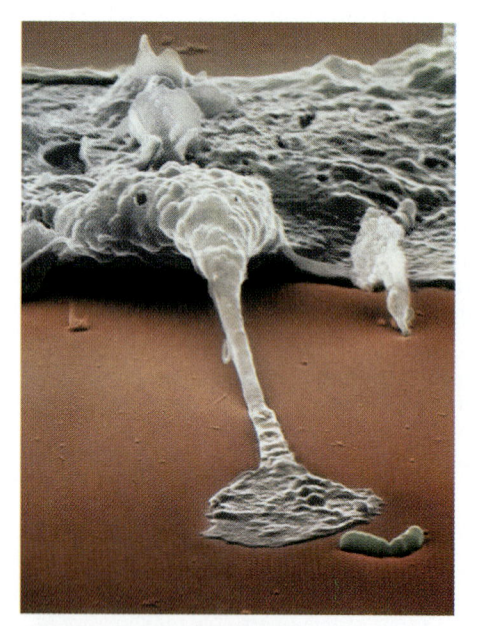

As noted in the chapter on biological aspects of psychology, components of the immune system act as the body's first line of defense by killing or deactivating foreign or harmful substances in the body, such as viruses and bacteria (Simpson, Hurtley, & Marx, 2000). This system plays a critical role in autoimmune diseases (in which the body falsely identifies its own cells as those of an invader) and chronic diseases such as AIDS, some cancers, and arthritis, as well as in fighting infectious diseases.

The role of physiological stress responses in altering the body's ability to fight disease was demonstrated more than a century ago. On March 19, 1878, at a seminar before the Académie de Médecine de Paris, Louis Pasteur showed his distinguished audience three chickens. One healthy bird, the control chicken, had been raised normally. A second bird had been intentionally infected with bacteria but given no other treatment; it was also healthy. The third chicken Pasteur presented was dead. It had been infected with the same bacteria as the second bird, but it had also been stressed by being exposed to cold temperatures; as a result, the bacteria had killed it (Kelley, 1985).

Research conducted since Pasteur's time has greatly expanded knowledge about how stressors affect the body's reaction to disease. **Psychoneuroimmunology** is the field that examines the interaction of psychological and physiological processes that affect the body's ability to defend itself against disease (Ader, 2001).

The Immune System and Illness
If the immune system is impaired—by stressors, for example—a person is left more vulnerable to colds, mononucleosis, and many other infectious diseases (Potter & Zautra, 1997). It is by disabling the immune system that HIV infection leads to AIDS and leaves the HIV-infected person defenseless against other infections or cancers.

There are many facets to the human immune system. One important component is the action of immune system cells, especially white blood cells, called *leukocytes* (pronounced "LU-koh-sites"), which are formed in the bone marrow and serve as the body's mobile defense units. Leukocytes are called into action when foreign substances are detected. Among the varied types of leukocytes are *B-cells*, which mature in the bone marrow, and *T-cells*, which mature in the thymus. Generally, T-cells kill other cells, and B-cells produce *antibodies*, which are circulating proteins that bind to specific toxins and other foreign cells and begin to deactivate them. *Natural killer cells*, another type of leukocyte, destroy a wide variety of foreign organisms, but they have particularly important antiviral and antitumor functions. Yet another type of immune system cell is the *macrophage* (pronounced "MACK-row-fayj). Macrophages engulf foreign cells and digest them in a process called *phagocytosis*,

The First Line of Defense A patrolling immune system cell sends out an extension known as a *pseudopod* (pronounced "SUE-doh-pod") to engulf and destroy a bacterial cell before alerting more defenders. Psychological stressors can alter immune system functions through a number of mechanisms. For example, they can activate neural connections between the sympathetic nervous system and organs of the immune system through response systems that have direct suppressant effects on immune function. These suppressant effects are due largely to the release of cortisol and other corticosteroid hormones from the adrenal cortex (see Figure 13.3).

or "eating cells." These scavengers are able to squeeze out of the bloodstream and enter organs, where they destroy foreign cells.

The activity of immune system cells can be either strengthened or weakened by a number of systems, including the endocrine system and the central and autonomic nervous systems. It is through these connections that stress-related psychological and emotional factors can affect the functioning of the immune system (see Figure 3.24 in the chapter on biological aspects of psychology). The exact mechanisms by which the nervous system affects the immune system are not yet fully understood. There is evidence, however, that the brain can influence the immune system indirectly by altering the secretion of hormones (including cortisol secretion by the adrenal gland) that modify circulating T-cells and B-cells, and directly by making connections with the immune organs, such as the thymus, where T-cells and B-cells are stored (Felten et al., 1991; Maier & Watkins, 2000).

The Immune System and Stress Researchers have found that people under stress are more likely than less stressed people to develop infectious diseases and to experience reactivation of latent viruses responsible for oral herpes (cold sores) or genital herpes (Cohen & Herbert, 1996). For example, Sheldon Cohen and his colleagues in the United Kingdom (Cohen et al., 1995) exposed 394 healthy adult volunteers either to one of five respiratory viruses or to a placebo. After being quarantined, the participants were asked about the number and severity of life stresses they had experienced in the previous year. After controlling for factors such as prior history of colds, exposure to other viruses, and health practices, the researchers found that the more stress the participants had experienced, the greater was the likelihood that their exposure to a virus would result in colds and respiratory infections.

These findings are supported by other research showing more directly that a variety of stressors lead to suppression of the immune system. The effects are especially strong in the elderly (Kiecolt-Glaser & Glaser, 2001), but they occur in everyone. For example, a study of first-year law students found that as these students participated in class, took exams, and experienced other stressful aspects of law school, they showed a decline in several measures of immune functioning (Segerstrom et al., 1998). Similarly, reduction in natural killer cell activity has been observed in both men and women following the death of their spouses (Irwin et al., 1987), and a variety of immune system impairments have been found in people suffering the effects of separation, divorce, lack of social support, and loneliness (Kiecolt-Glaser & Glaser, 1992). Providing care for an elderly relative who is mentally or physically incapacitated is a particularly stressful circumstance that has been reliably shown to diminish immune function (Cacioppo et al., 1998; Wu et al., 1999).

The relationship between stress and the immune system is especially important in persons who are HIV-positive but do not yet have AIDS. Because their immune systems are already seriously compromised, further stress-related impairments could be life-threatening. Research indicates that psychological stressors are associated with the progression of HIV-related illnesses (e.g., Antoni et al., 2000; Kemeny & Dean, 1995). Unfortunately, people with HIV (and AIDS) face a particularly heavy load of immune-suppressing psychological stressors, including bereavement, unemployment, uncertainty about the future, and daily reminders of serious illness. A lack of perceived control and resulting depression can further amplify their stress responses.

Moderators of Immune Function The effects of social support and other stress-moderating factors can be seen in the activity of the immune system. For example, immune system functioning among students who are able to get emotional assistance from friends during stressful periods appears better than among those with less-adequate social support (Cohen & Herbert, 1996).

> **psychoneuroimmunology** The field that examines the interaction of psychological and physiological processes that affect the ability of the body to defend itself against disease.

You Can't Fire Me—I Quit! For a time, researchers believed that anyone who displayed the pattern of aggressiveness, competitiveness, and nonstop work known as Type A behavior was at elevated risk for heart disease. More recent research shows, however, that the danger lies not in these characteristics alone but in hostility, a pattern seen in some, but not all, Type A people.

James Pennebaker and his colleagues (Pennebaker, 1993; Petrie, Booth, & Pennebaker, 1998) suggest that social support may help prevent illness by providing the person under stress with an opportunity to express pent-up thoughts and emotions. Keeping important things to oneself, says Pennebaker, is itself a stressor (Pennebaker, Colder, & Sharp, 1990). For example, the spouses of suicide or accidental-death victims who do not or cannot confide their feelings to others are most likely to develop physical illnesses during the year following the death (Pennebaker & O'Heeron, 1984). Disclosing, even anonymously, the stresses and traumas one has experienced is associated with enhanced immune functioning, reduced physical symptoms, and decreased use of health services (Petrie et al., 1995; Richards et al., 2000; Smyth et al., 1999). Suppressing the emotions associated with stressors can lead to impairment of the immune system (Pennebaker, Kiecolt-Glaser, & Glaser, 1988; Petrie et al., 1995, 1998). Future research in psychoneuroimmunology promises to reveal more about the complex chain of mental and physical events that determine whether people become ill or stay healthy.

Stress, Illness, and the Cardiovascular System

Earlier we discussed the role played by the sympatho-adreno-medullary (SAM) system in mobilizing the body during times of threat. Because the SAM system is linked to the cardiovascular system, its repeated activation in response to stressors has been linked to the development of coronary heart disease (CHD), high blood pressure (hypertension), and stroke. The link appears especially strong in people who display strong physical reactivity to stressors (Andre-Petersson et al., 2001; Kamarck et al., 1997; Stoney & Matthews, 1988; Treiber et al., 2001). For example, among healthy young adult research participants, those whose blood pressure rose most dramatically in response to a mild stressor were the ones most likely to develop hypertension over the next three decades (Kasagi, Akahoshi, & Shimaoki, 1995; Light et al., 1999; Menkes et al., 1989).

As also mentioned earlier, these physical reactions to stressors—and the chances of suffering stress-related health problems—depend partly on personality factors, especially on how people tend to think about stressors and about life in general. For example, hostility has been associated with the appearance of coronary heart disease (Friedman & Rosenman, 1959, 1974; Whiteman, Deary, & Fowkes, 2000).

THINKING CRITICALLY

Does Hostility Increase the Risk of Heart Disease?

Health psychologists see hostility as characterized by suspiciousness, resentment, frequent anger, antagonism, and distrust of others (Helmers & Krantz, 1996; Williams, 2001; Williams & Barefoot, 1988). The identification of hostility as a risk factor for coronary heart disease and *myocardial infarction,* or *MI* (commonly known as heart attack), could be an important breakthrough in better understanding the chief cause of death in the United States and most other Western nations (Hu et al., 2000). But is hostility as dangerous as health psychologists suspect?

- **What am I being asked to believe or accept?**

Many researchers contend that individuals displaying hostility are at increased risk for coronary heart disease and heart attack. This risk, they say, is independent of other risk factors such as heredity, diet, smoking, and drinking.

• What evidence is available to support the assertion?

The precise mechanism underlying the relationship between hostility and heart disease is not clear, but there are several possibilities (Helmers et al., 1995). The risk of CHD and MI may be elevated in hostile people because these people tend to be unusually reactive to stressors, especially when challenged (Suls & Wan, 1993). Under interpersonally challenging circumstances, for example, people predisposed to hostile behavior display not only overt hostility but also unusually large increases in blood pressure, heart rate, and other aspects of sympatho-adreno-medullary (SAM) reactivity (Suls & Wan, 1993). In addition, it takes hostile individuals longer than normal to get back to their resting levels of SAM functioning. Like a driver who damages a car by stepping on the accelerator and applying the brakes at the same time, these "hot reactors" may create excessive wear and tear on the arteries and the heart. Increased sympathetic nervous system activation not only puts stress on the coronary arteries but also leads to surges of stress-related hormones from the adrenal glands, including the catecholamines (adrenaline and noradrenaline). High levels of these hormones are associated with increases in cholesterol and other fatty substances that are deposited in arteries and contribute to atherosclerosis (hardening of the arteries) and CHD (Stoney & Hughes, 1999; Stoney et al., 1999a, 1999b). Plasma lipids, such as cholesterol and triglycerides, do appear to be elevated in hostile people, even when they are not under stress (Dujovne & Houston, 1991; Engebretson & Stoney, 1995).

Hostility might also affect heart disease risk less directly, through its impact on social support. Some evidence suggests that hostile people get fewer benefits from their social support network (Lepore, 1995a). Failure to use this support—and possibly offending potential supporters in the process—may intensify the impact of stressful events on hostile people. The result may be increased anger, antagonism, and ultimately, additional stress on the cardiovascular system (e.g., Hall & Davidson, 1996).

• Are there alternative ways of interpreting the evidence?

Studies suggesting that hostility causes CHD are not true experiments. Researchers cannot manipulate the independent variable, hostility, by creating it in some people but not others, nor can they create experimental conditions in which individuals who differ only in terms of hostility are compared on heart disease, the dependent variable. Accordingly, we have to consider other explanations of the hostility–CHD/MI relationship.

Some researchers suggest that higher CHD/MI rates among hostile people are due not to the impact of hostility on autonomic reactivity and hormone surges but, rather, to a third variable that accounts for the other two. Specifically, genetically determined autonomic reactivity might increase the likelihood of both hostility and heart disease (Krantz et al., 1988). Supporting this alternative interpretation is evidence that people with an inherited predisposition toward strong physiological responses to the stressors of everyday life not only have a higher risk for CHD but also tend to be more hostile (Cacioppo et al., 1998). It is at least plausible, then, that some individuals are biologically predisposed to exaggerated autonomic reactivity and to hostility, each of which is independent of the other.

• What additional evidence would help to evaluate the alternatives?

One way of testing whether hostile people's higher rates of CHD and MI are related to their hostility or to a more general tendency toward intense physiological arousal is to examine how hostile individuals react to stress when they are not angry. Researchers have done exactly this by observing the physiological reactions of hostile people as they undergo surgery. They have found that while enduring surgical stress under general anesthesia, hostile people show unusually strong autonomic reactivity (Krantz & Durel, 1983). Because these individuals are not conscious, it is more likely that oversensitivity to stressors, not hostile thinking, is causing this exaggerated response.

To more fully illuminate the role of hostility in the development of CHD and MI, future research will have to take into account a number of important possibilities: (1) Some individuals may be biologically predisposed to react to stress and challenge with hostility and increased cardiovascular activity, which in turn may contribute to heart disease; (2) hostile people may amplify and perpetuate their stress through aggressive thoughts and actions, which in turn may provoke others and elicit additional stressors; and (3) people high in hostility may harm their health to a greater extent than less hostile people by smoking, drinking, overeating, failing to exercise, and engaging in other high-risk behaviors (Houston & Vavac, 1991).

● **What conclusions are most reasonable?**

Although there is some inconsistency among various studies, most researchers continue to find that hostile individuals have a higher risk of heart disease and heart attacks than other people (Taylor, 1999). However, the causal relationship is probably more complex than researchers first thought; it appears that many interacting factors affect the relationship between hostility and CHD.

We must also keep in mind that the relationship between heart problems and hostility may not be universal. The relationship does appear to hold for women as well as men, and for individuals in various ethnic groups (e.g., Davidson, Hall, & MacGregor, 1996; Powch & Houston, 1996). However, final conclusions must await further research that examines the impact of gender, culture, and ethnicity on the link between hostility and CHD/MI.

Risking Your Life: Health-Endangering Behaviors

As we have seen, many of today's major health problems are caused or amplified by preventable behaviors such as those listed in Table 13.1.

Smoking

Smoking is the single most preventable risk factor for fatal illnesses in the United States (Centers for Disease Control and Prevention, 1999a). It accounts for 430,000 deaths each year—which is 20 percent of all U.S. deaths, and more than those caused by all other drugs, car accidents, suicides, homicides, and fires combined (Centers for Disease Control and Prevention, 1999a; U.S. Department of Health and Human Services, 2001b). Even nonsmokers who inhale "second-hand" smoke face an elevated risk for respiratory diseases, including lung cancer, and for cardiovascular diseases as well (Collins, 1997; Je et al., 1999; Otsuka et al., 2001), a fact that has fueled a militant nonsmokers' rights movement in North America.

A Deadly Habit The American Cancer Society has estimated that if people did not smoke cigarettes, 430,000 fewer U.S. citizens would die in the next twelve months, and 25 percent of all cancer deaths and thousands of heart attacks would never occur (Centers for Disease Control and Prevention, 1999a).

Although smoking is declining in the United States overall—only about 23.5 percent of adults now smoke—the habit is actually increasing in some groups, especially Latino men and women and young African American men (Centers for Disease Control and Prevention, 2000). Poorer, less educated people are particularly likely to smoke. Conversely, some American Indian tribes in the Southwest and most Asian American groups are less likely than other groups to smoke. In many other countries, smoking is still the rule rather than the exception (Lam et al., 2001). Smoking is a difficult habit to break; only about 10 to 40 percent of people participating in the stop-smoking programs available today show long-term success (Irvin et al., 1999; Klesges et al., 1999; USDHHS, 2000b). Improving this success rate and preventing adolescents from taking up smoking remain among health psychology's greatest challenges.

Alcohol   Like tobacco, alcohol is a potentially addicting substance that can lead to major health problems. More than 100,000 deaths occur each year in the United States as a result of excessive alcohol consumption (U.S. Surgeon General, 1999). In addition to its association with most leading causes of death, including heart disease, stroke, cancer, and liver disease, alcohol abuse contributes to permanent damage to brain tissue and to gastrointestinal illnesses, among many others (Centers for Disease Control and Prevention, 1999a). Both male and female alcohol abusers may experience disruption of their reproductive functions, such as early menopause in women and erectile disorder in men. Alcohol consumption by pregnant women is the most preventable cause of birth defects.

Unsafe Sex   According to the World Health Organization, about 36 million people worldwide are HIV-positive, and about 20 million have died from AIDS (Centers for Disease Control and Prevention, 2001a). As of December 2000, almost 775,000 people in the United States had been diagnosed as having AIDS, about 438,000 had died, and as many as 900,000 more had been infected with HIV (Centers for Disease Control and Prevention, 1999b, 2001b). With growing public awareness of how to prevent HIV infection, the number of new AIDS cases, as well as AIDS deaths, began to fall in the United States during the 1990s, but the rate of infection is now holding steady at about 40,000 cases per year (Centers for Disease Control and Prevention, 2001b). In short, not everyone is getting the message.

Unsafe sex—especially sexual relations without the use of a condom—greatly increases the risk of contracting HIV infection, yet many adolescents and adults continue this dangerous practice (Centers for Disease Control and Prevention, 1999c; Dodds et al., 2000). Like smoking and many other health-threatening behaviors, unprotected sex is disproportionately common among low-income individuals, many of whom are members of ethnic minority groups. Among African American men the risk of contracting AIDS is three times greater than it is among European American men; the risk for African American women is fifteen times higher than for European American women (Centers for Disease Control and Prevention, 1998).

Promoting Healthy Behavior

Health psychologists are deeply involved in the development of smoking cessation programs, in campaigns to prevent young people from taking up smoking, in alcohol-education efforts, and in the fight against the spread of HIV infection and AIDS (Kalichman, Cherry, & Browne-Sperling, 1999; Taylor, 1999). They have also helped promote early detection of disease. Encouraging women to perform breast self-examinations and men to do testicular self-examinations are just two examples of health psychology programs that can save thousands of lives each year (Taylor, 1999). Health psychologists have also explored the reasons behind some people's failure to follow treatment regimens that are vital to the control of diseases such as diabetes, heart disease, and high blood pressure. Understanding these reasons and devising procedures that encourage greater adherence to medical advice could speed recovery, prevent unnecessary suffering, and save many lives.

The process of preventing, reducing, or eliminating behaviors that pose risks to health and of increasing healthy behavior patterns is called **health promotion** (Taylor, 1999). Toward this end, many health psychologists have developed programs that teach children as young as nine or ten to develop healthy behaviors and avoid health-risky behaviors. School systems now offer a variety of these programs, including those that give children and adolescents the skills necessary to help them avoid cigarettes, drugs, and unprotected sex. To meet the more difficult challenge of modifying existing health-threatening behaviors, health psychologists go into workplaces and communities with the goal of altering diet, smoking, and exercise patterns and teaching stress-management techniques to help people develop healthier lifestyles (Langenberg et al., 2000; Tuomilehto et al., 2001). These programs may have the added advantage of creating savings in future medical treatment costs (Blumenthal et al., 2002; Kaplan, 1991).

In their health-promotion efforts, many health psychologists also conduct and apply research on the cognitive factors associated with the development and alteration of health-related behaviors. These psychologists have two goals: to better understand the thought processes that lead people to engage in health-endangering behaviors and to tailor intervention programs that alter those thought processes, or at least take them into account (Klepp, Kelder, & Perry, 1995).

Health Beliefs and Health Behaviors

The cognitive approach to health psychology is embodied in various *health-belief models*. One of the most influential of these models was developed by Irwin Rosenstock (1974). This model has been extensively tested (Aspinwall & Duran, 1999) and is based on the assumption that people's decisions about health-related behaviors (such as smoking) are guided by four main factors:

1. Perceiving a *personal threat* of, or susceptibility to, developing a specific health problem. (Do you believe that *you* will get lung cancer from smoking?)

2. Perceiving the seriousness of the illness and the severity of the consequences of having it. (How serious do *you* think lung cancer is, and what will happen if *you* get it?)

Doctor's Orders Despite their physicians' instructions, many patients fail to take their blood pressure medication and continue to eat a high-fat diet. Noncompliance with medical advice is especially common when cultural values and beliefs conflict with that advice. Aware of this problem, health psychologists are developing culture-sensitive approaches to health promotion and disease prevention (Kazarian & Evans, 2001).

3. The belief that a particular behavior change will reduce the threat. (Will *your* stopping smoking prevent *you* from getting lung cancer?)

4. A comparison of the *perceived costs* of enacting a health-related behavior change and the *benefits expected* from this change. (Will the reduced chance of getting cancer in the future be worth the discomfort and loss of pleasure associated with not smoking?)

This health-belief model suggests that the people most likely to quit smoking would be those who believe that they are susceptible to getting cancer from smoking, that cancer is serious and life-threatening, that giving up smoking will decrease their chances of getting cancer, and that the benefits of preventing cancer clearly outweigh the difficulties associated with quitting.

Other cognitive factors not included in Rosenstock's model may also be important, however. For example, people are unlikely to try to quit smoking unless they believe they can succeed. Thus, *self-efficacy*, the belief that one is able to perform some behavior, is an additional determinant of decisions about health behaviors (Bandura, 1992; Schwarzer, 2001). A related factor is the person's *intention* to engage in a behavior designed to improve health or protect against illness (Albarrican et al., 2001; Schwarzer, 2001).

Health-belief models have been useful in predicting a variety of health behaviors, including exercise (McAuley, 1992), safe-sex practices among gay men at risk for AIDS (Fisher, Fisher, & Rye, 1995), adherence to medical regimens among diabetic adolescents (Bond, Aiken, & Somerville, 1992), and the decision to undergo mammography screening for breast cancer (Champion & Huster, 1995). These models have also guided researchers in the development of interventions to reduce certain health-risky behaviors and promote health-enhancing actions. For example, interventions with individuals at high risk for AIDS, particularly adolescents and African American women, include programs to improve knowledge about the disease and skill in demanding safe sex (e.g., DiClemente & Wingood, 1995).

Changing Health Behaviors: Stages of Readiness

Changing health-related behaviors depends not only on a person's health beliefs but also on that person's readiness to change. According to James Prochaska and his colleagues, successful change involves five stages (Prochaska, DiClemente, & Norcross, 1992):

1. *Precontemplation.* The person does not perceive a health-related problem and has no intention of changing in the foreseeable future.

2. *Contemplation.* The person is aware of a health-related behavior that should be changed and is seriously thinking about changing it. People often get stuck here. Smokers, for example, have been known to spend years "thinking about" quitting.

health promotion The process of altering or eliminating behaviors that pose risks to health, as well as encouraging healthy behavior patterns.

3. *Preparation.* The person has a strong intention to change; has specific plans to do so; and may already have taken preliminary steps, such as cutting down on smoking.

4. *Action.* The person at this stage is engaging successfully in behavior change. Because "backsliding," or relapse, is so common when trying to change health-related behaviors, people must remain successful for up to six months before they officially reach the final stage.

5. *Maintenance.* The person uses skills learned along the way to continue the healthy behavior and to prevent relapse.

The path from precontemplation through maintenance is not a smooth one (Prochaska, 1994). Usually, people relapse and repeat one or more of the previous stages before finally achieving stability in the healthy behavior they desire (see Figure 13.5). For example, smokers typically require three to four cycles through the stages and up to seven years before they finally reach the maintenance stage.

What factors contribute to movement from one stage to the next? Prochaska and his colleagues found that the factors facilitating progress at one stage may be different from the most important factors at another stage. However, *decisional balance*—the outcome of weighing the pros and cons of changing—is important for predicting progress at any stage (Prochaska et al., 1994). Incorporating these factors into intervention programs has helped people seek mammography on a regular basis (Rakowski et al., 1996), participate in exercise programs (Bock, Marcus, & Pinto, 2001; Courneya, 1995), eat a low-fat diet (Laforge, Greene, & Prochaska, 1994), quit smoking (Adelman et al., 2001), and engage in other healthy behaviors (Prochaska & DiClemente, 1992).

Programs for Coping with Stress and Promoting Health

Tipping the decisional balance in favor of healthy change is but one strategy that health psychologists apply in their efforts to improve people's coping skills and promote healthier lifestyles. Let's consider a few specific procedures and programs used in this wide-ranging effort.

LINKAGES (a link to Treatment of Psychological Disorders)

Planning to Cope
Just as people with extra money in the bank have a better chance of weathering a financial crisis, those with effective coping skills may

figure 13.5

Stages of Readiness to Change Health Behaviors

Many health psychologists are guided by James Prochaska's theory that readiness to change health behaviors progresses through predictable stages. To help people quit smoking, for example, psychologists use persuasive communication during the contemplation stage and relapse-prevention techniques during the action stage. Tailoring interventions to each individual's history of progress through the stages of readiness may increase the likelihood of permanent changes in behavior (Kreuter & Holt, 2001).

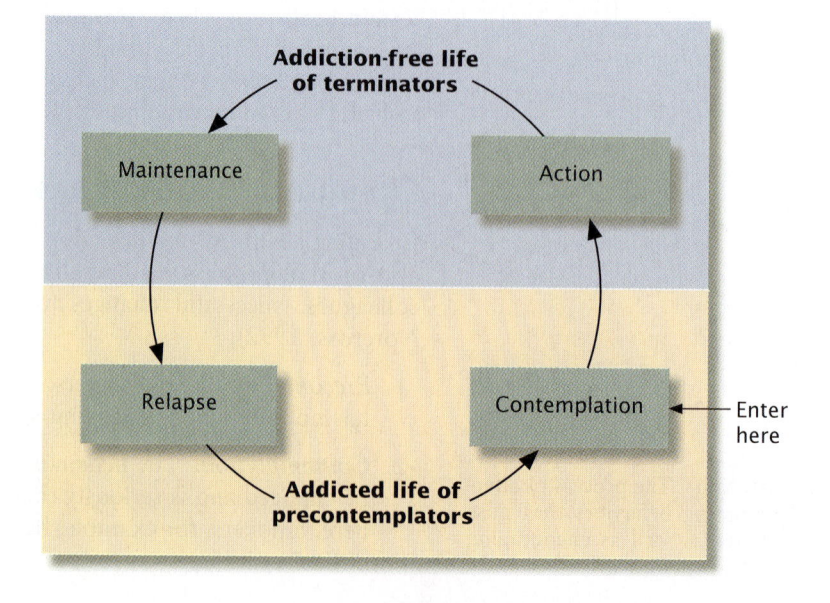

Many successful programs for systematically coping with stress guide people through several stages and are aimed at removing stressors that can be changed and at reducing responses to stressors that cannot be changed (Taylor, 1998a).

table 13.4
Stages in Coping with Stress

Stage	Task
1. Assessment	Identify the sources and effects of stress.
2. Goal setting	List the stressors and stress responses to be addressed. Designate which stressors are and are not changeable.
3. Planning	List the specific steps to be taken to cope with stress.
4. Action	Implement coping plans.
5. Evaluation	Determine the changes in stressors and stress responses that have occurred as a result of coping methods.
6. Adjustment	Alter coping methods to improve results, if necessary.

escape some of the more harmful effects of intense stress (Aspinwall & Taylor, 1997). Like family money, the ability to handle stress appears to come naturally to some people, but coping can also be learned.

The first step in learning to cope with stress is to make a systematic assessment of the degree to which stress is disrupting your life. This assessment involves (1) identifying the specific events and situations, such as conflicts or life changes, that are operating as stressors, and (2) noting the effects of these stressors, such as headaches, lack of concentration, or excessive drinking.

Table 13.4 lists the other steps in a program to cope with stress. Notice that the second step is to select an appropriate goal. Should you try to eliminate stressors or to alter your response to them? Knowing the difference between changeable and unchangeable stressors is important. Stress-related problems appear especially common among people who either exhaust themselves trying to change unchangeable stressors or miss opportunities to change stressors that can be changed (Folkman, 1984).

No single method of coping with stressors is universally successful. For example, denying the existence of an uncontrollable stressor may be fine in the short run but may lead to problems if no other coping method is used (Suls & Fletcher, 1985). Similarly, people who rely exclusively on an active problem-solving approach may handle controllable stressors well but find themselves nearly helpless in the face of uncontrollable ones (Murray & Terry, 1999). Individuals most successful at stress management may be those who are best able to adjust their coping methods to the demands of changing situations and differing stressors (Taylor, 1999).

Taking Time Out The workplace is the number one source of stress for many people in the United States. On January 1, 2000, Raymond Fowler, who was then chief executive officer of the American Psychological Association, joined the ranks of those whose elevated blood pressure, heart problems, and other physical stress responses necessitated a leave of absence from highly stressful jobs (Fowler, 2000). The National Institute for Occupational Safety and Health (1999) suggests a wide range of other behavioral coping options for stressed employees who cannot take time off.

Developing Coping Strategies Like stress responses, strategies for coping with stress can be cognitive, emotional, behavioral, or physical. *Cognitive coping strategies* change how people interpret stimuli and events. They help people to think more calmly, rationally, and constructively in the face of stress and may generate a more hopeful emotional state. For example, students with heavy course loads may experience anxiety, confusion, discouragement, lack of motivation, and the desire to run away from it all. Frightening, catastrophic thoughts about their tasks (for example, "What if I fail?") can amplify stress responses. Cognitive coping strategies replace catastrophic thinking with thoughts in which stressors are viewed as challenges rather than threats (Ellis & Bernard, 1985). This substitution process is often called *cognitive restructuring* (Lazarus, 1971; Meichenbaum, 1977). It can be done by practicing constructive thoughts such as "All I can do is the best I can." Cognitive coping does not eliminate stressors, but it can help people perceive them as less threatening and thus make them less disruptive (Antoni et al., 2000).

Seeking and obtaining social support from others are effective *emotional coping strategies*. The perception that you have such support, and that you are cared

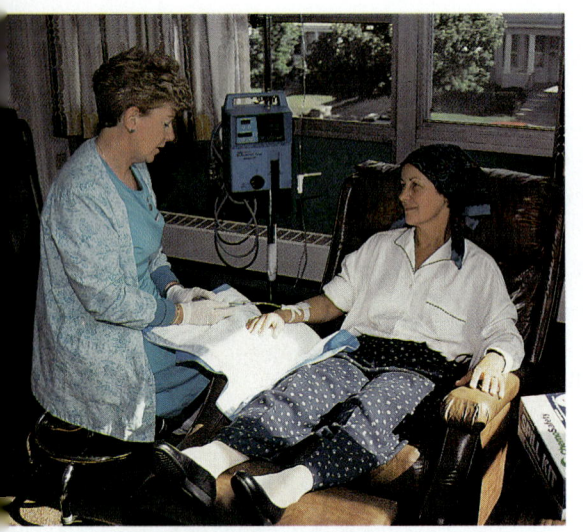

Dealing with Chemotherapy
Progressive relaxation training can be used to ease a variety of health-related problems. For example, one study found that this training resulted in significant reductions in anxiety, physiological arousal, and nausea following cancer chemotherapy (Burish & Jenkins, 1992).

for and valued by others, tends to be an effective buffer against the ill effects of many stressors (Taylor, 1999; Taylor et al., 2000b). With social support comes feedback from others, along with advice on how to approach stressors. Research suggests that having enhanced social support is associated with improved immune function (Kiecolt-Glaser & Glaser, 1992) and more rapid recovery from illness (Taylor, 1999).

Behavioral coping strategies involve changing behavior in ways that minimize the impact of stressors. Time management is one example. You might keep track of your time for a week and start a time-management plan. The first step is to set out a schedule that shows how you usually spend your time; then decide how to allocate your time in the future. A time-management plan can help control catastrophizing thoughts by providing reassurance that there is enough time for everything and a plan for handling it all.

Physical coping strategies are aimed at directly altering physical responses before, during, or after stressors occur. The most common physical coping strategy is some form of drug use. Prescription medications are sometimes an appropriate coping aid, especially when stressors are severe and acute, such as the sudden death of one's child. But if people depend on prescriptions or other drugs, including alcohol, to help them face stressors, they often attribute any success to the drug, not to their own skill. Furthermore, the drug effects that blunt stress responses may also interfere with the ability to apply coping strategies. The resulting loss of perceived control over stressors may make those stressors even more threatening and disruptive.

Nonchemical methods of reducing physical stress reactions and improving functioning include progressive relaxation training (Bernstein, Borkovec, & Hazlette-Stevens, 2000; Scheufele, 2000), physical exercise (Anshel, 1996), biofeedback (Sarafino & Goehring, 2000), and meditation and tai chi (Li et al., 2001), among others (Taylor, 1999).

Progressive relaxation training is one of the most popular physical methods for coping with stress. Edmund Jacobson developed the technique during the 1930s (Jacobson, 1938). Today, progressive relaxation is learned by tensing a group of muscles (such as the hand and arm) for a few seconds, then releasing the tension and focusing on the resulting feelings of relaxation. This procedure is repeated for each of sixteen muscle groups throughout the body (Bernstein, Borkovec, & Hazlette-Stevens, 2000). Once people develop some skill at relaxation, they can use it to calm themselves down anywhere and anytime, often without lying down. ("In Review: Methods for Coping with Stress" summarizes our discussion of stress-coping methods.)

progressive relaxation training A procedure for learning to relax that involves tensing muscles and then releasing the tension in those muscles.

in review	Methods for Coping with Stress
Type of Coping Method	**Examples**
Cognitive	Thinking of stressors as challenges rather than as threats; avoiding perfectionism.
Emotional	Seeking social support; getting advice.
Behavioral	Implementing a time-management plan; where possible, making life changes to eliminate stressors.
Physical	Progressive relaxation training; exercise; meditation.

LINKAGES

As noted in the chapter on introducing psychology, all of psychology's subfields are related to one another. Our discussion of posttraumatic stress disorder illustrates just one way in which the topic of this chapter, health, stress, and coping, is linked to the subfield of psychological disorders (which is the focus of the chapter by that name). The Linkages diagram shows ties to two other subfields as well, and there are many more ties throughout the book. Looking for linkages among subfields will help you see how they all fit together and help you better appreciate the big picture that is psychology.

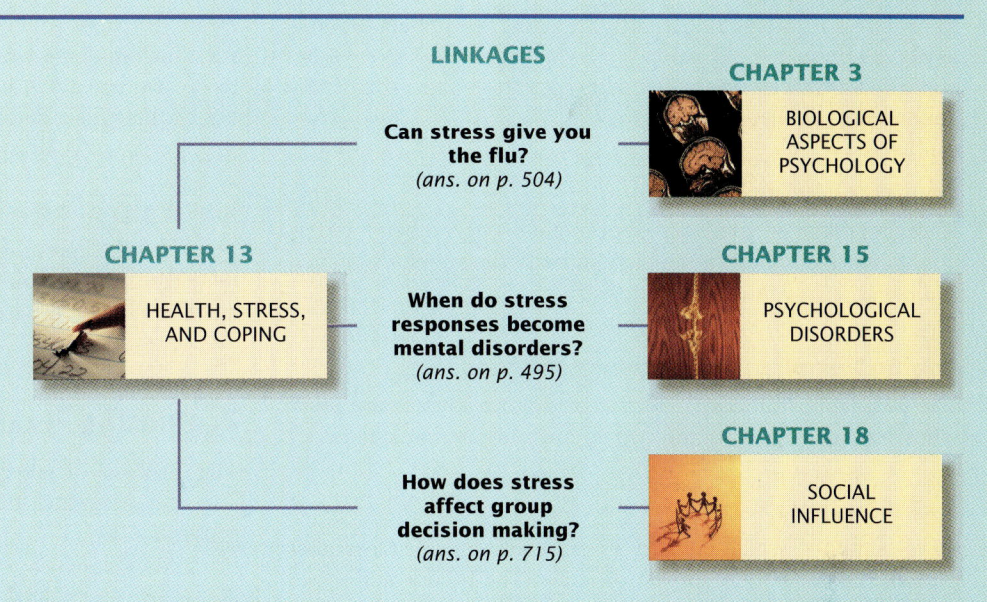

LINKAGES

CHAPTER 13 — HEALTH, STRESS, AND COPING

- Can stress give you the flu? (ans. on p. 504) → CHAPTER 3: BIOLOGICAL ASPECTS OF PSYCHOLOGY
- When do stress responses become mental disorders? (ans. on p. 495) → CHAPTER 15: PSYCHOLOGICAL DISORDERS
- How does stress affect group decision making? (ans. on p. 715) → CHAPTER 18: SOCIAL INFLUENCE

SUMMARY

Health Psychology

The development of *health psychology* was prompted by recognition of the link between stress and illness, as well as the role of behaviors such as smoking, in elevating the risk of illness. Researchers in this field explore how psychological factors are related to physical disease and vice versa. Health psychologists also help people behave in ways that prevent or minimize disease and promote health.

Stress and Stressors

The term *stress* refers in part to *stressors*, which are events and situations to which people must adjust. More generally, stress is viewed as an ongoing, interactive process that takes place as people adjust to, and cope with, their environment. Stressors may be physical or psychological.

Psychological Stressors

Psychological stressors include catastrophic events, life changes and strains, and daily hassles.

Measuring Stressors

Stressors can be measured by tests such as the Social Readjustment Rating Scale (SRRS) and the Life Experiences Survey (LES), as well as by surveys of daily hassles, but scores on such tests provide only a partial picture of the stress in an individual's life.

Stress Responses

Responses to stressors can be physical or psychological. They can occur alone or in combination, and the appearance of one response can stimulate others.

Physical Responses

Physical stress responses include changes in sympatho-adreno-medullary (SAM) activation, such as increases in heart rate, respiration, and many other processes, as well as hypothalamic-pituitary-adrenocortical (HPA) activation, including the release of corticosteroids. These responses may be viewed as part of a pattern known as the *general adaptation syndrome*, or *GAS*. The GAS has three stages: the alarm reaction, resistance, and exhaustion. The GAS helps people resist stress, but if present too long, it can lead to depletion of physiological resources, as well as to physical illnesses, which Hans Selye called *diseases of adaptation*.

Psychological Responses

Psychological stress responses can be emotional, cognitive, and behavioral. Cognitive stress reactions include ruminative thinking; catastrophizing; and disruptions in the ability to think clearly, remember accurately, and solve problems efficiently. Behavioral stress responses include irritability, aggression, absenteeism, and even suicide attempts. Extreme or chronic stressors can lead to *burnout* or *posttraumatic stress disorder (PTSD)*.

Stress Mediators: Interactions Between People and Stressors

The fact that different individuals react to the same stressors in different ways can be explained in part by stress mediators, such as the extent to which individuals can predict and control their stressors, how they interpret the threat involved, the social support they get, and their stress-coping skills.

How Stressors Are Appraised

Many stressors are not inherently stressful; their impact depends partly on how people perceive them. In particular, stressors appraised as threats are likely to have greater impact than those appraised as challenges.

Predictability and Control

Knowing that a particular stressor might occur but being uncertain whether it will occur tends to increase the stressor's impact, as does lack of control over stressors.

Coping Resources and Coping Methods

The people most likely to react strongly to a stressor are those whose coping resources and coping methods are inadequate.

Social Support

Social support, which consists of resources provided by other persons, can lessen the impact of stress. The friends and social contacts on whom a person can depend for support constitute that person's *social support network*.

Stress, Personality, and Gender

Certain personality characteristics help insulate people from the ill effects of stress. One such characteristic appears to be dispositional optimism, the belief or expectation that things will work out positively. Gender can also play a role in stress responses.

The Physiology and Psychology of Health and Illness

Stress, Illness, and the Immune System

Psychoneuroimmunology is the field that examines the interaction of psychological and physiological processes that affect the body's ability to defend itself against disease. When a person is under stress, some of the hormones released from the adrenal gland, such as cortisol, reduce the effectiveness of the cells of the immune system (for example, T-cells, B-cells, natural killer cells, and macrophages) in combating foreign invaders such as viruses.

Stress, Illness, and the Cardiovascular System

Heart disease is a major cause of death in most Western countries, including the United States. People who are hostile appear to be at greater risk for heart disease than other people, possibly because their heightened reactivity to stressors can damage their cardiovascular system.

Risking Your Life: Health-Endangering Behaviors

Many of the major health problems in Western cultures are related to preventable behaviors such as smoking and drinking alcohol. Having unsafe sex is a major risk factor for contracting HIV infection.

Promoting Healthy Behavior

The process of altering or eliminating health-risky behaviors and fostering healthy behavior patterns is called *health promotion*.

Health Beliefs and Health Behaviors

People's health-related behaviors are partly guided by their beliefs about health risks and what they can do about them.

Changing Health Behaviors: Stages of Readiness

The process of changing health-related behaviors may involve several stages, including precontemplation, contemplation, preparation, action, and maintenance. Understanding which stages people are in and helping them move through these stages are important tasks in health psychology.

Programs for Coping with Stress and Promoting Health

In order to cope with stress, people must recognize the stressors affecting them, note their effects, and develop ways of coping with them. Important coping skills include cognitive restructuring, as well as using emotional and behavioral means to minimize the intensity and impact of stressors. *Progressive relaxation training* and other physical coping strategies can reduce physical stress reactions. These coping procedures are often part of health psychologists' disease-prevention and health-promotion efforts.

Personality

14

The Psychodynamic Approach
The Structure and Development of Personality
Variations on Freud's Personality Theory
Contemporary Psychodynamic Theories
Evaluation of the Psychodynamic Approach

The Trait Approach
Allport's Trait Theory
The Big-Five Model of Personality
Biological Trait Theories
THINKING CRITICALLY: Are Personality Traits Inherited?
Evaluation of the Trait Approach

The Social-Cognitive Approach
Roots of the Social-Cognitive Approach
Prominent Social-Cognitive Theories
Evaluation of the Social-Cognitive Approach

The Humanistic Approach
Prominent Humanistic Theories
Evaluation of the Humanistic Approach

LINKAGES: Personality, Culture, and Human Development

FOCUS ON RESEARCH METHODS: Longitudinal Studies of Temperament and Personality

Assessing Personality
Objective Personality Tests
Projective Personality Tests
Personality Tests and Employee Selection

Linkages
Summary

It has been estimated that U.S. businesses lose more than $60 billion each year as a result of employee theft (Gatewood & Feild, 2001). Millions more are spent on security and surveillance designed to curb these losses, but it would be far better if companies could simply avoid hiring dishonest employees in the first place. Some firms have tried to screen out potential thieves by requiring prospective employees to take "lie detector" polygraph tests. As described in the chapter on motivation and emotion, however, these tests may not be reliable or valid; the federal government has banned their use in most kinds of employee selection.

Thousands of companies have turned instead to paper-and-pencil "integrity" tests designed to identify job applicants who are likely to steal or behave in other dishonest or irresponsible ways (Alliger & Dwight, 2000). Some of these tests simply ask applicants if they have stolen from previous employers and if they might steal in the future. Such questions can screen out people who are honest about their stealing, but most people who steal would probably also lie to conceal previous crimes or criminal intentions. Accordingly, some companies now use tests to assess applicants' general psychological characteristics and compare their scores with those of current or past employees. Applicants whose characteristics are most like the company's honest employees are hired; those who appear similar to dishonest employees are not hired.

Can employee honesty be predicted on the basis of such tests? To some extent, it can (Ones & Viswesvaran, 2001). For example, scores on the *Reliability Scale*—which includes questions about impulsivity and disruptive behavior during school years—are significantly correlated with a broad range of undesirable employee behaviors (Hogan & Ones, 1997). But psychological tests are far from perfect predictors of those behaviors. Although better than polygraph tests, psychological tests still fail to detect dishonesty in some people, or worse, they may falsely identify some honest people as potential thieves. The best that companies can hope for is to find tests that will help reduce the overall likelihood of hiring dishonest people.

The use of psychological tests to help select honest employees is a more formal version of the process that most of us use when we meet someone new. We observe the person's behavior, form impressions, and draw conclusions about how that person will act at other times or under other circumstances. Like the employer, we are looking for clues to *personality*. Although there is no universally accepted definition, psychologists generally view **personality** as the unique pattern of enduring thoughts, feelings, and actions that characterize a person. Personality research, in turn, focuses on understanding the origins or causes of the similarities and differences among people in their patterns of thinking, emotion, and behavior.

With such a large agenda, personality researchers must incorporate information from many other areas of psychology. In fact, personality psychology appears to lie at the crossroads of all psychological research (Funder, 2001a); it is the merging, in a particular individual, of all the psychological, behavioral, and biological processes discussed elsewhere in this book. To gain a comprehensive understanding of any individual's personality, for example, one must know about that person's developmental experiences (including cultural influences), genetic and other biological characteristics, perceptual and other information-processing habits and biases, typical patterns of emotional expression, and social skills. Psychologists also want to know about personality in general, such as how personality develops and changes across the life span, why some people are usually optimistic whereas others are usually pessimistic, and how consistent or inconsistent people's behavior tends to be from one situation to the next.

In this chapter we describe four approaches to the study of personality and some of the ways in which personality theory and research are being applied. We begin by presenting the psychodynamic approach, which was developed by Sigmund Freud and later modified by a number of people he influenced. Next, we describe the trait approach, which focuses on the consistent patterns of thoughts, feelings,

personality The pattern of psychological and behavioral characteristics by which each person can be compared and contrasted with others.

psychodynamic approach Freud's view that personality is based on the interplay of unconscious mental processes.

and actions that form individual personalities. Then we present the social-cognitive approach, which explores the roles of learning and cognition in shaping human behavior. Finally, we consider the humanistic approach, with its emphasis on personality as a reflection of personal growth and the search for meaning in life. After reviewing these approaches, we describe how psychologists measure and compare people's personalities. We also give some examples of how psychological tests are being used in personality research and in other ways as well.

The Psychodynamic Approach

Some people think they can understand personality by simply watching people. Someone with an "obnoxious personality," for example, shows it by acting obnoxiously. But is that all there is to personality? Not according to Sigmund Freud, who likened each individual's personality to an iceberg, whose tip is clearly visible but whose bulk remains hidden underwater.

Trained as a neurologist in the late nineteenth century, Freud spent most of his life in Vienna, Austria, treating patients who displayed "neurotic" disorders, such as blindness or paralysis for which there was no physical cause. Freud's experience with these patients, as well as his reading of the works of Charles Darwin and other scientists of his day, led him to believe that our personalities, behavior, and behavior disorders are determined mainly by basic drives and past psychological events (Schultz & Schultz, 2000). He proposed, further, that people may not know why they feel, think, or act the way they do, because these activities are partly controlled by the unconscious part of the personality—the part of which we are not normally aware (Funder, 2001b). From these ideas Freud created the **psychodynamic approach** to personality, which holds that the interplay of various unconscious psychological processes determines thoughts, feelings, and behavior.

The Structure and Development of Personality

Freud believed that people have certain basic impulses or urges—related not only to food, water, and air but also to sex and aggression. In most translations of his writings, the term *instinct* is used to describe these impulses and urges, though Freud did

Founder of the Psychodynamic Approach Here is Sigmund Freud with his daughter, Anna, who developed her own revised version of her father's psychodynamic theory of personality.

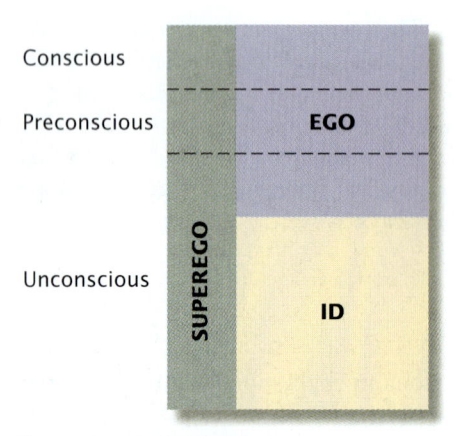

figure 14.1

Freud's Conception of the Personality Structure

According to Freud, some parts of the personality are conscious, whereas others are unconscious. Between these levels is the preconscious, which Freud saw as the location of memories and other material that is not usually in awareness but that can be brought into consciousness with little or no effort.

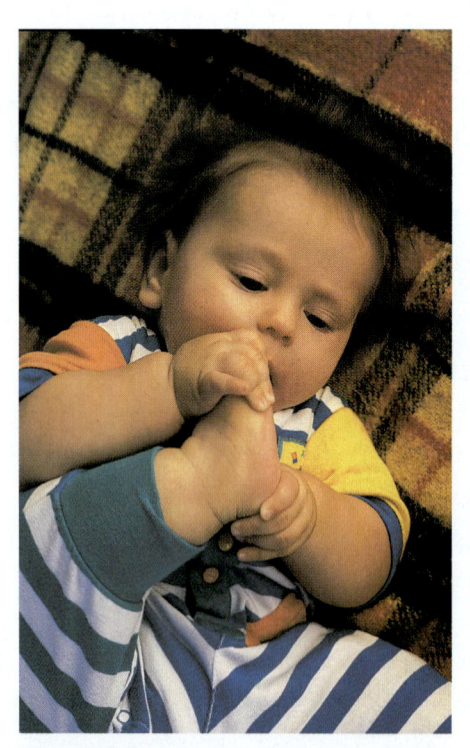

The Oral Stage According to Freud, personality develops in a series of psychosexual stages. At each stage, a different part of the body becomes the primary focus of pleasure. This baby would appear to be in the oral stage.

not believe that they are all inborn and unchangeable, as the word *instinct* might imply (Schultz & Schultz, 2001). He did believe, however, that our desires for love, knowledge, security, and the like are based on these more fundamental impulses. He said that each of us faces the task of figuring out how to satisfy basic urges; our own personality develops out of our struggle with that task, and it is reflected in the ways we go about satisfying a range of urges.

Id, Ego, and Superego

As shown in Figure 14.1, Freud described the structure of personality as having three major components: the id, the ego, and the superego.

He saw the **id** as the unconscious portion of personality, in which two kinds of "instincts" reside. There are life instincts, which he called *Eros;* they promote positive, constructive behavior and reflect a source of energy (sometimes called *psychic energy*) known as **libido**. There are also death instincts, or *Thanatos,* which Freud saw as responsible for aggression and destructiveness (Westen & Gabbard, 1999). The id operates on the **pleasure principle,** seeking immediate satisfaction of both kinds of instincts, regardless of society's rules or the rights or feelings of others. The hungry person who pushes to the front of the line at McDonald's would be satisfying an Eros-driven id impulse.

As parents, teachers, and others place ever greater restrictions on the expression of children's id impulses, a second part of the personality—the **ego**—develops from the id. The ego is responsible for finding ways to get what a person wants in the real world, as opposed to the fantasy world of the id. Operating on the **reality principle,** the ego makes compromises between the id's unreasoning demands for immediate satisfaction and the practical constraints imposed by the world. The ego would lead the hungry person at McDonald's to wait in line and think about what to order rather than risk punishment by pushing ahead.

As children learn about the rules and values of society, they tend to adopt them. This process of *internalizing* parental and cultural values produces the third component of personality: the **superego,** which tells us what we should and should not do. The superego is just as relentless and unreasonable as the id in its demand to be obeyed. It would make the pushy person at McDonald's feel guilty for even thinking about violating society's rules.

Conflicts and Defenses

Freud referred to the inner turmoil among the three personality components as *intrapsychic* or *psychodynamic conflicts,* and he believed that the number, nature, and outcome of these conflicts shape each individual's personality. The ego's primary function is to prevent the anxiety or guilt we would feel if we became aware of socially unacceptable id impulses or if we thought about violating the superego's rules (Funder, 2001b). Sometimes, the ego motivates realistic actions, as when a parent asks for help in dealing with impulses to abuse a child. However, the ego may also use **defense mechanisms,** which are unconscious tactics that protect against anxiety and guilt by either preventing threatening material from surfacing or disguising it when it does (see Table 14.1).

Stages in Personality Development

Freud proposed that personality develops during childhood in a series of **psychosexual stages.** Failure to resolve the problems and conflicts that arise at a given stage can leave a person *fixated*— that is, overly attached to, or unconsciously preoccupied with, the area of pleasure associated with that stage. Freud believed that the stage at which a person fixated in childhood can be seen in adult personality characteristics.

In Freud's theory, a child's first year or so is called the **oral stage,** because the mouth—which the infant uses to eat and explore—is the center of pleasure during this period. Freud said fixation at the oral stage can stem from weaning that is too early or too late and may result in adult characteristics ranging from overeating or childlike dependence (late weaning) to the use of "biting" sarcasm (early weaning).

TRY THIS According to Freud, defense mechanisms deflect anxiety or guilt in the short run, but they sap energy. Further, using them to avoid dealing with the source of problems can make those problems worse in the long run. Try listing some incidents in which you or someone you know might have used each of the defenses described here. What questions would a critical thinker ask to determine whether these behaviors were unconscious defense mechanisms or actions motivated by conscious intentions?

table 14.1
Ego Defense Mechanisms

Defense Mechanism	Description
Repression	Unconsciously pushing threatening memories, urges, or ideas from conscious awareness: A person may experience loss of memory for unpleasant events.
Rationalization	Attempting to make actions or mistakes seem reasonable: The reasons or excuses given (e.g., "I spank my children because it is good for them") sound rational, but they are not the real reasons for the behavior.
Projection	Unconsciously attributing one's own unacceptable thoughts or impulses to another person: Instead of recognizing that "I hate him," a person may feel that "He hates me."
Reaction formation	Defending against unacceptable impulses by acting opposite to them: Sexual interest in a married friend might appear as strong dislike instead.
Sublimation	Converting unacceptable impulses into socially acceptable actions, and perhaps symbolically expressing them: Sexual or aggressive desires may appear as artistic creativity or devotion to athletic excellence.
Displacement	Deflecting an impulse from its original target to a less threatening one: Anger at one's boss may be expressed through hostility toward a clerk, a family member, or even a pet.
Denial	Simply discounting the existence of threatening impulses: A person may vehemently deny ever having had even the slightest degree of physical attraction to a person of the same sex.
Compensation	Striving to make up for unconscious impulses or fears: A business executive's extreme competitiveness might be aimed at compensating for unconscious feelings of inferiority.

id The unconscious portion of personality containing basic impulses and urges.

libido The psychic energy contained in the id.

pleasure principle The id's operating principle, which guides people toward whatever feels good.

ego The part of the personality that mediates conflicts between and among the demands of the id, the superego, and the real world.

reality principle The operating principle of the ego that creates compromises between the id's demands and those of the real world.

superego The component of personality that tells people what they should and should not do.

defense mechanisms Psychological responses that help protect a person from anxiety and guilt.

psychosexual stages Periods of personality development in which conflicts focus on particular issues.

oral stage The first psychosexual stage, in which the mouth is the center of pleasure and conflict.

anal stage The second psychosexual stage, usually occurring during the second year of life, in which the focus of pleasure and conflict shifts from the mouth to the anus.

phallic stage The third psychosexual stage, in which the focus of pleasure and conflict shifts to the genital area.

The **anal stage** occurs during the second year as the demand for toilet training shifts the focus of pleasure and conflict to the anal area. According to Freud, toilet training that is too harsh or begins too early can produce a kind of anal fixation that appears in adulthood as stinginess or preoccupation with neatness (thus symbolically withholding feces). If toilet training is too late or too lax, however, the result could be another kind of anal fixation, which is reflected in adults who are disorganized or impulsive (symbolically expelling feces at will).

The most controversial stage in Freud's theory of personality development occurs between the ages of three and five, when the child's focus of pleasure is said to shift to the genitals. Because Freud emphasized male psychosexual development, he called this period the **phallic stage** (*phallus* is another word for *penis*). He believed that during this stage, a boy experiences sexual desire for his mother and a desire to eliminate, or even kill, his father, with whom the boy competes for the mother's affection. (Freud named this pattern of impulses the **Oedipus complex** because it echoes the plot of *Oedipus Rex,* the classical Greek play in which Oedipus, upon returning to his homeland, unknowingly slays his father and marries his mother.) The boy's fantasies make him fear that his powerful "rival" (i.e., his father) will castrate him. To reduce this fear, the boy's ego represses the incestuous desires and leads him to identify with, and be like, his father. It is during this stage that the male's superego begins to develop.

According to Freud, a girl begins the phallic stage with a strong attachment to her mother. When she realizes that boys have penises and girls don't, though, she supposedly develops *penis envy* and transfers her love to her father—a pattern known as the **Electra complex** because it parallels the plot of another classical Greek play. To avoid her mother's disapproval, the girl identifies with and imitates her, thus forming the basis for her own superego

Freud believed that unresolved conflicts from the phallic stage can lead to many problems in adulthood, including difficulties in dealing with authority figures and an inability to maintain a stable love relationship.

As the phallic stage draws to a close and its conflicts are dealt with by the ego, a peaceful interval known as the **latency period** occurs. When sexual impulses reappear during adolescence, the genitals again become the focus of pleasure, marking the beginning of the **genital stage,** which Freud said lasts until death.

Variations on Freud's Personality Theory

Freud's ideas—especially those involving the Oedipus and Electra complexes and the role of infantile sexuality—created an uproar in public and professional circles. Even many of Freud's followers disagreed with him. Some of these dissenters have been called *neo-Freudian* theorists, because though they differed from Freud on certain points and developed new theories of personality, their theories still contained many of the basic features of Freud's approach. Others are known as *ego psychologists,* because their ideas focused more on the ego than on the id (Westen & Gabbard, 1999).

Jung's Analytic Psychology

Carl Jung (pronounced "yoong") was the most prominent dissenter among Freud's early followers. Jung (1916) emphasized that libido is not just sexual instinct but rather a more general life force that includes an innate drive for creativity, for growth-oriented resolution of conflicts, and for the productive blending of basic impulses with real-world demands. Jung did not identify specific stages in personality development. He suggested instead that people develop, over time, differing degrees of *introversion* (a tendency to reflect on one's own experiences) or *extraversion* (a tendency to focus on the social world), along with differing tendencies to rely on specific psychological functions, such as thinking versus feeling. The combination of these tendencies, said Jung (1933), creates personalities that display distinctive and predictable patterns of behavior.

Jung also claimed there is a *collective unconscious,* which contains the memories we have inherited from our human and nonhuman ancestors (Carver & Scheier, 2000). According to Jung, we are not consciously aware of these memories, but they are responsible for our innate tendencies to react in particular ways to certain things. For example, Jung believed that our collective memory of mothers influences how each of us perceives our own mother. Although the notion of a collective unconscious is widely accepted by followers of Jung, there is no empirical evidence that it exists. In fact, Jung himself acknowledged that it would be impossible to objectively demonstrate the existence of a collective unconscious (Feist & Feist, 2001).

Other Neo-Freudian Theorists

Jung was not the first and not the only theorist to challenge Freud. Alfred Adler, once a loyal disciple of psychoanalysis, came to believe that the power behind the development of personality is

---

Oedipus complex A pattern described by Freud in which a boy has sexual desire for his mother and wants to eliminate his father's competition for her attention.

Electra complex A pattern described by Freud in which a young girl develops an attachment to her father and competes with her mother for his attention.

latency period The fourth psychosexual stage, in which sexual impulses lie dormant.

genital stage The last psychosexual stage, which begins during adolescence, when sexual impulses appear at the conscious level.

An Early Feminist After completing medical school at the University of Berlin in 1913, Karen Horney (1885–1952) trained as a Freudian psychoanalyst. She accepted some aspects of Freud's psychoanalytic views, including the idea of unconscious motivation, but she eventually developed her own neo-Freudian theory. She saw the need for security as more important than biological instincts in motivating infants' behavior. She also rejected Freud's notion that the psychological development of females is influenced by penis envy.

provided not by the id but by an innate desire to overcome infantile feelings of helplessness. Adler (1927) referred to this process as *striving for superiority,* by which he meant a drive for fulfillment as a person, not just a desire to do better than others. Other prominent neo-Freudians, including Erik Erikson, Erich Fromm, and Henry Stack Sullivan, focused on how people's personalities are shaped by those around them. They argued that once biological needs are met, the attempt to meet social needs (to feel protected, secure, and accepted, for example) is the primary influence on personality. The strategies people use to meet social needs, such as dominating other people or being dependent on them, thus become central aspects of the personality.

Another challenge to Freud came from the first feminist personality theorist, Karen Horney (pronounced "HORN-eye"), who disputed Freud's view that women's lack of a penis causes them to envy men and feel inferior to them. In fact, Horney (1937) argued that it is men who envy women: Realizing that they cannot bear children and that they often play only a small role in raising them, males see their lives as having less meaning or substance than women's. Horney called this condition *womb envy.* She argued further that when women feel inferior, it is because of the personal and political restrictions that men have placed upon them, not because of penis envy. Horney's position on this issue reflected her strong belief that cultural factors, rather than instincts, play a major role in personality development (Feist & Feist, 2001). This greater emphasis on cultural influences is one of the major theoretical differences between Freud and the neo-Freudians generally.

Contemporary Psychodynamic Theories

Today, some of the most influential psychodynamic approaches to personality focus on *object relations*—that is, on how people's perceptions of themselves and others influence their view of, and reactions to, the world (Westen & Gabbard, 1999). According to object relations theorists such as Melanie Klein (1991), Otto Kernberg (1984), Heinz Kohut (1984), and Margaret Mahler (1968), early relationships between infants and their love objects, usually the mother and other primary caregivers, are vitally important in the development of personality. These relationships, they say, shape a person's thoughts and feelings about social relationships later in life.

As described in the chapter on human development, children ideally form a secure early bond to the mother or some other caregiver, tolerate gradual separation from the object of attachment, and finally develop the ability to relate to others as an independent, secure individual (Ainsworth, 1989; Bowlby, 1973). Object relations theory argues that the nature of early child-parent attachments affects self-image, identity, security, and social relationships later in life (Mikelson, Kessler, & Shaver, 1997; Simpson & Rholes, 2000). In one study, women who had secure attachment to their parents in childhood were more likely to have happy marriages than women whose childhood attachment had been insecure (Klohnen & Bera, 1998). Another study found that people who had an avoidant attachment style in childhood were less supportive and comforting when they encountered a person in distress (Westmaas & Silver, 2001). A third study found that students whose attachments had been anxious or ambivalent tended to have shorter and less satisfying romances (Shaver & Clark, 1996).

Evaluation of the Psychodynamic Approach

Any overall evaluation of Freud and his theories will inevitably be mixed. There is no doubt that his views have influenced modern Western thinking about medicine, literature, religion, sociology, and anthropology, and his contributions to the field of psychology have been considerable. In fact, Freud's personality theory is probably the most comprehensive and influential psychological theory ever proposed. His ideas have also shaped a wide range of psychotherapeutic techniques and stimulated the development of several personality assessments, including the projective tests described later in this chapter. Further, contemporary theories and research have provided some limited support for certain aspects of Freud's theory. For example, psychologists have found that people do employ several of the defense mechanisms Freud described (Paulhus, Fridhandler, & Hayes, 1997), although it is unclear whether these always operate at an unconscious level. As mentioned in the chapter on consciousness, there is also evidence that events and experiences that people do not recall can influence their thoughts and actions (Andersen & Berk, 1998; Bargh & Ferguson, 2000). And some researchers believe that unconscious processes may affect people's health (Arndt et al., 2000).

However, Freud's psychodynamic theories have several weaknesses. For one thing, they are based almost entirely on case studies of a few individuals. As discussed in the chapter on research in psychology, conclusions drawn from case studies may not apply to people in general. Nor was Freud's sample representative of people in general. Most of his patients were upper-class Viennese women who not only had psychological problems but also were raised in a culture in which discussion of sex was considered to be uncivilized. Moreover, Freud's thinking about personality reflected Western European and North American values, which may or may not be helpful in understanding people in other cultures (Feist & Feist, 2001). For example, the concepts of ego and self that are so central to Freud's personality theory (and those of his followers) are based on the self-oriented values of individualist cultures and thus may be less illustrative of personality development in the more collectivist cultures of, say, Asia and South America (Matsumoto, 2000).

Freud's conclusions may have been distorted by other biases as well. Jeffrey Masson (1984) argued that Freud was afraid to accept his patients' accounts of sexual abuse by their parents because doing so would have brought him into conflict with those parents, many of whom had power and influence in Vienna. Instead, claimed Masson, Freud characterized the patients' reports as fantasies and wish fulfillment, not as memories of real events. Freudian scholars have largely rejected Masson's charges (Schultz & Schultz, 2001), but they do acknowledge other possible problems. They note, for example, that Freud might have modified reports of what happened during therapy to better fit his theory (Esterson, 2001; Kihlstrom, 1994). He may also have asked leading questions that influenced patients to "recall" events from their childhood that never really happened (Esterson, 2001; Showalter, 1997). Today, there are similar concerns that some patients who recover allegedly repressed memories about childhood sexual abuse by parents may actually be reporting false memories implanted by their therapists (Peiffer & Trull, 2000).

Freud's focus on male psychosexual development and his notion that females envy male anatomy have also caused both female and male feminists to reject some or all of his ideas. In the tradition of Horney, some contemporary female neo-Freudians have proposed theories that focus specifically on the psychosexual development of women (Sayers, 1991).

Finally, as judged by today's standards, Freud's theory is not very scientific. His definitions of id, ego, unconscious conflict, and other concepts lack the precision required for scientific measurement and testing (Feist & Feist, 2001). His belief that human beings are driven mainly by unconscious desires ignores evidence that much human behavior goes beyond impulse gratification. The conscious drive to attain personal, social, and spiritual goals is also an important determinant of behavior, as is learning from others.

Some of the weaknesses in Freudian theory have been addressed by those who have altered some of Freud's concepts and devoted more attention to social influences on personality. Attempts have also been made to increase precision and objectivity in the measurement of psychodynamic concepts (e.g., Barber, Crits-Christoph, & Paul, 1993). Research on psychodynamic theory is, in fact, becoming more sophisticated and increasingly reflects interest in subjecting psychodynamic principles to experimental tests (Westen & Gabbard, 1999). Still, the psychodynamic approach is better known for generating hypotheses about personality than for scientifically testing them. Accordingly, this approach to personality is now much less influential in mainstream psychology than it was in the past (Robins, Gosling, & Craik, 1999, 2000).

The Trait Approach

If you were to describe the personality of someone you know, it would probably take the form of a small number of descriptive statements. Here is an example:

She is a truly caring person, a real extravert. She is generous with her time, and very conscientious about everything she does. Yet sometimes I think she is not very assertive or confident. She is submissive to other people's demands because she wants to be accepted by them.

In other words, most people describe others by referring to the kind of people they are ("extravert," "conscientious"); to the thoughts, feelings, and actions that are most typical of them ("caring," "not very assertive," "generous"); or to their needs ("wants to be accepted"). Together, these statements describe personality *traits*—the inclinations or tendencies that help to direct how a person usually thinks and behaves (Johnson, 1997).

The **trait approach** to personality makes three basic assumptions:

1. Personality traits are relatively stable and therefore predictable over time. So a gentle person tends to stay that way day after day, year after year (Roberts & DelVecchio, 2000; Robins et al., 2001).

2. Personality traits are relatively stable across situations, and they can explain why people act in predictable ways in many different situations. A person who is fiercely competitive at work will probably also be competitive on the tennis court or at a party.

3. People differ in how much of a particular personality trait they possess; no two people are exactly alike on all traits. The result is an endless variety of unique human personalities.

Traits Versus Types
Theories about enduring differences in personality characteristics among people go back at least as far as Hippocrates, a physician of ancient Greece. He suggested that a certain temperament, or basic behavioral tendency, is associated with each of four bodily fluids, or humors: blood, phlegm, black bile, and yellow bile. Personality, said Hippocrates, depends on how much of each humor a person has. His terms for the four humor-driven personalities—sanguine (optimistic), phlegmatic (slow, lethargic), melancholic (sad, depressive), and choleric (angry, irritable)—still survive today.

Notice that Hippocrates was describing personality *types*, not traits. Traits involve *quantitative* differences among people—such as how much of a certain characteristic they possess. Types involve *qualitative* differences, such as whether someone possesses a certain characteristic at all. When people are "typed," they are said to belong to one class or another—such as male or female. Modern type theories of personality try to do the same by placing people in one category or another (Funder, 2001b). For example, Avashalom Caspi and his colleagues claim to have identified three qualitatively different basic personality types (Caspi, 1998; Robins et al., 1996). These include the *well-adjusted person,* who is flexible, resourceful, and successful with other people; the *maladjusted overcontrolling person,* who is too self-controlled to enjoy life and is difficult for others to deal with; and the *maladjusted undercontrolling person,* whose excessive impulsiveness can be dangerous both for the person and for others (see this chapter's Focus on Research Methods section for more on these types).

---

trait approach A perspective in which personality is seen as a combination of characteristics that people display over time and across situations.

Selecting a Jury Some psychologists employ type and trait theories of personality in advising prosecution or defense attorneys about which potential jurors are most likely to be sympathetic to their side of a court case.

Type theories are appealing to some personality researchers, but most do not think it is possible to compress the dazzling range of human characteristics into a just few discrete types. Accordingly, the trait approach to personality is much more influential. Trait theorists measure the relative strength of the many personality characteristics that they believe are present in everyone (see Figure 14.2).

Allport's Trait Theory

Gordon Allport (1961) spent thirty years searching for the traits that combine to form personality. He found nearly 18,000 dictionary terms that can be used to describe human behavior (Allport & Odbert, 1936), but he noticed that many of these terms referred to the same thing (e.g., *hostile*, *nasty*, and *mean* all convey a similar meaning). So if you were to jot down the personality traits that describe a close friend or relative, you would probably be able to capture that individual's personality using only about seven trait labels. Allport believed that the set of labels chosen to describe a particular person reflects that person's *central traits*—those that are usually apparent to others and that organize and control behavior in many different situations. Central traits are roughly equivalent to the descriptive terms used in letters of recommendation (*reliable* or *distractible*, for example) that are meant to convey what can be expected from a person most of the time (Schultz & Schultz, 2001). Allport also believed that people possess *secondary traits*—those that are more specific to certain situations and control far less behavior. "Dislikes crowds" is an example of a secondary trait.

Allport's research helped to lay the foundation for modern research on personality traits. However, his emphasis on the uniqueness of each individual personality made it difficult to draw conclusions about the structure of human personality in general (McAdams, 1997).

The Big-Five Model of Personality

In recent years, trait approaches have continued to focus on identifying and describing the core structure of personality. This work owes much to Allport and also to a British psychologist named Raymond Cattell. Cattell asked people to rate themselves and others on many of the trait-descriptive terms that Allport had identified. He then used a mathematical technique called *factor analysis* to study which of

figure 14.2
Two Personality Profiles

Trait theory describes personality in terms of the strength of particular dimensions, or traits. Here are trait profiles for Rodney, an inner-city social worker, and James, a sales clerk in a department store. Compared with James, Rodney is about equally industrious; more generous; and less nervous, extraverted, and aggressive. Just for fun, mark this figure to indicate how strong you think you are on each of the listed traits. Trait theorists suggest that this should be easy for you to do because, they say, virtually everyone displays a certain amount of almost any personality characteristic.

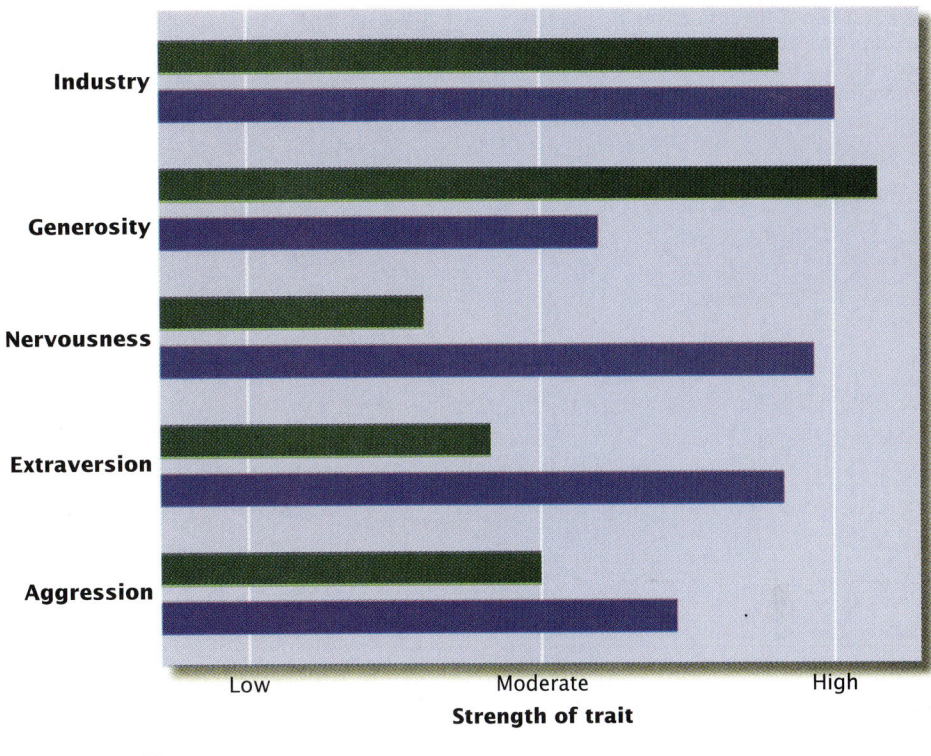

these terms were related to one another. Factor analysis can reveal, for example, whether someone who is moody is also likely to be anxious, rigid, and unsociable. Cattell believed that the sets of traits clustering together in this analysis would reflect a set of basic personality *factors* or dimensions. His analyses eventually identified sixteen such factors, including shy versus bold, trusting versus suspicious, and relaxed versus tense. Cattell believed that these factors are found in everyone, and he measured their strength using a test called the *Sixteen Personality Factor Questionnaire*, or *16PF* (Cattell, Eber, & Tatsuoka, 1970).

More recent factor analyses by researchers such as Paul Costa and Robert McCrae (1992) have led many trait theorists to believe that personality is organized around only five basic factors (McCrae & Costa, 1999). The components of this so-called **big-five model**, or five-factor model, of personality are *openness to experience, conscientiousness, extraversion, agreeableness,* and *neuroticism* (see Table 14.2). The importance of the big-five model is underscored by the fact that different investigators find these factors (or a set very similar to them) when they factor-analyze data from numerous sources, including personality inventories, peer ratings of personality characteristics, and checklists of descriptive adjectives (Costa & McCrae, 1995; John & Srivastava, 1999). The fact that some version of the big-five factors reliably appears in many countries and cultures—including Canada, China, the Czech Republic, Germany, Finland, India, Japan, Korea, the Philippines, Poland, and Turkey (McCrae & Costa, 1997; McCrae et al., 1998, 2000; Narayanan, Menon, & Levine, 1995)—provides further evidence that these few dimensions may represent the basic components of human personality.

Many trait theorists believe that the big-five model represents a major breakthrough in examining the personalities of people who come from different backgrounds, differ in age, and live in different parts of the world (Funder, 2001a). It has certainly enabled psychologists to provide a comprehensive description of the basic similarities and differences in people's personalities, and to explore how these factors are related to everything from personality disorders to happiness, or subjective well-being (e.g., Diener, 2000; DeNeve, 1999; Lynam & Widiger, 2001).

big-five model Five trait dimensions found in many factor-analytic studies of personality: neuroticism, extraversion, openness to experience, agreeableness, and conscientiousness.

Here is a list of the adjectives that define the big-five personality factors. You can more easily remember the names of these factors by noting that their first letters spell the word *ocean*.

table 14.2
The Big-Five Personality Dimensions

Dimension	Defining Descriptors
Openness to experience	Artistic, curious, imaginative, insightful, original, wide interests, unusual thought processes, intellectual interests
Conscientiousness	Efficient, organized, planful, reliable, thorough, dependable, ethical, productive
Extraversion	Active, assertive, energetic, outgoing, talkative, gesturally expressive, gregarious
Agreeableness	Appreciative, forgiving, generous, kind, trusting, noncritical, warm, compassionate, considerate, straightforward
Neuroticism	Anxious, self-pitying, tense, emotionally unstable, impulsive, vulnerable, touchy, worrying

Source: Adapted from McCrae & John (1992).

Biological Trait Theories

Some personality theorists are interested not only in what traits form the core of human personality but also in why people differ on these traits. Their research suggests that trait differences reflect the operation of some important biological factors.

Eysenck's Biological Trait Theory
Like Cattell, British psychologist Hans Eysenck (pronounced "EYE-sink") used factor analysis to study the structure of personality and thus helped lay the groundwork for the big-five model. Eysenck suggested that most people's traits could be described using two main dimensions—*introversion-extraversion* and *emotionality-stability* (Eysenck 1990a, 1990b; see Figure 14.3):

Animal Personalities The idea that personality can be described in terms of five main dimensions seems to hold for some animals, as well as humans. The five animal dimensions differ from, but are still related to, human traits. For example, hyenas differ from one another in terms of dominance, excitability, agreeableness (toward people), sociability (toward one another), and curiosity. Some of these same traits have been observed in a wide variety of other species, including chimpanzees and other primates (Gosling, 2001); dog and cat lovers often report such traits in their pets.

figure 14.3
Eysenck's Major Personality Dimensions

According to Eysenck, varying degrees of emotionality-stability and introversion-extraversion combine to produce predictable trait patterns. Notice that an introverted but stable person is likely to be controlled and reliable, whereas an introverted emotional person is likely to be rigid and anxious. (The traits appearing in the quadrants created by crossing these two personality dimensions correspond roughly to Hippocrates' four temperaments.) Eysenck also identified a less influential third dimension, called *psychoticism*. People who score high on psychoticism show such traits as cruelty, hostility, coldness, oddness, and rejection of social customs.

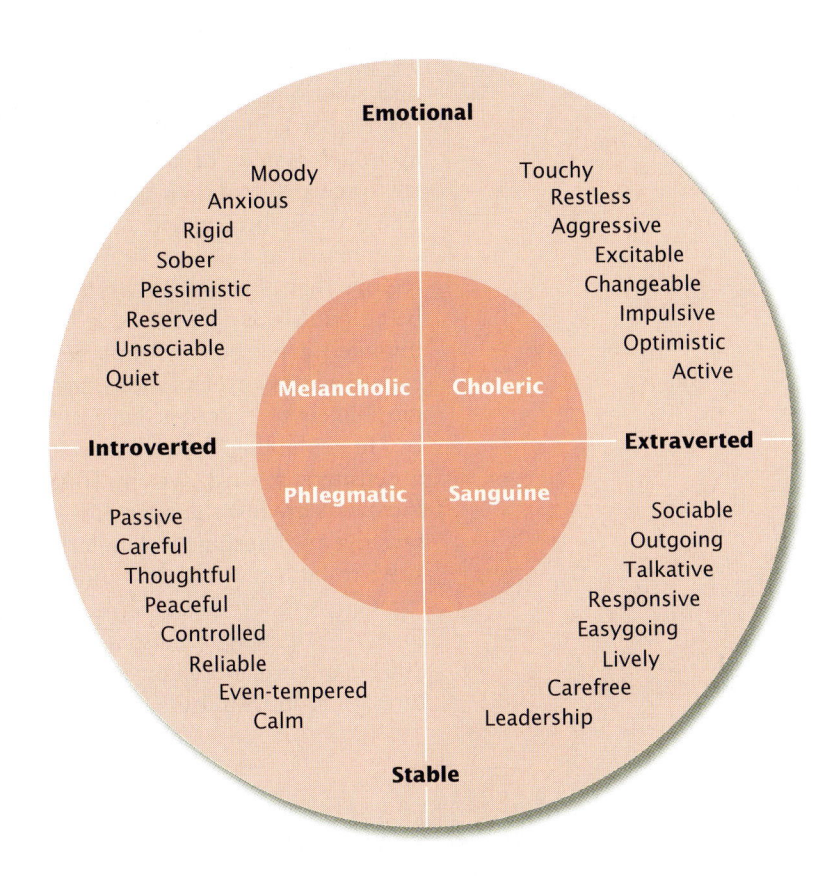

1. *Introversion-extraversion.* Extraverts are sociable and outgoing, enjoy parties and other group activities, take risks, and love excitement and change. Introverts tend to be quiet, thoughtful, and reserved, enjoying solitary pursuits and avoiding excitement and social involvement.

2. *Emotionality-stability.* People at one extreme of the emotionality-stability dimension display such characteristics as moodiness, restlessness, worry, anxiety, and other negative emotions. Those at the opposite extreme are calm, even-tempered, relaxed, and emotionally stable. (This dimension is also often called *neuroticism*.)

Eysenck argued that people fall at differing points along these two dimensions because of inherited differences in their nervous systems, especially in their brains. These biological differences, in turn, create variations in people's ongoing physiological arousal and sensitivity to stress and other environmental stimulation. For example, people who inherit a nervous system that normally operates at a low level of arousal (in terms of brain activity, heart rate, and muscle tension) will look constantly for excitement, change, and social contact in order to increase their arousal to some optimum level, as described in the chapter on motivation and emotion. As a result, these people will be *extraverted*. In contrast, people whose nervous system is normally "overaroused" will tend to avoid excitement, change, and social contact in order to reduce arousal to an optimum level. In short, they will be *introverted*. What about the emotionality-stability dimension? Eysenck said that people who score toward the stability side have nervous systems that are relatively insensitive to stress; those who are more emotional have nervous systems that react more strongly to stress.

Gray's Approach-Inhibition Theory
Jeffrey Gray, another British psychologist, agrees with Eysenck about the two basic dimensions of personality, but he offers a different explanation of the biological factors underlying them (Gray,

1991). According to Gray, differences among people in introversion-extraversion and emotionality-stability stem from two related systems in the brain: the behavioral approach system and the behavioral inhibition system. The *behavioral approach system,* or *BAS,* is made up of brain regions that affect people's sensitivity to rewards and their motivation to seek those rewards (Pickering & Gray, 1999). The BAS has been called a "go" system, because it is responsible for how impulsive or uninhibited a person is. The *behavioral inhibition system,* or *BIS,* involves brain regions that affect sensitivity to potential punishment and the motivation to avoid being punished. The BIS is a "stop" system that is responsible for how fearful or inhibited a person is. People with an active behavioral approach system tend to experience positive emotions; people with an active behavioral inhibition system are more likely to experience negative ones (Zelenski & Larsen, 1999).

In explaining Eysenck's personality dimensions, Gray sees extraverts as having a sensitive reward system (BAS) and an insensitive punishment system (BIS). Introverts are just the opposite—they are relatively insensitive to rewards but highly sensitive to punishment. Similarly, emotionally unstable people are much more sensitive to both rewards and punishments than are those who are emotionally stable.

Gray's theory has its critics, but it is now more widely accepted than Eysenck's theory—primarily because it is being supported by other research (e.g., Canli et al., 2001), and it is more consistent with what neuroscientists know about brain structures, neurotransmitters, and how they operate (Avila, 2001).

THINKING CRITICALLY

Are Personality Traits Inherited?

Gray's approach-inhibition theory is one of several new biologically oriented explanations of the origins of personality traits (e.g., Cloninger, 1998; Zuckerman, 1998). A related approach involves investigating the genetics of these traits. Consider the case of identical twins who were separated at five weeks of age and did not meet again for thirty-nine years. Both men drove Chevrolets, chain-smoked the same brand of cigarettes, had divorced a woman named Linda, were remarried to a woman named Betty, had sons named James Allan, had dogs named Toy, enjoyed similar hobbies, and had served as sheriff's deputies (Tellegen et al., 1988).

● **What am I being asked to believe or accept?**

Case studies like the one involving these twins have helped focus the attention of behavioral geneticists on the possibility that some core aspects of personality might be partly, or even largely, inherited (Krueger, 2000; Plomin & Caspi, 1999).

● **What evidence is available to support the assertion?**

The evidence and the arguments regarding this assertion are much like those presented in the chapter on cognitive abilities, where we discuss the origins of differences in intelligence. Stories about children who seem to "have" their parents' or grandparents' bad temper, generosity, or shyness are often presented in support of the heritability of personality. And in fact, family resemblances in personality do provide an important source of evidence. Several studies have found moderate but significant correlations between children's personality test scores and those of their parents and siblings (Davis, Luce, & Kraus, 1994; Loehlin, 1992).

Even stronger evidence comes from studies conducted around the world comparing identical twins raised together, identical twins raised apart, nonidentical twins raised together, and nonidentical twins raised apart (e.g., Loehlin & Martin, 2001; Saudino et al., 1999). Whether they are raised apart or together, identical twins (who have exactly the same genes) tend to be more alike in personality than nonidentical twins (whose genes are no more similar than those of other siblings).

Family Resemblance Do children inherit personality traits in the same direct way they inherit facial features, coloration, and other physical characteristics? Research in behavioral genetics suggests that personality is the joint product of genetically influenced behavioral tendencies and the environmental conditions each child encounters.

This research also shows that identical twins are more alike than nonidentical twins in general temperament, such as how active, sociable, anxious, and emotional they are (Pickering & Gray, 1999; Rowe, 1997). On the basis of such twin studies, behavioral geneticists have concluded that at least 30 percent, and perhaps as much as 60 percent, of the differences among people in terms of personality traits are due to genetic factors (Borkenau et al., 2001; Brody & Ehrlichman, 1998).

- **Are there alternative ways of interpreting the evidence?**

Family resemblances in personality could reflect genetic or social influence. An obvious alternative interpretation of this evidence, then, might be that family similarities come not from common genes but from a common environment, especially from the modeling that parents and siblings provide. Children learn many rules, skills, and behaviors by watching those around them; perhaps they learn their personalities as well (Funder, 2001b). The fact that nontwin siblings are less alike than twins may well result from what are called *nonshared environments* (Plomin & Caspi, 1999). A child's place in the family birth order, differences in the way parents treat each of their children, and accidents and illnesses that alter a particular child's life or health are examples of nonshared factors that can have a differential impact on each individual (Paulhus, Trapnell, & Chen, 1999). Nontwins are more likely than twins, especially identical twins, to be affected by nonshared environmental factors.

- **What additional evidence would help to evaluate the alternatives?**

One way to evaluate the degree to which personality is inherited would be to study people in infancy, before the environment has had a chance to exert its influence. If the environment were entirely responsible for personality, all newborns should be essentially alike. However, as discussed in the chapter on human development, they show immediate differences in *temperament*—varying markedly in activity, sensitivity to the environment, tendency to cry, and interest in new stimuli (Matthews & Dreary, 1998). These differences suggest biological and perhaps genetic influences.

To evaluate the relative contributions of nature and nurture beyond infancy, psychologists have examined characteristics of adopted children. The argument for genetic influences on personality would be stronger if adopted children are more like their biological parents than their adoptive parents. If they are more like their adoptive family, a strong role for environmental factors in personality would be suggested. In actuality, adopted children's personalities tend to resemble the personalities of their biological parents and siblings more than those of the families in which they are raised (Plomin et al., 1998).

Despite this finding, further research is needed to determine more clearly what aspects of the environment are most important in shaping personality (Turkheimer & Waldron, 2000). So far, the evidence suggests that elements in the shared environment affecting all children in the family to varying degrees (socioeconomic status, for example) are probably not the main reason why identical twins show similar personalities. As mentioned earlier, however, nonshared environmental influences may be very important in personality development (Halverson & Wampler, 1997; Harris, 2000; Plomin, 1994b). In fact, some researchers believe that nonshared influences must be considered even when trying to explain the greater similarities between identical twins reared apart than among nontwin siblings reared together. Additional research on the role of nonshared factors in personality development and the ways in which these factors might differentially affect twin and nontwin siblings' development is obviously vital. It will also be important to investigate the ways in which the personalities of individual children may affect the nature of the environment in which they are raised (Halverson & Wampler, 1997; see also the behavioral genetics appendix).

- **What conclusions are most reasonable?**

Even those researchers, such as Robert Plomin, who support genetic theories of personality caution that we should not replace "simple-minded environmentalism" with the equally incorrect view that personality is almost completely biologically determined (Plomin & Crabbe, 2000). As with cognitive abilities, it is pointless to talk about heredity versus environment as causes of personality, because nature and nurture always intertwine to exert joint and simultaneous influences. For example, we know that genetic factors affect the environment in which people live (e.g., their family) and how they react to their environment, but it also turns out that environmental factors can influence which of a person's genes are activated and how much those genes affect the person's behavior (Cacioppo et al., 2000; Pickering & Gray, 1999).

With these findings in mind, we would be well advised to draw rather tentative conclusions about the sources of differences in people's personalities. The evidence available so far suggests that genetic influences do appear to contribute significantly to personality differences. However, it is important to understand the implications of this statement. No single gene is responsible for a specific personality trait (Plomin & Crabbe, 2000). The genetic contribution to personality most likely comes through genes' influence on people's nervous systems and on their general predispositions toward certain temperaments (Buss, 1995). Temperamental factors—such as how active, emotional, and sociable a person is—then combine with environmental factors, such as a person's interactions with other people, to produce specific features of personality (Caspi & Roberts, 1999). For example, children who inherit a tendency toward emotionality might play less with other children, withdraw from social interactions, and thereby fail to learn important social skills (Eisenberg, Fabes, & Murphy, 1995). These experiences and tendencies, in turn, might lead to the self-consciousness and shyness seen in introverted personalities.

Notice, though, that genetic predispositions toward particular personality characteristics may or may not appear in behavior, depending on whether the environment supports or suppresses them. Changes in genetically influenced traits are not only possible but may actually be quite common as children grow (Cacioppo et al., 2000). So even though there is a strong genetic basis for shyness, many children learn to overcome this tendency and become rather outgoing (Rowe, 1997). In summary, it appears that rather than inheriting specific traits, people inherit the raw materials out of which personality is shaped by the world.

Evaluation of the Trait Approach

The trait approach, especially the big-five model, has gained such wide acceptance that it tends to dominate contemporary research in personality. Yet there are several problems and weaknesses associated with this approach.

For one thing, trait theories seem better at describing people than at understanding them. It is easy to say, for example, that Michelle is nasty to others because she has a strong hostility trait; but other factors, such as the way people treat her, could also be responsible. In short, trait theories say a lot about how people behave, but they don't always explain why (Funder, 2001a). Trait theories also don't say much about how traits are related to the thoughts and feelings that precede, accompany, and follow behavior. Do introverts and extraverts decide to act as they do, can they behave otherwise, and how do they feel about their actions and experiences? (Cervone & Shoda, 1999). Some personality psychologists are currently linking their research to that of cognitive psychologists in an effort to better understand how thoughts and emotions influence, and are influenced by, personality traits (e.g., Mischel & Shoda, 1999).

The trait approach has also been faulted for offering a short list of traits of varying strengths that provides, at best, a fixed and superficial description of personality that fails to capture how traits combine to form a complex and dynamic individual (Block, 2001; Funder, 2001a). Also, some people have questioned whether there are exactly five core dimensions of personality and whether they are exactly the same in all cultures (Cross & Markus, 1999; Zuckerman, 1998). And even if the big-five model is correct and universal, its factors are not all-powerful; situations also affect behavior. For example, people high in extraversion are not always sociable; whether they behave sociably depends, in part, on where they are and who else is present.

In fairness, early trait theorists, such as Allport, did implicitly acknowledge the importance of situations in influencing behavior, but it is only recently that consideration of person-situation interactions has become an explicit part of trait-based approaches to personality. This change is largely the result of research conducted by psychologists who have taken a social-cognitive approach to personality, which we describe next.

The Social-Cognitive Approach

The **social-cognitive approach** to personality differs from the psychodynamic and trait approaches in two important ways. First, social-cognitive theorists look to *conscious* thoughts and emotions for clues to how people differ from one another and what guides their behavior (Bandura, 2001). Second, the social-cognitive approach did not grow out of clinical cases or other descriptions of people's personalities, but out of the principles of animal and human learning described in the chapter on learning. In fact, the founders of the social-cognitive approach were originally known as *social learning theorists* because of their view that what we call *personality* consists mainly of the thoughts and actions we learn through observing and interacting with family and others in social situations (Bandura & Walters, 1963; Funder, 2001b).

Roots of the Social-Cognitive Approach

Elements of the social-cognitive approach can be traced back to the behaviorism of John B. Watson. As described in the chapter on introducing psychology, Watson (1925) used research on classical conditioning to support his claim that all human behavior, from mental disorder to scientific skill, is determined by learning. B. F. Skinner broadened the behavioral approach by emphasizing the importance of operant conditioning in learning. Through what he called **functional analysis,** Skinner sought to understand behavior in terms of the function it serves in obtaining rewards or avoiding punishment. For example, if observations show that a schoolboy's aggressive behavior occurs mainly when a certain teacher is present, it may be that the aggression is being rewarded by that teacher's attention. Rather than describing personality traits, then, functional analysis summarizes what people find rewarding, what they are capable of doing, and what skills they lack.

The principles of classical and operant conditioning launched social-learning explanations of personality, but because they were focused on observable behavior, they were of limited usefulness to researchers who wanted to explore the role of thoughts in guiding behavior. As the social-learning approach evolved into the social-cognitive approach, it incorporated learning principles, but also went beyond them.

Today, proponents of this very popular approach to personality seek to assess and understand how learned patterns of thoughts and feelings contribute to behavior and how behavior and its consequences alter cognitive activity, as well as future actions. In dealing with that aggressive schoolboy, for example, social-cognitive theorists would want to know not only what he has learned to do in certain situations (and how he learned it) but also what he thinks about himself, his teachers, his behavior—and his expectations about each (Mischel & Shoda, 1999).

social-cognitive approach An approach in which personality is seen as the patterns of thinking and behavior that a person learns.

functional analysis Analyzing behavior by studying what responses occur under what conditions of operant reward and punishment.

Prominent Social-Cognitive Theories

Julian Rotter, Albert Bandura, and Walter Mischel have presented the most influential social-cognitive personality theories.

Rotter's Expectancy Theory

Julian Rotter (1982) argued that learning creates cognitions, known as *expectancies*, that guide behavior. Specifically, he said that a person's decision to engage in a behavior is determined by (1) what the person expects to happen following the behavior and (2) the value the person places on the outcome. For example, people spend a lot of money on clothes to be worn at a job interview because (1) past learning leads them to expect that doing so will help get them the job, and (2) they place a high value on having the job. To Rotter, then, behavior is determined not only by the kinds of consequences that Skinner called *positive reinforcers*, but also by the expectation that a particular behavior will obtain those consequences (Mayer & Sutton, 1996).

Rotter himself focused mainly on how expectations shape particular behaviors in particular situations, but several of the researchers he influenced also examined people's more general ways of thinking about how life's rewards and punishments are controlled. Those researchers noticed that some people *(internals)* are inclined to expect events to be controlled by their own efforts. These people assume that what they achieve and the reinforcements they obtain are due to efforts they make themselves. Others *(externals)* are more inclined to expect events to be determined by external forces over which they have no control. When externals succeed, they are likely to believe that the success was due to chance or luck.

The research of psychologists influenced by Rotter has shown that differences in these generalized expectancies are related to differences in behavior. For example, in accordance with their belief that they can control what happens to them, internals are more likely than externals to buy bottled water and make other preparations when threatened with a hurricane or other natural disaster (Sattler, Kaiser, & Hittner, 2000). Internals also tend to work harder than externals at staying healthy. They are more likely to exercise and wear seat belts, and less likely to smoke, drink alcohol, or—if they do drink—to drive while intoxicated (Cavaiola & Desordi, 2000; Maddux, 1993; Phares, 1991). Among college students, internals tend to be better informed about the courses they take, including what they need to do to get a high grade. Perhaps as a result, students who are internals tend to get better grades than externals (Dollinger, 2000; Mayer & Sutton, 1996; Schultz & Schultz, 2001).

Bandura and Reciprocal Determinism

In his social-cognitive theory, Albert Bandura (1999) sees personality as shaped by the ways in which thoughts, behavior, and the environment interact and influence one another. He points out that whether people learn through direct experience with rewards and punishments or through the observational learning processes described in the chapter on learning, their behavior affects their environment, which in turn affects how they think, which then affects behavior, and so on in a constant web of mutual influence that Bandura calls *reciprocal determinism* (see Figure 14.4).

According to Bandura, an especially important cognitive element in this web of influence is **perceived self-efficacy**—the learned expectation of success. Bandura says that our overt behavior is largely controlled by our perception or belief that we can successfully perform that behavior. The higher our perceived self-efficacy in relation to a particular situation or task, the greater our actual accomplishments in that situation or task (Bandura, 2001). So going into a job interview with the belief that you have the skills necessary to be hired may lead to behaviors that help you get the job, or at least help you to deal with the impact of rejection.

Perceived self-efficacy about a specific behavior can interact with a person's expectancies about the consequences of behavior in general, thus helping to shape the person's psychological well-being (Bandura, 1986; Cozzarelli, 1993; see Figure 14.5).

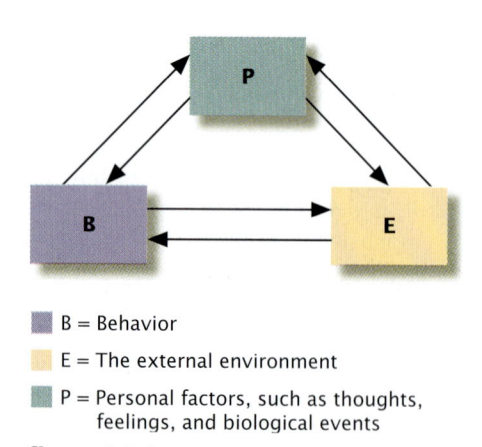

- B = Behavior
- E = The external environment
- P = Personal factors, such as thoughts, feelings, and biological events

figure 14.4
Reciprocal Determinism

Bandura's notion of reciprocal determinism suggests that personal factors (such as cognitions, or thoughts), behavior, and the environment are constantly affecting one another. For example, a person's hostile thoughts may lead to hostile behavior, which creates even more hostile thoughts. At the same time, the hostile behavior offends other people, which creates a threatening environment that causes the person to think and act in even more negative ways. As increasingly negative thoughts alter the person's perceptions of the environment, it seems to be more threatening than ever.

figure 14.5

Self-Efficacy and Psychological Well-Being

According to Bandura, if people with high self-efficacy perceive the environment as unresponsive to their best efforts, they may become resentful and socially active protesters. If they perceive the environment as responsive to their efforts, they are more likely to be both active and self-assured.

	Outcome expectation −	Outcome expectation +
Self-efficacy judgment +	Social activism, Protest, Grievance, Milieu change	Assured opportune action
Self-efficacy judgment −	Resignation, Apathy	Self-devaluation, Despondency

For example, if an unemployed person has low perceived self-efficacy about finding a job and also expects that nothing anyone does has much effect on the world, the result may be apathy. But if a person with low perceived self-efficacy also believes that other people are enjoying the benefits of their efforts, the result may be self-criticism and depression.

Mischel's Cognitive/Affective Theory Social-cognitive theorists argue that learned beliefs, feelings, and expectancies characterize each individual and make that individual different from other people. Walter Mischel calls these characteristics *cognitive person variables*; he believes that they outline the dimensions along which individuals differ (Mischel & Shoda, 1999).

The most important cognitive person variables, according to Mischel, are (1) *encodings* (the beliefs the person has about the environment and other people), (2) *expectancies* (what the person expects to follow from various behaviors and what the person believes he or she is capable of doing), (3) *affects* (feelings, emotions, and affective responses), (4) *goals and values* (the things a person believes in and wants to achieve), and (5) *competencies and self-regulatory plans* (the thoughts and actions the person is capable of, as well as the ability to engage in planned, self-controlled, and goal-directed behavior) (Mischel & Shoda, 1999).

To predict a person' behavior in a particular situation, says Mischel, we need to know about these cognitive person variables, as well as about the features of the situation the person will face. In short, the person and the situation interact to produce behavior. Mischel's ideas have been called an "if-then" theory (Mendoza-Denton et al., 2001), because if people encounter a particular situation, then they will engage in the characteristic behaviors (called *behavioral signatures*) they have learned to display in that situation.

Once highly critical of trait theories of personality, Mischel now sees his theory as generally consistent with that approach. In fact, the concept of behavioral signatures is quite similar to the concept of traits. However, Mischel still argues that trait theorists underestimate the power of situations to alter behavior and do not pay enough attention to the cognitive and emotional processes that underlie people's overt actions. Despite their remaining differences, most advocates of the trait and social-cognitive approaches are now focusing on the similarities between their views (Funder, 2001a). This trend toward reconciliation has helped to clarify the relationship between personal and situational variables and how they affect behavior under various conditions. Many of the conclusions that have emerged are consistent with Bandura's concept of reciprocal determinism:

1. Personal dispositions (which include traits and cognitive person variables) influence behavior only in relevant situations. The trait of anxiousness, for example, may predict anxiety, but only in situations where an anxious person feels threatened.

perceived self-efficacy According to Bandura, learned expectations about the probability of success in given situations.

The Impact of Situations Like the rest of us, former professional wrestler Jesse Ventura behaves differently in different situations, such as in the ring and in the office where he serves as the governor of Minnesota. Mischel's theory of personality holds that person-situation interactions are important in determining behavior.

2. Personal dispositions can lead to behaviors that alter situations that, in turn, promote other behaviors. For example, a hostile child can trigger aggression in others and thus start a fight.

3. People choose to be in situations that are in accord with their personal dispositions. Introverts, for instance, are likely to choose quiet environments, whereas extraverts tend to seek out livelier, more social circumstances.

4. Personal dispositions are more important in some situations than in others. Where many different behaviors would be appropriate—a picnic, for example—what people do may be predicted from their dispositions (extraverts will probably play games and socialize while introverts watch). However, in situations such as a funeral, where fewer options are socially acceptable, personal dispositions will not differentiate one person from another; everyone is likely to be quiet and somber.

Today, social-cognitive theorists devote much of their research to examining how cognitive person variables develop, how they are related to stress and health, and how they interact with situational variables to affect behavior.

Evaluation of the Social-Cognitive Approach

The original behavioral view of personality appealed to many people. It offered an objective, experimentally oriented approach that operationally defined its concepts, relied on empirical data for its basic principles, and based its applications on the results of empirical research (Pervin, 1996). However, its successor, the social-cognitive approach, has gained even wider acceptance because it blends theories from behavioral and cognitive psychology and applies them to such socially important areas as aggression, the effects of mass media on children, and the development of self-regulatory processes that enhance personal control over behavior. The popularity of this approach also stems from the ease with which its principles can be translated into treatment procedures for many types of psychological disorders (Clark & Fairburn, 1997; Goldfried & Davison, 1994; see the chapter on treatment of psychological disorders).

humanistic approach A view in which personality develops through an actualizing tendency that unfolds in accordance with each person's unique perceptions of the world.

Still, the social-cognitive approach has not escaped criticism. Psychodynamic theorists point out that social-cognitive theories leave no role for unconscious thoughts and feelings in determining behaviors (e.g., Westen, 1998). Some advocates of trait theory complain that social-cognitive theorists have focused more on explaining why traits are unimportant than on why situations are important, and that they have failed to identify what it is about specific situations that bring out certain behaviors (Funder, 2001a). The social-cognitive approach has also been faulted for failing to present a general theory of personality, offering instead a set of more limited theories that share certain common assumptions about the nature of personality (Feist & Feist, 2001). Most generally, the social-cognitive approach is deemed incapable of capturing the complexities, richness, and uniqueness that some critics see as inherent in human personality (Hall, Lindzey, & Campbell, 1998). According to these critics, a far more palatable alternative is provided by the humanistic approach to personality.

The Humanistic Approach

Unlike theories that emphasize the instincts and learning processes that humans seem to share with other animals, the **humanistic approach** to personality focuses on mental capabilities that set humans apart: self-awareness, creativity, planning, decision making, and responsibility. To those who adopt the humanistic approach, human behavior is motivated mainly by an innate drive toward growth that prompts people to fulfill their unique potential. And like the planted seed whose natural potential is to become a flower, people are seen as naturally inclined toward goodness, creativity, love, and joy. Humanistic psychologists also believe that to explain people's actions in any particular situation, it is more important to understand their view of the world than their instincts, traits, or learning experiences. To humanists, that world view is a bit different for each of us, and it is this unique *phenomenology*, or way of perceiving and interpreting the world, that shapes personality and guides behavior (Kelly, 1980). From this perspective, then, no one can

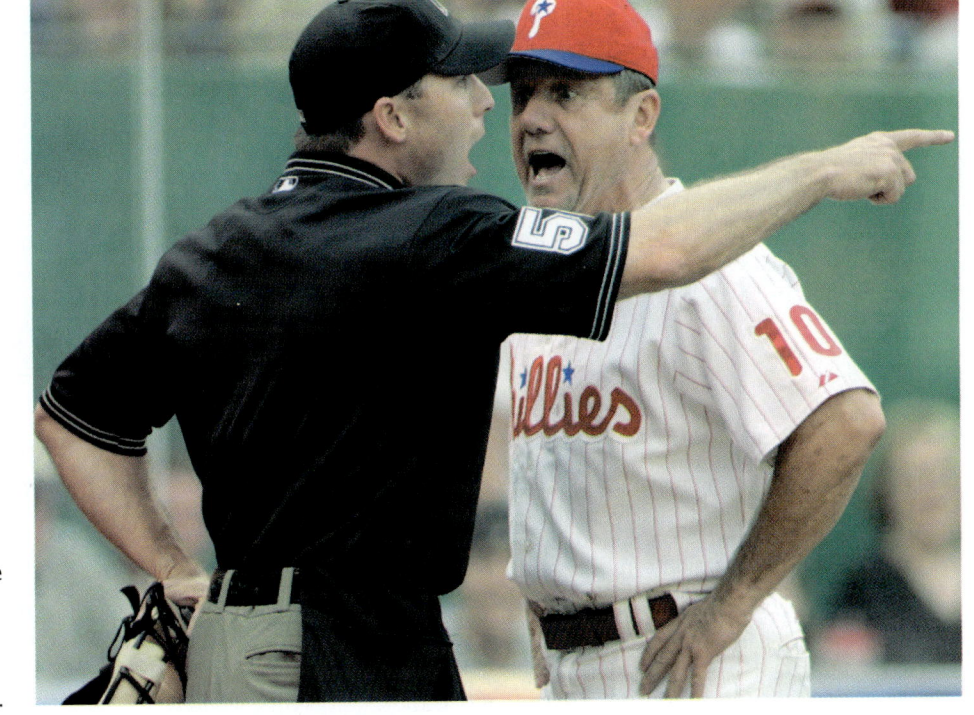

What Is Reality? Each of these people has a different perception of what happened during the play that started this argument—and each is sure he is right! Disagreement about the "same" event illustrates phenomenology, each person's unique perceptions of the world. The humanistic approach to personality sees these perceptions as shaping personality and guiding behavior. As described in the chapter on perception, our perceptions are often influenced by top-down processing; in this case, expectations and motivation stemming from differing loyalties are likely to influence reality—and reactions—for each team's players, coaches, and fans.

understand another person without somehow perceiving the world through that person's eyes. All behavior, even if it looks bizarre, is meaningful to the person displaying it.

The humanistic approach to personality has many roots. The idea that each person perceives a different reality reflects the views of existential philosophers such as Søren Kierkegaard and Jean-Paul Sartre. The idea that people actively shape their own reality stems in part from the Gestalt psychologists whose work is described in the chapter on perception and from George Kelly, a psychologist who also influenced social-cognitive theorists. We can also hear echoes of Alfred Adler and other psychodynamic theorists who emphasized the positive aspects of human nature and the importance of the ego in personality development.

Prominent Humanistic Theories

By far, the most prominent humanistic theories of personality are those of Carl Rogers and Abraham Maslow.

Rogers's Self Theory

In his prolific writings, Carl Rogers (e.g., 1961, 1970, 1980) emphasized the **actualizing tendency,** which he described as an innate inclination toward growth and fulfillment that motivates all human behavior and is expressed in a unique way by each individual (Raskin & Rogers, 2001; Rogers, 1980). To Rogers, then, personality is the expression of that actualizing tendency as it unfolds in each individual's uniquely perceived reality (Feist & Feist, 2001). The centerpiece of Rogers's theory is the *self,* the part of experience that a person identifies as "I" or "me." According to Rogers, those who accurately experience the self—with all its preferences, abilities, fantasies, shortcomings, and desires—are on the road to what Kurt Goldstein (1939) had called *self-actualization*. The progress of people whose experiences of the self become distorted, however, is likely to be slowed or stopped.

Rogers saw personality development beginning early, as children learn to need other people's approval, or as he called it, *positive regard*. Evaluations by parents, teachers, and others soon begin to affect children's self-evaluations. When these

Seeking Self-Actualization According to Rogers, conditions of worth can make it harder for children to become aware of and accept aspects of themselves that conflict with their parents' values. Progress toward self-actualization can be enhanced by associating with people whose positive regard is not conditional on displaying any particular pattern of behavior.

The Humanistic Approach

Parents are not usually this obvious about creating conditions of worth, but according to Rogers, the message gets through in many more subtle ways.

© The New Yorker Collection 2001 Pat Byrnes from cartoonbank.com. All rights reserved.

"Just remember, son, it doesn't matter whether you win or lose—unless you want Daddy's love."

evaluations are in agreement with a child's own self-evaluations, the child reacts in a way that matches, or is *congruent* with, self-experience. The child not only experiences positive regard but also evaluates the self as "good" for having earned approval. This positive self-experience becomes part of the **self-concept,** which is the way one thinks of oneself. But what if a positive self-experience is evaluated negatively by others, as when a little boy is teased by his father for having fun playing with dolls? In this case, the child must either do without a parent's positive regard or, more likely, reevaluate the self-experience—deciding perhaps that "I don't like dolls" or "Feeling good is bad."

In other words, said Rogers, personality is shaped partly by the actualizing tendency and partly by evaluations made by others. In this way, people come to like what they are "supposed" to like and to behave as they are "supposed" to behave. This socialization process is adaptive, because it helps people to function in society, but it often requires that they stifle their self-actualizing tendency and distort experience. Rogers argued that psychological discomfort, anxiety, or even mental disorder can result when the feelings people experience or express are *incongruent* with their true feelings.

Incongruence is likely, said Rogers, when parents and teachers act in ways that lead children to believe that their worth as a person depends on displaying the "right" attitudes, behaviors, and values. These **conditions of worth** are created whenever *people* are evaluated instead of their behavior. For example, parents who find their toddler smearing finger paint on the dog are unlikely to say, "I love you, but I don't approve of this particular behavior." They are more likely to shout, "Bad boy!" or "Bad girl!" thus suggesting that the child is lovable and worthwhile only when well behaved. As a result, the child's self-experience is not "I like painting Fang, but Mom and Dad don't approve," but instead, "Playing with paint is bad, and I am bad if I like it, so I don't like it," or "I like it, so I must be bad." The child may eventually display a degree of restraint that does not reflect the real self but, rather, is part of the ideal self dictated by the parents.

actualizing tendency According to Rogers, an innate inclination toward growth that motivates all people.

self-concept The way one thinks of oneself.

conditions of worth According to Rogers, the feelings an individual experiences when the person, instead of the person's behavior, is evaluated.

The Joys of a Growth Orientation
According to Maslow's theory of personality, the key to personal growth and fulfillment lies in focusing on what we have, not on what we don't have or on what we have lost. Rachel Barton could have let the accident that took her leg destroy her career as a concert violinist, and with it, her joy in life—but she didn't.

Like Freud's concept of superego, conditions of worth are first set up by external pressure but eventually become part of the person's belief system. To Rogers, rewards and punishments are important in personality development not just because they shape overt behavior, but also because they can so easily create distorted self-perceptions and incongruence.

Maslow's Growth Theory

Like Rogers, Abraham Maslow (1954, 1971) saw personality as the expression of a basic human tendency toward growth and self-actualization. In fact, Maslow believed that self-actualization is not just a human capacity but a human need; as shown in Figure 11.8, he described self-actualization as the highest in a hierarchy of motives, or needs. Yet, said Maslow, people are often distracted from seeking self-actualization because of needs that are lower on the hierarchy.

Maslow saw most people as controlled by a **deficiency orientation,** the preoccupation with perceived needs for material things. Ultimately, he said, deficiency-oriented people come to see life as a meaningless exercise in disappointment and boredom, and they may begin to behave in problematic ways. For example, in an attempt to satisfy the need for love and belongingness, people may focus on what love can give them (security), not on what they can give to another. This deficiency orientation may lead a person to be jealous and to focus on what is missing in relationships; as a result, the person will never truly experience either love or security.

In contrast, people with a **growth orientation** do not focus on what is missing but draw satisfaction from what they have, what they are, and what they can do. This orientation opens the door to what Maslow called *peak experiences,* in which people feel joy, even ecstasy, in the mere fact of being alive, being human, and knowing that they are utilizing their fullest potential.

Evaluation of the Humanistic Approach

The humanistic approach to personality is consistent with the way many people view themselves. It gives a central role to each person's immediate experiences and emphasizes the uniqueness of each individual. The humanistic approach and its phenomenological perspective has inspired the person-centered therapy of Rogers (see the chapter on treatment of psychological disorders), as well as short-term personal growth experiences—such as sensitivity training and encounter groups designed to

---

deficiency orientation A preoccupation with perceived needs for things a person does not have.

growth orientation Drawing satisfaction from what is available in life, rather than focusing on what is missing.

in review: Major Approaches to Personality

Approach	Basic Assumptions About Behavior	Typical Research Method
Psychodynamic	Determined by largely unconscious intrapsychic conflicts	Case studies
Trait	Determined by traits or needs	Analysis of tests for basic personality dimensions
Social-cognitive	Determined by learning, cognitive factors, and specific situations	Analysis of interactions between people and situations
Humanistic	Determined by innate growth tendency and individual perception of reality	Studies of relationships between perceptions and behavior

help people become more aware of themselves and the way they relate to others—and techniques to teach parents how to avoid creating conditions of worth while maximizing their children's potential.

Yet to its critics, the humanistic view is naive, romantic, and unrealistic. Are people all as inherently good and growth-oriented as this approach suggests? Humanistic personality theorists have also been faulted for underplaying the importance of inherited characteristics, learning, situational influences, and unconscious motivation in shaping personality. The idea that everyone is directed only by an innate growth potential is viewed by critics as an oversimplification. So, too, is the assumption that all human problems stem from blocked actualization. Like the trait approach, humanistic theories seem to do a better job of describing personality than explaining it. And like many of the concepts in psychodynamic theories, humanistic concepts seem too vague to be tested empirically. Accordingly, the humanistic approach is not very popular among psychologists who rely on empirical research to learn about personality (Funder, 2001a).

Finally, humanists' tendency to define ideal personality development in terms of personal growth, independence, and self-actualization has been criticized for emphasizing culture-specific ideas about mental health that may not apply outside North America and other Western cultures (Heine et al., 1999). As described in the next section, the individualist foundations of humanistic personality theories may be in direct conflict with the values of non-Western, collectivist cultures. ("In Review: Major Approaches to Personality" summarizes key features of the humanistic approach, along with those of the other approaches we have described.)

LINKAGES (a link to Human Development)

Personality, Culture, and Human Development

In many Western cultures, it is common to hear people encourage others to "stand up for yourself" or to "blow your own horn" in order to "get what you have coming to you." In middle-class North America, for example, the values of achievement and personal distinction are taught to children, particularly male children, very early in life (Markus & Kitayama, 1997). North American children are encouraged to feel special, to want self-esteem, and to feel good about themselves. (Many day-care centers, summer camps, and other children's programs support esteem building through names such as Starkids, Little Wonders, Superkids, and Precious Jewels). Those who learn and display these values tend to receive praise and encouragement for doing so.

As a result of this cultural training, many people in North America and Europe develop personalities that are largely based on a sense of high self-worth. In a study by Hazel Markus and Shinobu Kitayama (1991), for example, 70 percent of a sample of U.S. students believed they were superior to their peers, and 60 percent believed they were in the top 10 percent on a wide variety of personal attributes! This tendency toward self-enhancement is evident as early as age four.

As mentioned earlier, a sense of independence, uniqueness, and self-esteem is seen by many Western personality theorists as fundamental to mental health. Psychoanalyst Erik Erikson included the appearance of personal identity and self-esteem as part of normal psychosocial development (see the chapter on human development). Middle-class Americans who fail to value and strive for independence, self-promotion, and unique personal achievement may be seen as displaying a personality disorder, some form of depression, or other psychological problems.

Do these ideas reflect universal truths about personality development or, rather, the influence of the cultures that generated them? It is certainly clear that people in many non-Western cultures develop personal orientations very different from those of North Americans and Europeans (Cross & Markus, 1999). In China and Japan, for example, an independent, unique self is not emphasized (Ho & Chiu, 1998). Children there are encouraged to develop and maintain harmonious relations with others and not to stand out from the crowd, lest they diminish someone else. In fact, the Japanese word for "different" (*tigau*) also means "wrong" (Kitayama & Markus, 1992). So whereas children in the United States hear that "the squeaky wheel gets the grease," Japanese children are warned that "the nail that stands out gets pounded down" (Markus & Kitayama, 1997). From a very young age, they are taught to be modest, to play down the value of personal contributions, and to appreciate the joy and value of group work (Kitayama & Markus, 1992).

In contrast to the *independent* self-system prevalent in individualist cultures (e.g., the United States, Great Britain, and Switzerland), countries characterized by a more collectivist orientation (e.g., Japan, China, Brazil, and Nigeria) promote an *interdependent* self-system through which people see themselves as a fraction of a whole, as an entity that has little or no meaningful definition without reference

Culture and Personality In individualist cultures, most children learn early that personal distinction is valued by parents, teachers, and peers. In cultures where collectivist values prevail, a strong sense of personal self-worth tends to be seen as a less important characteristic. In other words, the features of "normal" personality development vary from culture to culture.

to the group. These differences in self-systems may produce differences in the way people experience well-being. In the United States, a sense of personal well-being is typically associated with the feeling of *having positive attributes,* whereas in Japan and other Asian countries it is more likely to be associated with the feeling of *lacking negative attributes* (Eliot et al., 2001). Similarly, the results of studies conducted around the world indicate that in collectivist cultures, life satisfaction is associated with social approval and harmonious relations with others, whereas in individualist cultures, life satisfaction is associated with high self-esteem and feeling good about one's own life (Uchida et al., 2001).

Given that cultural factors shape notions about ideal personality development, it is important to evaluate various approaches to personality in terms of how well they apply to cultures other than the one in which they were developed (Cross & Markus, 1999). Their applicability to males and females must also be considered. Even within North American cultures, for example, there are gender differences in the development of self-esteem. Females tend to display an interdependent self-system, achieving their sense of self and self-esteem from attachments to others. By contrast, males' self-esteem tends to develop in relation to personal achievement, in a manner more in keeping with an independent self-system (Cross & Madson, 1997). Cross-gender and cross-cultural differences in the nature and determinants of a sense of self underscore the pervasive effects of gender and culture on the development of many aspects of human personality.

FOCUS ON RESEARCH METHODS

Longitudinal Studies of Temperament and Personality

Studying the development of personality over the life span requires *longitudinal research,* in which the same people are followed from infancy to adulthood so that their characteristics can be assessed at different points in their lives. A number of studies have used this longitudinal methodology to explore a variety of questions about changes in personality over time.

● What was the researchers' question?

The specific question addressed by Avashalom Caspi and his colleagues was whether the temperament children display at birth and in their early years predicts their personality and behavior as adults (Caspi, 2000; Caspi & Silva, 1995; Caspi et al., 1997; Caspi et al., 1995). As discussed in the chapter on human development, it is generally agreed that differences in temperament are influenced more by heredity than by the environment (Rowe, 1997).

● How did the researchers answer the question?

Caspi's research team studied all the children born in Dunedin, New Zealand, between April 1972 and March 1973—a total of about a thousand individuals. When the children were three years old, an examiner gave each of them a test of their cognitive abilities and motor skills and, using a three-point scale, rated their reactions to the testing situation. Some of the children exhibited explosive or uncontrolled behaviors; some interacted easily; some were withdrawn and unresponsive. (To avoid bias while making their ratings, the examiners were told nothing about the children's typical behavior outside of the testing room.) Based on these ratings, each child was placed into one of three temperament categories: *undercontrolled* (impulsive, restless, emotional), *overcontrolled* (shy, fearful, easily distracted), and *well-adjusted* (comfortable, friendly, calm, well-controlled). The children were reexamined at ages five, seven, and nine; but each time, a different person did the ratings, thus eliminating the possibility that an examiner's earlier impressions might bias later ratings. Almost all correlations among the independent ratings made at various ages were positive and statistically significant, indicating that the temperament classifications were stable across time.

When the participants were eighteen years old, they completed a standard personality test. Finally, at the age of twenty-one, they were interviewed about the degree to which they engaged in risky and unhealthy behaviors such as excessive drinking, violent crime, unprotected sexual activity, and unsafe driving habits. To avoid bias, the interviewers were given no information about the participants' temperament when they were children or about their scores on the personality test.

What did the researchers find?

Several significant differences were found among the average personality scores for the three temperament categories. For example, participants classified as "undercontrolled" at the age of three were more aggressive, alienated, negative, and hostile as adults than the other temperament groups. Further, people originally classified as "well-adjusted" were more forceful and decisive than were the people classified as "overcontrolled." And young adults who, as children, had been classified as "well-adjusted" tended to be effective individuals who were likely to assume leadership roles. These findings held true for males and females alike.

Caspi and his colleagues also found small but significant correlations between early temperament and health-risk and criminal behaviors (Caspi, 2000). For example, people classified as "overcontrolled" were more likely to avoid dangerous and exciting activities at the age of twenty-one than were those who had been classified as "undercontrolled." In fact, participants classifed as "undercontrolled" were significantly more likely than either of the other groups to engage in risky behaviors and to have criminal records. The relationship between temperament in childhood and health-risk behaviors in young adulthood was not, however, a direct one. Statistical analyses revealed that temperament at age three affected personality at age eighteen, which in turn affected behavior patterns at age twenty-one.

What do the results mean?

The results of Caspi's studies provide persuasive empirical support for a hypothesis long endorsed by personality psychologists: that relatively accurate predictions can be made about people's personality and behavior as adults on the basis of information about their temperament as children. However, the strength of these results should not be overstated. The relationships between temperament and personality, and between temperament and various problematic behaviors, though statistically significant, were also relatively modest. For example, not all the participants classified as "undercontrolled" at age three turned out to be aggressive or violent at age twenty-one. The implication is that personality is influenced and shaped by temperament, but not completely determined by it.

The results of these studies also confirm a point made in the chapter on health, stress, and coping—that personality plays a significant role in health. Specifically, personality characteristics predispose people to engage in behaviors that can affect their mental and physical health.

What do we still need to know?

Caspi's research has revealed some continuity between temperament in childhood and personality in adulthood, but it also leaves some unanswered questions (Roberts & DelVecchio, 2000). For example, what factors underlie this continuity? The fact that there are individual differences in adult behavior within temperament groups shows that a child is not simply biologically programmed to exhibit certain personality traits later. One explanation offered by Caspi and his colleagues draws heavily on social-cognitive theories, particularly on Bandura's notion of *reciprocal determinism*. These researchers believe that long-term consistencies in behavior result from the mutual influence that temperament and environmental events have on one another. They propose, for example, that people tend to put themselves in situations that reinforce their temperament. So "undercontrolled" people might choose to spend time with people who accept and even encourage rude or impolite behavior. And when such behavior brings negative reactions, the world seems that much more hostile, and they become even more aggressive and negative. Caspi and his colleagues see the results of their studies as evidence that this process of mutual influence between personality and situations can continue over a lifetime (Caspi & Roberts, 1999).

Assessing Personality

Psychologists describe people's personalities using information from four main sources (Ozer, 1999): *life outcomes* (such as level of education, income, or marital status), *situational tests* (laboratory measurements of behavioral, emotional, and physiological reactions to conflict, frustration, and the like), *observer ratings* (judgments about a person made by family or friends), and *self-reports* (responses to interviews and personality tests). The data gathered through these methods are used for many purposes, including diagnosing psychological disorders, predicting dangerousness, selecting new employees, and even choosing astronaut candidates best suited to space travel (Butcher & Rouse, 1996; Groth-Marnat, 1997; Meyer et al., 2001; Nietzel et al., 2003).

Observer ratings and situational tests allow direct assessment of many aspects of behavior, including how often, how effectively, and how consistently various actions occur. *Interviews* provide a way to gather information about personality from the person's own point of view. Some interviews are *open-ended*, meaning that questions are tailored to the intellectual level, emotional state, and special needs of the person being interviewed. Others are *structured*, meaning that the interviewer asks a fixed set of questions about specific topics in a particular order. Structured interviews are routinely used in personality research because they are sure to cover matters of special interest to the researcher.

Personality tests offer a way of gathering self-report information that is more standardized and economical than interviews. To be useful, however, a personality test must be reliable and valid. As described in the chapter on cognitive abilities, reliability refers to how stable or consistent the results of a test are; validity reflects the degree to which a test measures what it is intended to measure and leads to correct inferences about people. The many personality tests available today are traditionally classified as either *objective* or *projective*.

Objective Personality Tests

Objective personality tests contain clearly stated items that relate to a person's thoughts, feelings, or behavior (such as "Do you like parties?"). The most common kind of objective personality test is similar in format to the multiple-choice or true-false examinations used in many classrooms. Like those exams, self-report personality tests can be administered to many people at the same time; they can also be machine scored. However, whereas there is only one correct answer for each item on a classroom exam, the "correct" answers to an objective personality test depend on who is taking it. Each person is asked to respond in a way that best describes him or her.

Ultimately, the person's responses to the objective test's items are combined into a score. That score can be used to draw conclusions about the respondent's personality, but only after it has been compared with the responses of thousands of other people who have taken the same test. For example, before interpreting your score of "77" on a self-report test of extraversion, a psychologist would compare the score with *norms*, or average scores from other individuals of your age and gender.

objective personality tests Personality tests containing direct, unambiguous items relating to the individual being assessed.

table 14.3
Sample Summary of Results from the NEO-PI-R

Compared with the responses of other people, your responses suggest that you can be described as:

☐ Sensitive, emotional, and prone to experience feelings that are upsetting.	☒ Generally calm and able to deal with stress, but you sometimes experience feelings of guilt, anger, or sadness.	☐ Secure, hardy, and generally relaxed even under stressful conditions.
☐ Extraverted, outgoing, active, and high-spirited. You prefer to be around people most of the time.	☐ Moderate in activity and enthusiasm. You enjoy the company of others, but you also value privacy.	☒ Introverted, reserved, and serious. You prefer to be alone or with a few close friends.
☐ Open to new experiences. You have broad interests and are very imaginative.	☐ Practical but willing to consider new ways of doing things. You seek a balance between the old and the new.	☒ Down-to-earth, practical, traditional, and pretty much set in your ways.
☐ Compassionate, good-natured, and eager to cooperate and avoid conflict.	☒ Generally warm, trusting, and agreeable, but you can sometimes be stubborn and competitive.	☐ Hardheaded, skeptical, proud, and competitive. You tend to express your anger directly.
☒ Conscientious and well organized. You have high standards and always strive to achieve your goals.	☐ Dependable and moderately well organized. You generally have clear goals but are able to set your work aside.	☐ Easygoing, not very well organized, and sometimes careless. You prefer not to make plans.

The NEO-PI-R assesses the big-five personality dimensions. In this example of the results a respondent might receive, the five factors scored are, from the top row to the bottom row, neuroticism, extraversion, openness, agreeableness, and conscientiousness. Because people with different NEO profiles tend to have different psychological problems, this test has been used to aid in the diagnosis of personality disorders (Trull & Sher, 1994).

Only if you were well above these averages would you be considered unusually extraverted.

Some self-report tests focus on one personality trait, such as optimism (Scheier et al., 1989); others measure a set of related traits, such as empathy and social responsibility (Penner, in press). Still others measure the strength of a wider variety of traits to reveal general psychological functioning. For example, the *Neuroticism Extraversion Openness Personality Inventory, Revised,* or *NEO-PI-R* (Costa & McCrae, 1992), is designed to measure the big-five personality traits described earlier. Table 14.3 shows how the test's results are presented. One innovative feature of the NEO-PI-R is its "private" and "public" versions. The first version asks for the respondent's self-assessment; the second version asks a person who knows the respondent to rate him or her on various dimensions. Personality descriptions derived from the two versions are often quite similar, but discrepancies may indicate problems. For example, if a person's self-ratings are substantially different from those of a spouse, marital problems may be indicated; in addition, the nature of the discrepancies could suggest a focus for marital therapy.

The NEO-PI-R is quite reliable (Viswesvaran & Ones, 2000), and people's scores on its various scales have been successfully used to predict a number of criteria, including performance on specific jobs and overall career success (Barrick & Mount, 1991; Siebert & Kraimer, 2001), social status (Anderson et al., 2001), and the likelihood of continued criminal behavior (Clower & Bothwell, 2001).

When the goal of personality testing is to diagnose psychological disorders, the most commonly used objective test is the *Minnesota Multiphasic Personality Inventory,* or the *MMPI* (Butcher & Rouse, 1996). This 566-item true-false test was originally developed during the 1930s at the University of Minnesota by Starke

LINKAGES (a link to Psychological Disorders)

figure 14.6

The MMPI: Clinical Scales and Sample Profiles

A score of 50 on the clinical scales of the MMPI is average. Scores at or above 65 mean that the person's responses on that scale are more extreme than at least 95 percent of the normal population. The green line represents the profile of Kenneth Bianchi, the infamous "Hillside Strangler" who murdered thirteen women in the late 1970s. His profile would be interpreted as characteristic of a shallow person with poor self-control and little personal insight who is sexually preoccupied and unable to reveal himself to others. The profile in purple comes from a more normal man, but it is characteristic of someone who is self-centered, passive, and unwilling to accept personal responsibility for his behavior, and who, when under stress, complains of numerous vague physical symptoms.

The clinical scales abbreviated in the figure are as follows:

1. Hypochondriasis (Hs; concern with bodily functions and symptoms).
2. Depression (D; pessimism, hopelessness, slowed thinking).
3. Hysteria (Hy; use of physical or mental symptoms to avoid problems).
4. Psychopathic deviate (Pd; disregard for social customs, emotional shallowness).
5. Masculinity/femininity (Mf; interests associated with a particular gender).
6. Paranoia (Pa; delusions, suspiciousness).
7. Psychasthenia (Pt; worry, guilt, anxiety).
8. Schizophrenia (Sc; bizarre thoughts and perceptions).
9. Hypomania (Ma; overactivity, excitement, impulsiveness).
0. Social introversion (Si; shy, insecure).

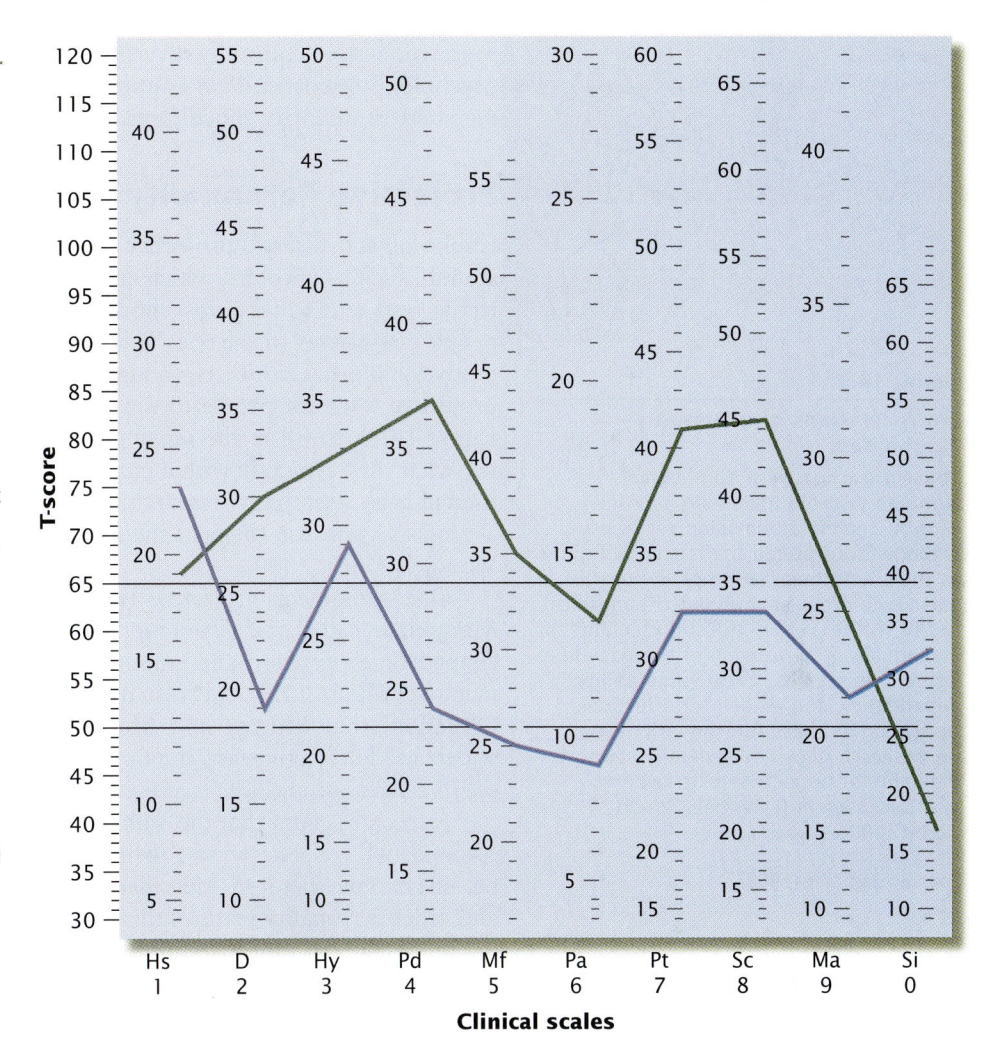

Hathaway and J. C. McKinley. It has subsequently been revised and updated to become the MMPI-2 (National Computer Systems, 1992). The MMPI's items are organized into ten *clinical scales*. These are groups of items that, in earlier research, had drawn a characteristic pattern of responses only from people who displayed particular psychological disorders or personality characteristics (see Figure 14.6).

Interpreting the MMPI is largely a matter of using computer programs to compare respondents' profiles—such as those shown in Figure 14.6—to the profiles of people already known to display certain personality characteristics. Respondents are presumed to share characteristics with the group whose profile most closely resembles theirs. So whereas a very high score on one scale, such as depression, might indicate a problem in the dimension measured by that scale, MMPI interpretation usually focuses on the overall *pattern* in the clinical scales—particularly on the combination of two or three scales on which a person has unusually high scores.

There is considerable evidence for the reliability and validity of MMPI clinical scales, but even the latest editions of the test are far from perfect measurement tools (Groth-Marnat, 1997; McIntire & Miller, 2000). The validity of MMPI interpretations may be particularly suspect when—because of cultural factors—the perceptions, values, and experiences of a respondent are notably different from those of the test developers and the people to whom the respondent's results are compared. A profile that looks typical of people with a certain disorder might reflect the culture-specific way the respondent interpreted the test items, not a mental problem (Groth-Marnat, 1997). Even though the MMPI-2 uses comparison norms that represent a more culturally diverse population than did those of the original MMPI, psychologists must remain cautious when interpreting profiles of people who are members of minority subcultures.

Projective Personality Tests

Unlike objective tests, **projective personality tests** contain relatively unstructured stimuli, such as inkblots, which can be perceived in many ways. Proponents of projective tests tend to take a psychodynamic approach to personality. They believe that people's responses to the tests' ambiguous stimuli are guided by unconscious needs, motives, fantasies, conflicts, thoughts, and other hidden aspects of personality. Some projective tests ask people to draw items such as a house, a person, or a tree (see Figure 14.7); to fill in the missing parts of incomplete pictures or sentences; or to say what they associate with a particular word. Projective techniques are sometimes used in basic personality research, but they are far more popular among clinical psychologists, who use them in the assessment of psychological disorders (Lilienfeld, Wood, & Garb, 2000).

One prominent projective test, developed by Henry Murray and Christina Morgan, is called the *Thematic Apperception Test*, or *TAT*. As described in the chapter on motivation and emotion, the TAT is used to measure need for achievement (see Figure 11.7). It is also used to assess other needs (e.g., needs for power or affiliation) that Murray and Morgan saw as the basis for personality. Another widely used projective test, the *Rorschach Inkblot Test*, asks people to say what they see in a series of inkblots (see Figure 14.8).

Advocates claim that the ambiguity of projective test items makes it difficult for respondents to detect what is being measured and what the "best" answers would be. They argue, therefore, that these tests can measure aggressive and sexual impulses and other personality features that people might otherwise be able to hide. However, in comparison to objective-test results, responses to projective tests are also much more difficult to translate into numerical scores for scientific analysis. In an effort to reduce the subjectivity involved in projective-test interpretation, some psychologists

figure 14.7

Interpretations of a Draw-a-Person Test

These drawings were done by an eighteen-year-old male who had been caught stealing a television set. A psychologist interpreted the muscular figure as the young man's attempt to boast of masculine prowess, but saw the muscles' "puffy softness" as suggesting feelings of inadequacy. The drawing of the baby-like figure was seen to reveal vulnerability, dependency, and a need for affection. Appealing as these interpretations may be, research does not generally support the value of projective tests in personality assessment (Lilienfield, Wood, & Garb, 2000).

Source: Hammer (1968).

figure 14.8

The Rorschach Inkblot Test

The Rorschach test consists of ten patterns—some in color, others in black and white. The respondent is asked to tell what the blot might be and then to explain why. This pattern is similar to one of those in the Rorschach test. What do you see? Most scoring methods focus on (1) what part of the blot the person responds to; (2) what details, colors, or other features appear to determine each response; (3) the content of responses (such as seeing animals, maps, or body parts); and (4) the popularity or commonness of the responses.

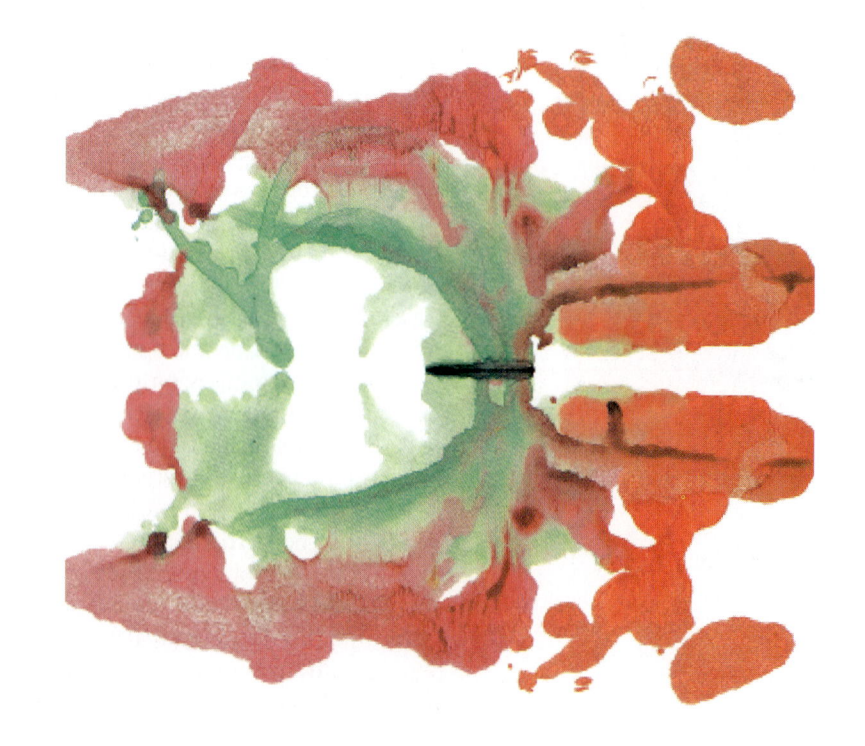

in review: Personality Tests

Type of Test	Characteristics	Advantages	Disadvantages
Objective	Asks direct questions about a person; quantitatively scored	Efficiency, standardization	Subject to deliberate distortion
Projective	Unstructured stimuli create maximum freedom of response; scoring is is subjective, though some objective methods exist	"Correct" answers not obvious; designed to tap unconscious impulses; flexible use	Reliability and validity lower than those of objective tests

have developed more structured—and thus potentially more reliable—scoring systems for instruments such as the Rorschach (Erdberg, 1990; Exner & Ona, 1995). There are in fact specific instances—as in studies assessing achievement motivation with the TAT—where projective tests show acceptable reliability and validity (Schultheiss & Brunstein, 2001), but overall, projective personality tests are substantially less reliable and valid than objective tests (Garb, Florio, & Grove, 1998; Lilienfeld, Wood, & Garb, 2000). Because of their generally low predictive validity, projective tests often add little information beyond what might be inferred from life outcome data, interviews, and objective personality tests (Lilienfeld, Wood, & Garb, 2000). ("In Review: Personality Tests" summarizes the characteristics of objective and projective tests, along with some of their advantages and disadvantages.)

Personality Tests and Employee Selection

How good are personality tests at selecting people for jobs? Most industrial/organizational psychologists believe these tests are valuable tools in the selection of good employees. The MMPI (and even some projective tests) are occasionally employed for such purposes (e.g., Bartol, 1991), but the majority of personality tests used by large organizations are those that measure the big-five personality dimensions or related characteristics (Borman, Hanson, & Wedge, 1997; Costa, 2001). Several researchers have found significant relationships between scores on these characteristics and measures of overall job performance and effective leadership (Barrick & Mount, 1991; Ones & Viswesvaran, 1996; Silverthorne, 2001). A more general review of studies involving thousands of people has shown that objective personality tests are of value in helping businesses reduce thefts and other disruptive employee behaviors (Ones & Viswesvaran, 2001).

Still, personality tests are far from perfect predictors of behavior, and as noted earlier, they sometimes lead to incorrect predictions. Many tests measure traits that may be too general to predict specific aspects of job performance (Furnham 2001), and in any case, personality characteristics may influence performance in some job situations but not in others (Ones & Viswesvaran, 2001). Further, some employees see personality tests as an invasion of their privacy. They worry also that test results in their personnel files might later be misinterpreted and hurt their chances for promotion or for employment by other companies. Lawsuits have resulted in a ban on the use of personality tests in the selection of U.S. federal employees. Concerns about privacy and other issues surrounding personality testing have also led the American Psychological Association and related organizations to publish ethical standards relating to procedures for the development, dissemination, and use of all psychological tests (American Educational Research Association, American Psychological Association, and National Council on Measurement in Education, 1999; American Psychological Association, 1992b). The goal is not only to improve the reliability and validity of tests but also to ensure that their results are properly used and do not infringe on individuals' rights (Turner et al., 2001).

projective personality tests Personality tests made up of unstructured stimuli that can be perceived and responded to in many ways.

LINKAGES

As noted in the chapter on introducing psychology, all of psychology's subfields are related to one another. Our discussion of cultural factors and personality illustrates just one way in which the topic of this chapter, personality, is linked to the subfield of developmental psychology (which is the focus of the chapter on human development). The Linkages diagram shows ties to two other subfields as well, and there are many more ties throughout the book. Looking for linkages among subfields will help you see how they all fit together and help you better appreciate the big picture that is psychology.

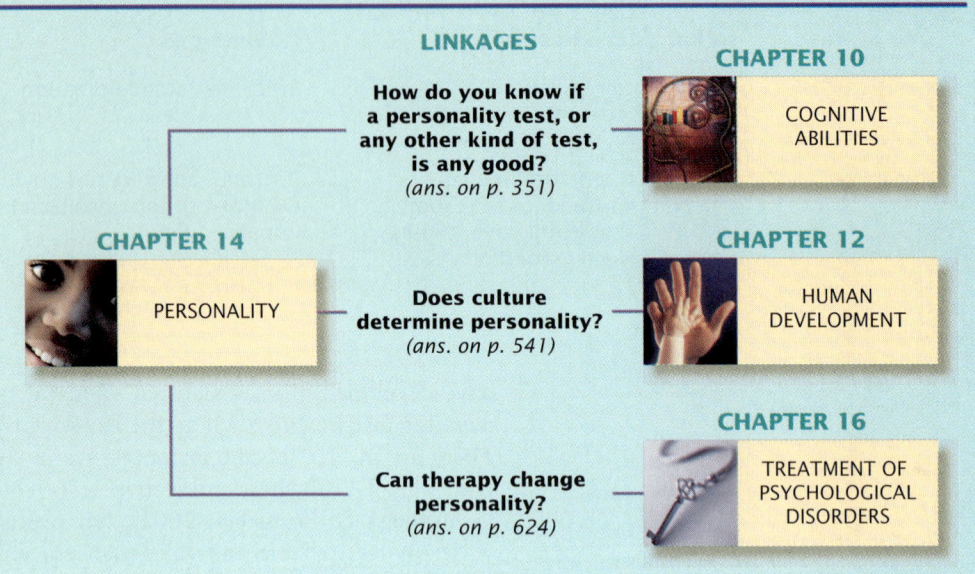

LINKAGES

CHAPTER 14 — PERSONALITY

- How do you know if a personality test, or any other kind of test, is any good? (ans. on p. 351) → **CHAPTER 10** COGNITIVE ABILITIES
- Does culture determine personality? (ans. on p. 541) → **CHAPTER 12** HUMAN DEVELOPMENT
- Can therapy change personality? (ans. on p. 624) → **CHAPTER 16** TREATMENT OF PSYCHOLOGICAL DISORDERS

SUMMARY

Personality refers to the unique pattern of psychological and behavioral characteristics by which each person can be compared and contrasted with other people. The four main theoretical approaches to personality are the psychodynamic, trait, social-cognitive, and humanistic approaches.

The Psychodynamic Approach

The *psychodynamic approach*, first proposed by Sigmund Freud, assumes that personality arises out of the interplay of various unconscious psychological processes.

The Structure and Development of Personality

Freud believed that personality has three components—the *id*, which has a reservoir of *libido* and operates according to the *pleasure principle*; the *ego*, which operates according to the *reality principle*; and the *superego*, which internalizes society's rules and values. The ego uses *defense mechanisms* to prevent unconscious conflicts among these components from becoming conscious and causing anxiety or guilt. Freud proposed that the focus of conflict changes as the child passes through *psychosexual stages* of development, called the *oral stage*, the *anal stage*, the *phallic stage* (during which the *Oedipus complex* or the *Electra complex* arises), the *latency period*, and the *genital stage*.

Variations on Freud's Personality Theory

Many of Freud's early followers developed new theories that differed from his. Among these theorists were Carl Jung, Alfred Adler, and Karen Horney. These and other theorists tended to downplay the role of instincts and the unconscious, emphasizing instead the importance of conscious processes, ego functions, and social and cultural factors. Horney also challenged the male-oriented nature of Freud's original theory.

Contemporary Psychodynamic Theories

Current psychodynamic theories are derived from the neo-Freudians' emphasis on family and social relationships. According to object relations theorists, personality development depends mainly on the nature of early interactions between individuals and their caregivers (objects).

Evaluation of the Psychodynamic Approach

Despite evidence in support of some psychodynamic concepts and recent attempts to test psychodynamic theories more precisely and objectively, critics still fault the approach for its lack of a scientific base and for its view of human behavior as driven by unmeasurable forces.

The Trait Approach

The *trait approach* to personality assumes that personality is made up of stable internal characteristics that appear at varying strengths in different people and guide their thoughts, feelings, and behavior.

Allport's Trait Theory

Gordon Allport believed that personality is created by a small set of central traits and a larger number of secondary traits in each individual. He analyzed language to try to identify those traits, thus laying the foundation for modern research on personality traits.

The Big-Five Model of Personality

Building on the work of Allport and Raymond Cattell, contemporary researchers have used factor analysis to identify five basic dimensions of personality, collectively referred to as the *big-five model,* or five-factor model. These dimensions, which have been found in many different cultures.

Biological Trait Theories

Hans Eysenck believed that differences in nervous system arousal are responsible for differences in core dimensions of personality, especially introversion-extraversion and emotionality-stability. Newer biological theories have largely supplanted Eysenck's theory, and they suggest instead that these differences are due to biological differences in the sensitivity of brain systems involved with responsiveness to rewards and to punishments.

Evaluation of the Trait Approach

The trait approach has been criticized for being better at describing personality than at explaining it, for failing to consider mechanisms that motivate behavior, and for underemphasizing the role of situational factors. Nevertheless, the trait approach—particularly the big-five model—currently dominates the field of personality.

The Social-Cognitive Approach

The *social-cognitive approach* to personality focuses on the thoughts and feelings that influence people's behavior and assumes that personality is a label that summarizes the unique patterns of thinking and behavior that a person learns in the social world.

Roots of the Social-Cognitive Approach

With roots in research on classical and operant conditioning (including Skinner's *functional analysis* of behavior), the social-cognitive approach has expanded on traditional behavioral approaches by emphasizing the role of cognitive factors, such as observational learning, in personality development.

Prominent Social-Cognitive Theories

Julian Rotter's theory focuses on cognitive expectancies that guide behavior, and it generated interest in assessing general beliefs about whether rewards occur because of personal efforts (internal control) or chance (external control). Albert Bandura believes that personality develops largely through cognitively mediated learning, including observational learning. He sees personality as reciprocally determined by interactions among cognition, environmental stimuli, and behavior. *Perceived self-efficacy*—the belief in one's ability to accomplish a specific task—is an important determinant of behavior. Walter Mischel emphasizes the importance of cognitive person variables and their interactions with the characteristics of particular situations in determining behavior. According to Mischel, we must look at both cognitive person variables and situational variables in order to understand human consistencies and inconsistencies.

Evaluation of the Social-Cognitive Approach

The social-cognitive approach has gained wide acceptance because it has merged theories from behavioral and cognitive psychology and used them to explain a wide range of important social behaviors. However, the approach has been criticized for failing to provide one coherent theory of personality and failing to capture the complexity, richness, and uniqueness of human personalities.

The Humanistic Approach

The *humanistic approach* to personality is based on the assumption that people are primarily motivated by a desire to fulfill their natural potential in a uniquely perceived version of reality. So to understand a person, you have to understand the person's view of the world, which serves as the basis for personality and guides behavior.

Prominent Humanistic Theories

Carl Rogers believed that personality development is driven by an innate *actualizing tendency,* but also that one's *self-concept* is shaped by social evaluations. He proposed that when people are free from the effects of *conditions of worth,* they will be psychologically healthy and achieve self-actualization. Abraham Maslow saw self-actualization as the highest in a hierarchy of needs. Personality development is healthiest, he said, when people have a *growth orientation* rather than a *deficiency orientation.*

Evaluation of the Humanistic Approach

Although it has a large following, the humanistic approach is faulted for being too idealistic, for failing to explain personality development, for being vague and unscientific, and for underplaying cultural differences in "ideal" personalities.

Assessing Personality

The information used in personality assessment comes from four main sources: life outcomes, situational tests, observer ratings, and self-reports. To be useful, personality assessments must be both reliable and valid.

Objective Personality Tests

Objective personality tests contain clearly worded items relating to the individual being assessed; their scores can be compared with group norms. The MMPI and the NEO-PI-R are examples of objective tests.

Projective Personality Tests

Based on psychodynamic theories, *projective personality tests* present ambiguous stimuli in an attempt to tap unconscious personality characteristics. Two popular projective tests are the TAT and the Rorschach Inkblot Test. In general, projective personality tests are less reliable and valid than objective personality tests.

Personality Tests and Employee Selection

Objective personality tests are often used to identify the people best suited for certain occupations. Although such tests can be helpful in this regard, those who use them must be aware of the tests' limitations and take care not to violate the rights of test respondents.

15 Psychological Disorders

Defining Psychological Disorders
What Is Abnormal?
Behavior in Context: A Practical Approach

Explaining Psychological Disorders
The Biopsychosocial Model
Diathesis-Stress as an Integrative Explanation

Classifying Psychological Disorders
A Classification System: *DSM-IV*
Purposes and Problems of Diagnosis

THINKING CRITICALLY: Is Psychological Diagnosis Biased?

Anxiety Disorders
Types of Anxiety Disorders
Causes of Anxiety Disorders

Linkages: Anxiety Disorders and Learning

Somatoform Disorders

Dissociative Disorders

Mood Disorders
Depressive Disorders
Bipolar Disorders
Causes of Mood Disorders

Schizophrenia
Symptoms of Schizophrenia
Categorizing Schizophrenia
Causes of Schizophrenia

Personality Disorders

FOCUS ON RESEARCH METHODS: Exploring Links Between Child Abuse and Antisocial Personality Disorder

A Sampling of Other Psychological Disorders
Psychological Disorders of Childhood
Substance-Related Disorders

Mental Illness and the Law

Linkages

Summary

During his first year at college, Mark began to worry about news stories describing the deadly diseases resulting from hantavirus, "flesh-eating" strep bacteria, and HIV. He took a blood test for HIV, the virus that causes AIDS, and was relieved when it showed no infection. But then he wondered if he might have contracted HIV after he took the test. Library research and a call to an AIDS hotline revealed that HIV antibodies may not appear until six months after infection. Mark took another blood test, also negative, but he still worried when he learned that the AIDS virus can live outside of the human body for anywhere from ten minutes to several hours or even days. He also read that no one can explain why hantavirus appears in new places or why some rare forms of bacteria cause deadly lesions.

Given this uncertainty, Mark concluded that HIV, hantavirus, and "flesh-eating" strep bacteria can live indefinitely outside of the body and could therefore be anywhere and everywhere. He decided that the only safe course was not just sexual abstinence but absolute cleanliness. Mark began to scrub himself whenever he touched doorknobs, money, walls, floors—anything. People with HIV or other deadly viruses or bacteria, he thought, could have touched these things, or they might have bled on the street and he might have tracked their infected blood into his car and house and bathroom. Eventually he felt the need to scrub everything around him up to forty times in each direction; it took him several exhausting hours just to shower and dress. He washed the shower knobs before touching them and, once in the shower, felt that he had to wash his body in cycles of thirteen strokes. If his feet touched the bare floor, he had to wash them again before putting on his underwear to ensure that his feet would not contaminate the fabric. He was sure that his hands, rubbed raw from constant washing, were especially susceptible to infection, so he wore gloves at all times except in the summer, when he wrapped his fingers in flesh-colored bandages. The process of protecting himself from infection was wearing him out and severely restricting his activities; he could not go anywhere without first considering the risk of infection.

Mark's case provides an example of someone who suffers from a psychological disorder, also called a *mental disorder* or *psychopathology*. **Psychopathology** is generally defined as patterns of thought, emotion, and behavior that result in personal distress or a significant impairment in a person's social or occupational functioning. Identifying psychopathology, then, is a social as well as a personal matter, and deciding who "has it" depends in part on how a particular culture defines *normal* and *abnormal* (Castillo, 1997).

In Western cultures, these terms are defined in such a way that a large number of people can be said to display some form of psychological disorder. Surveys reveal that in any given year in the United States alone, about 57 million people, or about 30 percent of the adult population, have displayed some form of mental disorder, and that as many as 48 percent have experienced a disorder at some point in their lives (Kessler et al., 1996; Regier et al., 1993a, 1993b; Robins & Regier, 1991; U.S. Surgeon General, 1999; see Figure 15.1). In addition, about 20 percent of U.S. children display significant mental disorders in any given year (Costello et al., 1988; U.S. Surgeon General, 1999). These overall rates of mental disorder are found, with only minor variations, in all segments of U.S. society, including males and females in all ethnic groups (Peterson et al., 1993). Bear in mind that the actual rates may be higher than the percentages just cited, because major survey studies have examined fewer than half of all known psychological disorders.

These psychological disorders are enormously costly in terms of human suffering, wasted potential, economic burden, and lost resources (Druss, Rosenheck, & Sledge, 2000; Lopez & Murray, 1998; Lyons & McLoughlin, 2001). In this chapter we discuss how abnormality is defined and classified. We also describe the major categories of psychological disorders, along with some of their possible causes, and we examine legal issues related to psychopathology.

psychopathology Patterns of thinking, feeling, and behaving that are maladaptive, disruptive, or uncomfortable for the person affected or for those with whom he or she comes in contact.

figure 15.1
Prevalence of Specific Psychological Disorders

Several large-scale surveys of adults throughout the United States revealed that about 30 percent of them experience some form of mental disorder in any given year, and that almost half of them have displayed a disorder at some time in life. The data shown here summarize these findings by category of disorder. The figures are somewhat lower if only the more severe cases are counted (Narrow et al., 2002), but these disorders still pose major problems for society. Worldwide, over 400 million people suffer from some form of psychological disorder (World Health Organization, 2001).

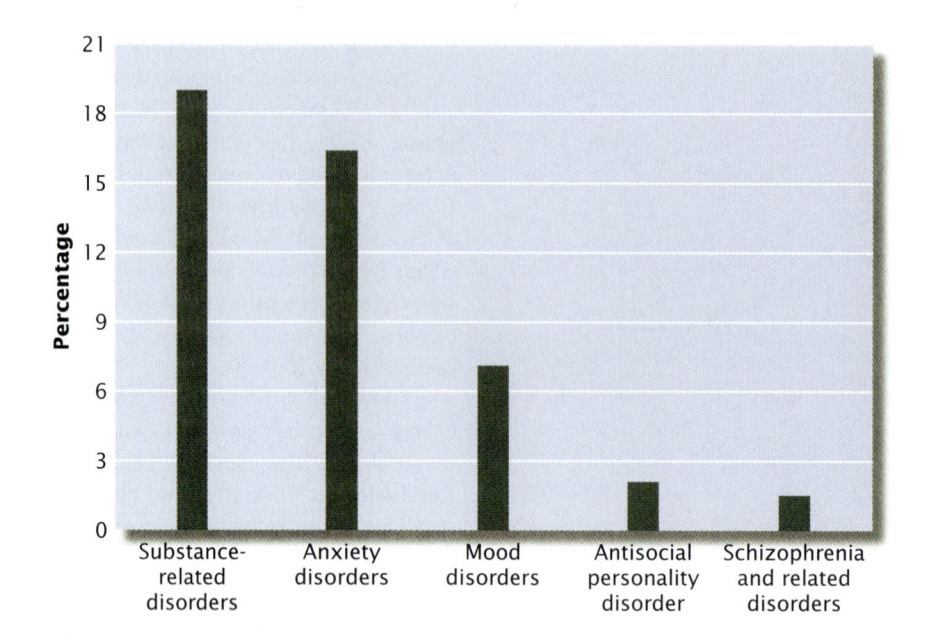

Defining Psychological Disorders

A woman's husband dies, and in her grief she stays in bed all day, weeping, refusing to eat, at times holding "conversations" with him. In India, a Hindu holy man on a pilgrimage rolls along the ground across a thousand miles of deserts and mountains, pelted by monsoon rains, until he reaches the sacred place he seeks. Eight percent of adults in the United States say they have seen a UFO (CNN/Time, 1997), and hundreds of people around the world claim to have been abducted by space aliens (Appelle et al., 2000). These examples and countless others raise the question of where to draw the line between normality and abnormality, between eccentricity and mental disorder (Kanner, 1995).

What Is Abnormal?

There are several criteria for judging whether people's thinking, emotions, or behaviors are abnormal. Each criterion has value, but also some flaws.

Infrequency
If we define *normality* as what most people do, an obvious criterion for abnormality is *statistical infrequency*—that which is unusual. By this criterion, the few people who believe that space aliens are stealing their thoughts would be judged abnormal; the many people who worry about becoming victims of crime or terrorism would not. Statistical infrequency alone is a poor criterion for abnormality, however, because some characteristics that appear only rarely—creative genius, extraordinary language skills, or world-class athletic ability, for example—may be highly valued. Further, because this definition implies that conformity with the majority is normal, equating rarity with abnormality can result in the oppression of nonconformists who express minority views in a society—as is reportedly occurring in China, for example (Eckholm, 2001). Finally, just how rare must a behavior be to warrant the designation of "abnormal"? The dividing line is not easy to locate.

Norm Violation
Abnormality can also be defined in terms of whether someone violates social norms—the cultural rules that tell us how we should and should not behave in various situations, especially in relation to others (see the chapter on social influence). According to this *norm violation* criterion, when

Is This Man Abnormal? This photo might have made you cringe. But whether unusual individuals are labeled "abnormal" and perhaps given treatment for psychological disorder depends on a number of factors, including how *abnormality* is defined by the culture in which they live, who is most directly affected by their behavior, and how much distress they suffer or cause.

people behave in ways that are bizarre, unusual, or disturbing enough to violate social norms, they may be described as abnormal.

Like the other criteria, however, norm violation alone is an inadequate measure of abnormality. For one thing, some norm violations are better characterized as eccentric or illegal than as abnormal (Weeks & Weeks, 1995). People who bathe infrequently or who stand too close during conversation violate social norms, but are they abnormal or merely annoying? Further, whose norms are we talking about? Social norms vary across cultures, subcultures, and historical eras, so behaviors that qualify as abnormal in one part of the world might be perfectly acceptable elsewhere.

Personal Suffering Another criterion for abnormality is *personal suffering*. In fact, experiencing distress is the criterion that people often use in deciding that their psychological problems are severe enough to require treatment. But personal suffering alone is an inadequate criterion for abnormality because it does not take into account the fact that some people's excessive distress may result from events or behaviors that are not pathological (e.g., the death of a loved one, or being homosexual). Conversely, people who display psychological disorders may experience little or no distress if the disorders have impaired their ability to recognize how maladaptive their behavior is. Those who sexually abuse children, for example, create far more distress in victims and their families than they suffer themselves.

Behavior in Context: A Practical Approach

Because no single criterion is entirely adequate for identifying abnormality, mental health practitioners and researchers tend to adopt a *practical approach* that combines aspects of all the criteria we've discussed. They consider the *content* of behavior (i.e., what the person does); the sociocultural *context* in which the person's behavior occurs; and the *consequences* of the behavior for that person, as well as for others. This practical approach pays special attention to whether a person's thoughts, behavior, or emotions cause **impaired functioning**—that is, difficulty in fulfilling appropriate and expected family, social, and work-related roles (U.S. Surgeon General, 1999; Wakefield, 1999).

What is "appropriate" and "expected" depends on age, gender, and culture, as well as on the particular situation and historical era in which people find themselves. For example, the same short attention span that is considered normal in a two-year-old would be considered inappropriate and problematic in an adult. There are gender-specific norms as well. In some countries, for example, it is more appropriate for women than for men to display emotion. Kisses, tears of happiness, and long embraces are common when women greet each other after a long absence; men tend to simply shake hands or, at most, hug briefly. Because of cultural differences, hearing a dead relative's voice calling from the afterlife would be more acceptable in certain North American Indian tribes than among, say, the families of suburban Toronto. Situational factors are important, too. Falling to the floor and "speaking in tongues" is considered appropriate, even desirable, during the worship services of certain religious groups, but the same behavior would be inappropriate, and a sign of disorder, in a college classroom. Finally, judgments about behavior are shaped by changes in social trends and cultural values. For example, the American Psychiatric Association once listed homosexuality as a mental disorder but dropped this category from its *Diagnostic and Statistical Manual of Mental Disorders* in 1973. In taking this step, it was responding to changing views of homosexuality that were prompted in part by the political and educational efforts of gay and lesbian rights groups.

In summary, it is difficult, and probably impossible, to define a specific set of behaviors that everyone, everywhere, will agree constitutes abnormality (Lilienfeld & Marino, 1999; Wakefield, 1999). The practical approach defines abnormality as including those patterns of thought, behavior, and emotional reaction that significantly impair people's functioning within their culture (Wakefield, 1992).

LINKAGES (a link to Social Influence)

impaired functioning Difficulty in fulfilling appropriate and expected family, social, and work-related roles.

Explaining Psychological Disorders

Since the dawn of civilization, people throughout the world have tried to understand the causes of psychological disorder. The earliest explanations of abnormal behavior focused on possession by gods or demons. Disordered people were seen either as innocent victims of evil spirits or as social or moral deviants suffering supernatural punishment. In Europe during the late Middle Ages, for example, disbelief in established religious doctrine and other unusual behaviors were viewed as the work of the devil or other evil beings. Hundreds of "witches"—mostly women—were burned at the stake, and exorcisms were performed to rid people of their demons. Supernatural explanations of psychological disorders are still invoked today in many cultures around the world—including certain ethnic and religious subcultures in North America (Nickell, 2001; Tagliabue, 1999).

The Biopsychosocial Model

More generally, however, researchers in Western cultures attribute the appearance of psychopathology to three other causes: biological factors, psychological processes, and sociocultural contexts. For many decades, there was controversy over which of these three causes is most important, but it is now widely agreed that they can all be important. Accordingly, researchers have adopted a **biopsychosocial model** in which mental disorders are seen as caused by the combination and interaction of biological, psychological, and sociocultural factors, each of which contributes in varying degrees to particular problems in particular people (U.S. Surgeon General, 1999).

Biological Factors

The *biological factors* thought to be involved in causing mental disorders include physical illnesses and disruptions or imbalances in bodily processes. This *medical model* of psychopathology has a long history. For example, the ancient Greek physician Hippocrates said that psychological disorders resulted from imbalances among four *humors,* or bodily fluids (blood, phlegm, black bile, and yellow bile). According to Hippocrates, depression ("melancholia") resulted from an excess of black bile. In ancient Chinese cultures, psychological disorders were seen as resulting from an imbalance of *yin* and *yang,* the dual forces of the universe flowing in the physical body.

As the medical model gained prominence in Western cultures after the Middle Ages, specialized hospitals for the insane were established throughout Europe. Treatment in these early asylums consisted mainly of physical restraints, laxative purges, bleeding of "excess" blood, and induced vomiting. Cold baths, fasts, and other physical discomforts were also used in efforts to "shock" patients back to normality.

The medical model gave rise to the concept of abnormality as *mental illness,* and to the view in Western cultures today that medical doctors are the proper source of help in the diagnosis and treatment of psychological disorders. The medical model is now more properly called the **neurobiological model,** because it explains psychological disorders in terms of particular disturbances in the anatomy and chemistry of the brain and in other biological processes. Neuroscientists and others who adopt a neurobiological approach study the causes and treatment of these disorders as they would study any physical illness, seeing problematic symptoms stemming primarily from an underlying illness that can be diagnosed, treated, and cured.

The importance of biological factors in psychopathology has been demonstrated in many psychological disorders (Spitzer et al., 1992). *Dementia,* for example, is characterized by a loss of intellectual functions, including disturbances in memory, personality, and cognitive abilities. The most frequent causes of dementia are progressive deterioration of the brain as a result of aging or long-term alcohol

---

biopsychosocial model A view of mental disorders as caused by a combination of interacting biological, psychological, and sociocultural factors.

neurobiological model A modern name for the medical model, in which psychological disorders are seen as reflecting disturbances in the anatomy and chemistry of the brain and in other biological processes.

An Exorcism Supernatural explanations of mental disorders, as well as supernaturally oriented cures, such as the exorcism being performed by this Buddhist monk in Thailand, remain influential among religious groups in many cultures and subcultures around the world—including some in the United States and other Western countries (Fountain, 2000).

abuse; acute diseases and disorders such as encephalitis, brain tumors, or head injury; and drug intoxication. Alzheimer's disease is a severe form of dementia seen mostly in the elderly. Research in neuroscience and behavioral genetics has also implicated biological factors in a number of other psychological disorders to be described later, including schizophrenia, bipolar disorders, some forms of anxiety disorder, and autism and attention deficit disorder (Kendler, 2001).

Psychological Processes If biological factors provide the "hardware" of mental disorders, the "software" includes psychological factors, such as our wants, needs, and emotions; our learning experiences; and our way of looking at the

Visiting Bedlam As shown here in William Hogarth's portrayal of "Bedlam" (the local name for London's St. Mary of Bethlehem hospital), most eighteenth-century asylums were little more than prisons. Notice the well-dressed visitors; in those days, members of the public could buy tickets to tour the cells and gawk at the patients.

world. The roots of this **psychological model** of mental disorders can be seen in ancient Greek literature and drama dealing with the *psyche,* or mind—especially with the struggles of the mind to resolve inner conflicts or to overcome the effects of stressful events. These ideas gained far greater prominence in the late 1800s, when Sigmund Freud challenged the assumption that psychological disorders had only physical causes. Freud's explanations of these disorders came as part of his more general *psychodynamic* approach, described in the chapter on personality. Freud viewed psychological disorders as the result of unresolved, mostly unconscious clashes between the desires of the id and the demands of the environment and society. These conflicts, he said, begin early in childhood. Contemporary versions of the psychodynamic model—such as *object relations* theory—focus less on unconscious urges and more on the role of attachment and other early interpersonal relationships (Schultz & Schultz, 2001).

Other theories discussed in the personality chapter suggest other psychological processes that can contribute to the appearance of mental disorders. For example, *social-cognitive* theorists see most psychological disorders as the result of past learning and current situations. Just as people learn to avoid hot grills after being burned, say these theorists, bad experiences in school or a dental office can "teach" people to fear such places. Social-cognitive theorists also emphasize how learned expectations, schemas, and other mental processes discussed in the chapter on cognition and language can influence the development of disorders. Depression, for example, is seen as stemming from negative events, such as losing a job, but also from the irrational or maladaptive thoughts that people have learned in relation to these events—thoughts such as "I never do anything right."

Finally, the *humanistic* approach to personality suggests that behavior disorders appear when a person's actualizing tendency is blocked, usually by a failure to be aware of, and to express, true feelings. When this happens, the person's perceptions of reality become distorted. The greater the distortion, the more serious the psychological disorder.

Sociocultural Context Understanding the neurobiological and psychological factors that contribute to most mental disorders has proven extremely helpful in explaining those disorders. Still, these factors relate mainly to causes residing within the individual. The **sociocultural model** of disorder suggests that we cannot fully explain all forms of psychopathology without also looking outside the individual—at the social and cultural factors that form the context, or background, of abnormal behavior. Looking for causes of disorders in this *sociocultural context* means paying attention to factors such as gender, age, and marital status; the physical, social, and economic situations in which people live; and the cultural values, traditions, and expectations in which they are immersed (Evans et al., 2000; Johnson et al., 1999; Whisman, 1999). Sociocultural context influences not only what is and is not labeled "abnormal" but also who displays what kind of disorder.

Consider gender, for instance. The greater tolerance in many cultures for open expression of emotional distress among women, but not men, may contribute to the higher rates of depression seen in women compared with men (Nolen-Hoeksema, Larson, & Grayson, 1999). And the view held in many cultures that excessive alcohol consumption is less appropriate for women than for men is a sociocultural factor that may help explain higher rates of alcohol abuse among men in those cultures (Helzer et al., 1990).

Sociocultural factors also influence the form that abnormality takes. For example, schizophrenia and depression are *culture-general* disorders—appearing virtually everywhere in the world—but their specific symptoms tend to differ depending on the disordered person's cultural background (Hopper & Wanderling, 2000). In Western cultures, where emotional and physical components of disorder are generally viewed separately, symptoms of depression tend to revolve around despair and other signs of emotional distress (Kleinman, 1991). But in China and certain other

LINKAGES (a link to Learning)

psychological model A view in which mental disorder is seen as arising from psychological processes.

sociocultural model A way of looking at mental disorders in relation to gender, age, ethnicity, and other social and cultural factors.

Asian cultures where emotional and physical experiences tend to be viewed as one, a depressed person is as likely to report stomach or back pain as to complain of sadness (Brislin, 1993; Parker, Gladstone, & Chee, 2001).

There are also *culture-specific* forms of disorder. For instance, Puerto Rican and Dominican Hispanic women sometimes experience *ataques de nervios,* a unique way of reacting to stress that includes heart palpitations, shaking, shouting, nervousness, depression, and on occasion, fainting or seizure-like episodes (Spiegel, 1994). Another example can be found in Southeast Asia, southern China, and Malaysia, where a disorder called *koro* is occasionally observed. Victims of this condition, who are usually male, fear that their penis will shrivel, retract into the body, and cause death (in females, the fear relates to shriveling of the breasts). *Koro* appears only in cultures holding the specific supernatural beliefs that explain it. In such cultures, epidemics of *koro* are often triggered by economic hard times (Tseng et al., 1992).

In short, as sociocultural factors create differing social roles, stressors, opportunities, and experiences for people who differ in age, gender, and cultural traditions, they help shape the disorders and symptoms to which certain categories of people are prone, and even help shape their response to treatment. For example, among people diagnosed with the severe disorder schizophrenia, those living in a developing country are much more likely to improve than those living in a more developed country (Hopper & Wanderling, 2000). What cultural factor might be responsible for the difference in outcome we do not yet know, but these data highlight the fact that any attempt to fully explain psychological disorders must take sociocultural factors into account.

Diathesis-Stress as an Integrative Explanation

The biopsychosocial model is currently the most comprehensive and influential approach to explaining psychological disorders. It is prominent partly because it encompasses so many important causal factors, including biological imbalances, genetically inherited characteristics, brain damage, enduring psychological traits, socioculturally influenced learning experiences, stressful life events, and many more.

How do all these factors interact to actually create disorder? Most researchers believe that inherited characteristics, biological processes, and early learning experiences combine to create a predisposition, or *diathesis* (pronounced "dye-A-thuh-sis"), for a psychological disorder. Whether or not a person actually develops symptoms of disorder depends on the nature and amount of *stress* the person encounters (National Advisory Mental Health Council, 1996; U.S. Surgeon General, 1999; Zuckerman, 1999). For example, a person may have inherited a biological tendency toward depression or may have learned depressing patterns of thinking, but these predispositions may be expressed as a depressive disorder only after the person is faced with a financial crisis or suffers the loss of a loved one. If such circumstances do not occur, or if the person has adequate skills for coping with stress, depressive symptoms may never appear, or they may be quite mild.

In summary, the **diathesis-stress approach** to explaining psychological disorders assumes that biological, psychological, and sociocultural factors can predispose us toward disorder, but that it takes a certain amount of stress to actually trigger a disorder. For people with a strong diathesis, relatively mild stress might be enough to create a problem. People whose predisposition is weaker might not show signs of disorder until stress becomes extreme or prolonged. Another way to think about the notion of diathesis-stress is in terms of *risk*: The more risk factors for a disorder a person has—whether in the form of genetic tendencies, personality traits, cultural traditions, or stressful life events—the more likely it is that the person will display a form of psychological disorder associated with those risk factors.

Table 15.1 provides an example of how the diathesis-stress approach and the factors contained in the biopsychosocial model of disorder might explain a particu-

diathesis-stress approach Viewing psychological disorders as arising when a predisposition for a disorder combines with sufficient amounts of stress to trigger symptoms.

Here are the factors that would be considered by the biopsychosocial model, and combined in the diathesis-stress approach, to explain the case of José, a fifty-five-year-old electronics technician. A previously healthy and vigorous father of two adult children, he was forced to take medical leave because of a series of sudden, uncontrollable panic attacks in which he experienced dizziness, heart palpitations, sweating, and fear of impending death. The attacks also kept him from his favorite pastime, scuba diving, but he has been able to maintain a part-time computer business out of his home. (Panic disorder is discussed in more detail later in this chapter; the outcome of this case is described in the chapter on treatment of psychological disorders.)

table 15.1
Explaining Psychopathology

Explanatory Domain	Possible Contributing Factors
Neurobiological/medical	José may have organic disorders (e.g., genetic tendency toward anxiety; brain tumor, endocrine dysfunction; neurotransmitter imbalance).
Psychological: psychodynamic	José has unconscious conflicts and desires. Instinctual impulses are breaking through ego defenses into consciousness, causing panic.
Psychological: social-cognitive	Physical stress symptoms are interpreted as signs of serious illness or impending death. Panic is rewarded by avoidance of work stress and the opportunity to stay home.
Psychological: humanistic	José fails to recognize his genuine feelings about work and his place in life, and he fears expressing himself.
Sociocultural	A culturally based belief that "a man should not show weakness" amplifies the intensity of stress reactions and delays José's decision to seek help.
Diathesis-stress summary	José has a biological (possibly genetic) predisposition to be overly responsive to stressors. The stress of work and extra activity exceeds his capacity to cope and triggers panic as a stress response.

lar case of psychopathology. Later in this chapter, you will see how the biopsychosocial model and the diathesis-stress approach are applied to understanding the causes of several other psychological disorders.

Classifying Psychological Disorders

Although definitions of abnormality differ somewhat within and across cultures, there is a set of culture-general and culture-specific behavior patterns that characterize what most mental health professionals consider to be psychopathology. Most of these behavior patterns qualify as disorders because they result in impaired functioning, a main criterion of the practical approach to defining abnormality. It has long been the goal of those who study abnormal behavior to establish a system of classifying such patterns in order to understand and deal with them.

In 1952 the American Psychiatric Association published the first edition of what has become the "official" North American diagnostic classification system, the *Diagnostic and Statistical Manual of Mental Disorders (DSM)*. Each subsequent edition of the *DSM* has included more categories of disorders. The latest editions, *DSM-IV* and *DSM-IV-TR* (which contains some text revisions), include more than three hundred specific diagnostic labels (American Psychiatric Association, 1994, 2000).

Mental health professionals outside North America diagnose mental disorders using the classification systems that appear in the tenth edition of the World Health Organization's *International Classification of Diseases (ICD-10)* and its companion volume, the second edition of the *International Classification of Impairments, Disabilities and Handicaps (ICIDH-2)*. To facilitate international communication about—and cross-cultural research on—psychopathology, *DSM-IV* was designed to be compatible with these manuals, and efforts are under way to remove inconsistencies existing between the systems (DeAngelis, 2001).

A Classification System: *DSM-IV*

DSM-IV describes the abnormal patterns of thinking, emotion, and behavior that define various mental disorders. For each disorder, the *DSM* provides specific criteria outlining the conditions that must be met before a person can be diagnosed as having that disorder. Diagnosticians using *DSM-IV* can evaluate troubled people on as many as five dimensions, or *axes*. In keeping with the biopsychosocial model, evaluations on all relevant dimensions are combined to create a broad outline of the person's biological and psychological problems, as well as of any sociocultural factors that might contribute to them. As shown in Table 15.2, major mental disorders, such as schizophrenia or major depressive disorder, are recorded on Axis I, whereas evidence of personality disorders or mental retardation are noted on Axis II. Any medical conditions that might be important in understanding the person's cognitive, emotional, or behavioral problems are listed on Axis III. On Axis IV the diagnostician notes any psychosocial and environmental problems (such as the loss of a loved one, physical or sexual abuse, discrimination, unemployment, poverty, homelessness, inadequate health care, or conflict with religious or cultural traditions) that are important for understanding the person's psychological problems. Finally, a rating (from 100 down to 1) of the person's current level of psychological, social, and occupational functioning appears on Axis V. Here is a sample *DSM-IV* diagnosis for a person who received labels on all five axes:

Axis I   Major depressive disorder, single episode; alcohol abuse.

Axis II   Dependent personality disorder.

Axis III Alcoholic cirrhosis of the liver.

Axis IV   Problems with primary support group (death of spouse).

Axis V   Global assessment of functioning = 50.

The terms neurosis and psychosis are no longer major categories in the *DSM* because they are not specific enough; however, some mental health professionals still sometimes use them as shorthand descriptions. *Neurosis* refers to conditions in which some form of anxiety is the major characteristic. *Psychosis* refers to conditions involving more extreme problems that leave people "out of touch with reality" or unable to function on a daily basis. The disorders once gathered under these headings now appear in various Axis I categories in the *DSM-IV*.

Further changes may appear in *DSM-V*, a new edition of the *DSM* that is currently under development. Some experts are proposing, for example, that future diagnoses should consist not only of specific labels, such as "major depression," but also of symptom clusters or symptom dimensions that would be rated in terms of severity (Vollebergh et al., 2001; Widiger & Clark, 2000). This *dimensional approach* would allow each symptom a person displays to be recognized and described, whether or not it is usually associated with a particular diagnostic category. For example, if a person displays symptoms of depression as well as anxiety, both would receive diagnostic attention. By rating the severity of the depressive mood and the intensity of the anxiety, the diagnostician using *DSM-V* would create an even more detailed picture of the problems a person is experiencing.

Purposes and Problems of Diagnosis

A major goal in diagnosing psychological disorders is to determine the nature of people's problems so that the characteristics of those problems can be described and understood, and the most appropriate treatment methods can be chosen. Diagnoses

table 15.2
The *Diagnostic and Statistical Manual of Mental Disorders (DSM)* of the American Psychiatric Association

Axis I (Clinical Syndromes)

1. ***Disorders usually first diagnosed in infancy, childhood, or adolescence.*** Problems such as hyperactivity, childhood fears, conduct disorders, frequent bed-wetting or soiling, and other problems in normal social and behavioral development. Autistic disorder (severe impairment in social, behavioral, and language development), as well as learning disorders.

2. ***Delirium, dementia, and amnestic and other cognitive disorders.*** Problems caused by physical deterioration of the brain due to aging, disease, drugs or other chemicals, or other possible unknown causes. These problems can appear as an inability to "think straight" (delirium) or as loss of memory and other intellectual functions (dementia).

3. ***Substance-related disorders.*** Psychological, behavioral, physical, social, or legal problems caused by dependence on, or abuse of, a variety of chemical substances, including alcohol, heroin, cocaine, amphetamines, hallucinogens, marijuana, and tobacco.

4. ***Schizophrenia and other psychotic disorders.*** Severe conditions characterized by abnormalities in thinking, perception, emotion, movement, and motivation that greatly interfere with daily functioning. Problems involving false beliefs (delusions).

5. ***Mood disorders (also called affective disorders).*** Severe disturbances of mood, especially depression, overexcitement (mania), or alternating episodes of each extreme (as in bipolar disorder).

6. ***Anxiety disorders.*** Specific fears (phobias); panic attacks; generalized feelings of dread; rituals of thought and action (obsessive-compulsive disorder) aimed at controlling anxiety; and problems caused by traumatic events, such as rape or military combat (see the chapter on health, stress, and coping for more on posttraumatic stress disorder).

7. ***Somatoform disorders.*** Physical symptoms, such as paralysis and blindness, that have no physical cause. Unusual preoccupation with physical health or with nonexistent physical problems (hypochondriasis, somatization disorder, pain disorder).

8. ***Factitious disorders.*** False mental disorders, which are intentionally produced to satisfy some psychological need.

9. ***Dissociative disorders.*** Psychologically caused problems of consciousness and self-identification—e.g., loss of memory (amnesia) or the development of more than one identity (multiple personality).

10. ***Sexual and gender identity disorders.*** Problems of (a) finding sexual arousal through unusual objects or situations (like shoes or exposing oneself), (b) unsatisfactory sexual activity (sexual dysfunction; see the chapter on motivation and emotion), or (c) identifying with the opposite gender.

11. ***Eating disorders.*** Problems associated with eating too little (anorexia nervosa) or binge eating followed by self-induced vomiting (bulimia nervosa). (See the chapter on motivation and emotion.)

12. ***Sleep disorders.*** Severe problems involving the sleep-wake cycle, especially an inability to sleep well at night or to stay awake during the day. (See the chapter on consciousness.)

13. ***Impulse control disorders.*** Compulsive gambling, stealing, or fire setting.

14. ***Adjustment disorders.*** Failure to adjust to, or deal well with, such stressors as divorce, financial problems, family discord, or other unhappy life events.

Axis II (Personality Disorders and Mental Retardation)

1. ***Personality disorders.*** Diagnostic labels given to individuals who may or may not receive an Axis I diagnosis but who show lifelong behavior patterns that are unsatisfactory to them or that disturb other people. These patterns may involve unusual suspiciousness, unusual ways of thinking, self-centeredness, shyness, overdependency, excessive concern with neatness and detail, or overemotionality, among others.

2. ***Mental retardation.*** As described in the chapter on cognitive abilities, the label of mental retardation is applied to individuals whose measured IQ is less than about 70 *and* who fail to display the skills at daily living, communication, and other tasks expected of people their age.

Axis I of the fourth edition *(DSM-IV)* lists the major categories of mental disorders. Personality disorders and mental retardation are listed on Axis II.

are also important for research on the causes of mental disorders. If researchers can accurately and reliably classify people into particular disorder categories, they will have a better chance of spotting genetic features, biological abnormalities, cognitive processes, and environmental experiences that people in the same category might share. And finding that people in one diagnostic category share a set of features that differs from those seen in people in other categories could provide clues to the relative importance of these features in the development of each disorder.

How good is the diagnostic system now in use? One way to evaluate *DSM-IV* is to consider *interrater reliability,* the degree to which different mental health professionals give the same person the same diagnostic label. Some studies indicate that interrater agreement is as high as 83 percent for schizophrenia and mood disorders; agreement on many other Axis I categories is also high (e.g., Foa & Kozak, 1995; Lahey et al., 1994; Nathan & Langenbucher, 1999). Still other categories, such as Axis II personality disorders, remain more difficult to diagnose reliably (Zanarini et al., 2000).

Overall, interrater agreement appears highest when diagnosis is based on structured or semistructured interviews that systematically address various areas of functioning and provide uniform guidelines for interpretation of the answers that people give (Rogers, 1995; Widiger & Sanderson, 1995). In one recent example, diagnosticians using a structured diagnostic interview schedule achieved good to excellent agreement about cases of anxiety and mood disorders (Brown et al., 2001).

Do diagnostic labels give accurate information that guides correct inferences about people? This *validity* question is difficult to answer because it is hard to find a fully acceptable standard for accuracy: Should one diagnosis be evaluated by comparing it with the judgments of experts? Or should it be judged by how well it predicts the diagnosed person's behavior? Still, there is evidence to support the validity of most *DSM* criteria (Clark, Watson, & Reynolds, 1995). And validity is likely to improve further as diagnostic labels—and the diagnostic system—are refined in *DSM-V* to reflect what researchers are learning about the characteristics, causes, courses, and cultural factors involved in various disorders.

The diagnostic system is far from perfect, however (Widiger & Sankis, 2000). First, people's problems often do not fit neatly into a single category. Second, the same symptoms may appear as part of more than one disorder. Third, diagnostic judgments are to some extent subjective, raising the possibility that personal bias might creep into the system. All of these factors can lead to misdiagnosis in some cases. Concern over this possibility is especially relevant as the nations of North America and Western Europe become increasingly multicultural, and as diagnosticians encounter people whose cultural backgrounds they may not fully understand or appreciate. Psychiatrist Thomas Szasz (pronounced "zaws") and other critics of the medical model (e.g., Caplan, 1995; Kutchins & Kirk, 1997) also argue that labeling people instead of describing problems is dehumanizing, because it ignores features that make each person unique. Calling people "schizophrenics" or "alcoholics," Szasz says, may actually encourage the behaviors associated with these labels and undermine the confidence of clients (and therapists) about the chances of improvement (Szasz, 1987).

In other words, it is unlikely that any shorthand label can fully describe a person's problems or predict exactly how that person will behave in the future. All that can be reasonably expected of a diagnostic system is that it allows informative, general descriptions of the types of problems displayed by people who have been placed in various categories.

THINKING CRITICALLY

Is Psychological Diagnosis Biased?

Some researchers and clinicians worry that problems with the reliability and validity of the diagnostic system are due partly to bias in its construction and use. They point out, for example, that if the research underlying the diagnostic criteria for a certain disorder focuses mainly on one culture, one gender, one ethnic group, or one age group, those criteria might not apply widely enough. Moreover, because diagnosticians, like other people, hold expectations and make assumptions about males versus females, and about individuals from differing cultures or ethnic groups, those cognitive biases could color their judgments. This "prejudging" process could lead them to apply diagnostic criteria in ways that are subtly, but significantly, different from one case to the next (Garb, 1997; Hartung & Widiger, 1998).

What am I being asked to believe or accept?

Here, we focus on ethnicity as a possible source of bias in diagnosing psychopathology. It is of special interest because there is evidence that, like social class and gender, ethnicity is an important sociocultural factor in the development of mental disorder. So the assertion to be considered is that clinicians in the United States base their diagnoses partly on clients' ethnic background and, more specifically, that there is bias in diagnosing African Americans.

What evidence is available to support the assertion?

Several facts suggest the possibility of ethnic bias in psychological diagnosis. African Americans receive the diagnosis of schizophrenia more frequently than European Americans do (Manderscheid & Barrett, 1987; Pavkov, Lewis, & Lyons, 1989). Further, relative to their presence in the general population, African Americans are overrepresented in public mental hospitals, where the most serious forms of disorder are seen, and underrepresented in private hospitals and outpatient clinics, where less severe problems are treated (Lindsey & Paul, 1989; Snowden & Cheung, 1990; U.S. Surgeon General, 1999).

Are there alternative ways of interpreting the evidence?

Differences among ethnic groups in diagnosis or treatment do not automatically indicate bias based on ethnicity. Perhaps real differences in psychological functioning are associated with different ethnic groups. For example, if, relative to other groups, African Americans are exposed to more risk factors for disorder, such as poverty, violence, or other major stressors, they could be more vulnerable to more serious forms of mental disorder. And poverty, not diagnostic bias, could be responsible for the fact that African Americans more often seek help at less expensive public hospitals than at more expensive private ones.

What additional evidence would help to evaluate the alternatives?

Do African Americans actually display more signs of mental disorder, or do diagnosticians just perceive them as more disordered? One way of approaching this question is to conduct experiments in which diagnosticians assign labels to clients on the basis of case histories, test scores, and the like. In some studies, the cases are selected so that pairs of clients show about the same objective amount of disorder, but one member of the pair is identified as European American and the other as African American. In other studies, the same case materials, identified as representing either African American or European American patients, are presented to different diagnosticians. Bias in diagnosis would be suggested if, for example, patients identified as African American were seen as more seriously disordered than others.

Most studies of this type have found little or no ethnic bias (e.g., Littlewood, 1992). These results are difficult to interpret, however, because the diagnosticians may be aware of the purpose of the study, and so may go out of their way to be unbiased (Abreu, 1999). In fact, researchers have found evidence of some diagnostic bias against African Americans when clinicians were unaware of the purpose of the research (e.g., Baskin, Bluestone, & Nelson, 1981; Jones, 1982).

Bias has also appeared in studies aimed at identifying the factors influencing clinicians' diagnostic judgments following extensive interviews with patients. One study conducted in a hospital setting found that in arriving at their diagnoses, psychiatrists were more likely to attribute hallucinations and paranoid thinking to African American patients than to patients who were not African American. Symptoms of mood disorders were more likely to be attributed to those who were not African American (Trierweiler et al., 2000). As noted earlier, these differences

---

anxiety disorder A condition in which intense feelings of apprehension are long-standing and disruptive.

could reflect ethnic differences in the rate of disorder in the population, but when people were interviewed in their own homes as part of large-scale mental health surveys, the diagnosis of schizophrenia was given only slightly more often to African Americans than to European Americans (Robins & Regier, 1991; Snowden & Cheung, 1990). In other words, ethnic bias is suggested, at least for some diagnoses, for patients who are evaluated in mental hospitals (Trierweiler et al., 2000).

● What conclusions are most reasonable?

Just as the diagnostic system is imperfect, so are those who use it. Cognitive biases and stereotypes affect human thinking to some extent in virtually every social situation (see the chapters on cognition and language and on social cognition), so it should not be surprising that they operate in diagnosis as well. But diagnostic bias does not necessarily reflect deliberate discrimination. At least one study has shown that, like the processes of prejudice discussed in the chapter on social cognition, diagnostic bias based on ethnicity can operate unconsciously, without the diagnostician's being aware of it (Abreu, 1999). So no matter how precisely researchers specify the criteria for assigning diagnostic labels, those biases and stereotypes are likely to threaten the objectivity of the diagnostic process (Funtowicz & Widiger, 1999; Trierweiler et al., 2000).

Minimizing diagnostic bias requires a better understanding of it. Toward this end, Hope Landrine (1991) suggests that diagnosticians focus more intently than ever on the fact that their concepts of "normality" and "abnormality" are affected by sociocultural values that they may not share with a given client. And Steven Lopez (1989) argues that diagnosticians must become more aware that the same cognitive shortcuts and biases (see the chapter on cognition and language) that affect everyone else's thinking and decision making can impair their own clinical judgments. In fact, studies of memory, problem solving, decision making, social attributions, and other aspects of culture and cognition may turn out to be key ingredients in reducing bias in the diagnosis of psychological disorders. Meanwhile, perhaps the best way to counteract clinicians' cognitive shortcomings is to teach them to base their diagnoses solely on published diagnostic criteria and statistically validated decision rules (aided, perhaps, by specialized computer programs) rather than relying on their potentially biased clinical impressions (Garb, 1997; Nietzel et al., 2003).

We do not have the space to cover all the *DSM-IV* categories, but we will sample several of the most prevalent and socially significant ones. As you read, try not to catch "medical student's disease." Just as medical students often think they have the symptoms of every illness they read about, some psychology students worry that their behavior (or that of a relative or friend) signals a mental disorder. Remember that everyone has problems sometimes. Before deciding that you or someone you know needs psychological help, consider whether the content, context, and functional impairment associated with the behavior would qualify it as abnormal according to the criteria of the practical approach.

Anxiety Disorders

If you have ever been tense before an exam, a date, or a job interview, you have some idea of what anxiety feels like. Increased heart rate, sweating, rapid breathing, a dry mouth, and a sense of dread are common components of anxiety. Brief episodes of moderate anxiety are a normal part of life for most people. But when anxiety is so intense and long-lasting that it impairs a person's daily functioning, it is called an **anxiety disorder.**

Phobia is the Greek word for "morbid fear," after the Greek god Phobos. Phobias are usually named using the Greek word for the feared object or situation, followed by the suffix *-phobia*.

table 15.3
Some Phobias

Name	Feared Stimulus	Name	Feared Stimulus
Acrophobia	Heights	Aerophobia	Flying
Claustrophobia	Enclosed places	Entomophobia	Insects
Hematophobia	Blood	Gamophobia	Marriage
Gephyrophobia	Crossing a bridge	Ophidiphobia	Snakes
Kenophobia	Empty rooms	Xenophobia	Strangers
Cynophobia	Dogs	Melissophobia	Bees

Types of Anxiety Disorders

Here we discuss four types of anxiety disorders: *phobia, generalized anxiety disorder, panic disorder,* and *obsessive-compulsive disorder.* Another type, called *post-traumatic stress disorder,* is described in the chapter on health, stress, and coping. Together, these are the most common psychological disorders in North America.

Phobia

An intense, irrational fear of an object or situation that is not likely to be dangerous is called a **phobia.** People who experience phobias usually realize that their fears are groundless, but the resulting discomfort and avoidance of the object or event may greatly interfere with daily life. Thousands of phobias have been described (see Table 15.3).

DSM-IV classifies phobias into specific, social, and agoraphobia subtypes. **Specific phobias** involve fear and avoidance of heights, blood, animals, automobile or air travel, and other specific stimuli and situations. In the United States, they are the most prevalent of the anxiety disorders, affecting 7 to 10 percent of adults and children (Kessler et al., 1994; Robins et al., 1984; U.S. Surgeon General, 1999). Here is an example:

> Mr. L. was a fifty-year-old office worker who became terrified whenever he had to drive over a bridge. For years, he avoided bridges by taking roundabout ways to and from work, and he refused to be a passenger in anyone else's car, lest they use a bridge. Even this very inconvenient adjustment failed when Mr. L. was transferred to a position requiring frequent automobile trips, many of which were over bridges. He refused the transfer and lost his job.

Social phobias involve anxiety about being negatively evaluated by others or acting in a way that is embarrassing or humiliating. The anxiety is so intense and persistent that it impairs the person's normal functioning. Common social phobias are fear of public speaking or performance ("stage fright"), fear of eating in front of others, and fear of using public restrooms (Kleinknecht, 2000). *Generalized social phobia* is a more severe form in which fear occurs in virtually all social situations (Mannuzza et al., 1995). Sociocultural factors can alter the form of social phobias. For example, in Japan, where cultural training emphasizes group-oriented values and goals, a common social phobia is *tai-jin kyofu sho,* fear of embarrassing those around you (Kleinknecht, 1994).

Agoraphobia is a strong fear of being away from a safe place, such as home; of being away from a familiar person, such as a spouse or close friend; or of being in

---

phobia A strong, irrational fear of an object or situation that does not objectively justify such a reaction.

specific phobias Phobias that involve fear and avoidance of heights, animals, and other specific stimuli and situations.

social phobias Strong, irrational fears relating to social situations.

agoraphobia A strong fear of being away from the security of home.

It's a Long Way Down Almost everyone is afraid of something, but as many as 10 percent of U.S. adults suffer from a specific phobia, in which fear interferes significantly with daily functioning. For example, people with acrophobia (fear of heights) would not do well in a job that requires being in this high position.

a place from which departure might be difficult or where help may be unavailable. Attempts to leave home lead to intense anxiety, so people who suffer severe agoraphobia may become housebound, seldom even trying to go out alone. Theaters, shopping malls, public transportation, and other potentially crowded places are particularly threatening. Most individuals who suffer from agoraphobia have a history of panic attacks, which we describe below. Their intense fear of public places occurs partly because they don't want to risk triggering an attack by going where they had one before or where they feel an attack would be dangerous or embarrassing.

Like other phobias in Western cultures, agoraphobia is more often reported by women. However, in other cultures, such as India, where being a housebound woman is considered less unusual than in the United States, those diagnosed as agoraphobic tend to be male (Raguram & Bhide, 1985). Although agoraphobia occurs less frequently than specific phobias (affecting about 5 percent of the population in the United States), it is the phobia that most often leads people to seek treatment, mainly because it so severely disrupts everyday life (U.S. Surgeon General, 1999).

Generalized Anxiety Disorder

Excessive and long-lasting anxiety that is not focused on any particular object or situation marks **generalized anxiety disorder**. Because the problem occurs in virtually all situations and because the person cannot pinpoint its source, this type of anxiety is sometimes called *free-floating anxiety*. For weeks at a time, the person feels anxious and worried, sure that some disaster is about to happen. The person becomes jumpy and irritable; sound sleep is impossible. Fatigue, inability to concentrate, and physiological signs of anxiety are also common. Generalized anxiety disorder affects about 3.4 percent of the U.S. population in any given year, and about 5 percent of the population at some point in their lives (Kessler et al., 1994; U.S. Surgeon General, 1999). It is more common in women, often accompanying other problems such as depression or substance abuse (Wittchen et al., 1994).

Panic Disorder

For some people, anxiety takes the form of **panic disorder**. Like the man described in Table 15.1, people suffering from panic disorder experience recurrent, terrifying *panic attacks* that seem to come without warning or obvi-

generalized anxiety disorder A condition that involves anxiety that is not focused on any particular object or situation.

panic disorder An anxiety disorder involving sudden panic attacks.

Anxiety and Depression People who experience anxiety disorders—particularly panic disorder, generalized anxiety disorder, or posttraumatic stress disorder—are likely to display some other mental disorder as well, most often depression (Kaufman & Charney, 2000; Roy-Byrne et al., 2000). Accordingly, the next edition of the *DSM* may include a new category, called *mixed anxiety-depression disorder*, to identify people whose symptoms of anxiety and depression combine to impair their daily functioning (Barlow & Campbell, 2000; Widiger & Clark, 2000).

ous cause. These attacks are marked by intense heart palpitations, pressure or pain in the chest, dizziness or unsteadiness, sweating, and a feeling of faintness. Often, victims believe they are having a heart attack. They may worry constantly about suffering future panic episodes and thus curtail activities to avoid possible embarrassment (Carter & Barlow, 1995). (As noted earlier, fear of experiencing panic attacks while alone or away from home can lead to agoraphobia.) Panic disorder may become a chronic problem, with periods of improvement followed by recurrence (Ehlers, 1995). As many as 30 percent of the people in the United States have experienced at least one panic attack within the past year (Ehlers, 1995), but only about 1.6 percent of the population develops full-blown panic disorder in any given year (Ehlers, 1995; U.S. Surgeon General, 1999). Here is one example:

> *Geri, a thirty-two-year-old nurse, had her first panic attack while driving on a freeway. Afterward, she would not drive on freeways. Her next attack occurred while with a patient and a doctor in a small examining room. A sense of impending doom flooded over her, and she burst out of the office and into the parking lot, where she felt immediate relief. From then on, fear of another attack made it impossible for her to tolerate any close quarters, including crowded shopping malls. She eventually quit her job because of terror of the examining rooms.*

Obsessive-Compulsive Disorder

Anxiety is also at the root of **obsessive-compulsive disorder (OCD)**, which affects about 2.4 percent of the U.S. population in any given year (U.S. Surgeon General, 1999). Like Mark, whose story opened this chapter, people displaying obsessive-compulsive disorder are plagued by persistent, upsetting, and unwanted thoughts—called *obsessions*—that often center on the possibility of infection, contamination, or doing harm to oneself or others. They do not actually carry out harmful acts, but the obsessive thoughts motivate ritualistic, repetitive behaviors—called *compulsions*—that the person performs in an effort to avoid some dreaded outcome or to reduce feelings of anxiety associated with the obsessions (Foa & Kozak, 1995). For example, Mark engaged in incessant, ritualized cleaning to protect himself from infection; other common compulsions include rituals such as checking locks; repeating words, images, or numbers; counting things; or arranging objects "just so." Obsessions and compulsions are much more intense than the familiar experience of having a repetitive thought or tune "in the back of your mind" or rechecking that a door is locked. In obsessive-compulsive

obsessive-compulsive disorder (OCD) An anxiety disorder involving repetitive thoughts and urges to perform certain rituals.

disorder, the obsessions and compulsions are intense, disturbing, and often bizarre intrusions that can severely impair daily activities. (*DSM-IV* defines compulsions as taking up more than one hour a day.) Many people who display this disorder recognize that their thoughts and actions are irrational, but they still experience severe agitation and anxiety if they try to interrupt their obsessions or give up their compulsive behaviors.

Causes of Anxiety Disorders

As with all the forms of psychopathology we will consider, the exact causes of anxiety disorders are a matter of debate. However, there is good evidence that biological, psychological, and social factors all contribute. Biological predispositions, distortions in thinking, and certain learning experiences appear to be particularly important (U.S. Surgeon General, 1999).

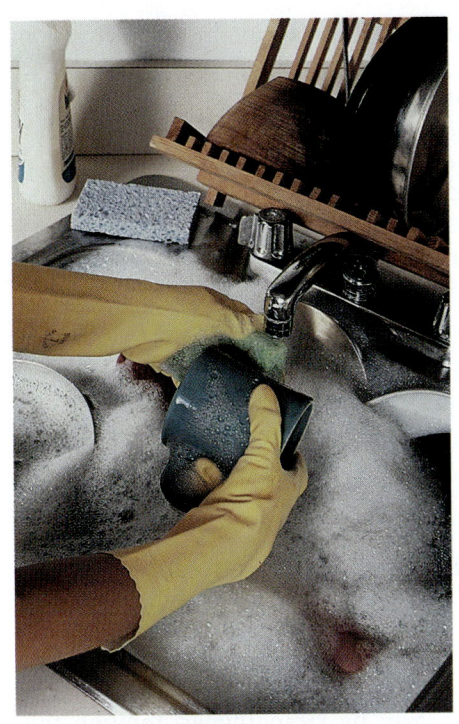

A Cleaning Compulsion Obsessive-compulsive disorder is diagnosed when a culturally expected degree of cleanliness evolves into an obsessive preoccupation with germs and a life-disrupting compulsion to clean things. Although learning and stress appear to play the major role in shaping and triggering this and other anxiety disorders, biological factors, including genetically inherited characteristics and deficiencies in certain neurotransmitters (see the chapter on biological aspects of psychology), may result in an oversensitive nervous system and a predisposition toward anxiety.

Biological Factors
Genetic influences on anxiety disorders are suggested by research showing that if one identical twin has an anxiety disorder, the other is more likely also to have an anxiety disorder than is the case in nonidentical twin pairs (Hettema, Neale, & Kendler, 2001; Kendler et al., 1992). In fact, most anxiety disorders, including panic disorder, obsessive-compulsive disorder, and generalized social phobia, appear to run in families (Kendler et al., 1995, 2001; Pauls et al., 1995; Skre et al., 2000; Wittchen et al., 1994). Some people who display these disorders may have inherited an autonomic nervous system that is oversensitive to stress, thus predisposing them to react with anxiety to a wide range of situations (Zinbarg & Barlow, 1996). There may be more specific predispositions as well. One study has found that identical twins were more likely than other siblings to share phobias of small animals and social situations, but not of heights or enclosed spaces (Skre et al., 2000).

A predisposition for developing anxiety disorders may also stem from abnormalities in the brain's neurotransmitter systems, which are discussed in the chapter on biological aspects of psychology. Excessive activity of norepinephrine in certain parts of the brain has been linked with panic disorder, and dysregulation of serotonin has been associated with obsessive-compulsive disorder. In addition, there is evidence that anxiety-generating neural impulses may run unchecked when the neurotransmitter GABA is prevented from exerting its normal inhibitory influence in certain neural pathways (Friedman, Clark, & Gershon, 1992; Zorumski & Isenberg, 1991).

Something may also be physically wrong in people with panic disorder. Unlike other people, many of these individuals have a panic episode after receiving an injection of lactate or caffeine, inhaling carbon dioxide, or taking yohimbine (a drug that blocks one type of norepinephrine receptor) (Papp et al., 1993). Because these substances all stimulate brainstem areas that control the autonomic nervous system, one hypothesis is that panic-disorder patients have hypersensitive brainstem mechanisms and are therefore especially prone to fear responses (Gorman et al., 1989).

Cognitive Factors
Although biological predispositions may set the stage for anxiety disorders, most researchers agree that environmental stressors and psychological factors, including cognitive processes and learning, are crucial to the development of most anxiety disorders (Ley, 1994; Schmidt, Lerew, & Jackson, 1997; Schmidt et al., 2000). Persons suffering from an anxiety disorder may exaggerate the dangers in their environment, thereby creating an unrealistic expectation that bad events are going to happen (Foa et al., 1996). In addition, they tend to underestimate their own capacity for dealing with threatening events, resulting in anxiety and desperation when feared events do occur (Beck & Emery, 1985).

As an example, consider the development of a panic attack. Whereas the appearance of unexplained symptoms of physical arousal may make a panic attack more likely, the person's cognitive interpretation of those symptoms can determine whether or not the attack actually develops (Clark et al., 1997; Schmidt, Lerew, & Jackson, 1999). One study, for instance, found that panic attacks were much less likely if panic-disorder patients believed they could control the source of their discomfort (Rapee et al., 1992). In another study, panic-disorder patients were asked to inhale carbon dioxide, which typically causes panic attacks in such patients. Those who inhaled this substance in the presence of a person they associated with safety were significantly less fearful than patients whose "safe person" was not present (Carter et al., 1995). Results like these suggest a role for cognitive factors in panic disorder.

LINKAGES (a link to Learning)

Anxiety Disorders and Learning

The learning principles discussed in the chapter on learning also play an important role in anxiety disorders. For example, upsetting thoughts—about money or illness, for example—often create anxiety and worry, especially when people are already under stress or feel incapable of dealing with their problems. As the thoughts become more persistent, anxiety increases. If, say, cleaning the kitchen temporarily relieves the anxiety, that action may be strengthened through the process of negative reinforcement discussed in the chapter on learning. But such actions do nothing to eliminate the obsessive thoughts, so they return, and the actions become compulsive, endlessly repeated rituals that keep the person trapped in a vicious circle of anxiety (Barlow, 1988). So to social-cognitive theorists, obsessive-compulsive disorder is a pattern that is sparked by distressing thoughts and maintained by operant conditioning.

Phobias may also be based in part on the principles of classical conditioning and observational learning described in the chapter on learning. The object of the

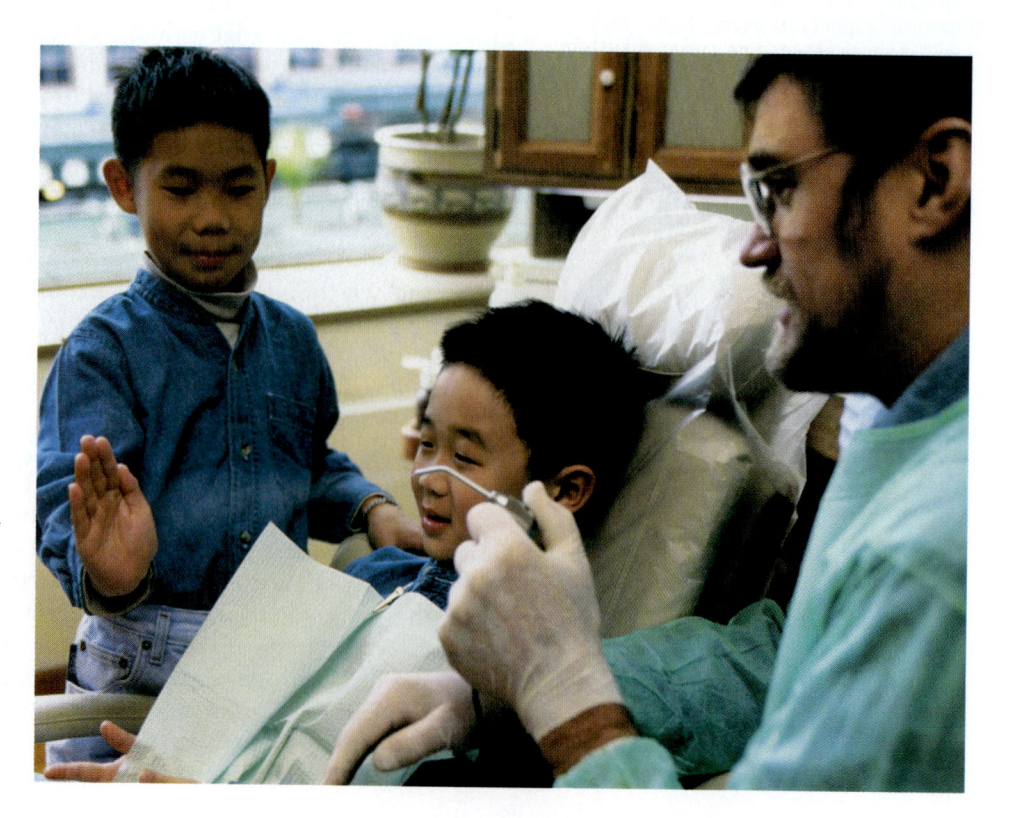

Learning by Watching Many phobias, including those of needles, blood, and medical-related situations, are acquired vicariously. Fear developed through observational learning can be as strong as fear developed through direct experience (Kleinknecht, 1991), though direct conditioning is the more common pathway to a phobia (Öst, 1992). Fearlessness can also be learned vicariously. By simply watching the boy in the dental chair as he learns to relax with his dentist, the other youngster is less likely to be distressed when it is his turn.

Biological Preparedness Having a predisposition to learn fear of snakes and other potentially dangerous stimuli makes evolutionary sense. Animals (and humans) who rapidly learn a fear response to objects or situations that they see frightening their parents or peers are more likely to survive to pass on their genes to the next generation. Make a list of the things that you might be especially afraid of. How did these fears develop? And how many of them appear to have "survival value"?

phobia becomes an aversive conditioned stimulus through association with a traumatic event that acts as an unconditioned stimulus (Öst, 1992). Fear of dogs, for example, may result from a dog attack. But just seeing or hearing about other people's bad experiences might produce the same result (most people who fear flying have never been in a plane crash). Once phobias are learned, avoiding the feared object or situation prevents the person from finding out that there is no need to be afraid. This cycle of avoidance helps explain why many phobias do not simply extinguish, or disappear, on their own.

Why are phobias about snakes and spiders so common, even though people are seldom harmed by them? And why are there so few cases of electrical-shock phobia, even though lots of people receive accidental electrical shocks? As discussed in the chapter on learning, the answer may be that people are *biologically prepared* to learn associations between certain stimuli and certain responses. These stimuli and responses, then, would be especially easy to link through conditioning (Hamm, Vaitl, & Lang, 1989). Specifically, people may be biologically prepared to learn to fear and to avoid stimuli that had the potential to harm their evolutionary ancestors (Skre et al., 2000; Staddon & Ettinger, 1989).

Some laboratory evidence supports the notion that people are biologically prepared to learn certain phobias. A group of Swedish psychologists attempted to classically condition people to fear certain stimuli by associating the stimuli with electrical shocks (Öhman, Dimberg, & Öst, 1985). The participants developed approximately equal conditioned anxiety reactions to photos of houses, human faces, and snakes. Later, however, when they were tested without shock, the reaction to snakes remained long after the houses and faces had lost their ability to elicit a fear response. A series of investigations with animals has also supported preparedness theory (Cook & Mineka, 1990). If a monkey sees another monkey behaving fearfully in the presence of a snake, it quickly develops a strong and persistent fear of snakes. However, if the snake is entwined in flowers, the observer monkeys come to fear only the snake, not the flowers. So fear conditioning was selective, focusing only on potentially dangerous creatures such as snakes or crocodiles (Zinbarg & Mineka, 1991), not on harmless objects. Data like these suggest that anxiety disorders probably arise through the combined effects of genetic predispositions and learning.

Somatoform Disorders

When an athlete's fainting spells prevented her from competing in track and field events, doctors examined her but could find nothing physically wrong. After a program of stress management, however, her symptoms disappeared, and she was able to rejoin her team (Lively, 2001). Sometimes people show symptoms of a *somatic*, or bodily, disorder, even though there is no physical cause. Because these conditions reflect psychological problems that take somatic form, they are called **somatoform disorders.** The classic example is **conversion disorder,** a condition in which a person appears to be, but is not, blind, deaf, paralyzed, or insensitive to pain in various parts of the body. (An earlier term for this disorder was *hysteria*.) Conversion disorders are rare, accounting for only about 2 percent of diagnoses (American Psychiatric Association, 1994, 2000). Although they can occur at any point in life, they usually appear in adolescence or early adulthood.

Conversion disorders differ from true physical disabilities in several ways. First, they tend to appear when a person is under severe stress. Second, they often help reduce that stress by enabling the person to avoid unpleasant or threatening situations. Third, the person may show remarkably little concern about what is apparently a rather serious problem. Finally, the symptoms may be physiologically impossible or improbable, as Figure 15.2 illustrates. One university student, for example, experienced visual impairment that began each Sunday evening and became total blindness by Monday morning. Her vision would begin to return on Friday evenings and was fully restored in time for weekend football games and other social activities. She expressed no undue concern over her condition (Holmes, 1991).

Can people who display a conversion disorder see and hear, even though they act as if they cannot? Experiments show that they can (Grosz & Zimmerman, 1970), but this does not necessarily mean that they are malingering, or lying. Research on consciousness suggests that people can use sensory input even when they are not consciously aware of doing so (e.g., Blake, 1998). Rather than destroying visual or auditory ability, the conversion process may prevent the person from being aware of information that the brain is still processing (Halligan & David, 1999).

Another somatoform disorder is **hypochondriasis** (pronounced "hye-poh-kon-DRY-a-sis"), a strong, unjustified fear that one has cancer, heart disease, AIDS, or other serious physical problems. The fear prompts frequent visits to physicians and reports of numerous symptoms. Their preoccupation with illness often leads hypochondriacs to become experts on their most feared diseases. In some ways, hypochondriasis resembles a phobic anxiety disorder, but whereas a phobic person might suffer irrational fear of getting a serious illness, the hypochondriac is excessively concerned about already *having* the illness. A related condition, called **somatization disorder,** is characterized by dramatic, but often vague, reports about a multitude of physical problems rather than any specific illness. Finally, **pain disorder** is marked by complaints of severe, often constant pain (typically in the neck, chest, or back) with no physical cause.

Some cases of somatoform disorder may be related to childhood experiences in which a person learns that symptoms of physical illness bring special attention, care, and nurturance (Barsky et al., 1994). Others, including conversion disorder, may be triggered by severe stressors (Spiegel, 1994). Based on such findings, many researchers have adopted a diathesis-stress approach rather than seeking a common cause for all somatoform disorders (e.g., Nietzel et al., 1998). The results of their work suggest that certain people may have biological and psychological traits that make them especially vulnerable to somatoform disorders, particularly when combined with a history of physical illness. Among these traits are self-consciousness and oversensitivity to physical sensations. If such people experience a number of long-lasting stressors, intense emotional conflicts, or severe traumas, they are more likely than others to display physical symptoms in association with emotional arousal (Nietzel et al., 1998).

---

somatoform disorders Psychological problems in which there are symptoms of a physical disorder without a physical cause.

conversion disorder A somatoform disorder in which a person displays blindness, deafness, or other symptoms of sensory or motor failure without a physical cause.

hypochondriasis A strong, unjustified fear of physical illness.

somatization disorder A somatoform disorder in which there are numerous physical complaints without verifiable physical illness.

pain disorder A somatoform disorder marked by complaints of severe pain with no physical cause.

figure 15.2
Glove Anesthesia
In glove anesthesia, a form of conversion disorder, lack of feeling stops abruptly at the wrist (Part B). But as shown in Part A, the nerves of the hand and arm blend, so if they were actually impaired, part of the arm would also lose sensitivity. Other neurologically impossible symptoms of conversion disorder include sleepwalking at night on legs that are "paralyzed" during the day.

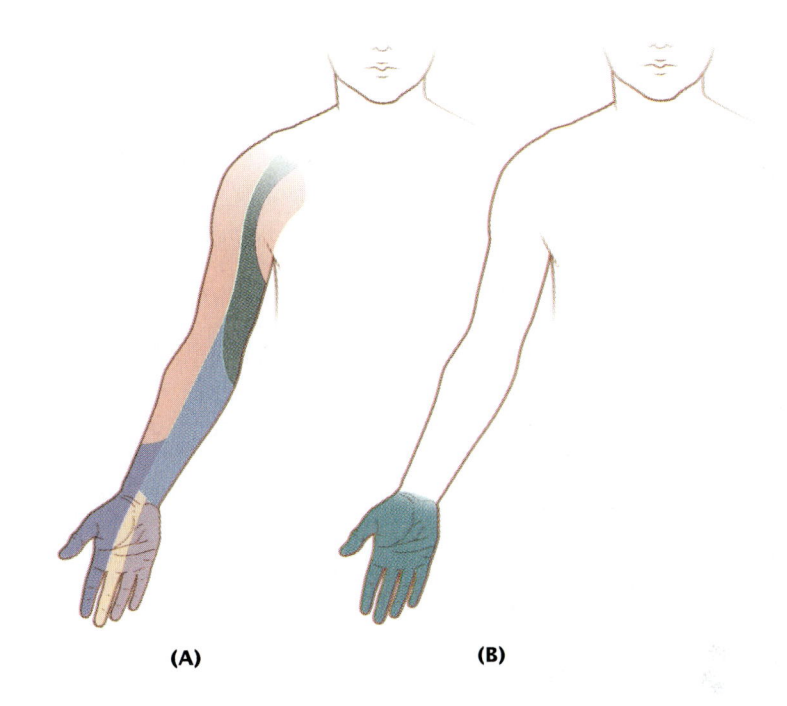

(A)   (B)

Sociocultural factors may also shape some somatoform disorders. For example, in many Asian, Latin American, and African cultures, it is not unusual for people to experience severe physical symptoms in association with psychological or interpersonal conflicts, whereas in North America such conflicts are more likely to result in anxiety or depression (Brislin, 1993). Genetic factors do not seem to be important in somatoform disorders.

Dissociative Disorders

If you have ever spent many hours driving on a boring highway, you may have suddenly realized that you had little or no recollection of what happened during the last half-hour. This common experience does not signal a mental disorder, but when disruptions in a person's memory, consciousness, or identity are more intense and long-lasting, they are known as **dissociative disorders**. These disruptions can come on gradually, but they usually occur suddenly and last from a few hours to many years.

Consider the case of John, a thirty-year-old computer manufacturing executive. John was a meek person who was dependent on his wife for companionship and emotional support. It came as a jolt when she announced that she was leaving him to live with his younger brother. John did not go to work the next day. In fact, nothing was heard from him for two weeks. Then he was arrested for public drunkenness and assault in a city more than three hundred miles from his home. The police discovered that during those two weeks, John lived under another name at a cheap hotel and worked selling tickets at a pornographic movie theater. When he was interviewed, John did not know his real name or his home address, could not explain how he had reached his present location, and could not remember much about the previous two weeks.

John's case illustrates the dissociative disorder known as **dissociative fugue**, which is characterized by a sudden loss of personal memory and the adoption of a new identity in a new locale. Another dissociative disorder, **dissociative amnesia**, also involves sudden memory loss. As in fugue, all personal identifying information may be forgotten, but the person does not leave home or create a new identity. These rare conditions attract intense publicity because they are so dramatic.

The most famous dissociative disorder is **dissociative identity disorder** (DID), formerly known as—and still commonly called—*multiple personality disorder*

dissociative disorders Rare conditions that involve disruptions in a person's memory, consciousness, or identity.

dissociative fugue A sudden loss of memory and the assumption of a new identity in a new locale.

dissociative amnesia A disorder marked by a sudden loss of memory.

dissociative identity disorder (DID) A dissociative disorder in which a person reports having more than one identity.

(MPD). Dissociative identity disorder is a condition in which a person appears to have more than one identity, each of which speaks, acts, and writes in a different way. Each personality seems to have its own memories, wishes, and (often conflicting) impulses. Here is a case example:

> *Mary, a pleasant and introverted thirty-five-year-old social worker, was referred to a psychiatrist for hypnotic treatment of chronic pain. At an early interview she mentioned the odd fact that though she had no memory of using her car after coming home from work, she often found that it had been driven fifty to one hundred miles overnight. It turned out that she also had no memory of large parts of her childhood. Mary rapidly learned self-hypnosis for pain control, but during one hypnotic session, she suddenly began speaking in a hostile manner. She told the doctor her name was Marian, and that it was "she" who had been taking long evening drives. She also called Mary "pathetic" for "wasting time" trying to please other people. Eventually, six other identities emerged, some of whom told of having experienced parental abuse in childhood. (Spitzer et al., 1994)*

A Famous Case of Dissociative Identity Disorder In this scene from the film *Sybil*, Sally Field portrays a woman diagnosed with dissociative identity disorder, previously known as multiple personality disorder, whose behavior created the appearance of as many as seventeen distinct personalities. The causes of such dramatic cases, and the reasons behind their increasing incidence in recent years, are a matter of intense debate.

How do dissociative disorders develop? Psychodynamic theorists see massive repression of unwanted impulses or memories as the basis for creating a "new person" who acts out otherwise unacceptable impulses or recalls otherwise unbearable memories (Ross, 1997). Social-cognitive theorists focus on the fact that everyone is capable of behaving in different ways, depending on circumstances (e.g., boisterous in a bar, quiet in a museum); but in rare cases, they say, this variation can become so extreme that an individual feels—and is perceived by others as being—a "different person." Further, dissociative symptoms may be strengthened by reward as people find that a sudden memory loss or shift in behavior allows them to escape stressful situations, responsibilities, or punishment for misbehavior (Lilienfeld et al., 1999).

Evaluating these hypotheses has been difficult, in part because of the rarity of dissociative disorders. Recently, however, dissociative identity disorder has been diagnosed more frequently, either because clinicians are looking for it more carefully or because the conditions leading to it are more prevalent. Research available so far supports three conclusions. First, many people displaying DID have experienced events they would like to forget or avoid. The majority (some clinicians believe all) have suffered severe, unavoidable, persistent abuse in childhood (Ross et al., 1991). Second, like Mary, most of these people appear to be skilled at self-hypnosis, through which they can induce a trance-like state. Third, most found that they could escape the trauma of abuse at least temporarily by creating "new personalities" to deal with stress (Spiegel, 1994). However, not all abused children display dissociative identity disorder, and there is evidence that some cases of dissociative identity disorder may have been triggered by media stories or by suggestions made to clients by their therapists (Spanos, 1996).

This evidence has led some skeptics to question the existence of multiple personalities (Acocella, 1998); others suggest that the increased incidence of dissociative identity disorder may simply reflect its status as a socioculturally approved method of expressing distress (Hacking, 1995; Spanos, 1994). In fact, it was observations such as these that prompted the change in its official designation from *multiple personality disorder* to *dissociative identity disorder*. The authors of *DSM-IV* made this change partly to avoid perpetuating the notion that people harbor multiple personalities that can easily be "contacted" through hypnosis or related techniques. The new name was chosen to suggest, instead, that dissociation, or separation, between one's memories and other aspects of identity can be so dramatic that people experiencing it may come to believe that they have more than one personality (Gleaves, May, & Cardena, 2001; Spiegel, 1994). Research on the existence and alleged effects of repressed memories—discussed in the chapter on memory—is sure to have an impact on our understanding of, and the controversy over, the causes of dissociative identity disorder. ("In Review: Anxiety, Somatoform, and Dissociative Disorders" presents a summary of our discussion of these disorders.)

Debate and skepticism about the nature and origins of dissociative identity disorder is not confined to professional journals. This cartoon appeared recently in the *New Yorker*.

"Would it be possible to speak with the personality that pays the bills?"

© The New Yorker Collection 2001 Leo Cullum from cartoonbank.com. All Rights Reserved.

in review: Anxiety, Somatoform, and Dissociative Disorders

Disorder	Subtypes	Major Symptoms
Anxiety disorders	Phobias	Intense, irrational fear of objectively nondangerous situations or things, leading to disruptions of behavior
	Generalized anxiety disorder	Excessive anxiety not focused on a specific situation or object; free-floating anxiety
	Panic disorder	Repeated attacks of intense fear involving physical symptoms such as faintness, dizziness, and nausea
	Obsessive-compulsive disorder	Persistent ideas or worries accompanied by ritualistic behaviors performed to neutralize the anxiety-driven thoughts
Somatoform disorders	Conversion disorder	A loss of physical ability (e.g., sight, hearing) that is related to psychological factors
	Hypochondriasis	Preoccupation with, or belief that, one has serious illness in the absence of any physical evidence
	Somatization disorder	Wide variety of somatic complaints that occur over several years and are not the result of a known physical disorder
	Pain disorder	Preoccupation with pain in the absence of physical reasons for the pain
Dissociative disorders	Dissociative fugue	Sudden, unexpected loss of memory, which may result in relocation and the assumption of a new identity
	Dissociative identity disorder (multiple personality disorder)	Appearance within the same person of two or more distinct identities, each with a unique way of thinking and behaving

Mood Disorders

Everyone's mood, or *affect*, tends to rise and fall from time to time. However, when people experience extremes of mood—wild elation or deep depression—for long periods, when they shift from one extreme to another, and especially when their moods are not consistent with the events around them, they are said to show a **mood disorder** (also known as *affective disorder*). We will describe two main types: depressive disorders and bipolar disorders.

Depressive Disorders

Depression can range from occasional, normal "down" periods to episodes severe enough to require hospitalization. A person suffering **major depressive disorder** feels sad and overwhelmed for weeks or months, typically losing interest in activities and relationships and taking pleasure in nothing (Coryell et al., 1993; Sloan, Strauss, & Wisner, 2001). Exaggerated feelings of inadequacy, worthlessness, hopelessness, or guilt are common. Despite the person's best efforts, everything from conversation to bathing is an unbearable, exhausting effort (Solomon, 1998). Changes in eating habits resulting in weight loss or weight gain often accompany major depressive disorder, as does sleep disturbance or, less often, excessive sleeping. Problems in working, concentrating, making decisions, and thinking clearly are also common. More often than not, there are also symptoms of an accompanying anxiety disorder (Zimmerman, McDermut, & Mattia, 2000). In extreme cases, depressed people may express false beliefs, or **delusions**—worrying, for example, that the government is planning to punish them. Major depressive disorder may come on suddenly or gradually. It may consist of a single episode or, more commonly, repeated depressive periods. Here is a case example:

> *Mr. J. was a fifty-one-year-old industrial engineer. . . . Since the death of his wife five years earlier, he had been suffering from continuing episodes of depression marked by extreme social withdrawal and occasional thoughts of suicide. . . . He drank and, when thoroughly intoxicated, would plead to his deceased wife for forgiveness. He lost all capacity for joy. . . . Once a gourmet, he now had no interest in food and good wine . . . and could barely manage to engage in small talk. As might be expected, his work record deteriorated markedly. Appointments were missed and projects haphazardly started and left unfinished. (Davison & Neale, 1990, p. 221)*

Depression is not always so extreme. In a less severe pattern of depression, called **dysthymic disorder**, the person experiences the sad mood, lack of interest, and loss of pleasure associated with major depression, but less intensely and for a longer period. (The duration must be at least two years to qualify as dysthymic disorder.) Mental and behavioral disruption are also less severe; people exhibiting dysthymic disorder rarely require hospitalization.

Major depressive disorder occurs sometime in the lives of up to 17 percent of the North American or European population; at any given time, about 6.5 percent of these people are affected (Blazer et al., 1994; Kessler et al., 1994; U.S. Surgeon General, 1999). Anyone can become depressed, but major depressive disorder is most likely to appear during the late teenage and early adult years (Burke et al., 1990); there is also evidence that rates of depression have increased among young people (Cross-National Collaborative Group, 1992; Fassler & Dumas, 1997). In the United States and other Western countries, women are two to three times more likely than men to experience major depressive disorder (Weissman et al., 1993). However, there are no reported gender differences in depression in some less economically developed countries in the Middle East, Africa, and Asia (Culbertson, 1997).

---

mood disorder A condition in which a person experiences extreme moods, such as depression or mania.

major depressive disorder A condition in which a person feels sad and hopeless for weeks or months.

delusions False beliefs, such as those experienced by people suffering from extreme depression.

dysthymic disorder A pattern of comparatively mild depression that lasts for at least two years.

Suicide and Depression Suicide is associated with a variety of psychological disorders, but it is most closely tied to depression; some form of depression has been implicated in 40 to 60 percent of suicides (Angst, Angst, & Stassen, 1999; Clark & Fawcett, 1992). In fact, thinking about suicide is a symptom of depressive disorders. Hopelessness about the future—another depressive symptom—and a desire to seek instant escape from problems are also related to suicide attempts (Beck et al., 1990; Brown et al., 2000).

About 31,000 people in the United States and Canada commit suicide each year, and 10 to 20 times that many people attempt it (Statistics Canada, 1998; U.S. Surgeon General, 1999). Worldwide, the annual death toll from suicide is 120,000. Suicide rates differ considerably depending on sociocultural factors such as age, gender, and ethnicity. The rate is as high as 25 per 100,000 individuals in some northern European countries and Japan (Lamar, 2000), and as low as 6 per 100,000 in countries with stronger religious prohibitions against suicide, such as Greece, Italy, Ireland, and the nations of the Middle East.

In the United States, where the overall suicide rate is about 10.6 per 100,000, suicide is most common among people 65 years old and older; the rate for those over 85 years old is 21 per 100,000 (Centers for Disease Control and Prevention, 1999d; Hoyert, Kochanek, & Murphy, 1999; U.S. Surgeon General, 1999). However, since 1950, suicide among adolescents—especially 15- to 19-year-olds—has tripled. It is now the third leading cause of death among adolescents (Centers for Disease Control and Prevention, 1999d). Suicide is the second leading cause of death among college students; about 10,000 try to kill themselves each year, and about 1,000 succeed. These figures are much higher than for 18- to 24-year-olds in general, but much lower than for the elderly (U.S. Surgeon General, 1999). Women attempt suicide 3 times as often as men, but men are 4 times as likely to actually kill themselves (Centers for Disease Control and Prevention, 1999). And among depressed people, men—at a rate of 65 per 100,000—are 10 times more likely than women to commit suicide (Blair-West et al., 1999; Centers for Disease Control and Prevention, 1999d).

Suicide rates also differ across ethnic groups in the United States (Oquendo et al., 2001; see Figure 15.3). For example, although there is wide variation from tribe to tribe, the overall rate for American Indians is 13.6 per 100,000, compared with 12.9 for European Americans, 9.1 for Asian Americans, 7.5 for Hispanic Americans, and 5.7 for African Americans (Centers for Disease Control and Prevention, 1999d; Garland & Zigler, 1993; Howard-Pitney et al., 1992; McIntosh,

figure 15.3

Suicide Rates in Various Ethnic Groups

The suicide rates among ethnic groups in the United States vary widely. For example, the rate among American Indians is more than twice that of African Americans. In 1997, more teenagers and young adults died from suicide than from cancer, heart disease, AIDS, birth defects, stroke, pneumonia and influenza, and chronic lung disease *combined* (Centers for Disease Control and Prevention, 1999d).

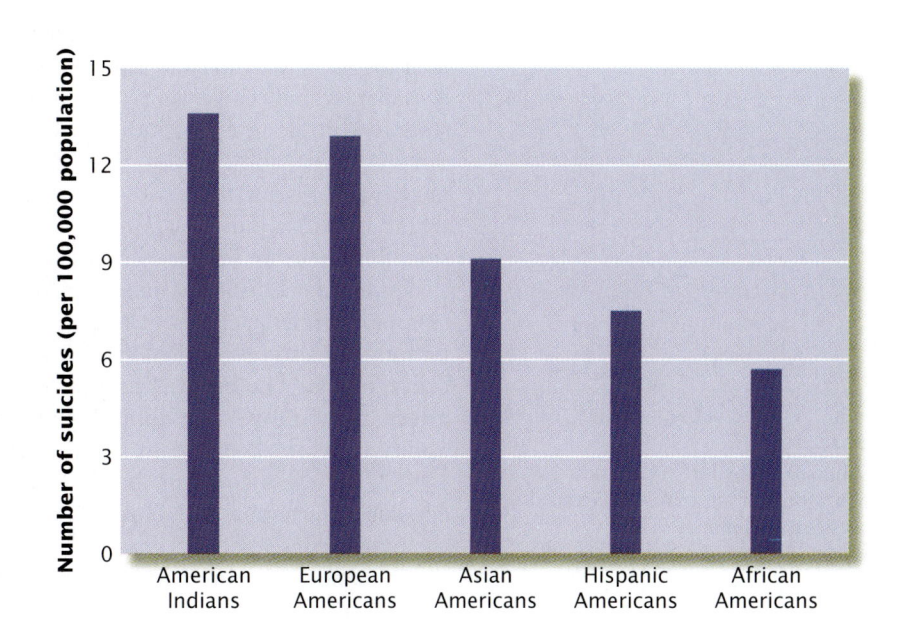

1992). The suicide rate among male European American teenagers, an alarming 16 per 100,000, has actually dropped from a high of 18 per 100,000 in 1986. However, the rate has increased from 7.1 to 11.4 per 100,000 for African American teens, and it stands at 62 per 100,000 among American Indian adolescents—the highest rate in the United States (Centers for Disease Control and Prevention, 1999d).

Predicting who will commit suicide is difficult. For one thing, suicidal thoughts are quite common—5.6 percent of all adults and as many as 10 percent of college students report having had such thoughts in the previous year (Brener, Hassan, & Barrios, 1999; Crosby, Cheltenham, & Sacks, 1999). Still, the results of hundreds of research studies provide some predictive guidelines. In the United States, at least, suicide is most likely among European American males, especially those over forty-five, single or divorced, and living alone. The risk of suicide is also heightened among people who have made a specific plan, have given away possessions (Clark et al., 1989), and are impulsive (Corruble, Damy, & Guelfi, 1999). Among the elderly, suicide is most common among men who are depressed about health problems (U.S. Surgeon General, 1999). A previous suicide attempt may not always be a good predictor of eventual suicide, because such attempts may have been help-seeking gestures, not failed efforts to die. In fact, although about 10 percent of unsuccessful attempters try again and succeed, most people who commit suicide had made no prior attempts (Clark & Fawcett, 1992).

One myth about suicide is that people who talk about it will never try it. On the contrary, those who say they are thinking of suicide are much more likely to attempt suicide than people from the general population. In fact, according to Edwin Schneidman (1987), 80 percent of suicides are preceded by some kind of warning, whether direct ("I think I'm going to kill myself") or vague ("Sometimes I wonder if life is worth living"). Although not everyone who threatens suicide follows through, if you suspect that someone you know is thinking about suicide, encourage the person to contact a mental health professional or a crisis hotline. If the danger is imminent, make the contact yourself, and ask for advice about how to respond. Many suicide attempts—including those triggered by other suicides in the same town or school—can be prevented by social support and other forms of help for people at high risk (Joiner, 1999). For more information, visit suicide-related web sites, such as that of the American Association of Suicidology (www.suicidology.org).

Bipolar Disorders

The alternating appearance of two emotional extremes, or poles, characterizes *bipolar I disorder*. We have already described one emotional pole: depression. The other is **mania**, which is a very agitated, usually elated, emotional state. People in a manic state tend to be utterly optimistic, boundlessly energetic, certain of having extraordinary powers and abilities, and bursting with all sorts of ideas. They become irritated with anyone who tries to reason with them or "slow them down." During manic episodes individuals may make impulsive and unwise decisions, including spending their life savings on foolish schemes.

In **bipolar I disorder,** manic episodes may alternate with periods of deep depression (sometimes, periods of relatively normal mood separate these extremes). This pattern has also been called *manic depression.* Compared with major depressive disorder, bipolar I disorder is rare; it occurs in only about 1 percent of adults, and it affects men and women about equally. However, it can severely disrupt a person's ability to work or maintain social relationships (Goldberg, Harrow, & Grossman, 1995). Even less common is *bipolar II disorder,* which features major depressive episodes alternating with episodes known as *hypomania,* which are less severe than the manic phases seen in bipolar I disorder.

A somewhat more common mood disorder is **cyclothymic disorder,** the bipolar equivalent of dysthymia. Cyclothymic disorder involves episodes of depression and

---

mania A very active, usually elated, emotional state.

bipolar I disorder A condition in which a person alternates between deep depression and mania.

cyclothymic disorder A form of bipolar disorder characterized by comparatively mild mood swings.

in review | Mood Disorders

Type	Typical Symptoms	Related Features
Major depressive disorder	Deep sadness, feelings of worthlessness, changes in eating and sleeping habits, loss of interest and pleasure	Lasts weeks or months; may occur in repeating episodes; severe cases may include delusions; danger of suicide
Dysthymic disorder	Similar to major depressive disorder, but less severe and longer lasting	Hospitalization usually not necessary
Bipolar I disorder	Alternating extremes of mood, from deep depression to mania, and back	Manic episodes include impulsivity, unrealistic optimism, high energy, severe agitation
Cyclothymic disorder	Similar to bipolar disorder, but less severe	Hospitalization usually not necessary

mania, but the intensity of both moods is less severe than in cases of bipolar I disorder. ("In Review: Mood Disorders" summarizes the main types of mood disorders.)

Causes of Mood Disorders

Research on the causes of mood disorders has focused on biological, psychological, and sociocultural risk factors. The more of these risk factors people have, the more likely they are to experience a mood disorder.

LINKAGES (a link to Biological Aspects of Psychology)

Biological Factors The role of genetics in mood disorders, especially in bipolar disorders, is suggested by twin studies and family studies (Kelsoe et al., 2001). For example, bipolar disorder is much more likely to be seen in both members of genetically identical twin pairs than in fraternal, or genetically nonidentical, twins (Bowman & Nurnberger, 1993; Egeland et al., 1987; NIMH, 1998a). Family studies also show that those who are closely related to people with a bipolar disorder are more likely than others to develop that disorder themselves (Winokur et al., 1995). Major depressive disorder is also more likely to be shared among family members, and especially by identical twins (Kendler et al., 1995; Klein et al., 2001; Nurnberger, 1993). This genetic influence is especially strong in female twins (Bierut et al., 1999). Researchers continue to look for the specific genes that might be involved in the transmission of elevated risk for mood disorders (Baron, 1997; U.S. Surgeon General, 1999).

Other potential biological causes of mood disorders include imbalances in the brain's neurotransmitter systems, malfunctioning of the endocrine system, disruption of biological rhythms, and according to a recent theory, reduced development in the brain's frontal lobes (Cotter et al., 2001), all of which may themselves be influenced by genetics. Neurotransmitters such as norepinephrine, serotonin, and dopamine were implicated decades ago, when scientists discovered that drugs capable of altering these brain chemicals also relieved mood disorders. Early research suggested that depression was triggered by too little of these neurotransmitters, whereas unusually high levels caused mania; but the neurochemical causes now appear more complex than that. Recent research suggests, for example, that mood disorders may result in part from changes in the sensitivity of the neuronal receptors at which these chemicals have their effects in the brain. The precise nature of these neurotransmitter-

Treating SAD Seasonal affective disorder (SAD) can often be relieved by exposure to full-spectrum light for as little as a couple of hours a day (Campbell & Murphy, 1998; Sato, 1997).

receptor mechanisms, and just how they affect mood, is not yet fully understood (Martinot et al., 2001; Schloss & Williams, 1998; U.S. Surgeon General, 1999).

Mood disorders have also been related to malfunctions of the endocrine system, especially the hypothalamic-pituitary-adrenocortical system (HPA), mentioned in the chapter on health, stress, and coping as being involved in the body's responses to stress. For example, research shows that as many as 70 percent of depressed people secrete abnormally high levels of the stress hormone *cortisol* (Dinan, 2001; Nemeroff, 1998; Posener et al., 2000).

The cyclical pattern seen in bipolar disorders and in recurring episodes of major depressive disorder suggests that mood disorders may be related to stressful triggering events (Miklowitz & Alloy, 1999), and perhaps to disturbances in the body's biological clock, which is described in the chapter on consciousness (Goodwin & Jamison, 1990). This second possibility seems especially likely to apply to the 15 percent of depressed people who consistently experience a calendar-linked pattern of depressive episodes known as *seasonal affective disorder (SAD)*. During months of shorter daylight, these people slip into severe depression, accompanied by irritability and excessive sleeping (Blehar & Rosenthal, 1989). Their depression tends to lift as daylight hours lengthen (Faedda et al., 1993). Disruption of biological rhythms is also suggested by the fact that many depressed people tend to have trouble sleeping—perhaps partly because during the day, their biological clocks are telling them it is the middle of the night. Resetting the biological clock through methods such as sleep deprivation or light stimulation has relieved depression in many cases (Kuhs & Tolle, 1991; Terman et al., 2001).

Psychological and Social Factors

Researchers have come to recognize that whatever biological causes are involved in mood disorders, their effects are always combined with those of psychological and social causes (U.S. Surgeon General, 1999). As mentioned earlier, the very nature of depressive symptoms can depend on the culture in which a person lives. Biopsychosocial explanations of mood disorders also emphasize the impact of anxiety, negative thinking, and the other psychological and emotional responses triggered by trauma, losses, and other stressful events (Monroe et al., 1999). For example, the higher incidence of depression among females—and especially among poor, ethnic minority, single mothers— has been attributed to their greater exposure to stressors of all kinds (Brown & Moran, 1997; Miranda & Green, 1999). Environmental stressors affect men, too, which may be one reason why gender differences in depression are smaller in countries where men and women face equally stressful lives (Bierut et al., 1999; Maier et al., 1999). Still, differing stressors may not be the only source of these gender differences (Kendler, Thornton, & Prescott, 2001).

A variety of social-cognitive theories suggest that the way people think about their stressors can increase or decrease the likelihood of mood disorders. One of these theories stemmed from the research on *learned helplessness* described in the chapter on learning. Just as animals become inactive and appear depressed when they have no control over negative events, humans may experience depression as a result of feeling incapable of controlling their lives, especially the stressors confronting them (Klein & Seligman, 1976; Seligman, 1991). But most of us have limited control; why aren't we all depressed? The ways in which people learn to *think* about events in their lives may hold the key. For example, Aaron Beck's (1967, 1976) cognitive theory of depression suggests that depressed people develop mental habits of (1) blaming themselves when things go wrong; (2) focusing on and exaggerating the negative side of events; and (3) jumping to overly generalized, pessimistic conclusions. Such cognitive habits, says Beck, are errors that lead to depressing thoughts and other symptoms of depression (Beck & Beck, 1995). Depressed people, in fact, do think about significant negative events in ways that are likely to increase or prolong their depression (Gotlib & Hammen, 1992).

Social-cognitive theories of depression are somewhat consistent with the psychodynamically oriented *object relations* approach discussed in the chapter on personality (Blatt & Maroudas, 1992). Both views suggest that negative patterns of thinking can be acquired through maladaptive experiences in childhood. For example, research indicates that children whose early relationships with parents or other primary caregivers were characterized by deprivation or abuse are especially likely to develop depression in later life (Gotlib & Hammen, 1992). It may be that close, protective, predictable, and responsive early relationships are necessary if children are to form healthy views of themselves, positive expectations about others, and a sense of control over the environment (Bowlby, 1980; Main, 1996).

Severe, long-lasting depression is especially common among people who attribute the lack of control or other problems they experience to a permanent, generalized personal failing rather than to a temporary lapse or external cause (Seligman et al., 1988). This *attributional style* may be another important cognitive factor in depression (Alloy, Abramson, & Francis, 1999; Ingram, Miranda, & Segal, 1998). People may be prone to depression when they attribute negative events to their own characteristics and believe they will never be capable of doing better. One study of adolescents, for example, found that those who strongly held such dysfunctional attitudes were more likely than other youngsters to develop depression when faced with stress later in life (Lewinsohn, Joiner, & Rohde, 2001).

Depressed people do hold more negative beliefs about themselves and their lives than other people, but the exact significance of these beliefs is not yet clear (Gara et al., 1993). For one thing, pessimistic beliefs may be a symptom of depression rather than its cause. Also, the negative beliefs held by some depressed persons appear to be an accurate reflection of these people's unfortunate life situations and experiences (Coyne & Whiffen, 1995).

In any case, the social-cognitive perspective suggests that whether depression continues or worsens depends in part on how people respond once they start to feel depressed. Those who ruminate, or continuously dwell, on negative events, on why they occur, and even on feeling depressed are likely to feel more and more depressed (Just & Alloy, 1997). According to Susan Nolen-Hoeksema (1990, 2001), this *ruminative style* is especially characteristic of women and may help explain gender differences in the frequency of depression. When men start to feel sad, she says, they tend to use a *distracting style*. That is, they engage in activity that distracts them from their concerns and helps bring them out of their depressed mood (Hankin & Abramson, 2001; Just & Alloy, 1997; Nolen-Hoeksema, Morrow, & Fredrickson, 1993).

Notice that social-cognitive explanations of depression are consistent with the diathesis-stress approach to disorder (Hankin & Abramson, 2001). These explanations suggest that certain cognitive styles constitute a predisposition (or diathesis) that makes a person vulnerable to depression, the occurrence of which is made more likely by stressors. In fact, most episodes of major depressive disorder are preceded by the onset of major stressors, such as the loss of a loved one. As suggested in the chapter on health, stress, and coping, the depressing effects of these stressors are likely to be magnified by lack of social support, inadequate coping skills, and the presence of other stressful conditions such as poverty.

Given the number and complexity of biological, psychological, social, and situational factors potentially involved in causing mood disorders, the biopsychosocial model and the diathesis-stress approach appear to be especially appropriate guides to future research. Studies based on these guides are already bearing fruit. One study looked at the role of genetics and stressful events in shaping mood disorders in a large group of female twin pairs. Both factors were associated with major depression; the women at highest genetic risk were also the most likely to become depressed following a significant stressor (Kendler, Thornton, & Gardner, 2000, 2001). Another study found that among adolescents already at risk for depression because of family history, the ones most likely to actually develop major depressive disorder were those who encountered significant stressors (personal losses and disappointments in the previous month) and who reacted most strongly to stress, as measured by cortisol and other stress-related hormones (Goodyer et al., 2000). In the final analysis, it may turn out that each subtype of mood disorder is caused by a unique combination of factors. The challenge for researchers is to identify these subtypes and map out their causal ingredients.

Schizophrenia

Here is part of a letter that arrived in the mail several years ago:

Dear Sirs:

Pertaining to our continuing failure to prosecute violations of minor's rights to sovereign equality which are occurring in gestations being compromised by the ingestation of controlled substances, . . . the skewing of androgyny which continues in female juveniles even after separation from their mother's has occurred, and as a means of promulflagitating my paying Governor Hickel of Alaska for my employees to have personal services endorsements and controlled substance endorsements, . . . the Iraqi oil being released by the United Nations being identified as Kurdistanian oil, and the July, 1991 issue of the Siberian Review spells President Eltsin's name without a letter y.

The disorganization and bizarre content of this letter suggest that its writer suffers from **schizophrenia** (pronounced "skit-so-FREE-nee-uh"), a pattern of extremely disturbed thinking, emotion, perception, and behavior that seriously impairs the ability to communicate and relate to others and disrupts most other aspects of daily functioning. Schizophrenia is one of the most severe and disabling of all mental disorders. Its core symptoms are seen virtually everywhere in the world, occurring in 1 to 2 percent of the population (American Psychiatric Association, 1994, 2000). In the United States, it appears about equally in various ethnic groups, but like most disorders, it tends to be diagnosed more frequently in economically disadvantaged populations. Schizophrenia is seen about equally in men and women, although in women it may appear later in life, be less severe, and respond better to treatment (American Psychiatric Association, 2000; U.S. Surgeon General, 1999).

schizophrenia A severe and disabling pattern of disturbed thinking, emotion, perception, and behavior.

Schizophrenia tends to develop in adolescence or early adulthood. The onset is gradual in some cases and more rapid in others. About 40 percent of people with schizophrenia improve with treatment and are able to function reasonably well; the rest show continuous or intermittent symptoms that permanently impair their functioning (Hegarty et al., 1994). It has been estimated that 10 to 13 percent of homeless individuals suffer from schizophrenia (Fischer & Breakey, 1991).

One of the best predictors of the course of schizophrenia is *premorbid adjustment,* the level of functioning a person had achieved before schizophrenic symptoms first appeared. Improvement is more likely in those who had attained higher levels of education and occupation, and who had established supportive relationships with family and friends (Watt & Saiz, 1991).

Symptoms of Schizophrenia

People displaying schizophrenia have problems in how they think and what they think. The nineteenth-century psychiatrist Eugen Bleuler coined the word *schizophrenia,* or "split mind," to refer to the peculiarities of schizophrenic thinking. However, schizophrenia does not mean "split personality," as in dissociative identity disorder (multiple personality disorder). It refers instead to a splitting of normally integrated mental processes, such as thoughts and feelings. For instance, some schizophrenics may giggle while claiming to feel sad.

LINKAGES (a link to Cognition and Language)

Schizophrenic thought and language are often disorganized. *Neologisms* ("new words" that have meaning only to the person speaking them) are common; the appearance of "promulflagitating" in the letter above is one example. That letter also illustrates *loose associations,* the tendency for one thought to be logically unconnected, or only superficially related, to the next. Sometimes the associations are based on double meanings or on the way words sound *(clang associations).* For example, "My true family name is Abel or A Bell. We descended from the clan of Abel, who originated the bell of rights, which we now call the bill of rights." In the most severe cases, a jumble of words known as *word salad* reflects utterly chaotic thoughts: "Upon the advisability of held keeping, environment of the seabeach gathering, to the forest stream, reinstatement to be placed, poling the paddleboat, of the swamp morass, to the forest compensation of the dunce" (Lehman, 1967, p. 627).

The *content* of schizophrenic thinking is also disturbed. Often it includes a bewildering assortment of delusions, especially delusions of persecution. Some patients claim that space aliens are trying to steal their internal organs, and they may interpret everything from TV commercials to casual hand gestures as part of the plot. Delusions that common events are somehow related to oneself are called *ideas of reference. Delusions of grandeur* may also appear; one young man was convinced that the president of the United States was trying to contact him for advice. Other types of delusions include (1) *thought broadcasting,* in which patients believe that their thoughts can be heard by others; (2) *thought blocking* or *withdrawal,* the belief that someone is either preventing thoughts or "stealing" them as they appear; and (3) *thought insertion,* the belief that other people's thoughts are appearing in one's own mind. Some patients may believe that their behavior, like a puppet's, is being controlled by others.

People with schizophrenia often report that they cannot focus their attention. They may feel overwhelmed as they try to attend to everything at once. Various perceptual disorders may also appear. The person may feel detached from the world and see other people as flat cutouts. The body may feel like a machine, or parts of it may seem to be dead or rotting. **Hallucinations,** or false perceptions, are common, often emerging as voices. These voices may sound like an overheard conversation, or they may urge the person to do or not to do things; they may also comment on, narrate, or (most often) harshly criticize the person's actions or characteristics. Hallucinations can also create sights, smells, tastes, and touches even when no external stimuli are present. (As shown in Figure 15.4, the brain areas activated during hallucinations are

hallucinations A symptom of disorder in which people perceive voices or other stimuli when there are no stimuli present.

figure 15.4
PET Scan Showing Areas of the Brain Activated During Hallucinations
This twenty-three-year-old schizophrenic patient hallucinated rolling, disembodied heads that gave him instructions. PET scans revealed heightened activity in the visual and auditory (language) *association* cortex, rather than in the *primary* cortex regions for these senses. Posterior cingulate cortex (part of the limbic system), which was also activated, is known to be affected by drugs that produce hallucinations (Silbersweig et al., 1995).

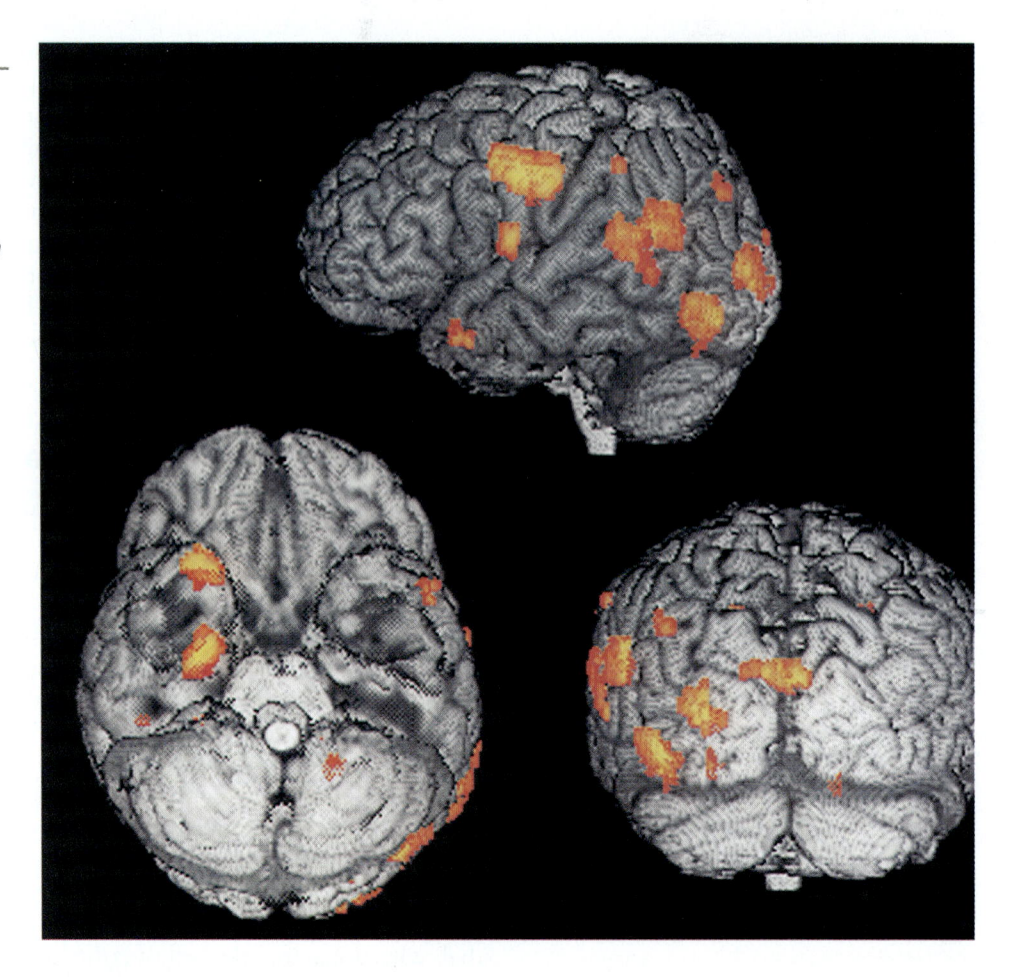

related to those that respond to real sights and sounds [Shergill et al., 2000].) The emotional expressiveness of people with schizophrenia is often muted, but when they do show emotion, it is frequently exaggerated or inappropriate. They may cry for no apparent reason or fly into a rage in response to a simple question.

Some schizophrenia patients are extremely agitated, ceaselessly moving their limbs, making facial grimaces, or pacing the floor in highly ritualistic sequences. Others become so withdrawn that they move very little. Lack of motivation and poor social skills, deteriorating personal hygiene, and an inability to function day to day are other common characteristics of schizophrenia.

Categorizing Schizophrenia

DSM-IV lists five major subtypes of schizophrenia: paranoid, disorganized, catatonic, undifferentiated, and residual (see Table 15.4). These subtype labels convey a certain amount of useful information. We know, for example, that the prognosis for paranoid schizophrenia is somewhat better than for the other subtypes (Fenton & McGlashan, 1991). However, subtype labels do not always provide accurate information about patients' behavior, because some symptoms appear in more than one subtype. Further, people originally diagnosed as suffering from disorganized schizophrenia might later display characteristics of the paranoid subtype. Finally, the *DSM-IV* subtypes may not be linked very closely to the various biological conditions thought to underlie schizophrenia (Fenton & McGlashan, 1991). With these concerns in mind, many researchers are now using methods of categorizing schizophrenia that focus more precisely on the kinds of symptoms that patients display.

One such method highlights the positive-negative symptom dimension in schizophrenia. Disorganized thoughts, delusions, and hallucinations are sometimes called

Mental health professionals still use these *DSM-IV* subtypes when diagnosing schizophrenia, but many researchers now tend to categorize patients in terms of whether positive or negative symptoms of schizophrenia predominate in a given case.

table 15.4
Subtypes of Schizophrenia

Type	Frequency	Prominent Features
Paranoid schizophrenia	40 percent of schizophrenics; appears late in life (after age 25–30)	Delusions of grandeur or persecution; anger; anxiety; argumentativeness; extreme jealousy; onset often sudden; signs of impairment may be subtle.
Disorganized schizophrenia	5 percent of all schizophrenics; high prevalence in homeless population	Delusions; hallucinations; incoherent speech; facial grimaces; inappropriate laughter/giggling; neglected personal hygiene; loss of bladder/bowel control.
Catatonic schizophrenia	8 percent of all schizophrenics	Disordered movement, alternating between total immobility (stupor) and wild excitement. In stupor, the person does not speak or attend to communication; also, the body is rigid or can be posed in virtually any posture (a condition called *waxy flexibility*).
Undifferentiated schizophrenia	40 percent of all schizophrenics	Patterns of disordered behavior, thought, and emotion that do not fall easily into any other subtype.
Residual schizophrenia	Varies	Applies to people who have had prior episodes of schizophrenia but are not currently displaying symptoms.

positive symptoms of schizophrenia, because they appear as undesirable *additions* to a person's mental life (Andreasen et al., 1995). In contrast, the absence of pleasure and motivation, lack of emotional reactivity, social withdrawal, reduced speech, and other deficits seen in schizophrenia are sometimes called **negative symptoms,** because they appear to *subtract* elements from normal mental life (Nicholson & Neufeld, 1993).

Describing patients in terms of positive and negative symptoms does not require that they be placed in one category or the other. In fact, many patients exhibit both positive and negative symptoms. However, it is important to know whether negative or positive symptoms predominate, because when symptoms are mainly negative, schizophrenia is generally more severe and less responsive to treatment. In such cases, patients typically experience long-term disability (e.g., Fenton & McGlashan, 1994).

Another way of categorizing schizophrenic symptoms focuses on whether they are *psychotic* (hallucinations, delusions), *disorganized* (incoherent speech, chaotic behavior, inappropriate affect), or *negative* (e.g., lack of speech or motivation). Some researchers believe that these categories of symptoms represent three separate dimensions of schizophrenia (Buchanan & Carpenter, 1994; Grube, Bilder, & Goldman,

positive symptoms Schizophrenic symptoms such as disorganized thoughts, hallucinations, and delusions.

negative symptoms Schizophrenic symptoms such as absence of pleasure, lack of speech, and flat affect.

1998; Johnstone & Frith, 1996). Not all studies have supported this interpretation (Dudgeon et al., 2001), but some research shows that patients' negative symptoms remain stable, and may even worsen, at the same time that their psychotic symptoms are being reduced through drug treatment (Andreasen et al., 1995).

The fact that, like positive and negative symptoms, the three dimensions of schizophrenia are to some extent independent from one another suggests to some researchers that each symptom cluster or dimension may ultimately be traceable to different causes, and that each may require different treatments (Tsuang, Stone, & Faraone, 2000).

Causes of Schizophrenia

The search for the causes of schizophrenia has been more intense than for any other psychological disorder. The findings so far confirm one thing for certain: As with other disorders, there are biological, psychological, and social factors at work in causing or worsening all forms of schizophrenia (U.S. Surgeon General, 1999).

Biological Factors
Research in behavioral genetics shows that schizophrenia runs in families (Asarnow et al., 2001; Gottesman, 1991). One longitudinal family study found, for instance, that 16 percent of the children of schizophrenic mothers—compared with 2 percent of those of nonschizophrenic mothers—developed schizophrenia themselves over a twenty-five-year period (Parnas et al., 1993). Even if they are adopted by nonschizophrenic families, the children of schizophrenic parents are ten times more likely to develop schizophrenia than adopted children whose biological parents are not schizophrenic (Kety et al., 1994). Still, it is unlikely that a single gene transmits schizophrenia (Kendler & Diehl, 1993). Among identical-twin pairs in which one member displays schizophrenia, 40 percent of the other members will, too; but 60 percent will not (McGue, 1992). It is more likely that some people inherit a genetic predisposition, or diathesis, for schizophrenia that then combines with other genetic and nongenetic factors to cause the disorder (Moldin & Gottesman, 1997).

The search for these more specific causes of schizophrenia focuses on a number of abnormalities in the structure, functioning, and chemistry of the brain that tend to appear in schizophrenics. For example, numerous brain imaging studies have shown that, compared with other mental patients, many schizophrenia patients have less tissue in thalamic regions, prefrontal cortex, and some subcortical areas (Baare et al., 2001; Byne et al., 2001; Gilbert et al., 2001; Pol et al., 2002; Sigmundsson et al., 2001). As shown in Figure 15.5, shrinkage of tissue in these regions leads to corresponding enlargement in the brain's fluid-filled spaces, called *ventricles*. The brain areas in which anatomical abnormalities have been found are active in emotional expression, thinking, and information processing—functions that are disordered in schizophrenia. Enlarged ventricles and reduced prefrontal cortex are more often found in patients whose schizophrenic symptoms are predominantly negative (Sigmundsson et al., 2001), and in one study, faster shrinkage appeared associated with more severe negative symptoms (Mathalon et al., 2001). Patients with mainly positive symptoms tend to have essentially normal looking brains (Andreasen, 1997).

Hundreds of studies of brain functioning in people diagnosed with schizophrenia provide general support for the idea that their impairments in information processing and other cognitive abilities are consistent with structural damage (Clementz, McDowell, & Zisook, 1994; Gur et al., 2000; Niznikiewicz et al., 1997). For example, patients with predominantly negative symptoms are especially likely to display cognitive deficits associated with the frontal-cortex problems often seen in these patients (Buchanan et al., 1994). This research provides important clues, but we still do not know the extent to which, or exactly how, specific structural abnormalities are related to the differing patterns of neurocognitive dysfunction seen in specific forms of schizophrenia (Allen, Goldstein, & Weiner, 2001). For one

Catatonic Stupor The symptoms of schizophrenia often occur in characteristic patterns. This woman's lack of motivation and other negative symptoms of schizophrenia are severe enough that she appears to be in a stupor. Such patients may become rigid or, as in this case, show a waxy flexibility that allows them to be posed in virtually any position. Diagnosticians using the traditional subtype system would probably label her as displaying catatonic schizophrenia.

figure 15.5
Brain Abnormalities in Schizophrenia

Here is a magnetic resonance imaging (MRI) comparison of the brains of identical twins. The schizophrenic twin (on the right) has greatly enlarged ventricles (see arrows) and correspondingly less brain tissue, including in the hippocampal area, a region involved in memory and emotion. The same results appeared in fourteen other identical-twin pairs; by contrast, no significant differences appeared between members of a seven-pair control group of normal identical twins (Suddath et al., 1990). These results support the idea that brain abnormalities are associated with schizophrenia and, because identical twins have the same genes, that such abnormalities may stem from nongenetic factors (Baare et al., 2001).

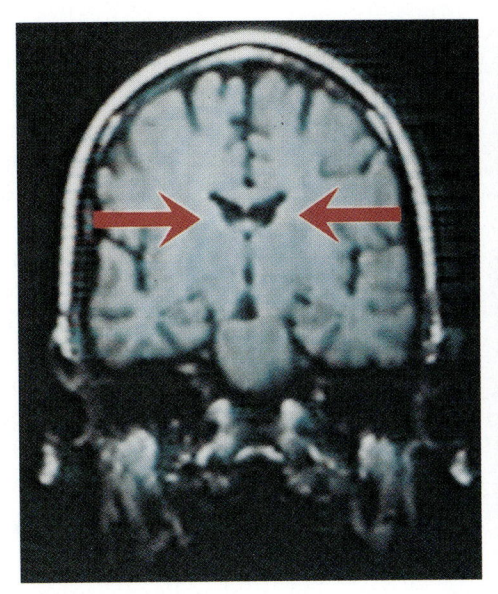

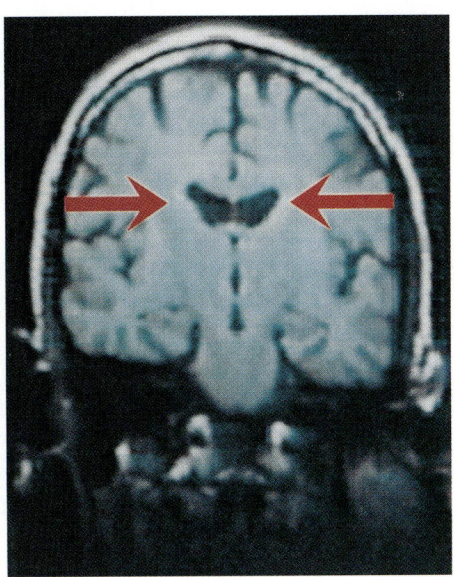

thing, not all schizophrenia patients show brain abnormalities, and some normal people do.

Researchers are also investigating the possibility that abnormalities in brain chemistry—especially in neurotransmitter systems that use dopamine—play a role in causing or intensifying schizophrenic symptoms. Because drugs that block the brain's dopamine receptors often reduce hallucinations, delusions, disordered thinking, and other positive symptoms of schizophrenia, some investigators speculate that schizophrenia results from excess dopamine. However, the relationship between dopamine and schizophrenia appears to be quite complex in several respects (Healy et al., 1998). First, excess dopamine is not always associated with schizophrenia. Second, schizophrenia may involve oversensitivity or undersensitivity of dopamine receptors, as well as an abnormal amount of dopamine itself. And third, schizophrenia might be related to *dysregulation* of dopamine mechanisms in several interconnected regions of the brain (e.g., Healy et al., 1998). Some research suggests, for example, that excessive activity in dopamine systems may be related to the appearance of hallucinations and other positive symptoms of schizophrenia, and that abnormally low dopamine system activity, especially in prefrontal brain areas, might be associated with negative symptoms such as withdrawal (Cohen & Servan-Schreiber, 1992; Davis et al., 1991). Negative symptoms have also been associated with dysfunctions in neural systems that use the neurotransmitter glutamate (Goff & Coyle, 2001).

Some researchers are integrating genetic and environmental explanations of schizophrenia by looking for *neurodevelopmental abnormalities* (Cannon et al., 2002; Gur et al., 2000; Loeber, Cintron, & Yurgelun-Todd, 2001; McGlashan & Hoffman, 2000; Walbeck et al., 2001). Perhaps, they say, some forms of schizophrenia arise from disruptions in brain development during the period from gestation through childhood, when the brain is growing and its various functions are maturing. Studies have shown, for instance, that prenatal exposure to viral infections or other physical traumas is associated with increased risk for developing schizophrenia (Malaspina et al., 2001; Takei et al., 1994). Similarly, children whose birth weight was low or who experienced oxygen deprivation during birth are more likely to have the brain abnormalities described earlier; these abnormalities are especially likely in children of schizophrenic parents (Cannon et al., 1993; Lawrie et al., 2001). Neurodevelopmental factors may help explain why children of schizophrenic parents tend to show the kinds of subtle cognitive and intellectual problems associated with brain abnormalities (Ashe, Berry, & Boulton; 2001; Cannon et al., 1994; McGlashan & Hoffman, 2000; Neumann et al., 1995).

It may be that the expression of a genetically transmitted predisposition for brain abnormality is also enhanced by environmental factors such as maternal drug use during pregnancy, complications during birth, and childhood malnutrition. As mentioned earlier, for example, the development of smaller-than-normal frontal lobes and other brain structures appears to constitute an inherited predisposition for schizophrenia. However, reduced brain growth alone does not appear to be sufficient to cause the disorder. Recent research shows that when only one member of an identical twin pair has schizophrenia, both tend to have unusually small brains, but that the schizophrenic twin's brain in each pair is the smaller of the two (Baare et al., 2001). This finding suggests that some environmentally based process caused degeneration in an already underdeveloped brain, making it even more prone to function abnormally.

Psychological and Social Factors Psychological factors alone are not considered to be primary causes of schizophrenia. Research does suggest, however, that psychological and social processes, including unfortunate learning experiences, dysfunctional cognitive habits, and maladaptive family communication patterns, can contribute to the appearance of schizophrenia and influence its course (Blackwood et al., 2001; Pitschel-Walz et al., 2001). For example, schizophrenia patients living with relatives who are critical, unsupportive, or emotionally overinvolved are especially likely to relapse following improvement (Rosenfarb et al., 2000; Wearden et al., 2000). Family members' negative attitudes may be a source of stress that actually increases the chances that disruptive or odd behaviors will persist or worsen (Rosenfarb et al., 1995). Patients who are helped to cope with these potentially damaging influences tend to have better long-term outcomes (Bustillo et al., 2001; Velligan et al., 2000).

Vulnerability Theory All the causal theories of schizophrenia we have discussed are consistent with the diathesis-stress approach, which assumes that various forms of stress can activate a person's predisposition for disorder (Fowles, 1992). ("In Review: Schizophrenia" summarizes these theories, as well as the symptoms of schizophrenia.) The diathesis-stress approach is embodied in the *vulnerability theory* of schizophrenia (Cornblatt & Erlenmeyer-Kimling, 1985). This theory suggests that (1) vulnerability to schizophrenia is mainly biological; (2) different people have differing degrees of vulnerability; (3) vulnerability is influenced partly by genetic influences on development and partly by neurodevelopmental abnormalities associated with environmental risk factors; and (4) psychological components—such as exposure to poor parenting or high-stress families, having inadequate coping skills, and the like—may help determine whether schizophrenia actually appears and also influence the course of the disorder (Walker & Diforio, 1998; Wearden et al., 2000).

Many different blendings of vulnerability and stress can lead to schizophrenia, as Figure 15.6 illustrates. People whose genetic characteristics or prenatal experiences leave them vulnerable to develop schizophrenia may be especially likely to do so if they are later exposed to learning experiences or family conflicts and other stressors that trigger and maintain schizophrenic patterns of thought and action. Those same experiences and stressors would not be expected to lead to schizophrenia in people who are less vulnerable to developing the disorder. In other words, schizophrenia is a highly complex disorder—probably more than one disorder (Kirkpatrick et al., 2001; Tsuang, Stone, & Faraone, 2000) whose origins appear to lie in numerous biological, psychological, and social domains, some of which are yet to be discovered (Thaker & Carpenter, 2001).

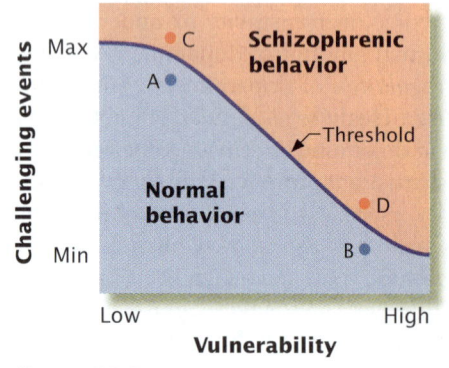

figure 15.6

The Vulnerability Theory of Schizophrenia

According to vulnerability theory, a person can cross the threshold into schizophrenia through many combinations of predisposition and stress. A strong predisposition for schizophrenia and little environmental stress (point D), a weak predisposition and a lot of stress (point C), or any other sufficiently potent combination can lead to the disorder. Points A and B represent combinations of vulnerability and stress that would probably not lead to schizophrenia.

in review: Schizophrenia

Aspect	Key Features
Common Symptoms	
Disorders of thought	Disturbed content, including delusions; disorganization, including loose associations, neologisms, and word salad
Disorders of perception	Hallucinations, or false perceptions; poorly focused attention
Disorders of emotion	Flat affect; inappropriate tears, laughter, or anger
Possible Causes	
Biological	Genetics; abnormalities in brain structure; abnormalities in dopamine systems; neurodevelopmental problems
Psychological	Learned maladaptive behavior; disturbed patterns of family communication

Personality Disorders

Personality disorders are long-standing, inflexible ways of behaving that are not so much severe mental disorders as dysfunctional styles of behavior. These disorders affect all areas of functioning and, beginning in childhood or adolescence, create problems for those who display them and for others (Millon & Davis, 1996). Some psychologists view personality disorders as interpersonal strategies (Kiesler, 1996) or as the extreme, rigid, and maladaptive expressions of personality traits (Widiger, 1997).

The ten personality disorders found on Axis II of *DSM-IV* are grouped into three clusters that share certain features (see Table 15.5). Here, we describe just a few of these disorders. The *odd-eccentric* cluster includes paranoid, schizoid, and schizotypal personality disorders. People diagnosed as having schizotypal personality disorder, for example, display some of the peculiarities seen in schizophrenia but are not disturbed enough to be labeled as schizophrenic. Rather than hallucinating, these people may report "illusions" of sights or sounds. They may also exhibit "magical thinking," including odd superstitions or beliefs (such as that they have extrasensory perception or that salt under the mattress will prevent insomnia). The *anxious-fearful* cluster includes dependent, obsessive-compulsive, and avoidant personality disorders. The avoidant personality disorder, for example, is akin to social phobia in the sense that persons labeled with this disorder tend to be "loners" with a long-standing pattern of avoiding social situations and of being particularly sensitive to criticism or rejection. They want to be with others but are too inhibited. Finally, the *dramatic-erratic* cluster includes the histrionic, narcissistic, borderline, and antisocial personality disorders. The main characteristics of narcissistic personality disorder, for example, are an exaggerated sense of self-importance, extreme sensitivity to criticism, a constant need for attention, and a tendency to arrogantly overestimate personal abilities and achievements. People displaying this disorder feel entitled to special treatment *by* others but are markedly lacking in empathy *for* others.

From the perspective of public welfare and safety, the most serious, costly, and intensively studied personality disorder is **antisocial personality disorder** (e.g., Scott et al., 2001). It is marked by a long-term pattern of irresponsible, impulsive, unscrupulous, even criminal behavior beginning in childhood or early adolescence. In the nineteenth century, this pattern was called *moral insanity,* because the people displaying it appear to have no morals or common decency; later, these people were

---

personality disorders Long-standing, inflexible ways of behaving that create a variety of problems.

antisocial personality disorder A disorder involving impulsive, selfish, unscrupulous, even criminal behavior.

Here are brief descriptions of the ten personality disorders listed on Axis II of *DSM-IV*.

table 15.5
Personality Disorders

Type	Typical Features
Paranoid	Suspiciousness and distrust of others, all of whom are assumed to be hostile.
Schizoid	Detachment from social relationships; restricted range of emotion.
Schizotypal	Detachment from, and great discomfort in, social relationships; odd perceptions, thoughts, beliefs, and behaviors.
Dependent	Helplessness; excessive need to be taken care of; submissive and clinging behavior; difficulty in making decisions.
Obsessive-compulsive	Preoccupation with orderliness, perfection, and control.
Avoidant	Inhibition in social situations; feelings of inadequacy; oversensitivity to criticism.
Histrionic	Excessive emotionality and preoccupation with being the center of attention; emotional shallowness; overly dramatic behavior.
Narcissistic	Exaggerated ideas of self-importance and achievements; preoccupation with fantasies of success; arrogance.
Borderline	Lack of stability in interpersonal relationships, self-image, and emotion; impulsivity; angry outbursts; intense fear of abandonment; recurring suicidal gestures.
Antisocial	Shameless disregard for, and violation of, other people's rights.

called *psychopaths* or *sociopaths*. The current "antisocial personality" label more accurately portrays them as troublesome but not "insane" by the legal standards we will discuss shortly. About 3 percent of men and about 1 percent of women in the United States fall into this diagnostic category (American Psychiatric Association, 1994, 2000).

At their least troublesome, people exhibiting antisocial personality disorder are a nuisance. They are often charming, intelligent, glib talkers who borrow money and fail to return it; they are arrogant and self-centered manipulators who con people into doing things for them, usually by lying and taking advantage of the decency and trust of others. A hallmark of people with antisocial personality disorder is a lack of anxiety, remorse, or guilt, whether they have wrecked a borrowed car or killed an innocent person (Hare, 1993). Fortunately, these individuals tend to become less active and dangerous after the age of forty (Stoff, Breiling, & Maser, 1997). No method has yet been found for permanently altering their behavior (Rice, 1997), but research suggests that identification of antisocial personalities prior to the development of their more treatment-resistant traits may offer the best hope for dealing with this disorder (Lynam, 1996; Stoff, Breiling, & Maser, 1997).

As for the causes of antisocial personality disorder, theories abound. Some studies suggest a genetic predisposition for the disorder (Slutske et al., 2001), possibly in the form of abnormal brain development or chronic underarousal of both the autonomic and central nervous systems (Patrick, Cuthbert, & Lang, 1994; Raine, Venables, & Williams, 1990; Raine et al., 2000). This underarousal may render peo-

A Classic Case of Antisocial Personality Disorder Alfred Jack Oakley meets women through personals ads, claiming to be a millionaire movie producer, pilot, and novelist. In reality, he is a penniless con artist who uses his smooth-talking charm to gain the women's trust so he can steal from them. In January 2000, upon being convicted of stealing a Florida woman's Mercedes, Oakley complimented the prosecutor's skills and the jury's wisdom, and claimed remorse. The judge appeared to see through this ploy ("I don't believe there is a sincere word that ever comes out of your mouth"), but it was still effective enough to get Oakley probation instead of jail time!

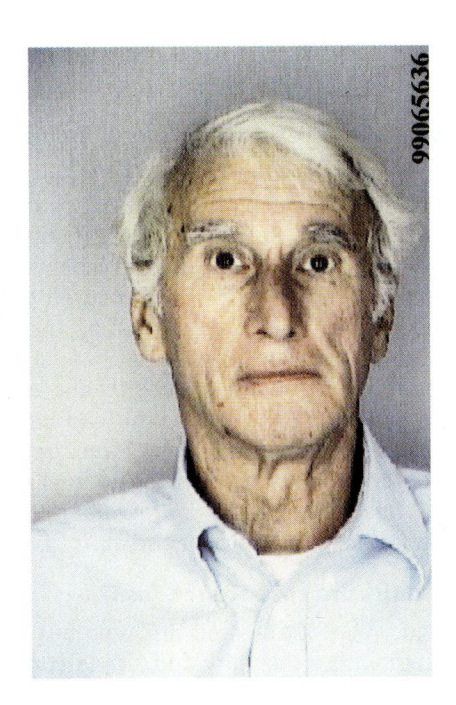

ple less sensitive to punishment and more likely to seek exciting stimulation than is normally the case (Herpertz et al., 2001; Stoff, Breiling, & Maser, 1997). Broken homes, rejection by parents, poor discipline, lack of good parental models, lack of attachment to early caregivers, impulsivity, conflict-filled childhoods, and poverty have all been suggested as psychological and social factors contributing to the development of antisocial personality disorder (Lahey et al., 1995; Raine, Brennan, & Mednick, 1994; Tremblay et al., 1994). The biopsychosocial model suggests that antisocial personality disorder results when these psychosocial and environmental conditions interact with genetic predispositions to low arousal and the sensation seeking and impulsivity associated with it (Rutter, 1997).

FOCUS ON RESEARCH METHODS

Exploring Links Between Child Abuse and Antisocial Personality Disorder

One of the most prominent environmental factors associated with the more violent forms of antisocial personality disorder is the experience of abuse in childhood (MacMillan et al., 2001). However, most of the studies that have found a relationship between childhood abuse and antisocial personality disorder were based on potentially biased reports (Monane, Leichter, & Lewis, 1984; Rosenbaum & Bennett, 1986). People with antisocial personalities—especially those with criminal records—are likely to make up stories of abuse in order to shift blame for their behavior onto others. Even if these people's reports were accurate, however, most of the studies lacked a control group of people from similar backgrounds who were not antisocial. Because of this research design flaw, it is virtually impossible to separate the effects of reported child abuse from the effects of poverty or other factors that might also have contributed to the development of antisocial personality disorder.

● **What was the researcher's question?**

Can childhood abuse cause antisocial personality disorder? To help answer this question and to correct some of the flaws in earlier studies, Cathy Widom (1989a) used a prospective research design, first finding cases of childhood abuse and then looking for the effects of that abuse on adult behavior.

● How did the researcher answer the question?

Widom began by identifying 416 adults whose backgrounds included official records of having been physically or sexually abused before the age of eleven. She then explored the stories of these people's lives, as told in police and school records, as well as in two-hour diagnostic interviews. To reduce experimenter bias and distorted reporting, Widom ensured that the interviewers remained "blind" to the purpose of the study and that the respondents were told only that the researchers wanted to learn about people who had grown up in a midwestern U.S. metropolitan area in the late 1960s and early 1970s. Widom also selected a comparison group of 283 people who had no history of abuse, but who were similar to the abused sample in terms of age, gender, ethnicity, hospital of birth, schools attended, and area of residence. Her goal was to obtain a nonabused control group that had been exposed to approximately the same environmental risk factors and socioeconomic conditions as the abused children.

● What did the researcher find?

First, Widom (1989a) tested the hypothesis that exposure to abuse in childhood is associated with criminality and/or violence in later life. She found that 26 percent of the abused youngsters went on to commit juvenile crimes, 29 percent were arrested as adults, and 11 percent committed violent crimes. These percentages were significantly higher than the figures for the nonabused group. The association between criminality and abuse was stronger for males than for females, and stronger for African Americans than for European Americans. And overall, victims of physical abuse were more likely to commit violent crimes as adults than were victims of sexual abuse.

Next, Widom tested the hypothesis that childhood abuse is associated with the development of antisocial personality disorder (Luntz & Widom, 1994). In fact, the abused group exhibited a significantly higher rate of antisocial personality disorder (13.5 percent) than did the comparison group (7.1 percent). The apparent role of abuse in antisocial personality disorder was particularly pronounced in men, and it remained strong even when other factors—such as age, ethnicity, and socioeconomic status—were accounted for in the statistical analyses. It is interesting to note that one other factor—failure to graduate from high school—was also strongly associated with the appearance of antisocial personality disorder, whether or not childhood abuse had occurred.

● What do the results mean?

Widom's research supported earlier studies in finding an association between childhood abuse and criminality, violence, and antisocial personality disorder. Further, although her study did not permit a firm conclusion that abuse alone causes antisocial personality disorder, the data from its prospective design added strength to the argument that abuse may be an important causal factor (Widom, 2000). The results suggest that there are probably other causes as well. For one thing, abuse is often part of a larger pool of experiences, such as exposure to deviant models, social rejection, poor supervision, and the like.

Finally, Widom's work offers yet another reason—as if more reasons were needed—why it is so important to prevent the physical and sexual abuse of children. The long-term consequences of such abuse can be tragic not only for its immediate victims but also for those victimized by the violence, criminal actions, and antisocial behavior perpetrated by some abused children as they grow up (Weiler & Widom, 1996).

● What do we still need to know?

Further research is needed to discover whether antisocial personality disorder stems from abuse itself, from one of the factors accompanying it, or from some other specific combination of known and still-unknown risk factors. For example,

Widom's study suggests that one or more of the factors leading teenagers to drop out (or be thrown out) of high school might be an independent cause of antisocial personality disorder.

In addition, because Widom's study found that violence, criminal behavior, and antisocial personality disorder are seen in only a minority of abused children, her results raise the question of what genetic characteristics or environmental experiences serve to protect some children from at least some of the devastating effects of abuse (Rind & Tromovitch, 1997; Rind, Tromovitch, & Bauserman, 1998). An understanding of these protective elements might go a long way toward the development of programs for the prevention of antisocial personality disorder.

A Sampling of Other Psychological Disorders

The disorders described so far represent some of the most prevalent and socially disruptive psychological problems encountered in cultures around the world. Several others are mentioned in other chapters. In the chapter on consciousness, for example, we discuss insomnia, night terrors, and other sleep disorders; mental retardation is covered in the chapter on cognitive abilities; sexual dysfunctions are mentioned in the chapter on motivation and emotion; and posttraumatic stress disorder is described in the chapter on health, stress, and coping. Here, we consider two other significant psychological problems: disorders of childhood and substance-related disorders.

Psychological Disorders of Childhood

The physical, cognitive, emotional, and social changes seen in childhood—and the stress associated with them—can create or worsen psychological disorders in children. Stress can do the same in adults, but childhood disorders are not just miniature versions of adult psychopathology. Because children's development is still incomplete and because their capacity to cope with stress is limited, children are often vulnerable to special types of disorders. Two broad categories encompass the majority of childhood behavior problems: externalizing disorders and internalizing disorders (Achenbach, 1997; Nigg, 2000).

The *externalizing*, or *undercontrolled*, category includes behaviors that are particularly disturbing to people in the child's environment. Lack of control shows up as *conduct disorders* in 4 to 10 percent of children, mostly boys (Martin & Hoffman, 1990). Conduct disorders are characterized by a relatively stable pattern of aggression, disobedience, destructiveness, and other problematic behaviors (Lahey et al., 1995). Often these behaviors involve criminal activity, and they may signal the development of antisocial personality disorder (Loeber & Stouthamer-Loeber, 1998). A genetic predisposition toward conduct disorders is suggested by the fact that many such children have parents who display antisocial personality disorder. There is no doubt, however, that environmental and parenting factors also help to shape these children's antisocial behavior (Lahey et al., 1995; U.S. Surgeon General, 1999).

Another kind of externalizing problem, also seen primarily in boys, is *attention deficit hyperactivity disorder (ADHD)*. This diagnosis is given to children who are impulsive and unable to concentrate on an activity as well as other children their age can (Nigg, 2001). Many of these children are *hyperactive*; they have great difficulty sitting still or otherwise controlling their physical activity. Their impulsiveness and lack of self-control contribute to significant impairments in learning, and to an astonishing ability to annoy and exhaust those around them (Henker & Whalen, 1989). Genetic predisposition, brain damage, poisoning from lead or other household substances, and ineffective parenting have all been proposed as possible causes

Active or Hyperactive? Normal behavior for children in one culture might be considered hyperactive in other cultures. Do people in the *same* culture disagree on what is hyperactive? To find out, ask two or three friends to join you in observing a group of children at a playground, a schoolyard, a park, or some other public place. Ask your friends to privately identify which children they would label as "hyperactive," and then count how many of their choices agree with yours and with the rest of the group.

of ADHD, but the role played by each of these factors is still uncertain (Daly et al., 1999; U.S. Surgeon General, 1999). Also uncertain is exactly what constitutes hyperactivity (Panksepp, 1998). Cultural standards about acceptable activity levels in children vary, so a "hyperactive" child in one culture might be considered merely "active" in another. In fact, when mental health professionals from four cultures used the same rating scales to judge the presence and severity of hyperactivity in a videotaped sample of children's behavior, the Chinese and Indonesians rated the children as significantly more hyperactive than did their American and Japanese colleagues (Mann et al., 1992). Such findings remind us again that sociocultural factors can be important determinants of what is acceptable, and thus what is abnormal, in various parts of the world.

A second group of child behavior problems falls into the *internalizing*, or *overcontrolled*, category. Children in this category experience distress, especially depression and anxiety, and may be socially withdrawn. Those displaying *separation anxiety disorder*, for example, constantly worry that they will be lost, kidnapped, or injured or that some harm may come to a parent (usually the mother). The child clings desperately to the parent and becomes upset or sick at the prospect of any separation. Refusal to go to school (sometimes called "school phobia") is often the result.

A few childhood disorders, such as *pervasive developmental disorders*, do not fall into either the externalizing or internalizing category. Children diagnosed with these disorders show severe deficits in communication and impaired social relationships; they also often display repetitive, stereotyped behaviors and unusual preoccupations and interests (American Psychiatric Association, 2000; Filipek et al., 1999). The disorders in this group, also known as *autistic spectrum disorders* (Filipek et al., 1999; Rutter & Schopler, 1992; U.S. Surgeon General, 1999), share many of these core symptoms, although the severity of the symptoms may vary. Estimates of the prevalence of autistic spectrum disorders range from 10 to 20 children per 10,000 births (Bryson & Smith, 1998; Filipek et al., 1999) to as high as 62 per 10,000 (Chakrabarti & Fombonne, 2001). About half of these children suffer *autistic disorder*, which can be the most severe disorder of the group. The earliest signs of autistic disorder usually occur within the first thirty months after birth, as these babies show little or no evidence of forming an attachment to their caregivers. Language development is seriously disrupted in most of these children; half of them never learn to speak at all. However, those who display high functioning autism or a less severe autistic spectrum disorder called *Asperger's disorder* are able to function adaptively and, in some cases, independently as adults (e.g., Grandin, 1996).

Possible biological roots of autistic disorder include genetic factors (Burac, 2001; Vastag, 2001) or neurodevelopmental abnormalities affecting language and communication (Courchesne et al., 2001; U.S. Surgeon General, 1999). The more specific causes of autistic disorder remain unknown, but it is likely that genetic influences, along with prenatal damage leading to structural brain abnormalities, are involved (Carper & Courchesne, 2000; Juul-Dam, Townsend, & Courchesne, 2001; Rodier, 2000; Szatmari et al., 1998; U.S. Surgeon General, 1999). Researchers today have rejected the once-popular hypothesis that autistic disorder is caused by cold and unresponsive parents.

Disorders of childhood differ from adult disorders not only because the patterns of behavior are distinct but also because their early onset renders childhood disorders especially capable of disrupting development. To take one example, children whose separation anxiety causes spotty school attendance may not only fall behind academically but also fail to form the relationships with other children that promote normal social development. Some children never make up for this deficit. They may drop out of school and risk a life of poverty, crime, and violence. Moreover, children are dependent on others to obtain help for their psychological problems, and all too often those problems may go unrecognized or untreated. For some, the long-term result may be adult forms of mental disorder.

Substance-Related Disorders

Childhood disorders, especially externalizing disorders, often lead to **substance-related disorders** in adolescence and adulthood. *DSM-IV* defines *substance-related disorders* as the use of psychoactive drugs for months or years in ways that harm the user or others. These disorders create major political, economic, social, and health problems worldwide. The substances involved most often are alcohol and other depressants (such as barbiturates), opiates (such as heroin), stimulants (such as cocaine or amphetamines), and hallucinogens (such as LSD).

As mentioned in the chapter on consciousness, one effect of using some substances (including alcohol, heroin, and amphetamines) is **addiction,** a physical need for the substance. *DSM-IV* calls addiction *physiological dependence*. Usually, addiction is evident when the person begins to need more and more of a substance to achieve the desired state; this is called building a *tolerance*. When addicted people stop using the substance, they experience painful, often terrifying, and potentially dangerous *withdrawal symptoms* as the body tries to readjust to a substance-free state. However, not all dependence is physiological in nature (Widiger & Smith, 1994). People can also display *psychological dependence*, sometimes called *behavioral dependence*; in such cases, a drug has become their primary source of reward, and their lives essentially revolve around getting and using it. People who are psychologically dependent on a drug often display problems that are at least as serious as, and sometimes more difficult to treat than, those exhibited by people who are physiologically addicted.

Even when use of a drug does not create psychological or physiological dependence, some people may use it in a way that is harmful to themselves or others. For example, they may rely on the drug to bolster self-confidence or to avoid depression, anger, fear, or other unpleasant feelings. However, the drug effects these people seek may also impair their ability to hold a job, care for their children, or drive safely. This pattern of behavior, defined in *DSM-IV* as *substance abuse*, creates significant social, legal, and interpersonal problems.

---

substance-related disorders Problems that involve the use of psychoactive drugs for months or years in ways that harm the user or others.

addiction The development of a physical need for a psychoactive drug.

In short, substance-related disorders can be extremely serious, even when they do not involve addiction. The chapter on consciousness includes a discussion of how consciousness can be affected by a wide range of psychoactive drugs. Here we focus more specifically on problems associated with the use of alcohol, heroin, and cocaine.

Alcohol Use Disorders

About 7.4 percent of U.S. adults—about 14 million people—display *alcohol dependence* or *alcohol abuse,* a pattern of continuous or intermittent drinking that may lead to addiction and almost always causes severe social, physical, and other problems (National Institute on Alcohol Abuse and Alcoholism, 2000). Males outnumber females in this category by a ratio of about three to one, although the problem is on the rise among women and among teenagers of both genders (Blum, Nielsen, & Riggs, 1998; U.S. Surgeon General, 1999). Prolonged overuse of alcohol can result in life-threatening liver damage, reduced cognitive abilities, vitamin deficiencies that can lead to an irreversible brain disorder called *Korsakoff's psychosis* (severe memory loss), and a host of other physical ailments. Many of these adverse effects appear to be due to the fact that excessive alcohol consumption causes deterioration in several brain areas (Hommer et al., 2001; Pfefferbaum et al., 2001).

Alcohol dependence or abuse, commonly referred to as **alcoholism**, has been implicated in half of all the traffic fatalities, homicides, and suicides that occur each year (NIAAA, 1998). Alcoholism also figures prominently in rape and child abuse, as well as in elevated rates of hospitalization and absenteeism from work, resulting in total costs to society of over $180 billion each year (Harwood, Fountain, & Livermore, 1998; NIAAA, 2000; U.S. Department of Justice, 1998). It is estimated that about half of U.S. adults have a close relative who is or was an alcoholic, and that about 25 percent of children are exposed to adults who display alcohol abuse or dependence (NIAAA, 2000). Children growing up in families in which one or both parents abuse alcohol are at increased risk for developing a host of mental disorders, including substance-abuse disorders (Sher et al., 1991). And, as described in the chapter on human development, children of mothers who abused alcohol during pregnancy may be born with fetal alcohol syndrome.

The biopsychosocial model suggests that alcohol use disorders stem from a combination of genetic characteristics (including inherited aspects of temperament such as impulsivity and emotionality) and what people learn in their social and cultural environment (Petry, 2001; Sher et al., 1991; Wall et al., 2001). For example, youngsters typically learn to drink by watching others (especially their friends), and by developing expectations that alcohol will make them feel good and help them cope with stressors (Koopmans & Boomsma, 1996). But alcohol use can become abuse, and often addiction, if drinking is a person's main coping strategy (NIAAA, 2000; see Table 15.6). The stress-reduction theory of alcoholism has been supported by studies showing that alcohol can reduce animals' learned fear of a particular location and that animals in a stressful conflict situation will choose to drink alcohol if it is available. The stress-reducing effects of alcohol have also been shown in humans, but not consistently (Burke & Stephens, 2000; Cooper et al., 1992a).

The importance of social and cultural learning is further suggested by evidence that alcoholism is more common among ethnic and cultural groups (such as the Irish and English) in which frequent drinking tends to be socially reinforced than among groups (such as Jews, Italians, and Chinese) in which all but moderate drinking tends to be discouraged (Wilson et al., 1996). Moreover, differing expressions of social support for drinking can result in differing consumption patterns within a cultural group. For example, one study found significantly more drinking among Japanese men living in Japan (where social norms for males' drinking are quite permissive) compared with those living in Hawaii or California, where excessive drinking is less strongly supported (Kitano et al., 1992). Learning would also help explain why the incidence of alcoholism is higher than average among people working as

alcoholism A pattern of drinking that may lead to addiction and almost always causes severe social, physical, and other problems.

Social drinking differs markedly from alcoholism, but it is all too easy for people to drift from social to alcoholic drinking patterns. Alcoholism can include heavy drinking on a daily basis, on weekends only, or in isolated binges lasting weeks or months (NIAAA, 2000).

table 15.6

Social Drinking Versus Alcoholism

Social Drinkers	Alcoholics
Sip drinks	Gulp drinks.
Usually drink in moderation and can control the amount consumed.	Drink increasing quantities (develop tolerance); sometimes drink until blacking out; may not recall events that occur while drinking.
Usually drink to enhance the pleasure of social situations.	Drink for the chemical effect, often to relieve tension or face problems; often drink alone, including in the morning to reduce hangover or to face the day.
Do not usually think about or talk about drinking in nondrinking situations.	Become preoccupied with getting their next drink, often sneaking drinks during working hours or at home.
Do not experience physical, social, or occupational problems caused by drinking.	Suffer physical disorders, damaged social relationships, and impaired capacity to work because of drinking.

bartenders and cocktail servers, as well as in other jobs where alcohol is available and drinking is socially reinforced, or even expected (Fillmore & Caetano, 1980). (Of course, it is also possible that attraction to alcohol led some of these people into such jobs in the first place.)

Learning, then, appears to be implicated in excessive drinking, but heredity may also play a role. For example, the children of alcoholics are more likely than others to become alcoholics themselves; and if the children are identical twins, both are at increased risk for alcoholism, even when raised apart (Kendler et al., 1992; McGue, 1999; Slutske et al., 1998). The role of genetics appears to be greatest among people who begin their alcoholic drinking pattern at an early age and display other conduct problems as teenagers (McGue, Pickens, & Svikis, 1992; Slutske et al., 1998). It is still unclear just what might be inherited or which genes are involved. One possibility involves inherited abnormalities in the brain's neurotransmitter systems or in the body's metabolism of alcohol (Devor, 1994; Kranzler & Anton, 1994; Nurnberger et al., 2001). Males who are alcoholics do tend to be less sensitive than other males to the effects of alcohol—a factor that may contribute to greater consumption (Pollack, 1992; Schuckit, 1998). The recently completed decoding of the human genome is guiding researchers to focus on a few specific chromosomes as the possible location of genes that predispose people to—or protect them from—the development of alcoholism (Foroud et al., 2000; NIAAA, 2000; Reich et al., 1998).

Heroin and Cocaine Dependence Like alcoholics, heroin and cocaine addicts suffer many serious physical problems, both as a result of the drugs themselves and of the poor eating and other unhealthy habits that drug use engenders. The risk of death from an overdose, contaminated drugs, or AIDS (contracted through blood in shared needles), as well as from suicide, is also always present. Dependence on these drugs tends to be more prevalent among males, especially young males (Warner et al., 1995).

Continued use or overdoses of cocaine can cause problems ranging from nausea and hyperactivity to paranoid thinking, sudden depressive "crashes," and even death. An estimated 1.5 million Americans have become physiologically dependent on cocaine, and millions more use it on occasion (National Institute on Drug Abuse,

1999). The widespread availability of crack, a powerful and relatively cheap form of cocaine, has made it one of the most dangerous and addicting drugs in existence. Pregnant women who use cocaine are much more likely than nonusers to lose their babies through spontaneous abortion, placental detachment, early fetal death, or stillbirth.

Although addiction to substances like heroin and cocaine is largely understood to be a biological process brought about by the physiological effects of the drugs, explaining why people first use them is more complicated. Beyond the obvious and immediate pleasure that these drugs provide, the causes of initial drug abuse are less well established than the reasons for alcohol abuse. One line of theorizing suggests that there might be a genetic tendency toward behavioral dysregulation or compulsion that predisposes some people to abuse many kinds of drugs, including alcohol (Holden, 1991; Smith et al., 1992). A study supporting this possibility found a link between alcoholism in biological parents and drug abuse in adopted-away sons (Cadoret et al., 1995). The same study also found a link between antisocial personality traits in biological parents and antisocial acts—including drug abuse—in the sons they had put up for adoption.

A number of psychological factors have been proposed as initial causes of substance abuse. One theory suggests that drug taking begins as self-medication for stress reactions or for the symptoms of anxiety, depression, schizophrenia, and other disorders that are seen in more than half of all substance abusers (Blanchard, 2000; U.S. Surgeon General, 1999). Other possible psychological causes include imitation of drug-using peers, impulsivity, thrill seeking, and social maladjustment. Research has still not established why drugs become a problem for some people and not for others, but as with so many other disorders, it is likely that some biological predisposition sets the stage on which specific psychological processes and stressors play out their roles in specific social and cultural contexts.

Mental Illness and the Law

Cheryl was barely twenty when she married Glen, a graduate student in biology. They moved into a large apartment complex near the university and within three years had two sons. Cheryl's friends had always been impressed by the attention and affection she showered on her boys; she seemed to be the ideal mother. She and Glen had serious marital problems, however, and she felt trapped and unhappy. One day Glen came home to find that Cheryl had stabbed both children to death. At her murder trial, she was found not guilty by reason of insanity and was placed in a state mental institution.

This verdict reflects U.S. laws and rules that protect people with severe psychological disorders when they are accused of crimes (Cassel & Bernstein, 2001). Similar laws and rules are in effect in many other countries as well. The protection takes two forms.

First, under certain conditions, people designated as mentally ill may be protected from prosecution. If, at the time of their trial, individuals accused of a crime are unable to understand the proceedings and charges against them or to assist in their own defense, they are declared to be *mentally incompetent to stand trial*. In such cases, defendants are sent to a mental institution until they are judged to have become mentally competent. If still not competent after a court-specified period—two years, in most cases—a defendant may be ruled permanently ineligible for trial and either committed in civil court to a mental institution or released. Release is rare, however, because competency to stand trial requires only minimal mental abilities. If drugs can produce even temporary mental competence, the defendant will usually go to trial (Nietzel, 1999).

Assessment of Mental Competence
Andrea Yates admitted to drowning all five of her children, one by one, in the bathtub of her Houston home in 2001. She had twice tried to kill herself in previous years, and she was reportedly depressed at the time of the murders. Accordingly, she pleaded not guilty by reason of insanity, but the first legal step in deciding her fate was to confine her in a mental institution for assessment of her mental competency to stand trial. Following the testimony of the psychologists who examined her, she was found competent, and ultimately sentenced to life in prison.

Second, mentally ill defendants may be protected from punishment. In most U.S. states, they may be judged *not guilty by reason of insanity* if, at the time of the crime, mental illness prevented them from (1) understanding what they were doing, (2) knowing that what they were doing was wrong, or (3) resisting the impulse to do wrong. The first two of these criteria—understanding the nature or wrongfulness of an act—are "cognitive" criteria known as the M'Naughton rule. This rule stems from an 1843 case in England in which a man named Daniel M'Naughton, upon hearing "instructions from God," tried to kill British prime minister Robert Peel; he was found not guilty by reason of insanity and put into a mental institution for life. The third criterion, which is based on a defendant's emotional state during a crime, is known as the irresistible-impulse test. All three criteria are combined in a rule proposed by the American Law Institute (ALI) in 1962 and now followed in about half of the U.S. states: "A person is not responsible for criminal conduct if at the time of such conduct as a result of mental disease or defect he lacks substantial capacity either to appreciate the criminality (wrongfulness) of his conduct or to conform his conduct to the requirements of law" (ALI, 1962, p. 66).

In 1984, after John Hinckley, Jr., was found not guilty by reason of insanity under the ALI rule for his attempted assassination of President Ronald Reagan, the U.S. Congress passed the Insanity Defense Reform Act, which eliminated the irresistible-impulse criterion from the definition of insanity in federal cases. Such laws highlight the fact that *insanity* is a legal term, not a psychiatric diagnosis; it does not appear in *DSM-IV* (Cassel & Bernstein, 2001). The responsibility falls on judges and juries to weigh evidence and testimony and decide whether or not a defendant should be held responsible for criminal acts. Defendants who are judged not guilty by reason of insanity and who still display a psychological disorder are usually required to receive treatment, typically through commitment to a hospital, until judged to be cured or no longer dangerous.

Insanity rules have been faulted on several grounds. Some critics argue that everyone, even those who meet legal criteria for insanity, should be held responsible for their actions and punished for their crimes. Others point out significant problems in the implementation of insanity rules. For one thing, different experts often give conflicting, highly technical testimony about a defendant's sanity at the time of a crime. (One expert said Cheryl was sane; another concluded she was insane.) Jurors are then left in the difficult position of deciding which expert to believe and what to make of the experts' diagnostic judgments. Their task is complicated by the fact that people suffering from mental disorders—even those as severe as schizophrenia—are still capable of some rational decision making and of controlling some aspects of their behavior (Grisso & Applebaum, 1995). Concern over such problems has led two U.S. states, Idaho and Montana, to abolish the insanity defense. Other states have tried less extreme reforms. In twelve states, it is now possible for juries to find defendants *guilty but mentally ill*. These defendants still serve a sentence, and although they are supposed to receive treatment while confined, they seldom do (Cassel & Bernstein, 2001). A second reform already noted is that federal courts no longer use the irresistible-impulse criterion in defining insanity. Third, federal courts and some state courts now require defendants to prove that they were insane at the time of their crime, rather than requiring the prosecution to prove that the defendants were sane.

Does the insanity defense allow lots of criminals to "get away with murder"? No. Although certain high-profile cases might suggest otherwise, the insanity plea is used in fewer than 1 of every 200 felony cases in the United States—usually when the defendant displays severe psychological disorder—and this plea is successful in only 2 of every 1,000 attempts (Silver, Cirincione, & Steadman, 1994). Further, the few defendants found not guilty by reason of insanity are usually hospitalized for two to nine times as long as they would have spent in prison had they been convicted (Silver, 1995; Steadman, 1993). For example, John Hinckley, Jr., has been in St. Elizabeth's hospital in Washington, D.C., since 1982, and in spite of his annual efforts to be released, he is unlikely to get out anytime soon.

In summary, legislators, victims' rights groups, civil liberties advocates, and ordinary citizens are constantly seeking the proper balance between protecting the rights of defendants and protecting society from dangerous criminals. In doing so, the sociocultural values that shape views about what is abnormal also influence judgments about the extent to which abnormality should relieve people of responsibility for criminal behavior.

LINKAGES

As noted in the chapter on introducing psychology, all of psychology's subfields are related to one another. Our discussion of how classical conditioning can lead to phobias illustrates just one way in which the topic of this chapter, psychological disorders, is linked to the subfield of learning (which is the focus of the chapter by that name). The Linkages diagram shows ties to two other subfields as well, and there are many more ties throughout the book. Looking for linkages among subfields will help you see how they all fit together and help you better appreciate the big picture that is psychology.

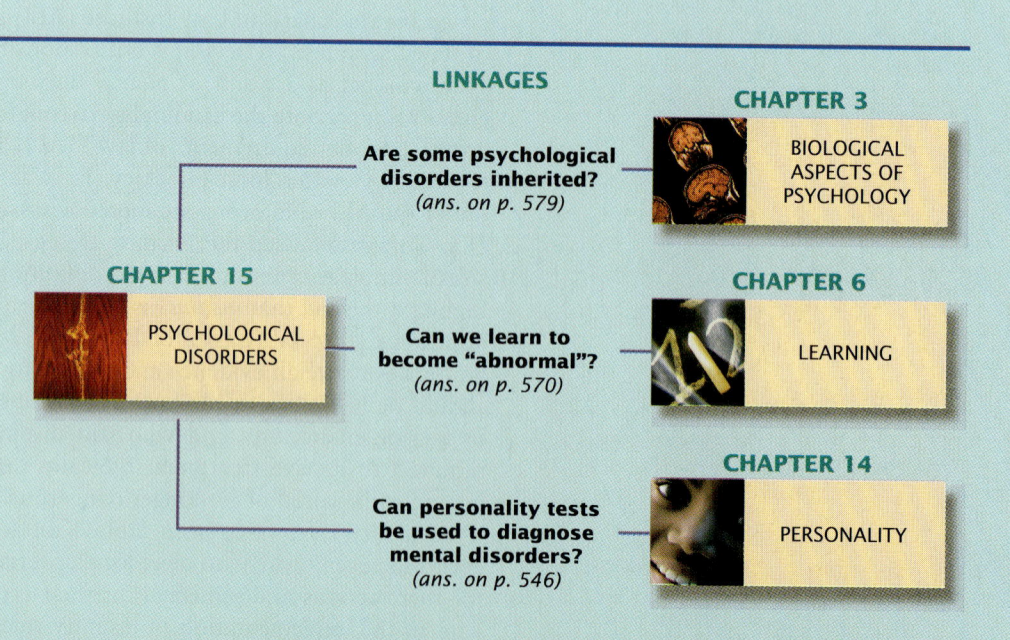

LINKAGES

CHAPTER 15 — PSYCHOLOGICAL DISORDERS

- Are some psychological disorders inherited? (ans. on p. 579) → **CHAPTER 3** BIOLOGICAL ASPECTS OF PSYCHOLOGY
- Can we learn to become "abnormal"? (ans. on p. 570) → **CHAPTER 6** LEARNING
- Can personality tests be used to diagnose mental disorders? (ans. on p. 546) → **CHAPTER 14** PERSONALITY

SUMMARY

Psychopathology involves patterns of thinking, feeling, and behaving that cause personal distress or that significantly impair a person's social or occupational functioning.

Defining Psychological Disorders

The definition of abnormality is largely determined by social and cultural factors.

What Is Abnormal?

The criteria for judging abnormality include statistical infrequency (a comparison with what most people do), norm violation, and personal suffering. Each of these criteria is flawed to some extent.

Behavior in Context: A Practical Approach

The practical approach to defining abnormality, which considers the content, context, and consequences of behavior, emphasizes the question of whether individuals show *impaired functioning* in fulfilling the roles appropriate for particular people in particular settings, cultures, and historical eras.

Explaining Psychological Disorders

Abnormal behavior has been attributed, at one time or another, to many different factors, including the action of supernatural forces.

The Biopsychosocial Model

In today's *biopsychosocial model,* mental disorders are attributed to the combination and interaction of biological, psychological, and sociocultural factors. Biological factors are emphasized by the medical, or *neurobiological model,* which sees psychological disorders as reflecting particular disturbances in the anatomy and chemistry of the brain and in other biological processes. The causal factors emphasized by the *psychological model* of mental disorders include unconscious conflicts, maladaptive cognitive schemas, learning, or blocked actualizing tendencies. The *sociocultural model* focuses on factors that help define abnormality and influence the form that disorders take in different parts of the world.

Diathesis-Stress as an Integrative Explanation

No single aspect of the biopsychosocial model can adequately explain all psychological disorders. However, the *diathesis-stress approach* takes all of them into account by suggesting that biological, psychological, and sociocultural characteristics create predispositions for disorder that are translated into symptoms in the face of sufficient amounts of stress.

Classifying Psychological Disorders

There seems to be a set of behavior patterns that roughly defines abnormality in most cultures.

A Classification System: DSM-IV

The dominant system for classifying abnormal behavior in North America is the *Diagnostic and Statistical Manual of Mental Disorders (DSM-IV)* of the American Psychiatric Association. It includes more than three hundred specific categories of mental disorders.

Purposes and Problems of Diagnosis

Diagnosis helps to identify the features, causes, and most effective methods of treating various psychological disorders. Research on the reliability and validity of *DSM-IV* shows that it is a useful, but imperfect, classification system.

Anxiety Disorders

Long-standing and disruptive patterns of anxiety characterize *anxiety disorders.*

Types of Anxiety Disorders

The most prevalent type of anxiety disorder is *phobia,* which includes *specific phobias, social phobias,* and *agoraphobia.* Other anxiety disorders are *generalized anxiety disorder,* which involves nonspecific anxiety; *panic disorder,* which brings unpredictable attacks of intense anxiety; and *obsessive-compulsive disorder (OCD),* in which uncontrollable repetitive thoughts and ritualistic actions occur.

Causes of Anxiety Disorders

The most influential explanations of anxiety disorders suggest that they may develop through the combination of a biological predisposition for strong anxiety reactions and the impact of fear-enhancing thought patterns and learned anxiety responses.

Somatoform Disorders

Somatoform disorders, including *conversion disorder,* involve physical problems that have no apparent physical cause. Other examples are *hypochondriasis,* an unjustified concern over becoming ill; *somatization disorder,* in which the person complains of numerous, unconfirmed physical complaints; and *pain disorder,* in which pain is felt in the absence of a known physical cause.

Dissociative Disorders

Dissociative disorders involve rare conditions such as *dissociative fugue, dissociative amnesia,* and *dissociative identity disorder,* or *DID* (multiple personality disorder), in which a person suffers memory loss or develops two or more identities.

Mood Disorders

Mood disorders, also known as affective disorders, involve extreme moods that may be inconsistent with events.

Depressive Disorders

Major depressive disorder is marked by feelings of inadequacy, worthlessness, and guilt; in extreme cases, *delusions* may also occur. Also seen is *dysthymic disorder*, which includes similar but less severe symptoms persisting for a long period. Suicide is often related to these disorders.

Bipolar Disorders

Alternating periods of depression and *mania* characterize *bipolar I disorder*, which is also known as manic depression. *Cyclothymic disorder*, an alternating pattern of less extreme mood swings, is more common.

Causes of Mood Disorders

Mood disorders have been attributed to biological causes such as genetics—which underlie disruptions in neurotransmitter and endocrine systems—and irregularities in biological rhythms. Both loss of significant sources of reward and maladaptive patterns of thinking are among the psychological causes proposed. A predisposition toward some of these disorders may be inherited, although their appearance may be determined by a diathesis-stress process.

Schizophrenia

Schizophrenia is perhaps the most severe and puzzling disorder of all.

Symptoms of Schizophrenia

Among the symptoms of schizophrenia are problems in thinking, perception (often including *hallucinations*), attention, emotion, movement, motivation, and daily functioning.

Categorizing Schizophrenia

Although *DSM-IV* lists five major subtypes of schizophrenia (paranoid, disorganized, catatonic, undifferentiated, and residual), many researchers today favor a descriptive system that focuses on whether patients display mainly *positive symptoms* (such as hallucinations and disorganized thoughts) or *negative symptoms* (such as lack of speech and restricted emotional expression). Each category of symptoms may be traceable to different causes; predominantly negative symptoms tend to be associated with more severe disorder and less successful treatment outcomes.

Causes of Schizophrenia

Genetic factors, neurotransmitter problems, abnormalities in brain structure and functioning, and neurodevelopmental abnormalities are biological factors implicated in schizophrenia. Psychological explanations have pointed to maladaptive learning experiences and disturbed family interactions. The diathesis-stress approach, often described in terms of the vulnerability model, remains a promising framework for research into the multiple causes of schizophrenia.

Personality Disorders

Personality disorders are long-term patterns of maladaptive behavior that may be disturbing to the person displaying them and/or to others. Examples include schizotypal, avoidant, narcissistic, and *antisocial personality disorders*.

A Sampling of Other Psychological Disorders

Psychological Disorders of Childhood

Childhood disorders can be categorized as externalizing disorders (such as conduct disorders or attention deficit hyperactivity disorder) and internalizing disorders (in which children show overcontrol and experience distress, as in separation anxiety disorder). Pervasive developmental disorders do not fall into either category and include the autistic spectrum disorders. In autistic disorder, which can be the most severe of these, children show no interest in, or attachment to, others.

Substance-Related Disorders

Substance-related disorders involving alcohol and other drugs affect millions of people. *Addiction* to, psychological dependence on, or abuse of these substances contributes to disastrous personal and social problems, including physical illnesses, accidents, and crime. Genetic factors may create a predisposition for *alcoholism*, but learning, cultural traditions, and other psychosocial processes are also important. In the case of dependence on heroin and cocaine, stress reduction, self-medication for other mental disorders, imitation, thrill seeking, and social maladjustment have been proposed as important causal factors, along with genetics. The exact causes of initial use of these drugs, however, are unknown.

Mental Illness and the Law

Current rules protect people accused of crimes from prosecution or punishment if they are mentally incompetent at the time of their trials or if they were legally insane at the time of their crimes. Difficulty in establishing the mental state of defendants and other knotty problems have created dissatisfaction with those rules and prompted a number of reforms, including the "guilty but mentally ill" verdict.

Treatment of Psychological Disorders

16

Basic Features of Treatment

Psychodynamic Psychotherapy
Classical Psychoanalysis
Contemporary Variations on Psychoanalysis

Humanistic Psychotherapy
Client-Centered Therapy
Gestalt Therapy

Behavior Therapy
Techniques for Modifying Behavior
Cognitive-Behavior Therapy

Group, Family, and Couples Therapy
Group Therapy
Family and Couples Therapy

Evaluating Psychotherapy

THINKING CRITICALLY: Are All Forms of Therapy Equally Effective?

FOCUS ON RESEARCH METHODS: Which Therapies Work Best for Which Problems?
Addressing the "Ultimate Question"
Cultural Factors in Psychotherapy
Rules and Rights in the Therapeutic Relationship

Biological Treatments
Electroconvulsive Therapy
Psychosurgery
Psychoactive Drugs
Evaluating Psychoactive Drug Treatments
Drugs and Psychotherapy

LINKAGES: Biological Aspects of Psychology and the Treatment of Psychological Disorders

Community Psychology: From Treatment to Prevention

Linkages

Summary

In the chapter on psychological disorders, we described José, a fifty-five-year-old electronics technician who had to take medical leave from his job after experiencing panic attacks (see Table 15.1). After four months of diagnostic testing turned up no physical problems, José's physician suggested that he see a psychologist. José resisted at first, insisting that his condition was not "just in his head," but he eventually began psychological treatment. Within a few months, his panic attacks had ceased, and José had returned to all his old activities. After the psychologist helped him reconsider his workload, José decided to retire from his job in order to pursue more satisfying work at his home-based computer business.

José's case is by no means unique. During any given year in the United States alone, about 15 percent of adults and about 21 percent of children are receiving some form of treatment for a psychological disorder (U.S. Surgeon General, 1999). Although the economic impact of mental disorders—in treatment costs, disability payments, and lost productivity—is a staggering $150 billion per year in the United States, the treatments that are available today for severe disorders can pay for themselves. In fact, the savings realized from treatment are actually greater than its costs (Clay, 2000; National Institute of Mental Health, 1998). In this chapter, we describe a variety of treatment methods, most of which are based on the theories of stress and coping, personality, and psychological disorders reviewed in the chapters on those topics. By spelling out proposed explanations for what can go wrong in the development of personality and behavior and the role of stress in both, those theories provide important guidelines for treatment.

First we examine the basic features common to all forms of treatment. Then we discuss approaches that rely on **psychotherapy,** the treatment of psychological disorders through psychological methods, such as talking about problems and exploring new ways of thinking and acting. These methods are based on psychodynamic, humanistic, or social-cognitive (behavioral) theories of disorder and treatment. We then consider biological approaches to treatment, which consist mainly of drugs and other physical therapies.

Although we discuss different psychotherapy methods in separate sections, keep in mind that the majority of mental health professionals see themselves as *eclectic* therapists; in other words, they might lean toward one set of methods, but when working with particular clients or particular problems, they employ other methods as well (Hayes & Harris, 2000; Jensen, Bergin, & Greaves, 1990; Northcut & Heller, 1999). Further, many clients receive psychoactive drugs in addition to psychotherapy during the course of psychological treatment (Sammons & Schmidt, 2001).

Basic Features of Treatment

All treatments for psychological, as well as physical, disorders share certain basic features. These common features include a *client* or patient, a *therapist* who is accepted as being capable of helping the client, and the establishment of a *special relationship* between the client and therapist. In addition, all forms of treatment are based on some *theory* about the causes of the client's problems. The theory may presume causes ranging from magic spells to infections and everything in between (Frank & Frank, 1991). The theory, in turn, leads to *procedures* for dealing with the client's problems. So traditional healers combat supernatural forces with ceremonies and prayers, medical doctors treat chemical imbalances with drugs, and psychologists focus on altering psychological processes through psychotherapy.

People receiving treatment for psychological disorders can be inpatients or outpatients. *Inpatients* are treated in a hospital or other residential institution. They are voluntarily or involuntarily committed to these institutions because their impairments are severe enough to constitute a threat to their own well-being or the safety of others. Depending on their level of functioning, inpatients may stay in the hospital for a few days or weeks or—in rare cases—several years. Their treatment almost

---

psychotherapy The treatment of psychological disorders through talking and other psychological methods.

psychiatrists Medical doctors who have completed special training in the treatment of psychological disorders.

psychologists Therapists whose education includes completion of a master's or (usually) a doctoral degree in clinical or counseling psychology, often followed by additional specialty training.

Basic Features of Treatment

Medieval Treatment Methods Methods used to treat psychological disorders have always been related to the presumed causes of those disorders. In medieval times, when demons were widely blamed for abnormal behavior, physician-priests tried to make the victim's body inhospitable to evil spirits. Here, we see a depiction of such spirits leaving an afflicted person's head as it is placed in an oven.

always includes psychoactive drugs. *Outpatients* receive psychotherapy and/or drugs while living in the community. Compared with inpatients, outpatients tend to be younger, are more likely to be female, and typically come from the middle or upper socioeconomic classes.

Those who provide psychological treatment are a diverse group. **Psychiatrists** are medical doctors who have completed specialty training in the treatment of psychological disorders. Like other physicians, they are authorized to prescribe drugs for the relief of psychological problems. **Psychologists** who offer psychotherapy have usually completed a doctoral degree in clinical or counseling psychology, often

Group Therapy for Vietnam Veterans Some psychotherapy occurs in one-to-one office sessions, but treatment might also be conducted with couples, families, and groups in hospitals, community health centers, and facilities for former mental hospital residents. Therapy is also provided at prisons, military bases, drug and alcoholism treatment centers, and many other places.

followed by additional specialized training. Except in New Mexico, psychologists are not authorized to prescribe drugs, although there is debate over proposals to extend prescription privileges to clinical psychologists elsewhere who have been specially trained for this function (Ax & Resnick, 2001; Kilby, 1999; Newman et al., 2000). Other therapy providers include *clinical social workers, marriage and family therapists,* and *licensed professional counselors,* all of whom typically hold a master's degree in their respective professions and provide treatment in a variety of settings, such as hospitals, clinics, and private practice. *Psychiatric nurses, substance abuse counselors,* members of the clergy working as *pastoral counselors,* and a host of paraprofessionals also provide therapy services, often as part of a hospital or outpatient treatment team (U.S. Surgeon General, 1999).

The general goal of treatment providers is to help troubled people change their thinking, feelings, and behavior in ways that relieve discomfort, promote happiness, and improve their overall functioning as parents, students, workers, and the like. To reach this goal, some therapists try to help clients gain insight into the hidden causes of problems, others seek to promote growth through more genuine self-expression, and still others help clients learn and practice new ways of thinking and acting. The particular methods used in each case—whether some form of psychotherapy, a drug treatment, or both—depend on the problems, preferences, and financial circumstances of the client; the time available for treatment; and the therapist's theoretical leanings, methodological preferences, and professional qualifications. Later, we will discuss drugs and other biological treatments; here, we consider several forms of psychotherapy, each of which is based on psychodynamic, humanistic, or behavioral explanations of mental disorder.

Psychodynamic Psychotherapy

The field of formal psychotherapy began in the late 1800s when, as described in the chapter on personality, Sigmund Freud established the psychodynamic approach to psychological disorders. Central to his approach, and to modern revisions of it, is the assumption that personality and behavior reflect the efforts of the ego to referee conflicts, usually unconscious, among various components of the personality.

Freud's method of treatment, **psychoanalysis,** was aimed at understanding these unconscious conflicts and how they affect the client. His one-to-one method of studying and treating people, his search for relationships between an individual's life history and current problems, his emphasis on thoughts and emotions in treatment, and his focus on the client-therapist relationship have influenced almost all forms of psychotherapy. We describe Freud's original methods first, and then consider some more-recently developed treatments that are rooted in his psychodynamic approach.

Classical Psychoanalysis

Classical psychoanalysis developed mainly out of Freud's medical practice. He was puzzled by patients who suffered from "hysterical" ailments—blindness, paralysis, or other symptoms that had no apparent physical cause. (As mentioned in the chapter on psychological disorders, these ailments are now considered to be symptoms of *conversion disorders.*) Inspired by his colleague Josef Breuer's dramatic success in using hypnosis to treat hysterical symptoms in a patient known as "Anna O." (Breuer & Freud, 1895/1974), Freud tried similar methods with other hysteria patients but found them to be only partially and temporarily successful. Eventually, Freud merely asked patients to lie on a couch and report whatever thoughts, memories, or images came to mind (a process Freud called *free association*).

The results of this "talking cure" were surprising. Freud came to believe that his patients' problems stemmed from childhood memories of sexual abuse, usually by a parent or other close relative (Esterson, 2001). Freud wondered whether child abuse

---

psychoanalysis A method of psychotherapy that seeks to help clients gain insight by recognizing and understanding unconscious thoughts and emotions.

Freud's Consulting Room During psychoanalytic sessions, Freud's patients lay on this couch, free-associating or describing dreams and everyday events, while he sat in the chair behind them. According to Freud, even apparently trivial or accidental behavior may hold important messages from the unconscious. Forgetting a dream or missing a therapy appointment might reflect a client's unconscious resistance to treatment. Even accidents may be meaningful. The waiter who spills hot soup on an elderly male customer might be seen as acting out unconscious aggressive impulses against a father figure.

was rampant in Vienna, whether he was getting a biased sample of patients, or whether the memories he believed he had found were being distorted by psychological factors. He ultimately concluded that his patients' memories of childhood abuse probably reflected childhood fantasies, not reality—a conclusion that, as described in the chapter on personality, has become quite controversial. In any case, Freud focused psychoanalysis on the exploration of unconscious impulses and fantasies. Hysterical symptoms, he said, developed out of conflicts about those impulses and fantasies.

Classical psychoanalytic treatment aims to help clients gain insight into their problems by recognizing unconscious thoughts and emotions, and then discover, or *work through*, the many ways in which those unconscious elements affect their everyday lives. The treatment may require as many as three to five sessions per week, usually over several years. Generally, the psychoanalyst tries to maintain a compassionate neutrality during treatment as the client slowly develops an understanding of how past conflicts determine current problems (Auld & Hyman, 1991).

To gain glimpses into the unconscious, Freud looked for unconscious meaning in his patients' free associations, their dreams, their everyday behaviors, and their relationship with him. He believed that hidden beneath the obvious or *manifest content* of dreams, there is *latent content* that reflects the wishes, impulses, and fantasies that the dreamer's defense mechanisms keep out of consciousness during waking hours. He focused also on "Freudian slips" of the tongue (such as saying *beast* instead of *best*) and other seemingly insignificant, but potentially meaningful, behaviors. Similarly, a patient's expression of tenderness, fear, dependency, hostility, or the like during therapy was viewed by Freud as part of an unconscious transference to the therapist of feelings and conflicts experienced in childhood in relation to parents and other significant people. Analysis of this *transference*, this "new edition" of the client's childhood conflicts and current problems, became another important psychoanalytic method; Freud believed that focusing on the transference allows clients to see how old conflicts haunt their lives and to resolve these conflicts (Arlow, 1995).

Contemporary Variations on Psychoanalysis

Although classical psychoanalysis is still practiced, it is not as prevalent as it was several decades ago (Horgan, 1996). The decline is due to many factors, including disenchantment with Freud's personality theory; the expense of classical

A Play Therapy Session Modern versions of psychoanalytic treatment include fantasy play and other techniques that make the approach more useful with children. A child's behavior and comments while playing with puppets representing family members, for example, are seen as a form of free association that the therapist hopes will reveal important unconscious material, such as fear of abandonment (Booth & Lindaman, 2000).

psychoanalysis (Moran, 2000); its limited usefulness with children; and the availability of many alternative forms of treatment, including variations on classical psychoanalysis.

Some of these variations were developed by the neo-Freudian theorists discussed in the chapter on personality. As noted there, those theorists tended to put less emphasis than Freud did on the past and on unconscious impulses stemming from the id. They also tended to stress the role of social relationships in clients' problems and how the power of the ego can be harnessed to solve those problems. *Ego analysis* (Hartmann, 1958; Klein, 1960), *interpersonal therapy* (Sullivan, 1954), and *individual analysis* (Adler, 1927/1963) were among the first treatments to be based on neo-Freudian theories; some were designed for treating children (A. Freud, 1946; Klein, 1960). More recent variants have come to be known as *short-term dynamic psychotherapy* because they aim to provide benefits in far less time than is required in classical psychoanalysis (Davanloo, 1999).

A particularly popular short-term dynamic approach is known as *object relations therapy* (Scharff & Scharff, 1998; St. Clair, 1999). (The term *object* refers to anything, including a person, that has had emotional significance in a client's life.) In object relations therapy, the powerful need for human contact and support takes center stage. In fact, object relations therapists believe that most of the problems that bring clients to treatment ultimately stem from this need and how it plays out in their relationships with others—especially with their mothers or other early caregivers. Psychotherapists who adopt an object relations perspective take a much more active role in therapy sessions than classical analysts do—particularly by directing the client's attention to evidence of certain conflicts, rather than waiting for free association or other more subtle methods to reveal these conflicts. Object relations therapists work to develop a nurturing relationship with their clients, providing a "second chance" for them to receive the support that might have been lacking in infancy and to counteract some of the consequences of maladaptive early attachment patterns (Lieberman & Pawl, 1988). One way they do this is to show that they will not abandon their clients, as might have happened to these people in the past.

Other variations on psychoanalysis retain more of Freud's ideas but alter the format of treatment so that it is less intense, less expensive, and more appropriate

Analysis of the transference would be quite a challenge in this parody of a psychoanalytic therapy relationship! Psychoanalysts focus not only on their clients' feelings toward them but also on their feelings toward clients—called *countertransference*. For example, if transference leads a client to treat the therapist as a mother, the therapist might, because of countertransference, unintentionally begin treating the client as her child.

"What do you think I think about what you think I think you've been thinking about?"

for a broader range of clients (Hoyt, 1995). For example, *psychoanalytically oriented psychotherapy* and *time-limited dynamic psychotherapy* employ classical psychoanalytic methods but use them more flexibly (Levenson & Strupp, 1997). The goal of treatment may range from giving psychological support to achieving basic changes in personality, and therapy may be completed in fewer than thirty sessions. A therapist using these briefer psychodynamic methods encourages clients to focus on concrete, specific goals. For example, the therapist might ask a client to describe how he or she would feel and act if a specific problem were suddenly solved.

Some version of transference analysis is seen in virtually all variations on classical psychoanalysis. In a short-term psychodynamic treatment called *supportive-expressive therapy*, for example, the therapist looks for a "core conflict" that appears repeatedly across a variety of relationships, including in the therapy relationship (Luborsky, 1997; Luborsky & Crits-Christoph, 1998). The core conflict in one young man, for example, centered on his desire to stand up for himself and his tendency to criticize himself for having that desire. (As a child, the client had been physically abused by his father.) The therapist watched for this core conflict to appear in the therapy relationship—as when tentative assertiveness was tempered by fear of having done wrong—and then helped the client see the links among his fear of asserting himself, his fantasies of getting even, and his childhood abuse experiences. This interpretation is part of transference analysis (Luborsky, 1997). At the same time, the therapist supported the client's attempts to be more assertive with authority figures without having violent fantasies.

With their focus on interpersonal relationships rather than instincts, their emphasis on clients' potential for self-directed problem solving, and the reassurance and emotional support they provide, contemporary variants on classical psychoanalysis have helped the psychodynamic approach retain its influence among mental health professionals (Westen & Gabbard, 1999).

Humanistic Psychotherapy

As discussed in the chapters on personality and psychological disorders, *humanistic psychologists* emphasize the subjective interpretations that people place on events. Humanists (sometimes called *phenomenologists*) view people as capable of consciously controlling their own actions and taking responsibility for their own decisions. Humanistic therapists believe that human behavior is motivated not by sexual or aggressive impulses but rather by an innate drive toward growth that is guided from moment to moment by the way people perceive their world. Disordered behavior, they say, reflects a blockage of natural growth brought on by distorted perceptions or lack of awareness of feelings. Accordingly, humanistic (or phenomenological) therapy operates on the following assumptions:

1. Treatment is an encounter between equals, not a cure provided by an expert. It is a way to help clients restart their natural growth and to feel and behave more in line with that growth.

2. Clients will improve on their own, given the right conditions. These ideal conditions promote clients' awareness, acceptance, and expression of their feelings and perceptions. So, like psychodynamic therapy, humanistic therapy promotes insight, but it is insight into current feelings and perceptions, not into unconscious childhood conflicts.

3. Ideal conditions in therapy can best be established through a relationship in which clients feel fully accepted and supported as human beings, no matter how problematic or undesirable their *behavior* may be. It is the client's experience of this relationship that brings beneficial changes. (As noted earlier, this assumption is also important in object relations therapy.)

4. Clients must remain responsible for choosing how they will think and behave.

Of the many humanistically oriented treatments in use today, the most influential are client-centered therapy, developed by Carl Rogers, and Gestalt therapy, developed by Frederick and Laura Perls.

Client-Centered Therapy

Carl Rogers was trained in psychodynamic methods during the 1930s, but he soon began to question their value. He especially disliked being a detached expert observer whose task was to "figure out" the client. He became convinced that a less formal approach would be more effective for the client and more comfortable for the therapist. Accordingly, Rogers developed *nondirective therapy,* which depends on the client's own drive toward growth or actualization. Rogers allowed his clients to decide what to talk about and when, without direction, judgment, or interpretation by the therapist (Raskin & Rogers, 1995). This approach, now called **client-centered therapy** or **person-centered therapy**, relies on the creation of a relationship that reflects three intertwined attitudes of the therapist: unconditional positive regard, empathy, and congruence.

Unconditional Positive Regard
The attitude Rogers called **unconditional positive regard** consists of treating the client as a valued person, no matter what. It is communicated through the therapist's willingness to listen to what the client has to say, without interrupting or evaluating it. The therapist doesn't have to approve of everything the client says, but must accept each statement as reflecting a part of the person who said it. Because they trust clients to solve their own problems, Rogerian therapists rarely give advice. Doing so, said Rogers, would send clients an unspoken message that they are incompetent, making them less confident and more dependent on help.

---

client-centered therapy A therapy that allows the client to decide what to talk about, without direction, judgment, or interpretation from the therapist.

unconditional positive regard A therapist attitude that conveys a caring for, and acceptance of, the client as a valued person.

A Client-Centered Therapy Group
Carl Rogers (shown here in shirtsleeves) believed that as successful treatment progresses, clients become more self-confident, more aware of their feelings, more accepting of themselves, more comfortable and genuine with other people, more reliant on self-evaluation than on the judgments of others, and more effective and relaxed.

Empathy Client-centered therapists try to appreciate how the world looks from the client's point of view. This involves far more than saying "I know what you mean." The therapist tries to replace an *external frame of reference*—looking at the client from the outside—with an *internal frame of reference* characterized by **empathy,** the emotional understanding of what the client might be thinking and feeling. Client-centered therapists convey empathy by showing that they are *actively listening* to the client. Like other skillful interviewers, they make eye contact with the client, nod in recognition as the client speaks, and give other signs of careful attention. They also use **reflection**, a paraphrased summary of the client's words that emphasizes the feelings and meanings that appear to accompany them; reflection confirms the communication, shows that the therapist is interested, and helps the client to perceive and focus on the thoughts and feelings being expressed. Here is an example:

CLIENT: This has been such a bad day. I've felt ready to cry any minute, and I'm not even sure what's wrong!

THERAPIST: You really do feel so bad. The tears just seem to well up inside, and I wonder if it is a little scary to not even know why you feel this way.

Notice that in rephrasing the client's statements, the therapist reflected back not only the obvious feelings of sadness but also the fear in the client's voice. Most clients respond to empathic reflection by elaborating on their feelings. In this example, the client went on to say, "It is scary, because I don't like to feel in the dark about myself. I have always prided myself on being in control." Clients do this, said Rogers, simply because the therapist expresses the desire to listen and understand without asking disruptive questions. Empathic listening tends to be so effective in promoting self-understanding and awareness that it is used across a wide range of therapies (Corsini & Wedding, 2001). Even outside the realm of therapy, people who are thought of as easy to talk to are usually "good listeners" who reflect back the important messages they hear from others.

Congruence Sometimes called *genuineness,* **congruence** refers to a consistency between the therapist's feelings and actions. When the therapist's unconditional

empathy The therapist's attempt to appreciate and understand how the world looks from the client's point of view.

reflection An active listening method in which a therapist conveys empathy by paraphrasing clients' statements and noting accompanying feelings.

congruence A consistency between the way therapists feel and the way they act toward clients.

Nonverbal Cues in Gestalt Therapy
Gestalt therapists pay particular attention to clients' "body language," especially when it conflicts with what they are saying. If this client had just said that she was looking forward to starting her new job, the therapist would probably challenge that statement in an effort to make the client more aware of her mixed feelings.

positive regard and empathy are genuine, the client is able to see that relationships can be built on openness and honesty. Ideally, this experience will help the client become more congruent in other relationships.

Here is an excerpt that illustrates the three therapist attitudes we have described.

CLIENT: *. . . I cannot be the kind of person I want to be. I guess maybe I haven't the guts or the strength to kill myself, and if someone else would relieve me of the responsibility or I would be in an accident I, I . . . just don't want to live.*

THERAPIST: *At the present time things look so bad that you can't see much point in living. [Note the use of empathic reflection and the absence of any criticism.]*

CLIENT: *Yes. I wish I'd never started this therapy. I was happy when I was living in my dream world. There I could be the kind of person I wanted to be. But now there is such a wide, wide gap between my ideal and what I am. . . . [Notice that the client responds to reflection by giving more information.]*

THERAPIST: *It's really a tough struggle digging into this like you are, and at times the shelter of your dream world looks more attractive and comfortable. [Note the use of reflection.]*

CLIENT: *My dream world or suicide. . . . So I don't see why I should waste your time—coming in twice a week—I'm not worth it—what do you think?*

THERAPIST: *It's up to you. . . . It isn't wasting my time. I'd be glad to see you whenever you come but it's how you feel about it. . . . [Note the congruence in stating an honest desire to see the client and the unconditional positive regard in trusting her capacity and responsibility for choice.]*

CLIENT: *You're not going to suggest that I come in oftener? You're not alarmed and think I ought to come in every day until I get out of this?*

THERAPIST: *I believe you are able to make your own decision. I'll see you whenever you want to come. [Note the unconditional positive regard.]*

CLIENT: *(Note of awe in her voice) I don't believe you are alarmed about—I see—I may be afraid of myself but you aren't afraid for me. [Here the client experiences the therapist's confidence in her. Happily, she did not kill herself.]* (Rogers, 1951, p. 49)

Gestalt Therapy

Frederick S. (Fritz) Perls, a European psychoanalyst, was greatly influenced by research in *Gestalt psychology*. (As noted in the chapter on perception, Gestalt psychologists emphasized the idea that people actively organize their perceptions of the world.) Perls believed that (1) people create their own versions of reality and (2) people's natural psychological growth continues only as long as they perceive, remain aware of, and act on their true feelings. Growth stops and symptoms appear, said Perls, when people are not aware of all aspects of themselves (Perls, 1969; Perls, Hefferline, & Goodman, 1951).

Perls and his wife, Laura, developed Gestalt therapy on the basis of these beliefs. Like client-centered therapy, **Gestalt therapy** seeks to create conditions in which clients can become more unified, self-aware, and self-accepting—and thus ready to grow again. However, Gestalt therapists use more direct and dramatic methods than do Rogerians. Often working in group settings, Gestalt therapists prod clients to become aware of feelings and impulses that they have disowned and to discard feelings, ideas, and values that are not really their own. For example, the therapist or other group members might point out inconsistencies between what clients say and how they behave. Gestalt therapists may also ask clients to engage in imaginary

Gestalt therapy An active treatment designed to help clients get in touch with genuine feelings and disown foreign ones.

"conversations" with other people, with parts of their own personalities, and even with objects. Like a shy person who can be socially outgoing only while in a Halloween costume, clients often find that these dialogues help to get them in touch with, and to express, their feelings (Paivio & Greenberg, 1995).

Behavior Therapy

Psychodynamic and humanistic approaches to therapy assume that if clients gain insight or self-awareness about underlying problems, the symptoms created by those problems will disappear. Behavior therapists emphasize a different kind of insight or self-awareness: They encourage clients to think about psychological problems as *learned behaviors* that can be changed without first searching for hidden meanings or underlying processes (Miltenberger, 2001).

For example, suppose you have a panic attack every time you leave home and find relief only when you return. Making excuses when friends invite you out eases your anxiety temporarily but does nothing to solve the problem. Could you reduce your fear without looking for its "underlying meaning"? *Behavior therapy* would offer just such an alternative by first identifying the learning principles that maintain your fear and then helping you to develop new responses in feared situations.

These goals are based on both the *behavioral approach* to psychology and the *social-cognitive approach* to personality and disorder. As described in the chapters on introducing psychology, on personality, and on psychological disorders, these approaches emphasize the role of learning in the development of personality, as well as in most psychological disorders. Accordingly, behaviorists tend to see those disorders as examples of the maladaptive thoughts and actions that a client has learned. For instance, behavior therapists believe that fear of leaving home (agoraphobia) develops through classically conditioned associations between being away from home and having panic attacks. The problem is maintained in part through operant conditioning: Staying home and making excuses for doing so are rewarded by reduced anxiety. Therapists adopting a behavioral approach argue that if learning experiences can create problems, they can also help to alleviate those problems. So even if the experiences that led to today's problems began in the client's childhood, behavior therapy seeks to solve those problems by creating beneficial new experiences using the principles discussed in the chapter on learning.

Inspired by John B. Watson, Ivan P. Pavlov, B. F. Skinner, and others who studied learning during the 1920s and 1930s, researchers in the late 1950s and early 1960s began to systematically apply the principles of classical conditioning, operant conditioning, and observational learning to alter disordered human behavior (Thorpe & Olson, 1997). By 1970, behavioral treatment had become a popular alternative to psychodynamic and humanistic methods.

Some of the most notable features of behavioral treatment include the following:

1. Development of a productive therapist-client relationship. As in other therapies, this relationship enhances clients' confidence that change is possible, makes it easier for them to be open about the nature and history of their problems, and increases their motivation to work toward improvement. In fact, behavior therapists see the therapeutic relationship as central to the success of treatment because it provides the context in which adaptive new learning can take place (Cahill, Carrigan, & Evans, 1998; Wilson, 1995).

2. A careful listing of the behaviors and thoughts to be changed. This assessment—and the establishment of specific goals—sometimes replaces the formal diagnosis used in some other therapy approaches. So instead of treating "depression" or "obsessive-compulsive disorder," behavior therapists work to change the specific thoughts, behaviors, and emotional reactions that led to these diagnostic labels.

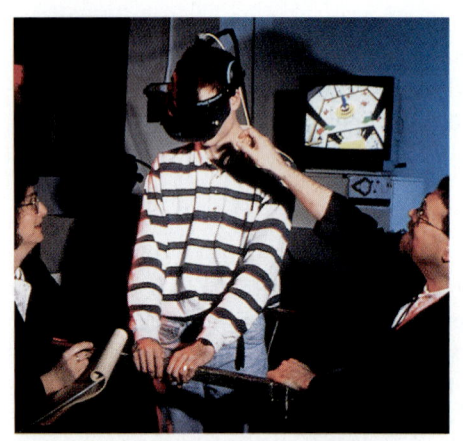

Virtual Desensitization A client who fears heights wears a virtual reality display that allows him to "experience" what he would see as a glass elevator gradually rises higher and higher. After learning to tolerate these realistic images without anxiety, clients are better able to fearlessly face the situations they once avoided.

3. A therapist who acts as a kind of teacher/assistant by providing learning-based treatments, giving "homework" assignments, and helping the client make specific plans for dealing with problems.

4. Continuous monitoring and evaluation of treatment, along with constant adjustments to any procedures that do not seem to be effective.

Behavioral treatment can take many forms. By tradition, those methods that rely mainly on *classical conditioning* principles are usually referred to as **behavior therapy.** Methods that focus on *operant conditioning* principles are usually called **behavior modification.** And behavioral treatment that focuses on changing thinking patterns as well as overt behaviors is called **cognitive-behavior therapy.**

Techniques for Modifying Behavior

Some of the most important and commonly used behavioral treatment techniques are systematic desensitization, modeling, positive reinforcement, extinction, aversive conditioning, and punishment.

Systematic Desensitization

Joseph Wolpe (1958) developed one of the first behavioral methods for helping clients overcome phobias and other forms of anxiety. Called **systematic desensitization,** it is a method in which the client visualizes a series of anxiety-provoking stimuli while remaining relaxed. Wolpe believed that this process gradually weakens the learned association between anxiety and the feared object, until the fear disappears.

Wolpe first arranged for clients to do something that is incompatible with being afraid. He often used *progressive relaxation training* (described in the chapter on health, stress, and coping) to prevent anxiety. Then, while relaxing, the client would be asked to imagine an item from a *desensitization hierarchy,* a sequence of increasingly fear provoking situations (see Table 16.1). The client would imagine one hierarchy item at a time, moving to a more difficult scene only after tolerating the previous one without distress. Wolpe found that once clients could calmly imagine being in feared situations, they were better able to deal with them in reality later on.

Desensitization appears especially effective if it slowly and carefully presents clients with real, rather than imagined, hierarchy items (Chambless, 1990; McGlynn et al., 1999). This *in vivo,* or "real life," desensitization was once difficult to arrange or control, especially in cases involving fear of flying, heights, or highway driving, for example. Recently, however, a technique known as *virtual reality graded exposure* is making it possible for clients to "experience" extremely vivid and precisely graduated versions of feared situations without actually being exposed to them. In one study, clients who feared heights wore a head-mounted virtual reality helmet that gave them the impression of standing on bridges of gradually increasing heights, on outdoor balconies at higher and higher floors, and in a glass elevator as it slowly rose forty-nine stories (Rothbaum et al., 1995). The same technology has been used successfully in the treatment of many other anxiety disorders, ranging from fear of spiders or air travel to posttraumatic stress disorder (Klein, 1999; Robbins, 2000; Rothbaum & Hodges, 1999; Rothbaum et al., 1999, 2000).

Exactly why systematic desensitization works is not clear. Traditionally, clinicians believed that change occurs because of basic learning processes—either through classical conditioning of a new, calmer response to the fear-provoking stimulus or through extinction, as the object or situation that had been a conditioned fear stimulus repeatedly occurs without being paired with pain or any other unconditioned stimulus (Rachman, 1990). More recent explanations emphasize that desensitization also modifies clients' cognitive processes, including their expectation that they can deal calmly and successfully with previously feared situations (Kehoe & Macrae, 1998).

behavior therapy Treatments that use classical conditioning principles to change behavior.

behavior modification Treatments that use operant conditioning methods to change behavior.

cognitive-behavior therapy Learning-based treatment methods that help clients change the way they think, as well as the way they behave.

systematic desensitization A behavioral treatment for anxiety in which clients visualize a graduated series of anxiety-provoking stimuli while remaining relaxed.

modeling Demonstrating desirable behaviors as a way of teaching them to clients.

assertiveness and social skills training A method for teaching clients how to interact with others more comfortably and effectively.

positive reinforcement A therapy method that uses rewards to strengthen desirable behaviors.

Desensitization hierarchies are lists of increasingly fear provoking situations that clients visualize while using relaxation methods to remain calm. Here are a few items from the beginning and the end of a hierarchy that was used to help a client overcome fear of flying.

table 16.1
A Desensitization Hierarchy

1. You are reading a newspaper and notice an ad for an airline.
2. You are watching a television program that shows a group of people boarding a plane.
3. Your boss tells you that you need to take a business trip by air.
4. You are in your bedroom packing your suitcase for your trip.

 .
 .
 .

12. Your plane begins to move as you hear the flight attendant say, "Be sure your seat belt is securely fastened."
13. You look at the runway as the plane is readied for takeoff.
14. You look out the window as the plane rolls down the runway.
15. You look out the window as the plane leaves the ground.

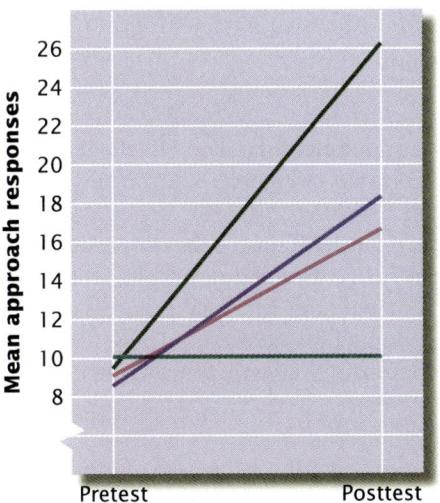

figure 16.1
Participant Modeling in the Treatment of Snake Phobia

In this study, participant modeling was compared with systematic desensitization, symbolic modeling (watching filmed models), and no treatment (control). Notice that compared with no treatment, all three methods helped snake-phobic clients approach live snakes, but participant modeling was clearly the best; 92 percent of the participants in that group were virtually free of any fear. The value of participant modeling has been repeatedly confirmed (e.g., Öst, Salkovskis, & Hellström, 1991).

Modeling Therapists often teach clients desirable behaviors by demonstrating those behaviors. In **modeling** treatments, the client watches the therapist or other people perform desired behaviors, thus learning skills vicariously, or at second hand, without going through a lengthy shaping process. In fear treatment, for example, modeling can teach the client how to respond fearlessly while vicariously extinguishing conditioned fear responses. For example, one therapist showed a twenty-four-year-old student with a severe spider phobia how to kill spiders with a fly swatter and had her practice this skill at home with rubber spiders (MacDonald & Bernstein, 1974). The combination of live modeling with gradual practice is called *participant modeling*; it is one of the most powerful treatments for fear (Bandura, Blanchard, & Ritter, 1969; Faust, Olson, & Rodriguez, 1991; see Figure 16.1).

Modeling is also a major part of **assertiveness training** and **social skills training**, which teach clients how to interact with people more comfortably and effectively. The goals of social skills training range from helping social-phobic singles make conversation on dates to rebuilding the abilities of mental patients to interact normally with people outside the hospital (Fairweather & Fergus, 1993; Trower, 1995; Wong et al., 1993). In assertiveness training, the therapist helps clients learn to be more direct and expressive in social situations. *Assertiveness* does not mean aggressiveness; it means clearly and directly expressing both positive and negative feelings and standing up for one's rights while respecting the rights of others (Alberti & Emmons, 1986; Ballou, 1995). Assertiveness training is often conducted in groups and involves both modeling and role playing of specific situations. For example, group assertiveness training has helped wheelchair-bound adults more comfortably handle the socially awkward situations in which they sometimes find themselves (Gleuckauf & Quittner, 1992; Weston & Went, 1999).

Positive Reinforcement Behavior therapists also use systematic **positive reinforcement** to alter problematic behaviors and to teach new skills in cases ranging from childhood tantrums and juvenile delinquency to schizophrenia and self-starvation. Using operant conditioning principles, they set up *contingencies*, or rules, that specify the behaviors to be strengthened through reinforcement. In one study, autistic children, who typically use very little language, were given grapes, popcorn, or other items they liked in return for saying "please," "thank you," and "you're welcome" while exchanging crayons and blocks with a therapist. The therapist first modeled the behavior by saying the appropriate words. The children

figure 16.2

Positive Reinforcement for an Autistic Child

During each pretreatment baseline period, the child rarely said "please," "thank you," or "you're welcome," but these statements began to occur once they were modeled and then reinforced. Did modeling and reinforcement actually cause the change? They probably did, because each type of response did not start to increase until the therapist began demonstrating it.

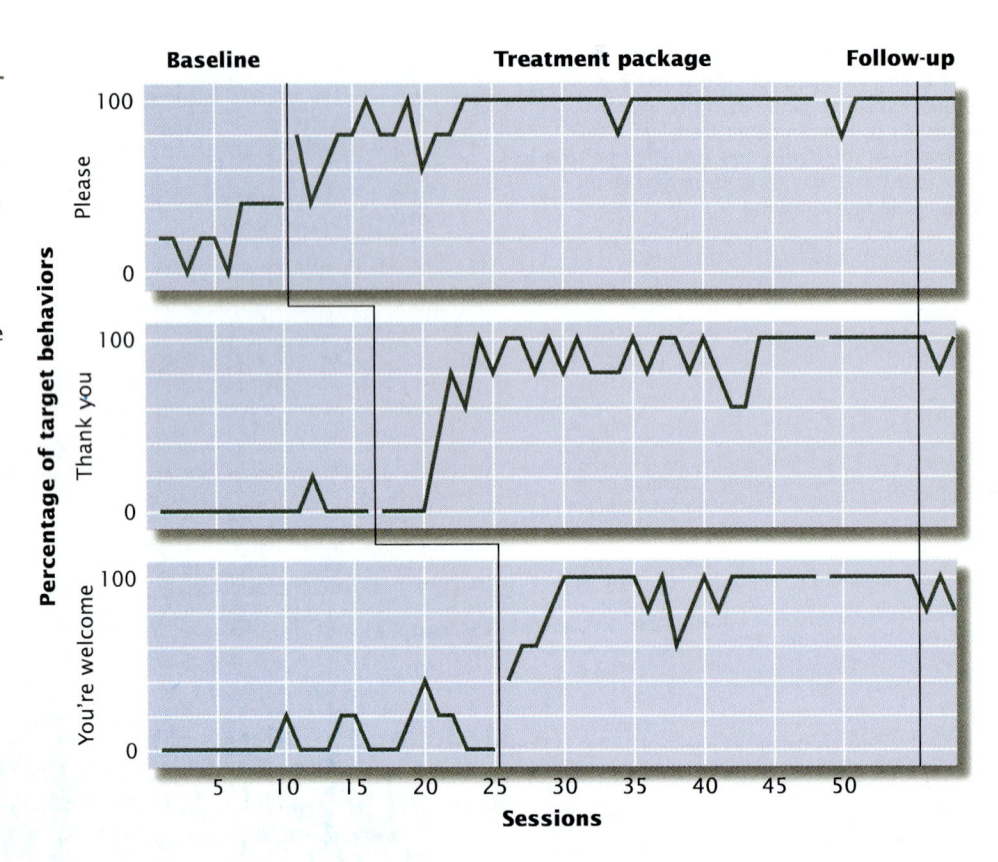

almost immediately began to utter the phrases spontaneously. The effects generalized to situations involving other toys, and as indicated in Figure 16.2, the new skills were still evident six months later (Matson et al., 1990).

For severely retarded or disturbed clients in institutions, behavior therapists sometimes establish a **token economy,** a system for reinforcing desirable behaviors with coin-like tokens or points that can be exchanged later for snacks, access to television, or other desired rewards (Ayllon, 1999; Ayllon & Azrin, 1968; Paul & Lentz, 1977). The goal is to shape behavior patterns that will persist outside the institution (Paul, 2000; Paul, Stuve, & Cross, 1997).

Extinction Just as reinforcement can make desirable behaviors more likely, other behavioral techniques can make undesirable behaviors less likely. In operant conditioning, **extinction** is the process of removing the reinforcers that normally follow a particular response. If you have ever given up telephoning someone whose line has been busy for hours, you know how extinction works: When a behavior does not "pay off," people usually stop it. Extinction changes behavior rather slowly, but it has been a popular way of treating children and retarded or seriously disturbed adults because it provides a gentle way to eliminate undesirable behaviors. For example, a client who gets attention by disrupting a classroom, damaging property, or violating hospital rules might be placed in a quiet, boring "time out" room for a few minutes in order to interrupt reinforcement for this misbehavior (e.g., Kee, Hill, & Weist, 1999; Reitman & Drabman, 1999).

Extinction is also the basis of a fear-reduction treatment called **flooding,** a procedure that keeps people in a feared but harmless situation, depriving them of their normally rewarding escape pattern (Barlow, 1988). (Flooding and related methods based on the extinction of classically conditioned fear responses are also called *exposure techniques.*) When someone is kept in contact with a fear-eliciting conditioned stimulus (a frog, say) without experiencing pain, injury, or any other aversive unconditioned stimulus, the fear-provoking power of the conditioned stimulus eventually fades, and the conditioned fear response extinguishes (Harris & Goetsch,

token economy A system for improving the behavior of institutionalized clients in which desirable behaviors are rewarded with tokens that can be exchanged for desired items or activities.

extinction The gradual disappearance of a conditioned response or operant behavior through nonreinforcement.

flooding A procedure for reducing anxiety that involves keeping a person in a feared, but harmless, situation.

1990; Öst et al., 2001). In one study, twenty clients who feared needles were exposed for two hours to the sight and feel of needles, including mild finger pricks, harmless injections, and blood samplings (Öst, Hellström, & Kåver, 1992). Afterward all the clients except one were able to have a blood sample drawn without experiencing significant anxiety.

Although often highly effective, flooding is equivalent to immediately exposing a fearful client to the most distressing item on a desensitization hierarchy. Therefore, some therapists and clients prefer more gradual exposure methods, especially in cases of agoraphobia and other problems in which a client's fear is not focused on a specific stimulus (Hecker & Thorpe, 1992). In dealing with agoraphobia, for instance, the therapist might provide gradual exposure by escorting the client away from home for increasing periods and eventually venturing into shopping malls and other previously avoided places (Kleinknecht, 1991; Zuercher-White, 1997). Clients can also practice gradual exposure methods on their own. They might be instructed, for example, to spend a little more time each day looking at photos of some feared animal or to spend some time alone in a dental chair or waiting room. In one study, clients suffering from various phobias made as much progress after six hours of instruction in gradual self-exposure methods and daily "homework" exercises as did those who received an additional nine hours of therapist-aided gradual exposure (Al-Kubaisy et al., 1992). Effective self-treatment using gradual exposure has also been reported in cases of panic disorder (Hecker et al., 1996) and obsessive-compulsive disorder (Fritzler, Hecker, & Losee, 1997).

Aversive Conditioning

Some unwanted behaviors—such as eating junk food or engaging in certain sexual offenses—can become so habitual and temporarily rewarding that they must be made less attractive if the client is to have any chance of giving them up in favor of a more desirable alternative. Methods for reducing the appeal of certain stimuli are known as **aversive conditioning** because they use classical conditioning principles to associate physical or psychological discomfort with behaviors, thoughts, or situations the client wants to stop or avoid (e.g., Clapham & Abramson, 1985).

One form of aversive conditioning, called *covert sensitization*, operates in a way that is the reverse of systematic desensitization. The client first visualizes the stimulus or situation that is to be made less attractive and is then exposed to frightening or disgusting stimuli. In one case, covert sensitization was used to treat a man who had been repeatedly arrested for making obscene phone calls. While imagining making an obscene call, the client heard vivid descriptions of his greatest fears: snakes, vomiting, and choking. Finally, he was told to imagine his mother walking in on him during a call. After a month of treatment, the thought of making obscene calls was no longer sexually arousing, and even two years later, the client had still not made any (Moergen, Merkel, & Brown, 1990).

Because aversive conditioning is unpleasant and uncomfortable and its effects are often temporary, behavior therapists use this method relatively rarely, only when it is the best treatment choice, and only long enough to allow the client to learn more desirable alternative behaviors.

Punishment

Sometimes the only way to eliminate a dangerous or disruptive behavior is to punish it with an unpleasant but harmless stimulus, such as a shouted "No!" or a mild electrical shock. Unlike aversive conditioning, in which the unpleasant stimulus occurs along with the behavior that is to be eliminated (a classical conditioning approach), **punishment** is an operant conditioning technique; it presents the unpleasant stimulus *after* the undesirable response occurs. (Although technically distinct, the two methods may overlap.) Before behavior therapists use mild shock or any other form of punishment with the institutionalized clients, other impaired adults, or children for whom it might be appropriate and beneficial, they must consider certain ethical questions. Among these are the following: Would the

Treating Fear Through Flooding
Flooding is designed to extinguish anxiety by allowing it to occur without the harmful consequences the person dreads. This man's fear of flying is obvious here, on takeoff, but is likely to diminish during and after uneventful flight. Like other behavioral treatments, flooding is based on the idea that phobias and other psychological disorders are learned and thus can be "unlearned."

aversive conditioning A method that uses classical conditioning to create a negative response to a particular stimulus.

punishment A therapy method that weakens undesirable behavior by following it with an unpleasant stimulus.

Albert Ellis Rational-emotive behavior therapy (REBT) focuses on altering the self-defeating thoughts that Ellis believes underlie people's behavior disorders. Ellis argues, for example, that students do not get upset because they fail a test but because they have learned to believe that failure is a disaster that indicates they are worthless. Many of Ellis's ideas have been incorporated into various forms of cognitive-behavior therapy, and they helped Ellis himself to deal rationally with the health problems he encountered when he reached his eighties (Ellis, 1997).

rational-emotive behavior therapy (REBT) A treatment designed to identify and change self-defeating thoughts that lead to anxiety and other symptoms of disorder.

cognitive therapy A treatment in which the therapist helps clients to notice and change negative thoughts associated with anxiety and depression.

client's life be in danger without treatment? Have all other methods failed? Has an ethics committee reviewed and approved the procedures? And has the client or a close relative formally agreed to the treatment? (Kazdin, 1994a). When the answer to these questions is yes, punishment can be an effective, sometimes lifesaving, treatment—as in the case illustrated in Figure 6.11 in the chapter on learning. Like extinction and aversive conditioning, punishment is best used only long enough to eliminate undesirable behavior and in combination with other behavioral methods designed to reward more appropriate behavior.

Cognitive-Behavior Therapy

Like psychodynamic and phenomenological therapists, behavior therapists recognize that depression, anxiety, and many other behavior disorders can stem from how clients think about themselves and the world. And like other therapists, behavior therapists also try to change their clients' troublesome ways of thinking. However, the methods used by behavior therapists—known collectively as *cognitive-behavior therapy*—rely on learning principles to help clients change the way they think (Goldfried et al., 1997; McMullin, 2000; Sperry, 1999). Suppose, for example, that a client suffers intense anxiety in social situations, in spite of having excellent social skills. In that case, social skills training would be unnecessary. Instead, the behavior therapist might combine relaxation training with cognitive-behavioral methods designed to help the client identify the habitual thoughts (such as "I shouldn't draw attention to myself") that get in the way of self-expression and create discomfort. Once these cognitive obstacles are brought to light, the therapist would encourage the client to develop more adaptive ways of thinking, as well as new ways of behaving in accordance with those new thoughts (Meichenbaum, 1995).

Rational-Emotive Behavior Therapy

One prominent form of cognitive-behavior therapy is **rational-emotive behavior therapy (REBT)**. Developed by Albert Ellis (1962, 1993, 1995), and originally called *rational-emotive therapy*, rational-emotive behavior therapy is based on the principle that anxiety, guilt, depression, and other psychological problems are caused by how people think about events. Ellis's therapy aims first at identifying self-defeating thoughts such as "I must be loved or approved by everyone" or "I must be perfectly competent, adequate, and achieving to be worthwhile." After the client learns to recognize thoughts like these and to see how they cause problems, the therapist uses modeling, encouragement, and logic to help the client replace these thoughts with more realistic and beneficial ones. Here is part of a rational-emotive behavior therapy session with a thirty-nine-year-old woman who suffered from panic attacks. She has just said that it would be "terrible" if she had an attack in a restaurant and that people "should be able to handle themselves!"

THERAPIST: *. . . The reality is that . . . "shoulds" and "musts" are the rules that other people hand down to us, and we grow up accepting them as if they are the absolute truth, which they most assuredly aren't.*

CLIENT: *You mean it is perfectly okay to, you know, pass out in a restaurant?*

THERAPIST: *Sure!*

CLIENT: *But . . . I know I wouldn't like it to happen.*

THERAPIST: *I can certainly understand that. It would be unpleasant, awkward, inconvenient. But it is illogical to think that it would be terrible, or . . . that it somehow bears on your worth as a person.*

CLIENT: *What do you mean?*

THERAPIST: *Well, suppose one of your friends calls you up and invites you back to that restaurant. If you start telling yourself, "I might panic and pass out and people might make fun of me and that would be terrible," . . . you might find you are dreading going to the restaurant, and you probably won't enjoy the meal very much.*

CLIENT: *Well, that is what usually happens.*

THERAPIST: *But it doesn't have to be that way. . . . The way you feel, your reaction . . . depends on what you choose to believe or think, or say to yourself.* (Masters et al., 1987)

Cognitive-behavior therapists use many techniques related to rational-emotive behavior therapy to help clients learn to think and act in more adaptive ways. Behavioral techniques aimed at replacing upsetting thoughts with alternative thinking patterns were originally called *cognitive restructuring* (Lazarus, 1971). Using these techniques, clients plan calming thoughts that they can employ during exams, tense discussions, and other anxiety-provoking situations. The calming thoughts might take a form such as "OK, stay calm; you can handle this if you just focus on the task and don't worry about being perfect" (Meichenbaum, 1977). Sometimes, the methods are expanded into *stress inoculation training*, in which clients imagine being in a stressful situation, then practice newly learned cognitive skills to remain calm (Meichenbaum, 1995).

Beck's Cognitive Therapy Many behavior therapists seek a different kind of cognitive restructuring using Aaron Beck's **cognitive therapy** (Beck, 1976, 1995; Beck & Beck, 1995). Beck's treatment approach is based on the idea that certain psychological disorders—especially those involving depression and anxiety—can often be traced to errors in logic (e.g., "If I fail my driver's test the first time, I will never pass it"), false beliefs (e.g., "Everyone ignores me"), and thoughts that minimize personal accomplishments (e.g., "Anyone could do that"). Beck says that over time, these learned *cognitive distortions* occur so quickly and automatically that the client never stops to consider that they might not be true.

Cognitive therapy is an active, structured, problem-solving approach in which the therapist helps clients notice how certain negative thoughts precede anxiety and depression (see Table 16.2). Then, much as in the five-step critical thinking system illustrated throughout this book, those thoughts and beliefs are treated as hypotheses to be tested rather than as assertions to be uncritically accepted. Accordingly, therapist and client take the role of "investigators" who develop ways to test beliefs such as "I'm no good around the house." They might decide on tasks that the client will attempt as "homework"—such as cleaning out the basement, cooking a simple meal, paying bills, or cutting the grass. Success at accomplishing even one of these

TRY THIS Here are just a few examples of the kinds of thoughts that cognitive-behavior therapists see as underlying anxiety, depression, and other behavior problems. After reading this list, try writing an alternative thought that clients could use to replace each of these ingrained cognitive habits. Then jot down a "homework assignment" that you would recommend to help clients challenge each maladaptive statement, and thus develop new ways of thinking about themselves.

table 16.2
Some Examples of Negative Thinking

"I shouldn't draw attention to myself."

"I will never be any good at this."

"It will be so awful if I don't know the answer."

"Everyone is smarter than I am."

"Nobody likes me."

"I should be able to do this job perfectly."

"What if I panic?"

"I'll never be happy."

"I should have accomplished more by this point in my life."

tasks provides concrete evidence to challenge a false belief that has supported depression, thus helping to reduce it (Beck et al., 1992). As therapy progresses, clients become more skilled at recognizing, and then correcting, the cognitive distortions related to their problems.

As mentioned in the chapter on psychological disorders, however, the cognitive roots of depression may involve more than specific thoughts and beliefs about certain situations. Depression may be associated with an overall cognitive style that leads people to expect that the worst will always happen to them and to assume that negative events occur because they are completely and permanently incompetent and worthless (Peterson, 1995; Peterson & Seligman, 1984). Accordingly, cognitive-behavior therapists also help depressed clients to develop more optimistic ways of thinking and to reduce their tendency to blame themselves for negative outcomes (Persons, Davidson, & Tompkins, 2001).

Group, Family, and Couples Therapy

Psychodynamic, humanistic, and behavioral treatments are often conducted with individuals, but they can also be adapted for use with groups of clients or with family units.

Group Therapy

Group therapy refers to the treatment of several unrelated clients under the guidance of a therapist who encourages helpful interactions among group members. Many groups are organized around a particular problem (such as alcoholism) or a particular type of client (such as adolescents). In most cases, six to twelve clients meet with their therapist at least once a week for about two hours. All group members agree to hold confidential everything that occurs during group sessions.

Group therapy offers several features not found in individual treatment (Yalom, 1995). First, group therapy allows the therapist to see clients interacting with one another. Second, clients discover that they are not alone as they listen to others and realize that many people struggle with difficulties at least as severe as their own. This realization tends to lift each client's expectations for improvement, a factor important in all forms of treatment. Third, group members can bolster one another's self-confidence and self-acceptance as they come to trust and value one another and develop group cohesiveness. Fourth, clients learn from one another. They share ideas for solving problems and give one another honest feedback about how each member "comes across." Fifth, perhaps through mutual modeling, the group experience makes clients more willing to share their feelings and more sensitive to other people's needs, motives, and messages. Finally, group therapy allows clients to try out new skills in a supportive environment.

Some of the advantages of group therapy are also put to use in *self-help*, or *mutual-help, organizations*. Self-help groups, such as Alcoholics Anonymous (AA), are made up of people who share some problematic experience and meet to help one another (Nowinski, 1999; Zimmerman et al., 1991). There are self-help groups for a wide range of problems, including alcohol and drug addiction, childhood sexual abuse, cancer, overeating, overspending, bereavement, compulsive gambling, and schizophrenia, among many others. The worldwide self-help movement has grown dramatically during the last two decades (Kurtz, 1997; O'Conner & Kratochwill, 1999), partly because many troubled people prefer to seek help from friends, teachers, or other "unofficial" helpers before turning to mental health practitioners (Swindle et al., 2000) and partly because some people have been dissatisfied with professional treatment. Dozens of self-help organizations operate through hundreds of thousands of local chapters, enrolling 10 million to 15 million participants in the United States and about half a million in Canada (Barlow et al., 2000; Norcross et al., 2000).

group therapy Psychotherapy involving several unrelated clients.

A Circle of Friends This meeting of Overeaters Anonymous is but one example of the self-help movement in North America, a rapidly growing network of inexpensive mental health and anti-addiction services offered by volunteer helpers, including friends and relatives of troubled people. A recent edition of one small-town Florida newspaper listed 104 local self-help groups focused on problems ranging from abuse to weight control. The services provided by nonprofessional groups like these make up about 20 percent of the total mental health and anti-addiction services offered in the United States (Borkman, 1997; Regier, Narrow, et al., 1993; Swindle et al., 2000).

Lack of reliable data makes it difficult to assess the value of many self-help groups, but available information suggests that active members may obtain some moderate improvement in their lives (Morganstern et al., 1997; Ouimette, Finney, & Moos, 1997). Some professional therapists view these groups with suspicion; others encourage clients to participate in them as part of their treatment or as a first step that might lead to more formal treatment (Haaga, 2000; Salzer, Rappaport, & Segre, 1999). This is especially true for clients with problems such as eating disorders, alcoholism, and other substance-related disorders (Dunne & Fitzpatrick, 1999).

Family and Couples Therapy

As its name implies, **family therapy** involves treatment of two or more individuals from the same family system, one of whom—often a troubled child or adolescent—is the initially identified client. The term *family system* highlights the idea that the problems displayed by one family member usually reflect problems in the entire family's functioning (Clarkin & Carpenter, 1995; Shlomo, 1999).

Ultimately, the family becomes the client, and treatment involves as many members as possible. In fact, the goal of family therapy is not just to alleviate the identified client's problems but also to create harmony and balance within the family by helping each member understand family interaction patterns and the problems they create (Goldenberg & Goldenberg, 1995). As with group therapy, the family format gives the therapist a chance to see how the initially identified client interacts with others, thus providing a basis for discussion of topics that are important to the family.

Family therapists who emphasize object relations theory point out that if the parents in a family have not worked out conflicts with their own parents, these conflicts will surface in relation to their spouses and children. Accordingly, these family therapy sessions might focus on the parents' problems with their own parents and, when possible, include members of the older generation (Nugent, 1994). A related approach, called *structural family therapy,* concentrates on family communication patterns (Minuchin & Fishman, 1981). It focuses on changing the rigid patterns and rituals that create alliances (such as mother and child against father) that perpetuate conflict and prevent the communication of love, support, or even anger.

family therapy Treatment of two or more individuals from the same family.

TRY THIS — Many forms of couples therapy help partners improve communication through establishing rules such as these. Think about your own experience in relationships or your observations of couples as they interact, and then write down some rules you would add to this list. Why do you think it would be important for couples to follow the rules on your list?

table 16.3
Some "Rules for Talking" in Couples Therapy

1. Always begin with something positive when stating a problem.
2. Use specific behaviors rather than derogatory labels or overgeneralizations to describe what is bothersome about the other person.
3. Make connections between those specific behaviors and feelings that arise in response to them (e.g., "It makes me sad when you . . .").
4. Admit your own role in the development of the problem.
5. Be brief; don't lecture or harangue.
6. Maintain a focus on the present or the future; don't review all previous examples of the problem or ask "why" questions, such as "Why do you always . . . ?"
7. Talk about observable events; don't make inferences about them (e.g., say, "I get angry when you interrupt me" rather than "Stop trying to make me feel stupid").
8. Paraphrase what your partner has said, and check out your own perceptions of what was said before responding. (Note that this suggestion is based on the same principle as Rogers's empathic listening.)

in review: Approaches to Psychological Treatment

Dimension	Classical Psychoanalytic	Contemporary Psychodynamic	Humanistic	Behavioral/Cognitive-Behavioral
Nature of the human being	Driven by sexual and aggressive urges	Driven by the need for human relationships	Has free will, choice, and capacity for self-actualization	Is a product of social learning and conditioning; behaves on the basis of past experience
Therapist's role	Neutral; helps client explore meaning of free associations and other material from the unconscious	Active; develops relationship with client as a model for other relationships	Facilitates client's growth; some therapists are active, some are nondirective	Teacher/trainer who helps client replace undesirable thoughts and behaviors; active, action oriented
Focus	Emphasizes unresolved unconscious conflicts from the distant past	Understanding the past, but focusing on current relationships	Here and now; focus on immediate experience	Current behavior and thoughts; may not need to know original causes to create change
Goals	Psychosexual maturity through insight; strengthening of ego functions	Correction of effects of failures of early attachment; development of satisfying intimate relationships	Expanded awareness; fulfillment of potential; self-acceptance	Changes in thinking and behaving in particular classes of situations; better self-management
Typical methods	Free association; dream analysis, analysis of transference	Analysis of interpersonal relationships, including the client-therapist relationship	Reflection-oriented interviews designed to convey unconditional positive regard, empathy, and congruence; exercises to promote self-awareness	Systematic desensitization, modeling, assertiveness and social skills training, positive reinforcement, extinction, aversive conditioning, punishment, cognitive restructuring

Structural family therapists argue that when dysfunctional communication patterns are eliminated, problematic behaviors decrease because they are no longer necessary for survival in the family system.

Behavior therapists often use family therapy sessions as meetings at which family members can discuss and agree on behavioral "contracts." Often based on operant conditioning principles, these contracts establish rules and reinforcement contingencies that help parents encourage their children's desirable behaviors (and discourage undesirable ones) and help spouses become more supportive of each other (O'Farrell, 1995; Sanders & Dadds, 1993).

Therapists of many theoretical persuasions also offer **couples therapy,** in which communication between partners is the most important focus of treatment (Cordova & Jacobson, 1993). Discussion in couples therapy sessions is usually aimed at identifying and improving the miscommunication or lack of communication that is interfering with a couple's happiness and intimacy. Often, the sessions revolve around learning to abide by certain "rules for talking," such as those listed in Table 16.3. Some therapists also focus on helping couples to accept each other as a way of becoming closer, and behavior therapists even offer programs designed to prevent marital problems in couples who are at high risk for developing such problems (Berger & Hannah, 1999; Jacobson et al., 2000). One such program, called *behavioral premarital intervention,* not only helps engaged couples head off relationship problems but also prepares them to deal effectively with problems that might arise. ("In Review: Approaches to Psychological Treatment" summarizes key features of the main approaches to treatment that we have discussed so far.)

Evaluating Psychotherapy

LINKAGES (a link to Introducing Psychology)

Psychotherapy has been available for more than a hundred years, yet people are still asking if it works. Most psychotherapists and their clients believe in psychotherapy's effectiveness (*Consumer Reports,* 1995); however, confirming this belief with experimental research has proved to be challenging and controversial (Brock, Green, & Reich, 1998; Dawes, 1994; DeRubeis & Crits-Christoph, 1998; Nathan, Stuart, & Dolan, 2000; Seligman, 1995, 1996).

The value of psychotherapy was first widely questioned in 1952, when British psychologist Hans Eysenck reviewed studies in which thousands of clients had received either traditional psychodynamic therapy, various other therapies, or no treatment. To the surprise and dismay of many therapists, Eysenck (1952) found that the percentage of clients who improved following any kind of psychotherapy was actually lower than that of people who received no treatment. Eysenck (1961, 1966) later supported his conclusions with additional evidence.

Critics argued that in drawing his conclusions, Eysenck had ignored studies that supported the value of psychotherapy and that he had misinterpreted his data (Bergin, 1971; de Charms, Levy, & Wertheimer, 1954; Luborsky, 1972). They pointed out, for example, that untreated clients may have been less disturbed than those in treatment, that untreated clients may have received informal treatment from their medical doctors, and that physicians who judged untreated clients' progress might have used less demanding criteria than the psychotherapists who rated their own clients. In fact, when some of these critics conducted their own "box score" counts of successes and failures, they concluded that psychotherapy tends to be more helpful than no treatment (Bergin, 1971).

Debate over Eysenck's findings—and the contradictory reports that followed them—highlighted several reasons why it is so difficult to definitively answer the apparently simple question, Does psychotherapy work? For one thing, there is the problem of how to measure improvement in psychotherapy. Should such assessment depend on psychological tests, behavioral observations, interviews, or a combination of all three? And what kinds of tests should be used? Where should clients be

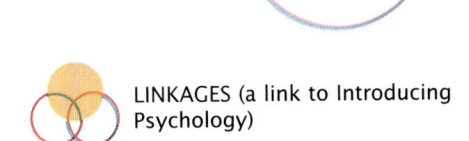

couples therapy A form of therapy focusing on improving communication between partners.

observed (and by whom)? And should equal weight be given to interviews with clients, friends, relatives, therapists, and teachers? The fact that all these measures tend to correlate only moderately with one another makes it that much harder for researchers to compare or combine the results of different studies and draw conclusions about the overall effectiveness of treatment (Lambert & Hill, 1994).

The question of effectiveness is further complicated by the broad range of clients, therapists, and treatments involved in the psychotherapy enterprise. Clients differ not only in terms of their problems but also in terms of their motivation to solve them. Therapists differ in skill, experience, and personality—and as we have seen, their treatment procedures can vary widely. To the extent that a client's improvement is influenced by all these factors, results from a study that evaluates one treatment may not apply to other clients and therapists (Kazdin, 1994b). Consider the example of a study in which "kindly college professors" were found to be as effective as experienced psychotherapists in helping people solve their problems (Strupp & Hadley, 1979). This result would appear relevant to the question of psychotherapy's effectiveness, but a careful reading of the study shows that the clients were college students with minor problems, not people with severe psychological disorders. Further, the fact that these students already had a relationship with their professors might have given the professors an edge over unfamiliar therapists (Chambless & Hollon, 1998). So the outcome of this study probably does not apply to the outcome of professional psychotherapy in general.

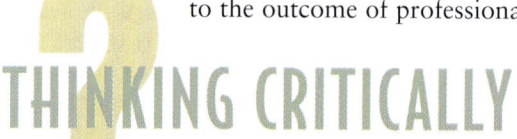

THINKING CRITICALLY

Are All Forms of Therapy Equally Effective?

LINKAGES (a link to Personality)

In short, the general question of whether psychotherapy "works" is difficult or impossible to answer scientifically in a way that applies to all therapies for all disorders. However, the findings of several research reviews (Anderson & Lambert, 1995; Galatzer-Levy et al., 2000; Shadish et al., 2000; Smith, Glass, & Miller, 1980; Weisz & Jensen, 1999) have bolstered therapists' beliefs that psychotherapy does work (see Figure 16.3). In fact, most therapists believe that the theoretical approach and treatment methods they use are superior to those of other therapists (e.g., Giles, 1990). They can't all be right, of course, so what is going on?

● **What am I being asked to believe or accept?**

Some researchers argue that theories about the causes of psychopathology, and the specific treatment methods based on them, don't have much to do with the success of psychotherapy. All approaches, they say, are equally effective. This has been called the "Dodo Bird Verdict," after the *Alice in Wonderland* creature who, when called upon to judge who had won a race, answered, "Everybody has won and all must have prizes" (Luborsky, Singer, & Luborsky, 1975).

figure 16.3

An Analysis of Psychotherapy's Effects

These curves show the results of one large-scale analysis of the effects of psychotherapy. Notice that on average, people who received therapy for their problems were better off than 80 percent of troubled people who did not. The overall effectiveness of psychotherapy has also been confirmed in a more recent analysis of ninety treatment outcome studies (Shadish et al., 2000).

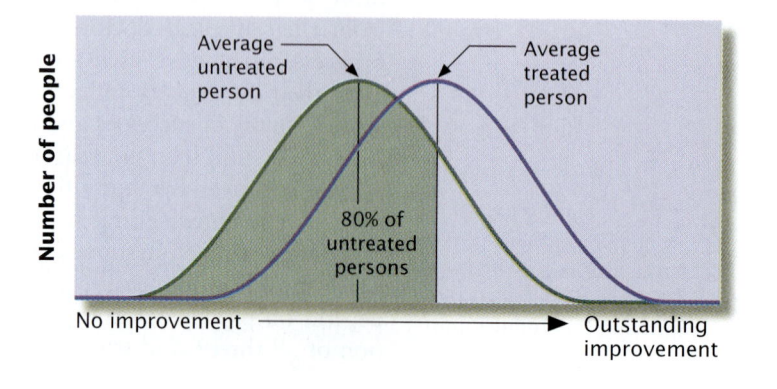

- **What evidence is available to support the assertion?**

Some evidence does suggest that there are no significant differences in the overall effectiveness of psychodynamic, humanistic, and behavioral therapies. Statistical methods, called *meta-analysis,* that combine the results of a large number of therapy studies have shown that the three treatment approaches are associated with about the same degree of success (Lambert & Bergin, 1994; Shadish et al., 2000; Smith, Glass, & Miller, 1980).

- **Are there alternative ways of interpreting the evidence?**

It is possible, however, that this evidence for the Dodo Bird Verdict is based on methods that cannot detect genuine differences among treatments. For example, a meta-analysis combining the results of many studies might not reveal important differences in the impact of particular treatments for particular problems (Eysenck, 1978; G. T. Wilson, 1985). It may also be that some specific techniques are more successful than others, but that when therapies are grouped by theoretical approach (psychodynamic, humanistic, or behavioral) rather than by specific procedures, the impact of those procedures might not be noticed (Giles, 1990; Marmar, 1990). For example, as described later, certain cognitive-behavioral techniques not used in other psychotherapy methods have been shown to be especially successful in the treatment of depression (DeRubeis & Feeley, 1990; DeRubeis et al., 1982; Feeley, DeRubeis, & Gelfand, 1999).

Further, differences among the effects of specific procedures might be overshadowed by the beneficial features shared by almost all forms of therapy—such as the support of the therapist, the hope and expectancy for improvement that therapy creates, and the trust that develops between client and therapist (Barber et al., 2000; Martin, Garske, & Davis, 2000). A therapist whose personal characteristics motivate a client to change might promote that change regardless of the therapeutic methods being used (Elkin, 1999; Hubble, Duncan, & Miller, 1999).

- **What additional evidence would help to evaluate the alternatives?**

The debate about whether all forms of psychotherapy are about equally effective on the average is likely to continue, but many researchers believe that it focuses on the wrong question. They believe that it is pointless to compare the effects of psychodynamic, humanistic, and behavioral methods in general. It is more important, they say, to address what Gordon Paul called the "ultimate question" about psychotherapy: "What treatment, by whom, is most effective for this individual with that specific problem, under what set of circumstances?" (Paul, 1969, p. 44).

- **What conclusions are most reasonable?**

Statistical analyses show that various treatment *approaches* appear to be about equally effective overall. But this does not mean that every specific psychotherapy method works in the same way, or that every psychotherapy experience will be equally beneficial. Potential clients must realize that the success of their treatment can still be affected by how severe their problems are, by the quality of the relationship they form with a therapist, and by the appropriateness of the therapy methods chosen for their problems.

Like those seeking treatment, many clinical psychologists, too, are eager for more specific scientific evidence about the effectiveness of particular therapies for particular kinds of clients and disorders. These empirically oriented clinicians are concerned that all too often, a therapist's choice of therapy methods depends more heavily on personal preferences or current trends than on scientific evidence of effectiveness (Davison, 1998; Nathan, Stuart, & Dolan, 2000). They believe that advocates of any treatment—whether it is object relations therapy or systematic desensitization—must demonstrate that its benefits are the result of the treatment itself and not just of the passage of time, the effects of repeated assessment, the

figure 16.4

Clinical Significance

Evaluations of psychological treatments must consider the clinical, as well as statistical, significance of observed changes. Here, the shaded area shows the range of deviant behaviors per minute displayed at home by normal boys. The solid line shows the average rate of deviant behaviors for boys in an operant conditioning treatment program for severe behavior problems. The improvement following reinforcement of appropriate behavior was not only statistically significant (compared with the pretreatment baseline) but also clinically significant, inasmuch as the once-deviant behavior came to resemble that of normal boys.

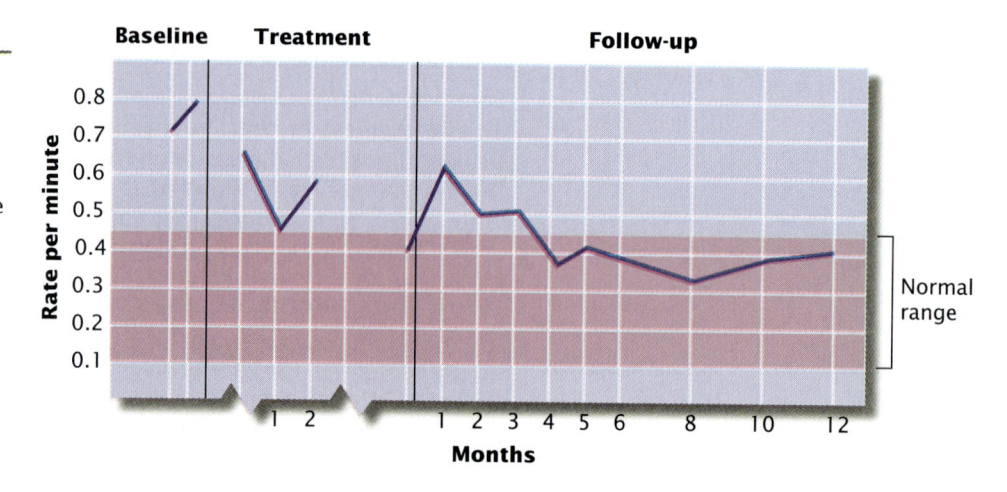

client's motivation and personal characteristics, or other confounding factors (Chambless & Hollon, 1998). They also want to see evidence that the benefits of treatment are *clinically significant*. To be clinically significant, therapeutic changes must be not only measurable but also substantial enough to make treated clients' feeling and actions similar to those of people who have not experienced these clients' disorders (Kendall, 1999; Kendall & Sheldrick, 2000). For example, a reduction in treated clients' anxiety test scores might be *statistically significant*, but if those clients do not now feel and act more like people without an anxiety disorder, the change is probably not clinically significant (see Figure 16.4). In recent years, the need to demonstrate the clinical significance of treatment effects has become clearer than ever as increasingly cost-conscious clients—and their health insurance companies—decide whether, and how much, to pay for various psychotherapy services (Dawes, 1994; Farberman, 1999).

By scientific tradition, the ideal way to evaluate treatment effects is through experiments in which clients are randomly assigned to various treatments or control conditions and their progress is objectively measured over time.

FOCUS ON RESEARCH METHODS

LINKAGES (a link to Research in Psychology)

Which Therapies Work Best for Which Problems?

To help clinicians select treatment methods on the basis of that kind of empirical evidence, the American Psychological Association's Division of Clinical Psychology created a task force on effective psychotherapies (Task Force on Promotion and Dissemination of Psychological Procedures, 1995).

● **What was the researchers' question?**

The question addressed by this task force was "What therapies have proven themselves most effective in treating various kinds of psychological disorders?"

● **How did the researchers answer the question?**

Working with other empirically oriented clinical psychologists, members of this task force examined the outcomes of thousands of experiments that evaluated psychotherapy methods used to treat mental disorder, marital distress, and health-related behavior problems in adults, children, and adolescents (Baucom et al., 1998; Chambless & Ollendick, 2001; Compas et al., 1998; DeRubeis & Crits-Christoph, 1998; Kazdin & Weisz, 1998; Kendall & Chambless, 1998).

● **What did the researchers find?**

The task force found that a number of treatments—known as **empirically supported therapies,** or **ESTs**—have been validated by controlled experimental

empirically supported therapies (ESTs) Treatments whose effects have been validated by controlled experimental research.

table 16.4
Some Empirically Supported Therapies

Problem	Efficacious and Specific	Efficacious	Possibly Efficacious
Major depressive disorder	Cognitive therapy	Behavior therapy; interpersonal therapy	Problem-solving therapy for depression
Generalized anxiety disorder	Cognitive therapy	Applied relaxation	
Social phobia	Exposure therapy; exposure plus cognitive restructuring		
Obsessive-compulsive disorder	Exposure and compulsive response prevention		Cognitive therapy
Agoraphobia	Exposure therapy		
Panic disorder	Panic control therapy; cognitive therapy	Exposure therapy; applied relaxation	
Posttraumatic stress disorder	Exposure therapy		Stress inoculation training; eye movement desensitization and reprocessing (see the chapter on research in psychology)
Schizophrenia			Social skills training
Alcohol abuse and dependence			Social skills training; cue exposure to drinking cues; cue exposure plus coping skills training
Substance dependence (Opiates)			Supportive-expressive therapy; cognitive therapy; behavior therapy (reinforcement)
(Cocaine)			Relapse prevention therapy

Treatments were listed by the American Psychological Association task force as "efficacious" (pronounced "eff-eh-KAY-shus"), or capable of helping clients, if they were superior to no treatment in at least two experiments by different research teams. Treatments listed as "efficacious and specific" were shown to produce clinically significant benefits that were superior to another form of therapy or a placebo control group. "Possibly efficacious" treatments have been found effective in only a single study or by a single research team (Chambless & Ollendick, 2001; DeRubeis & Crits-Christoph, 1998).

Source: DeRubeis & Crits-Christoph (1998).

research (DeRubeis & Crits-Christoph, 1998; Kendall & Chambless, 1998). As shown in Table 16.4, the therapies identified as effective for particular problems in adult clients are mainly behavioral, cognitive, and cognitive-behavioral methods, along with interpersonal therapy, a contemporary psychodynamic approach initially developed to treat depression (Klerman & Weissman, 1993; Markowitz & Swartz, 1997).

● **What do the results mean?**

The authors of the report on empirically supported therapies, as well as those who support their efforts, claim that relying on analysis of experimental research has constituted a scientific evaluation of various treatments and generated a list of methods from which clinicians and consumers can choose with confidence when facing specific disorders (e.g., Hunsley & Rumstein-McKean, 1999; Kendall & Chambless, 1998). Therapists are even being urged to follow the *treatment manuals* that were used in successful research studies to help them deliver empirically supported therapies exactly as they were intended (Addis, 1997; Wade, Treat, & Stuart, 1998).

Not everyone agrees with this interpretation or this recommendation. Critics argue that the list of empirically supported therapies is based on research that may not be relevant to clinicians practicing in the real world. They point out, for example, that experimental studies of psychotherapy have focused mainly on the therapeutic procedures used rather than on the characteristics and interactions of therapists and clients (Garfield, 1998; Hilliard, Henry, & Strupp, 2000). This emphasis on procedure is a problem, they say, because the outcome of therapy in these experiments might have been affected by whether the random assignment of clients to therapists resulted in a match or a mismatch on certain personal characteristics. These critics say that in real clinical situations, clients and therapists are not paired up at random (Hohmann & Shear, 2002; Persons & Silberschatz, 1998; Seligman, 1995). Finally, because therapists participating in experimental research were required to follow standard treatment manuals, they were not free to adapt treatment methods, as they normally would, to the needs of particular clients (Garfield, 1998). Perhaps, say these critics, when there is less experimental control over the treatment situation, all therapies are about equally effective, as suggested by the statistical analyses of outcome research we mentioned earlier (Shadish et al., 2000; Smith, Glass, & Miller, 1980).

In short, critics reject the empirically supported therapies list as a useful guide. In fact, some see it as an incomplete, irrelevant, and ultimately misleading document. They worry that it is based on research designed to evaluate treatment effects without adequately taking into account either the personal qualities and theoretical biases of those who offer therapy, or how those factors might interact with the characteristics of the clients who receive therapy (e.g., Henry, 1998). There is worry, too, that widespread use of treatment manuals would make psychotherapy too mechanical and less effective, and that it might suppress therapists' creativity in developing new treatment methods (Addis & Krasnow, 2000; Beutler, 2000; Garfield, 1998).

- **What do we still need to know?**

The efforts of the APA task force represent an important step in responding to Paul's (1969) "ultimate question" about psychotherapy: "What treatment, by whom, is most effective for this individual with that specific problem, under what set of circumstances?" We still have a long way to go, but—with research funding from the National Institute of Mental Health—empirically oriented clinical psychologists are determined to find scientific answers to this challenging question (Foxhall, 2000a). Their work will be focused not only on the efficacy of treatments in laboratory settings but also on the long-term effectiveness of treatment in more naturalistic situations (Nathan, Stuart, & Dolan, 2000; Westen & Morrison, 2001).

Addressing the "Ultimate Question"

The combinations of treatment methods and therapist and client characteristics that are best suited to remedying particular psychological problems have not yet been mapped out, but there are a few trends. For example, when differences show up in comparative studies of adult psychotherapy, they tend to reveal a small to moderate advantage for behavioral and cognitive-behavioral methods, especially in the treatment of phobias and certain other anxiety disorders (Barrowclough et al., 2001; Borkovec & Costello, 1993; DeRubeis & Crits-Christoph, 1998; Lambert & Bergin, 1994; Weisz et al., 1995), as well as bulimia nervosa, an eating disorder (Wilson, 1997). The same tends to be true for child and adolescent clients (Epstein et al., 1994; Weiss & Weisz, 1995; Weisz et al., 1995).

Further, the client-therapist relationship plays a consistent role in the success of all forms of treatment (Barber et al., 2000; Beutler, 2000; Brown & O'Leary, 2000; Elkin et al, 1999; Martin, Garske, & Davis, 2000). Certain people seem to be particularly effective in forming productive human relationships. Even without formal training, these people can sometimes be as helpful as professional therapists because of personal qualities that are inspiring, healing, and soothing to others (Stein & Lambert, 1995). Their presence in self-help groups may well underlie some of the success of those groups and, among professionals, may help account for the success of many kinds of formal therapy. (It would be ideal if we could learn more about these people's qualities and, if possible, train others to develop them, too.)

Before choosing a therapist and treatment approach, then, clients should keep Paul's "ultimate question" in mind. They should carefully consider (1) what treatment approach, methods, and goals they find most comfortable and appealing; (2) information about the therapist's "track record" of clinically significant success with a particular method for treating problems similar to those they face; and (3) the likelihood of forming a productive relationship with the therapist. This last consideration assumes special importance when client and therapist do not share similar cultural backgrounds.

Cultural Factors in Psychotherapy

Imagine that after moving to an unfamiliar country to pursue your education or career, you become severely depressed. A friend there refers you to a therapist who specializes in depression. At your first session the therapist stares at you intently, touches your head for a moment, and says, "You have taken in a spirit from the river, and it is trying to get out. I will help." The therapist then begins chanting softly and appears to go into a trance. What would you think? Would you return for a second visit? If you are like most people raised in a Western culture, you probably wouldn't continue treatment, because this therapist probably does not share your beliefs and expectations about what is wrong with you and what should be done about it.

Similar sociocultural clashes can also occur within a particular country if clients bring to therapy a cultural or subcultural world view that is not shared by their therapist. For example, if a therapist assumes that a client's unexplained abdominal pain is a learned reaction to stress but the client is sure that it comes as punishment for having offended a long-dead ancestor, the client may not easily accept a treatment based on the principles of stress management (Wohl, 1995). In the United States, cultural clashes may be partly to blame for the underuse of, or withdrawal from, mental health services by recent immigrants, as well as by African Americans, Asian Americans, Hispanic Americans, American Indians, and members of other minority populations (Sue, 1998; U.S. Department of Health and Human Services, 2001a). Often the problem lies in mismatched goals. A therapist who believes that people should confront and overcome life's problems may encounter a client who believes that one should work at calmly accepting such problems (Sundberg & Sue, 1989). The result may be much like two people singing a duet using the same music but different lyrics (Johnson & Thorpe, 1994).

In other words, cultural differences, including religious differences, can create enough miscommunication or mistrust to threaten the quality of the client-therapist relationship. Major efforts are under way to ensure that cultural differences between clients and therapists do not interfere with the delivery of treatment to anyone who wants or needs it (Richards & Bergin, 2000; Sue et al., 1999). Virtually every psychotherapy training program in North America is seeking to recruit more students from traditionally underserved minority groups in order to make it easier to match clients with therapists from similar cultural backgrounds (e.g., Hammond & Yung, 1993; Sleek, 1999).

In the meantime, minority group clients are still likely to encounter a therapist from a differing background, so researchers are also examining the value of matching therapy techniques with clients' culturally based expectations and preferences (Hays, 1995; Preciado, 1994; Tanaka-Matsumi & Higginbotham, 1994). For example, many clients from collectivist cultures—in which the emphasis is on meeting the expectations of family and friends rather than satisfying personal desires—might

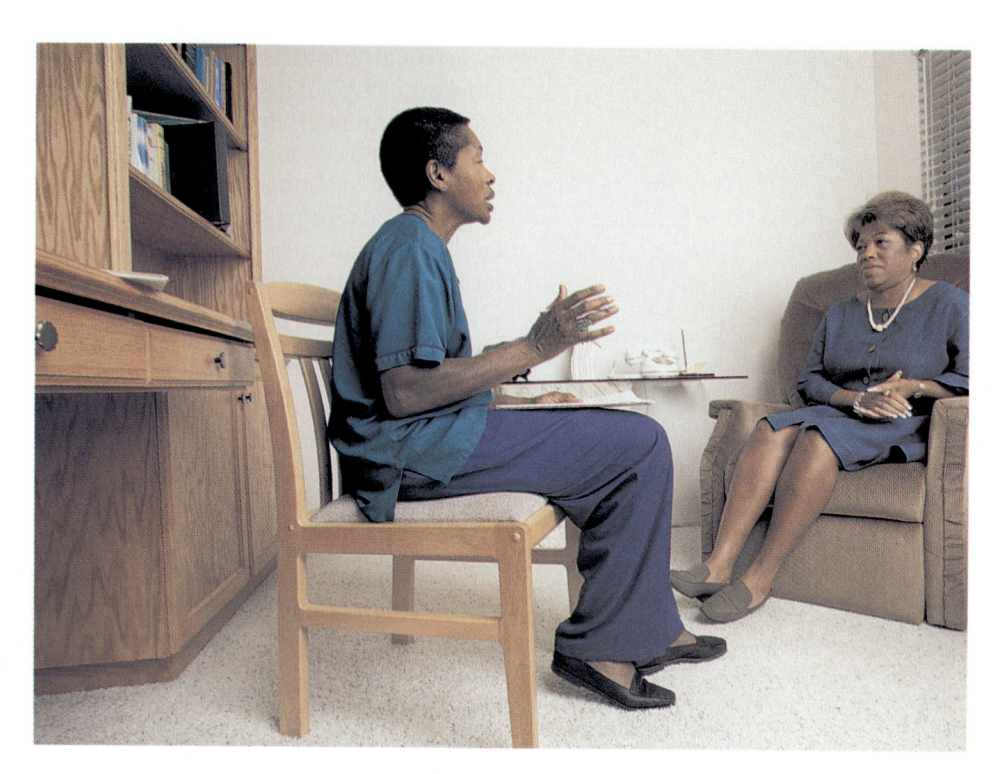

Preparing for Therapy Special pretreatment orientation programs may be offered to clients who, because of cultural or subcultural factors, are unfamiliar with the rules and procedures of psychotherapy. These programs provide a preview of what psychotherapy is, how it can help, and what the client is expected to do to make it more effective (Sue, Zane, & Young, 1994).

expect to receive instructions from a therapist about how to overcome problems. How would such clients respond to a therapist whose client-centered treatment emphasizes more individualist goals, such as being independent and taking responsibility for the direction of change? David Sue and his students have investigated the hypothesis that the collectivist values of Asian cultures would lead Asians and Asian Americans to prefer a directive, problem-solving approach over nondirective, client-centered methods. Sue (1992) found that a preference for directive treatment was highest among foreign-born Asians compared with American-born Asians and European Americans. However, there are always individual differences; two individuals from the same culture may react quite differently to a treatment that group research suggests should be ideal for both of them. In Sue's (1992) study, for example, more than a third of the foreign-born Asians preferred the nondirective approach, and 28 percent of the European Americans preferred the directive approach.

Today, psychotherapists are more sensitive than ever to the cultural values of particular groups and to the difficulties that can impair intercultural communication (Carrillo & Lopez, 2001; Hall, 2001; Mishina, 1999; Shlomo, 1999). Some U.S. states now require clinical and counseling psychologists to complete courses on the role of cultural factors in therapy before being licensed. This training helps clinicians appreciate, for example, that it is considered impolite in some cultures to make eye contact with a stranger; this helps them recognize that clients from those cultures are not necessarily depressed, lacking in self-esteem, or inappropriately submissive just because they look at the floor during an interview. Graduate students are receiving similar training and practical experience as part of their course work in clinical or counseling psychology (Clay, 2001; Neville et al., 1996). Research with these students suggests that the training increases their sensitivity to cultural factors in treatment but does not necessarily increase their competence in actually working with members of ethnic minorities (Pope-Davis et al., 1995; Quintana & Bernal, 1995; Ramirez et al., 1996). Nevertheless, by providing a cultural extension of Rogers's concept of empathy, cultural sensitivity training helps therapists to appreciate the client's view of the world and thus to set goals that are in harmony with that view (Sue, 1998; Yutrzenka, 1995). Minimizing the chances of cultural misunderstanding and miscommunication is one of the many ethical obligations that therapists assume whenever they work with a client (Tomes, 1999).

Rules and Rights in the Therapeutic Relationship

Treatment can be an intensely emotional experience, and the relationship established with a therapist can profoundly affect a client's life. Professional ethics and common sense require the therapist to ensure that this relationship does not harm the client. For example, the American Psychological Association's *Ethical Principles of Psychologists and Code of Conduct* forbids a sexual relationship between therapist and client—during treatment and for at least two years afterward—because of the severe harm it can cause the client (American Psychological Association, 1992b; Martin, 1999; Samuel & Gorton, 1998).

Ethical standards also require therapists, with a few exceptions, to keep strictly confidential everything a client says in therapy. Confidentiality is one of the most important features of a successful therapeutic relationship, because it allows the client to discuss unpleasant or embarrassing feelings, behaviors, or events without fear that the therapist might disclose this information to others. Professionals sometimes do consult with one another about their clients, but they are required not to reveal information to outsiders (including members of the client's family) without the client's consent. The next edition of the APA's code of ethics is sure to include new standards for protecting confidentiality for the growing number of clients who seek psychological services via *telehealth* channels, which include telephone, videophone, e-mail, or other Internet links (Budman, 2000; Foxhall, 2000b; Winzelberg et al., 2000). Among other things, these standards will probably require therapists to inform clients that others might be able to gain access to their e-mail messages, that no formal client-therapist relationship exists in e-mail exchanges, and perhaps that they should seek traditional therapy (Shapiro & Schulman, 1996).

Professional rules about confidentiality are backed up in most U.S. states by laws recognizing that information revealed in therapy—like information given to a priest, a lawyer, or a physician—is privileged communication. In 1996, a U.S. Supreme Court ruling also established psychotherapist-client privilege in the federal courts (DeBell & Jones, 1997; Knapp & VandeCreek, 1997). This means that by asserting *privilege*, a therapist can refuse, even in court, to answer questions about a client or to provide personal notes or tape recordings from therapy sessions. The law may require a therapist to violate confidentiality only under special circumstances, including those in which (1) the client is so severely disturbed or suicidal that hospitalization is needed, (2) the client uses his or her mental condition and history of therapy as part of a defense strategy in a civil or criminal trial, (3) the therapist must defend against the client's charge of malpractice, (4) the client reveals information about the sexual or physical abuse of a child or an incapacitated adult, and (5) the therapist believes the client may commit a violent act against a specific person.

The last condition poses a dilemma. Suppose a client says, "Someday I'm going to kill that brother of mine!" Should the therapist consider this a serious threat and warn the brother? In most cases, the danger is not real, but there have been tragic exceptions. For example, Prosenjit Poddar, a graduate student receiving therapy at the University of California at Berkeley in 1969, revealed his intention to kill Tatiana Tarasoff, a young woman whom he had dated the previous year but who later rejected him. The therapist took the threat seriously and consulted his supervisor and the campus police. It was decided that there was no real danger, so neither Tarasoff nor her parents were warned. After terminating therapy, the client killed Tarasoff. Her parents sued the university, the campus police, and the therapist. The parents won their case, thus setting an important precedent. Several U.S. states now have laws that make a therapist liable for failing to take steps to protect those who are threatened with violence by the therapist's clients (D.N. Bersoff, 1999). Other

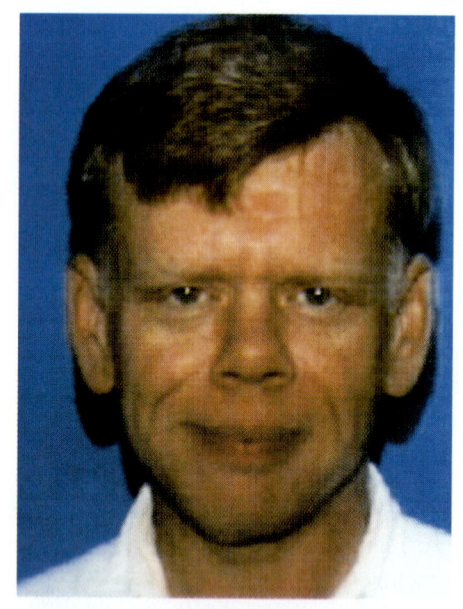

Rights of the Mentally Ill In 1996, after years of odd behavior—including vague threats against government officials and claims that the government was spying on him through TV satellite dishes—Russell Eugene Weston, Jr., was diagnosed as displaying paranoid schizophrenia. He was hospitalized for seven weeks, but he had to be released when doctors determined that he was not a threat to himself or others as long as he took his prescribed medication. He failed to do so, however, and in July 1998, Weston killed two police officers during an armed rampage at the U.S. Capitol. Cases like his are frustrating to mental health professionals, whose decisions about hospitalization must balance the rights of mental patients against those of the public.

states allow therapists discretion in warning or protecting potential victims (Stromberg, Schneider, & Joondeph, 1993).

In the United States, people are protected from being casually committed to mental hospitals. Federal court decisions have given clients threatened with commitment the right to have written notice; an opportunity to prepare a defense with the help of an attorney; a court hearing, with a jury if desired; and the right to take the Fifth Amendment to avoid self-incrimination. Furthermore, before people can be forcibly committed, the state must provide "clear and convincing" evidence that they are not only mentally ill but also gravely disabled or an "imminent danger" to themselves or others. Most states now require a periodic review of every committed person's records to determine whether release is appropriate.

While hospitalized, patients have the right to receive treatment, but they also have the right to refuse certain forms of treatment (Stromberg et al., 1988). These rules are designed to protect hospitalized mental patients from abuse, neglect, coercion, and exploitation, but they can also create difficulties and dangers. Consider Russell Eugene Weston, Jr., a former mental patient who was hospitalized after being charged with the murders of two police officers in 1998. Facing a possible death penalty but judged mentally incompetent to stand trial, he asserted his right to refuse drug treatment that would make him competent. After a long legal battle, Weston was forced to take medication. Prosecutors successfully argued that the right to refuse treatment does not extend to hospitalized patients who pose a danger to themselves or others.

Hospitalized patients who do not pose these dangers—including those whose dangerous impulses are being suppressed by drug treatment—have the right to be subjected to minimal restriction of their freedom. Accordingly, they are released from mental hospitals, usually with a supply of medication that they are to take on their own. Unfortunately, not all these patients follow doctors' orders. Like Weston, Andrew Goldstein was not considered dangerous as long as he took his antipsychotic medication, but after being released from a New York City mental hospital in December 1998, he stopped doing so. About two weeks later, Goldstein pushed Kendra Webdale to her death under the wheels of a subway train. Cases like these cause the staffs of mental health facilities to worry about being sued if they keep a patient unnecessarily confined or if they release a patient who then harms someone. In an effort to strike a balance between the rights of mental patients and those of the public, several states now have laws requiring outpatient treatment for people who are dangerous when not medicated. The New York statute is known as Kendra's Law.

Biological Treatments

Drugs that can ease the symptoms of psychological disorders are the latest in a long line of treatments based on the idea that psychological problems have physical causes. Hippocrates, a physician of ancient Greece, was among the first to propose this idea, and the treatments he prescribed included rest, special diets, laxatives, and abstinence from alcohol or sex. In the mental hospitals of Europe and North America during the sixteenth through eighteenth centuries, treatment of psychological disorders was based in part on Hippocrates' formulations and consisted mainly of physical restraints, laxative purges, draining of "excess" blood, and induced vomiting. Cold baths, hunger, and other physical discomforts were also used in efforts to shock patients back to normality (Jones, 1923). Biological treatments for psychological problems have advanced considerably since then, but they remain somewhat controversial. Here we review the three main biological treatments that appeared in the twentieth century: brain surgery; electroconvulsive therapy; and psychoactive drugs, which are by far the most common form of medical treatment today.

Hospital Restraints Here are examples of the chains, straitjackets, belts, and covered bathtubs that were used to restrain disruptive patients in North American and European mental hospitals in the 1800s and well into the 1900s. These devices were gentle compared with some of the methods endorsed in the late 1700s by Benjamin Rush. Known as the "father of American psychiatry," Rush advocated curing patients by frightening or disorienting them—for example, by placing them in a coffin-like box that was then briefly immersed in water.

Electroconvulsive Therapy

In the 1930s, a Hungarian physician named Ladislaus Von Meduna used a drug to induce convulsions in schizophrenics. He believed, incorrectly, that because schizophrenia and epilepsy rarely occur in the same person, epileptic-like seizures might combat schizophrenia. In 1938, Italian physicians Ugo Cerletti and Lucio Bini created seizures by passing an electric current through the brains of schizophrenia patients for one or two seconds. During the next twenty years or so, this procedure, called **electroconvulsive therapy (ECT)**, became a routine treatment for schizophrenia, depression, and sometimes mania. Upon awakening after an ECT session, the patient typically remembered nothing about the events just preceding the shock and experienced confusion. Although many patients improved, they often relapsed. The benefits of ECT also had to be weighed against its side effects, such as varying degrees of memory loss, speech disorders, and in some cases, death due to cardiac arrest or other problems (Lickey & Gordon, 1991; Shiwach, Reid, & Carmody, 2001).

To make ECT safer, patients are now given an anesthetic so that they are unconscious before the shock is delivered, along with a muscle relaxant to prevent bone fractures during convulsions. Also, the shock now lasts only about half a second and is usually delivered to only one side of the brain (e.g., Sackeim et al., 2000). Finally, in contrast to the dozens of treatments administered decades ago, patients now receive only about six to twelve shocks, one approximately every two days (Fink, 1999). Researchers have also recently begun experimenting with inducing seizures via repetitive transcranial magnetic stimulation (rTMS) instead of electrical shock (Lisanby et al., 2001; Wasserman & Lisanby, 2001).

Today, ECT is used mainly for patients with severe depression who do not respond to other treatments (Potter & Rudorfer, 1993; Rosenbach et al., 1997). It is also occasionally used with manic patients (e.g., Ciapparelli et al., 2001). ECT can be effective in such cases—especially when followed up with medication—and does not appear to cause brain damage (e.g., Ende et al., 2000; Sackeim et al., 2001; U.S. Surgeon General, 1999). However, no one knows for sure how ECT works (Rudorfer et al., 1997; Sackeim, 1994). Some suggest that it may somehow

electroconvulsive therapy (ECT) Brief electrical shock administered to the brain, usually to reduce depression that does not respond to drug treatments.

Electroconvulsive Therapy There are no national statistics on the use of ECT in the United States; estimates of the number of people receiving this treatment each year range from 30,000 to over 100,000 (Hermann et al., 1995). A survey in the United Kingdom suggests that about 12,000 patients a year are receiving ECT (U.K. Statistical Bulletin, 1999). Because of its dramatic and potentially dangerous nature, ECT remains a controversial method of treatment. Critics want it outlawed, but proponents of ECT argue that its benefits to certain patients outweigh its potential costs (Breggin, 1997; Fink, 1999).

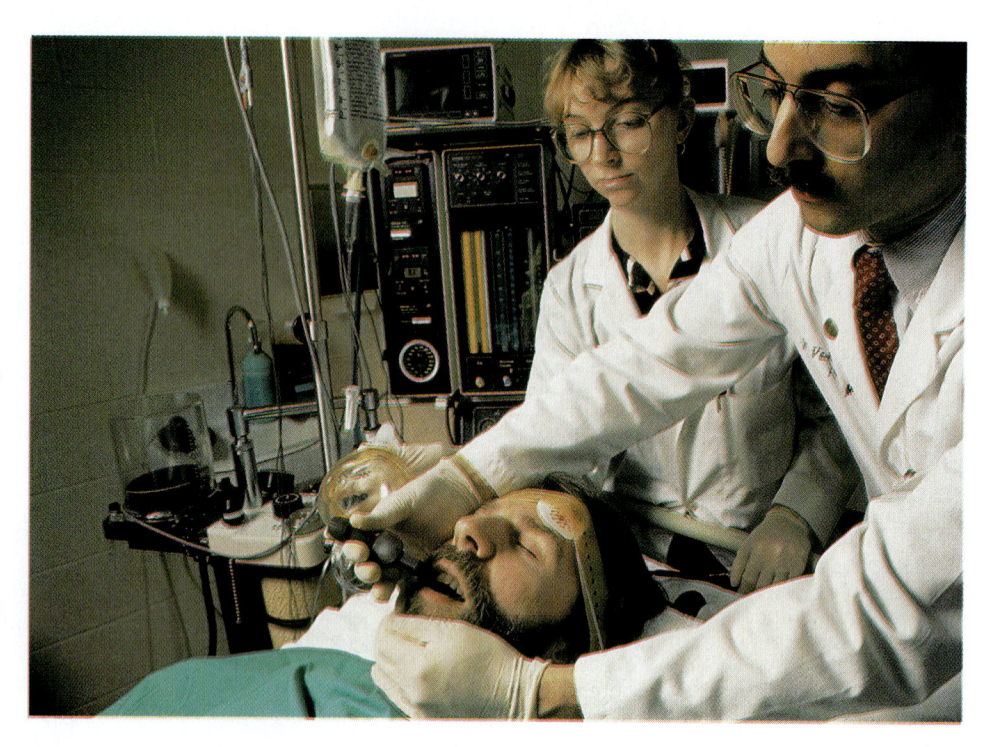

improve neurotransmitter functions and thereby alter mood (Julien, 2001; Kapur & Mann, 1993). Another view is that the neurotransmitters that help the brain recover from convulsions also reduce activity in areas of the brain associated with depression, thus relieving it (Nobler et al., 2001; Sackeim, 1985). Because shock affects many aspects of brain function, identifying the specific mechanisms underlying ECT's effects on depression is exceedingly difficult (Abrams, 1997).

Psychosurgery

Procedures known as **psychosurgery** involve the destruction of brain tissue for the purpose of treating mental disorder. Among the first to try these procedures was a Portuguese neurosurgeon named António Egas Moniz. In 1935 he developed a technique, called *prefrontal lobotomy,* in which small holes are drilled in the skull, and a sharp instrument is inserted and moved from side to side (Freeman & Watts, 1942; Moniz, 1948). The theory was that emotional reactions in disturbed people become exaggerated due to neural processes in the frontal lobes and that the lobotomy disrupts these processes. During the 1940s and 1950s, psychosurgery became almost routine in the treatment of schizophrenia, depression, anxiety, aggressiveness, and obsessive-compulsive disorder (Valenstein, 1980). Unfortunately, brain surgery is risky, and sometimes fatal; its benefits are uncertain; and its side effects and complications, including epilepsy, are irreversible (Martin et al., 2001). Today, psychosurgery is performed only in rare cases in which all else has failed, and—guided by brain-imaging techniques—it focuses on much smaller brain areas than those involved in lobotomies (Dougherty et al., 2002; Feldman & Goodrich, 2001).

Psychoactive Drugs

The use of psychosurgery and ECT declined after the 1950s, not only because of their complications and general distastefulness but also because *psychoactive drugs* had begun to emerge as more convenient and effective treatment alternatives. In the chapters on biological aspects of psychology and on consciousness, we discuss how psychoactive drugs affect neurotransmitter systems and consciousness. Here, we describe how drugs are used to combat schizophrenia, depression, mania, and anxiety.

psychosurgery Surgical procedures that destroy tissue in small regions of the brain in an effort to treat psychological disorders.

Neuroleptics

One group of drugs appearing in the early 1950s revolutionized the treatment of severe mental disorder. Called **neuroleptics** (or *antipsychotics*), these drugs dramatically reduced the intensity of psychotic symptoms such as hallucinations, delusions, paranoid suspiciousness, disordered thinking, and incoherence in many mental patients, especially those diagnosed with schizophrenia. As a result of taking these drugs, these patients became better able to care for themselves and more responsive to their environments. Thousands were able to leave the hospitals where they had been confined, some for many years. For those remaining, the drugs made straitjackets, padded cells, and other once-common restraints almost obsolete.

The most widely used neuroleptics are the *phenothiazines* (pronounced "fee-noh-THYE-uh-zeens"), of which the first, *chlorpromazine* (marketed as *Thorazine* in the United States and as *Largactil* in Canada and the United Kingdom), has been especially popular. Another neuroleptic called *haloperidol (Haldol)* is comparable to the phenothiazines in overall effectiveness, but it creates less sedation (Julien, 2001). Patients who do not respond to one of these neuroleptics may respond to the other. Between 60 and 70 percent of patients receiving these drugs show improvement, though fewer than 30 percent respond well enough to live entirely on their own.

Unfortunately, neuroleptics have problematic side effects, the mildest of which include dry mouth, blurred vision, urinary retention, dizziness, and skin pigmentation problems. More serious side effects include symptoms similar to those of Parkinson's disease, such as muscle rigidity, restlessness, tremors, and slowed movement (Kane, 1989). Some of these side effects can be treated with medication, but the most serious, *tardive dyskinesia*, is an irreversible disorder of the motor system that appears only after years of neuroleptic use. Affecting at least 25 percent of patients who take chlorpromazine or haloperidol for several years, tardive dyskinesia involves grotesque, uncontrollable, repetitive movements of the body, often including tic-like movements of the face and thrusting of the tongue. Sometimes the person's arms or legs flail unpredictably.

Among a newer generation of antipsychotic drugs (also called *atypical neuroleptics*) is *clozapine (Clozaril)*, which has effects similar to those of the phenothiazines but does not cause movement disorders. Although no more effective on average than the phenothiazines, clozapine has helped many patients who did not respond to the phenothiazines or haloperidol, and it may reduce suicide risk in schizophrenia (Green & Patel, 1996; Rabinowitz et al., 2001). Unfortunately, for about 1 or 2 percent of those who take it, clozapine greatly increases the risk of developing a fatal blood disease called *agranulocytosis*, which is marked by the loss of white blood cells and consequent susceptibility to infectious disease (Alvir et al., 1993). Weekly blood tests are required to detect early signs of this disease, thus greatly increasing the cost of using clozapine (Meltzer, 1997).

Several other atypical antipsychotics have been introduced recently, including *risperidone (Risperdal)*, *olanzapine (Zyprexa)* and *quetiapine (Seroquel)*. These newer medications are expensive and are not free of side effects, but they do not cause agranulocytosis. Like clozapine, they also appear to reduce the "negative" symptoms of schizophrenia, such as lack of emotion, social withdrawal, and reduced speech (e.g., Azorin et al., 2001; Conley & Mahmoud, 2001; Volavka et al., 2002).

Antidepressants

Soon after antipsychotic drugs appeared, they were joined by **antidepressants**, which, as their name suggests, were originally designed to relieve symptoms of depression. About 50 to 60 percent of patients who take these drugs show improved mood, greater physical activity, increased appetite, and better sleep. This degree of improvement is seen in only 10 to 20 percent of the most severe cases of psychotic depression, however (Agency for Healthcare Research and Quality, 1999; U.S. Surgeon General, 1999).

Curiously, although these drugs have almost immediate effects on neurotransmitters (usually increasing the availability of serotonin or norepinephrine), their

---

neuroleptics Drugs that alleviate the symptoms of severe disorders such as schizophrenia.

antidepressants Drugs that relieve depression.

effects on depressive symptoms do not occur for a week or two, and maximum effects take even longer. The mechanism underlying the effects of these drugs is consistent with some theories about the biology of depression discussed in the chapter on psychological disorders, but the time lag suggests that the effects occur through some sort of long-term compensatory process in the nervous system.

There are several classes of antidepressant drugs. The *monoamine oxidase inhibitors (MAOIs)* are effective in many cases of depression and in some cases of panic disorder, but they can produce severe hypertension if mixed with foods containing tyramine, a substance found in aged cheeses, red wine, and chicken livers (Julien, 2001). Fortunately, a new class of monoamine oxidase inhibitors is now available that does not carry this side effect risk (Julien, 2001).

Tricyclic antidepressants (TCAs) form another popular class of drugs for combating depression. The TCAs are prescribed more frequently than MAOI drugs because they seem to work somewhat better. They also have fewer side effects, though some patients stop taking tricyclics because of the sleepiness, dry mouth, dizziness, blurred vision, low blood pressure, constipation, and urinary retention they can cause. Further, the combination of tricyclics and alcohol can increase the effects of both, with potentially fatal results. Still, if side effects are controlled, tricyclics can be effective in cases of depression and can also reduce the severity and frequency of panic attacks in some cases of panic disorder.

Today, the most popular medications for depression are those that affect serotonin. The most prominent drug in this group is *fluoxetine (Prozac)*. Introduced in 1986, fluoxetine quickly became the most widely used antidepressant in the United States. Its popularity is due to the fact that it is as effective as older antidepressants and, in most cases, has milder side effects (Cookson & Duffett, 1998; *Harvard Mental Health Letter*, 1998; Stokes, 1998). An improved version of Prozac, containing a purer active ingredient called R-fluoxetine, is currently being developed. Other, even newer antidepressants, including *venlafaxine (Effexor)*, *nefazodone (Serzone)*, and *bupropion (Wellbutrin)*, show similar promise (Appleton, 2000; Croft et al., 1999; Quitkin et al., 2000).

Fluoxetine and other drugs that increase serotonin in the brain, such as *clomipramine (Anafranil)* and *fluvoxamine (Luvox)*, are also effective in treating panic disorder and obsessive-compulsive disorder (Julien, 2001; Koran et al., 2002; U.S. Surgeon General, 1999).

Another development in the pharmacological treatment of depression is the use of an herbal remedy from a plant called Saint-John's-wort (*Hypericum perforatum*). In Germany, where this treatment is covered by health insurance, it is more popular than Prozac. One of the active ingredients in Saint-John's-wort is *hypericin*, a substance that, like Prozac, is thought to affect serotonin. Some studies have found Saint-John's-wort to be as effective as Prozac and other antidepressants, especially in treating milder forms of depression (e.g., Brenner et al., 2000; Gaster & Holroyd, 2000; Volz & Laux, 2000; Woelk, 2000). The design of these studies has been questioned, however (e.g., Spira, 2001), and in any case, treatment effects appear less impressive in cases of major depression (Shelton et al., 2001). Final conclusions about the safety and effectiveness of Saint-John's-wort must await the results of further research (Ernst, 2000; U.S. Surgeon General, 1999).

Lithium and Anticonvulsants

Around 1970, it was discovered that a mineral salt of the element *lithium*, when taken regularly, could prevent both the depression and the mania associated with bipolar disorders in some patients. Administered as lithium carbonate, lithium is effective for 30 to 50 percent of patients with bipolar disorder (Baldessarini & Tondo, 2000; Manji, Bowden, & Belmaker, 2000; Zornberg & Pope, 1993). Without lithium, the typical bipolar patient has a manic episode about every fourteen months and a depressive episode about every seventeen months (Lickey & Gordon, 1991). With lithium, attacks of mania occur as rarely as every nine years (Bowden, 2000). The lithium dosage, however, must be exact and carefully controlled; taking too much can cause nausea, vomiting, tremor, fatigue, slurred speech, and if the overdose is severe, coma or death. Further, lithium is not useful for treating a manic episode in progress because, as in the case of antidepressants, it takes a week or two of regular use before its effects are seen. So, as with the antidepressants, lithium's effects probably occur through some form of long-term adaptation as the nervous system adjusts to the presence of the drug.

In recent years, anticonvulsant drugs such as *divalproex* (*Epival* or *Depakote*) have been used as an alternative to lithium in treating mania. These drugs appear to cause fewer side effects, are less dangerous at higher doses, and are easier to regulate (Bowden et al., 2000; Hirschfeld et al., 1999).

Anxiolytics

During the 1950s, a new class of drugs called *tranquilizers* was shown to reduce mental and physical tension and other symptoms of anxiety. The first of these drugs, called *meprobamate* (*Miltown* or *Equanil*), acts in a manner somewhat similar to barbiturates, meaning that overdoses can be fatal. Because they do not pose this danger, the *benzodiazepines*, particularly *chlordiazepoxide* (*Librium*) and *diazepam* (*Valium*), became the worldwide drug treatment of choice for anxiety (Blackwell, 1973). Today, these and other anti-anxiety drugs, now called **anxiolytics** (pronounced "ang-zee-oh-LIT-iks"), continue to be the most widely prescribed and used of all legal drugs. They have an immediate calming effect on anxiety and are quite useful in treating the symptoms of generalized anxiety disorder and posttraumatic stress disorder. One of the newest of the benzodiazepines, *alprazolam* (*Xanax*), has also become especially popular for the treatment of panic disorder and agoraphobia (Greenblatt, Harmatz, & Shader, 1993). Another benzodiazepine, *clonazepam* (*Klonopin*), is also being used, alone or in combination with other anxiolytics, in the treatment of anxiety ranging from phobias to panic disorder (Worthington et al., 1998). A number of antidepressant drugs, too—including *fluoxetine* (*Prozac*), *paroxetine* (*Paxil*), *clomipramine* (*Anafranil*), *fluvoxamine* (*Luvox*), and *sertraline* (*Zoloft*)—have also been found to be effective in treating anxiety-related problems such as panic disorder, social phobia, obsessive-compulsive disorder, and posttraumatic stress disorder in adults, and possibly in adolescents and children (Davidson et al., 2001; Todorov, Freeston, & Borgeat, 2000; Van Ameringen et al., 2001; Walkup et al., 2001).

Benzodiazepines can have bothersome side effects such as sedation, lightheadedness, and impaired psychomotor and mental functioning. Combining these drugs with alcohol can have fatal consequences, and continued use can lead to tolerance and physical dependence. After heavy or long-term use, attempts to stop taking benzodiazepines, particularly if the change is sudden, can result in severe withdrawal symptoms, including seizures and a return of anxiety more intense than the patient had initially experienced (Rickels et al., 1993).

An anxiolytic called *buspirone* (*BuSpar*) provides an alternative anxiety treatment that eliminates some of these problems, but it acts more slowly. As with the antidepressants, buspirone's effects do not occur for days or weeks after treatment begins; in fact, many patients stop taking it because they think it has no effect other than dizziness, headache, and nervousness (Lickey & Gordon, 1991). Yet buspirone can ultimately equal diazepam in reducing generalized anxiety (Schnabel, 1987; U.S. Surgeon General, 1999). Further, it does not seem to promote dependence, has fewer side effects than the benzodiazepines, and does not interact negatively with alcohol.

Table 16.5 lists the psychoactive drugs we have described, along with their uses, effects, and side effects.

Human Diversity and Drug Treatment

So far, we have talked about drug treatment effects in general ("In Review: Biological Treatments for Psychological Disorders" summarizes our discussion of drugs and other biological treatments), but there can be significant differences among members of various ethnic groups and between men and women in terms of the psychoactive drug dose

anxiolytics Drugs that reduce feelings of anxiety.

table 16.5
A Sampling of Psychoactive Drugs Used for Treating Psychological Disorders

For Schizophrenia: Neuroleptics (Antipsychotics)

Chemical Name	Trade Name	Effects and Side Effects
Chlorpromazine	Thorazine	Reduce hallucinations, delusions, incoherence, jumbled thought processes; cause movement-disorder side effects, including tardive dyskinesia
Haloperidol	Haldol	
Clozapine	Clozaril	Reduces psychotic symptoms; causes no movement disorders, but raises risk of serious blood disease
Risperidone	Risperdal	Reduces positive and negative psychotic symptoms without risk of blood disease

For Mood Disorders: Antidepressants and Mood Elevators

Tricyclics

Imipramine	Tofranil	Act as antidepressants, but also have antipanic action; cause sleepiness and other moderate side effects; potentially dangerous if taken with alcohol
Amitriptyline	Elavil, Amitid	

Other Antidepressants

Fluoxetine	Prozac	Have antidepressant, antipanic, and anti-obsessive action
Clomipramine	Anafranil	
Fluvoxamine	Luvox	
Sertraline	Zoloft	

Other Drugs

Lithium carbonate	Carbolith, Lithizine	Calms mania; reduces mood swings of bipolar disorder; overdose harmful, potentially deadly
Divalproex	Depakote	Is effective against mania, with fewer side effects

For Anxiety Disorders: Anxiolytics

Benzodiazepines

Chlordiazepoxide	Librium	Act as potent anxiolytics for generalized anxiety, panic, stress; extended use may cause physical dependence and withdrawal syndrome if abruptly discontinued
Diazepam	Valium	
Alprazolam	Xanax	Also has antidepressant effects; often used in agoraphobia (has high dependence potential)
Clonazepam	Klonopin	Is often used in combination with other anxiolytics for panic disorder

Other Anti-anxiety Agents

Buspirone	BuSpar	Has slow-acting anti-anxiety action; no known dependence problems

Psychoactive drugs have been successful in dramatically reducing the symptoms of many psychological disorders. Critics point out that drugs can have troublesome side effects, however, and they may create dependence, especially after years of use (e.g., Breggin, 1997). They note, too, that drugs do not "cure" psychological disorders (National Institute of Mental Health, 1995) and that symptom relief may make some patients less likely to seek a permanent solution to their anxiety, depression, or other psychological problems.

necessary to produce clinical effects (U.S. Surgeon General, 1999). For example, Keh-Ming Lin, director of the Research Center on the Psychobiology of Ethnicity at the University of California at Los Angeles, has demonstrated that compared with Asians, Caucasians need to take significantly higher doses of the benzodiazepines, haloperidol, clozapine, lithium, and possibly the tricyclic antidepressants in order to obtain equally beneficial effects (Lin & Poland, 1995; Matsuda et al., 1996). In addition, African Americans may show a faster response to tricyclic antidepressants than European Americans and respond to lower doses of lithium (Strickland et al., 1991). There is also some evidence that compared with European Americans or African Americans, Hispanic Americans require lower doses of antipsychotic drugs to get the same benefits (Ruiz et al., 1999). Some of these ethnic differences are

in review: Biological Treatments for Psychological Disorders

Method	Typical Disorders Treated	Possible Side Effects	Mechanism of Action
Electroconvulsive therapy (ECT)	Severe depression	Temporary confusion, memory loss	Uncertain
Psychosurgery	Schizophrenia, severe depression, obsessive-compulsive disorder	Listlessness, overemotionality, epilepsy	Uncertain
Psychoactive drugs	Anxiety disorders, depression, obsessive-compulsive disorder, mania, schizophrenia	Variable, depending on drug used: movement disorders, physical dependence	Alteration of neurotransmitter systems in the brain

thought to be a function of genetically regulated differences in drug metabolism, whereas others may be due to dietary practices.

Sex differences in drug response are also being investigated (e.g., Jensvold, 1996). In the past, much of our knowledge about drug effects in women—and about women's health in general—was based on studies of men. Because drug responses can differ in women and men, however, the male-oriented approach can be potentially dangerous for women. Fortunately, we are now seeing rapid growth in research focused specifically on matters relating to women's health, including their response to drugs (Vogeltanz, Sigmon, & Vickers, 1998). Some of this research suggests that women may maintain higher levels of therapeutic psychoactive drugs in their blood and show better response to neuroleptics, but they also may be more vulnerable to adverse effects such as tardive dyskinesia (Yonkers et al., 1992). It may be that hormonal and body-composition differences (such as the ratio of body fat to muscle) are among the factors responsible for sex differences in drug response (Dawkins & Potter, 1991; Yonkers et al., 1992). Continued research on these and other dimensions of human diversity will undoubtedly lead to more effective and safer drug treatments for psychological disorders (Thompson & Pollack, 2001).

Evaluating Psychoactive Drug Treatments

Despite the widespread success of psychoactive drugs in the treatment of psychological disorders, critics point out several problems with them. First, even if a disorder has physical components, drugs may mask the problem without curing it. This masking effect is desirable in treating otherwise incurable physical conditions such as diabetes, but it may divert attention from potentially effective nondrug approaches to psychological problems. For example, anti-anxiety drugs may be an aid to psychotherapy (Koenigsberg, 1994), but these drugs alone cannot teach people to cope with the source of their anxiety. Critics are concerned that psychiatrists, and especially general practitioners, rely too heavily on anxiolytics and other drugs to solve patients' psychological problems (Glenmullen, 2000). The antidepressant Prozac, for instance, is being widely prescribed—overprescribed, critics say—for problems ranging from hypersensitivity to criticism and fear of rejection to low self-esteem and premenstrual syndrome (Barondes, 1994). Second, abuse of some drugs (such as the anti-anxiety benzodiazepines) can result in physical or psychological dependence. Third, side effects present a problem. Some are merely annoying, such as the thirst and dry mouth produced by some antidepressants. Other side effects, such as tardive dyskinesia, are far more serious. Although these side effects occur in a minority of patients, some are irreversible, and it is impossible to predict in advance who will develop them.

Still, research on psychoactive drugs holds the promise of creating better drugs, a fuller understanding of the origin and nature of some psychological disorders, and

There is widespread concern that psychiatrists, and especially general practitioners, rely too heavily on drugs to deal with psychological problems. In one case, even a dramatic increase in medication failed to stop a paranoid schizophrenia patient from repeatedly running away from a mental hospital. But allowing him to use a telephone at a nearby shopping mall eliminated the problem. A psychologist discovered that the man had been afraid to use what he believed were "bugged" hospital phones and kept escaping to call his mother (Rabasca, 1999).

"I medicate first and ask questions later."

© The New Yorker Collection 2000 Frank Cotham from cartoonbank.com. All Rights Reserved.

more informed prescription practices. For example, advances in research on individual variations in the structure of the genes that create different types of dopamine receptors may explain why some schizophrenia patients respond to phenothiazines that bind primarily to one type of dopamine receptor, whereas others respond only to clozapine, which has a preference for another type of dopamine receptor (Van Tol et al., 1992). This research may guide the development of new drugs that are matched to specific receptors; the symptoms of schizophrenia then could be alleviated without the risk of movement disorders posed by the phenothiazines or the potentially lethal side effects of clozapine. Similarly, research on anxiolytics promises to reveal information about the chemical aspects of anxiety.

Drugs and Psychotherapy

We have seen that both drugs and psychotherapy can be effective in treating psychological disorders. Is one better than the other? Can they be effectively combined? A considerable amount of research is being conducted to address these questions.

Although occasionally a study does show that one approach or the other is more effective, there is no clear consensus; overall, neither form of therapy is clearly superior for treating problems such as anxiety disorders and major depressive disorder (Antonuccio, Danton, & DeNelsky, 1995). For example, large-scale studies of treatment for severe depression found that cognitive-behavior therapy was as effective as an antidepressant drug (DeRubeis et al., 1999). Cognitive-behavior therapy has also equaled drug effects in the treatment of phobias (Otto et al., 2000; Thom, Sartory, & Jöhren, 2000), panic disorder (Klosko et al., 1990), generalized anxiety disorder (Gould et al., 1997), and obsessive-compulsive disorder (Abramowitz, 1997; Kozak, Liebowitz, & Foa, 2000). Further, the benefits of many kinds of psychotherapy may last longer than those of drug therapies (e.g., Bovasso, Eaton, & Armenian, 1999; Segal, Gemar, & Williams, 2000; Thom, Sartory, & Jöhren, 2000).

What about combining drugs and psychotherapy? One research team compared the effects of gradual exposure treatment and an anti-anxiety drug (Xanax) in the treatment of agoraphobia. Clients receiving gradual exposure alone showed better short- and long-term benefits than those getting either the drug alone or a combination of the drug and gradual exposure (Echeburua et al., 1993). Other studies, too, have found that combining drugs and psychotherapy may produce surprisingly little advantage (e.g., Elkin, 1994; Spiegel & Bruce, 1997). However, the combination of drugs and psychotherapy has been shown to be more effective than either method alone in treating certain disorders, including attention deficit hyperactivity disorder, obsessive-compulsive disorder, alcoholism, stammering, compulsive sexual behavior, panic disorder, and chronic depression (Barlow et al., 2000; deBeurs et al., 1995; Engeland, 1993; Keller et al., 2000; Reynolds et al., 1999). This combined approach may be especially helpful for clients who are initially too distressed to cooperate in psychotherapy (Kahn, 1995). Another approach, already found successful with clients who have been taking drugs for panic disorder, is to use psychotherapy to prevent relapse and make further progress as drug treatment is discontinued (e.g., Bruce, Spiegel, & Hegel, 1999).

It has been suggested that the most conservative strategy for treating anxiety and depression is to begin with cognitive or interpersonal psychotherapy (which have no major negative side effects) and then to add or switch to drug treatment if psychotherapy alone is ineffective. Often, clients who do not respond to one method will be helped by the other.

LINKAGES (a link to Biological Aspects of Psychology)

Biological Aspects of Psychology and the Treatment of Psychological Disorders

As noted in the chapter on biological aspects of psychology, human feelings, thoughts, and actions—whether normal or abnormal—are ultimately the result of biological processes, especially those in the brain, and most especially those involving neurotransmitters and their receptors. Alterations in the availability of these neurotransmitters, in the sensitivity of their receptors, and thus in the activity of the neural circuits they influence affect the ebb and flow of neural communication, the integration of information in the brain, and ultimately, behavior and mental processes. Because different neurotransmitters are especially prominent in particular brain regions or circuits (see Figure 3.22), altering the functioning of particular neurotransmitter systems will have relatively specific psychological and behavioral effects.

Some of the drugs that we have described for the treatment of psychological disorders were developed specifically to alter a neurotransmitter system that biological theories suggest might be involved in those disorders; in other cases, causal theories evolved from (often accidental) findings that drugs known to affect certain neurotransmitter systems help patients who display some disorder.

Let's consider in a little more detail some of the ways in which therapeutic psychoactive drugs affect neurotransmitters and their receptors. As described in the chapter on biological aspects of psychology, a given neuron can receive excitatory ("fire") or inhibitory ("don't fire") signals via neurotransmitters that facilitate or inhibit firing. Some therapeutic drugs amplify excitatory signals, whereas others increase inhibition. For example, the benzodiazepines (e.g., Valium and Xanax) exert their anti-anxiety effects by helping the inhibitory neurotransmitter GABA bind to postsynaptic receptors and, thus, suppress neuronal firing. This enhanced inhibitory effect acts as a sort of braking system that slows the activity of GABA-sensitive neurons involved in the experience of anxiety. However, benzodiazepines also slow the action of all neural systems that use GABA, including those associated with motor activity and mental processing, which are located throughout the brain. The result is the decreased psychomotor coordination and clouded thinking that appear as benzodiazepine's side effects.

Other therapeutic drugs reduce postsynaptic activity by serving as receptor antagonists (see Figure 9.12 in the consciousness chapter), acting to block the receptor site normally used by a particular neurotransmitter. Some neuroleptics—the phenothiazines and haloperidol, for example—exert their antipsychotic effects

LINKAGES (a link to Biological Aspects of Psychology)

by blocking receptors for dopamine, a neurotransmitter that, as described in the chapter on biological aspects of psychology, is important for movement. These drugs compete with dopamine, blocking the firing of neurons that normally use it. The fact that dopamine blockage can normalize the disordered thinking processes of many schizophrenics suggests that, as discussed in the chapter on psychological disorders, schizophrenia may be partly due to excess dopamine activity. Unfortunately, reducing this activity can create severe disorders—such as tardive dyskinesia—in the movement systems that are also controlled by dopamine.

Psychoactive drugs can also exert their therapeutic influence by increasing the amount of a neurotransmitter available at receptors, thereby maximizing the effects of that neurotransmitter. This enhanced availability can be accomplished either by stimulating production of the neurotransmitter or, as is more common in therapeutic drugs, by keeping the neurotransmitter in circulation in the synapse. Normally, after a neurotransmitter has been released, it flows back to the presynaptic terminal, where it is stored for later use. If this *reuptake* process is blocked, the neurotransmitter remains in the synapse, ready to work. The tricyclic antidepressants, for example, operate by blocking the reuptake of norepinephrine. Fluoxetine, clomipramine, and several other of the newer antidepressants are called *selective serotonin reuptake inhibitors* (or *SSRIs*) because they block the reuptake of serotonin. Others, such as venlafaxine, slow the reuptake of both serotonin and norepinephrine. These effects are consistent with biological theories suggesting that some cases of depression are traceable to faulty norepinephrine or serotonin systems.

Community Psychology: From Treatment to Prevention

It has long been argued that even if psychologists knew exactly how to treat every psychological problem, there would never be enough mental health professionals to help everyone who needs them (Albee, 1968). This view fostered the rise of **community psychology,** a movement that aims both to treat troubled people in their home communities and to promote social and environmental changes that can minimize or prevent psychological disorders.

One aspect of community psychology, the *community mental health movement,* arose during the 1960s as an attempt to make treatment available to people in their own communities. As antipsychotic drugs became available, and as concern grew that patients were not improving—and might be getting worse—after years of confinement in mental hospitals, thousands of these patients were released. The plan was that they would receive drugs and other mental health services in newly funded community mental health centers. This *deinstitutionalization* process did spare patients the boredom and isolation of the hospital environment, but the mental health services available in the community never matched the need for them. Some former hospital patients and many people whose disorders might once have sent them to mental hospitals are now living in halfway houses and other community-based facilities where they receive *psychosocial rehabilitation.* These community support services are designed not to "cure" them but to help them cope with their problems and develop the social and occupational skills necessary for semi-independent living (Hunter, 1995; Liberman et al., 1998). All too many others with severe psychological disorders are to be found enduring the dangers of homelessness on city streets or of confinement in jails and prisons (Ditton, 1999; U.S. Department of Health and Human Services, 2001a).

Community psychology also attempts to prevent psychological disorders by addressing unemployment, poverty, overcrowded substandard housing, and other stressful social problems that may underlie some disorders (Albee, 1985; Bracken &

community psychology A movement to minimize or prevent psychological disorders through changes in social systems and through community mental health programs.

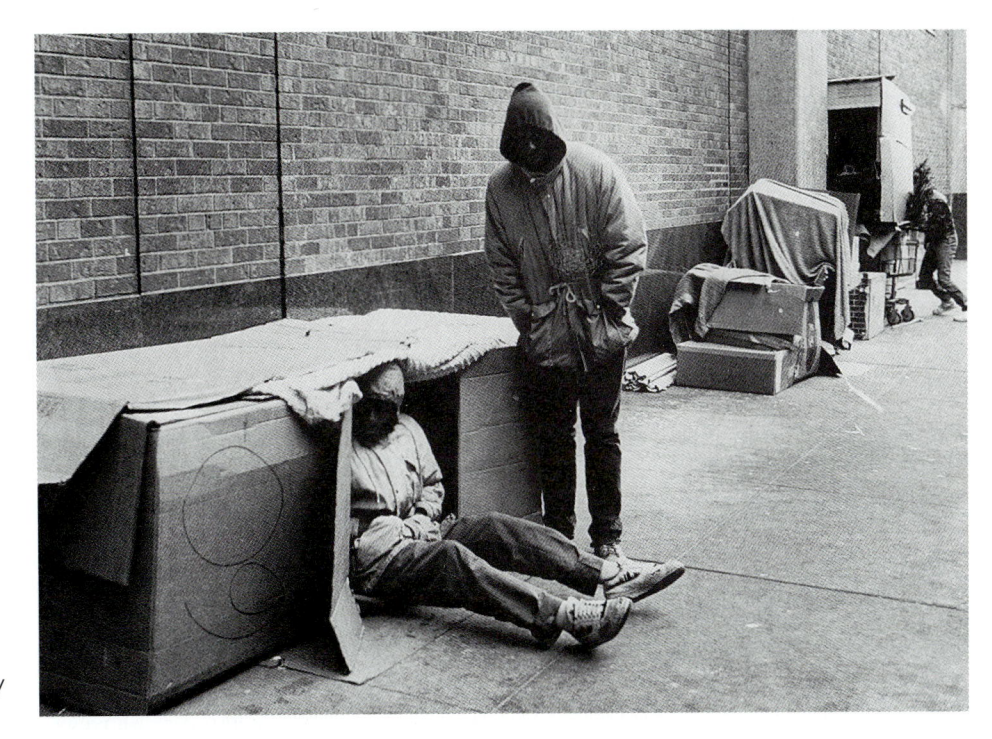

Community Psychology: From Treatment to Prevention

Community Mental Health Efforts
Professional and nonprofessional staff members of community mental health centers provide traditional therapy and mental health education, along with walk-in facilities or hotlines for people who are suicidal or in crises related to rape or domestic violence. They also offer day treatment to former mental patients, many of whom are homeless.

Thomas, 2001). Less ambitious, but perhaps even more significant, are efforts to detect psychological problems in their earliest stages and keep them from becoming worse, as well as to minimize the long-term effects of psychological disorders and prevent their recurrence (e.g., Dadds et al., 1997; Sanders et al., 2000). Examples include suicide prevention (Garland & Zigler, 1993); programs, including Head Start, that help preschoolers whose backgrounds hurt their chances of doing well in school and put them at risk for delinquency (Tremblay et al., 1995; Zigler, Taussig, & Black, 1992); identification of children who are at risk for disorder because of parental divorce or being rejected or victimized at school (e.g., Greenberg et al., 1999; Martinez & Forgatch, 2001); and interventions to head off anxiety or conduct disorders in children (August et al., 2001; Dadds et al., 1999).

LINKAGES

As noted in the chapter on introducing psychology, all of psychology's subfields are related to one another. Our discussion of treating psychological disorders through the use of psychoactive drugs illustrates just one way in which the topic of this chapter, the treatment of psychological disorders, is linked to the subfield of biological psychology (see the chapter on that topic). The Linkages diagram shows ties to two other subfields as well, and there are many more ties throughout the book. Looking for linkages among subfields will help you see how they all fit together and help you better appreciate the big picture that is psychology.

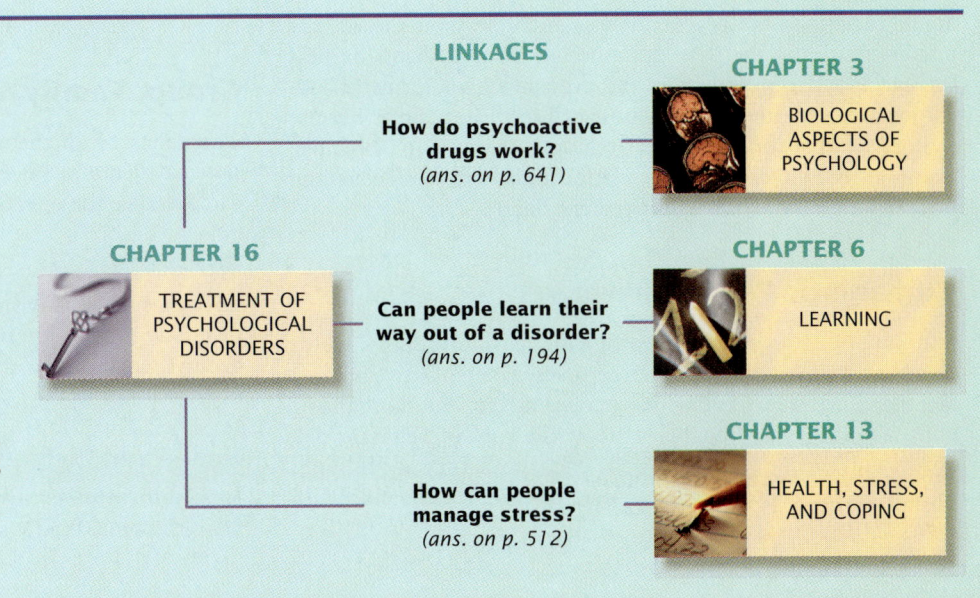

LINKAGES

CHAPTER 16 — TREATMENT OF PSYCHOLOGICAL DISORDERS

- How do psychoactive drugs work? (ans. on p. 641) — **CHAPTER 3** BIOLOGICAL ASPECTS OF PSYCHOLOGY
- Can people learn their way out of a disorder? (ans. on p. 194) — **CHAPTER 6** LEARNING
- How can people manage stress? (ans. on p. 512) — **CHAPTER 13** HEALTH, STRESS, AND COPING

SUMMARY

Psychotherapy for psychological disorders is usually based on psychodynamic, humanistic, or social-cognitive (behavioral) theories of personality and behavior disorder. Most therapists combine features of these theories in an eclectic approach. The biological approach is reflected in the use of drugs and other physical treatment methods.

Basic Features of Treatment

All forms of treatment for psychological disorders include a client; a therapist; an underlying theory of behavior disorder; a set of treatment procedures suggested by the underlying theory; and the development of a special relationship between the client and therapist, which may make it easier for improvement to occur. Therapy may be offered to inpatients and outpatients in many different settings by *psychologists, psychiatrists,* and other mental health professionals. The goal of treatment is to help people change their thinking, feelings, and behavior so that they will be happier and function better. This goal may be pursued by promoting insight into hidden causes of behavior problems, by fostering personal growth through genuine self-expression, or by helping clients learn new ways of thinking and acting.

Psychodynamic Psychotherapy

Psychodynamic psychotherapy, which began with Sigmund Freud's methods of *psychoanalysis,* seeks to help clients gain insight into unconscious conflicts and impulses and then to explore how those factors have created disorders.

Classical Psychoanalysis

Exploration of the unconscious is aided by the use of free association, dream interpretation, and analysis of transference.

Contemporary Variations on Psychoanalysis

Some variations on psychoanalysis focus less on the id, the unconscious, and the past and more on helping clients harness the ego to solve problems in the present. Other forms of psychodynamic treatment retain most of Freud's principles but use a more flexible format. Object relations therapy, for example, examines the effects of early relationships with caregivers and how those relationships affect current ones.

Humanistic Psychotherapy

Humanistic (or phenomenological) psychotherapy helps clients to become more aware of discrepancies between their feelings and their behavior. According to the humanistic approach, these discrepancies are at the root of behavior disorders and can be resolved by the client once they are brought to light in the context of a genuine, trusting relationship with the therapist.

Client-Centered Therapy

Therapists using Carl Rogers's *client-centered therapy,* also known as *person-centered therapy,* help mainly by adopting attitudes toward the client that express *unconditional positive regard, empathy,* and *congruence.* These attitudes create a non-judgmental atmosphere that facilitates the client's honesty with the therapist, with himself or herself, and with others. One way of creating this atmosphere is through *reflection.*

Gestalt Therapy

Therapists employing the *Gestalt therapy* of Fritz and Laura Perls use more active techniques than do Rogerian therapists, often confronting and challenging clients.

Behavior Therapy

Behavior therapy, behavior modification, and *cognitive-behavior therapy* use learning principles to reduce clients' undesirable patterns of thought and behavior and to strengthen more desirable alternatives.

Techniques for Modifying Behavior

Common behavioral treatments include *systematic desensitization, modeling, assertiveness training,* and *social skills training.* More generally, behavior therapists use *positive reinforcement* (sometimes in a *token economy*), techniques based on *extinction* (such as *flooding*), *aversive conditioning,* and *punishment* to make desirable behaviors more likely or problematic behaviors less likely.

Cognitive-Behavior Therapy

Many behavior therapists also employ cognitive-behavior therapy to help clients alter the way they think, as well as the way they behave. Among the specific cognitive-behavior therapy methods are *rational-emotive behavior therapy (REBT),* cognitive restructuring, stress inoculation training, and *cognitive therapy.*

Group, Family, and Couples Therapy

Therapists of all theoretical persuasions may offer therapy to several clients at once. Clients' interactions with one another can enhance the effects of treatment.

Group Therapy

Group therapy may involve a variety of people and problems, or it may focus on particular types of clients and problems. The group format is also adopted in many self-help, or mutual-help, organizations.

Family and Couples Therapy

Family therapy involves treatment of two or more individuals from the same family system. In *couples therapy,* the clients are spouses or other people in intimate partnerships. In both formats, treatment usually focuses on improving communication and other interactions between and among the people involved.

Evaluating Psychotherapy

There is little agreement about exactly how to measure improvement following psychotherapy and how best to ensure that observed improvement was actually due to the treatment itself and not to some other factor. Meta-analyses have found that clients who receive psychotherapy are better off than most people who receive no treatment but that no single approach is uniformly better than all others for all clients and problems. Still, some methods appear effective enough in the treatment of particular disorders to have been listed by an American Psychological Association task force as *empirically supported therapies (ESTs)*.

Addressing the "Ultimate Question"

Research is needed to discover which combinations of therapists, clients, and treatments are ideally suited to alleviating particular psychological problems. Several factors, including personal preferences, must be considered when choosing a treatment approach and a therapist.

Cultural Factors in Psychotherapy

The effects of cultural differences in values and goals between therapist and client have attracted increasing attention. Efforts are under way to minimize the problems that these differences can create.

Rules and Rights in the Therapeutic Relationship

Whatever the specific form of treatment, the client's rights include the right to confidentiality; the right to receive or, sometimes, to refuse treatment; and the right to protection from unnecessary confinement.

Biological Treatments

Biological treatment methods seek to relieve psychological disorders by physical rather than psychological means.

Electroconvulsive Therapy

In *electroconvulsive therapy (ECT)*, an electric current is passed through the patient's brain, usually in an effort to relieve severe depression.

Psychosurgery

Psychosurgery procedures once involved mainly prefrontal lobotomy; when used today, usually as a last resort, they focus on more limited areas of the brain.

Psychoactive Drugs

Today the most prominent form of biological treatment is the prescription of psychoactive drugs, including drugs that are used to treat schizophrenia (the *neuroleptics,* or *antipsychotics*), mood disorders (*antidepressants,* lithium, and anticonvulsants), and anxiety disorders *(anxiolytics)*. There appear to be significant differences among members of various ethnic groups and between men and women in the dosages of psychoactive drugs necessary to produce clinical effects.

Evaluating Psychoactive Drug Treatments

Psychoactive drugs have proven impressively effective in many cases, but critics point out a number of undesirable side effects associated with these drugs, the risks of abuse, and the dangers of overreliance on chemical approaches to human problems that might have other solutions.

Drugs and Psychotherapy

So far, neither psychotherapy nor drug treatment has been found clearly superior overall for treating problems such as anxiety or depression. Combining drugs and psychotherapy may help in some cases, but their joint effect may not be any greater than the effect of either one alone.

Community Psychology: From Treatment to Prevention

The realization that there will never be enough therapists to treat everyone who needs help prompted the development of *community psychology.* Community mental health programs and efforts to prevent mental disorders are the two main elements of community psychology.

Social Cognition

17

Social Influences on the Self
Social Comparison
FOCUS ON RESEARCH METHODS:
Self-Esteem and the Ultimate Terror
Social Identity Theory
Self-Schemas

Social Perception
The Role of Schemas
First Impressions
Explaining Behavior: Attribution
Biases in Attribution
The Self-Protective Functions of Social Cognition

Attitudes
The Structure of Attitudes
Forming Attitudes
Changing Attitudes

LINKAGES: Biological and Social Psychology

Prejudice and Stereotypes
Theories of Prejudice and Stereotyping
Reducing Prejudice

THINKING CRITICALLY: Is Ethnic Prejudice Too Ingrained Ever to Be Eliminated?

Interpersonal Attraction
Keys to Attraction
Intimate Relationships and Love

Linkages

Summary

At 8:48 A.M. on September 11, 2001, terrorists who had hijacked American Airlines Flight 11 crashed the plane into the north tower of New York City's World Trade Center. Fifteen minutes later, another team of hijackers flew United Airlines Flight 175 into the Trade Center's south tower. Both buildings ultimately collapsed. Forty-two minutes after the second crash, terrorists flew American Airlines Flight 77 into the Pentagon building, in Washington, D.C. Another target in Washington was spared only because courageous passengers on a fourth hijacked plane, United Airlines Flight 93, realized what was happening and attacked the hijackers. That plane crashed in a Pennsylvania field, killing all 45 people aboard. The loss of life in all 4 locations exceeded 3,000, the largest number of people to die violently on American soil in a single day since 1862, during the U.S. Civil War battle at Antietam.

Almost all of the questions being asked about this horrendous tragedy relate to human behavior. For example, what could lead people to kill themselves, along with thousands of innocent people, in the name of political or religious beliefs? Why did hundreds of firefighters, police officers, emergency medical workers, and others enter the World Trade Center's burning towers to save the lives of others while risking, and ultimately losing, their own? Why did some of the people who were fleeing the damaged buildings return to their offices after hearing an announcement telling them to do so? Is there any reason to hope that someday the hatred and distrust that brought about this disaster can be reduced or eliminated?

We may never have final answers to questions like these, but some partial answers may lie in the study of **social psychology,** the scientific study of how people's thoughts and feelings influence their behavior toward others, and how the behavior of others influences people's own thoughts, feelings, and behavior. In this chapter we focus on **social cognition,** the mental processes associated with the ways in which people perceive and react to other individuals and groups (Smith & Queller, 2001). Specifically, we will examine how people think about themselves and others, how they form and change attitudes, why and how they use stereotypes to judge other people (sometimes in unfair and biased ways), and why they like and dislike other people. In the chapter on *social influence,* we describe how social influences affect individuals, helping to shape behaviors that range from despicable acts of aggression to inspiring acts of heroism and self-sacrifice.

Social Influences on the Self

Each of us lives in both a private and a public world. You experience your thoughts and feelings privately, but they are products of the social and cultural environment, influenced by others in important ways, and they affect your public behaviors.

In the chapters on human development and personality, we describe how each individual develops within a cultural context, and the ways in which collectivist and individualist cultures emphasize different core values and encourage contrasting definitions of the self. In this section we look at the processes whereby the other people in the culture in which we live affect two important components of the self: **self-concept,** the beliefs we hold about who we are and what characteristics we have, and **self-esteem,** the evaluations we make about how worthy we are as human beings.

Social Comparison

People spend a lot of time thinking about themselves, trying to evaluate their own perceptions, opinions, values, abilities, and the like (Buunk & Oldersma, 2001). Decades ago, Leon Festinger (1954) noted that self-evaluation involves two distinct types of questions: those that can be answered by taking objective measurements and those that cannot. You can determine your height or weight by measuring it, but for

---

social psychology The study of how people's thoughts, feelings, and behavior influence, and are influenced by, the behavior of others.

social cognition Mental processes associated with people's perceptions of, and reactions to, other people.

self-concept The way one thinks of oneself.

self-esteem The evaluations people make about how worthy they are as human beings.

other types of questions—about mental ability, social skills, athletic prowess, or the quality of your relationships, for example—there are no objective criteria. In these cases, people make one of two types of comparisons: a **temporal comparison,** in which people consider their present condition in relation to how they were in the past (Wilson & Ross, 2000), or a **social comparison,** in which people evaluate themselves in relation to others. If you use others as a basis for evaluating how intelligent, interesting, or attractive you are, you are using social comparison (Oyserman, 2001).

Who serves as your basis of comparison? Festinger said that people usually look to others who are similar to themselves. For example, if you are curious about how good a swimmer you are, you are likely to compare yourself with the people against whom you compete, not with Olympic champions. That is, you tend to choose swimmers at your own level of experience and ability (Major, Sciacchtinano, & Crocker, 1993). The categories of people to which you see yourself belonging and to which you habitually compare yourself are called **reference groups.**

The performance of people in a reference group can influence your self-esteem (Baumeister, 1998). For example, if being a good swimmer is very important to you, knowing that someone in your reference group swims much faster than you do can lower your self-esteem. People use a wide variety of strategies to protect or maintain their self-esteem (Leary, 2001; Tesser, 2001). Sometimes they choose to compare themselves with those who are not doing as well, a strategy called *downward social comparison,* but they may also engage in *upward social comparison,* comparing themselves to people who do much better (Wood, Michele, & Giordano, 2000). Both kinds of social comparisons can improve people's feelings about themselves and their situation. For example, distressed people may come to feel better when they compare themselves with those whose situation is worse than their own—a fact that helps account for the popularity of television talk shows that present unpleasant, and even bizarre, family situations. But they may also feel better after comparing themselves with those whose lives or relationships are better than their own (Buunk & Oldersma, 2001). This latter effect may occur partly because seeing people who are better off can create optimism about improving one's own situation (Buunk & Oldersma, 2001).

Some people use a related tactic to maintain their self-esteem during upward social comparison: telling themselves that a superior performer is not similar enough to be in their reference group. They may even exaggerate the ability of the other person so that their own performance doesn't look so bad when viewed in light of such an able competitor (Alicke et al., 1997). If you can convince yourself that you lost every point during a tennis match because your opponent is as good as Pete Sampras, Venus Williams, or some other world-class champion, then you can believe that your performance wasn't so terrible, and that you would do just fine against someone with normal athletic skills.

An unfavorable comparison of your own status with that of others can produce a phenomenon known as **relative deprivation**—the belief that no matter how much you are getting in terms of recognition, status, money, and so forth, it is less than you deserve (Corning, 2000). The concept of relative deprivation explains why an actor who receives $5 million to star in a film feels abused if a co-star is receiving $10 million. If an average person constantly identifies very wealthy people as a reference group, the resulting relative deprivation can make that person feel depressed and anxious (Taylor & Lobel, 1989). And if a large group experiences relative deprivation, political unrest may follow. Social and political turmoil usually begins after the members of a deprived group experience some improvement in their lives and begin to compare their circumstances with those in other groups (Worchel et al., 2000). With this improvement comes elevated expectations about what they deserve. When these expectations are not met, violence may follow. A feeling among citizens of poor countries that the United States enjoys and exploits its great prosperity may have played a role in creating the hatred that led to the attack on the World Trade Center, a symbol of U.S. financial strength.

temporal comparison Using one's previous performance or characteristics as a basis for judging oneself in the present.

social comparison Using other people as a basis of comparison for evaluating oneself.

reference groups Categories of people to which people compare themselves.

relative deprivation The belief that, in comparison to a reference group, one is getting less than is deserved.

The Muhammad Ali Effect When former heavyweight boxing champion Muhammad Ali was once asked why he did so poorly on an intelligence test, he replied, "I only said I was the greatest, not the smartest." Recent research in the United States and in Holland suggests that most people, like Ali, consider it more important to be moral and honest than to be smart. They also believe that they are more honest than other people. This helps to maintain self-esteem (Van Lange & Sedikides, 1998).

FOCUS ON RESEARCH METHODS

Self-Esteem and the Ultimate Terror

Why is self-esteem so important to so many people? An intriguing answer to this question comes from the *terror management theory* proposed by Jeff Greenberg, Tom Pyszczynski, and Sheldon Solomon. This theory is based on the premise that humans are the only creatures capable of thinking about the future. One aspect of this ability is the realization that we will all eventually die, and the consequent experience of terror associated with it. We are unable to change this reality, but terror management theory suggests that humans cope with the anxiety it brings by developing a variety of self-protective psychological strategies, including efforts to establish and maintain high self-esteem (Greenberg, Pyszczynski, & Solomon, in press; Pyszczynski, Greenberg, & Solomon, 2001).

● **What was the researchers' question?**

In one series of experiments, Jeff Greenberg and his colleagues (1992) asked whether high self-esteem would, in fact, serve as a buffer against anxiety—specifically, the anxiety brought on by thoughts about death and pain.

● **How did the researchers answer the question?**

About 150 students at several North American universities participated in these studies, each of which followed a similar format. The first step in each experiment was to manipulate the independent variable, in this case the participants' self-esteem. To do this, the researchers gave the students feedback on a test they had taken earlier in the semester. Half the participants received feedback designed to increase their self-esteem (e.g., feedback that their scores indicated high intelligence or a stable personality). The other half received feedback that was neutral (i.e., neither flattering nor demeaning). Next, the students' self-esteem was measured to ensure that the positive feedback actually produced higher self-esteem than the neutral feedback (it did). In the third phase of each experiment, the researchers manipulated a second independent variable by provoking some anxiety in half of the participants in both the positive and neutral feedback groups. In one study, for example, anxiety was created by showing some students a film containing pictures of dead people and discussions of death. The others saw a neutral film that did not arouse emotion. In two other experiments, anxiety was created by leading some of the participants to believe (falsely) that they would be receiving a mild electrical shock. Afterward, anxiety was measured by participants' self-reports or by monitoring galvanic skin resistance (GSR), a measure of perspiration in their skin that reflects anxiety-related physiological arousal (Dawson, Scheel, & Fillon, 2000).

- **What did the researchers find?**

Self-reports or GSR measures revealed that participants in all three experiments were significantly less upset by an anxiety-provoking experience (the death film or the threat of shock) if they had first received esteem-building feedback about their previous test performance.

- **What do the results mean?**

The researchers concluded that these results offer converging support for the notion that self-esteem is important as a buffer against anxiety and other negative feelings. The results help explain why the maintenance of self-esteem is such a powerful human motive (Tesser, 2001). People do not like to feel anxious, and increased self-esteem reduces most people's anxiety.

- **What do we still need to know?**

These results support terror management theory, but they are not broad enough in and of themselves to confirm all of its assumptions. For example, the theory also predicts that when people are sensitized to the threat of death, they will seek to protect themselves by suppressing thoughts of death, denying personal vulnerability, and doing things that increase their acceptance (and thus support) by others in the society where they live. Other studies by Greenberg and his colleagues (e.g., Pyszczynski, Greenberg, & Solomon, 1999; Greenberg et al., 2001) show that people do, indeed, use these strategies. Increased patriotism, for example, is a common response in people concerned about death, as has been evident in the United States long after the September 11, 2001, terrorist attacks. Reliance on religious faith is another widespread response.

But we still need to know which strategies people are most likely to use, and why. Are some strategies more or less likely to be adopted at different times in a person's life or among people in certain cultures? And what forms of self-esteem are most important in different cultures? So far, most of the research on terror management theory has been done in individualistic cultures such as North America, where self-esteem is largely based on personal accomplishments. In more collectivist cultures, feelings of self-worth tend to be more closely tied to the performance and status of the groups to which people belong (Miller, 2001). So far, there has been little or no research that explicitly looks at whether a more collectivist brand of self-esteem might also buffer the anxiety created by thoughts of death and other threats. In short, it will take many more experiments to test all the predictions derived from terror management theory, and some of that research is now under way by Greenberg and his colleagues.

Social Identity Theory

Stop reading for a moment, and fill in the blank in the following sentence: "I am a(n) _____."

Some people complete the sentence by using characteristics such as "hard worker," "good sport," or some other aspect of their *personal* identity. However, many others identify themselves by using a word or phrase that reflects their nationality, gender, or religion. These responses reflect **social identity,** our beliefs about the groups to which we belong. Our social identity is thus part of our self-concept (Troop & Wright, 2001).

Our social, or group, identity permits us to feel part of a larger whole (Deaux & Martin, 2001). Its importance is seen in the pride that people feel when a member of

social identity The beliefs we hold about the groups to which we belong.

All in the Family Many people find that their place in their family is a central aspect of their social identity. For others, their role in a political, religious, cultural, or business organization might be most vital to that identity. Whatever the specifics, social identity is an important part of people's self-concept, or view of themselves.

their family graduates from college or when a local team wins a big game (Burris, Branscombe, & Klar, 1997). In wars between national, ethnic, or religious groups, individuals make sacrifices, and even die, for the sake of their group identity. A group identity is also one reason people donate money to those who are in need, support friends in a crisis, and display other helping behaviors toward those with whom they can identify. As we will see later, however, defining ourselves in terms of a group identity can foster an "us-versus-them" mentality that sets the stage for prejudice, discrimination, intergroup conflict, and even terrorism (Brewer, 2001).

Self-Schemas

Through social comparison and the formation of a social identity, people develop **self-schemas**, which are mental representations of their beliefs and views about themselves (Kenrick, Neuberg, & Cialdini, 2002). Like our social identity, self-schemas become part of our self-concept. Some people's self-schemas are relatively *unified;* they think of themselves as having more or less the same characteristics or attributes in every situation (at home, at a party, and so on) and in every role (as student, friend, or romantic partner). Other individuals have *differentiated* self-schemas; they think of themselves as having different attributes in different roles or situations.

Variations in the way people think about themselves have a strong impact on their emotional experiences (Clark, 1994). For example, students with unified self-schemas are likely to have an especially strong emotional reaction to failing an exam, because they would tend to interpret failure in this one area as implying incompetence in all areas (Niedenthal, Setterlund, & Wherry, 1992). After failing, they are likely to lower their opinions of themselves not only as students but also in a variety of other roles—as sons or daughters, for example. In contrast, people with more differentiated self-schemas may think less of themselves as students after failing an exam, but that failure will have fewer implications for the way they think of themselves in their other social roles (Kihlstrom & Klein, 1994).

Self-schemas contain information not only about what people are like at the moment but also about what they could be like in the future. Recognition of this *future self* or *possible self* can be a source of motivation to try harder to do better

---

self-schemas Mental representations that people form of themselves.

at various tasks. In one study, people who were told to think of themselves as successful at work persisted longer on a difficult task than people who were told to think of themselves as failing at work (Ruvolo & Markus, 1992). Unfortunately, feelings of depression can result in people who perceive an insurmountable discrepancy between the their present selves and some desired future self (Higgins, Vookles, & Tykocinski, 1992; Taylor, Peplau, & Sears, 2000).

Social Perception

There is a story about a company president who was having lunch with a man being considered for an executive position. When the man salted his food without first tasting it, the president decided not to hire him. The reason, she explained, was that the company had no room for a person who acted before collecting all relevant information. The candidate lost his chance because of **social perception**, the process through which people interpret information about others, form impressions of them, and draw conclusions about the reasons for their behavior. In this section we examine how and why social perception influences our thoughts, feelings, and actions.

The Role of Schemas

The perception of people follows many of the same laws that govern the perception of objects, including the Gestalt principles discussed in the chapter on perception. Consider Figure 17.1. Consistent with Gestalt principles, most people would describe it as "a square with a notch in one side," not as eight straight lines (Woodworth & Schlosberg, 1954). The reason is that they interpret new information using the mental representations, or *schemas*, they already have about squares; in short, they interpret this diagram as a square with a slight modification.

Schemas about people, too, can have a significant influence on our perception of them, because first of all, schemas influence what we pay attention to and what we ignore. Characteristics or events that are consistent with our schema about another person usually get more attention than those that are inconsistent with that schema. Accordingly, we tend to process information about the other person more quickly if it confirms our beliefs about that person's gender or ethnic group than if it violates those beliefs (Smith & Queller, 2001). Second, schemas influence what we remember about others. One study demonstrated that if people thought a woman they saw in a videotape was a waitress, they recalled that she had a beer with dinner and owned a TV set; if they thought she was a librarian, they remembered that she was wearing glasses and liked classical music (Cohen, 1981). Finally, schemas affect our judgment about the behavior of others (Fiske, 1995). Thomas Hill and his colleagues (1989) found that participants' ratings of male and female friends' sadness were influenced not only by the friends' actual behavior but also by the participants' general schemas about how much sadness men as opposed to women tend to experience.

In other words, through "top-down" processing, schemas can influence—and sometimes bias—person perception in the same manner in which schemas about objects can affect object perception. And just as they help us read sentences in which words have missing letters, schemas also allow us to efficiently "fill in the blanks" about people. Accordingly, medical patients and bus passengers do not usually ask their doctors or drivers for credentials. Their schemas about these people lead to perceptions that the person who examines them or drives their bus is competent, confident, skilled, and experienced. And usually these perceptions are correct. It is only when our expectations are violated that we realize that schemas can create errors in our judgment about other people.

figure 17.1

A Schema-Plus-Correction

People who see an object like this tend to use a pre-existing mental representation (their schema of a square) and then correct or modify it in some way (here, with a notch).

May I Help You? Schemas help us quickly categorize people and respond appropriately to them, but they can also create narrow-mindedness and, as we will see later, prejudice. If this woman does not fulfill your schema—your mental representation—of how carpenters are supposed to look, you might be less likely to ask her advice on your home improvement project. One expert carpenter who manages the hardware department of a large home improvement store told us that most customers walk right past her in order to ask the advice of one of her less-experienced male clerks.

First Impressions

The schemas we have about people act as lenses that shape our first impression of them. That impression, in turn, influences both our perceptions of their behavior and our reactions to that behavior. First impressions are formed quickly, usually change slowly, and typically have a long-lasting influence. No wonder first impressions are so important in the development of social relations (Smith & Mackie, 2000). How do people form impressions of other people? And why are they so resistant to change?

TRY THIS

Forming Impressions Think about your first impression of a close friend. It probably formed rapidly, because as mentioned earlier, existing schemas create a tendency to automatically infer a great deal about a person on the basis of limited information (Smith & Queller, 2001). An ethnic name, for example, might have caused you to draw inferences about your friend's religion, food preferences, or temperament. Clothing or hairstyle might have led you to make assumptions about your friend's political views or taste in music. These inferences and assumptions may or may not have been accurate; how many turned out to be true in your friend's case?

One schema has a particularly strong influence on our first impressions: the assumption that most people we meet hold attitudes and values similar to our own (Hoyle, 1993). All else being equal, then, we are initially inclined to like other people. However, it does not take much negative information to change our minds. The main reason for this is that most of us don't expect other people to act negatively toward us. When unexpectedly negative behaviors do occur, they capture our attention and lead us to believe that these behaviors reflect something negative about the other person (Taylor et al., 2000). For example, we know that there are many reasons why people might behave positively around us—because they are nice, they like us, they want to sell us insurance, our best friend likes them, and so on, but a negative act suggests to us only that they are unfriendly or have other undesirable personality traits (Coovert & Reeder, 1990). In short, negative behavior carries more weight in shaping first impressions than does positive information (Smith & Mackie, 2000).

social perception The processes through which people interpret information about others, draw inferences about them, and develop mental representations of them.

Noticeable features or actions help shape our impressions of others, which may or may not be correct.

DILBERT reprinted by permission of United Feature Syndicate, Inc.

Lasting Impressions Does your friend seem the same today as when you met? First impressions can change, but the process is usually very slow. One reason is that humans tend to be "cognitive misers" (Fiske, 1995). We maintain our existing beliefs about the world, often using our schemas to preserve a reality that fits our expectations. Holding on to existing impressions appears to be part of this effort. If your friend has recently said or done something that violates your expectations, your view of her probably did not change much, if at all. In fact, you may have acted to preserve your impression by thinking something like, "She is not herself today." In other words, impressions are slow to change because the meaning we give to new information about people is shaped by what we already know or believe about them (Sherman & Klein, 1994).

Self-Fulfilling Prophecies Another reason first impressions tend to be stable is that we often do things that cause others to confirm our impressions (Kenrick, Neuberg, & Cialdini, 2002). If teachers expect particular students to do poorly in mathematics, the students may sense this expectation, exert less effort, and perform below their ability level. In therapy, counselors can draw extraverted behavior from clients whom they believe to be extraverted, whether or not they actually are (Copeland & Snyder, 1995). When, without our awareness, schemas

Self-Fulfilling Prophecies in the Classroom As discussed in the chapter on cognitive abilities, first impressions of a student's potential can alter a teacher's behavior. If teachers inadvertently spend less time helping children who impressed them as "dull," those children may not learn as much, thus fulfilling the teachers' expectations. If the girl in the back row has not impressed this teacher as being bright, how likely do you think it is that she will be called on?

cause us to subtly lead people to behave in line with our expectations, a **self-fulfilling prophecy** is at work.

In one experiment on self-fulfilling prophecies, men and women participated in "get-acquainted" conversations over an intercom system. They could not see each other, but before the conversations took place, the men were shown photographs and told that they were pictures of their partners. Some saw a photograph of an obese woman, whereas others saw a picture of a woman of normal weight. In fact, the photographs bore no relationship to the women's actual appearance. Independent judges who had not seen any of the participants listened to tapes of the ensuing conversations and rated the women's behavior and personalities. The women who had been described as being of normal weight were judged as more articulate, lively, interesting, exciting, and fun to be with. Apparently, when the men thought their partners were of normal weight, they were more friendly and engaging, and this behavior drew more positive reactions from the women. In contrast, men who thought their partners were overweight behaved in ways that drew comparatively dull responses (Snyder & Haugen, 1995).

Self-fulfilling prophecies also help maintain judgments about groups. If you assume that members of a certain ethnic group are pushy or aggressive, for example, you might display defensiveness or even hostility toward them. Faced with this behavior, members of the group might become frustrated and angry. Their reactions would thus fulfill your prophecy and perpetuate the impressions that created it (Ross & Jackson, 1991).

Explaining Behavior: Attribution

So far, we have considered how people form impressions about the characteristics of other people. But perceptions of others include another key element: explanations of behavior. People tend to form *implicit theories* about why people (including themselves) behave as they do and about what behavior to expect in the future. Psychologists use the term **attribution** to describe the process people go through to explain the causes of behavior (including their own).

As an example, suppose a classmate fails to return borrowed notes on time. You could attribute the behavior to many causes, from an unanticipated emergency to simple selfishness. Which of these alternatives you choose is important because it will help you to *understand* your classmate's behavior, *predict* what will happen if this person asks to borrow something in the future, and decide how to *control* the situation should it arise again. Similarly, whether a person attributes a spouse's nagging to stress-induced irritability or to lack of love can influence whether that person will work on the marriage or work to dissolve it.

People tend to attribute behavior in a particular situation to either primarily internal causes (characteristics of the person) or primarily external (situational) causes (Aronson et al., 2002). For example, if you thought your classmate's failure to return notes was due to lack of consideration or laziness, you would be making an *internal attribution*. If you thought that the oversight was due to time pressure caused by an upcoming exam or a family crisis, you would be making an *external attribution*. Similarly, if you failed an exam, you could explain it by concluding either that you're not very smart (internal attribution) or that your work schedule left you too little time to study (external attribution). The attribution that you make, in turn, might determine how much you study for the next exam or even whether you decide to stay in school.

Sources of Attributions
Harold Kelley (1973) proposed an influential theory of how people (whom Kelley called *observers*) make attributions about the actions of other people (whom Kelley called *actors*). To illustrate this theory, suppose you are at home for the weekend. You want to invite your friend Ralph to stay for dinner, but your father says no. According to Kelley, understanding the reasons

---

self-fulfilling prophecy A process through which an initial impression of someone leads that person to behave in accordance with that impression.

attribution The process of explaining the causes of people's behavior, including one's own.

for your father's behavior requires information about three key variables: consensus, consistency, and distinctiveness (Kelley, 1973):

1. *Consensus* is the degree to which other people's behavior is similar to that of the actor—in this case, your father. If everyone you know avoids Ralph, your father's behavior has a high degree of consensus, and you would attribute his reaction to an external cause (probably something about Ralph). However, if everyone else likes being with Ralph, your father's negative response would have low consensus. Accordingly, you would probably attribute it to something about your father, such as his being a grouch or his personal dislike for Ralph.

2. *Consistency* is the degree to which the behavior is the same across time and/or situations. If your father has invited Ralph to dinner several times in the past but rejects him this time, the consistency of his behavior is low. Low consistency suggests that your father's behavior is attributable to external causes, such as the fact that Ralph has just returned from a camping trip and hasn't showered for two weeks. Conversely, if your father's behavior toward Ralph is always hostile, it has high consistency. But is your father's consistent behavior attributable to an internal cause (his consistent grouchiness) or to an external cause (Ralph's consistent offensiveness)? This question is difficult to answer without information about distinctiveness.

3. *Distinctiveness* concerns the extent to which similar stimuli draw the same behaviors from the actor. If your father is nasty to all your friends, his behavior toward Ralph has low distinctiveness. Behavior that is low in distinctiveness is usually attributable to internal causes, such as enduring personality traits. However, if your dad gets along with everyone except Ralph, his behavior has high distinctiveness, and your attribution about the cause of his behavior is likely to shift toward a cause other than your father's personality, such as how Ralph acts (or smells).

figure 17.2

Causal Attribution

Here are the most common patterns of consensus, consistency, and distinctiveness that lead people to attribute other people's behavior to internal or external causes.

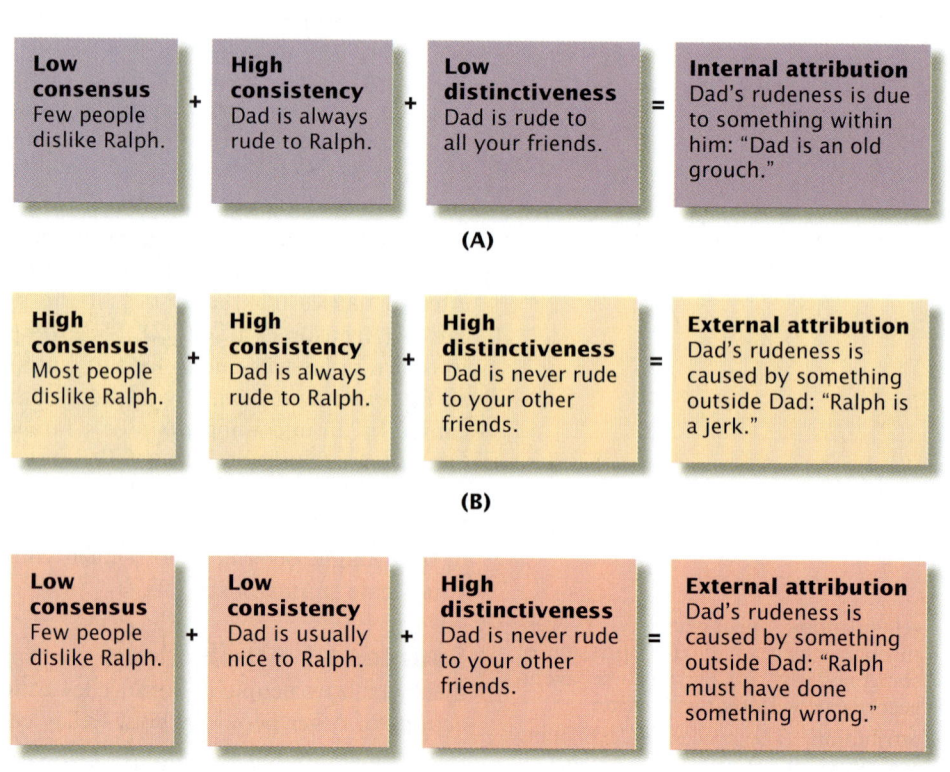

(A) **Low consensus** Few people dislike Ralph. + **High consistency** Dad is always rude to Ralph. + **Low distinctiveness** Dad is rude to all your friends. = **Internal attribution** Dad's rudeness is due to something within him: "Dad is an old grouch."

(B) **High consensus** Most people dislike Ralph. + **High consistency** Dad is always rude to Ralph. + **High distinctiveness** Dad is never rude to your other friends. = **External attribution** Dad's rudeness is caused by something outside Dad: "Ralph is a jerk."

(C) **Low consensus** Few people dislike Ralph. + **Low consistency** Dad is usually nice to Ralph. + **High distinctiveness** Dad is never rude to your other friends. = **External attribution** Dad's rudeness is caused by something outside Dad: "Ralph must have done something wrong."

In summary, Kelley's theory suggests that people are most likely to make internal attributions about an actor's behavior when there is low consensus, high consistency, and low distinctiveness. If you observe your boss insulting customers (a situation of low consensus, inasmuch as most people in business are polite to customers) every day (high consistency) no matter who the customers are (low distinctiveness), you would probably attribute this behavior to the boss's personality rather than to some external cause such as the weather or the customers' rudeness. But if you saw the boss on just one day (low consistency) being rude (low consensus) to one particular customer (high distinctiveness), you would be more likely to attribute the incident to the customer's behavior or some other external factor. External attributions are often made in response to other information patterns as well, as Figure 17.2 illustrates.

Culture and Attribution

Most theories of causal attribution were developed by North American psychologists who implicitly assumed that the same kinds of information lead to internal or external attributions all over the world. However, there is substantial evidence to suggest that this may not be true. For example, Joan Miller and David Bersoff (1994) found that students from the United States and students from India made very different attributions about the reasons why people would do a favor for someone who had just helped them. The Americans attributed the behavior to an external cause (feeling an obligation to repay a favor), but the Indians attributed it to an internal cause (liking to help people). Miller (1994) suggested that the differences in the two groups' responses reflected differences in their cultural experiences. The results of Miller and Bersoff's experiment highlight once again the danger of assuming that phenomena seen in European American cultures generalize to all cultures. Cross-cultural differences in attribution and other aspects of social cognition may help to explain why people in different cultures sometimes have so much difficulty in understanding one another.

Biases in Attribution

Whatever their background, most people are usually logical in their attempts to explain behavior (Trope, Cohen, & Alfieri, 1991). However, they are also sometimes prone to *attributional biases* that can distort their view of behavior (Gilbert, 1998).

Why Are They Helping? Helping occurs all around the world, but research shows that people's attributions, or explanations, about why it happens can differ from culture to culture.

Attributional Bias Men whose thinking is colored by the ultimate attribution error might assume that women who succeed at tasks associated with traditional male gender roles are just lucky, but that men succeed at those tasks because of their skill (Deaux & LaFrance, 1998). When this attributional bias is in operation, people who are perceived as belonging to an out-group, whether on the basis of their gender, age, sexual orientation, religion, ethnicity, or other characteristics, may be denied fair evaluations and equal opportunities.

fundamental attribution error A bias toward overattributing the behavior of others to internal causes.

actor-observer bias The tendency to attribute other people's behavior to internal causes while attributing one's own behavior (especially errors and failures) to external causes.

The Fundamental Attribution Error

North American psychologists have paid special attention to something they call the **fundamental attribution error**, a tendency to overattribute the behavior of others to internal factors, such as personality traits (Gilbert & Malone, 1995). Imagine that you hear a student give an incorrect answer in class. You are liable to attribute this behavior to an internal cause and assume that the person is not very smart. In doing so, however, you might be failing to consider the possible influence of various external causes (such as lack of study time).

A related form of cognitive bias is called the *ultimate attribution error,* in which both positive actions by members of an *out-group* (people we perceive as different) and negative actions by members of an *in-group* (people with whom we identify) are attributed to external situational factors rather than internal personal ones (Pettigrew, 1979). Because of the ultimate attribution error, members of the out-group receive little credit for their positive actions, and members of the in-group get little blame for their negative actions. Biases such as the ultimate attribution error help maintain people's negative views of out-groups and positive views of their own in-group (Fiske, 1998).

In recent years some psychologists have questioned the impact and pervasiveness of the fundamental attribution error (Sabini, Siepmann, & Stein, 2001). For example, they point out cross-cultural studies showing that the attributional tendencies seen Europeans and North Americans are not universal. People in collectivist cultures, such as India, China, Japan, and Korea, are less likely than those in the individualist cultures of North America and Europe to attribute people's behavior to internal causes; rather, they tend to see behavior as due to an interaction between individual characteristics and the situations or contexts in which the person is immersed (Miller, 2001; Norenzayan & Nisbett, 2000). There are also individual differences in attributional tendencies among people within Euro-American cultures. According to one study, for example, people raised in the southern United States are more inclined than northerners to make external attributions (Sims & Baumann, 1972).

Researchers also point out that when people from collectivist cultures do erroneously attribute other people's behaviors to internal causes, it is not necessarily because they fail to consider situational factors or other external influences on those behaviors. It may simply be that, given the information available, an internal attribution appears to be the most reasonable cognitive choice under the circumstances (Sabini, Siepmann, & Stein, 2001). Further, David Funder has argued that under many circumstances, we are capable of making quite accurate judgments of what people are like and what motivates them (Funder, 2001).

Other Attributional Biases

The inclination toward internal attributions is much less pronounced when people explain their own behavior. Here, in fact, another bias tends to come into play: the **actor-observer bias**. Whereas people often attribute other people's behavior to internal causes, they tend to attribute their own behavior to external factors, especially when the behavior is inappropriate or inadequate (Baumeister, 1998). For example, when you drive slowly, it is because you are looking for an address, not because you are a dimwitted loser like that jerk who crawled along in front of you yesterday.

The actor-observer bias occurs mainly because people have different kinds of information about their own and others' behavior. When *you* are acting in a situation—giving a speech, perhaps—the stimuli that are most noticeable to you are likely to be external and situational, such as the temperature of the room and the size of the audience. You also have a lot of information about other external factors, such as the amount of time you had to prepare your talk or the upsetting argument that occurred this morning. If your speech is disorganized and boring, you can easily attribute it to one or all of these external causes. But when you observe someone else, the most noticeable stimulus in the situation is *that person.* You do not know what happened to the person last night or this morning, so you are likely to attribute whatever he or she does to enduring internal characteristics (Gilbert, 1998).

Of course, people do not always attribute their own behavior to external forces. In fact, the degree to which they do so depends on whether the outcome of their behavior is positive or negative. In one study, researchers asked each of several students to work with a partner on a task and then, regardless of their actual performance, told half of the pairs that they had succeeded and half that they had failed. Students who were told that their team was successful took personal credit for the success; those who had supposedly failed blamed their partner (Sedikides et al., 1998). These students showed a **self-serving bias,** the tendency to take personal credit for success but to blame external causes for failure.

The Self-Protective Functions of Social Cognition

The self-serving bias occurs partly because, as noted earlier, people are motivated to maintain their self-esteem—and ignoring negative information is one way to do so. If you just failed an exam, it is painful to admit that your grade was fair, so you might blame your performance on an unreasonably demanding instructor. Other forms of social cognition also help people think about their failures and shortcomings in ways that protect their self-esteem (Tesser, 2001).

Unrealistic optimism is one example. Unrealistic optimism is the tendency to believe that positive events (such as financial success or having a gifted child) are more likely to happen to oneself than to others, and that negative events (such as being in an accident or having cancer) are more likely to happen to others than to oneself (Krueger, 1998; see "In Review: Some Biases in Social Perception").

Unrealistic optimism is fueled, in part, by another self-protective form of social cognition called *unique invulnerability.* For example, when motorcyclists in England were asked to estimate the chances that they would be in a serious traffic accident during the next twelve months, virtually all of them said that this was far less likely to happen to them than to other motorcycle riders (Rutter, Quine, & Albery, 1998).

in review: Some Biases in Social Perception

Bias	Description
Importance of first impression	Ambiguous information is interpreted in line with a first impression, and the initial schema is recalled better and more vividly than any later correction to it. Actions based on this impression may elicit behavior that confirms it.
Fundamental attribution error	The tendency to attribute the behavior of others to internal factors.
Actor-observer bias	The tendency for actors to attribute their own behavior to external causes and for observers to attribute the behavior of others to internal factors.
Self-serving bias	The tendency to attribute one's successes to internal factors and one's failures to external factors.
Unrealistic optimism	The tendency to assume that positive events are more likely, and negative events are less likely, to occur to oneself than to others.

self-serving bias The tendency to attribute one's successes to internal characteristics while blaming one's failures on external causes.

Unrealistic optimism tends to persist even in the face of evidence that contradicts it, and it can lead to potentially harmful behaviors. This phenomenon was illustrated by a study that found that people who were unrealistically optimistic about their health exercised infrequently and knew relatively little about how to prevent heart disease (Davidson & Prkachin, 1997).

Note that *unrealistic* optimism differs from the generally optimistic (but realistic) perspective on life that, as mentioned in the chapter on health, stress, and coping, is positively correlated with good physical and mental health. Unrealistic optimism can have the opposite effects. For example, one reason why people may engage in risky sexual behaviors (e.g., unprotected sex with multiple partners) is that they estimate the risks of unsafe sex to be much lower for themselves than for other people (Taylor et al., 1992).

Self-protective cognitive biases can help us temporarily escape from something painful, but they also set the stage for a somewhat unrealistic view of reality and, in the long run, can create problems. Like the defense mechanisms described in the chapter on personality, cognitive strategies such as unrealistic optimism may temporarily decrease anxiety and blunt the impact of stress. These strategies, though, may also keep people from taking the rational steps necessary for long-term protection of their health, well-being, and safety (Ayanian & Cleary, 1999).

Attitudes

People's views about health or safety reflect their *attitudes,* an aspect of social cognition that social psychologists have studied longer and more intensely than any other. An **attitude** is the tendency to think, feel, or act positively or negatively toward objects in our environment (Ajzen, 2001; Eagly & Chaiken, 1998). Attitudes are believed to play an important role in guiding how we react to other people, what political causes we support, which products we buy, and countless other daily decisions.

The Structure of Attitudes

Social psychologists have long viewed attitudes as having three components (Schwarz & Bohner, 2001; see Figure 17.3). The *cognitive* component is a set of beliefs about the attitude object. The emotional, or *affective,* component includes feelings about the object, and the *behavioral* component pertains to the way people act toward the object. Ideally, these components would be in harmony. We should be able to predict people's behavior in relation to preserving the natural environment, for example, on the basis of the thoughts or feelings they express and vice versa. This is often not the case, however (Bohner & Schwarz, 2001). Many people's positive thoughts and supportive emotions regarding the environment are never translated into actions aimed at, say, reducing pollution.

What determines whether people's behavior will be consistent with the cognitive and affective components of their attitudes? Several factors are important. For one thing, consistency is more likely when the cognitive and affective components are themselves in agreement (Lord, 1997). Second, consistency is more likely when the behavioral component of the attitude is in line with a *subjective norm,* our view of how important people in our lives want us to act. Conflict between attitudes and subjective norms may cause people to behave in ways that are inconsistent with their attitudes (Ajzen, 2001). For example, someone who believes that the rights of gay men and lesbians should be protected might not campaign for this cause because doing so would upset family members or co-workers who are against it. Third, attitude-consistent behavior is more likely when people have *perceived control,* the belief that they can actually perform such behavior (Ajzen & Fishbein, 2002). The cognitive and affective components of your attitude about protecting the envi-

---

attitude A predisposition toward a particular cognitive, emotional, or behavioral reaction to objects.

figure 17.3

Three Components of an Attitude
Various attitude components may or may not be consistent with one another. For example, people may deplore drunken driving (cognitive component) and be upset by its tragic consequences (affective component), yet not do anything to solve the problem. They may even get behind the wheel after drinking too much (behavioral component).

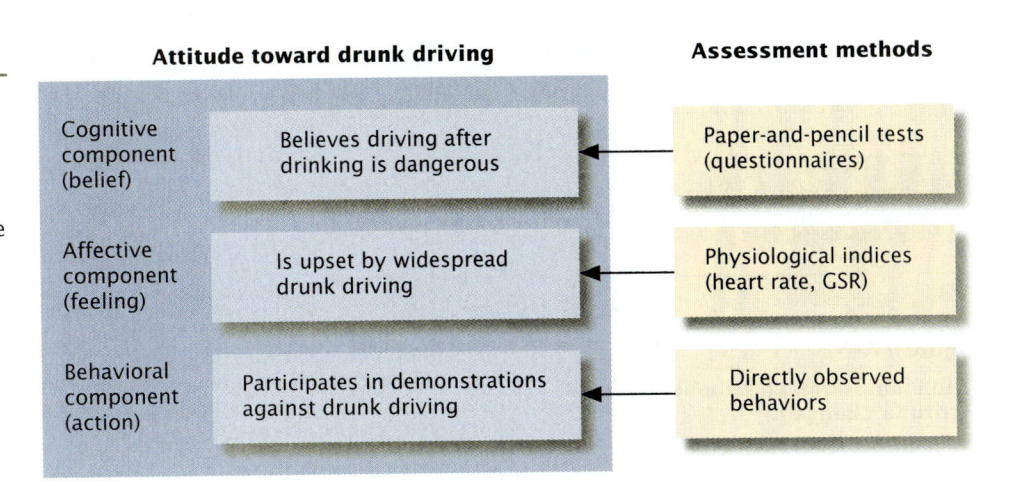

Attitude toward drunk driving		Assessment methods
Cognitive component (belief)	Believes driving after drinking is dangerous	Paper-and-pencil tests (questionnaires)
Affective component (feeling)	Is upset by widespread drunk driving	Physiological indices (heart rate, GSR)
Behavioral component (action)	Participates in demonstrations against drunk driving	Directly observed behaviors

ronment may be positive, but if you don't believe you can do anything about it, you are not likely to even try. Fourth, *direct experience* with the attitude object increases the likelihood of attitude-consistent behavior (Bohner & Schwarz, 2001). This is because attitudes based on direct experiences are more stable and memorable and, thus, more likely to come into play when the attitude object is present. Accordingly, you might be more likely to actively support, and perhaps even participate in, efforts to clean up a polluted river if you have fished in it than if you have only heard of it in news reports.

This last explanation of the consistency or discrepancy among the components of attitudes reflects the cognitive theories described in the chapters on learning and memory. According to this view, attitudes reside in networks of cognitions—interconnected evaluations and beliefs about attitude objects—that are stored in long-term memory (Tourangeau, Rips, & Rasinski, 2000; see also Figure 7.11 in the memory chapter). When you encounter an attitude object, the cognitions associated with it are activated. If your thoughts and feelings are well defined and come easily to mind, then your behavior is likely to be consistent with them; if not, there may be less consistency (Smith, 1998).

Forming Attitudes

People are not born with specific attitudes toward specific objects, but their attitudes about new objects begin to appear in early childhood and continue to emerge throughout life. How do attitudes form? As described in the chapters on human development and personality, inherited predispositions toward certain temperaments may create an indirect genetic basis for certain attitudes, but the formation of attitudes is influenced mainly by the principles of learning (Olson et al., 2001). In childhood, modeling and other forms of social learning are especially important. Children learn not only the names of objects but also what they should believe and feel about them and how they should act toward them. For example, a parent's words may teach a child not only that snakes are reptiles but also that they should be feared and avoided. So as children learn concepts such as "reptile" or "work," they learn attitudes about those concepts, too (Bohner & Schwarz, 2001).

Attitudes can also be influenced by classical and operant conditioning. In one study demonstrating this process, certain Pokémon cartoon characters were associated with positive words (e.g., *excellent*) and images (e.g., an ice cream sundae), whereas others were associated with negative words and images (Olson & Fazio, 2001). Afterward, participants in this study liked the characters associated with the positive stimuli much more than those associated with the negative ones. No wonder so many advertisers present enjoyable music or attractive images in association

TRY THIS — **A Reminder about Poverty** Photographs like this one are used by fund-raising organizations to remind people of the kind thoughts and charitable feelings they have toward needy people and other social causes. As a result, people may be more likely to behave in accordance with the cognitive and affective components of their attitudes and make a donation to these good causes. Browse through several popular magazines, and calculate the percentage of such photos you find in ads for charitable organizations.

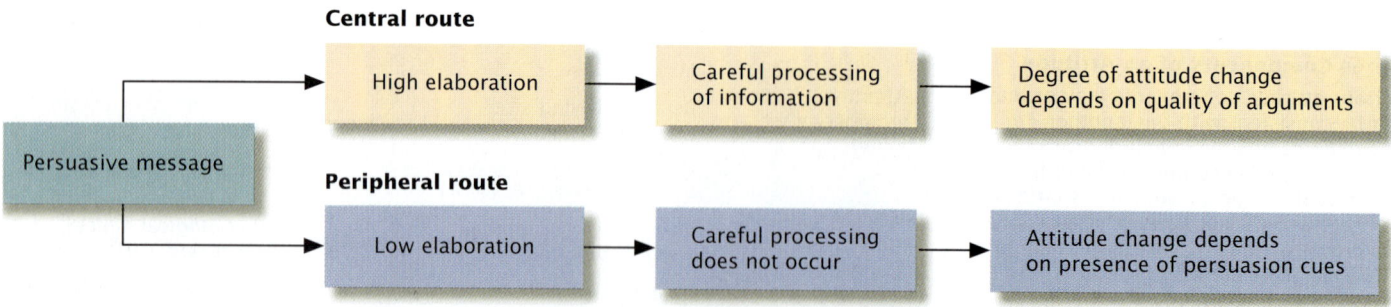

figure 17.4

The Elaboration Likelihood Model of Attitude Change

The central route to attitude change involves carefully processing and evaluating a message's content. The peripheral route involves reliance on persuasion cues, such as the attractiveness of the person making the argument, rather than on careful processing of the message (Cacioppo, Petty, & Crites, 1993).

[Diagram: Persuasive message → Central route: High elaboration → Careful processing of information → Degree of attitude change depends on quality of arguments. Peripheral route: Low elaboration → Careful processing does not occur → Attitude change depends on presence of persuasion cues.]

with the products they are trying to sell (Aronson, Wilson, & Akert, 2002; Pratkanis & Aronson, 1991)! As for operant conditioning, parents, teachers, and peers actively shape children's attitudes by rewarding them for stating particular views. The *mere-exposure effect* is influential as well: All else being equal, attitudes toward an object will become more positive the more frequently people are exposed to it (Seamon et al., 1997; Zajonc, 2001b). One study found that even newborns showed a preference for the passages their mother had repeatedly read aloud while they were still in the womb (Cacioppo, Berntson, & Petty, 1997). The mere-exposure effect helps explain why we sometimes come to like a song only after hearing it several times—and why commercials and political ads are aired over and over.

Changing Attitudes

The nearly $100 billion a year spent on advertising in the United States alone provides but one example of how people are constantly trying to change our attitudes. Stop for a moment and make a list of other examples, perhaps starting with the messages of groups concerned with abortion or recycling—and don't forget your friends who want you to think the way they do.

Two Routes to Attitude Change Whether a persuasive message succeeds in changing attitudes depends primarily on three factors: (1) the characteristics of the person communicating the message, (2) the content of the message, and (3) the audience who receives it (Bohner & Schwarz, 2001). The **elaboration likelihood model** of attitude change (illustrated in Figure 17.4) provides a framework for understanding when and how these factors affect attitude change. The model is based on the premise that persuasive messages can change people's attitudes through one of two main routes. The first is called the *peripheral route* because, when it is activated, we devote little attention to the actual content of the persuasive message and tend to be affected instead by the *persuasion cues* that surround it, such as the confidence, attractiveness, or other characteristics of the person delivering the message. Persuasion cues influence attitude change even though they say nothing about the logic or validity of the message content. Commercials in which movie stars or other attractive nonexperts endorse pain relievers are designed to operate via the peripheral route to attitude change. By contrast, when the *central route* to attitude change is activated, the content of the message becomes more important than the characteristics of the communicator in determining attitude change. A person following the central route uses logical steps—like those outlined in the Thinking Critically sections of this book—to rationally analyze the content of the persuasive message. This analysis considers the validity of the message's claims, determines whether the message leaves out pertinent information, assesses alternative interpretations of evidence, and so on.

elaboration likelihood model A model suggesting that attitude change can be driven by evaluation of the content of a persuasive message (central route) or by irrelevant persuasion cues (peripheral route).

cognitive dissonance theory A theory asserting that attitude change is driven by efforts to reduce tension caused by inconsistencies between attitudes and behaviors.

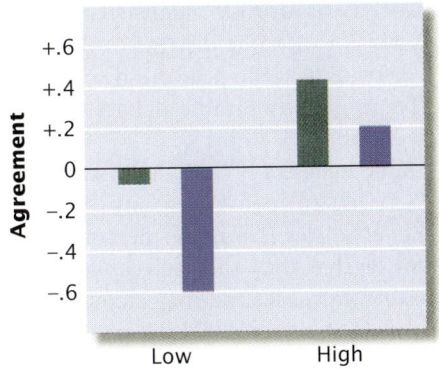

What determines which route people will follow? Personal involvement with message content is one important factor. The elaboration likelihood model proposes that the more personally involving a topic is, the more likely the central route will be activated (Petty & Wegener, 1998; Wood, 2000). Suppose, for example, that you heard someone advocating the termination of student loans in Chile. This message might persuade you via the peripheral route if it came from someone who looked attractive and sounded intelligent. However, you would be more likely to follow the central route if the message proposed terminating student loans at your own school. You might be persuaded, but only if the logic of the message was irrefutable (see Figure 17.5). This is why celebrity endorsements tend to be most effective when the products being advertised are relatively unimportant to the audience.

"Cognitive busyness" is another factor affecting which attitude-change route is activated. If you are busy thinking about other things while a message is being delivered, you will be unable to pay much attention to its content—in which case activation of the peripheral route becomes more likely. Personality characteristics are also related to attitude-change processes. For example, people with a strong *need for cognition* like to engage in thoughtful mental activities and are therefore more likely to use the central route to attitude change (Suedfeld & Tetlock, 2001). In contrast, people whose discomfort with uncertainty creates a *need for closure* are more likely to use the peripheral route (Cacioppo et al., 1996).

Persuasive messages are not the only means of changing attitudes. Another approach is to get people to act in ways that are inconsistent with their current attitudes, in the hope that they will adjust those attitudes to match their behavior. Often, such adjustments do occur. Cognitive dissonance theory and self-perception theory each attempt to explain why.

Cognitive Dissonance Theory

Leon Festinger's (1957) classic **cognitive dissonance theory** holds that people want their thoughts, beliefs, and attitudes to be consistent with one another and with their behavior. When people experience inconsistency, or *dissonance*, among these elements, they become anxious and are motivated to make them more consistent (Eliot & Devine, 1994; Harmon-Jones et al., 1996). For example, someone who believes that "smoking is bad" but must also acknowledge that "I smoke" would be motivated to reduce the resulting dissonance. Because it is often difficult to change behavior, people usually reduce cognitive dissonance by changing inconsistent attitudes: Rather than quit smoking, the smoker might decide that smoking is not so bad.

In one of the first studies of cognitive dissonance, Festinger and his colleague Merrill Carlsmith (Festinger & Carlsmith, 1959) asked people to turn pegs in a board, a very dull task. Later, some of these people were asked to persuade a person waiting to participate in the study that the task was "exciting and fun." Some were told that they would be paid $1 to tell this lie; others were promised $20. After they had talked to the waiting person, their attitudes toward the dull task were measured.

Figure 17.6 shows the surprising results. The people who were paid just $1 to lie liked the dull task more than those who were paid $20. Why? Festinger and Carlsmith (1959) argued that telling another person that a boring task is enjoyable will produce dissonance (between the thoughts "I think the task is boring" and "I am saying it is fun"). To reduce this dissonance, the people who were paid just $1 adopted a more favorable attitude toward the task, making their cognitions consistent: "I think the task is fun" and "I am saying it is fun." But if a person has adequate justification for the behavior, any dissonance that exists will be reduced simply by thinking about the justification. The participants who were paid $20 thought they had adequate justification for lying and so did not need to change their attitude toward the task.

Hundreds of other experiments have also found that when people publicly engage in behaviors that are inconsistent with their privately held attitudes, they are

figure 17.5

Personal Involvement and Routes to Attitude Change

In the study represented here, students' level of agreement (+) or disagreement (−) with messages advocating exit exams for seniors depended on whether they thought the policy would begin immediately (high involvement) or only after they had graduated (low involvement). In the low-involvement condition, students followed a peripheral route to attitude change, agreeing with messages from highly credible communicators regardless of how strong or weak the arguments were. Students who were more involved followed a central route, changing their minds only if the message contained a strong, logical argument.

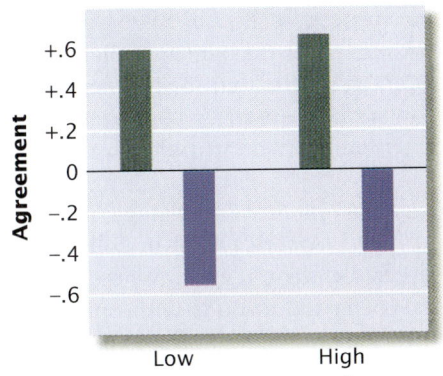

Source: Data from Petty, Cacioppo, & Goldman (1981); Petty, Cacioppo, & Schumann (1983).

Favorable

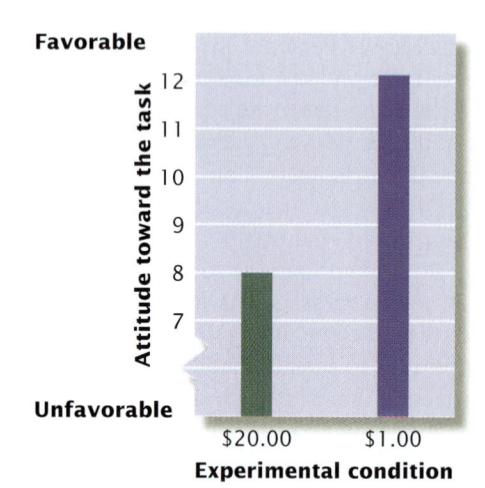

Unfavorable

■ High justification (low dissonance)
■ Low justification (high dissonance)

figure 17.6

Cognitive Dissonance and Attitude Change

According to cognitive dissonance theory, people who were paid $20 to say a boring task was enjoyable had clear justification for lying and should experience little dissonance between what they said and what they thought about the task. In fact, their attitude toward the task did not change much. However, participants who received just $1 had little justification to lie and reduced their dissonance mainly by displaying a more positive attitude toward the task.

self-perception theory A theory suggesting that attitudes can change as people consider their behavior in certain situations and then infer what their attitude must be.

likely to change their attitudes to be consistent with their behavior (Stone & Cooper, 2001). These experiments have also found that behavior-attitude inconsistency will produce attitude change when (1) the inconsistency causes some distress or discomfort in a person and (2) changing attitudes serves to reduce the person's discomfort or distress. But what causes the discomfort? There is considerable debate among attitude researchers about this question (Wood, 2000).

Currently, the most popular of several possible answers is that the discomfort is caused by an inconsistency between people's desire to maintain a positive self-concept and the fact that they have, for example, encouraged another person to do something that they themselves didn't believe in or that they themselves wouldn't do. This inconsistency makes most people feel uncomfortable, and they change their attitudes to reduce or eliminate such feelings (Stone & Cooper, 2001). If people can persuade themselves that they really believed in what they did, the perceived inconsistency disappears, and their positive self-concept is restored. Changing one's private attitude to match one's public actions is one way to accomplish this self-persuasion. Claude Steele's work on *self-affirmation* supports this explanation of why dissonance causes discomfort (e.g., Steele, Spencer, & Lynch, 1993). He has found that people will not change their attitudes after recognizing their own attitude-behavior inconsistency if they can do something else that makes them look good and feel good about themselves (e.g., showing how smart or competent they are). In other words, when people do not need to change their attitudes to reestablish a positive view of themselves, they don't.

The impact of attitude-behavior inconsistencies on attitude change may be greater in individualist cultures of Europe and North America than in collectivist cultures such as Japan and China (e.g., Heine & Lehman, 1997). Where group rather than individual identities are emphasized, behaving at odds with one's personal beliefs may create less discomfort—and thus less motivation for attitude change—because holding to those beliefs tends to be less important for self-esteem.

Self-Perception Theory Over the years, cognitive dissonance theory has been challenged by other explanations of why attitudes change when they are inconsistent with behavior (Dunning, 2001). The first and strongest of these challenges came from Daryl Bem's (1967) **self-perception theory**. Unlike dissonance theory, self-perception theory does not assume that people experience discomfort when their attitudes are inconsistent with their behaviors. According to Bem, situations often arise in which people are not quite sure about their attitudes. When this happens, Bem says, people look at their own behavior under particular circumstances and then infer what their attitude must be. The person says, "If I did that under those circumstances, my attitude must be this." This process makes their attitudes consistent with their behavior, but the process is not driven by tension or discomfort.

Self-perception explanations of attitude change seem reasonable, but two kinds of evidence are inconsistent with it. First, people actually do become physiologically aroused and feel uncomfortable when they experience an inconsistency between their attitudes and behavior, and their discomfort is reduced when they change their attitudes to match their behavior (Elliot & Devine, 1994). This finding suggests that some kind of internal tension is, in fact, created by cognitive dissonance. Second, people adjust their attitudes to match their behavior even when they are unable to reflect on that behavior—a process that is crucial to self-perception theory. In one experiment, for example, researchers studied the effects of attitude-behavior inconsistencies in people suffering from anterograde amnesia, a condition, described in the memory chapter, that leaves its victims unable to recall what they have said or done minutes earlier. Like the participants in other attitude-change experiments, these people, too, changed their attitudes to be more consistent with their behavior (Lieberman et al., 2001).

Although these results do not support self-perception theory, they do not entirely invalidate it. It may be that self-perception theory applies best either when

in review: Forming and Changing Attitudes

Type of Influence	Description
Modeling and conditioning	Attitudes are usually formed through observation of how others behave and speak about an attitude object, as well as through classical and operant conditioning.
Elaboration likelihood model	People change attitudes through either a central or peripheral route, depending on factors such as personal involvement, "cognitive busyness," and personality characteristics.
Cognitive dissonance and self-perception	Inconsistencies between attitudes and behaviors can produce attitude change, as can reviewing one's behavior in light of circumstances.

people have no prior attitude toward some object or when the discrepancy between their attitude and their behavior is slight. For instance, if you know you like Coca-Cola, but you also know that you just drank a Pepsi, this self-perception may drive an attitude change toward Pepsi even though you did not experience any dissonance. However, when attitudes are strong and clearly defined, and the inconsistency between them is larger and more important to one's self-concept, attitude change appears to occur mainly because of cognitive dissonance (Dunning, 2001). ("In Review: Forming and Changing Attitudes" summarizes some of the major processes through which attitudes are formed and changed.)

Biological and Social Psychology

Social psychologists' research on thoughts, feelings, and behaviors was once entirely separate from research on the biological processes that underlie those thoughts, feelings, and behaviors (Winkielman, Berntson, & Cacioppo, 2001). Social psychologists believed that it was not possible to reduce complex social psychological processes to the firing of neurons or the secretion of hormones. For their part, biological psychologists, more commonly known as *neuroscientists*, viewed the study of social psychology as having little, if any, relevance to the understanding of behavioral genetics or the functioning of the nervous, endocrine, or immune systems. Recently, however, scientists in both subfields have begun to take a closer look at each other's research and how their subfields are related. The result has been the emergence of a new specialty called *social neuroscience* or *social cognitive neuroscience* (Cacioppo et al., 2000; Frith & Frith, 2001; Ochsner & Lieberman, 2001). This new specialty focuses on the influence of social processes on biological processes and on the influence of biological processes on social psychological phenomena.

There are many reasons to believe that this approach will be valuable. For example, the chapter on health, stress, and coping contains numerous examples of how social stressors can have health-related biological consequences. Health psychologists have also found that the availability and quality of a person's social support network can affect biological processes ranging from blood pressure to the healing of wounds (Kiecolt-Glaser et al., 1998; Uchino, Cacioppo, & Kiecolt-Glaser, 1996). The social environment can even affect the way genes express themselves. In one study, for example, monkeys were selectively bred to react strongly to even mild stressors. These animals' hypersensitivity appeared to be

LINKAGES (a link to Biological Aspects of Psychology)

based on a specific gene, but researchers found it possible to modify the effects of this gene by changing the monkeys' social situation. When the animals were paired with a warm, nurturant foster mother, their hypersensitivity diminished significantly, and it remained low even when they were later separated from her (Suomi, 1991, 1999).

Researchers are also beginning to identify the biological underpinnings of many social processes. One example of this relationship is seen in studies of how the amygdala is related to the stereotypes and prejudice described in the next section. (As noted in the chapter on motivation and emotion, the amygdala is a brain structure that plays a significant role in emotion.) Using functional magnetic resonance imaging technology, researchers found that European Americans who were prejudiced against African Americans showed significantly more amygdala activity when looking at pictures of black people than when looking at pictures of white people (Hart et al., 2000; Phelps et al., 2000). Social neuroscientists have also used electroencephalography and other techniques to record the brain activity associated with positive and negative attitudes about people and objects. Their research has shown that these evaluative reactions are associated with activity in specific brain regions (Cacioppo, Crites, & Gardner, 1996).

Social cognitive neuroscience is still in its infancy; the first conference devoted to research in this specialty did not occur until April 2001 (Ochsner & Lieberman, 2001). However, that research shows great promise for creating a better understanding of the linkages among social, cognitive, and biological phenomena, as well as a better understanding of complex social and physiological processes.

Prejudice and Stereotypes

All of the principles that underlie impression formation, attribution, and attitudes come together to create prejudice and stereotypes. **Stereotypes** are the perceptions, beliefs, and expectations a person has about members of some group; they are schemas about entire groups of people (Dion, in press). Usually, they involve the false assumption that all members of a group share the same characteristics. Although the characteristics that make up the stereotype may be positive, they are usually negative. The most prevalent and powerful stereotypes focus on observable personal attributes, particularly ethnicity, gender, and age (Operario & Fiske, 2001). As discussed later, people may not be consciously aware of many of the stereotypes they hold (Banaji, Lemm, & Carpenter, 2001).

Stereotyping often leads to **prejudice,** which is a positive or negative attitude toward an individual based simply on his or her membership in some group (Dion, in press). The literal meaning of the word *prejudice* is "prejudgment." Many theorists believe that prejudice, like other attitudes, has cognitive, affective, and behavioral components. Stereotyped thinking is the cognitive component of prejudicial attitudes. The hatred, admiration, anger, and other feelings people have about stereotyped groups constitute the affective component. The behavioral component of prejudice involves **discrimination,** which is differential treatment of individuals who belong to different groups.

Theories of Prejudice and Stereotyping

Prejudice and stereotyping may occur for several reasons (Duckitt, 1994). Let's consider three explanatory theories, each of which has empirical support and accounts for some, but not all, instances of stereotyping and prejudice.

Motivational Theories For some people, prejudice against certain groups might enhance their sense of security and help them meet certain personal needs. This idea was first proposed by T. W. Adorno and his associates fifty years

---

stereotypes False assumptions that all members of some group share the same characteristics.

prejudice A positive or negative attitude toward individuals simply because of their membership in a group.

discrimination Differential treatment of individuals who belong to different groups; the behavioral component of prejudice.

ago (Adorno et al., 1950); it has since been revised and expanded by Bob Altemeyer (1988, 1996). Specifically, these researchers suggest that prejudice may be especially likely among people who display a personality trait called *authoritarianism*. According to Altemeyer, authoritarianism is composed of three elements: an acceptance of conventional or traditional values, a willingness to unquestioningly follow the orders of authority figures, and an inclination to act aggressively toward individuals or groups identified by these authority figures as threatening the values held by one's in-group. People with an authoritarian orientation tend to view the world as a threatening place (Winter, 1996), and one way to protect themselves from perceived threats is to identify strongly with their in-group and to reject, dislike, and perhaps even punish anyone who is a member of other groups. Looking down on, and discriminating against, out-groups—such as gay men and lesbians, African Americans, or Muslims, for example—may help people with authoritarian tendencies to feel safer, as well as better about themselves (Haddock & Zanna, 1998a).

A more recent motivational explanation of prejudice invokes the concept of social identity discussed earlier. Recall that whether they are authoritarian or not, most people are motivated to identify with their in-group and tend to see it as better than other groups (Brewer & Brown, 1998). As a result, members of an in-group often see all members of out-groups as less attractive and less socially acceptable than in-group members and may thus treat them badly (Jackson, in press). In other words, prejudice may result when people's motivation to enhance their own self-esteem causes them to disrespect other people.

Cognitive Theories

Stereotyping and prejudice may also result from the social-cognitive processes people use in dealing with the world. There are so many other people, so many situations in which one meets them, and so many possible behaviors they might perform that one cannot possibly attend to and remember them all. Therefore, people use schemas and other cognitive shortcuts to organize and make sense out of their social world (Fiske, 1998). Often these cognitive processes allow people to draw accurate and useful conclusions about other people, but sometimes they lead to inaccurate stereotypes. For example, one effective way to deal with social complexity is to group people into *social categories*. Rather than remembering every detail about everyone we have ever encountered, we tend to put other people into categories, such as doctor, senior citizen, Republican, student, Italian, and the like (Dovidio, Kawakami, & Gaertner, 2000). To further simplify perception of these categories, we tend to see their members as being quite similar

Schemas and Stereotypes The use of schemas to assign certain people to certain categories can be helpful when deciding who is a customer and who is a store employee, but it can also lead to inaccurate stereotypes. Following the September 11, 2001, terrorist attacks on New York City and Washington, D.C., many people in the United States began to think of all Muslims as potential terrorists, and to discriminate against them. This false assumption, and the problems it created for Muslims in the U.S., was one of the many awful side-effects of the terrorist attacks.

to one another. In fact, members of one ethnic group may find it harder to distinguish among specific faces within other ethnic groups than within their own group (Anthony, Cooper, & Mullen, 1992). People also tend to assume that all members of a different group hold the same beliefs and values and that those beliefs and values differ from their own (Dion, in press). Finally, as noted in the chapter on perception, people's attention tends to be drawn to distinctive stimuli. Noticeably rude behavior by even a few members of an easily identified ethnic group may lead other people to see an *illusory correlation* between rudeness and ethnicity (Hamilton & Sherman, 1994). As a result, they may incorrectly believe that all members of that group are rude.

Learning Theories Some prejudice results from conflicts between members of different groups, but people also develop negative attitudes toward groups with whom they have had little or no contact. Like other attitudes, prejudice can be learned vicariously. Learning theories suggest that children acquire prejudices just by watching and listening to the words and deeds of parents, peers, and others (Rohan & Zanna, 1996). Movies and television may also portray ethnic or other groups in ways that teach stereotypes and prejudice (Smith & Mackie, 2000). One study found, for example, that Hispanics were twice as likely as any other group to be portrayed as criminals in prime-time television shows (Purdue Exponent, 1994). Another study revealed that local news coverage often gives the impression that African Americans are responsible for a higher percentage of crimes than is actually the case (Romer, Jamieson, & de Cocteau, 1998). No wonder so many young children already know about the supposed negative characteristics of certain groups long before they ever meet members of those groups (Mackie et al., 1996; Quintana, 1998).

Reducing Prejudice

One clear implication of the cognitive and learning theories of prejudice and stereotyping is that members of one group are often ignorant or misinformed about the characteristics of people in other groups (Miller & Davidson-Podgorny, 1987). Before 1954, for example, most black and white children in the United States knew very little about one another because they went to separate schools. Then the Supreme Court declared that segregated public schools should be prohibited. By ruling segregation to be unconstitutional, the court created a real-life test of the **contact hypothesis,** which states that stereotypes and prejudice toward a group will diminish as contact with that group increases (Pettigrew & Tropp, 2000).

Did the desegregation of U.S. schools in the 1960s and 1970s confirm the contact hypothesis? In a few schools, integration was followed by a decrease in prejudice, but in most places either no change occurred or prejudice actually increased (Oskamp & Schultz, 1998). However, these results did not necessarily disprove the contact hypothesis. In-depth studies of schools in which desegregation was successful suggested that contact alone was not enough; integration reduced prejudice only when certain social conditions were created (Pettigrew & Tropp, 2000). First, members of the two groups had to be of roughly equal social and economic status. Second, school authorities had to promote cooperation and interdependence between the members of different ethnic groups by having them work together on projects that required reliance on one another to reach success. Third, the contact between group members had to occur on a one-on-one basis; it was only when people got to know one another as individuals that the errors contained in stereotypes became apparent. Finally, the members of each group had to be seen as typical and not unusual in any significant way. When these four conditions prevailed, the children's attitudes toward one another became more positive. These effects are not restricted to schoolchildren in the United States. In Italy, for example, people who had equal-status contact with black immigrants from North Africa displayed less prejudice against them than did Italians who had no contact with the immigrants (Kirchler & Zani, 1995).

contact hypothesis The idea that stereotypes and prejudice toward a group will diminish as contact with the group increases.

Fighting Ethnic Prejudice Negative attitudes about members of ethnic groups are often based on negative personal experiences or the negative experiences and attitudes people hear about from others. Cooperative contact between equals can help promote mutual respect and reduce ethnic prejudice.

Elliot Aronson (1995) describes a teaching strategy, called the *jigsaw technique*, that helps create the conditions that reduce prejudice. The strategy calls for children from several ethnic groups to work as a team to complete a task, such as writing a report about a famous figure in history. Each child learns, and provides the team with, a separate piece of information about this person, such as place of birth (Aronson, 1990). Studies show that children from various ethnic groups who are exposed to the jigsaw technique and other cooperative learning experiences show substantial reductions in prejudice toward other groups (Aronson, 1997). The success reported in these studies has greatly increased the popularity of cooperative learning exercises in classrooms in the United States. Such exercises may not eliminate all aspects of ethnic prejudice in children, but they seem to be a step in the right direction.

Can friendly, cooperative, interdependent contact reduce the more entrenched forms of prejudice seen in adults? It may. When equal-status adults work jointly toward a common goal, bias and distrust can be reduced. This is especially true if they come to see themselves as members of the same group rather than as belonging to opposing groups (Dovidio, Kawakami, & Gaertner, 2000; Fiske, 2000). The challenge to be met in creating such cooperative experiences in the real world is that the participants must be of equal status—a challenge made more difficult in many countries by the sizable status differences that still exist between ethnic groups (Pettigrew & Tropp, 2000).

In the final analysis, contact provides only part of the solution to the problems of stereotyping, prejudice, and discrimination. To reduce ethnic prejudice, we must develop additional educational techniques that address the social cognitions and perceptions that lie at the core of bigotry and hatred toward people who are different from us (Monteith, Zuwerink, & Devine, 1994).

THINKING CRITICALLY

Is Ethnic Prejudice Too Ingrained Ever to Be Eliminated?

There is little doubt that overt forms of ethnic prejudice have decreased dramatically in the United States over the past thirty to forty years. For example, in the 1950s fewer than half of European American college students surveyed said they were willing to live in integrated neighborhoods; today, about 95 percent say they would be willing to do so. And three decades ago, fewer than 40 percent of European Americans said they would vote for an African American presidential candidate; over 95 percent now say they might do so (Dovidio & Gaertner, 1998). Despite these welcome changes, research in social psychology suggests that more subtle manifestations of prejudice and discrimination may remain as entrenched in the United States today as they were ten or even fifteen years ago (Dovidio & Gaertner, 2000).

● What am I being asked to believe or accept?

Even people who see themselves as nonprejudiced and who disavow ethnic stereotypes and discrimination still hold negative stereotypes about ethnic out-groups and, in certain situations, will display prejudice and discrimination toward them (Dovidio, Kawakami, & Beach, 2001). Some people claim, therefore, that negative attitudes toward ethnic out-groups are so deeply ingrained in all of us that ethnic prejudice can never be eliminated.

● What evidence is available to support the assertion?

Evidence for this assertion focuses primarily on prejudice against African Americans by European Americans and comes, first, from studies testing the theory of *aversive racism* (Dovidio & Gaertner, 1998). This theory holds that even though many European Americans consider ethnic prejudice to be unacceptable, or aversive, they will still sometimes display it—especially when they can do so without admitting, even to themselves, that they are prejudiced. In one test of this theory, a male experimenter telephoned male and female European Americans who were known to believe in ethnic equality. The man claimed to be a stranded motorist who had misdialed from a pay phone while trying to call a service station for help. When told he had the wrong number, the man replied that he was out of coins and asked the person he'd reached to call a service station for him. If people listened long enough to learn of the man's problem, they were just as likely to contact the service station whether the caller "sounded" European American or African American. However, if the caller "sounded" African American, these supposedly unprejudiced people were almost five times as likely to hang up even before the caller could ask for help (Gaertner & Dovidio, 1986). In other studies, female European American college students were asked to help another female student who was doing poorly on some task. When the student's poor performance was described as being due to the task's difficulty, the students agreed to help, regardless of the other student's ethnicity. But if the problem was said to be due to lack of effort, help was offered much more often to European Americans than to African Americans (Frey & Gaertner, 1986; McPhail & Penner, 1995). These findings suggest that even people who do not display prejudice in most situations may do so in others.

A second line of evidence for the entrenchment of prejudice comes from research showing that many people hold negative stereotypes about ethnic minorities (and women) but are unaware that they do so. These negative stereotypes can also be *activated* without conscious awareness, even among people who believe they are free of prejudice (Banaji, Lemm, & Carpenter, 2001; Wheeler & Petty, 2001). To demonstrate these phenomena, researchers have used the priming procedures described in the chapter on consciousness to activate unconscious thoughts and feelings that can alter people's reactions to stimuli without their awareness. In one study, for example, white participants were exposed to subliminal presentations of pictures of black individuals (Chen & Bargh, 1997). The participants were not consciously aware that they had seen these pictures, but when they interacted with a black man soon thereafter, those who had been primed with the pictures acted more negatively toward him and saw him as more hostile than did people who had not been primed. Priming apparently activated these participants' negative ethnic stereotypes. It is also possible to prime unconscious negative stereotypes about other groups, including women and the elderly (Glick &

Fiske, 2001; Hense, Penner, & Nelson, 1996). All of these findings suggest that stereotypes are so well learned and so ingrained in people that they may be activated automatically and without their conscious awareness (Dovidio, Kawakami, & Beach, 2001).

- **Are there alternative ways of interpreting the evidence?**

The evidence presented so far suggests that it may be impossible to eliminate ethnic prejudice, because everyone harbors unconscious negative stereotypes about various groups. But this evidence does not necessarily mean that unconscious stereotypes affect everyone in the same way. Perhaps they have a greater impact on people who are more overtly prejudiced.

- **What additional evidence would help to evaluate the alternatives?**

One way to evaluate this possibility is to compare the responses of prejudiced and nonprejudiced people in various experimental situations. In one mock-trial study, for example, overtly prejudiced white jurors recommended the death penalty more often for black defendants than for white defendants found guilty of the same crime, but low-prejudice white jurors showed this bias only when they believed that a black member of the jury also favored giving the death penalty (Dovidio et al., 1997). Priming studies, too, show that although negative stereotypes can be primed in both prejudiced and nonprejudiced people, it is easier to do in people who openly display their ethnic bias (Dovidio, Kawakami, & Gaertner, 2000). Furthermore, activation of these stereotypes may be less likely to affect the conscious attitudes and behavior of nonprejudiced people. So when unconscious stereotypes are activated in nonprejudiced people, the effects tend to appear in subtle ways, such as in facial expressions or other nonverbal behaviors (Kawakami, Dion, & Dovidio, 1998; Lepore & Brown, 1997).

- **What conclusions are most reasonable?**

Taken together, research evidence presents a mixed picture regarding the possibility of eliminating ethnic prejudice. True, people in the United States are not nearly as colorblind as we might hope, and ethnic prejudice may be so ingrained in some people as to be subconscious. However, recent research suggests that it may still be possible to eliminate even subconscious stereotypes (Kawakami et al., 2000; Kurzban, Tooby, & Cosmides, 2001). It also appears that when nonprejudiced people are made aware of their negative beliefs about some target group, they will actively work to prevent those beliefs from influencing their behavior toward members of that group (Devine, Plant, & Buswell, 2000). In short, prejudice is ingrained, but it can also be reduced, and it makes sense to do everything possible to reduce it. In the United States, as in any multicultural country, survival as a civilized society requires that we all continue to fight against overt and covert forms of stereotyping, prejudice, and discrimination. This goal is more important than ever, as fear of, and the fight against, international terrorism can make it all too easy to misjudge and mistreat innocent people based on their ethnicity.

Interpersonal Attraction

Research on prejudice helps illuminate some of the reasons for which people, from childhood on, may come to dislike or even hate other people. An equally fascinating aspect of social cognition is why people like or love other people. Folklore tells us that "opposites attract," but it also maintains that "birds of a feather flock together." Although valid to some degree, each of these statements needs to be qualified in important ways. We begin our coverage of interpersonal attraction by discussing the factors that lead to initial attraction; we then examine how liking sometimes develops into more intimate relationships.

Keys to Attraction

Whether you like someone or not depends partly on situational factors and partly on personal characteristics.

The Environment One of the most important determinants of attraction is simple physical proximity (Berscheid & Reis, 1998). As long as you do not initially dislike a person, your liking for that person will increase with additional contact (Bornstein, 1992). For example, Richard Moreland and Scott Beach (1992) varied the number of times that several experimental assistants (posing as students) attended a class. Even though none of the assistants spoke to anyone in the class, they were rated by the other students as more likable the more often they attended. A more recent study found that such ratings generalized to individuals who resembled the people who had been present (Rhodes, Halberstadt, & Brajkovich, 2001). This proximity phenomenon—another example of the *mere-exposure effect* mentioned earlier—helps account for why next-door neighbors are usually more likely to become friends than people who live farther from one another. Chances are, most of your friends are people whom you met as neighbors, co-workers, or classmates.

The circumstances under which people first meet also influence attraction. In accordance with the conditioning principles discussed in the chapter on learning, you are much more likely to be attracted to a stranger if you meet in comfortable, rather than uncomfortable, physical conditions. Similarly, if you are rewarded in the presence of a stranger, the chances that you will like that stranger are increased, even if the stranger was not the one who gave the reward (Clark & Pataki, 1995). In one study, for example, an experimenter judged one person's creativity while another person watched. Compared with those who received a negative evaluation, participants who were evaluated positively tended to like the observer more (Griffitt & Guay, 1969). At least among strangers, then, liking can occur through associating someone with something pleasant.

Similarity People also tend to like those they perceive as similar to themselves on variables such as age, religion, smoking or drinking habits, or being a "morning" or "evening" person. As shown in Figure 17.7, similarity in attitudes is an especially important influence on attraction. This relationship has been found among children, college students, adult workers, and senior citizens (Brehm, Kassin, & Fein, 2002).

Similarity in attitudes toward mutual acquaintances is a particularly good predictor of liking, because in general, people prefer relationships that are *balanced*. As illustrated in Figure 17.8, if Zoe likes Abigail, the relationship is balanced as long as they agree on their evaluation of a third person, Samantha, regardless of whether they like or dislike that third person. However, the relationship will be imbalanced if Zoe and Abigail disagree on their evaluation of the third person.

One reason why we like people with similar views of the world is that we expect such people to think highly of us (Condon & Crano, 1988). Like many important relationships, it's hard to say whether attraction is a cause or an effect of similarity (Berscheid & Reis, 1998). For example, you might like someone because his attitudes are similar to yours, but it is also possible that as a result of liking him, your attitudes will become more similar to his (Davis & Rusbult, 2001). Even if your own attitudes do not change, you may change your *perceptions* of the liked person's attitudes such that those attitudes seem more similar to yours (Brehm, 1992).

Physical Attractiveness Physical characteristics are another important factor in attraction, particularly during the initial stages of a relationship (Berscheid & Reis, 1998). From preschool through adulthood, physical attractiveness is a key to popularity with members of both sexes (Aronson, Wilson, & Akert, 2002; Lemly,

TRY THIS — Proximity and Liking Research on environmental factors in attraction suggests that barring bad first impressions, the more often we make contact with someone—as neighbors, classmates, or co-workers, for example—the more we tend to like that person. Does this principle apply in your life? To find out, think about how and where you met each of your closest friends. If you can think of cases in which proximity did not lead to liking, what do you think interfered with the formation of friendship?

figure 17.7

Attitude Similarity and Attraction

This graph shows the results of a study in which participants learned about another person's attitudes. Their liking for that person was strongly related to the proportion of his or her attitudes that were similar to the participants' own.

Source: Adapted from Byrne & Nelson (1965).

figure 17.8

Balanced and Imbalanced Relationships

Here are some common examples of balanced and imbalanced patterns of relationships among three people. The plus and minus signs refer to liking and disliking, respectively. Balanced relationships are comfortable and harmonious; imbalanced ones often bring conflict.

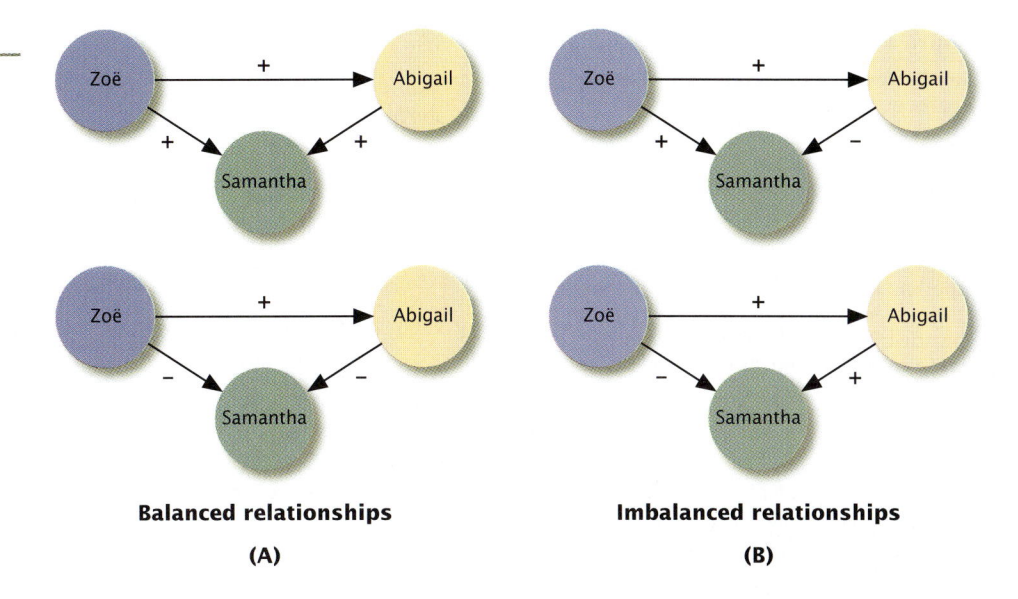

Balanced relationships
(A)

Imbalanced relationships
(B)

2000). Consistent with the **matching hypothesis** of interpersonal attraction, however, people tend to date, marry, or form other committed relationships with those who are similar to themselves in physical attractiveness (Yela & Sangrador, 2001). One possible reason for this outcome is that people tend to be most attracted to those with the greatest physical appeal, but they also want to avoid rejection by such individuals. In short, it may be compromise, not preference, that leads people to pair off with those who are roughly equivalent to themselves in physical attractiveness (Carli, Ganley, & Pierce-Otay, 1991).

Intimate Relationships and Love

There is much about intimate relationships that psychologists do not—and may never—understand, but they are learning all the time. As mentioned in the chapter on motivation and emotion, evolutionary psychologists suggest that men and women employ different strategies to ensure the survival of their genes, and that each gender looks for different attributes in a potential mate (Buss, 1999; Buss & Kenrick, 1998; Kenrick, Neuberg, & Cialdini, 2002). For example, women may be much more concerned than men about the intelligence level of their dating partners (Kenrick & Trost, 1997; see Figure 17.9).

Intimate Relationships
Eventually, people who are attracted to each other usually become *interdependent*, which means that the thoughts, emotions, and behaviors of one person affect the thoughts, emotions, and behaviors of the other (Rusbult, Arriaga, & Agnew, 2001). Interdependence is one of the defining characteristics of intimate relationships. It occurs in large measure as the thoughts and values of one person become part of the self-concept of the other (Agnew et al., 1998).

Another key component of successful intimate relationships is *commitment* to the relationship, which is the extent to which each party is psychologically attached to the relationship and wants to remain in it (Rusbult & Van Lange, 1996). People feel committed to a relationship when they are satisfied with the rewards they receive from it, when they have invested considerable resources (both tangible and intangible) in it, and when there are few attractive alternative relationships available to them (Bui, Peplau, & Hill, 1996).

Analyzing Love
Affection, emotional expressiveness, social support, cohesiveness, and sexuality—these characteristics of intimate relationships are likely to

matching hypothesis The notion that people are most likely to form long-term relationships with those who are similar to themselves in physical attractiveness.

figure 17.9

Sex Differences in Date and Mate Preferences

According to evolutionary psychologists, men and women have developed different strategies for selecting sexual partners. They say that women became more selective than men because they can have relatively few children and want a partner who has the ability to help care for those children. Here are some data supporting this idea. When asked about the intelligence of people they would choose for one-night stands, dating, and sexual relationships, women preferred much smarter partners than men did. Only when the choices concerned steady dating and marriage did the men's preference for bright partners equal that of the women. Critics of the evolutionary approach explain such sex differences as reflecting learned social norms and expectations of how men and women should behave (Eagly & Wood, 1999).

Source: Kenrick et al. (1993).

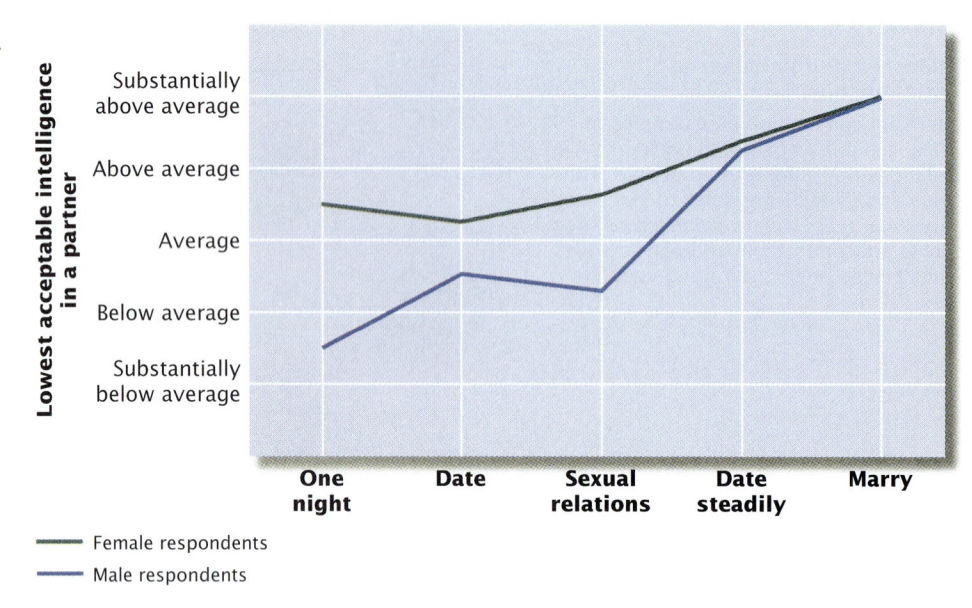

bring something else to mind: love. Yet *intimacy* and *love* are not synonymous. Most theorists agree that there are several different types of love (Brehm, Kassin, & Fein, 2002). One widely accepted view distinguishes between *passionate love* and *companionate love* (Hatfield & Rapson, 1995). Passionate love is intense, arousing, and marked by both strong physical attraction and deep emotional attachment. Sexual feelings are very strong, and thoughts of the other intrude on a person's awareness frequently. Companionate love is less arousing but psychologically more intimate. It is marked by mutual concern for the welfare of the other (Hendrick & Hendrick, 1986).

Robert Sternberg (1988a) has offered a more comprehensive analysis of love. According to his *triangular theory*, the three basic components of love are *passion*,

A Wedding in India Most people in Western cultures tend to marry a person they choose on the basis of love, sometimes without regard for discrepancies in religion, ethnicity, and financial or social status. In other cultures, however, these sociocultural considerations—and even arrangements made by parents—may largely determine who marries whom. What factors do you think might have brought this couple together?

**Liking =
Intimacy Alone**
(true friendship without passion
or long-term commitment)

**Romantic Love =
Intimacy + Passion**
(lovers physically
and emotionally
attracted to each
other but without
commitment, as in
a summer romance)

**Companionate
Love = Intimacy
+ Commitment**
(long-term committed
friendship such
as a marriage in
which the passion
has faded)

INTIMACY

**Consummate Love =
Intimacy + Passion
+ Commitment**
(a complete love
consisting of all three
components—an
ideal difficult to attain)

PASSION   COMMITMENT

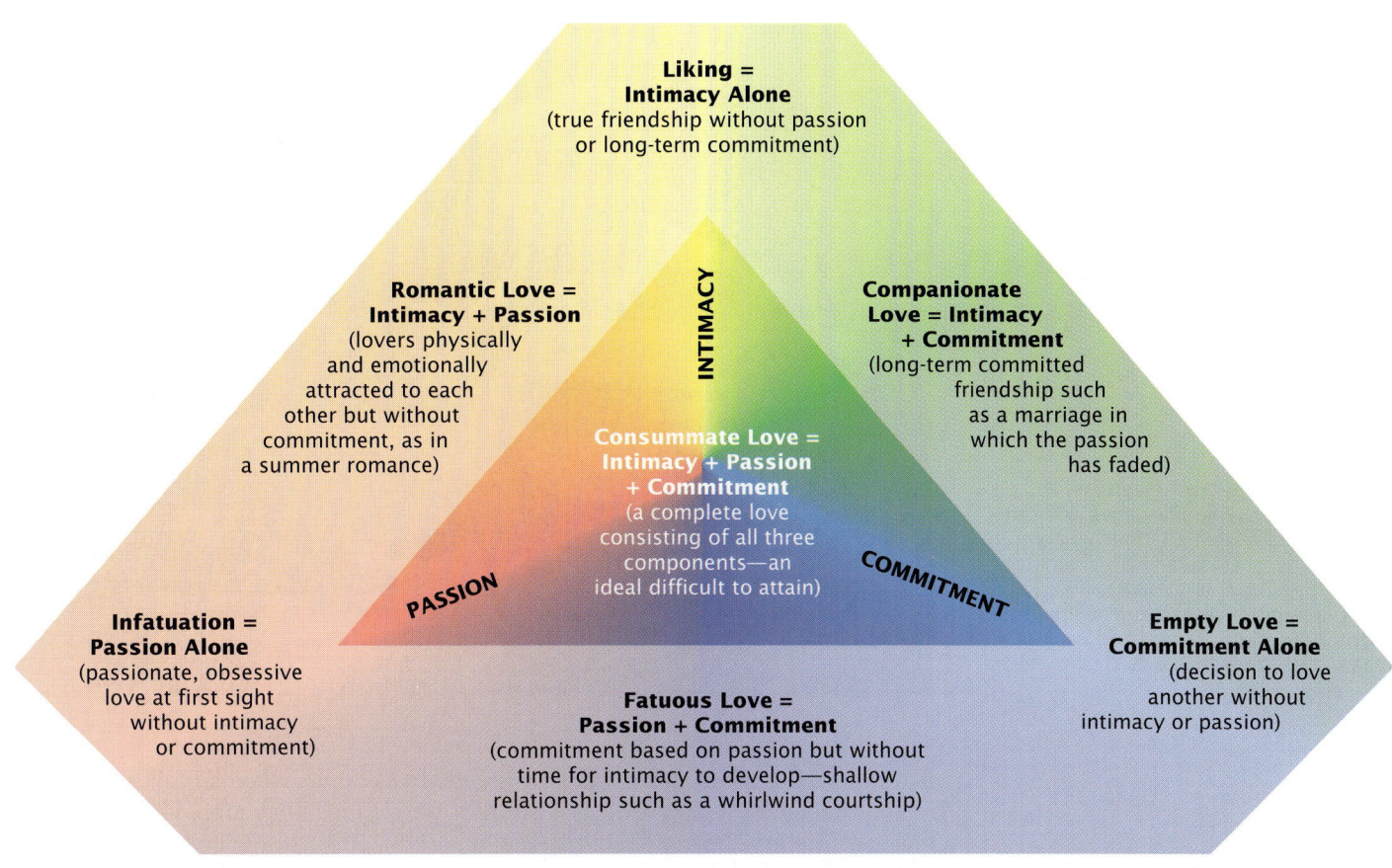

**Infatuation =
Passion Alone**
(passionate, obsessive
love at first sight
without intimacy
or commitment)

**Fatuous Love =
Passion + Commitment**
(commitment based on passion but without
time for intimacy to develop—shallow
relationship such as a whirlwind courtship)

**Empty Love =
Commitment Alone**
(decision to love
another without
intimacy or passion)

figure 17.10

A Triangular Theory of Love

According to Sternberg, different types of love result when the three basic components proposed in his triangular theory occur in different combinations. Sternberg has also begun to explore factors associated with falling in love (Sternberg, 2000; Sternberg, Hojjat, & Barnes, 2001). Preliminary results suggest that people who share similar views about what a loving relationship should be like are much more likely to fall in love with each other, and to remain committed to the relationship, than are people whose views on love are dissimilar.

Source: "Triangulating Love." In R. J. Sternberg & M. L. Barnes, *The Psychology of Love.* New Haven: Yale University Press. (pp. 500, 520)

intimacy, and *commitment.* Various combinations of these components result in quite different types of love, as illustrated in Figure 17.10. For example, Sternberg suggests that *romantic love* involves a high degree of passion and intimacy, yet lacks substantial commitment to the other person. *Companionate love* is marked by a great deal of intimacy and commitment but little passion. *Consummate love* is the most complete and satisfying. It is the most complete because it includes a high level of all three components, and it is the most satisfying because the relationship is likely to fulfill many of the needs of each partner.

Cultural factors have a strong influence on the value that people place on love. In North America and the United Kingdom, for example, the vast majority of people believe that they must love the person they marry. By contrast, in India and Pakistan, about half the people interviewed in a survey said they would marry someone they did not love if that person had other qualities that they desired (Levine et al., 1995). In Russia, only 40 percent of the people say that they married for love; rather, most married because of loneliness, shared interests, or an unplanned pregnancy (Baron & Byrne, 1994).

Strong and Weak Marriages

Long-term studies of successful and unsuccessful marriages suggest that premarital attitudes and feelings are predictive of

Happy and Healthy People in satisfying marriages and other long-term relationships tend to enjoy better physical and psychological health than those in unsatisfying relationships. In light of research described in the chapter on health, stress, and coping, make a list of reasons why this might be the case.

marital success. For example, one study found that couples who had a close, intimate relationship and similar attitudes when they were dating were more likely to still be married fifteen years later (Hill & Peplau, 1998). Also, still-married couples were more likely to have had a premarital relationship that was rewarding and balanced.

Among married couples, women—but not men—generally tend to be more satisfied with their marriage when the partners talk a lot about the relationship (Acitelli, 1992). Partners in successful marriages also tend to share each other's view of themselves and the other, even if that view is a negative one (Swann, De La Ronde, & Hixon, 1994). The perception that the relationship is fair or equitable also enhances marital satisfaction (Grote & Clark, 2001). After the birth of a first child, for example, many wives find that they have much more work than they had anticipated. If their husbands do not share this work to the degree they expected, wives' marital satisfaction tends to decrease (Hackel & Ruble, 1992).

Long-term studies of marriage have helped researchers identify some of the factors leading to divorce. Two of these factors, frequent conflicts and negative feelings toward one another, are especially associated with divorces that occur shortly after marriage. In these couples, the husband and wife trade increasingly nasty and hurtful remarks until communication breaks down (Gottman et al., 1998). A different picture emerges, however, in couples whose divorce occurs only after many years of marriage. These people do not necessarily display more negative emotions toward one another than couples who stay married, but they are less likely to express positive feelings and love toward one another. In other words, these later-divorcing couples may not dislike one another; they just don't love one another (Gottman & Levenson, 2000; Huston et al., 2001). These findings can help us understand why people in an apparently strong marriage suddenly announce that they are divorcing, and why they may remain friends afterward.

LINKAGES

As noted in the chapter on introducing psychology, all of psychology's subfields are related to one another. Our discussion of brain activity and attitudes illustrates just one way in which the topic of this chapter, social cognition, is linked to the subfield of biological psychology (see the chapter on biological aspects of psychology). The Linkages diagram shows ties to two other subfields as well, and there are many more ties throughout the book. Looking for linkages among subfields will help you see how they all fit together and help you better appreciate the big picture that is psychology.

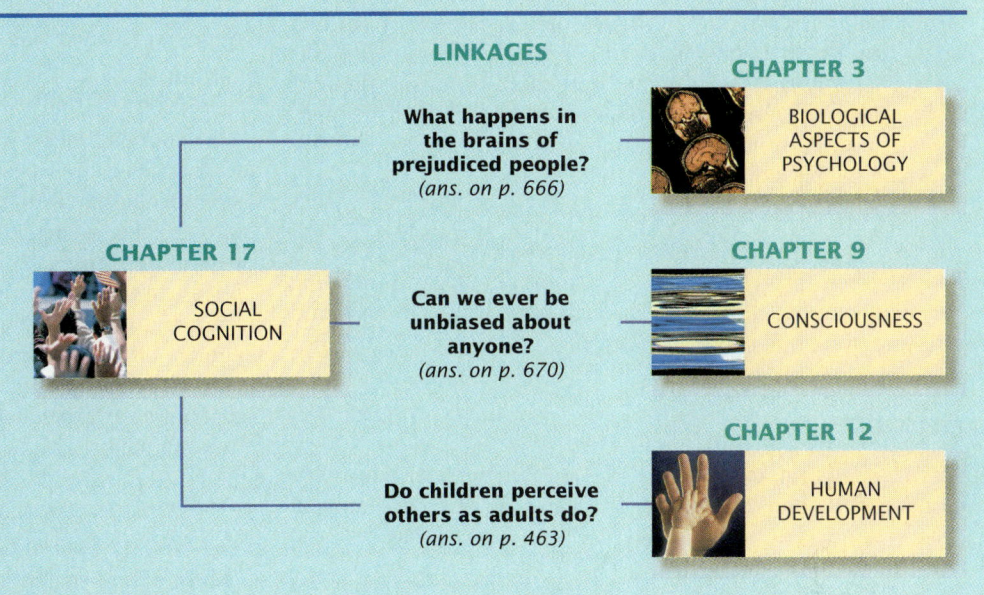

LINKAGES

CHAPTER 17: SOCIAL COGNITION

- What happens in the brains of prejudiced people? (ans. on p. 666) — **CHAPTER 3** BIOLOGICAL ASPECTS OF PSYCHOLOGY
- Can we ever be unbiased about anyone? (ans. on p. 670) — **CHAPTER 9** CONSCIOUSNESS
- Do children perceive others as adults do? (ans. on p. 463) — **CHAPTER 12** HUMAN DEVELOPMENT

SUMMARY

Social cognition (the mental processes through which people perceive and react to others) is one aspect of *social psychology* (the study of how people influence, and are influenced by, other people).

Social Influences on the Self

People's social and cultural environments affect their thoughts and feelings about themselves, including their *self-esteem* and their *self-concept*.

Social Comparison

When people have no objective criteria by which to judge themselves, they engage in *social comparison* (using others) or *temporal comparison* (using themselves at an earlier time) as their standard. Such comparison can affect self-evaluation, or self-esteem. Categories of people that are habitually used for social comparison are known as *reference groups*. Comparison to reference groups sometimes produces *relative deprivation*, which in turn can cause personal and social turmoil.

Social Identity Theory

A person's *social identity* is formed from beliefs about the groups to which the person belongs. Social identity affects the beliefs we hold about ourselves. It permits people to feel part of a larger group, engendering loyalty and sacrifice from group members but also potentially creating bias and discrimination toward people who are not members of the group.

Self-Schemas

Through social comparison and the formation of social identity, people develop mental representations of their views and beliefs about themselves. These mental representations, called *self-schemas*, are part of one's self-concept. Self-schemas can affect people's emotional reactions to events.

Social Perception

Social perception concerns the processes by which people interpret information about others, form impressions of them, and draw conclusions about the reasons for their behavior.

The Role of Schemas

Schemas, the mental representations about people and social situations that we carry into social interactions, affect what we pay attention to, what we remember, and how we judge people and events.

First Impressions

First impressions are formed easily and quickly, in part because people apply existing schemas to their perceptions of others. First impressions change slowly because people are "cognitive misers"; once we form an impression about another person, we try to maintain it. Schemas, however, can create *self-fulfilling prophecies*, leading people to act in ways that bring out in others behavior that is consistent with expectations.

Explaining Behavior: Attribution

Attribution is the process of explaining the causes of people's behavior, including one's own. Observers tend to attribute behavior to causes that are either internal or external to the actor. In general, they do this by looking at three aspects of the behavior: consensus, consistency, and distinctiveness. People from different cultures may sometimes reach different conclusions about the causes of an actor's behavior.

Biases in Attribution

Attributions are affected by biases that systematically distort one's view of behavior. The most common attributional biases are the *fundamental attribution error* (and its cousin, the ultimate attribution error), the *actor-observer bias,* and the *self-serving bias*. Personal and cultural factors can affect the extent to which people exhibit attributional biases.

The Self-Protective Functions of Social Cognition

People often protect themselves from admitting something threatening about themselves through unrealistic optimism and a feeling of unique invulnerability.

Attitudes

An *attitude* is the tendency to respond positively or negatively to a particular object. Attitudes affect a wide range of behaviors.

The Structure of Attitudes

Many theorists believe that attitudes have three components: the cognitive (beliefs), affective (feelings), and behavioral (actions) components. However, it is often difficult to predict a specific behavior from a person's beliefs or feelings about an object. Cognitive theories propose that attitudes consist of evaluations of an object that are stored in memory. This approach suggests that the likelihood of attitude-behavior consistency depends on the accessibility of evaluations in memory, on subjective norms, on perceived control over the behavior, and on prior direct experience with the attitude object.

Forming Attitudes

Attitudes can be learned through modeling, as well as through classical or operant conditioning. They are also subject to the mere-exposure effect: All else being equal, people develop greater liking for a new object the more often they are exposed to it.

Changing Attitudes

The effectiveness of a persuasive message in changing attitudes is influenced by the characteristics of the person who communicates it, by its content, and by the audience receiving it. The *elaboration likelihood model* suggests that attitude change can occur via either the peripheral or the central route, depending on a person's ability and motivation to carefully consider an argument. Another approach to attitude change is to change a person's behavior in the hope that the person's attitude will be adjusted to match the behavior. *Cognitive dissonance theory* holds that if inconsistency between attitudes and behavior creates discomfort related to a person's self-concept or self-image, the person will be motivated to reduce that discomfort. *Self-perception theory* suggests that such attitude changes occur in some cases as people look to their behavior for clues about what their attitudes are.

Prejudice and Stereotypes

Stereotypes often lead to *prejudice* and *discrimination*.

Theories of Prejudice and Stereotyping

Motivational theories of prejudice suggest that some people have a need to disrespect and dislike others. This need may stem from the trait of authoritarianism, as well as from a strong social identity. In either case, feeling superior to members of out-groups helps these people to feel better about themselves. As a result, in-group members tend to discriminate against out-groups. Cognitive theories suggest that people categorize others into groups in order to reduce social complexity. And learning theories maintain that stereotypes, prejudice, and discriminatory behaviors can be learned from parents, peers, and the media.

Reducing Prejudice

The *contact hypothesis* proposes that intergroup contact can reduce prejudice and lead to more favorable attitudes toward a stereotyped group—but only if the contact occurs under specific conditions, such as when there is equal status between group members. Helping diverse people to feel as if they belong to the same group can also reduce intergroup prejudice.

Interpersonal Attraction

Keys to Attraction

Interpersonal attraction is a function of many variables. Physical proximity is important because it allows people to meet. The situation in which they meet is important because positive or negative aspects of the situation tend to be associated with the other person. Characteristics of the other person are also important. Attraction tends to be greater when two people share similar attitudes and characteristics. Physical appearance plays a role in attraction; initially, attraction is strongest to those who are most physically attractive. But for long-term relationships, the *matching hypothesis* applies: People tend to choose others whose physical attractiveness is about the same as theirs.

Intimate Relationships and Love

A defining characteristic of intimate relationships is interdependence, and a key component of successful relationships is commitment. Commitment, in turn, is affected by the rewards coming from the relationship, by the resources invested in it, and by the possible alternatives open to each party. Robert Sternberg's triangular theory suggests that love is a function of three components: passion, intimacy, and commitment. Varying combinations of these three components create different types of love. Couples who have long and successful marriages are likely to perceive the relationship as fair to both parties, and they are likely to share warm and loving feelings for each other.

Social Influence 18

Social Influence
LINKAGES: Motivation and the Presence of Others
Conformity and Compliance
The Role of Norms
Why Do People Conform?
When Do People Conform?
Inducing Compliance
Obedience
Factors Affecting Obedience
Evaluating Milgram's Studies
Aggression
Why Are People Aggressive?
When Are People Aggressive?
THINKING CRITICALLY: Does Pornography Cause Aggression?
Altruism and Helping Behavior
Why Do People Help?
FOCUS ON RESEARCH METHODS: Does Family Matter?
Cooperation, Competition, and Conflict
Social Dilemmas
Fostering Cooperation
Interpersonal Conflict
Group Processes
Group Leadership
Groupthink
Linkages
Summary

In the days following the September 11, 2001, attacks on the World Trade Center and the Pentagon—and also after anthrax bacteria were mailed to news organizations and the U.S. Congress—cities throughout the United States experienced a substantial increase in false bomb threats, anthrax hoaxes, and other "copycat" crimes apparently inspired by the terrorists' actions. Unfortunately, this phenomenon is not unusual. After the murderous rampage at Columbine High School, for example, a number of students at other high schools were arrested for threatening similar acts of violence against their classmates. Well-publicized suicides, too, are often copied (Garland & Zigler, 1993; Phillips & Cartensen, 1986); after German television reported the case of a young man who killed himself by jumping in front of a train, there was a dramatic increase in railway suicides (Schmidtke & Hafner, 1988). Even telecasts of major professional boxing matches are typically followed by a small increase in murders.

Do these correlations mean that media coverage of violence triggers similar violence? As described in the chapter on learning, televised violence can play a causal role in aggressive behavior, but there are additional reasons to believe that when suicides and murders become media events, they stimulate people to imitate them. For one thing, many of the people who kill themselves soon after a notable suicide bear a strong similarity to the original victim (Cialdini, 2001). The copycat railway suicides in Germany, for example, were committed almost exclusively by other young German men. Further, murder victims in the days following a professional championship fight are more likely to be young white men if the losing boxer was white, and more likely to be young black men if the loser was black (Miller et al., 1991).

Copycat, or imitative, crimes illustrate the effects of *social influence,* the process whereby the words or actions of other people directly or indirectly influence a person's behavior. This chapter begins with a discussion of social influence itself, after which we consider several related aspects of how we are influenced by others, including the processes of conformity, compliance, and obedience. Then we explore the causes and consequences of aggression and altruism. Finally, we examine several different circumstances in which people jointly influence one another's behavior, especially circumstances in which people compete with one another for some scarce resource or work together in groups to solve some problem.

Social Influence

Copycat crimes are but one example of the fact that people can influence the way other people think, feel, and act, even without specifically trying to do so (Cialdini, 2001). The most pervasive, yet subtle, form of social influence is communicated through social norms.

Norms are learned, socially based rules that prescribe what people should or should not do in various situations (Cialdini & Trost, 1998). Norms are transmitted by parents, teachers, clergy, peers, and other agents of culture. Although they often cannot be verbalized, norms are so powerful that people usually follow them automatically. At movie theaters in North America, for example, norms tell us that we should get in line to buy a ticket rather than crowd around the ticket window; they also lead us to expect that others will do the same. By informing people of what is expected of them and others, norms make social situations less uncertain and more comfortable.

Robert Cialdini and his associates (1990) have described social norms as either descriptive or injunctive. *Descriptive norms* indicate how most other people actually behave in a given situation. They tell a person what actions are common in the situation and thereby implicitly give the person permission to act in the same way. The fact that most people do not cross a street until the green light or "walk" sign appears is an example of a descriptive norm. *Injunctive norms* give more specific information about the actions that others find acceptable and those that they find

norms Socially based rules that prescribe what people should or should not do in various situations.

Social Influence

unacceptable. Subtle pressure exists to behave in accordance with these norms. A sign that reads, "Do not cross on red" or the person next to you saying the same thing is an example of an injunctive norm.

A study by Raymond Reno and his colleagues (Reno, Cialdini, & Kallgren, 1993) illustrates the differing effects of these two types of norms. The participants were people who walked through a parking lot just after being handed an advertising leaflet. The experimenters arranged for the participants to see another person (who was working with the experimenters) either toss a paper bag on the ground or pick one up from the ground. On half the trials of this experiment, the parking lot was littered with paper; on the other half, the lot was clean. As shown in Figure 18.1, the descriptive norm—seeing another person litter in an already dirty environment—appeared to communicate that "many people do this," and a relatively high percentage of people dropped their own leaflet in the dirty parking lot. By contrast, the injunctive norm—seeing someone pick up litter—appeared to communicate that even though many people litter, one should not do so. When this norm was evident, fewer than 5 percent of the people dropped their leaflet in the dirty parking lot.

One very powerful injunctive norm is *reciprocity*, the tendency to respond to others as they have acted toward you (Cialdini & Trost, 1998). So when a researcher sent Christmas cards to strangers, most responded with a card of their own; some even added a personal note of good cheer (Kunz & Woolcott, 1976). But norms are not universal (Miller, 2001), as illustrated by the fact that people around the world differ greatly in terms of the physical distance they maintain between themselves and others while interacting. For example, people from South America usually stand much closer to one another than do people from North America. And as suggested in the chapter on psychological disorders, behavior considered normal and friendly in one culture may be seen as abnormal, and even offensive, in another.

The social influence exerted by norms creates orderly social behavior. But social influence can also lead to a breakdown in order. For example, **deindividuation** is a psychological state in which a person becomes "submerged in a group" and loses the sense of individuality (Prentice-Dunn & Rogers, 1989). When people experience deindividuation, they undergo heightened emotional arousal and intense feelings of cohesiveness with the group; they appear to become part of the "herd," and they may do things that they would not do otherwise. Deindividuation appears to be caused by two factors. The first is the belief that one cannot be held personally

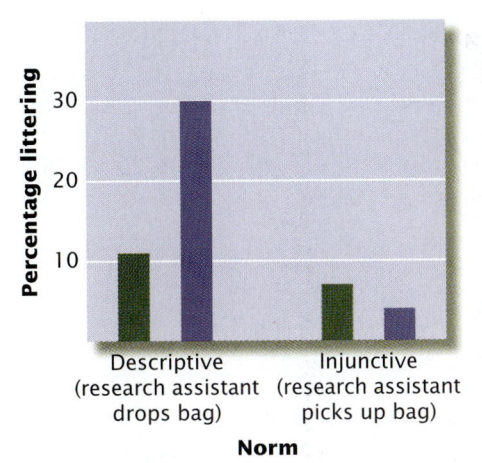

■ Clean environment
■ Littered environment

figure 18.1

Descriptive and Injunctive Norms
A descriptive norm, communicated by the littering of a messy parking lot, led many observers to litter, too. A clean lot changed the descriptive norm, leading fewer observers to imitate a litterer. An injunctive norm (communicated by the picking up of litter) was not altered significantly by the condition of the lot (Reno, Cialdini, & Kallgren, 1993). Research like this is being applied to combat alcohol abuse on college campuses. Rather than focusing on the dangers of alcohol, some student health campaigns create a descriptive norm for responsible drinking by citing statistics showing that most students drink in moderation (Zernike, 2000).

Source: Adapted from Reno, Cialdini, & Kallgren (1993).

deindividuation A psychological state occurring in group members that results in loss of individuality and a tendency to do things not normally done when alone.

Clothing and Culture The social norms that guide how people dress and behave in various situations are part of the culturally determined socialization process described in the chapter on human development. The process is the same worldwide—parents, teachers, peers, religious leaders, and others communicate their culture's social norms to children—but differences in those norms result in quite different behaviors from culture to culture.

Deindividuation Robes, hoods, and group rituals help create deindividuation in these Ku Klux Klansmen by focusing their attention on membership in their organization and on its values. The hoods also hide their identities, thus reducing their sense of personal responsibility and accountability and making it easier for them to engage in hate crimes and other cowardly acts of bigotry. Deindividuation operates in other groups, too, ranging from lynch mobs and terrorist death squads to political protesters and urban rioters. In short, people who feel themselves to be anonymous members of a group may engage in antisocial acts that they might not perform on their own.

accountable for one's actions. The second is a shifting of attention away from internal thoughts and standards and toward the external environment (Smith & Mackie, 2000). This shift of attention can be intensified when members of the group act in unison, such as by singing together or wearing uniforms (Ku Klux Klan robes, for example).

Deindividuation often results in antisocial acts, and the emotional arousal that it generates makes such behavior difficult to stop (Aronson, Wilson, & Akert, 2002). The greater the sense of anonymity, the more extreme the behavior. An analysis of newspaper accounts of lynchings in the United States over a fifty-year period showed that larger lynch mobs were more savage and vicious than smaller ones (Mullen, 1986). Deindividuation provides an example of how, given the right circumstances, quite normal people can engage in destructive, even violent, behavior.

LINKAGES

LINKAGES (a link to Motivation and Emotion

Motivation and the Presence of Others

In the chapter on motivation and emotion, we noted that social factors such as parental attitudes toward achievement often affect motivation. But a person's current motivational state is also affected by the mere presence of other people. As an illustration, consider what was probably the first experiment in social psychology, conducted by Norman Triplett in 1897.

Triplett noticed that bicycle racers tended to go faster when other racers were nearby than when they were alone. Did seeing one another remind the racers of the need to go faster to win? To test this possibility, Triplett arranged for bicyclists to complete a twenty-five-mile course under three conditions: riding alone in a race against the clock; riding with another cyclist, but not in competition; or competing directly with another rider. The cyclists went much faster when another rider was present than when they were simply racing against time. This was true even when they were not competing against the other person. Something about the presence of the other person, not just competition, produced increased speed.

social facilitation A phenomenon in which the presence of others improves a person's performance.

social impairment A reduction in performance due to the presence of other people.

The term **social facilitation** describes circumstances in which the mere presence of other people can improve performance (Aiello & Douthitt, 2001). This improvement does not always occur, however. The presence of other people sometimes hurts performance, a process known as **social impairment.** For decades

Social Facilitation On his way to a new home run record during the 2001 baseball season, Barry Bonds, shown here adding to his total, was able to perform at his best even though large crowds were present. In fact, the crowds probably helped him hit well, because the presence of others tends to increase arousal, which enhances the performance of familiar and well-learned skills, such as a batting swing. However, arousal created by an audience tends to interfere with the performance of unfamiliar and poorly developed skills. This is one reason why professional athletes who show flawless grace in front of thousands of fans are likely to freeze up or blow their lines in front of a small production crew when trying for the first time to tape a TV ad or a public service announcement.

these results seemed contradictory; then Robert Zajonc (pronounced "ZYE-onze") suggested that both effects could be explained by one process: arousal.

The presence of other people, said Zajonc, increases a person's general level of arousal or motivation (Zajonc, 1965). Why? One reason is that being watched by others increases our sense of being evaluated, producing apprehension that in turn increases emotional arousal (Penner & Craiger, 1992). Arousal increases the tendency to perform those behaviors that are most *dominant*—the ones we know best—and this tendency can either help or hinder performance. If you are performing an easy, familiar task, such as riding a bike, the increased arousal caused by the presence of others should allow you to ride even faster than normal. But if the task is hard or unfamiliar—such as trying new dance steps or playing a piano piece you just learned—the most dominant responses may be incorrect and cause your performance to suffer. In other words, the impact of other people on performance depends on whether the task is easy or difficult. Research shows that this is true even when the "other person" is a machine that records one's errors at a task (Aiello & Kolb, 1995).

The presence of others may affect performance in other ways as well. For example, having an audience may distract us from the task at hand or cause us to focus on only one part of it, thus impairing performance (Aiello & Douthitt, 2001).

What if a person is not merely in the presence of others but is actually working on a task with them? Research indicates that the impact of their presence changes slightly under these conditions (Sanna, 1992). In these situations, people typically exert less effort than they do when performing alone, a phenomenon termed **social loafing** (Karau & Williams, 1997). Whether the task is pulling on a rope, clapping as loudly as possible, or trying to solve intellectual puzzles, people tend to work harder when performing alone than with others (Baron, Kerr, & Miller, 1992; Geen, 1991). There are at least three reasons behind this social loafing phenomenon. First, it is usually much harder to evaluate the performance of individuals when they are working as part of a group (Szymanski, Garczynski, & Harkins, 2000). As a result, it is simply easier to "get away" with loafing when in a group. Second, rewards may come to a group whether or not every member exerts maximum effort. Third, a group's rewards are usually divided equally among its members rather than according to individual effort (Karau & Williams, 1997).

In North American and other Western countries, social loafing can be seen in groups of all sorts, from volunteer committees to search parties. Because social loafing can reduce productivity in business situations, it is important for managers to develop ways of evaluating the efforts of every individual in a work group, not

---

social loafing Exerting less effort when performing a group task than when performing the same task alone.

just the overall output of the team (Shepperd, 1993). Social loafing can also be reduced by strategies that cause people to like the group and identify with it (Karau & Williams, 1997).

Social loafing is much less common in Eastern cultures, such as those of China and Japan. In fact, in collectivist cultures, working in a group usually produces *social striving*—defined as greater individual effort when working in a group (Matsumoto, 2000). This difference in the effects of group membership on individual efforts probably reflects the value that collectivist cultures place on coordinated and cooperative group activities. This orientation serves to discourage social loafing.

Conformity and Compliance

Suppose you are with three friends. One says that Franklin Roosevelt was the greatest president in the history of the United States. You think that the greatest president was Abraham Lincoln, but before you can say anything, another friend agrees that it was Roosevelt, and then the other one does as well. What would you do? Disagree with all three? Maintain your opinion but keep quiet? Change your mind?

When people change their behavior or beliefs to match those of other members of a group, they are said to conform. **Conformity** occurs as a result of group pressure, real or imagined (Cialdini & Trost, 1998). You probably have experienced such group pressure when everyone around you stood to applaud a performance you thought was only mediocre. You might have conformed by standing as well, though no one told you to do so; the group's behavior creates a silent, but influential, pressure to follow suit. **Compliance,** in contrast, occurs when people adjust their behavior because of a request. The request can be either *explicit,* such as your brother saying, "Please pass the salt," or *implicit,* as when someone looks at you in a certain way to let you know it is time to start studying (Cialdini & Trost, 1998).

Mass Conformity The faithful who gather at Mecca, at the Vatican, and at other holy places around the world exemplify the power of religion and other social forces to produce conformity to group norms.

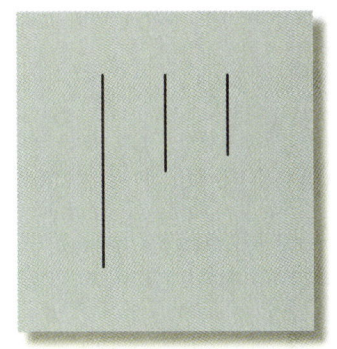

The Role of Norms

Conformity and compliance are usually generated by spoken or unspoken norms. In a classic experiment, Muzafer Sherif (1937) charted the formation of a group norm by taking advantage of a perceptual illusion, called the *autokinetic phenomenon*, whereby a stationary point of light in a pitch dark room appears to move. Estimates of the amount of movement tend to stay the same over time—if an observer is alone. But when Sherif tested several people at once, asking each person to say aloud how far the light moved on repeated trials, their estimates tended to converge; they had established a group norm. Even more important, when the individuals from the group were later tested alone, they continued to be influenced by this norm.

In another classic experiment, Solomon Asch (1956) examined how people would respond when they faced a norm that already existed but was obviously wrong. The participants in this experiment saw a standard line like the one in Figure 18.2(A); then they saw a display like that in Figure 18.2(B). Their task was to pick out the line in the display that was the same length as the one they had initially been shown.

Each participant performed this task in a small group of people who posed as fellow participants, but who were actually the experimenter's assistants. There were 2 conditions. In the control condition, the real participant responded first. In the experimental condition, the participant did not respond until after the assistants did. The assistants chose the correct response on 6 trials, but on the other 12 trials they all gave the same obviously incorrect response. So on 12 trials, each participant was confronted with a "social reality" created by a group norm that conflicted with the physical reality created by what the person could clearly see. Only 5 percent of the participants in the control condition ever made a mistake on this easy perceptual task. However, among participants who heard the assistants' responses before giving their own, about 70 percent made at least 1 error by conforming to the group norm. An analysis of 133 studies conducted in 17 countries reveals that conformity in Asch-type situations has declined somewhat in the United States since the 1950s, but it still occurs; it is especially likely in collectivist cultures, in which conformity to group norms is emphasized (Smith & Bond, 1999).

Pressure for conformity can even affect reports about personal experiences. In one study that used a procedure similar to Asch's, participants were shown a number of objects. Later, the same objects were shown again, along with some new ones, and the participants were asked to say whether they had seen each object in the previous display. When tested alone, the participants' memories were quite accurate, but hearing another person's opinion about which objects had or had not been shown before strongly affected their memory of which objects they had seen (Hoffman et al., 2001)

Why Do People Conform?

Why did so many people in Asch's experiment, and others like it, give incorrect responses when they were capable of near-perfect performance? One possibility is that they displayed *public conformity*, giving an answer they did not believe simply because it was the socially desirable thing to do. Another possibility is that they experienced *private acceptance*: Perhaps the participants used other people's responses as legitimate evidence about reality, were convinced that their own perceptions were wrong, and actually changed their minds. Morton Deutsch and Harold Gerard (1955) reasoned that if conformity disappeared when people gave their responses without identifying themselves, then Asch's findings must reflect public conformity, not private acceptance. In fact, conformity does decrease when people respond anonymously instead of publicly, but it is not eliminated (Deutsch & Gerard, 1955). People sometimes publicly produce responses that they do not believe, but hearing other people's responses also influences their private beliefs (Moscovici, 1985).

Standard line
(A)

Test lines
(B)

figure 18.2

Types of Stimulus Lines Used in Experiments by Asch

TRY THIS Participants in Asch's experiments saw a new set of lines like these on each trial. The middle line in Part B matches the line in Part A, but when several of Asch's (1956) assistants chose an incorrect line, so did many of the participants. Try re-creating this experiment with four friends. Secretly ask three of them to choose the line on the left in Part B when you show this drawing, and then see if the fourth person conforms to the group norm. If not, do you think it was something about the person, the length of the incorrect line chosen, or both that led to nonconformity? Would conformity be more likely if the first three people were to choose the line on the right? (Read on for more on this possibility.)

Source: Asch (1955).

conformity Changing one's behavior or beliefs to match those of others, generally as a result of real or imagined, though unspoken, group pressure.

compliance Adjusting one's behavior because of an explicit or implicit request.

Why do group norms wield such power? Research suggests three influential factors (Cialdini & Trost, 1998). First, people are motivated to be correct, and norms provide information about what is right and wrong. This factor may help explain why some extremely disturbed or distressed people consider stories about suicide to be "social proof" that self-destruction is a reasonable way out of their problems (Cialdini, 1993). Second, people are motivated to be liked by others, and we generally like those who agree with us. Finally, norms influence the distribution of social rewards and punishments (Cialdini, 1995). From childhood on, people in many cultures learn that going along with group norms is good and earns rewards. (These positive outcomes presumably help compensate for not always being able to say or do exactly what we please.) People also learn that breaking a norm may bring punishments ranging from scoldings for small transgressions to imprisonment for violation of norms that have been translated into laws.

When Do People Conform?

People do not always conform to social influence. In the original Asch studies, for example, nearly 30 percent of the participants did not go along with the research assistants' obviously erroneous judgments. Countless experiments have probed the question of what combinations of people and circumstances do and do not lead to conformity.

Ambiguity of the Situation

Ambiguity, or uncertainty, is very important in determining how much conformity will occur. As the physical reality of a situation becomes less certain, people rely more and more on others' opinions, and conformity to a group norm becomes increasingly likely (Aronson, Wilson, & Akert, 2002).

TRY THIS — You can demonstrate this aspect of conformity on any street corner. First, create an ambiguous situation by having several people look at the sky or the top of a building. When passersby ask what is going on, be sure everyone excitedly reports seeing something interesting but fleeting—perhaps a faint light or a tiny, shiny object. If you are especially successful, conforming newcomers will begin persuading other passersby that there is something fascinating to be seen.

Unanimity and Size of the Majority

If ambiguity contributes so much to conformity, why did so many of Asch's participants conform to a judgment that was unambiguously wrong? The answer has to do with the *unanimity* of the group's judgment and the number of people expressing it. Specifically, people experience great pressure to conform as long as the majority is unanimous. If even one other person in the group disagrees with the majority view, conformity drops greatly. When Asch (1951) arranged for just one assistant to disagree with the others, fewer than 10 percent of the real participants conformed. Once unanimity is broken, it becomes much easier to disagree with the majority, even if the other nonconformist does not agree with the person's own view (Turner, 1991).

Conformity also depends on the size of the group. Asch (1955) demonstrated this phenomenon by varying the number of assistants in the group from one to fifteen. Conformity to incorrect norms grew as the number of people in the group increased. But most of the growth in conformity occurred as the size of the majority rose from one to about three or four members; further additions had little effect. Several years after Asch's research, Bibb Latané (pronounced "lat-a-NAY") sought to explain this phenomenon with his *social impact theory*. This theory holds that a group's impact on an individual depends not only on group size but also on how important and close the group is to the person. And according to Latané (1981), the impact of increasing the size of a majority depends on how big the majority was originally. Increasing a majority from, say, two to three will have much more impact than increasing it from, say, sixty to sixty-one. The reason is that the increase from sixty to sixty-one is psychologically much smaller than the change from two to three; it attracts far less notice in relative terms. Does this explanation sound familiar? The principles underlying it are similar to those of Weber's law, which, as described in the chapter on perception, governs our experience of changes in brightness, weight, and other physical stimuli.

Minority Influence Conformity can also result from **minority influence,** by which a numerical minority in a group influences the behavior or beliefs of a majority (Taylor, Peplau, & Sears, 2000). This phenomenon is less common than majority influence, but minorities can be influential, especially when they persist in their views and show agreement with one another (Moscovici, 1994). William Crano and his associates have found that whereas majority influence tends to affect people immediately and directly, minority influence is indirect; that is, minority-influenced change often takes a while to occur and may involve only a moderate adjustment of the majority view in the direction favored by the minority (Alvaro & Crano, 1997; Crano & Chen, 1998).

Gender Early research on conformity suggested that women conform more than men, but this gender difference stemmed mainly from the fact that the tasks used in those experiments were often more familiar to men than to women. This fact is important because people are especially likely to conform when they are faced with an unfamiliar situation (Cialdini & Trost, 1998). No male-female differences in conformity have been found in subsequent research using materials that are equally familiar to both genders (Maupin & Fisher, 1989).

So why do some people still perceive women as more conforming than men despite evidence to the contrary? Part of the answer may lie in their perception of the relative social status of men and women. People who think of women as having lower social status than men in most social situations are likely to see women as easier to influence, even though men and women conform equally often (Eagly, 1987).

Inducing Compliance

In the conformity experiments we have described, the participants experienced psychological pressure to conform to the views or actions of others, even though no one specifically asked them to do so. In contrast, *compliance* involves changing what you say or do because of a request.

How is compliance brought about? Many people believe that the direct approach is always best: If you want something, ask for it. But salespeople, political strategists, social psychologists, and other experts have learned that often the best way to get something is to ask for something else. Three examples of this strategy are the foot-in-the-door technique, the door-in-the-face procedure, and the low-ball approach.

The *foot-in-the-door technique* works by getting a person to agree to a small request and then gradually presenting larger ones. In the original experiment on this strategy, homeowners were asked to do one of two things. Some were asked to allow a large, unattractive "Drive Carefully" sign to be placed on their front lawn. Approximately 17 percent of the people approached in this way complied with the request. In the foot-in-the-door condition, however, homeowners were first asked only to sign a petition supporting legislation aimed at reducing traffic accidents. Several weeks later, when a different person asked these same people to put the "Drive Carefully" sign on their lawn, 55 percent of them complied (Freedman & Fraser, 1966).

Why should the granting of small favors lead to granting larger ones? First, people are usually far more likely to comply with a request that costs little in time, money, effort, or inconvenience. Second, complying with a small request makes people think of themselves as being committed to the cause or issue involved (Cialdini

minority influence A phenomenon whereby members of a numerical minority in a group alter the view of the majority.

Sign Here, Please Have you ever been asked to sign a petition in favor of a political, social, or economic cause? Supporters of these causes know that people who comply with this small request are the best people to contact later with requests to do more. Complying with larger requests is made more likely because it is consistent with the signer's initial commitment to the cause. If you were contacted after signing a petition, did you agree to donate money or become a volunteer?

& Trost, 1998). This change occurs through the processes of self-perception and cognitive dissonance discussed in the chapter on social cognition. In the study just described, participants who signed the petition might have thought, "I must care enough about traffic safety to do something about it." Compliance with the higher-cost request (displaying the sign) thus became more likely, because it was consistent with these people's self-perceptions and past actions (Eisenberg et al., 1987).

The foot-in-the-door technique can be quite effective. Steven Sherman (1980) created a 700 percent increase in the rate at which people actually volunteered to work for a charity simply by first getting them to say that, in a hypothetical situation, they would volunteer if asked. For some companies, the foot in the door is a request that potential customers merely answer a few questions; the request to buy something comes later. Others offer a small gift, or "door opener," as salespeople call it. Acceptance of the gift not only allows a foot in the door, but also may invoke the reciprocity norm: Many people who get something free of charge feel obligated to reciprocate by buying something (Cialdini, 2001). Recent research suggests, however, that small favors don't always lead to bigger ones. Specifically, if the request for the larger favor comes immediately after the initial request, people may be unlikely to comply with it (Guadagno et al., 2001).

The *door-in-the-face procedure* offers a second way of obtaining compliance (Cialdini, 2001; Reeves et al., 1991). This strategy begins with a request for a favor that is likely to be denied. The person making the request then concedes that asking for the initial favor was excessive and substitutes a lesser alternative—which was what the person really wanted in the first place! Because the person appears willing to compromise and because the new request seems modest in comparison with the first one, it is more likely to be granted than if it had been made at the outset. In this case, compliance appears to be due to activation of the reciprocity norm. The door-in-the-face strategy is often the basis of bargaining among political groups and between labor and management.

A third technique for gaining compliance, called the *low-ball approach*, is commonly used by car dealers and other businesses (Cialdini, 2001). The first step in this strategy is to obtain a person's oral commitment to do something, such as to purchase a car at a certain price. Once this commitment is made, the cost of fulfilling it is increased, often because of an "error" in computing the car's price. Why do buyers end up paying much more than originally planned for "low-balled" items? Apparently, once people commit themselves to do something, they feel obligated to follow through, especially when the person who obtains the initial commitment also

OK, OK, I'll Be Home by Midnight! The door-in-the-face approach is sometimes used successfully by teenagers who want their parents to comply with many kinds of requests. A teen who normally has a 10 P.M. curfew on school nights might be allowed to stay out until midnight (a "compromise" that actually was the original goal) after first asking for permission to be away overnight.

makes the higher-cost request (Burger & Petty, 1981). In other words, as described in relation to cognitive dissonance theory in the chapter on social cognition, people like to be consistent in their words and deeds. In this instance, it appears that people try to maintain a positive self-image by behaving in accordance with their initial oral commitment, even though it may cost them a great deal to do so.

Obedience

Compliance involves a change in behavior in response to a request. In the case of **obedience**, the behavior change comes in response to a *demand* from an authority figure (Blass, 1999). In the 1960s, Stanley Milgram developed a laboratory procedure at Yale University to study obedience. In his first experiment, he used newspaper ads to recruit forty male volunteers between the ages of twenty and fifty. Among the participants were professionals, white-collar businessmen, and unskilled workers (Milgram, 1963).

Imagine you are one of the people who answered the ad. When you arrive for the experiment, you join a fifty-year-old gentleman who has also volunteered and has been scheduled for the same session. The experimenter explains that the purpose of the experiment is to examine the effects of punishment on learning. One of you—the "teacher"—will help the "learner" remember a list of words by administering an electrical shock whenever he makes a mistake. Then the experimenter turns to you and asks you to draw one of two cards out of a hat. Your card says "TEACHER." You think to yourself that this must be your lucky day.

Now the learner is taken into another room and strapped into a chair, as shown in Figure 18.3. Electrodes are attached to his arms. You are shown a shock generator with 30 switches. The experimenter explains that the switch on the far left administers a mild, 15-volt shock and that each succeeding switch increases the shock by 15 volts; the switch on the far right delivers 450 volts. The far left section of the shock generator is labeled "slight shock." Looking across the panel, you see "moderate shock," "very strong shock," and at the far right, "danger—severe shock." The last 2 switches are ominously labeled "XXX." The experimenter explains that you, the teacher, will begin by reading a list of word pairs to the learner. Then you will go through the list again, presenting just 1 word of each pair; the learner should indicate which word went with it. After the first mistake, you are to throw the switch to deliver 15 volts of shock. Each time the learner makes another mistake, you are to increase the shock by 15 volts.

You begin, following the experimenter's instructions. But after the learner makes his fifth mistake and you throw the switch to give him 75 volts, you hear a loud moan. At 90 volts, the learner cries out in pain. At 150 volts, he screams and asks to be let out of the experiment. You look to the experimenter, who says, "Proceed with the next word."

No shock was actually delivered in Milgram's experiments. The learner was always an accomplice of the experimenter, and the moans and other signs of pain came from a prerecorded tape. But you do not know that. What would you do in this situation? Suppose you continue and eventually deliver 180 volts. The learner screams that he cannot stand the pain any longer and starts banging on the wall. The experimenter says, "You have no other choice; you must go on." Would you continue? Would you keep going even when the learner begged to be let out of the experiment and then fell silent? Would you administer 450 volts of potentially deadly shock to a perfect stranger just because an experimenter demanded that you do so?

Figure 18.4 shows that only 5 participants in Milgram's experiment stopped before 300 volts, and 26 out of 40 participants (or 65 percent) went all the way to the 450-volt level. The decision to continue was difficult and stressful for the participants. Many protested repeatedly; but each time the experimenter told them to continue, they did so. Here is a partial transcript of what a typical participant said:

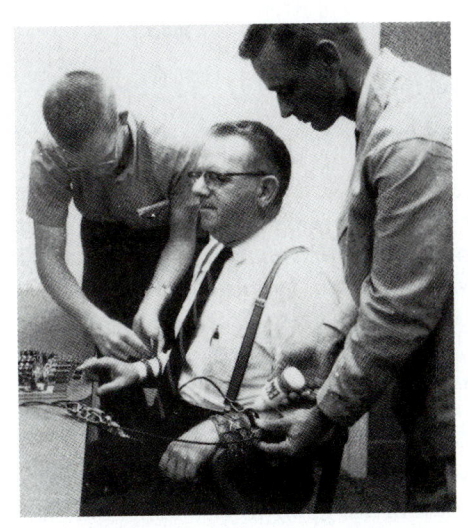

figure 18.3

Studying Obedience in the Laboratory
In this photograph from Milgram's original experiment, a man is being strapped into a chair with electrodes on his arm. Although participants in the experiment do not know it, the man is actually one of the experimenter's research assistants and receives no shock.

obedience Changing behavior in response to a demand from an authority figure.

figure 18.4

Results of Milgram's Obedience Experiment

When Milgram asked a group of undergraduates and a group of psychiatrists how participants in his experiment would respond, they estimated that fewer than 2 percent would go all the way to 450 volts. In fact, 65 percent of the participants did so. What do you think you would have done in this situation?

Source: Milgram (1963).

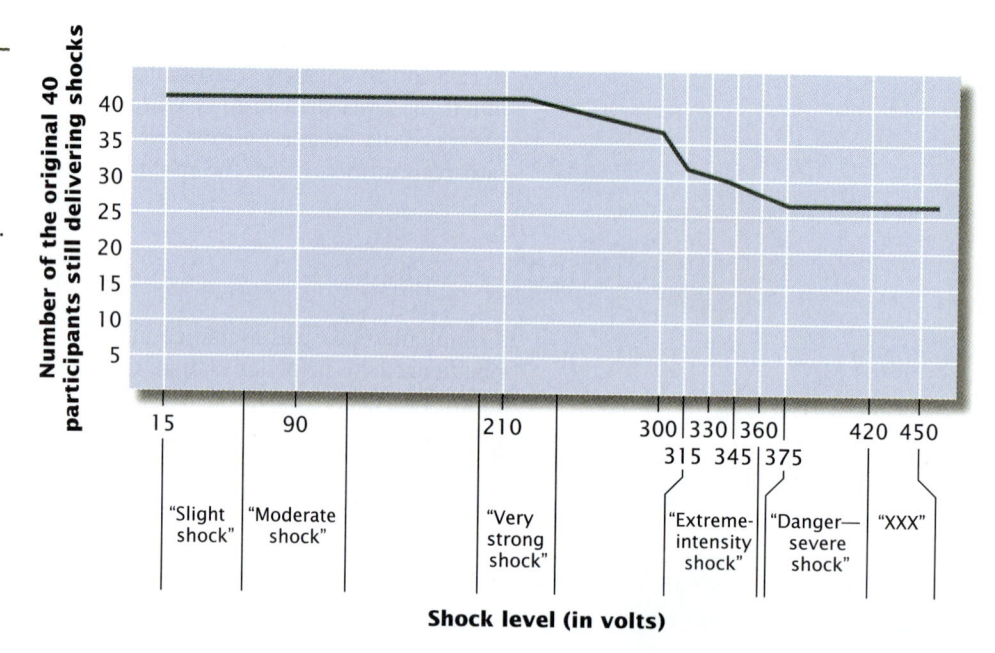

[After throwing the 180-volt switch:] *He can't stand it. I'm not going to kill that man in there. Do you hear him hollering? He's hollering. He can't stand it. What if something happens to him? I'm not going to get that man sick in there. He's hollering in there. Do you know what I mean? I mean, I refuse to take responsibility. He's getting hurt in there.... Too many left here. Geez, if he gets them wrong. There are too many of them left. I mean, who is going to take responsibility if anything happens to that gentleman?*

[After the experimenter accepts responsibility:] *All right....*

[After administering 240 volts:] *Oh, no, you mean I've got to keep going up the scale? No, sir, I'm not going to kill that man. I'm not going to give him 450 volts.*

[After the experimenter says, "The experiment requires that you go on":] *I know it does, but that man is hollering in there, sir.*

This participant administered shock up to 450 volts (Milgram, 1974, p. 74).

Factors Affecting Obedience

Milgram had not expected so many people to deliver such apparently intense shocks. Was there something about his procedure that produced this high level of obedience? To find out, Milgram and other researchers varied the original procedure in numerous ways. The overall level of obedience to an authority figure was usually quite high, but the degree of obedience was affected by several factors.

Experimenter Status and Prestige

In Milgram's original study, the experimenter's status and prestige as a Yale University professor created two kinds of social power that affected the participants. The first was *expert social power*, which is the ability to influence people because they assume the person in power is a knowledgeable and responsible expert. The second was *legitimate social power*, which is the ability to influence people because they assume the person in power has the right or legitimate authority to tell them what to do (Blass & Schmitt, 2001).

To test the effects of reduced status and prestige, Milgram rented an office in a rundown building in Bridgeport, Connecticut. He then placed a newspaper ad for people to participate in research sponsored by a private firm; there was no mention of Yale. In all other ways, the experimental procedure was identical to the original.

Proximity and Obedience Milgram's research found that the close proximity of an authority figure is one of several factors that can enhance obedience to authority (Rada & Rogers, 1973). This proximity principle is used in the military, where no one is ever far away from the authority of a higher-ranking person.

Under these less prestigious circumstances, the level of obedience dropped, but not as much as you might expect; 48 percent of the participants continued to the maximum level of shock, compared with 65 percent in the original study. Milgram concluded that people still would obey instructions that could cause great harm to another even if the authority figure was not associated with a prestigious institution. Evidently, people's willingness to follow orders from an authority operates somewhat independently of the setting in which the orders are given.

The Behavior of Others

To study how the behavior of fellow participants might affect obedience, Milgram (1965) created a situation in which there were apparently three teachers. Teacher 1 (in reality, a research assistant) read the words to the learner. Teacher 2 (another research assistant) indicated whether or not the learner's response was correct. Teacher 3 (the actual participant) was to deliver shock when mistakes were made. At 150 volts, when the learner began to complain that the shock was too painful, Teacher 1 refused to participate any longer and left the room. The experimenter asked him to come back, but he refused. The experimenter then instructed Teachers 2 and 3 to continue by themselves. The experiment continued for several more trials. However, at 210 volts, Teacher 2 said that the learner was suffering too much and refused to participate further. The experimenter then told Teacher 3 (the actual participant) to continue the procedure. In this case, only 10 percent of the participants (compared with 65 percent in the original study) continued to deliver shock all the way up to 450 volts. In other words, as research on conformity would suggest, the presence of others who disobey appears to be the most powerful factor in reducing obedience.

Personality Characteristics

Were the participants in Milgram's original experiment heartless creatures who would have given strong shocks even if there had been no pressure on them to do so? Quite the opposite; most of them were nice people who were influenced by experimental situations to behave in apparently antisocial ways. In a later demonstration of the same phenomenon, college students playing the role of prison guards behaved with aggressive heartlessness toward other students who were playing the role of prisoners (Zimbardo, 1973).

Still, not everyone is equally obedient to authority. For example, people high in *authoritarianism* (a characteristic discussed in the chapter on social cognition) are more likely than others to comply with an experimenter's request to shock the

Civil Disobedience Not everyone is blindly obedient to authority. In 1955, Rosa Parks was arrested and fingerprinted in Montgomery, Alabama, after refusing an order to move to the "colored" section in the back of a segregated bus. Her courageous act of disobedience sparked the civil rights movement in the United States.

learner (Blass, 1991). Real-world support for this idea comes from recent findings that German soldiers who may have obeyed orders to kill Jews during World War II were higher on authoritarianism than other German men of the same age and background (Steiner & Fahrenberg, 2000).

Evaluating Milgram's Studies

How relevant are Milgram's thirty-five-year-old studies in today's world? Consider this fact: The U.S. Federal Aviation Administration attributes many commercial airline accidents to a phenomenon it calls "captainitis." This phenomenon occurs when the captain of an aircraft makes an obvious error, but none of the other crew members is willing to challenge the captain's authority by pointing out the mistake. As a result, planes have crashed and people have died (Kanki & Foushee, 1990). A similar situation may have prevailed aboard the nuclear submarine USS *Greeneville* as it surfaced off the coast of Hawaii on February 9, 2001. The sub struck and sank a Japanese fishing boat, killing nine people, and a navy board of inquiry later found that crew members had been reluctant to challenge their captain's order to surface even though they felt he had not checked carefully enough for other vessels in the area (Myers, 2001). Obedience to authority may also have operated during the World Trade Center attack on September 11, 2001, when some people who had started for the exits returned to their offices after hearing an ill-advised public address announcement telling them to do so. Most of these people died as a result. Such events suggest that Milgram's findings are still relevant and important (Blass, 1999). Similar kinds of obedience have been observed in experiments conducted in many countries, from Europe to the Middle East, with female as well as male participants. In short, people appear to be as obedient today as they were when Milgram conducted his research (Blass, 1999; Smith & Bond, 1999).

Nevertheless, many aspects of Milgram's work still provoke debate. (For a summary of Milgram's results, plus those of studies on conformity and compliance, see "In Review: Types of Social Influence.")

Following Ghastly Orders When authority figures issue orders, they tend to be obeyed, even when they are inhumane. In this case, for example, fifteen people, including a pregnant woman, were executed in the Colombian village of Los Angeles by gunmen whose leaders told them that the victims were rebel collaborators. And when the Taliban militia ruled Afghanistan, soldiers routinely carried out their superiors' orders to beat, or even execute, women for "offenses" such as seeking an education, laughing in public, or leaving home alone.

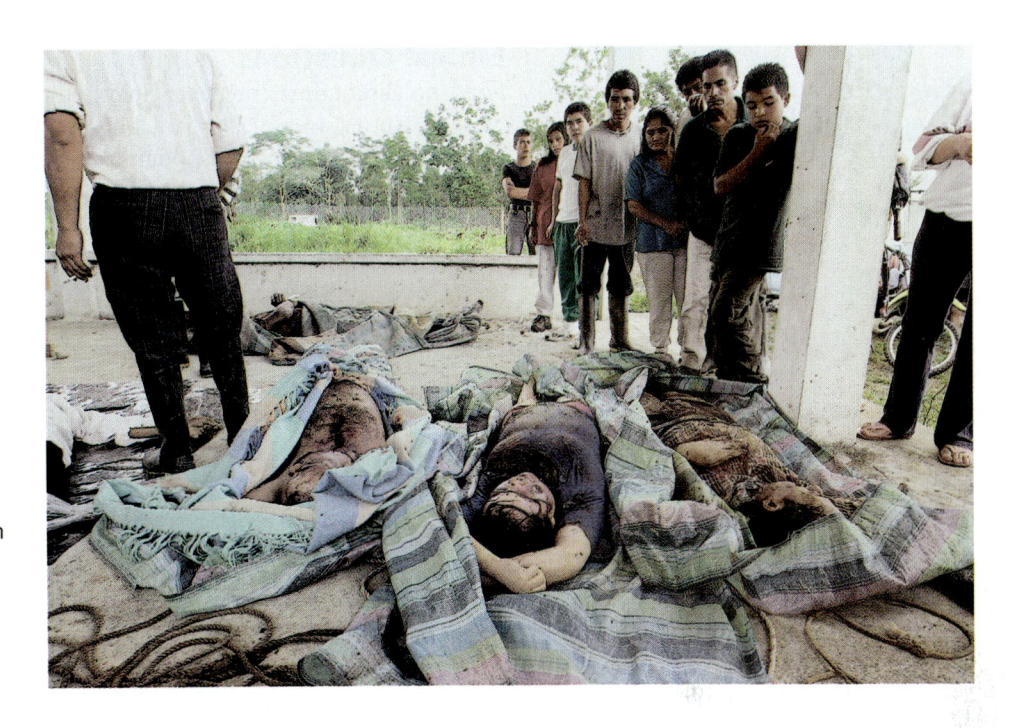

in review: Types of Social Influence

Type	Definition	Key Findings
Conformity	A change in behavior or beliefs to match those of others	In cases of ambiguity, people develop a group norm and then adhere to it.
		Conformity occurs because people want to be right, because they want to be liked by others, and because conformity to group norms is usually reinforced.
		Conformity usually increases with the ambiguity of the situation, as well as with the unanimity and psychological size of the majority.
Compliance	A change in what is said or done because of a request	Compliance increases with the foot-in-the-door technique, which begins with a small request and works up to a larger one.
		The door-in-the-face procedure can also be used. After making a large request that is denied, the person substitutes a less extreme alternative that was desired all along.
		The low-ball approach also elicits compliance. A person first obtains an oral commitment for something, then claims that only a higher-cost version of the original request will suffice.
Obedience	A change in behavior in response to an explicit demand, typically from an authority figure	People may inflict great harm on others when an authority demands that they do so.
		Even though people obey orders to harm another person, they often agonize over the decision.
		People are most likely to disobey orders to harm someone else when they see another person disobey.

LINKAGES (a link to Research in Psychology)

Ethical Questions
Although the "learners" in Milgram's experiment suffered no discomfort, the participants did. Milgram (1963) observed participants "sweat, stutter, tremble, groan, bite their lips, and dig their fingernails into their flesh" (p. 375). Against the potential harm inflicted by Milgram's experiments stand the potential gains. For example, people who learn about Milgram's work often take his findings into account when deciding how to behave in social situations (Sherman, 1980). But even if social value has come from Milgram's studies, the question remains: Was it ethical for Milgram to treat his participants as he did?

In the years before his death in 1984, Milgram defended his experiments (e.g., Milgram, 1977). He argued that his debriefing of the participants after the experiment prevented any lasting harm. For example, to demonstrate that their behavior was not unusual, Milgram told them that most people went all the way to the 450-volt level. He also explained that the learner did not experience any shock; in fact, the learner came in and chatted with each participant. On a later questionnaire, 84 percent of the participants said that they had learned something important about themselves and that the experience had been worthwhile. Milgram argued, therefore, that the experience was actually a positive one. Still, today's committees charged with protecting human participants in research would be unlikely to approve Milgram's experiments, and less controversial ways to study obedience have now been developed (Sackoff & Weinstein, 1988).

Questions of Meaning
Do Milgram's dramatic results mean that most people are putty in the hands of authority figures and that most of us would blindly follow inhumane orders from our leaders? Some critics have argued that other factors besides obedience to authority were responsible for the behavior of Milgram's participants and that the social-influence processes identified in his studies might not explain obedience in the real world. For example, Leonard Berkowitz (1999) pointed out that Milgram's studies cannot explain why, during World War II, many German concentration camp guards not only obeyed their superiors' orders to kill prisoners, but carried out those orders in the most sadistic and inhumane manner possible. Their actions, Berkowitz said, went far beyond simple obedience to authority.

Most psychologists believe that Milgram did more than highlight the phenomenon of obedience. He appears to have demonstrated a basic truth about human behavior—namely, that under certain circumstances, human beings are capable of unspeakable acts of brutality toward other humans. Sadly, examples abound. And one of the most horrifying aspects of human inhumanity—whether it is the Nazis' campaign of genocide against Jews sixty years ago or the campaigns of terror under way today—is that the perpetrators are not necessarily demented, sadistic fiends. Most of them are, in many respects, "normal" people who have been influenced by economic and political situations, and the persuasive power of their leaders, to behave in a demented and fiendish manner.

In short, inhumanity can occur even without pressure for obedience. For example, a good deal of people's aggressiveness toward other people appears to come from within. In the next section, we consider human aggressiveness and some of the circumstances that influence its expression.

Aggression

aggression An act that is intended to cause harm to another person.

Aggression is an action intended to harm another person. In the United States, the incidence of homicide and other violent crimes has dropped substantially in the last few years, but acts of violence are still all too common. In 1999, more than 8 million people in the United States were victims of violent crime. Just under 1 in every 1,000 women was raped and slightly more than 1 in every 1,000 young African American men was murdered (U.S. Department of Justice, 2001). One of the most frightening aspects of these figures is that many of the aggressors and victims were not strangers. About 45 percent of the murder victims knew their killers, and about 60 percent of rapists were romantic partners, friends, relatives, or acquaintances of their victims (U.S. Department of Justice, 2001). About one-third of married people in the United States display aggression toward each other that ranges from pushing, shoving, and slapping to beatings and the threatened or actual use of weapons (Archer, 2000; Heyman & Neidig, 1999).

LINKAGES (a link to Introducing Psychology)

Why Are People Aggressive?

An early theory of human aggression was offered by Sigmund Freud, who suggested it was partly due to *Thanatos,* the death instincts described in the chapter on personality. Freud proposed that aggression is an instinctive biological urge that gradually builds up in everyone and must be released. Sometimes, he said, release takes the form of physical or verbal abuse against others; at other times, the aggressive impulse is turned inward and leads to suicide or other self-damaging acts.

A slightly more complicated view is offered by evolutionary psychologists. As discussed in the introductory chapter, these psychologists believe that human social behavior is related to our evolutionary heritage. From this perspective, aggression is thought to have helped prehistoric people compete for mates, thus ensuring survival of their genes in the next generation. Through the principles of natural selection, then, aggressive tendencies were passed on through successive generations. Some evolutionary psychologists believe that even now, aggression sometimes occurs because it promotes the survival of the aggressor's genes (e.g., Malamuth & Addison, 2001).

Today, evolutionary theories of the origins of aggression are quite popular, but even ardent evolutionary theorists realize that "nature" alone cannot fully account for aggression. "Nurture," in the form of environmental factors, also plays a large role in when and why people are aggressive. How do we know this? For one thing, there are large differences in aggression from culture to culture. In the Philippines, for example, the murder rate is forty-six times higher than in China or Finland, and it is almost nine times higher in the United States than in those latter two countries (Triandis, 1994). In fact, the homicide rate is higher in the United States than in any other industrialized nation (Geen, 1998a). These data suggest that even if aggressive *impulses* are universal, the emergence of aggressive *behavior* reflects an interplay of nature and nurture (Malamuth & Addison, 2001). No equation can predict when people will be aggressive, but years of research have revealed a number of important biological, learning, and environmental factors that combine in various ways to produce aggression in various situations.

Genetic and Biological Mechanisms
The evidence for hereditary influences on aggression is strong, especially in animals (Cairns, Gariepy, & Hood, 1990). In one study, the most aggressive members of a large group of mice were interbred; then the most aggressive of their offspring were also interbred. After this procedure was followed for twenty-five generations, the resulting animals would immediately attack any mouse put in their cage. Continuous inbreeding of the least aggressive members of the original group produced animals that were so nonaggressive that they would refuse to fight even when attacked (Lagerspetz & Lagerspetz, 1983). Research on human twins reared together or apart suggests that there is a genetic component to aggression in people as well (Tellegen et al., 1988). However, other research suggests that people do not necessarily inherit the tendency to be aggressive; instead, they may inherit certain temperaments, such as impulsiveness, that in turn make aggression more likely (Baron & Richardson, 1994).

Several parts of the brain influence aggression (Anderson & Anderson, 1998). One is the limbic system, which includes the amygdala, the hypothalamus, and related areas (see Figure 3.14 in the chapter on biological aspects of psychology). Damage to these structures may produce *defensive aggression,* which includes heightened aggressiveness to stimuli that are not usually threatening or a decrease in the responses that normally inhibit aggression (Coccaro, 1989; Eichelman, 1983). The cerebral cortex may also be involved in aggression (e.g., Pietro et al., 2000; see Figure 3.16). One study found that the prefrontal area of the cortex metabolized glucose significantly more slowly in murderers than in nonmurderers (Raine et al., 1994).

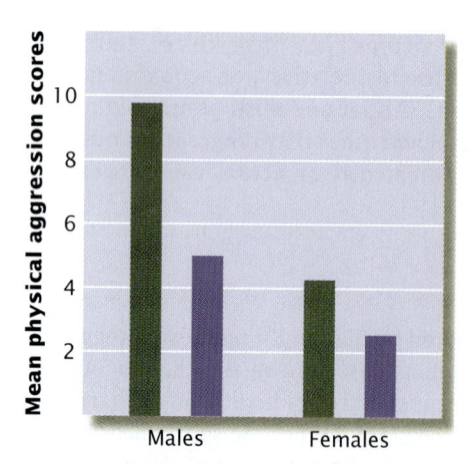

Hormones such as *testosterone*—the masculine hormone that is present in both sexes—may also play an important role in aggression (Dabbs & Dabbs, 2001). Experiments have shown that aggressive behavior increases or decreases dramatically with the level of testosterone in the human bloodstream (Pope, Kouri, & Hudson, 2000; Yates, 2000). Among criminals, those who commit violent crimes have higher levels of testosterone than those whose crimes are nonviolent. And among murderers, those with higher levels of testosterone are more likely than others to have known their victims and to have planned their crimes before committing them (Dabbs, Riad, & Chance, 2001).

Testosterone may have its most significant and durable influence not so much through its day-to-day variations as through its impact on early brain development. One natural test of this hypothesis occurred when pregnant women were given testosterone in an attempt to prevent miscarriages. Accordingly, their children were exposed to high doses of testosterone during prenatal development. Figure 18.5 shows that these children grew up to be more aggressive than their same-sex siblings who were not exposed to testosterone during prenatal development (Reinisch, Ziemba-Davis, & Sanders, 1991).

Drugs that alter central nervous system functioning can also affect the likelihood that a person will act aggressively. Alcohol, for example, can substantially increase some people's aggressiveness. Canadian researchers have found that in almost 70 percent of the acts of aggression they studied, the aggressors had been drinking alcohol. And the more alcohol the aggressors consumed, the more aggressive they were (Wells, Graham, & West, 2000). No one knows exactly why alcohol increases aggression, but research suggests that the drug may affect areas of the brain that normally inhibit aggressive responses (Lau, Pihl, & Peterson, 1995).

Research on the effects of other drugs on aggression has produced some surprising findings. One might expect, for example, that using stimulants would increase aggressiveness and that taking tranquilizers would reduce it, but the opposite appears to be true. Whereas amphetamine stimulants do not usually make people more aggressive, opiates (e.g., heroin and morphine) and some tranquilizers may do so (Taylor & Hulsizer, 1998). No one knows why heroin users are more likely than amphetamine users to be aggressive. Some have suggested that heroin addicts' aggression reflects their desperate need to get money, by any means, to buy more drugs. But if this were so, we should also see increased aggression among people who are addicted to amphetamines and cocaine—because these addictions, too, are very expensive. Further, ingesting opiates increases people's aggressiveness even in controlled laboratory settings (Taylor & Hulsizer, 1998), suggesting that these drugs have biochemical effects that lead directly to aggression. The nature of these effects is presently unknown.

Learning and Cultural Mechanisms
Cross-cultural research makes it clear that although biological factors may increase or decrease the likelihood of aggression, learning also plays a role. Aggressive behavior is much more common in individualist than in collectivist cultures, for example (Oatley, 1993). Cultural differences in the expression of aggression appear to stem in part from differing cultural values. For example, in contrast to many so-called "advanced" peoples, the Utku, an Inuit culture, view aggression in any form as a sign of social incompetence. In fact, the Utku word for "aggressive" also means "childish" (Oatley, 1993). The effects of culture on aggression can also be seen in the fact that the incidence of aggression in a given culture changes over time as cultural values change (Matsumoto, 2000).

figure 18.5

Testosterone and Aggression

In the study illustrated here, the children of women who had taken testosterone during pregnancy to prevent miscarriage became more aggressive than the mothers' other children of the same sex who had not been exposed to testosterone during prenatal development. This outcome held for both males and females.

Source: Data from Reinisch, Ziemba-Davis, & Sanders (1991).

Aggression can even differ in different areas of the same country. Consider the fact that more males in the southern U.S. states commit homicide than do males in the northern states (U.S. Department of Justice, 2001). As discussed later, this regional difference in the homicide rate may be related to the South's higher temperatures, but Richard Nisbett and his colleagues (Nisbett, 1993; Cohen & Nisbett, 1997) have proposed that it is due to a *culture of honor* that is more commonly endorsed by southern males. One key aspect of this cultural orientation is the need to defend one's honor, with violence if necessary, in response to a perceived insult. Studies testing this notion have in fact found that southern-born college students reacted much more angrily to a provocation than did northern-born students (Cassel & Bernstein, 2001; Cohen et al., 1996).

People also learn many aggressive responses by watching others (Bushman & Anderson, 2001). Children, in particular, learn and perform many novel aggressive responses that they see modeled by others (Bandura, 1983). Albert Bandura's "Bobo" doll experiments, which are described in the chapter on learning, provide impressive demonstrations of the power of observational learning. The significance of observational learning is highlighted by studies of the effects of televised violence, also discussed in that chapter. For example, the amount of violent content watched on television by eight-year-olds predicts aggressiveness in these children even fifteen years later (Huesmann et al., 1997). Fortunately, not everyone who sees aggression becomes aggressive; individual differences in temperament, the modeling of nonaggressive behaviors by parents, and other factors can temper the effects of violent television. Nevertheless, observational learning does play a significant role in the development and display of aggressive behavior (Bushman & Anderson, 2001).

Immediate reward or punishment can also alter the frequency of aggressive acts; people become more aggressive when rewarded for aggressiveness and less aggressive when punished for aggression (Geen, 1998a). In short, a person's accumulated experiences—including culturally transmitted teachings—combine with daily rewards and punishments to influence whether, when, and how aggressive acts occur (Baron & Richardson, 1994).

When Are People Aggressive?

LINKAGES (a link to Motivation and Emotion)

In general, people are more likely to be aggressive when they are both physiologically aroused and experiencing strong emotions such as anger (Geen, 1998b). People tend either to lash out at those who make them angry or to displace their anger onto

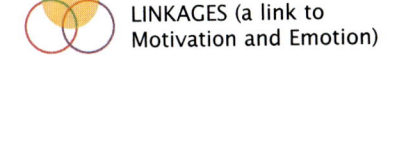

Following Adult Examples Learning to express aggression is especially easy for children, who, like this child at an anti-American demonstration in Pakistan in October 2001, see aggressive acts modeled for them all too often.

defenseless targets such as children or pets. However, aggression can also be made more likely by other forms of emotional arousal. One emotion that has long been considered to be a major cause of aggression is *frustration*, which occurs when we are prevented from reaching some goal.

Frustration and Aggression

Suppose that a friend interrupts your studying for an exam by coming over to borrow a book. If things have been going well that day and you are feeling confident about the exam, you are likely to be friendly and accommodating. But what if you are feeling frustrated because your friend's visit represents the fifth interruption in the last hour? Under these emotional circumstances, you may react aggressively, perhaps snapping at your startled visitor for not calling ahead.

Your aggressiveness in this situation conforms to the predictions of the **frustration-aggression hypothesis,** originally developed by John Dollard and his colleagues (Dollard et al., 1939). They proposed that frustration always results in aggression and, conversely, that aggression will not occur unless a person is frustrated. Research on this hypothesis, however, has shown that it is too simple and too general. For one thing, frustration sometimes produces depression and withdrawal, not aggression (Berkowitz, 1998). In addition, not all aggression is preceded by frustration (Berkowitz, 1994). In many of the experiments described earlier, for example, participants were not frustrated, but they still made aggressive responses.

After many years of research, Leonard Berkowitz (1998) suggested some substantial modifications to the frustration-aggression hypothesis. First, he proposed that it may be *stress* rather than frustration per se that can produce a readiness to act aggressively. Once this readiness exists, cues in the environment that are associated with aggression will often lead a person to behave aggressively. The cues might be guns or knives, televised scenes of people arguing, and the like. Neither stress alone nor the cues alone are sufficient to set off aggression. When combined, however, they often do set it off. Support for this aspect of Berkowitz's theory has been quite strong (Malamuth & Addison, 2001).

Second, Berkowitz argues that the direct cause of most kinds of aggression is *negative affect*, or unpleasant emotion, and that whether it is caused by frustrating circumstances or other sources, the greater the negative affect, the stronger is the readiness to respond aggressively (Berkowitz, 1998). For example, negative affect can stem from pain; and research suggests that people in pain do tend to become aggressive, no matter what caused their pain. In one study, female students whose hands were placed in painfully cold water became more aggressive toward other students than women whose hands were in water of room temperature (Berkowitz, 1998).

Generalized Arousal

Imagine you have just jogged three miles. You are hot, sweaty, and out of breath, but you are not angry. Still, the physiological arousal caused by jogging may increase the probability that you will become aggressive if, say, a passerby shouts an insult (Zillmann, 1988). Why? The answer lies in a phenomenon described in the chapter on motivation and emotion: Arousal from one experience may carry over to an independent situation, producing what is called *transferred excitation*. So the physiological arousal caused by jogging may intensify your reaction to an insult (Geen, 1998b).

By itself, however, generalized arousal does not lead to aggression. It is most likely to produce aggression when the situation contains some reason, opportunity, or target for aggression (Zillmann, 1988). In one study, for example, people engaged in two minutes of vigorous exercise. Then they had the opportunity to deliver electrical shock to another person. The participants chose high levels of shock only if they were first insulted (Zillmann, Katcher, & Milavsky, 1972). Apparently, the arousal resulting from the exercise made aggression more likely; the insult "released" it. These findings are in keeping with the notion that aggression is not

---

frustration-aggression hypothesis A proposition that frustration always leads to some form of aggressive behavior.

caused solely by a person's characteristics or by the particular situation a person is in; rather, the incidence and intensity of aggression are determined by the joint influence of individual characteristics and environmental circumstances.

THINKING CRITICALLY

Does Pornography Cause Aggression?

In both men and women, sexual stimulation produces strong, generalized physiological arousal, especially in the sympathetic nervous system. If arousal in general can make a person more likely to be aggressive (given a reason, opportunity, or target), could stimuli that create sexual excitement be dangerous? In particular, does viewing pornographic material make people more likely to be aggressive? Over the years, numerous scholars had concluded that there was no evidence for an overall relationship between any type of antisocial behavior and mere exposure to pornographic material (Donnerstein, 1984b). However, in 1986 the U.S. Attorney General's Commission on Pornography reexamined the question and concluded that pornography is dangerous.

- **What am I being asked to believe or accept?**

Specifically, the commission proposed that there is a causal link between viewing erotic material and several forms of antisocial behavior, including sexually related violent crimes.

- **What evidence is available to support the assertion?**

The commission cited several types of evidence in support of its conclusion. First, there was the testimony of men convicted of sexually related crimes. Rapists, for example, are unusually heavy consumers of pornography, and they often say that they were aroused by erotic material immediately before committing a rape (Silbert & Pines, 1984). Similarly, child molesters often view child pornography immediately before committing their crimes (Marshall, 1989).

In addition, the commission cited experimental evidence that men who are most aroused by aggressive themes in pornography are also the most potentially sexually aggressive. One study, for example, showed that men who said they could commit a rape became sexually aroused by scenes of rape and less aroused by scenes of mutually consenting sex; this was not true for men who said they could never commit a rape (Malamuth & Check, 1983).

Perhaps the most compelling evidence cited by the commission, however, came from transferred excitation studies. In a typical study of this type, men are told that a person in a separate room (actually a research assistant) will be performing a learning task and that they are to administer an electrical shock every time the person makes a mistake. The intensity of shock can be varied (no shock actually reaches the assistant), but participants are told that changing the intensity will not affect the speed of learning. So the shock intensity (and presumed pain) that the participants choose to administer is taken as an index of aggressive behavior. Some participants watch a sexually explicit film before beginning the learning trials, and some do not. The arousal created by the film appears to transfer into aggression, especially when the arousal is experienced in a negative way. For example, after watching a film in which several men have sex with the same woman, the participants became aroused but tended to label the experience as somewhat unpleasant. Their aggressiveness during the learning experiment was greater than that demonstrated by men who did not watch the film (Donnerstein, 1984b).

- **Are there alternative ways of interpreting the evidence?**

The commission's interpretation of evidence was criticized on several counts. First, critics argued that some of the evidence should be given little weight. In particular, how credible is the testimony of convicted sex offenders? It may reflect self-serving attempts to lay the blame for their crimes on pornography. These reports cannot establish that exposure to pornography causes aggression. In fact, it may be that pornography partially *satisfies* sex offenders' aggressive impulses rather than creating them (Aronson, Wilson, & Akert, 2002). Similarly, the fact that potential rapists are most aroused by rape-oriented material may show only that they prefer violence-oriented pornography, not that such materials *created* their impulse to rape.

What about the evidence from transferred excitation studies? To interpret these studies, you need to know that the pornography that led to increased aggression contained violence as well as sex; the sexual activity depicted was painful for, or unwanted by, the woman. So the subsequent increase in aggression could have been due to the transfer of sexual arousal, the effects of observing violent behavior, or the effects of seeing sex combined with violence (Donnerstein, Slaby, & Eron, 1995).

In fact, several careful experiments have found that highly arousing sexual themes, in and of themselves, do not produce aggression. When men in transferred excitation studies experience pleasant arousal by viewing a film depicting nudity or mutually consenting sexual activity, their subsequent aggression is actually less than when they viewed no film or a neutral film (Lord, 1997). In short, the transferred excitation studies might be interpreted as demonstrating not that sexually arousing material causes aggression but that portrayals of sexual *violence* influence aggressiveness.

● **What additional evidence would help to evaluate the alternatives?**

Two types of evidence are needed to understand more clearly the effects of pornography on aggression. First, because pornography can include sexual acts, aggressive acts, or both, the effects of each of these components must be more carefully examined. Second, factors affecting men's reactions to pornography, particularly pornography that involves violence, must be more clearly understood. Work is in progress on each of these fronts.

Aggressive themes—whether specifically paired with sexual activity or not—do appear to increase subsequent aggression (Bushman & Anderson, 2001). Research has focused on *aggressive pornography,* which contains sexual themes but also scenes of violence against women (Linz, Wilson, & Donnerstein, 1992). In laboratory experiments, men often administer higher levels of shock to women after viewing aggressive pornographic films as opposed to neutral films. Yet there is no parallel increase in aggression against other men, indicating that the films don't create a generalized increase in aggression but do create an increase in aggressiveness directed toward women (Aronson, Wilson, & Akert, 2002). Similarly, viewing aggressive pornography that depicts the *rape myth*—in which the victim of sexual violence appears to be aroused by the aggression—usually leads men to become less sympathetic toward the rape victim and more tolerant of aggressive acts toward women (Donnerstein & Linz, 1995). In general, sexually explicit films that do not contain violence have no effect on attitudes toward rape (Linz, Donnerstein, & Penrod, 1987).

Pornography is widely available, but are all men who view it equally likely to become rapists? The evidence available so far suggests that the answer is no. Whether aggressive pornography alters men's behavior and attitudes toward women depends to some extent on the men. A national study of more than 2,700 men in the United States examined how three factors—a history of sexual promiscuity, feelings of hostility toward women, and the consumption of pornography—were related to sexual aggression against women (Malamuth, 1998). Among men *low* in promiscuity and hostility, viewing pornography was not associated with sexual aggression; among men who were *high* in promiscuity and hostility, though, there was such an association. Specifically, 72 percent of the men who were high on all three factors had actually engaged in sexually aggressive acts (see Figure 18.6).

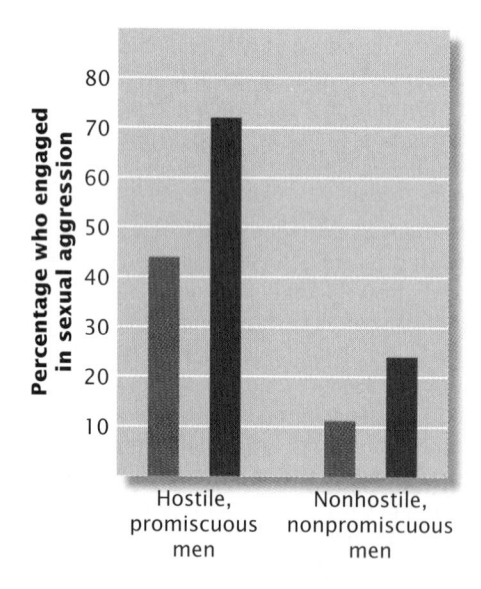

■ Small amount of pornography watched
■ Large amount of pornography watched

figure 18.6

Pornography and Sexual Aggression

Extensive exposure to pornography does not by itself make most men more likely to engage in sexual aggression. However, among men who are hostile toward women and have a history of sexual promiscuity, those who watch a lot of pornography are much more likely to engage in sexual aggression.

Source: Adapted from Malamuth (1998).

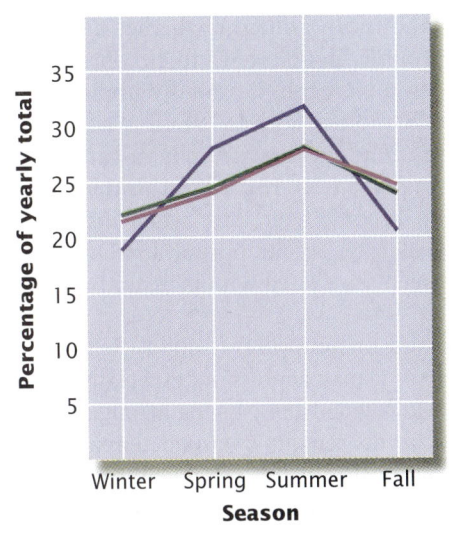

What conclusions are most reasonable?

The attorney general's commission appeared to ignore numerous studies showing that the relationship between sexual arousal and aggression is neither consistent nor simple (Seto, Maric, & Barabee, 2001). Analysis of this relationship reveals the importance of distinguishing between pornography in general and aggressive pornography in particular. Overall, there is no reason to assume that sexual arousal created by nonaggressive pornography is associated with aggressive behavior. In fact, for most people, sexual arousal and aggression remain quite separate. However, aggressive pornography is associated with violence against women, so there is reason for concern over the impact of sexual violence commonly seen on television and in films—especially "slasher" movies. Amazing as it may seem, in the United States such films are sometimes given less restrictive ratings (R or even PG-13) than films that are nonviolent but erotic.

Although pornography has little impact on most people, certain segments of the population do seem to be affected by it. Men who are inclined to abuse and exploit women are also inclined to watch a lot of pornography. And watching a lot of pornography can increase the likelihood of their sexually abusing a woman (Malamuth, Addison, & Koss, 2001). In short, pornography per se is probably not a cause of violence against women, but in combination with other factors it can play a role in sexual aggression.

figure 18.7

Effects of Temperature on Aggression
Studies from around the world indicate that aggressive behaviors are most likely to occur during hot summer months. These studies support the idea that environmental factors can affect aggression.

Source: Anderson & Anderson (1998).

Environmental Influences on Aggression The link between stress and aggressive behavior points to the possibility that stressful environmental conditions can make aggressive behavior more likely (Anderson, 2001). This possibility is one of the research topics in **environmental psychology,** the study of the relationship between people's physical environment and their behavior (Sommer, 1999). One aspect of the environment that clearly affects social behavior is the weather, especially temperature. High temperature is a source of stress and arousal, so it might be expected to correlate with aggressiveness. The results of many studies conducted in several countries show that many kinds of aggressive behavior are indeed more likely to occur during hot summer months than at any other time of the year (Anderson, et al., 2000; see Figure 18.7).

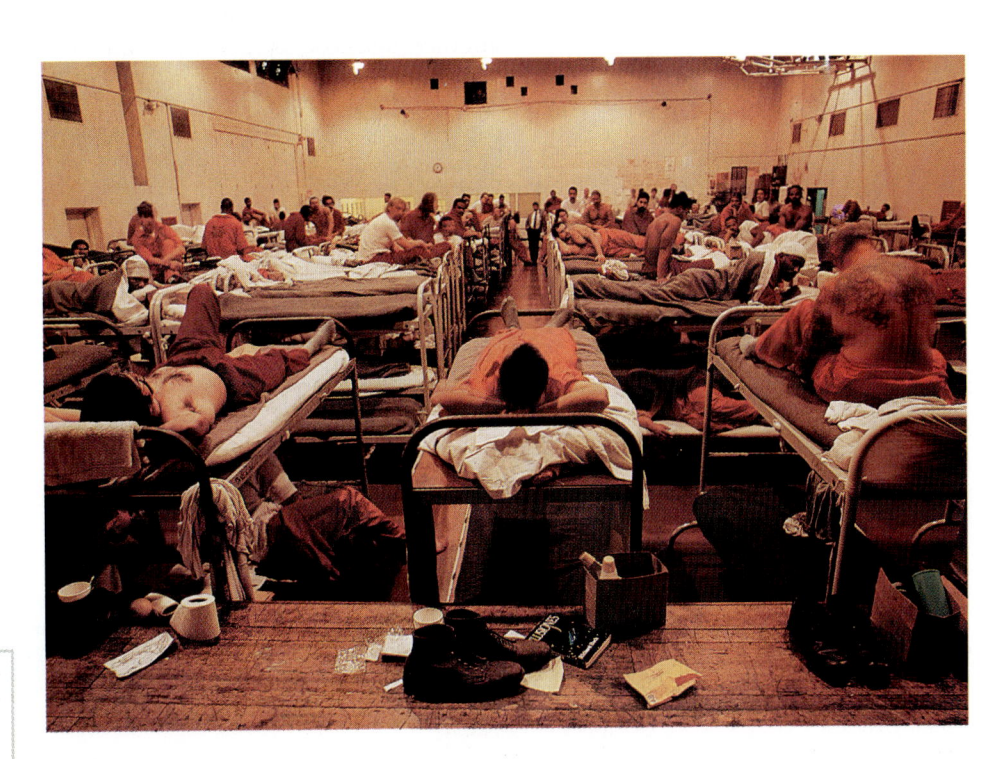

Crowding and Aggression Studies of prisons suggest that as crowding increases, so does aggression (Paulus, 1988). Accordingly, environmental psychologists are working with architects on the design of prisons that minimize the sense of crowding and that ideally may help prevent some of the violence that endangers staff and prisoners.

environmental psychology The study of the relationship between behavior and the physical environment.

Air pollution is another source of stress, and it can influence whether a person displays aggression (Holahan, 1986). For example, people tend to become more aggressive when breathing air that contains ethyl mercapton, a mildly unpleasant-smelling pollutant common in urban areas (Rotton et al., 1979). A study conducted in Dayton, Ohio, found that the frequency of aggressive family disturbances increased along with the ozone level in the air (Rotton & Frey, 1985). And in laboratory studies, nonsmokers are more likely to become aggressive when breathing smoke-filled rather than clean air (Zillmann, Baron, & Tamborini, 1981). Long-term exposure to toxins such as lead has also been associated with increased aggression (Needleman, 1996).

Noise—usually defined as any unwanted and uncontrollable sound (Bell et al., 1996)—also tends to make people more likely to display aggression, especially if the noise is unpredictable and irregular (Geen & McCown, 1984). Living arrangements, too, can influence aggressiveness. Compared with the tenants of crowded apartment buildings, those in buildings with relatively few residents are less likely to behave aggressively (Bell et al., 1996). This difference appears to be due in part to how people feel when they are crowded. Crowding tends to create physiological arousal and to make people tense, uncomfortable, and more likely to report negative feelings (Oskamp & Schultz, 1998). This arousal and tension can influence people to like one another less and to be more aggressive. One study of juvenile delinquents found that the number of behavior problems they displayed (including aggressiveness) was directly related to how crowded their living conditions had become (Ray et al., 1982).

Altruism and Helping Behavior

Like all acts of terrorism, the 2001 attacks on the World Trade Center and the Pentagon were horrifying examples of human behavior at its worst. But like all tragedies, they drew responses that provide inspiring examples of human behavior at its best. Michael Benfante and John Cerqueira were working in the World Trade Center when one of the hijacked planes struck their building. They headed for a stairwell, but they did not just save themselves. Although it slowed their own escape, they chose to carry Tina Hansen, a wheelchair-bound co-worker, down sixty-eight flights of stairs to safety. David Theall was in his Pentagon office when another hijacked plane hit not far from his desk. He could have escaped the rubble

Two of Many Heroes Along with his colleague Michael Benfante, John Cerqueira (shown here) risked his life on September 11, 2001, to help a handicapped co-worker escape from the 68th floor of the World Trade Center. Hundreds of other heroic acts of helping took place that day, and less dramatic examples occur every day, all over the world.

Photo courtesy of North Carolina State University, Cerqueira's alma mater.

A Young Helper Even before their second birthday, some children offer help to those who are hurt or crying by snuggling, patting, or offering food or even their own teddy bears.

immediately, but he first located a dazed officemate and led him, along with seven other co-workers, to safety. And no one will ever forget the heroism of the hundreds of New York City firefighters, police officers, and emergency workers who risked their lives, and lost their lives, while trying to save others. Acts of selflessness and sacrifice were common that day, and in the days and weeks and months that followed. Police officers, medical personnel, search-and-rescue specialists, and just ordinary people came to New York from all over the United States to help clear wreckage, look for survivors, and recover bodies. More than $1 billion in donations to the Red Cross and other charitable organizations poured in to help victims; one celebrity telethon raised $150 million in two hours.

All of these actions are examples of **helping behavior,** which is defined as any act that is intended to benefit another person. Helping can range from picking up dropped packages to donating a kidney. Closely related to helping is **altruism,** an unselfish concern for another's welfare (Dovidio & Penner, 2001). In the following sections we examine some of the reasons for helping and altruism, along with some of the conditions under which people are most likely to help others.

Why Do People Help?

The tendency to help others begins early, although at first it is not spontaneous. In most cultures, very young children generally help others only when they are asked to do so or are offered a reward (Grusec, 1991). Still, Carolyn Zahn-Waxler and her associates (1992) found that almost half of the two-year-olds they observed acted helpfully toward a friend or family member. As they grow older, children use helping behavior to gain social approval, and their efforts at helping become more elaborate. The role of social influence in the development of helping is seen as children follow examples set by people around them; their helping behaviors are shaped by the norms established by their families and the broader culture (Grusec & Goodnow, 1994). In addition, children are praised and given other rewards for helpfulness but are scolded for selfishness. Eventually children come to believe that being helpful is good and that they are good when they are helpful. By the late teens, people often help others even when no one is watching and no one will know that they did so (Cialdini, Baumann, & Kenrick, 1981). There are three major theories about why people help even when they cannot expect any external rewards for doing so.

Arousal: Cost-Reward Theory

One psychological model that attempts to explain why people help is called the **arousal: cost-reward theory** (Piliavin et al., 1981). This theory proposes that people find the sight of a victim distressing and anxiety provoking, and that this experience motivates them to do something to reduce the unpleasant arousal. Several studies have shown that all else being equal, the more physiologically aroused bystanders are, the more likely they are to help someone in an emergency (Dovidio et al., 1991; Schroeder et al., 1995). Before rushing to a victim's aid, however, the bystander will first evaluate two aspects of the situation: the costs associated with helping and the costs (to the bystander and the other person) of not helping. Whether or not the bystander actually helps depends on the outcome of this evaluation (Dovidio et al., 1991). If the costs of helping are low (as when helping someone pick up a dropped grocery bag) and the costs of not helping are high (as when the other person is physically unable to do this alone), the bystander will almost certainly help. However, if the costs of helping are high (as when the task is to load a heavy air conditioner into a car) and the costs of not helping are low (as when the person is strong enough to manage the task alone), the bystander is unlikely to offer help. This theory is attractive partly because it is comprehensive enough to provide a conceptual framework for explaining a number of research findings on the factors that affect helping. Let's consider some of these factors.

helping behavior Any act that is intended to benefit another person.

altruism An unselfish concern for another's welfare.

arousal: cost-reward theory A theory attributing people's helping behavior to their efforts to reduce the unpleasant arousal they feel in the face of someone's need or suffering.

One factor is the *clarity of the need for help,* which has a major impact on whether people provide help (Dovidio et al., 1991). In one study, undergraduate students were waiting alone in a campus building when a window washer appeared to suffer an accident. The man screamed as he and his ladder fell to the ground; then he began to clutch his ankle and groan in pain. All of the students looked out a window to see what had happened, but only 29 percent of them did anything to help. Other students experienced the same situation with one important difference: The man *said* he was hurt and needed help. In this case, more than 80 percent of the students came to his aid (Yakimovich & Saltz, 1971). Why? Apparently, this one additional cue eliminated any ambiguity about whether the person needed help. This cue also raised the perceived costs to the victim of not offering help; as these costs become higher, helping becomes more likely. If this laboratory study does not seem realistic enough, consider the case of a sixty-two-year-old woman in Darby, Pennsylvania, who was walking to the grocery store in March 2000 when she was pushed from behind by an attacker. She fended him off and then did her shopping as usual. It was only when she got home and her daughter saw the handle of a knife protruding from her back that she realized that the assailant had stabbed her! No one in the grocery store said anything to her about the knife, let alone offered to help. Why? Perhaps because the woman didn't say or do anything to suggest that help was needed.

The *presence of others* also has a strong influence on the tendency to help. However, their presence actually tends to inhibit helping behavior. One of the most highly publicized examples of this phenomenon was the Kitty Genovese incident, which occurred on a New York City street in 1964. During a thirty-minute struggle, a man stabbed Genovese repeatedly, but none of the dozens of neighbors who witnessed the attack intervened or even called the police until it was too late to save her life. A similar case occurred on November 27, 2000, in London, when a ten-year-old boy who had been stabbed by members of a street gang lay ignored by passersby as he bled to death. After each case, journalists and social commentators expressed dismay about the apathy and callousness that seems to exist among people who live in big cities. But psychologists believe that something about the situation surrounding such events deters people from helping.

The numerous studies of helping behavior stimulated by the Genovese case revealed a phenomenon that may explain the inaction of Genovese's neighbors and those passersby in London. This phenomenon is known as the *bystander effect*: usually, as the number of people who witness an emergency increases, the likelihood that one of them will help decreases (Dovidio & Penner, 2001). One explanation for why the presence of others often reduces helping is that each person thinks someone else will help the victim. That is, the presence of other bystanders allows each individual to experience a *diffusion of responsibility* for taking action, which lowers the costs of not helping (Schroeder et al., 1995).

The degree to which the presence of other people will inhibit helping may depend on who those other people are. When they are strangers, perhaps poor communication inhibits helping. People often have difficulty speaking to strangers, particularly in an emergency, and without speaking, they have difficulty knowing what the others intend to do. According to this logic, if people are with friends rather than strangers, they should be less uncomfortable, more willing to discuss the problem, and thus more likely to help.

In one experiment designed to test this idea, an experimenter left a research participant in a waiting room, either alone, with a friend, with a stranger, or with a stranger who was an assistant to the experimenter (Latané & Rodin, 1969). The experimenter then stepped behind a curtain into an office. For a few minutes, she could be heard opening and closing the drawers of her desk, shuffling papers, and so on. Then there was a loud crash, and she screamed, "Oh, my god . . . My foot, I . . . I can't move it. Oh, my ankle . . . I can't get this . . . thing off me." Then the participant heard her groan and cry.

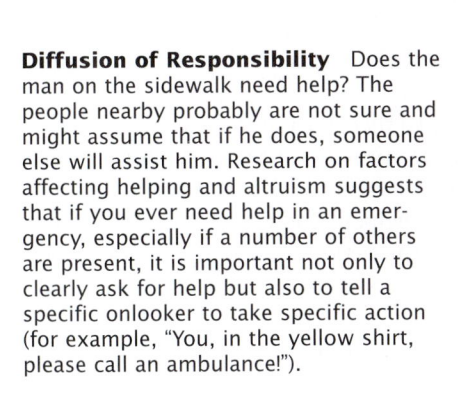

Diffusion of Responsibility Does the man on the sidewalk need help? The people nearby probably are not sure and might assume that if he does, someone else will assist him. Research on factors affecting helping and altruism suggests that if you ever need help in an emergency, especially if a number of others are present, it is important not only to clearly ask for help but also to tell a specific onlooker to take specific action (for example, "You, in the yellow shirt, please call an ambulance!").

Would the participant go behind the curtain to help? Once again, people were most likely to help if they were alone. When one other person was present, participants were more likely both to communicate with one another and to offer help if they were friends than if they were strangers. When the stranger was the experimenter's assistant (who had been instructed not to help), very few participants offered to help. Other studies have confirmed that bystanders' tendency to help increases when they know one another (Rutkowski, Gruder, & Romer, 1983).

Research suggests that the *personality of the helper* also plays a role in helping. Some people are simply more likely to help than others. Consider, for example, the Christians who risked their lives to save Jews from the Nazi Holocaust. Samuel and Pearl Oliner (1988) interviewed more than two hundred of these rescuers and compared their personalities with those of people who had a chance to save Jews but did not do so. The rescuers were found to have more empathy (the ability to understand or experience another's emotional state) (Davis, 1994), more concern about others, a greater sense of responsibility for their own actions, and a greater sense of self-efficacy (confidence in the success of their efforts, as discussed in the chapter on personality). Louis Penner and his associates (Penner & Finkelstein, 1998; Penner, in press) have found that these kinds of personality traits predict a broad spectrum of helping behaviors, ranging from the speed with which bystanders intervene in an emergency to the amount of time volunteers spend helping AIDS victims. Consistent with the arousal: cost-reward theory, these personality characteristics are also correlated with people's estimates of the costs of helping and not helping. For example, empathic individuals usually estimate the costs of not helping as high, and people with a sense of self-efficacy usually rate the costs of helping as low (Penner et al., 1995). These patterns of cost estimation may partially explain why such people tend to be especially helpful.

Other helping-related phenomena cannot be easily explained by the arousal: cost-reward theory. One of these is the impact of *environmental factors* on helping. Research conducted in several countries has revealed, for example, that people in urban areas are generally less helpful than those in rural areas (Aronson, Wilson, & Akert, 2002). Why? It is probably not the simple fact of living in a city but rather the stressors one finds there that tend to make some urban people less helpful. A study conducted in thirty-six North American cities found that people's tendency to

figure 18.8

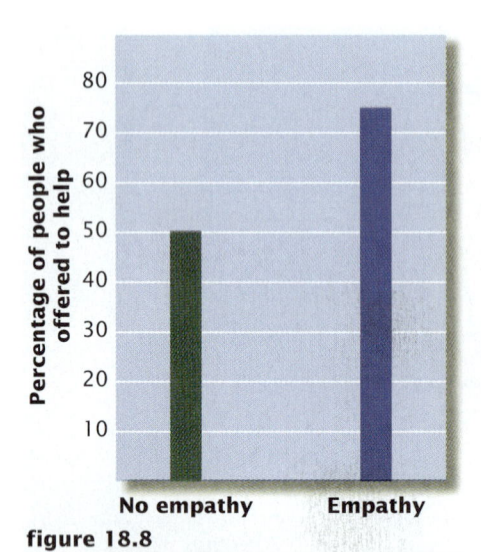

The Effect of Empathy on Helping
After hearing a staged interview with a woman who supposedly needed to raise money for her family, participants in this experiment were asked to help her. Those who were led to empathize with the woman were much more likely to offer to help her than those who did not empathize with her. These results are consistent with the empathy-altruism theory of helping.

Source: Adapted from Batson et al. (1997).

help was related more strongly to a community's *population density* (the number of people per square mile) than to the overall size of the city in which people lived (Levine et al., 1994). The higher the density, the less likely people were to help others. Similar results have been found in countries such as the United Kingdom, Saudi Arabia, and Sudan (Hedge & Yousif, 1992; Yousif & Korte, 1995). Two explanations have been suggested for this association between environmental stress and reduced likelihood of helping. The first is that stressful environments create bad moods—and generally speaking, people in bad moods are less likely to help (Salovey, Mayer, & Rosenhan, 1991). A second possibility is that noise, crowding, and other urban stressors create too much stimulation. To reduce this excessive stimulation, people may pay less attention to their surroundings, which might include individuals who need help.

It is also difficult for the arousal: cost-reward theory to predict what bystanders will do when the cost of helping and the cost of not helping are *both* high. In these instances, helping (or not helping) may depend on several situational factors and, sometimes, on the personality of the potential helper. There may also be circumstances in which cost considerations may not be the major cause of a decision to help or not help. A second approach to helping considers some of these circumstances.

Empathy-Altruism Theory The second approach to explaining helping is embodied in **empathy-altruism theory,** which maintains that people are more likely to engage in *altruistic,* or unselfish, helping—even when the cost of helping is high—if they feel empathy toward the person in need (Batson, 1998). In one experiment illustrating this phenomenon, C. Daniel Batson had participants listen to a recording of an interview with a female student. The student told the interviewer that her parents had been killed in an automobile accident, that they had no life insurance, and that she was now faced with the task of finishing college while taking care of a younger brother and sister. She said that these financial burdens might force her to quit school or give up her siblings for adoption. None of this was true, but the participants were told that it was. Further, before listening to the woman's story, half the participants were given other information about her that was designed to promote strong empathy. Later, all the participants were asked to help the woman raise money for herself and her siblings (Batson et al., 1997). The critical question was whether the participants who heard the empathy-promoting information would help more than those who did not. Consistent with the empathy-altruism theory, more participants in the empathy condition than in the nonempathy condition offered to help (see Figure 18.8).

Were those who offered help in this experiment being utterly altruistic, or could there be a different reason for their actions? This is a hotly debated question. Some researchers dispute Batson's claim that his study illustrated truly altruistic helping and suggest instead that people help in such situations for more selfish reasons, such as relieving the distress they experienced after hearing of the woman's problems (Cialdini et al., 1997). Although the final verdict on this question is not yet in, the evidence appears to support Batson's contention that empathizing with another person can sometimes lead to unselfish helping (Dovidio, Allen, & Schroeder, 1990).

Evolutionary Theory A third approach to explaining helping is based on the evolutionary approach to social psychology, which views many human social behaviors as echoes of actions that contributed to the survival of our prehistoric ancestors (Burnstein & Brannigan, 2001). At first glance, it might not seem reasonable to apply evolutionary theory to helping and altruism, because helping others at the risk of one's own well-being does not appear adaptive. If we die while trying to save others, it will be their genes, not ours, that will survive. In fact, according to Charles Darwin's concept of the survival of the fittest, helpers—and their genes—should have disappeared long ago. Contemporary evolutionary theorists suggest, however, that Darwin's thinking about natural selection focused too much on the

empathy-altruism theory A theory suggesting that people help others because of empathy with their needs.

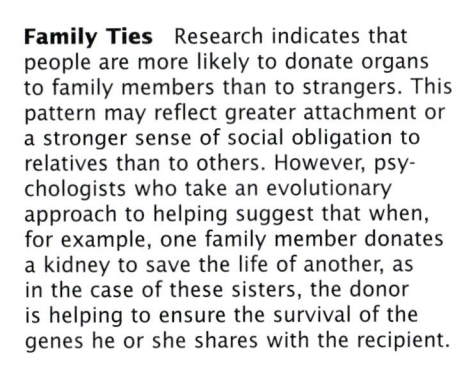

Family Ties Research indicates that people are more likely to donate organs to family members than to strangers. This pattern may reflect greater attachment or a stronger sense of social obligation to relatives than to others. However, psychologists who take an evolutionary approach to helping suggest that when, for example, one family member donates a kidney to save the life of another, as in the case of these sisters, the donor is helping to ensure the survival of the genes he or she shares with the recipient.

survival of the fittest *individuals* and not enough on the survival of their genes *in others*. Accordingly, the concept of survival of the fittest has been replaced by the concept of *inclusive fitness,* the survival of one's genes in future generations (Hamilton, 1964). Because we share genes with our relatives, helping or even dying for a cousin, a sibling, or above all, our own child potentially increases the likelihood that at least some of our genetic characteristics will be passed on to the next generation through the beneficiary's future reproduction (Burnstein & Brannigan, 2001). So *kin selection*—helping a relative to survive—may produce genetic benefits for the helper (McAndrew, 2002).

There is considerable evidence that kin selection occurs among birds, squirrels, and other animals. The more closely the animals are related, the more likely they are to risk their lives for one another. Studies in a wide variety of cultures show the same pattern of helping among humans (Buss, 1999). People in the United States are three times as likely to donate a kidney to a relative as to a nonrelative (Borgida, Conner, & Monteufel, 1992), and identical twins (who have exactly the same genes) are much more willing to help one another than are fraternal twins or siblings, who share only 50 percent of their genes (Segal, 1999).

FOCUS ON RESEARCH METHODS

Does Family Matter?

In and of themselves, data on kin selection do not confirm evolutionary theories of helping and altruism. For example, the greater tendency to donate organs to relatives could also be due to the effects of empathy toward more familiar people, pressure from family members, or other social influence processes. To control for the effects of these confounding variables, some researchers have turned to the laboratory to study the role of evolutionary forces in helping behavior.

● What was the researchers' question?

Eugene Burnstein, Christian Crandell, and Shinobu Kitayama (1994) wanted to know whether people faced with a choice of whose life to save would act in a manner consistent with the concept of kin selection. These investigators reasoned that if kin selection does affect helping, the more genetically related two people are—

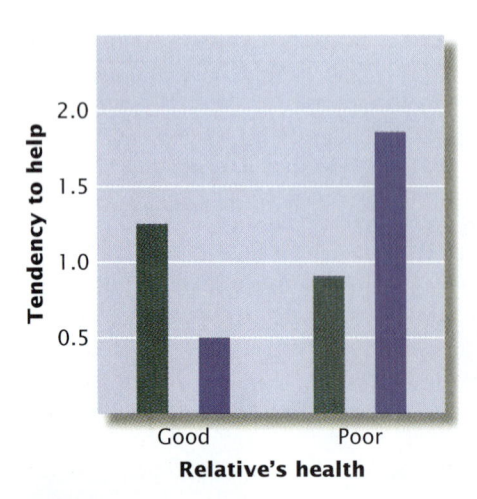

figure 18.9

Kin Selection and Helping

In this analogue experiment, students said they would be more likely to save the life of a healthy relative than a sick one, but more likely to do a favor for the sick relative. Results like these have been cited in support of evolutionary explanations of helping behavior (Burnstein, Crandell, & Kitayama, 1994).

Source: Burnstein, Crandell, & Kitayama (1994).

the more genes they share in common—the more inclined they should be to save each other's life. However, if the underlying reason for this kind of helping is actually to preserve one's genes in others, the tendency to save a close relative should be lessened if that relative is unlikely to produce offspring and thereby help preserve the helper's genes.

- **How did the researchers answer this question?**

The most direct way to test these predictions would be to put people's lives in danger and then observe which (if any) of their relatives try to save them. Such an experiment would be unthinkable, of course, so Burnstein and his colleagues used a simulation, or *analogue,* methodology. Specifically, they asked people to imagine a series of situations and then to say how they would respond if the situation were real.

The participants in their analogue experiment were 110 men and 48 women enrolled at universities in Japan and the United States. The first independent variable was the kind of help that was needed. On the basis of random assignment, some participants were asked to imagine life-or-death situations in which there was time to save only one of three people who were asleep in separate rooms of a burning house. The remaining participants were asked to imagine everyday situations in which they had time to help only one of three people who each needed a small favor. The other independent variables were the characteristics of the people needing help in each situation—their age, gender, physical health, and genetic relatedness to the potential helper. The dependent variable was the participants' choice of which person they would help.

- **What did the researchers find?**

In line with evolutionary theory, the participants were more than twice as likely to say they would save the life of a close relative than that of an unrelated friend. Also, the more closely related the endangered people were to the potential helpers, the more likely they were to be saved. Did these results occur simply because people tend to help closer relatives in any situation? Probably not; when the participants imagined situations in which only small favors were involved, they were only slightly more likely to help a close relative than a distant one.

The other major prediction of evolutionary theory was supported as well. Several different findings indicated that even close relatives might not be saved if they were unlikely to produce offspring. For example, the participants were more willing to do a small favor for a seventy-five-year-old relative than for a ten- or eighteen-year-old relative, but they were much more likely to save the lives of the younger relatives. Similarly, they were more likely to do a favor for a sick relative than for a healthy one; but in a life-or-death situation, they chose to save the healthy relative more often than the sick one (see Figure 18.9). Finally, the participants were more likely to save the life of a female relative than that of a male relative, unless the female was past childbearing age. There were no substantial differences between the responses of students in the United States and those in Japan.

- **What do the results mean?**

The results of this experiment generally support the concept of kin selection, which says that we are inclined to help close relatives because in the long run it helps us. Specifically, if we save the life of a relative and that relative is able to produce offspring, we have really helped ourselves, because more of our genes will be represented in the next generation. Evolutionary psychologists see these results as providing confirmation that kin selection affects the decisions people make about saving the life of another person, and thus that there is an evolutionary basis for helping.

- **What do we still need to know?**

The findings reported by Burnstein and his colleagues are consistent with the predictions of evolutionary theory, but they must be interpreted with caution and in light of the methods that were used to obtain them. Analogue studies give clues to behavior—and allow experimental control—in situations that approximate, but may not precisely duplicate, situations outside the laboratory. These studies tend to be used when it would be unethical or impractical to expose people to "the real thing." The more closely the analogue approximates the natural situation, the more confident we can be that conclusions drawn about behavior observed in the laboratory will apply, or generalize, to the world beyond the laboratory.

In an analogue experiment such as this one, we might question how closely the natural situation was approximated. For one thing, the participants predicted what their responses would be in hypothetical situations. Those responses might be different if the students were actually in the situations described. So although the analogue methodology in this study allowed the researchers to show that kin selection *could* play a role in human helping behavior; they did not demonstrate that it *did* play a role.

The study also failed to identify the mechanisms whereby biological tendencies are translated into thoughts that lead to helpful actions (Batson, 1998). It is highly unlikely that the participants were thinking, "I'll help a close relative because it will preserve my genes." So what conscious thoughts or feelings led to their choices? A recent analogue study by Josephine Korchmaros and David Kenny (2001) provides a partial answer to this question. In their simulation, the names of the people who needed help were those of the participants' actual family members. Further, the researchers measured the strength of the *emotional ties* between the participants and these particular people. The results suggested that genetic closeness was related to emotional closeness. Perhaps, then, emotional closeness provides the mechanism that drives the choice of whom to help. It may be that we are biologically predisposed to feel emotionally closer to closer relatives and thus more likely to help them if their lives are in danger. These feelings, in turn, serve to increase the chances that some of our genes will survive in those close relatives.

This is a reasonable possibility, but remember that even though evolutionary theory may explain some general human tendencies to help, it cannot predict the behavior of specific individuals in specific situations (Batson, 1998). Like all behavior, helping and altruism depend on the interplay of many genetic and environmental factors—including interactions between particular people and particular situations. (See "In Review: Theories of Helping Behaviors" for a summary of the major reasons why people help and the conditions under which they are most likely to do so.)

in review Theories of Helping Behaviors

Theory	Basic Premise	Important Variables
Arousal: cost-reward	People help in order to reduce the unpleasant arousal caused by another person's distress. They attempt to minimize the costs of doing this.	Factors that affect the costs of helping and of not helping.
Empathy-altruism	People sometimes help for utterly altruistic reasons. They are motivated by a desire to increase another person's well-being.	The amount of empathy that one person feels for another.
Evolutionary	People help relatives because it increases the chances that the helper's genes will survive in future generations.	The biological relationship between the helper and the recipient of help.

Cooperation, Competition, and Conflict

When people interact with one another while attempting to reach some goal, three kinds of behavior can result: cooperation, competition, or conflict. **Cooperation** is any type of behavior in which people work together to attain a goal. For example, several law students might form a study group to help one another pass a difficult exam. People can also engage in **competition**, trying to attain a goal for themselves while denying that goal to others. So those same students might later compete with one another for a single job opening at a prestigious law firm. Finally, **conflict** results when one person or group believes that another stands in the way of their achieving a goal. When the students become attorneys and represent opposing parties in a legal dispute, they will be in conflict. One way in which psychologists have learned about all three of these behaviors is by studying social dilemmas (Gifford & Hine, 1997b).

Social Dilemmas

Social dilemmas are situations in which an action that produces rewards for one individual will, if adopted by all others, produce negative consequences for everyone (Dawes & Messick, 2000). For instance, it might be in a factory owner's short-term self-interest to save the costs of pollution control by releasing untreated toxic waste; but if all factories do the same, the air and water will eventually become poisonous for everyone. One particular kind of social dilemma that psychologists have studied extensively is called the two-person "prisoner's dilemma."

The Prisoner's Dilemma
The **prisoner's dilemma** is based on a scenario in which two people are separated immediately after being arrested for a serious crime (Taylor, Peplau, & Sears, 2000). The district attorney believes they are guilty but does not have the evidence to convict them. Each prisoner can either confess or not. If they both refuse to confess, each will be convicted of a minor offense and will be jailed for one year. If they both confess, the district attorney will recommend a five-year sentence. However, if one prisoner remains silent and one confesses, the district attorney will allow the confessing prisoner to go free, whereas the other will serve the maximum ten-year sentence.

Cooperation, Competition, Conflict, and Cash Cooperation, competition, and conflict can all be seen on *Survivor*, a television series in which people try to win a million dollars by staying the longest in some remote location. Early on, contestants cooperate with members of their own teams, but as more and more people are eliminated, even team members compete with one another. When only two people remain, each stands in the way of the other's goal of winning, so they are in direct conflict.

Cooperation, Competition, and Conflict

A Social Dilemma If everyone in North America used public transportation or commuted in carpools, and if they drove small cars with fuel-efficient engines that minimized exhaust emissions, the problems of air pollution, traffic and parking, and highway construction and maintenance would be greatly reduced. However, most people like to drive to work alone, at the wheel of a car that is fun to drive and be seen in, but that may guzzle gas and take up a lot of space. In short, the choice of daily transportation reflects a social dilemma; what is good for the individual in the short run is bad for society in the long run.

cooperation Any type of behavior in which people work together to attain a goal.

competition Behavior in which individuals try to attain a goal for themselves while denying that goal to others.

conflict The result of a person's or group's belief that another person or group stands in the way of their achieving a valued goal.

social dilemmas Situations in which actions that produce rewards for one individual will produce negative consequences if adopted by everyone.

prisoner's dilemma A social dilemma in which mutual cooperation guarantees the best mutual outcome.

Each prisoner faces a dilemma. Figure 18.10(A) outlines the possible outcomes. Obviously, the strategy that will guarantee the best *mutual* outcome—short sentences for both prisoners—is cooperation: Both should remain silent. But the prisoner who remains silent runs the risk of receiving a long sentence if the other prisoner confesses, and the prisoner who confesses has the chance of gaining individually if the other prisoner does not talk. In other words, each prisoner has an incentive to compete for freedom by confessing. But if they both compete and confess, each will end up going to jail for longer than if nothing was said.

In the typical prisoner's dilemma experiment, two people sit at separate control panels. Each of them has a red button and a black button, one of which is to be pushed on each of many trials. Pressing the black button is a cooperative response; pressing the red button is a competitive response. For example, if, on a given trial, both participants press their black buttons, each wins $5. If both press their red buttons, they earn only $1. However, if one player presses the red button and the other presses the black button, the one who pressed the red button will win $10, and the other will win nothing.

Figure 18.10(B) shows the possible outcomes for each trial. Over the course of the experiment, the combined winnings of the players are greatest if each presses the black button—that is, if they cooperate. By pressing the black button, however, a player becomes open to exploitation, because on any trial the other might press the red button and take all the winnings. So each player stands to benefit the most individually by pressing the red button occasionally. The prisoner's dilemma is what psychologists call a *mixed-motive conflict*—there are good reasons to cooperate and also good reasons to compete.

What happens when people play this game? Overall, there is a strong tendency to respond competitively; people find it difficult to resist the competitive choice on any given trial (Komorita & Parks, 1995). This choice wins them more money on that trial, but in the long run they gain less than they would have gained through cooperation.

If acting competitively leads to smaller rewards in the long run, why do people persist in competing? There seem to be two reasons (Komorita, 1984). First, winning more than an opponent seems to be rewarding in itself. In the prisoner's dilemma game, many people want to outscore an opponent even if the result is that they win less money overall. Second, and more important, once several competitive responses are made, the competition seems to feed on itself (Insko et al., 1990). Each person becomes distrustful of the other, and cooperation becomes increasingly difficult. The more competitive one person acts, the more competitive the other becomes (McClintock & Liebrand, 1988).

Resource Dilemmas In recent years, psychologists interested in cooperation, competition, and conflict have concentrated on another kind of social dilemma, called a *resource dilemma* (Pruitt, 1998). In a **resource dilemma**, people share some common resource, thus creating inherent conflicts between the interests of the individual and those of the group, and also between people's short-term and long-term interests (Schroeder, 1995). There are two kinds of resource dilemmas. In the *commons dilemma,* people have to decide how much to take from a common resource; in the *public goods dilemma,* people must decide how much to contribute to a common resource. As an example of the commons dilemma, consider a situation in which farmers all draw water for their crops from the same lake. Each individual farmer would benefit greatly from unrestricted use of the water, but if all the farmers did the same, the water would soon be gone. Tax laws provide an example of the public goods dilemma. In the short run, you would benefit greatly if you did not pay taxes, but if everyone failed to pay, no one would have police and fire protection, highway repairs, national defense, or other vital government services. How can people facing such dilemmas be prompted to cooperate?

Fostering Cooperation

Communication can reduce people's tendency to act competitively (Pruitt, 1998). Unfortunately, however, not all communication increases cooperation, just as not all contact between ethnic groups reduces prejudice. If the communication takes the form of a threat, people apparently interpret the threat itself as a competitive response and are likely to respond competitively (Gifford & Hine, 1997b). Furthermore, the communication must be relevant. In one social dilemma study, cooperation increased only when people spoke openly about the dilemma and how they would be rewarded for various responses. Praising one another for past cooperation was most beneficial (Orbell, van de Kragt, & Dawes, 1988).

People can also communicate implicitly through the strategy they use. In the prisoner's dilemma, the most effective strategy for producing long-term cooperation is to use basic learning principles and play *tit-for-tat,* rewarding cooperative responses with cooperation and punishing exploitation with exploitative strategies of one's own. Cooperating after a cooperative response and competing after a competitive response produces a high degree of cooperation over time (Nowak, May, & Sigmund, 1995). Apparently, the players learn that the only way to come out ahead is to cooperate. There is even evidence from computer simulation studies that societies whose members use cooperative strategies with one another are more likely to survive and prosper than are societies whose members act competitively (Nowak, May, & Sigmund, 1995).

Interpersonal Conflict

In social dilemmas and other situations in which people are *interdependent*—that is, when what one person does always affects the other—cooperation usually leads to the best outcomes for everyone. This doesn't mean, however, that cooperation always occurs. People from collectivist cultures, in which cooperation is empha-

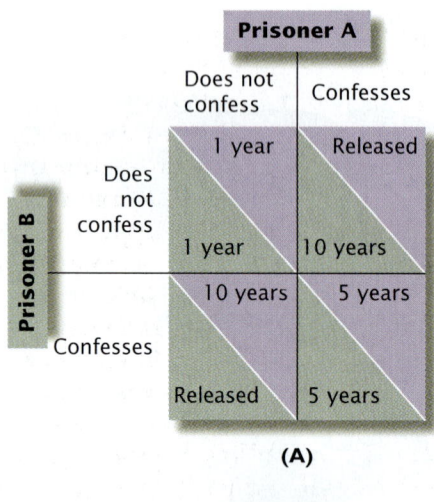

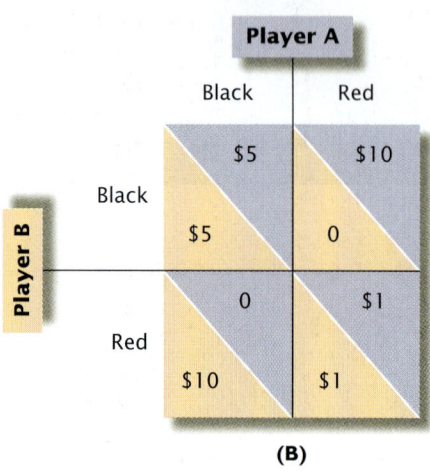

figure 18.10

The Prisoner's Dilemma

In the prisoner's dilemma, mutual cooperation benefits each person, and mutual competition is harmful to both, but one party can exploit the cooperativeness of the other. These diagrams show the potential payoffs for prisoners—and research participants—in prisoner's dilemma studies.

resource dilemma A situation in which people must share a common resource, creating conflicts between the short-term interests of individuals and the long-term interests of the group.

"There's quite a power struggle going on."

© 1999 Joseph Farris from cartoonbank.com. All Rights Reserved.

sized, are generally less likely to act selfishly in a social dilemma, but conflict in such situations does appear in all cultures (Smith & Bond, 1999). Conflict is especially likely when people are involved in a **zero-sum game**. This is a situation in which one person's gains are subtracted from the other person's resources; the sum of the gains and losses is zero. Election campaigns, lawsuits over a deceased relative's estate, and competition between children for a coveted toy are all examples of zero-sum games.

There are four major causes of interpersonal conflict (Baron & Byrne, 1994). One is *competition for scarce resources*. If a business has only five offices with windows, for example, employees will compete for them. Some managers report spending as much as 20 percent of their time dealing with interpersonal conflicts based on such competition (Thomas & Schmidt, 1976). A second major cause of interpersonal conflict is *revenge*. People reciprocate not only positive actions but also negative ones. Some people who feel exploited, deprived, or otherwise aggrieved spend months, or even years, plotting ways of getting back at those they hold responsible (Baron & Richardson, 1994).

Interpersonal conflict may also arise because people *attribute unfriendly or selfish motives to others* (Gifford & Hine, 1997a). For example, conflict is likely to emerge if people who must share some resource, such as printer paper, attribute a shortage of that resource to the other people's selfishness rather than to factors over which they have no control, such as an inadequate supply (Samuelson & Messick, 1995). Sometimes these attributions are accurate, but often conflict results from the kinds of attributional errors discussed in the chapter on social cognition.

Attributional errors are related to a final source of interpersonal conflict: *faulty communication*. A comment intended as a compliment is sometimes interpreted as a snide remark; constructive criticism is sometimes perceived as a personal attack. Such miscommunication may start a cycle of increasingly provocative actions, in which each person believes the other is being aggressive and unfair (Pruitt & Carnevale, 1993).

Managing Conflict

Interpersonal conflict can damage relationships among people and impair the effectiveness of organizations, but it can also lead to beneficial changes. Industrial/organizational psychologists have found that often it is much better to manage conflict effectively than to try to eliminate it. The most common way of managing organizational conflict is through *bargaining*. Each side—labor and management, for example—produces a series of offers and counteroffers until a solution that is acceptable to both sides emerges. At its best, bargaining can produce a win-win situation in which each side receives what is most important and gives up what is less important (Carnevale & Pruitt, 1992).

If bargaining fails, *third-party interventions* may be useful. Like a therapist working with a couple, an outside mediator can often help the two sides in an organizational conflict focus on important issues, defuse emotions, clarify positions and proposals, and make suggestions that allow each side to compromise without losing face (Pruitt, 1998).

Other techniques for managing conflict, especially conflict over resources, involve the introduction of *superordinate goals* or a *superordinate identity* (Williams, Jackson, & Karau, 1995). For example, if people who are competing for scarce resources can be made to feel that they are all part of the same group and share the same goals, they will act less selfishly and manage the limited resources more efficiently. Focusing on larger common goals was part of what created the unprecedented level of cooperation among people all over the United States following the September 11, 2001, terrorist attacks on New York City and Washington, D.C.

In short, although interpersonal conflict can be harmful if left unchecked, it can also be managed in a way that benefits the group. Much as psychotherapy can help people resolve personal conflict in a way that leads to growth, interpersonal conflict within an organization can be handled in a way that leads to innovations, increased loyalty and motivation, and other valuable changes.

zero-sum game A social situation in which one person's gains are subtracted from another person's resources, so that the sum of the gains and losses is zero.

Group Processes

Although Western industrialized cultures tend to emphasize individuals over groups, the fact remains that most important governmental and business decisions in those cultures and elsewhere are made by groups, not individuals (Cannon-Bowers & Salas, 1998). Sometimes group processes are effective, as when a team of doctors, nurses, specialists, and two parents brought the McCaughey septuplets into the world on November 19, 1997. At other times, group processes can have disastrous results, as we will see later. In the chapter on cognition and language, we describe some of the factors that influence the nature and quality of group decisions. Here, we consider some of the social psychological processes that often occur in groups to alter the behavior of their members and the quality of their collective efforts.

Group Leadership

A good leader can help a group pursue its goals; a poor one can impede a group's functioning. What makes a good leader? Early research suggested that the personalities of good and bad leaders were about the same, but we now know that certain personality traits often distinguish effective from ineffective leaders. For example, using tests similar to those that measure the big-five traits described in the chapter on personality, Colin Silverthorne (2001) examined the characteristics of leaders in the United States, Thailand, and China. He found that effective leaders in all three countries tended to score high on agreeableness, emotional stability, extraversion, and conscientiousness. Other researchers have found that in general, effective leaders are intelligent, success oriented, and flexible (Levine & Moreland, 1998).

Having particular personality traits does not guarantee good leadership ability, however. People who are effective leaders in one situation may be ineffective in another (Yukl & Van Fleet, 1992). The reason is that effective leadership also depends on the characteristics of the group members, the task at hand, and most important, the interaction between these factors and the leader's style.

Two main styles of leadership have been identified. **Task-oriented leaders** provide close supervision, lead by giving directives, and generally discourage group discussion (Yukl & Van Fleet, 1992). Their style may not endear them to group members. In contrast, **person-oriented leaders** provide loose supervision, ask for group members' ideas, and are generally concerned with subordinates' feelings. They are usually well liked by the group, even when they must reprimand someone (Taylor, Peplau, & Sears, 2000).

Research on leadership effectiveness and gender provides one explanation as to why one leadership style is not invariably better than another. According to Alice Eagly and her associates, men and women in Western cultures tend to have different leadership styles (Eagly & Johnson, 1990; Eagly, Karau, & Makhijani, 1995). Men tend to be more task oriented; women, more person oriented. One interpretation of these differences is that the gender-role learning processes described in the chapter on human development lead men and women to "specialize" in different leadership behaviors.

Overall, men and women are equally capable leaders, but men tend to be more effective when success requires a more task-oriented leader, and women tend to be more effective when success requires a more person-oriented leader. In other words, people of each gender tend to be most effective when they are acting in a manner consistent with gender-role traditions (Eagly & Karau, 1991; Eagly, Karau, & Makhijani, 1995). This may be one reason some people do not like female leaders who act in a "masculine" manner or occupy leadership positions traditionally held by men (Eagly, Makhijani, & Klonsky, 1992). In certain circumstances, such responses create bias against women leaders, particularly among male members of the groups they lead (Eagly, Makhijani, & Klonsky, 1992).

---

task-oriented leaders Leaders who provide close supervision, lead by directives, and generally discourage group discussion.

person-oriented leaders Leaders who provide loose supervision, ask for group members' ideas, and are concerned with subordinates' feelings.

A Team Effort How many people does it take to deliver a baby? Multiply your answer by seven, and you still won't come close to the number of medical professionals who, in 1997, worked as a well-organized team to ensure the healthy delivery of the McCaughey septuplets.

Most contemporary theories of leadership are known as *contingency theories* (Levine & Moreland, 1998) because they suggest that leadership effectiveness is contingent, or depends, on factors such as the leader's relations with group members and the nature of the group's task. They note, for example, that task-oriented leaders tend to be most effective when the group is working under time pressure, when the task is unstructured, and when circumstances make it unclear as to what needs to be done first and how the duties should be divided. People trapped in an elevator in a burning building, for example, need a task-oriented leader. Conversely, person-oriented leaders tend to be most effective when the task is structured and there are no severe time limitations (Chemers, 1987). These people would be particularly successful, for example, in managing an office in which the workers knew their jobs well.

Groupthink

The emphasis on group decisions in most large organizations is based on the belief that a group of people working together will make better decisions than will individuals working alone. As noted in the chapter on cognition and language, this belief is generally correct; yet under certain circumstances, groups have been known to make amazingly bad decisions (Levine & Moreland, 1998). Consider an example from 1986, when officials at the National Aeronautics and Space Administration (NASA) ignored engineers' warnings about the effects of cold weather and decided to launch the space shuttle *Challenger*. The spacecraft exploded seventy-three seconds after liftoff, killing everyone aboard. After analyzing disastrous decisions such as this one, Irving Janis (1989) proposed that they can be attributed to a phenomenon called **groupthink.** Groupthink occurs, he said, when group members are unable to realistically evaluate the options available to them or to fully consider the potential negative consequences of a contemplated decision. It is particularly likely when members of a group place a higher value on reaching a consensus than on being sure they have made the right decision.

LINKAGES (a link to Health, Stress, and Coping)

Trying to reach a consensus before a group acts is not necessarily a bad strategy. In fact, it usually produces a good decision and positive feelings about the group (Smith & Mackie, 2000). But the drive toward consensus is likely to produce groupthink and bad decisions when four conditions are present: (1) the consensus is not based on all the facts at hand, (2) group members all share certain biases, (3) members who express dissenting opinions are punished or even ejected from the group, and (4) the group leader puts pressure on the members to reach consensus (Ahlfinger & Esser, 2001; Smith & Mackie, 2000). This last condition appeared to play a crucial role in the U.S. government's decision to support a disastrously unsuccessful invasion of Cuba by anti-Castro Cubans in 1961. Before the final decision

groupthink A pattern of thinking in which group members fail to evaluate realistically the wisdom of various options and decisions.

was made, several advisers were told that President John F. Kennedy had made up his mind to support the invasion and that it was time to "close ranks with the president." This situation created enormous pressure for conformity (McCauley, 1989).

Some researchers have questioned the prevalence and dangers of groupthink (e.g., Aldag & Fuller, 1993; Park, 2000). Most researchers agree that groupthink does occur, though, and many of them have worked on developing techniques to help groups avoid it.

One way to avoid groupthink is to designate someone to take the unpopular role of "devil's advocate"—to constantly challenge the group's emerging consensus and offer additional alternatives. This person forces the group to consider all the facts and every possible decision option (Janis, 1985; Risen, 1998). Another technique is to encourage the expression of diverse opinions by allowing them to be presented anonymously. The group members might sit at separate computers and type out messages about all the options that occur to them. Each message is displayed for all to see on an electronic mail system that protects each sender's identity. This procedure allows the group to discuss the options via e-mail without knowing who is saying what. Research on this technique suggests that it is effective in stimulating logical debate and making people less inhibited about disagreeing with the group (O'Brien, 1991).

LINKAGES

As noted in the chapter on introducing psychology, all of psychology's subfields are related to one another. Our discussion of how the presence of other people affects a person's motivation to perform illustrates just one way in which the topic of this chapter, social influence, is linked to the subfield of motivation and emotion (see the chapter on that topic). The Linkages diagram shows ties to two other subfields as well, and there are many more ties throughout the book. Looking for linkages among subfields will help you see how they all fit together and help you better appreciate the big picture that is psychology.

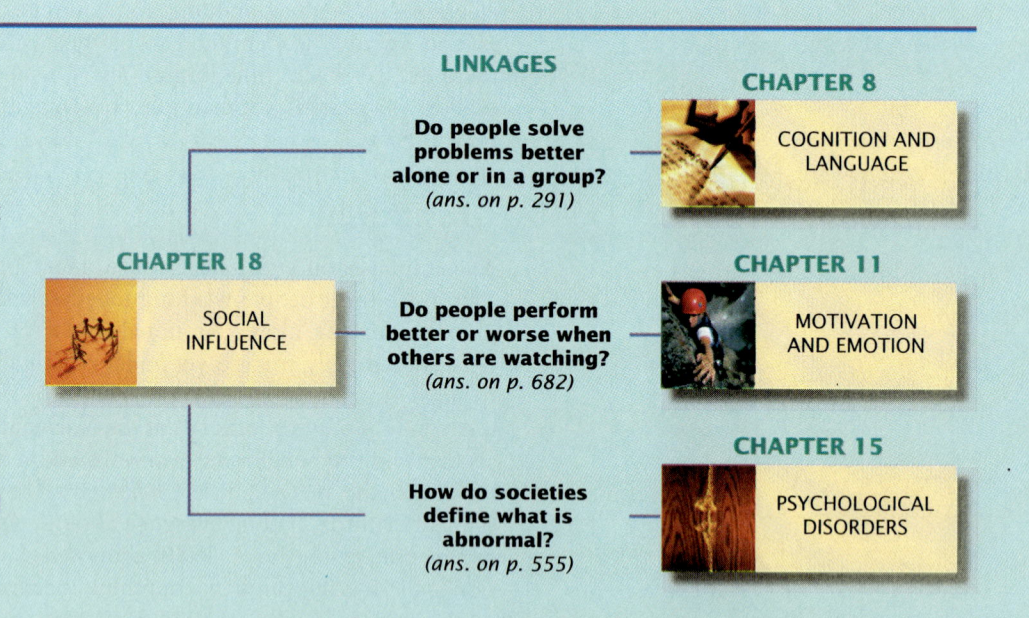

LINKAGES

CHAPTER 18 — SOCIAL INFLUENCE

- Do people solve problems better alone or in a group? (ans. on p. 291) — **CHAPTER 8** COGNITION AND LANGUAGE
- Do people perform better or worse when others are watching? (ans. on p. 682) — **CHAPTER 11** MOTIVATION AND EMOTION
- How do societies define what is abnormal? (ans. on p. 555) — **CHAPTER 15** PSYCHOLOGICAL DISORDERS

SUMMARY

Social Influence

Norms establish the rules for what should and should not be done in a particular situation. Descriptive norms indicate what most other people do and create pressure to do the same. Injunctive norms provide specific information about what others approve or disapprove of. *Deindividuation* is a psychological state in which people temporarily lose their individuality, their normal inhibitions are relaxed, and they may perform aggressive or illegal acts that they would not do otherwise.

Social facilitation, *social impairment*, and *social loafing* provide three other examples of how the presence of other people can affect an individual's behavior.

Conformity and Compliance

When behavior or beliefs change as the result of unspoken or implicit group pressure, *conformity* has occurred; when the change is the result of a request, *compliance* has occurred.

Summary

The Role of Norms
People tend to follow the normative responses of others, and groups create norms when none already exist.

Why Do People Conform?
People sometimes exhibit public conformity without private acceptance; at other times, the responses of other people have a genuine impact on private beliefs. People conform because they want to be right, because they want to be liked, and because they tend to be rewarded for doing so.

When Do People Conform?
People are most likely to conform when the situation is ambiguous, as well as when others in the group are in unanimous agreement. Up to a point, conformity usually increases as the number of people holding the majority view grows larger. Persistent and unanimous *minority influence* can also produce some conformity.

Inducing Compliance
Effective strategies for inducing compliance include the foot-in-the-door technique, the door-in-the-face procedure, and the low-ball approach.

Obedience
Obedience involves complying with an explicit demand, typically from an authority figure. Research by Stanley Milgram indicates that levels of obedience are high even when obeying an authority appears to result in pain and suffering for another person.

Factors Affecting Obedience
People obey someone who has certain kinds of social power. Obedience declines when the status of the authority figure declines, as well as when others are observed to disobey. Some people may be more likely to obey orders than others.

Evaluating Milgram's Studies
Because participants in Milgram's studies experienced considerable stress, the experiments have been questioned on ethical grounds. Nevertheless, Milgram's research showed that even apparently "normal" people can be influenced to inflict pain on others.

Aggression
Aggression is an act intended to harm another person.

Why Are People Aggressive?
Sigmund Freud saw aggression as due partly to self-destructive instincts. More recent theories attribute aggressive tendencies to genetic factors, brain dysfunctions, and hormonal influences. Learning is also important; people learn to display aggression by watching others and by being rewarded for aggressive behavior. There are wide cultural differences in the incidence of aggression.

When Are People Aggressive?
A variety of emotional factors play a role in aggression. The *frustration-aggression hypothesis* suggests that frustration can lead to aggression, particularly if cues that invite or promote aggression are present. Recent research indicates that stress and negative feelings play a major role in aggression. Arousal from sources unrelated to aggression, such as exercise, can also make aggressive responses more likely, especially if aggression is already a dominant response in that situation. Research in *environmental psychology* suggests that factors such as high temperature, air pollution, noise, and crowding increase the likelihood of aggressive behavior, particularly among people who are already angry.

Altruism and Helping Behavior
Human behavior is also characterized by *helping behavior* and *altruism*.

Why Do People Help?
There are three major theories of why people help others. According to the *arousal: cost-reward theory*, people help in order to reduce the unpleasant arousal they experience when others are in distress. Their specific reaction to a suffering person depends on the costs associated with helping or not helping. Helping behavior is most likely when the costs of helping are low and the costs of not helping are high. Perceptions of cost are affected by the clarity of the need for help, diffusion of responsibility, and personality traits. Environmental factors also affect willingness to help. The *empathy-altruism theory* suggests that helping can be truly unselfish if the helper feels empathy for the person in need. Evolutionary theory suggests that humans have an innate tendency to help others, especially relatives, because doing so increases the likelihood that family genes will survive.

Cooperation, Competition, and Conflict
Cooperation is behavior in which people work together to attain a goal; *competition* exists when individuals try to attain a goal while denying that goal to others; *conflict* occurs when a person or group believes that someone stands in the way of something of value.

Social Dilemmas
In *social dilemmas*, selfish behavior that benefits individuals in the short run may spell disaster in the long run if adopted by an entire group. Two kinds of social dilemmas are the *prisoner's dilemma* and *resource dilemmas*. When given a choice between cooperation and competition in a social dilemma, people often compete with one another. This is true even though they may receive fewer rewards for competing than for cooperating.

Fostering Cooperation
Communication between competing parties can increase cooperation, especially if the communication is nonthreatening and relevant to the situation. One of the most effective strategies for producing long-term cooperation in a prisoner's dilemma is

rewarding cooperative responses with cooperation and punishing exploitation by using exploitative strategies of one's own.

Interpersonal Conflict

In *zero-sum games*, competition is almost inevitable, because there can be only one winner. Competition for scarce resources, revenge, attribution of another's behavior to unfriendly motives, and faulty communication are frequent sources of interpersonal conflict. Bargaining, third-party interventions, and reminders about broader goals and shared identity are helpful procedures for managing conflict.

Group Processes

Many of the world's most important decisions are made by groups.

Group Leadership

No single personality type or behavioral style always results in good leadership. *Task-oriented leaders* are most effective when the task is unstructured and the group is working under time pressure. *Person-oriented leaders* are most effective when the task is structured and there are no severe time limitations. Contingency theories of leadership effectiveness propose that success depends on the extent to which a leader's style fits the characteristics of the group and its tasks.

Groupthink

The pattern of thinking called *groupthink* occurs when the desire to reach a consensus becomes more important than the need to reach the best decision.

APPENDIX

Behavioral Genetics

Think about some trait on which you are well above or well below average. Perhaps it relates to your skill at sports, languages, or music, or maybe to your fearfulness, sociability, or other aspects of personality. Have you ever wondered what made you the way you are? If you are shy, for example, it is easy to think of possible environmental explanations. Perhaps you are shy because as a child you had few opportunities to meet new children or because you had embarrassing or unpleasant experiences when you did meet them. Maybe you have shy parents who served as the role models you imitated. Such environmental explanations are certainly reasonable, but it is also possible that you inherited a disposition toward shyness from your parents.

Topics such as these are addressed by researchers in the field of *behavioral genetics,* the study of how genes affect behavior (see the chapter on research in psychology). These researchers have developed methods to explore genetic, as well as environmental, origins of behavioral differences among people. The results of behavioral genetics research make it clear that heredity has a surprisingly strong influence, not just on shyness but on personality more generally, on cognitive abilities, on psychological disorders, and on many other aspects of human behavior and mental processes. However, behavioral genetics is just as much the study of environment as of genetics. In the process of trying to disentangle genetic from environmental factors, researchers have made several important discoveries about the impact of the environment.

In this appendix, we discuss behavioral genetics in more detail than in the chapter on research in psychology. We begin with a review of the biochemical mechanisms underlying genetics and heredity. We then offer a brief history of genetic research in psychology, followed by a discussion of what research on genetic influences can and cannot tell us about the origins of human differences. Finally, we describe some findings from behavioral genetics research that illuminate several important aspects of human behavior and mental processes.

The Biology of Genetics and Heredity

What does it mean to say that someone has genetically inherited some physical feature or behavioral trait? The answer lies in **genetics,** the biology of inheritance. The story begins with the chemistry of the human body and with the chromosomes contained within each of the body's cells. Most human cells contain forty-six chromosomes, arranged in twenty-three matching pairs. These **chromosomes** are long, thin structures that are made up of thousands of genes. **Genes** are the biochemical units of heredity that govern the development of an individual by controlling the synthesis of protein. They are composed of **deoxyribonucleic acid (DNA)**—strands of sugar, phosphate, and four kinds of nitrogen-containing molecules twisted around each other in a double spiral (see Figure 1). It is the particular order in which the four nitrogen-containing molecules are arranged in the DNA that determines, through the production of *ribonucleic acid (RNA),* which protein each gene will produce. Protein molecules, in turn, form the physical structure of each cell and also direct the activity of the cell. So as a function of DNA, the genes contain a coded message that provides a blueprint for constructing every aspect of a physical human being, including eye color, height, blood type, inherited disorders, and the like—and all in less space than the period that ends this sentence.

New cells are constantly being produced by the division of existing cells. Most of the body's cells divide through a process called *mitosis,* in which the cell's

genetics The biology of inheritance.
chromosomes Long, thin structures in every biological cell that contain genetic information.
genes The biological instructions, inherited from both parents and located on the chromosomes, that provide the blueprint for physical development.
deoxyribonucleic acid (DNA) The molecular structure of a gene that provides the genetic code.

| The human body contains 100 trillion *cells*. | There is a *nucleus* inside each human cell (except red blood cells). | Each nucleus contains 46 *chromosomes*, arranged in 23 pairs. | One *chromosome* of every pair is from each parent. | The chromosomes are filled with tightly coiled strands of *DNA*. | Genes are segments of DNA that contain instructions to make proteins—the building blocks of life. |

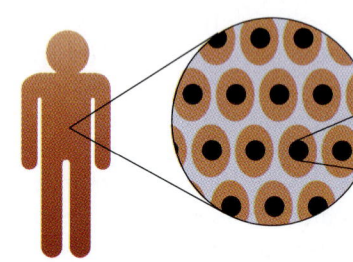

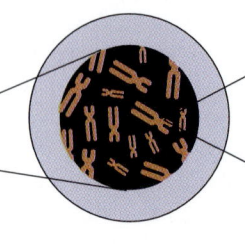

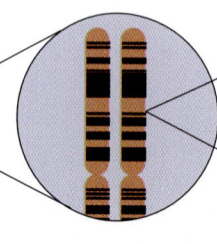

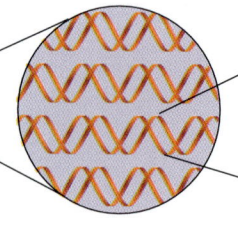

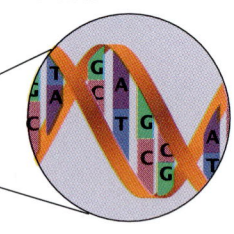

figure 1

Genetic Building Blocks

Only about 3 percent of DNA contains genes that guide the production of proteins, but it nevertheless determines all aspects of our physical bodies, and influences many of our behavioral characteristics, too.

"Genetic Building Blocks" from *Time*, January 17, 1994. Copyright © 1994 TIME, Inc. Reprinted with permission.

chromosomes duplicate themselves so that each new cell contains copies of the twenty-three pairs of chromosomes in the original.

A different kind of cell division occurs when a male's sperm cells and a female's egg cells (called *ova*) are formed. This process is called *meiosis*. In meiosis, the chromosome pairs are not copied. Instead, they are randomly split and rearranged, leaving each new sperm and egg cell with just one member of each chromosome pair, or twenty-three single chromosomes. No two of these special new cells are quite the same, and none contains an exact copy of the person who produced it. So at conception, when a male's sperm cell *fertilizes* the female's ovum, a truly new cell is formed. This fertilized cell, called a *zygote*, carries twenty-three pairs of chromosomes—half of each pair from the mother and half from the father. The zygote represents a unique heritage, a complete genetic code for a new person that combines genes from both parents. As described in the chapter on human development, the zygote divides first into copies of itself and then into the billions of specialized cells that form a new human being.

Whether or not genes express themselves in the individual who carries them depends on whether they are dominant or recessive. *Dominant* genes are outwardly expressed whenever they are present; *recessive* genes are expressed only when they are paired with a similar gene from the other parent. For example, phenylketonuria (PKU)—a disorder seen in about 1 in 10,000 newborns—is caused by a recessive gene. When inherited from both parents, this gene disrupts the body's ability to control phenylalanine, an amino acid found in milk and other foods. As a result, this acid is converted into a toxic substance that can cause severe mental retardation. (Discovery of this genetic defect made it possible to prevent retardation in children with PKU simply by making sure they did not consume foods high in phenylalanine.) PKU is one of more than 4,000 single-gene disorders, but in fact, relatively few human characteristics are controlled by just one gene. Most characteristics are **polygenic**, meaning that they are controlled by many genes. Even a person's eye color and height are affected by more than one gene.

The genes contained in the forty-six chromosomes inherited from parents make up an individual's **genotype**. Because identical twins develop from one fertilized egg cell, they are described as *monozygotic*; they have exactly the same genotype. So, why don't all identical twins look exactly alike? Because they do not have the same environment. An individual's **phenotype** is the set of observable characteristics that result from the interaction of heredity and environment. In twins and nontwins alike, the way people actually look and act is influenced by the combination of genes they carry, as well as by environmental factors—in other words, by both nature and nurture.

polygenic A term describing characteristics that are determined by more than one gene.

genotype The full set of genes, inherited from both parents, contained in twenty-three pairs of chromosomes.

phenotype How an individual looks and acts, which depends on how inherited characteristics interact with the environment.

A Brief History of Genetic Research in Psychology

The field now known as behavioral genetics began in the late 1800s with the work of Sir Francis Galton. A cousin of Charles Darwin, Galton was so impressed with Darwin's book on evolution that he decided to study heredity in the human species, especially as it related to human behavior. Galton suggested the family, twin, and adoption study designs that are the mainstays of human behavioral genetics research today (see the chapter on research in psychology). He even coined the phrase *nature-nurture* to refer to genetic and environmental influences. Galton's most famous behavioral genetics study was one in which he showed that genius runs in families. Unfortunately, Galton went too far in interpreting the evidence from this family study when he concluded that "nature prevails enormously over nurture" (Galton, 1883, p. 241). As noted in the chapter on research in psychology, family similarity can be due to environmental, as well as hereditary, factors. Still, Galton's work helped to stimulate psychologists' interest in the influence of genetics. The first twin and adoption studies were conducted in 1924. Both focused on IQ, and both suggested the existence of an important genetic contribution to intelligence.

However, research on the influence of genetics on behavior and mental processes was inhibited for a while because of two factors. The first was the impact of John B. Watson's behaviorism, which, as mentioned in the introductory chapter, suggested that we are what we learn. In 1925, Watson insisted "that there is no such thing as an inheritance of capacity, talent, temperament, mental constitution and characteristics. These things again depend on training that goes on mainly in the cradle" (Watson, 1925, pp. 74–75). The second factor discouraging attention to human genetics was its association with the view proclaimed by Adolf Hitler and his Nazis that certain groups of people were "genetically inferior." This view led to the Holocaust during World War II, a campaign of genocide during which millions of Jews and other allegedly "inferior" people were killed.

Genetic research on human behavior was reduced to a trickle during the 1930s and 1940s, but research with animals led, in 1960, to publication of the first behavioral genetics textbook (Fuller & Thompson, 1960) and to signs of increased interest in human genetics. In 1963 an influential article reviewed family, twin, and adoption findings and concluded that genetic factors are an important influence on IQ (Erlenmeyer-Kimling & Jarvik, 1963). Around the same time, the first adoption study of schizophrenia pointed to a strong genetic contribution to that disorder (Heston, 1966).

In the early 1970s, however, interest in human behavioral genetics among psychologists faded again, this time because of reactions to two publications. The first was a paper by Arthur Jensen suggesting that differences in average IQ between blacks and whites might be partly due to genetic factors (Jensen, 1969). The second was a book by Richard Herrnstein in which he argued that genetics might contribute to social class differences (Herrnstein, 1973). The furious public and scientific response to these publications—which included branding the authors as racists—inhibited genetic research in psychology, even though very few behavioral geneticists were studying ethnic or class differences. It was not until later in the 1970s and into the 1980s that major genetic studies were again conducted in psychology.

Today most psychologists recognize the role of both genetics and environment in behavior and mental processes, including the controversial area of cognitive abilities (Snyderman & Rothman, 1987). In fact, in 1992 the American Psychological Association selected behavioral genetics as one of two themes best representing the past, present, and especially the future of psychological research (Plomin & McClearn, 1993). To some, though, the study of human behavioral genetics still carries a hint of racism and class elitism. These concerns were resurrected nearly a decade ago by a book titled *The Bell Curve,* which considers the role of genetics in ethnic differences in intelligence and the implications of intelligence for social class structure (Herrnstein & Murray, 1994). Fortunately, reaction to that book has not altered the balanced perspective that recognizes the importance of nature as well as nurture in psychology (Neisser, 1997; Pinker, 2002).

The Focus of Research in Behavioral Genetics

Much of the controversy about behavioral genetics, and about nature and nurture in general, comes from misunderstandings about what behavioral genetics researchers study and, more specifically, what it means to say that genes influence behavior.

For one thing, behavioral genetics is the study of genetic and environmental factors responsible for *differences* among individuals or groups of individuals, not for the characteristics of a single individual. Consider height, for example. Identical twins are much more similar in height than are fraternal twins (who share no more genes than other siblings), and individuals who are genetically related but raised separately are just as similar in height as are relatives reared together. Further, genetically unrelated individuals reared together are no more similar in height than random pairs of individuals. These data suggest, not surprisingly, that height is highly *heritable*. This means that much of the *variability* in height that we see among people—actually about 80 percent of it—can be explained by genetic differences among them rather than by environmental differences. (It does not mean that a person who is six feet tall grew 80 percent of that height because of genes and the other 20 percent because of environment!) It also follows that if a person is, say, shorter than average, genetic reasons are probably the primary cause. We say "probably" because finding a genetic influence on height involves referring only to the origins of average individual differences in the population. So although the difference in people's heights is attributable mainly to genetic factors, a particular person's height could be due mainly to an early illness or other growth-stunting environmental factors.

To see how this logic applies to conclusions about psychological characteristics, suppose a researcher found that the heritability of a personality trait is 50 percent. This result would mean that approximately half of the differences among people on that trait are attributable to genetic factors. It would not mean that each person inherits half of the trait and gets the other half from environmental influences. As in our height example, behavioral geneticists want to know how much variability among people can be accounted for by genetic and environmental factors. The results of their research allow generalizations about the influence of nature and nurture on certain characteristics, but those generalizations do not necessarily apply to the origin of a particular person's characteristics.

Another misconception about genetic influences is that they are "hard-wired" and thus have inevitable effects. This is true in the case of single-gene disorders such as PKU, but more complex traits—intelligence, for example—are influenced by many genes, as well as by many environmental factors. So genetic influence means just that—influence (Plomin, Owen, & McGuffin, 1994). Genes can affect a trait without completely determining whether or not it will appear.

The Role of Genetic Factors in Psychology

It is no coincidence that the areas of psychology in which genes have been found to play an important role are areas that focus on individual differences—cognitive abilities, personality, and psychological disorders. Much less is known about individual differences in areas such as sensation, perception, consciousness, learning, memory, and motivation and emotion. Consequently, much less behavioral genetics research has been conducted on those variables. Nonetheless, enough is known about genetic factors to suggest that they probably influence every area of psychology to some extent. In the following sections, we consider behavioral genetics research results that tell a little more of the story about how genes can have an impact on behavior and mental processes.

Genetic Influences over the Life Span

One particularly interesting finding about genetic influences on general cognitive ability is that these influences continue to increase throughout the life span (McGue et al., 1993; Plomin, 1986). That is, the proportion of individual differences (variance) in IQ scores that can be explained by genetic factors increases from 40 percent in childhood to 60 percent in adolescence and young adulthood and then to 80 percent later in life. This increase in the magnitude of genetic influence can be seen, for example, in the expanding difference between IQ correlations for identical twins and those for fraternal twins: Identical twins become more similar in IQ over the life span, whereas fraternal twins become less similar as the years go by. This finding is all the more interesting for overturning the common assumption that environmental influences become increasingly important as accidents, illnesses, and other experiences accumulate throughout life. We still do not have enough data available to permit firm conclusions about whether the magnitude of genetic influences on other traits changes during development.

How can it be that genetic influences become more important over time? One possible explanation is that, as discussed later, genetic predispositions lead people to select, and even create, environments that foster the continued development of their genetically influenced abilities.

Genes Affecting Multiple Traits

Behavioral genetics research has also revealed that genes affecting one trait can sometimes affect others as well. For example, it appears that the same genetic factors affecting anxiety also affect depression (Kendler et al., 1992). So if we could identify specific genes responsible for genetic influences on anxiety, we would expect to find that the same genes were associated with the appearance of depression.

A similar finding has emerged for cognitive ability and scholastic achievement. Tests of scholastic achievement show almost as much genetic influence as do tests of cognitive ability. Moreover, tests of scholastic achievement correlate substantially with tests of cognitive ability. To what extent is a common set of genes responsible for this overlap? Research suggests that the answer is "almost entirely." It appears that the genes influencing performance on mental ability tests are the same ones that influence students' performance at school (Wadsworth, 1994).

Identifying Genes Related to Behavior

One of the most exciting new developments in behavioral genetics involves identifying the specific genes responsible for genetic influences in psychology (Plomin & Crabbe, 2000). As noted earlier, for example, there are hundreds of rare, single-gene disorders that affect behavior. One of these is *Huntington's disease*, an ultimately fatal disorder that involves loss of motor control and progressive deterioration of the central nervous system. Huntington's disease emerges only in adulthood, beginning with personality changes, forgetfulness, and other behavioral problems. It is caused by a single dominant gene whose identification in 1983 made it possible to determine who will get this disease—even though the mechanism for the disorder is still not understood, and prevention is not yet possible.

Researchers are also tracking down the several genes involved in the appearance of Alzheimer's disease. (As described in the chapter on biological aspects of psychology, Alzheimer's disease causes memory loss and increasing confusion in many older people.) One of these genes, a gene that contributes to the risk for late-onset Alzheimer's disease, was identified in 1993. This gene increases the risk for Alzheimer's disease about fivefold, but its presence is neither necessary nor sufficient for the disease to appear. That is, many people with Alzheimer's disease do not have the gene, and many people with the gene do not have the disease. Nonetheless, this gene is by far the strongest risk factor known for Alzheimer's disease, and its discovery marks the beginning of a new era in which specific genes—or regions of DNA near specific genes—will be identified as influencing disorders and psychological traits. Additional examples include reports of linkages between DNA and reading disability (Cardon et al., 1994), hyperactivity (Faraone et al., 2001), and autism (International Molecular Genetic Study of Autism Consortium, 1998). Progress in identifying specific genes in humans has been slower than expected in part because research ethics and common sense prevent the use of selective breeding. Accordingly, human studies have lacked the statistical power needed to detect relatively weak, but still potentially important, genetic influences on behavior (Plomin et al., 2002). However, the more powerful genetic research techniques available in studies of animals have identified several genes associated, for example, with fearfulness (Flint et al., 1995), with sensitivity to drugs such as alcohol (Crabbe et al., 1999), and with various aspects of learning and memory (Wahlsten, 1999).

Future efforts to identify genes related to human behavior will be aided by advances flowing from the Human Genome Project, which in early 2001 succeeded in identifying the sequence of most of the 3 billion "letters" of DNA in the human genome. One of the most surprising findings of that project so far is that the human genome appears to contain only about 30,000 to 40,000 genes—less than half the number expected, and a number that is similar to the estimates for animals such as mice and worms. Does this smaller-than-expected number of human genes mean that there are too few to influence all aspects of human behavior, and that the environment (nurture) must be even more important than we thought in this regard? Not necessarily. It may be that the greater complexity seen in human behavior versus, say, mouse behavior stems not from the number of genes we have but from the greater complexities involved in decoding our genes into proteins. Human genes, more than the genes of other species, are spliced in alternative ways to create a greater variety of proteins. It may be this more subtle *variation* in genes—not the number of genes—that is responsible for differences between mice and people. This possibility has important implications for behavioral genetics because if subtle DNA differences are responsible for the obvious differences between humans and other species, then individual differences within our species—in other words, among people—are likely to involve genetic factors that are even more subtle and hard to find.

Fortunately, new techniques are available that make it possible to detect DNA differences for many thousands of genes simultaneously. These techniques will help in identifying genes related to behavior, a process which will fill in the causal picture about a variety of characteristics and disorders that are influenced by many genes and many environmental factors.

Behavioral Genetics and Environmental Influences

As suggested earlier, research on genetic influences in psychology has also provided some of the best evidence for the importance of environmental influences. It has shown that even though genetic influences are important, they cannot explain everything about human behavior. We must always remember the crucial role of environmental influences—particularly now, when explanations for human behavior seem to increasingly favor nature over nurture.

For example, as already noted, twin and adoption studies have provided evidence of the importance of genetic factors in schizophrenia, and as a result, many researchers are now trying to identify the specific genes responsible. Enthusiasm for genetic explanations of schizophrenia makes it easy to forget, however, that environmental factors can be at least as important as genes. As described in the chapter on psychological disorders, when one member of an identical-twin pair is schizophrenic, the chances are about 40 percent that the other member of the pair is also schizophrenic. This result surely provides evidence of a strong genetic contribution to schizophrenia, but it also suggests that schizophrenia appears in both identical twins only 40 percent of the time. Most of the time, the identical twin of a person with schizophrenia will not display the disorder. Such differences within pairs of identical twins can be due only to the operation of environmental factors.

In fact, research generally suggests that genetic factors account for less than half of the variance among individuals for psychological characteristics such as personality and psychopathology. This means that at least half of the variance among individuals on these characteristics is due to environmental factors. These environmental—or more properly, *nongenetic*—factors encompass everything other than genetic inheritance. They include such biological factors as prenatal events, nutrition, and illnesses, as well as more traditional environmental factors such as parenting, schooling, and peer influences.

In short, one of the most important findings to emerge from behavioral genetics research has concerned not genetics but the environment. That research suggests that the most important environmental influences are likely to be those that different family members do not share (Plomin, Asbury, & Dunn, 2001). Psychologists need to find out more about these *nonshared factors* and how they act to create differences in children—twins or not—who grow up in the same family (Turkheimer & Waldron, 2000).

So far, research on this topic has shown that children growing up in the same family actually experience quite different environments, especially in relation to their parents. Siblings perceive that their parents treat them very differently—and indeed, observational studies back up such perceptions of differential treatment (Plomin, Asbury, & Dunn, 2001). Even events such as parental divorce, which would seem to be shared by all children in the family, appear to be experienced very differently by each child, depending especially upon age, personality, and the nature of the relationship with each parent.

Research is also beginning to focus on environmental influences beyond the family—such as relationships with teachers or friends—which are even more likely than home-related factors to vary among siblings. If you have a brother or sister, think about a psychological trait on which you and your sibling differ—confidence, for example. Why do you think you two are different on that trait? Perhaps one of you experienced a loss of self-confidence when faced with the demands of an impatient grade school teacher or after being betrayed by a childhood friend. Did these differing experiences occur randomly and thus make you considerably more confident or less confident than your sibling? Or is it possible that differences in your genetic makeups helped bring about these different experiences? Unless you and your sibling are identical twins, you share only about 50 percent of your genes. Perhaps genetically influenced differences between the two of you—in emotionality or other aspects of temperament, for example—caused parents, peers, and others to respond to each of you differently. This brings us to the second major discovery about the environment to emerge from research on behavioral genetics: Environmental influences that appear to cause differences between siblings might themselves be caused by genetic differences between the siblings.

In the past decade, most of the measures used by psychologists to assess environmental factors have been shown to be influenced by genetic factors (Plomin & Bergeman, 1991). These measures include, for example, adolescents' ratings of how their parents treated them, observations of parent-child interactions, and questionnaires about life events and social support. If scores on measures such as these reflected only environmental factors, then the scores of identical twins should be no more similar to each other than those of fraternal twins. By the same token, there should be little similarity in environmental-experience measures for genetically related individuals who grew up in different families.

The results reported by behavioral geneticists do not fit these expectations (Plomin, 1994b; Reiss et al., 2000). For example, parents differ in terms of how responsive they are to their children, but these differences in responsiveness correlate with the children's cognitive ability—a trait that has a clear genetic component. So, as described in the chapters on cognitive abilities and human development, parental responsiveness can influence cognitive development, and—as behavioral genetics research suggests—children's inherited cognitive abilities can alter the responsiveness of their parents. That is, parents tend to be more responsive to bright children who ask lots of questions and are interested in the answers.

Outside the family, too, genetic factors appear to play a role in generating environmental experiences (Harris, 1998). For example, research on the characteristics of children's peer groups shows that children tend to choose their friends—and to be chosen as friends—partly on the basis of genetically influenced traits, such as mental ability and temperament (Manke et al., 1995). Several studies also suggest that genetic factors can increase or decrease the likelihood of family conflicts and other social stressors that threaten one's physical and psychological well-being (Reiss et al., 2000).

An important implication of genetic influences on environmental events is that measuring the impact of family relationships, peer influences, and other environmental factors on behavior and mental processes may be more difficult than psychologists thought. A measure that is aimed at assessing an environmental factor may nonetheless be affected by the genetic characteristics of the people being studied.

In human development, nature and nurture work together. Children select, modify, and create environments that are correlated with their genetic inclinations. As developmental psychologists have long argued, children are not formless blobs of clay passively molded by the environment. Rather, they are active participants in their experiences. The new findings we have described here suggest that genetics plays an important role in those experiences (Plomin, 1994b).

SUMMARY

Behavioral genetics is the study of how genes affect behavior.

The Biology of Genetics and Heredity

Research on the ways in which nature and nurture interact to shape behavior and mental processes requires a knowledge of *genetics*, the biology of inheritance. The genetic code that transmits characteristics from one generation to the next is contained in the *deoxyribonucleic acid (DNA)* that makes up the *genes* that in turn make up *chromosomes*. Dominant genes are expressed whenever they are present; recessive genes are expressed only when inherited from both parents. Most human characteristics are controlled by more than one gene; they are *polygenic*. The genes in a person's forty-six chromosomes make up the *genotype*; the *phenotype*—how people actually look and act—is influenced by genes and the environment.

A Brief History of Genetic Research in Psychology

Sir Francis Galton's work in the nineteenth century helped to stimulate psychologists' interest in the influence of genetics on behavior. The popularity of research in this area has waxed and waned over the years, but today most psychologists recognize the role of genetic, as well as environmental, influences on many aspects of behavior and mental processes.

The Focus of Research in Behavioral Genetics

Behavioral genetics research identifies the genetic and environmental factors responsible for differences among individuals, not for the characteristics of a particular person. Although genes

Summary

can influence a trait, they may not completely determine whether that trait appears.

The Role of Genetic Factors in Psychology

Genetic factors probably influence, to some extent, every aspect of behavior and mental processes.

Genetic Influences over the Life Span

Genetic influences on general cognitive ability appear to increase over time, possibly because genetic predispositions lead people to select, and even create, environments that foster the continued development of abilities that are in line with those predispositions.

Genes Affecting Multiple Traits

Genes that affect one trait, such as anxiety, can sometimes also affect other traits, such as depression.

Identifying Genes Related to Behavior

Current research in behavioral genetics, aided by findings from the Human Genome Project, is identifying specific genes responsible for specific characteristics—especially rare, single-gene disorders such as Huntington's disease.

Behavioral Genetics and Environmental Influences

Research in behavioral genetics has actually provided evidence for the importance of environmental influences, too, because the research shows that genetics alone cannot account for such characteristics as intelligence, personality, and psychological disorders. Some of the most important environmental influences are likely to be those that members of the same family do not share. In short, neither nature nor nurture is conducting the performance of the other: They are playing a duet.

APPENDIX

Statistics in Psychological Research

Understanding and interpreting the results of psychological research depends on *statistical analyses,* which are methods for describing and drawing conclusions from data. The chapter on research in psychology introduced some terms and concepts associated with *descriptive statistics*—the numbers that psychologists use to describe and present their data—and with *inferential statistics*—the mathematical procedures used to draw conclusions from data and to make inferences about what they mean. Here, we present more details about these statistical analyses that will help you to evaluate research results.

Describing Data

To illustrate our discussion, consider a hypothetical experiment on the effects of incentives on performance. The experimenter presents a list of mathematics problems to two groups of participants. Each group must solve the problems within a fixed time, but for each correct answer, the low-incentive group is paid ten cents whereas the high-incentive group gets one dollar. The hypothesis to be tested is the **null hypothesis,** the assertion that the independent variable manipulated by the experimenter will have no effect on the dependent variable measured by the experimenter. In this case, the null hypothesis holds that the size of the incentive (the independent variable) will not affect performance on the mathematics task (the dependent variable).

Assume that the experimenter has obtained a random sample of participants, assigned them randomly to the two groups, and done everything possible to avoid the confounds and other research problems discussed in the chapter on research in psychology. The experiment has been run, and the psychologist now has the data: a list of the number of correct answers given by each participant in each group. Now comes the first task of statistical analysis: describing the data in a way that makes them easy to understand.

The Frequency Histogram

The simplest way to describe the data is to draw up something like Table 1, in which all the numbers are simply listed. After examining the table, you might discern that the high-incentive group seems to have done better than the low-incentive group, but the difference is not immediately obvious. It might be even harder to see if more participants had been involved and if the scores included three-digit numbers. A picture is worth a thousand words, so a more satisfactory way of presenting the same data is in a picture-like graphic known as a **frequency histogram** (see Figure 1).

Construction of a histogram is simple. First, divide the scale for measuring the dependent variable (in this case, the number of correct solutions) into a number of categories, or "bins." The bins in our example are 1–2, 3–4, 5–6, 7–8, and 9–10. Next, sort the raw data into the appropriate bin. (For example, the score of a participant who had 5 correct answers would go into the 5–6 bin, a score of 8 would go into the 7–8 bin, and so on.) Finally, for each bin, count the number of scores in that bin and draw a bar up to the height of that number on the vertical axis of a graph. The set of bars makes up the frequency histogram.

Because we are interested in comparing the scores of two groups, there are separate histograms in Figure 1: one for the high-incentive group and one for the low-incentive group. Now the difference between groups that was difficult to see in Table 1 becomes clearly visible: More people in the high-incentive group obtained high scores than in the low-incentive group.

---

null hypothesis The assertion that the independent variable manipulated by the experimenter will have no effect on the dependent variable measured by the experimenter.

frequency histogram A graphic presentation of data that consists of a set of bars, each of which represents how frequently different values of variables occur in a data set.

descriptive statistics Numbers that summarize a set of research data.

range A measure of variability that is the difference between the highest and the lowest value in a data set.

Here are the test scores obtained by thirteen participants performing under low-incentive conditions and thirteen participants performing under high-incentive conditions.

table 1
A Simple Data Set

Low Incentive	High Incentive
4	6
6	4
2	10
7	10
6	7
8	10
3	6
5	7
2	5
3	9
5	9
9	3
5	8

figure 1

Frequency Histograms
The height of each bar of a histogram represents the number of scores falling within each range of score values. The pattern formed by these bars gives a visual image of how research results are distributed.

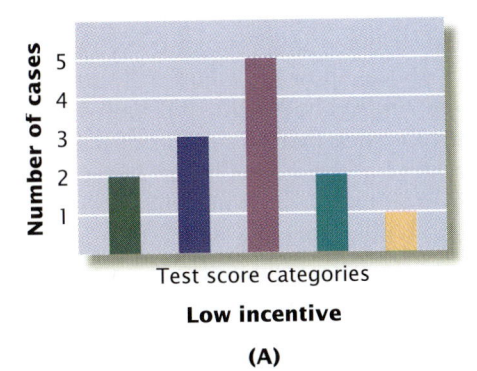

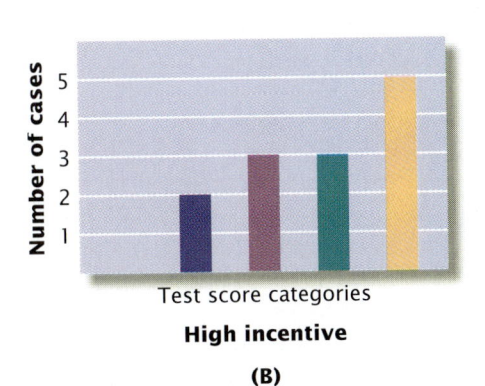

(A) Low incentive

(B) High incentive

■ 1–2 ■ 5–6 ■ 9–10
■ 3–4 ■ 7–8

Histograms and other pictures of data are useful for visualizing and better understanding the "shape" of research data, but in order to analyze data statistically, we need to use other ways of handling the data that make up these graphic presentations. For example, before we can tell whether two histograms are different statistically or just visually, the data they represent must be summarized using *descriptive statistics*.

Descriptive Statistics

The four basic categories of descriptive statistics (1) measure the number of observations made; (2) summarize the typical value of a set of data; (3) summarize the spread, or variability, in a set of data; and (4) express the correlation between two sets of data.

N The easiest statistic to compute, abbreviated as N, simply describes the number of observations that make up the data set. In Table 1, for example, $N = 13$ for each group, or 26 for the entire data set. Simple as it is, N plays a very important role in more sophisticated statistical analyses.

Measures of Central Tendency It is apparent in the histograms in Figure 1 that there is a difference in the pattern of scores between the two groups. But how much of a difference? What is the typical value, the *central tendency*, that represents each group's performance? As described in the chapter on research in psychology, there are three measures that capture this typical value: the mode, the median, and the mean. Recall that the *mode* is the value or score that occurs most frequently in the data set. The *median* is the halfway point in a set of data: Half the scores fall above the median, half fall below it. The *mean* is the arithmetic average. To find the mean, add the values of all the scores and divide by the number of scores.

Measures of Variability The variability, or spread, or dispersion of a set of data is often just as important as its central tendency. This variability can be quantified by measures known as the *range* and the *standard deviation*.

As described in the chapter on research in psychology, the **range** is simply the difference between the highest and the lowest value in a data set. For the data in Table 1, the range for the low-incentive group is $9 - 2 = 7$; for the high-incentive group, the range is $10 - 3 = 7$.

The **standard deviation**, or **SD**, measures the average difference between each score and the mean of the data set. To see how the standard deviation is calculated, consider the data in Table 2. The first step is to compute the mean of the set—in this case, 20/5 = 4. Second, calculate the difference, or *deviation* (*D*), of each score from the mean by subtracting the mean from each score, as in column 2 of Table 2. Third, find the average of these deviations. However, if you calculated the average by finding the arithmetic mean, you would sum the deviations and find that the negative deviations exactly balance the positive ones, resulting in a mean difference of 0. Obviously there is more than zero variation around the mean in the data set. So, instead of employing the arithmetic mean, we compute the standard deviation by first squaring the deviations (which removes any negative values), summing these squared deviations, dividing by *N*, and then taking the square root of the result. These simple steps are outlined in more detail in Table 2.

The Normal Distribution

Now that we have described histograms and reviewed some descriptive statistics, we will re-examine how these methods of representing research data relate to some of the concepts discussed elsewhere in the book.

In most subfields in psychology, when researchers collect many measurements and plot their data in histograms, the pattern that results often resembles that shown for the low-incentive group in Figure 1. That is, the majority of scores tend to fall in the middle of the distribution, with fewer and fewer occurring as one moves toward the extremes. As more and more data are collected, and as smaller and smaller bins are used (perhaps containing only one value each), the histograms tend to smooth out until they resemble the bell-shaped curve known as the **normal distribution**, or *normal curve*, which is shown in Figure 2(A). When a distribution of scores follows a truly normal curve, its mean, median, and mode all have the same value. Furthermore, if the curve is normal, we can use its standard deviation to describe how any particular score stands in relation to the rest of the distribution.

IQ scores provide an example. They are distributed in a normal curve, with a mean, median, and mode of 100 and an SD of 16—as shown in Figure 2(B). In such a distribution, half of the population will have an IQ above 100, and half will be below 100. The shape of the true normal curve is such that 68 percent of the area under it lies within one standard deviation above and below the mean. In terms of IQ, this means that 68 percent of the population has an IQ somewhere between 84 (100 minus 16) and 116 (100 plus 16). Of the remaining 32 percent of the

The standard deviation of a set of scores reflects the average degree to which those scores differ from the mean of the set.

table 2
Calculating the Standard Deviation

Raw Data	Difference from Mean = D	D^2
2	2 − 4 = −2	4
2	2 − 4 = −2	4
3	3 − 4 = −1	1
4	4 − 4 = 0	0
9	9 − 4 = 5	25
Mean = 20/5 = 4		$\Sigma D^2 = 34$

$$\text{Standard deviation} = \sqrt{\frac{\Sigma D^2}{N}} = \sqrt{\frac{34}{5}} = \sqrt{6.8} = 2.6$$

Note: Σ means "the sum of."

figure 2

The Normal Distribution

Many kinds of research data approximate the symmetrical shape of the normal curve, in which most scores fall toward the center of the range.

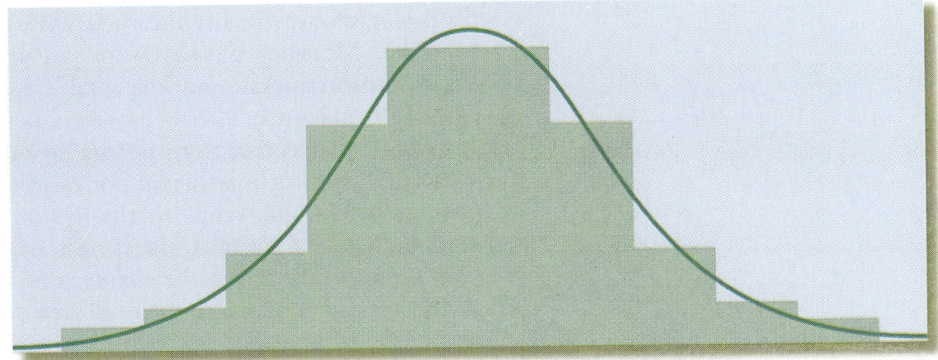

Normal distribution, showing the smoothed approximation to the frequency histogram

(A)

95% of the scores
68% of the scores

-2	-1	0	+1	+2

Standard deviations

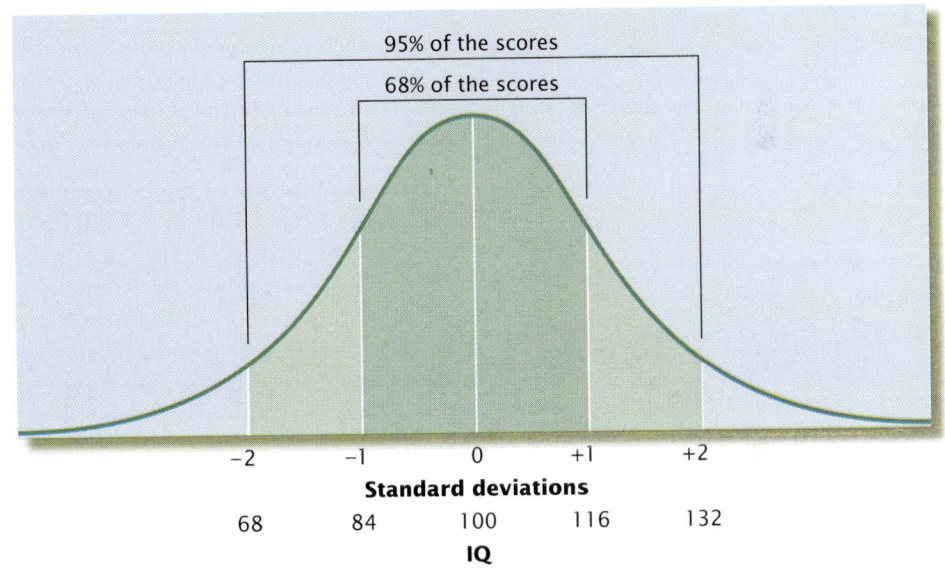

68	84	100	116	132

IQ

The normal distribution of IQ

(B)

---

population, half falls more than 1 SD above the mean, and half falls more than 1 SD below the mean. Thus, 16 percent of the population has an IQ above 116, and 16 percent scores below 84.

The normal curve is also the basis for percentiles. A **percentile score** indicates the percentage of people or observations that fall below a given score in a normal distribution. In Figure 2(B), for example, the mean score (which is also the median) lies at a point below which 50 percent of the scores fall. Thus, the mean of a normal distribution is at the 50th percentile. What does this say about IQ? If you score 1 SD above the mean, your score is at a point above which only 16 percent of the population falls. This means that 84 percent of the population (100 percent minus 16 percent) must be below that score; so this IQ score is at the 84th percentile. A score at 2 SDs above the mean is at the 97.5 percentile, because only 2.5 percent of the scores are above it in a normal distribution.

Scores may also be expressed in terms of their distance in standard deviations from the mean, producing what are called **standard scores**. A standard score of 1.5, for example, is 1.5 standard deviations from the mean.

Correlation

Histograms and measures of central tendency and variability describe certain characteristics of one dependent variable at a time. However,

---

standard deviation (SD) A measure of variability that is the average difference between each score and the mean of the data.

normal distribution A dispersion of scores such that the mean, median, and mode all have the same value. When a distribution has this property, the standard deviation can be used to describe how any particular score stands in relation to the rest of the distribution.

percentile score The percentage of people or observations that fall below a given score in a normal distribution.

standard score A value that indicates the distance, in standard deviations, between a given score and the mean of all the scores in a data set.

psychologists are often concerned with describing the *relationship* between two variables. Measures of correlation are frequently used for this purpose. We discussed the interpretation of the *correlation coefficient* in the chapter on research in psychology; here we describe how to calculate it.

Recall that correlations are based on the relationship between two numbers associated with each participant or observation. The numbers may represent, say, a person's height and weight or the IQs of a parent and child. Table 3 contains this kind of data for four participants from our incentives study who took the test twice. (As you may recall from the chapter on cognitive abilities, the correlation between their scores would be a measure of *test-retest reliability*.) The formula for computing the Pearson product-moment correlation, or r, is as follows:

$$r = \frac{\Sigma(x - M_x)(y - M_y)}{\sqrt{\Sigma(x - M_x)^2 \Sigma(y - M_y)^2}}$$

where:

x = each score on variable 1 (in this case, test 1)
y = each score on variable 2 (in this case, test 2)
M_x = the mean of the scores on variable 1
M_y = the mean of the scores on variable 2

The main function of the denominator in this formula is to ensure that the coefficient ranges from +1.00 to −1.00, no matter how large or small the values of the variables being correlated. The "action element" of this formula is the numerator. It is the result of multiplying the amounts by which each of two observations (x and y) differ from the means of their respective distributions (M_x and M_y). Notice that, if the two variables "go together" (so that, if one is large, the other is also large, and if one is small, the other is also small), then either both will tend to be above the mean of their distribution or both will tend to be below the mean of their distribution. When this is the case, $x - M_x$ and $y - M_y$ will both be positive, or they will both be negative. In either case, their product will always be positive, and the correlation coefficient will also be positive. If, on the other hand, the two variables go opposite to one another, such that, when one is large, the other is small, one of them is likely to be smaller than the mean of its distribution, so that either $x - M_x$ or $y - M_y$ will have a negative sign, and the other will have a positive sign. Multiplying these differences together will always result in a product with a negative sign, and r will be negative as well.

Though it appears complex, calculation of the correlation coefficient is quite simple. The resulting r reflects the degree to which two sets of scores tend to be related, or to co-vary.

table 3
Calculating the Correlation Coefficient

Participant	Test 1	Test 2	$(x - M_x)(y - M_y)$ [b]
A	1	3	$(1 - 3)(3 - 4) = (-2)(-1) = +2$
B	1	3	$(1 - 3)(3 - 4) = (-2)(-1) = +2$
C	4	5	$(4 - 3)(5 - 4) = (1)(1)\ \ \ = +1$
D	6	5	$(6 - 3)(5 - 4) = (3)(1)\ \ \ = +3$
	[a] $M_x = 3$	$M_y = 4$	$\Sigma(x - M_x)(y - M_y)\ \ \ = +8$

[c] $\Sigma(x - M_x)^2 = 4 + 4 + 1 + 9 = 18$
[d] $\Sigma(y - M_y)^2 = 1 + 1 + 1 + 1 = 4$

[e] $r = \dfrac{\Sigma(x - M_x)(y - M_y)}{\sqrt{\Sigma(x - M_x)^2 \Sigma(y - M_y)^2}} = \dfrac{8}{\sqrt{18 \times 4}} = \dfrac{8}{\sqrt{72}} = \dfrac{8}{8.48} = +.94$

Now compute the correlation coefficient for the data presented in Table 3. The first step (step a in the table) is to compute the mean (M) for each variable. M_x turns out to be 3 and M_y is 4. Next, calculate the numerator by finding the differences between each *x* and *y* value and its respective mean and by multiplying them (as in step b of Table 3). Notice that, in this example, the differences in each pair have like signs, so the correlation coefficient will be positive. The next step is to calculate the terms in the denominator; in this case, as shown in steps c and d in Table 3, they have values of 18 and 4. Finally, place all the terms in the formula and carry out the arithmetic (step e). The result in this case is an *r* of +.94, a high and positive correlation suggesting that performances on repeated tests are very closely related. A participant doing well the first time is very likely to do well again; a person doing poorly at first will probably do no better the second time.

Inferential Statistics

The descriptive statistics from the incentives experiment tell the experimenter that the performances of the high- and low-incentive groups differ. But there is some uncertainty. Is the difference large enough to be important? Does it represent a stable effect or a fluke? The researcher would like to have some *measure of confidence* that the difference between groups is genuine and reflects the effect of incentive on mental tasks in the real world, rather than the effect of random or uncontrolled factors. One way of determining confidence would be to run the experiment again with a new group of participants. Confidence that incentives produced differences in performance would grow stronger if the same or a larger between-group difference occurs again. In reality, psychologists rarely have the opportunity to repeat, or *replicate,* their experiments in exactly the same way three or four times. But **inferential statistics** provide a measure of how likely it was that results came about by chance. They put a precise mathematical value on the confidence or probability that rerunning the same experiment would yield similar (or even stronger) results.

Differences Between Means: The *t* Test

One of the most important tools of inferential statistics is the *t* test. It allows the researcher to ask how likely it is that the difference between two means occurred by chance rather than as a function of the effect of the independent variable. When the *t* test or other inferential statistic says that the probability of chance effects is small enough (usually less than 5 percent), the results are said to be *statistically significant.* Conducting a *t* test of statistical significance requires the use of three descriptive statistics.

The first component of the *t* test is the size of the observed effect, the difference between the means. Recall that the mean is calculated by summing a group's scores and dividing by the number of scores. In the example shown in Table 1, the mean of the high-incentive group is 94/13, or 7.23, and the mean of the low-incentive group is 65/13, or 5. Thus, the difference between the means for the high- and low-incentive groups is 7.23 − 5 = 2.23.

Second, the standard deviation of scores in each group must be known. If the scores in a group are quite variable, the standard deviation will be large, indicating that chance may have played a large role in producing the results. The next replication of the study might generate a very different set of group scores. If the scores in a group are all very similar, however, the standard deviation will be small, which suggests that the same result would probably occur for that group if the study were repeated. Thus, the *difference* between groups is more likely to be significant when each group's standard deviation is small. If variability is high enough that the scores of two groups overlap (in Table 1, for example, some people in the low-incentive group actually did better on the math test than some in the high-incentive group), the mean difference, though large, may not be statistically significant.

inferential statistics A set of procedures that provides a measure of how likely it is that research results came about by chance.

Third, we need to take the sample size, N, into account. The larger the number of participants or observations, the more likely it is that a given difference between means is significant. This is so because, with larger samples, random factors within a group—the unusual performance of a few people who were sleepy or anxious or hostile, for example—are more likely to be canceled out by the majority, who better represent people in general. The same effect of sample size can be seen in coin tossing. If you toss a quarter five times, you might not be too surprised if heads comes up 80 percent of the time. If you get 80 percent heads after one hundred tosses, however, you might begin to suspect that this is probably not due to chance alone and that some other effect, perhaps some bias in the coin, is significant in producing the results. (For the same reason, a relatively small correlation coefficient—between diet and grades, say—might be statistically significant if it was based on 50,000 students. As the number of participants increases, it becomes less likely that the correlation reflects the influence of a few oddball cases.)

To summarize, as the differences between the means get larger, as N increases, and as standard deviations get smaller, t increases. This increase in t raises the researcher's confidence in the significance of the difference between means.

Now we will calculate the t statistic and show how it is interpreted. The formula for t is:

$$t = \frac{(M_1 - M_2)}{\sqrt{\frac{(N_1 - 1)S_1^2 + (N_2 - 1)S_2^2}{N_1 + N_2 - 2} \left(\frac{N_1 + N_2}{N_1 N_2}\right)}}$$

where:

M_1 = mean of group 1
M_2 = mean of group 2
N_1 = number of scores or observations for group 1
N_2 = number of scores or observations for group 2
S_1 = standard deviation of group 1 scores
S_2 = standard deviation of group 2 scores

Despite appearances, this formula is quite simple. In the numerator is the difference between the two group means; t will get larger as this difference gets larger. The denominator contains an estimate of the standard deviation of the *differences* between group means; in other words, it suggests how much the difference between group means would vary if the experiment were repeated many times. Since this estimate is in the denominator, the value of t will get smaller as the standard deviation of group differences gets larger. For the data in Table 1,

$$t = \frac{(M_1 - M_2)}{\sqrt{\frac{(N_1 - 1)S_1^2 + (N_2 - 1)S_2^2}{N_1 + N_2 - 2} \left(\frac{N_1 + N_2}{N_1 N_2}\right)}}$$

$$= \frac{7.23 - 5}{\sqrt{\frac{(12)(5.09) + (12)(4.46)}{24} \left(\frac{26}{169}\right)}}$$

$$= \frac{2.23}{\sqrt{.735}} = 2.60 \text{ with 24 df}$$

To determine what a particular t means, we must use the value of N and a special statistical table called, appropriately enough, the t *table*. We have reproduced part of the t table in Table 4.

Inferential Statistics

This table allows the researcher to determine whether an obtained *t* value is statistically significant. If the *t* value is larger than the one in the appropriate row in the .05 column, the difference between means that generated that *t* score is usually considered statistically significant.

table 4
The *t* Table

df	p Value .10 (10%)	.05 (5%)	.01 (1%)
4	1.53	2.13	3.75
9	1.38	1.83	2.82
14	1.34	1.76	2.62
19	1.33	1.73	2.54
22	1.32	1.71	2.50
24	1.32	1.71	2.49

First, find the computed values of *t* in the row corresponding to the **degrees of freedom**, or **df**, associated with the experiment. In this case, degrees of freedom are simply $N_1 + N_2 - 2$ (or two less than the total sample size or number of scores). Since our experiment had 13 participants per group, df = 13 + 13 − 2 = 24. In the row for 24 df in Table 4, you will find increasing values of *t* in each column. These columns correspond to decreasing *p* values, the probabilities that the difference between means occurred by chance. If an obtained *t* value is equal to or larger than one of the values in the *t* table (on the correct df line), then the difference between means that generated that *t* is said to be significant at the .10, .05, or .01 level of probability. Suppose, for example, that an obtained *t* (with 19 df) was 2.00. Looking along the 19 df row, you find that 2.00 is larger than the value in the .05 column. This allows you to say that the probability that the difference between means occurred by chance was no greater than .05, or 5 in 100. If the *t* had been less than the value in the .05 column, the probability of a chance result would have been greater than .05. As noted earlier, when an obtained *t* is not large enough to exceed *t* table values at the .05 level, at least, it is not usually considered statistically significant.

The *t* value from our experiment was 2.60, with 24 df. Because 2.60 is greater than all the values in the 24 df row, the difference between the high- and low-incentive groups would have occurred by chance less than 1 time in 100. In other words, the difference is statistically significant.

Beyond the *t* Test

Many experiments in psychology are considerably more complex than simple comparisons between two groups. They often involve three or more experimental and control groups. Some experiments also include more than one independent variable. For example, suppose we had been interested not only in the effect of incentive size on performance but also in the effect of problem difficulty. We might then create six groups whose members would perform easy, moderate, or difficult problems with low or high incentives.

In an experiment like this, the results might be due to the incentive, the problem difficulty, or the combined effects (known as the *interaction*) of the two. Analyzing the size and source of these effects is typically accomplished through procedures known as *analysis of variance*. The details of analysis of variance are beyond the scope of this book; for now, note that the statistical significance of each effect is influenced by differences between means, standard deviation, and sample size in much the same way as described for the *t* test.

For more detailed information about how analysis of variance and other inferential statistics are used to understand and interpret the results of psychological

degrees of freedom (df) The total sample size or number of scores in a data set, less the number of experimental groups.

research, consider taking courses in research methods and statistical or quantitative methods.

SUMMARY

Psychological research generates large quantities of data. Statistics are methods for describing and drawing conclusions from data.

Describing Data

Researchers often test the *null hypothesis*, which is the assertion that the independent variable will have no effect on the dependent variable.

The Frequency Histogram

Graphic representations such as *frequency histograms* provide visual descriptions of data, making the data easier to understand.

Descriptive Statistics

Numbers that summarize a set of data are called *descriptive statistics*. The easiest statistic to compute is N, which gives the number of observations made. A set of scores can be described by two other types of descriptive statistics: a measure of central tendency, which describes the typical value of a set of data, and a measure of variability. Measures of central tendency include the mean, median, and mode; variability is typically measured by the *range* and by the standard deviation. Sets of data often follow a *normal distribution*, which means that most scores fall in the middle of the range, with fewer and fewer scores occurring as one moves toward the extremes. In a truly normal distribution the mean, median, and mode are identical. When a set of data shows a normal distribution, a data point can be cited in terms of a *percentile score*, which indicates the percentage of people or observations falling below a certain score, and in terms of *standard scores*, which indicate the distance, in standard deviations, that a score is located from the mean. Another type of descriptive statistic, a correlation coefficient, is used to measure the correlation between sets of scores.

Inferential Statistics

Researchers use *inferential statistics* to quantify the probability that conducting the same experiment again would yield similar results.

Differences Between Means: The *t* Test

One inferential statistic, the *t test*, assesses the likelihood that differences between two means occurred by chance or reflect the effect of an independent variable. Performing a *t* test requires using the difference between the means of two sets of data, the *standard deviation* of scores in each set, and the number of observations or participants. Interpreting a *t* test requires that *degrees of freedom* also be taken into account. When the *t* test indicates that the experimental results had a low probability of occurring by chance, the results are said to be statistically significant.

Beyond the *t* Test

When more than two groups must be compared, researchers typically rely on analysis of variance in order to interpret the results of an experiment.

REFERENCES

Abbott, B. B., Schoen, L. S., & Badia, P. (1984). Predictable and unpredictable shock: Behavioral measures of aversion and physiological measures of stress. *Psychological Bulletin, 96,* 45–71.

Abeles, N. (1985). Proceedings of the American Psychological Association, 1985. *American Psychologist, 41,* 633–663.

Abi-Hashem, N. (2000). Psychology, time, and culture. *American Psychologist, 55,* 342–343.

Abraham, H. D., & Wolf, E. (1988). Visual function in past users of LSD: Psychophysical findings. *Journal of Abnormal Psychology, 97,* 443–447.

Abramis, D. J. (1994). Work role ambiguity, job satisfaction, and job performance: Meta-analyses and review. *Psychological Reports, 75,* 1411–1433.

Abramowitz, J. S. (1997). Effectiveness of psychological and pharmacological treatments for obsessive-compulsive disorder: A quantitative review. *Journal of Consulting and Clinical Psychology, 65,* 44–52.

Abrams, R. (1997). *Electroconvulsive therapy* (3rd ed.). New York: Oxford University Press.

Abrams, R. L., & Greenwald, A. G. (2000). Parts outweigh the whole (word) in unconscious analysis of meaning. *Psychological Science, 11,* 118–124.

Abramson, L. Y., Metalsky, G. I., & Alloy, L. B. (1989). Hopelessness depression: A theory-based subtype. *Psychological Review, 96,* 358–372.

Abreu, J. M. (1999). Conscious and unconscious African American stereotypes: Impact on first impression and diagnostic ratings by therapists. *Journal of Consulting and Clinical Psychology, 67,* 387–393.

Abu-Elheiga, L., Matzuk, M. M., Abo-Hashema, K. A., & Wakil, S. J. (2001). Continuous fatty acid oxidation and reduced fat storage in mice lacking acetyl-CoA carboxylase 2. *Science, 291,* 2558–2559.

Achenbach, T. M. (1997). *Empirically based assessment of child and adolescent psychopathology.* Thousand Oaks, CA: Sage.

Acitelli, L. K. (1992). Gender differences in relationship awareness and marital satisfaction among young married couples. *Personality and Social Psychology Bulletin, 18,* 102–110.

Ackerman, D. (1995). *Mystery of the senses.* Boston: WGBH-TV/Washington, DC: WETA-TV.

Ackerman, M. J., Siu, B. L., Sturner, W. Q., Tester, D. J., Valdivia, C. R., Makielski, J. C., & Towbin, J. A. (2001). Postmortem molecular analysis of SCN5A defects in sudden infant death syndrome. *Journal of the American Medical Association, 286,* 2264–2269.

Ackerman, P. L. (1994). Intelligence, attention, and learning: Maximal and typical performance. In D. K. Detterman (Ed.), *Current topics in human intelligence* (Vol. 4, pp. 1–27). Norwood, NJ: Ablex.

Acocella, J. (1998, April 6). The politics of hysteria. *New Yorker,* pp. 64–79.

Addis, M. E. (1997). Evaluating the treatment manual as a means of disseminating empirically validated psychotherapies. *Clinical Psychology: Science and Practice, 4,* 1–11.

Addis, M. E., & Krasnow, A. D. (2000). A national survey of practicing psychologists' attitudes toward psychotherapy treatment manuals. *Journal of Consulting and Clinical Psychology, 68,* 331–339.

Adelman, W. P., Duggan, A. K., Hauptman, P., & Joffe, A. (2001). Effectiveness of a high school smoking cessation program. *Pediatrics, 107,* E50.

Ader, D. N., & Johnson, S. B. (1994). Sample description, reporting, and analysis of sex in psychological research: A look at APA and APA division journals in 1990. *American Psychologist, 49,* 216–218.

Ader, R. (2001). Psychoneuroimmunology. *Current Directions in Psychological Science, 10,* 94–98.

Ader, R., Felten, D., & Cohen, N. (1990). Interactions between the brain and the immune system. *Review of Pharmacology and Toxicology, 30,* 561–602.

Adler, A. (1963). *The practice and theory of individual psychology.* Paterson, NJ: Littlefield Adams. (Original work published 1927)

Adler, T. (1993, March). Bad mix: Combat stress, decisions. *APA Monitor,* p. 1.

Adolphs, R., Tranel, D., & Damasio, A. R. (1998). The human amygdala in social judgment. *Nature, 393*(6684), 470–474.

Adolphs, R., Tranel, D., & Damasio, H., & Damasio, A. (1994). Impaired recognition of emotion in facial expressions following bilateral damage to the human amygdala. *Nature, 372*(6507), 669–672.

Adorno, T. W., Frenkel-Brunswik, E., Levinson, D. J., & Sanford, R. N. (1950). *The authoritarian personality.* New York: Harper & Row.

Agarwal, D. P. (1997). Molecular genetic aspects of alcohol metabolism and alcoholism. *Pharmacopsychiatry, 30*(3), 79–84.

Agency for Healthcare Research and Quality (AHRQ). (1999). *Treatment of depression—newer pharmacotherapies* (Evidence Report/Technology Assessment, Number 7, Pub. No. 99-E014). Rockville, MD: Author.

Agnew, C. R., Van Lange, P. A. M., Rusbult, C. E., & Langston, C. A. (1998). Cognitive interdependence: Commitment and the mental representation of close relationships. *Journal of Personality and Social Psychology, 74,* 939–954.

Ahima, R. S., & Flier, J. S. (2000). Leptin. *Annual Review of Physiology, 62,* 413–437.

Ahlfinger, N. R., & Esser, J. K. (2001). Testing the groupthink model: Effects of promotional leadership and conformity. *Social Behavior and Personality, 29,* 31–41.

Ahmed, A., & Ruffman, T. (1998). Why do infants make A not B errors in a search task, yet show memory for the location of hidden objects in a nonsearch task? *Developmental Psychology, 34,* 441–453.

Aiello, J. R., & Douthitt, E. A. (2001). Social facilitation from Triplett to electronic performance monitoring. *Group Dynamics, 5,* 163–180.

Aiello, J. R., & Kolb, K. J. (1995). Electronic performance monitoring and social context: Impact on productivity and stress. *Journal of Applied Psychology, 80,* 339–353.

Aiken, L. R. (1994). *Psychological testing and assessment* (8th ed.). Boston: Allyn & Bacon.

Ainsworth, M. D. S. (1973). The development of infant-mother attachment. In B. M. Caldwell & H. N. Ricciuti (Eds.), *Review of child development research* (Vol. 3, pp. 1–94). Chicago: University of Chicago Press.

Ainsworth, M. D. S. (1989). Attachments beyond infancy. *American Psychologist, 44,* 709–716.

Ainsworth, M. D. S., Blehar, M. D., Waters, E., & Wall, S. (1978). *Patterns of attachment: A psychological study of the Strange Situation.* Hillsdale, NJ: Erlbaum.

Ajzen, I. (2001). Nature and operation of attitudes. *Annual Review of Psychology, 52,* 27–58.

Ajzen, I., & Fishbein, M. (2002). Attitudes and the attitude behavior relation: Reasoned and automatic processes. In W. Stroebe & M. Hewstone (Eds.), *European Review of Social Psychology.*

Alaimo, K., Olson, C. M., & Frongillo, E. A., Jr. (2001). Food insufficiency and American school-aged children's cognitive, academic, and psychosocial development. *Pediatrics, 108,* 44–53.

Albarracin, D., Johnson, B. T., Fishbein, M., & Muellerleile, P. A. (2001). Theories of reasoned action and planned behavior as models of condom use: A meta-analysis. *Psychological Bulletin, 127,* 142–161.

Albee, G. (1968). Conceptual models and manpower requirements in psychology. *American Psychologist, 23,* 317–320.

Albee, G. (1985, February). The answer is prevention. *Psychology Today,* pp. 60–64.

Albert, M. S., Savage, C. R., Blazer, D., Jones, K., Berkman, L., & Seeman, T. (1995). Predictors of cognitive change in older persons: MacArthur studies of successful aging. *Psychology and Aging, 10,* 578–589.

Alberti, R. E., & Emmons, M. L. (1986). *Your perfect right: A guide to assertive living* (5th ed.). San Luis Obispo, CA: Impact.

Aldag, R. J., & Fuller, S. R. (1993). Beyond fiasco: A reappraisal of the groupthink phenomenon and a new model of group decision processes. *Psychological Bulletin, 113,* 533–552.

Alderete, E., Eskenazi, B., & Sholtz, R. (1995). Effect of cigarette smoking and coffee drinking on time to conception. *Epidemiology, 6*(4), 403–408.

ALI (American Law Institute). (1962). *Model penal code: Proposed official draft*. Philadelphia: Author.

Alicke, M., LoSchiavo, F. M., Zerbst, J., & Zhang, S. (1997). The person who outperforms me is a genius: Maintaining perceived competence in upward social comparisons. *Journal of Personality and Social Psychology, 73*, 781–789.

Al-Kubaisy, T., Marks, I. M., Logsdail, S., Marks, M. P., Lovell, K., Sungur, M., & Araya, R. (1992). Role of exposure homework in phobia reduction: A controlled study. *Behavior Therapy, 23*, 599–621.

Allen, D. N., Goldstein, G., & Weiner, C. (2001). Differential neuropsychological patterns of frontal- and temporal-lobe dysfunction in patients with schizophrenia. *Schizophrenia Research, 48*, 7–15.

Allen, J. B., Kenrick, D. T., Linder, D. E., & McCall, M. A. (1989). Arousal and attraction: A response-facilitation alternative to misattribution and negative-reinforcement models. *Journal of Personality and Social Psychology, 57*, 261–270.

Allen, L. S., & Gorski, R. A. (1992). Sexual orientation and the size of the anterior commissure in the human brain. *Proceedings of the National Academy of Sciences of the United States of America, 89*, 7199–7202.

Allen, L. S., Hines, M., Shryne, J. E., & Gorski, R. A. (1989). Two sexually dimorphic cell groups in the human brain. *Journal of Neuroscience, 9*, 497–506.

Alliger, G. M., & Dwight, S. A. (2000). A meta-analytic investigation of the susceptibility of integrity tests to faking and coaching. *Educational & Psychological Measurement, 60*, 59–72.

Allison, D. B., Fontaine, K. R., Manson, J. E., Stevens, J., & VanItaillie, T. B. (1999). Annual deaths attributable to obesity in the United States. *Journal of the American Medical Association, 282*, 1530–1538.

Alloy, L. B., Abramson, L. Y., & Francis, E. L. (1999). Do negative cognitive styles confer vulnerability to depression? *Current Directions in Psychological Science, 8*, 128–132.

Allport, G. W. (1961). *Pattern and growth in personality*. New York: Holt, Rinehart & Winston.

Allport, G. W., & Odbert, H. S. (1936). Trait names: A psycholexical study. *Psychological Monographs, 47*(1, Whole No. 211).

Alston, J. H. (1920). Spatial condition of the fusion of warmth and cold in heat. *American Journal of Psychology, 31*, 303–312.

Altemeyer, B. (1996). *The authoritarian specter*. Cambridge: Harvard University Press.

Altemeyer, B. (1988). *Right-wing authoritarianism*. Winnipeg: University of Manitoba Press.

Altman, L. K. (2000, April 10). Company developing marijuana for medical uses. *New York Times* [On-line]. Available: http://www.mapinc.org/drugnews/v00/n474/a01.html

Aluja-Fabregat, A., & Torrubia-Beltri, R. (1998). Viewing of mass media violence, perception of violence, personality and academic achievement. *Personality and Individual Differences, 25*, 973–989.

Alvarez, F. J., Delrio, M. C., & Prada, R. (1995). Drinking and driving in Spain. *Journal of Studies on Alcohol, 56*(4), 403–407.

Alvarez-Buylla, A., Garcia-Verdugo, J. M., & Tramontin, A. D. (2001). A unified hypothesis on the lineage of neural stem cells. *National Review of Neuroscience, 2*, 287–293.

Alvaro, E. M., & Crano, W. D. (1997). Indirect minority influence: Evidence for leniency in source evaluation and counterargumentation. *Journal of Personality and Social Psychology, 72*, 949–964.

Alvir, J. M., Lieberman, J. A., Safferman, A. Z., Schwimmer, J. L., & Schaaf, J. A. (1993). Clozapine-induced agranulocytosis. Incidence and risk factors in the United States. *New England Journal of Medicine, 329*, 162–167.

Amabile, T. M. (1996). *Creativity in context: Update to "The Social Psychology of Creativity."* Boulder, CO: Westview.

Amabile, T. M. (2001). Beyond talent: John Irving and the passionate craft of creativity. *American Psychologist, 56*, 333–336.

Amabile, T. M., Goldfarb, P., & Brackfield, S. C. (1990). Social influences on creativity: Evaluation, coaction, and surveillance. *Creativity Research Journal, 3*, 6–21.

Amabile, T. M., Hennessey, B. A., & Grossman, B. S. (1986). Social influences on creativity: The effects of contracted-for reward. *Journal of Personality & Social Psychology, 50*, 14–23.

Amabile, T. M., Hill, K. G., Hennessey, B. A., & Tighe, E. M. (1994). The Work Preference Inventory: Assessing intrinsic and extrinsic motivational orientations. *Journal of Personality and Social Psychology, 66*(5), 950–967.

American Educational Research Association, American Psychological Association, and National Council on Measurement in Education. (1999). *Standards for Educational and Psychological Testing*. Washington, DC: American Educational Research Association.

American Psychiatric Association. (1994). *Diagnostic and statistical manual of mental disorders* (4th ed.). Washington, DC: Author.

American Psychiatric Association. (1999). Position statement on psychiatric treatment and sexual orientation. *American Journal of Psychiatry, 156*, 1131.

American Psychiatric Association. (2000). *Diagnostic and statistical manual of mental disorders* (4th ed., rev.). Washington DC: Author.

American Psychological Association. (1992). Ethical principles of psychologists and code of conduct. *American Psychologist, 47*, 1597–1611.

American Psychological Association. (1993). *Violence and youth: Psychology's response*. Washington, DC: Author.

American Society for Microbiology. (2000, September 18). *America's dirty little secret—our hands*. Washington, DC: Author.

Anastasi, A. (1997). *Psychological testing* (7th ed.). Upper Saddle River, NJ: Prentice-Hall.

Andersen, S. M., & Berk, M. S. (1998). The social-cognitive model of transference: Experiencing past relationships in the present. *Current Directions in Psychological Science, 7*, 109–115.

Anderson, A. K., & Phelps, E. A. (2000). Expression without recognition: Contributions of the human amygdala to emotional communication. *Psychological Science, 11*, 106–111.

Anderson, A. K., & Phelps, E. A. (2001). Lesions of the human amygdala impair enhanced perception of emotionally salient events. *Nature, 411*, 305–309.

Anderson, C., John, O. P., Keltner, D., & Kring, A. M. (2001). Who attains social status? Effects of personality and physical attractiveness in social groups. *Journal of Personality and Social Psychology, 81*, 116–132.

Anderson, C. A. (2001). Heat and violence. *Current Directions in Psychological Science, 10*, 33–38.

Anderson, C. A., & Anderson, K. P. (1998). Temperature and aggression: Paradox, controversy, and a (fairly) clear picture. In R. G. Geen & E. Donnerstein (Eds.), *Human aggression* (pp. 248–298). San Diego: Academic Press.

Anderson, C. A., Anderson, K. B., Dorr, N., DeNeve, K. M., & Flanagan, M. (2000). Temperature and aggression. In M. Zanna (Ed.), *Advances in experimental social psychology* (Vol. 32, pp. 63–133). New York: Academic Press.

Anderson, C. A., & Bushman, B. J. (2001). Effects of violent video games on aggressive behavior, aggressive cognition, aggressive affect, physiological arousal, and prosocial behavior: A meta-analytic review of the scientific literature. *Psychological Science, 12*, 353–359.

Anderson, C. A., & Dill, K. E. (2000). Video games and aggressive thoughts, feelings, and behavior in the laboratory and in life. *Journal of Personality and Social Psychology, 78*, 772–790.

Anderson, C. A., Lindsay, J. J., & Bushman, B. J. (1999). Research in the psychological laboratory: Truth or triviality? *Current Directions in Psychological Science, 8*, 3–9.

Anderson, E. M., & Lambert, M. J. (1995). Short-term dynamically oriented psychotherapy: A review and meta-analysis. *Clinical Psychology Review, 9*(6), 503–514.

Anderson, J. R. (1990). *Cognitive psychology and its implications* (3rd ed.). New York: Freeman.

Anderson, J. R. (1992). Problem solving and learning. *American Psychologist, 48*, 35–44.

Anderson, J. R. (1995). *Learning and memory: An integrated approach*. New York: Wiley.

Anderson, J. R. (2000). *Cognitive psychology and its implications* (5th ed). New York: Worth.

Anderson, M. C., & Green, C. (2001). Suppressing unwanted memories by executive control. *Nature, 410*, 366–369.

Andreasen, N. C. (1997). Linking mind and brain in the study of mental illnesses: A project for a scientific psychopathology. *Science, 275,* 1586–1593.

Andreasen, N. C., Arndt, S., Alliger, R., Miller, D., & Flaum, M. (1995). Symptoms of schizophrenia. *Archives of General Psychiatry, 52,* 341–351.

Andre-Petersson, L., Engstroom, G., Hagberg, B., Janzon, L., Steen, G., Lane, D. A., et al. (2001). Adaptive behavior in stressful situations and stroke incidence in hypertensive men: Results from prospective cohort study "Men Born in 1914" in Malmo, Sweden. *Stroke, 32,* 1712–1720.

Andrew, D., & Craig, A. D. (2001). Spinothalamic lamina I neurons selectively sensitive to histamine: A central neural pathway for itch. *Nature Neuroscience, 4,* 72–77.

Andrews, B., Brewin, C., Ochera, J., Morton, J., Bekerian, D. A., Davies, G. M., & Mollon, P. (2000). The timing, triggers, and quality of recovered memories in therapy. *British Journal of Clinical Psychology, 39,* 11–26.

Ang-Lee, M. K., Moss, J., & Yuan, C.-S. (2001). Herbal medicines and perioperative care. *Journal of the American Medical Association, 286,* 208–216.

Angst, J., Angst, F., & Stassen, H. H. (1999). Suicide risks inpatients with major depressive disorder. *Journal of Clinical Psychiatry, 60*(Suppl. 2), 57–62.

Anrep, G. V. (1920). Pitch discrimination in the dog. *Journal of Physiology, 53,* 367–385.

Anshel, M. (1996). Coping styles among adolescent competitive athletes. *Journal of Social Psychology, 136,* 311–323.

Anthony, M., & Bartlett, P. L. (1999). *Neural network learning: Theoretical foundations.* Cambridge: Cambridge University Press.

Anthony, T., Cooper, C., & Mullen, B. (1992). Cross-racial facial identification: Five studies of sex differences in facial prominence. *Personality and Social Psychology Bulletin, 18,* 296–301.

Antoni, M. H., Cruess, D. G., Cruess, S., Lutgendorf, S., Kumar, M., Ironson, G., et al. (2000). Cognitive-behavioral stress management intervention effects on anxiety, 24-hr urinary norepinephrine output, and t-cytotoxic/suppressor cells over time among symptomatic HIV-infected gay men. *Journal of Consulting and Clinical Psychology, 68,* 31–45.

Antonuccio, D. O., Danton, W. G., & DeNelsky, G. Y. (1995). Psychotherapy versus medication for depression: Challenging the conventional wisdom with data. *Professional Psychology: Research and Practice, 26,* 574–585.

APA Office of Ethnic Minority Affairs. (2000). *Guidelines for research in ethnic minority communities.* Washington, DC: American Psychological Association.

Appelle, S., Lynn, S. J., & Newman, L. (2000). Alien abduction experiences. In E. Cardena, S. J. Lynn, & S. Krippner (Eds.), *Varieties of anomalous experience: Examining the scientific evidence* (pp. 253–282). Washington, DC: American Psychological Association.

Appleton, W. S. (2000). *Prozac and the new antidepressants: What you need to know about Prozac, Zoloft, Paxil, Luvox, Wellbutrin, Effexor, Serzone, Vestra, Celexa, St. John's Wort, and others* (rev. ed.). New York: Plume Books.

Archambault, C. M., Czyzewski, D., Cordua y Cruz, G. D., Foreyt, F. P., & Mariotto, M. J. (1989). Effects of weight cycling in female rats. *Physiology and Behavior, 46,* 417–421.

Archer, J. (2000). Sex differences between heterosexual partners: A meta-analytic review. *Psychological Bulletin, 126,* 651–680.

Arenberg, D. (1982). Changes with age in problem solving. In F. I. M. Craik & S. Trehub (Eds.), *Aging and cognitive processes* (pp. 221–236). New York: Plenum.

Arendash, G. W., King, D. L., Gordon, M. N., Morgan, D., Hatcher, J. M., Hope, C. E., & Diamond, D. M. (2001). Progressive, age-related behavioral impairments in transgenic mice carrying both mutant amyloid precursor protein and presenilin-1 transgenes. *Brain Research, 891,* 42–53.

Arkes, H. R., & Ayton, P. (1999). The sunk cost and Concorde effects: Are humans less rational than lower animals? *Psychological Bulletin, 125,* 591–600.

Arlow, J. (1995). Psychoanalysis. In R. J. Corsini & D. Wedding (Eds.), *Current psychotherapies* (5th ed., pp. 15–50). Itasca, IL: Peacock.

Arndt, J., Goldenberg, J., Greenberg, J., Pyszcynski, T., & Solomon, S. (2000). Death can be hazardous to your health: Adaptive and ironic consequences of defenses against the terror of death. In R. P. Duberstein & J. Masling (Eds.), *Psychodynamic perspectives on sickness and health* (pp. 201–257). Washington, DC: American Psychological Association.

Arndt, J., Greenberg, J., Pyszcynski, T., & Solomon, S. (1997). Subliminal exposure to death-related stimuli increases defense of the cultural worldview. *Psychological Science, 8,* 379–385.

Arner, P. (2000). Obesity: A genetic disease of adipose tissue? *British Journal of Nutrition, 83,* S9–S16.

Arnett, J. J. (1999). Adolescent storm and stress, reconsidered. *American Psychologist, 54,* 317–326.

Arnett, J. J. (2000). Emerging adulthood: A theory of development from the late teens through the twenties. *American Psychologist, 55,* 469–480.

Aronoff, J., Barclay, A. M., & Stevenson, L. A. (1988). The recognition of threatening stimuli. *Journal of Personality and Social Psychology, 54,* 647–655.

Aronson, E. (1990). Applying social psychology to desegregation and energy conservation. *Personality and Social Psychology Bulletin, 16,* 118–132.

Aronson, E. (1995). *The social animal* (7th ed.). New York: Freeman.

Aronson, E. (1997). *The jigsaw classroom.* New York: Longman.

Aronson, E. (1999). *The social animal* (8th ed.). New York: Worth/Freeman.

Aronson, E., Wilson, T. D., & Akert, R. M. (1999). *Social psychology* (3rd ed.). New York: Longman.

Aronson, E., Wilson, T. D., & Akert, R. M. (2002). *Social psychology* (4th ed.). New York: Longman.

Arterberry, M., Yonas, A., & Bensen, A. S. (1989). Self-produced locomotion and development of responsiveness to textural gradients. *Developmental Psychology, 25,* 976–982.

Arterburn, D., & Noel, P. H. (2001). Obesity: Clinical review. *British Medical Journal, 322,* 1406–1409.

Asarnow, R. F., Nuechterlein, K. H., Fogelson, D., Subotnik, K. L., Payne, D. A., Russell, A. T., et al. (2001). Schizophrenia and schizophrenia-spectrum personality disorders in the first-degree relatives of children with schizophrenia: The UCLA family study. *Archives of General Psychiatry, 58,* 581–588.

Asch, S. E. (1951). Effects of group pressure upon the modification and distortion of judgments. In H. Guetzkow (Ed.), *Groups, leadership, and men* (pp. 177–190). Pittsburgh: Carnegie Press.

Asch, S. E. (1955). Opinions and social pressure. *Scientific American, 193,* 31–35.

Asch, S. E. (1956). Studies of independence and conformity: A minority of one against a unanimous majority. *Psychological Monographs, 70,* 1–70.

Ashcraft, M. H. (1989). *Human memory and cognition.* Glenview, IL: Scott, Foresman.

Ashcraft, M. H. (2002). *Cognition* (3rd ed.). Upper Saddle River, NJ: Prentice-Hall.

Ashe, P. C., Berry, M. D., & Boulton, A. A (2001). Schizophrenia, a neurodegenerative disorder with neurodevelopmental antecedents. *Progress in Neuro-Psychopharmacology and Biological Psychiatry, 25,* 691–707.

Asher, S. R., & Hopmeyer, A. (2001). Loneliness in childhood. In G. Bear, K. Minke, & A. Thomas (Eds.), *Children's needs II: Psychological perspectives.* Silver Spring, MD: National Association of School Psychologists.

Ashton, H. (1995). Protracted withdrawal from benzodiazepines: The postwithdrawal syndrome. *Psychiatric Annals, 25*(3), 174–179.

Aslin, R. N., Jusczyk, P. W., & Pisoni, D. B. (1998). Speech and auditory processing during infancy: Constraints on and precursors to language. In W. Damon (Ed.), *Handbook of child psychology* (5th ed., pp. 147–198). New York: Wiley.

Aspinwall, L. G., & Duran, R. E. F. (1999). Psychology applied to health. In A. Stec & D. Bernstein (Eds.), *Psychology: Fields of application.* Boston: Houghton Mifflin.

Aspinwall, L. G., & Taylor, S. E. (1992). Modeling cognition adaptation: A longitudinal investigation of the impact of individual differences and coping on college adjustment and performance. *Journal of Personality and Social Psychology, 63,* 989–1003.

Aspinwall, L. G., & Taylor, S. E. (1997). A stitch in time: Self-regulation and proactive coping. *Psychological Bulletin, 121,* 417–436.

Associated Press. (1997, October 22). Forty percent in senior classes fail at science. *Chicago Tribune.*

Associated Press. (1999, November 17). Stripes near Waldo mean slow down. *St. Petersburg Times.*

Aston-Jones, G., Chiang, C., & Alexinsky, T. (1991). Discharge of noradrenergic locus coeruleus neurons in behaving rats and monkeys suggests a role in vigilance. *Progress in Brain Research, 88,* 501–520.

Atkinson, J. W., & Raynor, J. O. (1974). *Personality, motivation, and achievement.* Washington, DC: Hemisphere.

Atkinson, R. C., & Shiffrin, R. M. (1968). Human memory: A proposed system and its control processes. In K. Spence (Ed.), *The psychology of learning and motivation* (Vol. 2, pp. 89–195). New York: Academic Press.

Au, T. K. (1992). Counterfactual reasoning. In G. R. Semin & K. Fiedler (Eds.), *Language, interaction and social cognition* (pp. 194–213). London: Sage.

August, G. J., Realmuto, G. M., Hektner, J. M., & Bloomquist, M. L. (2001). An integrated components preventive intervention for aggressive elementary school children: The early risers program. *Journal of Consulting and Clinical Psychology, 69,* 614–626.

Auld, F., & Hyman, M. (1991). *Resolution of inner conflict: An introduction to psychoanalytic therapy.* Washington, DC: American Psychological Association.

Averill, J. S. (1980). On the paucity of positive emotions. In K. R. Blankstein, P. Pliner, & J. Polivey (Eds.), *Advances in the study of communication and affect: Vol. 6. Assessment and modification of emotional behavior.* New York: Plenum.

Aviezer, O., Sagi, A., Joels, T., & Ziv, Y. (1999). Emotional availability and attachment representations in kibbutz infants and their mothers. *Developmental Psychology, 35,* 811–821.

Avila, C. (2001). *Journal of Personality and Social Psychology, 80,* 311–324.

Ax, R. K., & Resnick, R. J. (2001). Prescription privileges: An immodest proposal. *Monitor on Psychology, 32,* 53–54.

Ayanian, J., & Cleary, P. (1999). Perceived risks of heart disease and cancer among cigarette smokers. *Journal of the American Medical Association, 281,* 1019–1021.

Ayllon, T. (1999). *How to use token economy and point systems* (2nd ed.). Texas: Pro-Ed.

Ayllon, T., & Azrin, N. H. (1968). *The token economy: A motivational system for therapy and rehabilitation.* New York: Appleton-Century-Crofts.

Azar, B. (1995, January). DNA-environment mix forms intellectual fate. *American Psychological Association Monitor,* p. 24.

Azar, B. (1996, November). Project explores landscape of midlife. *APA Monitor,* p. 26.

Azorin, J.-M., Spiegel, R., Remington, G., Vanelle, J.-M., Pere, J.-J., Giguere, M., & Bourdeix, I. (2001). A double-blind comparative study of clozapine and risperidone in the management of severe chronic schizophrenia. *American Journal of Psychiatry, 158,* 1305–1313.

Baare, W. F. C., van Oel, C. J., Hushoff, H. E., Schnack, H. G., Durston, S., Sitskoorn, M. M., & Kahn, R. S. (2001). Volumes of brain structures in twins discordant for schizophrenia. *Archives of General Psychiatry, 58,* 33–40.

Baars, B. J. (1998). Metaphors of consciousness and attention in the brain. *Trends in Neuroscience, 21*(2), 58–62.

Babcock, R., & Salthouse, T. (1990). Effects of increased processing demands on age differences in working memory. *Psychology and Aging, 5,* 421–428.

Bacharach, V. R., & Baumeister, A. A. (1998). Direct and indirect effects of maternal intelligence, maternal age, income, and home environment on intelligence of preterm, low-birth-weight children. *Journal of Applied Developmental Psychology, 19,* 361–375.

Backman, L., & Nilsson, L. (1991). Effects of divided attention on free and cued recall of verbal events and action events. *Bulletin of the Psychonomic Society, 29,* 51–54.

Baddeley, A. (1982). *Your memory: A user's guide.* New York: Macmillan.

Baddeley, A. (1992). Working memory. *Science, 255,* 556–559.

Baddeley, A. (1998). *Human memory: Theory and practice.* Boston: Allyn & Bacon.

Bagley, C., & Tremblay, P. (1998). On the prevalence of homosexuality and bisexuality, in a random survey of 750 men aged 18–27. *Journal of Homosexuality, 36,* 1–18.

Bagwell, C. L., Newcomb, A. F., & Bukowski, W. M. (1998). Preadolescent friendship and peer rejection as predictors of adult adjustment. *Child Development, 69,* 140–153.

Bahrick, H. P., Bahrick, P. O., & Wittlinger, R. P. (1975). Fifty years of memory for names and faces: A cross-cultural approach. *Journal of Experimental Psychology: General, 104,* 54–75.

Bahrick, H. P., & Hall, L. K. (1991). Lifetime maintenance of high school mathematics content. *Journal of Experimental Psychology: General, 120,* 20–33.

Bahrick, H. P., Hall, L. K., & Berger, S. A. (1996). Accuracy and distortion in memory for high school grades. *Psychological Science, 7*(5), 265–271.

Bahrick, H. P., Hall, L. K., Noggin, J. P., & Bahrick, L. E. (1994). Fifty years of language maintenance and language dominance in bilingual Hispanic immigrants. *Journal of Experimental Psychology: General, 123,* 264–283.

Bailey, J. M., & Benishay, D. S. (1993). Familial aggregation of female sexual orientation. *American Journal of Psychiatry, 150,* 272–277.

Bailey, J. M., Bobrow, D., Wolfe, M., & Mikach, S. (1995). Sexual orientation of adult sons of gay fathers. *Developmental Psychology, 31*(1), 124–129.

Bailey, J. M., Dunne, M. P., & Martin, N. G. (2000). Genetic and environmental influences on sexual orientation and its correlates in an Australian twin sample. *Journal of Personality and Social Psychology, 78,* 524–536.

Bailey, J. M., & Pillard, R. C. (1991). A genetic study of male sexual orientation. *Archives of General Psychiatry, 48,* 1089–1096.

Baillargeon, R. (1994a). How do infants learn about the physical world? *Current Directions in Psychological Science, 3,* 133–139.

Baillargeon, R. (1994b). Physical reasoning in young infants: Seeking explanations for impossible events. *British Journal of Development Psychology, 12,* 9–33.

Baillargeon, R. (1995). Physical reasoning in infancy. In M. S. Gazzaniga (Ed.), *The cognitive neurosciences* (pp. 181–204). Cambridge: MIT Press.

Baillargeon, R. (1998). Infants' understanding of the physical world. In M. Sabourin et al. (Eds.), *Advances in psychological science: Vol. 2. Biological and cognitive aspects* (pp. 503–529). Hove, England: Taylor & Francis.

Baker, L. T., Vernon, P. A., & Ho, H. (1991). The genetic correlation between intelligence and speed of information processing. *Behavior Genetics, 21,* 351–367.

Baker, M. C. (2002). *The atoms of language: The mind's hidden rules of grammar.* New York: Basic Books.

Balaban, M. T. (1995). Affective influences on startle in five-month-old infants: Reactions to facial expressions of emotion. *Child Development, 66*(1), 28–36.

Baldessarini, R. J., & Tondo, L. (2000). Does lithium treatment still work? Evidence of stable responses over three decades. *Archives of General Psychiatry, 57,* 187–190.

Balestreri, R., Fontana, L., & Astengo, F. (1987). A double-blind placebo-controlled evaluation of the safety and efficacy of vinpocetine in the treatment of patients with chronic vascular senile cerebral dysfunction. *Journal of the American Geriatric Society, 35,* 425–430.

Ball, K., & Sekuler, R. (1992). Cues reduce direction uncertainty and enhance motion detection. *Perception and Psychophysics, 30,* 119–128.

Balleine, B., & Dickinson, A. (1994). Role of cholecystokinin in the motivational control of instrumental action in rats. *Behavioral Neuroscience, 108*(3), 590–605.

Ballou, M. (1995). Assertiveness training. In M. Ballou (Ed.), *Psychological interventions: A guide to strategies* (pp. 125–136). Westport, CT: Praeger.

Baltes, P. B. (1993). The aging mind: Potential and limits. *The Gerontologist, 33,* 580–594.

Baltes, P. B. (1994, August). *Life-span developmental psychology: On the overall landscape of human development.* Invited address presented at the annual meeting of the American Psychological Association, Los Angeles.

Baltes, P. B., Staudinger, U. M., Maercker, A., & Smith, J. (1995). People nominated as wise: A comparative study of wisdom-related knowledge. *Psychology and Aging, 10,* 155–166.

Banaji, M., Lemm, K. M., & Carpenter, S. J. (2001). The social unconscious. In A. Tesser & N. Schwarz (Eds.), *Blackwell handbook of social psychology: Intraindividual processes* (pp. 134–158). Oxford, England: Blackwell.

Bancroft, J. (1994). Homosexual orientation: The search for a biological basis. *British Journal of Psychiatry, 164,* 437–440.

Bancroft, J. (1997). *Researching sexual behavior: Methodological issues.* Bloomington, IN: Indiana University Press.

Bandura, A. (1965). Influence of a model's reinforcement contingencies on the acquisition of imitative responses. *Journal of Personality and Social Psychology, 1,* 589–595.

Bandura, A. (1969). *Principles of behavior modification.* New York: Holt, Rinehart & Winston.

Bandura, A. (1983). Psychological mechanisms of aggression. In R. G. Geen & C. I. Donnerstein (Eds.), *Aggression: Theoretical and empirical reviews* (Vol. 1, pp. 1–40). New York: Academic Press.

Bandura, A. (1986). *Social foundations of thought and action: A social cognitive theory.* Englewood Cliffs, NJ: Prentice-Hall.

Bandura, A. (1992). Self-efficacy mechanism in psychobiologic functioning. In R. Schwarzer (Ed.), *Self-efficacy: Thought control of action* (pp. 355–394). Washington, DC: Hemisphere.

Bandura, A. (1999). Social cognitive theory of personality. In L. Pervin & O. John (Eds.), *Handbook of personality: Theory and research* (2nd ed., pp. 154–198). New York: Guilford.

Bandura, A. (2001). Social cognitive theory: An agentic approach. *Annual Review of Psychology, 52,* 1–26.

Bandura, A., Blanchard, E. B., & Ritter, B. (1969). The relative efficacy of desensitization and modeling approaches for inducing behavioral, affective, and attitudinal changes. *Journal of Personality and Social Psychology, 13,* 173–199.

Bandura, A., Ross, D., & Ross, S. A. (1963). Imitation of film-mediated aggressive models. *Journal of Abnormal and Social Psychology, 66,* 3–11.

Bandura, A., & Walters, R. H. (1963). *Social learning and personality development.* New York: Holt, Rinehart & Winston.

Banich, M. (2003). *Neuropsychology: The neural bases of mental function.* Boston: Houghton Mifflin.

Banich, M. T., & Heller, W. (1998). Evolving perspectives on lateralization of function. *Current Directions in Psychological Science, 7,* 1–2.

Banich, M. T., Stolar, N., Heller, W., & Goldman, R. B. (1992). A deficit in right-hemisphere performance after induction of a depressed mood. *Neuropsychiatry, Neuropsychology, and Behavioral Neurology, 5*(1), 20–27.

Banks, W. P., & Krajicek, D. (1991). Perception. *Annual Review of Psychology, 42,* 305–332.

Bar, M., & Biederman, I. (1998). Subliminal visual priming. *Psychological Science, 9,* 464–469.

Baranano, D. E., Ferris, C. D., & Snyder, S. H. (2001). Atypical neural messengers. *Trends Neuroscience, 24,* 99–106.

Barber, J. P., Connolly, M. B., Crits-Christoph, P., Gladis, L., & Siqueland, L. (2000). Alliance predicts patients' outcome beyond in-treatment change in symptoms. *Journal of Consulting and Clinical Psychology, 68,* 1027–1032.

Barber, J. P., Crits-Christoph, P., & Paul, C. C. (1993). Advances in measures of psychodynamic formulations. *Journal of Consulting and Clinical Psychology, 61,* 574–585.

Barber, N. (1995). The evolutionary psychology of physical attractiveness: Sexual selection and human morphology. *Ethology and Sociobiology, 16,* 395–424.

Barclay, J. R., Bransford, J. D., Franks, J. J., McCarrell, N. S., & Nitsch, K. (1974). Comprehension and semantic flexibility. *Journal of Verbal Learning and Verbal Behavior, 13,* 471–481.

Bardo, M. T. (1998). Neuropharmacological mechanisms of drug reward: Beyond dopamine in the nucleus accumbens. *Critical Reviews of Neurobiology, 12*(1–2), 37–67.

Bardo, M. T., Donohew, R. L., & Harrington, N. G. (1996). Psychobiology of novelty-seeking and drug-seeking behavior. *Behavioral Brain Research, 77*(1–2), 23–43.

Bargh, J. A., Chen, M., & Burrows, L. (1996). Automaticity of social behavior: Direct effects of trait construct and stereotype activation on action. *Journal of Personality and Social Psychology, 71,* 245–262.

Bargh, J. A., & Ferguson, M. J. (2000). Beyond behaviorism: On the automaticity of higher mental processes. *Psychological Bulletin, 126,* 925–945.

Barinaga, M. (1999, November 26). Learning visualized, on the double. *Science, 286,* 1661.

Barker, L. M. (1997). *Learning and behavior: Biological, psychological, and sociocultural perspectives* (2nd ed.). Upper Saddle River, NJ: Prentice-Hall.

Barlow, D. H. (1988). *Anxiety and its disorders: The nature and treatment of panic and anxiety.* New York: Guilford.

Barlow, D. H., & Campbell, L. A. (2000). Mixed anxiety-depression and its implications for models of mood and anxiety disorders. *Comprehensive Psychiatry, 41,* 55–60.

Barlow, D. H., Gorman, J. M., Shear, M. K., & Woods, S. W. (2000). Cognitive-behavioral therapy, imipramine, or their combination for panic disorder: A randomized controlled trial. *Journal of the American Medical Association, 283,* 2529–2536.

Barlow, S. H., Burlingame, G. M., Nebeker, R. S., & Anderson, E. (2000). Meta-analysis of medical self-help groups. *International Journal of Group Psychotherapy, 50,* 53–69.

Barnett, W. S. (1998). Long-term cognitive and academic effects of early childhood education of children in poverty. *Preventative Medicine: An International Devoted Practice & Theory, 27,* 204–207.

Barnier, A. J., & McConkey, K. M. (1998). Posthypnotic responding away from the hypnotic setting. *Psychological Science, 9,* 256–263.

Baron, J., Roediger, H. L., III, & Anderson, M. C. (2000). Human factors and the Palm Beach ballot. *APS Observer, 13,* 5, 7.

Baron, M. (1997). Genetic linkage and bipolar affective disorder: Progress and pitfalls. *Molecular Psychiatry, 2,* 200–210.

Baron, R. A., & Byrne, D. (1994). *Social psychology: Understanding human interaction* (7th ed.). Boston: Allyn & Bacon.

Baron, R. A., & Richardson, D. C. (1994). *Human aggression* (2nd ed.). New York: Plenum.

Baron, R. S., Kerr, N. L., & Miller, N. (1992). *Group process, group decision, group action.* Pacific Grove, CA: Brooks/Cole.

Barondes, S. H. (1994). Thinking about Prozac. *Science, 263,* 1102–1103.

Barrick, M. R., & Mount, M. K. (1991). The Big Five personality dimensions and job performance: A meta-analysis. *Personnel Psychology, 44,* 1–26.

Barron, F., & Harrington, D. M. (1981). Creativity, intelligence, and personality. *Annual Review of Psychology, 52,* 439–476.

Barron, K. E., & Harackiewicz, J. M. (2001). Achievement goals and optimal motivation: Testing multiple goal models. *Journal of Personality and Social Psychology, 80,* 706–722.

Barrowclough, C., King, P., Colville, J., Russell, E., Burns, A., & Tarrier, N. (2001). A randomized trial of the effectiveness of cognitive-behavioral therapy and supportive counseling for anxiety symptoms in older adults. *Journal of Consulting and Clinical Psychology, 69,* 756–762.

Barsalou, L. W. (1991). Deriving categories to achieve goals. In G. H. Bower (Ed.), *The psychology of learning and motivation* (pp. 1–64). New York: Academic Press.

Barsalou, L. W. (1993). Flexibility, structure, and linguistic vagary in concepts: Manifestations of a compositional system of perceptual symbols. In A. F. Collins, S. E. Gathercole, M. A. Conway, & P. E. Morris (Eds.), *Theories of memory* (pp. 29–102). Hillsdale, NJ: Erlbaum.

Barsky, A. J., Wool, C., Barnett, M. C., & Cleary, P. D. (1994). Histories of childhood trauma in adult hypochondriacal patients. *American Journal of Psychiatry, 151,* 397–401.

Bartlett, J. C. (1993). Tonal structure of melodies. In T. J. Tighe & W. J. Dowling (Eds.), *Psychology and music.* Hillsdale, NJ: Erlbaum.

Bartol, C. (1991). Predictive validation of the MMPI for small-town police officers who fail. *Professional Psychology: Research and Practice, 22,* 127–132.

Bartoshuk, L. M. (1991). Taste, smell, and pleasure. In R. C. Bollef (Ed.), *The hedonics of taste*. Hillsdale, NJ: Erlbaum.

Bartoshuk, L. M. (2000). Comparing sensory experiences across individuals: recent psychophysical advances illuminate genetic variation in taste perception. *Chemical Senses, 25*, 447–460.

Bartoshuk, L. M., & Wolfe, J. M. (1990). Conditioned taste aversion in humans: Are there olfactory versions? *Chemical Senses, 15*, 551.

Bashore, T. R., & Ridderinkhof, K. R. (2002). Older age, traumatic brain injury, and cognitive slowing: Some convergent and divergent findings. *Psychological Bulletin, 128*, 151–198.

Baskin, D., Bluestone, H., & Nelson, M. (1981). Ethnicity and psychiatric diagnosis. *Journal of Clinical Psychology, 37*, 529–537.

Bass, E., & Davis, L. (1994). *The courage to heal* (3rd ed.). New York: Harper Perennial Library.

Bates, E. (1993, March). *Nature, nurture, and language development*. Paper presented at the biennial meeting of the Society for Research in Child Development, New Orleans.

Batson, C. D. (1998). Altruism and prosocial behavior. In D. Gilbert, S. T. Fiske, & G. Lindzey (Eds.), *Handbook of social psychology: Vol. 2* (4th ed., pp. 282–316). Boston: McGraw-Hill.

Batson, C. D., Sager, K., Garst, E., & Kang, M. (1997). Is empathy-induced helping due to self-other merging? *Journal of Personality and Social Psychology, 73*, 495–509.

Batson, C. D., & Thompson, E. R. (2001). Why don't moral people act morally?: Motivational considerations. *Current Directions in Psychological Science, 10*, 54–57.

Battaglia, G., Yeh, S. Y., & De Souza, E. B. (1988). MDMA-induced neurotoxicity: Parameters of degeneration and recovery of brain serotonin neurons. *Pharmacology, Biochemistry and Behavior, 29*, 269–274.

Baucom, D. H., Shoham, V., Mueser, K. T., Daiuto, A. D., & Stickle, T. R. (1998). Empirically supported couple and family interventions for marital distress and adult mental health problems. *Journal of Consulting and Clinical Psychology, 66*, 53–88.

Bauer, P. J. (1996). What do infants recall of their lives?: Memory for specific events by one- to two-year-olds. *American Psychologist, 51*, 29–41.

Baum, A., Gatchel, R. J., & Krantz, D. S. (1997). *Introduction to health psychology* (3rd ed.). New York: McGraw-Hill.

Baum, A., Revenson, T. A., & Singer, J. E. (Eds.). (2001). *Handbook of health psychology*. Mahwah, NJ: Erlbaum.

Baumeister, R. F. (1998). The self. In D. Gilbert, S. T. Fiske, & G. Lindzey (Eds.), *Handbook of social psychology* (4th ed., Vol. 1, pp. 680–740). Boston: McGraw-Hill.

Baumeister, R. F. (2000). Gender differences in erotic plasticity: The female sex drive as socially flexible and responsive. *Psychological Bulletin, 126*, 347–374.

Baumeister, R. F., & Leary, M. R. (1995). The need to belong: Desire for interpersonal attachments as a fundamental human motivation. *Psychological Bulletin, 117*(3), 497–529.

Baumrind, D. (1971). Current patterns of parental authority. *Developmental Psychology Monographs, 4*(1, part 2).

Baumrind, D. (1986). *Familial antecedents of social competence in middle childhood*. Unpublished monograph, Institute of Human Development, University of California, Berkeley.

Baumrind, D. (2001, August). *Does causally relevant research support a blanket injunction against the use of disciplinary spanking?* Paper presented at the annual convention of the American Psychological Association, San Francisco.

Beardsley, P. M., Sokoloff, P., Balster, R. L., & Schwartz, J. C. (2001). The D3R partial agonist, BP 897, attenuates the discriminative stimulus effects of cocaine and D-amphetamine and is not self-administered. *Behavioral Pharmacology, 12*, 1–11.

Beatty, J. (1995). *Principles of behavioral neuroscience*. Dubuque: Brown and Benchmark.

Beauchamp, G. K., Katahira, K., Yamazaki, K., Mennella, J. A., Bard, J., & Boyse, E. A. (1995). Evidence suggesting that the odortypes of pregnant women are a compound of maternal and fetal odortypes. *Proceedings of the National Academy of Sciences of the United States of America, 92*, 2617–2621.

Beauchamp-Turner, D. L., & Levinson, D. M. (1992). Effects of meditation on stress, health, and affect. *Medical Psychotherapy: An International Journal, 5*, 123–131.

Bechara, A., Damasio, H., & Damasio, A. R. (2000). Emotion, decision making, and the orbitofrontal cortex. *Cerebral Cortex, 10*, 295–307.

Beck, A. T. (1967). *Depression: Clinical, experimental and theoretical aspects*. New York: Harper & Row.

Beck, A. T. (1976). *Cognitive therapy and the emotional disorders*. New York: International Universities Press.

Beck, A. T. (1995). Cognitive therapy: A 30-year retrospective. In S. O. Lilienfeld (Ed.), *Seeing both sides: Classic controversies in abnormal psychology* (pp. 303–311). Pacific Grove, CA: Brooks/Cole. (Original work published 1991)

Beck, A. T., Brown, G., Berchick, R. J., Stewart, B. L., & Steer, R. A. (1990). Relationship between hopelessness and ultimate suicide: A replication with psychiatric outpatients. *American Journal of Psychiatry, 147*, 190–195.

Beck, A. T., & Emery, G. (1985). *Anxiety disorders and phobias: A cognitive perspective*. New York: Basic Books.

Beck, A. T., Sokol, L., Clark, D., Berchick, R., & Wright, F. (1992). A crossover study of focused cognitive therapy for panic disorder. *American Journal of Psychiatry, 149*, 778–783.

Beck, J. S., & Beck, A. T. (1995). *Cognitive therapy: Basics and beyond*. New York: Guilford.

Beck, M. (1992, December 7). The new middle age. *Newsweek*, pp. 50–56.

Becker, J. A. (1994). "Sneak-shoes," "sworders" and "nose-beards": A case study of lexical innovation. *First Language, 14*, 195–211.

Bedard, J., & Chi, M. T. H. (1992). Expertise. *Current Directions in Psychological Science, 1*, 135–139.

Begley, S. (1997, September 29). Hope for "snow babies." *Newsweek*, pp. 62–63.

Belin, P., Zatorre, R. J., Lafaille, P., Ahad, P., & Pike, B., (2000). Voice-selective areas in human auditory cortex. *Nature, 403*, 309–312.

Bell, B. E., & Loftus, E. F. (1989). Trivial persuasion in the courtroom: The power of (a few) minor details. *Journal of Personality and Social Psychology, 56*, 669–679.

Bell, P. A., Fisher, J. D., Baum, A., & Greene, T. (1996). *Environmental psychology* (4th ed.). Fort Worth, TX: Holt, Rinehart & Winston.

Belmont, J. M., & Butterfield, E. C. (1971). Learning strategies as determinants of memory deficiencies. *Cognitive Psychology, 2*, 411–420.

Belsky, J., & Kelly, J. (1994). *The transition to parenthood*. New York: Dell.

Belsky, J., Spritz, B., & Crnic, K. (1996). Infant attachment security and affective-cognitive information processing at age 3. *Psychological Science, 7*, 111–114.

Bem, D. J. (1967). Self-perception: An alternative interpretation of cognitive dissonance phenomena. *Psychological Review, 74*, 183–200.

Bem, D. J. (1996). Exotic becomes erotic: A developmental theory of sexual orientation. *Psychological Review, 103*, 320–335.

Benecke, M. (1999). Spontaneous human combustion: Thoughts of a forensic biologist. *Skeptical Inquirer, 22*, 47–51.

Benedetti, F., & Amanzio, M. (1997). The neurobiology of placebo analgesia: From endogenous opioids to cholecystokinin. *Progress in Neurobiology, 52*, 109–125.

Benedetti, F., Arduino, C., & Amanzio, M. (1999). Somatotopic activation of opioid systems by target-directed expectations of analgesia. *Journal of Neuroscience, 19*, 3639–3648.

Benight, C. C., Swift, E., Sanger, J., Smith, A., & Zeppelin, D. (1999). Coping self-efficacy as a mediator of distress following a natural disaster. *Journal of Applied Social Psychology, 29*, 2443–2464.

Benjamin, K., Wilson, S. G., & Mogil, J. S. (1999). *Journal of Pharmacology & Experimental Therapeutics, 289*, 1370–1375.

Benjamin, L. T., Jr. (2000). The psychology laboratory at the turn of the 20th century. *American Psychologist, 55*, 318–321.

Bennet, W. M. (1994). Marijuana has no medicinal value. *Hospital Practice, 29*(4), 26–27.

Bennett, H. L., Giannini, J. A., & Davis, H. S. (1985). Nonverbal response to intraoperational conversation. *British Journal of Anaesthesia, 57*, 174–179.

Ben-Shakhar, G., & Furedy, J. J. (1990). *Theories and applications in the detection of deception: A psychophysiological and international perspective.* New York: Springer-Verlag.

Benson, H. (1975). *The relaxation response.* New York: Morrow.

Berenbaum, S. A., & Resnick, S. M. (1997). Early androgen effects on aggression in children and adults with congenital adrenal hyperplasia. *Psychoneuroendocrinology, 22,* 505–515.

Berg, E. P., Engel, B. A., & Forrest, J. C. (1998). Pork carcass composition derived from a neural network model of electromagnetic scans. *Journal of Animal Science, 76,* 18–22.

Berger, A., Henderson, M., Nadoolman, W., Duffy, V., Cooper, D., Saberski, L., & Bartoshuk, L. (1995). Oral capsaicin provides temporary relief for oral mucositis pain secondary to chemotherapy/radiation therapy. *Journal of Pain and Symptom Management, 10,* 243–248.

Berger, R., & Hannah, M. T. (Eds.). (1999). *Preventative approaches in couples therapy.* Bristol, PA: Brunner/Mazel.

Bergin, A. E. (1971). The evaluation of therapeutic outcomes. In A. E. Bergin & S. L. Garfield (Eds.), *Handbook of psychotherapy and behavior change: An empirical analysis* (pp. 217–270). New York: Wiley.

Berkowitz, L. (1994). Is something missing? Some observations prompted by the cognitive-neoassociationist view of anger and emotional aggression. In L. R. Huesmann (Ed.), *Human aggression: Current perspectives* (pp. 35–60). New York: Plenum.

Berkowitz, L. (1998). Affective aggression: The role of stress, pain, and negative affect. In R. G. Geen & E. Donnerstein (Eds.), *Human aggression* (pp. 49–72). San Diego: Academic Press.

Berkowitz, L. (1999). Evil is more than banal: Situationism and the concept of evil. *Personality and Social Psychology Review, 3,* 246–253.

Berliner, D. L., Monti-Bloch, L., Jennings-White, C., & Diaz-Sanchez, V. (1996). The functionality of the human vomeronasal organ (VNO): Evidence for steriod receptors. *Journal of Steriod Biochemical Molecular Biology, 58,* 259–265.

Berman, R. F. (1991). Electrical brain stimulation used to study mechanisms and models of memory. L. Martinez & R. P. Kesner (Eds.), *Learning and memory: A biological view* (2nd ed.). San Diego: Academic Press.

Bermond, B., Fasotti, L., Nieuwenhuyse, B., & Schuerman, J. (1991). Spinal cord lesions, peripheral feedback and intensities of emotional feelings. *Cognition and Emotions, 5,* 201–220.

Bernard, L. L. (1924) *Instinct.* New York: Holt, Rinehart & Winston.

Bernat, J. A., Calhoun, K. S., Adams, H. E., & Zeichner, A. (2001). Homophobia and physical aggression toward homosexual and heterosexual individuals. *Journal of Abnormal Psychology, 110,* 179–187.

Berns, G. S., McClure, S. M., Pagnoni, G., & Montague, P. R. (2001). Predictability modulates human brain response to reward. *The Journal of Neuroscience, 21,* 2793–2798.

Bernstein, D. A. (1970). The modification of smoking behavior: A search for effective variables. *Behaviour Research and Therapy, 8,* 133–146.

Bernstein, D. A., Borkovec, T. D., & Hazlette-Stevens, H. (2000). *Progressive relaxation training: A manual for the helping professions* (2nd ed.). New York: Praeger.

Bernstein, D. M., & Roberts, B. (1995). Assessing dreams through self-report questionnaires: Relation with past research and personality. *Dreaming: Journal of the Association for the Study of Dreams, 5,* 13–27.

Berridge, K. C. (1999). Pleasure, pain, desire and dread: Biopsychological components and relations. In D. Kahneman, E. Diener, & N. Schwarz (Eds.), *Understanding the quality of life: Scientific perspectives on enjoyment and suffering.* New York: Russell Sage Foundation.

Berry, J. W., & Bennett, J. A. (1992). Cree conceptions of cognitive competence. *International Journal of Psychology, 27,* 73–88.

Berscheid, E., & Reis, H. T. (1998). Attraction and close relationships. In D. Gilbert, S. T. Fiske, & G. Lindzey (Eds.), *Handbook of social psychology* (Vol. 2, 4th ed., pp. 193–281). Boston: McGraw-Hill.

Bersoff, D. M. (1999). Why good people sometimes do bad things: Motivated reasoning and unethical behavior. *Personality and Social Psychology Bulletin, 25,* 28–39.

Bersoff, D. N. (1999). *Ethical conflicts in psychology* (2nd ed.). Washington, DC: American Psychological Association.

Berthoud, H. R., & Neuhuber, W. L. (2000). Functional and chemical anatomy of the afferent vagal system. *Autonomic Neuroscience, 85,* 1–17.

Besson, M., Faita, F., Peretz, I., Bonnel, A.-M., & Requin, J. (1998). Singing in the brain: Independence of lyrics and tunes. *Psychological Science, 9,* 494–498.

Best, J. B. (1999). *Cognitive psychology* (5th ed.) Belmont, CA: Brooks/Cole.

Bettman, J. R., Johnson, E. J., & Payne, J. W. (1990). A componential analysis of cognitive effort in choice. *Organizational Behavior and Human Decision Processes, 45,* 111–139.

Beutler, L. E. (2000). David and Goliath: When empirical and clinical standards of practice meet. *American Psychologist, 55,* 997–1007.

Bevan, S., & Geppetti, P. (1994). Protons: small stimulants of capsaicin-sensitive sensory nerves. *Trends in Neuroscience, 17,* 509–512.

Bevins, R. A. (2001). Novelty seeking and reward: Implications for the study of high-risk behaviors. *Current Directions in Psychological Science, 10,* 189–193.

Beyerstein, B. L. (1999). Pseudoscience and the brain: Tuners and tonics for aspiring superhumans. In S. Della Sala (Ed.), *Mind myths: Exploring popular assumptions about the mind and brain* (pp. 59–82). Chichester, England: Wiley.

Bickis, M., Kelly, I. W., & Byrnes, G. (1995). Crisis calls and temporal and lunar variables: A comprehensive study. *The Journal of Psychology, 129,* 701–711.

Biederman, I. (1987). Recognition by components. *Psychological Review, 94,* 115–147.

Biederman, I., Cooper, E. E., Fox, P. W., & Mahadevan, R. S. (1992). Unexceptional spatial memory in an exceptional memorist. *Journal of Experimental Psychology: Learning, Memory, and Cognition, 18,* 654–657.

Bierut, L. J., Heath, A. C., Bucholz, K. K., Dinwiddie, S. H., Madden, P. A., Statham, D. J., et al. (1999). Major depressive disorder in a community-based twin sample: Are there different genetic and environmental contributions for men and women? *Archives of General Psychiatry, 56,* 557–563.

Bigelow, A., MacLean, J., Wood, C., & Smith, J. (1990). Infants' responses to child and adult strangers: An investigation of height and facial configuration variables. *Infant Behavior and Development, 13,* 21–32.

Biklen, D. (1990). Communication unbound: Autism and praxis. *Harvard Educational Review, 60,* 290–314.

Billing, J., & Sherman, P. W. (1998). Antimicrobial functions of spices: Why some like it hot. *Quarterly Review of Biology, 73,* 3–49.

Binet, A., & Simon, T. (1905). Methodes nouvelles pour le diagnostic du niveau intellectuel des anormaux. *L'Annee Psychologique, 11,* 191–244.

Binzen, C. A., Swan, P. D., & Manore, M. M. (2001). Postexercise oxygen consumption and substrate use after resistance exercise in women. *Medicine and Science in Sports and Exercise, 33,* 932–938.

Bjork, R. A. (1979). An information-processing analysis of college teaching. *Educational Psychologist, 14,* 15–23.

Bjork, R. A. (1999). Assessing our own competence: Heuristics and illusions. In D. Gopher & A. Koriat (Eds.), *Attention and performance XVII. Cognitive regulation of performance: Interaction of theory and application* (pp. 435–459). Cambridge: MIT Press.

Bjork, R. A. (2000). Independence in scientific publishing: Reaffirming the principle. *American Psychologist, 55,* 981–984.

Bjork, R. A., & Vanhuele, M. (1992). Retrieval inhibition and related adaptive peculiarities of human memory. *Advances in Consumer Research, 19,* 155–160.

Bjorklund, D. F., & Green, B. L. (1992). The adaptive nature of cognitive immaturity. *American Psychologist, 47,* 46–54.

Bjorklund, D. F., & Shackelford, T. K. (1999). Differences in parental investment contribute to important differences between men and women. *Current Directions in Psychological Science, 8,* 86–89.

Black, J. E., & Greenough, W. T. (1991). Developmental approaches to the memory process. In J. L. Martinez & R. P. Kesner (Eds.), *Learning and memory: A biological view* (2nd ed.). San Diego: Academic Press.

Blackwell, B. (1973). Psychotropic drugs in use today. *Journal of the American Medical Association, 225,* 1637–1641.

Blackwood, N. J., Howard, R. H., Bentall, R. P., & Murray, R. M. (2001). Cognitive neuropsychiatric models of persecutory delusions. *American Journal of Psychiatry, 158,* 527–539.

Blagrove, M. (1996). Problems with the cognitive psychological modeling of dreaming. *Journal of Mind and Behavior, 17,* 99–134.

Blair-West, G. W., Cantor, C. H., Mellsop, G. W., & Eyeson-Annan, M. L. (1999). Lifetime suicide risk in major depression: Sex and age determinants. *Journal of Affective Disorders, 53,* 171–178.

Blake, J., & de Boysson-Bardies, B. (1992). Patterns in babbling: A crosslinguistic study. *Journal of Child Language, 19,* 51–74.

Blake, R. (1998). What can be "perceived" in the absence of visual awareness? *Current Directions in Psychological Science, 6,* 157–162.

Blakemore, S. J., Wolpert, D., & Frith, C. (2000). Why can't you tickle yourself? *Neuroreport, 11,* R-11–R-16.

Blakeslee, S. (2000, January 4). A decade of discovery yields a shock about the brain. *New York Times.*

Blakeslee, S. (2001, August 28). Therapies push injured brains and spinal cords into new paths. *New York Times* [Online]. Available: http://www.nytimes.com/2001./08/28/health/anatomy/28REHA.html

Blanchard, J. (2000). The co-occurrence of substance use in other mental disorders: Editor's introduction. *Clinical Psychology Review, 20,* 145–148.

Blascovich, J., Spencer, S. J., Quinn, D., & Steele, C. (2001). African Americans and high blood pressure: The role of stereotype threat. *Psychological Science, 12,* 225–229.

Blass, T. (1991). Understanding behavior in the Milgram obedience experiment: The role of personality, situations, and their interactions. *Journal of Personality and Social Psychology, 60,* 398–413.

Blass, T. (1999). The Milgram paradigm after 35 years: Some things we now know about obedience to authority. *Journal of Applied Social Psychology, 29,* 955–978.

Blass, T., & Schmitt, C. (2001). The nature of perceived authority in the Milgram paradigm: Two replications. *Current Psychology: Developmental, Learning, Personality, Social, 20,* 115–121.

Blatchford, P., Burke, J., Farquhar, C., & Plewis, I. (1989). Teacher expectations in infant school: Associations with attainment and progress, curriculum coverage and classroom interaction. *British Journal of Educational Psychology, 59,* 19–30.

Blatt, S. J., & Maroudas, C. (1992). Convergence of psychoanalytic and cognitive behavioral theories of depression. *Psychoanalytic Psychology, 9,* 157–190.

Blazer, D. G., Kessler, R. C., McGonagle, K. A., & Swartz, M. S. (1994). The prevalence and distribution of major depression in a national community sample: The national comorbidity survey. *American Journal of Psychiatry, 151,* 979–986.

Blehar, M., & Rosenthal, N. (1989). Seasonal affective disorders and phototherapy. *Archives of General Psychiatry, 46,* 469–474.

Block, J. (2001). Millennial contrarianism: The Five-Factor approach to personality description 5 years later. *Journal of Research in Personality, 35,* 98–107.

Block, J. A. (1971). *Lives through time.* Berkeley: Bancroft Books.

Block, R. I., & Ghoneim, M. M. (1993). Effects of chronic marijuana use on human cognition. *Psychopharmacology, 110*(1–2), 219–228.

Blood, A. J., & Zatorre, R. J. (2001). Intensely pleasurable responses to music correlate with activity in brain regions implicated in reward and emotion. *Proceedings of the National Academy of Science, 98,* 11818–11823.

Bloom, A. H. (1981). *The linguistic shaping of thought: A study of the impact of language on thinking in China and the West.* Hillsdale, NJ: Erlbaum.

Bloom, L. (1995). *The transition from infancy to language: Acquiring the power of expression.* New York: Cambridge University Press.

Blum, L. N., Nielsen, N. H., & Riggs, J. A. (1998). Alcoholism and alcohol abuse among women. *Journal of Women's Health, 7,* 861–871.

Blum, R. W., Beuhring, T., & Rinehart, P. M. (2000). *Protecting teens: Beyond race, income and family structure.* Minneapolis, MN: Center for Adolescent Health, University of Minnesota.

Blumberg, M. S., & Lucas, D. E. (1994). Dual mechanisms of twitching during sleep in neonatal rats. *Behavioral Neuroscience, 108*(6), 1196–1202.

Blume, E. S. (1998). *Secret survivors: Uncovering incest and its aftereffects in women.* New York: Ballantine.

Blumenthal, J. A., Babyak, M., Wei., J., O'Conner, C., Waugh, R., Eisenstein, E., et al. (2002). Usefulness of psychosocial treatment of mental stress-induced myocardial ischemia in men. *American Journal of Cardiology, 89,* 164–168.

Blundell, J. E., & Cooling, J. (2000). Routes to obesity: Phenotypes, food choices, and activity. *British Journal of Nutrition, 83,* S33–S38.

Blundell, J. E., & Halford, J. C. G. (1998). Serotonin and appetite regulation: Implications for the pharmacological treatment of obesity. *CNS Drugs, 9,* 473–495.

Bobko, P., Roth, P. L., & Potosky, D. (1999). Derivation and implications of a meta-analytic matrix incorporating cognitive ability, alternative predictors, and job performance. *Personnel Psychology, 52,* 561–590.

Bock, B. C., Marcus, B. H., & Pinto, B. M. (2001). Maintenance of physical activity following an individualized motivationally tailored intervention. *Annals of Behavioral Medicine, 23,* 79–87.

Bodian, S. (1999). *Meditation for dummies.* Indianapolis: IDG Books Worldwide.

Bogartz, R. S., Shinskey, J. L., & Speaker, C. J. (1997). Interpreting infant looking: The event set x event set design. *Developmental Psychology, 33,* 408–422.

Bogen, J. E. (1995). On the neurophysiology of consciousness: I. An overview. *Consciousness and Cognition, 4,* 52–62.

Bohner, G., & Schwarz, N. (2001). Attitudes persuasion and behavior. In A. Tesser & N. Schwarz (Eds.), *Blackwell handbook of social psychology: Intraindividual processes* (pp. 413–435). Oxford, England: Blackwell.

Bolger, K. E., & Patterson, C. J. (2001). Developmental pathways from child maltreatment to peer rejection. *Child Development, 72,* 549–568.

Bolles, R. C. (1975). *Theory of motivation* (2nd ed.). New York: Harper & Row.

Bomze, H. M., Bulsara, K. R., Iskandar, B. J., Caroni, P., & Skene, J. H. (2001). Spinal axon regeneration evoked by replacing two growth cone proteins in adult neurons. *Nature Neuroscience, 4,* 38–43.

Bond, G., Aiken, L., & Somerville, S. (1992). The Health Beliefs Model and adolescents with insulin-dependent diabetes mellitus. *Health Psychology, 11,* 190–198.

Bonk, V. A., France, C. R., & Taylor, B. K. (2001). Distraction reduces self-reported physiological reactions to blood donation in novice donors with a blunting coping style. *Journal of Psychosomatic Medicine, 63,* 447–452.

Bonner, R. (2001, August 24). Death row inmate is freed after DNA test clears him. *The New York Times.*

Bonwell, C. C., & Eison, J. A. (1991). *Active learning: Creating excitement in the classroom.* Washington, DC: George Washington University.

Booth, C., B., Clarke-Stewart, K. A., Vandell, D. L., McCartney, K., & Owen, M. T. (2002). Child-care usage and mother-infant "quality time." *Journal of Marriage and the Family.*

Booth, P. B., & Lindaman, S. (2000). Theraplay for enhancing attachment in adopted children. In H. G. Kaduson & C. Schaefer (Eds.), *Short-term play therapy for children.* New York: Guilford.

Borgida, E., Conner, C., & Monteufel, L. (1992). Understanding living kidney donors: A behavioral decision-making perspective. In S. Spacapan & S. Oskamp (Eds.), *Helping and being helped* (pp. 183–212). Newbury Park, CA: Sage.

Borkenau, P., Riemann, R., Angleitner, A., & Spinath, F. M. (2001). *Journal of Personality and Social Psychology, 80,* 655–668.

Borkman, T. J. (1997). A selected look at self-help groups in the U.S. *Health and Social Care in the Community, 5,* 357–364.

Borkovec, T. C., & Costello, E. (1993). Efficacy of applied relaxation and cognitive behavioral therapy in the treatment of generalized anxiety disorder. *Journal of Consulting and Clinical Psychology, 61,* 611–619.

Borkowski, J. G., Weyhing, R. S., & Turner, L. A. (1986). Attributional retraining and the teaching of strategies. *Exceptional Children, 53,* 130–137.

Borman, W. C., Hanson, M. A., & Hedge, J. W. (1997). Personnel selection. *Annual Review of Psychology, 48,* 299–337.

Bornstein, R. F. (1992). Subliminal mere exposure effects. In R. F. Bornstein & T. S. Pittman (Eds.), *Perception without awareness: Cognitive, clinical, and social perspectives* (pp. 191–210). New York: Guilford.

Bosma, H., Marmot, M. G., Hemingway, H., Nicholson, A. C., Brunner, E., & Stansfeld, S. A. (1997). Low job control and risk of coronary heart disease in Whitehall II (prospective cohort) study. *British Medical Journal, 314,* 558–565.

Boss, P. (1999). *Ambiguous loss: Learning to live with unresolved grief.* Cambridge: Harvard University Press.

Botwinick, J. (1961). Husband and father-in-law: A reversible figure. *American Journal of Psychology, 74,* 312–313.

Botwinick, J. (1966). Cautiousness in advanced age. *Journal of Gerontology, 21,* 347–353.

Botwinick, J. (1977). Intellectual abilities. In J. E. Birren & K. W. Schaie (Eds.), *Handbook of the psychology of aging.* New York: Van Nostrand Reinhold.

Bouchard, T. J., Jr., Lykken, D. T., McGue, M., Segal, N. L., & Tellegen, A. (1990). Sources of human psychological differences: The Minnesota study of twins reared apart. *Science, 250,* 223–228.

Bouton, M., Mineka, S., & Barlow, D. (2001). A modern learning theory perspective on the etiology of panic disorder. *Psychological Review, 107.*

Bovasso, G. B., Eaton, W. W., & Armenian, H. K. (1999). The long-term outcomes of mental health treatment in a population-based study. *Journal of Consulting and Clinical Psychology, 67,* 529–538.

Bowden, C. L. (2000). Efficacy of lithium in mania and maintenance therapy of bipolar disorder. *Journal of Clinical Psychiatry, 61,* 35–40.

Bowden, C. L., Calabrese, J. R., McElroy, S. L., Gyulai, L., Wassef, A., Petty, F., et al. (2000). A randomized, placebo-controlled 12-month trial of divalproex and lithium in treatment of outpatients with bipolar I disorder. *Archives of General Psychiatry, 57,* 481–489.

Bower, G. H. (1975). Cognitive psychology: An introduction. In W. K. Estes (Ed.), *Handbook of learning and cognitive processes* (Vol. 1, pp. 25–80). Hillsdale, NJ: Erlbaum.

Bower, J. E., Kemeny, M. E., Taylor, S. E., & Fahey, J. L. (1999). Cognitive processing, discovery of meaning, CD4 decline, and AIDS-related mortality among bereaved HIV-seropositive men. *Journal of Consulting and Clinical Psychology, 66,* 979–986.

Bowerman, M. (1996). The origins of children's spatial semantic categories: Cognitive versus linguistic determinants. In J. J. Gumperz & S. C. Levinson (Eds.), *Rethinking linguistic relativity: Studies in the social and cultural foundations of language* (No. 17, pp. 145–176). Cambridge: Cambridge University Press.

Bowlby, J. (1973). *Attachment and loss: Vol. 2. Separation.* New York: Basic Books.

Bowlby, J. (1980). *Loss: Sadness and depression.* New York: Basic Books.

Bowman, E. S., & Nurnberger, J. I. (1993). Genetics of psychiatry diagnosis and treatment. In D. L. Dummer (Ed.), *Current psychiatric therapy* (pp. 46–56). Philadelphia: Saunders.

Bozarth, M. A., & Wise, R. A. (1984). Anatomically distinct opiate receptor fields mediate reward and physical dependence. *Science, 224,* 516–518.

Bracken, B. A., & McCallum, R. S. (1998). *Universal Nonverbal Intelligence Test (UNIT).* Boston: Riverside.

Bracken, P., & Thomas, P. (2001). Postpsychiatry: A new direction for mental health. *British Journal of Psychiatry, 322,* 724–727.

Bradbury, T. N., Campbell, S. M., & Fincham, F. D. (1995). Longitudinal and behavioral analysis of masculinity and femininity in marriage. *Journal of Personality and Social Psychology, 68,* 328–341.

Bradley-Johnson, S., Graham, D. P., & Johnson, C. M. (1986). Token reinforcement on WISC-R performance for white, low-socioeconomic, upper and lower elementary-school-age students. *Journal of School Psychology, 24,* 73–79.

Brainerd, C. J., & Reyna, V. F. (1998). When things that were never experienced are easier to "remember" than things that were. *Psychological Science, 9,* 484–489.

Brainerd, C. J., Reyna, V. F., & Brandse, E. (1995). Are children's false memories more persistent than their true memories? *Psychological Science, 6,* 359–364.

Brandimonte, M. A., Hitch, G. J., & Bishop, D. V. M. (1992). Influence of short-term memory codes on visual image processing: Evidence from image transformation tasks. *Journal of Experimental Psychology: Learning, Memory, and Cognition, 18,* 157–165.

Brandtstadter, J., & Renner, G. (1990). Tenacious goal pursuit and flexible goal adjustment: Explication and age-related analysis of assimilative and accommodative strategies of coping. *Psychology and Aging, 5,* 58–67.

Bransford, J. D., Brown, A. L., & Cocking, R. R. (Eds.). (1999). *How people learn: Brain, mind, experience, and school.* Washington, DC: National Academy Press.

Bransford, J. D., & Johnson, M. K. (1972). Contextual prerequisites for understanding: Some investigations of comprehension and recall. *Journal of Verbal Learning and Verbal Behavior, 11,* 717–726.

Bransford, J. D., & Stein, B. S. (1993). *The ideal problem solver* (2nd ed.). New York: Freeman.

Braun, A. E., Balkin, T. J., & Wesensten, N. J. (1998). Dissociated pattern of activity in visual cortices and their projections during human rapid eye movement sleep. *Science, 279,* 91–95.

Bray, G. A., & Tartaglia, L. A. (2000). Medicinal strategies in the treatment of obesity. *Nature, 404,* 672–677.

Breedlove, S. M. (1994). Sexual differentiation of the human nervous system. *Annual Review of Psychology, 45,* 389–418.

Breggin, P. R. (1997). *Brain-disabling treatments in psychiatry: Drugs, electroshock, and the role of the FDA.* New York: Springer.

Bregman, A. S. (1990). *Auditory scene analysis.* Cambridge: MIT Press.

Brehm, S. (1992). *Intimate relationships.* New York: McGraw-Hill.

Brehm, S., Kassin, S., & Fein, S. (2002). *Social psychology* (5th ed.). Boston: Houghton Mifflin.

Breiter, H. C., Aharon, I., Kahneman, D., Dale, A., & Shizgal, P. (2001). Functional imaging of neural responses to expectancy and experience of monetary gains and losses. *Neuron, 30,* 619–639.

Brelsford, J. W. (1993). Physics education in a virtual environment. In *Proceedings of the 37th Annual Meeting of the Human Factors and Ergonomics Society.* Santa Monica, CA: Human Factors.

Bremner, J. D., Shobe, K. K., & Kihlstrom, J. F. (2000). False memories in women with self-reported childhood sexual abuse. *Psychological Science, 11,* 333–337.

Brener, N. D., Hassan, S. S., & Barrios, L. C. (1999). Suicidal ideation among college students in the United States. *Journal of Consulting and Clinical Psychology, 67,* 1004–1008.

Brennan, P. A., & Mednick, S. A. (1994). Learning theory approach to the deterrence of criminal recidivism. *Journal of Abnormal Psychology, 103,* 430–440.

Brennen, T., Baguley, T., Bright, J., & Bruce, V. (1990). Resolving semantically induced tip-of-the-tongue states for proper nouns. *Memory & Cognition, 18,* 339–347.

Brenner, L., & Ritter, R. C. (1995). Peptide cholecystokinin receptor antagonist increases food intake in rats. *Appetite, 24,* 1–9.

Brenner, R., Azbel, V., Madhusoodanan, S., & Pawlowska, M. (2000). *Clinical Therapeutics, 22,* 411–419.

Brenner, R. A., Trumble, A. C., Smith, G. S., Kessler, E. P., & Overpeck, M. D. (2001). Where children drown, United States, 1995. *Pediatrics, 108,* 85–89.

Breslin, P. A., & Beauchamp, G. K. (1997). Salt enhances flavour by suppressing bitterness. *Nature, 387,* 563.

Breuer, J., & Freud, S. (1974). Studies on hysteria. In J. A. Strachey (Ed. & Trans.), *The Pelican Freud library* (Vol. 3). Harmondsworth, England: Penguin. (Original work published 1875)

Brewer, J. B., Zhao, Z., Desmond, J. E., Glover, G. H., & Gabriel, J. D. E. (1998). Making memories: Brain activity that predicts how well visual experience will be remembered. *Science, 281,* 1185–1187.

Brewer, M. B. (2001). The many faces of social identity: Implications for political psychology *Political Psychology, 22,* 115–125.

Brewer, M. B., & Brown, R. J. (1998). Intergroup relations. In D. Gilbert, S. T. Fiske, & G. Lindzey (Eds.), *Handbook of social psychology* (Vol. 2, 4th ed., pp. 554–594). Boston: McGraw-Hill.

Brewer, W. F. (1977). Memory for the pragmatic implications of sentences. *Memory & Cognition, 5,* 673–678.

Brewer, W. F., & Treyens, J. C. (1981). Role of schemata in memory for places. *Cognitive Psychology, 13,* 207–230.

Brigham, C. C. (1923). *A study of American intelligence.* Princeton, NJ: Princeton University Press.

Brigham, C. C. (1930). Intelligence tests of immigrant groups. *Psychological Review, 37,* 158–165.

Brinckerhoff, L. C., Shaw, S. F., & McGuire, J. M. (1993). *Promoting postsecondary education for students with learning disabilities.* Austin, TX: Pro-Ed.

Brislin, R. (1993). *Understanding culture's influence on behavior.* Fort Worth: Harcourt, Brace, Jovanovich.

British Medical Association. (2000). *Acupuncture: Efficacy, safety, and practice.* London: Harwood Academic.

Brock, J. W., Farooqui, S. M., Ross, K. D., & Payne, S. (1994). Stress-related behavior and central norepinephrine concentrations in the REM sleep-deprived rat. *Physiology and Behavior, 55*(6), 997–1003.

Brock, T. C., Green, M. C., & Reich, D. A. (1998). New evidence of flaws in the Consumer Reports study of psychotherapy. *American Psychologist, 53,* 62–72.

Brody, J. E. (1998, September 15). Personal health: Teenagers and sex-Younger and more at risk. *New York Times* (Web Archive).

Brody, N., & Ehrlichman, H. (1998). *Personality psychology: The science of individuality.* Upper Saddle River, NJ: Prentice-Hall.

Bronstein, P., Duncan, P., Clauson, J., Abrams, C. L., Yannett, N., Ginsburg, G., & Milne, M. (1998). Preventing middle school adjustment problems for children from lower-income families: A program for aware parenting. *Journal of Applied Developmental Psychology, 19,* 129–152.

Brooks-Gunn, J., & Chase-Lansdale, P. L. (2002). Adolescent parenthood. In M. H. Bornstein (Ed.), *Handbook of parenting* (2nd ed). Mahwah, NJ: Erlbaum.

Brooks-Gunn, J., Klebanov, P. K., & Duncan, G. J. (1996). Ethnic differences in children's intelligence test scores: Role of economic deprivation, home environment, and maternal characteristics. *Child Development, 67,* 396–408.

Brown, A. L., Campione, J. C., Webber, L. S., & McGilly, K. (1992). Interactive learning environments: A new look at assessment and instruction. In B. Gifford & M. C. O'Connor (Eds.), *Changing assessments: Alternative views of aptitude, achievement, and instruction.* Boston: Kluever.

Brown, A. S. (1991). A review of the tip-of-the-tongue experience. *Psychological Bulletin, 109,* 204–233.

Brown, G. K., Beck, A. T., Steer, R. A., & Grisham, J. R. (2000). Risk factors for suicide in psychiatric outpatients: A 20-year prospective study. *Journal of Consulting and Clinical Psychology, 68,* 371–377.

Brown, G. W., & Moran, P. M. (1997). Single mothers, poverty and depression. *Psychological Medicine, 27,* 21–33.

Brown, J. (1958). Some tests of the decay theory of immediate memory. *Quarterly Journal of Experimental Psychology, 10,* 12–21.

Brown, J. D., & McGill, K. L. (1989). The cost of good fortune: When positive life events produce negative health consequences. *Journal of Personality and Social Psychology, 57,* 1103–1110.

Brown, P. D., & O'Leary, K. D. (2000). Therapeutic alliance: Predicting continuance and success in group treatment for spouse abuse. *Journal of Consulting and Clinical Psychology, 68,* 340–345.

Brown, R., & Kulik, J. (1977). Flashbulb memories. *Cognition, 5,* 73–99.

Brown, R., & McNeill, D. (1966). The "tip-of-the-tongue" phenomenon. *Journal of Verbal Learning and Verbal Behavior, 5,* 325–337.

Brown, R. A. (1973). *First language.* Cambridge: Harvard University Press.

Brown, T., DiNardo, P. A., Lehman, C, & Campbell, L. A. (2001). Reliability of DSM-IV anxiety and mood disorders: Implications for classification of emotional disorders. *Journal of Abnormal Psychology, 110,* 49–58.

Brownell, K. D., & Rodin, J. (1994). The dieting maelstrom: Is it possible and advisable to lose weight? *American Psychologist, 49*(9), 781–791.

Bruce, D., Dolan, A., & Phillips-Grant, K. (2000). On the transition from childhood amnesia to the recall of personal memories. *Psychological Science, 11,* 360–364.

Bruce, H. M. (1969). Pheromones and behavior in mice. *Acta Neurologica Belgica, 69,* 529–538.

Bruce, T. J., Spiegel, D. A., & Hegel, M. T. (1999). Cognitive-behavioral therapy helps prevent relapse and recurrence of panic disorder following Alpazolam discontinuation: A long-term follow-up of the Peoria and Dartmouth studies. *Journal of Consulting and Clinical Psychology, 67,* 151–156.

Bruck, M., Cavanagh, P., & Ceci, S. J. (1991). Fortysomething: Recognizing faces at one's 25th reunion. *Memory and Cognition, 19,* 221–228.

Brüning, J. C., Gautam, D., Burks, D. J., Gillette, J., Schubert, M., Orban, P. C., et al. (2000). Role of brain insulin receptor in control of body weight and reproduction. *Science, 289,* 2122.

Brunvald, J. H. (1989). *Curses! Broiled again! The hottest urban legends going.* New York: Norton.

Bruyer, R. (1991). Covert face recognition in prosopagnosia. *Brain and Cognition, 15,* 223–235.

Bryant, R. A., & McConkey, K. M. (1989). Hypnotic blindness: A behavioral and experiential analysis. *Journal of Abnormal Psychology, 98,* 71–77.

Bryson, S. E., & Smith, I. M. (1998). Autism. *Mental Retardation & Developmental Disabilities Research Reviews, 4,* 97–103.

Buchanan, R. W., & Carpenter, W. T. (1994). Domains of psychopathology: An approach to the reduction of the heterogeneity in schizophrenia. *Journal of Nervous and Mental Disease, 182,* 193–204.

Buchanan, R. W., Strauss, M., Kirkpatrick, B., Holstein, C., Breier, A., & Carpenter, W. T., Jr., (1994). Neuropsychological impairments in deficit vs. nondeficit forms of schizophrenia. *Archives of General Psychiatry, 51,* 804–811.

Buck, L. B. (1996). Information coding in the vertebrate olfactory system. *Annual Review of Neuroscience, 19,* 517–544.

Buckner, R. L., & Wheeler, M. E. (in press). The cognitive neuroscience of remembering. *Nature Reviews Neuroscience.*

Budman, S. H. (2000). Behavioral health care dot-com and beyond: Computer-mediated communications in mental health and substance abuse treatment. *American Psychologist, 55,* 1290–1300.

Budney, A. J., Hughes, J. R., Moore, B. A., & Novy, P. L. (2001). Marijuana abstinence effects in marijuana smokers maintained in their home environment. *Archives of General Psychiatry, 58,* 917–924.

Bugental, D. B., & Goodnow, J. J. (1998). Socialization processes. In W. Damon & N. Eisenberg (Eds.), *Handbook of child psychology: Vol. 3. Social, emotional, and personality development* (5th ed., pp. 389–462). New York: Wiley.

Bui, K.-V. T., Peplau, L. A., & Hill, C. T. (1996). Testing the Rusbult model of relationship commitment and stability in a 15-year study of heterosexual couples. *Personality and Social Psychology Bulletin, 22,* 1244–1257.

Bulik, C. M., Sullivan, P. F., Wade, T. D., & Kendler, K. S. (2000). Twin studies of eating disorders: A review. *International Journal of Eating Disorders, 27,* 1–20.

Bullough, V. L. (1995, August). Sex matters. *Scientific American,* pp. 105–106.

Burac, J. A. (2001). *Development of autism: Perspectives from theory and research.* Hillsdale, NJ: Erlbaum.

Burchard, R. E. (1992). Coca chewing and diet. *Current Anthropology, 33*(1), 1–24.

Burger, J. M., & Petty, R. E. (1981). The low-ball compliance technique: Task or person commitment? *Journal of Personality and Social Psychology, 40,* 492–500.

Burish, T., & Jenkins, R. (1992). Effectiveness of biofeedback and relaxation training in reducing the side effects of cancer chemotherapy. *Health Psychology, 11,* 17–23.

Burke, H. B., Hoang, A., Iglehart, J. D., & Marks, J. R. (1998). Predicting response to adjuvant and radiation therapy in patients with early-stage breast carcinoma. *Cancer, 82,* 874–877.

Burke, K. C., Burke, J. K., Jr., Regier, D. A., & Rae, D. S. (1990). Age at onset of selected mental disorders in five community populations. *Archives of General Psychiatry, 47,* 511–518.

Burke, R. S., & Stephens, R. S. (2000). Social anxiety and drinking in college students: A social cognitive theory analysis. *Clinical Psychology Review, 19,* 513–530.

Burleson, B. R., Albrecht, T. L., & Sarason, I. G. (Eds.). (1994). *Communication of social support: Messages, interactions, relationships, and community.* Thousand Oaks, CA: Sage.

Burleson, M. H., Gregory, W. L., & Trevarthen, W. R. (1995). Heterosexual activity: Relationship with ovarian function. *Psychoneuroendocrinology, 20*(4), 405–421.

Burnstein, E., & Branigan, C. (2001). Evolutionary analyses in social psychology. In A. Tesser & N. Schwarz (Eds.), *Blackwell handbook of social psychology: Intraindividual processes* (pp. 3–21). Oxford, England: Blackwell.

Burnstein, E., Crandell, C., & Kitayama, S. (1994). Some Neo-Darwinian decision rules for altruism: Weighing cues for inclusive fitness as a function of the biological importance of the decision. *Journal of Personality and Social Psychology, 67,* 773–789.

Burr, D. C., Morrone, C., & Fiorentini, A. (1996). Spatial and temporal properties of infant colour vision. In F. Vital-Durand, J. Atkinson, & O. J. Braddick (Eds.), *Infant vision* (pp. 63–77). Oxford: Oxford University Press.

Burris, C. T., Branscombe, N. R., & Klar, Y. (1997). Maladjustment implications of group gender-role discrepancies: An ordered distinction model. *European Journal of Social Psychology, 27,* 675–685.

Burton, A. M., Wilson, S., Cowan, M., & Bruce, V. (1999). Face recognition in poor-quality video: Evidence from security surveillance. *Psychological Science, 10,* 243–248.

Bushman, B. J. (1998). Priming effects of media violence on the accessibility of aggressive constructs in memory. *Personality and Social Psychology Bulletin, 24,* 537–545.

Bushman, B. J., & Anderson, C. A. (2001). Media violence and the American public: Scientific facts versus media misinformation. *American Psychologist, 56,* 477–489.

Buss, A. (1995). *Personality: Temperament, social behavior, and the self.* Boston: Allyn & Bacon.

Buss, A. H. (1989). Personality as traits. *American Psychologist, 44,* 1378–1388.

Buss, D. M. (1999). *Evolutionary psychology: The new science of the mind.* Boston: Allyn & Bacon.

Buss, D. M., & Kenrick, D. T. (1998). Evolutionary social psychology: Intergroup relations. In D. Gilbert, S. T. Fiske, & G. Lindzey (Eds.), *Handbook of social psychology* (Vol. 2, 4th ed., pp. 982–1026). Boston: McGraw-Hill.

Buss, D. M., & Schmitt, D. P. (1993). Sexual strategies theory: An evolutionary perspective on human mating. *Psychological Review, 100,* 204–232.

Bustillo, J. R., Lauriello, J., Horan, W. P., & Keith, S. J. (2001). The psychosocial treatment of schizophrenia: An update. *American Journal of Psychiatry, 158,* 163–175.

Butcher, J. N., & Rouse, S. V. (1996). Personality: Individual differences and clinical assessment. *Annual Review of Psychology, 47,* 87–111.

Butler, R. (1998). Information seeking and achievement motivation in middle childhood and adolescence: The role of conceptions of ability. *Developmental Psychology, 35,* 146–163.

Buunk, B., & Oldersma, F. L. (2001). Social comparisons and close relationships. In G. Fletcher & M. Clark (Eds.), *Blackwell handbook of social psychology: Interpersonal processes* (pp. 388–408). Oxford, England: Blackwell.

Buxhoeveden, D. P., Switala, A. E., Roy, E., Litaker, M., & Casanova, M. F. (2001). Morphological differences between minicolumns in human and nonhuman primate cortex. *American Journal of Physical Anthropology, 115,* 361–371.

Byrne, D., & Nelson, D. (1965). Attraction as a linear function of proportion of positive reinforcements. *Journal of Personality and Social Psychology, 1,* 659–663.

Byne, W., Buchsbaum, M. S., Kemether, E., Hazlett, E. A., Shinwari, A., Mitropoulou, V., & Siever, L. J. (2001). Magnetic resonance imaging of the thalamic mediodorsal nucleus and pulvinar in schizophrenia and schizotypal personality disorder. *Archives of General Psychiatry, 58,* 133–140.

Cabanac, M., & Morrissette, J. (1992). Acute, but not chronic, exercise lowers the body weight set-point in male rats. *Physiology and Behavior, 52*(6), 1173–1177.

Cabeza, R., & Nyberg, L. (2000). Imaging cognition II: An empirical review of 275 PET and MRI studies. *Journal of Cognitive Neuroscience, 12,* 1–47.

Cabeza, R., Rao, S. M., Wagner, A. D., Mayer, A. R., & Schacter, D. L. (2001). Can medial temporal lobe regions distinguish true from false? An event-related functional MRI study of veridical and illusory recognition memory. *Proceedings of the National Academy of Science, 98,* 4805–4810.

Cabot, P. J. (2001). Immune-derived opioids and peripheral antinociception. *Clinical and Experimental Pharmacology and Physiology, 28,* 230–232.

Cabral, G. A., & Dove Pettit, D. A. (1998). Drugs and immunity: Cannabinoids and their role in decreased resistance to infectious disease. *Journal of Neuroimmunology, 83,* 116–123.

Cacioppo, J. T., Berntson, G. G., & Petty, R. E. (1997). Persuasion. *Encyclopedia of human biology* (Vol. 6, pp. 679–690). San Diego: Academic Press.

Cacioppo, J. T., Berntson, G. G., Malarkey, W. B., Kiecolt-Glaser, J. K., Sheridan, J. F., Poehlmann, K. M., et al. (1998). Autonomic, neuroendocrine, and immune responses to psychological stress: The reactivity hypothesis. *Annals of the New York Academy of Sciences, 840,* 664–673.

Cacioppo, J. T., Berntson, G. G., Sheridan, J. F., & McClintock, M. K. (2000). Multilevel integrative analyses of human behavior: Social neuroscience and the complementing nature of social and biological approaches. *Psychological Bulletin, 126,* 829–843.

Cacioppo, J. T., Crites, S. L., & Gardner, W. L. (1996). Attitudes to the right: Evaluative processing is associated with lateralized late positive event-related brain potentials. *Personality and Social Psychology Bulletin, 22,* 1205–1219.

Cacioppo, J. T., Malarkey, W. B., Kiecolt-Glaser, J. K., Uchino, B. N., Sgoutas-Emch, S. A., Sheridan, J. F., et al. (1995). Heterogeneity in neuroendocrine and immune responses to brief psychological stressors as a function of autonomic cardiac activation. *Psychosomatic Medicine, 57,* 154–164.

Cacioppo, J. T., Petty, R. E., & Crites, S. L. (1993). Attitude change. In V. S. Ramachandran (Ed.), *Encyclopedia of human behavior* (pp. 261–270). San Diego: Academic Press.

Cadoret, R. J., Yates, W. R., Troughton, E., Woodworth, G., & Stewart, M. A. (1995). Adoption study demonstrating two genetic pathways to drug abuse. *Archives of General Psychiatry, 52,* 42–52.

Cahill, L., & McGaugh, J. L. (1998). Mechanisms of emotional arousal and lasting declarative memory. *Trends in Neuroscience, 21,* 294–299.

Cahill, S. P., Carrigan, M. H., & Evans, I. M. (1998). The relationship between behavior theory and behavior therapy: Challenges and promises. In J. J. Plaud & G. H. Eifert (Eds.), *From behavior theory to behavior therapy* (pp. 294–319). Boston: Allyn & Bacon.

Cairns, R. B., Gariepy, J., & Hood, K. E. (1990). Development, microevolution, and social behavior. *Psychological Review, 97,* 49–65.

Callen, D. J. A., Black, S. E., Gao, F., Caldwell, C. B., & Szalai, J. P. (2001). Beyond the hippocampus: MRI volumetry confirms widespread limbic atrophy in AD. *Neurology, 57,* 1669–1674.

Calvert, G. A., Bullmore, E. T., Brammer, M. J., Campbell, R., Williams, S. C., McGuire, P. K., et al. (1997). Activation of auditory cortex during silent lipreading. *Science, 276*(5312), 593–596.

Campbell, F. A., Pungello, E. P., Miller-Johnson, S., Burchinal, M., & Ramey, C. T. (2001). The development of cognitive and academic abilities: Growth curves from an early childhood educational experiment. *Developmental Psychology, 37,* 231–242.

Campbell, F. A., Tramer, M. R., Carroll, D., Reynolds, D. J., Moore, R. A., & McQuay, H. J. (2001). Are cannabinoids an effective and safe treatment option in the management of pain? A qualitative systematic review. *British Medical Journal, 323,* 13–16.

Campbell, S. B. (1986). Developmental issues. In R. Gittelman (Ed.), *Anxiety disorders of childhood* (pp. 24–57). New York: Guilford.

Campbell, S. S., & Murphy, P. J. (1998). Extraocular circadian phototransduction in humans. *Science, 279,* 396–399.

Campfield, L. A., Smith, F. J., Guisez, Y., Devos, R., & Burn, P. (1995). Recombinant mouse OB protein: Evidence for a peripheral signal linking adiposity and central neural networks. *Science, 269,* 546–549.

Campione, J. C., Brown, A. L., & Ferrara, R. A. (1982). Mental retardation and intelligence. In R. J. Sternberg (Ed.), *Handbook of human intelligence* (pp. 392–490). Cambridge: Cambridge University Press.

Campos, J. J. (1980). Human emotions: Their new importance and their role in social referencing. *Research and Clinical Center for Child Development, 1980–1981.* Annual Report. 1–7.

Canavero, S. Bonicalzi, V., De Lucchi, R., Davini, O., Podio, V., & Bisi, G (1998). Abolition of neurogenic pain by focal cortical ischemia. *Clinical Journal of Pain, 14,* 268–269.

Canli, T., Zhao, Z., Desmond, J. E., Kang, E., Gross, J., & Gabrieli, J. D. (2001). An fMRI study of personality influences on brain reactivity to emotional stimuli. *Behavioral Neuroscience, 115,* 33–42.

Cann, A., & Ross, D. A. (1989). Olfactory stimuli as context cues in human memory. *American Journal of Psychology, 102,* 91–102.

Cannon, T. D., Mednick, S. A., Parnas, J., Schulsinger, F., Praestholm, J., & Vestergaard, A. (1993). Developmental brain abnormalities in the offspring of schizophrenic mothers. *Archives of General Psychiatry, 50,* 551–564.

Cannon, T. D., van Erp, T. G. M., Rosso, I. M., Huttunen, M., Lonnqvist, J., Pirkola, T., et al. (2002). Fetal hypoxia and structural brain abnormalities in schizophrenic patients, their siblings, and controls. *Archives of General Psychiatry, 59,* 35–41.

Cannon, W. B. (1987). The James-Lange theory of emotions: A critical examination and an alternative theory. *American Journal of Psychology, 100*(3–4), 567–586. (Original work published 1927)

Cannon, W. B., & Washburn, A. L. (1912). An explanation of hunger. *American Journal of Physiology, 29,* 444–454.

Cannon-Bowers, J. A., & Salas, E. (1998). Team performance and training in complex environments: Recent findings from applied research. *Current Directions in Psychological Science, 7,* 83–87.

Cao, Y., Vikingstad, E. M., Huttenlocher, P. R., Towle, V. L., & Levin, D. N. (1994). Functional magnetic resonance studies of the reorganization of the human head sensorimotor area after unilateral brain injury in the perinatal period. *Proceedings of the National Academy of Sciences of the United States of America, 91,* 9612–9616.

Caplan, P. J. (1995). *They say you're crazy. How the world's most powerful psychiatrists decide who's normal.* Reading, MA: Addison-Wesley.

Capron, C., & Duyme, M. (1989). Assessment of effects of socio-economic status on IQ in a full cross-fostering study. *Nature, 340,* 552–553.

Caramazza, A., & Hillis, A. E. (1991). Lexical organization of nouns and verbs in the brain. *Nature, 349,* 788–790.

Cardinal, R. N., Pennicott, D. R., Sugathapala, C. L., Robbins, T. W., & Everitt, B. J. (2001, May 24). Impulsive choice induced in rats by lesions of the nucleus accumbens core. *Science* [Online]. Available: www.sciencemag.org

Cardon, L. R., & Fulker, D. W. (1993). Genetics of specific cognitive abilities. In R. Plomin, & G. McClearn (Eds.), *Nature, nurture, and psychology* (pp. 99–120). Washington, DC: American Psychological Association.

Cardon, L. R., Fulker, D. W., DeFries, J. C., & Plomin, R. (1992). Multivariate genetic analysis of specific cognitive abilities in the Colorado Adoption Project at age 7. *Intelligence, 16,* 383–400.

Cardon, L. R., Smith, S. D., Fulker, D. W., Kimberling, W. J., Pennington, B. F., & DeFries, J. C. (1994). Quantitative trait locus for reading disability on chromosome 6. *Science, 266,* 276–279.

Carli, L. L., Ganley, R., & Pierce-Otay, A. (1991). Similarity and satisfaction in romantic relationships. *Personality and Social Psychology Bulletin, 17,* 419–426.

Carlo, G. L., & Schram, M. (2001). *Cell phones: Invisible hazards in the wireless age: An insider's alarming discoveries about cancer and genetic damage.* New York: Carroll & Graf.

Carlo, G. L., & Thibodeau, P. M. (Eds.). (2001). *Wireless phones and health II: State of the science.* Boston: Kluwer Academic.

Carlson, N. R. (1998). *Physiology of behavior.* Boston: Allyn & Bacon.

Carlsson, K., Petrovic, P., Skare, S., Petersson, K. M., & Ingvar, M. (2000). Tickling expectations: Neural processing in anticipation of a sensory stimulus. *Journal of Cognitive Neuroscience, 12,* 691–703.

Carmichael, L. L., Hogan, H. P., & Walter, A. A. (1932). An experimental study of the effect of language on the reproduction of visually perceived form. *Journal of Experimental Psychology, 15,* 73–86.

Carmody, J. (1998, March 12). Sounds very familiar. *The Washington Post,* C5.

Carnegie Task Force on Learning in the Primary Grades. (1996). *Years of promise: A comprehensive learning strategy for America's children.* New York: Carnegie Corporation.

Carnevale, P. J., & Pruitt, D. G. (1992). Negotiation and mediation. *Annual Review of Psychology, 43,* 531–582.

Carney, R. M., McMahon, P., Freedland, K. E., Becker, L., Krantz, D. S., Proschan, M. A., Raczynski, J. M., Ketterer, M. W., Knatterud, G. L., Light, K., Lindholm, L., & Sheps, D. S. (1998). Reproducibility of mental stress-induced myocardial ischemia in the psychophysiological investigations of myocardial ischemia (PIMI). *Psychosomatic Medicine, 60,* 64–70.

Carper, R. A., & Courchesne, E. (2000). Inverse correlation between frontal lobe and cerebellum sizes in children with autism. *Brain, 123,* 836–844.

Carraher, T. N., Carraher, D., & Schliemann, A. D. (1985). Mathematics in the streets and in the schools. *British Journal of Developmental Psychology, 3,* 21–29.

Carrasco, M., & McElree, B. (2001). Covert attention accelerates the rate of visual information processing. *Proceedings of the National Academy of Science, 98,* 5363–5367.

Carrigan, M. H., & Levis, D. J. (1999). The contributions of eye movements to the efficacy of brief exposure treatment for reducing fear of public speaking. *Journal of Anxiety Disorders, 13,* 101–118.

Carrillo, E., & Lopez, A. (Eds.). (2001). *The Latino psychiatric patient: Assessment and treatment.* Washington, DC: American Psychiatric Press.

Carroll, J. B. (1993). The three-stratum theory of cognitive abilities. In D. P. & Flanagan, J. L. Genshaft (Eds.), *Contemporary intellectual measurement: Theories, tests, and issues* (pp. 122–130). New York: Guilford.

Carstensen, L. (1997, August). *Psychology and the aging revolution: Changes in social needs and social goals across the lifespan.* Paper presented at the annual convention of the American Psychological Association.

Carter, M. M., & Barlow, D. H. (1995). Learned alarms: The origins of panic. In W. T. O'Donohue & L. Krasner (Eds.), *Theories of behavior therapy: Exploring behavior change* (pp. 209–228). Washington, DC: American Psychological Association.

Carter, M. M., Hollon, S. D., Carson, R., & Shelton, R. C. (1995). Effects of a safe person on induced distress following a biological challenge in panic disorder with agoraphobia. *Journal of Abnormal Psychology, 104,* 156–163.

Cartwright, R. D. (1978). *A primer on sleep and dreaming.* Reading, MA: Addison-Wesley.

Cartwright, R. D. (1993). Who needs their dreams? The usefulness of dreams in psychotherapy. *Journal of the American Academy of Psychoanalysis, 21*(4), 539–547.

Carver, C. S., & Scheier, M. (2000). *Perspective on personality* (4th ed.). Boston: Allyn & Bacon.

Casagrande, M., Violani, C., Lucidi, F., Buttinelli, E., & Bertini, M. (1996). Variations in sleep mentation as a function of time of night. *International Journal of Neuroscience, 85,* 19–30.

Case, L., & Smith, T. B. (2000). Ethnic representation in a sample of the literature of applied psychology. *Journal of Consulting and Clinical Psychology, 68,* 1107–1110.

Caspi, A. (1998). Personality development across the life course. In W. Damon & N. Eisenberg (Eds.), *Handbook of child psychology: Vol. 3.*

Social, emotional, and personality development (5th ed., pp. 311–388). New York: Wiley.

Caspi, A. (2000). The child is the father of man: Personality continuities from childhood to adulthood. *Journal of Personality and Social Psychology, 78,* 158–172.

Caspi, A., Begg, D., Dickson, N., Harrington, H., Langley, J., Moffitt, T. E., & Silva, P. A. (1997). Personality differences predict health-risk behaviors in young adulthood: Evidence from a longitudinal study. *Journal of Personality and Social Psychology, 73,* 1052–1063.

Caspi, A., Henry, B., McGee, R. O., Moffitt, T. E., & Silva, P. A. (1995). Temperamental origins of child and adolescent behavior problems: From age 3 to Age 15. *Child Development, 66,* 55–68.

Caspi, A., & Roberts, B. (1999). Personality continuity and change. In L. Pervin & O. John (Eds.), *Handbook of personality: Theory and research* (2nd ed., pp. 300–326). New York: Guilford.

Caspi, A., & Silva, P. A. (1995). Temperamental qualities at age 3 predict personality traits in young adulthood: Longitudinal evidence from a birth cohort. *Child Development, 66,* 468–498.

Cassel, E., & Bernstein, D. A. (2001). *Criminal behavior.* Boston: Allyn & Bacon.

Castillo, R. (Ed.). (1997). *Meanings of madness.* Stamford, CT: Wadsworth.

Caterina, M. J., Schumacher, M. A., Tominaga, M., Rosen, T. A., Levine, J. D., & Julius, D. (1997). The capsaicin receptor: A heat-activated ion channel in the pain pathway. *Nature, 389,* 816–824.

Cattell, R. B. (1963). Theory of fluid and crystallized intelligence: A critical experiment. *Journal of Educational Psychology, 54,* 1–22.

Cattell, R. B., Eber, H. W., & Tatsuoka, M. (1970). *Handbook for the sixteen personality factor questionnaire (16PF).* Champaign, IL: Institute for Personality Testing.

Cavaiola, A. A., & Desordi, E. G. (2000). Locus of control in drinking driving offenders and nonoffenders. *Alcoholism Treatment Quarterly, 18,* 63–73.

Cavaliere, F. (1996, February). Bilingual schools face big political challenges. *APA Monitor,* p. 36.

Ceci, S. J., Huffman, M. L. C., Smith, E., & Loftus, E. F. (1994). Repeatedly thinking about a non-event: Source misattributions among preschoolers. *Consciousness and Cognition, 3,* 388–407.

Ceci, S. J., & Liker, J. K. (1986). A day at the races: A study of IQ, expertise and cognitive complexity. *Journal of Experimental Psychology: General, 115,* 255–266.

Centers for Disease Control and Prevention. (1998). *Trends in the HIV & AIDS epidemic.* Washington, DC: U.S. Government Printing Office.

Centers for Disease Control and Prevention. (1999a). *Chronic diseases and their risk factors.* Washington, DC: U.S. Government Printing Office.

Centers for Disease Control and Prevention. (1999b). *HIV/AIDS surveillance report.* Atlanta, Georgia: National Center for HIV, STD, and TB Prevention.

Centers for Disease Control and Prevention. (1999c). Increases in unsafe sex and rectal gonorrhea among men who have sex with men-San Francisco, California, 1994–1997. *Journal of the American Medical Association, 281,* 696–697.

Centers for Disease Control and Prevention. (1999d). *Suicide deaths and rates per 100,000* [Online]. Available at: http://www.cdc.gov/ncipc/data/us9794/suic.htm

Centers for Disease Control and Prevention. (2000). Cigarette smoking among adults: United States, 1998. *Morbidity and Mortality Weekly Report, 49,* 881–885.

Centers for Disease Control and Prevention. (2001a). The global HIV and AIDS epidemic, 2001. *Morbidity and Mortality Weekly Report, 50,* 434–439.

Centers for Disease Control and Prevention. (2001b). HIV and AIDS+United States, 1981–2000. *Morbidity and Mortality Weekly Report, 50,* 430–434.

Centerwall, L. (1990). Controlled TV viewing and suicide in countries: Young adult suicide and exposure to television. *Social Psychiatry and Social Epidemiology, 25,* 149–153.

Cerf, C., & Navasky, V. (1998). *The experts speak: The definitive compendium of authoritative misinformation.* New York: Villard.

Cervone, D., & Shoda, Y. (1999). *The coherence of personality: social cognitive bases of consistency, variability, and organization.* New York: Guilford.

Cha, J. H., Farrell, L. A., Ahmed, S. F., Frey, A., Hsiao-Ashe, K. K., Young, A. B., et al. (2001). Glutamate receptor dysregulation in the hippocampus of transgenic mice carrying mutated human amyloid precursor protein. *Neurobiological Disorders, 8,* 90–102.

Chaiken, A. L., Sigler, E., & Derlega, V. J. (1974). Nonverbal mediators of teacher expectancy effects. *Journal of Personality and Social Psychology, 30,* 144–149.

Chakrabarti, S., & Fombonne, E. (2001). Pervasive developmental disorders in preschool children. *Journal of the American Medical Association, 285,* 3093–3099.

Chamberlin, J. (2000). Easing children's psychological distress in the emergency room. *Monitor on Psychology, 31,* 40–42.

Chambless, D. L. (1990). Spacing of exposure sessions in the treatment of agoraphobia and simple phobia. *Behavior Therapy 21,* 217–229.

Chambless, D. L., & Hollon, S. D. (1998). Defining empirically supported therapies. *Journal of Consulting and Clinical Psychology, 66,* 7–18.

Chambless, D. L., & Ollendick, T. H. (2001). Empirically supported psychological treatments. *Annual Review of Psychology, 52,* 685–716.

Champion, V., & Huster, G. (1995). Effect of interventions on stage of mammography adoption. *Journal of Behavioral Medicine, 18,* 159–188.

Chan, S. F. (2000). Formal logic and dialectical thinking are not incompatible. *American Psychologist, 55,* 1063–1064.

Chance, P. (1988, April). Knock wood. *Psychology Today.*

Chao, R. K. (1994). Beyond parental control and authoritarian parenting style: Understanding Chinese parenting through the cultural notion of training. *Child Development, 65,* 1111–1119.

Chapman, P. F., Falinska, A. M., Knevett, S. G., & Ramsay, M. F. (2001). Genes, models and Alzheimer's disease. *Trends in Genetics, 17,* 254–261.

Chapman, S., & Morrell, S. (2000). Barking mad? Another lunatic hypothesis bites the dust. *British Medical Journal, 321,* 1561–1563.

Charleton, T., Gunter, B., & Coles, D. (1998). Broadcast television as a cause of aggression? Recent findings from a naturalistic study. *Emotional and Behavioral Difficulties, 3,* 5–13.

Charness, N. (1987). Component processes in bridge bidding and novel problem-solving tasks. *Canadian Journal of Psychology, 41,* 223–243.

Chase, T. N. (1998). The significance of continuous dopaminergic stimulation in the treatment of Parkinson's disease. *Drugs, 55*(Suppl. 1), 1–9.

Chastain, G., & Thurber, S. (1989). The SQ3R study technique enhances comprehension of an introductory psychology textbook. *Reading Improvement, 26,* 94–96.

Chemers, M. M. (1987). Leadership processes: Intrapersonal, interpersonal, and societal influences. In C. Hendrick (Ed.), *Group processes.* Newbury Park, CA: Sage.

Chen, M., & Bargh, J. A. (1997). Nonconscious behavioral confirmation processes: The self-fulfilling consequences of automatic stereotype activation. *Journal of Experimental Social Psychology, 33,* 541–560.

Chen, M. S., Huber, A. B., Van Der Haar, M. E., Frank, M., Schnell, L., Spillmann, A. A., Christ, F., & Schwab, M. E. (2000). Nogo-A is a myelin-associated neurite outgrowth inhibitor and an antigen for monoclonal antibody IN-1. *Nature, 403,* 434–439.

Cheng, Y., Kawachi, I., Coakley, E. H., Schwartz, J., & Colditz, G. (2000). Association between psychosocial work characteristics and health functioning in American women: Prospective study. *British Medical Journal, 320,* 1432–1436.

Cherkin, D. C., Eisenberg, D., Sherman, K. J., Barlow, W., Kaptchuk, T. J., Street, J., & Deyo, R. A. (2001). Randomized trial comparing traditional Chinese medical acupuncture, therapeutic massage, and self-care education for chronic low back pain. *Archives of Internal Medicine, 161,* 1081–1088.

Chi, M. T., Feltovitch, P. J., & Glaser, R. (1981). Representation of physics knowledge by novices and experts. *Cognitive Science, 5,* 121–152.

Chisholm, K. (1997, June). Trauma at an early age inhibits ability to bond. *APA Monitor,* p. 11.

Cho, Z. H., Chung, S. C., Jones, J. P., Park, J. B., Park, H. J., Lee, H. J., et al. (1998). New findings of the correlation between acupoints and corresponding brain cortices using functional MRI. *Proceedings of the National Academy of Sciences, 95,* 2670–2673.

Chomsky, N. (1986). *Knowledge of language: Its nature, origin, and use.* New York: Praeger.

Choo, K. L., & Guilleminault, C. (1998). Narcolepsy and idiopathic hypersomnolence. *Clinical Chest Medicine, 19*(1), 169–181.

Chorney, M. L., Chorney, K., Sense, N., Owen, M. J., Daniels, J., McGuffin, P., et al. (1998). A quantitative trait locus (QTL) associated with cognitive ability in children. *Psychological Science, 9,* 159–166.

Christensen, K. A., Stephens, M. A. P., & Townsend, A. L. (1998). Mastery in women's multiple roles and well-being: Adult daughters providing care to impaired parents. *Health Psychology, 17,* 163–171.

Chugani, H. T., & Phelps, M. E. (1986). Maturational changes in cerebral function in infants determined by 18FDG positron emission tomography. *Science, 231,* 840–843.

Chwalisz, K., Diener, E., & Gallagher, D. (1988). Autonomic arousal feedback and emotional experience: Evidence from the spinal cord injured. *Journal of Personality and Social Psychology, 54,* 820–828.

Cialdini, R. B. (1993). *Influence: Science and practice* (3rd ed.). New York: HarperCollins.

Cialdini, R. B. (1995). Principles and techniques of social influence. In A. Tesser (Ed.), *Advanced social psychology* (pp. 257–282). New York: McGraw-Hill.

Cialdini, R. B. (2001). *Influence: Science and practice* (4th ed.) Boston: Allyn & Bacon.

Cialdini, R. B., Baumann, D. J., & Kenrick, D. T. (1981). Insights from sadness: A three-step model of the development of altruism as hedonism. *Developmental Review, 1,* 207–223.

Cialdini, R. B., Brown, S. L., Lewis, C., & Neuberg, S. (1997). Reinterpreting the empathy-altruism hypothesis: When one into one equals oneness. *Journal of Personality and Social Psychology, 73,* 481–494.

Cialdini, R. B., Reno, R. R., & Kallgren, C. A. (1990). A focus theory of normative conduct: Recycling the concept of norms to reduce littering in public places. *Journal of Personality and Social Psychology, 58,* 1015–1026.

Cialdini, R. B., & Trost, M. (1998). Social influence: Social norms, conformity, and compliance. In D. Gilbert, S. T. Fiske, & G. Lindzey (Eds.), *Handbook of social psychology* (Vol. 2, 4th ed., pp. 151–192). Boston: McGraw-Hill.

Ciapparelli, A., Dell'Osso, L., Tundo, A., Pini, S., Chiavacci, M. C., Di Sacco, I., & Cassano, G. B. (2001). Electroconvulsive therapy in medication-nonresponsive patients with mixed mania and bipolar depression. *Journal of Clinical Psychiatry, 62,* 552–555.

Ciccocioppo, R., Sanna, P. P., & Weiss, F. (2001). Cocaine-predictive stimulus induces drug-seeking behavior and neural activation in limbic brain regions after multiple months of abstinence: Reversal by D1 antagonists. *Proceedings of the National Academy of Sciences 98,* 1976–1981.

Clancy, S. A., Schacter, D. L., McNally, R. J., & Pittman, R. K. (2000). False recognition in women reporting recovered memories of sexual abuse. *Psychological Science, 11,* 26–31.

Clapham, K., & Abramson, E. E. (1985). Aversive conditioning of junk food consumption: A multiple baseline study. *Addictive Behaviors, 10,* 437–440.

Clark, D. C., & Fawcett, J. (1992). Review of empirical risk factors for evaluation of the suicidal patient. In B. Bongar (Ed.), *Suicide: Guidelines for assessment, management, and treatment* (pp. 16–48). New York: Oxford University Press.

Clark, D. C., Gibbons, R. D., Fawcett, J., & Scheftner, W. A. (1989). What is the mechanism by which suicide attempts predispose to later suicide attempts? A mathematical model. *Journal of Abnormal Psychology, 98,* 42–49.

Clark, D. M., & Fairburn, C. G. (Eds.). (1997). *Science and practice of cognitive behavioral therapy.* New York: Oxford University Press.

Clark, D. M., Salkovskis, P. M., Ost, L.-G., Breitholtz, E., Koehler, K. A., Westling, B. E., Jeavons, A., & Gelder, M. (1997). Misinterpretation of body sensations in panic disorder. *Journal of Consulting and Clinical Psychology, 65,* 203–213.

Clark, E. V. (1983). Meanings and concepts. In P. H. Mussen, J. H. Flavell, & E. M. Markman (Eds.), *Handbook of child psychology: Vol. 3. Cognitive development* (4th ed., pp. 787–840). New York: Wiley.

Clark, E. V. (1993). *The lexicon in acquisition.* Cambridge: Cambridge University Press.

Clark, F., Azen, S. P., Carlson, M., Mandel, D., LaBree, L., Hay, J., Zemke, R., Jackson, J., & Lipson, L. (2001). Embedding health-promoting changes into the daily lives of independent-living older adults: Long-term follow-up of occupational therapy intervention. *Journal of Gerontology: Psychological Sciences, 56B,* 60.

Clark, L. A., Watson, D., & Reynolds, S. (1995). Diagnosis and classification of psychopathology: Challenges to the current system and future directions. *Annual Review of Psychology, 46,* 121–153.

Clark, M. (1994). Close relationships. In R. S. Wyer & T. K. Srull (Eds.), *Handbook of social cognition* (2nd ed.). Hillsdale, NJ: Erlbaum.

Clark, M. S., & Pataki, S. P. (1995). Interpersonal processes influencing attraction and relationships. In A. Tesser (Ed.), *Advanced social psychology* (pp. 283–332). New York: McGraw-Hill.

Clarke-Stewart, K. A. (1989). Infant day care: Maligned or malignant? *American Psychologist, 44,* 266–273.

Clarke-Stewart, K. A., & Fein, G. G. (1983). Early childhood programs. In P. H. Mussen (Ed.), *Handbook of child psychology: Vol. 2. Infancy and developmental psychobiology* (pp. 917–1000). New York: Wiley.

Clarkin, J. F., & Carpenter, D. (1995). Family therapy in historical perspective. In B. Bongar & L. E. Beutler (Eds.), *Comprehensive textbook of psychotherapy: Theory and practice* (pp. 205–227). New York: Oxford University Press.

Clausen, J., Sersen, E., & Lidsky, A. (1974). Variability of sleep measures in normal subjects. *Psychophysiology, 11,* 509–516.

Clay, R. (1996, December). Some elders thrive on working into late life. *APA Monitor,* p. 35.

Clay, R. (1997, July). Do hearing devices impair deaf children? *APA Monitor,* pp. 1, 29.

Clay, R. A. (2000). APA task force considers changes to proposed ethics code. *Monitor on Psychology, 31,* 86–87.

Clay, R. A. (2001). Training that's more than bilingual. *Monitor on Psychology, 32,* 70–72.

Clementz, B. A., McDowell, J. E., & Zisook, S. (1994). Saccadic system functioning among schizophrenia patients and their first-degree biological relatives. *Journal of Abnormal Psychology, 103,* 277–287.

Clendenen, V. I., Herman, C. P., & Polivy, J. (1995). Social facilitation of eating among friends and strangers. *Appetite, 23,* 1–13.

Clifton, R. K. (1992). The development of spatial hearing in human infants. In L. A. Werner & E. W. Rubel (Eds.), *Developmental psychoacoustics* (pp. 135–157). Washington, DC: American Psychological Association.

Clifton, R. K., Rochat, P., Litovsky, R., & Perris, E. (1991). Object representation guides infants' reaching in the dark. *Journal of Experimental Psychology: Human Perception and Performance, 17,* 323–329.

Clines, F. X. (2001, February 18). Death spurs laws against drivers on cell phones. *The New York Times.*

Cloninger, C. R. (1998). The genetics and psychobiology of the seven-factor model of personality. In K. R. Silk (Ed.), *Biology of personality disorders* (pp. 63–92). Washington, DC: American Psychiatric Press.

Clower, C. E., & Bothwell, R. K. (2001). An exploratory study of the relationship between the Big Five and inmate recidivism. *Journal of Research in Personality, 35,* 231–237.

Cnattingius, S., Signorello, L. B., Anneren, G., Clausson, B., Ekbom, A., Ljunger, E., Blot, W. J., McLaughlin, J. K., Petersson, G., Rane, A., & Granath, F. (2000). Caffeine intake and the risk of first-trimester spontaneous abortion. *New England Journal of Medicine, 343,* 1839–1845.

CNN/Time. (1997). 1997 poll: U.S. hiding knowledge of aliens. *CNN/Time* [Online]. Available: www-cgi.cnn.com/US/9706/15/ufo.poll/index.html

Coccaro, E. F. (1989). Central serotonin and impulsive aggression. *British Journal of Psychiatry, 155,* 52–62.

Cohen, C. E. (1981). Person categories and social perception: Testing some boundaries of the processing effects of prior knowledge. *Journal of Personality and Social Psychology, 40,* 441–452.

Cohen, D., & Nisbett, R. (1997). Field experiments examining the culture of honor: The role of institutions in perpetuating norms about violence. *Personality and Social Psychology Bulletin, 23,* 1188–1199.

Cohen, D., Nisbett, R. E., Bowdle, B. F., & Schwarz, N. (1996). Insult, aggression, and the southern culture of honor: An "experimental ethnography." *Journal of Personality and Social Psychology, 70,* 945–960.

Cohen, J. (1994). The earth is round ($p < .05$). *American Psychologist, 49,* 997–1003.

Cohen, J., & Servan-Schreiber, D. (1992). Context, cortex, and dopamine: A connectionist approach to behavior and biology in schizophrenia. *Psychological Review, 99,* 45–77.

Cohen, M. S. (1993). Three paradigms for viewing decision biases. In G. A. Klein, J. Orasanu, R. Calderwood, & C. E. Zasmbok (Eds.), *Decision making in action: Models and methods.* Norwood, NJ: Ablex.

Cohen, N. J., & Corkin, S. (1981). The amnesic patient H. M.: Learning and retention of a cognitive skill. *Neuroscience Abstracts, 7,* 235.

Cohen, S., Doyle, W. J., Skoner, D. P., Gwaltney, J. M., Jr., & Newsom, J. T. (1995). State and trait negative affect as predictors of objective and subjective symptoms of respiratory viral infections. *Journal of Personality and Social Psychology, 68,* 159–169.

Cohen, S., & Herbert, T. B. (1996). Health psychology: Psychological factors and physical disease from the perspective of human psychoneuroimmunology. *Annual review of psychology, 47,* 113–142.

Colby, A., Kohlberg, L., Gibbs, J., & Lieberman, M. (1983). A longitudinal study of moral judgment. *Monographs of the Society for Research in Child Development, 48*(1, Serial No. 200).

Cole, K. N., Mills, P. E., Dale, P. S., & Jenkins, J. R. (1991). Effects of preschool integration for children with disabilities. *Exceptional Children, 58,* 36–45.

Cole, R. A., & Jakimik, J. (1978). Understanding speech: How words are heard. In G. Underwood (Ed.), *Strategies of information processing* (pp. 67–116). London: Academic Press.

Coleman, D. (1992). Why do I feel so tired? Too little, too late. *American Health, 11*(4), 43–46.

Coles, M. (1989). Modern mind-brain reading: Psychophysiology, physiology & cognition. *Psychophysiology, 26,* 251–269.

Collacott, E. A., Zimmerman, J. T., White, D. W., & Rindone, J. P. (2000). Bipolar permanent magnets for the treatment of chronic low back pain: a pilot study. *Journal of the American Medical Association, 283,* 1322–1325.

College Board. (1994, August 25). *News from the college board* [Media release]. New York: College Board Publications.

Collins, A. M., & Loftus, E. F. (1975). A spreading activation theory of semantic processing. *Psychological Review, 82,* 407–428.

Collins, G. (1997, May 30). Trial near in new legal tack in tobacco war. *New York Times,* p. A10.

Collins, W. A., Maccoby, E. E., Steinberg, L., Hetherington, E. M., & Bornstein, M. H. (2000). Contemporary research on parenting: The case for nature and nurture. *American Psychologist, 55,* 218–232.

Colombo, M., D'Amato, M. R., Rodman, H. R., & Gross, C. G. (1990). Auditory association cortex lesions impair auditory short-term memory in monkeys. *Science, 247,* 336–338.

Coltrane, S. (2001). Research on household labor: Modeling and measuring the social embeddedness of routine family work. In R. M. Milardo (Ed), *Understanding families into the new millennium: A decade in review.* Minneapolis, MN: National Council on Family Relations.

Colwill, R. M. (1994). Associative representations of instrumental contingencies. *Psychology of Learning and Motivation, 31,* 1–72.

Compagnone, N. A., & Mellon, S. H. (2000). Neurosteroids: biosynthesis and function of these novel neuromodulators. *Frontiers of Neuroendocrinology, 21,* 1–56.

Compas, B. E., Haaga, D. A. F., Keefe, F. J., Leitenberg, H., & Williams, D. A. (1998). Sampling of empirically supported psychological treatments from health psychology: Smoking, chronic pain, cancer, and bulimia nervosa. *Journal of Consulting and Clinical Psychology, 66,* 89–112.

Condic, M. L. (2001). Adult neuronal regeneration induced by transgenic integrin expression. *Journal of Neuroscience, 21,* 4782–4788.

Condon, J. W., & Crano, W. D. (1988). Inferred evaluation and the relationship between attitude similarity and interpersonal attraction. *Journal of Personality and Social Psychology, 54,* 789–797.

Conley, R. R., & Mahmoud, R. (2001). A randomized double-blind study of risperidone and olanzapine in the treatment of schizophrenia or schizoaffective disorder. *The American Journal of Psychiatry, 158,* 765–774.

Conner, A. (2001a). They all answer to "psychologist." *APS Observer, 14,* 1, 8–9, 11.

Conner, A. (2001b). Territorial imperatives in psychological science. *APS Observer, 14,* 1, 16–17.

Connor, L. T., Balota, D. A., & Neely, J. H. (1992). On the relation between feeling of knowing and lexical decision: Persistent subthreshold activation of topic familiarity? *Journal of Experimental Psychology: Learning, Memory, and Cognition, 18,* 544–554.

Conrad, R. (1964). Acoustic confusions in immediate memory. *British Journal of Psychology, 55,* 75–84.

Consumer Reports. (1995, November). Mental health: Does therapy help? *Consumer Reports,* pp. 734–739.

Contrada, R. J., Ashmore, R. D., Gary, M. L., Coups, E., Egeth, J. D., Sewell, A., Ewell, K., Goyal, T. M., & Chasse, V. (2000). Ethnicity-related sources of stress and their effects on well-being. *Current Directions in Psychological Science, 9,* 136–139.

Cook, T., & Mineka, S. (1987). Second-order conditioning and overshadowing in the observational of fear in monkeys. *Behavior Research and Therapy, 25,* 349–364.

Cook, T., & Mineka, S. (1990). Selective association in the observational conditioning of fear in rhesus monkeys. *Journal of Experimental Psychology: Animal Behavior Processes, 16,* 372–389.

Cookson, J., & Duffett, R. (1998). Fluoxetine: therapeutic and undesirable effects. *Hospital Medicine, 59,* 622–626.

Cooper, H. (1979). Pygmalion grows up: A model for teacher expectation communication and performance influence. *Review of Educational Research, 49,* 389–410.

Cooper, M. L., Russell, M., Skinner, J. B., Frone, M. R., & Mudar, P. (1992). Stress and alcohol use: The moderating effects of gender, coping, and alcohol expectancies. *Journal of Abnormal Psychology, 101,* 139–152.

Cooper, R. M., & Zubek, J. P. (1958). Effects of enriched and restricted early environments on the learning ability of bright and dull rats. *Canadian Journal of Psychology, 12,* 159–164.

Coovert, M. D., & Reeder, G. D. (1990). Negativity effects in impression formation: The role of unit formation and schematic expectations. *Journal of Experimental Social Psychology, 26,* 49–62.

Copeland, J., & Snyder, M. (1995). When counselors confirm: A functional analysis. *Personality and Social Psychology Bulletin, 21,* 1210–1220.

Corbetta, M., Miezin, F. M., Dobmeyer, S., Shulman, G. L., & Peterson, S. E. (1991). Selective and divided attention during visual discrimination of shape, color, and speed: Functional anatomy by positron emission tomography. *Journal of Neuroscience, 11,* 2383–2402.

Cordova, J. V., & Jacobson, N. S. (1993). Couple distress. In D. H. Barlow (Ed.), *Clinical handbook of psychological disorders: A step-by-step treatment manual* (2nd ed., pp. 481–512). New York: Guilford.

Coren, S. (1999). Psychology applied to animal training. In A. Stec & D. Bernstein (Eds.), *Psychology: Fields of application.* Boston: Houghton Mifflin.

Cork, R. C., Kihlstrom, J. F., & Hameroff, S. R. (1992). Explicit and implicit memory dissociated by anesthetic technique. *Society for Neuroscience Abstracts, 22,* 523.

Cornblatt, B., & Erlenmeyer-Kimling, L. E. (1985). Global attentional deviance in children at risk for schizophrenia: Specificity and predictive validity. *Journal of Abnormal Psychology, 94,* 470–486.

Cornelius, R. R. (1996). *The science of emotion.* Upper Saddle River, NJ: Prentice-Hall.

Corning, A. F. (2000). Assessing perceived social inequity: A relative deprivation framework. *Journal of Personality and Social Psychology, 78,* 463–477.

Cornoldi, C., DeBeni, R., & Baldi, A. P. (1989). Generation and retrieval of general, specific, and autobiographic images representing concrete nouns. *Acta Psychologica, 72,* 25–39.

Corruble, E., Damy, C. & Guelfi, J. D., (1999). Impulsivity: A relevant dimension in depression regarding suicide attempts. *Journal of Affective Disorders, 53,* 211–215.

Corsini, R. J., & Wedding, D. (2001). *Current psychotherapies* (6th ed.). Itasca, IL: Peacock.

Coryell, W., Scheftner, W., Keller, M., Endicott, J., Maser, J., & Klerman, G. (1993). The enduring consequences of mania and depression. *American Journal of Psychiatry, 150,* 720–727.

Costa, P. (2001, June). *New insights on personality and leadership provided by the five-factor model.* Paper presented at Annual Convention of American Psychological Society, Toronto, Canada.

Costa, P. T., Jr., & McCrae, R. (1992). *Revised NEO Personality Inventory: NEO PI and NEO Five-Factor Inventory (NEO FFI: Professional Manual).* Odessa, FL: Psychological Assessment Resources.

Costa, P. T., Jr., & McCrae, R. R. (1995). Primary traits of Eysenck's P-E-N system: Three- and five-factor solutions. *Journal of Personality and Social Psychology, 69,* 308–317.

Costello, E., Costello, A., Edelbrock, C., Burns, B., Dulcan, M., Brent, D., & Janiszewski, S. (1988). Psychiatric disorders in pediatric primary care. *Archives of General Psychiatry, 45,* 1107–1116.

Costermans, J., Lories, G., & Ansay, C. (1992). Confidence level and feeling of knowing in question answering: The weight of inferential processes. *Journal of Experimental Psychology: Learning, Memory, and Cognition 18,* 142–150.

Cotter, D., Mackay, D, Landau, S. Kerwin, R., & Everall, I. (2001). Reduced glial cell density and neuronal size in the anterior cingulate cortex in major depressive disorder. *Archives of General Psychiatry, 58,* 545–553.

Courchesne, E., Karns, C. M., Davis, H. R., Ziccardi, R., Carper, R. A., Tigue, Z. D., et al. (2001). Unusual brain growth patterns in early life in patients with autistic disorder: An MRI study. *Neurology, 57,* 245–254.

Courneya, K. S. (1995). Understanding readiness for regular physical activity in older individuals: An application of the theory of planned behavior. *Health Psychology, 14,* 80–87.

Cowan, N. (1988). Evolving concepts of memory storage, selective attention, and their mutual constraints within the human information-processing system. *Psychological Bulletin, 104,* 163–191.

Cowey, A. (1994). Cortical visual areas and the neurobiology of higher visual processes. In M. J. Farah & G. Ratcliff (Eds.), *The neurophysiology of high-level vision: Collected tutorial essays* (pp. 3–31). Hillsdale, NJ: Erlbaum.

Coyne, J. C., & Whiffen, V. E. (1995). Issues in personality as diathesis for depression: The case of sociotropy-dependency and autonomy-self-criticism. *Psychological Bulletin, 4,* 278–287.

Cozzarelli, C. (1993). Personality and self-efficacy as predictors of coping with an abortion. *Journal of Personality and Social Psychology, 65,* 1224–1236.

Crabbe, J. C., Phillips, T. J., Buck, K. J., Cunningham, C. L., & Belknap, J. K. (1999). Identifying genes for alcohol and drug sensitivity: Recent progress and future directions. *Trends in Neuroscience, 22,* 173–179.

Craig, A. D., & Bushnell, M. C. (1994). The thermal grill illusion: Unmasking the burn of cold pain. *Science, 265,* 252–254.

Craik, F. I. M., & Lockhart, R. S. (1972). Levels of processing: A framework for memory research. *Journal of Verbal Learning and Verbal Behavior, 11,* 671–684.

Craik, F. I. M., Moroz, T. M., Moscovitch, M., Stuss, D. T., Winocur, G., Tulving, E., & Kapur, S. (1999). In search of the self: A positron emission topography study. *Psychological Science, 10,* 26–34.

Craik, F. I. M., & Rabinowitz, J. C. (1984). Age differences in the acquisition and use of verbal information. In H. Bouma & D. G. Bouwhuis (Eds.), *Attention and performance* (Vol. 10). Hillsdale, NJ: Erlbaum.

Craik, F. I. M., & Tulving, E. (1975). Depth of processing and the recognition of words in episodic memory. *Journal of Experimental Psychology: General, 104,* 268–294.

Cramer, E. P. (1999). Hate crime laws and sexual orientation. *Journal of Sociology & Social Welfare, 26,* 5–24.

Crandall, C. S., Preisler, J. J., & Aussprung, J. (1992). Measuring life event stress in the lives of college students: The Undergraduate Stress Questionnaire (USQ). *Journal of Behavioral Medicine, 15,* 627–662.

Crano, W. D., & Chen., X. (1998). The leniency contract and persistence of majority and minority influence. *Journal of Personality and Social Psychology, 74,* 1437–1450.

Crawford, H. J., Brown, A. M., & Moon, C. E. (1993). Sustained attentional and disattentional abilities: Differences between low and highly hypnotizable persons. *Journal of Abnormal Psychology, 102*(4), 534–543.

Crawford, J. (1989). *Bilingual education: History, politics, theory, and practice.* New York: Crane.

Crawford, J. G. (1998). Alzheimer's disease risk factors as related to cerebral blood flow: Additional evidence. *Medical Hypotheses, 50,* 25–36.

Crawley, J. N., & Corwin, R. L. (1994). Biological actions of cholecystokinin. *Peptides, 15*(4), 731–755.

Crick, F., & Koch, C. (1998). Consciousness and neuroscience. *Cerebral Cortex, 8,* 97–107.

Crick, N. (1997, June). Abused children have more conflicts with friends. *APA Monitor,* p. 32.

Crick, N. R., Casas, J. F., & Mosher, M. (1997). Relational and overt aggression in preschool. *Developmental Psychology, 33,* 579–588.

Crick, N. R., Werner, N. E., Casas, J. F., O'Brien, K. M., Nelson, D. A., Grotpeter, J. K., & Markon, K. (1999). Childhood aggression and gender: A new look at an old problem. In D. Bernstein (Ed.), *Nebraska Symposium on Motivation* (Vol. 44, pp. 75–141). Lincoln: University of Nebraska Press.

Critchley, E. M. (1991). Speech and the right hemisphere. *Behavioral Neurology, 4*(3), 143–151.

Croen, L. A., Grether, J. K., & Selvin, S. (2001). The epidemiology of mental retardation of unknown cause. *Pediatrics, 107,* 86.

Croft, H., Settle, E., Jr., Houser, T., Batey, S. R., Donahue, R. M., & Ascher, J. A. (1999). A placebo-controlled comparison of the antidepressant efficacy and effects on sexual functioning of sustained-release bupropion and sertraline. *Clinical Therapeutics, 21,* 643–658.

Cronbach, L. J. (1990). *Essentials of psychological testing* (5th ed.). New York: Harper & Row.

Crosby, A. E., Cheltenham, M. P., & Sacks, J. J. (1999). Incidence of suicidal ideation and behavior in the United States, 1994. *Suicide & Life Threating Behavior, 29,* 131–140.

Cross, S. E., & Madson, L. (1997). Models of the self: Self-construals and gender. *Psychological Bulletin, 122,* 5–37.

Cross, S. E., & Markus, H. R. (1999). The cultural constitution of personality. In L. Pervin & O. John (Eds.), *Handbook of personality research* (2nd ed., pp. 378–398). New York: Guilford.

Cross-National Collaborative Group. (1992). The changing rate of major depression: Cross-national comparisons. *Journal of the American Medical Association, 268,* 3098–3105.

Crowley, K., Callahan, M. A., Tenenbaum, H. R., & Allen, E. (2001). Parents explain more often to boys than to girls during shared scientific thinking. *Psychological Science, 12,* 258–261.

Crowther, J. H., Sanftner, J., Bonifazi, D. Z., & Shepherd, K. L. (2001). The role of daily hassles in binge eating. *International Journal of Eating Disorders, 29,* 449–454.

Cruz, A., & Green, B. G. (2000). Thermal stimulation of taste. *Nature, 403,* 889–892.

Crystal, D. S., Chen, C., Fuligni, A. J., Stevenson, H. W., Hsu, C.-C., Ko, H.-J., Kitamura, S., & Kimura, S. (1994). Psychological maladjustment and academic achievement: A cross-cultural study of Japanese, Chinese, and American high school students. *Child Development, 65,* 738–753.

Csikszentmihalyi, M. (1999). If we are so rich, why aren't we happy? *American Psychologist, 54,* 821–827.

Culbertson, F. M. (1997). Depression and gender. An international review. *American Psychologist, 52,* 25–31.

Cumsille, P. E., Sayer, A. G., & Graham, J. W. (2000). Perceived exposure to peer and adult drinking as predictors of growth in positive alcohol expectancies during adolescence. *Journal of Consulting and Clinical Psychology, 68,* 531–536.

Curcio, C. A., Sloan, D. R., Jr., Packer, O., Hendrickson, A. E., & Kalina, R. E. (1987). Distribution of cones in human and monkey retina: Individual variability and radial asymmetry. *Science, 236*, 579–582.

Curran, H. V., & Monaghan, L. (2001). In and out of the K-hole: A comparison of the acute and residual effects of ketamine in frequent and infrequent ketamine users. *Addiction, 96*, 749–760.

Cusack, K., & Spates, C. R. (1999). The cognitive dismantling of eye movement desensitization and reprocessing (EMDR) treatment of post-traumatic stress disorder (PTSD). *Journal of Anxiety Disorders, 13*, 87–99.

Cutler, W. B., Friedmann, E., & McCoy, N. L. (1998). Pheromonal influences on sociosexual behavior in men. *Archives of Sexual Behavior, 27*, 1–13.

Czeisler, C. A., Duffy, J. F., Shanahan, T. L., Brown, E. N., Mitchell, J. F., Rimmer, D. W., Ronda, J. M., Silva, E. J., Allan, J. S., Emens, J. S., Dijk, D.-J., & Kronauer, R. E. (1999). Stability, precision, and near 24-hour period of the human circadian pacemaker. *Science, 284*, 2177–2181.

D'Esposito, M., Detre, J. A., Alsop, D. C., & Shin, R. K. (1995). The neural basis of the central executive system of working memory. *Nature, 378*, 279–281.

Dabbs, J., & Dabbs, M. G. (2001). *Heroes, rogues, and lovers: Testosterone and behavior*. New York: McGraw-Hill.

Dabbs, J. M., Jr., Riad, J. K., & Chance, S. E. (2001). Testosterone and ruthless homicide. *Personality and Individual Differences, 31*, 599–603.

Dadds, M. R., Spence, S. H., Holland, D. E., Barrett, P. M., & Laurens, K. R. (1997). Prevention and early intervention for anxiety disorders: A controlled trial. *Journal of Consulting and Clinical Psychology, 65*, 627–635.

Dadds, M. R., Holland, D. E., Laurens, K. R., Mullins, M., Barrett, P. M., & Spence, S. H. (1999). Early intervention and prevention of anxiety disorders in children: Results at 2-year follow-up. *Journal of Consulting & Clinical Psychology, 67*, 145–150.

Dafilis, M. P., Liley, D. T. J., & Cadusch, P. J. (2001). Robust chaos in a model of the electroencephalogram: Implications for brain dynamics. *Chaos: An Interdisciplinary Journal of Nonlinear Science, 11*, 474–478.

D'Agostino, R. B., Sr., Grundy, S., Sullivan, L. M., & Wilson, P. (2001). Validation of the Framingham coronary heart disease prediction scores: Results of a multiple ethnic groups investigation. *Journal of the American Medical Association, 286*, 180–187.

Dale, P. S. (1976). *Language and the development of structure and function*. New York: Holt, Rinehart & Winston.

Daly, G., Hawi, Z., Fitzgerald, M., & Gill, M. (1999). Mapping susceptibility loci in attention deficit hyperactivity disorder: Preferential transmission of parental alleles at DAT1, DBH and DRD5 to affected children. *Molecular Biology, 4*, 192–196.

Daly, M., & Wilson, M. (1988). *Homicide*. New York: Aldine de Gruyter.

Damasio, A. R., Grabowski, T. J., Bechara, A., Damasio, H., Ponto, L. L. B., Parvizi, J., & Hichwa, R. D. (2000). Subcortical and cortical brain activity during the feeling of self-generated emotions. *Nature Neuroscience, 3*, 1049–1056.

Damasio, A. R. (1994). *Descartes' error*. New York: Putnam.

Damon, W., & Hart, D. (1982). The development of self-understanding from infancy through adolescence. *Child Development, 53*, 841–864.

Damos, D. (1992). *Multiple task performance*. London: Taylor & Francis.

Danner, D. D., Snowdon, D. A., & Friesen, W. V. (2001). Positive emotions in early life and longevity: Findings from the Nun Study. *Journal of Personality and Social Psychology, 80*, 804–813.

Dark, V. J., & Benbow, C. P. (1993). Cognitive differences among the gifted: A review and new data. In D. K. Detterman (Ed.), *Current topics in human intelligence* (Vol. 3, pp. 85–120). Norwood, NJ: Ablex.

Darkes, J., & Goldman, M. S. (1993). Expectancy challenge and drinking reduction. *Journal of Clinical and Consulting Psychology, 61*, 344–353.

Darwin, C. E. (1965). *The expression of emotions in man and animals*. Chicago: University of Chicago Press. (Original work published 1872)

Das, J. P. (2002). A better look at intelligence. *Current Directions in Psychological Science, 11*, 28–33.

Dasgupta, A. M., Juza, D. M., White, G. M., & Maloney, J. F. (1995). Memory and hypnosis: A comparative analysis of guided memory, cognitive interviews, and hypnotic hypermnesia. *Imagination, Cognition, and Personality 14*(2), 117–130.

Davanloo, H. (1999). Intensive short-term dynamic psychotherapy-central dynamic sequence: Phase of challenge. *International Journal of Short-Term Dynamic Psychotherapy, 13*, 237–262.

Davidson, J. K., & Moore, N. B. (1994). Guilt and lack of orgasm during sexual intercourse: Myth versus reality in college women. *Journal of Sex Education and Therapy, 20*(3), 153–174.

Davidson, J. M., Camargo, C. A., & Smith, E. R. (1979). Effects of androgen on sexual behavior in hypogonadal men. *Journal of Clinical Endocrinological Metabolism, 48*, 955–958.

Davidson, J. R. T., Rothbaum, B. O., van der Kolk, B. A., Sikes, C. R., & Farfel, G. M. (2001). Multicenter, double-blind comparison of sertraline and placebo in the treatment of posttraumatic stress disorder. *Archives of General Psychiatry, 58*, 485–492.

Davidson, K., Hall, P., & MacGregor, M. (1996). Gender differences in the relation between interview-derived hostility scores and resting blood pressure. *Journal of Behavioral Medicine, 19*, 185–201.

Davidson, K., & Prkachin, K. (1997). Optimism and unrealistic optimism have an interacting impact on health-promoting behavior and knowledge changes. *Personality and Social Psychology Bulletin, 23*, 617–625.

Davidson, R. J. (2000). Affective style, psychopathology, and resilience: Brain mechanisms and plasticity. *American Psychologist, 55*, 1196–1214.

Davidson, R. J., Ekman, P., Saron, C., Senulis, J., & Friesen, W. V. (1990). Approach-withdrawal and cerebral asymmetry: Emotional expression and brain physiology: I. *Journal of Personality and Social Psychology, 58*, 330–341.

Davies, C. (1999, April 21). Junior doctor is cleared in baby overdose death. *London Daily Telegraph*, p. 2.

Davies, R. J., & Stradling, J. R. (2000). The efficacy of nasal continuous positive airway pressure in the treatment of obstructive sleep apnea syndrome is proven. *American Journal of Respiratory Critical Care Medicine, 161*, 1775–1776.

Davis, J. A., & Smith, T. W. (1990). *General social surveys, 1972–1990: Cumulative codebook*. Chicago: National Opinion Research Center.

Davis, J. D., Gallagher, R. J., Ladove, R. F., & Turansky, A. J. (1969). Inhibition of food intake by a humoral factor. *Journal of Comparative and Physiological Psychology, 67*, 407–414.

Davis, J. L., & Rusbult, C. (2001). Attitude alignment in close relationships. *Journal of Personality and Social Psychology, 81*, 65–84.

Davis, K. D., Taylor, S. J., Crawley, A. P., Wood, M. L., & Mikulis, D. J. (1997). Functional MRI of pain- and attention-related activations in the human cingulate cortex. *Journal of Neurophysiology, 77*, 3370–3380.

Davis, K. L., Kahn, R. S., Ko, G., & Davidson, M. (1991). Dopamine in schizophrenia: A review and reconceptualization. *American Journal of Psychiatry, 148*, 1474–1486.

Davis, M., Falls, W. A., Campeau, S., & Kim, M. (1993). Fear-potentiated startle: A neural and pharmacological analysis. *Behavioural Brain Research, 58*(1–2), 175–198.

Davis, M. H. (1994). *Empathy: A social psychological approach*. Madison, WI: Brown and Benchmark.

Davis, M. H., Luce, C., & Kraus, S. J. (1994). The heritability of characteristics associated with dispositional empathy. *Journal of Personality, 60*, 369–391.

Davis, R. A., & Moore, C. C. (1935). Methods of measuring retention. *Journal of General Psychology, 12*, 144–155.

Davison, G. C. (1998). Being bolder with the Boulder Model: The challenge of education and training in empirically supported treatments. *Journal of Consulting and Clinical Psychology, 66*, 163–167.

Davison, G. C., & Neale, J. M. (1990). *Abnormal psychology* (5th ed.). New York: Wiley.

Davison, P. R., & Parker, K. C. H. (2001). Eye movement desensitization and reprocessing (EMDR): A meta-analysis. *Journal of Consulting and Clinical Psychology, 69*, 305–316.

Dawe, L. A., Platt, J. R., & Welsh, E. (1998). Spectral-motion aftereffects and the tritone paradox among Canadian subjects. *Perception and Psychophysics, 60*, 209–220.

Dawes, R. (1998). Behavioral judgment and decision making. In D. Gilbert, S. T. Fiske, & G. Lindzey (Eds.), *Handbook of social psychology* (Vol. 1, 4th ed., pp. 497–549). Boston: McGraw-Hill.

Dawes, R. M. (1994). *House of cards: Psychology and psychotherapy built on myth.* New York: Free Press.

Dawes, R. M., & Messick, D. M. (2000). Social dilemmas. *International Journal of Psychology, 35,* 111–116.

Dawkins, K., & Potter, W. (1991). Gender differences in pharmacokinetics and pharmacodynamics of psychotropics: Focus on women. *Psychopharmacology Bulletin, 27,* 417–426.

Dawson, D. A., Wadsworth, G., & Palmer, A. M. (2001). A comparative assessment of the efficacy and side-effect liability of neuroprotective compounds in experimental stroke. *Brain Research, 892,* 344–350.

Dawson, M., Schell, A. M., & Fillion, D. L. (2000). The electodermal system. In J. Cacioppo, L. Tassinary, & G. Bernston (Eds.), *Handbook of psychophysiology* (2nd ed., pp. 200–222). New York: Cambridge University Press.

Dawson-Basoa, M., & Gintzler, A. R. (1997). Involvement of spinal cord delta opiate receptors in the antinociception of gestation and its hormonal simulation. *Brain Research, 757,* 37–42.

DeAngelis, T. (1995). Firefighters' PTSD at dangerous levels. *APA Monitor,* pp. 36–37.

DeAngelis, T. (2000). School psychologists: In demand and expanding their reach. *Monitor on Psychology, 31,* 30–32.

DeAngelis, T. (2001). APA has lead role in revising classification system. *Monitor on Psychology, 32,* 54–56.

Deary, I. J., & Caryl, P. G. (1993). Intelligence, EEG and evoked potentials. In P. A. Vernon (Ed.), *Biological approaches to the study of human intelligence* (pp. 259–315). Norwood, NJ: Ablex.

Death Penalty Information Center. (2001, August 24). *Innocence: Freed from death row* [Online]. Available: http://www.deathpenaltyinfo.org/Innocentlist.html

Deaux, K., & LaFrance, M. (1998). Gender. In D. Gilbert, S. T. Fiske, & G. Lindzey (Eds.), *Handbook of social psychology* (Vol. 1, 4th ed., pp. 778–828). Boston: McGraw-Hill.

Deaux, K., & Martin, D. (2001). *Which context? Specifying levels of context in identity processes.* Paper presented at Indiana Conference on Identity Theory, Bloomington, Indiana.

DeBell, C., & Jones, R. D. (1997). As good as it seems? A review of EMDR experimental research. *Professional Psychology: Research and Practice, 28,* 153–163.

De Benedittis, G., Lornenzetti, A., & Pieri, A. (1990). The role of stressful life events in the onset of chronic primary headache. *Pain, 40,* 65–75.

DeBeurs, E., van Balkom, A. J. L. M., Lange, A., Koele, P., & van Dyck, R. (1995). Treatment of panic disorder with agoraphobia: Comparison of fluvoxamine, placebo, and psychological panic management combined with exposure and of exposure in vivo alone. *American Journal of Psychiatry, 152*(5), 683–691.

de Castro, J. M., & Goldstein, S. J. (1995). Eating attitudes and behaviors pre- and postpubertal females: Clues to the etiology of eating disorders. *Physiology and Behavior, 58*(1), 15–23.

de Charms, R., Levy, J., & Wertheimer, M. (1954). A note on attempted evaluations of psychotherapy. *Journal of Clinical Psychology, 10,* 233–235.

Deci, E. L, Koestner, R., & Ryan, R. M. (1999). The undermining effect is a reality after all—Extrinsic rewards, task interest, and self-determination: Reply to Eisenberger, Pierce, and Cameron (1999) and Lepper, Henderlong, and Gingras (1999). *Psychological Bulletin, 125,* 692–700.

Deci, E. L., Koestner, R., & Ryan, R. M. (2001). A meta-analytic review of experiments examining the effects of extrinsic rewards on intrinsic motivation. *Psychological Bulletin, 125,* 627–668.

De Houwer, A. (1995). Bilingual language acquisition. In P. Fletcher & B. MacWhinney (Eds.), *The handbook of child language* (pp. 219–250). Cambridge, MA: Blackwell.

de Lacoste-Utamsing, C., & Holloway, R. L. (1982). Sexual dimorphism in the human corpus callosum. *Science, 216,* 1431–1432.

Delmolino, L. M., & Romanczyk, R. G. (1995). Facilitated communication: A critical review. *The Behavior Therapist 18,* 27–30.

Dement, W. (1960). The effect of dream deprivation. *Science, 131,* 1705–1707.

Dement, W., & Kleitman, N. (1957). Cyclic variations in EEG during sleep and their relation to eye movements, body motility and dreaming. *Electroencephalography and Clinical Neurophysiology, 9,* 673–690.

Demo, D. H., Allen, K. R., & Fine, M. A. (Eds.). (2000). *Handbook of family diversity.* New York: Oxford University Press.

DeNeve, K. M. (1999). Happy as an extraverted clam? The role of personality for subjective well-being. *Current Directions in Psychological Science, 8,* 141–144.

Denmark, F., Russo, N. F., Frieze, I. H., & Sechzer, J. A. (1988). Guidelines for avoiding sexism in psychological research. *American Psychologist, 43,* 582–585.

Denton, G. (1980). The influence of visual pattern on perceived speed. *Perception, 9,* 393–402.

Denton, K., & Krebs, D. (1990). From the scene to the crime: The effect of alcohol and social context on moral judgment. *Journal of Personality and Social Psychology, 59,* 242–248.

de Rios, M. D. (1992). Power and hallucinogenic states of consciousness among the Moche: An ancient Peruvian society. In C. A. Ward (Ed.), *Altered states of consciousness and mental health: A cross-cultural perspective.* Newbury Park, CA: Sage.

Derogowski, J. B. (1989). Real space and represented space: Cross-cultural perspectives. *Behavior and Brain Sciences, 12,* 51–73.

Derryberry, D., & Tucker, D. M. (1992). Neural mechanisms of emotion. *Journal of Consulting and Clinical Psychology, 60,* 329–338.

DeRubeis, R. J., & Crits-Christoph, P. (1998). Empirically supported individual and group psychological treatments for adult mental disorders. *Journal of Consulting and Clinical Psychology, 66,* 37–52.

DeRubeis, R. J., & Feeley, M. (1990). Determinants of change in cognitive therapy for depression. *Cognitive Therapy & Research, 14,* 469–482.

DeRubeis, R. J., Gelfand, L. A., Tang, T. Z., & Simons, A. D. (1999). Medications versus cognitive behavior therapy for severely depressed outpatients: Mega-analysis of four randomized comparisons. *American Journal of Psychiatry, 156,* 1007–1013.

DeRubeis, R. J., Hollon, S. D., Evans, M. D., & Bemis, K. M. (1982). Can psychotherapies for depression be discriminated? A systematic investigation of cognitive therapy and interpersonal therapy. *Journal of Consulting and Clinical Psychology, 50,* 744–756.

Deschaumes, M. C., Dittmar, A., Sicard, G., & Vernet, M. E. (1991). Results from six autonomic nervous system responses confirm "autonomic response specificity" hypothesis. *Homeostasis in Health and Disease 33*(5–6), 225–234.

DeSchepper, B., & Treisman, A. (1996). Visual memory for novel shapes: Implicit coding without attention. *Journal of Experimental Psychology: Learning, Memory and Cognition 22,* 27–47.

de Silva, P. (1994). Psychological treatment of sexual problems. *International Review of Psychiatry, 6*(2–3), 163–173.

Deutsch, M., & Gerard, H. B. (1955). A study of normative and informative social influences on individual judgments. *Journal of Abnormal and Social Psychology, 51,* 629–636.

Devine, P., Plant, E. A., & Buswell, B. N. (2000). Breaking the prejudice habit: Progress and obstacles. In S. Oskamp (Ed.), *Reducing prejudice and discrimination* (pp. 175–190). Hillsdale, NJ: Erlbaum.

Devine, P. G. (1989). Stereotypes and prejudice: Their automatic and controlled components. *Journal of Personality and Social Psychology, 56,* 5–18.

Devinsky, O. (1997). Neurological aspects of the conscious and unconscious mind. *Annals of the New York Academy of Science, 835,* 321–329.

Devor, E. J. (1994). A developmental-genetic model of alcoholism: Implications for genetic research. *Journal of Consulting and Clinical Psychology, 62,* 1108–1115.

DeVries, R. (1969). Constancy of generic identity in the years three to six. *Monographs of the Society for Research in Child Development, 34*(3, Serial No. 127).

DeWitt, L. A., & Samuel, A. G. (1990). The role of knowledge-based function in music performance. *Journal of Experimental Psychology, 119,* 123–144.

DeWolff, M. S., & van IJzendoorn, M. H. (1997). Sensitivity and attachment: A meta-analysis on parental antecedents of infant attachment. *Child Development, 68,* 571–591.

Dhurandhar, N. V., Israel, B. A., Kolesar, J. M., Mayhew, G. F., Cook, M. E., & Atkinson, R. L. (2000). Increased adiposity in animals due to a human virus. *International Journal of Obesity, 24,* 989–996.

Diamond, M. (1993). Homosexuality and bisexuality in different populations. *Archives of Sexual Behavior, 22,* 291–310.

Dickinson, A. (2001). Causal learning: Association versus computation. *Current Directions in Psychological Science, 10,* 127–132.

DiClemente, R. J., & Wingood, G. M. (1995). A randomized controlled trial of an HIV sexual risk-reduction intervention for young African-American women. *Journal of the American Medical Association, 274,* 1271–1276.

Didier, A., Carleton, A., Bjaalie, J. G., Vincent, J. D., Ottersen, O. P., Storm-Mathisen, J., & Lledo, P. M. (2001). A dendrodendritic reciprocal synapse provides a recurrent excitatory connection in the olfactory bulb. *Proceedings of the National Academy of Science, 98,* 6441–6446.

Diener, E. (2000). Subjective well-being: The science of happiness and a proposal for a national index. *American Psychologist, 55,* 34–43.

Diener, E., & Diener, C. (1995). Most people are happy. *Psychological Science, 7,* 181–185.

Di Marzo, V., Goparaju, S. K., Wang, L., Liu, J., Batkai, S., Jarai, Z., Fezza, F., Miura, G. I., Palmiter, R. D., Sugiura, T., & Kunos, G. (2001). Leptin-regulated endocannabinoids are involved in maintaining food intake. *Nature, 410,* 822–825.

Dinan, T. G. (2001). Novel approaches to the treatment of depression by modulating the hypothalamic-pituitary-adrenal axis. *Human Psychopharmacology: Clinical and Experimental, 16,* 89–93.

Dion, K. L. (in press). Prejudice, racism, and discrimination. In M. Lerner (Ed.), *Personality and social psychology: Vol. 5. The comprehensive handbook of psychology.* New York: Wiley.

Ditton, P. M. (1999). *Mental health and treatment of inmates and probationers* (Special Report NCJ 174463). Washington, DC: U.S. Department of Justice.

Dixon, J. B., Schachter, L. M., & O'Brien, P. E. (2001). Sleep disturbance and obesity: Changes following surgically induced weight loss. *Archives of Internal Medicine, 161,* 102–106.

Dixon, M., Brunet, A., & Lawrence, J.-R. (1990). Hynotizability and automaticity: Toward a parallel distributed processing model of hynotic responding. *Journal of Abnormal Psychology, 99,* 336–343.

Dodds, J. P., Nardone, A., Mercey, D. E., & Johnson, A. M. (2000). Increase in high risk sexual behaviour among homosexual men, London 1996-98: Cross sectional, questionnaire study. *British Medical Journal, 320,* 1510–1511.

Dodson, C., & Reisberg, D. (1974). Indirect testing of eyewitness memory: The (non)effect of misinformation. *Bulletin of the Psychonomic Society, 29,* 333–336.

Dohrenwend, B. P., Raphael, K. G., Schwartz, S., Stueve, A., & Skodol, A. (1993). The structured event probe and narrative rating method for measuring stressful life events. In L. Goldenberger & S. Breznitz (Eds.), *Handbook of stress: Theoretical and clinical aspects* (2nd ed.). New York: The Free Press.

Dollard, J., Doob, L., Miller, N., Mowrer, O. H., & Sears, R. R. (1939). *Frustration and aggression.* New Haven, CT: Yale University Press.

Dollinger, S. J. (2000). Locus of control and incidental learning: An application to college students. *College Student Journal, 34,* 537–540.

Domhoff, G. W. (1996). *Finding meaning in dreams: A quantitative approach.* New York: Plenum.

Donegan, N. H., & Thompson, R. F. (1991). The search for the engram. In J. L. Martinez & R. P. Kesner (Eds.), *Learning and memory: A biological view* (2nd ed.). San Diego: Academic Press.

Donnerstein, E. (1984). Pornography: Its effects on violence against women. In N. M. Malamuth & E. Donnerstein (Eds.), *Pornography and sexual aggression.* New York: Academic Press.

Donnerstein, E., & Linz, D. (1995). The mass media: A role in injury causation and prevention. *Adolescent Medicine: State of the Art Reviews, 6,* 271–284.

Donnerstein, E., Shaby, R. G., & Eron, L. D. (1995). The mass media and youth aggression. In L. Eron, J. Gentry, & P. Schlegel (Eds.), *Reason to hope: A psychosocial perspective on violence and youth* (pp. 219–250). Washington, DC: American Psychological Association.

Dordain, G., & Deffond, D. (1994). Pyridoxine neuropathies: Review of the literature. *Therapie 49*(4), 333–337.

Dormehl, I. C., Jordaan, B., Oliver, D. W., & Croff, S. (1999). SPECT monitoring of improved cerebral blood flow during long-term treatment of elderly patients with nootropic drugs. *Clinical and Nuclear Medicine, 24,* 29–34.

Dougall, A. L., Craig, K. J., & Baum, A. S. (1999). Assessment of characteristics of intrusive thoughts and their impact on distress among victims of traumatic events. *Psychosomatic Medicine, 61,* 38–48.

Dougherty, D. D., Baer, L., Cosgrove, G. R., Cassem, E. H., Price, B. H., Nierenberg, A. A., et al. (2002). Prospective long-term follow-up of 44 patients who received cingulotomy for treatment-refractory obsessive-compulsive disorder. *American Journal of Psychiatry, 159,* 269–275.

Dovidio, J. F., Allen, J., & Schroeder, D. A. (1990). The specificity of empathy-induced helping: Evidence for altruism. *Journal of Personality and Social Psychology, 59,* 249–260.

Dovidio, J. F., & Gaertner, S. L. (1998). On the nature of contemporary prejudice: The causes, consequences, and challenges of aversive racism. In J. L. Eberhardt & S. T. Fiske (Eds.), *Confronting racism: The problem and the response* (pp. 3–32). Thousand Oaks, CA: Sage.

Dovidio, J. F., & Gaertner, S. L. (2000). Aversive racism and selection decisions: 1989 and 1999. *Psychological Science, 11,* 319–323.

Dovidio, J. F., Kawakami, K., & Beach, K. R. (2001). Implicit and explicit attitudes: Examination of the relationship between measures of intergroup bias. In R. Brown & S. Gaertner (Eds.), *Blackwell handbook of social psychology: Vol. 4. Intergroup relations* (pp. 175–197). Oxford, England: Blackwell.

Dovidio, J. F., Kawakami, K., & Gaertner, S. L. (2000). Reducing contemporary prejudice: Combating explicit and implicit bias at the individual and intergroup level. In S. Oskamp (Ed.), *Reducing prejudice and discrimination* (pp. 137–163). Hillsdale, NJ: Erlbaum.

Dovidio, J. F., & Penner, L. A. (2001). Helping and altruism. In G. Fletcher & M. Clark (Eds.), *Blackwell handbook of social psychology: Interpersonal processes* (pp. 162–195). Oxford, England: Blackwell.

Dovidio, J. F., Piliavin, J. A., Gaertner, S. L., Schroeder, D. A., & Clark, R. D., III. (1991). The arousal: cost-reward model and the process of intervention: A review of the evidence. In M. Clark (Ed.), *Review of personality and social psychology: Vol. 12. Prosocial behavior* (pp. 86–118). Newbury Park, CA: Sage.

Dovidio, J. F., Smith, J. K., Donnella, A. G., & Gaertner, S. L. (1997). Racial attitudes and the death penalty. *Journal of Applied Social Psychology, 27,* 1468–1487.

Downey, D. B. (2001). Number of siblings and intellectual development: The resource dilution explanation. *American Psychologist, 56,* 497–504.

Downey-Lamb, M. M., & Woodruff-Pak, D. S. (1999). Early detection of cognitive deficits using eyeblink classical conditioning. *Alzheimer's Reports, 2,* 37–44.

Dowson, D. I., Lewith, G. T., & Machin, D. (1985). The effects of acupuncture versus placebo in the treatment of headache. *Pain, 21,* 35–42.

Drayna, D., Manichaikul, A., de Lange, M., Snieder, H., & Spector, T. (2001). Genetic correlates of musical pitch recognition in humans. *Science, 291,* 1969–1972.

Dresner, R., & Grolnick, W. S. (1996). Constructions of early parenting, intimacy and autonomy in young women. *Journal of Social and Personal Relationships, 13,* 25–40.

Dreyfus, H. L., & Dreyfus, S. E. (1988). Making a mind versus modeling the brain: Intelligence back at a branchpoint. In S. R. Graubard (Ed.), *The artificial intelligence debate.* Cambridge: MIT Press.

Drucker, D. B., Ackroff, K., & Sclafani, A. (1994). Nutrient-conditioned flavor preference and acceptance in rats: Effects of deprivation state and non-reinforcement. *Physiology and Behavior, 56*(4), 701–707.

Druckman, D., & Bjork, R. A. (1994). *Learning, remembering, believing: Enhancing human performance.* Washington, DC: National Academy Press.

Drummond, S. P., Brown, G. G., Gillin, J. C., Stricker, J. L., Wong, E. C., & Buxton, R. B. (2000). Altered brain response to verbal learning following sleep deprivation. *Nature, 403,* 655–657.

Druss, B. G., Rosenheck, R. A., & Sledge, W. H. (2000). Health and disability costs of depressive illness in a major U.S. Corporation. *American Journal of Psychiatry, 157,* 1274–1278.

DuBois, D. L., Felner, R. D., Brand, S., Adan, A. M., & Evans, E. G. (1992). A prospective study of life stress, social support, and adaptation in early adolescence. *Child Development, 63,* 542–557.

DuBreuil, S. C., Garry, M., & Loftus, E. F. (1998). Tales from the crib: memories of infancy. In Lynn, S. J. & McConkey, K. M. (Ed.), *Truth in memory* (pp. 137–160). New York: Guilford.

Duckitt, J. H. (1994). *The social psychology of prejudice.* Westport, CT: Praeger.

Duclos, S. E., & Laird, J. D. (2001). The deliberate control of emotional experience through control of expressions. *Cognition and Emotion, 15,* 27–56.

Dudgeon, P., Mackinnon, A. J., Bell, R. C., & McGorry, P. D. (2001). Failure to confirm the 3 domains model of pPsychosis. *Archives of General Psychiatry, 58,* 94–96.

Duffy, V. B., & Bartoshuk, L. M. (2000). Genetic taste status associates with fat food acceptance and body mass index in adults. *Journal of the American Dietetic Association, 100,* 647–655.

Duffy, V. B., Fast, K., Cohen Z., Chodos, E., and Bartoshuk, L. M. (1999). Genetic taste status associates with fat food acceptance and body mass index in adults. *Chemical Senses.*

Dujovne, V., & Houston, B. (1991). Hostility-related variables and plasma lipid levels. *Journal of Behavioral Medicine, 14,* 555–564.

Duke, C. R., & Carlson, L. (1994). Applying implicit memory measures: Word fragment completion in advertising tests. *Journal of Current Issues and Research in Advertising, 15,* 1–14.

Duncan, G. J., Brooks-Gunn, J., & Klebanov, P. K. (1994). Economic deprivation and early childhood development. *Child Development, 65,* 296–318.

Duncan, J., & Owen, A. M. (2000). Common regions of the human frontal lobe recruited by diverse cognitive demands. *Trends in Neurosciences, 23,* 475–483.

Dunn, J., Brown, H., Slomkowski, C., Tesla, C., & Youngblade, L. (1991). Young children's understanding of other people's feelings and beliefs: Individual differences and their antecedents. *Child Development, 62,* 1352–1366.

Dunn, J., & Hughes, C. (2001). "I got some swords and you're dead!": Violent fantasy, antisocial behavior, friendship, and moral sensibility in young children. *Child Development, 72,* 491–505.

Dunn, N. R., Pearce, G. L., & Shakir, S. A. (2000). Adverse effects associated with the use of donepezil in general practice in England. *Journal of Psychopharmacology, 14,* 406–408.

Dunne, E., & Fitzpatrick, A. C. (1999). The views of professionals on the role of self-help groups in the mental health area. *Irish Journal of Psychological Medicine, 16,* 84–89.

Dunning, D. (2001). On the motives underlying social cognition. In A. Tesser & N. Schwarz (Eds.), *Blackwell handbook of social psychology: Intraindividual processes* (pp. 348–374). Oxford, England: Blackwell.

Düzel, E., Vargha-Khamdem, F., Heinze, H. J., & Mishkin, M. (2001). Brain activity evidence for recognition without recollection after early hippocampal damage. *Proceedings of the National Academy of Science, 98,* 8101–8106.

Dweck, C. S. (1998). The development of early self-conceptions: Their relevance for motivational processes. In J. Heckhausen & C. S. Dweck (Eds.), *Motivation and self-regulation across the life-span.* New York: Cambridge University Press.

Dweck, C. S., Chiu, C., & Hong, Y. (1995). Implicit theories and their role in judgements and reactions: A world from two perspectives. *Psychological Inquiry, 6,* 267–285.

Eacott, M. J. (1999). Memory of events of early childhood. *Current Directions in Psychological Science, 8,* 46–49.

Eagly, A. H. (1987). *Sex differences in social behavior: A social-role interpretation.* Hillsdale, NJ: Erlbaum.

Eagly, A. H. (1996). Differences between women and men: Their magnitude, practical importance, and political meaning. *American Psychologist, 51,* 158–159.

Eagly, A. H., & Chaiken, S. (1998). In D. Gilbert, S. T. Fiske, & G. Lindzey (Eds.), *Handbook of social psychology* (Vol. 1, 4th ed., pp. 269–322). Boston: McGraw-Hill.

Eagly, A. H., & Johnson, B. T. (1990). Gender and leadership style: A meta-analysis. *Psychological Bulletin, 108,* 233–256.

Eagly, A. H., & Karau, S. J. (1991). Gender and the emergence of leaders: A meta-analysis. *Journal of Personality and Social Psychology, 60,* 685–710.

Eagly, A. H., Karau, S. J., & Makhijani, M. G. (1995). Gender and the effectiveness of leaders: A meta-analysis. *Psychological Bulletin, 117,* 125–145.

Eagly, A. H., Makhijani, M. G., & Klonsky, B. G. (1992). Gender and evaluation of leaders: A meta-analysis. *Psychological Bulletin, 111,* 3–22.

Eagly, A. H., & Wood, W. (1999). The orgins of sex diffrences in human behavior: Evolved dispositions versus social roles. *American Psychologist, 54,* 408–423.

East, P. L., & Jacobson, L. J. (2001). The younger siblings of teenage mothers: A follow-up of their pregnancy risk. *Developmental Psychology, 37,* 254–264.

Eaton, M. J., & Dembo, M. H. (1997). Differences in the motivational beliefs of Asian American and non-Asian students. *Journal of Educational Psychology, 89,* 433–440.

Eberts, R., & MacMillan, A. C. (1985). Misperception of small cars. In R. Eberts & C. Eberts (Eds.), *Trends in ergonomics/human factors* (Vol. 2, pp. 30–39). Amsterdam: Elsevier.

Eccles, J., Lord, S., & Buchanan, C. M. (1996). School transitions in early adolescence: What are we doing to our young people? In J. A. Graber, J. Brooks-Gunn, & A. C. Peterson (Eds.), *Transitions through adolescence: Interpersonal domains and context* (pp. 251–284). Mahwah, NJ: Erlbaum.

Eccles, J. S., Lord, S. E., & Roeser, R. W. (1996). *Round holes, square pegs, rocky roads, and sore feet: The impact of stage-environment fit on young adolescents' experiences in schools and families.* Rochester: University of Rochester Press.

Echeburua, E., de Corral, P., Garcia Bajos, E., & Borda, M. (1993). Interactions between self-exposure and alprazolam in the treatment of agoraphobia without current panic: An exploratory study. *Behavioural and Cognitive Psychotherapy, 21,* 219–238.

Eckholm, E. (2001, February 18). Psychiatric abuse reportedly used to repress sect. *The New York Times.* Available: http://www.nytimes.com

Edinger, J. D., Wohlgemuth, W. K., Radtke, R. A., Marsh, G. R., & Quillian, R. E. (2001). Cognitive behavioral therapy for treatment of chronic primary insomnia. *Journal of the American Medical Association, 285,* 1865–1864.

Edwards, A. E., & Acker, L. E. (1972). A demonstration of the long-term retention of a conditioned GSR. *Psychosomatic Science, 26,* 27–28.

Edwards, G. (1987). The alcohol dependence syndrome: A concept as stimulus to enquiry. *British Journal of Addiction, 81,* 171–183.

Egbert, L. D., Battit, G. E., Welch, C. E., & Bartlett, M. K. (1964). Reduction of postoperative pain by encouragement and instruction of patients: A study of doctor-patient rapport. *New England Journal of Medicine, 270,* 825–827.

Egeland, J. A., Gerhard, D. S., Pauls, D. L., Sussex, J. N., Kidd, K. K., Allen, C. R., et al. (1987). Bipolar affective disorders linked to DNA markers on chromosome 11. *Nature, 325,* 783–787.

Ehlers, A. (1995). A 1-year prospective study of panic attacks: Clinical course and factors associated with maintenance. *Journal of Abnormal Psychology, 104,* 164–172.

Ehrlichman, H., & Halpern, J. N. (1988). Affect and memory: Effects of pleasant and unpleasant odors on retrieval of happy and unhappy memories. *Journal of Personality and Social Psychology, 55,* 769–779.

Eich, E. (1989). Theoretical issues in state dependent memory. In H. L. Roediger & F. I. M. Craik (Eds.), *Varieties of memory and consciousness.* Hillsdale, NJ: Erlbaum.

Eich, E., & Macaulay, D. (2000). Are real moods required to reveal mood-congruent and mood-dependent memory? *Psychological Science, 11,* 244–248.

References

Eich, E., & Metcalfe, J. (1989). Mood dependent memory for internal versus external events. *Experimental Psychology: Learning, Memory, and Cognition, 15,* 443–455.

Eich, J. E., Weingartner, H., Stillman, R. C., & Gillin, J. C. (1975). State dependent accessibility of retrieval cues in the retention of a categorized list. *Journal of Verbal Learning and Verbal Behavior, 14,* 408–417.

Eichelman, B. (1983). The limbic system and aggression in humans. *Neuroscience and Bio-behavioral Reviews, 7,* 391–394.

Eichenbaum, H., Otto, T., & Cohen, N. J. (1994). Two functional components of the hippocampal memory system. *Behavior and Brain Sciences, 17*(3), 449–517.

Eichorn, D. H., Clausen, J. A., Haan, N., Honzik, M. P., & Mussen, P. H. (1981). *Present and past in middle life.* New York: Academic Press.

Einhorn, H., & Hogarth, R. (1982). Prediction, diagnosis and causal thinking in forecasting. *Journal of Forecasting, 1,* 23–36.

Eisenberg, N. (1997, June). Consistent parenting helps children regulate emotions. *APA Monitor,* p. 17.

Eisenberg, N. (1998). Introduction. In W. Damon & N. Eisenberg (Eds.), *Handbook of child psychology: Vol. 3. Social, emotional, and personality development* (5th ed., pp. 1–24). New York: Wiley.

Eisenberg, N., Cialdini, R. B., McCreath, H., & Shell, R. (1987). Consistency-based compliance: When and why do children become vulnerable? *Journal of Personality and Social Psychology, 52,* 1174–1181.

Eisenberg, N., & Fabes, R. A. (1998). Prosocial development. In W. Damon & N. Eisenberg (Eds.), *Handbook of child psychology: Vol. 3. Social, emotional, and personality development* (5th ed., pp. 701–778). New York: Wiley.

Eisenberg, N., Fabes, R. A., & Murphy, B. C. (1995). Relations of shyness and low sociability to regulation and emotionality. *Journal of Personality and Social Psychology, 68,* 505–518.

Eisenman, R. (1994). Conservative sexual values: Effects of an abstinence program on student attitudes. *Journal of Sex Education and Therapy, 20*(2), 75–78.

Ekman, P. (1993). Facial expression and emotion. *American Psychologist, 48,* 384–392.

Ekman, P. (1994). Strong evidence for universals in facial expressions: A reply to Russell's mistaken critique. *Psychological Bulletin, 115*(2), 268–287.

Ekman, P., & Davidson, R. J. (1993). Voluntary smiling changes regional brain activity. *Psychological Science, 4*(5), 342–345.

Ekman, P., Davidson, R. J., & Friesen, W. V. (1990). The Duchenne smile: Emotional expression and brain physiology II. *Journal of Personality and Social Psychology, 58,* 342–353.

Ekman, P., Friesen, W. V., & Ellsworth, P. (1972). *Emotion in the human face: Guidelines for research and a review of findings.* New York: Pergamon Press.

Ekman, P., Levenson, R. W., & Friesen, W. V. (1983). Autonomic nervous system activity distinguishes among emotions. *Science, 221,* 1208–1210.

Elashoff, J. D. (1979). Box scores are for baseball. *Brain and Behavioral Sciences, 3,* 392.

Eldridge, L. L., Knowlton, B. J., Furmanski, C. S., Bookheimer, S. Y., & Engel, S. A. (2000). Remembering episodes: A selective role for the hippocampus during retrieval. *Nature Neuroscience, 3,* 1149–1152.

Eliot, A. J., Chirkov, V. I., Kim, Y., & Shelldon, K. M. (2001). A cross-cultural analysis of avoidance (relative to approach) personal goals. *Psychological Science, 12,* 505–510.

Elkin, I. (1994). The NIMH treatment of depression collaborative research program: Where we began and where we are. In A. E. Bergin & S. L. Garfield (Eds.), *Handbook of psychotherapy and behavior change* (pp. 114–139). New York: Wiley.

Elkin, I. (1999). A major dilemma in psychotherapy outcome research: Disentangling therapists from therapies. *Clinical Psychology: Science and Practice, 6,* 10–32.

Elkin, I., Yamaguchi, J. L., Arnoff, D. B., Glass, C. R., Sotsky, S. M., & Krupnick, J. L. (1999). "Patient-treatment fit" and early engagement in therapy. *Psychotherapy Research, 9,* 437–451.

Elliot, A. J., & Devine, P. G. (1994). On the motivational nature of cognitive dissonance: Dissonance as psychological discomfort. *Journal of Personality and Social Psychology, 67,* 382–394.

Elliott, C. L., & Greene, R. L. (1992). Clinical depression and implicit memory. *Journal of Abnormal Psychology, 101,* 572–574.

Ellis, A. (1962). *Reason and emotion in psychotherapy.* New York: Lyle Stuart.

Ellis, A. (1993). Reflections on rational-emotive therapy. *Journal of Consulting and Clinical Psychology, 61,* 199–201.

Ellis, A. (1995). Rational emotive behavior therapy. In R. J. Corsini & D. Wedding (Eds.), *Current psychotherapies* (5th ed., pp. 162–196). Itasca, IL: Peacock.

Ellis, A. (1997). Using rational emotive behavior therapy techniques to cope with disability. *Professional Psychology: Research and Practice, 28,* 17–22.

Ellis, A., & Bernard, M. E. (1985). *Clinical applications of rational-emotive therapy.* New York: Plenum.

Ellis, A. L., & Mitchell, R. W. (2000). Sexual orientation. In L. T. Szuchman & F. Muscarella (Eds.), *Psychological perspectives on human sexuality* (pp. 196–231). New York: Wiley.

Ellis, N. R. (1991). Automatic and effortful processes in memory for spatial location. *Bulletin of the Psychonomic Society, 29,* 28–30.

EMDR Institute. (2001, April 16). Description for professionals [Online]. Available: www.emdr.com/profess.htm

Emery, C. E., Jr. (2001). Cracked crystal balls?: Psychics' predictions for past year a litany of prognostive failures *Skeptical Inquirer, 25,* 7–8.

Ende, G., Braus, D. F., Walter, S., Weber-Fahr, W., & Henn, F. A. (2000). The hippocampus in patients treated with electroconvulsive therapy. *Archives of General Psychiatry, 57,* 937–943.

Engebretson, T. O., Stoney, C. M. (1995). Anger expression and lipid concentrations. *International Journal of Behavioral Medicine, 2,* 281–298.

Engel, A. K., Konig, P., Kreiter, A. K., Schillen, T. B., & Singer, W. (1992). Temporal coding in the visual cortex: New vistas on integration in the nervous system. *Trends in Neuroscience, 15,* 218–226.

Engel, S., Zhang, X., & Wandell, B. (1997). Colour tuning in human visual cortex measured with functional magnetic resonance imaging. *Nature, 388,* 68–71.

Engeland, H. V. (1993). Pharmacotherapy and behaviour therapy: Competition or cooperation? *Acta Paedopsychiatrica International Journal of Child and Adolescent Psychiatry, 56*(2), 123–127.

Engen, T., Gilmore, M. M., & Mair, R. G. (1991). Odor memory. In T. V. Getchell et al. (Eds.), *Taste and smell in health and disease.* New York: Raven Press.

Engle, R. W., & Oransky, N. (1999). The evolution from short-term to working memory: Multi-store to dynamic models of temporary storage. In R. Sternberg (Ed.), *The nature of human cognition* (pp. 514–555). Cambridge: MIT Press.

Enright, R. D., Lapsley, D. K., & Levy, V. M., Jr. (1983). Moral education strategies. In M. Pressley & J. R. Levin (Eds.), *Cognitive strategy research: Educational application.* New York: Springer-Verlag.

Epping-Jordan, M. P., Watkins, S. S., Koob, G. F., & Markou, A. (1998). Dramatic decreases in brain reward function during nicotine withdrawal. *Nature, 393,* 76–79.

Epstein, L. H., Valoski, A., Wing, R. R., & McCurley, J. (1994). Ten-year outcomes of behavioral family-based treatment for childhood obesity. *Health Psychology, 13,* 373–383.

Erdberg, P. (1990). Rorschach assessment. In G. Goldstein & M. Hersen (Eds.), *Psychological assessment* (2nd ed.). New York: Pergamon Press.

Erdelyi, M. H. (1985). *Psychoanalysis: Freud's cognitive psychology.* San Francisco: Freeman.

Ericsson, K. A., & Charness, N. (1994). Expert performance: Its structure and acquisition. *American Psychologist, 49,* 725–747.

Ericsson, K. A., & Simon, H. A. (1994). *Protocol analysis: Verbal reports as data* (rev. ed.). Cambridge: MIT Press.

Ericsson, K. A., & Staszewski, J. (1989). Skilled memory and expertise: Mechanisms of exceptional performance. In D. Klahr & K. Kotovsky (Eds.), *Complex information processing: The impact of Herbert A. Simon.* Hillsdale, NJ: Erlbaum.

Erikson, E. H. (1968). *Identity: Youth and crisis.* New York: Norton.

Eriksson, P. S., Perfilieva, E., Bjork-Eriksson, T., Alborn, A. M., Nordborg, C., Peterson, D. A., & Gage, F. H. (1998). Neurogenesis in the adult human hippocampus. *Nature Medicine, 4,* 1313–1317.

Erlenmeyer-Kimling, L., & Jarvik, L. F. (1963). Genetics and intelligence: A review. *Science, 142,* 1477–1479.

Ernst, E. (2000). Herbal medicines: Where is the evidence? *British Medical Journal, 321,* 395–396.

Ernst, M., Matochik, J. A., Heishman, S. J., Van Horn, J. D., Jons, P. H., Henningfield, J. E., & London, E. D. (2001). Effect of nicotine on brain activation during performance of a working memory task. *Proceedings of the National Academy of Science, 98,* 4728–4733.

Eron, L. D., Huesmann, L. R., Lefkowitz, M. M., & Walder, L. O. (1996). Does television violence cause aggression? In D. F. Greenberg (Ed.), *Criminal careers: Vol. 2. The international library of criminology, criminal justice and penology* (pp. 311–321). Aldershot, England: Dartmouth.

Essock, E. A., Sinai, M. J., McCarley J. S., Krebs, W. K., & DeFord, J. K. (1999). Perceptual ability with real-world nighttime scenes: Image-intensified, infrared, and fused-color imagery *Human Factors, 41,* 438–452.

Esterson, A. (2001). The mythologizing of psychoanalytic history: Deception and self-deception in Freud's account of the seduction theory episode. *History of Psychiatry, 12,* 329–352.

Evans, D. A., Hebert, L. E., Beckett, L. A., Scherr, P. A., Albert, M. S., Chown, M. J., et al. (1997). Education and other measures of socioeconomic status and risk of incident Alzheimer's disease in a defined population of older persons. *Archives of Neurology, 54,* 1399–1405.

Evans, G. W., Hygge, S., & Bullinger, M. (1995). Chronic noise and psychological stress. *Psychological Science, 6,* 333–338.

Evans, G. W., & Johnson, D. (2000). Stress and open-office noise. *Journal of Applied Psychology, 85,* 779–783.

Evans, G. W., Wells, N. M., Chan, H.-Y. E., & Saltzman, H. (2000). Housing quality and mental health. *Journal of Consulting and Clinical Psychology, 68,* 526–530.

Evans, J. St. B. T., Handley, S. J., Harper, C. N. J., & Johnson-Laird, P. N. (1999). Reasoning about necessity and possibility: A test of the mental model theory of deduction. *Journal of Experimental Psychology: Learning, Memory, and Cognition, 25,* 1495–1513.

Everaerd, W., & Laan, E. (1994). Cognitive aspects of sexual functioning and dysfunctioning. *Sexual and Marital Therapy, 9,* 225–230.

Everett, S. A., Warren, C. W., Santelli, J. S., Kann, L., Collins, J. L., & Kolbe, L. J. (2000). Use of birth control pills, condoms, and withdrawal among U.S. high school students. *Journal of Adolescent Health, 27,* 112–118.

Exner, J. E., Jr., & Ona, N. (1995). *RIAP-3: Rorschach Interpretation Assistance Program—version 3.* Odessa, FL: Psychological Assessment Resources.

Exton, M. S., von Auer, A. K., Buske-Kirschbaum, A., Stockhorst, U., Gobel, U., & Schedlowski, M. (2000). Pavlovian conditioning of immune function: animal investigation and the challenge of human application. *Behavior and Brain Research, 110,* 129–141.

Eysenck, H. J. (1952). The effects of psychotherapy: An evaluation. *Journal of Consulting Psychology, 16,* 319–324.

Eysenck, H. J. (1961). The effects of psychotherapy. In H. J. Eysenck (Ed.), *Handbook of abnormal psychology.* New York: Basic Books.

Eysenck, H. J. (1966). *The effects of psychotherapy.* New York: International Science Press.

Eysenck, H. J. (1978). An exercise in mega-silliness. *American Psychologist, 33,* 517.

Eysenck, H. J. (1986). What is intelligence? In R. J. Sternberg & D. K. Detterman (Eds.), *What is intelligence? Contemporary viewpoints on its nature and definition.* Norwood, NJ: Ablex.

Eysenck, H. J. (1987). Speed of information processing, reaction time, and the theory of intelligence. In P. A. Vernon (Ed.), *Speed of information-processing and intelligence* (pp. 21–67). Norwood, NJ: Ablex.

Eysenck, H. J. (1990a). Biological dimensions of personality. In L. A. Pervin (Ed.), *Handbook of personality: Theory and research* (pp. 244–276). New York: Guilford.

Eysenck, H. J. (1990b). Genetic and environmental contributions to individual differences: The three major dimensions of personality. *Journal of Personality, 58,* 245–261.

Eysenck, H. J. (1994). A biological theory of intelligence. In D. K. Detterman (Ed.), *Current topics in human intelligence* (Vol. 4). Norwood, NJ: Ablex.

Eysenck, M. W., & Keane, M. T. (1995). *Cognitive psychology: A student's handbook* (3rd ed.). Hillsdale, NJ: Erlbaum.

Fabes, R. A., Shepard, S. A., Guthrie, I. K., & Martin, C. L. (1997). Roles of temperamental arousal and gender-segregated play in young children's social adjustment. *Developmental Psychology, 33,* 693–702.

Faedda, G., Tondo, L., Teicher, M., Baldessarini, R., Gelbard, H., & Floris, G. (1993). Seasonal mood disorders: Patterns of seasonal recurrence in mania and depression. *Archives of General Psychiatry, 50,* 17–23.

Fagan, J. F. (2000). A theory of intelligence as processing. *Psychology, Public Policy, and Law, 26,* 168–179.

Fagot, B. I. (1995). Psychosocial and cognitive determinants of early gender-role development. *Annual Review of Sex Research, 6,* 1–31.

Fagot, B. I. (1997). Attachment, parenting, and peer interactions of toddler children. *Developmental Psychology, 33,* 489–499.

Fagot, B. I., & Gauvain, M. (1997). Mother-child problem solving: Continuity through the early childhood years. *Developmental Psychology, 33,* 480–488.

Fairweather, G. W., & Fergus, E. O. (1993). *Empowering the mentally ill.* Austin: Fairweather.

False Memory Syndrome Foundation. (1997). Outcome of recent malpractice suits against therapists brought by former patients claiming negligent encouragement or implantation of false memories. *FMSF Newsletter, 6,* 7–9.

Farah, M. J. (2000). *The cognitive neuroscience of vision.* Malden, MA: Blackwell.

Faraone, S. V., Doyle, A. E., Mick, E., Biederman, J. (2001). Meta-analysis of the association between the dopamine D4 gene 7-repeat allele and attention deficit hyperactivity disorder. *American Journal of Psychiatry, 158,* 1052–1057.

Farberman, R. (1999, February). As managed care grows, public unhappiness rises. *APA Monitor,* p. 14.

Farley, F. (1986). The big T in personality. *Psychology Today, 20,* 44–52.

Farooqi, I. S., Jebb, S. A., Langmack, G., Lawrence, E., Cheetham, C. H., Prentice, A. M., et al. (1999). Effects of recombinant leptin therapy in a child with congenital leptin deficiency. *The New England Journal of Medicine, 341,* 879–884.

Farooqi, I. S., Keogh, J. M., Kamath, S., Jones, S., Gibson, W. T., Trussel, R., et al. (2001). Metabolism: Partial leptin deficiency and human adiposity. *Nature, 414,* 34–35.

Fassler, D. G., & Dumas, L. S. (1997). *Help me, I'm sad: Recognizing, treating, and preventing childhood depression.* New York: Viking Press.

Faust, J., Olson, R., & Rodriguez, H. (1991). Same-day surgery preparation: Reduction of pediatric patient arousal and distress through participant modeling. *Journal of Consulting and Clinical Psychology, 59,* 475–478.

Faymonville, M. E., Laureys, S., Degueldre, C., DelFiore, G., Luxen, A., Franck, G., et al. (2000). Neural mechanisms of antinociceptive effects of hypnosis. *Anesthesiology, 92,* 1257–1267.

Federal Interagency Forum on Children and Family Statistics. (2001). *America's Children: Key National Indicators of Well-being 2001.* Washington, DC: Government Printing Office.

Feeley, M., DeRubeis, R. J., & Gelfand, L. A. (1999). The temporal relation of adherence and alliance to symptom change in cognitive therapy for depression. *Journal of Consulting and Clinical Psychology, 67,* 578–582.

Feinberg, L., & Campbell, I. G. (1993). Total sleep deprivation in the rat transiently abolishes the delta amplitude response to darkness: Implications for the mechanism of the "negative delta rebound." *Journal of Neurophysiology, 70*(6), 2695–2699.

Feingold, A., & Mazzella, R. (1998). Gender differences in body image are increasing. *Psychological Science, 9,* 190–195.

Feist, J., & Feist, G. (2001). *Theories of personality* (5th ed.). New York: McGraw-Hill.

Feldman, R. P., & Goodrich, J. T. (2001). Psychosurgery: A historical overview. *Neurosurgery, 48*, 647–657.

Felten, D. L., Cohen, N., Ader, R., Felten, S. Y., Carlson, S. L., & Roszman, T. L. (1991). Central neural circuits involved in neural-immune interactions. In R. Ader (Ed.), *Psychoneuroimmunology* (2nd ed.). New York: Academic Press.

Felten, S. Y., Madden, K. S., Bellinger, D. L., Kruszewska, B., Moynihan, J. A., & Felten, D. L. (1998). The role of the sympathetic nervous system in the modulation of immune responses. *Advances in Pharmacology, 42*, 583–587.

Feng-Chen, K. C., & Wolpaw, J. R. (1996). Operant conditioning of H-reflex changes synaptic terminals on primate motoneurons. *Proceedings of the National Academy of Science USA, 93*, 9206–9211.

Fenson, L., Dale, P. S., Reznick, J. S., & Bates, E. (1994). Variability in early communicative development. *Monographs of the Society for Research in Child Development, 59*, 173.

Fenton, W. S., & McGlashan, T. H. (1991). Natural history of schizophrenia subtypes: 1. Longitudinal study of paranoid, hebephrenic, and undifferentiated schizophrenia. *Archives of General Psychiatry, 48*, 969–977.

Fenton, W. S., & McGlashan, T. H. (1994). Antecedent, symptoms progression, and long-term outcome of the deficit syndrome in schizophrenia. *American Journal of Psychiatry, 151*, 351–356.

Fergusson, D. M., & Horwood, L. J. (1997). Early onset cannabis use and psychosocial adjustment in young adults. *Addiction, 92*, 279–296.

Fergusson, D. M., Lloyd, M., & Horwood, L. J. (1991). Family ethnicity, social background and scholastic achievement: An eleven-year longitudinal study. *New Zealand Journal of Educational Studies, 26*, 49–63.

Fernández-Dols, J.-M. & Ruiz-Belda, M.-A. (1995). Are smiles a sign of happiness?: Gold medal winners at the Olympic Games. *Journal of Personality and Social Psychology, 69*, 1113–1119.

Ferraro, R., Lillioja, S., Fontvieille, A. M., Rising, R., Bogardus, C., & Ravussin, E. (1992). Lower sedentary metabolic rate in women compared with men. *Journal of Clinical Investigation, 90*, 780–784.

Ferretti, R. P., & Butterfield, E. C. (1989). Intelligence as a correlate of children's problem solving. *American Journal of Mental Retardation, 93*, 424–433.

Feshbach, N., Katz, P., Huston, A. C., Fairchild, H. H., & Donnerstein, E. (1993). *Big world, small screen: The role of television in American society.* Lincoln: University of Nebraska Press.

Feske, U., & Goldstein, A. J. (1997). Eye movement desensitization and reprocessing treatment for panic disorder: A controlled outcome and partial dismantling study. *Journal of Consulting and Clinical Psychology, 65*, 1026–1035.

Festinger, L. (1954). A theory of social comparison processes. *Human Relations, 7*, 117–140.

Festinger, L. (1957). *A theory of cognitive dissonance.* Evanston, IL: Row, Petersen.

Festinger, L., & Carlsmith, J. M. (1959). Cognitive consequences of forced compliance. *Journal of Abnormal and Social Psychology, 58*, 203–210.

Field, A. E., Coakley, E. H., Must, A., Spadano, J. L., Laird, N., Dietz, W. H., Rimm, E., & Colditz, G. A. (2001). Impact of overweight on the risk of developing common chronic diseases during a 10-year period. *Archives of Internal Medicine, 161*, 1581–1586.

Field, T., Henteleff, T., Hernandez-Reif, M., Martinez, E., Mavunda, K., Kuhn, C., & Schangerg, S. (1998). Children with asthma have improved pulmonary functions after massage therapy. *Journal of Pediatrics, 132*, 854–858.

Field, T., Hernandez-Reif, M., Seligman, S., Krasnegor, J., Sunshine, W., Rivas-Chacon, R., et al. (1997). Juvenile rheumatoid arthritis: Benefits from massage therapy. *Journal of Pediatric Psychology, 22*, 607–617.

Field, T., Ironson, G., Scafidi, F., Nawrocki, T., Gonclaves, A., Burman, I., et al. (1996). Massage therapy reduces anxiety and enhances EEG pattern of alertness and math computations. *International Journal of Neuroscience, 86*, 197–205.

File, S. E., Fluck, E., & Fernandes, C. (1999). Beneficial effects of glycine (bioglycin) on memory and attention in young and middle-aged adults. *Journal of Clinical Psychopharmacology, 19*, 506–512.

Filipek, P. A., Accardo, P. J., Barancek, G. T., Cook, E. H., Jr., Dawson, G., Gordon, B., et al. (1999). The screening and diagnosis of autistic spectrum disorders. *Journal of Autism and Developmental Disorders, 29*, 439–484.

Fillmore, K. M., & Caetano, R. (1980, May 22). *Epidemiology of occupational alcoholism.* Paper presented at the National Institute on Alcohol Abuse and Alcoholism's Workshop on Alcoholism in the Workplace, Reston, VA.

Finer, N., James, W. P., Kopelman, P. G., Lean, M. E., & Williams, G. (2000). One-year treatment of obesity: A randomized, double-blind, placebo-controlled, multicentre study of orlistat, a gastrointestinal lipase inhibitor. *International Journal of Obesity and Related Metabolic Disorders, 24*, 306–313.

Fink, M. (1999). *Electroshock: Restoring the mind.* New York: Oxford University Press.

Fischer, K. W., & Bidell, T. (1991). Constraining nativist inferences about cognitive capacities. In S. Carey & R. Gelman (Eds.), *The epigenesis of mind: Essays on biology and cognition* (pp. 199–235). Hillsdale, NJ: Erlbaum.

Fischer, K. W., & Hencke, R. W. (1996). Infants' construction of actions in context: Piaget's contribution to research on early development. *Psychological Science, 7*, 204–209.

Fischer, P. J., & Breakey, W. R. (1991). The epidemiology of alcohol, drug, and mental disorders among homeless persons. *American Psychologist, 46*, 1115–1128.

Fischoff, B., & MacGregor, D. (1982). Subjective confidence in forecasts. *Journal of Forecasting 1*, 155–172.

Fischoff, B., & Slovic, P. (1980). A little learning.... Confidence in multi-cue judgment tasks. In R. Nickerson (Ed.), *Attention and performance* (Vol. 8). Hillsdale, NJ: Erlbaum.

Fisher, W. A., Fisher, J. D., & Rye, B. J. (1995). Understanding and promoting AIDS-preventive behavior: Insights from the theory of reasoned action. *Health Psychology, 14*, 255–264.

Fiske, A. P., Kitayama, S., Markus, H. R., & Nisbett, R. E. (1998). The cultural matrix of social psychology. In D. T. Gilbert, S. T. Fiske, & G. Lindzey (Eds.), *Handbook of social psychology* (Vol. 2, 4th ed., pp. 915–981). Boston: McGraw-Hill.

Fiske, S. (2000). Interdependence and the reduction of prejudice. In S. Oskamp (Ed.) *Reducing prejudice and discrimination* (pp. 115–135). Mahwah, NJ: Erlbaum.

Fiske, S. T. (1995). Social cognition. In A. Tesser (Ed.), *Advanced social psychology* (pp. 149–194). New York: McGraw-Hill.

Fiske, S. T. (1998). Stereotyping, prejudice, and discrimination. In D. Gilbert, S. T. Fiske, & G. Lindzey (Eds.), *Handbook of social psychology* (Vol. 2, 4th ed., pp. 357–414). Boston: McGraw-Hill.

Fitzgerald, T. E., Tennen, H., Affleck, G. S., & Pransky, G. (1993). The relative importance of dispositional optimism and control appraisals in quality of life after coronary artery bypass surgery. *Journal of Behavioral Medicine, 16*, 25–43.

Fitzpatrick, D. C., Olsen, J. F., & Suga, N. (1998). Connections among functional areas in the mustached bat auditory cortex. *Journal of Comparative Neurology, 391*, 366–396.

Fivush, R., Haden, C., & Adam, S. (1995). Structure and coherence of preschoolers' personal narratives over time: Implications for childhood amnesia. *Journal of Experimental Child Psychology, 60*, 32–56.

Flavell, J. E., Azrin, N., Baumeister, A., Carr, E., Dorsey, M., Forehand, R., Foxx, R., Lovaas, O. I., Rincover, A., Risley, T., Romanczyk, R., Russo, D., Schroeder, S., & Solnick, J. (1982). The treatment of self-injurious behavior. *Behavior Therapy, 13*, 529–554.

Flavell, J. H. (1996). Piaget's legacy. *Psychological Science, 7*, 200–203.

Flint, J., Corley, R., DeFries, J. C., Fulker, D. W., Gray, J. A., Miller, S., & Collins, A. C. (1995). A simple genetic basis for a complex psychological trait in laboratory mice. *Science, 269*, 321–327.

Flynn, J. T. (1999). Searching for justice: The discovery of IQ gains over time. *American Psychologist, 54*, 5–20.

Foa, E. B., Dancu, C. V., Hembree, E. A., Jaycox, L. H., Meadows, E. A., & Street, G. P. (1999). A comparison of exposure therapy, stress-inoculation training, and their combination for reducing posttraumatic stress disorder in female assault victims. *Journal of Consulting and Clinical Psychology, 67,* 194–200.

Foa, E. B., Franklin, M. E., Perry, K. J., & Herbert, J. D. (1996). Cognitive biases in generalized social phobia. *Journal of Abnormal Psychology, 105,* 433–439.

Foa, E. B., & Kozak, M. J. (1995). DSM-IV field trial: Obsessive-compulsive disorder. *American Journal of Psychiatry, 152,* 90–96.

Folk, C. L., Remington, R. W., & Wright, J. H. (1994). The structure of attentional control: Contingent attentional capture by apparent motion, abrupt onset, and color. *Journal of Experimental Psychology: Human Perception and Performance, 20,* 317–329.

Folkman, S. (1984). Personal control and stress and coping processes: A theoretical analysis. *Journal of Personality and Social Psychology, 46,* 839–852.

Folkman, S., & Lazarus, R. (1988). *Manual for the ways of coping questionnaire.* Palo Alto, CA: Consulting Psychologists Press.

Folkman, S., Lazarus, R., Dunkel-Shetteer, DeLongis, A., & Gruen, R. (1986). Dynamics of a stressful encounter: Cognitive appraisal, coping, and encounter outcomes. *Journal of Personality and Social Psychology, 50,* 992–1003.

Folkman, S., & Moskowitz, J. T. (2000). Stress, positive emotion, and coping. *Current Directions in Psychological Science, 9,* 115–118.

Foote, S. L., Bloom, F. E., & Aston-Jones, G. (1983). Nucleus locus coeruleus: New evidence of anatomical and physiological specificity. *Physiology Review, 63,* 844–914.

Forbes, D., Phelps, A., & McHugh, T. (2001). Treatment of combat-related nightmares using imagery rehearsal: A pilot study. *Journal of Traumatic Stress, 14,* 433–442.

Forbes, S., Bui, S., Robinson, B. R., Hochgeschwender, U., & Brennan, M. B. (2001). Integrated control of appetite and fat metabolism by the leptin-proopiommelanocortin pathway. *Proceedings of the National Academy of Science, 98,* 4233–4237.

Foreyt, J. P., Brunner, R. L., Goodrick, G. K., & Cutter, G. (1995). Psychological correlates of weight fluctuation. *International Journal of Eating Disorders, 17*(3), 263–275.

Foroud, T., Edenberg, H. J., Goate, A., Rice, J., Flury, L., Koller, D. L., et al. (2000). Alcoholism susceptibility loci: Confirmation studies in a replicate sample and further mapping. *Alcoholism: Clinical and Experimental Research, 24,* 933–945.

Fosse, R., Stickgold, R., & Hobson, J. A. (2001). Brain-mind states: Reciprocal variation in thoughts and hallucinations. *Psychological Science, 12,* 30–36.

Foster, M. D. (2000). Postive and negative responses to personal discrimination: Does coping make a difference? *Journal of Social Psychology, 140,* 93–106.

Foulke, E. (1991). Braille. In M. A. Heller & W. Shiff (Eds.), *The psychology of touch.* Hillsdale, NJ: Erlbaum.

Foulkes, D. (1985). *Dreaming: A cognitive-psychological analysis.* Hillsdale, NJ: Erlbaum.

Fountain, J. W. (2000, November 28). Exorcists and Exorcisms Proliferate Across U.S. *The New York Times.*

Fowler, R. D. (2000). A lesson in taking our own advice. *Monitor on Psychology, 31,* 9.

Fowles, D. (1992). Schizophrenia: Diathesis-stress revisited. *Annual Review of Psychology, 43,* 303–336.

Fox, A. S., & Olster, D. H. (2000). Effects of intracerebroventricular leptin administration on feeding and sexual behaviors in lean and obese female zucker rats. *Hormones and Behavior, 37,* 377–387.

Fox, N. (1997, June). Consistent parenting helps children regulate emotions. *APA Monitor,* p. 17.

Fox, P. T., Ingham, R. J., Ingham, J. C., Zamarripa, F., Xiong, J. H., & Lancaster, J. L. (2000). Brain correlates of stuttering and syllable production. A PET performance-correlation analysis. *Brain, 123,* 1985–2004.

Foxhall, K. (2000a). Research for the real world. *Monitor on Psychology, 31,* 28–36.

Foxhall, K. (2000b). How will the rules on telehealth be written? *Monitor on Psychology, 31,* 38.

Fozard, J., Wolf, E., Bell, B., Farland, R., & Podolsky, S. (1977). Visual perception and communication. In J. Birren & K. Schaie (Eds.), *Handbook of the psychology of aging.* New York: Van Nostrand Reinhold.

Fraenkel, P. (2001, October 28). Personal communication.

Frank, D. A., Augustyn, M., Knight, W. G., Pell, T., & Zuckerman, B. (2001). Growth, development, and behavior in early childhood following prenatal cocaine exposure: A systematic review. *Journal of the American Medical Association, 285,* 1613–1625.

Frank, J. D., & Frank, J. B. (1991). *Persuasion and healing: A comparative study of psychotherapy* (3rd ed.). Baltimore, MD: Johns Hopkins University Press.

Frank, M. G., Ekman, P., & Friesen, W. V. (1993). Behavioral markers and recognizability of the smile of enjoyment. *Journal of Personality and Social Psychology, 64*(1), 83–93.

Frank, M. G., Issa, N. P., & Stryker, M. P. (2001). Sleep enhances plasticity in the developing visual cortex. *Neuron, 30,* 275–287.

Frankenberg, W. K., & Dodds, J. B. (1967). The Denver developmental screening test. *Journal of Pediatrics, 71,* 181–191.

Freed, C. R., Greene, P. E., Breeze, R. E., Tsai, W. Y., DuMouchel, W., Kao, R., Dillon, S., Winfield, H., Culver, S., Trojanowski, J. Q., Eidelberg, D., & Fahn. S. (2001). Transplantation of embryonic dopamine neurons for severe Parkinson's disease. *New England Journal of Medicine, 344,* 710–719.

Freedland, R. L., & Bertenthal, B. I. (1994). Developmental changes in interlimb coordination: Transition to hands-and-knees crawling. *Psychological Science, 5,* 26–32.

Freedman, J. L. (1992). Television violence and aggression: What psychologists should tell the public. In P. Suedfeld & P. E. Tetlock (Eds.), *Psychology and social policy.* New York: Hemisphere.

Freedman, J. L., & Fraser, S. C. (1966). Compliance without pressure: The foot-in-the-door technique. *Journal of Personality and Social Psychology, 4,* 195–202.

Freedman, V. A., Aykan, H., & Martin, L. G. (2001). Aggregate changes in severe cognitive impairment among older Americans: 1993 and 1998. *Journal of Gerontology, 56B,* S100–S111.

Freeman, W., & Watts, J. W. (1942). *Psychosurgery.* Springfield, IL: Charles C. Thomas.

Fremgen, A., & Fay, D. (1980). Overextensions in production and comprehension: A methodological clarification. *Journal of Child Language, 7,* 205–211.

Freud, A. (1946). *The ego and the mechanisms of defense.* New York: International Universities Press.

Freud, S. (1900). The interpretation of dreams. In J. Strachey (Ed.), *The standard edition of the complete psychological works of Sigmund Freud* (Vol. 8). London: Hogarth Press.

Frey, P. L., & Gaertner, S. L. (1986). Helping and the avoidance of inappropriate interracial behavior: A strategy that perpetuates a nonprejudiced self-image. *Journal of Personality and Social Psychology, 50,* 1083–1090.

Fride, E., & Mechoulam, R. (1993). Pharmacological activity of the cannabinoid receptor agonist, anandamide, a brain constituent. *European Journal of Pharmacology, 231,* 313–314.

Fridlund, A., Sabini, J. P., Hedlund, L. E., Schaut, J. A., Shenker, J. I., & Knauer, M. J. (1990). Audience effects on solitary faces during imagery: Displaying to the people in your head. *Journal of Nonverbal Behavior, 14*(2), 113–137.

Fried, I., Wilson, C. L., MacDonald, K. A., & Behnke, E. J. (1998). Electric current stimulates laughter. *Nature, 391,* 650.

Fried, P. A., Watkinson, B., & Gray, R. (1992). A follow-up study of attentional behavior in 6-year-old children exposed prenatally to marijuana, cigarettes, and alcohol. *Neurotoxicity and Teratology, 14*(5), 299–311.

Friedman, E., Clark, D., & Gershon, S. (1992). Stress, anxiety, and depression: Review of biological, diagnostic, and nosologic issues. *Journal of Anxiety Disorders, 6,* 337–363.

Friedman, H. S., Tucker, J. S., Schwartz, J. E., Martin, L. R., Tomlinson-Keasey, C., Wingard, D. L., & Criqui, M. H. (1995a). Childhood conscientiousness and longevity: Health behaviors and cause of death. *Journal of Personality and Social Psychology, 68,* 696–703.

Friedman, H. S., Tucker, J. S., Schwartz, J. E., Tomlinson-Keasey, C., Martin, L. R., Wingard, D. L., & Criqui, M. H. (1995b). Psychosocial and behavioral predictors of longevity: The aging and death of the "Termites." *American Psychologist, 50,* 69–78.

Friedman, M. A., & Brownell, K. D. (1995). Psychological correlates of obesity: Moving to the next research generation. *Psychological Bulletin, 117*(1), 3–20.

Friedman, M., & Rosenman, R. H. (1959). Association of specific overt behavior patterns with blood and cardiovascular findings: Blood cholesterol level, blood clotting time, incidence of arcus senilis, and clinical coronary artery disease. *Journal of the American Medical Association, 169,* 1286–1296.

Friedman, M., & Rosenman, R. H. (1974). *Type A behavior and your heart.* New York: Knopf.

Frith, U., & Frith, C. (2001). The biological basis of social interaction. *Current Directions in Psychological Science, 10,* 151–155.

Fritzler, B. K., Hecker, J. E., & Losee, M. C. (1997). Self-directed treatment with minimal therapist contact: Preliminary findings for obsessive-compulsive disorder. *Behaviour Research and Therapy, 35,* 627–631.

Fromkin, V., & Rodman, R. (1992). *An introduction to language* (5th ed.). New York: Holt, Rinehart & Winston.

Fuller, J. L., & Thompson, W. R. (1960). *Behavior genetics.* New York: Wiley.

Funder, D. (2001a). Personality. *Annual Review of Psychology, 52,* 197–222.

Funder, D. (2001b). *The personality puzzle* (2nd ed.). New York: Norton.

Funder, D. C. (2001). The really, really fundamental attribution error. *Psychological Inquiry, 12,* 21–23.

Funtowicz, M. N., & Widiger, T. A. (1999). Sex bias in the diagnosis of personality disorders: An evaluation of DSM-IV criteria. *Journal of Abnormal Psychology, 108,* 195–201.

Furey, M. L., Pietrini, P., & Haxby, J. V. (2000). Cholinergic enhancement and increased selectivity of perceptual processing during working memory. *Science, 290,* 2315–2319.

Furnham, A. (2001). Personality and individual differences in the workplace: Person-organization-outcome fit. In R. Hogan & B. Roberts (Eds.), *Personality psychology in the workplace* (pp. 223–251). Washington, DC: American Psychological Association.

Furstenberg, F. F., Brooks-Gunn, J., & Chase-Lansdale, L. (1989). Teenaged pregnancy and childbearing. *American Psychologist, 44,* 313–320.

Fuson, K. C., & Kwon, Y. (1992). Effects on children's addition and subtraction of the system of number words and other cultural tools. In J. Bideaud & C. Meljac (Eds.), *Pathways to number.* Villeneuve d'Ascq, France: University de Lille.

Gabrieli, J. D. E. (1998). Cognitive neuroscience of human memory. *Annual Review of Psychology, 49,* 87–115.

Gabrieli, J. D. E., Fleischman, D. A., Keane, M. M., Reminger, S. L., & Morrell, F. (1995). Double dissociation between memory systems underlying explicit and implicit memory in the human brain. *Psychological Science, 6,* 76–82.

Gaertner, S. L., & Dovidio, J. F. (1986). The aversive form of racism. In J. F. Dovidio & S. L. Gaertner (Eds.), *Prejudice, discrimination, and racism* (pp. 61–89). Orlando, FL: Academic Press.

Galanter, E. (1962). Contemporary psychophysics. In R. Brown (Ed.), *New directions in psychology* (Vol. 1). New York: Holt, Rinehart, Winston.

Galatzer-Levy, R. M., Bachrach, H., Skolnikoff, A., & Waldron, S., Jr. (2000). *Does psychoanalysis work?* New Haven, CT: Yale University Press.

Galef, B. G., & Wright, T. J. (1995). Groups of naive rats learn to select nutritionally adequate foods faster than do isolated rats. *Animal Behaviour 49*(2), 403–409.

Gallagher, M. (1998, January 26). Day careless. *National Review,* pp. 37–41.

Gallagher, M., & Chiba, A. A. (1996). The amygdala and emotion. *Current Opinions in Neurobiology, 6*(2), 221–227.

Gallopin, T., Fort, P., Eggermann, E., Cauli, B., Luppi, P.-H., Rossier, J., et al. (2000). Identification of sleep-promoting neurons in vitro. *Nature, 404,* 992–995.

Galotti, K. M. (1999). *Cognitive psychology in and out of the laboratory* (2nd ed.). Belmont, CA: Brooks/Cole.

Galton, F. (1883). *Inquiries into human faculty and its development.* London: Macmillan.

Games, D., Adams, D., Alessandrini, R., Barbour, R., Berthelette, P., Blackwell, C., et al. (1995). Alzheimer-type neuropathology in transgenic mice overexpressing V717F beta-amyloid precursor protein. *Nature, 73,* 523–527.

Ganchrow, J. R., Steiner, J. E., & Daher, M. (1983). Neonatal facial expressions in response to different qualities and intensities of gustatory stimuli. *Infant Behavior and Development, 6,* 189–200.

Gangestad, S. W., & Thornhill, R. (1997). Human sexual selection and developmental stability. In J. A. Simpson & D. T. Kenrick (Eds.), *Evolutionary social psychology* (pp. 169–195). Mahwah, NJ: Erlbaum.

Gara, M. A., Woolfolk, R. L., Cohen, B. D., Goldston, R. B., Allen, L. A., & Novalany, J. (1993). Perception of self and other in major depression. *Journal of Abnormal Psychology, 102,* 93–100.

Garb, H. N. (1997). Race bias, social class bias, and gender bias in clinical judgment. *Clinical Psychology: Science and Practice, 4,* 99–120.

Garb, H. N., Florio, C. M., & Grove, W. M. (1998). The validity of the Rorschach and the Minnesota Multiphasic Personality Inventory: Results from meta-analyses. *Psychological Science, 9,* 402–404.

Garber, R. J. (1992). Long-term effects of divorce on the self-esteem of young adults. *Journal of Divorce and Remarriage, 17,* 131–138.

Garcia, J., & Koelling, R. A. (1966). Relation of cue to consequences in avoidance learning. *Psychonomic Science, 4,* 123–124.

Garcia, J., Rusiniak, K. W., & Brett, L. P. (1977). Conditioning food-illness aversions in wild animals: Caveat Canonici. In H. Davis & H. M. B. Hurwitz (Eds.), *Operant-Pavlovian interactions.* Hillsdale, NJ: Erlbaum.

Gardner, H. (1993). *Multiple intelligences: The theory in practice.* New York: Basic Books.

Gardner, H. (1998). Are there additional intelligences? The case for naturalistic, spiritual, and existential intelligence. In J. Kane (Ed.), *Education, information, and transformation* (pp. 111–131). Englewood Cliffs, NJ: Prentice-Hall.

Gardner, R., Heward, W. L., & Grossi, T. A. (1994). Effects of response cards on student participation and academic achievement: A systematic replication with inner-city students during whole-class science instruction. *Journal of Applied Behavior Analysis, 27,* 63–71.

Gardner, R. A., & Gardner, B. T. (1978). Comparative psychology and language acquisition. *Annals of the New York Academy of Science, 309,* 37–76.

Garfield, S. L. (1998). Some comments on empirically supported treatments. *Journal of Consulting and Clinical Psychology, 66,* 121–125.

Garland, A. F., & Zigler, E. (1993). Adolescent suicide prevention: Current research and social policy implications. *American Psychologist, 48,* 169–182.

Garris, P. A., Kilpatrick, M., Bunin, M. A., Michael, D., Walker, Q. D., & Wightman, R. M. (1999). Dissociation of dopamine release in the nucleus accumbens from intracranial self-stimulation. *Nature, 398,* 67–69.

Garry, M., & Loftus, E. (1994). Pseudomemories without hypnosis. *International Journal of Clinical and Experimental Hypnosis, 42*(4), 363–373.

Garry, M., & Polaschek, D. L. L. (2000). Imagination and memory. *Current Directions in Psychological Science, 9,* 6–10.

Gaster, B., & Holroyd, J. (2000). St. John's wort for depression: A systematic review. *Archives of Internal Medicine, 160,* 152–156.

Gatewood, R. D., & Feild, H. S. (2001). *Human resource selection* (5th ed.). Fort Worth, TX: Harcourt.

Gauvain, M. (2001). *The social context of cognitive development.* New York: Guilford.

Gawande, A. (1998, March 30). No mistake. *New Yorker.*

Gawande, A. (1998, September 21). The pain perplex. *New Yorker.*

Gazzaniga, M. S., Fendrich, R., & Wessinger, C. M. (1994). Blindsight reconsidered. *Current Directions in Psychological Science, 3*(3), 93–95.

Gazzaniga, M. S., & LeDoux, J. E. (1978). *The integrated mind.* New York: Plenum.

Ge, X., Conger, R., & Elder, G. H. (2001). Pubertal transition, stressful life events, and the emergence of gender differences in adolescent depressive symptoms. *Developmental Psychology, 37,* 404–417.

Geary, D. C. (1999). Evolution and developmental sex differences. *Current Directions in Psychological Science, 8,* 115–120.

Geary, D. C. (2000). Evolution and proximate expression of human paternal investment. *Psychological Bulletin, 126,* 55–77.

Geary, J. (1997, May 5). Should we just say no to smart drugs? *Time,* p. 149.

Geen, R. G. (1991). Social motivation. *Annual Review of Psychology, 42,* 377–399.

Geen, R. G. (1998a). Aggression and antisocial behavior. In D. Gilbert, S. T. Fiske, & G. Lindzey (Eds.), *Handbook of social psychology* (4th ed., Vol. 2, pp. 317–356). Boston: McGraw-Hill.

Geen, R. G. (1998b). Process and personal variables in affective aggression. In R. G. Geen & E. Donnerstein (Eds.), *Human aggression* (pp. 2–24). San Diego: Academic Press.

Geen, R. G., & McCown, E. J. (1984). Effects of noise and attack on aggression and physiological arousal. *Motivation and Emotion, 8,* 231–241.

Gellhorn, E., & Loofbourrow, G. N. (1963). *Emotions and emotional disorders.* New York: Harper & Row.

Gelman, R., & Baillargeon, R. (1983). A review of some Piagetian concepts. In P. H. Mussen (Ed.), *Handbook of child psychology* (Vol. 3, pp. 167–230). New York: Wiley.

George, M. S., Antonm, R. F., Bloomer, C., Teneback, C., Drobes, D. J., Lorberbaum, J. P., et al. (2001). Activation of prefrontal cortex and anterior thalamus in alcoholic subjects on exposure to alcohol-specific cues. *Archives of General Psychiatry, 58,* 345–352.

Gerin, W., Milner, D., Chawla, S., Pickering, T. G. (1995). Social support as a moderator of cardiovascular reactivity in women: A test of the direct effects and buffering hypotheses. *Psychosomatic Medicine, 57,* 16–22.

Gerken, L. (1994). Child phonology: Past research, present questions, future directions. In M. A. Gernsbacher (Ed), *Handbook of psycholinguistics* (pp. 781–820). San Diego: Academic Press.

Gerschman, J. A., Reade, P. C., & Burrows, G. D. (1980). Hypnosis and dentistry. In G. D. Burrows & L. Dennerstein (Eds.), *Handbook of hypnosis and psychosomatic medicine.* Amsterdam: Elsevier.

Geschwind, N. (1979). Specializations of the human brain. *Scientific American, 241,* 180–199.

Gessner, B. D., Ives, G. C., & Perham-Hester, K. A. (2001). Association between sudden infant death syndrome and prone sleep position, bed sharing, and sleeping outside an infant crib in Alaska. *Pediatrics, 108,* 923–927.

Gfeller, J. D. (1994). Hypnotizability enhancement: Clinical implications of empirical findings. *American Journal of Clinical Hypnosis, 37*(2), 107–116.

Gibbon, J., Malapani, C., Dale, C. L., & Gallistel, C. (1997). Toward a neurobiology of temporal cognition: Advances and challenges. *Current Opinion in Neurobiology, 7,* 170–184.

Gibson, E., Dembofsky, C. A., Rubin, S., & Greenspan, J. S. (2000). Infant sleep position practices 2 years into the "back to sleep" campaign. *Clinical Pediatrics, 39,* 285–289.

Gibson, E. J., & Walk, R. D. (1960). The visual cliff. *Scientific American, 202,* 64–71.

Gibson, J. J. (1979). *The ecological approach to visual perception.* Boston: Houghton Mifflin.

Gifford, R., & Hine, D. (1997a). "I'm cooperative, but you are greedy": Some cognitive tendencies in a common dilemma. *Canadian Journal of Behavioural Science, 29,* 257–265.

Gifford, R., & Hine, D. (1997b). Toward cooperation in the commons dilemma. *Canadian Journal of Behavioural Science, 29,* 167–178.

Gigerenzer, G., Todd, P. M., & ABC Research Group. (2000). *Simple heuristics that make us smart.* New York: Oxford University Press.

Gilbert, A. R., Rosenberg, D. R., Harenski, K., Spencer, S., Sweeney, J. A., & Keshavan, M. S. (2001). Thalamic volumes in patients with first-episode schizophrenia. *American Journal of Psychiatry, 158,* 618–624.

Gilbert, C. D. (1992). Horizontal integration and cortical dynamics. *Neuron, 9,* 1–13.

Gilbert, D. T. (1998). Ordinary personology. In D. Gilbert, S. T. Fiske, & G. Lindzey (Eds.), *Handbook of social psychology* (Vol. 2, 4th ed., pp. 89–150). Boston: McGraw-Hill.

Gilbert, D. T., & Malone, P. S. (1995). The correspondence bias. *Psychological Bulletin, 117,* 21–38.

Gilbert, D. T., & Wilson, T. D. (1998). Miswanting: Some problems in the forecasting of future affective states. In J. P. Forgas (Ed.), *Feeling and thinking: The role of affect in social cognition* (pp. 178–197). New York: Cambridge University Press.

Gilbert, R. M. (1984). Caffeine consumption. In G. A. Spiller (Ed.), *The methylxanthine beverages and foods: Chemistry, consumption, and health effects* (pp. 185–213). New York: Liss.

Gilbert, S. (1997, August 20). Two spanking studies indicate parents should be cautious. *New York Times Magazine.*

Gilboa-Schechtman, E., & Foa, E. B. (2001). Patterns of recovery from trauma: The use of intraindividual analysis. *Journal of Abnormal Psychology, 110,* 392–400.

Giles, T. R. (1990). Bias against behavior therapy in outcome reviews: Who speaks for the patient? *The Behavior Therapist, 13,* 86–90.

Gillette, M. U. (1986). The suprachiasmatic nuclei: Circadian phase-shifts induced at the time of hypothalamic slice preparation are preserved in vitro. *Brain Research, 379,* 176–181.

Gilligan, C. (1982). *In a different voice: Psychological theory and women's development.* Cambridge: Harvard University Press.

Gilligan, C. (1993). Adolescent development reconsidered. In A. Garrod (Ed.), *Approaches to moral development: New research and emerging themes.* New York: Teachers College Press.

Gilliland, F. D., Li, Y.-F., & Peters, J. M. (2001). Effects of maternal smoking during pregnancy and environmental tobacco smoke on asthma and wheezing in children. *American Journal of Respiratory and Critical Care Medicine, 163,* 429–436.

Gilmore, M. M., & Murphy, C. (1989). Aging is associated with increased Weber ratios for caffeine, but not for sucrose. *Perception and Psychophysics, 46,* 555–559.

Gilovich, T. (1997). Some systematic biases of everyday judgment. *Skeptical Inquirer, 21,* 31–35.

Givens, B. (1995). Low doses of ethanol impair spatial working memory and reduce hippocampal theta activity. *Alcoholism Clinical and Experimental Research, 19*(3), 763–767.

Gladue, B. A. (1994). The biopsychology of sexual orientation. *Current Directions in Psychological Science, 3*(5), 150–154.

Glanz, J. (1997). Sharpening the senses with neural "noise." *Science, 277,* 1759.

Glanzer, M., & Cunitz, A. (1966). Two storage mechanisms in free recall. *Journal of Verbal Learning and Verbal Behavior, 5,* 351–360.

Gleaves, D. H., May, M. C., & Cardena, E. (2001). An examination of the diagnostic validity of dissociative identity disorder. *Clinical Psychology Review, 21,* 577–608.

Gleitman, L., & Landau, B. (1994). *The acquisition of the lexicon.* Cambridge: MIT Press.

Glenmullen, J. (2000). *Prozac backlash: Overcoming the dangers of Prozac, Zoloft, Paxil, and other antidepressants with safe, effective alternatives.* New York: Simon & Schuster.

Gleuckauf, R., & Quittner, A. (1992). Assertiveness training for disabled adults in wheelchairs: Self-report, role-play, and activity pattern outcomes. *Journal of Consulting and Clinical Psychology, 60,* 419–425.

Glick, P. T., & Fiske, S. (2001). Ambivalent sexism. In M. Zanna (Ed.), *Advances in experimental social psychology* (Vol. 33, pp. 115–188). New York: Academic Press.

Glod, M. (1998, April 27). Springer mania: Too hot for parents and teachers. *Washington Post,* pp. A1, A10.

Glover, J. A., Krug, D., Dietzer, M., George, B. W., & Hannon, M. (1990). "Advance" advance organizers. *Bulletin of the Psychonomic Society, 28,* 4–6.

Goddard, H. H. (1917). Mental tests and the immigrant. *Journal of Delinquency, 2,* 243–277.

Goenjian, A. K., Molina, L., Steinberg, A. M., Fairbanks, L. A., Alvarez, M. L., Goenjian, H. A., & Pynoos, R. S. (2001). Posttraumatic stress and depressive reactions among Nicaraguan adolescents after hurricane Mitch. *American Journal of Psychiatry, 158,* 788–794.

Goff, D. C., & Coyle, J. T. (2001). The emerging role of glutamate in the pathophysiology and treatment of schizophrenia. *American Journal of Psychiatry, 158,* 1367–1377.

Gold, M. S. (1994). The epidemiology, attitudes, and pharmacology of LSD use in the 1990s. *Psychiatric Annals, 24*(3), 124–126.

Goldberg, J. F., Harrow, M., & Grossman, L. S. (1995). Course and outcome in bipolar affective disorder: A longitudinal follow-up study. *American Journal of Psychiatry, 152,* 379–384.

Goldblum, N. (2001). *The brain-shaped mind: A neural-network view: What the brain can tell us about the mind.* Cambridge: Cambridge University Press.

Goldenberg, I., & Goldenberg, H. (1995). Family therapy. In R. J. Corsini & D. Wedding (Eds.), *Current psychotherapies* (5th ed.). Itasca, IL: Peacock.

Goldfried, M. R., Castonguay, L. G., Hayes, A. M., Drozd, J. F., & Shapiro, D. A. (1997). A comparative analysis of the therapeutic focus in cognitive-behavioral and psychodynamic-interpersonal sessions. *Journal of Consulting and Clinical Psychology, 65,* 720–748.

Goldfried, M. R., & Davison, G. C. (1994). *Clinical behavior therapy.* New York: Wiley. Interscience.

Goldman, M. S., Darkes, J., & Del Boca, F. K. (1999). Expectancy mediation of biopsychosocial risk for alcohol use and alcoholism. In I. Kirsch (Ed.), *How expectancies shape experience* (pp. 233–262). Washington, DC: American Psychological Association.

Goldman, M. S., Del Boca, F. K., & Darkes, J. (1999). Alcohol expectancy theory: The application of cognitive neuroscience. In K. Leonard & H. Blane (Eds.), *Psychological theories of drinking and alcoholism* (2nd ed., pp. 203–246). New York: Guilford.

Goldman-Rakic, P. S. (1994). Specification of higher cortical functions. In S. H. Bromay & J. Grafman (Eds.), *Atypical cognitive deficits in developmental disorders.* Hillsdale, NJ: Erlbaum.

Goldstein, A. J., de Beurs, E., Chambless, D. L., & Wilson, K. A. (2000). EMDR for panic disorder with agoraphobia: Comparison with waiting list and credible attention-placebo control conditions. *Journal of Consulting and Clinical Psychology, 68,* 947–956.

Goldstein, E. B. (1999). *Sensation and perception* (5th ed.). Pacific Grove, CA: Brooks-Cole.

Goldstein, K. (1939). *The organism.* New York: American Book.

Goleman, D. (1995). *Emotional intelligence.* New York: Bantam Books.

Golomb, J., Kluger, A., De Leon, M. J., Ferris, S. H., Convit, A., Mittelman, M. S., et al. (1994). Hippocampal formation size in normal human aging: A correlate of delayed secondary memory performance. *Learning and Memory, 1,* 45–54.

Gonsalves, B., & Paller, K. A. (2000). Neural events that underlie remembering something that never happened. *Nature Neuroscience, 3,* 1316–1321.

Goode, K. T., Haley, W. E., Roth, D. L., & Ford, G. L. (1998). Predicting longitudinal changes in caregiver physical and mental health: A stress process model. *Health Psychology, 17,* 190–198.

Goodenough, F. L. (1932). Expression of the emotions in a blind-deaf child. *Journal of Abnormal and Social Psychology, 27,* 328–333.

Goodwin, F. K., & Jamison, K. R. (Eds.). (1990). *Manic-depressive illness.* New York: Oxford University Press.

Goodyer, I. M., Herbert J., Tamplin, A., & Altham, P. M. E. (2000). Recent life events, cortisol, dehydroepiandrosterone and the onset of major depression in high-risk adolescents. *British Journal of Psychiatry, 177,* 499–504.

Gorman, B. J. (1999). Facilitated communication: Rejected in science, accepted in court+a case study of the use of FC evidence under Frye and Daubert. *Behavioral Sciences and the Law, 17,* 517–541.

Gorman, J. M., Liebowitz, M. R., Fyer, A. J., & Stein, J. (1989). A neuroanatomical hypothesis for panic disorder. *American Journal of Psychiatry, 146,* 148–161.

Gosling, S. D. (2001). From mice to men: What can we learn about personality from animal research? *Psychological Bulletin, 127,* 45–86.

Gosling, S. D., & John, O. P. (1999). Personality dimensions in nonhuman animals: A cross-species review. *Current Directions in Psychological Science, 8,* 69–75.

Gotlib, I. H., & Hammen, C. L. (1992). *Psychological aspects of depression: Toward cognitive interpersonal integration.* Chichester, England: Wiley.

Gottesman, I. I. (1991). *Schizophrenia genesis.* New York: Freeman.

Gottfredson, L. S (1997). Why g matters: The complexity of everyday life. *Intelligence, 24,* 79–132.

Gottfried, A. (1997, June). Parents' role is critical to children's learning. *APA Monitor,* p. 24.

Gottlieb, B. H., & Peters, L. (1991). A national demographic portrait of mutual aid group participants in Canada. *American Journal of Community Psychology, 19,* 651–666.

Gottlieb, G. (2000). Environmental and behavioral influences on gene activity. *Current Directions in Psychological Science, 9,* 93–97.

Gottman, J. M., Coan, J., Carrere, S., & Swanson, C. (1998). Predicting marital happiness and stability from newlywed interactions. *Journal of Marriage and the Family, 60,* 5–22.

Gottman, J. M., & Levenson, R. W. (2000). The timing of divorce: Predicting when a couple will divorce over a 14-year period. *Journal of Marriage and the Family, 62,* 737–745.

Gould, E., Beylin, A., Tanapat, P., Reeves, A., & Schors, T. J. (1999). Learning enhances adult neurogenesis in the hippocampal formation. *Nature Neuroscience, 2,* 260–265.

Gould, E., Tanapat, P., Rydel, T., & Hastings, N. (2000). Regulation of hippocampal neurogenesis in adulthood. *Biological Psychiatry, 48,* 715–720.

Gould, R. A., Otto, M. W., Pollack, M. H., & Yap, L. (1997). Cognitive behavioral and pharmacological treatment of generalized anxiety disorder: A preliminary meta-analysis. *Behavior Therapy, 28,* 285–305.

Gould, S. J. (1983). *The mismeasure of man.* New York: Norton.

Grady, D. (1998, October 13). High chlamydia rates found in teenagers. *New York Times* (Web Archive).

Graham, S. (1992). "Most of the subjects were white and middle class." *American Psychologist, 47,* 629–639.

Grandin, T. (1996). *Thinking in pictures: And other reports from my life with autism.* New York: Vintage Press.

Grassi, L., Rasconi, G., Pedriali, A., Corridoni, A., & Bevilacqua, M. (2000). Social support and psychological distress in primary care attenders. *Psychotherapy and Psychosomatics, 69,* 95–100.

Gray, J. A. (1991). Neural systems, emotions, and personality. In J. Madden IV (Ed.), *Neurobiology of learning, emotion, and affect* (pp. 272–306). New York: Raven Press.

Gray-Little, B., & Hafdahl, A. R. (2000). Factors influencing racial comparisons of self-esteem: A quantitative review. *Psychological Bulletin, 126,* 26–54.

Green, A. I., & Patel, J. K. (1996). The new pharmacology of schizophrenia. *Harvard Mental Health Letter, 13*(6), 5–7.

Green, D. M., & Swets, J. A. (1966). *Signal detection theory and psychophysics.* New York: Wiley.

Green, J. T., & Woodruff-Pak, D. S. (2000). Eyeblink classical conditioning: Hippocampal formation is for neutral stimulus associations as cerebellum is for association response. *Psychological Bulletin, 126,* 138–158.

Green, M. (1991). Visual search, visual strains, and visual architecture. *Perception and Psychophysics, 50,* 388–404.

Green, R. A., Cross, A. J., & Goodwin, G. M. (1995). Review of the pharmacology and clinical pharmacology of 3,4-methylenedioxymethamphetamine (MDMA or "ecstacy"). *Psychopharmacology, 119,* 247–260.

Greenberg, J., Arndt, J., Schimel, J., Pyszczynski, T., & Solomon, S. (2001). Clarifying the function of mortality salience-induced worldview defense: Renewed suppression or reduced accessibility of death-related thoughts? *Journal of Experimental Social Psychology, 37,* 70–76.

Greenberg, J., Pyszczynski, T. & Solomon, S. (in press). A perilous leap from Becker's theorizing to empirical science: Terror management and research. In D. Leichty (Ed.), *Death and denial: Interdisciplinary essays: The legacy of Ernest Becker.* New York: Praeger.

Greenberg, J., Solomon, S., Pyszczynski, T., & Rosenblatt, A. (1992). Why do people need self-esteem? Converging evidence that self-esteem serves an anxiety-buffering function. *Journal of Personality and Social Psychology, 63,* 913–922.

Greenberg, M. T., Lengua, L. J., Coie, J. D., Pinderhughes, E. E., Bierman, K., Dodge, K. A., et al. (1999). Predicting developmental outcomes at school entry using a multiple-risk model: Four American communities. *Developmental Psychology, 35,* 403–417.

Greenblatt, D., Harmatz, J., & Shader, R. I. (1993). Plasma alprazolam concentrations: Relation to efficacy and side effects in the treatment of panic disorder. *Archives of General Psychiatry, 50,* 715–732.

Greene, E., & Loftus, E. F. (1998). Psycholegal research on jury damage awards. *Current Directions in Psychological Science, 7,* 50–54.

Greenfield, P. M. (1994). Video games as cultural artifacts. *Journal of Applied Developmental Psychology, 15,* 3–12.

Greenfield, P. M. (1995, Winter). Culture, ethnicity, race, and development: Implications for teaching theory and research. *Society for Research in Child Development Newsletter,* pp. 3ff.

Greenfield, P. M., & Childs, C. P. (1991). Developmental continuity in biocultural context. In R. Cohen & A. W. Siegel (Eds.), *Context and development* (pp. 135–159). Hillsdale, NJ: Erlbaum.

Greenough, W. T. (1997, November). We can't focus just on ages 0 to 3. *APA Monitor,* p. 3.

Greenough, W. T., Black, J. E., & Wallace, C. S. (1987). Experience and brain development. *Child Development, 58,* 539–559.

Greenwald, A. G., & Banaji, M. R. (1995). Implicit social cognition: Attitudes, self-esteem, and stereotypes. *Psychological Review, 102,* 4–27.

Greenwald, A. G., Draine, S. C., & Abrams, R. L. (1996). Three cognitive markers of unconscious semantic activation. *Science, 273,* 1699–1702.

Greenwald, A. G., Klinger, M. R., & Schuh, E. S. (1995). Activation by marginally perceptible ("subliminal") stimuli: Dissociation of unconscious from conscious cognition. *Journal of Experimental Psychology: General, 124*(1), 22–42.

Greenwald, J. (1991, December 22). Smart as you wanna be. *Los Angeles Times Magazine.*

Greenwald, R. (1999). Eye movement desensitization and reprocessing (EMDR): New hope for children suffering from trauma and loss. *Clinical Child Psychology & Psychiatry, 3,* 279–287.

Greer, A. E., & Buss, D. M. (1994). Tactics for promoting sexual encounters. *Journal of Sex Research, 31*(3), 185–201.

Gregg, V., Gibbs, J. C., & Basinger, K. S. (1994). Patterns of developmental delay in moral judgment by male and female delinquents. *Merrill-Palmer Quarterly, 40,* 538–553.

Griffitt, W. B., & Guay, P. (1969). "Object" evaluation and conditioned affect. *Journal of Experimental Research in Personality, 4,* 1–8.

Grinspoon, L. (1999). The future of medical marijuana. *Forsch Komplementarmed, 6,* 40–43.

Grinspoon, L., Bakalar, J. B., Zimmer, L., & Morgan, J. P. (1997). Marijuana addiction. *Science, 277,* 749, 750–752.

Grinspoon, S., Thomas, E., Pitts, S., Gross, E., Mickley, D., Killer, K., et al. (2000). Prevalence and predictive factors for regional osteopenia in women with anorexia nervosa. *Annals of Internal Medicine, 133,* 790–794.

Grisso, T., & Appelbaum, P. S. (1995). The MacArthur Treatment Competence Study: Vol. 3. Abilities of patients to consent to psychiatric and medical treatments. *Law and Human Behavior, 19,* 149–174.

Grob, C., & Dobkin-de-Rios, M. (1992). Adolescent drug use in cross-cultural perspective. *Journal of Drug Issues, 22*(1), 121–138.

Groopman, J. (2000, January 24). Second opinion. *The New Yorker,* pp. 40–49.

Gross, J. J. (2001). Emotion regulation in adulthood: Timing is everything. *Current Directions in Psychological Science, 10,* 214–219.

Grossberg, S. (1988). *Neural networks and natural intelligence.* Cambridge: MIT Press.

Grosz, H. I., & Zimmerman, J. (1970). A second detailed case study of functional blindness: Further demonstration of the contribution of objective psychological data. *Behavior Therapy 1,* 115–123.

Grote, N. K., & Clark, M. S. (2001). Perceiving unfairness in the family: Cause or consequence of marital distress? *Journal of Personality and Social Psychology, 80,* 281–293.

Grotevant, H. D. (1998). Adolescent development in family contexts. In W. Damon & N. Eisenberg (Eds.), *Handbook of child psychology: Vol. 3. Social, emotional, and personality development* (5th ed., pp. 1097–1150). New York: Wiley.

Groth-Marnat, G. (1997). *Handbook of psychological assessment* (3rd ed.). New York: Wiley.

Grube, B. S., Bilder, R. M., & Goldman, R. S. (1998). Meta-analysis of symptom factors in schizophrenia. *Schizophrenia Research, 31,* 113–120.

Grunberg, N. E. (1994). Overview: Biological processes relevant to drugs of dependence *Addiction, 89*(11), 1443–1446.

Grusec, J. E. (1991). Socialization of concern for others in the home. *Developmental Psychology, 27,* 338–342.

Grusec, J. E., & Goodnow, J. J. (1994). Impact of parental discipline methods on the child's internalization of values. *Developmental Psychology, 30,* 4–19.

Guadagno, R. E., Asher, T., Demaine, L. J., & Cialdini, R. B. (2001). When saying yes leads to saying no: Preference for consistency and the reverse foot-in-the-door effect. *Personality and Social Psychology Bulletin, 27,* 859–867.

Guerin, D. W., Gottfried, A. W., & Thomas, C. W. (1997). Difficult temperament and behaviour problems: A longitudinal study from 1. 5 to 12 years. *International Journal of Behavioral Development, 21,* 71–90.

Guerlain, S. (1993). Factors influencing the cooperative problem-solving of people and computers. *Proceedings of the Human Factors and Ergonomics Society 37th Annual Meeting* (pp. 387–391). Santa Monica, CA: Human Factors Society.

Guerlain, S. (1995). Using the critiquing approach to cope with brittle expert systems. *Proceedings of the Human Factors and Ergonomics Society 39th Annual Meeting, I* (pp. 233–237). Santa Monica, CA: Human Factors Society.

Guevara, M. A., Lorenzo, I., Ramos, J., & Corsi-Cabrera, M. (1995). Inter- and intra-hemispheric EEG correlation during sleep and wakefulness. *Sleep, 18*(4), 257–265.

Guilford, J. P. (1959). Traits of creativity. In H. H. Anderson (Ed.), *Creativity and its cultivation* (pp. 142–161). New York: Harper & Row.

Guilford, J. P., & Hoepfner, R. (1971). *The analysis of intelligence.* New York: McGraw-Hill.

Gunnoe, M. L., & Mariner, C. L. (1997). Toward a developmental-contextual model of the effects of parental spanking on children's aggression. *Archives of Pediatrics and Adolescent Medicine, 151,* 768–775.

Guntheroth, W. G., & Spiers, P. S. (1992). Sleeping prone and the risk of sudden infant death syndrome. *Journal of the American Medical Association, 267,* 2359–2362.

Gur, R. C., Mozley, L. H., Mozley, P. D., Resnick, S. M., Karp, J. S., Alavi, A., et al. (1995). Sex differences in regional cerebral glucose metabolism during a resting state. *Science, 267,* 528–531.

Gur, R. C., Skolnic, B. E., & Gur, R. E. (1994). Effects of emotional discrimination tasks on cerebral blood flow: Regional activation and its relation to performance. *Brain and Cognition, 25*(2), 271–286.

Gur, R. E., Cowell, P. E., Latshaw, A., Turetsky, B. I., Grossman, R. I., Arnold, S. E., et al. (2000). Reduced dorsal and orbital prefrontal gray matter volumes in schizophrenia. *Archives of General Psychiatry, 57,* 761–768.

Gura, T. (1999). Leptin not impressive in clinical trial. *Science, 286,* 881–882.

Gustavson, C. R., Garcia, J., Hawkins, W. G., & Rusniak, K. W. (1974). Coyote predation control by aversive conditioning. *Science, 184,* 581–583.

Guyer, B., Freedman, M. A., Strobino, D. M., & Sondik, E. J. (2000). Annual summary of vital statistics: Trends in the health of Americans during the 20th century. *Pediatrics, 106,* 1307–1317.

Ha, H., Tan, E. C., Fukunaga, H., & Aochi, O. (1981). Naloxone reversal of acupuncture analgesia in the monkey. *Experimental Neurology, 73,* 298–303.

Haaga, D. A. (2000). Introduction to the special section on stepped care models in psychotherapy. *Journal of Consulting and Clinical Psychology, 68,* 547–548.

Haber, R. N. (1979). Twenty years of haunting eidetic imagery: Where's the ghost? *The Behavioral and Brain Sciences, 2,* 583–629.

Haberlandt, K. (1999). *Human memory: Exploration and application.* Boston: Allyn & Bacon.

Haberstroh, J. (1995). *Ice cube sex: The truth about subliminal advertising.* South Bend, IN: Cross Cultural Publications/Crossroads.

Hackel, L. S., & Ruble, D. N. (1992). Changes in the marital relationship after the first baby is born: Predicting the impact of expectancy disconfirmation. *Journal of Personality and Social Psychology, 62,* 944–957.

Hacking, I. (1995). *Rewriting the soul: Multiple personality and the sciences of memory.* Princeton, NJ: Princeton University Press.

Hackman, J. R. (1998). Why don't teams work? In R. S. Tindale, J. Edwards, & E. J. Posavac (Eds.), *Applications of theory and research on groups to social issues*. New York: Plenum.

Haddock, G., & Zanna, M. P. (1998). Affect, cognition, and the prediction of social attitudes. In W. Stroebe & M. Hewstone (Eds.), *European review of social psychology* (Vol. 10). New York: Wiley.

Hagen, M. A. (2001). Damaged goods?: What, if anything, does science tell us about the long-term effects of childhood sexual abuse? *Skeptical Inquirer, 25*, 54–59.

Hahdahl, K., Iversen, P. M., & Jonsen, B. H. (1993). Laterality for facial expressions: Does the sex of the subject interact with the sex of the stimulus face? *Cortex, 29*(2), 325–331.

Hahn, C.-S., & DiPietro, J. A. (2001). In vitro fertilization and the family: Quality of parenting, family functioning, and child psychosocial adjustment. *Developmental Psychology, 37*, 37–48.

Haldeman, D. C. (1994). The practice and ethics of sexual orientation conversion therapy. *Consulting and Clinical Psychology, 62*(2), 221–227.

Halford, G. S., Maybery, M. R., O'Hare, A. W., & Grant, P. (1994). The development of memory and processing capacity. *Child Development, 65*, 1338–1356.

Halford, J. C., & Blundell, J. E. (2000). Pharmacology of appetite suppression. *Progress in Drug Research, 54*, 25–58.

Hall, C. C. I. (1997). Cultural malpractice: The growing obsolescence of psychology with the changing U.S. population. *American Psychologist, 52*, 642–651.

Hall, C. S., Lindzey, G., & Campbell, J. P. (1998). *Theories of personality* (4th ed.). New York: Wiley.

Hall, G. (1991). *Perceptual and associative learning*. Oxford: Clarendon Press.

Hall, G. C. N. (2001). Psychotherapy research with ethnic minorities: Empirical, ethical, and conceptual issues. *Journal of Consulting and Clinical Psychology, 69*, 502–510.

Hall, G. C. N., & Hirschman, R. (1991). Toward a theory of sexual aggression: A quadriparite model. *Journal of Consulting and Clinical Psychology, 59*, 662–669.

Hall, J. A. (1984). *Nonverbal sex differences*. Baltimore, MD: Johns-Hopkins University Press.

Hall, L. K., & Bahrick, H. P. (1998). The validity of metacognitive predictions of widespread learning and long-term retention. In G. Mazzoni & T. Nelson (Eds.), *Metacognition and cognitive neuropsychology: Monitoring and control processes* (pp. 23–36). Mahwah, NJ: Erlbaum.

Hall, P., & Davidson, K. (1996). The misperception of aggression in behaviorally hostile men. *Cognitive Therapy and Research, 20*, 377–389.

Hall, W. (1997). The recent Australian debate about the prohibition on cannabis use. *Addiction, 92*, 1109–1115.

Halligan, P. W., & David, A. S. (Eds.). (1999). *Conversion hysteria: Towards a cognitive neuropsychological account*. Hove, England: Psychology Press.

Halperin, D. (1992). *Sex differences in cognitive abilities*. Mahwah, NJ: Erlbaum.

Halpern, D. F. (1997). Sex differences in intelligence. *American Psychologist, 52*, 1091–1102.

Halverson, C. F., Jr., & Wampler, K. S. (1997). Family influences on personality development. In R. Hogan, J. Johnson, & S. Briggs (Eds.), *Handbook of personality psychology* (pp. 241–267). San Diego: Academic Press.

Hamilton, C. E. (2000). Continuity and discontinuity of attachment from infancy through adolescence. *Child Development, 71*, 690–694.

Hamilton, D. L., & Sherman, J. (1994). Social stereotypes. In R. S. Wyer & T. K. Srull (Eds.), *Handbook of social cognition* (2nd ed.). Hillsdale, NJ: Erlbaum.

Hamilton, W. D. (1964). The evolution of social behavior: Parts I and II. *Journal of Theoretical Biology 7*, 1–52.

Hamm, A. O., Vaitl, D., & Lang, P. J. (1989). Fear conditioning, meaning, and belongingness: A selective association analysis. *Journal of Abnormal Psychology, 98*, 395–406.

Hammer, E. (1968). Projective drawings. In A. I. Rabin (Ed.), *Projective techniques in personality assessment*. New York: Springer.

Hammond, W. R., & Yung, B. (1993). Minority student recruitment and retention practices among schools of professional psychology: A national survey and analysis. *Professional Psychology: Research and Practice, 24*, 3–12.

Han, S., & Shavitt, S. (1994). Persuasion and culture: Advertising appeals in individualist and collectivist societies. *Journal of Experimental Social Psychology, 30*, 326–350.

Hancock, E. (1996, February). High control at work makes for a healthy heart. *Johns Hopkins Magazine*, p. 31.

Haney, M., Ward, A. S., Comer, S. D., Foltin, R. W., & Fischman, M. W. (1999). Abstinence symptoms following smoked marijuana in humans. *Psychopharmacology, 141*, 395–404.

Hankin, B. L., & Abramson, L. Y. (2001). Development of gender differences in depression: An elaborated cognitive vulnerability-transactional stress theory. *Psychological Bulletin, 127*, 773–796.

Hannigan, S. L., & Reinitz, M. T. (2001). A demonstration and comparison of two types of inference-based memory errors. *Journal of Experimental Psychology: Learning, Memory, and Cognition, 27*, 931–940.

Hanson, G., & Venturelli, P. J. (1995). *Drugs and society* (4th ed.). Boston: Jones & Bartlett.

Hanson, S. J., & Burr, D. J. (1990). What connectionist models learn: Learning and representations in connectionist networks. *Behavioral and Brain Sciences, 13*, 471–518.

Happe, F. G. E., Winner, E., & Brownell, H. (1998). The getting of wisdom: Theory of mind in old age. *Developmental Psychology, 34*, 358–362.

Harasty, J., Double, K. L., Halliday, G. M., Kril, J. J., & McRitchie, D. A. (1997). Language-associated cortical regions are proportionally larger in the female brain. *Archives of Neurology, 54*, 171–176.

Hardimann, P. T., Dufresne, R., & Mestre, J. (1989). The relation between problem categorization and problem solving among experts and novices. *Memory & Cognition, 17*, 627–638.

Hare, R. D. (1993). *Without conscience: The disturbing world of the psychopaths among us*. New York: Pocket Books.

Harlow, H. F. (1949). The formation of learning sets. *Psychological Review, 56*, 51–65.

Harlow, H. F. (1959, June). Love in infant monkeys. *Scientific American*, pp. 68–74.

Harmon-Jones, E., Brehm, J. W., Greenberg, J., Simon, L., & Nelson, D. E. (1996). Evidence that the production of negative consequences is not necessary to produce cognitive dissonance. *Journal of Personality and Social Psychology, 72*, 515–525.

Harper, D. G., Stopa, E. G., McKee, A. C., Satlin, A., Harlan, P. C., Goldstein, R., & Volicer, L. (2001). Differential circadian rhythm disturbances in men with Alzheimer disease and frontotemporal degeneration. *Archives of General Psychiatry, 58*, 353–360.

Harper, R. C., Frysinger, J. D., Marks, J. X., & Zhang, R. B. (1988). Cardiorespiratory control during sleep. In P. J. Schwartz (Ed.), *The sudden infant death syndrome: Cardiac and respiratory mechanisms and interventions* (Annals of the New York Academy of Sciences, Vol. 533). New York: New York Academy of Sciences.

Harris, C. V., & Goetsch, V. L. (1990). Multi-component flooding treatment of adolescent phobia. In E. L. Feindler & G. R. Kalfus (Eds.), *Adolescent behavior therapy handbook* (Vol. 22). New York: Springer.

Harris, G. C., & Aston-Jones, G. (1995). Involvement of D2 dopamine receptors in the nucleus acumbens in opiate withdrawal syndrome. *Nature, 371*, 155–157.

Harris, J. R. (1995). Where is the child's environment? A group socialization theory of development. *Psychological Review, 102*, 458–489.

Harris, J. R. (1998). *The nurture assumption*. New York: Free Press.

Harris, J. R. (2000). Context-specific learning, personality, and birth order. *Current Directions in Psychological Science, 9*, 174–177.

Hart, A. J., Whalen, P. J., Shin, L. M., McInerney, S. C., Fischer, H. & Rauch, S. L. (2000). Differential response in the human amygdala to racial outgroup vs. ingroup face stimuli. *Neuroreport, 11*, 2351–2355.

Hart, D., & Yates, M. (1997). The interrelation of self and identity in adolescence: A developmental account. In R. Vasta (Ed.), *Annals of child development: Vol. 12. A research annual* (pp. 207–243). London: Jessica Kingsley.

Harter, S. (1998). The development of self representations. In W. Damon & N. Eisenberg (Eds.), *Handbook of child psychology: Vol. 3. Social, emotional, and personality development* (5th ed., pp. 553–618). New York: Wiley.

Hartmann, H. (1958). *Ego psychology and the problem of adaptation.* New York: International Universities Press.

Hartung, C. M., & Widiger, T. A. (1998). Gender differences in the diagnosis of mental disorders: Conclusions and controversies of DSM-IV. *Psychological Bulletin, 123,* 260–278.

Hartup, W. W., & Stevens, N. (1997). Friendships and adaptation in the life course. *Psychological Bulletin, 121,* 355–370.

Harvard Mental Health Letter. (1998a). Mood disorders: An overview—Part II. *Harvard Mental Health Letter, 14*(7), 1–5.

Harvard Mental Health Letter. (1998b). Mood disorders: An overview—Part III. *Harvard Mental Health Letter, 14*(8), 1–5.

Harvard Mental Health Letter. (2001). New treatments for cocaine addiction. *Harvard Mental Health Letter, 17,* 6–7.

Harwood, H., Fountain, D., & Livermore, G. (1998). *The economic costs of alcohol and drug abuse in the United States, 1992.* Bethesda, MD: National Institute on Drug Abuse and the National Institute on Alcohol Abuse and Alcoholism. Publication No. 98-4327.

Harwood, R. L., Schulze, P. A., & Wilson, S. P. (1995, March). *Cultural values and acculturation among lower-class Puerto Rican mothers living in the United States.* Poster presented at the biennial meeting of the Society for Research in Child Development, Indianapolis.

Haskell, I., & Wickens, C. D. (1993). Two- and three-dimensional displays for aviation. *International Journal of Aviation Psychology, 3*(2), 87–109.

Hastie, R., Penrod, S. D., & Pennington, N. (1984). *Inside the jury.* Cambridge: Harvard University Press.

Hatfield, E., & Rapson, R. L. (1995). *Love and sex: Cross-cultural perspectives.* Boston: Allyn & Bacon.

Hattori, M., Fujiyama, A., Taylor, T. D., Watanabe, H., Yada, T., Park, H. S., et al. (2000). The DNA sequence of human chromosome 21. *Nature, 405,* 311–319.

Hauptman, J., Lucas, C., Boldrin, M. N., Collins, H., & Segal, K. R. (2000). Orlistat in the long-term treatment of obesity in primary care settings. *Archives of Family Medicine, 9,* 160–167.

Hawkins, H. L., Kramer, A. R., & Capaldi, D. (1993). Aging, exercise, and attention. *Psychology and Aging, 7,* 643–653.

Haxby, J. V., Gobbini, M. I., Furey, M. L., Ishai, A., Schouten, J. L., & Pietrini, P. (2001). Distributed and overlapping representations of faces and objects in ventral temporal cortex. *Science, 293,* 2425–2430.

Hayes, A. M., & Harris, M. S. (2000). The development of an integrative therapy for depression. In S. L. Johnson & A. M. Hayes (Eds.), *Stress, coping, and depression* (pp. 291–306). Mahwah, NJ: Erlbaum.

Hays, P. A. (1995). Multicultural applications of cognitive-behavior therapy. *Professional Psychology: Research and Practice, 26,* 309–315.

Hays, W. L. (1981). *Statistics* (3rd ed). New York: Holt, Rinehart & Winston.

He, L. F. (1987). Involvement of endogenous opioid peptides in acupuncture analgesia. *Pain, 31,* 99–121.

Healy, D. J., Haroutunian, V., Powchik, P., Davidson, M., Davis, K. L., Watson, S. J., & Meador-Woodruff, J. H. (1998). AMPA receptor binding and subunit mRNA expression in prefrontal cortex and striatum of elderly schizophrenics. *Neuropsychopharmacology, 19,* 278–286.

Hebb, D. O. (1949). *The organization of behavior.* New York: Wiley.

Hebb, D. O. (1955). Drives and the C. N. S. (conceptual nervous system). *Psychological Review, 62,* 243–254.

Hecker, J. E., Losee, M. C., Fritzler, B. K., & Fink, C. M. (1996). Self-directed versus therapist-directed cognitive behavioral treatment for panic disorder. *Journal of Anxiety Disorders, 10,* 253–265.

Hecker, J. E., & Thorpe, G. L. (1992). *Agoraphobia and panic: A guide to psychological treatment.* Boston: Allyn & Bacon.

Hedge, A., & Yousif, Y. H. (1992). Effects of urban size, urgency, and cost of helpfulness: A cross-cultural comparison between the United Kingdom and the Sudan. *Journal of Cross-Cultural Psychology, 23,* 107–115.

Hegarty, J. D., Baldessarini, R. J., Tohen, M., Waternaux, C., & Oepen, G. (1994). One hundred years of schizophrenia: A meta-analysis of the outcome literature. *American Journal of Psychiatry, 151,* 1409–1416.

Heider, E. (1972). Universals of color naming and memory. *Journal of Experimental Psychology, 93,* 10–20.

Heim, C., Newport, J., Heit, S., Graham, Y. P., Wilcox, M., Bonsall, R., et al. (2000). Pituitary-adrenal and autonomic responses to stress in women after sexual and physical abuse in childhood. *Journal of the American Medical Association, 284,* 592–597.

Heine, S., Lehman, D., Markus, H. & Kitayama, S. (1999). Is there a universal need for positive regard? *Psychological Review, 106,* 766–794.

Heine, S. J., & Lehman, D. R. (1997). Culture, dissonance, and self-affirmation. *Personality and Social Psychology Bulletin, 23,* 389–400.

Hejmadi, A., Davidson, R. J., & Rozin, P. (2000). Exploring Hindu Indian emotion expressions: Evidence for accurate recognition by Americans and Indians. *Psychological Science, 11,* 183–187.

Helgesen, S. (1998). *Everyday revolutionaries: Working women and the transformation of American life.* New York: Doubleday.

Heller, W. (1993). Neuropsychological mechanisms of individual differences in emotion, personality, and arousal. *NeuroPsychology, 7*(4), 486–489.

Heller, W., Etienne, M. A., & Miller, G. A. (1993). Patterns of perceptual asymmetry in depression and anxiety: Implications for neuropsychological models of emotion and psychopathology. *Journal of Abnormal Psychology, 104*(2), 327–333.

Heller, W., Nitschke, J. B., & Miller, G. A. (1998). Lateralization in emotion and emotional disorders. *Current Directions in Psychological Science, 7,* 26–32.

Helmers, K. F., & Krantz, D. S. (1996). Defensive hostility, gender and cardiovascular levels and responses to stress. *Annals of Behavioral Medicine, 18,* 246–254.

Helmers, K. F., Krantz, D. S., Merz, C. N. B., Klein, J., Kop, W. J., Gottdiener, J. S., & Rozanski, A. (1995). Defensive hostility: Relationship to multiple markers of cardiac ischemia in patients with coronary disease. *Health Psychology, 14,* 202–209.

Helms, J. E. (1992). Why is there no study of cultural equivalence in standardized cognitive ability testing? *American Psychologist, 47,* 1083–1101.

Helson, R., & Moane, G. (1987). Personality change in women from college to midlife. *Journal of Personality and Social Psychology, 53,* 176–186.

Helzer, J. E., Canino, G. J., Yeh, E., Bland, R. C., Lee, C. K., Hwu, H., & Newman, S. (1990). Alcoholism—North America and Asia: A comparison of population surveys with the diagnostic interview schedule. *Archives of General Psychiatry, 47,* 313–319.

Henderson, B., & Bernard, A. (Eds.). (1998). *Rotten reviews and rejections.* Wainscott, NY: Pushcart Press.

Hendrick, C., & Hendrick, S. (1986). A theory and method of love. *Journal of Personality and Social Psychology, 50,* 392–402.

Henker, B., & Whalen, C. K. (1989). Hyperactivity and attention deficits. *American Psychologist, 44,* 216–223.

Henry, W. P. (1998). Science, politics, and the politics of science: The use and misuse of empirically validated treatment research. *Psychotherapy Research, 8,* 126–140.

Hense, R. L., Penner, L. A., & Nelson, D. L. (1995). Implicit memory for age stereotypes. *Social Cognition, 13,* 399–416.

Hepburn, M. A. (1995). TV violence: Myth and reality. *Social Education, 59,* 309–311.

Herbert, J. D., Lilienfeld, S. O., Lohr, J. M., Montgomery, R. W., O'Donohue, W. T., Rosen, G. M., & Tolin, D. F. (2000). Science and pseudoscience in the development of eye movement desensitization and reprocessing: Implications for clinical psychology. *Clinical Psychology Review, 20,* 945–971.

Hergenhahn, B. R., & Olson, M. (1997). *An introduction to theories of learning* (5th ed.). Upper Saddle River, NJ: Prentice-Hall.

Herman, L. M., Richards, D. G., & Wolz, J. P. (1984). Comprehension of sentences by bottlenosed dolphins. *Cognition, 16,* 129–219.

Hermann, R. C., Dorwart, R. A., Hoover, C. W., & Brody, J. (1995). Variation in ECT use in the United States. *American Journal of Psychiatry, 152,* 869–875.

References

Hernandez, D. J. (1997). Child development and the social demography of childhood. *Child Development, 68,* 149–169.

Herpertz, S. C., Werth, U., Lukas, G., Qunaibi, M., Schuerkens, A., Kunert, H.-J., et al. (2001). Emotion in criminal offenders with psychopathy and borderline personality disorder. *Archives of General Psychiatry, 58,* 737–745.

Herrmann, D. J., & Searleman, A. (1992). Memory improvement and memory theory in historical perspective. In D. Herrmann, H. Weingartner, A. Searlman, & C. McEvoy (Eds.), *Memory improvement: Implications for memory theory.* New York: Springer-Verlag.

Herrnstein, R. (1973). *I. Q. in the meritocracy.* Boston: Little, Brown.

Herrnstein, R. J., & Murray, C. (1994). *The bell curve: Intelligence and class structure in American Life.* New York: Free Press.

Herzog, D. B. (1982). Bulimia: The secretive syndrome. *Psychosomatics, 22,* 481–487.

Herzog, D. B., Dorer, D. J., Keel, P. K., Selwyn, S. E., Ekeblad, E. R., Flores, A. T., et al. (1999). Recovery and relapse in anorexia and bulimia nervosa: A 7. 5-year follow-up study. *Journal of the American Academy of Child and Adolescent Psychiatry, 38,* 829–837.

Herzog, D. B., Greenwood, D. N., Dorer, D. J., Flores, A. T., Ekeblad, E. R., Richards, A., et al. (2000). Mortality in eating disorders: A descriptive study. *International Journal of Eating Disorders, 28,* 20–26.

Hespos, S. J., & Baillargeon, R. (2001). Infants' knowledge about occlusion and containment events: A surprising discrepancy. *Psychological Science, 12,* 141–147.

Hess, R. D., Chih-Mei, C., & McDevitt, T. M. (1987). Cultural variations in family beliefs about children's performance in mathematics: Comparisons among People's Republic of China, Chinese-American, and Caucasian-American families. *Journal of Educational Psychology, 79,* 179–188.

Hesse, J., Mogelvang, B., & Simonsen, H. (1994). Acupuncture versus metropolol in migraine prophylaxis: A randomized trial of trigger point inactivation. *Journal of Internal Medicine, 235,* 451–456.

Heston, L. L. (1966). Psychiatric disorders in foster home-reared children of schizophrenic mothers. *British Journal of Psychiatry, 112,* 819–825.

Hetherington, E. M., & Clingempeel, W. G. (1992). Coping with marital transitions. *Monographs of the Society for Research in Child Development, 57*(2–3, Serial No. 227).

Hetherington, E. M., & Kelly, H. (2002). *For better or for worse: Divorce reconsidered.* New York: Norton.

Hetherington, E. M., & Stanley-Hagan, M. (2002). Parenting in divorced, single-parent, and stepfamilies. In M. H. Bornstein (Ed.), *Handbook of parenting* (2nd ed.). Mahwah, NJ: Erlbaum.

Hettema, J. M., Neale, M. C., & Kendler, K. S. (2001). A review and meta-analysis of the genetic epidemiology of anxiety disorders. *American Journal of Psychiatry, 158,* 1568–1578.

Heward, W. L. (1997). Four validated instructional strategies. *Behavior and Social Issues, 7,* 43–51.

Heyman, R. E., & Neidig, P. H. (1999). A comparison of spousal aggression prevalence rates in the U.S. army and civilian representative samples. *Journal of Consulting and Clinical Psychology, 67,* 239–242.

Heymsfield, S. B., Greenberg, A. S., Fujioa, K., Dixon, R. M., Kushner, R., Hunt, T., et al. (1999). Recombinant leptin for weight loss in obese and lean adults. *Journal of the American Medical Association, 282,* 1568–1575.

Hickok, G., Bellugi, U., & Klima, E. S. (1996). The neurobiology of sign language and its implications for the neural basis of language. *Nature, 381,* 699–702.

Higgins, E. T., Vookles, J., & Tykocinski, O. (1992). Self and health: How patterns of self-beliefs predict emotional and physical problems. *Social Cognition, 10,* 125–150.

Hilgard, E. R. (1965). *Hypnotic susceptibility.* New York: Harcourt, Brace & World.

Hilgard, E. R. (1977). *Divided consciousness: Multiple controls in human thought and action.* New York: Wiley.

Hilgard, E. R. (1979). *Personality and hypnosis: A study of imaginative involvement.* Chicago: University of Chicago Press.

Hilgard, E. R. (1980). Consciousness in contemporary psychology. *Annual Review of Psychology, 31,* 1–26.

Hilgard, E. R. (1982). Hypnotic susceptibility and implications for measurement. *International Journal of Clinical and Experimental Hypnosis, 30,* 394–403.

Hilgard, E. R. (1992). Divided consciousness and dissociation. *Consciousness and Cognition, 1,* 16–31.

Hilgard, E. R., & Marquis, D. G. (1936). Conditioned eyelid responses in monkeys, with a comparison of dog, monkey, and man. *Psychological Monographs, 47,* 186–198.

Hilgard, E. R., Morgan, A. H., & MacDonald, H. (1975). Pain and dissociation in the cold pressor test: A study of "hidden reports" through automatic key-pressing and automatic talking. *Journal of Abnormal Psychology, 84,* 280–289.

Hill, B. (1968). *Gates of horn and ivory.* New York: Taplinger.

Hill, C. T., & Peplau, L. A. (1998). Premarital predictors of relationship outcomes: A 15-year follow-up of the Boston Couples Study. In T. N. Bradbury (Ed.), *The developmental course of marital dysfunction* (pp. 237–278). New York: Cambridge University Press.

Hill, D. L., & Mistretta, C. M. (1990). Developmental neurobiology of salt taste sensation. *Trends in Neuroscience, 13,* 188–195.

Hill, D. L., & Przekop, P. R., Jr. (1988). Influences of dietary sodium on functional taste receptor development: A sensitive period. *Science, 241,* 1826–1828.

Hill, J. O., & Peters, J. C. (1998). Environmental contributions to the obesity epidemic. *Science, 280,* 1371–1374.

Hill, T., Lewicki, P., Czyzewska, M., & Boss, A. (1989). Self-perpetuating biases in person perception. *Journal of Personality and Social Psychology, 57,* 373–386.

Hilliard, R. B., Henry, W. P., & Strupp, H. H. (2000). An interpersonal model of psychotherapy: Linking patient and therapist developmental history, therapeutic process, and types of outcome. *Journal of Consulting and Clinical Psychology, 68,* 125–133.

Hilton, H. (1986). *The executive memory guide.* New York: Simon & Schuster.

Hinshaw, S. P., Zupan, B. A., Simmel, C., Nigg, J. T., & Melnick, S. (1997). Peer status in boys with and without attention-deficit hyperactivity disorder: Predictions from overt and covert antisocial behavior, social isolation, and authoritative parenting beliefs. *Child Development, 68,* 880–896.

Hinsz, V. B. (1990). Cognitive and consensus processes in group recognition memory performance. *Journal of Personality and Social Psychology, 59,* 705–718.

Hinton, J. (1967). *Dying.* Harmondsworth, England: Penguin.

Hintzman, D. (1991). Human learning and memory. *Annual Review of Psychology, 41,* 109–139.

Hiroto, D. S. (1974). Locus of control and learned helplessness. *Journal of Experimental Psychology, 102,* 187–193.

Hirschfeld, J. A. (1995). The "Back-to-Sleep" campaign against SIDS. *American Family Physician, 51*(3), 611–612.

Hirschfeld, R. M., Allen, M. H., McEvoy, J. P., Keck, P. E., Jr, & Russell, J. M. (1999). Safety and tolerability of oral loading divalproex sodium in acutely manic bipolar patients. *Journal of Clinical Psychiatry, 60,* 815–818.

Hirsch-Pasek, K., Treiman, R., & Schneiderman, M. (1984). Brown and Hanlon revisited: Mothers' sensitivity to ungrammatical forms. *Journal of Child Language, 11,* 81–88.

Ho, D. Y., & Chiu, C. (1998). Component ideas of individual, collectivism, and social organization. In U. Kim, C. Kagitcibasi, & H. C. Triandis (Eds.), *Individualism and collectivism: Theory, method, and applications.* Thousand Oaks, CA: Sage.

Hobson, J. (1997). Dreaming as delirium: A mental status analysis of our nightly madness. *Seminar in Neurology, 17,* 121–128.

Hobson, J. A., Pace-Schott, E. F., Stickgold, R., & Kahn, D. (1998). To dream or not to dream? Relevant data from new neuroimaging and electrophysical studies. *Current Opinions in Neurobiology, 8,* 239–244.

Hobson, J. A., & Stickgold, R. (1994). Dreaming: A neurocognitive approach. *Consciousness and Cognition, 3,* 1–15.

Hochhalter, A., Sweeney, W., Bakke, B. L., Holub, R. J., & Overmier, J. B. (2001). Improving face recognition in alcohol dementia. *Clinical Gerontologist, 22,* 3–18.

Hoffert, M. J. (1992). The neurophysiology of pain. In G. M. Aronoff (Ed.), *Evaluation and treatment of chronic pain*. Baltimore: Williams & Wilkins.

Hoffman, D. (1999, February 11). When the nuclear alarms went off, he guessed right. *International Herald Tribune*, p. 2.

Hoffman, H. G., Granhag, P. A., See, S. T. K., & Loftus, E. F. (2001). Social influences on reality-monitoring decisions. *Memory and Cognition, 29*, 394–404.

Hogan, R. J., & Ones, D. (1997). Conscientiousness and integrity at work. In R. Hogan, J. Johnson, & S. Briggs (Eds.), *Handbook of personality psychology* (pp. 849–873). San Diego: Academic Press.

Hogarth, R. M., & Einhorn, H. J. (1992). Order effects in belief updating: The belief adjustment model. *Cognitive Psychology, 24*, 1–55.

Hoglinger, G. U., Widmer, H. R., Spenger, C., Meyer, M., Seiler, R. W., Oertel, W. H., & Sautter, J. (2001). Influence of time in culture and BDNF pretreatment on survival and function of grafted embryonic rat ventral mesencephalon in the 6-OHDA rat model of Parkinson's disease. *Experimental Neurology, 167*, 148–157.

Hohman, A. A., & Shear, M. K. (2002). Community-based intervention research: Coping with the "noise" of real life in study design. *American Journal of Psychiatry, 159*, 201–207.

Hohmann, G. W. (1966). Some effects of spinal cord lesions on experienced emotional feelings. *Psychophysiology, 3*, 143–156.

Holahan, C. J. (1986). Environmental psychology. *Annual Review of Psychology, 37*, 381–407.

Holahan, C. J., Moos, R. H., Holahan, C. K., & Brennan, P. L. (1997). Social context, coping strategies, and depressive symptoms: An expanded model with cardiac patients. *Journal of Personality and Social Psychology, 72*, 918–928.

Holahan, C. K. (1994). Women's goal orientations across the life cycle: Findings from the Terman Study of the Gifted. In B. F. Turner & L. E. Troll (Eds.), *Women growing older* (pp. 35–67). Thousand Oaks, CA: Sage.

Holcomb, L., Gordon, M. N., McGowan, E., Yu, X., Benkovic, S., Jantzen, P., et al. (1998). Accelerated Alzheimer-type phenotype in transgenic mice carrying both mutant amyloid precursor protein and presenilin 1 transgenes. *Nature Medicine, 4*, 97–100.

Holden, C. (1991). Probing the complex genetics of alcoholism. *Science, 251*, 163–164.

Holden, C. (1996). Small refugees suffer the effects of early neglect. *Science, 274*, 1076–1077.

Holden, C. (1998). New clues to alcoholism risk. *Science, 280*, 1348–1349.

Hollis, K. A. (1997). Contemporary research on Pavlovian conditioning: A "new" functional analysis. *American Psychologist, 52*, 956–964.

Holman, B. R. (1994). Biological effects of central nervous system stimulants. *Addiction, 89*(11), 1435–1441.

Holmes, D. S. (1984). Meditation and somatic arousal reduction: A review of the experimental evidence. *American Psychologist, 39*, 1–10.

Holmes, D. S. (1991). *Abnormal psychology*. New York: HarperCollins.

Holway, A. H., & Boring, E. G. (1941). Determinants of apparent visual size with distance variant. *American Journal of Psychology, 54*, 31–37.

Hommer, D. W., Momenan, R., Kaiser, E., & Rawlings, R. R. (2001). Evidence for a gender-related effect of alcoholism on brain volumes. *The American Journal of Psychiatry, 158*, 198–204.

Hong, Y., Morris, M. W., Chiu, C., & Benet-Martinez, V. (2000). Multicultural minds: A dynamic constructivist approach to culture and cognition. *American Psychologist, 55*, 709–720.

Honts, C. R., & Quick, B. D. (1995). The polygraph in 1996: Progress in science and the law. *North Dakota Law Review, 71*, 997–1020.

Hood, M. Y., Moore, L. L., Sundarajan-Ramamurti, A., Singer, M., Cupples, L. A., & Ellison, R. C. (2000). Parental eating attitudes and the development of obesity in children: The Framingham children's study. *International Journal of Obesity, 24*, 1319–1325.

Hooker, E. (1993). Reflections of a 40-year exploration: A scientific view on homosexuality. *American Psychologist, 48*, 450–453.

Hopf, H. C., Muller, F. W., & Hopf, N. J. (1992). Localization of emotional and volitional facial paresis. *Neurology, 42*(10), 1918–1923.

Hopper, K., & Wanderling, J. (2000). Revisiting the developed versus developing country distinction in course and outcome in schizophrenia: Results from ISoS, the WHO Collaborative Followup Project. *Schizophrenia Bulletin, 26*, 835–846.

Hoptman, M. J., & Davidson, R. J. (1994). How and why do the two cerebral hemispheres interact? *Psychological Bulletin, 116*, 195–219.

Horgan, J. (1996, December). Why Freud isn't dead. *Scientific American*, pp. 106–111.

Horn, J. L. (1982). The theory of fluid and crystallized intelligence in relation to concepts of cognitive psychology and aging in adulthood. In F. I. M. Craik & S. Trehub (Eds.), *Aging and cognitive processes* (pp. 201–238). New York: Plenum.

Horne, J. A. (1988). *Why we sleep: The functions of sleep in humans*. Oxford: Oxford University Press.

Horney, K. (1937). *Neurotic personality of our times*. New York: Norton.

Horowitz, L. M., Rosenberg, S. E., & Bartholomew, K. (1993). Interpersonal problems, attachment styles, and outcome in brief dynamic psychotherapy. *Journal of Consulting and Clinical Psychology, 61*, 549–560.

Horwitz, P., & Christie, M. A. (2000). Computer-based manipulatives for teaching scientific reasoning: An example. In M. J. Jacobson & R. B. Kozuma (Eds.), *Innovations in science and mathematics education: Advanced designs for technologies of learning* (pp. 163–191). Mahwah, NJ: Erlbaum.

Houpt, T. R. (1994). Gastric pressure in pigs during eating and drinking. *Gastric pressure in pigs during eating and drinking, 56*(2), 311–317.

House, J. S., Landis, K. R., & Umberson, D. (1988). Structures and processes of social support. *Annual Review of Sociology, 14*, 293–318.

Houston, B., & Vavac, C. (1991). Cynical hostility: Developmental factors, psychosocial correlates and health behaviors. *Health Psychology, 10*, 9–17.

Howard, D. V. (1983). *Cognitive psychology*. New York: Macmillan.

Howard-Pitney, B., LaFramboise, T., Basil, M., September, B., & Johnson, M. (1992). Psychological and social indicators of suicide ideation and suicide attempts in Zuni adolescents. *Journal of Consulting and Clinical Psychology, 60*, 473–476.

Howe, M. J. A., Davidson, J. W., & Sloboda, J. A. (1998). Innate talent: Reality or myth? *Behavioral and Brain Sciences, 21*, 399–442.

Howe, M. L. (1995, March). *Differentiating cognitive and sociolinguistic factors in the decline of infantile amnesia*. Paper presented at the biennial meeting of the Society for Research in Child Development, Indianapolis.

Hoy, A. W. (1999). Psychology applied to education. In A. M. Stec & D. A. Bernstein (Eds.), *Psychology: The fields of application*. Boston: Houghton Mifflin.

Hoyert, D. L., Kochanek, K. D., & Murphy, S. L. (1999). *Deaths: Final data for 1997 National Vital Statistics Report* (DHHS Publication No. [PHS] 99-1120). Hyattsville, MD: National Center for Health Statistics.

Hoyle, R. H. (1993). Interpersonal attraction in the absence of explicit attitudinal information. *Social Cognition, 11*, 309–320.

Hoyt, M. F. (1995). Brief psychotherapies. In A. S. Gurman & S. B. Messer (Eds.), *Essential psychotherapies: Theory and practice* (pp. 441–487). New York: Guilford.

Hrobjartsson, A., & Gotzsche, P. C. (2001). Is the placebo powerless?: An analysis of clinical trials comparing placebo with no treatment. *The New England Journal of Medicine, 344*, 1594–1602.

Hser, Y. I., Hoffman, V., Grella, C. E., & Anglin, M. D. (2001). A 33-year follow-up of narcotics addicts. *Archives of General Psychiatry, 58*, 503–508.

Hsiao, K., Chapman, P., Nilsen, S., Eckman, C., Harigaya, Y., Younkin, S., et al. (1996). Correlative memory deficits, Abeta elevation, and amyloid plaques in transgenic mice. *Science, 274*, 99–102.

Hu, F. B., Stampfer, M. J., Manson, J. E., Grodstein, F., Colditz, G. A., Speizer, F. E., Willett, W. C. (2000). Trends in the incidence of coronary heart disease and changes in diet and lifestyle in women. *The New England Journal of Medicine, 343*, 530–537.

Hu, S., Patatucci, A. M. L., Patterson, C., Li, L., Fulker, D. W., Cherny, S. S., et al. (1995). Linkage between sexual orientation and chromosome Xq28 in males but not females. *Nature Genetics, 11*, 248–256.

Huang, L. & Li, C. (2000). Leptin: A multifunctional hormone. *Cell Research, 10*, 81–92.

Hubble, M. A., Duncan, B. L., & Miller, S. D. (Eds.). (1999). *The heart and soul of change: What works in psychotherapy*. Washington, DC: American Psychological Assocation.

Hubel, D. H., & Wiesel, T. N. (1979). Brain mechanisms of vision. *Scientific American, 241,* 150–162.

Hudson, J. A., & Sheffield, E. G. (1998). Deja vu all over again: Effects of reenactment on toddlers' event memory. *Child Development, 69,* 51–67.

Hudson, W. (1960). Pictorial depth in perception in subcultural groups in Africa. *Journal of Social Psychology, 52,* 183–208.

Hudspeth, A. J. (1997). How hearing happens. *Neuron, 19,* 947–950.

Huesmann, L. R. (1995). *Screen violence and real violence: Understanding the link.* Auckland, NZ: Media Aware.

Huesmann, L. R. (1998). The role of social information processing and cognitive schema in the acquisition and maintenance of habitual aggressive behavior. In R. G. Geen & E. Donnerstein (Eds.), *Human aggression.* San Diego: Academic Press.

Huesmann, L. R., & Eron, L. D. (1986). *Television and the aggressive child: A cross-national comparison.* Hillsdale, NJ: Erlbaum.

Huesmann, L. R., Moise, J., Podolski, C., & Eron, L. (1997, April). *Longitudinal relations between early exposure to television violence and young adult aggression: 1977–1992.* Paper presented at the annual meeting of the Society for Research in Child Development, Washington, DC.

Hughes, J. R., Higgins, S. T., & Bickel, W. K. (1994). Nicotine withdrawal versus other drug withdrawal syndromes: Similarities and dissimilarities. *Addiction, 89*(11), 1461–1470.

Hull, C. L. (1943). *Principles of behavior.* New York: Appleton-Century-Crofts.

Hull, C. L. (1951). *Essentials of behavior.* New Haven, CT: Yale University Press.

Humphreys, L. G. (1984). General intelligence. In C. R. Reynolds & R. T. Brown (Eds.), *Perspectives on bias in mental testing.* New York: Plenum.

Humphreys, L. G. (1988). Trends in levels of academic achievement of blacks and other minorities. *Intelligence, 12,* 183–197.

Hunsley, J., & Rumstein-McKean, O. (1999). Improving psychotherapeutic services via randomized trials, treatment manuals, and component analysis designs. *Journal of Clinical Psychology, 55,* 1507–1517.

Hunt, C. B. (1980). Intelligence as an information processing concept. *British Journal of Psychology, 71,* 449–474.

Hunt, D. M., Dulai, K. S., Bowmaker, J. K., & Mollon, J. D. (1995). The chemistry of John Dalton's color blindness. *Science, 267,* 984–988.

Hunt, E. (1983). On the nature of intelligence. *Science, 219,* 141–146.

Hunt, M. (1982). *The universe within.* New York: Simon & Schuster.

Hunt, M. (1999). *The new know-nothings: The political foes of the scientific study of human nature.* New Brunswick, NJ: Transaction.

Hunt, R., & Rouse, W. B. (1981). Problem solving skills of maintenance trainees in diagnosing faults in simulated power plants. *Human Factors, 23,* 317–328.

Hunter, J. E. (1986). Cognitive ability, cognitive aptitudes, job knowledge, and job performance. *Journal of Vocational Behavior, 29,* 340–362.

Hunter, J. N. (1997). Needed: A ban on the significance test. *Psychological Science, 8,* 3–7.

Hunter, R. H. (1995). Benefits of competency-based treatment programs. *American Psychologist, 50,* 509–513.

Hurt, H., Brodsky, N. L., Betancourt, L., & Braitman, L. E. (1995). Cocaine-exposed children: Follow-up through 30 months. *Journal of Developmental and Behavioral Pediatrics, 16*(1), 29–35.

Huston, A. C., & Wright, J. C. (1989). The forms of television and the child viewer. In G. Comstock (Ed.), *Public communication and behavior* (Vol. 2, pp. 103–159). San Diego: Academic Press.

Huston, T. L., Caughlin, J. P., Houts, R. M., Smith, S. E., & George, L. J. (2001). The connubial crucible: Newlywed years as predictors of marital delight, distress, and divorce. *Journal of Personality and Social Psychology, 80,* 237–252.

Huttenlocher, P. R. (1994). Synaptogenesis in human cerebral cortex. In G. Dawson & K. W. Fischer (Eds.), *Human behavior and the developing brain* (pp. 137–152). New York: Guilford.

Hyde, J. S. (1986). Gender differences in aggression. In J. S. Hyde & M. C. Linn (Eds.), *The psychology of gender: Advances through meta-analysis.* Baltimore: Johns Hopkins University Press.

Hyde, J. S. (1994). Can meta-analysis make feminist transformations in psychology? *Psychology of Women Quarterly, 18,* 451–462.

Hyde, J. S., & Durik, A. M. (2000). Gender differences in erotic plasticityn-Evolutionary or sociocultural forces? Comment on Baumeister. *Psychological Bulletin, 126,* 375–379.

Hyman, I. A. (1995). Corporal punishment, psychological maltreatment, violence, and punitiveness in America: Research, advocacy, and public policy. *Applied and Preventative Psychology, 4,* 113–130.

Hyman, I. E., Jr. (2000). The memory wars. In U. Neisser & I. E. Hyman Jr. (Eds.), *Memory observed* (2nd ed., pp. 374–379). New York: Worth.

Hyman, I. E., Jr., & Loftus, E. F. (1998). Errors in autobiographical memory. *Clinical Psychology Review, 18,* 933–948.

Hyman, I. E., & Pentland, J. (1996). The role of mental imagery in the creation of false childhood memories. *Journal of Memory and Language, 35,* 101–117.

Iacono, W. G., & Lykken, D. T. (1997). The validity of the lie detector: Two surveys of scientific opinion. *Journal of Applied Psychology, 82,* 426–433.

Igalens, J., & Roussel, P. (2000). A study of the relationships between compensation package, work motivation, and job satisfaction. *Journal of Organizational Behavior, 20,* 1003, 1025.

Ilgen, D. R., & Pulakos, E. D. (Eds.). (1999). *The changing nature of performance: Implications for staffing, motivation, and development.* San Francisco, CA: Jossey-Bass.

Inciardi, J. A., Surratt, H. L., & Saum, C. A. (1997). *Cocaine-exposed infants: Social, legal, and public health issues.* Thousand Oaks, CA: Sage.

Indovina, I., & Sanes, J. N. (2001). On somatotopic representation centers for finger movements in human primary motor cortex and supplementary motor area. *Neuroimage, 13,* 1027–1034.

Ingram, D. K. (2001). Vaccine development for Alzheimer's disease: A shot of good news. *Trends in Neuroscience, 24,* 305–307.

Ingram, R. E., Miranda, J., & Segal, Z. V. (1998). *Cognitive vulnerability to depression.* New York: Guilford.

Inoue-Nakamura, N., & Matsuzawa, T. (1997). Development of stone tool use by wild chimpanzees (Pan troglodytes). *Journal of Comparative Psychology, 111,* 159–173.

Inskip, P. D., Tarone, R. E., Hatch, E. E., Wilcosky, T. C., Shapiro, W. R., Selker, R. G., Fine, H. A., Black, P. M., Loeffler, J. S., & Linet, M. S. (2001). Cellular-telephone use and brain tumors. *The New England Journal of Medicine, 344,* 79–86.

Insko, C. A., Schopler, J., Hoyle, R. H., Dardis, G. J., & Graetz, K. A. (1990). Individual-group discontinuity as a function of fear and greed. *Journal of Personality and Social Psychology, 58,* 68–79.

International Association for the Evaluation of Education Achievement. (1999). *Trends in mathematics and science achievement around the world.* Boston: Lynch School of Education, Boston College.

International Human Genome Sequencing Consortium. (2001). Initial sequencing and analysis of the human genome. *Nature, 409,* 860–921.

International Molecular Genetic Study of Autism Consortium. (1998). A full genome screen for autism with evidence for linkage to a region on chromosome 7q. *Human Molecular Genetics, 7,* 571–578.

Inzlicht, M., & Ben-Zeev, T. (2000). A threatening intellectual environment: Why females are susceptible to experiencing problem-solving deficits in the presence of males. *Psychological Science, 11,* 365–371.

Irnich D., Behrens, N., Molzen, H., Konig, A., Gleditsch, J., Krauss, M., et al. (2001). Randomised trial of acupuncture compared with conventional massage and "sham" laser acupuncture for treatment of chronic neck pain. *British Medical Journal, 322,* 1574–1578.

Ironson, G., Wynings, C., Schneiderman, N., Baum, A., Rodriguez, M., Greenwood, D., et al. (1997). Posttraumatic stress symptoms, intrusive thoughts, loss, and immune function after Hurricane Andrew. *Psychosomatic Medicine, 59,* 128–141.

Irvin, J. E., Bowers, C. A., Dunn, M. E., & Wang, M. C. (1999). Efficacy of relapse prevention: A meta-analytic review. *Journal of Consulting and Clinical Psychology, 67,* 563–570.

Irwin, M., Daniels, M., Smith, T., Bloom, E., & Weiner, H. (1987). Impaired natural killer cell activity during bereavement. *Brain, Behavior, and Immunity, 1,* 98–104.

Ishai, A., Ungerleider, L. G., & Haxby, J. V. (2000). Distributed neural systems for the generation of visual images. *Neuron, 28,* 979–990.

Iversen, L. L., & Snyder, S. H. (2000). *The science of marijuana.* Oxford, England: Oxford University Press.

Iwahashi, K., Matsuo, Y., Suwaki, H., Nakamura, K., & Ichikawa, Y. (1995). CYP2E1 and ALDH2 genotypes and alcohol dependence in Japanese. *Alcoholism Clinical and Experimental Research, 19*(3), 564–566.

Iwamura, Y., Iriki, A., & Tanaka, M. (1994). Bilateral hand representation in the postcentral somatosensory cortex. *Nature, 369,* 554–556.

Izard, C. (1993). Organizational and motivational functions of discrete emotions. In M. Lewis and J. M. Haviland (Eds.), *Handbook of emotions.* New York: Guilford.

Izard, C., Fine, S., Schultz, D. Mostow, A., Ackerman, B., & Youngstrom, E. (2001). Emotion knowledge as a predictor of social behavior and academic competence in children at risk. *Psychological Science, 12,* 18–23.

Izard, C. E. (1977). *Human emotions.* New York: Plenum.

Jack, C. R., Jr., Petersen, R. C., Xu, Y. C., O'Brien, P. C., Smith, G. E., Ivnik, R. J., et al. (1999). Prediction of AD with MRI-based hippocampal volume in mild cognitive impairment. *Neurology, 52,* 1397–1403.

Jackson, J. J. (in press). The relationship between group identity and intergroup prejudice is moderated by sociocultural variation. *Journal of Applied Social Psychology.*

Jacob, S., & McClintock, M. K. (2000). Psychological state and mood effects of steroidal chemosignals in women and men. *Hormones and Behavior, 37,* 57–78.

Jacobs, G. D. (1999). *Say goodnight to insomnia.* New York: Holt.

Jacobs, M. K., & Goodman, G. (1989). Psychology and self-help groups: Predictions on a partnership. *American Psychologist, 44,* 536–545.

Jacobson, E. (1938). *Progressive relaxation.* Chicago: University of Chicago Press.

Jacobson, J. W., Mulick, J. A., & Schwartz, A. A. (1995). A history of facilitated communication. *American Psychologist, 50,* 750–765.

Jacobson, N. S., Christensen, A., Prince, S. E., Cordova, J., & Eldridge, K. (2000). Integrative behavioral couples therapy: An acceptance-based, promising new treatment for couple discord. *Journal of Consulting and Clinical Psychology, 68,* 351–355.

Jacoby, L. L., Marriott, M. J., & Collins, J. G. (1990). The specifics of memory and cognition. In T. K. Srull & R. S. Wyer (Eds.), *Advances in social cognition: Vol. 3. Content and process specificity in the effects of prior experiences.* Hillsdale, NJ: Erlbaum.

Jaffe, S., & Hyde, J. S. (2000). Gender differences in moral orientation: A meta-analysis. *Psychological Bulletin, 126,* 703–726.

Jagger, C., Clarke, M., & Stone, A. (1995). Predictors of survival with Alzheimer's disease: A community-based study. *Psychological Medicine, 25,* 171–177.

Jahnke, J. C., & Nowaczyk, R. H. (1998). *Cognition.* Upper Saddle River, NJ: Prentice-Hall.

James, W. (1884). Some omissions of introspective psychology. *Mind, 9,* 1–26.

James, W. (1890). *Principles of psychology.* New York: Holt.

James, W. (1892). *Psychology: brieffer course.* New York: Holt.

Jancke, L., & Kaufmann, N. (1994). Facial EMG responses to odors in solitude and with an audience. *Chemical Senses, 19*(2), 99–111.

Janik, V. M. (2000). Whistle matching in wild bottlenose dolphins. *Science, 289,* 1355–1357.

Janis, I. L. (1985). International crisis management in the nuclear age. *Applied Social Psychology Annual, 6,* 63–86.

Janis, I. L. (1989). *Crucial decisions: Leadership in policy making and crisis management.* New York: Free Press.

Janowiak, J. J., & Hackman, R. (1994). Meditation and college students' self-actualization and rated stress. *Psychological Reports, 75*(2), 1007–1010.

Janowitz, H. D. (1967). Role of gastrointestinal tract in the regulation of food intake. In C. F. Code (Ed.), *Handbook of physiology: Alimentary canal 1.* Washington, DC: American Physiological Society.

Je, J., Vupputuri, S., Allen, K., Prerost, M. R., Hughes, J., Whelton, P. K. (1999). Passive smoking and the risk of coronary heart disease—A meta-analysis of epidemiological studies. *The New England Journal of Medicine, 340,* 920–926.

Jenkins, G. D., Jr., Mitra, A., Gupta, N., & Shaw, J. D. (1998). Are financial incentives related to performance? A meta-analytic review of empirical research. *Journal of Applied Psychology, 83,* 777–787.

Jenkins, J. G., & Dallenbach, K. M. (1924). Oblivescence during sleep and waking. *American Journal of Psychology, 35,* 605–612.

Jenkins, M. R., & Culbertson, J. L. (1996). Prenatal exposure to alcohol. In R. L. Adams, O. A. Parsons, J. L. Culbertson, & S. J. Nixon (Eds.), *Neuropsychology for clinical practice: Etiology, assessment, and treatment of common neurological disorders* (pp. 409–452). Washington, DC: American Psychological Association.

Jenner, P. (2001). Parkinson's disease, pesticides and mitochondrial dysfunction. *Trends in Neuroscience, 24,* 245–246.

Jensen, A. R. (1969). How much can we boost IQ and scholastic achievement? *Harvard Educational Review, 39,* 1–123.

Jensen, A. R. (1993). Why is reaction time correlated with psychometric g? *Current Directions in Psychological Science, 2,* 53–55.

Jensen, J. P., Bergin, A. E., & Greaves, D. W. (1990). The meaning of eclecticism: New survey and analysis of components. *Professional Psychology: Research and Practice, 21,* 124–130.

Jensen, M., & Karoly, P. (1991). Control beliefs, coping efforts, and adjustment to chronic pain. *Journal of Consulting and Clinical Psychology, 59,* 431–438.

Jensvold, M. (Ed.). (1996). *Psychopharmacology and women: Sex, gender, and hormones.* Washington, DC: American Psychiatric Press.

Jevtovic-Todorovic, V., Wozniak, D. F., Benshoff, N. D., & Olney, J. W. (2001). A comparative evaluation of the neurotoxic properties of ketamine and nitrous oxide. *Brain Research, 895,* 264–267.

Jhanwar, U. M., Beck, B., Jhanwar, Y. S., & Burlet, C. (1993). Neuropeptide Y projection from the arcuate nucleus to the parvocellular division of the paraventricular nucleus: Specific relation to the ingestion of carbohydrate. *Brain Research, 631*(1), 97–106.

Johansen, J. P., Fields, H. L., & Manning, B. H. (2001). The affective component of pain in rodents: Direct evidence for a contribution of the anterior cingulate cortex. *Proceedings of the National Academy of Sciences, 98,* 8077–8082.

John, O., & Srivastava, S. (1999). The big five taxonomy: History, measurement, and theoretical perspectives. In L. Pervin & O. John (Eds.), *Handbook of personality: Theory and research* (2nd ed., pp. 102–138). New York: Guilford.

Johnson, J. (1997). Units of analysis for the description and analysis of behavior. In R. Hogan, J. Johnson, & S. Briggs (Eds.), *Handbook of personality psychology* (pp. 73–96). San Diego: Academic Press.

Johnson, J., & Vickers, Z. (1993). Effects of flavor and macronutrient composition of food servings on liking, hunger and subsequent intake. *Appetite, 21*(1), 25–39.

Johnson, J. G., Cohen, P., Dohrenwend, B. P., Link, B. G., & Brook, J. S. (1999). A longitudinal investigation of social causation and social selection processes involved in the association between socioeconomic status and psychiatric disorders. *Journal of Abnormal Psychology, 108,* 490–499.

Johnson, J. S., & Newport, E. L. (1989). Critical period effects in second language learning. *Cognitive Psychology, 21,* 60–99.

Johnson, L. E., & Thorpe, G. L. (1994). Review of psychotherapy and counseling with minorities: A cognitive approach to individual differences, by Manuel Ramirez. *Behavioural and Cognitive Psychotherapy, 22,* 185–187.

Johnson, M. A., Dziurawiec, S., Ellis, H., & Morton, J. (1991). Newborns' preferential tracking of face-like stimuli and its subsequent decline. *Cognition, 4,* 1–19.

Johnson, M. K., & Raye, C. L. (1998). False memories and confabulation. *Trends in Cognitive Sciences, 2,* 137–145.

Johnson, S. L., McPhee, L., & Birch, L. L. (1991). Conditioned preferences: Young children prefer flavors associated with high dietary fat. *Physiology and Behavior, 50,* 1245–1251.

Johnson, W. R., & Neal, D. (1998). In C. Jencks & M. Phillips (Eds.), *The black-white test score gap.* Washington, DC: Brookings Institute Press.

Johnson-Laird, P. N. (1983). *Mental models: Toward a cognitive science of language, inference, and consciousness.* Cambridge: Harvard University Press.

Johnstone, E. C., & Frith, C. D. (1996). Validation of three dimensions of schizophrenic symptoms in a large unselected sample of patients. *Psychological Medicine, 26,* 669–679.

Joiner, T. (1999). The clustering and contagion of suicide. *Current Directions in Psychological Science, 8,* 89–92.

Jones, E. E. (1982). Psychotherapists' impressions of treatment outcome as a function of race. *Journal of Clinical Psychology, 38,* 722–731.

Jones, G. V. (1990). Misremembering a common object: When left is not right. *Memory & Cognition, 18,* 174–182.

Jones, L. V., & Appelbaum, M. I. (1989). Psychometric methods. *Annual Review of Psychology, 40,* 23–44.

Jones, S. E. (2001). Ethics code draft published for comment. *Monitor on Psychology, 32,* 76.

Jones, W. H. S. (Ed. & Trans.). (1923). *Hippocrates* (Vol. 1). London: William Heinemann.

Jordan, N. C., Huttenlocher, J., & Levine, S. C. (1992). Differential calculation abilities in young children from middle- and low-income families. *Developmental Psychology, 28,* 644–653.

Josephson, W. L. (1987). Television violence and children's aggression: Testing the priming, social script, and disinhibition predictions. *Journal of Personality and Social Psychology, 53,* 882–890.

Joy, J. E., Watson, S. J., Jr., & Benson, J. A., Jr. (1999). *Marijuana and medicine: Assessing the science base.* Washington, DC: National Academy Press.

Julien, R. M. (1995). *A primer of drug action* (7th ed.). New York: Freeman.

Julien, R. M. (2000). *A primer of drug action: A nontechnical guide to the uses, and side effects of psychoactive drugs* (9th ed.). New York: Freeman.

Julien, R. M. (2001). *A primer of drug action* (9th ed.). New York: Freeman.

Jung, C. G. (1916). *Analytical psychology.* New York: Moffat.

Jung, C. G. (1933). *Psychological types.* New York: Harcourt, Brace and World.

Jusczyk, P. W., Smith, L. B., & Murphy, C. (1981). The perceptual classification of speech. *Perception and Psychophysics, 1,* 10–23.

Jussim, L. (1989). Teacher expectations: Self-fulfilling prophecies, perceptual biases, and accuracy. *Journal of Personality and Social Psychology, 57,* 469–480.

Just, M. A., Carpenter, P. A., Keller, T. A., Emery, L., Zajac, H., & Thulborn, K. R. (2001). Interdependence of nonoverlapping cortical systems in dual cognitive tasks. *Neuroimage, 14,* 417–426.

Just, N., & Alloy, L. B. (1997). The response styles theory of depression: Tests and an extension of the theory. *Journal of Abnormal Psychology, 106,* 221–229.

Juul-Dam, N., Townsend, J., & Courchesne, E. (2001). Prenatal, perinatal, and neonatal factors in autism, pervasive developmental disorder–not otherwise specified, and the general population. *Pediatrics, 107,* e63.

Kaas, J. H., & Hackett, T. A. (2000). Subdivisions of auditory cortex and processing streams in primates. *Proceedings of the National Academy of Sciences, 97,* 11793–11799.

Kadotani, H., Kadotani, T., Young, T., Peppard, P. E., Finn, L., Colrain, I. M., Murphy, G. M. Jr, & Mignot, E. (2001). Association between apolipoprotein E epsilon4 and sleep-disordered breathing in adults. *Journal of the American Medical Association, 285,* 2888–2890.

Kagan, J. R., Snidman, N., Arcus, D., & Resnick, J. S. (1994). *Galen's prophecy: Temperament in human nature.* New York: Basic Books.

Kahn, D. A. (1995). New strategies in bipolar disorder: Part II. Treatment. *Journal of Practical Psychiatry and Behavioral Health, 3,* 148–157.

Kahneman, D., & Tversky, A. (1984). Choices, values, and frames. *Choices, values, and frames, 29,* 341–356.

Kajiya, K., Inaki, K., Tanaka, M., Haga, T., Kataoka, H., & Touhara, K. (2001). Molecular bases of odor discrimination: Reconstitution of olfactory receptors that recognize overlapping sets of odorants. *Journal of Neuroscience, 21,* 6018–6025.

Kales, A., & Kales, J. (1973). Recent advances in the diagnosis and treatment of sleep disorders. In G. Usdin (Ed.), *Sleep research and clinical practice.* New York: Brunner/Mazel.

Kalichman, S. C., Cherry, C., & Browne-Sperling, F. (1999). Effectiveness of a video-based motivational skills-building HIV risk-reduction intervention for inner-city African American men. *Journal of Consulting and Clinical Psychology, 67,* 959–966.

Kalish, H. I. (1981). *From behavioral science to behavior modification.* New York: McGraw-Hill.

Kamarck, T. W., Annunziato, B., Amateau, L. M. (1995). Affiliation moderates the effects of social threat on stress-related cardiovascular responses: Boundary conditions for a laboratory model of social support. *Psychosomatic Medicine, 57,* 183–194.

Kamarck, T. W., Everson, S. A., Kaplan, G. A., Manuck, S. B., Jennings, J. R., Salonen, T., & Salonen, J. T. (1997). Exaggerated blood pressure responses during mental stress are associated with enhanced carotid atherosclerosis in middle-aged Finnish men. *Circulation, 96,* 3842–3848.

Kamphuis, J. H., & Emmelkamp, P. M. (2001). Traumatic distress among support-seeking female victims of stalking. *American Journal of Psychiatry, 158,* 795–798.

Kane, J. M. (1989). Current status of neuroleptic therapy. *Journal of Clinical Psychiatry, 50,* 322–328.

Kanki, B. J., & Foushee, H. C. (1990). Crew factors in the aerospace workplace. In S. Oskamp & S. Spacepan (Eds.), *People's reactions to technology* (pp. 18–31). Newbury Park, CA: Sage.

Kanner, B. (1995). *Are you normal?* New York: St. Martin's Press.

Kaplan, M. F. (1987). The influencing process in group decision making. In C. Hendrick (Ed.), *Group processes* (pp. 189–212). Newbury Park, CA: Sage.

Kaplan, M. F., & Miller, C. E. (1987). Group decision making and normative vs. informational influence: Effects of type of issue and assigned decision rule. *Journal of Personality and Social Psychology, 53,* 306–313.

Kaplan, R. M. (1991). Health-related quality of life in patient decision-making. *Journal of Social Issues, 47,* 69–90.

Kaptchuk, T. J. (2001). Methodological issues in trials of acupuncture. *Journal of the American Medical Association, 285,* 1015–1016.

Kapur, N. (1999). Syndromes of retrograde amnesia: A conceptual and empirical synthesis. *Psychological Bulletin, 125,* 800–825.

Kapur, S., & Mann, J. J. (1993). Antidepressant action and the neurobiologic effects of ECT: Human studies. In C. E. Coffey (Ed.), *The clinical science of electroconvulsive therapy.* Washington, DC: American Psychiatric Press.

Karau, S. J., & Williams, K. D. (1997). The effects of group cohesiveness on social loafing and social compensation. *Group Dynamics, 1,* 156–168.

Kardes, F. R. (1999). Psychology applied to consumer behavior. In A. M. Stec & D. A. Bernstein (Eds.), *Psychology: Fields of application* (pp. 82–97). Boston: Houghton Mifflin.

Karni, A., Meyer, G., Adams, M., Turner, R., & Ungerleider, L. G. (1994). The acquisition and retention of a motor skill: A functional MRI study of long-term motor cortex plasticity. *Abstracts of the Society for Neuroscience, 20,* 1291.

Karni, A., Meyer, G., Rey-Hipolito, C., Jezzard, P., Adams, M. M., Turner, R., & Ungerleider, L. G. (1998). The acquisition of skilled motor performance: Fast and slow experience-driven changes in primary motor cortex. *Proceedings of the National Academy of Science USA, 95,* 861–868.

Karon, B. P., & Widener, A. J. (1997). Repressed memories and World War II: Lest we forget. *Professional Psychology: Research and Practice, 28*(4), 338–340.

Karp, D. A. (1991). A decade of reminders: Changing age consciousness between fifty and sixty years old. In B. B. Hess & E. W. Markson (Eds.), *Growing old in America* (pp. 67–92). New Brunswick, NJ: Transaction.

Kasagi, F., Akahoshi, M., & Shimaoki, K. (1995). Relation between cold pressor test and development of hypertension based on 28-year follow-up. *Hypertension, 25,* 71–76.

Kass, S. (1999). Frequent testing means better grades, studies find. *APA Monitor, 30,* 10.

Kassin, S. M. (1997). The psychology of confession evidence. *American Psychologist, 52,* 221–233.

Kassin, S. M., Rigby, S., & Castillo, S. R. (1991). The accuracy-confidence correlation in eyewitness testimony: Limits and extensions of the retrospective self-awareness effect. *Journal of Personality and Social Psychology, 61,* 698–707.

Kassin, S. M., Tubb, V. A., Hosch, H. M., & Memon, A. (2001). On the "general acceptance" of eyewitness testimony: A new survey of the experts. *American Psychologist, 56,* 405–416.

Kastenbaum, R., Kastenbaum, B. K., & Morris, J. (1989). *Strengths and preferences of the terminally ill: Data from the National Hospice Demonstration Study.*

Kato, S., Wakasa, Y., & Yamagita, T. (1987). Relationship between minimum reinforcing doses and injection speed in cocaine and pentobarbital self-administration in crab-eating monkeys. *Pharmacology, Biochemistry, and Behavior, 28,* 407–410.

Katz, A. N., & Fodor, J. A. (1963). The structure of a semantic theory. *Language, 39,* 170–210.

Katz, S. E., & Landis, C. (1935). Psychologic and physiologic phenomena during a prolonged vigil. *Archives of Neurology and Psychiatry, 34,* 307–317.

Katzell, R. A., & Thompson, D. E. (1990). Work motivation: Theory and practice. *American Psychologist, 45,* 144–153.

Kauffman, N. A., Herman, C. P., & Polivy, J. (1995). Hunger-induced finickiness in humans. *Appetite, 24,* 203–218.

Kaufman, J., & Charney, D. (2000). Comorbidity of mood and anxiety disorders. *Depression and Anxiety, 12*(Suppl. 1), 69–76.

Kawakami, K., Dion, K. L., & Dovidio, J. F. (1998). Racial prejudice and stereotype activation. *Personality and Social Psychology Bulletin, 24,* 407–416.

Kawakami, K., Dovidio, J. F., Moll, J., Hermsen, S., & Russin, A. (2000). Just say no (to stereotyping): Effects of training in the negation of stereotypic associations on stereotype activation. *Journal of Personality and Social Psychology, 78,* 871–888.

Kawamura, N., Kim, Y., & Asukai, N. (2001). Suppression of cellular immunity in men with a past history of posttraumatic stress disorder. *American Journal of Psychiatry, 158,* 484–486.

Kawasaki, H., Adolphs, R., Kaufman, O., Damasio, H., Damasio, A. R., Granner, M., et al. (2001). Single-neuron responses to emotional visual stimuli recorded in human ventral prefrontal cortex. *Nature Neuroscience, 4,* 15–16.

Kaye, J. A., Swihart, T., Howieson, D., Dame, A., Moore, M. M., Karnos, T., et al. (1997). Volume loss of the hippocampus and temporal lobe in healthy elderly persons destined to develop dementia. *Neurology, 48,* 1297–1304.

Kaye, W. H., Gwirtsman, H. E., George, D. T., & Jimerson, D. C. (1988). CSF 5-HIAA concentrations in anorexia nervosa: Reduced values in underweight subjects normalize after weight gain. *Biological Psychiatry, 23*(1), 102–105.

Kaye, W. H., Klump, K. L., Frank. G. K. W., & Strober, M. (2000). Anorexia and bulimia nervosa. *Annual Review of Medicine: Selected Topics in the Clinical Sciences, 51,* 299–313.

Kazarian, S. S., & Evans, D. R. (Eds.). (2001). *Handbook of cultural health psychology.* New York: Academic Press.

Kazdin, A. E. (1994a). *Behavior modification in applied settings* (5th ed.). Pacific Grove, CA: Brooks/Cole.

Kazdin, A. E. (1994b). Methodology, design, and evaluation in psychotherapy research. In A. E. Bergin & S. L. Garfield (Eds.), *Handbook of psychotherapy and behavior change* (4th ed., pp. 19–71). New York: Wiley.

Kazdin, A. E., & Weisz, J. R. (1998). Identifying and developing empirically supported child and adolescent treatments. *Journal of Consulting and Clinical Psychology, 66,* 19–36.

Keane, T. M. (1998). Psychological and behavioral treatment of posttraumatic stress disorder. In P. Nathan & J. Gorman (Eds.) *Guide to treatments that work* (pp. 398–407). Oxford, England: Oxford University Press.

Keating, D. P. (1990). Adolescent thinking. In S. S. Feldman & G. R. Elliott (Eds.), *At the threshold: The developing adolescent* (pp. 4–89). Cambridge: Harvard University Press.

Kee, M., Hill, S. M., & Weist, M. D. (1999). School-based behavior management of cursing, hitting, and spitting in a girl with profound retardation. *Education and Treatment of Children, 22,* 171–178.

Keefe, F. J., & France, C. R. (1999). Pain: Biopsychosocial mechanisms and management. *Current Directions in Psychological Science, 8,* 137–141.

Keeling, P. J., & Roger, A. J. (1995). The selfish pursuit of sex. *Nature, 375,* 283.

Keesey, R. E., & Powley, T. L. (1986). The regulation of body weight. *Annual Review of Psychology, 37,* 109–133.

Kehoe, E. J., & Macrae, M. (1998). Classical conditioning. In W. O'Donohue (Ed.), *Learning and behavior therapy* (pp. 36–58). Boston: Allyn & Bacon.

Keinan, G., Friedland, N., & Ben-Porath, Y. (1987). Decision making under stress: Scanning of alternatives under physical threat. *Acta Psychologica, 64,* 219–228.

Keller, A., Ford, L. H., & Meacham, J. A. (1978). Dimensions of self-concept in preschool children. *Developmental Psychology, 14,* 483–489.

Keller, M. B., McCullough, J. P., Klein, D. N., Arnow, B., Dunner, D. L., Gelenberg, A. J., et al. (2000). A comparison of nefazodone, the cognitive behavioral-analysis system of psychotherapy, and their combination for the treatment of chronic depression. *The New England Journal of Medicine, 342,* 1462–1470.

Kelley, H. H. (1973). The processes of causal attribution. *American Psychologist, 28,* 107–128.

Kelley, K. W. (1985). Immunological consequences of changing environmental stimuli. In G. P. Moberg (Ed.), *Animal stress* (pp. 193–223). Bethesda, MD: American Physiological Society.

Kelley, W. M., Miezen, F. M., McDermott, K. B., Buckner, R. L., Raichle, M. E., Cohen, N. J., et al. (1998). Hemispheric asymmetry for verbal and nonverbal memory encoding in human dorsal frontal cortex. *Neuron, 20,* 927–936.

Kellman, P. J., & Banks, M. S. (1998). Infant visual perception. In W. Damon, D. Kuhn, & R. Siegler (Eds.), *Handbook of child psychology: Vol. 2. Cognition, language and perception* (5th ed., pp. 103–146). New York: Wiley.

Kellum, K. K., Carr, J. E., & Dozier, C. L. (2001). Response-card instruction and student learning in a college classroom. *Teaching of Psychology, 28,* 101–104.

Kelly, G. A. (1980). A psychology of the optimal man. In A. W. Landfield & L. M. Leitner (Eds.), *Personal construct psychology: Psychotherapy and personality.* New York: Wiley.

Kelly, T. H., Foltin, R. W., Emurian, C. S., & Fischman, M. W. (1990). Multidimensional behavioral effects of marijuana. *Progress in Neuro-Psychopharmacology and Biological Psychiatry, 14,* 885–902.

Kelsoe, J. R., Spence, M. A., Loetscher, E., Foguet, M., Sadovnick, A. D., Remick, R. A., et al. (2001). A genome survey indicates a possible susceptibility locus for bipolar disorder on chromosome 22. *Proceedings of the National Academy of Science, 98,* 585–590.

Kelter, D., & Buswell, B. N. (1996). Evidence for the distinctiveness of embarrassment, shame, and guilt: A study of recalled antecedents and facial expressions of emotion. *Cognition and Emotion, 10,* 117–125.

Kemeny, M. E., & Dean, L. (1995). Effects of AIDS-related bereavement on HIV progression among New York City gay men. *AIDS Education and Prevention, 7,* 36–47.

Kemper, S., Greiner, L. H., Marquis, J. G., Prenovost, K., & Mitzner, T. L. (2001). Language decline across the life span: Findings from the Nun Study. *Psychology and Aging, 16,* 227–239.

Kendall, P. C. (1999). Clinical significance. *Journal of Consulting and Clinical Psychology, 67,* 283–284.

Kendall, P. C., & Chambless, D. L. (Eds.). (1998). Special section: Empirically supported psychological therapies. *Journal of Consulting and Clinical Psychology, 66,* 3–167.

Kendall, P. C., & Sheldrick, R. C. (2000). Normative data for normative comparisons. *Journal of Consulting and Clinical Psychology, 68,* 767–773.

Kendler, K. S. (2001). Twin studies of psychiatric illness: An update. *Archives of General Psychiatry, 58,* 1005–1014.

Kendler, K. S., & Diehl, N. S. (1993). The genetics of schizophrenia: A current genetic-epidemiologic perspective. *Schizophrenia Bulletin, 19,* 87–112.

Kendler, K. S., Heath, A. C., Neale, M. C., Kessler, R. C., & Eaves, L. J. (1992). A population-based twin study of alcoholism in women. *Journal of the American Medical Association, 268,* 1877–1882.

Kendler, K. S., Kessler, R. C., Walters, E. E., MacLean, C., Neale, M. C., Heath, A. C., & Eaves, L. J. (1995). Stressful life events, genetic liability, and onset of an episode of major depression in women. *American Journal of Psychiatry, 152,* 833–842.

Kendler, K. S., Meyers, J., Prescott, C. A., & Neale, M. C. (2001). The genetic epidemiology of irrational fears and phobias in men. *Archives of General Psychiatry, 58,* 257–265.

Kendler, K. S., Neale, M. C., Kessler, R. C., Heath, A. C., & Eaves, L. J. (1992). Major depression and generalized anxiety disorder: Same genes, (partly) different environments? *Archives of General Psychiatry, 49,* 716–722.

Kendler, K. S., Thornton, L. M., & Gardner, C. O. (2000). Stressful life events and previous episodes in the etiology of major depression in women: An evaluation of the "kindling" hypothesis. *American Journal of Psychiatry, 157,* 1243–1251.

Kendler, K. S., Thornton, L. M., & Gardner, C. O. (2001). Genetic risk, number of previous depressive episodes, and stressful life events in predicting onset of major depression. *American Journal of Psychiatry, 158,* 582–586.

Kendler, K. S., Thornton, L. M., & Prescott, C. A. (2001). Gender differences in the rates of exposure to stressful life events and sensitivity to their depressogenic effects. *American Journal of Psychiatry, 158,* 587–593.

Kendler, K. S., Thornton, L. M., Gilman, S. E., & Kessler, R. C. (2000). Sexual orientation in a U.S. national sample of twin and nontwin sibling pairs. *American Journal of Psychiatry, 157,* 1843–1846.

Kenrick, D. T. (1994). Evolutionary social psychology: From sexual selection to social cognition. In M. Zanna (Ed.), *Advances in experimental social psychology* (Vol. 26, pp. 75–122). San Diego: Academic Press.

Kenrick, D. T., Groth, G., Trost, M., & Sadalla, E. K. (1993). Integrating evolutionary and social exchange perspectives on relationships: Effects of gender, self-appraisal, and involvement level on mate selection. *Journal of Personality and Social Psychology, 64,* 951–969.

Kenrick, D. T., & Trost, M. R. (1997). Evolutionary approaches to relationships. In S. Duck (Ed.), *Handbook of personal relationships: Theory, research, and interventions* (2nd ed., pp. 151–177) Chichester, England: Wiley.

Kenrick, D. T., Keefe, R. C., Bryan, A. Barr, A., & Brown, S. (1995). Age preferences and mate choice among homosexuals and heterosexuals: A case for modular psychological mechanisms. *Journal of Personality and Social Psychology, 69,* 1166–1172.

Kenrick, D. T., Neuberg, S. L., & Cialdini, R. B. (2002). *Social psychology: Unraveling the mystery* (2nd ed.). Boston: Allyn & Bacon.

Kent, S., Rodriguez, F., Kelley, K. W., & Dantzer, R. (1994). Reduction in food and water intake induced by microinjection of interleukin-1b in the ventromedial hypothalamus of the rat. *Physiology and Behavior, 56*(5), 1031–1036.

Kernberg, O. (1984). *Severe personality disorders: Psychotherapeutic strategies.* New Haven/London: Yale University Press.

Kerns, K. (1991). Data-link communication between controllers and pilots: A review and synthesis of the simulation literature. *International Journal of Aviation Psychology, 1,* 181–204.

Kessler, R. (1997). The effects of stressful life events on depression. *Annual Review of Psychology, 48,* 191–214.

Kessler, R. C., Berglund, P. A., Zhao, S., Leaf, P. J., Kouzis, A. C., Bruce, M. L., et al. (1996). The 12-month prevalence and correlates of serious mental illness In R. W. Manderscheid & M. A. Sonnenschein (Eds.), *Mental health, United States, 1996* (DHHS Publication No. [SMA] 96–3098, pp. 59–70). Washington, DC: U.S. Government Printing Office.

Kessler, R. C., McGonagle, K. A., Zhao, S., Nelson, C. B., Hughes, M., Eshleman, S., et al. (1994). Lifetime and 12-month prevalence of DSM-III-R psychiatric disorders in the United States. *Archives of General Psychiatry, 51,* 8–19.

Kety, S. S., Wender, P. H., Jacobsen, B., Ingraham, L. J., Jansson, L., Faber, B., & Kinney, D. K. (1994). Mental illness in the biological and adoptive relatives of schizophrenic adoptees. *Archives of General Psychiatry, 51,* 442–455.

Key, W. B. (1973). *Subliminal seduction: Ad media's manipulation of a not so innocent America.* Englewood Cliffs, NJ: Prentice-Hall.

Khan, J., Wei, J. S., Ringner, M., Saal, L. H., Ladanyi, M., Westermann, F., et al. (2001). Classification and diagnostic prediction of cancers using gene expression profiling and artificial neural networks. *Nature Medicine, 7,* 673–679.

Kiecolt-Glaser, J. K., & Glaser, R. (1992). Psychoneuroimmunology: Can psychological interventions modulate immunity? *Journal of Consulting and Clinical Psychology, 60,* 569–575.

Kiecolt-Glaser, J. K., & Glaser, R. (2001). Stress and immunity: Age enhances the risks. *Current Directions in Psychological Science, 10,* 18–21.

Kiecolt-Glaser, J. K., & Newton, T. L. (2001). Marriage and health: His and hers. *Psychological Bulletin, 127,* 472–503.

Kiecolt-Glaser, J. K., Page, G. G., Marucha, P. T., MacCallum, R. C. & Glaser, R. (1998). Psychological influences on surgical recovery: Perspectives from psychoneuroimmunology. *American Psychologist, 11,* 1209–1218.

Kiesler, D. J. (1996). *Contemporary interpersonal theory and research.* New York: Wiley.

Kiesler, S., & Sproull, L. (1992). Group decision making and communication technology. *Organizational Behavior & Human Decision Processes, 52,* 96–123.

Kiewra, K. A. (1989). A review of note-taking: The encoding storage paradigm and beyond. *Educational Psychology Review, 1,* 147–172.

Kihlstrom, J. F. (1994). Psychodynamics and social cognition: Notes on the fusion of psychoanalysis and psychology. *Journal of Personality, 62,* 681–696.

Kihlstrom, J. F. (1999). The psychological unconscious. In L. Pervin & O. John (Eds), *Handbook of personality* (pp. 424–442). New York: Guilford.

Kihlstrom, J. F., & Klein, S. B. (1994). The self as a knowledge structure. In R. S. Wyer & T. K. Srull (Eds.), *Handbook of social cognition* (2nd ed.). Hillsdale, NJ: Erlbaum.

Kilby, M. M. (1999, December). One academic's viewpoint on prescription privileges. *APA Monitor,* p. 11.

Kilgard, M. P., & Merzenich, M. M. (1998). Cortical map reorganization enabled by nucleus basalis activity. *Science, 279,* 1714–1718.

Kilts, C. D., Schweitzer, J. B., Quinn, C. K., Gross, R. E., Faber, T. L., Muhammad, F., et al. (2001). Neural activity related to drug craving in cocaine addiction. *Archives of General Psychiatry, 58,* 334–341.

Kimble, G. A. (1999). Functional behaviorism: A plan for unity in psychology. *American Psychologist, 54,* 981–988.

Kimble, G. A. (2000). Behaviorism and unity in psychology. *Current Directions in Psychological Science, 9,* 208–212.

Kimura, D. (1999). *Sex and cognition.* Cambridge: MIT Press.

King, J., & Pribram, K. H. (Eds.). (1995). *The scale of conscious experience: Is the brain too important to be left to specialists to study?* Mahwah, NJ: Erlbaum.

Kinney, H. C., Korein, J., Panigrahy, A., Dikkes, P., & Goode, R. (1994). Neuropathological findings in the brain of Karen Ann Quinlan: The role of the thalamus in the persistent vegetative state. *New England Journal of Medicine, 330*(21), 1469–1475.

Kinsey, A. C., Pomeroy, W. B., & Martin, C. E. (1948). *Sexual behavior in the human male.* Philadelphia: Saunders.

Kinsey, A. C., Pomeroy, W. B., Martin, C. E., & Gebhard, P. H. (1953). *Sexual behavior in the human female.* Philadelphia: Saunders.

Kircher, J. C., Horowitz, S. W., & Raskin, D. C. (1998). Meta-analysis of mock crime studies of the control question polygraph technique. *Law and Human Behavior, 12,* 79–90.

Kirchler, E., & Zani, B. (1995). Why don't they stay home? Prejudice against ethnic minorities in Italy. *Journal of Community and Applied Social Psychology, 5,* 59–65.

Kirkpatrick, B., Buchanan, R. W., Ross, D. E., & Carpenter, W. T., Jr. (2001). A separate disease within the syndrome of schizophrenia. *Archives of General Psychiatry, 58,* 165–171.

Kirsch, I. (1994a). Clinical hypnosis as a nondeceptive placebo: Empirically derived techniques. *American Journal of Clinical Hypnosis, 37*(2), 95–106.

Kirsch, I. (1994b). Defining hypnosis for the public. *Contemporary Hypnosis, 11*(3), 142–143.

Kirsch, I., & Braffman, W. (2001). Imaginative suggestibility and hypnotizability. *Psychological Science, 10*, 57–61.

Kirsch, I., & Lynn, S. J. (1995). The altered state of hypnosis: Changes in theoretical landscape. *The American Psychologist, 50*, 846–858.

Kishioka, S., Miyamoto, Y., Fukunaga, Y., Nishida, S., & Yamamoto, H. (1994). Effects of a mixture of peptidase inhibitors (Amastatin, Captopril and Phosphoramidon) on met enkephalin, betaa mixture of peptidase inhibitors (Amastatin, Captopril and Phosphoramidon) on met enkephalin, beta-endorphin, dynorphin (1–13) and electroacupun. *Japanese Journal of Pharmacology, 66*, 337–345.

Kitano, H., Chi, I., Rhee, S., Law, C., & Lubben, J. (1992). Norms and alcohol consumption: Japanese in Japan, Hawaii, and California. *Journal of Studies on Alcohol, 53*, 33–39.

Kitayama, S., & Markus, H. R (1992, May). *Construal of self as cultural frame: Implications for internationalizing psychology.* Paper presented to the Symposium on Internationalization and Higher Education, Ann Arbor.

Kjellberg, A., Landstrom, U., Tesarz, M., Soderberg, L., & Akerlund, E. (1996). The effects of nonphysical noise characteristics, ongoing task and noise sensitivity on annoyance and distraction due to noise at work. *Journal of Environmental Psychology, 16*, 123–136.

Klahr, D., & Simon, H. (1999). Studies of scientific discovery: Complementary approaches and convergent findings. *Psychological Bulletin, 125*, 524–543.

Klaus, M. H., & Kennell, J. H. (1976). *Maternal infant bonding: The impact of early separation or loss on family development.* St. Louis: Mosby.

Kleemola, P., Jousilahti, P., Pietinen, P., Vartiainen, E., & Tuomilehto, J. (2000). Coffee consumption and the risk of coronary heart disease and death. *Archives of Internal Medicine, 160*, 3393–3400.

Klein, D., Lewinsohn,. P. M., Seeley, J. R., & Rohde, P. (2001). A family study of major depressive disorder in a community sample of adolescents. *Archives of General Psychiatry, 58*, 13–20.

Klein, D. C., & Seligman, M. E. P. (1976). Reversal of performance deficits and perceptual deficits in learned helplessness and depression. *Journal of Abnormal Psychology, 85*, 11–26.

Klein, D. N. (1993). False suffocation alarms, spontaneous panics, and related conditions: An integrative hypothesis. *Archives of General Psychiatry, 50*, 306–316.

Klein, G. (1997). The recognition-primed decision (RPD) model: Looking back, looking forward. In C. E. Zsambok & G. Klein (Eds.), *Naturalistic decision making* (pp. 285–292). Mahwah, NJ: Erlbaum.

Klein, H. J., Wesson, M. J., Hollenbeck, J. R., & Alge, B. J. (1999). Goal commitment and the goal setting process: Conceptual clarification and empirical synthesis. *Journal of Applied Psychology, 84*, 885–896.

Klein, M. (1960). *The psychoanalysis of children.* New York: Grove Press.

Klein, M. (1991). The emotional life and ego-development of the infant with special reference to the depressive position. In P. King & R. Steiner (Eds.), *The Klein-Freud controversies: 1941–1945* (pp. 752–777). London: Tavistock/Routledge.

Klein, R. A. (1999). Treating fear of flying with virtual reality exposure therapy. In L. VandeCreek & T. L. Jackson (Eds.), *Innovations in clinical practice: A sourcebook* (Vol. 17, pp. 449–465). Sarasota, FL: Professional Resource Press.

Kleinknecht, R. A. (1991). *Mastering anxiety: The nature and treatment of anxious conditions.* New York: Plenum.

Kleinknecht, R. A. (2000). Social phobia. In M. Hersen & M. K. Biaggio (Eds.), *Effective brief Therapies: A clinician's guide.* New York: Academic Press.

Kleinknecht, R. A., Dinnel, D. L., Tanouye-Wilson, S., & Lonner, W. (1994). Cultural variation in social anxiety and phobia: A study of Taijin Kyofusho. *The Behavior Therapist, 17*, 175–178.

Kleinman, A. (1991, April). *Culture and DSM-IV: Recommendations for the introduction and for the overall structure.* Paper presented at the National Institute of Mental Health-sponsored Conference on Culture and Diagnosis, Pittsburgh, PA.

Klepp, K.-I., Kelder, S. H., & Perry, C. L. (1995). Alcohol and marijuana use among adolescents: Long-term outcomes of the class of 1989 study. *Annals of Behavioral Medicine, 17*, 19–24.

Klerman, G. L., & Weissman, M. M. (Eds.). (1993). *New applications of interpersonal therapy.* Washington, DC: American Psychiatric Press.

Klesges, R. C., Haddock, C. K., Lando, H., & Talcott, G. W. (1999). Efficacy of forced smoking cessation and an adjunctive behavioral treatment on long-term smoking rates. *Journal of Consulting and Clinical Psychology, 67*, 952–958.

Kline, S., & Groninger, L. D. (1991). The imagery bizarreness effect as a function of sentence complexity and presentation time. *Bulletin of the Psychonomic Society, 29*, 25–27.

Kling, K. C., Hyde, J. S., Showers, C. J., & Buswell, B. N. (1999). Gender differences in self-esteem: A meta-analysis. *Psychological Bulletin, 125*, 470–500.

Klintsova, A. Y., & Greenough, W. T. (1999). Synaptic plasticity in cortical systems. *Current Opinion in Neurobiology, 9*, 203–208.

Klohnen, E., & Bera, S. (1998). Behavioral and experiential patterns of avoidantly and securely attached women across adulthood: A 31-year longitudinal perspective. *Journal of Personality and Social Psychology, 74*, 211–223.

Klonoff-Cohen, H. S., & Edelstein, S. L. (1995). A case-control study of routine death scene sleep position in sudden infant death syndrom in Southern California. *Journal of the American Medical Association, 273*(10), 790–794.

Klosko, J. S., Barlow, D. H., Tassinari, R., & Cerny, J. A. (1990). A comparison of alprazolam and behavior therapy in treatment of panic disorder. *Journal of Consulting and Clinical Psychology, 58*, 77–84.

Kluger, A. N., & DeNisi, A. (1998). Feedback interventions: Toward the understanding of a double-edged sword. *Current Directions in Psychological Science, 7*, 67–72.

Knapp, S., & VandeCreek, L. (1997). Jaffee v. Redmond: The Supreme Court recognizes a psychotherapist-patient privilege in federal courts. *Professional Psychology: Research and Practice, 28*, 567–572.

Knapp, T. J. (1997). Behaviorism and public policy: B. F. Skinner's views on gambling. *Behavioral & Social Sciences, 7*, 129–139.

Koch, C., & Davis, J. L. (Eds.). (1994). *Large-scale neuronal theories of the brain.* Cambridge: MIT Press.

Koelega, H. S. (1993). Stimulant drugs and vigilance performance: A review. *Psychopharmacology, 111*(1), 1–16.

Koenigsberg, H. W. (1994). The combination of psychotherapy and pharmacotherapy in the treatment of borderline patients. *Journal of Psychotherapy Practice and Research, 3*(2), 93–107.

Koepp, M. J., Gunn, R. N., Lawrence, A. D., Cunningham, V. J., Dagher, A., Jones, T., et al. (1998). Evidence for striatal dopamine release during a video game. *Nature, 393*, 266–268.

Kohlberg, L., & Gilligan, C. (1971). The adolescent as a philosopher: The discovery of the self in a postconventional world. *Daedalus, 100*, 1051–1086.

Köhler, W. (1924). *The mentality of apes.* New York: Harcourt Brace.

Kohout, J. (2000). A look at recent baccalaureates in psychology. *Monitor on Psychology, 31*, 13.

Kohut, H. (1984). Selected problems of self-psychological theory. In J. D. Lichtenberg & S. Kaplan (Eds.), *Reflections on self psychology* (pp. 387–416). Hillsdale, NJ: Erlbaum.

Kok, M. R., & Boon, M. E. (1996). Consequences of neural network technology for cervical screening: increase in diagnostic consistency and positive scores. *Cancer, 78*, 112–117.

Kolata, G., & Markel, H. (2001, April 29). Baby not crawling? Reason seems to be less tummy time. *New York Times.*

Komatsu, S.-I., & Naito, M. (1992). Repetition priming with Japanese Kana scripts in word-fragment completion. *Memory & Cognition, 20*, 160–170.

Komorita, S. S. (1984). Coalition bargaining. In L. Berkowitz (Ed.), *Advances in experimental social psychology* (Vol. 18). New York: Academic Press.

Komorita, S. S., & Parks, C. D. (1995). Interpersonal relations: Mixed-motive interaction. *Annual Review of Psychology, 46*, 183–207.

Kondo, T., & Raff, M. (2000). Oligodendrocyte precursor cells reprogrammed to become multipotential CNS stem cells. *Science, 289*, 1754–1757.

Konkol, R. J., Murphey, L. J., Ferriero, D. M., Dempsey, D. A., & Olsen, G. D. (1994). Cocaine metabolites in the neonate: Potential for toxicity. *Journal of Child Neurology, 9*(3), 242–248.

Koob, G. F., & Bloom, F. E. (1988). Cellular and molecular mechanisms of drug dependence. *Science, 242*, 715–723.

Koob, G. F., Roberts, A. J., Schulteis, G., Parsons, L. H., Heyser, C. J., Hyytia, P., et al. (1998). Neurocircuitry targets in ethanol reward and dependence. *Alcohol: Clinical and Experimental Research, 22*(1), 3–9.

Koopmans, J. R., & Boomsma, D. I. (1996). Familial resemblance in alcohol use: Genetic or cultural transmission? *Journal of Studies in Alcoholism, 57*, 19–28.

Kop, W. J., Krantz, D. S., Howell, R. H., Ferguson, M. A., Papademetriou, V., Lu, D., et al. (2001). Effects of mental stress on coronary epicardial vasomotion and flow velocity in coronary artery disease: relationship with hemodynamic stress responses. *Journal of the American College of Cardiology, 37*, 1359–1366.

Kopelman, P. G. (2000). Obesity as a medical problem. *Nature, 404*, 635–643.

Koppenaal, L., & Glanzer, M. (1990). An examination of the continuous distractor task and the "long-term recency effect." *Memory & Cognition, 18*, 183–195.

Koran, L. M., Hackett, E., Rubin, A., Wolkow, R., Robinson, D. (2002). Efficacy of sertraline in the long-term treatment of obsessive-compulsive disorder. *American Journal of Psychiatry, 159*, 88–95.

Korchmaros, J. D., & Kenny, D. A. (2001). Emotional closeness as a mediator of the effect of genetic relatedness on altruism. *Psychological Science, 12*, 262–265.

Kordower, J. H., Emborg, M. E., Bloch, J., Ma, S. Y., Chu, Y., Leventhal, L., et al. (2000). Neurodegeneration prevented by lentiviral vector delivery of GDNF in primate models of Parkinson's disease. *Science, 290*, 767–773.

Kornhaber, M., Krechevsky, M., & Gardner, H. (1990). Engaging intelligence. *Educational Psychologist, 25*, 177–199.

Korteling, J. (1991). Effects of skill integration and perceptual competition on age-related differences in dual-task performance. *Human Factors, 33*, 35–44.

Kosslyn, S. M. (1988). Aspects of a cognitive neuroscience of mental imagery. *Science, 240*, 1621–1626.

Kosslyn, S. M. (1994). *Image and mind*. Cambridge: Harvard University Press.

Kotani, N., Hashimoto, H., Sato, Y., Sessler, D. I., Yoshioka, H., Kitayama, M., et al. (2001). Preoperative intradermal acupuncture reduces postoperative pain, nausea and vomiting, analgesic requirement, and sympathoadrenal responses. *Anesthesiology, 95*, 349–356.

Kouri, E. M., Pope, H. G., & Lukas, S. E. (1999). Changes in aggressive behavior during withdrawal from long-term marijuana use. *Psychopharmacology, 143*, 302–308.

Kozak, M. J., Liebowitz, M. R., & Foa, E. B. (2000). Cognitive behavior therapy and pharmacotherapy for obsessive-compulsive disorder: The NIMH-sponsored collaborative study. In W. K. Goodman, M. V. Rudorfer, & J. D. Maser (Eds.), *Obsessive-compulsive disorder: Contemporary issues in treatment* (pp. 501–530). Mahwah, NJ: Erlbaum.

Kraft, C. (1978). A psychophysical approach to air safety: Simulator studies of visual illusions in right approaches. In H. L. Picks, H. W. Leibowitz, J. E. Singer, A. Steinschneider, & H. W. Stevenson (Eds.), *Psychology: From research to practice*. New York: Plenum.

Krahn, L. E., Black, J. L., & Silber, M. H. (2001). Narcolepsy: new understanding of irresistible sleep. *Mayo Clinic Proceedings, 76*, 185–194.

Krakauer, J. (1997). *Into thin air*. New York: Villard.

Krakow, B., Hollifield, M., Johnston, L., Koss, M., Schrader, R., Warner, T. D., et al. (2001). Imagery rehearsal therapy for chronic nightmares in sexual assault survivors with posttraumatic stress disorder: a randomized controlled trial. *Journal of the American Medical Association, 286*, 537–545.

Kramer, A. F., Larish, J., Weber, T., & Bardell, L. (1999). Training for executive control: Task coordination strategies and aging. In D. Gopher & A. Koriat (Eds.), *Attention and Performance XVII*. Cambridge: MIT Press.

Krantz, D., Contrada, R., Hill, D., & Friedler, E. (1988). Environmental stress and biobehavioral antecedents of coronary heart disease. *Journal of Consulting and Clinical Psychology, 56*, 333–341.

Krantz, D., & Durel, L. (1983). Psychobiological substrates of the Type A behavior pattern. *Health Psychology, 2*, 393–411.

Kranzler, H. R., & Anton, R. F. (1994). Implications of recent neuropsychopharmacologic research for understanding the etiology and development of alcoholism. *Journal of Consulting and Clinical Psychology, 62*, 1116–1126.

Krause, N., & Shaw, B. A. (2000). Role-specific feelings of control and mortality. *Psychology and Aging, 15*, 617–626.

Krauzlis, R. J., & Lisberger, S. G. (1991). Visual motion commands for pursuit eye movements in the cerebellum. *Science, 253*, 568–571.

Krebs, R. L. (1967). *Some relations between moral judgment, attention, and resistance to temptation*. Unpublished doctoral dissertation, University of Chicago, Chicago, IL.

Kreuter, M. W., & Holt, C. L. (2001). How do people process health information?: Applications in an age of individualized communication. *Current Directions in Psychological Science, 10*, 206–209.

Kristof, N. D. (1997, August 17). Where children rule. *New York Times Magazine*.

Kronfol, Z., & Remick, D. G. (2000). Cytokines and the brain: Implications for clinical psychiatry. *American Journal of Psychiatry, 157*, 683–694.

Krosnick, J. A., Betz, A. L., Jussim, L. J., & Lynn, A. R. (1992). Subliminal conditioning of attitude. *Personality and Social Psychology Bulletin, 18*, 152–162.

Krueger, J. (1998). Enhancement bias in descriptions of self and others. *Personality and Social Psychology Bulletin, 24*, 505–516.

Krueger, J. (2001). Null hypothesis significance testing. *American Psychologist, 56*, 16–26.

Krueger, R. (2000). Phenotypic, genetic, and nonshared environment parallels the structure of personality: A view from the multidimensional personality questionnaire. *Journal of Personality and Social Psychology, 79*, 1057–1067.

Krumm, D. J. (2001). *Psychology at work: An introduction to industrial/organizational psychology*. New York: Worth.

Kryger, M. H., Roth, T., & Dement, W. C. (2000). *Principles and practice of sleep medicine* (3rd ed.). Philadelphia: Saunders.

Krykouli, S. E., Stanley, B. G., Seirafi, R. D., & Leibowitz, S. F. (1990). Stimulation of feeding by galanin: Anatomical localization and behavioral specificity of this peptide's effects in the brain. *Peptides, 11*(5), 995–1001.

Kübler-Ross, E. (1975). *Death: The final stage of growth*. Englewood Cliffs, NJ: Prentice-Hall.

Kuhs, H., & Tolle, R. (1991). Sleep deprivation therapy. *Biological Psychiatry, 29*, 1129–1148.

Kujala, T., Karma, K., Ceponiene, R., Belitz, S., Turkkila, P., Tervaniemi, M., & Naatanen, R. (2001). Plastic neural changes and reading improvement caused by audiovisual training in reading-impaired children. *Proceedings of the National Academy of Science, 98*, 10509–10514.

Kuncel, N. R., Hezlett, S. A., & Ones, D. S. (2001). A comprehensive meta-analysis of the predictive validity of the Graduate Records Examinations: Implications for graduate student selection and performance. *Psychological Bulletin, 127*, 162–181.

Kunkel, D., Wilson, B. J., Linz, D., Potter, J., Donnerstein, E., Smith, S. L., et al. (1996). *The national television violence study*. Studio City, CA: Mediascope.

Kunz, P. R., & Woolcott, M. (1976). Season's greetings: From my status to yours. *Social Science Research, 5*, 269–278.

Kurtz, L. F. (1997). *Self-help and support groups: A handbook for practitioners*. Thousand Oaks, CA: Sage.

Kurzban, R., & Leary, M. R. (2001). Evolutionary origins of stigmatization: The functions of social exclusion. *Psychological Bulletin, 127*, 187–208.

Kurzban, R., Tooby, J., & Cosmides, L. (2001). Can race be erased? Coalitional computation and social categorization. *Proceedings of the National Academy of Science, 98*, 15387–15392.

Kushner, M. G., Thuras, P., Kaminski, J., Anderson, N., Neumeyer, B., & Mackenzie, T. (2000). Expectancies for alcohol to affect tension and anxiety as a function of time. *Addictive Behaviors, 25*, 93–98.

Kutchins, H., & Kirk, S. A. (1997). *Making us crazy: The psychiatric bible and the creation of mental disorders.* New York: Free Press.

Kwan, M., Greenleaf, W. J., Mann, J., Crapo, L., & Davidson, J. M. (1983). The nature of androgen action on male sexuality: A combined laboratory-self-report study on hypogonadal men. *Journal of Clinical Endocrinology and Metabolism, 57,* 557–562.

Kwate, N. O. A. (2001). Intelligence or misorientation? *Journal of Black Psychology, 27,* 221–238.

Laan, E., Everaerd, W., Van Aanhold, M. T., & Rebel, M. (1993). Performance demand and sexual arousal in woman. *Behavior Research and Therapy, 31,* 25–36.

LaBar, K. S., Gatenby, J. C., Gore, J. C., LeDoux, J. E., & Phelps, E. A. (1998). Human amygdala activation during conditioned fear acquisition and extinction: A mixed-trial fMRI study. *Neuron, 20,* 937–945.

Labouvie-Vief, G. (1982). Discontinuities in development from childhood. In T. M. Field, A. Huston, H. C. Quay, L. Troll, & G. E. Finley (Eds.), *Review of human development.* New York: Wiley.

Labouvie-Vief, G. (1992). A new-Piagetian perspective on adult cognitive development. In R. J. Sternberg & C. A. Berg (Eds.), *Intellectual development.* New York: Cambridge University Press.

Lacayo, A. (1995). Neurologic and psychiatric complications of cocaine abuse. *Neuropsychiatry, Neuropsychology, and Behavioral Neurology, 8*(1), 53–60.

Ladd, G. W., & LeSieur, K. D. (1995). Parents and children's peer relationships. In M. H. Bornstein (Ed.), *Handbook of parenting: Vol. 4. Applied and practical parenting* (pp. 377–409). Mahwah, NJ: Erlbaum.

Laeng, B., & Caviness, V. S. (2001). Prosopagnosia as a deficit in encoding curved surface. *Journal of Cognitive Neuroscience, 13,* 556–576.

Laforge, R. G., Greene, G. W., & Prochaska, J. O. (1994). Psychosocial factors influencing low fruit and vegetable consumption. *Journal of Behavioral Medicine, 17,* 361–388.

Lagerspetz, K. M. J., & Lagerspetz, K. Y. H. (1983). Genes and aggression. In E. C. Simmel, M. E. Hahn, & J. K. Walters (Eds.), *Aggressive behavior: Genetic and neural approaches.* Hillsdale, NJ: Erlbaum.

Lahey, B. B., Applegate, B., Barkley, R., Garfinkel, B., McBurnett, K., Kerdyk, L., et al. (1994). DSM-IV Field Trials for oppositional defiant disorder and conduct disorder in children and adolescents. *American Journal of Psychiatry, 151,* 1163–1171.

Lahey, B. B., Loeber, R., Hart, E. L., Frick, P. J., & Applegate, B. (1995). Four-year longitudinal study of conduct disorder in boys: Patterns and predictors of persistence. *Journal of Abnormal Psychology, 104,* 83–93.

Lai, C. S. L., Fisher, S. E., Hurst, J. A., Vargha-Khadem, F., & Monaco, A. P. (2001). A forkhead-domain gene is mutated in severe speech and language disorder. *Nature, 413,* 519–523.

Lam, T. H., Ho, S. Y., Hedley, A. J., Mak, K. H., & Peto, R. (2001). Mortality and smoking in Hong Kong: case-control study of all adult deaths in 1998. *British Medical Journal, 323,* 361.

Lamar, J. (2000). Suicides in Japan reach a record high. *British Medical Journal, 321,* 528.

Lamb, M. E. (Ed.). (1997). *The role of the father in child development* (3rd ed.). New York: Wiley.

Lamb, M. E. (1998). Assessments of children's credibility in forensic contexts. *Current Directions in Psychological Science, 7,* 43–46.

Lambert, M. J., & Bergin, A. E. (1994). The effectiveness of psychotherapy. In A. E. Bergin & S. L. Garfield (Eds.), *Handbook of psychotherapy and behavior change* (4th ed.). New York: Wiley.

Lambert, M. J., & Hill, C. E. (1994). Assessing psychotherapy outcomes and processes. In A. E. Bergin & S. L. Garfield (Eds.), *Handbook of psychotherapy and behavior change* (4th ed.). New York: Wiley.

Lambert, N. M. (1999). Developmental trajectories in psychology: Applications to education and training. *American Psychologist, 54,* 991–1002.

Laming, P. R., Kimelberg, H., Robinson, S., Salm, A., Hawrylak, N., Muller, C., et al. (2000). Neuronal-glial interactions and behaviour. *Neuroscience and Biobehavioral Review, 24,* 295–340.

Landrine, H. (1991). Revising the framework of abnormal psychology. In P. Bronstein & K. Quina (Eds.), *Teaching a psychology of people.* Washington, DC: American Psychological Association.

Landsdale, M., & Laming, D. (1995). Evaluating the fragmentation hypothesis: The analysis of errors in cued recall. *Acta Psychologica, 88,* 33–77.

Lang, A. R., Goeckner, D. J., Adesso, V. J., & Marlatt, G. A. (1975). Effects of alcohol on aggression in male social drinkers. *Journal of Abnormal Psychology, 84,* 508–518.

Lang, P. J. (1995). The emotion probe: Studies of motivation and attention. *American Psychologist, 50*(5), 372–385.

Lang, P. J., & Melamed, B. G. (1969). Avoidance conditioning therapy of an infant with chronic ruminative vomiting. *Journal of Abnormal Psychology, 74,* 1–8.

Langenberg, P., Ballesteros, M., Feldman, R., Damron, D., Anliker, J., Havas, S. (2000). Psychosocial factors and intervention-associated changes in those factors as correlates of change in fruit and vegetable consumption in the Maryland WIC 5 a day promotion program. *Annals of Behavioral Medicine, 22,* 307–315.

Lanyon, R. I., & Goodstein, L. D. (1997). *Personality assessment* (3rd ed.). New York: Wiley.

Lapointe, L. (1990). *Aphasia and related neurogenic language disorders.* New York: Thieme Medical.

Larsen, J. R., Jr., Christensen, C., Franz, T. M., & Abbott, A. S. (1998). Diagnosing groups: The pooling, management, and impact of shared and unshared case information in team-based medical decision making. *Journal of Personality and Social Psychology, 75,* 93–108.

Larson, G. E., & Saccuzzo, D. P. (1989). Cognitive correlates of general intelligence: Toward a process theory of g. *Intelligence, 13,* 5–32.

Larson, M. C., Gunnar, M. R., & Hertsgaard, L. (1991). The effects of morning naps, car trips, and maternal separation on adrenocortical activity in human infants. *Child Development, 62,* 362–372.

Larson, R. W., & Verma, S. (1999). How children and adolescents spend time across the world: Work, play, and developmental opportunities. *Psychological Bulletin, 125,* 701–736.

Larzelere, R. E. (1996). A review of the outcomes of parental use of nonabusive or customary physical punishment. *Pediatrics, 98,* 824–828.

Lashley, K. S. (1950). In search of the engram. *Society of Experimental Biology, Symposium 4,* 454–482.

Latané, B. (1981). The psychology of social impact. *American Psychologist, 36,* 343–356.

Latané, B., & Rodin, J. (1969). A lady in distress: Inhibiting effects of friends and strangers on bystander intervention. *Journal of Experimental Social Psychology, 5,* 189–202.

Lau, M. A., Pihl, R. O., & Peterson, J. B. (1995). Provocation, acute alcohol intoxication, cognitive performance, and aggression. *Journal of Abnormal Psychology, 104,* 150–155.

Laughlin, P. L. (1999). Collective induction: Twelve postulates. *Organizational Behavior and Human Decision Processes, 80,* 50–69.

Laumann, E. O., Gagnon, J. H., Michael, R. T., & Michaels, S. (1994). *The social organization of sexuality: Sexual practices in the United States.* Chicago: University of Chicago Press.

Laumann, E. O., & Michael, R. T. (Eds.). (2000). *Sex, love, and health in America: Private choices and public policies.* Chicago, IL: University of Chicago Press.

Laumann, E. O., Paik, A., & Rosen, R. C. (1999). Sexual dysfunction in the United States: Prevalence and predictors. *Journal of the American Medical Association, 281,* 537–544.

Law, D. J., Pellegrino, J. W., & Hunt, E. B. (1993). Comparing the tortoise and the hare: Gender differences and experience in dynamic spatial reasoning tasks. *Psychological Science, 4,* 35–40.

Lawford, B. R., Young, R. M., Rowell, J. A., Qualichefski, J., Fletcher, B. H., Syndulko, et al. (1995). Bromocriptine in the treatment of alcoholics with the D2 dopamine receptor A1 allele. *Nature Medicine, 1*(4), 337–341.

Lawless, H. T., & Engen, T. (1977). Associations to odors: Interference, memories and verbal learning. *Journal of Experimental Psychology, 3,* 52–59.

Lawrie, S. M., Whalley, H. C., Abukmeil, S. S., Kestelman, J., Donnelly, L., Miller, P., et al. (2001). Brain structure, genetic liability, and psychotic symptoms in subjects at high risk of developing schizophrenia. *Biological Psychiatry, 49,* 811–823.

Lazarus, A. A. (1971). *Behavior therapy and beyond.* New York: McGraw-Hill.

Lazarus, R. S. (1966). *Psychological stress and the coping process.* New York: McGraw-Hill.

Lazarus, R. S. (1991). *Emotion and adaptation.* New York: Oxford University Press.

Lazarus, R. S. (1999). *Stress and emotion: A new synthesis.* New York: Springer.

Lazarus, R. S., & Folkman, S. (1984). *Stress, appraisal, and coping.* New York: Springer-Verlag.

Lazarus, R. S., Opton, E. M., Nomikos, M. S., & Rankin, M. O. (1965). The principle of short-circuiting of threat: Further evidence. *Journal of Personality, 33,* 622–635.

Leaper, C., Anderson, K. J., & Sanders, P. (1998). Moderators of gender effects on parents' talk to their children: A meta-analysis. *Developmental Psychology, 34,* 3–27.

Leary, M. (2001). The self-we know and the self we show: Self-esteem, self-presentation, and maintenance of interpersonal relationships. In G. Fletcher & M. Clark (Eds.), *Blackwell handbook of social psychology: Interpersonal processes* (pp. 457–477). Oxford, England: Blackwell.

LeDoux, J. E. (1995). Emotion: Clues from the brain. *Annual Review of Psychology, 46,* 209–235.

LeDoux, J. E. (1996). *The emotional brain.* New York: Simon & Schuster.

Lee, D. S., Lee, J. S., Oh, S. H., Kim, S. K., Kim, J. W., Chung, J. K., et al. (2001). Cross-modal plasticity and cochlear implants. *Nature, 409,* 149–150.

Lee, M. C., Schiffman, S. S., & Pappas, T. N. (1994). Role of neuropeptides in the regulation of feeding behavior: A review of cholecystokinin, bombesin, neuropeptide Y, and galanin. *Neuroscience and Biobehavioral Reviews, 18*(3) 313–323.

Lee, V. E., Brooks-Gunn, J., & Schnur, E. (1988). Does Head Start work? A 1-year follow-up comparison of disadvantaged children attending Head Start, no preschool, and other preschool programs. *Developmental Psychology, 24,* 210–222.

Lefcourt, H. M., Davidson, K., Prkachin, K. M., & Mills, D. E. (1997). Humor as a stress moderator in the prediction of blood pressure obtained during five stressful tasks. *Journal of Research in Personality, 31,* 523–542.

Legerstee, M., Anderson, D., & Schaffer, A. (1998). Five- and eight-month-old infants recognize their faces and voices as familiar and social stimuli. *Child Development, 69,* 37–50.

Lehman, H. E. (1967). Schizophrenia: IV. Clinical features. In A. M. Freedman, H. I. Kaplan, & H. S. Kaplan (Eds.), *Comprehensive textbook of psychiatry.* Baltimore: Williams & Wilkins.

Leibel, R. L., Rosenbaum, M., & Hirsch, J. (1995). Changes in energy expenditure resulting from altered body weight. *New England Journal of Medicine, 332*(10), 621–628.

Leibowitz, H. W., Brislin, R., Perlmutter, L., & Hennessy, R. (1969). Ponzo perspective illusion as a manifestation of space perception. *Science, 166,* 1174–1176.

Leigh, B. C., Schafer, J., & Temple, M. T. (1995). Alcohol use and contraception in first sexual experiences. *Journal of Behavorial Medicine, 18*(1), 81–95.

Leiner, H. C., Leiner, A. L., & Dow, R. S. (1993). Cognitive and language functions of the human cerebellum. *Trends in Neuroscience, 16,* 444–447.

Leippe, M. R., Manion, A. P., & Romanczyk, A. (1992). Eyewitness persuasion: How and how well do fact finders judge the accuracy of adults' and children's memory reports? *Journal of Personality and Social Psychology, 63,* 181–197.

Lejuez, C. W., Eifert, G. H., Zvolensky, M. J., & Richards, J. B. (2000). Preference among onset predictable and unpredictable administrations of 20% carbon-dioxide-enriched air: Implications for better understanding the etiology and treatment of panic disorder. *Journal of Experimental Psychology: Applied, 6,* 349–358.

Lemly, B. (2000, February). Isn't she lovely? *Discover,* 43–49.

Lennard, A. L., & Jackson, G. H. (2000). Stem cell transplantation. *British Medical Journal, 321,* 433–437.

Lenneberg, E. H. (1967). *Biological foundations of language.* New York: Wiley.

Leonard, B. E. (1992). *Fundamentals of psychopharmacology.* New York: Wiley.

Leonard, B. E. (1997). The role of noradrenaline in depression: A review. *Journal of Psychopharmacology, 11,* S39–S47.

Leonhardt, D. (2000, May 24). Makes sense to test for common sense. Yes? No? *New York Times.*

Lepore, L., & Brown, R. (1997). Category and stereotype activation: Is prejudice inevitable? *Journal of Personality and Social Psychology, 72,* 275–287.

Lepore, S. J. (1995a). Cynicism, social support, and cardiovascular reactivity. *Health Psychology, 14,* 210–216.

Lepore, S. J. (1995b). Measurement of chronic stressors. In S. Cohen, R. C. Kessler, & L. U. Gordon (Eds.), *Measuring stress: A guide for health and social scientists.* New York: Oxford University Press.

Lepore, S. J., Evans, G., & Schneider, M. (1991). Dynamic role of social support in the link between chronic stress and psychological distress. *Journal of Personality and Social Psychology, 61,* 899–909.

Lettvin, J. Y., Maturana, H. R., McCulloch, W. S., & Pitts, W. H. (1959). What the frog's eye tells the frog's brain. *Proceedings of the Institute of Radio Engineers, 47,* 1940–1951.

LeVay, S. (1991). A difference in hypothalamic structure between heterosexual and homosexual men. *Science, 253,* 1034–1037.

Levenson, H., & Strupp, H. H. (1997). Cyclical maladaptive patterns: Case formulation in time-limited dynamic psychotherapy. In T. D. Eells (Ed.), *Handbook of psychotherapy case formulation* (pp. 84–115). New York: Guilford.

Levenson, R. W., Ekman, P., & Friesen, W. V. (1990). Voluntary facial action generates emotion-specific autonomic nervous system activity. *Psychophysiology, 27*(4), 363–384.

Levenson, R. W., Ekman, P., Heider, K., & Friesen, W. V. (1992). Emotion and autonomic nervous system activity in the Minangkabau of West Sumatra. *Journal of Personality and Social Psychology, 62*(6), 972–988.

Levenstein, S., Smith, M. W., & Kaplan, G. A. (2001). Psychosocial predictors of hypertension in men and women. *Archives of Internal Medicine, 161,* 1341–1346.

Leventhal, T., & Brooks-Gunn, J. (2000). The neighborhoods they live in: The effects of neighborhood residence on child and adolescent outcomes. *Psychological Bulletin, 126,* 309–337.

Levine, J. M., & Moreland, R. L. (1998). Small groups. In D. Gilbert, S. T. Fiske, & G. Lindzey (Eds.), *Handbook of social psychology* (Vol. 2, 4th ed., pp. 415–469). Boston: McGraw-Hill.

Levine, R., Sato, S., Hashimoto, T., & Verna, J. (1995). Love and marriage in eleven cultures. *Journal of Cross-Cultural Psychology, 26,* 554–571.

Levine, R. V., Martinez, T. M., Brase, G., & Sorenson, K. (1994). Helping in 36 U.S. cities. *Journal of Personality and Social Psychology, 67,* 69–82.

Levine, S. (1999, February 1). In a loud and noisy world, baby boomers pay the consequences. *International Herald Tribune.*

Levinson, D. J., Darrow, C. N., Klein, E. B., Levinson, M. H., & McKee, B. (1978). *The seasons of a man's life.* New York: Knopf.

Levinson, S. C. (1996). Language and space. *Annual Review of Anthropology, 25,* 353–382.

Levinthal, C. F. (1996). *Drugs, behavior, and modern society.* Boston: Allyn & Bacon.

Levy, G. D., Taylor, M. G., & Gelman, S. A. (1995). Traditional and evaluative aspects of flexibility in gender roles, social conventions, moral rules, and physical laws. *Child Development, 66,* 515–531.

Levy, R. L., Cain, K. C., Jarrett, M., & Heitkemper, M. M. (1997). The relationship between daily life stress and gastrointestinal symptoms in women with irritable bowel syndrome. *Journal of Behavioral Medicine, 20,* 177–194.

Levy-Shiff, R. (1994). Individual and contextual correlates of marital change across the transition to parenthood. *Developmental Psychology, 30,* 591–601.

Lewicki, P. (1985). Nonconscious biasing of single instances of subsequent judgments. *Journal of Personality and Social Psychology, 48,* 563–574.

Lewicki, P. (1992). Nonconscious acquisition of information. *American Psychologist, 47,* 796–801.

Lewinsohn, P. M., Joiner, T. E., & Rohde, P. (2001). Evaluation of cognitive diathesis-stress models in precicting Major Depressive Disorder in adolescents. *Journal of Abnormal Psychology, 110,* 203–215.

Lewinsohn, P. M., & Rosenbaum, M. (1987). Recall of parental behavior by acute depressives, remitted depressives, and nondepressives. *Journal of Personality and Social Psychology, 52,* 611–619.

Lewis, C. E., Jacobs Jr., D. R., McCreath, H., Kiefe, C. I., Schreiner, P. J., Smith, D. E., & Williams, O. D. (2000). Weight gain continues in the 1990s: 10-year trends in weight and overweight from the CARDIA study. *American Journal of Epidemiology, 151,* 1172–1181.

Lewontin, R. (1976). Race and intelligence. In N. J. Block & G. Dworkin (Eds.), *The IQ controversy: Critical readings.* New York: Pantheon.

Ley, R. (1994). The "suffocation alarm" theory of panic attacks: A critical commentary. *Journal of Behavior Therapy and Experimental Psychiatry, 25,* 269–273.

Li, F., Harmer, P., McAuley, E., Duncan, T., Duncan, S. C., Chaumeton, N., & Fisher, K. J. (2001). An evaluation of the effects of Tai Chi exercise on physical function among older persons: A randomized controlled trail. *Annals of Behavioral Medicine, 23,* 139–146.

Liben, L. (1978). Perspective-taking skills in young children: Seeing the world through rose-colored glasses. *Developmental Psychology, 14,* 87–92.

Liberman, R. P., Wallace, C. J., Blackwell, G., Kopelowicz, A., Vaccaro, J. V., & Mintz, J. (1998). Skills training versus psychosocial occupational therapy for persons with persistent schizophrenia. *American Journal of Psychiatry, 155,* 1087–1091.

Lichstein, K. L., & Morin, C. M. (2000). *Treatment of late-life insomnia.* Thousand Oaks, CA: Sage.

Lichtenstein, P., Holm, N. V., Verkasalo, P. K., Iliadou, A., Kaprio, J., Koskenvuo, M., et al. (2000). Environmental and heritable factors in the causation of cancer-Analyses of cohorts of twins from Sweden, Denmark, and Finland. *New England Journal of Medicine, 343,* 78–85.

Lichtman, A. H., Dimen, K. R., & Martin, B. R. (1995). Systemic or intrahippocampal cannabinoid administration impairs spatial memory in rats. *Psychopharmacology, 119,* 282–290.

Lickey, M., & Gordon, B. (1991). *Medicine and mental illness: The use of drugs in psychiatry.* San Francisco: Freeman.

Lieberman, A., & Pawl, J. (1988). Clinical applications of attachment theory. In J. Bellsky & T. Nezworski (Eds.), *Clinical applications of attachment.* Hillsdale, NJ: Erlbaum.

Lieberman, M. A. (1996). Perspective on adult life crises. In V. L. Bengtson (Ed.), *Adulthood and aging: Research on continuities and discontinuities* (pp. 146–168). New York: Springer.

Lieberman, M. A., & Tobin, S. (1983). *The experience of old age.* New York: Basic Books.

Lieberman, M. D., Ochsner, K. N., Gilbert, D. T., & Schacter, D. L. (2001). Do amnesics exhibit cognitive dissonance reduction? The role of explicit memory and attention in attitude change. *Psychological Science, 121,* 135–140.

Lieberman, P. (1991). *Uniquely human.* Cambridge: Harvard University Press.

Liepert, J., Bauder, H., Miltner, W. H. R., Taub, E., & Weiller, C. (2000). Treatment-induced cortical reorganization after stroke in humans. *Stroke, 31,* 1210.

Light, K. C., Girdler, S. S., Sherwood, A., Bragdon, E. E., Brownley, K. A., West, S. G., & Hinderliter, A. L. (1999). High stress responsivity predicts later blood pressure only in combination with positive family history and high life stress. *Hypertension, 33,* 1458–1464.

Light, L. L. (1991). Memory and aging: Four hypotheses in search of data. *Annual Review of Psychology, 42,* 333–376.

Lilienfeld, S. O., & Marino, L. (1999). Essentialism revisited: Evolutionary theory and the concept of mental disorder. *Journal of Abnormal Psychology, 108,* 400–411.

Lilienfeld, S., Wood, J., & Garb, H. N. (2000). The scientific status of projective tests. *Psychological Science in the Public Interest, 1,* 27–66.

Lilienfeld, S. O., Lynn, S. J., Kirsch, I., Chaves, J. F., Sarbin, T. R., Ganaway, G. K., & Powell, R. A. (1999). Dissociative identity disorder and the sociocognitive model: Recalling the lessons of the past. *Psychological Bulletin, 125,* 507–523.

Lillywhite, A. R., Wilson, S. J., & Nutt, D. J. (1994). Successful treatment of night terrors and somnambulism with paroxetine. *British Journal of Psychiatry, 16,* 551–554.

Lin, K.-M. & Poland, R. E. (1995). Ethnicity, culture, and psychopharmacology. In F. E. Bloom & D. J. Kupfer (Eds.), *Psychopharmacology: The fourth generation of progress.* New York: Raven Press.

Lin, L., Umahara, M., York, D. A., & Bray, G. A. (1998). Beta-casomorphins stimulate and enterostatin inhibits the intake of dietary fat in rats. *Peptides, 19,* 325–331.

Lin, S., Thomas, T. C., Storlien, L. H., & Huang, X. F. (2000). Development of high fat diet-induced obesity and leptin resistance in C57BI/6J mice. *International Journal of Obesity and Related Metabolic Disorders, 24,* 639–646.

Lindsey, K. P., & Paul, G. L. (1989). Involuntary commitments to public mental institutions: Issues involving the overrepresentation of blacks and assessment of relevant functioning. *Psychological Bulletin, 106,* 171–183.

Lindvall, O., & Hagell, P. (2001). Cell therapy and transplantation in Parkinson's disease. *Clinical Chemistry and Laboratory Medicine, 39,* 356–361.

Lintern, G. (1991). An informational perspective on skill transfer in human-machine systems. *Human Factors, 33,* 251–266.

Linz, D., Donnerstein, E., & Penrod, S. (1987). The findings and recommendations of the Attorney General's Commission on Pornography: Do the psychological facts fit the political fury? *American Psychologist, 42,* 946–953.

Linz, D., Wilson, B. J., & Donnerstein, E. (1992). Sexual violence in the mass media: Legal solutions, warnings, and mitigation through education. *Journal of Social Issues, 48,* 145–172.

Lisanby, S. H., Schlaepfer, T. E., Fisch, H. U., & Sackeim, H. A. (2001). Magnetic seizure therapy of major depression. *Archives of General Psychiatry, 58,* 303–305.

Littlepage, G. E., Schmidt, G. W., Whisler, E. W., & Frost, A. G. (1995). An input-output analysis of influence and performance in problem-solving groups. *Journal of Personality and Social Psychology, 69,* 877–889.

Littlewood, R. (1992). Psychiatric diagnosis and racial bias: Empirical and interpretative approaches. *Social Science & Medicine, 34,* 141–149.

Liu, C., Weaver, D. R., Jin, X., Shearman, L. P., Pieschl, R. L., Gribkoff, V. K., & Reppert, S. M. (1997). Molecular dissection of two distinct actions of melatonin on the suprachiasmatic circadian clock. *Neuron, 19,* 91–102.

Liu, L. G. (1985). Reasoning counterfactually in Chinese: Are there any obstacles? *Cognition, 21,* 239–270.

Liu, Y., Gao, J.-H., Liu, H.-L., & Fox, P. (2000). The temporal response of the brain after eating revealed by functional MRI. *Nature, 405,* 1058–1062.

Lively, W. M. (2001). Syncope and neurologic deficits in a track athlete: A case report. *Medicine and Science in Sports and Exercise, 33,* 345–347.

Livingstone, M. S., & Hubel, D. H. (1987). Psychological evidence for separate channels for the perception of form, color, movement and depth. *Journal of Neuroscience, 7,* 3416–3468.

Lobaugh, N. J., Karaskov, V., Rombough, V., Rovet, J., Bryson, S., Greenbaum, R., et al. (2001). Piracetam therapy does not enhance cognitive functioning in children with down syndrome *Archives of Pediatrics & Adolescent Medicine, 155,* 442–448.

Locke, E. A., & Latham, G. P. (1990). *A theory of goal setting and task performance.* Englewood Cliffs, NJ: Prentice-Hall.

Lockhart, R. S., & Craik, F. I. M. (1990). Levels of processing: A retrospective commentary on a framework for memory research. *Canadian Journal of Psychology, 44,* 87–112.

Locurto, C. (1991a). Beyond IQ in preschool programs? *Intelligence, 15,* 295–312.

Locurto, C. (1991b). Hands on the elephant: IQ, preschool programs, and the rhetoric of inoculation-a reply to commentaries. *Intelligence, 15,* 335–349.

Loeber, R., & Stouthamer-Loeber, M. (1998). Development of juvenile aggression and violence. Some common misconceptions and controversies. *American Psychologist, 53,* 242–259.

Loeber, R. T., Cintron, C. M. B., & Yurgelun-Todd, D. A. (2001). Morphometry of individual cerebellar lobules in schizophrenia. *American Journal of Psychiatry, 158,* 952–954.

Loehlin, J. & Martin, N. G. (2001). Age changes in personality traits and their hertiabilities during the adult years: Evidence from Australian twin registry samples. *Personality and Individual Differences, 30,* 1147–1160.

Loehlin, J. C. (1989). Partitioning environmental and genetic contributions to behavioral development. *American Psychologist, 44,* 1285–1292.

Loehlin, J. C. (1992). *Genes and environment in personality development.* Newbury Park, CA: Sage.

Loewenstein, G. (1994). The psychology of curiosity: A review and reinterpretation. *Psychological Bulletin, 116*(1), 75–98.

Loftus, E. F. (1979). *Eyewitness testimony.* Cambridge: Harvard University Press.

Loftus, E. F. (1992). When a lie becomes memory's truth: Memory distortion after exposure to misinformation. *Psychological Science, 3,* 121–123.

Loftus, E. F. (1993). The reality of repressed memories. *American Psychologist, 48,* 518–537.

Loftus, E. F. (1997a). Memory for a past that never was. *Current Directions in Psychological Science, 6,* 60–65.

Loftus, E. F. (1997b). Repressed memory accusations: Devastated families and devastated patients. *Applied Cognitive Psychology, 11,* 25–30.

Loftus, E. F. (1998). The price of bad memories. *Skeptical Inquirer, 22,* 23–24.

Loftus, E. F., & Ketcham, K. (1991). *Witness for the defense.* New York: St. Martin's Press.

Loftus, E. F., & Ketcham, K. (1994). *The myth of repressed memory: False memories and allegations of sexual abuse.* New York: St. Martin's Press.

Loftus, E. F., & Palmer, J. C. (1974). Reconstruction of automobile destruction: An example of the interaction between language and memory. *Journal of Verbal Learning and Verbal Behavior, 13,* 585–589.

Loftus, G. R. (1996). Psychology will be a much better science when we change the way we analyze data. *Current Directions in Psychological Science, 5,* 161–171.

Loftus, T. M., Jaworsky, D. E., Frehywot, G. L., Townsend, C. A., Ronnet, G. V., Lane, M. D., & Kuhajda, F. P. (2000). Reduced food intake and body weight in mice treated with fatty acid synthase inhibitors. *Science, 288,* 2379–2381.

Logue, A. W. (1985). Conditioned food aversion in humans. *Annals of the New York Academy of Sciences, 104,* 331–340.

Longo, N., Klempay, S., & Bitterman, M. E. (1964). Classical appetitive conditioning in the pidgeon. *Psychonomic Science, 1,* 19–20.

Lopes, L. L. (1982). Procedural debiasing (Tech. Rep. WHIPP 15). Madison: University of Wisconsin, Human Information Processing Program.

Lopez, A. D., & Murray, C. C. J. L. (1998). The global burden of disease, 1990–2020. *Nature Medicine, 4,* 1241–1243.

Lopez, S. R. (1989). Patient variable biases in clinical judgment: Conceptual overview and methodological considerations. *Psychological Bulletin, 106,* 184–203.

Lopez-Lozano, J. J., Mata, M., & Bravo G. (2000). Neural transplants in Parkinson disease: Clinical results of 10 years of experience. *Review of Neurology, 30,* 1077–1083.

Lord, C. G. (1997). *Social psychology.* Fort Worth: Harcourt, Brace.

Lubinski, D., Benbow, C. P., Shea, D. L., Eftekhari-Sanjani, H., & Halverson, M. B. J. (2001). Men and women at promise for scientific achievement: Similarity not dissimilarity. *Psychological Science, 12,* 309–317.

Luborsky, L. (1972). Another reply to Eysenck. *Psychological Bulletin, 78,* 406–408.

Luborsky, L. (1997). The core conflictual relationship theme: A basic case formulation method. In T. D. Eells (Ed.), *Handbook of psychotherapy case formulation* (pp. 58–83). New York: Guilford.

Luborsky, L., & Crits-Christoph, P. (1998). *Understanding transference: The Core Conflictual Relationship Theme Method* (2nd ed.). Washington, DC: American Psychological Association.

Luborsky, L., Singer, B., & Luborsky, L. (1975). Comparative studies of psychotherapies: Is it true that everyone has won and all must have prizes? *Archives of General Psychiatry, 32,* 995–1008.

Luchins, A. S. (1942). Mechanization in problem solving: The effect of Einstellung. *Psychological Monographs, 54*(6, Whole No. 248).

Lue, T. F. (2000). Drug therapy: Erectile dysfunction *The New England Journal of Medicine, 342,* 1802–1813.

Lundqvist, D., Esteves, F., & Öhman, A. (1999). The face of wrath: Critical features for conveying facial threat. *Cognition and Emotion, 13,* 691–711.

Luntz, B. K., & Widom, C. S. (1994). Antisocial personality disorder in abused and neglected children grown up. *American Journal of Psychiatry, 151,* 670–674.

Luria, Z. (1992, February). *Gender differences in children's play patterns.* Paper presented at University of Southern California, Los Angeles.

Lustig, C., & Hasher, L. (2001). Implicit memory is not immune to interference. *Psychological Bulletin, 127,* 615–628.

Luthar, S. S., Cicchetti, D., & Becker, B. (2000). The construct of resilience: A critical evaluation and guidelines for future work. *Child Development, 71,* 543–562.

Lutz, D. J., & Sternberg, R. J. (1999). Cognitive development. In M. H. Bornstein & M. E. Lamb (Eds.), *Development psychology: An advanced textbook* (4th ed.). Mahwah, NJ: Erlbaum.

Lykken, D. T. (1992). Why (some) Americans believe in the lie detector while others believe in the guilty knowledge test. *Integrative Physiological and Behavioral Science, 26,* 214–222.

Lykken, D. T. (1998). *A tremor in the blood: Uses and abuses of the lie detector.* Cambridge, MA: Perseus Publishing.

Lykken, D. T. (1999). *Happiness: What studies on twins show us about nature, nuture, and the happiness set point.* New York: Golden Books.

Lynam, D. R. (1996). The early identification of chronic offenders: Who is the fledgling psychopath? *Psychological Bulletin, 120,* 209–234.

Lynam, D. R., & Widiger, T. A. (2001). Using the five-factor model to represent the DSM-IV personality disorders: An expert consensus approach. *Journal of Abnormal Psychology, 110,* 401–412.

Lynn, R. (1996). Racial and ethnic differences in intelligence in the U.S. on the Differential Ability Scale. *Personality and Individual Differences, 20,* 271–273.

Lynn, S. J., Myers, B., & Malinoski, P. (1997). Hypnosis, pseudomemories, and clinical guidelines: A sociocognitive perspective. In J. D. Read & D. S. Lindsay (Eds.), *Recollections of trauma: Scientific evidence and clinical practice. NATO ASI series: Series A: Life sciences* (Vol. 291, pp. 305–336). New York: Plenum Press.

Lynn, S. J., & Rhue, J. W. (1986). The fantasy-prone person: Hypnosis, imagination, and creativity. *Journal of Personality and Social Psychology, 51,* 404–408.

Lyons, D., & McLoughlin, D. M. (2001). Clinical review: Psychiatry. *British Medical Journal, 323,* 1228–1231.

Lyubomirsky, S., & Nolen-Hoeksema, S. (1995). Effects of self-focused rumination on negative thinking and interpersonal problem solving. *Journal of Personality and Social Psychology, 69,* 176–190.

MacAndrew, C., & Edgerton, R. B. (1969). *Drunken comportment.* Chicago: Aldine.

MacArthur Foundation. (1999). *Research network on successful midlife development.* The John D. and Catherine T. MacArthur Foundation, Vero Beach, FL.

MacDonald, M., & Bernstein, D. A. (1974). Treatment of a spider phobia with in vivo and imaginal desensitization. *Journal of Behavior Therapy and Experimental Psychiatry, 5,* 47–52.

MacEvoy, S. P., & Paradiso, M. A. (2001). Lightness constancy in primary visual cortex *Proceedings of the National Academy of Science, 98,* 8827–8831.

Mack, A., & Rock, I. (1998). *Inattentional blindness.* Cambridge: MIT Press.

MacKenzie, B. (1984). Explaining race differences in IQ: The logic, the methodology, and the evidence. *American Psychologist, 39,* 1214–1233.

Mackie, D. M., Hamilton, D. L., Susskind, S. J., & Rosselli, F. (1996). Social psychological foundations of prejudice. In C. N. Macrae, C. Stangor, & M. Hewstone (Eds.), *Stereotypes and stereotyping* (pp. 41–78). New York: Guilford.

MacMillan, H. L., Fleming, J. E., Streiner, D. L., Lin, E., Boyle, M. H., Jamieson, E., et al. (2001). Childhood abuse and lifetime psychopathology in a community sample. *American Journal of Psychiatry, 158,* 1878–1883.

Maddux, J. (1993). Social cognitive models of health and exercise behavior: An introduction and review of conceptual issues. *Journal of Applied Sport Psychology, 5,* 116–140.

Maess, B., Koelsch, S., Gunter, T. C., & Friederici, A. D. (2001). Musical syntax is processed in Broca's area: An MEG study. *Nature Neuroscience, 4,* 540–545.

Magee, J. C., & Johnston, D. (1997). A synaptically controlled, associative signal for Hebbian plasticity in hippocampal neurons. *Science, 275,* 209–213.

Maguire, T., Hattie, J., & Haig, B. (1994). Construct validity and achievement assessment. *Alberta Journal of Educational Research, 40*(2), 109–126.

Mahesh Yogi, M. (1994). *Science of being and art of living.* New York: NAL/Dutton.

Mahler, M. S. (1968). *On human symbiosis and the vicissitudes of individuation: Infantile psychosis.* New York: Basic Books.

Mahrer, A. R., & Nadler, W. P. (1986). Good moments in psychotherapy: A preliminary review, a list, and some promising research avenues. *Journal of Consulting and Clinical Psychology, 54,* 10–15.

Maier, S. F., & Watkins, L. R. (1998). Cytokines for psychologists: Implications of bidirectional immune-to-brain communication for understanding behavior, mood, and cognition. *Psychological Review, 105,* 83–107.

Maier, S. F., & Watkins, L. R. (2000). The immune system as a sensory system: Implications for psychology. *Current Directions in Psychological Science, 9,* 98–102.

Maier, W., Gansicke, M., Gater, R., Reziki, M., Tiemens, B. & Urzua, F. (1999). Gender differences in the prevalence of depression: A survey in primary care. *Journal of Affective Disorders, 53,* 241–252.

Main, M. (1996). Introduction to the special section on attachment and psychopathology: Vol. 2. Overview of the field of attachment. *Journal of Consulting and Clinical Psychology, 64,* 237–243.

Major, B., Sciacchtinano, A. M., & Crocker, J. (1993). In-group versus out-group comparisons and self-esteem. *Personality and Social Psychology Bulletin, 19,* 711–721.

Malamuth, N., & Addison, T. (2001). Helping and altruism. In G. Fletcher & M. Clark (Eds.), *Blackwell handbook of social psychology: Interpersonal processes* (pp. 162–195). Oxford, England: Blackwell.

Malamuth, N. M. (1998). The confluence model as an organizing framework for research on sexually aggressive men: Risk moderators, imagined aggression, and pornography consumption. In R. G. Geen & E. Donnerstein (Eds.), *Human aggression* (pp. 230–247). San Diego: Academic Press.

Malamuth, N. M., Addison, T., & Koss, M. (2000). Pornography and sexual aggression: Are there reliable effects and can we understand them? *Annual Review of Sex Research, 11,* 26–91.

Malamuth, N. M., & Check, J. V. P. (1983). Sexual arousal to rape depictions: Individual differences. *Journal of Abnormal Psychology, 92,* 55–67.

Malamuth, N. M., Sockloskie, R. J., Koss, M. P., & Tanaka, J. S. (1991). Characteristics of aggressors against women: Testing a model using a national sample of college students. *Journal of Consulting and Clinical Psychology, 59,* 670–681.

Malarkey, W. B., Kiecolt-Glaser, J. K., Pearl, D., & Glaser, R. (1994). Hostile behavior during marital conflict alters pituitary and adrenal hormones. *Psychosomatic Medicine, 56,* 41–51.

Malaspina, D., Goetz, R. R., Friedman, J. H., Kaufmann, C. A., Faraone, S. V., Tsuang, M., Cloninger, C. R., Nurnberger, J. I., Jr., & Blehar, M. C. (2001). Traumatic brain injury and schizophrenia in members of schizophrenia and bipolar disorder pedigrees. *American Journal of Psychiatry, 158,* 440–446.

Malberg, J. E., Eisch, A. J., Nestler, E. J., & Duman, R. S. (2000). Chronic antidepressant treatment increases neurogenesis in adult rat hippocampus. *Journal of Neuroscience, 20,* 9104–9110.

Malenka, R. C. (1995). LTP and LTD: Dynamic and interactive processes of synaptic plasticity. *The Neuroscientist, 1,* 35–42.

Malenka, R. C., & Nicoll, R. A. (1999). Long-term potentiation—a decade of progress? *Science, 285,* 1870–1874.

Malgrange, B., Rigo, J. M., Van de Water, T. R., Staecker, H., Moonen, G., & Lefebvre, P. P. (1999). Growth factor therapy to the damaged inner ear: Clinical prospects. *International Journal of Pediatric Otorhinolaryngology, 49*(Suppl. 1), S19–S25.

Malleret, G., Haditsch, U., Genoux, D., Jones, M. W., Bliss, T. V. P., Vanhoose, A. M., Weitlauf, C., Kandel, E. R., Winder, D. G., & Mansuy, I. M. (2001). Inducible and reversible enhancement of learning, memory, and long-term potentiation by genetic inhibition of calcineurin. *Cell, 104,* 675–686.

Manderscheid, R., & Barrett, S. (Eds.). (1987). *Mental health, United States, 1987* (DHHS Pub. No. ADM 87–1518). Bethesda, MD: National Institute of Mental Health.

Manji, H. K., Bowden, C. L., & Belmaker, R. H. (Eds.). (2000). *Bipolar medications: Mechanisms of action.* Washington, DC: American Psychiatric Press.

Manke, B., McGuire, S., Reiss, D., Hetherington, E. M., & Plomin, R. (1995). Genetic contributions to children's extrafamilial social interactions: Teachers, best friends, and peers. *Social Development, 4,* 238–256.

Mann, K., Roschke, J., Nink, M., Aldenhoff, J., Beyer, J., Benkert, O., & Lehnert, H. (1992). Effects of corticotropin-releasing hormone administration in patients suffering from sleep apnea syndrome. *Society for Neuroscience Abstracts, 22,* 196.

Mannuzza, M., Schneider, F. R., Chapman, T. F., Liebowitz, M. R., Klein, D. F., & Fyer, A. J. (1995). Generalized social phobia. *Archives of General Psychiatry, 52,* 230–237.

Mansfield, P. K., Voda, A., & Koch, P. B. (1995). Predictors of sexual response changes in heterosexual midlife women. *Health Values, 19*(1), 10–20.

Marcus, G. F. (1996). Why do children say "breaked"? *Current Directions in Psychological Science, 5,* 81–85.

Marenco, S., & Weinberger, D. R. (2000). The neurodevelopmental hypothesis of schizophrenia: Following a trail of evidence from cradle to grave. *Developmental Psychopathology, 12,* 501–527.

Markman, E. M. (1994). Constraints children place on word meanings. In P. Bloom (Ed.), *Language acquisition: Core readings* (pp. 154–173). Cambridge: MIT Press.

Markowitz, J. C., & Swartz, H. A. (1997). Case formulation in interpersonal psychotherapy of depression. In T. D. Eells (Ed.), *Handbook of psychotherapy case formulation* (pp. 192–222). New York: Guilford.

Markus, H. R., & Kitayama, S. (1991). Culture and the self: Implications for cognition, emotion, and motivation. *Psychological Review, 98,* 224–253.

Markus, H. R., & Kitayama, S. (1997). Culture and the self: Implications for cognition, emotion, and motivation. In L. A. Peplau & S. Taylor (Eds.), *Sociocultural perspectives in social psychology* (pp. 157–216). Upper Saddle River, NJ: Prentice-Hall.

Markus, H. R., Kitayama, S., & Heiman, R. J. (1996). Culture and "basic" psychological principles. In E. T. Higgins & A. W. Kruglanski (Eds.), *Social psychology: Handbook of basic principles* (pp. 857–913). New York: Guilford.

Marmar, C. R. (1990). Psychotherapy process research: Progress, dilemmas, and future directions. *Journal of Consulting and Clinical Psychology, 58,* 265–272.

Marrack, P., Kappler, J., & Kotzin, B. L. (2001). Autoimmune disease: Why and where it occurs. *Nature Medicine, 7,* 899–905.

Marshall, J., & Oberwinkler, J. (1999). The colourful world of the mantis shrimp. *Nature, 401,* 873–874.

Marshall, W. L. (1989). Pornography and sex offenders. In D. Zillmann & J. Bryant (Eds.), *Pornography: Research advances and policy considerations.* Hillsdale, NJ: Erlbaum.

Martin, B., & Hoffman, J. (1990). Conduct disorders. In M. Lewis & S. M. Miller (Eds.), *Handbook of developmental psychopathology.* New York: Plenum.

Martin, C. L., & Fabes, R. A. (2001). The stability and consequences of young children's same-sex peer interactions. *Developmental Psychology, 37,* 431–446.

Martin, D. J., Garske, J. P., & Davis, M. K. (2000). Relation of the therapeutic alliance with outcome and other variables: A meta-analytic review. *Journal of Consulting and Clinical Psychology, 68,* 438–450.

Martin, R., Gran, B., Zhao, Y., Markovic-Plese, S., Bielekova, B., Marques, A., et al. (2001). Molecular mimicry and antigen-specific t cell responses in multiple sclerosis and chronic cns lyme disease. *Journal of Autoimmunity, 16,* 187–192.

Martin, R. A. (2001). Humor, laughter, and physical health: Methodological issues and research findings. *Psychological Bulletin, 127,* 504–519.

Martin, R. C., Sawrie, S. M., Knowlton, R. C., Bilir, E., Gilliam, F. G., Faught, E., et al. (2001). Bilateral hippocampal atrophy: Consequences to verbal memory following temporal lobectomy. *Neurology, 57,* 597–604.

Martin, S. (1999, July/August). Revision of ethics code calls for stronger former client sex rule. *APA Monitor,* p. 44.

Martindale, C. (1981). *Cognition and consciousness.* Homewood, IL: Dorsey Press.

Martindale, C. (1991). *Cognitive psychology: A neural-network approach.* Pacific Grove, CA: Brooks/Cole.

Martinez, C. R., & Forgatch, M. S. (2001). Preventing problems with boys' noncompliance: Effects of a parent training intervention for divorcing mothers. *Journal of Consulting and Clinical Psychology, 69,* 416–428.

Martino, G., & Marks, L. E. (2001). Synesthesia: Strong and weak. *Current Directions in Psychological Science, 10,* 61–65.

Martinot, M.-L. P., Bragulat, V., Artiges, E., Dolle, F., Hinnen, F., Jouvent, R., & Martinot, J-L. (2001). Decreased presynaptic dopamine function in the left caudate of depressed patients with affective flattening and psychomotor retardation. *American Journal of Psychiatry, 158,* 314–316.

Marzuk, P. M., Tardiff, K., Leon, A. C., Hirsch, C. S., Stajic, M., Portera, L., et al. (1995). Fatal injuries after cocaine use as a leading cause of death among young adults in New York City. *New England Journal of Medicine, 332*(26), 1753–1757.

Masand, P., Popli, A. P., & Welburg, J. B. (1995). Sleepwalking. *American Family Physician, 51*(3), 649–653.

Maslach, C., & Goldberg, J. (1998). Prevention of burnout: New perspectives. *Applied and Preventive Psychology, 7,* 63–74.

Masling, J. (1992). What does it all mean? In R. F. Bornstein & T. Pittman (Eds.), *Perception without awareness* (pp. 259–276). New York: Guilford.

Masling, J., & Bornstein, R. F. (1991). Perception without awareness and electrodermal responding: A strong test of subliminal psychodynamic activation effects. *Journal of Mind and Behavior, 12,* 33–47.

Maslow, A. H. (1954). *Motivation and personality.* New York: Harper.

Maslow, A. H. (1970). *Motivation and personality* (2nd ed.). New York: Harper & Row.

Maslow, A. H. (1971). *The farther reaches of human nature.* New York: McGraw-Hill.

Mason, W. A. (1997). Discovering behavior. *American Psychologist, 52,* 713–720.

Massaro, D. W., & Cowan, N. (1993). Information processing models: Microscopes of the mind. *Annual Review of Psychology, 44,* 383–425.

Massaro, D. W., & Stork, D. G. (1998). Speech recognition and sensory integration. *American Scientist, 86,* 236–244.

Masson, J. M. (1983). *Assault on the truth: Freud's suppression of the seduction theory.* New York: Farrar, Straus, & Giroux.

Masson, M. E. J., & MacLeod, C. M. (1992). Reenacting the route to interpretation: Enhanced perceptual identification without prior perception. *Journal of Experimental Psychology: General, 121,* 145–176.

Masten, A. S., & Coatsworth, J. D. (1998). The development of competence in favorable and unfavorable environments: Lessons from research on successful children. *American Psychologist, 53,* 205–220.

Masters, J. C., Burish, T. G., Hollon, S. D., & Rimm, D. C. (1987). *Behavior therapy: Techniques and empirical findings* (3rd ed.). San Diego: Harcourt Brace Jovanovich.

Masters, W. H., & Johnson, V. E. (1966). *Human sexual response.* Boston: Little, Brown.

Mathalon, D. H., Sullivan, E. V., Lim, K. O., & Pfefferbaum, A. (2001). Progressive brain volume changes and the clinical course of schizophrenia in men: A longitudinal magnetic resonance imaging study. *Archives of General Psychiatry, 58,* 148–157.

Matlin, M. W. (1998). *Cognition* (4th ed.). Fort Worth, TX: Harcourt Brace.

Matson, J., Sevin, J., Fridley, D., & Love, S. (1990). Increasing spontaneous language in autistic children. *Journal of Applied Behavior Analysis, 23,* 227–223.

Matsuda, K. T., Cho, M. C., Lin, K. M., Smith, M. W., Young, A. S., & Adams, J. A. (1996). Clozapine dosage, serum levels, efficacy, and side-effect profiles: a comparison of Korean-American and Caucasian patients. *Psychopharmacol Bulletin, 32,* 253–257.

Matsumoto, D. (2000). *Culture and psychology: People around the world.* Belmont, CA: Wadsworth.

Matsumoto, D., & Ekman, P. (1989). American-Japanese cultural differences in intensity ratings of facial expressions of emotion. *Motivation and Emotion, 13,* 143–157.

Matte, T. D., Breshahan, M., Begg, M., & Susser, E. (2001). Influence of variation in birthweight within normal range and within sibships on IQ at 7 years: Cohort study. *British Medical Journal, 323,* 310–314.

Matthews, G., & Dreary, I. J. (1998). *Personality traits.* Cambridge, England: Cambridge University Press.

Matthies, E., Hoeger, R., & Guski, R. (2000). Living on polluted soil: Determinants of stress symptoms. *Environment and Behavior, 32,* 270–286.

Mattingly, J. B., Rich, A. N., Yelland, G., & Bradshaw, J. L. (2001). Unconscious priming eliminates automatic binding of colour and alphanumeric form in synaesthesia. *Nature, 410,* 580–582.

Maupin, H. E., & Fisher, J. R. (1989). The effects of superior female performance and sex-role orientation in gender conformity. *Canadian Journal of Behavioral Science, 21,* 55–69.

Mayer, D. J., & Price, D. D. (1982). A physiological and psychological analysis of pain: A potential model of motivation. In D. W. Pfaff (Ed.), *The physiological mechanisms of motivation.* New York: Springer-Verlag.

Mayer, F. S., & Sutton, K. (1996). *Personality: An integrative approach.* Upper Saddle River, NJ: Prentice-Hall.

Mayer, R. E. (1992). *Thinking, problem solving, and cognition* (2nd ed.). New York: Freeman.

Mazzoni, G. A., & Loftus, E. F. (1996). When dreams become reality. *Consciousness and Cognition, 5,* 442–462.

McAdams, D. P. (1997). A conceptual history of personality psychology. In R. Hogan, J. Johnson, & S. Briggs (Eds.), *Handbook of personality psychology* (pp. 4–40). San Diego: Academic Press.

McAndrew, F. T. (2002). New evolutionary perspectives on altruism. Multilevel-selection and costly-signaling theories. *Current Directions in Psychological Science, 11,* 79–82.

McAuley, E. (1992). The role of efficacy cognitions in the prediction of exercise behavior in middle-aged adults. *Journal of Behavioral Medicine, 15,* 65–88.

McCarty, M. F. (1995). Optimizing exercise for fat loss. *Medical Hypotheses, 44*(5), 325–330.

McCauley, C. (1989). The nature of social influence in groupthink: Compliance and internalization. *Journal of Personality and Social Psychology, 57,* 250–260.

McClelland, D. C. (1958). Risk-taking in children with high and low need for achievement. In J. W. Atkinson (Ed.), *Motives in fantasy, action, and society* (pp. 306–321). Princeton, NJ: Van Nostrand.

McClelland, D. C. (1985). *Human motivation.* Glenview, IL: Scott, Foresman.

McClintock, C. G., & Liebrand, W. B. G. (1988). Role of interdependence structure, individual value orientation, and another's strategy in social decision making: A transformational analysis. *Journal of Personality and Social Psychology, 55,* 396–409.

McCloskey, D. I. (1978). Kinesthetic sensibility. *Physiological Reviews, 58,* 763.

McClosky, M. (1983). Naïve theories of motion. In D. Gentner & K. Stevens (Eds.), *Mental models* (pp. 299–324). Northvale, NJ: Erlbaum.

McClure, E. B. (2000). A meta-analytic review of sex differences in facial expression processing and their development in infants, children, and adolescents. *Psychological Bulletin, 126,* 424–453.

McCormick, D. A., & Thompson, R. F. (1984). Cerebellum essential involvement in the classically conditioned eyelid response. *Science, 223,* 296–299.

McCrae, R. R., & Costa, P. T., Jr. (1997). Personality trait structure as a human universal. *American Psychologist, 52,* 509–516.

McCrae, R. R., & Costa, P. T. (1999). A five-factor theory of personality. In L. Pervin & O. John (Eds.) *Handbook of personality: Theory and research* (2nd ed., pp. 139–153). New York: Guilford.

McCrae, R. R., Costa, P. T., Jr., Osterndorf, F., Angleitner, A., Hrebickova, M., Avia, M. D., et al. (2000). Nature over nurture: Temperament, personality, and life-span development. *Journal of Personality and Social Psychology, 78,* 173–186.

McCrae, R., & John, O. (1992). An introduction to the five-factor model and its applications. *Journal of Personality, 60,* 175–215.

McCrae, R. R., Yik, M. S. M, Trapnell, P. D., Bond, M., & Paulhus, D. (1998). Interpreting personality profiles across cultures, bilingual, acculturation, and peer rating studies of Chinese undergraduates. *Journal of Personality and Social Psychology, 74,* 1041–1055.

McDermott, K. B. (2000). Implicit memory. A. E. Kazdin (Ed.), *The encyclopedia of psychology* (pp. 231–234). New York: American Psychological Association and Oxford University Press.

McDermott, K. B., & Buckner, R. L. (in press). Functional anatomic correlates of human memory retrieval. In L. R. Squire & D. L. Schacter (Eds.), *Neuropsychology of memory* (3rd ed.). New York: Guilford.

McDermott, K. B., & Roediger, H. L. (1998). Attempting to avoid illusory memories: Robust false recognition of associates persists under conditions of explicit warnings and immediate testing. *Journal of Memory and Language, 39,* 508–520.

McDonald, J. J., Teder-Salejarvi, W. A., & Hillyard, S. A. (2000). Involuntary orienting to sound improves visual perception. *Nature, 407,* 906–908.

McDougall, S. J. P., de Bruijn, O., & Curry, M. B. (2000). Exploring the effects of icon characteristics on user performance: The role of icon concreteness, complexity, and distinctiveness. *Journal of Experimental Psychology: Applied, 6,* 291–306.

McEwen, B. S. (1994). How do sex and stress hormones affect nerve cells? *Annals of the New York Academy of Science, 743,* 1–18.

McEwen, B. S. (1998). Protective and damaging effects of stress mediators. *New England Journal of Medicine, 338,* 171–179.

McEwen, B. S., & Seeman, T. (1999). Protective and damaging effects of mediators of stress: Elaborating and testing concepts of allostasis and allostatic load. *Annals of the New York Academy of Sciences, 896,* 30–47.

McFadden, D., & Pasanen, E. G. (1998). Comparison of the auditory systems of heterosexuals and homosexuals: Click-evoked otoacoustic emissions. *Proceedings of the National Academy of Science USA, 95,* 2709–2713.

McGarvey, R. (1989, February). Recording success. *USAIR Magazine,* pp. 94–102.

McGehee, D. S., Heath, M. J. S., Gelber, S., Devay, P., & Role, L. W. (1995). Nicotine enhancement of fast excitatory synaptic transmissions in CNS by presynaptic receptors. *Science, 269,* 1692–1696.

McGlashan, T. H., & Hoffman, R. E. (2000). Schizophrenia as a disorder of reduced synaptic connectivity. *Archives of General Psychiatry, 57,* 637–648.

McGlone, J. (1980). Sex differences in human brain asymmetry: A critical survey. *The Behavioral and Brain Sciences, 3,* 215–263.

McGlynn, F. D., Moore, P. M., Lawyer, S., & Karg, R. (1999). Relaxation training inhibits fear and arousal during in vivo exposure to phobia-cue stimuli. *Journal of Behavior Therapy and Experimental Psychiatry, 30,* 155–168.

McGue, M. (1992). When assessing twin concordance, use the probandwise not the pairwise rate. *Schizophrenia Bulletin, 18,* 171–176.

McGue, M. (1999). The behavioral genetics of alcoholism. *Current Directions in Psychological Science, 8,* 109–115.

McGue, M., Bouchard, T. J., Jr., Iacono, W. G., & Lykken, D. T. (1993). Behavioral genetics of cognitive ability: A life-span perspective. In R. Plomin & G. E. McClearn (Eds.), *Nature, nurture and psychology* (pp. 59–76). Washington, DC: American Psychological Association.

McGue, M., Pickens, R., & Svikis, D. (1992). Sex and age effects on the inheritance of alcohol problems: A twin study. *Journal of Abnormal Psychology, 101,* 3–17.

McGuire, M. T., Wing, R. R., Klem, M. L., Lang, W., & Hill, J. O. (1999). What predicts weight regain in a group of successful weight losers? *Journal of Consulting and Clinical Psychology, 67,* 177–185.

McIntire, S. A., & Miller, L. A. (2000). *Foundations of psychological testing.* New York: McGraw-Hill.

McIntosh, J. L. (1992). Suicide of the elderly. In B. Bonger (Ed.), *Suicide: Guidelines for assessment, management, and treatment.* New York: Oxford University Press.

McLaughlin, C. S., Chen, C., Greenberger, E., & Biermeier, C. (1997). Family, peer, and individual correlates of sexual experience among Caucasian and Asian-American late adolescents. *Journal of Research on Adolescence, 7,* 33–53.

McLeod, J. D., Kessler, R. C., & Landis, K. R. (1992). Speed of recovery from major depressive episodes in a community sample of married men and women. *Journal of Abnormal Psychology, 101,* 277–286.

McLeod, P., & Dienes, Z. (1996). Do fielders know where to go to catch the ball or only how to get there? *Journal of Experimental Psychology: Human Perception and Performance, 22,* 531–543.

McLoyd, V. C. (1998). Socioeconomic disadvantage and child development. *American Psychologist, 53,* 185–204.

McMahon, P. (2000, January 31). Oregon man leads life without frills, leaves $9 million to charities, children. *USA Today,* p. 4A.

McMullin, R. E. (2000). *The new handbook of cognitive therapy techniques.* New York: Norton.

McNally, R. J., Clancy, S. A., & Schacter, D. L. (2001). Directed forgetting of trauma cues in adults reporting repressed or recovered memories of childhood sexual abuse. *Journal of Abnormal Psychology, 110,* 151–156.

McNally, R. J., Clancy, S. A., Schacter, D. L., & Pittman, R. K. (2000a). Cognitive processing of trauma cues in adults reporting repressed, recovered, or continuous memories of childhood sexual abuse. *Journal of Abnormal Psychology, 109,* 355–359.

McNally, R. J., Clancy, S. A., Schacter, D. L., & Pittman, R. K. (2000b). Personality profiles, dissociation, and absorption in women reporting repressed, recovered, or continuous memories of childhood sexual abuse. *Journal of Consulting and Clinical Psychology, 68,* 1033–1037.

McNay, E. C., McCarty, R. C., & Gold, P. E. (2001). Fluctuations in brain glucose concentration during behavioral testing: Dissociations between brain areas and between brain and blood. *Neurobiology of Learning and Memory, 75,* 325–337.

McNeil, J. E., & Warrington, E. K. (1993). Prosopagnosia: A face-specific disorder. *Quarterly Journal of Experimental Psychology: Human Experimental Psychology, 46A(1),* 1–10.

McPhail, T. L., & Penner, L. A. (1995, August). *Can similarity moderate the effects of aversive racism?* Paper presented at the 103rd annual meeting of the American Psychological Association, New York.

McQuaid, J. R., Monroe, S. M., Roberts, J. E., Kupfer, D. J., & Frank, E. (2000). A comparison of two life stress assessment approaches: Prospective prediction of treatment outcome in recurrent depression. *Journal of Abnormal Psychology, 109,* 787–791.

Medin, D. L., & Bazerman, M. H. (1999). Broadening behavioral decision research: Multiple levels of cognitive processing. *Psychonomic Bulletin & Review, 6,* 533–546.

Medin, D. L., Ross, B. H., & Markman, A. B. (2001). *Cognitive psychology* (3rd ed.). Fort Worth, TX: Harcourt.

Mehle, T. (1982). Hypothesis generation in an automobile malfunction inference task. *Acta Psychologica, 52,* 87–116.

Meichenbaum, D. (1977). *Cognitive behavior modification: An integrative approach.* New York: Plenum.

Meichenbaum, D. H. (1995). Cognitive-behavioral therapy in historical perspective. In B. Bongar & L. E. Beutler (Eds.), *Comprehensive textbook of psychotherapy: Theory and practice* (pp. 140–158). New York: Oxford University Press.

Mellers, R. A., Schwartz, A., & Cooke, D. J. (1998). Judgments and decision making. *Annual Review of Psychology, 49,* 447–477.

Mello, N. K., Mendelson, J. H., Bree, M. P., & Lukas, S. E. (1989). Buprenorphine suppresses cocaine self-administration by rhesus monkeys. *Science, 245,* 859–862.

Meltzer, H. Y. (1997). Treatment-resistant schizophrenia: The role of clozapine. *Current Medical Research Opinion, 14,* 1–20.

Melzack, R. (1973). *The puzzle of pain.* New York: Basic Books.

Melzack, R., & Wall, P. D. (1965). Pain mechanisms: A new theory. *Science, 150,* 971–979.

Menaker, M., & Vogelbaum, M. A. (1993). Mutant circadian period as a marker of suprachiasmatic nucleus function. *Journal of Biological Rhythms, 8,* 93–98.

Mendoza-Denton, R., Ayduk, O., Mischel, W., Shoda, Y., & Testa, A. (2001). Person x situation interactionism in self-encoding (I am. . . when. . .): implications for affect regulation and social information processing. *Journal of Personality and Social Psychology, 80,* 533–544.

Menini, A., Picco, C., & Firestein, S. (1995, February 2). Quantal-like current fluctuations induced by odorants in olfactory receptor cell. *Nature, 373,* 435–437.

Menkes, M. S., Matthews, K. A., Krantz, D. S., Lundberg, V., Mead, L. A., Qaqish, B., Liang, K. Y., Thomas, C. B., Pearson, T. A. (1989). Cardiovascular reactivity to the cold pressor as a predictor of hypertension. *Hypertension, 14,* 524–530.

Mennella, J. A., & Beauchamp, G. K. (1996). The human infant's response to vanilla flavors in mother's milk and formula. *Infant Behavior and Development, 19,* 13–19.

Merzenich, M. M. (1996). Language comprehension in language-learning impaired children improved with acoustically modified speech. *Science, 271,* 81–84.

Mesquita, B., & Frijda, N. H. (1992). Cultural variations in emotions: A review. *Psychological Bulletin, 112,* 179–204.

Messick, S. (1982). Test validity and the ethics of assessment. *Diagnostica, 28*(1), 1–25.

Messick, S. (1989). Validity. In R. L. Linn (Ed.), *Educational measurement* (3rd ed., pp. 13–103). New York: Macmillan.

Messinger, A., Squire, L. R., Zola, S. M., & Albright, T. D. (2001). Neuronal representations of stimulus associations develop in the temporal lobe during learning. *Proceedings of the National Academy of Science, 98,* 12239–12244.

Metalsky, G. I., Joiner, T. E., Jr., Hardin, T. S., & Abramson, L. Y. (1993). Depressive reactions to failure in a naturalistic setting: A test of the hopelessness and self-esteem theories of depression. *Journal of Abnormal Psychology, 102,* 101–109.

Metzger, M. M. (2001). Glucose enhancement of a facial recognition task in young adults. *Physiology and Behavior, 68,* 549–553.

Metzinger, T. (Ed.). (2000). *Neural correlates of consciousness: Empirical and conceptual questions.* Cambridge: MIT Press.

Meyer, B. H. F. L., Ehrhardt, A. A., Rosen, L. R., & Gruen, R. S. (1995). Prenatal estrogens and the development of homosexual orientation. *Developmental Psychology, 31*(1), 12–21.

Meyer, G. J., Finn, S. E., Eyde, L. D., Kay, G. G., Moreland, K. L., Dies, R. R., et al. (2001). Psychological testing and psychological assessment: A review of evidence and issues. *American Psychologist, 56,* 128–165.

Meyer, J. D., & Salovey, P. (1997). What is emotional intelligence? In P. Salovey & D. Sluyter (Eds.), *Emotional development and emotional intelligence* (pp. 3–31). New York: Basic Books.

Meyer, R. G. (1975). A behavioral treatment of sleepwalking associated with test anxiety. *Behavior Therapy and Experimental Psychiatry, 6,* 167–168.

Meyers, C., & Jones, T. B. (1993). *Promoting active learning: Strategies for the college classroom.* San Francisco: Jossey-Bass.

Mezzacappa, E. S., Katkin, E. S. & Palmer, S. N. (1999). Epinephrine, arousal and emotion: A new look at two-factor theory. *Cognition and Emotion, 13,* 181–199.

Miceli, G., Fouch, E., Capasso, R., Shelton, J. R., Tomaiuolo, F., & Caramazza, A. (2001). The dissociation of color from form and function knowledge. *Nature Neuroscience, 4,* 662–667.

Michael, R. T., Wadsworth, J., Feinleib, J., Johnson, A. M., Laumann, E. O., & Wellings, K. (1998). Private sexual behavior, public opinion, and public health policy related to sexually transmitted diseases: A US-British comparison. *American Journal of Public Health, 88,* 749–754.

Michaud, D. S., Giovannucci, E., Willett, W. C., Colditz, G. A., Stampfer, M. J., & Fuchs, C. S. (2001). Physical activity, obesity, height, and the risk of pancreatic cancer. *Journal of the American Medical Association, 286,* 921–929.

Middlebrooks, J. C., Clock, A. E., Xu, L., & Green, D. M. (1994, May 6). A panoramic code for sound location by cortical neurons. *Science, 264,* 842–844.

Mikelson, K. D., Kessler, R. C., & Shaver, P. R. (1997). Adult attachment in a nationally representative sample. *Journal of Personality and Social Psychology, 72,* 1092–1106.

Miklowitz, D. J., & Alloy, L. B. (1999). Psychosocial factors in the course and treatment of bipolar disorder: Introduction to the special section. *Journal of Abnormal Psychology, 108,* 555–557.

Milberger, S., Biederman, J., Faraone, S. V., & Chen, L. (1997). Further evidence of an association between attention-deficit/hyperactivity disorder and cigarette smoking: Findings from a high-risk sample of siblings. *American Journal on Addictions, 6,* 205–217.

Milgram, S. (1963). Behavioral study of obedience. *Journal of Abnormal and Social Psychology, 67,* 371–378.

Milgram, S. (1965). Some conditions of obedience and disobedience to authority. *Human Relations, 18,* 57–76.

Milgram, S. (1974). *Obedience to authority.* New York: Harper & Row.

Milgram, S. (1977, October). Subject reaction: The neglected factor in the ethics of experimentation. *Hastings Center Report,* pp. 19–23.

Miller, C. L., Miceli, P. J., Whitman, T. L., & Borkowski, J. G. (1996). Cognitive readiness to parent and intellectual-emotional development in children of adolescent mothers. *Developmental Psychology, 32,* 533–541.

Miller, E. K., & Cohen, J. D. (2001). An integrative theory of prefrontal cortex function. *Annual Review of Neuroscience, 24,* 167–202.

Miller, G. (1956). The magical number seven, plus or minus two: Some limits on our capacity to process information. *Psychological Review, 63,* 81–97.

Miller, G. A. (1991). *The science of words.* New York: Scientific American Library.

Miller, J. (2001). The cultural grounding of social psychological theory. In A. Tesser & N. Schwarz (Eds.), *Blackwell handbook of social psychology: Intraindividual processes* (pp. 22–43). Oxford, England: Blackwell.

Miller, J. G. (1994). Cultural diversity in the morality of caring: Individually oriented versus duty-based interpersonal moral codes. *Cross-cultural Research, 28,* 3–39.

Miller, J. G. (1999). Cultural psychology: Implications for basic psychological theory. *Psychological Science, 10,* 85–91.

Miller, J. G., & Bersoff, D. M. (1994). Cultural influences on the moral status of reciprocity and the discounting of endogenous motivation. *Personality and Social Psychology Bulletin, 20,* 592–607.

Miller, K. F., Smith, C. M., Zhu, J., & Zhang, H. (1995). Preschool origins of cross-national differences in mathematical competence: The role of number-naming systems. *Psychological Science, 6,* 56–60.

Miller, L. K. (1999). The savant syndrome: Intellectual impairment and exceptional skill. *Psychological Bulletin, 125,* 31–46.

Miller, L. T., & Vernon, P. A. (1992). The general factor in short-term memory, intelligence, and reaction time. *Intelligence, 16,* 5–29.

Miller, L. T., & Vernon, P. A. (1997). Developmental changes in speed of information processing in young children. *Developmental Psychology, 33,* 549–554.

Miller, M. G., & Teates, J. F. (1985). Acquisition of dietary self-selection in rats with normal and impaired oral sensation. *Physiology and Behavior, 34*(3), 401–408.

Miller, N., & Davidson-Podgorny, G. (1987). Theoretical models of intergroup relations and the use of cooperative teams as an intervention for desegregated settings. In C. Hendrick (Ed.), *Group processes and intergroup relations* (pp. 41–67). Newbury Park, CA: Sage.

Miller, N. E. (1959). Liberalization of basic S-R concepts: Extensions to conflict behavior, motivation, and social learning. In S. Koch (Ed.), *Psychology: A study of science* (Vol. 2, pp. 196–292). New York: McGraw-Hill.

Miller, T. Q., Heath, L., Molcan, J. R., & Dugoni, B. L. (1991). Imitative violence in the real world: A reanalysis of homicide rates following championship prize fights. *Aggressive Behavior, 17,* 121–134.

Millon, T., & Davis, R. D. (1996). *Disorders of personality. DSM-IV and beyond* (2nd ed.). New York: Wiley.

Milner, B. (1965). Visually-guided maze learning in man: Effects of bilateral hippocampal, bilateral frontal, and unilateral cerebral lesions. *Neuropsychologia, 3,* 317–338.

Milner, B. (1966). Amnesia following operation on temporal lobes. In C. W. M. Whitty & O. L. Zangwill (Eds.), *Amnesia*. London: Butterworth.

Milner, D. (1983). *Children and race*. Beverly Hills, CA: Sage.

Miltenberger, R. G. (2001). *Behavior modification: Principles and procedures*. Pacific Grove, CA: Wadsworth.

Minimi, H., & Dallenbach, K. M. (1946). The effect of activity upon learning and retention in the cockroach. *American Journal of Psychology, 59*, 1–58.

Minuchin, S., & Fishman, H. (1981). *Family therapy techniques*. Cambridge: Harvard University Press.

Miranda, J., & Green, B. L. (1999). The need for mental health services research focusing on poor young women. *Journal of Mental Health Policy and Economics, 2*, 73–89.

Mischel, W., & Shoda, Y. (1999). Integrating dispositions and processing dynamics. In L. Pervin & O. John (Eds.) *Handbook of personality: Theory and research* (2nd ed., pp. 197–218). New York: Guilford.

Mishina, T. M. (1999). Russian group therapies mirror culture. *Psychology International, 10*, 1, 4–5.

Mitchell, D. B. (1991). Implicit memory, explicit theories. *Contemporary Psychology, 36*, 1060–1061.

Mitchell, K. J., & Zaragoza, M. S. (1996). Repeated exposure to suggestion and false memory: The role of contextual variability. *Journal of Memory and Learning, 35*, 246–260.

Miura, I. T., Okomoto, Y., Kim, C. C., Steere, M., & Fayol, M. (1993). First graders' cognitive representation of number and understanding of place value. *Journal of Educational Psychology, 81*, 109–114.

Moen, P., Erickson, W. A., Agarwal, M., Fields, V., & Todd, L. (2000). *The Cornell Retirement and Well-Being Study. Final Report*. Ithaca, NY: Cornell University.

Moergen, S., Merkel, W., & Brown, S. (1990). The use of covert sensitization and social skills training in the treatment of an obscene telephone caller. *Journal of Behavior Therapy and Experimental Psychiatry, 21*, 269–275.

Mogenson, G. J. (1976). Neural mechanisms of hunger: Current status and future prospects. In D. Novin, W. Wyrwicka, & G. Bray (Eds.), *Hunger: Basic mechanisms and clinical applications*. New York: Raven.

Mokdad, A. H., Bowman, B. A., Ford, E. S., Vinicor, F., Marks, J. S., & Koplan, J. P. (2001). The continuing epidemics of obesity and diabetes in the United States. *Journal of the American Medical Association, 286*, 1195–1200.

Mokdad, A. H., Serdula, M. K, Dietz, W. H., Bowman, B. A., Marks, J. S., & Koplan, J. P. (2000). The continuing epidemic of obesity in the United States. *Journal of the American Medical Association, 284*, 1650–1651.

Molden, D. C., & Dweck. C. S. (2000). Meaning and motivation. In C Sansone & J. M. Harackiewicz (Eds.), *Intrinsic and extrinsic motivation: The search for optimal motivation and performance*. San Diego: Academic Press.

Moldin, S. O., & Gottesman, I. I. (1997). At issue: Genes, experience, and chance in schizophrenia-positioning for the 21st century. *Schizophrenia Bulletin, 23*, 547–561.

Molsa, P. K., Marttila, R. J., & Rinne, U. K. (1995). Long-term survival and predictors of mortality in Alzheimer's disease and multi-infarct dementia. *Acta Neurologica Scandinavica, 91*, 159–164.

Monane, M., Leichter, D., & Lewis, O. (1984). Physical abuse in psychiatrically hospitalized children and adolescents. *Journal of the American Academy of Child and Adolescent Psychiatry, 23*, 653–658.

Moniz, E (1948). How I came to perform prefrontal leucotomy. *Proceedings of the first international congress of psychosurgery* (pp. 7–18). Lisbon: Edicoes Atica.

Monroe, S., Thase, M., & Simons, A. (1992). Social factors and psychobiology of depression: Relations between life stress and rapid eye movement sleep latency. *Journal of Abnormal Psychology, 101*, 528–537.

Monroe, S. M., Rohde, P., Seeley, J. R., & Lewinsohn, P. M. (1999). Life events and depression in adolescence: Relationship loss as a prospective risk factor for first onset of major depressive disorder. *Journal of Abnormal Psychology, 108*, 606–614.

Monteith, M. J., Zuwerink, J. R., & Devine, P. G. (1994). Prejudice and prejudice reduction: Classic challenges and contemporary approaches. In P. G. Devine, D. L. Hamilton, & T. M. Ostrom (Eds.), *Social cognition: Impact on social psychology* (pp. 324–346). San Diego: Academic Press.

Montmayeur, J. P., Liberles, S. D., Matsunami, H., & Buck, L. B. (2001). A candidate taste receptor gene near a sweet taste locus. *Nature Neuroscience, 4*, 492–498.

Moore, R. Y. (1997). Circadian rhythms: Basic neurobiology and clinical applications. *Annual Review of Medicine, 48*, 253–266.

Moran, A. (1996). *The psychology of concentration in sports performance: A cognitive analysis*. Hove, England: Psychology Press.

Moran, D. R. (2000, June). *Is active learning for me?* Poster presented at APS Preconvention Teaching Institute, Denver.

Moran, P. W. (2000). The adaptive practice of psychotherapy in the managed care era. *Psychiatric Clinics of North America, 23*, 383–402.

Moreland, R. L., & Beach, S. R. (1992). Exposure effects in the classroom: The development of affinity among students. *Journal of Experimental Social Psychology, 28*, 255–276.

Morgan, C. D., & Murray, H. A. (1935). A method for investigating fantasy: The thematic appreception test. *Archives of Neurology and Psychiatry, 34*, 289–306.

Morgan, D., Diamond, D. M., Gottschall, P. E., Ugen, K. E., Dickey, C., Hardy, J., et al. (2000). A beta peptide vaccination prevents memory loss in an animal model of Alzheimer's disease. *Nature, 408*, 982–985.

Morganstern, J., Labouvie, E., McCrady, B. S., Kahler, C. W., & Frey, R. M. (1997). Affiliation with Alcoholics Anonymous after treatment: A study of its therapeutic effects and mechanism of action. *Journal of Consulting and Clinical Psychology, 65*, 768–777.

Morgenthaler, J., & Dean, W. (1990). *Smart drugs and nutrients*. Santa Cruz, CA: B & J Publications.

Morisse, D., Batra, L., Hess, L., Silverman, R., & Corrigan, P. (1996). A demonstration of a token economy for the real world. *Applied and Preventative Psychology, 5*, 41–46.

Morris, C. D., Bransford, J. D., & Franks, J. J. (1977). Levels of processing versus transfer appropriate processing. *Journal of Verbal Learning and Verbal Behavior, 16*, 519–533.

Morris, J. S., DeGelder, B., Weiskrantz, L., & Dolan, R. J. (2001). Differential extrageniculostriate and amygdala responses to presentation of emotional faces in a cortically blind field. *Brain, 124*, 1241–1252.

Morris, J. S., Ohman, A., & Dolan, R. J. (1998). Conscious and unconscious emotional learning in the human amygdala. *Nature, 393*, 467–470.

Morris, L. (2000, December 5). Hold the anaesthetic. I'll hypnotise myself instead. *Daily Mail*, p. 25.

Morris, M. W., & Peng, K. (1994). Culture and cause: American and Chinese attributions for social and physical events. *Journal of Personality and Social Psychology, 67*, 949–971.

Mortimer, R. G., Goldsteen, K., Armstrong, R. W., & Macrina, D. (1988). *Effects of enforcement, incentives, and publicity on seat belt use in Illinois*. University of Illinois, Dept. of Health & Safety Studies, Final Report to Illinois Dept. of Transportation (Safety Research Report 88–11).

Moscovici, S. (1985). Social influence and conformity. In G. Lindzey & E. Aronson (Eds.), *The handbook of social psychology* (Vol. 2, 3rd ed.). New York: Random House.

Moscovici, S. (1994). Three concepts: Minority, conflict, and behavioral style. In S. Moscovici, A. Mucchi-Faina, & A. Maass (Eds.), *Minority influence* (pp. 233–251) Chicago: Nelson-Hall.

Most, S. B., Simons, D. J., Scholl, B. J., Jimenez, R., Clifford, E., & Chabris, C. F. (2001). How not to be seen: The contribution of similarity and selective ignoring to sustained inattentional blindness. *Psychological Science, 12*, 9–17.

Mroczek, D. K., & Kolarz, C. M. (1998). The effect of age on positive and negative affect: A developmental perspective on happiness. *Journal of Personality and Social Psychology, 75*, 1333–1349.

Muchinsky, P. (1993). *Psychology applied to work* (4th ed.). Pacific Grove, CA: Brooks/Cole.

Muir, J. L. (1997). Acetylcholine, aging, and Alzheimer's disease. *Pharmacological and Biochemical Behavior, 56*(4), 687–696.

Mullen, B. (1986). Atrocity as a function of lynch mob composition: A self-attention perspective. *Personality and Social Psychology Bulletin, 12*, 187–197.

Mumford, G. (2000). Interest in human factors peaks at medical error summit *APS Psychological Science Agenda, 13,* 11.

Munroe, R. H., & Munroe, R. L. (1994). Behavior across cultures: Results from observational studies. In W. J. Lonner & R. S. Malpass (Eds.), *Psychology and culture* (pp. 107–112). Boston: Allyn & Bacon.

Murray, B. (1995, June). Head Start sharpens focus on mental health. *APA Monitor,* p. 39.

Murray, B. (2000). Learning from real life. *APA Monitor, 31,* 72–73.

Murray, E. A., & Mishkin, M. (1985). Amygdalectomy impairs crossmodal association in monkeys. *Science, 228,* 604–606.

Murray, H. A. (1938). *Explorations in personality.* New York: Oxford University Press.

Murray, J. A., & Terry, D. (1999). Parental reactions to infant death: The effects of resources and coping strategies. *Journal of Social and Clinical Psychology, 18,* 341–369.

Murthy, C. V., & Panda, S. C. (1987). A study of intelligence, socioeconomic status and birth order among children belonging to SC-ST and non-SC-ST groups. *Indian Journal of Behaviour, 11,* 25–30.

Myers, B. J. (1987). Mother-infant bonding as a critical period. In M. H. Bornstein (Ed.), *Sensitive periods in development: Interdisciplinary perspectives.* Hillsdale, NJ: Erlbaum.

Myers, D. G. (2000a). *The American paradox: Spiritual hunger in an age of plenty.* New Haven, CT: Yale University Press.

Myers, D. G. (2000b). The funds, friends, and faith of happy people. *American Psychologist, 55,* 56–57.

Myers, M. G., Reeves, R. A., Oh, P. I., & Joyner, C. D. (1996). Overtreatment of hypertension in the community? *American Journal of Hypertension, 9,* 419–425.

Myers, P. I., & Hammill, D. D. (1990). *Learning disabilities: Basic concepts, assessment practices, and instructional strategies.* Austin, TX: Pro-Ed.

Myers, S. L. (2001, March 12). Sub's crew may have hesitated to question a trusted captain. *New York Times.*

Myerson, J., Rank, M. R., Raines, F. Q., & Schnitzler, M. A. (1998). Race and general cognitive ability. *Psychological Science, 9,* 139–142.

Nader, K., Bechara, A., & Van der Kooy, D. (1997). Neurobiological constraints on behavioral models of motivation. *Annual Review of Psychology, 48,* 85–114.

Nader, K., Schafe, G. E., & Le Doux, J. E. (2000). Fear memories require protein synthesis in the amygdala for reconsolidation after retrieval. *Nature, 406,* 722–726.

Naëgelé, B., Thouvard, V., Pépin, J.-L., Lévy, P., Bonnet, C., Perret, J. E., et al. (1995). Deficits of cognitive functions in patients with sleep apnea syndrome. *Sleep, 18*(1), 43–52.

Naglieri, J. A., Das, J. P., Stevens, J. J., & Ledbetter, M. F. (1991). Confirmatory factor analysis of planning, attention, simultaneous, and successive cognitive processing tasks. *Journal of School Psychology, 29,* 1–17.

Nagy, T. F. (1999). *Ethics in plain English: An illustrative casebook for psychologists.* Washington, DC: American Psychological Association.

Naito, M., & Miura, H. (2001). Japanese children's numerical competencies: Age-and schooling-related influences on the development of number concepts and addition skills. *Developmental Psychology, 37,* 217–230.

Nakamura, J., & Csikszentmihalyi, M. (2001). Catalytic creativity. *American Psychologist, 56,* 337–341.

Nakayama, K. (1994). James J. Gibson: An appreciation. *Psychological Review, 101,* 329–335.

Nalbantoglu, J., Tirado-Santiago, G., Lahsaini, A., Poirier, J., Goncalves, O., Verge, G., et al. (1997). Impaired learning and LTP in mice expressing the carboxy terminus of the Alzheimer amyloid precursor protein. *Nature, 387,* 500–505.

Narayanan, L., Menon, S., & Levine, E. L. (1995). Personality structure: A culture-specific examination of the five-factor model. *Journal of Personality Assessment, 64,* 51–62.

Narita, N., Narita, M., Takashima, S., Nakayama, M., Nagai, T., & Okado, N. (2001). Serotonin transporter gene variation is a risk factor for sudden infant death syndrome in the Japanese population. *Pediatrics, 107,* 690–692.

Narrow, W. E., Rae, D. S., Robins, L. N., & Regier, D. A. (2002). Revised prevalence estimates of mental disorders in the United States: Using a clinical significance criterion to reconcile 2 surveys' estimates. *Archives of General Psychiatry, 59,* 115–123.

Nathan, P. E., & Langenbucher, J. W. (1999). Psychopathology: Description and classification. *Annual Review of Psychology, 50,* 79–107.

Nathan, P. E., Stuart, S. P., & Dolan, S. L. (2000). Research on psychotherapy efficacy and effectiveness: Between Scylla and Charybdis? *Psychological Bulletin, 126,* 964–981.

National Advisory Mental Health Council. (1996). Basic behavioral science research for mental health: Vulnerability and resilience. *American Psychologist, 51,* 22–28.

National Cancer Institute. (1994). *National Cancer Institute fact book, 1994.* Washington, DC: U.S. Department of Health and Human Services.

National Center for Education Statistics. (1998). *Digest of Education Statistics, 1998.* Washington, DC: United States Department of Education.

National Center for Education Statistics. (2000). *National assessment of education progress.* Washington, DC: NCES.

National Center for Health Statistics. (1997). *Youth Risk Behavior Survey.* Washington, DC: Centers for Disease Control and Prevention.

National Center for Health Statistics. (2000). *Trends in pregnancies and pregnancy rates by outcome: Estimates for the United States, 1976–1996.* Washington, DC: Centers for Disease Control and Prevention.

National Center for Health Statistics. (2001). *Births, marriages, divorces, and deaths: Provisional data for January-December 2000.* Hyattsville, Maryland: Public Health Service.

National Computer Systems. (1992). *Catalog of assessment instruments, reports, and services.* Minneapolis: NCS.

National Drug Intelligence Center. (2001, October 6). *Information bulletin oxycontin diversion and abuse* [Online]. Available: http://www.usdoj.gov/ndic/pubs/651

National Information Center for Children and Youth with Disabilities. (2000, June 18). *NICHCY Fact Sheet #7.* Available: http://www.ldonline.org/ld_indepth/general_info/gen-2.html

National Institute for Occupational Safety and Health. (1999). *Stress at work.* Washington, DC: NIOSH Publication No. 99–101.

National Institute of Mental Health. (1995). *Medications.* Washington, DC: USDHHS.

National Institute of Mental Health. (1998). *Mental illness in America: The National Institute of Mental Health agenda.* Washington, DC: NIMH.

National Institute on Alcohol Abuse and Alcoholism. (2000). *Tenth special report to the U.S. Congress on alcohol and health.* Washington, DC: National Institutes of Health (Publication No. 00–1583).

National Institute on Drug Abuse. (1999). *Cocaine abuse and addiction.* Washington, DC: NIH Publication No. 99–4342.

National Institute on Drug Abuse. (2000a). *Epidemiologic trends in drug abuse: Advance report, December 1999.* Washington, DC: National Institutes of Health.

National Institute on Drug Abuse. (2000b). Facts about MDMA (Ecstasy). *NIDA Notes, 14* [On-line]. Available: http://165.122.78.61/NIDA_Notes/NNVol14N4/tearoff.html

National Joint Committee on Learning Disabilities. (1994). *Collective perspective on issues affecting learning disabilities.* Austin, TX: Pro-Ed.

National Science Foundation. (2000). *1999 survey of earned doctorates.* National Science Foundation: Arlington, VA.

National Science Foundation. (2001). *1999 survey of doctorate recipients.* National Science Foundation: Arlington, VA.

National Task Force on the Prevention and Treatment of Obesity. (2000). Dieting and the development of eating disorders in overweight and obese adults. *Archives of Internal Medicine, 160,* 2581–2589.

Needham, A., & Baillargeon, R. (1999). Effects of prior experience on 4.5 month-old infants' object segregation. *Infant Behavior and Development, 21,* 1–24.

Needleman, H. (1996). Bone lead levels and delinquent behavior. *Journal of the American Medical Association, 275,* 363–369.

Neher, A. (1991). Maslow's theory of motivation: A critique. *Journal of Humanistic Psychology, 31,* 89–112.

Nehlig, A., Daval, J. L., & Debry, G. (1992). Caffeine and the central nervous system: Mechanisms of action, biochemical, metabolic and psychostimulant effects. *Brain Research Review, 17,* 139–170.

Neisser, U. (1967). *Cognitive psychology.* New York: Appleton-Century-Crofts.

Neisser, U. (1997). Never a dull moment. *American Psychologist, 52,* 79–81.

Neisser, U. (1998). *The rising curve: Long-term gains in I.Q. and related measures.* Washington, DC: American Psychological Association.

Neisser, U. (2000). Memorists. In U. Neisser & I. E. Hyman Jr. (Eds.), *Memory observed* (2nd ed., pp. 475–478). New York: Worth.

Neisser, U., Boodoo, G., Bouchard, T. J., Boykin, A. W., Brody, N., Ceci, S. J., et al. (1996). Intelligence: Knowns and unknowns. *American Psychologist, 51,* 77–101.

Neitz, M., & Neitz, J. (1995, February 17). Numbers and ratios of visual pigment genes for normal red-green color vision. *Science, 267,* 1013–1016.

Nelson, C. A. (1997). The neurobiological basis of early memory development. In N. Cowan (Ed.), *The development of memory in childhood: Studies in developmental psychology* (pp. 41–82). Hove, England: Psychology Press/Erlbaum/Taylor & Francis.

Nelson, C. A., & Bloom F. E. (1997). Child development and neuroscience. *Child Development, 68,* 970–987.

Nelson, D. L. (1999). Implicit memory. In D. E. Morris & M. Gruneberg (Eds.), *Theoretical aspects of memory.* London: Routledge.

Nelson, D. L., McKinney, V. M., & Bennett, D. J. (1999). Conscious and automatic uses of memory in cued recall and recognition. In B. H. Challis & B. M. Velichkovsky (Eds.), *Stratification in cognition and consciousness* (p. 173–202). Amsterdam: John Benjamins.

Nelson, D. L., McKinney, V. M., Gee, N. R., & Janczura, G. A. (1998). Interpreting the influence of implicitly activated memories on recall and recognition. *Psychological Review, 105,* 299–324.

Nelson, E. C., Heath, A. C., Madden, P. A. F., Cooper, M. L., Dinwiddie, S. H., Bucholz, K. K., et al. (2002). Association between self-reported childhood sexual abuse and adverse psychosocial outcomes: Results from a twin study. *Archives of General Psychiatry, 59,* 139–145.

Nelson, K. (1986). Event knowledge and cognitive development. In K. Nelson (Ed.), *Event knowledge: Structure and function in development* (pp. 1–19). Hillsdale, NJ: Erlbaum.

Nelson, K. (1993). The psychological and social origins of autobiographical memory. *Psychological Science, 4,* 7–14.

Nelson, R. J., Demas, G. E., Huang, P. L., Fishman, M. C., Dawson, V. L., Dawson, T. M., & Snyder, S. H. (1995). Behavioral abnormalities in male mice lacking neuronal nitric oxide synthase. *Nature, 378,* 383–386.

Nelson-LeGall, S., & Resnick, L. (1998). Help seeking, achievement motivation, and the social practice of intelligence in school. In S. A. Karabenick (Ed.), *Strategic help seeking* (pp. 39–60). Mahwah, NJ: Erlbaum.

Nemeroff, C. B. (1998). Psychopharmacology of affective disorders in the 21st century. *Biological Psychiatry, 44,* 517–525.

Neugarten, B. L. (1977). Personality and aging. In J. E. Birren & K. W. Schaie (Eds.), *Handbook of the psychology of aging.* New York: Van Nostrand Reinhold.

Neumann, C. S., Grimes, K., Walker, E. F., & Baum, K. (1995). Developmental pathways to schizophrenia: Behavioral subtypes. *Journal of Abnormal Psychology, 104,* 558–566.

Neville, H. A., Heppner, M. J., Louie, C. E., Thompson, C. E., Brooks, L., & Baker, C. E. (1996). The impact of multicultural training on white racial identity attitudes and therapy competencies. *Professional Psychology: Research and Practice, 27,* 83–89.

Neville, H. J., Bavelier, D., Corina, D., Rauschecker, J., Karni, A., Lalwani, A., et al. (1998). Cerebral organization for language in deaf and hearing subjects: Biological constraints and effects of experience. *Proceedings of the National Academy of Science USA, 95,* 922–929.

Newcombe, N., & Fox, N. A. (1994). Infantile amnesia: Through a glass darkly. *Child Development, 65,* 31–40.

Newcombe, N. S., Drummey, A. B., Fox, N. A., Lie, E., & Ottinger-Alberts, W. (2000). Remembering early childhood: How much, how, and why (or why not). *Current Directions in Psychological Science, 9,* 55–58.

Newell, A., & Simon, H. A. (1972). *Human problem solving.* Englewood Cliffs, NJ: Prentice-Hall.

Newman, J. P., Wolff, W. T., & Hearst, E. (1980). The feature positive effect in adult human subjects. *Journal of Experimental Psychology: Human Learning and Memory, 6,* 630–650.

Newman, R., Phelps, R., Sammons, M. T., Dunivin, D. L., & Cullen, E. A. (2000). Evaluation of Psychopharmacology Demonstration Project: A retrospective analysis. *Professional Psychology: Research & Practice, 31,* 598–603.

Newsome, J. T. (1999). Another side to caregiving: Negative reactions to being helped. *Current Directions in Psychological Science, 8,* 183–187.

Newsome, J. T., & Schulz, R. (1998). Caregiving from the recipient's perspective: Negative reactions to being helped. *Health Psychology, 17,* 172–181.

NIAAA (National Institute on Alcohol Abuse and Alcoholism). (1998, May 13). News release.

NIAAA (National Institute on Alcohol Abuse and Alcoholism). (2000). *Tenth special report to the U.S. Congress on alcohol and health* (Publication No. 00–1583). Washington, DC: National Institutes of Health.

NICHD Early Child Care Research Network. (1997). The effects of infant child care on infant-mother attachment security: Results of the NICHD Study of Early Child Care. *Child Development, 68,* 860–879.

NICHD Early Child Care Research Network. (1998). Early child care and self-control, compliance and problem behavior at 24 and 36 months. *Child Development, 69,* 1145–1170.

NICHD Early Child Care Research Network. (1999). Chronicity of maternal depressive symptoms, maternal sensitivity, and child functioning at 36 months. *Developmental Psychology, 35,* 1297–1310.

NICHD Early Child Care Research Network. (2001, April). *Further explorations of the detected effects of quantity of early child care on socioemotional adjustment.* Paper presented at the biennial meetings of the Society for Research in Child Development, Minneapolis.

Nichols, R. (1978). Twin studies of ability, personality, and interests. *Homo, 29,* 158–173.

Nicholson, A. N., Pascoe, P. A., Spencer, M. B., Stone, B. M., Roehis, T., & Roth, T. (1986). Sleep after transmeridian fights. *Lancet, 2,* 1205–1208.

Nicholson, I. R., & Neufeld, R. W. J. (1993). Classification of the schizophrenias according to symptomatology: A two factor model. *Journal of Abnormal Psychology, 102,* 259–270.

Nickell, J. (1997, January/February). Sleuthing a psychic sleuth. *Skeptical Inquirer, 21,* 18–19.

Nickell, J. (2001). Exorcism! Driving out the nonsense. *Skeptical Inquirer, 25,* 20–24.

Nickerson, R. A., & Adams, M. J. (1979). Long-term memory for a common object. *Cognitive Psychology, 11,* 287–307.

Niedenthal, P. M., Setterlund, M. B., & Wherry, M. B. (1992). Possible self-complexity and affective reactions to goal-relevant evaluation. *Journal of Personality and Social Psychology, 63,* 5–16.

Nielsen Media. (1990). *1990 report on television.* New York: Author.

Niemela, M., & Saarinen, J. (2000). Visual search for grouped versus ungrouped icons in a computer interface. *Human Factors, 42,* 630–635.

Nienhuys, J. W. (2001). Spontaneous human combustion: Requiem for Phyllis. *Skeptical Inquirer, 25,* 28–34.

Nietzel, M. T. (1999). Psychology applied to the legal system. In A. M. Stec & D. A. Bernstein (Eds.), *Psychology: Fields of application.* Boston: Houghton Mifflin.

Nietzel, M. T., & Bernstein, D. A. (1987). *Introduction to clinical psychology* (2nd ed.). New York: Prentice-Hall.

Nietzel, M. T., Bernstein, D. A., Kramer, G, & Milich, R. (2003). *Introduction to clinical psychology* (6th ed.). Englewood Cliffs, NJ: Prentice-Hall.

Nietzel, M. T., Speltz, M. L., McCauley, E. A., & Bernstein, D. A. (1998). *Abnormal psychology.* Boston: Allyn & Bacon.

Nigg, J. T. (2000). On inhibition/disinhibition in developmental psychopathology: Views from cognitive and personality psychology and a working inhibition taxonomy. *Psychological Bulletin, 126,* 220–246.

Nigg, J. T. (2001). Is ADHD a disinhibitory disorder? *Psychological Bulletin, 127,* 571–598.

NIH Consensus Conference. (1998). Acupuncture. *Journal of the American Medical Association, 280,* 1518–1524.

Nijhawan, R. (1997). Visual decomposition of colour through motion extrapolation. *Nature, 386,* 66–69.

Nilsson, G. (1996). Some forms of memory improve as people age. *APA Monitor,* p. 27.

NIMH (National Institute of Mental Health). (1998). *Genetics and mental disorders: Report of the National Institute of Mental Health's genetics workgroup.* Rockville, MD: Author.

Nisbet, R. E., Peng, K., Choi, I., & Norenzayan, A. (2002). Culture and systems of thought. *Psychological Review.*

Nisbett, R. (1993). Violence and American regional culture. *American Psychologist, 48,* 441–449.

Niznikiewicz, M. A., O'Donnell, B. F., Nestor, P. G., Smith, L., Law, S., Karapelou, M., et al. (1997). ERP assessment of visual and auditory language processing in schizophrenia. *Journal of Abnormal Psychology, 106,* 85–94.

Noble, H. B. (2000, January 25). Outgrowth of new field of tissue engineering. *New York Times.*

Nobler, M. S., Oquendo, M. A., Kegeles, L. S., Malone, K. M., Campbell, C., Sackeim, H. A., & Mann, J. J. (2001). Decreased Regional Brain Metabolism After ETC. *American Journal of Psychiatry, 158,* 305–308.

Nolan, R. P., Spanos, N. P., Hayward, A. A., & Scott, H. A. (1995). The efficacy of hypnotic and nonhypnotic response-based imagery for self-managing recurrent headache. *Imagination, Cognition, and Personality, 14*(3), 183–201.

Nolen-Hoeksema, S. (1990). *Sex differences in depression.* Stanford, CA: Stanford University Press.

Nolen-Hoeksema, S. (2001). Gender differences in depression. *Current Directions in Psychological Science, 10,* 173–176.

Nolen-Hoeksema, S., Larson, J., & Grayson, C. (1999). Explaining gender differences in depression. *Journal of Personality and Social Psychology, 77,* 1061–1072.

Nolen-Hoeksma, S., Morrow, J., & Fredrickson, N. (1993). Response styles and the duration of episodes of depressed mood. *Journal of Abnormal Psychology, 102,* 20–28.

Noll, R. B. (1994). Hypnotherapy for warts in children and adolescents. *Journal of Developmental and Behavioral Pediatrics, 15*(3), 170–173.

Norcross, J. C., Santrock, J. W., Campbell, L. F., Smith, T. P., Sommer, R., & Zuckerman, E. L. (2000). *Authoritative guide to self-help resources in mental health.* New York: The Guilford Press.

Norenzayan, A., & Nisbett, R. E. (2000). Culture and causal cognition. *Current Directions in Psychological Science, 9,* 132–135.

Norman, D. A. (1988). *The psychology of everyday things.* New York: Basic Books.

Northcut, T. B., & Heller, N. R. (Eds.). (1999). *Enhancing psychodynamic therapy with cognitive-behavioral techniques.* Northvale, NJ: Aronson.

Nottebohm, F. (1985). Neuronal replacement in adulthood. *Annals of the New York Academy of Science, 457,* 143–161.

Novak, M. A. (1991, July). Psychologists care deeply about animals. *APA Monitor,* p. 4.

Nowak, M. A., Komarova, N. L., & Niyogi, P. (2001). Evolution of universal grammar. *Science, 291,* 114–118.

Nowak, M. A., May, R. M., & Sigmund, K. (1995). The arithmetics of mutual help. *Scientific American, 272,* 76–81.

Nowinski, J. (1999). Self-help groups for addictions. In B. S. McCrady & E. E. Epstein (Eds.), *Addictions: A comprehensive guidebook* (pp. 328–347). New York: Oxford University Press.

Nugent, F. (1994). *An introduction to the profession of counseling.* Columbus, OH: Merrill.

Nurnberger, J. (1993). Genotyping status report for affective disorder. *Psychiatric Genetics, 3,* 207–214.

Nurnberger, J. I., Jr., Foroud, T., Flury, L., Su, J., Meyer, E. T., Hu, K., et al. (2000). Evidence for a locus on chromosome 1 that influences vulnerability to alcoholism and affective disorder. *Journal of Psychiatry, 158,* 718–724.

Nyberg, L., Petersson, K. M., Nilsson, L. G., Sandblom, J., Aberg, C., & Ingvar, M. (2001). Reactivation of motor brain areas during explicit memory for actions. *Neuroimage, 14,* 521–528.

Oatley, K. (1993). Those to whom evil is done. In R. S. Wyer & T. K. Srull (Eds.), *Toward a general theory of anger and emotional aggression: Advances in social cognition* (Vol. 6). Hillsdale, NJ: Erlbaum.

O'Brien, T. L. (1991, September 2). Computers help thwart "groupthink" that plagues meetings. *Chicago Sun Times.*

Ochsner, K. N., & Lieberman, M. D. (2001). The emergence of social cognitive neuroscience. *American Psychologist, 56,* 717–734.

O'Conner, E. (2001). Psychology's diversity leaps "beyond 2000." *Monitor on Psychology, 32,* 36–38.

O'Conner, E. P., & Kratochwill, T. R. (1999). Self-help interventions: The reported practices of school psychologists. *Professional Psychology: Research and Practice, 30,* 147–153.

O'Connor, T. G., Rutter, M., Beckett, C., Keaveney, L., Kreppner, J. M., & the English and Romanian Adoptees Study Team. (2000). *Child Development, 71,* 376–390.

Oden, M. H. (1968). The fulfillment of promise: 40-year follow-up of the Terman gifted group. *Genetic Psychology Monographs, 17,* 3–93.

Oellerich, T. (2000). Rind, Tromovitch, and Bauserman: Politically incorrect-scientifically correct. *Sexuality and Culture 4,* 67–81.

Oettingen, G., Pak, H., & Schnetter, K. (2001). Self-regulation of goal setting: Turning free fantasies about the future into binding goals. *Journal of Personality and Social Psychology, 80,* 736–753.

O'Farrell, T. J. (1995). Marital and family therapy. In R. K. Hester & W. R. Miller (Eds.), *Handbook of alcoholism treatment approaches* (2nd ed., pp. 195–220). Boston: Allyn & Bacon.

Offenbach, S., Chodzko-Zajko, W., & Ringel, R. (1990). Relationship between physiological status, cognition, and age in adulot men. *Bulletin of the Psychonomics Society, 28,* 112–114.

O'Hare, D., & Roscoe, S. (1991). *Flight deck performance: The human factor.* Ames: Iowa University Press.

Ohira, H., & Kurono, K. (1993). Facial feedback effects on impression formation. *Perceptual and Motor Skills, 77*(3, Pt. 2), 1251–1258.

Öhman, A., Dimberg, U., & Öst, L. G. (1985). Animal and social phobias: A laboratory model. In S. Reiss & R. R. Bootzin (Eds.), *Theoretical issues in behavior therapy.* Orlando, FL: Academic Press.

Öhman, A., & Soares, J. F. (1994). "Unconscious anxiety": Phobic responses to masked stimuli. *Journal of Abnormal Psychology, 103*(2), 231–240.

Oishi, S., Diener, E., Lucas, R. E., & Suh, E. M. (1999). Cross-cultural variations in predictors of life-satisfaction: Perspectives from needs and values. *Personality and Social Psychology Bulletin, 25,* 980–990.

Okochi, M., Eimer, S., Bottcher, A., Baumeister, R., Romig, H., Walter, J., et al. (2000). A loss of function mutant of the presenilin homologue SEL-12 undergoes aberrant endoproteolysis in Caenorhabditis elegans and increases abeta 42 generation in human cells. *Journal of Biological Chemistry, 275,* 40925–40932.

Oldenberg, P.-A., Zheleznyak, A., Fang, Y.-F, Lagenaur, C. F., Gresham, H. D., & Lindberg, F. P. (2000). Role of CD47 as a marker of self on red blood cells. *Science, 288,* 2051–2054.

Olds, J. (1973). Commentary on positive reinforcement produced by electrical stimulation of septal areas and other regions of rat brain. In E. S. Valenstein (Ed.), *Brain stimulation and motivation: Research and commentary.* Glenview, IL: Scott Foresman.

Olds, J., & Milner, P. (1954). Positive reinforcement produced by electrical stimulation of septal areas and other regions of the rat brain. *Journal of Comparative and Physiological Psychology, 47,* 419–427.

Oliner, S. P., & Oliner, P. M. (1988). *The altruistic personality: Rescuers of Jews in Nazi Europe.* New York: Free Press.

Olio, K. A. (1994). Truth in memory. *American Psychologist, 49,* 442–443.

Olivares, R., Michalland, S., & Aboitiz, F. (2000). Cross-species and intraspecies morphometric analysis of the corpus callosum. *Brain and Behavior and Evolution, 55,* 37–43.

Olson, J. M., Vernon, P. A., Harris, J. A., & Jang, K. L (2001). The heritability of attitudes: A study of twins. *Journal of Personality and Social Psychology, 80,* 845–860.

Olson, L. (1997). Regeneration in the adult central nervous system. *Nature Medicine, 3,* 1329–1335.

Olson, M. A., & Fazio, R. H. (2001). Implicit attitude formation through classical conditioning. *Psychological Science, 12,* 413–417.

O'Neill, H. (2000, September 24). After rape, jail—a friendship forms. *St. Petersburg Times,* pp. 1A, 14A.

Ones, D., & Viswesvaran, C. (1996). Bandwidth-fidelity dilemma in personality measurement for personnel selection. *Journal of Organizational Behavior, 17,* 609–626.

Ones, D., & Viswesvaran, C. (2001). Personality at work: Criterion focused occupational personality scales used in personnel selection. In R. Hogan & B. Roberts (Eds.), *Personality psychology in the workplace* (pp. 63–92). Washington, DC: American Psychological Association.

Operario, D., & Fiske, S. T. (2001). Stereotypes: Processes, structures, content, and context. In R. Brown & S. Gaertner (Eds.), *Blackwell handbook in social psychology: Intergroup processes* (pp. 22–44). Oxford, England: Blackwell.

Oppel, S. (2000, March 5). Managing ABCs like a CEO. *St. Petersburg Times,* 1A, 12–13A.

Oquendo, M. A., Ellis, S. P., Greenwald, S., Malone, K. M., Weissman, M. M., & Mann, J. J. (2001). Ethnic and sex differences in suicide rates relative to major depression in the United States. *American Journal of Psychiatry, 158,* 1652–1658.

Oquendo, M. A., & Mann, J. J. (2000). The biology of impulsivity and suicidality. *Psychiatric Clinics of North America, 23,* 11–25.

Orbell, J. M., van de Kragt, A. J. C., & Dawes, R. M. (1988). Explaining discussioninduced cooperation. *Journal of Personality and Social Psychology, 54,* 811–819.

Orne, M. T., & Evans, F. J. (1965). Social control in the psychological experiment: Antisocial behavior and hypnosis. *Journal of Personality and Social Psychology, 1,* 189–200.

Orne, M. T., Sheehan, P. W., & Evans, F. J. (1968). Occurrence of posthypnotic behavior outside the experimental setting. *Journal of Personality and Social Psychology, 9,* 189–196.

Osborne, J. (1997). Race and academic disidentification. *Journal of Educational Psychology, 89,* 728–735.

Osherson, D., Perani, D., Cappa, S., Schnur, T., Grassi, F., & Fazio, F. (1998). Distinct brain loci in deductive versus probabilistic reasoning. *Neuropsychologia, 36,* 369–376.

Oskamp, S., & Schultz, P. W. (1998). *Applied social psychology* (2nd ed.). Upper Saddle River, NJ: Prentice-Hall.

Öst, L.-G. (1992). Blood and injection phobia: Background and cognitive, physiological and behavioral variables. *Journal of Abnormal Psychology, 101,* 68–74.

Öst, L.-G., Hellström, K., & Kåver, A. (1992). One- versus five-session exposure in the treatment of needle phobia. *Behavior Therapy, 23,* 263–282.

Öst, L.-G., Salkovskis, P. M., & Hellström, K. (1991). One-session therapist-directed exposure vs. self-exposure in the treatment of spider phobia. *Behavior Theapy, 22,* 407–422.

Öst, L. G., Svensson, L., Hellström, K., & Lindwall, R. (2001). One-session treatment of specific phobias in youths: A randomized clinical trial. *Journal of Consulting and Clinical Psychology, 69,* 814–824.

Otsuka, R., Watanabe, H., Hirata, K., Tokai, K., Muro, T., Yoshiyama, M., Takeuchi, K., & Yoshikawa, J. (2001). *Journal of the American Medical Association, 286,* 436–441.

Otto, M. W., Pollack, M. H., Gould, R. A., Worthington, J. J., III, McArdle, E. T., Rosenbaum, J. F., & Heimberg, R. G. (2000). A comparison of the efficacy of clonazepam and cognitive-behavioral group therapy for the treatment of social phobia. *Journal of Anxiety Disorders, 14,* 345–358.

Otto, R. K., & Heilbrun, K. (2002). The practice of forensic psychology: A look toward the future in the light of the past. *American Psychologist, 57,* 5–18.

Ouimette, P. C., Finney, J. W., & Moos, R. H. (1997). Twelve-step and cognitive-behavioral treatment for substance abuse: A comparison of treatment effectiveness. *Journal of Consulting and Clinical Psychology, 65,* 230–240.

Overmier, J. B., & Seligman, M. E. P. (1967). Effects of inescapable shock upon subsequent escape and avoidence learning. *Journal of Comparative and Physiological Psychology, 63,* 23–33.

Overton, D. A. (1984). State dependent learning and drug discriminations. In L. L. Iverson, S. D. Iverson, & S. H. Snyder (Eds.), *Handbook of psychopharmacology* (Vol. 18). New York: Plenum.

Overton, P. G., Richards, C. D., Berry, M. S. & Clark, D. (1999). Long-term potentiation at excitatory amino acid synapses on midbrain dopamine neurons. *Neuroreport, 10,* 221–226.

Oyserman, D., Coon, H. M., & Kemmelmeier, M. (2002). Rethinking individualism and collectivism: Evaluation of theoretical assumptions and meta-analyses. *Psychological Bulletin, 128,* 3–72.

Oysermann, S. (2001). Self-concept and identity. In A. Tesser & N. Schwarz (Eds.), *Blackwell handbook of social psychology: Intraindividual processes* (pp. 499–517). Oxford, England: Blackwell.

Ozer, D. J. (1999). Four principles of personality assessment. In L. Pervin & O. John (Eds.), *Handbook of personality: Theory and research* (2nd ed., pp. 671–689). New York: Guilford.

Paik, H., & Comstock, G. (1994). The effects of television violence on antisocial behavior: A meta-analysis. *Communication Research, 21,* 516–546.

Paivio, A. (1986). *Mental representations: A dual coding approach.* New York: Oxford University Press.

Paivio, S. C., & Greenberg, L. S. (1995). Resolving "unfinished business": Efficacy of experiential therapy using empty-chair dialogue. *Journal of Consulting and Clinical Psychology, 63,* 419–425.

Palmer, F. H., & Anderson, L. W. (1979). Long-term gains from early intervention: Findings from longitudinal studies. In E. Zigler & J. Valentine (Eds.), *Project Head Start: A legacy of the war on poverty.* New York: Free Press.

Palmer, S. E. (1999). *Vision science: Photons to phenomenology.* Cambridge: MIT Press.

Palmisano, M., & Herrmann, D. (1991). The facilitation of memory performance. *Bulletin of the Psychonomic Society, 29,* 557–559.

Paloski, W. H. (1998). Vestibulospinal adaptation to microgravity. *Otolaryngol Head and Neck Surgery, 118,* S39–S44.

Panksepp, J. (1998). Attention deficit hyperactivity disorders, psychostimulants, and intolerance of childhood playfulness: A tragedy in the making? *Current Directions in Psychological Science, 7,* 91–98.

Pantev, C., Oostenveld, R., Engelien, A., Ross, B., Roberts, L. E., & Hoke, M. (1998). Increased auditory cortical representation in musicians. *Nature, 392,* 811–814.

Paoletti, M. G. (1995). Biodiversity, traditional landscapes and agroecosystem management. *Landscape and Urban Planning, 31*(1–3), 117–128.

Papp, L., Klein, D., Martinez, J., Schneier, F., Cole, R., Liebowitz, M., et al. (1993). Diagnostic and substance specificity of carbon monoxide-induced panic. *American Journal of Psychiatry, 150,* 250–257.

Park, D. C. (2001, August). *The aging mind.* Paper presented at the annual convention of the American Psychological Association, San Francisco.

Park, J., White, A. R., & Ernst, E. (2001). New sham method in auricular acupuncture. *Archives of Internal Medicine, 161,* 894.

Park, W.-W. (2000). A comprehensive empirical investigation of the relationships among variables of the groupthink model. *Journal of Organizational Behavior, 21,* 873–887.

Parke, R. D. (2002). Fathers and families. In M. H. Bornstein (Ed.), *Handbook of parenting* (2nd ed., pp. 27–63). Mahwah, NJ: Erlbaum.

Parke, R. D., & Buriel, R. (1998). Socialization in the family: Ethnic and ecological perspectives. In W. Damon & N. Eisenberg (Eds.), *Handbook of child psychology: Vol. 3. Social, emotional, and personality development* (5th ed., pp. 463–552). New York: Wiley.

Parke, R. D., & Buriel, R. (2002). Socializing processes. In N. Smelser & P. B. Baltes (Eds.), *International encyclopedia of social sciences.* New York: Elsevier.

Parke, R. D., & O'Neil, R. (2000). The influence of significant others on learning about relationships: From family to friends. In R. S. L. Mills & S. Duck (Eds.), *The developmental psychology of personal relationships.* New York: Wiley.

Parker, G., Gladstone, G., & Chee, K. T. (2001). Depression in the planet's largest ethnic group: The Chinese. *American Journal of Psychiatry, 158,* 857–864.

Parker, J. G., Saxon, J. L., Asher, S. R., & Kovacs, D. M. (2001). Dimensions of children's friendship adjustment: Implications for understanding loneliness. In K. J. Rotenberg & S. Hymel (Eds.), *Loneliness in childhood and adolescence.* New York: Cambridge University Press.

Parkes, C. M. P., & Weiss, R. S. (1983). *Recovery from bereavement.* New York: Basic Books.

Parkin, A. J., & Walter, B. M. (1991). Aging, short-term memory, and frontal dysfunction. *Psychobiology, 19,* 175–179.

Parnas, J., Cannon, T., Jacobsen, B., Schulsinger, H., Schulsinger, F., & Mednick, S. (1993). Lifetime DSM-III-R diagnostic outcomes in the offspring of schizophrenic mothers. *Archives of General Psychiatry, 50,* 707–714.

Patel, A. D., & Balaban, E. (2001). Human pitch perception is reflected in the timing of stimulus-related cortical activity. *Nature Neuroscience, 4,* 839–844.

Patrick, C. J., Cuthbert, B. N., & Lang, P. J. (1994). Emotion in the criminal psychopath: Fear imaging processing. *Journal of Abnormal Psychology, 103,* 523–534.

Patterson, C. J. (2002). Lesbian and gay parenthood. In M. H. Bornstein (Ed.), *Handbook of parenting* (2nd ed., pp. 255–274). Mahwah, NJ: Erlbaum.

Pattie, F. A. (1935). A report of attempts to produce uniocular blindness by hypnotic suggestion. *British Journal of Medical Psychiatry, 15,* 230–241.

Pauk, W., & Fiore, J. P. (2000). *Succeed in college!* Boston: Houghton Mifflin.

Paul, G. L. (1969). Behavior modification research: Design and tactics. In C. M. Franks (Ed.), *Behavior therapy: Appraisal and status* (pp. 29–62). New York: McGraw-Hill.

Paul, G. L. (2000). Milieu therapy. In A. E. Kazdin (Ed.), *The encyclopedia of psychology.* Washington, DC: American Psychological Association.

Paul, G. L., & Lentz, R. J. (1977). *Psychosocial treatment of chronic mental patients: Milieu versus social learning programs.* Cambridge: Harvard University Press.

Paul, G. L., Stuve, P., & Cross, J. V. (1997). Real-world inpatient programs: Shedding some light-A critique. *Applied and Preventive Psychology, 6,* 193–204.

Paulhus, D. L., Fridhandler, B., & Hayes, S. (1997). Psychological defense: Contemporary theory and research. In R. Hogan, J. Johnson, & S. Briggs (Eds.), *Handbook of personality psychology* (pp. 544–588). San Diego: Academic Press.

Paulhus, D. L., Trapnell, P., & Chen, D. (1999). Birth order effects on personality and achievement within families. *Psychological Science, 10,* 482–488.

Pauls, D. L., Alsobrook, J. P., II, Goodman, W., Rasmussen, S., & Leckman, J. F. (1995). A family study of obsessive-compulsive disorder. *American Journal of Psychiatry, 152,* 76–84.

Paulus, P. B. (1988). *Prison crowding: A psychological perspective.* New York: Springer-Verlag.

Paus, T., Zijdenbos, A., Worsley, K., Collins, D. L., Blumenthal, J., Giedd, J. N., Rapoport, J. L., & Evans, A. C. (1999). Structural maturation of neural pathways in children and adolescents in vivo study. *Science, 283,* 1908–1911.

Pavkov, T., Lewis, D., & Lyons, J. (1989). Psychiatric diagnosis and racial bias: An empirical investigation. *Professional Psychology: Research and Practice, 20,* 364–368.

Payne, J. W., Bettman, J. R., & Johnson, E. J. (1992). Behavioral decision research: A constructive processing perspective. *Behavioral decision research: A constructive processing perspective, 43,* 87–131.

Peck, J. W. (1978). Rats defend different body weights depending on palatability and accessibility of their food. *Journal of Comparative and Physiological Psychology, 92,* 555–570.

Pederson, N. L., Plomin, R., Nesselroade, J. R., & McClearn, G. E. (1992). A quantitative genetic analysis of cognitive abilities during the second half of the life span. *Psychological Science, 3,* 346–353.

Peiffer, L. C., & Trull, T. J. (2000). Predictors of suggestibility and false-memory production in young adult women. *Journal of Personality Assessment, 74,* 384–399.

Penfield, W., & Rasmussen, T. (1968). *The cerebral cortex of man: A clinical study of localization of function.* New York: Hafner.

Pennartz, C. M., McNaughton, B. L., & Mulder, A. B. (2000). The glutamate hypothesis of reinforcement learning. *Progress in Brain Research, 126,* 231–253.

Pennebaker, J. W. (1993). Putting stress into words: Health, linguistic, and therapeutic implications. *Behaviour Research and Therapy, 31,* 539–548.

Pennebaker, J. W., Colder, M., & Sharp, L. K. (1990). Accelerating the coping process. *Journal of Personality and Social Psychology, 58,* 528–537.

Pennebaker, J. W., Kiecolt-Glaser, J. K., & Glaser, R. (1988). Disclosure of traumas and immune function: Health implications for psychotherapy. *Journal of Consulting and Clinical Psychology, 56,* 239–245.

Pennebaker, J. W., & O'Heeron, R. C. (1984). Confiding in others and illness rate among spouses of suicide and accidental death victims. *Journal of Abnormal Psychology, 93,* 473–476.

Penner, L. A. (in press). The causes of sustained volunteerism: An interactionist perspective. *Journal of Social Issues.*

Penner, L. A., & Craiger, J. P. (1992). The weakest link: The performance of individual group members. In R. W. Swezey & E. Salas (Eds.), *Teams: Their training and performance* (pp. 57–74). Norwood, NJ: Ablex.

Penner, L. A., Dovidio, J., & Albrecht, T. L. (2001). Helping victims of loss and trauma: A social psychological perspective. In J. Harvey & E. Miller (Eds.), *Loss and trauma: General and close relationship perspectives* (pp. 62–85). Philadelphia: Brunner Routledge.

Penner, L. A., & Finkelstein, M. A. (1998). Dispositional and structural determinants of volunteerism. *Journal of Personality and Social Psychology, 74,* 525–537.

Penner, L. A., Fritzsche, B. A., Craiger, J. P., & Friefeld, T. R. (1995). Measuring the prosocial personality. In J. Butcher & C. D. Spielberger (Eds.), *Advances in personality assessment* (Vol. 10, pp. 147–163). Hillsdale, NJ: Erlbaum.

Penner, L. A., Knoff, H., Batchshe, G., Nelson, D. L., & Spielberg, C. D. (Eds.). (1994). *Contribution of psychology to science and math education.* Washington, DC: American Psychological Association.

Penninx, B. W., Beekman, A. T., Honig, A., Deeg, D. J., Schoevers, R.A., van Eijk, J. T., van Tilburg, W. (2001). Depression and cardiac mortality: results from a community-based longitudinal study. *Archives of General Psychiatry, 58,* 221–227.

Pepeu, G. (1994). Memory disorders: Novel treatments, clinical perspective. *Life Sciences, 55,* 2189–2194.

Peppard, P. E., Young, T., Palta, M., Dempsey, J., & Skatrud, J. (2000). Longitudinal study of moderate weight change and sleep-disordered breathing. *Journal of the American Medical Association, 284,* 3015–3021.

Perls, F. S. (1969). *Ego, hunger and aggression: The beginning of Gestalt therapy.* New York: Random House.

Perls, F. S., Hefferline, R. F., & Goodman, P. (1951). *Gestalt therapy.* New York: Julian Press.

Peroutka, S. J., Newman, H., & Harris, H. (1988). The subjective effects of 3, 4-methylenedioxymethamphetamine in recreational users. *Neuro-Pharmacology, 1*(4), 273–277.

Perris, E. E., Myers, N. A., & Clifton, R. K. (1990). Long-term memory-for a single infancy experience. *Child Development, 61,* 1796–1807.

Persons, J. B., Davidson, J., & Tompkins, M. A. (2001). *Essential components of cognitive-behavior therapy for depression.* Washington, DC: American Psychological Association.

Persons, J. B., & Silberschatz, G. (1998). Are results of randomized controlled trials useful to psychotherapists? *Journal of Consulting and Clinical Psychology, 66,* 126–135.

Pervin, L. A. (1996). *The science of personality.* New York: Wiley.

Peterson, A., Compas, B., Brooks-Gunn, J., Stemmler, M., Ey, S., & Grant, K. (1993). Depression in adolescence. *American Psychologist, 48,* 155–168.

Peterson, A. C. (1987, September). Those gangly years. *Psychology Today,* pp. 28–34.

Peterson, C. (1995, April). *The preschool child witness: Errors in accounts of traumatic injury*. Paper presented at the biennial meeting of the Society for Research in Child Development, Indianapolis.

Peterson, C., & Barrett, L. C. (1987). Explanatory style and academic performance among university freshman. *Journal of Personality and Social Psychology, 53*, 603–607.

Peterson, C., Maier, S. F., & Seligman, M. E. (1993). *Learned helplessness: A theory for the age of personal control*. New York: Oxford University Press.

Peterson, C., & Seligman, M. E. P. (1984). Causal explanations as a risk factor for depression: Theory and evidence. *Psychological Review, 91*, 347–374.

Peterson, C., Seligman, M. E. P., Yurko, K. H., Martin, L. R., & Friedman, H. S. (1998). Catastrophizing and untimely death. *Psychological Science, 9*, 127–130.

Peterson, L. R., & Peterson, M. J. (1959). Short-term retention of individual verbal items. *Journal of Experimental Psychology, 58*, 193–198.

Petrie, K. J., Booth, R. J., Pennebaker, J. W. (1998). The immunological effects of thought suppression. *Journal of Personality and Social Psychology, 75*, 1264–1272.

Petrie, K. J., Booth, R. J., Pennebaker, J. W., & Davison, K. P. (1995). Disclosure of trauma and immune response to a Hepatitis B vaccination program. *Journal of Consulting and Clinical Psychology, 63*, 787–792.

Petrill, S. A., Plomin, R., Berg, S., Johansson, B., Pederson, N. L., Ahern, F., & McClearn, G. E. (1998). The genetic and environmental relationship between general and specific cognitive abilities in twins age 80 and older. *Psychological Science, 9*, 183–189.

Petrovic, P., Kalso, E., Petersson, K. M., & Ingvar, M. (2002). Placebo and opioid analgesia: Imaging a shared neuronal network. *Science, 295*, 1737–1740.

Petry, N. M. (2001). Substance abuse, pathological gambling and impulsivity. *Drug and Alcohol dependence, 63*, 29–38.

Pettigrew, T. F. (1979). The ultimate attribution error: Extending Allport's cognitive analysis of prejudice. *Personality and Social Psychology Bulletin, 5*, 461–476.

Pettigrew, T. F., & Tropp, L. R. (2000). Does intergroup contact reduce prejudice? Recent meta-analytic findings. In S. Oskamp (Ed.), *Reducing prejudice and discrimination* (pp. 93–114). Mahwah, NJ: Erlbaum.

Pettit, D. L., Shao, Z, & Yakel, J. L. (2001). Beta-amyloid(1–42) peptide directly modulates nicotinic receptors in the rat hippocampal slice. *Journal of Neuroscience, 21*, RC120.

Petty, R., Cacioppo, J., & Goldman, R. (1981). Personal involvement as a determinant of argument-based persuasion. *Journal of Personality and Social Psychology, 41*, 847–855.

Petty, R., Cacioppo, J. T., & Schumann, D. (1983). Central and peripheral routes to advertising effectiveness: The moderating role of involvement. *Journal of Consumer Research, 10*, 134–148.

Petty, R. E., & Wegener, D. T. (1998). Attitude change: Multiple roles for persuasion variables. In D. Gilbert, S. T. Fiske, & G. Lindzey (Eds.), *Handbook of social psychology* (Vol. 1, 4th ed., pp. 323–390). Boston: McGraw-Hill.

Pfefferbaum, A., Rosenbloom, M., Deshmukkh, A., & Sullivan, E., (2001). Sex differences in the effects of alcohol on brain structure. *The American Journal of Psychiatry, 158*, 188–197.

Phares, E. J. (1991). *Introduction to personality* (3rd ed.). New York: Harper-Collins.

Phelps, B. J., & Exum, M. E. (1992, Spring). Subliminal tapes: How to get the message across. *Skeptical Inquirer, 16*, 282–286.

Phelps, E. A., O'Connor, K. J., Cunningham, W. A., Funayama, E. S., Gatenby, J. C., Gore, J. C. & Banaji, M. (2000). Performance on indirect measures of race evaluation predicts amygdala activation. *Journal of Cognitive Neuroscience, 12*, 729–738.

Phelps, M. E., & Mazziotta, J. C. (1985). Positron emission tomography: Human brain function and biochemistry. *Science, 228*, 799–809.

Philip, P., Vervialle, F., Le Breton, P., Taillard, J., & Horne, J. A (2001). Fatigue, alcohol, and serious road crashes in France: factorial study of national data. *British Medical Journal, 322*, 829–830.

Phillips, D. P., & Cartensen, L. L. (1986). Clustering of teenage suicides after television news stories about suicide. *New England Journal of Medicine, 315*, 685–689.

Phillips, N. A. (2000). Female sexual dysfunction: Evaluation and treatment. *American Family Physician, 62*, 127–136, 141–142.

Phillips, R. L., Ernst, R. E., Brunk, B., Ivanova, N., Mahan, M. A., Deanehan, J. K., et al. (2000). The genetic program of hemotopoietic stems cells. *Science, 288*, 1635–1640.

Phinney, J. S. (1996). When we talk about American ethnic groups, what do we mean? *American Psychologist, 51*, 918–927.

Phinney, J. S., Ferguson, D. L., & Tate, J. D. (1997). Intergroup attitudes among ethnic minority adolescents: A causal model. *Child Development, 68*, 955–969.

Piaget, J. (1952). *The origins of intelligence in children*. New York: International Universities Press.

Pickering, A. D., & Gray, J. A. (1999). The neuroscience of personality. In L. Pervin & O. John (Eds.), *Handbook of personality: Theory and research* (2nd ed., pp. 277–299). New York: Guilford.

Pierce, G., Sarason, I., & Sarason, B. (1991). General and specific support expectations and stress as predictors of perceived supportivness: An experimental study. *Journal of Personality and Social Psychology, 63*, 297–307.

Pietro, P., Guazzeli, M., Basso, G., Jaffe, K., & Grafman, J. (2000). Neural correlates of imaginal aggressive behavior assessed by positron emission tomography in healthy subjects. *American Journal of Psychiatry, 157*, 1772–1781.

Piliavin, J. A., Dovidio, J. F., Gaertner, S. L., & Clark, R. D., III. (1981). *Emergency intervention*. New York: Academic Press.

Pillard, R. C., & Bailey, J. M. (1998). Human sexual orientation has a heritable component. *Human Biology, 70*, 347–365.

Pillemer, D. B. (1998). What is remembered about early childhood events? *Clinical Psychology Review, 18*, 895–915.

Pincus, T., & Morley, S. (2001). Cognitive-processing bias in chronic pain: A review and integration. *Psychological Bulletin, 127*, 599–617.

Pinel, J. P. J. (1993). *Biopsychology*. Boston: Allyn & Bacon.

Pinker, S. (1994). *The language instinct: How the mind creates language*. New York: Morrow.

Pinker, S. (in press). *The blank slate: the denial of human nature in modern intellectual life*. London: Penguin.

Pitschel-Walz, G., & Leutch, S., Bauml, J., Kissling, W., & Engel, R. R. (2001). The effect of family interventions on relapse and rehospitalization in schizophrenia: A meta-analysis. *Schizophrenia Bulletin, 27*, 73–92.

Plomin, R. (1986). *Development, genetics, and psychology*. Hillsdale, NJ: Erlbaum.

Plomin, R. (1994). *Genetics and experience: The developmental interplay between nature and nurture*. Newbury Park, CA: Sage.

Plomin, R., Asbury, K., & Dunn, J. F. (2001). Why are children in the same family so different? Nonshared environment a decade later. *Canadian Journal of Psychiatry, 46*, 225–233.

Plomin, R., & Bergeman, C. S. (1991). The nature of nurture: Genetic influence on "environmental" measures. *Behavioral and Brain Sciences, 14*, 373–427.

Plomin, R., & Caspi, A. (1999). Behavioral genetics and personality. In L. Pervin & O. John (Eds.), *Handbook of personality research* (2nd ed.) New York: Guilford.

Plomin, R., Corley, R., Caspi, A., Fulker, D. W., & DeFries, J. C. (1998). Adoption results for self-reported personality: Not much nature or nurture? *Journal of Personality and Social Psychology, 75*, 211–218.

Plomin, R., & Crabbe, J. C. (2000). DNA *Psychological Bulletin, 126*, 806–828.

Plomin, R., DeFries, J. C., Craig, I. C., & McGuffin, P. (Eds.). (2002). *Behavioral genetics in a postgenomic era*. Washington, DC: APA Books.

Plomin, R., DeFries, J. C., McClearn, G. E., & McGuffin, P. (2001). *Behavioral genetics* (4th ed.). New York: Worth.

Plomin, R., & McClearn, G. E. (Eds.). (1993). *Nature, nurture and psychology*. Washington, DC: American Psychological Association.

Plomin, R., Owen, M. J., & McGuffin, P. (1994). The genetic basis of complex human behaviors. *Science, 264*, 1733–1739.

Plous, S. (1996). Attitudes toward the use of animals in psychological research and education: Results from a national survey of psychologists. *American Psychologist, 51*, 1167–1180.

Plutchik, R., & Conte, H. R. (Eds.). (1997). *Circumplex models of personality and emotions.* Washington, DC: American Psychological Association.

Pol, H. E. H., Schnack, H. G., Bertens, M. G. B. C., van Haren, N. E. M., van der Tweel, I., Staal, W. G., et al. (2002). Volume changes in gray matter in patients with schizophrenia. *American Journal of Psychiatry, 159,* 244–250.

Pollack, I. (1953). The assimilation of sequentially coded information. *American Journal of Psychology, 66,* 421–435.

Pollack, V. (1992). Meta-analysis of subjective sensitivity to alcohol in sons of alcoholics. *American Journal of Psychiatry, 149,* 1534–1538.

Polusny, M. A., & Follette, V. M. (1995). Long-term correlates of child sexual abuse: Theory and review of the empirical literature. *Applied and Preventive Psychology, 4,* 143–166.

Polusny, M. A., & Follette, V. M. (1996). Remembering childhood abuse: A national survey of psychologists' clinical practices, beliefs, and personal experiences. *Professional Psychology: Research and Practice, 27,* 41–52.

Pomerantz, J. R., & Kubovy, M. (1986). Theoretical approaches to perceptual organization. In K. R. Boff, L. Kaufman, & J. P. Thomas (Eds.), *Handbook of perception and human performance* (pp. 36-1–36-46). New York: Wiley.

Pomerleau, C. S., & Pomerleau, O. F. (1992). Euphoriant effects of nicotine in smokers. *Psychopharmacology, 108,* 460–465.

Poole, D. A., Lindsay, D. S., Memon, A., & Bull, R. (1995). Psychotherapy and the recovery of memories of childhood sexual abuse: U.S. and British practitioners' opinions, practices, and experiences. *Journal of Consulting and Clinical Psychology, 63,* 426–437.

Pope, H. G., Gruber, A. J., Hudson, J. I., Huestis, M. A., Yurgelun-Todd, D. (2001). Neuropsychological performance in long-term cannabis users. *Archives of General Psychiatry, 58,* 909–915.

Pope, H. G., & Hudson, J. I. (1995). Can individuals "repress" memories of childhood sexual abuse? An examination of the evidence. *Psychiatric Annals, 25,* 715–719.

Pope, H. G., Jr., Kouri, E. M., & Hudson, J. I. (2001). Effects of supraphysiologic doses of testosterone on mood and aggression in normal men: A randomized controlled trial. *Archives of General Psychiatry, 57*(2), 133–140.

Pope, H. G., & Yurgelun-Todd, D. (1996). The residual cognitive effects of heavy marijuana use in college students. *Journal of the American Medical Association, 275,* 521–527.

Pope, H. G., Jr., Hudson, J. I., Bodkin, J. A., & Oliva, P. (1998). Questionable validity of "dissociative amnesia" in trauma victims: Evidence from prospective studies. *British Journal of Psychiatry, 172,* 210–215.

Pope, K. S. (1998). Pseudoscience, cross-examination, and scientific evidence in the recovered memory controversy. *Psychology, Public Policy, and Law, 4,* 1160–1181.

Pope-Davis, D. B., Reynolds, A. L., Dings, J. G., & Nielson, D. (1995). Examining multicultural counseling competencies of graduate students in psychology. *Professional Psychology: Research and Practice, 26,* 322–329.

Porges, S. W., Doussard, R. J. A., & Maita, A. K. (1995). Vagal tone and the physiological regulation of emotion. *Monographs of the Society for Research on Child Development, 59*(2–3), 167–186, 250–283.

Porkka-Heiskanen, T., Strecker, R. E., Thakkar, M., Bjorkum, A. A., Greene, R. W., & McCarley, R. W. (1997). Adenosine: A mediator of the sleep-inducing effects of prolonged wakefulness. *Science, 276,* 1265–1268.

Port, C. L., Engdahl, B., & Frazier, P. (2001). A longitudinal and retrospective study of PTSD among older prisoners of war. *American Journal of Psychiatry, 158,* 1474–1479.

Porte, H. S., & Hobson, J. A. (1996). Physical motion in dreams: One measure of three theories. *Journal of Abnormal Psychology, 105,* 329–335.

Porter, R. H. (1991). Human reproduction and the mother-infant relationship. In T. V. Getchell et al. (Eds.), *Taste and smell in health and disease.* New York: Raven Press.

Porter, R. H., Cernich, J. M., & McLaughlin, F. J. (1983). Maternal recognition of neonates through olfactory cues. *Physiology and Behavior, 30,* 151–154.

Porter, R. H., Makin, J. W., Davis, L. B., & Christensen, K. M. (1992). Breast-fed infants respond to olfactory cues from their own mother and unfamiliar lactating females. *Infant Behavior and Development, 15,* 85–93.

Porter, S., Birt, A. R., Yuille, J. C., & Lehman, D. R. (2000). Negotiating false memories: Interviewer and rememberer characteristics relate to memory distortion. *Psychological Science, 11,* 507–510.

Porter, S., Yuille, J. C., & Lehman, D. R. (1999). The nature of real, implanted, and fabricated memories for emotional childhood events: Implications for the recovered memory debate. *Law & Human Behavior, 23,* 517–537.

Posener, J. A., DeBattista, C., Williams, G. H., Kraemer, H. C., Kalehzan, B. M., & Schatzberg, A. F. (2000). 24-hour monitoring of cortisol and corticotropin secretion in psychotic and nonpsychotic major depression. *Archives of General Psychiatry, 57,* 755–760.

Posner, M. I. (1978). *Chronometric explorations of the mind.* Hillsdale, NJ: Erlbaum.

Posner, M. I., & DiGirolamo, G. J (2001). Cognitive neuroscience: Origins and promise. *Psychological Bulletin, 126,* 873–889.

Posner, M. I., Nissen, M. J., & Ogden, W. C. (1978). Attended and unattended processing modes: The role of set for spatial location. In H. L. Pick & I. J. Saltzman (Eds.), *Modes of perceiving and processing information.* Hillsdale, NJ: Erlbaum.

Posner, M. I., & Peterson, S. E. (1990). The attention system of the human brain. *Annual Review of Neurosciences, 13,* 24–42.

Posner, M. I., & Raichle, M. E. (1994). *Images of mind.* New York: Scientific American Books.

Potter, P. T., & Zautra, A. J. (1997). Stressful life events' effects on rheumatoid arthritis disease activity. *Journal of Consulting and Clinical Psychology, 65,* 319–323.

Potter, W. Z., & Rudorfer, M. V. (1993). Electroconvulsive therapy, a modern medical procedure. *New England Journal of Medicine, 328,* 882–883.

Pousset, F. (1994). Cytokines as mediators in the central nervous system. *Biomedical Pharmacotherapy, 48,* 425–431.

Powch, I. G., & Houston, B. K. (1996). Hostility, anger-in, and cardiovascular activity in White women. *Health Psychology, 15,* 200–208.

Pratkanis, A. R. (1992). The cargo-cult science of subliminal persuasion. *Skeptical Inquirer, 16,* 260–273.

Pratkanis, A. R., & Aronson, E. (1991). *Age of propaganda: The everyday use and abuse of persuasion.* New York: Freeman.

Pratkanis, A. R., Eskenazi, J., & Greenwald, A. G. (1994). What you expect is what you believe (but not necessarily what you get): A test of the effectiveness of self-help audiotapes. *Basic and Applied Social Psychology, 15,* 251–276.

Preciado, J. (1994). The empirical basis of behavior therapy applications with Hispanics. *The Behavior Therapist, 17,* 63–65.

Preece, J., Sharp, H., Benyon, D., Holland, S., & Carey, T. (1994). *Human-computer interaction.* Reading, MA: Addison-Wesley.

Premack, D. (1965). Reinforcement theory. In D. Levine (Ed.), *Nebraska symposium on motivation* (Vol. 13, pp. 123–180). Lincoln: University of Nebraska Press.

Premack, D. (1971). Language in chimpanzees? *Science, 172,* 808–822.

Premack, D., & Premack, A. J. (1983). *The mind of an ape.* New York: Norton.

Prentice-Dunn, S., & Rogers, R. W. (1989). Deindividuation and the self-regulation of behavior. In P. B. Paulus (Ed.), *Psychology of group influence* (2nd ed., pp. 87–109). Hillsdale, NJ: Erlbaum.

Prescott, J. W. (1996). The origins of human love and violence. *Pre- and Peri-Natal Psychology Journal, 10,* 143–188.

Price, R. (1992). Psychosocial impact of job loss on individuals and families. *Current Directions in Psychological Sciences, 1*(1), 9–11.

Prinzmetal, W. (1992). The word superiority effect does not require a T-scope. *Perception and Psychophysics, 51,* 473–484.

Prior, M. (1999). Resilience and coping: The role of individual temperament. In E. Frydenberg (Ed.), *Learning to cope: Developing as a person in complex societies.* New York: Oxford University Press.

Prochaska, J. O. (1994). Strong and weak principles for progressing from precontemplation to action on the basis of twelve problem behaviors. *Health Psychology, 13,* 47–51.

Prochaska, J. O., & DiClemente, C. C. (1992). Stages of change in the modification of problem behaviors. In M. Hersen, R. M. Eisler, & P. M. Miller (Eds.), *Progress in behavior modification.* Sycamore, IL: Sycamore Press.

Prochaska, J. O., DiClemente, C., & Norcross, J. (1992). In search of how people change: Application to addictive behaviors. *American Psychologist, 47,* 1102–1114.

Prochaska, J. O., Velicer, W. F., Rossi, J. S., Goldstein, M. G., Marcus, B. H., Rakowski, W., et al. (1994). Stages of change and decisional balance for 12 problem behaviors. *Health Psychology, 13,* 39–46.

Proctor, R., & Van Zandt, T. (1994). *Human factors in simple and complex systems.* Boston: Allyn & Bacon.

Pruitt, D. G. (1998). Social conflict. In D. Gilbert, S. T. Fiske, & G. Lindzey (Eds.), *Handbook of social psychology* (4th ed., Vol. 2, pp. 470–503). Boston: McGraw-Hill.

Pruitt, D. G., & Carnevale, P. J. (1993). *Negotiation in social conflict.* Pacific Grove, CA: Brooks/Cole.

Pryor, T. (1995). Diagnostic criteria for eating disorders: DSM-IV revisions. *Psychiatric Annals, 25*(1), 40–45.

Puca, A. A., Daly, M. J., Brewster, S. J., Matis, T. C., Barrett, J., Shea-Drinkwater, M., et al. (2001). A genome-wide scan for linkage to human exceptional longevity identifies a locus on chromosome 4. *Proceedings of the National Academy of Sciences, 10,* 1073.

Pugh, K. R., Mencl, W. E., Shaywitz, B. A., Shaywitz, S. E., Fulbright, R. K., Constable, R. T., et al. (2000). The angular gyrus in developmental dyslexia: Task-specific differences in functional connectivity within posterior cortex. *Psychological Science, 11,* 51–56.

Purcell, D. G., & Stewart, A. L. (1991). The object-detection effect: Configuration enhances perception. *Perception and Psychophysics, 50,* 215–224.

Purdue Exponent. (1994, September 7). *Study shows TV depiction of Latinos to be negative.*

Pyszczynski, T., Greenberg, J., & Solomon, S. (1999). A dual-process model of defense against conscious and unconscious death-related thoughts: An extension of terror management theory. *Psychological Review, 106,* 835–845.

Pyszczynski, T., Greenberg, J., & Solomon, S. (2001). Proximal and distal defense: A new perspective on unconscious motivation. *Current Directions in Psychological Science, 9,* 156–160.

Qizilbash, N., & Emre, M. (2001). Experimental approaches and drugs in development for the treatment of dementia. *Expert Opinion on Investigational Drugs, 10,* 607–617.

Quinn, G. E., Shin, C. H., Maguire, M. G., & Stone, R. A. (1999). Myopia and ambient lighting at night. *Nature, 399,* 113–114.

Quintana, S. M. (1998). Children's developmental understanding of ethnicity and race. *Applied and Preventive Psychology, 7,* 27–45.

Quintana, S. M., & Bernal, M. E. (1995). Ethnic minority training in counseling psychology: Comparisons with clinical psychology and proposed standards. *The Counseling Psychologist, 23*(1), 102–121.

Quitkin, F. M., Rabkin, J. G., Gerald, J., Davis, J. M., & Klein, D. F. (2000). Validity of clinical trials of antidepressants. *American Journal of Psychiatry, 157,* 327–337.

Rabasca, L. (1999, July/August). Behavioral interventions can cut the use of restraints. *APA Monitor,* p. 27.

Rabasca, L. (2000). Helping American Indians earn psychology degrees. *Monitor on Psychology, 31,* 52, 56.

Rabbitt, P. (1977). Changes in problem solving ability in old age. In J. E. Birren & K. W. Schaie (Eds.), *Handbook of the psychology of aging.* New York: Van Nostrand Reinhold.

Rabinowitz, J., Lichtenberg, P., Kaplan, Z., Mark, M., Nahon, D., & Davidson, M. (2001). Rehospitalization rates of chronically ill schizophrenic patients discharged on a regimen of risperidone, olanzapine, or conventional antipsychotics. *American Journal of Psychiatry, 158,* 266–269.

Rachlin, H. (2000). *The science of self-control.* Cambridge: Harvard University Press.

Rachman, S. J. (1990). *Fear and courage* (2nd ed.). San Francisco: Freeman.

Rada, J. B., & Rogers, R. W. (1973). *Obedience to authority: Presence of authority and command strength.* Paper presented at the annual convention of the Southeastern Psychological Association.

Radvansky, G. A. (1999). Aging, memory, and comprehension. *Current Directions in Psychological Science, 8,* 49–53.

Raeff, C., Greenfield, P. M., & Quiroz, B. (1995, March). *Developing interpersonal relationships in the cultural contexts of individualism and collectivism.* Paper presented at the biennial meeting of the Society for Research in Child Development, Indianapolis.

Raguram, R., & Bhide, A. (1985). Patterns of phobic neurosis: A retrospective study. *British Journal of Psychiatry, 147,* 557–560.

Raine, A., Brennan, P., & Mednick, S. (1994). Birth complications combined with early maternal rejection at age 1 year predispose to violent crime at age 18 years. *Archives of General Psychiatry, 51,* 984–988.

Raine, A., Buschbaum, M. S., Stanley, J., Lottenberg, S., Abel, L., & Stoddard, J. (1994). Selective reductions in prefrontal glucose metabolism in murderers. *Biological Psychiatry, 36,* 365–373.

Raine, A., Lencz, T., Bihrle, S., LaCasse, L., & Colletti, P. (2000). Reduced prefrontal gray matter volume and reduced autonomic activity in antisocial personality disorder. *Archives of General Psychiatry, 57,* 119–127.

Raine, A., Venables, P., & Williams, M. (1990). Relationships between central and autonomic measures of arousal at age 15 years and criminality at age 24 years. *Archives of General Psychiatry, 47,* 1003–1007.

Rainville, P., Duncan, G. H., Price, D. D., Carrier, B., & Bushnell, M. C. (1997). Pain affect encoded in human anterior cingulate but not somatosensory cortex. *Science, 277,* 968–971.

Rakowski, W., Ehrich, B., Dube, C., Pearlman, D. N., Goldstein, M. G., Peterson, K. K., et al. (1996). Screening mammography and constructs from the transtheoretical model: Associations using two definitions of the stages-of-adoption. *Annals of Behavioral Medicine, 18,* 91–100.

Ramachandran, V. S. (1988, August). Perceiving shape from shading. *Scientific American,* pp. 76–83.

Ramachandran, V. S., & Hubbard, E. M. (2001). Psychophysical investigations into the neural basis of synaesthesia. *Proceedings of the Royal Society London B Biological Sciences, 268,* 979–983.

Ramachandran, V. S., & Rogers-Ramachandran, D. (2000). Phantom limbs and neural plasticity *Archives of Neurology, 57,* 317–320.

Ramey, C. T. (1992). High-risk children and IQ: Altering intergenerational patterns. *Intelligence, 16,* 239–256.

Ramey, C. T., Campbell, F. A., Burchinal, M., Skinner, M. L., Gardner, D. M., & Ramey, S. L. (2000). Persistent effects of early childhood education on high-risk children and their mothers. *Applied Developmental Science, 4,* 2–14.

Ramey, C. T., & Ramey, S. L. (1998). Early intervention and early experience. *American Psychologist, 53,* 109–121.

Ramey, S. L. (1999). Head Start and preschool education: Toward continued improvement. *American Psychologist, 54,* 344–346.

Ramirez, S. Z., Wassef, A., Paniagua, F. A., & Linskey, A. O. (1996). Mental health providers' perceptions of cultural variables in evaluating ethnically diverse clients. *Professional Psychology: Research and Practice, 27,* 284–288.

Ranta, S., Jussila, J., & Hynynen, M. (1990). Recall of awareness during cardiac anaesthesia: Influence of feedback information to the anaesthesiologists. *Acta Aneasthesiolgia Scandinavica, 40,* 554–560.

Rapee, R., Brown, T., Antony, M., & Barlow, D. (1992). Response to hyperventilation and inhalation of 5.5% carbon dioxide-enriched air across DSM-III anxiety disorders. *Journal of Abnormal Psychology, 101,* 538–552.

Raskin, D. C. (1986). The polygraph in 1986: Scientific, professional and legal issues surrounding applications and acceptance of polygraph evidence. *Utah Law Review 1986,* 29–74.

Raskin, N. J., & Rogers, C. R. (1995). Person-centered therapy. In J. J. Corsini & D. Wedding (Eds.), *Current psychotherapies* (5th ed., pp. 128–161). Itasca, IL: Peacock.

Raskin, N. J., & Rogers, C. R. (2001). Person-centered therapy. In R. J. Corsini & D. Wedding (Eds.), *Current psychotherapies* (6th ed.) Itasca, IL: Peacock.

Ratcliff, R., & McKoon, G. (1989). Memory modesl, text processing, and cue-dependent retrieval. In H. L. Roediger & F. I. M. Craik (Eds.), *Varieties of memory and consciousness*. Hillsdale, NJ: Erlbaum.

Rathbone, D. B., & Huckabee, J. C. (1999). *Controlling road rage: A literature review and pilot study. The AAA Foundation for Traffic Safety*. Washington, DC: American Automobile Association.

Ratner, C. (1994). The unconscious: A perspective from sociohistorical psychology. *Journal of Mind and Behavior, 15*(4), 323–342.

Rauschecker, J. P. (1997). Processing of complex sounds in the auditory cortex of cat, monkey, and man. *Acta Oto-Laryngologia* (Suppl. 532–534), 34–38.

Rauscher, F. H., Shaw, G. L., Levine, L. J., Wright, E. L., Dennis, W. R., & Newcomb, R. L. (1997). Music training causes long-term enhancement of preschool children's spatial-temporal reasoning. *Neurological Research, 19,* 2–8.

Ray, D. W., Wandersman, A., Ellisor, J., & Huntington, D. E. (1982). The effects of high density in a juvenile correctional institution. *Basic and Applied Social Psychology, 3,* 95–108.

Rayner, G. (2000, July 14). Baby was given 100 times too much drug. *The Daily Mail,* p. 35.

Raynor, H. A., & Epstein, L. H. (2001). Dietary variety, energy regulation, and obesity. *Psychological Bulletin, 127,* 325–341.

Reber, A. S. (1992). The cognitive unconscious: An evolutionary perspective. *Consciousness and Cognition: An International Journal, 1*(2), 93–133.

Redd, M., & de Castro, J. M. (1992). Social facilitation of eating: Effects of social instruction on food intake. *Physiology and Behavior, 52,* 749–754.

Redd, W. H. (1984). Psychological intervention to control cancer chemotherapy side effects. *Postgraduate Medicine, 75,* 105–113.

Reder, L. M., & Ritter, F. E. (1992). What determines initial feeling of knowing? Familiarity with question terms, not the answer. *Journal of Experimental Psychology: Learning, Memory, and Cognition, 18,* 435–451.

Reed, G. M., Kemeny, M. E., Taylor, S. E., Wang, H.-Y. J., & Visscher, B. R. (1994). "Realistic acceptance" as a predictor of decreased survival time in gay men with AIDS. *Health Psychology, 13,* 299–307.

Reed, S. K. (2000). *Cognition* (5th ed.). Belmont, CA: Wadsworth.

Reedy, M. N. (1983). Personality and aging. In D. S. Woodruff & J. E. Birren (Eds.), *Aging: Scientific perspectives and social issues* (2nd ed.). Monterey, CA: Brooks/Cole.

Reeve, J. M. (1996). *Understanding motivation and emotion*. New York: Harcourt, Brace, Jovanovich.

Reeves, R. A., Baker, G. A., Boyd, J. G., & Cialdini, R. B. (1991). The door-in-the-face technique: Reciprocal concessions vs. self-presentational explanations. *Journal of Social Behavior and Personality, 6,* 545–558.

Regier, D. A., Farmer, M. E., Rae, D. S., Myers, J. K., Kramer, M., Robins, L. N., et al. (1993a). One-month prevalence of mental disorders in the United States and sociodemographic characteristics: The Epidemiologic Catchment Area study. *Acta Psychiatrica Scandinavica 88,* 35–47.

Regier, D. A., Narrow, W., Rae, D., Manderscheid, R., Locke, B., & Goodwin, F. (1993b). The de facto U.S. mental and addictive disorders service system: Epidemiologic catchment area prospective 1-year prevalence rates of disorders and services. *Archives of General Psychiatry, 50,* 85–94.

Reich, T., Edenberg, H. J., Goate, A., Williams, J. T., Rice, J. P., Van Eerdewegh, P., et al. (1998). Genome-wide search for genes affecting the risk for alcohol dependence. *American Journal of Medical Genetics, 81,* 207–215.

Reingold, E. M., Charness, N., Pomplun, M., & Stampe, D. M. (2001). Visual span in expert chess players: Evidence from eye movements. *Psychological Science, 12,* 48–55.

Reinisch, J. M., Ziemba-Davis, M., & Sanders, S. A. (1991). Hormonal contributions to sexually dimorphic behavioral development in humans. *Psychoneuroendocrinology, 16,* 213–278.

Reisberg, D. (1997). *Cognition: Exploring the science of the mind*. New York: Norton.

Reisenzein, R. (1983). The Schachter theory of emotion: Two decades later. *Psychological Bulletin, 94,* 239–264.

Reiss, A. J., & Roth, J. A. (1993). *Understanding and preventing violence*. Washington, DC: National Academy Press.

Reiss, D., & Marino, L. (2001). Mirror self-recognition in the bottlenose dolphin: A case of cognitive convergence. *Proceedings of the National Academy of Science, 98,* 5937–5942.

Reiss, D., Neiderhiser, J. M., Hetherington, E. M., & Plomin, R. (2000). *The relationship code: Deciphering genetic and social influences on adolescent development*. Cambridge: Harvard University Press.

Reitman, D., & Drabman, R. S. (1999). Multifaceted uses of a simple time-out record in the treatment of a noncompliant 8-year-old boy. *Education and Treatment of Children, 22,* 136–145.

Rendall, D., Cheney, D. L., & Seyfarth, R. M. (2000). Proximate factors mediating "contact" calls in adult female baboons (Papio cynocephalus ursinus) and their infants. *Journal of Comparative Psychology, 114,* 36–46.

Reneman, L., Lavalaye, J., Schmand, B., de Wolff, F. A., van den Brink, W., den Heeten, G. J., & Booij, J. (2001). Cortical serotonin transporter density and verbal memory in individuals who stopped using 3,4-methylenedioxymethamphetamine (MDMA or "ecstasy"). *Archives of General Psychiatry, 58,* 901–906.

Reno, R. R., Cialdini, R. B., & Kallgren, C. A. (1993). The transsituational influence of social norms. *Journal of Personality and Social Psychology, 64,* 104–112.

Rescorla, R. A. (1968). Probability of shock in the presence and absence of CS in fear conditioning. *Journal of Comparative and Physiological Psychology, 66,* 1–5.

Rescorla, L. A. (1981). Category development in early language. *Journal of Child Language, 8,* 225–238.

Rescorla, R. A. (1988). Pavlovian conditioning: It's not what you think it is. *American Psychologist, 43,* 151–159.

Rescorla, R. A., & Wagner, A. R. (1972). A theory of Pavlovian conditioning: Variations in the effectiveness of reinforcement and nonreinforcement. In A. H. Black & W. F. Prokasy (Eds.), *Classical conditioning II*. New York: Appleton Century Crofts.

Resnick, M. (1997). Protecting adolescents from harm: Findings from the National Longitudinal Study of Adolescent Health. *Journal of the American Medical Association, 278,* 823–832.

Reynolds, C. F., III, Frank, E., Perel, J. M., Imber, S. D., Cornes, C., Miller, M. D., et al. (1999). Nortriptyline and interpersonal psychotherapy as maintenance therapies for recurrent major depression: A randomized controlled trial in patients older than 59 years. *Journal of the American Medical Association, 281,* 39–45.

Reynolds, D. V. (1969). Surgery in the rat during electrical analgesia induced by focal brain stimulation. *Science, 164,* 444–445.

Rhodes, G., Halberstadt, J., & Brajkovich, G. (2001). Generalization of mere exposure effects to averaged composite faces. *Social Cognition, 19,* 57–70.

Rice, G., Anderson, C., Risch, H., & Ebers, G. (1999). Male homosexuality: Absence of linkage to microsatellite markers at Xq28. *Science, 284,* 665–667.

Rice, M. E. (1997). Violent offender research and implications for the criminal justice system. *American Psychologist, 52,* 414–423.

Richards, J. M., Beal, W. E., Seagal, J. D., & Pennebaker, J. W. (2000). Effects of disclosure of traumatic events on illness behavior among psychiatric prison inmates. *Journal of Abnormal Psychology, 109,* 156–160.

Richards, J. M., & Gross, J. J. (2000). Emotion regulation and memory: The cognitive costs of keeping one's cool. *Journal of Personality & Social Psychology, 79,* 410–424.

Richards, P. S., & Bergin, A. E. (Eds.). (2000). *Handbook of psychotherapy and religious diversity* (pp. 105–129). Washington, DC: American Psychological Association Press.

Richards, T. L., Corina, D., Serafini, S., Steury, K., Echelard, D. R., Dager, S. R., et al. (2000). Effects of a phonologically driven treatment for dyslexia on lactate levels measured by proton MR spectroscopic imaging. *American Journal of Neuroradiology, 21,* 916–922.

Richardson, P. H., & Vincent, C. A. (1986). Acupuncture for the treatment of pain: A review of evaluative research. *Pain, 24,* 15–40.

Richardson-Klavehn, A., & Bjork, R. A. (1988). Measures of memory. *Annual Review of Psychology, 39,* 475–543.

Rickels, K., Schweizer, E., Weiss, S., & Zavodnick, S. (1993). Maintenance drug treatment of panic disorder: II. Short- and long-term outcome after drug taper. *Archives of General Psychiatry, 50,* 61–68.

Ridley, M. (2000). *Genome: The autobiography of a species in 23 chapters.* New York: HarperCollins.

Riedel, W. J., & Jolles, J. (1996). Cognition enhancers in age-related cognitive decline. *Drugs and Aging, 8,* 245–274.

Riedy, C. A., Chavez, M., Figlewicz, D. P., & Woods, S. C. (1995). Central insulin enhances sensitivity to cholecystokinin. *Physiology and Behavior, 58*(4), 755–760.

Riegel, K. F. (1975). Toward a dialectical theory of development. *Human Development, 18,* 50–64.

Riger, S. (1992). Epistemological debates, feminist voices: Science, social values, and the study of women. *American Psychologist, 47,* 730–740.

Riggio, R. E. (1989). *Introduction to industrial/organizational psychology.* Glenview, IL: Scott, Foresman.

Rind, B., & Tromovitch, P. (1997). A meta-analytic review of findings from national samples on psychological correlates of child sexual abuse. *Journal of Sex Research, 34,* 237–255.

Rind, B., Tromovitch, P., & Bauserman, R. (1998). A meta-analytic examination of assumed properties of child sexual abuse using college samples. *Psychological Bulletin, 124,* 22–53.

Rinn, W. E. (1984). The neuropsychology of facial expressions: A review of the neurological and psychological mechanisms for producing facial expressions. *Psychological Bulletin, 95,* 52–77.

Rioult-Pedotti, M.-S., Friedman, D., & Donoghue, J. P. (2000). Learning-induced LTP in neocortex. *Science, 290,* 533–536.

Ripple, C. H., Gilliam, W. S., Chanana, N., & Zigler, E. (1999). Will fifty cooks spoil the broth? The debate over entrusting Head Start to the states. *American Psychologist, 54,* 327–343.

Rips, L. J. (1994). *The psychology of proof: Deductive reasoning in human thinking.* Cambridge, MA: MIT Press.

Risen, J. (1998, July 7). CIA seeks "curmudgeon" to signal its mistakes. *New York Times.*

Robbins, J. (2000, July 4). Virtual reality finds a real place as a medical aid. *New York Times.*

Robbins, T. W., & Everitt, B. J. (1999). Interaction of the dopaminergic system with mechanisms of associative learning and cognition. Implications for drug abuse. *Psychological Science, 10,* 199–202.

Roberts, B. W., & DelVecchio, W. F. (2000). The rank-order consistency of traits from childhood to old-age: A quantitative review of longitudinal studies. *Psychological Bulletin, 126,* 3–25.

Roberts, G. C., & Treasure, D. C. (1999). Sport psychology. In D. A. Bernstein & A. M. Stec (Eds.), *The psychology of everyday life.* Boston: Houghton Mifflin.

Robertson, I. H., & Murre, J. M. J. (1999). Rehabilitation of brain damage: Brain plasticity and principles of guided recovery. *Psychological Bulletin, 126,* 3–25.

Robertson, J., & Robertson, J. (1971). Young children in brief separation: A fresh look. *Psychoanalytic Study of the Child, 26,* 264–315.

Robins, L. N., Helzer, J. E., Weissman, M. M., Orvaschel, H., Gruenberg, E., Burke, J. D., Jr., & Regier, D. A. (1984). Lifetime prevalence of specific psychiatric disorders in three sites. *Archives of General Psychiatry, 41,* 949–958.

Robins, L. N., & Regier, D. A. (Eds.). (1991). *Psychiatric disorders in America: The Epidemiologic Catchment Area study.* New York: Free Press.

Robins, R., Fraley, R. C., Robert, B. W., & Trzesniewski, K. H. (2001). A longitudinal study of personality change in young adulthood. *Journal of Personality, 69,* 617–640.

Robins, R. W., Gosling, S. D., & Craik, K. H. (1999). An empirical analysis of trends in psychology. *American Psychologist, 54,* 117–128.

Robins, R. W., Gosling, S., & Craik, K. H. (2000). Trends in psychology: An Empirical issue. *American Psychologist, 55,* 277–278.

Robins, R. W., John, O. P., Caspi, A., Moffitt, T. E., & Stouthamer-Loeber, M. (1996). Resilient, overcontrolled, and undercontrolled boys: Three replicable personality types. *Journal of Personality & Social Psychology, 70,* 157–171.

Robinson, J. H., & Pritchard, W. S. (1995). "The scientific case that nicotine is addictive": Reply. *Psychopharmacology, 117*(1), 16–17.

Robinson, N. M., Zigler, E., & Gallagher, J. J. (2000). Two tails of the normal curve: Similarities and differences in the study of mental retardation and giftedness. *American Psychologist, 55,* 1413–1424.

Robinson, T. N., Wilde, M. L., Navracruz, L. C., Haydel, K. F., & Varady, A. (2001). Effects of reducing children's television and video game use on aggressive behavior: A randomized controlled trial. *Archives of Pediatrics & Adolescent Medicine, 155,* 17–23.

Rock, I. (1983). *The logic of perception.* Cambridge: MIT Press.

Rock, I., & Gutman, D. (1981). The effect of inattention on form perception. *Journal of Experimental Psychology: Human Perception and performance, 7,* 275–285.

Rodgers, J. (2000). Cognitive performance amongst recreational users of "ecstasy." *Psychopharmacology, 151,* 19–24.

Rodier, P. M. (2000). The early origins of autism. *Scientific American, 282,* 56–63.

Rodriguez, I., Greer, C. A., Mok, M. Y., & Mombaerts, P. (2000). A putative pheromone receptor gene expressed in human olfactory mucosa. *Nature Genetics, 26,* 18–19.

Rodriguez de Fonseca, F., Carrera, M. R. A., Navarro, M., Koob, G. F., & Weiss, F. (1997). Activation of corticotropin-releasing factor in the limbic system during cannabinoid withdrawal. *Science, 276,* 2050–2054.

Roediger, H. L., III. (1990). Implicit memory: Retention without remembering. *American Psychologist, 45,* 1043–1056.

Roediger, H. L., Buckner, R. L., & McDermott, K. B. (1999). Components of processing. In J. K. Foster & M. Jelicic (Eds.), *Memory: Systems, process, or function?* (pp. 31–65). Oxford: Oxford University Press.

Roediger, H. L., III, Guynn, M. J., & Jones, T. C. (1995). Implicit memory: A tutorial review. In G. d'Ydewalle, P. Eelen, & P. Bertelson (Eds.), *International perspectives on psychological science: Vol. 2. The state of the art* (pp. 67–94). Hove, England: Erlbaum.

Roediger, H. L., III, Jacoby, D., & McDermott, K. B. (1996). Misinformation effects in recall: Creating false memories through repeated retrieval. *Journal of Memory and Learning, 35,* 300–318.

Roediger, H. L., III, & McDermott, K. B. (1995). Creating false memories: Remembering words not presented in lists. *Journal of Experimental Psychology: Learning, Memory, and Cognition, 21,* 803–814.

Roediger, H. L., & McDermott, K. B. (2000). Tricks of memory. *Current Directions in Psychological Science, 9,* 123–127.

Roehrich, L., & Goldman, M. S. (1995). Implicit priming of alcohol expectancy memory processes and subsequent drinking behavior. *Experimental and Clincial Psychopharmocology, 3,* 402–410.

Roffwarg, H. P., Hermann, J. H., & Bowe-Anders, C. (1978). The effects of sustained alterations of waking visual input on dream content. In A. M. Arkin, J. S. Antrobus, & S. J. Ellman (Eds.), *The mind in sleep.* Hillsdale, NJ: Erlbaum.

Roffwarg, H. P., Muzio, J. N., & Dement, W. C. (1966). Ontogenetic development of the human sleep-dream cycle. *Science, 152,* 604–619.

Rogelberg, S. G., & Luong, A. (1998). Nonresponse to mailed surveys: A review and guide. *Current Directions in Psychological Science, 7,* 60–65.

Rogers, C. R. (1951). *Client-centered therapy.* Boston: Houghton Mifflin.

Rogers, C. R. (1961). *On becoming a person.* Boston: Houghton Mifflin.

Rogers, C. R. (1970). *Carl Rogers on encounter groups.* New York: Harper & Row.

Rogers, C. R. (1980). *A way of being.* Boston: Houghton Mifflin.

Rogers, J., Madamba, S. G., Staunton, D. A., & Siggins, G. R. (1986). Ethanol increases single unit activity in the inferior olivary nucleus. *Brain Research, 385,* 253–262.

Rogers, R. (1995). *Diagnostic and structured interviewing: A handbook for psychologists.* Odessa, FL: Psychological Assessment Resources.

Rogers, S. M., & Turner, C. F. (1991). Male-male sexual contact in the U.S.A.: Findings from five sample surveys, 1970–1990. *Journal of Sex Research, 28,* 491–519.

Rogers, T. B. (1995). *The psychological testing enterprise: An introduction.* Belmont, CA: Wadsworth.

Rogoff, B., & Waddell, K. J. (1982). Memory for information organized in a scene by children from two cultures. *Child Development, 53,* 1224–1228.

Rohan, M. J., & Zanna, M. P. (1996). Value transmission in families. In C. Seligman, J. M. Olson, & M. P. Zanna (Eds.), *The psychology of values: The Ontario symposium* (Vol. 8, pp. 253–276). Mahwah, NJ: Erlbaum.

Rolls, E. T. (1997). Taste and olfactory processing in the brain and its relation to the control of eating. *Critical Review of Neurobiology, 11*, 263–287.

Romer, D., Jamieson, K. H., & deCoteau, N. J. (1998). The treatment of persons of color in local television news: Ethnic blame discourse or realistic group conflict? *Communication Research, 25*, 286–305.

Rosch, E. (1975). Cognitive representations of semantic categories. *Journal of Experimental Psychology: General, 104*, 192–223.

Rosch, E., Mervis, C. B., Gray, W. D., Johnson, D. M., & Boyes-Braem, P. (1976). Basic objects in natural categories. *Cognitive Psychology, 8*, 382–439.

Rose, S. P. R. (1993, April 17). When to spank. *U.S. News & World Report*, pp. 52–58.

Rosellini, L. (1998, April 13). When to spank. *U.S. News and World Report*, pp. 52–58.

Rosen, B. C., & D'Andrade, R. (1959). The psychosocial origins of achievement motivation. *Sociometry, 22*, 188–218.

Rosen, G. M. (1999). Treatment fidelity and research on eye movement desinsitization and reprocessing (EMDR). *Journal of Anxiety Disorders, 13*, 173–184.

Rosen, R. (1991). *The healthy company*. Los Angeles: Tarcher.

Rosenbach, M. L., Hermann, R. C., & Dorwart, R. A. (1997). Use of electroconvulsive therapy in the Medicare population between 1987 and 1992. *Psychiatric Services, 48*, 1537–1542.

Rosenbaum, M., & Bennett, B. (1986). Homicide and depression. *American Journal of Psychiatry, 143*, 367–370.

Rosenbaum, R. S., Priselac, S. K., Black, S. E., Gao, F., Nadel, L., & Moscovitch, M. (2000). Remote spatial memory in an amnesiac person with extensive bilateral hippocampal lesions. *Nature Neuroscience, 3*, 1044–1048.

Rosenberg, M. B., Friedmann, T., Roberston, R. C., Tuszynski, M., Wolff, J. A., Breakefield, X. O., & Gage, F. H. (1988). Grafting genetically modifed cells to the damaged brain: Restorative effect of NGF expression. *Science, 242*, 1575–1578.

Rosenfarb, I. S., Goldstein, M. J., Mintz, J., & Nuechterlein, K. H. (1995). Expressed emotion and subclinical psychopathology observable within the transactions between schizophrenic patients and their family members. *Journal of Abnormal Psychology, 104*, 259–267.

Rosenfarb, I. S., Nuechterlein, K. H., Goldstein, M. J., & Subotnik, K. L. (2000). Neurocognitive vulnerability, interpersonal criticism, and the emergence of unusual thinking by schizophrenic patients during family transactions. *Archives of General Psychiatry, 57*, 1174–1179.

Rosenfeld, J. P. (1995). Alternative views of Bashore and Rapp's (1993) alternatives to traditional polygraphy: A critique. *Psychological Bulletin, 117*(1), 159–166.

Rosenstock, I. M. (1974). Historical origins of the health belief model. *Health Education Monographs, 2*, 328–335.

Rosenthal, R. (1994). Interpersonal expectancy effects: A 30-year perspective. *Current Directions in Psychological Science, 3*, 176–179.

Rosenthal, R. R. (1966). *Experimenter effects in behavioral research*. New York: Appleton-Century-Crofts.

Rosenthal, R. R., & Jacobson, L. (1968). *Pygmalion in the classroom*. New York: Holt, Rinehart & Winston.

Rosenzweig, M. R., & Bennett, E. L. (1996). Psychobiology of plasticity: Effects of training and experience on brain and behavior. *Behavioural Brain Research, 78*, 57–65.

Rosmond, R., Bouchard, C., & Björntorp, P. (2001). Tsp509I polymorphism in exon 2 of the glucocorticoid receptor gene in relation to obesity and cortisol secretion: Cohort study. *British Medical Journal, 322*, 652–653.

Ross, C. A. (1997). *Dissociative identity disorder: Diagnosis, clinical features, and treatment of multiple personality*. New York: Wiley.

Ross, C. A., Anderson, G., Fleisher, W. P., & Norton, G. R. (1991). The frequency of multiple personality disorder among psychiatric inpatients. *American Journal of Psychiatry, 148*, 1717–1720.

Ross, S. I., & Jackson, J. M. (1991). Teachers' expectations for Black males' and Black females' academic achievement. *Personality and Social Psychology Bulletin, 17*, 78–82.

Ross, S. M., & Ross, L. E. (1971). Comparison of trace and delay classical eyelid conditioning as a function of interstimulus interval. *Journal of Experimental Psychology, 91*, 165–167.

Roth, M. D., Arora, A., Barsky, S. H., Kleerup, E. C., Simmons, M., & Tashkin, D. P. (1998). Airway inflammation in young marijuana and tobacco smokers. *American Journal of Respiratory Critical Care Medicine, 157*, 928–937.

Rothbart, M. K., Ahadi, S. A., & Evans, D. E. (2000). Temperament and personality: Origins and outcomes. *Journal of Personality and Social Psychology, 78*, 122–135.

Rothbart, M. K., & Bates, J. E. (1998). Temperament. In W. Damon & N. Eisenberg (Eds.), *Handbook of child psychology: Vol. 3. Social, emotional, and personality development* (5th ed., pp. 105–176). New York: Wiley.

Rothbaum, B. O., & Hodges, L. F. (1999). The use of virtual reality exposure in the treatment of anxiety disorders. *Behavior Modification, 23*, 507–525.

Rothbaum, B. O., Hodges, L. F., Alarcon, R., Ready, D., Shahar, F., Graap, K., Pair, J., Hebert, P., Gotz, D., Wills, B., & Baltzall, D. (1999). Virtual reality exposure therapy for PTSD Vietnam veterans: A case study. *Journal of Traumatic Stress, 12*, 263–271.

Rothbaum, B. O., Hodges, L. F., Kooper, R., & Opdyke, D. (1995). Effectiveness of computer-generated virtual reality graded exposure in the treatment of acrophobia. *American Journal of Psychiatry, 152*, 626–628.

Rothbaum, B. O., Hodges, L., Smith, S., Lee, J. H., & Price, L. (2000). A controlled study of virtual reality exposure therapy for the fear of flying. *Journal of Consulting and Clinical Psychology, 68*, 1020–1026.

Rothbaum, F., Pott, M., Azuma, H., Miyake, K., & Weisz, J. (2000). The development of close relationships in Japan and the United States: Paths of symbiotic harmony and generative tension. *Child Development, 71*, 1121–1142.

Rottenstreich, Y., & Tversky, A. (1997). Unpacking, repacking, and anchoring: Advances in support theory. *Psychological Review, 104*, 406–415.

Rotter, J. (1982). *The development and application of social learning theory*. New York: Praeger.

Rotton, J. (1990). Individuals under stress. In C. E. Kimble (Ed.), *Social psychology: Living with people*. New York: Brown.

Rotton, J., & Frey, J. (1985). Air pollution, weather, and violent crimes: Concomitant time-series analysis of archival data. *Journal of Personality and Social Psychology, 49*, 1207–1220.

Rotton, J., Frey, J., Barry, T., Mulligan, M., & Fitzpatrick, M. (1979). The air pollution experience and physical aggression. *Journal of Applied Social Psychology, 9*, 397–412.

Rotton, J., & Kelly, I. W. (1985). Much ado about the full moon: A meta-analysis of lunar-lunacy research. *Psychological Bulletin, 97*, 286–306.

Rouéché, B. (1986, December 8). Cinnabar. *The New Yorker*.

Rovee-Collier, C. (1999). The development of infant memory. *Current Directions in Psychological Science, 8*, 80–85.

Rowe, D. C. (1997). Genetics, temperament, and personality. In R. Hogan, J. Johnson, & S. Briggs (Eds.), *Handbook of personality psychology* (pp. 367–386). San Diego: Academic Press.

Rowe, D. C., Jacobson, K. C., & Van den Oord, E. J. C. G. (1999). Genetic and environmental influences on vocabulary IQ: Parental education level as moderator. *Child Development, 70*, 1151–1162.

Roy-Byrne, P., Stang, P., Wittchen, H.-U., Ustun, B., Walters, E. E., & Kessler, R. (1999). Lifetime Panic-Depression comorbidity in the National Comorbidity Survey. *British Journal of Psychiatry, 176*, 229–235.

Rozin, P. (1982). "Taste-smell confusions" and the duality of the olfactory sense. *Perception and Psychophysics, 31*, 397–401.

Rozin, P. (1996). Sociocultural influences on human food selection. In E. D. Capaldi (Ed.), *Why we eat what we eat: The psychology of eating* (pp. 233–263). Washington DC: American Psychological Association.

Rozin, P., Dow, S., Moscovitch, M., & Rajaram, S. (1998). The role of memory for recent eating experiences in onset and cessation of meals. Evidence from the amnesic syndrome. *Psychological Science, 9*, 392–396.

Rubin, B. M. (1998, February 8). When he's retiring and she isn't. *Chicago Tribune*, Sect. 1, pp. 1ff.

Rubin, E. (1915). *Synsoplevede figure*. Copenhagen: Gyldendalske.

Rubin, K. H., Bukowski, W., & Parker, J. G. (1998). Peer interactions, relationships, and groups. In W. Damon & N. Eisenberg (Eds.), *Handbook of child psychology: Vol. 3. Social, emotional, and personality development* (5th ed., pp. 619–700). New York: Wiley.

Rubinow, D. R., & Schmidt, P. J. (1996). Androgens, brain, and behavior. *American Journal of Psychiatry, 153*, 974–984.

Rubinstein, S., & Caballero, B. (2000). Is Miss America an undernourished role model? *Journal of the American Medical Association, 283*, 1569.

Ruble, D. N., & Martin, C. L. (1998). Gender development. In W. Damon & N. Eisenberg (Eds.), *Handbook of child psychology: Vol. 3. Social, emotional, and personality development* (5th ed., pp. 933–1016). New York: Wiley.

Rudolph, K. D., Lambert, S. F., Clark, A. G., & Kurlakowsky, K. D. (2001). Negotiating the transition to middle school: The role of self-regulatory processes. *Child Development, 72*, 929–946.

Rudolph, M. C., Sahota, P., Barth, J. H., & Walker, J. (2001). Increasing prevalence of obesity in primary school children: Cohort study. *British Medical Journal, 322*, 1094–1095.

Rudorfer, M. V., Henry, M. E., & Sackheim, H. A. (1997). Electroconvulsive therapy. In A. Tasman, J. Kay, & J. A. Lieberman (Eds.), *Psychiatry* (pp. 1535–1556). Philadelphia: Saunders.

Rueckert, L., Baboorian, D., Stavropoulos, K., & Yasutake, C. (1999). Individual differences in callosal efficiency: Correlation with attention. *Brain and Cognition, 41*, 390–410.

Ruffman, T., Perner, J., Naito, M., Parkin, L., & Clements, W. A. (1998). Older (but not younger) siblings facilitate false belief understanding. *Developmental Psychology, 34*, 161–174.

Rugg, M. D., & Coles, M. G. H. (Eds.). (1995). *Electrophysiology of mind*. New York: Oxford University Press.

Rugg, M. D., & Wilding, E. L. (2000). Retrieval processing and episodic memory. *Trends in Cognitive Sciences, 4*, 108–115.

Ruiz, P., Varner, R. V., Small, D. R, & Johnson, B. A. (1999). Ethnic differences in the neuroleptic treatment of schizophrenia. *Psychiatric Quarterly, 70*, 163–172.

Rumbaugh, D. M. (Ed.). (1977). *Language learning by a chimpanzee: The Lana project*. New York: Academic Press.

Rumelhart, D. E., & McClelland, J. L. (1986). *Parallel distributed processing: Explorations in the microstructure of cognition: Vol. 1. Foundations*. Cambridge, MA: Bradford.

Rumelhart, D. E., & Todd, P. M. (1992). Learning and connectionist representations. In D. E. Meyer & S. Kornblum (Eds.), *Attention and performance XIV: Synergies in experimental psychology, artificial intelligence, and cognitive neuroscience* (pp. 3–30). Cambridge: MIT Press.

Rusbult, C. E., Arriagi, X. B., & Agnew, C. R (2001). Interdependence in close relationships. In G. Fletcher & M. Clark (Eds.), *Blackwell handbook of social psychology: Interpersonal processes* (pp. 359–387). Oxford, England: Blackwell.

Rusbult, C. E., & Van Lange, P. A. M. (1996). Interdependence processes. In E. T Higgins & A. W. Kruglanski (Eds.), *Social psychology: Handbook of basic principles* (pp. 564–596). New York: Guilford.

Ruscio, J. (2001). Administering quizzes at random to increase students' reading. *Teaching of Psychology, 28*, 204–206.

Rushton, J. P. (1990). Creativity, intelligence, and psychoticism. *Personality and Individual Differences, 11*, 1291–1298.

Russell, J. A. (1991). Culture and the categorization of emotions. *Psychological Bulletin, 110*, 426–450.

Russell, J. A. (1994). Is there universal recognition of emotion from facial expression? A review of the cross-cultural studies. *Psychological Bulletin, 155*(2), 102–141.

Russell, J. A. (1995). Facial expressions of emotion: What lies beyond minimal universality? *Psychological Bulletin, 118*, 379–391.

Rutkowski, G. K., Gruder, C. L., & Romer, D. (1983). Group cohesiveness, social norms, and bystander intervention. *Journal of Personality and Social Psychology, 44*, 545–552.

Rutter, D. R., Quine, L., & Albery, I. P. (1998). Perceptions of risk in motorcyclists: Unrealistic optimism, relative realism and predictions of behaviour. *British Journal of Psychology, 89*, 681–696.

Rutter, M., Pickles, A., Murray, R., & Eaves, L. (2001). Testing hypotheses on specific environmental causal effects on behavior. *Psychological Bulletin, 127*, 291–324.

Rutter, M., & Schopler, E. (1992). Classification of pervasive developmental disorders: Some concepts and practical considerations. *Journal of Autism and Developmental Disorders, 22*, 459–482.

Rutter, M. L. (1997). Nature-nurture integration: The example of antisocial behavior. *American Psychologist, 52*, 390–398.

Ruvolo, A. P., & Markus, H. R. (1992). Possible selves and performance: The power of self-relevant imagery. *Social Cognition, 10*, 95–124.

Ryan, A. M. (2001). The peer group as a context for the development of young adolescent motivation and achievement. *Child Development, 72*, 1135–1150.

Ryan, R. H., & Geiselman, R. E. (1991). Effects of biased information on the relationship between eyewitness confidence and accuracy. *Bulletin of the Psychonomic Society, 29*, 7–9.

Rymer, R. (1993a). *Genie: An abused child's flight from silence*. New York: HarperCollins.

Rymer, R. (1993b). *Genie: A scientific tragedy*. New York: HarperCollins.

Rynders, J., & Horrobin, J. (1980). Educational provisions for young children with Down's syndrome. In J. Gottlieb (Ed.), *Educating mentally retarded persons in the mainstream* (pp. 109–147). Baltimore: University Park Press.

Saarni, C., Mummer, D. L., & Campos, J. J. (1998). Emotional development: Action, communication, and understanding. In W. Damon & N. Eisenberg (Eds.), *Handbook of child psychology: Vol. 3. Social, emotional, and personality development* (5th ed., pp. 237–310). New York: Wiley.

Sabini, J., Siepmann, M., & Stein, J. (2001). The really fundamental attribution error in social psychological research, *Psychological Inquiry, 12*, 1–5.

Sachs, J. (1967). Recognition memory for syntactic and semantic aspects of connected discourse. *Perception and Psychophysics, 2*, 437–442.

Sack, R. L., Hughes, R. J., Edgar, D. M., & Lewy, A. J. (1997). Sleep-promoting effects of melatonin: At what dose, in whom, under what conditions, and by what mechanisms? *Sleep 20*, 908–915.

Sackeim, H. A. (1985, June). The case for ECT. *Psychology Today*, pp. 36–40.

Sackeim, H. A. (1994). Central issues regarding the mechanisms of action of electroconvulsive therapy: Directions for future research. *Psychopharmacology Bulletin, 30*, 281–308.

Sackeim, H. A., Haskett, R. F., Mulsant, B. H., Thase, M. E., Mann, J. J., Pettinati, H. M., et al. (2001). Continuation pharmacotherapy in the prevention of relapse following electroconvulsive therapy: A randomized controlled trial. *Journal of the American Medical Association, 285*, 1299–1307.

Sackeim, H. A., Prudic, J., Devanand, D. P., Nobler, M. S., Lisanby, S. H., Peyser, S., et al. (2000). A prospective, randomized, double-blind comparison of bilateral and right unilateral electroconvulsive therapy at different stimulus intensities. *Archives of General Psychiatry, 57*, 425–434.

Sackett, P. R., Schmitt, N., Ellington, J. E., & Kabin, M. B. (2001). High-stakes testing in employment, credentialing, and higher education: Prospects in a post-affirmative action world. *American Psychologist, 56*, 302–318.

Sackoff, J., & Weinstein, L. (1988). The effects of potential self-inflicted harm on obedience to an authority figure. *Bulletin of the Psychonomic Society, 26*, 347–348.

Sacks, O. (1985). *The man who mistook his wife for a hat*. New York: Summit Books.

Sacks, O. (1992, July 27). The landscape of his dreams. *The New Yorker*.

Saffran, J. R., Senghas, A., & Trueswell, J. C. (2001). The acquisition of language by children. *Proceedings of the National Academy of Science, 98*, 12874–12875.

Sakairi, Y. (1992). Studies on meditation using questionnaires. *Japanese Psychological Review, 35*(1), 94–112.

Salloum, I. M., Cornelius, J. R., Thase, M. E., Daley, D. C., Kirisci, L., & Spotts, C. (1998). Naltrexone utility in depressed alcoholics. *Psychopharmacological Bulletin, 34*, 111–115.

Salovey, P., Mayer, J. D., & Rosenhan, D. L. (1991). Mood and helping: Mood as a motivator of helping and helping as a regulator of mood. In M. S. Clark (Ed.), *Review of personality and social psychology: Vol. 12. Prosocial behavior* (pp. 215–237). Newbury Park, CA: Sage.

Salovey, P., Rothman, A. J., & Rodin, J. (1998). Health behavior. In D. Gilbert, S. T. Fiske, & G. Lindzey (Eds.), *Handbook of social psychology* (4th ed., Vol. 2, pp. 684–732). Boston: McGraw-Hill.

Salovey, P., Sieber, W. J., Smith, A. F., Turk, D. C., Jobe, J. B., & Willis, G. B. (1992). Reporting chronic pain episodes on health surveys. *Vital and health statistics* (Series 6, No. 6, 1–71, DHHS Publication No. 92–1081). Washington, DC: US Government Printing Office.

Salovey, P., & Sluyter, D. J. (Eds.). (1997). *Emotional development and emotional intelligence: Educational implications*. New York: Basic Books.

Salthouse, T. A. (1990). Working memory as a processing resource in cognitive aging. *Developmental Review, 10,* 101–124.

Salthouse, T. A. (1996). The processing-speed theory of adult age differences in cognition. *Psychological Review, 103,* 403–428.

Salthouse, T. A. (2000). Aging and measures of processing speed. *Biological Psychology, 54,* 35–54.

Salthouse, T. A., & Prill, K. A. (1987). Inferences about age impairments in inferential reasoning. *Psychology and Aging, 2,* 43–51.

Salvi, R. J., Chen, L., Trautwein, P., Powers, N., & Shero, M. (1998). Hair cell regeneration and recovery of function in the avian auditory system. *Scandinavian Audiology Supplement, 48,* 7–14.

Salzer, M. S., Rappaport, J., & Segre, L. (1999). Professional appraisal of professionally led and self-help groups. *American Journal of Orthopsychiatry, 69,* 536–540.

Sammons, M. T., & Schmidt, N. B. (2001). *Combined treatments for mental disorders: A guide to psychological and pharmacological interventions*. Washington, DC: American Psychological Association.

Sampson, E. E. (2000). Reinterpreting individualism and collectivism: Their religious roots and monologic versus dialogic person-other relationship. *American Psychologist, 55,* 1425–1432.

Samuel, A. G. (2001). Knowing a word affects the fundamental perception of the sounds within it. *Psychological Science, 12,* 348–351.

Samuel, S. E., & Gorton, G. E. (1998). National survey of psychology internship directors regarding education for prevention of psychologist-patient sexual exploitation. *Professional Psychology: Research and Practice, 29,* 86–90.

Samuelson, C. D., & Messick, D. M. (1995). When do people want to change the rules for allocating shared resources? In D. Schroeder (Ed.), *Social dilemmas: Perspectives on individuals and groups* (pp. 143–162). Westport, CT: Praeger.

Sanchez-Ramos, J., Song, S., Cardozo-Pelaez, F., Hazzi, C., Stedeford, T., Willing, A., et al. (2000). Adult bone-marrow stromal cells differentiate into neural cells in vitro. *Experimental Neurology, 164,* 247–256.

Sanders, M. R., & Dadds, M. R. (1993). *Behavioral family intervention*. Boston: Allyn & Bacon.

Sanders, M. R., Markie-Dadds, C., Tully, L. A., & Bor, W. (2000). The triple p-positive parenting program: A comparison of enhanced, standard, and self-directed behavioral family intervention for parents of children with early onset conduct problems. *Journal of Consulting and Clinical Psychology, 68,* 624–640.

Sanderson, W. C., Rapee, R. M., & Barlow, D. H. (1989). The influence of an illusion of control on panic attacks induced via inhalation of 5.5 carbon dioxide-enriched air. *Archives of General Psychiatry, 46,* 157–162.

Sandin, R. H., Enlund, G., Samuelsson, P., & Lennmarken, C. (2000). Awareness during anasthesia: A prospective case study. *Lancet, 355,* 707–711.

Sanna, L. J. (1992). Self-efficacy theory: Implications for social facilitation and social loafing. *Journal of Personality and Social Psychology, 62,* 774–786.

Sarafino, E. P., & Goehring, P. (2000). Age comparisons in acquiring biofeedback control and success in reducing headache pain. *Annals of Behavioral Medicine, 22,* 1–9.

Sarason, B. R., Sarason, I. G., & Gurung, R. A. R. (1997). Close personal relationships and health outcomes: A key to the role of social support. In S. Duck (Ed.), *Handbook of personal relationships* (pp. 547–573). New York: Wiley.

Sarason, I. G. (1984). Stress, anxiety, and cognitive interference: Reactions to tests. *Journal of Personality and Social Psychology, 46*(4), 929–938.

Sarason, I. G., Johnson, J., & Siegel, J. (1978). Assessing impact of life changes: Development of the life experiences survey. *Journal of Clinical and Consulting Psychology, 46,* 932–946.

Sarason, I. G., Sarason, B. R., Keefe, D. E., Hayes, B. E., & Shearin, E. N. (1986). Cognitive interference: Situational determinants and traitlike characteristics. *Journal of Personality and Social Psychology, 51,* 215–226.

Sasaki, Y., Jadjikhani, N., Fischl, B., Liu, A. K., Marret, S., Dale, A. M., & Tootell, R. B. H. (2001). Local and global attention are mapped retinotopically in human occipital cortex. *Proceedings of the National Academy of Science, 98,* 2077.

Sato, T. (1997). Seasonal affective disorder and phototherapy: A critical review. *Professional Psychology: Research and Practice, 28,* 164–169.

Sattler, D. N., Kaiser, C. F., & Hittner, J. B. (2000). Disaster preparedness: Relationships among prior experience, personal characteristics, and distress. *Journal of Applied Social Psychology, 30,* 1396–1420.

Saudino, K. J., Gagne, J. R., Grant, J., Ibatoulina, A., Marytuina, T., & Whitfield, K. (1999). Genetic and environmental influences in adult Russian twins. *International Journal of Behavioral Development, 23,* 375–389.

Saufley, W. H., Otaka, S. R., & Bavaresco, J. L. (1985). Context effects: Classroom tests and context independence. *Memory & Cognition, 13,* 522–528.

Sauter, S., Murphy, L., Colligan, M., Swanson, N., Hurrell, J., Jr., Scharf, F., Jr., et al. (1999). *Stress at work* (DHHS [NIOSH] Publication No. 99–101). Washington, DC: National Institute on Occupational Health and Safety.

Savage-Rumbaugh, E. S. (1990). Language acquisition in a non-human species: Implications for the innateness debate. *Developmental Psychology, 23,* 599–620.

Savage-Rumbaugh, E. S., Murphy, J., Sevcik, R. A., Brakke, K. E., Williams, S. L., & Rumbaugh, D. M. (1993). Language comprehension in age and child. *Monographs of the Society for Research in Child Development, 58*(3–4).

Savage-Rumbaugh, E. S., Pate, J. L., Lawson, J., Smith, S. T., & Rosenbaum, S. (1983). Can a chimpanzee make a statement? *Journal of Experimental Psychology: General, 112,* 469–487.

Savage-Rumbaugh, S., & Brakke, K. E. (1996). Animal language: Methodological and interpretive issues. In M. Bekoff & D. Jamieson (Eds.), *Readings in animal cognition* (pp. 269–288). Cambridge: MIT Press.

Savage-Rumbaugh, S., Shanker, S. G., & Taylor, T. J. (1999). *Apes, language and the human mind*. New York: Oxford University Press.

Saveliev, S. V., Lebedev, V. V., Evgeniev, M. B., & Korochkin, L. I. (1997). Chimeric brain: theoretical and clinical aspects. *International Journal of Developmental Biology, 41,* 801–808.

Savelkoul, M., Post, M. W. M., de Witte, L. P., & van den Borne, H. B. (2000). Social support, coping, and subjective well-being in patients with rheumatic diseases. *Patient Education and Counseling, 39,* 205–218.

Savin-Williams, R. C., & Demo, D. H. (1984). Developmental change and stability in adolescent self-concept. *Developmental Psychology, 20,* 1100–1110.

Sawamoto, K., Nakao, N., Kakishita, K., Ogawa, Y., Toyama, Y., Yamamoto, A., et al. (2001). Generation of dopaminergic neurons in the adult brain from mesencephalic precursor cells labeled with a nestin-GFP transgene. *Journal of Neuroscience, 21,* 3895–3903.

Saxe, L., & Ben-Shakhar, G. (1999). Admissibility of polygraph tests: The application of scientific standards post-Daubert. *Psychology, Public Policy, and Law, 5,* 203–223.

Sayers, J. (1991). *Mother of psychoanalysis*. New York: Norton.

Scarr, S. (1998). How do families affect intelligence? Social environmental and behavior genetic prediction. In J. J. McArdle & R. W. Woodcock (Eds.), *Human cognitive abilities in theory and practice* (pp. 113–136). Mahwah, NJ: Erlbaum.

Scarr, S., & Carter-Saltzman, L. (1982). Genetics and intelligence. In R. Sternberg (Ed.), *Handbook of human intelligence* (pp. 792–896). Cambridge, England: Cambridge University Press.

Scarr, S., & Weinberg, R. A. (1976). IQ test performance of black children adopted by white families. *American Psychologist, 31,* 726–739.

Schachar, R., & Logan, G. (1990). Impulsivity and inhibitory control in normal development and childhood psychopathology. *Developmental Psychology, 26,* 710–720.

Schachter, S., & Singer, J. (1962). Cognitive, social and physiological determinants of emotional state. *Psychological Review, 69,* 379–399.

Schacter, D. L. (1999). The seven sins of memory: Insights from psychology and cognitive neuroscience. *American Psychologist, 54,* 182–203.

Schacter, D. L. (2001). *The seven sins of memory.* Boston: Houghton Mifflin.

Schacter, D. L., & Badgaiyan, R. D. (2001). Neuroimaging of priming: New perspectives on implicit and explicit memory. *Current Directions in Psychological Science, 10,* 1–4.

Schacter, D. L., Chiu, C.-Y. P., & Ochsner, K. N. (1993). Implicit memory: A selective review. *Annual Review of Neuroscience, 16,* 159–182.

Schacter, D. L., Church, B., & Treadwell, J. (1994). Implicit memory in amnesic patients: Evidence for spared auditory priming. *Psychological Science, 5,* 20–25.

Schacter, D. L., & Cooper, L. A. (1993). Implicit and explicit memory for novel visual objects: Structure and function. *Journal of Experimental Psychology: Learning, Memory, and Cognition, 19*(5), 995–1009.

Schacter, D. L., Cooper, L. A., Delaney, S. M., Peterson, M. A., & Tharan, M. (1991). Implicit memory for possible and impossible objects: Constraints on the construction of structural descriptions. *Journal of Experimental Psychology: Learning, Memory, and Cognition, 17,* 3–19.

Schacter, D. L., Norman, K. A., & Koutstaal, W. (1998). The cognitive neuroscience of constructive memory. *Annual Review of Psychology, 49,* 289–318.

Schaefer, J., Sykes, R., Rowley, R., & Baek, S. (1988). *Slow country music and drinking.* Paper presented at the 87th annual meetings of the American Anthropological Association, Phoenix, AZ.

Schafer, J., & Brown, S. A. (1991). Marijuana and cocaine effect expectancies and drug use patterns. *Journal of Consulting and Clinical Psychology, 59,* 558–565.

Schaffer, C. E., Davidson, R. J., & Saron, C. (1983). Frontal and parietal EEG asymmetry in depressed and non-depressed subjects. *Biological Psychiatry, 18,* 753–762.

Schaie, K. W. (1993). The Seattle logitudinal study of adult intelligence. *Current Directions in Psychological Science, 2*(6), 171–175.

Schaie, K. W. (1996). Intellectual development in adulthood. In J. E. Birren, K. Schaie, R. P. Abeles, M. Gatz, & T. A. Salthouse (Eds.), *Handbook of the psychology of aging* (4th ed., pp. 266–286). San Diego: Academic Press.

Scharff, C., Kirn, J. R., Grossman, M., Macklis, J. D., & Nottebohm, F. (2000). Targeted neuronal death affects neuronal replacement and vocal behavior in adult songbirds. *Neuron, 25,* 481–492.

Scharff, J. S., & Scharff, D. E. (1998). *Object relations individual psychotherapy.* Northvale, NJ: Aronson.

Schaubroeck, J., Jones, J. R., & Xie, J. J. (2001). Individual differences in utilizing control to cope with job demands: effects on susceptibility to infectious disease. *Journal of Applied Psychology, 86,* 265–278.

Scheck, B., Neufeld, P., & Dwyer, J., (2000). *Actual innocence: Five days to execution and other dispatches from the wrongly convicted.* New York: Doubleday.

Scheerer, M., Rothmann, R., & Goldstein, K. (1945). A case of "idiot savant": An experimental study of personality organization. *Psychology Monograph, 58*(4), 1–63.

Scheier, M. F., Matthews, K. A., Owens, J. F., Magovern, G. J., Lefebvre, R. C., Abbott, R. A., & Carver, C. S. (1989). Dispositional optimism and recovery from coronary artery bypass surgery: The beneficial effects on physical and psychological well-being. *Journal of Personality and Social Psychology, 57,* 1024–1040.

Schenck, C. H., & Mahowald, M. W. (1992). Motor dyscontrol in narcolepsy: Rapid eye movement (REM) sleep without atonia and REM sleep behavior disorder. *Annals of Neurology, 32*(1), 3–10.

Scheufele, P. M. (2000). Effects of progressive relaxation and classical music on measurements of attention, relaxation, and stress responses. *Journal of Behavioral Medicine, 23,* 207–228.

Schiff, M., Duyme, M., Dumaret, A., Stewart, J., Tomkiewicz, S., & Feingold, J. (1978). Intellectual status of working class children adopted early into upper-middle class families. *Science, 200,* 1503–1504.

Schiller, P. H. (1996). On the specificity of neurons and visual areas. *Behavior and Brain Research, 76,* 21–35.

Schloss, P., & Williams, D. C. (1998). The serotonin transporter: A primary target for antidepressant drugs. *Journal of Psychopharmacology, 12,* 115–121.

Schmidt, N. B., Lerew, D. R., & Jackson, R. J. (1997). The role of anxiety sensitivity in the pathogenesis of panic: Prospective evaluation of spontaneous panic attacks druing acute stress. *Journal of Abnormal Psychology, 106,* 355–364.

Schmidt, N. B., Lerew, D. R., & Jackson, R. J. (1999). Prospective evaluation of anxiety sensitivity in the pathogenesis of panic: Replication and extension. *Journal of Abnormal Psychology, 108,* 532–537.

Schmidt, N. B., Storey, J., Greenberg, B. D., Santiago, H. T., Li, Q., & Murphy, D. L. (2000). Evaluating gene x psychological risk factor effects in the pathogenesis of anxiety: A new model approach. *Journal of Abnormal Psychology, 109,* 308–320.

Schmidt, R. A., & Bjork, R. A. (1992, July). New conceptualizations of practice: Common principles in three paradigms suggest new concepts for training. *Psychological Science, 3*(4), 207–217.

Schmidtke, A., & Hafner, H. (1988). The Werther effect after television films: New evidence for an old hypothesis. *Psychological Medicine, 18,* 665–676.

Schmolck, H., Buffalo, E. A., & Squire, L. R. (2000). Memory distortions over time: Recollections of the O. J. Simpson trial verdic after 15 and 32 months. *Psychological Science, 11,* 39–47.

Schnabel, T. (1987). Evaluation of the safety and side effects of antianxiety agents. *American Journal of Medicine, 82*(Suppl. 5A), 7–13.

Schnapf, J. L., Kraft, T. W., & Baylor, D. A. (1987). Spectral sensitivity of human cone photoreceptors. *Nature, 325,* 439–441.

Schneider, B. (1985). Organizational behavior. *Annual Review of Psychology, 36,* 573–611.

Schneider, B. H., Atkinson, L., & Tardif, C. (2001). Child-parent attachment and children's peer relations: A quantitative review. *Developmental Psychology, 37,* 86–100.

Schneider, W., & Bjorklund, D. F. (1998). Memory. In W. Damon, D. Kuhn, & R. Siegler (Eds.), *Handbook of child psychology: Vol. 2. Cognition, language and perception* (5th ed., pp. 467–521). New York: Wiley.

Schneiderman, B. (1992). *Designing the user interface* (2nd ed.) Reading, MA: Addison-Wesley.

Schneidman, E. S. (1987). A psychological approach to suicide. In G. VandenBos & B. K. Bryant (Eds.), *Cataclysms, crises, and catastrophes: Psychology in action. The master lectures* (Vol. 6, pp. 147–183). Washington, DC: American Psychological Association.

Schnurr, P. P., Ford, J. D., Friedman, M. J., Green, B. L., Dain, B. J., & Sengupta, A. (2000). Predictors and outcomes of posttraumatic stress disorder in World War II veterans exposed to mustard gas. *Journal of Consulting and Clinical Psychology, 68,* 258–268.

Schreiber, G. B., Robins, M., Striegel-Moore, R., Obarzanek, E., Morrison, J. A., & Wright, D. J. (1996). Weight modification efforts reported by black and white preadolescent girls: National Heart, Lung, and Blood Institute Growth and Health Study. *Pediatrics, 98,* 63–70.

Schroeder, D. A. (1995). An introduction to social dilemmas. In D. Schroeder (Ed.), *Social dilemmas: Perspectives on individuals and groups* (pp. 1–13). Westport, CT: Praeger.

Schroeder, D. A., Penner, L. A., Dovidio, J. F., & Piliavin, J. A. (1995). *The psychology of helping and altruism: Problems and puzzles.* New York: McGraw-Hill.

Schuckit, M. A. (1998). Biological, psychological, and environmental predictors of alcoholism risk: A longitudinal study. *Journal of Studies in Alcoholism, 59,* 485–494.

Schultheiss, O., & Brunstein, J. C. (2001). Assessment of implicit motives with a research version of the TAT: Picture profiles, gender differences, and relations to other personality measure. *Journal of Personality Assessment, 77,* 71–86.

Schultz, D. P., & Schultz, S. E. (1998). *A history of modern psychology* (7th ed.). Fort Worth, TX: Harcourt Brace.

Schultz, D. P., & Schultz, S. E. (2000). *A history of modern psychology* (7th ed.). Fort Worth, TX: Harcourt Brace.

Schultz, D. P., & Schultz, S. E. (2001). *Theories of personality.* Pacific Grove, CA: Brooks Cole.

Schulz, R. (1978). *The psychology of death, dying, and bereavement.* Reading, MA: Addison-Wesley.

Schulz, R., Beach, S. R., Lind, B., Martire, L. M., Zdaniuk, B., Hirsch, C., et al. (2001). Involvement in caregiving and adjustment to death of a spouse findings from the caregiver health effects study. *Journal of the American Medical Association, 285,* 3123–3129.

Schulz-Hardt, S., Frey, D., Luthgens, C., & Moscovici, S. (2000). Biased information search in group decision making. *Journal of Personality and Social Psychology, 78,* 665–669.

Schwab, M. E. (2002). Repairing the injured spinal cord. *Science, 295,* 1029–1031.

Schwartz, B., & Reisberg, D. (1991). *Learning and memory.* New York: Norton.

Schwartz, B., & Robbins, S. J. (1995). *Psychology of learning and behavior* (4th ed.). New York: Norton.

Schwartz, C., Kagan, J., & Snidman, N. (1995, May). *Inhibition from toddlerhood to adolescence.* Paper presented at the annual meeting of the American Psychiatric Association, Miami.

Schwartz, M. W., Woods, S. C., Porte, D., Jr., Seeley, R. J., & Baskin, D. G. (2000). Central nervous system control of food intake. *Nature, 404,* 661–671.

Schwarz, N. (1999). Self-reports: How the questions shape the answers. *American Psychologist, 54,* 93–105.

Schwarz, N., & Bohner, G. (2001). The construction of attitudes. In A. Tesser & N. Schwarz (Eds.), *Blackwell handbook of social psychology: Intraindividual processes* (pp. 436–457). Oxford, England: Blackwell.

Schwarzer, R. (2001). Social-cognitive factors in changing health-related behaviors. *Current Directions in Psychological Science, 10,* 47–51.

Schweinhart, L. J., & Weikart, D. P. (1991). Response to "Beyond IQ in preschool programs?" *Intelligence, 15,* 313–315.

Schwender, D., Klasing, D., Daunderer, M., Maddler, C., Poppel, E., & Peter, K. (1995). Awareness during general anesthetic: Definition, incidence, clinical relevance, causes, avoidance, and medicolegal aspects. *Anaesthetist, 44,* 743–754.

Schwenk, K. (1994, March 18). Why snakes have forked tongues. *Science, 263,* 1573–1577.

Scott, S., Knapp, M., Henderson, J., & Maughan, B. (2001). Financial cost of social exclusion: follow up study of antisocial children into adulthood. *British Medical Journal, 323,* 191.

Scribner, S. (1977). Modes of thinking and ways of speaking: Culture and logic reconsidered. In P. N. Johnson-Laird & P. C. Watson (Eds.), *Thinking: Readings in cognitive science.* New York: Cambridge University Press.

Seamon, J. G., Ganor-Stern, D., Crowley, M. J., & Wilson, S. M. (1997). A mere exposure effect for transformed three-dimensional objects: Effects of reflection, size, or color changes on affect and recognition. *Memory and Cognition, 25,* 367–374.

Searle, L. V. (1949). The organization of hereditary maze-brightness and maze-dullness. *Genetic Psychology Monographs, 39,* 279–325.

Sears, R. (1977). Sources of satisfaction of the Terman gifted men. *American Psychologist, 32,* 119–128.

Secord, D., & Peevers, B. (1974). The development and attribution of person concepts. In T. Mischel (Ed.), *Understanding other persons.* Oxford: Blackwell.

Sedikides, C., Campbell, W. K., Reeder, G., & Elliot, A. J. (1998). The self-serving bias in relational context. *Journal of Personality and Social Psychology, 74,* 378–386.

Segal, L., & Suri, J. F. (1999). Psychology applied to product design. In A. M. Stec & D. A. Bernstein (Eds.), *Psychology: Fields of application.* Boston: Houghton Mifflin.

Segal, N. L. (1999). *Entwined lives.* New York: Dutton.

Segal, Z. V., Gemar, M., & Williams, S. (2000). Differential cognitive response to a mood challenge following successful cognitive therapy or pharmacotherapy for unipolar depression. *Journal of Abnormal Psychology, 108,* 3–10.

Segall, M. H., Dasen, P. R., Berry, J. W., & Poortinga, Y. H. (1990). *Human behavior in global perspective: An introduction to cross-cultural psychology.* Elmwood, NY: Pergamon Press.

Segerstrom, S. C., Taylor, S. E., Kemeny, M. E., & Fahey, J. L. (1998). Optimism is associated with mood, coping, and immune change in response to stress. *Journal of Personality and Social Psychology, 74,* 1646–1655.

Seiger, A., Nordberg, A., Vonholst, H., Backman, L., Ebendal, T., Alafuzoff, I., et al. (1993). Intracranial infusion of purified nerve growth factor to an Alzheimer patient: the 1st attempt of a possible future treatment strategy. *Behavioral Brain Research, 57,* 255–261.

Sejnowski, T. J., Chattarji, S., & Stanton, P. K. (1990). Homosynaptic long-term depression in hippocampus and neocortex. *Seminars in the Neurosciences, 2,* 355–363.

Sejnowski, T. J., & Destexhe, A. (2000). Why do we sleep? *Brain Research, 886,* 208–223.

Sekuler, R., & Blake, R. (1994). *Perception* (3rd ed.). New York: McGraw-Hill.

Seligman, M. E. P. (1975). *Helplessness: On depression, development, and death.* San Francisco: Freeman.

Seligman, M. E. P. (1991). *Learned optimism.* New York: Knopf.

Seligman, M. E. P. (1995). The effectiveness of psychotherapy: The Consumer Reports study. *American Psychologist, 50,* 965–974.

Seligman, M. E. P. (1996). Good news for psychotherapy: The Consumer Reports study. *Independent Practitioner, 16,* 17–20.

Seligman, M. E. P., Castellon, C., Cacciola, J., Shulman, P., Luborsky, L., Ollove, M., & Downing, R. (1988). Explanatory style change during cognitive therapy for unipolar depression. *Journal of Abnormal Psychology, 97,* 13–18.

Seligman, M. E. P., & Csikszentmihalyi, M. (2000). Positive psychology: An introduction. *American Psychologist, 55,* 5–14.

Seligman, M. E. P., Klein, D. C., & Miller, W. R. (1976). Depression. In H. Leitenberg (Ed.), *Handbook of behavior modification and behavior therapy.* Englewood Cliffs, NJ: Prentice-Hall.

Seligman, M. E. P., & Schulman, P. (1986). Explanatory style as a predictor of productivity and quitting among life insurance agents. *Journal of Personality and Social Psychology, 50,* 832–838.

Sell, R. L., Wells, J. A., & Wypij, D. (1995). The prevalence of homosexual behavior and attraction in the United States, the United Kingdom, and France: Results of national population-based samples. *Archives of Sexual Behavior, 24*(3), 235–248.

Selye, H. (1956). *The stress of life.* New York: McGraw-Hill.

Selye, H. (1976). *The stress of life* (2nd ed.). New York: McGraw-Hill.

Senghas, A., & Coppola, M. (2001). Children creating language: How Nicaraguan sign language acquired a spatial grammar. *Psychological Science, 12,* 323–328.

Seppa, N. (1997, June). Children's TV remains steeped in violence. *APA Monitor,* p. 36.

Serpell, R. (1994). The cultural construction of intelligence. In W. J. Lonner & R. S. Malpass (Eds.), *Psychology and culture.* Boston: Allyn & Bacon.

Serpell, R. (2000). Intelligence and culture. In R. J. Sternberg (Ed.), *Handbook of intelligence* (pp. 549–577). New York: Cambridge University Press.

Servan-Schreiber, E., & Anderson, J. R. (1990). Learning artificial grammars with competitive chunking. *Journal of Experimental Psychology: Learning, Memory, and Cognition, 16,* 592–608.

Service, R. F. (1994, October 14). Neuroscience: Will a new type of drug make memory-making easier? *Science, 266,* 218–219.

Seto, M. C., Maric, A., & Barbaree, H. E. (2001). The role of pornography in the etiology of sexual aggression. *Aggression and Violent Behavior, 6,* 35–53.

Sevcik, R. A., & Savage-Rumbaugh, E. S. (1994). Language comprehension and use by great apes. *Language and Communication, 14,* 37–58.

Seybold, K. S., & Hill, P. C. (2001). The role of religion and spirituality in mental and physical health. *Current Directions in Psychological Science, 10,* 21–24.

Shadish, W. R., Cook, T. D., & Campbell, D. T. (2002). *Experimental and quasi-experimental designs for generalized causal inference.* Boston: Houghton Mifflin.

Shadish, W. R., Matt, G. E., Navarro, A. M., & Phillips, G. (2000). The effects of psychological therapies under clinically representative conditions: A meta-analysis. *Psychological Bulletin, 126,* 512–529.

Shaffer, D. R. (1973). *Social and personality development* (Box 4-2). Pacific Grove, CA: Brooks/Cole.

Shahinfar, A., Kupersmidt, J. B., & Matza, L. S. (2001). The relation between exposure to violence and social information processing among incarcerated adolescents. *Journal of Abnormal Psychology, 110,* 136–141.

Shalev, A. Y., Bonne, M., & Eth, S. (1996). Treatment of posttraumatic stress disorder: A review. *Psychosomatic Medicine, 58,* 165–182.

Shalev, A. Y., Peri, T., Brandes, D., Freedman, S., Orr, S. P., & Pitman, R. K. (2000). Auditory startle response in trauma survivors with posttraumatic stress disorder: A prospective study. *American Journal of Psychiatry, 157,* 255–261.

Shams, L., Kamitani, Y., & Shimojo, S. (2000). Illusions: What you see is what you hear. *Nature, 408,* 788.

Shand, M. A. (1982). Sign-based short-term memory coding of American Sign Language and printed English words by congenitally deaf signers. *Cognitive Psychology, 14,* 1–12.

Shapiro, A. F., Gottman, J. M., & Carrere, S. (2000). The baby and the marriage: Identifying factors that buffer against decline in marital satisfaction after the first baby arrives. *Journal of Family Psychology, 14,* 59–70.

Shapiro, D. E., & Schulman, C. E. (1996). Ethical and legal issues in e-mail therapy. *Ethics and Behavior, 6,* 107–124.

Shapiro, D. H., & Walsh, R. N. (Eds.). (1984). *Meditation: Classical and contemporary perspectives.* New York: Aldine.

Shapiro, F. (1989a). Eye movement desensitization: A new treatment for post-traumatic stress disorder. *Journal of Behavior Therapy and Experimental Psychiatry, 20,* 211–217.

Shapiro, F. (1989b). Efficacy of the eye movement desensitization procedure in the treatment of traumatic memories. *Journal of Traumatic Stress, 2,* 199–223.

Shapiro, F. (1991). Eye movement desensitization and reprocessing procedure: From EMD to EMD/R-A new treatment model for anxiety and related traumata. *The Behavior Therapist, 15,* 133–135.

Shapiro, F. (1995). *Eye movement desensitization and reprocessing: Basic principles, protocols, and procedures.* New York: Guilford.

Shapiro, F. (1999). Eye movement desensitization and reprocessing (EMDR): Accelerated information processing and affect-driven constructions. *Crisis Intervention and Time-Limited Treatment, 4,* 145–157.

Shaver, P. R., & Clark, C. L. (1996). Forms of adult romantic attachment and their cognitive and emotional underpinnings. In G. G. Noam & K. W. Fischer (Eds.), *Development and vulnerability in close relationships: The Jean Piaget symposium series* (pp. 29–58). Mahwah, NJ: Erlbaum.

Shaw, J. S., III. (1996). Increases in eyewitness confidence resulting from persistent questioning. *Journal of Experimental Psychology: Applied, 2,* 126–146.

Shaw, S. F., Cullen, J. P., McGuire, J. M., & Brinckerhoff, L. C. (1995). Operationalizing a definition of learning disabilities. *Journal of Learning Disabilities, 28,* 586–597.

Shaywitz, B. A., Shaywitz, S. E., Pugh, K. R., Constable, R. T., Skudlarski, P., Fulbright, R. K., et al. (1995). Sex differences in the functional organization of the brain for language. *Nature, 373,* 607–609.

Sheldon, K. M., Eliot, A. J., Kim, Y., & Kasser, T. (2001). What is satisfying about satisfying events? Testing 10 candidate psychological needs. *Journal of Personality and Social Psychology, 80,* 325–339.

Sheldon, K. M., & Kasser, T. (2001). Getting older, getting better? Personal striving and psychological maturity across the life span. *Developmental Psychology, 37,* 491–501.

Sheldon, K. M., & King, L (2001). Why positive psychology is necessary. *American Psychologist, 56,* 216–217.

Shelton, R. C., Keller, M. B., Gelenberg, A., Dunner, D. L., Hirschfeld, R., Thase, M. E., et al. (2001). Effectiveness of St. John's Wort in major depression. *Journal of the American Medical Association, 285,* 1978–1986.

Shepard, R. N., & Metzler, J. (1971). Mental rotation of three-dimensional objects. *Science, 171,* 701–703.

Shepherd, C. (1994, March 31). News of the weird. *Daily Illini.*

Shepherd, C., Kohut, J. J., & Sweet, R. (1989). *News of the weird.* New York: New American Library.

Shepperd, J. A. (1993). Productivity loss in performance groups: A motivation analysis. *Psychological Bulletin, 113,* 67–81.

Sher, K. J., Walitzer, K., Wood, P., & Brent, E. (1991). Characteristics of children of alcoholics: Putative risk factors, substance use and abuse, and psychopathology. *Journal of Abnormal Psychology, 100,* 427–448.

Shergill, S. S., Brammer, M. J., Williams, S. C., Murray, R. M., & McGuire, P. K. (2000). Mapping auditory hallucinations in schizophrenia using functional magnetic resonance imaging. *Archives of General Psychiatry, 57,* 1033–1038.

Sherif, M. (1937). An experimental approach to the study of attitudes. *Sociometry, 1,* 90–98.

Sherin, J. E., Shiromani, P. J., McCarley, R. W., & Saper, C. B. (1996). Activation of ventrolateral preoptic neurons during sleep. *Science, 271,* 216–219.

Sherman, J. W., & Bessenoff, G. R. (1999). Stereotypes as source-monitoring cues: On the interaction between episodic and semantic memory. *Psychological Science, 10,* 106–110.

Sherman, J. W., & Klein, S. B. (1994). Development and representation of personality impressions. *Journal of Personality and Social Psychology, 67,* 972–983.

Sherman, S. J. (1980). On the self-erasing nature of errors of prediction. *Journal of Personality and Social Psychology, 39,* 211–221.

Sherwin, B. B., & Gelfand, M. M. (1987). The role of androgen in the maintenance of sexual functioning in oophorectomized women. *Psychosomatic Medicine, 49,* 397–409.

Shiffman, S., Engberg, J. B., Paty, J. A., & Perz, W. G. (1997). A day at a time: Predicting smoking lapse from daily urge. *Journal of Abnormal Psychology, 106,* 104–116.

Shiller, R. J. (2001). *Irrational exuberance.* Princeton, NJ: Princeton University Press.

Shimamura, A. P., Berry, J. M., Mangels, J. A., Rusting, C. L., & Jurica, P. J. (1995). Memory and cognitive abilities in university professors: Evidence for successful aging. *Psychological Science, 6,* 271–277.

Shimizu, E., Tang, Y.-P., & Tsien, J. Z. (2000). NMDA receptor-dependent synaptic reinforcement as a crucial process for memory consolidation. *Science, 290,* 1170–1174.

Shin, L. M., Kosslyn, S. M., McNally, R. J., Alpert, N. M., Thompson, W. L., Rauch, S. L., et al. (1997). Visual imagery and perception in post-traumatic stress disorder: A positron emission tomographic investigation. *Archives of General Psychiatry, 54,* 233–241.

Shiwach, R. S., Reid, W. H., & Carmody, T. J. (2001). An analysis of reported deaths following electroconvulsive therapy in Texas, 1993–1998. *Psychiatric Services, 52,* 1095–1097.

Shlomo, A. (1999). *Culturally competent family therapy: A general model.* Westport, CT: Praeger.

Showalter, E. (1997). *Hystories: Hysterical epidemics and modern culture.* New York: Columbia University Press.

Shreeve, J. (1993, June). Touching the phantom. *Discover,* pp. 35–42.

Shweder, R. A., Much, N. C., Mahapatra, M., & Park, L. (1994). The "big three" of morality (autonomy, community, and divinity), and the "big three" explanations of suffering, as well. In A. Brandt & P. Rozin (Eds.), *Morality and health.* Stanford, CA: Stanford University Press.

Siddle, D. A. T., Packer, J. S., Donchin, E., & Fabiani, M. (1991). Mnemonic information processing. In J. R. Jennings & M. G. H. Coles (Eds.), *Handbook of cognitive psychophysiology: Central and autonomic nervous system approaches* (pp. 449–510). Chichester, England: Wiley.

Siebert, S. E., & Kraimer, M. L. (2001). The five-factor model of personality and career success. *Journal of Vocational Behavior, 58,* 1–21.

Siegal, M. (1997). *Knowing children: Experiments in conversation and cognition* (2nd ed.). Hove, England: Psychology Press/Erlbaum/Taylor & Francis.

Siegel, J. M., & Rogawski, M. A. (1988). A function for REM sleep: Regulation of noradrenergic receptor sensitivity. *Brain Research Review, 13,* 213-233.

Siegel, S., Hirson, R. E., Krank, M. D., & McCully, J. (1982). Heroin "overdose" death: The contribution of drug associated environmental cues. *Science, 216,* 430-437.

Siegler, R. S. (1994). Cognitive variability: A key to understanding cognitive development. *Current Directions in Psychological Science, 3,* 1-4.

Siegler, R. S. (1995). Children's thinking: How does change occur? In W. Schneider & F. Weinert (Eds.), *Memory performance and competencies: Issues in growth and development*. Hillsdale, NJ: Erlbaum.

Sigmundsson, T., Suckling, J., Maier, M., Bullmore, E., Greenwood, K., Ron, M., & Toone, B. (2001). Structural abnormalities in frontal, temporal, and limbic regions and interconnecting white matter tracts in schizophrenic patients with prominent negative symptoms. *The American Journal of Psychiatry, 158,* 234-243.

Silber, M. H. (2001). Sleep disorders. *Neurology Clinics, 19,* 173-186.

Silbersweig, D. A., Stern, E., Frith, C., Cahill, C., Holmes, A., Grootoonk, S., et al. (1995). A functional neuroanatomy of hallucinations in schizophrenia. *Nature, 378,* 176-179.

Silbert, M. H., & Pines, A. M. (1984). Pornography and sexual abuse of women. *Sex Roles, 10,* 857-868.

Silver, E. (1995). Punishment or treatment? Comparing the lengths of confinement of successful and unsuccessful insanity defendants. *Law and Human Behavior, 19,* 375-388.

Silver, E., Cirincione, C., & Steadman, H. J. (1994). Demythologizing inaccurate perceptions of the insanity defense. *Law and Human Behavior, 18,* 63-70.

Silverman, K., Evans, A. M., Strain, E. C., & Griffiths, R. R. (1992). Withdrawal syndrome after the double-blind cessation of caffeine consumption. *New England Journal of Medicine, 327,* 1109-1114.

Silverman, K., Svikis, D., Robles, E., Stitzer, M. L., & Bigelow, G. E. (2001). A reinforcement-based therapeutic workplace for the treatment of drug abuse: Six-month abstinence outcomes. *Experimental and Clinical Psychopharmacology, 9,* 14-23.

Silverstein, L. B. (1996). Evolutionary psychology and the search for sex differences. *American Psychologist, 51,* 160-161.

Silverthorne, C. (2001). Leadership effectiveness and personality: A cross cultural evaluation. *Personality & Individual Differences, 30,* 303-309.

Simons, D. J., & Chabris, C. F. (1999). Gorillas in our midst: Sustained inattentional blindness for dynamic events. *Perception, 28,* 1059-1074.

Simons, D. J., & Levin, D. T. (1997). Failure to detect changes to attended objects. *Investigative Ophthalmology and Visual Science, 38,* S747.

Simonton, D. K. (1984). *Genius, creativity and leadership*. Cambridge: Harvard University Press.

Simonton, D. K. (1999). Creativity and genius. In L. Pervin & O. John (Eds.), *Handbook of personality research* (2nd ed., pp. 629-652). New York: Guilford.

Simpson, J. A., & Kenrick, D. T. (1997). *Evolutionary social psychology*. Mahwah, NJ: Erlbaum.

Simpson, J. A., & Rholes, W. S. (2000). Caregiving, attachment theory, and the connection theoretical orientation. *Psychological Inquiry, 11,* 114-117.

Simpson, S., Hurtley, S. M., & Marx, J. (2000). Immune cell networks. *Science, 290,* 79.

Sims, J. H., & Baumann, D. D. (1972). The tornado threat: Coping styles of the north and south. *Science, 17,* 1386-1392.

Sinclair, R. C., Hoffman, C., Mark, M. M., Martin, L. L., & Pickering, T. L. (1994). Construct accessibility and the misattribution of arousal. *Psychological Science, 5*(1), 15-19.

Singer, L. T., Arendt, R., Minnes, S., Salvator, A., Siegel, C., & Lewis, B. A. (2001). Developing language skills of cocaine-exposed infants. *Pediatrics, 107,* 1057-1064.

Sinha, P., & Poggio, T. (1996). I think I know that face. *Nature, 384,* 404.

Sinha, R., & Parsons, O. A. (1996). Multivariate response patterning of fear and anger. *Cognition and Emotion, 10,* 173-198.

Sirvio, J. (1999). Strategies that support declining cholinergic neurotransmission in Alzheimer's disease patients. *Gerontology, 45,* 3-14.

Skinner, B. F. (1938). *The behavior of organisms*. New York: Appleton.

Skinner, B. F. (1961). *Cumulative record* (3rd ed.). Englewood Cliffs, NJ: Prentice-Hall.

Skre, I., Onstad, S., Toregersen, S., Lyngren, S., & Kringlin, E. (2000). The heritability of common phobic fear: A twin study of a clinical sample. *Journal of Anxiety Disorders, 14,* 549-562.

Slamecka, N. J., & McElree, B. (1983). Normal forgetting of verbal lists as a function of their degree of learning. *Journal of Experimental Psychology: Learning, Memory, and Cognition, 9,* 384-397.

Slater, A., Mattock, A., Brown, E., & Bremmer, J. G. (1991). Form perception at birth. *Journal of Experimental Child Psychology, 51,* 395-406.

Sleek, S. (1999, February). Programs aim to attract minorities to psychology. *APA Monitor,* p. 47.

Sloan, D. M., Strauss, M. E., & Wisner, K. L. (2001). Diminished response to pleasant stimuli by depressed women. *Journal of Abnormal Psychology, 110,* 488-493.

Slomkowski, C., & Dunn, J. (1996). Young children's understanding of other people's beliefs and feelings and their connected communication with friends. *Developmental Psychology, 32,* 442-447.

Slovic, P. (1984). *Facts versus fears: Understanding perceived risk*. Paper presented at science and public policy seminar sponsored by the Federation of Behavioral and Psychological and Cognitive Sciences, Washington, DC.

Slutske, W., Eisen, S., Xian, H., True, W., Lyons, M. J., Goldberg, J., & Tsuang, M. (2001). A twin study of the association between pathological gambling and antisocial personality disorder. *Journal of Abnormal Psychology, 110,* 297-308.

Slutske, W. S., Heath, A. C., Dinwiddie, S. H., Madden, P. A., Bucholz, K. K., Dunne, M. P., et al. (1998). Common genetic risk factors for conduct disorder and alcohol dependence. *Journal of Abnormal Psychology, 107,* 363-374.

Small, B. J., & Bäckman, L. (1999). Time to death and cognitive performance. *Current Directions in Psychological Science, 8,* 168-172.

Small, G. W., Rabins, P. V., Barry, P. P., Buckholtz, N. S., DeKosky, S. T., Ferris, S. H., et al. (1997). Diagnosis and treatment of Alzheimer's disease and related disorders: Consensus statement of the American Association for Geriatric Psychiatry, the Alzheimer's Association, and the American Geriatrics Society. *Journal of American Medical Association, 278,* 1363-1371.

Smit, A. B., Syed, N. I., Schaap, D., van Minnen, J., Klumperman, J., Kits, K. S., et al. (2001). A glia-derived acetylcholine-binding protein that modulates synaptic transmission. *Nature, 411,* 261-268.

Smith, A., & Weissman, M. (1992). Epidemiology. In E. S. Paykel (Ed.), *Handbook of affective disorders* (2nd ed., pp. 111-129). New York: Guilford.

Smith, A. M., Malo, S. A., Laskowski, E. R., Sabick, M., Cooney, W. P., III, Finnie, S. B., et al. (2000). A multidisciplinary study of the 'yips' phenomenon in golf: An exploratory analysis. *Sports Medicine, 30,* 423-437.

Smith, A. P., & Maben, A. (1993). Effects of sleep deprivation, lunch, and personality on performance, mood, and cardiovascular function. *Physiology and Behavior, 54*(5), 967-972.

Smith, B. W., Pargament, K. I., Brant, C., & Oliver, J. M. (2000). Noah revisited: Religous coping by church members and the impact of the 1993 Midwest flood. *Journal of Community Psychology, 28,* 169-186.

Smith, E. (1998). Mental representation and memory. In D. Gilbert, S. T. Fiske, & G. Lindzey (Eds.), *Handbook of social psychology* (4th ed., Vol. 1, pp. 391-445). Boston: McGraw-Hill.

Smith, E., & Mackie, D. (2000). *Social psychology* (2nd ed.). Philadelphia: Taylor & Francis.

Smith, E., & Queller, S. (2001). Mental representations. In A. Tesser & N. Schwarz (Eds.), *Blackwell handbook of social psychology: Intraindividual processes* (pp. 499-517). Oxford, England: Blackwell.

Smith, E. E. (2000). Neural bases of human working memory. *Currents Directions in Psychological Science, 9,* 45-49.

Smith, E. E., Geva, A., Jonides, J., Miller, A., Reuter-Lorenz, P., & Koeppe, R. A. (2001). The neural basis of task-switching in working memory:

Effects of performance and aging. *Proceedings of the National Academy of Sciences, 98,* 2095–2100.

Smith, J. (1993). *Understanding stress and coping.* New York: Macmillan.

Smith, J., & Baltes, P. B. (1990). A study of wisdom-related knowledge: Age/cohort differences in responses to life-planning problems. *Developmental Psychology, 26,* 494–505.

Smith, L. B., & Sera, M. D. (1992). A developmental analysis of the polar structure of dimensions. *Cognitive Psychology, 24,* 99–142.

Smith, M. (1988). Recall of spatial location by the amnesic patient HM. Special issue: Single case studies in amnesia-Theoretical advances. *Brain and Cognition, 7,* 178–183.

Smith, M. L., Glass, G. V., & Miller, T. I. (1980). *The benefits of psychotherapy.* Baltimore: Johns Hopkins University Press.

Smith, M. U., & DiClemente, R. J. (2000). STAND: A peer educator training curriculum for sexual risk reduction in the rural South. Students Together Against Negative Decisions. *Preventative Medicine, 30,* 441–449.

Smith, P., & Yule, W. (1999). Eye movement desensitization and reprocessing. In W. Yule (Ed.) *Posttraumatic stress disorders: Concepts and therapy.* Chichester, England: Wiley.

Smith, P. B., & Bond, M. H. (1999). *Social psychology across cultures: Analysis and perspectives* (2nd ed.). Boston: Allyn & Bacon.

Smith, P. K., & Drew, L. M. (2002). Grandparenthood. In M. H. Bornstein (Ed.), *Handbook of parenting* (2nd ed.). Mahwah, NJ: Erlbaum.

Smith, S., & Freedman, D. G. (1983, April). *Mother-toddler interaction and maternal perception of child temperament in two ethnic groups: Chinese-American and European-American.* Paper presented at the meeting of the Society for Research in Child Development, Detroit, MI.

Smith, S. L., & Donnerstein, E. (1998). Harmful effects of exposure to media violence: Learning of aggression, emotional desensitization, and fear. In R. G. Geen & E. Donnerstein (Eds.), *Human aggression* (pp. 230–247) San Diego: Academic Press.

Smith, S. M., Glenberg, A. M., & Bjork, R. A. (1978). Environmental context and human memory. *Memory & Cognition, 6,* 342–355.

Smith, S. M., Vela, E., & Williamson, J. E. (1988). Shallow input processing does not induce environmental context-dependent recognition. *Bulletin of the Psychonomic Society, 26,* 537–540.

Smith, S. S., O'Hara, B. F., Persico, A. M., Gorelick, D. A., Newlin, D. B., Vlahov, D., et al. (1992). Genetic vulnerability to drug abuse. The D2 dopamine receptor Taq i B1 restriction fragment length polymorphism appears more frequently in polysubstance abusers. *Archives of General Psychiatry, 49,* 723–727.

Smith, V. L. (1991). Prototypes in the courtroom: Lay representations of legal concepts. *Journal of Personality and Social Psychology, 44,* 787–797.

Smyth, J. M., Stone, A. A., Hurewitz, A., & Kaell, A. (1999). Effects of writing about stressful experiences on symptom reduction in patients with asthma or rheumatoid arthritis. *Journal of the American Medical Association, 281,* 1304–1309.

Smythies, J. (1997). The functional neuroanatomy of awareness: With a focus on the role of various anatomical systems in the control of intermodal attention *Consciousness and Cognition, 6,* 455–481.

Snarey, J. (1987). A question of morality. *Psychological Bulletin, 97,* 202–232.

Snodgrass, S. R. (1994). Cocaine babies: A result of multiple teratogenic influences. *Journal of Child Neurology, 9*(3), 227–233.

Snow, R. E. (1995). Pygmalion and intelligence? *Current Directions in Psychological Science, 4,* 169–171.

Snowden, L. R., & Cheung, F. (1990). Use of inpatient mental health services by members of ethnic minority groups. *American Psychologist, 45,* 347–355.

Snyder, A. W., & Mitchell, D. J. (1999). Is integer arithmetic fundamental to mental processing?: The mind's secret arithmetic. *Proceedings of the Royal Society of London, 266,* 587–592.

Snyder, M., & Haugen, J. A. (1995). Why does behavioral confirmation occur? A functional perspective on the role of the target. *Personality and Social Psychology Bulletin, 21,* 963–974.

Snyderman, M., & Rothman, S. (1987). Survey of expert opinion on intelligence and aptitude testing. *American Psychologist, 42,* 137–144.

Soetens, E., Casaer, S., D'Hooge, R., & Hueting, J. E. (1995). Effect of amphetamine on long-term retention of verbal material. *Psychopharmacology, 119,* 155–162.

Sokoloff, L. (1981). Localization of functional activity in the central nervous system by measurement of glucose utilization with radioactive deoxyglucose. *Journal of Cerebral Blood Flow and Metabolism, 1,* 7–36.

Solomon, A. (1998, January 12). Anatomy of melancholy. *New Yorker,* pp. 46–61.

Solomon, R. L. (1980). The opponent-process theory of acquired motivation: The costs of pleasure and the benefits of pain. *American Psychologist, 35,* 691–712.

Solomon, R. L., & Corbit, J. D. (1974). An opponent-process theory of motivation: I. Temporal dynamics of affect. *Psychological Review, 81,* 119–145.

Solomon, R. L., Kamin, L. J., & Wynne, L. C. (1953). Traumatic avoidance learning: The outcomes of several extinction procedures with dogs. *Journal of Abnormal and Social Psychology, 48,* 291–302.

Solowij, N., Stephens, R. S., Roffman, R. A., Babor, T., Kadden, R., Miller, M., et al. (2002). Cognitive functioning of long-term heavy cannabis users seeking treatment. *Journal of American Medical Association, 287,* 1123–1131.

Sommer, R. (1999). Applying environmental psychology. In D. A. Bernstein & A. M. Stec (Eds.), *The psychology of everyday life.* Boston: Houghton Mifflin.

Sora, I., Hall, F. S., Andrews, A. M., Itokawa, M., Li, X. F., Wei, H. B., et al. (2001). Molecular mechanisms of cocaine reward: combined dopamine and serotonin transporter knockouts eliminate cocaine place preference. *Proceedings of the National Academy of Science, 98,* 5300–5305.

Sorce, J., Emde, R., Campos, J., & Klinnert, M. (1981, April). *Maternal emotional signaling: Its effect on the visual cliff behavior of one-year-olds.* Paper presented at the meetings of the Society for Research in Child Development, Boston, MA.

Sorrentino, R. M., & Roney, C. J. R. (2000). *The uncertain mind: Individual differences in facing the unknown.* Philadelphia: Psychology Press.

Sowell, E. R., Delis, D., Stiles, J., & Jernigan, T. L. (2001). Improved memory functioning and frontal lobe maturation between childhood and adolescence: A structural MRI study. *Journal of the International Neuropsychological Society, 7,* 312–322.

Spangler, G., Fremmer-Bombik, E., & Grossman, K. (1996). Social and individual determinants of infant attachment security and disorganization. *Infant Mental Health Journal, 17,* 127–139.

Spanos, N. P. (1994). Multiple identity enactments and multiple personality disorder: A sociocognitive perspective. *Psychological Bulletin, 116,* 143–165.

Spanos, N. P. (1996). *Multiple identities and false memories: A sociocognitive perspective.* Washington, DC: American Psychological Association.

Spanos, N. P., Burnley, M. C. E., & Cross, P. A. (1993). Response expectancies and interpretations as determinants of hypnotic responding. *Journal of Personality and Social Psychology, 65*(6), 1237–1242.

Spearman, C. E. (1904). General intelligence objectively determined and measured. *American Journal of Psychology, 15,* 201–293.

Spearman, C. E. (1927). *The abilities of man.* New York: Macmillan.

Spelke, E. S., Breinlinger, K., Macomber, J., & Jacobson, K. (1992). Origins of knowledge. *Psychological Review, 99,* 605–632.

Spencer, S., Steele, C. M., & Quinn, D. (1997). *Under suspicion on inability: Stereotype threats and women's math performance.* Unpublished manuscript.

Sperry, L. (1999). *Cognitive behavior therapy of DSM-IV personality disorders: Highly effective interventions for the most common personality disorders.* Bristol, PA: Bruner/Mazel.

Sperry, R. W. (1968). Hemisphere deconnection and unity in conscious awareness. *American Psychologist, 23,* 723–733.

Sperry, R. W. (1974). Lateral specialization in the surgically separated hemispheres. In F. O. Schmitt & F. G. Wordon (Eds.), *The neurosciences third study program.* Cambridge: MIT Press.

Spiegel, D. (Ed.). (1994). *Dissociation: Culture, mind, and body.* Washington, DC: American Psychiatric Press.

Spiegel, D. A., & Bruce, T. J. (1997). Benzodiazepines and and exposure-based cognitive behavior therapies for panic disorder: Conclusions from combined treatment trials. *American Journal of Psychiatry, 151,* 876–881.

Spira, J. L. (2001). Study design casts doubt on value of St. John's wort in treating depression. *British Medical Journal, 322,* 493.

Spitz, H. H. (1991). Commentary on Locurto's "Beyond IQ in preschool programs?" *Intelligence, 15,* 327–333.

Spitz, H. H. (1997). *Nonconscious movements: From mystical messages to facilitated communication.* Hillsdale, NJ: Erlbaum.

Spitzer, R., First, M., Williams, J., Kendler, K., Pincus, A., & Tucker, G. (1992). Now is the time to retire the term "Organic Mental Disorders." *American Journal of Psychiatry, 149,* 240–244.

Spitzer, R. L., Gibbon, M., Skodol, A. E., & Williams, J. B. W., & First, M. B. (Eds.). (1994). *DSM-IV casebook: A learning companion to the Diagnostic and Statistical Manual of Mental Disorders, fourth edition.* Washington, DC: American Psychiatric Association.

Spitzer, R. L., Skodol, A. E., Gibbon, M., & Williams, J. B. W. (1983). *Psychopathology: A casebook.* New York: McGraw-Hill.

Sprecher, S., Hatfield, E., Anthony, C., & Potapova, E. (1994). Token resistance to sexual intercourse and consent to unwanted sexual intercourse: College students' dating experiences in three countries. *Journal of Sex Research, 31*(2), 125–132.

Springer, K., & Belk, A. (1994). The role of physical contact and association in early contamination sensitivity. *Developmental Psychology, 30*(6), 864–868.

Springer, S. P., & Deutsch, G. (1989). *Left brain, right brain.* San Francisco: Freeman.

Squire, L. (1987). *Memory and brain.* New York: Oxford University Press.

Squire, L. R. (1986). Mechanisms of memory. *Science, 232,* 1612–1619.

Squire, L. R. (1992). Memory and the hippocampus: A synthesis from findings with rats, monkeys, and humans. *Psychological Review, 99,* 195–231.

Squire, L. R., Amara, D. G., & Press, G. A. (1992). Magnetic resonance imaging of the hippocampal formation and mamillary nuclei distinguish medial temporal lobe and diencephalic amnesia. *Journal of Neuroscience, 10,* 3106–3117.

Squire, L. R., & McKee, R. (1992). The influence of prior events on cognitive judgments in amnesia. *Journal of Experimental Psychology: Learning, Memory, and Cognition, 18,* 106–115.

Squire, L. R., & Zola, S. M. (1996). Structure and function of declarative and nondeclarative memory systems. *Proceedings of the National Academy of Sciences, USA 93*(24), 13515–13522.

Srinivas, K. (1993). Perceptual specificity in nonverbal priming. *Journal of Experimental Psychology: Learning, Memory, and Cognition 19,* 582–602.

Srivastava, A., Locke, E. A., & Bartol, K. M. (2001). Money and subjective well-being: It's not the money, it's the motives. *Journal of Personality and Social Psychology, 80,* 959–971.

St. Clair, M. (1999). *Object relations and self-psychology: An introduction.* Pacific Grove, CA: Brooks/Cole.

Stacey, J., & Biblarz, T. J. (2001). (How) Does the sexual orientation of parents matter? *American Sociological Review, 66,* 159–183.

Staddon, J. E. R., & Ettinger, R. H. (1989). *Learning: An introduction to the principles of adaptive behavior.* San Diego: Harcourt Brace Jovanovich.

Standing, L., Conezio, J., & Haber, R. N. (1970). Perception and memory for pictures: Single-trial learning of 2500 visual stimuli. *Psychonomic Science, 19,* 73–74.

Stankov, L. (1989). Attentional resources and intelligence: A disappearing link. *Personality and Individual Differences, 10,* 957–968.

Stanley, B. G., Willett, V. L., Donias, H. W., & Ha-Lyen, H. (1993). The lateral hypothalamus: A primary site mediating excitatory aminoacid-elicited eating. *Brain Research, 63*(1–2), 41–49.

Stanton-Hicks, M., & Salamon, J. (1997). Stimulation of the central and peripheral nervous system for the control of pain. *Journal of Clinical Neurophysiology, 14,* 46–62.

Stapleton, S. (2001, February 19). Miles to go before I sleep: America is becoming a culture of sleeplessness. *Amednews* [Online]. Available: http://www.ama-assn.org/sci-pubs/amnews/pick_01/hlsa0219.htm

Stasser, G. (1991). Pooling of unshared information during group discussion. In S. Worchel, W. Wood, & J. Simpson (Eds.), *Group processes and productivity.* Beverly Hills, CA: Sage.

Stasser, G., Stewart, D., & Wittenbaum, G. M. (1995). Expert roles and information exchange during discussion: The importance of knowing who knows what. *Journal of Experimental Social Psychology, 31,* 244–265.

Statistics Canada. (1998). *Causes of death, 1995.* Ottawa: Ministry of Industry, Science, and Technology, Health Statistics Division.

Staudt, M., Grodd, W., Niemann, G., Wildgruber, D., Erb, M., & Krageloh-Mann, I. (2001). Early left periventricular brain lesions induce right hemispheric organization of speech. *Neurology 2001, 57,* 122–125.

Steadman, H. J. (1993). *Reforming the insanity defense: An evaluation of pre- and post- Hinckley reforms.* New York: Guilford.

Stec, A. M., & Bernstein, D. A. (Eds.). (1999). *Psychology: Fields of application.* Boston: Houghton Mifflin.

Steele, C. M. (1997). A threat in the air: How stereotypes shape intellectual identity and performance. *American Psychologist, 52,* 613–629.

Steele, C. M., & Aronson, J. (1995). Stereotype threat and the intellectual performance of African-Americans. *Journal of Personality and Social Psychology, 69,* 797–811.

Steele, C. M., & Aronson, J. (2000). Stereotype threat and the intellectual test performance of African Americans. In C. Stangor (Ed.), *Stereotypes and prejudice: Essential readings* (pp. 369–389). Philadelphia: Psychology Press/Taylor & Francis.

Steele, C. M., Spencer, S. J., & Lynch, M. (1993). Self-image resilience and dissonance: The role of affirmational resources. *Journal of Personality and Social Psychology, 64,* 885–896.

Steele, T. D., McCann, U. D., & Ricaurte, G. A. (1994). 3,4-methylenedioxy-methamphetamine (MDMA, ecstacy): Pharmacology and toxicology in animals and humans. *Addiction, 89*(5), 539–551.

Steiger, H., Young, S. N., Ng Ying Kin, N. M. K., Koerner, N., Israel, M., Lageix, P., & Paris, J. (2001). Implications of impulsive and affective symptoms for serotonin function in bulimia nervosa. *Psychological Medicine, 31,* 85–95.

Stein, D. M., & Lambert, M. J. (1995). Graduate training in psychotherapy: Are therapy outcomes enhanced? *Journal of Consulting and Clinical Psychology, 63,* 182–196.

Stein, E. (1999). *The mismeasure of desire: The science, theory and ethics of sexual orientation.* New York: Oxford University Press.

Stein, K. D., Goldman, M. S., & Del Boca, F. K. (2000). The influence of alcohol expectancy priming and mood manipulation on subsequent alcohol consumption. *Journal of Abnormal Psychology, 109,* 106–115.

Stein, M. A. (1993, November 30). Spacewalking repair team to work on Hubble flaws; shower head inspires a device to improve focusing ability. *Los Angeles Times,* A1, A5.

Steinberg, L. (1990). Autonomy, conflict, and harmony in the family relationship. In S. S. Feldman & G. R. Elliott (Eds.), *At the threshold: The developing adolescent* (pp. 255–276). Cambridge: Harvard University Press.

Steinberg, L., Dornbusch, S. M., & Brown, B. B. (1992). Ethnic differences in adolescent achievement: An ecological perspective. *American Psychologist, 47,* 723–729.

Steinberg, L., Lamborn, S. D., Darling, N., Mounts, N. S., & Dornbusch, S. M. (1994). Over-time changes in adjustment and competence among adolescents from authoritative, authoritarian, indulgent, and neglectful families. *Child Development, 65,* 754–770.

Steiner, J. M., & Fahrenberg, J. (2000). Authoritarianism and social status of former members of the Waffen-SS and SS and of the Wehrmacht: An extension and reanalysis of the study published in 1970. *Koelner Zeitschrift fuer Soziologie und Sozialpsychologie, 52,* 329–348.

Stella, N., Schweitzer, P., & Piomelli, D. (1997). A second endogenous cannabinoid that modulates long-term potentiation. *Nature, 388,* 773–778.

Stepanski, E. J., & Perlis, M. L. (2000). Behavioral sleep medicine. An emerging subspecialty in health psychology and sleep medicine. *Journal of Psychosomatic Research, 49,* 343–347.

Stephens, R. S., Roffman, R. A., & Simpson, E. E. (1994). Treating adult marijuana dependence: A test of the relapse prevention model. *Journal of Consulting and Clinical Psychology, 62*(1), 92–99.

Steriade, M., & McCarley, R. W. (1990). *Brainstem control of wakefulness and sleep*. New York: Plenum.

Stern, K., & McClintock, M. K. (1998). Regulation of ovulation by human pheromones. *Nature, 392*(6672), 177–179.

Stern, Y., Tang, M. X., Denaro, J., & Mayeux, R. (1995). Increased risk of mortality in Alzheimer's disease patients with more advanced educational and occupational attainment. *Annals of Neurology, 37*, 590–595.

Sternberg, E. M. (2001). Neuroendocrine regulation of autoimmune/inflammatory disease. *Journal of Endocrinology, 169*, 429–435.

Sternberg, R. (2000, July/August). What's your story? *What's your story?*, 52–59.

Sternberg, R. J. (1985). *Beyond IQ: A triarchic theory of human intelligence*. Cambridge, England: Cambridge University Press.

Sternberg, R. J. (1996). *Successful intelligence*. New York: Simon & Schuster.

Sternberg, R. J. (1988a). Triangulating love. In R. J. Sternberg & M. L. Barnes (Eds.), *The psychology of love*. New Haven: Yale University Press.

Sternberg, R. J. (1988b). *The triarchic mind*. New York: Cambridge University Press.

Sternberg, R. J. (1989). Domain generality versus domain specificity: The life and impending death of a false dichotomy. *Merrill-Palmer Quarterly, 35*, 115–130.

Sternberg, R. J. (1999). Ability and expertise: It's time ot replace the current model of intelligence. *American Educator Spring 1999*, pp. 10–51.

Sternberg, R. J. (2000). Patterns of giftedness: A triarchic analysis. *Roeper Review, 22*, 231–236.

Sternberg, R. J. (2001). What is the common thread of creativity?: Its dialectical relation to intelligence and wisdom. *American Psychologist, 56*, 360–362.

Sternberg, R. J., Castejon, J. L., Prieto, M. D., Hautamaeki, J., & Grigorenko, E. L. (2001). Confirmatory faculty analysis of the Sternberg Triarchic Abilities Test in three international samples: An empirical test of the triarchic theory of intelligence. *European Journal of Psychological Assessment, 17*, 1–16.

Sternberg, R. J., & Dess, N. K. (2001). Creativity for the new millennium. *American Psychologist, 56*, 332.

Sternberg, R. J., Hojjat, M., & Barnes, M. L. (2001). Empirical tests of aspects of a theory of love as a story. *European Journal of Personality, 15*, 199–218.

Sternberg, R. J., & Kaufman, J. C. (1998). Human abilities. *Annual Review of Psychology, 49*, 479–502.

Sternberg, R. J., & Lubert, T. I. (1992). Buy low and sell high: An investment approach to creativity. *Current Directions in Psychological Science, 1*(1), 1–5.

Sternberg, R. J., & O'Hara, L. A. (1999). Creativity and intelligence. In R. J. Sternberg et al. (Eds.), *Handbook of creativity* (pp. 251–272). New York: Cambridge University Press.

Sternberg, R. J., Wagner, R. K., Williams, W. M., & Horvath, J. A. (1995). Testing common sense. *American Psychologist, 50*, 912–927.

Sternberg, R. J., & Williams, W. M. (1997). Does the graduate record examination predict meaningful success of graduate training of psychologists? A Case Study. *American Psychologist, 52*, 630–641.

Stevens, A. (1996). *Private myths: Dreams and dreaming*. Cambridge: Harvard University Press.

Stevens, D. G. (1995, July 29). New Doppler radar off to stormy start. *Chicago Tribune*.

Stevens, J. C., & Hooper, J. E. (1982). How skin and object temperature influence touch sensation. *Perception and Psychophysics, 32*, 282–285.

Stevens, R. (1999, April 21). Personal communication.

Stevenson, S. (1992). *A long way from being number one: What we can learn from East Asia*. Washington, DC: Federation of Behavior, Psychological and Cognitive Sciences.

Stewart, R. E., DeSimone, J. A., & Hill, D. L. (1997). New perspectives in a gustatory physiology: Transduction, development, and plasticity. *American Journal of Physiology, 272*, C1–C26.

Stice, E. (2001). A prospective test of the dual-pathway model of bulimic pathology: Mediating effects of dieting and negative affect. *Journal of Abnormal Psychology, 110*, 124–135.

Stickgold, R., James, L., & Hobson, J. A. (2000). Visual discrimination learning requires sleep after training. *Nature Neuroscience, 3*, 1237–1238.

Stickgold, R., Malia, A., Maguire, D., Roddenberry, D., & O'Connor, M. (2000). Replaying the game: hypnagogic images in normals and amnesics. *Science, 290*, 350–353.

Stickgold, R., Rittenhouse, C. D., & Hobson, J. A. (1994). Dream splicing: A new technique for assessing thematic coherence in subjective reports of mental activity. *Consciousness and Cognition, 3*(1), 114–128.

Stipek, D. J., & Ryan, R. H. (1997). Economically disadvantaged preschoolers: Ready to learn but further to go. *Developmental Psychology, 33*, 711–723.

Stoff, D. M., Breiling, J., & Maser, J. D. (Eds.). (1997). *Handbook of antisocial behavior*. New York: Wiley.

Stokes, P. E. (1998). Ten years of fluoxetine. *Depression and Anxiety, 8*, 1–4.

Stone, J., & Cooper, J. (2001). A self-standards model of cognitive dissonance. *Journal of Experimental Social Psychology, 37*, 228–243.

Stoney, C. M., Bausserman, L., Niaura, R., Marcus, B., & Flynn, M. (1999). Lipid reactivity to stress: II. Biological and behavioral influences. *Health Psychology, 18*, 251–261.

Stoney, C. M., & Finney, M. L. (2000). Social support and stress: Influences on lipid reactivity. *International Journal of Behavioral Medicine, 7*, 111–126.

Stoney, C. M., & Hughes, J. W. (1999). Lipid reactivity among men with a parental history of myocardial infarction. *Psychophysiology, 36*, 484–490.

Stoney, C. M., & Matthews, K. A. (1988). Parental history of hypertension and myocardial infarction predicts cardiovascular responses to behavioral stressors in middle-aged men and women. *Psychophysiology, 25*, 269–277.

Stoney, C. M., Niaura, R., Bausserman, L., & Matacin, M. (1999). Lipid reactivity to stress: Comparison of chronic and acute stress responses in middle-aged airline pilots. *Health Psychology, 18*, 241–250.

Strain, E. C., Mumford, G. K., Silverman, K., & Griffiths, R. R. (1994). Caffeine dependence syndrome: Evidence from case histories and experimental evaluations. *Journal of the American Medical Association, 272*(13), 1043–1048.

Strang, J., Witten, J., & Hall, W. (2000). Improving the quality of the cannibis debate: Defining the different domains. *British Medical Journal, 320*, 108–110.

Strass, R. S., & Pollack, H. A. (2001). Epidemic increases in childhood overweight: 1986–1998. *Journal of the American Medical Association, 286*, 2845–2848.

Strathearn, L., Gray, P. H., O'Callaghan, M. J., & Wood, D. O. (2001). Childhood neglect and cognitive development in extremely low birth weight infants: A prospective study. *Pediatrics, 108*, 142–151.

Strayer, D. L., & Johnston, W. A. (2001). Driven to distraction: Dual-task studies of simulated driving and conversing on a cellular phone. *Psychological Science, 12*, 462–466.

Streissguth, A. P., Barr, H. M., Bookstein, F. L., Sampson, P. D., & Olson, H. C. (1999). The long-term neurocognitive consequences of prenatal alcohol exposure: A 14-year study. *Psychological Science, 10*, 186–190.

Strickland, T., Ranganath, V., Lin, K.-M., Poland, R., Mendoza, R., & Smith, M. (1991). Psychopharmacologic considerations in the treatment of Black American populations. *Psychopharmacology Bulletin, 27*, 441–448.

Stromberg, C., Schneider, J., & Joondeph, B. (1993, August). Dealing with potentially dangerous patients. *The Psychologist's Legal Update*, No. 2, pp. 3–12.

Stromberg, C. D., Haggarty, D. J., Leibenluft, R. F., McMillian, M. H., Mishkin, B., et al. (1988). *The psychologist's legal handbook*. Washington, DC: Council for the National Register of Health Service Providers in Psychology.

Strongman, K. T., & Kemp, S. (1991). Autobiographical memory for emotion. *Bulletin of the Psychonomic Society, 29*, 195–198.

Stroop, J. R. (1935). Studies of interference in serial verbal reactions. *Journal of Experimental Psychology, 18*, 643–662.

Strupp, H. H., & Hadley, S. W. (1979). Specific versus non-specific factors in psychotherapy. *Archives of General Psychiatry, 36*, 1125–1136.

Stuart, G. J., & Hausser, M. (2001). Dendritic coincidence detection of EPSPs and action potentials. *Nature Neuroscience, 4*, 63–71.

Stunkard, A. J., & Wadden, T. A. (1992). Psychological aspects of severe obesity. *American Journal of Clinical Nutrition, 55*, 524S–532S.

Sturchler-Pierrat, C., Abramowski, D., Duke, M., Wiederhold, K. H., Mistl, C., Rothacher, S., et al. (1997). Two amyloid precursor protein transgenic mouse models with Alzheimer's disease-like pathology. *Proceedings of the National Academy of Science USA, 94,* 13287–13292.

Sturm, R., & Wells, K. B. (2001). Does obesity contribute as much to morbidity as poverty or smoking? *Public Health, 115,* 229–235.

Subrahmanyam, K., & Greenfield, P. M. (1994). Effect of video game practice on spatial skills in girls and boys. *Journal of Applied Developmental Psychology, 15,* 13–32.

Suddath, R. L., Christison, G. W., Torrey, E. F., Casanova, M. F., & Weinberger, D. R. (1990). Anatomical abnormalities in the brains of monopsychotic twins discordant for schizophrenia. *New England Journal of Medicine, 322,* 789–794.

Sue, D. (1992). *Asian and Caucasian subjects' preference for different counseling styles.* Unpublished manuscript, Western Washington University.

Sue, D. W., Bingham, R. P., Porché-Burke, L., & Vasquez, M. (1999). The diversification of psychology: A multicultural revolution. *American Psychologist, 54,* 1061–1069.

Sue, S. (1998). In search of cultural competence in psychotherapy and counseling. *American Psychologist, 53,* 440–448.

Sue, S., & Okazaki, S. (1990). Asian-American educational achievements: A phenomenon in search of an explanation. *American Psychologist, 45,* 913–920.

Sue, S., Zane, N., & Young, K. (1994). Research on psychotherapy with culturally diverse populations. In A. E. Bergin & S. L. Garfield (Eds.), *Handbook of psychotherapy and behavior change.* New York: Wiley.

Suedfeld, P., & Tetlock, P. (2001). Individual differences in information processing. In A. Tesser & N. Schwarz (Eds.), *Blackwell handbook of social psychology: Intraindividual processes* (pp. 284–304). Oxford, England: Blackwell.

Suh, E., Diener, E., & Fujita, F. (1996). Events and subjective well-being: Only recent events matter. *Journal of Personality and Social Psychology, 70,* 1091–1102.

Suinn, R. M. (2001). The terrible twos: Anger and anxiety. *American Psychologist, 56,* 27–36.

Sullivan, H. S. (1954). *The psychiatric interview.* New York: Norton.

Sullivan, L., & Stankov, L. (1990). Shadowing and target detection as a function of age: Implications for the role of processing resources in competing tasks and in general intelligence. *Australian Journal of Psychology, 42,* 173–185.

Sullivan, P. F. (1995). Mortality in anorexia nervosa. *American Journal of Psychiatry, 152,* 1073–1074.

Suls, J., & Fletcher, B. (1985). The relative efficacy of avoidant and nonavoidant coping strategies: A meta-analysis. *Health Psychology, 4,* 249–288.

Suls, J., & Wan, C. K. (1993). The relationship between trait hostility and cardiovascular reactivity: A quantitative review and analysis. *Psychophysiology, 30,* 1–12.

Summala, H., & Mikkola, T. (1994). Fatal accidents among car and truck drivers: Effects of fatigue, age, and alcohol consumption. *Human Factors, 36*(2), 315–326.

Sundberg, N., & Sue, D. (1989). Research and research hypotheses about effectiveness in intercultural counseling. In P. Pederson, J. Draguns, W. Lonner, & J. Trimble (Eds.), *Counseling across cultures* (3rd ed.). Honolulu: University of Hawaii Press.

Suomi, S. J. (1991). Primate separation models of affective disorders. In J. Madden (Ed.), *Neurobiology of learning, emotion and affect* (pp. 195–213). New York: Raven Press.

Suomi, S. (1991). Up-tight and laid-back monkeys: Individual differences in the response to social challenges. In S. Brauth, W. Hall, & R. Dooling (Eds.), *Plasticity of development* (pp. 27–56). Cambridge: MIT Press.

Suomi, S. (1999). Attachment in Rhesus monkeys. In J. Cassidy & P. R. Shaver (Eds.), *Handbook of attachment* (pp. 181–197). New York: Guilford.

Suzdak, P. D., Glowa, J. R., Crawley, J. N., Schwartz, R. D., Skolnick, P., & Paul, S. M. (1986). A selective imidazobenzodiazepine antagonist of ethanol in the rat. *Science, 234,* 1243–1247.

Suzuki, L. A., & Valencia, R. R. (1997). Race-ethnicity and measured intelligence. *American Psychologist, 52,* 1103–1114.

Swaab, D. E., & Hofman, M. A. (1990). An enlarged suprachiasmatic nucleus in homosexual men. *Brain Research, 537,* 141–148.

Swaab, D. E., & Hofman, M. A. (1995). Sexual differentiation of the human hypothalamus in relation to gender and sexual orientation. *Trends in Neuroscience, 18*(6) 264–270.

Swan, G. E. (1996, December). Some elders thrive on working into late life. *APA Monitor,* p. 35.

Swan, G. E., & Carmelli, D. (1996). Curiosity and mortality in aging adults: A 5-year follow-up of the Western Collaborative Group Study. *Psychology and Aging, 11,* 449–453.

Swann, W. B., Jr., De La Ronde, C., & Hixon, J. G. (1994). Authenticity and positivity strivings in marriage and courtship. *Journal of Personality and Social Psychology, 66,* 857–869.

Sweller, J., & Gee, W. (1978). Einstellung: The sequence effect and hypothesis theory. *Journal of Experimental Psychology: Human Learning and Memory, 4,* 513–526.

Swets, J. A. (1992). The science of choosing the right decision threshold in high-stakes diagnostics. *American Psychologist, 47,* 522–532.

Swets, J. A., Dawes, R. M., & Monahan, J. (2000). Psychological science can improve diagnostic decisions. *Psychological Science in the Public Interest, 1,* 1–26.

Swindle, R., Jr., Heller, K., Pescosolido, B., & Kikuzawa, S. (2000). Responses to nervous breakdowns in America over a 40-year period: Mental health policy implications. *American Psychologist, 55,* 740–749.

Swithers, S. E., & Hall, W. G. (1994). Does oral experience terminate ingestion? *Appetite, 23*(2), 113–138.

Symons, D. (1995). Beauty is in the adaptations of the beholder: The evolutionary psychology of human female sexual attractiveness. In P. R. Abramson & S. D. Pinkerton (Eds.), *Sexual nature, sexual culture* (pp. 80–118). Chicago: University of Chicago Press.

Szasz, T. S. (1987). *Insanity: The idea and its consequences.* New York: Wiley.

Szatmari, P., Jones, M. B., Zwaigenbaum, L., & MacLean, J. E. (1998). Genetics of autism: Overview and new directions. *Journal of Autism and Developmental Disorders, 28,* 351–368.

Szymanski, K., Garczynski, J., & Harkins, S. (2000). The contribution of the potential for evaluation to coaction effects. *Group Processes and Intergroup Relations, 3,* 269–283.

Tagliabue, J. (1999, January 28). Devil gets his due, but Catholic church updates exorcism rites. *International Herald Tribune,* p. 6.

Takayama, Y., Sugishita, M., Kido, T., Ogawa, M., & Akiguchi, I. (1993). A case of foreign accent syndrome without aphasia caused by a lesion of the left precentral gyrus. *Neurology, 43,* 1361–1363.

Takei, N., Sham, P., O'Callaghan, E., Murray, G. K., Glover, G., & Murray, R. M. (1994). Prenatal exposure to influenza and the development of schizophrenia: Is the effect confined to females? *American Journal of Psychiatry, 151,* 117–119.

Takeuchi, A. H., & Hulse, S. H. (1993). Absolute pitch. *Psychological Bulletin, 113,* 345–361.

Tallal, P., Miller, S. L., Bedi, G., Wang, X., Nagarajan, S. S., Schreiner, C., et al. (1996). Language comprehension in language-learning impaired children improved with acoustically modified speech. *Science, 271,* 81–84.

Tanaka-Matsumi, J., & Higginbotham, H. N. (1994). Clinical application of behavior therapy across ethnic and cultural boundaries. *The Behavior Therapist, 17,* 123–126.

Tanda, G., Pontieri, F. E., & Di Chiara, G. (1997). Cannabinoid and heroin activation of mesolimbic dopamine transmission by a common mu1 opioid receptor mechanism. *Science, 276,* 2048–2050.

Tannen, D. (1994). *Gender and discourse.* New York: Oxford University Press.

Tanner, J. M. (1978). *Foetus into man: Physical growth from conception to maturity.* London: Open Books.

Tanner, J. M. (1992). Growth as a measure of nutritional and hygienic status of a population. *Hormone Research, 38,* 106–115.

Tarr, S. J., & Pyfer, J. L. (1996). Physical and motor development of neonates/infants prenatally exposed to drugs in utero: A meta-analysis. *Adapted Physical Activity Quarterly, 13,* 269–287.

Tartaglia, L. A., Dembski, M., Weng, X., Deng, N., Culpepper, J., Devos, R., et al. (1996). Identification and expression cloning of a leptin receptor, OB-R. *Cell, 83,* 1263–1271.

Task Force on Promotion and Dissemination of Psychological Procedures. (1995). Training in and dissemination of empirically validated psychological treatments: Report and recommendations. *Clinical Psychologist, 48,* 3–23.

Tasker, F., & Golombok, S. (1995). Adults raised as children in lesbian families. *American Journal of Orthopsychiatry, 65*(2), 203–215.

Taub, A. (1998). Thumbs down on acupuncture. *Science, 279,* 159.

Taubenfeld, S. M., Milekic, M. H., Monti, B., & Alberini, C. M. (2001). The consolidation of new but not reactivated memory requires hippocampal C/EBPb. *Nature Neuroscience, 4,* 813–818.

Taubes, G. (1998). Weight increases worldwide? *Science, 280,* 1368.

Tavris, C. (1998, September 13). Peer pressure. *New York Times Book Review,* 14.

Taylor, H. A., & Tversky, B. (1992). Spatial mental models derived from survey and route descriptions. *Journal of Memory and Language, 31,* 261–292.

Taylor, R. L., & Richards, S. B. (1991). Patterns of intellectual differences of Black, Hispanic, and White children. *Psychology in the Schools, 28,* 5–8.

Taylor, S., Peplau, A. & Sears, R. (2000). *Social psychology* (10th ed.) Upper Saddle River, NJ: Prentice-Hall.

Taylor, S. E. (1998). *Health psychology* (4th ed.). New York: McGraw-Hill.

Taylor, S. E. (1999). *Health psychology* (4th ed.). New York: McGraw-Hill.

Taylor, S. E., & Aspinwall, L. G. (1996). Mediating processes in psychosocial stress: Appraisal, coping, resistance, and vulnerability. In H. B. Kaplan (Ed.), *Psychosocial stress: Perspectives on structure, theory, life course, and methods* (pp. 71–110). New York: Academic Press.

Taylor, S. E., Kemeny, M. E., Aspinwall, L. G., Schneider, S. G., Rodriguez, R., & Herbert, M. (1992). Optimism, coping, psychological distress, and high-risk sexual behavior among men at risk for acquired immunodeficiency syndrome (AIDS). *Journal of Personality and Social Psychology, 63,* 460–473.

Taylor, S. E., Kemeny, M. E., Reed, G. M., Bower, J. E., & Gruenewald, T. L. (2000a). Psychological resources, positive illusions, and health. *American Psychologist, 55,* 99–109.

Taylor, S. E., Klein, L. C., Lewis, B. P., Gruenewald, T. L., Gurung, R. A. R., & Updegraff, J. A. (2000b). Biobehavioral responses to stress in females: Tend-and-befriend, not fight-or-flight. *Psychological Review, 107,* 411–429.

Taylor, S. E., & Lobel, M. (1989). Social comparison activity under threat: Downward evaluation and upward contacts. *Psychological Review, 96,* 569–575.

Taylor, S. P., & Hulsizer, M. R. (1998). Psychoactive drugs and human aggression. In R. G. Geen & E. Donnerstein (Eds.), *Human aggression* (pp. 139–167). San Diego: Academic Press.

Tecott, L. H., Sun, L. M., Akana, S. F., Strack, A. M., Lowenstein, D. H., Dallman, M. F., & Julius, D. (1995). Eating disorder and epilepsy in mice lacking 5-HT2C serotonin receptors. *Nature, 374,* 542–546.

Teghtsoonian, R. (1992). In defense of the pineal gland. *Behavioral and Brain Sciences, 15,* 224–225.

Teigen, K. H. (1994). Yerkes-Dodson: A law for all seasons. *Theory and Psychology, 4*(4), 525–547.

Tellegen, A., Lykken, D. T., Bouchard, T. J., Wilcox, K. J., Segal, N. L., & Rich, S. (1988). Personality similarity in twins reared apart and together. *Journal of Personality and Social Psychology, 54,* 1031–1039.

Terman, J. S., Terman, M., Lo, E. S., & Cooper, T. B. (2001). Circadian time of morning light administration and therapeutic response in winter depression. *Archives of General Psychiatry, 58,* 69–75.

Terman, L. M. (1916). *The measurement of intelligence.* Boston: Houghton Mifflin.

Terman, L. M., & Oden, M. H. (1947). *The gifted child grows up: Vol. 4. Genetic studies of genius.* Stanford, CA: Stanford University Press.

Terman, L. M., & Oden, M. H. (1959). *The gifted group at midlife.* Stanford, CA: Stanford University Press.

Terrace, H. S., Petitto, L. A., Sanders, D. L., & Bever, J. G. (1979). Can an ape create a sentence? *Science, 206,* 891–902.

Ter Riet, G., Kleijnen, J., & Knipschild, P. (1990). Acupuncture and chronic pain: A criteria-based meta-analysis. *Journal of Clinical Epidemiology, 43,* 1191–1199.

Tesser, A. (2001). Self-esteem: The frequency of temporal-self and social comparisons in people's personal appraisals. In A. Tesser & N. Schwarz (Eds.), *Blackwell handbook of social psychology: Intraindividual processes* (pp. 479–498). Oxford, England: Blackwell.

Thaker, G. K., & Carpenter, W. T., Jr. (2001). Advances in schizophrenia. *Nature Medicine, 7,* 667–671.

Thanos, P. K., Volkow, N. D., Freimuth, P., Umegaki, H., Ikari, H., Roth, G., et al. (2001). Overexpression of dopamine D2 receptors reduces alcohol self-administration. *Journal of Neurochemistry, 78,* 1094–1103.

Thelen, E. (1995). Motor development: A new synthesis. *American Psychologist, 50,* 79–95.

Theofilopoulos, S., Goggi, J., Riaz, S. S., Jauniaux, E., Stern, G. M., & Bradford, H. F. (2001). Parallel induction of the formation of dopamine and its metabolites with induction of tyrosine hydroxylase expression in foetal rat and human cerebral cortical cells by brain-derived neurotrophic factor and glial-cell derived neurotrophic factor. *Brain Research: Developmental Brain Research, 127,* 111–122.

Theunisson, E. (1994). Factors influencing the design of perspective flight path displays for guidance and navigation. *Displays, 15,* 241–254.

Thom, A., Sartory, G., & Jöhren, P. (2000). Comparison between one-session psychological treatment and benzodiazepine in dental phobia. *Journal of Consulting and Clinical Psychology, 68,* 378–387.

Thomas, A., & Chess, S. (1977). *Temperament and development.* New York: Brunner/Mazel.

Thomas, E. L., & Robinson, H. A. (1972). *Improving reading in every class: A sourcebook for teachers.* Boston: Allyn & Bacon.

Thomas, K. W., & Schmidt, W. H. (1976). A survey of managerial interests with respect to conflict. *Academy of Management Journal, 19,* 315–318.

Thompson, D. S., & Pollack, B. G. (2001, August 26). Psychotropic metabolism: Gender-related issues. *Psychiatric Times* [Online], *14.* Available: http://www.mhsource.com/pt/p010147.html

Thompson, J. K. (1996a). Eating disorders: Introduction. In J. K. Thompson (Ed.), *Body image, eating disorders, and obesity* (pp. 173–176) Washington DC: American Psychological Association.

Thompson, J. K. (1996b). Introduction: Assessment and treatment of binge eating disorder. In J. K. Thompson (Ed.), *Body image, eating disorders, and obesity* (pp. 1–22). Washington, DC: American Psychological Association.

Thompson, J. K., & Stice, E. (2001). Thin-ideal internalization: Mounting evidence for a new risk factor for body-image disturbance and eating pathology. *Current Directions in Psychological Science, 10,* 181–183.

Thompson, P. M., Giedd, J. N., Woods, R. P., Macdonald, D., Evans, A. C., & Toga, A. W. (2000). Growth patterns in the developing brain detected by using continuum mechanical tensor maps *Nature, 404,* 190–193.

Thompson, R. A. (1998). Early sociopersonality development. In W. Damon & N. Eisenberg (Eds.), *Handbook of child psychology: Vol. 3. Social, emotional, and personality development* (5th ed., pp. 25–104). New York: Wiley.

Thompson, S. C., Sobolow-Shubin, A., Galbraith, M. E., Schwankovksy, L., & Cruzen, D. (1993). Maintaining perceptions of control: Finding perceived control in low control circumstances. *Journal of Personality and Social Psychology, 64,* 293–304.

Thompson, W. G. (1995). Coffee: Brew or bane. *American Journal of the Medical Sciences, 308*(1), 49–57.

Thomson, C. P. (1982). Memory for unique personal events: The roommate study. *Memory & Cognition, 10,* 324–332.

Thorndike, E. L. (1898). Animal intelligence: An experienced study of the associative process in animals. *Psychological Monographs, 2*(Whole No. 8).

Thorndike, R. M. & Dinnel, D. L. (2001). *Basic statistics for the behavioral sciences.* Upper Saddle River, NJ: Prentice-Hall.

Thorndike, R. M., Hagen, E., & Sattler, J. (2001). *Stanford-Binet Intelligence Scale* (4th ed.). Boston: Riverside.

Thorpe, G. L., & Olson, S. L. (1997). *Behavior therapy: Concepts, procedures, and applications* (2nd ed.). Boston: Allyn & Bacon.

Tian, H.-G., Nan, Y., Hu, G., Dong, Q.-N., Yang, X.-L., Pietinen, P., & Nissinen, A. (1995). Dietary survey in a Chinese population. *European Journal of Clinical Nutrition, 49,* 27–32.

Tidwell, M. C. O., Reis, H. T., & Shaver, P. R. (1996). Attachment, attractiveness, and social interaction: A diary study. *Journal of Personality and Social Psychology, 71,* 729–745.

Tiihonen, J., Kuikka, J., Bergstrom, K., Hakola, P., Karhu, J., Ryynänen, O.-P., & Föhr, J. (1995). Altered striatal dopamine re-uptake site densities in habitually violent and non-violent alcoholics. *Nature Medicine, 1*(7), 654–657.

Tiller, J., Schmidt, U., Ali, S., & Treasure, J. (1995). Patterns of punitiveness in women with eating disorders. *International Journal of Eating Disorders, 17*(4), 365–371.

Timberlake, W. (1980). A molar equilibrium theory of learned performance. In G. H. Bower (Ed.), *The psychology of learning and motivation* (Vol. 14, pp. 1–58). San Diego: Academic Press.

Timberlake, W., & Farmer-Dougan, V. A. (1991). Reinforcement in applied settings: Figuring out ahead of time what will work. *Psychological Bulletin, 110*(3), 379–391.

Tinbergen, N. (1989). *The study of instinct.* Oxford: Clarendon.

Todorov, C., Freeston, M. H., & Borgeat, F. (2000). On the pharmacotherapy of obsessive-compulsive disorder: Is a consensus possible? *Canadian Journal of Psychiatry, 45,* 257–262.

Toh, K. L., Jones, C. R., He, Y., Eide, E. J., Hinz, W. A., Virshup, D. M., et al. (2001). An hPer2 phosphorylation site mutation in familial advanced sleep phase syndrome. *Science, 291,* 1040–1043.

Tolman, E. C., & Honzik, C. H. (1930). Introduction and removal of reward and maze performance in rats. *University of California Publication in Psychology, 4,* 257–265.

Tomasello, M. (2000). Culture and cognitive development. *Current Directions in Psychological Science, 9,* 37–40.

Tomes, H. (1999, April). The need for cultural competence. *APA Monitor,* p. 31.

Toni, N., Buchs, P. A., Nikonenko, I., Bron, C. R., & Muller, D. (1999). LTP promotes formation of multiple spine synapses between a single axon terminal and a dendrite. *Nature, 402,* 421–425.

Torasdotter, M., Metsis, M., Henriksson, B. G., Winblad, B., & Mohammed, A. H. (1998). Environmental enrichment results in higher levels of nerve growth factor mRNA in the rat visual cortex and hippocampus. *Behavior and Brain Research, 93,* 83–90.

Tourangeau, R., Rips, L. J., & Rasinski, K. (2000). *The psychology of the survey response.* Cambridge, England: Cambridge University Press.

Townsend, J. M., Kline, J., & Wasserman, T. H. (1995). Low-investment copulation: Sex differences in motivational and emotional reactions. *Ethology and Sociobiology, 16*(1), 25–51.

Trabasso, T. R., & Bower, G. H. (1968). *Attention in learning.* New York: Wiley.

Tramer, M. R., Carroll, D., Campbell, F. A., Reynolds, D. J., Moore, R. A., & McQuay, H. J. (2001). Cannabinoids for control of chemotherapy induced nausea and vomiting: quantitative systematic review. *British Medical Journal, 323,* 16–21.

Treiber, F. A., Musante, L., Kapuku, G., Davis, C., Litaker, M., & Davis, H. (2001). Cardiovascular (CV) responsivity and recovery to acute stress and future CV functioning in youth with family histories of CV disease: A 4-year longitudinal study. *International Journal of Psychophysiology, 41,* 65–74.

Treisman, A. (1988). Features and objects: The 14th Bartlett memorial lecture. *Quarterly Journal of Experimental Psychology, 40,* 201–237.

Tremblay, A., & Bueman, B. (1995). Exercise-training, macronutrient balance and body weight control. *International Journal of Obesity, 19*(2), 79–86.

Tremblay, R. E., Pagani-Kurtz, L., Mâsse, L., Vitaro, F., & Pihl, R. O. (1995). A bimodal preventive intervention for disruptive kindergarten boys: Its impact through mid-adolescence. *Journal of Consulting and Clinical Psychology, 63,* 560–568.

Tremblay, R. E., Pihl, R. O., Vitaro, F., & Dobkin, P. (1994). Predicting early onset of male antisocial behavior from preschool behavior. *Archives of General Psychiatry, 51,* 732–739.

Triandis, H. C. (1964). Cultural influences upon cognitive processes. In L. Berkowitz (Ed.), *Advances in experimental social psychology.* New York: Academic Press.

Triandis, H. C. (1994). *Culture and social behavior.* New York: McGraw-Hill.

Triandis, H. C. (1996). The psychological measurement of cultural syndromes. *American Psychologist, 51,* 407–415.

Triandis, H. C. (1998). Vertical and horizontal individualism and collectivism: Theory and research implications for international management. In J. L. C. Cheng, R. B. Peterson, et al. (Eds.), *Advances in international comparative management.* Stamford, CT: JAI Press.

Trierweiler, S. J., Neighbors, H. W., Munday, C., Thompson, E. E., Binion, V. J., & Gomez, J. P. (2000). Clinician attributions associated with the diagnosis of schizophrenia in African American and non-African American patients. *Journal of Consulting and Clinical Psychology, 68,* 171–175.

Trillin, A. S. (2001, January 29). Betting your life. *The New Yorker,* pp. 38–41.

Trivers, R. L. (1972). Parental investment and sexual selection. In B. Campbell (Eds.), *Sexual selection and the descent of man: 1871–1971* (pp. 136–179). Chicago: Aldine.

Tronick, E. Z. (1989). Emotions and emotional communication in infants. *American Psychologist, 44,* 112–119.

Troop, L. R., & Wright, S. (2001). In group identification as the inclusion of ingroup in the self. *Personality and Social Psychology Bulletin, 27,* 585–600.

Trope, Y., Cohen, O., & Alfieri, T. (1991). Behavior identification as a mediator of dispositional inference. *Journal of Personality and Social Psychology, 61,* 873–883.

Trower, P. (1995). Adult social skills: State of the art and future directions. In W. O'Donohue & L. Krasner (Eds.), *Handbook of psychological skills training: Clinical techniques and applications* (pp. 54–80). Boston: Allyn & Bacon.

Trujillo, C. M. (1986). A comparative evaluation of classroom interactions between professors and minority and non-minority college students. *American Educational Research Journal, 23,* 629–642.

Trujillo, K. A., & Akil, H. (1991). Inhibition of morphine tolerance and dependence by the NMDA receptor antagonist MK-801. *Science, 251,* 85–87.

Trull, T. J., & Sher, K. J. (1994). Relationship between the five-factor model of personality and Axis I disorders in a nonclinical sample. *Journal of Personality and Social Psychology, 103,* 350–360.

Tryon, R. C. (1940). Genetic differences in maze-learning ability in rats. *Yearbook of the National Society for the Study of Education, 39,* 111–119.

Tseng, W., Kan-Ming, M., Li-Shuen, L., Guo-Qian, C., Li-Wah, O., & Hong-Bo, Z. (1992). Koro epidemics in Guangdong China. *Journal of Nervous and Mental Disease, 180,* 117–123.

Tsuang, M. T., Stone, W. S., & Faraone, S. V. (2000). Toward reformulating the diagnosis of schizophrenia. *American Journal of Psychiatry, 157,* 1041–1950.

Tulving, E. (1983). *Elements of episodic memory.* New York: Oxford University Press.

Tulving, E. (1993). Self-knowledge of an amnesic individual is represented abstractly. In T. K. Srull & R. S. Wyer (Eds.), *The mental representation of trait and autobiographical knowledge about the self: Advances in social cognition* (Vol. 5). Hillsdale, NJ: Erlbaum.

Tulving, E. (1995). Organization of memory: Quo vadis? In M. S. Gazzaniga (Ed.), *The cognitive neurosciences* (pp. 839–853). Cambridge: MIT Press.

Tulving, E. (in press). Episodic memory: From mind to brain. *Annual Review of Psychology.*

Tulving, E., Hayman, C. A. G., & Macdonald, C. A. (1991). Long-lasting perceptual priming and semantic learning in amnesia: A case experiment.

Journal of Experimental Psychology: Learning, Memory, and Cognition, 17, 595–617.

Tulving, E., & Psotka, J. (1971). Retroactive inhibition in free recall: Inaccessibility of information available in the memory store. *Journal of Experimental Psychology, 87,* 1–8.

Tulving, E., & Schacter, D. L. (1990). Priming and human memory systems. *Science, 247,* 301–306.

Tulving, E., Schacter, D. L., & Stark, H. (1982). Priming effects in word-fragment completion are independent of recognition memory. *Journal of Experimental Psychology: Learning, Memory, and Cognition, 8,* 336–342.

Tuomilehto, J., Lindstrom, J., Eriksson, J. G., Valle, T. T., Hamalainen, H., Ilanne-Parikka, P., et al. (2001). Prevention of type 2 diabetes mellitus by changes in lifestyle among subjects with impaired glucose tolerance. *New England Journal of Medicine, 344,* 1343–1350.

Turiel, E. (1998). The development of morality. In W. Damon & N. Eisenberg (Eds.), *Handbook of child psychology: Vol. 3. Social, emotional, and personality development* (5th ed., pp. 863–932). New York: Wiley.

Turkheimer, E., & Waldron M. (2000). Nonshared environment: A theoretical, methodological, and quantitative review. *Psychological Bulletin, 126,* 78–108.

Turkington, C. (1987). Special talents. *Psychology Today,* pp. 42–46.

Turkkan, J. S. (1989). Classical conditioning: The new hegemony. *Behavioral & Brain Sciences, 12,* 121–179.

Turner, B. G., Beidel, D. C., Hughes, S., & Turner, M. W. (1993). Test anxiety in African-American school children. *School Psychology Quarterly, 8,* 140–152.

Turner, C. F., Miller, H. G., & Rogers, S. M. (1998). Survey measurement of sexual behaviors: Problems and progress. In J. Bancroft (Ed.), *Researching sexual behavior* (pp. 37–60). Bloomington: Indiana University Press.

Turner, J. C. (1991). *Social influence.* Pacific Grove, CA: Brooks/Cole.

Turner, S. M., DeMers, S. T., Fox, H. R., & Reed, G. M. (2001). APA's guidelines for test user qualifications: An executive summary. *American Psychologist, 56,* 1099–1113.

Tversky, A. (1972). Elimination by aspects: A theory of choice. *Psychological Review, 79,* 281–299.

Tversky, A., & Kahneman, D. (1974). Judgment under uncertainty: Heuristics and biases. *Science, 185,* 1124–1131.

Tversky, A., & Kahneman, D. (1981). The framing of decisions and the psychology of choice. *Science, 211,* 453–458.

Tversky, A., & Kahneman, D. (1991). Loss aversion in riskless choice: A reference dependent model. *Quarterly Journal of Economics, 106,* 1039–1061.

Tversky, A., & Kahneman, D. (1993). Probabilistic reasoning. In A. Goldman (Ed.), *Readings in philosophy and cognitive science* (pp. 43–68). Cambridge: MIT Press.

Tversky, B., & Tuchin, M. (1989). A reconciliation of the evidence on eyewitness testimony: Comments on McCloskey and Zaragoza. *Journal of Experimental Psychology: General, 118,* 86–91.

U.K. Statistical Bulletin. (1999). *Electro convulsive therapy: Survey covering the period from January 1999 to March 1999, England.* London: Department of Health.

U.S. Bureau of the Census. (2001). *Population by race and Hispanic or Latino origin for the United States, summary file for states, Table PL 1.* Washington, DC: U.S. Bureau of the Census, Population Division.

U.S. Census Bureau. (2000). *Current population survey: Poverty highlights, 1999.* Washington, DC: U.S. Government Printing Office.

U.S. Census Bureau. (2001). *Poverty in the United States: 2000.* Washington, DC: U.S. Government Printing Office.

U.S. Department of Health and Human Services. (1996). *Physical activity and health: A report of the Surgeon General.* Atlanta: Centers for Disease Control and Prevention.

U.S. Department of Health and Human Services. (2000a). *National health and nutrition examination survey, 1999.* Washington, DC: National Center for Health Statistics.

U.S. Department of Health and Human Services. (2000b). *Reducing tobacco use: A report of the Surgeon General.* Atlanta, GA: Centers for Disease Control and Prevention.

U.S. Department of Health and Human Services. (2001a). *Mental health: Culture, race, and ethnicity. A supplement to mental health: A report of the Surgeon General.* Washington, DC: United States Public Health Service.

U.S. Department of Health and Human Services. (2001b). *Women and smoking: A report of the Surgeon General.* Atlanta: Centers for Disease Control and Prevention.

U.S. Department of Justice. (1997). *Lifetime likelihood of going to state or federal prison.* Washington DC: Bureau of Justice Statistics.

U.S. Department of Justice. (1998). *Alcohol and crime: An analysis of national data on the prevalence of alcohol involved in crime.* Washington, DC: Author.

U.S. Department of Justice. (1999). *Eyewitness evidence: A guide for law enforcement.* Washington, DC: National Institute of Justice.

U.S. Department of Justice. (2001). *Bureau of Justice statistics.* Washington, DC: United States Government.

U.S. Surgeon General. (1999). *Mental health: A report of the surgeon general.* Rockville, MD: U.S. Department of Health and Human Services.

Uchida, Y., Kitayama, S., Mesquita, B., & Reyes, J. A. (2001, June). *Interpersonal sources of happiness: The relative significance in Japan, the Philippines, and the United States.* Paper presented at Annual Convention of American Psychological Society, Toronto, Canada.

Uchino, B. N., Cacioppo, J. T. & Kiecolt-Glaser, J. K. (1996). The relationship between social support and physiological process: A review with emphasis on underlying mechanisms and implications for health. *Psychological Bulletin, 119,* 488–531.

Uchino, B. N., Uno, D., & Holt-Lunstad, J. (1999). Social support, physiological processes, and health. *Current Directions in Psychological Science, 8,* 145–148.

Uhl, G., Sora, I., & Wang, Z. (1999). *Proceedings of the National Academy of Sciences, 96,* 7752–7755.

Ullian, E. M., Sapperstein, S. K., Christopherson, K. S., & Barres, B. A. (2001). Control of synapse number by glia. *Science, 291,* 657–661.

Ungless, M. A., Whistler, J. L., Malenka, R. C., & Bonci, A. (2001). Single cocaine exposure in vivo induces long-term potentiation in dopamine neurons. *Nature, 411,* 583–587.

Valencia-Flores, M., Castano, V. A., Campos, R. M., Rosenthal, L., Resendiz, M., Vergara, P., et al. (1998). The siesta culture concept is not supported by the sleep habits of urban Mexican students. *Journal of Sleep Research, 7,* 21–29.

Valenstein, E. S. (Ed.). (1980). *The psychosurgery debate.* San Francisco: Freeman.

Valent, F., Brusaferro, S., & Barbone, F. (2001). A case-crossover study of sleep and childhood injury. *Pediatrics, 107,* e23.

Valenza, E., Simion, F., Assia, V. M., & Umilta, C. (1996). Face preference at birth. *Journal of Experimental Psychology: Human Perception & Performance, 22,* 892–903.

Van Ameringen, M. A., Lane, R. M., Walker, J. R., Bowen, R. C., Chokka, P. R., Goldner, E. M., et al. (2001). Sertraline treatment of generalized social phobia: A 20-week, double-blind, placebo-controlled study. *American Journal of Psychiatry, 158,* 275–281.

Van Bezooijen, R., Otto, S. A., & Heenan, T. A (1983). Recognition of vocal expression of emotion: A three-nation study to identify universal characteristics. *Journal of Cross-Cultural Psychology, 14,* 387–406.

Van Essen, D. C., Anderson, C. H., & Felleman, D. J. (1992). Information processing in the primate visual system: An integrated systems perspective. *Science, 255,* 419–423.

van IJzendoorn, M. H. (1995). Adult attachment representations, parental responsiveness, and infant attachment: A meta-analysis on the predictive validity of the Adult Attachment Interview. *Psychological Bulletin, 117,* 387–403.

Van Lange, P. A. M., & Sedikides, C. (1998). Being more honest but not necessarily more intelligent than others: Generality and explanations for the Muhammad Ali effect. *European Journal of Social Psychology, 28,* 675–680.

van Praag, H., Christie, B. R., Sejnowski, T. J., & Gage, F. H. (1999). Running enhances neurogenesis, learning, and long-term potentiation in mice. *Proceedings of the National Academy of Sciences, 96,* 13427–13431.

van Reekum, R., Black, S. E., Conn, D., & Clarke, D. (1997). Cognition-enhancing drugs in dementia: A guide to the near future. *Canadian Journal of Psychiatry, 42*(Suppl. 1), 35S–50S.

Van Sickel, A. D. (1992). Clinical hypnosis in the practice of anesthesia. *Nurse Anesthesiologist, 3*, 67–74.

Van Tol, H., Caren, M., Guan, H.-C., Ohara, K., Bunzow, J., Civelli, O., et al. (1992). Multiple dopamine D4 receptor variants in the human population. *Nature, 358*, 149–152.

Vastag, B. (2001). Brain gene for autism? *Journal of the American Medical Association, 285*, 23.

Vattano, F. (2000). *The mind: Video teaching modules* (2nd ed.). Fort Collins, CO: Colorado State University and Annenberg/CPB.

Velligan, D. I., Bow-Thomas, C. C., Huntzinger, C., Ritch, J., Ledbetter, N., Prihoda, T. J., & Miller, A. L. (2000). Randomized controlled trial of the use of compensatory strategies to enhance adaptive functioning in outpatients with schizophrenia. *American Journal of Psychiatry, 157*, 1317–1328.

Venter, J. C., et al. (2001). The sequence of the human genome. *Science, 291*, 1304–1351.

Verfaellie, M., & Cermak, L. S. (1991). *Neuropsychological issues in amnesia.* In J. L. Martinez & R. P. Kesner (Eds.), *Learning nad memory: A biological view* (2nd ed.). San Diego: Academic Press.

Vernet, M. E., Robin, O., & Dittmar, A. (1995). The ohmic perturbation duration, an original temporal index to quantify electrodermal responses. *Behavioural Brain Research, 67*(1), 103–107.

Vernon, P. A. (Ed.). (1987). *Speed of information-processing and intelligence.* Norwood, NJ: Ablex.

Vincent, C. A., & Richardson, P. H. (1986). The evaluation of therapeutic acupuncture: Concepts and methods. *Pain, 24*, 1–13.

Vincent, K. R. (1991). Black/White IQ differences: Does age make a difference? *Journal of Clinical Psychology, 47*, 266–270.

Vink, T., Hinney, A., van Elburg, A. A., van Goozen, S. H. M., Sandkuijl, L. A., Sinke, R. J., et al. (2001). Association between an agouti-related protein gene polymorphism and anorexia nervosa. *Molecular Psychiatry, 6*, 325–328.

Vioque, J., Torres, A., & Quiles, J. (2000). Time spent watching television, sleep duration, and obesity in adults living in Valencia, Spain. *International Journal of Obesity, 24*, 1683–1688.

Viswesvaran, C., & Ones, D. S. (2000). Measurement error in "Big Five factors" personality assessment: Reliability generalization across studies and measures. *Educational & Psychological Measurement, 60*, 224–235.

Voelker, R. (1997). "Decent research and closure" needed on medical marijuana, says head of NIH panel. *Journal of the American Medical Association, 278*, 802.

Vogeltanz, N. D., Sigmon, S. T., & Vickers, K. S. (1998). Feminism and behavior analysis: A framework for women's health research and practice. In J. J. Plaud & G. H. Eifert (Eds.), *From behavior theory to behavior therapy* (pp. 269–293). Boston: Allyn & Bacon.

Vokey, J. R., & Read, J. D. (1985). Subliminal messages: Between the devil and the media. *American Psychologist, 40*, 1231–1239.

Volavka, J., Czobor, P., Sheitman, B., Lindenmayer, J. P., Citrome, L., McEvoy, J. P., et al. (2002). Clozapine, olanzapine, risperidone, and haloperidol in the treatment of patients with chronic schizophrenia and schizoaffective disorder. *American Journal of Psychiatry, 159*, 255–262.

Volkow, N. D., Chang, L., Wang, G. J., Fowler, J. S., Franceschi, D., Sedler, M. J., et al. (2001). Higher cortical and lower subcortical metabolism in detoxified methamphetamine abusers. *American Journal of Psychiatry, 158*, 383–389.

Vollebergh, W. A. M., Iedema, J., Bijl, R. V., de Graaf, R., Smit, F., & Ormel, J. (2001). The Structure and stability of common mental disorders: The NEMESIS study. *Archives of General Psychiatry, 58*, 597–603.

Volz, H. P., & Laux, P. (2000). Potential treatment for subthreshold and mild depression: A comparison of St. John's wort extracts and fluoxetine. *Comprehensive Psychiatry, 41*, 133–137.

Volz, J. (2000). Successful aging. The second 50. *APA Monitor, 31*, 24–28.

von Bekesy, G. (1960). *Experiments in hearing.* New York: McGraw-Hill.

Von Wright, J. M., Anderson, K., & Stenman, U. (1975). Generalization of conditioned GSRs in dichotic listening. In P. M. A. Rabbitt & S. Dornic (Eds.), *Attention and performance V.* New York: Academic Press.

Vorel, S. R., Liu, X., Hayes, R. J., Spector, J. A., & Gardner, E. L. (2001). Relapse to cocaine-seeking after hippocampal theta burst stimulation. *Science, 292*, 1175–1178.

Vyse, S. A. (1997). *Believing in magic: The psychology of superstition.* New York: Oxford University Press.

Wagenaar, W. A. (1989). *Paradoxes of gambling behavior.* Hove, England: Erlbaum.

Wadden, T. A., Berkowitz, R. I., Sarwer, D. B., Prus-Wisniewski, R., & Steinberg, C. (2001). Benefits of lifestyle modification in the pharmacologic treatment of obesity: A randomized trial. *Archives of Internal Medicine, 161*, 218–227.

Wade, C. (1988, April). *Thinking critically about critical thinking in psychology.* Paper presented at the annual meeting of the Western Psychological Association, San Francisco, CA.

Wade, T., Martin, N. G., & Tiggemann, M. (1998). Genetic and environmental factors for the weight and shape concerns characteristic of bulimia nervosa. *Psychological Medicine, 28*, 761–771.

Wade, W. A., Treat, T. A., & Stuart, G. L. (1998). Transporting an empirically supported treatment for panic disorder to a service clinic setting: A benchmarking strategy. *Journal of Consulting & Clinical Psychology, 66*, 231–239.

Wadsworth, S. (1994). School achievement. In J. C. DeFries, R. Pomin, & D. W. Fulker (Eds.), *Nature and nurture during middle childhood* (pp. 86–101). Cambridge, MA: Blackwell.

Wadsworth, S. J., Olson, R. K., Pennington, B. F., & DeFries, J. C. (2000). Differential genetic etiology of reading disability as a function of IQ. *Journal of Learning Disabilities, 33*, 192–200.

Waelti, P., Dickinson, A., & Schultz, W. (2001). Dopamine responses comply with basic assumptions of formal learning theory. *Nature, 412*, 43–48.

Wagner, A. D. (1999). Working memory contributions to human learning and remembering. *Neuron, 22*, 19–22.

Wagner, A. D., Schacter, D. L., Rotte, M., Koutstaal, W., Maril, A., Dale, A., et al. (1998). Building memories: Remembering and forgetting of verbal experiences as predicted by brain activity. *Science, 281*, 1188–1191.

Wagner, U., Gais, S., & Born, J. (2001). Emotional memory formation is enhanced across sleep intervals with high amounts of rapid eye movement sleep. *Learning and Memory, 8*, 112–119.

Wahlsten, D. (1999). Single-gene influences on brain and behavior. *Annual Review of Psychology, 50*, 599–624.

Wakefield, J. C. (1992). The concept of mental disorder: On the boundary between biological facts and social values. *American Psychologist, 47*, 373–388.

Wakefield, J. C. (1999). Evolutionary versus prototype analyses of the concept of disorder. *Journal of Abnormal Psychology, 108*, 374–399.

Walbeck, K., Forsen, T., Osmond, C., Barker, D. J., & Ericksson, J. G. (2001). Association of schizophrenia with low maternal body mass index, small size at birth, and thinness during childhood. *Archives of General Psychiatry, 58*, 48–52.

Walberg, H. J. (1987). Studies show curricula efficiency can be attained. *NASSP Bulletin, 71*, 15–21.

Waldrop, M. M. (1987). The working of working memory. *Science, 237*, 1564–1567.

Walker, E. F., & Diforio, D. (1998). Schizophrenia: A neural diathesis-stress model. *Psychological Review, 104*, 667–685.

Walker, L. (1991). The feminization of psychology. *Psychology of Women Newsletter of Division 35*, 1, 4.

Walker, L. J. (1989). A longitudinal study of moral reasoning. *Child Development, 60*, 157–166.

Walker, L. J. (1995). Sexism in Kohlberg's moral psychology? In W. M. Kurtines & J. L. Gewirtz (Eds.), *Moral development: An introduction* (pp. 83–107). Boston: Allyn & Bacon.

Walker-Andrews, A. S., Bahrick, L. E., Raglioni, S. S., & Dias, I. (1991). Infants' bimodal perception of gender. *Ecological Psychology, 3*, 55–75.

Walkup, J. T., Labellarte, M. J., Riddle, M. A., Pine, D. S., Greenhill, L., Klein, R., et al. (2001). Fluvoxamine for the treatment of anxiety disorders in children and adolescents. *The New England Journal of Medicine, 344,* 1279–1285.

Wall, T. L., Shea, S. H., Chan, K. K., & Carr, L. G. (2001). A genetic association with the development of alcohol and other substance use behavior in Asian Americans. *Journal of Abnormal Psychology, 110,* 173–178.

Wallace, R. K., & Benson, H. (1972). The physiology of meditation. *Scientific American, 226,* 84–90.

Wallen, K., & Lovejoy, J. (1993). Sexual behavior: Endocrine function and therapy. In J. Shulkin (Ed.), *Hormonal pathways to mind and brain.* New York: Academic Press.

Waller, D. (2000). Individual differences in spatial learning from computer-simulated environments. *Journal of Experimental Psychology: Applied, 6,* 307–321.

Wallerstein, J. S., Lewis, J. M., & Blakeslee, S. (2000). *The unexpected legacy of divorce.* New York: Hyperion.

Wallis, G., & Bülthoff, H. H. (2001). Effects of temporal association on recognition memory. *Proceedings of the National Academy of Sciences, 98*(8), 4800–4804.

Wallis, J. D., Anderson, K. C., & Miller, E. K. (2001). Single neurons in prefrontal cortex encode abstract rules. *Nature, 411,* 953–956.

Wallman, J., Gottlieb, M. D., Rajaram, V., & Fugate-Wentzek, L. A. (1987). Local retinal regions control local eye growth and myopia. *Science, 237,* 73–76.

Walton, G. E., Bower, N. J. A., & Bower, T. G. R. (1992). Recognition of familiar faces by newborns. *Infant Behavior and Development, 15,* 265–269.

Wang, C.-H. C., & Phinney, J. S. (1998). Differences in child rearing attitudes between immigrant Chinese mothers and Anglo-American mothers. *Early Development & Parenting, 7,* 181–189.

Wang, X., Merzenich, M. M., Sameshima, K., & Jenkins, W. M., (1995). Remodelling of hand representation in adult cortex determined by timing of tactile stimulation. *Nature, 378,* 71–75.

Warburton, D. M. (1995). Effects of caffeine on cognition and mood without caffeine abstinence. *Psychopharmacology, 119,* 66–70.

Ward, C. (1994). Culture and altered states of consciousness. In W. J. Lonner & R. S. Malpass (Eds.), *Psychology and culture.* Boston: Allyn & Bacon.

Ward, L. M. (1997). Involuntary listening aids hearing. *Psychological Science, 8,* 112–118.

Warner, L., Kessler, R., Hughes, M., Anthony, J., & Nelson, C. (1995). Prevalence and correlates of drug use and dependence in the United States. *Archives of General Psychiatry, 52,* 219–229.

Warot, D., et al. (1991). Comparative effects of ginko biloba extracts on psychomotor performances and memory in healthy subjects. *Therapies, 46,* 33–36.

Warrington, E. K., & Weiskrantz, L. (1970). The amnesic syndrome: Consolidation of retrieval? *Nature, 228,* 626–630.

Wasik, B. H., Ramey, C. T., Bryant, D. M., & Sparling, J. J. (1990). A longitudinal study of two early intervention strategies: Project CARE. *Child Development, 61,* 1682–1696.

Wasserman, E. M., & Lisanby, S. H. (2001). Therapeutic application of repetitive transcranial magnetic stimulation: A review. *Clinical Neurophysiology, 112,* 1367–1377.

Watanabe, K., & Shimojo, S. (2001). When sound affects vision: Effects of auditory grouping on visual motion perception. *Psychological Science, 12,* 109–116.

Watanabe, S., Sakamoto, J., & Wakita, M. (1995). Pigeons' discrimination of paintings by Monet and Picasso. *Journal of Experimental Analysis of Behavior, 63,* 165–174.

Watanabe, T., Náñez, J. E., & Sasaki, Y. (2001). Perceptual learning without perception. *Nature, 413,* 844–848.

Watanabe, T., & Sugita, Y. (1998). REM sleep behavior disorder (RBD) and dissociated REM sleep. *Nippon Rinsho, 56*(2), 433–438.

Waterman, A. S. (1982). Identity development from adolescence to adulthood: An extension of theory and a review of research. *Developmental Psychology, 18,* 341–358.

Waters, E., Merrick, S., Treboux, D., Crowell, J., & Albersheim, L. (2000). Attachment security in infancy and early adulthood: A twenty-year longitudinal study. *Child Development, 71,* 684–689.

Watson, J. B. (1925). *Behaviorism.* London: Kegan Paul, Trench, Trubner.

Watson, R. I. (1963). *The great psychologists: From Aristotle to Freud.* Philadelphia: Lippincott.

Watt, N. F., & Saiz, C. (1991). Longitudinal studies of premorbid development of adult schizophrenics. In E. F. Walker (Ed.), *Schizophrenia: A life-course in developmental perspective* (pp. 157–192). San Diego: Academic Press.

Watts, R. L., Subramanian, T., Freeman, A., Goetz, C. G., Penn, R. D., Stebbins, G. T., et al. (1997). Effect of stereotaxic intrastriatal cografts of autologous adrenal medulla and peripheral nerve in Parkinson's disease: Two-year follow-up study. *Experimental Neurology, 147,* 510–517.

Wearden, A. J., Tarrier, N., Barrowclough, C., Zastowny, T. R., & Rahill, A. A. (2000). A review of expressed emotion research in health care. *Clinical Psychology Review, 20,* 633–666.

Wechsler, D. (1939). *The measurement of adult intelligence.* Baltimore: Williams & Wilkins.

Wechsler, D. (1949). *The Wechsler Intelligence Scale for Children.* New York: Psychological Corporation.

Weekes, J. R., Lynn, S. J., Green, J. P., & Brentar, J. T. (1992). Pseudomemory in hypnotized and task-motivated subjects. *Journal of Abnormal Psychology, 101,* 356–360.

Weeks, D., & Weeks, J. (1995). *Eccentrics: A study of sanity and strangeness.* New York: Villard.

Weiler, B. L., & Widom, C. S. (1996). Psychopathy and violent behavior in abused and neglected young adults. *Criminal Behaviour & Mental Health, 6,* 253–271.

Weinberg, J., & Levine, S. (1980). Psychobiology of coping in animals: The effects of predictability. In S. Levine & H. Ursin (Eds.), *Coping and health.* New York: Plenum.

Weinberg, R. A. (1989). Intelligence and IQ: Landmark issues and great debates. *American Psychologist, 44,* 98–104.

Weinberg, R. A., Scarr, S., & Waldman, I. D. (1992). The Minnesota transracial adoption study: A follow-up of IQ test performance at adolescence. *Intelligence, 16,* 117–135.

Weiner, B. (1980). *Human motivation.* New York: Holt, Rinehart & Winston.

Weiner, B. (1993). On sin versus sickness: A theory of perceived responsibility and social motivation. *American Psychologist, 48*(9), 957–965.

Weinfield, N. S., Sroufe, L. A., & Egeland, B. (2000). Attachment from infancy to early adulthood in a high-risk sample: continuity, discontinuity, and their correlates. *Child Development, 71,* 695–702.

Weinraub, M., Horuath, D., & Gringlas, M. (2002). Single parenthood. In M. H. Bornstein (Ed.), *Handbook of parenting* (2nd ed., pp. 65–87). Mahwah, NJ: Erlbaum.

Weinstein, D. (1999, July 24). Who are you? *Sunday Telegraph Magazine,* pp. 24–26.

Weiss, B., & Weisz, J. R. (1995). Relative effectiveness of behavioral versus nonbehavioral child psychotherapy. *Journal of Consulting and Clinical Psychology, 63,* 317–320.

Weiss, F., Ciccocioppo, R., Parsons, L. H., Katner, S., Liu, X., Zorrilla, E. P., et al. (2001). Compulsive drug-seeking behavior and relapse. Neuroadaptation, stress, and conditioning factors. *Annals of the New York Academy of Science, 937,* 1–26.

Weissman, M. M., Bland, R., Joyce, P. R., Newman, S., Wells, J. E., & Wittchen, H. U. (1993). Sex differences in rates of depression: Cross-national perspectives. *Journal of Affective Disorders, 29,* 77–84.

Weisstein, N., & Harris, C. S. (1974). Visual detection of line segments: An object superiority effect. *Science, 186,* 752–755.

Weisz, J. R., & Jensen, P. S. (1999). Efficacy and effectiveness of psychotherapy and pharmacotherapy with children and adolescents. *Mental Health Services Research, 1,* 125–157.

Weisz, J. R., Weiss, B., Han, S. S., Granger, D. A., & Morton, T. (1995). Effects of psychotherapy with children and adolescents revisited: A meta-analysis of treatment outcome studies. *Psychological Bulletin, 117,* 450–468.

Wells, G. L., & Bradfield, A. L. (1999). Distortions in eyewitness' recollections: Can the postidentification-feedback effect be moderated? *Psychological Science, 10,* 138–144.

Wells, G. L., Malpass, R. S., Lindsay, R. C. L., Fisher, R. P., Turtle, J. W., & Fulero, S. M. (2000). From the lab to the police station: A successful application of eyewitness research. *American Psychologist, 55,* 581–598.

Wells, S., Graham, K., & West, P. (2000). Alcohol-related aggression in the general population. *Journal of Studies on Alcohol, 61,* 626–632.

Weltzin, T. E., Bulik, C. M., McConaha, C. W., & Kaye, W. H. (1995). Laxative withdrawal and anxiety in bulimia nervosa. *International Journal of Eating Disorders, 17*(2), 141–146.

Werker, J. F., Lloyd, V. L., Pegg, J. E., & Polka, L. (1996). Putting the baby in the bootstraps: Toward a more complete understanding of the role of input in infant speech processing. In J. L. Morgan & K. Demuth (Eds.), *Signal to syntax* (pp. 427–447). Mahwah, NJ: Erlbaum.

Wertheimer, M. (1987). *A brief history of psychology* (3rd ed.). New York: Holt, Rinehart & Winston.

Westen, D. (1998). The scientific legacy of Sigmund Freud: Toward a psychodynamically informed psychological science. *Psychological Bulletin, 124,* 333–371.

Westen, D., & Gabbard, G. O. (1999). Psychoanalytic approaches to personality. In L. Pervin & O. John (Eds), *Handbook of personality: Theory and research* (2nd ed., pp. 57–101). New York: Guilford.

Westen, D., & Morrison, K. (2001). A multidimensional meta-analysis of treatments for depression, panic, and generalized anxiety disorder: An empirical evaluation of the status of empirically supported therapies. *Journal of Consulting and Clinical Psychology, 69,* 875–899.

Westmaas, J. L., & Silver, R. C. (2001). The role of attachment in responses to victims of life crises. *Journal of Personality and Social Psychology, 80,* 425–438.

Weston, C., & Went, F. (1999). Speaking up for yourself: Description and evaluation of an assertiveness training program for people with learning disabilities. *Mental Handicap, 27,* 110–115.

Whalen, P. J. (1998). Fear, vigilance, and ambiguity: Initial neuroimaging studies of the human amygdala. *Current Directions in Psychological Science, 7,* 177–188.

Whalley, L. J., & Deary, I. J. (2001). Longitudinal cohort study of childhood IQ up to age 76. *British Medical Journal, 322,* 819.

Whalley, L. J., Starr, J. M., Athawes, R., Hunter, D., Pattie, A., & Deary, I. J (2000). Childhood mental ability and dementia. *Neurology, 55,* 1455–1459.

Wharton, C. M., Grafman, J., Flitman, S. S., Hansen, E. K., Brauner, J., Marks, A., & Honda, M. (2000). Toward neuroanatomical models of analogy: A positron emission tomography study of analogical mapping. *Cognitive Psychology, 40,* 173–197.

Wheeler, S. C., & Petty, R. E. (2001). The effects of stereotype activation on behavior: A review of possible mechanisms. *Psychological Bulletin, 127,* 797–826.

Whimbey, A. (1976). *Intelligence can be taught.* New York: Bantam.

Whisman, M. A. (1999). Marital dissatisfaction and psychiatric disorders: Results from a national comorbidity study. *Journal of Abnormal Psychology, 108,* 701–706.

Whitam, F. L., Diamond, M., & Martin, J. (1993). Homosexual orientation in twins: A report on 61 pairs and three triplet sets. *Archives of Sexual Behavior, 22*(3), 187–206.

Whitbourne, S. K., Zuschlag, M. K., Elliot, L. B., & Waterman, A. D. (1992). Psychosocial development in adulthood: A 22-year sequential study. *Journal of Personality and Social Psychology, 63,* 260–271.

White, D. E., & Glick, J. (1978). *Competence and the context of performance.* Paper presented at the meeting of the Jean Piaget Society, Philadelphia.

White, F. J. (1998). Nicotine addiction and the lure of reward. *Nature Medicine, 4,* 659–660.

Whiteman, M. C., Deary, I. J., & Fowkes, F. G. R. (2000). Personality and social predictors of atherosclerotic progression: Edinburgh Artery Study. *Psychosomatic Medicine, 62,* 703–714.

Whitman, T. L., Borkowski, J. G., Keogh, D. A., & Week, K. (2001). *Interwoven lives: Adolescent mothers and their children.* Mahwah, NJ: Lawrence Erlbaum.

Whitney, P. (1998). *The psychology of language.* Boston: Houghton Mifflin.

Whitney, P. (2001). Schemas, frames, and scripts in cognitive psychology. In N. J. Smelser & P. B. Baltes (Eds.), *International encyclopedia of the social and behavioral sciences.* The Netherlands: Elsevier.

Whorf, B. L. (1956). *Language, thought, and reality.* Cambridge/New York: MIT Press/Wiley.

Wickens, C. D. (1989). Attention and skilled performance. In D. Holding (Ed.), *Human skills* (pp. 71–105). New York: Wiley.

Wickens, C. D. (1992). *Engineering psychology and human performance* (2nd ed.) New York: HarperCollins.

Wickens, C. D., & Carswell, C. M. (1997). Information processing. In G. Salvendy (Ed.), *Handbook of human factors and ergonomics* (2nd ed., pp. 89–122) New York: Wiley. Interscience.

Wickens, C. D., Gordon, S. E., & Liu, Y. (1998). *An introduction to human factors engineering.* New York: Longman.

Wickens, C. D., Stokes, A., Barnett, B., & Hyman, F. (1992). The effects of stress on pilot judgment in a MIDIS simulator. In O. Svenson & J. Maule (Eds.), *Time pressure and stress in human judgment and decision making* (pp. 271–292). New York: Plenum.

Widiger, T. A. (1997). The construct of mental disorder. *Clinical Psychology: Science and Practice, 4,* 262–266.

Widiger, T. A., & Clark, L. A. (2000). Toward DSM-V and the classification of psychopathology. *Journal of Abnormal Psychology, 126,* 946–963.

Widiger, T. A., & Sanderson, C. J. (1995). Assessing personality disorders. In J. N. Butcher (Ed.), *Clinical personality assessment: Practical approaches* (pp. 380–394). New York: Oxford University Press.

Widiger, T. A., & Sankis, L. M. (2000). Adult psychopathology: Issues and controversies. *Annual Review of Psychology, 51,* 377–404.

Widiger, T. A., & Smith, G. T. (1994). Substance use disorder: Abuse, dependence, and dyscontrol. *Addiction, 89,* 267–282.

Widom, C. S. (1989). The cycle of violence. *Science, 244,* 160–166.

Widom, C. S. (2000). Childhood victimization: Early adversity, later psychopathology. *National Insitute of Justice Journal, 19,* 2–9.

Wiebe, D. J., & Smith, T. W. (1997). Personality and health: Progress and problems in psychomatics. In R. Hogan, J. Johnson, & S. Briggs (Eds.), *Handbook of personality psychology* (pp. 891–918). San Diego: Academic Press.

Wiedenfeld, S., O'Leary, A., Bandura, A., Brown, S., Levine, S., & Raska, K (1990). Impact of perceived self-efficacy in coping with stressors on components of the immune system. *Journal of Personality and Social Psychology, 59,* 1082–1094.

Wiener, E., & Nagel, D. (1988). *Human factors in aviation.* Orlando, FL: Academic Press.

Wiertelak, E. P., Maier, S. F., & Watkins, L. R. (1992). Cholecystokinin antianalgesia: Safety cues abolish morphine analgesia. *Science, 256,* 830–833.

Wigfield, A., & Eccles, J. S. (2000). Expectancy-value theory of achievement motivation. *Contemporary Educational Psychology, 25,* 68–81.

Williams, R. B. (2001). Hostility and heart disease: Williams et al. (1980). *Advances in Mind-Body Medicine, 17,* 52–55.

Williams, D. A., Butler, M. M., & Overmier, J. B. (1990). Expectancies of reinforcer location and quality as cues for a conditional discrimination in pigeons. *Journal of Experimental Psychology, 16,* 3–13.

Williams, G. V., & Goldman-Rakic, P. S. (1995). Modulation of memory fields by dopamine D1 receptors in prefrontal cortex. *Nature, 376,* 572–575.

Williams, J. E., & Best, D. L. (1990). *Measuring stereotypes: A multination study* (rev. ed.). Newbury Park, CA: Sage.

Williams, K. D., Jackson, J. M., & Karau, S. J. (1995). In D. Schroeder (Ed.), *Social dilemmas: Perspectives on individuals and groups* (pp. 117–142). Westport, CT: Praeger.

Williams, K. D., & Sommer, K. L. (1997). Social ostracism by coworkers: Does rejection lead to loafing or compensation? *Personality and Social Psychology Bulletin, 23,* 693–706.

Williams, L. M. (1994). What does it mean to forget child sexual abuse? A reply to Loftus, Garry, and Feldman (1994). *Journal of Consulting and Clinical Psychology, 62,* 1182–1186.

Williams, R. B., Jr., & Barefoot, J. C. (1988). Coronary-prone behavior: The emerging role of the hostility complex. In B. K. Houston & C. R. Snyder (Eds.), *Type A behavior pattern: Current trends and future directions* (pp. 189–221). New York: Wiley.

Williams, S. (2000). What does it pay to be a psychologist? *Monitor on Psychology, 31*, 13.

Williams, T. J., Pepitone, M. E., Christensen, S. E., Cooke, B. M., Huberman, A. D., Breedlove, T. J., et al. (2000). Finger length patterns and human sexual orientation. *Nature, 404*, 455–456.

Willing, A. E., Othberg, A. I., Saporta, S., Anton, A., Sinibaldi, S., Poulos, S. G., et al. (1999). Sertoli cells enhance the survival of co-transplanted dopamine neurons. *Brain Research, 822*, 246–250.

Willis, S. L., & Schaie, K. W. (1999). Intellectual functioning in midlife. In S. L. Willis & J. D. Reid (Eds.), *Life in the middle: Psychological and social development in middle age* (pp. 233–247). San Diego: Academic Press.

Willis, W. D., Jr. (1988). Dorsal horn neurophysiology of pain. *Annals of the New York Academy of Science, 531*, 76–89.

Wills, T. A., Sandy, J. M., Yaeger, A., & Shinar, O. (2001). Family risk factors and adolescent substance use: Moderation effects oft temperament dimension. *Developmental Psychology, 37*, 283–297.

Wilson, A. E., & Ross, M. (2000). The frequency of temporal-self and social comparisons in people's personal appraisals. *Journal of Personality and Social Psychology, 78*, 928–942.

Wilson, D. L., Silver, S. M., Covi, W. G., & Foster, S. (1996). Eye movement desensitization and reprocessing: Effectiveness and autonomic correlates. *Journal of Behaviour Therapy and Experimental Psychiatry, 27*, 219–229.

Wilson, G. T. (1997). Dissemination of cognitive behavioral treatments: Commentary. *Behavior Therapy, 28*, 473–475.

Wilson, G. T. (1985). Limitations of meta-analysis in the evaluation of the effects of psychological therapy. *Clinical Psychology Review, 5*, 35–47.

Wilson, G. T. (1995). Behavior therapy. In R. J. Corsini & D. Wedding (Eds.), *Current psychotherapies* (5th ed., pp. 197–228). Itasca, IL: Peacock.

Wilson, G. T., Loeb, K. L., Walsh, B. T., Labouvie, E., Petkova, E., Liu, X., & Waternaux, C. (1999). Psychological versus pharmacological treatments of bulimia nervosa: Predictors and processes of change. *Journal of Consulting and Clinical Psychology, 67*, 451–459.

Wilson, G. T., Nathan, P. E., O'Leary, K. D., & Clark, L. A. (1996). *Abnormal psychology*. Boston: Allyn & Bacon.

Wilson, R. S., Mendes de Leon, C. F., Barnes, L. L., Schneider, J. A., Bienias, J. L., Evans, D. A., & Bennett, D. A. (2002). Participation in cognitively stimulating activities and risk of incident Alzheimer disease. *Journal of the American Medical Association, 287*, 742–748.

Wilson, W. J. (1997). *When work disappears: The world of the new urban poor*. New York: Vintage Books.

Winkielman, P., Bernston, G. G., & Cacioppo, J. T. (2001). The psychophysiological perspective on the social mind. In A. Tesser & N. Schwarz (Eds.), *Blackwell handbook of social psychology: Intraindividual processes* (pp. 89–109). Oxford, England: Blackwell.

Winn, P. (1995). The lateral hypothalamus and motivated behavior: An old syndrome reassessed and a new perspective gained. *Current Directions in Psychological Science, 4*, 182–187.

Winner, E. (2000). Giftedness: Current theory and research. *Current Directions in Psychological Science, 9*, 153–156.

Winokur, G., Coryell, W., Keller, M., Endicott, J., & Leon, A. (1995). A family study of manic-depressive (Bipolar I) disease. *Archives of General Psychiatry, 52*, 367–373.

Winson, J. (1990, November). The meaning of dreams. *Scientific American*, pp. 86–96.

Winter, D. G. (1996). *Personality: Analysis and interpretation of lives*. New York: McGraw-Hill.

Winzelberg, A. J., Eppstein, D., Eldredge, K. L., Wilfley, D., Dasmahapatra, R., Dev, P., & Taylor, C. B. (2000). Effectiveness of an internet-based program for reducing risk factors for eating disorders. *Journal of Consulting and Clinical Psychology, 68*, 346–350.

Wise, R. A., & Rompre, P. P. (1989). Brain dopamine and reward. *Annual Review of Psychology, 40*, 191–225.

Wiseman, R., West, D., & Stemman, R. (1996, January/February). Psychic crime detectives: A new test for measuring their successes and failures. *Skeptical Inquirer, 21*, 38–58.

Witt, S. D. (1997). Parental influence on children's socialization to gender roles. *Adolescence, 32*, 253–259.

Wittchen, H. U., Zhao, S., Kessler, R. C., & Eaton, W. W. (1994). DSM-III-R: Generalized anxiety disorder in the national comorbidity survey. *Archives of General Psychiatry, 51*, 355–364.

Wittenbaum, G. M., & Stasser, G. (1996). Management of information in small groups. In J. L. Nye & A. M. Brower (Eds.), *What's social about cognition? Social cognition in small groups* (pp. 3–28). Newbury Park, CA: Sage.

Woelk, H. (2000). Comparison of St. John's wort and imipramine for treating depression: Randomised controlled trial. *British Medical Journal, 321*, 536–539.

Wohl, J. (1995). Traditional individual psychotherapy and ethnic minorities. In J. F. Aponte, R. Y. Rivers, & J. Wohl (Eds.), *Psychological interventions and cultural diversity* (pp. 74–91). Boston: Allyn & Bacon.

Wolfe, J. M., Alvarez, G. A., & Horowitz, T. S. (2000). Attention is fast but volition is slow. *Nature, 406*, 691.

Wolman, C., van den Broek, P., & Lorch, R. F. (1997). Effects of causal structure and delayed story recall by children with mild mental retardation, children with learning disabilities, and children without disabilities. *Journal of Special Education*.

Wolpe, J. (1958). *Psychotherapy by reciprocal inhibition*. Stanford, CA: Stanford University Press.

Wolpe, J., & Plaud, J. J. (1997). Pavlov's contributions to behavior therapy: The obvious and the not so obvious. *American Psychologist, 52*, 966–972.

Wong, B. Y. L. (1986). Metacognition and special education: A review of a view. *Journal of Special Education, 20*, 9–29.

Wong, S. E., Martinez-Diaz, J. A., Massel, H. K., Edelstein, B. A., Wiegand, W., Bowen, L., & Liberman, R. P (1993). Conversational skills training with schizophrenic inpatients: A study of generalization across settings and conversants. *Behavior Therapy, 24*, 285–304.

Wood, J. V., Michela, J. L., & Giordano, C. (2000). Downward comparison in everyday life: Reconciling self-enhancement models with the mood-cognition priming model. *Journal of Personality and Social Psychology, 79*, 563–579.

Wood, W. (2000). Attitude change: Persuasion and social influence. *Annual Review of Psychology, 51*, 539–570.

Woodbury, D., Schwarz, E. J., Prockop, D. J., & Black, I. B. (2000). Adult rat and human bone marrow stromal cells differentiate into neurons. *Journal of Neuroscience Research, 61*, 364–370.

Woodhead, M. (1988). When psychology informs public policy: The case of early childhood intervention. *American Psychologist, 43*, 443–454.

Woods, S. C., Schwartz, M. W., Baskin, D. G., & Seeley, R. J. (2000). Food intake and the regulation of body weight. *Annual Review of Psychology, 51*, 255–277.

Woods, S. C., Seeley, R. J., Porte, D., Jr., & Schwartz, M. W. (1998). Signals that regulate food intake and energy homeostasis. *Science, 280*, 1378–1383.

Woodworth, R. S., & Schlosberg, H. (1954). *Experimental psychology*. New York: Holt.

Woolfolk-Hoy, A. (1999). Psychology applied to education. In A. Stec & D. Bernstein (Eds.), *Psychology: Fields of application* (pp. 61–81). Boston: Houghton Mifflin.

Woolley, J. D. (1997). Thinking about fantasy: Are children fundamentally different thinkers and believers from adults? *Child Development, 68*, 991–1011.

Worchel, S., Cooper, J., Goethals, G. R., & Olson, J. (2000). *Social psychology*. Belmont, CA: Wadsworth.

World Health Organization. (2001). *World Health Report*. Geneva, Switzerland: WHO.

Worthington, J. J., III, Pollack, M. H., Otto, M. W., McLean, R. Y., Moroz, G., & Rosenbaum, J. F. (1998). Long-term experience with clonazepam in patients with a primary diagnosis of panic disorder. *Psychopharmacology Bulletin, 34*, 199–205.

Wren, C. S. (1998, September 22). For crack babies, a future less bleak. *New York Times* (Web Archive).

Wren, C. S. (1999, February 24). U.N. drug board urges research on marijuana as medicine [Online]. *New York Times.*

Wright, B. A., & Fitzgerald, M. B. (2001). Different patterns of human discrimination learning for two interaural cues to sound location. *Proceedings of the National Academy of Science, 98,* 12307–12312.

Wright, E. F., Voyer, D., Wright, R. D., & Roney, C. (1995). Supporting audiences and performance under pressure: The home-ice disadvantage in hockey championships. *Journal of Sport Behavior, 18,* 21–28.

Wright, G. N., & Phillips, L. D. (1980). Cultural variation in probabilistic thinking: Alternative ways of dealing with uncertainty. *International Journal of Psychology, 15,* 239–257.

Wu, H. W., Cacioppo, J. T., Glaser, R., Kiecolt-Glaser, J. K., & Malarkey, W. B. (1999). Chronic stress associated with spousal caregiving of patients with Alzheimer's dementia is associated with downregulation of B-lymphocyte GH mRNA. *Journals of Gerontology, 54A,* M212–M215.

Wurtman, R. J., & Wurtman, J. J. (1995). Brain serotonin, carbohydrate-craving, obesity and depression. *Obesity Research, 3*(Suppl. 4), 477S–480S.

Wynn, K., & Chiang, W.-C. (1998). Limits to infants' knowledge of objects: The case of magical appearance. *Psychological Science, 9,* 448–455.

Yaffe, K., Barnes, D., Nevitt, M., Lui, L.-Y., & Covinsky, K. (2001). A prospective study of physical activity and cognitive decline in elderly women. *Archives of Internal Medicine, 161,* 1703–1708.

Yahr, P., & Jacobsen, C. H. (1994). Hypothalamic knife cuts that disrupt mating in male gerbils sever efferents and forebrain afferents of the sexually dimorphic area. *Behavioral Neuroscience, 108*(4), 735–742.

Yakimovich, D., & Saltz, E. (1971). Helping behavior: The cry for help. *Psychonomic Science, 23,* 427–428.

Yalom, I. D. (1995). *The theory and practice of group therapy* (4th ed.). New York: Basic Books.

Yantis, S. (1993). Stimulus-driven attentional capture. *Current Directions in Psychological Science, 2,* 156–161.

Yates, J. F., Lee, J. W., & Shinotsuka, H. (1992). *Cross-national variation in probability judgment.* Paper presented at the 33rd annual meeting of the Psychonomic Society, St. Louis.

Yates, J. F., Zhu, Y., Ronis, D. L., Wang, D. F., Shinotsuka, H., & Masanao, T. (1989). Probability judgment accuracy: China, Japan, and the United States. *Organizational Behavior and Human Decision Processes, 43,* 145–171.

Yates, W. R. (2000). Testosterone in psychiatry. *Archives of General Psychiatry, 57,* 155–156.

Yela, C., & Sangrador, J. L. (2001). Perception of physical attractiveness throughout loving relationships. *Current Research in Social Psychology, 6,* 57–75.

Yerkes, R. M. (Ed.). (1921). Psychological examining in the U.S. Army. *Memoirs of the National Academy of Sciences,* No. 15.

Yesavage, J. A., Leirer, V. O., Denari, M., & Hollister, L. E. (1985). Carry-over effects of marijuana intoxication on aircraft pilot performance: A preliminary report. *American Journal of Psychiatry, 142,* 1325–1329.

Yonas, A., Arterberry, M. E., & Granrud, C. D. (1987). Space perception in infancy. In R. Vasta (Ed.), *Annals of child development* (Vol. 4, pp. 1–34). Greenwich, CT: JAI Press.

Yonkers, K., Kando, J., Cole, J., & Blumenthal, S. (1992). Gender differences in pharmacokinetics and pharmacodynamics of psychotropic medication. *American Journal of Psychiatry, 149,* 587–595.

York, J. L., & Welte, J. W. (1994). Gender comparisons of alcohol consumption in alcoholic and nonalcoholic populations. *Journal of Studies on Alcohol, 55*(6), 743–750.

Young, A. W., & De Haan, E. H. F. (1992). Face recognition and awareness after brain injury. In A. D. Milner & M. D. Rugg (Eds.), *The neuropsychology of consciousness* (pp. 69–90). San Diego: Academic Press.

Young, A. W., Aggleton, J. P., Hellawell, D. J., & Johnson, M. (1995). Face processing impairments after amygdalotomy. *Brain, 118*(1), 15–24.

Young, M. (1971). Age and sex differences in problem solving. *Journal of Gerontology, 26,* 331–336.

Youniss, J., & Yates, M. (1997). *Community service and social responsibility in youth.* Chicago: University of Chicago Press.

Younkin, S. G. (2001). Amyloid beta vaccination: reduced plaques and improved cognition. *Nature Medicine, 7,* 18–19.

Yousif, Y., & Korte, C. (1995). Urbanization, culture, and helpfulness: Cross-cultural studies in England and the Sudan. *Journal of Cross-Cultural Psychology, 26,* 474–489.

Yukl, G., & Van Fleet, D. D. (1992). Theory and research on leadership in organizations. In M. D. Dunnette & L. M. Hough (Eds.), *Handbook of industrial and organizational psychology* (Vol. 3, 2nd ed., pp. 147–198). Palo Alto, CA: Consulting Psychologists Press.

Yukl, G. A., Latham, G. P., & Purcell, E. D. (1976). The effectiveness of performance incentives under continuous and variable ratio schedules of reinforcement. *Personnel Psychology, 29,* 221–232.

Yutrzenka, B. A. (1995). Making a case for training in ethnic and cultural diversity in increasing treatment efficacy. *Journal of Consulting and Clinical Psychology, 63,* 197–206.

Zadnik, K. (2001). Association between night lights and myopia: True blue or a red herring? *Archives of Ophthalmology, 119,* 146.

Zahn-Waxler, C., Friedman, R. J., Cole, P. M., Mizuta, I., & Hiruma, N. (1996). Japanese and United States preschool children's responses to conflict and distress. *Child Development, 67,* 2462–2477.

Zahn-Waxler, C., Radke-Yarrow, M., Wagner, E., & Chapman, M. (1992). Development of concern for others. *Developmental Psychology, 28,* 1038–1047.

Zahrani, S. S., & Kaplowitz, S. A. (1993). Attributional biases in individualistic and collectivist cultures: A comparison of Americans with Saudis. *Social Psychology Quarterly, 56*(3), 223–233.

Zajonc, R. B. (1965). Social facilitation. *Science, 149,* 269–274.

Zajonc, R. B. (1998). Emotions. In D. Gilbert, S. T. Fiske, & G. Lindzey (Eds.), *Handbook of social psychology* (Vol. 1, 4th ed., pp. 591–634). Boston: McGraw-Hill.

Zajonc, R. B. (2001a). The family dynamics of intellectual development. *American Psychologist, 56,* 490–496.

Zajonc, R. B. (2001b). Mere exposure: A gateway to the subliminal. *Current Directions in Psychological Science, 10,* 224–228.

Zakzanis, K. K., & Young, D. A. (2001). Memory impairment in abstinent MDMA ("Ecstasy") users: A longitudinal investigation. *Neurology, 56,* 966–969.

Zanarini, M. C., Skodol, A. E., Bender, D., Dolan, R., Sanislow, C., Schaefer, E., et al. (2000). The collaborative longitudinal personality disorders study: Reliability of axis I and II diagnoses. *Journal of Personality Disorders, 14,* 291–299.

Zaragosa, M. S., Payment, K. E., Ackil, J. K., Drivdahl, S. B., & Beck, M. (2001). Interviewing witnesses: Forced confabulation and confirmatory feedback increase false memories. *Psychological Science, 12,* 473–477.

Zeki, S. (1992). The visual image in mind and brain. *Scientific American, 267,* 68–76.

Zelenski, J. M., & Larsen, R. J. (1999). Susceptibility to affect: A comparison of three taxonomies. *Journal of Personality, 67,* 761–791.

Zelinski, E., Schaie, K. W., & Gribben, K. (1977). *Omission and commission errors: Task-specific adult lifespan differences.* Paper presented at the convention of the American Psychological Association, San Francisco.

Zernike, K. (2000, October 3). Colleges shift emphasis on drinking. *New York Times.*

Zhang, G., & Simon, H. A. (1985). STM capacity for Chinese words and idioms: Chunking and acoustical loop hypothesis. *Memory & Cognition, 13,* 193–201.

Zhang, Y., Proenca, R., Maffei, M., Barone, M., Leopold, L., & Friedman, J. M. (1994). Positional cloning of the mouse obese gene and its human homologue. *Nature, 372,* 425–432.

Zhou, J.-N., Hofman, M. A., Gooren, L. J. G., & Swaab, D. F. (1995). A sex difference in the human brain and its relation to transsexuality. *Nature, 378,* 68–70.

Zigler, E., & Seitz, V. (1982). Social policy and intelligence. In R. J. Sternberg (Ed.), *Handbook of human intelligence* (pp. 586–641). Cambridge, England: Cambridge University Press.

Zigler, E., & Styfco, S. J. (1994). Head Start: Criticisms in a constructive context. *American Psychologist, 49*(2), 127–132.

Zigler, E., Taussig, C., & Black, K. (1992). Early childhood intervention: A promising preventive for juvenile delinquency. *American Psychologist, 47,* 997–1006.

Zigler, E. F., & Stevenson, M. F. (1993). *Children in a changing world* (2nd ed.). Pacific Grove, CA: Brooks/Cole.

Zillmann, D. (1984). *Connections between sex and aggression.* Hillsdale, NJ: Erlbaum.

Zillmann, D. (1988). Cognition-excitation interdependencies in aggressive behavior. *Aggressive Behavior, 14,* 51–64.

Zillmann, D., Baron, R. A., & Tamborini, R. (1981). Social costs of smoking: Effects of tobacco smoke on hostile behavior. *Journal of Applied Social Psychology, 11,* 548–561.

Zillmann, D., Katcher, A. H., & Milavsky, B. (1972). Excitation transfer from physical exercise to subsequent aggressive behavior. *Journal of Experimental Social Psychology, 8,* 247–259.

Zimbardo, P. G. (1973). The psychological power and pathology of imprisonment. In E. Aronson & R. Helmreich (Eds.), *Social psychology.* New York: Van Nostrand.

Zimmerman, M., McDermut, W., & Mattia, J. I. (2000). Frequency of anxiety disorders in psychiatric outpatients with major depressive disorder. *American Journal of Psychiatry, 157,* 1337–1340.

Zimmerman, M., Reischl, T., Seidman, E., Rappaport, J., Toro, P., & Salem, D. (1991). Expansion strategies of a mutual help organization. *American Journal of Community Psychology, 19,* 251–279.

Zinbarg, R. E., & Barlow, D. H. (1996). Structure of anxiety and the anxiety disorders: A hierarchical model. *Journal of Abnormal Psychology, 105,* 181–193.

Zinbarg, R. E., & Mineka, S. (1991). Animal models of psychopathology: II. Simple phobia. *The Behavior Therapist, 14,* 61–65.

Zoellner, L. A., Foa, E. B., Brigidi, B. D., & Przeworski, A. (2000). Are trauma victims susceptible to "false memories"? *Journal of Abnormal Psychology, 109,* 517–524.

Zornberg, G. L., & Pope, H. G., Jr. (1993). Treatment of depression in bipolar disorder: New directions for research. *Journal of Clinical Psychopharmacology, 13,* 397–408.

Zorumski, C., & Isenberg, K. (1991). Insights into the structure and function of GABA-benzodiazepine receptors: Ion channels and psychiatry. *American Journal of Psychiatry, 148,* 162–173.

Zou, Z., Horowitz, L. F., Montmayeur, J.-P., Snapper, S., & Buck, L. B. (2001). Genetic tracing reveals a stereotyped sensory map in the olfactory cortex. *Nature, 414,* 173–179.

Zsambok, C. E., & Klein, G. (1997). *Naturalistic decision making.* Hillsdale, NJ: Erlbaum.

Zuckerman, M. (1979). *Sensation seeking: Beyond the optimal level of arousal.* Hillsdale, NJ: Erlbaum.

Zuckerman, M. (1984). Sensation seeking: A comparative approach to a human approach. *The Behavioral and Brain Sciences, 7,* 413–471.

Zuckerman, M. (1990). Some dubious premises in research and theory on racial differences. *American Psychologist, 45,* 1297–1303.

Zuckerman, M. (1996). "Conceptual clarification" or confusion in "The study of sensation seeking" by J. S. H. Jackson and M. Maraun. *Personality and Individual Differences, 21,* 111–114.

Zuckerman, M. (1998). Psychobiological theories of personality. In D. F. Barone, M. Hersen, & V. B. Hassselt (Eds.), *Advanced personality* (pp. 123–154). New York: Plenum.

Zuckerman, M. (1999). *Vulnerability to psychopathology: A biosocial model.* Washington, DC: American Psychological Association.

Zuercher-White, E. (1997). *Treating panic disorder and agoraphobia: A step-by-step clinical guide.* Oakland, CA: New Harbinger.

Zuger, A. (1998, July 28). A fistful of aggression is found among women. *New York Times,* pp. B8, B12.

CREDITS

PHOTOGRAPHS

Chapter 1: p. 1: © 2002 PhotoDisc, Inc. p. 3: B. A. Shaywitz, et al. 1995 NMR/Yale Medical School. p. 5: AP/Wide World Photos. p. 6: (*top*) Will & Deni McIntyre/Photo Researchers. (*bottom*) AP/Wide World Photos. p. 7: © Corbis Stock Market/Charles Gupton 2002. p. 10: Photofest. p. 12: Psychology Archives—The University of Akron. p. 13: Courtesy of the Harvard University Archives. p. 16: (*top*) Courtesy of the Wellesley College Archives, photo by Partridge. (*bottom*) Courtesy Robert W. Levenson, Ph.D. p. 17: (*top*) Archives and Special Collections, Rembert E. Stokes Learning Resources Center, Wilberforce University. (*bottom*) Michael Newman/PhotoEdit. p. 18: © 2002 PhotoDisc, Inc. p. 19: Bob Daemmrich/The Image Works. p. 20: Will & Deni McIntyre/Photo Researchers. p. 22: Chip Hires/Getty Images.

Chapter 2: p. 25: © 2002 PhotoDisc, Inc. p. 29: © 2002 PhotoDisc, Inc. p. 39: Mason Morfit/Getty Images. p. 31: AP/Wide World Photos. p. 33: © 1998 Joel Gordon. p. 34: (*top*) Tomas McAvoy/TimePix. (*bottom*) David Young-Wolff/PhotoEdit. p. 35: Everett Collection. p. 36: David Young-Wolff/PhotoEdit. p. 38: Steven Peters/Getty Images. p. 39: AP/Wide World Photos. p. 40: © 2002 PhotoDisc, Inc. p. 41: Christopher Bissell/Getty Images. p. 44: Robert Earnest/Getty Images. p. 49: A. Ramey/PhotoEdit. p. 51: INS News Group.

Chapter 3: p. 54: © Don Carstens/Brand X Pictures/PictureQuest. p. 60: Micrograph produced by John E. Heuser of Washington University School of Medicine. p. 63: AP/Wide World Photos. p. 65: Don Fawcett/Photo Researchers. p. 69: (*top*) D. N. Levin, H. Xiaoping, K. K. Tan, S. Galhotra, C. A. Palizzare, G. T. Y. Chen, R. N. Beck, C. T. Chen, M. D. Cooper, J. F. Mullan, J. Hekmatpanah, and J. P. Spire (1989). The brain: Integrated three-dimensional display of MR and PET images. *Radiology*, 172: 783–789. (*bottom left and right*) From "New findings of the correlation between acupoints and corresponding brain cortices using functional MRI," by Cho et al., *Proceedings of the National Academy of Sciences*, Vol. 95, March 1998, page 2671. Copyright 1998 National Academy of Sciences, U.S.A. p. 71: Bachmann/The Image Works. p. 73: © 2002 Dr. D. Dickson/Peter Arnold, Inc. p. 75: Valina L. Dawson, Department of Neurology, Johns Hopkins School of Medicine. p. 78: Cleveland FES Center, Cleveland VA Medical Center, Case Western Reserve University, Cleveland, Ohio. p. 81: © Dan McCoy/Rainbow. p. 83: Will & Deni McIntyre/Photo Researchers, Inc. p. 94: © 2002 Luiz C. Marigo/Peter Arnold, Inc. p. 96: Terry Wild Studio.

Chapter 4: p. 99: © 2002 PhotoDisc, Inc. p. 103: © Corbis Stock Market/Ed Bock 2002. p. 105: Photo provided by NCT Group, Inc., Stamford, CT. p. 106: Ed Roy. p. 108: Scanning electron micrographs by Robert Preston and Joseph E. Hawkins, Kresge Hearing Research Institute, University of Michigan. p. 110: AP/Wide World Photos. p. 111: © David Young-Wolff/PhotoEdit. p. 114: Courtesy of Dr. Frank Schaeffel. p. 115: Omikron/Photo Researchers. p. 122: Fritz Goro/TimePix. p. 125: Vienot, Brettel, Mollon, MNHN, CRNS. p. 127: © 2002 Gary Braasch. p. 129: (*top*) Omikron/Photo Researchers. (*bottom*) L. M. Bartoshuk and V. B. Duffy. p. 132: Alain Evrard/Photo Researchers. p. 134: (*top*) J. D. Sloane/Index Stock Imagery. (*bottom*) Peter Southwick/Stock Boston. p. 136: Bob Daemmrich/The Image Works. p. 137: Alain Evrard/Getty Images.

Chapter 5: p. 143: © Steve Allen/Brand X Pictures/PictureQuest. p. 145: Stephen R. Swinburne/Stock Boston. p. 150: David Frazier/Photo Researchers. p. 152: Farrell Grehan/Photo Researchers. p. 157: (*top*) Frank Whitney/Rainbow. (*bottom*) M. C. Escher's "Waterfall" © 1999 Cordon Art B.V.–Baam–Holland. p. 159: (*top*) AP/Wide World Photos. (*bottom*) Ira Kirschenbaum/Stock Boston. p. 161: David Weintraub/Stock Boston. p. 162: Courtesy George Eastman House. p. 163: Jim Anderson/Woodfin Camp. p. 167: John Chiasson/Getty Images. p. 169: (*top*) © 2001 stellarimages.com/Mark D. Phillips. (*bottom*) Eabin/Anrs/The Image Works. p. 172: Mark Richards/PhotoEdit. p. 176: Courtesy Ron Rensink, University of British Columbia. p. 179: Larry Mulvehill/Rainbow. p. 180: © 2002 PhotoDisc, Inc.

Chapter 6: p. 184: © 2002 Eyewire, Inc. p. 186: Jonathan Nourok/PhotoEdit. p. 187: Photofest. p. 192: © Herb Lingl/aerialarchives.com. p. 193: Steven Needham/Envision. p. 195: © 2002 Gerard Lacz/Peter Arnold, Inc. p. 196: (*left*) Psychology Archives—The University of Akron. (*bottom*) Nina Leen/TimePix. p. 199: Frank Lotz Miller/Black Star. p. 201: (*top*) Bob Daemmrich/The Image Works. (*bottom*) Rick Smolan/Stock Boston. p. 202: Courtesy of The Lincoln Electric Company. p. 204: AP/Wide World Photos. p. 206: Lang and Melamed, 1969. p. 208: Lawrence Migdale/Stock Boston. p. 212: *The Mentality of Apes* by W. Kohler, 1976, courtesy of Routledge. p. 213: Paul Chesley/Getty Images. p. 214: Albert Bandura, Stanford University. p. 219: Charles Gupton/Stock Boston. p. 220: (*top*) Hank Morgan/Rainbow. (*bottom*) M. Ferguson/PhotoEdit. p. 221: Rhoda Sidney/Stock Boston.

Chapter 7: p. 224: © corbisstockmarket.com p. 227: (*top*) Mary Kate Denny/Getty Images. (*bottom*) J. Greenberg/The Image Works. p. 233: Frank Siteman/Stock Boston. p. 235: AP/Wide World Photos. p. 238: (*left*) Franco Magnani. (*right*) Susan Schwarzenberg/The Exploratorium. p. 240: Jeff Dunn/Index Stock Imagery. p. 242: William F. Brewer. Originally appeared in *Cognitive Psychology*, 1981, 13, p. 211, published by Academic Press. p. 244: Todd Warshaw/Getty Images. p. 247: AP/Wide World Photos. p. 251: Paul Conklin. p. 254: Courtesy of Professor Dominique Muller. p. 257: AP/Wide World Photos. p. 259: Robert Burke/Getty Images.

Chapter 8: p. 264: © 2002 Eyewire, Inc. p. 267: Frank Siteman/PhotoEdit. p. 268: Bob Daemmrich/Stock Boston. p. 269: From *Cognitive Psychology and its Implications* by John R. Anderson © 2000, 1995, 1985, 1980, by Worth Publishers and W. H. Freeman and Company. p. 271: (*left*) NASA. (*right*) Joe Sohm/Chromosohm/Stock Boston. p. 272: Jeff Greenberg/PhotoEdit. p. 277: Paul Howell/Getty Images. p. 280: AP/Wide World Photos. p. 281: Wharton, C. M., Grafman, J., Flitman, S. S., Hansen, E. K., Brauner, J., Marks, A., and Honda, M. Toward neuroanatomical models of analogy: A positron emission tomography study of analogical mapping. *Cognitive Psychology*, Vol. 40, No. 3, May 1, 2000. p. 287: Reuters/Barbara L. Johnston/Getty Images. p. 290: AP/Wide World Photos. p. 292: Lawrence Migdale. p. 296: Peter W. Jusczyk, Linda B. Smith, & Christopher Murphy (1981). The perceptual classification of speech, *Perception and Psychophysics*, 30(1), 10–23, Figure 1, p. 13. Courtesy of Ann M. Jusczyk. p. 297: (*top*) Eastcott/Momatiuk/The Image Works. (*bottom*) Joe McNally/Sygma. p. 300: © Jeff Greenberg/Rainbow. p. 303: Dr. Ronald H. Cohn/Gorilla Foundation/Koko.org.

Chapter 9: p. 308: © 2002 PhotoDisc, Inc. p. 309: © Wildlife Conservation Society, headquartered at the Bronx Zoo. p. 315: AP/Wide World Photos. p. 318: (*left*) Jacques Jangoux/Photo Researchers. (*right*) Nathan Benning/National Geographic Image Collection. p. 319: Will & Deni McIntyre/Photo Researchers. p. 320: Bob Daemmrich/The Image Works. p. 322: David Young-Wolff/PhotoEdit. p. 324: Patrick Ward/Stock Boston. p. 327: David Parker/Photo Researchers. p. 329: Grant Mason/Manni Mason's Pictures. p. 334: Photo by Jules Asher at NIMH. p. 335: Kenneth Murray/Photo Researchers. p. 336: Barry King/Getty Images. p. 337: L. Mulvehill/The Image Works. p. 338: © Joel Gordon 1994. p. 340: A. Ramey/Stock Boston. p. 341: www.danielsmithphotography.com.

Chapter 10: p. 344: Corbis/Royalty Free. p. 348: Records of the Public Health Service, National Archives. p. 349: Simulated items similar to those in the Wechsler Intelligence Scales for Adults and Children. Copyright 1949,

C-1

1955, 1974, 1981, 1991, 1997 by The Psychological Corporation. Reproduced by permission. All rights reserved. Photo © Dan McCoy/Rainbow. **p. 353:** Jeff Greenberg/The Image Works. **p. 360:** Andy Sacks/Getty Images. **p. 362:** Bob Daemmrich. **p. 367:** Stephen Collins/Photo Researchers. **p. 369:** Jim Cummins/Getty Images. **p. 371:** Skjold/The Image Works. **p. 376:** Fraser Hale/St. Petersburg Times. **p. 377:** U. S. Department of the Interior, National Park Service, Edison National Historic Site.

Chapter 11: **p. 380:** © 2002 PhotoDisc, Inc. **p. 382:** AP/Wide World Photos. **p. 383:** Dwight Kuhn. **p. 385:** AP/Wide World Photos. **p. 386:** Okoniewski/The Image Works. **p. 391:** Richard Howard. **p. 392:** Peter Menzel/Stock Boston. **p. 394:** AP/Wide World Photos. **p. 396:** Bill Aron/PhotoEdit. **p. 402:** AP/Wide World Photos. **p. 404:** Reprinted with permission of the publisher from Henry A. Murray, *Thematic Apperception Test*, Cambridge, Mass.: Harvard University Press, Copyright © 1943 by the President and Fellows of Harvard College. © 1971 by Henry A. Murray. **p. 405:** Mary Kate Denny/PhotoEdit. **p. 407:** © Corbis Stock Market/Ariel Skelley 2002. **p. 408:** David Joel/Getty Images. **p. 412:** Joe Hoyle/The Daily Illini. **p. 415:** From *The Neurological Examination*, 4th edition, by R. N. Dejong, New York: Lippincott/Harper & Row, 1979. **p. 420:** Robert E. Daemmrich/Getty Images. **p. 424:** Reuters/Antonio Guevara/Getty Images. **p. 425:** (*left*) Eastcott/Momatiuk/Woodfin Camp. (*center*) Rick Smolan/Stock Boston. (*right*) Jonathan Blair/Woodfin Camp.

Chapter 12: **p. 431:** © Jean-Yves Bruel/Wonderfile. **p. 433:** Les Stone/Sygma. **p. 434:** (*top*) B. Anderson/Photo Researchers. (*bottom*) C. Salvador/Sygma. **p. 436:** Photo Lennart Nilsson/Albert Bonniers Fortag AB, *Behold Man*, Little Brown and Company. **p. 437:** Reproduced, with permission, from Nelson, C. A. (1987). The recognition of facial expressions in the first two years of life: Mechanisms of development. *Child Development*, 58, 889–909. **p. 438:** Petit Format/J. DaCunha/Photo Researchers. **p. 441:** George Zimbel. **p. 442:** Courtesy of Carolyn Rovee Collier. **p. 446:** Pedrick/The Image Works. **p. 451:** © Corbis Stock Market/Jose L. Pelaez 2002. **p. 452:** Jose Polleross/The Image Works. **p. 453:** David Young-Wolff/PhotoEdit. **p. 455:** Martin Rogers/Stock Boston. **p. 457:** Michael Newman/PhotoEdit. **p. 458:** B. Mahoney/The Image Works. **p. 462:** David Young-Wolff/PhotoEdit. **p. 463:** David Grossman/PhotoEdit. **p. 465:** Jeff Greenberg/Photo Researchers. **p. 467:** AP/Wide World Photos. **p. 470:** Mary Kate Denny/PhotoEdit. **p. 477:** Steve Liss/TimePix. **p. 479:** Penny Tweedie/Getty Images. **p. 481:** Reuters/Joe Skipper/Getty Images.

Chapter 13: **p. 485:** © 2002 PhotoDisc, Inc. **p. 487:** Lori Adamski Peek/Getty Images. **p. 489:** AP/Wide World Photos. **p. 490:** Piet Van Lier. **p. 493:** AP/Wide World Photos. **p. 494:** Photofest. **p. 496:** David Alan Harvey/Woodfin Camp. **p. 500:** Laruen Greenfield/Sygma. **p. 504:** Boehringer Ingelheim, International GmbH/photo Lennart Nilsson, *The Incredible Machine*, National Geographic Society. **p. 506:** Esbin-Anderson/The Image Works. **p. 508:** Huntly Hersch/Index Stock Imagery. **p. 510:** Gustavo Gilabert/Corbis SABA. **p. 513:** Bachrach. **p. 514:** Leslie O'Shaughnessy/Medical Images, Inc.

Chapter 14: **p. 517:** © 2002 PhotoDisc, Inc. **p. 519:** Mary Evans Picture Library. **p. 520:** Bob Daemmrich/Stock Boston. **p. 523:** Corbis-Bettmann. **p. 526:** John Neubauer/PhotoEdit. **p. 528:** Robert Caputo/Aurora. **p. 531:** Bruce Plotkin/Getty Images. **p. 536:** (*left*) Titan Sports/Sygma. (*right*) Andy King/Sygma. **p. 537:** Reuters/Tim Shaffer/Getty Images. **p. 538:** Karen Thomas/Stock Boston. **p. 540:** Steve Kagan/TimePix. **p. 542:** AP/Wide World Photos. **p. 548:** Charlotte Miller.

Chapter 15: **p. 552:** Corbis/Royalty Free. **p. 554:** © Jim Cornfield/Corbis. **p. 557:** (*top*) J. L. Dugast/Sygma. (*bottom*) Culver Pictures. **p. 567:** David Woo/Stock Boston. **p. 568:** Michael Banks/Getty Images. **p. 569:** Abe Rezny/The Image Works. **p. 570:** © 2002 PhotoDisc, Inc. **p. 571:** Dr. Susan Mineka. **p. 574:** Photofest. **p. 580:** © Dan McCoy/Rainbow. **p. 584:** Dr. Silberswieg/E. Stern, Cornell Medical Center.

p. 586: Grunnitus/Photo Researchers. **p. 587:** Office of Scientific Information, National Institute of Mental Health. **p. 591:** Hillsboro County Sheriff, Tampa, Florida. **p. 594:** Bob Daemmrich/The Image Works. **p. 599:** AP/Wide World Photos.

Chapter 16: **p. 603:** © 2002 PhotoDisc, Inc. **p. 605:** (*top*) Stock Montage. (*bottom*) © Hank Morgan/Rainbow. **p. 607:** Edmund Engleman. **p. 608:** M. Grecco/Stock Boston. **p. 611:** Michael Rougier/TimePix. **p. 612:** Zigy Kaluzny/Getty Images. **p. 614:** Georgia Tech photo by Gary Meek. **p. 617:** Rick Friedman/Black Star. **p. 618:** Courtesy Albert Ellis, Institute for Rational-Emotive Therapy. **p. 621:** James Wilson/Woodfin Camp. **p. 630:** Spencer Grant/PhotoEdit. **p. 632:** Reuters/Montana Department of Justice/Getty Images. **p. 633:** The Medical History Museum of the University of Zurich. **p. 634:** Will & Deni McIntyre/Photo Researchers. **p. 643:** Joseph Sohm: ChromoSohm, Inc./Corbis.

Chapter 17: **p. 646:** © 2002 PhotoDisc, Inc. **p. 649:** AP/Wide World Photos. **p. 651:** Bob Daemmrich/The Image Works. **p. 653:** Michael Newman/PhotoEdit. **p. 654:** © Tom McCarthy/Rainbow. **p. 657:** Peter Ginter/Material World. **p. 658:** Bob Daemmrich/The Image Works. **p. 661:** David Woo/Stock Boston. **p. 667:** Bonnie Kamin/PhotoEdit. **p. 669:** Robert Brenner/PhotoEdit. **p. 672:** Michelle Bridwell/PhotoEdit. **p. 674:** D.P.A./The Image Works. **p. 676:** Myrleen Ferguson/PhotoEdit.

Chapter 18: **p. 679:** © 2002 PhotoDisc, Inc. **p. 681:** AP/Wide World Photos. **p. 682:** David Leeson/The Image Works. **p. 683:** AP/Wide World Photos. **p. 684:** (*left*) Nabeel Turner/Getty Images. (*right*) Corbis-Bettmann. **p. 688:** (*top*) Jonathan Nourok/PhotoEdit. (*bottom*) David Young-Wolff/PhotoEdit. **p. 689:** From the film *Obedience* © 1965 Stanley Milgram and distributed by Penn State Media Sales. **p. 691:** John Chiasson/Getty Images. **p. 692:** AP/Wide World Photos. **p. 693:** Reuters/TimePix. **p. 697:** Chris Hondros/Getty Images. **p. 701:** Edward Citrinblum/Outline. **p. 702:** Courtesy of North Carolina State University. **p. 703:** Ellen Senisi/The Image Works. **p. 705:** Benali/Getty Images. **p. 707:** Mark C. Burnett/Photo Researchers. **p. 710:** CBS Photo Archive. **p. 711:** Michael Newman/PhotoEdit. **p. 715:** Najilah Feanny/Corbis SABA.

TABLES AND ILLUSTRATIONS

Figure 1.2, p. 4: *Social and Personality Development* by D. R. Shaffer (Box 4-2) published in 1973. Reprinted by permission of D. R. Shaffer. **Figure 1.3, p. 5:** "Husband and Father-in-Law: A Reversible Figure" by J. Botinwick in *American Journal of Psychology*, 1961, 74: 312–313. Copyright © 1961 by the Board of Trustees of the University of Illinois. Used by permission of the University of Illinois Press. **Figure 1.4, p. 11:** *Source:* Morris, Michael W. and Kaiping Peng (1994). Culture and Cause: American and Chinese Attributions for Social and Physical Events. *Journal of Personality and Social Psychology*, Vol. 67, No. 6, 949–997. Adapted from figure 8, p. 965. Copyright © 1994 by the American Psychological Association. Adapted with permission.

Figure 3.12, p. 69: *Source:* Cho, Z. H., Chung, S. C., Jones, J. P., Park, J. B., Park, H. J., Lee, H. J., Wong, E. K., & Min, B. I. (1996). New findings of the correlation between acupoints and corresponding brain cortices using functional MRI. *Proceedings of the National Academy of Science USA*, 95, 5, pp. 2670–2573. **Figure 3.17, p. 77:** From *The Cerebral Cortex of Man* by Wilder Penfield and Theodore Rasmussen. Copyright 1950 Macmillan Publishing Company; copyright renewed © 1978 Theodore Rasmussen, copyright © 2002 Gale Group. Reprinted by permission of Gale Group. **Figure 3.18, p. 79:** *Eye, Brain and Vision* by D. Hubel, New York: Scientific Library, pp. 138–139, W. H. Freeman & Co. **Figure 3.21, p. 85:** Reprinted by permission of the publisher from *The Postnatal Development of the Human Cerebral Cortex*, Vol. I-VIII by Jesse LeRoy Conel, Cambridge, Mass.: Harvard University Press, Copyright © 1993–1975 by the President and Fellows of Harvard College.

Table 4.1, p. 106: From *Fundamentals of Sensation and Perception* by M. W. Levine and J. M. Shefner, Addison Wesley, 1981. Reprinted by permission of the author. **Figure 4.6, p. 109:** G. L. Rasmussen and W. F. Windle, *Neural Mechanisms of the Auditory and Vestibular Systems*, 1960. Courtesy of Charles C. Thomas, Publisher, Springfield, Illinois. **Figure 4.12, p. 117:** From *Sensation and Perception* by H. R. Schiffman, Copyright © 1990 John Wiley, & Sons, p. 275, Figure 14.6. This material is used by permission of John Wiley & Sons, Inc. **Figure 4.22, p. 126:** V. S. Ramachandran & E. M Hubbard (2001), Psychophysical investigations into the neural basis of synaesthesia. Proceedings of the Royal Society London, *Biological Sciences, 268*, 979–963. (figure #3). Reprinted by permission of E. M. Hubbard.

Figure 5.5, p. 153: *Seeing: Illusion, Brain and Mind*, pp. 14 and 105 by Frisby, J. P., Oxford, Oxford University Press 1980. Roxby Press. **Figure 5.15, p. 166:** Illustration from *Sensation and Perception*, Fourth Edition by Stanley Coren, Lawrence M. Ward, and James T. Enns, p. 393, copyright © 1994 John Wiley & Sons. This material is used by permission of John Wiley & Sons, Inc. **Figure 5.23, p. 170:** Rumelhart, D. E., and McClelland, J. L. (1986). Parallel Distributing Processing Volume 1: Foundations. Cambridge, MA: MIT Press. Copyright © 1986 by the Massachusetts Institute of Technology. Reprinted by permission. **Figure 5.24, p. 172:** Johnson, M. A., Dziurawiec, S., Ellis, H., and Morton, J. (1991). "Newborns' Preferential Tracking of Face-Like Stimuli and Decline." *Cognition*, 4, 1–19. Reprinted by permission Elsevier Science Publishing.

Figure 6.7, p. 198: From *The Psychology of Learning and Memory* by Hintzman. Copyright © 1978 W. H. Freeman and Company. Used with permission. **Figure 6.9, p. 203:** Adapted from "Teaching Machines" by B. F. Skinner. Copyright © 1961 by Scientific American, Inc. All rights reserved.

Figure 7.2, p. 229: Tulving, Schacter, & Stark (1982). Printing effects in word-fragment completion are independent of recognition memory. *Journal of Experimental Psychology, Learning, Memory, and Cognition*, 8, 336–342, figure 1, adapted, p. 339. Copyright © 1982 by the American Psychological Association. **Figure 7.5, p. 232:** From "Contextual Prerequisites for Understanding: Some Investigations of Comprehension and Recall" by Bransford and Johnson. *Journal of Verbal Learning and Verbal Behavior*, Volume 61, pp. 717–726, copyright 1972, Elsevier Science (USA), reproduced by permission of the publisher. **Figure 7.6, p. 234:** *Cognitive Psychology: Memory Language and Thought*, by Howard, Darlene, V., © 1967, Prentice-Hall, Inc. Upper Saddle River, NJ. Reprinted by permission of the author. **Figure 7.8, p. 237:** From "Long-Term Memory For a Common Object," by R. S. Nickerson and M. J. Adams in *Cognitive Psychology*, Volume 11, 187–307, copyright 1979, Elsevier Science (USA), reproduced by permission of the publisher. **Figure 7.17, p. 250:** Tulving and Psotka, "Retroactive Inhibition in Free Recall: Inaccessibility of Information Available in the Memory Store." *Journal of Experimental Psychology*, 87, pp. 1–8, 1971, figure 1, p. 339. Copyright © 1971 by the American Psychological Association. Adapted with permission.

Figure 8.6, p. 273: Excerpt from P. Whitney, 1998, The Psychology of Language. See attached. A Mental Script for Eating at a Restaurant. Copyright © 1998 by Houghton Mifflin. Used with permission. **Figure 8.8, p. 274:** From "Mental Rotation of Three-Dimensional Objects," R. Shepard et al., *Science*, Vol. 171, #3972, pp. 701–703, figure on p. 702, 19 February 1971. Copyright © 1971 by the American Association for the Advancement of Science. **Figure 8.9, p. 281:** Figure from *Cognitive Psychology Journal*, Vol. 40, page 179. Comparing Stimulus Patterns; Wharton, C. M. et al. Toward neuroanatomical models of analogy: A positron emission tomography study of analogical mapping. Copyright 2000, Elsevier Science (USA), reproduced by permission of the publisher. **Figure 8.10, p. 281:** Figure from *Cognitive Psychology Journal*, Vol. 40, page 184. Brain Activity During Analogical Mapping: Comparing Stimulus Patterns; Wharton, C. M. et al. Toward neuroanatomical models of analogy: A positron emission tomography study of analogical mapping. Copyright 2000, Elsevier Science (USA), reproduced by permission of the publisher.

Figure 9.2, p. 313: D. L. Schacter, L. A. Cooper, S. M. Delaney, M. A. Peterson, and M. Tharan's article "Implicit Memory for Possible and Impossible Objects: Constraints on the Construction of Structural Descriptions," (1991) from *Journal of Experimental Psychology: Learning Memory and Cognition*, 17, 3–19. Copyright © 1991 by the American Psychological Association. Reprinted with permission. **Figure 9.3, p. 313:** John A. Bargh, Mark Chen, and Lara Burrows, "Automaticity of Social Behavior: Direct Effects of Train Construction and Stereotype Activation on Action," *Journal of Personality and Social Psychology*, 1996, Vol. 71, No. 2, 230–244, Figure 1, p. 235. Copyright © 1996 by the American Psychological Association. Adapted with permission. **Figure 9.5, p. 319:** Horne, J. A. *Why We Sleep: The Functions of Sleep in Humans and Other Mammals.* Copyright © 1998 James Horne. Reprinted by permission of Oxford University Press. **Figure 9.6, p. 320:** Adapted from Cartwright, *A Primer of Sleep and Dreaming*, Reading, Mass.: Addison-Wesley, 1978. Reprinted by permission. **Figure 9.7, p. 321:** Reprinted with permission from "Ontogenic Development of the Human Sleep Dream Cycle," Roffwarg et al. *Science*, Vol. 152, page 606, 29 April 1966 (revised 1969). Copyright © 1966 by the American Association for the Advancement of Science. **Figure 9.10, p. 328:** Pattie, F. A. (1935). "A Report at Attempts to Produce Uniocular Blindness by Hypnotic Suggestion," *British Journal Medical Psychiatry*, 15, 230–241. Reprinted by permission. **Figure 9.11, p. 328:** From *Hypnotic Age Susceptibility* by Ernest R. Hilgard, copyright 1965 by Harcourt Brace Jovanovich, Inc. Reprinted by permission of the author. **Figure 9.13, p. 333:** Laurie Roehrich and Mark S. Goldman, Implicit Priming of Alcohol Expectancy Memory Processes and Subsequent Drinking Behavior, *Experimental and Clinical Psychopharmacology*, 1995, Vol. 3, No. 4, 402–410. Figure 1, p. 406: Copyright © 1995 by the American Psychological Association. Adapted with permission.

Figure 10.4, p. 358: Figure: The Curve Moves Higher. *Source:* Neisser, 1998/NYT Pictures. **Figure 10.6, p. 364:** Figure 1, p. 620, from Steele, C. M., "A threat in the air: How stereotypes shape intellectual identity and performance," *American Psychologist*, June 1997, Vol. 52, No. 6, 613–629. Copyright © 1997 by the American Psychological Association. Adapted with permission.

Figure 11.2, p. 384: Douglas T. Kenrick, Richard C. Keefe, Angela Bryan, Alicia Barr, and Stephanie Brown, "Age Preference and Mate Choice Among Homosexuals and Heterosexuals: A Case for Modular Psychological Mechanisms," *Journal of Personality and Social Psychology*, 1995. Vol. 89, No. 6, 1166–1172, Figure 1, p. 1169. Copyright © 1995 by the American Psychological Association. Adapted with permission. **Figure 11.5, p. 390:** Adapted with permission from Schwartz, M. W., Woods, S. C., Porte, Jr., D., Seeley, R. J., & Baskin, D. G. (2000). Central nervous system control of food intake. *Nature*, 404, 661–671. Reprinted with permission of Dr. M. W. Schwartz. **Figure 11.6, p. 399:** Adapted from W. H. Masters and V. E. Johnson, *Human Sexual Response*, p. 5 (Boston: Little, Brown and Company, 1966). **Figure 11.13, p. 419:** Figure 3 from "Voluntary Facial Action Generates Emotion-Specific Autonomic Nervous System Activity," by R. W. Levenson, P. Ekman, and W. V. Friesen. *Psychophysiology*, 1990, 24, 363–384. Copyright © 1990 the Society for Psychophysiological Research. Reprinted with permission of the author and the publisher from Levenson, Ekman, and Friesen, 1990. **Figure 11.14, p. 426:** Aronoff, J., Barclay, A. M., and Stevenson, L. A. "The Recognition of Threatening Facial Stimuli," 1988. *Journal of Personality and Social Psychology*, 54, pp. 647–655, figure p. 651. Copyright © 1988 by the American Psychological Association. Adapted with permission.

Figure 12.5, p. 444: Baillargeon, R. (1992). "A model of physical reasoning in infancy." in C. Rovee-Collier & L. P. Lipsitt (eds.). *Advances in infancy research*. Norwood, N.J., ABLEX Publishing Corp., pp. 305–371. Reprinted by permission.

Figure 13.2, p. 491: "The General Adaptation Syndrome" from *Stress Without Distress* by Hans Selye, M.D. Copyright © 1974 by Hans Selye, M.D. Reprinted by permission of HarperCollins Publishers. **Figure 13.4, p. 497:** Adapted from Lazarus, Opton, Nornikos, and Rankin, *Journal of Personality*, 33:4. Copyright © 1965 Duke University Press. Reprinted with permission. **Figure 13.5, p. 512:** Prochaska, W., DeClementi, C., and Norcoss, J., "In Search of How People Change: Application to Addictive Behaviors," *American Psychologist*, 47, 1102–1114, Figure 1, p. 104. Copyright © 1992 by the American Psychological Association. Adapted with permission.

Figure 14.1, p. 520: Adapted from *Personality: Strategies and Issues*, by Robert M. Liebert and Michael D. Spiegler. Copyright © 1990 by Wadsworth, Inc. Reprinted by permission of Brooks/Cole Publishing Company, Pacific Grove, CA, 93950. **Figure 14.3, p. 529:** Eysenck, H. J., Rachman, S.: "The Causes and Cures of Neurosis: An Introduction to Modern Behavior Therapy Based on Learning Therapy and the Principle of Conditioning." 1965. *Edits*. Reprinted with permission. **Figure 14.4, p. 534:** Reprinted from *Journal of Behavior Therapy and Experimental Psychiatry*, 13, A. Bandura, "The Assessment and Predictive Generality of Self-Precepts of Efficacy," pp. 195–199. Copyright © 1982 by Pergamon Press. Reprinted with permission of Elsevier Science. **Figure 14.5, p. 535:** Reprinted from *Journal of Behavior Therapy and Experimental Psychiatry*, 13, A. Bandura, "The Assessment and Predictive Generality of Self-Precepts of Efficacy," pp. 195–199. Copyright © 1982, with kind permission from Pergamon Press, Ltd., Headington Hill-Hall, Oxford OX3 OBW, UK. **Table 14.3, p. 546:** Reproduced by special permission of the publisher, Psychological Assessment Resources, Inc., Odessa, FL 33556. From the "NEO Personality Inventory" by Paul Costa and Robert McCrae. Copyright © 1978, 1985, 1989, 1991 by PAR, Inc. **Figure 14.6, p. 547:** Minnesota Multiphasic Personality Inventory-2 (MMPI-2) Profile for Basic Scales. Copyright © 1989 by the Regents of the University of Minnesota. All rights reserved. Used by permission of the University of Minnesota Press. "MMPI-2" and "Minnesota Multiphasic Personality Inventory-2" are trademarks owned by the University of Minnesota. **Figure 14.7, p. 548:** Emmanuel F. Hammer, Ph.D., "Projective Drawings," in Rabin, ed. *Projective Techniques in Personality Assessment*, pp. 375–376. Copyright © 1968 by Springer Publishing Company, Inc., New York. Used by permission.

Figure 15.6, p. 588: J. Zubin and B. Spring, 1977, "A New View of Schizophrenia," *Journal of Abnormal Psychology*, 86, pp. 103–126. Copyright © 1977 by the American Psychological Association. Adapted with permission.

Figure 16.2, p. 616: After Matson, J., Sevin, J., Fridley, and Love, S. (1990). "Increasing Spontaneous Language in Autistic Children," *Journal of Applied Behavior Analysis*, 23, pp. 227–233. **Figure 16.4, p. 626:** G. R. Patterson, "Intervention for Boys with Conduct Problems: Multiple Settings, Treatments, and Criteria," *Journal of Consulting and Clinical Psychology*, 1974, 42, 471–481, figure 1, p. 476. Copyright © 1974 by the American Psychological Association. Adapted with permission.

Figure 17.6, p. 664: L. Festinger and J. M Carlsmith, "Cognitive Consequences of Forced Compliance," *Journal of Abnormal and Social Psychology*, 58, 203–210. **Figure 17.7, p. 672:** C. Byrne and D. Nelson, "Attraction as a Linear Function of Proportion of Positive Reinforcements," *Journal of Personality and Social Psychology*, 1, 659–663, figure 1, p. 661. Copyright © 1965 by the American Psychological Association. Adapted with permission.

Figure 18.1, p. 681: Reno, R. R., Cialdini, R. B., & Kallgren, C. A. "The transitional influence of social norms," *Journal of Personality and Social Psychology*, 64, 104–112, figure 1, p. 106. Copyright © 1993 by the American Psychological Association. Adapted with permission. **Figure 18.4, p. 690:** Courtesy of Alexandra Milgram. From S. Milgram, "Behavioral Study of Obedience," *Journal of Abnormal Social Psychology*, 67, 371–378. Copyright © 1963 by the American Psychological Association. Adapted by permission of the publisher and literary executor. **Figure 18.7, p. 701:** Figure from Anderson, C. A., & Anderson, K. P., "Temperature and aggression: Paradox, controversy, and a (fairly) clear picture." In R. G. Green & E. Donnerstein (Eds.), *Human aggression theories: Research and implications for social policy*, p. 279, Figure 10.9. Copyright 1998, Elsevier Science (USA), reproduced by permission of the publisher.

NAME INDEX

Abbott, B. B., 497
Abeles, N., 421
Abi-Hashem, N., 22
Abraham, H. D., 338
Abramis, D. J., 407
Abramowitz, J. S., 640
Abrams, R., 634
Abrams, R. L., 148, 313
Abramson, E. E., 617
Abramson, L. Y., 210, 581, 582
Abreu, J. M., 6, 564, 565
Abu-Elheiga, L., 394
Achenbach, T. M., 593
Acker, L. E., 194
Ackerman, D., 107
Ackerman, M. J., 322
Ackerman, P. L., 366
Ackroff, K., 392
Acocella, J., 574
Adam, S., 449
Adams, M. J., 237
Addis, M. E., 627, 628
Addison, T., 695, 698, 701
Adelman, W. P., 512
Ader, D. N., 33
Ader, R., 96, 504
Adler, A., 522–523, 538, 608
Adler, T., 496
Adolphs, R., 414
Adorno, T. W., 666–667
Agarwal, D. P., 334
Agency for Healthcare Research and Quality, 635
Agnew, C. R., 673
Ahadi, S. A., 454
Ahima, R. S., 389
Ahlfinger, N. R., 715
Ahmed, A., 442
Aiello, J. R., 682, 683
Aiken, L. R., 350, 356, 511
Ainsworth, M. D. S., 456, 523
Ajzen, I., 660
Akahoshi, M., 506
Akert, R. M., 7, 284, 662, 672, 682, 686, 700, 705
Akil, H., 337
Alaimo, K., 361
Albarrican, D., 511
Albee, G., 642
Albert, M. S., 476
Alberti, R. E., 615
Albery, I. P., 659
Albrecht, T. L., 499
Aldag, R. J., 716
Alderete, E., 336
Alexinsky, T., 70
Al-Fayed, D., 257
Alfieri, T., 657
Alicke, M., 648
Al-Kubaisy, T., 617
Allen, D. N., 586
Allen, J. B., 422, 706
Allen, K. R., 478
Allen, L. S., 81, 401
Alliger, G. M., 518

Allison, D. B., 393
Alloy, L. B., 210, 580, 581
Allport, G. W., 526
Alston, J. H., 17
Altemeyer, B., 667
Altman, L. K., 341
Aluja-Fabregat, A., 216
Alvarez, F. J., 333
Alvarez, G. A., 175
Alvarez-Buylla, A., 84
Alvaro, E. M., 687
Alvir, J. M., 635
Alzheimer, A., 73
Amabile, T. M., 373–374, 374, 407
Amanzio, M., 135
Amara, D. G., 257
Amateau, L. M., 500
American Educational Research Association, 351, 352, 354, 549
American Law Institute (ALI), 599
American Psychiatric Association, 332, 375, 376, 400, 403, 560, 572, 582, 590, 594
American Psychological Association, 8, 215, 216, 351, 352, 549, 631
American Psychological Association and National Council on Measurement in Education, 354
American Psychological Association Office of Ethnic Minority Affairs, 32
American Society for Microbiology, 36
Anastasi, A., 351
Andersen, S. M., 524
Anderson, A. K., 414, 421
Anderson, C. A., 215, 216, 217, 546, 697, 700, 701
Anderson, C. H., 116
Anderson, D., 449
Anderson, E. M., 624
Anderson, J. R., 231, 235, 259, 269, 272, 273, 279, 285, 288, 514
Anderson, K., 312
Anderson, K. C., 269
Anderson, K. J., 465
Anderson, K. P., 701
Anderson, L. W., 362
Anderson, M. C., 5, 218, 251
Andreasen, N. C., 585, 586
Andre-Peterson, L., 506
Andrew, D., 134
Andrews, B., 251
Ang-Lee, M. K., 91
Angst, F., 577
Angst, J., 577
Annan, K., 235
Annunziato, B., 500
Anrep, G. V., 188
Ansay, C., 242
Anshel, M., 514
Anthony, T., 668
Anton, R. F., 597

Antoni, M. H., 505, 513
Antonuccio, D. O., 640
Appelbaum, M. I., 354, 355
Appelle, S., 554
Applebaum, M. I., 354, 355
Applebaum, P. S., 600
Appleton, W. S., 636
Archambault, C. M., 394
Archer, J., 695
Arduino, C., 135
Arenberg, D., 475
Arendash, G. W., 74
Aristotle, 11, 275
Arkes, H. R., 289, 290
Arlow, J., 607
Armenian, H. K., 640
Armstrong, N., 104
Arndt, J., 313, 524
Arnett, J. J., 469, 474
Aronoff, J., 425
Aronson, E., 7, 284, 655, 662, 669, 672, 682, 686, 700, 705
Aronson, J., 364
Arriaga, X. B., 673
Arterberry, M. E., 173
Arterburn, D., 394
Arvee, F., 100
Asarnow, R. F., 586
Asbury, K., A-7
Asch, S. E., 685, 686
Ascraft, M. H., 276, 285
Ashe, P. C., 587
Asher, S. R., 463
Ashton, H., 321
Aslin, R. N., 437
Aspinwall, L. G., 498, 501, 510, 513
Associated Press, 144, 218
Astengo, F., 91
Aston-Jones, G., 70, 332
Asukai, N., 495
Atkinson, J. W., 359
Atkinson, L., 457
Atkinson, R. C., 231
Au, T. K., 304
August, G. J., 643
Auld, F., 607
Aussprung, 489
Averill, J. S., 419
Aviezer, O., 457
Avila, C., 530
Ax, R. K., 606
Ayanian, J., 660
Aykan, H., 476
Ayllon, T., 208, 616
Ayton, P., 289, 290
Azaar, B., 479
Azorin, J.-M., 635
Azrin, N. H., 616
Baare, W. F. C., 586, 587, 588
Baars, B. J., 311, 316
Babcock, R., 372
Bacharach, W. R., 359
Bäckman, L., 245, 246, 481
Baddeley, A., 226, 230, 233, 256

Badia, P., 497
Bagley, C., 400
Bagwell, C. L., 463
Bahrick, H. P., 237, 247, 449
Bahrick, P. O., 449
Bailey, J. M., 400, 401, 402, 403
Baillargeon, R., 442, 443–444, 447
Baker, L. T., 366
Balaban, E., 110
Balaban, M. T., 425
Baldessarini, R. J., 636
Baldi, A. P., 234
Baldwin, J. M., 13
Balestreri, R., 91
Balkin, T. J., 326
Ball, K., 175
Balleine, B., 387
Ballou, M., 615
Balota, D. A., 242
Baltes, P. B., 475, 476
Banaji, M. R., 229, 666, 670
Bancroft, J., 396
Bandura, A., 214, 215, 511, 533, 534–535, 697
Banich, M. T., 35, 82, 415
Banks, M. S., 437
Banks, W. P., 167
Bar, M., 313
Barabee, H. E., 701
Baranano, D. E., 89
Barber, J. P., 524, 625, 628
Barber, N., 384
Barbone, F., 324
Barclay, J. R., 239
Bard, P., 421
Bardo, M. T., 385, 421
Barefoot, J. C., 506
Bargh, J. A., 6, 313, 524, 670
Barker, L. M., 186, 197
Barlow, D., 193
Barlow, D. H., 498, 568, 569, 570, 616, 620, 641
Barnett, W. S., 361
Barnier, A. J., 328
Baron, J., 5
Baron, M., 579
Baron, R. A., 675, 695, 697, 702, 713
Baron, R. S., 683
Barondes, S. H., 639
Barrett, L. C., 210
Barrett, S., 564
Barrick, M. R., 546, 549
Barrios, L. C., 578
Barron, F., 374
Barron, K. E., 405
Barrowclough, C., 628
Barsalou, L. W., 270
Barsky, A. J., 572
Bartholomew, K., 478
Bartlett, P. L., 218
Bartol, C., 549
Bartol, K. M., 409
Bartoshuk, L. M., 129, 130
Basinger, K. S., 473

NI-1

Baskin, D., 564
Bass, E., 252
Bates, E., 300
Bates, J. E., 464
Batson, C. D., 474, 706, 709
Battaglia, G., 337
Baucom, D. H., 626
Bauer, P. J., 449
Baum, A. S., 494
Baum, A., 487, 488
Baumann, D. D., 658
Baumann, D. J., 703
Baumeister, A. A., 359
Baumeister, R. F., 382, 399, 410, 658
Baumrind, D., 460–461
Bauserman, R., 593
Bavaresco, J. L., 240
Baylor, D. A., 122
Bazerman, M. H., 277
Beach, K. R., 314, 670
Beach, S., 672
Beardsley, P. M., 336
Beatty, J., 167
Beauchamp, G. K., 128, 129, 438
Beauchamp-Turner, D. L., 330
Bechara, A., 387
Beck, A. T., 569, 577, 581, 619–620
Beck, J. S., 581, 619
Beck, M., 479
Becker, B., 466
Becker, J. A., 298
Bedard, J., 285
Begley, S., 436
Belin, P., 110
Belk, A., 392
Bell, B. E., 246
Bell, P. A., 702
Bellugi, U., 91
Belmaker, R. H., 636
Belmont, J. M., 376
Belsky, J., 457, 478
Bem, D. J., 401, 664
Benbow, C. P., 375
Benecke, M., 27
Benedetti, F., 135
Benfante, M., 702
Benight, C. C., 498
Benishay, D. S., 401
Benjamin, K., 135
Benjamin, L. T., Jr., 11
Bennet, W. M., 340
Bennett, B., 591
Bennett, D. J., 229
Bennett, E. L., 254, 255
Bennett, H. L., 312
Bennett, J. A., 355
Ben-Porath, Y., 494
Ben-Shakhar, G., 420
Benson, H., 329, 330
Benson, J. A., Jr., 341
Ben-Zeev, T., 364
Bera, S., 523
Berenbaum, S. A., 93
Berg, E. P., 66
Bergeman, C. S., A-7

Berger, A., 134
Berger, R., 623
Berger, S. A., 237
Bergin, A. E., 604, 623, 628, 629
Berk, M. S., 524
Berkeley, G., 11
Berkowitz, L., 694, 698
Berliner, D. L., 128
Berman, R. F., 257
Bermond, B., 420
Bernal, M. E., 630
Bernard, A., 286
Bernard, L. L., 383
Bernard, M. E., 513
Bernat, J. A., 400
Berns, G. S., 205, 385
Bernstein, D. A., 7, 9, 13, 28, 34, 40, 207, 288, 321, 347, 465, 514, 545, 598, 600, 615, 697
Bernstein, D. M., 326
Berntson, G. G., 662, 665
Berridge, K. C., 387
Berry, J. W., 355
Berry, M. D., 587
Berscheid, E., 672
Bersoff, D. M., 473, 657
Bersoff, D. N., 49, 631
Bertenthal, B. I., 438
Berthoud, H. R., 65
Bessenoff, G. R., 243
Besson, M., 78
Best, D. L., 464
Best, J. B., 226, 232, 234, 248
Bettman, J. R., 285, 289, 290
Beuhring, T., 468
Beutler, L. E., 628
Bevan, S., 134
Beyerstein, B. L., 330
Bhide, A., 567
Bianchi, K., 547
Biblarz, T. J., 402
Bickel, W. K., 336
Bickis, M., 27
Bidell, T., 442
Biederman, I., 167–168, 225, 313
Bierut, L. J., 579, 581
Bigelow, A., 462
Biklen, D., 47
Bilder, R. M., 585
Billing, J., 130
Binet, A., 346, 347, 363
Binzen, C. A., 394
Bishop, D. V. M., 233
Bitterman, M. E., 191
Bjork, R. A., 48, 219, 221, 225, 239–240, 259
Bjorklund, D. F., 259, 384, 447, 449
Björntorp, P., 393
Black, J. E., 86, 254
Black, K., 643
Blackwell, B., 637
Blackwood, N. J., 588
Blagrove, M., 326
Blair-West, G. W., 577
Blake, J., 297
Blake, R., 116, 572

Blakemore, S. J., 56
Blakeslee, S., 82, 84, 466
Blanchard, J., 598
Blascovich, J., 364
Blass, T., 689, 690, 692
Blatchford, P., 363
Blatt, S. J., 581
Blazer, D. G., 576
Blehar, M., 580
Bleuler, E., 583
Block, J., 532
Block, J. A., 479
Block, R. I., 340
Blood, A. J., 205
Bloom, A., 304
Bloom, F. E., 70, 334, 475
Bloom, L., 299
Bluestone, H., 564
Blum, L. N., 596
Blum, R. W., 468
Blumberg, M. S., 320
Blundell, J. E., 391, 393, 394
Bobko, P., 354
Bock, B. C., 512
Bodian, S., 329
Bogartz, R. S., 443
Bogen, J. E., 315
Boggs, W., 204
Bohner, G., 660, 661, 662
Bolger, K. E., 463
Bolles, R. C., 385
Bomze, H. M., 82
Bond, G., 511
Bond, M. H., 22, 685, 692, 713
Bonds, B., 683
Bonicalzi, V., 134
Bonk, V. A., 487
Bonne, M., 496
Bonner, R., 246
Bonwell, C. C., 219
Boomsma, D. I., 596
Boon, M. E., 288
Boor, Sister M. E., 477
Booth, C. B., 479
Booth, P. B., 608
Booth, R. J., 506
Borgeat, F., 637
Borgida, E., 707
Boring, E. G., 163
Borkenau, P., 531
Borkman, D. A., 621
Borkovec, T. C., 628
Borkovec, T. D., 321, 514
Borkowski, J. G., 376
Borman, W. C., 353, 549
Bornstein, R. F., 148, 672
Bosma, H., 498
Boss, P., 497
Bothwell, R. K., 546
Botwinick, J., 5, 371
Bouchard, C., 393
Bouchard, T. J., Jr., 357
Boulton, A. A., 587
Bouton, M., 193
Bovasso, G. B., 640
Bowden, C. L., 636, 637
Bowe-Anders, C., 326

Bower, G. H., 235, 270
Bower, J. E., 499
Bower, N. J. A., 453
Bower, T. G. R., 453
Bowerman, M., 450
Bowlby, J., 455, 523, 581
Bowman, E. S., 579
Bozarth, M. A., 337
Bracken, B. A., 355
Bracken, P., 642–643
Brackfield, S. C., 373
Bradbury, T. N., 33
Bradfield, A. L., 246
Bradley-Johnson, S., 355, 359
Braffman, W., 327
Brainerd, C. J., 251
Brajkovich, G., 672
Brakke, K. E., 302
Brandimonte, M. A., 233
Brandse, E., 251
Brandtstadter, J., 481
Brannigan, C., 706, 707
Branscombe, N. R., 651
Bransford, J. D., 219, 230, 232, 279
Braun, A. E., 326
Bravo, G., 83
Bray, G. A., 394
Breakey, W. R., 583
Breedlove, S. M., 398
Breggin, P. R., 634, 638
Bregman, A. S., 157
Brehm, S., 23, 672, 674
Breiling, J., 590, 591
Breiter, H. C., 205, 385
Brelsford, J. W., 220
Bremner, J. D., 252
Brener, N. D., 578
Brennan, P., 591
Brennan, P. A., 207
Brennen, T., 242
Brenner, L., 389
Brenner, R., 636
Brenner, R. A., 37
Breslin, P. A., 129
Brett, L. P., 194
Breuer, J., 13, 606
Brewer, J. B., 255, 257
Brewer, M. B., 667
Brewer, W. F., 236, 243
Brigha, C. C., 348
Brinckerhoff, L. C., 377
Brislin, R., 559, 573
British Medical Association, 136
Broca, P., 78
Brock, J. W., 325
Brock, T. C., 623
Brody, J. E., 469
Brody, N., 353, 531
Bronstein, P., 469
Brooks-Gunn, J., 360, 361, 452, 462, 469
Brown, A. L., 219, 376
Brown, A. M., 327
Brown, A. S., 242
Brown, B. B., 360, 461, 470
Brown, G. K., 577

Name Index

Brown, G. W., 580–581
Brown, J., 236
Brown, J. D., 488
Brown, P. D., 628
Brown, R., 229, 242, 253, 314, 671
Brown, R. A., 298
Brown, R. J., 667
Brown, S., 617
Brown, S. A., 332
Brown, T., 563
Brownell, H., 476
Brownell, K. D., 393
Browne-Sperling, 509
Bruce, D., 449
Bruce, H. M., 127
Bruce, T. J., 641
Bruck, M., 237
Bruijn, O., 180
Brunet, A., 327
Brüning, J. C., 389
Brunstein, J. C., 549
Brunvald, J. H., 27
Brusaferro, S., 324
Bruyer, R., 316
Bryant, R. A., 328
Bryson, S. E., 594
Buchanan, C. M., 468
Buchanan, R. W., 585, 586
Buck, L. B., 126
Buckner, R. L., 229, 257–258
Budman, S. H., 631
Budney, A. J., 340
Bueman, B., 394
Buffalo, E. A., 237–238
Bugental, D. B., 461
Bui, K.-V., 673
Bukowski, W. M., 462, 463
Bulik, C. M., 394
Bullinger, M., 488
Bullough, V. L., 400
Bülthoff, H. H., 163
Burac, J. A., 595
Burchard, R. E., 392
Burger, J. M., 689
Buriel, R., 461
Burish, T., 514
Burke, H. B., 66
Burke, K. C., 576
Burke, R. S., 596
Burleson, B. R., 499
Burleson, M. H., 398
Burnley, M. C. E., 327
Burnstein, E., 706, 707–709
Burr, D. C., 171
Burr, D. J., 218
Burris, C. T., 651
Burrows, G. D., 329
Burrows, L., 313
Burton, A. M., 169
Busbult, C. E., 673
Bushman, B. J., 215, 216, 217, 697, 700
Bushnell, M. C., 132
Buss, A., 532
Buss, A. H., 384
Buss, D. M., 17, 384, 396, 466, 673, 707

Bustillo, J. R., 588
Buswell, B. N., 419, 671
Butcher, J. N., 545, 546
Butler, M. M., 190
Butler, R., 405, 406
Butterfield, E. C., 376
Buunk, B., 647, 648
Buxhoeveden, D. P., 300, 303
Byne, W., 586
Byrne, D., 672, 675, 713
Byrnes, G., 27
Cabanac, M., 390
Cabeza, R., 253, 258
Cabot, P. J., 135
Cabral, G. A., 341
Cacioppo, J., 663
Cacioppo, J. T., 16, 488, 491, 505, 507, 532, 662, 663, 665, 666
Cadoret, R. J., 598
Cadusch, P. J., 9
Caetano, R., 597
Cahill, L., 94
Cahill, S. P., 613
Cairns, R. B., 695
Calkins, M. W., 16
Calvert, G. A., 111
Camargo, C. A., 398
Campbell, D. T., 39
Campbell, F. A., 340, 362, 452
Campbell, I. G., 325
Campbell, J. P., 410, 537
Campbell, L. A., 568
Campbell, S. B., 364
Campbell, S. M., 33
Campbell, S. S., 580
Campfield, L. A., 389
Campione, J. E., 376
Campos, J. J., 427, 464
Canavero, S., 134
Canli, T., 530
Cann, A., 240
Cannon, T. D., 587
Cannon, W., 418, 421–422, 423
Cannon, W. B., 388
Cannon-Bowers, J. A., 714
Cao, Y., 82
Capaldi, D., 475, 476
Caplan, P. J., 563
Capron, C., 357
Caramazza, A., 79
Cardinal, R. N., 205
Cardon, L. R., 357, A-6
Carli, L. L., 673
Carlo, G. L., 29
Carlsmith, M., 663
Carlson, L., 229
Carlson, N. R., 338, 401
Carlsson, K., 56
Carmelli, D., 482
Carmichael, L. L., 244
Carmody, J., 278
Carmody, T. J., 633
Carnegie Task Force, 218
Carnevale, P. J., 713
Carney, R. M., 492
Carpenter, D., 621
Carpenter, S. J., 666

Carpenter, W. T., Jr., 585, 588
Carper, R. A., 595
Carr, B., 381
Carr, J. E., 220
Carraher, D., 367
Carraher, T. N., 367
Carrasco, M., 175
Carrere, S., 478
Carrigan, M. H., 40, 613
Carrillo, E., 630
Carroll, J. B., 366
Carstensen, L., 481
Carswell, C. M., 173, 268
Cartensen, L. L., 680
Carter, M. M., 568, 570
Carter-Saltzman, L., 356, 357
Cartwright, R. D., 320, 326
Carver, C. S., 522
Caryl, P. G., 366
Casagrande, M., 326
Casas, J. F., 465
Case, L., 32
Casell, E., 9
Caspi, A., 434, 477, 525, 530, 531, 532, 543–545
Cassel, E., 28, 207, 465, 598, 600, 697
Castillo, S. R., 245
Caterina, M. J., 130
Cattell, R. B., 365, 526–527
Cavaiola, A. A., 534
Cavaliere, R., 301
Cavanagh, P., 237
Caviness, V. S., 316
Ceci, S. J., 237, 252, 367
Centers for Disease Control and Prevention, 467, 486, 487, 508, 509, 577, 578
Centerwall, L., 216
Cerf, C., 286
Cermak, L. S., 257
Cernich, J. M., 128
Cerqueira, J., 702
Cervone, D., 532
Cha, J. H., 89
Chabris, C. F., 177
Chaiken, A., 363
Chaiken, S., 660
Chakrabarti, S., 594
Chamberlin, J., 498
Chambless, D. L., 614, 624, 626, 627
Champion, V., 511
Chan, S. F., 304
Chance, P., 204
Chance, S. E., 696
Chapman, P. F., 74
Chapman, S., 27
Charleton, T., 217
Charness, N., 221, 372
Charney, D., 568
Chase, T. N., 88
Chase-Lansdale, L., 469
Chase-Lansdale, P. L., 469
Chastain, G., 259
Chattarji, S., 254
Check, J. V. P., 699

Chee, K. T., 559
Cheltenham, M. P., 578
Chemers, M. M., 715
Chen, D., 531
Chen, M., 6, 313, 670
Chen, M. S., 82
Chen, X., 687
Cheney, D. L., 301
Cheng, Y., 498
Cherkin, D. C., 136
Cherry, C., 509
Chess, S., 454
Cheung, F., 564
Chi, M. T. H., 285
Chiang, C., 70
Chiang, W.-C., 443–444
Chiba, A. A., 255, 257
Chih-Mei, C., 406
Childs, C. P., 454
Chisholm, K., 456
Chiu, C., 210, 542
Chiu, C.-Y. P., 227, 251
Cho, Z. H., 69, 135
Chodzko-Zajko, W., 476
Chomsky, N., 293–294, 299–300
Choo, K. L., 321
Chorney, M. L., 358
Christensen, K. A., 498
Christie, M. A., 220
Chugani, H. T., 85
Church, B., 229
Chwalisz, K., 420
Cialdini, R. B., 276, 471, 494, 651, 680, 681, 684, 686, 687–688, 703, 706
Ciapparelli, A., 633
Cicchetti, D., 466
Ciccocioppo, R., 205
Cintron, C. M. B., 587
Cirincione, C., 600
Clancy, S. A., 251, 252, 253
Clapham, K., 617
Clark, C. L., 523
Clark, D., 569
Clark, D. C., 577, 578
Clark, D. M., 536, 570
Clark, D. N., 676
Clark, E. V., 298
Clark, F., 482
Clark, L. A., 561, 563, 568
Clark, M. S., 651, 672
Clarke, M., 476
Clarke-Stewart, K. A., 458
Clarkin, J. F., 621
Clausen, J., 320
Clay, R., 107, 480
Clay, R. A., 604, 630
Cleary, P., 660
Clementz, B. A., 586
Clendenen, V. I., 392
Clifton, R. K., 437, 442, 449
Clines, F. X., 180
Clingempeel, W. G., 461
Clinton, B., 35–36
Cloninger, C. R., 530
Clower, C. E., 546
Cnattingius, S., 336

CNN/Time, 554
Coady, B., 329
Coatsworth, J. D., 466
Coccaro, E. F., 696
Cocking, R. R., 219
Cohen, C. E., 652
Cohen, D., 697
Cohen, G. J., 269
Cohen, J., 47, 587
Cohen, M. S., 290
Cohen, N., 96
Cohen, N. J., 256, 317
Cohen, O., 657
Cohen, S., 505
Colby, A., 473
Colder, M., 506
Cole, K. N., 476
Cole, R. A., 295
Coleman, D., 324
Coles, D., 217
Coles, M. G. H., 268, 269
Collacott, E. A., 40
College Board, 361
Collins, A. M., 241
Collins, G., 508
Collins, J. G., 229
Collins, W. A., 462
Colombo, M., 257
Coltrane, S., 479
Colwill, R. M., 195
Compagnone, N. A., 94
Compas, B. E., 626
Comstock, G., 216
Condic, M. L., 82
Condon, J. W., 672
Conel, J. L., 85
Conger, R., 467
Conley, R. R., 635
Conner, A., 3, 8
Conner, C., 707
Connor, L. T., 242
Conrad, R., 234
Consumer Reports, 623
Conte, H. R., 385
Contrada, R. J., 490
Cook, T., 215, 571
Cook, T. D., 39
Cooke, D. J., 277, 289
Cookson, J., 636
Cooley, T., 225
Cooling, J., 393
Cooper, C., 668
Cooper, H., 363
Cooper, J., 664
Cooper, L. A., 313
Cooper, M. L., 313, 495, 596
Cooper, R. M., 50
Coovert, M. D., 653
Copeland, J., 654–655
Coppola, M., 299
Corbetta, M., 178
Corbit, J. D., 411
Coren, S., 201
Cork, R. C., 312
Corkin, S., 256
Cornblatt, B., 588
Cornelius, R. R., 422, 423

Corning, A. F., 648
Cornoldi, C., 234
Corruble, E., 578
Corsini, R. J., 611
Corwin, R. L., 389
Coryell, W., 576
Costa, P., 549
Costa, P. T., Jr., 527, 546
Costello, E., 628
Costermans, J., 242
Cotter, D., 579
Cotton, R., 245, 246
Courchesne, E., 595
Courneya, K. S., 512
Cowan, N., 231, 238
Cowey, A., 167
Coyle, J. T., 587
Coyne, J. C., 581
Cozzarelli, C., 534
Crabbe, J. C., 52, 532, A-5, A-6
Craig, A. D., 132, 134
Craig, K. J., 494
Craiger, J. P., 385, 683
Craik, F. I. M., 225, 229, 230, 475
Craik, K. H., 15, 525
Cramer, E. P., 403
Crandell, C., 707–709
Crandall, C. S., 489
Crano, W. D., 672, 687
Crawford, H. J., 327
Crawford, J., 301
Crawford, J. G., 92
Crawley, J. N., 389
Criak, K. H., 18
Crick, F., 309, 310–311
Crick, N. R., 463, 465
Critchley, E. M., 415
Crites, S. L., 662, 666
Crits-Christoph, P., 5, 524, 609, 623, 626, 627, 628
Crnic, K., 457
Crocker, J., 280–281, 648
Croen, L. A., 376
Croft, H., 636
Cronbach, L. J., 350
Crosby, A. E., 578
Cross, A. J., 337
Cross, J. V., 616
Cross, P. A., 327
Cross, S. E., 21, 434, 533, 542, 543
Cross-National Collaborative Group, 576
Crowley, K., 363
Crowther, J. H., 395
Cruz, A., 130
Crystal, D. S., 451
Csikszentmihalyi, M., 5, 374, 408, 409
Culbertson, F. M., 576
Culbertson, J. L., 436
Cumsille, P. E., 332
Curcio, C. A., 114
Curran, H. V., 338
Curry, M. B., 180
Cusack, K., 40
Cuthbert, B. N., 590
Cutler, W. B., 128

Czeisler, C. A., 323
Da Vinci, L., 377
Dabbs, J., 696
Dabbs, M. G., 696
Dadds, M. R., 623, 643
Dafilis, M. P., 9
D'Agostino, R. B., Jr., 487
Daher, M., 437
Dale, P. S., 298
Dallenbach, K., 249
Dalton, J., 125
Daly, G., 594
Daly, M., 465
Damasio, A., 265, 267
Damasio, A. R., 414, 419
Damon, W., 470
Damos, D., 177
Damy, C., 578
D'Andrade, R., 405
Danton, W. G., 640
Dark, V. J., 375
Darkes, J., 332, 333, 334
Darwin, C., 13, 14, 17, 31, 185, 519, 706–707, A-3
Dasgupta, A. M., 328
Daval, J. L., 336
Davanloo, H., 608
David, A. S., 572
Davidson, J., 620
Davidson, J. K., 403
Davidson, J. M., 398
Davidson, J. R. T., 637
Davidson, J. W., 221
Davidson, K., 507, 508, 660
Davidson, R. J., 82, 414, 415, 420, 425, 426
Davidson-Podgorny, G., 668
Davies, C., 493
Davies, R. J., 322
Davine, P. G., 663
Davis, H. S., 312
Davis, J. A., 389, 397
Davis, J. L., 66, 672
Davis, K. D., 133
Davis, K. L., 587
Davis, L., 252
Davis, M., 414
Davis, M. H., 530, 705
Davis, M. K., 625, 628
Davis, R. A., 247
Davis, R. D., 589
Davison, G. C., 536, 576, 625
Davison, P. R., 40
Dawe, L. A., 110
Dawes, R. M., 288, 289, 290, 623, 626, 710, 712
Dawkins, K., 639
Dawson, D. A., 89
Dawson, M., 650
Dawson-Basoa, M., 135
De Boysson-Bardies, B., 297
De Castro, J. M., 392, 394
De Charms, R., 623
De Cocteau, N. J., 668
De Haan, E. H. F., 316
De La Ronde, C., 676
De Lacoste-Utamsing, C., 81

De Rios, M. D., 318
De Rubeis, R. J., 628
De Silva, P., 403
De Souza, E. B., 337
Dean, L., 505
Dean, W., 90, 91
DeAngelis, T., 7, 496, 561
Deary, I. J., 366, 374, 506
Death Penalty Information Center, 246
Deaux, K., 650, 658
DeBell, C., 631
DeBenedittis, G., 490
DeBeni, R., 234
DeBeurs, R. J., 641
Debry, G., 336
Deci, E. L., 374
Deffond, D., 140
DeHouwer, A., 300
Del Boca, F. K., 332, 333, 334
Delmolino, L. M., 47
Delrio, M. C., 333
DelVecchio, W. F., 525, 544
Dembo, M. H., 406
Dement, W. C., 320, 321, 325, 326
Demo, D. H., 471, 478
DeNelsky, G. Y., 640
DeNeve, K. M., 527
DeNisi, A., 408
Denmark, F., 32
Denton, G., 144
Denton, K., 474
Derogowski, J. B., 165
Derryberry, D., 421
DeRubeis, R. J., 5, 623, 625, 626, 627, 640
Descartes, R., 11, 310
Deschaumes, M. C., 385
Deschepper, B., 177
DeSimone, J. A., 128
Desordi, E. G., 534
D'Esposito, M., 257
Dess, N. K., 373, 374
Destexhe, A., 325
Deutsch, G., 80, 91
Deutsch, M., 685
Devine, P., 671
Devine, P. G., 229, 664, 669
Devinsky, O., 310
Devor, E. J., 597
DeVries, R., 445
DeWitt, L. A., 169
DeWolff, M. S., 457
Dhurandhar, N. V., 393
Di Chiara, G., 340
Di Marzo, V., 391
Diamond, M., 400, 401
Diana, Princess of Wales, 257
Dickinson, A., 205, 209, 387
DiClemente, C. C., 511, 512
DiClemente, R. J., 399, 511
Didier, A., 60
Diehl, N. S., 586
Diener, C., 409
Diener, E., 408, 409, 420, 527
Diforio, D., 588
Dill, K. E., 215

Dimberg, U., 571
Dimen, K. R., 340
Dinan, T. G., 580
Dinnel, D. L., 351
Dion, K. L., 666, 671
DiPietro, J. A., 478
Dittmar, A., 415
Ditton, P. M., 642
Dixon, J. B., 322
Dixon, M., 327
Dobkin-de-Rios, M., 318
Dodds, J. B., 433
Dodson, C., 246
Dohrenwend, B. P., 490
Dolan, A., 449
Dolan, S. L., 623, 625, 628
Dollard, J. J., 698
Dollinger, S. J., 534
Domhoff, G. W., 326
Donegan, N. H., 257
Donezio, J., 237
Donnerstein, E., 215, 217, 699, 700
Donoghue, J. P., 254
Donohew, R. L., 385
Dordain, G., 140
Dordova, J. V., 623
Dormehl, I. C., 91
Dornbusch, S. M., 360, 461, 470
Dougell, A. L., 494
Douglas, M., 385
Doussard, R. J. A., 416
Douthitt, E. A., 682, 683
Dove Pettit, D. A., 341
Dovidio, J. F., 314, 499, 667, 669, 670, 671, 703, 704, 706
Dow, R. S., 70
Downey, D. B., 359
Downey-Lamb, M. M., 195
Dowson, D. I., 135
Dozier, C. L., 220
Drabman, R. S., 616
Draine, S. C., 148
Drayna, D., 110
Dreary, I. J., 531
Dresner, R., 478
Drew, L. M., 480
Dreyfus, H. L., 287
Dreyfus, S. E., 287
Drucker, D. B., 392
Druckman, D., 221
Drummond, S. P., 324, 325
DuBois, D. L., 468
DuBreuil, S. C., 252
Duckitt, J. H., 666
Duclos, S. E., 419
Dudgeon, P., 586
Duffett, R., 636
Duffy, V. B., 129
Dufresne, R., 285
Dujovne, V., 507
Duke, C. R., 229
Dumas, L. S., 576
Duncan, B. L., 625
Duncan, G. J., 360, 452
Duncan, J., 269
Dunn, J., 462, 463, A-7

Dunn, N. R., 91
Dunne, E., 621
Dunne, M. P., 401, 403
Dunning, D., 664, 665
Duran, R. E. F., 510
Durel, L., 507
Durik, A. M., 399
Duyme, M., 357
Dweck, C. S., 210, 404, 406
Dwight, S. A., 518
Dwyer, J., 246
Düzel, E., 317
Eacott, M. J., 450
Eagly, A. H., 464, 501, 660, 674, 687, 714
East, P. L., 469
Easton, M. J., 406
Eaton, W. W., 640
Ebbinghaus, H., 12, 247, 248
Eber, H. W., 527
Eberts, R., 163
Eccles, J. S., 406, 468
Echeburua, E., 640
Eckholm, E., 554
Edelstein, S. L., 322
Edenberg, H., 597
Edgerton, R. B., 332, 333
Edinger, J. D., 320
Edison, T., 377
Edwards, A. E., 194
Egeland, B., 457
Egeland, J. A., 579
Ehlers, A., 568
Ehrlichman, H., 240, 353, 531
Eich, E., 240
Eich, J. E., 240
Eichelman, B., 696
Eichenbaum, H., 317
Eichhorn, D. H., 475
Einhorn, H., 191
Einhorn, H. J., 278
Eisenberg, N., 461, 463, 464, 532, 688
Eisenman, R., 399
Eison, J. A., 219
Ekman, P., 419, 420, 425, 426, 427
Elashoff, J. D., 363
Elder, G. H., 467
Eldridge, L. L., 258
Eliot, A. J., 543, 663
Eliot, G. F., 286
Elkin, I., 625, 628, 641
Elliot, A. J., 664
Elliott, C. L., 229
Ellis, A., 513, 618
Ellis, A. L., 400
Ellis, N. R., 236
Ellsworth, P., 427
Elwood, G., 272
EMDR Institute, 26
Emery, C. E., Jr., 27
Emery, G., 569
Emmelkamp, P. M., 495
Emmons, M. L., 615
Emre, M., 92
Ende, G., 633
Engdahl, B., 495

Engebretson, T. O., 507
Engel, A. K., 118
Engel, B. A., 66
Engel, S., 124
Engeland, H. V., 641
Engen, T., 127
Engle, R. W., 233
Enright, R. D., 473
Epping-Jordan, M. P., 336
Epstein, L. H., 391, 628
Erdberg, P., 549
Erdelyi, M. H., 251
Ericsson, K. A., 14, 221, 235
Erikson, E., 459, 460, 470–471, 478, 479–480, 481, 523, 542
Eriksson, P. S., 82, 84
Erlenmeyer-Kimling, L. E., 588, A-3
Ernst, E., 136, 636
Ernst, M., 336
Eron, L. D., 215, 216, 700
Eskenazi, B., 336
Eskenazi, J., 149
Esser, J. K., 715
Essock, E. A., 180
Esteves, F., 425
Eth, S., 496
Etienne, M. A., 415
Ettinger, R. H., 193, 571
Evans, D. A., 92
Evans, D. E., 454
Evans, D. R., 510
Evans, F. J., 328
Evans, G., 500
Evans, G. W., 488, 558
Evans, I. M., 613
Evans, J. St. B. T., 276
Everaerd, W., 403
Everett, S. A., 399
Everitt, B. J., 332
Exner, J. E., Jr., 549
Exton, M. S., 96
Exum, M. E., 221
Eysenck, H. J., 366, 528–529, 530, 623, 625
Eysenck, M. W., 233
Fabes, R. A., 461, 464, 465, 532
Faedda, G., 580
Fagan, J. F., 354
Fagot, B. I., 452, 457, 465
Fahrenberg, J., 692
Fain, C., 246
Fairburn, C. G., 536
Fairweather, G. W., 615
False Memory Syndrome Foundation, 252
Farah, M. J., 273
Faraone, S. V., 586, 588, A-6
Farberman, R., 626
Farley, F., 385
Farmer-Dougan, V. A., 204
Farooqi, I. S., 389
Fassler, D. G., 576
Faust, J., 615
Fawcett, J., 577, 578
Fay, D., 298
Faymonville, M. E., 329
Fazio, R. H., 661

Fechner, G., 11, 153
Federal Interagency Forum on Children and Family Statistics, 467
Feeley, M., 625
Feild, H. S., 518
Fein, G. G., 458
Fein, S., 23, 672, 674
Feinberg, L., 325
Feingold, P., 394
Feist, G., 522, 523, 524, 537, 538
Feist, J., 522, 523, 524, 537, 538
Feldman, R. P., 634
Felleman, D. J., 116
Felten, D., 96
Felten, D. L., 505
Felten, S. Y., 96
Feltovitch, P. J., 285
Fendrich, R., 312
Feng-Chen, K. C., 82
Fenson, L., 297
Fenton, W. S., 584, 585
Fergus, E. O., 615
Ferguson, D. L., 470
Ferguson, M. J., 524
Fergusson, D. M., 341, 358
Fernandes, C., 91
Fernández-Dols, J.-M., 426
Ferrara, R. A., 376, 393
Feshbach, N., 215
Feske, V., 40
Festinger, L., 647–648, 663
Field, A. E., 393
Field, T., 132
Fields, H. L., 134
File, S. E., 91
Filipek, P. A., 594
Fillmore, K. M., 597
Fillon, D. L., 650
Fincham, F. D., 33
Fine, M. A., 478
Finer, N., 394
Fink, M., 633, 634
Finkelstein, M. A., 705
Finney, J. W., 621
Fiore, J. P., 260
Fiorentini, A., 171
Firestein, S., 126
Fischer, K. W., 439, 442
Fischer, P. J., 583
Fischoff, B., 285, 290
Fishbein, M., 660
Fisher, I., 286
Fisher, J. D., 511
Fisher, J. R., 687
Fisher, W. A., 511
Fishman, H., 621
Fiske, A. P., 21, 22, 201
Fiske, S. T., 470, 652, 654, 658, 666, 667, 669, 670
Fitzgerald, M. B., 110
Fitzgerald, T. E., 501
Fitzpatrick, A. C., 621
Fitzpatrick, D. C., 110
Fivush, R., 449
Flavell, J. E., 206
Flavell, J. H., 434

Fletcher, B., 513
Flier, J. S., 389
Flint, J., A-6
Florio, C. M., 549
Fluck, E., 91
Flynn, J. T., 358, 359
Foa, E. B., 495, 496, 563, 568, 569, 640
Fodor, J. A., 270
Folk, C. L., 175
Folkman, S., 493, 497, 498, 499, 501, 513
Follette, V. M., 252, 495
Fombonne, E., 594
Fontana, L., 91
Foote, S. L., 70
Forbes, D., 322
Forbes, S., 389
Ford, L. H., 470
Foreyt, J. P., 394
Forgatch, M. S., 643
Foroud, T., 597
Forrest, J. C., 66
Fosse, R., 326
Foster, M. D., 499
Foulke, E., 131
Foulkes, D., 326
Fountain, D., 596
Fountain, J. W., 557
Foushee, H. C., 692
Fowkes, F. G. R., 506
Fowler, R. D., 513
Fowles, D., 588
Fox, A. S., 389
Fox, N., 464
Fox, P. T., 71
Foxhall, K., 10, 247, 628, 631
Fozard, J., 474
Fraenkel, P., 40
France, C. R., 134, 487
Francis, E. L., 581
Frank, D. A., 436
Frank, J. B., 604
Frank, J. D., 604
Frank, M. G., 325, 426
Frankenberg, W. K., 433
Franklin, G., 250, 252
Franklin-Lipsker, E., 250
Franks, J. J., 230
Fraser, S. C., 687
Frazier, P., 495
Fredrickson, N., 581
Freed, C. R., 83
Freedland, R. L., 438
Freedman, D. G., 454
Freedman, J. L., 217, 687
Freedman, V. A., 476
Freeman, W., 634
Freeston, M. H., 637
Fremgen, A., 298
Freud, A., 519, 608
Freud, S., 12–13, 15, 18, 31, 34, 310, 312, 313, 326, 519–525, 540, 558, 606–607, 695
Frey, J., 702
Frey, P. L., 670
Fride, E., 338

Fridhandler, B., 524
Fridlund, A., 426
Fried, I., 415
Fried, P. A., 341
Friedland, N., 494
Friedman, D., 254
Friedman, E., 569
Friedman, H., 502–503
Friedman, H. S., 466, 479, 482
Friedman, M., 506
Friedman, M. A., 393
Friedmann, E., 128
Friesen, W. V., 419, 426, 427
Frijda, N. H., 426
Frith, C. D., 586
Fritzler, B. K., 617
Fromkin, V., 293
Fromm, E., 523
Frongillo, E. A., Jr., 361
Fujita, F., 409
Fulker, D. W., 357
Fuller, J. L., A-3
Fuller, S. R., 716
Funder, D., 518, 525, 527, 531, 532, 533, 535, 537, 541, 658
Funtowicz, M. N., 565
Furedy, J. J., 420
Furey, M. L., 255
Furnham, A., 549
Furstenberg, F. F., 469
Fuson, K. C., 450
Gabbard, G. O., 520, 522, 523, 524, 609
Gabrieli, J. D. E., 229, 257
Gaertner, S. L., 667, 670
Galanter, 146
Galatzer-Levy, R. M., 624
Galef, B. G., 391
Gallagher, D., 420
Gallagher, J. J., 374
Gallagher, M., 255, 257, 457
Gallopin, T., 324
Galotti, K. M., 273, 280
Galton, F., A-3
Games, D., 74
Ganchrow, J. R., 437
Gangestad, S. W., 384
Ganley, R., 673
Gara, M. A., 581
Garb, H. N., 548, 549, 564, 565
Garber, R. J., 466
Garcia, J., 193, 194
Garczynski, J., 683
Gardner, A., 301
Gardner, B. T., 301, 302
Gardner, C. O., 582
Gardner, H., 369–370
Gardner, R., 220
Gardner, R. A., 302
Gardner, W. L., 666
Garfield, S. L., 628
Gariepy, J., 695
Garland, A. F., 577, 643, 680
Garris, P. A., 332
Garry, M., 252, 329
Garske, J. P., 625, 628
Gaster, B., 636

Gatchel, R. J., 488
Gatewood, R. D., 518
Gatiss, J., 282–283
Gauvain, M., 450, 452
Gawande, A., 134, 286
Gazzaniga, M. S., 79, 80, 312
Ge, X., 467
Geary, D. C., 17, 383, 465
Geary, J., 90
Geen, R. G., 216, 683, 695, 697, 698, 702
Geiselman, R. E., 246
Gelfand, L. A., 625
Gelfand, M. M., 398
Gellhorn, E., 417
Gelman, R., 447
Gemar, M., 640
Genovese, K., 704
George, M. S., 332
Geppetti, P., 134
Gerard, H. B., 685
Gergin, A. E., 625
Gerin, W., 500
Gerken, L., 296
Gerschman, J. A., 329
Gershon, S., 569
Geschwind, N., 78
Gesell, A., 433
Gessner, B. D., 322
Gfeller, J. D., 327
Ghoneim, M., 340
Giannini, J. A., 312
Gibbon, J., 70
Gibbs, J. C., 473
Gibson, E., 322
Gibson, E. J., 172
Gibson, J. J., 146, 179
Gifford, R., 710, 712, 713
Gigerenzer, G., 277
Gilbert, A. R., 586
Gilbert, C. D., 118
Gilbert, D. T., 409, 657, 658, 659
Gilbert, R. M., 330
Gilbert, S., 206
Gilboa-Schechtman, E., 495
Giles, T. R., 624, 625
Gillette, M. U., 323
Gilligan, C., 472, 473
Gilliland, F. D., 436
Gilmore, M. M., 127, 152
Gilovich, T., 289
Gintzler, A. R., 135
Giordano, C., 648
Givens, B., 334
Gladstone, G., 559
Gladue, B. A., 401
Glanz, J., 138
Glanzer, M., 239
Glaser, R., 285, 505, 506, 514
Glass, G. V., 624, 625, 628
Gleaves, D. H., 574
Gleitman, L., 298
Glenberg, A. M., 239–240
Glenmullen, J., 639
Gleuckauf, R., 615
Glick, J., 450
Glick, P. T., 670

Glod, M., 217
Glover, J. A., 259
Goddard, H., 347
Goehring, P., 514
Goenjian, A. K., 495
Goetsch, V. L., 616
Goff, D. C., 587
Gold, M. S., 338
Gold, P. E., 173
Goldberg, J., 495
Goldberg, J. F., 578
Goldblum, N., 218
Golden, A., 433
Goldenberg, H., 621
Goldenberg, I., 621
Goldfarb, R., 373
Goldfried, M. R., 536, 618
Goldman, M. S., 332, 333, 334
Goldman, R., 663
Goldman, R. S., 585
Goldman-Rakic, P. S., 256, 257
Goldstein, A., 632
Goldstein, A. J., 40, 46
Goldstein, E. B., 107, 172, 173
Goldstein, G., 586
Goldstein, K., 369, 538
Goldstein, S. J., 394
Goleman, D., 464
Golomb, J., 72
Golombok, S., 402
Gonsalves, B., 258
Goode, K. T., 496
Goodenough, F. L., 425
Goodman, P., 612
Goodnow, J. J., 461, 703
Goodrich, J. T., 634
Goodstein, L. D., 352
Goodwin, F. K., 580
Goodwin, G. M., 337
Goodyer, I. M., 582
Gordon, B., 633, 636, 637
Gordon, S. E., 261, 266, 267
Gorman, B. J., 48
Gorman, J. M., 569
Gorski, R. A., 401
Gorton, G. E., 631
Gosling, S. D., 15, 18, 525, 528
Gotlib, I. H., 581
Gottesman, I. I., 586
Gottfredson, L. S., 353
Gottfried, A. W., 452, 454
Gottlieb, G., 50
Gottman, J. M., 478, 676
Gotzsche, P. C., 40
Gould, E., 84
Gould, S. J., 348
Grady, D., 469
Graham, D. P., 355, 359
Graham, J. W., 332
Graham, K., 696
Graham, S., 21
Grandin, T., 595
Granrud, C. D., 173
Grassi, L., 499
Gray, J. A., 529–530, 531, 532
Gray, R., 341
Gray-Little, B., 32

Grayson, C., 558
Greaves, D. W., 604
Green, A. I., 635
Green, B. G., 130
Green, B. L., 259, 581
Green, C., 251
Green, D. M., 150
Green, J. T., 194–195
Green, M., 145
Green, M. C., 623
Green, R. A., 337
Greenberg, J., 649–650
Greenberg, L. S., 613
Greenberg, M. T., 643
Greenblatt, D., 637
Greene, E., 278
Greene, G. W., 512
Greene, R. L., 229
Greenfield, P. M., 452, 454, 459, 460, 465
Greenough, W. T., 85, 86, 254, 452
Greenwald, A. G., 148, 149, 229, 313
Greenwald, J., 90
Greenwald, R., 26
Greer, A. E., 396
Gregg, V., 473
Gregory, W. L., 398
Grether, J. K., 376
Gribben, K., 354
Griffith, J., 225
Griffith-Barwell, P., 256
Griffitt, W. B., 672
Gringlas, M., 478
Grinspoon, L., 341
Grinspoon, S., 394
Grisso, T., 600
Grob, C., 318
Grolnick, W. S., 478
Groninger, L., 258
Groopman, J., 284
Gross, J. J., 251, 413
Grossberg, S., 171
Grossi, T. A., 220
Grossman, B. S., 373, 374
Grossman, L. S., 578
Grosz, H. I., 572
Grote, N. K., 676
Grotevant, H. D., 471
Groth-Marnat, G., 545, 547
Grove, W. M., 549
Grube, B. S., 585
Gruder, C. L., 705
Grunberg, N. E., 332
Grusec, J. E., 703
Guadagno, R. E., 688
Guay, P., 672
Guelfi, J. D., 578
Guerin, D. W., 454
Guerlain, S., 288
Guevara, M. A., 318
Guilford, J. P., 373
Guilleminault, C., 321
Gunnar, M. R., 456
Gunnoe, M. L., 206
Gunter, B., 217
Guntheroth, W. G., 322

Gur, R. C., 81, 415
Gur, R. E., 415, 586, 587
Gura, T., 389
Gurung, R. A. R., 499
Guski, R., 497
Gustavson, C. R., 194
Gutman, D., 177
Guyer, B., 487
Guynn, M. J., 229
Ha, H., 136
Haaga, D. A., 621
Haber, R. N., 237, 238
Haberlandt, K., 248
Haberstroh, J., 148
Hackel, L. S., 676
Hackett, T., 109
Hacking, I., 574
Hackman, J. R., 292
Hackman, R., 330
Haddock, G., 667
Haden, C., 449
Hadley, S. W., 624
Hafdahl, A. R., 32
Hafner, H., 680
Hagan, E., 349
Hagell, P., 83
Hagen, M. A., 48
Hahdahl, K., 415
Hahn, C.-S., 478
Haig, B., 354
Halberstadt, J., 672
Haldeman, D. C., 400
Halford, G. S., 447
Halford, J. C., 394
Halford, J. C. G., 391
Hall, C. C. I., 32
Hall, C. S., 410, 537
Hall, G., 13, 192
Hall, G. C. N., 630
Hall, J. A., 425
Hall, L. K., 237, 247
Hall, P., 507, 508
Hall, W., 339
Hall, W. G., 391
Halligan, P. W., 572
Halperin, D., 91
Halpern, D. F., 464, 466
Halpern, J. N., 240
Halverson, C. F., Jr., 531
Hameroff, S. R., 312
Hamilton, C. E., 457
Hamilton, D. L., 668
Hamilton, M., 204
Hamilton, W. D., 707
Hamm, A. O., 571
Hammen, C. L., 581
Hammer, E., 548
Hammill, D. D., 377
Hammond, W. R., 629
Han, S., 23
Hancock, E., 498
Haney, M., 340
Hankin, B. L., 581, 582
Hannah, M. T., 623
Hannigan, S. L., 237
Hansen, T., 702
Hanson, G., 333

Hanson, M. A., 353, 549
Hanson, S. J., 218
Happe, F. G. E., 476
Harackiewicz, J. M., 405
Harasty, J., 81
Hardimann, P. T., 285
Hare, R. D., 590
Harkins, S., 683
Harlow, H. F., 213, 455–456
Harmatz, J., 637
Harmon-Jones, E., 663
Harper, D. G., 323
Harper, R. C., 322
Harrington, N. G., 385
Harris, C. S., 170
Harris, C. V., 616
Harris, G. C., 332
Harris, H., 337
Harris, J. R., 461, 531, A-8
Harris, M. S., 604
Harrow, M., 578
Hart, A. J., 666
Hart, D., 470, 471
Harter, S., 468
Hartmann, H., 608
Hartung, C. M., 564
Hartuup, W. W., 462
Harvard Mental Health Letter, 336, 636
Harwood, H., 596
Harwood, R. L., 460
Hasher, L., 229
Haskell, I., 179
Hassan, S. S., 578
Hastie, R., 291
Hatfield, E., 674
Hathaway, S., 546–547
Hattie, J., 354
Hattori, M., 375
Haugen, J. A., 655
Hauptman, J., 394
Hausser, M., 59
Hawkins, H. L., 475, 476
Haxby, J. V., 167, 255
Hayes, A. M., 604
Hayes, S., 524
Hayman, C. A. G., 256
Haymsfield, S. B., 389
Hays, P. A., 629
Hays, W. L., 45
Hazlette-Stevens, H., 321, 514
He, L. F., 136
Healy, D. J., 587
Hearst, E., 199
Hebb, D. O., 253, 254, 255, 385
Hecker, J. E., 617
Hedge, A., 706
Hedge, J. W., 353
Heenan, T. A., 426
Hefferline, R. F., 612
Hegarty, J. D., 583
Hegel, M. T., 641
Heider, E., 304
Heim, C., 495
Heiman, R. J., 291
Heine, S., 541
Heine, S. J., 664

Hejmadi, A., 425, 426
Helgesen, S., 481
Heller, N. R., 604
Heller, W., 82, 415
Hellström, K., 615, 617
Helmers, K. F., 506, 507
Helms, J. E., 354
Helson, R., 479
Helzer, J. E., 558
Hencke, R. W., 439
Henderson, B., 286
Hendrick, C., 674
Hendrick, S., 674
Henker, B., 593
Hennessey, B. A., 373, 374
Henrick, S., 674
Henry, W. P., 628
Hense, R. L., 314, 670–671
Hepburn, M. A., 215
Herbert, J. D., 28, 31, 40
Herbert, T. B., 505
Hergenhahn, B. R., 204, 217, 254
Hering, F., 123, 124
Herman, C. P., 392, 393
Herman, L. M., 302
Hermann, J. H., 326
Hernandez, D. J., 478
Herpertz, S. C., 591
Herrmann, D. J., 258, 259
Herrnstein, R. J., 354, 358, A-3, A-4
Hertsgaard, L., 456
Hertz, H., 104
Herzog, D. B., 394, 395
Hespos, S. J., 442
Hess, R. D., 406
Hesse, J., 136
Hetherington, E. M., 461, 466, 479
Hettema, J. M., 569
Heuper, W. C., 286
Heward, W. L., 219, 220
Heyman, R. E., 695
Hezlett, S. A., 350
Hickok, G., 91
Higginbotham, H. N., 629
Higgins, E. T., 652
Higgins, S. T., 336
Hilgard, E. L., 327, 328
Hilgard, E. P., 329
Hilgard, E. R., 194, 317, 327
Hill, C. E., 624
Hill, C. T., 673, 676
Hill, D. L., 128, 129
Hill, J. O., 388, 393
Hill, P. C., 499
Hill, S. M., 616
Hill, T., 652
Hilliard, R. B., 628
Hillis, A. E., 79
Hillyard, S. A., 125
Hilton, H., 258
Hinckley, J., Jr., 599, 600
Hine, D., 710, 712, 713
Hinshaw, S. P., 461
Hinsz, V. B., 292
Hinton, J., 481
Hintzman, D., 217, 218

Hippocrates, 525, 556, 632
Hiroto, D., 209–210
Hirsch, J., 393
Hirsch-Pasek, K., 299
Hirschfeld, J. A., 322
Hirschfeld, R. M., 637
Hitch, G. J., 233
Hitler, A., A-3
Hittner, J. B., 534
Hixon, J. G., 676
Ho, D. Y., 542
Ho, H., 366
Hobson, J. A., 325, 326
Hochhalter, A., 208
Hodges, L. F., 614
Hoeger, R., 497
Hoepfner, R., 373
Hoffert, M. J., 134
Hoffman, D., 285
Hoffman, H. G., 685
Hoffman, J., 593
Hoffman, R. E., 587
Hofman, M. A., 401
Hofmann, A., 338
Hogan, H. P., 244
Hogan, R. J., 518
Hogarth, R., 191
Hogarth, R. M., 278
Hogarth, W., 557
Hoglinger, G. U., 83
Hohmann, G. W., 420
Holahan, C. J., 499, 702
Holahan, C. K., 481
Holcomb, L., 74
Holden, C., 456, 598
Hollis, K. A., 190
Hollon, S. D., 624, 626
Holloway, R. L., 81
Holman, B. R., 335
Holmes, D. S., 330, 572
Holmes, T., 489
Holroyd, J., 636
Holt, C. L., 512
Holt-Lunstad, J., 500
Holway, A. H., 163
Hommer, D. W., 596
Hong, Y., 210, 300
Honts, C. R., 420
Honzik, C. H., 211
Hood, K. E., 695
Hood, M. Y., 393
Hooker, E., 400
Hooper, J. E., 132
Hopf, H. C., 414
Hopf, N. J., 414
Hopmeyer, A., 463
Hopper, K., 558, 559
Hoptman, M. J., 82
Horgan, J., 607
Horn, J. L., 371
Horne, J. A., 319
Horney, K., 523, 524
Horowitz, L. M., 478
Horowitz, S. W., 420
Horowitz, T. S., 175
Horrobin, J., 376
Horuath, D., 478

Horwitz, P., 220
Horwood, L. J., 341, 358
Houpt, T. R., 388
House, J. S., 499
Houston, B. K., 507, 508
Howard, D. V., 234
Howard-Pitney, B., 577
Howe, M. J. A., 221
Hoyert, D. L., 577
Hoyle, R. H., 653
Hoyt, M. F., 609
Hrobjartsson, A., 40
Hser, Y. I., 337
Hsiao, K., 74
Hu, F. B., 506
Hu, S., 400
Huang, L., 389
Hubbard, E. M., 125, 126
Hubble, M. A., 625
Hubel, D. H., 118, 119, 166
Huckabee, J. C., 490
Hudson, J. A., 449
Hudson, J. I., 251, 696
Hudson, W., 165
Hudspeth, A. J., 108
Huesmann, L. R., 215, 216, 217, 697
Hughes, C., 462
Hughes, J. R., 336
Hughes, J. W., 507
Hull, C. L., 385
Hulse, S. H., 105
Hulsizer, M. R., 696
Hume, D., 11
Humphreys, L. G., 356, 359
Hunsley, J., 627
Hunt, C. B., 366
Hunt, D. M., 125
Hunt, E., 366
Hunt, E. B., 465
Hunt, M., 48, 225
Hunt, R., 285
Hunter, J. E., 353
Hunter, J. N., 47
Hunter, R. H., 642
Hurt, H., 336
Hurtley, S. M., 504
Huster, G., 511
Huston, A. C., 215
Huston, T. L., 676
Huttenlocher, J., 358
Huttenlocher, P. R., 85
Hyde, J. S., 399, 465, 473
Hygge, S., 488
Hyman, I. A., 207
Hyman, I. E., Jr., 250, 251
Hyman, M., 607
Hynynen, M., 309
Iacono, W. G., 421
Igalens, J., 407
Ilgen, D. R., 408
Ilzendoorn, M. H., 457
Inciardi, J. A., 436
Indovina, I., 78
Ingram, D. K., 74
Ingram, R. E., 581
Inoue-Nakamura, N., 214

Inskip, P. D., 29
Insko, C. A., 712
International Human Genome Sequencing Consortium, 52
International Molecular Genetic Study of Autism Consortium, A-6
Inzlicht, M., 364
Iriki, A., 132
Irnich, D., 136
Ironson, G., 495
Irvin, J. E., 509
Irwin, M., 505
Isenberg, K., 569
Ishai, A., 310
Iversen, L. L., 339
Iversen, P. M., 415
Ives, G. C., 322
Iwahashi, K., 334
Iwamura, Y., 132
Izard, C. E., 427, 463
Jack, C. R., 73
Jackson, G. H., 84
Jackson, J. J., 667
Jackson, J. M., 655, 713
Jackson, R. J., 569, 570
Jacob, S., 128
Jacobs, G. D., 208
Jacobsen, C. H., 398
Jacobson, E., 514
Jacobson, J. W., 47
Jacobson, K. C., 358
Jacobson, L., 362–363
Jacobson, L. T., 469
Jacobson, N. S., 623
Jacoby, D., 246
Jacoby, L. L., 229
Jaffe, S., 473
Jagger, C., 476
Jahnke, J. C., 230, 270, 274
Jakimik, J., 295
James, W., 13, 16, 311, 417–421, 423
Jamieson, K. H., 668
Jancke, L., 426
Janik, V. M., 301
Janis, I. L., 715, 716
Janowiak, J. J., 330
Janowitz, H. D., 388
Jarvik, L. F., A-3
Je, J., 508
Jenkins, G. D., Jr., 408
Jenkins, J. G., 249
Jenkins, M. R., 436
Jenkins, R., 514
Jenner, P., 88
Jensen, A. R., 366, A-3
Jensen, J. P., 604
Jensen, M., 497
Jensen, P. S., 624
Jensvold, M., 639
Jevtovic-Todorovic, V., 338
Jhanwar, U. M., 391
Johansen, J. P., 134
John, O., 527, 528
Johnson, B. T., 714
Johnson, C. M., 355, 359
Johnson, D., 488

Johnson, E. J., 285, 289, 290
Johnson, J., 391, 490, 525
Johnson, J. G., 558
Johnson, J. S., 300
Johnson, L. E., 629
Johnson, M. A., 172, 437
Johnson, M. K., 232, 252
Johnson, S. B., 33
Johnson, V. E., 396, 398, 399
Johnson, W. R., 353
Johnson-Laird, P. N., 272
Johnston, D., 59
Johnston, W. A., 181
Johnstone, E. L., 586
Jöhren, P., 640
Joiner, T., 578
Jolles, J., 91
Jones, B., 220
Jones, E. E., 564
Jones, G. H., 17
Jones, G. V., 237
Jones, J. R., 488
Jones, L. V., 354, 355
Jones, R. D., 631
Jones, S. E., 49
Jones, T. C., 229
Jones, W. H. S., 632
Jonsen, B. H., 415
Joondeph, B., 632
Jordan, N. C., 358
Josephson, W. L., 216
Joy, J. E., 341
Julien, R. M., 337, 338, 634, 635, 636
Jung, C., 522
Jusczyk, P. W., 296, 437
Jussila, J., 309
Jussim, L., 363
Just, M. A., 177, 178, 181
Just, N., 581
Juul-Dam, N., 595
Kaardes, F., 289
Kaas, J. H., 109
Kadotani, H., 322
Kagan, J., 454
Kahn, D. A., 641
Kahn, J., 286
Kahneman, D., 212, 277–278, 283, 289, 290, 305, 475
Kaiser, C. F., 534
Kajiya, K., 126
Kales, A., 334
Kales, J., 334
Kalichman, S. C., 509
Kalish, H. I., 201
Kallgren, C. A., 681
Kamarck, T. W., 500, 506
Kamin, L. J., 199
Kamitani, Y., 125
Kamphuis, J. H., 495
Kane, J. M., 635
Kanki, B. J., 692
Kanner, B., 554
Kaplan, G. A., 488
Kaplan, M. F., 292
Kaplan, R. M., 510
Kaplowitz, S. A., 405

Name Index

Kappler, J., 95
Kaptchuk, T. J., 136
Kapur, N., 256
Kapur, S., 634
Karau, S. J., 683, 684, 713, 714
Kardes, F. R., 6
Karni, A., 94, 325
Karoly, P., 497
Karon, B. P., 251
Karp, D. A., 480
Kasagi, F., 506
Kasparov, G., 287
Kass, S., 219
Kasser, T., 480
Kassin, S., 23, 672, 674
Kassin, S. M., 9, 245
Kastenbaum, B. K., 481
Kastenbaum, R., 481
Katcher, A. H., 698
Katkin, E. S., 422
Kato, S., 336
Katz, A. N., 270
Katz, S. E., 324
Katzell, R. A., 407–408
Kauffman, N. A., 393
Kaufman, J., 568
Kaufman, J. C., 356, 367
Kaufmann, N., 426
Kåver, A., 617
Kawakami, K., 314, 667, 670, 671
Kawamura, N., 495
Kawasaki, H., 415
Kaye, J. A., 72
Kaye, W. H., 394
Kazarian, S. S., 510
Kazdin, A. E., 618, 624, 626
Keane, M. T., 233
Keane, T. M., 31
Keating, D. P., 471
Kee, M., 616
Keefe, F. J., 134
Keeling, P. J., 395
Keesey, R. E., 393
Kehoe, E. J., 614
Keinan, G., 494
Kelder, S. H., 510
Keller, A., 470
Keller, M. B., 641
Kelley, H., 466, 655–657
Kelley, H. H., 656
Kelley, K. W., 504
Kelley, W. M., 237
Kellman, P. J., 437
Kellum, K. K., 220
Kelly, G. A., 537, 538
Kelly, I. W., 27
Kelly, J., 478
Kelly, T. H., 339
Kelsoe, J. R., 579
Kelter, D., 419
Kelvin, L., 286
Kemeny, M. E., 505
Kemp, S., 253
Kemper, S., 476
Kendall, P. C., 626, 627
Kendler, K. S., 569

Kendler, K. S., 400, 557, 579, 581, 582, 586, 597, A-5
Kennedy, J. F., 716
Kennell, J. H., 453
Kenny, D. A., 709
Kenrick, D. T., 384, 465, 651, 654, 673, 674, 703
Kent, S., 390
Kernberg, O., 523
Kerns, K., 179
Kerr, N. L., 683
Kessler, R., 488
Kessler, R. C., 500, 523, 566, 567, 576
Ketcham, K., 245, 250, 252
Kety, S. S., 586
Key, W. B., 148
Kiecolt-Glaser, J. K., 491, 498, 499, 505, 506, 514, 665
Kierkegaard, S., 538
Kiesler, D. J., 589
Kiesler, S., 292
Kiewra, K. A., 260
Kihlstrom, J. F., 251, 252, 312, 524, 651
Kilby, M. M., 606
Kilgard, M. P., 77, 87
Kilts, C. D., 332
Kim, Y., 495
Kimble, G. A., 15
Kimura, D., 398
King, J., 309
King, L., 408
King, M. L., 410
Kinney, H. C., 315
Kinsey, A. C., 396, 403
Kircher, J. C., 420
Kirchler, E., 668
Kirk, S. A., 563
Kirkpatrick, B., 588
Kirsch, I., 327, 328, 329
Kirsch, J., 327
Kishioka, S., 136
Kitano, H., 596
Kitayama, S., 291, 541, 542, 707–709
Kjellberg, A., 497
Klahr, D., 373
Klar, Y., 651
Klaus, M. H., 453
Klebanov, P. K., 360, 452
Kleemola, P., 336
Kleijnen, J., 136
Klein, D. C., 210, 579, 581
Klein, D. N., 213
Klein, G., 290, 291
Klein, H. J., 408
Klein, M., 523, 608
Klein, R. A., 614
Klein, S. B., 651, 654
Kleinknecht, R. A., 44, 193, 215, 566, 570, 617
Kleinman, A., 558
Kleitman, N., 326
Klempay, S., 191
Klepp, K.-I., 510
Klerman, G. L., 627

Klesges, R. C., 509
Klima, E. S., 91
Kline, J., 384
Kline, S., 258
Kling, K. C., 468
Klinger, M. R., 149
Klintsova, A. Y., 85
Klohnen, E., 523
Klonoff-Cohen, H. S., 322
Klonsky, B. G., 714
Klosko, J. S., 640
Kluger, A. N., 408
Knapp, S., 631
Knapp, T. J., 203
Knipschild, P., 136
Koch, C., 66, 309, 310–311
Koch, P. B., 403
Kochanek, K. D., 577
Koelega, H. S., 335
Koelling, R. A., 193
Koenigsberg, H. W., 639
Koepp, M. J., 385
Koestner, R., 374
Koffka, K., 12
Kohlberg, L., 472–473
Köhler, W., 12
Kohout, J., 8
Kohut, H., 523
Kohut, J. J., 420
Kok, M. R., 288
Kolarz, C. M., 480
Kolata, G., 438
Kolb, K. J., 683
Komarova, N. L., 299
Komatsu, S.-I., 228
Komorita, S. S., 711, 712
Kondo, T., 84
Konkol, R. J., 336
Koob, G. F., 333, 334
Koopmans, J. R., 596
Kopelman, P. G., 392
Koppenaal, L., 239
Korchmaros, J. D., 709
Kordower, J. H., 83
Kornhaber, M., 370
Korte, C., 706
Korteling, J., 475
Koss, M., 701
Kosslyn, S. M., 119, 311
Kotani, N., 136
Kotzin, B. L., 95
Kouri, E. M., 340, 696
Koutstaal, W., 243
Kozak, M. J., 563, 568, 640
Kraft, C., 179
Kraft, T. W., 122
Krahn, L. E., 321
Kraimer, M. L., 546
Krajicek, D., 167
Krakauer, J., 280
Krakow, B., 322
Kramer, A. F., 372
Kramer, A. R., 475, 476
Krantz, D. S., 488, 506, 507
Kranzler, H. R., 597
Krasnow, A. D., 628
Kratochwill, T. R., 620

Kraus, S. J., 530
Krause, N., 482, 498
Krauzlis, R. J., 70
Krebs, D., 474
Krechevsky, M., 370
Kreuter, M. W., 512
Kristof, N. D., 219
Kronfol, Z., 96
Krosnick, J. A., 148
Krueger, J., 47, 659
Krueger, R., 530
Krumm, D. J., 6
Kryger, M. H., 322
Kübler-Ross, E., 486
Kubovy, M., 156
Kuhl, P., 297
Kühler, W., 212–213
Kuhs, H., 580
Kujala, T., 377
Kulik, J., 253
Kuncel, N. R., 350
Kunitz, A., 239
Kunkel, D., 215
Kunz, P. R., 681
Kupersmidt, J. B., 19
Kurono, K., 419
Kurtz, L. F., 620
Kurzban, R., 17
Kushner, M. G., 334
Kutchins, H., 563
Kwan, M., 398
Kwate, N. O. A., 354, 361
Kwon, Y., 450
Laan, E., 403
LaBar, K. S., 414
Labouvie-Vief, G., 475
Lacayo, A., 336
Ladd, G. W., 463
Laeng, B., 316
Laforge, R. G., 512
LaFrance, M., 658
Lagerspetz, K. M. J., 695
Lagerspetz, K. Y. H., 695
Lahey, B. B., 563, 591, 593
Lai, C. S. L., 300
Laird, J. D., 419
Lam, T. H., 509
Lamar, J., 577
Lamb, M. E., 246, 456
Lambert, M. J., 624, 625, 628, 629
Lambert, N. M., 218
Laming, D., 251
Laming, P. R., 58
Landau, B., 298
Landis, C., 324
Landis, K. R., 499, 500
Landrine, H., 565
Landsdale, M., 251
Lang, A. R., 332
Lang, P. J., 206, 421, 571, 590
Lange, C., 417
Langenberg, P., 510
Langenbucher, J. W., 563
Lanyon, R. I., 352
Lapointe, L., 78
Lapsley, D. K., 473
Larsen, R. J., 530

Larson, G. E., 366
Larson, J., 558
Larson, J. R., Jr., 292
Larson, M. C., 456
Larzelere, R. E., 206
Lashley, K. S., 253–254
Latan, B., 686
Latané, B., 704
Latham, G. P., 202, 408
Lau, M. A., 696
Laughlin, P. L., 292
Laumann, E. D., 397, 398, 400, 403
Laux, P., 636
Law, D. J., 465
Lawford, B. R., 333
Lawless, H. T., 127
Lawrence, J.-R., 327
Lawrie, S. M., 587
Lazarus, A. A., 513, 619
Lazarus, R. S., 423, 493, 496, 497, 498
Le Doux, J. E., 257
Leaper, C., 465
Leary, M., 648
Leary, M. R., 17, 382, 410
LeDoux, J. E., 72, 80, 414, 421
Lee, D. S., 107
Lee, J. W., 290
Lee, M. C., 391
Lee, V. E., 361
Lefcourt, H. M., 499
Legerstee, M., 449
Lehman, D. R., 251, 664
Lehman, H. E., 583
Leibel, R. L., 393
Leibowitz, H. W., 146, 165
Leichter, D., 591
Leigh, B. C., 399
Leiner, A. L., 70
Leiner, H. C., 70
Leippe, M. R., 246
Lejuez, C. W., 497
Lemly, B., 672
Lemm, K. M., 666
Lennard, A. L., 84
Lenneberg, E. H., 300
Lentz, R. J., 616
Leonard, B. E., 70, 338
Leonhardt, D., 367
Lepore, L., 229, 314, 671
Lepore, S. J., 499, 500, 507
Lerew, D. R., 569, 570
LeSieur, K. D., 463
Lettvin, J. Y., 100
LeVay, S., 401
Levenson, H., 609
Levenson, R. W., 419, 676
Levenstein, S., 488
Leventhal, T., 462
Levin, D. T., 176
Levine, E. L., 527
Levine, J. M., 292, 714, 715
Levine, R., 675
Levine, R. V., 706
Levine, S., 107, 497
Levine, S. C., 358

Levinson, D. J., 479
Levinson, D. M., 330
Levinson, S. C., 450
Levinthal, C. F., 330
Levis, D. J., 40
Levy, G. D., 465
Levy, J., 623
Levy, R. L., 490
Levy, V. M., Jr., 473
Levy-Shiff, R., 478
Lewicki, P., 228, 312
Lewinsky, M., 35
Lewinsohn, P. M., 240, 581
Lewis, C. E., 392, 393
Lewis, D., 564
Lewis, J. M., 466
Lewis, O., 591
Lewith, G. T., 135
Lewontin, R., 359
Ley, R., 569
Li, C., 389
Li, F., 514
Li, Y.-F., 436
Liben, L., 447
Liberman, R. P., 642
Lichstein, K. L., 208
Lichtenstein, P., 487
Lichtman, A. H., 340
Lickey, M., 633, 636, 637
Lidsky, A., 320
Lieberman, A., 608
Lieberman, M. A., 477, 481
Lieberman, M. D., 664, 665
Lieberman, P., 301
Liebowitz, M. R., 640
Liebrand, W. B. G., 712
Liepert, J., 82
Light, K. C., 492, 506
Light, L. L., 228
Liker, J. K., 367
Liley, D. T., 9
Lilienfeld, S. O., 548, 549, 555, 574
Lillywhite, A. R., 322
Lin, K.-M., 638
Lin, L., 391
Lin, S., 389
Lindaman, S., 608
Lindsay, G., 410
Lindsay, J. A., 216
Lindsey, K. P., 564
Lindvall, O., 83
Lindzey, G., 537
Lintern, G., 179
Linz, D., 700
Lisanby, S. H., 633
Lisberger, S. G., 70
Littlepage, G. E., 292
Littlewood, R., 564
Liu, C., 323
Liu, L. G., 304
Liu, Y., 261, 266, 267, 393
Lively, W. M., 572
Livermore, G., 596
Livingstone, M. S., 118
Lloyd, M., 358
Lobaugh, N. J., 91

Lobel, M., 648
Locke, E. A., 408, 409
Locke, J., 11, 432
Lockhart, R. S., 229, 230
Locurto, C., 361, 362
Loeber, R., 593
Loeber, R. T., 587
Loehlin, J., 530
Loehlin, J. C., 358
Loewenstein, G., 385
Loewi, O., 87
Loftus, E. F., 241, 245, 246, 250, 251, 252, 253, 278, 329
Loftus, G. R., 47
Loftus, T. M., 394
Logue, A. W., 193
Longo, N., 191
Loofbourrow, G. N., 417
Lopes, L. L., 285
Lopez, A., 630
Lopez, S. R., 565
Lopez-Lozano, J. J., 83
Lorch, R. F., 218
Lord, C. G., 660, 700
Lord, S. E., 468
Lorenz, K., 34
Lories, G., 242
Lornenzetti, A., 490
Losee, M. C., 617
Lovejoy, J., 398
Lubert, T. I., 373
Lubinski, D., 375
Luborsky, L., 609, 623, 624
Lucas, D. E., 320
Luce, C., 530
Luchins, A., 283–284
Lue, T. F., 403
Lukas, S. E., 340
Luntz, B. K., 592
Luong, A., 36
Luria, Z., 465
Lustig, C., 229
Luthar, S. S., 466
Lutz, D. J., 475
Lykken, D. T., 5, 409, 420, 421
Lynam, D. R., 527, 590
Lynch, M., 664
Lynn, R., 354
Lynn, S. J., 327, 329
Lyons, J., 564
Lyubomirsky, S., 493
Maben, A., 324
McAdams, D. P., 526
MacAndrew, C., 332, 333
MacArthur, E., 280
MacArthur Foundation, 479
Macaulay, D., 240
McAuley, E., 511
McCallum, R. S., 355
McCann, U. D., 337
McCarley, R. W., 325
McCarty, M. F., 394
McCarty, R. C., 173
McCauley, C., 716
McClelland, D. C., 404, 405, 406
McClelland, J. L., 170, 230, 244

McClintock, C. G., 712
McClintock, M. K., 128
McCloskey, D. I., 137
McClosky, M., 273
McClure, E. B., 425
McConkey, K. M., 328
McCormick, D. A., 70
McCown, E. J., 702
McCoy, N. L., 128
McCrae, R., 527, 528, 546
McDermott, K. B., 227, 229, 246, 251, 258
McDermut, W., 576
McDevitt, T. M., 406
Macdonald, C. A., 256
MacDonald, H., 328
McDonald, J. J., 125
MacDonald, M., 615
McDougall, S. J. P., 180
McDougall, W., 383
McDowell, J. E., 586
McElree, B., 175, 247
MacEvoy, S. P., 164
McEwen, B. S., 92, 492, 496
McFadden, D., 401
McGarvey, R., 148
McGaugh, J. L., 94
McGehee, D. S., 336
McGill, K. L., 488
McGlashan, T. H., 584, 585, 587
McGlone, J., 81
McGlynn, F. D., 614
MacGregor, D., 290
MacGregor, M., 508
McGue, M., 586, 597, A-5
McGuffin, P., A-4
McGuire, J. M., 377
McGuire, M. T., 393
McGuire, N. L., 357
Machin, D., 135
McIntire, S. A., 547
McIntosh, J. L., 577
Mack, A., 176
McKee, R., 256
MacKenzie, B., 359
Mackie, D. M., 668, 682, 715
McKinley, J. C., 547
McKinney, V. M., 229
McKoon, G., 250
McLaughlin, C. S., 469
McLaughlin, F. J., 128
McLearn, G. E., A-3
MacLeod, C. M., 227
McLeod, J. D., 500
McLeod, P., 162
McLoyd, V. C., 358, 452
McMahon, P., 272
MacMillan, H. L., 591
MacMillan, A. C., 163
McMullin, R. E., 618
McNally, R. J., 252, 253
McNay, E. C., 173
McNeil, J. E., 316
McNeill, D., 242
McPhail, T. L., 670
McQuaid, J. R., 490

Name Index

Macrae, M., 614
Maddux, J., 534
Madson, L., 543
Maess, B., 79
Magee, J. C., 59
Magnani, F., 238
Maguire, T., 354
Mahadevan, R., 225
Mahler, M., 523
Mahmoud, R., 635
Mahowald, M. W., 322
Maier, S. F., 96, 135, 210, 505
Maier, W., 581
Main, M., 581
Mair, R. G., 127
Maita, A. K., 416
Major, B., 648
Makhijani, M. G., 714
Makie, D., 653
Malamuth, N. M., 695, 698, 699, 700, 701
Malarkey, W. B., 500
Malaspina, D., 587
Malberg, J. E., 84
Malenka, R. C., 254–255
Malgrange, B., 107
Malinoski, P., 329
Malleret, G., 255
Malone, P. S., 658
Manderscheid, R., 564
Manion, A. P., 246
Manji, H. K., 636
Manke, B., A-8
Mann, J. J., 88, 634
Mann, K., 594
Manning, B. H., 134
Mannuzza, M., 566
Manore, M. M., 394
Mansfield, P. K., 403
Marcus, B. H., 512
Marcus, H. R., 298
Marenco, S., 88
Maric, A., 701
Mariner, C. L., 206
Marino, L., 301, 309, 555
Markel, H., 438
Markman, A. B., 241, 273, 285
Markman, E. M., 298
Markowitz, J. C., 627
Marks, L. E., 126
Markus, H. R., 21, 291, 298, 434, 533, 541, 542, 543, 652
Marmar, C. R., 625
Maroudas, C., 581
Marquis, D. G., 194
Marrack, P., 95
Marriott, M. J., 229
Marshall, J., 124
Marshall, W. L., 699
Martin, B., 593
Martin, B. R., 340
Martin, C. E., 396
Martin, C. L., 465
Martin, C. R., 634
Martin, D., 650
Martin, D. J., 625, 628
Martin, J., 401

Martin, L. G., 476
Martin, N. G., 395, 401, 403, 530
Martin, R., 59
Martin, R. A., 499
Martin, S., 631
Martindale, C., 233, 243, 244, 317
Martinez, C. R., 643
Martino, G., 126
Martinot, M.-L. P., 580
Marttila, R. J., 476
Marx, J., 504
Marzuk, P. M., 336
Masand, P., 322
Maser, J. D., 590, 591
Maslach, C., 495
Masling, J., 148
Maslow, A. H., 20, 409–410, 540
Mason, W. A., 49
Massaro, D. W., 231, 295
Masson, J., 524
Masson, M. E. J., 227
Masten, A. S., 466
Masters, J. C., 618–619
Masters, W. H., 396, 398, 399
Mata, M., 83
Mathalon, D. H., 586
Matlin, M. W., 237, 241, 247
Matson, J., 616
Matsuda, K. T., 638
Matsumoto, D., 426, 524, 684, 696
Matsuzawa, T., 214
Matte, T. D., 358
Matthews, G., 531
Matthews, K. A., 506
Matthies, E., 497
Mattia, J. I., 576
Mattingly, J. B., 125
Matza, L. S., 19
Maupin, H. E., 687
May, M. C., 574
May, R. M., 712
Mayer, D. J., 134
Mayer, F. S., 352, 404, 406, 534
Mayer, J. D., 706
Mayer, R. E., 285
Mazzella, R., 394
Mazziotta, J. C., 81
Mazzoni, G. A., 252
Meacham, J. A., 470
Mechoulam, R., 338
Medin, D. L., 241, 273, 277, 285
Mednick, S., 591
Mednick, S. A., 207
Mehle, T., 283
Meichenbaum, D., 513
Meichenbaum, D. H., 618, 619
Melamed, B. G., 206
Mellers, R. A., 277, 289
Mello, N. K., 336
Mellon, S. H., 94
Meltzer, H. Y., 635
Melzack, R., 134, 488
Menaker, M., 323
Mendoza-Denton, R., 535
Menini, A., 126
Menkes, M. S., 506
Mennella, J. A., 438

Menson, S., 527
Merkel, W., 617
Merzenich, M. M., 77, 87, 111
Mesmer, F. A., 327
Mesquita, B., 426
Messick, D. M., 710, 713
Messick, S., 354
Messinger, A., 218
Mestre, J., 285
Metalsky, G. I., 210
Metcalfe, J., 240
Metzger, M. M., 91
Metzinger, T., 309
Metzler, J., 273, 274
Meyer, B. H. F. L., 401
Meyer, G. J., 545
Meyer, J. D., 370
Meyer, R. G., 322
Meyers, C., 220
Mezzacappa, E. S., 422
Miceli, G., 257
Michael, R. T., 398
Michaud, D. S., 393
Michele, J. L., 648
Middlebrooks, J. C., 110
Mikelson, K. D., 523
Mikkola, T., 324
Miklowitz, D. J., 580
Milavsky, B., 698
Milberger, S., 436
Milgram, S., 689–694
Milich, R., 13, 34, 288, 545
Miller, C. E., 292
Miller, C. L., 469
Miller, E. K., 269
Miller, G., 235
Miller, G. A., 293, 415
Miller, H. G., 36
Miller, J., 650, 657, 658, 681
Miller, J. G., 23
Miller, K. F., 450
Miller, L. A., 547
Miller, L. K., 35, 369
Miller, L. T., 366, 447
Miller, M. G., 391
Miller, M. I., 269, 628
Miller, N., 668, 683
Miller, N. E., 410
Miller, S. D., 625
Miller, T. I., 624, 625
Miller, T. Q., 680
Miller, W. R., 210
Millon, T., 589
Milner, B., 316, 317
Milner, D., 470
Milner, P., 204–205, 421
Miltenberger, R. G., 613
Mineka, S., 193, 215, 571
Minimi, H., 249
Minuchin, S., 621
Miranda, J., 581
Mischel, W., 532, 533, 535–536
Mishina, T. M., 630
Mishkin, M., 72
Mistretta, C. M., 129
Mitchell, D. B., 228
Mitchell, D. J., 35

Mitchell, K. J., 246
Mitchell, R. W., 400
Miura, H., 451
Miura, I. T., 304
Moane, G., 479
Moen, P., 481
Moergen, S., 617
Mogelvang, B., 136
Mogenson, G. J., 389
Mogil, J. S., 135
Mokdad, A. H., 392
Molden, D. C., 404
Moldin, S. O., 586
Molsa, P. K., 476
Monaghan, L., 338
Monahan, J., 288
Monane, M., 591
Moniz, A. E., 634
Monroe, S., 490
Monroe, S. M., 580
Monteith, M. J., 669
Monteufel, L., 707
Montmayeur, J. P., 128
Moon, C. E., 327
Moore, C. C., 247
Moore, N. B., 403
Moos, R. H., 621
Moran, A., 175
Moran, D. R., 219
Moran, P. M., 580–581
Moran, P. W., 608
Moreland, R., 672
Moreland, R. L., 292, 714, 715
Morgan, A. H., 328
Morgan, C., 548
Morgan, C. D., 404
Morgan, D., 74
Morganstern, J., 621
Morgenthaler, J., 90, 91
Morin, C. M., 208
Morisse, D., 208
Morley, S., 134
Morrell, S., 27
Morris, C. D., 230
Morris, J., 481
Morris, J. S., 312, 421
Morris, L., 329
Morris, M., 10, 11
Morrissette, J., 390
Morrone, E., 171
Morrow, J., 581
Mortimer, R. G., 202
Moscovici, S., 685, 687
Mosher, M., 465
Moskowitz, J. T., 498, 501
Moss, J., 91
Most, S. B., 176
Mount, M. K., 546, 549
Mroczek, D. K., 480
Muchinsky, P., 202
Muir, J. L., 255
Mulick, J. A., 47
Mullen, B., 668, 682
Muller, F. W., 414
Mumford, G., 4
Mummer, D. L., 464
Munroe, R. H., 21

Munroe, R. L., 21
Murphy, B. C., 532
Murphy, C., 152
Murphy, P. J., 580
Murphy, S. L., 577
Murray, B., 219
Murray, C., 354, 358, A-4
Murray, E. A., 72
Murray, H., 548
Murray, H. A., 404
Murray, J. A., 513
Murre, J. M. J., 82
Murthy, C. V., 358
Muzio, J. N., 320, 321, 325
Myers, B., 329
Myers, B. J., 453
Myers, D. G., 409
Myers, M. G., 192
Myers, N. A., 449
Myers, P. I., 377
Myers, S. L., 692
Myerson, J., 362
Nader, K., 257, 387
Naëgelé, B., 322
Nagel, D., 179
Naglieri, J. A., 366
Nagy, T. F., 49
Naito, M., 228, 451
Nakamura, J., 374
Nakayama, K., 146
Nalbantoglu, J., 74
Náñez, J. E., 185
Narayanan, L., 527
Narita, N., 322
Narrow, W., 621
Nathan, P. E., 563
Nathan, P. E., 623, 625, 628
National Advisory Mental Health Council, 559
National Cancer Institute, 487
National Center for Education Statistics, 8
National Center for Health Statistics, 469, 479
National Computer Systems, 547
National Council on Measurement in Education, 351, 352, 549
National Information Center for Children and Youth with Disabilities, 476
National Institute for Occupational Safety and Health, 513
National Institute of Alcohol Abuse and Alcoholism (NIAAA), 596, 597
National Institute of Mental Health, 579, 604, 638
National Institute on Drug Abuse, 337, 339, 597
National Institutes of Health, 136
National Joint Committee on Learning Disabilities, 377
National Task Force on the Prevention and Treatment of Obesity, 394
Navasky, V., 286
Neal, D., 353

Neale, M. C., 569
Neale, J. M., 576
Needham, A., 443–444
Neely, J. H., 242
Neher, A., 410
Nehlig, A., 336
Neidig, P. H., 695
Neisser, U., 235, 247, 258, 265, 354, 358, 359, 367, A-4
Neitz, J., 123
Neitz, M., 123
Nelson, C. A., 439, 475
Nelson, D., 672
Nelson, D. L., 227, 229, 314, 438, 670–671
Nelson, K., 229, 450
Nelson, M., 564
Nelson, R. J., 75
Nelson-LeGall, S., 359
Nemeroff, C. B., 580
Neuberg, S. L., 651
Neufeld, P., 246
Neufeld, R. W. J., 585
Neugarten, B. L., 480
Neuhuber, W. L., 65
Neumann, C. S., 587
Neville, H. A., 630
Neville, H. J., 111
New York Times, 36
Newcomb, A. F., 463
Newcombe, N. S., 450
Newell, A., 279, 286
Newman, H., 337
Newman, J. P., 199
Newman, R., 606
Newport, E. L., 300
Newsome, J. T., 500
Newton, T. L., 499
NICHD Early Child Care Research Network, 458, 459
Nichols, R., 374
Nicholson, A. N., 323
Nicholson, I. R., 585
Nickell, J., 27, 556
Nickerson, R. A., 237
Nicoll, R. A., 255
Niedenthal, P. M., 651
Nielsen, N. H., 596
Nielsen Media, 215
Niemela, M., 180
Nienhuys, J. W., 27
Nietzel, M. T., 7, 13, 34, 288, 347, 545, 565, 572, 598
Nigg, J. T., 593
Nijhawan, R., 161
Nilsson, G., 476
Nilsson, L., 245, 246
Nisbett, R. E., 304, 658, 697
Nissen, M. J., 174–175
Nitschke, J. B., 415
Niyogi, P., 299
Niznikiewicz, M. A., 586
Noble, H. B., 83
Nobler, M. S., 634
Noël, P. H., 394
Nolan, R. P., 329
Nolen-Hoeksema, S., 493, 558, 581

Noll, R. B., 328
Norcross, J., 511–512
Norcross, J. C., 620
Norenzayan, A., 658
Norman, D. A., 261
Norman, K. A., 243
Northcut, T. B., 604
Nottebohm, F., 82
Novak, M. A., 49
Nowaczyk, R. H., 230, 270, 274
Nowak, M. A., 299, 712
Nowinski, J., 620
Nugent, F., 621
Nurnberger, J. I., 579
Nutt, D. J., 322
Nyberg, L., 253, 258
Oakley, A. J., 591
Oatley, K., 696
Oberwinkler, J., 124
O'Brien, P. E., 322
O'Brien, T. L., 716
Ochsner, K. N., 227, 251, 665
O'Conner, E., 15
O'Conner, E. P., 620
O'Conner, T. G., 451
Odbert, H. S., 526
Oden, M. H., 353, 374, 502
Oellerich, T., 48
Oettingen, G., 406
O'Farrell, T. J., 623
Offenbach, S., 476
Ogden, W. C., 174–175
O'Hara, L. A., 374
O'Hare, D., 179
O'Heeron, R. C., 506
Ohira, H., 419
Öhman, A., 148, 425, 571
Oishi, S., 410
Okazaki, S., 355
Okochi, M., 57
Oldersma, F. L., 647, 648
Olds, J., 204–205, 421
O'Leary, K. D., 628
Oliner, P., 705
Oliner, S., 705
Olio, K. A., 252
Olivares, R., 81
Olsen, J. F., 110
Olson, C. M., 361
Olson, J. M., 661
Olson, K., 286
Olson, L., 82
Olson, M., 254
Olson, M. A., 661
Olson, M. H., 204, 217
Olson, R., 615
Olson, S. L., 613
Olster, D. H., 389
Ona, N., 549
O'Neil, R., 463
O'Neill, H., 245
Ones, D. S., 350, 518, 546, 549
Operario, D., 666
Oppel, S., 219
Oquendo, M. A., 88
Oransky, N., 233
Orbell, J. M., 712

Orne, M. T., 328
Osborne, J., 468
Osherson, D., 281
Oskamp, S., 668, 702
Öst, L.-G., 570, 571, 615, 617
Otaka, S. R., 240
Otsuka, R., 508
Otto, M. W., 640
Otto, S. A., 426
Otto, T., 317
Ouimette, P. C., 621
Overmier, J. B., 190, 209
Overton, D. A., 240
Overton, P. G., 332
Owen, A. M., 269
Owen, M. J., A-4
Oyserman, S., 648
Ozer, D. J., 545
Paik, A., 403
Paik, H., 216
Paivio, A., 237
Paivio, S. C., 613
Pak, H., 406
Paller, K. A., 258
Palmer, F. H., 362
Palmer, J. C., 245
Palmer, S., 156
Palmer, S. N., 422
Palmisano, M., 258
Paloski, W. H., 137
Panda, S. C., 358
Panksepp, J., 594
Pantev, C., 110
Paoletti, M. G., 392
Papp, L., 569
Pappas, T. N., 391
Paradiso, M. A., 164
Park, D. C., 475, 476
Park, J., 136
Park, W-W., 716
Parke, R. D., 456, 461, 463, 479
Parker, G., 559
Parker, J. G., 462, 463
Parker, K. C. H., 40
Parkes, C. M. P., 497
Parkin, A. J., 372
Parks, C. D., 711
Parnas, J., 586
Parsons, O. A., 419
Pasanen, E. G., 401
Pasteur, L., 504
Pataki, S. P., 672
Patel, A. D., 110
Patel, J. K., 635
Patrick, C. J., 590
Patterson, C. J., 463, 479
Patterson, P., 303
Pattie, F. A., 328
Pauk, W., 260
Paul, C. C., 524
Paul, G. L., 564, 616, 625, 628, 629
Paulhus, D. L., 524, 531
Pauls, D. L., 569
Paus, T., 84
Pavkov, T., 564
Pavlov, I. P., 14, 187–190, 195, 613

Name Index

Pawl, J., 608
Payne, J. W., 285, 289, 290
Peck, J. W., 391, 393
Peevers, B., 470
Peiffer, L. C., 524
Pellegrino, J. W., 465
Penfield, W., 77, 133
Peng, K., 10, 11
Pennartz, C. M., 89
Pennebaker, J. W., 498, 506
Penner, L. A., 218, 314, 385, 499, 546, 670–671, 683, 703, 704, 705
Penninx, B. W., 501
Pennngton, N., 291
Penrod, S. D., 291, 700
Pentland, J., 251
Pepeu, G., 91
Peplau, A., 652
Peplau, L. A., 673, 676, 710
Peppard, P. E., 322
Perham-Hester, K. A., 322
Perlis, M. I., 321
Perls, F. S., 610, 612
Perls, L., 610, 612
Peroutka, S. J., 337
Perris, E. E., 449
Perry, C. L., 510
Persons, J. B., 620, 628
Pervin, L. A., 313, 536
Peters, J. C., 388, 393
Peters, J. M., 436
Peterson, A. C., 469
Peterson, C., 210, 501, 502, 620
Peterson, J. B., 696
Peterson, L. R., 236
Peterson, M. J., 236
Peterson, S. E., 178
Petrie, K. J., 506
Petrill, S. A., 358
Petrov, S., 284–285
Petry, N. M., 596
Pettigrew, T. F., 658, 668, 669
Pettit, D. L., 255
Petty, R., 663
Petty, R. E., 662, 663, 670, 689
Pfefferbaum, A., 596
Phares, E. J., 534
Phelps, B. J., 221
Phelps, E. A., 414, 421, 666
Phelps, M. E., 81, 85
Philip, P., 324
Phillips, D. P., 680
Phillips, L. D., 290
Phillips, N. A., 403
Phillips, R. L., 84
Phillips-Grant, K., 449
Phinney, J. S., 22, 461, 470
Piaget, J., 434, 439–442, 445–447, 450, 471, 475
Picco, C., 126
Pickens, R., 597
Pickering, A. D., 530, 531, 532
Pienes, Z., 162
Pierce, G., 500
Pierce-Otay, A., 673
Pieri, A., 490

Pietrini, P., 255
Pietro, P., 696
Pihl, R. O., 696
Piliavin, J. A., 703
Pillard, R. C., 400, 401
Pincus, T., 134
Pinel, J. P. J., 186
Pines, A. M., 699
Pinker, S., 296, A-4
Pinto, P. M., 512
Piomelli, D., 339
Pisoni, D. B., 437
Pitschel-Walz, G., 588
Plant, E. A., 671
Plato, 11
Platt, J. R., 110
Plaud, J. J., 194
Plomin, R., 50, 52, 358, 434, 530, 531–533, 532, A-3, A-4, A-5, A-6, A-7, A-8
Plous, S., 49
Plutchik, R., 385
Poddar, P., 631
Poggio, T., 167
Poland, R. E., 638
Polaschek, D. L. L., 252
Polivy, J., 392, 393
Pollack, B. G., 639
Pollack, I., 235
Pollack, V., 597
Polusny, M. A., 252, 495
Pomerantz, J. R., 156
Pomerleau, C. S., 336
Pomerleau, O. F., 336
Pomeroy, W. B., 396
Pontieri, F. E., 340
Poole, D. A., 252
Pope, H. G., 251, 253, 340, 636, 696
Pope, K. S., 251, 253
Pope-Davis, D. B., 630
Popli, A. P., 322
Porges, S. W., 416
Porkka-Heiskanen, T., 325
Port, C. L., 495
Porte, H. S., 326
Porter, R. H., 128, 438
Porter, S., 251, 252
Posener, J. A., 580
Posner, M. I., 174–175, 178, 267
Potosky, D., 354
Potter, P. T., 504
Potter, W. Z., 633, 639
Pousset, F., 96
Powch, I. G., 508
Powley, T. L., 393
Prada, R., 333
Pratkanis, A. R., 148, 149, 662
Preciado, J., 629
Preece, J., 180
Preisler, J. J., 489
Premack, A. J., 301, 302
Premack, D., 204, 301, 302
Prentice-Dunn, S., 681
Prescott, C. A., 581
Prescott, J. W., 456
Press, G. A., 257

Pribram, K. H., 309
Price, D. D., 134
Price, R., 488
Prill, K. A., 372
Prinzmetal, W., 170
Prior, M., 501
Pritchard, W. S., 336
Prkachin, K., 660
Prochaska, J. O., 511, 512
Proctor, R., 268
Pruitt, D. G., 712, 713
Pryor, T., 395
Przekop, P. R., Jr., 129
Psotka, J., 249, 250
Puca, A. A., 482
Pugh, K. R., 377
Pulakos, E. D., 408
Purcell, D. G., 170
Purcell, E. D., 202
Purdue Exponent, 668
Pyfer, J. L., 436
Pyszczynski, T., 649–650
Qizilbash, N., 92
Queller, S., 647, 652, 653
Quick, B. D., 420
Quiles, J., 393
Quine, L., 659
Quinlan, K. A., 315
Quinn, D., 364
Quinn, G. E., 113
Quintana, S. M., 630, 668
Quiroz, B., 460
Quitkin, F. M., 636
Quittner, A., 615
Rabasca, L., 15, 640
Rabbitt, P., 372
Rabinowitz, J., 635
Rabinowitz, J. C., 475
Rachlin, H., 208
Rachman, S. J., 614
Rada, J. B., 691
Radvansky, G. A., 475
Raeff, C., 460
Raff, M., 84
Raguram, R., 567
Rahe, R., 489
Raichle, M. E., 178
Raine, A., 590, 696
Rainville, P., 133
Rakowski, W., 512
Ramachandran, V. S., 100, 125, 126, 160
Ramey, C. T., 361, 452
Ramey, S. L., 361, 452
Ramirez, S. Z., 630
Ramona, G., 252
Ranta, S., 309
Rapee, R., 570
Rapee, R. M., 498
Rappaport, J., 621
Rapson, R. L., 674
Rasinski, K., 661
Raskin, D. C., 420
Raskin, N. J., 538, 610
Rasmussen, T., 77, 133
Ratcliff, R., 250
Rathbone, D. B., 490

Ratner, C., 312
Rauschecker, J. P., 109
Rauscher, F. H., 452
Raye, C. L., 252
Rayner, G., 4
Raynor, H. A., 391
Raynor, J. O., 359
Read, J. D., 314–315
Reade, P. C., 329
Reagan, R., 599
Reber, A. S., 311
Redd, M., 392
Redd, W. H., 329
Reder, L. M., 242
Reed, G., 486
Reed, S. K., 273, 278
Reeder, G. D., 653
Reedy, M. N., 481
Rees-Jones, T., 257
Reeve, C., 63, 83
Reeve, J. M., 381, 405
Reeves, R. A., 688
Regier, D. A., 565
Reich, D. A., 623
Reich, T., 597
Reid, W. H., 633
Reingold, E. M., 285
Reinisch, J. M., 696
Reinitz, M. T., 237
Reis, H. T., 478, 672
Reisberg, D., 19, 201, 218, 246
Reisenzein, R., 422
Reiss, A. J., 215, 216
Reiss, D., 301, 309, 461, A-8
Reitman, D., 616
Remick, D. G., 96
Remington, R. W., 175
Rendall, D., 301
Reneman, L., 337
Renner, G., 481
Reno, R. R., 681
Rescorla, L. A., 298
Rescorla, R. A., 190, 191, 218
Resnick, L., 359
Resnick, M., 468
Resnick, R. J., 606
Resnick, S., 93
Revenson, T. A., 487
Reyna, V. F., 251
Reynolds, C. F., III, 641
Reynolds, D. V., 134
Reynolds, S., 563
Rhodes, G., 672
Rholes, W. S., 523
Rhue, J. W., 327
Riad, J. K., 696
Ricaurte, G. A., 337
Rice, G., 400
Rice, M. E., 590
Richards, D. G., 302
Richards, J. M., 251, 506
Richards, P. S., 629
Richards, S. B., 350, 354
Richards, T. L., 377
Richardson, D. C., 695, 697, 713
Richardson, P. H., 135
Richardson-Klavehn, A., 240

Rickels, K., 637
Ridley, M., 300
Riedel, W. J., 91
Riedy, C. A., 389
Riegel, K. F., 475
Rigby, S., 245
Riger, S., 33
Riggio, R. E., 407
Riggs, J. A., 596
Rind, B., 593
Rinehart, P. M., 468
Ringel, R., 476
Rinn, W. E., 414
Rinne, U. K., 476
Rioult-Pedotti, M.-S., 254
Rips, L. J., 275, 661
Risen, J., 716
Rittenhouse, C. D., 326
Ritter, F. E., 242
Ritter, R. C., 389
Robbins, J., 5, 614
Robbins, S. J., 209
Robbins, T. W., 332
Roberts, B. W., 326, 525, 532, 544, 545
Roberts, G. C., 7
Robertson, I. H., 82
Robertson, J., 458
Robin, O., 415
Robins, L. N., 565, 566
Robins, P. W., 15
Robins, R. W., 18, 525
Robinson, H. A., 259
Robinson, J. H., 336
Robinson, N. M., 374
Robinson, T. N., 217
Rock, I., 146, 169, 176, 177
Rodgers, J., 337
Rodier, P. M., 595
Rodin, J., 210, 393, 704
Rodman, R., 293
Rodriguez de Fonseca, F., 340
Rodriguez, H., 615
Rodriguez, I., 128
Roediger, H. L., III, 5, 228, 229, 231, 246, 251
Roehrich, L., 333
Roeser, R. W., 468
Roffman, R. A., 340
Roffwarg, H. P., 320, 321, 325, 326
Rogawski, M. A., 325
Rogelberg, S. G., 36
Roger, A. J., 395
Rogers, C. R., 20, 538, 540, 610, 611, 612, 630
Rogers, J., 334
Rogers, R., 346, 347, 350
Rogers, R. W., 681, 691
Rogers, S. M., 36
Rogers, T. B., 563
Rogers-Ramachandran, D., 100
Rogoff, B., 448
Rohan, M. J., 668
Rolls, E. T., 128, 129
Romanczyk, A., 246
Romanczyk, R. G., 47

Romer, D., 668, 705
Rompre, P. P., 88, 421
Roney, C. J. R., 497
Rosch, E., 270, 298, 304
Roscoe, S., 179
Rose, S., 91
Rosellini, L., 206
Rosen, B. C., 405
Rosen, G. M., 40
Rosen, R. C., 403, 407
Rosenbach, M. L., 633
Rosenbaum, M., 240, 393, 591
Rosenberg, M. B., 84
Rosenberg, S. E., 478
Rosenfarb, I. S., 588
Rosenfeld, J. P., 420
Rosenhan, D. L., 706
Rosenman, R. H., 506
Rosenstock, I. M., 510
Rosenthal, N., 580
Rosenthal, R., 40–41, 362–363
Rosenzweig, M. R., 254, 255
Rosmond, R., 393
Ross, B. H., 241, 273, 285
Ross, C. A., 574
Ross, D., 214
Ross, L. E., 191
Ross, M., 648
Ross, S. A., 214
Ross, S. I., 655
Ross, S. M., 191
Roth, J. A., 215, 216
Roth, P. L., 354
Rothbart, M. K., 454, 464
Rothbaum, B. O., 614
Rothbaum, F., 457
Rothman, A. J., 210
Rothman, S., A-3
Rothmann, R., 369
Rottenstreich, Y., 277
Rotter, J., 534
Rotton, J., 27, 495, 702
Rouéché, B., 265
Rouse, S. V., 545, 546
Rouse, W. B., 285
Rousseau, J.-J., 432
Roussel, P., 407
Rovee-Collier, C., 442, 450
Rowe, D. C., 358, 531, 532, 543
Roy-Byrne, P., 568
Rozin, P., 129, 391, 392, 425, 426
Rubin, B. M., 480
Rubin, E., 155
Rubin, K. H., 462, 463
Rubinow, D. R., 93
Ruble, D. N., 465, 676
Rudolph, K. D., 468
Rudolph, M. C., 392
Rudorfer, M. V., 633
Rueckert, L., 82
Ruffman, T., 442, 463
Rugg, M. D., 258, 268, 269
Ruiz, P., 638
Ruiz-Belda, M.-A., 426
Rumbaugh, D., 301
Rumelhart, D. E., 170, 230, 244
Rumstein-McKean, O., 627

Rusbult, C. E., 672, 673
Ruscio, J., 203
Rush, B., 633
Rushton, J. P., 374
Rusiniak, K. W., 194
Russell, J. A., 412, 426, 427
Rutkowski, G. K., 705
Rutter, D. R., 659
Rutter, M. L., 50, 591, 594
Ruvolo, A. P., 652
Ryan, A. M., 468
Ryan, R. H., 246, 452
Ryan, R. M., 374
Rye, B. J., 511
Rymer, R., 300, 451
Rynders, J., 376
Saarinen, J., 180
Saarni, C., 453, 464
Sabini, J., 658
Saccuzzo, D. P., 366
Sachs, J., 236
Sack, R. L., 323
Sackeim, H. A., 633, 634
Sackett, P. R., 354, 356, 359
Sackoff, J., 694
Sacks, J. J., 578
Sacks, O., 34–35, 139, 140, 238
Saffran, J. R., 296
St. Clair, M., 608
Saiz, C., 583
Sakairi, Y., 330
Sakamoto, J., 200
Salamon, J., 134
Salas, E., 714
Salkovskis, P. M., 615
Salloum, I. M., 333
Salovey, P., 210, 370, 464, 488, 706
Salthouse, T. A., 372
Saltz, E., 704
Salvi, R. J., 107
Salzer, M. S., 621
Sammons, M. T., 604
Sampson, E. E., 23
Samuel, A. G., 169, 295
Samuel, S. E., 631
Samuelson, C. D., 713
Sanchez-Ramos, J., 84
Sanders, M. R., 623, 643
Sanders, P., 465
Sanders, S. A., 696
Sanderson, L. A., 563
Sanderson, W. C., 498
Sandin, R. H., 309
Sanes, J. N., 78
Sangrador, J. L., 673
Sankis, L. M., 563
Sanna, L. J., 683
Sanna, P. P., 205
Sarafino, E. P., 514
Sarason, B. R., 499, 500
Sarason, I. G., 387, 490, 493, 499, 500
Saron, C., 415
Sartory, G., 640
Sartre, J.-S., 538
Sasaki, Y., 178, 185
Sato, T., 580

Sattler, D. N., 534
Sattler, J., 349
Saudino, K. J., 530
Saum, C. A., 436
Sauter, S., 495
Savage-Rumbaugh, E. S., 302, 303
Savage-Rumbaugh, S., 301, 302, 303
Saveliev, S. V., 83
Savelkoul, M., 499
Savin-Williams, R. C., 471
Sawamoto, K., 83
Saxe, L., 420
Sayer, A. G., 332
Sayers, J., 524
Scarr, S., 356, 357, 360
Schachter, L. M., 322
Schachter, S., 418, 422–423
Schacter, D. L., 225, 227, 228–229, 243, 251, 253, 313
Schaefer, J., 45
Schafe, G. E., 257
Schafer, J., 332, 399
Schaffer, A., 449
Schaffer, C. E., 415
Schaie, K. W., 354, 371, 372, 475, 476
Scharff, C., 82
Scharff, D. E., 608
Scharff, J. S., 608
Schaubroeck, J., 488
Scheck, B., 246
Scheel, A. M., 650
Scheerer, M., 369
Scheier, M. F., 501, 522, 546
Schenck, C. H., 322
Scheufele, P. M., 514
Schiff, M., 357
Schiffman, S. S., 391
Schiller, P. H., 120
Schliemann, A. D., 367
Schlosberg, H., 652
Schloss, P., 580
Schmidt, N. B., 569, 570, 604
Schmidt, P. J., 93
Schmidt, R. A., 221
Schmidt, W. H., 713
Schmidtke, A., 680
Schmitt, C., 690
Schmitt, D. P., 384
Schmolck, H., 237–238
Schnabel, T., 637
Schnapf, J. L., 122
Schneider, B., 177
Schneider, B. H., 457
Schneider, J., 632
Schneider, M., 500
Schneider, W., 447, 449
Schneiderman, B., 180
Schneiderman, M., 299
Schneidman, E. S., 578
Schnetter, K., 406
Schnur, E., 361
Schnurr, P. P., 495
Schoen, L. S., 497
Schopler, E., 594
Schram, M., 29

Schroeder, D. A., 215, 703, 704, 706, 712
Schuckit, M. A., 597
Schuh, E. S., 149
Schulman, C. E., 631
Schulman, P., 210
Schultheiss, O., 549
Schultz, D. P., 11–12, 15, 346, 347, 495, 519, 520, 524, 526, 534, 558
Schultz, P. N., 668
Schultz, P. W., 702
Schultz, S. E., 11–12, 15, 346, 347, 495, 519, 520, 524, 526, 534, 558
Schultz, W., 205
Schulz, R., 481, 497, 500
Schulze, P. A., 460
Schulz-Hardt, S., 292
Schumann, D., 663
Schwartz, A. A., 47, 277, 289
Schwartz, B., 201, 209, 218
Schwartz, C., 454
Schwartz, M. W., 389, 390
Schwarz, N., 35, 660, 661, 662
Schwarzer, R., 511
Schweinhart, L. J., 361
Schweitzer, P., 339
Schwender, D., 309
Schwenk, K., 127
Sciacchtinano, A., 648
Sclafani, A., 392
Scott, S., 589
Scribner, S., 471
Seamon, J. G., 662
Searle, L. V., 50
Searleman, A., 259
Sears, D. O., 710
Sears, R., 374, 652
Secord, D., 470
Sedikides, C., 649, 659
Seeman, T., 496
Segal, L., 4, 261, 268
Segal, N. L., 707
Segal, Z. V., 581, 640
Segall, M. H., 355
Segerstrom, S. C., 501, 505
Segre, L., 621
Seiger, A., 84
Seitz, V., 359, 361
Sejnowski, T. J., 254, 325
Sekuler, R., 116, 175
Seligman, M. E., 210
Seligman, M. E. P., 5, 209, 210, 408, 581, 620, 623, 628
Sell, R. L., 400
Selvin, S., 376
Selye, H., 491
Senghas, A., 296, 299
Seppa, N., 215
Sera, M. D., 298
Serpell, R., 354, 355, 361
Sersen, E., 320
Servan-Schreiber, D., 587
Servan-Schreiber, E., 235
Service, R. F., 91
Seto, M. C., 701

Setterlund, M. B., 651
Sevcik, R. A., 303
Seybold, K. S., 499
Seyfarth, R. M., 301
Shackelford, T. K., 384
Shader, R. I., 637
Shadish, W. R., 39, 624, 625, 628
Shaffer, D. R., 4
Shahinfar, A., 19
Shalev, A. Y., 495, 496
Shams, L., 125
Shand, M. A., 234
Shankar, S. G., 302, 303
Shao, Z., 255
Shapiro, A. F., 478
Shapiro, D. E., 631
Shapiro, D. H., 329
Shapiro, F., 26, 28, 30–31, 34, 37, 38, 40
Sharp, L. K., 506
Shaver, P. R., 478, 523
Shavitt, S., 23
Shaw, B. A., 482, 498
Shaw, J. S., III, 246
Shaw, S. F., 377
Shaywitz, B. A., 3, 81
Sheehan, P. W., 328
Sheffield, E. G., 449
Sheldon, K. M., 408, 410, 480
Sheldrick, R. C., 626
Shelton, R. C., 31, 636
Shepard, B. B., 420
Shepard, R., 273
Shepard, R. N., 274
Shepherd, C., 381
Shepperd, J. A., 684
Sher, K. J., 546, 596
Shergill, S. S., 584
Sherif, M., 685
Sherin, J. E., 324
Sherman, J., 668
Sherman, J. W., 243, 654
Sherman, P. W., 130
Sherman, S. J., 688, 694
Sherwin, B. B., 398
Shiffman, S., 336
Shiffrin, R. M., 231
Shiller, R. J., 289
Shimamura, A. P., 476
Shimaoki, K., 506
Shimizu, E., 257
Shimojo, S., 125
Shin, L. M., 72
Shinotsuka, H., 290
Shinskey, J. L., 443
Shiwach, R. S., 633
Shlomo, A., 621, 630
Shobe, K. K., 252
Shoda, Y., 532, 533, 535
Sholtz, R., 336
Showalter, E., 524
Shreeve, J., 100
Shweder, R. A., 473
Siddle, D. A. T., 269
Siebert, S. E., 546
Siegal, M., 447
Siegel, J., 490

Siegel, J. M., 325
Siegel, S., 186
Siegler, R. S., 447
Siepmann, M., 658
Sigmon, S. T., 639
Sigmund, K., 712
Sigmundsson, T., 586
Silber, M. H., 322
Silberschatz, G., 628
Silbersweig, D. A., 3, 584
Silbert, M. H., 699
Silva, P. A., 543
Silver, E., 600
Silver, R. C., 523
Silverman, K., 208, 336
Silverstein, L. B., 385
Silverthorne, C., 714
Simon, H., 373
Simon, H. A., 14, 234, 279, 286
Simon, T., 346, 347
Simons, A., 490
Simons, D. J., 176, 177
Simonsen, H., 136
Simonton, D. K., 373, 374
Simpson, E. E., 340
Simpson, J. A., 465, 523
Simpson, O. J., 237–238
Simpson, S., 504
Sims, J. H., 658
Sinclair, R. C., 422, 423
Singer, B., 624
Singer, J., 422, 423
Singer, J. E., 487
Sinha, P., 167
Sinha, R., 419
Sirvio, J., 255
Skinner, B. F., 14, 15, 196, 197, 202, 203, 533, 613
Skolnic, B. E., 415
Skre, I., 569, 571
Slaby, R. G., 700
Slamecka, N. J., 247
Slater, A., 171, 172
Sloan, D. M., 576
Sloboda, J. A., 221
Slomkowski, C., 463
Slovic, P., 278, 285
Slutske, W., 590, 597
Sluyter, D. J., 464
Small, B. J., 481
Small, G. W., 73
Smit, A. B., 58
Smith, A., 332
Smith, A. P., 324
Smith, B. W., 499
Smith, E., 271, 647, 652, 653, 661, 668, 682, 715
Smith, E. E., 253, 257, 475
Smith, E. R., 398
Smith, F. L., 246
Smith, G. T., 595
Smith, I. M., 594
Smith, J., 475, 504
Smith, L. B., 298
Smith, M., 317
Smith, M. L., 624, 625, 628
Smith, M. U., 385, 399

Smith, M. W., 488
Smith, P., 26
Smith, P. B., 22, 685, 692, 713
Smith, P. K., 480
Smith, S., 454
Smith, S. L., 217
Smith, S. M., 239–240
Smith, S. S., 598
Smith, T. B., 32
Smith, T. W., 210, 397
Smith, V. L., 278
Smyth, J. M., 506
Smythies, J., 70
Snarey, J., 473
Snidman, N., 454
Snodgrass, S. R., 336
Snow, R. E., 363
Snowden, L. R., 564, 565
Snyder, A. W., 35
Snyder, M., 654–655
Snyder, S. H., 339
Snyderman, M., A-3
Soares, J. F., 148
Socrates, 11
Soetens, E., 335
Sokoloff, L., 57
Solomon, A., 576
Solomon, R. L., 186, 199, 411–412
Solomon, S., 649–650
Somerville, S., 511
Sommer, K. L., 292
Sommer, R., 7, 701
Sora, I., 75, 135
Sorce, J., 427
Sorrentino, R. M., 497
Sowell, E. R., 85
Spangler, G., 457
Spanos, N. P., 327, 574
Spates, C. R., 40
Speaker, C. J., 443
Spearman, C., 365
Spelke, E. S., 442
Spencer, S., 364
Spencer, S. J., 664
Sperry, L., 618
Sperry, R., 79, 80
Spiegel, D., 559, 572, 574
Spiegel, D. A., 641
Spiers, P. S., 322
Spira, J. L., 636
Spitz, H. H., 47, 361
Spitzer, R. L., 495, 556, 574
Sprecher, S., 399
Springer, K., 392
Springer, S. P., 80, 91
Spritz, B., 457
Sproull, L., 292
Squire, L. R., 72, 229, 237–238, 255, 256, 257
Srinivas, K., 237
Srivastava, A., 409
Srivastava, S., 527
Sroufe, L. A., 457
Stacey, J., 402
Staddon, J. E. R., 193, 571
Standing, L., 237
Stankov, L., 366

Stanley-Hagan, M., 479
Stanton, P. K., 254
Stanton-Hicks, M., 134
Stapleton, S., 324
Stark, H., 228–229
Stassen, H. H., 577
Stasser, G., 292
Staszewski, J., 235
Statistics Canada, 577
Staudt, M., 82
Steadman, H. J., 600
Stec, A. M., 7
Steele, C. M., 355, 364, 664
Steele, T. D., 337
Steiger, H., 395
Stein, B. S., 279
Stein, D. M., 629
Stein, E., 403
Stein, J., 658
Stein, K. D., 332
Stein, M. A., 281
Steinberg, L., 360, 461, 469, 470
Steiner, J. E., 437
Steiner, J. M., 692
Stella, N., 339
Stemman, R., 27
Stenman, U., 312
Stepanski, E. J., 321
Stephens, M. A. P., 498
Stephens, R. S., 340, 596
Steriade, M., 325
Stern, K., 128
Stern, Y., 476
Sternberg, E. M., 96
Sternberg, R., 346, 366–368, 369
Sternberg, R. J., 356, 367, 373, 374, 447, 475, 674–675
Stevens, A., 326
Stevens, D. G., 151
Stevens, J. C., 132
Stevens, N., 462
Stevens, R., 23
Stevens, S. S., 153
Stevenson, L. A., 425
Stevenson, M. F., 467
Stevenson, R. L., 325
Stewart, A. L., 170
Stewart, D., 292
Stewart, R. E., 128
Stice, E., 394, 395
Stickgold, R., 325, 326
Stills, S., 107
Stipek, D. J., 452
Stoff, D. M., 590, 591
Stone, A., 476
Stone, J., 664
Stone, W. S., 586, 588
Stoney, C. M., 506, 507
Stork, D. G., 295
Stouthamer-Loeber, M., 593
Stradling, J. R., 322
Strain, E. C., 336
Strang, J., 339
Strasser, G., 291
Strathearn, L., 358

Strauss, M. E., 576
Strayer, D. L., 181
Streissguth, A. P., 436
Strickland, T., 638
Stromberg, C. D., 632
Strongman, K. T., 253
Stroop, J. R., 177
Strupp, H. H., 609, 624, 628
Stuart, G. J., 59
Stuart, G. L., 627
Stuart, S. P., 623, 625, 628
Stunkard, A. J., 393
Sturchler-Pierrat, C., 74
Sturm, R., 393
Stuve, P., 616
Styfco, S. J., 362
Subrahmanyam, K., 452
Suddath, R. L., 587
Sue, D., 629, 630
Sue, D. W., 21
Sue, S., 355, 629, 630, 631
Suedfeld, P., 663
Suga, N., 110
Sugita, Y., 322
Suh, E., 409
Suinn, R. M., 501
Sullivan, H. S., 523, 608
Sullivan, P. F., 394
Suls, J., 507, 513
Summala, H., 324
Sundberg, N., 629
Suomi, S., 666
Suri, J. F., 4, 261, 268
Surratt, H. L., 436
Sutton, K., 352, 404, 406, 534
Suzdak, P. D., 333
Suzuki, L. A., 359
Svikis, D., 597
Swaab, D. E., 401
Swan, G. E., 480, 482
Swan, R. D., 394
Swann, W. B., Jr., 676
Swartz, H. A., 627
Sweet, R., 420
Swets, J. A., 150, 151, 288
Swindle, R., Jr., 620, 621
Swithers, S. E., 391
Symons, D., 384
Szasz, S., 563
Szatmari, P., 595
Szymanski, K., 683
Tagliabue, J., 556
Takayama, Y., 79
Takei, N., 587
Takeuchi, A. H., 105
Tallal, P., 111
Tamborini, R., 702
Tanaka, M., 132
Tanaka-Matsumi, J., 629
Tanda, G., 340
Tang, Y.-P., 257
Tannen, D., 23
Tanner, J. M., 55, 467
Tarasoff, T., 631
Tardif, C., 457
Tarr, S. J., 436
Tartaglia, L. A., 389, 394

Task Force on Promotion and Dissemination of Psychological Procedures, 626
Tasker, F., 402
Tate, J. D., 470
Tatsuoka, M., 527
Taub, A., 136
Taubenfeld, S. M., 257
Taubes, G., 392
Taussig, C., 643
Tavris, C., 48
Taylor, B. K., 487
Taylor, H. A., 273
Taylor, R. L., 354, 358
Taylor, S. E., 210, 486, 487, 488, 495, 498, 499, 501, 508, 509, 510, 513, 514, 648, 652, 653, 660, 687, 710, 714
Taylor, S. P., 696
Taylor, T. J., 302, 303
Teates, J. F., 391
Tecott, L. H., 75
Teder-Salejarvi, W. A., 125
Teghtsoonian, R., 310
Teigen, K. H., 385, 387
Tellegen, A., 409, 530, 695
Temple, M. T., 399
Ter Riet, G., 136
Teresa, Mother, 410
Terman, L. M., 346, 347, 353, 374, 502–503, 580
Terrace, H. S., 301, 302
Terry, D., 513
Tesser, A., 648, 650, 659
Tetlock, P., 663
Thaker, G. K., 588
Thanos, P. K., 333
Thase, M., 490
Theall, D., 702–703
Thelen, E., 438
Theofilopoulos, S., 83
Theunisson, E., 179
Thibodeau, P. M., 29
Thom, A., 640
Thomas, A., 454
Thomas, C. W., 454
Thomas, E. L., 259
Thomas, K. W., 713
Thomas, P., 642–643
Thompson, D. E., 407–408
Thompson, D. S., 639
Thompson, E. R., 474
Thompson, J., 245, 246
Thompson, J. K., 394, 395
Thompson, P. M., 84
Thompson, R. A., 456
Thompson, R. F., 70, 257
Thompson, S. C., 498
Thompson, W. G., 336
Thompson, W. R., A-3
Thomson, C. P., 247
Thorndike, E. L., 195–196, 197, 213
Thorndike, R. M., 349, 351
Thornhill, R., 384
Thornton, L. M., 581, 582
Thorpe, G. L., 613, 617, 629

Thunberg, 132
Thurber, S., 259
Thurstone, L. L., 365, 371
Tian, H.-G., 392
Tidwell, M. C. O., 478
Tiggemann, M., 395
Tiihonen, J., 333
Tiller, J., 394
Timberlake, W., 204
Tinbergen, N., 382, 383
Titchener, E., 12, 13, 15
Tobin, S., 481
Todd, P. M., 170
Todorov, C., 637
Toh, K. L., 323
Tolle, R., 580
Tolman, E., 211
Tomasello, M., 451
Tomes, H., 631
Tompkins, M. A., 620
Tondo, L., 636
Toni, N., 254
Torasdotter, M., 85
Torres, A., 393
Torrubia-Beltri, R., 216
Tourangeau, R., 661
Townsend, A. L., 498
Townsend, J., 595
Townsend, J. M., 384
Townshend, P., 107
Trabasso, T. R., 270
Tramer, M. R., 340
Tranel, D., 414
Trapnell, P., 531
Treadwell, J., 229
Treasure, D. C., 7
Treat, T. A., 627
Treiman, R., 299
Treisman, A., 177, 178
Tremblay, A., 394
Tremblay, P., 400
Tremblay, R. E., 591, 643
Trevarthen, W. R., 398
Treyens, J., 243
Triandis, H. C., 21, 22, 23, 695
Trierweiler, S. J., 564, 565
Trillin, A. S., 284
Triplett, N., 682
Trivers, R. L., 384
Tromovitch, P., 593
Tronick, E. Z., 453
Troop, L. R., 650
Trope, Y., 657
Tropp, L. R., 668, 669
Trost, M., 673, 680, 681, 684, 686, 687–688
Trower, P., 615
Trueswell, J. C., 296
Trujillo, C. M., 363
Trujillo, K. A., 337
Trull, T. J., 524, 546
Tryon, R., 50
Tseng, W., 559
Tsien, J. Z., 257
Tsuang, M. T., 588, 589
Tuchin, M., 246
Tucker, D. M., 421

Name Index

Tulving, E., 227, 228–229, 239, 249, 250, 256
Tuomilehto, J., 510
Turiel, E., 473
Turkheimer, E., 531, A-7
Turkington, C., 376
Turkkan, J. S., 186
Turner, B. G., 364
Turner, C. D., 40
Turner, C. F., 36
Turner, J. C., 686
Turner, L. A., 376
Tversky, A., 212, 277–278, 289, 290, 305, 475
Tversky, B., 246, 273
Tversky, P., 283
Tykocinski, O., 652
Uchida, Y., 543
Uchino, B. N., 500, 665
Uhl, G., 135
Ullian, E. M., 82
Umberson, D., 499
Ungless, M. A., 335
U.S. Census Bureau, 360
U.S. Department of Health and Human Services (USDHHS), 336, 392, 393, 487, 508, 509, 629, 642
U.S. Department of Justice, 10, 207, 246–247, 596, 694, 695, 697
U.S. Surgeon General, 73, 320, 375, 394, 395, 509, 555, 556, 559, 564, 566, 567, 568, 569, 576, 577, 579, 580, 582, 586, 593, 595, 596, 598, 604, 606, 633, 635, 636, 637, 638
Uno, D., 500
Vaitl, D., 571
Valencia, R. R., 359
Valencia-Flores, M., 320
Valenstein, E. S., 634
Valent, F., 324
Valenza, E., 437
Van Ameringen, M. A., 637
Van Bezooijen, R., 426
Van de Kragt, A. J. C., 712
Van den Broek, P., 218
Van den Oord, E. J. C. G., 358
Van der Kooy, D., 387
Van Essen, D. C., 116
Van Fleet, D. D., 714
Van Ijzendoorn, M. H., 478
Van Lange, P. A. M., 649, 673
Van Praag, H., 84
Van Reekum, R., 91
Van Sickel, A. D., 329
Van Zandt, T., 268
VandeCreek, L., 631
Vanhuele, M., 225
Vastag, B., 595
Vattano, F., 256
Vavac, C., 508
Vela, E., 240
Velligan, D. I., 588
Velpeau, A., 286
Venables, P., 590

Venter, J. C., 52
Ventura, J., 536
Venturelli, P. J., 333
Verfaellie, M., 257
Vernet, M. E., 415
Vernon, P. A., 366, 447
Vicary, J., 147
Vickers, K. S., 639
Vickers, Z., 391
Vincent, C. A., 135
Vincent, K. R., 361
Vink, T., 394
Vioque, J., 393
Viswesvaran, C., 518, 546, 549
Voda, A., 403
Voelker, R., 340
Vogelbaum, M. A., 323
Vogeltanz, N. D., 639
Vokey, J. R., 314–315
Volkow, N. D., 335
Vollebergh, W. A. M., 561
Volz, H. P., 636
Volz, J., 480, 481
Von Bekesy, G., 108
Von Helmholtz, H., 11, 122
Von Meduna, L., 633
Von Wright, J. M., 312
Vookles, J., 652
Vorel, S. R., 332
Vygotsky, L., 450
Vyse, S. A., 315
Waagenaar, W. A., 290
Waddell, K. J., 448
Wadden, T. A., 393, 394
Wade, C., 28
Wade, T., 395
Wade, W. A., 627
Wadsworth, J. S., 377
Wadsworth, S., A-5
Waelti, P., 205
Wagner, A. D., 231, 255
Wagner, A. R., 218
Wagner, U., 325
Wahlsten, D., A-6
Wakasa, Y., 336
Wakefield, J. C., 555
Wakita, M., 200
Walbeck, K., 587
Walberg, H. J., 219
Waldman, I. D., 357, 360
Waldron, M., 531, A-7
Waldrop, M. M., 235
Walk, R. D., 172
Walker, E. F., 588
Walker, L., 21
Walker, L. J., 473
Walker-Andrews, A. S., 442
Walkup, J. T., 637
Wall, P. D., 134
Wall, T. L., 596
Wallace, C. S., 86
Wallace, Dr., 288
Wallace, J., 265, 266
Wallace, R. K., 330
Wallen, K., 398
Waller, D., 91
Wallerstein, J. S., 466

Wallis, G., 163
Wallis, J. D., 269
Wallman, J., 114
Walsh, R. N., 329
Walter, A. A., 244
Walter, B. M., 372
Walters, R. H., 533
Walton, G. E., 453
Wampler, K. S., 531
Wan, C. K., 507
Wandell, B., 124
Wanderling, J., 558, 559
Wang, C.-H. C., 461
Wang, X., 402
Wang, Z., 135
Warburton, D. M., 336
Ward, C., 317
Ward, L. M., 312
Warner, L., 597
Warot, D., 91
Warrington, E. K., 228, 316
Washburn, A. L., 388
Washburn, M., 16
Wasik, B. H., 361
Wasserman, E. M., 633
Wasserman, T. H., 384
Watanabe, K., 125
Watanabe, S., 200
Watanabe, T., 185, 322
Waterman, A. S., 471
Waters, E., 457
Watkins, L. R., 96, 135, 505
Watkinson, B., 341
Watson, D., 563
Watson, J. B., 14, 15, 18, 433, 533, 613, A-3
Watson, R. I., 12
Watson, S. J., Jr., 341
Watt, N. F., 583
Watts, J. W., 634
Watts, R. L., 83
Wearden, A. J., 588
Webdale, K., 632
Weber, E., 152
Wechsler, D., 348
Wedding, D., 611
Wedge, J. W., 549
Weekes, J. R., 329
Weeks, D., 555
Weeks, J., 555
Wegener, D. T., 663
Weikart, D. P., 361
Weiler, B. L., 592
Weinberg, J., 497
Weinberg, R. A., 357, 360, 361
Weinberger, D. R., 88
Weiner, B., 382, 405
Weiner, C., 586
Weinfield, N. S., 457
Weinraub, M., 478
Weinstein, D., 256
Weinstein, L., 694
Weiskrantz, L., 228
Weiss, B., 628
Weiss, F., 205, 332
Weiss, R. S., 497
Weissman, M. M., 576, 627

Weisstein, N., 170
Weist, M. D., 616
Weisz, J. R., 624, 626, 628
Welburg, J. B., 322
Wells, G. L., 246, 247
Wells, J. A., 400
Wells, K. B., 393
Wells, S., 696
Welsh, E., 110
Welte, J. W., 334
Weltzin, T. E., 395
Went, F., 615
Werker, J. F., 297
Wernicke, C., 78
Wertheimer, M., 11, 12, 623
Wesensten, N. J., 326
Wessinger, C. M., 312
West, D., 27
West, P., 696
Westen, D., 520, 522, 523, 524, 537, 609
Westmaas, J. L., 523
Weston, C., 615
Weston, R. E., Jr., 631, 632
Weyhing, R. S., 376
Whalen, C. K., 593
Whalen, P. J., 72
Whalley, L. J., 476
Whalley, L. T., 374
Wharton, C. M., 281, 282
Wheeler, M. E., 257–258
Wheeler, S. C., 670
Wherry, M. B., 651
Whiffen, V. E., 581
Whimbey, A., 259
Whisman, M. A., 558
Whitam, F. L., 401
Whitbourne, S. K., 478
White, A. R., 136
White, D. E., 450
White, F. J., 336
Whiteman, M. C., 506
Whitman, T. L., 469
Whitney, P., 272, 273
Whorf, B., 303–304
Wickens, C. D., 152, 173, 177, 179, 221, 261, 266, 267, 268, 285
Widener, A. J., 251
Widiger, T. A., 527, 561, 563, 564, 565, 568, 589, 595
Widom, C. S., 591–593
Wiebe, D. J., 210
Wiedenfeld, S., 497
Wiener, E., 179
Wiertelak, E. P., 135
Wiesel, T. N., 119, 166
Wigfield, A., 406
Wilding, E. L., 258
Williams, D. A., 190
Williams, D. C., 580
Williams, G. V., 256
Williams, J. E., 464
Williams, K. D., 292, 683, 684, 713
Williams, L. M., 251
Williams, M., 590

Williams, R. B., 506
Williams, R. B., Jr., 506
Williams, S., 8, 640
Williams, T. J., 401
Williams, W. M., 367
Williamson, J. E., 240
Willing, A. E., 83
Willis, S. L., 475, 476
Willis, W. D., Jr., 134
Wills, T. A., 467
Wilson, A. E., 648
Wilson, B. J., 700
Wilson, D. L., 317, 596
Wilson, G. T., 395, 403, 467, 613, 625, 628
Wilson, M., 465
Wilson, S. G., 135
Wilson, S. J., 322
Wilson, S. P., 460
Wilson, T., 662, 672
Wilson, T. D., 7, 284, 409, 682, 686, 700, 705
Wilson, W. J., 360
Wingood, G. M., 511
Winkielman, P., 665
Winn, P., 391
Winner, E., 375, 476
Winokur, G., 579
Winson, J., 326
Winter, D. G., 404, 667
Winzelberg, A. J., 631
Wise, R. A., 88, 337, 421
Wiseman, R., 27
Wisner, K. L., 576
Witt, S. D., 465
Wittchen, H. U., 567, 569
Witten, J., 339
Wittenbaum, G. M., 291, 292
Wittlinger, R. P., 449
Wohl, J., 629

Wolf, E., 338
Wolfe, J. M., 130, 175
Wolff, W. T., 199
Wolman, C., 218
Wolpaw, J. R., 82
Wolpe, J., 194, 614
Wolz, J. P., 302
Wong, B. Y. L., 376
Wong, S. E., 615
Wood, J., 548, 549
Wood, J. V., 648
Wood, W., 501, 663, 664, 674
Woodhead, M., 361, 362
Woodruff-Pak, D. S., 194–195
Woods, S. C., 389, 390
Woods, T., 434
Woodworth, R. S., 652
Woolcott, M., 681
Woolfolk-Hoy, A., 218, 219
Woolley, J. D., 447
Worchel, S., 648
World Health Organization, 554
Worthington, J. J., III, 637
Wren, C., 336, 341
Wright, B. A., 110
Wright, E. F., 385
Wright, G. N., 290
Wright, J. C., 215
Wright, J. H., 175
Wright, S., 650
Wright, T. J., 391
Wu, H. W., 505
Wundt, W., 11–12, 13, 15
Wurtman, J. J., 88
Wurtman, R. J., 88
Wynn, K., 443–444
Wynne, L. C., 199
Wypij, D., 400
Xie, J. J., 488
Yaffe, K., 482

Yahr, P., 398
Yakel, J. L., 255
Yakimovich, D., 704
Yalom, I. D., 620
Yamagita, T., 336
Yantis, S., 175
Yates, A., 599
Yates, J. F., 290
Yates, M., 471, 474
Yates, W. R., 696
Yeh, S. Y., 337
Yela, C., 673
Yerkes, R. M., 348, 387
Yesavage, J. A., 340
Yogi, M., 329
Yonas, A., 173
Yonkers, K., 639
York, J. L., 334
Young, A. W., 134, 316
Young, D. A., 337
Young, K., 630
Young, M., 372
Young, T., 122
Youniss, J., 474
Younkin, S. G., 74
Yousif, Y. H., 706
Yuan, C.-S., 91
Yuille, J. C., 251
Yukl, G. A., 202, 714
Yule, W., 26
Yung, B., 629
Yurgelun-Todd, D. A., 587
Yutrzenka, B. A., 631
Zachman, Sister M., 477
Zadnik, K., 113
Zahn-Waxler, C., 464, 703
Zahrani, S. A., 405
Zajonc, R. B., 359, 424, 425, 683
Zakzanis, K. K., 337
Zanarini, M. C., 563

Zane, N., 630
Zani, B., 668
Zanna, M. P., 667, 668
Zaragoza, M. S., 246
Zatorre, R. J., 205
Zautra, A. J., 504
Zeki, S., 119
Zelenski, J. M., 530
Zelinski, E., 354
Zernike, K., 681
Zeta-Jones, C., 385
Zhang, G., 234
Zhang, X., 124
Zhang, Y., 389
Zhou, J.-N., 398
Ziemba-Davis, M., 696
Zigler, E., 359, 361, 362, 374, 577, 643, 680
Zigler, E. F., 467
Zillmann, D., 422, 698, 702
Zimbardo, P. G., 691
Zimmerman, J., 572
Zimmerman, M., 576, 620
Zinbarg, R. E., 569, 571
Zisook, S., 586
Zoellner, L. A., 252
Zola, S. M., 255
Zornberg, G. L., 636
Zorumski, C., 569
Zou, Z., 127
Zsambok, C. E., 290, 291
Zubek, J. P., 50
Zuckerman, M., 359, 385, 530, 533, 559
Zuercher-White, E., 617
Zuger, A., 465
Zuwerink, J. R., 669

SUBJECT INDEX/GLOSSARY

Key terms, which appear in **boldface**, *are followed by their definitions.*

Abecedarian Project, 361–362
Abnormality, 554–555. *See also* Psychological disorders
Absolute threshold *The minimum amount of stimulus energy that can be detected 50 percent of the time,* 146, 147–149
Abuse, false memories and, 250, 251, 252, 253
Academic achievement
 genetics and, A-5
 language and, 450–451
 socioeconomic status and, 451–452
Accessory structures *Structures, such as the lens of the eye, that modify a stimulus,* 101
Accidental reinforcement, 204
Accommodation *(in cognitive development) The process of modifying schemas as an infant tries out familiar schemas on objects that do not fit them,* 441
Accommodation *(in eye structure) The ability of the lens to change its shape and bend light rays so that objects are in focus,* 112–113, 160, 173
Acetylcholine *A neurotransmitter used by neurons in the peripheral and central nervous systems in the control of functions ranging from muscle contraction and heart rate to digestion and memory,* 87, 90, 91, 255, 336, 416
Achievement motivation, 404–409
 development of, 405–406
 goal setting and, 406–407
 individual differences in, 404–405
 need for achievement and, 404–406
 subjective well-being and, 408–409
 success in workplace and, 407–408
Achievement tests *Measures of what a person has accomplished or learned in a particular area,* 350
Acoustic encoding *The mental representation of information as a sequence of sounds,* 226, 233–234
Acquired immune deficiency syndrome (AIDS), 95, 396, 399, 469, 486, 501, 504, 505, 509, 511
Acrophobia, 566, 567
ACT, *see* American College Testing Assessment
Action potential *An abrupt wave of electrochemical changes traveling down an axon when a neuron becomes depolarized,* 58–60, 61, 102
Activation-synthesis theory, 326
Active learning, 219–220
Actor-observer bias *The tendency to attribute other people's behavior to internal causes while attributing one's own behavior (especially errors and failures) to external causes,* 658–659
Actualizing tendency *According to Rogers, an innate inclination toward growth that motivates all people to seek the full realization of their highest potential,* 538, 539

Acuity *Visual clarity, which is greatest in the fovea because of its large concentration of cones,* 114
Acupuncture, 69, 135–136
Adam, *see* MDMA
Adaptation *The process through which responsiveness to an unchanging stimulus decreases over time,*
 dark, 113–114
 diseases of, 492
 general adaptation syndrome and, 491–492, 501
 learning and, 185
 sensory systems and, 101, 131
Addiction *Development of a physical need for a psychoactive drug,* 332, 595. *See also* Psychoactive drugs
Additive color mixing, 121
A-delta fibers, 133
Adenosine, 325, 336
ADHD, *see* Attention deficit hyperactivity disorder
Adolescence, 467–474
 cognitive development in, 440, 446, 471, 480
 depression in, 576, 581, 582
 early, 467, 480
 eating disorders in, 394–395
 genital stage in, 522
 identity formation in, 460, 469–471
 late, 471, 480
 moral reasoning in, 472–474
 peer relationships in, 461, 468
 physical development in, 468, 469, 480
 pregnancy in, 469
 puberty and, 398, 467–469
 sexual behavior in, 399, 469
 sleep in, 321
 social and emotional development in, 457, 460, 462, 467–471, 480
 suicide in, 578
Adoption studies, 51–52, A-3
Adrenal glands, 93, 94, 95, 505, 507
 general adaptation syndrome and, 491, 492
Adrenaline, *see* Epinephrine
Adrenocorticotropic hormone (ACTH), 94, 95
 general adaptation syndrome and, 491–492
Adulthood, 474–482
 cognitive changes in, 84–86, 370–372, 440, 471, 474–477, 480, 481
 early, 474, 475, 478–479
 middle, 474, 475, 479–480
 moral reasoning in, 472, 473
 physical changes in, 474, 480
 social and emotional changes in, 460, 477–481
 see also Late adulthood
Advertising
 cultural differences and, 23, 304
 errors in formal reasoning and, 276
 memory and, 229
 subliminal, 147–149

Aerophobia, 566, 614, 617
Affective disorder, *see* **Mood disorder**
Afferent neurons, 67
Afghanistan, Taliban and, 693, 697
Afterimages, 123, 124
Age regression, hypnosis and, 327, 328, 329
Aggression *An act that is intended to cause harm or damage to another person,* 694–702
 acquaintances and, 694–695
 alcohol and, 332, 334
 androgens and, 93
 arousal and, 698–701
 biological approach to, 695–696
 cognitive approach to, 19
 copycat crimes and, 680
 culture and, 208, 695, 696–697
 day care and, 37
 defensive, 695–696
 environment and, 695, 697, 698–699, 701–702
 evolutionary approach to, 17, 383, 695
 frustration and, 698
 humanistic approach to, 19
 learning and, 696–697
 observational learning and, 214
 physical punishment and, 206
 pornography and, 37, 699–701
 prevalence of, 694
 psychodynamic approach to, 18, 520
 reasons for, 695–697
 serotonin and, 88
 as stress response, 495
 television and, 37, 215–217, 697
 temperature and, 697, 701
Aging, *see* Late adulthood
Agonists *Drugs that mimic the effects of the neurotransmitter that normally binds to a neural receptor,* 331
Agoraphobia *A strong fear of being alone or away from the security of home,* 566–567, 568, 617, 627, 637, 640
Agranulocytosis, 635
Agreeableness, as big-five personality factor, 528
AI, *see* **Artificial intelligence**
AIDS, *see* Acquired immune deficiency syndrome
Air pollution, aggression and, 702
Alarm reaction, general adaptation syndrome and, 491
Alcohol, 332, 333–334, 335
 aggression and, 696
 alcohol use disorders and, *see* **Alcoholism**
 cerebellum and, 71
 fetal alcohol syndrome and, 436, 509, 596
 health problems and, 509
 social drinking and, 597
Alcoholics Anonymous (AA), 620
Alcoholism *A pattern of drinking that may lead to addiction and almost always causes severe social, physical, and other problems,* 558, 596–597, 598, 620, 621, 627, 641, A-6

SIG-1

Algorithms *Systematic procedures that cannot fail to produce a solution to a problem*, 274, 277
Alpha waves, 318
Alprazolam (Xanax), 637, 638, 640, 641
Altered state of consciousness *A condition in which changes in mental processes are extensive enough that a person or others notice significant differences in psychological and behavioral functioning*, 317
Altruism *An unselfish concern for another's welfare*, 702–703. *See also* Altruism/helping behavior
Altruism/helping behavior, 702–709
　arousal: cost-reward theory of, 703–706, 709
　children and, 703
　empathy-altruism theory of, 706, 709
　evolutionary approach to, 383, 706–709
　examples of, 702–703
Alzheimer's disease, 55, 57, 73–75, 84, 87, 89, 91, 92, 194–195, 255, 323, 371, 474, 476–477, 557, A-5–A-6
American Association of Suicidology, 578
American Cancer Society, 508
American College Testing Assessment (ACT), 350
American Law Institute (ALI), 599
American Medical Association, 341
American Psychiatric Association, 400, 555, 560
American Psychological Association, 16, 49, 352, 513, 549, 626–628, 631, A-3
American Psychological Association Commission on Violence and Youth, 215
American Sign Language, 111, 301, 303
Amitid, *see* Amitriptyline
Amitriptyline (Elavil; Amitid), 638
Amnesia, 229, 562
　anterograde, 256, 257, 316, 317
　dissociative, 573
　infantile, 449–450
　posthypnotic, 327
　retrograde, 256, 257
Amphetamines, 335, 386, 696
Amplitude *The difference between the peak and the baseline of a waveform*, 104, 105, 106
Amygdala *A structure in the forebrain that, among other things, associates features of stimuli from two sensory modalities, such as linking the shape and feel of objects in memory*, 72–73, 86, 127, 414, 666
Amyloid vaccines, 74
Anabolic effects, 390
Anafranil, *see* Clomipramine
Analgesia *The absence of the sensation of pain in the presence of a normally painful stimulus*, 134–135
Analogical representations, 273
Analogies, 280–282, 285
Analogue methodology, 707–709
Anal stage *The second of Freud's psychosexual stages, usually occurring during the second year of life, in which the focus of pleasure and conflict shifts from the mouth to the anus*, 521

Analysis of variance, A-17–A-18
Analytic intelligence, 366, 367, 368
Analytic psychology, 522
Anandamide, 338
Anchoring heuristic *A mental shortcut that involves basing judgments on existing information*, 277–278
Androgens *Masculine hormones that circulate in the bloodstream and regulate sexual motivation in both sexes; relatively more androgens circulate in men than in women*, 93, 398, 401
Anesthesia, consciousness and, 309, 312
Anger, facial expression of, 425
Animal studies
　of acupuncture, 136
　of addiction, 332, 336, 340
　of aggression, 695
　of brain plasticity, 85
　of consciousness, 309
　of dopamine, 88
　of dreams, 326
　of emotion, 421
　ethics and, 49
　of gene manipulation in animal models of human disease, 73–75
　of genetic influences on behavior, A-6
　of hunger and satiety, 389, 390, 391
　of insight, 212–213
　of language use, 301–303
　of latent learning, 211
　of learned helplessness, 209
　of nootropic drugs, 90–91
　of olfaction, 127
　of pain, 134, 135
　of personality, 528
　selective breeding and, 50
　of sex hormones, 93
　of sexual behavior, 396, 398, 401
　social cognitive neuroscience and, 665–666
　of stress, 96
　of synaptic plasticity, 82–84
　of taste, 129–130, 193
　of touch, 132
　of vision, 116
　of wanting and liking, 387
　of weight loss, 393–394
Animal Welfare Act, 49
Animism, 445
"Anna O.," 606
Anorexia nervosa *An eating disorder characterized by self-starvation and dramatic weight loss*, 394
Antagonists *Drugs that bind to a receptor and prevent the normal neurotransmitter from binding*, 331
Anterior cingulate cortex, 133
Anterograde amnesia *A loss of memory for any event that occurs after a brain injury*, 256, 257, 316, 317
Anti-anxiety agents, *see* **Anxiolytics**
Antibodies, 95, 504
Anticonvulsant drugs, 637, 638
Antidepressants *Drugs that relieve depression*, 635–636, 638, 641, 642
Antipsychotics, *see* **Neuroleptics**

Antisocial personality disorder *A disorder involving impulsive, selfish, unscrupulous, even criminal behavior*, 554, 589–593
Anvil, *see* Incus
Anxiety disorder *A condition in which intense feelings of apprehension are long-standing or disruptive*, 557, 562, 565–571, 575, 576, 627, 628
　antidepressants for, 636, 637, 638
　anxiolytics for, 637, 638, 640
　biological factors in, 569, 571
　causes of, 569–570
　cognitive factors in, 569–570
　depression and, 568
　eye movement desensitization and reprocessing for, 26, 28, 30–31, 34, 37, 38, 40, 41, 42, 43, 46–47
　generalized, 567, 575, 627, 640
　incidence of, 554
　learning and, 569, 570–571
　observational learning and, 215
　obsessive-compulsive disorder, 553, 568–569, 570, 575, 617, 627, 634, 636, 637, 640, 641
　panic disorder, 337, 498, 560, 567–568, 569–570, 575, 604, 613, 617, 618–619, 627, 636, 637, 640, 641
　phobias, 566–567, 569, 570–571, 575, 614, 615, 616–617, 627, 628, 637, 640
　posttraumatic stress disorder, 72, 194, 252, 309, 322, 495–496, 568, 614, 627, 637
　psychosurgery for, 634
　psychotherapy for, 640, 641
　separation, 594, 595
　treatment of, *see* **Behavior therapy**
　see also **Behavior therapy**
Anxiolytics *Drugs that reduce feelings of anxiety*, 637
Anxious-fearful cluster, of personality disorders, 589, 590
Aphasia, 78
Appetite, 391
Applied relaxation, 627
Approach-approach conflicts, 411
Approach-avoidance conflicts, 411
Approach-inhibition theory, 529–530
Aptitude tests *Tests designed to measure a person's capacity to learn certain things or perform certain tasks*, 350
Aricept, 91
Army Alpha and Beta tests, 347–348
Arousal *A general level of activation that is reflected in several physiological systems and can be measured by electrical activity in the brain, heart action, muscle tension, and the state of many other organ systems*, 386–387
　aggression and, 698–701
　altruism/helping behavior and, 703–706, 709
　presence of other people and, 682–684
Arousal: cost-reward theory *A theory attributing people's helping behavior to their efforts to reduce the unpleasant arousal they feel in the face of someone's need or suffering*, 703–706, 709
Arousal disorder, 403

Arousal theories *Theories of motivation stating that people are motivated to behave in ways that maintain what is, for them, an optimal level of arousal,* 386–387, 388
Arthritis, 95
Artificial insemination, 478–479
Artificial intelligence (AI) *The field that studies how to program computers to imitate the products of human perception, understanding, and thought,* 286–288
ASL, *see* American Sign Language
Asperger's disorder, 595
Assertiveness and social skills training *Methods for teaching clients how to interact with others more comfortably and effectively,* 615
Assimilation *The process of trying out existing schemas on objects that fit those schemas,* 440–441
Association cortex *Those parts of the cerebral cortex that receive information from more than one sense or combine sensory and motor information to perform such complex cognitive tasks,* 76, 78–79, 81, 104
Associations, neural network models and, 217–218
Associative learning, *see* **Classical conditioning; Operant conditioning**
Astringent, 128
Ataques de nervios, 559
Attachment *A deep and enduring relationship with the person with whom a baby has shared many experiences,* 128, 453, 455–459, 478, 523
Attention *The process of directing and focusing certain psychological resources to enhance information processing, performance, and mental experience,* 173–178
  aging and, 372
  automatic processing and, 177–178
  brain and, 178
  classical conditioning and, 191–192
  covert, 173, 174–175
  directing, 175
  divided, 177
  effort and, 173, 178
  ignoring, 176–177
  intelligence and, 366
  limits of, 173, 178
  mental functioning and, 173, 178
  selective, 233
Attention deficit hyperactivity disorder (ADHD), 557, 594, 641
Attitude *A predisposition toward a particular cognitive, emotional, or behavioral reaction to objects,* 660–665
  affective component of, 660, 661
  behavioral component of, 660, 661
  changes in, 662–665
  cognitive component of, 660, 661
  cognitive dissonance theory and, 663–664, 665
  consistency and, 660–661
  elaboration likelihood model and, 662–663, 665

  first impressions and, 653
  formation of, 661–662
  interpersonal attraction and, 672, 673
  self-perception theory and, 664–665
  structure of, 660–661
Attraction, *see* Interpersonal attraction
Attribution *The process of explaining the causes of people's behavior, including one's own,* 422, 655–659
  biases in, 657–659
  culture and, 657
  decision making and, 289, 291
  depression and, 581
  external, 655
  internal, 655
  sources of, 655–657
Attributional biases, 657–659
Atypical neuroleptics, *see* **Neuroleptics**
Auditory cortex, 76, 109–110, 111
Auditory nerve *The bundle of axons that carries stimuli from the hair cells of the cochlea to the brain,* 106, 107, 109, 110, 137
Auditory pathways, 109–111
Auditory scene analysis *The perceptual process through which sounds are mentally represented and interpreted,* 157
Auditory streams, 157
Authoritarian parents *Firm, punitive, and unsympathetic parents who value obedience from the child and authority for themselves,* 460, 461
  obedience and, 691–692, 693
  prejudice and, 667
Authoritative parents *Parents who reason with the child, encourage give and take, are firm but understanding,* 460–461, 462
Autistic disorder, 557, 594–595, 616
  biological approach to, 595, A-6
  facilitated communication for, 47, 48
Autistic savants, 35
Autistic spectrum disorders, 594–595
Autoimmune disorders *Physical problems caused when cells of the body's immune system attack normal body cells as if they were foreign invaders,* 95, 504
Autokinetic phenomenon, 685
Automatic thinking, 267
Autonomic nervous system (ANS) *A subsystem of the peripheral nervous system that carries messages between the central nervous system and the heart, lungs, and other organs and glands,* 65–66, 95, 96
  amphetamines and, 335
  antisocial personality disorder and, 590–591
  anxiety disorder and, 569
  emotion and, 415–417
  general adaptation syndrome and, 491, 492
  immune system and, 505
  nicotine and, 336
  parasympathetic system and, 65, 87, 416
  sympathetic system and, 65, 88, 416–417
  vestibular system and, 137
Autonomy *versus* shame and doubt, 459, 460
Availability heuristic *A mental shortcut through which judgments are based on information that is most easily brought to mind,* 278, 290

Aversive conditioning *A method that uses classical conditioning to create a negative response to some stimulus,* 617
Aversive racism, 670
Aviation psychology, 179
Avoidance-avoidance conflicts, 411
Avoidance conditioning *A type of learning in which an organism responds to a signal in a way that avoids exposure to an aversive stimulus,* 198–199, 209
Avoidant attachment, 523
Avoidant personality disorder, 589, 590
Axons *Fibers that carry signals from the cell body of a neuron out to where communication occurs with other neurons,* 58, 59, 60, 61, 63, 82
Babblings *The first sounds infants make that resemble speech,* 297
Backward conditioning, 191
Balance, 131, 137
Balanced bilinguals, 300
Barbiturates, 333, 334–335
Bargaining, conflict management and, 713
BAS, *see* **Behavioral approach system**
Base rates, 278
Basilar membrane *The floor of the fluid-filled duct that runs through the cochlea,* 106, 107, 108, 109, 110
B-cells, 504, 505
Bedlam, 557
Behavior
  evolutionary approach to, 17
  genetics and, A-5–A-6
  subliminal stimuli and, 147–149
Behavioral approach *An approach to psychology emphasizing that human behavior is determined mainly by what a person has learned, especially from rewards and punishments the person has experienced in interacting with other people; also called behavioral model,* 18, 20, 613
  classical and operant conditioning and, 208–209
  to motivation, 382
  see also **Behavior therapy**
Behavioral approach system (BAS) *Brain regions that affect people's sensitivity to rewards,* 530
Behavioral coping strategies, 514
Behavioral dependence, 595
Behavioral genetics *The study of the effect of genes on behavior,* A-1–A-9
  adoption studies in, 51–52, A-3
  environment and, A-6–A-8
  family studies in, 50, 51, A-3
  Human Genome Project and, 52, A-6
  research and, 49–52, A-3–A-4
  see also **Genetics**
Behavioral inhibition system (BIS) *Brain regions that affect people's sensitivity to punishment,* 530
Behavioral premarital intervention, 623
Behavioral stress responses, 488, 494–496, 503
Behaviorism, 14, 15, 18, 309, A-3

Behavior modification *Treatments that use operant conditioning methods to change behavior,* 613, 614–618, 622
Behavior therapy *Treatments that use classical conditioning principles to change behavior,* 613–620, 622
  aversive conditioning, 617
  behavior modification, 613, 614–618, 622
  cognitive-behavior therapy, 614, 618–620, 622, 625, 626–628, 640
  cognitive therapy, 619–620, 626–628, 641
  effectiveness of, 625, 626–628
  extinction, 616–617
  modeling, 615
  positive reinforcement, 615–616
  punishment, 617–618
  rational-emotive behavior therapy, 618–619
  systematic desensitization, 614–615
Bell Curve, The, A-3–A-4
Belongingness motives, 409, 410
Benzodiazepines, 637, 638, 639, 641
Beta-amyloid, 73–75
Beta-amyloid precursor protein, 73–75
Bias(es)
  in attribution, 657–659
  confirmation, 30, 276, 284, 285, 292
  in decision making, 289–291, 292
  experimenter, 40–41
  in IQ tests, 354–356, 358–361, 363
  in psychological diagnosis, 563–565
  in sampling, 32
Biased sample *A group of research participants selected from a population each of whose members did not have an equal chance of being chosen,* 32
Big-five model *Five trait dimensions found in many factor-analytic studies of personality: neuroticism, extraversion, openness to experience, agreeableness, and conscientiousness,* 526–528, 532, 533
Bilingualism, 300–301
Binocular disparity *A depth cue based on the difference between two retinal images of the world,* 160, 161
Biological approach *An approach to psychology in which behavior and behavior disorders are seen as the result of physical processes, especially those relating to the brain and to hormones and other chemicals; also called* biological model, 16–17, 20, 56
  to aggression, 695–696
  to anxiety disorder, 569
  to arousal, 386
  to autistic disorder, 595, A-6
  to eating, 388–389
  to emotion, 413–417, 418, 421–422, 423–424
  to hunger, 395
  to incentives, 387
  to language acquisition, 299–300
  to memory, 253–258, A-6
  to mood disorder, 579–580, 582
  to motivation, 382
  to prejudice/stereotypes, 666
  to psychological disorders, 556–557, 641–642
  to reinforcement, 204–205
  to schizophrenia, 586–588, A-6–A-7
  to sexual behavior, 398–399
  to sexual orientation, 400–403
  social cognitive neuroscience and, 665–666
  trait theories and, 526, 527, 533
  see also Biology; **Genetics**; Nature and nurture
Biological clock, 580
Biological motives, 409, 410
Biological preparedness, 571
Biological psychologists *Psychologists who analyze the biological factors influencing behavior and mental processes; also called* physiological psychologists, 3, 8, 9
Biological psychology *The psychological specialty that researches the physical and chemical changes that cause, and occur in response to, behavior and mental processes,* 55
Biological rhythms, 71
Biological treatments, 632–634
  electroconvulsive therapy, 633–634, 639
  psychosurgery, 634, 639
  see also Psychoactive drugs
Biology, 54–55. *See also* **Biological approach**; **Endocrine system**; **Genetics**; **Immune system**; **Nervous system**; **Sensory systems**
Biopreparedness, 192–193
Biopsychosocial model *A view of mental disorders as caused by a combination of interacting biological, psychological, and sociocultural factors,* 556–559, 560
  alcohol use disorders and, 596
  antisocial personality disorder and, 591
Biotechnology, 14
Bipolar cells, 114, 116
Bipolar disorders, 557, 578–579, 580
  lithium and anticonvulsants for, 636–637, 638
Bipolar I disorder *A condition in which a person alternates between deep depression and mania,* 578
Bipolar II disorder, 578
BIS, *see* **Behavioral inhibition system**
Bisexual *People who engage in sexual activities with partners of both sexes,* 400, 401, 402–403
Blindness, 138
  hypnosis and, 328
  touch and, 131
Blindsight, 312
Blind spot *The light insensitive point at which axons from all of the ganglion cells converge and exit the eyeball,* 116, 118
Blood, hunger and, 389, 391, 393, 395
Blood-brain barrier *A feature of blood vessels supplying the brain that allows only certain substances to leave the blood and interact with brain tissue,* 331
BMI (body-mass index), 392
Body-kinesthetic intelligence, 369–370
Body language, in Gestalt therapy, 612
Bone marrow, 95
Borderline personality disorder, 589, 590
Bottom-up processing *Aspects of recognition that depend first on the information about the stimulus that comes up to the brain from the sensory receptors,* 165–168, 169, 171, 295
Braille, 131
Brain, 55, 64, 66, 68–86, 114
  acupuncture and, 69
  addicts and, 332
  in adulthood, 84–86, 370–372, 440, 471, 474–477, 480, 481
  aggression and, 695–696
  alcohol consumption and, 596, 597
  analogies and, 281–282
  antisocial personality disorder and, 590
  association cortex and, 76, 78–79, 81, 104
  attention and, 178
  autistic disorder and, 595
  autonomic nervous system and, 65
  cells of, 57
  corpus callosum and, 79, 81–82, 86
  decision making and, 269
  dreams and, 326
  electroconvulsive therapy and, 633–634, 639
  emotion and, 414–415, 418, 421–422, 423–424
  forebrain and, 70, 71–73, 86, 87, 88
  functions of, 56, 63
  general adaptation syndrome and, 491–492
  hearing and, 109–110
  hemispheres of, 75, 79–82
  hindbrain and, 68–71, 86, 88
  hormones and, 94–95
  human development and, 84–86
  hunger and, 389, 390–391, 393, 394, 395
  immune system and, 505
  in infancy, 437, 438, 439
  information-processing tasks of, 60
  intelligence and, 366, 367, 369
  kinesthesia and, 137–138
  language and, 111
  lateralization of, 80–82
  learning disabilities and, 377
  locus coeruleus and, 69–70, 88, 325, 334
  memory and, 253–258
  midbrain and, 70, 71, 86, 87, 88
  motor cortex and, 76, 77–78
  neural networks in, 62
  neuropsychology and, 34–35
  of newborn, 437
  number of cells in, 70
  olfaction and, 127
  pain and, 133–135
  parallel distributed processing and, 66
  plasticity of, 82–86
  prejudice/stereotypes and, 666
  problem solving and, 269
  psychosurgery and, 634, 639
  recognition and, 166–167
  reinforcement and, 204–205
  retrieval and, 257–258
  schizophrenia and, 584, 586–588
  sensory cortex and, 76–77, 102, 103
  sensory system and, 101, 102, 103–104, 110, 113
  sexual behavior and, 398
  sexual orientation and, 401
  sleep and, 323, 324, 325
  somatosensory cortex and, 76, 77, 138
  spinal cord and, 67

split-brain studies and, 79–80
techniques for studying, *see* Neuroimaging
vestibular sense and, 131, 137
vision and, 113, 116–117, 118–119, 120
see also **Cerebellum; Cerebral cortex;**
  Cognitive development; Consciousness;
  Electroencephalograph; **Hippocampus;**
  Hypothalamus; Intelligence;
  Neurotransmitters; Psychoactive drugs;
  Thalamus
Brain damage
  consciousness and, 315–317
  dementia and, 73, 556–557, 562, *see also*
    Alzheimer's disease
  emotion and, 414–415
  epilepsy and, 89
  gender differences in, 81
  Huntington's disease and, 88–89, A-5
  Korsakoff's syndrome and, 256–257
  language and, 78–79
  memory and, 255–257
  multiple sclerosis and, 59
  nootropic drugs and, 90–92
  olfactory neuron regeneration and, 126
  Parkinson's disease and, 83, 84, 88
  prosopagnosia and, 316–317
  split-brain patients and, 79–80
  strokes and, 89, 138
  synaptic plasticity and, 82–84
  vision and, 119
  see also Amnesia
Brainstorming, 292
Brain surgery, *see* **Psychosurgery**
Brain waves, 330. *See also*
  Electroencephalograph
Brightness *The overall intensity of all of the wavelengths that make up light,* 120, 121
Brightness constancy, 164–165
Broca's aphasia, 78
Broca's area, 76, 78, 79
Brown-Peterson procedure *A method for determining how long unrehearsed information remains in short-term memory,* 236
BSTc, 398
Bulimia nervosa *An eating disorder that involves eating massive quantities of food and then eliminating the food by self-induced vomiting or the use of strong laxatives,* 394–395, 628
Buprenorphine, 336
Bupropion (Wellbutrin), 636
Burnout *A gradually intensifying pattern of physical, psychological, and behavioral dysfunctions in response to a continuous flow of stressors,* 495, 496
Buspirone (BuSpar), 637, 638
Bystander effect, 704
Caffeine, 330, 336
Cannabis, see Marijuana
Cannon-Bard theory, 418, 421–422, 423
Capsaicin, 130, 132–133, 134
Captainitis, 692
Carbolith, *see* Lithium
Carbon monoxide, as neurotransmitter, 89
Case study *A research method involving the intensive examination of some phenomenon in a particular individual, group, or situation. It is especially useful for studying complex or relatively rare phenomena,* 31, 34–35, 42, 139–140, 314–315
Catabolic effects, 390
Catastrophic events, as stressors, 488, 489
Catastrophizing, 493–494, 513
Catecholamines, 87–88, 491, 507
Cause-and-effect relationships, 31, 37
CCK, *see* Cholecystokinin
Cell assembly, 254
Cell body, of neuron, 57
Cell division, A-1–A-2
Cell phones, driving and, 180–181
Center-off ganglion cells, 116
Center-on ganglion cells, 116, 117
Center-surround receptive fields, 116, 117, 119
Central nervous system (CNS) *The part of the nervous system encased in bone, including the brain and the spinal cord,* 66–86
  antisocial personality disorder and, 590–591
  depressants and, 332, 333–335, 339
  function of, 66–67
  neural networks and, 66
  nuclei of, 66
  synaptic plasticity and, 82–84
  see also Brain; **Nervous system; Spinal cord**
Central route, in elaboration likelihood model, 662, 663
Central tendency, measures of, 42–44, A-11
Central theory, *see* Cannon-Bard theory
Central traits, 526
Cerebellum *The part of the hindbrain whose function is to control finely coordinated movements and to store learned associations that involve movement,* 70–71, 86
  alcohol and, 334
  vestibular system and, 137, 138
Cerebral cortex *The outer surface of the brain,* 70, 72, 75–79, 84–85, 86, 87, 88, 89, 102, 103–104
  alcohol and, 334
  emotion and, 414–415
  memory and, 255
  pain and, 133
  sensory systems and, 102, 103–104
Cerebral hemispheres *The left and right halves of the rounded, outermost part of the brain,* 75
C fibers, 133
Challenger, 715
Channels, acupuncture and, 135–136
Chaos theory, 9
Characteristic frequency, 108
Chemical senses, *see* **Gustation; Olfaction**
Child abuse, 620
  antisocial personality disorder and, 591–593
  classical psychoanalysis and, 606–607
  depression and, 581
  dissociative disorders and, 574
  pornography and, 699
Childhood
  altruism/helping behavior in, 703
  attitude formation in, 661–662
  cognitive development in, 440, 441, 445–450, 447
  gender roles in, 464–466
  information processing in, 447–449
  latency period in, 522
  memory in, 447–450
  moral reasoning in, 472–473
  peer relationships in, 461–463
  phallic stage in, 521–522
  psychological disorders in, 562, 593–595
  risk and resilience in, 466–467
  social and emotional development in, 457, 459–467, 480
  social skills in, 463–464
  temperament in, 543–545
Chinese Psychiatric Association, 400
Chlordiazepoxide (Librium), 637, 638
Chlorpromazine (Thorazine; Largactil), 635, 638
Cholecystokinin (CCK), 389, 395
Cholesterol, 507
Cholinergic neurons, 87
Chromosomes *Long, thin structures in every biological cell that contain genetic information,* A-1–A-2
Chronic stressors, 488
Chronological age, 346
Chunks *Stimuli that are perceived as one unit or a meaningful grouping of information,* 235–236, 261, 285
Cingulate cortex, 133, 134
Circadian rhythm *A cycle, such as waking and sleeping, that repeats about once a day,* 323, 324
Circle of thought, 266–267, 279
Civil disobedience, 692
Clang associations, schizophrenia and, 583
Clarity
  depth cues and, 159, 160
  as MDMA, 337
Classical conditioning *A procedure in which a neutral stimulus is paired with a stimulus that elicits a reflex or other response until the neutral stimulus alone comes to elicit a similar response,* 14, 187–195
  acquisition and, 187–188, 194
  Alzheimer's disease and, 194–195
  attention and, 191–192
  attitudes and, 661–662
  avoidance conditioning and, 198
  behavioral approach to, 208–209
  biopreparedness and, 192–193
  extinction and, 189, 190, 194
  Pavlov's discovery and, 187–188
  phobias and, 5, 193–194, 570–571
  predator control and, 194, 195
  predictability and, 191
  second-order conditioning and, 192
  signaling of significant events and, 190–193
  signal strength and, 191
  spontaneous recovery and, 189, 190
  stimulus generalization and discrimination and, 190, 194
  timing and, 191
  see also **Behavior therapy**
Claustrophobia, 566
Client-centered therapy (person-centered therapy) *A therapy that allows the client to decide what to talk about, without direction,*

judgment, or interpretation from the therapist, 540, 610–612
Client-therapist relationships, *see* Therapeutic relationship
Clinical psychologists *Psychologists who seek to assess, understand, and correct abnormal behavior,* 5, 8
Clinical social workers, 606
Clomipramine (Anafranil), 633, 636, 637, 642
Clonazepam (Klonopin), 637, 638
Cloning, animals and, 39
Closure, as Gestalt law, 155, 156, 157
Clozapine (Clozaril), 635, 638, 640
CNS, *see* **Central nervous system**
Cocaine, 88, 205, 332, 335–336, 436, 597–598, 627
Cocaine babies, 336
Cochlea *A fluid-filled spiral structure in the ear in which auditory transduction occurs,* 106, 107–108
Cochlear implants, 107
Coding *Translating the physical properties of a stimulus into a pattern of neural activity that specifically identifies those properties,* 101, 102
  hearing and, 108–110
  kinesthesia and, 138–140
  touch and, 132
Cognition, learning and , 208–218. See also Social cognition
Cognitive ability *The capacity to reason, remember, understand, solve problems, and make decisions,* 345–346
  creativity and, 373–374
  giftedness and, 374–375
  learning disabilities and, 376–377
  mental retardation and, 375–376
  over life span, 370–372
  parental responsiveness and, 452, A-8
  see also **Intelligence; Intelligence quotient; IQ test**
Cognitive/affective theory, 535–536
Cognitive appraisal theories, 423, 424
Cognitive approach *A way of looking at human behavior that emphasizes research on how the brain takes in information, creates perceptions, forms and retrieves memories, processes information, and generates integrated patterns of action,* 18–19, 20
  to anxiety disorder, 569–570
  to attitudes, 661
  to emotion, 418, 422–423
  to health psychology, 510–511
  to incentives, 387
  to learning, 209–218
  to motivation, 382
  to prejudice/stereotypes, 667–668
  see also **Cognitive-behavior therapy; Cognitive therapy; Social-cognitive theories**
Cognitive-behavioral approach, 18, 19
Cognitive-behavior therapy *Treatment methods that help clients change the way they think as well as the way they behave,* 614, 618–620, 622, 625, 626–628, 640
Cognitive busyness, attitude change and, 663
Cognitive coping strategies, 513
Cognitive development, 432, 439–452

  in adolescence, 440, 471, 480
  in adulthood, 471, 474–477, 480, 481
  in childhood, 440, 441, 445–450, 480
  concrete operational period of, 440, 446, 448
  cultural differences in, 450–451
  environment and, 357, 358, 359, 361, 451–452
  formal operational period of, 440, 446, 471, 475
  genetics and, A-5
  in infancy, 439–444, 448
  nature and nurture and, 448–449, A-3
  preoperational period of, 440, 445–446, 447
  sensorimotor period of, 440, 441–442
  stages of, 439, 440, 441–442, 445–447
  see also **Intelligence; Memory**
Cognitive dissonance theory *A theory asserting that attitude change is driven by efforts to reduce tension caused by inconsistencies between attitudes and behaviors,* 663–664, 665, 688, 689
Cognitive distortions, 619
Cognitive map *A mental representation of familiar parts of the environment,* 211–212, 273, 275
Cognitive neuroscientists, 258, 269
Cognitive person variables, 535
Cognitive psychologists *Psychologists who study the mental processes underlying judgment, decision making, problem solving, imagining, and other aspects of human thought or cognition,* 4, 5, 8
  case studies and, 35
  consciousness and, 310
  information processing and, 269
  law and, 9, 10
  mental images and, 273
  traumatic memories and, 253
Cognitive psychology *The study of the mental processes by which information from the environment is modified, made meaningful, stored, retrieved, used, and communicated to others,* 219, 265. See also **Language; Thought**
Cognitive restructuring, 513, 619, 627
Cognitive scientists, 19
Cognitive stress responses, 488, 493–494, 503
Cognitive theory, of depression, 581
Cognitive therapy *A treatment in which the therapist helps clients to notice and change negative thoughts associated with anxiety and depression,* 619–620, 626–628, 641
Cognitive unconscious, 311
Cohort effect, 370
Collective unconscious, 522
Collectivist cultures, 21, 22
  achievement motivation and, 405
  aggression and, 696
  attitude change and, 664
  conflict and, 712–713
  decision making and, 291
  fundamental attribution error and, 658
  moral reasoning and, 473
  personality and, 542–543
  psychodynamic approach to, 524
  psychotherapy and, 629–630
  self-esteem and, 650

  socialization and, 459–460
  social loafing and, 684
Color
  depth cues and, 159–160
  infants' perception of, 171, 173
  see also **Vision**
Colorado Adoption Project, 357
Colorblindness, 125
Color circle, 121, 123
Color vision, 111, 120–125
  colorblindness and, 125
  opponent-process theory of, 122–123, 124
  trichromatic theory of, 122–124
  wavelengths and color sensations and, 120–122
Columbine High School, 680
Commitment
  intimate relationships and, 673
  love and, 674–675
Common fate, as Gestalt law, 155, 157
Common region, grouping and, 156
Commons dilemma, 712
Communication
  cooperation and, 712
  gender differences in, 23
  interpersonal conflict and, 713
Community mental health movement, 642
Community psychologists *Psychologists who work to obtain psychological services for people in need of help and to prevent psychological disorders by changing social systems,* 5–6
Community psychology *A movement to minimize or prevent psychological disorders through changes in social systems and through community mental health programs,* 642–643
Companionate love, 674, 675
Compensation, 521
Competition *Behavior in which individuals try to attain a goal for themselves while denying that goal to others,* 710
  resource dilemmas and, 712
  social dilemmas and, 710–712
Complementarity, 446
Complementary colors, 123
Compliance *Adjusting one's behavior because of an explicit or implicit request,* 684, 693
  inducing, 687–689
  norms and, 685
Compulsions, 568–569. *See also* **Obsessive-compulsive disorder**
Computational approach *An approach to perception that focuses on how computations by the nervous system translate raw sensory stimulation into an experience of reality,* 145, 161, 163, 171
Computational neuroscientists, 66
Computers, 14
  artificial intelligence and, 286–288
  human interaction and, 180
  problem solving and, 286–288
Concepts *Categories of objects, events, or ideas that have common properties,* 270–271, 275
Concrete operations *According to Piaget, the third stage of cognitive development, during*

which children's thinking is no longer dominated by visual appearances, 440, 446, 448

Conditioned reinforcer, *see* **Secondary reinforcer**

Conditioned response (CR) *In classical conditioning, the response that the conditioned stimulus elicits,* 188, 189–190, 191, 198

Conditioned stimulus (CS) *In classical conditioning, the originally neutral stimulus that, through pairing with the unconditioned stimulus, comes to elicit a conditioned response,* 188, 189, 190, 191, 198

Conditioning
 aversive, 617
 avoidance, 198–199, 207
 escape, 197–198, 207
 instrumental, 196–197, *see also* **Operant conditioning**
 interpersonal attraction and, 672
 language acquisition and, 299
 vicarious, 214
 see also **Classical conditioning; Operant conditioning**

Conditions of worth *According to Rogers, the feelings an individual experiences when the person, instead of behavior, is evaluated,* 539–540

Condoms, 399, 509

Conduct disorders, 593
 attention deficit hyperactivity disorder, 557, 593, 641

Conduction deafness, 106

Cones *Photoreceptors in the retina whose color-sensitive photopigment helps us to distinguish colors,* 114, 115, 122, 123, 124, 173

Confidentiality, in therapeutic relationship, 631–632

Confirmation bias *The tendency to pay more attention to evidence in support of one's hypothesis than to evidence that refutes that hypothesis,* 30, 276, 284, 285, 292

Conflict *The result of a person or group believing that another person or group stands in the way of achieving a valued goal,* 710
 interpersonal, 712–713
 management of, 713
 mixed-motive, 711
 resource dilemmas and, 712
 social dilemmas and, 710–712

Conformity *Changing one's behavior or beliefs to match those of other group members, generally as a result of real or imagined, though unspoken, group pressure,* 684–689, 693
 ambiguity of situation and, 686
 gender differences and, 687
 mass, 684
 minority influence and, 687
 norms and, 685, 686
 private acceptance and, 685
 public, 685
 reasons for, 685–686
 unanimity and size of majority and, 686–687
 see also **Compliance**

Confounding variable *In an experiment, any factor that affects the dependent variable along with or instead of the independent variable. Confounding variables include random variables, the placebo effect, and experimenter bias,* 38–41

Congruence *A consistency between the way therapists feel and the way they act toward clients,* 611–612

Connectedness, grouping and, 156

Connectionist models, *see* **Neural networks; Parallel distributed processing (PDP) models**

Conscientiousness, as big-five personality factor, 528

Conscious level *The level at which mental activities that people are normally aware of occur,* 311–312

Consciousness *Awareness of external stimuli and one's own mental activity,* 309–318
 altered state of, 317
 analysis of, 309–310
 anesthesia and, 309, 312
 behaviorism and, 14
 cognitive processes and, 15
 functionalism and, 13
 functions of, 310–311
 Gestalt psychologists and, 12
 hypnosis and, 12, 133, 327–329
 levels of, 311–312
 meditation and, 329–330
 memory and, 311, 329
 mental processing without awareness and, 312–314
 neuropsychology of, 315–317
 opiates and, 337
 psychoanalysis and, 12–13
 states of, 311, 317–318, *see also* **Psychoactive drugs; Sleep**
 subliminal stimuli and, 147–149, 314–315
 unconscious and, 310, 312, 313–314, 326
 Wundt and, 11–12

Consensus, attribution and, 656, 657

Consequences Test, 373

Conservation *The ability to recognize that the important properties of a substance remain constant despite changes in shape, length, or position,* 445–446, 447, 448

Consistency, attribution and, 656, 657

Constructive memory, 242, 243–247, 257

Constructivist approach *A view of perception taken by those who argue that the perceptual system uses fragments of sensory information to construct an image of reality,* 145–146, 156, 161, 163, 179

Consummate love, 675

Contact hypothesis *The idea that stereotypes and prejudice toward a group will diminish as contact with the group increases,* 668

Content validity, 352

Context-dependent *Referring to memories that can be helped or hindered by similarities or differences between the context in which they are learned and that in which they are recalled,* 240

Contingencies, 615

Contingency theories, of leadership, 715

Continuity, as Gestalt law, 155, 156

Continuous reinforcement schedule *In operant conditioning, a pattern in which a reinforcer is delivered every time a particular response occurs,* 202

Contralateral representations, 103

Control
 in research, 31, 33, 38, 39, 74, 91, 592–593
 of stressors, 498

Control group *In an experiment, the group that receives no treatment or provides some other base line against which to compare the performance or response of the experimental group,* 38, 39

Conventional moral reasoning *Reasoning that reflects the belief that morality consists of following rules and conventions,* 472–473

Convergence *A depth cue involving the rotation of the eyes to project the image of an object on each retina,* 160, 173

Convergent thinking *The ability to apply the rules of logic and knowledge to narrow down the number of possible solutions to a problem or perform some other complex cognitive task,* 374

Conversion disorder *A somatoform disorder in which a person displays blindness, deafness, or other symptoms of sensory or motor failure without a physical cause,* 572, 573, 575, 606

Cooperation *Any type of behavior in which several people work together to attain a goal,* 710
 fostering, 712
 resource dilemmas and, 712
 social dilemmas and, 710–712

Coping, with stress, 488, 498–499, 501, 503, 512–514

Copycat crimes, 680

Cornea *The curved, transparent, protective layer through which light rays enter the eye,* 112, 113

Corpus callosum *A massive bundle of fibers that connects the right and left cerebral hemispheres and allows them to communicate with each other,* 79, 81–82, 86

Correlation *In research, the degree to which one variable is related to another; the strength and direction of the relationship is measured by a correlation coefficient,* 44–46, 461, A-13–A-15

Correlation coefficient *A statistic, r, that summarizes the strength and direction of a relationship between two variables,* 44–46, 351, A-13–A-15

Corticosteroids, 504

Cortisol, 94, 95, 492, 504, 505, 580

Counseling psychologists, *see* **Clinical psychologists**

Counterfactual arguments, 304

Countertransference, 609

Couples therapy *A form of therapy focusing on improving communication between partners,* 605, 622, 623

Covert orienting, 173, 174–175

Covert sensitization, 617

CR, *see* **Conditioned response**
Crack, 336, 598
Crawling, 438
Creative intelligence, 366–367, 368
Creativity *The capacity to produce new, high quality ideas or products,* 373–374
Criminal justice
  anchoring heuristic and, 278
  confirmation bias and, 276
  effectiveness of, 207
  eyewitness testimony and, 245–247
  false memories and, 250–253, 258, 329
  informal reasoning and, 276
  lie detection and, 420–421
  and memory, 9, 10, 245–247, 250–253, 258, 329
  memory and, 9, 10
  mentally ill and, 631–632
  psychological disorders and, 598–600
  representativeness heuristic and, 278
Criterion, 352
Criterion validity, 352
Critical period *An interval during which certain kinds of growth must occur if development is to proceed normally*
  in language acquisition, 300
  in prenatal development, 436
Critical thinking *The process of assessing claims and making judgments on the basis of well-supported evidence,* 26–31, 47–48
Cross-cultural research, *see* Cultural differences
Cross-sectional study, 370
Cross-sequential with resampling design, 371
Crystallized intelligence *The specific knowledge gained as a result of applying fluid intelligence,* 365, 371, 475
CS, *see* **Conditioned stimulus**
Cultural differences, 21–23
  in achievement motivation, 405–406
  in advertising, 23, 304
  in aggression, 208, 695, 696–697
  in alcoholism, 596
  in attachment, 457
  in attitude change, 664
  in attribution, 657
  in cognitive development, 450–451
  in decision making, 290, 291
  in depression, 581
  in drug affects, 332
  in eating, 392
  in emotions, 412, 426, 427
  in explanations of other people's behavior, 10
  in fundamental attribution error, 658
  in gender roles, 464
  in hunger, 395
  in intelligence quotient, 354–356, 358–361
  in language and thought, 303–305
  in learning, 218–219
  in love, 674, 675
  in moral reasoning, 473
  in motor development, 433
  in norms, 681
  in parenting styles, 461
  in perception, 165, 169
  in personality, 527, 541–543
  in phobias, 566, 567
  in pitch, 110
  psychodynamic approach to, 524
  in psychological disorders, 555, 556, 557, 558–559
  in psychotherapy, 629–631
  in secondary reinforcement, 201
  in self-esteem, 650
  in self-regulation, 464
  in sexual behavior, 399, 469
  in sleep, 320
  in smoking, 509
  in socialization, 459–460
  in social loafing, 683–684
  in somatoform disorders, 573
  in states of consciousness, 317–318
  in suicide, 577
  in temperament, 454
  see also Collectivist cultures; Ethnic group differences; Individualist cultures
Culture *The accumulation of values, rules of behavior, forms of expression, religious beliefs, occupational choices, and the like, for a group of people who share a common language and environment,* 21, 22
Culture-fair tests, 355, 356
Culture-specific tests, 355
Cycling, weight loss and, 393–394
Cyclothymic disorder *A form of bipolar disorder characterized by comparatively mild mood swings,* 578–579
Cynophobia, 566, 571
Cytokines, 95, 96
Daily hassles, as stressors, 488, 490
Dark adaptation *The increasing ability to see in the dark as time in the dark increases,* 113–114
Data *Numbers that represent research findings and provide the basis for research conclusions,* 30
  frequency histogram and, A-10–A-11
  See also **Descriptive statistics; Inferential statistics**
Data set, *see* **Data**
Day care
  aggression and, 37
  emotional development and, 457–459
Daydreaming, 317
Deaf community, 107
Deafness, 106–107, 111, 138, 328
Death and dying, 481
  attitude toward, 486
  coping with, 498–499
  lifestyle behaviors and, 486–487, 508–509
  sudden, 497
  terror management theory and, 649–650
Death instincts, 520
Decay *The gradual disappearance of the mental representation of a stimulus,* 248–249
Decibels (dB), 105, 106
Decision making, 266, 267, 288–292
  biases and flaws in, 289–291, 292
  brain and, 269
  comparing attributes in, 289, 291
  estimating probabilities in, 289, 290
  evaluating options in, 288–289
  group processes in, 291–292
  groupthink and, 715–716
  language and, 304–305
  naturalistic, 291
Decomposition, *see* **Means-end analysis**
Deductive reasoning, *see* **Formal reasoning**
Deep structure *An abstract representation of the underlying meanings of a given sentence,* 293–294, 295
Defense mechanisms *According to Freud, psychological responses that help protect a person from anxiety and guilt,* 520, 521, 524
Defensive aggression, 695–696
Deficiency orientation *According to Maslow, a preoccupation with perceived needs for things a person does not have,* 409, 540
Degrees of freedom (df) *The total sample size or number of scores in a data set, less the number of experimental groups,* A-17
Deindividuation *A psychological state occurring in group members that results in loss of individuality and a tendency to do things not normally done when alone,* 681–682
Deinstitutionalization, 642
Delirium, 562
Delusions *False beliefs, such as those experienced by people suffering from schizophrenia or extreme depression,* 576
  of grandeur, 583
Dementia, 73, 556–557, 562. *See also* Alzheimer's disease
Demerol, 337
Dendrites *Neuron fibers that receive signals from the axons of other neurons and carry that signal to the cell body,* 58, 59, 60, 62, 63, 82, 84–85
Denial, 521
Deoxyribonucleic acid (DNA) *The molecular structure of a gene that provides the genetic code,* A-1, A-2
  and Human Genome Project, 52, A-6
Depakote, *see* **Divalproex**
Dependent personality disorder, 589, 590
Dependent variable *In an experiment, the factor affected by the independent variable,* 37
Depressants *Psychoactive drugs that inhibit the functioning of the central nervous system,* 332, 333–335, 339
Depression, 84, 558–559, 576–578
  in adolescence, 467, 576, 581, 582
  antidepressants for, 635–636, 638, 641, 642
  anxiety and, 568, 576
  brain and, 70
  causes of, 210
  cognitive-behavior therapy for, 625, 640, 641
  cognitive therapy for, 619–620, 627, 641
  diathesis-stress approach to, 582
  dysthymic disorder and, 576, 579
  earliest explanations of, 556
  electroconvulsive therapy for, 633
  gender differences in, 576, 580–582
  genetics and, A-5
  herbal remedy for, 636
  interpersonal therapy for, 627, 641
  major depressive disorder and, 576, 579, 580, 582, 627, 640
  memory and, 229

present *versus* future self and, 652
problem-solving therapy for, 627
psychosurgery and, 634
seasonal affective disorder and, 580
sleeping and, 580
social-cognitive theories of, 558, 581–582
social support and, 500
sociocultural context and, 558–559
stress and, 496
suicide and, 577–578
Depth perception *Perception of distance, one of the most important factors underlying size and shape constancy,* 158–161, 164, 165, 172–173, 437
Description, in research, 31, 33
Descriptive norms, 680, 681
Descriptive statistics *Numbers that summarize a set of research data,* 42–46, A-10, A-11–A-15
 correlation and correlation coefficients and, 42, 44–46, 351, A-13–A-15
 mean and, 43–44, 46, A-11
 measures of central tendency and, 42–44, A-11
 measures of variability and, 42, 43, 44, A-11–A-12
 median and, 42–43, 46, A-11
 mode and, 42, 46, A-11
 N and, A-11
 normal distribution and, 349, 350, A-12–A-13
 range and, 44, 46, A-11–A-12
 standard deviation and, 44, 46, A-11, A-12
Desensitization, *see* Systematic desensitization
Desensitization hierarchy, 614, 615
Developmental disability, *see* Mental retardation
Developmental psychologists *Psychologists who seek to understand, describe, and explore how behavior and mental processes change over the course of a lifetime,* 4, 7–8, 9. *See also* Human development
Developmental psychology *The psychological specialty that documents the course of people's social, emotional, moral, and intellectual development over the life span and explores how development in different domains fits together, is affected by experience, and relates to other areas of psychology,* 432. *See also* Cognitive development; Emotional development; Moral development; Social development; Human development
df, *see* Degrees of freedom
Diabetes, 95
Diagnostic and Statistical Manual of Mental Disorders (DSM)
 homosexuality and, 400, 555
 IV–TR, 560
 –V, 561, 568
 see also Diagnostic and Statistical Manual of Mental Disorders–IV
Diagnostic and Statistical Manual of Mental Disorders–IV (DSM-IV), 560–561, 562, 563
 dissociative identity disorder and, 574
 personality disorders and, 589, 590

phobia and, 566
schizophrenia and, 584, 585
substance abuse and, 595
substance-related disorders and, 595
Dialectical thinking, 475
Diathesis-stress approach *Viewing psychological disorders as arising when a predisposition for disorder combines with sufficient amounts of stress to trigger symptoms,* 496, 559–560
 to depression, 582
 to schizophrenia, 588
 to somatoform disorders, 572
Diazepam (Valium), 637, 638, 641
DID, *see* Dissociative identity disorder
Diet, serotonin and, 88
Dietary supplements, sharpened mind and, 90–92
Differences, perception of, 152
Difference threshold, *see* Just-noticeable difference
Differentiated self-schemas, 651
Difficult babies, 454
Diffusion of responsibility, 704, 705
Discipline, *see* Punishment
Discrimination *Differential treatment of various groups; the behavioral component of prejudice,* 666. *See also* Prejudice/stereotypes
Discriminative stimuli *Stimuli that signal whether reinforcement is available if a certain response is made,* 199, 208
Diseases of adaptation *Illnesses that are caused or promoted by stressors,* 492
Disequilibrium hypothesis, 204
Dishabituation, 171
Dispersion, *see* Variability, measures of
Displacement, 521
 forgetting and, 248
Dispositional optimism, 501
Dissociation theory *A theory defining hypnosis as a socially agreed-upon opportunity to display one's ability to let mental functions become dissociated,* 328–329
Dissociative amnesia *A disorder marked by a sudden loss of memory,* 573
Dissociative disorders *Rare conditions that involve sudden and usually temporary disruptions in a person's memory, consciousness, or identity,* 562, 573–575
Dissociative fugue *A sudden loss of memory and the assumption of a new identity in a new locale,* 573, 575
Dissociative identity disorder (DID) *A dissociative disorder in which a person reports having more than one identity,* 573–574, 575
Distance, perception of, *see* Depth perception
Distinctiveness, attribution and, 656, 657
Distracting style, depression and, 581–582
Distributed practice, 259
Divalproex (Depakote; Epival), 637, 638
Divergent thinking *The ability to think along many alternative paths to generate many different solutions to a problem,* 373, 374
Diversity, *see* Cultural differences
Divorce, 466, 477, 479, 676

DNA, *see* Deoxyribonucleic acid
DNA evidence, 246
Dodo Bird Verdict, 624–625
Dominant genes, A-2
Door-in-the-face procedure, compliance and, 688
Dopamine *A neurotransmitter used in the parts of the brain involved in regulating movement and experiencing pleasure,* 88, 90, 91
 alcohol and, 333
 emotion and, 421
 memory and, 256
 mood disorder and, 579
 neuroleptics and, 641–642
 psychoactive drugs and, 332, 335, 336, 337
 schizophrenia and, 587, 640, 642
 stimulants and, 386
Dopamine systems, reinforcers and, 205
Double-blind design *A research design in which neither the experimenter nor the participants know who is in the experimental group and who is in the control group,* 41
Down syndrome, 375, 376
Downward social comparison, 648
Dramatic-erratic cluster, of personality disorders, 589–593
Dreams *Story-like sequences of images, sensations, and perception occurring mainly during REM sleep,* 317, 321, 322, 324, 325–326, 607
Drive *In drive reduction theory, a psychological state of arousal, created by an imbalance in homeostasis that prompts an organism to take action to restore the balance and, in the process, reduce the drive,* 385
 need and, 385, 409–410
 primary, 385–386
 secondary, 385–386
Drive reduction theory *A theory of motivation stating that much motivation arises from constant imbalances in homeostasis,* 385–386, 388. *See also* Drive; Homeostasis.
Drug abuse, *see* Substance abuse
Drugs, *see* Psychoactive drugs
DSM, *see Diagnostic and Statistical Manual*
Dual coding theory, 237
Dualism, consciousness and, 310
Duchenne smile, 426
Dyscalculia, 377
Dysgraphia, 377
Dyslexia, 377
Dysphasia, 377
Dysthymic disorder *A pattern of comparatively mild depression that lasts for at least two years,* 576, 579
E, *see* MDMA
Ear, 105, 106–108, 110. *See also* Hearing
Ear canal, 106, 107
Eardrum, *see* Tympanic membrane
Early intervention
 community psychology and, 643
 intelligence quotient and, 358, 361–362
Easy babies, 454
Eating, *see* Hunger
Eating disorders, 467, 562, 620, 621
 anorexia nervosa, 394

bulimia nervosa, 394–395, 628
obesity, 389, 392–394
subliminal stimuli and, 148
Eclectic therapists, 604
Ecological approach *An approach to perception maintaining that humans and other species are so well adapted to their natural environment that many aspects of the world are perceived automatically, without requiring higher-level analysis and inferences,* 146, 156, 159, 161, 179, 180
Ecstasy, *see* MDMA
ECT, *see* Electroconvulsive therapy
Edges, center-surround receptive fields and, 116, 117
Education
active learning and, 219–220
cognitive psychology and, 219
cultural differences in learning and, 218–219
operant conditioning and, 219
see also Learning
Educational psychologists *Psychologists who study methods by which instructors teach and students learn, and who apply their results to improving such methods,* 6–7, 8
EEG, *see* Electroencephalograph
Efferent neurons, 67
Effexor, *see* Venlafaxine
Ego *According to Freud, the part of the personality that mediates conflicts between and among the demands of the id, the superego, and the real world,* 520, 524
Ego analysis, 608
Egocentric, children as, 445, 447
Ego psychologists, 522
Eidetic imagery, 238
Elaboration likelihood model *A model suggesting that attitude change can be driven by evaluation of the content of a persuasive message (central route) or by irrelevant persuasion cues (peripheral route),* 662–663, 665
Elaborative rehearsal *A memorization method that involves thinking about how new information relates to information already stored in long-term memory,* 229, 230, 259
Elavil, *see* Amitriptyline
Electra complex *A pattern described by Freud in which a young girl develops an attachment to her father and competes with her mother for his attention,* 522
Electrochemical potential, 58
Electroconvulsive therapy (ECT) *Brief electric shock administered to the brain, usually to reduce depression that does not respond to drug treatments,* 633–634, 639
Electroencephalograph (EEG), 68, 268, 269, 318–320, 325, 330, 666
Electromagnetic radiation, light and, 111, 112
E-mail, group problem solving and decision making and, 292
Embryo *The developing individual from the fourteenth day after fertilization until the end of the second month after conception,* 435, 436
EMDR, *see* Eye movement desensitization and reprocessing

EMDR Institute, Inc., 26
Emotion *A transitory positive or negative experience that is felt as happening to the self, is generated, in part, by the cognitive appraisal of a situation, and is accompanied by both learned and reflexive physical responses,* 412–427
autonomic nervous system and, 415–417
biology of, 413–417, 418, 421–422, 423–424
brain and, 72, 73, 414–415, 418, 421–422, 423–424
Cannon-Bard theory of, 418, 421–422, 423
characteristics of, 412–413
cognitive theories of, 418, 422–423
communication and, 424–425
facial expressions and, 414, 415, 419, 420, 424–427
gustation and, 129–130
innate expressions of, 425
IQ tests and, 364–365
James-Lange theory of, 417–421, 423
learning and, 426–427
motivation and, 382, 410–411
olfaction and, 127, 128, 129–130
opponent-process theory and, 411–412
pain and, 134
social and cultural influences on, 426–427
social referencing and, 427
subliminal information and, 148
theories of, 417–424
Emotional coping strategies, 513–514
Emotional development
in adolescence, 457, 460, 462, 467–471, 480
in adulthood, 460, 477–481
in childhood, 457, 459–467, 480
in infancy, 453–459, 460
see also Social development
Emotional intelligence, 370
Emotionality-stability, 528–529
Emotional signals, ability to detect and interpret, 463
Emotional stress responses, 488, 493, 503
Emotion culture, 427
Emotion-focused coping, 498, 499, 501
Empathy *The effort or ability, emphasized in client-centered therapy, to appreciate another person's point of view and feelings,* 464
altruism/helping behavior and, 705, 706
in client-centered therapy, 611, 612, 630–631
Empathy-altruism theory *A theory suggesting that people help others because of empathy with their needs,* 706, 709
Empirically supported therapies (ESTs) *Treatments whose effects have been validated by controlled experimental research,* 626–628
Empirical research, 9. See also Research methods
Empiricism, 9, 11
Employment, personality tests and, 545, 548, 549
Encoding *The process of putting information into a form that the memory system can accept and use,* 225–226, 231, 233–234, 236–237, 245
Encoding specificity principle *A principle stating that the ability of a cue to aid retrieval depends on the degree to which it*

taps into information that was encoded at the time of the original learning, 239
Encounter groups, 540–541
Endocannabinoids, 391
Endocrine system *Cells that form organs called glands and communicate with one another by secreting chemicals called hormones,* 92–95
immune system and, 505
mood disorder and, 580
see also Hormones
Endorphin *One of a class of neurotransmitters that bind to opiate receptors and moderate pain,* 89, 90, 92
acupuncture and, 136
alcohol and, 333
opiates and, 337
pain and, 134–135
Engineering psychologists, 179, 180
Engineering psychology *A field in which psychologists study human factors in the use of equipment, and help designers create better versions of that equipment,* 4, 5
Enterostatin, 391
Entomophobia, 566
Envelope, of waves, 108
Environment
aggression and, 695, 697, 698–699, 701–702
altruism/helping behavior and, 705–706
behavioral genetics and, A-6–A-8
behaviorism and, 14
intelligence and, 354–362, 363, 435, 451–452
interpersonal attraction and, 672
mental retardation and, 375, 376
personality tests and, 530–532
schizophrenia and, 587–588, A-7
sexual orientation and, 402
see also Behavioral genetics; Nature and nurture
Environmental psychologists *Psychologists who study the effects of the physical environment on behavior and mental processes,* 7
Environmental psychology *The study of the relationship between behavior and the physical environment,* 701
Ephedrine, 91
Epilepsy, 89, 133
split-brain patients and, 79–80
Epinephrine (adrenaline), 88, 96, 417, 491, 492, 507
Episodic memory *Memory of an event that happened while one was present,* 226, 227, 243–244, 476
Epival, *see* Divalproex
EPSP, *see* Excitatory postsynaptic potential
Equanil, *see* Meprobamate
Equipotentiality, 193
Erectile disorder, 403
Eros, 520
Escalation effect, 206
Escape and avoidance tactics, as stress responses, 495
Escape conditioning *A type of learning in which an organism learns to make a*

particular response in order to terminate an aversive stimulus, 197–198, 207
Essence, *see* MDMA
Esteem motives, 410. *See also* **Self-esteem**
Estradiol, 398
Estrogens *Feminine hormones that circulate in the bloodstream of both men and women; relatively more estrogens circulate in women,* 92–93, 398, 474
ESTs, *see* **Empirically supported therapies**
Ethical Principles of Psychologists and Code of Conduct (American Psychological Association), 49, 631
Ethics
   psychological tests and, 549
   in research, 39, 48–49
   therapeutic relationship and, 631
Ethnic group differences, 23
   in abnormality, 555
   in alcoholism, 596
   in intelligence quotient, 354–356, 358–361
   in psychoactive drugs, 638–639
   in psychological diagnosis, 563–565
   in sexual behavior, 509
   in smoking, 509
   in suicide, 577, 578
   see also Cultural differences
Ethnic identity *The part of a person's identity associated with the racial, religious, or cultural group to which the person belongs,* 470
Ethnic minorities, *see* Cultural differences; Ethnic group differences
Ethnic minorities, in psychology, 15, 17. *See also* Cultural differences; Ethnic group differences
Ethnic prejudice, 314, 470, 668–671
Ethology, 34
Evoked brain potential *A small, temporary change in EEG voltage that is evoked by some stimulus,* 268–269
Evolution, 13, 14, 17, 31
Evolutionary approach *An approach to psychology that emphasizes the inherited, adaptive aspects of behavior and mental processes,* 17, 20
   to aggression, 695
   to altruism/helping behavior, 706–709
   to gender roles, 466
   to intimate relationships, 673, 674
   to motivation, 383–384
   to sexual behavior, 383–385
Exams, studying for, 258–260
Excitatory postsynaptic potential (EPSP) *A postsynaptic potential that depolarizes the neuronal membrane, bringing the cell closer to threshold for firing an action potential,* 61
Excitement phase, of sexual response cycle, 399
Exhaustion stage, of general adaptation syndrome, 492
Exorcism, 557
Expectancy, reaction time and, 268
Expectancy theory, 534
Expectations, self-fulfilling prophesies and, 654–655

Expected value *The total benefit to be expected if a decision were to be repeated several times,* 289
Experience
   naturalistic decision making and, 291
   openness to as big-five personality factor, 528
   perception and, 165
   problem solving and, 285–286
Experimental group *In an experiment, the group that receives the experimental treatment; its performance or response is compared with that of one or more control groups,* 38, 39
Experimental psychologists *Psychologists who conduct experiments aimed at understanding learning, memory, perception, and other basic behavioral and mental processes,* 4
Experimenter bias *A confounding variable that occurs when an experimenter unintentionally encourages participants to respond in a way that supports the hypothesis,* 40–41
Experimenter expectancies, 40–41
Experiments *Situations in which the researcher manipulates one variable and then observes the effect of that manipulation on another variable, while holding all other variables constant,* 36–41, 42
   analogue, 707–708
   cause-and-effect relationships and, 31, 37
   control in, 32, 38, 74
   on developing minds, 443–444
   double-blind design and, 41
   empirical, 9, 626–628
   experimental method and, 37–39
   experimenter bias and, 40–41
   on explicit *versus* implicit memory, 228–229
   in mind reading, 174–175
   participants' expectations and, 39–40, 41
   on self-esteem, 649–650
   two-factor, 209–210
   variables and, 30, 38–41
Expert systems, computerized, 286
Explanation, in research, 31, 33
Explicit memory *The process in which people intentionally try to remember something,* 227–229
Exposure techniques, 616. *See also* **Flooding**
Exposure therapy, 627
External attribution, 655
Externalizing disorders, of childhood, 593
Externals, 534
Extinction *The gradual disappearance of a conditioned response or operant behavior due to elimination either of the association between conditioned and unconditioned stimuli or of rewards for certain behaviors,* 208, 616
   classical conditioning and, 190, 194
   operant conditioning and, 203–204
Extrapyramidal motor system, 414
Extraversion, 522
   as big-five personality factor, 528
Extrinsic motivation, 404
Eye, 112–113, 114, 120
   of newborn, 437

   retina and, 112, 113, 114–117, 118, 160, 161
   see also Vision
Eye blink conditioning, Alzheimer's disease and, 194–195
Eye movement desensitization and reprocessing (EMDR), 26, 28, 30–31, 34, 37, 38, 40, 41, 42, 43, 46–47, 627
Eyewitness Evidence: A Guide for Law Enforcement, 246–247
Eyewitness testimony, 245–247
Faces
   infants' perception of, 172, 437
   prosopagnosia and, 316–317
Facial expressions, emotion and, 414, 415, 419, 420, 424–427
Facial feedback hypothesis, 420
Facilitated communication, for autistic disorder, 47, 48
Facilitated Communication Institute, 48
Factor analysis, 526–527, 528
False memories, 251–253, 257, 329, 524, 574
False Memory Syndrome Foundation, 252, 253
Familial retardation, 376
Families, changes in, 478–479
Family studies, 50, 51
Family system, 621
Family therapy *Treatment of two or more individuals from the same family,* 605, 621, 623
Farsightedness, 112–113
Fathers
   attachment to, 456
   child care and, 17, 478, 479
   see also Parents and parenting
Fear
   aging and, 44–45
   conditioned, 192, 193
   genetics and, A-6
   see also Phobia
Feature analysis, 166, 167, 173
Feature detectors *Cells in the cortex that respond to a specific feature of an object,* 119, 166, 167, 169
Fechner's law, 153
Feedback system, 67
   hormones and, 94–95
   negative, 94–95
   reflexes and, 67, 71
   skill learning and, 221
Feeling-of-knowing experience, 242
Fertilization, A-2
   in vitro, 478
Fetal alcohol syndrome *A pattern of physical and mental defects found in babies born to women who abused alcohol during pregnancy,* 436, 509, 596
Fetus *The developing individual from the third month after conception until birth,* 435–436
Fiber tracts *Axons that travel together in bundles; also called* pathways, 66
Field sobriety test, 71
Fight-or-flight syndrome *Physical reactions initiated by the sympathetic nervous system that prepare the body to fight or to run from a threatening situation,* 94, 417, 491, 503

Figure-ground organization, 155, 164
Fingertips, touch and, 131
First impressions, 653–655, 659
Fissures, *see* Sulci
Fixation, 520, 521
Fixed action pattern, 383
Fixed-interval (FI) schedule *In operant conditioning, a type of partial reinforcement schedule that provides reinforcement for the first response that occurs after some fixed time has passed since the last reward,* 202, 203
Fixed-ratio (FR) schedule *In operant conditioning, a type of partial reinforcement schedule that provides reinforcement following a fixed number of responses,* 202–203
Flashbacks, posttraumatic stress disorder and, 495
Flashbulb memories, 253
Flavor, 129–130
   eating and, 391–392
   hunger and, 395
Flooding *A procedure for reducing anxiety that involves keeping a person in a feared, but harmless, situation,* 616–617
Fluid intelligence *The basic power of reasoning and problem solving,* 365, 371, 475
Fluoxetine (Prozac), 636, 637, 638, 639, 642
Fluvoxamine (Luvox), 636, 637, 638
Flying phobia, *see* Aerophobia
Food culture, 392
Foot-in-the-door technique, compliance and, 687–688
Forebrain *The most highly developed part of the brain; it is responsible for the most complex aspects of behavior and mental life,* 70, 71–73, 86, 87, 88
Foreign accent syndrome, 79
Forensic psychologists *Psychologists who create criminal profiles, assist in jury selection, evaluate defendants' mental competence to stand trial, and deal with other issues involving psychology and the law,* 7
Forgetting, 225, 247–253
   causes of, 248–250
   curve of, 247, 248
   decay and, 248–249
   interference and, 248–250
   retrieval failure and, 249–250
   in short-term memory, 236, 248
   traumatic memories and, 250–253
Formal concepts *Concepts that can be clearly defined by a set of rules or properties,* 270
Formal operational period *According to Piaget, the fourth stage in cognitive development, usually beginning around age eleven,* 440, 446, 471, 475
Formal reasoning *The process of following a set of rigorous procedures for reaching valid conclusions,* 274–276
Forward conditioning, 191
Fourier analysis, 105
Fovea *A region in the center of the retina where cones are highly concentrated,* 114, 117, 173

Fragile X syndrome, 375
Free association, 606, 607
Free-floating anxiety, *see* Generalized anxiety disorder
Free nerve endings, 131
Frequency *The number of complete waveforms, or cycles, that pass by a given point in space every second*
   hearing and, 104, 105, 106, 108–110
Frequency histogram *A graphic presentation of data that consists of a set of bars, each of which represents how frequently different values of variables occur in a data set,* A-10–A-11
Frequency matching *The view that some sounds are coded in terms of the frequency of neural firing; also called* volley theory, 108–109
Freudian slips, 607
Freudian theory, *see* **Psychoanalysis**
Friends, *see* Peer relationships
Frigidity, *see* Arousal disorder
Frontal lobe, 75, 76
Frustration-aggression hypothesis *A proposition that frustration always leads to some form of aggressive behavior,* 698
Functional analysis *Analyzing behavior by studying what responses occur under what conditions of operant reward and punishment,* 14, 533
Functional fixedness *A tendency to think about familiar objects in familiar ways that may prevent using them in other ways,* 284, 494
Functionalism, 13, 15
Functional magnetic resonance imaging (fMRI), *see* Magnetic resonance imaging
Fundamental attribution error *A bias toward overattributing the behavior of others to internal causes,* 658, 659
Fundamental frequency, 105
Future self, 651–652
g *A general intelligence factor that Charles Spearman postulated as accounting for positive correlations between people's scores on all sorts of mental ability tests,* 365, 366
GABA *A neurotransmitter that inhibits the firing of neurons,* 89, 90, 333, 334, 569, 641
Galanin, 391
Galvanic skin resistance (GSR), 148, 650
Gambler's fallacy, 290
Gamma-amino butyric acid, *see* **GABA**
Gamophobia, 566
Ganglion cells *Cells in the retina that generate action potentials,* 114, 116, 117, 118, 119, 124
GAS, *see* General adaptation syndrome
Gases, as neurotransmitters, 89, 90
GATB, *see* General Aptitude Test Battery
Gate control theory *A theory suggesting that a functional gate in the spinal cord can either let pain impulses travel upward to the brain or block their progress,* 134
Gender differences, 23
   in abnormality, 555
   in alcohol effects, 334
   in brain laterality, 81–82

   in color vision, 124
   in communication, 23
   in communication of emotions, 424–425
   in conformity, 687
   in depression, 576, 580–582
   hormones and, 93–94
   in leadership, 714
   in longevity, 481–482
   in mate-selection preferences, 17, 673, 674
   in moral reasoning, 473
   in psychoactive drug response, 639
   in retirement, 481–482
   in self-esteem, 543
   in sexual behavior, 383–385
   in stress responses, 501
   in suicide, 577
   in test scores, 363, 364
Gender nonconformity, 401
Gender roles *Patterns of work, appearance, and behavior that a society associates with being male or female,* 464–466
   rewards and punishments and, 207–208
   sexual behavior and, 399
Gender schemas *The generalizations children develop about what toys, activities, and occupations are "appropriate" for males versus females,* 465
General adaptation syndrome (GAS) *A three-stage pattern of responses triggered by the effort to adapt to any stressor,* 491–492, 501
General Aptitude Test Battery (GATB), 350
Generalizations, spontaneous, 244
Generalized anxiety disorder *A condition that involves relatively mild but long-lasting anxiety that is not focused on any particular object or situation,* 567, 575, 627, 637, 640
Generalized social phobia, 566, 569
Generativity *Adult concerns about producing or generating something,* 460, 479–480
Genes *The biological instructions, inherited from both parents and located on the chromosomes, that provide the blueprint for physical development,* A-1, A-2
   dominant, A-2
   evolutionary approach to, 17
   manipulation of in animal models of human disease, 73–75
   recessive, A-2
   synaptic plasticity and, 82
   variation in, A-6
   see also **Genetics**
Genetics *The biology of inheritance,* A-1–A-2, A-4–A-6
   aggression and, 695
   alcohol and, 334, 596, 597, 598, A-6
   anorexia nervosa and, 394
   anxiety disorder and, 569, 571, A-5
   autistic disorder and, 595, A-6
   behavior and, A-5–A-6
   cloning and, 39
   conduct disorders and, 593
   drug abuse and, 598
   emotions and, 425
   fearfulness and, A-6
   gustation and, 129
   hyperactivity and, A-6
   intelligence over life span and, A-5

language and, 300
learning and, A-6
learning disability and, A-6
longevity and, 482
memory and, A-6
mental retardation and, 375, 376
mood disorder and, 579, 582
multiple traits and, A-5
obesity and, 393
over life span, A-5
personality traits and, 530–532, A-4
pitch and, 110
schizophrenia and, A-6–A-7, 586, 587–588, A-3
sexual orientation and, 400–403
stress and, 507
subjective well-being and, 409
temperament and, 543
see also Behavioral genetics; Biological approach; Genes; Nature and nurture
Genital stage *The last of Freud's psychosexual stages, which begins during adolescence when sexual impulses appear at the conscious level,* 522
Genius, A-3
Genotype *The full set of genes, inherited from both parents, contained in twenty-three pairs of chromosomes,* A-2
Geons, 167, 168
Gephyrophobia, 566
German measles (rubella), 375, 436
Germinal stage, 435
Gestalt laws, 155, 156, 157
social perception and, 652
Gestalt psychologists, 12, 15, 155, 212
Gestalt therapy *An active treatment designed to help client's get in touch with genuine feelings and to disown foreign ones,* 610, 612–613
Giftedness, 374–375, 452
Ginkgo biloba, 90, 91
Glands *Organs that secrete hormones into the bloodstream,* 92–95
Glial cell line-derived neurotrophic factor (GDNF), 83
Glial cells *Cells in the nervous system that hold neurons together and help them communicate with one another,* 58, 82
Glove anesthesia, 573
Glucose, 389
Glutamate *An excitatory neurotransmitter that helps strengthen synaptic connections between neurons,* 89, 91, 255, 333, 336, 587
Glutamate receptor, 337
Goal setting, achievement motivation and, 406–407
Graduate Records Examination (GRE), 350
Grammar *A set of rules for combining the words used in a given language,* 293, 294, 298, 299
Grandparenthood, 480
Grasping reflex, 438
GRE, *see* Graduate Records Examination
Greeneville, USS, 692
Group assertiveness training, 615
Group identity, *see* Social identity

Grouping, perceptual organization and, 154, 155–157, 164
Group polarization, 292
Group processes, 714–716
groupthink and, 715–716
leadership and, 714–715
problem solving and decision making and, 291–292
social loafing and, 683–684
Group therapy *Psychotherapy involving several unrelated clients,* 605, 620–621, 629
Groupthink *A pattern of thinking in which group members fail to evaluate realistically the wisdom of various options and decisions,* 715–716
Growth factors
brain-tissue grafts and, 83
hair cell regeneration and, 107
Growth orientation *According to Maslow, drawing satisfaction from what is available in life, rather than focusing on what is missing,* 540
Growth theory, 540, 541
GSR, *see* Galvanic skin resistance
Guilty but mentally ill, 600
Gustation *The sense that detects chemicals in solutions that come into contact with receptors inside the mouth; the sense of taste,* 128–130
absolute thresholds and, 146
in newborn, 437, 438
taste aversions and, 193
Gyri, 75, 76
Habituation *The process of adapting to stimuli that do not change,* 171
fetus and, 435
learning and, 186
psychoactive drugs and, 186–187
Hair cells, of organ of Corti, 106, 107, 108, 110
Hallucinations *A symptom of disorder in which people perceive voices or other stimuli when there are no stimuli present,* 317, 326, 583–584
Hallucinogens *Psychoactive drugs that alter consciousness by producing a temporary loss of contact with reality and changes in emotion, perception, and thought,* 332, 337–341, 391
Haloperidol (Haldol), 635, 638, 641–642
Hammer, *see* Malleus
Happiness, 412
subjective well-being and, 408–409
Head, vestibular sense and, 131, 137
See also Brain
Headaches, acupuncture and, 135–136
Head Start, 361, 362, 643
Health-belief models, 510–511
Health promotion *The process of (a) altering or eliminating behaviors that pose risks to health and (b) encouraging healthy behavior patterns,* 509–514
Health psychologists *Psychologists who study the effects of behavior and mental processes on health and illness, and vice versa,* 6, 8
Health psychology *A field in which psychologists conduct and apply research aimed at promoting human health and preventing illness,* 486–487
alcohol and, 509
coping and, 512–514
health belief models and, 510–511
health promotion and, 509–514
personality and health and, 501–503, 506–508, 544
readiness to change and, 511–512
smoking and, 508–509, 510–511, 512
stress and, 492, 498, 499, 501–503, 504–508
unsafe sex and, 509, 511
see also under Stress
Hearing, 101, 104–111
absolute thresholds and, 146
in adulthood, 474
auditory pathways and, 109–111
coding and, 108–110
deafness and, 106–107, 111, 138, 328
ear and, 105, 106–108, 110
frequency and, 104, 105, 106, 108–110
frequency matching and, 108–109
grouping principles and, 157
language and, 110–111
memory and, 257
in newborns, 437, 438
place theory and, 108, 109
representations of, 103–104, 109–111
sound and, 104–106, 109–111, 157–158
vision and, 125–126
Heart disease, 487
in adulthood, 474–475
stress and, 492, 498, 501, 506
Height in the visual field *A depth cue whereby more distant objects are higher in the visual field than those nearby,* 158, 159
Heinz dilemma, 472
Helping behavior *Any act that is intended to benefit another person,* 702–703. See also Altruism/helping behavior
Hematophobia, 566, 570
Hemispheres, of brain, 75, 79–82
Heredity, *see* Genetics
Hermann grid, 117
Heroin, 89, 186, 332, 337, 597–598, 696
Herpes virus, 505
Hertz (Hz), 104, 105
Heterosexual *Sexual motivation that is focused on members of the opposite sex,* 400, 402–403
Heuristics *Time-saving mental shortcuts used in reasoning,* 277–278, 290
Hierarchical processing of visual information, 117, 119–120
Hierarchy of needs, 20, 409–410
High blood pressure, 492, 506
Hindbrain *An extension of the spinal cord contained inside the skull where nuclei control blood pressure, heart rate, breathing, and other vital functions,* 68–71, 86, 88
Hippocampus *A structure in the forebrain associated with the formation of new memories,* 72–73, 84, 86, 87, 88, 89
alcohol and, 334
Alzheimer's disease and, 194–195
memory and, 255–256, 257
problem solving and, 269

History effect, 371
Histrionic personality disorder, 589, 590
HIV, see Human immunodeficiency virus
Homeostasis *The tendency for organisms to keep their physiological systems at a stable, steady level by constantly adjusting themselves in response to change,* 385, 386, 393
Homosexual *Sexual motivation that is focused on members of one's own sex,* 400–403
    Diagnostic and Statistical Manual of Mental Disorders and, 555
    parenthood and, 478–479
Homunculus, 76–78
Horizontal-vertical illusion, 153
Hormones *Chemicals secreted by glands into the bloodstream, which carries them throughout the body,* 92–95, 95
    hunger and, 389
    immune system and, 505
    sympathetic system and, 507
    see also Endocrine system; Sex hormones
Hostility, heart disease and, 506–508
HPA, *see* Hypothalamic-pituitary-adrenocortical system
Hubble Space Telescope, 280–281
Hue *The essential color determined by the dominant wavelength of light,* 120, 121
Human development, 432–435
    attachment and, 128
    brain and, 84–86
    perception and, 171–173
    reproduction and, 128, A-1–A-2
    see also Adolescence; Adulthood; Childhood; Infancy; Prenatal development
Human differences, *see* Cultural differences; Ethnic group differences; Gender differences
Human factors psychology, *see* Engineering psychology
Human Genome Project, 52, A-6
Human immunodeficiency virus (HIV), 486, 501, 504, 505, 509
Humanistic approach *An approach to psychology that views behavior as controlled by the decisions that people make about their lives based on their perceptions of the world; a view in which personality is seen as developing through an actualizing tendency which unfolds in accordance with each person's unique perceptions of the world,* 19–21, 537–543
    collectivist cultures and, 541–543
    evaluation of, 540–541
    growth theory and, 540, 541
    to psychological disorders, 558, 560
    self-theory and, 538–540
    see also Humanistic psychotherapy
Humanistic psychotherapy, 610–613, 622
    client-centered therapy, 610–612
    effectiveness of, 625
    Gestalt therapy, 610, 612–613
Humor, stress and, 499
Humors, 525, 556
Hunger *The general state of wanting to eat,* 388–395
    appetite and, 391
    biological signals and, 388–389, 395
    blood-borne signals and, 389, 391, 393, 395
    brain and, 389, 390–391, 393, 395
    culture and, 392, 395
    flavor and, 391–392, 395
    incentive theory and, 387
    learning and, 392
    satiety and, 388–390
    specific, 391
    stomach cues and, 388
    see also Eating disorders
Huntington's disease, 88–89, A-5
Hyperactivity, 593, A-6. *See also* Attention deficit hyperactivity disorder
Hypericin, 636
Hypnosis *A phenomenon brought on by special induction techniques and characterized by varying degrees of responsiveness to suggestions for changes in experience and behavior,* 12, 133, 327–329
Hypnotic susceptibility, 327, 329
Hypochondriasis *A strong, unjustified fear of physical illness,* 572, 575
Hypocretin, narcolepsy and, 321
Hypomania, 578
Hypothalamic-pituitary-adrenocortical (HPA) system
    general adaptation syndrome and, 491–492
    mood disorder and, 580
Hypothalamus *A structure in the forebrain that regulates hunger, thirst, and sex drives,* 72, 86, 88, 93, 94, 96
    general adaptation syndrome and, 491–492
    hunger and, 390–391, 393, 395
    sexual behavior and, 398
    sexual orientation and, 401
    sleep and, 323, 324
Hypothesis *In scientific research, a prediction stated as a specific, testable proposition about a phenomenon,* 29–30, 283
Hysteria, 606, 607. *See also* Conversion disorder
ICD-10, *see* International Classification of Disease
ICIDH-2, *see* International Classification of Impairments, Disabilities and Handicaps
Id *In Freud's psychodynamic theory, the unconscious portion of personality containing basic impulses and urges,* 520, 524
Ideas of reference, schizophrenia and, 583
Identity crisis *A phase during which an adolescent attempts to develop an integrated self image,* 460, 469–471
Identity *versus* role confusion, 460, 470–471
Imagery therapy, nightmares and, 322
Images *Mental representations of visual information,* 273, 275
Imipramine (Tofranil), 638
Imitation
    language acquisition and, 299
    observational learning and, 213–217
Immediate memory span *The maximum number of items a person can recall perfectly after one presentation of the items,* 234–235
Immune system *The body's system of defense against invading substances and microorganisms,* 95–96, 492
Impaired functioning *Difficulty in fulfilling appropriate and expected family, social and work-related roles,* 555
Implicit memory *The unintentional influence of prior experiences,* 227–229, 256, 449
Impotence, *see* Erectile disorder
Impressions, 653–655, 659
Impulse control, serotonin and, 88
Inattentional blindness, 176–177
Incentive theory *A theory of motivation stating that behavior is directed toward attaining desirable stimuli and avoiding unwanted stimuli,* 387–388
Inclusive fitness, 707
Incus, 106, 107, 110
Independent variable *The variable manipulated by the researcher in an experiment,* 37
Individual analysis, 608
Individualist cultures, 21, 22
    achievement motivation and, 405
    aggression and, 696
    attitude change and, 664
    decision making and, 291
    fundamental attribution error and, 658
    personality and, 541–542
    psychodynamic approach to, 524
    self-esteem and, 650
    social loafing and, 683–684
Inductive reasoning, *see* Informal reasoning
Industrial/organizational psychologists *Psychologists who study ways to improve efficiency, productivity, and satisfaction among workers and the organizations that employ them,* 6, 9, 202, 713
Industry *versus* inferiority, 460
Infancy
    anal stage in, 521
    attachment in, 128, 453, 455–459, 478, 523
    brain in, 84, 85, 439
    cognitive development in, 439–444, 448
    day care and, 457–459
    emotions in, 425, 426, 427
    language development in, 296–298
    marital satisfaction and, 478
    memory in, 442
    motor development in, 433, 438
    oral stage in, 520–521
    peer relationships in, 462
    perception in, 171–173
    sleep in, 320, 321, 325
    social and emotional development in, 453–459, 460, 462
    sudden infant death syndrome and, 322
    temperament in, 454, 531, 543–545
    thinking in, 442
    see also Newborn
Infantile amnesia, 449–450
Inferences, 274
Inferential statistics *A set of procedures that provides a measure of how likely it is that research results came about by chance,* 46–47, A-10
    analysis of variance and, A-17–A-18
    statistically significant and, 46, 47, A-15
    t test and, A-15–A-16
Inflections, 299

Informal reasoning *The process of evaluating a conclusion, theory, or course of action on the basis of the believability of evidence,* 276–278
Information processing, 14
 in childhood, 447–449
 cognitive approach to, 19
 in late adulthood, 372
 learning disabilities and, 377
 without awareness, 312
Information-processing approach *An approach to the study of intelligence that focuses on mental operations, such as attention and memory, that underlie intelligent behavior,* 366, 367, 369
Information-processing model *A model of memory in which information is seen as passing through sensory memory, short-term/working memory, and long-term memory,* 231–232
 of thought, 266–267, 270, 274
 see also **Long-term memory; Sensory memory; Short-term memory**
Information-processing system *Mechanisms for receiving, mentally representing, and manipulating information,* 266–267
 measurement of, 267–269
In-group
 prejudice and, 667
 ultimate attribute error and, 658
Inhibitory postsynaptic potential (IPSP) *A postsynaptic potential that hyperpolarizes the neuronal membrane, making a cell less likely to fire an action potential,* 61
Initiative *versus* guilt, 460
Injunctive norms, 680–681
Inpatients, 604–605
Insanity, 599–600
Insanity Defense Reform Act, 599
Insecure attachment, 457, 458–459, 478, 523
Insight *In problem solving, a sudden understanding about what is required to produce a desired effect,* 212–213
Insomnia *A sleep disorder in which a person feels tired during the day because of trouble falling asleep or staying asleep at night,* 208, 320–321
Instincts *Innate, automatic dispositions toward responding in a particular way when confronted with a specific stimulus; instincts produce behavior over which an organism has no control,* 383, 519–520
Instinct theory *A view that explains human behavior as motivated by automatic, involuntary, and unlearned responses,* 383–385, 388
Instrumental conditioning *A process through which responses are learned that help produce some rewarding or desired effect,* 196–197. *See also* Operant conditioning
Insulin, 389, 390, 395
Integrity *versus* despair, 460, 481
Intelligence *Those attributes that center around reasoning skills, knowledge of one's culture, and the ability to arrive at innovative solutions to problems,* 346, 365–370
 analytic, 366, 367, 368

 creativity and, 366–367, 368, 374
 crystallized, 365, 371, 475
 definition of, 346
 fluid, 365, 371, 475
 genetics over life span and, A-5
 improvements in, 452
 information-processing approach to, 366, 367, 369
 in late adulthood, 476
 multiple, 369–370
 nature and nurture and, 354–362, 363, 435, 451–452, A-3–A-4
 practical, 367, 368
 psychometric approach to, 365–366, 369
 triarchic theory of, 366–368, 369
 see also **Cognitive ability;** Cognitive development; **Intelligence quotient; IQ test**
Intelligence quotient *An index of intelligence that reflects the degree to which a person's score on an intelligence test deviates from the average score of others in the same age group,* 346, 349–350, 356–365
 in classroom, 362–363
 conditions raising, 358, 361–362
 group differences in, 354–356, 358–361, 364
 influences on, 353–354
 as measure of innate ability, 356–358
 nature and nurture and, 354–362, 363
 normal distribution of, 349, 350, A-12–A-13
 socioeconomic differences and, 357, 358, 359, 361, 451–452
 see also **IQ test**
Intelligence test, *see* **IQ test**
Intensity, of touch, 132
Interdependence, intimate relationships and, 673
Interference *The process through which either the storage or the retrieval of information is impaired by the presence of other information,* 248–250
Intermittent reinforcement schedules, *see* **Partial reinforcement schedule**
Internal attribution, 655
Internalization, 520
Internalizing disorders, of childhood, 593
Internals, 534
International Classification of Diseases (ICD-10), 400, 560
International Classification of Impairments, Disabilities and Handicaps (ICIDH-2), 560
Interneurons, 115
Interpersonal attraction, 671–676
 environment and, 672
 intimate relationships and, 671, 673, 674
 love and, 673–675
 matching hypothesis of, 673
 mate selection and, 17, 383–385
 physical attractiveness and, 672–673
 similarity and, 672, 673
 see also Marriage
Interpersonal intelligence, 370
Interpersonal psychotherapy, 641
Interpersonal therapy, 608, 627
Interposition *A depth cue whereby closer objects block one's view of things farther away,* 159
Interrater reliability, 563
Intervening variable, motivation as, 381–382

Interviews, personalities assessed with, 545
Intimacy
 versus isolation, 460, 478
 in love, 674–675
Intimate relationships, 671, 673, 674. *See also* Interpersonal attraction
Intrapersonal intelligence, 370
Intrapsychic (psychodynamic) conflicts, 520
Intrinsic motivation, 404
Introspection, 11–12
Introversion, 522
Introversion-extraversion, 386, 528–529
In vitro fertilization, 478
Iodopsin, 114
IPSP, *see* **Inhibitory postsynaptic potential**
IQ score, *See* Intelligence quotient
IQ test *A test designed to measure intelligence on an objective, standardized scale,* 346–356
 aptitude and achievement tests and, 350
 Army Alpha and Beta tests, 347–348
 emotionality and, 364–365
 evaluation of, 350–356
 fairness of, 354–356, 358–361
 history of, 346–348
 reliability of, 352–353
 Stanford-Binet, 346, 347, 349
 today, 348–350
 validity of, 353–354
 Wechsler scales, 348–350
 see also **Intelligence quotient**
Iris *The colorful part of the eye that constricts or relaxes to adjust the amount of light entering it,* 112, 113
Irresistible-impulse test, 599, 600
James-Lange theory, 417–421, 423
Jet lag *A syndrome of fatigue, irritability, inattention, and sleeping problems caused by air travel across several time zones,* 323
Jigsaw technique, 669
JND, *see* **Just-noticeable difference**
Judgment, subliminal information and, 148
Just-noticeable difference (JND) *The smallest detectable difference in stimulus energy,* 152
Kava, 333
Kendra's Law, 632
Kenohobia, 566
Ketamine, 338
Kinesthesia *The sense that tells you where the parts of your body are with respect to one another,* 131, 137–140
Kinesthetic encoding, 234
Kin selection, altruism/helping behavior and, 707–709
Klonopin, *see* Clonazepam
Koro, 559
Korsakoff's syndrome, 256–257, 596
Ku Klux Klan, 682
Language *Symbols and a set of rules for combining them that provides a vehicle for communication,* 265, 292–305
 acquisition of, 299–303
 aphasia and, 78
 bilingualism and, 300–301
 biological approach to, 299–300
 brain and, 70–71, 76, 78–79, 80–81, 111
 cognitive development and, 450–451
 conditioning and, 299

culture and thought and, 303–305
deep structure in, 293–294, 295
development of, 296–298, 445, 448
grammar in, 293, 298, 299
hearing and, 110–111
imitation and, 299
nonhumans and, 301–303
nonverbal, 295
sentences in, 293, 295, 298
sequencing and, 70–71
sounds in, 293, 294–295
speech and, 294–296
stuttering and, 71
surface structure in, 293–294, 295
symbols in, 293, 445, 448
See also **Words**
Largactil, *see* Chlorpromazine
Late adulthood, 480–482
cognitive changes in, 84–86, 370–372, 440, 471, 474–477, 480, 481
death and dying in, 481
fears in, 44–45
longevity and, 481–482
nootropic drugs and, 91
physical changes in, 480
prejudice and, 314
retirement in, 480–481
sexual behavior in, 9
sleep in, 320, 321
social and emotional changes in, 460, 480–481
suicide in, 577, 578
vision in, 112–113
Latency period *The fourth of Freud's psychosexual stages, in which sexual impulses lie dormant,* 522
Latent learning *Learning that is not demonstrated at the time it occurs,* 211–212
Lateral geniculate nucleus (LGN) *A region of the thalamus in which axons from most of the ganglion cells in the retina end and form synapses,* 116, 118, 119
Lateral hypothalamus, 390
Lateral inhibition *The enhancement of the sensation of contrast that occurs when greater response to light in one photoreceptor cell suppresses the response of a neighboring cell,* 115–116
Lateralized *Referring to the tendency for one cerebral hemisphere to excel at a particular function or skill compared to the other hemisphere,* 80–82
Law, *see* Criminal justice
Law of effect *A law stating that if a response made in the presence of a particular stimulus is followed by a reward, that same response is more likely to be made the next time the stimulus is encountered. Responses that are not rewarded are less likely to be performed again,* 196
LCUs, *see* Life change events
Leadership, in groups, 714–716
Learned expectations, psychoactive drugs and, 332–333, 334
Learned helplessness *A failure to try to exert control over the environment when an organism has, or believes that it has, no such control,* 209–210
mood disorder and, 581
Learning *The modification through experience of pre-existing behavior and understanding,* 184–223
active, 219–220
aggression and, 696–697
alcohol use disorders and, 596–597
anxiety disorder and, 569, 570–571
attitudes and, 661–662
behaviorism and, 18, 19
cognitive approach to, 209–218
cognitive maps and, 211–212
connections between neurons and, 59
cultural differences in, 218–219
eating and, 392
emotions and, 426–427
genetics and, A-6
glutamate and, 89
immune responses and, 96
insight and, 212–213
latent, 211–212
learned helplessness and, 209–210
mental retardation and, 376
motivation and, 385
neural networks and, 217–218
nonassociative, 186–187
observational, 213–217
opponent-process theory and, 411–412
research on, 185
skills and, 220–221
sleep deprivation and, 324–325
stimuli and, 186–187
see also Conditioning
Learning approach, to prejudice/stereotypes, 668
Learning disabilities, 376–377, A-6
Learning goals, 404, 405
Learning memory, synaptic plasticity and, 82–84
Lecture notes, effectiveness of, 260
Length, illusions of, 153, 154
Lens *The part of the eye behind the pupil that bends light rays, focusing them on the retina,* 112, 113
Leptin, 389, 390, 393, 395
LES, *see* Life Experiences Survey
Leukocytes, 504
Levels-of-processing model *A view stating that how well something is remembered depends on the degree to which incoming information is mentally processed,* 229–230, 232
LGN, *see* **Lateral geniculate nucleus**
Libido *According to Freud, the psychic energy contained in the id,* 520
Librium, *see* Chlordiazepoxide
Licensed professional counselors, 606
Lie detection, 420–421
Life change events (LCUs), 488, 489
Life Experiences Survey (LES), 490
Life outcomes, personalities assessed with, 545
Lifestyle, death and, 486–487, 508–509
Light, 111–113, 120. See also Vision
Light intensity *A physical dimension of light waves that refers to how much energy the light contains; it determines the brightness of light,* 112

Light wavelength *The distance between peaks in light waves; at a given intensity, different wavelengths produce sensations of different colors,* 112
Likelihood principle, 154, 156, 157
Liking, wanting *versus*, 387–388
Limbic system *A set of brain structures that play important roles in regulating emotion and memory,* 72, 73, 87, 94
aggression and, 695–696
emotion and, 414
Linear perspective *A depth cue whereby objects closer to the point where two lines appear to converge are perceived as being at a greater distance,* 159
Linguistic determinism, 303–304
Linguistic intelligence, 369, 370
Lip reading, 111
Lithium carbonate (Carboleth, Lithizine), 636–637, 638
Lobotomy, *see* **Psychosurgery**
Local review committees, 48–49
Location
perception of, 157–158, 164
of touch, 132
Locus coeruleus *A small nucleus in the reticular formation that contains about half of the cell bodies of neurons in the brain that use norepinephrine,* 69–70, 88, 325, 334
Logic, *see* **Rules of logic**
Logical-mathematical intelligence, 369, 370
Logical reasoning, *see* **Formal reasoning**
Longevity, 481–482
Longitudinal research, 370–371, 501–503, 543–545
Long-term memory (LTM) *A relatively long-lasting stage of memory whose capacity to store new information is believed to be unlimited,* 231, 236–239, 257
in childhood, 447–448
encoding in, 236–237, 245
episodic, 226, 227, 243–244, 476
forgetting from, 248–250
procedural, 226, 227, 256
retrieval from, 239–240
savings in, 247
semantic, 226, 227
short-term *versus*, 238–239
storage capacity of, 237–238
thought and, 267
see also Memory
Long-term potentiation, 254
Long-wavelength cones, 122
Looming *A motion cue involving a rapid expansion in the size of an image so that it fills the available space on the retina,* 161
Loose associations, schizophrenia and, 583
Loss aversion, 289
Loudness *A psychological dimension of sound determined by the amplitude of a sound wave,* 105, 106, 108
Love motives, 409, 410
Love, 673–675. See also Interpersonal attraction
Low-ball approach, compliance and, 688–689
LSD, 338
LTM, *see* **Long-term memory**

Luchins jar problem, 283–284
Lucid dreaming *Awareness that a dream is a dream while it is happening,* 326
Luvox, *see* Fluvoxamine
Lysergic acid diethylamide, *see* LSD
Macrophages, 504–505
Magnetic resonance imaging (MRI), 3, 68, 69, 71, 72, 84, 85, 93–94, 133, 178, 255, 269, 332, 587, 666
Magnetoencephalography (MEG), 68
Magnitude estimation, 153–154
Mainstreaming, 376
Maintenance, in working memory, 133
Maintenance rehearsal *Repeating information over and over to keep it active in short-term memory,* 229–230
Major depressive disorder *A condition in which a person feels sad and hopeless for weeks or months,* 576, 579, 580, 582, 627, 640. See also Depression
Maladjusted overcontrolling person, 525
Maladjusted undercontrolling person, 525
Malleus, 106, 107, 110
Mania *An elated, very active emotional state,* 578, 633, 635, 636–637, 638
Manic depression, 578
Manipulation, in working memory, 133
Mantra, 330
MAOIs, *see* Monoamine oxidase inhibitors
Marijuana *(cannabis),* 332, 338–341, 391
Marriage, 478, 479
   aggression and, 695
   attachment in infancy and, 523
   and changes in family life, 478
   couples therapy and, 622, 623
   and divorce, 466, 477, 479
   strong and weak, 675–676
Marriage and family therapists, 606
Massage, 132
Massed practice, 259
Matching hypothesis *The notion that people are most likely to form relationships with those who are similar to themselves in physical attractiveness,* 673
Materialism, consciousness and, 310
Mate selection
   evolutionary explanation of, 383–385
   gender differences in, 17
   see also Interpersonal attraction; Marriage
Mathematics, cultural differences and, 450–451
Maturation *Natural growth or change that unfolds in a fixed sequence relatively independent of the environment,* 433, 438, 448
MDMA, 337
Mean *A measure of central tendency that is the arithmetic average of the scores in a set of data; the sum of the values of all the scores divided by the total number of scores,* 43–44, 46, A-11
Means-end analysis, 279
Median *A measure of central tendency that is the halfway point in a set of data: Half the scores fall stimuli such as pain,* 42–43, 46, A-11
Mediators, conflict management and, 713
Medical model, of psychopathology, 530, 556

Medical model, of psychological disorders, 530, 556, 563
Meditation, 329–330
Medium-wavelength cones, 122
Medulla *An area in the hindbrain that controls blood pressure, heart rate, breathing, and other vital functions,* 68, 70, 86
Meiosis, A-2
Melatonin, 323
Melissophobia, 566
Melodic intonation therapy, 78
Memory, 224–263
   alcohol and, 334
   attitudes and, 661
   biochemistry of, 254–255
   biological approach to, 253–258, A-6
   brain and, 72, 73, 253–258
   capacity of, 225
   in childhood, 447–450
   connections between neurons and, 59
   consciousness and, 311
   consolidation and, 257
   constructive, 242, 243–247, 257
   context-dependent, 240
   criminal justice and, 9, 10, 245–247, 250–253, 258, 329
   design of electronic and mechanical devices and, 260–261
   encoding and, 225–226, 231, 233–234, 236–237, 245
   episodic, 226, 227, 243–244, 476
   explicit, 227–229
   eyewitness, 245–247
   false, 251–253, 257, 329, 524, 574
   forgetting and, 225, 226
   formation of, 254–255
   glutamate and, 89
   hypnosis and, 329
   implicit, 227–229, 256, 449
   improving, 258–260
   in infancy, 442
   information-processing model of, 231–232, *see also* **Long-term memory; Sensory memory; Short-term memory**
   intelligence and, 366
   ketamine and, 338
   in late adulthood, 476
   levels-of-processing model of, 229–230, 232
   mental retardation and, 376
   mnemonics and, 258, 260
   models of, 229–232
   nitric oxide and, 89, 90
   nootropic drugs and, 90–92
   olfaction and, 127, 128
   parallel distributed processing models of, 230–231, 232, 243–244, 254
   photographic, 238
   procedural, 226, 227, 256
   processes of, 225–226, *see also* **Retrieval**
   rehearsal and, 229–230, 248
   as selective, 225
   semantic, 226, 227, 240–244, 276, 476
   sensory, 232–233, 239
   state-dependent, 240
   storage and, 226
   transfer-appropriate processing model of, 230, 231, 232

   types of, 226–227
   working, 233, 239, 256, 261, 267, 276, 372, *see also* **Short-term memory**
   see also Alzheimer's disease; Amnesia; Forgetting; **Long-term memory; Retrieval; Short-term memory**
Memory codes, 226
Menopause *The process whereby a woman's reproductive capacity ceases,* 474
Menstrual cycle, 398, 474
Menstrual synchrony, 128
Mental age, 346
Mental chronometry, 267–268
Mental hospitals
   commitment to, 632
   in history, 632, 633
Mental illness, *see* Psychological disorders
Mentally challenged, *see* Mental retardation
Mentally incompetent to stand trial, 598, 599
Mental model *A cluster of propositions representing our understanding of objects and processes that guides our interaction with those things,* 272–273, 274, 275
Mental processing, without awareness, 312–314
Mental representations, 190
   in infants, 441, 442, 443–444
Mental retardation, 375–376
   fetal alcohol syndrome and, 436, 509, 596
   phenylketonuria and, 375, A-2, A-4
Mental set *The tendency for old patterns of problem solving to persist, even when they might not always be the most efficient alternative,* 283–284
   stress and, 494
Meprobamate (Miltown, Equanil), 637
Mere-exposure effect, 662
   interpersonal attraction and, 672
Meta-analysis, 625
Metabolism, obesity and, 393, 394
Metacognition *The knowledge of what strategies to apply, when to apply them, and how to deploy them in new situations so that new specific knowledge can be gained and different problems mastered,* 376
Metamemory, 376
Method of loci, 258
Method of savings *Measuring forgetting by computing the difference between the number of repetitions needed to learn, and after a delay, relearn, the same material,* 247, 248
Midbrain *A small structure, between the hindbrain and forebrain, that relays information from the eyes, ears, and skin, and controls certain types of automatic behaviors in response to information received through those senses,* 70, 71, 86, 87, 88
Midlife transition *A point at around age forty when adults take stock of their lives,* 479
Mild mental retardation, 375
Miltown, *see* Meprobamate
Mind-body problem, consciousness and, 310
Mind reading, 174–175
Minimally acceptable solution, 291
Minnesota Multiphasic Personality Inventory (MMPI), 546–548, 549
Minorities, *see* Ethnic minorities

Minority influence *A phenomenon whereby members of a numerical minority in a group alters the view of the majority,* 687
Mitochondria, 57, 60
Mitosis, A-1–A-2
Mixed anxiety-depression disorder, 568
Mixed-motive conflict, 711
MMPI, *see* Minnesota Multiphasic Personality Inventory
M'Naughton rule, 599
Mnemonics *Strategies for placing information in an organized context in order to remember it,* 258, 260
Modafinil, 322
Mode *A measure of central tendency that is the value or score that occurs most frequently in a data set,* 42, 46, A-11
Modeling *Demonstrating desirable behaviors as a way of teaching them to clients*
   aggression and, 697
   attitudes and, 661–662
   in behavior therapy, 615
Moderate mental retardation, 375
Monoamine oxidase inhibitors (MAOIs), 636
Monozygotic, A-2
Mood, serotonin and, 88
Mood congruency effects, 240
Mood disorder *Conditions in which a person experiences extreme moods, such as depression or mania,* 562, 576–582
   biological factors in, 579–580, 582
   bipolar disorders, 557, 578–579, 580
   causes of, 579–582
   cyclothemic disorder, 578–579
   diagnosis of, 563, 564
   incidence of, 554
   lithium and anticonvulsants for, 636–637, 638
   mania, 578, 633, 635, 636–637, 638
   psychological and social factors in, 580–582
   see also Depression
Moral action, moral reasoning and, 473–474
Moral development, 472–474
Moral insanity, 589. *See also* Antisocial personality disorder
Morpheme *The smallest unit of language that has meaning,* 293
Morphine, 89, 337, 696
Mortality effect, 371
Mothers, single, 478. *See also* **Attachment**; Parents and parenting
Motion, perception of, 161–162
Motion parallax *A depth cue whereby a difference in the apparent rate of movement of different objects provides information on the relative distance of those objects,* 160
Motion sickness, 162
Motivation *The influences that account for the initiation, direction, intensity, and persistence of behavior*
   arousal theories and, 386–387, 388
   biological factors in, 382
   cognitive factors in, 382
   creativity and, 373–374
   drive reduction theory and, 385–386, 388
   emotion and, 382, 410–411
   extrinsic, 404

   hierarchy-of-needs theory of, 20
   incentive theory and, 387–388
   instinct theory and, 383–385, 388
   intelligence quotient and, 354–355, 359, 361, 363
   as intervening variable, 381–382
   intrinsic, 404
   IQ tests and, 364
   learning and, 385
   opponent-process theory and, 411–412
   perception and, 170
   prejudice/stereotypes and, 666–667
   presence of others and, 682–684
   relations and conflicts among motives and, 409–412
   social factors in, 382
   sources of, 382
   see also Achievement motivation; **Hunger**; Sexual behavior
Motive *A reason or purpose for behavior,* 381, 410–411. *See also* **Motivation**
Motor cortex *The part of the cerebral cortex whose neurons control voluntary movements in specific parts of the body,* 76, 77–78
Motor development, in infancy, 433, 438, 448
Motor systems *The parts of the nervous system that influence muscles and other organs to respond to the environment in some way,* 63
Mouth, gustation and, 128–130
MPD (multiple personality disorder), *see* Dissociative identity disorder
MRI, *see* Magnetic resonance imaging
MS, *see* Multiple sclerosis
Muhammad Ali Effect, 649
Müller-Lyer illusion and variation, 153
Multiculturalism, 21–22. *See also* Cultural differences
Multiple approach-avoidance conflicts, 411
Multiple intelligences *Howard Gardner's theory that people are possessed of eight semi-independent kinds of intelligence, only three of which are measured by standard IQ tests,* 369–370
Multiple personality disorder, *see* Dissociative identity disorder
Multiple sclerosis (MS), 59, 95
Musical intelligence, 369, 370
Muslims, terrorist attacks and, 647, 648, 650, 667, 680, 692, 702–703, 713
Myelin *A fatty substance that wraps around some axons and increases the speed of action potentials,* 59
N, A-11
Naloxone, 136, 333
Naltrexone, 333
Narcissistic personality disorder, 589, 590
Narcolepsy *A daytime sleep disorder in which a person switches abruptly from an active, often emotional waking state into several minutes of REM sleep,* 321–322
National Academy of Science, 215
National Aeronautics and Space Administration (NASA), 715
National Health and Social Life Survey, 397–398, 400
National Institute of Medicine, 341

National Institute of Mental Health, 628
National Institutes of Health, 49
Natural concepts *Concepts that have no fixed set of defining features but instead share a set of characteristic features,* 270–271
Naturalistic decision making, 291
Naturalistic intelligence, 370
Naturalistic observation *The process of watching without interfering as a phenomenon occurs in the natural environment,* 31, 33–34, 42
Natural killer cells, 504
Natural selection, 17, 111
Nature and nurture, 49–50, 55, A-2
   brain plasticity and, 85–86
   cognitive development and, 448–449, A-3
   creativity and, 374
   gender roles and, 464
   history of research on, A-3–A-4
   human development and, 432–435
   and intelligence, 354–362, 363, 435, 451–452, A-3–A-4
   intelligence and, 354–362, 363, 435
   perception and, 172, 173
   personality and, 530–532
   prenatal development and, 435–436
   temperament and, 454
   vision and, 113
   see also **Behavioral genetics**
Nearsightedness, 113, 114
Necker cube, 311
Need *In drive reduction theory, a biological requirement for well-being that is created by an imbalance in homeostasis,* 385
   hierarchy of, 409–410
   see also **Drive**
Need achievement *A motive influenced by the degree to which a person establishes specific goals, cares about meeting those goals, and experiences feelings of satisfaction by doing so; it is often measured by the Thematic Apperception Test,* 404–406
Nefazodone (Serzone), 636
Negative affect, aggression and, 698
Negative correlation, 45, 46
Negative feedback system *An arrangement in which the output of a system is monitored and maintained at some particular level,* 95
Negative priming, 177
Negative reinforcers *The removal of unpleasant stimuli such as pain,* 197, 198, 207
Negative symptoms *Schizophrenic symptoms such as absence of pleasure, lack of speech, and flat affect,* 585, 586, 587
Negative thinking, 619–620
Neo-Freudian theorists, 522–523, 524
   contemporary psychoanalysis and, 608–609, 622
Neologisms, schizophrenia and, 583
NEO-PI-R, *see* Neuroticism Extraversion Openness Personality Inventory
Nerve deafness, 106–107, 108
Nerve growth factor, brain damage and, 83–84
Nervous system *A complex combination of cells whose primary function is to allow an organism to gain information about what is*

Subject Index/Glossary

going on inside and outside the body and to respond appropriately, 55–64
    action potentials and, 58–60, 61, 102
    in adulthood, 474–475
    cells of, 56–58
    communication between cells and, 60–62, *see also* **Neurotransmitters**
    definition of, 55–56
    endocrine system and, 95
    excitatory and inhibitory signals and, 61–62
    functions of, 56
    immune system and, 95, 96
    organization and functions of, 62–64
    synapses and, 58, 60, 61, 63, 84, 85–86
    see also **Brain; Central nervous system; Peripheral nervous system**
Network processing, pattern recognition and, 170–171
Neural networks *Neurons that operate together to perform complex functions,* 62–63, 66
    artificial intelligence and, 287–288
    learning and, 217–218
    parallel distributed processing models of memory and, 218, 231
Neural stem cell, 84
Neurobiological model *A modern name for the medical model, in which psychological disorders are seen as reflecting disturbances in the anatomy and chemistry of the brain and other biological processes,* 556, 560
Neurodevelopmental abnormalities, schizophrenia and, 587–588
Neuroimaging, 3, 68, 269
    addiction and, 332
    analogical thinking and, 280–282
    attention and, 178
    dopamine system and, 386
    dreams and, 326
    electroencephalograph and, 68, 268, 269, 318–320, 325, 330, 666
    emotion and, 414
    hypnosis and, 329
    information processing and, 269
    magnetic resonance imaging (MRI) and, 3, 68, 69, 71, 72, 84, 85, 93–94, 133, 178, 255, 269, 332, 587, 666
    magnetoencephalography and, 68
    meditation and, 330
    memory and, 229, 255
    paint, 133
    parallel processing of visual properties and, 119
    positive emission tomography (PET scans) and, 68, 69, 80, 81, 84, 119, 178, 255, 269, 280–282, 584
    prejudice/stereotypes, 665–666
    schizophrenia and, 584, 586, 587
    sleep and, 318–320, 325
Neuroleptics (antipsychotics) *Drugs that alleviate the symptoms of severe disorders such as schizophrenia,* 635, 638, 639, 640, 641–642
Neuromodulators, 87, 390, 395
Neuromuscular junction, 64–65

Neurons *Fundamental units of the nervous system; nerve cells,* 57–58, 59–60, 61, 62, 67, 82
    afferent, 67
    efferent, 67
    synaptic plasticity and, 82–84
Neuropeptide Y, 391
Neuropsychology, case studies in, 34–35
Neuroscience, 8–9
Neuroscientists, 665–666
Neurosis, 561
Neuroticism, as big-five personality factor, 528
Neuroticism Extraversion Openness Personality Inventory, Revised (NEO-PI-R), 546
Neurotransmitters *Chemicals that transfer signals from one neuron to another,* 60–62, 63, 86–90, 569
    alcohol use disorders and, 597
    anorexia nervosa and, 394
    antidepressants and, 635–636
    electroconvulsive therapy and, 634
    gases and, 89, 90
    gene manipulation and, 75
    hormones *versus,* 92
    hunger and, 389, 390, 391, 395
    memories and, 255
    mood disorder and, 579–580
    neuromodulators and, 87
    neuromuscular junction and, 64–65
    nootropic drugs and, 90–92
    pain and, 133
    peptides and, 89, 90
    psychoactive drugs and, 330–331, 332, 334, 335, 336, 337, 338, 641–642
    receptors and, 62
    schizophrenia and, 587
    small-molecule, 87–89, 90
    vision and, 116
    see also specific neurotransmitters
Neurotransmitter system *A group of neurons that communicates by using the same neurotransmitter,* 86
Neurotrophic factors, brain-tissue grafts and, 83
Neutral stimulus, 188, 189, 191
Newborn
    as blank slate *(tabula rasa),* 11, 432
    motor skills in, 438, 448
    reflexes in, 438, 448
    sensory abilities in, 436–437, 448
    see also **Infancy**
Nicotine, 336, 337
Nicotine withdrawal syndrome, 336
Nightmares *Frightening, sometimes recurring dreams that take place during REM sleep,* 322
Night terrors *Rapid awakening from stage 4 sleep accompanied by a horrific dream that causes the dreamer to experience intense fear for up to thirty minutes,* 322
Nine-dot problem, 283, 285
Nitric oxide, as neurotransmitter, 89, 90
Nogo, 82
Noise, 105, 106, 107
    aggression and, 702
    sensitivity and, 149, 150
Nonassociative learning, 186–187

Nonconscious level *A level of mental activity that is inaccessible to conscious awareness,* 311
Nondirective therapy, 610. *See also* **Client-centered therapy**
Nonlinear dynamics, 138
Non-REM sleep, *see* **Slow-wave sleep**
Nonverbal cues, understanding speech and, 295
Nootropic drugs, 90–92
Noradrenaline, *see* **Norepinephrine**
Norepinephrine *A neurotransmitter involved in arousal, as well as in learning and mood regulation; also called* noradrenaline, 88, 90, 92, 416–417
    antidepressants and, 635–636, 642
    general adaptation syndrome and, 491
    heart disease and, 507
    mood disorder and, 579
    panic disorder and, 569
    psychoactive drugs and, 335
    sleep and, 325
Norm *A description of the frequency at which a particular score occurs, which allows scores to be compared statistically,* 351
Normal distribution, A-12–A-13
    intelligence quotient and, 349, 350, A-12–A-13
Norms *Socially based rules that prescribe what people should or should not do in various situations*
    abnormality and violation of, 554–555
    altruism/helping behavior and, 703
    conformity and compliance and, 685, 686
    social influence and, 680–682
    subjective, 660
Nose, olfaction and, 126–128, 129–130
Not guilty by reason of insanity, 599
NREM sleep, *see* **Slow-wave sleep**
Nuclei *Collections of nerve cell bodies in the central nervous system,* 57, 66, 86
Null hypothesis *The assertion that the independent variable manipulated by the experimenter will have no effect on the dependent variable measured by the experimenter,* A-10
Nun Study, 476, 477
Nutrients, 391–392
    hunger and, 389
Obedience *A form of compliance in which people comply with a demand, rather than with a request,* 689–694
    behavior of others and, 691
    civil disobedience and, 692
    Milgram's study of, 689–694
    personality and, 691–692, 693
    proximity and, 691
    status and power and, 690–691
Obesity *A condition in which a person is severely overweight, as measured by a body mass index above 30,* 389, 392–394
Objective tests *Personality tests containing direct, unambiguous items relating to the individual being assessed,* 545–548, 549
Object permanence *The knowledge that objects exist even when they are not in view,* 442, 448

Object relations theory, 523, 558, 581
  family therapy and, 621
Object relations therapy, 608
Object superiority effect, 170, 171
Observation, see **Naturalistic observation**
Observational learning *Learning how to perform new behaviors by watching the behavior of others,* 213–217
  aggression and, 697
Observer ratings, personalities assessed with, 545
Obsessions, 568–568. See also **Obsessive-compulsive disorder**
Obsessive-compulsive disorder (OCD) *An anxiety disorder involving repetitive thoughts and urges to perform certain rituals,* 553, 568–569, 570, 575, 617, 627, 634, 636, 637, 640, 641
Obsessive-compulsive personality disorder, 589, 590
Occipital lobe, 75, 76
Occlusion, see **Interposition**
OCD, see **Obsessive-compulsive disorder**
Odd-eccentric cluster, of personality disorders, 589, 590
Oedipus complex *A pattern described by Freud in which a boy has sexual desire for his mother and wants to eliminate his father's competition for her attention,* 522
Olanzapine (Zyprexa), 635
Olfaction *The sense that detects chemicals that are airborne, or volatile; the sense of smell,* 126–128, 129–130, 146
  in newborn, 437–438
Olfactory bulb *The brain structure that receives messages regarding olfaction,* 127
One-word stage *A stage of language development during which children tend to use one word at a time,* 298
Open-ended interviews, 545
Operant *A response that has some effect on the world,* 197
Operant conditioning *A process through which an organism learns to respond to the environment in a way that produces positive consequences,* 14, 195–208
  applications of, 207–208
  attitudes and, 661–662
  avoidance conditioning and, 198–199, 207
  behavioral approach to, 208–209
  behavior modification and, 613, 614
  delay and size of reinforcement and, 201–202
  discriminative stimuli and stimulus control and, 199–200, 208
  education and, 219
  escape conditioning and, 197–198, 207
  explanation for reinforcement and, 204–205
  extinction and, 203–204, 208
  instrumental conditioning and, 196–197
  operants and, 197
  phobia and, 215, 570–571
  punishment and, 205–208
  puzzle box and, 195–196, 197
  reinforcers and, 197, 207
  schedules of reinforcement and, 202–204
  secondary reinforcement and, 201
  shaping and, 200–201
  Skinner box and, 196, 197

Operational definitions *Statements that define variables describing the exact operations or methods used in research,* 29
Ophdophobia, 566, 571, 615
Opiates *Psychoactive drugs, such as opium, morphine, or heroin, that produce both sleep-inducing and pain-relieving effects,* 332, 337, 338, 339, 627
  aggression and, 696
  peptides and, 89–90
Opium, 337
Opponent-process theory *A theory of color vision stating that color sensitive visual elements are grouped into red-green, blue-yellow, and black-white elements,* 122–123, 124, 186, 411–412
Optical flow, 161
Optic chiasm *Part of the bottom surface of the brain where half of each optic nerve's fibers cross over to the opposite side of the brain,* 116, 118
Optic nerve *A bundle of fibers composed of axons from ganglion cells that carries visual information to the brain,* 113, 114, 116, 118
Optimism
  stress response and, 501
  unrealistic, 659, 660
Optimistic explanatory style, 210
Oral stage *The first of Freud's psychosexual stages, in which the mouth is the center of pleasure,* 520–521
Orbitofrontal cortex, 129–130
Organ of Corti, 106, 107, 108, 110
Orgasmic phase, of sexual response cycle, 399
Origin of Species (Darwin), 17
Otis-Lennon Mental Abilities Test, 350
Otoacoustic emissions, 401
Otoliths *Small crystals in the fluid-filled vestibular sacs of the inner ear that, when shifted by gravity, stimulate nerve cells that inform the brain of the position of the head relative to the earth,* 137
Outer membrane, of neuron, 57
Out-group
  prejudice and, 667
  ultimate attribute error and, 658
Ova, A-2
Oval window, 106, 107, 108, 110
Ovaries, 93
Overcontrolled disorders, of childhood, 594
Overeaters Anonymous, 621
Overt orienting, 173
Oxycodone (OxyContin), 338
Oxytocin, 501
Pain, 131, 132–136, 138
  acupuncture and, 135–136
  control over, 497, 498
  emotional aspects of, 134
  hypnosis and, 328–329
  as information sense, 132–133
  modulation of, 134–135
  morphine and, 337
  representations of, 103–104
Pain disorder *A somatoform disorder marked by complaints of severe pain with no physical cause,* 572, 575
Pancreas, 93

Panic attack, 498, 560, 567–568, 569–570, 604, 613, 618–619
Panic disorder *An anxiety disorder involving sudden panic attacks,* 337, 498, 560, 567–568, 569–570, 575, 604, 613, 617, 618–619, 627, 636, 637, 640, 641
Papillae *Structures on the tongue containing groups of taste receptors, or taste buds,* 128, 129, 130
PAPNET, 288
Paradoxical sleep, see **Rapid eye movement (REM) sleep**
Parallel distributed processing (PDP) models *An approach to understanding object recognition in which various elements of the object are thought to be simultaneously analyzed by a number of widely distributed but connected neural units in the brain; memory models in which new experiences change one's overall knowledge base,* 66
  of consciousness, 310
  of memory, 230–231, 232, 243–244
  of perception, 170–171, 218
Parallel processing, 117, 118–119, 177
Paranoid personality disorder, 589, 590
Paranoid schizophrenia, 335, 631, 640
Parasympathetic system *The subsystem of the autonomic nervous system that typically influences activity related to the protection, nourishment, and growth of the body,* 65, 87, 416
Parents and parenting, 478–479
  cognitive ability and, 452, A-8
  depression and, 581
  differential treatment of siblings and, A-7–A-8
  sexual orientation and, 478–479
  styles of, 459–462
  training programs for, 462
  working, 479
  see also **Attachment**; Fathers; Mothers
Parietal lobe, 75, 76
Parkinson's disease, 83, 84, 88
Paroxetine (Paxil), 637
Partial reinforcement extinction effect *A phenomenon in which behaviors learned under a partial reinforcement schedule are more difficult to extinguish than those learned on a continuous reinforcement schedule,* 203–204
Partial reinforcement schedule *A pattern of reinforcement in which a reinforcer is administered only some of the time after a particular response occurs,* 202–204
Participant modeling, 615
Participants' expectations, in experiments, 39–40, 41
Passion, in love, 674–675
Passionate love, 674
Pastoral counselors, 606
Pathways, see **Fiber tracts**
Pattern recognition, see **Recognition**
Paxil, see **Paroxetine**
PDP, see **Parallel distributed processing (PDP) models**
Peak experiences, 540

Pearson product-moment correlation (r), A-14–A-15
Peer relationships
  in adolescence, 462, 468
  in childhood, 461–463
  gender roles and, 465
  genetics and, A-8
  influence of, A-7
  in late adulthood, 481
  social support network and, 488, 499–503
Penalty, 205. *See also* **Punishment**
Penile erection, nitric oxide and, 89, 90
Penis envy, 522, 524
Pentagon attack (9/11/01), 647, 650, 667, 680, 702–703, 713
Peptides, 89, 90
Perceived self-efficacy *According to Bandura, learned expectations about the probability of success in given situations,* 534–535
Percentile score *The percentage of people or observations that fall below a given score in a normal distribution,* A-13
Perception *The process through which people take raw sensations from the environment and interpret them, using knowledge, experience, and understanding of the world, so that the sensations become meaningful experiences,* 143–183
  approaches to, 145–146, 156, 159, 161, 163, 171, 179, 180
  aviation psychology and, 179
  definition of, 144
  errors in, 144–145
  eyewitness testimony and, 245–247
  human-computer interaction and, 180
  human development and, 171–173
  parallel distributed processing models of, 170–171, 218
  psychophysics and, 11
  research applications and, 174–175, 178–181
  sensation *versus*, 100
  traffic safety and, 180–181
  see also **Attention; Neural networks; Perceptual organization; Psychophysics; Recognition; Sensory systems**
Perceptual constancy *The perception of objects as constant in size, shape, color, and other properties despite changes in their retinal image,* 162–165
Perceptual organization *The task of determining what edges and other stimuli go together to form an object,* 154–165
  auditory scene analysis and, 157
  brightness constancy and, 164–165
  cultural differences and, 165, 169
  depth perception and, 158–161, 164, 165, 172–173, 437
  experience and, 165
  figure-ground organization and, 155, 164
  grouping and, 154, 155–157, 164
  location perception and, 157–158, 164
  motion perception and, 161–162
  perceptual constancy and, 162–165
  shape constancy and, 163–164
  size constancy and, 163
Perceptual set, 169
Percodan, 337

Perfect pitch, 105
Performance goals, 404–405
Peripheral nervous system (PNS) *The parts of the nervous system not housed in bone,* 64–66, 87
  somatic nervous system and, 64–65
  see also **Autonomic nervous system; Nervous system**
Peripheral route, in elaboration likelihood model, 662, 663
Peripheral theory, *see* James-Lange theory
Permissive parents *Those who give their child great freedom and lax discipline,* 460, 461
Personality *The pattern of psychological and behavioral characteristics by which each person can be compared and contrasted with others,* 518–551
  adoption studies of, 51–52
  altruism/helping behavior and, 705
  approaches to study of, *see* **Humanistic approach; Psychodynamic approach; Social-cognitive approach; Trait approach**
  assessment of, 545, see also Personality tests
  attitude change and, 663
  cultural differences and, 541–543
  explanations of other people's behavior and, 10, 11
  health and, 501–503, 506–508, 544
  longevity and, 482
  obedience and, 691–692, 693
  stress and, 501
  temperament and, 531, 532, 543–545
Personality disorders *Long-standing, inflexible ways of behaving that create a variety of problems,* 562, 589–593
  antisocial, 554, 589–593
  anxious-fearful cluster of, 589, 590
  diagnosis of, 563, see also Personality tests
  dramatic-erratic cluster of, 589–593
  odd-eccentric cluster of, 589, 590
Personality psychologists *Psychologists who study the characteristics that make individuals similar to, and different from, one another,* 5
Personality tests, 545–549
  employee selection and, 518, 545, 549
  objective, 545–548, 549
  projective, 524, 548–549
Person-centered therapy, 540, *see* **Client-centered therapy**
Person-oriented leaders *Leaders who provide loose supervision, ask for group members' ideas, are concerned with subordinates' feelings, and are usually well liked by those they lead,* 714, 715
Persuasion cues, in elaboration likelihood model, 662, 663
Pervasive developmental disorders, 594–595
Pessimism, stress response and, 501
Pessimistic explanatory style, learned helplessness and, 210
PET scans, *see* Positive emission tomography
Phagocytosis, 504–505
Phallic stage *The third of Freud's psychosexual stages, in which the focus of pleasure shifts to the genital area,* 521–522

Phenomenological approach, *see* **Humanistic approach**
Phenomenologists, 610. See also Humanistic psychotherapy
Phenomenology, 537
Phenothiazines, 368, 635, 640, 641–642
Phenotype *How an individual looks and acts, which depends on how inherited characteristics interact with the environment,* A-2
Phenylketonuria (PKU), 375, A-2, A-4
Pheromones *Chemicals released by one animal and detected by another that shape the second animal's behavior or physiology,* 127–128
Phobia *Strong, irrational fear of an object or situation that does not objectively justify such a reaction,* 566–567, 575
  behavior therapy for, 614, 615, 616–617, 618, 640
  biology and, 569
  classical conditioning and, 5, 193–194, 570–571
  observational learning and, 215, 570–571
  psychoactive drugs for, 637, 640
Phoneme *The smallest unit of sound that affects the meaning of speech,* 293
Photographic memory, 238
Photopigments *Chemicals in photoreceptors that respond to light and assist in converting light into neural activity,* 113, 114, 124
Photoreceptors *Nerve cells in the retina that code light energy into neural activity,* 113–114, 115–116, 117, 120, 123
Physical attractiveness, interpersonal attraction and, 672–673
Physical coping strategies, 514
Physical dependence *Development of a physical need for a psychoactive drug,* 332. *See also* **Psychoactive drugs**
Physical development
  in adolescence, 468, 469, 480
  in adulthood, 477–480
Physical therapy, proprioception and, 138
Physiological dependence, 595. *See also* **Addiction**
Physiological psychologists, *see* **Biological psychologists**
Pinna, 106, 107, 110
Piracetam, 90
Pitch *How high or low a tone sounds,* 105, 106, 108, 110
Pituitary gland, 93, 94, 95
  general adaptation syndrome and, 491–492
PKU, *see* Phenylketonuria
Placebo *A physical or psychological treatment that contains no active ingredient but produces an effect because the person receiving it believes it will. In an experiment, the placebo effect (a confounding variable) occurs when the participant responds to the belief that the independent variable will have an effect, rather than to the actual effect of the independent variable,* 39–40
Placebo effect, 39–40
  acupuncture and, 136
  endorphins and, 135
  nootropics and, 91

Placenta, 435
Place theory *A theory that hair cells at a particular place on the basilar membrane respond most to a particular frequency of sound,* 108, 109
Plaques, Alzheimer's disease and, 73, 74
Plasticity, *see* **Synaptic plasticity**
Plateau phase, of sexual response cycle, 399
Play
   in childhood, 462, 463, 464
   gender roles and, 465
   sleep deprivation and, 324
Pleasure principle *In Freud's psychodynamic theory, the id's operating principle which guides people toward whatever feels good,* 520
PNS, *see* **Peripheral nervous system**
Polygenic *Describing characteristics that are determined by more than one gene,* A-2
Polygraphs, 420–421
Ponzo illusion, 153, 165
Pop psychologists, 31
Pornography, aggression and, 37, 699–701
Positive correlation, 45, 46
Positive psychology, 5, 408
Positive regard, 538–549
Positive reinforcement *A therapy method using rewards to strengthen desirable behaviors,* 615–616
Positive reinforcers *Stimuli that strengthen a response if they follow that response,* 197, 198, 207, 208, 534
Positive symptoms *Schizophrenic symptoms such as disorganized thoughts, hallucinations, and delusions,* 585
Positron emission tomography (PET), 68, 69, 80, 81, 84, 119, 178, 255, 269, 280–282, 584
Possessions, deficiency orientation and, 540
Possible self, 651–652
Postconventional moral reasoning *Reasoning that reflects moral judgments based on personal standards or universal principles of justice, equality, and respect for human life,* 472, 473
Posthypnotic amnesia, 327
Posthypnotic suggestion, 327, 328
Postsynaptic cell, 60, 61
Postsynaptic potential *The change in the membrane potential of a neuron that has received stimulation from another neuron,* 61
Posttraumatic stress disorder (PTSD) *A pattern of adverse and disruptive reactions following a traumatic event,* 72, 194, 252, 309, 322, 495–496, 568, 614, 627, 637
PQ4R method, 259–260
Practical intelligence, 367
Practice, skill learning and, 221
Preconscious level *A level of mental activity that is not currently conscious, but of which we can easily become conscious,* 311
Preconventional moral reasoning *Reasoning that is not yet based on the conventions or rules that guide social interactions in society,* 472
Prediction, in research, 31, 33
Predictive validity, 352

Prefrontal lobotomy, 634
Pregnancy
   in adolescence, 469
   alcohol and, 509
   caffeine and, 336
   cocaine and, 336
   endorphins and, 135
   single-motherhood and, 478
   technological advances in, 478–479
Prejudice *A positive or negative attitude toward an entire group of people. See* Prejudice/stereotypes
Prejudice/stereotypes, 666–671
   age discrimination and, 314
   amygdala and, 666
   cognitive theories of, 667–668
   contact hypothesis and, 668
   ethnic prejudice and, 314, 470, 668–671
   learning theories of, 668
   memory and, 229
   motivational theories of, 666–667
   psychological diagnosis and, 565
   reduction of, 668–671
   schemas and, 653
   self-fulfilling prophecies and, 655
   stimulus discrimination and generalization and, 200
Premack principle, 204
Premarital relationships, 675–676
Premature ejaculation, 403
Premises, 275–276
Premorbid adjustment, schizophrenia and, 583
Prenatal development, 435–436
   autistic disorder and, 595
   fetal alcohol syndrome and, 436, 509, 596
   gender roles and, 466
   psychoactive drugs and, 336, 436, 598
   risks in, 435–436
   schizophrenia and, 587–588
   sexual orientation and, 401, 402, 403
   stages of, 435
   see also Newborn
Preoperational period *According to Piaget, the second stage of cognitive development, during which children begin to use symbols to represent things that are not present,* 440, 445–446, 447
Presenilin, 74, 75
Primacy effect *A characteristic of memory in which recall of the first two or three items in a list is particularly good,* 238–239
Primary auditory cortex *The area in the brain's temporal lobe that is first to receive information about sounds,* 109, 110, 111
Primary cortex, 103
Primary drives *Drives that arise from basic biological needs,* 385–386
Primary mental abilities (PMA), 365, 371
Primary reinforcers *Reinforcers that meet an organism's most basic needs, such as food, water, air, and moderate temperatures,* 201, 204, 385
Primary visual cortex *An area at the back of the brain, to which neurons in the lateral geniculate nucleus relay visual input,* 116, 117
Priming, 227–228, 313–314, 333
   prejudice/stereotypes and, 670–671

Prisoner's dilemma *A social dilemma in which mutual cooperation guarantees the best mutual outcome,* 710–712
Privacy, personality tests and, 549
Private acceptance, 685
Proactive interference *A cause of forgetting in which information already in long-term memory interferes with the ability to remember new information,* 248, 249
Probabilities, decision making and, 289, 290
Problem-focused coping, 498, 499, 501
Problem solving, 279–288
   analogies and, 280–282, 285
   brain and, 269
   computer and, 286–288
   confirmation bias and, 284, 285
   experience and, 285–286
   group processes in, 291–292
   ignoring negative evidence and, 284–285
   improving, 285–286
   language and, 304–305
   late adulthood and, 372
   means-end analysis and, 279
   memory and, 229
   mental retardation and, 376
   mental sets and, 283–284
   multiple hypotheses and, 283
   obstacles to, 282–285
   steps in, 282, 287
   strategies for, 279–282
   working backward and, 279–280
Problem-solving therapy, 627
Procedural memory *A type of memory containing information about how to do things,* 226, 227, 256
Profound mental retardation, 375
Progesterone, 398, 474
Progestins *Feminine hormones that circulate in the bloodstream of both men and women; relatively more progestins circulate in women,* 398
Progressive relaxation training *A procedure for learning to relax that involves tensing then releasing muscles,* 514, 614
Projection, 521
Projective tests *Personality tests made up of unstructured stimuli that can be perceived and responded to in many ways,* 524, 548–549
Propositions *Mental representations of the relationship between concepts,* 271, 275
Proprioceptive senses *The sensory systems that allow us to know about where we are and what each part of our body is doing,* 137–140
   kinesthesia and, 131, 137–140
   vestibular system and, 131, 137
Prosopagnosia, 316–317
Prospective research design, 591–593
Prototype *A member of a natural concept that possesses all or most of its characteristic features,* 271
Proximity
   as Gestalt law, 155, 156
   interpersonal attraction and, 672
   and obedience, 691
Prozac, *see* Fluoxetine

Psyche, 558
Psychedelics, *see* Hallucinogens
Psychiatric nurses, 606
Psychiatrists *Medical doctors who have completed special training in the treatment of mental disorders,* 605, 639, 640. See also **Psychoactive drugs**
Psychiatry, 633
Psychic energy, 520
Psychoactive drugs *Substances that act on the brain to create some psychological effect,* 87, 317, 330–341, 632
    aggression and, 696
    antidepressants, 635–636, 638, 641, 642
    anxiolytics, 637, 638, 639, 640, 641
    cocaine, 88, 205, 332, 335–336, 436, 597–598, 627
    depressants, 332, 333–335, 339
    evaluation of for treatment, 639–640
    expectations and effects of, 332–333, 334
    habituation and, 186–187
    hallucinogens, 332, 337–341, 391
    heroin, 89, 186, 332, 337, 597–598, 696
    human diversity and, 637–639
    lithium and anticonvulsants, 636–637
    neuroleptics, 635, 638, 639, 640, 641–642
    neurotransmitters and, 641–642
    opiates, 89–90, 332, 337, 338, 339, 627, 696
    prenatal development and, 336, 436, 598
    psychiatrists and, 605, 639, 640
    psychopharmacology of, 330–331
    psychotherapy and, 604, 640–641
    stimulants, 330, 332, 335–337, 339, 386, 696
    substance-related disorders and, 554, 595–598
    therapeutic, 634–642
    tranquilizers, 696
    varying effects of, 331–333
    see also specific drugs
Psychoanalysis *A method of psychotherapy that seeks to help clients gain insight by recognizing and understanding unconscious thoughts and emotions,* 12–13, 15, 31
    case studies in, 34
    classical, 606–608, 622
    contemporary, 607–609, 622, 627
    dreams and, 326
    unconscious and, 313, 326, 606–608, 622
Psychoanalytically oriented psychotherapy, 609
Psychobiological models, 493
Psychodynamic approach *A view developed by Freud that emphasizes the interplay of unconscious mental processes in determining human thought, feelings, behavior, and personality; also called psychodynamic model,* 18, 20, 519–525, 541
    conflicts and defenses and, 520, 521, 524
    to depression, 581
    to dissociative disorders, 574
    evaluation of, 523–525
    id, ego, and superego and, 520
    neo-Freudian theorists and, 522–523, 524
    object relations and, 523
    to psychological disorders, 558, 560
    social-cognitive approach to, 537
    stages in personality development and, 520–522
    structure and development of personality and, 519–522
    see also **Psychoanalysis**; Psychodynamic psychotherapy
Psychodynamic model, *see* **Psychodynamic approach**
Psychodynamic psychotherapy, 606–609, 622
    classical psychoanalysis, 606–608, 622
    contemporary, 607–609, 622, 627
    effectiveness of, 625
Psychological dependence *A condition in which a person uses a drug despite adverse effects, needs the drug for a sense of well-being, and becomes preoccupied with obtaining it,* 332, 595. See also **Psychoactive drugs**
Psychological disorders, 552–602
    abnormality and, 554–555, 556
    biological factors in, 641–642
    biopsychosocial model of, 556–559, 560
    of childhood, 562, 593–595
    classification of, 532, 560–561, *see also Diagnostic and Statistical Manual of Mental Disorders*
    costs of, 553
    criminal justice and, 598–600
    cultural differences in, 555, 556, 557, 558–559
    definition of, 554–555
    desensitization and, 194
    diagnosis of, 561–565, *see also* Personality tests
    diathesis-stress approach to, 559, 560
    dissociative disorders, 562, 573–575
    earliest explanations of, 554
    explanation of, 554–560
    incidence of, 554
    medical model of, 530, 556, 563
    neurobiological model of, 556, 560
    practical approach to, 555
    prevalence of, 553
    psychological model of, 557–558, 560
    sociocultural model of, 559–560
    somatoform disorders, 562, 572–573, 575
    stress and, 495–496
    substance-abuse disorders, 562
    substance-related disorders, 554, 595–598
    supernatural explanations of, 556, 557
    see also **Anxiety disorder; Mood disorder; Personality disorders; Schizophrenia;** Treatment, of psychological disorders
Psychological model *A view in which mental disorder is seen as arising from inner turmoil or other psychological processes,* 557–558, 560
Psychological stressors, 488–489
Psychologists *Among therapists, those whose education includes completion of a master's or doctoral degree in clinical or counseling psychology, often followed by additional specialty training,* 605–606. See also **Psychotherapy**
Psychology *The science of behavior and mental processes*
    and academic disciplines, 8–9
    approaches to, 16–21, *see also* **Behavioral approach; Biological approach; Cognitive approach; Evolutionary approach; Humanistic approach; Psychodynamic approach**
    cultural differences and, 21–23
    current status of, 14–15
    definition of, 2–3, 15
    history of, 11–14, 15
    subfields of, 3–9
    unity in, 15
    women and minorities in, 15, 16, 17
Psychometric approach *A way of studying intelligence that emphasizes analysis of the products of intelligence, especially scores on intelligence tests,* 365–366, 369
Psychoneuroimmunology *The field that examines the interaction of psychological and physiological processes that affect the ability of the body to defend itself against disease,* 504, 506
Psychopathology *Patterns of thinking and behaving that are maladaptive, disruptive, or uncomfortable for the person affected or for those with whom he or she comes in contact,* 523. See also **Psychological disorders**
Psychopaths, 589–590. See also **Antisocial personality disorder**
Psychopharmacology *The study of psychoactive drugs and their effects,* 330–331. See also **Psychoactive drugs**
Psychophysics *An area of research focusing on the relationship between the physical characteristics of environmental stimuli and the psychological experience those stimuli produce,* 11, 146–154
    absolute thresholds and, 146, 147–149
    judging differences and, 152
    magnitude estimation and, 153–154
    signal-detection theory and, 146, 149–152
    subliminal stimuli and, 147–149
    supraliminal stimuli and, 147, 148
Psychosexual stages *In Freud's psychodynamic theory, periods of personality development in which conflicts focus on particular issues,* 520–521
Psychosis, 561
Psychosocial development, 459, 460, 470–471, 478, 479–480, 481, 542
Psychosocial rehabilitation, 642
Psychosurgery *Surgical procedures that destroy tissue in small regions of the brain in an effort to treat psychological disorders,* 634, 639
Psychotherapy *The treatment of psychological disorders through talking and other psychological methods,* 604
    beginnings of, 606
    cultural factors in, 629–631
    drug therapy with, 604, 640–641, *see also* **Psychoactive drugs**
    empirically supported therapies and, 626–628
    evaluation of, 623–632
    inpatients and, 604–605
    outpatients and, 605
    providers of therapy and, 605–606

therapeutic relationship in, 613, 628–629, 631–632
see also **Behavior therapy; Couples therapy; Family therapy; Group therapy;** Humanistic psychotherapy; Psychodynamic psychotherapy
Psychoticism, 529
Psychotomimetics, *see* **Hallucinogens**
PTSD, *see* **Posttraumatic stress disorder**
Puberty *The condition of being able for the first time to reproduce,* 398, 467–469
Public conformity, 685
Public goods dilemma, 712
Punishment *The presentation of an aversive stimulus or the removal of a pleasant stimulus; punishment decreases the frequency of the immediately preceding response; in therapy, weakening undesirable behavior by following it with an unpleasant stimulus,* 205–208
aggression and, 697
in behavior therapy, 617–618
discipline and, 461
Pupil *An opening in the eye, just behind the cornea, through which light passes,* 112, 113
Puzzle box, 195–196, 197
Pyramidal motor system, 414
Pyridoxine, *see* **Vitamin B6**
Quetiapine (Seroquel), 635
r, see Pearson product-moment correlation
Rainbow, 120
Rain Man, 35
Random assignment *The procedure by which random variables are evenly distributed in an experiment by putting participants into various groups by means of a coin flip or other random process,* 39
Random sample *A group of research participants selected from a population in which all members had an equal chance of being chosen for study,* 32, 39
Random variables *In an experiment, confounding variables in which uncontrolled or uncontrollable factors affect the dependent variable along with or instead of the independent variable,* 39
Range *A measure of variability that is the difference between the highest and the lowest value in a data set,* 44, 46, A-11–A-12
Range theory, hunger and, 390
Rape, pornography and, 699–701
Rapid eye movement (REM) sleep *A stage of sleep in which EEG and other functions resemble the waking state, but is accompanied by rapid eye movements and virtual muscle paralysis,* 319–320, 321, 322, 325, 326
Rational-emotive therapy (REBT) *A treatment designed to identify and change self-defeating thoughts that lead to anxiety and other symptoms of disorder,* 618–619
Rationalization, 521
Reaction formation, 521
Reaction time *The time between the presentation of a stimulus and an overt response to it,* 267–268
Readiness to change health behaviors, 511–512

Reality principle *According to Freud, the operating principle of the ego that creates compromises between the id's demands and those of the real world,* 520
Reasoning *The process by which people evaluate and generate arguments and reach conclusions,* 274–278
anchoring heuristic and, 277–278
availability heuristic and, 278
deductive, 274–275
formal, 274–276
informal, 276–278
language and, 304–305
representativeness heuristic and, 278
REBT, *see* **Rational-emotive behavior therapy**
Recall, 226, 238–239. See also **Retrieval**
Recency effect *A characteristic of memory in which recall is particularly good for the last few items on a list,* 239
Receptive field *The portion of the world that affects a given sensory neuron,* 116
Receptors *Sites on the surface of cells that allow only one type of neurotransmitter to fit into them, triggering a chemical response that may lead to an action potential,* 60, 62, 63
psychoactive drugs and, 330–331
Recessive genes, A-2
Reciprocal determinism, 534–535, 544–545
Reciprocal teaching, 219
Reciprocity, 681
Recognition, 165–171, 226
bottom-up processing and, 165–168, 169, 171
network processing and, 170–171
top-down processing and, 165, 168–170, 169, 171
see also **Retrieval**
Reconditioning *The relearning of a conditioned response following extinction,* 189
Reference groups *Categories of people to which people compare themselves,* 648
Reflection *An active listening method in which a therapist conveys empathy by paraphrasing clients' statements and noting accompanying feelings,* 611, 612
Reflexes *Involuntary, unlearned reactions in the form of swift, automatic, and finely coordinated movements in response to external stimuli,* 67, 71, 188
in adulthood, 474–475
in newborn, 438, 448
vestibular, 137
Refractory period *A short rest period between action potentials,* 60
Refractory phase, of sexual response cycle, 399
Rehabilitative medicine, proprioception and, 138
Rehearsal, 248
memory and, 229–230
Reinforcement/reinforcer *A stimulus event that increases the probability that the response that immediately preceded it will occur again,* 201
accidental, 204
continuous, 202
delay and size of, 201–202
explanation for, 204–205

extinction and, 203–204, 208
negative, 197, 198, 207
partial, 202–204
positive, 197, 198, 207, 208
primary, 201, 204
schedules of, 202–204
secondary, 201, 204
shaping and, 200–201
Relapse prevention therapy, 627
Relative deprivation *The belief that one is not doing as well as others in one's reference group,* 648
Relative size *A depth cue whereby larger objects are perceived as closer than smaller ones,* 158, 159
Relaxation
applied, 627
progressive relaxation training and, 514, 614
Reliability *The degree to which a test can be repeated with the same results,* 30, 351
interrater, 563
of IQ tests, 352–353
of personality tests, 545
Reliability Scale, 518
REM behavior disorder *A sleep disorder in which a person does not lose muscle tone during REM sleep, allowing the person to act out dreams,* 322
REM sleep, *see* **Rapid eye movement (REM) sleep**
Repetition, memory and, 259
Repetitive transcranial magnetic stimulation (rTMS), 633
Representation
sensory systems and, 103–104, 109–111
visual, 117–120
Representativeness heuristic *A mental shortcut that involves judging whether something belongs in a given class on the basis of its similarity to other members of that class,* 278
Representative sample, 32
Repression, 521
traumatic memories and, 250–253
Reproduction, A-1–A-2
pheromones and, 128
Research methods, 9–11, 31–53
adoption studies and, 51–52, A-3
analogue, 707–709
behavioral genetics and, 49–52, A-3–A-4
case studies and, 31, 34–35, 42, 139–140, 314–315
control in, 33, 38, 39, 41, 74, 91, 592–593
critical thinking and, 26–31, 47–48
cross-sectional studies and, 370
cross-sequential with resampling design and, 371
data in, 30, *see also* **Descriptive statistics; Inferential statistics**
ethics and, 39, 48–49
family studies and, 50
goals in, 31–32, 33
hypothesis in, 29–30
longitudinal studies and, 370–371, 501–503, 543–545
naturalistic observation and, 31, 33–34, 42
neuroimaging and, 280–282
prospective research design and, 591–593

sampling and, 32–33, 39
social impact of, 47, 48
surveys and, 31, 35–36, 42, 396–398
theories and, 30–31
twin studies and, 50–51, A-3
variables in, 30, 38–41
see also Animal studies; **Experiments**; Statistics
Resilience *A quality allowing children to develop normally in spite of severe environmental risk factors*, 466-467
Resistance stage, general adaptation syndrome and, 492
Resolution phase, of sexual response cycle, 399
Resource dilemma *A situation in which people must share a common resource, creating conflicts between the short-term interests of individuals and the long-term interests of the group*, 712
Response
 conditioned, 188, 189-190, 191, 198
 unconditioned, 188, 189, 191
Response criterion *The internal rule a person uses to decide whether or not to report a stimulus*, 150, 151, 152
Reticular formation *A network of cells and fibers threaded throughout the hindbrain and midbrain that alters the activity of the rest of the brain*, 69, 70, 86
Retina *The surface at the back of the eye onto which the lens focuses light rays*, 112, 113, 114–117, 118, 160, 161
Retirement, 480–481
Retrieval *The process of recalling information stored in memory*, 226, 239-253
 brain and, 257-258
 constructive memory and, 242, 243–247, 257
 context and state dependence and, 240
 encoding specificity and, 239, 240
 eyewitness testimony and, 245–247
 forgetting and, 249–250
 of incomplete knowledge, 242
 recall and, 226, 238–239
 recognition and, 226
 of repressed memories, 250-253, 257
 retrieval cues and, 239, 240
 schemas and, 244–245
 from semantic memory, 240-243
 semantic networks and, 241–242
Retrieval cues *Stimuli that allow people to recall or recognize information stored in memory*, 239, 240, 249
Retroactive interference *A cause of forgetting in which new information placed in memory interferes with the ability to recall information already in memory*, 248, 249
Retrograde amnesia *A loss of memory for events prior to a brain injury*, 256, 257
Reuptake process, 642
Reversibility, 446
Reversible figures, 155
Rewards, aggression and, 697
Ribonucleic acid (RNA), A-1
Risperidone (Risperdal), 635, 638
RNA, *see* Ribonucleic acid
Rock music, subliminal messages in, 314–315

Rods *Highly light-sensitive, but color insensitive photoreceptors in the retina that allow vision even in dim light*, 114, 115
Role theory *A theory that hypnotized people act in accordance with a special social role that provides a socially acceptable reason to follow the hypnotist's suggestions*, 328, 329
Romantic love, 675
Rooting reflex, 438
Rorshach Inkblot Test, 548, 549
Rubella (German measles), 375, 436
Rules of logic *Sets of statements that provide a formula for drawing valid conclusions*, 274–276
Ruminative style, depression and, 581
Ruminative thinking, 493–494
s *A group of special abilities that Charles Spearman saw as accompanying general intelligence* (**g**), 365
SAD, *see* Seasonal affective disorder
Safety motives, 409, 410
Saint-John's-wort (*Hypericum perforatum*), 636
SAM, *see* Sympathoadrenomedullary system
Sampling *The process of selecting participants who are members of the population that the researcher wishes to study*, 32–33
 biased, 32
 random, 32, 39
Sanders illusion, 153
SAT (Scholastic Aptitude Test), 350, 364
Satiety factors, 389
Satiety *The condition of no longer wanting to eat*, 388-390. *See also* **Hunger**
Saturation *The purity of a color*, 120, 121
Savings, method of, 247
Scatterplot, 45
Schachter-Singer theory, 422–423
Schemas *Mental representations of what we know and have come to expect about categories of objects, events, and people; generalizations based on experience that form the basic units of knowledge*, 169, 271–272, 273, 275
 cognitive development and, 439–441
 in social perception, 652–653
 prejudice/stereotypes and, 667
 retrieval and, 244–245
 self-, 651–652
Schizoid personality disorder, 589, 590
Schizophrenia *A severe and disabling pattern of disturbed thinking, emotion, perception, and behavior*, 88, 557, 562, 582–589, 615, 620, 627, 631
 biological factors in, 586-588, 589, A-3, A-6–A-7
 catatonic, 584, 585, 586
 categorization of, 584–586
 causes of, 586–589
 diagnosis of, 563, 565
 disorganized, 584, 585
 electroconvulsive therapy for, 633
 environment and, 587-588, A-7
 family and twin studies of, 50, 51
 incidence of, 554
 neuroleptics for, 635, 638, 640, 641–642
 paranoid, 335, 584, 585

 positive-negative symptom dimension in, 584–585
 psychological and social factors in, 588, 589
 psychosurgery and, 634
 psychotic/disorganized/negative symptoms of, 585–586
 residual, 584, 585
 sociocultural context and, 558, 559
 stress and, 496
 symptoms of, 582, 583–586, 587, 589
 undifferentiated, 584, 585
 vulnerability theory of, 589
Schizotypal personality disorder, 589, 590
Scholastic Aptitude Test, *see* SAT
School phobia, 594
School psychologists *Psychologists who test IQs, diagnose students' academic problems, and set up programs to improve students' achievement*, 7
School Sisters of Notre Dame, 476, 477
Scientific psychology, 11
Scientific research, *see* Research methods
SCN, *see* **Suprachiasmatic nuclei**
Scores, 351
 percentile, A-13
 standard, A-13
 see also **Intelligence quotient**
Scripts *Mental representations of familiar sequences of activity*, 272, 273, 275, 450
SD, *see* **Standard deviation**
Seasonal affective disorder (SAD), 580
Seattle Longitudinal Study, 371
Secondary drives *Stimuli that acquire the motivational properties of primary drives through classical conditioning or other learning mechanisms*, 385-386
Secondary reinforcer *A reward that people or animals learn to like*, 201, 204
Secondary traits, 526
Second-order conditioning *A phenomenon in learning when a conditioned stimulus acts like a UCS, creating conditioned stimuli out of events associated with it*, 192
Secure attachment, 456-457, 478, 523
Seizures, 89. *See also* Epilepsy
Selective attention *The focusing of mental resources on only part of the stimulus field*, 233
Selective-breeding studies, animals and, 50
Selective serotonin reuptake inhibitors (SSRIs), 642
Self-actualization, 410, 538
Self-affirmation, 664
Self-concept *The way one thinks of oneself*, 539, 647
 intimate relationships and, 673
 memory and, 229
 social identity and, 650–651
Self-efficacy
 health behaviors and, 511
 perceived, 534–535
Self-esteem *The evaluations people make about how worthy they are as human beings*, 543, 647, 648–650
 achievement and, 404
 in adolescence, 468

Self-fulfilling prophecy *A process through which an initial impression of someone leads that person to behave in accordance with that impression,* 654–655
Self-help books, positive reinforcement and, 208
Self-help groups, 629
  group therapy and, 620–621
Self-perception theory *A theory suggesting that attitudes can change as people consider their behavior in certain situations, then infer what their attitude must be,* 664–665
  compliance and, 688
Self-regulation *The ability to control one's emotions and behavior,* 464
Self-reports, personalities assessed with, 545
Self-schemas *Mental representations that people form of themselves,* 651–652
Self-serving bias *The tendency to attribute one's successes to internal characteristics while blaming one's failures on external causes,* 659
Self, social influences on, 647–652
  self-esteem and, 647, 649–650
  self-schemas and, 651–652
  social comparison and, 647–650
  social identity theory and, 650–651
Self theory, 538–540
Semantic encoding *The mental representation of an experience by its general meaning,* 226, 231, 236–237, 245
Semantic memory *A type of memory containing generalized knowledge of the world,* 226, 227, 240–244, 276, 476
Semantic memory networks, 241–242
Semantics *Rules governing the meaning of words and sentences,* 293
Semicircular canals *Arc-shaped tubes in the inner ear containing fluid that, when shifted by head movements, stimulate nerve cells that provide information to the brain about the rate and direction of those movements,* 137
Sensations *Messages from the senses which comprise the raw information that affects many kinds of behavior and mental processes,* 100
Sense *A system that translates information from outside the nervous system into neural activity,* 100
Sensitivity *The ability to detect a stimulus,* 149–150, 151–152
Sensitivity training, 540–541
Sensitization, 186–187
Sensorimotor period *The first of Piaget's stages of cognitive development, when the infant's mental activity is confined to sensory perception and motor skills,* 440, 441–442
Sensory cortex *The parts of the cerebral cortex located in the parietal, occipital, and temporal lobes that receives stimulus information from the skin, eyes, and ears, respectively,* 76–77, 102, 103
Sensory memory *A type of memory that holds large amounts of incoming information very briefly, but long enough to connect one impression to the next,* 231, 232–233, 239
Sensory receptors *Specialized cells that detect certain forms of energy,* 101

Sensory registers *Memory systems that hold incoming information long enough for it to be processed further,* 232–233
Sensory systems *The parts of the nervous system that provide information about the environment,* 63, 99–142
  in adulthood, 474
  biology and, 103–104
  brain and, 76–77
  elements in, 101–102
  memory and, 257
  reality and, 100
  see also **Coding; Gustation; Hearing; Olfaction;** Pain; **Perception; Proprioceptive senses;** Temperature; Touch; Vision
Sentences, 293, 295
  telegraphic, 298
Separation anxiety disorder, 594, 595
Septum, 72
Serial position, 238
Serial-position curve, 238
Seroquel, *see* Quetiapine
Serotonin *A neurotransmitter used by cells in parts of the brain involved in the regulation of sleep, mood, and eating,* 88, 90, 91
  antidepressants and, 635–636
  hunger and, 391
  mood disorder and, 579
  obsessive-compulsive disorder and, 569
  pain and, 134
  psychoactive drugs and, 333, 337, 338
Sertraline (Zoloft), 632, 637
Serzone, *see* Nefazodone
Set point
  hunger and, 390
  weight loss and, 393
Severe mental retardation, 375
Sex differences, *see* Gender differences
Sex education programs, 399
Sex hormones *Chemicals in the blood of males and females that have both organizational and motivational effects on sexual behavior,* 398, 399, 401, 402, 403, 474
  aggression and, 696
  androgens, 93, 398, 401
  estrogens, 92–93, 398, 474
Sexual abuse, false memories and, 524
Sexual behavior, 395–404
  in adolescence, 469
  in adulthood, 9, 478–479
  aggression and, 37, 699–701
  autonomic system and, 417
  biology of sex and, 128, 398–399
  evolutionary approach to, 383–385
  sexual dysfunctions and, 403
  sexual orientation and, 400–403
  social and cultural factors and, 399
  surveys of, 396–398
  unsafe sex and, 509, 511
Sexual dysfunctions *Problems with sexual motivation, arousal, or orgasmic response,* 403
Sexually dimorphic areas, 398
Sexually transmitted diseases (STDs), 396, 469. *See also* Acquired immune deficiency syndrome
Sexual orientation, 400–403
  parenthood and, 478–479

Sexual response cycle *The pattern of arousal during and after sexual activity,* 398–399
Sexual scripts, 396
Shadows, depth cues and, 158, 159, 160
Shape constancy, 163–164
Shaping *A procedure that involves reinforcing responses that come successively closer to the desired response,* 200–201
Short-term dynamic psychotherapy, 608, 609
Short-term memory (STM) *The maintenance component of working memory which holds unrehearsed information for about eighteen seconds,* 231, 233–236, 239, 257
  in childhood, 447
  chunking and, 235–236, 261, 285
  duration of, 236
  encoding in, 233–234
  forgetting in, 236, 248
  logical errors and, 276
  long-term memory *versus,* 238–239
  mental retardation and, 376
  multiple hypotheses and, 283
  storage capacity of, 234–235
  thought and, 267
  see also Memory
Short-wavelength cones, 122
Shuttle box, 198
SIDS, *see* **Sudden infant death syndrome**
Signal-detection theory *A mathematical model of what determines a person's report that a near-threshold stimulus has or has not occurred,* 146, 149–152
Signaling, classical conditioning and, 190–193
Sign language, 111
Similarity
  as Gestalt law, 155, 156
  interpersonal attraction and, 672, 673
Simplicity principle, 154, 156–157
Simultaneous conditioning, 191
Sine wave, 104, 105
Single-motherhood, 478
Single photon emission computed tomography, *see* SPECT
Situational tests, personalities assessed with, 545
Situation awareness, 291
Sixteen Personality Factor Questionnaire (16PF), 527
Size constancy, 163
  in newborns, 437
Skill learning, 220–221
Skinner box, 196, 197, 205
Skin, 131–132, 138. *See also* Somatic senses
Sleep, 318–326
  anesthesia and, 309, 312
  barbiturates and, 334–335
  brain and, 325
  as circadian rhythm, 323, 324
  depression and, 580
  deprivation of, 324–325
  disorders, 320–322
  dreams and, 317, 321, 322, 324, 325–326
  functions of, 324–325
  night's sleep and, 320
  over lifespan, 320, 321, 325
  rapid eye movement (REM), 319–320, 321, 322, 325, 326

reasons for, 322–325
serotonin and, 88
slow-wave, 318–319, 320, 321, 322, 325, 326
stages of, 318–320
Sleep apnea *A sleep disorder in which people briefly but repeatedly stop breathing during the night,* 322
Sleep disorders, 320–322, 562
Sleepwalking *A phenomenon primarily occurring in non-REM sleep in which people walk while asleep,* 322
Slow-to-warm-up babies, 454
Slow-wave sleep *Sleep stages 1 through 4, which are accompanied by slow, deep breathing; a calm, regular heartbeat; and reduced blood pressure,* 318–319, 320, 321, 322, 325, 326
Small-molecule neurotransmitters, 87–89, 90
Smart drugs, *see* Nootropic drugs
Smell, *see* Olfaction
Smile, facial expression of, 425, 426
Smoking, 487
  cessation of, 510–511, 512
  discriminative stimuli and, 208
  health problems and, 508–509
  nicotine and, 336, 337
  prenatal development and, 436
Snake phobia, *see* Ophdophobia
Social categories, 667–668
Social cognition *Mental processes associated with people's perceptions of and reactions to other people,* 646–678
  self-protective functions of, 659–660
  see also **Attitude; Attribution;** Interpersonal attraction; Prejudice/stereotypes; Self, social influences on; **Social perception**
Social-cognitive approach *An approach in which personality is seen as the patterns of thinking and behavior that a person learns,* 18, 533–537, 541, 613
  cognitive/affective theory and, 535–536
  evaluation of, 536–537
  expectancy theory and, 534
  reciprocal determinism and, 534–535, 544–545
  roots of, 533
  see also **Behavior therapy**
Social cognitive neuroscience, 665–666
Social-cognitive theories
  dissociative disorders and, 574
  mood disorder and, 581–582
  obsessive-compulsive disorder and, 570
  psychological disorders and, 558, 560
Social comparison *Using other people as a basis of comparison for evaluating oneself,* 647–650
Social development
  in adolescence, 457, 460, 462, 467–471, 480
  in adulthood, 457, 460, 477–481
  in childhood, 457, 459–467, 460
  in infancy, 453–459, 460, 462
  see also Emotional development
Social dilemmas *Situations in which actions that produce rewards for one individual will produce negative consequences if adopted by everyone,* 710–712

Social facilitation *A phenomenon in which the presence of others improves a person's performance,* 682–683
Social identity *The beliefs we hold about the groups to which we belong,* 650–651
  prejudice and, 667
Social impact theory, 686–687
Social impairment *A reduction in performance due to the presence of other people,* 682–683
Social influence, 647, 679–718
  cooperation, competition, and conflict and, 710–713
  copycat crimes and, 680
  motivation and, 682–684
  norms and, 680–682
  schizophrenia and, 588
  social loafing and, 292, 683–684
  see also **Aggression;** Altruism/helping behavior; **Compliance; Conformity;** Group processes; **Obedience;** Self, social influences on; Social-cognitive theories
Socialization, 459–460, 466
  actualizing tendency and, 538, 539
  gender roles and, 465
  learning and, 218
  observational learning and, 215
Social learning, *see* **Observational learning**
Social learning theorists, 533. *See also* **Social-cognitive approach**
Social loafing *Exerting less effort when performing a group task than when performing the same task alone,* 292, 683–684
Social perception *The processes through which people interpret information about others, draw inferences about them, and develop mental representations of them,* 652–655
  first impressions and, 653–655, 659
  schemas and, 652–653
  see also **Attribution**
Social phobias *Strong, irrational fears relating to social situations,* 566, 627, 637
Social psychologists *Psychologists who study how people influence one another's behavior and attitudes, individually and in groups,* 6, 8, 9
  group problem solving and decision making and, 292
  implicit memory and, 229
Social psychology *The study of how people's thoughts, feelings, and behavior influence, and are influenced by, the behavior of others,* 647
  motivation and presence of others and, 682
  social cognitive neuroscience and, 665–666
  see also **Social cognition;** Social influence
Social Readjustment Rating Scale (SRRS), 489–490
Social referencing *A phenomenon in which other people's facial expressions, tone of voice, and bodily gestures serve as guidelines for how to proceed in uncertain situations,* 427, 453
Social skills, in childhood, 463–464
Social skills training, 615, 627
Social striving, 684

Social support network *The friends and social contacts on whom one can depend for help and support,* 488, 499–503, 505–506, 507, 513–514
Sociocultural factors, 21, 23. *See also* Cultural differences; Ethnic group differences; Gender differences
Sociocultural model *A way of looking at mental disorders in relation to gender, age, ethnicity and other social and cultural factors,* 558–559
Socioeconomic differences, cognitive development and, 357, 358, 359, 361, 451–452
Sociopaths, 589–590. *See also* **Antisocial personality disorder**
Somatic nervous system *The subsystem of the peripheral nervous system that transmits information from the senses to the central nervous system and carries signals from the CNS to the muscles that move the skeleton,* 64–65
Somatic senses *Senses, including touch, temperature, pain, and kinesthesia; also called* somatosensory systems, 130–131. *See also* Pain; Temperature; Touch; **Kinesthesia**
Somatization disorder *Somatoform disorders in which there are numerous physical complaints without verifiable physical illness,* 572, 575
Somatoform disorders *Psychological problems in which there are symptoms of a physical disorder without a physical cause,* 562, 572–573, 575
Somatosensory cortex, 76, 77, 138
Somatosensory systems, *see* **Somatic senses**
Sound *A repetitive fluctuation in the pressure of a medium such as air,* 104–106, 109–110, 157–158. *See also* Hearing
Spanking, 206
Spatial codes *Coding attributes of a stimulus in terms of the location of firing neurons relative to their neighbors,* 102
Spatial intelligence, 369, 370
Special K, *see* Ketamine
Specific hungers, 391
Specific nerve energies *A doctrine stating that stimulation of a particular sensory nerve provides codes for that sense, no matter how the stimulation takes place,* 102
Specific phobias *Phobias that involve fear and avoidance of heights, animals, and other specific stimuli and situations,* 566, 567
SPECT (single photon emission computed tomography), 68
Speech, 294–296. *See also* **Language**
Speech spectrograms, 296
Speed, *see* Amphetamines
Speed-accuracy tradeoff, reaction time and, 268
Spider phobia, 614, 615
Spinal cord *The part of the central nervous system within the spinal column that receives signals from peripheral senses and relays them to the brain. It also conveys messages from the brain to the rest of the body,* 62, 64, 66, 67, 70, 82
  emotions and injuries to, 420

kinesthesia and, 138
  pain and, 133, 134
Spinal injuries, and emotions, 420
Spines, 254
Spleen, 95, 96
Split-brain studies, 79–80
Split-half method, 351
Spontaneous recovery *The reappearance of the conditioned response after extinction and without further pairings of the conditioned and unconditioned stimuli,* 189, 190
Sport psychologists *Psychologists who explore the relationships between athletic performance and such psychological variables as motivation and emotion,* 7
  motion perception and, 161–162
Spread, *see* Variability, measures of
Spreading activation *A principle that explains how information is retrieved in semantic network theories of memory,* 241
SRRS, *see* Social Readjustment Rating Scale
SSRIs, *see* Selective serotonin reuptake inhibitors
Standard deviation (SD) *A measure of variability that is the average difference between each score and the mean of the data set,* 44, 46, A-11, A-12
Standardized test, 350-351. *See also* **IQ test**
Standard scores *A value that indicates the distance, in standard deviations, between a given score and the mean of all the scores in a data set,* A-13
Stanford-Binet *A test for determining a person's intelligence quotient, or IQ,* 346, 347, 349
Stapes, 106, 107, 110
State-dependent *Referring to memories that are aided or impeded by a person's internal state,* 240
State of consciousness *The characteristics of consciousness at any particular moment,* 311, 317–318. *See also* **Hypnosis; Psychoactive drugs; Sleep; Meditation**
State theory *A theory that hypnosis is an altered state of consciousness,* 328, 329
Statistically significant *In statistical analysis, a term used to describe the results of an experiment when the outcome of a statistical test indicates that the probability of those results occurring by chance is small (usually less than 5 percent),* 46, 47, A-15
Statistics, 30, A-10–A-18
  critical thinking and, 47
  see also **Data; Descriptive statistics; Inferential statistics**
STDs, *see* Sexually transmitted diseases
Stem cells, Parkinson's disease and, 83
Stepping reflex, 438
Stereotypes *False assumptions that all members of some group share the same characteristics. See* **Prejudice/stereotypes**
Stereotype threat, 364
Stevens's power law, 153
Stimulants *Psychoactive drugs that have the ability to increase behavioral and mental activity,* 330, 332, 335–337, 339, 386, 696

Stimulus
  conditioned, 188, 189, 190, 191, 198
  control and, 199, 208
  discriminative, 199, 208
  learning about, 186–187
  neutral, 188, 189, 191
  subliminal, 147–148, 314–315
  supraliminal, 147, 148
  unconditioned, 188, 189, 190, 191, 192, 193, 198
  see also **Classical conditioning; Stimulus discrimination; Stimulus generalization**
Stimulus control, 199, 208
Stimulus control therapy, insomnia and, 320
Stimulus discrimination *A process through which individuals learn to differentiate among similar stimuli and respond appropriately to each one*
  classical conditioning and, 190, 194
  operant conditioning and, 199–200, 208
Stimulus generalization *A phenomenon in which a conditioned response is elicited by stimuli that are similar but not identical to the conditioned stimulus*
  classical conditioning and, 190, 194
  operant conditioning and, 199–200
Stimulus-response compatibility, reaction time and, 268
Stirrups, *see* Stapes
STM, *see* **Short-term memory**
Stomach, hunger and satiety and, 388
Storage *The process of maintaining information in memory over time,* 226
Strange Situation Test, 456–457, 458
Stress *The process of adjusting to circumstances that disrupt, or threaten to disrupt, a person's equilibrium,* 487–488
  conflicting motives and, 410–411
  disease processes and, 96
  endorphins and, 135
  fight-or-flight syndrome and, 94, 417, 491, 503
  health and, 492, 498, 499, 501–503, 504–508
  hormones and, 94–95
  meditation and, 329–330
  obesity and, 393, 394
  process of, 488, *see also* Stress mediators; Stressors; Stress responses
  substance abuse and, 598
Stress inoculation training, 619, 627
Stress management techniques, insomnia and, 321
Stress mediators, 488, 496–504
  appraisal, 488, 496–497, 503
  control, 488, 498, 503
  coping and, 488, 498–499, 501, 503, 512–514
  immune system and, 505–506
  predictability, 488, 497, 503
  social support, 488, 499–503, 505–506, 507, 513–514
Stressors *Events or situations to which people must adjust,* 487–490
  aggression and, 701–702
  altruism/helping behavior and, 706
  catastrophic events, 488, 489
  chronic, 488

  daily hassles, 488, 490
  depression and, 582
  diseases of adaptation and, 492
  genetics and, A-8
  life changes and strains, 488, 489
  measurement of, 489–490
  mood disorder and, 580–581
  personality and, 501–503
  psychological, 488–489
  social cognitive neuroscience and, 665–666
  see also **Diathesis-stress approach**
Stress-reduction theory, of alcoholism, 596
Stress responses, 488, 490–496, 503
  behavioral, 488, 494–496, 503
  cognitive, 488, 493–494, 503
  cognitive influences on, 496–497
  disease and, 504
  emotional, 488, 493, 503
  gender differences in, 501
  personality and, 501–503
  physical, 488, 490–492, 495–496, 503
  psychological, 488, 490–491, 493–496, 503
  psychological disorders and, 495–496
Striatum *A structure within the forebrain that is involved in the smooth initiation of movement,* 71, 84, 87, 88
Stroboscopic motion *An illusion in which lights or images flashed in rapid succession are perceived as moving,* 162, 233
Strokes, 82, 89
  proprioception and, 138
Stroop task, 177
Structural family therapy, 621, 623
Structuralism, 12, 15
Structured interviews, personalities assessed with, 545
Studying, guidelines for, 258–260
Stuttering, 71
Subconscious, *see* **Unconscious level**
Subcultures, 21–22. *See also* Cultural differences
Subjective contours, 154
Subjective norm, 660
Subjective well-being *A combination of a cognitive judgment of satisfaction with life, the frequent experiencing of positive moods and emotions, and the relatively infrequent experiencing of unpleasant moods and emotions,* 408–409
Sublimation, 521
Subliminal priming, 148
Subliminal stimuli *Stimuli that are too weak or brief to be consciously perceived,* 147–149
  in rock music, 314–315
Substance abuse *The self-administration of psychoactive drugs in ways that deviate from a culture's social norms,* 332, 595
  in adolescence, 467, 468, 469
  operant conditioning and, 208
  primary reinforcement and, 204
  see also **Psychoactive drugs**
Substance abuse counselors, 606
Substance-abuse disorders, 541, 562, 620, 621, 627
Substance-related disorders *Problems that involve use of psychoactive drugs for months or years in ways that harm the user or others,* 554, 595–598. *See also* **Alcoholism**

Substantia nigra *An area of the midbrain involved in the smooth initiation of movement,* 71, 86, 88
Subtractive color mixing, 121
Sucking reflex, 438
Sudden infant death syndrome (SIDS) *A disorder in which a sleeping baby stops breathing and suffocates,* 322, 438
Suicide
  in adolescence, 467, 468
  copycat suicides and, 680
  depression and, 577–578
  norms and, 686
  prevention of, 643
Sulci, 75, 76
Superego *According to Freud's psychodynamic theory, the component of personality that tells people what they should and should not do,* 520, 540
Superiority, striving for, 523
Supernatural, psychological disorders and, 556, 557
Superordinate goals/identity, conflict management and, 713
Superstition, partial reinforcement and, 204
Supertasters, 129
Supportive-expressive therapy, 609, 627
Suprachiasmatic nuclei (SCN) *Nuclei in the hypothalamus that generate biological rhythms,* 72, 323, 324
Supraliminal stimuli *Stimuli that fall above the absolute threshold and thus are consistently perceived,* 147, 148
Surface structures *The order in which words are arranged in sentences,* 293–294, 295
Survey *A research method that involves giving people questionnaires or special interviews designed to obtain descriptions of their attitudes, beliefs, opinions, and intentions,* 31, 35–36, 42, 396–398
Survival of the fittest, 706–707
Sybil (film), 574
Syllogisms *Arguments made up of two propositions, called premises, and a conclusion based on those premises,* 275, 276
Symbols, in childhood, 293, 445, 448
Sympathetic system *The subsystem of the autonomic nervous system that usually prepares the organism for vigorous activity,* 65, 88, 416–417
Sympatho-adreno-medullary (SAM) system, general adaptation syndrome and, 491, 492, 506, 507
Sympathy, 464
Synapse *The tiny gap between neurons across which the neurons communicate,* 58, 60, 61, 63, 84, 85–86
  memories and, 254–255
Synaptic plasticity *The ability to create synapses and to change the strength of synapses,* 82–84
Synchrony, grouping and, 156
Synesthesia *A blending of sensory experience that causes some people to "see" sounds or "taste" colors, for example,* 125–126

Syntax *The set of rules that govern the formation of phrases and sentences in a language,* 293, 299
Systematic desensitization *A behavioral treatment for anxiety in which clients visualize a graduated series of anxiety-provoking stimuli while remaining relaxed,* 194, 614–615
Tabula rasa, 11, 432
Tacrine, 91
Taliban, 693, 697
Tangles, Alzheimer's disease and, 73, 74
Tardive dyskinesia, 635, 639, 642
Target organs, 92, 94, 416, 417
Task-oriented leaders *Leaders who provide close supervision, lead by directives, and generally discourage group discussion,* 714, 715
Taste, *see* **Gustation**
Taste buds, 128, 130
TAT, *see* Thematic Apperception Test
Tau, Alzheimer's disease and, 73–75
TCAs, *see* Tricyclic antidepressants
T-cells, 504, 505
Teachers
  expectancies of and intelligence quotient, 362-363
  influence of, A-7
Teh-ch'i, 135
Telegraphic sentences, 298
Telehealth channels, 631
Television, aggression and, 37, 215–217, 697
Temperament *An individual's basic disposition, evident from infancy,* 454
  attitudes and, 661
  parenting style and, 461
  personality and, 531, 532, 543–545
Temperature, 130, 132, 138
  flavor of food and, 130
  representations of, 103–104
Temporal codes *Coding attributes of a stimulus in terms of changes in the timing of neural firing,* 102
Temporal comparison, 648
Temporal lobe, 75, 76
Teratogens *Harmful substances that can cause birth defects,* 436
Terman Life Cycle Study of Intelligence, 502–503
Terminal drop *A sharp decline in mental functioning that tends to occur in late adulthood, a few years or months before death,* 481
Terror management theory, 649–650
Test *A systematic procedure for observing behavior in a standard situation and describing it with the help of a numerical scale or a category system,* 350–352
  reliability and, 351
  stereotype threat and, 364
  test anxiety and, 364–365
  validity and, 351–352
  see also **Achievement tests; IQ test; Personality tests**
Test anxiety, IQ tests and, 364–365
Testes, 93
Testosterone, 93, 398, 696

Test-retest method, 351
Test-retest reliability, A-14
Tetrahydrocannabinol (THC), 338–339. *See also* Marijuana (cannabis)
Textbook, remembering material in, 258–260
Texture gradient *A graduated change in the texture, or grain, of the visual field, whereby changes in texture across the retinal image are perceived as changes in distance; objects with finer, less detailed textures are perceived as more distant,* 158, 159
Thalamus *A forebrain structure that relays signals from most sense organs to higher levels in the brain and plays an important role in processing and making sense out of this information,* 72, 84, 86
  consciousness and, 315–316
  emotion and, 418, 421–422, 423
  hearing and, 109
  kinesthesia and, 138
  memory and, 255, 257
  pain and, 134
  sensory systems and, 101, 102, 104, 110
  vision and, 118, 119
Thanatos, 520, 695
Thematic Apperception Test (TAT), 404, 548, 549
Theory *An integrated set of propositions that can be used to account for, predict, and suggest ways of controlling certain phenomena,* 30–31
Therapeutic relationship, 604, 607, 609, 613, 628–629, 631–632. *See also* **Psychotherapy**
Thinking *The manipulation of mental representations,* 266
  in adulthood, 475–476
  convergent, 374
  divergent, 373, 374
  negative, 619–620
  ruminative, 493, 494
  see also Thought
Thinking strategies, *see* **Reasoning**
Third-party interventions, conflict management and, 713
Thorazine, *see* Chlorpromazine
Thought, 265–274
  circle of, 266–267, 279
  cognitive maps and, 273, 275
  concepts and, 270–271, 275
  culture and language and, 303–305
  evoked brain potential and, 268–269
  functions of, 266–267
  images and, 273, 274, 275
  in infancy, 441–442
  information-processing model and, 266–267, 270, 274
  ingredients of, 270–273, 275
  measuring information processing in, 267–269
  mental chronometry and, 267–268
  mental models and, 272–273, 275
  propositions and, 271, 275
  scripts and, 272, 273, 275
  see also Decision making; Problem solving; **Reasoning; Schemas**
Thought blocking/withdrawal, schizophrenia and, 583

Thought broadcasting, schizophrenia and, 583
Thought insertion, schizophrenia and, 583
Thymus, 95, 505
Thyroid, 93
Timbre *The mixture of frequencies and amplitudes that make up the quality of sound,* 105
Time-limited dynamic psychotherapy, 609
Tinnitus, 105, 108
Tip-of-the-tongue phenomenon, 242
Tissue engineering, 82
Tofranil, *see* Imipramine
Token economy *A system for improving the behavior of institutionalized clients in which desirable behaviors are rewarded with tokens that can be exchanged for desired items or activities,* 616
Tolerance *A condition in which increasingly larger drug doses are needed to produce a given effect,* 332, 595
Tongue, papillae and, 128, 129, 130
Top-down processing *Those aspects of recognition that are guided by higher-level cognitive processes and psychological factors such as expectations,* 165, 168–170, 171
  understanding speech and, 295
Topographical representations, 103
Touch, 130, 131–132, 138
  absolute thresholds and, 146
  adaptation and, 101
  representations of, 103–104
  vision and, 100
Traffic safety, perception and, 180–181
Trait approach *A perspective in which personality is seen as a combination of characteristics that people display over time and across situations,* 525–533, 541
  Allport's trait theory and, 526, 527, 533
  approach-inhibition theory and, 529–530
  big-five model and, 526–528, 532, 533
  biological trait theory and, 528–529
  evaluation of, 532–533
  genetics and, 530–532
  social-cognitive approach to, 537
  types *versus,* 525–526, 543–545
Tranquilizers, 637, 696. See also **Anxiolytics**
Transduction *The process of converting incoming energy into neural activity through receptors,* 101
  auditory, 106, 107
  visual, 113
Transfer-appropriate processing model *A model of memory that suggests that a critical determinant of memory is how well the retrieval process matches the original encoding process,* 230, 231, 232
Transference, 607, 609
Transferred excitation *The process of carrying over arousal from one experience to an independent situation,* 422–423, 698, 699, 700
Transsexual, 398
Traveling wave theory, *see* **Place theory**
Treatment, of psychological disorders, 603–645
  basic features of, 604–606
  community psychology and, 642–643
  costs of, 604

  eclectic, 604
  in history, 556, 557, 605, 632, 633
  see also Biological treatments; **Psychoactive drugs**; **Psychotherapy**
Triangular theory, of love, 674–675
Triarchic Abilities Test, 374
Triarchic theory of intelligence *Sternberg's theory that describes intelligence as having analytical, creative, and practical dimensions,* 366–368, 369
Trichromatic theory *A theory of color vision identifying three types of visual elements, each of which is most sensitive to different wavelengths of light,* 122–124
Tricyclic antidepressants (TCAs), 635, 638, 642
Triglycerides, 507
Trust *versus* mistrust, 459, 460
Tryptophan, 88
t table, A-16–A-17
t test, A-15–A-16
Twin studies, 50–51, A-3
Two-factor experiment, on learned helplessness, 209–210
Tympanic membrane *A membrane in the middle ear that generates vibrations that match the sound waves striking it,* 106, 107, 110
Type A people, 506
Type personality theories, 525–526, 543–545
Tyramine, 636
UCR, *see* **Unconditioned response**
UCS, *see* **Unconditioned stimulus**
Ultimate attribution error, 658
Umami, 128
Unconditional positive regard *A therapist attitude that conveys a caring for and acceptance of the client as a valued person,* 610
Unconditioned response (UCR) *The automatic or unlearned reaction to a stimulus,* 188, 189, 191
Unconditioned stimulus (UCS) *A stimulus that elicits a response without conditioning,* 188, 189, 190, 191, 192, 193, 198
Unconscious, 12
  classical psychoanalysis and, 313, 326, 606–608, 622
  collective, 522
  see also **Psychodynamic approach**
Unconscious level *A level of mental activity that influences consciousness, but is not conscious,* 310, 312, 313–314
Undercontrolled disorders, of childhood, 593
Undergraduate Stress Questionnaire, 489
Unified self-schemas, 651
Unique invulnerability, 659
United Nations, 341
U.S. Attorney General's Commission on Pornography, 699–701
U.S. Federal Aviation Administration, 692
Universal grammar, 299
Universal Nonverbal Intelligence Test, 355
Unrealistic optimism, 659, 660
Uppers, *see* **Amphetamines**
Upward social comparison, 648
Utility *A subjective measure of value,* 289–290

Validity *The degree to which a test measures what it is supposed to measure, and leads to correct inferences about people,* 30, 351–352
  of IQ test, 353–354
  of personality tests, 545
Valium, *see* Diazepam
Variability, measures of, 42, 43, 44, A-11–A-12
Variable-interval (VI) schedule *A type of partial reinforcement schedule that provides reinforcement for the first response after some varying period of time,* 202, 203
Variable-ratio (VR) schedule *A type of partial reinforcement schedule that provides reinforcement after a varying number of responses,* 202–203
Variables *Specific factors or characteristics that can take on different values in research,* 30
  confounding, 38–41
  dependent, 37
  independent, 37
  intervening, 381–382
Vasopressin, 90
Venlafaxine (Effexor), 636, 642
Ventricles, of brain, 586
Ventromedial nucleus, 390, 391
Vesicles, 60
Vestibular-ocular reflexes, 137
Vestibular sacs *Organs in the inner ear that connect the semicircular canals and the cochlea, and contribute to the body's sense of balance,* 137
Vestibular sense *The proprioceptive sense that provides information about the position of the body in space and about its movements,* 131, 137
Viagra, 403
Vicarious conditioning *Learning the relationship between a response and its consequences (either reinforcement or punishment) or the association between a conditioned stimulus and a conditioned response by watching others,* 214
Virtual reality graded exposure, 614
Visible light *Electromagnetic radiation that has a wavelength from about 400 nanometers to about 750 nanometers,* 111, 112
Vision, 101, 111–120
  absolute thresholds and, 146, 147
  in adulthood, 474
  blindness and, 131, 138, 328
  converting light into, 113–116
  depth perception and, 158–161, 164, 165, 172–173, 437
  development of, 173
  eye and, 112–113, 114, 120
  focusing light and, 112–113
  ganglion cells and, 114, 116, 117, 118, 119, 124
  grouping principles and, 157
  hearing and, 125–126
  hierarchical processing of visual information and, 117, 119–120
  light and, 111–112, 120
  in newborns, 437, 438
  parallel processing of visual properties and, 117, 118–119

photoreceptors and, 113–114, 115–116, 117, 120
representations and, 103–104, 117–120
retina and, 112, 113, 114–117, 118, 160, 161
touch and, 100
vestibular system and, 137
visual pathways and, 116–117, 120
without awareness, 312
see also Color vision
Visual-cliff studies, 172, 427
Visual cortex, 76, 118, 119
Visual dominance, 158
Visual encoding *The mental representation of stimuli as images,* 226, 237
Visual pathways, 116–117, 120
Vitamin B6, kinesthetic disorders and, 140
Volatile odorants, in foods, 391–392
Volley theory of frequency coding, *see* Frequency matching
Vomeronasal organ *A portion of the mammalian olfactory system that is sensitive to pheromones,* 127, 128
Vulnerability theory, of schizophrenia, 589
WAIS-III, *see* Wechsler Adult Intelligence Scale-Third Edition
Wanting, liking *versus,* 387–388
Wave, sound and, 104, 105
Waveform, 104, 105
Wavelength *The distance from one peak to the next in a waveform*
color sensations and, 120–122
light, 112
sound, 104

Ways of Coping questionnaire, 499
Weber's constant (Weber's fraction), 152
Weber's law *A law stating that the smallest detectable difference in stimulus energy is a constant fraction of the intensity of the stimulus,* 152, 153, 687
Wechsler Adult Intelligence Scale-Third Edition (WAIS-III), 348–349
Wechsler Intelligence Scale for Children (WISC-III-R), 348, 349
Well-adjusted person, 525
Wellbutrin, *see* Bupropion
Wernicke's aphasia, 78
Wernicke's area, 76, 78, 79
"What" system, 118
"Where" system, 118
White blood cells, 504
White coat hypertensives, 192, 193
Wild Boy of Aveyron, 450, 451
Williams syndrome, 375
WISC-III-R, *see* Wechsler Intelligence Scale for Children
Wisdom, 475–476
Wish fulfillment, 326
Witches, 556
Withdrawal symptoms, 595
Withdrawal syndrome *Symptoms associated with discontinuing the use of a habit-forming substance,* 332
Womb envy, 523
Women, in psychology, 15, 16
Wonderlic Personnel Test, 350
Words *Units of language composed of one or more morphemes,* 293, 295

recognition of, 170–171
see also **Language**
Word salad, schizophrenia and, 583
Word superiority effect, 170, 171
Working-backward strategy, for problem solving, 279–280
Working memory *The part of the memory system that allows us to mentally work with, or manipulate, information being held in short-term memory,* 233, 239, 256, 261, 267, 276, 372. See also **Short-term memory**
Working parents, 479
Workplace, achievement and success in, 407–408
World Health Organization, 392, 400, 509, 560
World Trade Center attack (9/11/01), 647, 648, 650, 667, 680, 692, 702–703, 713
Xanax, *see* Alprazolam
X chromosome, 375
Xenophobia, 566
XTC, *see* MDMA
Yerkes-Dodson law, 387
Yin and *yang,* 556
Young-Helmboltz theory, *see* **Trichromatic theory**
Zero-sum game *A social situation in which one person's gains are subtracted from another person's resources, so that the sum of the gains and losses is zero,* 713
Zoloft, *see* Sertraline
Zygote *A new cell, formed from a father's sperm and a mother's ovum, that carries the genetic heritage of each,* 435, A-2
Zyprexa, *see* Olanzapine